Here is the work that made all other puzzle dictionaries obsolete. Its unique Instant Finders System saves you time-consuming searches through the long, jumbled paragraphs of words that are so common in other crossword puzzle dictionaries.

Suppose your clue is a seven-letter word for MIX: just turn to that entry and your eye immediately picks out the bold number 7. Now you can pick your answer from just five words, ignoring the 38 others that *can't* fit.

Down and across, SWANFELDT spells SUCCESS for the stumped crossword fan.

5TH EDITION

ANDREW SWANFELDT
CROSSWORD PUZZLE DICTIONARY

HarperPaperbacks

A Division of HarperCollinsPublishers

HarperPaperbacks *A Division of* HarperCollins*Publishers*
10 East 53rd Street, New York, N.Y. 10022

First HarperPaperbacks printing: June 1990

Printed in the United States of America

HarperPaperbacks and colophon are trademarks of HarperCollins*Publishers*

40

Editor's Preface

Since its first appearance in 1940, the *Crossword Puzzle Dictionary*, compiled by the late Andrew Swanfeldt, has acquired a widespread and loyal following among crossword puzzle fans. Each successive edition improved and expanded the original. The third edition introduced the Instant Finder System, in which answer words are listed according to the number of letters. In this fifth edition, the editors have responded to many reader requests by providing separate lists for prefixes, suffixes, and combining forms, lists that can be found at the back of the book. To this fifth edition thousands of new words, both clue words and answer words, have been added and the book has been completely reset in larger type for easier reading. This fifth edition more than adequately reflects today's crossword puzzle clues and answers.

We are greatly indebted to Mr. John Willig, who began and completed a substantial amount of the revisions for this fifth edition. Mr. Willig died during his work on the book, and will be remembered with great fondness and deep gratitude. Ms. Ruth Adler took over the task of revising the book with admirable drive and attention to detail. She has our sincere thanks for a superb job.

Abbreviations Used in This Book

abbr.	abbreviation	It.	Italian
anc.	ancient	L.	Latin
Ar.	Arabic	mas.	masculine
c.	capital	O.T.	Old Testament
comb. form	combining form	pert. to	pertaining to
D.	Dutch	P.I.	Philippine Islands
F.	French	pl.	plural
fem.	feminine	Russ.	Russian
G.	German	Sc.	Scottish
Gr.	Greek	Sp.	Spanish
her.	heraldic	W.	Welsh
Ind.	Indian	Yid.	Yiddish
Ir.	Irish		

CROSSWORD
PUZZLE
DICTIONARY

A

aa: 4 lava 9 aphrolite

aal, al: 8 mulberry
  dye: 8 morindin

aalii: 4 tree, wood

aardvark: 4 anteater, earth pig, edentate

Aaron: 10 high priest
  associate: Hur
  brother: 5 Moses
  builder of: 10 golden calf
  burial place: Hor
  father: 5 Amram
  sister: 6 Miriam
  son: 5 Abihu, Nadab 7 Eleazar, Ithamar

Aaron's rod: 7 mullein

aba: 4 robe 5 cloth 6 fabric 7 garment

abaca: 4 hemp 5 fiber, lupis

aback: 6 behind 8 unawares 10 by surprise

abaculus: 4 tile 7 tessera

abacus: 4 slab 10 calculator
  Chinese: 7 suan pan

abaddon: pit 4 hell 5 hades

Abadite, Ibidite: 6 Muslim

abaft: 4 back 5 arear 6 astern, behind 8 rearward

abalone: 5 awabi, ormer, shell 6 sea ear 7 mollusk

abandon: 4 drop, flee, junk, quit 5 ditch, leave, scrap, waive, yield 6 abjure, desert, disuse, give up, maroon, reject, resign, vacate 7 discard, forsake 8 abdicate, forswear, rashness, renounce 9 surrender 10 enthusiasm, exuberance, relinquish

abandoned: bad 4 left, lost 6 wanton 7 corrupt, forlorn 8 derelict, flagrant, forsaken, stranded 9 desolated, destitute, dissolute, shameless, unbridled 10 dissipated, profligate 12 unrestrained

abandonment instrument: 6 waiver

abase: 5 shame 6 defame, demean, demote, grovel, humble, lessen, reduce 7 degrade, put down 9 denigrate, humiliate 10 depreciate

abash: 5 shame, upset 6 dismay, put out 7 chagrin, mortify 8 bewilder, confound 9 discomfit, embarrass, humiliate 10 disconcert

abashed: 7 ashamed 8 sheepish, red-faced

abate: ebb, end 4 ease, fall, omit, slow, void, wane 5 allay, annul, let up, lower,

quash, relax, remit, slake 6 deduct, lessen, reduce, recede 7 abolish, assuage, die down, nullify, slacken, subside 8 decrease, diminish, mitigate, moderate 9 alleviate

abatement: 6 rebate 8 decrease 9 allowance, deduction, reduction 10 diminution, relaxation, subsidence

abatis: 8 obstacle 9 barricade 13 fortification

abba: 6 father

abbey: 6 priory 7 convent, nunnery 8 cloister 9 monastery, sanctuary
  head: 5 abbot 6 abbess
  assistant: 5 prior 8 prioress
  pert. to: 8 abbatial

abbreviate: cut 4 clip, dock 5 prune 6 digest 7 abridge, curtail, cut back, shorten 8 contract, condense, truncate 9 make brief

ABC's: 6 basics 9 rudiments

abdicate: 4 cede, quit 5 demit, leave 6 disown, forego, resign, retire, vacate 7 abandon, lay down 8 disclaim, renounce 9 surrender 10 relinquish

abdomen: gut, pot 5 belly 6 paunch 7 midriff, stomach 9 bay window
  crustacean: 5 pleon
  pert. to: 6 pelvic 7 gastric, ventral 8 visceral

abduct: 5 seize 6 kidnap, snatch

abecedarian: 4 tyro 6 novice 7 learner 8 beginner, neophyte 9 fledgling 10 tenderfoot 12 alphabetical

abecedarium: 6 primer 12 alphabet book
  relative: 8 acrostic

abed: 4 sick 7 resting, retired 8 sleeping

Abel: *brother:* 4 Cain, Seth
  parent: Eve 4 Adam
  slayer: 4 Cain

Abelard's beloved: 7 Heloise

abele: 6 poplar

aberrant: odd 7 deviant, unusual 8 abnormal, atypical, peculiar, straying 9 unnatural, wandering

aberration: 4 slip 5 error, fault, lapse, mania, quirk 8 delusion, insanity 9 deviation 12 eccentricity 13 hallucination

abet: aid 4 back, goad, help 5 egg on 6 assist, foment, incite, second, uphold 7 espouse, further, support, sustain 8 befriend 9 encourage, instigate 11 countenance

abettor: 6 patron 8 advocate, promoter 9 accessory, auxiliary, supporter 10 accomplice 11 confederate, conspirator

abeyance: 4 stay 5 break, letup, pause 7 respite 10 on the shelf, suspension

abhor: 4 hate, shun 6 detest, loathe 7 despise, dislike 8 execrate 9 abominate

abhorrence: 5 odium 6 hatred 7 disgust 8 aversion 9 antipathy, revulsion 10 repugnance 11 detestation

Abi: *father:* 9 Zechariah

husband: 4 Ahaz

mother: 8 Hezekiah

abide: 4 bear, last, live, stay 5 await, brook, delay, dwell, exist, pause, stand, tarry 6 accept, endure, linger, remain, reside, submit, suffer 7 sojourn, sustain 8 continue, tolerate 9 acquiesce, withstand

Abiel's son: Ner

a bientot(F.): 6 so long

abies: 4 firs 5 trees 10 evergreens

Abigail: *husband:* 5 David, Nabal

son: 5 Amasa

ability: 5 force, knack, power, skill 6 energy, talent 7 caliber, faculty, knowhow, prowess 8 aptitude, capacity, facility, strength 9 dexterity, ingenuity 10 capability, competence, efficiency 11 proficiency

abject: low 4 base, mean, meek, poor 6 humble, paltry, sordid 7 hangdog, ignoble, servile, slavish 8 beggarly, contrite, cringing, degraded, wretched 9 miserable 10 submissive

abjure: 4 deny 5 avoid, spurn 6 eschew, give up, recall, recant, reject, resign, revoke 7 abandon, disavow, retract 8 abnegate, disclaim, forswear, renounce, take back, withdraw 9 repudiate

ablate: 8 melt away, vaporize 12 disintegrate

ablation: 7 erosion, removal 11 evaporation

ablaze: 5 afire, lit up 6 ardent, aflame 7 burning, glowing, ignited, radiant 8 inflamed

able: apt, fit 4 up to 5 adept, smart 6 au fait, clever, facile, strong, suited 7 capable 8 dextrous, skillful, suitable, talented, vigorous 9 competent, dexterous, effective, efficient, qualified, versatile 10 proficient

ablution: 4 bath 10 church rite

abnegate: 4 deny 5 forgo 6 abjure, forego, refuse, reject 7 disavow 8 disclaim, forswear, renounce 10 relinquish

Abner: *cousin:* 4 Saul

father: Ner

abnormal: 5 queer 7 deviant, erratic, offbeat, unusual 8 aberrant, uncommon 9 anomalous, eccentric, irregular, unnatural 9 out-of-line 10 exorbitant 11 exceptional 13 extraordinary

aboard: 4 onto 6 on deck 7 astride, present 9 alongside

abode: flat, home 5 house, manor 6 estate 7 cottage, mansion 8 domicile, dwelling, tenement 9 apartment, residence 10 habitation

animal: zoo 9 menagerie

of Dead: Dar 4 Aaru, Hell 5 Aralu, Hades, Orcus, Sheol 6 Heaven 9 Purgatory

of gods: 4 Meru 6 Asgard 7 Asgarth, Olympus 8 Asgardhr

abolish: end 4 kill 5 abate, annul, erase, quash 6 cancel, repeal, revoke, vacate 7 destroy, nullify, rescind, wipe out 8 abrogate 9 eradicate 10 annihilate, do away with, invalidate 11 discontinue, exterminate

aboma: boa 6 python 8 anaconda

abominable: 4 vile 6 horrid, odious 9 atrocious, execrable, loathsome, revolting 10 unpleasant 12 disagreeable

abominable snowman: 4 yeti 7 monster

habitat: 9 Himalayas

abominate: 4 hate 5 abhor 6 detest, loathe 8 execrate

abomination: 4 evil 5 crime, curse 6 infamy, horror, plague 7 outrage 8 anathema, atrocity, disgrace 9 antipathy 10 abhorrence, odiousness, repugnance 11 detestation

à bon marché(F.): 5 cheap

aboriginal: 5 first 7 endemic 8 primeval 9 primitive 10 indigenous

aborigine: 6 Indian, native, savage 10 autochthon

abortion: 7 failure 8 misbirth 11 miscarriage, monstrosity

abortive: 4 idle, vain 6 futile, no good 9 fruitless 12 unproductive, unsuccessful

abound: 4 teem 5 crawl, swarm 8 overflow

abounding: 4 rife 5 alive, flush 6 full of, jammed, packed 7 replete, teeming 8 abundant, thronged 9 plentiful

about: 4 as to, in re, near, some 5 anent, astir, circa 6 active, almost, around 7 apropos, close to 9 as regards 10 concerning, relative to, respecting, throughout 11 surrounding 13 approximately

about-face: 6 switch 8 flip-flop, reversal 9 turnabout 12 change of mind

above: oer 4 atop, over, past, upon 5 aloft 6 beyond, higher, on high 7 on top of 8 overhead, superior 9 exceeding 12 transcendent

above all: 6 indeed, mostly 7 chiefly 9 in the main, primarily

aboveboard: 4 open 5 frank, overt 6 honest, square 8 bona fide 9 in the open 10 on the level

above water: 4 safe 5 clear 7 solvent 9 out of debt

abracadabra: 5 charm, spell 6 jargon 10 hocus-pocus 11 incantation

abrade: rub 4 file, fret, gall, rasp, sand, wear 5 chafe, erode, grate, grind 6 scrape 7 corrode, eat away 8 irritate 9 excoriate

Abraham: 9 patriarch
  bosom: 6 heaven 8 paradise
  brother: 5 Nahor
  concubine: 5 Hagar
  father: 5 Terah
  grandfather: 5 Nahor
  grandson: 4 Esau
  newphew: Lot
  shrine: 5 Caaba, Kaaba
  son: 5 Isaac, Medan, Shuah 6 Midian, Zimran 7 Ishmael
  wife: 4 Sara 5 Hagar, Sarah 7 Keturah

abrasive: 4 sand 5 emery 6 pumice, quartz 8 annoying, corundum 9 sandpaper, provoking

abraxas: gem 5 charm

abreast: 4 even, up to 5 abeam 6 beside 8 parallel 9 alongside 10 side by side
  of the times: 6 modern 7 popular 8 up to date 9 au courant(F.) 12 contemporary

abri: 6 dugout 7 shelter

abridge: cut 5 limit, 6 reduce, shrink 7 capsule, curtail, cut back, shorten 8 compress, condense, contract, diminish, retrench 10 abbreviate

abridgement: 4 brief 6 digest, precis, sketch 7 epitome, summary 8 abstract, synopsis 9 lessening 10 compendium, diminution

abroad: off 4 asea, away 5 astir 6 afield, astray 7 distant 8 overseas

abrogate: 4 undo, void 5 annul, quash, remit 6 cancel, repeal, revoke 7 abolish, nullify, rescind 8 overrule, set aside

abrupt: 4 curt, fast, rude 5 bluff, blunt, brief, brisk, gruff, hasty, jerky, quick, sharp, sheer, short, steep, terse 6 sudden 7 brusque, headlong 8 vertical 9 impetuous 10 unexpected 11 precipitous 13 unceremonious

Absalom: *captain:* 5 Amasa
  father: 5 David
  sister: 5 Tamar
  slayer: 4 Joab

abscess: 4 boil 5 ulcer 6 fester, lesion

abscond: fly, run 4 bolt, flee, quit, skip 5 scram 6 decamp, escape 7 make off 8 clear out 12 absquatulate

absence: 4 lack, void, want 5 leave 6 vacuum 7 truancy 8 furlough, omission 10 deficiency, withdrawal 13 nonappearance, nonattendance

absent: off, out 4 away, gone 7 lacking, missing 10 not present

absent-minded: 7 bemused, far away 8 distrait, dreaming, unseeing 9 oblivious 10 abstracted 11 inattentive

absent without leave: 4 AWOL

absolute: 4 pure, rank, real, true 5 sheer, stark, total, utter, whole 6 actual, entire, simple 7 perfect, plenary 8 complete, despotic, explicit, implicit, outright, positive 9 arbitrary, downright, out and out, undoubted 10 autocratic, peremptory 11 categorical, unalienable 13 unconditional

absolutely: yea, yes 4 amen 5 quite, truly 6 wholly, for sure, utterly 8 of course 9 certainly, perfectly 10 positively, thoroughly 13 unequivocally

absolution: 6 pardon 7 amnesty 9 acquittal, cleansing, remission 11 exculpation, forgiveness

absolve: 4 free 5 clear, remit 6 acquit, excuse, exempt, let off, pardon, shrive 7 forgive, release 8 dispense, liberate, overlook 9 discharge, exculpate, exonerate, vindicate

absorb: 5 merge, unite 6 engage, imbibe, soak up, take in 7 combine, consume, drink in, engross, immerse, occlude 8 take over 10 assimilate 11 incorporate

absorbed: 4 rapt 5 intent, lost in 7 riveted 8 immersed, involved 9 engrossed, wrapped up 10 abstracted 11 preoccupied

absquatulate: 5 scram 6 decamp 7 abscond

abstain: 4 deny, fast 5 forgo, spurn, waive 6 desist, eschew, forego, pass up, refuse, reject 7 forbear, refrain 8 hold back, keep from, let alone, teetotal 9 do without

abstemious: 5 sober 7 ascetic, austere, sparing 8 moderate 9 abstinent, temperate

abstinence: 8 sobriety 10 self-denial 12 renunciation

abstract: 4 cull, deed, pure 5 brief, ideal, steal 6 deduct, divert, precis, remove 7 abridge, excerpt, purloin, summary 8 abstruse, detached, separate, synopsis, withdraw 9 difficult, epitomize, recondite, summarize 10 compendium 11 theoretical
  art: 6 unreal 12 non-objective 13 expressionism
  being: ens 4 esse 5 entia(pl.)

abstracted: 7 bemused, far away, pensive 8 absorbed 9 engrossed 11 preoccupied 12 absent-minded

abstruse: 4 deep 6 mystic, remote, subtle, 7 obscure 8 abstract, esoteric, profound

9 recondite 10 mysterious 11 hard to grasp

absurd: 4 wild 5 crazy, droll, inane, inept, silly, wacky 6 stupid 7 asinine, foolish 9 fantastic, ludicrous, senseless 10 irrational, ridiculous 11 meaningless, nonsensical 12 inconsistent, preposterous

abundance: 4 lots 5 store 6 oodles, plenty, riches, wealth 8 fullness, opulence, plethora 9 affluence, amplitude, plenitude, profusion 10 quantities

abundant: 4 lush, much, rich, rife 5 ample, thick 6 common, lavish 7 copious, fertile, profuse, replete, riotous, teeming 8 fruitful, generous, numerous, prolific 9 abounding, bountiful, luxuriant, plenteous, plentiful, prevalent 11 overflowing

abuse: mar, tax 4 flay, harm, hurt, maul, 5 curse, fault, scold, wrong 6 berate, defile, injure, insult, misuse, punish, revile 7 affront, bedevil, calumny, exploit, obloquy, outrage, pervert, slander, upbraid, violate 8 maltreat, misapply, mistreat, 9 blaspheme, contumely, desecrate, disparage, invective, objurgate 10 impose upon, manipulate, opprobrium, scurrility 12 vituperation

abusive: 4 foul 5 rough 6 savage 7 corrupt, profane 8 insolent, libelous 9 offensive, perverted 10 calumnious, scurrilous 11 blasphemous 12 vituperative

abut: 4 join 5 touch 6 adjoin, border, rest on 10 end against

abysmal: 4 deep 6 dreary 8 profound, unending, wretched 10 bottomless

abyss: pit 4 deep, gulf, hell, void 5 chasm, Hades 6 bottom, depths, vorago 7 gehenna, inferno 9 perdition

Abyssinia: See **Ethiopia**

acacia: 4 tree 5 babul, boree, cooba, myall 6 locust, wattle 7 catechu 9 boobyalla, gum arabic

academic: 5 rigid 6 formal, unreal 7 bookish, classic, erudite, learned 8 pedantic 9 scholarly, professor 11 quodlibetic, theoretical 12 conventional

division: 4 term 7 quarter 8 semester

academy: 5 lyceum, manege, school 7 college, society 8 seminary 9 institute 10 university

service: 4 Army (West Point), Navy (Annapolis) 8 Air Force (Colorado) 10 Coast Guard (New London) 14 Merchant Marine (Long Island)

Acadian: 5 Cajun

acajou: 6 cashew 8 mahogany 9 laurel oak

acaleph: 9 jellyfish

acarid: 4 mite, tick 6 insect

acaudal: 7 anurous 8 tailless

accede: let 5 agree, allow, grant, yield 6 assent, attain, comply, concur, give in 7

approve, consent 9 acquiesce 10 take office 11 acknowledge

accelerate: rev, gun 4 race, 5 hurry 6 hasten 7 advance, forward, further, quicken, speed up 8 dispatch, expedite, go faster, increase, step on it 9 move ahead, stimulate 11 precipitate

accelerator: 8 throttle 9 activator, cyclotron

accent: 4 beat, burr, mark, tone 5 ictus, drawl, pitch, pulse, sound, throb, twang 6 brogue, rhythm, stress 7 cadence 8 emphasis 9 underline 10 inflection, intonation

mark: 5 acute, grave 10 circumflex

accented: 7 marcato

syllable: 5 arsis

accentuate: 6 set off 7 sharpen 8 bring out 9 emphasize, intensify

accept: buy, see 4 take 5 admit, adopt, agree, allow, bow to, grant, honor 6 assent, endure, take in 7 approve, believe, embrace, espouse, receive 8 tolerate 9 acquiesce 10 understand 11 acknowledge

acceptable: 6 decent, not bad, viable 7 average, welcome 8 adequate, all right, pleasant, suitable 9 palatable 10 good enough 12 satisfactory

accepted: 5 valid 6 proper 7 correct, routine, popular 8 credited, orthodox, standard 9 canonical, customary, prevalent 10 sanctioned 12 conventional, countenanced

access: way 4 adit, door, gate, path, road 5 entry, onset, route, spell 6 attack, avenue, entree, portal, street 7 flare-up 8 approach, entrance, eruption, increase, outburst, paroxysm 9 admission 10 admittance, passageway, right of way

accessible: 4 near, open 5 handy 6 at hand, patent, public 8 pervious 9 available, reachable 10 attainable, convenient, easy to meet, obtainable, procurable 12 approachable, unrestricted

accession: 5 enter 7 arrival 8 addition, approach, increase 9 adherence, agreement, inaugural, increment, induction 11 acquisition 12 installation

accessory: 4 aide, ally, tool 5 extra 6 helper 7 abettor, adjunct 8 additive, a party to, trapping 9 appendage, assistant, auxiliary, secondary 10 accomplice, attachment, incidental, subsidiary, supplement 11 additional, concomitant, confederate, contingency, subservient, subordinate, unessential 12 appurtenance, contributory 13 accompaniment

accident: hap 4 case, fate, luck 5 event, fluke, wreck 6 chance, hazard, mishap 7 fortune 8 calamity, disaster, incident

9 mischance 10 misfortune 11 catastrophe, contingency, contretemps 12 misadventure

accidental: 6 casual, chance, random 9 extrinsic, haphazard, secondary, unplanned, unwitting 10 extraneous, fortuitous, incidental, unexpected, unforeseen, unintended 11 conditional, inadvertent, subordinate 12 adventitious, nonessential 13 unintentional 14 unpremeditated

acclaim: 4 clap, fame, hail, laud 5 cheer, eclat, extol, honor, kudos 6 praise, repute, salute 7 applaud, approve, commend, glorify, root for, ovation 8 plaudits 9 pay homage 10 compliment 11 approbation

acclimate: 5 inure 6 harden, season 7 toughen 8 accustom 9 condition, habituate

acclivity: 4 hill, rise 7 incline 11 upward slope

accolade: 5 award, honor, medal 6 eulogy, salute 7 laurels, tribute 8 ceremony, citation, encomium 9 laudation, panegyric 10 decoration, salutation 11 distinction

accommodate: fit 4 give, hold, lend, suit 5 adapt, board, defer, favor, house, lodge, put up, serve, yield 6 adjust, attune, billet, change, comply, oblige, orient, settle 7 conform, contain, quarter 9 make agree, reconcile

accompany: 4 join, lead 5 add to, pilot 6 assist, attend, convey, convoy, escort, follow, go with, squire 7 coexist, conduct 8 chaperon 10 supplement

accomplice: 6 helper 7 abettor, cohort, partner 9 accessory, assistant, associate, colleague 11 confederate 12 participator 13 co-conspirator

accomplish: end, win 5 reach 6 attain, effect, finish, fulfil, manage, make it 7 achieve, execute, fulfill, furnish, perfect, perform, produce, realize, succeed 8 bring off, complete, dispatch, engineer 9 put across 10 consummate

accomplished: apt 4 able, done 5 adept, ended 6 expert 7 skilled 8 finished, talented 9 versatile 10 proficient

accomplishment: art 4 deed, feat 5 craft, skill 7 success 8 learning 10 attainment 11 achievement, performance

accord: 4 jibe 5 agree, allot, grant, tally, unity 6 accede, adjust, bestow, concur, treaty 7 concede, concert, consent, rapport 8 affinity, volition 9 give as due, harmonize, reconcile 10 compliance, conformity, correspond

accordant: 7 attuned 8 agreeing, coherent, suitable 9 congruous, consonant 10 compatible, consistent, harmonious 11 conformable 13 correspondent

accordingly: 4 ergo, then, thus 5 hence 9 therefore, thereupon, wherefore 12 consequently, in the same way

accost: 4 hail, meet 5 greet, speak 6 call to, halloo, salute, waylay 7 address, solicit, speak to 8 approach, bid hello, confront 9 encounter 10 button-hole

account: tab, use 4 bill, deem, item, rate, tale, view 5 basis, score, story, value, worth 6 client, detail, esteem, profit, reason, record, report, repute 7 history, invoice, recital 8 business, customer, estimate 9 advantage, chronicle, discourse, inventory, narrative, reckoning, statement 10 commentary, importance, recitation 11 description, explanation

book: 6 ledger

accountable: 6 liable 10 answerable, explicable 11 responsible 12 attributable

accountant: CPA 5 clerk 7 auditor 8 reckoner 10 bookkeeper, controller

accoutre, accouter: arm, rig 4 gird 5 array, dress, equip 6 attire, clothe, outfit 7 costume, furnish, turn out 8 decorate

accoutrements, accouterments: 4 gear 7 regalia 8 fittings, materiel 9 equipment, trappings

accredit: 4 okay 6 ratify 7 approve, ascribe, certify, confirm, empower, endorse, license 8 deputize, notarize, sanction, validate, vouch for 9 attribute, authorize 10 commission

accretion: 4 gain 6 growth 8 addition, increase 9 coherence, increment 11 enlargement 12 accumulation

accrue: add 4 earn, gain, grow 5 swell 6 collect, fall due, redound 8 cumulate, increase, multiply, snowball

accumulate: 4 grow, save 5 amass, hoard, lay in 6 accrue, garner, gather, muster, pile up 7 collect, compile, store up 8 assemble, increase 9 stockpile

accumulation: 4 bank, fund, heap, mass, pile 5 stack, store 7 backlog, cumulus, nest egg 8 dividend, interest, treasure 9 inventory 10 acervation 11 aggregation

accurate: 4 true 5 exact, right 7 certain, correct, precise 8 reliable 9 authentic, errorless, on the nose, veridical 10 dependable

accursed: fey(Sc.) 6 damned, doomed 7 hellish 9 abhorrent, execrable 10 abominable, detestable

accuse: tax 4 cite 5 blame 6 allege, attack, charge, defame, finger, indict 7 arraign, censure, impeach 8 denounce, reproach 9 inculpate 10 calumniate 11 bring to book, incriminate, recriminate

falsely: 5 libel

accuser: 7 charger, delator 8 libelant 9 plaintiff 10 prosecutor 11 complainant

accustom: use 5 adapt, enure, drill, inure, train 6 orient, season 7 toughen 9 acclimate, condition, get used to, habituate 11 familiarize

ace: jot, one, pip 4 a-one, card, hero, mark, star, tops, unit 5 adept, basto, flyer, point 6 expert 7 aviator 8 particle, topnotch 9 first-rate, hole-in-one 11 crackerjack, hairbreadth, tennis score

acerbic: 4 acid, sour, tart 5 acrid, harsh, sharp, 6 bitter, severe 7 caustic 9 corrosive, sarcastic 10 astringent 11 acrimonious

acerbate: vex 7 envenom 8 embitter, irritate, infuriate 10 exasperate

acetaldehyde: 5 ethyl 7 ethanol

acetic acid: 7 vinegar
salt: 7 acetate

acetylene: 5 tolan 6 alkyne, ethyne, tolane

ache: 4 hurt, long, pain, pang, pine 5 bleed, smart, throb, throe 6 desire, grieve, hunger, stitch, suffer, twinge 7 anguish 8 soreness, yearn for

achieve: get, win 4 earn, gain 5 reach 6 afford, attain, effect, finish, obtain 7 compass, execute, fulfill, produce, realize, succeed, triumph 8 complete, conclude, contrive 9 terminate 10 accomplish, consummate

achievement: act 4 coup, deed, feat 6 action 7 exploit 9 execution, 11 performance, tour de force 14 accomplishment

Achilles: *advisor:* 6 Nestor
charioteer: 9 Automedon
father: 6 Peleus
fought in: 9 Trojan War
friend: 9 Patroclus
hero of: 5 Iliad
horse: 7 Xanthus
lover and captive: 7 Briseis
mother: 6 Thetis
slayer: 5 Paris
soldier: 8 Myrmidon
teacher: 6 Chiron 7 Centaur
victim: 6 Hector
vulnerable part: 4 heel

achromatic: 7 neutral 8 diatonic 9 colorless

acid: dry, LSD 4 keen, sour, tart 5 acerb, acrid, harsh, sharp 6 biting, bitter 7 acetose, acetous, pungent, vinegar 9 corrosive 11 acrimonious
in fruit: 5 malic 6 citric 8 tartaric
kind of: 5 amino, boric, iodic, oleic 6 acetic, cyanic, formic 7 stearic 8 carbolic
neutralizer: 6 alkali
nitric: 10 aquafortis
radical: 4 acyl 6 acetyl 7 malonyl, benzoyl
used in dyeing: 6 citric, oxalic 7 benzoic
used in tanning: 6 lactic, tannic

acid rain: 7 fallout 12 air pollutant

Acis: *father:* 6 Faunus
lover: 7 Galatea
slayer: 10 Polyphemus

acknowledge: nod, own 4 aver, avow 5 admit, allow, grant, thank, yield 6 accept, affirm, answer, avouch, reveal 7 concede, confess, declare, divulge, own up to, profess 8 disclose 9 recognize

acme: cap, top 4 apex, peak 5 crest 6 apogee, climax, crisis, height, heyday, summit, vertex, zenith 8 pinnacle 11 culmination

acolyte: 6 helper, novice, server 8 altar boy, follower 9 attendant

aconite: 9 monkshood, wolfsbane
poison from: 4 bikh

acorn: 4 mast 6 oak nut
dried: 6 camata 8 camatina
edible: 7 ballote, bellote

acouchi: 5 elemi, resin

acquaint: 4 tell 5 teach 6 advise, clue in, fill in, inform, notify 7 apprise, present 8 disclose 9 enlighten, introduce

acquaintance: 4 kith 6 friend 9 associate, companion, knowledge 11 familiarity

acquainted: 4 up on 6 au fait, versed 8 informed 9 in the know

acquiesce: bow 5 abide, agree, yield 6 accede, accept, assent, comply, concur, submit 7 concede, conform, consent

acquire: add, buy, get, win 4 earn, gain, grab, reap 5 amass, learn, reach 6 garner, gather, obtain, pick up, secure, take on 7 collect, develop, procure 8 contract 9 cultivate

acquisitive: 4 avid 6 greedy 8 covetous, grasping 10 avaricious

acquit: 4 free 5 clear 6 excuse, let off, pardon, parole 7 absolve, amnesty, comport, conduct, release 8 liberate 9 discharge, exculpate, exonerate, vindicate

acreage: 4 land 5 tract 6 realty 7 grounds 8 property 11 landholding

acrid: 4 sour 5 harsh, rough, sharp, 6 biting, bitter 7 caustic, pungent, reeking 8 unsavory, virulent 9 acidulous, corrosive 10 astringent, irritating

acrimonious: mad 5 angry, gruff, harsh, irate, sharp, surly, testy, wroth 6 bitter, cranky 7 caustic 8 stinging 9 rancorous, resentful 11 contentious, quarrelsome

acroamatic: 4 oral 8 esoteric

acrobat: 7 gymnast, tumbler 8 balancer, stuntman 9 aerialist, trapezist 13 contortionist
garment: 6 tights 7 leotard

acrogen: 4 fern, moss 9 liverwort

acropolis: 4 fort, hill 7 citadel

across: 4 over 6 beyond, facing 7 athwart

8 opposite 9 astraddle 10 transverse

the board: all 5 total 6 in toto, wholly 8 sweeping 11 altogether

acrostic: 4 game 6 phrase, puzzle 7 acronym 11 composition

act: law 4 bill, deed, fake, feat, move, skit, turn, work 5 doing, edict, emote, feign, put-on, serve, stunt 6 behave, bestir, decide, decree 7 comport, exploit, perform, portray, pretend, statute 8 function, play part, 9 dissemble, ordinance, represent 10 observance 11 impersonate, performance 12 have an effect

by turns: 9 alternate

act for: 5 front, spell 7 relieve 8 pinch-hit 9 represent

act like: ape 4 copy, echo 5 mimic 7 imitate 8 simulate

act on: 4 rule 6 affect 9 influence, take steps

act up: 7 carry on, show off 9 misbehave

action: 4 case, deed, fray, step, work 5 cause, fight, means 6 affair, battle 7 conduct, process 8 behavior, conflict, function, goings-on, maneuver, movement 9 animation, 10 deportment, enterprise, proceeding 11 transaction

field of: 4 bowl 5 arena, stage 7 stadium

legal: res 4 suit 6 trover 8 replevin 10 litigation

out of: 7 dormant 8 disabled, unused 9 sidelined 10 broken down, on the blink 11 inoperative

activate: 6 arouse, charge 7 start up 8 energize, mobilize, vitalize

active: 4 busy, spry 5 agile, alert, brisk, in use, quick, zippy 6 hearty, lively, moving, nimble 7 dynamic, kinetic, moving 8 animated, athletic, spirited, vigorous 9 energetic, sprightly, 10 productive, up and about 11 functioning, industrious

activity: ado 4 life, stir, work 6 bustle, doings 8 business, exercise, function, movement 10 occupation

actor: 4 doer, mime 5 mimic 6 mummer, player, 7 artiste, histrio, trouper 8 comedian, stroller, thespian 9 performer, tragedian 11 barnstormer, entertainer

cue: 4 hint, word 6 prompt

group of: 4 cast 6 troupe 7 company

incompetent: ham 6 emoter

lines: 4 role, side

part: 4 hero, lead, role, star 5 heavy, 7 heroine, villain 8 juvenile

substitute: 7 stand-in 10 understudy

supporting: bit 5 extra, super 8 walk-on

actress: 4 diva 7 ingenue 9 soubrette 10 comedienne

actual: 4 real, true 6 extant 7 current, genuine 8 bona fide, concrete, existing, material, physical, positive, tangible 9 authentic, veritable 11 substantial

actuality: 4 fact 5 being 6 verity 7 reality 9 existence, substance

actuate: 4 move, stir 5 drive, enact, impel, spark, start 6 arouse, incite, set off 7 agitate, animate, enliven, inspire, provoke, trigger 8 motivate 9 instigate 11 put in motion

acumen: wit 7 insight 8 keenness, sagacity 9 acuteness, sharpness 10 astuteness, perception, shrewdness 11 discernment 12 perspicacity 14 discrimination

acupuncture: 7 therapy 11 anaesthesia, perforation

acute: 4 dire, keen 5 quick, sharp, smart 6 astute, severe, shrewd, shrill, subtle, urgent 7 crucial, extreme, intense, pointed 8 critical, incisive, piercing 9 ingenious, sensitive 10 discerning, perceptive 11 high-pitched, intelligent, penetrating, quick-witted 13 perspicacious

ad-lib: 9 improvise 11 extemporize

ad patres: 4 dead 8 deceased

adage: saw 5 axiom, maxim, motto 6 byword, dictum, homily, saying, truism 7 bromide, precept, proverb 8 aphorism, apothegm

Adah: *husband:* 4 Esau 6 Lamech

son: 5 Jabal, Jubal

Adam: *grandson:* 4 Enos 5 Enoch

rib: Eve

son: 4 Abel, Cain, Seth

teacher: 6 Raisel

wife, first: 6 Lilith

Adam-and-Eve: 9 puttyroot

Adam Bede author: 5 Eliot

adamant: 4 firm, hard 5 rigid, stony 8 obdurate 9 immovable, unbending 10 inflexible, relentless, unyielding

adapt: fit 4 suit 5 alter, inure, shape 6 adjust, change, comply, gear to, modify, tailor, temper 7 arrange, conform, convert, qualify 8 attemper, 9 acclimate, harmonize, reconcile 11 accommodate

adaptable: 6 pliant, supple 8 flexible 9 all-around, malleable, resilient, tractable, versatile 10 adjustable, changeable 11 conformable 12 reconcilable

add: sum, tot 4 fuse, join, tote 5 affix, annex, put in, tally, total, unite 6 append, attach, figure, reckon 7 augment, combine, compile, compute, connect, say more, subjoin 9 calculate

to: 5 mix in 6 blow up, expand, tack on 7 amplify 8 increase 9 strengthen 10 supplement

up: 5 recap 6 be okay, go over, 8 ring true 9 summarize

adda: 5 skink 6 lizard

adder: 5 krait, snake, viper 7 serpent

addict: fan 4 buff, user 5 hound, slave 6 votary 7 deliver, devotee, fanatic, habitue, hophead, pothead 8 acidhead 9 mainliner 10 aficionado, enthusiast

addiction: 5 habit 9 surrender 10 attachment 11 disposition, enslavement

addition: ell 4 plus, wing 5 annex, rider 6 prefix suburb, suffix 7 adjunct, codicil, joining 8 addendum, increase 9 accession, accretion, amendment, appendage, expansion, extension

in: 4 also, else 7 besides, further

additional: new 4 else, more 5 extra, fresh, other 9 auxiliary 12 supplemental

addled: 4 asea 5 dizzy, giddy, upset 7 mixed up 8 confused 9 befuddled, flustered 10 bewildered

address: aim, sue, woo 4 call, hail, home, tact, talk, 5 abode, court, greet, poise, skill 6 accost, adjust, aplomb, appeal, eulogy, manner, speech 7 lecture, oration, speak to 8 approach, dispatch, harangue, mail drop, petition, presence 9 dexterity, discourse, residence, statement 10 allocution, peroration 11 take a stance

adduce: 4 cite, name 5 offer, quote 6 allege, submit, tender 7 advance, mention, present, suggest 11 give as proof

adeps: fat 4 lard

adept: ace, apt 4 A-one, able, deft, whiz, up on 5 handy, sharp 6 adroit, artist, expert, good at, master 7 capable, 8 skillful 9 dexterous, masterful, tolerable 10 acceptable, consummate, proficient

adequate: 4 fair, okay 5 ample, 6 decent, enough, not bad, plenty 8 all right, possible, suitable 9 competent, effective 10 answerable, sufficient 12 commensurate, satisfactory

a deux: 6 for two, 8 intimate

adhere: 5 cling, stick, 6 cleave, cohere 8 hold fast 12 stay together

adherence: 7 loyalty 8 devotion, fidelity 9 constancy 10 allegiance, attachment

adherent: 4 ally 6 votary 8 believer, disciple, follower, henchman, partisan, servitor, upholder 9 supporter

adhesive: gum, wax 4 bond, glue, tape 5 epoxy, paste 6 cement, gluten, mastic, sticky, viscum 7 stickum 8 birdlime, mucilage 9 tenacious

adhibit: 5 admit, affix, let in 6 attach

adieu: 5 adios, aloha 6 good-by, so long 7 good-bye 8 au revoir, farewell 11 leavetaking, valediction

adipose: fat 4 suet 5 fatty 6 tallow

adit: 5 stulm 6 access, tunnel 7 opening, passage 8 approach, entrance 9 admission, mine entry 10 passageway

adjacent: 4 near, next, nigh 5 close, handy 6 beside, hard by 7 against, meeting 8 abutting, touching 9 adjoining, bordering 10 contiguous, juxtaposed 11 neighboring 12 conterminous

adjective: 8 modifier 9 dependent, qualifier

demonstrative: 4 that, this 5 these, those

limiting: the

verbal: 9 gerundive

adjoin: add 4 abut, 5 touch, verge 6 append, attach, border, butt on 7 contact 8 be next to, neighbor 9 juxtapose

adjourn: end 4 stay 5 close, defer, delay 6 put off, recess 7 disband, suspend 8 dissolve, hold over, postpone, prorogue 9 terminate 11 discontinue

adjudge: 4 deem, find, rule 5 award, grant 6 decide, decree, settle 7 referee 9 arbitrate, determine

adjunct: 4 aide, part 5 annex 6 helper 7 quality 8 addition, appanage, appendix 9 accessory, appendage, associate, auxiliary, colleague 10 complement 11 subordinate 12 appurtenance

adjure: ask, beg, bid 5 plead, 6 appeal, charge 7 beseech, command, implore, entreat

adjust: fit, fix, set 4 bend, suit, trim, true, tune 5 adapt, align 6 attune, change, line up, settle, temper, 7 address, arrange, balance, conform, correct, justify, rectify, work out 8 modulate, regulate, set right 9 harmonize 10 concinnate, coordinate, straighten 11 accommodate, systematize

adjutage: 4 tube 5 spout 6 nozzle

adjutant: 4 aide, 5 stork 6 helper 7 officer 9 assistant, auxiliary

bird: 5 crane, stork 6 argala 7 marabou

admeasure: 5 allot 7 mete out, apportion

Admetus' wife: 8 Alcestis

administer: run 4 dose, rule 5 apply, issue, treat 6 direct, give to, govern, manage 7 conduct, control, deal out, execute, furnish, 8 carry out, dispense 9 look after, supervise 10 distribute 11 superintend

administrator: 7 manager, officer, trustee 8 director, executor 9 executrix

admirable: 5 brave, great 6 worthy 7 capital 8 laudable, splendid 9 deserving, estimable, excellent

name meaning: 7 Miranda

Admiralty Island: 5 Manus

capital: 8 Lorengau

admire: 4 like 5 adore, honor, prize, value 6 esteem, regard, revere, 7 approve, idolize, respect 8 venerate, look up to 11 think well of

admirer: fan 4 beau, buff 5 lover 6 backer, patron 7 booster, devotee, fancier

admission: fee 4 adit 6 access, charge, entree, ticket **7** ingress **8** entrance **10** admittance, concession, confession, disclosure **15** acknowledgement

receipts: **4** gate, take **9** box-office

admit: own **4** avow **5** agree, allow, enter, grant, let in, own up **6** accept, avouch, enroll, induct, permit, take in **7** adhibit, concede, confess, include, profess, receive **8** initiate **9** come clean, recognize **11** acknowledge

admonish: **4** warn **5** alert, chide, scold **6** advise, enjoin, exhort, notify, rebuke, remind **7** caution, counsel, lecture, monitor, reprove **8** reproach **9** reprehend, reprimand, sermonize

ado: **4** fuss, stir, to-do **5** bother, bustle, flurry, hassle, hubbub, pother, ruckus **7** trouble, turmoil **9** commotion, confusion **10** excitement, hullabaloo

adobe: **4** clay **5** brick, house **6** mudcap

adolescence: **5** teens, youth **6** nonage **7** puberty **8** minority **9** salad days

adolescent: lad **4** girl, lass **5** green, minor, young, **6** subdeb **8** immature, juvenile, teenager, youthful **9** pubescent

Adonis: *beloved:* **9** Aphrodite

slayer of: **4** boar

adopt: **4** pass **5** enact **6** accept, assume, borrow, choose, employ, take up **7** approve, embrace, espouse, receive, support **8** advocate, maintain, practice **9** affiliate **10** naturalize **11** appropriate

adorable: **4** cute **5** sweet **6** lovely **7** angelic, lovable, winsome **8** charming, kissable **9** appealing **10** cuddlesome, delightful

adoration: **6** homage **8** devotion, idolatry

adore: **4** love **5** honor **6** admire, dote on, esteem, praise, revere **7** cherish, glorify, idolize, respect, worship **8** hold dear, venerate, **9** delight in

adorn: **4** deck, gild, trim **5** array, begem, grace, primp, prink **6** bedeck, doll up, emboss, enrich, set off **7** bedizen, dignify, dress up, enhance, furbish, garnish, **8** beautify, decorate, emblazon, ornament, trick out **9** bespangle, caparison, embellish, glamorize

ad rem: **8** relevant **9** pertinent **10** to the point

Adriana's servant: **4** Luce

Adriatic: *city:* **6** Venice

island: Bua, Eso **7** Lagosta, Lastovo

peninsula: **6** Istria

port: **4** Bari, Pola **5** Fiume **6** Ancona, Rimini **7** Trieste

resort: **4** Lido **5** Split

river into: **4** Reno **5** Adige, Bosna, Drini, Kerka, Piave

wind: **4** bora **10** tramontana, tramontane (pl.)

adrift: **4** asea, lost **5** loose **6** afloat, astray,

aweigh **8** derelict, homeless, unmoored **9** wandering **10** unanchored

adroit: apt **4** deft, **5** adept, handy, sharp, smart **6** artful, brainy, clever, expert, facile, habile **7** cunning **8** dextrous, skillful **9** dexterous, ingenious, masterful **10** proficient **11** quick-witted, resourceful

adulate: **7** idolize, lionize **8** enshrine, fawn upon, soft-soap **10** slaver over, overpraise

adulator: fan **5** toady **6** yes-man **9** flatterer, sycophant **10** bootlicker

adult: **4** aged, ripe **5** imago, **6** mature, nubile **7** grown-up, tempered **8** seasoned **9** developed, full-blown

adulterate: cut, mix **5** alloy, alter, spike **6** debase, dilute, doctor, weaken **7** falsify, thin out **8** denature **10** tamper with

adulterated: cut **6** impure **8** spurious **11** counterfeit, watered down

adumbrate: **4** bode **5** augur **6** darken, hint at, sketch **7** obscure, outline, portend, presage, suggest **8** indicate, intimate, rough out **10** foreshadow

adust: **6** burned, gloomy, sallow **7** parched **8** scorched **9** sunburned

advance: aid **4** cite, help, lend, loan, rise **5** boost, get on, raise, serve **6** adduce, allege, assign, better, foster, hasten, move up, prepay **7** bring up, elevate, forward, further, improve, proceed, promote, propose, upgrade **8** increase, overture, progress, put forth **9** encourage, get nearer, push ahead **10** accelerate, aggrandize, appreciate **11** improvement, make headway

guard: van **6** patrol **7** outpost

slowly: **4** inch, worm **5** crawl, creep

advanced: **5** ahead, early **7** liberal **8** tolerant **9** premature **10** avant-garde, precocious **11** enlightened, progressive

equally: **7** abreast

most: **8** farthest, foremost, headmost

advantage: use **4** boot, edge, gain, odds **5** asset, favor, start, stead **6** behalf, behoof, profit **7** account, benefit, **8** handicap, interest, leverage, overplus **9** upper hand **11** opportunity, superiority

advantageous: **6** useful **9** expedient, favorable, strategic **10** auspicious, beneficial, commodious, profitable, propitious **11** encouraging

advent: **6** coming **7** arrival **8** approach **11** incarnation

adventitious: **6** casual **7** foreign **8** acquired, episodic **9** extrinsic **10** accidental, fortuitous, incidental **12** nonessential

adventure: **4** feat, lark, risk **5** event, geste, quest **6** chance, danger, hazard **7** exploit **8** escapade **10** enterprise, experience 11 undertaking

adventurer: 7 gambler 9 daredevil, mercenary 13 fortune hunter

adventurous: 4 bold, rash 5 brash 6 daring, errant 8 intrepid, reckless 9 audacious, foolhardy, hazardous, imprudent

adversaria: ana 5 memos, notes 10 miscellany 12 commentaries

adversary: foe 5 enemy, rival 8 opponent 9 assailant 10 antagonist, competitor

adverse: con 4 anti 7 against, counter, harmful, hostile 8 contrary, critical, inimical, negative, opposing, opposite, untoward 9 diametric 11 conflicting, detrimental, disinclined, unfavorable 12 inauspicious, unpropitious

adversity: woe 5 trial 6 misery, sorrow 7 setback, tragedy, trouble 8 calamity, distress, hardship 9 suffering 10 affliction, ill-fortune, misfortune

advert: 4 note 5 refer 6 allude, attend 7 bring up, observe 8 consider, point out

advertise: 4 plug, puff, push 5 bruit 6 blazon, inform, notify, report 7 build up, declare, display, exploit, promote, publish 8 announce, ballyhoo, proclaim 9 broadcast, publicize 10 promulgate

advertisement: 4 bill, sign, spot 6 dodger, insert, notice, teaser 7 affiche, handout, leaflet, release, stuffer, placard 8 circular, handbill 9 broadside, throwaway 10 commercial

book jacket: 5 blurb 11 testimonial

outdoor: 5 flyer 6 banner, poster 9 billboard 10 skywriting 11 marquee sign

advice: tip 4 news, word 6 notice 7 caution, counsel, opinion, pointer, tidings 8 guidance 9 direction 10 admonition, suggestion 11 instruction 12 intelligence, word to the wise 14 recommendation

seek: 5 confer 6 huddle 7 consult

advisable: 4 wise 6 proper 7 politic, prudent 9 befitting, desirable, expedient

advise: 4 read, post, tell, warn 5 coach, guide 6 inform, notify 7 apprise, caution, counsel, suggest 8 acquaint, admonish, advocate, disclose 9 encourage, recommend

adviser, advisor: 4 tout 5 coach, guide 6 nestor 7 monitor, tipster 9 confidant, counselor 10 admonisher, consultant, Dutch uncle, instructor

advisory: 6 notice, report 7 warning 9 hortatory

body: 5 board, panel 7 cabinet, council 9 committee, think tank 10 brain trust

advocate: pro 4 abet, back, urge 5 favor, plead 6 advise, defend, friend, lawyer 7 endorse, espouse, promote, support 8 argue for, champion, hold with, partisan 9 counselor, paraclete, proponent,

recommend 11 intercessor

of new laws: 9 neonomian

adytum: 6 shrine 7 sanctum 9 sanctuary

adz, adze: axe 7 hatchet

relative: 6 pickax

Aeacus: *father:* 4 Zeus

son: 6 Peleus 7 Telamon

Aeetes: *kingdom:* 7 Colchis

daughter: 5 Medea

keeper of: 12 Golden Fleece

Aegean Sea: *ancient peoples:* 5 Psara, Psyra 6 Samian 7 Leleges, Samiote

gulf: 5 Saros 7 Argolis, Corinth, Saronic

island group: 8 Cyclades, Sporades 10 Dodecanese

river into: 6 Struma, Vardar 7 Marista

rock: Aex

Aegeon's wife: 7 Aemilia

Aegir's wife: Ran

aegis, egis: 6 shield 7 auspices, backing, control, defense 8 guidance 9 patronage 10 protection 11 sponsorship

Aegisthus: *father:* 8 Thyestes

mother: 7 Pelopia

slayer: 7 Orestes

victim: 6 Atreus 9 Agamemnon

Aegyptus: *brother:* 6 Danaus

father: 5 Belus

mother: 8 Anchinoe

Aello: 5 Harpy

Aeneas: *beloved:* 4 Dido

companion: 7 Achates

father: 8 Anchises

grandfather: 5 Capys

great-grandson: 4 Brut

mother: 9 Aphrodite

rival: 6 Turnus

son: Iulus 8 Ascanius

wife: 6 Creusa 7 Lavinia

Aeneid: *author:* 6 Vergil, Virgil

archer: 7 Acestes

first word: 4 arma

hero: 6 Aeneas

king slain by Aeneas: 6 Turnus

second word: 8 virumque

steersman: 9 Palinurus

third word: 4 cano

Aengus' mother: 5 Boann

Aeolian lyricist: 6 Sappho

Aeolus' daughter: 6 Canace 8 Halcyone

aeon, eon: age 5 kalpa(Ind.) 8 eternity 12 billion years 14 geologic period

aeonian, eonian: 7 eternal, forever 8 infinite 11 everlasting

aerate: 6 add air, aerify, charge 7 inflate 9 oxygenate, ventilate 11 expose to air

aerial: 4 aery, airy 5 lofty 6 high up, unreal 7 antenna 8 antennae(pl.), ethereal 9 imaginary 10 light as air 11 atmospheric 13 unsubstantial

aerie, eyrie: 4 nest 5 brood 9 penthouse 10 cliff house

aeriform: 6 unreal 7 gaseous 10 intangible

aerobatics: 4 loop, roll 5 stunt 11 flying feats

aerolite: 9 meteorite 10 brontolite

aeronaut: 5 pilot 7 aviator 10 balloonist

aerose: 6 brassy

aerostat: 7 airship, balloon 8 zeppelin 9 dirigible

aerugo: 4 rust 9 verdigris

aes: 4 coin 6 bronze

Aesculapius' teacher: 6 Chiron

Aeson: *brother:* 6 Pelias

son: 5 Jason

Aesop work: 6 Fables

character: ox; ant, ass, dog, fox 4 frog, hare, lion 5 eagle, mouse 8 tortoise 11 grasshopper

aesthete: 8 virtuoso 10 dilettante 11 cognoscente, connoisseur

aesthetic, esthetic: 8 artistic, pleasing, tasteful 9 beautiful 11 well-composed

aet, aetat(L.): 7 of an age

Aeta: Ita 8 Filipino 10 Philippino

Aether's father: 6 Erebus

Aetolian prince: 6 Tydeus

afar: off 4 away, 6 remote 7 distant

affable: 4 open 5 civil, 6 benign, genial, urbane 7 amiable, cordial, likable 8 charming, friendly, gracious, pleasant, sociable 9 agreeable, convivial, courteous 10 accessible 11 complaisant, good-natured 12 easy to talk to

affair: 5 event, issue, thing 6 action, matter 7 concern, lookout 8 business, endeavor, interest, intrigue, occasion 10 engagement, proceeding 11 transaction 12 circumstance

love: 5 amour, tryst 7 liaison, romance 8 intrigue 10 attachment

social: 4 ball, gala 5 party 6 at home, soiree 7 blowout, shindig 9 gathering 11 get together

affect: hit 4 move, stir, sway 5 act on, alter, fancy, feign, touch 6 assume, change, strike, 7 concern, impress, operate, pretend, profess 8 bear upon, frequent, interest, simulate, soften up 9 cultivate, influence 11 counterfeit, hypothecate

each other: 8 interact

affectation: 4 airs, pose, sham 5 put-on 6 façade, fakery 7 pietism 8 artifice, pretense 9 hypocrisy, mannerism 10 false front

affected: 5 moved, stagy 6 chi-chi, tootoo 7 mincing, stilted, studied, touched 8 disposed, involved, mannered, precious 9 unnatural 10 artificial, influenced 11 pretentious 13 grandiloquent

affection: 4 love 5 amour, fancy 6 liking, esteem, malady, regard 7 ailment, emotion, feeling 8 fondness, weakness 10 attachment, friendship, propensity, tenderness

affectionate: 4 fond, warm 6 ardent, doting, loving, soft on, tender 7 amorous, devoted 8 attached 11 sentimental

affianced: 7 engaged 8 intended, plighted, promised 9 betrothed, bride-to-be, groom-to-be 10 set to marry

affiant: 8 deponent

affidavit: 9 statement 10 deposition 11 attestation

affiliate: 4 ally, join, 5 merge, unite 6 attach, branch, relate 7 chapter, connect 9 associate, tie up with 10 subsidiary 11 combine with, group member

affinity: 4 bias 6 accord, liking 7 kinship, rapport 8 relation, sympathy 10 attraction, connection, fellowship, preference, similarity 11 propinquity, resemblance 12 predilection

affirm: 4 aver, avow 5 posit, swear 6 allege, assert, attest, avouch, depose, ratify, uphold, verify 7 declare, profess, testify 8 maintain, validate 9 predicate, pronounce 10 asseverate 11 state as true

affirmative: aye, nod, yea, yep, yes 4 amen, yeah 7 hopeful 8 dogmatic, thumbs up, positive 9 assertive 10 optimistic 11 declarative, predicative

affix: add 4 join, nail, seal 5 annex, pin on, stamp, unite 6 anchor, append, attach, clip to, fasten, staple 7 adhibit, connect, impress, subjoin

afflatus: 6 vision 10 creativity 11 inspiration

afflict: try, vex 4 hurt, pain, rack 5 beset, gripe, grill, harry, wound 6 burden, grieve, harass, pester, plague 7 oppress, torment, trouble 8 distress

afflicted: sad 6 ailing, woeful 7 grieved, doleful, put-upon 8 impaired, stricken, troubled 9 depressed, lacerated, suffering 10 in distress

affliction: rue, woe 4 care, evil, loss, pain 5 cross, grief, trial 6 duress, misery, ordeal, sorrow 7 anguish, disease, illness, scourge, trouble 8 calamity, distress, hardship, sickness 9 adversity, martyrdom 10 heartbreak, misfortune 11 tribulation 12 wretchedness

affluence: 4 flow 6 afflux, influx, riches, wealth 7 fortune 8 opulence 9 abundance, plenitude, profusion, substance 10 prosperity

affluent: fat 4 rich 5 flush, river 6 loaded, stream 7 copious, well off 8 in clover, well-to-do 9 flowing to, tributary 10 in the money, well-heeled 12 on easy street

afford: 4 bear, give, lend, risk 5 grant, incur, spare, stand, yield 6 manage, supply 7 furnish, provide 10 pay the cost

affray: row 4 feud, riot 5 brawl, clash, fight, melee 6 attack, battle, fracas, ruckus, strife, tumult 7 assault, contest, quarrel, scuffle, 9 encounter 10 donnybrook, free-for-all 11 disturbance

affright: awe, cow 5 alarm, daunt, dread, scare, spook 7 startle, terrify 8 frighten 10 intimidate

affront: cut 4 defy, slap, snub 5 abuse, beard 6 insult, jeer at, nettle, offend, slight 7 outrage, provoke, put down 8 disgrace, illtreat, irritate 9 humiliate, indignity, stand up to 10 defamation

afghan: 5 shawl, throw 7 blanket 8 coverlet

Afghan fox: 6 corsac

Afghanistan: *capital:* 5 Kabul
city: 5 Herat, Qalat, Tagab, Tigri 6 Gardez, Ghazni, Kunduz, Maidan 7 Baghlan, Qala Nau 8 Charikar, Kandahar
language: 6 Pashto, Pashtu, Turkic 7 Persian
monetary unit: pul 7 afghani
mountain pass: 6 Khyber, Peiwar
mountain peak: 7 Sikaram 10 Shah Fuladi
mountain range: 8 Koh-i-Baba, Safed Koh 9 Hindu Kush
people: 5 Tajik, Uzbek 6 Hazara, Pathan 7 Pashtun, Sistani 8 Pashtoon
province: 4 Ghor 5 Balkh, Farah, Herat, Logar, Zabul 6 Bamian, Faryab, Ghazni, Kunduz, Paktia, Parwan, Takhar, Wardak
river: 5 Kabul, Kunar 7 Hari Rud, Helmand 8 Amu Darya

aficionado: fan 4 buff 5 freak 7 admirer, devotee 8 follower 10 enthusiast

afield: 4 away 6 abroad, astray, beyond 11 at a distance

afire: 5 aglow, eager 6 ablaze, alight, ardent 7 burning, flaming, ignited

afloat: 4 asea 5 awash 6 adrift, buoyed, natant 7 flooded, rumored 9 operating 10 above water, going about 11 circulating

afoot: 5 about, a pied, astir 6 abroad 7 brewing, walking 8 under way 9 happening 10 in the works, shanks mare

aforesaid: 5 ditto 10 prior named 13 last mentioned

aforethought: 7 planned 10 deliberate 12 premeditated

afraid: rad(Sc.) 4 wary 5 loath, timid 6 aghast, averse, craven, scared 7 alarmed, anxious, fearful 8 cowardly, hesitant, skittish 9 concerned, reluctant, terrified 10 frightened 12 apprehensive, fainthearted 13 pusillanimous

afreet, afrit, afrite: 4 ogre 5 demon,

giant, jinni 7 monster

afresh: 4 anew, over 5 again, newly 6 de novo(L.), encore 8 once more 10 repeatedly 11 from scratch

Africa (see also specific countries):
city: 4 Oran 5 Accra, Cairo, Dakar, Lagos, Rabat, Tunis 6 Bangui, Durban, Harare, Ibadan 7 Algiers, Conakry, Mombasa, Nairobi, Tripoli, Yaounde 8 Cape Town, Freetown, Khartoum, Kinshasa, Monrovia, Pretoria 9 Salisbury, Timbuctoo 10 Addis Ababa, Alexandria, Casablanca 11 Brazzaville, Dar es Salaam 12 Johannesburg, Leopoldville 14 Elisabethville
country: 4 Chad, Mali, Togo 5 Benin, Congo, Egypt, Gabon, Ghana, Kenya, Libya, Niger, Sudan, Venda, Zaire 6 Angola, Gambia, Guinea, Malawi, Rwanda, Uganda, Zambia 7 Algeria, Burundi, Comoros, Lesotho, Liberia, Morocco, Nigeria, Senegal, Somalia, Tunisia 8 Botswana, Cameroon, Djibouti, Ethiopia, Tanzania, Transkei, Zimbabwe 9 Cape Verde, Mauritius, Swaziland 10 Ivory Coast, Madagascar, Mauritania, Mozambique, Seychelles, Upper Volta 11 Sierra Leone, South Africa 12 Guinea-Bissau
desert: 6 Libyan, Nubian, Sahara 8 Kalahari
gulf: 4 Aden 5 Gabes, Sidra 6 Guinea
island: 6 Azores, Djerba 7 Comoros, Madeira, Reunion 8 Canaries, St. Helena 9 Ascension, Cape Verde, Mauritius 10 Fernando Po, Madagascar, Seychelles
lake: 4 Chad, Tana 5 Abaya, Kyoga, Mweru, Ngami, Nyasa, Tumba 6 Albert, Chilwa, Dilolo, Kariba, Moeris, Rudolf, Shirwa 7 Leopold, Turkana 8 Victoria 9 Bangweulu 10 Tanganyika
language: Gur, Ibo, Kwa, Twi 4 Akan, Geez, Saho, Taal 5 Bantu, Fanti, Galla, Hausa, Tigre 6 Arabic, Berber, Gurage 7 Amharic, Argobba, Khoisan, Swahili 8 Cushitic, Kingwana, Tigrinya 9 Afrikaans
mountain: 4 Pare 5 Atlas, Elgon, Kenya 7 Cathkin 8 Cameroon 9 Champagne 11 Drakensberg, Kilimanjaro
people: Edo, Ewe, Fon, Ibo, Ijo, Kru, Vai, Vei, Yao 4 Agau, Agni, Akim, Akka, Akra, Alur, Arab, Asha, Bari, Beja, Boer, Boni, Copt, Efik, Egba, Ekoi, Fula, Hutu, Igbo, Kafa, Lozi, Luri, Madi, Moor, Nama, Nuba, Nupe, Qung, Riff, Saho, Sara, Yaka, Zulu 5 Bantu, Bassa, Batwa, Dinka, Fanti, Felup, Galla, Grebo, Gurma, Hausa, Inkra, Kafir, Masai, Mande, Mossi, Pygmy, Rundi, Shluh, Temne, Tutsi 6 Bariba, Basuto, Berber, Damara, Dorobo, Dyerma, Fu-

lani, Hamite, Harari, Herero, Kabyle, Kikuyu, Nilote, Senufo, Somali, Tuareg, Ubangi, Watusi, Yoruba, Zenaga 7 Akwamba, Ashango, Ashanti, Bedouin, Dahoman, Malinke, Sandawe, Songhai, Swahili 8 Hottentot, Mandingo

river: Nun, Omo 4 Athi, Geba, Nile, Ruvu, Tana 5 Benue, Binue, Chari, Chobe, Congo, Niger, Shari, Volta 6 Atbara, Bafing, Gambia, Joliba, Orange, Ruvuma, Sabaki, Ubangi, 7 Calabar, Limpopo, Lualaba, Luapula, Semliki, Senegal, Zambezi 9 Crocodile

Afrikaans: 4 Boer, Taal

Afro: 6 hair-do

aft: 4 back 6 astern, behind 9 posterior, to the rear

opposite of: 4 fore

after: for 4 next, past 5 since, apres(F.) 6 behind, beyond, hinder 8 in back of, rearward 9 following, in spite of 10 concerning, looking for, subsequent

a fashion: 6 in a way, partly 7 somehow 9 to a degree

all: but, yet 5 still 6 though 7 besides, however 9 in any case 10 just the same 11 nonetheless

awhile: 4 anon, soon 5 later

after-dinner: 12 postprandial

aftermath: 5 issue 6 effect, payoff, result, sequel, upshot 7 outcome 8 follow-up 11 consequence

afternoon nap: 6 siesta

afternoon performance: 7 matinee

afterthought: 9 added idea 10 doubletake 15 late inspiration

in letter: 10 postscript

afterwards: 4 then 5 later 7 by and by 9 thereupon 11 in the future 12 subsequently

aga, agha: 4 lord 5 chief, title 6 leader 8 official 9 commander

wife: 5 begum

agacella: 8 antelope

Agag's slayer: 6 Samuel

again: bis(F.) 4 anew, more, over 6 afresh, de novo(L.), encore 7 besides, further 8 moreover, once more 12 additionally

against: con 4 anti, from, near, upon 6 beside, facing, next to, versus 7 opposed, vis-a-vis 9 counter to, in spite of 10 concerning, respecting

against the law: 7 illegal, illicit 12 unauthorized

agal: 4 cord, rope

agalloch: 5 garoo 8 calambac 9 aloeswood, calambour, eaglewood

Agamemnon: *avenger:* 7 Orestes

brother: 8 Menelaus

daughter: 7 Electra 9 Iphigenia

father: 6 Atreus

rival: 9 Aegisthus

son: 7 Orestes

wife: 12 Clytemnestra

agape: 4 agog, ajar, open 6 amazed 7 yawning 9 awestruck 10 bewildered, confounded, slack-jawed 11 dumbfounded, open-mouthed

agar, agar-agar: 6 gelose 12 algae extract 13 culture medium

agate: mib, taw 4 ruby 6 achate, marble, quartz 8 type size 10 chalcedony

agave: 4 aloe 5 amole, datil 6 maguey, mescal, pulque 9 amaryllis

fiber: 4 pita 5 istle, sisal

age: eld, eon, era 4 aeon, grow, time 5 cycle, epoch, ripen, years 6 mature, mellow, period, siecle(F.), wither 7 century, develop 8 blue moon, duration, eternity, lifetime, majority 10 generation

geological: See **geology:** age

modern: 5 space 6 atomic

of one's age: 5 aetat.(L.)

same: 6 coeval

aged: old 4 ripe 5 anile, dated, hoary, passe 6 feeble, infirm, mature, senile 7 ancient, elderly 8 seasoned, timeworn 9 senescent, up in years, venerable 10 antiquated

ageless: 7 eternal 8 enduring, timeless

agency: 4 firm, hand 5 cause, force, lever, means, proxy 6 bureau, medium, office 7 company, vehicle 9 influence, operation 10 instrument

agenda: 4 card, list 5 slate 6 record, docket 7 program 8 calendar, schedule 10 memorandum

Agenor: *daughter:* 6 Europa

father: 7 Antenor

son: 6 Cadmus

agent: fed, spy 4 doer, g-man, T-man 5 actor, buyer, cause, envoy, force, means, organ, proxy 6 broker, dealer, deputy, factor, medium, seller 7 bailiff, channel, facient, steward 8 assignee, emissary, executor, operator, promoter, salesman 9 go-between 10 commissary, instrument 11 facilitator 12 intermediary 14 representative

appoint: 6 depute 8 deputize

drug: 4 nark

insurance: 11 underwriter

agger: 4 road, tide 5 mound 7 rampart 9 earthwork 10 prominence

agglomerate: 4 heap, lump, mass, pile, 7 cluster 9 aggregate 10 collection 12 volcanic rock

agglutination: 5 union 8 adhesion

aggrandize: 4 lift 5 boost, exalt, raise 7 advance, augment, build up, dignify, elevate, enlarge, ennoble, glorify, magnify, promote 8 increase

aggravate: irk, nag, vex 4 gall, rile 5 anger, annoy, peeve 6 nettle, pester, worsen 7 enhance, enlarge, incense, magnify, provoke 8 aggrieve, heighten, increase, irritate 9 intensify, make acute 10 exacerbate, exasperate 11 fan the flame, get one's goat

aggregate: all, sum 4 bulk, mass 5 add up, bunch, gross, total, unite, whole 6 amount, volume 9 accretion, composite 10 accumulate 11 agglomerate

aggregation: 4 herd 5 flock, group, hoard 7 cluster, company 8 quantity 9 congeries, gathering 10 assemblage, collection, cumulation 11 association, combination

aggression: war 4 raid 6 attack, injury 7 assault, offense 8 invasion 9 intrusion 10 initiative 11 provocation 12 encroachment

aggressive: 4 bold 5 pushy 7 scrappy 8 militant, bellicose 10 pugnacious 11 hard-hitting 12 enterprising

aggressor: 7 invader 8 attacker 9 assailant

aggrieve: try 4 harm, hurt, pain 5 harry, wrong 6 injure, offend 7 afflict, oppress, trouble 8 distress 9 aggravate, persecute

aghast: 6 afraid 7 shocked, stunned 8 appalled 9 horrified, petrified, stupefied, terrified 11 scared stiff

agile: 4 deft, fast, spry, wiry 5 alert, brisk, light, lithe, quick 6 active, adroit, limber, lively, nimble, supple, valant 7 lissome, springy 8 dextrous

agio: 7 premium 10 banking fee

agitate: fan, irk, jar, vex 4 move, rile, rock, roil, seek 5 alarm, churn, drive, harry, rouse, shake, upset 6 debate, excite, foment, harass, incite, rattle, ruffle 7 discuss, disturb, fluster, inflame, perturb, provoke, push for, trouble 8 activate, convulse, disquiet, distress 9 make waves 10 discompose

agitation: 4 flap, stew 5 furor, storm 6 bustle, energy, flurry, tumult, unrest, uproar 7 ferment, flutter, rampage, tempest, turmoil 8 paroxysm, upheaval, violence 9 commotion, confusion 10 excitement, turbulence 11 trepidation

prone to: 9 emotional

Aglaia: 5 Grace

aglet, aiglet: pin, tag 8 metal tip 9 fancy stud 11 shoelace tip

agley: 4 awry 5 askew, wrong 6 aslant

agnate: 4 akin 6 allied 7 connate, kindred 8 paternal

agnomen: 5 alias 7 epithet 8 nickname

agnostic: 7 doubter, infidel, skeptic 8 nescient 10 unbeliever 11 freethinker

agnus dei: 4 hymn, lamb 6 prayer 8 mass part

ago: 4 back, erst, past, syne(Sc.), yore 5 since

agog: 4 avid, keen 5 eager 6 lively 7 all eyes, excited, popeyed 8 bursting, worked up 9 expectant, impatient 10 breathless

agon: 6 debate 7 contest 8 conflict, struggle 11 competition

agonize: 4 bear, rack 6 strain, writhe 10 excruciate

agony: 4 hell, pain 5 dolor, grief, throe, trial 6 misery 7 anguish, despair, torment, torture, travail 8 distress, 9 heartache, nightmare, suffering 11 tribulation

agora: 8 assembly 11 market place

agouti, agouty: 6 rodent

relative: 4 paca 9 guinea pig

Agra tomb: 8 Taj Mahal

agrafe, agraffe: 4 hook 5 clamp, clasp 6 eyelet 9 fastening, sculpture

agrarian: 5 rural 8 agrestic, pastoral 10 campestral 12 agricultural, land reformer

agree: fit 4 jibe, side, suit 5 admit, allow, grant, match, tally, yield, unite 6 accede, accord, assent, comply, concur, square, submit 7 arrange, comport, concede, conform, consent, promise 8 check out, coincide, get along, quadrate 9 acquiesce, be willing, congruous, cooperate, harmonize, reconcile 10 correspond, homologate

agreeable: 4 nice 5 ready, sweet 7 amiable, welcome, willing 8 amenable, charming, pleasant, pleasing, sociable, suitable 9 appealing, compliant, consonant 10 acceptable, compatible, convenient 11 consentient

render: 7 dulcify

agreement: nod 4 bond, deal, pact 5 lease 6 treaty, unison 7 bargain, compact, consent, entente, harmony, rapport 8 contract, covenant 9 concordat, indenture 10 accordance 11 arrangement, concordance, concurrence 13 understanding

in opinion: 9 consensus, unanimity

secret: 5 covin 9 collusion 10 conspiracy

written: 6 cartel 8 contract

agremens, agrements: 6 graces 8 niceties 9 amenities

agrestic: 5 rural 6 rustic 7 bucolic 10 unpolished

agriculture: 7 farming, tillage 8 agronomy 9 husbandry

area: 11 breadbasket

college student: 5 aggie

establishment: 4 farm 5 grove, ranch 7 orchard 8 vineyard

god: 4 Nabu, Nebo, Thor 6 Faunus,

Tammuz 8 Amaethon

goddess: Ops 5 Ceres 7 Demeter

machine: 4 disk, plow 5 baler, drill, mower 6 binder, harrow, header, reaper, seeder, tedder 7 combine, tractor 8 thrasher, thresher 9 separator 10 cultivator 11 caterpillar

pert to: 7 georgic 8 geoponic

science: 8 agrology 11 arviculture

agriculturist: 6 farmer, grower 7 planter, rancher 10 husbandman, orchardist

Agrippina: *brother:* 8 Caligula

husband: 8 Claudius

son: 4 Nero

aground: 6 ashore 7 beached 8 stranded

agrypnia: 8 insomnia 13 sleeplessness

agua: 4 toad

aguacate: 7 avocado

ague: 5 chill, fever 7 malaria

ague tree: 9 sassafras

agueweed: 7 boneset, comfrey, gentian 10 eupatorium

Ahab: *daughter* 7 Athalia 8 Athaliah

father: 4 Omri

wife: 7 Jezebel

Ahasuerus: *minister:* 5 Haman

wife: 6 Vashti

Ahaz: *son:* 8 Hezekiah

wife: Abi

Ahaziah's sister: 9 Jehosheba 11 Jehosobeath

ahead: 4 fore 5 early 6 before, onward 7 betimes, forward, in front, leading, one up on 8 advanced, anterior 9 in the lead, preceding 10 beforehand

Ahinoam: *husband:* 4 Saul 5 David

son: 5 Ammon

Aholibamah's husband: 4 Esau

Ahriman's angel: div 4 deev, deva

ahu: 5 mound 7 gazelle 8 boundary, memorial 9 stone heap

ahuehuete: 5 cedar 6 sabino 7 cypress

ai: 5 sloth 8 edentate

aid: 4 abet, back, help 5 allay, boost, coach, favor, grant, serve, treat 6 assist, relief, remedy, rescue, succor, uphold 7 advance, be of use, forward, further, subsidy, support 8 befriend 9 alleviate, auxiliary, give a hand 10 facilitate, go to bat for 11 collaborate

Aida: *composer:* 5 Verdi

father: 8 Amonasro

lover: 7 Radames

rival: 7 Amneris

aide: 6 deputy, second 7 officer, orderly 8 adjutant 9 assistant, attendant, man Friday 11 subordinate

aigrette: 5 egret, heron, plume, spray 8 feathers

ail: 4 ache, fail, pain 6 affect, bother, falter, suffer 7 decline, feel ill 8 take sick 10 feel poorly

ailment (see also **disease**): 6 malady 7 disease, illness 8 disorder, sickness, weakness 9 affection, complaint, infirmity 10 affliction, disability 13 indisposition

aim: end, try 4 bent, goal, head, plan 5 essay, level, point, sight, train 6 aspire, design, direct, intend, intent, scheme, strive, target 7 address, attempt, go after, propose, purpose, resolve 8 ambition, consider, endeavor, estimate, shoot for, zero in on 9 calculate, intention, objective 11 destination

aimless: 4 idle 5 blind 6 chance, random 7 erratic 8 drifting 9 desultory, haphazard, hit-or-miss, senseless 10 undirected 11 to no purpose

aimlessness: 8 flanerie

aine: 5 elder 6 senior

air: sky 4 aria, aura, lilt, mien, pose, song, tell, tune, vent 5 ether, ozone, style, voice 6 aerate, aerify, allure, aspect, broach, cachet, expose, manner, melody, regard, vanity, welkin 7 bearing, display, exhibit, publish 8 attitude, behavior, carriage, demeanor, proclaim 9 broadcast, semblance 10 appearance, atmosphere, deportment 11 affectation, haughtiness

containing: 9 pneumatic

current: 4 wind 5 draft 6 breeze 7 draught

downward motion (pert. to): 9 katabatic

element: 4 neon 5 argon, xenon 6 helium, oxygen 7 krypton 8 nitrogen

up in the: 5 aloft, angry 6 agitated 9 unsettled 10 in suspense, not decided

overcast: 4 haze, smog 5 smaze 7 pea soup 10 cloudiness

air plant: 8 epiphyte

air pressure: 5 baric

air propeller: fan

air spirit: 5 Ariel, sylph

aircraft (see also **spacecraft**): 4 kite 5 blimp, plane 6 copter, glider 7 balloon, chopper 8 aerostat, airplane, autogyro, zeppelin 9 dirigible 10 helicopter

carrier: 7 flattop

group: 4 wing 5 fleet 6 flight 10 escadrille

fleet formation: 7 echelon

manufacturer: 4 Lear, Vega 5 Astra, Piper 6 Bendix, Boeing, Cessna, Hughes, United, Vultee, Wright 7 Convair, Curtiss, Douglas, Grumman, Tupolev 8 Ilyushin, Lockheed, Northrop, Republic 9 McDonnell 11 DeHavilland

motorless: 6 glider

part: fin 4 keel, tail, wing 5 cabin 6 cabane 7 aileron, cockpit, nacelle 8 fusilage 9 empennage

pilotless: 5 drone

route: 6 skyway

route marker: 5 pylon

shelter: 6 hangar

vapor: 8 contrail

airing: 4 walk 6 pasear 8 exposure

airplane: jet, MIG, SST 4 gyro, zero 5 avion(F., Sp.), liner 6 bomber, copter, glider 7 clipper, fighter 9 transport

battle: 8 dogfight

dropper of A-bomb: 8 Enola Gay

inventor: 6 Wright

maneuver: dip 4 buzz, dive, loop, roll 8 hedgehop, nosedive, sideslip, tailspin 10 barrel roll

operator: 5 flier, flyer, pilot 7 aviator 8 aeronaut

Supersonic transport: 8 Concorde

airport: 5 drome 8 airdrome, airfield 9 aerodrome

area: 5 apron, tower 6 runway 7 taxiway

Airport terminal:

Amsterdam: 8 Schiphol

Berlin: 5 Gatow, Tegel 9 Tempelhof

Boston: 7 Logan

Chicago: 5 O'Hare

Copenhagen: 7 Kastrup

Denver: 9 Stapleton

Dublin: 7 Shannon

London: 7 Croydon, Gatwick 8 Heathrow

Newfoundland: 6 Gander

New York: JFK 7 Kennedy 9 La Guardia

Paris: 4 Orly 8 De Gaulle 9 Le Bourget

Rome: 7 Da Vinci 8 Ciampino 9 Fiumicino

Tokyo: 6 Atsugi, Narita

Scotland: 9 Prestwick

Washington: 6 Dulles 8 National

airs: 4 show 7 hauteur 8 pretense 9 arrogance 10 uppishness, affectation

airtight: 6 sealed 8 hermetic 9 foolproof 12 impenetrable, invulnerable

airy: gay 4 cool, rare, thin 5 empty, light, lofty, merry 6 aerial, breezy, jaunty, jocund, lively 7 haughty 8 affected, animated, debonair, delicate, ethereal, flippant, graceful, trifling, volatile 9 sprightly, visionary, vivacious 11 atmospheric 13 insubstantial, unsubstantial

aisle: way 4 lane, path, walk 5 alley 7 passage 8 corridor 10 passageway

ait: oat(Sc.) 4 eyot, holm, isle 5 islet

ajar: 4 open 10 discordant

Ajax's father: 7 Telamon

ajonjoli: 6 sesame

akia: 5 shrub 6 poison

akimbo: 4 bent 6 angled 7 crooked

akin: sib 4 near 5 alike, close 6 agnate, allied 7 cognate, connate, related, similar 9 analogous 10 comparable, correlated 11 consanguine

aku: 6 bonito 10 victorfish

akule: 4 fish, scad 7 goggler

ala: 4 axil, drum, wing 6 axilla, recess

Alabama: *capital:* 10 Montgomery

city: Opp 4 Elba, Troy 5 Ozark, Piper, Selma 6 Dothan, Jasper, Mobile 7 Cullman, Gadsden, Opelika 8 Anniston 10 Birmingham, Huntsville, Tuscaloosa

county: Lee 4 Bibb, Clay, Dale, Hale, Pike 5 Coosa, Lamar 6 Blount, Elmore, Etowah, Greene, Shelby, Sumter 7 Autauga, Chilton, Colbert, Marengo, Pickens, Winston 8 Escambia

explorer: 6 De Soto

Indian tribe: 5 Creek 6 Tohome 7 Choctaw, Koasati

motto: 21 We dare defend our rights

mountain: 6 Cheaha 7 Lookout, Raccoon

river: Pea 5 Coosa 6 Cahaba, Mobile, Sipsey, Tensaw 7 Alabama, Conecuh, Sepulga 9 Tennessee, Tombigbee

state bird: 12 yellowhammer

state fish: 6 tarpon

state flower: 8 camellia

state nickname: 12 Heart of Dixie

state tree: 4 pine

alabaster: 6 gypsum 7 calcite 9 aragonite

alacrity: 4 zest 5 haste, speed 8 celerity, dispatch, rapidity 9 briskness, eagerness, readiness 10 enthusiasm, promptness 11 willingness

Aladdin's lamp spirits: 4 jinn 5 genni

a la diable: 7 deviled 8 seasoned

alameda: 4 mall, walk 9 promenade

Alamo: 4 fort 5 aspen 6 battle, poplar, shrine 7 mission 10 cottonwood

hero: 5 Bowie 8 Crockett

a la mode: 4 chic 7 stylish 11 fashionable

alant: 10 sneezeweed

alar: 6 pteric, winged 8 axillary, winglike 10 wing-shaped

opposite of: 7 apteral

alarm: din, SOS 4 bell, fear 5 alert, clock, noise, panic, scare, siren, upset 6 alarum, appall, buzzer, dismay, excite, outcry, signal, tocsin 7 disturb, startle, warning 8 frighten, surprise 9 commotion 11 disturbance, trepidation 13 consternation

alarmist: 9 Cassandra, pessimist, worrywart 11 scaremonger 13 prophet of doom

alas: ach, woe 5 alack 6 ochone(Sc.) 8 welladay, wellaway 9 alackaday 12 interjection

Alaska: *borough:* 5 Kenai, Sitka 6 Haines, Juneau, Kodiak 10 Bristol Bay, North Slope

capital: 6 Juneau

city: Eek 4 Nome 5 Sitka 6 Barrow,

Bethel, Chevak, Kodiak, Naknek 9 Anchorage, Fairbanks, Ketchikan
discovered by: 11 Vitus Bering
glacier: 4 Muir 8 Columbia
highway: 5 Alcan
island: 4 Adak, Atka, Attu 5 Kiska, Umnak 6 Agattu, Kodiak, Shuyak 7 Afognak, Baranof, Diomede, Nunivak
island group: Fox, Rat 4 Near 7 Fur Seal 8 Aleutian, Pribilof 9 Alexander, Andreanof
mountain peak: 4 Bona 5 Spurr 6 Katmai 7 Foraker, St. Elias 8 McKinley 9 Michelson
mountain range: 5 Baird 6 Brooks, De Long 7 Chugach 8 Wrangell
native: Auk 4 Dene, Tena 5 Aleut, Inuit 6 Ahtena, Eskimo, Innuit 7 Ingalik, Khotana, Koyukon, Tlingit
peninsula: 5 Kenai 6 Seward
purchase (1867): 12 "Seward's Folly"
river: 5 Chena, Kobuk, Yukon 6 Copper, Innoko, Noatak, Tanana 7 Koyukuk, Susitna 9 Kuskokwim, Matanuska, Porcupine
sea: 6 Bering 7 Chukchi
state bird: 9 ptarmigan
state fish: 6 salmon
state flower: 11 forget-me-not
state motto: 16 North to the future
state tree: 6 spruce
unofficial nickname: 12 Last Frontier
volcano: 5 Kukak 6 Griggs, Mageik, Seguam 7 Redoubt, Torbert
alate: ant 5 aphid 6 insect, winged
alb, albe: 7 camisia 8 vestment
albacore: 4 tuna 5 tunny 6 germon
Albania: *capital:* 6 Tirana
city: 5 Berat, Vlore 6 Avlona, Durres, Valona 7 Chimara, Coritza, Durazzo, Elbasan, Koritza, Prevesa, Scutari 8 Tepeleni
dialect: Geg 4 Cham, Gheg, Tosc, Tosk 7 Ghegish, Toskish
former king: Zog
lake: 5 Ohrid 6 Prespa 7 Scutari
monetary unit: lek 6 qintar
mountain: 4 Alps 6 Pindus
river: 4 Arta, Drin 5 Buene, Seman 6 Vijose
soldier: 7 palikar
albatross: 4 bird 5 nelly 6 fabric, gooney 9 hindrance, mallemuck 11 encumbrance
albeit: but, tho 5 altho, while 6 though 8 although 10 for all that 15 notwithstanding
Alberta: *capital:* 8 Edmonton
city: 4 Olds 5 Banff, Edson 7 Calgary 10 Lethbridge 11 Medicine Hat
lake: 4 Cold 5 Slave 6 Legend, Louise, Pigeon 8 Peerless

mountain peak: 5 Trout 6 Robson 7 Wallace 8 Columbia 10 Eisenhower
mountain range: 7 Rockies
province of: 6 Canada
provincial bird: 9 horned owl
provincial flower: 8 wild rose
resort: 5 Banff 6 Jasper 10 Lake Louise
river: Bow 4 Milk 5 Peace, Smoky 6 Battle, Oldman, Wapiti 7 Red Deer, Wabasca 9 Athabasca
Albion: 6 Anglia 7 England
albula: 5 chiro 8 bonefish
album: ana 4 book 6 record 8 register 9 anthology, scrapbook 10 collection
albumen 8 egg white
albuminoid: 7 elastin, keratin, protein 8 collagen
alburnum: 7 sapwood
alcazar: 6 castle, palace 8 fortress
Alcestis: *father:* 6 Pelias
husband: 7 Admetus
rescuer: 8 Heracles, Hercules
alchemy: *art* 5 magic 7 sorcery 11 thaumaturgy 13 transmutation
god: 6 Hermes
Alcidice: *husband:* 9 Salmoneus
daughter: 4 Tyro
Alcinous: *daughter:* 8 Nausicaa
wife: 5 Arete
Alcmaeon: *father:* 10 Amphiaraus
wife: 10 Callirrhoe
Alcmene's husband: 10 Amphitryon
alcohol: 5 booze, ethyl, vinyl 6 liquor, methyl 7 ethanol, spirits 8 methanol
aromatic: 8 farnesol, geraniol, linalool
crystalline: 6 guaiol, 7 menthol, talitol 8 mannitol
liquid: 5 allyl, butyl 6 pentyl 7 butanol 8 glycerol
radical: 4 amyl
solid: 5 cetyl 6 sterol 11 cholesterol
standard: 5 proof
alcoholic: 6 addict 9 spiritous 11 dipsomaniac 12 intoxicating
alcoholic drink: ale, gin, rum 4 beer, grog, wine 5 julep, negus, toddy, vodka 6 brandy, liquor, whisky 7 liqueur, whiskey 8 cocktail, highball, vermouth
Alcott heroine: Amy, Meg 4 Beth
alcove: bay 4 nook 5 arbor, bower, niche, oriel 6 cranny, gazebo, recess 7 cubicle, dinette, pergola 8 alhacena(Sp.) 11 compartment
al dente: 13 firm to the bite, not overcooked
alder: arn(Sc.) 4 tree 5 shrub
genus: 5 alnus
ale: mum 4 beer, bock, brew 5 lager, nappy(Sc.), stout 6 porter, stingo 8 beverage
mixed with sweetener: 4 flip 7 bragget

ale mug: 4 toby 5 stein

Alea: 6 Athena

alee: 5 ahead 7 leeward

opposite of: 5 stoss 8 windward

alehouse: bar, pub 4 cafe 6 bistro, saloon, tavern 7 taproom 8 grogshop 10 beer garden 11 rathskeller

alembic: 5 still 6 retort, vessel 7 refiner 9 distiller

Alençon product: 4 lace

alert: 4 gleg(Sc.), warn, wary 5 agile, alarm, alive, awake, brisk, eager, ready, sharp, siren 6 active, bright, lively, nimble, tocsin 7 wakeful 8 vigilant, watchful 9 observant, wide-awake 11 circumspect

alette: 4 wing 8 abutment

Aleutian Island: 4 Adak, Atka, Attu 5 Amlia, Kiska, Umnak 6 Akutan, Amukta, Kodiak, Seguam 7 Kagamil 8 Amchitka, Unalaska

group: Fox, Rat 4 Near 9 Andreanof

alewife: 4 fish 6 allice 7 herring, pompano, walleye

Alexander: *birthplace:* 5 Pella

father: 6 Philip

horse: 10 Bucephalus

kingdom: 9 Macedonia

mistress: 8 Campaspe

tutor: 9 Aristotle

victory: 4 Gaza, Tyre 5 Egypt, Issus 6 Arbela, Persia 7 Babylon

Alexandria: *bishop:* 10 Athanasius

magistrate: 8 alabarch

patriarch: 4 papa

theologian: 5 Arius

Alexandria Quartet: *author:* 7 Durrell

books: 4 Clea 7 Justine 9 Balthazar 10 Mountolive

narrator: 6 Darley

alfalfa: hay 6 fodder, lucern 7 lucerne

alforja: bag 5 pouch 6 wallet 9 saddlebag

alga: 4 kelp, nori 6 desmid, diatom, lichen 7 seaweed 8 plankton, rockweed 9 stonewort

genus: 5 dasya 6 alaria, nostoc, padina

study: 8 algology

algarroba: 5 carob 8 mesquite, raintree

Algeria: *capital:* 7 Algiers

city: 4 Oran 5 Blida, Medea, Setif 6 Biskra 7 Tlemcen 11 Constantine

department: 4 Oran 5 Alger, Batna, Oasis, Saida, Setif 6 Annaba, Saoura, Tiaret 7 Al Asnam 11 Constantine

desert: 6 Sahara

known to Romans as: 7 Numidia

measure: pik 5 rebis, tarri 6 termin

monetary unit: 5 dinar 7 centime

mountain: 5 Atlas

people: 5 Arabs 7 Berbers, Kabyles

river: 7 Cheliff, Sheliff

seaport: 4 Oran 6 Annaba 7 Algiers,

weight: 4 rotl

algid: 4 cold, cool 6 chilly, clammy

Alhambra: 6 palace 7 citadel

site: 7 Granada

Ali: *descendant:* 7 fatimid 8 fatimite

wife: 6 Fatima

Ali Baba: *brother:* 6 Cassim

password: 6 sesame

slave: 8 Morgiana 10 woodcutter

alias: AKA 7 epithet, pen name 9 pseudonym 10 nom de plume 11 assumed name

alibi: 4 plea 6 excuse 7 pretext 10 offer an out

Alice in Wonderland: *author:* 7 Carroll

cat of Alice: 5 Dinah

character: 5 Queen 6 Walrus 7 Duchess 8 Dormouse 9 Carpenter, Mad Hatter, March Hare 11 Cheshire cat, White Rabbit

alien: 5 fremd 6 exotic 7 foreign, hostile, invader, opposed, strange 8 outsider, stranger 9 different, extrinsic, foreigner, immigrant, outlander, unrelated

alienate: 4 part, wean 6 convey, devest 8 disunite, estrange, separate, transfer 9 disaffect 10 cause a rift

alienist: 6 shrink 12 psychiatrist

aliform: 8 winglike 10 wing-shaped

alight: sit 4 land, rest 5 aglow, lodge, perch, roost 6 arrive, bright, settle 7 deplane, descend, lighted, radiant 8 dismount 9 disembark, touch down

align, aline: 4 true 5 array, level 6 adjust, even up 7 marshal 8 regulate 10 straighten, join up with

alike: 4 akin, same 5 equal, twins 7 similar, uniform 8 of a piece 9 congruent, duplicate, identical 10 comparable

aliment: pap 4 food 6 viands 7 pabulum, rations 9 nutriment, substance 10 sustenance 11 nourishment

alimony: 4 keep 9 allowance 10 settlement 11 maintenance 12 support money

alive: 4 keen, spry, vive(F.) 5 alert, astir, aware, brisk, quick, vital, vivid 6 active, extant, living 7 dynamic, vibrant 8 animated, existent, swarming 9 breathing, sprightly, unexpired 10 not out of it, unforgotten

alkali: lye, reh 4 kali, salt, soda, usar

volatile: 7 ammonia

alkaline: *remedy:* 7 antacid

salt: 5 borax

alkaloid: 6 conine, heroin, eserin 7 caffein, cocaine, codeine 7 quinine 8 atropine, caffeine, morphine 10 strychnine

all: sum 5 gross, quite, total, whole 6 entire, in toto, solely, wholly 7 plenary 8 entirely, everyone, totality 9 aggregate, everybody 10 altogether, completely, everything, thoroughly 11 exclusively

all-fired: 7 extreme 9 excessive 10 inordinate

all in: 4 beat 5 tired, weary 6 bushed, pooped 7 worn out 9 exhausted

all-knowing: 10 omniscient

all out: 7 utterly 9 full scale 10 unreserved

all over: 4 done 5 ended 8 finished 9 universal 10 everywhere, throughout

all right: yes 4 okay 6 agreed 9 hunkydory

all there: 4 sane

allay: 4 calm, cool, ease, lull 5 abate, quell, quiet, still 6 pacify, reduce, soften, soothe, temper 7 appease, assuage, comfort, compose, lighten, mollify, relieve 8 mitigate, palliate 9 alleviate

allege: 4 aver, avow, cite 5 claim, offer, plead, state 6 affirm, assert, charge 7 advance, ascribe, declare, present, profess 8 maintain 9 attribute 10 asseverate

allegiance: tie 4 duty 5 honor 6 fealty, homage 7 loyalty, tribute 8 devotion, fidelity 9 constancy, obedience 10 obligation

violation of: 7 treason 9 defection

allegory: 4 myth, tale 5 fable, story 7 parable 8 apologue

alleviate: aid 4 ease, help 5 abate, allay, salve, slake 6 lenify, lessen, soften 7 assuage, lighten, relieve 8 diminish, mitigate, moderate, palliate

alley: via, way 4 lane, mall, path, walk 5 byway 6 vennel(Sc.) 7 passage

back: 4 slum

blind: 7 dead end 8 cul-de-sac

alliance: 4 pact 5 union 6 accord, fusion, league, treaty 7 compact, entente, society 8 affinity, agnation, covenant 9 coalition 10 federation, fellowship 11 affiliation, association, confederacy, partnership

allice, allis: 4 shad

allied: 4 akin 6 agnate, in with, joined, linked, united 7 cognate, connate, germane, kindred, related, similar 9 analogous, connected

alligator: 6 caiman, cayman, jacare, yacare 9 crocodile

alligator pear: 7 avocado 8 aguacate

allium: 4 leek 5 onion 6 chives, garlic

allmouth: 6 angler

allocate: 5 allot, allow, award, share 6 assign 7 earmark, mete out 8 set aside 9 apportion 10 distribute

allonge: 5 rider 12 ballet stance

allot: tag 4 give 5 award, grant, share 6

accord, assign, bestow, design, ordain, ration 7 deal out, dole out, let have, present, pro-rate, reserve, specify 8 allocate 9 apportion, parcel out, prescribe 10 distribute

allow let 4 bear, lend 5 admit, defer, grant, stand, yield 6 accept, assign, endure, permit, suffer 7 approve, concede, confess, own up to, suppose 8 consider, sanction, tolerate 9 authorize, give leave 11 acknowledge

allowance: fee 4 agio, edge, gift, odds, part 5 leave, quota, share 6 bounty, margin, salary 7 aliment, alimony, measure, pension, portion, stipend 8 discount, handicap, quantity, sanction 9 advantage, allotment, deduction, reduction, tolerance 10 concession, permission

short: 6 ration 9 scrimping

traveling: 7 mileage

weight: 4 tare, tret 7 scalage

alloy: mix 4 fuse 5 blend 7 mixture 8 compound 9 composite 10 adulterate, amalgamate

carbon and iron: 5 steel

Chinese: 7 paktong 8 packtong

copper and aluminum: 9 duralumin

copper, iron and zinc: 4 aich 7 rheotan

copper and tin: 6 bronze, oreide, ormolu, oroide, pewter

copper and zinc: 5 brass 6 tombac 8 arsedine

costume jewelry: 4 aich 6 oreide, ormolu, oroide, tombac 8 arsedine

fusible: 6 solder

gold and silver: 4 asem 8 electrum

gold-like: 4 aich 6 oreide, ormolu, oroide 8 arsedine

heat resistant: 6 cermet 7 ceramal

Japanese: 5 mokum

lead and tin: 5 calin, terne 6 pewter

mercurial: 7 amalgam

nickel and silver: 8 alfenide

nickel and iron: 7 elinvar

nonferrous: 4 tula

pewter-like: 5 bidri

silver with copper or tin: 6 billon

sulfuric: 6 niello

All's Well That Ends Well character: 5 Diana, Lafeu 7 Bertram

allspice tree: 7 pimento

allude to: 5 imply, infer 6 advert, hint at, relate 7 bring up, connote, mention, refer to, suggest, touch on 8 indicate, intimate, point out 9 insinuate

allure: air, woo 4 bait, draw, lead, lure, move, sway 5 angle, charm, court, decoy, snare, tempt 6 entice, entrap, glamor, induce, seduce 7 attract, beguile, ensnare 8 blandish, inveigle, persuade 9 captivate, fascinate, influence

allusion: 4 hint 7 mention 8 innuendo, instance 9 quotation, reference 10 intimation

alluvial: *clay:* 5 adobe

deposit: mud 4 sand, silt, wash 5 delta, drift, geest 6 gravel, placer

fan: 5 delta

alluvion: 4 flow, wash 5 flood 10 inundation

ally: pal 4 aide, join 5 unite 6 backer, friend, helper 7 connect, partner 8 adherent, relate to 9 affiliate, assistant, associate, auxiliary, colleague, supporter, take sides 10 accomplice 11 confederate

almanac: 4 ordo 8 calendar, yearbook 9 chronicle, ephemeris

almandine: 6 spinel, garnet

almighty: 5 great 7 extreme 8 powerful, puissant 10 omnipotent 12 irresistible

Almighty: God 7 Creator

almond: nut 5 badam 6 kanari

paste: 8 marzipan

pert. to: 10 amygdaline

served with: 8 amandine

syrup: 6 orgeat

almost: 4 nigh 5 about, close 6 all but, feckly(Sc.), nearly 8 as good as, not quite 9 virtually 13 approximately

alms: 4 dole, gift 6 aumous(Sc.) 7 charity, handout 8 donation, offering, pittance 11 benefaction 12 contribution

chest: 4 arca 7 poor box

dispenser: 7 almoner, almsman 11 eleemosynar

almsman: 6 beggar, pauper

almuce: 4 hood 6 tippet 9 headdress

aloe: 4 pita 5 agave 6 maguey

compound: 5 aloin

extract: 5 orcin 7 orcinol

powder: 5 picra

aloes: 6 tonic 8 agalloch 10 agallochum

aloft: 4 high 5 above 6 upward 7 skyward 8 airborne, in the air, overhead

aloha: 4 love 5 hello 7 goodbye 8 farewell, greeting, kindness 9 affection 10 salutation

alone: 4 bare, lorn, only, sole, solo 5 aloof, apart, solus 6 single, unique 8 desolate, detached, isolated, separate, solitary 9 matchless 11 exclusively 12 incomparable, unparalleled 13 unaccompanied

along: 4 near, with 5 ahead 6 as well, beside, onward 7 forward, in a line 8 advanced, on the way, together 10 lengthwise 11 approaching 12 in accord with

alongside: 6 beside, next to 7 abreast, against, close by 8 parallel

Alonso's son: 9 Ferdinand

aloof: shy 4 cold, cool 5 alone, apart,

proud 6 frosty, remote, silent 7 social, distant, removed 8 detached, reserved, reticent 10 withdrawn 11 at a distance, indifferent, standoffish

alopecia: 8 baldness 11 phalacrosis

alopecoid: 7 foxlike, vulpine

alouatte: 6 monkey

aloud: 4 oral 5 vocal 7 audible

alp: 4 peak 5 mount 8 mountain

alpaca: 4 paco, wool 5 cloth

habitat: 4 Peru 5 Andes 7 Bolivia

relative of: 5 llama 7 guanaco

alpha: 5 chief, first, start 11 Greek letter

and omega: all 5 whole 6 entire 15 beginning and end

alphabet (see also **Arabic, Greek, Hebrew):** 4 ABC's 5 order 6 basics, primer 7 letters 9 rudiments 10 abecedarium

character: 4 ogam, ogum, rune 5 ogham

pert. to: 11 abecedarian

Runic: 7 futharc, futhork

alpha rhythm: 9 brain wave

Alpine: *antelope:* 7 chamois

climber: 10 alpestrian

dance: 5 gavot

dress: 6 dirndl

dwelling: 6 chalet

goat: 4 ibex 5 steinbok

herdsman: 4 senn

pass: col 7 Brenner, Splugen 9 St. Bernard

plant: 9 edelweiss

primrose: 8 auricula

wind: 4 bise, bora 5 foehn

Alps: *Austrian:* 5 Tirol, Tyrol

division of: 5 Noric, Savoy 7 Bernese, Pennine 8 Maritime 9 Lepontine

Italian: 9 Dolomites

peak: 4 Rosa 5 Blanc, Eiger, Leone 7 Bernina 8 Jungfrau 10 Matterhorn

tunnel: 5 Blanc, Cenis 7 Arlberg, Simplon 10 St. Gotthard

Yugoslav: 7 Julian 7 Dinaric

already: now 6 before 7 earlier 8 even then, formerly 9 previously 10 beforehand, by this time

also: and, too, yet 4 erst, more, plus 5 again, ditto 6 as well 7 besides, further 8 likewise, moreover 9 similarly 10 in addition

also-ran: dud 5 loser 7 failure, washout

altar: 5 table 6 shrine 7 chantry 9 sanctuary

area: 4 apse 7 chancel

boy: 6 server 7 acolyte

cloth: 4 pall 7 frontal

curtain: 6 riddel, riddle

enclosure: 4 bema

hanging: 6 dorsal, dossal, dossel

ledge: 6 gradin 7 retable

platform: 8 predella

portable: 10 superaltar

screen: 7 reredos

top: 5 mensa

vessel: pyx 5 cruet, paten 7 chalice, piscina 8 ciborium 10 monstrance

alter: 4 geld, redo, spay, turn, vary, veer 5 adapt, amend, emend, reset, shift 6 adjust, change, modify, mutate, neuter, revamp, revise, temper 7 convert 9 transform

alter ego: 5 agent 6 friend 8 henchman 9 confidant, other self

altercation: row 4 spat, tiff 5 brawl, fight, scrap, set-to 6 strife, tussle 7 dispute, quarrel, wrangle 8 argument, squabble 10 contention, falling out 11 controversy

alternate: sub 4 else, sway, vary 5 other, proxy, recur, shift 6 change, deputy, rotate, seesaw 8 intermit 9 oscillate, take turns 11 interchange, reciprocate

alternative: 6 choice, either, option, way out 8 elective, loophole 10 preference

word introducing: 7 whether

Althaea's husband: 6 Oeneus

although: 5 while 6 albeit 7 despite, whereas 11 granted that 15 notwithstanding

altitude: 6 height 7 ceiling 9 elevation, loftiness

measuring device: 8 orometer 9 altimeter

altitude sickness: 7 soroche

alto: 4 part 6 singer 7 althorn, saxhorn 8 vocalist

altogether: 5 quite 6 in toto, wholly 7 en masse, totally, utterly 8 all in all, entirely 10 by and large, completely, thoroughly 12 collectively

in the: 4 bare, nude 5 naked 8 stripped 9 au naturel

altruism: 7 charity 10 generosity 11 benevolence 12 philanthropy 13 unselfishness

alum: 7 styptic 10 astringent

rock: 7 alunite

alumina: 4 clay 5 argil 8 corundum

aluminum: *calcium silicate:* 7 epidote

discoverers: 4 Davy 6 Wohler

hydrousphosphate: 9 wavellite

oxide: 7 alumina

sulfate: 4 alum

alumnus: 4 grad 5 pupil 8 graduate

alveolate: 6 pitted 11 honeycombed, having holes

always: e'er 4 ever 6 semper(L.) 7 forever, for good 8 evermore 9 eternally, uniformly 10 constantly, habitually, invariably 11 continually, perpetually, unceasingly 12 till doomsday 13 everlastingly

ama: 5 amula 9 candlenut

Amadis' beloved: 6 Oriana

amadou: 4 fuse, punk 6 tinder 9 touchwood

amah: 5 nurse 7 servant

amain: 7 greatly 8 forcibly, speedily 9 violently 10 vigorously 11 exceedingly

Amalekite king: 4 Agag

amalgamate: mix 4 fuse, join 5 alloy, blend, merge, unite 6 mingle 7 combine 8 coalesce, compound 11 consolidate

Amaltheia: 4 goat

horn: 10 cornucopia

nursling: 4 Zeus

amanita: 6 agaric, fungus

amanuensis: 6 penman, scribe, typist 8 recorder 9 scrivener, secretary 11 transcriber 12 stenographer

Amasa's father: 6 Jether

amass: 4 save 5 gross, hoard, stack, store 6 gather, heap up, pile up 7 collect, compile 8 assemble 9 stockpile 10 accumulate

amateur: ham 4 tiro, tyro 6 novice, votary 7 admirer, dabbler, devotee, fancier 8 beginner, neophyte 9 greenhorn 10 dilettante, aficionado 15 nonprofessional

Amati: 6 violin 11 violin maker

birthplace: 7 Cremona

amative: 6 ardent, erotic, loving 7 amorous 10 passionate

amaze: awe 4 stun 7 astound, stagger, stupefy 8 astonish, bowl over, confound, surprise 9 dumbfound, overwhelm 11 flabbergast

amazement: 6 wonder 8 unbelief 12 astonishment 13 consternation

Amazon: 5 river 12 woman warrior

discoverer: 6 Pinzon

early explorer: 8 Orellana, Teixeira

estuary: 4 Para

headstream: 7 Maranon

queen: 9 Hippolyta 12 Penthesileia

tributary: Ica 4 Napo, Paru 5 Jurua, Jutai, Negro, Xingu

amazon: ant 5 harpy, shrew, vixen, 6 parrot, virago 11 hummingbird

ambari: 4 hemp 5 fiber 7 cordage

ambassador: 5 agent, envoy 6 deputy, legate, nuncio 8 diplomat, emissary, minister 9 messenger 12 intermediary 14 representative 15 plenipotentiary

pert. to: 8 legatine

amber: 5 resin 6 yellow 8 amberoid

amberfish: 6 kahala 10 yellowtail

ambiance, ambience: 6 milieu 10 atmosphere 11 environment 12 surroundings

ambiguity: 7 duality, evasion, paradox 9 duplexity, duplicity, looseness, obscurity 10 hesitation 12 doubtfulness 13 inconsistency

ambiguous: 4 dark 5 vague 6 unsure 7

cryptic, dubious, unclear 8 doubtful 9 equivocal, uncertain, unsettled 10 indefinite, indistinct 11 problematic 12 questionable 13 indeterminate

ambit: 5 limit, scope, space 6 bounds, extent, sphere 7 circuit, compass 8 boundary, precinct 13 circumference

ambition: aim 4 goal, hope, mark, wish 5 dream, drive 6 desire 7 purpose 9 intention, objective 10 aspiration

ambitious: 4 avid, bold, keen 5 eager, showy 7 emulous 8 aspiring 9 energetic, on the make 10 aggressive 11 power-hungry 12 enterprising

amble: 5 mosey 6 dawdle, stroll 7 meander, saunter 9 poke along

ambo: 4 desk 6 pulpit

Amboina button: 4 yaws

ambrosia: 5 honey 6 nectar 7 dessert 8 red-brown

ambrosial: 5 sweet, tasty 6 divine 8 fragrant, heavenly, luscious, perfumed 9 delicious 13 fit for the gods

ambry: 4 safe 5 chest, niche 6 closet, recess 10 repository

ambulatory: 7 movable, walking

ambush: mug 4 lurk, trap 5 await, blind, snare 6 lay for, waylay 7 assault 8 surprise 12 take unawares

ameliorate: 4 ease, help, mend 6 better, uplift 7 improve, promote 8 mitigate

amen: yea, yes 5 truly 6 assent, verily, sobe-it 7 exactly 8 approval, response, sanction 9 assuredly, certainly 10 that's right

Amen-Ra's wife: Mut

amenable: 4 open 6 docile, liable, pliant 7 willing 9 receptive, tractable 10 responsive 11 accountable 12 in the mood for

amend: 4 edit 5 alter 6 better, change, reform, remedy, repair, revise 7 correct, improve, rectify, redress 8 put right, work over

amends: 7 apology, redress 9 atonement, expiation 10 recompense, reparation 11 restitution 12 compensation 13 peace offering

amenities: 7 manners 8 agremens, comforts, niceties 9 agrements, etiquette 10 civilities, courtesies 11 formalities 12 conveniences, pleasantries

ament: 5 idiot, moron 6 catkin 7 cachrys, cattail, gosling 8 imbecile, nucament

amerce: 4 fine 6 punish 8 penalize

American: 4 Yank 6 Gringo, Yankee, Yanqui

colonists: 5 Dutch 8 pilgrims, puritans

American Indian: See Indian (American)

Amerind: 6 Eskimo, Indian

amethyst: gem 7 onegite

Amfortas' father: 7 Titurel

ami(F.): 5 lover 6 friend

amiable: 4 kind, warm 6 genial 7 affable, cordial, lovable, winsome 8 charming, engaging, friendly, gracious, sociable 9 agreeable, courteous 11 good-humored, good-natured, kind-hearted

amicable: 8 friendly 9 peaceable 10 harmonious, neighborly 12 well-disposed

amice: 4 cape, cowl, hood 5 ephod 6 almuce, tippet, vakass 8 vestment

amid: 5 among, midst 6 during 7 between 10 surrounded 11 encompassed

amino acid: 7 protein

amino compound: 7 diamide, diamine 8 triamine

amiss: ill 4 awry, bias 5 agley, askew, wrong 6 astray, faulty 7 haywire 8 improper 9 erroneous, incorrect 10 inaccurate

amity: 5 peace 6 accord 7 concord, harmony 8 goodwill 10 friendship 12 friendliness

ammonia: 9 hartshorn 11 refrigerant

derivative: 5 amide, amine 6 anilid 7 anilide, diamine

ammoniac: 8 gum resin

ammunition: 4 ammo, arms, shot 5 bombs 6 powder, shells 7 bullets rockets, weapons 8 grenades, materiel, missiles, ordnance, shrapnel 9 resources, artillery

case: 9 bandolier

depot: 4 dump 7 armory, arsenal 8 magazine

amnesia: 5 fugue 8 blackout 11 memory lapse 13 forgetfulness

amnesty: 6 pardon 10 absolution 11 forgiveness

amoeba, ameba: olm 7 proteus 8 organism 9 protozoon

amok, amuck: mad 5 crazy 6 crazed 7 violent 8 frenzied 12 uncontrolled

amole: 4 salt, soap 5 agave, plant

Amon's son: 6 Josiah

among: 4 amid, with 5 midst 7 between, betwixt 8 to each of 12 in the thick of

amor: 4 Eros, love 5 Cupid

amoral: 7 neutral 9 objective, shameless, unethical

amorous: 4 fond 6 ardent, erotic, loving, tender 7 amatory, fervent 10 passionate 12 affectionate

amorphous: 5 vague 8 formless, inchoate 9 irregular, shapeless, undefined 12 lacking unity 14 uncrystallized

amortize: 6 pay off 8 alienate, settle up, write off 9 liquidate 12 pay gradually

Amos: 6 O.T. book 7 prophet

amotion: 7 ousting, removal 11 deprivation

amount: gob, sum, tab 4 bulk, cost, dose,

part, unit 5 add up, chunk, equal, price, reach, stack, store, tally, total, whole 6 extent, number 7 measure, portion, signify 8 comprise, quantity 9 aggregate

fixed: 4 rate 8 set price 11 fixed charge

indefinite: any 4 some

made: lot 5 batch

relative: 5 ratio 6 degree

small: bit, jot, tot 4 dash, drop, iota, lick, mite, whit, wisp 5 grain, pinch, shred, speck, taste, trace 6 morsel, trifle 7 dribble, driblet, modicum, smidgen 8 fragment, molecule, particle

amour propre: 5 pride 6 egoism, vanity 7 conceit 8 self-love 10 narcissism

ampere unit: 4 volt, watt

ampersand: and 4 also, plus 9 character

amphetamine: 5 benny, upper 7 pep pill 8 inhalant 9 nose spray, stimulant

amphibian: eft, olm 4 frog, hyla, newt, rana, toad 7 caudate, proteus 8 tree toad 9 caecilian 10 salamander 14 land-water craft

family: 7 Hylidae, Pipidae, Ranidae 9 Bufonidae, Proteidae, Sirenidae

order of: 5 anura 6 eryops 7 aglossa, caudata 9 salientia

young: 7 tadpole 8 polliwog

amphibole: 7 edenite, oralite, uralite 9 tremolite 10 hornblende

Amphion: *father:* 4 Zeus 5 Iasus

mother: 7 Antiope

twin brother: 6 Zethus

wife: 5 Niobe

amphitheater: 4 bowl, oval 5 arena, cavea 6 circus 7 stadium 10 auditorium

Amphitrite: *father:* 6 Nereus

husband: 8 Poseidon

mother: 5 Doris

son: 6 Triton

Amphitryon's wife: 7 Alcmena, Alcmene

amphora: jar, urn 4 vase 6 pelike

ample: 4 full, good, much, rich, wide 5 broad, great, large, roomy 6 enough, plenty 7 copious, liberal, opulent 8 abundant, adequate, generous, handsome, spacious 9 bounteous, bountiful, capacious, extensive, plentiful, unstinted 10 munificent, sufficient

amplify: pad 5 swell, widen 6 dilate, expand, extend, stress 7 augment, enlarge 8 increase, lengthen, multiply 9 add detail 10 exaggerate

amputate: cut, lop 5 prune, sever 6 excise 7 chop off, curtail 9 eliminate

amula: ama 6 vessel 7 wine cup

amulet: gem 4 juju, mojo 5 charm, saffi, token 6 fetish, grigri, saphie 7 periapt 8 greegree, ornament, talisman 10 lucky piece, protection

Amulius' brother: 7 Numitor

amuse: wow 6 divert, engage, please, regale, tickle 7 beguile, delight, disport, enliven, gratify 8 distract 9 entertain, knock dead 10 exhilarate 11 play the fool

amusement: fun 4 game, jest, play 5 mirth, sport 7 pastime 8 pleasure 9 avocation, diversion, merriment 10 recreation, relaxation 13 divertisement, entertainment

place 4 fair, park 5 movie 6 casino, cinema, circus, midway 7 theater 8 carnival

amusing: 5 droll, funny 7 comical, risible 8 humorous, pleasant 9 laughable, ludicrous, priceless, quizzical 10 ridiculous 11 rib-tickling

Amy's sisters: Meg 4 Beth

Amycus: *enemy:* 5 Lycus 8 Dascylus

father: 8 Poseidon

friend: 8 Hercules

mother: 5 Melie

amyl: 6 pentyl, starch 7 alcohol

an: one 7 article

ana: 6 events 7 sayings 9 anecdotes, anthology 10 collection, miscellany 11 memorabilia

anabasis: 7 advance, headway, on-going 8 progress 10 expedition 11 forward march

anabatic: 9 ascending 12 upward moving

anaconda: boa 5 snake

Anacreon's birthplace: 4 Teos

anadem: 5 crown 6 diadem, fillet, wreath 7 chaplet, coronet, garland

anagogic: 7 occult 8 abstruse, mystical

anagram: 4 game 5 rebus 6 puzzle 9 logogriph

analgesic: 5 opium 6 codein 7 anodyne, aspirin, codeine 8 sedative 10 anesthetic, pain-killer

analogous: 4 akin, like 5 alike 6 allied 7 cognate, related, similar 8 parallel 10 comparable, equivalent 11 correlative 13 correspondent

analogy: 8 metaphor 10 comparison, congruence, similarity, similitude 11 resemblance

analysis: 4 test 5 audit, study 8 exegesis 9 breakdown, criticism, reduction, titration 10 dissection 11 examination 14 interpretation

analyze: 4 sift 5 assay, parse, study, weigh 7 break up, dissect, examine 8 diagnose, separate 9 determine, reason out, take apart, subdivide

ananas: 7 pinguin 9 pineapple

Ananias: 6 liar 6 fibber 12 prevaricator

wife: 8 Sapphira

anarchist: 5 rebel 7 radical 8 mutineer, nihilist 9 insurgent 13 revolutionary

anarchy: 4 riot 5 chaos 6 revolt 7 license, misrule, mob rule 8 disorder, lynch law, nihilism 9 confusion 11 lawlessness

anathema: ban 4 oath 5 curse 6 pariah, phobia 7 censure, outcast 9 bete noire 10 abhorrence, hated thing 11 imprecation, malediction 12 denunciation

anatomy: 4 body 8 analysis, skeleton 9 structure 10 dissection, morphology
animal: 7 zootomy
cell: 8 cytology
microscopic: 9 histology
plant: 9 phytotomy
research: 11 vivisection

Anaximander's principle: 7 apeiron

ancestor: 4 Adam, 8 forebear, 9 patriarch, precursor, prototype 10 forefather, forerunner, progenitor 11 predecessor
having common: 14 consanguineous
of a family branch: 6 stirps
worship: 6 manism

ancestry: 4 race 5 stock 6 family, origin 7 descent, lineage 8 breeding, heredity, pedigree 9 genealogy 10 bloodlines, extraction, family tree 11 antecedents
relating to: 6 atavic 9 atavistic

Anchises' son: 6 Aeneas

anchor: fix 4 bind, hook, moor 5 berth, bower, kedge, rivet 6 attach, drogue, secure 7 chaplet, connect, grapnel, killick, support 8 make fast 10 come to rest
bill: 4 peak
hoist: cat 7 capstan
part: arm 4 palm 5 fluke, shank, stock
position: 5 atrip
rest: 9 billboard
shaped: 8 ankyroid
timber: 7 grouser

anchorage: 4 dock, port, rade(Sc.) 5 haven 6 harbor, refuge 7 mooring 8 mainstay

anchorite: 4 monk 6 hermit 7 ascetic, eremite, recluse, stylite

anchorman: key 5 emcee 8 mainstay 11 commentator

anchovy: 6 sprat 7 herring

ancient: old 4 aged, auld(Sc.) 5 hoary 6 bygone, 7 antique, archaic, classic, elderly 8 historic, Noachian, obsolete, primeval 9 primitive 10 antiquated 11 patriarchal 12 along in years

ancilla: aid 6 helper 7 adjunct 8 handmaid 9 accessory

ancillary: 7 related 9 auxiliary 10 subsidiary 11 subordinate 13 supplementary

ancon: 5 elbow 6 corbel 7 console 9 olecranon

and: ant, too 4 also, plus 7 besides, further 8 moreover 10 connective 11 furthermore

and so forth: etc 4 more 6 others 8 etcetera

Andean: 5 grand, lofty 8 Peruvian

andiron: dog 7 firedog, hessian

Andorra: *capital:* 14 Andorra la Vella
language: 7 Catalan
monetary unit: 5 franc 6 peseta 7 centime, centimo
mountain: 8 Pyrenees
river: 6 Valira

andradite: 6 aplome, garnet

android: 5 robot 9 automaton

Andromache's husband: 6 Hector

Andromeda: 5 heath, plant 13 constellation
father: 7 Cepheus
husband: 7 Perseus
mother: 10 Cassiopeia

ane(Sc.): one 4 once

anecdote: 4 joke, tale, yarn 5 story 6 sketch 9 narrative
Collection: ana

anele: 5 bless 6 anoint, shrive

anemia: 4 fern 9 emptiness 11 lack of blood

anemic: wan 4 pale 6 watery 8 lifeless 10 exsanguine 12 without vigor

anemone: 9 buttercup 10 windflower

anent: 4 in re 5 about, as for 7 apropos 9 regarding 10 concerning 13 in reference to

aneroid: 9 barometer

anesthetic: gas 5 ether, 6 obtuse, opiate 7 anodyne, cocaine, dulling, menthol 8 morphine, sedative 9 analgesic, novocaine 10 chloroform, palliative 12 unperceptive

anew: 4 over 5 again 6 afresh 8 once more, recently

anfractuous: 6 spiral 7 turning, sinuous, winding 8 tortuous

angel: 4 dear, lamb 6 backer, cherub, patron, seraph, spirit, sponsor 8 guardian 9 harbinger, messenger 13 heavenly being
apostate prince: 5 Eblis 7 Lucifer
biblical: 5 Uriel 7 Chamuel, Gabriel, Jophiel, Michael, Raphael, Zadkiel
bottomless pit: 7 Abaddon 8 Apollyon
hierarchy: 6 Powers 7 Thrones, Virtues 8 Cherubim, Seraphim 9 Dominions
of death: 6 Azrael 7 Sammael
Paradise Lost: 5 Uriel 6 Belial 7 Ariocha
worship: 5 dulia

angelic: 4 pure 7 saintly 8 cherubic, heavenly, innocent 9 celestial, spiritual

angelus: 4 bell 6 prayer 8 devotion
painter: 7 Millet

anger: ire, irk, vex 4 bile, fury, gall, rile, roil 5 annoy, pique, wrath 6 choler, dander, enrage, nettle, offend, rancor, spleen, stir up, temper 7 burning, dudgeon, incense, inflame, passion, provoke 8 acrimony, irritate, vexation 9 aggravate, infuriate 10 antagonize, exasperate, resentment 11 displeasure, indignation

Angevin: 11 Plantagenet

angle: aim, ell, tee 4 bend, bias, fish, fork, hook 5 bevel, crook, facet, phase, point, quoin, slant, twist 6 aspect, jockey, scheme, zigzag 7 gimmick, perigon 8 fishhook, intrigue, position 10 standpoint

equal (pert. to): 8 isogonal, isogonic

external: 4 cant

having no: 6 agonic

mathematical: 5 acute, right 6 obtuse 7 oblique

measuring device: 6 octant 7 sextant 10 semicircle

of branch and leaf: 4 axil

of keel and bowsprit: 6 steeve

of ore vein: 4 hade

salient: 5 arris

angler: 7 lophiid, rodster, schemer, troller 8 allmouth, piscator 9 fisherman, goosefish, trickster

the compleat: 11 Izaak Walton

Anglo Saxon: *armor:* 7 hauberk 9 habergeon

army: 4 fyrd

assembly: 4 moot 5 gemot 6 gemote

coin: ora 5 sceat, styca 6 mancus

confederacy: 9 heptarchy

deity: Ing 4 Frey, Wyrd 5 Freyr

epic: 7 Beowulf

freeman: 7 thane, thegn

king: Ine 4 Edwy, Edred 6 Alfred, Egbert, Harold 8 Ethelred

king's council: 5 witan 11 witenagemot

letter: edh, eth, wyn 4 wynn 5 thorn

nobleman: 4 earl 8 atheling

poet: 4 scop

sheriff: 5 reeve 6 gerefa

slave: 4 esne

tax: 4 geld

village: ham

writer: 4 Bede

Angola: *capital:* 6 Luanda

city: 6 Lobito 7 Lubango, Malange 8 Benguela

monetary unit: 4 lwei 6 kwanza

mountain peak: 4 Moco

river: 5 Congo, Cuito, Kasai 6 Cuando, Cunene, Kwango

tribe: 5 Bantu, Kongo

angora: cat 4 goat, hair, wool, yarn 6 mohair, rabbit

angry: mad 4 grim, sore, 5 cross, huffy, irate, livid, vexed, wroth 6 fuming, ireful, put out 7 furious, painful, teed off, uptight 8 burned up, choleric, inflamed, 9 in a temper, indignant, irascible, resentful 11 exasperated, fit to be tied

anguilla: eel

anguish: rue, woe 4 ache, pain, pang 5 agony, dolor, grief, throe 6 misery, sorrow 7 torment, torture 8 distress 10 heartbreak

angular: 4 bony, lank, lean thin 5 gaunt, sharp 6 abrupt 7 jutting, pointed, scraggy, scrawny 8 rawboned 13 sharpcornered

ani: 6 cuckoo 9 blackbird

anil: dye 6 indigo

anile: old 5 silly 6 doting, feeble, infirm, senile, simple 7 flighty, foolish 9 doddering 11 old-womanish

anima: 4 life, soul 6 psyche 9 inner self 10 vital force

animadversion: rap 4 slur 5 blame, knock 7 censure, obloquy, reproof 8 reproach 9 aspersion, criticism 10 perception, raking over 11 observation 12 faultfinding

animal (see also **amphibian, bird, carnivore, fish, insect, invertebrate, mammal, reptile, vertebrate**): 5 beast, biped, brute, gross, lusty 6 carnal, fleshy, mammal, rodent 7 sensual 8 creature, organism, physical 9 marsupial, quadruped

arboreal: 4 unau 5 chimp, koala, lemur, sloth 6 gibbon, marten, monkey 7 dasyure, opossum, raccoon, tarsier 8 kinkajou, marmoset, squirrel 10 orangutan

Biblical: 4 reem 8 behemoth

body: 4 soma

burrowing: 4 mole 6 badger, gopher, marmot, rabbit, wombat 7 echidna 9 armadillo, groundhog, woodchuck

class: 5 genus 6 genera(pl.)

coat: fur 4 fell, hair, hide, pelt, skin, wool 6 pelage

collection: zoo 9 menagerie

crawling: 4 worm 5 snake

cross-bred: 4 mule 5 hinny 6 hybrid

doctor: vet 12 veterinarian

draft: 4 mule, oxen(pl.) 5 horse 8 elephant

enclosure: pen, run, sty 4 barn, cage, coop, cote, fold, yard 5 hutch, kraal, stall 6 corral 7 pasture, paddock

equine: ass 5 horse, zebra

extinct: 4 dodo, urus 8 dinosaur, mastodon

fat: 4 lard, suet 5 cetin 6 tallow 7 lanolin

feline: cat 4 lion, lynx, puma 5 tiger 6 jaguar, ocelot 7 cheetah, leopard, panther

female: cow, dam, doe, ewe, gyp, hen, roe, sow 4 hind, mare, slut 5 bitch, filly, jenny, nanny, vixen 6 heifer 7 lioness, tigress

footless: 5 apoda

group: pod 4 herd, pack 5 drove, flock, pride, swarm 6 gaggle, school *hibernating:* 4 bear 9 groundhog, woodchuck

life: 4 bios 5 fauna

life (god of): 6 Faunus

lover: 8 zoophile 10 zoophilist

lupine: 4 wolf

male: cob, ram, tom 4 boar, buck, bull, cock, jack, stag, stud 5 billy, steer 6 gander 7 rooster 8 stallion

many-footed: 7 decapod, hexapod 8 multiped 9 centipede, millipede

marine: orc 4 brit, fish, inia, seal 5 coral, otter, polyp, salpa, whale 6 dugong, walrus 7 dolphin, manatee, rotifer 9 jellyfish 10 ctenophore, ctenophran

meat-eating: 9 carnivore

microscopic: 5 ameba, monad 6 acarid, amoeba 8 rhizopod 9 protozoan 10 animalcule

monkey-like: 5 lemur, loris

mythical: 4 faun, yeti 5 Hydra, snark 6 bagwyn, bunyip, dragon, garuda, Geryon, kraken, sphinx 7 centaur, griffin, mermaid, phoenix, unicorn 8 basilisk, Cerberus, Loch Ness, Minotaur 10 cockatrice

nocturnal: bat, owl 4 coon 5 lemur, ratel, tapir 6 possum 7 opossum 9 armadillo

one-celled: 5 ameba, monad 6 amoeba 9 protozoan

ovine: 5 sheep

pack: ass 4 mule 5 burro, camel, horse, llama 6 donkey

parasitic: 8 entozoon

plant-eating: 9 herbivore

porcine: hog, pig, sow 4 boar

pouched: 6 possum 7 opossum 8 kangaroo 9 marsupial

rabbit-like: 4 pika 6 marmot

ruminant: cow 4 deer, goat 5 camel, sheep 8 antelope

science: 7 zoology 8 ethology

symbol: 5 totem

track: pug 4 slot 5 spoor

undersized: 4 runt

ursine: 4 bear

vulpine: fox

young: cub, kid, pup 4 brit, calf, colt, fawn, foal, lamb, parr 5 bruin, chick, filly, puppy, shoat, whelp 6 cygnet, heifer, kitten 7 gosling 8 suckling, yearling 9 fledgling

animal and plant life: 5 biota

Animal Farm author: 6 Orwell

animalcule: 5 ameba, monad 6 amoeba 7 microbe, no-see-um, rotifer 9 protozoan

animate: 4 move, perk, stir 5 liven, rouse 6 ensoul, excite, fire up, living, vivify 7 actuate, enliven, inspire, quicken 8 activate, energize, vitalize 9 stimulate 10 exhilarate, invigorate 12 give motion to

animated: gay 5 brisk, peppy, vivid, vital 6 active, blithe, lively 7 buoyant, jocular 8 spirited, vigorous 9 sprightly, vivacious 10 full of zest 12 enthusiastic

animation: vim 4 dash, elan, life, zing 5 verve 6 esprit, spirit

anime: 5 copal, elemi, resin 9 oleoresin

animism: 8 naturism

animosity: 4 hate, 6 enmity, malice, rancor 7 dislike 9 antipathy, hostility 10 antagonism, resentment

animus: 4 mind, soul 6 effort, rancor, spirit, temper 7 ill will 8 attitude 9 intention, objective 10 antagonism 11 disposition, inclination

anion: ion 8 particle

opposed to: 6 cation

anisette: 7 cordial, liqueur

Anius' daughter: 5 Elais

ankle: 4 coot(Sc.) 5 talus 6 tarsus

pert. to: 6 tarsal

anlage: 4 base 6 embryo, source 8 blastema, rudiment 10 primordium

anna: 9 Hindu coin

annals: 6 record 7 history 8 archives 10 chronicles 11 publication 13 year by year log

annalist: 6 writer 7 diarist 8 recorder 9 historian 12 chronologist

Annapolis student: 4 pleb 5 plebe 10 midshipman

annatto, annotto, arnatto: dye 4 tree 5 urucu 6 salmon 7 achiote

derivative: 5 bixin 7 orellin

anneal: 4 bake, fuse, heat 5 smelt 6 temper 7 toughen 10 strengthen

annelid: 4 worm

fresh water: 4 naid

marine: 9 autolytus

annex: add, ell 4 wing 5 affix, seize, unite 6 append, attach, fasten, obtain, pick up, secure 7 acquire, preempt, procure 8 addition, arrogate, take over 9 extension 11 appropriate

Annie Oakley: 4 pass 6 ticket 7 freebie

annihilate: end 4 kill, raze, rout, slay 5 crush, erase, wreck 6 devour, murder, negate, squash 7 abolish, destroy, expunge, nullify, wipe out 8 decimate, demolish, massacre 9 eradicate, extirpate 10 extinguish, obliterate 11 exterminate 12 reduce to ruin

anniversary: 4 fete 7 jubilee 8 birthday, ceremony 11 celebration 13 commemoration

hundredth: 10 centennial

one hundred fiftieth: 16 sesquicentennial

tenth: 9 decennial

third: 9 triennial

thousandth: 10 millennial 11 millenniary

twentieth: 12 vigentennial

wedding: see **wedding:** *anniversary*

annotate: 4 edit, note 5 gloss 6 remark 7

comment, explain 9 elucidate 10 illustrate

announce: bid, cry 4 call, tell 5 bruit, state 6 assert, blazon, herald, inform, report, reveal 7 declare, divulge, publish, usher in 8 foretell, proclaim 9 advertise, broadcast, enunciate, introduce, make known 10 promulgate 11 give the word

announcement: 5 blurb, edict 6 decree, dictum, notice 7 message 8 bulletin 9 broadcast, manifesto, statement 11 declaration 12 notification, proclamation

of marriage: 5 banns

announcer: 4 page 5 crier, emcee

of coming events: 4 seer 6 herald 7 prophet 9 harbinger

annoy: bug, dun, ire, irk, nag, try, vex 4 bait, bore, fret, gall, nark, pain, rile 5 chafe, harry, peeve, pique, spite, tease, upset, worry 6 badger, harass, heckle, molest, needle, nettle, offend, pester, rattle 7 bedevil, disturb, provoke, trouble 8 distress, irritate 9 aggravate, displease, embarrass 10 exasperate 13 inconvenience

annoyance: 4 drag, pain, pest 5 thorn, trial, worry 8 headache, nuisance, vexation 11 disturbance 13 inconvenience

annual: 4 book 5 plant 6 flower, yearly 7 etesian 8 yearbook 11 publication

annul: 4 undo, void 5 blank, elide, erase, quash, remit 6 cancel, negate, recall, repeal, revoke 7 abolish, blot out, nullify, rescind 8 abrogate, derogate, dissolve, overrule 9 disaffirm 10 annihilate, extinguish, invalidate, neutralize, obliterate 11 countermand

annular: 6 banded, cyclic, ringed 8 cingular, circular

annulet: 4 ring 5 ridge 6 fillet 7 molding

anoa: 6 wild ox 8 sapiutan

relative: 7 buffalo

anode: 5 plate 8 terminal 9 electrode

deposit: 9 ascending

anodic: 9 ascending

anodyne: 4 balm 6 opiate 7 soother 8 narcotic, sedative 9 analgesic 10 anesthetic, painkiller, palliative

anoesia, anoia: 6 idiocy

anoint: oil 5 anele 6 grease 9 apply balm 10 consecrate

anole: 6 lizard

anomalous: odd 6 off-key 7 deviant, foreign, strange, unusual 8 aberrant, abnormal, atypical, peculiar 9 eccentric, irregular 11 incongruous 12 out of keeping 13 contradictory

anomy: 7 miracle

anon: 4 soon, then 5 again, later 6 afresh 7 by and by, shortly 8 in a while 9

afterward, presently

anonym: 5 alias 10 nom-de-plume

anonymous: 7 unknown 8 nameless, unavowed, unsigned 9 incognito

anorexia: 7 fasting 14 self-starvation

another: new 4 more 5 fresh 6 second 7 further, one more 9 different 10 additional, not the same

anserine: 5 silly 6 stupid 7 foolish 9 gooselike

answer: 4 meet, plea, suit 5 avail, react, reply, serve 6 refute, result, retort, return 7 defense, fulfill, riposte, satisfy 8 rebuttal, repartee, response, solution 9 conform to, rejoinder 11 acknowledge

opposite of: ask 7 inquire 8 question

answerable: 6 liable 8 amenable 9 obligated 11 accountable, responsible

ant: 5 emmet 7 pismire, termite

genus: 6 eciton 7 formica 8 myrmecia

kind: 4 army 6 amazon, driver 7 soldier 9 carpenter

leaf-cutting: 4 atta

male: 8 micraner 9 ergataner

nest: 4 hill 5 mound 6 colony 9 formicary

nonworker: 5 drone

queen: 4 gyne

stinging: 5 kelep 8 ponerine

worker: 6 ergate

ant bear: 8 aardvark, edentate, tamanoir

ant cow: 5 aphid

anta: 4 pier 5 tapir 8 pedestal, pilaster

Antaeus: *enemy:* 8 Hercules

father: 8 Poseidon

mother: 4 Gaea

antagonism: 6 animus, enmity, rancor 7 dislike 8 friction 9 animosity, antipathy, hostility 10 opposition

antagonist: foe 5 enemy, rival 7 battler, warrior 8 opponent 9 adversary 10 competitor

antagonistic: 4 anti 6 at odds 7 counter, hostile, opposed 8 contrary, inimical 9 dissonant 11 dead against

Antarctica: *bird:* 4 skua 7 penguin

explorer: 4 Byrd, Cook, Ross 5 Scott 6 Mawson 7 Wilkins 8 Amundsen

land areas: 5 Coats, Oates 6 Adelie, Graham, Wilkes 7 Enderby 8 Victoria 9 Queen Maud

mountain: 5 Siple 9 Admiralty

sea: 4 Ross 7 Weddell 8 Amundsen

seal: 4 Ross 9 sterrinck

ante: *pay* 5 price 9 poker term 10 come up with 11 initial cost

anteater: 5 tapir 6 animal 7 echidna 8 aardvark, aardwolf, edentate, tamandua, tamanoir

scaly: 5 manis 8 pangolin

antecedent: 4 fore 5 cause, prior 6 former, reason 7 premise 8 ancestor, anterior, previous 9 foregoing, precursor, prototype 10 forerunner 11 predecessor

antedate: 7 precede 10 come before 11 make earlier

antediluvian: 10 antiquated

antelope: gnu 4 puku 5 eland, takin, yakin 6 dik-dik, impala 7 gazelle 8 steenbok 9 pronghorn 10 hartebeest

brown: 5 nagor

extinct: 7 blaubok

female: doe

forest: 5 bongo

four-horned: 6 chouka 7 chikara 10 chousingha

gazelle-like: 5 beira 7 gerenuk

genus: 4 oryx

goat-like: 5 goral, serow 7 chamois

golden: 6 impala

harnessed: 4 guib

large: gnu 4 aste, kudu, oryx 5 addax, beisa, bongo, eland 6 impala, koodoo, nilgai, nilgau 7 bubalis, defassa, gemsbok, sassaby 10 hartebeest

male: 4 buck

mountain: 7 chamois

mythical: 4 yale

pied: 6 bontebok

pronghorn: 6 cabrree, cabrie, cabret, cabrit

reddish: 7 grysbok

royal: 5 ipete 9 kleeneboc

sheep-like: 5 saiga

short-maned: gnu 6 nilgau

small: 6 duiker, grimme 7 grysbok 9 duikerbok

tawny: 5 oribi

tiger-like: 8 agacella

young: kid

antelope-like: 5 bovid 6 bovine

antenna: 4 palp 6 aerial, feeler, lead-in

insect: 5 clava

radar: 7 scanner

Antenor: *father:* 8 Aesyetes

son: 6 Agenor 11 Archelochus

wife: 6 Theano

anterior: 5 front, prior 6 atloid, former, before 7 earlier, ventral 8 atlantal, previous 9 foregoing, preceding 10 antecedent

anteroom: 4 hall 5 foyer, lobby 8 entrance 9 vestibule 11 antechamber

anthelion: 4 halo 6 nimbus 7 antisun, aureole 10 countersun

anthem: 4 hymn, song 5 motet, psalm 7 choral 9 antiphony, offertory 10 responsory

anther: 10 stamen part

anthesis: 9 full bloom 13 efflorescence

anthill: 4 bank 5 mound 9 formicary

anthology: ana 4 book 5 album 6 corpus 7 garland 8 excerpts 9 potpourri 10 collection, miscellany 11 compilation

Anthony Adverse author: 5 Allen

anthozoan: 5 coral, polyp 7 anemone

anthropoid: ape 5 orang 6 gibbon, monkey, simian 7 gorilla, primate, siamang 9 orangutan 10 chimpanzee, troglodyte

anthropophagite: 8 cannibal

anti: con, foe 6 contra 7 against, opposed

anti-aircraft: *fire:* 4 flack

gun: 5 archy 6 pom-pom

antic: 4 dido, lark 5 caper, comic, droll, prank, stunt 6 gambol 7 caprice, gambado 9 ludicrous 10 frolicsome, shenanigan, tomfoolery 11 monkeyshine

anticipate: 4 balk, hope 5 augur, await 6 divine, expect, prepay, thwart 7 counter, foresee, obviate, portend, prepare, presage, prevent 8 do before, forecast, outguess 9 apprehend, forestall, foretaste 10 enjoy ahead 11 precipitate 13 look forward to

anticipation: 6 augury 9 foresight, intuition 10 expectancy 12 presentiment

anticipating: 8 pregnant

antidote: 4 cure 6 remedy 10 corrective, preventive 11 neutralizer, restorative

Antigone: *father:* 7 Oedipus

mother: 7 Jocasta

sister: 6 Ismene

Antilles: *god:* 4 Zeme

native: 5 Ineri

pearl: 4 Cuba

antimacassar: 4 tidy 5 doily

antimony: 4 kohl 7 stibium

pert. to: 7 stibial

Antioch proselyte: 7 Nicolas

antipasto: 6 relish 9 appetizer 11 hors d'oeuvre

antipathy: 6 enmity, nausea, rancor 7 allergy, dislike 8 aversion, distaste, loathing 9 animosity, hostility 10 abhorrence, antagonism, repugnance

antipodal: 7 opposed 8 contrary, opposite 9 diametric 10 across from

antiquated: old 4 aged 5 fusty, hoary, passe 6 old hat 7 ancient, archaic 8 obsolete, outdated, outmoded 9 primitive 12 antediluvian 13 superannuated

antique: old 5 relic, virtu 7 classic, hasbeen 8 artifact, heirloom, type face 9 out of date, venerable 12 old-fashioned

antiseptic: 4 dull 5 vapid 6 iodine, phenol 7 alcohol, camphor, sterile 8 creosote, hygienic, peroxide, sanitary 9 boric acid, germicide, purifying 10 overly neat 12 disinfectant

powder: 6 formin

antisocial: 7 hostile 8 solitary 9 reclusive 11 anarchistic, stand-offish 12 misanthropic

antithesis: 7 reverse 8 antipode, contrast 10 opposition 13 exact opposite

antitoxin: 4 sera(pl.) 5 serum

antler: 4 horn

branch: bay 4 brow, snag, tine 5 crown, royal 7 speller 8 surroyal, trestine 9 bezantler

knob: 6 croche

main stem: 4 beam

skin surrounding: 6 velvet

unbranched: dag 5 spike 7 pricket 9 greenhorn

Antony and Cleopatra character: 4 Eros, Iras 5 Menas, Philo 6 Gallus, Taurus 7 Agrippa

anuran: 4 toad 10 salientian

anurous: 8 tailless

Anu's consort: 4 Anat

anvil: 5 forge 6 smithy, stithy 7 bickern 8 beakiron

bone: 4 amos 5 incus 7 incudes(pl.)

point: 4 horn, beak

tinsmith's: 5 teest

anxiety: 4 care, fear 5 alarm, anger, doubt, dread, panic, worry 7 caution, chagrin, concern, scruple, trouble 8 disquiet, suspense 9 misgiving 10 foreboding, perplexity, solicitude, uneasiness 12 apprehension

anxious: 4 agog 5 eager 6 uneasy 7 carking, unquiet 8 desirous, restless, watchful 9 disturbed, expectant, impatient

any: 4 much, part, some 8 quantity, whatever 9 one or more

anybody: one 7 someone

anyway: 11 at all events 12 nevertheless

Anzac: 12 Australian 12 New Zealander

A-OK: 4 fine 9 excellent 10 all in order

A-one: 4 tops 5 prime 8 superior 9 first rate, top-drawer

aorist: 9 verb tense

aoristic: 10 indefinite 12 undetermined 13 indeterminate

aorta: 6 artery

auodad: 4 arui 5 sheep

apa: 4 tree 7 wallaba

apace: 4 fast 7 quickly, rapidly, swiftly 8 speedily

Apache: 4 Yuma 6 Indian 10 Chiricahua

beverage: 6 tiswin

chief: 7 Cochise 8 Geronimo

jacket: 6 bietle

apar: 9 armadillo

apart: 4 away 5 alone, aloof, aside, riven, solus, split 7 asunder, enisled, removed 8 detached, divorced, in pieces, isolated, reserved, secluded, separate 9 divergent 10 abstracted 11 dissociated 12 individually

from: 6 but for 7 barring, save for 9 excepting, excluding, outside of

apartment: 4 digs, flat 5 abode, rooms, suite 6 rental, walk-up 7 chamber 8 building, dwelling, tenement

upper: 5 solar 6 sollar

apathetic: 4 dull, limp, logy 5 inert, stoic 6 torpid, supine 7 unmoved 8 listless, sluggish 9 impassive, incurious, unfeeling 10 insensible, phlegmatic 11 indifferent, unemotional 12 uninterested 13 dispassionate

apathy: 6 acedia, phlegm, torpor 7 languor 8 doldrums, lethargy 9 lassitude, unconcern 12 indifference

ape (see also **anthropoid**): 4 boor, copy, lout, mime 5 magot, mimic 6 baboon, gelada, gibbon, monkey, parrot, simian 7 emulate, imitate, portray, primate, take off 9 orangutan 10 chimpanzee 11 impersonate

family: 8 pongidae

largest: 7 gorilla

like animal: 5 lemur

apeak: 8 vertical

apeman: 6 Tarzan

aper: 4 boar, mime 5 mimic 7 buffoon, copycat

apercu: 6 digest, precis, sketch 7 insight, outline 10 conspectus 11 brief survey

aperitif: 4 whet 5 drink 8 cocktail 9 appetizer

aperture: gap 4 hole, leak, pore, rima, slit, slot, vent 5 chasm, cleft, crack, stoma 6 window 7 fissure, opening, orifice, ostiole 8 loophole, spiracle 11 perforation

apex: tip, top 4 acme, cusp, noon, peak 5 crest, crown, point, spire 6 apogee, climax, summit, vertex, zenith 8 meridian, pinnacle 9 fastigium 11 culmination, ne plus ultra 12 quintessence

covering: epi 6 finial

elbow: 5 ancon

pert. to: 6 apical

rounded: 6 retuse

Aphareus: *brother:* 7 Lynceus

son: 4 Idas

aphid: 5 louse 8 parasite

aphorism: saw 5 adage, axiom, gnome, maxim, motto 6 dictum, saying 7 epigram, precept, proverb 8 apothegm

Aphrodite: 5 Venus 8 Cytherea 9 butterfly

consort: 4 Ares

father: 4 Zeus

mother: 5 Dione

priestess: 4 Hero

son: 4 Eros 5 Eneas 6 Aeneas

temple site: 6 Paphos

apiary: 4 hive, skep 8 beehouse

apiece: per 4 each 6 singly 8 one by one 9 severally 11 for every one 12 individually, respectively

apish: 5 silly 7 foppish, slavish 8 affected

apishamore: 7 blanket

aplomb: 4 ease, elan, tact 5 nerve, poise 6 surety 8 coolness 9 assurance, composure, sangfroid 10 confidence, equanimity 11 nonchalance, savoir faire

apocalypse: 6 vision 8 prophecy 10 prediction, revelation

apocopate: 5 elide 7 shorten

apocryphal: 4 sham 5 false 6 unreal, untrue 7 dubious 8 doubtful, spurious 10 fictitious, not genuine 11 counterfeit, uncanonical, unauthentic

Apocryphal book: 5 Tobit 6 Baruch, Esdras, Judith 9 Maccabees

apodal: 8 footless

apogee: 4 acme, apex, peak 6 climax, summit, zenith 12 highest point

apograph: 4 copy 10 transcript

Apollo: 6 Delius 7 Phoebus
abode of: 7 Helicon
beloved of: 6 Cyrene, Daphne 8 Calliope
birthplace: 5 Delos
father: 4 Zeus 7 Jupiter
festival: 5 Delia 6 Carnea
instrument: 4 lute, lyre
mother: 4 Leto 6 Latona
oracle site: 6 Delphi
priest: 7 Calchas
sacred vale: 5 Tempe
sister: 5 Diana 7 Artemis
son: Ion 7 Orpheus
traveler: 6 Abaris
twin: 5 Diana

Apollyon: 5 Satan, devil 7 Abaddon, Lucifer 9 archfiend, Beelzebub
evil spirit of: 16 Pilgrim's Progress
vanquished by: 9 Christian

apologetic: 5 sorry 8 contrite, penitent 9 defensive, regretful 10 remorseful

apologue: 4 myth 5 fable, story 7 parable 8 allegory

apology: 4 plea 5 alibi 6 excuse, regret 7 defense 8 mea culpa 9 penitence 11 explanation, vindication 13 justification 14 acknowledgment

apostate: 7 traitor, seceder 8 deserter, disloyal, recreant, renegade, turncoat 9 faithless 10 recidivist

apostle: 4 John, Jude, Paul 5 James, Judas, Peter, Silas, Simon 6 Andrew, Philip, Thomas 7 Matthew, teacher 8 Barnabas, disciple, follower, Matthias, preacher 9 messenger 10 evangelist, missionary 11 Bartholomew
of Indies: 6 Xavier
pert. to: 7 petrine
to Franks: 4 Remi
to Gauls: 5 Denis
to Goths: 7 Ulfilas

apothecary: 7 chemist 8 druggist, gallipot 10 pharmacist
weight: 4 dram 5 grain, pound 7 scruple

apothegm: saw 5 adage, axiom, gnome, maxim 6 dictum, saying, truism 7 proverb 8 aphorism

apotheosize: 5 deify, exalt 7 ennoble, glorify, idolize 8 enshrine, idealize 10 consecrate

Appalachian range: 6 Ramapo

appall, appal: awe 4 stun 5 daunt, shock 6 dismay, 7 depress, horrify, terrify 8 frighten 10 scare stiff 11 make shudder 13 give the creeps

appalling: 5 awful 7 awesome, fearful 8 alarming, dreadful, terrible 9 frightful, unearthly 10 petrifying

appanage: 5 grant 7 adjunct 9 allowance, endowment, privilege 10 perquisite 11 prerogative

apparatus (see also **device, instrument**): rig 4 gear, tool 5 gizmo 6 dingus, gadget, outfit, system 7 utensil 8 material 9 appliance, equipment, machinery, mechanism, trappings 10 furnishing 11 contrivance 12 appurtenance

apparel (see also **dress, vestment**): 4 duds, garb, gear, robe, togs, wear 5 adorn, array, dress, equip 6 attire, clothe, outfit 7 costume, deck out, garment, raiment, vesture 8 clothing, wardrobe 9 embellish 11 furnishings, habiliments

apparent: 4 open 5 clear, overt, plain 6 patent 7 evident, glaring, obvious, seeming, visible 8 distinct, manifest, palpable, probable 9 easy to see, noticeable 10 ostensible, plain as day 11 discernible, perceptible, unconcealed 12 unmistakable

apparition: 5 ghost, haunt, shade, spook 6 shadow, spirit, sprite, wraith 7 eidolon, fantasy, phantom, specter, spectre 8 illusion phantasm, revenant 9 hobgoblin 10 appearance, phenomenon 13 hallucination

appeal: ask, beg 4 call, plea, seek, suit 5 charm, plead 6 adjure, allure, prayer, summon, turn to 7 address, beseech, entreat, glamour, implore, request, solicit 8 approach, petition 9 importune 10 attraction, supplicate

appealing: 4 cute 6 catchy 7 winsome 8 engaging, fetching, pleading, pleasant 9 agreeable, imploring 10 attractive, entrancing

appear: 4 come, look, loom, seem 5 arise, enter, issue, occur 6 arrive, emerge, show up 7 compear(Sc.), develop, emanate 11 materialize

appearance: air, hue 4 form, idea, look, mien, show, view 5 front, guise, sight 6 aspect, facade, manner, 7 arrival, bearing, display 8 demeanor, illusion, presence, pretense 9 semblance 10 disclosure, phenomenon 11 countenance 13 manifestation

first: 5 debut 8 premiere 9 unveiling

appease: 4 calm, ease, hush 5 allay, mease(Sc.), quiet, slake 6 buy off, pacify, please, soften, slake 6 buy off, pacify, please, soften, soothe 7 assuage, content, gratify, mollify, placate, satisfy 8 mitigate 9 sweet-talk 10 conciliate, propitiate 11 tranquilize

appellation: nom(F.), tag 4 name 5 label, title 7 epithet, moniker 8 cognomen, nickname 9 sobriquet 11 designation

appellee: 9 defendant 10 respondent

append: add 4 clip, hang 5 affix, annex, pin to, tag on 6 attach 7 subjoin 8 fasten to

appendage: arm, awn, ear, fin, leg, tab, tag 4 aril, barb, flap, limb, tail, wing 5 canda, extra, rider 6 branch, suffix 7 adjunct, antenna, codicil 8 addition, hanger-on, offshoot, parasite, tentacle 9 accessory 10 dependency

appendix: 4 organ 7 addenda(pl.) 8 addendum, epilogue 10 supplement

appertain: 4 bear on, belong 7 apply to, concern, refer to 8 relate to 12 have to do with

appetite: yen 4 lust, urge, zest 5 gusto, taste 6 desire, hunger, liking, orexis, relish 7 craving, longing, passion, wanting 8 cupidity, penchant, tendency 10 preference, propensity

abnormal: 4 pica 7 bulimia

excessive: 5 greed 8 gluttony, gulosity 10 polyphagia

pert. to: 7 oretic

voracious: 7 edacity 8 rapacity

appetizer: 5 snack 6 canape, relish, savory, tidbit 8 aperitif, cocktail 9 antipasto 11 hors d'oeuvre

applaud: 4 clap, hail 5 cheer, extol 6 praise 7 acclaim, approve, commend, endorse, root for 10 compliment

applauders: 6 claque

applause: 4 hand 5 eclat, kudos 6 bravos, cheers, huzzas, salvos 7 hurrahs, ovation 8 clapping, plaudits 11 approbation

apple: 4 crab, pome 6 Esopus, pippin, russet 7 Baldwin, Fameuse, Winesap, Wealthy 8 Ben Davis, Cortland, Greening, Jonathan, McIntosh 9 Delicious, Oldenberg 10 Rome Beauty 11 Granny Smith, Gravenstein, Northern Spy, Spitzenburg 12 Yellow Newton, York Imperial 17 Yellow Transparent

acid: 5 malic

blight: 5 aphid 8 eriosoma

crushed pulp: 6 pomace

drink: 5 cider 8 Calvados

genus: 5 malus

immature: 6 codlin 7 codling

pastry: 7 strudel

ribbed: 7 costard

seed: pip

wild: 4 crab

apple knocker: 4 hick 5 yokel 6 rustic 7 bumpkin, hayseed 9 greenhorn

apple of one's eye: 7 darling 8 favorite

apple-polish: 4 fawn 5 toady 7 flatter 8 kowtow to 10 curry favor

applesauce: 4 bunk, pulp 5 hokum, hooey 6 relish 7 baloney, dessert, rubbish 8 nonsense 9 poppycock

appliance (see also **tool**): 4 gear 6 device, gadget 7 utensil 9 implement 10 instrument 11 contrivance

applicable: apt, fit 4 meet 5 ad rem(L.) 6 proper, useful 7 apropos, fitting, germane 8 apposite, relative, relevant, suitable 9 pertinent 10 to the point 11 appropriate

applicant: 8 prospect 9 candidate, solicitor

application: use 4 form 5 study 6 appeal, effort 7 request 8 dressing, industry, petition, sedulity 9 diligence, relevance 11 mental labor 12 perseverance

applique: 6 design 7 overlay 8 ornament, trimming 10 decoration

apply: ask, fit, use 5 put on, rub on 6 appeal, bear on, bestow, betake, devote, direct, employ, impose, relate 7 conform, overlay, pertain, request, solicit, utilize 8 carry out, petition, put in for, spread on 9 persevere 10 administer 11 superimpose 13 put into effect

appoggiatura: 9 grace note

appoint: fix, set 4 name 5 allot, elect, equip 6 assign, decree, detail, direct, outfit 7 confirm, furnish, mark out 8 delegate, nominate 9 authorize, designate, prescribe 10 commission

as agent: 6 depute 8 delegate, deputize

appointment: 4 date, post 5 berth, tryst 6 billet, office 7 meeting, station 8 position 9 selection 10 assignment, engagement, rendezvous 11 assignation

apportion: 5 allot, award, grant, share, split 6 assess, assign, divide, parcel, ration 7 divvy up, dole out, mete out, prorate 8 allocate 10 distribute

apportionment: 4 deal 8 dividend, division 9 allowance 12 distribution

appose: 9 place near 11 put opposite 13 put side by side

apposite: apt 6 timely 7 germane 8 relevant, suitable 9 pertinent 11 appropriate

appraise: 4 rate 5 assay, gauge, judge 6 assess, survey 7 analyze, examine 8 estimate, evaluate 10 adjudicate 11 put a price on

appreciable: 7 evident, obvious 8 apparent, palpable, tangible 10 noticeable 11 discernible, perceptible

appreciate: 4 feel, love 5 judge, prize, value 6 admire, esteem 7 advance, cherish, realize, respect 8 increase, treasure 9 be aware of 10 understand 11 go up in worth

appreciation: 5 gusto 6 thanks 7 tribute 8 judgment 9 enjoyment, gratitude 11 recognition, testimonial 12 gratefulness

apprehend: nab, see 4 know, view 5 catch, grasp, seize 6 arrest, detain, divine, fathom, wise up 7 capture, foresee, make out, realize 8 conceive, perceive 9 recognize 10 anticipate, comprehend

apprehensible: 5 lucid 6 noetic 7 sensate 8 knowable 12 intelligible

apprehension: 4 fear, idea 5 doubt, dread, worry 6 arrest, dismay, notion 7 anxiety, capture, concern 8 distrust, mistrust, suspense 9 misgiving, suspicion 10 conception, foreboding, perception, solicitude, uneasiness 11 premonition 12 anticipation, intellection, presentiment 13 understanding

apprehensive: apt 5 aware, jumpy 6 morbid 7 fearful, nervous 9 cognizant, conscious 10 discerning

apprentice: 4 tyro 6 novice, rookie 7 learner, trainee 8 beginner, neophyte 9 greenhorn, novitiate 10 tenderfoot

apprise, apprize: 4 tell, warn 5 value 6 advise, inform, notify, reveal 8 acquaint, disclose 10 appreciate

apprised: 5 aware 7 knowing

approach: try 4 loom, near 5 essay, verge 6 access, accost, advent, coming, impend 7 address, advance, close in, get warm, landing, solicit 8 overture 9 draw close, procedure 11 approximate, break the ice 12 narrow the gap

approbation: 4 okay 5 favor 6 assent, esteem, praise, regard, repute 7 plaudit, respect 8 applause, approval, blessing, sanction 10 admiration 12 commendation

appropriate: apt, due, use 4 grab, meet, take 5 annex, claim, right, steal, usurp 6 assign, assume, borrow, pilfer, pirate, proper, timely, worthy 7 apropos, condign, convert, fitting, germane, impound, preempt, purloin, related 8 accroach, arrogate, becoming, deserved, relevant, suitable 9 pertinent 10 applicable, confiscate, convenient, felicitous, plagiarize 11 set apart for

appropriation: 5 grant 7 stipend, subsidy 9 allotment, allowance 11 special fund

approval: 4 amen 5 eclat 6 assent 7 go

ahead, support 8 blessing, sanction 10 imprimatur 11 approbation, benediction

approve: 4 back, like, okay, pass 5 adopt, allow, clear, favor, value 6 accept, admire, concur, ratify 7 applaud, certify, commend, confirm, consent, endorse, initial, vote for 8 accredit, sanction 9 authorize 10 compliment 11 countenance, think well of

approximate: 4 near 5 about, circa, close 8 approach, resemble 9 come close

approximately: 4 nigh 5 about 6 almost, around, nearly 7 roughly 9 virtually 10 more or less 11 practically

appurtenance: 4 gear 5 annex 7 adjunct 8 appendix 9 accessory, apparatus, appendage, appliance, belonging

après: 5 after 10 afterwards

apricot: ume 4 ansu, tree 5 color, fruit 8 Blenheim

confection: 5 mebos 6 meebos

cordial: 7 perisco 8 periscot

vine: 6 maypop

a priori: 9 deductive 11 conditional, inferential, presumptive, reasoned out

apron: bib 4 tier 5 cover, smock 6 runway, shield, tarmac 8 pinafore 10 protection

leather: 4 dick 8 barmskin, lambskin 9 forestage

apropos: apt 4 as to, in re, meet 5 about, anent 6 timely 7 fitting, germane 8 by the way, relevant, suitable 9 opportune, pertinent 10 to the point 11 appropriate, in respect to

apse: 5 niche 6 recess 10 orbit point, projection

apt: fit, pat 4 able, deft, keen 5 adept, alert, prone, quick, ready 6 clever, liable, likely 7 apropos, capable, fitting 8 apposite, dextrous, disposed, inclined, skillful, suitable, tendency 9 competent, consonant, dexterous, pertinent 10 proficient 11 appropriate

apteral: 8 wingless

opposite of: 4 alar 5 alate

apteryx: 4 bird, kiwi

aptitude: art 4 bent, gift, turn 5 craft, flair, knack 6 genius, talent 7 ability, faculty, leaning 8 instinct 10 propensity 11 disposition

aquamarine: gem 4 blue 5 beryl, color

aquarium: 4 bowl, pool, pond, tank 5 globe

aquatic plant: 4 lily 5 coral, lotus 6 enalid, sugamo 7 elatine, seaweed 10 hydrophyte

aqueduct: 5 canal 7 channel, conduit, passage 9 conductor, water pipe

of Sylvius: 4 iter

aquila: 5 eagle
aquiline: 6 hooked 7 curving 9 eagle-like, prominent
Aquinas work: 5 Summa
aquosity: 7 wetness 8 moisture 10 wateriness
ara: 5 macaw
arab: 4 waif 5 gamin, nomad 6 urchin 8 wanderer
araba: cab 5 coach 6 monkey 8 carriage
Arabian: *abode:* dar 4 tent
  alphabet: See **Arabic:** *alphabet*
  antelope: 5 addax
  author: 6 lokman
  banquet: 5 diffa
  bazaar: suq
  bird: 7 phoenix
  caliph: Ali 6 sharif, sherif 7 shareef, shereef
  caravan: 6 cafila
  cloak: aba
  coffee: 5 mocha
  coin: 4 lari 5 carat, dinar, kabik, riyal
  cosmetic: 4 kohl
  demon: 4 jinn 5 afrit, genie, jinni 6 afreet, jinnee
  dish: 8 couscous
  drink: 4 bosa, boza 5 bozah 6 lebban
  drum: 9 tara-booka
  fabric: aba 4 haik
  father: abu 4 abba, abou
  flour source: 4 samh
  garment: aba 4 haik 6 cabaan 7 burnous 8 burnoose
  gazelle: 4 cora 5 ariel
  goddess: 5 Allat
  grammar: 7 ajrumya
  horse: anezeh 8 kadischi, palomino
  infantryman: 5 askar
  jasmine: 4 bela 10 sampaquita
  judge: 4 cadi
  land: 6 feddan
  measure: den, saa 4 ferk, foot, kist 5 achir, barid, cadba, cafiz, covid, cuddy, makuk, mille, qasab, teman, woibe, zudda 6 artaba, assbaa, covido, feddan, gariba, ghalva 7 caphite, farsakh, farsang, kiladja, marhale, nusfiah
  palm: 4 doom, doum
  peasant: 6 fellah
  philosopher: 6 Farabi 8 Averroes
  plant: kat 5 retem
  prince (see also ruler below): 6 sherif 7 shereef
  raiders: 8 fedayeen
  river bed: 4 wadi, wady
  romance: 5 antar 6 antara
  ruler: 4 amir, emir 5 ameer, emeer, sheik 6 sultan
  shrub: kat 5 alhaj, retem
  tambourine: 4 taar 5 daira

  tea shrub: kat
  tent encampment: 5 douar
  vessel: 4 dhow 6 boutre, sambuk
  weight: 4 rotl 5 cheki, kella, nasch, nevat, occque, oukia, ratel, toman, vakia 6 bokard, dirhem, miskal, tomand 8 farsalah
  wind: 6 simoom, simoon
Arabian Nights: *bird:* roc 4 aqib
  character: Ali 4 Sidi 5 Amina 7 Zobeide
  dervish: 4 Agib
  merchant: 7 Sindbad
  poet: Kab 5 Antar
  prince: 7 Alasnam
  sailor: 6 Sinbad 7 Sindbad
  sorceress: 5 Amine
  youth: 7 Aladdin
Arabic: *alphabet:* tha, jim, kha, dal, zay, sin, sad, dad, ayn, qaf, kaf, lam, mim, nun, waw 4 alif, dhal, shin 5 ghayn
  script: 5 cufic, kufic, neski 6 neshki
arable: 7 fertile 8 plowable, tillable
aracanga: 5 macaw
aracari: 6 toucan
arachnid: 4 crab, mite, tick 6 acarus, spider 8 scorpion 9 tarantula
Aram: 12 ancient Syria
Aramaic: 6 Syriac 9 Samaritan
araneous: 4 thin 5 delicate, gossamer 9 arachnoid 10 cobweblike
araphorostic: 7 unsewed 8 seamless
araponga: 8 bellbird
Arawakan: *Indian:* 4 Uran 5 Araua, Bares, Guana, Moxos, Piros 6 Campas 7 Atorais, Banivas, Jucunas, Lucayos, Tacanan, Ticunan 8 Lorenzan
  language: 5 Taino
arbiter: 5 judge 6 umpire 7 referee 8 dictator 9 moderator 11 adjudicator
arbitrary: 4 rash 6 random, thetic 7 willful 8 absolute, despotic 9 imperious 10 autocratic, capricious, highhanded, peremptory, tyrannical 11 dictatorial 12 unreasonable 13 irresponsible
arbitrate: 6 decide, settle 7 adjudge, mediate 9 determine, intercede
arbitrator: 8 mediator 9 ombudsman 11 conciliator
arbor: bar, rod 4 axle, beam 5 bower, shaft 6 gazebo 7 mandrel, pergola, retreat, spindle, trellis
arbustum: 5 copse 7 orchard 10 plantation
arc: bow 4 bend, halo 5 curve, orbit 7 rainbow 8 spotlight 10 circle part
  chord of: 4 sine
  horizon: 7 azimuth
arc lamp rod: 6 carbon
arca: box 5 chest, paten 9 reliquary
arcade: 6 loggia 7 gallery, portico 8 arcature 9 colonnade 10 passageway

Arcadia: 4 Eden 6 Arcady 8 paradise
huntress: 8 Atalanta
princess: 4 Auge
town: 4 Alea
woodland spirit: Pan
arcadian: 5 ideal, rural 6 rustic, simple 7 bucolic, idyllic 8 pastoral, shepherd
arcane: 6 hidden, occult 8 esoteric 10 cabalistic, mysterious
arcanum: 6 elixir, remedy, secret 7 mystery
Arcas: *father:* 4 Zeus
mother: 8 Callisto
son: 4 Azan 8 Apheidas
arch: bow, coy, sly 4 bend, hump, span 5 chief, curve, great, prime, saucy, vault 6 camber, clever, fornix, impish, instep 7 cunning, eminent, roguish, support, waggish 9 principal 11 mischievous
inner curve of: 8 intrados
kind of: 4 flat 5 round, Tudor 6 lancet 7 rampant, trefoil 9 horseshoe, primitive, segmental 10 shouldered 11 equilateral 12 basket-handle, four-centered 13 three-cornered
memorial: 6 pailoo, pailou, pailow
molding: 9 accolade
part: 8 keystone, springer, voussoir
pointed: 4 ogee 5 ogive 6 Gothic
arch-enemy: 5 devil, Satan
archaic: old 7 ancient 8 historic, obsolete 9 venerable 10 antiquated 12 old-fashioned
archangel: 5 Satan, Uriel 7 Gabriel, Michael, Raphael
archer: 4 Clym, Egil, Tell 5 cupid 6 bowman 9 Robin Hood 11 Sagittarius
archery: *deity:* 6 Apollo 7 Artemis
locker: 6 ascham
lover: 11 toxophilite
target: 4 wand 5 clout
archetype: 4 idea 5 ideal, model 7 example, paragon, pattern 8 exemplar, original, paradigm 9 prototype 10 pilot model
architect: 5 maker 6 artist, author 7 artisan, builder, creator, planner 8 designer 9 draftsman
architectural: 8 tectonic
architecture: *convexity:* 7 entasis
order: 5 Doric, Ionic 10 Corinthian
ornament: ove 5 gutta 6 dentil, rosace 7 rosette
style: 5 Doric, Greek, Ionic, Tudor 6 French, Gothic, Lancet, Modern, Norman 7 Baroque, Cape Cod, English, Italian, Moorish, Spanish 8 Academic, Colonial, Egyptian, Etruscan, Georgian 9 Byzantine, Palladian 10 Corinthian, Romanesque 11 Renaissance
archive: 5 annal 6 museum, record 7 library 8 document, register 9 chronicle

archon: 5 ruler 8 dictator, official 10 magistrate
arctic: icy 4 cold, cool, shoe 5 gelid, polar 6 boreal, chilly, frigid, galosh 8 northern, overshoe
Arctic: *base:* 4 Etah
bird: auk 9 ptarmigan
canoe: 5 kayak, umiak 6 oomiak
current: 8 Labrador
dog: 5 husky 7 samoyed 8 malamute
explorer: Nay, Rae 4 Byrd, Eric, Kane, Ross 5 Davis, Peary 6 Baffin, Bering, Button, Greely, Hudson, Nansen, Nobile 7 McClure, Wilkins, Wrangel 8 Amundsen 9 Frobisher, Rasmussen, Stefansson 10 Willoughby
gull (genus): 4 xema
headland: 5 Odden
inhabitant: 4 Lapp 5 Aleut, Inuit 6 Eskimo, Indian 7 Alaskan 9 Laplander
island: 5 Banks, Devon 6 Baffin 7 Wrangel 8 Bathurst
jacket: 5 parka 6 anorak
musk ox: 6 ovibos
plain: 6 tundra
plant: 5 ledum
sea: 4 Kara 6 Laptev 7 Barents, Chukchi, Lincoln 8 Beaufort
sea animal: 6 narwal, walrus 8 narwhale
snowstorm: 5 purga
Arcturus: 4 star
arcuate: 4 bent 5 bowed 6 arched, curved, hooked
ardent: hot 4 avid, fond, keen, warm 5 eager, fiery, rethe(Sc.) 6 ablaze, fervid 7 amorous, earnest, feeling, fervent, flaming, intense, shining, zealous 8 desirous, vehement 9 impetuous, perfervid 11 inflammable 12 enthusiastic
ardor: 4 dash, elan, glow, heat, love, zest 5 gusto, verve 6 desire, fervor, mettle, spirit 7 passion 8 devotion, vivacity 9 animation, calenture 10 enthusiasm
arduous: 4 hard 5 lofty, steep 6 trying 7 onerous 8 exacting, tiresome, toilsome 9 difficult, laborious, strenuous 10 exhausting
area: 4 belt, size, zone 5 field, range, realm, scene, scope, space, tract 6 extent, locale, region, sector, sphere 7 expanse, purlieu 8 district, province 9 bailiwick, territory 12 neighborhood
measure: are 4 acre, road 6 orpent 7 hectare
pert. to: 7 spatial
areca: 4 palm 5 betel
arena: pit 4 bowl, oval, ring, rink 5 court, field, stage 6 sphere 7 stadium, theater 8 coliseum, province 10 hippodrome 12 amphitheater
sports: See **field:** *athletic*
arenaceous: 5 sandy 6 gritty 8 sabulous

areola: pit 4 area, ring, spot 5 space 9 periphery 10 interstice

areometer: 10 hydrometer

Ares: 4 Mars
father: 4 Zeus
mother: 4 Enyo, Hera
sister: 4 Eris
son: 6 Cycnus

arete: 4 crag 5 crest, ridge, valor 6 virtue 9 manliness 10 excellence

argali: 5 sheep 6 aoudad

argent: 4 coin 5 money, white 6 silver 7 shining, silvery 9 whiteness

Argentina: *capital:* 11 Buenos Aires
capital suburb: 5 Lanus, Moron 7 Quilmes
city: 4 Azul, Goya 5 Jujuy, Salta 6 Parana 7 Cordoba, La Rioja, Mendoza, Posadas, San Juan, Santa Fe, Tucuman 8 Santiago
estuary: 7 La Plata
explored by: 5 Cabot 11 Juan de Solis
falls: 6 Iguacu, Iguazu 7 Iguassu
former dictator: 9 Juan Peron 11 Isabel Peron
Indian: 4 Lule 7 Guarani
measure: 4 sino, vara 5 legua 6 cuadra, fanega 7 manzana
monetary unit: 4 peso 7 centavo
mountain pass: 9 Uspallata
mountain peak: 4 Mayo 5 Cachi, Laudo 6 Bonete, Pissis, Rincon 9 Aconcagua, Incahuasi, Tupungato
mountain range: 5 Andes
port: 6 Rawson, Viedma 7 La Plata, Rosario 8 Gallegos 11 Bahia Blanca, Buenos Aires
province: 5 Chaco, Jujuy, Pampa, Rioja, Salta 6 Chubut 7 Cordoba, Formosa, Mendoza, Neuquen, Rio Negro, San Juan, San Luis, Santa Fe, Tucuman 8 Misiones, Santiago 9 Catamarca, Entre Rios
river: 4 Coig 5 Atuel, Chico, Dulce, Limay, Negro, Teuco 6 Chubut, Parana, Quinto, Salado 7 Bermejo 8 Colorado, Gallegos 9 Rio Grande
southern steppes: 9 Patagonia
volcano: 5 Lanin, Maipo 6 Domuyo 7 Peteroa
weight: 4 last 5 grano 7 quintal 8 tonelada

argil: 4 clay 7 alumina

argillaceous: 5 loamy 6 clayey, doughy, earthy, spongy

Argonaut: 5 Jason 8 wanderer 10 adventurer

Argos: *king:* 4 Abas 6 Danaus 7 Lynceus 8 Acrisius, Adrastus
princess: 5 Danae

argosy: 4 boat, ship 5 craft, fleet 6 supply, vessel 7 galleon 10 storehouse

argot: 4 cant 5 flash, lingo, slang 6 jargon, patois 7 dialect

argue: 4 moot, show, spar 5 cavil, claim, clash 6 bicker, debate, induce, reason 7 contend, contest, discuss, dispute, quarrel, wrangle 8 indicate, maintain, persuade 11 expostulate, remonstrate

argument: row 4 case, fuss, idea, plea, plot, text 5 set to, theme 6 combat, debate, hassle, reason 7 defense, polemic, rhubarb, summary 8 abstract 9 discourse, statement 10 difference 11 altercation, controversy
conclusive: 6 corker 7 crusher 8 clincher 9 knockdown 11 sockdolager, sockdologer
fallacious: 7 sophism
negative side: con
positive side: pro
specious: rot 8 claptrap, nonsense 9 sophistry 10 paralogism
starting point: 7 premise

argumentative: 7 eristic 8 forensic 10 rhetorical 11 indicative, contentious, presumptive 12 disputatious 13 controversial

argute: 5 acute, sharp 6 shrewd, shrill 8 saw-edged 9 sagacious

arhat: 4 monk 5 lohan, saint

aria: air 4 solo, song, tune 6 melody 7 sortita

arid: dry 4 bald, bare, dull, lean 6 barren, jejune, meager 7 parched, sterile 8 withered 9 unfertile, waterless 10 desiccated, siccaneous 12 moistureless 13 uninteresting

ariel: 7 gazelle

Aries: ram
mother: 4 Enyo

aril: pod 7 coating 8 covering 9 appendage 10 integument

ariose: 7 melodic 8 songlike 9 melodious

arise: 4 flow, lift, rear, soar 5 begin, get up, issue, mount, raise, stand, surge, tower, waken 6 accrue, amount, appear, ascend, come up, derive, emerge, happen, spring 7 develop, emanate, proceed 8 stem from 9 come about, originate, take place

arista: 4 awn 5 beard 9 appendage

aristocracy: 5 elite 8 nobility 9 oligarchy 10 ruling class, upper crust

aristocrat: 4 peer 7 Brahmin 8 nobleman 9 blue-blood, patrician 12 thoroughbred

Aristophanes *work:* 5 Birds, Frogs 6 Clouds, Plutus

Aristotle: 5 Greek 11 philosopher
birthplace: 6 Thrace 7 Stagira
category: 4 time 5 place 6 action 7 quality 8 position, quantity, relation 9 pas-

sivity, substance 10 possession
disciple: 11 Peripatetic
father: 10 Nicomachus
school: 6 Lyceum
teacher: 5 Plato
works: 7 De Anima, Organon, Poetico 8 Politics, Rhetoric
Arizona: *capital:* 7 Phoenix
city: Ajo 4 Mesa, Yuma 5 Tempe 6 Bisbee, Tucson 7 Nogales 8 Prescott 9 Flagstaff
county: 4 Gila, Pima 5 Pinal 6 Apache, Graham, Mohave, Navajo 7 Cochise, Yavapai 8 Coconino, Maricopa
dam: 6 Hoover 7 Boulder 8 Coolidge, Tailings 9 Roosevelt
desert: 7 Painted
early explorer: 6 De Niza 8 Coronado
forest: 6 Kaibab 9 Petrified
gorge: 11 Grand Canyon
Indian: 4 Hopi, Pima, Yuma 6 Apache, Navaho, Navajo, Papago
Indian war chiefs: 7 Cochise 8 Geronimo
lake: 4 Mead 6 Havasu 9 Roosevelt, San Carlos
mountain peak: 5 Lemon 6 Graham 7 Hualpai, Pastora 8 Mazatzal 9 Humphreys
mountain range: 5 Black 8 Gila Bend 13 Santa Catalina
river: 4 Gila, Salt 5 Verde 8 Colorado, San Pedro 9 San Carlos
site of noted battle: 8 O.K. Corral (Tombstone)
state bird: 10 cactus wren
state flower: 7 saguaro
state motto: 9 Ditat Deus (God enriches)
state nickname: 11 Grand Canyon
state tree: 9 paloverde
ark: bin, box 4 boat, ship 5 barge, chest, hutch 6 basket, coffer, refuge, wangan 7 retreat, shelter, wanigan 8 flatboat
builder: Noe 4 Noah
resting place: 6 Ararat
Arkansas: *capital:* 10 Little Rock
city: 4 Hope, Mena 5 Salem, Wynne 6 Des Arc, Lonoke, Searcy 7 De Queen 9 Fort Smith, Pine Bluff 10 Hot Springs
county: Lee 4 Clay, Drew, Pike, Poke, Pope, Yell 5 Izard, Sharp, Stone 6 Baxter, Chicot, Conway, Sevier 7 Pulaski 8 Poinsett
explored by: 6 de Soto, Joliet 7 La Salle 9 Marquette
Indian tribe: 5 Caddo 6 Quapaw
lake: 7 Greeson, Norfork
mountain: 4 Blue 6 Boston, Walker 8 Magazine
plateau: 5 Ozark
river: Red 5 Black, White 6 Saline 8 Arkansas, Cimarron, Ouachita 11 Mississippi

spa: 10 Hot Springs
state bird: 11 mockingbird
state flower: 12 apple blossom
state motto: 13 Regnat Populus (The people rule)
state nickname: 17 Land of Opportunity
state tree: 4 pine
unique mine product in U.S.: 8 diamonds
arkose: 9 sandstone
arm: bay, fin 4 limb, spur, wing 5 bough, equip, fiord, firth, fjord, force, inlet, might, power 6 branch, energy, member, outfit, sleeve, weapon 7 flipper, fortify, furnish, prepare, protect, provide, support 8 strength 9 appendage, extension 10 instrument, projection
bone: 4 ulna 6 radius 7 humerus
hollow at bend: 8 chelidon
joint: 4 ares 5 elbow, wrist
muscle: 6 biceps 7 triceps
part: 4 ares 5 elbow, wrist
pert. to: 8 brachial
armada: 4 navy 5 fleet 8 flotilla, squadron, warships 9 task force
armadillo: 5 poyou 6 mulita 7 tatouay 8 pangolin 10 pichiciago
giant: 4 tatu 8 tatou 6 peludo
small: 4 peba 11 quirquincho
three banded: 4 apar 5 apara 6 mataco
armament: 7 defense 8 ordnance, security, weaponry 9 munitions, safeguard 12 military gear
armamentarium: 4 data 5 store 6 armory 7 arsenal 9 apparatus, equipment 10 collection
armband: 7 maniple 8 brassard
Armenia: 14 Soviet Republic
ancient name: 5 Minni 8 Anatolia
capital: 7 Yerevan
lake: 5 Sevan
mountain: 7 Aragats
river: 5 Araks 6 Razdan (Zanga)
armet: 6 helmet
armistice: 4 lull 5 peace, truce 9 cessation 10 suspension
armoire: 8 cupboard, wardrobe 12 clothespress
armor: 4 egis, mail 5 guard, plate, byrnie, sheath, shield 7 cuirass, defense, hauberk 8 covering 10 protection
arm: 8 brassard, brassart 9 gardebras
armpit: 8 pallette
bearer: 8 squire 7 armiger, custrel
cap: 10 cerveliere
elbow guard: 9 cubitiere
face: 6 beaver 7 ventail 8 aventail
foot: 8 sabbaton, solleret
hand: 8 gauntlet
head: 4 coif 6 helmet 7 basinet
horse: 5 barde 6 crinet 7 peytrel, poitrel 8 chamfron
knee: 11 genouillere

leg: 4 boot, jamb 5 jambe 6 greave 7 chausse, jambeau

shoulder: 7 ailette 8 pauldron, pouldron 9 epauliere

skirt: 4 tace 5 tasse 6 taslet, tasset 11 braconniere

thigh: 5 cuish 6 cuisse, tuille 8 cuissard

throat: 6 camail, gorget

armored: 6 mailed, plated 8 ironclad, shielded 9 panoplied, protected 11 encuirassed

armpit: ala(L.) 5 oxter(Sc.) 6 axilla 7 axillae(pl.)

pert. to: 7 axillar

armory: 4 dump 5 depot 7 arsenal 8 magazine 9 warehouse

army: 4 here, host 5 array, crowd, force, horde 6 cohort, legion, number, throng, troops 7 militia 8 soldiers, warriors 9 multitude

chaplain: 5 padre

commission: 6 brevet

engineer: 6 sapper 7 pioneer

enlisted man: NCO 5 GI Joe 7 private 8 doughboy

mascot: 4 mule

meal: 4 chow, mess

NCO: PFC 8 corporal, sergeant

officer: 5 major 7 captain, colonel, general 8 sergeant 10 lieutenant

pert. to: 7 martial 8 military

post: 4 base, camp, fort

postal abbreviation: APO

school: OCS, OTS 7 academy 9 West Point

storehouse: 5 depot 6 armory 7 arsenal

unit: 4 corps, squad, troop 5 detail, outfit 7 brigade, company, platoon 8 division, regiment, battalion, task force 10 detachment

vehicle: 4 jeep, tank 9 half-track

army ant: 6 driver 9 legionary

aroid: 4 taro 5 apium, tania 6 tanier 8 araceous

aroma: 4 odor 5 nidor, savor, scent, smell 6 flavor 7 bouquet, perfume 9 fragrance, redolence

aromatic: 5 balmy, spicy, sweet 6 fruity, savory 7 odorous, piquant, pungent 9 ambrosial

gum: 5 myrrh

herb: 4 dill, mint, nard 5 anise, basil, clary, nondo, thyme 8 lavender, rosemary

seed: 5 anise, cumin 6 nutmeg

spice: 4 mace 5 clove 8 cinnamon

tree: 6 balsam, laurel 8 huisache 9 sassafras

weed: 5 tansy

around: 4 near 5 about, alive, circa 6 in turn 7 close by, through 10 encircling, enveloping, everywhere, on all sides

12 here and there

around-the-clock: 8 constant, unending 9 incessant, perpetual 10 continuous 11 day and night

arouse: 4 call, fire, move, spur, stir, whet 5 alarm, awake, evoke, pique, raise, rally, rouse 6 excite, foment, incite, kindle, revive, summon, thrill, work up 7 actuate, agitate, animate, enliven, incense, inflame 9 stimulate

arpeggio: 7 roulade, flourish 10 musical run

arraign: try 4 cite 6 accuse, charge, indict 7 impeach 8 denounce 9 challenge 11 incriminate 13 call to account

arrange: fix, set 4 edit, file, form, plan, sort 5 adapt, align, array, drape, frame grade, group, score, space 6 adjust, codify, design, devise, settle 7 catalog, compose, dispose, gradate, marshal, prepare, seriate, work out 8 classify, conclude, organize, regulate, tabulate 9 collocate 10 put in order 11 alphabetize, orchestrate

mutually: 5 agree 7 concert

arrangement: 4 deal 5 index, order, set-up 6 format, layout, scheme, system, treaty 7 pattern 8 contract, sequence 9 direction, structure 10 allocation 11 composition, disposition 12 dispensation

arrant: bad 5 utter 6 brazen 7 blatant, vagrant 8 rascally 9 confirmed, downright, itinerant, notorious, out and out, shameless 11 unmitigated 13 thoroughgoing

arras: 7 drapery, hanging 8 tapestry

array: 4 garb, host, robe, show 5 adorn, align, dress, habit, order 6 attire, bedeck, clothe, draw up, finery, series 7 apparel, arrange, company, deck out, display, furnish, marshal 8 accouter, grouping 10 assemblage

arrears: 4 IOU's 9 liability 11 unpaid bills 12 indebtedness

arrest: nab 4 curb, grab, halt, hold, jail, stay, stop 5 catch, check, delay, pinch, seize 6 collar, detain, hinder, lock up, retard, thwart 7 capture, custody, suspend 8 imprison, slow down, obstruct, restrain 9 apprehend, intercept, interrupt 11 incarcerate

arresting: 8 gripping, pleasing, striking 10 impressive, noticeable

arret: 5 edict 6 decree 8 decision, judgment

arrie: auk 5 murre 9 guillemot, razorbill

arris, aris: 4 pien 5 angle, piend

arrive: 4 come, land, show 5 reach 6 appear, attain, make it, turn up 7 prosper, succeed 8 get there

arrogance: 5 pride 6 hubris, hybris 7

conceit, disdain, egotism, hauteur **9** insolence **10** effrontery **11** affectation

arrogant: 5 lofty, proud **6** lordly, uppish **7** haughty **8** affected, assuming, cavalier, fastuous, insolent, superior **9** conceited, insulting, presuming **10** disdainful, hoity-toity **11** dictatorial, domineering, highfalutin, impertinent, overbearing, **12** contemptuous, contumelious, presumptuous, supercilious

arrogate: 4 grab, take **5** claim, seize, usurp **6** assume **7** preempt **8** take over **10** commandeer, confiscate

arrondissement: 4 ward **8** division

arrow: pin, rod **4** bolt, dart, reed **5** shaft **6** sprite, weapon **7** missile, pointer **9** indicator

case: **6** quiver

feathered: **4** vire

maker: **6** bowyer **8** fletcher

part: **4** barb, butt, head, nock **5** shaft, stele **7** feather

point: neb **4** barb

poison: **4** haya, inee, upas **5** urali **6** antiar, curare, sumpit, wagogo **7** woorali

rotating: **4** vire

arrow-shaped: 6 beloid **8** sagittal **9** sagittate

Arrowsmith author: 5 Lewis

arrowstone: 9 belemnite

arrowwood: 5 alder **9** buckthorn **10** burrobrush

arroyo: 5 brook, creek, gulch, gully, hondo, zanja **6** ravine, stream **7** channel **11** watercourse

ars artium: 5 logic

arsenal: 6 armory, supply **8** dockyard, magazine **10** storehouse **13** armamentarium

arsenate: *copper:* **7** erinite

hydrous zinc: **7** adamite

red manganese: **9** sarkinite

arsenic: 6 poison **8** chemical

antimony: **10** allemonite

sulfide: **7** realgar

trisulfide: **8** orpiment

arsenillo: 9 atacamite

arsenopyrite: 7 danaite

arsis: 4 beat **5** ictus **6** accent, rhythm

opposed to: **6** thesis

arson: 12 incendiarism

arsonist: 7 firebug **10** pyromaniac

art: ars(L.) **4** wile **5** craft, knack, magic, skill, trade **7** calling, cunning, faculty, finesse, science **8** business, learning **9** dexterity, duplicity, ingenuity **10** profession **11** contrivance, cultivation

black: **5** magic **7** alchemy **8** wizardry **9** diablerie **10** demonology, necromancy **11** conjuration

fancier of: **6** votary **7** esthete, devotee **10** dilettante **11** connoisseur

gallery: **5** salon **6** museum

manual: **5** craft, sloid, slojd, sloyd

school: **4** Dada **5** Dutch **6** ashcan, French, Paduan **7** Bauhaus, Flemish, Italian, Lombard, Umbrian **8** American, eclectic, Milanese, Scottish **9** Bolognese **10** Raphaelite

style: pop **4** Dada **5** genre **6** cubism **7** baroque, fauvism, realism **10** surrealism **11** objectivism, primitivism, romanticism **13** impressionism **14** abstractionism

Artemis: 5 Diana

birthplace: **5** Delos

brother: **6** Apollo

father: **4** Zeus

mother: **4** Leto

priestess: **9** Iphigenia

artel: 5 union **11** association, cooperative

artery: way **4** path, road **5** route **6** course, street, vessel **7** anonyma, conduit, highway **9** maxillary

trunk: **5** aorta **6** aortae(pl.)

head: **7** carotid

heart: **8** coronary

pulsation: **5** ictus

artful: apt, sly **4** foxy, wily **5** suave **6** adroit, clever, crafty, facile, shrewd, smooth, tricky **7** crooked, cunning, politic, vulpine **8** slippery, stealthy **9** deceitful, deceptive, designing, dexterous, practical

Artful Dodger: 7 Dawkins (Jack)

artfulness: 8 subtlety **9** diplomacy, duplicity, strategem **10** refinement

arthritis: 4 gout

arthron: 5 joint **12** articulation

Arthur: See King Arthur

artichoke: 5 plant **6** Cynara **7** chorogi

leafstalk: **5** chard

relative: **7** cardoon

article: one, the **4** item, term **5** essay, paper, piece, plank, point, story, theme, thing **6** clause, detail, object, report **7** feature **8** causerie, doctrine **9** condition, statement **10** particular **11** composition, stipulation

French: les, une

German: das, der, die, ein

Spanish: las, los, una

articulate: say **5** speak, utter, vocal **6** fluent, verbal **7** express, jointed **8** distinct **9** enunciate, pronounce, talkative **10** formulated, meaningful, say clearly **12** intelligible

artificer: 4 hoax, plot, ploy, ruse, wile **5** blind, cheat, dodge, feint, fraud, guile, skill, trick **6** deceit, device, gambit **7** cunning, evasion, finesse **8** intrigue, maneuver, pretense **9** deception, expedient, ingenuity, invention, stratagem **10** subterfuge **11** machination

artificial: 4 mock, sham **5** bogus, faked, false **6** ersatz, forced, pseudo, unreal **7**

assumed, feigned 8 affected, falsetto, spurious 9 insincere, pretended, simulated, synthetic, unnatural 10 factitious, fictitious, theatrical 11 counterfeit

artillery: 4 arms, guns 6 cannon 7 rockets 8 missiles, ordnance
emplacement: 7 battery
fire: 5 salvo 6 rafale 7 barrage
wagon: 6 camion 7 caisson

artilleryman: 6 gunner, lascar 8 topechee 9 cannoneer 10 bombardier

artiodactyl: ox; pig 4 deer, goat 5 camel, sheep 6 artiad 7 giraffe 8 antelope 12 hippopotamus

artisan: 6 expert 9 craftsman 12 professional 13 skilled worker

artist: 4 star 5 actor 6 dancer, expert, master, singer, wizard 7 painter 8 designer, musician, sculptor, virtuoso 9 performer 12 professional

artless: 4 naif, open 5 frank, naive, plain 6 candid, rustic, simple 7 natural 8 innocent, trusting 9 childlike, guileless, ingenuous, untutored 10 unaffected 11 undesigning 15 unsophisticated

arty: 5 showy 9 imitative, overblown 11 pretentious, superficial

arui: 5 sheep 6 aoudad

arum: 4 taro 5 aroid, plant 10 cuckoopint
family: 7 araceae
water: 5 calla

arundinaceous: 5 reedy

Aryan: 11 Indo-Iranian 12 Indo-European
deity: 6 Ormazd, Ormuzd
god of fire: 4 Agni
language: 5 Latin 7 Persian 8 Sanskrit
of India: 5 Hindu

as: for, qua 4 like, that, thus, when 5 equal, since, while 7 because, equally, similar 9 therefore
a rule: 7 usually 8 commonly 9 generally 10 ordinarily
good as: 5 about 6 all but, almost, nearly
if: 5 quasi 9 seemingly
long as: 5 since 7 because 10 seeing that 11 considering

As You Like It character: 5 Celia, Phebe 6 Jaques, Oliver 7 Charles, Orlando 8 Rosalind
clown: 10 Touchstone
forest: 5 Arden
Rosalind's alias: 8 Ganymede

Asa: 6 healer 9 physician
father: 4 Abia
son: 11 Jehoshaphat

asafetida: 4 hing 6 ferula 8 gum resin

ascend: 4 rise, soar 5 climb, mount, scale, tower 7 clamber 8 escalate, progress 12 gain altitude

ascendancy: 4 sway 5 power 7 control, mastery, success 8 dominion, prestige, whip hand 9 authority, dominance, influence, supremacy 11 sovereignty, superiority

ascent: 4 hill, ramp, rise 5 slope 6 stairs 7 incline, upgrade, upswing 8 eminence, gradient, progress 9 acclivity, elevation 11 advancement

ascertain: get 5 learn 6 dig out 7 find out, seek out, unearth 8 discover 9 determine

ascetic: nun 4 monk, yogi 5 fakir, stark, stoic, Yogin 6 Essene, severe, strict 7 austere, eremite, recluse, stylite 8 anchoret 9 abstinent, anchorite 10 abstemious 11 disciplined, self-denying
Buddhist: 7 bhikshu

ascot: tie 5 scarf 6 cravat 7 necktie 9 racetrack
relative: bib 6 choker 7 bolo tie

ascribe: lay 4 cite 5 blame, infer, refer 6 accuse, allege, assign, attach, charge, credit, impute 8 accredit 9 attribute

ascription: 6 prayer 11 declaration
of praise: 6 gloria
popular: 6 repute

ascus: bag, sac

asea: 4 lost 6 addled, adrift, in a fog 7 puzzled, sailing 8 confused 9 befuddled, uncertain 10 bewildered, ocean-going

aseptic: 4 cold 5 clean 6 barren 7 sterile 8 detached, lifeless 9 purifying

Asgard: *bridge to:* 7 Bifrost
watchman: 8 Heimdall

ash: ase(Sc.) 4 cite, tree 5 ember, rowan 6 cinder 7 clinker, residue
receptacle: bin, box, urn
reduce to: 7 cremate
tobacco: 6 dottel, dottle

ashamed: 7 abashed, hangdog 8 contrite, red-faced 9 mortified 10 humiliated, remorseful 11 embarrassed

Ashanti pepper: 5 cubeb

ashen: wan 4 gray, grey, pale 5 waxen 6 pallid 7 ghastly 8 blanched 9 cinereous

Asher: *daughter:* 5 Serah 6 Beriah
father: 5 Jacob
son: 4 Usui 6 Jimnah

ashkoko: 4 cony, hare 5 daman, hyrax

Asia: 6 Orient 9 continent
country: 4 Iran, Iraq, Laos, Oman 5 Burma, China, Egypt(part), India, Japan, Nepal, Qatar, Syria, Yemen 6 Bhutan, Brunei, Cyprus, Israel, Jordan, Kuwait, Russia(part), Taiwan, Turkey(part) 7 Bahrain, Lebanon 8 Cambodia, Malaysia, Maldives, Mongolia, Pakistan, Sri Lanka, Thailand 9 Indonesia, Singapore 10 Bangladesh, North Korea, South Korea 11 Afghanistan, Philippines, Saudi Arabia 12 Arab Emirates, North Vietnam, South Vietnam
desert: 4 Gobi, Thar (India) 6 Syrian 7 Arabian 10 Takla Makan (China)

ethnic group: Han, Lao, Mon, Tai 4 Arab, Kurd, Shan, Thai, Turk 5 Karen, Khmer, Malay, Tajik, Tamil, Uzbek 6 Indian, Lepcha, Manchu, Mongol, Sindhi 7 Baluchi, Bengali, Persian, Punjabi, Tibetan 8 Armenian, Kanarese 9 Chungchia, Dravidian, Indo-Aryan, Sinhalese

lake: 6 Baikal 7 Aral Sea 8 Balkhash, Tungting 10 Caspian Sea

mountain pass: 6 Burzil 8 Baroghil

mountain peak: 4 Fang 5 Jannu, Kamet 6 Batura, Cho Oyu, Kailas, Kungpu, Nuptse, Pobeda, Trivor 7 Everest 9 Annapurna

mountain range: 5 Altai, Kumon, Sayan 6 Elburz, Kunlun, Pamirs, Zagros 7 Khingan, Kumgang 8 Tien Shan 9 Himalayas, Hindu Kush

river: Hsi, Ili 4 Amur, Lena, Onon, Ural, Yalu 5 Indus 6 Ganges, Irtysh, Mekong, Tigris, Yellow 7 Salween, Yangtze 8 Irrawaddy 9 Euphrates

Asia Minor (see also Asia): 8 Anatolia 9 peninsula

ancient city: 4 Myra, Myus, Teos, Troy 5 Issus, Perga 6 Mylasa, Patara, Priene, Sardis, Tarsus 7 Ephesus, Miletus 8 Colophon

ancient kingdom: 5 Caria, Ionia, Lydia, Mysia, Troad, Troas 6 Pontus 7 Cilicia, Phrygia, Pisidia 8 Bithynia, Pergamum

mountain: Ida

mountain range: 6 Sultan, Taurus

river: 5 Halys 8 Monderez

sea: 5 Black 6 Aegean 7 Marmara

aside: off 4 away, gone 5 aloof, apart 6 aslant 7 private, whisper 8 reserved, secretly, separate 9 obliquely, stage ploy 10 digression 11 parenthesis

aside from: 4 save 7 barring, besides 9 except for, excluding, outside of

asinine: 4 dull 5 crass, dense, inept, silly 6 absurd, obtuse, simple, stupid 7 doltish, fatuous, foolish, idiotic 9 gooselike, senseless

ask: beg, bid, sue 4 pray, quiz, seek 5 claim, crave, exact, plead, query, speer(Sc.), utter 6 adjure, demand, expect, invite 7 beseech, consult, entreat, implore, inquire, request, require, solicit 8 petition, question 11 interrogate

askance: 4 awry 5 askew 7 crooked 8 sideways 9 doubtfully, obliquely 11 skeptically 13 distrustfully, with suspicion

askew: 4 alop, awry 5 agley, amiss, atilt 6 aslant 7 asquint, cockeyed, crooked 9 distorted, out of line, to one side

asleep: out 4 dead, idle 6 dozing, latent, numbed 7 dormant, napping, unaware

8 off-guard 9 unfeeling 10 motionless, slumbering 11 not on the job, unconscious

asomatous: 10 immaterial 11 incorporeal

asp: 5 adder, aspen, snake, viper 7 serpent 8 ophidian

representative headdress: 6 uraeus

asparagus: 5 sprue

aspect: air 4 face, look, mien, side, view 5 angle, facet, guise, phase 6 manner, visage 7 bearing, feature, outlook 8 carriage, prospect 9 semblance 10 appearance 11 countenance

aspen: 4 tree 6 poplar 7 quaking 9 quivering, trembling, tremulous

asperity: ire 5 rigor 8 acerbity, acrimony, hardness, severity, sourness, tartness 9 briskness, harshness, roughness 10 bitterness, difficulty, unevenness 11 crabbedness 16 disagreeableness

asperse: 4 slur 5 abuse, decry, libel 6 defame, malign, revile 7 baptize, detract, slander, traduce 8 besmirch, christen, sprinkle 9 denigrate, discredit, disparage

aspersion: 7 baptism, calumny 8 innuendo 9 invective 12 vituperation

aspersorium: 4 font 5 basin, stoup

asphalt: 7 bitumen 8 blacktop, uintaite 10 wurtzilite

asphyxia: 5 apnea 6 apnoea 11 suffocation

aspic: gel 4 mold 5 jelly 7 gelatin 8 lavender

aspirant: 7 hopeful 9 applicant, candidate

aspiration: aim 4 goal, hope 5 ideal 8 ambition

aspire: try 4 hope, long, rise, seek, soar, wish 5 tower, yearn 6 ascend, desire 11 be ambitious

ass: 4 dolt, duff, fool 5 burro, chump, dunce, idiot, kiang, kulan 6 donkey, koulan, onager, quagga 8 imbecile 9 blockhead, simpleton 10 nincompoop

female: 5 jenny

male: 4 jack

assail: 4 beat, pelt 5 assay, beset, stone, storm, whack 6 accuse, attack, impugn, invade, malign, molest, scathe 7 assault, belabor, bombard 8 fall upon 9 encounter

assailant: 6 mugger 8 attacker 9 aggressor

Assam: 11 Indian state

capital: 8 Shillong

city: 4 Ledo 7 Gauhati, Nowgong

hills: 4 Abor, Garo, Miri, Naga 5 Khasi 6 Lushai

rubber: 7 rambong

silkworm: eri 4 eria

tribesman: Aka 4 Ahom, Garo, Naga 5 Lhota

assassin: gun **5** bravo **6** hit man, killer, slayer **8** murderer **9** cut-throat **10** hatchet man

Abel's: **4** Cain
Archduke Ferdinand's: **7** Princip
Gandhi's: **5** Godse
Garfield's: **7** Guiteau
J. F. Kennedy's: **6** Oswald
John Lennon's: **7** Chapman
Lincoln's: **5** Booth
Martin Luther King's: Ray
McKinley's: **8** Czolgosz
R. F. Kennedy's: **6** Sirhan

assault: mug **4** beat, raid, slug **5** beset, onset, pound, smite, storm **6** affray, assail, attack, buffet, breach, charge, fall on, invade **7** bombard, violate **8** outburst **9** incursion, onslaught **10** aggression **11** impinge upon

assay: try **4** test **5** prove **6** try out **7** analyze, examine **8** analysis, appraise, evaluate **9** determine **10** experiment

assemblage: **4** army, crew, herd, host, mass, pack **5** bunch, crowd, drove, flock, swarm **6** convoy, galaxy, hookup, throng **7** cluster, turnout **9** community **11** aggregation **12** congregation

art: **7** collage

assemble: fit **4** call, mass, meet **5** amass, piece, rally, unite **6** couple, gather, huddle, muster, summon **7** collect, convene, convoke, recruit **10** foregather **11** put together

assembly: hui **4** bevy, diet, feis, moot, raad **5** forum, group, junta, party, press, setup, troop **6** gemote, pow-wow, senate **7** comitia, company, council, husting, meeting, session, society **8** audience, conclave, congress, tribunal **10** convention, parliament **11** convocation, legislature

ecclesiastical: **5** synod **10** consistory
full: **5** plena
of witches: **5** coven
place: **5** agora
room: **4** hall **10** auditorium

assent: aye, bow, nod, yea, yes **4** amen **5** admit, agree, yield **6** accede, accept, accord, chorus, comply, concur, submit **7** approve, concede, conform, consent **8** adhesion, sanction **9** acquiesce, subscribe **10** compliance, condescend **11** acknowledge

assert: say **4** aver, avow, cite **5** claim, plead, posit, state, utter, vaunt, voice **6** affirm, allege, assure, avouch, defend, depone, depose, uphold **7** advance, betoken, contend, declare, protest, support **8** advocate, champion, maintain **9** predicate, vindicate

positively: **5** swear **10** asseverate

assertive: **8** dogmatic, positive **8** cock-

sure, forceful **9** defensive, pragmatic **10** aggressive **11** affirmatory

assess: tax **4** cess, levy, rate, scot, toll **5** price, value **6** charge, impose **7** measure **8** appraise, estimate **9** apportion

assessment: fee, tax **4** duty, levy **5** tithe **6** impost, surtax, tariff **7** scutage **9** valuation

assessor: **5** judge **11** adjudicator

asset: **9** advantage **11** distinction, strong point

assets: **5** goods, means, money, worth **6** credit, wealth **7** capital, effects **8** accounts, property **9** resources, valuables

assiduous: **4** busy **6** active **7** devoted **8** diligent, sedulous, studious **9** laborious, unwearied **10** persistent **11** hardworking, industrious, painstaking, persevering, unremitting **13** indefatigable

assign: fix, set **4** cede, give, rate, seal, sign **5** allot, allow, award, endue, order, refer **6** adduce, affect, allege, charge, convey, depute, detail, reckon, select, settle **7** adjudge, advance, appoint, ascribe, consign, dispose, mete out, specify, tribute **8** allocate, delegate, transfer **9** apportion, attribute, designate, determine **10** commission, distribute **11** appropriate

assignation: **4** date **5** tryst **7** meeting **10** rendezvous **11** appointment

assignment: job **4** duty, task **5** chore, stint **6** lesson **11** appointment

assimilate: **4** fuse **5** alter, blend, learn, liken, merge **6** absorb, digest, imbibe, take in **7** compare **8** resemble **9** transform **10** comprehend, metabolize, understand **11** appropriate, incorporate

assist: aid **4** abet, back, help **5** avail, boost, coach **6** back up, succor **7** benefit, be of use, relieve, support, sustain **8** befriend **9** give a hand **10** facilitate

assistant: **4** aide, ally, hand, zany **5** valet **6** deputy, lackey, minion, second **7** abettor, orderly, partner **8** adjutant, adjuvant, henchman, servitor **9** associate, auxiliary, secretary **10** accomplice **11** confederate, subordinate

to pastor: **6** curate

assistants: **4** crew **5** staff

assize: **4** rate, rule **5** court, edict, trial **6** decree **7** hearing, inquest, measure, precept, session, sitting, statute **8** assembly, standard, tribunal **9** enactment, ordinance **10** regulation

associate: mix, pal **4** aide, ally, chum, join, link, mate, peer, yoke **5** buddy, crony **6** cohort, fellow, friend, helper, hobnob, mingle, relate, spouse **7** adjunct, bracket, comrade, connect, consort, partner **8** copemate, federate, identify, intimate **9** affiliate, assistant, attendant, coadjutor, colleague, companion, secondary, socialize 10 fraternize 11 concomitant

in crime: 10 accomplice

association: 4 body, bond, clan, club, coop 5 artel 6 cartel, league, pledge 7 company, consort, society 8 alliance, converse, intimacy, overtone, sodality 9 coalition, syndicate 10 assemblage, connection, fellowship, sisterhood 11 aggregation, brotherhood, combination, confederacy, conjunction, connotation, partnership

criminal: mob 4 gang, ring

literary: 6 lyceum 9 athenaeum

merchants': 5 hanse

political: 4 axis, bund 5 junta, party 7 machine

secret: 5 cabal, lodge

student: 7 council 8 sorority 10 fraternity

workers': 5 guild, union

assonance: pun 5 rhyme 8 paragram 11 resemblance

assort: 4 file, rank, type 5 group 8 classify 10 put in order

assortment: lot, set 4 olio 5 batch, group, suite 6 medley 7 melange, mixture, variety 8 pastiche 9 potpourri 10 collection, miscellany

assuage: 4 calm, ease 5 abate, allay, slake 6 lessen, modify, pacify, quench, reduce, soften, solace, soothe, temper 7 appease, comfort, mollify, relieve, satisfy 8 diminish, mitigate, moderate 9 alleviate 11 tranquilize

assuasive: 7 calming 8 soothing

as such: 5 per se 8 in itself 9 basically, in the main 11 in its own way

assume: don 4 dare, mask, sham 5 adopt, cloak, elect, feign, indue, infer, put on, raise, seize, usurp 6 accept, affect, clothe 7 believe, pretend, receive, suppose, surmise 8 accroach, arrogate, take over, simulate 9 undertake 11 appropriate, counterfeit

assumed: 5 alias, false 8 affected, supposed 9 fictional, uncertain 10 artificial, fictitious 12 hypothetical, supposititious

assumed name: 5 alias 9 pseudonym 11 nom de guerre

assuming: 5 lofty 8 arrogant, superior 11 pretentious 12 presumptuous

different form: 7 protean

assurance: 4 word 5 brass, faith, nerve 6 aplomb, belief, credit, pledge, safety, surety 7 courage, promise 8 audacity, boldness, coolness, security 9 certainty, certitude, cockiness, guarantee, impudence 10 confidence, effrontery 12 self-reliance

assure: 4 aver 6 assert, avouch, secure 7 confirm, declare, hearten 8 convince, embolden 9 encourage, vouchsafe 10 asseverate, certiorate, strengthen, underwrite 13 say positively

assuredly: 4 amen 6 surely, verily 10 truthfully 11 indubitably, undoubtedly

Assyria: 5 Ashur, Assur 6 Asshur

capital: 5 Calah 7 Nineveh

city: 4 Hara, Opis 5 Al Sur 6 Arbela, Asshur, Kalakh 9 Dur Sargon

god: El, Zu; Ira, Sin 4 Adad, Anet, Nebo 5 Ashur, Hadad, Ninip 6 Asshur, Nergal, Shamas

goddess: 4 Nana, Nine 5 Istar 6 Allatu, Ishtar 9 Sarpanitu

king: Pul 5 Belus 6 Sargon 9 Sennacherib

measure: 4 cane, foot 5 makuk, gasab 6 artaba, gariba, ghalva 7 mansion

queen: 9 Semiramis

river: 6 Tigris

astart: 8 suddenly

asterisk: 4 star 13 reference mark

Asterius: 8 argonaut, minotaur

father: 10 Hyperasius

mother: 8 Pasiphae

wife: 6 Europa

astern: aft 4 back 6 behind 9 in the rear

asteroid: 4 Eros, Hebe, Iris, Juno 5 Ceres, Flora, Irene, Metis, Vesta 6 Astrea, Egeria, Europa, Hygeia, Pallas, planet, Psyche, Thetis 7 Eunomia, Fortuna, Lutetia 8 Massalia, starfish, starlike, Victoria 9 Melpomene, planetoid 10 Parthenope, star-shaped

first: 5 Ceres

nearest earth: 4 Eros

asthmatic: 5 pursy 6 wheezy 7 panting, puffing

astir: 5 about, afoot, alert 6 active, moving, roused 8 out of bed 10 up and doing

Astolat's Lily Maid: 6 Elaine

astonish: awe 4 daze 5 amaze 7 astound, impress, startle 8 bewilder, confound, surprise 11 flabbergast

astonished: 5 agape

astonishing: 8 fabulous 9 wonderful 10 incredible, stupendous 11 spectacular

astound: 5 amaze, appal, shock 6 appall 7 stagger, terrify 8 astonish, confound 9 overwhelm

astragalus: 5 talus 9 anklebone

astrakhan: 5 cloth 7 caracul, karakul

astral: 6 remote, starry 7 stellar 8 sidereal, starlike 9 visionary

astray: 4 awry, lost 5 agley, amiss, aside, wrong 6 abroad, afield, errant, erring, faulty 7 sinning 8 mistaken 9 wandering

astride: 4 atop 7 à cheval, mounted 8 bridging, spanning 9 astraddle 10 straddling

astringent: 4 acid, alum, sour, tart 5 acerb, harsh, stern 6 severe, tannin 7 austere, binding, styptic 11 acrimonious, compressive, contracting 12 constrictive
extract: 7 catechu
gum: 4 kino

astrologer: 4 Josh 6 Merlin 7 diviner 10 star reader 11 Nostradamus

astronaut: 9 cosmonaut
American: 4 Bean, Duke 5 Glenn, Irwin, Roosa, Scott, White, Young 6 Aldrin, Anders, Borman, Cernan, Conrad, Gordon, Kerwin, Lousma, Lovell, Worden 7 Collins, Grissom, Schirra, Shepard 8 McDivitt, Mitchell, Stafford 9 Armstrong, Mattingly 10 Cunningham
first in orbit: 5 Glenn
first on moon: 9 Armstrong
first space walker: 5 White
on longest mission: 4 Carr 5 Pogue 6 Gibson
on first space shuttle: 5 Young 7 Crippen
on rendezvous with Soviets: 5 Brand 7 Slayton 8 Stafford
Soviet: 7 Gagarin, Komarov

astromoner: 10 Hipparchus

astronomical: far 4 huge 5 great 6 uranic 7 distant, immense 8 colossal, infinite
instrument: aba 9 telescope 10 equatorial
measurement: 5 apsis 7 azimuth
Muse: 4 Clio 6 Urania

astute: sly 4 foxy, keen, wily 5 acute, canny, quick, sharp, smart 6 clever, crafty, shrewd 7 cunning, skilled 9 sagacious 10 discerning 14 discriminating

asunder: 5 apart, split 7 divided 8 divorced 9 separated

asylum: ark 4 home 5 altar, cover, haven 6 bedlam, harbor, refuge 7 alsatia, hospice, retreat, shelter 9 sanctuary 11 institution

asymmetric: 4 skew 9 distorted 10 unbalanced

asymmetry: 13 disproportion

at: 5 there 7 located
at all: 4 ever 5 aught, nohow 6 anyway
at hand: 4 near, nigh 7 close by, present
at last: 7 finally 10 ultimately
at once: now, PDQ 4 anon 5 amain 6 presto 9 forthwith, instantly, right away 11 immediately

Ata, Aeta: Ita 7 Negrito

Atahualpa: 4 Inca 6 Indian

ataman: 5 chief, judge 6 hetman 7 Cossack, headman

atap: 8 nipa palm

atavism: 9 reversion

atavus: 8 ancestor 11 grandfather

atelier: 6 studio 7 bottega 8 workshop

ates: 8 sweetsop

Athamas: *daughter:* 5 Helle

son: 7 Phrixos, Phrixus 8 Learchus
wife: Ino

athanor: 4 oven 7 furnace

Athapascan Indian: 4 Dene, Hupa, 5 Hoopa

atheist: 7 doubter 8 agnostic 11 nonbeliever

Athena, Athene: 4 Alea, Auge, Nike 5 Areia 6 Ergane, Hippia, Hygeia, Itonia, Pallas, Polias 7 Minerva 8 Apaturia, Athenaia 9 Parthenos, Poliuchos, Promachos 10 Chalinitis
pert. to: 9 Palladian
temple: 9 Parthenon

Athens (see also **Greece**): *alien resident:* 5 metic
ancient capital of: 6 Attica
assembly: 4 pnyx 5 boule
assembly platform: 4 bema
astronomer: 5 Meton
clan: obe
coin: 5 oboli 6 obolus 7 chalcus, chalkos
festival: 8 Apaturia, Athenaea 11 Scirophoria
founder: 7 Cecrops
general: 6 Nicias 7 Phocion 8 Zenophon
hill: 9 Acropolis 10 Lycabettus
hill where Paul preached: 9 Areopagus
historian: 8 Xenophon
king: 6 Codrus 7 Cecrops, Pandion
lawgiver: 5 Draco, Solon
magistrate: 5 draco 6 archon, dicast
marketplace: 5 agora
mountain: 6 Parnes
orator: 9 Isocrates
philosopher: 5 Plato 8 Socrates 9 Aristotle
platform: 4 bema 6 bemata(pl.)
rival: 6 Sparta
sculptor: 7 Phidias
seaport: 7 Piraeus
statesman: 8 Pericles 9 Aristides
temple: 4 Nike 9 Parthenon
theater: 5 Odeum
youth center: 6 Lyceum

athlete: pro 4 jock, star 5 boxer 7 amateur, acrobat, gymnast, tumbler 8 wrestler 9 aerialist
athlete's foot: 8 ringworm 10 skin fungus

athletic: 5 agile, burly, lusty, vital 6 brawny robust, sinewy, strong 8 muscular, powerful, vigorous 9 acrobatic, energetic, strapping
contest: 4 agon, game, meet, race 5 match 8 Olympics
field: 4 oval, ring, rink 5 arena, court, green 6 course 7 diamond, stadium 8 gridiron
prize: cup 5 medal, purse, 6 ribbon, trophy

athletics: 5 games, sport 8 exercise

athwart: 4 over 6 across, aslant 7

against, oblique 9 crosswise **10** perversely

atlantal: 6 atloid **8** anterior, cephalic

Atlantides: 8 Pleiades **10** Hesperides

atlas: 4 bone, book, list, maps, tome **5** titan **8** mainstay

Atlas: *daughter:* **4** Maia **6** Merope **7** Alcyone, Calypso, Electra, Kelaine, Taygete **8** Asterope, Pleiades
mother: **7** Clymeme

atmosphere: air **4** aura, mood, tone **5** ether **6** miasma, nimbus, welkin **7** climate, feeling **8** ambiance **10** background **11** environment
disturbance: **5** storm **6** static
gas: **5** argon **6** oxygen **8** nitrogen
phenomenon: **6** aurora, meteor
pressure: **10** barometric

atole: 4 mush **5** gruel **8** corn meal, porridge

atoll: 4 reef **6** island
Pacific: **4** Beru, Ebon, Mili **5** Makin, Wotho **6** Bikini, Canton, Jaluit, Likiep, Majuro, Tarawa **8** Eniwetok

atom: ace, bit, jot **4** iota, mite, mote, whit **5** monad, shade, speck, tinge **8** molecule, particle, quantity **9** corpuscle, scintilla
electrically charged: ion **5** anion **6** cation
nucleus: **6** proton **7** neutron

atomic: 4 tiny **6** minute **7** nuclear **9** molecular **13** infinitesimal
particle: **4** beta, pion **5** alpha, meson, quark **6** photon, proton **7** neutron **8** electron
physicist: **4** Bohr, Rabi **5** Fermi, Pauli **7** Compton, Meitner **8** Einstein
pile: **7** reactor
submarine: **5** Sargo, Skate **6** Triton **8** Nautilus
theory originator: **6** Dalton

atomize; 5 grate, spray **6** reduce **8** nebulize, vaporize **9** devastate, pulverize

atomy: 4 atom, mite, mote **5** pygmy **8** skeleton

atone: 6 repent **7** expiate **10** compensate, make amends

atonement: 7 penance **10** reparation **12** satisfaction

atonic: 7 unheard **9** voiceless **10** unaccented

atrabilious: 4 glum **6** gloomy, morose, sullen **10** melancholy

atramentous: 4 ebon, inky **5** black

Atreus: *brother:* **8** Thyestes
father: **6** Pelops
half brother: **6** Chrysippus
mother: **10** Hippodamia
slayer: **9** Aegisthus
son: **8** Menelaus **9** Agamemnon **11** Pleisthenes
wife: **6** Aerope

atrio: 6 valley **10** depression

atrip: 6 aweigh

atrium: 4 hall **5** court **6** cavity **7** auricle, chamber, passage **8** entrance

atrocha: 5 larva

atrocious: bad **4** dark, rank, vile **5** awful, black, cruel, gross **6** brutal, odious, savage, wicked **7** heinous, ungodly, violent **8** grievous, horrible, terrible **9** execrable, frightful, nefarious **10** abominable, villainous

atrophy: 6 shrink, starve, wither **9** waste away **10** emaciation **11** deteriorate

Atropos: 4 Fate

attach: add, fix, tag, tie **4** bind, glue, join, link, take, vest, weld **5** affix, annex, hitch, paste, seize, unite **6** accuse, addict, adhere, adjoin, append, arrest, cement, fasten, indict **7** adhibit, appoint, ascribe, connect, subjoin **9** affiliate, associate, garnishee

attached: 4 aide **8** diplomat

attached: 4 fond **6** doting
at base: **7** sessile
to the land: **8** praedial, agrarian

attachment: 4 love **8** devotion, fondness **9** accessory, addiction, adherence, affection **10** engagement, friendship **11** inclination

attack: fit **4** bout, fray, pang, raid, rush **5** assay, begin, beset, blitz, drive, fight, foray, ictus, onset, sally, spasm, storm **6** accuse, action, affray, assail, battle, charge, invade, onrush, pounce, sortie, strike, stroke, thrust **7** assault, besiege, censure, offense, potshot, seizure **8** paroxysm **9** incursion, onslaught **10** aggression
deceptive: **5** feint **9** diversion
suicidal: **8** kamikaze

attain: get, hit, win **4** earn, gain, rise **5** reach, touch **6** accede, amount, arrive, aspire, effect, secure, strike **7** achieve, acquire, compass, procure, succeed **8** overtake **10** accomplish, comprehend

attainment: 4 feat **5** skill **6** wisdom **14** accomplishment

attar: oil **7** essence, perfume

attempt: try **4** dare, seek, shot, stab, wage **5** assay, begin, essay, frame, start **6** effort **7** venture **8** endeavor, exertion **9** undertake **10** enterprise, experiment

attend: see **4** go to, hear, heed, mind, tend, wait **5** await, guard, nurse, serve, treat, visit, watch **6** assist, convoy, follow, harken, listen, shadow **7** care for, consort **8** champion, chaperon, minister **9** accompany

attendance: 4 gate **6** number, regard **8** presence **9** attention **11** application, expectation

attendant: aid **4** maid, page, zany **5** guide,

usher, valet 6 escort, helper, minion, porter, squire, waiter 7 courier, orderly, pageboy 8 chasseur, follower, henchman 9 assistant, associate, attentive, companion 10 consequent, subsequent 11 chamberlain, concomitant 12 accompanying

attendants: 5 suite, train 7 cortege, retinue 9 entourage

attention: ear 4 care, heed, hist, note 5 study 6 notice, regard 7 achtung(G.), respect 8 courtesy 9 diligence, obedience, vigilance 10 observance 11 observation 13 concentration, consideration

attentive: 4 wary 5 alert, awake, civil 6 intent, polite 7 careful, gallant, mindful 8 studious, watchful 9 advertent, assiduous, courteous, listening 10 interested 11 circumspect

attenuate: sap 4 thin 5 water 6 dilute, lessen, rarefy, reduce, weaken 7 slender 8 decrease, diminish, enfeeble, tapering 9 subtilize

attest: 5 prove, swear, vouch 6 adjure, affirm, invoke 7 certify, confirm, testify, witness 9 subscribe 12 authenticate

attic: 4 loft 6 garret 8 cockloft

Attic: 5 Greek 8 Athenian

Attic salt: wit

Attila: Hun 5 Etzel

attire: See **dress**

attitude: air, set 4 bias, mien, mood, pose 5 angle, phase, slant, stand 6 action, aspect, manner 7 bearing, feeling, posture 8 behavior, position 11 disposition

attorney: 5 agent, proxy 6 deputy, factor, lawyer 7 proctor 8 advocate 9 barrister, counselor, solicitor 10 counsellor

attract: 4 bait, draw, lure, pull 5 catch, charm, court, fetch, tempt 6 allure, engage, entice, invite, seduce 8 interest 9 captivate, fascinate, influence, magnetize

attraction: 4 card 6 magnet 7 gravity 8 affinity, penchant, witchery

attractive: 4 chic, cute, fair 5 bonny 6 lovely, pretty, taking 7 winning, winsome 8 alluring, charming, fetching, graceful 9 beautiful

attribute: fix, owe 4 mark, sign, type 5 asign, badge, blame, place, power, refer 6 allege, allude, assert, bestow, charge, impute, symbol 7 ascribe, pertain, quality 8 accredit, property 10 reputation 11 peculiarity 14 characteristic

attribution: 6 theory 8 etiology

attrition: 4 wear 5 grief 6 regret, sorrow 7 penance, remorse 8 abrasion, friction 9 weakening

attune: key 4 tune 5 adapt, agree 6 accord, adjust, temper 7 prepare 9 harmonize

atua: 5 being, demon 6 spirit

au fait(F.): 6 expert, versed 8 informed 9 competent, in the know 10 proficient

au fond(F.): 8 at bottom 9 basically

au naturel(F.): raw 4 nude 5 naked 6 unclad 8 stripped 9 in the buff

auberge: inn 7 albergo

auction: 4 cant, roup(Sc.), sale, sell, vend 5 trade 6 barter, bridge 8 disposal

hammer: 5 gavel

platform: 5 block

price: bid 5 upset

audacious: 4 bold 5 brash, hardy, saucy 6 brazen, cheeky, daring 7 forward 8 arrogant, fearless, impudent, insolent, intrepid, spirited 9 barefaced, impenitent, shameless 10 courageous 11 adventurous, impertinent, venturesome 12 presumptuous

audacity: 4 gall, grit, guts 5 brass, cheek, nerve, spunk, valor 7 courage 8 boldness, temerity 9 assurance, cockiness, derring-do, hardihood, impudence, insolence, sauciness 10 effrontery 12 impertinence

audible: 5 aloud, clear, heard 8 distinct

audience: 4 fans 5 house 6 public 7 gallery, hearing 8 assembly, audition, tribunal 9 following, interview, reception 10 spectators

audio-visual aid: 4 film, tape 5 slide 10 television

audit: 4 scan 5 check, probe 6 reckon, survey, verify 7 examine, inquire, inspect 8 analysis, estimate 10 accounting 11 investigate

audition: 4 test 5 trial 6 tryout 7 hearing

auditor: CPA 6 censor, hearer 8 listener 10 accountant, bookkeeper 11 comptroller

auditorium: 4 hall, room 5 cavea, odeum 7 theater

auditory: 4 otic 5 aural 8 acoustic

auger: bit 4 bore, tool 5 grill 6 gimlet, wimble

aught: 4 zero 5 zilch 6 cipher, 7 nothing 8 anything, goose egg

Augie March creator: 6 Bellow

augite: 8 pyroxene

augment: add, eke 4 grow 5 exalt, swell 6 append, dilate, expand, extend 7 amplify, enhance, enlarge, improve, magnify 8 heighten, increase, multiply 9 increment 10 aggrandize

augur: 4 bode, omen, seer 6 auspex, divine 7 betoken, foresee, portend, predict, presage, prophet, promise, signify 8 forebode, foreshow, foretell, forewarn, indicate, prophesy 9 auspicate 10 anticipate, conjecture, soothsayer 13 prognosticate

augury: 4 rite, sign 5 token 6 herald, ritual 7 warning 8 ceremony, forecast 9 harbinger, sortilege 10 divination, foreboding, forerunner

august: 5 awful, grand, noble 6 solemn 7 exalted, stately 8 imposing, majestic 9 dignified, venerable 11 magisterial

Augustus' death place: 4 Nola

auk: 4 loom 5 arrie, lemot, noddy 6 puffin, rotche 7 dovekey, dovekie 9 guillemot

family: 7 alcidae

genus: 4 alca, alle

razorbill: 4 falk 5 murre

aula: 4 hall, room 5 court 6 emblic

aumildar(Ind.): 5 agent 6 factor 7 manager 9 collector

aura: air 4 glow, halo, mood, odor 5 aroma 6 nimbus 7 essence, feeling, quality 8 mystique 9 emanation 10 atmosphere, exhalation

aural: 4 otic 7 audible 9 auricular

appendage: ear

aureate: 6 gilded, golden, ornate, rococo, yellow 8 splendid 9 brilliant

aureole: 4 halo 5 crown, glory, light 6 corona, nimbus 8 gloriole

auricle: ear 5 pinna 6 atrium, earlet 7 trumpet

part: 7 earlobe

auricular: 4 otic 7 hearsay 12 confidential

aurochs: 4 urus 5 bison 6 wisent

Aurora: Eos 4 dawn 7 morning, sunrise

auroral: 4 eoan, rosy 7 eastern, radiant

aurum: 4 gold

auscultate: 6 listen

auspex: 5 augur 7 diviner, prophet 10 forecaster, soothsayer

auspicate: 5 augur 7 portend, predict 8 initiate 10 inaugurate

auspices: 4 care, egis 5 aegis 7 backing, support 8 guidance 9 patronage 10 protection 11 sponsorship

auspicious: 4 fair, good 6 dexter 9 favorable, fortunate, opportune 10 propitious, prosperous 12 advantageous

Aussie: 10 Australian

austere: 4 cold, grim, hard 5 bleak, grave, gruff, harsh, rigid, rough, sharp, stern, stiff 6 bitter, formal, severe, simple, somber, strict 7 ascetic, earnest, spartan, serious 8 rigorous 9 unadorned, unsmiling 10 astringent, forbidding, relentless 13 unembellished

Australia: *capital:* 8 Canberra

city: Ayr 4 Yass 5 Dubbo, Perth, Weipa 6 Casino, Hobart, Mackay, Sydney 7 Kogarah, Mildura 8 Adelaide, Brisbane, Toowomba 9 Melbourne, Newcastle 10 Wagga Wagga

desert: 6 Gibson, Tanami 8 Victoria 10 Great Sandy

explored by: 13 Capt. James Cook

island: 5 Cocos, Heard 6 Fraser 7 Ashmore, Cartier 8 Kangaroo, Thursday 9 Christmas

lake: 4 Eyre 5 Carey, Cowan, Frome 6 Austin, Barlee, Mackay 7 Amadeus, Eyerard, Torrens 8 Carnegie

monetary unit: 4 cent 6 dollar

mountain peak: 4 Hale 5 Bruce 6 Cradle, Morgan 7 Bogong, Painter 9 Kosciusko

mountain range: 6 Stuart 7 Darling, Gregory 8 Flinders, Musgrave, St. George 9 Petermann

native: 6 Binghi 9 aborigine

peninsula: 4 Eyre 8 Cape York

port: 5 Pirie 6 Darwin, Kembla 7 Geelong, Jackson, Lincoln 8 Adelaide, Brisbane 9 Fremantle

river: Ord 4 Avon, Daly, Swan 5 Namoi, Paroo, Roper, Yarra 6 Barwon, Bulloo, Calgoa, Hunter, Isaacs, Murray 7 Darling, Fitzroy, Lachlan, Staaten 8 Burdekin, Flinders, Gascoyne, Georgina, Goulburn

sea: 5 Coral, Timor 6 Tasman 7 Arafura

state: 8 Tasmania, Victoria 10 Queensland 13 New South Wales

strait: 4 Bass 6 Torres

Australian: *animal:* 4 tait 5 koala, panda 6 bunyip, cuscus, wombat 7 dasqure, wallaby 8 duckbill, kangaroo, platypus 9 bandicoot, phalanger

apple: 6 colane

badger: 6 wombat

bag: 5 dilli

bear: 5 koala

beefwood: 5 belar

beverage: 4 kava

bird: emu 4 emeu, lory 5 arara, crake, grebe, stint 6 gannet, leipoa 7 bittern, boobook, bustard, figbird 8 berigora, dabchick, dotterel, lorikeet, lyrebird, morepork, whimbrel 9 bower-bird, cassowary, coachwhip, friarbird, stipiture 10 paradalote, partincole, sanderling

boomerang 5 kiley, kilie

brushwood: 6 millee

bush: ake

bustard: 7 bebilya

cake: 6 damper 7 brownie

call: 5 cooee, cooey

cat: 7 dasyure

catfish: 6 tandan

cattle stealer: 6 duffer

cedar: 4 toon

clover fern: 6 nardoo

cockatoo: 5 galah

coin: 4 dump

colonist: 8 sterling

countryman: 8 Billijim

crayfish: 5 yabby 6 yabbie

cycad: 5 banga

dog: 5 dingo 6 Kelpie
duckbill: 8 platypus
eucalyptus: 6 bimbil, mallee 7 carbeen
fern: 5 nardu 6 nardoo
fish: 4 dart, mado, mako 5 yabby 6 tandan, yabbie
fruit: 5 nonda
gum tree: 4 kari 6 tewart, tooart, touart
herb: 8 piripiri
horse: 7 brumbee 8 yarraman
hut: 6 miamia
insect: 4 laap, lerp
kangaroo: 4 joey 5 tungo 7 bettong
kiwi: roa
lizard: 6 goanna
lorikeet: 6 parrot, warrin
mahogany: 6 jarrah 7 gunning
marsupial: 4 tait 5 koala 6 wombat 8 kangaroo
measure: 4 saum
mile: 4 naut
moth: 6 bogong
no: 4 baal, bail, bale
owl: 7 boobook 8 morepoke, morepork
palm: 8 bangalow
parakeet: 6 budgie 7 corella 10 budgerigar
parrot: 4 lory 7 corella, lorilet 8 lorikeet 9 cockateel, cockatiel
pepper: 4 arva, kava, yava 6 ava-ava
petrel: 4 titi
phalanger: 5 ariel
plant: 5 lakea 6 correa 7 calomba, waratah 8 warratau
pine: 5 kauri, kaury
pond: 9 billabong
rat: 8 hapalote 9 hapalotis
ratite: 4 emeu
rifleman: 5 yager
rustler: 6 duffer
shark: 4 mako
shield: 8 heelaman, heilaman, hielaman, yeelaman
snake: 6 elapid
soldier: 5 Anzac 6 digger, swaddy 8 Billijim
sorcerer: 5 boyla 6 boolya
spear: 7 wommera, woomera
talk: 6 yabber
thicket: 6 mallee
throwing stick: 5 kiley, kylie 7 wommera, woomera 9 boomerang
toy: 8 weet-weet
tree: 4 toon 5 belah, belar, boree, gidya, penda 6 gidgea, gidgee, gidyea, marara 7 alipata 8 beefwood, curajong, flindosa, flindosy, ironbark 9 koorajong 10 bunya-bunya
tulip: 7 waratah 8 warratau
war club: 5 waddy
weapon: 5 hulla, waddy 6 hullah 7 liangle 8 leeangle 10 hullanulla

wilderness: 7 outback
wombat: 5 koala
wood: emu
workman: 8 Billijim
Austria: *capital:* 6 Vienna
city: 4 Graz, Linz, Wels 5 Steyr 7 Bregenz 8 Salzburg 9 Innsbruck 10 Klagenfurt
ethnic group: 5 Croat 7 Slovene
lake: 5 Atter, Traun 9 Constance 10 Neusiedler
monetary unit: 8 groschen 9 schilling
mountain pass: 5 Loibl 7 Brenner, Plocken 9 Semmering
mountain peak: 9 Hochstuhl, Hochvogel 10 Hochfeiler, Wildspitze 13 Grossglockner
mountain ranges of Alps: 6 Allgau, Carnic 8 Bavarian, Otztaler 10 Hohe Tauern
river: Inn, Mur 4 Enns, Lech, Murz, Raba 5 Drava, Steyr, Traun 6 Danube 7 Salzach
state (lander): 5 Tirol 6 Styria, Vienna 8 Salzburg 9 Carinthia 10 Burgenland, Vorarlberg 12 Lower Austria, Upper Austria
Austrian: *coin:* 5 ducat, krone 6 florin, heller, zehner
composer: 4 Berg 5 Haydn 6 Mahler, Mozart, Webern 7 Strauss 8 Bruckner, Schubert
conductor: 6 Mahler 7 Karajan
dance: 6 dreher
former ruling family: 8 Habsburg, Hapsburg
measure: 4 fass, fuss, joch, mass, muth, yoke 5 halbe, linie, meile, metze, pfiff, punkt 6 achtel, becher, seidel 7 klafter, viertel 8 dreiling 10 muthmassel 12 futtermassel
measure of weight: 4 marc, saum, unze 5 denat, karch, pfund, stein 7 centner, pfennig 8 vierling 9 quentchen
nobility: 6 Ritter 9 Esterhazy
playwright: 7 Nestroy 10 Schnitzler 11 Grillparzer
psychiatrist: 5 Adler, Freud
violinist: 8 Kreisler
austringer: 8 falconer
Austronesian language: 4 Niue 7 Tagalog
autarch: 6 despot 8 autocrat
auteur: 8 director, virtuoso 9 film-maker
authentic: 4 pure, real, sure, true 5 exact, right, valid 6 actual, proper 7 correct, genuine 6 bonafide, credible, official, original, reliable 9 veritable 10 authorized 11 trustworthy 13 authoritative
authenticate: 4 seal 5 prove 6 attest, verify 7 bear out, confirm, endorse 8 validate, vouch for
author: 4 doer 5 maker 6 father, framer,

parent, source, writer 7 creator, founder 8 ancestor, begetter, compiler, composer, inventor, novelist, producer 9 architect, initiator 10 playwright, instigator, originator

authoritative: 5 sound 7 factual, learned 8 dogmatic, official, oracular, positive 9 authentic, canonical, effectual, imperious, masterful, scholarly 10 conclusive, convincing, legitimate, peremptory 11 dictatorial, ex cathedra, magisterial

authority: 4 rule, sway 5 force, might, power, right 6 artist, expert, source, weight 7 command, control, warrant 8 dominion, prestige, sanction 9 influence 10 competence, importance, specialist 12 jurisdiction 13 justification

judicial: 4 banc

preponderant: 8 hegemony

symbol: 7 scepter

woman's: 7 distaff

authorize: let 4 vest 5 allow 6 clothe, permit, ratify 7 approve, empower, endorse, entitle, indorse, justify, license, warrant 8 accredit, delegate, legalize, sanction 10 commission, legitimize

authorless: 8 unsigned 9 anonymous

auto court: inn 5 motel

auto race: 4 drag 5 derby

driver: 4 Foyt 5 Petty, Sneva, Unser 8 Andretti 10 Rutherford, Yarborough

kind: 4 road 7 formula 8 stock car

notable: 7 Daytona 9 Grand Prix 12 Indianapolis

autobiography: 4 vita 5 diary 6 memoir

autochthonous: 6 native 7 edaphic, endemic 10 aboriginal, indigenous

autocrat: 4 czar, tsar, tzar 5 mogul 6 Caesar, despot 7 autarch, monarch 8 dictator 9 sovereign

autocratic: 8 absolute, arrogant, despotic 9 arbitrary 10 tyrannical

autograph: ink 4 name, sign 9 signature 11 John Hancock

automatic: 7 routine 8 habitual 10 mechanical, push-button, self-acting 11 instinctive, involuntary, spontaneous

automation: 5 golem, robot 7 android, machine

automobile: car 4 heap, jeep 5 coupe, crate, racer, sedan 6 jalopy 7 flivver, machine, phaeton 8 roadster 11 convertible

army: 4 jeep

British: AC, MG 5 Alvis, Riley, Rover 6 Allard, Anglia, Austin, Consul, Humber, Jaguar, Jowett, Morgan, Morris, Rapier, Singer, Zephyr 7 Bentley, Daimler, Hillman, Sunbeam, Triumph 8 Berkeley, Vauxhall 10 Rolls-Royce 11 Austin-Healy, Hillman-Minx, Morris-Minor 12 Metropolitan 13 Sunbeam-Talbot

Czech: 5 Skoda

early: EMF, Reo 4 Alco, Benz, Cord, Knox, Moon, Olds, Sear, Star 5 Brush, Regal, Stutz 6 Auburn, Dupont, Duryea, Graham, Haynes, Kissel, Lozier, Marmon, Mercer, Saxson, Thomas, Winton 7 Autocar, Bugatti, La Salle, Maxwell, Oakland, Premier, Rambler, Simplex, Stevens, Tourist 8 Apperson, Chalmers, Chandler, Franklin, Mercedes, National, Overland, Peerless 9 Hupmobile 10 Cunningham, Duesenberg, Jackrabbit, Locomobile 11 Graham-Paige, Pierce-Arrow 12 Crane-Simplex, Owen-Magnetic, Pope-Hartford, White-Steamer 13 Baker-Electric, Ofeldt-Steamer, Stevens-Duryea, Wills-St. Claire 14 Stanley-Steamer 16 Columbia-Electric 22 International Auto Buggy

Europe: BMW 4 Benz 5 Aston, Metro, Prinz, Skoda 6 Martin, Denzel, Isetta, Zodiac 7 Bugatti, Prefect 9 Facel-Vega

French: 5 Simca 7 Citroen, Panhard, Peugeot, Renault 8 Dauphine

German: DKW 4 Opel 6 Taunus 7 Goliath, Porsche, Weidner 8 Borgward, Rometsch, Wartburg 10 Golomobile, Lloyd-Wagon, Volkswagen 12 Mercedes-Benz

Italian: 4 Fiat 6 Lancia 7 Ferrari 8 Maserati 9 Alfa-Romeo

Japanese: 5 Honda, Mazda 6 Datsun, Subaru, Toyota 13 Pringe-Skylark

part: 4 hood 5 motor, trunk 6 engine 7 chassis, magneto, tonneau 8 ignition

Russian: Zim 6 Pobeda 9 Moskvitch

Swedish: 4 Saab 5 Volvo

supercharged: 6 hot rod

United States: 4 Ford, Jeep, Nash, Nova, Vega 5 Buick, Capri, Comet, Dodge, Pinto 6 Cougar, De Soto, Duster, Hudson, Impala, LeMans, Torino, Willys 7 Caprice, Lincoln, Mercury, Montego, Mustang, Packard, Pontiac, Rambler, Ventura 8 Cadillac, Chrysler, Corvette, Imperial, Maverick, Plymouth 9 Chevrolet 10 Oldsmobile, Studebaker 11 Continental, Thunderbird

autonomous: 4 free 8 separate 9 sovereign 11 independent 12 self-governed

autopsy: 8 necropsy 10 dissection 11 examination

autumn: 4 fall 6 season 8 maturity 11 harvest-time

auxiliary: aid, sub 4 aide, ally 6 backup, branch, helper 7 abetter, abettor, adjunct, partner, reserve 8 adjutant 9 accessory, adminicle, ancillary, assistant, coadjutor, secondary, tributary 10 additional, subsidiary, supporting 11 subordinate, subservient 13 supplementary

ava: 4 kava 5 shrub 6 pepper

avail: aid, use 4 help 5 serve, stead, value 6 profit 7 account, benefit, purpose, service, success, suffice, utilize 9 advantage 10 assistance

available: fit 4 free, open 5 handy, on tap, ready 6 usable 7 present 9 effectual, practical 10 accessible, attainable, convenient, obtainable, up for grabs 11 efficacious

avalanche: 4 heap, mass, pile 5 flood, slide 6 deluge 7 torrent 9 landslide, snowslide 10 inundation

Avalon, Avilion: 4 isle 6 island

tomb: 6 Arthur

avant-garde: new 7 leaders, offbeat 8 advanced, original, pioneers, vanguard 10 innovative 12 trendsetting, trailblazing

avarice: 7 avidity 8 cupidity, rapacity, venality 9 money-lust

spirit of: 6 Mammon

avaricious: 5 close 6 greedy, hungry, stingy 7 miserly 8 covetous, grasping 9 niggardly, penurious 12 parsimonious

avast: 4 halt, hold, stay, stop 5 cease

avatar: 8 epiphany 10 embodiment 11 incarnation

ave: 4 hail 8 farewell, greeting 10 salutation

Ave Maria: 6 prayer 8 Hail Mary 10 rosary bead

avenge: 5 repay 6 injure, punish 7 pay back, redress, requite, revenge 8 chastise 9 retaliate, vindicate 10 get even for

avenger: 7 nemesis 10 vindicator

avenue: rue(F.), way 4 gate, mall, pike, road 5 drive, entry 6 access, arcade, artery, course, outlet, street 7 opening 9 boulevard 10 passageway 12 thoroughfare

aver: say 5 claim, prove, state, swear 6 affirm, allege, assert, assure, avouch, depose, insist, verify 7 certify, contend, declare, justify, protest 8 maintain, proclaim 9 predicate 10 asseverate 11 acknowledge

average: par, sum 4 fair, mean, norm, so-so 5 ratio, usual 6 common, medial, median, medium, middle, normal, not bad 7 typical 8 mediocre, moderate, ordinary, standard 10 proportion 12 run-of-the-mill 13 approximation

averse: 5 balky, loath 7 against, opposed 8 hesitant, inimical 9 reluctant, unwilling 11 disinclined, ill-disposed, unfavorable 12 recalcitrant

aversion: 4 hate 5 odium 6 enmity, hatred, horror 7 disdain, disgust, dislike 8 distaste 9 antipathy 10 repugnance 11 abomination 12 estrangement 14 disinclination

avert: 4 bend, fend, foil 5 avoid, deter, dodge, evade, parry, twist 6 thwart 7 deflect, prevent, ward off 8 preclude, stave off 9 forestall, frustrate, keep at bay, turn aside

aviary: 4 cage 6 volary 8 dovecote, ornithon 9 birdhouse, columbary

keeper: 8 aviarist

aviation: 6 flying 10 airplaning 11 aeronautics

aviator: ace 5 flier, flyer, pilot 6 airman, fly-boy 7 birdman

notable: 7 Earhart 8 Corrigan 9 Chennault, Doolittle, Lindbergh 10 Richthofen (Red Baron), Rickenbacker

signal: out 4 over 5 roger

avid: 4 agog, keen, warm 5 eager, rabid 6 ardent, greedy, hungry 7 anxious, athirst, devoted 8 covetous, desirous, grasping 9 impatient, voracious

avidity: 7 avarice, craving, longing 8 cupidity 10 greediness

avifauna: 5 birds, ornis

avocado: 4 coyo, pear, tree 5 palta 6 chinin 13 alligator pear

avocation: 5 hobby 7 pastime 8 sideline 9 amusement, diversion 10 recreation

avocet: 4 bird 5 stilt 6 godwit

avoid: 4 duck, shun 5 annul, avert, dodge, elude, evade, hedge, parry, shirk, skirt, spair(Sc.) 6 bypass, escape, eschew 7 abstain, boycott, forbear, forsake, refrain 8 keep from, sidestep 10 steer clear 11 fight shy of

avoidance: 8 escapism 9 annulment 10 withdrawal

avoirdupois weight: ton 4 dram 5 ounce, pound 7 long ton

a votre sante(F.): 5 skoal, toast 6 prosit(G). 12 to your health

avow: own 5 admit, state, swear 6 affirm, assert, avouch, depose 7 confess, declare, justify, profess 8 maintain, proclaim 11 acknowledge

avowal: 4 word 8 averment 9 assurance 10 profession 14 representation

awa: 4 kava 8 milkfish

awabi: 8 abalone

await: 4 bide, pend, 5 abide, tarry 6 attend, expect, impend 8 mark time, watch for 10 anticipate, be ready for

awake: 5 alert, alive, astir, aware, rouse 6 active, arouse, excite, revive 7 careful, heedful 8 open-eyed, vigilant 9 attentive, conscious 10 up and about

awakening: 7 letdown 9 debunking, eye-opener 13 enlightenment

award: 4 give 5 allot, grant, honor, medal, prize 6 accord, assign, bestow, confer 7 adjudge, appoint, mete out, present, tribute 8 accolade, judgment, sentence 9 apportion, determine 10 decoration

academic: 6 degree 7 diploma 8 cum laude 9 sheepskin 12 Phi Beta Kappa 13 magna cum laude

broadcasting: 7 Peabody
cinema: 5 Oscar
detective story: 5 Edgar
Off-Broadway: 4 Obie
recording: 6 Grammy
science fiction: 4 Hugo
television: 4 Emmy
theatre: 4 Tony

aware: hep, hip 4 wary 5 alert, alive 7 knowing, mindful 8 apprised, apprized, informed, sensible, vigilant, watchful 9 au courant, cognizant, conscious 11 intelligent

away: awa(Sc.), fro, off, out, via 4 gone 5 along, apart, aside, forth, hence 6 abroad, absent, at once, begone, onward, thence 7 distant 8 directly, right off 9 elsewhere, forthwith

awe: cow 4 fear 5 alarm, amaze, daunt, scare 6 fright, regard, terror, wonder 7 buffalo, respect 8 astonish, bewilder, overcome 9 fascinate, overpower, reverence 10 intimidate, veneration

aweigh: 5 atrip

awesome: 4 eery 5 awful, eerie, weird 6 solemn 7 dreaded, ghostly, uncanny 8 imposing, terrible 9 appalling, unearthly 12 spell-binding

awful: bad 4 dire, ugly 6 august, horrid 7 awesome, fearful 8 dreadful, majestic, shocking, terrible 9 appalling, frightful 10 impressive, tremendous

awfully: 4 very 5 quite 7 greatly 9 extremely

awkward: 5 gawky, inapt, inept 6 clumsy, gauche, rustic, uneasy 7 boorish, loutish, stilted, uncouth, unhandy 8 bungling, lubberly, ungainly, untoward, unwieldy 9 difficult, graceless, ill at ease, inelegant, lumbering, maladroit, ponderous 10 backhanded, blundering, cumbersome, ungraceful, unskillful 11 heavyhanded 12 embarrassing, inconvenient

awl: 4 tool 5 punch 6 gimlet

awn: ear 4 barb 5 beard 6 arista 7 bristle 9 appendage

awning: 4 hood 6 canopy, screen, shield 7 shelter 8 velarium
fastening: 6 earing
relative: 7 marquee

awry: 5 agley(Sc.), amiss, askew, wrong 6 faulty, uneven 7 askance, asquint, crooked, haywire, oblique 8 cockeyed 9 distorted 11 out of kilter

ax: adz 4 adze, fire, sack 6 twibil 7 cleaver, dismiss, hatchet, kick out, twibill 8 tomahawk 9 discharge
blade: bit
butt: 4 poll
handle: 5 helve

axial: 7 central, midmost, pivotal

axilla: 6 armpit 8 shoulder

axiom: saw 5 adage, dicta(pl.), maxim, motto 6 byword, dictum, saying, truism 7 precept, proverb 8 aphorism, apothegm, sentence 9 principle 11 proposition

axis: 4 axle, deer, stem 5 pivot 6 chitra 7 fulcrum, spindle 8 alliance

axle: bar, cod, pin 4 axis 5 arbor, shaft 7 mandrel, spindel

axolotl: 4 newt 10 salamander

ayah: 4 maid 5 nurse 9 nursemaid

aye, ay: pro, yea, yes 4 ever, okay, vote 6 always, assent 7 forever 11 affirmative, continually

aye-aye: 5 lemur 6 will do 10 understood

Azerbaijan: *capital:* 4 Baku

Azores: *district:* 5 Horta 12 Ponta Delgada
island: 4 Pico 5 Corvo, Faial 6 Flores
port: 5 Horta
volcano: 4 Pico

Aztec: *ball game:* 8 tlachtli
emperor: 9 Moctezuma, Montezuma
god: 4 Xipe 9 Xipetotic 11 Xiuhtecutli
language: 7 Nahuatl
myth: 4 Nana, Nata
stone: 9 temelactl 12 chalchihuitl
temple: 6 teopan 8 teocalli

azure: 4 bice, blue 8 cerulean 9 cloudless, unclouded

azygous: odd 6 single

B

baa: 5 bleat
baahling: 4 lamb
Baal: 4 idol 5 deity 8 false god
  consort: 6 Baltis
baba: 5 child(Ind.) 7 rumcake
babacoote: 5 lemur
babassu: oil 4 palm, soap
Babbitt: 5 alloy, metal 9 bourgeois 10
  philistine 11 materialist
  author: Lewis
babblative: 9 garrulous, talkative 10 loquacious
babble: yak 4 chat 5 prate, run on 6 cackle, drivel, gibber, gossip, murmur 7
  blabber, blather, chatter, clatter, prattle, twaddle 8 nonsense 11 stultiloquy
babel: din 5 clang, tower 6 hubbub, jargon, medley, racket, tumult 7 discord 9
  charivari, confusion 10 hullabaloo
babiche: 6 lacing, thongs
babillard: 4 bird 11 whitethroat
baboon: ape 4 papa 5 drill 6 chaema 7
  babuina 8 mandrill
babul: gum, lac 4 tree, wood 6 acacia, mimosa
  pod: 5 garad
babushka: 5 scarf 8 kerchief 11 grandmother
  relative of: 8 bandanna
baby: tot 4 baba, babe, doll 5 bairn(Sc.),
  child, humor, spoil 6 coddle, fondle, infant, moppet, pamper, weanie(Sc.) 7
  bambino(It.), papoose 9 youngster
  bed: 4 crib 6 cradle 8 bassinet
  carriage: 4 pram 5 buggy 6 gocart 8
  stroller 12 perambulator
  christening robe: 7 chrisom, chrysom
  cry: mew 6 squall
  food: pap 4 milk 6 pablum
  outfit: 7 layette
  shoe: 6 bootee
babyish: 6 simple 7 puerile 8 childish
Babylonia: abode of the dead: 5 Aralu
  capital: 7 Babylon
  city: 5 Erech, Larsa 6 Calneh, Cunaxa,
  Cuthah, Lagash, Nippur, Sippar
  cycle of moon: sar 5 saros
  divison: 5 Akkad, Sumer
  god: Anu, Aya, Bel, Hea, Hes, Ira, Ler,
  Sin, Utu 4 Adad, Anat, Apsu, Baal,
  Gula, Irra, Nebo, Utug 5 Alala, Alalu,
  Dagan, Enlil, Etana, Ninib, Nusku,

Siris, Urash 6 Ishtar, Nergal, Oannes,
  Tammuz 7 Ninurta, Shamash 8 Mero-
  dach 10 Adramelech 11 Adrammelech
  goddess: Aya 4 Erua, Nana, Nina 5 Belit,
  Istar 6 Belili, Beltis, Ishtar 7 Mylitta
  hero of myth: 5 Adapa, Etana 9 Gilga-
  mesh
  king: 5 Gudea 6 Sargon 8 Naram-Sin 9
  Hammurabi
  language: 8 Akkadian, Sumerian
  mountain: 6 Ararat
  New: 7 Chaldea
  priestess: 5 Entum
  river: 6 Tigris 9 Euphrates
  Jewish exile ruler: 8 Exilarch
  sun god's attendant: 6 Bunene
  tower: 5 Babel 7 zikurat 8 ziggurat
  waters: 4 Apsu
  weight: 4 mina 5 maneh
Babylonian: 6 lavish, wicked 7 opulent
bacalao: 5 murre 7 codfish, grouper 9
  guillemot
bacca: 5 berry
baccalaureate: 6 degree, sermon 7 address, service 14 bachelor of arts
baccarat: 4 game
  player: 6 punter
  term: 5 banco
  variety of: 11 chemin-de-fer
baccate: 5 pulpy 7 berried
bacchanal: 4 orgy 7 debauch, reveler 8
  carouser
Bacchanal's cry: 4 evoe 5 evohe
bacchante: 6 maenad 9 priestess
bachelor: 7 unmated 8 celibate
  recently married: 8 benedict
bachelor button: 8 milkwort 10 bluebottle
bacillus: 4 germ 5 virus 7 microbe
back: aid, tub, vat 4 abet, hind, nata, rear,
  tail 5 angel, bet on, dorsa(pl.), notum,
  spine, splat, stern 6 assist, dorsum, second, uphold, verify 7 endorse, finance,
  sponsor, support, sustain 8 bankroll,
  rearward 9 encourage, posterior, reinforce 10 strengthen
  at the: aft 5 abaft, arear 6 astern 7 postern
  lower part of: 4 loin
  of neck: 4 nape 6 scruff
  pain: 7 lumbago
  pert. to: 6 dorsal, lumbar, tergal

back off: ebb 6 recede, retire 7 retreat, reverse 10 give ground, retrograde

back out: 4 funk 5 welsh 6 renege 8 crawfish, withdraw

back scratcher: 7 strigil

back-street: 6 secret 8 on the sly 13 surreptitious

Back Street author: 5 Hurst

back talk: lip 4 guff, sass 9 insolence

backbite: 5 abuse 6 defame, vilify 7 asperse, slander

backbone: 4 grit, guts 5 nerve, pluck, spine, spunk 6 mettle, spirit 7 stamina, support 8 mainstay, vertebra

backer: 5 angel 6 patron 7 sponsor 8 promoter

backgammon: *old relative:* 7 pachisi
term: 4 blot 6 double
variation: 10 acey-deucey

background: 4 rear 6 offing 7 setting 8 distance, training 9 education

backing: aid 6 lining, refuse 7 support 9 financing 10 embankment 11 endorsement

backlash: 6 recoil 8 reaction

backlog: 7 reserve, surplus 12 accumulation

backslide: 4 fall 5 lapse 6 desert, revert 7 relapse 11 deteriorate

backup: 4 help 5 spare 9 alternate 10 substitute, supporting

backward: shy 4 dull, slow 5 arear, loath 6 astern, averse, behind, bygone, stupid 7 bashful, laggard, lagging, reverse 8 dilatory, hesitant 9 recessive, reluctant, to the rear, unwilling 10 behindhand, hesitating 11 into the past 13 retrogressive, retrospective

backwater: ebb 5 bayou 7 retract, retreat

backwoodsman: 4 hick 9 hillbilly

backwort: 7 comfrey

bacon: pig 4 pork 5 prize
Canadian: 4 loin
fat: 5 speck
side: 6 flitch, gammon
slice: 6 rasher, collop

Bacon work: 6 Essays, 11 New Atlantis 12 Novum Organum

bacteria, bacterium: 4 germ 6 aerobe 7 microbe 8 organism 10 aerobacter
chain: 6 torula 7 torulae(pl.)
culture: 4 agar 8 agar-agar
dissolver: 5 lysin
free from harmful: 7 asepsis, aseptic
rod-shaped: 7 bacilli(pl.) 8 bacillus
spherical: 5 cocci(pl.) 6 coccus
spiral: 8 spirilla(pl.) 9 spirillum
vaccine: 8 bacterin

bactrian: 5 camel

bad: big, ill, sad 4 evil, full, lewd, poor, sick, vile 5 nasty, sorry, wrong 6 arrant, faulty, rotten, severe, sinful, wicked 7 baleful, baneful, corrupt, harmful, hurtful, immoral, inutile, naughty, spoiled, tainted, unlucky, unsound, vicious 8 annoying, criminal, depraved, flagrant, inferior, unsuited 9 abandoned, atrocious, blemished, dangerous, defective, incorrect, injurious, offensive, perverted, worthless 10 aggravated, distressed, inadequate, iniquitous, pernicious 11 deleterious, displeasing, inopportune, unfavorable 12 disagreeable, inauspicious

bad blood: 4 hate 5 anger 6 enmity 10 bitterness, ill-feeling, resentment

bad debt: 7 default

bad habit: 4 vice 5 fault 7 frailty 8 weakness

bad luck: 7 ill wind 9 adversity 10 misfortune, tough break

badderlocks: 6 murlin 7 henware, seaweed

badge: pin 4 mark, sign 5 token 6 emblem, ensign, symbol 8 insignia 10 cognizance

badger: nag 4 bait, 5 annoy, brock, chivy, hound, tease, worry 6 bother, chivvy, harass, heckle, pester, teledu, wombat 7 torment 8 carcajou, huckster, irritate 9 bandicoot, mistonusk
group: 4 cete

Badger State: 9 Wisconsin

badigeon: 5 paste 6 cement 11 composition

badinage: 6 banter 7 joshing, kidding, teasing 8 raillery, repartee 11 give and take

badly: 4 illy 6 poorly, unwell 7 harshly 8 faultily, severely 9 seriously 10 shamefully 11 imperfectly 12 unskillfully 13 unfortunately

bad-mouth: 4 slur 7 run down 9 criticize, disparage

Baedeker: 9 guidebook 10 tourist aid

baffle: 4 balk, foil, pose 5 elude, evade, fling, stump 6 defeat, delude, outwit, puzzle, thwart 7 confuse, deceive, grating, mystify, nonplus 8 bewilder, confound 9 confusion, deflector, discomfit, frustrate 10 circumvent, disconcert

bag: cod, net, pod, pot 4 gain, poke, sack, trap 5 bulse, catch, forte, pouch, purse, seize, snare, steal 6 budget, cavity, entrap, hang-up, pocket, sachet, wallet 7 alforja, balloon, capture, reticle, satchel 8 reticule 9 cartridge, container, gladstone, haversack, specialty, way of life 10 collection, pocketbook 11 portmanteau
botanic: sac 4 asci 5 ascus, spore
canvas: 7 musette
fishing net: 4 bunt, fyke

hop: 7 sarpler

muslin: 6 tillot

traveling: 4 grip 6 valise 8 backpack, knapsack, suitcase

bagatelle: 4 game 5 verse 6 trifle

baggage: 4 arms, gear, minx 5 huzzy, nasty, tents, trash, wench 6 harlot, refuse, trashy, trunks 7 clothes, effects, rubbish, valises 8 carriage, rubbishy, utensils 9 munitions, viaticals, worthless 10 prostitute 11 impedimenta

baggy: 5 loose 6 flabby, puffed

Baghdad: *capital:* 4 Iraq

  merchant; 6 Sinbad 7 Sindbad

  river: 6 Tigris

bagnio: 4 bath 5 bagne 6 prison 7 brothel 8 hothouse

bagpipe: 5 drone 7 musette 8 zampogna 10 doodlesack, sordellina

  mouthpiece: 4 muse

  pipe: 6 drones 7 chanter

  play: 5 skirl

  player: 5 piper 7 doodler

  sound: 5 skirl

  tune: 4 port

bah: foh, pah, rot 5 faugh, pshaw 8 nonsense

Bahama Islands: Cat 4 Long 5 Abaco, Exuma, Grand, Turks 6 Andros, Bimini, Caicos, Inagua 7 Acklins, Crooked 9 Eleuthera

  capital: 6 Nassau

  native indian: 7 Lucayan

bahia: bay

Bahrain: 11 archipelago

  capital: 6 Manama

  gulf: 7 Persian

  islands: 5 Sitra 7 Bahrain 8 Muharraq

  monetary unit: 4 fils 5 dinar

bail: dip 4 bond, hoop, lade, lave, ring, rynd, yoke 5 ladle, scoop, throw, vouch 6 bucket, handle, secure, surety 7 custody, deliver, release 8 bailsman, bulwarks, security 9 guarantee

bailiff: 5 agent 6 deputy 7 steward 8 overseer 9 constable 10 magistrate 12 court officer

bailiwick: 4 area 6 domain, office 8 home base, province 9 territory 12 jurisdiction

bairn: 5 child

bait: bad 4 bite, chum, feed, halt, lure 5 decoy, tempt, worry 6 allure, attack, badger, entice, harass, repast 7 fulcrum, gudgeon, provoke, torment 9 persecute 10 allurement, enticement, exasperate, inducement, temptation 11 refreshment

  artificial: 9 hackle fly

baize: 6 fabric 7 drapery

bake: dry 4 cook, fire 5 batch, broil, grill, parch, roast 6 anneal, harden 7 biscuit

baker: 4 oven 6 baxter 7 furnace, roaster, utensil

  sheet: pan

  shovel: 4 pale, peel

  tool: 4 pale, peel

baker's dozen: 8 thirteen

baker's itch: 4 rash 9 psoriasis

baking chamber: 4 kiln, oast, oven

baking dish: 7 cocotte, ramekin

baking soda: 9 saleratus

Bakongo goddess: 6 Nyambe, Nzambi

Balaam's beast: ass 6 donkey

balance: 4 even, rest 5 poise, scale, weigh 6 adjust, equate, offset, sanity, stasis 7 residue 8 equality, equalize, serenity 9 composure, equipoise, remainder, stability 10 neutralize, steadiness 11 equilibrium 12 counterpoise

  lose: 4 trip 7 stagger

  weighing: 6 auncel

balancer: 7 acrobat, athlete, gymnast

balcony: 5 oriel, porch 6 piazza, sollar 7 balagan, gallery, mirador, pergola, terrace 8 brattice, verandah

  church singer: 8 cantoria

  projecting: 6 gazabo, gazebo

bald: 4 bare, base 5 crude, naked, plain, stark 6 callow, paltry, pilled, shaven, smooth 7 epilose, literal, sheared 8 glabrous, hairless 9 unadorned, uncovered 11 undisguised, unvarnished

Balder, Baldur: *father:* 4 Odin

  mother: 5 Frigg

  murder weapon: 9 mistletoe

  slayer: 4 Hoth, Loke 5 Hothr

  son: 7 Forsete, Forseti

  wife: 5 Nanna

balderdash: rot 5 bilge, trash 6 drivel, jargon 8 claptrap, malarkey, nonsense 9 rigmarole 10 flumdiddle

baldicoot: 4 coot, monk

baldmoney: 7 gentian 8 spicknel

baldness: 8 alopecia 11 phalacrosis

baldric, baldrick: 4 belt 6 girdle, zodiac 7 balteus, support 8 baltheous, necklace

bale: woe 4 evil, harm 5 crate, death 6 bundle, sorrow 7 package 8 compress, disaster 9 influence, suffering

  of wool: 7 sarpler

Balearic Island: 5 Ibiza 7 Cabrera, Majorca, Minorca 8 Mallorca 10 Formentera

  language: 7 Catalan

  measure: 5 palmo 6 misura, quarta, quarte 7 quartin 8 barcella, quartera

  port: 5 Palma

  weight: 5 artal, artel, cargo, corta, libra, mayor, ratel, rotel 8 quartano

baleen: 5 whale 9 whalebone

baleful: bad 4 evil 6 deadly, malign 7 noxious, ruinous 8 sinister, wretched 10 calamitous, pernicious 11 destructive

balk: jib, shy 4 beam, bilk, foil, loft 5 block, check, demur, hunch, rebel, reest(Sc.), ridge, waver 6 baffle, defeat, falter, hinder, impede, outwit, rafter, recoil, refuse, thwart 7 quibble 8 hang back 9 discomfit, frustrate, stop short 14 disappointment

Balkan: 9 Mountains, Peninsula

peak: 5 Botev

people: 4 Serb, Slav 5 Croat 8 Albanian, Romanian

states: 6 Greece, Turkey(part) 7 Albania, Romania 8 Bulgaria 10 Yugoslavia

balky: 6 mulish 8 stubborn 9 obstinate

ball: bal(F.), bob, orb, toy 4 bead, pill 5 dance, globe, glome 6 bullet, muddle, pellet, pompon, rundle, sphere 7 confuse, mandrel, ridotto 8 spheroid 11 glomeration

lofted: fly, lob

low: 5 liner

minced meat: 5 pinda 7 rissole

wooden: 4 knur

ball and chain: 4 wife 6 burden

ball club: 4 nine, team 6 eleven

ball game: cat 5 rugby 6 pelota, soccer, tennis 7 cricket

ball of fire: 4 whiz 6 genius, dynamo 7 hustler 8 go-getter, live wire 11 eager beaver

ball up: 5 snarl 7 confuse, perplex

ballad: lai(F.) 4 lied, lilt, poem, song 5 derry 6 sonnet 7 canzone

ballast: 4 load, trim 5 poise, stone 6 burden, gravel, weight 7 balance 9 saburrate

ballerina: 6 dancer 8 coryphee, danseuse

ballet: 5 dance, drama 9 pantomime 12 choreography

knee bend: 4 plie

leap 4 jete 9 entrechat, pas de chat

movement: pas 5 brise 8 glissade

posture: 6 pointe 9 arabesque

wear: 4 tutu 6 tights 7 leotard

whirl: 9 pirouette

ballistic missile: 4 ICBM, IRBM

balloon: bag 5 blimp 6 expand, gasbag 7 airship, distend, inflate 8 aerostat 9 dirigible

basket: car 7 gondola, nacelle

ballot: 4 poll, vote 5 elect, voice 6 billet, choice, ticket

ballyhoo: 4 plug, tout 6 hoopla, puff up 7 promote, trumpet 9 publicity

balm: oil 5 salve 6 lotion, relief, solace 7 anodyne, comfort, perfume, soother, unguent 8 ointment 9 fragrance

horse: 10 citronella

of Gilead: 6 balsam, poplar

balmy: 4 mild, soft 5 bland, daffy, moony, spicy, sunny, sweet 6 gentle, insane 7 healing, lenient 8 aromatic, fragrant,

soothing 9 assuaging 10 refreshing 11 odoriferous

baloney: 4 bunk 5 hooey 6 humbug 8 nonsense

balsa: 4 raft, tree, wood 5 float

balsam: 4 riga, tree, tolu 6 storay 7 copaiba 8 bdellium, ointment

apple: 4 vine 7 creeper 8 amargosa, amargoso, ampalaya

Baltic native: 4 Lett 7 Latvian 8 Estonian 10 Lithuanian

Baltic Sea: *canal:* 4 Kiel

gulf: 4 Riga 6 Danzig 7 Bothnia, Finland

island: 4 Dago 5 Faron, Oland, Visby 6 Karlso, Sarema 7 Gotland 8 Bornholm

port: 4 Abo 5 Kiel, Riga 6 Gdansk, Gdynia 7 Tallinn 8 Klaipeda 9 Stockholm

river: 4 Oder, Odra 5 Dvina, Neman 7 Vistula

balustrade: 7 barrier, parapet, railing 8 banister

Balzac character: 4 Nana 6 Goriot

Bambi: 4 deer 7 animal

bambino: 4 baby 5 child 6 infant

bamboo: 4 cane, reed, tree

sacred: 6 nandin

sprouts: 5 achar

sugar: 9 tabasheer

woven: 6 sawali

bamboozle: 4 dupe 5 cheat, cozen, grill 6 cajole, humbug 7 buffalo, defraud, deceive, mystify, swindle 8 hoodwink 11 hornswoggle

ban: bar 4 tabu, veto 5 block, taboo 6 enjoin, forbid, hinder, invoke, outlaw 7 condemn, exclude 8 anathema, denounce, execrate, prohibit 9 proscribe 11 malediction 12 denunciation, interdiction 15 excommunication

Bana: *conqueror:* 7 Krishna

daughter: 4 Usha

banal: 4 flat 5 corny, inane, silly, stale, trite, vapid 6 jejune 7 insipid, trivial 9 hackneyed 10 pedestrian 11 commonplace 13 platitudinous

phrase: 6 cliche

banana: 4 musa 6 ensete 7 platano(Sp.) 8 plantain

bunch 4 hand, stem

family: 4 musa 6 pesang 8 musaceae

leaf: 5 frond

spider: 9 tarantula

wild: fei

banana fish: 6 albula 8 ladyfish

banana oil: 7 blarney 8 soft soap

bananas: mad 4 crazy 5 batty

band: tie 4 belt, cord, crew, fess, gang, girt, hoop, ring, zone 5 group, label, strap, strip, tribe, unite 6 armlet, bundle, collar, collet, fillet, girdle, streak, string, stripe, team up, troupe 7 binding, circlet, company, garland, orphrey 8 bracelet, cincture, ligament, symphony, tressure 9 aggregate, orchestra 10 collection

armed: 5 posse

armor: 6 tonlet

brain: 6 ligula 7 ligulae(pl.)

narrow: 4 tape 5 stria 6 striae(pl.)

small: 5 combo

bandage: 4 bind, tape 5 blind, clout, dress, sling, truss 6 fettle, fillet, ligate, swathe 8 cincture, ligature 9 blindfold

fastener: 7 ligator

nose: 9 accipiter

surgical: 5 spica 6 fascial, spicae(pl.) 7 fasciae(pl.)

bandeau: 4 strip 6 fillet 9 brassiere 10 hair ribbon

bandicoot: rat 6 badger

bandikai: 4 okra

bandit: 4 caco 5 bravo, thief 6 banish, outlaw, robber 7 bandido, brigand, ladrone 8 marauder, picaroon 10 highwayman

bandleader: 6 master 7 choragi, maestro 8 choragus 9 conductor

bandmaster: 5 Sousa

bandy: 4 cart, swap 5 trade 6 banter, bowed 7 chaffer, discuss 8 carriage, exchange 9 toss glibly, use glibly 11 give and take 12 treat lightly

bane: woe 4 evil, harm, kill, pest, ruin 5 curse, death, venom 6 injury, murder, poison, slayer 7 nemesis, scourge 8 mischief, murderer, nuisance

baneful: bad, ill 4 evil, vile 7 harmful, hurtful, noxious, ruinous 8 venomous 9 sinistral 10 pernicious

bang: rap 4 beat, blow, dash, dock, drub, slam 5 clash, drive, excel, force, impel, pound, sound, thump, whack, whang 6 bounce, cudgel, energy, strike, thrash, thwack 7 sardine, surpass 8 forelock 9 explosion

into: hit 5 crash 7 collide

bang-up: 5 crack 6 tiptop 9 first-rate

Bangladesh: *bay:* 6 Bengal

capital: 5 Dacca

city: 5 Bogra 6 Khulna, Mungla, Sylhet 7 Barisal 8 Chandput 10 Chittagong

language: 6 Bangla

monetary unit: 4 taka 5 paisa

river: 5 Padma 6 Ganges, Jamuna(Brahmaputra)

bangle: 4 flap, roam 5 droop, waste 7 circlet, fritter, trinket 8 bracelet, ornament

Bani's son: Uel 4 Amzi 5 Amram

banish: ban 5 eject, exile, expel, fleme 6 bandit, deport, dispel, forsay, outlaw 7 abandon, condemn, dismiss, exclude 8 displace, relegate 9 ostracize, proscribe, transport 10 expatriate, repatriate

banister: 7 railing 10 balustrade

bank: bar, bay, cop, rim, row 4 bink, brae, brew, caja, dike, dune, dyke, edge, hill, mass, pile, ramp, rive, sand, seat, tier, weir 5 banco, bench, bluff, brink, fence, levee, marge, mound, ridge, stack, share, shelf, shoal, shore, slope, stage, trust 6 causey, degree, depend, margin, reckon, rivage, strand 7 anthill, deposit, pottery, shallow 8 barranca, barranco, platform 9 acclivity, 10 depository, elevation, embankment

clerk: 6 teller

examiner: 10 accountant

requirement: 5 funds, money 6 assets 7 surplus 8 deposits

river: 4 ripa

bankroll: wad 4 back 5 funds 7 finance 8 currency 9 grubstake, subsidize

bankrupt: sap 4 bung 5 broke, drain, smash, strip 6 busted, devour, quisby, ruined 7 failure 8 beggarly, depleted 9 destitute, insolvent 12 impoverished

banner: 4 fane, flag, jack 5 color 6 ensign, fannon, pennon 7 leading, pennant, salient 8 banderol, foremost, gonfalon, standard, vexillum 9 banderole, exemplary, oriflamme 10 surpassing

banns: 6 notice 12 proclamation

banquet: 4 fete, meal 5 feast 6 dinner, junket, regale, repast 8 carousal, festival

room: 8 cenacula(pl.) 9 cenaculum

banquette: way 4 seat 5 shelf 7 footway 8 platform, sidewalk 10 embankment

banshee: fay 5 fairy, sidhe 6 goblin

bantam: 4 cock 5 saucy, small 6 little 7 chicken 9 combative 10 diminutive

breed: 8 Sebright

banter: kid, rag, rib 4 fool, jest, joke, josh, mock 5 chaff, jolly, tease 8 badinage, raillery 10 persiflage, pleasantry 11 give and take, playfulness

bantling: 5 child 6 infant

Bantu: *dialect:* 6 Chwana 8 Sechuana

language: 4 Ila 4 Suto 5 Ronga 6 Thonga 7 Nyanja 8 Nyamwezi 10 Wanymawezi

people: 4 Baya, Bihe, Bule, Fang, Gogo, Gola, Guha, Hehe, Jaga, Luba, Maka, Nama, Vira, Yaka, Zulu 5 Duala, Kafir 6 Banyai, Damara, Kaffir, Waguha, Yakala 7 Swahili, Wachaga 8 Bechuana

banxring: 6 mammal, tupaya 7 pentail 9 tree shrew

genus: 4 tana

look-alike: 8 squirrel

banzai: cry 6 attack

baobab: 4 tree 7 tebeldi

baptism: 9 aspersion, cleansing, immersion 11 christening

robe: 7 chrisom

vessel: 4 font 6 fontal, spring 7 piscina

water: 5 laver

baptize: dip 4 full, name 5 heave 6 purify

7 cleanse 8 christen, sprinkle

bar: ban, dam, fid, gad, law, rod 4 axle, band, bank, beam, bolt, cake, gate, hide, joke, lock, oust, pole, rail, reef, save, shut, stop 5 arbor, bench, bilco, block, close, court, deter, estop, fence, hedge, lever, perch, shade, shaft, strap, strip 6 billet, bistro, brooch, except, fasten, grille, hinder, meagre, saloon, stripe 7 barrage, barrier, confine, counter, leave out, exclude, pass over, prevent 8 conclude, handicap, obstacle, obstruct, preclude, prohibit, restrain, restrict, surround, tribunal 9 barricade, fastening, gatehouse, hindrance, interpose, ostracize 10 crosspiece, difficulty, impediment, inhibition, portcullis 11 obstruction

acrobat: 7 trapeze
bullion: 5 ingot
millstone: 4 rynd
resisting pressure: 5 strut
supporting: fid, rod 9 stanchion
tamping: 7 stemmer
window: 5 jemmy, jimmy 7 forcing

barb: awn, bur, jag, mow 4 burr, clip, file, flue, hair, herl, hook, jagg 5 beard, horse, point, ridge, shaft 6 pigeon 7 bristle 8 kingish 9 appendage 10 projection

anchor: 4 flue
feather: 4 harl, herl 5 ramus 7 pinnula, pinnule 8 pinnulae

Barbados: *capital:* 10 Bridgetown
bay: 4 Long 7 Oistins 8 Carlisle
liquor: rum
member: 12 Commonwealth
monetary unit: 4 cent 6 dollar
native: Bim
peak: 9 Mt. Hillaby
sovereign: 11 Elizabeth II
town: 5 Rouen 6 Kendal 7 Maxwell 8 Hastings

barbarian: Hun 4 boor, Goth, rude, wild 5 alien, brute 6 savage, vandal 7 ruffian 9 foreigner, untutored 10 Philistine, unlettered 11 uncivilized

barbarism: 4 cant 8 savagism, solecism 10 savageness

barbarity: 6 ferity 7 cruelty 8 ferocity, rudeness, savagery 9 brutality 10 inhumanity

barbarous: 4 fell, rude, wild 5 cruel 6 brutal 7 foreign, Hunnish, inhuman, slavish, uncivil 8 ignorant 9 ferocious, primitive 10 illiterate, outlandish, tramontane, unpolished 11 uncivilized 12 uncultivated

barbary ape: 5 magot 6 monkey

Barbary Coast States: 5 Tunis 7 Algiers, Morocco, Tripoli

barbecue: 4 bake 5 broil, grill

rod: 4 spit 6 skewer

barbed: 4 bent 6 hooked 8 uncinate

barber: 6 Figaro, poller, shaver, tonsor 7 scraper, tonsure 11 chirotonsor

barber's itch: 8 ringworm

bard: 4 poet, scop 5 druid, runer, scald 6 singer 8 minstrel, musician
India: 4 bhat

Bard of Avon: 11 Shakespeare

bare: 4 bald, mere, nude 5 alone, crude, empty, naked, plain, stark, strip 6 barren, callow, denude, divert, divest, expose, histie, meager, meagre, paltry, pilled, reveal, simple 7 divulge, exposed, unarmed, uncover 8 desolate, disclose, stripped 9 in the buff, unadorned, uncovered, worthless 10 threadbare 11 defenseless, unconcealed, unfurnished 13 unaccompanied

barefaced: 4 bold 6 brazen 7 blatant, glaring 8 impudent 9 audacious, out-and-out, shameless 11 undisguised

barefooted: 6 unshod 9 discalced

barely: 4 only 5 faint 6 hardly, merely, poorly 8 scantily, scarcely, slightly 13 unqualifiedly 14 insufficiently

barf: 5 vomit 7 upchuck

barfly: 5 drunk, stiff 8 carouser

bargain: 4 deal, huck, pact, sale 5 cheap, steal 6 barter, dicker, haggle, palter 7 chaffer, compact, contend, contest 8 contract, covenant, giveaway, struggle 9 agreement, negotiate, situation, stipulate 10 engagement 11 come to terms, transaction

bargain-basement: 5 cheap 6 tawdry

bargain for: 6 expect 7 count on

barge: ark, tow 4 bark, boat, raft, scow 5 lunge, lurch 6 barque, lumber, thrust, tender, vessel 7 lighter 8 flagship, flatboat 9 intrude on 12 move clumsily
charge: 10 lighterage
coal: 4 keel

bark: bag, bay, rub, wap, yap, yip 4 boat, coat, howl, husk, peel, pelt, pill, rind, ross, ship, skin, yawp 5 balat, barca, barge, cough, shell, shout, strip 6 abrade, cortex, girdle, vessel 7 solicit, tanbark 8 cortices, covering
aromatic: 6 sintoc 7 canella 9 sassafras
at: 5 scold 6 rebuke
cloth: 4 tapa 5 tappa 8 mulberry
covered with: 9 corticate 10 corticated
medicinal: 4 coto 5 casca, madar, nudar, niepa 7 quinine 8 cinchona 9 sassafras
outer: 8 periderm
pert. to: 8 cortical
remove: 4 ross 5 scale
resembling: 8 cortical
rough: 4 ross
tanning: 5 alder
up the wrong tree: err 5 stray

barker: dog 4 tout 7 spieler 8 pitchman 9 solicitor

barking deer: 7 muntjac, muntjak

barley: 5 grain
ground: 6 tsamba
pert. to: 11 hordeaceous
steep: 4 malt
variety: big 4 bere, bigg

barmy: 5 foamy, kooky, silly 6 frothy, screwy, yeasty 7 flighty, foolish, idiotic

barn: 4 byre 6 stable 10 storehouse
part: bay, mow 4 loft 5 stall 7 hayloft

barn dance: 7 hoedown
official: 6 caller

barnacle: 5 leech 8 hanger-on, parasite 9 appendage, shellfish 11 encumbrance

barnstorm: 4 tour 5 stump 6 troupe

barometric line: 6 isobar

baron: 4 peer 5 mogul 6 tycoon 7 magnate

baroque: 6 ornate, rococo 9 grotesque, irregular 11 extravagant 13 overdecorated

barrack: 4 camp 6 casern 7 cuartel(Sp.) 8 quarters

barracuda: 4 fish, kaku, spet 5 barry, pelon 6 becuna, picuda, sennet 10 guaguanche 12 guanchepelon

barrage: 4 hail 5 burst, salvo 6 attack, volley 7 barrier 9 broadside, cannonade, fusillade 10 obtruction, outpouring 11 bombardment

barranca, barranco: 4 bank 5 bluff 6 ravine

barrel: fat, keg, tun, vat 4 butt, cade, cask, drum, knag 6 runlet, tierce, vessel 7 cistern, rundlet 8 cylinder, hogshead 9 container, kilderkin
herring: 4 cade
maker: 6 cooper
part: 4 side, hoop 5 stave
raising device: 9 parbuckle
stopper: 4 bung
support: 4 hoop 6 gantry 7 gauntry

barren: dry 4 arid, bare, dull 5 empty, gaunt, stark, stern 6 desert, effete, fallow, jejune, meager 7 sterile 8 desolate, devoid of, impotent, treeless 9 childless, exhausted, fruitless, infertile 10 unfruitful 12 unproductive, unprofitable

barren oak: 9 blackjack

barren privet: 7 alatern 9 houseleek

barrette: bar 8 ornament

Barrie character: 5 Peter, Wendy

barrier: bar, dam 4 door, gate, line, wall, weir 5 bound, chain, fence, hedge, limit 6 abatis, hurdle, screen 7 barrage, defense, parapet, railing 8 boundary, fortress, frontier, stockade 9 barricade, palisades, restraint, roadblock 10 difficulty 11 obstruction
movable: 4 bars, door 5 blind, shade 6 screen 7 curtain 8 shutters

barring: 6 save for 9 aside from, excepting, outside of

barrio: 4 slum 6 ghetto 7 village

barrister: 6 barman, lawyer 7 counsel 8 advocate, attorney 9 solicitor

barroom: pub 4 cafe 6 lounge, tavern, saloon 7 cantina(Sp.), doggery 8 dramshop

barrow: hod, hog 4 bank, dune, hill, mote 5 grave, gurry, mound 6 tumuli 7 hillock, trolley, tumulus 8 mountain

barter: 4 chap, chop, cope, coup, hawk, sell, swap, vend 5 corse, trade, troke, truck 6 dicker 7 bargain, cambium, permute, traffic 8 commerce, exchange 9 excambion 11 reciprocate

Bartered Bride composer: 7 Smetana

bas: low

bas-relief: 9 plaquette

basal: 5 basic 7 basilar 11 fundamental

basalt: 6 marble, navite 7 pottery

base: bed, low 4 clam, evil, foot, foul, lewd, mean, poor, root, stem, step, vile 5 basis, cheap, dirty, muddy, petty, snide 6 abject, bottom, common, ground, menial, paltry, podium, shabby, sordid, vulgar 7 bastard, bedrock, caitiff, comical, hangdog, housing, ignoble, lowdown, servile, slavish, support 8 degraded, infamous, inferior, pedestal, scullion, shameful, stepping, unworthy, wretched 9 absorbent, degrading, establish, predicate, worthless 10 despicable, foundation, villainous 11 ignominious 12 contemptible, dishonorable, disreputable 13 dishonourable
architectural: 5 socle 6 plinth
attached by: 7 sessile
military: HDQ 4 camp 5 depot 12 headquarters
structural: 6 plinth

base on balls: 4 pass, walk

baseball: *field:* 7 diamond
founder: 9 Doubleday
glove: 4 mitt
hit: 4 bunt
official: ump 5 coach 6 umpire 7 manager
players: Ott (Mel) 4 Cobb (Ty), Dean (Dizzy), Ford (Whitey), Foxx (Jimmy), Mays (Willie), Rose (Pete), Ruth (Babe) 5 Aaron (Hank), Banks (Ernie), Bench (Johnny), Berra (Yogi), Brock (Lou), Grove (Lefty), Kiner (Ralph), Maris (Roger), Spahn (Warren), Young (Cy) 6 Feller (Bob), Gehrig (Lou), Gibson (Bob), Hunter (Catfish), Koufax (Sandy), Mantle (Mickey), Musial (Stan), Seaver (Tom), Wagner (Honus) 7 Hornsby (Rogers), Hubbell (Carl), Jackson (Reggie), Johnson (Walter), Speaker (Tris) 8 Clemente (Roberto),

DiMaggio (Joe), Robinson (Jackie), Williams (Ted) **9** Alexander (Grover), Killebrew (Harmon) **10** Campanella (Roy) **11** Yastrzemski (Carl)

team: **4** nine

teams (American League): **5** Twins (Minnesota) **6** Angels (Cal.), Red Sox (Boston), Royals (Kansas City), Tigers (Detroit) **7** Brewers (Milwaukee), Indians (Cleveland), Orioles (Baltimore), Rangers (Texas), Yankees (N.Y.) **8** Blue Jays (Toronto), Mariners (Seattle), White Sox (Chicago) **9** Athletics (Oakland)

teams (National League): **4** Cubs (Chicago), Mets (N.Y.), Reds (Cincinnati) **5** Expos (Montreal) **6** Astros (Houston), Braves (Atlanta), Giants (San Francisco), Padres (San Diego) **7** Dodgers (Los Angeles), Pirates (Pittsburgh) **8** Phillies (Philadelphia) **9** Cardinals (St. Louis)

term: bag, bat, box, fan, fly, hit, lob, low, out, peg, RBI, run, tap, top **4** ball, bean, beat, bunt, burn, deck, foul, high, hill, hole, home, hook, miss, pill, pole, sack, save, turn, walk, wild **5** alley, apple, bench, booth, clout, coach, count, curve, drive, error, field, first, force, frame, glove, homer, lined, mound, pitch, plate, popup, punch, score, slide, swing, third **6** assist, batter, bungle, bottom, charge, clutch, double, dugout, groove, hitter, inside, lifted, lumber, middle, popout, putout, rubber, runner, screen, second, series, single, sinker, stance, strike, string, target, triple, wind-up **7** arbited, arbiter, battery, blooper, bullpen, circuit, cleanup, diamond, fielder, floater, infield, manager, nothing, outside, pitcher, side-arm, squeeze, stretch, thumbed **8** delivery, grounded, grounder, knuckler, outfield, pinch-hit, powdered, soupbone, spitball **9** full-count, hot corner, sacrifice, smothered, strikeout, two-bagger **10** scratch-hit **11** three-bagger

baseless: 4 idle **9** unfounded, untenable **10** gratuitous, groundless **11** unsupported

bash: bat, lam **4** beat, blow, dent, mash, swat, wham, whop **5** party, smash **6** bruise, strike, wallop **7** blowout, hit hard **8** wingding

Bashemath's husband: 4 Esau

bashful: coy, shy **5** blate(Sc.), mousy, timid **6** demure, modest **7** daunted **8** backward, blushing, dismayed, retiring, sheepish **9** diffident, shrinking

Bashkir capital: Ufa

basic: 5 chief, vital **7** central **9** elemental, principal **10** underlying **11** fundamental, rudimentary **13** indispensable

basically: 8 at bottom **9** in essence, primarily **11** essentially

basil: 4 herb **5** plant, royal **6** fetter

basilica: 6 church, shrine, temple **7** Lateran

part of: **4** apse, nave

basin: cwm, pan **4** bowl, dish, dock, ewer, font, sink, tank **5** laver, stoup **6** cirque, crater, marina, valley, vessel **7** cuvette, piscina **8** lavatory, receptor, washbowl **9** reservoir **10** depression **11** aspersorium

geological: **4** tala

basis: 4 root **5** axiom **6** bottom, ground, reason **7** essence, footing, premise, support **10** foundation, groundwork

bask: sun **4** beek(Sc.), warm **5** acrid, bathe, enjoy, revel **6** bitter **7** rejoice **9** luxuriate

basket: ark, fan, ped **4** kipe, trug **5** cassy(Sc.), cesta, chest, crate, scull **6** cassie(Sc.), dosser, hamper, hoppet, panier **7** canasta, hanaper, pannier, scuttle **9** container **10** receptacle

coal mine: **4** corf

eel: **4** buck

fig: **4** caba **5** frail **6** tapnet

fire: **5** grate **7** cresset

fish: pot **4** caul, cawl, corf, hask, skip, weel **5** creel, crate, maund **6** courge

fruit: **6** pottle **7** prickle

material: **4** cane, rush **5** osier, otate **6** willow

twig: **6** wattle

water-tight: **7** wattape

wicker: cob **4** cobb, coop **5** willy **6** hamper **7** hanaper **8** bassinet

work: **4** caba **5** cabas, slath **6** slarth

basketball

inventor: **8** Naismith

official: ref **6** umpire **7** referee

players: **4** Reed (Willis), West (Jerry) **5** Cousy (Bob) **6** Baylor (Elgin), Pettit (Bob), Cowens (Dave) **7** Bellamy (Walt), Frazier (Walt) **8** Havlicek (John) **9** Robertson (Oscar) **11** Chamberlain (Wilt)

positions: **5** cager, guard **6** center **7** forward **8** hoopster

pro teams (NBA): **4** Jazz (Utah), Nets (New Jersey), Suns (Phoenix) **5** Bucks (Milwaukee), Bulls (Chicago), Hawks (Atlanta), Kings (Kansas City), 76ers (Philadelphia), Spurs (San Antonio) **6** Knicks (New York), Lakers (Los Angeles), Pacers (Indiana) **7** Bullets (Washington), Celtics (Boston), Nuggets (Denver), Pistons (Detroit), Rockets (Houston) **8** Clippers (San Diego), Warriors (Golden State) **9** Cavaliers (Cleveland), Mavericks (Dallas)

11 Supersonics (Seattle) 12 Trail Blazers (Portland)

team: 4 five 7 cagemen, quintet

term: gun, key 4 cage, dunk, pass 5 lay-up, stuff, tip-in 6 freeze, tap-off 7 dribble, rebound, time-out 8 jump ball 9 backboard, backcourt, field goal, free throw 11 ball control

Basque: *bay:* 6 Biscay

cap: 5 beret

city: 4 Irun 5 Eibar 6 Bermeo, Bilbao, Sestao, Tolosa 7 Vitoria

dance: 8 zortzico

game: 6 pelota 7 jai alai

language: 9 Euskarian

mountains: 8 Pyrenees 10 Cantabrian

petticoat: 8 basquine

province: 5 Alava 7 Vizcaya 9 Guipuzcoa

bass: low 4 deep, fish 5 voice 6 singer 7 achigan, jewfish

bassinet: 4 crib 6 cradle 7 baby bed

basswood: lin 4 bast 5 tilia 6 linden

bast: 4 bark, flax, hemp, jute 5 fiber, ramie 6 phloem 8 piassava

bastard: 4 base 5 false 6 cannon, galley, hybrid, impure 7 byspell, lowbred, mongrel 8 bantling, spurious 10 artificial 11 adulterated 12 illegitimate

baste: sew 4 beat, cane, cook, drub, lard, tack 6 cudgel, punish, stitch, thrash

bastion: *defensive:* 4 fort 13 fortification

shoulder: 6 epaule

bat: hit, wad 4 bate, beat, blow, club, gait, lump, mass, swat, wink 5 binge, brick, piece, speed, spree, stick 6 aliped, backie(Sc.), baston, beetle, cudgel, racket, strike, stroke, wander 7 flutter, noctule, vampire 8 bludgeon, serotine 9 reremouse 10 battledore, chiroptera, packsaddle 11 rattlemouse 12 chauvesouris, flittermouse 🖘

around: 4 roam 6 ponder 7 debate

European: 9 barbastel 11 barbastelle

species: 9 pipistrel 11 pipistrelle

Bataan: *bay:* 5 Subic

city: 7 Balanga

batch: lot 4 mass, mess, sort 5 group 6 bundle 7 mixture 8 quantity 10 collection

bate: 6 deduct, except 7 decrease, exclude

bateau: 4 boat

batfish: 6 diablo

bath: dip 4 bate, pert 5 therm 6 plunge, shower 7 balneum 8 ablution 10 natatorium

pert. to: 7 balneal

public: 7 piscine

sponge: 5 luffa 6 loofah

treatment by: 13 balneotherapy

Bath river: 4 Avon

bathe: bay, tub 4 bask, lave, stew, wash 5 embay 6 enwrap 7 immerse, pervade,

suffuse 8 permeate

bathhouse: 6 cabana 8 balneary

bathing suit: 6 bikini, trunks 7 maillot

bathos: 8 comedown 10 anticlimax

bathroom: W.C.(abbr.) 6 hammam 8 sudatory 10 sudatorium 11 water closet

Bathsheba: *husband:* 5 Uriah

son: 7 Solomon

baton: rod 4 bend 5 staff, stick 6 baston, cudgel 7 bourdon, scepter, sceptre 9 truncheon

batrachian: 4 frog, toad

batten: 6 enrich, fatten, thrive 9 fertilize

batter: ram 4 beat, dent, maim 5 clour, dinge, frush, paste, pound 6 bruise, hammer, hitter, pummel 7 bombard, cripple, destroy, shatter, striker 8 demolish

battery: *floating:* 4 cell 5 praam 7 parapet 9 artillery 11 bombardment

plate: 4 grid

terminal: 5 anode 7 cathode

battle: war 4 duel, fray, meet, tilt 5 brush, fight, joust, onset 6 action, affray, combat 7 bombard, contend, contest, hosting 8 conflict, skirmish, warfare 9 encounter 10 engagement, struggle 11 competition, hostilities

area: 5 arena, front 6 sector 7 terrain

cry: 6 slogan 9 catchword

formation: 5 herse 6 deploy

line: 5 front

order: 7 regalia 8 battalia

royal: 5 melee 7 scrimmage

site: 6 Shiloh 7 Bull Run 8 Manassas 10 Armageddon, Gettysburg

trophy: 5 medal, scalp 6 ribbon

Battle Hymn of the Republic author: 4 Howe

battleship: 7 carrier 11 dreadnaught 16 superdreadnaught

batty: 5 crazy, silly 7 foolish

bauble: bow, toy 4 bead 6 button, gewgaw, trifle 7 trinket 8 gimcrack 9 plaything 10 knickknack

bauxite derivative: 8 aluminum

Bavaria: 6 Bayern(G.)

capital: 6 Munich

city: Hof 5 Furth 6 Passau 8 Augsburg, Bayreuth, Nurnberg, Wurzburg 9 Nuremberg 10 Regensburg

lake: 5 Ammer, Chiem 9 Starnberg

mountain: 10 Allgau Alps 11 Wetterstein 14 Bohemian Forest

peak: 5 Arber 9 Zugspitze

river: Alz, Ilz, Inn, Nab 4 Eger, Isar, Lech, Main 5 Amper, Iller, Regen, Saale 6 Danube 7 Altmuhl, Regnitz

Wagner festival site: 8 Bayreuth

bawd: 4 aunt, hare 5 dirty 6 defile 7 commode 8 procurer 9 procuress 10 fruitwoman

bawdy: 4 foul, lewd 5 dirty 7 obscene 8 unchaste

bawl: cry 4 howl 5 golly, shout 6 bellow, boohoo, outcry 8 glaister 10 vociferate
out: 5 scold 9 reprimand

bay: dam, ria, voe 4 bank, bark, cove, gulf, hole, hope, howl, loch(Sc.), roan, tree, yaup, yawp 5 bahia(Sp.), berry, bight, color, creek, fiord, fjord, fleet, haven, horse, oriel, sinus 6 laurel, recess, window 7 enclose, estuary, silanga, ululate 11 compartment, indentation
bird: 5 snipe 6 curlew, godwit, plover
camphor: 6 laurin

Bay of Biscay: *island:* Yeu 5 Belle, Groix 6 Oleron
resort: 7 Hendaye 8 Biarritz
river to: 5 Adour, Loire 7 Garonne

Bay State: 13 Massachusetts

bayard: 5 horse

Baylor University site: 4 Waco

bayonet: 4 stab 5 knife 6 pierce, weapon

bayou: 5 brook, creek, inlet, river 6 outlet, stream 7 rivulet 9 backwater

Bayou State: 11 Mississippi

bazaar, bazar: 4 fair, fete, sale 5 agora, burse 6 market 7 canteen 8 emporium 9 bezesteen 10 exposition

bazoo: 4 talk 5 kazoo, mouth

be: are 4 live 5 abide, exist, occur 6 remain 7 breathe, subsist 8 continue

beach: 4 bank, moor, ripa, sand 5 coast, plage(F.), playa(Sp.), shore 6 ground, shilla, strand 7 hardway, seaside, shingle

beachcomber: 7 vagrant 8 vagabond

beachhead: van 7 landing 8 foothold

beacon: 4 mark, sign 5 baken, fanal, guide, phare 6 ensign, pharos, signal 7 cresset, seamark, warning 8 signpost 10 lighthouse, watchtower
light: 7 cresset, lantern

Beaconsfield: 8 Disraeli

bead: 4 drop, foam 5 sewan, sight 6 bauble, bubble, prayer, wampum 7 globule, molding, rosary, trinket
string: 6 rosary 7 chaplet 8 necklace

beady: 5 round, small 8 globular 10 glistening

beak: neb, nib 4 bill, nose, peak 5 snout, spout 7 rostrum 8 mandible 9 proboscis, schnozzle 10 promontory
ship's: bow, ram 4 prow
without: 9 erostrate

beaker: cup 4 tass 5 bocal, bouse, glass 6 bareca, bareka, vessel

be-all and end-all: 4 acme, A to Z 8 entirety, sum total, ultimate, whole bit 9 aggregate 10 everything 11 ne plus ultra 13 alpha and omega

beam: bar, ray 4 balk, emit, glow, I-bar, sile(Sc.), stud, T-bar 5 arbor, caber, flash, gleam, gleed, joist, light, shine, smile 6 binder, girder, rafter, timber, walker 7 bumpkin, chevron, radiate, support, trimmer 10 architrave

beaming: gay 4 rosy 6 bright, lucent, joyous 7 radiant, shining 8 all aglow, cheerful

beamy: 5 broad 7 massive 8 mirthful

bean: urd 4 chap, gram, head 5 brain, skull 6 caster, collar, fellow, kidney, lentil, nipple, noggin, strike, thrash, trifle 7 calabar, frijole(Sp.) 11 castigation
Asian: 4 gram, mung
climbing: 4 lima, pole
cluster: 4 guar
curd: 4 tofu
eye: 4 hila 5 hilum
kind: goa, soy, wax 4 lima, navy, snap 5 cacao, green, jelly, pinto 6 castor, coffee, kidney, string 7 calabar, jumping
lima: 4 haba 5 sieva
locust: 5 carob
lubricant: ben
Mexican: 6 frejol, frijol 7 frijole
poisonous 4 loco 7 calabar

bean shooter: 8 catapult 9 slingshot

Beantown: 6 Boston

bear: cub, lug 4 gest, tote 5 abide, allow, beget, breed, bring, brook, brown, bruin, carry, drive, geste, koala, Polar, press, stand, yield 6 afford, behave, endure, pierce, render, suffer, thrust, uphold 7 comport, conduct, forbear, grizzly, produce, support, sustain, undergo 8 forebear, tolerate 9 carnivore, transport 13 constellation
Alaskan: 6 kadiak, kodiak
genus: 5 ursus

bear bush: 8 inkberry

bear cat: 4 paud 9 binturong

bear down: 5 exert, press 6 stress 8 approach

bear-shaped: 8 ursiform

bear upon: 6 affect 7 concern

beard: 4 barb, defy 5 brave 6 arista, goatee 7 Vandyke 8 confront, face up to, hair tuft, whiskers 9 challenge 11 mutton chops
grain: awn

bearded: 5 hairy 6 barbed 7 barbate, hirsute 9 whiskered 11 barbigerous
grain: rye 5 awned, wheat 8 aristate

beardless: 5 young 6 callow

bearing: aim, air 4 gest, mien, port 5 birth, front, geste, habit, poise, trend 6 allure, apport, aspect, course, gerent, manner, orient, thrust 7 address, conduct, meaning, posture, purport, support 8 amenance, attitude, behavior, carriage, demeanor, pressure, relation, tendency, yielding 9 direction, gesta-

tion, influence, personage, producing
10 cognizance, deportment 11 comportment, countenance 12 significance
fine: 6 belair
heraldic: 4 ente, orle 5 pheon
plate: gib
beast: 4 bete(F.) 5 brute 6 animal, savage
7 monster 8 blighter 9 quadruped
   mythical: roc 5 harpy, Hydra 6 dragon,
   Garuda, Geryon, gorgon, Kraken,
   Orthos, Scylla, Sphinx, Triton 7 centaur, chimera, Echidna, figfaun, griffin,
   griffon, Midgard, phoenix 8 Cerberus,
   chimaera, Minotaur 9 Charybdis, Sasquatch 10 Jabberwock
   pertaining to: 7 leonine
   royal: 4 lion
beast of burden: ass, yak 4 oxen(pl.) 5
burro, camel, horse, llama 6 donkey,
onager
beastly: 5 feral, gross 6 animal, brutal 7
bestial, brutish, inhuman, swinish 9 offensive 10 abominable, disgusting
beat: bat, cob, dad(Sc.), fan, fib, tap, taw,
tew 4 baff, bang, bash, bate, belt, best,
blow, bolt, bray, cane, chap, club, daud,
ding, dint, drub, dump, dunt, fell, flap,
flax, flog, frat, haze, lash, lump, maul,
mill, pant, pelt, prat, rout, scat, slam,
tack, tick, whip, whop 5 baste, berry,
churn, clink, douse, fight, filch, flail,
knock, pound, pulse, round, scoop,
strap, throb, thump, trump, whang,
worst 6 accent, batter, beetle, buffet,
cotton, cudgel, defeat, fettle, hammer,
hamper, larrup, outrun, pummel, raddle,
rhythm, squash, strike, stroke, swinge,
switch, thrash, threap(Sc.), thresh 7 assault, battuta, belabor, blister, cadence,
canvass, conquer, contuse, exhaust, fatigue, pulsate, shellac, surpass, trounce,
vibrate 8 belabour, fatigued, lambaste,
overcome, shellack, vanquish 9 exhausted, pulsation, throbbing 10 assignment
   back: 5 repel 7 repulse 8 drive off
   down: 5 crush 7 wear out 8 dispirit, suppress 10 make abject
   into plate: 8 malleate
beat it: 4 scat 5 scram 7 vamoose
beater: rab 4 maul, seal 5 caner, lacer 6
dasher, mallet 8 thresher 9 scrutcher
beatify: 6 hallow 7 glorify 8 sanctify
beatitude: joy 5 bliss 7 benison 9 happiness 11 blessedness
beau: 5 beaux(pl.), blade, dandy, flame,
lover, spark, swell 6 garcon, escort, fellow, steady, suitor 7 admirer, bravery,
courter, coxcomb, cupidon, gallant 8
follower 9 boyfriend
Beau Brummell: fop 5 dandy 7 coxcomb
beau geste: 5 favor

beau ideal: 5 model 8 paradigm 14 shining example
beau monde: 7 fashion, society
beaut: 4 lulu
beautician: 10 beautifier, cosmetiste(F.)
11 cosmetician
beautifier: 8 cosmetic
beautiful: 4 fair, fine, glad, mear, meer,
mere 5 belle, bonny 6 blithe, bonnie,
choice, comely, decore, freely, lovely,
poetic, pretty 7 elegant 8 charming,
delicate, fairsome, gorgeous, graceful,
handsome, stunning 9 exquisite 10
good-looking
   people: 5 elite 6 jet set 9 haut monde 11
   high society
beautify: 4 gild 5 adorn, grace, hight,
preen, primp, prune 6 bedeck 7 adonize, garnish 8 decorate 9 embellish,
glamorize
beauty: 5 belle, charm, grace 6 eyeful,
looker, polish 8 knockout 10 comeliness, goodliness, loveliness 11 pulchritude
   goddess: Sri 5 Freya, Venus 6 Freyja 7
   Lakshmi 9 Aphrodite
   lover: 7 esthete 8 aesthete
beaver: hat 4 coin 6 castor, rodent
   cloth: 6 kersey
   eater: 9 wolverine
   skin: 4 plew
Beaver State: 6 Oregon
because: for 4 that 5 since 8 inasmuch, as
long as
because of that: 7 thereby 9 therefore
becken: 7 cymbals
beckon: bow, nod 4 wave 6 curtsy, summon 7 bidding, command, curtsey, gesture 10 salutation
becloud: 4 hide 5 bedim 6 darken, perplex, puzzle 7 confuse, mystify, obscure
8 befuddle, overcast
become: get, wax 4 grow, pass, suit 5
adorn, befit, grace 6 accord, befall, beseem, betide, change 7 behoove, flatter
becoming: 4 good 5 right 6 comely, gainly 7 decorum, farrand, farrant 8 decorous, handsome, suitable, tasteful 10
attractive, convenient, flattering 11 appropriate
becscie: 9 merganser
becuna: 9 barracuda
bed: cot, pad 4 base, bunk, doss, lair, plot
5 basis, berth, couch, layer 6 bottom,
couche(F.), cradle, litter, matrix, pallet,
strata, tuck in 7 channel, lodging, stratum 8 matrices, plancher, rollaway 9
basegrave, stretcher 10 apishamore,
foundation
   feather: tye
   small: cot 4 crib 6 cradle, pallet 7 hammock, truckle, trundle 8 bassinet

straw: 9 shakedown
bed stay: 4 slat
bedbug: 5 cimex 6 chinch 7 cimice(pl.) 8 conenose
bedding: 6 quilts, sheets 8 blankets 10 bedclothes
bedeck: gem 4 lard, trim 5 adorn, array, dight, grace 7 dress up 8 ornament 9 embellish
bedevil: 5 abuse, annoy, worry 6 muddle, pester 7 bewitch, confuse, torment
bedim: fog 4 mist 5 cloud 6 darken 7 becloud, obscure
bedizen: 4 daub 5 adorn, array, dizen 6 bedaub 9 overdress
bedlam: 4 riot 5 noise, rudas(Sc.) 6 asylum, madman, tumult, uproar 7 lunatic, madness 8 madhouse 9 confusion
Bedouin: 4 Arab, Moor 5 nomad
head cord: 4 agal
official: 4 cadi 5 sheik
tribe: 4 Harb
bedridden: ill 6 ailing, laid up 8 confined 13 incapacitated
bedrock: 5 basis, nadir 6 bottom
bedroll: 6 bindle
bedroom: 4 flat 5 berth, cabin 7 boudoir 11 compartment
bee: dor, fly 4 apis, idea, ring 5 party 6 dingar, insect, notion, torque 7 caprice, stinger 9 gathering 11 hymenoptera 12 hymenopteron
colony of: 5 swarm, yeast
family: 5 apina 6 apidae
female: 5 queen
genus: 5 apis
girl named for: 7 Melissa
house: gum 4 butt, hive, scap, skep 6 apiary 7 alveary, bee-butt 9 alvearium
house covering: 6 hackle
male: 5 drone
nose: 4 lora(pl.) 5 lorum
pert. to: 8 apiarian
pollen brush: 5 scopa 6 scopae(pl.) 9 sarothrum
beebread: 8 ambrosia
beech: 4 buck, tree 6 myrtle
genus: 5 fagus
beechnut: 4 mast
beef: 4 meat 5 gripe 8 complain
cut: 4 loin, rump, side 5 baron, chine, chuck, flank, roast, round, shank, steak 6 cutlet, muscle, saddle 7 brisket, knuckle, quarrel, quarter, sirloin 8 short-rib, shoulder 9 aitchbone, rattleran 11 porterhouse
dried: 5 bucan, jerky, vifda, vivda 6 buccan 7 charqui
pickled: 5 bully
salted: 4 junk
spiced: 8 pastrami, pastroma, pastromi
beefeater: 6 warden, yeoman

beefy: 5 hefty, heavy, husky 6 brawny, fleshy, stolid
Beehive State: 4 Utah
beekeeper: 8 apiarist, skeppist 12 apiculturist
beep: 4 tone, toot 6 signal
beer: ale, mum 4 bock, brew, grog, scud(Sc.) 5 kvass, lager, stout 6 liquor, porter, stingo, swanky 8 beverage
barley: 5 chang
cask: 4 butt
ingredient: 4 hops, malt 5 yeast 6 barley
king: 9 Gambrinus
maize: 5 chica 6 chicha
maker: 6 brewer
mug: see *vessel,* below
Russian: 5 kvass
shop: pub 6 saloon, tavern
unfermented: 4 wort
vessel: mug 4 Toby 5 stein 6 flagon, seidel, tanker 8 schooner 9 blackjack
beer and skittles: fun 4 play
beery: 7 maudlin, muddled
beeswax substitute: 7 ceresin
beet: 5 chard, sugar 6 mangel 8 beetrave 9 vegetable
genus: 4 beta
soup: 7 borscht
Beethoven: *birthplace:* 4 Bonn
opera: 7 Fidelio
symphony: 5 fifth, first, ninth, sixth, third 6 Choral, eighth, Eroica, fourth, second 7 seventh 8 Pastoral
beetle: bat, bug, jut, ram 4 beat, goga, gogo, hang, maul, stag 5 amara, bulge, drive, gogga, hispa, meloe 6 chafer, golach, goloch, jutout, mallet, pestle, scarab, weevil 7 prinoid, project 8 lowering, overhang 9 prioninae(pl.) 10 battledore, projecting
bark: 5 borer
bright: 7 ladybug
family: 10 elateridae 11 clavicornes, clavicornia
fire: 6 cucuyo
genus: 5 fidia
grain: 7 cadelle
grapevine: 6 thrips
ground: 5 amara
horny substance of: 6 chitin
mustard: 8 blackjack
rhinoceros: 4 uang
sacred: 6 scarab
wing cover: 5 shard
wood: 6 sawyer
beetle-browed: 6 morose 8 scowling
beetle-head: 5 dunce 6 plover 9 blockhead
befall: hap 4 come 5 occur 6 astart, become, betide, happen 7 come off, pertain 8 bechance
befit: dow 4 suit 5 beset 6 become, be-

hove, beseem, betide 7 behoove 9 agree with 10 go together

befog: 5 cloud 6 obsane, puzzle 7 confuse, mystify

before: ere 4 said, up to 5 ahead, afore, avant, coram(L.), first, forby, front, prior 6 facing, forbye, former, rather, sooner 7 already, earlier, forward 8 anterior, hitherto, in advance 10 beforehand, heretofore, in time past, previously

before long: 4 anon, soon 9 presently

before now: ere 4 gone, over 6 erenow

befoul: 4 soil 5 dirty 6 bemire, defile, malign 7 pollute 8 entangle 11 contaminate

befriend: aid 4 abet, help 5 favor 6 assist, favour, foster, succor 7 benefit, support, sustain 11 countenance

befuddle: 4 daze 5 addle, besot 6 muddle 7 becloud, confuse, fluster, mystify, stupefy

beg: ask, bid, sue, woo 4 coax, pray, sorn(Sc.) 5 cadge, crave, mooch, plead 6 adjure, appeal 7 beseech, entreat, implore, request, solicit 8 petition 9 importune, panhandle 10 supplicate

beget: ean 4 bear, sire 5 breed, yield 6 author, create, father 7 acquire, engraff 8 engender, generate 9 germinate, procreate

begetter: 4 sire 6 author, father, mother, parent

beggar: 4 ruin 5 asker, randy, rogue 6 alsman, bacach, bidder, canter, devour, mumper, pariah, pauper, wretch 8 palliard, stroller 9 maunderer, mendicant, schnorrer, suppliant 10 impoverish, panhandler, petitioner, starveling, supplicant 12 hallan-shaker

saint: 5 Giles

speech: 4 cant

beggarly: 4 mean, poor 5 cheap, petty, sorry 6 abject, paltry 8 bankrupt, indigent, wretched 10 despicable 12 contemptible

Beggar's Opera author: Gay 6 Brecht

begin: 4 fang, lead, open, rise 5 arise, enter, start 6 attack, get off, spring 7 commence, embark on, inchoate, initiate 9 institute, introduce, originate 10 embark upon, inaugurate

begin again: 4 anew, over 5 renew 6 resume 7 restart

beginner: 4 boot, tiro, tyro 5 rooky 6 novice, rookie 7 amateur, entrant, noviate, recruit, trainee, student 8 freshman, neophyte 9 candidate, debutante, novitiate, postulate 10 apprentice

beginning: egg 4 dawn, edge, germ, rise, root, seed 5 alpha, birth, debut, start 6 outset, setout, source 7 genesis, geneses(pl.), initial, nascent 8 entrance, exordium, inchoate, rudiment 9 day spring, embryonic, inception, incipient, the word go 10 conception, elementary, foundation, incunabula(pl.), initiation, opening gun 11 incunabulum 12 commencement

begone: off, out 4 away, scat, shoo 5 scoot, scram 6 aroint, avaunt, depart, get out 7 vamoose

begrudging: 6 loathe, grudge 7 envious, grumble 9 reluctant

beguile: fox 4 coax, foil, gull, lure 5 amuse, charm, cheat, cozen, elude, evade, trick 6 brique, delude, divert, entrap, seduce 7 deceive, ensnare, flatter, mislead 9 entertain 10 manipulate

behalf: 4 part, sake, side 5 stead 6 affair, matter, profit 7 benefit, defence, defense, support 8 interest 9 advantage

behave: act 4 bear, go on, quit, work 5 carry, react, treat 6 acquit, demean, deport, handle 7 comport, conduct, gesture, manager 8 function, regulate, restrain

behavior, behaviour: air 4 port, mien 5 guise, tenue 6 action, manner 7 bearing, comport, conduct, decorum 8 amenance, breeding, carriage 9 demeanour 10 deportment, governance

behead: 9 decollate 10 decapitate, guillotine

behemoth: 4 huge 5 beast, giant, hippo 7 monster

behest: bid, law 4 hest, rule 5 order 6 demand 7 command, mandate 9 prompting 10 injunction 9 solicitation

behind: aft 4 past, rear, ward, rump 5 abaft, abaft, after, ahind(Sc.), arear, later, passe, tardy 6 arrear, astern 8 backward, buttocks, dilatory 9 posterior 10 afterwards

behold: eye, see, spy 4 ecce, espy, gaze, hold, keep, look, scan, stop, view, wait 5 sight, voila, watch 6 descry, regard, retain 7 discern, observe, witness 8 consider, maintain, perceive

beholden: 7 obliged 8 indebted

behoof: use 6 profit 7 benefit 8 interest 9 advantage

behoove: dow, fit 4 need, suit 5 befit, ought 6 belong, proper 7 require 8 suitable 9 incumbent

beige: tan 4 ecru 5 color, grege(F.) 10 unbleached

being: ens 4 etre(F.), self 5 entia, gnome, human, thing, troll 6 animal, entity, extant, living, mortal, person 7 because, essence, present, reality 8 creature, ontology, standing 9 actuality, existence 11 subsistence 12 constitution

abstract: ens 5 entia

actual: 4 esse
celestial: 5 angel 6 cherub, seraph 8 divinity
in front: 6 anteal
physiological: 4 bion
science of: 8 ontology
Bela's son: Ard, Iri 4 Uzzi 5 Ezbon
Bel's wife: 5 Belit 6 Beltis
belabor, belabour: ply 4 beat, drub, lash, work 6 assail, batter, buffet, cudgel, hammer, hamper, thrash, thwack
belated: 7 tardy 7 delayed, overdue 12 old-fashioned
belay: 5 beset 6 invest, waylay 7 besiege 8 encircle
belaying pin: 5 kevel 7 bollard
belch: 4 boke, bolk, burp, galp, rasp 5 eruct 8 eructate 10 eructation
beldam, beldame: hag 4 fury 5 crone, jixen 6 alecto, erinys, virago 7 Jezebel 8 ancestor 9 Tisiphone 11 grandmother
beleaguer: 5 belay, beset 6 invest 7 assault, besiege 8 blockade, surround 9 encompass
belfry: 4 shed 5 tower 7 clocher 9 campanile
Belgian: 7 Fleming, Walloon
Belgium: *canal:* 5 Union 6 Albert 7 Campine
capital: 8 Brussels
city: Ans, Huy, Spa 4 Gand, Mons 5 Alost, Ciney, Eupen, Ghent, Ieper, Jumet, Liege, Namur, Ypres 6 Bruges, Brugge, Deurne, Lierre, Ostend, Turnai 7 Antwerp, Berchem, Herstal, Hoboken, Ixelles, Louvain, Malmedy, Mechlin, Roulers, Seraing 8 Bastogne, Courtrai, Muscron, Turnhout, Verviers, Waterloo
coin: 5 belga, franc 7 centime
commune: Ath, Ely, Hal, Mol, Spa 4 Aath, Boom, Geel, Genk, Lier, Niel, Roux, Zele 5 Aalst, Evere, Genck, Halle, Jette, Ronse, Uccle, Ukkel
endive: 7 witloof
Gaul tribe: 4 Remi 6 Belgae, Nervii
horse: 9 Brabancon
kings: 6 Albert 7 Leopold 8 Baudouin
language: 6 French 7 Flemish
marble: 5 rance
measure: vat 4 aune, last, pied 5 carat 6 perche 8 boisseau
province: 5 Liege, Namur 7 Antwerp, Brabant, Hainaut, Limburg 9 Luxemburg 12 East Flanders, West Flanders
river: Lys 4 Dyle, Leie, Maas, Yser 5 Demer, Dijle, Lesse, Meuse, Nethe, Rupel, Senne 6 Dender, Ourthe, Sambre 7 Ambieve, Schelde, Scheldt
seaport: 6 Ostend 7 Antwerp
tribe: 9 Bellovaci

violinist: 5 Ysaye
weight: 4 last 5 carat, livre, pound 6 charge 7 chariot 8 esterlin
Belial: 5 devil, Satan
belie: 4 hide 6 belong, defame 7 besiege, falsify, pertain, slander, traduce 8 disguise, negative, strumpet, surround 9 encompass 10 calumniate, contradict, contravene 11 counterfeit 12 misrepresent
belief: fay, ism 4 mind, sect, view 5 credo, creed, dogma, faith, tenet, troth, trust 6 credit 7 opinion 8 credence, doctrine, reliance 9 assurance, certainty 10 confidence, conviction, persuasion
liable to: 7 credent 9 credulous
believe: buy, wis 4 deem, trow, ween 5 judge, think, trust 6 accept, credit 7 suppose, swallow 8 accredit, consider, credence
believer: ist 8 adherent
in all religions: 7 omnist
in God: 5 deist 6 theist
in predestination: 13 particularist
Belili's brother: 6 Tammuz
belittle: 5 decry, dwarf, sneer 6 slight 7 detract 8 minimize 9 criticize, denigrate, discredit, disparage 10 depreciate, 13 underestimate
Belize: *capital:* 9 Belmopan
city: 10 Belize City
monetary unit: 6 dollar
peak: 8 Victoria
bell: 4 call, fair, gong, peal, ring, roar, toll 5 chime, cloak, codon, flare, knell, swell 6 bellow, bubble(Sc.), crotal, curfew, tocsin 7 blossom, campana, campane, corolla 9 beautiful 13 tintinnabulum
alarm: 6 tocsin
axle bearing: cod
clapper: 6 tongue
kind of: cow 4 door, gong, hand 5 ship's 6 church, jingle, school 8 electric
ringer: 6 sexton, toller 12 carillonneur
ringer of fiction: 9 Quasimodo
shaped: 10 campanula 11 campanulate
sound: 4 ding, dong, toll 5 knell 6 tinkle
tower: 6 belfry 9 campanine
bell, book, and candle: 15 excommunication
bell bottoms: 5 pants 8 trousers
bell ear: 6 cannon
Bell for Adano author: 6 Hersey
belladonna: 5 dwale, plant 6 remedy 7 manicon 8 narcotic 9 dwayberry 10 nightshade
extract: 7 atropin 8 atropine
bellbird: 6 shrike 8 arapunga
bellboy: 4 page 6 porter, redcap
Bellerophon: *father:* 7 Glaucus
spring: 7 Pelrene
belles-lettres: 10 literature

bellicose: mad 5 irate 7 hostile, warlike 8 militant 10 pugnacious 11 belligerent

belligerent: hot 7 hostile, warlike 8 choleric, fighting, jingoist 9 bellicose, combative, irascible, litigious, wrangling 10 pugnacious 11 contentious, hot-tempered, quarrelsome 12 disputatious, antagonistic

Bellini: *opera:* 5 Norma 9 I Puritani 12 La Sonnambula

sleepwalker: 5 Amina

bellow: cry, low, moo, yap 4 bawl, beal, bell, roar, rout, yaup, yawp 5 belve, blart, croon, roust(Sc.), shout 6 buller, clamor 7 bluster, ululate 10 vociferate

bellwether: 5 sheep 6 leader

belly: bag, cod, gie(Sc.), gut, pod 4 bouk, kyte(Sc.) 5 bingy, bulge, pleon 6 hunger, paunch 7 abdomen, stomach 8 appetite

belong: fit, set 4 bear, vest 5 apply, belie 6 inhere, relate 7 pertain 9 appertain

belongings: 4 gear 5 goods, traps 6 assets, estate 7 effects 8 chattels, property 9 household 10 appendages 11 possessions 13 appurtenances

beloved: 4 dear, idol 5 cheri(F.) 6 adored, cherie(F.) 7 darling 8 precious 9 boy friend, inamorata, valentine 10 girl friend, sweetheart

below: 4 down 5 infra, sotto(It.), under 7 beneath 8 downward, inferior 10 downstairs, underneath

belt: 4 area, band, beat, blow, cest, gird, mark, ring, sash, zone 5 girth, strap, strip, tract, whack, zonar 6 bodice, cestus, cingle, fettle, girdle, invest, region, strait, stripe, zonnar, zonule 7 baldric, circuit, passage 8 ceinture, cincture, encircle, surround 9 bandoleer, encompass 10 cummerbund

conveyor: 5 apron

ecclesiastical: 7 baldric, balteus 8 baltheus, baldrick

non-Mohammedan: 5 zonar

belted: 6 zonate 7 girdled 9 cinctured

bema: 4 pace, step 7 chancel

bemired: 5 dirty, muddy, stuck 10 bogged down

bemoan: 4 wail 6 grieve, lament, sorrow 7 deplore

bemuse: 5 addle 7 confuse 8 distract

bench: bar, pew 4 banc, seat 5 board, judge, ledge, stool 6 settee 7 discard

church: pew, pue 6 sedile(L.)

bench hook: 5 clamp

benchmark: 5 model 8 standard 13 comparison aid

bend: bow, nid, ply, sag 4 arch, flex, kink, turn 5 angle, baton, bulge, crimp, crook, curve, stoop, twist 6 buckle, cotice, cotise, crouch, direct, divert, fasten, inflex, submit 7 bendlet, incline, refract 9 genuflect

backward: 6 retort

in timber: sny

bender: leg 5 binge, drunk, spree 7 whopper 8 guzzling, sixpence

bending: 5 lithe 6 pliant, supple 7 anfract, crooked, flexion 8 flection

beneath: 5 below, lower, under 11 underground

Benedictine: 4 monk 7 Cluniac, liqueur

title: dom

benediction: 4 amen 5 grace 6 prayer 7 benison 8 approval, blessing 10 invocation

benefaction: 4 alms, boon, gift 5 grant 7 present 8 donation, gratuity 11 approbation

benefactor: 5 agent, angel, donor 6 friend, helper, patron, savior 8 promoter 14 philanthropist

beneficence: 6 bounty 7 charity 8 donation, goodness, kindness

beneficial: 4 good 6 useful 7 helpful 8 salutary 9 desirable, enjoyable, favorable, healthful, lucrative, wholesome 10 profitable, salubrious 11 serviceable 12 advantageous, remunerative

beneficiary: 4 heir, user 5 donee 6 vassal 7 legatee 9 feudatory

benefit: aid, use 4 boon, boot, gain, gift, help, prow, sake 5 avail, boost 6 assist, behalf, behoof, better, profit, usance 7 advance, bespeak, concert, deserve, improve, service, utility, welfare 8 befriend, interest 9 advantage, charity do, emolument 11 performance 12 contribute to

benevolent: 4 good, kind 6 benign, loving 7 amiable, liberal 8 generous 10 altruistic, charitable, munificent 13 philanthropic, tenderhearted

benign: 4 boon, good, kind, mild 5 bland 6 genial, gentle 7 affable 8 benedict, gracious, salutary 9 benignant, favorable, wholesome 10 benevolent, charitable, favourable, propitious, salubrious

Benin: *capital:* 9 Porto Novo

ethnic group: 4 Fons 5 Adjas, Mahis 7 Baribas, Yorubas

gulf: 6 Guinea

monetary unit: 5 franc 7 centime

mountain: 7 Atakora

port: 7 Cotonou

river: 4 Mono 5 Niger

town: 6 Abomey, Ouidah 7 Parakou

benison: 8 blessing, 9 beatitude 10 invocation 11 benediction

Benjamin: *descendant:* 4 Aher

grandson: Iri

son: Ehi 4 Gera, Rosh

benne: 6 sesame

bent: aim, bow, set 4 bias, gift, turn 5
bound, bowed, crank, crump, flair,
knack, prone, taste, trend 6 akimbo, biased, braced, courbe, course, curved, energy, genius, hooked, swayed, talent 7
crooked, curvant, decided, flexion, flexure, impetus, leaning, leveled, pronate,
purpose, stooped, tension 8 aptitude,
declined, flection, penchant, tendency 9
curvature, direction, prejudice 10 determined, proclivity, propensity 11 disposition, inclination 13 prepossession
14 predisposition

benthonic plant: 6 enalid

benthos: 5 fauna, flora

benumb: nip 4 daze, dunt, numb, stun 5
daver 6 cumber, deaden 7 fretish, fre-
tize, stupefy

benzine derivative: 6 phenol

Beowulf: 4 epic, poem

bequeath: 4 give, will 5 endow, leave, offer 6 bestow, commit, demise, devise,
legate, quethe 7 bequest, commend 8
hand down, transmit 9 testament

bequest: 4 gift, will 6 legacy 8 bequeath,
heritage, pittance 9 endowment

berate: jaw, nag 4 lash, rail 5 abuse,
chide, scold, score 6 revile 7 censure,
reprove, upbraid 8 chastise 10 vitupe-
ate

Berber: 4 Moor 6 Hamite, Kabyle 7 Har-
atin
 chief: 4 caid, qaid
 dialect: 6 Tuareg
 tribe: 4 Daza, Riff, Tibu 6 Tuareg

bereave: rob 5 strip 6 divest, sadden 7
deprive, despoil 10 dispossess

bereft: orb 4 lorn, lost, poor 7 forlorn 8
bereaved 9 destitute 12 dispossessed

beret: cap, hat, tam 7 biretta, chapeau 8
berretta, chapeaux(pl.), headgear

berg: ice 4 floe 6 barrow 8 eminence,
mountain

bergamot: 4 bose, mint, pear 5 snuff 6
orange 7 Bergama, essence, perfume

Berlin park: 10 Tiergarten

berm, berme: 4 bank, edge, path 5 ledge,
shelf 7 terrace

Bermuda: 10 archipelago
 capital: 8 Hamilton
 monetary unit: 6 dollar

Bermuda cedar: 7 juniper

Bermuda grass: 4 doob

berry: bay, dew, haw 4 beat, cran, rasp 5
acini, bacca, black, fruit, mound, salal,
savin 6 acinus, baccae, burrow, sabine,
thresh 7 currant, hillock
 disease: 8 bluestem
 medicinal: 5 cubeb
 oil: 5 olive

berry-like: 7 baccate

berserk: mad 5 bravo 6 pirate 7 enraged,
warrior 8 frenzied, maniacal

berth: bed, job 4 bunk, dock, slip 5 place,
wharf 6 billet, office 7 lodging, mooring
8 position 9 anchorage, situation 11
appointment

bertha: 4 cape 6 cannon, collar

beryl: gem 5 jewel 7 emerald 10 aquamarine
 green: 11 davidsonite
 yellow: 8 heliodor

beseech: ask, beg, sue 4 pray 5 crave,
plead 6 adjure, appeal, obtest 7 entreat,
implore, solicit 9 impetrate, obsecrate
10 supplicate

beseeching: 9 precative

beset: ply 4 sail, stud 5 allot, belay, harry,
siege, spend 6 assail, attack, harass, infest 7 arrange, bejewel, besiege, perplex
8 blockade, encumber, obstruct, surround 9 beleaguer

beside: by 4 hear 5 along, aside 6 next to
7 abreast 8 adjacent
 comb. form: 4 para 5 juxta

besides: by; and, but, too, yet 4 also, else,
over, then 6 beyond, except, withal 8
moreover 10 additional 11 furthermore

besiege: 4 gird, girt 5 belay, belie, beset,
siege, storm 6 attack, invest, pester,
plague 7 solicit 8 blockade, surround 9
beleaguer

besmirch: 4 soil 5 smear, sully, taint 7
asperse, blacken 8 discolor

besom: map 4 drab(Sc.) 5 broom, sweep 6
sloven(Sc.) 7 heather

besot: 4 dull 6 muddle, stupid 7 stupefy 8
befuddle 9 infatuate

bespangle: dot 4 star, stud 5 adorn 8
sprinkle

bespatter: 4 blot, dash, soil, spot 5 muddy, plash, stain, sully 6 malign, sparge
7 asperse, scatter 8 reproach, sprinkle

bespeak: ask 4 cite, hint, show 5 argue,
imply, order, speak 6 accost, attest, engage, steven 7 address, arrange, benefit,
betoken, discuss, exclaim, reserve 8
foretell, indicate, put in for 9 stipulate

best: ace 4 a-one, beat, most, pick, tops,
wale 5 cream, elite, excel, worst 6
choice, defeat, finest, flower, outwit, utmost 7 conquer, largest, optimum, paragon, surpass 8 greatest, nonesuch, out-
match, outstrip, vanquish 9 excellent,
overmatch 11 superlative

bestial: low 4 vile, wild 5 feral 6 brutal,
filthy 7 brutish, inhuman 8 depraved

bestir: 5 rouse

bestow: add, put, use 4 deal, dote, give 5
allot, allow, apply, award, beset, grant,
lodge, place 6 accord, beteem, confer,
demise, devote, divide, donate, employ,
entail, extend, harbor, impart, render 7
collate, dispose, instate, present, quar-

ter, tribute **8** bequeath **11** communicate

bestride: 5 mount **6** stride **8** straddle

bet: 4 lay, pot **4** ante, gage, play, plot, risk, wage **5** hedge, stake, wager **6** gamble, pledge

broker: **6** bookie **9** bookmaker

fail to pay: **5** welch, welsh

faro: **7** sleeper

roulette: bas **4** noir **5** carre **6** milieu **7** dernier, encarre, enplein

betake: hie **4** move **5** apply, catch, grant **6** assume, commit, repair, remove, resort **7** commend, journey

bete noire: 4 hate **5** dread **6** terror **7** bugaboo, bugbear **11** abomination

betel: 4 ikmo, itmo, siri **6** pupulo

leaf: pan **4** buyo

betel palm: 5 areca

extract: **7** catechu

masticatory: pan **4** buyo

seed: **8** betel nut

Betelgeuse: 4 star

bethel: 6 chapel

Bethesda: 4 pool **6** chapel

bethink: 5 think **6** devise, recall **7** reflect **8** consider, remember **9** recollect **10** deliberate

Bethlehemite: 4 Boaz

Beth's sister: Amy, Meg

Bethuel's son: 5 Laban

betide: hap **5** befit, occur, trite **6** become, befall, chance, happen **7** betoken, presage

betimes: 4 anon, rath, soon **5** early, rathe **8** speedily **9** forthwith, sometimes **10** seasonally **11** prematurely **12** occasionally

betise: 7 folly **9** silliness, stupidity

betoken: 4 mark, note, show **5** augur **6** assert, betide, denote, evince, import **7** bespeak, express, oblique, portend, presage, signify **8** forebode, foreshow, indicate **10** symbolize **13** prognosticate

betray: 4 blab, blow, boil, gull, sell, sile, sing, tell, undo, wray **5** peach, snare, spill **6** accuse, delude, descry, reveal, seduce, sell out, snitch, squeal, turn in **7** beguile, deceive, falsify, mislead **8** disclose, discover **11** double-cross

betrayer: rat **5** Judas, skunk **7** seducer, traitor **8** derelict, informer

betroth: 4 affy **6** assure, engage, ensure, pledge, plight **7** espouse, promise **8** affiance, contract, handfast

better: 4 aid, top **4** good, mend, more **5** amend, emend, excel, safer, wiser **6** bigger, choice, exceed, reform **7** advance, choicer, correct, greater, improve, promote, rectify, relieve, support, surpass **8** increase, superior **9** desirable, melio-

rate, upper hand **10** ameliorate, preferable

better half: 4 wife

betting: *adviser:* **4** tout

figures: **4** odds

odds: **5** price

between: 4 amid **5** amell, among, entre(F.) **7** average, betwixt **12** intermediate

law: **5** mesne

between the lines: 6 latent, secret

bevel: 4 blow(Sc.), cant, edge, push(Sc.) **5** angle, bezel, miter, mitre, slant, slope **6** aslant **7** chamfer, incline, oblique **8** diagonal

corners: **5** splay

end of timber: **5** snape

out: **4** ream

beverage: ade, ale, nog, pop, tea **4** beer, grog, mead, milk, soda, wine **5** cider, cocoa, draft, drink, lager, leban, negus, morat, punch, treat, water **6** coffee, eggnog, liquid, liquor, nectar, posset **7** potable **8** cocktail, potation **9** metheglin **10** melicratum

alcoholic: See **alcoholic drink**

container: vat **6** kettle **7** charger **9** separator

extract: **4** kola

malted wheat: **6** zythem, zythum

mixed: **5** negus, punch, smash **6** bishop

mulberry and honey: **5** morat

Oriental: rak **4** sake **5** rakee **6** arrack

pepper: **4** kava

Polynesian: **4** kava

South American: **4** mate

bevy: 4 herd, pack **5** covey, drove, flock, group, swarm **6** flight, school **7** company **8** assembly **9** gathering, multitude **10** collection

bewail: 4 cry, rue **4** keen, moan, sigh, wail, weep **5** mourn **6** bemoan, grieve, lament, plaint, sorrow **7** deplore **8** complain

beware: 4 cave, heed, shun **5** avoid, spend **6** eschew **7** look out, warning **8** take care, watch out

bewilder: fog **4** daze, foil, gaum **5** abash, addle, amaze, amuse, deave **6** baffle, bemist, bother, dazzle, muddle, puzzle **7** buffalo, confuse, fuddle, muddle, mystify, perplex, stagger, stupefy **8** astonish, confound, distract, entangle, surprise **9** embarrass, obfuscate **10** spifficate **11** spifficate

bewildered: 4 asea, lost, mang **5** agape, dazed **8** confused, helpless **9** perplexed

bewilderment: awe, fog **4** daze **9** amazement, confusion **10** perplexity **11** distraction **13** embarrassment

bewitch: hex **5** charm, fasci, spell, trick **6** enamor, entice, glamor, grigri, hoodoo, thrill, voodoo 7 attract, bedevil, delight, enchant, glamour 8 ensorcel, forspeak, greegree 9 captivate, ensorcell, fascinate

Beyle's penname: 8 Stendhal

beyond: 4 free, over, past 5 above, after, aside, forby, ultra 6 forbye, yonder 7 besides, further, outside 8 superior 9 hereafter 10 too deep for

the sea: 11 ultramarine

the threshold: 12 ultraliminal

bezel, basil: rim 4 edge, ouch, seal 5 bevil, crown, facet 6 chaton, flange 8 template

bhagavat: 7 blessed

bhakta: 7 devotee 9 worshiper

bhalu: 4 bear

bhang, bang: 7 hashish 8 narcotic 10 intoxicant

product of: 6 majoon

bhangi: 6 mehtar 7 sweeper

bharal: tur 5 sheep 6 nahoor

bhat: 4 bard 8 minstrel

bhikku: 4 monk 5 friar 6 priest 9 mendicant

bhikshu: 5 friar 7 ascetic 9 mendicant

bhoosa: 6 chaff, husks, straw

b'hoy: 5 rowdy 8 gangster

bhut: 5 demon, ghost 6 goblin

Bhutan: *capital:* 6 Thimbu 7 Thimphu

ethnic group: 6 Bhotia, Lepcha

monetary unit: 8 chhetrum, ngultrum

mountain: 9 Himalayas

plain: 4 Duar

bias: 4 awry, bent, sway 5 amiss, color, slant, slope 7 bigotry, incline, leaning, oblique 8 clinamen, diagonal, tendency 9 clinamina(pl.), prejudice, procedure 10 favoritism, partiality, prepossess, propensity 11 declination, disposition, favouritism, inclination 12 predetermine, predilection 13 prepossession

biased 6 warped 7 partial 8 one-sided 9 jaundiced 11 tendentious

bib: sip 4 brat, fish 5 apron, drink 6 tipple, tucker 7 bavette(F.) 9 neckpiece 10 protection

bibelot: 5 curio 7 trinket 8 ornament 10 knickknack

Bible: *angel:* 5 Micah 7 Raphael

animal: 4 reem 5 daman 6 hydrax 8 behemoth

apocrypha: 5 Tobit 6 Baruch, Esdras, Jeremy, Judith, Syriac, Wisdom 7 Vulgate 8 Manasses 9 Maccabees 10 Septuagint 14 Ecclesiasticus

ascetic order: 6 Essene

battle scene: 10 Armageddon

book: Job 4 Acts, Amos, Ezra, Joel, John, Jude, Luke, Mark, Ruth 5 Hosea, James, Jonah, Kings, Micah, Peter, Titus 6 Daniel, Esther, Exodus, Haggai, Isaiah, Joshua, Psalms, Romans, Samuel 7 Ezekiel, Genesis, Hebrews, Matthew, Numbers, Obadiah, Timothy 8 Habakkuk, Jeremiah, Nehemiah, Philemon, Proverbs 9 Apocrypha, Ephesians, Galatians, Leviticus, Zechariah 10 Chronicles, Colossians, Revelation 11 Corinthians, Deuteronomy, Philippians 12 Ecclesiastes, Lamentations 13 Song of Solomon, Thessalonians

character: see *name* below

charioteer: 4 Jehu

city: Ain, Dan 4 Arad, Aven, Cana, Elim, Elon, Gath, Gaza, Geba, Maon, Rome, Tyre, Zoar 5 Akkad, Arvad, Ashur, Assur, Joppa, Sidon, Sodom 6 Bethel, Biblos, Gadara, Jerico, Tarsus 7 Babylon, Nineveh 8 Gomorrah, Nazareth 9 Jerusalem

clan: 6 Shelah

country: Nod, Pul 4 Aram, Bela, Edam, Elam, Gath, Hali, Moab, Seba, Seir 5 Ammon 6 Canaan 7 Galilee, Samaria

desert: 5 Sinai

garden: 4 Eden 8 Paradise

giant: 4 Anak, Emim 7 Goliath

giant killer: 5 David

hill: 4 Zion

hunter: 6 Nimrod

judge: 4 Agog, Elon 6 Gideon, Samson 8 Jephthah

king: Asa, Gog, Iva 4 Agag, Ahab, Ahaz, Amon, Bera, Jehu, Omri, Reba, Saul 5 David, Herod, Hiram, Joram, Nadab, Rezin, Tidal, Zimri 6 Birsha, Hezion, Japhia, Jotham, Uzziah 7 Jehoram, Solomon

kingdom: 4 Elam, Moab 5 Judea, Judah 6 Israel 8 Chaldeae

land of plenty: 6 Goshen

liar: 7 Ananias

money: 4 beka 5 bekah 6 shekel

mountain: Hor 4 Ebal, Nebo, Peor, Sina, Sion, Zion 5 Heres, Horeb, Sinai, Tabor 6 Ararat, Gilead, Moriah, Olivet, Pisgah

name: Ahi, Asa, Eri, Eve, Evi, Hor, Iri, Koa, Lot, Ner, Ono, Reu, Toi, Uel, Uri 4 Abel, Acan, Acub, Adam, Ader, Adna, Ador, Agee, Aher, Aman, Anak, Anam, Aner, Aram, Arem, Arie, Asan, Asom, Ater, Aven, Azal, Cain, Cana, Dura, Edar, Edec, Edes, Eker, Enan, Enos, Eran, Esau, Etam, Gera, Irad, Iram, Isac, Mary, Neri, Obal, Omar, Oreb, Oren, Paul, Reba, Sami, Sara, Seth, Suba, Ucal, Vale 5 Ahlab, Alian, Amasa, Aroer, Bedan, Besai, Caleb, Elias, Ephai, Esrom, Hadad, Hanes, Isaac, Mered, Nahum, Oseas, Peleg, Rahad, Tarah, Vania 6 Naaman, Pilate, Ramath 7 Abadias, Abigail, Antioch, Elmodam, Idithum, Sidrach, Tabitha *navigator:* 4 Noah

ornament: 4 urim 7 thummin

patriarch: Reu 4 Seth, Shem 5 Jacob, Nahor, Peleg 6 Israel, Lamech

people: 4 Moab, Phut, Seba 5 Ammon 6 Hamite, Hivite, Kenite, Levite 7 Amorite, Dodanim, Moabite

plain: 4 Maab 5 Mamre 7 Jericho

plotter: 5 Haman

poem: 5 psalm

pool: 6 Siloam

priest: Eli 5 Aaron 6 Levite

pronoun: thy 4 thee, thou 5 thine

prophet: Zab 4 Amos, Ezra 5 Elias, Hosea, Jonah, Micah, Nahum 6 Elijah, Isaiah 7 Ezekial 8 Jeremiah

psalmist: 5 David

queen: Abi 5 Sheba 6 Esther, Vashti 7 Jezebel

region: 4 Enon 5 Ophir, Perea 6 Bashan

reproach: 4 raca

river: Zab 4 Nile 5 Abana, Arnon 6 Kishon, Jordan

ruler: see *king* above

scholar: 7 Biblist 9 Biblicist

sea: Red 4 Dead 7 Galilee 8 Tiberias 10 Gennesaret

shepherd: 4 Abel 5 David

spice: 5 myrrh 6 cassia, stacte 12 frankincense

spy: 5 Caleb

stone: 4 ezel 6 ligure

tower: 4 Edar 5 Babel

town: see *city* above

tree: 5 cedar

tribe: see *people* above

valley: 4 Baca, Elah 6 Shaveh, Siddim

version: 4 Geez 5 Douay, Itala 6 Syriac 7 Vulgate 8 Bohairic 9 Apocrypha, King James 10 New English 15 Revised Standard

weed: 4 tare

witch's home: 5 Endor

Bible society: 7 Gideons

Biblical: 10 scriptural

bicker: war 4 bowl, spar, tiff 5 argue, brawl, cavil, fight 6 assail, attack, battle, rattle 7 contend, dispute, quarrel, wrangle 8 pettifog, skirmish, squabble 10 contention

bicycle: 4 bike 5 wheel 10 two-wheeler

for two: 6 tandem

rider: 7 cyclist

ten-speed: 10 derailleur

bid: beg 4 call, hist, pray 5 clepe, offer, order 6 adjure, charge, direct, enjoin, invite, reveal, summon, tender 7 command, declare, entreat, proffer, request 8 announce, proclaim, proposal

biddable: 6 docile 8 obedient

biddy: hen 7 chicken

bide: 4 face, stay, wait 5 abide, await,

dwell, tarry 6 endure, remain, reside, suffer 7 sojourn 8 continue, tolerate 9 encounter, withstand

bidonville: 10 shantytown

bier: 4 pyre 5 frame, grave 6 coffin, hearse, litter 7 support 10 catafalque, handbarrow

biff: 4 blow 6 strike

bifid: 6 forked

bifocal: 4 lens

bifold: 6 double 7 twofold

bifurcation: wye 4 fork 5 split 6 branch 8 division

big: 4 bold, huge, vast 5 bulky, chief, grand, great, gross, hefty, large 6 mighty 7 bumping, eminent, leading, massive, pompous, violent 8 boastful, bouncing, enormous, generous, gigantic, imposing, pregnant 9 notorious 10 tremendous 11 magnanimous, outstanding, pretentious, threatening

Big Dipper: *constellation:* 9 Ursa Major

star: 5 Alcor, Dubhe, Merak, Mizar 6 Alioth, Alkoid, Megrez, Phecda

big shot: VIP 5 mogul, wheel 6 tycoon 7 notable 8 brass hat 9 celebrity 11 heavyweight 13 high-muck-a-muck

big toe: 6 hallux

bigener: 4 mule 6 hybrid

bigfoot: 4 omah 9 sasquatch

bighorn: 5 sheep 6 argali, aoudad 8 cimarron

bight: bay 4 bend, coil, gulf, loop 5 angle, curve, inlet, noose 6 corner, hollow

bignou, biniou: bagpipe

bigot: 6 cafard, zealot 7 fanatic 9 hypocrite

bigoted: 6 biased, narrow 9 hidebound, illiberal, sectarian 10 intolerant, prejudiced 12 narrow-minded

bijou: 5 jewel 7 trinket

bile: 4 boil, gall, hump 5 venom 6 choler, growth

bilge: 4 scum 5 bouge, bulge 8 nonsense

bilingual: diglot

bilk: gyp 4 balk, hoax 5 cheat, cozen, dodge, shake, trick 6 delude, escape, fleece 7 deceive, defraud, swindle 9 frustrate 10 disappoint

bill: act, dun, law, neb, nib, tab 4 beak, note, peck, rise 5 libel, score, visor 6 caress, charge, indict, pecker, pickax, poster, strike 7 invoice, lampoon, mattock, placard, statute 8 billhook, document, headland, petition 9 memoranda(pl.), reckoning, statement 10 broadsword, memorandum, promontory 13 advertisement

anchor: pee

five dollar: fin, vee

one dollar: 4 buck 8 frogskin

ten dollar: 7 sawbuck

bill of fare: 4 card, menu 5 carte
billet: bar, gad, log 4 loop, note, pass, post 5 berth, enrol, house, lodge, order, put up, stick, strap 6 ballot, canton, enroll, harbor, letter, notice, ticket 7 bearing, epistle, harbour, missive, pollack, quarter 8 coalfish, document, firewood, ornament, position, quarters 11 appointment, requisition
billet-doux: 8 mash note 10 love letter
opposite: 12 Dear John note
billiards: 4 game, pool
player's turn: 6 inning
play to open: lag 6 string
shot: run 4 miss 5 break, carom, masse 6 cannon 7 bricole, cushion, scratch
stick: cue
term: 4 rack, spot 5 chalk 6 bridge, pocket 7 English 8 balkline, rotation 9 eight ball 10 object ball
billibi: 10 mussel soup
relative: 12 bouillabaise
billingsgate: 5 abuse 7 obloquy 8 ribaldry 12 vituperation
billow: sea 4 wave 5 bulge, float, surge, swell 6 ripple, roller 7 breaker 8 undulate
billowing: 5 tidal 7 surging
billy: caw 4 chap, club, goat, mate 6 cudgel, fellow 7 brother, comrade 8 billikin, bludgeon 9 blackjack
billycock: 5 derby 6 bowler
bin: ark, box, cub 4 bing, cart, crib, vina 5 frame, hutch, pungi, stall, store, wagon 6 basket, bunker, hamper, manger, trough, within 9 container 10 receptacle
coal: 6 bunker
fish: 5 canch, kench
binary: 6 hydrid 7 twofold
binate: 4 dual 6 double, paired 7 coupled, twofold
bind: jam, tie 4 gird, hold, tape 5 stick 6 cement, fetter, secure 7 confine 9 constrict, indenture, make stick 11 predicament
tightly: 4 frap
to secrecy: 4 tile, tyle
wings of a bird: 5 truss 6 pinion, skewer
binder: 4 band, beam, bond, cord, rope 5 baler, cover, frame, lever 6 fillet, folder, girder, header 9 bondstone
binding: 4 band, cord, rope, tape 5 valid 6 edging, ribbon 7 galloon, mousing, webbing 9 stringent 10 astringent, obligatory 11 restraining, restrictive
limp: 4 yapp
bindle stiff: 4 hobo 5 tramp 8 vagabond
binge: bat, bow, hit 4 blow, bust, soak, toot 5 beano, party, spree 6 bender, cringe 7 indulge 8 carousal 9 obeisance 10 indulgence

bingo: 4 game, keno 5 lotto 6 brandy
bioclean: 7 aseptic 8 germ-free
biography: 4 life, vita(It.) 6 memoir 7 account, history, memoire(F.), recount
saint's: 11 hagiography
biological class: 5 genus, order, phyla(pl.) 6 family, genera(pl.), phylum 7 species
bionomics: 7 ecology
biota: 13 flora and fauna
biotic community: 5 biome
biotite: 4 mica 7 anomite
birch: 4 cane, flog, tree, whip 5 canoe 6 betula 7 hickory
bird: ani, daw, nun, pie, tit 4 avis(L.), crow, kite, lark, ruff, tern, wren 5 brant, egret, finch, hobby, pewee, pewit, raven, robin, snipe, terek, vireo 6 bulbul, dunlin, falcon, hoopoe, linnet, marten, mocker, oriole, phoebe, plover, shrike, thrush 7 bluejay, bustard, buzzard, catbird, flicker, halcyon, irrisor, jackdaw, kinglet, ortolan, peacock, redwing, skylark, sparrow, swallow, tanager, warbler, waxwing 8 airplane, bluebird, boatbill, bobolink, bobwhite, chicadee, grosbeak, kingbird, pheasant, redstart, starling, thrasher 9 blackbird, blackcock, brambling, bullfinch, goldfinch, partridge, phalarope, sandpiper 10 bufflehead, meadowlark, tropicbird, woodpecker 11 butcherbird, hummingbird 12 yellowhammer
adjutant: 5 stork 6 argala 7 hurgila, marabou
African: 4 taha 6 quelea 7 touraco 8 umbrette
American: 4 sora 5 robin, vireo 6 darter, fulmar, turkey 7 grackle, tanager 8 cardinal 10 bufflehead
Antarctic: 4 skua 7 penguin
aquatic: 4 duck, gull, loon, swan, tern 5 goose, grebe, small, terne 7 penguin 8 dabchick, flamingo
aquiline: 5 eagle
Arabian Nights: roc
Arctic: 4 auk 6 fulmar
Asiatic: 4 mine, myna 5 pitta 7 hilltit 8 dotterel 9 brambling, feng-huang, fenghwang
Attic: 11 nightingale
Australian: emu, roa 4 emeu, lory 5 arara 6 leipoa 7 boobook, bustard, waybung 8 bellbird, lorikeet, lyrebird, manucode 9 cassowary, coachwhip, friarbird, pardalote
black: ani, ano, daw, pie 4 crow 5 merle, raven 6 oriole 7 jackdaw 8 starling
brilliant plumage: 4 tody 5 jalep 6 oriole, trogon 7 jacamar, tanager 8 pheasant
Central American: daw 4 crow, rave, rook 5 raven 6 magpie 7 corvine, jacamar 8 puffbird

crane-like: 5 wader 6 chunga

crocodile: 9 trochilus

crow-family: daw, jay, pie 4 craw 5 raven 6 magpie 7 jackdaw

crying: 6 ramage 7 limpkin

diving: auk 5 grebe

dressing of feathers: 5 preen

emu-like: 9 cassowary

European: ani, daw, emu, mew, qua 4 cirl, darr, emeu, gled, kite, mall, moro, osel, rook, stag, whim, yite 5 amsel, boonk, glede, mavis, merle, ousel, ouzel, sacer, saker, serin, tarin, terek, terin, whaup 6 avocet, avoset, cushat, gaylag, godwit, linnet, loriot, marten, merlin, missel, redcap, whewer, windle, winnel, wranny 7 bittern, bustard, haybird, kestrel, motacil, ortolan, sakeret, starnel, whiskey, winnard, witwall 8 bargoose, chepster, dotterel, garganey, redstart, wheybird, whimbrel, wrannock, yoldring 9 brambling, gallinule, goldfinch, goosander, peregrine, swinepipe, wheybeard 10 chiffchaff, lammegeyer, turtledove, whitterick 11 capercailie, lammergeier 12 capercailzie

extinct: moa 4 dodo, jibi, mamo 7 offbird

finch-like: 7 chewink, tanager

fish-catching: 6 osprey 9 cormorant

flightless: emu, moa 4 dodo, emeu, kiwi, rhea 7 apteryx, ostrich, penguin, ratitae 9 solitaire

fly-catching: 8 redstart 9 solitaire

flying backwards: 7 swallow, humming

food: hen 5 capon 6 pullet, turkey 7 chicken, rooster

frigate: ioa, iwa 6 tropic

gallinaceous: 6 peahen 7 peacock, peafowl

game: 5 quail, snipe 6 grouse, turkey 8 pheasant, woodcock 9 merganser

genus: 4 alca, crax, otis 7 certhia 9 apatornis

gull-like: 4 tern 6 jaeger

Hawaiian: ava, ioa, iwa 4 iiwi, koae, mamo, moho

heron family: 4 benu, ibis 7 bittern

honey eater: 4 moho

humming: ava 5 carib 7 colibri

insectivorous: owl 5 vireo

jay: gae 6 magpie

large: emu 4 emeu, guan, rhea 5 eagle 6 curlew, willet 7 bustard, megapod, ostrich, pelican, seriema 8 curassow, shoebill 11 lammergeier

largest: 7 ostrich

lark-like: 5 pipit

long-billed: 5 snipe 7 pelican

long-legged: io 4 sora 5 heron, snipe, stilt, wader 6 avocet, avoset, curlew 7 seriema

long-necked: 4 swan 5 agami, crane, goose, geese(pl.), stork 7 ostrich

male: cob, tom 4 cock 5 drake 6 gander 7 peacock, rooster 11 chanticleer

marsh: 4 sora 5 snipe, stilt

meadow: 8 bobolink

Mexican: 6 jacana, towhee 7 jacamar

mythological: roc 5 hansa 6 simurg 7 phoenix, simurgh

New Zealand: kea, moa 4 kaka, kiwi, kulu, ruru, titi, weka 6 kakapo 7 apterix, apteryx 8 morepork, notornis 10 blightbird

nonpasserine: 4 tody 6 hoopoe, motmot 8 hornbill 10 kingfisher

Northern: auk, 6 gannet, puffin

of Athena: owl

of Juno: 7 peacock

of paradise: 8 manucode

of peace: 4 dove

of prey: owl 4 hawk, kite 5 eagle, elant, owlet 6 eaglet, elanet 7 goshawk, vulture 9 accipiter

of Zeus: 5 eagle

oldest known: 13 archaeopteryx

oscine: 4 chat 6 dronge, oriole 7 tanager

ostrich-like: emu, moa 4 emeu, rhea 10 cassowarie

parrot-like: 11 budgereegah, buddgerygah

parson: poe, tue, tui

parts of body: neb, nib 4 bill, cere, knee, lora, mala 5 lores 6 pecten, pileum, pinion, rostra, syrinx 7 ambiens 8 pectines(pl.)

passerine: 5 finch 7 sparrow, starnel 9 chatterer, coachwhip

pert. to: 5 avian, avine 8 ornithic 9 volucrine

pink: 8 flamingo

plover-like: 5 drome 7 lapwing

Poe's: 5 raven

predatory: owl 4 kite 5 yager 6 falcon, shrike 9 cormorant

protuberance at base of bill: 4 cere

rare: 8 rara avis

ratite: emu, moa 4 emeu 7 ostrich 10 cassowary

red-tailed: 4 koae

sacred: 4 ibis

sea: auk, ern 4 erne, gony, gull, smew, tern 5 eider, solan 6 gannet, petrel, puffin 7 pelican 9 albatross 10 shearwater

shore: ree 4 rail, sora 5 snipe, stilt, wader 6 avocet, avoset, curlew, plover, willet

Sindbad's: roc 4 rock, rukh

singing: 4 lark, wren 5 finch, mavis, robin, shama, veery, vireo 6 canary, linnet, mocker, oriole, oscine, thrush 7 mocking, robinet 8 bobolink, redstart 12 whippoorwill

small: tit 4 tody, wren 5 dicky, pipit, vireo 6 dickey, linnet, siskin, todies(pl.), tomtit 7 creeper, humming, sparrow, titlark, wheater 8 starling 9 didappers

South American: 4 guan, mina, myna 5 chaja, mynah 6 barbet, becard, toucan 7 cariama, oilbird 8 bellbird, boatbill, caracara, guacharo, hoactzin, puffbird
swallow-like: 4 cran 5 swift
swimming: 4 loon 5 grebe
talking: 4 crow, mina, mino, myna 5 mynah 6 parrot
tall: 6 avocet, avoset
tropical: ani 4 koae, tody 6 barbet, motmot, toucan, trogon
unfledged: gor 4 eyas 6 gorlin 8 bubbling, nestling
Vishnu's: 6 Garuda
wading: 4 hern, ibis, rail, sora 5 crane, heron, snipe, stilt, stork 6 avocet, jacana 8 flamingo, shoebill 9 sandpiper
web-footed: 4 duck, swan 5 drake, goose 6 avocet, avoset, gander
West Indies: ani 4 tody
white-tailed: ern 4 erne 5 egret
woodcock: 5 pewee
young: eya 4 gull 5 piper 7 flapper, nestler 8 birdikin, nestling 9 fledgling
bird cage: 6 aviary, pinjra, volary, volery 7 paddock
bird clapper: 9 scarecrow
bird crest: 4 tuft
bird eye: 12 cuckoo flower
bird nest: 4 aery, eyry 5 aerie, eyrie
bird of passage: 8 wanderer 9 transient
bird route: 6 flyway
birdman: 5 pilot 6 airman 7 aviator 13 ornithologist
birds: 4 aves
collective: 4 fowl
domesticated: 7 poultry
bird's-eye view: 6 apercu
bird-witted: 5 giddy
birdwoman: 8 aviatrix 9 aviatress, aviatrice
biretta, berretta: cap 5 beret 8 skullcap 13 clergyman's cap
biri: 9 cigarette
birl: 4 spin, toss, whir 5 whirr 6 rattle, rotate 7 revolve
birma: 6 calaba
birr: bur 4 blow, burr, push, rush, wind 5 force, storm, vigor 6 energy, thrust, onrush 7 impetus
birth: 4 bear 6 burden, origin, spring 7 descent, genesis, lineage 8 delivery, geniture, nascency, nativity 9 beginning, naissance, parentage 10 extraction
after: 9 postnatal
before: 8 prenatal
by: nee
goddess: 5 Parca
help with: 8 accouche
new: 10 renascence 11 Renaissance
nobleness: 6 eugeny
pert. to: 5 natal 13 primogenitive

birth control: 7 the pill 9 vasectomy 13 contraception
birth flower: *April:* 5 daisy
August: 9 gladiolus
December: 10 poinsettia
February: 8 primrose
January: 9 carnation
July: 8 sweet pea
June: 4 rose
March: 6 violet
May: 15 lily of the valley
November: 13 chrysanthemum
October: 6 dahlia
September: 5 aster
birth stone: *April:* 7 diamond 8 sapphire
August: 9 carnelian
December: 9 turquoise
February: 8 amethyst
January: 6 garnet
July: 4 ruby
June: 5 agate
March: 6 jasper 10 bloodstone
May: 7 emerald
November: 5 topaz
October: 5 beryl
September: 10 chrysolite
birthday: 11 anniversary, celebration
ode: 12 genethliacon
pert. to: 10 genethliac 12 genethliacal
birthmark: 4 mole 5 naeve, nevus 6 naveus 7 blemish, feature, spiloma 14 characteristic
pert. to: 7 naevoid
birthplace: 10 incunabula(pl.) 11 incunabulum
birthrate: 8 natality
birthright: 8 heritage
bis: 5 again, twice 6 encore, repeat 7 replica 9 duplicate
biscuit: bun 4 bake(Sc.), roll, rush, snap 5 scone, wafer 6 cookie 7 cracker, pentile, pretzel 8 hardtack 9 porcelain 11 earthenware
bisect: 4 fork 5 cross, halve, split 6 cleave, divide 8 separate
bisexual: 13 hermaphrodite
bishop: 4 pope 5 angel 6 archer, bustle, priest 7 pontiff, prelate, primate 8 director, overseer 9 clergyman, inspector 3 administrator 14 superintendent
apron: 7 gremial
assistant: 6 verger 9 coadjutor
buskin: 6 caliga 7 caligae(pl.)
cap: 4 hura 5 miter, mitre 7 biretta 8 berretta, mitrella
first year revenue: 5 annat 6 annate
jurisdiction: see 7 diocese
private room: 9 accubitus
robe: 6 chimar, chimer 7 chimere
staff: 7 crosier
stave: 6 baculi(pl.) 7 baculus
throne: 4 apse 8 cathedra

title: 4 abba, anba 7 prelate, primate

vestment: alb 4 cope 6 chimer, rochet 7 gremial, tunicle 8 dalmatic 10 omophorion

bishopric: see 7 diocese 10 episcopacy, episcopate

bishop's weed: 4 ammi 6 ammeos 8 bolewort, goutweed

bison: 6 bovine 7 aurochs, bonasus, buffalo

bisque: 4 soup 5 point 8 ceramics

bistro: bar 4 café 6 tavern 9 nightclub 10 restaurant

bisulcate: 6 cloven

bit: ace, end, jot, ort, wee 4 atom, bite, curb, doit, food, iota, item, mite, mote, part, snap, tool, whit 5 blade, check, crumb, drill, pezzo, piece, scrap, shred, speck, while 6 bridle, cannon, eating, morsel, smidge, splice, tittle, trifle 7 morceau(F.), portion, scatche, smidgen, smidgin, smigeon, snaffle 8 fraction, fragment, particle, quantity, restrain, smitchin, victuals 9 restraint

horse's curb: 6 pelham

Irish: 7 traneen

bit by bit: 9 gradually

bit part: 6 walk-on

bite: bit, cut, eat, nip 4 bait, cham, chew, food, gash, gnap, gnaw, hold, knap, meal, snap 5 chack, chamm, champ, cheat, chomp, pinch, seize, share, smart, snack, sting, trick 6 crunch, morsel, nibble, pierce 7 cheater, corrode, impress, partake, sharper, slander 8 lacerate, puncture, victuals 9 denticate, masticate

bite one's tongue: 6 regret

bite the bullet: 8 face up to 10 meet head-on 14 do it regardless

biting: 4 acid, hoar, keen 5 acrid, sharp, snell 6 bitter, rodent, severe 7 caustic, cutting, mordant, nipping, pungent 8 clear-cut, incisive, poignant, scathing, stinging 9 corrosive, sarcastic, trenchant, vitriolic

biting dragon: 8 tarragon

biting of nails: 12 phaneromania

bito: 4 balm, tree 7 hajilij

oil: 6 zachun

bitt: 4 post 5 block

bitter: bad 4 acid, bask, gall, keen, sore, sour, tart 5 acerb, acrid, amara, bleak, harsh, irate, sharp 6 biting, picric, severe 7 austere, caustic, crabbed, cutting, galling, hostile, painful, pungent, satiric 8 grievous, poignant, stinging, virulent 9 malicious, offensive 10 afflictive 11 acrimonious, distressful 12 antagonistic

bitter apple: 9 colocynth

bitter bush: 9 snakeroot

bitter-ender: 7 diehard

bitter gentian: 9 baldmoney

bitter grass: 9 colicroot

bitter oak: 6 cerris

bitter spar: 8 dolomite

bitter vetch: ers 5 vicia

bitter wintergreen: 10 pipsissewa

bitterly: 4 hard, sour 8 cursedly

bittern: 4 bump 5 boonk, heron 6 kakkak

bitterness: rue 4 acor, bile, fell, gall 5 atter 6 enmity, malice, rancor 7 amarity 8 acerbity, acrimony, severity 9 amaritude, hostility, poignancy, virulence 11 malevolence

bitters: 4 amer(F.) 5 tonic 6 liquor

pert. to: 9 amaroidal

bittersweet: 10 confection, nightshade

bitterweed: 7 ragweed 9 horseweed 10 sneezeweed

bitterwort: 7 felwort 9 dandelion

bitumen: tar 5 pitch 7 asphalt 8 alkitran 9 alchitran, elaterite

bivalve: 4 clam, spat 6 cockle, diatom, mussel, oyster 7 mollusk, Pandora, scallop 10 brachipod

genus: 5 pinna 6 anomia 7 toheroa 12 gastrochaena

bivocal: 9 diphthong

bivouac: 4 camp 5 etape, watch 6 encamp 7 shelter 10 encampment

biwa: 6 loquat

bizarre: odd 5 antic, dedal, outre, queer 6 quaint 7 curious, strange 8 fanciful 9 eccentric, fantastic, grotesque 10 ridiculous 11 extravagant

Bizet opera: 6 Carmen

blab: 4 chat 5 blart, blate, clack 6 babble, betray, gossip, reveal, tattle 7 blabber, chatter 8 telltale

black: jet 4 calo, dark, ebon, foul, inky, onyx 5 dirty, dusky, murky, Negro, noire(F.), raven, sable, slate, sooty 6 atrous, dismal, gloomy, pitchy, sullen 7 melanic, Negrito, piceous, swarthy, unclean 8 charcoal, mournful 9 atrocious 10 blackamoor, calamitous, forbidding

and white: 11 chiaroscuro

black and blue: 5 livid

spot: 6 bruise, shiner 10 ecchymosis

black art: 5 magic 7 alchemy 8 wizardry 10 necromancy 11 conjuration

black cod: 6 beshow

black death: 6 plague

black diamond: oil 4 coal 8 hematite

black earth: 4 mold 9 chernozem

black elder: 9 hackberry

black eye: 5 shame 6 bruise, shiner 7 scandal

black-eyed Susan: 6 ketmia 10 coneflower

black grunt: 10 tripletail

black hole: 4 cell 7 dungeon 8 solitary

13 collapsed star
black plague: 7 bubonic
Black Sea: *ancient name:* 6 Pontus
  arms: 9 Sea of Azov 12 Sea of Marmara
  connecting straits: 5 Kerch 8 Bosporus
    11 Dardanelles
  peninsula: 6 Crimea
  ports: 5 Varna 6 Batumi, Burgas, Odessa
    8 Istanbul 9 Constanta 10 Sevastopol
  river to: Bug, Don 5 Kuban 6 Danube 7
    Dnieper, Sakarya 8 Dniester
black sheep: 7 deviate 9 reprobate
black widow: 6 spider 7 pokomoo
blackamoor: 5 bleck, Negro 7 negress
blackball: 4 pill, vets 6 ballot 7 boycott,
  exclude, heeball 9 ostracize
blackberry: 6 agawam 8 dewberry
blackbird: ani, daw, pie 4 crow, merl 5
  amsel, colly, merle, ousel, ouzel, raven 6
  colley 7 jackdaw
blackboard: 5 slate
blackcap: 4 gull 7 warbler 8 chicadee, titmouse 9 raspberry
blackdamp: 9 chokedamp
blacken: ink, tar 4 char, soot 5 bleck,
  cloud, japan, sully 6 darken, defame,
  malign, vilify 7 asperse, slander, traduce 8 besmirch 10 calumniate
black eye: 5 mouse 6 shiner, stigma 9
  contusion
blackface: 5 actor, comic, sheep 8 boldface, minstrel
blackfin: 4 fish 5 cisco, sesis
blackfish: 5 whale 6 tautog 10 nigrescent
  school: 5 grind
blackguard: 4 shag 5 gamin, guard, snuff
  7 vagrant, villain 8 criminal, hanger-
  on, vagabond 9 scoundrel
blackhead: 4 clam 6 comedo, mussel
blackjack: oak 4 club, duck, flag, game,
  jack 5 billy 6 beetle, jerkin, vessel,
  weapon 7 tankard
blackleg: 4 scab, snob 7 disease, gambler
  8 apostate, swindler 13 strikebreaker
blacklist: ban 4 veto
blackmail: 5 bribe 6 coerce, extort 7 payment, tribute
blackmailer: 5 ghoul 7 leecher
blackmailing: 8 chantage 9 extortion
Blackmore heroine: 10 Lorna Doone
blackout: 5 faint 6 darken 8 darkness,
  scrounge 11 suppression
blacksmith: gow 5 shoer, smith 6 plover,
  smithy, stithy 7 farrier, striker 10
  horseshoer
  shop: 5 anvil, stith 6 smithy, stithy 8
  smithery
blacksnake: 4 whip 5 racer, quirt
blackthorn: haw 4 sloe, tree
blackwort: 8 comfrey
bladder: sac 7 blister, inflate, vesicle

comb. form: 4 asco
blade: bit, fop, oar 4 blow, bone, edge, leaf,
  shiv 5 blood, dandy, fluke, grain, knife,
  spark, spear, spire, sword 6 cutter, lamina, scythe, sickle 7 gallant, lamin-
  ae(pl.), scapula 9 propeller
blague: lie 4 hoax 6 humbug 8 claptrap,
  nonsense, raillery
blah: 4 bunk, dull 8 nonsense
blahs: 5 dumps, ennui 7 boredom, malaise
  8 doldrums
Blake's symbol: 4 Zoas
blamable: 6 faulty 8 culpable 11 blameworthy 13 reprehensible
blame: 4 call, hurt, onus, twit 5 chide,
  fault, guilt, odium, shend 6 accuse,
  charge, dirdum, impute, rebuke, revile,
  scance 7 ascribe, censure, condemn, obloquy, reproof, reprove, upbraid 8 reproach 9 challenge, criticism, inculpate,
  liability 10 accusation 11 culpability,
  reprobation 12 reprehension 13 animadversion
  deserving: 8 culpable
blameless: 4 good 7 perfect 8 innocent,
  spotless 9 faultless, righteous 13 unimpeachable 14 irreproachable
blanch: 4 fade, pale 5 chalk, scald, white
  6 argent, bleach, blench, whiten 8 etiolate 9 whitewash
bland: 4 kind, mild, oily, open, soft 5
  suave 6 benign, genial, gentle, smooth,
  urbane 7 affable, amiable, insipid, lenient 8 gracious 9 benignant, courteous
  10 wishy-washy 11 good-natured 12
  ingratiating
blandish: 4 coax 5 charm 6 allure,
  blanch, cajole 7 beguile, flatter, wheedle
  10 compliment
blank: 4 bare, flan, form, shot, void 5 annul, blind, break, clean, empty, range,
  space 6 vacant 7 nonplus, unmixed,
  vacuous 8 omission, unfilled 9 colorless, downright, fruitless, frustrate
blanket: 4 brot, wrap 5 cotta, cover, layer,
  manta, quilt, sheet, throw 6 afghan,
  poncho, serape 8 coverlet 10 barraclade
  cowboy: 5 sugan 6 soogan, sougan, su-
  gann
  goat's hair: 6 cumbly
  horse: 5 manta
  Indian: 6 stroud
blare: 4 peal 5 blast, blaze, noise 6 blazon, scream 7 fanfare, tantara, trumpet
  11 flamboyance
blarney: 4 coax 5 stone 6 butter 7 flatter,
  wheedle 8 flattery
blasé: 5 bored, sated, weary 8 satiated 9
  surfeited 11 indifferent
blasphemy: 7 calumny, cursing, impiety
  8 anathema, swearing 9 profanity, sac-

rilege 10 execration 11 imprecation, irreverence, malediction 12 vilification

blast: bub, nip, wap 4 bang, blow, gale,
gust, ruin, wind 5 party, split, stunt 6
attack, blight, wither 7 blowout, bluster, explode, shatter, shindig, shrivel 8
dynamite, outburst, proclaim 9 criticize, discharge, explosion 10 detonation

blast furnace: *lower part:* 4 bosh
nozzle: 6 tuyere

blat: 5 bleat, blurt 7 exclaim

blatant: 4 glib, loud 5 gaudy, gross, noisy,
silly, vocal 6 coarse, vulgar 8 brawling
9 bellowing, clamorous, inelegant, obtrusive, shameless 10 vociferous

blather: 4 stir 5 bleat 6 babble 7 blither,
prattle 8 nonsense 9 commotion

blaubok: 5 etaac 8 antelope

blaze: 4 burn, fire, glow, mark, shot 5
flame, flare, flash, glare, gleam, glory,
shine, torch, 6 bleeze 7 bonfire, declare,
pioneer, sparkle 8 splendor 9 firebrand
10 effulgence, illuminate 11 coruscation 13 conflagration

blazer: 6 jacket

blazon: 4 deck, show 5 adorn, blare, boast
6 depict, shield 7 declare, display, exhibit, publish 8 emblazon, inscribe 9
delineate, embellish 11 description,
publication 14 representation

bleach: sun 5 chalk 6 blanch, blench,
chlore, purify, whiten 7 decolor, lighten
8 etiolate

bleachers: 5 seats, stand 8 scaffold 10
grandstand

bleaching vat: 4 keir, kier

bleak: dim, raw 4 blae, blay, cold, gray
grim, pale 5 sprat 6 bitter, bleach, dismal, dreary, frigid, gloomy, pallid 7 cutting 8 desolate 9 cheerless 10 depressing

fish: 4 blay, bley 5 sprat

blear: dim 4 blur, dull 5 faint 6 darken 7
deceive, mislead 8 hoodwink, protrude

bleared: 4 inky 5 dusky 6 rheumy

bleat: baa 4 blat, blea 5 blart, gripe 7
blather, bluster, whicker

bleb: 4 blob 5 bulla 6 bubble 7 blister,
pustule, vesicle 8 swelling

bleed: 4 flow, leak, shed 5 exude 6 escape,
extort, fleece 7 agonize

bleeding heart: 8 dicentra

bleep, blip: 8 high note 10 TV deletion
11 shrill sound, video signal

blemish: mar 4 blot, blur, dent, flaw, gall,
lack, mark, rift, scar, slur, spot, vice,
want, wart 5 blame, breck, crack, fault,
mulct, speck, sully, tache, taint 6
blotch, breach, defame, defect, impair,
injure, macula, macule, smirch, stigma,
blister 7 default, failing, fissure, macu-

lae(pl.) 8 pockmark 9 birthmark, deformity, discredit, disfigure 10 deface-
ment, deficiency 12 imperfection 13
disfigurement

wood: 4 mote

wound: 4 scar 8 cicatrix 9 cicatrice

blend: mix 4 blot, fuse, join, meng 5 blind,
cream, merge, shade, spoil, stain, tinge,
unite 6 commix, dazzle, mingle 7 combine, confuse, corrupt, deceive, mixture,
pollute 8 coalesce, tincture 9 admixture, associate, commingle, harmonize,
integrate 10 amalgamate 11 incorporate

blended: 5 fondu, mixed 6 merged 7 mingled 9 confluent

blesbok: 5 nunni 8 antelope

bless: 4 keep, sain, wave 5 adore, anele,
bensh(Yid.), extol, favor, guard, thank,
wound 6 favour, hallow, praise, thrash
7 approve, beatify, glorify, protect 8
dedicate, macarize, preserve, sanctify
10 consecrate, felicitate

blessed: 4 holy 5 happy 6 divine, joyful,
sacred 8 benedict, bhagavat, blissful,
hallowed 9 beatified, benedight 11 consecrated

blessing: 4 boon, gift 5 bliss, grace 6
praise 7 benison, worship 8 felicity 9
beatitude 10 benedicite, beneficent 11
benediction

blight: nip 4 ruin, rust, smut 5 blast, frost
6 mildew, wither 7 destroy 9 frustrate

blimp: 7 airship, balloon, colonel

blind: bet, pot 4 ante, dark, daze, dull,
hood 5 blank, blend, decoy, dunch,
front, shade, stake, wager 6 ambush,
bisson, dazzle, screen, secret 7 aimless,
bandage, benight, eclipse, execate, eyeless, obscure, pretext, shutter 8 abortive, artifice, bayardly, blinding, hoodwink, ignorant, involved, jalousie,
outshine, purblind, unseeing 9 benight-
ed, concealed, deceitful, defective, insensate, intricate, senseless, sightless
10 incomplete, misleading, subterfuge
11 intoxicated 12 shortsighted

as a hawk: 4 seel

part of: 4 slat

printing for: 7 braille

blind alley: 7 dead end, impasse 8 cul-de-
sac

blind god: 4 Hoth 5 Hoder, Hothr

blind spot: 6 hang-up 7 bigotry

blind staggers: gid 7 vertigo

blind worm: 5 orvet

blinder: 4 flap 5 bluff 7 blinker 8 hoodwink 9 blindfold 11 obstruction

blindfold: 4 dark 5 blink, bluff 7 bandage, blinder, obscure 8 heedless, hoodwink, reckless 9 concealed

blindness: 6 bisson, cecity 7 ablepsy, anopsia 8 oblepsia 9 ignorance
color: 13 achromatopsia 14 monochromatism
day: 11 hemeralopia
partial: 7 meropia 10 cecutiency
snow: 14 chiona-blepsia

blink: 4 shun, wink 5 blush, cheat, flash, gleam, shine, trick 6 glance, ignore, obtuse 7 blinter, condone, flicker, glimmer, glimpse, neglect, nictate, sparkle, twinkle 9 blindfold
at: 7 condone 8 overlook
on the: 7 haywire 10 out of order, out of whack 11 inoperative, in disrepair

blinker: eye 5 bluff, light 6 signal 7 blinder, goggles 8 coquette, hoodwink, mackerel

blinking: 5 utter 6 damned 8 blooming, complete

blintze: 7 pancake

blip: 4 echo

bliss: joy 4 Eden, kaif, seil(Sc.) 5 glory 6 heaven 7 delight, ecstasy, gladden, rapture 8 felicity, gladness, paradise, pleasure 9 happiness 11 contentment
place of: 4 Eden 6 Utopia 7 Elysium 8 Paradise

blissful: 4 holy 5 happy 6 blithe, elated 7 blessed, Elysian, Utopian 8 ecstatic, euphoric 9 beatified, glorified

blister: 4 beat, bleb, blob, lash 5 blain, bulge 6 bubble, scorch 7 vesicle 8 lambaste, vesicate 10 vesicatory

blithe: gay 4 glad 5 bonny, happy, jolly, merry 6 bonnie, jovial, joyous, lively 7 gaysome, jocular, winsome 8 cheerful, gladsome 9 sprightly

blitzkrieg: 4 raid 6 attack 11 bombardment

blizzard: 4 blow, gale, wind 5 purga 6 retort 9 snowstorm, squelcher

bloat: 5 puffy, swell 6 expand, tumefy 7 distend, ferment, inflate 8 drunkard

bloated: 5 bloat, cured 6 sodden, turgid 7 pompous

blob: lip, wen 4 bleb, blot, boil, daub, drop, lump, mark, mass 6 bubble, pimple, splash 7 blemish, blister, blossom, globule, pustule, splotch 8 globular

bloc: 4 ring 5 cabal, party, union 6 clique 7 faction 11 combination

block: ame, bar, cob, dam, hob, nog, row, vol 4 bloc, cake, clog, cube, fill, foil, head, mass, stop 5 annex, check, chump, deter, nudge, parry, shape, spike, stump 6 hamper, hinder, impede, oppose, outwit, square, street, stymie, tablet, thwart 7 buckler, inhibit, outline, prevent 8 blockade, obstacle, obstruct, stoppage 9 barricade, blockhead,

frustrate, hindrance, intercept 11 obstruction
architectural: 6 dentil, mutule
electrically insulated: 6 taplet
football: 4 clip
for shaping metal objects: ame
ice: 4 cube 5 serac
mechanical: 6 pulley
metal type: 4 quad, quod
nautical: 7 deadeye
perforated: nut
small: 7 tessera

blockade: bar, dam 5 beset, block, siege 6 whisky 7 embargo 8 obstruct 9 beleaguer, moonshine 11 obstruction, restriction

blockhead: ass, oaf 4 bust, coof, dolt, fool, mome 5 block, chump, cuddy, dunce, idiot, ninny 6 noodle 7 dizzard, halfwit, tomfool 8 beefhead, clodpate, gamphrel, hardhead 9 blockpate, grouthead, hoddy-peak, numbskull, screwball, simpleton 10 beetlehead, dunderhead, hoddy-doddy

blockhouse: 4 fort

bloke: guy, man 4 chap, toff 6 fellow 9 personage

blonde: 4 fair 5 light, straw 6 flaxen, golden, yellow 9 towheaded

blood: kin, sap 4 gore, life, mood, race 5 blade, fluid, serum, stock 6 claret, indred 7 gallant, kinship, kinsman, lineage, youstir(Sc.) 8 relation 9 lifeblood 14 consanguineous
cell: red 5 white 8 hemocyte 9 leukocyte 10 erythrocyte
clot: 8 thrombus
deficiency: 6 anemia 7 anaemia
disease: 8 leukemia
fluid part: 5 serum 6 plasma 7 opsonin
mixed: See **hybrid**
of the gods: 4 icor 5 ichor
particle in: 7 embolus
poisoning: 6 pyemia 7 pyaemia, toxemia 10 septicemia
pressure: 8 systolic 9 diastolic
serum: 6 plasma
stagnation: 4 clot 5 cruor, grume 6 stasis, stases
strain: 4 race 5 stock 6 family
testing instrument: 13 hemabarometer 14 haemabarometer

blood and thunder: 6 uproar 8 violence 9 melodrama

blood brother: 6 friend 8 intimate

blood feud: 8 vendetta

blood fine: cro(Sc.) 4 eric 7 galanas, wergild 9 bloodwite

blood horse: 12 thoroughbred

blood money: cro 7 breaghe

blood pudding: 7 sausage

blood relationship: 7 kinsman 8 relative 13 consanguinity

blood vessel: 4 vein 5 hemad 6 artery 9 capillary

comb. form: vas

rupture: 6 rhexis

bloodbath: 7 carnage 8 massacre 9 slaughter

bloodcurdling: 4 gory 8 horrible 10 terrifying

blooded: 9 pedigreed 12 thoroughbred

bloodhound: 4 lyam, lyme

bloodless: 4 dead, pale 6 anemic 7 anaemic, inhuman 8 lifeless 9 colorless, unfeeling 10 exsanguine

bloodroot: 7 puccoon 10 tetterwort

bloodshed: 5 death 7 carnage 8 violence 9 slaughter

bloodshot: red 8 inflamed

bloodstone: 10 chalcedony

bloodsucker: 5 leech 7 sponger, vampire 11 extortioner

bloodthirsty: 6 bloody, carnal 9 ferocious, murderous 10 sanguinary

bloody: 4 gory, grim 5 cruel 6 cruent 7 imbrued 8 bleeding, hematose, infamous 9 cruentous, ferocious, haematose, merciless, murderous, red-handed 10 sanguinary 11 ensanguined 12 bloodstained, bloodthirsty, contemptible

bloom (see also **flower**): dew 4 blow 5 flush 7 blossom, blowing 8 floreate, flourish 13 efflorescence

bloomer: 5 error 6 blower 7 blunder, failure

blooming: 4 rosy 5 flush, fresh, green 6 abloom, damned, florid

blooper: 5 error, radio 7 blunder, blowing, faux pas, roseate 8 blinking 10 prospering

blossom (see also **flower**): bud 4 blob, open 5 bloom 7 burgeon, prosper 8 flourish 13 efforesce 13 efflorescence

small: 8 floweret

blot: mar 4 blob, blue, daub, flaw, soil, spot 5 blend, erase, smear, speck, stain, sully 6 blotch, cancel, damage, defect, efface, impair, macula, shadow, smirch, smudge, smutch, stigma 7 blemish, eclipse, expunge, maculae(pl.), obscure, tarnish 8 disgrace, reproach 9 bespatter 10 obliterate, stigmatize 12 obliteration 13 disfigurement

out: 5 annul, erase 6 efface 7 abolish 10 annihilate

blotch: dab 4 blot, gout, spot 5 patch, smear, stain 6 macula, mottle, smirch, stigma 7 blemish, maculae(pl.), pustule, splotch 8 eruption, maculate

blotto: 11 intoxicated

blouse: 5 shirt, smock, tunic 7 casaque 10 shirtwaist

bushman's: 5 bluey

blow: bob, cob, cop, dub, fan, jab, pat, rap, tap, wap 4 ande, baff, bang, bash, beat, belt, biff, birr, blad, blaw, brag, buff, bump, chap, conk, crig, cuff, daud, dint, dird, drub, dunt, dush, fleg, gale, gowf, huff, jolt, knap, lash, mint, oner, pant, plug, puff, scud, slam, slap, slug, sock, wind 5 binge, blade, blast, blizz, bloom, boast, botch, break, brunt, burst, clink, clour, clout, clump, crump, curse, douse, dowse, filip, flack, flick, gowff, ictus, impel, knock, peise, shock, skite, slipe, sound, spend, storm, swipe, thump, treat, waste, whack, whang 6 bensel, bensil, betray, bounce, buffet, depart, dirdum, expand, fillip, flower, frolic, larrup, wallop 7 assault, attaint, bensail, bensall, bensell, blossom, blowout, bluster, boaster, destroy, inflate, publish, shatter, whample 8 boasting, calamity, confound, disaster, disclose 9 bastinado

in: 4 come 5 enter 6 arrive

mock: 5 feint

one's mind: 4 flip 5 go ape 6 turn on 8 freak out 10 overexcite 11 hallucinate

over: end 4 pass 7 subside

to: 5 treat

up: 4 bomb 5 scene 7 explode, inflate 8 dynamite, outburst

blow-by-blow: 8 detailed, itemized, thorough 10 particular

blower: fan 5 whale 6 puffer 7 bloomer 8 braggart 9 swellfish 11 sacheverell

blowfish: 6 puffer

blowfly: 10 bluebottle

blowgun: 10 peashooter

blowhard: 8 braggart

blowhole: 7 nostril 8 spiracle

blown: 5 stale, tired 6 opened 7 blossom, swollen, tainted 8 betrayed, flyblown, inflated 9 distended, exhausted, worthless

blowout: 4 blow, feed, meal 6 valley 7 shindig 10 depression

blowzy: 5 dowdy 6 frowzy 10 disheveled, slatternly

blub: 4 bulb 5 dwell 6 puffed 7 blubber, swollen

blubber: cry, fat 4 blub, foam, wail, weep 5 swell, thick, whine 6 bubble, flitch, medusa, nettle, seethe 7 blobber, bluster, swollen, whimper 9 disfigure

remove: 6 flense

whale: 5 fenks, speck 6 muktuk

blubbery: fat 5 obese 7 swollen 9 quivering 10 gelatinous 11 protuberant

bludgeon: bat, hit 4 club, mace 5 billy, stick 6 coerce, cudgel, weapon

blue: low, sad, sky 4 aqua, bice, glum 5
azure, livid, ocean, perse, risqué, small
6 cobalt, gloomy, indigo, severe 7 celeste, gentian, learned, lobelia 8 cerulean, cynanine, dejected, downcast, literary 9 turquoise 10 despondent,
melancholy

asbestos: 11 crocidolite

gray: 5 merle, pearl, slate 7 cesious 8 caesious

green: 4 aqua, bice, teal 5 beryl 8 calamine 9 turquoise

red: 5 smalt 6 mallow 8 gridelin, mazar-
ine 9 gris-de-lin

sheep: 6 bharal

sky: 5 azure 8 cerulean

blue blood: 5 noble 9 gentleman 10 aristocrat 12 bluestocking

blue boneset: 4 Scot 10 cornflower, mist-
flower

blue catalpa: 9 paulownia
blue-chip: 9 exemplary 11 prestigious
blue dandelion: 7 chicory
blue dye herb: 4 woad
Blue Eagle agency: NRA
blue earth: 10 kimberlite
Blue Grotto site: 5 Capri(Italy)
blue gum: 4 tree 10 eucalyptus
Blue Hen State: 8 Delaware
blue huckleberry: 11 tangleberry
blue jaundice: 9 cyanosis
blue jeans: 5 levis 6 denims
blue Joe: 8 bluegill
blue John: 4 milk
Blue Law State: 11 Connecticut
blue-pencil: 4 edit 6 delete, redact, revise
blue peter: 4 coot, flag 9 gallinule
blue-ribbon: top 4 best 6 Grade A 7 supreme 8 top-notch

Bluebeard's wife: 6 Fatima
bluebonnet: cap 4 Scot 7 bluecap 8
Scotsman 10 cornflower

bluebottle: 5 bluet 7 barbeau, blowfly 8
hyacinth

bluecap: 4 Scot 10 bluebonnet
bluefish: 4 bass, tuna 5 saury 8 weakfish
bluegill: 7 sunfish
bluegrass: 12 country music
Bluegrass State: 8 Kentucky
bluejacket: gob, tar 6 sailor
bluejoint: 6 redtop
bluenose: 4 snob 5 prude 8 moralist 11
Nova Scotian

bluepoint: 6 oyster
blueprint: map 4 plan, plot 5 chart, draft,
trace 6 sketch 7 diagram, outline 8
game plan, strategy 9 cyanotype

bluer: 4 anil
bluerocket: 9 monkshood
blues: 4 song 5 dumps 6 cafard 7 megrims, sadness 10 melancholy, mulligrubs 11 despondency

bluestocking: 5 woman 12 intellectual
bluet: 5 plant 10 bluebottle 11 farkle-
berry

bluethroat: 7 warbler
bluff: 4 bank, brag, curt, fool, rude 5
blunt, burly, cliff, frank, gruff, short,
surly, trick 6 abrupt, assume, crusty 7
blinder, blinker, brusque, deceive, uncivil 8 barranca, barranco, churlish,
hoodwink, impolite 9 blindfold, outspoken, precipice 13 unceremonious

Bluff King Hal: 5 Henry
blunder: err, mix 4 balk, bull, flub, gaff,
roil, slip, stir 5 boner, botch, break, error, fault, lapse, misdo 6 blotch, boggle,
bumble, bungle, gazabo, gazebo, mingle,
muddle, wallow 7 bloomer, confuse, derange, failure, faux pas, mistake, stumble 8 solecism 9 confusion, mismanage
11 disturbance

blunderbuss: gun 9 espingole 10 stumblebum

blunge: mix 5 blend 10 amalgamate
blunt: 4 bald, curt, damp, dull, flat 5 bluff,
brusk, inert, plain, plump, stunt 6
clumsy, deaden, obtund, obtuse, stupid,
weaken 7 brusque 8 hebetate 9 depressed, downright 10 point-blank 11
insensitive 13 unceremonious

mentally: 8 hebitate
blur: dim, hum 4 blob, blot, mist, soil,
spot 5 blear, cloud, smear, stain, sully,
taint 6 mackle, macule, smudge, stigma
7 blemish, confuse, obscure 9 disfigure

blurb: ad 4 puff, rove 5 brief 6 notice 7
write-up 12 announcement, commendation 13 advertisement

blush: 4 glow, look, rose 5 blink, color,
flush, gleam, rouge, tinge 6 glance,
mantle, redden 7 crimson 8 likeness 10
appearance, rubescence

blushing: red 4 rosy 5 ruddy 7 roseate 8
flushing 9 rosaceous 10 erubescent 11
embarrassed

bluster: 4 blow, huff, rage, roar, rant 5
blast, bleat, boast, bully, noise, storm,
swank 6 babble, bellow, bounce, hector,
huffle, tumult 7 blubber, bravado, gauster, roister, swagger 8 boasting, bullying, threaten 9 confusion, gasconade
10 intimidate, swaggering, turbulence
11 fanfaronade, rodomontade

boa: 5 aboma, scarf, snake 8 anaconda 9
neckpiece

boa contrictor: 5 snake 6 giboia, python
Boadicea's people: 5 Iceni
boar: hog, sus 4 aper 5 swine 6 barrow,
hogget 8 sanglier 9 hoggaster

head: 4 hure

wound: 4 gore 5 ganch
board: 4 deal, diet, eats, fare, keep, lath,
slat 5 enter, found, get on, house, lodge,

meals, panel, plank, stage, table 6 accost, embark, planch, shield 7 cabinet, council, duoviri, emplane, enplane, entrain, planche 8 approach, tribunal 9 authority, shipboard 10 commission, management, provisions 11 switchboard 13 entertainment

boast: gab 4 blaw, blow, brag, crow, pomp, rave 5 brave, extol, exult, glory, prate, roose, scold, skite, vapor, vaunt 6 bounce, clamor, extoll, flaunt, menace(Sc.), outcry, splore 7 bluster, clamour, display, glorify, show off, swagger 8 flourish, threaten 9 gasconade 11 rodomontade

boaster: 5 skite 6 crower, gascon, pedant 7 bouncer, bravado, cracker, ruffler 8 blowhard, braggart, cacofogo, fanfaron, glorioso, jingoist, rodomont 9 cacafuego 11 braggadocio

boastful: big 6 parado 8 fanfaron 9 cocka-hoop, gasconade, kompology 11 rodomontade, swellheaded, thrasonical

boat (see also canoe, ship, vessel): ark, cat, cot, gig, tub 4 bark, brig, carv, dory, junk, raft, scow, ship, skag, tack, trow, yawl 5 aviso, barca, barge, bully, canoe, coble, craft, dingy, ferry, ketch, liner, shell, skiff, skift, smack, xebec, zebec 6 baidak, bateau, carvel, chebec, cruise, cutter, dinghy, dugout, garvey, packet, vessel, zebeck 7 bateaus, chebeck, coracle, gondola, lighter, nacelle, pinnace, scooter, steamer 8 pessoner, schooner 9 submarine, transport 10 watercraft

Chinese: 4 junk 6 sampan
coal cargo: 7 collier
deck: 4 poop 5 orlop
fishing: 8 bracozzo
flat-bottomed: arc, bac 4 dory, keel, punt, scow 5 barge 6 bateau
freight: 7 lighter
front: 4 prow
garbage: 6 hopper
harbor: tug 5 barge 7 bumboat
Italian: 7 gondola
joint: 4 jerl
landing: LST
merchant: 6 argosy, holcad
ornamental: 9 navicella
part: bow 4 beam, deck, hold, keel, prow 5 bilge, cabin, stern 6 bridge, gunnel, kelson, saloon, thwart 7 capstan, gunwale, keelson, painter, scupper 12 companionway
pin: 5 thole
post: poy 4 biff 7 bollard, capstan 9 sternpost
power: tug
propellant: oar, row 4 pole 5 motor, scull
racing: gig 5 scull
ride: row 4 sail 6 cruise

round: 4 gufa 5 goofa 6 goofah
sailing: 4 pram, proa, yawl 5 praam, prahu, skiff, sloop, yacht
twin-hulled: 9 catamaran
undersea: sub 9 submarine 11 submersible

boatman: 5 poler 6 barger, Charon 7 hobbler, hoveler, huffler 8 hoveller 9 gondolier 10 barcajuolo

boatswain: 5 bosun 6 serang
whistle: 4 pipe

Boaz: *son:* 4 Obed
wife: 4 Ruth

bob: bow, cut, dab, job, rap, tap 4 ball, blow, buff, calf, clip, coin, cork, duck, grub, jeer, jerk, jest, knob, mock, worm 5 bunch, cheat, dance, filch, float, flout, shake, taunt, trick 6 bingle, buffet, curtsy, delude, pommel, strike, weight 7 bobsled, bobtail, cluster, curtesy, haircut, pendant, refrain 8 shilling 9 bobsleigh

bobac: 6 marmot

bobber: 4 cork, duck 5 float 6 bobfly 7 dropper 8 deadhead

bobbery: row 4 fray 5 brawl, fight, melee 6 hubbub, tumult 8 squabble 9 commotion 11 disturbance

bobbie, bobby: cop 4 bull 6 peeler 7 officer 9 policeman

bobbin: pin 4 cord, pirn, reel 5 braid, quill, spool 7 ratchet, spindle 8 cylinder 10 cuckoopint
frame: 5 creel
pin: 7 spindle

bobble: dib 4 mess 5 gum up 6 fumble

bobby: 7 officer 9 policeman

bobcat: 4 lynx

bobolink: 4 bird, reed 7 bunting, ortolan 10 butterbird

bobsled: bob 6 ripper

bobtail: bob, cur 4 dock 6 rabble, strunt(Sc.) 7 curtail 8 sheepdog 9 deficient 11 abbreviated

bobwhite: 4 bird 5 colin, quail 9 partridge

bocardo: 6 dokhma, 7 bokardo

Boccaccio work: 9 Decameron

bode: 4 omen, stop 5 augur, offer 6 herald 7 message, portend, presage 8 forebode, forecast, foreshow, foretell, indicate 9 messenger 10 inaugurate 13 foreshadowing, prognosticate

bodice: 4 jupe 5 choli, gilet, waist 6 basque, corset

bodiless: 9 trunkless 10 immaterial 11 incorporeal

bodily: 5 solid 6 actual, carnal 7 fleshly, sensual, somatic 8 corporal, entirely, material, physical 9 corporeal 10 completely 11 corporeally, substantial

bodily motion: 5 shrug 7 gesture

boding: 7 ominous 9 foretoken 10 foreboding, prediction, prognostic

bodkin: awl, pin 6 dagger, needle 7 hairpin, poniard 8 stiletto 9 eyeleteer

body: 4 bole, bouk, bulk, form, mass, nave, rupa, soma, stem 5 flesh, group, stiff, torso, trunk 6 corpse, corpus, extent, licham, object, person 7 cadaver, carcass, company 8 extensum, majority 9 aggregate, curcurbit, substance 10 assemblage, foundation 11 association, corporation

anterior part of: 7 prosoma

armor: 4 tace 6 corium

away from center: 6 distal

cavity: 5 sinus 6 coelom 7 coelome

fluid: 5 blood, lymph, serum 6 plasma, saliva

heavenly: sun 4 luna, moon, star 5 comet 6 meteor, planet 8 asteroid, luminary

joint: hip 4 knee 5 elbow, wrist 8 shoulder

motion: 7 gesture

of men: 5 posse 10 authorized

of persons: 5 corps, posse

of students: 5 class

of water: bay, sea 4 gulf, lake, pond, pool 5 ocean 6 lagoon, sealet 9 reservoir

path: 5 orbit

pert. to: 5 somal 8 physical, systemic

wagon: box

wall: 6 paries, septum

body politic: 4 weal 5 state 6 nation 9 community

bodyguard: 5 thane 6 escort 7 retinue, trabant 9 attendant, lifeguard, protector

Boeotia: *capital:* 6 Thebes

region: 5 Ionia

boeotian: 10 philistine

Boer: *dialect:* 4 Taal

general: 5 Botha

boffo: 10 successful 11 sensational 13 extraordinary 14 out of this world

bog: bug, car, fen, gog, hag 4 bold, carr, cess, mire, moor, moss, ooze, sink, slew, slue, syrt 5 marsh, saucy, swamp 6 morass, muskeg, slough 7 forward 8 quagmire 9 conceited

bog down: 4 mire 5 stall 6 bemire

bogey: bug, cow, hag 5 bogie, bogle, devil, gnome 6 boggle, booger, goblin 7 boggard, boggart, bugaboo, bugbear, gnomide, specter, spectre 9 hobgoblin, scarecrow 10 bullbeggar

in golf: 10 one over par

in the sky: UFO

boggle: jib, shy 4 balk, foil, stop 5 alarm, botch, demur, scare, start 6 baffle, bungle, goblin, shrink 7 bauchle, blunder, perplex, scruple, stagger 8 frighten, hesitate 9 dissemble, dumbfound, embarrass

boggy: wet 4 miry, soft 5 gouty, fenny, haggy, mossy 6 quaggy, swampy 7 boggish, quechy

bogus: 4 fake, sham 5 false, phony 6 forged 8 spurious 9 imitation 10 fictitious 11 counterfeit

bogy: See bogey

Bohemian: 4 arty 5 gipsy, gypsy 6 Picard 8 maverick 12 nonconformist

dance: 6 redowa

boil: sty 4 bile, blob, buck, coct, cook, rage, sore, stew, stye, teem 5 anger, botch, brede, poach, steam 6 betray, bubble, buller, burble, decoct, seethe, simmer 7 anthrax, estuate, inflame 8 aestuate, ebullate 10 ebbulliate, effervesce

almost: 5 scald

down: 6 decoct 8 simplify 10 streamline

boiler: 4 reef 6 copper, kettle, retort 7 alembic, caldron, furnace 8 cauldron

plate: 4 sput

tube scaler: 6 sooter

boisterous: 4 gurl, loud, rude 5 burly, gurly, noisy, rough, windy 6 coarse, stormy, strong, unruly 7 furious, massive, roaring, violent 8 cumbrous, strident, vehement 9 clamorous, excessive, excitable, turbulent 10 blustering, tumultuous, unyielding, vociferous

bold: big, bog, yep 4 derf, pert, rash, rude, wise, yepe 5 bardy, bield, brash, brave, brent, frack, freak, freck, gally, hardy, large, manly, nervy, peart, saucy, steep, stout 6 abrupt, audace, brassy, brazen, crouse, daring, fierce, heroic, strong 7 assured, dashing, defiant, forward, grivois, haughty, massive, valiant 8 arrogant, familiar, fearless, grivoise, immodest, impudent, insolent, intrepid, malapert, powerful, resolute 9 audacious, bodacious, confident, dauntless, imprudent, undaunted 10 courageous, forritsome 11 venturesome 12 enterprising, overassuming, presumptuous, stout-hearted 13 overconfident

boldness: 4 brow 5 bield, nerve, vigor 6 daring 7 bravery, chutzpa, courage 8 audacity, chutzpah, temerity 9 assurance, hardiesse, hardihood, hardiness 10 brazenness, confidence, effrontery 11 intrepidity, presumption 13 dauntlessness

bole: 4 clay, dose, stem 5 bolus, crypt, trunk 7 opening

bolero: 5 dance, waist 6 jacket

Bolero composer: 5 Ravel

bolide: 6 meteor 7 missile

Bolivia: *capitals:* 5 La Paz, Sucre

city: 5 Oruro, Uyuni 6 Camiri, Potosi, Robore, Viacha 8 Trinidad 9 Santa Cruz

district: 5 La Paz, Oruro, Pando 6 Elbeni,

Potosi, Tarija 9 Santa Cruz 10 Chuquisaca, Cochabamba

Indian: Uro, Uru 4 Iten, Moxo, Uran 6 Arawak, Aymara, Charca, Chicha, Tacana 7 Aymaran, Puquina, Sirione 10 Chiriguano

lake: 5 Poopo 8 Titicaca

liberator: 5 Sucre 7 Bolivar

measure: 6 league 7 celemin

monetary unit: 4 peso 7 centavo 9 boliviano

mountain: 5 Cuzco 6 Sajama, Sorata 7 Illampu 8 Illimani

plateau: 9 Altiplano

river: 4 Beni 5 Abuna, Orton 6 Baures, Mamore, Yacuma 7 Guapore, Madeira 9 Pilcomayo, San Miguel 11 Madre de Dios

weight: 5 libra, macro

boll: pod 4 bulb, grow, knob 5 onion 6 bubble 7 capsule, measure 8 pericarp 12 protuberance

boll weevil: 6 picudo

bollix: 4 flub, mess 5 botch, gum up 6 bungle

bollard: 4 bitt, post

bolo: 4 knife 7 machete, sundang 8 pacifist 9 defeatist

Bolshevist: 7 Russian 9 socialist

leader: 5 Lenin

bolster: aid, pad 6 pillow 7 cushion, support 8 compress, maintain 9 reinforce 10 strengthen

bolt: bar, pen, pin, rod, run 4 beat, dart, flee, gulp, lock, pawl, rush, sift 5 arrow, bilbo, close, elope, flash, gorge, latch, rivet, shaft 6 assort, decamp, desert, fasten, flight, garble, pintle, purify, refine, secure, strong, toggle, winnow 7 missile, shackle, thunder 8 fastener, separate, stampede 9 lightning

bolus: cud 4 bole, clop, lump, mass, pill, rock

bomb: dud, egg 4 flop 5 blare, shell 6 ashcan 7 bombard, failure, grenade, marmite 8 fall flat 9 pineapple 10 projectile 11 blockbuster

guide: fin

hole: 6 crater

bombard: 4 bomb 5 blitz, crump, shell 6 batter, bottle, strafe, vessel

bombardier: 6 gunner 12 artilleryman

bombardment: 5 blitz, siege 6 attack, rafale, strafe 7 barrage 9 cannonade

bombardon: 4 oboe, tuba 7 bassoon

bombast: gas, pad 4 rage, rant, rave 5 stuff 6 padded 7 bluster, stuffed, tympany 8 boasting, rhetoric 9 turgidity 11 rodomontade 12 altiloquence 14 grandiloquence

bombastic: 5 tumid, vocal 6 fluent, heroic, turgid 7 bombast, flowery, fustian, orotund, pompous, ranting, stilted 8 inflated 9 expansive, flatulent, grandiose, plethoric 10 lexiphanic, rhetorical 12 magniloquent

bombinate: hum 4 boom

bombproof chamber: 8 casemate

bombyx: eri 4 eria, moth 8 silkworm

bon ami: 5 lover 6 friend 10 sweetheart

bon mot: pun 4 jest, quip 9 witticism

bonafide: 7 genuine 9 authentic, veritable

bonanza: 4 mint 6 eureka 7 jackpot 8 eldorado, Golconda, gold mine

Bonanza State: 7 Montana

bonbon: 5 candy, cream 6 dainty 7 caramel 8 confetto, confetti 9 sugarplum

bond: tie, vow 4 bail, band, duty, glue, knot, link, note, yoke 5 bound, chain, nexus 6 binder, cement, connex, engage, escrow, fetter, league, pledge 7 husband, manacle, shackle 8 adhesive, contract, covenant, guaranty, ligament, ligature, mortgage, security, vinculum 9 agreement, composure, guarantee 10 constraint, husbandman, obligation 11 association, householder

chemical: 5 diene 7 valence

bondage: 4 yoke 7 helotry, peonage, serfdom, slavery 9 captivity, restraint, servitude, thralldom

bondsman: 4 carl, esne, peon, serf 5 churl, Helot, slave 6 stooge, surety, thrall, vassal 7 chattel, peasant, servant, villein

bone: rib 4 ossa(pl.), core, cram 5 blade 6 fillet, radius 7 humerus, utterly

ankle: 5 talus 6 tarsus

anvil: 5 incus 7 incudes(pl.)

arm: 4 ulna 6 radius 7 humerus

back: 5 spine 8 vertebra

breast: 6 sterna(pl.) 7 sternum

cartilage: 6 ossein

cavity: 5 antra(pl.), sinus 6 antrum

cell: 10 osteoblast

change into: 6 ossify

collar: 8 clavicle

dorsal: 4 ilia(pl.) 5 ilium

elbow: 4 ulna

formation: 7 ostosis 10 parostosis

girdle: 12 sphenethmoid

manipulator: 9 osteopath

pert. to: 6 osteal 7 osseous

scraper: 6 xyster

thigh: 5 femur

bonefish: 6 ladyfish

bonelet: 7 ossicle

boner: 5 error 7 blooper, blunder, faux pas, mistake

bones: 4 dice, ossa 8 skeletoa

boneset: 7 comfrey 8 hempweek 12 thoroughwort

boneyard: 5 stock, store 6 supply 9 scrap heap

bonfire: 5 blaze

bongo: 4 drum 8 antelope

boniata: yam

boniface: 8 landlord 9 barkeeper, innkeeper 12 saloonkeeper

bonito: aku, atu 4 fish, nice 5 cobia 6 bonita, pretty, robalo 8 albacore, mackerel, skipjack

Bonjour Tristesse author: 5 Sagan

bonkers: mad 5 crazy 6 insane

bonne: 5 nurse 9 nursemaid 11 maidservant

bonnet: cap, hat 4 hood 5 cover, decoy, toque 6 capote, slouch 7 chapeau, coronet 8 headgear 9 headdress 10 accomplice, chinquapin

brim: 4 poke

string: 5 bride

bonnet monkey: 4 zati 5 munga

bonny, bonnie: gay 4 fine 5 merry, plump 6 blithe, pretty, strong 7 healthy 8 budgeree, handsome 9 beautiful 11 goodlooking

bonton: 5 elite

bonus: tip 4 gift, meed 5 award, bribe, bunce, pilon, prize, spiff 6 reward 7 cumshaw, premium, subsidy 8 dividend, lagnappe 9 allowance, lagniappe 12 compensation

bon vivant: 5 sport 7 epicure

bony: 4 hard, lank, lean, thin 5 stiff, tough 6 osteal, skinny 7 osseous 8 skeletal

boo: 4 hoot, jeer 5 decry, grass 9 marijuana

boob: ass 4 fool 5 dunce, goony, neddy 6 nitwit

boobook: owl 6 cuckoo

booby: 5 dunce, idiot, loser, prize 6 sleigh, stupid 8 goosecap 9 simpleton

booby hatch: 4 jail 6 asylum

boodle: 4 swag 5 cheat, crowd, graft 6 noodle 7 plunder 8 caboodle

boohoo: sob 4 hoot, weep 5 shout 8 sailfish

boojum: 5 snark

book: log, mss. 4 opus, text, tome 5 Bible, canto, diary, divan, enter, folio, liber, libri(pl.) 6 manual, record, volume 7 blotter, catalog, writing 8 brochure, document, libretto, register 9 catalogue, pot-boiler

accounts: day 5 bilan, liber 6 ledger 7 journal

alphabet: 9 abecedary

Apocrypha: 5 Tobit

back: 5 spine

best selling: 5 Bible

binding material: 5 cloth, paper 6 canvas 7 buckram, leather

blank: 5 album, diary 6 tablet

church music: 6 hymnal

collector: 12 bibliomaniac

cover ornamentation: 7 tooling

covering: 6 jacket 7 binding

design: 6 format, layout

destroyer: 11 biblioclast

devotional: 5 Bible 6 gospel, missal 7 diurnal, psalter

division: 7 chapter

elementary reading: 6 primer

fiction: 5 novel

group: 7 trilogy

Islam: 5 kitab, Koran

jacket notice: 5 blurb

kept in print: 8 backlist

large: 4 tome 5 folio

lover: 11 bibliophile

make-up: 6 format

manuscript: 5 codex, draft 7 codices(pl.)

map: 5 atlas

mass: 6 missal

navigator's: log 7 logbook 9 portolano

obscene: 11 pornography

of hours: 4 Hora 5 Horae(pl.)

of masses: 6 missal

of nobility: 7 peerage

of psalms: 7 psalter

of rules: 5 Hoyle

page: 5 folio

palm: 4 tara 7 taliera

part: 4 leaf, page 5 cover 7 binding, chapter, section 9 signature

pert. to: 13 bibliographic

school: 6 primer, reader 7 grammar, speller 9 geography 10 arithmetic

size: 6 octavo, quarto 8 twelvemo 9 duodecimo

title page: 6 rubric

translation: 4 pony

words of opera: 8 libretto

yearbook: 7 almanac

Zoroastrian: 6 Avesta

book dealer: 10 bibliopole 11 bouguiniste

bookbinder: 12 bibliopegist

bookcase: 5 forel 6 forrel

bookish: 8 highbrow, pedantic

bookkeeper: 7 auditor 10 accountant

bookkeeping term: 4 loss, post 5 audit, debit, entry 6 credit 9 statement

booklet: 8 brochure 10 literature

bookman: 6 bookie, dealer 7 scholar 9 publisher 11 litterateur

bookplate: 8 exlibris

bookworm: 6 reader 7 scholar 11 bibliophile

boom: jib 4 bang, bump, crib, pole, roar, spar 5 croon 7 bumpkin, resound, support 8 bowsprit, flourish 9 bombilate, bombinate 10 prosperity

boomerang: 5 kiley, kalie 6 recoil 7 rebound 8 backfire, ricochet

boon: gay 4 bene, gift, good, kind 5 favor, grant, merry, order 6 benign, bounty, favour, goodly, jovial, prayer 7 benefit, command, present 8 blessing, intimate, petition 9 congenial, convivial, favorable 10 concession, prosperous 11 benefaction

boon companion: pal 4 chum 5 buddy

boondocks: 6 sticks 9 backwoods 10 hinterland, wilderness

boondoggle: 6 trifle 7 goof off 9 goldbrick

boor: cad, oaf 4 Boer, carl, lout, pill 5 chuff, churl, clown, looby, slave, yokel 6 carlot, clunch, hoblike, lubber, lummox, rustic 7 cauboge, grobian, peasant, villein 8 bosthoon 9 barbarian, roughneck 10 clodhopper, countryman, husbandman, tramontane

boorish: 4 rude 5 gawky, rough, surly 6 clumsy, coarse, rustic, sullen, vulgar 7 awkward, crabbed, hoblike, ill-bred, loutish, roister, uncouth 8 churlish, cloddish, clownish, lubberly, ungainly 9 bourgeois 10 uncultured, unmannerly

boost: aid 4 abet, back, help, lift, plug, push, rise 5 coach, exalt, hoist, raise 6 assist, rear up 7 advance, commend, elevate, endorse, indorse, promote 8 increase 9 encourage 10 assistance 12 commendation

booster: 4 shot 9 injection 10 enthusiast

boot: pac, use 4 cure, gain, help, kick, shoe, sock 5 avail, booty, eject, jemmy, kamik, spoil 6 bootee, buskin, casing, crakow, enrich, fumble, galosh, novice, sheath, thrill 7 benefit, dismiss, galoshe 8 chassure(F.), covering 9 advantage, discharge, dismissal

half: pac 4 pack 6 buskin, cocker 7 blucher, bottine 8 cothurni(pl.) 9 cothurnus

heavy: pac 5 stogy 6 Brogan 8 Balmoral

high-water: 5 wader

loose-topped: 10 wellington

riding: 5 jemmy 7 gambado, jodhpur

small: 7 bottine 8 bottekin

Boot: 5 Italy

booted: 4 shod 7 ocreate

booth: 4 loge, shed, shop, sook, souk 5 bothy, cabin, crame, house, stall, stand 6 tienda 7 balagan

bootleg: 7 illegal, illicit, smuggle 11 clandestine 12 illegitimate 13 surreptitious

bootless: 6 futile 7 useless 9 incurable, worthless 10 remediless, unavailing 12 unprofitable

bootlick: 4 fawn 5 toady 7 flatter 9 brownnose 11 apple-polish

booty: 4 gain, loot, pelf, prey, swag 5 cheat, graft, prize 6 spoils 7 despoil, pillage, plunder 10 chevisance

booze: 4 bout 5 budge, drink, spree 6 fuddle, liquor

boozer: pub 5 toper 6 bouser 8 drunkard

bora: 4 wind

borax: 6 tincal

Bordeaux wine (see also **wine**): 5 Bourg, cosne, medoc 6 claret 7 Margauz

border: hem, rim 4 abut, brim, dado, eave, edge, line, nark, orle, rand, roon, rund(Sc.), side, trim 5 bound, braid, brink, coast, costa, flank, forel, frame, limit, march, marge, plait, skirt, strip, touch, verge 6 adjoin, costae, edging, forrel, fringe, impale, margin, purfle, set off stripe 7 bordure, confine, outline, selvage 8 boundary, frontier, neighbor, surround, tressour, tressure 9 extremity, periphery 10 sidepieces 11 come close to

fluted: 5 frill

ornamental: 4 dado 5 frame 6 fringe

wall: 4 dado, ogee 7 cornice

bordering: 6 edging 8 abutting, adjacent

bore: bit, irk, tap 4 drag, gaze, hole, pall, poke, push, ream, size, tide, tire, tool 5 annoy, augur, chink, drill, eagre, ennui, gauge, prick, punch, tewel, trick, weary 6 befool, gimlet, pierce, thrust, tunnel 7 caliber, calibre, carried, crevice, opening 8 aiguille, diameter 9 annoyance, penetrate, perforate, terebrate 10 put to sleep 11 perforation 12 buttonholder

Boreas: 4 wind 7 norther

son: 5 Butes 6 Calais

borecole: 4 kail, kale

bored: 7 ennuyee(F.)

boredom: 5 ennui 6 tedium 7 fatigue 9 weariness

borer: 6 insect 7 hagfish, termite 8 shipworm

boric acid salt: 6 borate

boring: dry 4 flat 6 broach, tiring 7 tedious 8 irksome, piercing, tiresome 9 wearisome 11 displeasing, penetrating 13 uninteresting

boring tool: bit 5 auger, drill 6 gimlet, wimble

born: nee(F.) 6 innate 7 nascent, natural 8 inherent 9 delivered

dead: 9 stillborn

prematurely: 8 abortive

well: 4 free 5 noble 7 eugenic

borne (see also **bear**): 4 rode 6 narrow 7 carried, endured

by the wind: 6 eolian

boron 5 borax, boric 7 ulexite

borough: 4 burg, town 5 brush, burgh 6 burgus, castle 7 citadel, village 8 fortress, township

borrow: 4 copy, loan, take 5 adopt, steal 6 pledge, surety 7 chevise, hostage, tithing 11 frankpledge

bosc: 4 pear

boscage: 4 wood 5 grove 7 thicket

bosh: end, rot 4 joke, show, talk, tosh 5

trash 6 bushwa, figure, flaunt, humbug, trivia 8 nonsense 9 poppycock

bosky: 5 bushy, tipsy, woody 7 fuddled 11 intoxicated

Bosnian native: 4 Slav 5 Croat

bosom: 4 barm(Sc.) 5 close, heart, sinus 6 breast, cavity, recess 7 beloved, embrace, inclose 8 intimate 9 cherished 11 inclination, indentation 12 confidential

boss: bur, pad 4 baas, buhr, burr, knob, stud 5 bully, chief, empty, knosp, order, owner 6 brooch, button, direct, emboss, hollow, leader, manage, master, shield 7 capataz, cushion, foreman, hassock, headman, manager, phalera 8 director, domineer, overseer 9 supervise 10 politician, supervisor 12 protuberance 14 superintendent

African: 5 bwana

logging camp: 5 bully

political: 7 cacique

shield: 4 umbo

bossy: cow 4 calf 9 masterful 11 dictatorial, domineering

Boston: 4 game 5 waltz 8 Beantown

district: Hub 7 Back Bay

leader: 7 Brahmin

bot: 5 larva

botany: *angle:* 4 axil

cell: 5 spore

depression: 5 fovea 7 variole

botch: dub, mar, mux 4 boil, mend, mess, sore 5 bitch, bodge, spoil 6 boggle, bumble, bungle, cobble, jumble, repair 7 blunder, louse up 8 swelling 10 hodgepodge

botcher: 6 grilse, salmon 7 bungler, butcher, clouter, cobbler

both: two 7 equally

handed: 12 ambidextrous

bother: ado, ail, nag, vex 4 fuss 5 annoy, deave, tease, worry 6 badger, bustle, dither, flurry, gravel, harass, meddle, moider, molest, pester, pother, puzzle, tamper 7 confuse, disturb, perplex, trouble 8 bewilder, irritate, nuisance 10 discompose 13 inconvenience

Botswana: *capital:* 8 Gaborone

desert: 8 Kalahari

ethnic group: 5 Bantu 7 Bushmen

lake: 5 Ngami

monetary unit: 4 pula 5 thebe

river: 8 Okavango

town: Kanye 7 Mochudi

bottle: jug 4 vial 5 cruet, cruse, flask, glass, gourd, house, phial 6 bundle, carafe, carboy, corner, fiasco, flagon, magnum, vessel 7 canteen, costrel 8 building, decanter, demijohn, jeroboam, preserve, restrain 9 aryballos, aryballus, container

sealer: 6 capper

size: 4 pint, pipe 5 fifth, quart 6 magnum 8 jeroboam

small: 4 vial 5 ampul, cruet, phial 6 doruck, flacon 7 ampoule, costrel 8 decanter 11 vinaigrette

bottleneck: 7 barrier 8 blockade

bottom: bed 4 base, dale, foot, fund, holm, lees, root 5 abyss, basis, belly, dregs, floor, nadir 6 ground 7 bedrock, essence, grounds, lowland, support, surface 8 buttocks, sediment 10 foundation, groundwork 11 fundamental

bottom line: 12 crucial point, profit or loss 13 the whole story

boudoir: 4 room, cabin 7 bedroom, cabinet

bouffant, bouffante: 4 full 6 puffed 7 bulging

bough: arm, leg 4 limb, twig 5 shoot, spray, sprig 6 branch, ramage 7 gallows 8 offshoot, shoulder

bouillabaisse: 4 stew 7 chowder

bouillon: 4 soup 5 broth 8 consomme

boulder: 4 rock 5 stone

monument: 8 megalith

transported by ice: 7 erratic

boulevard: way 6 avenue, street 7 highway 12 thoroughfare

boulevardier: 4 roue 5 dandy, idler

bounce: 4 bang, blow, brag, bump, fire, jump, leap, sack 5 boast, bound, bully, carom, chuck, eject, knock, scold, thump, verve 6 spirit, spring, strike 7 address, bluster, dismiss, rebound, swagger 8 proclaim, ricochet 9 discharge, explosion, expulsion, terminate 10 resilience

bouncing: big 5 buxom, lusty, stout 7 healthy 9 excessive

bound: dap, end, hop 4 bent, bind, bond, brow, butt, dart, girt, jump, leap, mere, ramp, scud, skip, stem 5 ambit, bourn, going, limit, ready, stend, sting, tiled, vault, verge 6 border, bounce, bourne, curvet, define, domain, finish, finite, hurdle, oblige, prance, spring 7 barrier, certain, chained, closure, confine, costive, delimit, dressed, rebound, saltate, secured, trussed 8 boundary, confined, destined, enclosed, frontier, handfast, landmark, precinct, prepared, shackled 9 compelled, inhibited, obligated 10 borderland, indentured 11 apprenticed, constrained, termination 12 circumscribe 13 circumference

back: 5 carom 6 resile

by a vow: 6 votary

boundary: ahu, end, rim 4 dole, dool, edge, line, mear, meer, mere, meta, mete, term, wall 5 ambit, bourn, fence, hedge, limit, march, metae, mound, verge 6 border, bourne, define 7 barrier,

bounder, termini(pl.), environs 8 frontier, precinct, terminus 9 demarcate, perimeter 11 termination 13 circumference

bounder: cad, cur 4 boor, rake, roue

boundless: 4 vast 6 untold 7 endless, eternal 8 infinite 9 limitless, unlimited 10 immoderate, unconfined, unmeasured 11 illimitable, measureless 12 immeasurable, interminable

bountiful: 4 good, lush, rich 5 ample 6 freely, lavish 7 liberal, profuse 8 abundant, generous 9 bounteous, plenteous, plentiful 10 munificent

bounty: 4 boon, gift, meed 5 award, bonus, grant, valor, worth 6 reward, virtue 7 largess, premium, present, prowess, subsidy 8 goodness, gratuity, kindness 9 allowance 10 generosity, liberality, recompense 11 beneficence, munificence

Bounty captain: 5 Bligh

bouquet, boquet: 4 aura, odor, posy 5 aroma, cigar, posey, spray 7 corsage, nosegay 9 fragrance 10 compliment 11 boutonniere

bourgeois: 6 common, stupid 7 boorish, burgher 8 mediocre 9 hidebound 12 capitalistic, conservative

bourn, bourne: 4 brook 6 stream 7 rivulet

bout: job 4 turn 5 booze, essay, fight, match, round, set-to, siege, spell, trial 6 attack, fracas 7 attempt, carouse, circuit, contest, debauch, outside, without 8 conflict 10 knobkerrie

drinking: bat 4 bust, toot 5 binge, spree 6 bender 7 carouse

boutique: 4 shop

boutonniere: 7 bouquet 10 buttonhole

bovine: bos, cow 4 bull, calf, dull, neat, slow, zebu 5 bison, steer 6 oxlike 7 patient, taurine 8 longhorn, sluggish

hybrid: 4 mule 6 catalo

genus: bos

bow: arc, nod, tie 4 arch, beck, bend, bent, duck, fold, knot, prow, stem, turn, wend 5 binge, conge, crush, curve, defer, kneel, noued, stoop, yield 6 archer, assent, bauble, buckle, curtsy, fiddle, ribbon, salaam, submit, swerve, weapon 7 depress, incline, inflict, rainbow 8 crescent, greeting 9 obeisance, prostrate 10 capitulate 11 buckle under

facing sea: 4 atry

of ship: 4 beak, prow, stem

oriental: 5 salam 6 salaam

toward: 5 afore

wood for: yew

bow-shaped: 6 arcate

bowdlerize: 6 censor, screen 9 expurgate

bowed: 4 bent 5 kneed 6 arcate, curved 7 bulging

bowels: gut 5 belly, colon 8 entrails 10 compassion 11 disembowels, eviscerates

bower: 4 jack, nook 5 abode, arbor, joker, knave 6 anchor 7 berceau, chamber, cottage, embower, enclose, pergola, retreat, shelter

bowfin: 4 amia 6 lawyer 7 grindle, mudfish

bowie: tub 4 bowl, cask, pail 5 knife

bowl: cap, cup, pan 4 coup 5 arena, basin, bowie, depas, phila, rogan 6 beaker, crater, syphus, tureen, vessel 7 stadium, whiskin

bowlegged: 5 bandy 6 curved 9 misshapen

bowler: hat 5 derby 6 kegler 8 trundler

bowling: 7 tenpins

division: 5 frame

pin: 7 ninepin, skittle

place: 5 alley

score: 5 spare 6 strike

bowman: 5 cupid 6 archer

box: bin, lug, pix, pyx 4 arca, cage, caja, case, cist, crib, cuff, cyst, loge, pack, scob, seat, slap, slug, spar, stow, till, tray 5 barge, boist, buist, buxus, caddy, chest, clout, crate, fight, hutch, punch, shrub, stall, trunk, TV set 6 arcana(pl.), buffet, bunker, carton, casket, coffin, hopper, shrine, strike 7 arcanum, cabinet, caisson, casquet, cassone, confine, enclose, fostell, hanaper, package, trummel 9 container, fisticuff 10 receptacle

alms: 4 arca

ammunition: 7 caisson 9 bandoleer, bandolier

document: 7 hanaper

tea: 8 canister

box office: 4 gate 6 income 8 receipts

boxcar: 7 carrier

boxer: dog, hat, pug 5 champ 6 bantam 7 bruiser, fighter, sparrer 8 pugilist 11 heavyweight

hand covering: 5 cesti, glove 6 cestus

boxing: 4 bout 5 match 8 pugilism 10 fisticuffs 13 prize-fighting

blow: jab 5 feint, punch

knockout: TKO

boxwood: 4 tree 5 seron

boy: bub, lad, son, tad 4 chap, nino(Sp.), page, puer(L.) 5 buddy, chabo, child, gamin, knave, rogue, valet, youth 6 garcon, nipper, rascal, shaver, urchin 7 gossoon, servant 8 henchboy 9 shaveling, stripling, youngster

boy friend: 4 beau 5 beaux(pl.), lover 6 steady 8 paramour 9 inamorato 10 sweetheart

boycott: 4 shun 5 avoid, debar 9 blackball 10 ostracized

brabble: 5 argue 7 chatter, quarrel

brace: leg, tie, two 4 bind, case, frap, gird, mark, pair, prop, stay 5 nerve, strut 6 clench, couple, crutch, fasten, fathom, splint 7 embrace, refresh, stiffen, support 8 buttress, encircle 9 reinforce, stimulate, suspender 10 strengthen 11 mantelpiece

bracelet: 4 band, ring 5 chain, charm, slave 6 armlet, bangle, grivna 7 armilla, circlet, manacle, poignet 8 handcuff 10 calombigas

bracer: 5 drink, tonic 6 breeze 9 stimulant

brachyuran: 4 crab 10 crustacean

bracing: 5 crisp, quick, tonic 10 salubrious 11 stimulating 12 invigorating 13 strengthening

bracken: 4 fern 5 plaid

bracket: 4 join 5 brace, class, level, shelf, strut 6 corbel, couple, sconce 7 console, fixture, spotted 8 category, speckled 9 merganser

brackish: 5 foist, salty 6 bracky, saline 7 saltish 8 nauseous 11 distasteful

bract: 5 glume, palea, palet 6 spadix, spathe

brad: pin 4 nail 5 rivet, sprig

brag: 4 blaw, blow, crow, defy, huff, yelp 5 bluff, boast, flird, preen, strut, vaunt 6 bounce, splore 7 display, gauster, roister, swagger 8 braggart, flourish, pretense, threaten 9 gasconade 11 rodomontade

braggadocio: 7 boaster 8 braggart, rodomont 9 swaggerer 10 cockalorum, pretension

braggart: 4 brag 5 boast 6 blower, crower, gasbag, gascon, potgun 7 boaster, cracker, ruffler, windbag 8 bangster, blowhard, fanfaron, rodomont 9 loudmouth, renommist 10 burgullian 11 braggadocio, rodomontade

Bragi's wife: 4 Idun 6 Ithunn

Brahma: 5 Hindu 7 creator
first woman created by: 6 Ahalya

Brahman: 4 zebu 5 Aryan, Hindu, 6 priest, pundit 9 Bostonian
land grant: 5 sasan
precept: 5 sutra, sutta
title: aya

Brahmin: 7 egghead 8 highbrow 12 intellectual

braid: cue 4 band, jerk, lace, plat, trim 5 brede, fancy, freak, jiffy, lacet, onset, plait, pleat, queue, start, tress, trick, twine, vomit, weave 6 bobbin, border, cordon, moment, plight, ribbon, sennet, snatch, string 7 caprice, entwine, upbraid 8 brandish, ornament, reproach, soutache, trimming 9 deceitful, interlace 10 interweave
gold and silver: 5 orris

hemp: 5 tagal
knotted: 5 lacet

brain: mad 4 bean, harn(Sc.), mind, utac, wits 5 skull 6 psyche 7 furious 8 cerebrum(L.), computer 9 intellect
box: pan 5 skull 7 cranium
layer: 4 obex 6 cortex
membrane: 4 tela 8 meninges
operate on: 6 trepan
orifice: 4 lura
part: 4 aula 8 cerebrum 10 encephalon 11 pericranium
passage: 4 iter
pert. to: 8 cerebral 10 cerebellar, encephalic
tumor: 6 glioma
white matter: pia 4 alba, dura

brain trust: 5 panel 7 council 8 advisers

brainchild: 4 opus, work 9 invention

brainless: 5 silly 6 stupid 7 foolish, witless 11 thoughtless

brainstorm: 4 idea 11 inspiration

brake: 4 cage, curb, drag, fern, rack, slow, trap 5 block, check, copse, delay, deter, stop, snare, vomit 6 bridle, harrow, hinder, retard 7 dilemma, thicket 9 brushwood

bramble: 5 brier, thorn 6 bumble 10 cloudberry

brambly: 5 spiny 6 thorny 7 prickly

bran: 5 treat 6 cereal, chisel

branch: arm, bow, 4 brog, bush, chat, fork, limb, part, rame, rami, snag, spur, stem, twig 5 bough, creek, ramus, shoot, spray, sprig, vimen, withe 6 divide, member, outlet, raddle, ramage, ramify, stolon, stream 7 diverge, tendril 8 district, offshoot 10 department 11 bifurcation 12 ramification
angle of: 4 axil
of nerves: 4 rami(pl.) 5 ramus

branched: 6 forked, ramate, ramose 7 cladose

branchia: 4 gill

brand: 4 birn, blot, burn, flaw, kind, mark, sear, smit, sort 5 buist, stain, stamp, sword, taint, torch 6 stigma 8 flambeau 9 cauterize, character, trademark 10 stigmatize
on stolen cattle: 4 duff
sheep: 4 smit

brandish: 4 dart, show, wave 5 bless, braid, shake, swing, wield 6 flaunt, hurtle 7 flutter, glitter, swagger, trot out, vibrate 8 flourish 9 coruscate, irradiate

brandling: 4 parr 9 earthworm

brandy: 4 marc 5 bingo 6 cognac 11 aguardiente(Sp.)
and soda: peg
cocktail: 7 sidecar, stinger 9 alexander
mastic: 4 raki 5 rakee
plum: 9 slivovitz

brannigan: 5 brawl, spree **6** bender, ruckus **10** falling out **11** altercation

brant: 4 rout **5** erect, goose, proud, quink, sheer, steep **7** steeply **8** straight

brash: 4 bold, rash **5** brazen, hasty, saucy, storm **6** attack **7** brittle, forward **8** cocksure, impudent, tactless **9** irascible **11** thoughtless **12** presumptuous

brass: 4 cash **5** alloy, money, nerve **6** brazen **7** officer **9** impudence, insolence **10** effrontery

brass hat (army slang): **7** general, officer **8** superior

brass tacks: 5 facts **10** essentials

brassard, brassart: 5 badge **6** bracer **7** armband

brassbound: set **5** rigid **10** inflexible

brassica: 4 cole, rape **6** turnip

brassy: 4 bold **6** aerose, brazen **8** impudent

brat: bib, imp **4** film, scum **5** apron, bairn, bilsh, child, cloak **6** infant, mantle, urchin **7** garment **8** clothing **9** offspring

bravado: 4 pomp **5** brave, pride, storm **6** bravor, hector **7** bluster, bombast, bravade, bravery, swagger **9** gasconade

brave: 4 bold, braw(Sc.), dare, defy, face, fine, game, good, prow **5** adorn, boast, bravo, bully, gutsy, hardy, manly, Roman, stout, vaunt **6** breast, chin-up, daring, heroic, manful, plucky **7** bravado, gallant, soldier, swagger, valiant, venture, warrior **8** cavalier, defiance, embolden, fearless, intrepid, stalwart, superior, valorous, virtuous **9** challenge, dauntless, excellent, undaunted **10** courageous **11** venturesome **12** stouthearted

Brave New World author: 6 Huxley

bravery: 4 grit **5** valor **6** spirit, valour **7** bravado, bravura, courage, heroism **8** boldness **9** fortitude, gallantry, gentleman, hardihood

bravo: ole(Sp.), rah **4** thug, viva **5** brave, bully **6** bandit, Indian **7** bravado, villain **8** applause, assassin **9** cutthroat, desperado

brawl: din, row **4** clem, fray, riot **5** broil, fight, melee, revel, scold **6** affray, bicker, fracas, habble, revile, rumpus, shindy, strife, tumult, uproar **7** brabble, discord, dispute, quarrel, scuffle, wrangle **8** complain, squabble **10** contention, donnybrook, free-for-all **11** altercation, disturbance

brawling: 5 noisy **7** blatant **9** clamorous **10** clamourous, vociferous **11** quarrelsome

brawn: 4 boar **5** flesh **6** fatten, muscle **8** strength **10** headcheese

brawny: 5 beefy **6** fleshy, robust, sinewy, strong, sturdy **7** callous **8** muscular, powerful, stalwart

bray: cry, mix, rub **4** beat, rout, tool **5** grind, noise, pound **6** bruise, heehaw, outcry, pestle, thrash, whinny

brazen: 4 bold, pert **5** brass, harsh, sassy **6** brassy **7** callous, forward **8** immodest, impudent, insolent, metallic **9** shameless

Brazil: *capital:* **8** Brasilia

city: **5** Belem, Natal **6** Cuiaba, Macapa, Maceio, Manaus, Santos **7** Aracaju, Goiania, Sao Luis **8** Boa Vista, Curitiba, Sao Paulo **10** Pernambuco **12** Rio de Janeiro

coffee plantation: **7** fazenda

dance: **5** samba **6** maxixe **9** bossa nova

discoverer: **6** Cabral

drink: **5** assai

emperor: **6** Pedro I **7** Pedro II

estuary: **4** Para

falls: **6** Iguacu **11** Paulo Afonso

fiber: **4** imbe

fish: **8** arapaima

forest: **5** matta, selva

grasslands: **6** campos

Indian: **4** Anta **5** Arara, Bravo, Carib, Guana **6** Arawak, Caraja, Tupian **7** Tariana **8** Araquaju, Botocudo

island: **6** Maraca, Marajo **7** Caviana, Mexiana

measure: pe **4** moio, pipa, sack, vara **5** braca, fanga, legoa, milha, passo, tonel **6** canada, covado, cuarta, league, quarto, tarefa **7** alquier, garrafa **8** alqueire **9** pollegada, quartilho

monkey: sai **6** miriki **9** belzebuth

monetary unit: **4** reis **5** conto, dolra **7** centavo, milreis **8** cruzeiro

mountain: Mar **5** Geral **6** Acarai, Orgaos, Parima **7** Paracis **8** Estrondo, Roncador, Tombador **10** Tumuc-Humac

palm: **4** jara **5** assai, inaja, tucum **6** babaca, jupati **7** babassu, cassava **9** barriguda

paste: **7** guarana

plant: **4** imbe, para, yage, yaje **5** caroa **7** ayapana, seringa **9** jaborandi

plateau: **8** planalto

promontory: **4** frio

river: **4** Para, Paru **5** Negro, Purus, Verde, Xingu **6** Amazon, Parana **7** Madeira, Tapajos, Uruguay **8** Paraguay, Parnaiba **9** Tocantins **12** Sao Francisco

rubber: ule **4** hule, Para **6** caucho

seaport: Rio **5** Belem, Natal **6** Recife, Santos **7** Pelotas, Vitoria **8** Salvador **9** Fortaleza; Rio Grande **11** Porto Alegre

state: **4** Acre, Para **5** Bahia, Ceara, Goias, Piaui **6** Parana **7** Alagoas, Sergipe, Paraiba **8** Amazonas, Maranhao, Sao Paulo **10** Mato Grosso, Pernambuco **11** Minas Gerais **13** Espirito Santo, Santa

Catarina 14 Rio Grande do Sul 16 Rio
Grande do Norte

tree: apa, ule 4 anda, assu, uhle 5 araca,
tingi 6 biriba, brauna, satine 7 araroba,
becuiba, gomavel, paraiba, seringa, wallaba 8 bakupari 10 barbatimao, dal
guarabu

weight: bag 4 onca 5 libra 6 arroba, oitava 7 arratel, quilate, quintal 8 tonelada

wood: 6 embuia 8 kingwood

breach: gap 4 chap, flaw, gool, rent, rift 5
brack, breck, chasm, cleft, crack, pause,
split, wound 6 bruise, harbor, hernia,
hiatus, inroad, schism 7 assault, blemish, dispute, fissure, opening, quarrel,
rupture 8 breaking, fraction, fracture,
interval, trespass 9 violation 10 disruption, infraction 12 infringement, interruption 14 nonfulfillment 16 misunderstanding

of etiquette: 4 gaffe 8 solecism

breach pin: 4 tige

bread: bun 4 diet, fare, food, loaf, pone,
roll 5 dough, money 6 staple 7 aliment,
bannock(Sc.) 10 livelihood, sustenance

boiled: 4 cush 6 panada

browned: 5 toast 6 sippet 7 crouton

communion: 4 azym, host 5 azyme, wafer

crust: 4 rind

dry and crisp: 4 rusk 8 zwieback 10 melba toast

leavened: 5 kisra 6 cocket

Passover: 5 matzo 6 matzoh, matzos(pl.),
matzot(pl.) 7 matzoth(pl.)

pert. to: 6 panary

unleavened: 4 azym 5 azyme 6 matzos 7
bannock, matzoth 8 afikomen

bread-and-butter: 5 basic 8 everyday,
ordinary

pert. to: 6 living 7 support 8 daily job 12
note of thanks

bread spread: jam 4 oleo 5 jelly 6 butter
9 margarine, marmalade 13 oleomargarine

breadth: 4 span 5 brede, scope, width 6
extent 8 diameter, distance, latitude 9
amplitude, dimension

breadwinner: 6 earner, worker

break: gap 4 boon, bust, dash, hint, knap,
pick, plow, rend, rent, rift, rive, ruin,
rush, slip, snap, stop, tear 5 alter,
blank, burst, cleft, crack, craze, frush,
lapse, pluck, sever, smash, wound 6
bruise, change, cleave, defeat, hiatus,
impair, lacuna, pierce 7 blunder, caesura, crackle, crevice, crumble, destroy,
disable, dispart, disrupt, exhaust, fissure, lacunae(pl.), opening, respite, rupture, shatter 8 caesurae, fraction, fracture, interval, separate 9 interrupt,
penetrate 10 invalidate 12 interruption

14 discontinuance

down: 7 debacle, failure 8 collapse 9 cataclysm 10 catabolism

in: 5 stave, train 7 intrude 8 initiate 9
interrupt 13 enter forcibly

of day: 4 dawn, morn 5 sunup 7 morning

out: 5 erupt 6 escape 10 bring forth

up: 4 part 5 split 7 disband, disrupt 8
disperse, dissolve, separate 9 take apart
10 put a stop to

breakable: 7 brittle, bruckle, friable 8
delicate

breakbone fever: 6 dengue

breaker: 4 surf, wave 6 billow, comber,
roller

breakwater: cob, dam 4 cobb, dike, mole,
pier, pile, quay 5 jetty 6 refuge 11 obstruction

bream: tai 4 fish, scup 5 broom 7 sunfish

sea: 4 shad 6 sargus

breast: 4 crop 5 bosom, brave, chest 6
thorax 9 encounter

ornament: 8 pectoral

breastbone: 6 sterna(pl.) 7 sternum, xiphoid 9 gladiolus

pert to: 7 sternal

breastplate: *armor:* 4 urim 6 gorget, lorica, shield 7 poitrel, thummin 8 poitrail

ecclesiastical: 4 urim

breastwork: 4 fort 5 redan 7 brattle, bulwark, parapet, rampart 10 forecastle

breath: 4 ande, gasp, hint, huff, life, pant,
pech, puff, sigh, wind 5 pause, scent,
smell, vapor, whiff 6 breeze, pneuma 7
halitus, instant, respite 10 exhalation

breathe: 4 ande, live, pant, pech, puff,
sigh 5 exist, speak, utter 6 aspire, exhale, inhale, wheeze 7 afflate, emanate,
respire, suspire

hard: 4 gasp, pant

breather: 4 rest 5 break, pause, truce 6
recess 7 respite 9 armistice

breathing: 5 alive 7 gasping 9 spiration
11 respiration

difficult: 7 dyspnea 8 dyspnoea

harsh: 4 rale

impairment of: 9 emphysema

orifice: 4 nose, pore 5 mouth, nares 7
nostril 8 spiracle

smooth: 4 lene

sound: 4 rale 5 snore, snort 7 stridor

breathless: 4 dead 5 stale, tense 6 stuffy
10 motionless

Brecht (Bertolt): *play:* 7 Galileo 8 Man
Is Man 9 Mahagonny 13 Mother Courage 15 Threepenny Opera

breech: 4 bore, butt, doup 5 block 7 drod-
dum 8 buttocks, derriere 9 posterior

breeches: 5 chaps, jeans, levis 8 jodhpurs,
knickers, trousers 10 pantaloons

breeching: 4 rope 7 harness

breed: ilk 4 bear, kind, race, rear, sort,

type 5 beget, brood, caste, cause, class, hatch, raise, stock, train 6 create, strain 7 educate, nourish, produce, progeny, species, variety 8 engender, instruct, multiply 9 offspring, originate, propagate 10 generation

breeding: 6 origin 7 culture, descent 8 behavior, civility, training 9 education, gestation 10 deportment, extraction 11 development, instruction

science: 8 eugenics

breeze: air, zip 4 aura, blow, flaw, gale, gust, pirr, stir, wind 5 blast, rumor, waltz 6 breath, report, zephyr 7 freshen, quarrel, whisper 11 disturbance

land: 6 terral

breezy: 4 airy 5 brisk, fresh, windy 6 airish 9 easygoing, vivacious

bressumer: 4 beam 6 girder, lintel 7 support

breve: 4 bird, mark, note, writ 5 brief, order 6 letter 7 compose, precept 8 syllable

brevet: 6 confer 9 promotion 10 commission

breviary: 4 ordo 6 digest, portas 7 coucher, epitome, summary 8 abstract 10 compendium 11 abridgement

brevity: 8 laconism 9 briefness, shortness, terseness 11 conciseness 12 succinctness

brew: ale, mix 4 beer, boil, loom, make, plot, pour 5 hatch 6 devise, dilute, foment, gather, liquor, seethe 7 concoct, incline, prepare 8 beverage, contrive 9 potpourri 10 miscellany

brewer: *grain:* rye 4 corn, malt 6 barley

vat: tun

yeast: 4 barm 6 leaven

briar: saw 4 pipe

bribe: fee, fix, oil, rob, sop, tip 4 bait, gift, hire, meed 5 bonus, cuddy, graft, offer, steal, sugar, tempt 6 buy off, extort, grease, payola, suborn 7 corrupt 8 gratuity 10 allurement

bric-a-brac: 5 curio, vertu, virtu 7 bibelot 11 knickknacks

brick: 4 pave, tile 5 block, quarl, stone 6 fellow, quarle

handler: 6 hacker

oven: 4 kiln

sun-baked: bat 5 adobe

tray: hod

vitrified: 7 clinker

wood: nog 4 dook 6 scutch

bridal: 7 nuptial, wedding 8 espousal, marriage

bride: bar, tie 4 loop, rein, rose 6 bridle, kallah

bridesmaid: 9 attendant

bridge: way 4 game, link, pons, pont, span 5 cross 6 ponton 7 auction, bascule, connect, pontoon, trestle, viaduct 8 contract, traverse 9 alcantara, gangplank

combination: 6 tenace

forerunner: 5 whist

lever: 7 bascule

of musical instrument: 5 magas 10 ponticello

part: 4 arch, deck, pier 5 cable, pylon 7 caisson 8 spandrel

player: 4 east, west 5 north, south

pontoon plank: 5 chess

score: leg

support: 4 pier 5 truss

term: bid, bye, leg, set 4 book, game, pass, ruff, slam, suit, void 5 dummy, raise, trick, trump 6 double, renege, revoke, rubber 7 finesse, jump bid, no-trump, overbid 8 contract, redouble 9 grandslam, overtrick, part score, singleton 10 little slam, vulnerable

bridle: bit 4 curb, rein, rule 5 brake, brank, bride, check, guard, guide, strut 6 direct, govern, halter, master, simper, subdue 7 blinder, control, repress, snaffle, swagger 8 restrain, suppress 9 restraint

noseband: 6 musrol 8 cavesson

brief: few 4 curt, life, writ 5 blurb, breve, charm, pithy, quick, short, terse 6 abrupt, common, letter 7 abridge, compact, compose, concise, invoice, laconic, mandate, outline, precept, summary 8 breviate, condense, fleeting, succinct, syllabus 9 catalogue, condensed, ephemeral, memoranda(pl.), prevalent 10 abridgment, compendium, memorandum, transitory 11 compendious 12 condensation

briefness: 7 brevity

brier, briar: 4 barb, pipe 5 erica, thorn 6 smilax

briery: 5 sharp, spiny

brig: 4 boat, jail 6 prison, vessel 8 stockade 10 guardhouse

brigand: 5 thief 6 bandit, pirate, robber 7 cateran, ladrone, soldier 8 marauder, picaroon 10 highwayman

bright: apt, gay 4 fine, glad, rosy 5 acute, aglow, alert, anime, beamy, clear, fresh, gemmy, light, lucid, nitid, quick, riant, sharp, smart, sunny, vivid, witty 6 cheery, clever, florid, garish, limpid, lively, lucent, orient 7 forward, fulgent, radiant, ringing, shining 8 animated, cheerful, colorful, flashing, gleaming, luminous, lustrous, splendid, splendor 9 brilliant, cloudless, effulgent, favorable, refulgent, sparkling 10 brightness, epiphanous, glistening, glittering, precocious 11 illustrious, intelligent, resplendent, transparent

brighten: 4 gild 5 cheer, clear, light, liven, shine 6 cantle, engild, polish 7 animate, burnish, enliven, furbish, lighten 8 illumine 9 irradiate

brightness: 5 eclat, flame, gleam, gloss, nitor, sheen 6 acumen, bright, fulgor, luster 7 clarity, fulgour, sparkle 8 splendor 9 clearness 10 brilliance, effulgence 13 distinguished

brilliance: 4 fame 5 eclat, flame, glory 8 keenness, radiance, splendor 10 brightness, effulgence

brilliant: gay 4 good, keen, sage, wise 5 breme 6 bright, clever, signal 7 eminent, erudite, flaming, learned, radiant, shining 8 dazzling, glorious, luminous 9 effective, prismatic, refulgent, sparkling 10 glittering 11 prismatical, resplendent 13 distinguished

brim: lip, rim, rut, sea 4 edge 5 bluff, brink, marge, ocean, verge, water 6 border, margin 8 copulate, strumpet 9 periphery

brimming: big 4 full

brimstone: 6 sulfur, virago 7 sulphur 8 spitfire

brindled: 5 tawny 7 branded, flecked 8 streaked

brine: sea 4 main, salt 5 ocean, tears 6 pickle 8 marinade

preserve in: 4 corn, cure, salt

brine shrimp: 7 artemia

bring: 4 bear, sell, take 5 carry, fetch 6 convey, deduce 7 conduce, convert, procure, produce 8 accompany, transport

about: 5 cause 6 create, effect 7 achieve 10 accomplish

back: 6 effect, recall, return, revive 7 produce, restore 8 occasion, retrieve, transact 9 instigate 10 consummate

forth: ean(Sc.) 4 bear 5 educe, hatch, incur 6 adduce, beteem 7 produce

forward: 7 present 9 introduce

in: 4 earn 5 usher, yield 6 import, report, return 9 introduce

near to: 6 appose

off: 7 achieve, succeed 8 complete

on: 6 induce

out: 7 display, publish

to: 11 resuscitate

to earth: 4 land

to light: 6 elicit, reveal 7 unearth 8 disclose, discover

to naught: 4 dash 6 negate 7 confute 9 frustrate

together: 4 join 5 unite 7 compile 11 consolidate

up: 4 rear, stop 5 nurse, raise, refer, train, vomit 6 broach 7 educate 11 regurgitate

up to date: 4 post 5 brief 6 inform

brink: end, eve, lip, rim, sea 4 bank, brim,
edge, foss 5 marge, shore, verge 6 border, margin

briny: 5 brack, ocean, salty 6 saline

brioche: 4 roll 6 stitch 7 cushion, pudding, savarin

Briseis' lover: 8 Achilles

brisk: gay 4 busy, fast, keen, pert, racy, spry, yern 5 agile, alert, alive, budge, crisp, fresh, frisk, peart, perky, quick, sharp, smart, yerne 6 active, adroit, breezy, cocket, crouse, lively, nimble, snappy 7 allegro 8 animated, friskful, spirited 9 energetic, sprightly, vivacious 11 stimulating 12 effervescing

bristle: awn 4 barb, hair, seta, tela 5 anger, birse, brush, parch, preen, setae, strut, toast 6 chaeta, palpus, ruffle, setula 7 chaetae, setulae, stubble

surgical: 4 seta 5 seton

bristled: 7 horrent 9 echinate

bristlelike: 5 setal 8 setiform

bristling: 5 rough 6 hispid, horrid, setose, thorny 7 horrent, scrubby

brit, britt: 5 sprat 7 herring 10 crustacean

Britain: See **England**

British Columbia: *capital:* 8 Victoria

city: 6 Duncan 7 Kitimat, Nanaimo, Quesnel 8 Kamloops, Smithers 9 Vancouver

explored by: 4 Cook 5 Drake 10 Juan de Fuca

Indian: 5 Haida 7 Shuswap

island: 9 Vancouver

lake: 6 Babine, Chilko, Fraser, Muncho, Stuart 7 Thutade

mountain: 5 Coast, Rocky 7 Cariboo, Purcell, Selkirk 8 Monashee

river: 4 Nass 5 Liard, Peace 6 Fraser, Skeena 7 Parsnip 8 Columbia

strait: 6 Hecate

Britomartis: 7 Artemis 8 Dictynna

mother: 5 Carme

brittle: 4 frow, weak 5 brash, candy, crisp, crump, eager, frail, frowy, frush, short 6 crispy, crumpy, feeble, fickle, frough, infirm, slight 7 brickle, bruckle, fragile, friable, froughy 8 delicate, snappish 9 breakable, crumbling, frangible, irritable 10 perishable

broach: air, awl, cut, pin, rod, tap 4 open, ouch, shed, spit, spur, stab, veer, vent 5 begin, dress, drift, prick, rimer, spool, voice 6 boring, brooch, launch, pierce, reamer 7 bring up, enlarge, publish, spindle, suggest, violate 8 approach, broacher, deflower, incision 9 introduce 11 perforation

broad: 4 deep, free, vast, wide 5 ample, beamy, large, plain, roomy, thick, woman 6 coarse, risqué 7 evident, general, grivois, liberal, obvious, platoid 8 grivoise, spacious, tolerant 9 capacious, expansive, extensive, outspoken 12 unrestrained 3 comprehensive

broad-footed: 8 platypod

broad-minded: 7 lenient, liberal 8 catholic, tolerant

broadbill: 4 bird, gaya, raya 5 scaup 8 shoveler 9 swordfish

broadcast: sow 4 seed, send 5 radio, strew 6 spread 7 declare, publish, scatter 8 announce, televise, transmit 9 advertise

broadside: 4 bill 5 salvo 7 barrage 8 circular

broadsword: 4 bill, kris 6 glaive, spatha 7 cutlass, Ferrara 8 claymore, scimitar

brobdingnagian: big 4 huge 5 giant 8 colossal, gigantic

brocade: 5 cloth 6 broche, kincab 8 baudekin 9 baldachin

brocard: 4 gibe, rule 5 maxim, moral 6 speech 7 sarcasm 8 aphorism 9 principle

brochure: 4 book 5 tract 8 pamphlet, treatise

brocket: 4 deer, pita, stag 5 brock 7 spitter

brogue: 4 hose, shoe 5 fraud, trick 6 accent, brogan 7 dialect 8 trousers

broil: row 4 burn, char, feud, fray, heat 5 alarm, brawl, grill, melee, scrap 6 affray, birsle, braise, splore, tumult 7 brulyie(Sc.), contest, discord, dispute, embroil, garboil, quarrel 8 conflict, grillade 10 contention, dissension 11 altercation, disturbance

broiling: hot 6 torrid 8 sizzling, steaming 9 scorching 10 sweltering

broke: 4 poor 8 bankrupt 9 insolvent, penniless

broken: 4 rent, torn 5 burst, gappy, rompu(F.), rough, tamed 6 hackly, ruined, shaken 7 crushed, fracted, reduced, subdued 8 outlawed, ruptured, weakened 9 cashiered, dispersed, fractured, shattered 10 incoherent, incomplete 11 fragmentary 12 disconnected, intermittent

down: 6 shabby 7 haywire

broker: 5 agent 6 corser, dealer, factor, jobber 7 brogger, changer, courser, peddler, realtor, scalper 8 broacher, huckster, merchant 9 go-between 10 pawnbroker

brokerage: fee 4 agio 10 commission

brolly: 8 umbrella

bromide: 5 trite 8 compound, sedative 9 platitude 11 commonplace

bronco: 5 horse 6 cayuse 7 broncho, mustang 9 estrapade(Sp.)

bronco buster: 6 cowboy, ginete

Bronte: 4 Anne 5 Emily 9 Charlotte
hero: 9 Rochester 10 Heathcliff
novels: 8 Jane Eyre 16 Wuthering Heights
pen name: 9 Ellis Bell

Bronx cheer: boo 9 raspberry

bronze: aes(L.), tan 4 bust 5 alloy, brown 6 statue
film: 6 patina
gilded: 6 ormolu
nickel: 11 cupronickel
pert. to: 7 aeneous

brooch: bar, pin 4 boss, clip, ouch 5 cameo, clasp 6 fibula, plaque, shield 8 ornament 9 brochette

brood: fry, nye, set, sit 4 mope, nest, nide, race, weep 5 aerie, breed, covey, flock, group, hatch, issue, sedge, worry, young 6 cletch, clutch, family, litter, ponder 7 progeny, species 8 cogitate, incubate, meditate 9 multitude, offspring 11 contemplate

brook: run 4 bear, beck, burn, ghyl, gill, rill, rush, sike 5 abide, bayou, bourn, creek, stand 6 arroyo(Sp.), bourne, canada, endure, gutter, rindle, rivose, runlet, stream, suffer 7 comport 8 quebrada, tolerate 11 watercourse

brooklet: 4 beck, rill 6 rillet, runnel 7 rillock, rivulet 9 arroyuelo(Sp.)

broom: mop 4 fray, swab 5 besom, bream, brush, spart, sweep, whisk 8 splinter

broom plant: 5 hirse, spart 6 whisk 7 cyticus, genista, heather 8 deerweed

broomcorn millet: 5 hirse

broth: 4 bree, broo, soup 5 stock 6 brewis, jussal, jussel 7 pottage 8 bouillon, consomme, jusshell

brothel: 4 crib, stew 6 bagnio, bordel 8 bordello 10 bawdy house

brother: bub, fra, kin, pal, sib 4 mate, monk, peer 5 billy, buddy, cadet, frere(F.), friar 6 fellow, fraile, frater(L.) 7 comrade, sibling
pert. to: 9 fraternal

brotherhood: 4 gild 5 guild, lodge 6 friary 8 bratstro, sodality 10 fellowship, fraternity 11 association 13 brotherliness, companionship, confraternity

brotherly: 4 kind 6 tender 9 fraternal 12 affectionate

brougham: 8 carriage

brought up: 4 cade

brouhaha: din 5 babel, furor 6 furore, racket, rumpus, tumult 9 commotion 10 hullabaloo 11 pandemonium

brow: top 4 brae, bree, edge, mien, snab(Sc.) 5 bound, brink, crest, front, ridge, slope 8 boldness, forehead 9 acclivity, gangplank 10 effrontery 11 countenance

browbeat: 5 abash, bully 6 hector 7 depress 10 disconcert, intimidate

brown: dun, tan 4 coin, cook, dark, sear 5 dusky, penny, sedge, sepia, tawny, tenne, toast, umber 6 gloomy, russet, sennet, tanned 9 half-penny

cocoa: 6 sahara
dark: 5 sepia, umber 6 bister, bistre 9 chocolate
light: tan 4 ecru, fawn 5 beige, khaki, tenne
purple: 4 puce
red: bay 4 cuba, roan 5 henna, sepia 6 auburn, russet, sorrel 8 chestnut
yellow: 6 almond, bronze 12 butterscotch
brown Betty: 7 pudding 10 coneflower
brown study: 7 reverie 10 absorption 11 abstraction
brownie: elk, nis 4 cake 5 cooky, fairy, nisse, urisk 6 goblin, uruisg(Sc.) 9 sandpiper
brownnose: 9 sycophant
browse: 4 brut, crop, feed 5 graze 6 forage, nibble, peruse 7 dip into, pasture
bruin: 4 bear
bruise: 4 bash, bray, dent, dunt, hurt, maim, maul 5 black, break, crush, curry, delve, dinge, pound 6 batter, breach, hatter, injury, mangle, shiner 7 contuse, dammish, disable 9 pulverize, triturate
bruiser: 5 boxer 8 pugilist
bruit: din 4 fame, hint, rale, tell 5 noise, rumor, sound 6 blazon, clamor, report 7 declare, hearsay 8 intimate
brume: fog 4 haze, mist, smog 5 vapor
brumous: 5 foggy, misty 6 hiemal, sleety 7 wintery
brunette: 4 dark 5 brown, brune, gipsy, gypsy 9 swarthy
brunt: jar 4 blow, jolt 5 clash, force, onset, shock 6 attack, effort, impact 7 assault 8 outburst
brush: 4 comb, fray, skim 5 broom, clash, clean, copse, fight, graze, sweep, touch 6 badger, battle, brosse(F.), stroke 7 thicket 8 skirmish 9 brushwood, encounter, sideswipe 11 undergrowth
brushwood: 4 rone 5 brake, brush, copse, frith, scrog, scrub 6 rammel 7 coppice, thicket
brusque: 4 curt, rude 5 bluff, blunt, brusk, gruff, hasty, rough, short 6 abrupt 7 violent 8 cavalier, impolite 12 discourteous
brut: dry 6 browse
brutal: 5 cruel, feral, gross 6 carnal, coarse, savage, severe 7 bestial, beastly, brutish, caddish, inhuman 8 ruthless 9 atrocious, barbarous, ferocious, insensate
brute: 5 beast, yahoo 6 animal, savage 7 ruffian 9 scoundrel
bryophyte: 4 moss 5 plant 9 liverwort
Brython: 5 Welsh 6 Celtic 7 Cornish
god: Dea, Ler 4 Brian 5 Dylan, Lludd 8 Amaethon
goddess: Don 8 Rhiannon 9 Arianrhod
bubal: 4 topi 8 antelope

bubble: air, bub 4 bead, bell(Sc.), bleb, blob, boil, bull, dupe, foam, glob, seed, suds 5 caper, cheat, empty, slosh 6 burble, delude, seethe, trifle 7 blister, blubber, deceive, globule 8 delusive 9 pipe dream 10 effervesce 11 speculation
bubbling: gay 8 effusive 9 sparkling
buccal: 4 oral
buccaneer: 6 pirate, rifler, robber, viking 7 corsair, mariner, spoiler 8 Picaroon 10 freebooter
standard: 5 roger
Bucephalus: 5 steed 7 charger
buck: fob, ram 4 boil, butt, deer, dude, male, pass, prig, rear, soak, stag, toff, wash 5 carry, dandy, steep 6 basket, dollar, oppose, resist 7 sawbuck 8 antelope, prickett, sawhorse 9 buckwheat, pulverize
first year: 4 fawn
fourth year: 4 sore
buck up: 5 brace 7 comfort
buckaroo: 6 cowboy 8 horseman
buckboard: 8 carriage
bucket: tub 4 bail, bowk, cage, pail 5 cheat, hurry, scoop, skeel 6 bailer, barrel, drench, hoppet, situla(L.), vessel 7 swindle 8 cannikin
handle: 4 bail
molten glass: 7 cuvette
Buckeye State: 4 Ohio
buckle: bow 4 bend, curl, kink, tach, warp 5 clasp, marry, twist, yield 6 fibula(L.) 7 contend, fermail, fibulae(L.pl.), grapple 8 fastener, struggle 10 distortion
down: 5 set to 7 address, pitch in
part: 5 chape 6 tongue
under: bow 5 yield 6 cave in 10 capitulate
buckler: 4 crab 5 block 6 shield 7 rotella, roundel, shutter
buckram: 6 fabric 7 precise 10 cuckoopint, stiffening 11 muscle-bound
buckthorn: 5 rhamn 7 alatern, cascara 8 lotebush 9 alaternus, chaparral
buckwheat: 4 buck 8 sarrazin
buckwheat tree: 4 titi 6 teetee
bucolic: 4 idyl 5 local, naive, rural 6 farmer, rustic, simple 7 cowherd, ecologue 8 agrestic, herdsman, pastoral
bud: eye, gem, imp, pip 4 bulb, cion, germ, girl, grow, knop, seed 5 child, graft, scion, shoot, youth 6 button, flower, germin, sprout 7 blossom, brother, gemmule 8 bourgeon 9 germinate
arrangement: 11 aestivation
social: deb 8 debutant 9 debutante
Buddha: Foh 7 Gautama 10 Shakyamuni
cause of infinite existence: 6 nidana
center: 5 Lassa, Lhasa
chant: 6 mantra
church: 4 Tera

column: lat
disciple: 6 Ananda
doctrine: 7 trikaya
dryad: 6 Yakshi
enlightenment: 5 bodhi
evil spirit: 4 Mara
fate: 5 karma
fertility spirit: 6 Yaksha, Yakshi
festival: bon
final beatitude: 4 raga 7 nirvana
for justice: 6 dharna, dhurna
gateway: 5 toran, torii 6 torana
god: 4 deva
greater: 8 Mahayana
hatred: 4 dosa
hell: 6 Naraka
Japanese image: 8 Daibutsu
language: 4 Pali
lesser: 8 Hinayana
life cycle: 6 anicca
mendicant: 6 bhikku 7 bhikshu
monastery: 4 Tera 6 Vihara
monk: 4 lama 5 arhat, yahan, 7 poongee
  8 poonghee, poonghie, talapoin
monument: 5 stupa
mother: 4 Maya
novice: 5 goyim
paradise: 4 Jodo
passion: 4 raga
prayer: 4 mani
priest: 4 lama 7 mahatma
relic mound: 5 stupa
retribution: 5 karma
rock temple: 4 rath 5 ratha
sacred city: 5 Lassa, Lhasa
school: 5 ritsu
scripture: 5 sutra
sect: Zen 6 tendai 7 Jodo-shu
shrine: 4 tope 5 stupa 6 dagoba 7 chorten
son: 6 Rahula
spiritual leader: 4 guru 9 Dalai Lama
stupa site: 9 Amaravati
throne: 5 asana
title: 7 Mahatma
tree: 5 pipal 6 botree
will to live: 5 Tanha
buddy: boy, pal 4 chum, mate 5 crony 7
  brother, comrade 9 companion
buddy-buddy: 4 cozy 5 close 8 intimate
budge: fur 4 move, stir 5 booze, brisk,
  stiff, thief 6 jocund, liquor 8 movement
  11 nervousness
budget: bag 4 body, boot, pack, plan, roll
  5 batch, bunch, stock, store 6 bottle,
  bundle, parcel, socket, wallet 7 program
  12 accumulation
buds: 8 burgeons, dehisces
pickled: 6 capers
buff: fan, rub 4 coat 5 shine 6 addict, polish 7 leather 8 nonsense 10 enthusiast
in the: 4 nude 5 naked
buffalo: ox 5 anoa, buff, stag 5 bison, bu-

gle 6 buffle, hamper 7 caribao, caribou,
gazelle, nonplus, overawe, timarau, za-
mouse 8 bewilder 9 bamboozle, frustrate
large: 4 arna, arni 5 arnee
meat: 7 biltong
wild: 4 arna, arni 5 arnee 8 seladang
buffalo gourd: 11 calabazilla
buffalo tree: 10 rabbitwood
buffer: dog, pad 6 bumper, fender, pistol
  7 cushion
buffet: bar, bob, box 4 beat, blow, buff,
  cuff, slap, toss 5 filip, smite, stool 6
  abacus, batter, fillip, strike, strive,
  thrash 7 contend, counter, hassock 8
  credence, credenza, cupboard, lambaste
  9 footstool, sideboard 10 affliction
bufflehead: 4 duck, fool 5 clown, dunce 6
  buffle 9 merrywing
buffleheaded: 4 dull 6 simple, stupid
buffoon: dor, wag, wit 4 aper, fool, jape,
  mime, mome 5 actor, antic, buffo,
  clown, comic, drole, droll, mimer 6 harlot, jester, mummer, stooge 7 playboy 8
  balatron, gracioso, humorist, merryman, ridicule 9 harlequin 10 harlequina, hobby-horse 11 merry-andrew,
  Punchinello
bug: bog, dor 4 flaw, germ, idea, mite, wire
  5 annoy, bogey, bulge, roach 6 beetle,
  chinch, elater, insect, scheme 7 bellied,
  bugbear, forward, pompous, wiretap 8
  hemipter, hobbyist 9 conceited, hide a
  mike, hobgoblin, prominent 10 enthusiast, flashlight 11 hunchbacked
June: dor
lightning: 7 firefly
needle: 7 ranatra
bugaboo: 4 bogy, fear, goga, gogo, ogre 5
  alarm, bogey, bogie, gogga 6 bodach,
  goblin 7 bugbear, specter, spectre 8
  worricow(Sc.) 9 hobgoblin, scarecrow,
  worriecow(Sc.) 10 mumbo-jumbo
bugbane: 4 herb 9 hellebore 10 rattleroot
bugger: 4 chap 5 scamp 6 fellow, rascal
buggy (see also **carriage**): 4 cart, shay,
  trap 5 nutty 7 caboose, foolish, vehicle
  8 demented, infested, stanhope 9 gladstone
bughouse: 5 crazy, nutty 6 asylum, insane
bugle: 4 bead, horn 5 black 7 buffalo,
  bullock, clarion, trumpet
blare: 7 tanatara
call: 4 taps 6 alerte(F.), sennet, tattoo 7
  retreat 9 reveille
note: mot
yellow: iva
bugleweed: 4 mint 6 indigo
bug off: 5 leave, scram 6 go away 7 buzz
  off, get lost
build: big 4 bigg, form, make, rear 5 edify,

erect, found, frame, raise, set up, shape 6 create, graith 7 fashion 8 assemble, increase, physique 9 construct, establish, fabricate

nest: 6 nidify

up: 5 erect 7 enhance 8 increase 9 publicity 10 strengthen

builder: 5 maker 7 erector 8 tectonic 9 carpenter 11 constructor

labyrinth: 8 Daedalus

of wooden horse: 5 Epeus 6 Epeius

building: hut 4 casa(Sp.), pile 5 aedes, hotel, house 6 biggin, bottle, fabric 7 edifice, factory 8 dwelling 9 apartment, structure 10 storehouse 11 edification

addition to: ell 4 apse, wing 5 annex 6 lean-to

dilapidated: 7 rookery 8 firetrap, tenement

exhibition: 6 museum

farm: 4 barn, crib, shed, silo

gateway: 5 pylon

material: 4 iron, wood 5 brick, glass, steel 6 cement

medieval: 6 castle

part: ell 4 apse

projection: bay, ell 4 apse, wing 5 annex 6 dormer, lean-to 7 cornice

public: 5 edile 6 aedile, casino, church, museum, temple 7 capitol, library, theater 10 auditorium

rib: 9 tierceron

round: 6 rotunda

sacred: 4 fane 6 church, mosque, temple 7 edicule 8 pantheon 9 cathedral

stately: 6 castle, palace 7 edifice, mansion

bulb: bud 4 blub, corm, knob, lamp, root, seed 5 globe, onion, swell, tuber 6 bulbus, crocus 9 expansion 12 protuberance

edible: yam 4 sego 5 onion 6 garlic, potato

segment: 5 clove

bulbous: 5 round 7 swollen

bulbul: 4 bird, kala

Bulgaria: *capital:* 5 Sofia

city: 4 Ruse 5 Varna 6 Burgas, Pleven 7 Plovdiv

former kings: 5 Boris 6 Simeon 9 Ferdinand

monetary unit: lev 8 stotinka

mountain: 7 Balkans, Rhodope

peak: 6 Musala

province: 5 Vidin 6 Lovech, Pernik, Shumen, Sliven, Vratsa, Yambol 7 Gagrovo, Razgrad, Smolyan

river: 5 Mesta 6 Danube, Struma 7 Maritsa

weight: oka, oke 5 tovar

bulge: bag, bug, jut 4 bump, cask, hump, knob, lump 5 belly, bilge, bloat, bouge, flask, pouch, swell 6 billow, cockle, di-

late, extend, pucker, wallet 7 blister, distend 8 protrude, swelling 9 convexity, gibbosity 10 projection 11 indentation 12 protuberance

bulging: 4 full 5 bombe, bowed, pudgy 6 convex 7 gibbous 8 bouffant

bulk: 4 body, heap, hold, hulk, hull, lump, mass, pile, size 5 cargo, gross, might, power, stall, swell 6 expand, extent, figure, volume 7 bigness 8 majority, quantity 9 aggregate, dimension, largeness, magnitude 11 massiveness

bulkhead: 5 check 7 battery 9 partition, structure

bulky: big 5 burly, gross, large, stout 6 clumsy, sturdy 7 hulking, massive, weighty 8 unwieldy 9 corpulent, policeman, ponderous

bull: cop 4 apis, jest, male, seal, slip, toro(Sp.), zebu 5 bobby, boner, drink, edict, error 6 bovine, letter, peeler, taurus(L.) 8 cajolery, document, flattery, nonsense 9 detective, policeman, quadruped 10 zapaterito(Sp.)

angry: 5 gorer

castrated: 4 stot 5 steer 7 bullock

half man: 8 minotaur

hornless: 5 doddy 6 doddie

pert. to: 7 taurine

young: 4 stot(Sc.) 5 stirk 7 bullock

bull-like: taurine

Bull Run: *battle:* 8 Manassas

hero: Lee

bull session: 4 talk 7 rapping 10 discussion

bulla: 4 bleb, case, seal 5 blain 7 vesicle

bullate: 8 puckered

bulldoze: cow, dig, ram 5 bully, force, push, scoop 6 coerce, menace, pistol 7 browbeat, restrain, threaten 10 intimidate

bulldozer: 5 bully 6 grader 7 machine

bullet: 4 ball, lead, shot, slug 5 hurry 6 pellet, sinker, tracer 7 missile

diameter: 7 caliber

fake: 6 pellet

bulletin: 4 memo 6 notice, poster, report 7 program 9 statement 11 publication 12 announcement

bullfight cheer: ole

bullfighter: 6 torero 7 matador, picador 8 capeador, matadore, toreador

foot: 6 torero

mounted: 8 toreador

bullfinch: alp, olp 4 monk, nope, olph, pope 5 hedge

bullheaded: 6 stupid 8 stubborn 9 obstinate 10 headstrong

bullion: bar 5 ingot, metal 6 billot

bullock: 4 stot 5 bugle, steer, stirk 6 bovine 9 quadruped

bull's eye: 6 target

bully: 4 boat, boss, fine, good, huff, mate, punk 5 brave, bravo, great, tough 6 bounce, harass, hector, jovial, menace, tyrant 7 bluster, bouncer, bullock, darling, dashing, gallant, gauster, huffcap, roister, ruffian 8 bangster, barrater, barrator, browbeat, bulldoze, domineer, frampler, harasser 9 blusterer, bulldozer, companion, excellent, scrimmage 10 burgullian, intimidate, sweetheart

bulrush: 4 reed, rush, tule 5 sedge 6 bumble 7 cattail, papyrus, scirpus

bulwark: 4 bail, fort, wall 5 fence, mound 6 defend, shield 7 bastion, defence, defense, parapet, protect, rampart 10 breakwater, stronghold 12 propugnacula(L.pl.) 13 propugnaculum(L.)

bum: beg, din 4 hobo, idle 5 drink, drone, idler, mooch, tramp 6 frolic, guzzle, sponge 7 guzzler 8 vagaband

bumble: bee 4 veil 5 botch, drone, idler 6 beadle, bungle, jumble, muffle 7 bittern, blunder, bramble, bulrush, bungler

bummer: 4 flop 7 bad trip, washout 12 bad situation

bump: hit, jar 4 bang, blow, bust, jolt, lump, oust, thud, whop 5 bulge, clash, knock, thump 6 bounce, demote, nodule, strike 7 collide, pothole, replace 8 swelling 9 downgrade, hip thrust 12 protuberance

bump into: 4 meet 7 collide 8 come upon 9 encounter, run across, sideswipe

bump off: 4 do in, kill 6 murder, rub out 7 put away 9 liquidate

bumper: 4 fine 5 glass, large, guard 6 buffer, fender, goblet 8 carangid, doorstop 10 successful

bumpkin: oak, yap 4 clod, gawk, hick, lout, rube 5 churl, yahoo, yokel 6 lummox, rustic 7 hayseed 9 chawbacon

bumptious: 5 cocky 8 insolent 9 obtrusive

Bumppo, Natty: *alias:* 7 Hawkeye 10 Deerslayer, Pathfinder
companion: 12 Chingachgook
novels: 20 Leatherstocking Tales
writer: 6 Cooper

bumpy: 5 rough 6 uneven 7 jolting

bun: jag 4 buzz, roll 7 biscuit, chignon 8 hair knot

bunch: lot, set 4 body, crew, herd, lump, pack, tuft 5 batch, clump, crowd, flock, group 6 bundle, circle 7 cluster 8 assemble, quantity, swelling 9 aggregate 10 collection

bunco: con, gyp 5 cheat, trick 7 defraud, swindle

bund: 4 band 6 league 7 society 10 embankment, federation 11 confederacy

bundle: lot, pot, wad 4 band, hank, pack, pile, roll 5 bunch, group 6 bindle, pack-

et, parcel, wrap up 7 package 10 collection

bundle of: *arrows:* 5 sheaf 6 quiver
grain: 5 sheaf 6 shock
hay: 4 bale
sticks: 5 fagot 6 faggot 7 fascine
straw: 4 bolt

bung: 4 cork, plug 5 spile 7 stopper, stopple, tampion

bungle: err 4 flub, goof, muff 5 botch, fluff, gum up, spoil 6 boggle, bumble, foozle, fumble, mess up 7 blunder, louse up 9 mismanage 10 pull a boner

bungling: 6 clumsy 7 awkward 8 slipshod 9 maladroit, unskilled 10 blundering

bunk: bed, cot 5 berth, hokum, hooey, lodge, put up, sleep 7 billet, trough 7 baloney, twaddle 8 log truck, nonsense

bunker: bin 4 crib, hold 6 dugout, hazard 7 shelter 8 obstacle, sandtrap 10 difficulty 11 compartment

bunkum: rot 4 jazz 6 drivel, humbug 7 hogwash 8 buncombe 9 poppycock 10 balderdash, doubletalk

bunt: tap 4 butt, push 5 shove 6 strike 8 sail part 9 wheat smut, spearhead

bunting: 4 bird, flag, pape 5 finch 6 fabric, towhee 7 cowbird, garment, ortolan 8 bobolink

buoy: dan 5 elate, float, raise 6 hold up, marker, signal 7 support, sustain 8 deadhead
mooring: 7 dolphin

buoyant: gay 5 happy, light, on air 6 blithe, lively 7 elastic, hopeful, lilting, springy 8 animated, cheerful, floating, sanguine, spirited, volatile 9 resilient, vivacious 12 lighthearted

burble: yak 4 boil, gush 5 run on 6 bubble, gurgle, jabber 7 chatter, prattle

burbot: 4 fish, ling 6 lawyer 7 ellpout
genus: 4 lota
relative: cod

burden: tax, vex 4 birn(Sc.), care, cark, clog, duty, load, onus, 5 cargo, theme, worry 6 charge, hamper, impose, lading, saddle, weight 7 afflict, ballast, freight, oppress, refrain, trouble 8 capacity, encumber, handicap, overhead 9 aggravate, grievance 10 imposition 14 responsibility
of complaint: 8 gravamen

burden bearer: 5 Atlas 9 worry wart

burdensome: 5 heavy 7 arduous, irksome, onerous, weighty 8 cumbrous, grievous, grinding 9 demanding, difficult 10 oppressive 11 importunate, troublesome

bureau: 4 desk 5 chest 6 agency, office 7 dresser 10 chiffonier, department, escritoire

bureaucrat: 8 stickler 12 civil servant 13 petty official

bureaucratese: 4 cant 6 jargon 12 gobbledygook

burg: 4 city, town 6 hamlet 7 village 8 hick town 11 whistle-stop

burgeon: bud 4 grow 5 bloom 6 expand, flower, sprout 7 shoot up 8 increase, put forth

burglar: 4 yegg 5 crook, thief 6 cat man, robber 8 peterman

burglary: 5 caper, heist, theft 7 break-in, larceny, robbery 8 stealage

burgomaster: 4 gull 5 mayor 7 alcalde 10 magistrate

burgoo: 4 soup, stew 5 gruel 6 picnic 8 porridge

burial: 9 interment 10 deposition
case: box, urn 6 casket, coffin
ceremony: 7 funeral
litter: 4 bier
mound: low 6 barrow 7 tumulus
pile: 4 pyre
place: 4 tomb 5 grave 7 pyramid 8 catacomb, cemetery, golgotha 9 graveyard, mausoleum, sepulcher 10 necropolis 12 potter's field

burin: 4 tool 6 graver

burl: 4 knot, lump 5 bulge 6 growth, veneer 11 excrescence
in mahogany: roe

burlap: 5 gunny 6 fabric 7 bagging, sacking 8 wrapping
fiber: 4 hemp, jute

burlesque: ape 4 mock, mime 5 farce, mimic, revue 6 comedy, overdo, parody, satire 7 ham it up, lampoon, overact, takeoff 8 ridicule, travesty 9 slapstick 10 caricature, exaggerate *comedian* 9 top banana
serenade: 8 shivaree 9 charivari

burly: big 5 beefy, bulky, heavy, hefty, husky 6 brawny, hearty, stocky, sturdy 8 muscular, thickset 9 strapping

Burma: *bay:* 6 Bengal 7 Hunter's 10 Combermere
canopy: 7 tauzaung
capital: 7 Rangoon
city: 4 Paan, Pegu 5 Falam, Manle, Prome 6 Lashio, Loikaw, Sittwe 7 Bassein, Henzada 8 Mandalay, Moulmein
coin: pya 4 kyat
dagger: dah, dao, dow 4 dout
deer: 6 thamin 7 thameng
demon: nat
district: 7 Toungoo
division: 4 Chin, Pegu 5 Magwe 6 Arakan 7 Rangoon, Sagaing 8 Mandalay 9 Irrawaddy 10 Tenasserim
garment: 6 tamein
gate: 5 toran
gibbon: lar
girl: 4 mima
gulf: 8 Martaban

hill dweller: Lai
language: Lai 4 Chin, Pegu 6 Kachin
measure: dha, lan, tha 4 byee, dain, seit, taim, teng 6 palgat
musical instrument: 4 turr 5 tarau
official: wun 4 woon 6 sawbwa
peak: 4 Popa 8 Victoria
people: Lai, Mon, Tai 4 Chin, Kadu, Naga, Shan 5 Karen, Lhota 6 Kachin, Khamti, Peguan 7 Karenni 8 Chingpaw
range: 4 Pegu 5 Dawna 6 Arakan
river: Uyu 4 Mali, Nmai, Pegu 6 Salwin, Shweli 7 Kaladan, Myitnge, Salween, Sittang 8 Chindwin 9 Irrawaddy
robber: 6 dacoit
ruined city: Ava
sash: 7 tubbeck
sea: 7 Andaman
states: 4 Shan 5 Kayah 6 Kachin 8 Kawthule
traveler's shed: 5 zayat
tree: 4 acle 7 yamanai
weight: mat, moo, vis 4 kait, ruay, viss 5 candy, tical, ticul

burn: 4 brew, char, fire, plot, raze, rill, sear, sere 5 adust, anger, blaze, broil, brook, cense, flame, parch, scald, singe, waste, water 6 scorch, stream, tingle 7 combure, combust, consume, cremate, flicker, oxidize, rivulet, smolder 8 squander 9 cauterize 10 incinerate
midnight oil: 6 stay up 9 lucubrate
surface: 5 singe 6 scorch 7 blister

burn up the road: 5 speed

burned: 5 baked 6 seared 7 charred 8 ustulate

burner: 6 Bunsen, censer 8 thurible

burning: hot 4 fire 5 afire, angry, blaze, calid, eager, fiery, flame, gledy 6 ablaze, ardent, fervid, torrid, urgent 7 caustic, cautery, fervent, flaming, glaring, glowing, mordant, shining 8 arduous, exciting, inustion 9 consuming, cremating, inflaming 10 combustion, phlogistic 13 conflagration
bush: 5 wahoo
malicious: 5 arson
mountain: 7 volcano
taste: 5 acrid

burnish: rub 4 buff 5 glaze, gloss, shine 6 luster, patina, polish 7 furbish

burnisher: 4 tool 5 agate 6 buffer 7 frottom 8 polisher

burnoose, burnous: 5 cloak 7 garment 8 albornoz

burnsides: 5 beard 8 whiskers

burnt work: 10 pyrography

burr: nut, pad, rib 4 barb, birr, boss, buzz, halo, knob, ring, whir 5 briar, whirr 6 banyan, circle, corona, tunnel, washer 7 sticker 8 parasite 9 whet-

stone 10 sweetbread
burro: ass 6 donkey 9 quadruped 10 pack
animal
burrow: den, dig 4 heap, hole, mine, mole,
root, tube 5 berry, couch, mound 6 furrow, tunnel 7 passage, shelter 8 excavate
bursa: sac 4 hall, sack 5 pouch 6 cavity 9
residence
bursar: 6 purser, terrar 7 cashier 9 paymaster, treasurer 10 controller
burst: 4 blow, bust, loss, rend, scat 5
blast, break, erupt, flash, go off, salvo,
split 6 broken, damage, injury, volley 7
explode, flare up, rupture, shatter 8
outbreak, sundered 9 interrupt
forth: 5 erupt, sally 9 blasted
inward: 7 implode
out: 5 blurt 7 exclaim 9 ejaculate
bursting: 8 erupting 10 dehiscence
Burundi: *capital:* 9 Bujumbura
ethnic group: Twa 4 Hutu 5 Tutsi
lake: 10 Tanganyika
monetary unit: 5 franc 7 centime
town: 5 Ngozi 6 Gitega, Ruyigi
bury: 4 hide, sink 5 inter, inurn 6 cover,
entomb, inhume, shroud 7 conceal, engross, immerse, repress, secrete 8 inundate, submerge 9 overwhelm, stash
away
bus: 6 jitney 7 vehicle 9 charabanc
busby: cap, wig 6 fur hat 8 bearskin 9
headdress
bush: tod 4 buss, butt 5 bosch, clump,
grove, shrub 6 branch, tavern 7 boscage, cluster, thicket 11 advertising
bushed: 4 worn 5 spent 6 dog-tired 9 exhausted
bushel: foo(Sc.), gob, lot 4 full
quarter of: 4 peck
forty: wey
bushing: 5 drill 6 collet, lining 7 padding
machine: 6 sleeve
bush-league: 6 non-pro 7 amateur 8 inferior 10 second-rate
bushman: (pl.) 4 gung, saan(pl.) 5
bushy 6 Abatoa, Abatua, Abatwa, rustic
8 woodsman
blanket: 5 bluey
bushmaster: 5 snake, viper
bushwa: 4 bosh, bull, bunk 5 hooey, trash
7 baloney, hogwash, rubbish 8 nonsense
bushwacker: 5 papaw 6 pawpaw, scythe,
sniper 8 guerilla
bushy: 5 bosky 6 dumose, dumous 7 bushman, queachy
hair: 4 shag
heap: tod
business: ado, art, job 4 care, firm, fuss,
game, line, task, work 5 cause, trade 6
affair, custom, matter, metier, office 7

calling, concern, trading, traffic 8 activity, commerce, industry, vocation 9 diligence, following, patronage, rickmatic
10 employment, enterprise, occupation,
solicitude 11 disturbance, importunity,
intercourse, transaction 13 attentive-
ness, establishment
custom: 9 patronage
memorandum: 4 note 7 agendum
place of: 4 mart, shop 5 store 6 market,
office, shoppe 8 emporium
businessman: 9 executive
powerful: 6 tycoon
buskin: 4 boot, shoe 7 bottine, tragedy 8
cothurni(L.pl.), half-boot, stocking 9
brodequin, cothurnus(L.)
buss: 4 boat, bush, calf, deck, kiss 5 dress,
smack 6 vessel 9 transport
bussu: 4 palm 7 troolie
bust: 4 fail, raid, ruin, tame 5 bosom,
break, burst, chest, flunk, lemon, loser,
spree 6 arrest, bronze, demote, reduce,
statue 7 degrade, dismiss, failure 8
bankrupt 9 blockhead, sculpture 10 depression
bust-up: 5 party, split 7 failure 8 collapse
11 dissolution
bustard: 4 bird, kori 5 crane, paauw 7 bebilya, houbara 8 gompaaum
genus: 4 otis 6 otidae
buster: 4 crab, wind 5 blade, child 6 fellow
bustle: ado 4 fuss, stir, todo, whir 5 frisk,
haste, whirr 6 clamor, fistle, flurry,
hubbub, hustle, pother, racket, tumult,
unrest, uproar 7 clatter, turmoil 8 activity, tournure 9 agitation, commotion, whirlwind 10 hurly-burly
woman's: 6 bishop
busy: 4 nosy 5 brisk 6 active, at work, intent, lively, occupy 7 engaged, humming, on the go, operose 8 diligent, employed, occupied, sedulous, tireless,
untiring 9 assiduous, attentive, detective, laborious, officious 11 distracting,
industrious 13 indefatigable
busybody: 5 snoop, yenta(Yid.) 6 gossip
7 marplot, meddler, snooper 8 factotum, quidnunc 10 pragmatist, rubberneck
but: sed(L.), yet 4 mere, only, save 5 still
6 except, unless 7 besides, howbeit,
however 11 nonetheless 12 nevertheless
butcher: 4 kill, slay 5 botch, spoil 6 bungle, murder 8 mutilate 9 slaughter 10
meat vendor 11 executioner
hook: 7 gambrel
rabbi: 8 shochtim
tool: saw 5 knife, steel 7 cleaver
butcher-bird: 6 shrike
butchery: 6 murder 7 carnage 8 abattoir,

massacre, shambles **9** bloodbath, slaughter

butler: 7 servant, spencer, steward **8** factotum, retainer **9** major-domo **10** manservant

butt: end, jut, pit, ram, tun **4** buck, bunt, cart, cask, fool, goad, goat, jolt, push, rump, stub **5** hinge, joint, mound, stump **6** adjoin, breech, target, thrust **7** fall guy, project **8** derriere, flatfish, flounder **13** laughing stock

cigar or cigarette: **5** snipe

in: **6** meddle **7** intrude **9** interfere, interrupt, intervene

butte: 4 hill **7** picacho **8** mountain

butter: fat, oil **4** food **6** beurre(F.), cajole, spread **7** blarney, flatter

artificial: **4** oleo **9** butterine, margarine **13** oleomargarine

serving of: pat

pert. to: **7** butyric

semifluid: ghi **4** ghee

shea: **5** galam **6** bambui, bambuk **7** bambara

tree: **4** shea **5** fulwa **8** phulwara

tub: **6** firkin

without solids: **5** drawn **9** clarified

butter-and-eggs: 6 clover **7** ransted **8** ramstead, toadflax

butterball: 6 chubby **8** roly-poly

buttercup: 6 flower **7** anemone **8** crowfoot, reindeer **10** butter-rose

fruit: **6** achene

butterfingered: 6 clumsy **7** awkward **9** all-thumbs

butterfish: 5 coney **6** blenny, gunnel

butterfly: 4 kiho **5** satyr **6** idalia, morpho, ursula **7** admiral, buckeye, monarch, skipper, vanessa, viceroy **8** arthemis, cecropia, grayling **9** aphrodite, underwing **10** fritillary, lepidopter, swim stroke

expert: **13** lepidopterist

fish: **6** blenny, chiton **7** gurnard

genus: **8** melitaea **10** heliconius

larva: **11** caterpillar

lily: **4** sego **8** mariposa

butterweed: 9 steepweed

buttery: 6 larder, pantry, spence **9** storeroom, wheedling **10** flattering

button: bud: **4** boss, chin, hook, knob, knop **5** badge, catch, pearl **6** bauble, buckle **8** fastener, lapel pin

ornamental: **4** stud

part: **4** hole **5** shank

three jewel: **6** troche

button-down: 6 proper, square **8** orthodox, straight **10** unoriginal **12** conservative, conventional

buttonhole: 4 loop, slit **6** accost, detain, eyelet **11** boutonniere, get the ear of

buttress: 4 pier, pile, prop, stay **5** brace **7** support **8** abutment **11** counterfort

buxom: 5 busty, hefty, jolly, plump, prone, sonsy **6** bosomy, florid, sonsie **7** shapely **8** bouncing **10** curvaceous **11** full-figured

buy: 4 chap, coff(Sc.), coup, gain, shop **5** bribe, trade, fling, phone, rumor **6** notion **7** whisper **9** bombinate, telephone

back: **6** redeem

cheaply: **5** steal **7** bargain

to sell at a profit: **7** regrate

buyer: 5 agent **6** client, patron **7** shopper **8** customer, prospect **9** purchaser

beware: **12** caveat emptor

stolen property: **5** fence

buzz: hum **4** burr, call, hiss, ring, whir **5** fancy, fling, phone, rumor **6** notion **7** whisper **9** bombinate, telephone

bald: **6** osprey

honey: **4** pern

buzzer: bee **4** bell **5** alarm, badge **6** signal

buzz off: 5 leave **6** depart, pull out

by: ago, per, via **4** near, past **5** apart, aside, close **6** beside, nearby, next to, toward **7** besides, through **9** alongside **10** concerning **11** according to

and by: **4** anon, soon **5** later **7** shortly

means of: per **4** from, with **7** through

mouth: **4** oral

bypass: 4 miss, shun **5** evade, shunt, skirt **6** detour **7** circuit **8** sidestep

bygone: 4 past, yore **5** olden **6** former **7** ancient, elapsed **8** backward, departed

byname: 6 byword **7** surname **8** cognomen, nickname **9** sobriquet

bypath: 4 lane **5** byway

Byron character: 4 Inez, Lara **6** Haidee **7** Don Juan

bystander: 7 witness **9** spectator

byway: 4 lane, path **5** alley

byword: saw **5** axiom, motto **6** byname, phrase, saying **7** epithet, proverb **8** nickname **9** catchword

Byzantine: 6 tricky **7** devious **8** involved **9** intricate

C

C: 7 hundred

Caaba: 6 shrine

caama: fox 4 asse 10 hartebeest

cab: 4 hack, taxi 6 hansom

cab driver: 5 cabby 6 cabbie, cocher(F.) 7 cochero(Sp.)

cabal: 4 camp, plot, ring 5 junta, party 6 brigue, circle, clique, scheme 7 coterie, council, faction, in group 8 intrigue 10 conspiracy 11 machination

pert. to: 9 factional

cabalistic: 6 mystic 10 mysterious

caballero: 6 escort, knight 8 cavalier, horseman 9 gentleman

cabana: 7 shelter 9 bathhouse

cabaret: 4 cafe 6 tavern 8 late spot 9 nightclub 10 restaurant, supper club

cabbage: 4 chou, crib, kale 5 filch, steal 6 pilfer, 7 bowkail(Sc.), purloin 8 borecole, colewort

daisy: 11 globeflower

salad: 4 slaw 8 coleslaw

seed: 5 colza

soup: 4 kale(Sc.) 7 borscht

tree: 7 angelin 8 palmetto

variety: 4 cale, kale 5 colza, savoy 8 colewort, kohlrabi

cabbagehead: 5 dunce 9 screwball

cabbageworm: 6 looper 7 cutworm

cabin: cot, den, hut 4 shed 5 booth, coach, hovel, lodge, shack 6 shanty 7 cottage 9 stateroom

cabin boy: 7 grummet

cabin car: 7 caboose

cabinet: box 4 case 5 habut, board, chest 6 bureau, closet, vanity 7 almirah (Ind.), armoire, commode, console, council, etagere, whatnot 8 cellaret, cupboard, ministry 10 chiffonier

cable: 4 boom, link, rope, wire 5 chain 6 stitch 8 telegram

lifter: 7 wildcat

post: 4 bitt

cable car: 4 tram 6 telfer 7 telpher

Cable TV: 13 shared antenna

cabochon: gem 5 stone 8 ornament 10 style of cut

caboodle: kit, lot 10 collection

caboose: cab, car 5 buggy 6 galley

cabotin: 5 actor 9 charlatan

cabotinage: 7 emoting 9 ham acting, theatrics

cabrilla: 4 bass 7 grouper

cacao: 4 bean, seed, tree 5 broma, cocoa 6 arriba 9 chocolate

cache: 4 bury, hide 5 store 7 conceal, secrete 8 treasure 10 storehouse, hiding place

cachepot: jar, urn 7 planter

cachet: 4 seal 5 stamp, wafer 6 status 8 prestige 11 distinction

cachexia: 7 illness, wasting 9 morbidity 2 malnutrition

cacholong: 4 opal

cackle: gab, jaw 4 blab, chat 5 clack, laugh 6 babble, gabble, giggle, gossip, titter 7 chackle, chatter, prattle, twaddle 8 laughter

cacoethes: 4 itch, mania 6 desire

cacography: 11 misspelling

opposite: 11 orthography

cacophonous: 5 harsh 7 raucous 8 jangling, strident 9 dissonant 10 discordant 11 unmelodious

cactus: 4 bleo 5 dildo, nopal, plant 6 cereus, chaute, chende, cholla, mescal 7 airampo, opuntia, saguaro 8 chichipe 11 prickly pear

drug: 6 peyote

fruit: 6 cochal

plantation: 7 nopalry

cad: cur 4 boor, heel 5 churl, creep 6 rascal, rotter 7 bounder, dastard 9 scoundrel

cadaver: 4 body 5 stiff 6 corpse 7 carcass 8 skeleton

cadaverous: 4 pale 5 gaunt 6 wasted 7 ghastly, haggard 9 emaciated

caddow: 5 quilt 7 jackdaw 8 coverlet

caddy: box, boy, can 4 case 5 chest 9 container

cade: keg, pet 4 cask, lamb 6 barrel, coddle 7 indulge, juniper

cadence: 4 beat, lilt, pace, tone 5 meter, metre, pulse, sound, swing, throb 6 rhythm 8 clausula 10 inflection, modulation

cadet: 5 plebe, youth 6 embryo, junior 7 student 10 midshipman 11 West Pointer

cadew: 4 worm

cadge: beg, bum 4 bind, hawk 5 carry, mooch 6 peddle, sponge 8 scrounge 9 panhandle

Cadmus: *daughter:* Ino **5** Agave **6** Semele **7** Autonoe
father: **6** Agenor
sister: **6** Europa
wife: **8** Harmonia

cadre: **4** cell, core, unit **5** frame, group **6** scheme, nucleus **9** framework

caduceus: **4** wand **5** staff **6** emblem, symbol **7** insigne, scepter, sceptre

caducity: **5** lapse **8** senility **10** feebleness **14** perishableness

Caesar: **6** tyrant **7** emperor
assassin: **6** Brutus **7** Cassius
capital: **4** Roma
colleague: **7** Bibulus
country conquered by: **4** Gaul
eulogist: **7** Antony
fatal day: **4** Ides
message: **12** veni, vidi, vici
place of victory: **6** Actium
river crossed by: **7** Rubicon
sister: **4** Atia
site of famous message: **4** Zela
wife: **7** Pompeia **8** Cornelia **9** Calpurnia

caesura: **4** rest, stop **5** pause **8** interval **10** verse break **12** interruption

cafard: **5** blues **6** apathy **7** boredom **10** depression **12** listlessness

cafe: **5** diner **6** saloon **7** barroom, cabaret **8** teahouse **9** nightclub **10** restaurant **11** coffeehouse

caffeine: **5** thein **6** theine **8** alkaloid **9** stimulant

cage: box, car, mew, pen **4** coop, jail **5** brake **6** aviary, basket, bucket, chapel, prison, shut in **7** chantry, confine **8** imprison, scaffold, strainer **9** enclosure, inclosure **11** incarcerate

cage hawk: mew **5** meute

cagey, cagy: sly **4** foxy, wily, wary **6** astute, shrewd **7** cunning

cahoots: **6** league **9** collusion **11** partnership

caiman: **6** jacare **9** crocodile

Cain: **8** murderer **10** fratricide
brother: Pur **4** Abel, Seth
descendant: **6** Lamech
father: **4** Adam
killer of: **4** Abel
land: Nod
mother: Eve
nephew: **4** Enos
son: **5** Enoch

Caine Mutiny: *author:* **4** Wouk (Herman)
character: **5** Queeg
ship: **11** mine sweeper

cairn: **8** landmark, monument **9** stone heap **11** trail marker

cairngorm: **6** quartz

caisson: box **5** chest, float, wagon **7** chamber, pontoon
disease: **5** bends

caitiff: **4** base, mean, vile **6** wicked **8** cowardly **10** despicable

cajole: con **4** coax **5** jolly, tease **6** entice, whilly(Sc.) **7** beguile, flatter, wheedle **8** blandish, butter up **9** sweet talk

cake: bar, bun set **4** lump, mass **5** block, crust, patty, wedge **6** harden, nacket(Sc.), pastry **7** bannock **8** solidify **9** coagulate
almond: **8** macaroon
boiled in honey: **8** teiglech
coffee: **6** kuchen
corn: **4** pone **7** fritter **8** tortilla
custard: **6** eclair **9** creampuff
dough: **6** batter
fat free: **9** angel food
filled: **4** flan **9** enchilada
fried: **7** cruller **8** doughnut
griddle: **7** bannock(Sc.), crumpet, hotcake, oatcake, pancake
plum: **4** baba
rich: **5** torte **7** stollen **8** madeline **9** madeleine
sacrificial: **6** hallah
seed: wig **4** wiff
small: bun **4** tart **6** cookie, muffin **7** cupcake
tea: **5** scone
thin: **5** scone, wafer
topping: **5** icing **8** frosting
unleavened: **5** matzo **6** damper **8** tortilla

cakewalk: **5** dance, march, strut **6** prance

calaba: **4** tree **5** birma

calabash: **5** gourd **6** curuba

calaboose: jug **4** brig, gaol, jail **5** clink **6** cooler, lockup, prison **8** hoosegow

caladium: **4** taro

calamanco: **6** fabric **7** garment

calamitous: sad **4** dire, evil **5** black, fatal **6** bitter, dismal, tragic, woeful **7** adverse, baleful, direful, hapless, ruinous, unhappy, unlucky **8** grievous, wretched **9** miserable **10** afflictive, deplorable, disastrous **11** distressful, unfortunate

calami: pen **5** quill **9** sweetflag

calamity: **4** blow, evil, ruin **5** storm **6** misery, sorrow **7** scourge, tragedy **8** accident, disaster, fatality **9** adversity, cataclysm **10** affliction, misfortune **11** catastrophe **12** misadventure, wretchedness

calangay: **8** cockatoo

calash: **6** calesa **8** carriage **10** woman's hood **11** Asian Seaman

calcar: **4** oven, spur **7** furnace

calced: **4** shod

calcite: *animal:* **8** skeleton
deposit: **4** spar, tufa **5** tatar **10** stalactite, stalagmite
soil with: **4** marl

calcium: *carbonate:* **4** tufa
oxide: **9** quicklime

101

call

sulfate: 6 gypsum 14 plaster of paris
calculate: aim 4 plan, rate, tell 5 count,
  think 6 assess, expect, figure, number,
  reckon 7 average, compute, prepare 8
  consider, estimate, evaluate 9 determine, enumerate
calculation: 4 care 7 caution 8 forecast,
  prudence 9 deduction, logistics, reckoning 10 adjustment, estimation 11 computation
calculating: sly 4 wily 6 crafty, shrewd 7
  cunning, guarded 8 cautious, scheming
calculator: 5 table 6 abacus 7 soroban 8
  computer 10 accountant
Calder: 6 artist
  work: 7 mobiles
caldron, cauldron: pot, vat 6 boiler, kettle, vessel 8 red color
Caleb's son: Hur, Iru
Caledonia: 8 Scotland
calefy: 4 heat, warm
calembour: pun
calendar: log 4 card 5 diary, slate 6 agenda, docket 7 almanac, journal, program
  8 menology, register, schedule
  church: 4 ordo
  former: 6 Julian
  French revolution: 6 Nivose 7 Floreal,
    Ventose 8 Brumaire, Fervidor, Gernu-
    bak, Messidor, Pluviose, Prairial 9
    Fructidor, Thermidor 11 Vendemiaire
  modern: 9 Gregorian
calenture: 4 fire, glow, zeal 5 ardor, fever
  7 passion 9 sunstroke
calf: boy, leg 4 dolt 5 bobby, bossy, youth
  6 bovine, muscle 7 fatling
  flesh: 4 veal, veau(F.)
  hide: kip
  motherless: 4 dogy 5 dogie
  muscle: 9 plantaris
  pert. to: 5 sural
  unbranded: 8 maverick
Caliban: 5 beast, slave
  adversary of: 8 Prospero
  deity of: 7 Setebos
  witch mother: 9 Sycorax
caliber: 4 bore, rank 5 class, worth, value
  6 degree, talent 7 ability, breadth, compass, quality, stature 8 capacity, diameter
calibrate: 5 grade 7 measure 11 standardize
calico: 4 girl 5 cloth, woman 7 spotted 8
  goldfish 9 womankind 12 multicolored
  bass: 7 crappie
  horse: 5 pinto 7 piebald
California: capital: 10 Sacramento
  city: 7 Oakland, San Jose 8 San Diego 9
    Long Beach 10 Los Angeles 12 San
    Francisco
  county: 4 Napa 5 Butte, Glenn, Kings 6
    Merced, Orange, Shasta, Sierra 7 Ala-

meda 8 Del Norte, Monterey 9 Riverside, San Joaquin 10 Sacramento, Santa Clara 13 San Bernardino, San Luis
  Obispo
desert: 6 Mojave 8 Colorado
fault zone: 10 San Andreas
Indian tribe: 4 Hupa, Pomo, Seri, Juma 5
  Hoopa, Yorok
lake: 5 Owens, Tahoe 6 Salton
motto: 6 Eureka
mountain peak: 6 Lassen, Shasta
national park: 8 Yosemite
nickname: 11 Golden State
observatory: 4 Lick 7 Palomar 8 Mt. Wilson
pass: 6 Donner, Sonora
peninsula: 8 Monterey
prison: 8 Alcatraz
state animal: 11 grizzly bear
state bird: 11 valley quail
state fish: 5 trout
state flower: 11 golden poppy
state tree: 9 butterfly
river: Eel, Mad, Pit 4 Kern 5 Kings,
  Smith 6 Merced, Salmon 7 Feather,
  Klamath, Russian, Salinas, Trinity 10
  Sacramento, San Jacinto, Stanislaus
shrub: 5 salal 7 chamise, chamiso, tarbush 9 chaparral, manzanita
town: 4 Asti, Napa 5 Tracy 6 Arcata, Eureka, Fresno 7 Alameda, Arcadia, Salinas
tree: 6 torrey 7 redwood, sequoia 12
  Wellingtonia
valley: 4 Napa
wine area: 4 Napa
caliginous: dim 4 dark 5 murky 7 obscure
Caligula's horse: 9 Incitatus
caliph, calif: Abu, Ali 4 Bekr, Imam,
  Omar 8 Othman 9 caliphate
  descendant: 5 Alide 7 Fatamid 8 Fata-
    mite
  fourth: Ali
calix: cup 7 chalice
calk, caulk: nap 6 fill in 7 occlude 9 shoe
  plate, stop leaks 14 make water-tight
calking: 5 oakum
call: bid, cry, dub 4 cite, dial, hail, name,
  page, stop, term, yell 5 claim, clepe,
  clock, elect, phone, rouse, shout, style,
  utter, visit, waken, yodel, yodle 6 accuse, appeal, arouse, demand, invite, invoke, muster, quethe, summon 7 address, appoint, collect, command,
  convene, convoke, entitle, impeach 8
  announce, assemble, nominate, proclaim, vocation 9 challenge, reprimand,
  telephone, terminate 10 denominate
  back: 6 revoke 8 retrieve 10 phone again
    11 ask to return
  distress: S.O.S.

down: 5 scold 6 berate, invoke, rebuke 7 censure, reprove 8 denounce, execrate 9 reprimand

for: 4 page 5 exact 6 demand 7 predict, request, require

forth: 5 evoke 6 arouse, elicit, invoke, signal, summon 7 evocate

off: end 4 kill 5 count 6 cancel

on: ask, bid 4 urge 5 visit 6 drop in 8 appeal to

out: 5 ascry, shout 6 holler, muster 11 give voice to

to: 4 hail 5 ascry 6 accost, halloo 7 address

to attention: hop 6 remind

to mind: 4 cite 6 recall 8 remember

together: 6 muster 7 convene, convoke

call-in: 9 radio show 12 phone protest

Call of the Wild author: 6 London

calligrapher: 6 penman, writer 7 copyist 9 engrosser

calling: art, job 4 rank 5 trade 6 career, metier, naming, outcry 7 pursuit, station, summons 8 business, function, position, shouting, vocation 9 condition, summoning, utterance 10 employment, invitation, occupation, profession 11 appellation, convocation, undertaking 13 circumstances

Calliope's son: 7 Orpheus

Callisto's son: 5 Arcas

callous: 4 hard 5 horny, tough 6 brawny, obtuse, torpid 8 obdurate 9 indurated, unfeeling 11 hardhearted, indifferent 4 pachydermatous

callow: raw 4 bald, bare 5 crude, green 6 marshy 7 meadow 8 immature, juvenile, unformed, youthful 9 unfledged 13 inexperienced 15 unsophisticated

calm: lee 4 cool, dill, easy, fair, hush, lull, mees(Sc.), mild, rest 5 abate, allay, charm, mease, peace, quell, quiet, sober, still, stoic 6 defuse, docile, gentle, irenic, pacify, placid, sedate, serene, smooth, soothe, steady 7 appease, assuage, halcyon, mollify, pacific, patient, placate, restful, unmoved 8 composed, decorous, peaceful, restrain, tranquil 9 collected, impassive, temperate, unexcited, unruffled 10 halcyonian, phlegmatic, unconfused 11 complacence, tranquilize, undisturbed 13 dispassionate, imperturbable 15 undemonstrative

calmness: 5 poise 6 repose 8 ataraxia, serenity 9 composure, placidity, quietness, sang-froid, stillness 10 equanimity 11 self-control, tranquility 12 peacefulness 13 impassiveness

calorie, calory: 5 therm 10 energy unit

calotte: 6 ice cap 7 glacier 8 skull cap 11 snowy summit

calumet: 4 pipe

calumniate: 4 slur 5 belie, libel, smear 6 accuse, attack, defame, malign, revile, vilify 7 asperse, blacken, slander, traduce 9 blaspheme

calyx: 4 leaf 5 sepal

helmet-shaped: 5 galea

of flower: 8 perianth

cam: cog 4 awry, lobe 5 askew, catch, wiper 6 tappet 7 crooked, trippet 8 perverse

camalig (P.I.): hut 5 cabin 10 storehouse

camaraderie: 7 jollity 9 good cheer 10 fellowship 11 sociability 12 friendliness

camarilla: 4 cell, ring 5 cabal, junta 6 clique

Cambodia: *capital:* 9 Phnom Penh

city: 6 Angkor, Kratie 8 Siem Reap 10 Battambang

ethnic group: 5 Khmer

gulf: 4 Siam

lake: 8 Tonle Sap

monetary unit: sen 4 riel

one-time rulers: 6 Lon Nol, Pol Pot 8 Sihanouk

port: 6 Kampot

river: 6 Mekong

temple: 9 Angkor Wat

Cambria: See Wales

cambric: 5 linen 7 batiste

Cambridge: *boat races:* 4 Lent

college official: 6 bedell

council: 5 caput

honor examination: 6 tripos

student: 5 sizar, spoon 6 optime

camel: 6 mehari 8 ruminant 9 dromedary

driver: 6 sarwan 8 cameleer

two-humped: 8 Bactrian

camellia: 8 japonica

camelopard: 7 giraffe

Camelot: *lord:* 6 Arthur

magician: 6 Merlin

camel's hair: aba 5 cloth 6 camlet 8 cameline

garment: aba

cameo: gem 7 carving, relievo, rilievo, phalera 8 anaglyph 9 sculpture

cutting tool: 5 spade

stone: 4 onyx 8 sardonyx

camera: 7 chamber 10 department, instrument

part: 4 lens 6 finder 7 bellows, shutter

platform: 5 dolly

cameraman: 8 camerist, operator 12 photographer 13 projectionist

Cameroon: *Capital:* 7 Yaounde

city: 4 Buea, Edea 5 Kribi 6 Douala

ethnic group: 5 Bantu 7 Hamitic

gulf: 6 Guinea

monetary unit: 5 franc 7 centime

port: 6 Douala 8 Victoria

river: 5 Nyong 6 Sanaga

camion: bus 4 dray 5 truck, wagon 7 motorbus

camlet: 6 Angora, fabric, mohair 9 camelteen, camletine

Camorra: 5 Mafia

camouflage: 4 fake, hide 6 muffle, screen 7 conceal 8 disguise 9 deception

camp: 4 pest, tent 5 etape(F.), horde, siege, tabor 7 barrack, bivouac, shelter 8 quarters 10 settlement

follower: 5 bidar(Ind.) 6 gudget(Sc.)

pert. to: 7 castral

provision seller: 6 sutler

campaign: 5 drive, plain 7 canvass, crusade, solicit 9 champaign, operation

campanero: 8 arapunga, bellbird

campanile: 5 tower 6 belfry 7 clocher, steeple

camphol: 7 borneol

camphor: 7 menthol, asarone

campus: 4 quad 5 field 7 grounds

campy: 5 outre 7 extreme 8 affected 11 exaggerated

Camus work: 5 Rebel 6 Plague 8 Caligula, Stranger 12 State of Siege

can: cup, jug, may, tin 4 able, fire, jail 5 caddy, could eshin, skill 6 vessel 7 ability, capable, dismiss 8 conserve, preserve 9 competent, container, discharge, knowledge 10 cleverness, receptacle

Canada: *capital:* 6 Ottawa

bay: 5 Fundy, James 6 Baffin, Hudson, Ungava

city: 5 Banff 6 London, Oshawa, Regina 7 Calgary, Halifax, Toronto, Windsor 8 Edmonton, Montreal, Victoria, Winnipeg 9 Carstairs, Saskatoon, Vancouver

early explorer: 5 Cabot 7 Cartier, Erikson

emblem: 9 maple leaf

island: 5 Banks 6 Baffin 8 Victoria 9 Vancouver 11 Southampton

lake: 6 Louise 8 Winnipeg 9 Great Bear 10 Great Slave

measure: ton 5 minot, perch, point 6 arpent 7 chainon

monetary unit: 4 cent 6 dollar

mountain: 7 Cascade, Rockies 10 Laurentian

native group: 5 Inuit (Eskimo), Metis 6 Indian

peninsula: 5 Foxe, Gaspe 6 Ungava 7 Boothia 8 Melville

province: 6 Quebec 7 Alberta, Ontario 8 Manitoba 10 Nova Scotia 12 New Brunswick, Newfoundland, Saskatchewan 15 British Columbia 18 Prince Edward Island (see also entry for province)

river: Red 5 Yukon 6 Nelson, Ottawa 8 Columbia 9 Mackenzie 10 St. Lawrence

territory: 5 Yukon 9 Northwest (see also entry for province)

U.S. border lake: 4 Erie 5 Huron 7 Ontario 8 Superior

Canadian: 6 Canuck

canadine: 8 alkaloid

canaille: mob 5 flour 6 rabble 7 riffraff

canal: cut 4 cano, duct, tube 5 ditch, drain, fossa(L.), graff, zanje 6 fossae(L.pl.), groove, strait, trench 7 acequia(Sp.), channel, conduit, raceway, towpath 8 aqueduct 10 waterspout 11 watercourse

dredging machine: 7 couloir

famous: Soo 4 Erie, Kiel, Suez 6 Morris, Panama 7 Welland

footpath: 7 towpath

Canal Zone: *city:* 6 Balboa

lake: 5 Gatun

canape: 5 relish 9 appetizer 11 hors d'oeuvre

canard: 4 hoax 9 grapewine 11 fabrication

canary: 4 bird, fink 5 dance 6 singer, snitch, stoolie 8 informer, squealer

forerunner of: 5 serin

canary broom: 7 genista

Canary Islands: 4 Roca 5 Ferro, Lobos, Palma, Clara 6 Gomero 7 Inferno 8 Graciosa, Rocca Sta., Tenerife 9 Lanzarote, Teneriffe 10 Allegranza 11 Grand Hierro 13 Fuerteventura

city: 6 Laguna 9 Santa Cruz(c.)

commune: 4 Icod

measure: 8 fanegada

mountain: 6 La Cruz 8 El Cumbre, Tenerife 9 Teneriffe 11 Gran Canaria

canary yellow: 6 meline

canasta: 4 game 5 cards, crate 6 basket, hamper

play: 4 meld

cancel: 4 blot, dele, omit 5 annul, erase, quash, remit 6 delete, efface, recall, remove, revoke 7 abolish, call off, destroy, expunge, nullify, rescind, retract, scratch 8 abrogate 10 obliterate 11 countermand

cancer: 5 tumor 7 sarcoma 9 carcinoma

cancion: 4 song 5 lyric

candent: hot 7 fervent, glowing

candescent: 7 glowing 8 dazzling 11 luminescent

Candia: 5 Crete

candid: 4 fair, just, open, pure 5 blunt, clear, frank, naive 6 honest 7 artless, sincere 8 splendid 9 guileless, honorable, impartial, ingenuous, outspoken 10 aboveboard, immaculate 11 unconcealed 15 straightforward

candidate: 7 nonimee 8 aspirant, prospect 9 applicant

list: 4 leet 5 slate 6 roster

religious: 9 postulant
winning: 7 electee
Candiot, Candiote: 6 Cretan
candle: dip, wax 5 light, taper 6 cierge(F.) 9 chandelle
holder: 6 lampad, sconce, sconse, spider 7 menorah 9 girandole 10 candelabra 11 candlestick
kind of: 8 bayberry
place of keeping: 9 chandlery
wax: 5 taper 6 bougie
candlelight: 4 dusk 8 twilight 9 nightfall
candlelighter: 5 spill 7 acolyte
candlenut tree: ama 5 kukui 6 bankul
candlestick: 6 lampad, sconce 8 flambeau, standard 9 flambeaux(pl.)
bracket: 6 sconce, sconse
branched: 5 jesse 8 dicerion, dikerion 9 girandole, tricerion, trikerion 10 chandelier 11 candelabrum
candlewood: 4 tree 5 shrub 9 coachwhip
candor, candour: 6 purity 8 fairness, kindness 9 frankness, innocence, integrity, unreserve, whiteness 10 brightness, brilliance, kindliness 12 impartiality 13 outspokenness
candy: 5 fudge, gundy, lolly, sweet, taffy 6 bonbon, comfit, nougate 7 brittle, caramel, congeal, fondate, flatter, sweeten 8 lollipop, sourball 9 chocolate, granulate, jelly bean, sweetmeat 10 confection 11 crystallize
base: 7 fondant
medicated: 7 lozenge 9 cough drop
mixture: 6 fourre
nut: 7 praline
pulled sugar: 5 taffy 6 penide
sugar: 7 fondant 8 alphenic
candy striper: 10 nurse's aide
candytuft: 5 plant 6 flower, iberis
cane: rod 4 beat, dart, flog, pipe, reed, stem, tube, whip 5 birch, lance, staff, stick 6 bamboo, punish, rattan 7 calamus, hickory, malacca, scourge 9 crabstick
dense growth: 7 canebrake
knife: 7 machete
part: 7 ferrule
sugar: 7 sucrose
Canfield: 8 Klondike 9 solitaire
cangle: 7 dispute, quarrel, wrangle
canine (see also **dog**): cur, dog, fox, pup 4 fisc, wolf 5 canis(L.), hound, pooch 7 doglike
tooth: 7 laniary
caning: 6 rattan 8 birching
canister: box 9 container
canker: 4 rust 5 stain 6 infect 7 consume, corrode, corrupt, pervert, tarnish 9 verdigris
cannabis: 4 hemp
drug: 5 bhang 7 hashish 9 marijuana

Cannery Row author: 9 Steinbeck
cannibal: 6 savage 15 anthropophagite
cannikin: can, cup 4 pail 6 bucket
cannon: bit, gun 5 crack, thief 6 mortar, pom-pom 7 bastard 8 howitzer, ordnance 9 artillery 10 pickpocket
breech-end knob: 8 cascabel
early: 5 aspic, saker 7 robinet
fire: 7 barrage
firing stick: 8 linstock
fodder: 8 infantry
handle: 4 anse
muzzle plug: 7 tampion
part: 4 bore 5 chase 6 breech, muzzle 7 chamber, rimbase 8 cascabel, trunnion
shot: 5 grape
support: 8 trunnion
cannon fodder: 8 infantry, soldiers
cannonade: 5 blitz, burst, salvo 6 volley 7 barrage
cannoneer: 12 artilleryman
cannot: 6 unable
cannular: 6 hollow 7 tubular
canny: 4 sly 4 cozy, snug, wary, wily, wise 5 lucky, pawky, quiet 6 clever, frugal, gentle, shrewd 7 careful, cunning, knowing, prudent, quietly, thrifty 8 cautious, skillful, watchful 9 carefully, dexterous, fortunate, sagacious 10 cautiously 11 comfortable, sharpwitted
canoe: 4 boat, kiak, pahi, proa, waka 5 birch, kayak, prahu, skiff, umiak, waapa 6 ballam, dugout, oomiak, pitpan 7 almadia, bidarka, coracle, currane, pirogue
bark: 7 cascara
dugout: 5 banca 6 baroto, corial 7 pirogue, piroque 12 pambanmanche
large: pah 5 bungo
sailing: 4 proa 5 prahu
skin-covered: 4 kiak 5 bidar, kayak 7 baidara
war: 4 proa
canon: law 4 code, hymn, laud, list, rule, song 5 axiom, gorge, gulch, model, table, tenet 6 decree 7 precept, statute 8 decision, standard 9 catalogue, clergyman, criterion 10 regulation 12 constitution
enigmatical: 4 nodi(pl.) 5 nodus
resident: 8 stagiary
canonical: 8 accepted, orthodox 10 sanctioned 13 authoritative
hour: 4 laud, none, sext 5 matin, prime 6 tierce 7 vespers 8 compline
canonicals: alb 4 cope, cowl, robe 5 stole 9 vestments
canopy: sky 4 ceil, cope, dais, hood 5 shade, vault 6 awning, celure, finial, tester 7 marquee, shelter 8 covering 9 baldachin, baldaquin, pavillion 11 baldacchino

altar: **7** ciboria(pl.) **8** baldakin, ciborium **9** baldachin, ciborium **9** baldachin, baldaquin **10** baldachino **11** baldacchino

bed: **6** tester **7** sparver

canorous: **5** clear **7** musical **8** sonorous **9** melodious **10** euphonious

cant: tip **4** coax, heel, lean, list, nook, sing, tilt, turn **5** argot, bevel, chant, hield, idiom, lingo, lusty, merry, niche, pitch, share, slang, slant, slope, whine **6** careen, corner, herald, intone, jargon, lively, patois, patter, snivel **7** auction, incline, portion, singing, wheedle **8** cheerful, pretense, vigorous **9** barbarism, hyprocrisy, vulgarism **10** intonation, vernacular **13** colloquialism **17** sanctimoniousness

cantabank: **6** singer **7** chanter

cantaloupe 9 muskmelon

cantankerous: **6** ornery **8** perverse **9** irritable, malicious **10** brabagious **11** contentious **12** crossgrained

cantata: **4** mote, poem **8** serenata **11** composition

cantatrice: **6** singer **9** chanteuse

canteen: K.T., P.X., bar **5** bazar, flask **6** bazaar **7** cantina

canter: jog, run **4** gait, lope, pace, rack **5** rogue **6** beggar, whiner **8** vagabond **10** street arab

Canterbury: *archbishop:* Odo **4** Lang **6** Anselm, Becket **7** Cranmer, Dunstan **9** Augustine

gallop: **5** aubin

canticle: ode **4** hymn, laud, song **5** canto **6** anthem, hirmos **7** bravura

church: **6** Te Deum, Venite **10** Magnificat

cantilena: **6** legato, melody **8** graceful

cantillate: hum **5** chant **6** intone, recite

cantina: bar, pub **5** pouch, store **6** pocket, pommel, saloon, tavern **7** canteen, gin mill **8** groggery

canting: **5** atrip, pious **12** hypocritical

cantle: **4** join, nook, part **5** cheer, piece, raise, slice **6** corner **7** portion, segment **8** brighten, fragment **11** cornerpiece

canto: air, fit **4** book, pace, song **5** verse **6** melody, passus

canton: **4** part **5** angle **6** billet, corner **7** portion, quarter, section **8** district, division

cantor: **5** hazan **6** leader, singer **7** chanter, chazzan, soloist **9** precentor

cantoria: **7** balcony, gallery

cantrip: **5** charm, spell, trick

cantus: **4** song **5** chant

canty: **6** lively **8** cheerful **9** sprightly

Canuck: **5** Canadian

canvas: **4** duck, sail, tarp, tent, tewk **5** scrim **6** burlap **7** picture, poldavy **8** painting

waterproof: **9** tarpaulin

canvasback: **4** duck **6** cheval

canvass: **4** beat, hawk, poll, sift **5** randy, study **6** debate, peddle, search **7** agitate, discuss, examine, solicit, trounce **8** campaign, consider **10** scrutinize **11** electioneer, investigate

canvasser: **5** agent **6** poller, rodman **7** counter **8** salesman

canyon: **5** cajon, chasm, gorge, gulch **6** arroyo, ravine

mouth: **4** abra

small: **6** canada

canzonet: air **4** song **5** canto **6** ballad **7** canzona, canzone **8** madrigal

caoba: **5** quira **8** mahogany, muskwood

caoutchouc: **6** rubber

source: ule **6** caucho

cap: fez, hat, lid, taj, tam, tip, top **4** acme, best, coif, cork, dome, eton, hood, hure, mate, pass, topi **5** beret, chief, cover, crown, excel, match, outdo, seize, topee, trump **6** arrest, beanie, bonnet, climax, cornet, helmet, puzzle, summit, top off, turban **7** commode, ferrule, overlie, overtop, perplex, surpass **8** headgear, surprise, tarboosh **9** detonator, headpiece **11** mortarboard

child's: **5** mutch, toque **6** biggin, bonnet

close-fitting: **4** coif **5** toque **6** cloche **7** calotte

covering: **8** havelock

ecclesiastical: **5** beret, miter **6** barret **7** biretta, galerum, galerus **8** barretta **9** zucchetto

hunter's: **7** montero

ignition: **4** fuse, fuze

knitted: **5** toque

military: **4** kepi **5** busby, shako

muslin: **5** mutch

part: **4** bill, peak **5** visor

Roman: **6** pileus

Scotch: tam **8** balmoral **9** glengarry **11** tamoshanter

sheepskin: **6** calpac **7** calpack

skull: **5** beame **6** callot, pileus **7** calotte, yamilke **8** yarmulka

steel: **10** cerveliere

cap-a-pie: **7** utterly **10** throughout

capa: **5** cloak **6** mantle

capability: art **5** craft, skill **6** stroil **7** ability **8** capacity **9** potential **10** competence, efficiency

capable: apt, can, fit **4** able **5** adept **6** expert **7** skilled **9** competent, effective, efficient, qualified **10** proficient **12** accomplished

of being cut: **7** sectile **8** scissile

of being defended: **7** tenable

of being heard: **7** audible

of being molded: **7** plastic

of being touched: **8** tangible

of endurance: 4 wiry 5 tough

of extension: 7 tensile

of flying: 6 volant

of suffering: 8 passible 9 sensitive
render: 6 enable

capacious: 4 full, wide 5 ample, broad, large, roomy 6 goodly 8 captious, spacious 9 extensive 10 commodious 12 considerable

capacitate: 7 qualify

capacity: 4 bent, gift, size, turn 5 knack, power, skill, space 6 burden, extent, spread, talent, volume 7 ability, caliber, calibre, content, faculty, fitness 8 aptitude, strength 9 continent, endowment, intellect 10 capability, competence

Capaneus: *father:* 9 Hipponous

mother: 8 Astynome

slayer: 4 Zeus

son: 9 Sthenelus

wife: 6 Evadne

caparison: 4 deck, trap 8 clothing, covering 9 adornment 10 decoation

cape: ras 4 cope, gape, head, look, neck, ness, writ 5 amice, cappa, cloak, fanon, fichu, orale, point, sagum, stare, stole, talma 6 bertha, chapel, mantle, sontag, tabard, tippet 7 leather, manteel 8 headland, lambskin, mantilla, pelerine 9 inverness, peninsula, sheepskin 10 projection, promontory

crocheted: 6 sontag

lace: 5 fichu 6 bertha 8 collaret

Cape anteater: 8 aardvark

Cape armadillo: 8 pangolin

Cape Colony plateau: 5 karoo 6 karroo

Cape Dutch: 9 Afrikaans

Cape elk: 5 eland

Cape gooseberry: 4 poha 12 ground cherry

Cape jasmine: 8 gardenia

Cape lancewood: 7 assagai

cape merchant: 10 supercargo

Cape polecat: 5 zoril 8 muishond

Cape Province: *people:* 4 Xosa 5 Pondo

Cape ruby: 6 garnet, pyrope

Cape Verde: *capital:* 5 Praia

island: Sal 4 Fago

native: 5 Brava, Serer

Capek: *play:* RUR

creature: 5 robot

capel: 4 rock, wall 5 horse 6 quartz

capelin: 5 smelt 7 ice fish

caper: hop 4 dido, jump, lark, leap, romp, skip, skit 5 antic, brank, dance, flisk, frisk, prank, sauce, shrub 6 cavort, frisco, frolic, gambol, gamond, prance, spring, tittup, vagary 7 corsair, courant, friscal, gambado 8 capricci(pl.), capriole, devilment, marigold 9 capriccio, condiment, privateer 11 monkeyshine, waggishness

family: 13 capparidaceae

capercaillie: 4 cock 6 grouse

courtship: lak

capernoited: 7 crabbed, peevish 9 irritable 11 intoxicated 12 muddleheaded

capernoitie: 4 head 6 noddle

capeskin: 7 leather 9 sheepskin

capful: 4 puff 8 quantity

capias: 4 writ 7 process

capillary: 6 minute 7 slender 8 filiform, hairlike 11 blood vessel

capillus: 4 hair

capilotade: 4 stew 5 sauce 6 ragout

capital: cap, top 4 cash, city, good, main, rare, seat 5 basic, chief, fatal, great, major, money, stock, vital 6 deadly, letter, mortal, primal, wealth 7 central, chattel, leading, radical, serious, weighty 9 copacetic, excellent, paramount, principal, prominent 10 first-class, pre-eminent 11 scrumptious

ancient: 4 Roma

gambler's: 5 stake

impairment of: 7 deficit 9 depletion

inadequate: 10 shoestring

provide: 4 back 5 angel 7 finance

capital punishment: 7 hanging 8 shooting 12 death penalty 13 electrocution

capitalist: 8 investor 9 financier, plutocrat

capitalize: 4 back, fund, help 5 stake 7 finance, sponsor 8 bankroll 9 subsidize

capitano: 5 chief 7 captain, headman, soldier

capitate: 8 headlike, headshaped

Capitol Hill group: 5 House 6 Senate

capitulate: 4 fall 5 agree, title, yield 8 headline 9 enumerate, surrender 11 buckle under

caporal: 7 foreman, tobacco 8 overseer

capote: 4 hood 5 cloak 6 bonnet, mantle, topper 8 overcoat

cappuccino: 14 espresso coffee

capric acid salt: 7 rutate

caprice: fad 4 kink, mood, whim 5 antic, braid, fancy, freak, humor, quirk 6 maggot, notion, temper, vagary, whimsy 7 boutade, conceit, crochet, impulse, whimsey 9 capriccio 12 inconsistent

capricious: 5 dizzy, doddy, fluky, moody 6 fickle 7 comical, erratic, flighty, wayward 8 fanciful, freakish, humorous, unsteady, volatile 9 arbitrary, crotchety, fantastic, humorsome, whimsical 10 changeable, inconstant

Capricorn: 4 Goat 6 beetle 13 Constellation

star within: 5 Deneb

capriole: 4 leap 5 caper 6 spring 9 headdress

capripede: 4 goat 5 satyr

caprylate: 4 acid, salt 5 ester 7 octoate

capsize: 4 coup, keel 5 upset 8 overturn

capstan: 4 drum 5 hoist, lever 8 cylinder, windlass
catch: 4 pawl

capstone: 4 acme, apex, peak 6 apogee, climax 8 pinnacle 11 culmination

capsule: pod 4 boll, casc, pill 5 shell, theco, wafer 6 ampule, sheath 7 ampoule 8 pericarp 9 cartridge, detonator 10 repository

captain: boh 4 head 5 chief 6 leader, master 7 capitan, foreman, headman, manager, skipper 8 capitano, governor 9 centurion, commander, principal 14 superintendent
boat: gig
fictional: 4 Ahab, Nemo 5 Bligh, Queeg
pirate: 4 Kidd

caption: 5 title 6 leader, legend 7 cutline, heading 8 headline, overline, subtitle 9 underline

captious: 5 testy 6 crafty, severe 7 carping, cynical, fretful, peevish 8 alluring, caviling, contrary, critical, perverse, petulant 9 capacious, insidious, irascible 10 capricious, censorious 12 faultfinding 13 hypercritical

captivate: win 4 take 5 catch, charm 6 allure, enamor, please, ravish, subdue 7 attract, bewitch, capture, enamour, enchant 8 enthrall, overtake 9 enrapture, fascinate, infatuate

captive: 5 slave 6 enamor 7 caitiff, hostage 8 prisoner

captivity: 4 bond 6 duress 7 bondage, serfdom, slavery 9 servitude, thralldom 10 subjection 11 confinement 12 imprisonment

captor: 5 taker 6 victor 7 catcher

capture: bag, cop, get, nab, net, win 4 fang, grab, hook, land, prey, take, trap, tree 5 catch, prize, raven, seize 6 arrest, collar, obtain 9 apprehend, captivate 10 circumvent 12 apprehension

capuche: 4 cowl, hood

Capuchin: 5 friar 6 monkey, pigeon

caput: top 4 head 7 chapter, council, section 8 divison 9 paragraph

capybara: 6 rodent

car: (see also **automobile**): box, bus, van 4 auto, jeep, rath 5 buggy, coach, hutch, ratha, sedan, train, wrong 6 basket, hotrod 7 awkward, chariot, trailer, trolley, vehicle 8 roadster, sinister 10 automobile, left-handed 11 convertible 12 station wagon
aerial cable: 6 telfer 7 telpher
armored:
railroad: box, oil 4 club, flat, mail, tank 5 chair, coach, diner 6 buffet, hopper, parlor 7 baggage, caboose, express, freight, gondola, pullman, sleeper, tour-ist 9 furniture, passenger 12 refrigerator

car barn: 5 depot

carabao: 5 mango 7 buffalo

caracara: 4 hawk

caract: See **character**

carafe: 6 bottle

caramel: 5 candy, sweet 6 bonbon 9 flavoring 10 confection

carapace: 5 crust, shell 6 lorica

carara: 9 coronopus

caravan: van 4 trek, trip 5 fleet 6 cafila, convoy, safari, travel 7 journey, vehicle
slave: 6 coffle

caravansary: inn 4 chan, khan 5 hotel, serai 6 hostel, imaret 8 choultry, hostelry 9 resthouse

carbine: gun 5 rifle 6 musket, weapon 7 escopet 9 escopette

carbohydrate: 5 sugar 6 starch 8 dextrose 9 cellulose

carbon: 4 coal, coke, copy, soot 6 crayon 7 replica 8 graphite
deposit: 4 soot
point: 6 crayon

carbonate: 4 burn, char, fizz 6 aerate, alkali 7 enliven 9 carbonize, energizer

carborundum: 5 emery 8 abrasive

carboy: jug 6 bottle

carbuncle: 4 boil 5 jewel 6 garnet 7 abscess, pustule

carcajou: 4 lynx 6 badger, cougar 9 wolverine

carcanet: 5 chain 6 collar 8 headband, necklace

carcass: 4 body 6 corpse 7 carrion

carcoon: 5 clerk 7 manager

card: map, pam, wag 4 comb, menu, plan 5 chart, fiche, joker, tease 6 cartel, ticket 7 program 8 schedule 9 character, eccentric 10 attraction, pasteboard
spot: pip
wool: tum 4 comb, rove, toom

card game: lu; gin, hoc, loo, pam 4 bank, faro, hock, keno, ruff, skat, slam, snap, solo, spin, vint 5 beast, chico, cinch, comet, crimp, decoy, gilet, gleek, monte, omber, ombre, pedro, pique, pitch, poker, rummy, stuss, trump, two-up, waist, whist 6 basset, boston, bridge, casino, commit, ecarte, euchre, fantan, flinch, hearts, masset, piquet, rounce, sledge, smudge 7 baccara, bezique, cayenne, Chicago, canasta, cooncan, old maid, sevenup 8 baccarat, commerce, conquian, contract, cribbage, handicap, Napoleon, patience, pinochle, tresillo, vederuff 9 Newmarket, panguinui, solitaire 10 blackstone 11 everlasting, speculation 14 spite and malice
bid: 4 slam 6 misere
fortune-telling: 5 tarot

cardigan

holding: 6 tenace
old: hoc, loo, pam 4 brag, ruff 5 comet,
gilet, omber, ombre, trump 7 primero,
reversi 8 penneech, penneeck
player who cuts: 4 pone
playing card: ace, pam, ten 4 jack, king,
trey 5 basto(Sp.), deuce, joker, knave,
queen, taroc, tarot
term: bid, bue, cat, pic 4 book, card, deal,
hand, meld, pair, pass, suit 5 flush,
raise, trump 6 renege, tenace, tricon 8
sequence, straight 9 doubleton, singleton 10 Yarborough
widow: 4 skat
wild: 5 joker

cardigan: 6 fabric, jacket, wampus 7
sweater

cardinal: red 4 bird, main 5 basic, chief,
cloak, color, vital 6 cleric 7 radical 9
principal 10 underlying
assembly at Rome: 7 college
hat: 8 gallerum
notification of elevation: 9 biglietto
office: hat 6 datary 7 dataria
title: 8 eminence

cards (see also **card game**): 4 deck, pack,
suit

care: 4 cark, cure, duty, fret, heed, mind,
reck, soin(F.), tend, wish, yeme 5 grief,
guard, nurse, pains, worry 6 burden, desire, grieve, lament, regard, sorrow 7
anxiety, auspice, caution, cherish, concern, keeping, scruple, thought, tuition
8 business 9 attention, diligence, direction, oversight 10 management, solicitude 11 calculation, heedfulness 12
watchfulness 14 responsibility
for: 4 like, mind, tend 5 guard, nurse,
treat 6 foster, relish
requiring: 7 fragile 8 ticklish
under another's: 4 ward 6 charge 7 protege 10 apprentice

careen: tip 4 cant, heel, keel, list, sway,
tilt, veer 5 lurch, slope, swing, weave 7
incline

career: run, way 4 life, road 5 trade 6
charge, course, gallop 7 calling, pursuit,
running 8 business, vocation 10 occupation, profession, racecourse 11
achievement

care for: 4 like, mind, tend 5 nurse 6 foster 7 nurture

carefree: 4 easy 5 frank, happy 6 breezy
8 reckless 10 insouciant 12 happy-go-
lucky, lighthearted

careful: 4 wary 5 canny, chary, exact 6
frugal, intent 7 anxious, guarded, heedful, prudent, thrifty 8 accurate, cautious, diligent, discreet, dreadful, gingerly, mournful, troubled, vigilant,
watchful 9 advertent, attentive, exquisite, observant, provident 10 economi-

cal, meticulous, respectful, respective,
scrupulous, solicitous, thoughtful 11
circumspect, considerate, painstaking,
punctilious

carefully: 7 charily 8 gingerly

careless: lax 4 cool, easy, lash, rash 5
slack 6 casual, overly, remiss, supine,
untidy, unwary 7 languid 8 heedless,
listless, reckless, slattern, slipshod, slovenly 9 forgetful, haphazard, negligent,
unheeding, unmindful 10 delinquent,
neglectful, nonchalant, regardless 11
inadvertent, inattentive, indifferent,
perfunctory, spontaneous, thoughtless,
unconcerned 13 irresponsible

caress: coy, hug, pat, pet 4 bill, dant(Sc.),
kiss, neck 6 coddle, cosset, fondle, pamper, stroke 7 cherish, embrace 10 endearment

caretaker: 6 keeper 7 janitor 9 custodian
11 housekeeper

Carew's love: 5 Celia

careworn: 5 jaded, lined 7 haggard,
pinched 8 troubled 10 distressed

carfuffle: 6 flurry, ruffle 8 disorder 9 agitation 10 disarrange

cargador: 6 porter 7 carrier 9 stevedore

cargo: 4 bulk, load 6 burden, lading 7
freight, payload 8 property, shipment
10 freightage
discarded: 6 jetsam
loader: 9 stevedore
space in ship: 4 hold
stabilizer: 7 ballast
take on: 4 lade, load
wrecked ship: 7 flotsam

Caribbean: *bird:* 4 tody
gulf: 4 Darien
island: 4 Cuba 5 Aruba, Haiti 6 Nassau,
Tobago 7 Curacao, Grenada, Jamaica 8
Dominica, Trinidad 10 Hispaniola,
Puerto Rico 12 Santo Domingo
island group: 7 Leeward 8 Antilles, Windward

caribe: 4 fish 6 pirana, piraya 7 piranha

caribou: 4 deer 8 reindeer

carica: 4 tree 6 papaya, pawpaw

caricature: ape 4 copy, mock, skit 5
farce, libel, mimic, squib 6 overdo, parody, satire 7 cartoon, lampoon 8 travesty 9 burlesque 12 exaggeration

caries: 5 decay 10 ulceration 11 saprodontia

carillon: 5 bells 6 chimes 9 bell tower 12
glockenspiel

cark: ail, vex 4 care, heed, load, stew 5
cavil, pains, worry 6 burden, charge,
harass 7 anxiety, perplex, trouble 8 distress

carling: 6 rafter 7 support

Carmelite: 4 monk 5 friar
barefoot: 8 Teresian

carmen: 4 poem, song 11 incantation

Carmen composer: 5 Bizet

carmine: red 7 crimson, scarlet 8 coloring

carnage: 6 murder, pogrom 8 butchery, massacre 9 bloodshed, slaughter

carnal: 4 crow, lewd 6 animal, bodily, sexual, worldly 7 brutish, earthly, fleshly, secular, sensual 8 material, temporal 9 corporeal 11 unspiritual 12 bloodthirsty, unregenerate

carnation: 4 pink 5 flake 6 flower 7 picotee 9 grenadine(F.)

carnelian: 4 sard 10 chalcedony

carnival: 4 fete 7 revelry 8 festival 11 merrymaking
  attraction: 4 ride 6 midway 8 sideshow 10 concession
  performer: 4 geek

carnivore: cat, dog, fox 4 bear, coon, lion, lynx, mink, puma, seal, wolf 5 civet, coati, genet, hyena, otter, panda, pekah, ratel, sable, stoat, tiger 6 cougar, ermine, feline, ferret, jackal, jaguar, marten, ocelot, possum, serval, weasel 7 dasyure, genette, glutton, leopard, opossum, polecat, raccoon, tigress 8 mongoose 9 ichneumon

carnose: 6 fleshy

carob: 4 tree 6 locust 9 algarroba

carol: lay 4 noel, sing, song 5 ditty, yodel, yodle 6 alcove, ballad, warble 8 madrigal

Caroline island: Yap 4 Truk 5 Palau 6 Kusaie, Ponape

carom: 4 shot 6 bounce, glance, strike 7 rebound 8 ricochet

carousal: 4 lark, orgy, riot, romp, toot 5 binge, drunk, feast, randy, revel, spree 6 frolic, shindy, splore 7 banquet, carouse, wassail 8 festival, jamboree 9 bacchanal

carouse: 4 bout, hell, riot 5 birle(Sc.), bouse, drink, revel, quaff, spree, toast 7 wassail 8 carousal

carp: nag 4 fish, sing, snag, talk, yerk 5 cavil, prate, scold, speak 6 censor, nibble, peck at, recite 7 censure, chatter, henpeck, quibble 8 complain, goldfish 9 criticize, discourse

carpel: 9 carpophyll 10 carpophyll

carpenter: ant, bee 6 framer, joiner, wright 7 artisan, builder 8 tectonic 9 artificer 10 woodworker 12 cabinetmaker
  machine: 5 lathe 6 planer, shaper
  ship: 5 chips
  tool: adz, awl, saw 4 adze 5 level, plane 6 gimlet, hammer, square 7 hatchet

carpet: mat, rug 4 kali 5 scold, tapet, tapis 6 fabric 8 covering
  on the: 11 reprimanded
  design: 9 medallion

variety: 4 Agra 6 velvet, Wilton 7 ingrain 8 Brussels, moquette, Venetian 9 Axminster, broadloom

carping: 6 jawing 7 blaming 8 captious, caviling, critical 10 censorious 12 faultfinding 13 hypercritical

carplike fish: 4 dace, rudd

carpus: 5 wrist

carr, car: bog, fen 4 pool 5 grove

carrack, carack: 4 boat 7 galleon

carrageen: 4 alga, moss 7 seaweed

carriage: air, gig 4 gait, garb, hack, load, mien, shay 5 bandy, brake, break, buggy, coach, front, midge, poise, wagon 6 burden, convoy, landau, manner, surrey 7 baggage, bearing, conduct, gesture, hackney, phaeton, vecture, vehicle 8 behavior, demeanor, dormeuse, equipage, portance 9 behaviour, execution 10 conveyance, deportment, management 14 administration
  baby: 4 pram 5 buggy 6 gocart 8 stroller 12 perambulator
  closed: cab 4 hack, taxi 6 calash 7 caleche 8 brougham, clarence
  covered: 6 Berlin, landau 7 ricksha 8 carryall, dearborn, stanhope
  driver: 4 hack 5 cabby 8 coachman
  four-wheeled: 5 coupe 6 surrey, whisky 7 phaeton, whiskey 8 barouche, clarence, rockaway, victoria 9 chariotee, gladstone
  French: 6 fiacre
  one-horse: fly, gig 4 ekka(Ind.), shay, trap 5 sulky 6 dennet 7 cariole, dogcart 8 carriole
  open: 7 dogcart, dos-a-dos 8 sociable
  portable: 5 sedan
  three-horse: 6 troika
  two-seated: 6 tandem
  two-wheeled: gig 4 shay, trap 5 essed, sulky, tonga 6 chaise, cisium, esseda, hansom 7 carreta, chariot, tilbury 8 carretta 9 caretella, carromata 11 jinrickshaw

carriage trade: 7 society

carried: 5 borne, giddy, toted 6 carted, lugged, wafted 8 drifting, ravished 10 abstracted 11 transported

carrier (see also conveyance): hod 4 ship 5 hamal, macer, plane 6 bearer, cadger, hamaul, hammal, khamal, porter 7 airline, courier, drayman, flattop, hammaul, postman, remover 8 cargador, portator, railroad, teamster 9 messenger

carrion: 4 vile 6 corpse, refuse, rotten 7 carcass, corrupt 9 loathsome

Carroll character: 5 Alice 6 hatter, rabbit 7 duchess 8 Dormouse 9 March Hare 10 Mock Turtle 11 White Rabbit 12 Humpty Dumpty

carrot: 4 root 5 plant 6 daucus 10 enticement
deadly: 5 drias
family: 8 ammaicea
genus: 5 carum
top: 7 red-head
wild: 8 hilltrot 10 laceflower

carrousel: 4 ride 12 merry-go-round

carry: hug, jag, lug 4 bear, cart, gest, hold, lead, take, tote, tump 5 bring, cadge, geste, guide, poise 6 behave, convey, convoy, delate, derive, extend 7 conduct, contain, produce, support, sustain, undergo 8 continue, transfer, transmit 9 prosecute, transport 11 comportment
away: 4 kill, take 5 eloin, reave, steal 6 eloign, remove 7 transport
off: win 4 kill 6 kidnap 7 succeed
on: 4 rant, rave, wage 5 manage 7 conduct, perform, proceed 8 continue, maintain, transact 9 misbehave, prosecute
out: 6 effect 7 execute, perform, sustain 8 complete
over: 4 tide 5 table 6 extend, shelve 8 contango, postpone, transfer
the day: win 7 prevail

carryall: bag, bus 4 case 8 carriage

carrying: 6 gerent 9 gestation

cart: 4 butt, char, dray, haul, tote, wain 5 araba, bandy, bogie, carry, sulky, tonga, wagon 6 charet, convey 7 chariot, hackery, trolley, trundle, tumbler, tumbrel, tumbril, vehicle 8 charette
farmer: 7 morfrey 8 morphrey
freight: 8 carreton
horse: 8 cartaver(Sc.)
license: 6 caroon 7 caroome, carroon
racing: 5 sulky
rope: 5 wanty(Sc.)
strong: 4 dray
two-wheeled: bin, gig 4 shay 5 dandy, sulky, tonga 6 reckla 7 tumbril 8 carretta(Sp.)

cartage: 7 drayage, haulage

carte: map 4 card, list, menu 5 chart 7 charter, diagram

carte du jour: 4 menu

cartel: 4 card, defy, pact, pool, ship 5 paper, trust 6 corner, letter, treaty 8 contract 9 agreement, challenge, syndicate 10 convention

carter: 7 drayman, trucker 8 horseman, teamster

Carthage: *citadel:* 5 Bursa, Byrsa
emblem: 4 palm
foe: 4 Cato
founder: 4 Dido
general: 5 Hanno 8 Hannibal
god: 6 Moloch
goddess: 5 Tanit 6 Tanith

language: 5 Punic
magistrate: 7 suffete
pert. to: 5 Punic
queen: 4 Dido
subject: 6 Libyan
victor at Zama: 6 Scipio

Carthusian: 4 monk 7 eremite
monastery: 5 Pavia 7 Certosa
noted: 4 Hugh
superior: 5 prior

cartilage: 6 tissue 7 gristle
ossified: 4 bone

cartload: 6 fother

cartograph: map 4 plat 5 chart

carton: box 4 case 9 container 10 receptacle

cartoon: 10 caricature

cartoonist: 4 Arno, Capp, Ding, Nast, Szep 5 Gould, Kelly, Young 6 Addams, Disney, Schultz 7 Mauldin, Trudeau 8 Goldberg

cartridge: bag 4 case 5 shell 7 capsule 8 cylinder
holder: 4 clip

cartwheel: 4 coin 6 tumble 10 handspring

carucate: 4 hide, land 5 carve, field

caruncle: 4 comb, gill 6 growth, wattle

carve: cut 4 face, sculp, sever, slice, split 6 chisel, sunder 7 dissect 9 sculpture

carving: *in stone:* 5 cameo 8 intaglio 10 engrailing
pert. to: 7 glyphic, glyptic
relief: 5 cameo

carya: 5 pecan 6 pignut 9 bitternut

caryatid: 6 figure 9 priestess
male: cap 7 telamon

casa: 5 house 8 building, dwelling

casaba: 5 melon 9 muskmelon

Casanova: 4 rake, roue, wolf 5 lover, Romeo 6 chaser 7 Don Juan 8 lothario, paramour 9 ladies' man

cascade: 5 falls, spout, force(Sc.) 8 cataract 9 waterfall

case: bag, box, hap, pod 4 bunk, burr, deed, file, pack, pair, suit 5 brace, bulla, burse, casus, cover, crate, event, folio, state, theca, trial 6 action, affair, binder, carton, chance, coffin, couple, matter, quiver, sheath, survey 7 cabinet, capcase, capsule, enclose, envelop, example, holster, inclose, lawsuit, oddball, satchel 8 accident, argument, cupboard, envelope, instance, pomander, situated 9 cartridge, condition, container, happening 10 occurrence, receptacle, sabretache 11 contingency
cigar: 7 humidor
cosmetic: 7 compact
document: 7 hanaper
explosive: 5 shell 6 petard 11 firecracker

grammatical: 6 dative 8 ablative, genitive, vocative 9 objective 10 accusative, nominative

small: tye 4 etui 5 bulla, etwee 6 trouse

toiletries: 4 etui 5 etwee

case history: 5 story 6 record 7 example 12 illustration

casement: 6 window 8 covering

cash: 4 coin, cush, dump, dust, jack, jake 5 blunt, brass, bread, clink, darby, dough, funds, money 6 specie 7 capital, hemlock 8 currency 10 ready money, spondulics

keeper: 6 bursar, teller 7 cashier 9 treasurer

cashbox: 4 till 6 coffer

cashew: nut 4 tree 7 maranon

cashier: 6 reject, purser 7 destroy, discard, dismiss, kick out 8 throw out 9 terminate

casing: 4 boot, shoe, tire 5 gaine 6 coffin, collet, lining, sheath 8 covering 9 framework

cask: keg, tub, tun, vat 4 butt, cade, cowl, knag, pipe 5 bowie, bulge, foist 6 bareca, bareka, barrel, cardel, casque, firkin, tierce 7 barrico, fostell 8 cassette, hogshead, puncheon 9 kilderkin

bulge: 5 bilge

oil: 4 rier

orifice: 8 bunghole

rim: 5 chimb, chime

stave: lag

wine: fat, tun 4 butt, fust, pipe 6 tierce

casket: box, pix, tye 4 case, cask, cist, till, tomb 5 chest 6 Accera, chasse, coffer, coffin 7 casquet, fostell 8 cassette 9 reliquary

Caspian Sea: 5 Tates

ancient region: 7 Parthia

harbor: 4 Baku

river to: 4 Kura, Ural 5 Terek, Volga

casque: hat 4 cask 5 armor 6 helmet 9 headdress

Cassandra: 7 prophet, seeress

father: 4 Priam

husband: 9 Agamemnon

mother: 6 Hecuba

slayer: 12 Clytemnestra

cassation: 8 quashing 9 annulling, canceling 10 abrogation

cassava: 4 aipi, juca 5 aipim 6 casiri, manioc 7 tapioca

casserole: 4 dish 6 tureen

cassette: 6 casket, holder, sagger 9 cartridge 10 tape holder

cassia: 4 drug, herb, tree 5 senna, shrub

bark: 8 cinnamon

cassie: 6 basket 8 huisache

Cassiopeia: *daughter:* 9 Andromeda

husband: 7 Cepheus

kingdom: 8 Ethiopia

cassock: 4 gown 5 gippo 6 priest 7 pelisse, soutane 9 clergyman

cassone: box 5 chest

cassowary: emu 4 bird 5 murup 6 moorup

cast: 4 hurl, mold, molt, shed, spew, tint, toss 5 eject, fling, found, heave, mould, pitch, shade, sling, throw, tinge 7 cashier, deposit, discard

about: 4 hunt, seek 9 ferret out, search out

aside: see *away* below

away: 4 jilt, junk, shed 5 scrap, wreck 6 maroon, reject 7 abandon, discard, dismiss 8 squander 9 shipwreck

down: 5 abase 6 abattu, deject, sadden 7 abattue, depress, destroy 8 demolish, dispirit 9 woebegone 10 discourage, dispirited 11 crestfallen 12 disconsolate

lots: 5 cavel

off: 4 free 5 untie 6 disown, unmoor 7 discard 9 eliminate

out: 5 eject, expel 6 banish

up: add 5 total, count 6 reckon 7 compute, measure 8 reproach

castaway: 4 waif 5 tramp 6 pariah, reject 7 outcast 8 derelict, stranded 9 shipwreck

caste: 4 rank 5 breed, class, grade, order 6 degree, status

group: 5 varna

merchant: 6 banian, banyan

priestly: 4 magi(pl.) 5 magus

caster: 4 vial 5 cruse, cruet, phial, wheel 6 castor, hurler, roller 7 pitcher, trundle

castigate: 4 lash 5 emend, scare 6 berate, punish, revise, strafe, subdue 7 censure, chasten, correct, reprove 8 chastise, lambaste 9 criticize 10 tongue-lash

castigatory: 5 penal 8 punitive 10 corrective

Castile: *hero:* Cid

province: 5 Avila, Soria

river: 4 Ebro, Esla 5 Douro, Duero

Castilian: 7 Spanish

casting: *mold:* die 6 matrix 7 matrice

rough: pig

castle: 4 fort, rock, rook 5 abode, morro 7 bastile, chateau, citadel 8 bastille, castillo, fastness, fortress 10 stronghold 13 fortification

gate: 10 portcullis

in the air: 5 dream 6 vision 7 fantasy 8 daydream 9 imagining

ledge: 7 rampart

part: 4 bawn, moat 6 donjon 10 drawbridge

tower: 4 keep 6 turret

wall: 6 bailey 10 battlement

warden: 6 disdar, dizdar 9 castellan

castor: hat 4 bean, star 6 beaver 7 leather

Castor: *and Pollux:* 5 twins 6 Gemini 8 Dioscuri

brother: 6 Pollux 10 Polydeuces

father: 4 Zeus 9 Tyndareus

horse: 8 Cyllaros

mother: 4 Leda

sister: 5 Helen

slayer: 4 Idas

castor oil: 9 cathartic

castrate: gib 4 geld, spay, swig 5 alter, capon, prune 6 eunuch, neuter 7 evirate 8 caponize, mutilate 10 emasculate

casual: 5 stray 6 chance, random 7 cursory, natural, offhand 8 informal 9 easy-going, haphazard, uncertain 10 accidental, contingent, fortuitous, incidental, nonchalant, occasional 11 indifferent, low-pressure 14 unconventional, unpremeditated

casualty: 4 loss 5 death 6 chance, hazard, injury, mishap 8 accident, disaster 9 mischance 10 misfortune 11 contingency 12 misadventure

casus: 4 case 5 event 6 occasion

cat: 4 flog, lion, lynx, pard, puma, puss 5 civet, felid, gatol(Sp.), kitty, moggy, ounce, pussy, tiger 6 cougar, feline, jaguar, malkin, mawkin, ocelot, tibert 7 caracal, cheetah, leopard, panther, tigress, wildcat 8 baudrons(Sc.) 9 carnivore, grimalkin 11 caterpillar 12 catamountain, mountain lion

breed: 4 Manx 5 alley, tabby 6 Angora, Calico 7 Maltese, Persian, Siamese

civetlike: 5 genet

cry: mew 4 hiss, meow, miau, purr 5 miaou, miaow, miaul

disease: 9 distemper

Eugene Field's: 6 calico

female: 9 grimalkin

genus: 5 felis 7 felidae(pl.)

cat-o-nine-tails: 4 lash, whip 7 cattail

catachresis: 10 word misuse

cataclysm: 5 flood 6 deluge 7 debacle 8 disaster, overflow, upheaval 11 catastrophe

catacomb: 4 tomb 5 crypt, vault 8 cemetery

catafalque: 4 bier 6 coffin

cataian: 5 thief 7 sharper 9 scoundrel

catalepsy: 9 trance 7 seizure

catalog, catalogue: 4 book, list, roll, rota 5 brief, canon, flyer, index 6 record, roster 7 arrange, itemize 8 classify, register, schedule 9 enumerate, repertory 10 prospectus 11 systematize

of books: 11 bibliotheca

of goods: 9 inventory

of saints: 9 hagiology

Catalonia: *dance:* 7 sardana

marble: 8 brocatel 10 brocatelle

catalyst: 4 goad, spur 7 impetus 8 stimulus 9 incentive 10 motivation

catamaran: 4 raft, trow 6 balsa, float 6 vessel 8 auntsary

catamount: 4 lynx, puma 6 cougar

cataplasm: 8 poultice

catapult: 5 throw 6 launch, onager 7 bricole 8 ballista, crossbow 9 slingshot

cataract: lin 4 linn 5 falls, flood 6 deluge 7 cascade, Niagara 8 Victoria 9 waterfall 10 eye disease

cataria: 6 catnip

catarrh: 4 cold 5 rheum

catastrophe (see also **cataclysm**): 8 accident, calamity, disaster, fatality 10 denouement, misfortune

catbird: 7 mimidae

catcall: boo 4 hoot, razz 6 deride 8 poohpooh 10 Bronx cheer

catch: bag, cop, get, nab, net 4 draw, hasp, haul, hawk, hold, hook, land, nail, pawl, snap, stop, trap, tree 5 grasp, hitch, ketch, knack, seize, snare, trick 6 button, clutch, corner, detect, detent, engage, enmesh, entrap, snatch 7 attract, capture, ensnare, grapnel 8 entangle, overtake, surprise 9 intercept 12 come down with

fire: 6 ignite, kindle

one's breath: 4 gasp 5 chink

sight of: 4 espy, spot 6 descry

up with: 8 overtake

catchall: bag 6 basket 10 receptacle

catchfly: 5 plant 6 silence 7 campion

catching: 6 taking 8 alluring 10 contagious, entrapping, infectious 11 captivating

catchword: cue, tag 5 motto 6 byword, phrase, slogan

catchy: 6 fitful, tricky 9 appealing

cate: 4 food 6 viands 8 dainties 10 delicacies, provisions

catechism: 5 guide 6 manual 8 carritch 9 questions 10 carritches(Sc.)

catechumen: 5 pupil 7 audient, auditor, convert, student 8 beginner, neophyte

categorical: 8 absolute, explicit 11 dictatorial, unequivocal, unqualified

category: 4 rank 5 class, genus, genre(pl.), order 6 family 7 species 8 division 12 denomination 14 classification

catena: 4 link 5 chain 6 series 7 excerpt

cater: 4 feed 5 humor, serve, treat 6 pander, purvey, supply 7 provide

caterpillar: cat 4 muga 5 aweto, eruca, larva 6 canker, erucae(pl.), risper, woubit 7 tractor

caterwaul: cry 4 wail 5 miaul

catface: 4 scar

catfish: mud 4 cusk, elod, pout, raad, shal 5 bagre, raash 6 docmac, hassar,

raasch, tandau 7 candiru 8 bullhead 9
sheatfish
genus: 13 saccobranchus
catgut: 4 cord, ropp 5 tharm 6 string, violin
cathartic: 8 lapactic, laxative 9 cleansing,
purgative
cathedral: dom 5 duomo 6 church
passage: 5 slype
cathode: 9 electrode
catholic: 5 broad, papal 6 cosmic, global 7
general, liberal 8 tolerant 9 universal
10 ecumenical
Catholic: See Roman Catholic
catkin: 5 ament, spike
catlike: 6 feline 8 stealthy 9 noiseless
catmint: nep, nip 4 herb
catnap: 4 doze 6 siesta, snooze
catnip: nep 6 catnep 7 cataria, catwort
Catoism: 9 austerity, harshness
Catreus: *daughter:* 6 Aerope 7 Clymene 9
Apemosyne
father: 5 Minos
mother: 8 Pasiphae
cat's-cradle: 7 ribwort
cat's-paw: 4 dupe, gull, pawn, tool 5 cully
cattail: 4 flag, musk, rush 5 ament, cloud,
raupo, reree 6 catkin 7 bulrush, ma-
treed
family: 9 typhaceae
cattle: 4 cows, dhan(Ind.), kine, neat,
oxen 5 beefs, bulls, stock 6 beasts,
beeves, steers 7 bovines
assemblage: 4 herd 5 drove
brand: 4 duff 5 buist
breed: 4 Nata, Zobo 5 Angus, Devon,
Dutch, Niata(dwarf) 6 Durham, Belted,
Jersey, Sussex 7 Brahman, Brangus,
Kerries 8 Ayrshire, Bradford, Char-
bray, Guernsey, Hereford, Holstein,
Longhorn 9 Red Polled, Shorthorn,
Teeswater 10 Beefmaster, Brown Swiss
11 Charollaise, Dutch Belted 14
French Canadian, Santa Gertrudis
call: 4 sook
castrated: 5 steer
dealer: 6 drover, herder
dehorned: 5 muley 6 mulley
female: cow
genus: bos
goddess: 8 Bubona
group: 4 herd 5 drove 7 creaght(Ir.)
plague: 10 rinderpest
shelter: 4 byre 5 barth
tick: 8 carapato
yard: 6 cancha
cattleman: 6 cowboy 7 byreman 8 stockman
catty: 4 mean 8 spiteful 9 malicious
catwalk: 7 footway, walkway
catwort: 6 catnip
Caucasian: *goat:* tur

ibex: zac
language: Laz, Udi 4 Andi, Avar, Laze,
Lazi, Udic 5 Udish 7 Semitic 9 Itrani-
can
race: 5 Aryan, Osset 6 Ossete
rug: 4 baku, kuba 5 chila 7 derbend
tribe: 4 Imer, Kurd, Laze, Lazi, Svan 5
Pshav 7 Kubachi
caucho: ule 4 tree 6 rubber
caucus: 7 council, meeting, primary 8
election
caudal: 4 rear 9 posterior
appendage: 4 tail
caudata: 4 newt 5 snake 10 salamander
cauk: 5 chalk 9 limestone
caul: web 4 cawl, trug, veil 7 network,
omentum 8 membrane, tressour, tressure
cauldron: See caldron
cauliflower: 7 cabbage 8 broccoli 9 disfigure
caulk, calk: 4 cork, fill, flag 6 chinse 7
chintze
cause: aim, gar(Sc.), key 4 case, chat,
move, root, spur, suit 5 agent, basis,
breed 6 create, effect, gossip, ground,
induce, malady, motive, object, origin,
reason, source, spring 7 concern, disease, lawsuit, produce, provoke 8 business, engender, movement, occasion 9
originate, wherefore 10 bring about,
mainspring, prime mover
causerie: 4 chat, plea, talk 6 debate 10
discussion 12 conversation
causes, science of: 8 etiology
causeuse: 4 sofa 9 tete-a-tete
causeway: way 4 dike, road 7 chaus-
se(F.), highway
causey: dam, way 4 bank, pave, road 5
mound 6 street 7 highway 8 sidewalk
caustic: lye 4 tart 5 acrid, sharp 6 biting,
bitter, severe 7 burning, cutting, erodent, mordant, pungent, satiric 8 alkaline, scathing, snappish, stinging 9 corrosive, sarcastic, satirical, vitriolic 10
malevolent 11 acrimonious
agent: 7 cautery, erodent
cauterize: 4 burn, char, fire, sear 5 brand,
inust, singe 9 sterilize
caution: 4 care, heed, warn 6 advice, cautel, caveat, exhort 7 anxiety, counsel,
precept, proviso 8 admonish, forecast,
monition, prudence, wariness 9 diligence, vigilance 10 admonition, precaution, providence 11 calculation, forethought, reservation 12 watchfulness
cautious: 4 wary 5 alert, canny, chary,
siker 6 fabian, sicker 7 careful, guarded, prudent 8 discreet, vigilant 10 scrupulous 11 circumspect
cavalcade: 4 raid, ride 5 march 6 parade,
safari 7 journey, pageant 10 procession

cavalier: gay 4 curt, easy, fine 5 brave, frank, lofty, proud, rider 6 escort, knight 7 brusque, gallant, haughty, offhand, soldier 8 Royalist 9 caballero, chevalier 10 disdainful 12 high-spirited, supercilious 13 high-and-mighty

Cavalleria Rusticana character: 4 Lola 5 Alfio 7 Turiddu

cavalry: 6 horses, troops 8 horsemen 10 knighthood
horse: 6 lancer
weapon: 5 lance, saber

cavalryman: 5 spahi 6 hussar, lancer, spahee 7 courier, dragoon, soldier, trooper 8 gendarme, horseman

cave: den, tip 4 café, cove, hole, lair, rear, sink, toss, weem 5 antre, cavea, crypt, speos, store, upset 6 beware, cavern, cavity, cellar, forgou, grotto, hollow, larder, luster, pantry, plunge 7 reserve, spelunk 8 collapse, overturn 9 storeroom 10 wine cellar
dweller: 10 troglodyte
researcher: 9 spelunker 12 speleologist
science of researching: 10 speleology

cave in: 5 stove, yield 6 submit 8 collapse

caveat: 6 beware, notice 7 caution, warning

cavern: den 4 cave, grot, hole, lair, weem 5 antra(pl.), croft 6 antrum, cavity, grotto, hollow 7 spelunk

cavernous: 4 vast 6 gaping, hollow 10 sepulchral 11 reverberant

cavetto: 7 gorge 7 molding

caviar: ova, roe 4 eggs, ikra 5 ikary 6 relish 8 delicacy
source: 6 beluga 7 sterlet 8 sturgeon

cavie: 4 cage, coop 7 hencoop

cavil: 4 cark, carp, haft 6 haggle 7 quibble 9 criticise, criticize, exception, objection

caviling: 4 mean 5 fussy, small 8 captious, picayune

cavity: bag, pit, sac 4 abri, cave, dalk, dent, hole, mine, vein, void 5 antra(pl.), atria(pl.), fossa, geode, lumen, mouth, sinus 6 antrum, atrium, camera, cavern, fossae(pl.), grotto, hollow, vacuum 7 cistern, vesicle 8 cul-de-sac 10 depression, excavation
anatomical: 5 antra(pl.), fossa 6 antrum, fossae(pl.)
brain: 6 coelia
gun: 4 bore
heart: 7 auricle 9 ventricle
lode: 4 voog, vugg, vugh
pert. to: 5 sinal 6 atrial, geodic
sac-like: 5 bursa 6 bursae(pl.)
skull: 4 aula 5 fossa, sinus
stone: 5 geode

cavort: 4 play, romp 5 bound, caper, cut up 6 curvet, gambol, prance 11 horse around

cavy: 4 paca, pony 6 agouti, aperea, cayuse, rodent 8 capybara 9 guinea pig

caw: cry 4 call, cawl 5 croak, quark, quawk 6 squall, squawk

cawl: 4 trug 6 basket

caxi: 4 fish 7 snapper

cay: See key

cayenne: 5 whist 6 canary, pepper 8 capsicum

cayuse: 4 cavy, pony 6 bronco 7 broncho

cease: end 4 halt, liss, quit, rest, stop 5 avast, douse, dowse, lisse, pause, peter 6 desist, devall, finish 7 abstain, refrain 8 intermit, knock off, leave off 9 terminate 11 discontinue

cease-fire: 5 truce 9 armistice

ceaseless: 4 ever 7 endless 8 unending 9 continual, incessant, unceasing 11 never-ending

ceasing: 9 cessation

Cecrops' daughter: 5 Herse 8 Aglauros

cecum: pit 4 pore 6 cavity

cedar: 4 toon, tree 5 savin 6 deodar, sabina, sabine, savine 7 waxwing
camphor: 6 cedrol
green: 5 cedre(F.), color
moss: 8 hornwort

cede: 4 cess, give 5 award, grant, leave, waive, yield 6 assign, resign, submit 8 hand over, renounce, sign over, transfer 9 surrender 10 relinquish

cedula: 8 document, schedule 11 certificate

ceil: 4 line 7 overlay 8 wainscot

ceiling: 6 lining, screen, soffit 7 curtain, testudo 8 covering, paneling 10 testudines(pl.) 11 wainscoting
covering: 9 calcimine, kalsomine
decorated: 7 plafond
division: 5 trave
mine: 5 astel
wooden: 8 plancher

Celebes: *bovine:* ox 4 anoa
island: 4 Muna
people: 6 toraja 7 toradja

celebrate: 4 keep, sing 5 extol, honor, revel 6 extoll, praise 7 glorify, observe 8 emblazon, eulogize, proclaim 9 solemnize 11 commemorate

celebrated: 4 kept 5 famed, noted 6 famous 7 eminent, feasted, renomme 8 glorious, observed, renowned 9 distingue, prominent 10 solemnized 11 conspicuous, illustrious 13 distinguished

celebration: 4 fete, rite 6 renown 7 jubilee 8 jamboree 9 celebrity, festivity

celebrity: VIP 4 fame, lion, name, star 5 eclat 6 renown, repute 9 superstar 11 celebration

celerity: 5 haste, hurry, speed 8 dispatch, rapidity, velocity 9 prestezza, quickness, swiftness

celery: *family:* 6 pascal
　relative of: 6 carrot 7 parsnip
　wild: 8 smallage
celestial: 4 holy 6 divine, uranic 7 angel-
　ic, Chinese, ethered 8 beatific, empyre-
　al, ethereal, heavenly, Olympian
　being: 5 angel 6 cherub, seraph 8 sera-
　phim(pl.)
　body: sun 4 moon, star 5 comet 6 meteor,
　nebula, planet 8 asteroid 9 satellite
　elevation of mind: 7 anagoge
　matter: 6 nebula
celibacy: 8 chastity
celibate: 6 chaste, single 8 bachelor, spin-
　ster 9 unmarried
cell: egg 4 cage, germ, jail 5 cabin, crypt,
　group, vault 6 cytode, prison 7 cellule,
　chamber, cubicle, dungeon 9 hermitage
　10 ergastulum 11 compartment
　blood: red 5 white 8 hemocyte 9 leuko-
　cyte 11 erythrocyte
　bull: 5 toril 7 toriles(pl.)
　coloring: 10 endochrome
　colorless: 10 achroacyte, lymphocyte
　connecting: 10 heterocyst
　division: 7 spireme
　generative: 6 gamete
　group: 6 ceptor 7 cascade 8 blastema
　layer: 8 blastula 10 blastoderm
　lens-shaped: 8 lenticel
　migratory: 9 leucocyte
　pert. to: 6 cytoid
　photoelectric: eye
　star-shaped: 10 astroblast
　structural unit: 7 energid, nucleus 10 pro-
　toplast
　study of: 8 cytology
　substance: 5 linin
cell-like: 6 cytoid
cella: 4 naos
cellar: 4 cave 5 vault 7 hypogee 8 base-
　ment 9 storeroom
cellaret: 4 case 7 cabinet 9 sideboard
cellophane: 7 wrapper 9 packaging
cellular: 6 porous 7 areolar 9 alveolate
celluloid: 4 film 6 plastic 8 xylonite
cellulose: *acetate:* 7 acetose
　elastic: 5 rayon
Celsius: 10 centigrade 11 thermometer
Celt: 4 Gael, Gaul, Manx 5 Irish, Welsh 6
　Breton, Briton, Eolith 7 Cornish
Celtic: 4 Erse, Gael 7 Scotch
　abbot: 5 coarb
　chariot: 5 essed
　chieftain: 6 tanist
　divinity: 7 Taranis
　foot soldier: 4 kern
　giant: 5 Fomor
　god: Ler 4 Leir, Llyr
　harp: 5 telyn 11 clairschach
　hero: 5 Fionn
　language: 4 Erse, Manx 5 Irish, Welsh 6

Celtic, Cymric, Gaelic 9 Brythonic
　peasant: 4 kern
　priest: 5 Druid
　sword: sax 4 seax
cembalo: 8 dulcimer 11 harpsichord
cement: fix 4 glue, join, knit, lime, lute 5
　imbed, paste, putty, stick, unify, unite
　6 cohere, fasten, gulgul(Ind.), mortar,
　solder 7 asphalt 8 adhesive, concrete,
　hadigeon(F.), solidify 11 agglutinate
　hydraulic: 4 paar
　infusible substance: 4 lute
　mixer: 8 temperer
　plastic: 8 albolite, albolith
　quick-drying: 6 mastic
　substance: 6 celite
　window glass: 5 putty
cemetery: 6 litten 7 charnel 8 catacomb,
　Golgotha 9 graveyard 10 necropolis 11
　polyandrium
　underground: 8 catacomb
cenchrus: 5 grass 6 millet
cenobite: nun 4 monk 5 friar 6 essene 7
　recluse 8 monastic 9 anchorite
cenoby: 5 abbey 6 priory 7 convent
cense: 4 rank 6 assess, rating 7 perfume,
　thurify 8 estimate, position
censer: 8 thurible
censor: 4 blip, edit 6 critic, cut out 7
　clean up 8 restrict, suppress 9 detrac-
　tor, blue-pencil
censorious: 6 severe 7 carping 8 blame-
　ful, captious, critical 9 satirical 10 de-
　nouncing 11 reproachful 12 fault find-
　ing
censurable: 5 amiss, wrong 8 blamable,
　culpable 13 reprehensible
censure: 4 carp, flay 5 blame, chide, de-
　cry, judge, slate 6 accuse, berate,
　charge, rebuff, rebuke, remord, tar-
　gue(Scot.), tirade 7 chasten, condemn,
　impeach, inveigh, reprove 8 disallow,
　reproach 9 challenge, criticize, repri-
　mand 10 animadvert, exprobrate, vitu-
　perate 11 disapproval 12 reprehension
　13 animadversion 15 discommendation
census: 4 list, poll 5 count 11 enumeration
cent: 4 coin 5 penny 6 copper
centaur: 6 Chiron, Nessus 8 horseman
　father: 5 Ixion
Centennial State: 8 Colorado
center, centre: cor, hub, mid 4 axis, core,
　foci(pl.), nave, seat 5 focus, heart,
　midst, pivot, spine 6 middle 7 lineman,
　nucleus 8 centrate 10 focal point 12
　headquarters
　away from: 6 distal
　toward: 4 orad 5 entad 10 centerward
centerpiece: 7 epergne
centigrade: 5 scale 7 Celsius 11 ther-
　mometer
centipede: 4 veri 6 earwig, golach, goloch

8 chilopod, myriapod 9 arthropod, geophilus

central: key, mid 5 axial, basic, chief, focal, prime 6 median, middle 7 capital, centric, leading, pivotal, primary 8 dominant 11 equidistant 12 all-absorbing

Central Africa: See Africa

Central America: *agave:* 5 sisal
  ant: 5 kelep
  bird: 7 jacamar 8 puffbird
  canoe: 6 pitpan
  country: 6 Belize, Panama 8 Honduras, Salvador 9 Costa Rica, Guatemala, Nicaragua 10 El Salvador
  ethnic group: 6 Indian 7 Mestizo
  fishing boat: 6 cayuco
  gopher: 7 quachil
  Indian: 4 Maya 5 Carib
  language: 7 Nahuatl, Spanish
  measure: 7 cantaro, manzana
  monkey: 4 mono
  mullet: 4 bobo
  rodent: 4 paca
  snake: 10 bushmaster
  stockade: 4 boma
  tragon: 4 bird 6 quezal 7 quetzal
  tree: ebo, ule 4 eboe 5 amate 9 sapodilla
  village: 4 boma
  weight: 5 libra

Central Asia: See Asia

centric: 5 focal 6 middle, tarete 7 central 9 clustered 11 cylindrical 12 concentrated

centrifugal: 8 efferent 9 radiating

centripetal: 8 afferent, unifying 12 centralizing

century: age 6 siecle(F.)
  ten: 7 chiliad 10 millennium

century plant: 4 aloe 5 agave 6 maguey 7 tequila
  fiber: 4 pita, pito

ceorl: 5 churl, thane 7 freeman, villein

cepa: 5 onion

cephalagia: 8 headache

cephalic: 8 atlantal, cerebral

cephalopod: 5 squid 6 cuttle 7 inkfish, octopus
  secretion: ink

Cepheus: *daughter:* 9 Andromeda
  wife: 10 Cassiopeia

ceral: 4 waxy 7 waxlike

ceramics: 5 tiles 7 pottery 9 stoneware
  oven: 4 kiln
  sieve: 4 laun

cerate: wax 4 lard 5 salve 8 ointment

ceratoid: 5 horny

Cerberus: dog 7 monster 8 guardian 9 custodian

cere: wax 4 sere, wrap 6 anoint, embalm

cereal: rye 4 bean, bran, corn, mush, oats, rice 5 grain, maize, spelt, wheat 6 barley, farina, hominy 7 oatmeal, soybean 8 porridge 9 buckwheat
  coating: 4 bran
  grass: oat, rye 4 ragi, rice 5 grain, wheat 6 barley, raggee
  seed: 6 kernel
  spike: ear

cereal grass genus: 6 secale

cerebral: 6 mental 7 psychic 8 highbrow

cerebration: 7 thought 9 brainwork 10 reflection

cerement: 6 shroud 9 cerecloth

ceremonial fuss: 10 panjandrum

ceremonious: 5 grand, lofty, stiff 6 formal, proper, solemn 7 precise, stately, studied 10 respectful 11 punctilious 12 conventional

ceremony: 4 fete, form, pomp, rite, show, sign 5 state 6 augury, parade, powwow, review, ritual 7 display, pageant, portent, prodigy 8 accolade, function, marriage, occasion 9 formality, solemnity 10 observance 11 celebration

Ceres: 7 Demeter
  daughter: 10 Persephone, Proserpina
  father: 6 Cronus, Saturn
  mother: Ops 4 Rhea

cerise: red 6 cherry

cerite: 7 mineral 8 allanite

cernuous: 7 nodding 8 drooping 9 pendulous

cero: 4 fish 6 sierra 7 cavallo, pintado 8 mackerel

certain: 4 firm, real, sure, true 5 bound, clear, exact, fixed, plain, siker(Sc.) 6 actual, sicker, stated 7 assured, precise, settled 8 absolute, apparent, constant, official, positive, reliable, resolved, unerring 9 confident, steadfast, undoubted 10 dependable, inevitable, infallible, undeniable 11 determinate, indubitable, trustworthy 12 indisputable 13 incontestable 14 unquestionable 16 incontrovertible

certainly: 4 amen, ywis 5 iwiss, truly 6 certes, indeed, verily 7 hardily 8 forsooth

certainty: 8 firmness, sureness 9 assurance, dogmatism 10 confidence, conviction

certificate: 4 bond 5 check, libel, scrip 6 attest, ticket, verify 7 diploma, voucher 9 statement, testimony 10 credential 11 attestation, declaration, testimonial 13 certification
  cargo: 8 navicert
  debt: IOU 9 debenture
  land: 6 amparo(Sp.)
  medical, for ill student: 8 aegrotat
  money owed: 9 debenture

certify: 4 avow, vise 5 swear 6 affirm, assure, depose, evince, verify 7 endorse,

license, testify **9** determine, guarantee
    under oath: 6 attest
certiorari: 4 writ 6 review
cerulean: 4 blue 5 azure 6 coelin 7 sky-
    blue
cervine: elk 4 deer, stag 5 moose 6 cervid
    8 cervidae(pl.), reindeer
cervix: 4 neck
cespitose: 6 matted, tufted 7 tangled
cess: bog, tax 4 cede, duty, levy, luck, rate,
    tyrf 5 slope, yield 6 impost 7 measure
    9 surrender 10 assessment, estimation
cessation: end 4 halt, liss, lull, rest, stay,
    stop 5 letup, lisse, pause, truce 6 recess
    7 ceasing, respite 8 interval, stoppage,
    surcease 9 armistice, remission 10 con-
    clusion 11 termination 12 intermis-
    sion, interruption 14 discontinuance
    of being: 8 desition
cession: 8 yielding 9 surrender 10 com-
    pliance, concession
cesspool: den, sty 4 sump 7 cistern
cetacean: orc 4 cete, orca 5 whale 6 belu-
    ga 7 dolphin, grampus 8 porpoise
    blind: 4 susu
    genus: 4 inia
cete: 5 whale 7 cetacea
Ceylon: *aborigine:* 4 Toda 5 Vedda 6
    Veddah
    bay: 4 Palk
    boat: 4 done, doni 5 balsa, dhoni, doney
        11 warkamoowee
    capital: 7 Colombo
    coin: 4 cent
    Dravidian: 5 Tamil
    garment: 6 sarong
    gooseberry: 10 ketembilla
    governor: 6 disawa
    hemp: 6 sina-wa
    hill dweller: 4 Toda
    language: 4 Pali 5 Tamil
    measure: 4 para 5 parra 6 amunam, par-
        rah
    modern name: 8 Sri Lanka
    monkey: 4 maha 5 toque 6 langur, rilawa,
        rillow 10 wanderoock
    moss: 4 agar, alga 5 jaffa 7 gulaman
    native: 5 Vedda 6 Veddah
    oak: 5 kusam
    palm: 7 talipat, talipot
    rat: 9 bandicoot
    resthouse: 6 abalam
    rice: 4 padi 5 paddy
    rose: 8 cleander
    seaport: 5 Galle
    sedan: 6 tomjon, tonjon
    skirt: 6 reddha
    snake: 7 adjiger
    soldier: 4 peon
    tea: 5 pekoe
    tree: 4 doon, hara, palu, tala 7 talipot
Chablis: 4 wine 8 Burgundy

chack: 4 bite, snap 5 clack, snack 8
    wheatear
chackle: 6 cackle, rattle 7 chatter
chacma: 6 baboon
chacra: 4 farm 5 milpa, ranch
Chad: *capital:* 8 N'Djamena
    monetary unit: 5 franc
    river: 5 Chari 6 Logone
chaeta: 4 seta 5 spine 7 bristle
chafe: irk, rub, vex 4 fret, frig, frot, fume,
    gall, heat, josh, rage, warm, wear 5 an-
    ger, annoy, grind, scold 6 abrade, ban-
    ter, excite, fridge, harass, injury, nettle
    7 incense, inflame 8 friction, irritate,
    raillery
chaff: guy, hay, kid, pug 4 bran, caff(Sc.),
    guff, joke, josh, quiz, twit 5 borak,
    chyak, dross, glume, hulls, husks, straw,
    tease, trash 6 banter, bhoosa, chyack,
    refuse 7 tailing 8 raillery, ridicule
chaffer: 5 bandy, sieve, wares 6 buying,
    dicker, haggle, higgle, market 7 bargain,
    chatter, selling, traffic 8 exchange 9 ne-
    gotiate 11 merchandise
chaffinch: 7 robinet
chaffy: 5 scaly 7 acerose, acerous, paleate,
    trivial 9 bantering, worthless 10 palea-
    ceous
Chaillot resident: 8 madwoman
chain: guy, row, set, tew, tie, tye 4 bind,
    bond, file, gyve, join, link 5 cable, leash,
    suite, train 6 catena, chigon, collar, fas-
    ten, fetter, hobble, secure, series, string,
    tether 7 bobstay, catenae(pl.), connect,
    embrace, enslave, manacle, network,
    shackle 8 bracelet, restrain 9 constrain
    10 chatelaine 13 concatenation
    collar: 4 tore 6 torque
    key: 10 chatelaine
    of quotations: 6 catena
    of rocks: 4 reef
    ornamental: 10 chatelaine
    pert. to: 8 catenary
    set with precious stones: 7 sautoir
chain-like: 8 catenate
chains: 7 bondage, serfdom
    lady in: 9 Andromeda
chair: 4 seat 5 sedan, stool 6 office, pul-
    pit, rocker 7 preside
    back: 5 splat
    bishop's official: 8 cathedra
    cover: 4 tidy 12 antimacassar
    decoration: 8 claw foot
    easy: 6 morris, rocker
    folding: 9 faldstool
    litterlike: 4 kago
    occupy: 7 preside
    portable: 5 sedan
    type: 4 club, easy 6 morris 7 rocking 8
        captain's 9 reclining
chairperson: 4 head 5 emcee 7 speaker 8
    director 9 moderator 10 supervisor

chaise: gig 4 shay 7 curicle 8 carriage

chaise longue: 6 daybed

chalcedony: 4 onyx, opal, sard 5 agate 6 jasper, quartz 7 opaline 9 carnelian 10 bloodstone 11 chrysoprase

orange: 4 sard

Chalcodon: *father:* 4 Abas

son: 9 Elephenor

Chaldea: 9 Babylonia

measure: 4 cane, foot 5 makuk, qasab 6 artaba, gariba, ghalva 7 mansion

river: 6 Tigris 9 Euphrates

chalet: hut 5 cabin, house 7 cottage 8 lavatory

chalice: ama, cup 4 bowl 5 calix, grail 6 goblet 7 calices(pl.)

cover: 4 pall 8 animetta

chalk: 4 cauk, pale, scar, talc, tick 5 creta, score 6 blanch, bleach, crayon, credit, rubble, whiten 7 account 9 limestone, reckoning

out: 6 sketch 8 block out, rough out 11 skeletonize

up: get, win 6 pick up 7 acquire

challenge: 4 call, dare, defy, gage 5 blame, brave, claim, query, stump 6 accuse, appeal, cartel, charge, dacker, daiker, demand, forbid, impugn, invite, take on 7 arraign, censure, impeach, provoke, reprove, summons 8 question, reproach 9 exception, objection 10 controvert 11 impeachment

judge: 6 recuse

to a duel: 6 cartel

challenger: 5 rival 7 duelist 8 pugilist 9 adversary, contender 10 competitor

chamber: oda 4 cell, fiat, hall, kiva, room 5 atria(pl.), bower, solar, soler 6 atrium, camara, camera, hollow, sollar 7 bedroom, caisson, cubicle, lochlus 9 apartment, camarilla, vestibule 11 compartment

annealing: 4 leer

bombproof: 8 casemate

council: 10 consistory

drying: 4 kiln, oven

judge's: 6 camera

pert. to: 7 cameral

private: 5 adyta(pl.) 6 adytum 7 sanctum 8 conclave

underground: 4 cave 5 crypt 6 cavern 7 hypogee

chamberlain: 6 factor 7 officer, servant, steward 9 attendant, chamberer, treasurer 10 camerlengo 14 superintendent

papal: 10 camerlengo, camerlingo

chambray: 5 cloth 6 fabric 7 gingham

chameleon: 5 anole, anoli 6 lizard

chameleonic: 6 fickle 10 changeable, inconstant

chamfer: 5 bevel, flute 6 furrow, groove 7 channel 11 countersink

chamois: 4 gems, skin 5 cloth, gemse 6 chammy, shammy, shamoy 7 leather 8 antelope, ruminant

male: 7 gemsbok

champ: 4 bite, chaw, firm, hard, mash 5 field, gnash 7 trample 8 ruminate 9 masticate 11 battlefield

champagne: 4 wine 5 color 6 bubbly

champignon: 6 fungus 8 mushroom

champion: ace, aid 4 abet, back, defy, hero 6 assert, attend, defend, squire, victor 7 espouse, fighter, protect 8 advocate, defender 9 challenge, combatant, firstrate 10 blue-ribbon, unexcelled 11 outstanding, titleholder

championship: 5 crown, title 7 defense, pennant 8 advocacy 9 supremacy 10 leadership

champleve: 6 enamel, inlaid

chance: die, hap, lot 4 case, dint, fate, luck, odds, risk, tide 5 ettle, stake 6 betide, casual, gamble, happen, hazard, mishap, random 7 aimless, fortune, stumble, venture 8 accident, casualty, fortuity 9 adventure, haphazard, happening, mischance 10 contingent 11 contingency, opportunity, probability

by: 5 haply

even: 6 tossup

favorable: 4 odds

chancellor: 5 judge 7 adviser, officer 8 minister

chancery: 5 court 6 office 8 registry

chandelier: 6 pharos 7 fixture 11 candelabrum

chandler: 6 dealer 8 merchant, provider 9 tradesman

change: mew 4 move, swap, turn, vary, veer 5 adapt, alter, amend, break, coins, shift 6 modify, mutate, remove, revamp, revise, switch 7 commute, convert, deviate 8 castrate, revision, transfer 9 diversity, permutate, rearrange, transform, transmute, transpose, variation 10 alteration, correction, difference, transition 11 desexualize, vicissitude 13 metamorphosis 15 diversification

appearance: 6 obvert

back: 6 return, revert

character of: 8 denature

color: dye 5 blush 6 redden

course: 4 tack, turn, veer 5 sheer

into: 6 become

music: 4 muta

subject to: 7 mutable 8 amenable, variable

sudden: 8 peripety

changeable: 5 eemis, giddy, immis 6 fickle, fitful, mobile 7 bruckle, erratic, mutable, protean, variant 8 amenable, catching, unstable, volatile 9 alterable, irregular, mercurial, uncertain, unsettled **10** capricious, inconstant, irresolute **11** chameleonic

in form: **9** metabolic

changeless: **5** fixed **6** steady **8** constant **9** steadfast **10** invariable

changeling: oaf **4** dolt, fool **5** child, dunce, idiot **7** waverer **8** imbecile, renegade, turncoat **9** simpleton **10** substitute

changeover: **5** shift **10** alteration, conversion

changing: *color:* **11** allochrous

pattern and color: **13** kaleidoscopic

channel: gat, ree, rut **4** cano, cava, dike, duct, dyke, gool, gote, gout, pipe, vein, wadi, wady **5** canal, chase, ditch, drain, drill, flume, flute, glyph, media(pl.), regal, rigol, river, sinus, stria **6** arroyo, artery, furrow, groove, gutter, medium, rabbet, rivose, sluice, strait, stream, striae(pl.), trough **7** conduct, conduit, passage, rivulet, silanga, tideway **8** aqueduct, guideway **10** instrument **11** watercourse

artificial: gat **4** leat **5** canal, drain, flume **6** sluice **7** drainer

brain: **4** iter

formed by cutting: **5** scarf

longitudinal: **6** rabbet

marker: **4** buoy

narrow: **6** furrow, strait

near port: **5** deeps

river: bed **6** alveni(pl.) **7** alvenus

ship: gat

vertical: **5** glyph

vital: **6** artery

water: gat **4** gote, gurt, leat, pipe, race **5** canal, drain, gurt **6** sluice **7** conduit **8** aqueduct, millrace, tailrace

Channel Island: **4** Sark **8** Guernsey

measure: **4** cade **5** cabot

seaweed: **5** vraic

channelbill: **9** rainfowl

channeled: **6** fluted **7** voluted **8** furrowed **9** chamfered

channels: **5** media **6** striae

chanson: **4** song **5** lyric **6** ballad **7** refrain

chant: **4** cant, sing, song, tune **5** carol, psalm **6** anthem, cantus, intone, warble **7** introit, worship **8** vocalize **10** cantillate

Gregorian: **9** plainsong **12** cantus firmus

Jewish: **6** Hallel

chantage: **9** extortion **12** blackmailing

chanter: **6** cantor, singer **7** bagpipe **8** songster **9** chorister

chanteuse: **6** singer **10** cantatrice

chantey, chanty: **4** song

chanticleer: **4** cock **7** rooster

Chantilly: **4** lace

chantry: **4** cage **5** altar **6** chapel, shrine

chanty, chantey: **4** song

chaos: pie **4** gulf, mess, void **5** abyss, babel, chasm **6** jumble **7** anarchy, mixture **8** disorder, shambles **9** confusion **10** unruliness **11** lawlessness

primordial: **4** Apsu

utter: **6** tophet **7** topheth

Chaos: *Babylonian:* **4** Apsu

daughter: Nox, Nyx

Maori: **4** kore

son: **6** Erebus

chaotic: **5** snafu **7** muddled **8** confused, formless

chap: boy, buy, man, rap **4** bean, beat, blow, chip, chop, cove, duck, gent, kibe, mash **5** billy, bloke, bully, buyer, chink, cleft, crack, knock, lover, split, trade, youth **6** barter, breach, bugger, callan, choose, fellow, shaver, strike, stroke **7** callant, chapman, chappie, fissure, husband, roughen **8** blighter, customer, division

odd: **6** galoot

old: **6** geezer

young: **6** gaffer

chaparral: **7** thicket **9** buckthorn

chapel: **4** cage, cape, cope, cowl, hood **5** cloak **6** bethel, church, shrine **7** chantry, service **8** bethesda **9** reliquary, sanctuary

private: **7** oratory

sailor's: **6** bethel

chaperon: **4** hood **6** attend, duenna(Sp.), escort, matron **7** oversee, protect **8** guardian, trapping **10** escutcheon **11** gouvernante(F.)

chaplain: **5** padre **8** sky pilot **9** clergyman

chaplet: **4** bead, orle **5** crown **6** anadem, anchor, circle, fillet, rosary, trophy, wreath **7** coronal, coronet, garland **8** moulding, necklace, ornament

chapman: **5** buyer **6** dealer, hawker, trader **7** peddler **8** customer, merchant

chaps: **4** boys, jaws, lads **5** flews **8** breeches, leggings, overalls

chapter: **4** body, cell, post **5** caput, lodge **6** branch **7** correct, meeting, section **8** assembly **9** reprimand **10** contingent

char: **4** burn, cart, sear **5** broil, chark, chore, singe, trout **6** scorch **7** blacken, chariot **8** sandbank **9** carbonize

charabanc: bus **5** coach **7** vehicle

character: **4** bent, card, kind, mark, mold, note, part, rune, sign, sort, tone **5** brand, fiber, stamp, tenor, token, trait, write **6** caract, emblem, figure, letter, mettle, nature, repute, stripe, symbol **7** edition, essence, engrave, impress, quality **8** inscribe **9** agreement, ampersand **10** reputation **11** disposition

assumed: **4** role

bad: **5** drole(F.)

chief: 4 hero, lead, star 7 heroine 11 protagonist

group: 5 ethos

of a people: 5 ethos

vein: 6 streak

word-representing: 8 logogram 9 logograph

characteristic: 4 cast, mark, mien 5 trait 6 nature 7 feature, impress, quality, typical 8 property, symbolic 9 attribute, lineament 11 distinctive, pathognomic, peculiarity

individual: 9 idiopathy

characterize: 4 mark 6 define, depict 7 engrave, entitle, imprint, portray 8 describe, indicate, inscribe 9 delineate, designate, represent 11 distinguish

charade: 6 enigma, puzzle, riddle 7 pageant, picture, tableau 8 disguise, pretense 11 make-believe

charcoal: 5 carbo, chark 6 carbon, fusain, pencil 7 blacken, drawing

animal: 9 boneblack

reduce to: 4 char

chard: 4 beet 7 thistle 9 artichoke

chare, char: job 4 lane, task, turn 5 alley, chore 6 finish, street 7 perform

charge: fee 4 bill, cark, cost, duty, fill, lien, load, onus, rate, rush, toll, ward 5 debit, onset, order, price, refer 6 accuse, adjure, allege, assess, attack, burden, career, credit, defame, demand, enjoin, impute, indict, tariff, weight 7 arraign, ascribe, assault, average, censure, command, concern, custody, expense, impeach, keeping, mandate, mission 8 chastise, overload, price tag 9 challenge, oversight 10 commission, impetition, impregnate, injunction, management 11 arraignment, encumbrance, incriminate, instruction 14 responsibility

customary: 4 dues

grazing: 5 agist

with gas: 6 aerate

chargeable: 6 costly, liable 7 weighty 9 expensive, important, momentous 10 burdensome 11 responsible, troublesome

charged: 5 tense 9 emotional, on the cuff 10 purposeful

with electricity: 4 live

chargeman: 7 blaster, foreman 10 batteryman

charger: 4 dish 5 horse, mount, plate, steed 6 vessel 7 accuser, courser, platter 8 war-horse

charges: *boat carrying:* 7 boatage

legal: 4 dues, fees 5 costs 9 retainers

repairs to barrister's quarters: 9 detriment

charily: 8 frugally, gingerly 9 carefully 10 cautiously

chariness: 7 caution 8 prudence 9 frugality, integrity 11 heedfulness, sparingness

chariot: car 4 cart, char, wain 5 buggy, essed, wagon 6 charet, esseda, essede 7 vehicle 8 carriage, charette

for carrying image of god: 4 rath 5 ratha

Greek: 8 quadriga

Roman: 5 essed 6 esseda, essede

two-horse: 4 biga

charioteer: 5 pilot 6 auriga, driver 7 wagoner 9 charioter

charisma: 5 charm, power 6 allure, appeal, glamor, impact 8 urtchery 9 magnetism 11 fascination

charitable: 4 kind 6 benign, humane 7 lenient, liberal 8 generous 9 favorable, forgiving, indulgent 10 beneficent, benevolent 12 eleemosynary 13 compassionate, philanthropic

charity: 4 alms, dole, gift, love, pity, ruth 5 mercy 6 bounty 7 handout, largess 8 lenience 9 affection 10 almsgiving, generosity, liberality, tenderness 12 philanthropy

dispenser: 7 almoner

charivari: 5 babel 6 medley 8 serenade, shivaree 10 callithump 11 celebration

chark: cup 4 burn, char, coal, coke 5 glass 6 cinder, noggin 8 charcoal

charlatan: 4 sham 5 cheat, faker, fraud, quack 7 cabotin, empiric 8 imposter, magician 9 pretender 10 medicaster, mountebank

Charlemagne: *brother:* 8 Carloman

conquest: 5 Avars

court hero: 6 Roland

father: 5 Pepin

knight: 4 Gano 7 Ganelon, Paladin

nephew: 6 Roland 7 Orlando

peer: 6 Oliver 7 Paladin

pert. to: 8 Caroline

sword: 7 Joyeuse

Charles' Wain: 4 Bear, Ursa 9 Big Dipper

Charlie Chan creator: 7 Biggers

charlock: 4 weed 5 kraut 7 mustard, yellows

charlotte: 7 custard, dessert

Charlotte Corday's victim: 5 Marat

charm: obi 4 calm, juju, jynx, mojo, play, song 5 allay, freet, freit, grace, obeah, magic, saffi, safie, spell, weird 6 allure, amulet, beauty, caract, enamor, entice, fetich, fetish, glamor, grigri, melody, please, scarab, saphie, soothe, subdue, summon 7 assuage, attract, beguile, bewitch, cantrip, conjure, control, delight, enamour, enchant, enthral, flatter, glamour, periapt, singing, sorcery 8 breloque, enthrall, entrance, greegree, practice, talisman 9 agreeable, captivate, fascinate, seduction 10 attraction, demonifuge 11 incantation

protective: 6 amulet

charmer: 5 siren 8 exorcist, magician, sorcerer 9 sorceress 11 spellbinder

charming: 7 amiable, eyesome, winning, winsome 8 adorable, delicate 9 agreeable, beautiful, glamorous 10 attractive, glamourous

charnel: 7 ghastly 8 cemetery 10 sepulchral

house: 7 ossuary 8 mortuary

Charon: 7 boatman 8 ferryman

father: 6 Erebus

mother: Nox

payment to: 4 obol 6 obolus

river: 4 Styx

Charpentier opera: 6 Louise

charqui: 4 beef, meat 5 jerky 6 xarque

chart: map 4 card, plan, plat, plot 5 carte, graph 6 design, devise, record, scheme 7 diagram, dope out, explore, outline, project 8 document, platform 9 blueprint 10 cartograph

charter: let 4 deed, hire, rent 5 carte, chart, grant, lease 6 charta, permit 9 privilege 10 commission, conveyance

chary: shy 4 dear, safe, wary 5 chere, scant 6 frugal, prized, skimpy 7 careful, guarded, sparing 8 cautious, hesitant, precious, reserved, vigilant 9 diffident, reluctant, treasured 10 economical, fastidious, scrupulous 11 circumspect

Charybdis rock: 6 Scylla

chase: 4 hunt, shag, sick 5 annoy, catch, chevy, chivy, harry, score 6 chivvy emboss, follow, frieze, furrow, gallop, groove, harass, hollow, indent, pursue, quarry, scorse, trench 7 channel, engrave, kick out, pursuit 8 ornament

away: 4 rout, shoo 5 drive

goddess: 4 Dian 5 Diana

chaser: ram 4 wolf 5 drink 6 masher 7 Don Juan 8 airplane, engraver

chasm: gap, pit 4 gulf, rift 5 abyss, blank, canon, chaos, cleft, gorge 6 breach, canyon, hiatus 7 fissure 8 aperture, crevasse, interval

glacial: 7 crevass 8 crevasse

chasse: 4 slip, step 5 glide 6 liquor, sashay, shrine 7 dismiss 9 relinquary

chassepot: 5 rifle

chasseur: 6 hunter 7 footman 8 huntsman 9 attendant

chassis: 5 frame

chaste: 4 pure 5 clean, moral 6 decent, honest, modest, proper, severe, vestal 7 refined 8 celibate, innocent, virtuous 9 continent, undefiled 10 immaculate

chasten: 4 rate 5 abase, smite, smote, sober 6 humble, punish, refine, subdue, temper 7 afflict, censure, correct 8 chastise, moderate, restrain 9 castigate, humiliate, reprimand 10 discipline

chastise: 4 beat, flog, lash, slap, trim, whip 5 amend, blame, scold, spank, strap, taunt 6 accuse, anoint, berate, charge, punish, purify, rebuke, refine, swinge, temper, thrash 7 chasten, correct, reprove, scourge, suspect 9 castigate 10 discipline

chastity: 5 honor 6 purity, virtue 7 modesty 8 celibacy, goodness 9 innocence

chasuble: 6 deacon, planet 8 vestment

chat: mag 4 bird, chin, cone, coze, gist, talk, tove, twig 5 ament, cause, dally, point, prate, speak, spike 6 babble, branch, catkin, confab, gabble, gibber, gossip, jabber, potato, samara 7 chatter, prattle 8 causerie, converse, spikelet, strobile 9 dalliance 11 confabulate 12 conversation

chateau: 5 house, manor, villa 6 castle 7 mansion 8 fortress

Chateaubriand work: 4 René 5 Atala 10 Les Natchez

chatelaine: pin 4 etui, hook 5 chain, clasp, etwee, purse 6 brooch 8 mistress

chaton: 5 basil, bezel, bezil 7 setting

chattel: 4 gear 5 goods, money, slave, wares 7 capital 8 bondsman, property 9 livestock, principal

chatter: gab, jaw, mag, yap 4 blab, carp, chat, hack, rick, talk, tear, yirr 5 cabal, clack, garre, haver, prate, shake 6 babble, gabble, gibber, gossip, jabber, palter, rattle, shiver, tattle, yammer, yatter 7 blabber, brabble, chackle, chaffer, chipper, chitter, clitter, nashgob, prabble, prattle, shatter 8 schmoose, verbiage 9 small talk 11 goosecackle

conjurer's: 10 hanky-panky

chatterbox: jay, mag 4 piet 5 clack 6 gossip, magpie 8 quidnunc 10 chatterbag, chattermag 12 blabbermouth 13 chatterbasket

chattering: 8 babbling 9 prattling, talkative 10 loquacious

chauffeur: 5 drive 6 driver 8 operator 9 transport

chaussee: 4 road 6 street 7 highway 8 causeway

chaussure: 4 boot, shoe 7 slipper 8 footgear

chauvinism: 8 jingoism 10 patriotism 11 nationalism

chaw: jaw, vex 4 chew, envy, mull 5 champ, grind 6 ponder 7 portion 8 ruminate 9 chawbacon, masticate

chawbacon: 4 chaw, lout 5 yokel 6 rustic 7 bumpkin

cheap: low 4 base, poor, vile 5 close, gaudy, kitch, price, tacky, tight, tinny, value 6 abject, common, kitsch, plenty, shoddy, sordid, stingy, tawdry, trashy 7 bargain, dealing 8 inferior, purchase 9 innkeeper, low-priced 10 despicable 11 depreciated, inexpensive 12 contemptible

cheap jack: 6 hawker, monger, pedlar, pedler, vendor 7 peddler 8 huckster 9 Cheap-John

cheat: do; bam, bob, cog, con, fob, gip, gum, gyp, nip 4 bilk, bite, clip, dupe, fake, flam, geck, gull, hoax, jilt, jouk, liar, mump, rook, sell, sham, skin 5 bunco, bunko, cozen, cully, dodge, faker, fling, foist, fraud, gouge, guile, knave, mulct, rogue, scamp, spoil, trick, welsh 6 baffle, chiaus, chisel, daddle, delude, deride, doodle, duffer, fiddle, fleece, grease, humbug, illude, jockey, outwit, raddle, renege, shaver 7 abusion, beguile, deceive, defraud, escheat, finesse, foister, gudgeon, juggler, mislead, plunder, quibble, sharper, swindle 8 artifice, delusion, dry-shave, hoodwink, imposter 9 bamboozle, hypocrite, imposture, scoundrel, strategem, victimize 10 mountebank 15 prestidigitator

cheater: 4 bite, gull 5 knave 6 bilker, topper 7 sharper 9 trickster

check: bit, dam, nab, nip, tab 4 balk, curb, damp, rein, snub, stay, stem, stop, stub, test, twit, were 5 abort, allay, block, brake, catch, chide, chink, choke, crack, daunt, delay, deter, draft, limit, quell, repel, stall, still, stunt, tally, taunt, token 6 arrest, attack, baffle, bridle, defeat, detain, detent, gravel, hinder, impede, oppose, outwit, quench, rabbet, rebate, rebuff, rebuke, scotch, stifle, ticket, verify 7 backset, command, control, inhibit, monitor, refrain, repress, reproof, reprove, repulse, setback 8 bulkhead, encumber, obstruct, restrain, withhold 9 constrain, frustrate, interrupt, overpower, reprimand, restraint, supervise 10 difficulty 11 certificate, counterfoil, examination

check growth of: 5 stunt 7 shorten

check in: 6 arrive 8 register

check out: die 5 leave 6 depart 7 confirm 11 investigate

check over: 5 study 7 examine, inspect 10 scrutinize

checkerboard: 7 dambrod 8 damboard

marked like: 10 tessellate

checkered: 4 pied, vair 5 diced, plaid 6 motley 10 changeable, variegated 11 diversified

checkers: 4 game 6 damrod, drafts 8 draughts

move: 4 dyke, fife, huff 5 cross 7 bristol

opening: 6 souter

term: 4 king 5 block, crown

checkerwork: 7 tessera 8 tesserae(pl.)

inlay: 6 mosaic

checklist: 7 catalog 9 catalogue, inventory

checkmate: 4 gain, lick, stop, undo 6 baffle, corner, defeat, outwit, stymie, thwart 9 frustrate

checkrein: 4 curb 7 saccade

cheddar: 6 cheese

cheek: 4 chap, gall, gena, jole, jowl, leer, sass 5 bucca, chyak, crust, genae(pl.), nerve, sauce 6 chyack, haffet, haffit 8 audacity, temerity 9 brashness, impudence

bone: 5 malar 6 zygoma

distended: 7 buccate

muscle: 10 buccinator

pert. to: 5 genal, malar 6 buccal

cheep: pip, yap, yip 4 hint(Sc.), peep, pule 5 chirp, creak(Sc.), tweet 6 squeak, tattle 7 chirrup, twitter

cheer: ole(Sp.), rah 4 fare, food, root, viva, yell 5 bravo, elate, feast, heart, huzza, mirth, shout, whoop 6 cantle, gaiety, hurrah, huzzah, solace, viands 7 acclaim, animate, applaud, cherish, comfort, console, enliven, gladden, hearten, jollity, refresh, rejoice 8 applause, brighten, inspirit, pheasant, vivacity 9 animation, encourage, merriment 10 exhilarate, invigorate 11 acclamation, hospitality 13 entertainment, hospitability

burst: 5 salvo

cheerful: gay 4 cant, glad, gleg(Sc.), rosy 5 cadgy, canty, chirk, douce, happy, jolly, merry, peart, ready, sunny 6 blithe, bright, cheery, chirpy, crouse, genial, hearty, hilary, jocund, lively 7 buoyant, chipper 8 cheering, gladsome, homelike, sanguine 9 contented, lightsome, sprightly 10 enlivening 11 comfortable 12 lighthearted

cheerless: sad 4 cold, drab, glum, gray 5 bleak, drear 6 dismal, dreary, gloomy 7 forlorn, joyless 8 dejected 10 dispirited, melancholy 11 comfortless 12 disconsolate

cheerio: 5 adieu 6 bye-bye 7 good-bye

cheese: 4 Brie, Edam, Jack 5 cream, Gouda, Swiss, Ziega 6 Barrie, Dunlop, Glarus, mysost, Zieger 7 Cheddar, cottage, Gruyere, Stilton 8 American, Parmesan 9 Camembert, Gammelost, Limburger, Roquefort 10 Gorgonzola, Neufchatel 11 Liederkranz

brown: 6 mysost

curdy: 4 trip

dish: 4 cake 6 fondue, omelet 7 rarebit, souffle

green: 7 sapsago

large: 7 kebbock, kebbuck

milk whey: 5 ziega 6 zieger

Normandy: 7 angelot

pert. to: 6 caseic 7 caseous

poached: 10 gnocchetti

white: 11 Neufchatel

cheese maggot: 7 skipper
cheesecake: 7 dessert 10 photograph
cheeseparing: 6 penury 9 parsimony 10 stinginess
cheesy: 4 fine, poor 5 cheap, smart 6 shabby, sleazy 7 caseous 8 inferior 9 excellent, worthless
cheetah: cat 5 youse, youze 7 guepard 8 gueparde
chef: 4 cook 7 saucier 9 cuisinier 10 cuisiniere
chef d'oeuvre: 7 classic 9 showpiece, work of art 11 masterpiece, tour de force
chela: 4 claw 5 slave 6 pincer 7 servant 8 disciple
chelicera: 8 mandible 9 appendage
chelonian: 6 turtle 8 tortoise
chemical: 4 acid, salt 6 alkali 8 catalyst 10 alchemical 13 iatrochemical
  agent: 8 catalyst
  compound: 4 acid, base, diol, imin 5 amide, azine, ceria, ester, imine, purin 6 boride 7 inosite, leucine, metamer
  element: See **element:** *chemical*
  measure: 4 dram, gram 5 liter, titer
  salt: sal
chemise: 5 shift, shirt, smock 6 camisa 8 lingerie
chemisette: 4 sham 6 guimpe
chemist: 7 analyst 8 druggist 9 alchemist 10 apothecary, pharmacist
  vessel: 4 vial 5 ampul, cupel, flask, phial 6 aludel, ampule, beaker, retort 7 ampoule 8 bolt head, test tube
  workroom: lab 10 laboratory
cheri, cherie: 4 dear 7 beloved, darling 9 cherished 10 sweetheart
cherish: aid, hug, pet 4 dote, hope, like, love, save 5 adore, cheer, cling, enjoy, nurse, prize, value 6 caress, esteem faddle, fondle, foster, harbor, nestle, pamper, pettle, revere 7 comfort, embosom, embrace, indulge, nourish, nurture, protect, support, sustain 8 enshrine, inspirit, preserve, treasure 9 cultivate, encourage, entertain
cheroot: 5 cigar
cherry: 4 bing, duke, gean 5 morel 7 capulin, chapman, lambert, morello, oxheart 8 amarelle, napoleon 9 bigarreau
  acid: 7 cerasin
  color: red 6 cerise
  extract: 8 cerasein
  sour: 8 amarelle
  sweet: 4 bing 7 lambert, oxheart
  wild: 4 gean 7 marasca, mazzard 10 maraschino
cherry finch: 8 hawfinch
cherry holly: 5 islay
cherry laurel: 7 cerasus
cherry orange: 7 kumquat

cherrystone: 4 clam 6 quahog
cherub: 5 angel 6 seraph, spirit 8 seraphim(pl.)
chervil: bun 4 herb
Cheshire district: 4 Hale 5 Hoole 6 Marple
chess: *draw game:* 9 stalemate
  finish: 4 draw, mate 7 endgame 9 checkmate, stalemate
  Japanese: 5 shogi
  move: 5 debut 6 castle, fidate, gambit 10 fianchetto
  opening: 5 debut 6 gambit 10 fianchetto
  pert. to: 8 scacchic
  piece: man 4 king, pawn, rook 5 horse, queen 6 bishop, castle, knight
chest: ark, box, kit 4 arca, bust, cist, cyst, fund, safe 5 ambry, bahut, front, hoard, hutch, trunk 6 basket, breast, bunker(Sc.), bureau, casket, coffer, coffin, hamper, locker, shrine, stripe, thorax 7 caisson, capcase, cassone(It.), commode, deposit, dresser, enclose, highboy 8 cupboard, treasury 9 container, strongbox 10 chiffonier, contention, receptacle, repository 11 controversy, gardeviance
  alms: 6 almoin 7 almoign
  animal: 7 brisket
  bone: 5 costa
  human: 6 breast, thorax
  meal: 6 girnal, girnel
  pert. to: 8 thoracic
  sacred: ark 4 arca, cist
  sound: 4 rale 7 rhonchi(pl.) 8 rhonchus
  stone: 4 cist, kist
  supply: 6 wangan, wangun 7 wanigan 8 wannigan
chesterfield: 4 coat, sofa 5 divan 8 overcoat 9 davenport
chestnut: 4 joke, ling, rata, tree 5 brown, horse 6 cliche, marron(F.), sativa 7 crenata, dentata
  and gray: 4 roan
  dwarf: 9 chincapin 10 chinquapin
  genus of: 8 castanea
  water: 4 ling 5 trapa
chevalier: 5 noble 6 knight 7 gallant 8 cavalier, horseman 9 gentleman 10 greenshank
cheverel, cheveril: 6 pliant 7 elastic, kidskin 8 flexible
chevet: 4 apse 11 termination
chevisance: 5 booty, issue, spoil 6 remedy, supply 8 chivalry, resource 9 expedient, substance 10 enterprise, provisions 11 achievement, transaction
chevron: 4 beam, mark 5 glove 6 rafter, stripe, zigzag 7 molding 10 gravystain
chevrotain: 4 napu 7 deerlet, kanchil, tragule
chew: cud 4 bite, cham, chaw, gnaw, quid

5 chamm, grind, munch, rumen 6 mumble 8 meditate, ruminate 9 denticate, manducate, masticate

inability to: 8 amasesis

on: 8 consider

out: jaw 5 scold 7 bawl out, tell off 10 tongue-lash

the rag: 6 gossip 7 chatter

chewing gum base: 6 chicle

chewink: 4 bird 5 finch, joree 6 towhee

chiastolite: 5 macle 10 andalusite

chiaus: 5 cheat 8 sergeant, swindler 9 messenger

Chibcha: 4 zipa 5 zaque 6 Indian, zacqua 7 muisca

chic: 4 pert, posh, trig, trim 5 natty, nifty, smart 6 dapper, modish 9 elegant, stylish

chicadee: 8 titmouse

Chicago district: 4 Loop

chicanery: 4 ruse, wile 5 feint, trick 8 artifice, intrigue, trickery 9 deception, duplicity, sophistry, stratagem

chichi: 5 showy, swank 7 splashy 8 affected 11 pretentious

chick: 4 girl, tick 5 child, natty 6 moppet, screen, sequin, sprout 7 chicken 8 young one

chick-pea: 4 gram, herb 5 chich, cicer 8 garbanzo, garvance, garvanzo 9 garavance

chickadee: 8 titmouse

chickaree: 8 squirrel

chicken: hen 4 cock, fowl 5 biddy, capon, chick, child, chuck, fryer, layer, manoc, poult 6 chicky, pullet 7 broiler, rooster 8 cockerel 11 chickabiddy

breed: 7 Leghorn 9 Wyandotte 11 Rhode Island

castrated: 5 capon

cooking: 5 fryer 7 broiler, roaster

pen: 4 coop

raising device: 7 brooder

young: 5 chick, fryer, poult 6 pullet 7 broiler

chicken out: 4 quit 6 renege

chicken snake: 4 boba

chickenhearted: 5 timid 8 cowardly

chickweed genus: 6 alsine

chicle: gum 5 latex

chicory: 4 bunk, root 5 plant 6 endive 7 succory, witloof

family: 12 cichoriaceae

chide: 4 rail, rate 5 blame, check, flite, flyte, scold 6 berate, rebuff, rebuke, threap, threep, threpe 7 censure, reprove, upbraid, wrangle 8 admonish, call down, reproach 9 objurgate, reprehend, reprimand

chief: aga, big, boh, cap, cob, dux, mir 4 agha, arch, boss, duce, duke, head, high, khan, main, rais, raja, reis, tyee 5 alder, elder, first, great, major, prime, rajah, ruler, thane, titan, vital 6 adalid, cabeza, leader, master, rector, sachem, staple 7 capital, captain, central, eminent, foreman, overman, palmary, prelate, premier, supreme 8 big wheel, dominant, especial, foremost, intimate, sagamore 9 chieftain, commander, number one, paramount, principal, prominent 11 predominant

chiffonier: 5 chest 6 bureau 7 cabinet, commode, dresser

chigger: 4 mite 6 chigoe, insect, jigger, red-bug

chignon: bun 4 knot 5 chain, twist 6 collar

chigoe: 4 flea 7 chigger

chilblain: 4 kibe, mule(F.), sore 5 blain 6 pernio 8 swelling 12 inflammation

child (see also **children**): ben (Heb.), boy, bud, imp, kid, son, tad, tot 4 baba, babe, baby, bata, brat, chit, girl, page, tike, tyke 5 bairn(Sc.), chick, chiel(Sc.), gamin, issue, minor, youth 6 cherub, enfant, filius(L.), infant, moppet, urchin 7 bambino(It.), progeny 8 bantling, chiseler(Ir.), daughter 9 firstling, offspring, youngster 10 adolescent, descendant 11 chickabiddy

advancement: 9 precocity

chubby: 8 rolypoly 10 butterball

dainty: elf 5 fairy

gifted: 7 prodigy

homeless: 4 waif

illegitimate: 6 by-blow 7 bastard

killer: 11 infanticide

parentless: 6 orphan

patron saint: 8 Nicholas

pert. to: 6 filial

puckish: imp

roguish: 6 urchin

spoiled: 4 brat 5 mardy 7 cockney

street: 5 gamin

tiny: tot 4 babe, baby, tyke 6 infant, peewee

unmannerly: 7 smatche(Sc.)

childbirth: 5 labor 7 lying-in, travail 11 confinement, parturition

goddess: 4 Apet, Auge, Upis 5 Damia 6 Lucina 7 Auxesia

childish: 4 slow, weak 5 naive, petty, silly 6 puling, simple, weanly(Sc.), young 7 asinine, babyish, foolish, kiddish, puerile, unmanly 8 bairnish, brattish, immature, juvenile 9 credulous, childlike, infantile, kittenish

childish talk: 7 prattle

childish walk: 6 toddle

childless: 6 barren 7 sterile

childlike: 4 meek 6 docile, filial 7 babyish, dutiful 8 childish, innocent, trusting 9 confiding, frivolous 10 submissive

children: 7 progeny 9 offspring

dislike of: 9 misopedia 10 misopaedia

medical science: 10 pediatrics 11 paediatrics

room: 7 nursery

study: 8 pedology 9 paedology

tender of: 4 amah 6 sitter 9 nursemaid

Chile: *capital:* 8 Santiago

chief export: 6 copper

city: 6 Arauco, Cobija, Serena 7 Caldera, Copiapo 8 Coquimbo, Valdivia 10 Concepcion, Valparaiso

coastal wind: 5 sures

conqueror: 8 Valdivia

desert: 7 Atacama

Indian: Ona 4 Auca, Inca, Onan 6 Arauca, Chango

island: 5 Byron, Guafo, Hoste

measure: 4 vara 5 legua, linea 6 cuadra, fanega

monetary unit: 4 peso 5 libra 6 condor, escudo

mountain: 4 Maco, Toro 5 Maipu, Pular, Torre, Yogan

mountain range: 5 Andes

national police: 11 carabineros

province: 5 Arica, Aysen, Maule, Nuble, Talca 6 Bio-Bio, Cautin, Chiloe, Curico 7 Atacama

river: Loa 5 Itata, Maipu, Maule 6 Bio-Bio, Chuapa, Lontue 7 Illapel 8 Valdivia

rodent: 10 chinchilla

seaport: 4 Lota, Tome 5 Arica 8 Coquimba

shrub: 5 lithi 6 pepino

tree: 4 brea, pelu, ulmo 5 coleu, rauli, roble 6 alerce, alerse, coigue, muermo

volcano: 5 Lanin, Maipo 6 Antuco, Lascar, Llaima 7 Calbuco

weight: 5 grano, libra 7 quintal

workman: 4 roto

chill: ice, raw 4 ague, cold, cool, dazy(Sc.) 5 algor, gelid, rigor, shake 6 frappe, freeze, frigid, frosty, shiver 7 depress, frisson, glacial, malaria 8 coldness 11 refrigerate

chiller: 7 shocker 8 thriller

chilling: 4 eery 5 eerie 6 wintry 7 glacial

chills and fever: 4 ague 7 malaria

chilly: raw 4 cold, cool, lash 5 algid, bleak, hunch 6 arctic, frosty 9 cauldrife

chimaera: 7 ratfish

chime: din, rim 4 bell, edge, peal, ring, suit, ting 5 agree, prate 6 accord, cymbal, jingle, melody 7 concord, harmony 8 singsong

chime in: 4 tell 5 state, offer 6 chip in

chimera: 5 dream, fancy 6 mirage 8 illusion 9 pipe dream

chimerical: 4 vain, wild 6 absurd, unreal 7 utopian 8 delusive, fanciful, romantic 9 fantastic, imaginary, unfounded, visionary

chimes: 5 bells 8 carillon

chimney: lum 4 flue, pipe, tube, vent 5 gully, stack, tewel 6 funnel 7 fissure, opening, orifice 10 smokestack

cover: 4 cowl 7 turncap

deposit: 4 soot

piece: 5 parel 6 mantel

post: 5 speer

chimney corner: 8 fireside 9 inglenook

chimpanzee: ape 5 jacko, pigmy 10 anthropoid, troglodyte

chin: jaw, rap 4 chat 5 menta(pl.) 6 mentum

double: 4 fold 7 buccula

china: 4 ware 6 dishes 7 ceramic, pottery 8 Cinchona, crockery 9 porcelain 11 earthenware

fine: 5 Spode 6 Sevres 7 Dresden, Limoges, Meissen 8 Wedgwood

China: *aborigine:* Yao 4 Mans, Miao 6 Mantzu, Yaomin 7 Miaotse, Miaotze

alloy: 7 paktong 8 packtong

ancient name: 4 Tsao 5 Seres 6 Cathay

antelope: 6 dzeren

arch: 6 pailoo, pailou, pailow

artichoke: 7 chorogi

bamboo: 7 whangee

banker: 6 shroff

bean: soy 6 cowpea

black tea: 6 oolong

boat: 4 bark, junk 6 sampan

brigand: 9 hunghutze, hunghutzu

Buddha: Fo; Foh

Buddhist paradise: 7 Chingtu

cabbage: 7 pakchoi

calculator: 7 suan pan, swan pan

canton: Fu 5 Hsein

capital: 6 Peking 7 Beijing

city: Nom, Ude 4 Amoy, Luta, Tsin, Wuhu 5 Jehol, Macao, Macau, Pekin 6 Canton, Fachan, Fuchau, Hankau, Hankow, Huchau, Kalgan, Mukden, Nankin, Ningpo, Suchau, Swatow, Tsinan, Yunnan 7 Chengte, Chengtu, Chingtu, Fatshan, Foochow, Hanyang, Kaifeng, Lanchau, Nanking, Paoting, Taiyuen, Tunkuan, Wenchau, Wuchang, Yenping 8 Changsha, Chaochau, Fancheng, Hangchau, Hangchow, Kiaochau, Nanchang, Shanghai, Shenyang, Shaohing, Siangtan, Tengchau, Tientsin, Tungchau, Tunghwan, Yanphing 9 Changchau, Chinkiang, Chungking, Lienkiang 10 Chingkiang, Kingtechen

city (Pinyin spelling): 4 Luda (Luta) 7 Beijing (Peking), Chengdu (Chengtu), Nanjing (Nanking), Tianjin (Tientsin) 8 Quingdao (Tsingtao) 9 Chongqing (Chungking), Guangzhou (Canton)

civet: 5 rasse

clay: 6 kaolin

cloth: sha 4 moxa, pulo, silk 6 nankin 7 nankeen

cloth-stiffening gelatin: 7 haitsai

coin: le, pu; fan, neu, sen 4 cash, cent, mace, tael, tiao, yuan 5 liang, tsien 6 dollar, ticket 9 candareen 10 Kuping-tael 11 Haikwantael

cooking style: 5 Hunan 6 Fukien, Peking 8 Szechuan 9 Cantonese

cosmic order: tao

customs collector: 5 hoppo

deer: 8 elaphure

department: Fu 5 Hsien

desert: 4 Gobi

dialect: 4 Amoy 5 Hakka 6 Canton, Ningpo, Swatow 7 Foochow, Wenchow

dish: 4 rice 7 fooyung 8 fooyoung

divison: 4 chow, Miao 5 Hsien 6 canton 8 province

dog: 4 chow, peke

dragon: 6 chilin

drink: 6 samshu

duck eggs: 5 pidan

dulcimer: 7 yang-kin

dynasty: Han, Sui, Wei, Yin 4 Chin, Chou, Hsia, Ming, Sung, Tang, Tsin, Yuan 5 Shang 6 Manchu

exchange medium: 5 sycee

factory: 4 hong

festival: 9 Ching Ming

feudal state: Wei

figurine: 5 magot

fir: 5 nikko

fish: 7 trepang

flute: che 4 tche

fruit: 6 lichee, litchi

ginger: 9 galingale

god: 4 Ghos, Joss, Shen 5 Kuant

gong: 6 tamtam

gooseberry: 9 carambola

grass: bon 5 ramie

grass linen: 8 barandos

gruel: 6 congee, conjee

herb: tea 7 ginseng

herb genus: 7 nandina

houseboat: 5 tanka

idol: 4 joss 6 pagoda

indigo: 6 isatis

isinglass: 4 agar 8 agar-agar

island: 4 Amoy 5 Macao 6 Hainan, Taiwan 7 Formosa

jute: 7 chingma

laborer: 6 coolie

lake: 6 Po-yang 8 Tung-ting

language: 4 Shan 8 Mandarin 9 Cantonese

largest city: 8 Shanghai

leaders (Communist): Mao 9 Mao Zedong (Mao Tse-tung), Zhou Enlai (Chou En-lai) 10 Hua Guofeng (Hua Kuo-feng) 12 Deng Xiaoping (Teng Hsiao-ping)

leaders (Republic): 9 Sun Yat-sen 13 Chiang Kai-shek

lemon: 6 citron

magistrate: 8 mandarin

magnolia: 5 yulan

mandarin's residence: 6 oyamen

measure: cho, fen, tou, yan, yin 4 chih, fang, kish, quei, shih, teke, tsan, tsun 5 chang, ching, sheng, shing 6 kung ho, kung li, kung mu, tching, tchung 7 kung fen 8 kung chih, kung shih 9 kung ching, kung sheng

measure of distance: li

measure of weight: 4 chin 5 catty

money (see also coin above): fen 4 mace, tael, tiao, yuan 5 sycee, tsien

mountain: Omi 4 Omei, Sung 5 Tsins 6 Inshan, Kunlun, Pu-ling 7 Alashan, Kuliang 8 Tien Shan 9 Funiu-shan, Tsing-Ling

musical instrument: kin 5 cheng, sheng 7 samisen

Nationalist Party: 11 Kuomintang

noodles: 4 mein

nurse: ama 4 amah

official: 4 kuan, kwan 5 amban

oil: 4 tung

old name: 6 Cathay

orange: 7 kumquat 8 mandarin

ounce: 4 tael

ox: 4 zebu

pagoda: taa 4 taag

parasol tree: 6 aogiri

peony: 6 moutan

pert. to: 4 Sino

philosopher: 4 Moti 5 Motzu 6 Laotse, Laotzu 9 Confucius

plant: tea, udo 4 rice, tche 5 ramie 7 ginseng

poet: 4 Li Po 7 Li Tai-Po

pony: 7 griffin

porcelain: 7 Celadon, Nankeen

porcelain glaze: 7 eelskin

porgy: tai

port: 4 Amoy, Wuhu 5 Aigun, Shasi 6 Antung, Canton, Chefoo, Dairen, Harbin, Ichang, Ningpo, Pakhoi, Swatow, Szemao, Wuchow, Yochow 7 Foochow, Hangkow, Hunchun, Lungkow, Mengtsz, Nanking, Nanning, Samshui, Santuao, Soochow, Wenchow 8 Changsha, Hangchow, Kiukiang, Kongmoon, Lungchow, Shanghai, Tengyueh, Tientsin, Tsingtao, Wanhsien 9 Chinkiang, Chungking, Kiungchow, Newchwang 10 Chiankiang 12 Chingwangtao

port (Pinyin spelling): 6 Fuzhou (Foochow), Suzhou (Soochow), Xiamen (Amoy) 7 Qingdao (Tsingtao), Tianjin (Tientsin) 8 Hangzhou (Hangchow), Jiujiang (Kiukiang) 9 Chongqing (Chungking)

positive principle: 4 yang

pottery: 4 Kuan, Ming, Ting 5 Chien 7 boccaro, Tzuchou

pound: 5 catty

prefecture: fu

province: 4 Amur 5 Chili, Honan, Hunan, Hupeh, Kansu 6 Fokien, Fukien, Shansi, Shensi, Yunnan 7 Kiangsi, Kiangsu, Kwangsi, Nganhui 8 Che-Kiang, Kweichau, Shantung, Szechuan, Szechwan 9 Kwangtung, Manchuria

province (Pinyin spelling): 5 Anhui (Anhwei), Gansu (Kansu), Hebei (Hopei), Henan (Honan), Hubei (Hupeh), Jilin (Kirin) 6 Fujian (Fukien), Shanxi (Shansi) 7 Guizhou (Kweichow), Jiangsu (Kiangsu), Jiangxi (Kiangsi), Ginghai (Chinghai), Shaanxi (Shensi), Sichuan (Szechwan) 8 Shandong (Shantung), Zhejiang (Chekiang) 9 Guangdong (Kwangtung) 12 Heilongjiang (Heilungkiang)

provincial chief: 6 taoyin

puzzle: 7 tangram

race: 4 Lolo 5 Sinic, Soyot 6 Mongol

region: 5 Tibet 7 Kwangsi, Ningsia 8 Mongolia, Sinkiang

religion: 6 Taoism 8 Buddhism 12 Confucianism

river: Han, Hsi, Ili, Kan, Min, Pei, Wei 4 Hwai, Tung, Yuan, Yuen 5 Hwang, Peiho, Pieho, Tarim 6 Yellow 7 Hoangho, Sikiang, Yangtze 12 Yangtsekiang

roller: 7 sirgang

salutation: bow 6 kowtow

sauce: soy

secret society: hui 4 tong

sedge: 4 mati

shrub: tea 5 ramie

silk: sha 5 pekin, tasar 6 pongee, tussah 7 taysaam, tsatlee 8 shantung

silkworm: 4 sina 6 tussah, tusser 10 ailanthus

silver: 5 sycee

skiff: 6 sampan

sky: 4 tien

sleeping platform: 4 kang

society: 4 Hoey, Huey, Hung, Tong 5 Triad

squash: 6 cushaw

state(anc.): 4 Tsao 6 Cathay

stocks: 6 cangue

strait: 6 Hainan, Taiwan 7 Formosa

street: 6 hutung

student: 9 sinologue

sugar cane: 5 sorgo

taa: 6 pagoda

Tartar tribe: 4 Toda

tax: 5 likin

tea: cha 4 Tsia 5 bohea, congo, congu, Emesa, hyson

temple: taa 6 pagoda

toy: 7 tangram

treaty port: 4 Amoy

tree: 5 nikko 6 kinkan, litchi 7 gingkgo, hagbush, kumquat 9 bandoline, soapberry

tribe: 4 Shan, Toba

vegetable: udo

vine: 5 kudzu 7 yangtao

walking stick: 7 whangee

warehouse: 4 hong

wax: 4 cere, pela

weight: fen, hao, kin, ssu, tan, yin 4 chee, chin, mace, shih, tael 5 catty, chien, liang, picul, tsien 6 kung li 7 haikwan, kung fen, kung ssu, kung tun 8 king chin 9 candareen 10 kuping tael 11 haikwan tael

wind instrument: 5 cheng, sheng

wormwood: 4 moxa

China Sea: *gulf:* 4 Siam

island: 6 Hainan 7 Formosa

Chinaberry: 5 lilac 9 soapberry

chinch: 6 bedbug

chine: 4 back, grow 5 chink, crack, crest, ridge, spine 6 cleave, ravine, sprout 7 crevice, fissure 8 backbone

Chinese (see also **China**): 5 Cerai, Seres, Seric, Sinic 6 Mongol, Sinico 7 Asiatic, Cataian, Sangley 9 Celestial

pert. to: 5 Seric 6 Serian 7 Sinitic 8 Senesian

chink: gap 4 bore, cash, coin, kink, rent, rift, rime 5 boore, check, chine, cleft, crack, grike, money 6 cranny, jingle, sprain 7 chinkle, crevice, fissure 8 aperture 9 chaffinch 10 interstice

chinky: 5 rifty 6 rimose

Chinook: 4 wind 6 indian 8 Flathead

chief: 4 Tyee

god: 8 tamanoas

people: 7 tilikum 8 tillicum

powwow: 4 wawa

salmon: 7 quinnat

woman: 10 klootchman

Chinook State: 10 Washington

chinquapin: oak 6 bonnet 8 chestnut, wankapin 9 rattlenut

chintzy: 4 mean 5 cheap, petty 6 stingy

chip: bit, cut, hew, nig 4 chap, clip, knap, nick, pare 5 crack, flake, piece, scrap, spale, spalt, waste 6 chisel 7 counter 8 fragment, splinter

in: 10 contribute 11 come through

of stone: 5 spall 6 gallet

chipmunk: 6 chippy, backee, rodent 8 squirrel

chipper: gay 4 spry 5 chirp, perky 6 babble, cockey, lively 7 chatter, chirrup, twitter 8 cheerful

chirk: gay 6 lively 7 chirrup 8 cheerful, embolden 9 encourage

chirm: din, hum 5 chirp, croon, noise 6 clamor

chirography: 6 script 7 writing 10 engrossing 11 handwriting

chiromancy: 9 palmistry 10 chirognomy

chirp: pip 4 peek, peep, pipe 5 cheep, chelp, chirk, chirl, chirm, chirt, tweet 7 chipper, chirrup, chitter, rejoice, twitter, wheetle

chirrup: 5 chirk, chirp, tweet 7 chitter, twitter

chisel: cut, gad, gyp 4 chip, form, pare, tool 5 burin, carve, cheat, gouge, hardy 6 gravel, haggle 7 bargain, defraud, engrave, quarrel, shingle 9 sculpture

ancient stone: 4 celt

engraving: 7 scooper, scorper

mine: gad 6 peeker

sculpture: 7 gradine 9 ebauchoir

stonemason's: 5 drove

toothed: 6 jagger

chiseler: 5 cheat, crook 6 gouger 9 bargainer

chiselled: 8 clearcut

chiselly: 6 gritty 8 gravelly 10 unpleasant 12 disagreeable

chit: dab, IOU, kid 4 bill, girl, mind, note, rice 5 child, draft, shoot 6 infant, letter, moppet, sprout 7 voucher 8 young one 9 offspring 10 memorandum

chitchat: 4 talk 6 banter, gossip 9 small talk 12 conversation

chiton: 4 gown, robe 5 tunic 7 mollusk

chitter: 4 peep 5 chirp 6 shiver 7 chatter, twitter

chivalrous: 4 brave, civil, noble 6 gentle, polite 7 gallant, genteel, valiant, warlike 8 knightly 9 courteous, honorable

chive: cut 4 stab 5 clout, clove, knive, onion 6 bulbet

chivy, chivvy: run, vex 4 hunt, race 5 chase, tease 6 badger, flight, harass, pursue 7 pursuit, scamper, torment 8 maneuver 9 confusion

chlamys: 5 cloak 6 mantle 7 garment

Chloe: 11 shepherdess

beloved: 7 Daphnis

chloride: 4 salt 5 ester 7 calomel, muriate 8 compound

chlorine: 6 bleach

chloroform: 4 kill 10 anesthetic

discoverer: 6 Liebig 7 Guthrie 9 Soubeiran

ingredient: 7 acetone

liquid used: 7 acetone

chobdar: 5 usher 9 attendant

chock: 5 block, chuck, cleat, wedge

chocolate: bar 5 candy, cocoa 8 beverage

family: 13 sterculiaceae

machine: 6 conche

powder: 5 cocoa 6 pinola

seed: 5 cacao

stick for mixing: 7 molinet

tree: 4 cola 5 cacao

choice: 4 a-one, best, fine, pick, rare, wale, weal, will 5 cream, elite, prime, voice 6 chosen, dainty, flower, option, picked, select 8 delicate, druthers, election, eximious, uncommon, volition 9 excellent, exquisite, recherche 10 preferable, preference 11 alternative

choicy: 5 fussy, picky 6 choosy 7 finicky 10 fastidious 11 persnickety

choir: 5 quire 6 chorus

leader: 6 cantor 9 precentor

member: 4 alto, bass 5 basso 7 songman, soprano 9 chorister

vestment: 4 gown 5 cotta 8 surplice

choke: dam, gag 4 clog, fill, plug, quar 5 check, close, grane 6 hinder, impede, stifle 7 congest, querken, repress, silence, smother 8 obstruct, stoppage, strangle, suppress, throttle 9 constrict, neckcloth, suffocate 10 asphyxiate, extinguish

choler: ire 4 fury, rage 5 anger, wrath 6 spleen, temper 9 distemper, ill temper 10 resentment 11 biliousness 12 irascibility

choleric: mad 5 angry, cross, fiery, huffy, testy 6 fumish, touchy 7 bilious, enraged, iracund, peevish, peppery, waspish 8 wrathful 9 impatient, irascible 10 passionate 11 belligerent, hot-tempered, quarrelsome 13 quick-tempered

render: 6 enrage

chomp: 4 bite, chew 5 munch 6 crunch 8 ruminate 9 masticate

choose: opt 4 chap, cull, pick, vote, wale, weal 5 adopt, chuse, elect 6 prefer, select 7 embrace, espouse 9 single out

choosy, choosey: 7 finical, finicky 9 selective 10 fastidious

chop: cut, hew, jaw, lop 4 chap, dice, gash, hack, hash, jowl, rive, slit 5 carve, cleft, crack, knock, mince, slash, stamp, trade, truck, whang 6 barter, change, cleave, incise 8 exchange 9 cotolette

down: 4 fell, raze 5 level

off: lop 4 drib 5 prune 8 amputate

chop-chop: 7 quickly 8 promptly 9 posthaste 12 lickety-split

chophouse: 10 restaurant

Chopin: 7 pianist 8 composer

birthplace: 6 Poland

lover: 4 Sand (George)

chopping block: 7 hacklog

chopping tool: axe 7 cleaver, hatchet

choppy: 5 rough

choragus: 6 leader 10 bandleader

chord: 4 cord, tone 5 nerve, triad 6 string, tendon 7 harmony 8 filament 9 harmonize

arc: 4 sine

harplike: 8 arpeggio

musical: 5 major, minor

ninth: 4 none

seventh: 6 tetrad
succession: 7 cadence
chore: job 4 duty, task 5 stint 6 errand 9 housework 10 assignment
choreography: 7 dancing
chorister: 6 singer 7 chanter 8 choirboy
chorography: 9 map-making
chortle: 5 laugh, snort 7 chuckle
chorus: 4 song 5 choir 6 accord, assent, unison 7 concert, concord, harmony, refrain, singers 8 response
girl: 6 dancer, singer 7 chorine
leader: 7 choragi(pl.) 8 choragus 9 conductor
chosen: 5 elect, elite 7 elected 8 selected
Chosen: 5 Korea
chosen people: 10 Israelites
chough: 4 bird, crow
chouse: 4 dupe, gull, sham 5 chase, cheat, trick 6 harass 7 defraud, swindle 8 swindler 10 imposition
chow: dog 4 eats, food, grub, meal 6 fodder
chowchow: dog 4 bird, hash, olio 7 mixture 8 mishmash 10 hodgepodge, miscellany
chowderhead: 4 dope 5 dunce 6 noodle 7 schnook 9 lame-brain
Christ: 4 Lord 7 Messiah, Saviour
christen: 4 name 7 baptize 10 denominate
Christian: 7 Gentile 8 Nazarene
denomination: 6 Mormon, Quaker 7 Baptist 8 Anglican, Catholic, Lutheran 9 Calvinist, Methodist 12 Episcopalian
early 8 Galilean
Eastern: 6 Uniate
Egyptian: 4 Copt
persecuted: 6 martyr
unity: 7 irenics
Christian Science founder: 4 Eddy
Christiania: 4 Oslo
Christianity: *heretical sect:* 7 Docetae
love feast: 5 agape
martyr: 7 Stephen
symbol: 5 cross, orant 7 lehthus
theologian: 4 Kuhn 7 Aquinas, Niebuhr, Tillich 8 Bultmann 9 Augustine, de-Chardin 10 Bonhoeffer 11 Kierkegaard
writer: 6 Origen
Christmas: 4 noel, yule 7 holiday 8 festival, nativity, yuletide
carol: 4 noel 5 nowel
crib: 6 creche
decoration: 5 holly 6 tinsel 9 mistletoe
midnight mass supper: 9 reveillon
Christmas Carol: *author:* 7 Dickens
character: Tim 7 Scrooge
Christmas rose: 9 hellebore
Christ's thorn: 4 nabk, nubk 5 shrub 6 jujube

chromium: 7 element, mineral
group element: 7 uranium 8 tungsten 10 molybdenum
chromolithograph: 7 picture
chronic: 5 fixed, usual 6 severe 7 intense, routine 8 constant 9 confirmed, continual, customary, lingering, prolonged 10 continuous, inveterate 12 disagreeable
chronicle: 5 annal, diary, story 6 record 7 account, archive, history, recital 8 register 9 narrative
chronicler: 6 writer 8 compiler, recorder 9 historian 11 memorialist
chronology: 6 record 11 arrangement 14 classification
according to: 5 datal
error in: 9 prolepsis 11 anachronism
chronometer: 4 dial 5 clock, watch 7 metronome, timepiece 10 timekeeper
chrysalis: 4 kell, pupa 5 pupae(pl.)
chrysolite: 7 olivine, peridot
chrysoprase: 10 chalcedony
chthonian: 6 Hadean 8 infernal, plutonic 10 sulphurous
chub: 4 dace, dolt, fool, lout 5 chopa 6 chevin, shiner 8 fallfish, mackerel 9 hornyhead, squawfish
chubby: 5 chuff, fubsy, plump, pudgy, round, tubby 6 choaty, rotund 8 roly-poly
chuck: hen, log, pig 4 beef, cast, food, fowl, grub, hurl, jerk, lump, shed, toss 5 chock, cluck, ditch, pitch, throw 6 bounce 7 chicken, discard 9 dismissal
chuckle: 5 cluck, exult, laugh 6 giggle, titter 7 chortle
chuff: fat 4 boor, glum, ugly 5 brick, churl, cross, miser, proud, sound, sulky, surly 6 chubby, elated, rustic 8 swollen 9 conceited 11 ill-tempered
chug: 4 puff
chum: cad, pal 4 bait, mate, pard 5 buddy, butty, crony 6 cobber, copain, friend 8 roommate 9 associate, companion
around: 6 hobnob
chump: ass, oaf, sap 4 boob, dolt, head 5 block 7 fall guy 8 lunkhead 9 blockhead, schlemiel, schlemihl
chunk: dab, gob, pat, wad 4 junk, slug 5 claut, piece, throw, whang
chunky: 4 game 5 lumpy, plump, squat, stout, thick
church: 4 cult, sect, tera(Jap.) 5 creed, faith 6 temple 7 edifice 9 sanctuary, structure 10 house of God 13 house of prayer
adjunct: 6 belfry 7 steeple 9 bell tower
altar end: 4 apse
altar offering: 8 altarage
attendant: 8 altarboy, choirboy
balcony: 8 cantoria
bench: pew, pue 4 seat

bishopric: see 7 diocese 10 episcopacy, episcopate
body of: 4 nave
calendar: 4 ordo
caretaker: 6 sexton
chapel: 7 oratory
congregation: 7 synaxis
council: 5 synod 6 Nicene
court: 4 Rota
deputy: 5 vicar 6 curate
dignitary: 4 dean, pope 5 abbot, canon 6 bishop 7 prelate, primate
dissenter: 7 sectary
district: 6 parish 7 diocese
dominion of: 11 sacerdotium
doorkeeper: 7 ostiary
early Christian: 8 basilica
endowed: 8 benefice
entrance chapel: 7 galilee
episcopacy: 7 prelacy
field: 5 glebe
government: 9 hierarchy
home: 5 manse 7 deanery 8 convento 9 parsonage
law: 5 canon
member: 11 communicant
morning service: 5 matin
officer: 5 elder, vicar 6 beadle, deacon, lector, sexton, warden 7 prelate, sacrist 8 reverend 9 clergyman, moderator, presbyter, sacristan 11 headborough
part of: 4 apse, bema, nave 5 altar, solea 7 chancel, narthex 8 cantoria, transept 10 clearstory, clerestory
pertaining to: 9 ecclesial 14 ecclesiastical
prayer: 5 kyrie 12 kyrie eleison
property: 5 glebe
reader: 6 lector
recess: 4 apse
revenue: 5 tithe 8 benefice
Roman: 7 lateran 8 basilica
room: 6 vestry 7 galilee 8 sacristy
seat: pew, pue 5 bench 6 sedile 7 sedilia(pl.)
service: 4 mass, rite 5 matin 7 vespers, nocturn 8 evensong 9 communion
stand: 4 ambo
stipend: 7 prebend
vault: 5 crypt
vessel: ama, pyx 4 font 5 amula 7 columba, piscina 9 colymbion 10 monstrance
vestry room: 8 sacristy
wall: 6 cashel
warden's aide: 7 hoggler
wing: 5 aisle
churchgoer: 11 communicant
churchly: 9 religious, spiritual
churchyard: 6 litten 8 cemetery 9 graveyard
churl: cad, man 4 boor, carl, gnof, hind, lout, serf 5 carle, ceorl, chuff, gnoff, knave, miser 6 bodach, carlot, lubber,

rustic, vassal, yeoman 7 bondman, freeman, haskard, husband, niggard, peasant, villain, villein 10 countryman, curmudgeon
churlish: 4 mean 5 bluff, gruff, rough, surly 6 crabby, rustic, sordid, sulkly, sullen, vulgar 7 boorish, crabbed, uncivil, violent 9 illiberal 10 ungracious, unyielding 12 cross-grained
churn: 4 beat, kirn(Sc.), stir 5 drill, shake 7 agitate
part: 6 dasher
chute: 4 rush, tube 5 flume, hurry, rapid, shoot, slide 6 hopper, trough 7 cascade, decline, descent 8 downfall, stampede 9 waterfall
cibol: 5 onion 7 shallot
ciborium: pix, pyx 6 canopy, coffer, vessel
cicada: 6 cagale, cigala, locust 11 grasshopper
noise: 5 chirr
cicatrix: eye 4 mark, scab, scar, seam
cicatrization: 8 scarring
cicely: 5 myrrh
Cicero's target: 8 Catiline 10 Mark Antony
cicerone: 5 guide, pilot 6 mentor, orator 7 courier 9 conductor
cid: Ruy 4 epic, hero, poem 5 Bivar, chief, title 9 commander
sword of: 6 colada, tizona
cider: 5 perry 6 perkin, swanky 8 beverage
pulp: 6 pomace
cigar: 4 toby, weed 5 claro, smoke, stogy 6 boquet, Corona, maduro, stogie 7 bouquet, cheroot, culebra 8 perfecto 9 Belvedere
case: 7 humidor
crude: 7 cheroot, culebra
long thin: 8 panatela, panetela 9 panatella, panetella
cigarette: fag 4 biri, butt, pill 5 cubeb, smoke 6 gasper, reefer 9 cigarillo 10 coffin nail
cigarfish: 4 scad 8 quiaquia
cilium: 4 hair, lash 7 eyelash 8 barbicel
cima: See cyma
cimarron: 5 slave 6 maroon 7 bighorn
cimbia: 4 band 6 fillet
cimex: 6 bedbug, insect
cimmerian: 4 inky 5 black 6 gloomy 7 stygian 8 infernal 9 plutonian
cinch: 4 belt, gird, grip, pipe, snap 5 girth 6 fasten 8 sinecure 9 certainty
cinchona: 4 bark, tree
extract: 7 quinine
cinct: 4 girt 9 encircled
cincture: 4 band, belt, gird, halo, list, ring 5 girth 6 cestus, collar, fillet, girdle 7 baldric, compass 8 encircle 9 enclosure 11 environment, surrounding

cinder: ash 4 gray, slag 5 chark, dross, ember 6 scoria 7 clinker, lapilla, residue

cinders: 5 gleed, track

cinema (see also **motion picture**): 4 film, show 5 flick, movie 6 screen 7 picture 13 motion picture

cinerarium: urn 8 mortuary

cinerator: 6 ashery 9 crematory

cinerous: 4 gray 5 ashen

cingular: 7 annular 8 circular

cingulum: 4 band 5 ridge 6 girdle

cinnabar: ore 7 mineral 9 vermilion
color: red
derivative: 11 quicksilver

cinnamic acid derivative: 7 sinapic

cinnamon: 4 tree 5 canel, spice 6 canela, canell, canelo, cassia 7 canella, canelle 8 barbasco

cinnamon apple: 8 sweetsop

cinnamon oak: 8 bluejack

cinnamon stone: 6 garnet 8 essonite

cinquefoil: 5 clover 7 frasier 8 cowberry

cion: bud 5 graft, scion, shoot, uvula 10 descendant

Cipango: 5 Japan 6 Nippon

cipher: key, nil 4 code, null, zero 5 aught, ought 6 device, decode, figure, letter, naught, nought, number, symbol 8 goose egg 9 nonentity 10 cryptogram

cippus: 6 pillar 8 landmark 10 gravestone

circa: 5 about 6 around 13 approximation

Circassian: *dialect:* 6 Adighe 8 Cherkess 9 Abkhasian, Kabardian
king: 9 Sacripant

Circe: 5 siren 7 tempter 9 sorceress 11 enchantress
brother: 6 Aeetes
father: Sol 6 Helios
island: 5 Aeaea
lover: 7 Ulysses 8 Odysseus
niece: 6 Medea
son: 5 Comus 9 Telegonus

circle: lap, set 4 disk, gyre, halo, hoop, loop, maru(Jap.), orbe, ring, rink, turn 5 class, crown, cycle, frame, group, monde, realm, rhomb, rigol, round, swirl, twirl 6 bezant, cirque, clique, collet, cordon, corona, diadem, girdle, rotate, rundle, spiral, system 7 chukkar, chukker, circlet, circuit, company, compass, coronet, coterie, enclose, revolve, ringlet 8 encircle, surround 9 circulate, encompass 10 associates, companions 13 circumference
around sun or moon: 6 corona
geographic: 6 tropic
graph: 8 pie chart
heraldry: 7 annulet
inner: 5 bosom
longest chord: 8 diameter
luminous: 4 aura, halo 6 corona, nimbus

part of: arc 5 chord 6 degree, radius, secant, sector 7 segment

circlet: 4 band, hoop, ring 6 bangle, cirque 7 circuit 8 bracelet, headband
of light: 7 aureola, aureole

circuit: lap 4 area, bout, iter, loop, tour, zone 5 ambit, cycle, orbit, round, route 6 ambage, circle, detour 7 compass, itinera(pl.) 8 district 10 revolution 13 circumference
auxiliary: 5 relay
court: 4 eyre

circuitous: 4 mazy 6 curved 7 crooked, devious, oblique, sinuous, twisted, vagrant, winding 8 circular, flexuous, indirect, rambling, tortuous 9 ambagious, ambiguous, deceitful, underhand, wandering 10 roundabout, serpentine 12 disingenuous, labyrinthine

circular: 4 bill 5 libel, orbed, round 6 ringed 7 annular, cycloid, discoid, perfect 8 cingular, complete, encyclic, globular, pamphlet 9 orbicular 10 circuitous, roundabout 11 publication
indicator: 4 dial
motion: 4 eddy, gyre 5 whirl 8 gyration
plate: 4 disc, disk

circulate: air, mix 4 move, turn 6 rotate, spread 7 diffuse, publish 8 propagate 10 promulgate 11 disseminate
publicly: 6 report 9 broadcast

circumference: arc, rim 4 ambi 5 girth 6 border, bounds, limits 7 circuit 8 boundary, surround 9 dimension, perimeter, periphery

circumlocution: 6 ambage 7 winding 8 verbiage 10 periphrase, redundancy, roundabout

circumscribe: 5 bound, fence, limit 6 define 7 confine, enclose, environ 8 encircle, restrain, restrict, surround 9 encompass

circumscribed: 6 narrow 7 insular, limited

circumspect: 4 wary, wise 5 alert, chary 7 careful, guarded, prudent 8 cautious, discreet, watchful 9 attentive 10 deliberate

circumstance: fix 4 fact, item 5 event, phase, state 6 affair, detail, factor, pickle 7 element, episode 8 incident, position 9 condition, situation 10 occurrence, particular 11 environment, opportunity 12 surroundings

circumstantial: 5 exact 6 minute 7 precise 8 detailed 9 pertinent 10 incidental, particular 11 inferential 12 nonessential

circumstantiate: 7 support 8 evidence

circumvent: 4 balk, dupe, foil 5 cheat, check, cozen, evade, trick 6 baffle, delude, entrap, outwit, thwart 7 capture,

deceive, defraud, ensnare, prevent 8
surround 9 encompass, frustrate, overreach, underfong

circus: 4 ring 5 arena 6 circle, cirque 9
spectacle 10 hippodrome 12 amphitheater 13 entertainment
arena wall: 5 spina
attraction: 5 freak 8 sideshow
column: 4 meta
employee: 5 clown, tamer
gear: 4 tent 5 rings 7 trapeze
rider: 8 desultor

cirque: 5 basin 6 circle, circus, corrie, recess 7 circlet, erosion

cirrus: 5 cloud 7 tendril 8 filament

cisco: 8 blackfin, whitefin

cist: box 4 tomb 5 chest 6 casket 7 chamber 9 cistavaen

cistern: sac, tub, vat 4 tank, well 6 cavity
7 cuvette 8 cisterna 9 reservoir, impluvium

cit: 8 townsman 9 tradesman 10 shopkeeper

citadel: arx 4 fort, hall 5 alamo, tower 6
castle 7 borough 8 fastness, fortress 10
stronghold 13 fortification
of Carthage: 5 Bursa, Byrsa
of Moscow: 7 Kremlin

citation: 6 notice 7 mention, summons 8
encomium, monition 9 quotation, reference 10 allegation 11 enumeration

cite: 4 call, tell 5 allay, quote, refer 10 accite, accuse, adduce, allege, arouse,
avouch, excite, notify, repeat, summon
7 arraign, bespeak, excerpt, extract,
mention 8 indicate

citizen: cit 5 voter 6 native 7 burgess,
burgher, citoyen(F.), denizen, elector,
freeman, oppidan 8 civilian, commoner,
occupant, resident 9 citoyenne(F.) 10
inhabitant

citizenship: *admission to:* 14 naturaliza-
tion 15 enfranchisement
pert. to: 5 civic

citrine: 5 color 7 rhubarb

citron: 4 lime 5 lemon 6 cedrat, yellow

citrullus: 7 pumpkin 10 watermelon

citrus: *belt:* 7 Florida 10 California
disease: 8 buckskin
drink: ade 5 juice
fruit: 4 lime, ugli 5 lemon 6 citron, orange 7 kumquat, tangelo 8 mandarin,
shaddock 9 tangerine 10 grapefruit
pest: 7 red mite

city: 4 burg, dorp, town, urbs(L.) 5 ville 6
ciudad, staple 9 community 10 metropolis 12 municipality
celestial: 4 Zion
district: 4 slum 6 barrio, ghetto, uptown
8 business, downtown, red-light 11 residential 12 neighborhood
eternal: 4 Roma, Rome

hanging gardens: 7 Babylon
holy: 5 Mecca 6 Medina 9 Jerusalem
leaning tower: 4 Pisa
official: 5 mayor 7 manager, marshal 8
alderman 10 councilman
oldest inhabited: 8 Damascus
pert. to: 5 civic, urban 7 oppidan 9 mu-
nicipal 12 metropolitan
planner: 8 urbanist
problem: 4 riot, slum, smog 5 crime 6
ghetto 7 poverty, traffic
section: 4 slum, ward 5 block, plaza 6
ghetto, square 8 downtown, red light
11 residential 12 neighborhood
slicker: 4 dude
wicked: 5 Sodom 8 Gomorrah

City: *of Bells:* 9 Strasburg 10 Strasbourg
of Bridges: 6 Bruges
of Brotherly Love: 12 Philadelphia
of Churches: 8 Brooklyn
of David: 9 Jerusalem
of God: 6 church, heaven 8 Paradise
of God author: 9 Augustine
of Hundred Towers: 5 Pavia
of Kings: 4 Lima
of Lilies: 8 Florence
of Masts: 6 London
of Rams: 6 Canton
of Refuge: 6 Medina
of Saints: 8 Montreal
of Seven Hills: 4 Rome
of Violet Crown: 6 Athens
of Victory: 5 Cairo

city-state: 5 polis 7 civitas

Cius: 6 Gemlik

civet: cat, cit 5 rasse, zibet 6 bondar, musang, zibeth 7 fossane, nandine

civet-like animal: 5 genet

civic: lay 5 civil, suave, urban 6 polite,
public, urbane 7 secular

civil: 4 hend 5 hende, suave 6 polite, urbane 7 affable, courtly, elegant, politic,
refined 8 discreet, gracious, obliging,
polished, wellbred 9 civilized, courteous
10 cultivated, respectful 11 complaisant 13 condescending

civil rights *(extinction of):* 9 attainder

Civil War: *admiral:* 8 Farragut
battle: 6 Shiloh 8 Antietam
commander: Lee 4 Pope 5 Ewell, Grant,
Meade, Sykes 7 Forrest, Jackson

civil wrong: 4 tort

civilian: cit 5 civvy 7 citizen, teacher 12
noncombatant, practitioner
dress: 5 mufti

civility: 6 comity 7 amenity, decorum 8
courtesy 9 propriety 10 affability, compliance, politeness 11 complacence 12
complaisance

civilization: 6 kultur(G.) 7 culture 10 refinement 11 cultivation

civilize: 4 tame 5 teach, train 6 polish,

refine 7 educate 8 humanize, urbanize 9 cultivate 11 domesticate

clabber: mud 4 mire 6 curdle, lopper 12 bonnyclabber

clack: gab, jaw, yak 4 blab 5 chack, cluck, crack 6 cackle, gossip, rattle, tongue 7 chatter, clacket, clatter, prattle 10 chatterbox

clad: 5 drest, robed 6 beseen, decked 7 adorned, arrayed, attired, clothed, covered, dressed 8 sheathed

cladose: 6 ramose 8 branched

clag: mud 4 clog, clot, daub, mire 5 fault, stick 6 adhere, burden

claggum: 5 taffy 7 treacle 8 molasses 9 sweetmeat

claim: ask 4 aver, call, case, lien, mine, name 5 exact, right, shout, title 6 assert, demand, elicit 7 acclaim, derecho, pretend, profess, require 8 maintain, pretence, pretense, proclaim 9 challenge, homestead, postulate, vindicate 11 encumbrance

claimant: 7 usurper 9 pretender, arrogator

clairvoyance: ESP 7 insight 8 sagacity 10 divination 11 discernment, penetration

clairvoyant: 4 seer 6 omener 7 prophet, seeress

clam: 4 base, clog, daub, glam, hush, mean 5 clamp, crash, glaum, grasp, grope, smear, stick 6 adhere, clutch, sticky 7 bivalve, clangor, mollusk, steamer 8 adhesive

genus of: mya

kinds of: 4 mega 5 blunt, chama, razor, solen 6 gweduc, quahog 7 geoduck, quahaug 10 little neck

clamant: 4 dire, loud 6 crying, urgent 9 clamorous 10 imperative

clamber: 5 climb, scale 6 claver 7 rammack 8 scramble, struggle

clamjamfry: mob 5 crowd 6 rabble 7 rubbish

clammy: 4 damp, dank, soft, wack 5 moist, sammy 6 sticky, waughy

clamor: cry, din, hue 4 bere, bunk, roar, rout, to-do, wail 5 blare, boast, bruit, noise, shout 6 bellow, hubbub, outcry, racket, tumult, uproar 7 stashie 10 hullabaloo, hurly-burly, vociferate

clamorous: 4 loud 5 noisy 7 blatant, clamant, yelling 8 brawling, decrying 9 clamatory, turbulent 10 boisterous 11 openmouthed

clamp: lug, nip, pin 4 bolt, glam, grip, hold, nail, vise 5 block, clasp, glaum 6 fasten 7 grapple 8 fastener, holdfast 10 clothespin

clan: set, sib 4 cult, race, sect, sept, unit 5 class, group, horde, party, tribe 6

clique, family 7 coterie, society 8 division 10 collection, fraternity

emblem: xat 5 totem

head of: 5 chief, elder, thane

pert. to: 6 tribal

clancular: 6 secret 11 clandestine

clandestine: bye, sly 4 foxy 5 privy 6 artful, covert, hidden, secret 7 bootleg, furtive, illicit 8 phratria, stealthy 9 clancular, concealed 10 fraudulent 12 hugger-mugger 13 surreptitious, under-the-table

clang: din 4 ding, peal, ring 5 clank, clash, noise 6 jangle, timbre

clangor: din 4 clam, roar 5 clang 6 hubbub, uproar

clank: 4 ring 5 sound 6 rackle

clannish: 5 close 6 secret, tribal, united

clap: 4 bang, flap, peal, slap 5 cheer, clink, crack 6 poster, strike, stroke 7 applaud, chatter, plaudit 9 explosion 11 thunderpeal

clapper: 6 rattle, tongue 7 knacker, knocker

support: 7 baldric 8 baldrick

claptrap: 4 bull 5 hokum, trash 6 blague, device, drivel, humbug 7 fustian 8 malarkey, nonsense, trickery 10 pretension 11 insincerity

clarify: 5 clean, clear 6 purify, refine, render, settle 7 cleanse, explain, glorify 8 depurate, eliquate, simplify 10 illuminate 11 transfigure 13 straighten out

clarinet: 4 reed, wind 10 instrument

mouthpiece: 4 birn

snake charmer's: 4 been

clarion: 5 clear, sharp 7 ringing, trumpet

clarity: 5 glory 8 accuracy, literacy, splendor 9 clearness 10 brightness, brilliance 11 pellucidity

claro: 4 mild 5 cigar 12 light-colored

clash: jar 4 bang, bolt, dash, news, slam 5 brawl, brunt, crash, fight, occur, prate, shock 6 affray, differ, gossip, hurtle, impact, strife, strike, tattle 7 collide, discord, scandal 8 argument, conflict 9 collision, interfere

clasp: hug, pin 4 fold, grab, grip, hasp, hold, hook, hoop, ouch, tach 5 cling, grasp, morse, preen, seize, tache 6 agrafe, brooch, buckle, clench, clutch, enfold, enwrap, fasten, fibula, gimmer, gimmor, infold 7 agrafe, amplect, embrace, entwine, fermail, tendril 8 barette, fastener, surround 9 constrain, safety-pin 10 chatelaine

class: ilk 4 clan, kind, race, rank, sect, sort, type 5 breed, caste, genus, genre, grade, group, order, tribe 6 circle, family, gender, rating 7 seminar, species, variety 8 category, division 9 abteilung 11 description 12 denomination

animal: 5 genus 6 genera
biological: 5 genus 6 genera(pl.)
member: 4 coed 6 junior, senior 8 freshman 9 sophomore
middle: 11 bourgeoisie
pert. to: 7 generic
working: 11 proletariat
classic: top 4 book 5 model 7 ancient, vintage 8 standard, top-notch 9 venerable 11 composition, masterpiece, tour de force
classical: 4 pure 5 Attic, Greek, Latin, Roman 6 chaste 8 academic, masterly 9 firstrate
classification: 4 file, rank, rate, sort 5 genre, genra(pl.), genus, grade, order, taxis 6 genera(pl.), rating, system 8 analysis, category, division, taxonomy 12 confidential, distribution
classify: 4 list, rank, rate, size, sort, type 5 grade, group, label, range 6 assort, codify, divide, ticket 7 arrange, catalog, dispose, marshal 8 register 9 catalogue, segregate 10 categorize, distribute, pigeonhole
classy: 4 tony 5 nifty, slick, smart 7 stylish 11 fashionable
clatter: din, jar 5 clack, noise, rumor 6 babble, gabble, gossip, rackle, rattle, tattle, uproar 7 blatter, chatter, clutter, prattle, reeshie 9 commotion 10 hurlyburly 11 disturbance
Claudia's husband: 6 Pilate
claudicant: 4 lame 7 limping
Claudius: 7 emperor
nephew: 6 Hamlet
slayer: 6 Hamlet 9 Agrippina
wife: 9 Messalina
successor: 4 Nero
clause: 4 part 5 close, plank, rider 6 phrase 7 article, passage, proviso 8 sentence 9 condition, provision 10 conclusion 11 stipulation
additional: 5 rider
claut: 4 hand, lump, rake, tear 5 chunk 6 clutch, scrape 7 handful, scratch
clavecin: 11 harpsichord
claver: 5 prate 6 clover, gossip 7 chatter, chamber
clavichord: 6 spinet
clavicle: 4 bone 10 collarbone
clavis: key 8 glossary
clavus: 4 band, corn 5 strip 6 bunion, callus
claw: dig 4 clee, fawn, hand, hook, nail, pull, sere, tear, unce 5 chela, cloof, clufe, court, grasp, griff, seize, talon, uncus 6 clutch, nipper, scrape, ungula 7 crubeen, flatter, scratch, wheedle 8 lacerate
clay: cob, pug 4 bole, galt, loam, lute, marl, mire 5 argil, brick, cloam, earth, gault,

loess, ochre, rabat, tasco 6 cledge, clunch, kaolin 8 lifeless 9 inanimate
bed: 5 gault
box: 6 saggar, sagger
building: 5 adobe, tapia
casting: 4 slip
constituent: 7 alumina
covered with: 6 lutose
deposit: 4 marl
fragment: bat
friable: 4 bole
layer: 4 lias 5 sloam
lump: 4 clag, clod
made of: 7 fictile
mineral: 7 nacrite
mold: dod
musical instrument: 7 ocarina
pert. to: 5 bolar
piece: 4 tile
pottery: 6 kaolin 7 kaoline
tropical: 8 laterite
claybrained: 4 dull 6 stupid
clayey: 5 bolar, heavy, malmy, marly 6 cledgy, lutose 9 argillous 12 argillaceous
clay pigeon: 6 target
clead: 8 attire, clothe
clean: fay, fey, hoe, mop 4 dust, fair, pure, smug, swab, trim, wash, wipe 5 bream, clear, curry, empty, feigh, grave, scour, scrub, smart 6 chaste, clever, kosher, purify 7 apinoid, cleanse, clearly, furbish, perfect 8 absterge, brightly, dextrous, entirely, renovate, spotless, unsoiled 9 destitute, dexterous, guiltless, speckless, undefiled 10 immaculate 11 butterworth, untarnished 12 spick-and-span, straighten up 13 unadulterated
Hebrew: 6 kosher
cleaner: 4 soap 5 borax, purer 6 ramrod 8 cleanser 9 detergent 10 dentifrice
fish: 6 scaler
cleaning implement: mop 4 swab 5 broom 6 ramrod, vacuum 7 sweeper
cleanly: 4 pure 5 adroit, artful, chaste 7 correct, elegant 8 innocent, skillful 9 dexterous
cleanse: 4 farm, heal, soap, wash 5 brush, clean, dight, purge, rinse, scour, scrub 6 purify, refine 7 baptize, clarify, deterge, sweeten 8 renovate 9 disinfect, expurgate, sterilize
cleanser: lye 9 detergent 10 clarifiant
cleansing: 4 bath 7 abluent, clysmic, washing 8 ablution, lavation 9 acquittal, cathartic, purgation 10 emundation 12 purification
cleansing process: 4 bath 7 washing
clear: net, rid 4 free, gain, open, over, pure, quit 5 atrip, breme, brent, clean, erase, lucid, plain, prune, sharp, vivid 6 acquit, assoil, bright, candid, clever, ex-

empt, fluted, limpid, lucent, patent, purify, settle, smooth 7 absolve, clarion, clarify, crystal, deliver, evident, glaring, graphic, lighten, obvious, release, rule out 8 apparent, brighten, definite, distinct, explicit, manifest, pellucid, relevant, scot-free, shake off 9 cloudless, discharge, disengage, elucidate, enigmatic, exculpate, exonerate, extricate, vindicate 10 see-through, unconfused 11 disentangle, open-and-shut, perspicuous, transparent 12 intelligible

as crystal: 7 evident, obvious

away: fay, fey 5 feigh 6 dispel 8 evacuate 9 eliminate, expurgate

out: 5 scram 6 decamp, desert 7 skidoo, take off

up: 5 solve 6 settle

clear-cut: 5 exact, lucid, sharp 7 concise 8 chiseled, definite, distinct, incisive 9 chiselled 10 unconfused 11 categorical 12 unquestioned

clear-eyed: 10 discerning

clear-headed: 10 perceptive

clear-sighted: 10 discerning 13 perspicacious

clearing: *in woods:* 5 glade, tract 8 slashing

of land: 4 sart 6 assart

cleat: 4 bitt 5 block, chock, kevel, wedge 6 batten 7 bollard, coxcomb, support 9 butterbur

cleavage: 5 chasm, cleft, split 6 schism 7 fission, fissure 8 division 9 partition 10 separation

cleave: cut, rip 4 chop, hold, join, link, part, rely, rend, rift, rive, slit, tear 5 break, carve, chawn, chine, clave, cleft, cling, clove, crack, sever, shear, split, stick 6 adhere, bisect, cohere, divide, pierce, sunder 7 dispart, fissure 8 separate

cleaver: axe 4 froe, frow

cleche: 4 urde 5 urdee 11 cross-shaped

cleek: 4 club, hook, link 5 crook, pluck, seize 6 clutch, snatch 8 fishhook, golf club

clef: key 9 character

bass: eff

treble: gee

cleft: gap 4 chap, chop, fent, flow, reft, rift, rima, rive 5 break, chasm, chawn, chink, clove, crack, crena, riven, split 6 breach, cleave, cloven, cranny, crotch, divide, recess 7 crevice, divided, fissure, opening 8 aperture, fracture

cleft-lip: 7 harelip

Cleite: *father:* 6 Merops

husband: 7 Cyzicus

clemency: 4 pity 5 mercy 6 lenity 7 quarter 8 kindness, leniency, mildness 10 compassion, indulgence

clement: 4 easy kind, mild, soft, warm 6 gentle 7 lenient 8 merciful 9 forgiving, indulgent 10 benevolent 13 compassionate

clench: 4 fist, grip, grit, hold 5 brace, clasp, clint, close, grasp 6 clinch, clutch 9 interlock 10 strengthen

cleome: 5 caper

Cleopatra: *attendant:* 4 Iras 8 Charmian

killer: asp

lover: 6 Antony, Caesar 10 Mark Antony

river: 7 Nile

sister: 7 Arsinoe

Cleopatra's Needle: 7 obelisk

clepsydra: 9 timepiece 10 water clock

clergy: 4 cloth 8 ministry

body of: 6 pulpit 7 college

clergyman: 4 abba, abbe, dean, Papa 5 canon, clerk, padre, pilot, prior, rabbi, vicar 6 bishop, cleric, curate, deacon, divine, domine, parson, pastor, priest, rector 7 cassock, prelate 8 cardinal, chaplain, minister, preacher, reverend 9 blackcoat, dignitary, presbyter 12 ecclesiastic

office: 4 cure 6 curacy 8 ministry 9 pastorate, priorship, rectorate

residence: 5 manse 6 priory 7 rectory 8 vicarage 9 parsonage

traveling: 12 circuit rider

clergywoman: nun 8 rectress 9 priestess 10 religieuse

cleric: See **clergyman**

clerical: 10 of the cloth

clerical clothing: alb 5 rabat, stole, amice, cloth, fanon, orale 6 collar 7 biretta

clerk: nun 4 monk 5 agent, steno, write 6 cleric, commis, hermit, layman, priest, scribe, teller, yeoman 7 carcoon, compose, gomasta, scholar 8 employee, greffier(F.), recorder, salesman 9 assistant, clergyman, registrar, secretary 10 accountant 11 salesperson 12 ecclesiastic, stenographer

court: 11 protonotary 12 prothonotary

hotel: 7 deskman

passenger ship: 6 purser

clerkly: 7 learned, scribal 9 scholarly

clever: apt, sly 4 able, cute, deft, fine, gnib, hend, keen 5 agile, alert, clean, clear, handy, hende, lithe, quick, slick, smart, witty 6 active, adroit, artful, astute, bright, expert, habile, heppen, neatly, nimble, pretty, shrewd 7 amiable, cunning, parlous 8 dextrous, handsome, obliging, skillful, talented 9 dexterous, ingenious 10 well-shaped 11 clean-limbed, dexterously, intelligent, quick-witted 13 scintillating

cleverness: can 4 tact 5 skill 6 esprit 9 dexterity, ingenuity 10 adroitness, astuteness clevis: 4 hake 5 copse 6 muzzle 7 fitting 10 connection

clew, clue: 4 ball, hint 5 globe, blome, skein 6 hurdle, thread

cliche: 6 truism 7 bromide 8 banality 9 hackneyed, platitude 11 stereotyped

click: 4 pawl, tick 5 agree, catch 6 detent 7 come off, ratchet

click beetle: 6 elater

client: 5 ceile 6 patron 7 patient 8 customer, henchman, retainer 9 dependent

clientele: 6 public 9 following

cliff: hoe 4 crag, hill, rock, scar 5 bluff, cleve, heuch, heugh, scarp, shore, slope 6 cleeve, height 7 clogwyn 8 hillside, palisade 9 precipice

cliff-hanger: 7 suspense 9 melodrama

climate: 4 mood 5 region, temper 8 attitude 9 condition

control chamber: 7 biotrin

climax: cap, top 4 acme, apex, near, peak, shut 5 mount, scale, tight 6 apogee, ascend, finish, opogee, summit, zenith 9 gradation 11 culmination

climb: gad 4 ramp, rise, shin 5 creep, grimp, mount, scale, speed(Sc.), twine 6 ascend, ascent, shinny 7 clamber

climb down: 7 descend 8 dismount

climb on: 5 mount, scale

climber: 6 rigger, scaler 11 mountaineer 12 alpenstocker

climbing device: 6 ladder

climbing plant: ivy 4 vine 5 liana, liane 7 creeper

clime: See climate

clinch: fix, get, hug 4 bind, grip, nail, seal 5 clamp, cling, clink, clint, grasp, rivet, seize 6 clench, clutch, fasten, secure, snatch 7 confirm, embrace, grapple, scuffle 8 complete, conclude, holdfast 9 establish

cling: hug 4 bank, hang, hold, rely 5 clasp, stick, trust 6 adhere, cleave, clinch, cohere, depend, fasten, shrink, wither 7 cherish, embrace, shrivel 8 contract 9 persevere

clingfish: 6 testar

clink: ale, jug, put, rap 4 beat, blow, brig, cash, clap, coin, jail, move, ring, slap 5 latch, money, rhyme, seize 6 clinch, jingle, lockup, moment, prison, strike, tinkle 7 instant 8 hoosegow 9 assonance, calaboose 10 guardhouse

clinker: 4 slag 5 waste

clinquant: 5 clink, showy 6 tinsel 8 tinseled 10 glittering

Clio: See Muse

clip: bob, cut, dod, hug, lip, lop, mow, nip 4 barb, flap, coll, crop, dock, dodd, hold, pace, pare, poll, snip, trim 5 clasp, force, prune, shear 6 clutch, fasten, hinder, holder 7 curtain, curtail, cut down,

embrace, scissor, shorten 8 diminish, encircle, mark down 9 encompass 10 abbreviate, overcharge

clipper: 4 boat, ship 6 vessel 7 shearer, workman

clique: cot, mob, set 4 bloc, clan, club, gang, ring 5 cabal, group, junto, write 6 circle, cletch 7 coterie, faction, in-group 8 conclave, sodality 9 camarilla 11 combination

clitter: 5 noise 6 rattle 7 chatter 10 stridulate

cloak: aba 4 brat, capa, cape, hide, mant, mask, pall, rail, robe, veil, wrap 5 capot, cover, guise, manta, manto, sagum 6 assume, bautta, capote, caster, chapel, dolman, mantle, mantua, pharos, screen, serape, shield, shroud, tabard, visite 7 bavaroy, chlamys, conceal, garment, manteau, manteel, pelisse, pretext, shelter, zimarra 8 albornoz, burnoose, disguise, intrigue, mantilla, palliate 9 dissemble 10 camouflage, roquelaure 11 portmanteau

African: 5 jelab 6 jellab

Arabian: 7 feridgi, ferigee, ferijee 8 feridjee

baptismal: 7 chrisom

bishop's: 10 mantelleta

ecclesiastical: 4 cope

Greek: 6 abolla 7 chlamys

hooded: 6 camail 8 burnoose

Indian: 5 choga

Jewish: 6 kittel 9 gaberdine

large-sleeved: 10 witzchoura

loose: 5 palla

monk's: 8 analabos

Punjabi: 5 choga

Roman: 5 sagum 7 alicula, paenula

Roman military: 10 paludament 11 paludamenta(pl.) 12 paludamentum

sleeveless: aba 6 dolman 7 paenula

Spanish: 4 capa 5 manta 6 mantle

Turkish: 6 dolman

waterproof: 6 poncho

worn over armor: 6 tabard

clobber: 4 beat, belt, slug 5 patch, pound, smear 6 cobble, defeat, strike, wallop

cloche: hat, jar 4 bell 5 cover

clocher: 6 belfry 9 bell tower, campanile

clock: nef 4 bell, call, dial, gong, time 5 cluck, hatch, hurry, meter, watch 6 beetle, Big Ben, crouch 8 horologe, incubate, ornament, recorder 9 clepsydra, hourglass, indicator, taximeter, timepiece 11 chronometer, speedometer

ancient water: 9 clepsydra

astronomical: 8 sidereal

maker: 9 horologer 10 horologist

part of: 4 dial 5 bundy 6 detent, foliot 8 pendulum, recorder

regulating body: 8 pendulum 10 escapement

ship-shaped: nef
water: 5 clepsydra
weight: 5 peise

clocker: 5 timer 8 railbird 11 embroiderer

clockmaker: 9 horologer

clockwise: 6 deasil, dessil 7 deiseal 8 positive

clod: sod 4 clat, clot, dolt, dull, lout, lump, turf 5 clout, clown, divot, earth, glebe, gross, knoll, yokel 6 dimwit, ground, stupid 7 bumpkin 9 blockhead, coagulate 10 clodhopper

cloddish: 5 gross 6 stupid 7 boorish, ill-bred

clodhopper: 4 boor, clod, shoe 6 rustic 7 bumpkin, plowman

clodpate: 4 clot, dolt, fool 7 ramhead 8 clodpole, clodpoll, imbecile 9 blockhead

clog: gum, jam, log 4 clag, clam, cloy, curb, load, lump, shoe, skid, stop 5 block, check, choke, dance, sabot 6 adhere, burden, chopin, fetter, galosh, hamper, hobble, hog-tie, impede, pattern, remora, sandal, secque, weight 7 galoshe, perplex, shackle, trammel 8 coalesce, encumber, obstruct, overshoe, restrain 9 embarrass, hindrance, restraint 10 difficulty 11 encumbrance
with mud: 4 daub 6 daggle

cloggy: 5 heavy, lumpy 6 sticky

clogwyn: 5 cliff 9 precipice

cloister: 4 hall, stoa 5 abbey, aisle, stoae(pl.) 6 arcade, friary, immure, piazza, priory 7 closter, convent, nunnery, seclude 9 cloistral, enclosure, hermitage, monastery, sanctuary, sequester 11 ambulatoria(pl.) 12 ambulatorium
pert. to: 9 claustral, cloistral

Cloister and the Hearth author: 5 Reade

cloistered: 7 recluse 11 sequestered

clone: 4 copy, dupe 6 double 7 replica 9 duplicate 13 identical twin

cloof, clufe: 4 claw, hoof 6 cleave

clop: 4 limp 5 sound 6 hobble

close: cap, end, hot 4 clit, firm, hard, hide, near, nigh, quit, seal, shut, slam, snug, stop 5 anear, block, cease, cheap, dense, finis, garth, gross, muggy, thick, tight 6 clause, clench, effect, expiry, finale, finish, narrow, nearby, period, stingy, strait 7 adjourn, compact, context, extreme, miserly, occlude, similar 8 accurate, adjacent, complete, conclude, familiar, imminent, intimate, taper off 9 barricade, extremity, niggardly, terminate 10 avaricious, conclusion, nip-and-tuck 11 termination 12 parsimonious
a hawk's eyes: 4 seel
firmly: bar 4 lock, seal 5 tight 6 batten, cement

closefisted: 4 near 6 stingy 7 miserly 8 handfast 9 niggardly

closely: 4 just 6 almost, barely, narrow, nearly 9 carefully, compactly

closemouthed: 6 secret, silent

closeness: 7 secrecy 8 fidelity, intimacy 9 parsimony, proximity 10 stinginess, strictness 11 conciseness, literalness 14 oppressiveness

closest: 4 next 7 nearest 9 proximate

closet: 4 ewry, room, safe 5 ambry, cuddy 6 armary, locker, pantry, secret 7 cabinet, conceal, private 8 conclave, cupboard, gardevin, wardrobe 9 gardevine 12 confidential

closing device: 4 lock 6 zipper

closure: end, gag 5 bound, limit 7 cloture 8 clausure 9 agreement, enclosure 10 conclusion 9 confinement, containment 12 entrenchment

clot: dot, gel 4 clag, clat, clod, gout, jell, lump, mass 5 clart, group, grume 6 balter, cotter 7 clodder, congeal, embolus, thicken 8 clodplate, coagulum, concrete, solidify 9 blockhead, coagulate 12 crassamentum

cloth (see also **fabric,** and name of individual fabrics: **cotton, linen, silk,** etc.): rag 5 bluet, toile(F.), tweed, twill 6 canvas, clergy, drapet, fabric, livery, napkin 7 acetate, drapery, garment, raiment, textile, worsted 8 dwelling, material, sheeting 10 cassinette
baptismal: 7 chrisom
bark: 4 tapa 9 tapa cloth
blemish: yaw 4 snag, tear 5 amper
camel's hair: aba 6 camlet
coarse: 4 duck 5 crash, gunny 6 burlap, linsey
crinkled: 5 crape, crepe 10 seersucker
dealer: 6 draper, mercer
decorative: see *ornamental* below
dryer: 6 tenter
dye method: tie 5 batik
fine-textured: 4 mull, pima, silk 7 percale
finisher: 7 beetler
flaw in: 4 rase
flaxen: 5 linen
glazed: 5 tammy
goat's hair: 5 tibet 6 camlet, mohair
heavy: 9 petersham
hemp: 4 jute 5 gunny 6 baline, burlap, canamo
homespun: 4 kelt
instrument: 8 ringhead
knitted: 6 jersey, tricot
light: 6 tissue 7 challis, etamine
lining: 6 serge 8 sarcenet, sarsenet
measure: ell 4 nail
mesh: net 5 super, tulle 11 cheesecloth
metallic: 4 acca, tash
mourning: 5 crape, crepe

muslin: 5 adati

narrow: 4 tape 5 braid 6 edging, ribbon

old kind: 4 acca, tuke 5 tewke 6 samite

ornamental: 4 gimp, lace 6 lampas, riband 8 tapestry

poplin: 7 tabinet 8 tabbinet

print: 6 calico 7 percale

printer: 7 candroy

raised design: 7 brocade

remnant: 4 fent

ridge in: 4 wale

roll: 4 bolt

rug: mat 7 matting

satin: See **fabric:** *satin*

shop: 7 mercery

silk: See **fabric:** *silk*

soft: 5 panne, plush, surah 6 fleece 9 montagnac

stiff: 7 taffeta 9 crinoline

stretcher: 6 tenter

synthetic: 5 nylon, rayon 6 dacron 7 acetate

toweling: 5 terry

twilled: rep 4 jean 5 denim, serge

used as a dressing: 5 stupe

velvet: 5 panne

weatherproof: 4 tarp 6 canvas

woolen: 6 kersey

clothe: don, dub, rig, tog 4 deck, dress, garb, gird, gown, robe, vest 5 adorn, array, clead, cleed, dress, endow, endue, frock, habit 6 attire, enrobe, invest, swathe 7 apparel, vesture 8 accouter, accoutre 9 authorize, represent

clothes (see also **dress**): 4 duds, garb, gear, suit, tack, wear 5 get-up, habit 6 attire 7 apparel, baggage, costume, raiment, regalia, toggery, vesture 8 clothing, frippery, garments 9 vestments 10 bedclothes 11 habiliments

basket: 6 hamper

civilian: 5 mufti

collection: 8 wardrobe

dealer: 6 ragman 7 fripper 9 fripperer

informal: 5 smock 6 halter, shorts, slacks, trunks

pert. to: 8 vestiary 10 habilatory

presser: 7 sadiron

clothesmoth: 5 tinea

clothespress: kas 5 chest 7 armoire 8 wardrobe

clothing: (see also **garment**): 4 wear 6 attire 7 apparel

coarse: 4 brat 5 burel

protective: 5 armor

woman's: 6 fardel

cloud: fog, nue(F.) 4 blur, dust, haze, hide, mist 5 bedim, befog, gloom, nubia, stain, sully, swarm, taint, vapor 6 cirrus, damage, darken, deepen, defame, nebula, nimbus, screen, shadow, stigma 7 blacken, confuse, cumulus, eclipse,

obscure, perplex, tarnish 8 befuddle, overcast 9 obfuscate 11 thunderhead

form: 6 nebule 7 stratus 9 mare's tail

morning: 4 velo

pert. to: 7 nebular 12 nephological

study of: 9 nephology

wind-driven: 4 rack, scud

cloudburst: 6 deluge 9 rainstorm

cloudless: 5 azure, clear 6 bright

cloudy: dim 4 dark, dull, hazy 5 filmy, murky, shady 6 gloomy, lowery, opaque 8 overcast 10 indistinct, lackluster

clough: 5 cleft 6 ravine, valley

clour: 4 blow, bump, dint 5 thump 6 batter

clout: bat, box, hit 4 beat, blow, bump, clod, club, cuff, join, mend, nail, pull, slap, slug, swat 5 patch, power, smite 6 strike, target, thrash, washer 7 bandage 8 bosthoon 9 influence 11 what it takes 12 handkerchief

clouter: 7 botcher, cobbler

clove: bud 4 bulb, tree 5 spice 6 ravine

cloven: 5 cleft, split 9 bisulcate

cloven-footed: 8 fissiped

clover: red 5 lotus, medic, nardu 6 alsike, luxury, nardoo 7 alfalfa, comfort, lucerne, melilot, trefoil 10 prosperity

cloverleaf: fan 7 freeway 8 crossway 11 interchange

clown: hob, oaf 4 aper, boor, fool, goff, joey, lout, mime, mome, zany 5 churl, comic, mimer, punch, zanni(It.) 6 august, bodach, hobbil, jester, lubber, rustic, stooge 7 buffoon, bumpkin, peasant, playboy 8 merryman 9 harlequin, joculator 10 bufflehead, countryman, harlequina 11 Emmet Kelly, merry-andrew, punchinello 13 pickle-herring

clownish: raw 4 rude, zany 5 gawky, rough 6 clumsy, coarse, rustic 7 awkward, boorish, hoblike, ill-bred, loutish, uncivil 8 ungainly 9 untutored

cloy: 4 clog, glut, nail, pall, sate 5 gorge, prick 6 pierce 7 satiate, satisfy, surfeit

club: bat, hit, set 4 beat, cane, join, mace, maul, polt, team 5 billy, bunch, clout, kebby, lodge, order, staff, stick, unite, yokel 6 clique, cudgel, kebbie, menage, weapon 8 bludgeon, sorority, spontoon 9 blackjack, truncheon 10 fraternity, knobkerrie, shillelagh 11 association

famous: 5 Lambs 6 Friars 7 Garrick

golf: 4 iron, wood 5 wedge 6 putter 7 sand wedge

club moss: 8 buckhorn

club-shaped: 7 clavate

clubfoot: 7 talipes 9 deformity

clubfooted: 7 taliped

clubs: 4 suit 5 cards, basto

clubstart: 5 stoat

cluck: hen 4 call, fuss 5 chuck, clack,

click, clock, sound 9 dumb bunny 13 featherweight

clue: key, tip 4 ball, clew, hint, idea 5 guide, twine 6 thread 7 inkling 8 innuendo 10 indication, intimation, suggestion 11 fingerprint

clump: tod 4 blow, bush, heap, lump, mass, mott, tope, tuft 5 bunch, group, grove, patch, tread 6 clunch, dollop 7 cluster, thicket 10 hodgepodge

clumsy: 4 rude 5 blunt, bulky, gawky, hulky, inapt, inept, stiff 6 gauche 7 awkward, boorish, ill-made, unhandy 8 bungling, tactless, ungainly, unwieldy 9 all thumbs, lumbering, maladroit 10 cumbersome 11 heavy-handed 13 inappropriate

Cluny product: 4 lace

cluster: bog 4 bush, cyme, knot, lump, tuft 5 bunch, clump, group 7 bourock, cluther, package 8 fascicle 9 glomerule 10 collection 11 agglomerate, aggregation

fern spore: 4 sori(pl.) 5 sorus

fiber: nep

flower: 4 cime, cyme 5 ament, umbel 6 raceme 7 panicle 8 anthemia

flower-like: 7 rosette

growing in: 8 acervate

of seven stars: 8 Pleiades

clustered: 6 tufted 8 racemose 9 aciniform, aggregate, glomerate 10 coacervate

clutch: nab 4 clam, claw, clem, clip, fist, glam, grab, grip, nest 5 brood, catch, clasp, claut, cleek, glaum, grasp, gripe, hatch, lever, power, seize, talon 6 cleach, clench, cletch, clinch, retain, snatch 7 control 8 coupling

clutter: 4 mess 6 bustle 7 clatter 8 disorder 9 confusion 10 disarrange, hodgepodge

Clymene: *father:* 7 Oceanus

husband: 7 Iapetus

mother: 6 Tethys

son: 5 Atlas 10 Prometheus

Clytemnestra: *daughter:* 7 Electra 9 Iphigenia

father: 9 Tyndareus

half-sister: 5 Helen

husband: 9 Agamemnon

mother: 4 Leda

paramour: 7 Aegisthus

son: 7 Orestes

victim: 9 Agamemnon, Cassandra

cnemis: 4 shin 5 tibia 7 legging

coach: bus, car 4 hack, help 5 araba, cabin, prime, teach, train, tutor 6 advise, direct, fiacre(F.), mentor, saloon 7 adviser, prepare, tallyho 8 carriage, dormeuse, instruct 10 instructor, stagecoach

railway: 7 Pullman, sleeper

coach dog: 9 Dalmatian

coachman: fly 4 fish, jehu, whip 5 pilot 6 driver 7 coachee, coacher 8 yemschik

assistant: 10 postillion

Russian: 7 yamshik 8 yemschik 9 yamstchik

coadjutor: 4 aide 6 bishop 7 partner 8 coworker 9 assistant, associate

coagulant: 4 curd 6 rennet 7 styptic 8 gelatine

coagulate: gel, set 4 cake, clod, clot, curd, jell 5 quail 6 cotter, curdle, posset 7 clabber, congeal, thicken 8 solidify

coagulation: 4 gout 7 clotter

coal: 4 bass, fuel 5 chark, ember, gleed, stoke 6 carbon, cinder

agent: 6 fitter

bed: 4 seam

block: jud

carrying box: hod 7 scuttle

constituent: 4 goaf 6 carbon, ethene, phenol, pyrene 7 benzene 8 creosote 11 naphthalene

distillate: tar

dust: 4 coom, culm, smut, soot, swad 6 coomb

immature form of: 7 lignite

kind of: jud 4 dant, hard, soft 6 cannel 7 lignite 9 tasmanite 10 anthracite, bituminous

lump: cob

mine explosive: 9 Bobbinite

miner: 7 collier

miner's disease: 11 anthrocosis

mining implement: 7 breaker

oil: 8 kerosene

refuse: 4 coke, dust, slag 6 cinder 7 backing, clinker

size: cob, egg, nut, pea 4 lump 5 slack, stove 6 broken 8 chestnut 9 buckwheat

wagon: 4 corb, carf, tram

worker: 7 collier, geordie 8 chaffman

coal car part: 6 hopper

coalbin: 6 bunker

coalesce: mix 4 fuse, join 5 blend, merge, unite 6 embody 7 combine 10 amalgamate

coalescence: 5 union 6 fusion, league 11 combination

coalfish: sey 4 parr 5 cuddy 6 beshow, billet, cudden, podler, sarthe 7 baddock, glashan, pollack

coalition: 4 bloc 5 trust, union 6 fusion, league, merger 8 alliance 11 combination, confederacy, conjunction 13 confederation

coarse: low, raw 4 dank, hard, hask, lewd, loud, rank, rude, vile 5 bawdy, broad, crass, crude, dirty, gross, harsh heavy, loose, randy, routh, thick 6 brutal, callow, common, earthy, impure, ribald, rustic, vulgar **7** blatant, fulsome, goatish, obscene, raucous, sensual **8** clownish, homespun, immodest, indecent, unchaste **9** inelegant, offensive, unrefined **10** boisterous, indelicate, unpolished **12** scatological

food: **6** fodder

coast: 4 bank, land, ripa **5** beach, blide, shore, slide **6** adjoin, border, rivage, strand **7** seaside **8** approach, littoral, seaboard, seashore

area: **7** seaside **8** seacoast **9** coastline, shoreline

dweller: **7** orarian

pert. to: **7** coastal, orarian **8** littoral, riparian

projection: **4** cape, ness **8** headland **9** peninsula

Coast Guard: *boat:* **6** cutter

service-woman: **4** Spar

coaster: 4 mat **4** sled **5** trout **8** toboggan **9** container

coat (see also **cloak**)**: 4** bark, daub, husk, rind, zinc **5** cloth, cover, crust, glaze, habit, layer, paint, plate, shell, terve **6** enamel, jacket, mantle, parget, pelage, veneer **7** garment, incrust, overlay, plaster, vesture **8** membrane, tegument **9** petticoat **10** integument

animal: fur **4** hair, hide, pelt, wool **6** pelage

arctic: **5** parka

fastener: **4** frog **6** button

Irish: **9** coatamore

kind of: car, pea **4** cape, jupe, mail, robe, sack, toga **5** armor, simar, tails **6** coatie, duster, jerkin, kirtle, mantle, reefer, rocket, topper **7** cassock, cutaway, haubeck, paletot, pelisse, surcoat, surcote, surtout **8** benjamin, mackinaw, overcoat **9** gaberdine, newmarket, redingote **12** chesterfield

neck: **6** george

part: **4** cuff **5** lapel, skirt **6** collar, george, pocket, sleeve

seaman's: **5** grego

soldier's: **5** tunic

coat of arms: 5 crest

pert to: **8** heraldic

coati: 5 nasua **6** animal, narica

coating: 4 aril, film **6** patina, veneer **8** mucilage

coax: beg, coy, pet **4** cant, dupe, fawn, lure, urge **5** tease **6** cajole, cuitle, entice **7** beguile, cuittle, flatter, implore, wheedle **8** blandish, butter up, collogue, inveigle, persuade, soft soap **9** influence **10** manipulate

coaxial: 12 conterminous

cob: ear, mew **4** beat, blow, gull, loaf, lump, mole, mule, pier, pony, swan, toss **5** block, break, chief, excel, horse, out-

do, piece, stump, throw, thump **6** basket, cobnut, leader, muffin, peapod, spider, strike **7** beating, seagull, surpass, threash **8** dumpling **10** breakwater

cobble: 4 darn, make, mend, pave **5** botch, patch, stone **6** bungle, repair **7** clobber, snarl up **11** cobblestone

cobbler: pie **4** snob **5** sheep, soler, sutor **6** souter **7** botcher, catfish, crispin, dessert, pompano, saddler **8** chuckler, scorpion **9** killifish, shoemaker

pitch: **4** code

cobia: 4 fish **6** bonito

cobra: asp, nag **4** naga, naja **5** snake, viper **6** uraeus

genus: **4** naja

tree: **5** mamba

cobweb: net **4** trap **5** snare, wevet **8** gossamer **9** intricacy

cocaine: 4 snow **8** alkaloid, narcotic **10** anesthetic

source: **4** coca

coccyx: 8 tailbone

cochleate: 6 spiral **11** shell-shaped

cock: tap **4** bank, fowl, heap, kora, pile, rick **5** fugie, fight, gallo, shock, stack, strut, valve, yowle **6** faucet, leader **7** chicken, contend, gorcock, rooster, swagger **8** gamecock, malemass **10** cockalorum **11** chanticleer

gun: nab

of the walk: **8** kingfish

weather: **4** vane

cock-a-hoop: 4 awry **5** askew **6** elated, lively **8** boastful, cockeyed

cock-and-bull story: lie **6** canard **7** untruth **9** falsehood

cockade: 4 knot **5** badge **7** rosette

Cockaigne: 6 utopia **8** paradise

cockatoo: ara **5** arara, cocky, galah, macaw **6** abacay, cockie, parrot **8** calangay, ganggang

genus: **7** cacatua, kakatoe

cockatrice: 7 serpent **8** basilisk

cockboat: cog **7** rowboat

cockchafer: 6 beetle

cocker: dog, pet **4** shoe **6** coddle, fondle, pamper, quiver, reaper **7** cater to, fighter, indulge, legging, nurture, spaniel

cockerel: 4 cock, slip **6** bantam

cockeyed: 4 alop, awry **5** askew **10** inebriated **11** intoxicated

cockfight: 4 game, spar **5** match **7** contest

cockfighting: 13 alectryomachy

cockhorse: 5 lofty, proud **7** astride, upstart **8** exultant

cockle: 4 boat, gall, gith, kiln, oast **5** bulge, shell, stove **6** darnel, pucker, ripple, wabble **7** mollusk, wrinkle **9** whimsical

cocklebur: 5 plant **7** burdock

cockpit: pit 4 ring, rink, well 5 arena, cabin, field 7 gallera

cocksure: 4 sure 5 cocky 7 certain 8 confident, positive

cocktail: 5 Bronx, drink 7 apertif, martini, sidecar 8 daiquiri 9 appetizer, Manhattan, Margarita 10 Bloody Mary

cocky: 4 pert 6 crouse, farmer, jaunty 8 arrogant, insolent 9 conceited 11 smart alecky

cocoa, coco: 4 head, palm, tary 5 broma 6 yuntia 9 chocolate

coconut: 7 coquito

dried meat: copra

fiber: 4 coir, kyar

cocoon: pod 4 clew, clue 5 shell 11 incunabulum

cod: bag, cor, pod 4 axle, bank, cusk, fish, fool, hoax, husk, rock 5 belly, pouch, scrod, torsk 6 burbot, codger, cultus, fellow, pillow 7 bacaloa, cushion

family: 7 gadidae

genus: 5 gadus

related fish: 7 rattail 9 grenadier

young: 5 scrod, sprag 7 codling

cod-like: bib 4 hake, ling 5 gadus

coda: 4 part 5 rondo 6 finale 10 conclusion

coddle: pet 4 baby, cade, cook 5 humor, nurse, spoil 6 caress, cocker, cosset, cotton, fondle, pamper, cater to 7 indulge, parboil

code: law 4 flag 5 canon, codex 6 cipher, digest, secret, signal 7 precept

inventor: 5 Morse

message: 6 cipher 10 cryptogram

coded message: 10 cryptogram

codex: 4 code 5 annal 9 formulary 10 manuscript

codger: cod 5 churl, crank, miser 6 fellow 7 niggard

codicil: 5 rider 6 sequel 8 appendix 10 supplement

codify: 5 index 6 digest 8 classify 11 systematize

coerce: cow 4 curb, make, urge 5 bully, check, drive, force 6 compel, menace 7 concuss, enforce, repress 8 bludgeon, bulldoze, restrain, restrict 9 blackmail, constrain, terrorize 10 intimidate

coercion: 5 force 6 duress

coeval: 12 contemporary

coffee: *after dinner:* 9 demitasse

alkaloid: 7 caffein

bean: nib

beverage: Rio 4 Java, Kona 5 Milds, Mocha 6 Bogota, Brazil, Santos 7 Sumatra 8 Medellin 9 Maracaibo

cake: 6 kuchen

French: 4 café

grinder: 4 mill

kind: 4 drip, java 5 mocha, Sanka 7 arabica, instant 8 espresso

maker: urn 5 silex 10 percolator

refuse: 6 triage

coffee shop: 5 diner 8 snack bar 9 lunchroom 12 luncheonette

coffeeberry: 6 jojoba 7 cascara, soybean 8 peaberry 9 buckthorn, chaparral

coffeepot: 6 biggin 9 cafetiere

coffer: ark, box, dam 5 chest, hutch, trunk 6 casket, forcer, trench 7 caisson 8 ciborium, standard

coffin: 4 bier, case, cist, mold 6 basket, casing, casket 11 sarcophagus

cloth: 4 pall 5 cloak

support: 4 bier

cog: cam, lie 4 gear, jest 5 catch, cheat, cozen, tenon, tooth, trick, wedge, wheel 6 cajole 7 deceive, produce, quibble, wheedle 8 cockboat 9 fabricate, falsehood

cogent: 5 pithy, valid 6 potent, strong 7 telling 8 forcible, powerful 9 trenchant 10 conclusive, convincing, legitimate, persuasive

cogitate: 4 mull, muse, plan 5 think 6 ponder 7 connate, reflect 8 consider, meditate

cognate: kin 4 akin 5 alike 6 allied 7 kindred, related, similar 8 bandhava, relative

cognizance: ken 4 heed, mark 5 badge, crest 6 emblem, notice 7 bearing, cockade 9 knowledge 11 observation, recognition 12 apprehension

cognizant: 4 onto, ware 5 awake, aware 8 sensible 9 conscious 10 conversant 11 intelligent 12 apprehensive

cognize: 4 know 5 grasp 6 fathom 8 perceive 9 apprehend, recognize 10 appreciate, understand

cognomen (see also **name**): 4 name 5 style, title 6 byname 7 agnomen, moniker, surname 8 nickname, patronym 11 appellation

cognoscente: 5 judge 6 critic, expert 9 authority 10 specialist

cohabit: 4 live 5 dwell 6 occupy 8 accustom 9 accompany

cohere: fit 4 glue, suit 5 agree, cling, stick, unite 6 adhere, cement, cleave 7 connect 8 coincide 9 glutinate

coherence: 5 union 8 cohesion 9 congruity 10 accordance, connection, continuity 11 consistency

cohort: 4 band, mate 6 fellow 7 company 9 associate

coif, coiffe: cap 4 hood 6 beggin, burlet, hairdo 7 arrange 8 skullcap 9 headdress

coiffure: 6 hairdo 9 headdress

coign: 5 wedge 6 corner 8 position 10 projection

coil: ado, wip 4 ansa, clew, curl, fuss, hank, loop, roll, wind 5 helix, querl, tense, twine, twist 6 rundle, spiral, tumult, windup 7 haycock, ringlet, trouble 8 encircle 9 confusion, encounter 10 difficulty 11 convolution

electric: 6 teaser

coin: die, ori 4 cash, dime, make, mint 5 angle, brown, chink, clink, metal, money, quoin, shape, stamp, token, wedge 6 change, corner, create, invent, specie, strike 7 convert 8 currency 9 fabricate, neologize, originate 11 cornerstone

ancient: 4 obol 6 obolus

box: pyx 4 till 5 meter 8 register

collector: 11 numismatist

copper: 4 cent 5 penny, bodle, brown

counterfeit: 9 brummagem

difference: 5 value 11 seigniorage

edge corrugation: 7 reeding

front: 4 head 7 obverse

imperfectly minted: 8 brockage

kind of: lap, ora 4 dime, doit, mite, rial, rosa 5 cuyne, daric, disme, ducat, eagle, groat 6 bawbee, beaver, besant, bezant, cunzie 7 bezzant, carolus, crocard, louleau 8 bezantee, crockard 10 castellano

pert. to: 10 numismatic 12 numismatical

reverse side: 4 tail 5 verso

roll: 7 rouleau

science: 11 numismatics

silver: 4 batz, dime, dump, pina, tara 5 bezzo 6 tester, teston

stamper: 4 mill

weight: 6 shekel

coinage: 7 fiction, mintage 9 neologism

collector: 11 numismatist

coincide: gee 4 jibe 5 agree, tally 6 concur 9 harmonize 10 correspond

coincidence: 9 concourse 11 concurrence 12 concomitance, simultaneity

coincident: 4 even 8 together 9 consonant 10 concurrent 11 concomitant 12 contemporary 15 contemporaneous

coiner of new words: 9 neologian, neologist

coition: 7 meeting 10 attraction 11 conjunction

coke: aks 4 coal, core, dope 5 chark 7 cocaine

col: 4 pass 10 depression

colander: 5 sieve 7 utensil 8 strainer

Colchis: *king:* 6 Aeetes

  princess: 5 Medea

cold: flu 4 dead, dull 5 algid, bleak, frore, gelid, rheum, virus 6 arctic, chilly, frigid, frosty, wintry 7 catarrh, chilled, distant, glacial 8 reserved, rhigosis, unheated 9 apathetic, cheerless 10 insensible, spiritless 11 hyperborean, indifferent, unemotional 12 unresponsive 13 dispassionate, marblehearted 15 undemonstrative

instrument to apply: 9 cryoprobe

pert. to: icy 5 gelid 6 frigid, frozen 10 frigorific

remedy: 13 antihistamine

cold and damp: raw 4 dank 5 bleak

cold-blooded: 7 callous 9 unfeeling

cold feet: 4 fear 5 alarm, doubt 9 cowardice 12 apprehension

cold mist: 4 drow

cold-shoulder: cut 4 snub 6 ignore, rebuff

cold steel: 5 sword 6 dagger 7 bayonet

cold sweat: 4 fear 5 shock 11 trepidation

colder: 4 husk 6 refuse 7 rubbish

coleoptera insect: 6 beetle, insect, weevil

Coleridge's sacred river: 4 Alph

Colette: 8 novelist

  characters: 4 Gigi 5 Cheri 8 Claudine

colewort: 4 cole, kale 7 cabbage

colic: 5 gripe 9 bellyache 10 mulligrubs

coliseum: 4 bowl, hall 7 stadium, theater 8 building 12 amphitheater

collaborate: aid 9 cooperate

collagen: 7 protein 10 albuminoid

collapse: 4 cave, fall, fold 5 crash, slump, wreck 6 bust-up 7 crumple, debacle, deflate, failure, flummox, smashup 8 contract, downfall 9 breakdown, telescope 11 prostration

collar: nab 4 band, eton, gill, grab, ring, ruff 5 chain, fichu, ruche, seize 6 bertha, gorget, tackle, torque 7 capture, chignon, circlet, shackle 8 cincture, neckband, necklace 9 neckpiece

horse: 6 hounce

jeweled: 8 carcanet

kind of: 4 cowl, ruff 5 fanon, jabot, orale, phano, ruche, rabat, V-neck 6 cangue, carcan, rabato, rebato 7 bargham, panuelo 8 carcanet, Peter Pan 10 chevesaile, turtleneck

collarbone: 8 clavicle

collate: 6 bestow, confer, verify 7 arrange, bracket, compare, emamine 9 integrate

collateral: 4 side 8 indirect, parallel, security 9 ancillary 10 subsidiary 11 concomitant, subordinate

collation: tea 4 meal 5 lunch 6 repast, sermon 7 address, reading 8 dejeuner, parallel, treatise 10 collection, comparison, conference 12 consultation, contribution

colleague: 4 aide, ally 6 deputy 7 adjunct, consort, partner 8 confrere 9 assistant, associate

collect: tax 4 call, heap, levy, pile, pool, save 5 amass, glean, group, hoard, raise 6 accoil, accrue, confer, garner, gather, muster, prayer, sheave 7 compile, engross, impound, round up 8 assemble, contract 9 aggregate 10 accumulate, congregate, simmer down 11 agglomerate

collected: 4 calm, cool 5 sober 6 serene 8

composed **9** aggregate, clustered **10** coacervate **11** agglomerate, unflappable **13** dispassionate

collection: ana **4** bevy, clan, olio **5** batch, group, store, suite **6** bundle, conger, sorite **8** assembly, caboodle **9** aggregate, anthology, collation, repertory **10** assemblage, assortment, cancionero
animals: zoo **9** menagerie
clothes: **8** wardrobe
facts: **4** data
literary: ana **7** library **8** analects
miscellaneous: **4** olio **6** fardel, jumble, medley
poems: **5** divan, sylva **9** anthology **10** cancionero
proper names: **11** onomasticon

collector: *bird egg:* **8** oologist
book: **11** bibliophile
coin: **11** numismatist
item: **5** curio **11** collectible
stamp: **11** philatelist

colleen: **4** girl, lass, miss **5** belle **6** damsel, lassie, maiden

college (see also **university**): **5** lycee **6** school **7** academy **8** seminary **10** assemblage, university **11** institution **12** organization
accounts: **6** battel
building: gym, lab
campus: **4** quad **10** quadrangle
course: **5** major, minor **7** seminar
court: **4** quad
degree: B.L.S., B.Sc., LL.B., LL.D., M.Sc., S.C.B., Ph.D. **5** Litt.D.
girl: **4** coed
graduate: **6** alumna, doctor, master **7** alumnus **8** bachelor
kind of: **9** electoral
living quarters: **4** dorm, hall **9** dormitory
official: **4** dean **5** prexy **6** beadle, bursar, regent **7** proctor **9** president, registrar
pert. to: **8** academic **10** collegiate
professor: don **6** docent, doctor
session: lab **5** class **7** lecture, seminar **8** tutorial
song: **9** alma mater
student group: **4** frat **8** sorority **10** fraternity
term: **8** semester
treasurer: **6** bursar
U.S. oldest: **7** Harvard
U.S. woman's oldest: **9** Mt. Holyoke

collet: **4** band, ring **5** chuck **6** casing, circle, collar, flange, socket **7** bushing, ferrule **8** neckband

collide: hit, ram **4** bump, dash, hurt **5** carom, clash, crash, wreck **6** hurtle, strike

collier: fly **4** boat **5** miner **6** plover, vessel **7** geordie
boy: **6** hodder
lung disease: **11** anthracosis

colliery: **4** mine

collision: **5** clash, crash, shock **7** crackup, smashup **8** clashing **9** encounter **10** opposition, percussion **12** interference

collocate: set **5** place **7** arrange **8** position

colloquial: **6** patois **8** familiar, informal **9** unstudied **10** vernacular **14** conversational

colloquy: **4** chat, talk **6** parley **8** dialogue **9** discourse **10** conference **12** conversation

colluctation: **8** struggle **10** contention

collude: **4** plot **6** scheme **7** connive **8** collogue, conspire

collusion: **6** deceit **7** cahoots, secrecy **9** agreement, complicity **10** connivance
law: **5** covin

collusive: **8** convinous **10** fraudulent

Cologne: *German spelling:* **4** Koln
king: **6** Caspar, Jaspar

Colombia: *capital:* **6** Bogota
city: **4** Cali **5** Neiva, Pasto, Tunja **6** Cucuta, Ibaque, Quibdo **7** Leticia, Popayan **8** Medellin **9** Cartagena, Manizales, San Andres **10** Santa Maria **12** Barranquilla
coin: **4** peso, real **6** condor, peseta **7** centavo
gulf: **6** Darien
Indian: **5** Boros **6** Betoya, Chitas, Tahami, Yahuna **7** Tunebos
highest peak: **9** Cristobal
mahogany: **7** albarco
measure: **4** vara **7** celemin
monetary unit: **4** peso
mountains: **5** Andes
plant: **5** yocco
province: **5** Cauca, Choco, Huila, Valle **6** Boyaca, Caldas, Narina, Tolima, Vaupes **7** Bolivar
river: **4** Sinu, Tomo **6** Atrato, Atroto, Pattia, Yapura **7** Orinoco
seaport: **6** Lorica **9** Cartagena **10** Santa Marta
volcano: **5** Huila, Pasto **6** Purace
weight: bag **4** saco **5** carga, libra **7** quilate, quintal

Colonel Blimp: **10** fuddy-duddy **12** stuffed shirt

colonial teak: **8** flindosa

colonist: **7** pioneer, settler **8** emigrant

colonize: **5** found **6** gather, settle **7** migrate **9** establish

colonizer: ant **6** oecist **7** settler

colonnade: row **4** stoa **7** pergola, portico, terrace **9** peristyle

colony: **5** swarm **9** community **10** dependency, settlement

colophon: **6** device, emblem

colophonite: **6** garnet **9** andradite

colophony: **5** resin, rosin

color: (see also next entry): dye, hue **4**

blee, cast, flag, tint, tone 5 badge, blush, paint, shade, stain, tenne, tinge 6 banner, ensign, redden 7 distort, pennant, pigment 8 standard, tincture 10 complexion

achromatic: 4 gray 5 black, white

change: 8 iridesce, opalesce

dull: dun 4 drab 5 terne

full of: 9 chromatic

graduation: 5 shade

healthy: tan

light: 4 tint

line of: 6 streak

malachite: 4 bice

mat white: 9 alabaster

mulberry: 7 morello

neutral: 4 ecru, gray 5 beige, black, white

painter: 6 Titian

pale: 6 pastel

primary: red 4 blue 5 black, white 6 yellow

quality: 4 tone

secondary: 5 green 6 orange, purple

shade of difference: 6 nuance

unhealthy 6 sallow

uniform in: 4 flot

value: see *quality* above

varying: 10 iridescent, opalescent

color: For colors see their names: **red, green, purple,** etc.; for shades see main color. EXAMPLES: "reddish brown": see **brown**; "grayish green": see **green.**

color bar: 11 segregation 14 discrimination

color blindness: 9 Daltonism 13 achromatopsia 14 monochromatism

color organ: 8 clavilux

color photography inventor: 4 Ives

Colorado: *capital:* 6 Denver

city: 5 Aspen, Delta, Lemar 6 Aurora, Pueblo 7 Boulder, Greeley, Manassa 8 Lakewood, Trinidad

county: Ada 4 Baca, Bent, Mesa, Yuma 5 Otero, Ouray, Routt 6 Custer, Gilpin, Moffat 7 Crowley, Chaffee

fort: 5 Logan

Indian: Ute 8 Arapahoe

motto: 13 Nil sine Numine

mountain peak: 5 Longs, Pikes 6 Elbert

mountain range: 5 Rocky

nickname: 10 Centennial

park: 5 Estes 9 Mesa Verde

resort: 4 Vail 5 Aspen 7 Manitou 15 Colorado Springs

river: 4 Bear 5 Green, White 7 Laramie 9 Rio Grande 11 South Platte

state bird: 11 lark bunting

state flower: 9 columbine

state tree: 10 blue spruce

colorant: dye 4 anil 7 pigment

coloratura: 6 singer 7 soprano 8 vocalist

colored: 6 biased 9 distorted, prismatic 14 misrepresented

partly: 4 pied 6 motley 7 piebald 10 variegated

colorful: gay 5 vivid 9 brilliant

colorimeter: 10 tintometer

coloring: *cell:* 10 endochrome

matter: dye 5 morin 7 pigment 8 clorofil 10 endochrome 11 chlorophyll

colorless: wan 4 drab, dull, pale 5 ashen, blake, blank, plain 6 pallid 7 hueless, neutral 8 blanched 9 impartial 10 achromatic 11 transparent 13 uninteresting

colors, set of: 7 palette

colossal (see also **huge**): big 4 huge, vast 5 great, large 7 immense, mammoth, titanic 8 enormous, gigantic 9 monstrous

colossus: 5 giant, titan 6 statue 7 monster, prodigy

colporteur: 6 hawker 7 apostle, peddler 10 evangelist, missionary 11 distributor

colt: gun 4 foal, tyro 5 filly 6 pistol 8 beginner, neophyte 9 quadruped, youngster

coluber: 5 snake 7 serpent

colubrine: 6 crafty 7 cunning 9 snakelike

Columbia River rapids: 6 Dalles

columbine: 4 bird, dodo 5 plant 6 flower 8 dovelike

Columbus: *birthplace:* 5 Genoa

burial place: 7 Seville

companion: 5 Ojeda

embarkation port: 5 Palos

patron: 8 Isabella 9 Ferdinand

ship: 4 Nina 5 Pinta 10 Santa Maria

son: 5 Diego

column: lat, row 4 file, line, post 5 shaft, stela, stele 6 pillar 7 support 8 cylinder, pilaster 9 formation

arrange in: 8 tabulate

base: 6 plinth 9 stylobate

female figure: 8 caryatid

male figure: 5 Atlas 7 telamon

part: 4 anta, fust 5 galbe, socle, scape, shank 6 plinth 7 entasis, capital 8 pilaster

pert to: 8 columnar

shaped like human figure: 7 telamon 8 atlantes, caryatid

small: 5 stele

support: 5 socle

type of: 5 Doric, Ionic 10 Corinthian

columnar: 6 terete 7 stelene 8 vertical

columnist: 6 writer 7 analyst

columns: *series of:* 9 colonnade

set in: 7 tabular

without: 7 astylar

coma: 4 tuft 5 bunch, carus, sleep 6 stupor, torpor, trance 7 cluster 8 lethargy 13 insensibility

comate: 5 hairy

comatose: out 6 drowsy 9 lethargic 10 insensible

comb: 4 card, lash, rake 5 brush, clean, crest, curry, tease 6 smooth 11 disentangle

flax: 6 hackle, heckle 7 hatchel

horse: 5 curry

comb-like: 8 pectinal 9 pectinate

combat: war 4 bout, cope, duel, fray, meet, rush, tilt 5 clash, fight, joust, repel, set-to 6 action, battle, oppose, resist, strife 7 contend, contest, counter, scuffle 8 argument, conflict, struggle 9 encounter, withstand 10 antagonize, contention

challenge to single: 6 cartel

code: 6 duello

place: 5 arena

combatant: 6 dueler 7 battler, fighter 8 champion 10 contestant

combative: 8 militant 9 agonistic 10 pugnacious 11 agonistical, belligerent

comber: 4 wave 7 breaker 11 beachcomber

combination: key 4 bloc, gang, pact, pool, ring 5 cabal, junto, party, trust, union 6 cartel, clique, corner, merger 7 combine, consort, coterie, faction 8 alliance, ensemble 9 aggregate, camarilla, coalition, composite, composure, synthesis 10 concoction, conspiracy 11 association, coalescence, composition, confederacy, conjunction, corporation, unification 12 undergarment 13 incorporation

combine: add, mix, wed 4 bloc, join, pool 5 blend, marry, merge, total, unite 6 absorb, concur, embody, merger, mingle, splice 7 conjoin, conjure, machine 8 coalesce, compound, concrete, condense, contract, federate 9 construct, cooperate 11 amalgamate 11 combination, consolidate 12 conglomerate

combining form: See list page 826

comboy: 6 sarong

combust: 4 burn 5 burnt 8 consumed 10 incinerate

combustible: 4 fuel, peat 5 fiery 9 irascible 10 accendible 11 inflammable

material: gas, oil 4 coal, coke, peat 6 tinder

combustion: 4 fire, heat 5 therm 6 tumult 7 burning 8 volatile 9 agitation, confusion, consuming, cremation, oxidation 12 inflammation

residue: ash, gas 7 clinker

come: 4 grow 5 arise, issue, occur, reach 6 accrue, appear, arrive, befall, emerge, happen, spring 7 advance, develop, emanate 8 approach, practice 9 eventuate

a cropper: 4 fail, fall

across: 4 find, meet 9 encounter 10 contribute

after: 5 ensue 6 follow 7 succeed

again: 6 return

along: 4 fare 7 improve 8 progress

apart: 5 break 12 disintegrate

at: 6 attack

before: 7 precede, prevene 8 antecede

between: 8 alienate 9 interpose

by: get 4 gain 6 obtain 7 acquire, inherit

clean: 7 confess

down with: 5 catch 8 contract

forth: 6 appear, emerge

from: 5 ensue 6 derive, result

in: 5 crash, enter 6 arrive 7 intrude

into view: 4 loom 6 appear, emerge

of age: 6 mature

off: 5 break, click, occur 6 go over, pan out 7 develop, succeed

on: 4 bait, lure 5 decoy, snare

out: 6 appear, emerge, emerse, extend 8 protrude

to: 5 total 6 arrive, awaken, revive 7 recover

to a head: 6 climax 9 suppurate

to nothing: end 4 stop 5 cease

to terms: 4 join 5 agree 6 assent, settle 7 approve, consent 8 coincide 9 acquiesce

together: 4 bump, join, meet 5 clash, merge 7 collide, convene 8 assemble, converge

under: 7 subvene

up: 5 arise, occur 6 appear

comeback: 5 rally 6 answer, retort, return 7 rebound 9 recovery, repartee

comedian: wag, wit 4 card 5 actor, antic, clown, comic 6 jester 7 buffoon

comedown: 4 fall, land 5 crash 6 alight, bathos 7 descend 8 collapse

comedy: 5 drama, farce, revue 8 comoedia(L.), travesty 9 burlesque, slapstick

muse: 6 Thalia

symbol: 4 sock

comely: 4 fair, hend, pert 5 bonny, hende 6 decent, goodly, liking, lovely, pretty, proper 7 farrant 8 becoming, decorous, graceful, handsome, pleasing, suitable 9 agreeable, beautiful 10 gratifying, personable 11 good-looking

comestible: 4 food 5 manna, viand 6 edible 7 eatable, victual 8 esculent

comet: 6 meteor

discoverer: 5 Biela, Encke, Swift 6 Donati, Halley, Olbers 8 Kohoutek

part: 4 coma

tail: 8 streamer

comeuppance: due 6 rebuke 7 deserts 12 chastisement

comfit: 5 candy 7 confect, praline 8 conserve, preserve 9 sweetmeat 10 confection

comfort: aid 4 ease, rest 5 bield(Sc.),

cheer 6 buck up, endure, relief, repose, solace, soothe, succor 7 animate, assuage, cherish, confirm, console, enliven, gladden, refresh, relieve, support, sustain 8 inspirit, nepenthe, pleasure, reassure 9 encourage, well-being 10 strengthen 11 consolation

comfortable: 4 bein, bien, cosh, cozy, easy, like, snug, trig 5 comfy 7 relaxed 8 cheerful, euphoric, well-to-do 9 contented 10 acceptable, commodious, complacent, gratifying 11 consolatory, encouraging

comforter: 4 puff 5 cover, quilt, scarf 6 tippet 7 cheerer 8 pacifier

comfortless: 7 forlorn 8 desolate 9 cheerless 12 inconsolable

comfrey: 5 daisy 9 blackwort

comic: wag, wit 5 droll, funny 8 comedian, farcical 9 burlesque, laughable, ludicrous

strip: 7 funnies

comical: low 4 base, zany 5 droll, funny, queer, witty 7 amusing, jocular, risible, strange, trivial 8 humorous, ticklish 9 diverting, laughable, ludicrous, quizzical, whimsical 10 capricious

coming: due 4 next 6 advent, future 7 arrival, forward 8 deserved 9 impending 11 approaching

coming out: 5 debut 8 issuance

comma: 4 lull 5 pause 8 interval

command: bid 4 beck, bode, boon, call, fiat, hest, rule, sway 5 beken, check, edict, exact, force, hight, order, power, ukase 6 adjure, behest, charge, compel, degree, demand, direct, enjoin, govern, impose, master, ordain 7 appoint, behight, bidding, control, dictate, mandate, officer, precept, require 8 domineer, restrain 9 authority, direction, influence, ordinance, prescribe 10 commission 11 appointment

supreme: 9 hegemony

to a horse: gee, haw, hup 4 whoa

to go: 4 mush 6 begone, giddap

to stop: 4 whoa 5 avast

commander: cid, cio 4 head 5 chief 6 leader, master, rammer 7 captain, drungar, emperor, general, officer 10 commandant 11 commendador(Sp.) 13 generalissimo

of a thousand men: 9 chiliarch

commanding: 8 dominant, imposing 9 imperious, masterful 10 imperative 13 authoritative

commandment: law 4 rule 5 edict, order 7 precept

commando: 6 raider, ranger

comme il faut: 7 proper 7 fitting

commemorate: 7 observe 9 celebrate, solemnize 11 memorialize

commemoration: 5 award, medal 6 plaque 7 service 8 memorial 11 celebration 13 solemnization

commence: 4 fall, open 5 arise, begin, found, start 6 incept, spring 7 take off kick off, lead off 8 initiate 9 institute, originate

commencement: 4 dawn 5 alpha, birth, onset, start 7 genesis, opening 9 beginning

commencer: 4 tyro 8 beginner

commencing: 7 initial, nascent 9 incipient

commend: pat 4 give, laud 5 adorn, boost, extol, grace, offer 6 bestow, betake, commit, praise, resign 7 applaud, approve, bespeak, deliver, entrust, intrust 8 bequeath 9 predicate, recommend 10 compliment, ingratiate

highly: 5 extol 8 eulogize 10 panegyrize

to favor: 10 ingratiate

commendable: 4 good 6 worthy 8 laudable 9 exemplary, honorable 12 praiseworthy

commensurate: 4 even 5 equal 6 enough 8 adequate 10 answerable, convenient 11 appropriate 12 proportional 13 corresponding, proportionate

comment: 4 note, talk, word 5 aside, gloss, gloze 6 notate, postil, remark 7 descant, discuss, explain, expound, observe 9 criticise, criticism, criticize, discourse 10 animadvert, annotation, commentary 12 obiter dictum 13 animadversion

commentary: 5 gloss 6 memoir 7 account 8 glossary, treatise

commentator: 6 critic, glozer 7 analyst 9 annotator, expositor, glossator, scholiast 10 glossarist 13 glossographer

commerce: 5 trade 6 barter 7 traffic 8 business, exchange 10 connection 11 interchange

vehicle: 5 truck

commercial: 9 mercature 10 mercantile 13 advertisement

commingle: mix 4 fuse, join 5 blend, merge, unite 7 combine, embroil 10 amalgamate

comminute: 4 mill 5 crush, grind 9 pulverize, triturate

commiseration: 4 pity 7 empathy 8 sympathy 10 compassion, condolence

commission: 4 send, task 5 board, trust 6 brevit, charge, demand, depute, errand, office, ordain, permit 7 command, consign, empower, mandate, mission, warrant 8 delegate, encharge 9 allowance, authority, authorize, brokerage, establish 10 constitute 11 instruction 12 compensation, dispensation, perpetration 13 authorization

commissioner: 5 envoy 7 officer 8 delegate

commissure: 4 seam 5 joint, miter, mitre 8 juncture 10 miter joint

commit: 4 give 5 allot, refer 6 assign, betake, remand 7 command, confide, consign, deposit, entrust, intrust 8 bequeath, delegate, imprison, relegate, turn over 9 recommend 10 perpetrate

committee: 4 body 5 board, group, junta 7 council 9 executors, guardians

commixture: 6 fusion 7 mixture 8 compound 9 composite

commode: cap 5 chest 8 cupboard 10 chiffonier

commodious: fit 5 ample, roomy 6 proper, useful 8 spacious, suitable 9 capacious 10 beneficial, convenient 11 comfortable, serviceable 12 advantageous

commodity: 4 item, ware 5 goods 6 staple 7 article

common: low 4 base 5 banal, brief, cheap, joint, stale, trite, usual 6 coarse, mutual, ornery, vulgar 7 average, current, general, generic, natural, popular, regular, trivial, unnoble 8 all right, familiar, frequent, habitual, mediocre, ordinary, pandemic, plebeian, trifling 9 bourgeois, customary, defective, hackneyed, prevalent, universal, unrefined 10 second-rate 11 commonplace 12 matter-of-fact

common effort: 8 teamwork

common fund: pot 4 pool 5 purse

common law: 6 custom 9 tradition

common man: 4 pleb 8 plebeian

common sense: 6 wisdom 8 gumption, judgment

common stock: 8 security

commoner: 5 ceorl, plebe 7 burgess, citizen, student 8 roturier 12 participator

commonly: *accepted:* 7 popular, vulgate
thought: 7 reputed 8 putative

commonplace: 4 dull, fade, worn 5 banal, daily, plain, prose, stale, trite, usual 6 common, garden, truism 7 humdrum, prosaic, tedious, trivial 8 ordinary 9 hackneyed 11 stereotyped, unimportant 13 unexceptional
remark: 6 cliche, truism 9 platitude

commonwealth: 5 state 6 public 9 community 10 federation, res publica

Commonwealth country: 6 Canada 8 Zimbabwe 9 Australia 10 New Zealand

commotion: ado, din 4 bree, fray, fuss, heat, riot, stir, to-do, whir 5 alarm, flare, hurry 6 bustle, cathro(Sc.), fracas, flurry, garray, mutiny, pother, tumult, unrest, welter 7 clatter, tempest, turmoil 8 brouhaha, disorder, upheaval, uprising 9 agitation, confusion 10 concussion, convulsion, ebullition, excitement, turbulence 11 disturbance, pandemonium 12 perturbation

commune: 4 area, talk 5 argue, realm, share, treat 6 advise, confer, debate, import, parley, reveal 7 consult, discuss, divulge 8 converse, district, township 11 communicate, intercourse, participate 12 conversation
Israeli: 7 kibbutz
Russian: mir 7 kolkhoz

communicable: 4 open 5 frank 8 catching, sociable 9 expansive, garrulous, talkative 10 contagious, diffusible, infectious 13 communicative

communicant: 6 member 8 adherent 9 informant

communicate (see also **commune**): 4 tell 6 bestow, convey, impart, inform, reveal, signal 7 declare, dictate, divulge 8 converse

communication: 4 note 5 favor 6 favour, letter 7 message 8 telegram 9 directive 10 communique, connection 11 interchange 12 conversation
means: 4 drum, flag, note, post 5 phone, radio, smoke 6 letter, movies, speech, tomtom 9 telegraph, telephone 10 television

communion: 4 cult, host, mass, sect, talk 5 creed, faith, share, unity 6 church, homily 7 concord 8 antiphon, converse, viaticum 9 agreement, eucharist, sacrament 10 confession, fellowship 11 intercourse 12 conversation, denomination 13 communication, participation
case: 5 burse
cloth: 8 corporal 9 corporale
consecrated food: 5 hagia
cup: ama 7 chalice
plate: 5 paten
table: 5 altar
vessel: pyx

communique: 6 report 7 message 12 announcement 13 communication

communism: 8 Leninism 10 Bolshevism

communist: Red 5 pinko 6 Soviet 7 comrade, Marxist

community: mir 4 body, burg, city 5 firca, state, thorp 6 cenoby, colony, hamlet, nation, polity, public 7 enclave, society, village 8 district, likeness, province, township 9 frequency 10 commonness 12 commonwealth, neighborhood
pert. to: 8 societal

commute: 5 alter 6 change, travel 7 convert 8 exchange 10 substitute 11 interchange

Comoros: *capital:* 6 Moroni
island: 6 Moheli 7 Anjouan, Mayotte 12 Grande Comoro

monetary unit: franc

comose: 5 hairy 6 tufted

compact: 4 bond, case, firm, hard, knit, pact, plot, snug, trim 5 brief, close, dense, gross, pithy, solid, terse, thick 6 vanity 7 bargain, concise, concord, serried 8 alliance, condense, contract, covenant, solidify, succinct 9 agreement, concordat 10 compaction, compressed, conspiracy, federation 11 compendious, concentrate, confederacy, consolidate, sententious 13 understanding

compadre: pal 5 buddy 6 friend 9 companion

companion: pal 4 chum, fere, mate, peer, twin, wife 5 buddy, bully, butty, crony, cully, matey 6 comate, escort, fellow, friend, spouse 7 compeer, comrade, consort, husband, partner 8 compadre, helpmate 9 associate, attendant 11 concomitant 12 acquaintance

constant: 6 shadow

equal: 4 peer 7 compeer

faithful: dog 7 Achates

companionable: 6 social 7 amiable, cordial 8 gracious, sociable 9 agreeable

company: mob, set 4 band, bevy, body, core, crew, fare, fere, firm, gang, gest, ging, host, rout, team 5 coven, covey, crowd, flock, geste, group, guest, horde, party, squad, troop 6 actors, circle, clique, cohort, covine, curney(Sc.), throng, troupe 7 battery, college, consort, society, visitor 8 assembly 9 camarilla, cavalcade, concourse, gathering 10 fellowship 11 association, partnership 13 companionship

comparable: 4 like 7 similar 8 parallel 9 analogous

comparative: 4 than 5 equal, rival 7 compeer 8 relative 11 approximate

compare: vie 4 even 5 apply, liken, match, scale 6 confer, relate 7 collate, examine, senible 8 contrast, estimate 10 assimilate

comparison: 6 simile 7 analogy, parable 8 likeness, likening, metaphor 9 collation 10 conference, similitude 11 examination

compartment: bay, bin 4 cell, part 5 abode, stall, 6 alcove, bunker, region 7 cellule, chamber, section 8 division 9 apartment 10 pigeonhole

granary: 8 grintern

compass: 4 area, gain, room, size 5 admit, field, gamut, range, reach, scope 6 arrive, attain, bounds, circle, degree, device, effect, extent, sphere 7 achieve, caliber, circuit, confine, divider, enclose, environ, go round, horizon, pelorus 8 boundary, cincture, circuity, surround 10 accomplish, comprehend

beam: 7 trammel

card: 4 rose

housing: 8 binnacle

ink leg: pen

kind of: sun 4 gyro 5 solar

part: pen 4 airt, vane 5 rhumb 6 gimbal, needle 7 gimbals, trammel 8 trammels

pocket: 6 diacle

point: E.N.E., E.S.E., N.N.E., N.N.W., S.S.E., S.S.W., W.N.W., W.S.W. 4 airt 5 airth, rhumb 7 azimuth

sight: 4 vane

suspender: 6 gimbal

compassion: rue 4 pity, ruth 5 heart, grace, mercy, sorry 6 lenity 7 remorse 8 clemency, humanity, sympathy 10 condolence 12 misericordia 13 commiseration

compatible: 8 suitable 9 accordant, agreeable, congenial, congruous, consonant 10 consistent, harmonious 16 noncontradictory

compatriot: 9 associate, colleague 10 countryman

compeer: 4 mate, peer, rank 5 equal, match 7 comrade 9 colleague, companion 11 comparative

compel: gar(Sc.) 4 make, move, urge 5 cause, drive, exact, force, impel, press 6 coerce, enjoin, extort, incite, oblige 7 actuate, command, dragoon, enforce, require 9 constrain, influence, instigate, overpower 11 necessitate, subjudicate

compelled: has 4 must 5 bound

compelling: 6 cogent 7 telling 8 forceful 9 demanding 10 conclusive, convincing, persuasive

compendious: 5 brief, short 6 direct 7 compact, concise 8 succinct 9 condensed 11 expeditious 13 comprehensive, short and sweet

compendium: 4 list 5 brief 6 apercu, digest, precis, sketch 7 catalog, compend, epitome, medulla, outline, summary 8 abstract, breviary, syllabus, synopsis 10 abridgment 11 compilation, composition, contraction 12 abbreviation

compensate: pay 4 jibe 5 agree, atone, repay, tally 6 recoup, reward, square 7 correct, redress, requite, restore, satisfy 9 indemnify 10 recompense, remunerate 11 contervail 12 counterpoise 14 counterbalance

compensation: fee, pay, utu 4 hire 5 bonus, wages 6 amends, angild, gersum, offset, reward, salary 7 damages, payment, redress, stipened 8 pittance, requital 9 emolument, indemnity 10 recompense 11 restitution 12 counterpoise, remuneration, satisfaction 15 indemnification

compete: pit, vie 4 cope, tend 5 match,

rival 6 strive 7 contend, contest, emulate

competent: apt, can, fit 4 able, good, meet, sane 5 adept, capax, smart 6 worthy 7 capable, endowed, skilled 8 adequate, suitable 9 effective, efficient, qualified 10 proficient, sufficient

competition: 4 game, heat 5 match, trial 7 contest, rivalry 8 conflict, tug-of-war 9 emulation 10 contention, free-for-all, opposition

competitor: foe 5 enemy, rival 6 player 7 entrant 8 opponent 9 adversary, candidate, combatant 10 antagonist, contestant

Compiegne's river: 4 Oise 5 Aisne

compilation: ana 4 book, code 5 cento 8 digest 9 accretion 10 collection, compendium, confection

compile: add 4 edit 5 amass 6 gather, select 7 arrange, collect, compose, prepare 8 assemble 11 anthologize

compiler: 6 author, editor

complacent: 4 calm, smug 7 fatuous 9 satisfied 11 comfortable 13 self-satisfied

complain: ail, yip 4 beef, carp, fret, fuss, kick, moan, rule, wail, yelp, yirn 5 brawl, croak, croon, gripe, whine 6 bewail, charge, cotter, grieve, grizze, grouse, murmur, repine, yammer 7 deplore, grumble, protest 9 bellyache 11 expostulate

complainant: 5 asker 7 accuser, querent, relator 9 plaintiff

complaining: 9 plaintive, querulous

complaint: ill 6 lament, malady, plaint 7 ailment, disease, illness, protest 8 disorder, gravamen, jeremiad 9 exception, grievance 10 accusation 11 lamentation

complaisant: 4 able, easy, kind 5 buxom, civil, suave 6 polite, smooth, urbane 7 affable, amiable, lenient 8 gracious, obliging, pleasing 9 compliant, courteous, favorable 10 favourable 12 ingratiating

complement: 4 crew, gang 5 force 6 amount 7 adjunct, obverse 10 completion, supplement 11 counterpart 13 accompaniment

complete: all, end 4 dead, deep, fill, full 5 close, every, plumb, quite, ripen, total, utter, whole 6 effect, entire, finish, intact, mature 7 achieve, execute, fullfill, germane, perfect, plenary, realize 8 absolute, blinking, circular, conclude, implicit, thorough 9 implement, surfeited, terminate 10 accomplish, consummate, effectuate 11 unqualified 12 wholehearted

completely: all 5 quite

completeness: 5 depth 9 entelechy

completion: end 6 finish 9 plenitude

complex: 4 hard, mazy 5 mixed 6 knotty 7 network, tangled, twisted 8 involved, manifold, syndrome 9 composite, difficult, entangled, intricate, perplexed 10 interlaced 11 complicated 12 labyrinthine 13 heterogeneous, sophisticated

complexion: hue 4 blee, look, rudd, tint 5 color, humor, state, tenor, tinge 6 aspect, temper 10 appearance

compliance: 7 harmony 8 civility 9 obedience 10 concession, submission 11 application 12 acquiescence, complaisance, tractability

compliant: 4 easy, oily 6 pliant, supple 7 ductile, dutiful, willing 9 indulgent 10 applicable, manageable, obsequious, sequacious 11 complaisant

complicate: 5 mix up 6 intort, puzzle, tangle 7 involve, perplex 8 bewilder

complicated: 4 hard 6 knotty, prolix 7 complex, gordian, snarled, tangled 8 involved 9 difficult, elaborate, embroiled, intricate, plexiform 10 disordered

complication: 4 node, plot 5 nodus, snarl 9 complexus, confusion, intricacy 10 difficulty, perplexity

compliment: 4 gift, laud 5 extol 6 boquet, eulogy, praise 7 adulate, applaud, bouquet, commend, flatter, tribute 8 encomium, flummery, gratuity 9 adulation, panegyric 12 blandishment, commendation, congratulate

comply: 4 cede, mind, obey 5 abide, adapt, agree, apply, yield 6 accede, accord, assent, enfold, submit 7 conform, embrace, observe 9 acquiesce 11 accommodate

component: 4 item, part, unit 6 factor, member 7 element 8 integral 10 compounder, ingredient 11 constituent

comport: act 4 bear, jibe, suit 5 agree, brook, carry, tally 6 accord, acquit, behave, demean, endure, square 7 conduct 9 behaviour, harmonize 10 correspond, deportment 11 comportance

comportable: 8 suitable 9 endurable, tolerable 10 consistent

comportment: 4 mien 7 conduct, dealing 8 behavior, demeanor 9 behaviour, demeanour 10 deportment

compose: pen, set 4 calm, dite, form, lull, make 5 allay, brief, clerk, dight, order, write 6 accord, adjust, create, design, indite, settle, soothe 7 arrange, compone, concoct, conform, dispose, fashion, produce 8 compound, comprise, comprize, regulate 9 alleviate, construct, formulate 10 constitute 11 tranquilize

compose type: set

composed: 4 calm, cool 5 quiet, sober, wrote 6 demure, placid, sedate, serene 7 written 8 compound, decorous, tranquil 9 collected, composite, unruffled 11 unflappable 13 dispassionate, self-possessed

composer: 4 bard, poet 5 odist 6 author, writer 7 elegist 8 monodist, musician 10 compositor, typesetter

composition (see also **musical composition**): ana 4 mass, opus, work 5 cento, ditty, drama, essay, paper, piece, poesy, theme 6 accord, lesson, make-up, thesis 7 article, concept, mixture, picture, writing 8 acrostic, compound, fantasia 9 admixture, aggregate, composure, congruity, formation, invention, structure, synthesis 10 adjustment, compendium, composture, confection, manuscript 11 arrangement, combination, composture, conjunction 12 constitution, construction

art of: 8 rhetoric

for two: 4 duet 6 duetto

literary: 4 book 5 cento, drama, essay, novel, theme 6 satire, thesis 7 tragedy 8 treatise

metrical: 4 poem, rime 5 poesy, rhyme

mournful: 5 dirge

compositor: 7 caseman, printer 10 type setter

compos mentis: 4 sane 5 lucid 6 normal

compost: 4 soil 6 mingle 7 compote, mixture 8 compound 10 fertilizer 11 composition

composure: 4 bond, mien 5 quiet, union 6 repose 7 balance, posture 8 calmness, serenity 9 sangfroid 10 composture, equanimity, sedateness 11 combination, composition, tranquility

compote, compot: 4 bowl 5 fruit 7 dessert

compound: 4 fill, join 5 alloy, blend, ester, unite 6 adjust, jumble, medley, settle 7 amalgam, combine, complex, compone, compose, compost 8 ceromide 9 admixture, aggregate, composite, enclosure 10 amalgamate, commixture, compromise, concoction, confection, constitute, hodge-podge, settlement

alkaline: 4 soda

amorphous: 7 phenose

chemical: 4 amid, amin, azin, imid, imin 5 amide, amine, azine, azola, borid, ceria, ester, imide, imine, osone 6 borids 7 inosite, metamer, leucine 8 chloride

containing double bonds: 5 diene 6 triene

containing two hydroxyl groups: 4 diol

crystalline: 5 aloin, oscin 6 amarin, anisil, phenol 7 tropine

hypnotic: 7 trional

organic: 4 amin 5 amine, ester, ketol 6 ketole, ketone

compound interest: 9 anatocism

comprehend: get, see 4 know 5 grasp, imply, savvy, seize, sense 6 attain, digest, embody, fathom, follow, take in, uptake 7 contain, discern, embrace, enclose, imagine, include, involve, realize 8 comprise, comprize, conceive, conclude, perceive 9 apprehend 10 appreciate, understand

comprehensible: 8 exoteric, included 9 comprised, scrutable 11 conceivable 12 intelligible

comprehension: 4 hold 5 grasp 6 noesis 7 epitome, knowing, summary 9 inclusion, intension 10 conception 11 connotation

comprehensive: big 4 full, wide 5 broad, grand, large 7 concise, generic 8 encyclic, spacious 9 all-around, expansive, extensive, panoramic 11 compendious 12 encyclopedic

compress: nip, tie 4 bale, bind, firm, wrap 5 cling, cramp, crowd, crush, press 6 gather, shrink 7 abridge, bolster, compact, curtail, embrace, deflate, flatten, repress, squeeze 8 astringe, condense, contract, restrain 9 condense, constrain, epitomize 11 consolidate

medical: 5 stupe 7 bandage, pledget

compressor: 4 pump 6 device 7 machine 9 condenser

comprise, comprize: 4 hold 5 cover, imply, seize 6 attach, confer, embody 7 compose, contain, embrace, enclose, include, involve 8 conceive, perceive 10 comprehend, constitute

comprised: 4 rapt 8 included 9 engrossed 14 comprehensible

compromise: 8 compound, endanger 9 surrender 10 concession 12 middle ground

opposition to: 13 intransigence

comptroller: 7 auditor, officer 10 controller

compulsion: 4 need, urge 5 force 6 duress, stress 7 impulse 8 coaction, coercion 9 necessity 10 constraint

compulsory: 8 coercive, forcible 10 imperative, obligatory

compulsory service: 6 angary 7 angaria, slavery

compunction: 5 qualm 6 regret, sorrow 7 remorse, scruple 9 misgiving 10 conscience, contrition, repentance

compute: add, sum 4 cast, rate 5 count, tally 6 assess, figure, number, reckon 7 account 8 estimate 9 calculate, enumerate

computer: 5 brain 6 abacus, univac 7 machine 10 calculator 13 adding machine

algebraic language: **5** algol
bank: **6** memory
correct: **5** debug
data: **7** readout **8** software
information: **4** data **5** input **6** output
inventor: **7** Babbage
lag in getting information: **10** access time
plan for action: **7** program
program symbol: **5** block
symbol system: **4** code
type: **6** analog **7** digital
worker: **9** programer **10** programmer

comrade: pal **4** ally, chum, mate, peer **5** billy, buddy, crony **6** copain(F.), digger, fellow, frater, friend, hearty **7** brother **8** copemate **9** associate, companion

comte: **5** count

comtesse: **8** countess

con: rap **4** anti, know, lead, look, pore, read, scan **5** cheat, guide, knock, learn, steer, study **6** direct, peruse, regard, versus **7** against, deceive, examine, inspect, opposed, swindle **10** understand

conation: **4** will **8** tendency, volition **11** inclination

concatenate: **4** join, link **5** chain, unite **7** connect

concave: **4** void **6** arched, dished, hollow **7** bowlike, vaulted **8** incurved **9** depressed

concavity: dip, pit **4** bowl, dent, hole **6** crater, hollow **10** depression

conceal: **4** bury, hide, mask, sile, veil **5** cache, cloak, couch, cover, feign **6** closet, emboss, pocket, screen, shroud **7** secrete **8** bescreen, disguise, ensconce, withhold **9** dissemble **10** camouflage
  goods: **5** cache, eloin **6** eloign

concealed: **4** dern(Sc.) **5** blind **6** buried, covert, hidden, latent, occult, perdue, secret, veiled **7** covered, larvate **8** abstruse **9** blindfold, disguised, insidious, recondite, withdrawn **11** clandestine

concealing: **9** designing **10** obvelation

concede: own **4** cede **5** admit, agree, allow, grant, own up, waive, yield **6** accord, assent **7** confess **9** surrender, vouchsafe **10** condescend **11** acknowledge

conceit: ego **4** idea **5** fancy, pride **6** notion, vagary, vanity **7** caprice, egotism, tympany **9** arrogance, conundrum **10** conception, self-esteem **11** swelled head

conceited: bug **4** fess, vain **5** chuff, cocky, flory, huggy, proud **6** clever **8** arrogant, dogmatic, priggish, snobbish **9** pragmatic, whimsical **11** coxcombical, egotistical, opinionated **12** narcissistic

conceive: **4** form, make, plan, ween **5** begin, brain, dream, fancy, frame, think **6** devise, ideate, ponder **7** imagine, realize, suppose, suspect **8** comprise, com-

prize, contrive **9** apprehend, formulate **10** comprehend, understand

concent: **9** agreement, harmonize **10** accordance **11** consistency

concentrate: aim, fix **4** mass, pile **5** coact, exalt, focus, unify **6** arrest, attend, center, gather **7** compact, essence, thicken **8** approach, assemble, condense, contract **9** intensify **10** centralize **11** consolidate **12** conglomerate

concentration: **7** extract **8** fixation **10** absorption **11** application

concentration camp: **6** prison, stalag

concept: **4** idea **5** fancy, image **7** opinion, thought **11** disposition

conception: ens **4** idea **5** fancy, fetus, image, start **6** belief, design, embryo **7** conceit, purpose **8** notation **9** beginning **10** cogitation, impression **12** apprehension **13** comprehension

conceptual: **5** ideal **8** abstract

concern: **4** bear, care, firm, reck, sake **5** apply, cause, event, grief, touch, worry **6** affair, affect, behold, charge, employ, matter, regard **7** anxiety, article, company, disturb, involve, pertain, respect, trouble **8** business, interest **9** implicate, rickmatic **10** solicitude **11** corporation, distinguish **12** apprehension **13** consideration, establishment

concerned: **6** intent **7** anxious, worried **8** affected, bothered, involved

concerning: for **4** in-re **5** about, anent, as for **9** regarding

concert: **4** plan, tune **5** unite **6** accord, chorus, concur, devise **7** arrange, benefit, concent, concord, consort, consult, harmony, recital **9** agreement **11** performance **13** entertainment

concert hall: **5** odeon, odeum **10** auditorium

concertina: **9** bandonion

concession: **4** boon **5** favor, grant, lease **6** assent, favour, gambit **7** cession **9** admission, allowance, privilege **10** compliance, compromise **12** acquiescence **13** condescension **15** acknowledgement

conch: **5** shell **6** cockle, mussel **7** mollusk

concierge: **6** porter, warden **7** doorman, janitor **9** attendant **10** doorkeeper

conciliate: get **4** calm, ease **5** atone **6** adjust, pacify, soothe **7** acquire, appease, concile, mollify, placate, satisfy **9** reconcile **10** propitiate **11** tranquilize

conciliatory: **4** mild, soft **6** gentle, giving, irenic **7** lenient, pacific, winning **8** irenical, lenitive **9** forgiving **10** mollifying **12** propitiating

concilium: **7** council

concise: **4** curt, neat **5** brief, crisp, pithy, short, terse **7** compact, laconic, pointed, precise, serried **8** mutilate, pregnant,

succinct 9 condensed 10 compedious,
contracted 11 sententious 12 epigram-
matic 13 comprehensive, short and
sweet

concision: 6 schism 7 faction 8 division
10 cutting off, mutilation

conclave: 6 closet 7 chamber, meeting 8
assembly 13 secret meeting

conclude: bar, end 4 rest 5 close, estop,
infer, judge, limit 6 clinch, deduce, figure, finish, gather, reason, settle, wrap
up 7 achieve, arrange, confine, embrace,
enclose, resolve, suppose 8 complete,
dispatch, graduate, restrain 9 determine, speculate, terminate 10 comprehend

conclusion: end 4 amen, coda, last 5 finis
6 finale, finish, period, result, upshot 7
finding, outcome 8 epilogue, judgment
9 diagnosis, inference 10 conjecture,
settlement 11 probability, termination

conclusive: 4 last 5 final, valid 6 cogent
7 certain, extreme, telling 8 decisive,
definite, ultimate 10 convincing, peremptory 11 irrefutable 12 unanswerable 13 determinative

concoct: mix 4 brew, cook, plan, plot,
vamp 5 fame, hatch 6 decoct, devise,
digest, invent, refine, scheme 7 compose, dream up, perfect, prepare 8 compound, intrigue 9 fabricate, originate
10 assimilate

concomitant: 4 mate 6 fellow 7 consort 9
accessory, associate, attendant, attend-
ing, companion, conjoined, cooperant
10 coincident, concurrent 11 synchronous 12 accompanying 13 accompaniment, supplementary

concord: 4 pact 5 agree, amity, peace, union, unity 6 treaty, unison 7 compact,
concert, consent, harmony, oneness 8
covenant 9 agreement, communion,
congruity 10 accordance, consonance

concordant: 8 unisonal 9 agreeable, congruous, consonant 10 harmonious 13
correspondent

concourse: 5 crowd, place, point 6 throng
7 company 8 assembly 9 affluence, frequency, gathering 10 assemblage, confluence 11 coincidence, concurrence,
conjunction, cooperation

concrete: 4 clot, firm, hard, knot, mess,
real 5 beton, solid, unite 6 actual 7
combine, congeal, special 8 coalesce,
compound, solidify, tangible 9 con-
cresce 10 particular

component: 4 sand 5 water 6 gravel

construction: 6 tremie 7 caisson

concretion: 4 clot, mess 5 pearl 6 nodule
8 calculus

concubine: 5 woman 7 adalisk 8 mistress
9 odalisque

concur: 4 jibe, join 5 agree, chime, unite
6 accede, accord, assent 7 approve,
combine, consent, go along 8 coincide,
converge 9 acquiesce, cooperate 10 correspond

concurrence: 5 union 6 assent, bestow 7
consent, consort, meeting 8 adhesion 9
adherence, agreement, concourse 10
conspiracy 11 coincidence, conjunction

concurrent: 6 coeval, united 7 meeting
10 associated, coincident 11 concomitant, synchronous 12 accompanying,
simultaneous

concuss: jar 4 jolt 5 clash, force, shake,
shock 6 coerce 7 agitate

condalia: 9 chaparral

condemn: ban 4 damn, doom, file, fine 5
blame, decry, judge 6 amerce, attain,
awreak, banish, detest 7 adjudge, censure, convict 8 denounce, reproach,
sentence 10 confiscate, disapprove

condemnation: 4 doom 5 blame 7 censure, decrial 11 reprobation 13 animadversion 4 disapprobation

condense: cut 5 brief, unite 6 decoct, digest, harden, lessen, narrow, reduce,
shrink 7 abridge, combine, compact,
deflate, distill, shorten, thicken 8 compress, diminish, solidify 9 constrict,
epitomize, evaporate, intensify 11 concentrate, consolidate

condensed: 4 curt 5 brief 7 compact, concise 8 absorbed 11 compendious

condenser: 4 cric 6 aludel

condescend: 6 deign, favor, grant, stoop 6
assent, oblige, submit, unbend 7 concede, descend 9 patronize, vouchsafe

condescension: 7 disdain 8 courtesy 10
affability, concession 12 complaisance

condiment: rea, soy 4 herb, kari, mace,
sage, salt 5 caper, gurry, sauce, spice,
thyme 6 catsup, cloves, pepper, relish 7
chutney, cuminos, ketchup, mustard,
paprika, vinegar 8 allspice, turmeric 9
appetizer, seasoning 10 mayonnaise

container: 5 cruet

stand: 6 caster

condisciple: 7 student 12 schoolfellow

condition: 4 case, mode, rank, rote, term
5 angle, birth, cause, class, estre, facet,
place, stage, state 6 estate, fettle, gentry, morale, plight, status 7 article, calling, premise, proviso, station 8 covenant, occasion, position 9 agreement
exception, provision, requisite, situation 10 limitation, sine qua non 11
predicament, stipulation 13 circumstances

critical: 9 emergency

favorable: 4 odds

conditional: 4 iffy 9 qualified, tentative
10 accidental

conditioned: 6 finite 7 limited

condolence: 4 pity, ruth 7 empathy 8 sympathy 10 compassion 13 commiseration

condone: 5 blink, remit 6 acquit, excuse, forget, ignore, pardon 7 absolve, forgive 8 overlook

condor: 4 coin 6 tiffin 7 vulture 8 gymnogyp

conduce: aid 4 help, hire, lead, tend 5 bring, guide 6 confer, effect, engage 7 advance, conduct, further, redound 10 contribute

conduct: act, run 4 bear, deed, gest, lead, mien, rule, wage 5 carry, geste, guard, guide, usher 6 action, attend, behave, convey, convoy, demean, deport, direct, escort, govern, manage, squire 7 bearing, channel, comport, conduce, conduit, control, execute, officer, operate 8 behavior, carriage, chaplain, demeanor, guidance, regulate, transact 9 accompany, behaviour, demeanour, supervise 10 administer, deportment, governance, government, proceeding 11 comportment, countenance, superintend

scandalous: 9 esclandre(F.)

conductor: cad 4 gude 5 guard 6 convoy, copper, escort, leader 7 cathode, maestro 8 aqueduct, cicerone, conveyor, director, employee 10 bandleader, impresario, propagator

stick: 5 baton

conduit: 4 duct, main, pipe, tube, wire 5 cable, canal, sewer 6 trough 7 channel, conduct, culvert, passage 8 aqueduct, pipeline

cone: 4 chat 5 crack, solid, spire 6 bobbin, object 7 cluster, fissure, strobil 8 strobile 9 container

section: 8 parabola

cone-shaped: 5 conic 6 pineal 7 conical

conenose: 6 bedbug

coney: See cony

confab: 4 chat, talk 6 powwow 7 prattle 10 conference 11 confabulate 12 conversation

confect: mix 4 form, make 6 pickle 7 prepare 8 preserve 9 construct

confection: 5 candy, dulce, sweet 6 bonbon, comfit, cimbal, dainty, nougat 7 caramel, confect, fondant, mixture, praline, sherbet, succade 8 compound, delicacy, marzipan, preserve, sherbert 9 confiture, marmalade, sweetmeat 10 concoction 11 bittersweet, compilation, composition, preparation

Confederacy: *banknote:* 8 blueback

capital: 8 Richmond

general: Lee 4 Hill, Hood 5 Bragg, Price 6 Morgan 7 Jackson, Pickett 10 Beauregard, Longstreet

guerrilla: 11 bushwhacker

president: 5 Davis

soldier: reb

vice-president: 8 Stephens

victory: 7 Bull Run 11 Chickamauga 16 Chancellorsville

confederate: aid, pal, reb 4 ally 5 rebel, stall, unite 6 league 7 abetter, abettor, conjure, fedarie, federal, partner 8 conspire, federate 9 accessory, assistant, associate, auxiliary 10 accomplice 12 collaborator

confederation: 4 band, body 5 union 6 league 7 compact, society 8 alliance, covenant 9 coalition 10 conspiracy, federation 11 association

confer: dub 4 give, meet, talk 5 award, endow, grant, treat 6 advise, bestow, donate, impart, invest, parley, powwow 7 commune, compare, conduce, consult, counsel, discuss, instate, present 8 comprise, converge 10 contribute, deliberate

conference: rap 4 talk 5 synod, trust 6 confab, huddle, parley, pow-wow 7 council, meeting, palaver 8 colloque, colloquy, congress 9 collation, comparing, discourse, interview 10 comparison, discussion 11 association 12 consultation, conversation

technique: 13 brainstorming

confess: own 4 avow, sing 5 admit, grant 6 attest, avouch, beknow, recant, reveal, shrive 7 concede, divulge 8 disclose, discover, manifest 11 acknowledge

confession: 5 credo, creed 6 avowal, shrift, shrive 9 admission, communion, statement 10 profession

confetti: 4 tape 5 candy 7 bonbons 9 sweetmeat 10 confection

container: 8 cascaron

confidant: 6 friend 8 intimate

confide: 4 rely, tell 5 trust 6 commit, depend 7 believe, consign, entrust, intrust 8 turn over

confidence: 4 hope 5 bield, faith, trust 6 aplomb, belief, credit, mettle, morale, secret, spirit 7 courage 8 affiance, boldness, credence, reliance, sureness 9 assurance, certitude, hardihood, hardiness 10 effrontery 11 presumption 12 impertinence

game: 4 scam 5 bunco, bunko 6 sting 7 swindle

lack: 10 diffidence

confident: 4 bold, smug, sure 5 hardy, siker 6 crouse, secure, sicker 7 assured, certain, hopeful, reliant 8 constant, fearless, impudent, sanguine, trustful 9 dependent, undaunted 10 dogmatical 11 trustworthy 12 presumptuous 13 self-possessed

confidential: 5 bosom, privy 6 covert, secret 7 private, subrosa 8 esoteric, intimate 9 auricular 11 trustworthy

law: 9 fiduciary

configuration: 4 cast, form 5 shape 6 figure 7 contour, outline 10 topography

confine: bar, box, dam, hem, new, pen, pin, sty, tie 4 bind, cage, coop, hasp, jail, keep, lock, seal 5 bound, cramp, delay, impen, limit, pinch, stint 6 border, compas, corral, fetter, forbar, hamper, hurdle, immure, impale, intern, pinion, pocket, tether 7 astrict, impound 8 boundary, conclude, imprison, restrain, straiten 9 carcerate, constrain, restraint 11 incarcerate 12 circumscribe

confined: ill 4 pent 5 bound, caged 6 sealed 7 cramped, cribbed, limited 8 impended, interned 9 impounded 10 cloistered 13 incommunicado

to select group: 8 esoteric

confinement: mew 7 lying-in 8 clausure, firmance 9 captivity, restraint 10 childbirth, constraint, internment 11 contraction 12 accouchement, imprisonment

place of: mew, pen 4 brig, cage, coop, goal, jail, stir 5 limbo 6 asylum, corral, prison 7 dungeon 9 calaboose 12 penitentiary

confirm: fix, set 4 firm, seal 5 prove 6 affirm, assent, assure, attest, avouch, clinch, ratify, settle, verify 7 approve, comfort, endorse, fortify, sustain 8 accredit, convince, sanction, validate 9 approbate, establish 10 corroborate, strengthen 11 corroborate, countersign 12 adminiculate, authenticate, substantiate

confirmed: set 5 fixed 6 arrant, stable 7 chronic 8 habitual, ratified 9 fortified, initiated 10 encouraged, inveterate 11 established

confiscate: 4 grab 5 seize, usurp 7 condemn, preempt 8 arrogate 9 sequester 11 appropriate

conflagration: 4 fire 5 blaze, fever 7 burning, inferno 9 holocaust 10 combustion 12 inflammation

conflict: war 4 bout, duel, fray, rift 5 broil, brush, clash, fight, grips, mix-up 6 action, battle, combat, mutiny, oppose, strife 7 contend, contest, discord, warfare 8 disagree, militate, struggle, tug-of-war 9 collision, encounter, rebellion 10 contentin 11 competition, controversy

final: 10 Armageddon

conflicting: 7 adverse, warring 8 clashing 10 contending 12 incompatible, inharmonious

confluence: 5 crowd 7 conflux, meeting 8 junction 9 concourse 12 assimilation

conform: fit 4 lean, obey, suit 5 adapt, agree, apply, yield 6 accede, adjust, assent, comply, settle, submit 7 compose 9 acquiesce, harmonize, reconcile 10 correspond 11 accommodate

conformist: 6 pedant 7 babbitt 9 precisian 10 philistine 11 reactionary

conformity: 7 decorum, harmony 9 affinity, likeness, symmetry 9 agreement, congruity, obedience 10 accordance, compliance, similarity, submission 11 affirmative 12 acquiescence, complaisance

to law: 6 dharma 8 legality

confound: mix 4 blow, dash, maze, rout, stam, stun 5 abash, addle, amaze, spend, spoil, waste 6 baffle, dismay, muddle, rattle 7 astound, confuse, confute, corrupt, destroy, flummox, perplex, stupefy 8 astonish, bewilder, distract, surprise 9 discomfit, dumbfound, embarrass, frustrate, overthrow 10 disconcert 11 intermingle

confraternity: 4 body 5 union 7 society 11 brotherhood

confrere: 6 fellow 7 comrade 9 colleague

confront: 4 defy, face, meet 5 beard, brave 6 oppose, resist 7 affront, compare 8 envisage, face up to, threaten 9 challenge, encounter

confuse: mix 4 dash, daze, maze, muss, rout 5 abash, addle, amaze, befog, blend, cloud, snarl 6 baffle, bemuse, bother, burble, caddle, flurry, fuddle, jumble, muddle, puzzle, rattle 7 bedevil, blunder, derange, fluster, mystify, nonplus, perplex, stupefy 8 befuddle, bewilder, confound, distract 9 barbulyie, discomfit, dumbfound, obfuscate 10 demoralize, disarrange, discompose, disconcert

confused: 4 asea, lost 5 foggy, muddy, vague 6 doiled, doited 7 chaotic, mixed up, obscure 8 deranged 9 chagrined 10 bewildered, hurly-burly, topsy-turvy, tumultuous 13 helter-skelter

confusion: din 4 coil, dust, fuss, harl, mess, moil, riot 5 babel, chaos, chevy, chivy, deray, mix-up, snafu, snarl, strow 6 babble, bedlam, caddle, chivvy, habble, hubbub, huddle, jabble, jumble, muddle, pother, rabble, rumpus, tophet, tumult, uproar, welter 7 blunder, bluster, clutter, farrage, flutter, garboil, topheth, turmoil, widdrim 8 disarray, disorder 9 agitation, commotion 10 hullabaloo, hurly-burly 11 disturbance, trepidation 12 hugger-mugger, perturbation, razzle-dazzle 13 embarrassment

confute: 4 deny 5 rebut 6 expose, refute 7 silence 8 confound, convince, disprove, infringe, overcome 9 overwhelm

conge: bow 5 adieu 6 curtsy 7 license, molding 8 farewell, passport 9 clearance, dismissal 10 permission 11 leavetaking

congeal: gel, ice, set 4 jell 5 candy 6 cotter, curdle, freeze, harden 7 stiffen, thicken 8 concrete, solidify 9 coagulate 10 gelalinize 11 crystallize

congealing agent: 6 pectin 8 gelatine

congee: 9 departure 11 leave-taking

congener: 4 kind, race 5 class, genus

congenial: 4 boon 5 natal 6 native 7 connate, kindred 10 compatible 11 sympathetic

conger: eel 4 pike

congeries: 4 mass, ruck 5 group 6 muster 8 assembly 9 gathering 10 collection

congestion: jam 4 heap 8 crowding, stoppage 9 gathering 12 accumulation

conglobation: 4 ball

conglomerate: 4 heap, mass, pile, rock 5 stack 6 cartel 7 combine 9 clustered 10 assemblage 11 agglomerate 12 concentrated

Congo (see also **Zaire**): *capital:* 11 Brazzaville

  tribe: 4 Susa 6 Wabuma 7 Bangala

  monetary unit: franc

  tributary: 4 Uele 6 Ubangi 7 Aruwima

congou: tea

congratulate: 4 laud 5 greet 6 salute 8 macarize 10 compliment, felicitate

congregate: 4 herd, mass, meet, teem 5 group, swarm, troop 6 gather, muster 7 collect, convene 8 assemble

congregation: 4 body, fold, host, mass 5 flock, swarm 6 church, parish 7 meeting, synaxes 8 assembly, brethren 9 gathering 10 collection 11 convocation

congress: 4 dail, diet 5 synod 7 council, meeting 8 assembly, conclave 10 conference, convention, parliament 11 convocation, legislature

Congress: *building:* 7 Capitol

  member: 7 senator 14 representative

  upper house: 6 Senate

congressman: 7 senator 8 delegate 10 legislator 14 representative

congruity: 6 accord 7 concord, fitness, harmony 8 symmetry 9 agreement, coherence 10 conformity, consonance 11 composition, consistency, correctness, suitability 13 compatibility 14 correspondence

conical: 8 tapering

conifer: fir, yew 4 pine, tree 5 cedar, larch 6 spruce 7 pinacle, pinales

conium: 7 hemlock

conjecture: aim 4 plot, shot, view 5 augur, ettle, fancy, guess, opine 6 belief, divine, theory 7 imagine, opinion, presume, suppose, surmise, suspect 9 inference, speculate, suspicion 10 conclusion, estimation 11 contrivance, speculation, supposition

conjoined: wed 6 joined, linked, united 7 related 8 conjunct, touching 11 concomitant

conjoint: 6 mutual, shared 8 combined 9 conjoined 10 associated 11 correlative 12 simultaneous

conjugal: 6 wedded 7 marital, nuptial 9 connubial 11 matrimonial

conjugate: 5 yoked 6 joined, united 7 coupled

conjunction: and, but, nor, tie 4 than 5 joint, since, union 6 either, hookup 7 coition, consort 9 coalition, concourse 10 connection 11 association, combination, composition, concurrence

conjuration: art 4 rune 5 charm, magic, spell, trick 6 voodoo 10 necromancy 11 incantation, legerdemain

conjure: beg 4 pray 5 charm, crave, halse 6 adjure, invent, invoke 7 beseech, combine, entreat, imagine 8 conspire, contrive, exorcise, exorcize 9 importune 10 supplicate 11 confederate

conjuror: 4 mage, sear 6 pellar, shaman, wizard 7 juggler, warlock 8 magician, sorcerer 9 coswearer, enchanter 15 prestidigatator

conk: die, hit 4 fail, head, nose, swat 5 faint, knock, stall 7 decease 8 pass away

Conlaech: *father:* 10 Cuchulainn

  mother: 5 Aoife

connate: 4 akin, born 5 fused 6 allied, inborn, innate 7 cognate, kindred, related 9 congenial 10 congenital, deep-seated

connect: tie, wed 4 ally, bind, glue, join, knit, link 5 affix, chain, marry, unite 6 attach, bridge, cement, cohere, connex, couple, fasten, relate 7 combine 8 continue 9 affiliate, associate, correlate, interlock 11 communicate

Connecticut: *capital:* 8 Hartford

  city: 4 Avon 6 Bethel, Darien 7 Meriden 8 New Haven, Stamford 9 Greenwich, Waterbury 10 Bridgeport

  county: 7 Tolland 8 Hartford 9 Fairfield, Middlesex

  Indian: 6 Pequot 7 Mohegan, Niantic

  nickname: 6 Nutmeg

  river: 10 Housatonic

  seaport: 6 Mystic

  state bird: 5 robin

  state flower: 6 laurel

  state song: 12 Yankee Doodle

  state tree: oak

connection: tie 4 bond, link 5 nexus, union 6 family 7 contact, kinship 8 affinity, alliance, commerce, intimacy, junction, relative, syndetic 9 coherence, reference, relevance 10 catenation, continuity 11 affiliation, association, conjunction, intercourse 12 articulation, relationship 13 communication

connective: and, nor 6 either 7 neither 8 syndetic 11 conjunction

connective tissue: 6 fascia

conniption fit: 7 tantrum

connive: 4 abet, plot, wink 5 blink, cabal 6 assent, foment, incite, scheme 7 collude 8 intrigue, overlook 9 machinate

connoisseur: 5 judge 6 critic, expert 7 epicure, gourmet 8 gourmand 9 collector 11 cognoscente

connotation: 4 hint 6 intent 7 meaning 10 denotation 13 comprehension, signification

connote: 5 imply 7 add up to 8 indicate

connubial: 6 wedded 7 marital 8 conjugal, domestic 11 matrimonial

conquer: get, win 4 beat, best, down, gain, lick, rout, tame 5 crush, daunt 6 defeat, evince, humble, master, reduce, subdue, victor 7 acquire, prevail, subject, triumph 8 overcome, surmount, vanquish 9 checkmate, discomfit, overpower, overthrow, overwhelm, subjugate

conqueror: 4 hero 6 victor, winner 12 conquistador

conquest: 7 mastery, triumph, victory

conquistador: 6 Cortez 9 conqueror

consanguineous: 4 akin 6 carnal 7 kindred, related

consanguinity: 5 blood, nasab 7 kinship 8 affinity 12 relationship

conscience: 5 grace, heart, inwit, qualm, sense 6 erinys, psyche, virtue 7 monitor, probity, scruple, thought 9 casuistry, punctilio 11 compunction

conscienceless: 6 amoral, shifty, tricky, unfair 7 devious 12 unprincipled

conscientious: 4 fair, just 5 exact, rigid 6 honest, strict 7 dutiful, upright 8 faithful 9 honorable 10 scrupulous 11 punctilious

conscious: 4 keen 5 alive, awake, aware 7 feeling, knowing 8 rational, sensible, sentient 9 attentive, cognizant, concerned 10 perceptive 12 apprehensive

consciousness: 9 awareness

loss of: 4 coma 5 faint 8 apoplexy

consciousness-altering: 11 psychedelic

conscript: 5 draft, enrol 6 enlist, muster 7 recruit

consecrate: vow 4 fain, seal 5 bless, deify, devot 6 anoint, hallow, ordain 8 sanctify, dedicate 10 inaugurate 11 apotheosize

consecrated: 4 holy 5 blest 6 oblate, sacred, votive 8 hallowed

cloth: 11 antimension

oil: 6 chrism

thing: 6 sacrum

consent: let 5 agree, allow, grant, yield 6 accede, accord, assent, beteem, comply, permit 7 approve 9 recognize 10 permission 11 concurrence 12 acquiescence 13 authorization

consequence: end 4 bore 5 event, fruit, issue, worth 6 effect, import, moment, repute, result, sequel, weight 7 concern, outcome 8 aftering, interest, occasion 9 aftermath, emanation, inference 10 importance 11 aftereffect, consecution 13 consideration

consequently: 4 ergo, then, thus 5 hence, later 8 pursuant 9 therefore 11 accordingly 12 subsequently 13 consecutively

conservative: 4 safe, Tory 5 staid 6 stable 7 diehard 8 moderate, old-liner 9 bourgeois 11 reactionary, right-winger 12 preservative

conservatory: 6 school 7 academy 10 glasshouse, greenhouse

conserve: can, jam 4 save 5 guard, jelly 6 defend, keep up, secure, shield, uphold 7 husband, protect, sustain 8 maintain, preserve 9 confiture, sweetmeat

consider: see 4 deem, heed, mull, muse, rate 5 ettle, judge, study, think, weigh 6 behold, debate, expend, impute, ponder, reason, reckon, regard 7 account, believe, canvass, examine, inspect, reflect, suppose 8 cogitate, estimate, look upon, meditate, ruminate 9 calculate, entertain, speculate 10 adjudicate, deliberate, think about 11 contemplate

considerable: 5 geyan(Sc.), large, smart, 7 notable, several 9 capacious, important 10 cognizable, noteworthy, remarkable 11 perceptible, significant

considerate: 4 kind, mild 6 gentle 7 careful, heedful, prudent, serious 8 delicate 9 attentive, observant, regardful 10 deliberate, reflective, respectful, thoughtful 11 sympathetic, warm-hearted

consideration: 4 sake 5 price, topic 6 aspect, esteem, motive, notice, reason, regard 7 respect, thought 9 attention, deference, incentive, influence 10 importance, inducement, recompense, reputation 11 consequence

considering: for 5 since 6 seeing

consign: 4 doom, give, mail, send, ship 5 allot, award, dight, remit, shift, yield 6 assign, commit, devote, remand, resign 7 address, confide, deliver, deposit, intrust, intrust 8 delegate, relegate, transfer, turn over 9 recommend 10 commission

consignee: 5 agent 8 receiver

consist: lie 4 hold 5 exist, stand 6 inhere, reside 7 contain, embrace 8 comprise, dovetail 9 harmonize

consistency: 4 body 5 union 6 degree 7 concord, harmony 8 firmness, solidity, symmetry 9 adherence, coherence, congruity 10 consonance, uniformity 11 composition, persistency 14 correspondence, substantiality

consistent: 4 firm 7 durable, logical, uniform 8 coherent, enduring, suitable 9 accordant, congruous, consonant, unfailing, unvarying 10 changeless, compatible, persisting

consociate: 9 associate 11 confederate

consolation: sop 4 fine 6 relief, solace 7 comfort 10 booby prize

console: 4 calm 5 allay, ancon, cheer, organ, table 6 buck up, solace, soothe 7 bracket, cabinet, comfort, relieve, support, sustain 9 alleviate, encourage

consolidate: mix 4 fuse, knit, mass, pool, weld 5 blend, merge, unify, unite 6 harden, mingle 7 combine, compact 8 coalesce, compress, condense, organize, solidify 10 amalgamate, strengthen 11 concentrate

consomme: 4 soup

consonance: 6 accord 7 harmony 9 resonance

consonant: 6 dental, fortis, letter, sonant 7 palatal, phoneme, spirant, unified 8 harmonic, in accord, suitable 9 accordant, agreeable, congruous 10 coincident, compatible, concordant, consistent, harmonious
hard: 6 fortis
hissing: 8 sibilant
pert. to: 7 palatal 9 fricative
smooth: 4 lene 5 lenis
voiceless: 4 lene, surd 6 atonic 7 spirate

consort: cot 4 aide, ally, join, mate, wife 5 agree, group, tally, unite 6 accord, attend, escort, mingle, spouse 7 company, concert, husband, partner 8 accustom, assembly 9 accompany, associate, colleague, companion, forgather 10 foregather 11 association, combination, concurrence, conjunction

consortium: 5 group, guild, order, union 8 alliance, congress

conspectus: 4 list 5 brief 6 survey 7 outline 8 synopsis 11 abridgement

conspicuous: 5 clear, famed, plain 6 extant, famous, marked, patent, signal 7 eminent, glaring, notable, obvious, pointed, salient, visible 8 apparent, manifest, striking 9 egregious, prominent 10 celebrated, noticeable 11 discernible, distinctive, illustrious, outstanding, perspicuous 13 distinguished

conspiracy: 4 coup, plan, plot, ring 5 cabal, covin, junto 6 scheme 7 compace 8 intrigue 9 agreement, champerty 11 combination, concurrence, confederacy, machination

conspire: 4 abet, plot 5 unite 6 league, scheme 7 collude, complot, conjure 8 contrive 9 cooperate 11 confederate

constable: cop 4 bull 6 beadle, harman, keeper, warden 7 bailiff, officer 8 tipstaff 9 policeman

constancy: 4 zeal 5 ardor 6 fealty 7 loyalty 8 devotion, fidelity 9 adherence, diligence, eagerness, integrity, stability 10 allegiance, attachment 11 earnestness 12 perseverance
symbol of: 6 garnet

constant: set 4 even, fast, firm, leal, true 5 fixed, loyal, solid, still, tried 6 stable, steady 7 certain, chronic, durable, forever, lasting, regular, staunch, uniform 8 enduring, faithful, positive, resolute 9 confident, continual, immovable, incessant, permanent, perpetual, steadfast, unvarying 10 consistent, continuous, invariable, persistent, unwavering

Constantine: *birthplace:* 4 Nish
mother: 6 Helena
son: 7 Crispus
victim: 6 Fausta 7 Crispus
wife: 6 Fausta

Constantinople: See Istanbul

constantly: 4 ever 6 always 10 invariably 11 perpetually 12 continuously

constate: 6 assert 9 establish

constellation (see also **star**): 5 group 6 dipper 7 cluster, pattern 10 assemblage 13 configuration
altar: Ara
archer: 11 Sagittarius
Argo division: 4 Vela
arrow: 7 Sagitta
balance: 5 Libra
Big Dipper: 9 Ursa Major
bird of paradise: 5 Apus
bull: 6 Taurus
Champion: 7 Perseus
charioteer: 6 Auriga
Charles' Wain: 6 Dipper
clock: 10 Horologium
compass: 5 Pyxis 8 Circinus
crab: 6 Cancer
crane: 4 Grus
cross: 4 Cruz
crow: 6 Corvus
crown: 6 Corona
dog: 5 Canis
dolphin: 9 Delphinus
dove: 7 Columba
dragon: 5 Draco
eagle: 6 Aquila
fish: 6 Pisces
goat: 9 Capricorn
herdsman: 6 Bootes
hunter: 5 Orion

lady, chained: 9 Andromeda
lady in the chair: 10 Cassiopeia
lion: Leo
Little Dipper: 9 Ursa Minor
lyre: 4 Lyra
maiden: 5 Virgo
northern: Leo 4 Coma, Lynx, Lyra, Ursa 5 Aries, Canes, Draco 6 Aquila, Auriga, Bootes, Cancer, Cygnus, Gemini, Taurus 7 Cepheus, Lacerta, Pegasus, Sagitta 8 Hercules 9 Andromeda, Delphinus, Vulpecula 10 Cassiopeia
peacock: 4 Pavo
rabbit: 5 Lepus
ram: 5 Aries
sails: 4 Vela
southern: Ara 4 Apus, Argo, Crux, Grus, Pavo, Vela 5 Canis, Cetus, Hydra, Indus, Lepus, Libra, Mensa, Musca, Norma, Virgo 6 Antlia, Carina, Corvus, Crater, Dorado, Fornax, Pictor, Pisces, Puppis, Tucana, Volans 7 Columba, Phoenix, Sextans 8 Aquarius, Circinus, Sculptor, Scorpius 9 Centaurus, Chameleon, Monoceros, Reticulum 10 Horologium 11 Capricornus, Sagittarius, 12 Microscopium
stern: 6 Puppis
swan: 6 Cygnus
twins: 6 Gemini
water bearer: 8 Aquarius
whale: 5 Cetus
winged horse: 7 Pegasus
wolf: 5 Lupus
consternation: 4 fear 5 alarm, dread, panic 7 dismay, fright, horror, terror 9 amazement, confusion, trepidity 11 distraction, trepidation 12 befuddlement
constituent: 4 item, part 5 piece, voter 6 detail, factor, matter, member 7 elector, element 9 component 10 ingredient
constitute: fix, set 4 form, make 5 enact, forge, found, set up, shape 6 depute, graith, ordain 7 appoint, compose, station 8 compound, comprise 9 determine, establish 10 commission
constitution: law 4 code 5 being, canon, humor, state 6 custom, health, nature, temper 7 charter 8 physique 9 enactment, ordinance, structure 11 composition, disposition 12 organization 13 establishment
Constitution: 9 Ironsides
Constitution State: 11 Connecticut
constitutional: 4 walk 6 inborn, innate 8 exercise 9 essential, organical 10 congenital, deep-seated
constrain: 4 bend, bind, curb, fain, urge 5 chain, check, clasp, cramp, deter, drive, force, impel, limit, press 6 coerce, compel, hold in, oblige, ravish, secure 7 as-

trict, confine, enforce, oppress, repress, violate 8 compress, distress, hold down, restrain 9 constrict 10 constringe 11 necessitate
constraint: 4 bond 5 force 6 duress, stress 7 reserve 8 coercion, distress, pressure 9 captivity, restraint, stiffness 10 compulsion, obligation 11 compression, confinement
constrict: tie 4 bind, curb, grip 5 choke, cramp, limit 6 hamper, shrink, strait 7 astrict, deflate, squeeze, tighten 8 astringe, compress, condense, contract, restrict 9 constrain 10 constipate, constringe
breath: 8 strangle
constrictor: boa 5 snake 6 muscle, python 8 anaconda 9 sphincter, strangler
construct: 4 form, make, rear 5 build, dight, erect, frame, model, set up 6 devise 7 arrange, combine, compose, confect, fashion 8 construe, engineer 9 fabricate, originate 11 put together
construction: 6 design, makeup 7 synesis 8 building, erection
constructive: 7 helpful 8 creative, implicit, inferred
construe: 5 infer, parse 6 render 7 analyze, dissect, explain, expound, resolve 8 spell out 9 construct, interpret, translate
consuetude: use 4 wont 5 habit, usage 6 custom 8 practice
consul's recognition: 9 exequatur
consult: ask 5 cabal, refer 6 advise, confer, decree, devise 7 concert, counsel, discuss, meeting 8 consider, contrive, decision 9 agreement, determine 10 deliberate
consultant: 6 expert 7 adviser, counsel
consultation: 6 advice 7 council, counsel 9 collation, interview 10 conference, discussion 12 deliberation
consume: eat, use 4 burn, fret, rust, wear 5 drink, raven, spend, use up, waste 6 absorb, absume, bezzle, canker, devour, engage, expend, feed on, perish 7 corrode, destroy, dwindle, engross, exhaust, swallow 8 gobble up, squander 9 dissipate 10 incinerate, monopolize
consumer: 4 usee, user
consummate: end 4 fine, full, ripe 5 ideal, sheer, utter 6 arrant, effect, finish, wind up, wrap up 7 achieve, consume, crowned, perfect, perform 8 absolute, complete 9 culminate, exquisite, out-and-out 10 accomplish
consumption: use 5 decay, waste 7 expense 8 phthisis 11 destruction, expenditure, white plague 12 tuberculosis
contact: 4 abut, join, meet 5 touch, union 6 arrive, impact, syzygy 7 meeting, rap-

port, taction 8 junction, tangency, touching 10 connection, contiguity 11 contingency 13 juxtaposition

contagion: pox 5 taint, virus 6 miasma, poison 7 disease 9 infection 13 contamination

preventative: 4 shot 8 antidote 10 alexiteric 11 prophylaxis

contagious: 7 noxious 8 catching 9 pestilent, spreading 10 infectious 12 communicable

contain: 4 have, hold, keep 5 carry, check, cover, house 6 embody, retain, take in 7 embrace, enclose, include, subsume, sustain 8 comprise, restrain 10 comprehend, simmer down

container: bag, bin, box, can, cup, jug, keg, pan, pod, pot, tin, tub, urn, vat 4 cage, case, cask, crib, ewer, sack, silo, tank, vase 5 crate, cruet, gourd, pouch 6 barrel, basket, bottle, carboy, carton, hamper, hatbox, holder, shaker 7 bandbox, capsule, hanaper, inkwell 8 canister, decanter, demijohn, hogshead, puncheon 10 receptacle

containing: For all phrases beginning with this word, see under the main word or phrase. EXAMPLE: "containing air": see air *containing*.

contaminate: 4 foul, harm, slur, soil 5 stain, sully, taint 6 befoul, debase, defile, infect, injure, poison 7 corrupt, debauch, pollute, tarnish, vitiate 8 dishonor 9 desecrate 10 adulterate

conte: 4 tale 5 story 9 narrative, novelette

contemn: 4 hate 5 flout, scorn, spurn 6 reject, slight 7 despise, disdain 8 contempt, look down

contemplate: 4 muse, plan, scan, view 5 deign, study, think, weigh 6 look at, ponder, regard, survey 7 propose, reflect 8 consider, meditate 9 speculate, think over

contemplation: 5 study 6 musing, prayer, regard, theory 7 request 8 petition 9 intention 10 meditation 11 speculation 12 deliberation 13 consideration

contemporaneous: 6 coeval, living, modern 7 current 8 existing, up-to-date 10 coincident 12 contemporary, simultaneous

contemporary: 6 coeval 7 current

contempt: 5 scorn, shame, sneer 6 slight 7 contemn, disdain, mockery 8 derision, disgrace 9 contumacy, contumely 10 disrespect 11 indignation

exclamation of: bah, foh 4 pooh

contemptible: low 4 base, mean, vile 5 cheap, petty, sorry 6 abject, paltry, scurvy, shabby, sordid, yellow 7 pitiful, scorned 8 beggarly, infamous, inferior, sneaking, unworthy, wretched 9 groveling, worthless 10 despicable 11 ignominious 12 dishonorable 13 insignificant

contemptuous: 7 haughty 8 arrogant, flouting, insolent, scornful 9 hubristic, insulting 10 despicable, disdainful 12 contemptible, supercilious

contend: say vie, war 4 cope, race, wage 5 argue, bandy, brawl, claim, fight 6 assert, battle, bicker, buffet, bustle, combat, debate, oppose, reason, strive 7 bargain, compete, contest, dispute, quarrel 8 conflict, contrive, cope with, maintain, militate, squabble, struggle

contender: 7 entrant 10 contestant 11 protagonist

content: 4 calm, ease, gist, paid 5 happy 6 amount, at ease, please 7 appease, gratify, replete, satiate, satisfy, suffice, willing 8 capacity 9 satisfied 12 satisfaction

contented: 4 cozy 5 sated 8 cheerful 9 satisfied

contention: war 4 bait, bate, feud, riot, tiff 5 broil 6 combat, debate, strife 7 contest, discord, dispute, opinion, quarrel, rivalry, wrangle 8 argument, conflict, squabble, struggle, variance 9 rebellion 10 dissension, litigation 11 altercation, competition, controversy 12 disagreement

contentious: 7 carping, peevish 8 perverse 9 bellicose, litigious, wrangling 10 pugnacious 11 belligerent, quarrelsome 12 cantankerous, disputatious

contentment: 4 ease 5 bliss 8 pleasure 9 happiness 11 complacence 12 satisfaction 13 gratification

conterminous: 4 next 8 adjacent, proximal, touching 9 adjoining, bordering

contest: bee, sue, try, vie 4 agon, bout, cope, duel, feud, fray, game, pitt, race, spar, tiff, tilt 5 broil, clash, fight, set-to, trial 6 action, adjure, affray, battle, combat, debate, defend, oppose, resist, strife, strive 7 bargain, brabble, compete, contend, dispute, protest, tourney, warfare 8 argument, conflict, skirmish, struggle, tug-of-war 9 champerty, encounter 10 controvert, tournament 11 altercation

kind of: 6 tryout 7 lawsuit 10 litigation

narrowly won: 8 squeaker

contestant: 4 vier 5 rival 6 player 7 agonist, entrant 8 finalist, prospect 9 combatant, candidate, contender, defendant, plaintiff 10 competitor 12 participator

contiguous: 4 next, nigh 6 nearby 7 close by 8 abutting, adjacent, touching 9 adjoining, immediate, proximate 10 contacting, near-at-hand 11 neighboring

continence: 6 virtue 8 chastity, sobriety 10 abstinence, moderation, temperance 13 self-restraint

continent: 4 Asia, land, mass 5 sober 6 Africa, chaste, Europe 7 content 8 capacity, mainland, moderate 9 Australia, Greenland, temperate 10 Antarctica, New Zealand receptacle, restrained 12 North America, South America

hypothetical: 8 Cascadia

lost: 8 Atlantis

contingency: 4 case 5 event 6 chance 7 adjunct, contact 8 fortuity, incident, prospect 9 accessory, emergency 10 crossroads 11 possibility, uncertainty

contingent: 6 casual, chance 8 doubtful, touching 9 dependent 10 accidental, fortuitous 11 provisional

on discretion: 9 arbitrary

continual: 7 endless, lasting, regular, undying, uniform 8 constant, enduring, unbroken 9 ceaseless, connected, incessant, perennial, permanent, unceasing 10 continuous, invariable 11 everlasting, unremitting 12 imperishable 13 unintermitted, uninterrupted

continually: aye 4 ever 6 always, hourly, steady 7 endless, eternal, forever 9 perpetual 10 constantly 11 incessantly, unceasingly

continuance: 4 stay 5 delay 6 sequel 8 duration 9 endurance, procedure 10 continuity 11 adjournment 12 postponement, perseverance

continue: be 4 bide, dure, go on, last, live, stay 5 abide, carry, exist, unite 6 beleve, endure, extend, remain, resume, take up 7 beleave, carry on, connect, persist, proceed, prolong, sustain 8 protract 9 persevere

continued: 5 still 6 serial 7 chronic 8 constant 9 extending 10 protracted

continuity: 6 script 8 cohesion, scenario 9 coherence 10 connection

contort: wry 4 bend, coil, turn, warp 5 gnarl, screw, twist, wrest 6 deform, writhe 7 distort, pervert 8 obvolute 9 convolute

contortionist: 7 acrobat

contour: 4 form, line 5 curve, graph, shape 6 figure 7 outline, profile 9 lineament 10 appearance, silhouette 13 configuration

contra: 6 offset 7 against, counter, opposed 8 opposite 9 opposed to, vice versa 11 contrasting 12 contrariwise

contraband: 6 banned 7 illegal, illicit 8 hot goods, smuggled, unlawful

contract: get 4 bond, knit, pact 5 catch, cramp, incur, lease, limit 6 cartel, engage, lessen, narrow, pledge, pucker, reduce, shrink, treaty 7 abridge, bargain, compact, crumple, curtail, promise, shorten, shrivel, wrinkle 8 condense, covenant, restrict 9 agreement, betrothal, constrict, indenture 10 abbreviate, constringe, convention, obligation, sicken with 11 arrangement, concentrate, stipulation 12 come down with

addition to: 5 rider 7 codicil

furnishing slaves: 8 assiento

maritime: 8 bottomry

part: 6 clause 7 article, proviso

unlawful: 10 chevisance

contraction: tic 5 cramp, spasm 6 intake, twitch 7 elision, epitome 9 gathering, reduction, shrinkage, stricture 10 abridgment, compendium, limitation 11 conciseness, confinement 12 abbreviation

common: een, eer, oer, oft, tis 5 arent, shant

heart: 8 systolic

contractor: 7 builder, remover 8 supplier

contradict: 4 deny 5 belie, rebut 6 forbid, impugn, negate, oppose, recant, refute 7 counter, dispute, gainsay 8 disprove 9 disaffirm 10 contravene, controvert

contradiction: 6 denial 7 paradox 8 antilogy, negation 10 gainsaying

contradictory: 6 oppose 8 antipode, contrary 9 dissonant 12 incompatible, inconsistent

contraption: rig 4 tool 6 device, gadget 7 machine 11 contrivance

contrary: 5 balky, polar, snivy 6 averse, contra, ornery, snivey 7 adverse, counter, hostile, opposed, reverse, wayward 8 captious, contrair, inimical, opposite, perverse, petulant 9 refactory, repugnant, unpopular, vexatious 10 discordant, discrepant 11 prejudicial, unfavorable 12 antagonistic, cantankerous, cross-grained 13 insubordinate

to fact: 5 false

to law: 7 illegal 16 unconstitutional

to reason: 6 absurd

contrast: 6 strife 7 compare, contend 8 opposite 9 diversity 10 difference, divergence

contravene: 4 defy, deny 6 hinder, oppose, thwart 7 dispute, violate 8 infringe, obstruct 9 disregard, repudiate 10 contradict, transgress

contravention: sin 4 vice 5 crime 6 breach 7 offense 9 violation 13 contradiction, transgression

contretemps: 4 slip 5 boner, hitch 6 mishap, scrape 8 accident 9 mischance 10 occurrence

music: 11 syncopation

contribute: aid 4 ante, give, help, tend 5

cause, grout 6 assist, bestow, chip in, concur, confer, donate, supply, tender 7 conduce, further, pitch in 9 cooperate, subscribe

contribution: sum, tax 4 alms, boon, gift 5 essay, share 6 impost 7 article, largess, payment, present, renewal, writing 8 donation, offering 9 collation 10 imposition

contrite: 4 worn 5 sorry 6 humble, rueful 8 penitent 9 repentant, sorrowful 10 apologetic, remorseful

contrition: 7 penance, remorse

contrivance: art, gin 4 gear, plan, tool 5 shift 6 deceit, design, device, gadget, scheme 7 fiction, machine, project 8 adaption, artifice, resource 9 apparatus, appliance, doohickey, invention 10 conjecture, instrument 11 contraption

contrive: 4 brew, make, plan, plot 5 frame, fudge, hatch, weave 6 afford, design, devise, divine, invent, make up, manage, scheme, wangle 7 achieve, agitate, concoct, consult, contend, dream up, fashion, procure, project, work out 8 conspire, engineer, intrigue 9 fabricate, machinate 10 accomplish

contrived: pat 5 hokey 10 artificial

contriver: 8 Daedalus 9 architect 10 originator

control: law, run 4 curb, hold, rein, rule, sway 5 charm, check, grasp, gripe, guide, power, skill, steer 6 bridle, direct, empire, govern, handle, manage, regime, subdue 7 command, conduct, mastery, preside 8 attemper, dominate, dominion, hegemony, regulate, restrain 9 influence, ordinance, prescribe 10 ascendancy, discipline, domination, manipulate, moderation, possession, regulation 11 predominate, superintend 12 jurisdiction

controversial: 7 eristic 9 debatable, polemical 12 disputatious 13 argumentative

controversy: row 4 spat, suit, tiff 5 chest 6 debate, strife 7 dispute, quarrel, wrangle 8 argument 10 contention, difference, difficulty, discussion, fallingout, litigation 11 altercation 12 disagreement

controvert: 4 deny, face, moot 5 argue 6 debate, oppose, oppugn, refute 7 contest, dispute, gainsay 9 challenge 10 contradict

contumacious: 6 unruly 7 riotous 8 insolent, mutinous, perverse, stubborn 9 obstinate, seditious 10 disdainful, headstrong, rebellious, refractory, unyielding 11 disobedient, intractable 13 insubordinate

contumely: 5 abuse, scorn 6 contek, insult 7 conteck, disdain 8 contempt, rudeness 9 arrogance 10 opprobrium 11 humiliation

contuse: 4 beat 5 pound 6 bruise, injure 7 squeeze

contusion: 4 blow, bump 6 bruise

conundrum: pun 4 whim 6 enigma, puzzle, riddle 7 conceit 8 crotchet

convalesce: 4 mend 7 improve, recover 10 recuperate

convene: sit 4 call, meet, open 5 unite 6 gather, muster, summon 7 convoke 8 assemble, converge 10 congregate, foregather

convenience: 4 ease 6 toilet 7 benefit, comfort 8 plumbing 9 appliance

convenient: fit 5 handy, ready 6 proper, useful 7 adapted, close-by, helpful 8 becoming, suitable 9 agreeable, available, congruous, favorable, opportune 10 accessible, commodious, near-at-hand 11 appropriate 12 commensurate

convent: 5 abbey 6 priory 7 meeting 8 cloister 9 community, monastery, sanctuary

  head: 5 abbot 6 abbess 8 hegumene 10 hegumeness

  member: nun 4 monk 8 cenobite

  pert. to: 6 friary

  reception room: 8 arlatory

  room: 9 parlatory

  superior: see *head* above

convention: 4 diet, feis, mise, rule 5 synod, usage 6 cartel, caucus, custom, treaty 7 decorum, meeting 8 assembly, congress, contract, covenant, practice 9 agreement, gathering, tradition 10 conference 11 convocation

conventional: 4 more 5 nomic, right, trite, usual 6 decent, formal, modish, proper 7 correct, regular 8 academic, accepted 9 customary, hidebound 10 ceremonial, stipulated 11 contractual

conventionalize: 5 adapt 7 conform, stylize

converge: 4 join, meet 5 focus 6 concur 8 approach, focalize

conversant: 5 adept, awake, aware 6 busied, expert, versed 7 skilled 8 familiar, occupied, up-to-date 9 concerned, practiced 10 acquainted, proficient

conversation: 4 chat, talk 6 confab, parley 7 conduct, palaver 8 behavior, chitchat, colloquy, dialogue, parlance 9 discourse, tete-a-tete 10 conference 11 association, interchange, intercourse 13 communication, interlocution

  of three: 7 trialog 9 trialogue

  private: 7 celidh(Sc.) 8 collogue 9 tete-a-tete

converse: 4 chat, chin, live, move, talk 5 dwell, speak 6 confer, homily, parley 7 commune, obverse, reverse 8 colloque, exchange, opposite 9 discourse 11 association, confabulate

convert: 4 turn 5 alter, amend, apply, renew 6 change, decode, direct, novice 7 restore, reverse 8 converse, neophyte, persuade 9 acetalize, proselyte, transform, translate, transmute, transpose 10 regenerate 11 proselytize 12 metamorphose, transmogrify

convertible: 4 auto 7 soft-top 10 automobile, changeable, equivalent, reciprocal, synonymous 15 interchangeable

convex: 5 bowed 6 arched, camber, curved 7 bulging, gibbous, rounded 9 cymbiform 11 protuberant
molding: 5 ovolo, torus

convey: 4 bear, cart, cede, deed, lead, mean, pass, send, take, tote, will 5 bring, carry, ferry, grant, guide, hurry, steal 6 assign, convoy, delate, demise, devise, eloign, impart, import, pass on, remove 7 auction, conduct, deliver, dispone, dispose 8 alienate, bequeath, transfer, transmit 9 accompany, transport 11 communicate

conveyance: bus, car, sak 4 auto, cart, deed, sled, taxi, tram 5 grant, stage, theft, train, wagon 6 demise 7 charter, conduct, rattler, trailer, trolley, vecture, vehicle, waftage 8 carriage, carrying, stealing, transfer 9 transport 10 automobile 11 transmittal
public: bus, car 4 taxi, tram 5 train 6 subway 7 omnibus, ricksha, steamer 8 airplane, elevated, railroad, rickshaw 10 jinricksha, jinrikisha

convict: 4 find 5 argue, felon, lifer, prove 6 attain, termer, trusty 7 attaint, captive, condemn, culprit 8 criminal, jailbird, prisoner, sentence 10 malefactor

conviction: 4 mind, view 5 creed, dogma, faith, tenet 6 belief, credit 7 opinion 8 sentence 9 assurance 10 confidence

convince: get 4 draw 5 assure, prompt 7 win over 8 talk into 9 prevail on 11 bring around

convinced: 4 sold, sure 6 assure, subdue 7 certain 8 absolute, positive 9 persuaded

convincing: 5 sound, valid 6 cogent, potent 7 telling 8 forcible 10 conclusive, persuasive

convivial: gay 4 boon 6 festal, genial, jovial, lively, social 7 festive, jocular 8 reveling 9 vivacious

convocation: 4 diet 5 synod 7 calling, council, meeting 8 assembly, congress 9 gathering 10 convention 12 congregation

convoke: bid, sit 4 call, cite, meet 6 gather, muster, summon 7 convene 8 assemble 10 congregate

convolute: 4 coil, roll, wind 5 twist 6 tangle, writhe 7 contort 8 obvolute

convolution: 4 coil, curl, fold 5 gyrus, whorl 9 sinuosity
of brain: 5 gyrus

convolve: 5 twist 6 enwrap, enfold, infold, writhe

convolvulus: 4 vine 12 morning glory

convoy: 4 lead 5 carry, guard, guide, pilot, watch 6 attend, convey, escort, manage 7 conduct 9 accompany, conductor, safeguard

convulse: 4 rock, stir 5 shake 6 excite 7 agitate, disturb

convulsion: fit 5 shrug, spasm, throe 6 attack, tumult, uproar 8 laughter, paroxysm 9 agitation, commotion 11 disturbance

cony: das 4 hare, pika 5 daman, dassy, ganam, hutia, hyrax, lapen 6 burbot, dassie, gazabo, gazebo, rabbit 7 ashkoko
catcher: 5 cheat 7 sharper 8 swindler

coo: 4 curr(Sc.), woot 6 murmur

cook: fix, fry 4 bake, boil, chef, make, sear, stew 5 broil, grill, poach, roast, saute, shirr, steam 6 braise, decoct, seethe, simmer 7 dream up, prepare, process, servant 8 barbecue, contrive, cusinero, magirist 9 cuisinier
in simmering liquid: 4 poach
one's goose: 5 spoil 6 defeat
partially: 7 parboil

cooked: 4 done

cookery: 7 cuisine, science 8 magirics

cookie, cooky: 4 cake, snap 6 hermit 7 brownie, oatcake 8 seedcake 10 confection, gingersnap

cooking: *art:* 7 cuisine 8 magirics
device: 4 etna 5 range, stove 7 brazier, griddle 10 rotisserie
odor: 5 nidor
pert. to: 8 culinary
room: 5 cuddy 6 galley 7 kitchen
vessel: pan, pot 4 etna, olla 6 caster, chafer, spider, tureen 7 broiler, griddle, roaster, skillet, steamer 8 colander, fleshpot 9 autoclave

cool: air, fan, ice 4 calm, cold 5 algid, allay, chill, fresh, gelid, nervy, sober, staid, whole 6 chilly, go easy, placid, quench, sedate, serene 7 unmoved 8 careless, cautious, composed, mitigate, moderate, tranquil 9 apathetic, collected, officious, temperate, unruffled 10 deliberate, nonchalant, simmer down, unfriendly 11 indifferent, refrigerate, unconcerned 12 unresponsive 13 dispassionate, imperturbable, self-possessed 15 undemonstrative *one's heels:* 4 wait

cooled: 6 frappe

cooler: fan 4 icer, jail, olla 5 drink 6 icebox, lockup, prison 11 refrigerant 12 refrigerator

coolie: 7 changar

cooling device: fan 7 freezer 12 refrigerator 14 air-conditioner

coolness: 5 nerve 6 aplomb 8 serenity 9 assurance 10 equanimity

coony: sly 4 cute, foxy 6 clever, crafty

coop: cot, cub, mew, pen, pot 4 cage, cote, jail 5 cramp, hutch 6 basket, corral 7 confine 9 enclosure 11 cooperative

cooperate: 4 tend 5 agree, coact, unite 6 concur 7 combine, conduce, connive 8 coadjute, conspire 10 contribute 11 collaborate

cooperation; 8 teamwork

cooperator: 9 auxiliary, colleague 10 accomplice

coordinate: 5 adapt, equal 6 adjust 7 arrange, syntony 8 classify 9 harmonize, integrate, reconcile 10 concurrent

coordination: 4 bond 5 skill 7 harmony, liaison 12 relationship

inability: 6 abasia

lack: 8 asynergy

coot: 4 duck, fowl, rail 5 smyth 6 beltie, person, scoter 7 henbil 13 phalacrocorax

cooter: 4 idle 6 loiter, turtle 8 tortoise

cootie: nit 4 bowl, game 5 louse 6 vessel 8 grayback

cop: bag, nab, rob 4 bank, blow, bull, head, heap, lift, pile, trap, tube 5 catch, crest, filch, mount, quill, shock, snare, steal, stock, swipe 6 peeler, spider, strike 7 capture 9 patrolman, policeman

cop-out: 6 excuse 7 retreat 9 defection

copacetic: 4 fine 5 dandy, prime 6 snappy 7 capital 12 satisfactory

copaiba: 4 tree 6 balsam 9 oleoresin

copal: 5 anime, resin

cope: vie, war 4 cape, duty, face 5 cappa, cloak, cover, dress, equal, flight, match, notch, rival, vault, wield 6 barter, canopy, chapel, combat, make do, mantel, muzzle, oppose, strike, strive 7 contend, contest 8 complete, deal with, exchange, struggle, vestment 9 encounter

Copenhagen: *park:* 6 Tivoli

shopping district: 7 Stroget

copestone: 5 crown, stone 6 coping 11 culmination

copier: 4 stat 5 Xerox 6 scribe

copious: 4 full, good, lush, rich 5 ample, large 6 fluent, lavish, plenty 7 diffuse, flowing, fulsome, profuse, replete, teeming, uberous 8 abundant, affluent, numerous 9 exuberant, plenteous, plentiful, redundant 11 overflowing

copper: cop 4 bull, cent 5 bobby, metal, penny 6 cuprum, peeler 9 butterfly, policeman

alloy: 5 brass 6 oroide 7 rheotan

arsenic sulfide: 8 enargite

coin: 4 cent 5 brown, penny

engraving: 9 mezzotint

sulfate: 7 vitriol

copperhead: 5 snake, viper

coppice: 4 bosk, wood 5 copse, firth, grove 6 forest, growth 7 thicket 9 brushwood, underwood

Corpreus: *father:* 6 Pelops

son: 10 Periphetes

victim: 7 Iphitus

copse: cut, hag 4 hasp, trim 6 clevis 7 coppice, shackle

Copt: 8 Egyptian 9 Christian 11 monophysite

dialect: 8 Bohairic

title: 4 anba

copula: 4 band, link 5 union 7 coupler

copy: ape 4 echo, edit, mime 5 dummy, image, mimic 6 ectype, effigy, follow, record 7 emulate, estreat, imitate, redraft, replica, reprint, tracing 8 apograph, likeness 9 abundance, antigraph, duplicate, imitation, reproduce 10 transcribe, transcript 11 counterpart 12 reproduction

exact: 5 tenor

kind of: 6 carbon, ectype 7 estreat, extract, pattern, replica 9 duplicate, facsimile

true: 7 estreat

copying: 7 mimicry 8 mimetism

copyist: 6 sribe 7 copycat 10 plagiarist 12 calligrapher

pert. to: 8 clerical

copyread: edit

copyright: 6 patent

infringe: 6 pirate 10 plagiarize

coque: bow 4 loop 8 trimming

coquet: toy 5 dally, flirt 6 lead on 11 string along

coquette: toy 4 vamp 5 dally, flirt 6 trifle 9 philander 11 hummingbird

coquettish: coy 4 arch 7 roguish

cora: 7 gazelle

coral: red 4 pink 5 polyp 6 palule 8 skeleton, zoophyte 9 limestone, madrepore, millepore 10 stalactite

division: 7 aporosa

formation: 5 palus

island: key 4 reef 5 atoll

corbel: 4 knot 5 ancon 6 timber 10 projection

corbie: 4 crow 5 raven

cord: rib 4 band, bind, bond, welt 5 nerve, twine 6 bobbin, sennet, string, tendon, thread 7 amentum, measure 10 aiguilette, cordeliere

drapery: 7 torsade
goat's hair: 4 agal
parachute: 7 ripcord
twisted: 7 torsade

cordage: 4 rope, coir, eruc, feru, hemp, imbe, jute 5 fiber 6 sennit 7 rigging

Corday's victim: 5 Marat

corded: 4 tied 6 repped, ribbed, welted 7 stacked, twilled

Cordelia: *father:* 4 Lear
sister: 5 Regan 7 Goneril

cordelle: tow 4 cord, rope 7 towline, tow-rope

cordial (see also *liqueur*): 4 real, warm 5 shrub 6 ardent, elixir, genial, hearty 7 liqueur, sincere, zealous 8 anisette, friendly, gracious, vigorous 9 courteous, unfeigned 10 hospitable
apricot: 8 periscot
flavoring: 7 aniseed

cordiality: 5 ardor 6 regard, warmth 10 friendship, heartiness

cordon: 4 lace 5 braid, group, guard 6 ribbon
bleu: 4 chef, cook 6 ribbon 10 decoration
sanitary: 10 quarantine

core: cob, hub, nut 4 coke, gist, nave, pith 5 focus, heart, nowse, spool 6 cener, centre, kernel, matrix, middle, nodule 7 company, corncob, essence, nucleus 9 substance

corge: 5 score 6 twenty

coriander: 4 herb

corinne: 7 gazelle

corium: 5 layer 6 dermis

cork: oak 4 plug, seal, stop 5 float, shive 6 bobber 7 soberin, stopper, stopple
pert. to: 7 suberic
tissue: 5 suber
wax: 5 cerin

corker: 4 lulu 5 dandy 8 knockout 9 humdinger

corking: 4 fine 8 pleasing 9 excellent

corkscrew: 4 coil, wind 5 twist 6 spiral

corkwood: 5 balsa 6 blolly 8 harefoot

cormorant: 4 bird, shag 5 norie, scart 6 gormaw, scarth 7 glutton 8 ravenous 13 phalacrocorax
young: 7 shaglet

corn: zea 4 salt, samp 5 grain, maize, mealy 6 clavis, heloma, kernel 7 callous 8 preserve 9 granulate
bread: 4 pone
dealer: 10 cornmonger
ear: cob 5 mealy 6 mealie, nubbin
food: 6 hominy
ground: 4 meal 5 grist
hulled: 4 samp 6 hominy
Indian: zea
knife: 7 machete
spike: cob, ear

corn bread: 4 pone 8 tortilla

Corncracker State: 8 Kentucky

corndodger: 4 pone 5 bread 8 dumpling

corned: 6 salted

cornel: 4 tree 6 cherry 7 dogwood 8 red-brush

corner: box, get, wro 4 bend, cant, coin, nook, pool, trap, tree 5 angle, bight, catch, coign, elbow, herne, ingle, niche, quoin, trust 6 cantle, canton, coigne, cranny, recess 8 monopoly

cornerpiece: 6 bumper, cantle

cornerstone: 5 basis, coign 6 coigne 7 support 9 curbstone 10 foundation

cornet: 4 horn 8 woodwind 10 instrument

cornflower: 7 barbeau 10 bluebonnet, bluebottle

cornhouse: 7 granary 8 corncrib

Cornhusker State: 8 Nebraska

cornice: cap 4 band, drip, eave 5 crown 6 geison 7 molding 8 astragal
basket: 4 caul
diamond: 6 quartz
support: 5 ancon
underside: 6 soffit 8 plancier
wolframite: cal

cornmeal: 4 masa, samp 5 atole 7 hoecake 10 johnnycake

cornsilk: 5 floss

cornucopia: 4 horn 9 abundance 12 horn of plenty

Cornwall: *castle:* 8 Tintagel
mine: bal 5 wheal
ore: 5 whits

Cornwallis *adversary:* 6 Greene
surrender site: 8 Yorktown

corny: 5 banal, stale, trite 6 old hat 11 sentimental

corolla: 4 bell 8 perianth
part: 5 galea, petal

corollary: 5 dogma 6 result, truism 7 adjunct, theorem 9 deduction, inference, end product 11 consequence, proposition
geometric: 6 porism

corona: 4 halo 5 cigar, crown, glory 6 circle, fillet, rosary, wreath 7 aureole, circlet, garland, scyphus

coronation: 9 inaugural
stone: 5 Scone

coroner: 6 elisor 7 officer 8 examiner

coronet: 4 band, burr 5 crown, tiara 6 anadem, circle, diadem, timbre, wreath 7 chaplet

coronopus: 4 herb 6 carara

corporal: NCO 4 fano 5 fanon, fanum, phano 6 bodily

corporal punishment: 5 death 7 penalty 8 spanking, whipping

corporate: 6 united 8 combined 9 aggregate

corporation: 4 body, firm 5 trust 10 fellowship, foundation 11 association, combination

corporeal: 4 real 5 hylic, somal 6 actual, bodily, carnal 7 somatic 8 material, physical, tangible 11 substantial

corpse: DOA 4 body 5 mummy, relic, stiff 7 cadaver, carcass, carrion
fat of: 9 adipocere
pert. to: 7 deathly 10 cadaverous

corpulent: fat 5 bulky, burly, husky, obese, plump, stout 6 fleshy, portly, rotund 7 adipose, bellied, weighty 8 roly-poly 10 overweight

corpus: 4 body, bulk, mass 8 writings 10 literature

corpuscle: 4 cell 9 leucocyte
lack of red: 6 anemia
red blood: 7 hematid 8 haematid 11 polkilocyte, schistocyte

corral: pen, sty 4 coop 5 atajo, pound 7 confine, enclose 8 stockage, surround 9 enclosure, inclosure

correct: due, fit, fix 4 edit, lean, nice, okay, smug, true 5 amend, check, emend, exact, right 6 adjust, better, change, inform, proper, punish, rebuke, reform, remedy, repair, revamp, revise, strict 7 chasten, improve, perfect, precise, rectify, redress, reprove 8 accurate, chastise, definite, emendate, make over, regulate, rigorous, truthful 9 castigate, faultless 10 immaculate, particular, scrupulous 11 comme il faut, punctilious 12 conventional

correctable: 10 corrigible

correction: 10 discipline, punishment 11 castigation

correlated: 4 akin 7 matched, related

correlative: nor 4 then 5 equal, still 6 either, mutual 7 neither 8 analogue, conjoint 9 analogous 10 reciprocal 11 correspondent

correspond: fit, gee 4 jibe, suit 5 agree, match, tally, write 6 accord, concur, square 7 comport, respond 8 coincide, parallel, quadrate 9 analogous, harmonize 11 communicate

correspondence: 4 mail 7 analogy, letters, traffic 8 homology 9 assonance, congruity 10 similarity

correspondent: 5 match 6 pen pal, writer 8 quadrate, suitable 9 accordant, analogous, congruous 10 accomplice, concordant, equivalent 11 conformable, contributor, correlative

corresponding: 4 akin 5 alike 7 similar
in sound: 5 rimic 6 rhymic
part: 7 isomere

corrida: 9 bullfight
shout: olé

corridor: 4 hall 5 aisle, oriel 6 arcade 7 couloir, gallery 8 coulisse 10 passageway

corrie: 6 cirque, hollow

corrigible: 8 amenable 10 corrective, punishable 11 correctable

corroborant: 5 tonic 10 supporting 12 invigorating 13 strengthening

corroborate: 5 prove 7 bear out, confirm, support, sustain 8 validate 9 establish 11 countersign 12 substantiate

corrode: eat 4 bite, burn, etch, gnaw, rust 5 decay, erode, waste 6 be-gnaw, canker, impair 7 consume, eat away 8 wear away

corrosive: 4 acid 6 ardent, biting 7 caustic, erosive, fretful, mordant 9 sarcastic 11 destructive 14 disintegrating

corrugate: 5 crimp 6 furrow, rumple 7 crinkle, crumple, wrinkle

corrugation: 4 fold 6 crease, pucker 7 wrinkle

corrupt: bad, low, rot 4 evil, vile 5 blend, bribe, spoil, stain, sully, taint, venal 6 augean, canker, debase, impure, poison, putrid, ravish, rotten 7 abusive, attaint, carrion, crooked, defiled, degrade, deprave, envenom, falsify, immoral, pervert, pollute, putrefy, violate, vitiate 8 confound, empoison, two-faced 9 abandoned, dishonest 10 adulterate, demoralize, flagitious, profligate 11 contaminate, purchasable 13 double-dealing

corsage: 5 waist 6 bodice 7 bouquet, flowers

corsair: bug 6 pirate, robber 8 picaroon, rockfish 9 buccaneer, sea robber 10 freebooter
body: 5 armor, cover

corset: 4 belt, busk 6 bodice, girdle 7 support
covering: 8 camisole
strip: 4 bone, busk

Corsica: *seaport:* 6 Bastia
town: 5 Calvi, Corte 7 Ajaccio(c.)

corslet: 6 bodice 8 corselet 11 breastplate

cortege: 4 pomp 5 suite, train 6 parade 7 retinue 10 procession

cortex: 4 bark, peel, rind 8 peridium

corundum: 4 ruby, sand 5 emeru, emery 7 alumina 8 abrasive, sapphire

coruscate: 5 blaze, flash, gleam, shine 7 glisten, glitter, radiate, sparkle 8 brandish 11 scintillate

corviform: 7 corvine 8 crowlike

corvine bird: daw 4 crow, rook 5 raven

coryza: 4 cold
symptom: 6 sneeze

cos: 7 lettuce, romaine

cosa nostra: 5 Mafia 9 syndicate

cosh: 4 neat, snug, tidy 5 happy, quiet, still 6 attack, lively, strike, weapon 7 assault 8 familiar, friendly 11 comfortable

cosher: pet 4 chat 5 feast, visit 6 pamper, sponge

cosmetic: 5 cream, henna, liner, paint, rouge 6 enamel, pomade, powder 7

blusher, mascara 8 lipgloss, lipstick 9
eye shadow 10 nail polish
medicated: 6 lotion
paste: 4 pack
white lead: 6 ceruse
cosmic: 4 vast 6 global 7 orderly 8 catholic, infinite 9 universal 10 harmonious
12 cosmopolitan
opposed to: 7 chaotic
cosmonaut: See astronaut
cosmopolitan: 6 global, smooth, urbane 8
ecumenic 10 ecumenical 13 sophisticated
cosmos: 5 earth, globe, order, realm, world
6 flower, nature 7 harmony 8 creation,
universe
opposed to: 5 Chaos
Cossack: 4 Turk 5 tatar 6 ataman, hetman, tartar 7 Russian 10 cavalryman
captain: 6 Sotnik
chief: 6 ataman, hetman
district: 6 voisko
mount: 5 steed 7 charger
regiment: 4 polk, pulk
squadron: 6 sotnia, sotnya
village: 8 stanitza
whip: 5 knout
cosset: pet 4 baby, love 6 caress, coddle,
cuddle, fondle, pamper
cossette: 4 chip 5 slice, strip 9 schnitzel
cossid: 9 messenger
cost: 4 loss, pain 5 price, value 6 charge,
outlay 7 expense 8 estimate 9 detriment, sacrifice, suffering 11 deprivation, expenditure 14 characteristic
business: 8 overhead
costa: rib 4 side, vein 5 ridge 6 border,
mid-rib
Costa Rica: *capital:* San Jose
city: 7 Cartago, Heredia 8 Alajuela 9
Guadalupe
measure: 6 fanega, tercia 7 cajuela, manzana 10 caballeria
monetary unit: 5 colon 7 centimo
mountain: 6 Blanco 8 Chirripo
people: 6 Guaymi 7 Guaymie
port: 10 Puerto Limon 11 Punta Arenas
volcano: 5 Barba, Irazu
weight: bag 4 caja
costate: 6 ribbed
costly 4 dear, fine, high, rich 6 lavish 8
gorgeous, precious, prodigal, splendid 9
dearthful, expensive, priceless, sumptuous 10 exorbitant, invaluable 11 extravagant
costmary: 4 herb 5 plant, tansy 7 alecost
costume (see also dress, vestment): rig 4
garb, robe, sari, suit 5 dress, getup, habit 6 attire, outfit 7 apparel, clothes, raiment, uniform 8 clothing, ensemble 10
habiliment
costus root: 4 herb 6 pachak, pochok
cot: bed, hut, mat, pen 4 boat, coop, cote,

fold 5 abode, cabin, couch, cover, house,
stall 6 pallet, sheath, tangle 7 charpai,
charpoy, cottage, shelter 8 bedstead,
dwelling 9 sheepfold, stretcher 11 fin-
gerstall
cote: cot, hut 4 coop, fold, shed, wine 5
house, quote 7 cottage, shelter 8 hillside, outstrip, vineyard 9 inclosure,
sheepfold
Cote d'Azur: 7 Riviera
coterie: set 4 ring 5 junto, monde 6 circle,
clique, galaxy 7 platoon, society 9 camarilla
cothamore: 8 overcoat 9 greatcoat
cothurnus: 4 boot 6 buskin
cotillion: 5 dance 9 quadrille, solitaire
cotta: 5 stole 6 mantle 7 blanket 8 surplice, vestment
cottage: hut 4 bari, cosh 5 bower, cabin,
house, lodge, shack 6 bohawn, cabana,
chalet, shanty 7 shelter 8 bungalow 9
hosthouse 10 guesthouse
partition: 5 speer 6 hallan
Russian: 5 dacha
Swiss: 6 chalet
cottage cheese: 9 smearcase
cotter, cottar: mat, pin, vex 4 clot 6 fasten, potter, pucker, shrink, toggle, wither 7 congeal, cottier, peasant, shrivel,
villein 8 cottager, cotterel, entangle 9
coagulate
cotton: 4 beat, flog 5 agree, fiber, toady 6
coddle, fabric 7 algodon, garment, succeed 8 perceive 9 harmonize 10 fraternize, understand
and linen: 7 fustian
cleaner: 5 willy 6 willow
cloth: 4 baft, jean, lawn, leno, susi 5
bafta, bluet, denim, doria, khaki, lisle,
manta, surat, terry, vichy, wigan 6 baline, calico, cangan, hum-hum 7 cam-
boye, cotonia, galatea, jaconet, nankeen,
percale, silesia
cloth blemish: nit
Egyptian: sak 4 Pima 5 sakel
extraction: 5 bolly
fabric: 4 leno
fiber: 4 lint, noil 6 stapel
flowered: 6 chintz
fuzz remover: 6 linter
gauze: 4 leno
handkerchief: 7 malabar
knot in: nep 4 slub
lawn: 7 batiste
light: 7 etamine
long-staple: 4 maco
measure: lea 4 hank
printed: 6 calico
refuse: 8 grabbots
seed pod: 4 boll 5 bolly
seed remover: gin
sheeting: 5 manta 6 muslin 7 percale 8
drilling

striped: 5 bezan 7 express
strong: 4 duck 5 scrim 6 canvas
thread: 5 lisle
twilled: 4 jean 7 silesia
up to: 10 ingratiate
waste: 4 noil 6 linter
cotton gin inventor: 10 Eli Whitney
Cotton State: 7 Alabama
cottonseed kernel: 4 meat 7 oil cake
cottontail: 4 hare 7 leveret
cottonwood: 4 tree 5 alamo 6 poplar
couch: bed, cot, lie, put 4 hide, lair, lurk,
sofa 5 divan, inlay, lodge, press, skulk,
slink, sneak, squat, stoop, utter 6 burrow, litter, pallet, settee 7 conceal, express, overlay, recline 8 disguise 9 accu-
bitus(L.), davenport, embroider
couch grass: 5 quack, quick 6 quitch,
scutch
couchant: 4 abed 5 prone 6 supine 7
lurking 9 crouching, squatting
cougar: cat 4 puma 7 panther 9 catamount
cough: 4 bark, hack 5 hoast 6 tussis 9
pertussis
pert. to: 7 tussive
cough drop: 6 pastil, troche 7 lozenge 8
pastille
cough up: 4 ante 5 yield 10 contribute
coulee: 4 lava 5 gorge, gulch 6 cooley, ravine
couloir: 5 gorge, gully 7 hallway, passage
8 corridor
council: 4 body, dael, diet, rede 5 board,
boule, cabal, divan, junta, junto, synod
6 senate 7 cabinet, consult, meeting 8
assembly, conclave, congress, hustling,
ministry 10 conference, consistory, federation 11 convocation 12 consultation
church: 5 synod 10 consistory
pert. to: 7 cameral
political: 5 cabal, junta
table cover: 5 tapis
counsel: 4 lore, rede, rule, urge, warn 5
chide 6 advice, advise, confer 7 caution,
suggest 8 admonish, advocate, attorney,
prudence 9 barrister, counselor, recommend 10 counsellor 11 exhortation, instruction 12 consultation, deliberation
counselor, counsellor: 4 sage 6 lawyer,
mentor, nestor 7 adviser, advisor, counsel, proctor 8 attorney 9 barrister
counselor-at-law: 9 barrister
count: add, sum, tot 4 bank, cast, earl,
foot, graf, name, rely, tell, tote 5 com-
te(F.), judge, score, tally 6 census, depend, esteem, figure, impute, number,
reckon, rely on 7 account, ascribe, compute, trust in 8 numerate, sanction 9
ascertain, calculate, enumerate 10 depend upon
Count of Monte Cristo: 6 Dantes
count on: 4 lean, rely 6 depend, expect

count out: bar 6 except 7 rule out 9 eliminate
countenance: aid, mug 4 abet, brow, face,
mien, puss, show, vult 5 favor, front 6
aspect, favour, visage 7 approve, bearing, conduct, endorse, feature, proffer,
support 8 befriend, demeanor, hold
with, sanction 9 demeanour, encourage,
semblance 10 appearance 11 physiognomy
counter: bar, vie 4 chip, dump, eddy,
pawn 5 shelf, stand, table 6 combat,
marker, oppose 7 adverse, contend, current 8 contrary, opposite 10 contradict
12 football play 13 contradictory
counter-irritant: 4 moxa 5 seton, stupe
6 arnica, ginger, iodine, pepper 7 mustard 8 liniment
counteract: 5 annul, check 6 oppose, resist, thwart 7 balance, correct, destroy,
nullify 8 antidote, negative 9 frustrate
10 compensate, neutralize 11 countermand 12 counterpoise
counterattack: 6 answer, charge
countercurrent: 4 eddy 5 swirl 7 backset
9 whirlpool
counterfeit: tin 4 base, copy, coin, duff,
fake, mock, sham 5 belie, bogus, dummy, false, feign, forge, fudge, phony,
queer 6 affect, assume, forged, pseudo,
tinsel 7 falsify, feigned, imitate 8 deformed, simulate, spurious 9 brummagem, disguised, dissemble 10 adulterate, artificial, fictitious, fraudulent
counterfoil: 4 stub 5 check
countermand: 4 stop 5 annul 6 cancel,
forbid, recall, revoke 7 abolish, rescind,
reverse 8 abrogate, prohibit 9 frustrate
10 counteract
counterpane: 6 spread 8 bedcover, coverlet 9 bedspread
counterpart: 4 copy, like, mate, twin 5
image, match 6 double 7 obverse, vis-á-
vis 8 parallel 9 duplicate, facsimile 10
complement, equivalent, similitude
counterpoint: 4 foil 7 descant 8 contrast
11 arrangement 13 juxtaposition
counterpoise: 6 make up, offset, set off 7
balance 8 equalize 10 compensate,
counteract 13 counterweight 14 counterbalance
countersign: 4 mark, seal, sign 6 signal 7
confirm, endorse 8 consign, password,
sanction 9 signature, watchword 11
corroborate
countersink: 4 ream 5 bevel 7 chamfer
countertenor: 4 alto 8 falsetto
counting frame: 6 abacus
countless: 8 infinite 10 numberless 12
incalculable
country: 4 home, land, pais(Sp.) 5 realm,
rural, state, tract, weald 6 ground, nation, people, region, sticks 7 bucolic,

outland 8 district, homeland 9 champaign, territory 10 fatherland 12 commonwealth

ancient: 4 Aram, Elam, Elis 5 Sheba

dance: 4 reel

home: 5 manor, ranch, villa 8 hacienda

man: 4 jake, rube 5 swain, yokel 6 farmer, rustic 7 bumpkin, hayseed, plowman 10 compatriot, inhabitant

mythical: 6 Utopia

open: 4 wold 5 heath, weald

pert. to: 5 rural 6 rustic 7 predial 8 agrestic, pastoral, praedial

place: 4 farm, peat 5 ranch, villa

reside in: 9 rusticate

road: 4 lane, path 5 byway

county: 4 seat 5 shire 6 domain, parish 7 borough 8 district

coup: buy 4 blow, plan, play 5 scoop, upset 6 attack, barter, putsch, strike, stroke 7 capsize, traffic 8 overturn, takeover 9 stratagem

coup de grace: end 7 quietus 9 deathblow

coup d'etat: 9 stratagem 10 revolution

couple: duo, tie, two 4 bond, case, dyad, join, link, mate, pair, span, team, twin, yoke 5 brace, leash, marry, twain, unite 7 bracket, connect 8 assemble

coupled: 5 yoked 6 joined, wedded 7 gemalad 8 geminate 9 conjugate

coupler: 4 link, ring 7 drawbar, shackle, tirasse

couplet: 4 pair, poem 5 brace 7 distich

coupon: 4 form, slip, stub 5 check, stamp 7 portion

courage: 4 grit, guts, prow, sand, soul 5 heart, nerve, pluck, spine, spunk, valor 6 daring, mettle, spirit 7 bravery, heroism, prowess 8 audacity, backbone, boldness, firmness, tenacity 9 assurance, fortitude, gallantry, hardihood 10 resolution

symbol of: 10 bloodstone

courageous: 4 bold, game 5 brave, hardy, manly, stout 6 daring, heroic, manful, plucky 7 gallant, spartan, staunch, valiant 8 fearless, intrepid, valorous 9 undaunted 11 adventurous 12 enterprising, high-spirited

courante: 4 romp 5 caper, dance, music 6 letter 7 current, gazette, running 9 messenger, newspaper

courier: 4 post 5 envoy, guide, scout 7 estafet, orderly, postboy, soilage 8 cicerone, dragoman, estafeet, horseman 9 attendant, go-between, messenger 10 cavalryman

courlan: 4 bird 7 limpkin

course: lap, run, way 4 bent, flow, game, heat, line, mode, path, race, rill, rink, road, rote, went 5 cycle, drift, orbit, route, tenor, track, trail, trend 6 artery,

career, cursus, gallop, manner, method, series, stream, street, system 7 beeline, conduct, highway, passage, pathway, process, routine, running, subject, traject 8 curricle, progress, sequence, tendency 9 direction 10 curriculum, proceeding, racecourse, succession 11 watercourse

alter: 4 veer 6 detour

dinner: 5 salad 6 entrée 7 dessert 9 blue plate

easy: 4 pipe, snap 5 cinch 8 sinecure

habitual: rut, way 4 rote 7 regimen, routine

of action: 6 career 8 demarche 9 procedure

of study: 7 seminar 8 syllabus 10 curriculum

roundabout: 6 detour 11 indirection

courser: 5 horse, racer, steed 7 charger 8 war-horse

court: bar, bid, see, sue, woo 4 area, body, quad, rota, seek, yard 5 arena, curea, curry, favor, forum, judge, patio, space, spark, tempt, train 6 allure, atrium, gemote, homage, invite, palace 7 address, attract, retinue, solicit 8 hustings, serenade, tribunal 9 attention, enclosure 10 quadrangle

action: 4 case, suit 5 trial

attendant: 5 staff 6 elisor, staves

bring into: sue 4 sist 6 arrest

calendar: 6 docket

call to: 4 oyes, oyez 7 summons 8 subpoena 11 arraignment

circuit: 4 eyre, iter

crier: 6 beadle

cry: 4 oyes, oyez

decision: 6 assize 7 finding, verdict 8 judgment

ecclesiastical: 5 Curia 10 consistory

exemption: 6 essoin

hearing: 4 oyer, suit 5 trial 6 action

inner: 5 patio

Mikado's: 5 dairi

minutes: 4 acta

of equity: 8 chancery

official: 5 clerk, crier, macer(Sc.) 7 bailiff

old: 4 leet 5 gemot 6 gemote 8 woodmote

order: 4 nisi, rule, writ 6 decree

panel: 4 jury

participant: 4 jury 5 crier, judge 6 elisor 7 pleader 8 advocate, talesman 9 defendant, plaintiff

pert. to: 5 aulic 10 fornaneous

session: set 4 oyer 6 assize 7 sitting 8 sederunt 11 downsitting

writ: 6 capias 7 summons 8 subpoena

court game: 6 tennis 9 badminton

court-martial: 8 drumhead

courteous: 4 fair 5 buxom, civil, suave 6 polite, urbane 7 affable, cordial, gallant, genteel, gentile, refined 8 debonair, gracious 9 attentive 10 complaisant, respectful 11 considerate, gentlemanly 12 well mannered

courtesan: 5 whore 6 geisha, madame 10 prostitute

courtier: 4 beau 5 beaux(pl.), wooer 7 courter 8 courtman 9 attendant, courtling, flatterer

courtly: 4 hend, prim 5 aulic, civil, hende, lofty 6 polite 7 elegant, refined, stately 8 gracious, polished 9 dignified

courtship: 4 suit 7 romance 8 sparking

courtyard: 4 area, quad 5 patio 7 cortile 9 curtilage 10 quadrangle

cousin: coz, kin 4 akin 5 allied 8 relative

couthie: 4 smug 6 kindly, smooth 8 friendly, pleasant 9 agreeable 11 comfortable

couturier, couturiere: 8 designer 10 dressmaker

cove: bay, den 4 cave, chap, gill, hole, nook, pass 5 basin, bight, creek, inlet 6 fellow, hollow, recess, valley 7 molding

covenant: 4 bind, bond, mise, pact 5 agree 6 accord, cartel, engage, pledge, treaty 7 bargain, compact, concord, promise 8 alliance, contract, document 9 agreement, concordat, condition, stipulate, testament, undertake 10 convention 11 confederacy, stipulation, transaction

cover: cap, lid 4 coat, hide, mask, pave, roof, span, veil 5 drape, hatch, put-on 6 mantle, screen, shield 7 obscure, overlay, shelter

a bet: 4 fade

a fire: 4 bank

a hatch: 6 batten

ground: 5 speed 7 advance

the eyes: 9 blindfold

up: 4 hide 7 conceal

up for: 6 shield 7 protect

with mud: 6 belute

with straw: 6 thatch

with strips of bacon: 4 lard

coverall: 4 gown 6 jumper 10 boiler suit

covered: 4 clad, shod 5 mossy 6 covert, hidden 7 encased 8 screened 9 cleithral, concealed, panoplied, sheltered

covering: fur, hap 4 aril, bark, boot, case, hood, hull, husk, mask, pall, roof, tarp, tile 5 apron, armor, crust, quilt, shell, testa 6 awning, canopy, drapet, facing, heling, helmet, jacket, pelage, screen, sheath, shroud 7 capsule, ceiling, healing, overlay, pericap, wrapper 8 casement, clothing, coverlet, umbrella 9 coverture, operculum 10 integument 11 smokescreen

defensive: 5 armor 6 helmut 10 camouflage 11 smokescreen

seed: 4 aril

thin: 4 film 6 veneer

coverlet: 5 quilt, rezai, throw 6 afghan, caddow, spread 7 blanket 8 coverlid 9 comforter 11 counterpane

covert: den, lie, sly 4 lair 5 niche, privy 6 asylum, harbor, hidden, latent, masked, refuge, secret 7 covered, defense, harbour, private, shelter, subrosa, thicket 8 hush-hush 9 concealed, disguised, insidious, shrubbery 10 underbrush 12 confidential 13 under-the-table

covet: 4 ache, envy, pant, want, wish 5 crave, yearn 6 desire, grudge, hanker

covetous: 4 avid, gair, gare, keen 5 eager, itchy 6 frugal, greedy, stingy 7 miserly 8 desirous, grasping 9 mercenary 10 avaricious 12 parsimonious

covey: 4 bevy 5 brood, bunch, flock, hatch 7 company 8 assembly

cow: awe 4 beef, bogy, cowl, cush, faze, kine, vaca 5 abash, alarm, bossy, brock, bully, daunt, dompt, moggy, scare 6 bovine, goblin, heifer, subdue 7 bluster, bugbear, depress, dragoon, overtop, squelch, terrify 8 browbeat, dispirit, frighten, threaten 9 quadruped, strongarm 10 intimidate

barn: 5 byre 7 vaccary

barren: 5 drape

cud: 5 rumen

dung: 4 upla

French: 5 vache

group: 4 herd, kine 6 cattle

hornless: not 4 moil 5 doddy, muley 6 doddie, mulley 7 pollard

hybrid: 7 cattabu, cattalo

pasture: 7 vaccary

pen: 6 corral

sound: low, moo

Spanish: 4 vaca

young: 4 calf 5 stirk 6 heifer

cow-headed deity: 4 Isis

cow pilot: 4 fish 9 chirivita 10 damselfish

coward: 6 pigeon 7 caitiff, chicken, quitter 9 jellyfish 10 scaredy-cat 11 lily-livered

cowardly: shy 4 argh 5 timid 6 afraid, cowish, craven, yellow 7 caitiff, chicken 11 lily-livered 12 fainthearted 13 pusillanimous

cowbird: 7 bunting 9 blackbird

cowboy: 5 rider, roper, waddi 6 drover, gaucho, herder 7 llanero, puncher, vaquero 8 buckaroo, buckayro, herdsman, wrangler 9 cattleman 10 cowpuncher 12 broncobuster

breeches: 5 chaps, levis 8 jodhpurs

contest: 5 rodeo

rope: 5 lasso, riata 6 lariat

cowcatcher: 5 guard, pilot

cowed: 8 downcast 11 crestfallen

cower: 4 fawn 5 quail, stoop, toady, wince 6 coorie, cringe, crouch, hurkle, shrink 11 apple-polish

cowfish: 4 toro 7 grampus, manatee, sirenia

cowherd: 8 herdsman, neatherd

cowl: cap, lid, tub 4 hood, monk 6 bonnet, vessel 7 capuche

cowled: 6 hooded 9 cucullate

cowpea: 5 sitao

cowpuncher: See cowboy

cowslip: 8 auricula, cyclamen, marigold, primrose

coxa: hip 6 haunch

coxcomb: fop, nob 4 buck, dude, fool, toff 5 cleat, dandy, hinge 7 princox 8 popinjay 12 lounge lizard

coy: pal, shy 4 arch, coax, nice 5 aloof, chary, decoy, quiet, still 6 allure, caress, demure, modest, proper 7 bashful, distant 8 reserved 9 diffident 10 coquettish, disdainful, hesitating 12 self-effacing

Coyote State: 11 South Dakota

coypu: 6 nutria, rodent

coze: 4 chat, talk 6 gossip 8 converse

cozen, cosen: cog, con, gyp 4 bilk, gull 5 cheat, trick 6 chisel 7 beguile, deceive, defraud, swindle 8 hoodwink 9 bamboozle 11 double-cross

cozy: 4 easy, safe, snug 5 bield 6 chatty, secure, toasty 8 covering, familiar, homelike, sociable 9 contented, gemutlich, talkative 10 buddy-buddy, palsy-walsy 11 comfortable

cozy retreat: den 4 lair, nest, nook 5 ingle

crab: gin 4 beef, fuss, yawp 5 anger, gripe, maian, racer, winch 6 buster, cancer, grouse, hermit, peeler 7 buckler, fiddler, grumble 8 arachnid, irritate, windlass 9 horseshoe 10 crosspatch, crustacean, curmudgeon

abdomen: 5 apron

claw: 5 chela 6 nipper

constellation: 6 Cancer

fiddler: uca

genus: uca 6 birgus 7 limulus, squilla

resembling: 8 cancroid

suborder: 9 brachyura

crab apple: 5 malus, scrog

crabbed: 4 dour, glum, ugly 5 cabby, cross, testy 6 bitter, cranky, crusty, morose, rugged, sullen, trying 7 boorish, cramped, cornish, crooked, gnarled, knotted, obscure, peevish 8 churlish, contrary, petulant, vinegary 9 difficult, fractious, intricate, irregular 10 perplexing 11 intractable

crabgrass: 4 weed 9 digitaria

crabstick: 4 cane 5 crank, stick 6 cudgel

crabwood: 8 andiroba

crack: gag, pop 4 a-one, bang, blow, chap, chip, chop, clap, cone, flaw, jest, jibe, joke, kibe, leak, quip, rend, rift, rime, snap, yerk 5 brack, break, check, chine, chink, clack, cleft, craze, split 6 cleave, cranny 7 blemish, crackle, crevice, crevise, fissure 8 fracture 9 witticism 10 proficient

crack down on: 5 quash 6 attack 7 repress 10 discipline

crack up: 5 amuse, crash, extol, smash 8 collapse 9 break down

crackbrain: 8 crackpot 9 ding-a-ling, screwball

crackbrained: 5 crazy, kooky, nutty 7 erratic 12 unreasonable

cracker: 4 bake, liar 5 wafer 7 biscuit, boaster, breaker, burster, redneck, saltine, snapper 8 braggart, Georgian 11 firecracker

Cracker State: 7 Georgia

crackle: 4 snap 5 break, crack 7 brustle, crinkle, sparkle, sputter 9 crackling, crepitate

crackpot: nut 4 kook, loon 5 crank 7 erratic, lunatic 9 screwball

cracksman: 4 yegg 7 burglar, peteman

cradle: bed, cot 4 crib, rest, rock 5 cader, frame 6 creche 7 berceau, shelter 8 bassinet, cunabula 9 framework 11 incunabulum

song: 7 lullaby 8 berceuse

craft (see also boat): art, job 4 boat 5 fraud, guile, skill, trade 6 deceit, metier, talent, vessel 7 ability, know-how 8 aptitude, artifice, vocation 9 dexterity 10 employment, occupation 12 skillfulness

craftsman: 4 hand 5 navvy 6 artist, potter, weaver, writer 7 artisan, builder, workman 8 mechanic 9 artificer, carpenter

crafty: sly 4 arch, foxy, wily 5 adept 6 adroit, astute, callid, shrewd, subtle, tricky 7 cunning, vulpine 8 captious, fetching 9 cautelous, deceitful, ingenious 10 fallacious, fraudulent 13 Machiavellian 15 Mephistophelean

crag: tor 4 craw, neck, rock, scar, spur 5 arete, brack, cliff 6 throat 9 precipice

craggy: 5 harsh, rough 6 abrupt, knotty, rugged

crake: 4 bird, crow, rail, rook 5 raven 8 railbird

cram: wad 4 bone, fill, glut, pack, stow, urge 5 crowd, crush, drive, force, gorge, grind, learn, press, study, stuff, teach 6 bone up, review 7 jam-pack, squeeze

cramp: 4 coop, kink, pain 5 crick, crowd, pinch, stunt 6 hamper, hinder, knotty 7 confine 8 compress, contract, restrain, restrict 9 constrict, difficult 11 contraction *one's style:* 5 queer 9 frustrate

cranberry: 7 pembina 8 bilberry, foxberry 9 mossberry, sourberry
habitat: bog

crane: job 4 bird, grus 5 davit, heron, jenny, raise, wader 6 sarsus 7 derrick, stretch 9 cormorant 10 wading bird
arm: gib, jib 6 gibbet 7 ramhead
charges: 7 cranage
genus: 4 grus
Malayan: 5 sarus
neck: 4 gaze 5 stare
pert. to: 6 gruine
ship: 5 davit
small: 10 demoiselle
traveling: 5 jenny, titan 7 goliath

crane fly: 6 tipula

cranial nerve: 4 vagi(pl.) 5 vagus
root: 5 radix 5 radices(pl.)

cranium: pan 4 head 5 skull 8 brainpan
nerve root: 5 radix
part: 7 calotte 8 calvaria
pert. to: 7 cranial

crank: wit 4 bent, crab, kook, sick, weak, whim, wind 5 brace, loose, rogue, shaky, winch 6 ailing, boldly, grouch, handle, infirm 7 awkward, bracket, fanatic, lustily 8 crackpot, grumbler, sourpuss 9 distorted, eccentric, sprightly 10 get started, monomaniac, vigorously

cranky: 4 ugly 5 crazy, cross, lusty, shaky, testy 6 ailing, infirm, sickly 7 crooked, grouchy 8 tortuous 9 crotchety, difficult, irritable 10 ill-humored 11 hot-tempered 12 disagreeable

cranny: 4 hole, nook 5 chink, cleft, crack, niche 6 corner 7 crevice, fissure

crap: 5 dregs, money 7 gallows, greaves, rubbish 8 nonsense, sediment

crape: 4 band, curl, friz 5 crepe, crimp, drape, gauze 6 shroud 8 mourning

crapehanger: 7 killjoy 10 spoilsport

crapulence: 7 surfeit 8 gluttony 11 overfeeding 12 intemperance, intoxication

crash: 4 fail, fall 5 blast, burst, cloth, crush, shock, smash, sound, wreck 6 fiasco 7 failure, shatter, smashup 8 collapse, splinter 9 collision

crass: raw 4 dull, rude 5 crude, dense, gross, rough, thick 6 coarse, obtuse, stupid 9 unrefined

crate: box, car 4 case, crib 5 plane, seron 6 basket, cradle, encase, hamper, hurdle 7 canasta, vehicle 9 container 10 receptacle
bar: 4 slat

crater: cup, pit 4 cone, hole 5 fovea 6 cavity, hollow 7 caldera 10 depression
edge: lip

cravat: tie 4 neck 5 ascot, scarf, stock 7 bandage, necktie, overlay 8 crumpler 9

neckcloth 10 fourinhand 11 neckerchief

crave: ask, beg 4 long, need, pray, seek 5 covet, yearn 6 desire, hanker, hunger, thirst 7 beseech, entreat, implore, request, require, solicit 10 supplicate

craven: 6 afraid, coward, scared 7 dastard 8 cowardly, defeated, overcome, poltroon, recreant, sneaking 10 vanquished 11 lily-livered 12 fainthearted

craw: maw 4 crop 7 stomach 9 ingluvies

crawl: lag 4 drag, fawn, inch, ramp, swim 5 creep, kraal 6 cringe, grovel, scride 7 slither

crayfish: 4 crab 5 yabby 6 yabbie 7 crawdad, lobster 8 cambarus, crawfish 9 ecrevisse 10 crustacean

crayon: 4 plan 5 chalk 6 pastel, pencil, sketch 7 drawing

craze: fad 4 flaw, mode, rage 5 break, crack, crush, furor, mania, vogue 6 defect, impair, madden, weaken, whimsy 7 derange, destroy, fashion, shatter, whimsey 8 distract 9 bedlamize, infirmity 10 dernier cri 11 infatuation

crazed: mad, ree 4 amok, loco, wild, wood, zany 5 balmy, batty, daffy, dotty, manic, nutty, potty, wacky 6 coocoo, dottle, insane, looney 7 lunatic 8 deleerit, delieret, demented, deranged 10 crackbrain, distraught

crazy: mad 4 gaga, luny, nuts 5 batty, daffy, goofy, silly, wacky 6 absurd, cuckoo, insane, looney, maniac, teched 7 bananas, bonkers, cracked, lunatic 8 crackpot, demented 9 possessed 10 crackbrain, unbalanced 11 harebrained 12 preposterous

creak: gig 4 rasp, yirr 5 cheep(Sc.), croak, grind, groan 6 squeak 8 complain

cream: 4 beat, best, pick, whip 5 creme, elite, froth, sauce 6 bonbon 8 emulsion, ointment

cream of tartar: 5 argol

cream puff: 6 pastry 8 weakling

creamery: 5 dairy

creamy: 4 rich 5 reamy 6 smooth 8 luscious

crease: 4 fold, lirk, ruck, ruga, seam 5 crimp, pleat 6 furrow, rimple 7 crumple, wrinkle

create: 4 coin, form, make, plan 5 build, cause, forge, shape, write 6 design, invent 7 compose, fashion, imagine, produce 8 generate 9 establish, originate

creation: 5 world 6 cosmos, effect 7 fashion, product 8 creature, universe 9 macrocosm 10 production 11 masterpiece

creative: 9 demiurgic, inventive 10 innovative, productive 12 constructive

creativity: 6 genius

creator: 5 maker 6 author 7 founder 8 designer 9 architect 10 originator

creature (see also **animal**): man 4 tool 5 beast, being, slave, thing 6 animal, minion, person, wretch 8 hellicat(Sc.) 9 dependent 10 animalcule, individual

fabled: elf 4 puck 5 gnome 6 dragon, merman 7 centaur, mermaid

ogre: 5 pixie 6 wyvern

creche: 4 crib 6 manager 7 nursery

credence: 5 faith, trust 6 belief, buffet, credit 8 credenza 10 acceptance, confidence 11 reliability 15 trustworthiness

credential: 7 voucher 8 credence 11 certificate, testimonial

credenza: 5 niche, shelf, table 6 buffet 8 credence, cupboard 9 sideboard

credible: 6 likely 7 credent 8 probable 9 authentic, plausible, reputable 11 trustworthy 12 satisfactory

credit: 4 deem, feel, loan 5 asset, chalk, faith, honor, merit, tenet, trust 6 belief, charge, esteem, impute, renown, repute, weight 7 ascribe, believe 8 accredit, credence 10 estimation 11 recognition

credulous: 4 fond 5 naive 6 unwary 8 credible, gullible

creed: ism 4 cult, sect 5 credo, dogma, faith, tenet 6 belief 7 trowing 8 doctrine 10 confession

Christian: 6 Nicene 8 Apostle's

creek: bay, ria, rio 4 burn(Sc.), cove, kill, pill, rill, slue 5 bayou, bight, bogue, brook, crick, fleet, inlet, zanja 6 arroyo, estero, Indian, slough, stream 7 estuary, freshet, rivulet 11 watercourse

creel: 4 caul, cawl, rack, trap 6 basket, junket

creep: 4 fawn, inch, ramp 5 crawl, prowl, skulk, slink, steal 6 cringe, grovel, scride 7 cramble, gumshoe 9 pussyfoot

creeper: ivy 4 shoe, vine, worm 5 snake 6 ipecac, romper, tecoma

creeping: 4 slow 7 reptant, servile 9 reptilian 11 reptatorial

creese: 4 kris, stab 5 sword 6 dagger, weapon

cremate: 4 burn 9 incremate 10 incinerate

Cremona: 5 Amati 6 violin

crena: 5 cleft, notch 7 scallop 11 indentation

crenic acid salt: 7 crenate

creole: 6 patois 7 mestizo

Creole State: 9 Louisiana

crepe: 4 fabric 7 frizzed, pancake 8 crinkled, wrinkled

crepey cloth: 6 plissé

crepitate: 4 snap 6 rattle 7 crackle

crepuscule: 8 twilight

crescent: 4 horn, lune, moon, rool 5 curve, lunar 6 lunule 7 lunette, menis-

ci(pl.) 8 meniscus 10 semicircle

point: 4 cusp

crescent-shaped: 6 bicorn, lunate 7 lunated, lunular 9 semilunar

crescive: 7 growing 10 increasing

cresset: 5 torch 6 basket, beacon, signal 7 furnace 8 flambeau

crest: cop, tip, top 4 acme, apex, comb, edge, knap, peak, seal, tuft 5 chine, crown, plume, ridge 6 apogee, climax, copple, crista, finial, height, helmet, summit 7 bearing 8 pinnacle, whitecap 10 cognizance 11 culmination

rugged: 6 arete

crested: 6 muffed 7 crisate, crowned 8 pileated 9 coronated

crestfallen: low 4 blue, down 5 cowed 8 dejected 10 dispirited 11 downhearted 12 disconsolate

creta: 5 chalk

cretaceous: 6 chalky

Crete: 6 Candia

cape: 4 krio 5 krios

city: Hag 5 Canea(c.), Khora 6 Kisamo, Malemi, Mallia, Meleme, Retimo 7 Kasteli 8 Nikolacs, Sphakion 9 Heraclion, Tympakion 11 Palaiokhora

earth spirit: 6 Curete

flier: 6 Icarus

goddess: 8 Dictynna 11 Britomartis

king: 5 Minos 9 Idomeneus

language: 6 Minoan

man of brass: 5 Talos

maze: 9 labyrinth

monster: 8 minotaur

mountain: Ida 5 Dikte 9 Psiloriti

princess: 7 Ariadne

seaport: 5 Canea 6 Candia, Khania

Cretheus: *son:* 8 Amythaon

wife: 7 Biadice

cretin: 5 idiot

Creusa: *father:* 5 Priam

husband: 6 Aeneas

mother: 6 Hecuba

son: 8 Ascanius

crevasse: 5 chasm, split 8 cleavage

crevice: 4 bore, leak, nook, seam, vein 5 break, chine, chink, cleft, crack, grike 6 cranny 7 fissure, opening 8 cleavage, crevasse, peephole 10 interstice

crew: men, mob, set 4 band, gang, herd, oars, team 5 covey, group, hands, party, squad, staff 6 seamen, throng 7 company, faculty, members, retinue 8 equipage, mariners 10 assemblage, complement

crewel: 6 caddis 7 caddice 10 crewelwork, embroidery

crib: bed, bin, box, cab, cot, cub, hut, key 4 boom, dive, pony, rack, raft, trot 5 boose, boosy, cheat, crate, frame, hovel, stall, steal 6 bunker, cratch, creche,

manger, pilfer 7 purloin 8 cribbage 9
enclosure 10 plagiarize, storehouse
cribbage score: nob, peg
crick: 4 kink 5 creek, hitch, spasm, twist
cricket: 4 game, grig 6 insect
genus: 7 gryllus
run: bye
side: ons
sound: 5 chirp 12 stridulation
team: 6 eleven
term: off, ons, rot 4 over 5 smick 6 yorker
crier: 4 huer 5 cryer 6 beadle, herald,
wailer 7 muezzin
crime: act, sin 4 evil 5 abuse, arson,
blame, wrong 6 felony, murder, piacle 7
misdeed, offense 8 iniquity 9 violation
10 wickedness 11 abomination, malefaction, misdemeanor 13 transgression
ecclesiastical: 6 simony
goddess of: Ate
organized: 10 underworld
scene of: 5 venue
Crimea: 4 Krym
capital: 10 Simferopol
city: 5 Kerch, Yalta 10 Sevastopol
people: 6 Tauri
river: 4 Alma
sea: 4 Azof, Azov
seaport: 9 Balaklava
criminal: bad 4 yegg 5 crook, felon 6
guilty, inmate, nocent, slayer, wicked 7
convict, culprit, illegal 8 culpable, gangster 9 desperado, wrongdoer 10 blackguard, deplorable, flagitious, malefactor,
malfeasant 11 blameworthy, disgraceful
13 reprehensible
habitual: 8 repeater 10 recidivist
refuge: 7 Alsatia 11 Whitefriars
criminology branch: 8 penology
crimp: bit, rub 4 bend, curl, fold, friz,
pote, wave, weak 5 cramp, flute, frizz,
pinch, plait 6 goffer, hold in, ruffle 7
crinkle, friable, gauffer, wrinkle 8 hold
back, obstacle 9 corrugate 12 inconsistent
crimson: dye, lac, red 4 pink, rose 5
blush, color, rouge 6 bloody, maroon,
modena 7 carmine, scarlet
crine: 4 hair, mane 6 shrink 7 shrivel
cringe: bow 4 bend, fawn, jouk 5 binge,
cower, crawl, quail, sneak, stoop, toady,
wince, yield 6 crouch, grovel, shrink,
submit 7 crinkle, distort, truckle 8
bootlick 11 apple-polish
cringing: 6 abject 7 hangdog
cringle: orb 4 disk 6 eyelet, terret 7
grommet
crinite: 6 hairy 6 fossil
crinitory: 5 hairy 7 crinose
crinkle: 4 bend, curl, kink, turn, wind 5
crimp, plica, ridge 6 pucker, ripple,
ruck up, rumple, rustle 7 crackle, wrin-

kle 9 corrugate 11 convolution
cripple: mar 4 halt, harm, hurt, lame,
main, wing 6 bacach, hobble, impair,
injure, scotch, spavin, weaken 7 crap-
ple, crumpet, disable, lamiter(Sc.) 8 enfeeble, handicap, mutilate, paralyze 9
hamstring 12 incapacitate
crisis: 4 acme, crux, pass, turn 5 panic,
peril, pinch, trial 6 strait 8 decision,
juncture 9 criterion, emergency, crossroads 11 conjunction 12 turning point
having no: 9 acritical
crisp: new 4 cold 5 brisk, clear, curly,
fresh, nippy, pithy, sharp, short, stiff,
terse 6 biting, bright, lively 7 bracing,
brittle, concise, cutting, friable 8 clear-
cut 9 crackling, trenchant
crispin: 4 coat 9 shoemaker
crisscross: 4 awry 7 network 8 confused
9 intersect
cristate: 6 ridged, tufted 7 crested
criterion: low 4 norm, rule, test, type 5
axiom, canon, gauge, nodel, proof 6
metric 7 measure 8 standard 9 yardstick 10 indication, touchstone
critic: 4 booer, judge, momus 6 carper,
censor, expert, slater 8 collator, reviewer 9 detractor, literator, muckraker, nit-
picker 11 connoisseur, criticaster,
faultfinder
critical: 4 dire, edge 5 acute, exact 6 urgent 7 carping, exigent 8 captious, decisive, exacting 10 censorious, fastidious
12 faultfinding 14 discriminating
mark: 6 obelus 7 obelisk
study: 6 examen 8 exegesis
criticism: 5 blame 6 review 7 comment 8
critique, diatribe, judgment 9 stricture
10 assessment, commentary 13 animadversion
criticize: hit, pan, rap, rip 4 carp, flay,
slam, slur, yelp 5 blame, blast, cavil,
judge, knock, roast 6 jeer at, rebuke, review 7 censure, comment, examine 8
critique 9 castigate 10 animadvert
Crius: *father:* 6 Uranus
mother: 4 Gaea, Gaia
sister: 7 Eurybia
son: 8 Astraeus
croak: caw, die 4 gasp, kill 5 creak, quark,
speak, 6 grouch, grouse 7 forbode,
grumble 8 complain
Croatia: *capital:* 5 Agram 6 Zagreb
city: 5 Fiume, Rieka, Split 6 Osijek, Rijeka
mountain: 6 Kapela
people: 4 Serb, Slav, Sorb, Wend 5 Sclav 6
Hrvati 7 Hervati, Slovene 8 Croatian,
European
crochet: 4 hoot, knit 5 braid, plait, weave
crock: jar, pig, pot 4 bull, smut, soil, soot
5 stool 6 critch, smudge 8 potsherd 11
earthenware

crockery: 5 china, cloam 6 dishes, plates 11 earthenware

crocodile: goa 5 gator 6 cayman, gavial, jacare, mugger 7 reptile 9 alligator
genus: 11 goniopholis

crocus: 4 irid, lily 7 saffron

Croesus: 4 king 9 moneybags, plutocrat
country: 5 Lydia

croft: 4 farm 5 crypt, field, garth, vault 6 bleach, cavern

cromlech: 5 quoit 6 circle, dolmen 7 gorsedd 9 cyclolith

Cromwell: 4 Noll 6 Oliver
regiment: 9 Ironsides
son: 7 Richard
son-in-law: 6 Ireton
victory site: 6 Naseby

crone: hag 4 cive 5 biddy, witch 6 beldam 7 beldame 9 cailleach, cailliach

Cronus: 5 Titan
daughter: 4 Hera 6 Hestia 7 Demeter
father: 6 Uranus
mother: 4 Gaea
sister: 6 Cybele, Tethys
son: 4 Zeus 5 Hades 7 Jupiter, Neptune 8 Poseidon
wife: 4 Rhea 6 Cybele

crony: pal 4 chum 9 associate, companion

crook: 4 bend, turn, warp 5 cheat, cleek, crump, curve, pedum, staff, thief, trick 6 robber 7 crosier, crozier 8 artifice, swindler 10 camshachle(Sc.)

crooked: cam 4 agee, awry, bent 5 agley(Sc.), askew, false, gleed, lying, snaky, snide 6 akimbo, artful, aslant, crabby, crafty, curved, errant, shifty, tricky, zigzag 7 askance, asquint, corrupt, crabbed, oblique, turning, twisted, winding 8 tortuous 9 dishonest, distorted, irregular 10 circuitous, fraudulent, misleading 12 dishonorable, unscrupulous

croon: hum, low 4 boom, lull, sing, wail 5 chirm, whine 6 lament, murmur 8 complain

crop: cut, maw, top 4 clip, craw, knap, reap, trim, whip 5 fruit, quirt, shear 6 gather, gebbie, silage 7 curtail, harvest, tillage 8 gleaning, inglutes
goddess of: 5 Annona
second growth: 5 rowen
year's: 6 annona

cropper: 8 collapse, disaster

croquet: 5 roque

croquette: 5 cecil, 6 oyster

crosier, crozier: 5 crook, cross, staff

cross: go; mix 4 ford, rood, span 5 angry, testy, trial 6 bisect, crabby, cranky, crouch, emblem, gibbet, grumpy, outwit, signum, sullen, symbol, thwart, touchy 7 athwart, crabbed, fretful, froward, oblique, peevish, pettish, potence,

sell out 8 crotched, crucifix, petulant, snappish, suastica, swastika, traverse, vexillum 9 frustrate, half-breed, intersect, irritable, plaintive 10 affliction, ill-humored, transverse 12 disagreeable 13 quick-tempered
barred: 11 trabeculate
fiery: 8 crantara 9 crostarie
Greek: 6 fylfot
stroke: 5 serif 6 ceriph
swords: 4 dael 5 fight 6 combat
tau: 4 crux 5 ankih
type: 5 Greek, Latin, Papal 6 Celtic, fleuré, formée, moline 7 Maltese 8 Egyptian
wires: 9 confuse

cross-examine: 5 grill 8 question 11 interrogate

cross-eye: 6 squint 9 esotropia 10 strabismus

cross-grained: 7 gnarled 8 churlish, perverse 9 irascible 12 cantankerous

cross out: 4 dele 5 blank, erase 6 cancel, delete 9 eliminate

cross-rib: 4 arch 6 lierne

cross section: 4 part 14 representation

crossbar: 4 axle, rung 5 round 10 horizontal

crossbeam: bar 5 trave 6 girder

crossbow: 6 weapon 8 arbalest

crossbreed: 5 husky 6 hybrid 9 hybridize

crosshatch: 7 engrave

crossing: 7 passage 8 opposing

crosspatch: 4 bear, crab 6 grouch

crosspiece: bar 4 spar, yoke 5 grill 7 crossarm 10 doubletree

crossroads: 4 pass 5 pinch 6 crisis 8 zero hour 9 carrefour 12 interaction, turning point
goddess: 6 Hecate, Hekate, Trivia

crossruff: 6 seesaw 9 alternate

crosswise: 6 across 7 athwart 8 acrostic, diagonal

crotch: 4 fork, pole, post 5 cleft, notch, stake 9 stanchion

crotchet: fad 4 hook, kink, whim 5 fancy 6 vagary 9 conundrum 11 peculiarity 12 eccentricity

crotchery: 6 cranky 10 capricious

crotch: 4 bend, fawn, ruck 5 cower, hunch, squat, stoop 6 cringe 7 scrooch

crouching: 8 couchant

crouton: bit 5 toast 7 garnish

crow: aga, caw, cry, daw, jay 4 bird, brag, rook 5 boast, exult, raven, vaunt 6 carnal, corvas, magpie 7 grapnel, jackdaw, swagger 9 blackbird
colony: 7 rookery
cry: caw
pert. to: 7 corvine

crow-like: 7 corvine

crowbar: pry 5 jemmy, jimmy, lever 7

gablock 8 gavelock

crowd: jam, mob, set 4 bike, cram, herd, host, pack, push, rock, rout, stow, swad 5 bunch, cramp, crush, drove, flock, group, horde, posse, press, serry, shoal, swarm, three, wedge 6 boodle, clique, hubble, huddle, jostle, rabble, throng 7 bourock(Sc.), company, squeeze 9 multitude 10 assemblage, clamjamfry(Sc.), confluence

penetrate: 5 elbow 6 needle

crowded: 4 full 5 close, dense, thick 6 filled, jammed, loaded, packed 7 bunched, compact, serried, stipate, stuffed, teeming 9 chock-full, congested

crowder: 6 loader 7 fiddler 8 thatcher

crown: cap, top 4 coin, pate, peak, poll 5 adorn, basil, bezel, bezil, crest, miter, mitre, tiara 6 anadem, circle, climax, corona(L.), diadem, fillet, invest, laurel, potong, reward, summit, trophy, wreath 7 aureole, chaplet, coronet, garland, install 8 coronate, enthrone, pinnacle, surmount 9 finish off, headdress, sovereign

pert. to: 8 coronal

crown prince: 4 heir 8 atheling

cru: 8 vineyard

crucial: 4 dire 5 acute, vital 6 severe, trying 7 pivotal, telling 8 critical, decisive 9 important, necessary

crucible: pot 4 dish, etna, test 6 cruset, ordeal, retort 7 furnace 10 affliction 11 climacteric

crucifix: pax 4 rood 5 cross

crucify: vex 4 hang, kill 5 harry 6 martyr 7 mortify, torment, torture 8 cruciate 9 persecute

crud: goo 4 curd, gook, gunk, junk 5 filth, slime, trash 6 refuse 7 thicken

crude: raw 4 bald, bare, rude 5 crass, green, harsh, rough 6 callow, coarse, savage, unripe, vulgar 7 uncouth 8 immature, impolite 9 primitive, unglossed, unrefined, untrained 10 incomplete, unpolished 11 undeveloped 13 inexperienced

cruel: 4 fell, hard 5 harsh 6 bloody, brutal, fierce, savage, severe, unjust, unkind 7 bestial, brutish, inhuman, neronic 8 barbaric, diabolic, fiendish, inhumane, pitiless, ruthless, sadistic, tyrannic 9 atrocious, draconian, ferocious, heartless, merciless, rapacious, unfeeling 10 diabolical, sanguinary, vindictive 11 hardhearted

cruet: ama, jar, jug 4 vial 5 cruse 6 bottle, caster, guttus, vessel 7 ampulla, burette 9 container

cruise: 4 boat, sail, trip 6 voyage 9 excursion

cruiser: 4 ship 6 vessel 7 warship 9 patrol car, powerboat

cruising: 4 asea

cruller: 7 olycook, olykoek 8 doughnut 9 friedcake

crumb: bit, ort 5 piece, scrap, shred 6 little, morsel 7 remnant, smidgen, smidgin 8 fragment, particle

crumb covered: 7 breaded

crumble: rot 5 break, crush, decay, slake, spoil 6 molder, perish 7 moulder 9 break down, decompose, pulverize 12 disintegrate

crumbly: 7 friable

crumpet: 4 cake 6 muffin 7 pikelet

crumple: 4 fold, muss 5 crush 6 crease, furrow, raffle, rumple 7 crunkle, wrinkle 8 collapse, contract 9 corrugate

crunch: 4 bite, chew 5 chomp, crump, crush, gnash, grind, munch, press 6 cranch 7 craunch, scrunch 8 ruminate 9 masticate

cruor: 4 gore 5 blood

crural joint: 4 knee

crus: 5 shank

crusade: war 5 jehad, jihad 8 campaign 10 expedition

crusader: 7 pilgrim, Templar 8 reformer

enemy: 7 Saladin, Saracen

port: 4 Acre

crush: bow, jam 4 cram, dash, mash, mill, mull 5 brake, break, crash, craze, crowd, force, grind, press, quash, quell, smash, tread, unman 6 bruise, burden, crunch, squash, subdue, thwack 7 conquer, crumple, depress, destroy, oppress, overrun, repress, scrunch, scrunge, shatter, squeeze, squelch 8 bear down, compress, demolish, overcome, suppress 9 overpower, overwhelm, pulverize 10 annihilate, obliterate

crust: 4 cake, hull, rind 5 shell 6 eschar, harden 7 coating 8 pellicle

crustacean: 4 crab, flea, scud 5 louse, prawn 6 endite, isopod, shrimp 7 lobster, squilla 8 barnacle 9 water flea 10 whale louse

appendage: 5 exite 6 endite 7 pleopod

claw: 5 chela 6 pincer

feeler: 7 antenna

genus: 5 eryon, hippa 6 tripos

group: 7 caridea

larva: 5 alima, 8 nauplius

limb: 6 podite 8 podomere

small: 6 isopod 7 copepod 8 barnacle

ten-footed: 4 crab

crusty: 4 curt 5 bluff, blunt, crisp, gruff, surly, testy 6 morose 7 crabbed, peevish, pettish 8 choleric, snappish 11 illtempered

crux: nub 4 ankh, core, gist, pith 5 cross, point 6 kernel, puzzle, riddle 7 problem 9 substance 10 difficulty cry (see also **exclamation**): boo, caw, cri(F.), fad, hue, ole, sob, yip 4 bawl, bump, call, evoe, hawk, hoot, howl, keen, mewl, pule, rage, scry, wail, weep, yell, yelp 5 clepe, crede, greet, groan, rumor, shout, sound, utter, vogue, whewl, whine 6 bellow, boohoo, clamor, demand, lament, outcry, quethe, scream, shriek, slogan, snivel, squeal, squall, wimick, yammer 7 clamour, exclaim, fashion, screech 8 proclaim 11 acclamation, lamentation

court: 4 oyes, oyez

derisive: bah, boo 4 hiss, hoot 6 phooey 7 catcall

for: 4 need 6 demand, desire

gang's signal: 4 whyo

havoc: 8 mobilize

of approval: ole, rah 5 bravo

of pain: 4 ouch

of relief: 4 phew, whew

of sorrow: woe 4 alas 5 alack

of triumph: aha 6 hurrah

out: bay 4 bawl, hoot, howl 5 blame, crake, deery 7 censure, exclaim, protest 8 complain, denounce

political: 6 slogan 10 shibboleth

Cry the Beloved Country author: 5 Paton

crying: 4 dire 6 urgent 7 burning, clamant, heinous 8 pressing, recreant 9 notorious 11 exclamatory

crying bird: 7 limpkin

crying hare: 4 pika

crying out: 10 childbirth 11 confinement

crypt: pit 4 cave, cell 5 croft, vault 6 cavern, grotto, recess 7 chamber 8 follicle 10 depression

cryptic: 4 dark 5 murky, vague 6 hidden, occult, secret 7 obscure 9 enigmatic, recondite 10 mysterious 12 hieroglyphic

cryptogram: 4 code 6 cipher 11 cryptograph

crystal: ice 4 dial, hard 5 clear, glass, lucid 6 limpid, pebble 7 acicula, diamond 8 clear-cut, pellucid 11 crystalline, transparent

gazer: 4 seer 7 seeress

ice: 6 frazil

twin: 5 macle

crystalline: 4 pure 7 crystal 8 pellucid 11 transparent

acid: 7 alanine

compound: 5 alban 6 anisil, oscine 7 aconite, amarine 8 atropine

mineral: 4 mica, spar 6 quartz 7 apatite 8 boracite, elaterin

phenol: 5 orcin 6 orcine

pine tar: 6 retene

salt: 5 borax 8 analgene, racemate

structure: 6 sparry 8 siderite

substance: 4 urea 6 dulcin 9 scopoline

crystallize: 5 candy, sugar 7 congeal 8 solidify 9 granulate

cub: fry, pen 4 bear, coop, shed 5 stall, whelp 6 lionet, novice 7 codling 8 reporter 9 youngster

Cuba: *bay:* 4 Nipe, Pigs 10 Guantanamo

beverage: 4 pina

bird: 6 trogon 8 tocororo

capital: 6 Havana

carriage: 7 volante

castle: 5 Morro

chief export: 5 sugar

cigar: 6 Havana

city: 6 Guines 7 Palmira 8 Camaguey, Matanzas, Santiago 10 Cienfuegos, Santa Clara 14 Puerto Principe

dance: 5 conga, rumba 6 danzon, rhumba

dollar: 6 gourde

fish: 6 diablo 7 viajaca

hutia: 6 pilori

measure: 4 vara 5 bocoy, tarea 6 cordel, fanega 10 caballeria

monetary unit: 4 peso 7 centavo 8 cuarenta

mountain: 6 Copper 11 Pinar del Rio 12 Guaniguanico 13 Pico Turquinos

premier: 6 Castro

province: 6 Havana 7 Oriente 8 Camaguey, Matanzas 10 Santa Clara 11 Pinar del Rio

rodent: 5 hutia 6 pilori

root: 7 malanga

rum: 7 Bacardi

secret police: 5 porra

snake: 4 juba

storm: 6 bayamo

tobacco: 4 capa 6 vuelta

U.S. naval base: 10 Guantanamo

tree: 4 cuya 5 culla, jique

ward: 6 barrio

weapon: 7 machete

weight: 5 libra 6 tercio

cubbyhole: 5 nook

cube: cut, die 4 dice 5 block, solid 10 hexahedron

cube spar: 9 anhydrite

cubic: 5 solid 9 isometric

decimeter: 5 liter, litre

meter: 5 stere

shape: 6 cuboid

cubicle: bay 4 cell, room 5 booth, niche 6 alcove

cubitus: 4 ulna 7 forearm

Cuchulain, Cuchullin: 7 warrior

father: Lug

foe: 5 Maeve

kingdom: 6 Ulster

mother: 8 Dechtire

son: 8 Conlaoch

wife: 4 Emer 5 Eimer

cuckoo: ani 4 bird, fool, gowk, koel 5 clock, crazy, silly 7 boobook 8 rainfowl 10 road runner
kind: 6 coucal, kobird 7 dowbird, wryneck 8 coccyzus

cuckoopint: 4 arum 5 aaron, plant 6 bobbin, dragon 7 buckram 8 mandrake 9 wake-robin

cucullate: 6 cowled, hooded 7 covered 10 hood-shaped

cucumber: 4 cuke, pepo, gourd 6 conger, pepino(Sp.), pickle 7 gherkin 9 elaterium

cud: chew, quid 5 bolus, rumen 6 cudgel

cuddle: hug, pet 6 caress, cosset, fondle, nestle 7 embrace, snuggle

cuddy: ass 4 lout 5 bribe, cabin 6 donkey, galley, pantry 9 blockhead

cudgel: bat 4 beat, cane, club, drub, rack 5 baste, drive, kebby, kevel, staff, stave, stick 6 alpeen, ballow, baston, kebbie, thrash, weapon 7 belabor, bourdon 8 bludgeon, shillala 9 bastinado, blackjack, crabstick, fustigate, truncheon 10 nightstick, shillelagh

cue: nod, tip 4 hint, mast, tail, wink 5 braid, cluff, plait, queue, twist 6 prompt, signal 7 pigtail 9 catchword 10 intimation

cuff: box 4 bank, blow, gowf, slam, slap, slug, swat 5 clout, fight, gowff, miser, smite, spank 6 buffet, codger, mitten, strike, wallop 7 scuffle 8 gauntlet, handcuff

cuirass: 4 mail 5 armor, loric, plate 6 lorica, thorax

cuisine: 4 food, menu 5 table 7 cookery

cul-de-sac: 6 pocket, strait 7 deadend, impasse 10 blind alley, difficulty

culicid: 8 mosquito

cull: opt 4 dupe, gull, pick, sift, sort 5 elect, glean, pluck 6 assort, choose, gather, remove, select 8 separate 9 single out

culm: 5 slack 6 refuse 7 deposit

culmen: top 4 acme 5 ridge

culmination: end 4 acme, apex, noon, peak 5 crown 6 apogee, climax, summit, vertex, zenith 10 completion 11 ne plus ultra 12 consummation

culpa: 5 fault, guilt 10 negligence 2 carelessness

culpable: 6 faulty, guilty, laches 7 immoral 8 criminal 10 censurable 11 blameworthy 5 reprehensible

culprit: 5 felon 7 convict 8 criminal, offender 10 malefactor

cult: 4 clan, sect 5 creed, faith 6 church, ritual, school 7 worship 8 religion 12 denomination

cultivate: ear, hoe 4 disk, farm, grow, plow, rear, tend, till, work 5 nurse,

raise, study, train 6 affect, foster, harrow, plough 7 acquire, cherish, educate, husband, improve, nourish, prepare 8 civilize 9 encourage

cultivated: 5 civil 6 polite 7 genteel, refined 8 cultured, well-bred 12 domesticated
land: 4 farm 5 arada, tilth

cultivation: 6 polish 7 culture, tillage 9 culturing, husbandry 10 refinement 12 civilization
art: 9 geoponics

cultivator: 6 farmer, harrow, tiller 7 grubber, husband 10 husbandman

culture: art 4 agar 5 taste 6 polish 7 tillage 9 knowledge 10 discipline, refinement 11 savoir faire 12 civilization 13 enlightenment
medium: 4 agar

culver: 4 dove 6 pigeon

culvert: 5 drain, sluit 6 bridge 7 conduit 8 overpass

cumbersome: 5 heavy 6 clumsy 7 awkward, onerous, weighty 8 cumbrous, unwieldy 10 burdensome

cumbrous: 8 clogging, unwieldy 9 difficult, vexatious 10 burdensome, cumbersome

cumin: 5 anise, cumic

cummerbund: 4 band, belt, sash

cumshaw: tip 5 bonus 6 thanks 7 present 8 gratuity

cumulate: 4 heap 5 amass, lay up 6 gather 7 combine 9 stockpile 10 accumulate

cunabula: 6 cradle

cuneal: 7 cuneate 11 wedge-shaped

cuneiform: 4 bone 6 wedged 7 writing 8 sphenoid

cunner: 5 canoe 6 nipper, wrasse

cunning: sly, wit 4 arch, cute, foxy, keen, wily 5 downy, guile, sharp, smart 6 adroit, artful, astute, callid, clever, crafty, deadal, deceit, shrewd, subtle, tricky, wisdom 7 curious, finesse, know-how, politic, vulpine 8 dextrous, skillful, stealthy 9 chicanery, colubrine, designing, dexterity, ingenious, knowledge, sagacious 10 fraudulent, witchcraft 3 Machiavellian

cup: ama, dop, mug, tyg 4 tass, toby 5 bouse, calix, cruse, glass, grail, phial, stein, tazza 6 beaker, crater, goblet, noggin, potion, vessel 7 chalice, stirrup, tankard
assay: 4 test 5 cupel 6 beaker
diamond cutting: dop
eared: 6 quaich, quaigh
earthenware: mug
fungus: 6 aecium
handle: ear, lug
holder: 4 zarf

horn-shaped: 6 holmos

large: 5 grail, jorum

looped handles: 5 kylix 9 cantharus, kantharos

loving: tyg 5 award, prize

of tea: 5 forte, thing 6 metier

pastry: 7 dariole

resembling: 9 oalicular

small: 4 shot 5 chark, cruse 6 noggin 8 cannikin 9 demitasse

sports: 5 Davis, Ryder 6 Curtis 7 Stanley 8 America's, Wightman

two-handled: tig, tyg 5 depas

cup-shaped: 8 pezizoid, scypliate 10 cyathiform

cupbearer of the gods: 4 Hebe 8 Ganymede

cupboard: kas 4 case, safe 5 ambry, cuddy 6 buffet, closet, larder, pantry 7 armoire, cabinet, dresser 8 credenza 9 sideboard

cupel: 4 burn, test 6 refine

Cupid: Dan 4 Amor, Eros, love 7 Amorino

beloved of: 6 Psyche

mother: 5 Venus

cupidity: 4 lust 5 greed 6 desire 7 avarice, avidity, longing 8 appetite 12 covetousness

demon of: 6 Mammon

cupola: 4 dome, kiln 5 vault 6 turret 7 furnace, lantern, lookout

cur: cad, dog, yap 4 fice, mutt, tike, toad, tyke 5 feist 6 canine, messan, messin, rotter 7 bobtail, mongrel 9 goldeneye, yellow dog

curacao: 7 liqueur

Curacao island: 5 Aruba

curare: 5 urare, urari 6 oorali, poison

curassow: 4 crax, mitu 8 game bird

curate: cur 4 abbe 5 agent 7 dominie, vicaire 8 minister 9 assistant, clergyman

curative: 7 healing 8 remedial, salutary, sanative 9 medicinal 11 restorative, therapeutic 12 invigorating

curator: 6 keeper 7 manager, steward 8 guardian, overseer 9 custodian 14 superintendent

curb: bit 4 foil, rein 5 brake, check, curve, guard, limit 6 arrest, bridle, govern, hamper, thwart 7 control, inhibit, repress, shackle 8 hold back, hold down, moderate, restrain, restrict, withhold 9 constrain, hindrance 10 hamshackle

curculio: 4 turk 6 weevil

curd: See **curdle**

curdle: 4 clot, earn(Sc.), leep, quar, sour, yern 5 quail, quarl, spoil 6 posset, quarle 7 clabber, congeal, thicken 8 condense 9 coagulate

agent causing: 6 rennet

cure: age, 4 boot, care, heal, heed, help, jerk, salt, save 5 reest, smoke 6 charge,

curacy, physic, remedy, season 7 restore, therapy 8 antidote, preserve

by smoking: 6 gammon, smudge

in sun: 6 rizzar

skins: 5 dress

cure-all: 4 balm 5 avens 6 elixir, remedy 7 nostrum, panacea 10 catholicon

curfew: 4 bell 6 signal

curio: 5 relic, virtu 6 bauble, gewgaw 7 bibelot 8 keepsake, souvenir 9 bric-a-brac, curiosity, objet d'art 10 knickknack

curious: odd 4 nosy, rare 5 queer 6 prying, quaint 7 cunning, strange, unusual 8 freakish, meddling, peculiar, singular 9 intrusive, wondering 11 inquisitive

curl: 4 bend, coil, kink, lock, roll, wave, wind 5 acker, crisp, tress, twist 6 buckle, frowse, ripple, spiral, writhe 7 crimple, flexure, ringlet, tendril 11 convolution 12 heartbreaker

curled: 5 fuzzy, kinky 7 savoyed

curlew: 4 bird, fute 5 kioea, snipe, whaup 6 marlin, smoker 7 bustard

curlicue: ess 5 caper, curve 6 paraph, squirl 7 souggle 8 flourish, purlicue, squiggle

curling mark: tee

curly: 4 wavy 5 crisp 7 rippled 8 crinkled

curmudgeon: 4 crab 5 churl, miser 6 grouch 7 niggard

currant: 5 berry 6 raisin, rizzar

genus: 5 ribes

currency: 4 cash, coin 5 bills, lucre, money, scrip 6 specie 10 greenbacks 11 legal tender

current: now, way 4 eddy, flow, flux, ford, rife, tide 5 drift, going, rapid, tenor, trend, usual 6 coeval, common, course, living, motion, moving, recent, stream 7 counter, flowing, general, ongoing, present, running, thermal, torrent 8 frequent 9 prevalent 10 prevailing 11 electricity 15 contemporaneous

generator: electromotor

measuring device: 7 ammeter

ocean: 7 riptide 8 undertow 9 maelstrom, whirlpool

pert. to: 7 voltaic

currish: 4 base 7 cynical, ignoble 8 snarling 12 mean-spirited

curry: 4 comb, drub 5 clean, dress, groom 6 bruise, cajole, powder 7 prepare 9 condiment, seasoning

favor: 4 fawn 6 cajole, smooge

curse: ban 4 bane, blow, damn, oath 5 spell, swear 6 malign 7 beshrew, malison 8 anathema 9 blaspheme, imprecate, maranatha 10 execration, vituperate 11 deprecation, malediction 12 anathematize 13 excommunicate

cursed: bad 6 damned, odious 8 blighted,

virulent 9 execrable 13 blankety-blank

cursory: 4 fast 5 brief, hasty, quick, short 6 fitful, speedy 7 passing, shallow, sketchy 8 careless, rambling 9 desultory, irregular, transient 10 discursive, evanescent 11 superficial

curt: 4 rude, tart 5 bluff, blunt, brief, brusk, short, terse 6 abrupt 7 brusque, concise 8 cavalier, succinct 9 condensed

curtail: cut, lop 4 clip, crop, dock, pare, stop 5 abate, short, slash, stunt 6 lessen, reduce, teaser 7 abridge, bobtail, shorten 8 diminish, minorate, retrench 9 decurtate, epitomize 10 abbreviate

curtain: end 4 boom, drop, mask, veil, wall 5 blind, drape, shade 6 purdah, screen, shroud 7 ceiling, conceal, drapery 8 portiere

half: 4 bise, cafe 5 brise

holder: rod

raiser: 9 forepiece

curtains: end 5 death 6 demise 7 decease, drapery

curtilage: 4 quad, yard 5 court 9 enclosure 10 fenced area

curtsy, curtsey: bob, bow 4 beck 5 conge 9 obeisance

curvaceous: 7 endowed, rounded, shapely, stacked 9 well-built

curvature (see also **curve**): arc 4 bool, curl 8 kyphosis, lordosis 9 arcuation, scoliosis

center locus: 7 evolute

convex: 6 camber

surface: 5 plane

curve: arc, bow, ess 4 arch, bend, curb, ogee, turn, veer 5 ambit, bight, crook, crump, swirl, twist 6 bought, spiral 7 circuit, concave, contour, curvity, ellipse, flexure, inflect, sinuate 8 parabola, sinusaid, twisting 9 convexity, curvature

cusp: 7 spinode

double point of: 6 acnode

kind: 9 parabolic 10 memniscate

mathematical plane: 5 polar

parallel to an ellipse: 6 toroid

S-shaped: ess 4 agee 7 sigmoid

curved: 4 bent 5 round, wound 6 convex, hamate, turned 7 arcuate, arrondi, crooked, curvant 8 anchoral, aquiline, arciform

inward: 5 adunc 6 hooked 8 aduncous

curvet: hop 4 leap, turn 5 bound, caper, frisk, 6 cavort, frolic, gambol, gyrate, prance 8 corvetta(F.) 9 courbette, horse leap

Cush: *father:* Ham

son: 4 Seba 6 Nimrod

cushat: 4 bird, dove 6 pigeon

cushion: bag, cod, mat, pad 4 boss, seat 5 gaddi, squab 6 buffer, insole, jockey, pillow, sachet 7 bolster, hassock 9 upholster

stuffing: 4 baru, down 5 kapok 8 feathers

cusk 4 fish, tusk 5 torsk 6 burbot

cusp: tip 4 apex, horn, peak 5 angle, point, tooth 6 corner 8 paracone 10 projection

cuspid: 11 canine tooth

custard: 4 flan 5 flawn 6 doucet, dowcet, dowset 8 flummery 9 charlotte

custard apple: 5 anona 6 annona, pawpaw 8 sweetsop

custodian: 5 guard 6 bailee, keeper, warden 7 curator, janitor 8 cerberus, guardian 9 caretaker, protector 10 supervisor

custody: 4 care, ward 5 trust 6 charge 7 control, durance, keeping, tuition 11 safekeeping 12 guardianship

custom: fad, law, mos(L.), tax, use 4 duty, form, garb, mode, more, rite, rote, rule, toll, wont 5 habit, haunt, usage, vogue 6 dastur, impost, ritual 7 costume, fashion, tribute 8 business, practice 9 costumbre, patronage 10 consuetude, convention, observance, tailor-made 12 constitution

of peoples: 5 mores

with force of law: mos

customary: 5 nomic, usual 6 common 7 general 8 familiar, habitual, orthodox 10 accustomed 11 traditional 12 conventional 14 consuetudinary

customer: 4 chap 5 buyer 6 client, patron 7 callant, patient, shopper 8 consumer, prospect 9 purchaser

group: 9 clientele

steady: 7 habitue, regular

customs: tax 4 cess, duty, levy, rate, toll 5 mores 6 impost, tariff 7 trewage

officer: 8 douanier

cut: bob, hew, lop, mow, nip, rit 4 bite, chip, chop, clip, crop, dock, fell, gash, hack, knap, mode, nick, pare, raze, slit, snee, snip, snub, trim 5 carve, flick, knife, lance, mince, notch, piece, prune, razee, scarp, sever, share, shear, shorn, slash, slice, snick, split 6 ablate, bisect, broach, chisel, cleave, dilute, divide, excise, haggle, ignore, incise, lessen, mangle, reduce, slight, swinge 7 affront, curtail, shorten, whittle 8 lacerate, mark down, retrench 9 engraving

a melon: 5 allot 8 dispense

a rug: 5 dance

across: 5 slice 8 transect 9 intersect, transcend

along: go 5 speed

back: 4 clip, pare, trim 5 lower, shave, slash 6 reduce 8 mark down

capable of being: 7 sectile

down: 4 pare 5 clear, slash 9 economize

in: mix 6 horn in 7 intrude 9 interpose, interrupt, introduce

in half: 5 halve 6 bisect, secant 8 dimidate

in small pieces: 4 dice, hash 5 mince 6 sliver

off: lop, nig 4 clip, crop, drib, poll 5 elide, roach, shave 7 deprive, divorce, exscind 8 amputate, truncate 9 apocopate, intercept 10 disinherit

out: 4 dele 5 elide 6 exsect, remove 7 exscind 9 eliminate

roughly: jag 4 hack, snag 7 butcher

short: bob 4 clip, crop, dock, poll 5 abort, check, clipt 6 arrest 7 curtail

slanting: 4 bias 5 bevel, miter, mitre

with die: 4 dink

with shears: 4 snip 5 shirl

wool: dod 4 dodd 5 shear

cut and dried: 5 trite 7 routine 8 foregone

cutaneous: 6 dermal

cutaway: 4 coat

cute: coy 4 keen 5 coony, dinky, sharp 6 clever, pretty, shrewd 7 cunning 8 affected 10 attractive

cuticle: 4 hide, skin 8 membrane, pellicle 9 epidermis 10 integument

blister: 4 bleb 5 bulla

ingredient: 5 cutin

cutis: 4 skin 6 corium, dermis

cutlass: 5 sword 6 dusack, tesack 7 machete

cutout: 9 decoupage

cutpurse: 5 thief 10 pickpocket

cutter: 4 beef, boat, sled 5 bravo, sloop, smack 6 cotter, editor, sleigh, slicer 7 clipper, incisor, ruffian 9 cutthroat, foretooth

cutthroat: 5 bravo, cruel 6 hit man 7 ruffian 8 ruthless

cutting: hag, raw 4 curt, keen, kerf, slip, tart, twig 5 acute, bleak, crisp, scion, scrap, scrow, sharp 6 biting, bitter, secant, severe 7 caustic, mordant, painful, satiric 8 chilling, incisive, piercing, poignant, wounding 9 sarcastic, trenchant 10 blustering 11 abridgement, curtailment 12 adulteration

edge: 5 blade

implement: ax, axe, bit, hob, saw 4 adze 5 knife, lathe, mower, plane, razor 6 chisel, reaper, scythe, shears 8 scissors

of last letter: 7 apocope

remark: dig 4 gibe 5 taunt 7 put-down

cuttlefish: 5 sepia, squid 7 octopus, scuttle

ink: 5 sepia

cutup: wag 5 devil, scamp 7 show off 9 prankster

cuvette: pot, tub 4 tank 5 basin 6 bucket, trench 7 cistern

Cybele: 4 Rhea

brother: 6 Cronus

father: 6 Uranus

mother: 4 Gaea

son: 4 Zeus 7 Jupiter, Neptune 8 Poseidon

sweetheart: 5 Attis

Cyclades Island: Ios, Zea 4 Keos, Milo, Nios, Sira, Syra 5 Delos, Melos, Naxia, Naxos, Paros, Syros, Tenos, Tinos 6 Andros 7 Amorgos

cycle: age, eon, era 4 aeon, bike 5 chain, epoch, pedal, round, saros, wheel 6 circle, course, period, series 7 bicycle, circuit, vehicle 8 tricycle 10 revolution, two-wheeler

cyclone: 4 gale, gust, wind 5 blast, storm 6 baguio 7 tornado, twister, typhoon 9 hurricane, whirlwind, windstorm

cyclopean: 4 huge, vast 6 strong 7 massive, titanic 8 colossal, gigantic 9 herculean

Cyclopes: 5 Arges 7 Brontes 8 Steropes 10 Polyphemus

Cyclops: 5 giant 7 monster

feature: 6 one eye

cyclostome: 7 hagfish, lamprey

cygnet: pen 4 fowl, swan

cylinder: 4 beam, drum, pipe, tube 6 barrel, bobbin, gabian, piston, platen, roller 8 lock part

cylindrical: 5 round 6 terete 7 centric, tubular

cyma: 4 gola, gula, ogee 7 molding

cymar, simar: 4 robe 5 shift

cymbal: tal, zel 8 doughnut 10 brass plate

cymbals: 6 becken, piatti

Cymbeline's daughter: 6 Imogen

Cymric: 5 Welsh

god of dead: 5 Pwyll

god of sky: 7 Gwydion

god of sun: 4 Lleu, Llew

god of underworld: 4 Gwyn

cynic: 5 Timon 7 doubter, knocker 9 pessimist 11 misanthrope

cynical: 6 ironic, sullen 7 currish, doglike 8 captious, downbeat, negative, sardonic, snarling

cynosure: 8 lodestar, polestar

cypress: 9 belvedere

Cyprus: *capital:* Nicosia

city: 6 Paphos 7 Limasol 9 Famagusta

measure: oka, oke, pik 4 cass 5 donum, kouza 6 gomari, kartos 7 medimno

monetary unit: 4 para 5 pound 7 piaster

mountain: 7 Troodos

weight: oka, oke 5 moosa 6 kantar

Cyrano: 4 poet 7 duelist

author: 7 Rostand

feature: 4 nose

cyrenaic: 7 hedonic 10 hedonistic

Cyrus: *daughter:* 6 Atossa

treasurer: 10 Mithredath

cyst: bag, sac, wen 5 pouch 6 ranulá 7 vesicle

Cyzicus: *mother:* 6 Aenete
　slayer: 5 Jason
　wife: 6 Cleite

czar: 4 Ivan, king, Paul 5 baron, noble, Peter 6 prince, tycoon 7 emperor 8 Nicholas
　daughter: 8 czarevna, tsarevna
　son: 10 czarevitch, tsarevitch
　wife: 7 czarina, tsarina

Czechoslovakia: *capital:* 5 Praha 6 Prague
　city: 4 Asch, Brno, Eger, Hron 5 Opava, Plzen, Tuzla 6 Aussig, Kosice 7 Bud-

weis, Ostrava, Teplitz 10 Bratislava
　coin: 5 ducat, haler 6 heller, koruna
　county: Ung
　dance: 5 polka 6 redowa 7 furiant
　leader: 5 Benes 7 Masaryk
　measure: lan, sah 4 mira 5 latro, liket, stopa 6 merice
　mountain: 5 Tatra
　munitions plant: 5 Skoda
　province: 7 Bohemia, Moravia
　reformer: 4 Huss
　river: Vag, Vah 4 Eger, Elbe, Gran, Hron, Isar, Iser, Labe, Oder, Ohre, Waag 5 Nitra 6 Moldau, Vltava

czigany: 5 gypsy

D

dab: hit, pat 4 blow, chit, lump, peck, spot 5 clout, smear 6 blotch, strike 7 portion, splotch 8 flatfish, flounder

dabble: dib 4 mess 5 dally 6 dibble, meddle, paddle, potter, splash, tamper, trifle 7 moisten, spatter 8 sprinkle

dabbler: 7 amateur 10 dilettante

dabchick: 5 grebe 9 helldiver

dace: 4 chub

dacoit: 6 robber 8 criminal 9 plunderer

dactyl: toe 6 finger 10 metric foot

dactylogram: 11 fingerprint

dactylopodite: 5 thumb 6 pollex

dactyloscopy: 14 classification, identification

Dadaism: 14 artistic revolt
　followers: Arp 4 Ball 5 Tzara 6 Aragon, Breton 7 Duchamp
　forerunner of: 10 surrealism

daddy longlegs: 5 stilt 7 spinner, tipulid 8 arachnid

dado: 6 groove 7 solidum 11 wall molding

daedal: 4 rich 6 varied 7 bizarre 8 artistic, skillful 9 ingenious, intricate 10 variegated

Daedalus: *son:* 6 Icarus
　constructor of: 9 labyrinth
　victim: 5 Talos

daemon (see also **demon**)**:** 8 eudaemon

daffodil: 5 dilly

daft: mad 4 luny, wild 5 balmy, crazy, gid-

dy, potty, silly 6 cuckoo, insane 7 cracked, foolish, idiotic 8 imbecile

Dag's horse: 8 Hrimfaxi 9 Skinfaksi

Dagda's kin: 5 Boann 6 Aengus, Brigit

dagger: 4 dirk, itac(P.I.), kris, snee 5 crise, katar(Ind.), skean(Ir.) 6 anlace, bodkin, coutel, creese, diesis, kreese, stylet, weapon 7 dudgeon, poniard 8 stiletto 10 misericord
　Burmese: dah, dow
　handle: 4 hilt
　Malay: 4 kris
　stroke: 4 stab 8 stoccado

daily: 4 a day 7 diurnal 9 hodiernal, newspaper, quotidian

daintily: 8 gingerly

dainty: 4 cate, nice, rare 5 acate, denty 6 bonbon, choice, costly, friand, mignon, minion, picked, scarce 7 elegant, finicky, minikin 8 delicacy, delicate, migniard 9 exquisite, squeamish 10 confection, fastidious

dairy: 7 vaccary 8 creamery
　food: 4 milk 5 cream 6 butter, cheese, yogurt
　tool: 9 separator

dais: 4 seat 5 bench, podia(pl.), stage, table 6 canopy, podium, settle 7 estrade, terrace 8 chabutra, platform

daisy: 5 gowan, oxeye 6 shasta 7 comfrey 10 moonflower

dak: 4 post

Dakota Indian: 4 Crow 5 Omaha, Osage, Sioux, Teton 6 Mandan 7 Arikara 8 Arikaree

Daksha's father: 6 Brahma

Dalai Lama: 5 ruler 13 reincarnation

dale: 4 dell, dene, glen, vale 5 spout 6 bottom, dingle, trough, valley

dalles: 6 rapids

dally: toy 4 chat, fool, idle, play, wait 5 delay, flirt, sport, tarry 6 dabble, dawdle, lead on, linger, loiter 10 trifle with 11 string along

dam: bar, bay 4 mare, stay, stem, stop, weir 5 block, check, choke, garth, mound 6 anicut, causey 7 annicut, barrier 8 blockade, obstacle, obstruct, restrain

dama: 5 addra 7 gazelle

damage: mar 4 blot, cost, harm, hurt, loss, ruin, teen 5 burst, cloud, spoil, wound 6 charge, deface, defect, impair, injure, scathe 7 expense, scratch 8 accident, disserve, mischief, sabotage 9 detriment, disprofit, vandalism 11 deleterious, impeachment 12 disadvantage

pert. to: 5 noxal

damages: 5 award 7 payment

daman: 5 hyrax

damask: 5 color 6 fabric 8 deep pink

correlative: 4 sire

dammar: 5 resin, rosin

damn: 4 ruin 5 curse 7 condemn, swear at

damnable: 6 odious 8 infernal 9 execrable 10 detestable, outrageous

damnation: 9 perdition

damned: 4 lost 6 doomed 8 accursed

damnum: 4 harm, loss 9 detriment

damourite: 4 mica 9 muscovite

damp: deg, fog, wet 4 dank, dewy, dull, mist, roky 5 dabby, humid, moist, muggy, musty, rafty, rainy, soggy 6 clammy, deaden, muffle, quench, stupor 7 depress 8 dejected, dispirit 10 discourage

damper: 5 bread 7 checker 8 register

damsel: 4 girl, lass, miss 6 maiden 8 donzella, princess 10 demoiselle

Dan: *prince:* 7 Ahiezer

town: 4 Elon

Danae's kin: 4 Zeus 7 Perseus 8 Acrisius

dance: bal(F.), bob, hop, jig 4 ball, frug, haka, hoof, prom, shag 5 caper, frisk, rumba, tango, tread, stomp, twist, waltz 6 Boston, masque, minuet, monkey 7 foxtrot, saltate 8 fandango 9 cotillion, farandole, jitterbug 10 roundabout

ballroom: 5 polka, rumba, waltz 6 chacha 7 foxtrot, mazurka, twostep 10 Charleston, Turkey Trot

Brazilian: 5 samba 6 maxixe 9 bossa nova

ceremonial: 6 areito

chorus: 5 strut 6 cancan, kordax

college: 5 prom

country: hay 7 hoedown 8 haymaker 10 villanella

designer: 13 choreographer

drama: 6 ballet

English: 6 althea, morris

exhibition: tap 6 apache

fads: 4 frug, pony, shag 5 Lindy, twist 6 monkey 12 mashed potato

formal: 4 prom 5 pavan 7 mazurka 9 farandole

German: 9 allemande

gypsy: 7 farruca 8 flamenco 10 zingaresca

Hawaiian: 4 hula

Hebrew: 4 hora

India: 6 nautch

Italian: 8 courante 9 rigoletto 10 tarantella

Latin American: 5 conga, mambo, rumba, samba, tango 6 chacha, maxixe 7 carioca, criolla

lively: jig 4 juba, reel, trot 5 fling, galop, gavot, polka 6 bolero, branle, canary 8 galliard, rigadoon 9 cotillion, shakedown, tambourin 10 corybantic 11 schottische

masked: 7 ridotto

Muse: 11 Terpsichore

nineteenth-century: 7 tempete

old: 5 loure, rondo 6 bource, carole, cebell, corant, minuet 7 boutade, coranto, furlana, lavolta 8 chaconne 9 horedance, sarabande 10 tarantella

Peruvian: 5 cueca

shoes: 4 taps 5 pumps 8 slippers, toeshoes

slow: 6 adagio, minuet, valeta

Spanish: 8 fandango

square: 7 argeers, lancers 9 quadrille

strut: 8 cakewalk

sword: 8 matachin 11 Flamborough

voluptuous: 5 belly 8 habanera

dance of death: 7 macabre

dancer: 6 artist, hoofer 7 danseur 9 chorus boy 11 terpsichore

Biblical: 6 Salome

female: 4 pony 7 artiste, chorine 8 bayadere, coryphee, danseuse, devadasi 9 ballerina

dandelion: 7 chicory 10 bitterwort

stalk: 5 scape

dander: 5 anger, scurf 6 stroll, temper, wander 7 passion, saunter

dandle: pet 4 love 6 caress, fondle, pamper 9 knee-swing

dandruff: 5 scurf 6 furfur

dandy: fop 4 beau, buck, dude, fine, jake, prig, toff, yawl 5 nifty, swell 7 capstan, coxcomb, foppish, jessamy 8 popinjay, sailboat **9** first-rate, exquisite **11** scrumptious **12** Beau Brummell, crackerjack

danger: 4 fear, risk **5** doubt, peril **6** hazard **7** pitfall, venture **8** distress, jeopardy **9** adventure

signal: **4** bell **5** alarm, siren **6** tocsin

dangerous: bad, rum **5** nasty, risky **6** unsafe **7** parlous **8** insecure **9** hazardous **10** precarious

dangle: lop **4** hang, loll **5** droop, swing **7** shoggle, suspend

Danish: 4 roll **6** pastry

anatomist: **5** Steno

astronomer: **5** Brahe

author: **8** Andersen

composer: **4** Gade

physicist: **4** Bohr

statesman: **5** Bajer, Brake

dank: wet **4** damp **5** humid, moist **6** clammy, coarse **7** drizzle

danta: **5** tapir

Dante: *beloved:* **8** Beatrice

birthplace: **8** Florence

circle of hell: **5** Caina

illustrator: **4** Dore

patron: **5** Scala

verse form: **7** sestina

work: **8** Commedia, Convivio, Eclogues, Epistles **9** Vita Nuova

Danube: *start:* **11** Black Forest

city on: Lom, Ulm **4** Baja, Linz, Ruse **6** Braila, Mohacs, Passau, Vienna **8** Belgrade, Budapest

delta: **8** Black Sea

tributary: Inn, Olt, Vah **4** Enns, Hrow, Isar, Lech, Naab, Prut, Raba, Sava **5** Arges, Drava, Iller, Iskur, Nitra, Tisza, Traun **6** Leitha, Morava **7** Altmuhl, Siretul

Danzig: *coin:* **6** gulden **7** pfennig

liqueur: **7** ratafia

dap: dab, dib, dip **4** skip **6** bounce, dibble **7** rebound

Daphne: 8 Mezereon

father: **5** Ladon

mother: **6** Creusa

pursued by: **6** Apollo

turned into: **10** laurel tree

Daphnis' lover: **5** Chloe

dapper: 4 neat, trim **5** natty **6** spruce **7** finical, foppish

dappled: 6 dotted **7** flecked, mottled, spotted **8** freckled **10** variegated

darbies: 8 manacles **9** handcuffs

Dardanelles: 10 Hellespont

dare: 4 dast, defy, face, osse, risk **5** brave **6** assume **7** attempt, venture **9** challenge, undertake

daredevil: 6 madcap **12** swashbuckler

daresay: 5 agree **7** believe, presume, suppose **13** think probable

dargah, durgah(Ind.): 4 tomb **5** court **6** mosque, shrine

daring: 4 bold, rash **5** brave, hardy, manly, nerve **6** heroic **7** courage **8** devilish, fearless **9** audacious **10** courageous **11** adventurous, venturesome

dariole: cup **5** shell

Darius: *father:* **9** Ahasuerus

prince: **6** Daniel

dark: dim, sad, wan **4** ebon **5** black, blind, brown, dingy, dusky, faint, murky, shady, sooty, unlit, vague **6** brunet, closed, cloudy, dismal, gloomy, opaque, wicked **7** melanic, obscure, rayless, stygian, swarthy **8** abstruse, ignorant, lowering, sinister **9** ambiguous, Cimmerian, infuscate, recondite, secretive, shuttered, tenebrous, uncertain **10** caliginous, indistinct, mysterious

dark-complexioned: 5 dusky **7** swarthy

dark horse: 7 unknown **9** candidate **10** contestant **14** unlikely winner

darken: dim **4** dull **5** bedim, shade, sully, umber **6** deepen, shadow **7** becloud, benight, blacken, eclipse, obscure, opacate, tarnish **8** overcast **9** obfuscate, overcloud **10** overshadow

darkness: 4 dusk, murk **5** gloom, night, shade **6** shadow **7** dimness, privacy, secrecy **8** gloaming, iniquity, twilight **9** blackness **10** wickedness

realm: Po **6** Erebus

darling: joe(Sc.), pet **4** cute, dear, duck **5** aroon(Ir.), deary, honey, sweet **6** cherie, cuddly, moppet **7** beloved **8** adorable, favorite **9** attractive, delightful, sweetheart

darn: 4 mend **5** patch **6** cussed, damned, repair **7** blasted, doggone

darnel: 4 tare, weed **5** grass **6** cockle

darner: 6 needle

dart: 4 bolt, flit, leap **5** bound, fling, scoot, shaft, speed, start **6** scurry, spring, sprint **7** missile **9** flechette **11** move quickly **12** stitched fold

barbed: **10** banderilla

dart-like: 8 spicular

D'Artagnan: *companion:* **5** Athos **6** Aramis **7** Porthos

creator: **5** Dumas

Dartmouth College location: 7 Hanover

Darwin: 10 naturalist

ship: **6** Beagle

theory: **9** evolution

teacher in evolution trial: **10** John Scopes

work: **12** Descent of Man **15** Origin of Species

das: 4 fish **6** dassie **9** blacktail **12** Hindu servant

Das Kapital author: 4 Marx

dash: pep **6** bang, ding, elan, gift, hurl, line, pelt, race, ruin, rush, show, slam **5**

abash, ardor, break, clash, crash, crush, fling, knock, smash, speed, spice, style, swash, throw 6 energy, hurtle, hyphen, shiver, spirit, splash, sprint, stroke, thrust 7 bravura, collide, depress, display, shatter, spatter, splotch 8 confound, gratuity, splinter 9 animation, bespatter, frustrate, overthrow

dasheen: 4 taro

dashiki: 7 garment 12 African shift
relative: 6 muu-muu

dashing: gay 4 bold, chic 5 bully, showy 6 jaunty, lively, swanky, veloce 7 stylish 8 spirited 11 fashionable

dastard: cad, sot 5 sneak 6 coward, craven 7 dullard 8 poltroon

dastardly: 4 base, mean, foul 5 nasty 6 rotten 10 despicable

data: 5 facts 8 material 11 information

date: age, day, era, woo 5 epoch, fruit 6 escort 7 take out 9 originate 10 engagement, extend from, rendezvous 11 anniversary, appointment
erroneous: 11 anachronism
on coin: 7 exergue

dated: 5 passe 6 demode, old hat 7 archaic 8 outmoded 12 old-fashioned 13 unfashionable

dateless: 8 timeless 10 immemorial

dating: 6 timing 8 courting

daub: 4 blob, blot, clag, clam, clat, coat, gaum, soil 5 clart, cleam, cover, paint, slake, smear 6 bedaub, grease 7 besmear, plaster, splotch 8 slaister

daughter: 4 bint 5 fille, filly 6 alumna 7 cadette
pert. to: 6 filial

Daughter of Moon: 7 Nokomis

daunt: awe, cow, daw 4 daze, faze, stun, tame 5 abash, break, check, deter 6 dismay, subdue 7 conquer, control, overawe, repress, stupefy, terrify 8 dispirit, overcome 10 disconcert, discourage, dishearten, intimidate

dauntless: 4 bold, good 5 brave, gutsy 7 aweless 8 fearless, intrepid, unafraid 10 courageous 11 indomitable, lionhearted

davenport: 4 desk, sofa 5 couch, divan 12 chesterfield
small: 8 love seat

David: *chief ruler:* Ira
companion: 6 Hushai
daughter: 5 Tamar
employer: 5 Nabal
favorite son: 7 Absalom
friend: 5 Ittai
kin: 5 Jesse, Tamar 6 Michal 7 Abigail, Absalom, Solomon
man of: Ira 4 Igal 7 Shammah
musician: 5 Asaph
prophet: 6 Nathan
scribe: 7 Shavsha

traitor to: 10 Ahithophel
valley of Goliath's death: 4 Elah

David Copperfield character: 4 Dora 5 Agnes, James 6 Barkis, Betsey, Dartle 8 Micawber, Peggotty, Traddles 9 Wickfield, Uriah Heep 10 Steerforth

Davy: 4 lamp

dawdle: lag 4 idle, loaf, poke 5 dally 6 diddle, linger, loiter, putter, trifle 8 lollygag 9 waste time 10 fool around

dawn: 4 morn 5 sunup 6 aurora 7 morning, sunrise 8 daybreak 9 beginning
goddess: Eos 5 Ushas 6 Aurora
pert. to: 4 eoan 7 auroral
symbol: dew
toward the: 8 eastward

day: yom(Heb.) 4 date, time 5 epoch 6 period 8 lifetime
before: eve 9 yesterday
father of: 6 Erebus
god of: 5 Horus
hot: 8 scorcher
joyful: 8 festival
judgment: 8 doomsday
of Atonement: 9 Yom Kippur
pert. to: 6 ferial

day blindness: hemeralopia

daydream: 4 muse 6 vision 7 reverie

days: *fateful:* 4 Ides
fifty: 13 quinquagesima
fourteen: 9 fortnight
gone by: 4 yore 7 long ago 8 old times 9 antiquity 10 yesteryear 11 past history

daze: fog 4 stun 5 daunt 6 bemuse, benumb, dazzle, muddle, trance 7 confuse, stupefy 8 befuddle, bewilder 9 dumbfound

dazed: 4 asea 5 dizzy, dopey, woozy 6 addled, groggy 7 stunned 9 in a stupor 10 punch-drunk

dazzle: 4 daze 5 blind, shine 7 eclipse 8 bewilder, outshine, surprise

dazzling: 5 vivid 6 bright, garish 7 fulgent, glaring, radiant 8 gorgeous 9 brilliant, sparkling 10 candescent, foudroyant 11 pyrotechnic

deaccession: 10 museum sale

deacon: 5 adept 6 cleric, doctor, layman, master 10 adulterate
prayers: 6 ectene
stole: 7 orarion

dead: 4 cold, dull, flat, gone, mort(F.), numb, tame 5 amort, inert, quiet, slain 6 asleep, lapsed 7 defunct, expired, extinct, sterile, tedious 8 absolute, complete, deceased, departed, inactive, lifeless, obsolete 9 apathetic, bloodless, inanimate, nerveless, unsalable 10 breathless, lusterless, monotonous, motionless, spiritless, unexciting 11 indifferent, ineffectual, inoperative 12 extinguished, unproductive, unprofitable *house of:* 4 tomb 5 grave 6 morgue 7 ossuary 8 mortuary 9 crematory, ossuarium

mass for: 7 requiem

region of: Po 5 Hades 6 Erebus

dead duck: 5 goner 9 sure loser 13 hopeless cause

Dead Souls author: 5 Gogol

deadbeat: bum 7 sponger 8 parasite 10 free-loader

deaden: 4 dull, kill, mute, numb, stun 5 blunt 6 benumb, dampen, muffle, obtund, opiate, retard, weaken 7 petrify, repress, stupefy 8 paralyze 10 devitalize

dead end: 4 stop 7 impasse 8 cul-de-sac 9 blank wall 10 blind alley

deadfall: 4 trap 9 brush pile

deadhead: 6 bobber 8 non-payer 12 lacking cargo

deadline: 5 limit 8 boundary

deadlock: tie 4 draw 7 impasse 9 stalemate 10 standstill

deadly: 4 dire, fell 5 fatal 6 lethal, mortal 7 capital, fateful, ruinous 8 venomous, virulent 9 pestilent 10 implacable, pernicious 11 destructive, internecine

deadpan: 4 blank 6 vacant 9 impassive

deaf: 8 heedless 9 unmindful

deal: 4 dole, part, sale 5 allot, board, plank, sever, share, trade, wield 6 bestow, divide, handle, parcel 7 bargain, deliver, inflict, portion, scatter, wrestle 8 dispense, separate 9 apportion, negotiate 10 administer, distribute 11 transaction

great: 4 lots 5 loads 6 oodles 8 very much 9 big amount

with: 4 cope 6 handle 10 take care of

dealer: 5 agent 6 badger, broker, cadger, jobber, monger, seller, trader 8 merchant, operator 9 middleman, tradesman 10 negotiator, trafficker 11 distributor

secondhand goods: 10 pawnbroker

dealing: 7 trading, traffic 8 exchange 11 intercourse

shrewd: 6 deceit 9 chicanery

dean: 5 doyen 6 senior, verger 8 official

dear: pet 4 agra(Ir.), cara(It.), cher(F.), fond, high, lief, near 5 honey, loved 6 costly, scarce, worthy 7 beloved, darling, lovable 8 esteemed, glorious, precious, valuable 9 cherished, expensive, heartfelt, honorable, important 10 sweetheart 12 affectionate

dearly: 6 deeply, keenly, richly 8 heartily 9 earnestly

dearth: 4 lack, want 6 famine 7 paucity, poverty 8 scarcity 10 deficiency

death: end 4 bale, bane, doom, mort(F.) 5 decay 6 demise 7 decease, quietus 8

biolysis, curtains, rawbones 9 bloodshed, departure 10 expiration, extinction, grim reaper

after: 10 posthumous

angel of: 6 Azrael

aware of portending: fey

bringing: 6 funest

goddess: Hel 4 Dana, Danu

march: 7 cortege, funeral

meditation: 11 thanatopsis

mercy: 10 euthanasia

notice: 4 obit 8 obituary

personification: 4 Mors 5 Ankou 6 Charos, Charus

put to: gas 4 hang, kill, slay 5 choke, lynch 6 murder, starve, stifle 7 garrote 8 strangle 9 suffocate 11 assassinate, electrocute

rate: 9 mortality

rattle: 4 rale

register: 9 necrology

song: 5 dirge, elegy 8 threnody

symbol of: 5 orant

death-defying: 4 bold, rash 6 heroic 9 audacious, imprudent

deathless: 7 abiding, eternal, undying 8 immortal 12 imperishable

deathly: 5 fatal 6 deadly, grisly, lethal, mortal 7 ghastly, macabre 8 gruesome, moribund 10 cadaverous 11 destructive

debacle: 4 rout 5 wreck 6 defeat 7 beating, failure 8 collapse 9 breakdown, cataclysm

debar: 4 deny, tabu 5 estop, taboo 6 forbid, hinder, refuse 7 boycott, deprive, exclude, prevent, suspend 8 preclude, prohibit 9 foreclose, interdict 10 disqualify

debark: 4 land

debase: 5 alloy, lower, stoop 6 defile, demean, humble, impair, reduce, revile, vilify 7 cheapen, degrade, deprave, devalue, pervert, traduce, vitiate 8 dishonor 9 brutalize 10 adulterate, degenerate, depreciate 11 deteriorate

debased: low 4 vile 7 corrupt

debatable: 4 moot 8 arguable 9 uncertain 10 in question

debate: 4 agon, moot 5 argue, fight 6 reason, strife 7 agitate, canvass, contend, contest, discuss, dispute, examine, palaver, quarrel, wrangle 8 argument, consider, militate, question 9 dialectic, quodlibet 10 contention, deliberate 11 controversy 12 dissertation

pert. to: 8 forensic

place of: 5 forum 6 Lyceum

stoppage of: 7 cloture

debauch: 4 bout, orgy 5 spree, taint 6 defile, guzzle, seduce 7 corrupt, deprave, mislead, pollute, violate 9 bacchanal, dissipate 10 hellbender, lead astray, saturnalia 11 contaminate

debauched: 4 lewd 6 wanton 9 dissolute

debauchee: rip 4 rake, roue 6 lecher 8 rake-hell 9 libertine

debilitated: 4 weak 5 seedy 6 feeble, infirm, sapped 9 burned out, enervated

debility: 5 atony 7 languor, malaise 8 weakness 9 infirmity, lassitude 10 feebleness

debit: 4 loss 6 charge

debonair: 4 airy 6 jaunty, polite, urbane 7 affable 8 graceful, gracious

Deborah's husband: 8 Lapidoth

debouche: 4 exit 6 outlet 7 opening, passage 9 emergence

debris: 5 scree, talus, trash, waste 6 refuse, rubble 7 rubbish 8 detritus

debt: sin 5 debit, fault 7 arrears 8 trespass 9 arrearage, liability 10 obligation
acknowledgment: IOU 4 bill, note
without: 7 solvent 11 unobligated

debunk: 6 expose, show up, unmask 8 disabuse 11 disillusion, set straight 12 tell the truth

debut: 7 opening 8 entrance, premiere 9 beginning, coming out 12 introduction

decad: ten

decade: 9 decennium

decadent: 6 effete, rotten, sinful, wicked 7 decayed 9 declining 10 degenerate, iniquitous, retrograde 12 deteriorated 13 retrogressive

decamp: 4 bolt 5 elope, scoot 6 depart, levant, mizzle 7 abscond, run away, take off, vamoose 8 clear out 9 skedaddle 10 hightail it

decant: 4 emit, pour 6 unload 8 transfer

decanter: 6 carafe

decapitate: 6 behead 10 guillotine

decapod: 4 crab 5 prawn, squid 7 lobster 10 crustacean

decay: ebb, rot 4 conk, dote, doze, fade, fail, ruin 5 death, spoil, waste 6 caries, mildew, wither 7 decline, failure 8 decrease 9 adversity, decadence, decompose 11 destruction, deteriorate, dissolution 12 dilapidation, disintegrate, putrefaction
dental: 6 caries
in fruit: 4 blet

deceased: 4 dead 7 defunct 8 departed

deceitful: shy 4 foxy 5 false, lying 6 fickle, hollow, shifty, sneaky 7 sirenic 8 tortuous 9 dishonest, faithless, insidious, insincere 10 circuitous, fallacious, mendacious 11 underhanded 13 machiavellian

deceivable: 8 gullible

deceive: con, lie 4 bilk, dupe, fool, gaff, gull, hoax, jilt 5 abuse, blind, bluff, catch, cheat, cozen, dodge, hocus, trick 6 baffle, betray, delude, humbug, illude 7 beguile, defraud, mislead 8 flimflam, hoodwink 9 bamboozle, frustrate 11 doublecross 12 misrepresent

deceiver: 6 trepan 7 juggler, sharper, warlock 8 magician

decelerate: 4 slow 5 brake 11 reduce speed

decency: 7 decorum 9 propriety

decennium: 6 decade

decent: 4 fair, good, pure 5 clean 6 chaste, comely, honest, modest, proper, seemly 7 correct, fitting, shapely 8 adequate, decorous 10 acceptable, conforming, sufficient 11 appropriate, respectable

deception: gyp 4 gaff, ruse, sham, scam, wile 5 cheat, covin, craft, fraud, guile, magic, trick 6 cautel, deceit, humbug 7 blaflum(Sc.), cunning, evasion, fallacy, fiction, knavery, pretext, sleight, slyness 8 artifice, falsedad(Sp.), intrigue, prestige, subtlety, trickery, trumpery 9 chicanery, collusion, duplicity, falsehood, hypocrisy, imposture, mendacity, sophistry, treachery 10 artfulness, camouflage, dishonesty, subterfuge 11 contrivance, counterfeit, dissembling 13 deceitfulness, dissimulation

deceptive: 5 false 8 delusive, illusory 10 fallacious, misleading

decided: 4 firm, flat, sure 5 fixed 6 all set, formed 7 certain, settled 8 clear-cut, decisive, definite, resolved 10 determined 11 established 14 unquestionable

decima: 5 tenth, tithe

decimal base: ten

decimate: 5 wreck 7 destroy, wipe out 8 demolish, massacre 9 slaughter 10 annihilate

decipher: 4 read 5 break, solve 6 decode, detect, reveal 7 analyze, unravel 8 discover, indicate 9 translate

decision: 4 fiat 5 arret, canon 6 crisis, decree, ruling 7 verdict 8 finality, judgment, sentence 9 precedent 10 conclusion, resolution 12 adjudication 13 determination
maker: 5 judge 6 umpire 7 referee 9 executive
sudden: 4 whim 7 impulse

decisive: 5 final 6 crisic 7 crucial 8 critical 10 conclusive, peremptory

deck: tog 4 buss, dink, heap, pink, trig 5 adorn, array, cover, dress, equip, floor, prink, store 6 blazon, clothe, fettle 7 apparel, bedight, bedizen, feather 8 beautify, decorate, platform 9 embellish 11 pack of cards
kind: gun 4 boat, main, spar 5 berth, upper 6 bridge 7 shelter 8 platform, splinter 9 hurricane, promenade 10 forecastle

high: 4 poop

lowest: 5 orlop

part: 7 scupper

deckle-edged: 5 erose

declaim: 4 rant, rave 5 orate, speak, spout 6 recite 7 elocute, inveigh 8 denounce, harangue, perorate 9 discourse

declaration: 4 word 6 oracle, placet 9 affidavit, assertion, statement 10 allegation, deposition, disclosure, exposition 11 affirmation 12 announcement, asseveration, proclamation 13 advertisement, pronouncement

declare: bid, say, vow 4 aver, avow, deny, tell 5 posit, state, voice 6 affirm, allege, assert, assure, avouch, blazon, depone, herald, indict, notify, relate 7 behight, express, profess, protest, signify, testify 8 announce, denounce, describe, indicate, maintain, manifest, proclaim 9 advertise, nuncupate, pronounce 10 annunciate, asseverate, promulgate 11 acknowledge, communicate

in cards: bid 4 meld

declination: 4 bias 5 slope 7 descent 8 swerving 9 deviation 10 declension 11 inclination 13 deterioration

decline: dip, ebb, set 4 bend, fade, fail, fall, flag, sink, turn, wane 5 chute, droop, lower, repel, slope, slump, stoop, stray 6 debase, refuse, reject, weaken 7 descend, descent, deviate, disavow, dwindle, failure, forbear 8 decrease, languish, withdraw 9 decadence, declivity, recadence, repudiate 10 retrograde 13 deterioration

declivity: dip 4 drop, fall 5 cliff, scarp, slope 6 calade 7 decline, descent 8 gradient 9 precipice

decoct: 5 smelt, steep 6 reduce, refine 7 extract 8 boil down, condense

decoction: 7 essence, extract

decode: 5 crack 8 decipher 9 figure out

decompose: rot 5 decay, spoil 7 putrefy

decor: 7 setting 10 background, design plan 11 furnishings, style scheme

decorate: 4 bind, cite, deck, pink, trim 5 adorn, dress, inlay, panel 6 emboss, parget 7 festoon, garnish, miniate 8 ornament, titivate 9 embellish

decorated: 6 ornate 7 damasse, honored, wrought 9 sigillate 10 beribboned

decoration: 4 bahl 5 medal 6 frieze, plaque, tinsel 7 epergne, garnish, regalis 8 applique, fretwork, ornament 9 furniture 10 chambranle, decorament

metalware: 4 tole

military: DSC, DSM, DSO 5 medal 6 ribbon

pert. to: 8 medallic

decorous: 4 calm, good, prim 5 grave, quiet, sober, staid 6 decent, demure, mod-

est, polite, proper, sedate, seemly, serene, steady 7 fitting, orderly, regular, settled 8 becoming, composed, mannerly 9 befitting, dignified, unruffled 11 appropriate

decorticate: 4 flay, hull, husk, pare, peel, pill, skin 5 strip 6 denude 9 excoriate

decorum: 7 decency 9 etiquette, propriety 10 convention

decoy: 4 bait, lure, tole 5 drill, plant, shill, tempt 6 allure, entice, entrap, pigeon 8 inveigle 9 shillaber

decrease: ebb 4 drop, fall, loss, sink, wane 5 abate, decay, taper, waste 6 impair, lessen, shrink 7 decline, dwindle, slacken, subside 8 diminish, moderate, retrench 9 decession, decrement 10 diminution

decree: act, law 4 rule, will 5 edict, enact, order, tenet, ukase 6 arrest, assize, decern(Sc.), dictum, indict, ordain 7 adjudge, appoint, command, mandate, statute 8 decision, rescript, sentence 9 determine, enactment, ordinance 10 adjudicate, plebiscite 12 adjudication, announcement

authoritative: 5 arret, canon

imperial: 4 fiat

Oriental: 5 irade 6 firman

papal: 4 bull

decrement: 4 loss 5 waste 8 decrease 10 diminution

decrepit: 4 lame, weak 6 feeble, infirm, senile, shabby 7 failing, invalid, rundown, unsound 9 bedridden 10 broken down 11 in disrepair

decretum: 4 rule 5 canon 7 precept 10 regulation

decry: boo 4 slur 5 lower 6 lessen 7 asperse, censure, condemn, degrade, detract 8 belittle, derogate 9 deprecate, discredit, disparage, down-grade, underrate 10 depreciate, undervalue

decuple: 7 tenfold

decussate: 5 cross 7 form an X 9 intersect

dedicate: vow 6 devote, direct, hallow, oblate 7 ascribe 8 inscribe 9 nuncupate 10 consecrate

deduce: 4 draw, lead 5 bring, drive, infer, trace 6 derive, elicit, evolve, gather 7 extract, make out 8 conclude

deduct: 4 bate, dock, take 5 abate, allow 6 defalk, remove 7 curtail 8 abstract, discount, separate, subtract, take away

deduction: 4 agio 6 rebate 7 reprise 8 illation, write-off 9 inference 10 conclusion

deed: act 4 case, fact, feat, fiat, gest 5 chart, doing, title 6 action, convey, escrow, pottah, remise 7 charter, exploit 8 document, contract, transfer 9 adventure 10 instrument 11 achievement, performance, tour de force 14 accomplishment

benevolent: 4 boon 5 favor 8 benefice

evil: sin 11 malefaction

deeds: 4 acta 9 res gestae

deem: say 4 hope, reck, tell 5 judge, opine, think 6 esteem, expect, ordain, reckon, regard 7 account, adjudge, believe, surmise 8 announce, consider, judgment, proclaim 10 adjudicate

deep: low, sea 4 howe, rapt 5 abyss, grave, great, gruff, heavy, ocean 6 hollow, intent 7 abysmal, intense, serious, unmixed 8 absorbed, abstruse, complete, powerful, profound, thorough 9 entangled, insidious, recondite 11 far-reaching

deep-dyed: 6 rooted 7 long-set, old-line 9 colorfast, confirmed, hard-shell, indelible, ingrained 10 inveterate

deepen: 5 cloud 6 darken 7 enhance, thicken 9 intensify 10 strengthen

deep-seated: 6 inbred, innate, primal 8 inherent 9 intrinsic 10 congenital, entrenched, in the blood 11 instinctive

deer: 4 hind 6 animal, cervid, mammal 8 ruminant

Asian: 4 axis, maha, napu, shou, sika 5 maral 6 chitra, hangul, sambar 10 barasingha, chevrotain

barking: 7 muntjac, muntjak

cry: 4 bell

European: red 6 fallow 9 white-tail

fallow: 4 dama

family: 8 cervidae

female: doe 4 hind

genus of: 6 cervus

large: elk 5 moose 6 wapiti 7 caribou

male: 4 buck, hart, spay, stag 7 roebuck

meat: 5 jerky 7 charqui, venison

North American: elk 5 moose 6 wapiti

path: run 4 slot 5 trail

pert. to: 6 damine 7 cervine

small: roe 7 roebuck

South American: 4 pudu 6 guemal, vanada 7 brocket

young: kid 4 fawn, spay 7 spitter

de-escalate: 6 weaken 8 decrease, diminish, slow down

deface: mar 4 foul, ruin, scar 5 spoil 6 damage, defoil, deform, injure 7 blemish, detract, distort 8 mutilate 9 disfigure, vandalize

de facto: 7 in being 8 existing 10 unofficial

defalcation: 9 pilferage 10 peculation 12 embezzlement

defame: 4 foul 5 abase, cloud, libel, smear 6 injure, malign, vilify 7 asperse, blacken, blemish, detract, slander, traduce 8 dishonor 9 discredit, denigrate 10 calumniate

default: 4 fail, flaw, lack, omit, want 7 blemish, failure, forfeit, mistake, neglect 8 omission 10 negligence 11 delinquency, dereliction 12 imperfection 13 nonappearance

defeasance: 6 defeat 7 undoing 9 overthrow, annulment

defeat: win 4 balk, beat, best, drub, foil, loss, rout, ruin, undo 5 break, check, floor, skunk, worst 6 baffle, cumber, master, thwack 7 conquer, deprive, destroy, preempt, reverse, shellac 8 overcome, vanquish, Waterloo 9 discomfit, frustrate, overpower, overthrow, overwhelm 10 defeasance, disappoint 12 discomfiture

at chess: 4 mate 9 checkmate

narrowly: nip 4 edge 7 nose out

defeatist: 7 kill-joy 8 fatalist 9 Cassandra, pessimist

defect: 4 flaw, lack, vice, want 5 craze, fault, minus 6 damage, desert, injury 7 blemish, failing, forsake 8 drawback, renounce, weakness 10 deficiency 11 shortcoming 12 imperfection

in timber: 4 knot

without: 5 sound 7 perfect

defective: bad, ill 4 poor 6 faulty 7 halting, unsound 8 impaired, vitiated 9 deficient, imperfect 10 disordered, inaccurate, incomplete

defector: 6 bolter 8 apostate, deserter, renegade 9 turnabout 10 repudiator

defend: 4 back, hold, save, wear 5 guard, watch 6 assert, forbid, screen, secure, shield, uphold 7 contest, espouse, justify, prevent, protect, shelter 8 advocate, champion, conserve, maintain, preserve, prohibit 9 exculpate, vindicate

defendant: 7 accused 8 appellee

answer: 4 plea 14 nolo contendere

defender: 8 advocate, champion, guardian, upholder 9 proponent, protector

of the people: 7 tribune 10 ombudsman

defense: 4 egis, fort 5 aegis, alibi, fence, grith 6 answer, behalf, covert, excuse, sconce 7 bulwark, shelter 8 apologia, boundary, security 9 coverture, safeguard 10 protection 11 maintenance

position: 7 rampart 10 bridgehead

unit: AAF 4 army, NATO, navy 5 SEATO 7 marines

defenseless: 4 bare 5 naked 7 unarmed 8 helpless 9 unguarded

defensible: 7 tenable 9 excusable

defensive: 9 shielding 10 apologetic

defer: bow 4 wait 5 delay, yield 6 put off, shelve, submit 7 suspend 8 lay aside, postpone, prorogue, protract 9 hold off on 10 capitulate 12 knuckle under 13 procrastinate

deference: 6 homage, regard 7 respect 8

courtesy 9 obeisance

defiant: 4 bold 5 brave 6 daring 8 insolent 11 challenging

deficiency: 4 lack, want 5 fault, minus 6 dearth, defect 7 absence 8 scarcity, shortage 10 inadequacy, scantiness 13 insufficiency

deficient: 5 short 6 meager 7 bobtail

deficit: 8 shortage 9 arrearage, income gap 11 debit excess 12 business loss

defile: 4 pass, soil 5 abuse, dirty, gorge, smear, sully, taint 6 debase, infect, ravish 7 corrupt, deprave, passage, pollute, tarnish, violate 8 dishonor, maculate 9 desecrate 11 contaminate

defiled: 6 impure 7 unclean 8 maculate

definable: 6 finite

define: end, fix, set 4 mere, term 5 bound, limit 6 decide 7 clarify, delimit, explain, expound 8 describe, discover 9 demarcate, determine, interpret, prescribe 11 distinguish 12 characterize, circumscribe

definite: 4 sure 5 clear, final, fixed, sharp 7 certain, limited, precise 8 distinct, explicit, limiting 10 conclusive 11 determinate, determining, unequivocal 12 determinable, unmistakable

definitive: 5 final 8 clear-cut, explicit, specific 10 conclusive

deflect: 4 bend, warp 5 parry 6 divert, swerve 8 deviate, refract 8 turn away

deflower: 6 ravage, ravish 7 despoil, violate

Defoe character: 4 Moll, Xury 6 Crusoe, Friday, Roxana 7 Mrs. Veal

deform: mar 4 maim, warp 6 deface 7 contort, cripple, distort 8 misshape 9 disfigure 10 disarrange

deformed: 7 crooked, hideous 8 formless 9 amorphous, loathsome, monstrous, shapeless, unshapely 11 counterfeit

deformity: 4 flaw 6 defect 7 blemish 13 disfigurement
of foot: 5 varus 7 talipes

defraud: rob 4 bilk, fake, gull, rook, trim 5 cheat, cozen, gouge, mulct, trick 6 chouse, fleece 7 swindle 9 bamboozle

defray: pay 6 expend, prepay 7 finance 10 stand treat 11 foot the bill, pay expenses 12 pick up the tab

deft: 4 neat, trim 5 agile, handy, quick 6 adroit, expert, nimble, spruce 8 dextrous, skillful 9 dexterous

defunct: 4 dead 7 extinct 8 deceased, departed, finished

defy: 4 dare, face 5 beard, brave, flout, scorn, stump 6 oppose, resist 7 affront, outface 8 champion 9 stand up to

dégagé: 6 casual 7 relaxed 8 detached, informal 10 uninvolved 11 free and easy 13 unconstrained

degenerate: rot 6 debase, effete, worsen 7 corrupt 8 decadent, depraved 10 go downhill 11 deteriorate

degradation: 7 descent 8 ignominy

degrade: 4 bust 5 abase, decry, lower, shame, strip 6 debase, demean, demote, depose, humble, reduce, vilify 7 corrupt, decline, depress 8 disgrace, dishonor 9 disparage, humiliate 10 degenerate, depreciate 11 deteriorate

degraded: 5 seamy 6 abject, fallen 7 debased 10 degenerate, diminished

degrading: 4 base 6 menial 8 shameful

degree: 4 bank, heat, rank, rate, rung, step, term, tier 5 class, grade, honor, order, pitch, point, stage, stair 6 extent, medium, soever 7 measure, station 8 quantity, standing 9 gradation 10 attainment
academic: B.L.S., B.Sc., L.L.B., L.L.D., M.Sc., Ph.D. 4 D.Lit. 5 Litt.D.
honorary: 8 laureate
kind of: nth 5 third
of academic excellence: 8 cum laude 13 magna cum laude, summa cum laude
seeker: 9 candidate
slight: ace, nth 4 hair, inch 5 shade 8 slightly 9 gradation

degust, degustate: 5 savor, taste 6 relish

dehydrate: dry 9 desiccate, evaporate

deific: 6 divine 7 godlike

deification: 10 apotheosis

deify: 5 exalt 7 glorify, idolize 10 consecrate 11 apotheosize

deign: 5 stoop 9 vouchsafe 10 condescend

deigning: 11 patronizing

deity (see also **god** and **goddess** under appropriate country or function): god 4 deva, idol, muse 6 genius 7 creator, demigod, godling, godhead 8 Almighty, divinity, 12 supreme being
half-fish: 6 Oannes
half-goat: 4 faun
hawk-eyed: 5 Horus 6 Sokari 7 Sokaris
jackal-headed: 6 Anubis
tutelary: 5 genie, lares, numen 7 Hershef, penates

deja vu: 8 illusion 10 paramnesia, seen before

de jure: 7 by right 8 lawfully

deject: 5 abase, lower 6 humble, lessen 7 flatten 8 dispirit 9 overthrow 10 demoralize, discourage, dishearten

dejected: low, sad 4 blue, down, glum, sunk 6 abased, gloomy, pining 7 humbled, unhappy 8 repining, wretched 9 cheerless, depressed, prostrate, woebegone 10 despondent, spiritless 11 crestfallen, downhearted 12 disconsolate, disheartened, fainthearted

dejection: 5 dumps 7 despair 10 melancholy

dejeuner: 5 lunch 9 breakfast, collation

Delaware: *capital:* 5 Dover
  bay: 8 Delaware, Rehoboth 11 Indian River
  city: 5 Lewes 6 Newark 7 Chester, Milford, Seaford, Smyrna 9 New Castle, 10 Wilmington
  county: 4 Kent 6 Sussex 9 New Castle
  Indian: 6 Lenape
  river: 6 Indian 7 Leipsic 8 Delaware 9 Broadkill, Christina, Nanticoke
  state bird: 7 blue hen
  state flower: 12 peach blossom
  state insect: 7 ladybug
  state nickname: 5 First 7 Diamond
  state tree: 5 holly

delay: lag 4 slow, stay, stop, wait 5 allay, check, dally, defer, demur, deter, dwell, stall, tarry 6 arrest, dawdle, detain, hinder, impede, linger, loiter, put off, retard, temper, weaken 7 assuage, prolong, respite 8 demurral, hesitate, macerate, mitigate, obstruct, postpone, reprieve, stoppage 9 detention, hindrance, lingering 10 cunctation, moratorium, suspension 13 procrastinate

delayed: 4 late 5 tardy 7 belated, overdue

delaying: 8 dilatory

dele: 4 omit 5 erase 6 cancel, delete, efface, remove 7 expunge 9 eradicate, extirpate 10 obliterate

delectable: 5 tasty 8 pleasing 9 delicious, desirable, diverting, enjoyable 10 delightful 11 pleasurable

delegate: 4 name, send 6 assign, commit, depute, deputy, legate, nuncio 7 appoint, consign, empower, entrust 8 emissary, transfer 9 authorize, surrogate 10 commission 12 commissioner 14 representative

delegation: 7 mission 9 committee 10 deputation

delete: 4 dele, omit 5 erase, purge 6 cancel, remove 7 destroy, expunge 9 eliminate, eradicate 10 obliterate
  opposite of: 4 stet 7 put back, restore

deleterious: bad 7 harmful, hurtful, noxious 8 damaging 9 injurious, malignant 10 pernicious 11 destructive, detrimental, prejudicial

Delian god: 6 Apollo

deliberate: 4 cool, pore 5 study, think, weigh 6 advise, confer, debate, ponder 7 consult, planned, reflect, resolve 8 consider, measured, meditate, mull over 9 determine, leisurely, speculate, voluntary 10 purposeful, thought out 11 circumspect, intentional 12 premeditated 13 dispassionate

deliberation: 7 counsel 10 reflection
  without: 4 rash 8 headlong 9 on impulse

Delibes ballet: 5 Naila 6 Kassya 8 Coppelia, La Source

opera: 5 Lakme

delible: 10 eradicable

delicacy: roe 4 cate, ease, tact 5 taste 6 caviar, dainty, luxury, nicety 7 finesse 8 niceness, pleasure, subtlety 9 exactness, precision 10 daintiness, femininity, refinement 11 savoir faire 13 gratification
  lacking: 5 gross 7 boorish 9 unrefined

delicate: 4 airy, fine, lacy, nice 5 frail, light, silky 6 dainty, minion, petite, puling, queasy, slight, tender 7 elegant, finical, fragile, minikin, refined, subtile, tenuous 8 araneose, araneous, charming, ethereal, graceful, luscious, migniard, pleaseant 9 agreeable, beautiful, exquisite, sensitive 10 delightful, fastidious 11 comfortable, considerate

delicatessen: 11 charcuterie

delicious: 5 tasty, yummy 6 savory 8 heavenly 9 ambrosial, exquisite, luxurious, nectarous, toothsome 10 delectable, delightful 11 scrumptious

delight: joy 4 glee, love 5 bliss, charm, feast, mirth, revel 6 admire, divert, liking, please, ravish, regale 7 ecstasy, enchant, gladden, gratify, rapture, rejoice 8 entrance, gladness, pleasure, savoring 9 delectate, enjoyment, enrapture, happiness 11 delectation
  in: 6 relish

delightful: 4 nice 6 dreamy 7 elysian 8 adorable, delicate, glorious 9 delicious 10 delectable, enchanting, entrancing 11 pleasureful

Delilah's paramour: 6 Samson

delimit: See **define**

delineate: map 4 draw, limn, line 5 trace 6 blazon, depict, design, sketch, survey 7 outline, picture, portray 8 describe 9 represent 12 characterize

delineation: 5 image 7 account 10 expression

delinquency: 7 default, failure, misdeed, offense 8 omission 9 violation 10 misconduct 11 dereliction, malfeasance, misdemeanor

delinquent: lax 6 remiss 7 overdue 8 behind in 9 negligent 12 teen offender

deliquesce: 4 thaw, melt 7 liquefy 8 dissolve

delirious: mad 4 wild 5 manic 6 insane, raving 7 frantic, lunatic 8 deranged, ecstatic frenetic, frenzied 9 rapturous 10 irrational 11 lightheaded

delirium: 5 fever, mania 10 aberration 13 hallucination

delirium tremens: 6 shakes 7 horrors

delitescent: 6 latent 10 obfuscated

deliver: rid 4 bail, deal, free, give, save, tell 5 bring, serve, speak, utter 6 commit, convey, redeem, render, rescue, resign, succor, unbind 7 consign, declaim, dictate, present, release, relieve 8 dispatch, hand over, liberate 9 enunciate, pronounce, surrender 10 bring forth, emancipate 11 come through

delivery: 5 birth 6 rescue 7 address 8 shipment 9 rendition 11 deliverance, parturition 12 accouchement

dell: 4 dale, glen, vale 6 dingle, ravine, valley

Delphi: 6 oracle, shrine

god: 6 Apollo

priestess: 5 Pythia

Delphic: 5 vague 7 cryptic, obscure 9 ambiguous, enigmatic

delphinium: 8 larkspur

delta: 8 alluvium, triangle

delude: 4 bilk, dupe, fool 5 cheat, evade, trick 6 take in 7 beguile, deceive, mislead 8 hoodwink 10 circumvent, lead astray

deluge: sea 4 flow 5 flood, swamp 6 engulf 7 niagara, torrent 8 downpour, inundate, overflow, submerge 9 cataclysm, overpower, overwhelm 10 cloudburst

delusion: 5 dream, trick 6 mirage, vision 7 chimera, fallacy, fantasy 8 illusion, phantasm 9 deception 13 appersonation, hallucination

Buddhist: 4 moha

of grandeur: 11 megalomania

partner of: 5 snare

delusive: 5 false 6 unreal 7 seeming 8 fanciful, illusory 9 deceiving, imaginary

deluxe: 5 plush, super 6 choice 7 elegant, opulent 8 palatial 9 extra fine, luxurious, sumptuous

delve: dig, dip 4 mine, seek 5 plumb, probe 6 search 7 dig into, explore 11 investigate

demagogic: 8 factious

demagogue, demagog: 6 leader 8 agitator, fomenter 10 instigator 12 rabble rouser

demand: ask, cry 4 call, need 5 claim, exact, order, query 6 charge, elicit, expect, summon 7 command, inquire, mandate, request, require 8 question 9 challenge 10 commission 11 requisition

demandable: due

demarcate: 5 bound, limit 6 define 7 mark off 8 separate 12 circumscribe, discriminate

demean: 5 abase, lower 6 debase 7 degrade 8 belittle, maltreat 9 disparage, humiliate

demeanor: 4 mien, 5 habit 6 action 7 bearing, conduct 8 behavior, carriage, portance 9 treatment 10 deportment, management 11 comportment, countenance

demented: mad 4 luny 5 buggy, crazy, nutty 6 insane 7 fatuous 8 deranged

demerit: 5 fault 7 bad mark 11 short-

coming 12 imperfection

Demeter: 5 Ceres

daughter: 4 Kore 10 Persephone, Proserpina, Proserpine

headdress: 5 polos

mother: 4 Rhea

shrine: 9 anaktoron

demigod: 4 hero 7 godling

pert. to: 7 satyric

sylvan: 4 faun 5 satyr

demirep: 11 adventuress

demise: 5 death 7 decease 8 bequeath 13 pass by descent

demit: 5 lower 6 resign 8 abdicate, withdraw 10 relinquish 11 resignation

demiurgic: 8 creative 9 formative

demo: 5 model 7 display, protest 13 show of feeling, test recording

demobilize: 7 break up, disband 9 muster out 12 demilitarize

democratic: 7 popular 10 self-ruling 11 egalitarian, not snobbish

demode: 5 passe 8 outdated 12 old-fashioned

demoiselle: 5 crane 7 kaikara

demolish: 4 raze, ruin 5 level, waste, wreck 6 batter 7 destroy 8 devastate, overthrow

demon: hag, imp, nat 4 aitu, atua, ogre 5 devil, fiend, genie, lamia, Satan, witch 6 Abigor, afreet 7 villain, warlock 10 evil spirit

assembly of: 6 sabbat

drive out: 8 exorcize

female: 8 succubus

Hebrew: 8 Asmodeus

Iroquois: 5 otkon

person possessed by: 9 energumen

prince of: 9 Beelzebub

worship of: 9 diabolism

Zoroastrian: 5 daeva

demoniac: 7 satanic 8 devilish, diabolic, fiendish, infernal 10 diabolical

demonstrate: 4 show 5 prove 7 display, explain, portray 8 manifest

demonstration: 4 show, sign 5 proof 9 portrayal 10 apparition 11 mass protest 12 illustration 13 manifestation

demonstrative: 4 that, this 5 these, those 8 effusive, outgoing 9 emotional, expansive, ostensive 12 unrestrained

demoralize: 6 weaken 7 confuse, corrupt, deprave, pervert, unnerve 8 disspirit 9 undermine 10 discourage, dishearten 11 disorganize

Demosthenes: *follower:* 5 Bryan 6 orator

oration: 9 philippic

demote: 4 bust 6 reduce 9 downgrade

demotic: 6 common 7 popular

demulcent: 8 soothing 9 softening 10 mollifying

demur: 4 stay 5 delay, doubt, pause 6 boggle, linger, object 7 protest, scruple

8 hesitate, question 9 challenge 12 irresolution

demure: coy, shy 4 prim 5 grave, staid 6
modest, sedate 8 composed, decorous

den: mew 4 cave, cove, dell, dive, glen,
hole, lair, nest, room 5 bield, cabin,
couch, haunt, study 6 burrow, cavern,
covert, grotto, hollow, ravine 7 retreat
8 hideaway, snuggery, workroom

denary: 7 tenfold

dendroid: 8 tree-like 11 arborescent

dendrophilous: 8 arboreal

denial: See deny

denigrate: 5 libel 6 defame, malign 7 disdain, put down, slander 8 ridicule 9
deprecate, disparage 10 speak ill of

denizen: 6 native 7 citizen, dweller, habi-
tué 8 resident 10 inhabitant

Denmark: capital: 10 Copenhagen

   city: 5 Arhus 6 Alborg, Odense 7 Esbjerg
8 Elsinore, Gentofte

   county: Fyn 4 Ribe 5 Arhus, Vejle 6 Vi-
borg 8 Bornholm

   fjord: Ise, Lim 8 Mariager, Roskilde

   flag: 9 Dannebrog

   island: Als, Fyn 4 Aero 5 Samso 7 Falster, Lolland 8 Bornholm 9 Langeland

   measure: ell, fod, mil, pot 4 alen, favn,
rode 5 album, kande, linje, paegl,
tomme 6 achtel, paegel, paegle, skeppe
7 landmil, oltonde, skieppe, viertel 8
fjerding 9 korntonde, ottingkar

   monetary unit: ore 5 krone

   parliament: 9 Folketing

   peninsula: 7 Jutland

   river: 4 Omme, Stor 5 Varde 6 Gudena

   ruler: 4 Cnut, Eric, Knut 5 Sweyn 6 Canute 8 Waldemar 9 Christian, Mar-
grethe

   sea: 5 North 6 Baltic

   sea inlet: 8 Kattegat 9 Skagerrak

   territory: 9 Greenland 13 Faeroe Islands

   weight: es; lod, ort, vog 4 eser(pl.), last,
mark, pund, unze 5 carat, kvint, pound,
quint, tonde 6 toende 7 centner, lispund, quintin 8 lispound, skippund 9
ship pound, skibslast 10 bismerpund

dennet: gig 8 carriage

denominate: 4 call, name 5 title 6 denote
8 christen, indicate, nominate 9 designate

denomination: 4 cult, sect 5 class, title,
value 6 church 7 society 8 category 9
communion 10 persuasion 11 appellation

   religious: 7 Baptist 8 Lutheran 9 Methodist, Unitarian 12 Episcopalian, Presbyterian 14 Congregational

denotation: 4 sign 5 token

denote: 4 give, mark, mean, name, show 6
import 7 betoken, express 8 indicate 9
designate, recommend, represent 10 denominate

denouement: end 6 answer, result 7 outcome 8 solution 11 explanation

denounce: 6 accuse, delate, descry, menace, scathe 7 arraign, condemn, upbraid
8 threaten 9 fulminate 10 stigmatize
13 inform against

de novo: 4 anew 5 again, newly 6 afresh 8
once more 12 from the start

dense: 4 firm 5 close, foggy, gross, heavy,
murky, silly, solid, thick 6 obtuse, stupid 7 compact, crowded, serried 11
thickheaded 12 impenetrable

density: 4 mass 11 compactness

dent: 4 bash, dint, nick 5 dinge, notch,
tooth 6 batter, hallow, indent 7 blemish, depress 10 depression, impression
11 indentation

dentate: 6 jagged 7 serrate, toothed

dentil: 5 block

dentin, dentine: 5 ivory 6 enamel

dentistry: appliance: dam 4 burr

   branch: 9 exodontia 11 orthodontia 12
orthodontics

   plastic: 6 cement

   tool: 6 scaler 7 forceps

denture: 5 plate 10 set of teeth

denude: 4 bare 5 scalp, strip 6 divest 11
decorticate

denunciation (see also denounce): 7
censure 8 diatribe 9 philippic 10 accusation 11 malediction 12 condemnation

deny: nay 5 debar, repel 6 abjure, disown,
forbid, impugn, negate, refuse, refute,
rejec. renege 7 confute, deprive, disavow, dispute, forsake, gainsay, protest
8 abnegate, disclaim, forswear, renounce, withhold 9 disaffirm 10 contradict, contravene, controvert

deodar: 5 cedar

depart: die 4 blow, exit, pass, quit, vary 5
found, leave, mosey, sever 6 begone, decamp, demise, desist, divide, perish, recede, retire, sunder 7 abscond, deviate,
forsake, get away, pull out, retreat, take
off, vamoose 8 farewell, separate, withdraw

department: 4 part 5 realm 6 branch, bureau, sphere 7 portion 8 division, province 11 subdivision

departure: 4 exit 5 death, going, twist 6
egress, exodus 7 decease 9 deviation 10
difference, divergence 11 abandonment, leavetaking

   words of: 4 ta-ta 5 aloha 6 so long 7
goodbye 8 farewell

depend: 4 bank, hang, lean, rely, rest, turn
5 count, hinge, trust 7 confide

dependable: 4 sure 5 loyal, solid 6 secure,
steady 7 certain 8 faithful, reliable 11
responsible, trustworthy

dependency: 6 colony 7 apanage, mandate 8 appanage

dependent: 4 ward 5 child 6 client, minion, vassal 7 subject 8 clinging, follower 9 reliant on 10 contingent, sequacious 11 conditional, provisional, subordinate

depict: 4 draw, limn 5 paint 6 blazon 7 picture, portray 8 describe 9 delineate, represent 12 characterize

depilate: 4 husk 5 shave

depilatory: 5 rusma

depilous: 8 hairless

deplete: 5 drain, empty, use up 6 reduce, unload 7 exhaust 8 diminish 10 impoverish

deplorable: sad 8 grievous, terrible, wretched 10 calamitous, lamentable 11 distressing, unfortunate

deplore: rue 4 moan, sigh, wail 5 mourn 6 bemoan, bewail, grieve, lament, regret 10 disapprove

deploy: 6 unfold 7 display 9 spread out

deplume: 5 pluck, strip

depone: 5 swear 7 testify 11 bear witness

deport: 5 evict, exile, expel 6 banish, behave, demean 7 bearing, conduct 8 send away 9 transport

deportment: air 4 gest, mien 5 geste, havit 6 action, manner 7 address, bearing, conduct 8 behavior, breeding, carriage, demeanor

depose: 4 aver, oust 5 abase 6 affirm, assert, divest, remove 7 degrade, dismiss, testify 8 dethrone, displace 10 dispossess

deposit: lay, set 4 bank, cast, dump, fund, hock, pawn 5 chest, lodge, place, store 6 entomb, pledge, repose, settle 7 consign, entrust, put down 8 security 11 part payment 12 accumulation

alluvial: 5 delta, geest

black: 4 soot

earthy: 4 gobi, marl, sand, silt 5 loess, trona 6 sludge 8 alluvium

geyser: 6 sinter 10 travertine

glacial: 4 kame 5 eskar, esker 7 moraine

gold-containing: 6 placer

gravel: 4 apron

marine: 5 coral

mineral: bed 4 lode, vein 5 manto

roric: dew

teeth: 6 tartar

wine cask: 6 tartar

deposition: 6 burial 7 deposit, opinion 8 sediment 9 affidavit, statement, testimony 10 allegation 11 declaration 12 displacement 13 precipitation

depository: 4 bank, safe 5 attic, chest, vault 6 locker 7 ossuary 9 strongbox

depot: 4 base, gare(F.) 6 aurang(Ind.), aurung 7 arsenal, station 8 magazine, terminal, terminus 9 warehouse 10 storehouse

deprave: 5 taint 6 debase, defile, malign,

revile 7 corrupt, pervert, vitiate 10 degenerate, depreciate

depraved: bad 4 evil, ugly, vile 6 rotten, wicked 7 bestial, immoral, vicious 9 abandoned, graceless 10 profligate 11 demoralized 12 incorrigible

depravity: 4 vice 8 villainy

deprecate: 8 play down 9 denigrate, underrate 10 depreciate, disapprove

depreciate: 4 fall 5 abase, decry, slump 6 lessen, reduce, shrink 7 cheapen, degrade, depress, detract, devalue 8 belittle, derogate, diminish, minimize 9 disparage, dispraise, downgrade 10 undervalue

depredate: rob 4 prey, raze, sack 5 spoil 6 thieve, ravage 7 despoil, destroy, pillage, plunder 8 lay waste, prey upon

depress: bow, cow 4 dash, dent, fall, sink 5 abase, appal, chill, crush, lower, slump 6 appall, dampen, dismay, humble, indent, lessen, sadden, weaken 7 degrade, flatten 8 browbeat, diminish, dispirit, enfeeble 9 subjugate 10 depreciate, discourage, dishearten

depressed: low, sad 4 blue, down, glum 6 gloomy, hollow, lonely, oblate, somber, triste 8 dejected, downcast 9 afflicted, heartsore 10 in the dumps, spiritless 11 downhearted, melancholic

depressing: 5 bleak 6 dismal, dreary

depression: dip, pit 4 fall, foss, howe(Sc.) 5 atrio, basin, cowal, crypt, dinge, fossa, fosse, nadir 6 cafard, cavity, crater, dismay, gulley, ravine, valley 7 alveola, blowout 8 doldrums 9 dejection 11 despondency

between mountains: col

pert. to: 6 bathic

deprivation: 4 loss, want 6 penury 7 amotion, poverty 8 hardship 11 destitution

deprive: rob 4 deny 5 strip 6 depose, divest, hinder, remove 7 bereave, cashier, despoil 9 dismantle, relieve of 10 dispossess

deprived: 4 reft 5 needy 12 impoverished

depth: 5 abyss 8 deepness, strength 9 abundance, intensity 10 profundity 11 perspective 12 abstruseness, completeness, profoundness

in: 8 thorough 13 comprehensive

without: 4 thin 7 cursory, shallow, sketchy 11 superficial

depth charge: 4 bomb, mine 10 projectile

depths: 5 heart 7 lowness 10 inmost part

deputation: 7 mission 10 delegation

depute: 4 send 5 allot 6 assign, devote 7 appoint 8 de'egate 10 commission, constitute

deputy: 4 aide 5 agent, envoy, proxy, vicar 6 commis, legate 7 bailiff 8 delegate

9 assistant, surrogate, vigilante 10 substitute

deracinate: 6 uproot 9 eradicate, extirpate

derange: 5 upset 7 confuse, disturb, perturb 8 disorder, displace, unsettle 9 interrupt 10 discompose 11 disorganize

deranged: mad 5 crazy 6 insane 8 demented, maniacal 10 distraught, unbalanced

derby: hat 4 race, town 5 shire 6 bowler

deregulate: 8 end curbs 9 decontrol 11
free of rules

derelict: bum, lax 4 hobo, wino 5 dingy,
seedy, tramp 6 remiss, shabby 7 drifter,
run down, vagrant 8 castaway, deserted, forsaken 9 abandoned 10 delinquent, neglectful

deride: 4 geck(Sc.), gibe, hoot, jape, jeer,
mock, twit 5 fleer, rally, scoff, scorn,
taunt 6 illude 8 ridicule 9 make fun of

de rigueur: 5 right 6 proper 7 correct 8
required 11 fashionable

derision: 8 contempt

sound of: boo 4 hiss 5 snort

derivation: 6 origin, source 9 etymology
10 wellspring

derivative: 7 spin-off 8 offshoot 9 outgrowth, traceable 10 unoriginal

derive: get 4 draw, stem 5 carry, infer,
trace 6 deduce, evolve, gather, obtain 7
extract, proceed, receive 9 originate

derm: 4 skin 7 cuticle

dermal filament: 4 hair

dernier cri: 4 mode, rage 5 craze, style,
vogue 7 fashion 8 last word

derogate: 5 annul, decry 6 lessen, repeal
7 detract, slander 8 restrict, withdraw
9 disparage 10 depreciate

derrick: rig 4 lift, spar 5 crane, davit,
hoist 6 tackle

part: jib, leg 4 boom

derring-do: 7 bravado, courage 8 audacity

derringer: 6 pistol, weapon

dervish: 5 fakir 9 mendicant

cap: taj

of Arabian Nights: 4 Agib

practice: 7 dancing, howling 8 whirling

descant: 4 sing, song 6 melody, remark,
warble 7 comment 9 discourse 11 observation 12 counterpoint, dissertation
13 accompaniment

descend: 4 fall, sink 5 avale, lower, stoop
6 alight, derive, go down 7 decline 9
originate 10 spring from

by rope: 6 rappel

descendant: son 4 cion, heir, seed 5 child,
scion 7 spin-off 8 offshoot 9 offspring

descendants: 4 seed 5 issue 7 progeny 9
posterity 10 generation

descended from same mother: 5 enate
6 enatic

descent: 4 drop, fall 5 birth, chute, issue,
scarp, slope, stock 6 escarp, strain 7 assault, decline, lineage 8 ancestry, breeding, downfall, pedigree 9 avalanche, declivity, onslaught 10 declension,
derivation, extraction, generation 11
declination, degradation, inclination

airplane: 8 approach

skier's: 6 schuss

describe: 4 tell 6 define, depict, relate, report 7 declare, explain, express, narrate,
outline, picture, portray, recount 9 delineate, designate, discourse, enumerate,
represent 10 illustrate 12 characterize

description: ilk 4 kind, sort, type 7 account, recital, variety, version 9 chronicle 12 presentation

descry: see, spy 4 espy 5 sight 6 behold,
detect, reveal, turn up 7 discern, display
8 disclose, discover, perceive 9 determine 11 distinguish

Desdemona: *husband:* 7 Othello

servant: 6 Emilia

slayer: 7 Othello

traducer: 4 Iago

desecrate: 5 abuse 6 defile 7 pollute, profane, violate 8 unhallow 11 contaminate

desecration: 9 blasphemy, sacrilege

desert: due, rat 4 bolt, fail, flee, sand 5
merit, waste 6 decamp, defect, go
AWOL, renege, reward 7 abandon, abscond, badland, demerit, forsake, hor-
nada 8 renounce 9 backslide, wasteland
10 punishment, relinquish, wilderness

area: 4 Gobi 6 Libyan, Mohave, Nubian,
Sahara 7 Arabian, Painted

area of shifting sand: erg

beast: 5 camel 9 dromedary

dweller: 4 Arab 5 nomad 7 Bedouin

hallucination: 6 mirage

pert. to: 6 eremic

rat: 10 prospector

region: erg

science: 9 eremology

ship: 5 camel

shrub: 5 retem 6 alhagi, cactus, raetam
10 camel thorn

train: 7 caravan

valley: 6 bolson

vehicle: 9 dune buggy

watering spot: 5 oasis

wind: 6 samiel, simoom 7 sirocco

desert candle: 5 plant 8 ocotillo

desert-like: dry 4 arid, sere

deserted: 6 lonely, 7 forlorn 8 desolate,
forsaken 9 abandoned 11 uninhabited

deserter: rat 6 bolter 8 apostate, defector,
fugitive, recreant, renegade

deserve: 4 earn, rate 5 merit 10 be worthy of

desiccate: dry 4 sear 5 drain, parch 6

wither 7 shrivel 9 dehydrate

desideratum: 4 need 6 desire

design: aim, end, map 4 draw, goal, idea, mean, plan, plot 5 allot, decor, drift, ettle, mean, motif, shape 6 device, intend, intent, invent, layout, object, sketch 7 destine, diagram, fashion, outline, pattern, project, propose, purpose 8 contrive 9 calculate, delineate, intention 10 conception 11 contemplate, contrivance

inlaid: 6 mosaic 8 intarsia

of scattered objects: 4 seme

open: 8 filigree, fretwork

perforated: 7 stencil

raised: 8 repousse 9 bas relief

skin: 6 tattoo

sunken: 8 intaglio

designate: set 4 mark, mean, name, show 5 label, style, title 6 assign, denote, intend, settle 7 appoint, entitle, specify 8 describe, identify, indicate 9 appellate, nuncupate 10 denominate 11 distinguish 12 characterize

designed: 8 prepense 10 thought out 11 intentional 12 premeditated

designer: 7 planner, plotter, schemer 8 engineer 9 architect, couturier

designing: 6 artful, crafty 7 cunning 8 planning, plotting, scheming 10 foreseeing, fraudulent

desinential: 8 terminal

desipient: 5 silly 7 foolish

desirable: 7 welcome 8 eligible, pleasing, salutary 9 agreeable, excellent 10 attractive, beneficial, worthwhile

desire: yen 4 care, hope, itch, lust, need, urge, want, will, wish 5 ardor, covet, crave, mania, yearn 6 affect, aspire, hanker, hunger, prefer, thirst, yammer 7 craving, fantasy, inkling, longing, passion 8 appetite, cupidity 9 appetency, cacoethes 10 desiderium

want of: 11 inappetence

desirous: 4 fain, fond 5 eager 6 ardent, greedy 7 envious, wishful 8 covetous 10 solicitous 11 acquisitive

desist: 4 ease, halt, quit, stop 5 cease 7 abstain, forbear, hold off 11 discontinue, refrain from

desk: pew 4 ambo 5 board, table 6 pulpit 7 lectern 8 prie-dieu 9 davenport, monocleid, secretary 10 escritoire, monocleide

desman: 4 mole 7 muskrat

Desmanthus: 5 Acuan

desmid: 4 alga 5 algae(pl.)

desolate: sad 4 bare, lorn, ruin, sack, sole 5 alone, bleak, gaunt 6 dreary, gloomy, lonely, ravage 7 destroy, forlorn, lacking 8 deprived, deserted, forsaken, solitary 9 abandoned, destitute, dissolute,

woebegone 11 comfortless, uninhabited 12 disconsolate

desolation: woe 5 grief, havoc 6 sorrow 7 sadness 10 melancholy 11 destruction, devastation

area of: 5 waste 6 desert

Desmodium: 7 trefoil

despair: 5 gloom 6 give up 8 lose hope 10 melancholy 11 despondency 12 hopelessness

desperado: 6 bandit, outlaw 7 ruffian 8 criminal 10 lawbreaker

desperate: mad 4 rash 7 extreme, frantic 8 headlong, hopeless, perilous, reckless 9 dangerous 10 despairing, desperado, infuriated, outrageous 11 precipitate 13 irretrievable

despicable: low 4 base, mean, vile 5 cheap, dirty 6 abject, paltry, scurvy, shabby, sordid 7 caitiff, ignoble 8 unworthy, wretched 9 loathsome, miserable 11 ignominious 12 contemptible, contemptuous

despise: 4 defy, hate 5 scorn, scout, spurn 6 detest, loathe, slight 7 contemn, disdain 8 misprize, vilipend 9 abominate, disregard 10 look down on

despite: 4 hate, snub 6 injury, insult, malice 7 ill will 8 aversion, contempt 12 regardless of

despoil: rob 4 raid, ruin, sack 5 harry, reave, rifle, strip 6 divest, fleece, ravage, ravish, remove 7 bereave, deprive, disrobe, pillage, plunder 8 deflower, disarray, unclothe 9 depredate

Despoina: 4 Kore 10 Persephone

despondency: 6 misery 7 despair 10 depression, melancholy 11 desperation

despondent: sad 4 blue 8 dejected, downcast, hopeless 9 woebegone 10 dispirited 11 discouraged 12 disconsolate, heavyhearted

despot: 4 czar, tsar, tzar 6 satrap, tyrant 7 autarch, monarch 8 autocrat, dictator 9 strong man

despotic: 6 lordly 8 absolute, dominant 9 arbitrary 10 tyrannical

dessert: ice, pie 4 cake 5 fruit, glace(Fr.) 6 eclair, mousse, pastry, sweets 7 banquet, pudding, sherbet, strudel 8 ice cream, Napoleon, sillabub 9 pound cake, sweetmeat 10 blanc-mange

destination: aim, end 4 fate, goal 7 address 8 terminus 9 objective 12 end of the line

destine: 6 decree, direct, doom to, intend 9 devise for, fix before, preordain 11 assign ahead, set aside for 12 predetermine

destiny: lot 4 doom, fate 5 karma 6 future, kismet 7 fortune 8 God's will 13 inevitability

destitute: 4 poor 5 clean, needy 6 bereft, devoid, wasted 7 forlorn, lacking, wanting 8 bankrupt, beggared, defeated, deprived, desolate, forsaken, helpless, indigent 9 abandoned, defaulted, driftless 10 devastated, frustrated 12 disappointed, impoverished

destroy: eat, end, gut 4 blow, full, raze, ruin, rush, slay, undo 5 break, craze, erase, erode, quell, smash, smite, spoil, wrack, wreck 6 blight, cumber, deface, defeat, efface, famish, ravage 7 abolish, consume, expunge, overrun 8 amortize, confound, decimate, demolish, desolate, dissolve, mutilate, overturn, sabotage 9 depredate, devastate, dismantle, eradicate, extirpate, liquidate, overthrow 10 annihilate, counteract, extinguish 11 assassinate, exterminate

destroyed: 5 kaput

destroyer: hun 6 vandal 7 warship 8 saboteur

Destroyer: 4 Siva

Destroying Angel: *fungus:* 7 amanita *Mormon:* 6 Danite

destruction: end 4 bane, doom, loss, ruin 5 decay, havoc, waste 7 Abaddon(Heb.) 8 downfall, excision, shambles 9 holocaust, perdition 10 extinction, subversion
god: 4 Siva
goddess: Ara
of species: 8 genocide

destructive: 4 fell 5 fatal 6 deadly, mórtal 7 baleful, deathly, fateful, harmful, hurtful, noisome, noxious, ruinous 8 wasteful 9 poisonous, truculent 10 catawampus, pernicious 11 deleterious, internecine

desuetude: 6 disuse 7 neglect 12 obsolescence 14 discontinuance

desultory: 4 idle 5 hasty, loose 6 casual, fitful, random, roving 7 aimless, cursory 8 rambling, unsteady, wavering 9 irregular, unsettled 10 discursive, incidental, inconstant 12 disconnected

detach: 5 sever 6 cut off 7 disjoin, divorce, isolate 8 disunite, separate, unfasten, withdraw 9 disengage 10 disconnect

detached: 4 free 5 alone, aloof, apart 7 neutral, removed 8 taken off, unbiased 10 impersonal 11 unconcerned, unconnected 13 disinterested, dispassionate

detail: 4 item 6 assign, nicety, relate 7 account, appoint, article, itemize, minutia, narrate, specify 8 rehearse, salience, spell out 9 enumerate, narrative 10 particular 11 stipulation 12 circumstance

detailed: 4 full 6 minute, prolix 8 itemized, thorough, tiresome 9 wearisome

10 meticulous, protracted

detain: 4 hold, keep, stay, stop 5 check, delay 6 arrest, hinder, retard 8 imprison, restrain, withhold
in time of war: 6 intern

detect: see, spy 4 espy, find, spot 5 catch 6 descry, divine, expose, reveal 7 develop, discern, nose out, uncover 8 decipher, discover

detection device: 5 radar, sonar 6 dowser 11 divining rod

detective: tec 4 bull, dick 6 sleuth, tracer 7 gumshoe, scenter, spotter 8 flatfoot, operator, Sam Spade, The Saint 9 James Bond, Nero Wolfe 10 Martin Kane, Miss Marple, Nick Carter, Perry Mason, Peter Salem, Philo Vance 11 Charlie Chan, Ellery Queen, Green Hornet, Nick Charles 12 investigator, Simon Templar 13 Hercule Poirot, Michael Shayne, Philip Marlowe 14 Sherlock Holmes
story writer: 8 Rex Stout 10 Ian Fleming 11 Ellery Queen 14 Agatha Christie 15 Dashiell Hammett, Raymond Chandler 16 Arthur Conan Doyle 18 Erle Stanley Gardner

detector: 7 reagent
storm: 7 sferics
weather change: 9 barometer

detent: dog 4 pawl 5 catch, click

detente: 8 easement 13 rapprochement

detention: 5 delay 7 capture 9 hindrance, restraint 10 arrestment

deter: bar 5 block, check, delay 6 hinder, retard 7 prevent 8 dissuade, keep from, restrain 9 constrain 10 discourage, dishearten, intimidate

detergent: 4 soap 7 purging, smectic, solvent 8 cleanser 9 cleansing

deteriorate: 4 fail 5 decay, spoil 6 debase, impair, weaken 7 decline, wear out 9 backslide 10 degenerate

determinable: 5 fixed 8 definite 9 judicable 10 mensurable

determinate: 7 certain 8 definite, resolute, resolved, specific 9 arbitrary 10 invariable 11 established

determinative: 5 final 7 shaping 8 limiting 9 directing 10 conclusive 13 authoritative

determine: end, fix, get 4 test 5 assay, award 6 assess, assign, decide, decree, define, descry, settle 7 adjudge, analyze, appoint, arrange, dispose, resolve 8 conclude 9 admeasure, arbitrate, ascertain, calculate 10 adjudicate, constitute, deliberate, predestine

determined: set 4 bent, firm 6 dogged, intent, mulish, sturdy 7 decided, settled 8 foregone, perverse, resolute, resolved, stubborn 9 obstinate, pigheaded 10 persistent, unyielding

deterrent: 5 block 6 hurdle 8 obstacle 9 hindrance 14 discouragement

detest: 4 damn, hate 5 abhor, curse 6 loathe 7 condemn, despise, dislike 8 denounce, execrate 9 abominate

detestable: 4 foul, vile 6 horrid, odious 7 heinous 8 infamous 9 nefarious 10 despicable 12 antipathetic

dethrone: 6 depose, divest

detonate: 4 fire 5 blast 6 blow up, set off 7 explode 9 fulminate

detonator: cap 7 torpedo 9 explosive

detour: 5 avoid, skirt 6 bypass 7 circuit 8 go around 9 deviation

detract: 5 decry 6 defame, divert, vilify 7 asperse, traduce 8 belittle, derogate, minimize 9 disparage 10 depreciate

detraction: 7 calumny, scandal, slander

detriment: 4 cost, hurt, loss 5 damna(pl.), wound 6 damage, injury 8 mischief 9 disprofit 10 impediment 12 disadvantage

detrimental: 7 adverse, harmful, hurtful 9 injurious 10 pernicious 11 deleterious

detritus: 4 tuff 5 chaff, scree, waste 6 debris 7 garbage, rubbish

de trop: 6 excess 7 too much, surplus 8 in the way, unwanted 11 superfluous

deva: 5 angel, deity

Devaki's son: See 7 Krishna

devalue: See depreciate

devastate: 6 ravage 7 destroy, pillage, plunder, scourge 8 demolish, lay waste 10 depopulate

develop: 4 form, grow 5 arise, ripen 6 appear, detect, evolve, expand, flower, mature, reveal, unfold, unfurl 7 educate, enlarge, expound, uncover 8 disclose, discover, engender, generate, manifest 9 elaborate, germinate, transpire 11 come to light, materialize

development: 6 growth 7 stature 8 breeding, increase 9 evolution, expansion, formation, unfolding 11 elaboration

arrested: 7 aplasia

full: 8 maturity, ripeness

going back: 13 retrogression

Devi: *beneficent:* 5 Guari

consort: 4 Siva

fierce: 4 Kali

light: Uma

malignant: 5 Durga

riding a tiger: 6 Chandi

deviate: err, vary 4 lean, miss, vary, veer 5 drift, lapse, sheer, stray 6 change, depart, detour, recede, squint, swerve, wander 7 decline, deflect, digress, diverge

from the norm: 6 mutate

from the vertical: 4 hade 5 angle, slant 10 out of plumb

deviation: 7 anomaly 11 declination

device: gin, mot 4 tool 5 drift, meter, motto, shift 6 design, emblem, gadget, scheme 7 compass, fiction, impresa, imprese, project, vehicle 8 artifice, fastener, gimcrack 9 apparatus, appliance, doohickey, expedient, invention, regulator, stratagem 10 concoction, instrument 11 contraption, contrivance

curve measuring: 9 rotameter

holding: 4 vise 5 clamp

devil: imp 4 Deil(Sc.), haze, mahu 5 annoy, bogey, demon, fiend, Satan, tease 6 dybbuk, pester 7 Amaimon, clootie, dickens, gremlin, Lucifer, Old Nick, torment, warlock 8 Apollyon, diabolus, Mephisto 9 archfiend, Beelzebub, cacodemon, scoundrel

Dante's: 8 Cagnazzo

pert. to: 7 satanic 10 diabolical

printer's: 10 apprentice

ruler: 10 diabolarch

tree: 4 dita

worship: 8 satanism

devil's bones: 4 dice

devil-may-care: gay 4 fast, rash 5 blasé 6 madcap 7 raffish 8 heedless, reckless 9 imprudent 10 nonchalant 11 harumscarum

deviled: 9 a la diable

devilfish: ray 5 manta

devilish: 6 daring, rakish, wicked 7 demonic, extreme, hellish, inhuman, satanic 8 demoniac, diabolic, fiendish, infernal 9 excessive 10 diabolical 15 Mephistophelian

devilkin: imp

devious: sly 4 foxy 6 crafty, errant, roving, shifty, tricky 7 vagrant, winding 8 indirect, rambling, tortuous 9 eccentric, irregular 10 circuitous, farfetched, roundabout

devise: 4 plan, plot, will 5 array, frame, forge, weave 6 convey, cook up, design, invent, scheme 7 appoint, arrange, bethink, concoct, consult, dream up, prepare 8 bequeath, contrive 9 construct, fabricate, formulate 11 put together

devitalize: 6 deaden 10 eviscerate

devoid: 4 bare 5 empty 6 barren, free of, vacant 7 lacking, wanting 9 destitute

devoir: 4 duty, task 6 effort

devolve: 4 pass 8 overturn, transfer, transmit 11 change hands

devote: vow 4 ally, avow, doom, give 5 apply 6 addict, attach, bestow, depute, resign 7 address, consign, destine 8 dedicate, venerate 10 consecrate 11 appropriate

devoted: 4 true 5 liege, loyal, pious 6 devout, fervid **7** adoring, arduous, zealous **8** attached, constant, faithful **9** assiduous, religious **10** obsequious, venerating **11** whole-souled **12** affectionate, wholehearted

devotee: fan, nun **4** buff, monk **6** votary, zealot **7** admirer, amateur, fanatic **8** follower, partisan **9** supporter **10** aficionado, enthusiast

devotion: 4 aves(pl.) **6** fealty, prayer **7** loyalty, passion, worship **8** fidelity **9** adoration, reverence **10** allegiance

excessive: **13** ecclesiolatry

object of: **4** idol **5** totem **6** fetich, fetish

period of: **4** Lent **6** novena

devour: eat **4** fret **5** raven, waste **6** engulf **7** consume, engorge **10** annihilate

devout: 4 good, holy, warm **5** godly, pious **6** hearty, solemn **7** cordial, devoted, godlike, saintly, sincere **8** reverent **9** religious, righteous, spiritual **13** sanctimonious

dew: 4 rime **8** moisture **9** hoarfrost

dewlap: 4 jowl **7** wattles

dewy: 4 damp **5** moist, roric **6** gentle **9** sparkling **10** glistening, refreshing

dexter: 5 right **6** honest **9** fortunate **10** auspicious **15** straightforward

dexterity: art **5** craft, knack, skill **7** ability, address, agility, aptness, cunning, finesse, sleight **8** aptitude, deftness, facility **9** adeptness, diplomacy, quickness, readiness **10** adroitness, cleverness, expertness, nimbleness

dextral: 10 auspicious **11** right-handed

dey: 5 pasha, ruler

dhan: 6 cattle, wealth **8** property

diabetes remedy: 7 insulin

diablerie: 7 devilry, sorcery **8** mischief **10** black magic, demonology, witchcraft

diabolical, diabolic: 5 cruel **6** wicked **7** hellish, inhuman, satanic, violent **8** demoniac, devilish, fiendish, infernal

diacritic: 4 mark **5** tilde **6** umlaut **11** distinctive

diadem: 5 crown, tiara **6** anadem, circle, emblem, fillet **7** coronet **8** headband **11** sovereignty

diagnose: 7 analyze **8** identify, pinpoint

diagonal: 4 bias **7** slanted **13** catercornered

diagram: map **4** plan **5** chart, epure(F.), graph **6** design **7** outline, schema **8** blueprint

dial: 4 disk, face **6** tune in **7** control, crystal **8** horologe **9** indicator, telephone

dialect: 5 argot, idiom, lingo **6** brogue, debate, patois, patter, speech **8** language **10** vernacular **11** phraseology

Georgia: **6** Gullah

London: **7** cockney

Louisiana: **5** Cajun

most prestigious: **8** acrolect

dialogue: 4 chat, talk **6** parley **10** discussion **12** conversation

having nature of: **13** interlocutory

diameter: 4 bore **14** circle bisector

half: **5** radii(pl.) **6** radius

diametric: 7 counter **8** contrary, opposite

diamond: gem, ice **4** rock **5** field, jager, jewel **7** lozenge **8** corundum **9** brilliant, briolette, sparkling

crystal: **7** glassie

cutter: **12** brilliandeer

element: **6** carbon

famous: See **stone:** *famous*

fragments: **5** chips

glazier's: **6** emeril

holding device: dop **4** dopp

imitation: **5** paste **9** schlenter

industrial: **4** bort **5** bortz

necklace: **7** riviere(F.)

surface: **5** facet

unit of weight: **5** carat

diamond-hard: 7 adamant

Diamond State: 8 Delaware

Diana: 7 Artemis

father: **7** Jupiter

mother: **6** Latona

twin: **6** Apollo

diana monkey: 7 roloway

diaphanous: 5 filmy, gauzy, sheer **8** gossamer **11** transparent

diaphragm: 7 midriff

pert. to: **7** phrenic

diary: log **6** record **7** journal **8** register **9** ephemeris

diaskeuast: 6 editor **7** reviser

diastase: 4 malt **6** enzyme

diatribe: 6 tirade **8** harangue **9** criticism, invective, philippic **12** denunciation

Diaz de Bivar's title: Cid

dibble: dib **7** dip bait **10** garden tool

dibs: 5 claim, share, syrup **6** rights

dice: 4 cube **5** bones **6** gamble **7** checker

game: **5** craps

losing throw: **5** three **7** boxcars **9** snake eyes

throw of six: **4** sice

dicey: 5 risky **6** chancy **9** uncertain

dichotomize: 4 part **5** sever **6** divide **7** break up **8** separate **10** split in two

dick: tec **6** copper **8** flatfoot **9** detective, policeman

Dickens's title: *character:* Pip, Tim **4** Dora, Nell **5** Fagin **6** Cuttle **7** Dorritt, Podsnap **9** Bill Sikes, Uriah Heep

pen name: Boz

dicker: 4 deal, swap **5** daker **6** barter, haggle **7** bargain, chaffer **8** exchange **9** agreement, negotiate

dickey: 4 weak 5 shaky 10 shirt front

dictate: say 4 tell 5 order, utter 6 decree, enjoin, impose, ordain 7 command, deliver, mandate, require 9 prescribe, principle 11 communicate

dictatorial: 6 lordly 7 pompous 8 arrogant, despotic, dogmatic, positive 9 imperious, masterful 10 autocratic, peremptory, tyrannical 11 doctrinaire, domineering, magisterial, opinionated, overbearing 13 authoritative

diction: 5 style 6 phrase 7 wording 8 language, parlance, verbiage 10 vocabulary 11 enunciation, phraseology

dictionary: 7 lexicon 8 wordbook 10 vocabulary 11 onomasticon

compiler: 13 lexicographer

geographical: gazetteer

poet's: 6 gradus

dictum: 5 adage, axiom, edict 6 decree, saying 7 opinion 8 apothegm 9 principle, statement 13 pronouncement

Dictynna: 11 Britomartis

didactic: dry 7 preachy 8 pedantic 10 moralistic 11 instructive

didacticism: 6 homily 8 pedantry

diddle: gyp 4 hoax 5 cheat 6 befool, dawdle, jiggle, loiter, trifle 7 swindle 9 waste time

dido: 5 antic, caper, frill, prank, trick 6 gewgaw 7 trinket 8 furbelow, gimcrack

Dido: *father:* 5 Belus

founder of: 8 Carthage

husband: 7 Acerbas

sister: 4 Anna

wooer: 6 Aeneas

die: ebb 4 cube, dado, fade, mold, seal, wane 5 abate, croak, stamp, yearn 6 chance, depart, expire, finish, perish, vanish, wither 7 decease, succumb 8 languish, puncheon 9 grow faint

loaded: 6 fulham, fullam

symbol: ace

die-hard: 4 Tory 7 old fogy 8 hardnose, mossback, rightist, stubborn 9 dogmatist, obstinate, pigheaded 11 reactionary 12 conservative

Dies Irae(L.): 4 hymn 8 mass part 10 day of wrath

diet: 4 fare, fast, food 5 board 6 reduce, viands 7 regimen 8 congress 10 convention 11 convocation, legislature

difference: 5 clash 6 change 7 discord, dispute 8 conflict, division, variance 10 alteration, dissension, unlikeness 11 controversy, discrepancy, distinction 12 disagreement

different: 5 other 6 divers, sundry, unlike 7 diverse, several, unalike, unusual, variant, various 8 distinct, manifold, separate 9 disparate, divergent 10 dissimilar, variegated 11 diversified

differentiate: 8 contrast 11 distinguish 12 discriminate

difficult: 4 hard 5 fussy, rough, tough 6 crabby, cranky, knotty, rugged, uphill 7 arduous, labored, not easy, obscure, painful, practic 8 abstract, puzzling, stubborn 9 intricate, laborious 11 complicated, troublesome

difficulty: ado, fix, jam, rub 4 snag 5 fight, nodus 6 hassle, pickle, plight, scrape, strait 7 barrier, dilemma, dispute, pitfall, problem, quarrel, trouble 8 asperity, obstacle, severity, struggle 9 hindrance, objection 10 impediment 11 controversy, obstruction, vicissitude 12 complication, disagreement

diffidence: 5 doubt 7 modesty, reserve, shyness 8 distrust, humility, timidity 9 suspicion 10 hesitation 11 bashfulness 12 apprehension

diffuse: 4 full, shed 5 strew, wordy 6 divide, expand, extend, prolix, spread 7 copious, pervade, pour out, publish, radiate, scatter, verbose 8 disperse 9 circulate, dissipate, expatiate, garrulous, irradiate, propagate 10 widespread 11 disseminate

diffusion: 7 osmosis 10 outpouring

dig: get, hoe 4 claw, gibe, grub, hole, like, mine, poke, root 5 delve, nudge, probe, spade, taunt 6 burrow, exhume, plunge, quarry, shovel, thrust 7 approve, unearth 8 excavate, scoop out 10 understand

dig out: 6 go into 7 uncover 10 do research 11 investigate

digest: 4 code 5 ripen 6 absorb, codify, mature, precis 7 concoct, epitome, pandect, summary 8 condense, synopsis 10 abridgment, assimilate, compendium, comprehend

digestion: 7 eupepsy 8 eupepsia

agent: 6 pepsin, rennin 7 maltase

ailment: 5 colic 6 gripes 7 pyrosis 9 dyspepsia 12 constipation

having good: 8 eupeptic

digging, fitted for: 7 fodient

digit: toe 4 unit 5 thumb 6 figure, finger, number 7 integer, numeral

podal: toe

shield for: cot 5 stall 7 thimble

vestigial: 7 dewclaw

diglot: 9 bilingual

dignified: 5 grand, lofty, noble, staid 6 august, sedate, solemn 7 courtly, stately 8 majestic 11 magisterial

dignify: 5 adorn, exalt, grace, honor 7 elevate, ennoble, promote

dignitary: VIP 5 nabob 6 big gun, leader 7 notable 8 brass hat, luminary, official

dignity: 4 rank 5 honor, pride, worth 6 repute 7 bearing, decorum, fitness, gravity, majesty, station 8 elegance, prestige, standing 9 nobleness 10 excellence

digress: 4 veer 5 drift, stray 6 swerve, wander 7 deviate, diverge 8 divagate 10 depart from

digression: 7 episode 8 excursus 9 excursion

dike, dyke: 4 bank, pond, pool 5 digue, ditch, levee 7 channel 8 causeway 10 embankment 11 watercourse

dilapidated: 5 dingy 6 beat-up, shabby 7 damaged, run-down 10 threadbare 12 falling apart

dilapidation: 4 ruin 5 decay 9 disrepair 10 raggedness 14 disintegration

dilate: 5 swell, widen 6 expand, extend 7 amplify, broaden, distend, enlarge, inflate, prolong, stretch 8 increase, lengthen, protract 9 discourse, expatiate

dilatory: 4 slow 5 slack, tardy 6 fabian, remiss 8 backward, delaying, inactive, sluggish 10 behindhand 15 procrastinating

dilemma: fix 4 node 5 poser 7 problem 8 quandary 10 perplexity 11 predicament 12 complication 13 Hobson's choice

dilettante: 5 lover 7 admirer, amateur, dabbler, dabster, esthete 8 aesthete

diligence: 4 heed 6 effort 7 caution 8 industry 9 constancy 11 application, earnestness, heedfulness

diligent: 4 busy 6 active, eident, steady 7 careful, earnest, heedful, operose 8 sedulous 9 assiduous 11 hardworking, industrious, painstaking, persevering

dill: 4 herb 6 pickle 9 flavoring, seasoning

dilly: pip 4 darb, lulu 5 beaut, dandy 9 humdinger

dillydally: lag, toy 4 loaf 5 stall 6 loiter, trifle 9 vacillate

dilute: cut 4 thin 5 alter 6 debase, modify, reduce, weaken 8 diminish 9 attenuate, water down

dim: wan 4 blur, dark, dull, fade, gray, hazy, mist, pale, veil 5 bleak, blear, dusky, faint, foggy, misty 6 cloudy, darken, gloomy, obtuse 7 eclipse, obscure, shadowy, tarnish 8 overcast 9 obfuscate 10 indistinct, mysterious 11 crepuscular

dime: 4 coin 5 disme

dimension: 4 bulk, size 5 scope 6 aspect, extent, height, length 7 breadth, quality 9 magnitude, thickness 10 importance, proportion
fourth: 4 time

diminish: ebb 4 ease, fade, melt, pare, sink, wane, wear 5 abate, lower 6 dilute, lessen, reduce, subdue, wither 7 abridge, assuage, curtail, deplete, dwindle, subside 8 condense, decrease, derogate, minimize, moderate, peter out, retrench, taper off 9 alleviate, epitomize, extenuate

diminution: 8 decrease 9 abatement, decrement, lessening 11 attenuation, curtailment

diminutive: wee 4 tiny 5 dwarf, petty, runty, small 6 bantam, little, petite 9 miniature, minuscule 11 lilliputian 12 teensy-weensy

dimness: 5 gloom 8 darkness 9 obscurity

dimple: 6 hollow, ripple 11 indentation

dim-witted: 4 dull, slow 5 dopey 6 obtuse 8 backward 11 thick-headed

din: bum 4 riot 5 alarm, bruit, clang, noise 6 clamor, hubbub, racket, rattle, steven, tumult, uproar 7 clangor, clatter, discord, turmoil 9 commotion, confusion 10 hullabaloo

dine: eat, sup 5 feast 6 regale

diner: 4 cafe 5 eatery 8 train car 10 coffee shop, restaurant 11 greasy spoon 12 luncheonette

dinette: 6 alcove 10 kitchen set

ding: 4 beat, dash, push, ring 5 clang, drive, excel, fling, knock, pound, thump 6 stroke, thrash, thrust

dingbat: 4 fool 5 dunce 6 dimwit 9 dumb cluck 12 featherbrain

dinge: 4 dent, dint 6 batter, bruise 10 depression

dinghy: 4 boat 5 skiff 7 rowboat, shallop

dingle: 4 dale, dell, glen, vale 6 valley

dingo: 7 wild dog

dingus: 5 gizmo 6 gadget 9 doohickey 11 thingamajig

dingy: dun 4 dark, drab, mean 5 dirty, dusky, grimy, seedy, smoky, tacky 6 gloomy, shabby 7 run-down, squalid 8 smirched 11 dilapidated

dinky: 4 cute, neat, poor, small 8 trifling 13 insignificant

dinner: 4 meal 5 feast 6 repast 7 banquet
after: 12 postprandial
course: 4 nuts, soup 5 fruit, salad 6 entree 7 dessert 9 appetizer
pert. to: 8 cenatory

dint: 4 beat, blow, dent, nick 5 clour, delve, dinge, force, notch, onset, power, press, shock 6 attack, chance, effort, strike, stroke 7 imprint 8 efficacy, striking 10 impression 11 indentation

diocese: see 8 district 9 bishopric
division: 6 parish

Dione: *consort:* 4 Zeus
daughter: 9 Aphrodite

Dionysus: *attendant:* 6 Maenad
festival: 7 Agronia 8 Agrionia

mother: 6 Semele
pert. to: 7 Bromian
diopside: 7 alalite 8 pyroxene
diorite: 7 diabase
Dioscuri: 5 twins 6 Anaces, Castor, Gemini, Pollux
  father: 4 Zeus 9 Tyndareus
  mother: 4 Leda
  sister: 5 Helen 12 Clytemnestra
dip: sag, sop 4 bail, drop, dunk, lade, sink, soak 5 delve, ladle, lower, sauce, slope 6 candle, go down, hollow, plunge 7 decline, immerse, moisten 8 decrease, downturn, submerge 10 depression, pickpocket
  in water: 5 douse, rinse, souse
diploma: 6 degree 7 charter 11 certificate
diplomacy: 4 tact 5 poise 7 finesse 8 delicacy 9 dexterity 10 artfulness
diplomat: 4 dean 6 consul 7 attache 8 minister 10 ambassador
  office of: 7 embassy
dipody: 6 syzygy
dipper: 5 ladle, scoop 8 songbird
dippy: mad 5 silly, wacky 6 absurd 7 foolish 9 screwball
dipsomania: 7 potomania 10 alcoholism
dipteran: fly 4 gnat 8 mosquito
  lobe of wing: 5 alula
dire: 4 dern, evil 5 awful, fatal 6 deadly, dismal, funest, tragic, woeful 7 doleful, drastic, fearful 8 dreadful, horrible, terrible, ultimate 10 calamitous, oppressive, portentous 12 overpowering
direct: aim, bid, con 4 airt, bain, bend, boss, edit, even, flat, head, helm, lead, open, rein, sway, turn 5 apply, blank, coach, frank, guide, order, point, refer, steer, teach, train, utter, write 6 ensign, govern, handle, honest, impart, lineal, manage 7 address, appoint, command, conduct, control, convert, execute, express, officer, preside 8 dedicate, instruct, marshall, regulate, straight 9 categoric, downright, immediate 10 administer, forthright, point-blank 11 categorical, compendious, superintend, superscribe 15 straightforward
direction: way 4 bent, care, duct, east, road, rule, west 5 north, route, south, trend 6 course 7 address, bearing, command, control, mandate, precept 8 guidance, tendency 10 management, regulation 11 arrangement, inclination, information, instruction 13 determination
  biblical: 5 selah
  court: 5 order
  line of: 5 range
  musical: See **musical direction**
  pole to pole: 5 axial
  printer's: 4 stet

  without: 7 astatic
direction finder: 7 compass
directive: 5 edict, order 6 decree, ruling 10 injunction, memorandum 13 pronouncement
directly: 4 now 6 at once 8 promptly 9 instantly, presently, right away 11 immediately, straightway
director: 4 boss, head 5 coach, guide, pilot 6 archon, bishop, leader, rector 7 manager, prefect, trainer 8 governor, producer 9 conductor 10 supervisor 13 administrator 14 superintendent
directory: 4 list, ordo 5 guide, index 9 phonebook
dirge: 4 keen, song 5 elegy 6 lament 7 requiem, epicede 8 epicedia(pl.), threnody 9 epicedium
dirigible: 5 blimp 7 airship 8 zeppelin
dirk: 4 snee, stab 5 skean, sword 6 dagger, weapon
dirndl: 5 dress, skirt
dirt: fen, mud 4 dust, gore, muck, nast, smut, soil 5 earth, filth, grime, trash 6 gossip, gravel, ground, refuse 7 lowdown, mullock, squalor 11 scuttlebutt
dirty: low 4 base, clat, foul 5 bawdy, cabby, dingy, foggy, grimy, gusty, horry, muddy, nasty, stain, sully 6 bemire, clarty, defile, filthy, greasy, grubby, impure, mussed, smutty, soiled, sordid, stormy 7 begrime, brookie, bruckle, clouded, muddied, obscene, squalid, sullied, tarnish, unclean 10 despicable
dirty dig: 4 gibe 5 taunt
dirty look: 5 frown, glare, scowl
dirty pool: 5 trick 5 foul play 9 chicanery, duplicity 10 unfairness 13 double-dealing
Dis: 5 Pluto
disability: 8 drawback, handicap 10 limitation 12 disadvantage
disable: 4 lame, maim 5 break, wreck 6 bruise, dismay, weaken 7 cripple 9 hamstring 10 disqualify 12 incapacitate
disabuse: 4 free 6 debunk, expose, show up 8 set right 9 enlighten 10 disenchant
disaccharide: 5 biose 7 lactose, maltose, sucrose 10 saccharose
disadvantage: 4 hurt, loss, risk 6 damage, injury 7 penalty 8 handicap 9 detriment
disadvantageous: 7 adverse, hurtful 11 detrimental, prejudicial, unfavorable
disaffected: 5 false 6 untrue 8 disloyal, forsworn, mutinous, perjured, recreant 9 estranged, faithless, insidious 10 perfidious, traitorous 11 treacherous
disaffection: 6 deceit 7 disease, disgust, dislike 8 disorder 9 distemper, hostility

10 disloyalty, alienation, discontent 13 indisposition 14 disinclination

disaffirm: 4 deny 5 annul 6 negate 7 reverse 9 repudiate 10 contradict

disagree: 4 vary 5 argue, clash 6 differ 7 dissent, quarrel 8 conflict

disagreeable: bad 4 sour, vile 5 cross, harsh, nasty 6 cranky 7 hateful, peevish 8 annoying, petulant 9 invidious, irritable, offensive, repugnant 10 forbidding, unpleasant 11 displeasing, distasteful

disagreement: 5 clash, fight 7 discord, dispute, dissent, wrangle 8 argument, variance 9 diversity 10 contention, difference, difficulty, dissension, divergence, unlikeness 11 contrariety, controversy, discrepancy, displeasure, incongruity 16 misunderstanding

disallow: 4 deny, veto 6 forbid, refuse, reject 7 censure 8 disclaim, prohibit 10 disapprove

disappear: fly 4 fade, flee 6 vanish 7 evanish 8 evanesce

disappoint: 4 balk, bilk, fail, fall, mock, undo 6 baffle, defeat, delude, outwit, thwart 7 deceive, destroy, nullify, let down 9 frustrate

disapproval: 7 censure, dislike, dissent 9 disliking 10 opposition 14 disapprobation

sound of: boo 4 hiss, hoot 7 catcall 9 raspberry 10 Bronx cheer

disapprove: 4 veto 6 reject, resent 7 condemn, protest 8 disallow, turn down 9 deprecate

disarm: 5 charm 6 defuse, subdue 7 win over 10 demilitarize, make harmless

disarming: 4 glib 5 suave 6 smooth 8 unctuous 10 soft-spoken 12 ingratiating

disarrange: 4 muss 5 upset 6 deform, ruffle 7 clutter, confuse, disturb 8 dishevel, unsettle 9 dislocate 10 discompose, disconcert 11 disorganize

disarray: 4 mess 5 strip 6 jumble, muddle 8 disorder 9 confusion 10 dishabille

disassociate: 4 part 5 break up, pull out 8 separate 11 cut ties with 12 withdraw from 14 sever relations

disaster: woe 4 bale, blow, evil, ruin 6 mishap 7 tragedy 8 accident, calamity, casualty, fatality 9 cataclysm, extremity, mischance 10 misfortune 11 catastrophe 12 misadventure

disavow: 4 deny 6 abjure, disown, recant, refuse, reject 7 decline, retract 8 abnegate, disclaim, renounce 9 repudiate

disband: part 7 break up, dismiss, release, scatter 8 disperse, dissolve, separate 9 discharge 12 disintegrate

disbelieve: 5 doubt 6 reject 7 suspect 8 question 9 discredit

disbeliever: 5 cynic 7 atheist, heretic, skeptic

disburden: rid 4 ease 7 relieve 8 get rid of, jettison 9 exonerate 11 disencumber

disburse: 5 spend 6 defray, expend, lay out, pay out 8 dispense 10 distribute

disc: See disk

discalced: 6 unshod 8 barefoot

discard: 4 dump, jilt, junk, omit, oust, shed 5 chuck, ditch, scrap, shuck, sluff 6 disuse, divest, reject 7 abandon, cashier, dismiss, forsake 9 cast aside, eliminate, repudiate, throw away

pile: 4 heap 5 trash 8 boneyard

discern: see 4 espy, read 6 behold, descry, detect, notice 7 observe 8 discover, perceive 10 understand 11 distinguish

discernible: 7 evident, visible 8 apparent, manifest 11 conspicuous, perceptible 15 distinguishable

discerning: 4 wise

discernment: 4 tact 5 flair, taste 6 acumen 7 insight 8 sagacity 9 sharpness 10 astuteness, divination, perception, shrewdness 11 penetration 12 clairvoyance, perspicacity 14 discrimination

discharge: can 4 boot, dump, emit, fire, free, pour, sack 5 eject, empty, expel, exude, shoot 6 acquit, bounce, defray, effect, exempt, let out, unlade, unload 7 absolve, cashier, disband, dismiss, execute, give off, release, relieve 8 disgorge, displace, evacuate 9 explosion, muster out, exculpate, exonerate, liquidate 10 liberation

disciple: ite 4 John, Jude, Mark 5 James, Judas, Peter, Simon 6 Andrew, Philip, Thomas 7 apostle, Matthew, scholar, student 8 adherent, believer, follower

disciplinarian: 4 czar, tsar 6 tyrant 7 trainer 8 martinet 10 taskmaster

discipline: 4 whip 5 drill, inure, teach, train 6 punish, school 7 chasten, control, scourge 8 chastise, instruct, regiment, regulate, restrain, training 9 obedience 10 keep in line, strictness 11 hold in check, self-control

disclaim: 4 deny 6 abjure, disown, refuse 7 disavow 8 abdicate, abnegate, disallow, renounce 9 repudiate

disclose: 4 bare, blow, open, tell 5 admit, utter 6 betray, descry, expose, impart, reveal, shrive, unseal, unveil 7 confess, develop, display, divulge, exhibit, uncover 8 discover, indicate 9 make known

disclosure: 6 expose 10 revelation

discolor: run 4 fade, spot 5 stain, smear, tinge 6 streak 7 tarnish 8 besmirch

discoloration: 4 mark, spot 5 stain

discomfit: irk, vex 4 rout 5 abash, annoy, upset 6 baffle, defeat, rattle 7 confuse, disturb, perturb 8 confound 9 embarrass, frustrate 10 disconcert

discomfort: 4 pain 6 dismay, grieve, sorrow, unease 7 disturb 8 distress 9 annoyance, embarrass 10 discourage, uneasiness 11 displeasure 13 inconvenience 14 discouragement

discommode: 5 upset 6 bother, put out 7 trouble 13 inconvenience

discompose: 4 fret 5 upset 6 flurry, ruffle 7 agitate, confuse, derange, disturb, fluster, perturb 8 disorder, displace, disquiet, unsettle 9 discharge 10 disarrange, disconcert

disconcert: 4 faze 5 abash, daunt, feeze, upset, worry 6 baffle, blench, rattle 7 confuse, disturb, nonplus, perplex, perturb 8 bewilder, confound 9 discomfit, embarrass 10 disarrange, discompose

disconnect: 4 undo 5 sever 6 unplug 7 disjoin 8 dissolve, disunite, separate, uncouple

disconnected: 6 abrupt, broken 7 cursory 8 rambling 9 desultory, scattered 10 abstracted, disjointed, incoherent

disconsolate: sad 6 gloomy, woeful 7 forlorn 8 dejected, desolate, hopeless 9 cheerless, miserable, sorrowful 10 dispirited, melancholy

discontent: 8 disquiet 9 dysphoria 10 uneasiness 11 displeasure, unhappiness 12 restlessness

discontinue: end 4 drop, quit, stop 5 break, cease, let up 6 desist, disuse, give up 9 terminate

discord: din, jar 5 clash 6 strife 7 faction 8 conflict, variance 9 cacophony, diversity 10 contention, difference, dissension, dissonance 12 disagreement

goddess of: Ate 4 Eris

discordant: 5 harsh 6 hoarse 7 jarring 8 contrary, jangling 10 discrepant, mismatched 11 incongruous, quarrelsome 12 antagonistic, incompatible, inconsistent, inharmonious

musically: 8 scordato

serenade: 9 charivari

Discordia: 4 Eris

discotheque: 7 cabaret 9 nightclub

discount: 4 agio 5 batta(Ind.) 6 ignore, rebate 7 dismiss 8 minimize 9 allowance, deduction, disregard, reduction 10 brush aside, disbelieve 11 sell for less 12 depreciation

discourage: 4 carp 5 daunt, deter 6 dampen, deject, hinder 7 depress, inhibit, prevent 8 dispirit, dissuade, restrain 10 discomfort, dishearten

discourse: 4 talk, tell 5 orate, paper, speak, tract 6 eulogy, homily, parley, preach, sermon 7 account, address, comment, declaim, discuss, dissert, lecture, oration, prelect 8 argument, colloquy, converse, parlance, treatise 9 expatiate, narration, panegyric, soliloquy 10 commentate 11 description 12 conversation, dissertation

art of: 8 rhetoric

long: 6 screed, tirade 7 descant 9 philippic

discourteous: 4 rude 6 scurvy 7 ill-bred, uncivil 8 impolite, ungentle 10 unmannerly 11 ill-mannered 13 disrespectful

discover: see, spy 4 espy, find 5 learn 6 define, descry, detect, expose, invent, locate, reveal 7 confess, discern, display, divulge, explore, find out, uncover, unearth 8 decipher, disclose, manifest, perceive 9 apprehend, ascertain

discoverer: spy 5 scout 8 explorer, inventor 10 originator

discovery: 4 find 5 trove 6 espial, strike 10 disclosure, revelation

discredit: 5 decry, doubt 6 damage, expose, show up 7 asperse, blemish, impeach, scandal, suspect 8 belittle, disgrace, dishonor, distrust, ignominy 9 disparage, disrepute 10 disbelieve

discreet: 4 wary 5 civil 6 polite, silent 7 careful, guarded, politic, prudent 8 cautious, reserved, reticent 11 circumspect

discrepant: 8 contrary 9 different, divergent 10 discordant 11 conflicting, disagreeing 12 inconsistent

discrete: 8 detached, distinct, separate 9 unrelated

discretion: 4 tact 6 wisdom 7 caution 8 judgment, prudence 9 restraint 13 secretiveness

discriminate: 5 favor 8 perceive, show bias 9 demarcate 10 place apart 11 distinguish 13 differentiate, play favorites

discriminating: 6 astute 7 careful, choosey 8 critical 9 selective 10 discerning, prejudiced

discrimination: 5 taste 6 acumen 8 inequity 10 partiality 11 discernment

discursive: 6 roving 7 cursory 8 rambling 9 desultory 10 digressive

discus: 4 disk 5 quoit

thrower: 10 discobolus

discuss: air 4 moot 5 argue, bandy 6 confer, debate, parley 7 agitate, bespeak, consult, dispute, examine 8 talk over 9 discourse 10 deliberate

discussion: rap 6 confab, huddle, parley, powwow 8 causerie 10 conference 11 bull session

group: 5 class, panel 7 seminar 10 round table

medium of: 5 forum

open to: 4 moot 9 debatable

disdain: 5 flout, scorn, spurn 7 contemn, despise, put down, ridicule, sneer at 8 contempt, derision 9 arrogance 11 haughtiness

disease: bug 4 harm 5 virus 6 malady 7 ailment, illness, trouble 8 debility, distress, sickness 9 complaint, infirmity 10 discomfort, pestilence, uneasiness 12 disaffection

animal: coe, pip 5 braxy, colic, farcy, hoose, hooze, mange 6 amoeba, garget 7 spavins 8 glanders, sacbrood 9 distemper, tularemia

local: 7 endemic

plant: fen 4 bunt, rust, scab, smut 5 ergot, speck 6 calico, coleur, mildew 7 erinose, viruela, walloon 8 brindled, melanose

prediction about: 9 prognosis

recognition of: 9 diagnosis

skin: 4 acne, rash 5 favus, hives, psora, tinea 6 dartre, eczema, herpes, lichen, tetter 7 scabies 8 impetigo, ringworm 9 psoriasis, xeroderma 11 scleroderma

wide-spreading: 8 epidemic

disembark: 4 land 6 alight 8 go ashore

disembodiment: 4 soul 6 spirit

disembowel: gut 4 hulk 6 paunch 8 gralloch 10 eviscerate

disembroil: 6 free of 8 untangle 9 extricate

disenchanted: 5 blase 7 knowing, let down, unhappy 9 turned off 11 enlightened, put straight, worldly-wise

disencumber: rid 4 ease 7 lighten, relieve 8 unburden 9 disengage

disengage: 4 free 5 clear, untie 6 detach, — loosen 7 release, retreat, unravel 8 liberate, uncouple, unfasten 9 extricate

disentangle: 4 comb 5 clear, loose 6 evolve 7 unravel 8 separate 9 extricate 13 straighten out

disfavor: 5 odium 7 dislike, umbrage 9 bad repute, disesteem 11 displeasure

disfigure: mar 4 scar 5 spoil 6 deface, deform, injure, mangle 7 blemish 8 mutilate

disgorge: 4 spew, vent 5 eject, empty, expel, vomit 7 bring up 9 discharge 10 relinquish

disgrace: 4 blot, slur, soil, spot 5 abase, crime, odium, shame, stain 6 infamy, stigma 7 affront, attaint, degrade, scandal, slander 8 contempt, dishonor, ignominy, reproach 9 discredit, disesteem, humiliate 10 opprobrium 11 humiliation

disgruntled: 4 sore 5 upset 7 peevish

disguise: 4 hide, mask, veil 5 belie, cloak, feign 6 facade, masque 7 conceal, obscure, pretend 8 artifice, pretense 9 coverture, dissemble, incognito 10 camouflage, false front, masquerade 11 dissimulate

disgust: 5 repel, shock 6 degout(F.), horror, nausea, offend, revolt, sicken 8 aversion, distaste, loathing, nauseate 9 antipathy 10 abhorrence, repugnance 11 abomination 12 disaffection

disgusting: 4 foul, vile 5 nasty 6 filthy 7 beastly, fulsome, hateful, noisome, obscene 8 shocking

dish (see also **food**): cup 4 bowl, food 5 basin, nappy, paten, plate 6 critch, looker, patera, saucer, tureen 7 charger, plateau, platter, ramekin 8 favorite 9 casserole, container 10 preference

gravy: 4 boat

main: 6 entree

dishabille: 8 disarray, disorder 13 partly dressed

Dishan's son: 4 Aran

dishearten: 5 daunt 6 deject 7 depress, flatten, unnerve 8 dispirit 10 demoralize, discourage

disheartened: 6 gloomy 8 downcast 10 despondent 11 discouraged

disheveled: 5 messy 6 sloppy, untidy 7 ruffled, rumpled, tousled, unkempt 8 mussed up, slovenly, uncombed 10 disarranged, disorderly, in disarray

dishonest: 5 false, lying 7 corrupt, crooked, knavish 8 cheating, two-faced 9 deceitful 10 fraudulent, perfidious, untruthful 13 untrustworthy

dishonor: 5 shame, stain 6 defame, defile 7 degrade, obloquy, violate 8 disgrace, ignominy 9 discredit, disparage, disrepute 10 opprobrium

dishonorable: 4 base, foul 5 shady 7 corrupt, ignoble 8 infamous, shameful, unsavory 9 unethical 12 unscrupulous

disillusion: 10 disenchant

disinclination: 7 dislike 8 aversion, distaste 9 antipathy 10 reluctance, repugnance 12 disaffection

disinclined: 6 averse 9 reluctant, unwilling 10 indisposed

disinfect: 7 cleanse 9 sterilize

disinfectant: 5 iodin 6 iodine, phenol 9 germicide 10 antiseptic

disingenuous: 4 wily 5 false 6 artful, tricky 7 devious 8 indirect, specious 9 insincere 10 circuitous

disinherit: 6 cut off 7 deprive 10 exheredate

disintegrate: 4 melt 5 decay, erode 7 crumble, disband 8 dissolve, separate 9 decompose

disinter: 5 dig up 6 exhume 7 unearth

disinterested: 4 fair 8 unbiased, uncaring 9 apathetic, impartial 11 unconcerned

disjoin: 4 part, undo 5 sever 6 detach, sunder, break up 8 dissolve, disunite, separate 10 disconnect, dissociate

disjointed: 7 muddled 8 inchoate, unhinged 10 disordered, incoherent 12 disconnected, lacking unity

disk: 4 chip, dial 5 cakra, medal, paten, plate, sabot, wheel 6 bezant, chakra, harrow, record, washer 7 medalet, phalera 9 cultivate, faceplate, medallion, millstone

hockey: 4 puck

metal: 4 flan, gong 6 ghurry, sequin 8 zecchino

pert. to: 6 discal 7 discoid

solar: 4 Aten

dislike: 4 loth, mind 6 detest, loathe 8 aversion, distaste 9 antipathy, disrelish, prejudice 10 repugnance 11 displeasure 12 disaffection

object of: 8 anathema

of children: 9 misopedia

dislocate: 5 splay 7 disrupt 8 disjoint, displace 10 disarrange

dislodge: 5 expel 6 remove 8 force out

disloyal: 5 false 6 untrue 9 faithless 10 inconstant, perfidious, traitorous, unfaithful 11 disaffected, treacherous

dismal: sad, wan 4 dark, dire, dull, glum, gray 5 black, bleak, drear, sorry 6 dreary, gloomy, triste 7 doleful, ghastly, joyless, ominous, unhappy 8 dolorous, funereal, lonesome 9 cheerless, sorrowful 10 acherontic, calamitous, lugubrious, melancholy 11 unfortunate

dismantle: 4 rase, raze 5 annul, strip 6 divest 7 deprive, destroy, rescind, uncloak 8 dismount, take down 10 do away with

dismay: 4 fear, ruin 5 alarm, appal, daunt, dread 6 appall, fright, subdue, terror 7 depress, deprive, horrify, terrify 8 affright, confound 9 dejection 10 depression, discomfort, discourage 11 trepidation 12 apprehension 13 consternation

dismember: 4 maim, part, rend 5 sever 6 mangle 7 dissect 8 disjoint, mutilate

dismiss: can 4 boot, bust, drop, oust 5 chuck, eject 6 banish, bounce, reject, remove 7 cashier, disband, discard 8 relegate 9 discharge, overthrow

dismissal: 5 conge 6 ouster 7 removal 9 discharge

dismount: 6 alight, get off 9 dismantle, take apart

Disney (Walt): 10 cartoonist

character: 4 Huey, Puff 5 Daisy, Dewey, Dumbo, Goofy, Louie, Pluto 6 Donald, Mickey, Minnie

film classic: 5 Bambi 8 Fantasia 9 Pinocchio, Snow White 15 Reluctant Dragon, Steamboat Willie

disobedient: 6 unruly 7 forward, naughty, wayward, willful 8 mutinous 10 rebellious, refractory 11 intractable 12 contumacious 13 insubordinate

disoblige: 6 offend 7 affront

disorder: 4 mess, muss, riot 5 chaos, snafu 6 burble, jumble, litter, malady, mucker, muddle, ruffle, tousle, tumult 7 ailment, clutter, confuse, derange, disturb, embroil, flutter, illness, misdeed, perturb, trouble 8 disarray, disherel 9 commotion, complaint, confusion, distemper 10 disarrange, discompose, disconcert, misconduct 11 disorganize, misdemeanor 13 indisposition

visual: 10 strabismus

disorderly: 5 randy 6 unruly 8 slipshod, slovenly 10 topsy-turvy 12 huggermugger, ungovernable, unmanageable

disorganize: 5 upset 7 confuse, derange, disband, disrupt 8 disorder, dissolve 10 disarrange

disown: 4 deny 6 reject 7 disavow, retract 8 abdicate, disclaim, renounce 9 repudiate

disparage: 4 slur 5 abuse, decry, lower 6 slight 7 degrade, depress, detract, impeach 8 belittle, derogate, dishonor, disprize, minimize 9 discredit 10 depreciate

disparate: 7 unequal 8 separate 9 different 10 dissimilar 16 disproportionate

dispassionate: 4 calm, cool, fair 5 stoic 6 sedate, serene 8 composed, moderate 9 collected, impartial, temperate, unruffled 10 deliberate, unimpaired 12 unprejudiced

dispatch: rid 4 free, kill, mail, note, post, send 5 haste, hurry, speed 6 hasten 7 deliver, depeche(F.), dispose 8 celerity, conclude, expedite 9 quickness 10 accelerate, accomplish, promptness

dispatch boat: 5 aviso 6 packet

dispel: 7 scatter 8 disperse 9 dissipate, drive away 10 make vanish

dispendious: 6 costly 9 expensive 11 extravagant

dispensation: 4 plan 6 scheme 7 license, release 9 allotment, exemption 10 indulgence 12 distribution

dispense: 4 deal 5 forgo 6 effuse, excuse, exempt, forego, manage 7 absolve, arrange, dole out, hand out, provide 9 apportion 10 administer, distribute

with: 5 chuck, scrap 7 discard 8 get rid of 9 eliminate, toss aside

disperse: sow 4 rout 5 strew 6 dispel, spread, vanish 7 break up, diffuse, scatter 8 separate, squander 9 dissipate 10 distribute 11 disseminate

dispirit: cow 4 damp 5 daunt 6 deject 7 depress, flatten 10 discourage, dishearten, intimidate

dispirited: low, sad 4 blue 6 abattu(F.) 7

abbattue(F.) 8 downcast 9 cheerless, woebegone 11 crestfallen 12 disconsolate

displace: 6 banish, depose, mislay, remove 7 push out 8 dislodge, take over, supplant 9 discharge, dislocate, supersede

display: air 4 pomp, show, wear 5 boast, scene, sight, sport 6 blazon, evince, expose, extend, flaunt, parade, reveal, unfold, unveil 7 etalage, exhibit, pageant, trot out, uncover 8 ceremony, disclose, discover, emblazon, exercise, flourish, indicate, manifest, splendor 9 spectacle, spread out 10 exhibition 11 affectation 13 demonstration

displease: vex 4 miff 5 anger, annoy, pique 6 offend 7 provoke 8 irritate 9 discontent, dissatisfy

displeasing: bad 7 irksome 9 offensive 10 unpleasant 11 distasteful 12 disagreeable

displeasure: ire 5 anger 6 injury 7 dislike, offense, umbrage 8 disfavor, distaste, vexation 10 discomfort, discontent, resentment, uneasiness 11 indignation

show: cry 4 pout 5 frown, scowl

disport: 4 play 5 amuse, frisk 6 divert, frolic, gambol

disposal: 4 sale 8 riddance 9 clearance 11 arrangement, transferral

dispose: set 4 bend, give, mind 5 array, order, place 6 adjust, attire, bestow, settle 7 appoint, arrange, prepare 8 dispatch, organize, regulate 9 determine 10 distribute

disposed: apt 5 fixed, prone, ready 7 tending 8 arranged, inclined

disposition: 4 bent, bias, mood, turn 5 humor 6 affect, animus, health, nature, temper 7 concept 8 aptitude, attitude, disposal 9 affection, character, diathesis 10 adjustment, management, proclivity, propensity 11 arrangement, inclination, temperament 12 constitution, distribution, organization 14 relinquishment

dispossess: 4 oust 5 eject, evict, expel, strip 6 depose, divest 7 bereave, deprive

dispraise: 5 blame 7 censure 9 disparage 10 depreciate 11 detract from

disproportion: 9 disparity 10 inequality

disproportionate: 6 uneven 7 unequal 8 lopsided 9 irregular, overblown 10 asymmetric, unbalanced

disprove: 5 rebut 6 negate, refute 7 confute, explode 8 overturn 9 discredit 10 controvert

disputable: 4 moot 5 vague 6 unsure 7 dubious, fallible 8 doubtful, insecure 9 uncertain 10 indefinite, precarious

disputant: 6 arguer 7 debater

disputation: 7 polemic 8 argument 9 dialectic 10 discussion 11 controversy

dispute: 4 deny, feud, fuss, moot, spat 5 argue, brawl, cabal 6 barney, bicker, debate, differ, haggle 7 brabble, contend, contest, faction, gainsay, quarrel, wrangle 8 argument, question, squabble 9 argy-bargy, encounter 10 contravene, controvert, litigation 11 altercation, controversy 12 disagreement

disqualify: 5 debar 6 outlaw 7 disable, rule out 8 prohibit 9 indispose 11 invalidate 12 incapacitate

disquiet: vex 4 fear, fret, pain 6 excite, stir up, unease, unrest 7 agitate, anxiety, disturb, fluster, trouble, turmoil 10 discompose, discontent 12 inconvenience, restlessness

disquisition: 5 essay 8 treatise 10 discussion

disregard: 4 omit 5 waive 6 forget, ignore, pass by, slight 7 neglect 8 discount, overlook 9 pretermit 10 contravene 11 inattention 12 indifference

disrelish: 7 dislike 8 distaste 9 antipathy

disreputable: low 4 base, hard 5 seamy, shady 7 raffish 8 shameful, unsavory 9 notorious 13 discreditable

disrepute: 5 odium 7 bad name 8 disgrace, dishonor, ignominy, reproach 9 disesteem

disrespect: 8 rudeness 9 insolence 10 incivility 11 discourtesy

disrespectful: 7 uncivil 8 impolite, impudent 10 irreverent 11 impertinent

disrobe: 5 strip 6 divest 7 take off, undress

disrupt: 4 rend, tear 5 break 7 disrump 11 discontinue, disorganize

dissatisfaction: 8 distaste 9 annoyance 10 discontent 11 displeasure

dissect: 5 carve, cut up 7 analyze 9 anatomize, dismember

dissemble: 4 hide, mask 5 cloak, feign 6 boggle 7 conceal 8 disguise, simulate 11 counterfeit, dissimulate

dissembler: 5 actor 9 hypocrite

disseminate: sow 5 stew 6 effuse, spread 7 diffuse, publish, scatter, send out 8 disperse 9 broadcast, circulate, propagate 10 distribute

dissent: 4 vary 6 differ 7 protest 8 disagree 9 exception, objection 10 dissidence 12 disagreement 13 nonconformity 14 nonconcurrence

signal of: nay

dissenter: 7 heretic, sectary 8 recusant 9 protestor 10 Protestant, schismatic, separatist, unbeliever 13 nonconformist

dissentious: 8 factious 11 contentious

dissert: 7 discuss 9 discourse

dissertation: 5 essay, theme, tract 6 debate, thesis, theses(pl.) 7 descant, lecture 8 treatise 9 discourse 10 discussion

Dissertation on a Roast Pig author: 11 Charles Lamb

disservice: 4 harm 6 damage, injury 8 mischief

dissever: 4 part 6 sunder 8 disunite

dissidence: 6 schism, strife 7 dissent 8 conflict 10 contention 12 disagreement 13 nonconformity

dissimilar: 6 unlike 7 difform, diverse 9 anomalous, different, disparate 13 heterogeneous

dissimulate: 5 feign 7 deceive, pretend 8 disguise 9 dissemble

dissipate: 5 spend, waste 6 dispel, expend 7 diffuse, scatter, shatter 8 disperse, dissolve, evanesce, squander 9 evaporate 11 fritter away, overindulge

dissocial: 10 unfriendly 11 standoffish

dissociate: 5 sever 7 disjoin 8 disunite, separate

dissolute: lax 4 wild 5 loose, slack 6 rakish, wanton 7 immoral, lawless 8 uncurbed 9 abandoned, debauched, unbridled 10 licentious, profligate 12 unrestrained

dissolution: end 4 ruin 5 decay 6 bust-up, demise 7 breakup, decease, divorce 10 abrogation 11 adjournment, termination 14 disintegration

comb. form: lys

dissolve: 4 fade, fuse, melt, thaw, void 5 annul 6 relent, unbind 7 adjourn, destroy, disband, disjoin, divorce, liquefy 8 discandy, disunite, separate 9 decompose, dissipate 10 deliquesce 12 disintegrate

dissolved: 6 solute

dissolving: 7 diluent

dissonant: 5 harsh 7 grating, jarring 8 jangling 10 discordant 11 cacophonous, incongruous, unmelodious 12 inconsistent, inharmonious 13 contradictory

dissuade: 5 deter 6 dehort, divert 10 discourage, disincline

distaff: 5 woman 6 female 12 maternal side

distal: 6 remote 7 distant 8 terminal
  angle: 4 axil
  opposite of: 8 proximal

distance: 4 step 5 depth, range, space 7 farness, mileage, reserve, yardage 8 interval, outstrip 10 background, remoteness
  measuring device: 6 stadia 8 odograph, odometer, viameter 9 pedometer, telemeter

  on earth's surface: 8 latitude 9 longitude

distant: far, off 4 afar, away, cold 5 aloof 6 remote, yonder 7 faraway, foreign, removed 8 reserved 9 separated 10 discrepant

distaste: 7 disgust, dislike 8 aversion 9 disrelish 11 displeasure 14 disinclination

distasteful: 7 hateful 8 brackish, nauseous, unsavory 9 loathsome, offensive, repugnant, repulsive 10 unpleasant 11 unpalatable 12 disagreeable

distemper: 4 soak 5 steep 6 choler, dilute, malady 7 ailment, disease, illness 8 disorder, sickness, unsettle 12 disaffection 13 indisposition

distend: 4 fill, grow 5 bloat, plump, swell, widen 6 dilate, expand, extend, spread 7 balloon, enlarge, inflate, stretch

distended: 4 wide 5 blown 8 patulous

distich: 7 couplet

distill, distil: 4 emit 6 infuse 7 trickle

distillation: 7 essence 10 refinement
  device: 6 retort 7 alembic, matrass

distinct: 5 clear, plain, vivid 7 diverse, legible, obvious, special 8 apparent, separate 9 different 10 articulate, individual 11 well-defined 13 distinguished

distinction: 4 note, rank 5 glory, honor 6 laurel, luster, renown 9 variation 10 prominence, reputation, separation 14 discrimination 15 differentiation

distinctive: 8 peculiar, talented 9 prominent 11 conspicuous, outstanding 14 characteristic, discriminating
  air: 6 cachet

distingué: 6 urbane 7 eminent 8 cultured, polished 10 cultivated

distinguish: 6 define, descry 7 discern 8 perceive, separate 9 designate, punctuate 10 discrepate 12 characterize, discriminate 13 differentiate

distinguished: 5 noted 6 famous, marked 7 eminent, notable, special 8 distinct, laureate, renowned 9 brilliant, prominent 10 celebrated 11 conspicuous, illustrious 13 extraordinary

distort: 4 warp 5 slant, twist 6 deform, garble 7 falsify, pervert 8 misstate 10 disfeature 12 misrepresent

distorted: 4 awry 5 askew 7 colored, crooked, deviant, gnarled 9 misshapen 10 anamorphic 11 anamorphous

distract: 5 addle, amuse, mix up 6 bemuse, divert, harass, puzzle 7 agitate, confuse, disturb, embroil, perplex 8 bewilder, confound

distraught: mad 6 crazed 7 frantic 8 deranged, harassed

distress: ail 4 hurt, need, pain 5 agony, anger, annoy, dolor, grief, gripe, worry, wound 6 danger, grieve, harass, harrow, misery, sorrow 7 afflict, anguish, anxiety, oppress, perplex, torture, trouble 8 aggrieve, calamity, straiten 9 adversity, constrain, martyrdom, necessity 10 affliction, constraint, discomfort 11 tribulation

call: SOS 6 mayday

signal: 5 alarm, flare, siren

distressing: sad 6 woeful 7 fearful, painful 9 sorrowful 10 deplorable, lamentable 11 troublesome

distribute: 4 deal, dole, mete, sort 5 allot, issue, share 6 assign, assort, divide, expend, impart, parcel 7 arrange, dispose, prorate 8 allocate, classify, dispense, disperse, separate 9 apportion, partition 10 administer 11 disseminate

distributively: 4 each 6 apiece 9 severally 10 separately 12 individually, respectively

distributor: 6 dealer, jobber 8 auto part 10 colporteur

district: 4 area, slum, ward 5 tract, vicus(L.) 6 canton, parish, region 7 circuit, country, demesne, diocese, quarter 8 locality, precinct, province 9 community, territory 12 neighborhood

theater: 6 rialto

District of Columbia: See Washington, D.C.

distrust: 4 fear 5 doubt 7 suspect 8 be wary of 9 suspicion 12 apprehension

distrustfully: 7 askance 11 skeptically

disturb: vex 4 rile, roil 5 alarm, annoy, freeze, rouse, upset 6 harass, molest, ruffle 7 agitate, derange, perturb, trouble 8 disquiet, distract, unsettle 9 discomfit, interfere, interrupt, make waves 10 disarrange, discompose, disconcert

disturbance: 4 riot, rout 5 alarm, brawl 6 affray, bother, fracas, hubbub, pother, rumpus, tumult, uproar 7 clatter, ferment, trouble, turmoil 8 disorder 9 agitation, annoyance, commotion, confusion 10 excitement 11 derangement, distraction, trepidation 12 discomposure, interruption, perturbation 13 collie-shangie(Sc.), inconvenience

atmospheric: 5 storm 7 cyclone, thunder, tornado 9 hurricane, lightning

emotional: 8 neurosis

ocean: 7 tsunami

disunite: 4 part 5 sever, untie 6 detach, divide, sunder 7 disband, disjoin, dissent, divorce, split up, unravel 8 alienate, dissever, dissolve, estrange, separate 10 disconnect, dissociate

disuse: 7 abandon, discard 9 desuetude 12 obsolescence

disyllabic foot: 7 trochee

ditch: rut, dike, junk, moat 5 canal, scrap 6 gutter, trench 7 abandon, channel 8

get rid of, jettison 9 throw away 10 excavation

side: 5 scarp

dither: 4 flap 5 panic, shake, waver 6 babble, shiver 7 tremble, twitter 9 vacillate 10 act nervous 12 shilly-shally

dithyrambic: 4 wild 10 boisterous

ditto: 4 same 6 repeat 8 likewise 9 duplicate

ditty: lay 4 poem, song 6 melody

diurnal: 5 daily 9 ephemeral

opposite: 9 nocturnal

divagate: 5 stray 6 wander 7 digress

divan: 4 sofa 5 couch 6 lounge, settee 9 davenport 11 smoking room 13 Muslim council

divaricate: 6 forked 7 diverge 11 spread apart

dive: den 4 dump, fall, jump, leap 5 joint, lunge, swoop 6 plunge 7 descend, hangout 8 submerge, tailspin

kind of: 4 swan 6 gainer 9 jackknife

dive into: try 5 begin, start

diver: 4 loon 7 pearler, plunger 9 submarine

disease: 5 bends 12 aeroembolism

gear: 4 mask, tank 5 scuba 7 flipper, snorkel, wet suit

diverge: 6 branch, differ, divide, ramify, spread 7 deviate, digress 8 disagree

divers: 4 many 6 sundry 7 several, various

diverse: 6 motley, sundry, unlike, varied 8 distinct, separate 9 different, multiform 10 dissimilar 13 heterogeneous

diversion: jeu 4 game, play 5 feint, hobby, sport 7 pastime 9 amusement, avocation, merriment 10 deflection, digression, recreation, relaxation 11 distraction 13 divertisement, entertainment

diversity: 6 change 7 variety 10 difference, unlikeness 11 variegation

divert: 5 amuse, relax 7 beguile, deflect, delight 8 dissuade, distract 9 entertain, turn aside

diverting: 5 droll 8 pleasant 9 laughable

divest: 4 bare, doff 5 spoil, strip 6 denude, depose 7 bereave, deprive, despoil, disrobe, uncover 8 denature, dethrone, take away, unclothe 9 dismantle 10 dispossess

of sham: 6 debunk

divide: cut, lot 4 deal, fork, part, rift, zone 5 cleft, divvy, ridge, sever, share, slice, space, split 6 branch, cleave, differ, parcel, ramify, sunder 7 aliquot, diverge, fissure, prorate 8 alienate, allocate, classify, disunite, graduate, separate 9 apportion, dismember, intersect, multisect, partition, watershed 10 distribute

into feet: 4 scan

into parts: 4 paly 6 bisect, gobbet 7 quarter, trisect 9 bifurcate, septinate

divided: 4 reft 7 fissate, partite 8 areolate, camerate 10 incomplete

dividend: 5 bonus 6 return, reward 12 extra portion

divider: 6 screen 7 compass 9 partition

divination: 4 omen 6 augury 8 prophecy 9 good guess 11 discernment 12 clairvoyance

ability: ESP
by dreams: 11 oneiromancy
by figures: 8 geomancy
by fire: 9 pyromancy
by the hands: 9 palmistry
by lots: 9 sortilege
by numbers: 10 numerology
by rods: 7 dowsing
by stars: 9 astrology
manual: 6 I Ching

divine: 4 holy 5 guess, pious 6 detect, devise, priest, sacred 7 blessed, foresee, godlike, portend, predict, presage 8 forebode, foreknow, foretell, heavenly, immortal, minister, perceive 9 ambrosial, celestial, clergyman, religious 10 anticipate, conjecture, superhuman, theologian 12 supernatural

artificer: 8 tvashtar, tvashtri
being: 4 deva
communication: 6 oracle
gift: 5 grace
messenger: 7 apostle
render: 5 deify
spirit: 5 numen
word: 5 logos
work: 7 theurgy

Divine Comedy author: 5 Dante

diviner: 4 seer 5 augur, sibyl 7 prophet 8 haruspex 10 soothsayer 11 clairvoyant 14 prognosticator

diving: 8 plunging 10 acrobatics, submerging

bird: 4 auk 4 loon 5 grebe 6 osprey

divinity (see also **god, goddess**): 5 candy 8 theology

division: 4 chap, clan, dole, neat, part, rift 5 group, realm, share 6 canton, schism, sector 7 roulade, section 8 arpeggio, category, cleavage 9 Abteilung, allotment, concision, departure, partition 10 department 11 bifurcation, compartment, disjunction 13 apportionment, disconnection, dismemberment

athletic contest: lap, set 4 half, heat 5 round 6 inning, period 7 chukker, quarter

between torrid and temperate zones: 6 tropic

Bible: 4 book 5 verse
play: act 5 scene
poem: 5 canto 6 stanza

political: 4 city, ward 5 state 6 county, parish 7 borough 8 district, province

religious: 4 sect 6 schism

result: 8 fraction, quotient

social: 4 clan 5 caste, class, tribe

time: day, eon, era 4 aeon, hour, week, year 5 month, night 6 decade, minute, moment, second 7 weekend 9 fortnight

word: 8 syllable

divisional: 10 fractional, separative

divorce: 5 sever 6 sunder 7 break up 8 dissolve, disunion, disunite, separate 10 separation 11 dissolution

Jewish law: get 4 gett
mill: 4 Reno

divot: 10 lump of turf

divulge: 4 bare, show, tell 5 voice 6 impart, reveal, spread, unfold 7 publish, uncover 8 disclose, discover, give away, proclaim

divvy: 5 share 6 divide 7 portion

Dixie Land: 5 South

dizziness: 6 megrim 7 vertigo 9 giddiness

with headache: 10 scotodinia

dizzy: 4 daze 5 crazy, giddy 6 fickle, stupid 7 foolish 8 swimming, unsteady 10 capricious 11 lightheaded, vertiginous

Djibouti: *capital:* 8 Djibouti

city: 5 Obock 6 Dikhil
gulf: 4 Aden
monetary unit: 5 franc 7 centime
native: 5 Afars, Issas

DNA: 4 gene 11 nucleic acid 14 heredity factor

segment: 7 cistron

Dnieper: *tributary:* 4 Psel, Sozh, Sula 5 Desna, Psiol 7 Pripyat

cities on: 4 Kiev, 5 Orsha 7 Kherson, Mogilev, Nikopol 8 Smolensk

do: act 4 bilk, dost, make, suit 5 avail, cheat, guise, serve, trick 6 answer, finish, render, wind up, work at 7 achieve, arrange, clean up, execute, perform, produce, satisfy, suffice 8 carry out, transact 10 accomplish, administer

do away with: rid 4 drop 7 abolish 8 dissolve 9 liquidate 11 discontinue

do in: 4 kill 6 defeat 7 destroy, exhaust

do out of: 5 cheat, cozen 7 defraud

do-re-mi: 4 song 5 money

do up: tie 4 wrap 5 clean 7 arrange, prepare

do well: 7 prosper, succeed

do without: 5 forgo 6 forego, pass up, refuse

dobbin: 4 mare

docent: 5 guide 7 teacher 8 lecturer

docile: 4 calm, meek, tame 6 gentle 7 ductile, dutiful 8 biddable 9 tractable 10 manageable

dock: cut 4 bang, clip, moor, pier, quay 5 basin, wharf 6 marina 7 bobtail, cur-

tail, shorten 12 prisoner's box
post: 4 pile 7 bollard
ship's: 4 slip 5 basin, berth
worker: 9 stevedore
yard: 7 arsenal
docket: 4 card 6 agenda 7 program 8 calendar, schedule 13 police blotter
doctor: 4 dose 5 fix up, treat 6 healer, medico, repair 7 dentist, scholar 8 sawbones 9 internist, physician, adulterate 11 aesculapian
aide: 5 nurse
animal: vet 10 veterinary 12 veterinarian
oath of: 11 hippocratic
specialist: 7 oculist, surgeon 9 otologist 10 podiatrist 11 chiropodist, neurologist, optometrist, orthopedist 12 chiropractor, gynecologist, obstetrician, orthodontist, pediatrician, psychiatrist
doctrine: ism 4 doxy, lear, rule 5 credo, creed, dogma, maxim, tenet 6 belief, gospel, theory 7 article, opinion, precept 8 position 9 principle 10 discipline
pert. to: 10 dogmatical 12 teleological
secret: 7 esotery
single principle: 6 henism, monism
specific: 6 cabala, heresy, malism, Mishna 7 Mishnah 8 fatalism, hedonism 10 agathology, pragmatism 13 monarchianism
spreader: 12 propagandist
document: 4 bill, book, cite, deed, writ 5 lease, paper 6 record, verify 7 bear out, confirm, missive, precept, writing 8 contract, covenant, mortgage, validate 9 indenture 10 manuscript 11 corroborate
addition: 5 rider 7 codicil 9 amendment
file: 7 dossier
original record: 8 protocol
permissive: 7 license
provisional: 5 scrip
receptacle: 7 hanaper
signed by all parties: 8 syngraph
storehouse: 8 archives
travel: 8 passport
true copy: 7 estreat
Dodecanese Island: Kos 4 Syme 5 Kasos, Leros, Telos 6 Khalke, Lipsos, Patmos, Rhodes 7 Nisyros, Piscopi 8 Kalymnos 9 Karpathos
dodder: 5 shake 6 totter 7 tremble
doddering: old 5 inane 6 infirm, senile 7 foolish
dodge: 4 duck, jink, ruse 5 avoid, cheat, elude, parry, shift, shirk, trick 6 escape 7 deceive, evasion 8 artifice, sidestep 9 expedient 10 equivocate
dodger: 7 haggler 8 circular, handbill 13 advertisement
corn: 4 pone

dodo: 7 old fogy 8 mossback 10 back number, fuddy-duddy 11 extinct bird
doe: roe, teg 4 fawn, hind 6 female
doer: 6 dynamo, worker 7 hustler 8 activist, go-getter, live wire 9 performer 10 ball of fire
doff: 5 douse 6 remove 7 discard 8 put aside
dog: cur, mut, pug, pup 4 mutt, tyke 5 canis(L.), frank, lemon, pooch, puppy, trail, whelp 6 bowwow, canine, detent, rascal, shadow, wiener 7 mongrel 9 carnivore
African: 7 basenji
Australian: 5 dingo
breed: pug 4 Dane 5 boxer, hound, Husky, spitz 6 Afghan, basset, beagle, borzoi, Briard, collie, Eskimo, poodle, Saluki, setter 7 Basenji, bulldog, griffon, harrier, Maltese, mastiff, pointer, Scottie, Shih Tzu, spaniel, terrier, whippet 8 Airedale, Alsatian, chow chow, coach dog, Doberman, elkhound, foxhound, keeshond, Labrador, Malamute, Malemute, Malinois, papillon, Pekinese, Pyrenees, Samoyede, Sealyham, shepherd, springer 9 Chihuahua, dachshund, Dalmatian, deerhound, Great Dane, greyhound, kerry blue, Lhasa apso, St. Bernard, schnauzer, wolfhound, Yorkshire 10 Bedlington, bloodhound, Boston bull, Chesapeake, Manchester, otter hound, Pomeranian, Rottweiler, schipperke, weimaraner 11 bull terrier, Groenendael, ruby spaniel, Skye terrier 12 cairn terrier, Gordon setter, Newfoundland, water spaniel, Welsh terrier 13 Boston terrier, cocker spaniel, Great Pyrenees, Prince Charles 15 Brussels griffon, highland terrier, Riesenschnauzer 17 Bouvier de Flandres
close-haired: pug 5 boxer
Dorothy's: 4 Toto
Eskimo: 5 husky 7 Samoyed 8 Malamute, Malemute, Samoyede
famous: 4 Asta, Fala, King, Tige, Toby 5 Benji, Devil 6 Feller, Lassie 8 Checkers 9 Old Yeller, Rin-Tin-Tin 11 Strongheart
FDR's: 4 Fala
fox-like: 6 colpeo
genus: 5 canis
German origin: 5 boxer 8 Doberman 9 Drahthaar 10 Weimaraner
hauling: 5 husky 7 Samoyed 8 Malamute, Malemute, Samoyede 9 Dalmatian
house: 6 kennel
howling of: 9 ululation
hunting: 5 hound, toler 6 basset, beagle, borzoi, saluki, setter, talbot 7 courser, harrier, pointer 8 elkhound 9 retriever,

wolfhound 10 bloodhound

iron: 7 firedog

large: 4 Dane 5 boxer 6 briard, collie, police 7 mastiff 12 Newfoundland

long-haired: 4 alco, chow 7 spaniel

Orphan Annie's: 5 Sandy

small: Pom, pug, pup 4 alco, Peke 8 Pekinese 9 Chihuahua, Pekingese 10 Pomeranian

space traveler: 5 Leika

underworld: 8 Cerberus

upper lip: 5 flews

Welsh: 5 corgi 8 Sealyham

wild: 5 adjag, dhole, dingo 6 jackal 7 agouara 8 cimarron

dog days: 8 canicule

dog rose: 9 eglantine

fruit: hip

dog star: 6 Sirius

constellation: 10 Canis Major

dogfight: 5 brawl, melee, scrap 9 air battle 10 free-for-all

dogfish: 5 shark 6 bowfin

dogged: 8 stubborn 9 obstinate, tenacious 10 determined, persistent, purposeful 11 persevering

doggerel: 6 jingle 10 light verse

doggish: 5 showy, sulky 7 stylish 8 snappish, snarling

doggone: 4 damn, darn, drat 5 blast 6 shucks 9 son of a gun

dogie: 9 stray calf

dogma: 5 canon, credo, creed, tenet 6 belief, dictum 8 doctrine 10 conviction, philosophy

dogmatic: 6 biased 7 a priori 9 arbitrary, assertive, doctrinal 10 intolerant, peremptory, pontifical, prejudiced 11 dictatorial, opinionated

do-gooder: 8 altruist, idealist 9 soul saver 10 fixer-upper 13 bleeding heart

Dogpatch depicter: 4 Capp (Al)

dogs: 4 feet

dogwood: 5 osier, sumac 6 cornel

flowering: 7 boxwood

genus: 6 cornus

doily: 4 mat 6 napkin

kin: 7 coaster

do in: 4 kill, ruin 6 finish, murder 7 exhaust, wear out 9 liquidate

doings: 5 deeds 6 events 7 actions 9 functions 10 activities

doldrums: 5 blues, dumps, ennui 6 apathy, tedium 7 boredom 10 depression, low spirits, ocean calms

dole: 4 alms 5 allot 6 relief 7 charity, deal out, handout, mete out 8 dispense 9 apportion 10 distribute

doleful: sad 5 drear, heavy 6 dismal, dreary, rueful 7 flebile 8 downcast, mournful 9 plaintive, sorrowful 10 lugubrious, melancholy 12 disconsolate

dolent: 9 sorrowful

doll: toy 4 babe, baby 5 array, puppe(G.) 6 maumet, moppet, muneca(Sp.), poupee(F.), puppet 8 mistress 9 golliwogg 10 sweetheart

doll up: 5 adorn, dress 11 put on the dog

dollar: one 4 buck 8 frogskin, simoleon

dollop: bit, tot 4 blob, dash, lump 5 snort 6 jigger, splash 10 tiny amount

Doll's House heroine: 4 Nora

dolly: car 4 cart 5 truck 7 carrier 12 wheeled frame 14 camera platform

dolor: 5 grief 6 sorrow 7 anguish, sadness 8 distress, mourning 11 lamentation

dolorous: sad 6 dismal 7 doleful 8 grievous 9 sorrowful

dolphin: 4 fish 6 dorado 8 bollard 8 moor spar, porpoise 10 bottlenose

movie: 7 Flipper

river: 5 bouto

dolt: ass, oaf 4 clod, fool 5 chump, dummy, dunce, idiot 7 bluntie(Sc.), dullard, half-wit 8 imbecile, numskull 9 blockhead, ignoramus, simpleton 10 dunderhead

doltish: 4 dull 5 dense, thick 6 stupid 7 foolish 8 blockish 11 thickheaded

domain: 4 area 5 realm, world 6 empire, estate, sphere 7 demesne 8 dominion, province 9 bailiwick, territory

Dombey and Son author: 7 Dickens

character: 4 Paul 5 Edith 6 Carker 9 Walter Gay

dome: cap 4 cima 6 cupola 7 calotte, edifice

domed: 7 vaulted

domestic: 4 cook, maid 6 native 7 servant 8 homebred, homemade 9 home-grown 11 housewifely

establishment: 6 menage

domesticate: 4 tame 5 train 6 master 7 reclaim 8 civilize 10 housebreak

domicile: 4 home 5 abode, house 6 menage 8 dwelling 9 residence 10 habitation

identification: 9 doorplate

dominant: 5 bossy, chief 6 ruling 7 central, regnant, supreme 8 superior 9 ascendant, imperious, paramount, prevalent, principal 10 commanding, preeminent, prevailing 11 outweighing 12 preponderant 13 overbalancing

dominate: 4 rule 5 reign 6 govern 7 control 8 stand out 9 tower over

domination: 4 sway 5 power 7 command, control, mastery 9 supremacy 11 sovereignty

domineer: cow 4 boss, rule 5 bully 7 command, oppress 8 bulldoze, ride over, walk over 12 crack the whip

domineering: 5 bossy 6 lordly 7 haughty 8 arrogant 9 imperious, masterful 10 tyrannical 11 dictatorial, magisterial, overbearing

Dominica: *capital:* 6 Roseau
city: 6 Roseau 10 Portsmouth
island group: 8 Windward
member: 12 Commonwealth
monetary unit: 4 cent 6 dollar

Dominican: 9 Predicant

Dominican Republic: *bay:* 4 Ocoa, Yuma 5 Neiba 6 Rincon, Samana 7 Isabela 8 Escocesa
cape: 5 Beata, Falso, Viejo 6 Engano
capital: 12 Santo Domingo
city: 4 Bani, Moca 5 Neiba 8 Barahona, La Romana, Santiago
dictator: 8 Trujillo (Rafael)
ethnic group: 5 Negro 7 mulatto 9 Caucasian
Indian: 5 Carib 6 Arawak
island: 10 Hispaniola
island possession: 5 Beata, Saona 8 Catalina
lake: 10 Enriquillo
monetary unit: 4 peso 7 centavo
mountain peak: 4 Tina 5 Gallo 10 Pico Duarte
mountain range: 10 Cordillera
peninsula: 6 Samana
port: 11 Puerto Plata 12 Santo Domingo
province: 4 Azua 6 Duarte, La Vega, Samana 7 Dajabon, Peravia, Salcedo, San Juan 8 Bahoruco, Barahona, Santiago, Valverde
river: 4 Yuna 5 Yaque

dominie: 6 pastor 9 clergyman, pedagogue 12 schoolmaster

dominion: 4 rule, sway 5 realm, reign 6 domain, empire 7 control, dynasty, regency 9 authority, hierarchy, ownership, supremacy 10 ascendancy 11 sovereignty 12 jurisdiction
church: 11 sacerdotium
joint: 11 condominium

domino: die 4 mask

dominoes: 4 game 5 bones 7 ivories

domus: 4 home 5 house

don: 4 wear 5 array, dress, put on 6 assume, clothe, invest 7 get into 8 nobleman 9 gentleman, professor 10 instructor

Don Carlos: *author:* 8 Schiller
opera composer: 5 Verdi

Don Giovanni composer: 6 Mozart

Don Juan: 4 rake 6 masher 7 seducer 9 libertine 10 lady-killer, profligate

Don Quixote: *companion:* 11 Sancho Panza
steed: 9 Rosinante, Rozinante

Donar: 4 Thor

donate: gie(Sc.) 4 give 6 bestow 7 hand out, present, provide 10 contribute

donation: 4 gift 5 grant 7 bequest, present 8 offering 11 benefaction 12 contribution

done: 4 over 5 baked, ended 6 cooked 7 through 8 finished 9 completed, exhausted 12 accomplished

donee: 7 heritor 8 receiver 9 recipient 11 beneficiary

done for: 4 dead 5 goner, kaput 6 licked, ruined 7 wrecked 8 bankrupt 10 on the ropes

done in: 4 beat 5 spent 6 pooped, used up 7 worn out 8 frazzled 9 played out

donkey: ass 4 fool 5 burro, jenny, neddy 6 onager 8 imbecile, numskull
cry: 4 bray 6 heehaw

donkey engine: 6 yarder 10 locomotive 11 cargo lifter

donna: 4 lady, wife 5 madam, woman 8 mistress

donor: 5 giver 10 benefactor 11 contributor 14 philanthropist

doodle: 4 dolt, draw 5 cheat 6 putter 7 cartoon, trifler 8 scribble 10 nincompoop

doodlesack: 7 bagpipe

doohickey: 6 doodad, gadget 11 thingamabob

dooly, doolie: 6 litter 9 palanquin

doom: law, lot 4 damn, fate, ruin 5 death 6 decree, kismet 7 condemn, destine, destiny, fortune, statute 8 calamity, decision, judgment, sentence 9 ordinance, preordain 10 adjudicate, predestine 11 destruction 12 condemnation

doomed: fey 5 fatal 6 accursed 9 sentenced

door: 4 exit, gate 5 entry, hatch 6 portal 7 barrier, opening, passage 11 entranceway
back: 7 postern
crosspiece: 6 lintel
fastener: bar 4 bolt, hasp, lock 5 catch, latch
frame: 4 jamb
holder: 5 hinge
holy: 11 amphithyron
part: 4 jamb, knob, sill 5 panel 6 alette
storm: 6 dingle
trap: 4 drop

doorkeeper: 5 guard 6 porter, warden 7 ostiary 9 concierge(F.)

doormat: rug 8 weakling 10 pantywaist

dope: hop 4 drug 5 dunce, opium, paste 6 heroin, opiate 7 cocaine, predict, stupefy 8 narcotic 9 marijuana

doped: 4 high 6 stoned 7 drugged 8 hopped-up 9 spaced out

dope out: 5 crack, solve 6 decode, fathom 7 clear up 10 unscramble 12 get the answer

dopester: 4 tout 7 tipster 10 forecaster

dopey, dopy: 4 dull 5 dazed, woozy 6

groggy, torpid 8 sluggish 9 lethargic 10 punch drunk

doppelganger: 6 double, spirit, wraith 10 apparition 11 counterpart

dor: bee 6 beetle 11 drumbledore

dorcas: 7 gazelle

dorian: 6 simple

Dorian festival: 6 Carnea 7 Carneia

doric: 6 rustic

Doric: *frieze bottom:* 6 taenia

frieze slab: 6 metope

Doris' king: 8 Aegimius

dormancy: 6 torpor 8 abeyance 10 quiescence

dormant: 6 fixed, quiet 6 asleep, latent, torpid 7 resting 8 inactive, sleeping 9 unaroused 10 stationary

dormer: 6 window 7 lucarne

dormitory: 12 sleeping room 13 residence hall

monastery: 6 dorter 7 dortour

dormouse: 4 loir 5 lerot

pert. to: 7 myoxine

dornick: 5 linen 6 damask

dorsal: 5 notal 6 aboral, tergal 7 abaxial 9 posterior

opposed to: 7 ventral

dorsum: 4 back

dose: 4 bole 5 draft, treat 6 doctor, drench, potion 7 draught 8 quantity

doss: 7 bed down 12 lodging house

dot: 4 clot, lump, mote, peck 5 dowry, point, speck 6 period 7 speckle, stipple 8 particle, sprinkle 9 bespangle 10 besprinkle, distribute

over the letter i: 6 tittle

dotage: 6 old age 7 anility 8 senility 10 feebleness 11 senectitude

dote on: 5 adore, fancy 6 pamper, revere 7 idolize, worship 10 love dearly 11 be partial to

doting: 4 fond 6 loving 7 devoted, doddery, fatuous 8 overfond 13 overindulgent

dotterel: 6 plover 7 lapwing 9 turnstone

dotty: 5 crazy, wacky, spotty 8 obsessed 9 eccentric 12 feebleminded

Douay Bible: 4 Aree

double: ply 4 dual, fold, twin 5 duple, fetch, twice 6 binary, binate, clench, duplex 7 twofold 8 geminate 9 ambiguous, duplicate, look-alike 11 counterpart

double-cross: 5 cheat 6 betray 7 deceive, sell out, swindle 9 treachery

double dagger: 6 diesis

double dealing: 6 deceit 8 trickery 9 duplicity

double-edged: 9 ancipital

doubled: 5 gemel 6 paired 7 twinned

doublespeak: 9 ambiguity, vague talk 12 equivocation 13 foggy language

double-talk: 5 hokum 7 twaddle 8 nonsense 9 gibberish 12 gobbledygook

doubt: 4 fear 5 demur, dread, qualm, query, waver 7 scruple, suspect 8 distrust, hesitate, mistrust, question 9 discredit, misgiving, suspicion 10 diffidence, disbelieve, indecision 11 uncertainty 12 apprehension

doubter: 5 cynic 7 skeptic 10 unbeliever

doubtful: 4 iffy 6 unsure 7 dubious, fearful 8 wavering 9 ambiguous, diffident, equivocal, uncertain, undecided 10 apocryphal, hesitating, irresolute, suspicious 11 distrustful, vacillating 12 apprehensive, questionable, undetermined 13 problematical

douceur: sop 4 gift 5 bonus 7 present 8 gratuity 9 pourboire

dough: 4 cash 5 money, paste 7 cabbage 10 green staff

doughnut: 6 sinker 7 cruller

relative: 7 fritter 9 friedcake

doughty: 4 fell 5 brave 7 valiant 8 intrepid

doughy: 4 ashy, soft 5 pasty 6 flabby, pallid 7 viscous

dour: 4 glum, grim, hard, sour 5 rough, stern 6 gloomy, morose, severe, strong, sullen 7 ominous 9 obstinate 10 inflexible

douse, dowse: 4 doff, duck, dunk, stow 5 rinse, slosh 6 drench, plunge, put out, strike 7 immerse 8 downpour 9 drenching 10 extinguish

douzepers: 4 Ivon, Otton 5 Ivory, Gerin, Ogier, peers 6 Anseis, Gerier, nobles, Oliver, Roland, Samson, Turpin 7 knights 8 Engelier, paladins 9 Berengier 17 Gerard de Rousillon

dove: 5 color 6 culver, pigeon 7 namaqua 8 pacifist 11 conciliator

home: 4 cote 9 columbary

pert. to: 9 columbine

political opposite: 4 hawk

sound: coo 4 curr

dovekey, dovekie: auk 9 guillemot

dovelike: 4 pure 6 gentle 7 lovable 9 columbine

dovetail: fit 4 jibe, mesh 5 agree, tally, tenon 6 go with 8 check out 10 correspond

dovish: 7 antiwar 9 peaceable 10 nonviolent

dowager: 6 matron 9 matriarch 10 grande dame

dowdy: 4 drab 5 seedy, tacky 6 blowzy, shabby, untidy 8 slovenly 9 unstylish 10 slatternly

woman: 5 frump

dowel: peg, pin 4 coak 6 pintle

dower: dot 5 endow 6 talent 9 endowment 13 bride's portion

dowitcher: 5 snipe

down: 4 dowl, fell, flix, flue, fuzz, hill, lint 5 below, dowle, floor, fluff 7 hillock, plumage 9 overthrow

down at the heel: 5 seamy, seedy

down in the mouth: 4 glum 7 unhappy 8 dejected 9 depressed 11 discouraged

down under: 8 Tasmania 9 antipodes, Australia 10 New Zealand

down with: 4 a bas

downbeat: 4 grim 5 bleak 6 dismal, gloomy 8 negative 11 pessimistic

downcast: sad 6 abject, gloomy, morose 7 forlorn 8 hopeless 10 despondent, dispirited, melancholy 11 discouraged 12 disheartened

downer: 6 bummer 7 bad trip 10 depressant 11 barbiturate

downfall: pit 4 fate, ruin, trap 5 abyss 7 .escent, undoing 8 collapse 9 precipice, ruination 11 destruction, ecroulement 12 degringolade

downgrade: dip 4 bust, drop 5 lower 6 debase, demote, lessen, reduce 7 decline, descent, devalue 9 declivity

downpour: 4 rain 6 deluge 7 torrent 10 cloudburst

downright: 4 flat, pure, rank 5 blank, blunt, plain, plumb, sheer, stark 6 arrant, direct 8 absolute, complete, positive, thorough 9 out-and-out 10 forthright 11 unmitigated

downstairs: 5 below

downtrend: dip, sag 4 drop, fall, slip 5 slide, slump 7 decline

downwind: 7 leeward

downy: 4 soft 5 mossy, nappy, pilar, quiet 6 fluffy, placid 7 cunning, knowing 8 soothing

dowry: See dower

doxy: ism 5 wench 6 harlot 7 opinion 8 doctrine

doyen: 4 dean 6 expert 8 virtuoso 9 authority 10 past master 12 senior member

doze: nap, nod 5 decay, sleep 6 catnap, drowse, snooze 7 slumber, snoozle

drab: 4 bawd, dull 5 dingy, mousy, wench, whore 6 dreary 7 prosaic 8 lifeless 9 colorless 10 monotonous, prostitute 13 uninteresting

drachma: 4 coin, dram
one-sixth: 4 obol

draconian: 5 cruel 6 severe, strict

Dracula: 7 vampire
author: 10 Bram Stoker

draff: 4 lees 5 dregs, drink 6 refuse 7 hogwash

draft: nip, sip 4 dose, dram, gust, levy, plan, swig, toot 5 drink, epure, swipe 6 call up, devise, drench, potion, redact, scroll, sketch 7 draught, drawing, outline, pattern, project 8 beverage 9 conscript 10 air current
evader: 6 dodger

draftsman, draughtsman: 6 drawer 7 tippler 9 architect

drag: lug, tow, tug 4 bore, draw, haul, pull, swig, tear, tump 5 brake, delay, drawl, trail, trawl 6 anchor, burden, linger, taigle(Sc.) 7 grapnel 9 lag behind 10 wet blanket
out: 6 elicit, extend 7 prolong 8 protract

dragnet: 5 trawl 7 grapnel

dragoman: 5 agent, guide 11 interpreter

dragon: 7 monster 8 basilisk
biblical: 5 Rahab
biting: 8 tarragon
Chinese: 5 lung
French: 8 Tarasque
killer: 6 Cadmus, Sigurd 7 Beowulf, Perseus 8 St. George, St. Martha
Norse: 6 Fafner, Fafnir
Vedic: Ahi

dragonfly order: 8 odonata

dragoon: 6 coerce 9 force into 10 cavalryman

drain: dry, gaw, sap 4 fade, milk, pump, sink, tire, tube 5 canal, empty, gully, sewer, spout 6 burden, furrow, guzzle, outlet, siphon, trench 7 acequia, channel, deplete, draw off, exhaust 9 drink down, undermine 11 watercourse
arched: 7 culvert

drainage: 11 waste system
area: 5 basin

drained: 5 all in, spent 6 used up 7 worn out 8 depleted 10 cleaned out, gulped down

drainpipe: 6 leader

dram: nip 4 mite, slug 5 draft, drink 6 drachm 7 snifter 8 potation, quantity

drama: 4 play 5 opera 7 theater, tragedy 8 conflict, pastoral, the stage 11 composition
court: 5 trial
father of: 7 Thespis
Japanese: noh
main act: 8 epitasis
television: 9 soap opera
unspoken: 9 pantomime

dramatic: 4 wild 5 vivid 6 scenic 10 theatrical 12 melodramatic
expession system: 8 delsarte

dramatist: 5 actor 10 playwright

drape: 4 hang 5 adorn, cover 6 sprawl, swathe 7 curtain, hanging, valance 8 spraddle 10 fall in folds, wrap around

drapeau: 4 flag 8 standard

draper: 6 tailor

drastic: 4 dire 5 harsh 6 severe 7 extreme, radical 8 rigorous

draught: See draft

Dravidian (see also India): 4 Gond, Kota, Toda, Tulu 5 Arava, Gondi, Khond, Malto, Oraon, Tamil 6 Andhra,

Brahui, Kodagu, Kurukh, Telegu, Telugu 8 Kanarese 9 Malayalam
demon: 4 bhut
tribe: 6 Badaga 7 Collery
draw: lug, tie, tow, tug 4 drag, duct, hale,
haul, lade, limn, lure, pull 5 catch,
educe, train 6 allure, deduce, depict, derive, design, elicit, entice, induce, inhale, select, sketch 7 attract, detract,
extract, inspire, portray 8 inveigle,
standoff 9 allowance, delineate, reproduce, statement
again: 5 remap 6 replat
away from: 6 shrink
back: 5 wince 6 cringe, recede, recoil, resile, retire, shrink 7 retract, retreat
close: 4 near 8 approach, come nigh
finely: 4 etch
forth: 5 educe, evoke 6 elicit 7 pull out
off: sap 5 drain 6 siphon 7 extract 8 abstract
out: 4 pump 5 educe 6 elicit, extend 7 extract, prolong 8 lengthen, protract 11
interrogate 12 cross-examine
tight: 4 frap, furl, lace 5 brace, cinch
up: 4 halt, stop 5 frame 7 prepare 9 formulate
drawback: 6 defect 8 handicap 9 detriment, hindrance 12 disadvantage
draw game: 9 stalemate
drawer: 4 till
drawers: 5 pants 6 shorts 7 panties 9
long johns, underwear
chest of: 6 bureau 7 commode 10 chiffon-
nier
drawing: 4 plan 5 draft, epure 7 hauling,
picture, pulling 10 attracting, extract-
ing 11 delineation, centripetal
absent-minded: 8 doodling
by number: 7 lottery
exaggerated: 7 cartoon 10 caricature
instrument: 9 eidograph 10 pantograph
watercolor: 4 wash
drawing room: 5 salon 6 parlor, saloon
drawl: 5 drant 6 loiter
drawn: wan 4 worn 6 peaked 7 haggard
drawstring: 5 latch
dray: 4 cart 5 wagon 6 camion
drayage: 7 cartage, haulage
drayman: 6 carter 7 carrier, wagoner
dread: awe 4 fear 5 alarm 6 dismay, horror, terror 7 anguish, anxiety 8 affright
12 apprehension
dreadful: 4 dire 5 awful 6 grisly, horrid 7
direful, fearful, ghastly, grimful, hideous
8 doubtful, horrible, shocking, terrible
9 frightful 10 formidable
dreadnaught, dreadnought: 4 tank 7
warship 8 fearless 10 battleship
dream: 4 hope, muse, reve(F.) 5 fancy 6
vision 7 chimera, fantasy, imagine, reverie, romance 8 illusion, phantasm 9
nightmare 10 apparition, aspiration

god of: 8 Morpheus
pert. to: 7 oneiric, somnial 9 oneirotic
dreamer: 4 poet 5 mystic 7 fantast 8 idealist 9 visionary 10 ideologist
dreaminess: 7 languor 8 euphoria
dreamy: kef 4 soft 5 great, super, vague 6
divine, groovy 7 faraway, pensive 8
fanciful, soothing 9 beautiful, marvelous 11 imaginative
dreary: sad 4 dire, dull, flat 5 bleak, cruel,
ourie(Sc.) 6 boring, deadly, dismal,
gloomy, somber, lonely 7 doleful 8
grievous 9 cheerless, sorrowful 10 depressing, monotonous, oppressive, pedestrian 11 distressful
dredge: dig, mop 4 coat, sift 5 scoop 6
deepen 8 excavate 9 search for
dredger: 6 duster 9 sprinkler
dregs: 4 lees, scum 5 draff, dross 6 bottom, dunder, rabble, refuse 7 deposit,
grounds, residue 8 remnants, riffraff,
sediment, settling 10 subsidence 12
crassamentum
drench: 4 dose, hose, sink, soak 5 douse,
draft, drink, drown, souse, steep 6 imbrue 7 immerse 8 permeate, saturate,
submerge
drenched: wet 4 asop 6 soaked 7 sopping
dress (see also garment, gown, robe,
vestment): don, dub, fig, ray, rig, tog 4
garb, gear, gown, hone, knap, mill, rail,
robe, suit, tire, trim, wear 5 adorn, array, curry, equip, fix up, frock, groom,
guise, habit, prink, prune, treat 6 attire,
clothe, enrobe, invest, outfit, revest, toilet 7 apparel, bandage, clothes, costume, deck out, garment, garnish, raiment, toggery, vesture 8 clothing,
decorate, ornament, vestment 9 embellish, equipment, vestiture 10 habiliment 12 accouterment
clerical: 5 cloth
court: 4 robe
feathers: 5 preen
gaudily: 5 primp, prink 7 bedizen
in full armor: 7 panoply
informal: 6 shorts, slacks 8 negligee 9
blue-jeans
kind of: alb 4 huke 5 crape, crepe, ephod,
mufti, tails, tenue, tunic, weeds 6
dirndl, finery, gaiter, kirtle, livery, tuxedo 7 regalia 8 lava-lava, peignoir 9 canonical, decollete, polonaise
leather: tan, taw, tew 5 curry
mean: 4 rags
odd: rig 5 getup
ornament: 4 frog, lace 5 jabot, ruche 6 sequin, zequin 7 ruching 8 chequeen, zecchino 10 embroidery
riding: 5 habit 8 breeches, jodhpurs
stone: nig 5 nidge, spall 7 scabble
trimming: 4 gimp, lace 5 braid
dress down: 5 scold 6 berate 7 bawl out,

tell off 9 castigate 10 tongue-lash

dressed: 4 clad 5 bound 7 habited

well: 4 braw 5 smart 6 modish 7 soignee, stylish 9 spruced-up

dresser: 5 chest, rober 6 bureau 7 modiste 8 cupboard 10 chiffonier, escritoire

leather: 7 currier 8 levanter

scrupulous: fop 4 dude 5 dandy 8 macaroni 11 Beau Brummell

dressing: 5 sauce 7 bandage 8 stuffing

dressing stone: 9 scotching

dressmaker: 5 sewer 7 modiste 8 stitcher 9 couturier 10 couturiere, seamstress

form: 7 manikin 8 mannikin 9 mannequin

dribble: 4 drip, drop 5 drool 6 bounce 7 slobber, trickle 11 fritter away

driblet: bit 6 trifle 8 pittance, small sum

drift: sag, 4 dene, dune, ford, herd, plot, tide, till 5 drove, fleet, float, flock, tenor, trend 6 broach, course, design, device, scheme, tunnel 7 impetus, impulse, pasture, purport 8 tendency 9 deviation 10 propulsion

along: 4 tide 5 float 10 move slowly

sidewise: 4 skid 8 crescent

driftage: 6 jetsam 7 flotsam 8 wreckage

drifter: bum 4 hobo 5 tramp 7 floater, vagrant 8 vagabond, wanderer 12 rolling stone

drill: gad, saw, tap 4 bore, spud 5 auger, borer, churn, decoy, train, tutor, twirl, whirl 6 allure, entice, furrow, pierce, school, seeder, stoper 7 channel 8 exercise, instruct, practice 9 perforate

drilling: 5 denim

drink (see also **beverage**): bib, lap, sip, tea 4 brew, grog, horn, swig, tiff, tope 5 booze, draft, punch, quaff, toast 6 absorb, bracer, chaser, coffee, drench, guzzle, hooker, imbibe, liquid; potion, tipple 7 draught, potable, swallow 8 beverage, cocktail, highball, libation, potation 10 intoxicant

alcoholic: ale, gin, rum, rye 4 beer, beno, bosa, boza, chia, flip, mead, nipa, nogg, soma, swig 5 airah, bombo, bozah, bubud, bumbo, julep, lager, negus, posca, sling, vodka, zombi 6 brandy, casiri, caudle, fuddle, mescal, posset, rickey, zombie 7 cobbler, guarapo, martini, sidecar, tequila 8 aperitif, rumbarge, sangaree, tequilla 9 cointreau, margarita 11 screwdriver

carbonated: 4 fizz, soda 9 ginger ale

Christmas: nog 6 eggnog 7 wassail

drugged: 6 mickey

farinaceous: 6 ptisan

frozen: 6 frappe

fruit: ade 5 assai, bland, julep, morat 6 rickey 7 ratafia

honey: 4 mead

hot: 5 cocoa, negus, toddy 6 caudle

magic: 8 nepenthe

molasses and vinegar: 6 swanky

of gods: 6 nectar

Oriental: 4 sake

portion: 4 shot 5 ounce 6 dollop, jigger

Russian: 5 vodka

sassafras: 6 saloop

small: nip, peg, tot 4 dram, pony, shot, slug 5 snort 6 chaser, jigger 7 snifter

Tatar: 6 kumiss

drinker: sot 4 lush 5 toper 7 imbiber, intaker, quaffer 8 drunkard 9 inebriate

drinking: 8 guzzling, tippling 9 carousing

bout: bum 4 orgy, toot 5 binge, spree 6 bender

horn: 6 rhyton

salutation: 5 skoal 6 prosit 7 wassail 11 a votre sante

vessel: cup, mug 4 bowl, tass(Sc.) 5 glass, gourd, hanap, jorum, stein 6 beaker, cappie(Sc.), dipper, goblet, noggin, patera 7 canikin, snifter, tankard 8 cannikin, schooner

drip: sie 4 bore, drop, leak, pill 5 eaves 7 dribble, trickle 10 wet blanket

frozen: 6 icicle

drippy: 5 soupy 6 slushy 7 drizzly, insipid, maudlin 10 unpleasant 11 sentimental

drive: run 4 bang, bear, butt, goad, herd, push, ride, send, spur, urge 5 chase, crowd, force, hurry, impel, press, shove, sweep, vigor 6 attack, compel, cudgel, hasten, plunge, propel 7 impulse, operate, overtax 9 constrain 10 get-up-and-go

away: 4 shoo 5 chase, repel 6 banish, dispel 7 repulse

down: 4 tamp

frantic: 7 bedevil

out: 4 rout 5 exile, expel 8 exorcise 9 eradicate

public: 9 esplanade

too close: 8 tailgate

drive-in: 7 open-air 10 restaurant

drivel: 4 dote 5 drool 6 dotage, slaver 7 twaddle 8 claptrap, nonsense

driver: 4 jehu 5 drabi(Ind.) 6 cabbie, hackie, caller, jarvey, hammer, mallet 7 catcher, spanker 8 coachman, engineer, golf club, motorist, overseer, teamster 9 chauffeur, propeller 10 charioteer, taskmaster

of golden chariot: 6 Helios

drizzle: 8 sprinkle 9 misty rain

droll: odd 5 comic, funny, merry, queer 6 jocose 7 amusing, comical, jocular, strange 8 farcical, humorous 9 diverting, laughable, ludicrous, whimsical 10 ridiculous

drollery: wit 4 jest 5 farce, humor 6 japery 10 buffoonery 11 waggishness

dromedary: 5 camel

dromond: 6 galley 7 warship

drone: bee, bum, hum 4 drum, slug 5 drant, idler, snail 6 bumble, draunt, lubber 7 bagpipe, humming, shirker, sleeper, speaker 8 loiterer, sluggard 9 bombilate

dronish: 4 slow 8 indolent, sluggish

drool: 6 drivel, slaver 7 slobber

droop: sag 4 bend, drop, flag, hang, loll, pine, sink, wilt 5 slump 6 slouch, wither 7 decline 8 languish

drooping: 4 limp 5 tired, weary 6 flaggy, 7 nodding 8 dejected, downcast 10 disspirited

of eyelid: 6 ptosis

on one side: 4 alop

drop: dap 4 bead, blob, drib, drip, fall, omit, shed, sink, stop 5 droop, lower, plump, plunk, slump 6 plunge 7 abandon, curtain, descent, dismiss, dribble, forsake, globule, plummet, release 8 decrease, quantity 10 relinquish 11 discontinue

lachrymal: 4 tear

syllable: 5 elide 7 elision

drop in: 5 enter, visit 6 arrive, call on, stop by 8 surprise

drop off: nap 4 doze 5 sleep 8 decrease

droplet: 7 globule

dropout: 6 misfit 8 maverick 11 social rebel 13 school quitter

dropped: 6 fallen 7 left off, lowered 8 released, went down 11 had done with

dropper: 7 pipette

dropsy: 5 edema

dross: 4 lees, scum, slag 5 chaff, dregs, sprue, waste 6 garble, refuse, scoria, sinter 7 cinders 8 leavings 9 recrement

iron: 6 sinter

drought, drouth: 6 thirst 7 aridity, dryness

drought plant: 9 xerophyte

drove (see also **drive**): mob 4 herd 5 atajo(Sp.), crowd, flock, horde 6 chisel, pushed, throng 7 steered 10 assemblage

drown: 5 flood 6 drench 8 get rid of, inundate 9 overwhelm

drowse: nod 4 doze 5 sleep 6 catnap, snooze 7 slumber

drowsiness: 8 dullness, lethargy 9 oscitancy 10 sleepiness 12 sluggishness

drowsy: 4 dull, logy 5 noddy 6 sleepy, stupid, supine 7 lulling 8 comatose, indolent, oscitant, sluggish 9 somnolent, soporific 11 heavy-headed

drub: tap 4 bang, beat, drum, lick, trim, whip 5 pound, stamp 6 berate, cudgel, pummel, thrash 7 belabor, shellac 8 lambaste

drubbing: 4 rout 7 debacle 9 thrashing, trouncing, walloping

drudge: 4 grub, moil, plod, toil 5 grind, scrub, slave 6 digger, endure, slavey, suffer 7 plodder 9 workhorse

literary: 4 hack

drudgery: 4 moil, toil, work 5 labor 10 tedious job 11 irksome task

drug: 4 dope, dull, numb 5 hocus, opium 6 heroin, opiate 7 cocaine, stupefy 8 medicine, narcotic, sedative 9 analgesic, marijuana 10 pain killer, put to sleep 11 barbiturate

addict: 6 junkie 7 sniffer 8 snowbird 9 acid freak, mainliner

and ship: 8 shanghai

container: bag 4 deck 6 packet 7 capsule

depressant: 6 downer, heroin 7 cocaine, codeine 8 atropine

emetic: 5 senna 6 ipecac

hallucinogenic: LSD 4 hemp 6 mescal, peyote 7 cocaine 9 marijuana

of forgetfulness: 5 opium 7 hashish 8 nepenthe

stimulant: 7 pep pill, zedoary 9 digitalis 11 amphetamine

drugged: 4 high 5 hyped 6 zonked 7 freaked, on a trip 8 turned on 9 spaced out 10 insensible

drugget: mat, rug

druggist: 10 apothecary, pharmacist

bible: USP

drugstore: 8 pharmacy

druid: 6 priest

priestess of opera: 5 Norma

stone: 6 sarsen

symbol: 9 mistletoe

drum: 4 cask, drub 5 bongo, drone, gumbe, gumby, tabor 6 barrel, tambor, tom-tom, tympan 7 capstan, tambour, timbrel 8 bamboula, cylinder 9 reiterate, tambourin 10 tambourine

kettle: 5 naker 6 atabal, nagara, timbal 7 timpani(pl.), tympani(pl.) 9 darabukka, tambourone

string: 5 snare

tighten cords: 4 frap

drumbeat: 6 ruffle 8 berloque

at hour for sleep: 6 tattoo

drumbeater: 8 advocate, promoter 9 supporter 10 press agent, tub-thumper

drumfire: 5 salvo 6 volley 7 barrage 9 fusillade 11 bombardment

drummer: 8 salesman 13 percussionist

drumstick: 6 tampon

drunkard: sot 4 soak 5 dipso, rummy, souse, toper 6 boozer 7 fuddler, tippler, tosspot 8 borachio 9 alcoholic, inebriate 11 dipsomaniac

drunken: 4 gone 5 tight, tipsy 6 blotto, loaded 7 pickled, pie-eyed, sottish 8 squiffed 10 inebriated 11 intoxicated

drupelet: 5 acini(pl.) 6 acinus, kernel

dry: sec, ted 4 arid, brut, dull, sere, wipe 5 baked, drain, prosy, vapid, wizen 6 barren, boring, jejune 7 insipid, parched, sapless, sub-arid, sterile, thirsty, xerotic 8 tiresome 9 dehydrate, drinkless, exsuccous, fruitless, pointless, sarcastic, waterless 10 evaporated, siccaneous, teetotaler 11 displeasing 12 moistureless, unprofitable 13 uninteresting

grass: hay

leather: sam

out: 5 steam, toast 6 rizzar(Sc.) 7 sober up 8 detoxify

up: 6 shrink, wither 7 shrivel 9 dehydrate, desiccate, evaporate, exsiccate, keep quiet 10 dehumidify

dry goods: 4 wear 6 linens, napery 7 fabrics 8 clothing, textiles

dry run: try 8 maneuver 9 rehearsal

dry shave: cheat 7 defraud

dry spell: 7 drought

dryad: 5 nymph 6 yaksha, yakshi

dual: 4 twin 6 binary, double 7 twofold

dub: rub 4 call, flub, muff, name, poke 5 botch, fluff 6 duffer, goof up, thrust 7 entitle 8 add sound, beginner, nickname, rerecord 9 schlemiel 10 poor player

dubious: 8 doubtful 9 ambiguous, equivocal, uncertain, unsettled 10 disputable, precarious 12 questionable, undetermined

ducal: 5 noble

duck: bob, bow, pet 4 dive, dunk, fowl, jouk 5 avoid, dodge, douse, evade, shirk, souse 6 plunge 7 darling, odd chap 8 sidestep 11 shy away from

Asiatic: 8 mandarin

black: 9 blackjack

bluebill: 5 scaup

brood: 4 team

dead: 5 goner

diving: 4 smew 9 goldeneye 10 bufflehead, butterball

eating: 5 Pekin

eider: 4 colk, wamp

eggs in brine: 5 pidan

freshwater: 5 teal

freshwater genus: aix

genus: 4 anas 7 nettion

group: 4 sord, team 5 skein

heraldic: 4 cannet 8 cannette

hooked-bill: 9 merganser

hunter's screen: 5 blind

male: 5 drake

Muscovy: 4 pato

old squaw: 6 quandy

Old World: 7 pochard 9 sheldrake

pert. to: 7 anatine

pintail: 4 smee, smew 8 piketail 11 querquedule

rare: 4 merse

ring-necked: 5 bunty

river: 4 smee, teal 7 pintail, widgeon 8 piketail, shoveler 9 greenwing

ruddy: 6 bobber 9 blackjack

sea: 4 coot 5 eider, scaup 6 scoter 7 scooter 9 harlequin

tree: 7 yaguaza

wild: 4 teal 5 scaup 7 gadwall, mallard 10 canvasback

wooden: 5 decoy

yellow-billed: 7 geelbec 8 geelbeck

duck out: 4 flee 7 escape 9 disappear 10 go suddenly 11 take a powder

duckbill: 8 platypus 10 mallangong

duckweed: 5 lemna

duck soup: 4 snap 5 cinch 6 breeze 8 pushover 9 easy as pie 10 child's play

duct: vas 4 main, pipe, tube, vasa(pl.) 5 canal 7 channel, conduit, passage, trachea 8 aqueduct

ductile: 4 soft 6 docile, facile, pliant 7 plastic, pliable, tensile 8 flexible, tractile 9 compliant, malleable, tractable 10 manageable, sequacious

ductless gland: 6 pineal, thymus

dud: 4 bomb, bust, flop 5 lemon 6 fizzle, turkey 7 failure, washout

dude: fop 5 dandy, swell 7 coxcomb, peacock 8 macaroni 11 Beau Brummell 12 clotheshorse, fashion plate

rancher: 9 Easterner 10 tenderfoot

dudeen: 8 clay pipe

dudgeon: ire 4 fury, huff, rage 5 anger, pique, wrath 7 umbrage 8 ill humor 10 resentment

duds: 4 togs 6 attire 7 apparel, clothes 8 garments 10 belongings

due: 4 debt, just, meed, owed 5 merit, owing 6 extent, lawful, mature, proper, unpaid 7 deserts, exactly, fitting, payable 8 adequate, deserved, directly, rightful, suitable 9 scheduled 10 sufficient 11 appropriate 12 attributable

duel: 4 tilt 5 fence, fight 6 combat 7 contest, dispute 8 conflict 13 affair of honor

duelist: 9 combatant, principal

aide: 6 second

duende: 5 charm 6 allure 9 magnetism

duenna: 8 chaperon 9 governess

dues: 4 fees 5 taxes, tolls 7 charges 8 payments 11 assessments

duet: duo 4 pair 11 piece for two

ballet: 6 adagio

lower part: 7 secondo

upper part: 5 primo

duff: 5 humus, slack 7 pudding 8 coal dust

duffer: dub 4 dope 5 dunce 6 geezer 10 stumblebum 11 incompetent

dugong: 6 sea cow 7 manatee

dugout: 4 abri, boat, cave 5 banca, banka, canoe 6 cayuca, cayuco 7 foxhole, pirogue, shelter 10 excavation

dulcet: 5 sweet 8 pleasing, soothing 9 agreeable, melodious, organ stop 10 harmonious

dulcimer: 7 cembalo 9 pantaleon 10 instrument
  Chinese: 7 yang-kin
  gypsy: 8 cimbalom
  Persian: 6 santir
dull: dim, dry, dun, sad 4 blah, dead, drab, dumb, flat, gray, logy, mopy, numb, poky, slow, tame 5 blear, blind, blunt, dingy, foggy, heavy, inert, mopey, murky, muted, prosy, stale, vapid 6 boring, cloudy, dampen, darken, deaden, dismal, dreary, drowsy, gloomy, leaden, lessen, muffle, obtund, obtuse, somber, stodgy, stolid, stuffy, stupid, torpid, weaken 7 doltish, humdrum, insipid, prosaic, tedious, vacuous 8 boeotian, lifeless, listless, overcast, sluggish, tiresome 9 apathetic, colorless, inanimate, lethargic, pointless 10 indistinct, insensible, lackluster, monotonous, pedestrian, slow-witted, uninspired 11 thickheaded 13 unimaginative
  become: 4 fade, pall, rust 7 cloud up, tarnish 8 hebetate
  finish: mat 5 matte
  noise: 4 klop, thud
dullard: 4 clod, dolt, dope 5 dunce, idiot, moron 6 dimwit 8 dumbbell 9 lamebrain, simpleton
dullness: 6 apathy, torpor 7 languor 8 hebetude, lethargy, monotony 9 bluntness 10 mediocrity
dullsville: 4 drag 7 boredom, the pits 11 for the birds
dulse: 5 algae 7 seaweed
duly: 7 rightly 8 properly 9 fittingly, regularly 13 appropriately
Dumas fils: *character:* 7 Camille
Dumas père: *character:* 5 Athos 6 Aramis, Dantes 7 Porthos 9 D'Artagnan
dumb: mum 4 dull, mute 6 silent, stupid 7 asinine, idiotic 8 ignorant 9 senseless 10 speechless, tongue-tied 11 meaningless 12 inarticulate
dumbbell: 4 boob, dope, fool 6 nitwit 7 dullard, fathead 9 exerciser
dumbfound: 4 daze, stun 5 amaze 6 boggle 7 nonplus, stagger, surprise 8 astonish 11 flabbergast
dummy: 4 copy, dolt, fake, sham 5 dunce, front 6 effigy, layout 9 ignoramus, imitation, simpleton 10 fictitious, figurehead, substitute
  in bridge: 11 exposed hand
  magazine: 7 paste-up
  window: 7 manikin 9 mannequin
dump: 4 beat, coin, drop, fire, junk 5 chuck, ditch, empty, hovel, let go, scrap 6 pigsty, unload 7 deposit 8 get rid of, jettison 11 storage area
dumpling: 5 blimp, knish 7 darling, gnoc-

chi(pl.) 8 doughboy, quenelle 10 butterball
dumps: 5 blues 8 doldrums, the blahs 9 dejection 10 depression, melancholy 11 despondency
dumpy: 5 pudgy, squat 6 stubby 8 thickset 9 shapeless
dun: tan 4 dark, drab, dull 5 annoy, brown, dingy, sepia 6 pester, plague 8 pressure 9 importune 13 demand payment
dunce: ass, oaf 4 boob, dodo, dope, fool 5 chump, idiot 6 dimwit 7 jackass 8 bonehead, dumbbell, imbecile, lunkhead, numskull 10 dunderhead, nincompoop
dune: 5 ridge 7 barchan, barkhan 8 sand hill
dungarees: 5 jeans, pants 6 slacks 8 overalls, trousers
  fabric: denim
dungeon: 4 cell, jail 5 vault 6 donjon, prison 9 oubliette 10 ergastulum(L.)
  of Calcutta: 9 Black Hole
dunk: dip, sop 4 soak 5 douse, steep 6 drench 7 immerse, moisten 8 saturate
dunlin: 4 stib 9 sandpiper
duo: 4 duet, dyad, pair 6 couple 7 twosome
dupe: con, fob, mug 4 bilk, fool, gull, hoax, tool 5 cheat, patsy, trick 6 delude, outwit, pigeon, sucker, victim 7 cat's-paw, deceive, defraud, mislead, swindle 8 flimflam, hoodwink 9 bamboozle
  genetic: 5 clone
duple: 4 dual 6 binary, double 7 twofold
duplicate: 4 copy, mate, same 5 alike, ditto, spare 6 carbon, double, repeat 7 do again, estreat, replica 9 facsimile, identical, reproduce 10 transcript, bridge game 11 counterpart
duplicity: 5 fraud, guile 6 deceit 7 cunning, perfidy 8 trickery 9 deception, falsehood, treachery 13 dissimulation, double-dealing
durable: 4 firm 5 hardy, tough, stout 6 stable, staple, strong 7 lasting 8 constant, enduring 9 long-lived, permanent 10 consistent
duration: age, run 4 span, term, time 5 space 6 length, period 8 lifetime 9 longevity
  denoting: 4 time 5 clock, timer 9 stopwatch
  of ministerial charge: 9 pastorate
  of position: 6 tenure
  without beginning or end: 8 eternity
D'Urberville lass: 4 Tess
duress: 5 force 6 coercion, hardship, pressure 9 necessity 10 compulsion, constraint
durgah: See **dargah**

during: 4 amid 5 while 7 pending 10 throughout 11 at the time of

durra: 4 corn 6 millet 7 sorghum

durst: 8 ventured

dusk: eve 5 gloom 6 darken 7 dimness 8 darkness, gloaming, twilight

dusky: dim 4 dark 5 brown, murky, tawny 6 gloomy, somber 7 obscure, shadowy, swarthy, unclear 8 blackish, blue-gray 11 dark-skinned

dust: ash 4 coat, dirt, soot, smut 5 clean, earth, flour, pouce, stive(Sc.), strew 6 pollen, powder 7 eburine, fall-out, remains, turmoil, wipe off 8 levigate, sprinkle 9 commotion, confusion

measuring device: 9 koniscope

reduce to: 4 mull 9 pulverize

speck: 4 mote

dust off: 4 redo 8 renovate 9 bring back, refurbish

dusty: dim, dry 4 arid 7 clouded, powdery

dustup: row 4 tiff 7 quarrel 8 argument

Dutch: See Netherlands

Dutch ware: 5 delft

Dutch uncle: oom 6 mentor 7 adviser

dutiful: 5 loyal 6 docile 7 willing 8 faithful, obedient, reverent 9 compliant 10 respectful, submissive 11 reverential 13 conscientious

duty: job, lot, tax 4 care, onus, role, task, toll 5 chore, stint, trust 6 burden, charge, devoir, exitus(L.), impost, office, tariff 7 purpose, respect, service, station, tribute 8 function 10 allegiance, obligation

on commodities: 6 excise

shirk: 6 truant 7 goof off 8 goldbrick

tour of: 4 turn 5 hours, shift, trick, watch

dwarf: elf 4 grig, runt, tiny 5 crowl(Sc.), gnome, midge, pigmy, pygmy, scrub, stunt, troll 6 midget, peewee 7 manikin 8 belittle, decrease, diminish, minimize, Tom Thumb 9 make small, tower over 10 diminutive, homunculus, overshadow 11 lilliputian

in Snow White: Doc 5 Dopey, Happy 6 Grumpy, Sleepy, Sneezy 7 Bashful

king: 8 Alberich

male: 9 nannander

race: 8 Nibelung

dwarfish: 4 tiny 5 elfin, runty, small, squat 6 nanoid 7 stunted

dwarfishness: 6 nanism

dwell: lie 4 bide, live, stay 5 abide, delay, exist, lodge, pause, tarry 6 remain, reside 7 inhabit

dwell on: 5 brood, nurse 6 repeat 7 belabor, prolong 10 linger over

dweller: 5 liver 6 tenant 7 denizen 8 habitant, occupant, resident 9 addressee 10 inhabitant

around city: 11 suburbanite

cave: 10 troglodyte

city: 7 slicker 8 townsman, urbanite

desert: 4 Arab 5 nomad 7 Bedouin

earth: 9 tellurian

institutional: 6 inmate

lone: 6 hermit 7 eremite, recluse

monastic: nun 4 monk 5 abbot 6 abbess 8 cenobite

temporary: 6 lodger, roomer 7 boarder 9 transient

dwelling: hut 4 casa, digs, flat, home, slum, tent 5 abode, cabin, condo, hotel, house, hovel, motel, villa 6 castle, chalet, duplex, palace, shanty 7 chateau, cottage, lodging, mansion, trailer, triplex 8 building, bungalow, domicile, tenement 9 apartment, residence 10 habitation, pied-a-terre

dwindle: ebb 4 melt, pine, wane 5 abate, waste 6 lessen, shrink 7 decline 8 decrease, diminish, peter out, taper off

dye: aal 4 anil, tint 5 color, eosin, fucus, imbue, stain, tinge 6 litmus, madder 7 aniline, pigment, toluene 8 colorant

blue: 4 anil, woad 6 indigo

brown: 5 sumac 6 sumach

coal-tar: 7 magenta

hair: 5 henna 6 rastik

purple: 6 archil, orchil 8 murexide

quercitron bark: 6 flavin

red: 5 aurin, eosin 7 annatto, magenta 8 rhodamin 9 rhodamine 10 orseilline

red-brown: 5 henna

red-orange: 5 chica 7 fuchsin 8 morindin

source: 5 murex

violet: 7 gallein 8 thionine

yellow: 4 woad 5 arusa

yellow-red: 7 annatto

dyeing apparatus: vat 4 ager

scrape: 6 harass

dying 8 moribund

dynamic: 5 vital 6 active, potent 7 driving, intense 8 forceful, spirited, vigorous 9 energetic

dynamite: TNT 5 blast 6 blow up 9 explosive

kind of: 6 dualin 7 dualine 9 fulgurite 10 kieselguhr

inventor: 5 Nobel

dynamo: 7 hustler 8 go-getter, live wire 9 generator

in distributing system: 7 booster

inventor: 7 Faraday

part: 5 rotor 7 brushes 8 armature 10 commutator

dynast: 5 ruler 6 prince 8 governor

dynasty: 5 realm 8 dominion 10 line of rule

dyspeptic: 6 crabby 7 grouchy 10 ill-humored 11 bad-tempered

dysphoria: 7 anxiety 10 discomfort, discontent

dystopia: 10 living hell 13 dreadful place

E

Ea's daughter: 4 Nina

each: all, per 5 every 6 apiece 8 everyone

eager: hot 4 agog, avid, keen, sour, warm, wave 5 afire, agasp, itchy, ready, sharp 6 ardent, greedy, intent 7 anxious, athirst, brittle, burning, excited, fervent 8 desirous, spirited, vigorous, yearning 9 desireful, impatient, impetuous, strenuous 12 enthusiastic, forereaching

eagerness: 4 elan, zeal 5 ardor 6 fervor 7 ardency, avidity 8 alacrity, cupidity, fervency 9 alertness, constancy, readiness 10 enthusiasm, impatience 13 impetuousness

eagle: 6 aquila 8 allerion, bateleur, berghaan, insignia, U.S. emblem 9 golf score
- *biblical:* 4 gier
- *constellation:* 6 Aquila
- *genus of:* 10 Haliaeetus
- *nest:* 4 aery, eyry 5 aerie, eyrie
- *relative:* 4 hawk 6 falcon
- *sea:* ern 4 erne

eaglestone: 7 aetites

eagre: 4 bore, wave

ear: lug(Sc.) 4 hear, heed, obey, plow, till 5 auris(L.), spike 7 listen 7 auricle, hearing 8 audience 9 attention, cultivate
- *absence of:* 6 anotia
- *bone:* 5 ambos, incus 6 stapes 7 malleus, stirrup
- *canal:* 5 scala
- *cavity:* 6 meatus 7 cochlea
- *cleaning device:* 8 aurilave
- *covering:* lap 4 flap, muff
- *doctor:* 9 otologist
- *inflammation of:* 6 otitis
- *middle:* 4 drum 8 tympanum
- *near:* 7 parotic
- *part of:* 4 burr, lobe 5 helix, pinna 6 tragus
- *pert. to:* 4 otic 5 aural 7 entotic 9 auricular
- *plug:* 7 stopple
- *science of:* 7 otology

ear shell: 7 abalone

earache: 7 otalgia

eardrop: 7 earring, pendant

eared seal: 5 otary

earl: 4 peer 8 nobleman
- *wife of:* 8 countess

earlier: ere 4 erst 5 elder 6 before, sooner

8 formerly, previous

early: old 5 prior 6 timely 7 ancient, betimes, too soon 9 in advance, matutinal, premature 10 beforehand

earmark: tag 5 allot, label, stamp, trait 7 feature 8 set aside 10 reserve for 14 identification

earn: get, win 4 gain, rate 5 gross, merit 6 obtain 7 achieve, acquire, deserve, realize 8 drag down

earner: 6 worker 11 breadwinner

earnest: 4 hard 5 grave, sober, staid 6 ardent, hearty, intent, sedate, solemn 7 engaged, forward, serious, sincere, zealous 8 diligent, emphatic 9 heartfelt 10 expressive, thoughtful 12 affectionate, wholehearted

earnest money: 5 token 6 pledge 7 deposit 8 security

earnings: pay 5 wages 6 income, salary 7 profits, returns 9 dividends

earring: 4 grip 8 ornament 9 girandole

earshot: 5 sound 7 hearing

earsplitting: 4 loud 5 shrill 8 piercing

earth: erd(Sc.), orb 4 bury, clay, dirt, fill, grit, land, loam, marl, muck, soil, turf 5 glebe, globe, loess, terra(L.), world 6 ground, planet 7 topsoil 10 terra firma
- *compound:* 7 tierras
- *crust constituent:* 6 silica
- *deposit:* 4 marl, silt 5 loess 8 alluvium
- *dweller:* 9 tellurian
- *god:* Geg, Keb, Seb 5 Dagan
- *goddess:* 4 Gaea 5 Ceres, Terra 6 Semele 7 Demeter
- *layer of:* 5 sloam
- *lump of:* 4 clod
- *metallic:* ore
- *opposite side of:* 9 Antipodes
- *pert. to:* 4 geal 5 terra 8 telluric 9 planetary 11 terrestrial
- *pigment:* 5 ochre, umber
- *prepare for seeding:* 4 plow 5 spade 6 harrow 9 cultivate
- *ridge of:* 4 kame 6 rideau
- *satellite of:* 4 moon
- *science:* 7 geodesy, geology 9 geography

earth bob: 4 grub 6 maggot

earth hog: 8 aardvark

earth lodge: 5 hogan

earthdrake: 6 dragon

earthenware: 4 delf 5 china, delft 7 bis-

cuit, faience, pottery 8 crockery 9 porcelain 10 terra-cotta
maker: 6 potter
piece of: 5 shard
earthfall: 9 landslide
earthling: 5 human 6 mortal
earthly: 6 carnal 7 mundane, secular, terrene, worldly 8 material, physical, possible, temporal 11 conceivable, terrestrial
earthnut: 5 arnot, chufa 6 peanut 7 truffle
earthquake: 5 seism, shock 6 tremor 7 temblor
intensity scale: 7 mercali, Richter
measuring device: 10 seisometer
pert. to: 7 seismic
point directly above: 9 epicenter
science: 10 seismology
earthstar: 6 fungus 7 geaster
earthwork: 5 agger 7 rampart 10 breastwork, embankment 13 fortification
earthworm: ess 7 annelid, ipomoea
earthy: low 5 gross 6 coarse, fleshy 7 sensual 9 practical, realistic, unrefined 11 terrestrial
earwax: 7 cerumen
earwig: 6 golach(Sc.) 9 centipede 12 eavesdropper
ease: 4 calm, rest 5 allay, knack, peace, quiet, relax 6 loosen, pacify, reduce, relief, repose, smooth, soften, soothe 7 appease, assuage, comfort, faculty, freedom, leisure, liberty, lighten, relieve, slacken 8 diminish, facility, mitigate, moderate, palliate, pleasure, security, unburden 9 alleviate, disburden, enjoyment 10 ameliorate, facilitate, relaxation, solicitude 11 contentment, naturalness, tranquility 12 satisfaction, tranquillity
at: 6 degage, otiose 7 relaxed, resting
ease off: 4 slow 5 slack
easel: 5 frame 7 support
easily: 6 gently, glibly 7 handily, readily 8 smoothly 13 without effort
east: 4 Asia 6 Levant, Orient
pert. to: 4 eoan 8 oriental
Easter: 5 Pasch 6 Eostre, Pascha
first Sunday after: 9 Quasimodo
pert. to: 7 paschal
Sunday before: 4 Palm
Eastern Church: *bishop:* 4 abba
choir platform: 5 solea
convent head: 8 hegumene
festival day: 8 apodosis
monk: 7 caloyer
prayer: 6 ectene, ektene
East Germany (see also **German, West Germany**): *capital:* 10 East Berlin
city: 5 Halle 6 Erfurt 7 Dresden, Leipzig, Rostock 9 Frankfurt

ethnic group: 5 Wends
island: 5 Rugen 6 Usedom
monetary unit: 4 mark 7 pfennig
mountain: 4 Harz 10 Erzgebirge 11 Fichtelberg
province: 4 Gera, Suhl 5 Halle 6 Erfurt 7 Cottbus, Dresden, Potsdam, Rostock 8 Schwerin 9 Frankfurt
river: 4 Elbe, Oder 5 Havel, Saale, Spree
easy: 4 calm, cozy, glib, mild 5 cushy, light, suave 6 facile, gentle, secure, simple 7 lenient, natural 8 carefree, careless, familiar, graceful, homelike, moderate, tranquil, unforced 9 compliant, indulgent, tractable, unhurried 10 manageable, unaffected 11 comfortable, complaisant, susceptible, unconcerned 13 unconstrained
easy job: 4 pipe, snap 5 cinch 8 sinecure
easy mark: 4 dupe 5 chump 6 pigeon, sucker 7 fall guy 9 soft touch
easygoing: 4 calm 5 homey 6 casual, placid 7 relaxed 8 carefree, informal 10 unaffected 11 low-pressure 12 happy-go-lucky
eat: sup 4 bite, dine, fare, feed, fret, gnaw, grub, rust 5 erode, feast, lunch, munch, taste 6 absorb, devour, ingest, ravage 7 consume, corrode, destroy, swallow 8 wear away 9 breakfast, partake of
between meals: 5 snack
by regimen: 4 diet
grass: 5 graze 6 forage 7 pasture
greedily: 4 cram, wolf 5 gorge, raven 6 gobble 10 gormandize
sumptuously: 5 feast 6 regale 7 banquet
eatable: 6 edible 8 esculent 10 comestible
eater: 8 consumer
big: 7 glutton 8 gourmand 11 trencherman
fastidious: 7 epicure, gourmet 8 Lucullus 10 gastronome
eating-place: inn 4 cafe 5 diner, grill, hotel 6 tavern 7 automat, beanery, tearoom 8 grubbery 9 cafeteria, chophouse, lunchroom 10 restaurant 11 greasy spoon 12 luncheonette
institutional: 9 refectory 10 dining hall
military: 8 mess hall
eave: 7 cornice
ebb: 4 fail, sink, wane 5 abate, decay 6 recede, reflux, retire 7 decline, subside 8 decrease, diminish 9 backwater
ebb and flow: 5 estus 6 aestus
Eber's son: 6 Joktan
Eblis: 5 Devil, Satan
before the fall: 6 Azazel
son: Sut, Tir 4 Awar 5 Dasim 8 Zalambur
ebon: 4 dark, inky 5 black, raven, sable
ebony: 5 black 8 hard wood
eboulement: 9 landslide
ebullience: 4 zest 6 gaiety 8 vitality 9

animation 10 enthusiasm, exuberance 11 high spirits

ebullient: 5 brash 6 lively 7 boiling 8 agitated 12 effervescent

ebullition: 7 ferment 8 outburst 9 agitation, commotion 10 excitement 12 fermentation 13 effervescence

ecaudate: 8 tailless

ecce(L.): 6 behold

eccentric: odd 4 card, kook 5 crank, queer, weird 7 bizarre, devious, erratic, strange 8 abnormal, peculiar, singular 9 anomalous, character, irregular, quizzical, screwball

eccentricity: 5 quirk 6 oddity 8 crotchet 9 queerness 10 aberration 11 peculiarity, strangeness 12 idiosyncrasy

ecclesiastic: 4 abbe 5 abbot, clerk 6 divine, parson, pastor, priest 7 prelate 8 minister, reverend 9 clergyman

belt: 7 balteus 8 baltheus

council: 5 synod

court: 4 rota

garment: alb 4 cope 5 amice, fanon, orale, stole, cappa, rabat 6 callot 7 cassock, biretta, calotte 8 berretta

head: 6 rector

land: 5 glebe

living: 8 benefice

military: 5 padre 8 chaplain

ruler: 8 hierarch

service: 5 matin

unit: 6 parish

ecdysiast: 6 peeler 8 stripper 11 stripteaser

echelon: 4 rank 5 level 6 lineup 8 maneuver 9 formation

echidna: 8 anteater

three-toed: 6 nodiak

echinate: 5 spiny 7 bristly, prickly

echinoderm: 8 starfish 9 sea urchin

echo: 4 ring 6 repeat, second 7 imitate, iterate, resound, respond, revoice 8 response 9 imitation 10 repetition 11 reverberate 13 reverberation

eciton: ant

eclat: 4 fame, pomp 5 glory, kudos 6 praise, renown, repute 7 acclaim 8 applause, facility, splendor 9 notoriety 10 brilliancy 11 distinction, ostentation

eclectic: 5 broad, mixed 6 choosy, varied 7 blended, diverse, jumbled 8 catholic, combined 9 many-sided, selective

eclipse: dim 4 bind, blot, hide 5 blind, cloud, shade, sully 6 darken, dazzle, exceed 7 obscure, travail 8 outrival 10 extinguish, overshadow 11 obscuration, occultation

demon of: 4 Rahu

shadow: 8 penumbra 9 penumbrae(pl.)

eclogue: 4 idyl, poem 5 idyll 7 bucolic

ecology, oecology: 9 bionomics

economical: 5 chary 6 frugal, saving 7 careful, prudent, thrifty 9 provident

economics: *element:* 9 commodity

theoretical: 9 plutology

economize: 4 save 5 skimp, stint 6 scrimp 7 husband, utilize 8 retrench

ecostate: 7 ribless

ecru: 5 beige, linen 10 unbleached

ecstasy: joy 5 bliss 6 heaven, trance 7 delight, emotion, madness, rapture 8 euphoria, paradise 9 happiness 10 exaltation

ecstatic: 4 rapt 8 glorious 9 enchanted, entranced, rhapsodic 10 enraptured

ectad: 5 outer 7 outward 8 exterior

opposite of: 5 entad

ectype: 9 imitation

ecu: 4 coin 6 shield

Ecuador: *capital:* 5 Quito

city: 4 Loja, Nono, Puyo, Tena 5 Chone, Daule, Guano 6 Ambato, Cuenca, Ibarra, Pujili, Tulcan 7 Azogues, Cayambe, Machala, Pelileo, Pillaro 8 Babahoyo, Guaranda, Riobamba 9 Guayaquil

conquered by: 7 Pizarro

Indian: 4 Cara, Inca 5 Palta 6 Canelo, Jibaro

island: 4 Puna 9 Galapagos

measure: 5 libra 6 cuadra, fanega

monetary unit: 5 sucre 7 centavo

mountain peak: 5 Altar 6 Sangay 7 Cayambe 8 Cotopaxi, Illiniza

mountain range: 5 Andes

port: 5 Manta 7 Salinas 9 Guayaquil

province: 4 Loja, Napo 5 Azuay, Canar, El Oro 6 Carchi, Guayas, Manabi 7 Bolivar, Los Rios, Pastaza 8 Cotopaxi, Imbabura 9 Galapagos, Pichincha 10 Chimborazo, Esmeraldas, Tungurahua

river: 4 Coca, Napo 5 Daule, Paute, Tigre 6 Blanco, Guayas, Macuma, Zamora 7 Curaray, Pastaza 10 Esmeraldas

volcano: 8 Antisana

ecumenical: 6 global 7 liberal 8 catholic, tolerant, unifying 9 universal, worldwide 12 all-inclusive, cosmopolitan

ecumenical council: 4 Lyon 5 Lyons, Trent 6 Nicaea 7 Vatican 9 Chalcedon

eczema: 6 herpes, tetter 9 malanders 10 dermatitis

edacity: 8 appetite, gluttony, voracity 12 ravenousness

Edda: 4 saga

Eddaic god: 4 Odin

eddo: 4 taro

eddy: 4 purl, weel(Sc.) 5 gurge, shift, swirl, whirl 6 vortex 7 backset 9 maelstrom, whirlpool 12 contrary flow 14 countercurrent

edema: 5 tumor 6 dropsy 8 swelling 9 puffiness 12 intumescence

Eden: 6 heaven, utopia 7 arcadia, elysium 8 paradise

edentate: 5 sloth 7 ant bear 8 aardvark, anteater, pangolin, tamandua 9 armadillo, toothless

Edessa's king: 5 Abgar

edge: hem, jag, lip, rim 4 bank, bite, brim, brow, hone, rand, side, trim, whet 5 arris, bevel, blade, brink, crest, frill, ruler, sidle, splay, sting, verge 6 adjoin, border, flange, fringe, impale, margin 7 nose out, sharpen, selvage 8 boundary, keenness, selvedge 9 advantage, beginning, perimeter, periphery, sharpness 10 escarpment
run along: 5 skirt
sharp: 5 beard
uneven: 4 wany 5 waney

edged: 5 sharp, erose 7 crenate, cutting, trimmed

edge in: 7 intrude, sneak by 9 gain entry 10 infiltrate 11 slip through

edging: hem 4 lace 5 frill, picot 6 border, fringe 7 binding 8 rickrack 10 embroidery
loop: 5 picot

edgy: 5 sharp, tense 6 touchy 7 angular, jittery, nervous, uptight 8 critical, snappish 9 irritable

edible: 7 eatable 8 esculent 9 palatable 10 comestible
arum: 4 taro
fungus: 5 morel
gallingale: 5 chufa
mollusk: 4 clam 6 oyster 7 scallop
parts of fruit: 4 pulp
rush: 5 chufa
seaweed: 4 agar 5 dulse, laver 6 delisk 8 agaragar
seed: nut, pea 4 bean
tuber root: oca, uva, yam 4 beet, eddo, taro 6 turnip 7 parsnip 8 rutabaga

edict: act, ban, law 4 bull, fiat 5 arret, bando, bulla, irade, order, ukase 6 decree, dictum, notice 7 command, embargo, program, statute 9 ordinance, programma 12 announcement, proclamation
papal: 4 bull

edifice: 4 dome 6 church 8 building 9 structure
kind: 6 castle, museum, palace, temple 7 capitol, mansion 8 monument 9 cathedral 10 tabernacle

edify: 5 teach 6 better, inform 7 educate, improve 8 instruct 9 enlighten, make clear 10 illuminate

edile: 10 magistrate

edit: 5 emend 6 direct, redact, review, revise 7 arrange, compile, correct, prepare, publish, rewrite 8 copyread 9 supervise

edition: 4 kind 5 issue, print, stamp 6 source 7 version 9 character 10 extraction
kind of: 5 extra 7 revisal, reprint

editor: 8 redactor 9 emendator, publisher, redacteur 10 diaskeuast, journalist
room: 7 sanctum

Edom: 7 Idumaea
chieftain: 4 Iram
district: 5 Teman
king: 5 Hadad
mountain: Hor

Edomite's ancestor: 4 Esau

educate: 4 rear 5 teach, train 6 inform, school 7 develop, nurture 8 instruct 9 cultivate, enlighten 10 discipline, strengthen 12 indoctrinate

educated: 4 bred 6 taught 7 learned, trained 8 lettered, literate, well-read 11 experienced 13 knowledgeable

education: 7 nurture 8 breeding, learning, pedagogy, training 9 erudition 10 background, discipline 11 scholarship
institution: 6 school 7 college 8 seminary 10 university
organization: PTA 6 lyceum

educator: 5 tutor 7 teacher 9 pedagogue, professor 10 instructor

educe: 6 evoke 6 elicit, evolve 7 extract 9 eliminate

eel: 4 grig 5 elver, moray, siren 6 conger 7 lamprey, muraena 8 anguilla, wriggler 9 snipefish
cut and cooked: 10 spitchcock
fish for: 7 sniggle
marine: 6 conger
migration: 7 eelfare
sand: 6 launce
young: 5 elver

eel-like: 10 anguilloid

eel-shaped: 12 anguilliform

eelboat: 6 schuit

eelpot: 4 trap

eelpout: 6 burbot, guffer, yowler 10 muttonfish

eelworm: 4 nema

eely: 7 elusive, evasive, wriggly 8 slippery, slithery 9 wriggling

eerie, eery: 5 scary, timid, weird 6 dismal, gloomy, spooky 7 awesome, ghostly, macabre, strange, uncanny 8 eldritch, ghoulish 9 unearthly, unnatural, unworldly 10 frightened 11 phantomlike

efface: 4 dele, raze 5 erase 6 cancel, rub out 7 blot out, destroy, expunge 9 eradicate, extirpate 10 obliterate

effacement: 7 erasure 10 withdrawal

effect: 4 make 5 cause, close, eclat, enact 6 intent, result, sequel 7 achieve, acquire, compass, conduce, emotion, execute, fulfill, operate, outcome, perform, produce, purport, realize 8 complete 9 influence 10 accomplish, bring about, consummate, expression, impression 11 consequence 13 manifestation

of past experience: 5 mneme

effective: 4 able, real 5 sound 6 active, actual, causal, potent 7 capable, telling 8 adequate, forceful, powerful, striking, vigorous 9 brilliant, competent, effectual, efficient 10 perficient 11 efficacious, influential

effectiveness: 5 force, power, punch 8 strength, validity 10 efficiency

effects: 5 goods 7 baggage 8 chattels, movables property 10 belongings 11 possessions

effectual: 5 valid 6 useful 7 capable 8 adequate, workable 9 effective, efficient 10 does the job, functional, productive 13 authoritative

effeminate: 4 weak 5 timid 6 chichi, prissy 7 unmanly 8 oversoft, womanish 9 emolliate, not virile, sissified 12 nicenellyish, overdelicate 13 overemotional

effervesce: 4 fizz, foam, huff 6 bubble 7 enthuse, ferment, sparkle 8 rave over

effervescent: gay 4 airy 6 breezy, bubbly, frothy, lively, snappy, yeasty 7 buoyant 8 animated, bouncing, spirited, volatile 9 ebullient, exuberant, full of pep, vivacious

effete: 4 sere 5 spent 6 barren 8 decadent, moribund 9 exhausted

efficacious: 5 valid 6 mighty, potent 8 forcible, powerful, vigorous, virtuous 9 available, effective, officious, prevalent 10 legitimate 11 efficiently

efficient: 4 able 5 adept 6 expert 7 capable 8 powerful, skillful 9 competent, effective, effectual 11 efficacious

effigy: 5 dummy, image 8 likeness 9 jack-straw

efflorescence: 8 anthesis, blooming 9 flowering 10 burgeoning 11 fulfillment

effluvium: 4 aura, odor 5 vapor 9 emanation 10 exhalation

efflux: 7 outflow 8 effusion 9 effluence, emanation

effort: try 4 task, toil, work 5 chore, drive, essay, force, labor, nisus, pains, power, trial 6 energy, strain, stress 7 attempt, trouble 8 endeavor, exertion, struggle 9 diligence 11 application, undertaking

effortless: 4 easy 6 facile, simple, smooth 8 painless

effrontery: 4 gall 5 brass, cheek, nerve 8 audacity, boldness, temerity 9 hardihood, impudence, insolence, sauciness 10 confidence, incivility 11 presumption

effulgence: 5 blaze, glory 8 radiance,

splendor 10 brightness, brilliance

effulgent: 6 bright 7 radiant 8 luminous

effuse: 4 flow, gush, shed 7 emanate 9 pour forth, spread out 11 disseminate

effusive: 5 gushy 6 smarmy 7 cloying, profuse 8 bubbling 9 exuberant, rhapsodic 12 unrestrained 13 demonstrative

eft: 4 newt 6 lizard, triton 10 salamander

egad: 8 mild oath 9 expletive

egeran: 8 idocrase 11 vesuvianite

egeria: 12 woman adviser

egest: 4 void 7 excrete

egg: 4 ova(pl.) 5 abet, goad, ovum, prod, seed, spur, urge 5 ovule, spore 6 incite 7 actuate, 9 instigate

before maturation: 6 oocyte

case: 5 shell 6 ovisac 7 ootheca

collector: 8 oologist

fertilized: 6 zygote 7 oosperm, oospore

fish: roe 5 berry 6 caviar

insect: nit

measuring device: 7 oometer

nest: 6 clutch

part of: 4 yolk 5 shell, white 7 albumen, latebra

Philippine duck: 5 balut

small: 5 ovule

tested: 7 candled

unfertilized: 8 oosphere

white of: 5 glair 7 albumen

yolk: 6 yellow 8 vitellus

egg-shaped: 4 ooid, oval 5 ovate, ovoid 6 ooidal 7 obovoid, ovaloid, oviform

egger: 4 moth

egghead: 7 Brahmin 8 highbrow 12 intellectual

eggnog: nog 8 beverage

eggplant: 7 brinjal 8 brinjaul 9 aubergine

eggshell: *confetti-filled:* 8 cascaron

Egil's brother: 6 Volund

egis: See aegis

Eglah: *husband:* 5 David

son: 7 Ithream

eglantine: 8 woodbine 10 sweetbrier 11 honeysuckle

Eglon's king: 5 Debir

ego: 4 self 6 psyche 7 conceit 9 number one 11 personality, selfishness

egotism: 5 pride 6 vanity 7 conceit 8 self-love 9 arrogance 10 self-esteem, narcissism

egotistic: 4 smug 5 cocky 7 selfish, stuck-up 8 boastful, superior 9 conceited 11 swell-headed 12 self-centered, vainglorious 13 self-important

egregious: 4 rank 5 gross 7 blatant, glaring, heinous 8 flagrant, shocking 10 deplorable, outrageous

egress: 4 exit 5 issue 6 outlet 7 outgate, passage 9 departure

egret: 5 heron, plume 6 gaulin 8 gaulding

Egypt: *capital:* 5 Cairo
city: 4 Giza, Qena, Suez 5 Asyut, Benha, Luxor, Tanta 7 Al Arish 8 Port Said 9 El Mansura 10 Alexandria
dam: 5 Aswan
desert: 5 Libyan 7 Arabian, Western
ethnic group: 6 Nubian 7 Bedouin
governorate: 4 Giza, Qena, Suez 5 Aswan, Asyut, Cairo, Minya, Sinai 6 Faiyum, Matruh, Red Sea, Sawhaj 7 Beheira 8 Beni Suef, Damietta, Ismailia, Port Said
lake: 6 Bitter, Nasser 7 Manzala 8 Burullus 11 Birket Qarun
monetary unit: 5 pound 7 piaster
mountain peak: 5 Sinai 6 Gharib, Nugrus 9 Katherina
mountain range: 9 Gebel Musa
oasis: 4 Siwa 6 Dakhla, Dunqul, Kharga 7 Farafra 8 Bahariya
peninsula: 5 Sinai
river: 4 Nile, Qena 7 Rosetta 8 Damietta
waterway: 9 Suez Canal

Egyptian: 4 Arab, Copt 5 Nilot
air god: Shu
animal: fox 4 adda, lynx 5 genet, hyena 6 jackal, jerboa 7 gazelle 9 ichneumon
antelope: 5 bubal
army chieftain: 6 sirdar
beer: 6 zythum
beetle: 6 scarab
bird: 6 sicsac
boat: 5 baris 8 dahabeah
bottle: 6 doruck
bull: 4 apis
burial jar: 7 Canopus
calendar: 4 Ahet, Apap, Tybi 5 Choik, Payni, Shemu, Thoth 6 Hathor, Mechir, Mesore, Paophi 7 Pachons 9 Phamenoth, Pharmuthi
cap: fez
cat-headed goddess: 4 Bast 5 Pakht
Christian: 4 Copt
civilization: 6 Tasian
clover: 7 berseem
cobra: 4 haje
concubine: 5 Hagar
cosmetic: 4 kohl
cotton: Sak 4 pima
crocodile-headed god: 4 Sobk 5 Sebek
cross: 4 ankh
crown: 4 atef
dam: 4 sudd
dancers: 7 ghawazi 8 ghawazee
deity: Hor, Mut, Nut 4 Anta, Apet, Bast, Isis, Maat, Sati 5 Anaka 6 Hathor, Seshat, Tefnut 7 Nepthys 8 Nechebit
descendant: 4 copt 6 fellah
dog: 6 saluki
drink: 4 bosa, boza 5 bozah
drug: 8 nepenthe
elysium: 4 Aalu

emblem: 4 aten 5 lotus
gateway: 5 pylon
god: Set 4 Ptah, Seth 5 Thoth 6 Anubis 7 Serapis
goddess: Mut, Nut 4 Bast, Isis 5 Pakht 6 Sekhet 8 Nekhebet
guard: 6 ghafir 7 ghaffir
guide: 8 dragoman
hawk-headed god: 5 Horus
herb: 5 anise
instrument: 7 arghool, arghoul, sistrum
judge of the dead: 6 Osiris
king: Tut 4 Fuad, Mena 5 Menes 6 Ramses 7 Ptolemy, Rameses 9 Amenhotep 11 Tutankhamen
laborer: 5 aperu
lighthouse: 6 pharos
lily: 6 calla, lotos, lotus
lion-headed goddess: 4 Bast 5 Pakht 6 Sekhet
lizard: 4 adda 5 scink, skink
love goddess: 6 Hathor
lute: 5 nabla
maternity goddess: 4 Apet
measure: apt, dra, hen, rob 4 dira, draa, kada, khet, ocha, roub, theb 5 abdat, ardab, ardeb, cubit, farde, keleh, kilah, sahme 6 artaba, aurure, baladi, kantar, kedlah, robhah, schene 7 choryos, daribah, malouah, roubouh, toumnah 8 kassabah, kharouba 10 dira baladi, dira mimari, kerat kamel, nief keddah 11 feddan nasri
monarch: 7 Pharaoh
monument: 7 obelisk
official: 5 mudir
paper: 6 papyri 7 papyrus
peasant: 6 fellah
Pharaoh's headdress: 7 pschent
plant: 5 cumin 6 cummin, lentil
pyramids at Giza: 6 Cheops (Khufu), Khafre 7 Menkure
queen: 9 Cleopatra, Nefertiti, Nofretete
relic: 5 mummy
ruined cities: 5 Tanis 6 Abydos, Karnak, Thebes 7 Memphis
sacred bird: 4 ibis
sacred bull: 4 apis
sacred flower: 5 lotos, lotus
sanctuary: 5 secos, sekos
seal: 6 scarab
serpent: 5 apepi
shrub: kat
solar disk: 4 Aten
stone: 7 rosetta
sun god: Tem, Tum 4 Atmu, Atum
symbol: uta 4 ankh 6 scarab
talisman: 5 angle
temple: 4 Idfu 5 Luxor 6 Abydos, Karnak, Osiris 7 Dendera
tomb: 7 mastaba, pyramid
underworld: 4 Aaru, Duat 6 Amenti

vase: 7 canopic

viper: 8 cerastes

vulture-headed goddess: Mut 8 Nekhebet

weight: ket, oka, oke 4 dera, heml, khar, okia, rotl 5 artal, artel, deben, kerat, okieh, ratel, uckia 6 hamlah, kantar 7 drachma, quintal

wind: 6 kamsin 7 chamsin, kamseen, khamsin 8 khamseen

Ehud's son: 6 Naaman

eider duck: 4 colk

eidetic: 5 vivid

eidolon: 4 icon 5 ghost, image 7 phantom 10 apparition

eight: eta(G.) 6 ogdoad

group of: 5 octad, octet 6 octave 7 octette

eight-sided: 9 octagonal

eighth: *circle:* 6 octant

day after nones: 4 ides

note: 6 quaver

order: 5 octic

eighty: 9 fourscore

Eire: 4 Erin 5 Ierne 7 Ireland 8 Hibernia

Eireannach: 8 Irishman

ejaculate: 5 blurt, eject 7 exclaim

ejaculation: 7 begorra 8 uttering 11 exclamation

eject: 4 boot, cast, emit, oust, spat, spew, spit, void 5 erupt, evict, expel, spout, spurt, vomit 6 banish, bounce 7 dismiss, exclude, extrude, obtrude 8 disgorge 9 discharge, ejaculate 10 disembogue, dispossess

ejection: 6 ouster 8 eviction 9 expulsion

eke: 7 augment, enlarge, husband, stretch 8 increase, lengthen 10 supplement

el: 4 bend

El Salvador: *capital:* 11 San Salvador

city: 8 Santa Ana 9 San Miguel, Sonsonate 12 Villa Delgado

department: 5 La Paz 7 Cabanas, La Union, Morazan 8 Usulutan 9 Cuscatlan, Sonsonate 10 Ahuachapan, San Vicente

Indian: 5 Pipil

lake: 5 Guija 8 Ilopango

monetary unit: 5 colon 7 centavo

mountain peak: 8 Santa Ana 9 San Miguel 10 San Vicente 11 San Salvador

river: 5 Lempa

volcano: 6 Izalco

elaborate: 5 fancy 6 expand, ornate 7 amplify, develop, enlarge, explain 8 detailed 9 embellish, intricate 11 complicated, extravagant, painstaking

Elam: *capital:* 4 Susa

king: 12 Chedorlaomer

elan: 4 dash 5 ardor, gusto, verve 6 spirit, warmth 7 potency 9 eagerness 10 enthusiasm

elanet: 4 kite

elapse: 4 pass, slip 6 expire

elasmobranch fish: ray

elastic: 6 garter, spongy 7 buoyant, springy 8 cheverel, cheveril, flexible, stretchy 9 expansive, resilient 10 propulsive

fluid: gas

material from whales: 6 baleen

elastin: 10 albuminoid

elate: 4 buoy 5 cheer, exalt, exult, flush, lofty, raise 6 excite, please, thrill 7 elevate, gladden, inflate, success 8 elevated, heighten, inspirit 9 stimulate 10 exhilarate

elated: 5 happy, vogie(Sc.) 6 jovial 7 excited, jocular 8 exultant, jubilant 9 cock-a-hoop, overjoyed

elater: 6 beetle 8 skipjack

elaterite: 7 bitumen

Elatha's son: 4 Bres

Elatus' daughter: 6 Caenis 7 Caeneus

Elbe tributary: 4 Eger, Elde, Iser 5 Havel, Mulde, Saale 6 Elster

elbow: 4 bend 5 ancon, joint, nudge, shove 6 jostle

bend an: 5 drink 6 imbibe

bone: 4 ulna 5 ulnae(pl.)

pert. to: 4 ulnad 8 anconeal

elbowroom: 6 leeway 10 ample space

elcaja: 6 mafura

eld: 9 antiquity

elder: iva 4 aine(F.) 5 prior 6 senior 7 oldster 8 ancestor, danewort, superior, 9 presbyter 10 forefather

elderly: old 4 aged, gray 6 senile 7 ancient 9 up in years, venerable 11 over the hill

eldritch: 4 eery 5 eerie, weird 7 uncanny 9 frightful

Eleanor's husband: 7 Henry II

elect: 4 call, pick 6 assume, choose, chosen, decide, opt for, prefer, select, vote in 7 embrace, espouse, pick out 9 legislate

election: 6 choice 9 balloting 10 plebiscite 11 alternative

majority of votes: 9 plurality

nominating: 7 primary

to break the: 6 runoff

electioneer: 5 stump 8 campaign, politick 9 seek votes

elective: 8 optional 9 voluntary

elector: 5 voter 6 elisor 7 chooser 11 constituent

Electra: *brother:* 7 Orestes

father: 9 Agamemnon

husband: 7 Thaumas

mother: 1 Klytemnestra

son: 8 Dardanus

electric: 6 static 8 magnetic

appliance: 4 iron, oven 5 dryer, mixer, stove 6 heater, washer 7 blender, broiler, toaster *carrier:* 9 conductor

circuit regulator: 7 booster

coil: 5 tesla

current: 6 direct 11 alternating

current meter: 7 ammeter 9 voltmeter

current moderator: 5 coder 9 rheometer 10 attenuator

device: 4 plug 6 dynamo, switch 7 battery 8 resistor, rheostat 9 amplifier, capacitor, condenser

generator: 6 dynamo

light: arc 4 neon 12 incandescent

measuring unit: amp, ohm, rel 4 volt, watt 5 barad, farad, henry, joule 6 ampere, proton 7 coulomb 8 kilowatt

motor part: 10 commutator

particle: ion

pole: 5 anode 7 cathode

power: 7 wattage

resistance: 6 ohmage

safety device: 4 fuse

strength: 8 amperage

transmission: 5 radio

wave meter: 9 ondometer

electrify: jar 4 jolt 5 amaze 6 dazzle, fire up, thrill 7 astound, stagger, startle 8 astonish 9 galvanize

electronic tube: 6 triode 7 tetrode 8 klystron

electrum: 5 amber

Electryon: *brother:* 6 Mestor

daughter: 7 Alcmene

father: 7 Perseus

mother: 9 Andromeda

wife: 5 Anaxo

eleemosynary: 4 free 9 dependent 10 charitable, gratuitous

elegance: 4 chic 5 grace, style, taste 6 finery, luxury, polish 7 dignity 8 courtesy, grandeur, richness, splendor 9 propriety 10 concinnity, refinement 12 gracefulness

elegant: 4 chic, fine, posh 5 swank 6 dainty, dressy, superb, urbane 7 courtly, genteel, refined, stately 8 delicate, graceful, handsome, polished, tasteful 9 admirable, beautiful, excellent, exquisite, recherche, sumptuous 10 concinnous, fastidious

elegiac: sad 8 mournful 9 plaintive

elegist: 4 Gray, poet 6 Milton 10 Propertius

elegit: 4 writ

elegy: 4 poem, song 5 dirge 6 lament 7 epicede 9 epicedium 11 lamentation

element: air 4 fire 5 basic, earth, group, metal, water 6 matter 7 essence, quality 8 rudiment 9 component 10 ingredient 11 constituent, environment, fundamental

chemical: tin(Sn) 4 gold(Au), Iron(Fe), lead(Pb), neon(Ne), zinc(Zn) 5 argon(A), boron(B), radon(Rn), xenon(Xe) 6 barium(Ba), carbon(C), cerium(Ce), cesium(Cs), cobalt(Co), copper(Cu), erbium(Er), helium(He), indium(In), iodine(I), nickel(Ni), osmium(Os), oxygen(O), radium(Ra), silver(Ag), sodium(Na), sulfur(S.) 7 arsenic(As), bismuth(Bi), bromine(Br), cadmium(Cd), calcium(Ca), gallium(Ga), hafnium(Hf), holmium(Ho), iridium(Ir), krypton(Kr), lithium(Li), mercury(Hg), niobium(Cb), rhenium(Re), rhodium(Rh), silicon(Si), terbium(Tb), thorium(Th), thulium(Tm), uranium(U), yttrium(Y) 8 actinium(Ac), aluminum(Al), antimony(Sb), astatine(At), chlorine(Cl), chromium(Cr), Europium(Eu), fluorine(F), hydrogen(H), illinium(Il), lutecium(Lu), masurium(Ma), nitrogen(N), platinum(Pt), polonium(Po), rubidium(Rb), samarium(Sm), scandium(Sc), selenium(Se), tantalum(Ta), thallium(Tl) titanium(Ti), tungsten(W), vanadium(V) 9 beryllium(Be), columbium(Cb), germanium(Ge), lanthanum(La), magnesium(Mg), manganese(Mn), neodymium(Nd), palladium(Pd), potassium(K), ruthenium(Ru), strontium(Sr), tellurium(Te), virginium(Vi), ytterbium(Yb), zirconium(Zr) 10 dysprosium(Dy), gadolinium(Gd), molybdenum(Mo), phosphorus(P) 12 praseodymium(Pr) 13 protoactinium(Pa)

combining power: 7 valence

decomposed: 5 anion

different weight: 7 isotope

even valence: 6 artiad

family: 7 halogen

minute: 5 monad

nonmetallic: 5 boron 6 bromin, iodine 7 bromine, silicon

nonvolatile: 6 barium

of air: 5 argon 6 oxygen 8 nitrogen

poisonous: 7 arsenic

rare earth: 6 erbium

elemental spirit: 5 genie

elementary: 5 basic, crude, plain 6 simple 7 initial, primary 8 inchoate, original 9 primitive 10 rudimental, uncombined 11 fundamental, rudimentary

organism: 5 monad

reader: 6 primer

elemi: 5 anime, resin 9 oleoresin

elephant: 5 hathi 6 tusker, muckna 7 mammoth 8 mastodon 9 pachyderm

call: 4 barr 7 trumpet

dentin: 5 ivory

driver: 6 mahout

ear: 4 taro

enclosure: 5 kraal

extinct: 8 mastodon

female: cow
goad: 5 ankus
group: 4 herd
male: 4 bull
maverick: 5 rogue
pert. to: 11 pachydermic
seat: 6 howdah
trap: 6 keddah
trappings for: 5 jhool
trunk: 9 proboscis
tusk: 5 ivory 9 scrivello
young: 4 calf
elephant boy: 4 Sabu
elephantine: 4 huge 6 clumsy 8 colossal,
     enormous, gigantic, ungainly 9 ponder-
     ous
goddess: 4 Sati
elevate: 4 lift, rear, rise 5 elate, erect, ex-
     alt, extol, heave, hoist, raise, setup, tow-
     er 6 uplift 7 advance, dignify, enhance,
     ennoble, glorify, promote 8 heighten,
     inspirit 10 exhilarate
elevated: 4 high 5 great, lofty, noble, ris-
     en, steep 6 elate, raised 7 boosted, ex-
     alted, moved up 8 majestic, towering,
     uplifted 9 dignified 10 high-minded
elevation: 4 bank, hill, rise 5 mound,
     ridge 6 ascent, height 8 altitude, emi-
     nence, highness, mountain 9 acclivity
     10 exaltation, prominence 11 advance-
     ment
of mind: 7 anagoge
reference point: 9 benchmark
to sainthood: 12 canonization
elevator: bin 4 cage, lift, silo 5 hoist 9
     ascenseur
elf: fay, hob, imp, pug 4 peri, pixy 5 dwarf,
     fairy, gnome, ouphe, pixie 6 goblin,
     sprite 7 brownie, incubus, succubi 8
     succubus 10 changeling, leprechaun
elfin: 4 tiny 6 impish 7 puckish, tricksy 8
     delicate, prankish 9 fairylike
elfwort: 10 elecampane
Elgin marbles: 10 sculptures
Eli: 4 Yale
son: 6 Hophni 8 Phinehas
Elia: 11 Charles Lamb
Eliam's daughter: 9 Bathsheba
Elian: 8 Eretrian
elicit: 4 draw, milk, pump 5 claim, educe,
     evoke, exact, wrest, wring 6 deduce, de-
     mand, entice, extort, induce 7 extract 8
     bring out 9 call forth
elide: 4 omit, skip 5 annul 6 ignore 7 nul-
     lify 8 slur over, suppress 9 apocopate
eligible: fit 6 proper, worthy 8 suitable 9
     desirable, qualified 10 acceptable
Elijah: 5 Elias 7 prophet 8 Tishbite
eliminate: 4 drop, oust 5 erase, expel,
     purge 6 cut out, delete, except, ignore,
     remove 7 abolish, exclude, silence, weed
     out 8 get rid of 9 eradicate

Eliot: *hero:* 6 Marner
heroine: 6 Romola
Elisha: *father:* 7 Shaphat
home: 11 Abelmeholah
servant: 6 Gehazi
elision mark: 10 apostrophe
Elissa: See Dido
elite: 4 best 6 choice, flower, gentry, select
     7 quality, society 9 haut monde, top
     drawer 10 blue bloods, uppercrust 11
     aristocracy 12 quintessence
gathering: 6 galaxy
elixir: 6 potion, spirit 7 arcanum, cordial,
     cure-all, nostrum, panacea
of life: 7 amrita 7 amreeta
Elizabeth I: 4 Bess 6 Oriana
mother: 6 Boleyn
elk: 4 deer 5 eland, moose 6 sambar, wa-
     piti
genus of: 5 Alces
ell: 4 wing 5 annex 8 addition 9 extension
ellipse: 4 oval
elliptical: 4 oval 5 ovate 7 concise 8
     abridged, cut short 10 contracted
elm: *family of:* 8 Ulmaceae
fruit of: 6 samara
rock: 5 wahoo
Elmo's fire: See **Saint Elmo's fire**
elocute: 7 declaim
elocution: 7 oratory 9 eloquence
elocutionist: 6 reader 7 reciter, speaker
eloge: 6 eulogy 7 oration 8 encomium 9
     panegyric
elongate: 6 extend 7 draw out, stretch 8
     lengthen, protract
elongated: 4 lank 6 linear 7 prolate, slen-
     der 9 stretched, strung out
elope: 4 flee 6 decamp 7 run away
eloquence: 7 fluency, oratory 8 rhetoric 9
     elocution, facundity, loftiness
eloquent: 5 vivid 6 fervid, moving, poetic
     8 stirring 10 expressive, meaningful,
     oratorical, persuasive 11 impassioned
else: 4 more 5 other 7 besides, further, in-
     stead 9 otherwise 10 additional
elsewhere: 4 away 7 not here 12 another
     place
elucidate: 5 clear 7 clarify, explain 8 sim-
     plify, spell out 9 interpret 10 illustrate
elude: 4 duck, flee, foil 5 avoid, dodge,
     evade 6 baffle, befool, delude, escape 7
     beguile, deceive 9 frustrate
elusive: 4 eely 5 cagey 6 subtle, tricky 7
     evasive 8 baffling 10 impalpable, lubri-
     cious 11 hard to grasp
elute: 5 rinse 7 cleanse, soak out 8 dis-
     solve 10 use solvent
elver: eel
Elysian: 8 beatific, blissful 10 delightful
Elysium: 4 Eden 8 Paradise
elytrum of beetle: 4 wing 5 shard
emaciated: 4 lean 5 gaunt 6 peaked, skin-

ny, wasted 7 scrawny, wizened 8 starving, underfed 10 cadaverous

emanate: 4 flow 5 arise, issue 6 effuse 7 breathe, give off, proceed, radiate 8 stem from 9 come forth, originate

emanation: 4 aura 5 radon 6 efflux 7 outcome 8 emission 9 ectoplasm, effluence 10 exhalation 11 consequence

emancipate: 4 free 5 loose 6 unbind 7 manumit, release 8 liberate, unfetter 11 enfranchise

emancipator: 5 freer, Moses 7 Lincoln 9 deliverer

emasculate: 4 geld 6 soften, weaken 8 castrate, enervate 10 devitalize 12 make impotent

embalm: 7 mummify, perfume 8 preserve

embankment: 4 bund, dike, fill, quay 5 digue, levee, mound, revet 6 staith 7 backing 9 banquette

embargo: 5 edict, order 8 blockade, stoppage 9 restraint 10 impediment, inhibition 11 prohibition, restriction

embark: 5 begin, board, start 6 take up 7 enter on 8 commence, engage in 11 venture upon

embarrass: 4 faze 5 abash, annoy, shame, upset 6 hamper, hinder, impede 7 confuse, flummox, nonplus 8 bewilder, confound, dumfound, encumber, entangle, handicap, obstruct, straiten 9 discomfit, dumbfound 10 complicate, disconcert

embarrassment: fix 5 shame 6 unease 7 chagrin 8 distress 9 confusion 10 discomfort, perplexity 11 humiliation 12 bewilderment, discomposure, entanglement 13 inconvenience, mortification

embassy: 5 envoy 7 mission 8 legation 10 ambassador 13 foreign office

embattled: 8 fighting 9 embroiled, fortified 10 crenelated 11 hardpressed

embattlement: 7 parapet

embay: 7 shelter 8 encircle, surround

embed: 5 infix, inlay, set in 7 implant, ingrain 8 entrench

embellish: 4 deck, gild, trim 5 add to, adorn, dress, grace 6 bedeck, blazon, emboss, enrich, flower 7 apparel, bedrape, garnish, magnify 8 beautify, decorate, ornament 9 elaborate, embroider 10 exaggerate

embellished: 6 florid, gested, ornate

ember: ash 4 coal, slag 6 cinder 7 clinker

embezzle: 4 rook 5 steal 6 thieve 7 defraud, swindle 8 peculate

embitter: 4 sour 7 acidify, envenom 8 acerbate 9 acidulate 10 exacerbate, exasperate

emblaze: 5 adorn, honor 6 kindle 9 embellish

emblazon: 4 laud 5 adorn, extol 7 deck

out, display, exhibit, glorify 9 celebrate

emblem: bar 4 mace, orle, sign, star, type 5 badge, crest, image, token 6 device, figure, symbol 7 scepter 8 allegory, colophon, insignia 9 character, coat of arms

of authority: 4 mace

of Christianity: 5 cross

of clan: 5 totem

of U.S.: 5 eagle

emblematic: 7 typical 8 symbolic 10 figurative

emblic: 4 aula 5 aulae(pl.)

embodiment: map 6 avatar 7 epitome 11 incarnation 15 personification

of Ptah: 4 Apis

embody: 4 fuse 5 blend, merge, unite 6 mirror, take in, typify 7 contain, embrace, include 8 coalesce, organize 9 incarnate, personify, represent 10 comprehend 11 incorporate

embolden: 4 abet 5 brave, nerve 6 assure, buck up 7 bolster, hearten, inspire, support 9 encourage, enhearten

embolism: 8 stoppage 9 occlusion 11 obstruction 13 intercalation

embolus: 4 clot

embosom: 6 foster 7 cherish, embrace, enclose, shelter 8 surround

emboss: 5 adorn, chase 6 indent 8 ornament 9 embellish, embroider 10 do in relief

embossing: 8 celature

embouchure: 10 mouthpiece, river mouth

embowed: 6 arched 7 vaulted

embower: 6 enclose 9 shelter in

embrace: hug 4 clip, fold, love, neck, side 5 adopt, bosom, chain, clasp, cling, enarm, grasp 6 accept, caress, clinch, comply, cradle, cuddle, embody, enfold, huddle, inclip, infold, plight 7 cherish, contain, enclose, espouse, include, involve, welcome 8 comprise, encircle 9 encompass 10 comprehend 11 incorporate

embrangle: 7 confuse, perplex

embrocation: 6 arnica 8 liniment

embroider: tat 4 lace 5 couch, panel 6 emboss, frieze, pad out, stitch 7 build up 8 ornament 9 elaborate, embellish 10 exaggerate

embroidery: 4 lace 6 bonnaz, edging, hedebo 7 orphrey 8 arrasene 10 needlework

figure: 6 etoile

frame: 7 taboret

hole: 6 eyelet

machine-made: 6 bonnaz

thread: 5 floss

embroil: 5 mix up 6 muddle 7 confuse, involve 8 distract, entangle 9 commingle, implicate 12 get in trouble

embroilment: 4 spat, tiff 5 fight 6 fracas 7 dispute, quarrel 8 argument, squabble 11 altercation

embrown: tan 6 darken

embryo: 4 germ, seed 5 fetus, ovule 6 foetus 9 peritroch

young: 8 blastula

emcee: 4 host 8 director 9 moderator 10 run the show

eme(Sc.): 5 uncle 6 friend 8 relative

emend: 4 edit 5 alter 6 better, reform, repeal, revise 7 correct, improve, rectify, redress

emendator: 6 editor

emerald: gem 5 beryl, green 7 smaragd

Emerald Isle: 4 Eire, Erin 7 Ireland

emerge: 4 loom, rise 5 issue 6 appear, evolve 7 develop 9 come forth 10 come in view 11 materialize

emergence: 4 need 8 debouche, exigence 9 occurrence, outgrowth

emergency: fix 5 pinch 6 crisis, crises(pl.), crunch, strait 8 exigency, juncture 11 contingency

money: 5 scrip 8 reserves

signal: SOS 5 flare, siren

emergent: 6 rising

Emerson: *friend:* 7 Thoreau

philosophy: 17 transcendentalism

work: 6 Brahma, Merlin 8 Threnody

emery: 8 abrasive, corundum 11 carborundum

emetic holly: 6 yaupon

emeute: 4 riot 6 tumult 8 outbreak, uprising

emigrant: 7 exodist, settler 8 colonist, stranger

emigre: 5 alien, exile 7 evacuee, refugee 10 expatriate

eminence: 4 hill, note, rank, rise 5 knoll 6 ascent, esteem, height, renown, repute 8 standing 9 elevation, loftiness 10 projection, promontory 11 distinction

eminent: big 4 high 5 great, lofty, noble, noted 6 famous, marked, signal 8 glorious, renowned, singular, towering 9 egregious 10 celebrated, noteworthy 11 conspicuous, illustrious, outstanding 13 distinguished

emir, emeer: 5 noble, ruler, title 6 leader, prince 8 governor 9 chieftain, commander

province: 7 emirate

emissary: spy 5 agent, envoy, scout 6 deputy, legate 7 courier 8 delegate

emission: 4 flow 8 ejection, issuance 9 discharge, radiation

emissive: 8 exhalant

emit: 4 beam, cast, give, pour, send, shed, vent 5 eject, exude, fling, issue, utter 6 exhale, expire, let out 7 give off, radiate, release 8 throw off, transmit 9 discharge 10 disembogue

heat: 4 glow

light: 4 glow 9 luminesce

offensive odors: 4 reek

emmer: 5 spelt, wheat

emmet: ant 7 pismire 8 formicid

Emmy: 7 TV award 9 statuette

emolliate: 6 soften, weaken

emollient: 4 balm 5 salve 6 lotion 8 lenitive, soothing

emolument: 4 fees 5 wages 6 income, profit, salary 7 benefit, stipend 9 advantage 12 compensation

Emory University site: 7 Atlanta

emote: act, mug 4 gush, rant 7 ham it up, overact 12 be theatrical

emotion: ire, joy 4 fear, hate, love 5 agony, anger, grief, heart 6 relief, sorrow 7 ecstasy, feeling passion 8 jealousy, movement, surprise 9 affection, agitation, sensation, sentiment 11 disturbance, sensibility 14 susceptibility

without: 9 apathetic

emotional: 6 moving 8 stirring, touching 9 rhapsodic, sensitive 10 hysterical, passionate, responsive

emotionless: 4 cold 5 staid 6 frigid, torpid 7 deadpan, distant 8 reserved 9 apathetic, impassive, unfeeling 11 coldblooded

empathy: 4 pity, ruth 6 accord 7 rapport 8 affinity, sympathy 13 understanding

emperor: 4 czar, king, tsar 5 ruler 6 caesar, sultan 7 monarch 9 imperator, sovereign

Holy Roman: 4 Otho, Otto

emphasis: 5 focus 6 accent, stress, weight 8 salience

emphasize: 6 play up 7 dwell on, feature 8 pinpoint, point out 9 highlight, punctuate 10 accentuate, underscore

emphatic: 7 certain, decided, earnest, marcato 8 absolute, decisive, definite, distinct, enfatico, forcible, positive 9 energetic

empire: 4 rule, sway 5 power, realm, reign, state 6 domain 7 control, kingdom 8 dominion 11 sovereignty

Empire State: 7 New York

empirical: 7 factual 12 experimental 13 observational, trial-and-error

emplacement: 7 battery 8 platform

employ: use 4 hire 5 apply 6 bestow, engage, occupy, retain, supply, take on 7 concern, enclose, involve, service, utilize 8 exercise

employed: 4 busy 6 unidle 7 engaged, working

employee: 4 hand, help 6 worker 8 hireling 9 jobholder 10 wage earner *bank:* 5 clerk, guard 6 teller 7 cashier 8 watchman 10 bookkeeper

minor: cog 6 helper, minion 7 servant 9 assistant, underling

slaughterhouse: 5 sider

employer: 4 boss, user 6 gaffer 7 manager 12 entrepreneur

employment: use 4 task, toil, work 5 craft, trade, usage 7 calling, purpose 8 business, vocation 10 engagement, occupation, profession

empoison: 7 envenom 10 make bitter

emporium: 4 mart, shop 5 bazar, store 6 bazaar, market

empower: 6 enable 7 entitle, license 8 accredit, delegate, deputize, sanction 9 authorize 10 commission

empress: 5 queen, ruler

Austrian: 12 Maria Theresa

Byzantine: 5 Irene 7 Endocia

French: 7 Eugenie 9 Josephine

of India: 8 Victoria

Russian: 4 Anna 7 czarina, tsarina 9 Catherine, Elizabeth

empress tree: 9 paulownia

emptiness: 4 void 6 hunger, vacuum 7 inanity, vacancy, vacuity

empty: rid 4 bare, dump, free, idle, pour, toom(Sc.), void 5 blank, drain, expel 6 barren, devoid, hollow, unload, vacant, vacate 7 deplete, exhaust, untaken 8 disgorge, evacuate, unfilled 9 discharge 10 unburdened, unoccupied

empty-headed: 5 silly, vapid 6 jejune, simple, stupid 7 fatuous, moronic, witless 8 ignorant 11 bird-brained

Empusa: 7 specter 9 hobgoblin

empyreal: 7 sublime 9 celestial

empyrean: 5 ether 7 heavens 9 firmament

emu: 4 rhea 6 ratite 9 cassowary

relative: 7 ostrich

emulate: ape, vie 4 copy 5 equal, excel, rival 7 compete, imitate

emulation: 6 strife 7 contest 10 contention 11 competition

emulsive: 9 softening

emyd: 6 turtle

enable: let 5 allow 6 permit 7 empower, entitle, qualify 9 authorize 12 make possible

enact: 4 pass 6 decree, effect, ordain 7 actuate, appoint, execute, perform, portray 9 legislate, personate, represent 10 bring about, constitute

enactment: law 6 assize, decree 7 passage, statute 9 ordinance 14 representation

enamel: 5 glaze, gloss, paint 6 aumail 7 dentine, schmelz 8 cosmetic, schmelze

enameled: 6 inlaid 10 variegated

enamored: 6 soft on 7 charmed, smitten 9 bewitched, entranced 10 captivated,

crazy about, fascinated, infatuated, in love with

Enan's son: 5 Ahira

en bloc: 5 as one 8 as a whole 11 all together

en brochette: 8 skewered

encamp: 4 tent 5 lodge 7 bivouac

encase: box 5 cover 7 inclose

enceinte: 8 pregnant 9 expectant, with child

enchain: 4 bind 5 tie up 6 fetter

enchant: 5 charm 6 delude 7 bewitch, delight 8 ensorcel, enthrall 9 captivate, enrapture, fascinate, hypnotize, mesmerize, spellbind

enchantment: hex 5 charm, magic, spell 7 gramary, sorcery 8 gramarye, wizardry 10 necromancy, witchcraft 11 fascination, incantation

enchantress: 5 Circe, fairy, Medea, siren, witch 9 sorceress 11 Morgan le Fay

encharge: 7 entrust 10 commission

enchase: 5 inlay 7 engrave 8 decorate, ornament

enchiridion: 6 manual 8 handbook

enchorial: 6 native 7 demotic 8 domestic 11 of the people

encina: oak

encipher: 4 code

encircle: 4 band, belt, gird, girt, ring 5 embay, embow, hem in, inorb, orbit 6 emball, engirt, enlace, girdle 7 embrace, enclose, environ, wreathe 8 cincture, ensphere, surround 9 encompass, loop about 10 wrap around 12 circumscribe 13 circumference

encircling band: 4 halo, ring, zone 6 choker 8 bracelet, necklace

enclose: box, hem, mew, pen, rim 4 cage, gird, pale 5 bound, bower, fence, hedge, house 6 circle, corral, encase, encyst, enfold, enlock, enwrap, picket, pocket, shut in 7 contain, embosom, embrace, envelop, harness 8 comprise, conclude, encircle, imprison, palisade, surround 9 encompass, put inside 12 circumscribe

enclosure: haw, mew, pen, sty 4 bawn, cage, cell, coop, cote, fold, wall, weir, yair, yard 5 atajo, booly, court, crawl, fence, kraal, pound, stall 6 aviary, corral, cowpen, garden, hurdle, kennel, paling, prison, runway 7 paddock 8 cincture, cloister, sepiment, stockade 9 cofferdam 10 quadrangle

encomiast: 8 eulogist 10 panegyrist

encomium: 5 eloge 6 eulogy, praise 7 plaudit, tribute 8 accolade, citation 9 panegyric 10 compliment, salutation 12 commendation

encompass: 4 be-go, belt, clip, gird, ring, wall 5 belie, beset 6 begird, circle, embody, engird, take in 7 contain, embrace, enclose, environ, include 8 comprise, encircle, engirdle, surround 9 beleaguer, circulate 10 circumvent 12 circumscribe

encore: bis 5 again 6 recall, repeat 10 repetition

anti: boo 4 hiss 7 catcall

encounter: 4 bout, espy, face, meet 5 brush, fight, force, incur, onset 6 accost, affray, assail, attack, battle, breast, combat, oppose 7 address, affront, contest, dispute, hosting, run in 8 come upon, conflict, confront, skirmish 9 collision, forgather, interview 10 engagement, foregather, occurrence, tournament

courageously: 5 beard, brave 7 weather

group: 12 therapy sit-in 13 confrontation

encourage: 4 abet, back 5 boost, cheer, egg on, impel, nerve 6 advise, assure, buck up, exhort, foment, foster, incite, induce, second, uphold 7 advance, animate, cherish, comfort, confirm, console, enliven, forward, further, hearten, inspire, promote, support, sustain 8 embolden, inspirit, reassure 9 instigate, stimulate 10 give hope to, strengthen 11 countenance

encouragement: 4 lift, push 5 boost 6 praise 7 support 8 approval 9 incentive, patronage 12 pat on the back

encouraging: 4 good, rosy 6 likely 7 helping, hopeful 9 favorable, promising 11 comfortable, inspiriting 12 advantageous

encroach: 5 poach 6 invade 7 impinge, intrude 8 entrench, infringe, overstep, trespass

encroachment: 6 inroad 10 aggression, infraction

encuirassed: 7 armored 8 loricate

encumber: tax 4 clog, load 5 beset, check 6 burden, hamper, hinder, impede, retard, saddle 7 involve, oppress 8 entangle, handicap, obstruct, overcome, overload, slow down 9 embarrass, weigh down 10 overburden

encumbrance: 4 clog, lien, load 5 claim 6 burden, charge 7 trouble 8 handicap, hardship, mortgage 9 albatross 10 impediment 13 embarrassment, inconvenience

encyclic: 8 circular 13 comprehensive

encyclopedic: 7 erudite 8 complete 9 extensive, scholarly 10 exhaustive 11 wide-ranging 12 all-inclusive 13 comprehensive

end: aim, tip 4 fate, goal, heel, stop, tail 5 amend, cease, close, death, ensue, finis, issue, limit, napoo, omega, raise, scrap, stash 6 define, design, expire, finale, finish, napooh, object, period, upshot, windup 7 abolish, achieve, closure, destroy, lineman, purpose, remnant 8 boundary, complete, conclude, dissolve, finality, surcease, terminal, terminus 9 cessation, determine, extremity, intention, objective, terminate 10 completion, conclusion, denouement, expiration 11 consequence, destruction, discontinue, termination 12 consummation 14 accomplishment

loose: tag 6 thread

musical: 4 coda, fine

on: 7 upright 8 vertical

remove: tip 4 clip

tending to: 5 telic

upper: tip 4 apex, head

End of World: 15 Gotterdammerung

end result: 7 outcome, product

end-all: 6 killer 7 quietus 8 clincher 9 last straw 11 coup de grace

endanger: 4 risk 6 hazard, menace 7 imperil 10 compromise, jeopardize

endearing: 5 sweet 7 lovable

endearment: 6 caress 9 sweet talk 10 loving word

term of: hon, pet 5 angel, lover, sugar 7 darling, sweetie 8 baby doll, precious

endeavor: aim, job, try 4 best, seek, work 5 assay, essay, exert, labor, study, trial 6 affair, effort, strife, strive 7 afforce, attempt 8 exertion, interest, struggle 9 undertake 10 enterprise

ended: 4 done, over, past 8 finished

endemic: 5 local

endive: 7 chicory 8 escarole

endless: 7 eternal, forever, undying 8 immortal, infinite 9 boundless, ceaseless, continual, incessant, perpetual, unceasing 10 continuous 11 everlasting, measureless 12 interminable 13 uninterrupted

endlong: 10 lengthwise 14 longitudinally

endmost: 4 last 8 farthest, remotest

endorse: 4 back, okay, sign 5 boost 6 second 7 approve, certify, stand by, support 8 advocate, sanction, vouch for 9 authorize, guarantee 11 countenance

endorsement: 4 fiat, visa 5 rider 7 backing 8 approval 9 signature

endow: 4 fund, will 5 award, bless, endue, equip, found, grace, grant, leave 6 clothe, enrich, invest, supply 7 furnish, provide 8 bequeath

with bodily form: 11 materialize

with power: 8 energize

endowment: 4 gift 5 dower, dowry 6 talent 7 ability, chantry 8 appanage, dotation 9 mentality 10 foundation

endue: 5 endow, teach 6 clothe, invest 8 instruct

endurable: 7 livable 8 bearable 9 tolerable 10 sufferable 11 supportable

endurance: 5 pluck 7 stamina 8 gameness, patience, strength, tenacity 9 fortitude, hardihood, suffering 10 resolution 11 continuance, persistence, resignation 12 perseverance

endure: 4 bear, bide, last, live, wear 5 abide, allow, brook, stand 6 drudge, harden, remain, suffer 7 comfort, forbear, persist, prevail, sustain, toughen, undergo, weather 8 continue, forebear, tolerate 9 withstand 10 strengthen 11 bear up under

endured: 5 borne

enduring: 4 fast 6 biding 7 durable, eternal, lasting, staunch 8 immortal 9 continual, perennial, permanent 11 everlasting 12 imperishable

Endymion: *mother:* 6 Calyce
son: 7 Aetolus
loved by: 6 Selene

enemy: fae, foe 4 Axis, feid 5 devil, fiend, Satan 6 foeman 7 hostile 8 opponent 9 adversary, ill-wisher 10 antagonist, backfriend

energetic: 4 fast, hard, spry 5 brisk, peppy 6 active, hearty, lively 7 arduous 8 emphatic, forceful, forcible, full of go, vigorous 9 dynamical, strenuous 10 expressive 11 hardworking 12 enterprising

energize: 7 animate 8 activate 10 invigorate

energumen: 7 fanatic 8 demoniac 10 enthusiast

energy: pep, vim, zip 4 bang, bent, birr, life 5 drive, force, might, nerve, power, steam, vigor 6 effort, intake, output, spirit 7 potency 8 activity, strength, vitality 9 animation
lack: 5 atony 7 inertia 9 lassitude
measuring device: 11 dynamometer
unit: erg 4 dyne 5 joule 7 quantum 8 watt hour 9 megajoule 10 horsepower

enervate: sap 6 weaken 7 exhaust, tire out, unnerve 8 enfeeble 10 debilitate, devitalize

enfant terrible: 4 brat 5 devil, scamp, whelp 6 terror 7 hellion 12 troublemaker

enfeeble: 4 numb 5 drain 6 deaden, deplete, impair, soften, weaken 8 enervate 9 attenuate, undermine 10 debilitate

enfilade: 4 rake

enfold: hug 4 wrap 5 clasp, cover 6 cuddle, enlace, enwrap, swathe 7 embrace, enclose, envelop, squeeze 8 encircle, surround

enforce: 5 exact 6 coerce, compel 7 execute, implant 8 carry out, insist on 9 constrain, prosecute 10 administer

enfranchise: 4 free 6 let vote, manumit, release 8 liberate 10 emancipate

engage: 4 book, hire, join, mesh, rent, sign 5 agree, catch, enter, lease, trade 6 absorb, arrest, embark, employ, enlist, induce, oblige, occupy, pledge, take on 7 bespeak, betroth, conduce, engross, involve, promise 8 contract, covenant, entangle, interest, persuade, set about 9 interlock, undertake

engaged: 4 busy 5 hired 6 bonded, meshed 7 assured, earnest, entered, pledged, versant 8 employed, involved, occupied, promised 9 affianced, betrothed

engagement: job 4 aval, date 5 fight 6 affair, battle, escrow 7 booking, contest, meeting 8 skirmish 9 betrothal, encounter 10 attachment, employment 11 appointment, involvement

engager: 6 surety

engaging: 5 sapid 6 taking 7 winning 10 attractive 11 interesting

engender: 5 beget, breed, cause 6 excite 7 develop, produce 8 generate, occasion 9 procreate, propagate

engine: gas 5 motor, steam 7 turbine 8 gasoline 10 locomotive
covering: 4 cowl
kind of: gin, ram 4 goat 5 dinky, mogul 6 diesel, helper, mallet, pusher 7 turbine 8 dollbeer 10 locomotive
military: ram 4 tank 6 onager 7 robinet 8 ballista, helepole 9 espringal 11 ribaudequin
part: cam 4 gear 6 boiler, piston, stator 8 cylinder 9 crankcase 10 carburetor 12 differential, transmission
speed up: rev

engineer: 4 plan 6 driver, manage 7 planner, plotter 8 contrive, designer, inventor, maneuver 9 construct 10 accomplish 11 constructor, superintend

engirdle: 8 surround 9 encompass

engirt: 7 envelop 8 encircle

England: 6 Albion 7 Britain 9 Britannia
capital: 6 London
city: 4 Bath, Hull, York 5 Derby, Leeds, Luton 6 Exeter, Oldham 7 Bristol, Croydon, Ipswich, Preston, Reading 8 Brighton, Coventry, Plymouth 9 Liverpool, Sheffield 10 Birmingham, Manchester
county: 4 Avon, Kent 5 Devon, Essex, Salop 6 Dorset, Durham, Surrey 7 Cumbria, Norfolk, Suffolk 8 Cheshire, Somerset 9 Cleveland, Hampshire, Wiltshire 10 Derbyshire, East Sussex, Humberside, Lancashire, West Sussex
invader of: 4 Dane 5 Norse, Roman, Saxon 6 Norman
island: Man 4 Holy 5 Farne, Lundy, Wight 6 Scilly, Thanet, Walney 7 Sheppey

lake: 8 Coniston 9 Ullswater 10 Windermere

mountain peak: 7 Scafell, Snowdon 9 Cross Fell

mountain range: 7 Pennine 8 Cumbrian 9 Cotswolds 12 Cheviot Hills 13 Cotswold hills, Coniston Fells

port: 4 Hull 5 Dover 6 London 7 Preston 8 Plymouth 9 Liverpool 10 Portsmouth 11 Southampton

river: Exe, Lea 4 Aire, Avon, Foss, Hull, Nene, Ouse, Tyne 5 Stour, Trent 6 Humber, Kennet, Mersey, Severn, Thames 7 Derwent, Welland

English: 7 British

aborigine: 4 Pict

actor: 4 Tree 5 Donat, Evans 6 Arliss, Irving 7 Burbage, Gielgud, Olivier 8 Guinness

actress: 4 Gwyn 5 Leigh, Terry 6 Whitty 7 Langtry

admiral: 6 Nelson, Ramsey, Rodney, Vernon

admirer of: 10 anglophile

air force: RAF

Antarctic explorer: 5 Scott

apartment: 4 flat

apple: 6 beefin, biffin, coling, rennet 7 beaufin, costard 8 coccagee 9 guarenden, guarender

apron: 8 barmskin

archbishop: 4 Lang, Laud 6 Becket 7 Cranmer

architect: 4 Wren 10 Inigo Jones

bailiff: 5 reeve

bed: 4 doss

biologist: 6 Huxley

boat: 7 coracle

cattle tender: 7 byreman

charity school scholar: 8 blue coat

cheese: 7 stilton, truckle

chinaware: 5 Spode 8 Wedgwood

church caretaker: 6 verger

church officer: 6 beadle

circuit court: 4 eyre

class: 4 form

clergyman: 4 Inge 5 Donne, Oates 6 Becket, Newman 7 Latimer

coin: ora 4 rial, ryal 5 ackey, angel, crown, groat, pence, pound 6 bawbee, florin, guinea, seskin, teston 7 angelet, carolus 8 farthing, shilling, sixpence, twopence 9 dandiprat, fourpence, halfcrown, halfpenny, sovereign 10 threepence

composer: 4 Arne 5 Elgar, Neale 6 Delius, Handel 7 Britten, Stainer 8 Williams

conductor: 5 Boult 7 Beecham 10 Barbirolli

conservative: 4 Tory

conspirator: 6 Fawkes

court: 4 eyre, leet 5 gemot 6 gemote 8 hustling

crown tax: 4 geld

dance: 6 morris

dandy: 4 toff

diarist: 5 Pepys 6 Evelyn

dramatist: 4 Shaw 5 Peele, Reade, Wilde 6 Coward, Dryden, Pinero 7 Marlowe 8 Beaumont, Fletcher 11 Shakespeare

early conqueror: 5 Horsa 7 Hengist

economist: 4 Mill 6 Angell, Keynes 7 Gresham, Malthus, Ricardo

elevator: 4 lift

emblem: 4 lion

entertainment: 4 busk 7 ridotto

essayist: 4 Elia, Lamb, Lang 5 Bacon 6 Steele 7 Addison

estate: 4 este

explorer: 4 Cook, Ross 5 Cabot, Drake, Scott 6 Hudson

field: 5 croft

food dealer: 12 costermonger

forest: 5 Arden 8 Sherwood

freeman: 5 ceorl

game: 5 darts, rugby 6 soccer 7 cricket

gold: 4 rial, ryal

gun carrier: 4 bren

historian: 4 Bede 5 Acton, Grote 7 Toynbee 8 Macaulay

humorist: 4 Lear

jacket: 4 Eton

king: Hal, Lud 4 Bran, Brut, Cnut, Cole, Knut, Lear 5 Brunt, Henry, James, Sweyn 6 Alfred, Arthur, Bladud, Cnaute, Edward, Egbert, George 7 Artegal, Elidure, Richard, Stephen, William 8 Gorboduc

laborer: 5 navvy

land: 5 laine

law: 4 soke 6 esnecy 7 danelaw

lawyer: 7 bencher 9 barrister, solicitor

liberal: 4 Whig

lunch: 6 tiffin

machine gun: 4 Bren, Sten

magistrate: 4 beak

man: 6 Briton 8 John Bull 9 Britisher

measure: ell, pin, rod, ton, tun, vat 4 acre, bind, boll, comb, cran, foot, gill, goad, hand, hide, inch, last, line, mile, once, palm, peek, pint, pipe, pole, pool, rood, sack, span, trug, wist, yard, yoke 5 bodge, carat, chain, coomb, cubit, digit, float, floor, fluid, hutch, minim, perch, point, prime, quart, skein, stack, truss 6 barrel, bovate, bushel, cranne, fathom, firkin, gallon, hobbet, jugrum, league, manent, oxgang, pottle, runlet, strike, sulung, thread, tieree 7 furlong, hobbitt, quarter, quarten, rundlet, spindle, tertian, virgate 8 carucate, chaldron, hogshead, landyard, puncheon, quadrant, standard 9 kilderskin, shaftment, shaftmont **10** barleycorn, barn gallon, winchester **13** tablespoonful

minister: **4** Peel, Pitt **7** Walpole **8** Disraeli

molasses: **7** treacle

monk: **4** Beda, Bede **5** Baeda

news agency: **7** Reuters

novelist: **5** Arlen, Eliot, Hardy, Reade, Waugh, Wells **6** Austen, Bronte, Butler, Huxley, Sterne **7** Bennett, Dickens, Forster **8** Fielding, Forester, Trollope

officer's civilian dress: **5** mufti

old letter: wen **5** thorn

order: **6** Garter

painter: **4** Opie **6** Turner **7** Hogarth, Millais, Poynter **8** Reynolds **9** Constable **12** Gainsborough

pamphleteer: Defoe, Swift

Parliament houses: **5** Lords **7** Commons

Parliament proceedings: **7** Hansard

party member: **4** Tory, Whig **7** Liberal **8** Laborite **9** Labourite **12** Conservative

patron saint: **6** George

peasant: **5** churl

pert. to: **8** Anglican **10** Anglo-Saxon

philosopher: **4** Hume **5** Bacon, Locke **6** Hobbes **7** Russell, Spencer **9** Whitehead

pirate: **4** Kidd **5** Drake **6** Morgan **7** Hawkins

poet: **4** Gray, Pope **5** Auden, Blake, Byron, Carew, Donne, Eliot, Keats **6** Brooke, Cowper, Dryden, Landor **7** Barrett, Caedmon, Chaucer, Shelley, Spenser **8** Browning **9** Coleridge, Masefield **11** Shakespeare

policeman: **5** bobby **6** copper, peeler

prairie: **4** moor **5** heath

printer: **7** Caxton

prison: **4** gaol

public school: **4** Eton **5** Rugby **6** Harrow **9** Sandhurst

queen: **4** Anne, Mary **8** Victoria **9** Elizabeth

racing town: **5** Ascot **10** Epsom Downs

rebel: **5** Essex, Tyler **8** Cromwell **10** Washington

resort: **4** Bath **8** Brighton

rifle: **7** Enfield

royal house: **4** York **5** Tudor **6** Stuart **7** Hanover, Windsor **8** Lancaster **11** Plantagenet

royal household officer: **7** equerry

royal residence: **7** Windsor

scientist: **6** Darwin, Huxley **7** Boyd-Orr

seaman: **5** limey **6** rating

serf: **6** thrall

settler: **4** Jute, Pict **5** Angle, Saxon **6** Norman

sheep: **8** cotswold

shoemaker: **4** snob

sixpence: **5** sprat

slave: **4** esne

socialist: **6** Fabian

soldier: **5** tommy **7** redcoat **8** fusileer, fusilier

spy: **5** Andre

stable: **4** mews

statesman: **4** Eden, Grey, Peel, Pitt **5** Bevin, Simon **6** Attlee **7** Asquith, Baldwin **8** Disraeli **9** Churchill, Gladstone, MacDonald, Macmillan **10** Walsingham **11** Chamberlain, Lloyd George

stone monument: **8** cromlech

streetcar: **4** tram

tavern: pub

tea muffin: **7** crumpet

thicket: **7** spinney

thrush: **5** mavis

title: **4** dame, duke, earl, king, lady, lord, peer **5** baron, noble, queen **6** knight, prince **7** baronet, duchess, marquis **8** baroness, countess, marquess, princess, viscount **11** marchioness, viscountess

tourist: **7** tripper

tribe: **5** Iceni

truck: **5** lorry

tutor: don

university: **5** Leeds **6** London, Oxford **9** Cambridge

uplands: **5** downs

weight: **5** stone

engorge: **4** glut **5** gorge **6** devour

engrave: cut **4** etch **5** carve, chase, print, sculp **6** chisel, incise **7** enchase, impress, imprint, stipple **8** inscribe, ornament **9** character, sculpture

by dots: **7** stipple

engraver: **6** chaser, etcher **7** artisan **13** siderographer

tool of: **5** burin

notable: **5** Durer **7** Hogarth

engraving: *wax:* **8** intaglio **9** cerograph, xylograph **11** glyptograph

instrument: **6** stylet

pert. to: **7** glyphic, glyptic

engross: **4** bury, grip, hold **6** absorb, engage, occupy **7** immerse **8** enthrall **9** fascinate, overwhelm, preoccupy

engrossed: **4** rapt **6** intent

engrosser: **7** copyist **12** calligrapher

engulf: **5** flood, swamp, whelm **6** deluge, devour **7** swallow **8** inundate, submerge **9** overwhelm

enhance: **4** lift **5** enarm, exalt, raise **6** deepen **7** augment, elevate, enlarge, greaten, improve, sharpen **8** heighten, increase **9** aggravate, intensify **10** exaggerate

enhearten: **8** embolden

enigma: **5** rebus **6** puzzle, riddle, sphinx **7** mystery, problem **9** conundrum

enigmatic: **6** mystic **7** cryptic, elusive,

obscure 8 baffling, mystical, puzzling 9 equivocal 12 inexplicable

enisle: 6 cut off 7 isolate 8 separate

enisled: 5 alone, apart 8 solitary

enjoin: bid 5 order 6 decree, forbid 7 command, dictate, require 8 admonish, prohibit

enjoy: own 4 have, like 5 eat up, fancy, savor 7 command, possess 11 think well of

enjoyment: fun, use 4 ease, zest 5 gusto 6 liking, relish 7 delight 8 felicity, pleasure 9 happiness 11 delectation 12 satisfaction 13 gratification

enkindle: 5 light 6 arouse, excite, ignite, stir up 7 incense, inflame 9 set on fire

enlace: tie 5 twine, twist, weave 6 enfold 7 entwine 8 encircle, entangle 10 interweave

enlarge: add, eke(Sc.) 4 grow, huff, ream 5 add to, swell, widen 6 broach, dilate, expand, extend, spread 7 amplify, augment, broaden, build up, develop, distend, enhance, greaten, magnify, stretch 8 increase, lengthen, 9 elaborate, expatiate, intumesce 10 aggrandize, exaggerate, make bigger

enlarged: 8 varicose

enlargement: 6 growth 8 addition, swelling 9 accretion, expansion, inflation 13 magnification

enlarging gradually: 5 evase

enlighten: 5 edify, teach 6 inform 7 apprise, educate 8 acquaint, instruct 9 irradiate 10 illuminate 11 disillusion

enlightened person: 10 illuminato

enlightenment: 5 bodhi 6 wisdom

enlist: 4 join 5 enter 6 embark, engage, enroll, induct, sign up 7 impress, recruit 8 register 9 volunteer

enlisted man: GI

enlistment: 5 hitch 11 service time

enliven: 4 warm 5 cheer, pep up, rouse 6 revive 7 animate, comfort, inspire, refresh 8 brighten, inspirit 9 encourage, stimulate 10 exhilarate, invigorate

enlivening: 5 vital 6 genial 9 sprightly

enlock: 7 enclose

en masse: 5 as one 8 as a whole, in a group 11 all together

enmesh: 4 trap 5 catch 7 ensnare 8 entangle

enmity: 5 spite 6 hatred, malice, rancor 7 dislike, ill will 8 aversion, bad blood 9 animosity, antipathy, hostility 10 antagonism, repugnance, resentment 11 malevolence

ennead: 4 nine 8 ninefold

ennoble: 5 exalt, honor, raise 6 uplift 7 dignify, elevate, glorify

ennui: 6 apathy, tedium 7 boredom, languor 8 doldrums 9 lassitude, weariness 12 indifference, listlessness

Enoch: *father:* 4 Cain 5 Jared
son: 4 Irad 10 Methuselah

enormous: big 4 huge, vast 5 great, large 6 heroic, mighty 7 immense, mammoth, massive 8 abnormal, colossal, gigantic 9 excessive, monstrous 10 gargantuan, prodigious, stupendous, tremendous 11 elephantine

Enos: *father:* 4 Seth
grandfather: 4 Adam
grandmother: Eve
uncle: 4 Abel, Cain

enough: 4 enow 5 ample, basta 6 fairly, plenty 8 adequate, passably 9 tolerably 10 sufficient 12 satisfactory

enounce: say 5 state, utter 8 proclaim 9 enunciate

enrage: 5 anger 6 grieve, madden 7 incense, inflame 9 infuriate 10 exasperate

enraged: 5 irate 7 berserk 8 choleric, maddened, wrathful

enrapture: 5 charm 6 ravish, thrill 7 beguile, bewitch, delight, enchant 8 enravish, enthrall, entrance 9 captivate, fascinate, transport

enrich: 5 adorn, endow 6 fatten 7 enhance, fortify, improve 8 decorate, ornament 9 embellish, fertilize 10 make better 11 add vitamins

enrobe: 6 attire, clothe

enroll, enrol: 4 join, list 5 enter, write 6 enfold, enlist, induct, record, sign up 7 impanel, recruit 8 inscribe, register 11 matriculate

enroot: 7 implant

en route: 8 on the way 9 in transit

ens: 5 being 6 entity 9 existence

ensconce: 4 hide 5 cover 6 settle 7 conceal, shelter 9 establish 11 place snugly

ensemble: 5 decor, getup, whole 6 outfit, troupe 7 company, costume 9 aggregate 11 combination

enshrine: 7 cherish 10 hold sacred

enshroud: 4 hide, veil, wrap 5 cloak 7 conceal, envelope, obscure

ensiform: 6 ensate 7 xiphoid

ensign: 4 flag, sign 5 badge 6 banner, signal, symbol 7 officer, pennant 8 gonfalon, standard 9 oriflamme
of Othello: 4 Iago
of sovereignty: 7 regalia
papal: 8 gonfalon

ensilage: 4 feed 6 fodder

enslave: 5 chain 7 shackle 8 enthrall 9 subjugate

enslavement: 7 bondage, serfdom 9 addiction, servitude, thralldom

ensnare: net, web 4 mesh, trap 5 benet, catch, noose, snarl 6 allure, enmesh, entoil, entrap 7 beguile, springe 8 entangle 10 intertwine

ensorcell, ensorcel: 5 charm 7 bewitch, enchant 9 fascinate

ensoul, insoul: 7 animate

ensuing: 4 next 9 following, resulting 10 subsequent, succeeding

ensure: 5 guard 6 clinch, secure 7 protect, warrant 8 make safe 9 guarantee

entad: 6 inward

opposite of: 5 ectad

entail: 6 demand, impose 7 call for, include, involve, require 11 necessitate

ental: 5 inner

opposite of: 5 ectal

entangle: knot, mesh, mire, trap 5 catch, ravel, snafu, snare 6 engage, enlace, enmesh, entrap, foul up, muddle, puzzle 7 confuse, embroil, ensnarl, involve, perplex 8 bewilder, encumber 9 embarrass, implicate 10 intertwine, interweave

entangled: 7 complex 9 intricate, twisted up 10 interwoven 11 complicated

entanglement: web 4 knot 6 affair 7 liaison 8 obstacle 13 embarrassment

entellus: 6 monkey 7 hanuman

entente: 6 treaty 8 alliance 9 agreement, coalition 13 understanding

enter: 4 join, post 5 admit, share 6 appear, arrive, engage, enlist, enroll, entrer(F.), pierce, record 7 get into, intrude 8 initiate, inscribe, register 9 introduce, penetrate, sign up for 11 matriculate

militarily: 6 invade

enter into: 8 take part 10 participate

enter upon: 5 begin 6 embark

enteric: 10 intestinal

enterprise: job 4 firm, push, task, zeal 5 drive, essay, vigor 6 action, effort, spirit 7 attempt, project, venture 8 business, endeavor, gumption 9 adventure, operation 10 initiative, management 11 undertaking

enterpriser: 12 entrepreneur

enterprising: 4 bold 5 alert 6 active, daring 7 driving 8 hustling 9 ambitious, energetic, wide-awake 10 aggressive, courageous 11 hardworking, industrious, progressive

entertain: 5 amuse, treat 6 divert, harbor, regale 7 beguile, cherish 8 consider, interest, play host 10 think about 11 contemplate

entertainer: 4 host, mime 5 actor 6 amuser, dancer, singer 7 actress, hostess, regaler, speaker, trouper 8 comedian, magician, minstrel 9 performer, soubrette(F.) 10 comedienne

entertainment: fun 4 fair, fete, gala, play 5 cheer, feast, opera, revue, sport, treat 6 kermis, shivvo 7 banquet, ceilidh(Ir.), concert, pastime, ridotto 8 function,

musicale 9 amusement, diversion, enjoyment, festivity, reception 10 recreation

place: 4 park 5 movie 6 casino, cinema, circus, midway, resort 7 cabaret, theater 10 playground

enthrall: 4 grip 5 charm 6 absorb 7 engross, enslave 8 intrigue 9 captivate, fascinate, spellbind

enthrone: 5 crown, exalt

enthusiasm: 4 elan, fire, zeal, zest 5 ardor, mania, verve 6 fervor, spirit 7 ardency, passion 9 animation, eagerness 10 ebullience, fanaticism

enthusiast: bug, fan, nut 4 buff 5 freak, lover 6 addict, maniac, rooter, zealot 7 devotee, fanatic 8 follower 9 supporter 10 aficionado

enthusiastic: 4 keen 5 rabid 6 ardent, gung ho 8 hipped on 10 forthgoing

enthymeme: 8 argument 9 syllogism

entice: 4 bait, coax, draw, lure, tole, wile 5 charm, decoy, tempt 6 allure, cajole, incite, induce, invite, seduce 7 attract, bewitch, wheedle 8 inveigle, persuade

entire: all 4 full 5 every, gross, sound, total, utter, whole 6 choate, intact 7 perfect, plenary 8 absolute, complete, integral, unbroken 9 undivided 10 unimpaired 11 unqualified 12 all-inclusive, undiminished

entirely: 4 only 5 alone, quite 6 solely, wholly 7 utterly 10 altogether, thoroughly 11 exclusively

entitle: dub 4 call, name, term 5 allow 6 enable, permit 7 empower, qualify 8 nominate 9 authorize, designate 10 denominate 12 characterize, make eligible

entity: ens 4 body, unit 5 being, thing 7 essence, integer 9 existence, structure 10 individual

entomb: 4 bury 5 inter, inurn 6 inhume

entourage: 5 court, staff, train 7 retinue 9 following, retainers 10 associates, attendants, sycophants

entracte: 8 interval 9 interlude 12 intermission

entrails: 6 vitals 7 giblets, innards, insides, viscera

entrain: 5 board

entrance: 4 adit, boca(Sp.), door, gate, hall 5 charm, debut, entry, foyer, mouth, stulm, toran, way in 6 access, atrium(L.), entree, portal, ravish, zaguan 7 delight, gateway, hallway, ingress, postern 9 admission, beginning, enrapture, fascinate, incursion, induction, overpower, threshold, vestibule 10 admittance, appearance 12 introduction

entranced: 4 rapt 8 ecstatic 10 mesmerized

entrant: 7 starter 8 beginner 10 competitor, contestant 11 participant

entrap: bag, net 5 catch, decoy, snare 6 allure, ambush, taigle(Sc.), trepan 7 beguile 8 entangle, inveigle

entre(F.): 7 between

entreat: ask, beg, bid, sue 4 pray, seek, urge 5 crave, plead 6 adjure, appeal, exhort, invoke 7 beseech, conjure, implore, prevail, request, solicit 8 persuade, petition 9 impetrate, importune 10 supplicate

entreaty: 4 plea, suit 8 petition 9 treatment 11 importunity, negotiation

entree: 5 entry 6 access 8 entrance 9 admission 10 acceptance, main course, permission

entrench, intrench: fix, set 5 dig in, embed 6 anchor, invade 7 implant 8 encroach, infringe, trespass 9 establish

entrenchment: 7 closure

entrepot: 5 depot 9 warehouse 10 storehouse

entrepreneur: 7 manager 8 employer, operator 10 impresario 11 enterpriser

entresol: 9 mezzanine

entrust: 4 give 6 assign, commit 7 address, commend, confide, consign, deposit 8 delegate, encharge, hand over 11 give custody

entry: 4 adit, hall, item, memo, note 5 debit 6 credit, entree, postea, record 7 ingress, passage 8 entrance, notandum, register 9 vestibule 10 adjustment, contestant, enlistment, enrollment

entwine: 4 coil, lace 5 braid, twist, weave 6 enlace 7 wreathe 9 interlace 10 interweave

enumerate: 4 tell 5 add up, count 6 detail, number, recite, reckon, relate 7 compute, itemize, recount, tick off 8 estimate 9 calculate 13 particularize

enumeration: 4 list 5 tally 6 census 7 account, catalog 9 catalogue

enunciate: say 5 state, utter, voice 7 declare, enounce 8 announce, proclaim 9 pronounce 10 articulate

enure: See **inure**

envelop: 4 hide, mask, veil 5 cloak, cover 6 bemist, encase, enfold, engirt, enwrap, invest, muffle, sheath, shroud, swathe 7 blanket, conceal, enclose, environ, obscure 8 surround 9 encompass

envelope: 4 coma, husk, rind 5 shell 6 jacket 7 wrapper 8 covering 10 integument

envenom: 6 poison 7 corrupt, vitiate 8 embitter 12 fill with hate

envious: 7 jealous 8 covetous 9 invidious, resentful 10 begrudging

environ: hem 4 gird 5 limit 6 girdle 7 envelop, inclose 8 encircle, surround 9 encompass 12 circumscribe

environment: 6 medium, milieu 7 climate, element, habitat, setting 8 ambiance, ambience 10 background 12 surroundings

science of: 7 ecology

environs: 7 suburbs 8 vicinity 9 outskirts 10 nearby area

envisage: 4 face 8 confront 9 visualize

envision: 5 dream 7 imagine, picture 8 conceive 9 conjure up 11 bring to mind

envoy: 5 agent, envoi(F.) 6 deputy, legate 7 courier 8 emissary 9 messenger 10 ambassador 12 commissioner 14 representative 15 plenipotentiary

envy: 5 covet 6 grudge 8 begrudge, jealousy

enwrap: 4 roll 5 clasp 6 enfold 7 enclose, envelop

enzyme: 6 cytase, lipase, olease, papain, pepsin, rennin, urease 7 adenase, amylase, case18ase, diatase, erepsin, guanase, inulase, maltase, pectase, pepsine, tannase 8 catalase, cytolist, eraptase, esterase, protease 9 biogenase, deamidase, deaminase, invertase, trehalase 10 amygdalase

leather-making: 7 tannase

opposite of: 5 azyme

eoan: 7 auroral

eolith: 4 celt 5 flint

eon: age 8 eternity

eonic: 4 eral

epee: 4 foil 5 blade, sword

epergne: 5 stand 11 centerpiece

ephah: 7 measure

one-tenth: 4 omer

ten: 5 homer

ephelis: 7 freckle

ephemeral: 5 brief, vague 7 passing 8 fleeting 9 temporary, transient 10 evanescent, short-lived, transitory 11 impermanent

Ephialtes' slayer: 6 Apollo 8 Hercules

Ephraim's descendant: 7 Resheph

epi: 6 finial

epic: 4 Edda, epos, saga 5 grand, Iliad, noble 6 Aeneid, epopee, heroic 7 Beowulf, Odyssey 8 epyllion, imposing, majestic, Ramayana 9 narrative

epicarp: 4 husk, rind

epicedium: ode 4 song 5 dirge, elegy

epicene: 7 sexless, unmanly 10 effeminate

epichoric: 5 local

Epictetus: 4 Stoic 10 philosopher

birthplace: 10 Hierapolis

expelled from: 4 Rome

home: 6 Epirus

epicure: 7 glutton, gourmet 8 gourmand 9 bon vivant, high liver 10 gastronome 11 connoisseur epicurean: 4 rich 6 lavish 7 Apician, sensual 8 hedonist, Lucullan 9 libertine, luxurious, sybaritic 10 voluptuous

epidemic: 4 rash 6 plague 8 outbreak 10 pestilence, widespread

epiderm appendage: 4 horn

epidermis: 4 skin 7 cuticle

epigram: 4 poem 6 bon mot, saying

epigramatic: 5 terse, witty 7 concise, piquant, pointed

epigraph: 5 motto 7 imprint 9 quotation 11 inscription

epilogue, epilog: 8 appendix, follow-up, postlude 10 conclusion

Epimetheus: daughter: 7 Pyrrha
wife: 7 Pandora

epinard: 7 spinach

Epiphany: 10 Twelfth Day

episcopacy: 9 bishopric

Episcopal parish head: 6 rector

episode: 5 event, scene, story 8 incident 9 happening 10 occurrence

episperm: 5 testa

epistaxis: 9 nosebleed

epistle: 4 note 6 letter 7 message, missive

epitaph: 8 hicjacet 11 inscription

epithet: 4 name, term 5 title 6 insult, phrase 7 agnomen 9 expletive, sobriquet 11 abusive word, appellation

epitome: 5 brief 6 digest, precis, resume 7 summary 8 abstract, synopsis, ultimate 10 abridgment 12 condensation, quintessence

epitomize: 5 sum up 6 embody, typify 8 boil down, compress, condense 9 exemplify, summarize 10 abbreviate

epoch: age, era 4 date, time 5 event 6 period

epochal: 4 eral

epopee: 4 epic, epos

epoptic: 6 mystic, secret

epure: 5 draft 7 diagram, drawing, pattern

equable: 4 calm, even, just 6 placid, serene, smooth, stable, steady 7 regular, uniform 8 constant, tranquil, unvaried 9 easygoing, unruffled

equal: tie 4 cope, egal(F.), even, isos(Gr.), like, meet, peer, same 5 alike, match, rival 7 abreast, compeer, emulate, uniform 8 adequate, 9 identical 10 equivalent, tantamount 11 comparative, counterpart 12 commensurate, counterpoise

equal-angled figure: 6 isogon

equality: par 6 equity, parity 7 balance, egality 8 evenness, fairness 12 impartiality
legal: 7 isonomy

Equality State: 7 Wyoming

equally: 5 alike 6 evenly, justly 8 likewise 9 similarly 10 fifty-fifty

equanimity: 4 cool 5 poise 6 aplomb 7 egality 8 calmness, evenness, serenity 9 composure 11 tranquility 12 tranquillity

equate: 5 match 7 balance, compare, even out 8 equalize

equatorial: 8 tropical

Equatorial Guinea: capital: 6 Malabo
city: 4 Bata 11 Santa Isabel
ethnic group: 4 Bubi, Fang 6 Pangwe
island: 5 Bioko 6 Elobey, Pagalu 7 Corisco
mainland area: 7 Rio Muni
monetary unit: 6 ekuele 7 centimo
mountain peak: 11 Santa Isabel
river: 4 Ntem 6 Benito

equestrian: 5 rider 7 vaquero(Sp.) 8 horseman

equidistant: 7 central, halfway

equilibrium: 5 poise 7 balance 9 equipoise

equine: 4 colt, foal, mare 5 filly, horse, zebra

equine water sprite: 5 kelpy 6 kelpie

equip: arm, rig 4 deck, gear, gird, heel 5 array, dress, enarm, endow 6 attire, fit out, outfit 7 apparel, appoint, furnish, prepare, qualify, turn out 8 accouter, accoutre 10 habilitate

equipment: 4 gear 5 goods 6 attire, tackle 7 harness, panoply 8 armament, materiel 10 provisions 12 appointments 13 paraphernalia

equipoise: 7 balance 13 counterweight

equitable: 4 even, fair, just 5 equal, right 6 honest 7 upright 9 impartial, objective, righteous 10 reasonable

equitation: 12 horsemanship

equity: law 7 honesty, justice 8 equality, fairness 9 cash value, rectitude 10 investment 11 uprightness

equivalent: 4 akin, same 5 alike, match 8 of a piece, parallel 9 identical, the same as 10 comparable, synonymous, tantamount

equivocal: 4 hazy 5 vague 7 dubious, obscure 8 doubtful 9 ambiguous, enigmatic, uncertain 10 ambivalent, indecisive 11 problematic 12 questionable, undetermined 13 indeterminate, problematical

equivocate: fib, lie 5 dodge, evade, hedge, parry, shift, stall 6 escape, palter, weasel 7 quibble, shuffle 8 sidestep 9 pussyfoot 10 mince words 11 prevaricate

equivoque: mot, pun 4 quip 9 witticism 10 paronomasia

era: age 4 aeon, date, time 5 epoch, stage 6 period

eradicate: 4 dele, raze 5 erase 6 delete, remove, uproot 7 abolish, destroy, wipe out 8 demolish 9 extirpate 10 annihilate, deracinate 11 exterminate

eral: 7 epochal

erase: 4 blot, dele 5 annul 6 cancel, delete, efface, excise, remove, rub out 7 destroy, expunge, scratch 9 eliminate, eradicate 10 obliterate

ere: 6 before 10 sooner than, rather than

Erebus: *parent:* 5 Chaos
sister: Nox
son: 6 Charon

erect: 4 make, rear, step 5 build, exalt, raise, put up, set up 6 unbent 7 elevate, upended, upright 8 standing, straight, vertical 9 construct, establish, fabricate, institute 10 upstanding 13 perpendicular

erelong: 4 anon, soon

eremite: 6 hermit 7 ascetic, recluse 8 anchoret 9 anchorite
hut: 4 cell

Erewhon: 6 utopia
author: 6 Butler

ergo: 5 hence 9 as a result, therefore

ergot: 6 fungus 12 grain disease

Erin: 4 Eire 7 Ireland 8 Hibernia 9 Innisfail

Erinys: 4 Fury 6 Alecto 7 Megaera 9 Tisiphone

Eriphyle: *brother:* 8 Adrastus
daughter: 8 Eurydice
father: 6 Talaus
son: 7 Alcmeon

Eris: *brother:* 4 Ares
daughter: Ate
goddess of: 6 strife 7 discord
missile: 5 apple

eristic: 12 disputatious 13 controversial

ermine: fur 5 stoat 6 weasel 7 miniver
relative: 4 mink

erode: 4 rust 5 decay 6 abrade 7 corrode, destroy, eat into 8 wear away 9 undermine 11 deteriorate 12 disintegrate

Eros: 4 Amor 5 Cupid
beloved: 6 Psyche
brother: 7 Anteros
father: 6 Hermes 7 Mercury
mother: 5 Venus 9 Aphrodite

erose: 6 uneven 9 irregular

erotic: 4 lewd, sexy 5 bawdy 6 ardent, carnal, loving, ribald 7 amatory, amorous, sensual 8 immodest, indecent, prurient 9 salacious

err: sin 4 miss, slip 5 lapse, stray 6 bungle, wander 7 blunder, deviate, misplay, mistake 8 misjudge 10 transgress 12 miscalculate, misinterpret

errand: 5 chore 7 journey, mission

errand boy: 4 page 5 gofer 7 bellhop, courier 9 messenger

errant: 6 astray 8 shifting 9 deviating,

itinerant, wandering 10 journeying 11 adventurous

erratic: odd 4 wild 5 queer, wacky 6 fitful 7 strange, vagrant, wayward 8 aberrant, peculiar, unstable, variable 9 eccentric, irregular, wandering 10 capricious, changeable 12 inconsistent 13 unpredictable

erratum: 5 error 7 mistake

errhine: 6 sneeze

erroneous: 5 amiss, false, wrong 6 faulty, untrue 7 unsound 8 mistaken 9 incorrect, misguided 10 fallacious, inaccurate

error: sin 4 bull, flub, muff, slip 5 bevue, boner, fault, fluff, lapse 6 fumble, miscue 7 bloomer, blunder, default, erratum, fallacy, falsity, misplay, misstep, mistake, offense, rhubarb 8 solecism 9 violation 10 inaccuracy 12 irregularity, malformation
measuring device: 11 aberrometer

ers: 5 vetch 9 kersenneh

ersatz: 4 fake, sham 5 phony 9 imitation, synthetic 10 artificial, substitute 11 replacement

Erse: 5 Irish 6 Celtic, Gaelic 8 Scottish

erstwhile: 6 former, whilom 7 one-time 8 formerly 10 heretofore

eruca: 11 caterpillar

eruct: 4 burp, spew 5 belch 8 disgorge

erudition: 4 lore 6 wisdom 7 letters 8 learning, literacy 9 education, knowledge 11 instruction, scholarship

erupt: 4 emit, gush, spew 5 burst, eject, expel, spout 6 blow up 7 cast out, explode 8 throw off 9 discharge, pour forth

eruption: 4 rush 5 storm 7 flare-up 8 outbreak, outburst 9 commotion, explosion
skin: 4 acne, rash 5 rupia 6 blotch, pimple 9 festering

Eryx: *father:* 5 Butes
mother: 5 Venus 9 Aphrodite

Esau: 4 Edom
brother: 5 Jacob
country: 4 Edom
descendant: 7 Edomite
father: 5 Isaac
father-in-law: 4 Elon
grandson: 6 Amalek
mother: 7 Rebekah
son: 5 Korha, Reuel 7 Eliphaz
wife: 4 Adah 10 Aholibamah

escalate: 4 grow, go up, rise 5 climb, mount, swell 6 expand, extend, step up 7 advance, broaden 8 increase 9 intensify

escapade: 4 lark 5 antic, caper, fling, prank, sally 9 adventure, excursion

escape: lam 4 bolt, flee, jink(Sc.), miss,

skip, slip 5 avoid, dodge, elope, elude, evade, issue, spill 6 eschew, outlet 7 get away, leakage, outflow, take off 8 break out, get loose 9 disappear, diversion, evaporate 10 fly the coop 11 distraction

means: 8 loophole

escargot: 5 snail

escarole: 6 endive

escarp: 5 cliff, slope

eschalot: 5 onion

eschar: 4 scab 5 crust

eschew: 4 shun 5 avoid 6 escape 7 abstain

escolar: 8 mackerel

escort: see 4 beau, lead, show 5 guard, usher 6 attend, convoy, squire 7 conduct, consort, gallant 8 cavalier, chaperon 9 accompany, attendant, bodyguard, safeguard

escritoire: 4 desk 6 bureau 9 secretary

escrow: 4 bond, deed, fund 7 deposit

esculent: 6 edible 7 eatable 10 comestible

escutcheon: 6 shield
band: 4 fess 5 fesse
cord: 10 cordeliere

Esdras' angel: 5 Uriel

esker, eskar: 4 kame 5 mound, ridge

Eskimo: Ita 4 Yuit 6 Innuit
bird: 4 fute
boot: 5 kamik
canoe: 5 cayak, kayak, umiak 6 oomiac, oomiak 7 oomiack
coat: 5 parka 6 parkee, temiak
dog: 5 husky 8 malamute, malemute
dwelling: 4 iglu 5 igloo, topek, tupek, tupik 9 barrabora
goddess: 5 Sedna
knife: ulu
medicine man: 7 angakok, angakut, angekok, angekut 8 angekkok
mountain: 7 nunatak
settlement: 4 Etah
sledge: 7 komatik

esne: 4 serf 7 bondman 8 hireling

esodic: 8 afferent

esophagus: 6 gullet 7 pharynx

esoteric: 5 inner 6 mystic, secret 7 private 8 abstruse 9 recondite 10 acroamatic, mysterious 12 confidential

esoteric doctrine: 6 cabala

esoteric knowledge: 6 gnosis

ESP: 9 intuition 12 clairvoyance

espadon: 9 swordfish

espalier: 7 lattice, railing, trellis

Español: 7 Spanish

espantoon: 4 club 8 spontoon

esparto: 4 alfa 5 grass

especial: 4 dear 5 chief, close 8 intimate, peculiar, specific, uncommon 10 particular 11 exceptional, outstanding

especially: 6 mainly, really 7 notably 8 uniquely 9 expressly, primarily 10 singularly 11 exclusively

espial: 6 notice 9 discovery 11 observation

espionage: 6 spying 12 surveillance
agent: spy

esplanade: 4 walk 5 drive 6 maidan 7 roadway 9 promenade

espouse: wed 4 back, mate, tout 5 adopt, boost, marry 6 defend, take up 7 betroth, embrace, further, husband, promote, support 8 advocate, champion, maintain

esprit: wit 4 elan, zing 5 verve 6 spirit 10 cleverness 12 intelligence

esprit de corps: 9 team unity 10 group pride, solidarity

espy: see 4 spot 5 sight, watch 6 behold, descry, detect, locate, notice 7 discern, observe 8 discover

esquire: 7 armiger

ess: 4 worm 5 curve, sigma 7 sigmoid 8 curlicue, curlycue

essay: try 4 seek 5 chria(L.), paper, theme, tract, trail 6 effort, satire, take on, thesis 7 article, attempt, venture, writing 8 endeavor, exertion, treatise 9 undertake 10 enterprise, experiment 11 make a stab at 12 disquisition, dissertation

essayist: 4 Elia, Lamb 5 Paine 6 Holmes, Steele 7 Addison, Emerson

esse: 5 being 9 existence

essence: ens 4 core, crux, gist, odor, pith, soul 5 attar, being, heart, ousia(G.) 6 entity, nature, spirit 7 element, extract, meaning, perfume 9 existence, principle, substance 10 extraction 11 concentrate

Essene: 6 mystic 7 ascetic

essential: key 4 main 5 basic, vital 7 crucial, leading, needful 8 cardinal, inherent 9 intrinsic, necessary, principal, requisite 10 sine qua non 11 fundamental 13 indispensable

essonite: 6 garnet

establish: fix, set 4 base, rear, rest, show 5 build, erect, found, plant, prove, set-up, start 6 avouch, clinch, create, ground, locate, ordain, ratify, settle, verify 7 appoint, approve, confirm, install, instate, justify, provide, situate, sustain 8 colonize, constate, ensconce, identify, initiate, organize, radicate, regulate, validate 9 determine, institute, originate 10 accomplish, constitute 11 corroborate

established: 4 fast, firm, sure 7 certain

establishment: 4 mill 5 elite, house, plant 6 ecesis, menage 7 company, concern dounset(Sc.) 8 business, factory, Old Guard 10 enterprise 11 institution, ruling class 12 control group

estancia(Sp.): 4 farm 5 ranch

estate: 4 fief, home, rank 5 acres, class, finca, manor, order, taluk 6 assets, domain, ground, legacy, status 7 demesne, dignity, fortune 8 allodium, freehold, hacienda, position, property, standing 9 condition, situation 10 belongings, plantation 11 latifundium
fourth: 5 press 9 newspaper
manager: 7 steward 8 executor, guardian

esteem: 4 deem 5 adore, count, favor, honor, pride, prize, value, worth 6 credit, regard, repute 7 account, cherish, opinion, respect 8 approval, venerate 9 deference, reckoning, reverence 10 admiration, appreciate, estimation 13 consideration

ester: 6 oleate 7 acetate, tropate 8 compound, stearate

estero: 5 inlet 7 channel, estuary

Esther: 8 Hadassah
festival: 5 Purim
foster father: 7 Mordecai
husband: 6 Xerxes 9 Ahasuerus

esthesiometer: 10 tactometer

esthetic: See **aesthetic**

estimable: 4 good 5 solid 6 worthy 8 laudable 9 admirable, honorable 10 worthwhile 11 meritorious, respectable

estimate: set 4 rank, rate 5 assay, gauge, guess, judge, prize, think, value 6 assess, figure, reckon 7 average, believe, surmise 8 appraise, consider, evaluate 9 calculate 11 computation
smallest: 7 minimum
too high: 8 overrate
too low: 10 undervalue

estimation: 4 fame, view 5 honor 6 belief, regard, repute 7 opinion 8 judgment

estivate: 6 summer
opposite of: 9 hibernate

estoc: 5 sword

estop: 6 bar 5 debar 6 hinder, impede 7 prevent 8 preclude, prohibit

estrade: 4 dais 8 platform

estrange: part, wean 6 divert 7 break up 8 alienate, disunite 9 disaffect 10 antagonize, drive apart

estrangement: 6 schism 7 divorce 10 falling out, separation

estray: 4 waif 5 dogie

estreat: 4 copy, fine 5 exact 6 record 7 extract 9 duplicate

estuary: ria 5 firth, frith, inlet 6 estero 10 river mouth, tidal basin

esurient: 6 greedy, hungry 9 voracious

et al: 6 others 9 elsewhere

etaac: 7 blaubok 8 antelope

etagere: 7 whatnot 12 display stand

etat: 5 state

etch: 6 incise 7 engrave, impress 8 inscribe

Eteocles: *father:* 7 Oedipus
kingdom: 6 Thebes

mother: 7 Jocasta
son: 8 Laodamas

eternal: 6 eterne 7 ageless, endless, lasting, undying 8 constant, enduring, immortal, timeless 9 boundless, continual, deathless, immutable, perpetual, unceasing 10 perdurable 11 everlasting 12 imperishable, interminable, unchangeable 13 uninterrupted

Eternal City: 4 Rome

eternally: 6 always 7 forever 11 in perpetuum

eternity: age, eon 4 aeon 8 infinity 9 afterlife 12 the hereafter

etesian: 6 annual 8 periodic
pert. to: 4 wind

ethenol: 7 alcohol

etheostomoid: 4 fish 6 darter

ether: air, gas, sky 5 ozone 7 heavens, solvent 8 empyrean 10 anesthetic, atmosphere

ethereal: 4 aery, airy 5 filmy 6 aerial 7 fragile, slender 8 delicate, gossamer, heavenly 9 celestial, unearthly 10 spiritlike

ethical: 5 moral 7 upright 8 virtuous 9 righteous 10 aboveboard

ethics: 6 morals, values 9 moral code, standards 10 conscience, principles

Ethiopia: 9 Abyssinia
capital: 10 Addis Ababa
city: 4 Dese, Goba, Gore, Jima 5 Asela, Harer 6 Asmara, Gonder, Mekele 7 Nekemte 8 Dire Dawa
desert: 4 Haud 7 Danakil
emperor: 4 Negus 6 Memnon 7 Menelik 8 Selassie
ethnic group: 4 Afar, Arab 5 Galla, Tigre 6 Amhara, Harari, Sidama, Somali
lake: 4 Abbe, Tana, Zwai 5 Abaya, Chamo 6 Assale, Rudolf 8 Stefanie
measure: tat 4 cubi, kuba 5 derah, messe 6 cabaho, sinjer, sinzer, tanica 7 entelam, farsakh, tanega, ghebeta
monetary unit: 4 birr 6 santim
mountain peak: 9 Ras Dashan
mountain range: 5 Simen
old coin: 4 besa 6 talari
province: 4 Bale, Kefa, Welo 5 Arusi, Gojam, Harer, Shewa, Tigre 6 Sidamo, Welega 7 Eritrea 8 Gemu Gefa
river: Omo 4 Abay (Blue Nile) 5 Awash 6 Tekeze
weight: pek 4 kasm, natr, oket, rotl 5 alada, artal, mocha, neter, ratel, wakea 6 wogiet 8 farasula 9 mutagalla

etiolate: 4 pale 6 bleach, weaken

etiquette: 4 form, Post 5 usage 7 conduct, decorum, manners 8 courtesy, protocol 9 amenities, propriety 10 civilities 12 good behavior
breach of: 8 solecism

etna: 4 lamp 7 volcano

Etruria: *city:* 4 Veii
  god: 5 Tinia
  goddess: Uni 6 Menfra
  king: 4 Lars 7 Porsena
  pert. to: 8 Etruscan
  pottery: 8 bucchero
etui, etwee: 4 case 8 reticule 10 needle-case
etymology: 10 word change, word origin
etymon: 4 root 5 radix 7 radical
eucalyptus: 4 yate 6 jarrah 8 messmate, iron bark
  eater: 5 koala
  gum: 4 kino
  insect secretion: 4 laap, lerp
Eucharist: *box:* pix, pyx
  bread plate: 5 paten
  cloth: 4 fano 5 fanon
  cup: 5 calix 7 chalice
  wafer vessel: 8 ciborium
  wine vessel: ama 5 amula
eugenic: 8 wellborn
eulogistic: 9 laudatory 11 encomiastic, panegyrical 12 commendatory
eulogize: 4 laud 5 extol 7 glorify 9 celebrate
eulogy: 5 eloge, paean 6 hesped(Heb.), homage, praise 7 address, oration, tribute 8 encomium 9 panegyric 11 composition
eunuch: 5 spado 7 gelding 8 castrato
euphonium: 4 tuba
euphony: 5 meter 6 melody 7 harmony
euphorbia: 5 plant 6 spurge
euphoria: 4 ease 7 comfort, elation 9 well-being 12 exhilaration
Euphrates tributary: 6 Balikh, Khabur
euplexoptera: 6 earwig
Eurasia: *range:* 4 Ural 5 Urals
eureka red: 4 puce
Euripides: *play:* Ion 5 Helen, Medea 6 Hecuba 7 Electra, Orestes 8 Alcestis 10 Andromache, Hippolytus 11 Trojan Women
euripus: 6 strait 7 channel
Europa: *father:* 6 Agenor
  husband: 8 Asterius
Europe: See also **individual countries**
  countries: 5 Italy, Malta, Spain 6 Cyprus, France, Greece, Monaco, Norway, Poland, Russia (part), Sweden, Turkey (part) 7 Albania, Andorra, Austria, Belgium, Denmark, Finland, Hungary, Iceland, Ireland, Romania 8 Bulgaria, Portugal 9 San Marino 10 Luxembourg, Yugoslavia 11 East Germany, Netherlands, Switzerland, West Germany, Vatican City 12 Great Britain 13 Liechtenstein 14 Czechoslovakia
  islands: Fyn 5 Crete, Malta, Oland, Rugen 6 Aegean, Cyprus, Ionian, Orkney, Rhodes, Sicily 7 Britain, Corsica, Faeroes, Falster, Gotland, Iceland, Ireland, Lofoten, Lolland, Vaigach 8 Balearic, Hebrides, Kolguyev, Sardinia, Shetland, Svalbard
  lake: 4 Como 5 Garda, Onega 6 Geneva, Ladoga, Peipus, Vanern, Zurich 7 Balaton, Malaren, Scutari, Vattern 8 Maggiore 9 Constance, Neuchatel
  mountain: 4 Alps, Ural 6 Balkan, Kjolen 7 Rhodope, Sudetic 8 Caucasus, Pyrenees 9 Apennines 10 Carpathian, Erzgebirge 14 Bohemian Forest
  peninsula: 6 Balkan 7 Crimean, Iberian, Italian, Jutland
  people: 4 Dane, Finn, Lapp, Lett, Pole, Serb, Slav, Turk, Wend 5 Croat, Czech, Dutch, Greek, Gypsy, Irish, Swede, Swiss, Welsh 6 Basque, French, German, Magyar, Scotch, Slovak 7 Catalan, Cypriot, English, Flemish, Italian, Russian, Slovene, Spanish, Walloon 8 Albanian, Andorran, Armenian, Romanian 9 Bulgarian, Hungarian, Icelander, Norwegian, Ukrainian 10 Monegasque 12 Byelorussian, Scandinavian
  river: Don 4 Ebro, Elbe, Oder 5 Dvina, Loire, Rhine, Rhone, Seine, Tagus, Tiber, Volga 6 Danube, Thames 7 Dnieper, Vistula 8 Dniester
  sea: 4 Azov 5 Black, North, White 6 Aegean, Baltic, Ionian 7 Barents, Caspian 8 Adriatic, Ligurian 9 Norwegian 10 Tyrrhenian 13 Mediterranean
Eurydice's husband: 7 Orpheus
Eurytus's daughter: 4 Iole
eutaxy: 4 form 8 dispatch, tidiness 9 good order 10 management
Euterpe: 4 Muse
  lover: 7 Strymon
  son: 6 Rhesus
evacuant: 6 emetic 8 diuretic, emptying 9 cathartic, purgative
evacuate: 4 void 5 empty, expel, leave 6 desert, remove, vacate 7 abandon, move out 12 withdraw from
evade: 4 bilk, duck, foil, shun 5 avert, avoid, dodge, elude, hedge, parry, shirk 6 baffle, escape, eschew 7 fend off 10 equivocate
evaluate: 4 rank, rate 5 class, grade 6 assess, ponder 8 appraise
evaluation: 5 assay, worth 8 critique, judgment 9 appraisal 10 estimation
evanesce: 4 fade 5 empty 6 vanish 9 disappear, dissipate, evaporate
evanescent: 7 cursory, evasive 8 fleeting, fugitive 9 ephemeral, fugacious, transient, vanishing 11 impermanent
evangel: 6 gospel
Evangeline's home: 6 Acadia
evangelist: 4 John, Luke, Mark 6 Graham, Sunday, writer 7 apostle, Ed-

wards, Matthew, Roberts 8 crusader, disciple 9 McPherson, patriarch 10 missionary, revivalist

evaporate: 5 dry up 8 condense, evanesce, fade away 9 dehydrate, disappear

evasion: 5 dodge, shift 6 escape 9 avoidance 10 subterfuge 12 equivocation

evasive: sly 4 eely 5 dodgy 6 shifty 7 devious, elusive, elusory, unclear 8 slippery 9 deceitful 12 tergiversate

eve: 4 dusk 6 sunset 7 sundown 9 threshold

Eve: rib 6 female

even: een, tie 4 fair, just 5 aline, equal, exact, flush, grade, level, match, plain, rival, suant 6 direct, placid, smooth, square, steady 7 abreast, balance, equable, flatten, regular, uniform 8 moderate, parallel 9 equitable, impartial 10 coincident 15 straightforward

even if: tho 8 although

even-tempered: 4 calm, mild 6 placid, serene 11 slow to anger, unflappable

evener: 7 leveler 9 equalizer 10 doubletree

evening: eve 4 ereb(Heb.), sera(It.), soir(F.) 5 abend(G.) 6 sunset 8 eventide, twilight

  dress: tux 4 gown 5 tails 6 formal, tuxedo 8 black tie, white tie

  party: 6 soiree

  pert. to: 11 crepuscular

  prayer: 7 vespers

  primrose: 7 fuchsia

  song: 8 serenade

  star: 5 Venus 6 Hesper, Vesper 8 Hesperus

evenness: 7 balance 8 equality 10 equanimity, uniformity 11 consistency

event: hap 4 case, fact, fate, feat, tilt 5 casus(L.), doing, match 6 factum(L.), result 7 contest, episode 8 incident, landmark, occasion 9 adventure, happening, milestone 10 experience, occurrence, phenomenon 11 competition, consequence 12 circumstance

first: 5 debut 6 opener, prelim 8 premiere

eventful: 7 notable 8 historic 9 important, memorable, momentous 11 significant

eventide: 6 vesper 7 evening

eventual: 4 last 5 final, later 6 future 7 ensuing 8 ultimate

eventually: 6 one day 7 finally 8 in the end, sometime 10 ultimately 13 sooner or later

eventuate: 5 occur 6 happen, result

ever: aye, eer 6 always 7 forever 8 in any way 9 at any time 10 constantly 11 continually, perpetually

Everglades: 5 marsh, swamp

evergreen: fir, ivy 4 ilex 5 heath, holly,

savin 6 laurel, savine 7 jasmine 9 mistletoe 12 rhododendron

  genus of: 4 Olax 9 Cupressus 11 Pittosporum

  .tree: fir, yew 4 pine 5 carob, cedar 6 balsam, calaba, larche

Evergreen State: 10 Washington

everlasting: 6 eterne 7 durable, endless, eternal, forever, lasting, tedious, undying 8 constant, enduring, immortal, infinite, timeless 9 continual, incessant, perpetual, unceasing, wearisome 10 perdurable 12 imperishable 13 uninterrupted

everlasting flower: 6 orpine

evermore: 6 always 9 eternally 10 constantly

every: all, ilk(Sc.) 4 each 6 entire 8 complete

everybody: all 8 everyone

everyday: 5 usual 6 common 7 mundane, prosaic, routine 8 ordinary

everything: all

evict: 4 oust 5 eject, expel 6 remove 7 kick out 10 dispossess

evidence: 4 show 5 proof, token, trace 6 attest, reveal 7 display, exhibit, support 8 argument, indicate, manifest, muniment 9 testimony 10 illustrate

evident: 5 broad, clear, plain 6 patent 7 glaring, obvious, visible 8 apparent, manifest, palpable 10 noticeable 11 discernible, indubitable, transparent 12 demonstrable

evil: bad, ill, sin 4 base, foul, harm, vice, vile 5 crime, malum(L.), wrong 6 menace, wicked 7 adverse, baleful, corrupt, heinous, hurtful, immoral, misdeed, noxious, satanic, vicious 8 calamity, depraved, devilish, disaster, iniquity, mischief, sinister 9 injurious, malicious, malignant, malignity, nefarious, offensive, worthless 10 malevolent, misfortune, pernicious 11 malefaction

  incarnation of: 5 Satan

evil eye: hex 4 jinx 5 curse, Jonah 6 hoodoo, whammy 11 malediction

evil spirit: imp 5 demon, devil, fiend

  Hebrew: 8 Asmodeus

  Iroquois: 5 otkon

  Zoroastrian: 5 daeva

evildoer: 5 cheat, crook, felon 6 sinner 7 culprit, villain 8 criminal 9 miscreant 10 malefactor

evince: 4 show 5 prove 6 subdue 7 conquer, display, exhibit 8 indicate, manifest

eviscerate: gut 10 devitalize, disembowel, exenterate

evocative: 6 moving 8 stirring 9 remindful 10 suggestive 11 reminiscent, stimulating

evoke: 5 educe, waken 6 arouse, elicit, excite, summon 9 stimulate 10 bring forth

evolution: 6 change, growth 7 biogeny 8 progress 11 development

evolve: 4 emit, grow 5 ripen 6 derive, expand, mature 7 develop, enlarge 8 increase 10 show change 11 disentangle

ewe: teg 5 sheep
    old: 5 crone

ewer: jug 5 basin 7 pitcher 9 container

ewest: 4 next 7 nearest

ex: 6 former 9 strike out

ex cathedra: 8 official 13 authoritative

exacerbate: irk 5 tease 6 enrage, excite, worsen 7 provoke 8 embitter, increase, irritate 9 aggravate, infuriate 10 exasperate

exact: ask 4 even, fine, levy, true 5 wreak, wrest 6 compel, demand, elicit, extort, formal, minute, square, strict 7 careful, certain, command, correct, enforce, estreat, extract, literal, precise, regular, require 8 accurate, critical, explicit, rigorous, specific 9 identical 10 methodical, meticulous, scrupulous 11 painstaking, punctilious 13 hypercritical
    satisfaction: 6 avenge 7 revenge

exacting: 5 fussy 6 severe, strict, trying 7 arduous, exigent, finicky, onerous 8 pressing, rigorous 9 demanding, stringent 10 burdensome

exactly: 4 just 5 fully, quite, spang, truly 6 evenly, just so, wholly 7 totally 8 entirely, of course 9 assuredly, certainly, on the nose 10 absolutely, altogether, positively

exactness: 8 accuracy 9 precision, rightness

exaggerate: 6 extend, overdo 7 amplify, enhance, enlarge, magnify, romance, stretch 8 increase 9 aggravate, embroider, overstate

exaggerated: 5 outre 6 padded 7 blown up, extreme 8 inflated, prodigal 11 extravagant

exaggeration: 9 hyperbole 10 caricature 13 embellishment, overstatement

exalt: 4 laud 5 extol, honor, raise 6 praise, uplift 7 acclaim, advance, dignify, elevate, enhance, ennoble, glorify, inspire, magnify, promote 8 enthrone, heighten 9 intensify 10 aggrandize

exaltation: 5 bliss 7 ecstasy, elation, rapture 9 elevation, transport 10 apotheosis 11 deification

exalted: 4 high 5 grand, noble 6 august, lordly 7 haughty, sublime 8 glorious 11 illustrious, high-ranking

examen: 7 inquiry 11 examination 13 investigation

examination: 4 exam, oral, quiz, test 5

assay, audit, check, trial 6 examen, review, survey 7 autopsy, inquest, inquiry 8 research, scrutiny 10 comparison, inspection 11 exploration, inquisition 13 consideration, investigation 14 reconnaissance
    judicial: 13 interrogation
    physical: 7 checkup
    taker: 6 testee

examine: con, try 4 feel, scan, sift, view 5 assay, probe, quest 6 candle, ponder 7 analyze, canvass, explore, inspect, observe, palpate 8 look over, overhaul 10 scrutinize 11 inquire into, interrogate, reconnoiter

examiner 6 censor, conner 7 analyst, auditor, coroner 9 inspector 10 inquisitor

example: 4 case 5 ideal, model 6 sample 7 pattern 8 exemplar, foregoer, instance, paradigm, specimen 9 precedent 11 description, case history 12 illustration 15 exemplification

exanimate: 4 dead 8 lifeless 10 spiritless

exasperate: ire, irk 4 bait, gall, rile 5 annoy 6 enrage, excite, nettle, stir up 7 agitate, inflame, provoke, roughen 8 irritate 9 aggravate

exasperated: 5 wroth 9 indignant

excavate: dig 4 mine, mole 5 dig up, scoop 6 burrow, dredge, tunnel 9 hollow out

excavation: cut, pit 4 hole 5 grave 6 cavity, groove, trench
    for ore: 4 mine 5 stope 6 quarry

exceed: top 4 best, pass 5 excel, outdo, outgo 6 better, outrun, outvie, overdo 7 eclipse, overtax, surpass 8 go beyond, outstrip, overstep, surmount 9 overshoot, transcend 11 predominate

exceedingly: 4 tres(F.), very 5 amain 7 parlous 9 extremely 10 remarkably, strikingly

excel: cap, top 4 best 5 outdo, shine 6 better, exceed 7 surpass 8 outclass, outrival 10 be expert at, tower above

excellence: 5 arete(Gr.), merit, worth 6 virtue 7 quality 8 goodness 10 perfection 11 distinction, superiority

excellent: 4 braw(Sc.), fine, good, tops 5 brave, bully, great, prime, super 6 choice, famous, grade A, select, spiffy, worthy 7 capital, corking, elegant 8 generous, peerless, sterling, superior, top-notch, valuable 9 admirable, first-rate 10 inimitable, preeminent, sans pareil 12 transcendent

except: bar, but 4 bate, omit, only, save 6 exempt, unless 7 besides, exclude, rule out 9 eliminate, other than

exception: 5 demur 7 dissent, offense 9 complaint, condition, objection

exceptional: 4 rare 7 notable, special, unusual 8 singular, superior, uncommon 9 wonderful 10 remarkable 11 outstanding 13 extraordinary

excerpt: 4 cite 5 quote, scrap 7 extract, pick out, portion, section 10 select from

excess: 4 glut, over, plus, riot 5 flood 7 nimiety, overage, surfeit, surplus 8 overmuch, plethora 9 profusion 10 exuberance, redundancy 11 prodigality, superfluity 12 intemperance 13 overabundance

of solar year: 5 epact

excessive: too 4 over 5 enorm(Sc.), undue 6 de trop(F.) 7 extreme, nimious 8 enormous, overmuch 9 exuberant 10 exorbitant, immoderate, inordinate 11 extravagant, intemperate 12 extortionate, unreasonable

exchange: set 4 mart, swap 5 bandy, store, trade, truck 6 barter, bourse, dicker, excamb(Sc.), market, rialto, switch 7 commute, traffic 9 tit for tat, transpose 10 quid pro quo, substitute 11 reciprocate 12 headquarters

exchequer: 5 funds, money 6 coffer 8 finances, treasury

excise: tax 4 duty, toll 6 cut out, impost, remove, resect 7 exscind, extract 8 alcabala(Sp.) 9 extirpate, surcharge

officer: 8 revenuer

excision: cut 7 erasure 10 exsection 11 amputation, rooting out 11 eradication, extirpation

excite: 4 fire, spur, stir, whet 5 elate, impel, pique, rouse 6 arouse, awaken, foment, incite, kindle, thrill, turn on 7 agitate, animate, inflame, provoke 8 disquiet 9 electrify, galvanize, stimulate, titillate

excited: hot 4 agog 5 eager, moved 6 heated 7 frenzied, frantic 8 atwitter, worked up 9 steamed up 11 carried away

excitement: ado 4 stir, to-do 5 fever, furor 6 hubbub, warmth 7 turmoil 8 hysteria 9 commotion 10 hullabaloo 11 disturbance

exclaim: 6 cry out 8 burst out 9 ejaculate 10 vociferate 12 say violently

exclamation: aha, aie, bah, boo, fie, foh, hep, hey, hic, huh, och, oho, pah, poh, suz, tut, ugh, wow, yah 4 adad, ahem, alas, arra(Ir.), drat, egad, evoe, garn, hech, heck, hein(F.), hist, hoch(G.), hola, phew, pish, psha, pugh, rats, rivo, tush, wugg 5 alack, arrah(Ir.), bravo, faugh, feigh, heigh, holla, humph, ohone(Ir.), pshaw 6 clamor, hurrah, indeed, ochone(Ir.), outcry 7 hosanna 9 alackaday, expletive 12 interjection

of contempt: foh, pah

of disgust: ugh 4 rats

of exhilaration: 4 evoe

of pain: 4 ouch

of sorrow: 4 alas 9 alackaday

of surprise: aha, gee, oho, wow

of reproach: fie

exclude: ban, bar 5 debar, eject, expel 6 banish, except, exempt, reject 7 keep out 8 prohibit 9 blackball, eliminate, ostracize 13 excommunicate

exclusive: 4 only, rare, sole 5 alone, aloof, elite, scoop, whole 6 entire, select, single 7 private 8 cliquish, complete, snobbish 10 restricted

excommunicate: 8 unchurch

excoriate: 4 flay, gall 5 chafe, score, strip 6 abrade 8 denounce, lambaste 9 lash out at 11 decorticate

excrescence: 4 burl, lump, wart 6 pimple 8 tubercle 9 outgrowth

excruciating: 5 acute 6 fierce, severe 7 extreme, intense, painful, racking 9 agonizing, torturous 10 tormenting, unbearable 12 insufferable

exculpate: 4 free 5 clear, remit 6 acquit, excuse, pardon 7 absolve, forgive, justify, release 8 palliate 9 discharge, exonerate, vindicate

excursion: row 4 ride, sail, tour, trek, trip 5 jaunt, sally, tramp 6 cruise, junket, outing, ramble, safari, sortie, voyage 7 journey 8 campaign, escapade 10 digression, expedition

excusable: 6 venial 7 tenable 9 allowable 10 defensible, pardonable 11 justifiable

excuse: 4 plea 5 alibi, remit 6 acquit, copout, defend, let off, pardon 7 absolve, apology, condone, forgive, indulge, pretext 8 dispense, occasion, overlook, pass over 9 exculpate, exonerate, extenuate, vindicate, whitewash

execrable: bad 4 base, foul, vile 8 accursed, damnable, wretched 9 atrocious, monstrous, revolting 10 abominable, detestable, horrifying

execrate: 4 damn, hate 5 abhor, curse 6 detest, loathe, revile 8 denounce 9 imprecate, objurgate 12 anathematize

execute: act 4 hang, kill, obey, play, slay 5 lynch 6 direct, effect, finish, manage 7 conduct, enforce, perform 8 carry out, complete 9 discharge 10 accomplish, administer 11 electrocute

execution: 7 garrote, killing 8 garrotte 9 rendition, technique 10 completion 11 achievement, fulfillment, transaction

executive: 4 dean 5 mayor 7 manager, officer, premier 8 director, governor, official, overseer 9 president 10 supervisor 12 entrepreneur 13 administrator

executor: 4 doer 5 agent 8 enforcer 9 performer 13 administrator\

exegesis: 10 exposition 11 explanation 14 interpretation

exegete: 6 critic 11 interpreter

exemplar: 5 model 7 example, pattern 9 archetype 12 illustration

exemplary: 5 ideal, model 6 worthy 7 typical 8 laudable, sterling 9 admirable, emulative 11 commendable 12 praiseworthy

exemplify: 6 embody, typify 9 epitomize, represent, symbolize 10 illustrate

exempt: 4 free 5 clear, spare 6 excuse, fidate 7 exclude, release, relieve 8 excepted 9 discharge 12 not subject to

exemption: 7 freedom 8 immunity 12 dispensation

exequy: 4 rite 7 obsequy 8 ceremony 10 procession

exercise: ply, use, vex 5 drill, etude, exert, train, wield 6 employ, harass, lession, parade, praxis, push-up, school 7 aufgabe, display, prepare, practice, provoke, utilize, work out 8 activity, maneuver, practice 9 athletics 10 exhibition, gymnastics, recitation 12 calisthenics 14 constitutional

system of: 8 aerobics

exerciser: 5 groom

exert: use 5 apply, wield 6 employ, strain 8 exercise, put forth

exertion: 4 toil, work 5 essay, labor, trial 6 action, effort, energy 7 trouble 8 endeavor, industry, strength, struggle 11 elbow grease

exfoliate: 5 scale 8 flake off 10 desquamate

exhalation: 5 steam 9 effluvium, emanation 10 expiration 11 evaporation

exhale: 4 emit 6 expire 7 blow out, respire 10 breathe out

exhaust: sap 5 drain, empty, use up 6 expend, overdo, weaken 7 deplete, fatigue, wear out 8 enervate 9 discharge 10 impoverish

exhausted: 4 beat, dead, done, worn 5 all in, spent, tired, weary 6 barren, beaten, bushed, effete, pooped 7 emptied 8 consumed, dog-tired 9 washed out

exhausting: 7 arduous

exhaustion: 7 fatigue 8 collapse 9 depletion, inanition, lassitude 11 prostration

exhaustive: 6 all-out 8 complete, sweeping, thorough 9 intensive 13 comprehensive

exheridate: 10 disinherit

exhibit: air 4 fair, show 5 stage 6 evince, expose, ostend, parade, reveal 7 display, perform, produce, trot out 8 disclose, evidence, manifest 9 represent 11 demonstrate

exhibition: 4 fair, show 5 sight 7 display, pageant 8 showcase 9 cosmorama, spectacle 10 exposition 12 presentation 13 demonstration

exhilarate: 5 cheer, elate, pep up 6 excite, uplift 7 animate, enliven, gladden 10 invigorate

exhilaration: 6 gaiety 7 jollity 8 gladness, hilarity 9 merriment 10 joyousness

exhort: bid 4 goad, prod, spur, urge, warn 5 egg on, plead 6 advise, incite, preach 7 beseech, caution 8 admonish, appeal to 9 encourage

exhume: dig 5 delve 7 unearth 8 disinter

exigency: fix, jam 4 need, want 5 pinch 6 crisis, plight 7 urgency 8 juncture, pressure, quandary 10 difficulty 11 requirement

exigent: 5 vital 8 critical, exacting, pressing 9 demanding, necessary 10 imperative 13 indispensable

exiguity: 7 paucity

exiguous: 4 tiny 5 scant, small, spare 6 meager, sparse 7 slender 10 diminutive

exile: 4 oust 5 eject, expel 6 deport, outlaw, pariah 7 outcast, refugee 8 drive out, fugitive 9 nonperson, ostracize 10 banishment, expatriate 12 proscription

exist: am, are 4 live 6 endure, remain 7 breathe, survive

passively: 7 subsist 8 vegetate

existence: ens 4 esse, life 5 being 6 entity, inesse 7 essence, reality 9 actuality

beginning of: 5 birth, origin 9 nascency

having no: 4 dead, null, void 7 defunct

pert. to: 5 ontic

existent: 4 real 5 alive, being 6 extant 7 present 9 living now

at same time: 15 contemporaneous

in name only: 7 nominal, titular

Existentialist leader: 6 Sartre

exit: 4 door, gate 5 going, leave, split 6 egress, exodus, outlet, way out 7 buzz off, outgate, passage, pull out, retreat 9 debouche 9 departure 10 withdrawal

area without: 8 cul-de-sac 10 blind alley

exode: 5 farce 8 travesty 10 afterpiece

exodus: 7 migration 10 mass flight

Exodus author: 4 Uris (Leon)

exonerate: 4 free 5 clear 6 acquit, excuse, 7 absolve, relieve 9 disburden, discharge, exculpate, vindicate 12 find innocent

exorbitant: 5 undue 8 abnormal 9 excessive, out of line 10 immoderate, outrageous, overpriced 11 extravagant 12 extortionate, unreasonable

exorcism: 5 charm, spell 9 expulsion 11 incantation

exordium: 7 preface, prelude 8 foreword, preamble, prologue 9 beginning 12 introduction

exoteric: 6 layman 7 popular 8 external,

outsider 13 easily grasped

exotic: 5 alien 7 foreign, strange, unusual 8 enticing, striking 9 different, glamorous 10 extraneous, outlandish

expand: wax 4 grow, open 5 splay, swell, widen 6 dilate, extend, unfold, unfurl 7 amplify, augment, balloon, broaden, develop, distend, enlarge, inflate, magnify, stretch 8 increase, lengthen 9 expatiate, explicate, intumesce, spread out 10 make bigger

expanded: 8 patulous

expanse: 4 area, room 5 range, reach, space, sweep, tract 6 extent, spread 7 stretch 8 distance 9 magnitude

vast: 5 ocean 6 desert, empire

expansion: 6 growth 8 increase 9 extension 10 dilatation, distention 11 development, enlargement

expansive: 4 free, wide 5 ample, broad, large 6 genial 7 elastic, liberal 8 effusive, outgoing, spacious 9 bombastic, extensive, grandiose 11 extroverted 13 demonstrative

expatiate: 6 wander 7 descant, dwell on, enlarge 11 elaborate on 12 talk at length

expatriation: 5 exile 10 banishment

expect: 4 deem, hope 5 await, guess 6 assume, plan on, reckon 7 believe, foresee, look for, presume, suppose 8 envision 9 calculate 10 anticipate

expectant: 4 agog 5 alert, eager 7 hopeful, waiting 8 pregnant, sanguine 11 watching for

expectation: 4 hope 6 belief 7 surmise 8 prospect 10 confidence 12 anticipation

expectorate: 4 spit

expedient: 4 wise 5 dodge 6 proper 7 politic, stopgap 9 advisable, makeshift 10 profitable 12 advantageous

expedite: 4 free 5 hurry, speed 6 hasten 7 quicken 8 dispatch 10 accelerate, facilitate 11 move quickly

expedition: 4 trek, trip 5 drave(Sc.), haste, hurry 6 safari, voyage 7 crusade, journey, mission 8 alacrity, progress 9 excursion

expeditious: 4 fast 5 hasty, quick, rapid, ready, swift 6 prompt, speedy 9 effective, immediate

expel: 4 oust 5 eject, evict, exile 6 banish, deport 7 cast out, exclude 8 dislodge, forjudge 9 discharge, eliminate, forejudge 10 dispossess, expatriate

expend: 5 spend, use up, waste 6 pay out 7 consume 8 disburse, dispense, shell out, squander 9 dissipate 10 distribute

expenditure: 4 cost 5 outgo 6 outlay 11 consumption 12 disbursement

expense: 4 cost, loss 5 batta(Ind.), price 6 charge, outlay 8 overhead 11 consumption, expenditure 12 disbursement

expensive: 4 dear, high 6 costly, lavish 10 high-priced 11 dispendious, extravagant

experience: see 4 feel, have, know, live, meet, view 5 assay, event, skill, taste, trial 6 affair, endure, ordeal, suffer 7 calvary, feeling, know-how, undergo 8 training 9 adventure, encounter, go through, knowledge 10 background

experienced: met 4 able, wise 6 expert 7 veteran 9 practiced, qualified, underwent

experiment: try 4 test 5 assay, essay, trial 7 analyze 8 research

experimental: 9 empirical, tentative

expert: ace, pro 4 deft, good 5 adept 6 adroit, artist, au fait, clever, habile 7 artiste(F.), capable, skilled 9 authority 10 proficient 11 experienced 12 professional

expertness: 5 knack, savvy, skill 7 ability, mastery 8 facility 9 dexterity

expiate: 5 atone, avert 7 redress 10 make amends, propitiate

expiatory: 8 piacular 9 purgative

expiration: end 5 death 10 exhalation, extinction 11 termination

expire: die, end 5 cease, expel, lapse 6 run out, perish

expiry: 5 close, death 10 extinction 11 termination

explain: 5 solve 6 define, expand, unfold 7 clarify, expound, justify, unravel 8 describe, manifest, spell out 9 elucidate, explicate, interpret, make clear 10 account for, illuminate

explanation: key 5 cause 6 answer, motive, reason 7 account, apology, meaning 8 exegesis 9 rationale 10 exposition 11 description 13 clarification

expletive: 4 oath 5 curse 9 swear word 11 exclamation

explicate: 6 expand, unfold 7 amplify, explain, expound 9 interpret

explicit: 4 open 5 clear, exact, fixed, plain 7 express, obvious, precise 8 absolute, clear-cut, definite, positive, specific 9 categoric, outspoken 10 plain to see 11 categorical, unambiguous, unequivocal 13 unconditional

explode: 4 fire 5 blast, burst, erupt, go off 6 blow up, refute 7 deflate 8 detonate, disprove, dynamite 9 fulminate

exploding meteor: 6 bolide

exploding star: 4 nova

exploit: act 4 deed, feat, gest, milk 5 abuse, geste, stunt 6 misuse 7 utilize 8 impose on, profit by, put to use 9 adventure, heroic act 10 manipulate 11 achievement, tour de force

exploration: 5 probe 6 search 11 examination 13 investigation

explore: map, try 4 test 5 chart, probe, scout 6 search 7 examine, feel out 8 look into 9 range over 11 investigate

explorer: 4 Cook, Eric 5 Bruce, Cabot, Davis, diver, Drake 6 Baffin, Carter, Cortes, De Soto, Hearne, Hudson 7 pioneer, Pizarro, Raleigh 8 Amundsen, Columbus, Magellan, Vespucci 9 Frobisher 10 Chancellor, discoverer

explosion: pop 5 blast 6 blow-up, report 8 outburst 10 detonation

explosive: TNT 4 bomb, mine 5 tense 6 amatol, powder, tonite 7 ammonal, lyddite, melnite 8 cheddite, critical, dynamite, eruptive, unstable, volatile 9 fulminate, guncotton, plastique 10 ammunition, detonative 11 hot-tempered 13 nitroglycerin 15 trinitrotoluene

coal mine: 9 Bobbinite

device: cap 6 petard 9 initiator

high: TNT 7 cordite

igniter: 4 fuse

picric acid: 7 lyddite

projectile: 5 shell 6 rocket 7 grenade, missile 9 cartridge

sound: 4 bang, boom, chug 5 pluff, vroom

exponent: 6 backer 8 advocate, champion, promoter 9 expounder, supporter

expose: 4 bare, open, risk 5 strip 6 betray, detect, reveal, unmask 7 display, exhibit, pillory, publish, uncover, unearth 8 disclose, discover, muckrake, ridicule, satirize, unclothe 10 jeopardize

exposed: 6 unsafe 11 unprotected

exposition: 4 fair, mart, show 5 tract 6 bazaar 7 account 8 analysis, exegesis, treatise 10 exhibition 11 declaration, explanation 14 interpretation

ex post facto: 5 later 9 done after 10 subsequent 11 retroactive 12 after the fact

expostulate: 5 argue 6 object, oppose 7 discuss, dispute, examine, protest 8 complain 11 remonstrate

exposure: 5 vista 7 outlook 9 discovery, publicity, unmasking 10 divulgence, laying bare 11 orientation 12 helplessness

expound: 5 state, treat 6 define 7 develop, explain, exposit, express 8 construe 9 elucidate, explicate, hold forth, interpret

express: 4 vent 5 emote, opine, rapid, speak, state, utter, voice 6 convey, denote, direct, phrase, reveal 7 declare, dictate, expound, nonstop, testify 8 definite, describe, explicit, manifest 9 expatiate, high-speed 10 articulate, particular, peremptory

appreciation: 5 thank

approval: 6 praise 7 applaud

pity: 6 bemoan

regret: 9 apologize

expression: 4 form, pose, show, sign, term, word 5 idiom, token, voice 6 byword, oracle, phrase, symbol 8 laconism 9 euphemism, statement, utterance 10 holophrase 11 delineation, holophrasis 13 manifestation 14 representation

facial: 4 grin, leer 5 frown, scowl, smile, sneer, wince 7 grimace

hackneyed: 6 cliche 7 bromide 8 banality

mathematical: 8 equation

metaphorical: 6 figure

of approval: 4 clap 5 smile 7 ovation 8 applause

of assent: aye, nod, yea, yes 4 amen, okay 6 placet, righto, so be it 8 of course 9 sure thing

of contempt: bah, fie 4 geck, hiss 5 pshaw, sneer

of gratitude: 12 thanksgiving

of incredulity: 6 indeed

of opinion: 4 poll, vote

of sorrow: ay 4 alas 11 lamentation

of weariness: 4 sigh

expressionless: 5 stony 6 vacant 7 deadpan 9 impassive 11 inscrutable

expressive: 5 vivid 6 poetic 7 graphic 8 eloquent, emphatic 10 indicative 11 significant

expressly: 4 just 6 namely 7 clearly, plainly 9 specially

expressway: 4 road 7 freeway, highway 8 turnpike

expropriate: 4 take 5 seize 7 preempt 10 commandeer, confiscate

expulsion: 5 exile 7 ousting, removal 8 ejection, eviction 9 debarment, discharge 10 banishment

expunge: 4 dele 5 erase 6 cancel, delete, efface, excise 7 blot out, destroy, scratch 9 eradicate 10 annihilate, obliterate

expurgate: cut 4 blip 5 purge 6 censor, remove 10 blue-pencil

exquisite: fop 4 dude, nice 5 dandy, exact 6 choice, dainty 7 careful, elegant, refined 8 affected, delicate 9 beautiful, delicious, excellent, matchless, perfected, recherche 10 consummate, fastidious 12 accomplished 4 discriminating

exsanguine: 6 anemic 9 bloodless

exscind: 5 cut out 6 excise 9 extirpate

exsert: 8 protrude, stick out 11 thrust forth

exsiccate: dry 4 sear 5 parch 9 dehydrate

exsuccous: 7 dried up, sapless 8 withered 9 juiceless

extant: 5 alive, being 6 living 8 existing, manifest

extemporaneous: 6 ad-lib 7 offhand 9

impromptu **10** improvised, off-the-cuff **11** unrehearsed **14** unpremeditated

extend: eke, lie, run **4** grow, rise, span **5** bulge, cover, offer, range, reach, renew, widen **6** accord, deepen, dilate, expand, spread, strain **7** amplify, broaden, display, distend, draw out, enlarge, overlap, overrun, proffer, prolong, radiate, stretch **8** continue, increase, lengthen, protract, protrude **10** exaggerate, generalize, outstretch

extension: **4** area **5** scope **8** addendum, addition, duration, increase **9** expansion **11** enlargement **12** augmentation **13** amplification

building: ell **4** wing, annex **6** lean-to

of time: **4** stay **7** respite **8** reprieve

trench: sap

extensive: **4** vast, wide **5** ample, broad, large **7** immense **8** expanded **9** capacious **10** widespread **11** far-reaching, wide-ranging **13** comprehensive

extent: due, tax **4** area, body, bulk, levy, size, writ **5** ambit, limit, range, reach, scope, space, sweep **6** amount, degree, spread **7** acreage, breadth, compass, expanse **8** increase, latitude, duration **9** dimension, extension, magnitude, territory, valuation **10** assessment

extenuate: **4** thin **5** gloze **6** excuse, lessen, temper, weaken **7** justify **8** diminish, mitigate, palliate **9** alleviate, gloss over, whitewash **10** depreciate

exterior: **4** ectad, ectal, outer, shell **6** facade **7** outside, outward, surface **8** external

exterminate: **4** kill **6** uproot **7** abolish, destroy, wipe out **9** eradicate, extirpate **10** annihilate, extinguish

external: out **5** alien, outer **7** foreign, outside, outward **8** exterior **9** extrinsic **10** peripheral **11** superficial

extinct: **4** dead, gone, lost **7** defunct **8** quenched, vanished **11** disappeared, nonexistent **12** extinguished

extinction: **5** death **6** expiry **9** abolition **10** expiration **11** destruction **12** annihilation, obliteration

extinguish: end **5** choke, douse, quash, quell **6** cancel, put out, quench, stifle **7** destroy, expunge, smother **8** snuff out, suppress **9** suffocate **10** annihilate

extirpate: **4** dele **5** erase, expel **6** excise, uproot **7** destroy, exscind **8** demolish **9** eradicate **10** annihilate, deracinate **11** exterminate

extol: **4** laud **5** bless, exalt **6** praise **7** applaud, commend, elevate, enhance, glorify **8** emblazon, eulogize **9** celebrate

extort: **5** exact, force, wrest, wring **6** compel, elicit, wrench **7** extract **9** blackmail

extortion: **6** ransom **7** tribute **8** chantage, coercion, exaction **9** shakedown **10** overcharge

extortionate: **9** excessive **10** exorbitant

extra: odd **4** more, orra(Sc.), over, plus **5** added, spare **7** adjunct, special, surplus **8** superior **9** accessory, lagniappe, unusually **10** additional, uncommonly **12** supplemental

information: **4** pump, **5** grill **8** question

extract: dig, pry **4** cite, draw **5** educe, exact, quote, steep, wring **6** decoct, deduce, derive, elicit, evulse, extort, obtain, pull out, remove, render **7** essence, estreat, excerpt, exhaust **8** separate, withdraw **9** decoction, quotation **11** concentrate

extraction: **5** birth, stock **6** origin **7** descent, essence **8** breeding, tincture **9** parentage

extraneous: **5** outer **6** exotic **7** foreign **9** extrinsic, unrelated **10** accidental, immaterial, irrelevant

extraordinary: odd **4** rare **6** signal **7** amazing, notable, special, strange, unusual **8** abnormal, singular, uncommon **9** irregular, monstrous, unheard of, wonderful **10** additional, incredible, phenomenal, remarkable, surprising, tremendous **11** exceptional **13** distinguished

extravagant: **4** wild **5** outre **6** costly, heroic, lavish **7** baroque, bizarre, fanatic, nimious, profuse, vagrant **8** prodigal, reckless, romantic, wanderer, wasteful **9** excessive, expensive, fantastic, luxurious **10** exorbitant, thriftless **11** dispendious **12** preposterous, unreasonable, unrestrained

extreme: end **4** last **5** final, great, limit, ultra, undue, utter **6** far out, heroic, severe, utmost **7** advanced, drastic, forward, howling, intense, outward, violent **8** devilish, farthest, greatest, terrible, terrific **9** desperate, excessive, nth degree, outermost, stringent, uttermost **10** avant-garde, conclusive, immoderate

extremely: **4** very **6** mighty **8** terribly **9** unusually **11** exceedingly

extremist: **5** basic **7** fanatic, radical **11** fundamental **13** revolutionary

extremity: arm, end, leg, tip, toe **4** foot, hand, limb, need, tail **5** limit, verge **6** border, finger, margin **8** boundary, disaster, terminus **9** bitter end

extricate: **4** free **5** clear, loose **6** rescue **8** liberate, untangle **9** disengage **10** disembroil **11** disentangle **12** wriggle out of

extrinsic: **5** alien **7** foreign, outward **8** external **10** accidental, extraneous, incidental **11** unessential **12** adventitious, nonessential

extroverted: 7 affable 8 friendly, outgoing, sociable 10 gregarious

extrude: 4 spew 5 eject, expel 7 project 8 force out

exuberance: 4 life, zest 5 vigor 6 energy, spirit 8 buoyancy, vivacity 9 animation 10 enthusiasm

exuberant: 6 lavish, lively 7 copious, fertile 8 effusive 9 abounding, excessive, luxuriant, plentiful, vivacious 10 flamboyant 11 uninhibited 12 unrestrained

exudation: gum, lac, sap, tar 5 pitch, resin, rosin 9 discharge, secretion

exude: 4 emit, ooze, seep, weep 5 sweat 7 secrete 8 perspire 9 discharge, percolate

exult: 4 brag, crow, leap 5 boast, gloat, glory 7 rejoice

exultant: 6 elated, joyous 8 jubilant 10 triumphant

exuviate: 4 molt, shed 5 moult 6 slough

eyas: 4 bird 8 nestling

eye: ee(Sc.); orb 4 disc, gaze, glim, lamp, loop, mien, ogle, scan, view 5 glare, watch 6 behold, goggle, oculus(L.), peeper, regard, vision 7 blinker, observe, witness 10 scrutinize 11 contemplate

black: 5 mouse 6 shiner
cavity: 5 oribt
colored portion: 4 iris
cosmetic: 4 kohl, kuhl 5 liner 6 shadow
covering: 6 eyelid 9 blindfold
defect: 4 cast 6 anopia, myopia 11 astigmatism
disease: 6 iritis 8 glaucoma, trachoma 14 conjunctivitis
doctor: 15 ophthalmologist
hollow: 5 orbit 6 socket
instrument for examining: 8 otoscope 14 ophthalmoscope

opening in: 5 pupil
part: 4 disc, iris, uvea 5 pupil 6 areola, cornea, retina
pert. to: 5 irian, optic 7 areolar, corneal, retinal 9 ocellated
protector: 5 patch, visor 7 blinker
pupil dilater: 8 atropine 10 belladonna
science: 13 ophthalmology
simple: 6 ocelli(pl.) 7 ocellus

eyebrow: 4 bree(Sc.) 11 supercilium

eye-catching: 6 marked 9 prominent 10 noticeable 11 conspicuous

eyedropper: 7 pipette

eyeglasses: 5 specs 6 lenses 7 lorgnon, nippers 8 monocles, pince-nez 9 lorgnette

eyelash: 5 cilia(pl.) 6 cilium
dye: 7 mascara
loss: 9 madarosis

eyeless: 5 blind 9 sightless

eyelet: 6 agrafe, gromet, oillet 7 agraffe 8 peephole 10 buttonhole 11 perforation

eyeleteer: 6 bodkin

eyelid: *drooping of:* 6 ptosis
pert. to: 9 blepharal

eye-popping: 7 amazing 8 exciting, stirring 9 thrilling 11 astonishing

eyer: 8 beholder 9 spectator

eyeshot: 5 range, reach

eyesight: 4 view 5 sight 11 observation

eyesore: 4 mess 6 defect 7 blemish

eyetooth: 6 cuspid

eyewash: rot 5 bilge 6 bunkum, drivel, excuse 8 claptrap, flattery

eyot: ait 5 islet

eyra: 7 wildcat

eyrie: See aerie

Ezekiel: *father:* 4 Buzi
four beasts: 5 Aniel 6 Azriel, Haniel 7 Kafziel

F

fabian: 8 cautious, dilatory
fabiform: 10 bean-shaped
fable: 4 myth, tale 5 story 6 legend 7 fiction, parable, untruth 8 allegory, apologue 9 falsehood, narrative
animal of: 6 dragon 7 centaur, unicorn
being of: 4 ogre 5 dwarf, giant, troll
bird of: roc 7 phoenix
collection: 8 bestiary
serpent of: 8 basilisk
fabric: rep, web 4 felt, repp 5 baize, beige, build, crepe, frame, lisle, rayon, serge, terry, tulle 6 creton, etoile 7 bunting, etamine, parable, texture 8 cretonne, material 9 construct, cottonade, structure
calico: 5 sallo 6 sallco
coarse: 4 mat 5 crash 6 burlap
corded: rep 4 repp 5 pique
cotton: 4 susi 5 pique, wigan 6 burrah 7 buckram, galatea, hickory 8 bourette
cotton knit: 10 balbriggan
cotton of light quality: 4 leno 7 jaconet, organza 9 silkaline
cotton mixture: 6 mashru 7 delaine, satinet, zanella 9 bombasine, bombazine, grusaille
cotton print: 6 calico 7 percale 8 cretonne
cotton twilled: 5 denim, sallo 6 salico 7 fustian, silesia
cotton with silk embroidery: 8 agabanee
curtain material: 4 leno 5 scrim 6 moreen, velvet 7 silesia
dealer: 6 draper, mercer
finisher: 6 beetle
flag material: 7 buntine, bunting
heavy: 6 denim 6 canvas
linen: 4 crea(Sp.), ecru 5 carde, crash 6 barras 7 buckram, drabbet, sinelon
linen and cotton: 9 huckaback
linen of light quality: 4 lawn 5 scrim
lustrous: 6 poplin, sateen
medieval: 4 acca 6 samite
metallic: 4 lamé
old: 9 ciclatoun
plaid: 6 tartan
printed: 5 batik 6 calico 7 challis
satin: 5 pekin 6 etoile
satin imitation: 6 sateen
sheer: 4 lawn 5 gauze, voile 6 dimity 7 batiste, chiffon, organdy
silk: 4 alma, gimp, gros, ikat 5 caffa, carde, crepe, ninon, rumal, satin, surah

6 blatta, camaka, patola, samite 7 alamode, chiffon, taffeta, Xmantua 8 barathea, bourette, sarcenet, sarsenet 9 charmeuse, levantine, matelasse 10 bombay-cine
silk (thin): 4 moff 5 tulle 6 pongee 7 hernani 8 eolienne
silk and cotton: 6 crepon, gloria 9 bombasine, bombazine
silk and linen: 8 brocatel 10 brocatelle
silk and wool: 6 crepon, gloria 7 challie, challis 8 eolienne
silk imitation: 5 rayon 7 satinet
silk mixture: kin 4 acca 5 balda 6 mashru 7 grogram 9 baldachin, baldaquin, farandine
silk-ribbed: rep 4 repp 6 faille 7 epingle 8 marocain
silk yarn: 7 schappe
straw: mat 7 matting
striped: aba 7 galatea, ticking
suiting: 6 dacron 7 acrilan, acrylic
surface: nap
synthetic: 5 nylon, orlon, rayon 6 dacron 7 acrilan, acrylic, plastic 9 polyester
textile: rep 5 moire 7 etamine
texture: 4 woof
thin: 5 gauze 8 gossamer, tarlatan 9 grenadine
towel: 4 huck 5 terry
Turkish: 6 agaric 7 chekmak 8 cottonee 10 terry cloth
twilled: 4 alma, jean 5 denim, sallo, serge, surah 6 coburg, sallco 8 corduroy, dungaree, shalloon, whipcord 9 bombasine, bombazine, gabardine, levantine, messaline, tricotine 10 broadcloth, kerseymere
unbleached: 5 beige
upholstery: rep 4 repp 6 frieze 7 tabaret
velvet-like: 5 panne 6 velure 8 duvetine 9 velveteen
waste material: 5 mungo
watered silk: 5 moire
waterproof: 8 burberry
white: 8 coteline
wide: 6 cotele
wool: 5 baize, beige, casha, serge, tweed 6 burnet, frisca, moreen 7 bolivia, debeige, delaine, droguet, frisado, frizado, hernani, worsted 8 cataloon, harateen, rattinet, zibeline 9 catalowne, gabar-

dine, grenadine, harrateen, montagnac, zibelline

wool (coarse): 6 djersa, duffel, kersey, witney 7 blocking

wool dress: 5 beige 7 delaine 8 wildbore 9 grenadine

wool mixture: 7 delaine, zanella 9 grisaille

wool-ribbed: rep 4 repp 8 marocain

worsted: 7 etamine

woven: 4 lamé 5 tweed, twill 6 tissue, tricot 7 blanket, damasse, textile

fabricate: 4 coin, form, make, mint 5 build, frame 6 devise, invent, make up 7 concoct, fashion, produce 8 contrive 9 construct 11 manufacture

fabrication: lie 7 fiction, forgery, untruth 8 pretense 9 falsehood

fabricator: 4 liar 6 forger 12 manufacturer

fabula: 5 story

fabulist: 4 liar 5 Aesop, Grimm 6 fabler 8 Andersen 10 parabolist

fabulous: 7 amazing, feigned 8 mythical, romantic 9 legendary 10 apocryphal, fictitious, incredible, phenomenal, remarkable 11 astonishing

facade: 4 face, mask 5 front, put-on 8 pretense

face: map, mug, pan 4 dare, defy, dial, leer, line, meet, moue 5 cover, front, stand 6 facade, oppose, veneer, visage 7 feature, grimace, surface 8 confront, envisage 9 encounter, semblance, stand up to 11 countenance, physiognomy

artery: 9 maxillary

bone: 5 malar 6 zygoma 7 maxilia 8 mandible

covering: 4 mask, veil

defect: 7 harelip

false: 4 mask

guard: 6 beaver

ornament: 4 veil 5 jewel, patch 9 cosmetics

paint: 4 fard 6 parget

part: eye, jaw, lid, lip 4 brow, chin, nose 5 cheek

with masonry: 5 revet

face eastward: 9 orientate

face-off: 8 showdown 13 confrontation

face-to-face: 7 affront, vis-a-vis

face value: par

facer: 6 bumper 7 tankard

facet: 4 side 5 angle, bezel, culet, phase 6 aspect

facetious: 5 comic, droll, funny, witty 6 jocose 7 amusing, jocular 8 humorous, polished 9 laughable 12 wisecracking

facia: 5 plate 6 tablet

facient: 4 doer 5 agent

facile: 4 able, easy, glib 5 adept, quick, ready, slick 6 expert, fluent 7 shallow

facilitate: aid 4 ease, help 5 speed 6 assist 8 expedite

facility: art 4 ease 5 eclat, knack, skill 7 address, freedom 9 dexterity, readiness 10 adroitness, expertness, pliability

facing: 5 front, panel 6 veneer 7 surface 8 covering, opposite

downward: 5 prone

inward: 8 introrse

outward: 8 extrorse

upward: 6 supine

facsimile: 4 copy 5 model 7 replica 9 duplicate, imitation 10 similitude 11 counterpart

fact: 4 data(pl.), deed, fait(F.) 5 datum, event, truth 7 keynote, lowdown, reality 9 actuality, thing done 12 circumstance

support: 15 circumstantiate

faction: 4 bloc, sect, side 5 cabal, junto, party 6 circle, clique, schism 7 coterie, dispute, quarrel 8 intrigue, offshoot 9 concision 11 combination

factious: 9 seditious 11 dissentious

factitious: 4 sham 9 unnatural 10 artificial

factor: gen 4 doer, gene 5 agent, cause, maker 6 author, detail 7 bailiff, steward 8 adherent, aumildar, gomashta, gomastah 11 chamberlain, constituent

factory: 4 mill, shop 5 plant 6 aurang, aurung 8 building, fabrique(F.), officina (Sp.), workshop 11 manufactory 13 establishment

book: 7 bindery

factotum: 5 agent 7 servant 8 handyman

factual: 4 real, true 7 genuine, literal

faculty: wit 4 ease, gift, flair, knack, power, skill, staff 6 talent 7 ability 8 aptitude, capacity

fad: 4 rage, whim 5 craze, fancy, hobby 7 crochet, fashion 9 amusement

faddle: 6 trifle 8 nonsense

fade: die, dim 4 dull, pale, wilt 5 decay 6 perish, vanish, wither 7 decline, lighten 8 diminish, discolor, dissolve, evanesce, languish 9 lose color 11 become faint

camera device: 4 iris 9 diaphragm

Faerie Queen: *author:* 7 Spenser

character: ate, Una 4 Alma 5 Guyon 6 Amoret 7 Artegal 8 Calidore, Florimel, Gloriana 11 Britomartis

Fafnir: *brother:* 5 Regin

slayer: 6 Sigurd 7 Sigurth 9 Siegfried

fag: 4 flag, tire, toil 5 droop, weary 6 drudge, menial 7 exhaust, fatigue, frazzle 9 cigarette

faik(Sc.): 6 lessen

fail: ebb 4 flag, fold, lose, sink, wane 5 flunk 6 desert, falter 7 exhaust, flicker, founder 8 languish, peter out

failing: 5 fault 6 foible 7 blemish, frailty, weakness 9 infirmity 10 deficiency 11 delinquency, diminishing 12 imperfection

fail-safe: 8 riskless 9 foolproof 10 error-proof

failure: dud 4 bust, flop, lack, loss, miss 5 bilge, decay, fault, lapse, lemon 6 fiasco, fizzle 7 bloomer, debacle, decline, default, neglect 8 abortion, collapse, omission 10 bankruptcy, deficiency 11 delinquency, miscarriage, shortcoming 13 deterioration 14 disappointment

fain: 4 fond, glad 5 eager 7 pleased, willing 8 desirous, inclined 11 constrained

faineant: 4 idle, lazy 5 idler 8 inactive, sluggard

faint: dim 4 dark, pale, pall, soft, weak 5 fuzzy, swoon, vague 6 evanid, feeble, hushed, sickly 7 blurred, languid, obscure, syncope 8 delicate, languish, listless, sluggish 9 simulated 10 indistinct

fainthearted: 5 timid 6 afraid, craven 8 cowardly, timorous

fair: 4 calm, even, just, mart 5 bazar, blond, clear, feria(L.), right 6 bazaar, blonde, decent, honest, kermis 7 exhibit, kermess 8 distinct, middling, unbiased 9 beautiful, equitable, impartial 10 auspicious, exhibition, reasonable 12 unprejudiced 13 disinterested, dispassionate

fair game: 4 butt, dupe 6 victim

fair-haired: 5 blond 6 blonde 8 favorite

fairest: 6 flower

fairly: 4 well 7 plainly 8 properly, suitably 9 favorably, tolerably 10 handsomely 12 legitimately

fairness: 6 equity 7 honesty, justice 8 equality 12 impartiality

fairy: elf, fay, hob, imp 4 peri, perl, pixy, puck 5 dwarf, gnome, pixie 6 goblin, spirit, sprite, yaksha, yakshi 7 banshee, gremlin, sylphid 10 leprechaun 11 enchantress

abode: 4 shee 5 sidhe

air: 5 sylph

chief: 4 Puck

king: 6 Oberon

of the Tempest: 5 Ariel

queen: Mab, Una 7 Titania

shoemaker: 10 leprechaun

spirit of death: 7 banshee

tricky: 4 Puck

fairy-like: 5 elfin

fait: 4 deed, fact

faith: 4 cult, sect 5 certy(Sc.), creed, troth, trust 6 belief, certie(Sc.), church, credit, pledge 7 promise 8 affiance, reliance, religion 9 bona fides 10 confidence, conviction

article: 5 tenet 9 credendum

faithful: 4 fast, feal, firm, leal, true 5 liege, loyal, pious, tried 6 honest, steady, trusty 7 devoted, sincere 8 accurate, constant 9 steadfast, veracious 13 conscientious

faithfulness: 8 fidelity

faithless: 5 false, punic 6 fickle, hollow, unjust, untrue 7 atheist 8 apostate, delusive, disloyal, shifting, unstable 9 deceptive, mercurial 10 inconstant, perfidious 11 disaffected, incredulous, treacherous 12 unsatisfying

faithlessness: 7 falsity, perfidy, untruth 8 betrayal 10 infidelity

fake: 4 hoax, sham 5 bogus, cheat, dummy, false, feign, fudge, phony 7 falsify, furbish, pretend, swindle, trump up 8 simulate, spurious 9 imitation 10 fictitious, fraudulent 11 counterfeit, manufacture

faker: 5 quack 6 humbug 7 peddler 9 charlatan, pretender

fakir: 4 monk, yogi 7 ascetic, dervish 9 mendicant

falbala: 7 flounce 8 furbelow, trimming

falcon: 4 hawk 6 hobby, saker 6 lanner, luggar, lugger, merlin, musket, tercel 7 kestrel 9 peregrine

bait: 4 lure

blind: 4 seel

genus: 5 Falco

male: 6 tercel 7 tiercel

nestling: 4 eyas

strap for: 4 jess

falconer: 6 hawker 8 ostreger 10 austringer

fall: sag 4 drip, drop, flop, plop, ruin, ruse, sile, sink, slip 5 abate, cloit(Sc.), crash, hance, lapse, plump, rapid, shoot, slump 6 autumn, happen, perish, recede, season, topple, tumble 7 cascade, decline, degrade, depress, descend, devolve, dribble, escheat, plummet, retreat, stumble, subside 8 cataract, collapse, commence, decrease 9 backslide, prostrate, surrender 10 capitulate, depreciate, disappoint 11 precipitate

back: 6 recede 7 relapse, retreat

behind: lag 5 lapse, trail 6 follow 8 straggle 10 lose ground

flat: die 4 fail, goof 6 bungle 7 misfire 9 fizzle out

in: 4 cave 5 agree 6 concur, line up 9 terminate

short: shy 4 fail, lack, miss

fall guy: 4 butt, dupe, gull 5 chump, patsy 6 pigeon, sucker 9 scapegoat

fallacious: sly 6 untrue 8 delusive, guileful, illusory 9 deceitful, deceptive, insidious 10 fraudulent, misleading 11 treacherous

fallacy: 4 flaw 5 error 6 idolum 7 mistake, pitfall 11 false notion

fallal: 4 ruff 6 finery, gewgaw

fallen: 5 loose, slain 6 ousted, sinful 7 debased, deposed, immoral

fallfish: 4 chub

fallible: 5 human 6 faulty, unsure 7 errable 9 imperfect 10 unreliable

falling: 6 cadent 8 prolapse, windfall 10 subsidence

fallout: 9 by-product, radiation 12 chance result

fall out: row 4 spat, tiff 5 scrap 6 bicker 7 wrangle 8 disagree

fallow: 4 pale 6 barren 9 yellow-red, yellowish 12 uncultivated

fallow deer: 6 damine

false: 4 fake, sham 5 bogus, fause(Sc.), paste, phony, wrong 6 fickle, hollow, pseudo, untrue 7 bastard, crooked, feigned 8 disloyal, illusive, recreant, spurious 9 deceitful, deceptive, dishonest, erroneous, faithless, incorrect, insincere, irregular, pretended 10 apocryphal, artificial, calumnious, fictitious, groundless, mendacious, misleading, perfidious, traitorous, untruthful 11 counterfeit, disaffected, treacherous, unveracious 12 hypocritical

falsehood: cog, fib, lie 4 flam, tale 5 fable, story 6 canard 7 fiction, perfidy, romance, untruth 8 roorback 9 deception, duplicity, imposture, mendacity, treachery 10 pseudology 11 fabrication

falsify: lie 4 fake 5 belie, feint, forge 6 betray, doctor 7 violate 9 dissemble 10 adulterate 11 counterfeit

Falstaff: *follower:* Nym
ancient: 6 Pistol
opera composer: 5 Verdi
play: 7 Henry IV
playwright: 11 Shakespeare
prince: Hal

falter: 4 fail 5 pause, waver 6 boggle, flinch, totter 7 fribble, stumble, tremble 8 hesitate

Fama: 5 rumor

fame: 4 bruit, glory, honor, kudos, rumor 6 renown, report, repute 7 hearsay 9 celebrity 10 reputation

familiar: 4 bold, cozy, easy, free, tosh 5 usual 6 common, homely, versed 7 affable 8 frequent, habitual, intimate, sociable 9 customary, household, presuming, well-known 10 accustomed, conversant 12 acquaintance 13 unconstrained

familiarize: 4 haft 8 accustom 9 habituate, make known 10 naturalize

family: kin 4 clan 5 class, flesh, group, house 6 cletch 7 kindred, lineage, progeny 8 category 9 household 10 generation
head: 7 goodman, husband 9 patriarch 11 householder 13 pater familias(L.)
pert. to: 7 nepotic 12 genealogical

famine: 6 dearth, hunger 8 scarcity 10 starvation 11 destitution

famished: 6 hungry 7 starved 8 ravenous

famous: 5 grand, known, noted 6 namely 7 eminent, namable, notable 8 renowned 9 excellent, notorious, prominent 10 celebrated 11 conspicuous, illustrious, outstanding 13 distinguished

famulus: 7 servant 9 attendant

fan: 4 beat, buff, cool 5 punka 6 basket, blower, colmar, punkah, rooter, shovel, spread, winnow 7 admirer, devotee 8 follower 9 flabellum, propeller 10 enthusiast

alluvial: 5 delta

form of: 7 plicate

fan-shaped: 10 flabellate

fanatic: mad 5 bigot, crazy, rabid, ultra 6 zealot 7 devotee 8 frenetic 9 energumen, extremist, phrenetic 10 enthusiast, monomaniac 11 extravagant

fancied: 6 unreal 7 dreamed 9 imaginary 10 fictitious

fanciful: odd 5 ideal, queer 6 dreamy, quaint, unreal 7 bizarre, strange 8 romantic 9 conceited, fantastic, grotesque, visionary, whimsical 10 capricious, chimerical, notionable 11 imaginative, unrealistic

fancy: fad 4 idea, love, maze, ween, whim 5 dream, freak, guess, humor 6 deluxe, ideate, liking, megrim, notion, ornate, vagary, vision, whimsy 7 caprice, chimera, conceit, elegant, fantasy, romance, suspect 8 conceive, illusion, phantasm, phantasy 9 capriccio 10 conception, conjecture, decorative, impression, ornamental 11 hanker after, imagination, inclination

fandango: 4 ball, tune 5 dance

fanfare: 4 pomp, show 5 salvo 7 display, panoply, tantara 8 flourish, ceremony

fanfaronade: 7 bluster 8 boasting, bragging 10 swaggering 11 ostentation

fanfoot: 5 gecko 6 lizard

fang: 4 earn, take, tusk, vang 5 begin, seize, snare, tooth 6 assume, obtain 7 capture, procure 9 undertake

fanion: 4 flag 6 guidon

fanlight: 7 transom

fanon: 4 cape 5 orale 7 maniple

fantast: 7 dreamer 9 visionary

fantastic: odd 5 queer, weird 6 absurd, quaint, unreal 7 bizarre 8 fanciful, freakish, romantic, singular 9 grotesque, whimsical 10 capricious, chimerical, ridiculous 11 extravagant, imaginative 12 unbelievable

fantasy: 4 idea, whim 5 dream, fancy 6 desire, vision 7 caprice, chimera, phantom, romance 8 illusion, phantasm 9 odd notion 10 apparition 11 imagination, inclination 13 hallucination

fantocinni: 5 shows 7 puppets

fantod: pet 4 fuss 7 anxiety

far: 4 long 6 remote 7 distant

across: 4 wide

down: 4 deep

far-out: 7 extreme, radical 8 advanced 10 avant-garde, unorthodox 11 in left field

far-reaching: 4 deep, vast 7 intense 8 profound

faraway: 6 dreamy, remote 7 distant, removed 9 oblivious 10 abstracted, star-gazing

farce: 4 mime 5 stuff 6 comedy 7 mockery 8 drollery, pretense 9 forcemeat

farceur: wag 5 joker

farcical: 5 comic, droll 7 Atellan 9 ludicrous 10 ridiculous

fare: eat 4 diet, food, path, rate, wend 5 cheer, going, price, track, viand 6 happen, travel 7 journey, passage, proceed, prosper 8 progress 9 equipment, passenger, provision, sagaciate 10 expedition 11 nourishment 13 entertainment

farer: 8 traveler

farewell: ave(L.) 4 vale(L.) 5 adieu, adios, aloha, conge, final 7 goodbye, leaving, parting 9 bon voyage, departure 11 valedictory

farfetched: 6 forced 7 devious, dubious 8 doubtful, strained, unlikely 9 recherche 10 improbable, roundabout

farina: 4 meal 5 flour 6 starch

farinaceous food: oat, rye 4 meal 5 flour, grain, salep, spelt, wheat 6 barley, cereal 7 pudding 10 cornstarch

farm: 4 till 5 croft, ranch, range 6 grange, rancho, spread 7 hennery, potrero 8 estancia, hatchery, hacienda 9 cultivate, farmstead 10 plantation

building: 4 barn, crib, shed, silo

Israeli collective: 7 kibbutz

Russian collective: 7 kolkhoz

farm out: let 4 hire

farmer: 4 tate 6 grower, tiller, yeoman 7 granger, hayseed, planter, plowman, rancher 8 producer 9 hacendero(Sp.), ploughman 10 cultivator, husbandman 13 agriculturist

Egyptian: 6 fellah 8 fellahin(pl.)

migratory: 4 Okie

South African: 4 Boer

tenant: 6 cotter 7 cottier 12 sharecropper

farming: 9 husbandry

farnesol: 7 alcohol

faro: 5 monte

bet: 7 sleeper

card: 4 soda

card combination: 5 split 6 cathop

player: 6 punter

farouche: 4 wild 5 surly 6 fierce, savage 7 boorish 10 unsociable

farrago: 6 medley 7 mixture 10 hodgepodge

farrier: 5 shoer, smith 10 blacksmith,

horseshoer 12 veterinarian

farrow: 9 pig litter

farseeing: 10 telescopic

farsighted: 6 shrewd 9 hyperopia, provident, sagacious 13 hypermetropic

farther: 6 longer 7 remoter 10 in addition

farthest: 7 endmost, extreme, farmost, longest, outmost 9 remotest

farthing: 4 coin 8 quadrans

fascia: 4 band, sash 6 fillet 7 molding

fascicle: 6 bundle 7 cluster

fascinate: 5 charm 6 allure, enamor 7 attract, bewitch, enchant, engross 8 entrance, interest, intrigue 9 captivate, enrapture, spellbind

fascinating: 9 glamorous 10 attractive

fascination: 5 charm, spell 6 allure

Fascism: 6 Nazism 7 Falange 12 dictatorship

leaders of: 6 Franco, Hitler 9 Mussolini

fashion: fad, ton(F.) 4 form, make, mode, mold, rage 5 craze, forge, frame, guise, model, mould, shape, style, vogue 6 create, custom, design, fangle, invent, manner, method 7 compose, portray 8 contrive 9 construct, fabricate

fashionable: 4 chic 5 smart 6 modish, with it 7 a la mode, dashing, stylish 9 an courant

fashioned: 6 carved 7 wrought

fast: 4 diet, firm 5 agile, apace, bawdy, brisk, fixed, fleet, hasty, loose, quick, rapid, stuck, swift 6 lively, secure, speedy, stable, starve 7 abiding, settled 8 enduring, faithful, reckless 9 immovable, indelible, lecherous, steadfast, unfadable, velocious 10 abstinence, stationary, unyielding 11 expeditious

day of: 5 Ember

period of: 4 Lent

fasten: bar, fix, pen, pin, tag, tie 4 bend, bind, bolt, clip, gird, girt, glue, knit, lace, lash, link, lock, moor, nail, rope, seal, snib, soud, weld, wire 5 affix, annex, belay, brace, chain, clamp, clasp, cling, latch, paste, rivet, seize, strap, truss 6 anchor, attach, batten, cement, clinch, picket, secure, solder, staple, tether 7 connect, padlock 8 transfix

fastener: bar, big, nut, pin 4 agal, bolt, frog, hasp, lock, nail, snap 5 catch, clamp, clasp, latch, rivet, screw, strap, thong 6 buckle, button, hatpin, staple, zipper 7 latchet, padlock 8 staylace

fastidious: 4 fine, nice 5 chary, fussy, natty 6 choicy, choosy, dainty 7 choosey, elegant, finical, finicky, haughty, refined 8 critical, delicate, exacting, overnice, scornful 9 exquisite, squeamish 10 meticulous, particular

fastigate: 7 conical, pointed

fastness: 4 fort 6 castle 7 citadel, sanctum 8 fortress 10 stronghold

fastuous: 5 lofty 7 haughty 8 arrogant 11 pretentious 12 ostentatious

fat: oil, tub 4 lard, lipa, rich, suet 5 adeps, brosy, cetin, chuff, ester, fleck, gross, lipid, lipin, obese, plump, podgy, pudgy, pursy, squab, stout, thick 6 fleshy, grease, lipide, oleate, portly, pubble, stocky, tallow 7 adipose, blubber, fertile, fulsome, lanolin, opulent, pinguid, stearin 8 extended, fruitful, lanoline, stearate, stearine, unctuous 9 corpulent 10 profitable 11 flourishing

hard: 4 suet

liquid: 5 olein 6 oleine

wool: 7 lanolin 8 lanoline

fat farm: 9 health spa 10 diet resort

fat person: 4 lump 5 blimp, squab, tubby 8 roly-poly 12 humpty-dumpty

fata morgana: 6 mirage

fatal: fey 4 dire 6 deadly, doomed, lethal, mortal 7 ominous, ruinous 8 destined 9 condemned, prophetic 10 calamitous, disastrous, pernicious, portentous 11 destructive

fatality: 5 death 8 calamity, disaster

fatback: 8 menhaden, salt pork, sowbelly

fatbird: 9 guacharo

fate: end, lot 4 doom, ruin 5 event, karma 6 chance, kismet 7 destiny, fortune, outcome 8 downfall 9 predestination

goddess: Ker 4 Nona, Norn 5 Morta, Tyche 8 Adrastea 9 Adrasteia

fated: 6 doomed 7 decreed 8 destined 10 inevitable

fateful: 7 crucial 8 critical, decisive 9 momentous, prophetic 10 inevitable, portentous 11 destructive, predestined

Fates: *Greek:* 5 Moera, Moira 6 Clotho, Moerae 7 Atropos 8 Lachesis

Roman: 4 Nona 5 Decum, Morta, Parca 6 Parcae

fathead: oaf 4 boob, dolt 5 chump, dunce 6 dimwit 8 numskull

father: abu(Ar.), ama, dad, pop 4 abba, abou(Ar.), baba(Ar.), bapu, papa, pere(F.), sire 5 adopt, babbo, beget, daddy, friar, padre(Sp.), pater(L.), vader(Dan.) 6 author, create, old man, parent, priest 7 founder, tatinek (Czech.) 8 beaupere(F.), generate, inventor 9 confessor, originate, paternity, procreate 11 acknowledge

of English learning: 4 Bede

of geometry: 6 Euclid

of gods and men: 4 Zeus

of human race: 4 Adam

of plenty: 8 Abiathar

pert. to: 6 agnate 8 paternal

Father of Waters: 11 Mississippi

Father Time: *personified:* 6 old man

implements: 6 scythe 9 hourglass

fatherhood: 9 paternity

fatherly: 6 kindly 8 paternal 10 protective

fathom: 5 brace, delve, solve 7 measure 9 penetrate, ferret out 10 understand

fathomless: 7 abysmal 16 incomprehensible

fatidic: 9 prophetic

fatigue: fag 4 jade, tire 5 spend, weary 6 overdo, taigle(Sc.) 7 exhaust, wear out

fatigued: 4 beat 5 spent 7 drained 11 tuckered out

Fatima: *husband:* Ali 9 Bluebeard

descendant: 7 Fatimid 8 Fatimite

sister: 4 Anne

stepbrother: Ali

fatten: 4 lard 6 batten, enrich, thrive

fatty: 4 oily 5 suety 6 greasy 7 adipose 8 blubbery

fatuous: 5 inane, silly 6 stupid, unreal 7 foolish, idiotic, witless 8 demented, illusory, imbecile 9 frivolous, insensate

faucet: tap 4 cock 5 valve 6 spigot 7 hydrant

faugh: bah, fie, ugh

Faulkner: *character:* 4 Anse, Cash, Darl 5 Addie, Caddy, Jason, Jewel 6 Bayard, Dilsey, Popeye, Sutpen 7 Quentin 9 Dewey Dell

family: 7 Bundren, Compson 8 Sartoris

trilogy: 7 The Town 9 The Hamlet 10 The Mansion

work: 5 Pylon 6 A Fable 8 Sartoris 9 Sanctuary 11 As I Lay Dying 14 Absalom Absalom

fault: sin 4 debt, flaw, flub, lack, slip, vice 5 abuse, blame, culpa(L.), error, guilt, lapse, tache(Sc.) 6 defect, foible, vitium(L.) 7 blemish, blunder, default, demerit, failure, frailty, mistake, neglect, offense 10 peccadillo 11 culpability, delinquency, misdemeanor 12 imperfection 13 transgression

in mining: 3 hade

faultfinder: 5 momus 6 carper, critic 7 caption, knocker, nagster

faultless: 4 pure 5 right 7 correct, perfect, precise 8 flawless 9 blameless 10 impeccable 13 unimpeachable 14 irreproachable

faulty: bad, ill 5 amiss, unfit, wrong 9 incorrect 10 inaccurate

faun: 5 satyr

of Praxiteles: 6 marble

fauna and flora: 5 biota

Faunus: *grandfather:* 6 Saturn

son: 4 Acis

Faust: *author:* 6 Goethe

composer: 6 Gounod

faux pas: 4 bull, slip 5 boner, error, gaffe, lapse 6 boo-boo, bungle 7 blooper, misstep, mistake
faveolate: 9 alveolate 11 honeycombed
favonian: 4 mild 6 gentle
favor: aid, for, pro 4 boon, face, gree, help 5 bless, grace, leave, spare 6 esteem, letter, uphold 7 advance, feature, forward, support 8 advocacy, befriend, goodwill, kindness, resemble 9 party gift, patronage, privilege, subscribe 10 assistance, concession, indulgence, permission 11 accommodate, approbation, countenance 13 communication
pay: woo 5 court
favorable: 4 good, kind, rosy 5 clear 6 benign 7 benefic, optimal, popular 8 friendly, gracious, pleasing 9 approving, opportune 10 auspicious, charitable, convenient, propitious 12 advantageous
favored: 6 gifted 9 fortunate, preferred
favorite: pet 6 minion 7 darling, popular
favoritism: 4 bias 8 nepotism 9 prejudice
fawn: 4 buck, deer, jouk 5 color, cower, crawl, kotow, toady, whelp 6 cringe, grovel, kotow, shrink 7 adulate, flatter, hangdog, servile, truckle 9 parasitic, sycophant 10 ingratiate
skin: 6 nebris
fay: elf 5 fairy, pixie 6 sprite
faze: 5 abash, daunt, worry 6 bother, rattle 7 confuse, nonplus, perplex 8 irritate 9 embarrass 10 disconcert
fealty: 6 homage 7 loyalty 8 fidelity 9 constancy, obeisance 10 allegiance
fear: awe 5 alarm, doubt, dread, panic 6 danger, dismay, fright, horror, phobia, terror 7 anxiety, suspec 9 affright, disquiet, distrust, venera 9 agitation, reverence, revulsion 10 s ctitude 12 apprehension 13 consternation
of animals: 9 zoophobia
of being alone: 10 monophobia
of burial alive: 11 taphephobia
of cats: 12 aelurophobia, ailurophobia
of crowds: 11 ochlophobia
of darkness: 10 nyctophobia
of dirt: 10 mysophobia
of drafts: 10 aerophobia
of enclosed places: 14 claustrophobia
of fire: 10 pyrophobia
of great heights: 10 acrophobia
of open spaces: 11 agoraphobia
of pain: 10 algophobia
of poisons: 10 toxiphobia
of strangers: 10 xenophobia
of thunder: 12 brontophobia 13 tonitrophobia
of water: 11 hydrophobia
fearful: 4 dire 5 awful, timid 6 afraid 7 ghastly, nervous, panicky, worried 8

cautious, doubtful, dreadful, grewsome, gruesome, horrible, horrific, shocking, terrible, timorous 9 appalling, frightful, trembling 10 formidable, horrendous, meticulous 11 distressing 12 apprehensive
fearless: 4 bold 5 brave 6 daring, heroic 8 intrepid 9 audacious, confident, dauntless, undaunted 10 courageous
feasible: 6 likely, viable 8 possible, probable, suitable 9 practical 10 reasonable
feast: eat, foy(Sc.), sup 4 dine, fete, luau, meal 5 festa, treat 6 regale, repast 7 banquet, delight, festino, gratify 8 festival, potlatch 10 burrakhana
January 6: 8 Epiphany
of lanterns: 7 Hanukka 8 Chanukah, Hanukkah
of lights: 7 Hanukka 8 Chanukah, Hanukkah
of lots: 5 Purim
of nativity: 9 Christmas
of tabernacles: 7 Succoth
of weeks: 8 Shabuoth
passover: 5 seder
feasting: 9 epulation
companion: 7 convive
feat: act 4 deed, gest 5 geste, stunt, trick 7 exploit miracle, venture 11 achievement, performance, tour de force 14 accomplishment
feather: 4 deck, down, vane 5 adorn, penna, pinna(L.), pluma(L.), plume, quill 6 clothe, fledge, fletch, hackle, pinion
barb: 4 harl, herl 7 pinnula
down: 4 dowl 5 dowle 7 plumule
mature: 10 teleoptile
quill: 5 remex 7 calamus
shaft: 5 scape
shank: 4 boot
shoulder: 4 cape
feather key: 6 spline
feather star: 8 comatula 9 comatulae(pl.), comatulid
featherbrained: 5 giddy, silly 7 flighty, foolish 9 frivolous 11 empty-headed
feathered: 7 pennate, pinnate
feathers: 5 dress 6 attire 7 plumage
shed: 4 molt 5 moult
featherweight: 5 dunce, light 7 trivial 10 of no matter
feathery: 4 soft 5 light 6 fluffy
featly: 6 neatly, nimbly 8 properly
feature: 4 face 5 favor, motif, token, trait 6 aspect, detail, play up, stress 7 amenity, element, outline 8 salience 9 attribute, character, emphasize, lineament 11 countenance 14 characteristic
natural: 9 geography
febris: 5 fever
feckless: 4 weak 8 careless 9 shiftless, worthless 10 unreliable 11 ineffective,

thoughtless 13 irresponsible

fecund: 7 fertile 8 fruitful, prolific

fecundate: 9 fertilize, pollinate 10 impregnate

fed up: 5 bored 7 wearied 8 satiated 9 disgusted, surfeited

federation: 5 union 6 league 8 alliance 9 coalition 11 association, confederacy

fedora: hat

fee: 4 dues, cost, feal, feul(Sc.), fier, hire, rate, wage 5 price 6 charge, reward, salary 7 expense, payment, stipend, tribute, tuition 8 gratuity, malikana, retainer 9 allowance, bienvenne, emolument, pourboire 10 assessment, honorarium, perquisite, recompense 12 compensation

bridge: 4 toll

money-changing: 4 agio

trucking: 4 cartage

wharf: 7 quayage

feeble: 4 lame, mean, poor, puny, weak 5 faint 6 flabby, flimsy, infirm, scanty, sickly 7 fragile, invalid, languid 8 decrepit, impotent, inferior, thewless(Sc.), yielding 9 miserable 10 inadequate, indistinct 11 debilitated

feebleminded: 5 anile, dotty 7 moronic 10 irresolute 11 vacillating

feed: eat, hay 4 bait, bran, fill, grub, meal, oats, sate 5 grass, graze, nurse 6 fodder, foster, repast, suckle, supply 7 blowout, furnish, gratify, herbage, indulge, nourish, nurture, satiate, satisfy, sustain 9 replenish

the kitty: 4 ante

to excess: 4 glut 5 gorge, stuff 7 surfeit 8 overfill 9 crapulate

feeder: 6 branch 9 tributary

fire: 6 stoker

feel: paw 4 deem 5 grope, probe, sense, touch 6 finger, fumble, handle 7 believe, examine, explore, texture 8 perceive 9 be moved by 10 appreciate, experience

feeler: 4 palp 6 palpus 7 antenna, smeller 8 proposal, tentacle 12 trial balloon

feeling: 4 pity, tact, view 5 humor, touch 6 morale 7 emotion, opinion, passion 8 attitude 9 affection, sensation, sentiment 10 atmosphere, experience, perception 11 sensibility 13 consciousness 14 susceptibility

capable of: 8 sentient

evocative of: 7 emotive

lack of: 6 apathy 8 numbness 9 unconcern 10 anesthesia 13 insensibility

feet (see also **foot**): 4 dogs

feign: act 4 fake, seem, sham 5 avoid, fable, shape, shirk 6 affect, assume, invent 7 conceal, fashion, imagine, pretend, romance 8 disguise, simulate 9 dissemble, personate 11 counterfeit, dissimulate, make-believe

ignorance: 7 connive

sickness: 8 malinger

feigned: 5 false, put on 6 pseudo 9 insincere 10 artificial, fictitious

feint: 4 hoax, ploy, ruse, wile 5 bluff, dodge, shift, trick 6 gambit 8 pretense 9 diversion

in fencing: 5 appel

feis: 8 assembly, festival 10 convention

feisty: 6 lively 8 snappish, spirited 9 energetic 10 aggressive 11 belligerent, quarrelsome

feldspar: 6 albite, gneiss 7 odinite, syenite 9 anorthite 11 labradorite

yield: 6 kaolin

felicitate: 6 salute 12 congratulate

felicitous: apt 5 happy 6 joyous 7 apropos, fitting 8 pleasing 11 appropriate

felicity: joy 9 happiness, well-being

felid: cat

feline: cat, sly, tom 4 lion, lynx, pard, puma 5 civet, tiger 6 jaguar 7 cheetah, leonine, leopard, sinuous, wildcat 9 stealthy 9 grimalkin 11 treacherous

breathing: 4 purr

fell: cut, fen, hew 4 down, hide, hill, moor, pelt, ruin, skin, very 5 cruel, eager, field, great, sharp 6 deadly, fierce, fleece, intent, mighty, savage, shrewd 7 brutish, crashed, doughty, hideous, inhuman, tumbled 8 mountain, spirited 9 barbarous, ferocious, marshland, momentous, prostrate 11 destructive

fellah: 7 peasant

fellow (see also **man, person**): guy, lad, man 4 bean, beau, bozo, chap, cove, dick, duck, hind, mate, peer 5 billy, bloke, match 6 bugger, codger, hombre(Sp.), person, sirrah 7 chappie, comrade, partner 8 neighbor 9 associate, companion 10 sweetheart 12 contemporary

awkward: 4 oaf 4 lout 5 booby, clown 6 galoot 7 bumpkin 11 hobble-de-hoy

brutish: 5 yahoo

conceited: 7 egotist 8 braggart 9 know-it-all

craven: 6 coward

dissolute: 4 rake, roue 9 debaucher

dull: 4 drip, fogy 5 fogey

fat: 7 glutton

fine: 5 brick, bully 8 bonhomme(F.)

funny: wag, wit 4 card 5 clown

honest: 6 trusty

lazy: bum 6 loafer 9 drawlatch

little: bub 5 caddy 6 birkie, caddie, shaver 9 dandiprat

mean: cad 4 boor 5 bucko, churl 8 blighter

old: 6 geezer, gleyde

old-fashioned: 4 fogy

queer old: 6 geezer 10 curmudgeon

ragged: 10 ragamuffin 14 tatterdemalion

reckless: 4 buck 5 blade 9 daredevil, hell-raker

rowdy: 6 roarer 8 larrikin

shrewd: 6 gazabo, gazebo

silly: 8 dotterel

stupid: ass 4 clod, dolt, simp 5 dunce, moron 9 blockhead

tricky: 5 knave, scamp 6 rascal

vain: fop

worthless: bum, cur 5 rogue, scamp 7 brothel 9 schlemiel(Yid.), scoundrel

fellowship: 5 guild, union 7 company 8 alliance 9 communion 10 fraternity, membership 11 association, brotherhood, camaraderie, comradeship, corporation, familiarity, intercourse, partnership 12 friendliness 13 companionship

felly: 7 cruelly 8 savagely 11 barbarously 13 destructively

felo-de-se: 7 suicide

felon: 4 base 5 cruel 6 wicked 7 convict, culprit, whitlow 8 criminal, offender 10 lawbreaker, malefactor

felony: 5 crime 7 offense

felt: hat 6 fabric, sensed

felwort: 7 gentian

female: 4 girl 5 woman 7 womanly 8 feminine, ladylike, womanish 9 womanlike 10 effeminate

 animal: cow, dam, doe, ewe, hen, sow 4 mare, slut 5 bitch, filly, jenny, tabby 6 heifer 7 lioness, tigress

 assistant: 8 adjutrix 9 adjutrice

 camel: 4 naga

 figure: 5 orant 8 caryatid

 fish: 4 raun

 fox: 5 vixen

 monster: 6 gorgon

 principle: 5 Sakti

 red deer: 4 hind

 sandpiper: 5 reeve

 sheep: ewe

 slave: 7 odalisk 9 odalisque

 spirit: 7 banshee

 warrior: 6 Amazon

feminine: 4 soft, weak 6 female, tender 8 womanish 10 effeminate

femme fatale: 5 siren 7 Lorelei 9 temptress 10 seductress

femoral: 6 crural

femur: 9 thighbone

fen: bog 4 carr, fowl, moor 5 marsh, snipe, swamp 6 morass 8 quagmire

fence: bar 4 coop, duel, gird, rail, wall 5 dodge, guard, hedge, parry, pen in 6 paling, picket, rasper 7 barrier, bulwark, defense 8 encircle, palisade, surround 9 enclosure 12 circumscribe, dealer in loot 14 buy stolen goods

fish: net 4 weir

interwoven: 6 raddle

mending: 11 politicking

on the: 9 undecided 11 uncommitted

picket: 6 paling

sunken: 4 ha-ha

fencer: 7 duelist, parrier 9 gladiator, swordsman

 cry of: 6 touche 7 en garde

fencing: 9 swordplay

 attack: 7 reprise

 breastplate: 8 plastron

 cry: 4 sasa

 hit: 5 punto

 maneuver: 5 appel

 movement: 4 volt

 position: 5 carte, prime, sixte, terce 6 octave, quarte, quinte, tierce 7 seconde, septime

 position of hands: 9 pronation 10 supination

 redoubling of attack: 7 reprise

 term: 4 bind 5 lunge 6 thrust, touche

 thrust: 7 riposte

 weapon: 4 epee, foil 5 saber, sabre, sword 6 rapier

fend: 4 ward 5 avert, avoid, parry 6 defend, manage, resist 7 keep off, provide, support 8 push away 10 take care of

fender: 5 guard 6 buffer, bumper, shield 8 mudguard 11 splashboard

fenestra: 6 window 7 foramen, opening 8 aperture, fontanel

fennel: 4 herb 9 seasoning

 relative: 7 parsley

fer-de-lance: 5 snake

feracious: 8 fruitful

feral, ferine: 4 wild 6 deadly, savage 7 bestial, untamed 8 unbroken 11 uncivilized 14 undomesticated

Ferdinand's wife: 8 Isabella

feria: 4 fair 6 fiesta 7 holiday

fermail: 5 clasp 6 buckle

ferment: 4 barm, heat, turn, work, zyme 5 fever, yeast 6 enzyme, seethe, tumult, uproar 7 agitate 8 disorder 10 ebullition, exacerbate, excitement, turbulence

fermenting mixtue: bub

fern: 4 tara, weki 5 brake 7 bracken, woodsia 8 polypody 10 maidenhair

 climbing: 4 nito

 edible: roi 4 tara

 genus: 7 Onoclea, Osmunda 8 Psilotum

 leaf: 5 frond

 royal: 6 osmund

 scale: 7 ramenta(pl.) 8 ramentum

fern-like: 7 pteroid

ferocious: 4 fell, grim, wild 5 cruel, feral 6 bloody, brutal, fierce, raging, savage 7 inhuman, ominous, violent 8 pitiless, ravenous, ruthless 9 barbarous, malignant, merciless, murderous, rapacious,

truculent **10** implacable, malevolent, relentless, sanguinary **11** remorseless **12** bloodthirsty
ferret: 4 tape **6** weasel **7** polecat
male: hob
ferret out: 4 hunt, seek **5** probe **6** elicit **7** uncover **9** search for
ferric oxide: 5 rouge **6** powder
ferrotype: 7 tintype
ferrule: cap **4** ring, virl(Sc.) **6** collet, pulley, verrel **7** bushing, verrell
ferry: 4 pont, scow **7** traject
ferryman: 6 Charon
fertile: fat **4** rank, rich **5** gleby **6** fecund, hearty **7** teeming **8** abundant, fruitful, generous, prolific **9** exuberant, feracious, inventive, luxuriant, plenteous, plentiful **10** productive, profitable
render: **6** enrich
fertility god: 4 Frey **5** Freyr
fertilize: 6 batten, enrich **8** fructify **9** fecundate **10** impregnate, inseminate
fertilizer: 4 marl **5** guano, humus **6** alinit, manure, pollen, potash **7** compost, nitrate **8** nitrogen **11** phosphorous **14** superphosphate
ferule: rod **5** ruler **6** fennel **10** discipline
fervent: hot **4** keen, warm **5** eager, fiery **6** ardent, bitter, fierce, raging, savage **7** boiling, burning, glowing, intense **8** vehement **9** impetuous, religious **10** passionate **11** impassioned
fervor: 4 fire, heat, love, rage, zeal **5** ardor **7** ecstasy, feeling, passion **8** ardency **9** eagerness, vehemence **10** enthusiasm, excitement **11** earnestness
fess: bar **4** band
fester: rot **4** grow **6** rankle **7** blister, inflame, pustule, putrefy, smolder **8** embitter, ulcerate
festival: bee **4** fair, fete, gala **5** feast, feria, festa, revel **6** fiesta **7** banquet, holiday **8** carnival, carousal, jamboree **11** celebration
church: **4** Lent **6** Easter **9** Christmas
epiphany: **7** uphelya
festive: gay **4** gala **5** merry **6** festal, genial, joyous **7** jocular, playful **8** mirthful, sportive **9** convivial **10** frolicsome **11** celebratory
festivity: 4 gala **5** mirth, randy, revel **6** gaiety, splore **7** jollity, jubilee, whoopee **8** function **10** joyfulness **11** celebration, merrymaking **12** conviviality **13** entertainment, glorification
god: **5** Comus **7** Bacchus **8** Dionysus
festoon: 4 loop, swag **6** wreath **7** garland **8** decorate
fetch: get **4** gasp, tack, take **5** bring, sweep, trick **6** double, elicit, obtain, wraith **7** achieve, attract, go after, realize, sell for **8** artifice, interest, retrieve **9** stratagem

round: **6** revive **8** convince, persuade
fetching: 4 cute **8** alluring, charming, pleasing **10** attractive **11** fascinating
fete: 4 fair, gala **5** bazar, feast **6** bazaar, fiesta, regale **7** banquet, holiday **8** ceremony, festival **9** entertain **11** celebration
fetid: 4 foul, olid, rank **5** fusty, musty **6** putrid, rancid, rotten, virose **7** miasmic, noisome, noxious **8** mephitic, stinking **9** offensive **10** malodorous
fetish, fetich: obi **4** idol, joss, juju, obia **5** charm, huaca, image, obeah, obiah, totem **6** amulet, grigri, voodoo **7** sorcery **8** fixation, greegree, idee fixe, talisman **10** mumbo jumbo
fetter: 4 band, bind, bond, gyve, iron **5** basil, chain, tie up **6** anklet, garter, hamper, hobble, hog-tie, hopple, impede **7** confine, enchain, manacle, shackle, trammel **8** handcuff, restrain **9** restraint
fettle: 4 mend, trim **5** dress, groom, order, shape **6** repair, strike **7** fitness, harness, spirits **9** condition
feud: 4 fief, fray **5** broil **6** affray, enmity, strife **7** contest, dispute, quarrel **8** conflict **9** hostility **10** contention
blood: **8** vendetta
feudal: 6 lordly **8** manorial, medieval **9** imperious **10** oligarchic
estate: **4** fief **5** feoff
jurisdiction: soc **4** soke
lord: **7** vavasor **8** suzerain, vavasour
penalty: **7** sursise
pert. to: **5** banal
tenant: **6** vassal **7** homager
tenure: **6** socage
fever: 4 fire **6** febris(L.) **7** ferment **9** calenture **10** excitement **11** temperature **13** conflagration
kind of: **4** ague **5** octan, swamp **6** dengue, sextan, sodoku **7** malaria, quartan, scarlet, spotted **8** undulant
without: **8** apyretic
feverish: 5 fiery **6** hectic **7** excited, febrile, flushed, frantic, parched **8** inflamed, restless **9** overeager **11** impassioned
few: 4 less, some, thin **5** scant **6** scarce, skimpy **7** limited, not many, several **8** exiguous
fewness: 7 paucity
fey: odd **5** queer **7** puckish **9** eccentric, visionary, whimsical **12** otherworldly
fez: hat **8** tarboosh
fiacre: 4 hack **5** coach **8** carriage
fiance: 8 intended **9** betrothed
fiasco: 4 bomb, flop **6** fizzle **7** debacle, failure, washout **8** disaster
fiat: 5 edict, order **6** decree **7** comand **8** decision, sanction **9** ordinance **12** announcement, proclamation

fib: lie 5 hedge, story 7 untruth 9 falsehood 10 equivocate 11 prevaricate

fiber, fibre: 4 root 5 grain 6 nature, thread, tissue 7 quality 9 character

band: 6 fillet

bark: 5 olona, terap

hat: 5 datil

kind of: nap, nep, tal, tow 4 adad, aloe, bast, buri, coir, eruc, feru, flax, hemp, ixle, jute, kyar, lint, marl, noil, pita, silk, sola, wool 5 abaca, civil, erizo, floss, istle, istli, ixtle, kapok, linen, mudar, oakum, ramee, ramie, sisal 6 amiray, cotton, manila, raffia, staple 7 castuli, haurizo, sabutan 8 filament, fibrilla, keratose 9 gamelotte 10 anodendron, escobadura

knot: nep

palm: 4 eruc 6 raffia 7 coquita, coquito

synthetic: 5 nylon, orlon, rayon 6 dacron 7 acetate, acrilan

yarn: 6 strand

fibril: 4 hair 8 filament

fibrin: 6 gluten

fibrous: 4 ropy, wiry 6 sinewy 7 stringy

fibula: 5 clasp 6 brooch, buckle 7 leg bone

fickle: 5 dizzy, giddy 6 shifty 7 erratic, flighty 8 unstable, unsteady, variable, volatile, wavering 9 faithless, frivolous, mercurial, unsettled 10 capricious, changeable, inconstant, irresolute 11 vacillating 12 inconsistent

fictile: 6 molded 7 plastic

fiction: 4 tale, yarn 5 fable, novel 6 deceit, device, fabula, legend 7 coinage, fantasy, figment, forgery, romance 9 falsehood, invention 10 concoction, pretending 11 contrivance, dissembling, fabrication 14 counterfeiting

fictitious: 4 fake, sham 5 bogus, dummy, false, phony 6 untrue 7 assumed, feigned 8 fabulous, fanciful, mythical, spurious 9 imaginary, imitative, pretended, trumped up 10 apocryphal, artificial, not genuine 11 counterfeit

fid: 9 splice pin 10 topmast bar

fiddle: bow 4 viol 5 cheat 6 doodle, fidget, putter, tinker, trifle, violin 7 swindle 10 fool around

fiddler: 4 crab 7 scraper 8 sixpence 9 violinist

fiddler crab: uca

fiddlesticks: 4 bosh 5 pshaw 8 nonsense

Fidelio: *composer:* 9 Beethoven

hero: 9 Florestan

heroine: 7 Leonora

fidelity: 5 troth, truth 6 fealty 7 honesty 8 adhesion, devotion, veracity 9 adherence, closeness, constancy 10 allegiance 12 faithfulness

symbol of: 5 topaz 7 diamond

fidgety: 5 fussy, jumpy 6 uneasy 7 jittery, nervous, restive, twitchy, unquiet 8 restless 9 impatient, irritable

fiducial: 4 firm 7 trusted 8 reliable 9 confident 11 trustworthy 12 solid as a rock

fiduciary: 7 trustee

field: lea, lot 4 acre, area, mead 5 campo, croft, paddy, plain, range, realm, rowen, sawah 6 campus, domain, ground, meadow, sphere 7 compass, entries, paddock, pasture, terrain 8 clearing 9 grassland 10 department

athletic: 4 oval, ring, rink 5 arena, court, green 6 course, stadia(pl.) 7 diamond, stadium 8 gridiron

common share: 4 dale

extensive: 7 savanna 8 savannah

god: 4 Faun

goddess: 5 Fauna

hand: 4 hoer 5 sower 6 picker, plower 7 laborer

pert. to: 8 agrarian, agrestic 10 campestral

questions: 11 reply glibly

Roman: 4 ager

stubble: 5 rowen

field mouse: 4 vole

field of blood: 8 Aceldama

fieldwork: 5 redan 7 lunette 13 fortification

fiend: 5 beast, brute, demon, devil, Satan 6 addict, expert, maniac, wizard 7 fanatic, monster 9 succubus 10 evil spirit

fiendish: 5 cruel 6 wicked 7 demonic, inhuman, vicious 8 demoniac, devilish, diabolic, infernal 9 barbarous 10 diabolical

fierce: 4 bold, fell, grim, wild 5 cruel 6 ardent, gothic, raging, savage 7 brutish, fervent, furious, intense, violent 9 ferocious, impetuous, truculent 10 catawampus, forbidding, passionate 12 disagreeable, uncontrolled

fiery: hot, red 5 adust 6 ablaze, ardent, fervid, torrid 7 burning, fervent, flaming, furious, glowing, igneous, parched, peppery, violent 8 choleric, feverish, inflamed, spirited, vehement 9 excitable, hotheaded, impetuous, irascible, irritable 10 mettlesome, passionate 11 combustible, inflammable

fiesta: 4 fete 5 feria, party 7 holiday 8 festival 9 festivity

fife: 4 pipe 5 flute

fifty-fifty: 4 even 7 equally 11 half and half

fig: rig 5 array, dress, fruit, shape 6 trifle 7 furbish 9 condition, little bit 10 tinker's dam

basket: 5 cabas

crate: 5 seron

family tree: 8 mulberry

genus: 5 ficus

sacred: 5 pipal

Smyrna: 5 eleme, elemi

fig-shaped: 8 ficiform

Figaro: 6 barber

author: 12 Beaumarchais

character: 6 Rosina 7 Susanna 8 Almaviva 9 Dr. Bartolo 10 Don Basilio

opera composers: 6 Mozart 7 Rossini

fight: box, war 4 bout, duel, fray, grit, spat, tiff, tilt 5 argue, brawl, clash, melee, pluck, scrap, set-to 6 affair, affray, battle, bicker, combat, debate, fracas, mettle, oppose, resist, spirit, strife, tussle 7 contend, contest, dispute, quarrel, ruction, scuffle, wrangle 8 conflict, militate, skirmish, squabble, struggle 9 encounter, pugnacity 11 altercation 12 disagreement

against the gods: 9 theomachy

fighter: pug 4 vamp 5 boxer 6 cocker 7 battler, duelist, soldier, warrior 8 andabata, barrater, barrator, champion, pugilist, guerilla, scrapper 9 combatant, guerrilla

fighting: 7 warlike 8 militant 10 pugnacious 11 belligerent

street: 4 riot 5 brawl 10 free-for-all

fighting fish: 5 betta

figment: 7 fiction 9 invention 11 fabrication

figuration: 4 form 5 shape 7 outline 9 symbolism 10 appearance

figurative: 6 florid 7 flowery 8 symbolic 9 allegoric 10 not literal, rhetorical 12 metaphorical

use of words: 5 trope

figure: sum 4 body, cost, form, rate 5 add up, build, digit, guess, image, judge, motif, price, shape, total, value 6 amount, design, emblem, number, reckon, symbol 7 chiffer, compute, contour, notable, numeral, outline 8 likeness 9 calculate, character, personage, play a part, quotation 13 configuration

geometrical: 4 cone, cube, lune 5 prism, rhomb, solid 6 circle, gnomon, oblong, sector, square 7 ellipse, lozenge, rhombus 8 crescent, pentacle, triangle 9 rectangle

human form: 4 nude 5 dummy 6 statue 7 manikin, telamon 8 atlantes, caryatid

many-sided: 4 cube 6 isogon 7 decagon, hexagon, nonagon, octagon, polygon 8 pentagon, tetragon 10 hexahedron, octahedron

of speech: 5 trope 6 aporia, simile 7 imagery 8 metaphor, metonymy

ornamental: 7 topiary 8 gargoyle

praying: 5 orant

symbolic: 6 emblem

figure out: 4 dope 5 crack, solve 6 decode 7 clear up, resolve, unravel 10 unscramble 12 get the answer

figured: 7 adorned, faconne(Fr.) 8 computed 9 patterned

figurehead: 4 tool 5 dummy, front 6 puppet, stooge 7 stand-in

figurine: 7 tanagra 9 statuette

motion picture: 5 Oscar

Fiji: *capital:* 4 Suva

cities: 5 Nandi 7 Lambasa, Lautoka

ethnic: 10 Polynesian

islands: 4 Koro, Ngau 8 Tavenuni, Viti-Levu 9 VanuaLevu

monetary unit: 6 dollar

mountains: 6 Nararu 8 Monavatu

filament: 4 hair, harl, wire 5 fiber, fibre 6 mantle, strand, thread

lamp: 8 tungsten

filbert: 8 hazelnut

filch: bob, nim, rob 4 lift 5 pinch, steal, swipe 6 pilfer 7 purloin

file: row 4 line, rank, rasp, tool 5 index, label 6 folder, record, smooth 7 arrange, cabinet 8 apply for, register 9 grind down 10 procession

combmaker's: 6 carlet

document: 7 dossier

nail: 10 emery board

filet: net 4 lace

filial: 9 childlike 10 respectful

filibeg: 4 kilt 5 skirt

filibuster: 9 talkathon 14 political stall 15 talk against time

filigree: 4 mesh 7 network, tracery 8 fretwork, lacelike

filing: 5 lemel 8 limation

Filipino: See **Philippines**

fill: pad 4 cram, feed, glut, heap, load, pack, sate 5 earth, gorge 6 blow up, charge, occupy, supply 7 distend, enlarge, execute, fraught, inflate, perfect, perform, pervade, satiate, satisfy, suffuse 8 complete, compound, permeate 9 replenish 10 accomplish, embankment, take care of 11 sufficiency

cracks: 4 calk, plug, shim 5 caulk, putty

in: 5 brief, spell 6 inform 7 put wise 8 acquaint 10 substitute 13 bring up to date

with zeal: 7 enthuse

fille: 4 girl 8 daughter

filled: SRO 4 full 5 sated, solid 6 loaded 7 replete 9 saturated 10 carried out

fillet: 4 band, bone, orle, orlo, tape 5 crown, miter, snood, stria, strip, tiara 6 anadem, binder, diadem, ribbon, striae(pl.), turban, wreath 7 bandeau, chaplet, garland, molding 8 headband, tressure 9 sphendone

architectural: 6 cimbia, fascia, listel, quadra, reglet, regula, taenia 8 bandelet, cincture

filling: *dental:* 5 inlay

fabric: 4 weft, woof

fillip: tap 4 blow, flip, snap 5 boost, twist 6 buffet, charge, jazz up 8 stimulus 9 extra dash, stimulate

filly: tap 4 colt, foal, girl, mare 9 youngster

film (see also **motion picture**): 4 blur, brat(Sc.), haze, mist, scum, skin, veil 5 flake, layer 6 lamina, patina 7 coating 8 beeswing, negative, pellicle 10 photograph

filmy: 4 hazy 5 gauzy, misty, wispy 6 cloudy 7 clouded 8 gossamer 13 unsubstantial

filter: 4 sift 5 drain, sieve 6 purify, refine, screen, strain 8 strainer 9 percolate

sugar: 4 clay

filth: 4 dirt, dung, muck, slop, smut 5 offal 6 ordure, refuse, vermin 7 garbage, squalor 9 obscenity

filthy: low 4 foul, miry, vile 5 dirty, gross, nasty 6 impure, rotten, sordid 7 bestial, immoral, obscene, raunchy, squalid, unclean 8 indecent, sluttish 9 polluting, repulsive, revolting 10 disgusting, licentious 11 disgraceful

fimbriate: 7 fringed

fin: arm 4 hand 5 fiver, pinna 7 acantha, airfoil, flipper 10 stabilizer

fin-footed: 8 pinniped

finagle: 5 cheat, trick 6 wangle 7 connive, deceive 9 machinate

final: 4 last 6 latter 7 dernier, extreme, outmost 8 decisive, definite, eventual, farewell, ultimate 9 uttermost 10 concluding, conclusive, definitive 11 terminating 13 determinating

final outcome: 5 issue 6 payoff, upshot

finale: end 4 coda 5 close, finis 6 ending, windup 7 closing 8 swan song 9 cessation 10 conclusion 11 termination

finally: 8 at length, in the end 10 ultimately 11 irrevocably 12 in conclusion 13 once and for all

finance: tax 4 back 5 endow, stake 6 pay for 7 banking 8 bankroll 9 subsidize 10 underwrite

finances: 5 funds, money 8 accounts, supports 9 economics, exchequer

financial: 6 fiscal 8 monetary 9 pecuniary

finch: 4 fink, moro, pape 5 serin, terin 6 burion, citril, linnet, siskin, towhee 7 chewink, redpoll, senegal, tanager 8 amadavat 9 snowflake

find: get 5 catch 6 locate 8 discover

by keen search: 5 probe 6 ferret

find fault: nag 4 carp, crab, fret 5 cavil, scold 8 complain 9 bellyache, criticize

find guilty: 7 convict

find out: 4 hear 5 learn 6 detect 7 unearth 8 discover 9 ascertain, determine

fine: rum, tax 4 good, jake, levy, nice, pure, thin 5 bonny, brave, bully, clear, dandy, frail, nifty, noble, sharp, sheer, silky, swell 6 amerce, bonnie, bright, choice, finish, ornate, proper, slight, spiffy, subtle, tender 7 elegant, forfeit, fragile, penalty, perfect, precise, tenuous 8 absolute, all right, delicate, handsome, penalize, pleasant, skillful, splendid, superior, top-grade, very well 9 beautiful, excellent, ingenious, sensitive 10 assessment, consummate, fastidious, pulverized, punishment, surpassing

for misdemeanor: 5 mulct

record of: 7 estreat

finery: 6 frills 7 clothes, gaudery, gewgaws, regalia 8 frippery, glad rags 9 showiness, trappings 10 fancy dress, Sunday best

finesse: art 4 tact 5 guile, skill, taste 7 cunning 8 artifice, delicacy, subtlety 9 dexterity, stratagem 10 artfulness, bridge play, manipulate, refinement, shrewdness 11 sensitivity 12 one-upmanship

Fingal's cave: *island:* 6 Staffa

kingdom: 6 Morven

fingent: 7 pliable 8 flexible, yielding

finger: paw, tap, toy 4 feel 5 digit, index, pinky, thumb, touch 6 handle, pilfer, pinkie 7 purloin 8 identify, indicate, inform on, point out

bone: 7 phalanx

guard for: cot 5 stall 7 thimble

little: 7 minimus

inflammation of: 5 felon 7 whitlow

pert. to: 7 digital 8 digitate

snap with: 6 fillip

finger board: 4 fret

fingerlike: 6 dactyl

fingerling: 4 parr 8 troutlet

fingernail moon: 6 lunule

fingerprint: 11 dactylogram

mark: 4 arch, loop 5 whorl 9 composite

science: 12 dactyloscopy

Finger Lakes: 5 Keuka 6 Cayuga, Owasco, Seneca 11 Skaneateles

finial: epi 5 crest 8 ornament, pinnacle

finical: 4 nice 5 fussy 6 choosy, dainty, dapper, jaunty, prissy, spruce 7 choosey, finicky, foppish, mincing 8 delicate 9 squeamish 10 fastidious, meticulous 11 overprecise 14 overscrupulous

finis: end 4 goal 5 close 10 conclusion

finish: die, end 4 char, mill 5 bound, cease, chare, cheve, close, enden(G.), glaze, limit 6 fulfil, windup 7 achieve, execute, fulfill, perfect, surface 8 complete, conclude, terminal 9 erudition, terminate 10 accomplish, completion, conclusion, consummate, perfection

dull: mat 5 matte

glossy: 6 enamel

finished: did, oer, pau 4 done, fine, gone, over, ripe 5 ended, kaput 6 closed, ornate 7 refined, stopped 8 climaxed, lustered, polished 9 completed, concluded, perfected, performed 10 terminated 11 consummated 12 professional

finisher: 4 eyer 5 ender 7 beetler 8 enameler

finishing line: 4 tape

finite: 7 limited 9 definable 10 restricted, terminable 11 conditioned

fink: 8 informer, squealer 13 strikebreaker

Finland: 5 Suomi
  bathhouse: 5 sauna
  capital: 8 Helsinki
  city: 4 OuLu 5 Espoo, Lahti, Turku 7 Tampere
  composer: 8 Sibelius
  dialect: 5 Karel
  division: 5 Ijore 9 Villipuri
  forest god: 5 Tapio
  fortress: 11 Suomenlinna
  god: 6 Jumala
  harp: 7 kantele
  island: 5 Aland, Karlo 6 Kimito 9 Vallgrund
  isthmus: 7 Karelia
  lake: 5 Enare 6 Saimaa 7 Keitele 8 Piefinen 9 Oulujarvi
  language: 4 Avar, Lapp 5 Ugric 6 Magyar, Ostyak, Tarast 7 Samoyed 8 Estonian
  measure: 5 kannu, tunna, verst 6 fathom, sjomil 7 tunland 8 ottinger, skalpund, tunnland
  monetary unit: 5 peññi 6 markka
  mountain: 13 Haltiatunturi
  parliament: 9 Eduskunta
  pert. to: 6 Suomic 7 Suomish
  rivers: 4 Kemi, Oulu
  town: 5 Enare
  tribe: 4 Veps, Wote 5 Vepse 6 Ugrian

Finlandia composer: 8 Sibelius

Finnegan's Wake author: 5 Joyce

fiord, fjord: ise 5 inlet

fir: 9 evergreen
  genus: 5 abies

Firbolg queen: 6 Tailte 7 Talitiu

fire: can, feu(F.) 4 bale, burn, heat, zeal 5 ardor, arson, fever, gleed, light, shoot, stoke 6 arouse, excite, fervor, ignite, incite, kindle, spirit 7 animate, burning, dismiss, explode, fervour, glimmer, inflame, inspire 8 detonate, illumine, irritate, vivacity 9 calenture, cauterize, discharge, holocaust, terminate 10 combustion, enthusiasm, illuminate 12 inflammation 13 conflagration
  artillery: 7 barrage
  basket: 5 grate 7 cresset
  containing: 7 igneous

fighter: 4 vamp

god: 4 Agni, Loki 6 Vulcan 10 Hephaestus

military: 4 flak 5 salvo 6 rafale 7 barrage

particle: arc 5 spark

pert. to: 7 igneous

sacrificial: 4 agni

set: 6 accend, ignite, kindle 7 inflame 8 enkindle, irritate

worshiper: 5 Parsi 6 Parsee 9 pyrolater 10 ignicolist

firearm: gun 5 piece, rifle 6 musket, pistol 7 demihag 8 revolver

fireback: 7 reredos 8 pheasant

fireboat: 8 palander

firebrand: 5 blaze 6 bleery

firebug: 10 incendiary, pyromaniac

firecracker: 5 squib 6 petard 7 cracker, snapper 9 skyrocket

firedamp: gas 7 methane

firedog: 7 andiron

fireman: 4 vamp 6 stoker, tizeur 9 fireeater

fireplace: 5 focus, fogon, forge, foyer, ingle 6 heath 8 cheminee
  part: hob 6 mantel 9 ingleside 11 hearthstone

fireplug: 7 hydrant

firer: 6 stoker 10 incendiary

fireside: 9 ingleside 11 hearthstone

firestone: 5 flint

firewood: 4 lena 5 fagot 6 billet, billot

fireworks: 4 gerb 5 gerbe 7 fizgigs, rockets 9 sparklers 10 girandoles 11 tourbillion 12 pyrotechnics
  resembling: 11 pyrotechnic

firing: 4 fuel

firm: hui 4 buff, fast, hard, sure, trig 5 champ, dense, exact, firma, fixed, hardy, house, loyal, rigid, solid, sound, stith, stout, tight 6 hearty, secure, settle, sinewy, stable, stanch, steady, stolid, strong 7 adamant, certain, compact, company, confirm, context, decided, durable, staunch, unmoved 8 constant, faithful, fiducial, obdurate, resolute, unshaken 9 backboned, establish, immovable, immutable, standfast, steadfast 10 consistent, determined, unslipping, unwavering, unyielding 11 established, partnership, substantial, substantive, well-founded 13 establishment

firmament: sky 7 heavens 8 empyrean

firmly fixed: 6 rooted, stable

firmness: 4 iron 7 courage, resolve 8 solidity, strength, tenacity 9 constancy, stability 10 immobility, steadiness 11 consistency 13 determination 15 indissolubility

firn: ice 4 neve, snow

first: 4 erst, head, high, main 5 alpha, chief, forme, nieve, prime 6 primal, primus **7** highest, initial, leading, primary **8** earliest, foremost, original **9** primitive, principal **10** aboriginal, primordial

appearance: **5** debut **8** premiere

firstborn: **4** heir **5** eigne **6** eldest

first class: **5** prime **9** excellent, topdrawer **10** first-cabin

first-rate: **4** A-one, good, jake **5** prime **6** tiptop **7** skookum **8** clipping, top-notch **9** admirable, excellent

firth: **4** kyle **5** frith, inlet **7** coppice, estuary

Firth of Clyde island: **4** Bute

fiscal: **8** monetary **9** financial

fiscus: **8** treasury

fish: net **4** cast, quab **5** angle, drail, seine, troll **7** poisson(F.)

Alaska: **6** iconnu

ascending river from sea: **7** anadrom

Atlantic Coast: **4** opah, pogy **6** bunker, salema **7** alewife, bugfish, bughead, fatback, oldwife **8** bonyfish, menhaden **9** greentail **10** mossbunker

Australian: **4** mado **6** groper **7** grouper

bait: **5** killy **9** killifish

barbed tail: **8** stingray **9** stingaree

California: **4** rena **5** reina **6** rasher **8** bocaccio **9** garibaldi

carangoid: **4** scad **5** jurel

carp: id; ide, orf

catfish: **6** hassar **9** sheatfish

caviar-yielding: **7** sterlet **8** sturgeon

cod: bib **4** cusk, hake, ling **5** torsk **6** gadoid **7** bacalao, beardie

colorful: **4** opah

cyprinoid: id; ide **4** dace

devil: ray **5** manta

eel-like: **4** link, opah **6** conger, cuchia **7** eelpout, lamprey

electric: **4** raad **7** torpedo

elongated: eel, gar **6** saurel

European: id; ide, rud **4** boce, dace, rudd, spet **5** alose, bleak, bream, sprat **6** angler, barbel, braice, meagre, plaice **7** gudgeon, lavaret, picarel

female: **4** raun **7** henfish

flat: dab, ray **4** butt, dace, sole **5** bream, fluke, skate **6** plaice, turbot **7** halibut, sanddab, sunfish, torpedo **8** flounder

Florida: **5** crunt **6** atinga, salema **7** burfish, tomtate **8** burrfish

food: cod, eel, gar, iki, sey **4** bass, boga, carp, haik, hake, scup, shad, sole, stew, tile, tuna **5** bolti, cisco, hilsa, jurel, siera, skate, smelt, trout **6** baleen, groupa, hilsah, mullet, pompon, salema, salmon, tautog, wahoo, weever, wrasse **7** alewife, escolar, garlopa, halibut, herring, pompano, pompoon, sardine, snapper **8** mackerel, sea trout **9** barracuda **10** barracouta

freshwater: id; gar, ide, orf **4** bass, carp,

chub, dace, orfe, pike, rudd **5** bream, loach, roach, tench **6** darter, redeye, sucker **7** crappie, mooneye

game: **4** bass, cero, pike, tuna **5** perch, trout **6** grilse, marlin, salmon, tarpon **8** grayling **9** swordfish

grunt: **5** ronco **10** bluestripe

Hawaiian: aku **4** ulua **5** akule, lania

herring: **4** shad, brit **5** sprat, sprot **7** alewife **8** pilchard

Japanese: tai, ayu

kind of: cat, cod, dab, eel, gar, ide, orf **4** bass, carp, chub, dace, dorn, hake, hiku, jocu, lant, lija, ling, mado, masu, meat, mero, mola, opah, orfe, pega, peto, pike, pogy, pout, rena, roud, rudd, ruff, scad, scup, shad, sier, skil, sole, spot, spet, tope, ulua **5** bream, lance, midge, otter, perch, pogie, porgy, prane, roach, ruffe, scrod, seine, skate, smelt, trout, umbra, wahoo **6** barbel, caribe, launce, mullet, porgie, sauger, saurel, shiner, timcod, turbot, wrasse **7** alewife, grunion, haddock, machete, pegador, pintado, piranha, poisson **8** gourhead, hardhead, pilchard, sturgeon **9** teleostei **10** candlefish

large: **4** cusk, opah **5** chiro, sargo, shark **6** bichir, tarpon **7** escolar, gourami, sennett **8** arapaima, sturgeon **10** blanquillo, maskalonge, maskinonge **11** muskellunge

little: see *small* below

long: eel, gar **7** lamprey

mackerel-like: **4** cero **5** tunny **6** coelho **7** escolar, pintado

Mediterranean: **5** porgy, sargo **6** chivey **9** menominee

nest-building: **5** acara **11** stickleback

New England: **4** hake

New Zealand: ihi **5** hikus

newly hatched: fry

Nile: **4** erse **5** saide

olive green: **7** lutfisk **8** ludefisk

one-horned: **9** monoceros

parasitic: **6** remora

pert. to: **7** piscine **8** ichthyic **9** piscatory

pike: gar **4** lude

pilot: **6** romero

raw: **7** sashimi

ray-like: **5** skate

river: **8** arapaima **10** barramunda

rock: **4** rena **5** reina **8** buccaina

scaleless: **9** alepidote

serpentine: eel

shark-eating: som **4** pega **7** catfish

shell: **7** abalone

small: fry, ide, ihi **4** brit, dace, goby, spet **5** saury, sprat **6** blenny, cunner, limpet, minnow, riggle, sennet, shiner **7** sardine **8** halfbeak, seahorse, spearing

small bait: **5** killy **9** killfish

South American: 4 gogy, mapo 5 acara 6 acoupa, aimara, almara, caribe

sparoid: tai 5 porgy, sargo

spear-snouted: gar

star: 7 asteria

sucking: 6 remora

teleost: eel 6 iniomi

toad: 4 sapo 6 slimer

toothed: 7 piranha

total haul: 4 mess 5 catch

tree-climbing: 6 anabas

tropical: 8 coachman

tunny: 4 tuna

voracious: 4 pike 5 shark 6 caribe 9 barracuda

West Indies: 4 Boga, cero, sier 5 chopa 7 Blanco 7 guapena 12 walleyed pike

young: fry 4 parr 6 alevin

fish basket: pot 4 caul 5 creel, slath

fish gig: 5 spear

fish handler: 4 icer

fish hawk: 6 osprey

fish hide: 7 eelskin

fish limb: fin

fish peddler: 6 ripier, ripper 7 rippier

fish pole: pew

fish preserve: 6 warren

fish relish: 7 botargo

fish roe: 6 caviar 7 caviare

fish sauce: 4 alec 5 garum

fish spear: gig 7 trident

fish trap: 4 coop, fyke, weel, weir 5 willy 6 eelpot

fisher: 5 eeler, pecan 6 seiner, wejack 7 trawler, troller

fisherman: 5 eeler 6 angler, seiner 7 prawner, trawler 8 peterman, piscator 9 harpooner 11 Izaak Walton

fishery: 7 piscary 9 piscation

fishhook: gig 5 angle, Kirby 6 Sproat 7 Kendall 8 Aberdeen, barbless, Carlisle, limerick

feathered: fly 5 sedge 9 hackle

fishing duck: 9 merganser

fishing gear: lam, rod, tew 4 cork, flew, flue, gaff, gimp, hook, line, reel, trot 5 cadar, cader, float, sedge, seine, snell, shood 8 trotline

fishing ground: 4 haaf

fishing vessel: 5 smack 6 seiner 7 trawler

fishlike: 8 ichthyic

fishline: 5 snell 7 boulter

fishmonger: 8 pessoner

fishnet: 4 bunt 5 seine, trawl 6 sagene

fishnet line: 5 meter

fishnet mender: 8 beatster

fishpond: 7 piscina

fishwife: 9 buttwoman

fishy: 4 dull 6 vacant 10 improbable, lusterless, suspicious, unreliable 11 extravagant

fissile rock: 5 shale

fission: 8 breaking, cleavage, cleaving 9 splitting 12 reproduction

fissure: gap 4 chap, cone, flaw, gool, leak, lode, rent, rift, rima, rime, seam, vein, vent 5 break, chasm, chine, chink, cleft, crack 6 cleave, cranny, divide, lesion 7 blemish, crevice, opening 8 aperture, cleavage, coloboma, crevasse, quebrada

fissured: 6 rimate 7 fissate, rimosed

fist: job 4 nave 5 grasp, nieve 6 clench, clutch, daddle, effort, strike 7 attempt 8 puffball, tightwad 11 handwriting

fistic: 10 pugilistic

fisticuffs: 4 ring 6 boxing 8 pugilism 13 prizefighting

fistula: 4 pipe, reed, tube 5 sinus 6 cavity

fit: apt, fay, gee, pan, rig 4 able, ague, good, hard, meet, ripe, suit, well, whim 5 adapt, adept, besit, chink, fancy, ictus, ready, right, spasm 6 adjust, attack, become, behove, besort, go with, habile, heppen, proper, seemly, stroke, strong, suited 7 adapted, behoove, capable, condign, conform, correct, healthy, prepare, qualify, tantrum 8 adequate, apoplexy, becoming, dovetail, eligible, glooming, idoneous(L.), outbreak, paroxysm, passable, suitable, syncopes 9 befitting, competent, congruous, convenable, opportune, pertinent, qualified 10 applicable, commodious, correspond, convenient, go together 11 accommodate, appropriate

out: 6 outfit 7 habille, prepare 9 equipment

together: fay 4 mesh, nest 5 panel 8 dovetail

fitful: 4 gery 7 cursory, flighty 8 restless, unstable, variable 9 impulsive, irregular, spasmodic, uncertain 10 capricious, convulsive 12 intermittent

fitly: pat 4 duly 6 gladly, meetly 7 happily 8 properly, suitably

fitness: 7 aptness, decency, decorum, dignity 8 aptitude, capacity, justness 9 rectitude 10 competence 11 suitability

fitout: 6 outfit 9 equipment

fitted: apt 4 able 6 suited 7 adapted 8 adjusted 9 qualified 10 convenient

for digging: 7 fodient, laniary

fitting: apt, due, pat 4 meet 5 happy 6 become, proper, seemly 8 decorous, graceful, suitable 9 befitting 10 adjustment, answerable, habiliment 11 appropriate

five: 4 cinq(F.), funf(G.) 6 cinque(It.) 7 epsilon(Gr.), quinque(L.)

group of: 6 pentad

five-dollar bill: "V"; fin, vee

five-finger: 4 fish 5 oxlip, plant 10 cinquefoil

Five Nations: 7 Cayugas, Mohawks, Oneidas, Senecas 9 Onondagas

founder: 8 Hiawatha

five-year period: 6 pentad 7 lustrum

fivefold: 9 quintuple

fix: peg, pin, set 4 glue, mend, moor, nail, seal 5 affix, allot, found, imbed, limit, tryst 6 adjust, anchor, arrest, assign, assize, attach, buy off, cement, clinch, define, fasten, ficche, freeze, make up, repair, revamp, settle, temper 7 appoint, arrange, confirm, delimit, dilemma, impress, imprint, prepare, station 8 renovate, transfix 9 determine, establish, stabilize 10 constitute 11 predicament, recondition, reconstruct 13 embarrassment

firmly: set 4 moor 5 brace, grave, imbed, stamp 6 anchor, cement, enroot 7 engraff

fixed: pat, set 4 fast, firm 5 siker, staid 6 frozen, intent, mended, sicker, stable 7 certain, dormant, settled, statary 8 arranged, attached, constant, definite, explicit, fastened, immobile, moveless, resolute, stubborn 9 immovable, indelible, inerratic, permanent 10 stationary 12 determinable, refrigerated

amount: 4 rate 6 ration 7 stipend 10 remittance

star: 4 Vega

fixer: 8 handyman

fixture: 5 annex 7 bracket, shelves 8 counters, shelving 10 furnishing

fizgig: 9 fireworks, whirligig

fizzle: 4 fuss 6 barney 7 failure, flivver, hissing 9 agitation

flabby: lax 4 fozy, lash, limp, weak 5 frush 6 feeble 7 flaccid

flaccid: 4 limp 6 flabby, flaggy 8 yielding

flabellate: 9 fan-shaped

flack: 4 blow, flap 5 throb 6 stroke 7 flutter

flag: fag, sag, sod 4 fail, fane, pine, tire, turf, waif, wilt 5 droop, woman 6 banner, colors, ensign, flower, pennon, signal 7 ancient, cattail, decline, drapeau, pennant 8 banderol, brattach, languish, standard, streamer, vexillum 9 banderole, flagstone, fourpence

kind of: 5 Roger 6 burgee, colors, danger, ensign, fanion, guidon, muleta 7 calamus, curtain, pennant 8 banderol, brattach, masthead, standard, streamer, vexillum 9 banderole, blackjack 10 Jolly Roger

flagellants: 4 albi

flagellate: 4 beat, flog, lash, whip 5 throw 6 thrash 7 flutter, scourge

flagellum: 4 whip 5 shoot 6 runner 7 scourge

flageolet: 4 pipe 6 zufolo 7 basaree, zuffolo

Hindu: 7 basaree

flagging: 4 weak 7 languid 10 spiritless

flagitious: 6 rotten, sinful, wicked 7 corrupt, heinous 8 criminal, flagrant, grievous 10 scandalous, villainous

flagon: cup, mug 5 stoup 6 bottle, vessel 7 flacket

flagrant: bad 4 rank 5 gross 6 odious, wanton, wicked 7 glaring, hateful, heinous, scarlet, violent 8 shameful 9 abandoned, atrocious, egregious, monstrous, nefarious, notorious 10 flagitious, outrageous, profligate, villainous

flagstone: 5 shale, slate

flagstone layer: 5 paver

flail: 4 beat, flog, whip 6 thrash, thresh

part: 7 swingle

flair: ray 4 bent, odor 5 skate, smell, taste 6 talent 7 leaning 8 aptitude 11 discernment

flak: 9 criticism 10 opposition

flake: nut 4 chip, film, flaw, rack, snow 5 fleck, flock, scale, strip 6 hurdle, lamina, paling 7 flaught 8 fragment 9 screwball

flaky: 5 scaly 7 laminar 8 laminose

flam: 4 whim 5 cheat, false, freak, trick 6 cajole, humbug, untrue 7 deceive, pretext, rubbish 8 drumbeat, illusory, nonsense, pretense 9 deception, deceptive, falsehood

flambeau: 5 torch 6 kettle 11 candlestick

flamboyant: 5 showy, swank 6 florid, ornate 7 flaming 9 flamelike 10 extravagant 11 resplendent

flame: 4 beau, fire, glow 5 ardor, blaze, flare, flash, glare, gleed, light 7 burning 9 affection 10 brightness, brilliance, sweetheart

fire without: 4 punk

movement: 4 dart, lick

flaming: 5 afire, fiery, vivid 6 ardent, flambe 7 blazing, burning, flaring 9 brilliant, consuming, flamelike 10 flamboyant, passionate 12 illuminating

Flanders capital: 5 Ghent

flanerie: 6 stroll 7 loafing 8 idleness 9 aimlessly, strolling 10 pillowcase

flaneur: 6 loafer 7 trifler

flank: 4 leer, side 5 thigh 6 border

flannel: 4 lana 6 stamin

flap: rob, tab, tag, wap 4 clap, flip, fuss, loma, slam, slap, waff 5 alarm, flack, fiaff, flipe, lapel, skirt 6 bangle, faffle, lappet, strike, tongue 7 aileron, blinder, flounce, flutter, swindle 8 hang down 9 appendage, operculum 10 epiglottis

furnished with: 5 lobed

flapper: 7 snicket 9 backfisch 10 backfische

flare: 4 bell, flue 5 blaze, flame, flash, fleck, fusee, light, torch 6 signal, spread

7 flicker 8 outburst 10 illuminate 11 ostentation

flaring: 4 bell, flue 5 evase(F.), gaudy 7 flaming, glaring 8 dazzling

flash: 4 pool, rush 5 blash, blaze, burst, flare, flame, fluff, glaik, gleam, glent, glint, marsh, spark 6 bottle, fillip, glance 7 fouldre, glimmer, glimpse, glisten, glitter, instant, shimmer, sparkle 11 coruscation, fulguration, scintillate

flashing: 6 bright, flashy 7 forward 8 meteoric, snapping 9 fulgurant, fulgurous

flashy: gay 4 flat, gaud, loud 5 fiery, gaudy, showy 6 frothy, garish, ornate, slangy, sporty 7 insipid, tinhorn 8 dazzling, vehement 9 impetuous 10 spiritless

flask: 4 olpe 5 betty, bulge, girba 6 bottle, fiasco, flacon, guttus 7 ampulla, canteen, matrass 8 cucurbit 9 aryballos

flask-shaped: 10 lageniform

flat: 4 dead, dull, even, fade, plat, tame 5 abode, aflat, banal, bland, blunt, level, molle, plane, prone, vapid 6 boring, dreary, flashy 7 decided, insipid, platoid, prosaic, uniform 8 directly, dwelling, lifeless, unbroken 9 apartment, downright, prostrate, tasteless 10 homaloidal, horizontal, monotonous, unanimated 12 unmistakable 13 uninteresting

flat-nosed: 6 simous

flatboat: ark 4 scow 5 barge

flatfish: dab, ray 4 butt, dace, sole 5 bream, fluke 6 acedia, plaice, turbot 7 sanddab, sunfish, torpedo 8 flounder

flatiron: 7 sadiron

flatten: 4 even 5 level 6 deject, smooth 7 depress 8 compress, dispirit 9 prostrate 10 complanate, discourage, dishearten

flattened: 6 oblate 7 planate

flatter: 4 bull, claw, coax, fage, fume, palp 5 charm, float, gloze, honey, smalm 6 become, cajole, fickle, fleech, fraise, glaver, smooge, soothe 7 adulate, beguile, blarney, flether, flutter, wheedle 8 blandish, bootlick, butter up, collogue 10 compliment, ingratiate

flatterer: 6 cogger, glozer 7 soother 8 courtier 9 sycophant 10 assentator, greasehorn

flattering: 7 buttery, candied 11 assentatory

flattery: 4 bull, bunk 5 fraik, gloze, salve, taffy 6 butter, fleech 7 blarney, fawning, flether, palaver 8 cajolery 9 adulation 10 compliment 14 obsequiousness

flatulent: 5 gassy, windy 6 turgid 7 pompous, ventose 8 inflated 9 bombastic

flaunt: 4 bosh, wave 5 boast, vaunt 6 parade, trapes 7 display, flutter, traipse 8 brandish

flavor: 4 gamy, odor, rasa, salt, tang, zest 5 aroma, devil, sapid, sapor, sauce, savor, scent, taste, tinge 6 asarum, relish, season 7 perfume 8 hautgout, piquancy 9 fragrance

flavorable: 5 sapid, sipid 6 savory 9 palatable

flavoring material: 4 mint, sage 6 orgeat 7 cumarin 8 coumarin, cumarone 9 coumarone

flavorless: 5 stale, vapid 9 tasteless

flaw: fib, gap, lie, mar 4 gall, hole, rase, rift, spot, wind 5 brack, cleft, crack, craze, fault, flake 6 breach, defect 7 blemish, default, fissure, nullify, violate, whitlow 8 fracture, fragment, gendarme 10 intoxicate 12 imperfection

flawless: 5 sound 7 perfect 9 faultless

flax: pob, tow 4 card, harl, lint 5 hards, hurds, linen, linin, pouce 6 bobbin

filament: 4 harl

holder: 7 distaff

prepare: ret

refuse: pob

remove seed: 6 ribble

tool: 7 hatchel, swingle

flaxen: 5 blond, straw 6 golden

flaxen-haired: 4 bawn

flaxseed: 7 linseed

flay: 4 skin 5 slash, strip 6 assail, attack, fleece 7 censure, pillage, reprove 9 excoriate 11 decorticate

flea: 6 chigoe 10 sandhopper

genus: 5 pulex

fleck: fat 4 flea, flit, spot, tuft 5 flake, flare 6 dapple, streak, stripe 7 flutter, speckle 8 particle 9 variegate

fledgling, fledgeling: 5 squab

flee: fly, lam, run 4 bolt, fleg, loup, shun 5 elude, speed 6 escape, vanish 7 abandon, abscond, forsake 8 liberate 9 disappear, skedaddle

fleece: abb, jib, teg 4 bilk, fell, flay, gaff, wool 5 cheat, fleck, pluck, shear 6 toison 7 despoil

fleecy: 5 wooly 6 linten, woolly

fleeing: 7 fugient 8 fugitive

fleer: 4 gibe, grin, jeer, leer, mock 5 flout, laugh, scoff, sneer, taunt 7 grimace 8 derision

fleet: bay 4 fast, flit, navy, sail, skim, swim 5 creek, drain, drift, evand, float, flote, hasty, inlet, quick, rapid, swift 6 abound, argosy, armada, hasten, nimble, speedy 7 estuary 8 flotilla 10 evanescent, transitory

fleeting: 5 brief 6 caduke, volage 7 flighty, passing 8 caducous, fugitive, volatile 9 ephemeral, fugacious, transient **10** evanescent, short-lived, transitory **11** impermanent

Flemish: *geographer:* **8** Mercator

painter: **5** Bouts **6** Mabuse, Massys, Rubens **7** Gossart, Memling, Patinir, van Eyck **8** Breughel, Brueghel, Gossaert, van Cleve **12** van der Weyden

flesh: kin **4** body, meat, race **5** stock **6** family, muscle **7** kindred, mankind **8** humanity **9** mortality **10** sensuality

appendage: **5** palpi(pl.) **6** palpus

colored mineral: **9** sarcoline

formation: **8** sarcosis

kind of: **5** brawn **6** chevon, chiver **7** carrion

pert. to: **7** sarcoid

resembling: **7** sarcoid

fleshbrush: **7** strigil

flesh-eating: **11** carnivorous

fleshy: fat **5** beefy, gross, human, obese, plump, pulpy, stout **6** animal, bodily, brawny, carnal **9** corpulent

fruit: **4** pear, pome **5** berry, drupe, melon **6** tomato

fleur-de-lis: lis, lys **4** iris, liss, luce, lucy

fleuret: **4** epee **5** sword **6** flower

flex: **4** bend **5** tense

flexible: **4** limp, lush, soft **5** buxom, lithe, withy **6** limber, pliant, supple **7** ductile, elastic, flexile, lissome, plastic, pliable, springy, willowy **8** cheverel, cheveril, yielding **9** tractable, versatile **10** manageable

shoot: **4** bine

tube: **4** hose

flexuous: **5** snaky **6** zigzag **7** relaxed, sinuous, winding **8** softened, tortuous, wavering **9** adaptable **10** circuitous, flickering, serpentine, undulating

flexure: **4** bend, bent, curl, fold **5** curve

flick (see also **motion picture**): cut, hit **4** blow, flip, flit, snap, toss, whip **5** flisk, throw **6** flitch, propel **7** flutter

flicker: **4** fail, flit **5** flare, flunk, waver **6** fitter, shiver, yucker **7** blinter, flimmer, flitter, flutter, tremble, twinkle **8** flichter **9** flaughter, palpitate **10** woodpecker

flickering: **7** flabent, lambent **8** flexuous, unsteady

flier: ace **5** pilot **6** airman **7** aviator **8** operator

female: **8** aviatrix **9** aviatress, aviatrice

flight: hop, lam **4** bolt, rout **5** chevy, chivy, flock, floor, scrap, story, volee **6** chivvy, exodus, hegira, hejira **7** flaught, getaway, migrate, mission, scamper **8** stampede, swarming **9** agitation, migration **12** perturbation

in: **8** on the lam

of fancy: **5** sally

of steps: **4** rise **5** stoop **6** perron

of wild fowl: **5** skein

pert. to: **5** volar

put to: **4** rout

flightiness: **9** lightness

flightless bird: emu, moa **4** dodo, kiwi, weka **7** ostrich, penguin

flighty: **5** barmy, giddy, swift **6** fitful, nimshi, volage, whisky **7** foolish, giggish **8** fleeting, freakish **9** transient **10** capricious **11** harum-scarum **13** shuttlewitted

flim-flam: fob **5** freak, trick **6** humbug, tricky, trifle **7** swindle **8** nonsense, trifling **9** deception, deceptive **11** nonsensical

flimmer: **7** flicker, glimmer

flimsy: **4** limp, vain, weak **5** frail, gaudy **6** feeble, paltry, sleazy, slight **7** shallow, tenuous **10** gossamered **11** superficial **13** insubstantial, unsubstantial

flinch: **4** funk, game **5** feign, start, wince **6** blench, falter, flense, recoil, shrink

fling: **4** buzz, cast, dart, dash, ding, emit, fleg, gibe, hurl, kick, toss **5** cheat, dance, flirt, pitch, sling, sneer, throw, whang **6** baffle, effuse, hurtle, plunge, rebuff, spirit **7** flounce, repulse, sarcasm, scatter, swindle **9** overthrow

flint: **5** chert, miser, silex **6** quartz **9** firestone, skinflint

flintlock: **6** musket

flinty: **4** hard **5** cruel **8** obdurate

flip: tap **4** flap, glib, pert, snap, toss, trip **5** flick, flirt, slirt **6** fillip, limber, nimble, pliant, propel **7** journey **10** somersault

flippant: **4** airy, glib **6** fluent, limber, nimble **9** talkative

flipper: arm, fin, paw **4** hand

flip through: **4** scan **6** browse **7** dip into **8** glance at

flirt: tap, toy **4** dart, fike, flip, gibe, jeer, jest, joke, mash, mock, play, toss **5** dally, flick, fling, throw **6** coquet, fillip, lead on, masher, spring, trifle **7** trifler **9** philander

flirtatious: coy **4** arch **10** coquettish

flit: **4** dart, flow, scud **5** fleck, fleet, flick, float, flurr, hover, quick, scoot, swift **6** nimble **7** flicker, flutter, migrate

flitter: rag **5** droop, hover, piece, waver **6** tatter **7** flicker, flutter, shuffle **8** fragment

flittermouse: bat

float: bob, fly, sea **4** buoy, cork, flow, flux, hove, pont, raft, ride, sail, scow, soar, swim, waft, wave **5** balsa, drift, fleet, flood, hover, ladle **6** billow, bobber, bungey, ponton **7** flatter, flotter, pontoon **8** overflow **9** catamaran, negotiate, podoscaph *aloft:* 4 soar

floating: 4 free 5 awash, loose 6 adrift, afloat, flying, natant 7 movable 8 drifting, fluitant, shifting, variable 9 wandering

flocculent: 6 woolly

flock: mob 4 bevy, fold, herd, pack 5 brood, bunch, charm, covey, crowd, drift, drove, flake, fleck, group, sedge, shoal, swarm 6 flight, hirsel 7 company 9 multitude 10 assemblage 11 aggregation

kind of: nid, nye, pod 4 nide, sord 5 covey, sedge, tribe

of geese: 6 gaggle

of lions: 5 pride

pert. to: 6 gregal

flocks (god of): Pan

floe: 4 raft

flog: cat, tan 4 beat, cane, hide, lash, toco, toko, wale, whip 5 birch, excel, fight, flail, linge, quilt, skeeg 6 cotton, larrup, strike, switch, thrash 7 baleise, belabor, scourge, sjambok, surpass, trounce 8 slaister 10 flagellate

flood: sea 4 bore, flow, flux 5 eagre, float, spate 6 deluge, excess 7 debacle, freshet, torrent 8 alluvion, inundate, overflow 9 cataclysm 10 inundation, outpouring 14 superabundance

flooded: 5 awash 6 afloat 10 surrounded

floodgate: 5 hatch 6 sluice

floodlight: 5 klieg

floor: 4 drop, flat 5 level, story 6 defeat, ground, lay low 7 planche 8 bowl over 9 knock down

floor covering: mat, rug 4 tile 5 tapis(Fr.) 6 carpet, planks 8 linoleum, oilcloth

flop: dud 4 bomb, bust, fail, fall, whop 5 lemon, loser 6 fizzle 7 failure

flora: 6 plants 9 florilege 10 vegetation 11 florilegium

flora and fauna: 5 biota

floreate: 5 bloom

Florence: *bridge:* 12 Ponte Vecchio
cathedral: 5 Duomo
coin: 6 florin 7 ruspone
devotees: 4 neri
family: 6 Medici
gallery: 5 Pitti 6 Uffizi
iris: 5 ireos, orris

Florentine (see also Florence): 4 gold 6 finish

floret bract: 5 palea, palet

florid: 5 buxom, fresh, ruddy 6 ornate 7 flowery 8 blooming, rubicund, vigorous 10 figurative, flamboyant, rhetorical 11 embellished, full-blooded

Florida: *capital:* 11 Tallahassee
city: 5 Miami, Ocala, Tampa 7 Key West, Orlando, Palatka, Pompano 8 Sarasota

county: Bay, Lee 4 Dade, Gulf, Lake, Leon, Levy, Polk 5 Pasco
discoverer: 11 Ponce de Leon
key: 4 West 5 Largo 8 Biscayne
motto: 12 In God We Trust
nickname: 8 Sunshine
region: 10 Everglades
state bird: 11 mockingbird
state flower: 13 orange blossom
state tree: 8 palmetto

floss: 5 fluff, skein, waste 6 sleave, stream

flotage: 8 buoyancy

flotilla: 5 fleet

Flotow opera: 6 Martha

flotsam: 6 jetsam 8 driftage, wreckage 9 driftwood

flounce: 4 flap, slam 5 fling, frill 6 ruffle 7 falbala, falbelo 8 flounder, furbelow, struggle

flounder: dab 4 butt, keel, roll, toss 5 bream, fluke, megin 6 grovel, muddle, plaice, turbot, wallow 7 flounce, plounce, stumble, sunfish, topknot, vaagmar, vaagmer 8 flatfish, struggle, vaagmaer

flour: 4 atta, meal 5 clear 6 patent, powder, red dog
bleach: 5 agene
diabetic: 9 aleuronat
maker: 6 miller
sifter: 6 bolter
sprinkle with: 6 dredge
testing device: 11 farinometer
wheat: 4 atta

flourish: 4 boom, brag, grow, riot, rise, show, wave 5 adorn, bloom, boast, cheve, gloss, quirk, vaunt 6 parade, paraph, thrive 7 blossom, display, enlarge, fanfare, prosper, roulade 8 arpeggio, brandish, curlicue, curlycue, increase, ornament 9 embellish 10 decoration 11 ostentation

flourishing: fat 4 frim 5 green, palmy 7 florent 8 thriving 10 prosperous, successful

floury: 4 meal

flout: bob 4 gibe, jeer, mock 5 fleer, flite, flyte, frump, scoff, scorn, scount, sneer, taunt 6 deride, insult, quip at 7 jeering, mockery 8 betongue

flow: ebb, jet, run 4 bore, flit, flux, fuse, gush, hale, lava, lave, melt, pour, roll, shed, sile, teem, well 5 avale, drain, eagre, exude, fleam, float, flood, glide, issue, river, spill, spurt 6 abound, afflux, deluge, recede, stream 7 current, emanate, flutter, meander, spurtle 8 alluvion, inundate 9 streaming 10 menstruate, outpouring 12 menstruation

flower (see also plant): bud 4 best, blow, flag, iris, ixia, pink, posy, rose 5 aster, bloom, elite, lilac, pansy, tulip 6 azalia, crocus, dahlia, orchid, posies(pl.), unfold 7 blethia, blossom, develop, fairest, gentian 8 camellia, choicest, daffodil, freshest, gardenia, geranium, hyacinth, ornament 9 carnation, embellish, gladiolus 10 upper class, upper crust 13 chrysanthemum

appendage: 5 bract
artificial: 7 rosette 8 gloxinia
band: 6 wreath
bell-shaped: 4 lily 5 tulip
blooming once a year: 6 annual
blue: 6 lupine 8 harebell
bud: 5 ament, caper 6 spadix
cluster: 4 cime, cyme 5 ament, bract, umbel 6 corymb, raceme 7 panicle 9 glomerule
of death: 8 asphodel
desert: 6 cactus
extract: 4 atar, otto 5 attar, ottar
fall: 5 aster 6 cosmos
of forgetfulness: 5 lotus
garden: 4 iris, ixia, lily, pink, rose 5 aster, canna, daisy, lilac, pansy, peony, phlox, tulip 6 asalia, olivia, orchid, violet 7 freesia, petunia, verbena 8 bletilla, camellia, daffodil, gloxinia, hyacinth, primrose 9 buttercup, carnation, gladiolus, narcissus 10 heliotrope, ranunculus 11 honeysuckle
goddess: 5 Flora
imaginary: 7 amarant 8 amaranth
large: 5 canna, peony
late-blooming: 5 aster
mass: 8 anthemia
meadow: 5 bluet
modest: 6 violet
obsolete: 5 pense
part: 5 calyx, sepal 6 anther, pistil, stamen 7 nectary, petiole 8 peduncle, perianth, pericarp
passion: 6 maypop
pink: 4 rose 7 rhodora
prickly: 4 burr
purple: 5 lilac, pense
receptacle: 4 vase 5 torus
spring: 4 iris 5 lilac, peony, tulip 7 arbutus 8 hepatica
stand: 7 epergne
stylized: lis
unfading: 7 amarant 8 amaranth
unknown kind: 8 belamour
white: 5 gowan
wild: 4 sage 5 bluet, daisy 6 lupine 7 anemone, arbutus 8 bluebell, hepatica 9 buttercup, innocence
wind: 7 anemone
yellow: 5 daisy, gowan, pense 7 jonquil 8 daffodil, marigold 9 buttercup
flower holder: pot 4 frog, vase 5 lapel
flowering: 7 flowery 8 anthesis, blooming 11 florescence

flowering plant: rue 4 arum 5 avens, calla, canna, orpin, phlox, yucca, zamia 6 azalea, bareta, cosmos, oxalis, spirea, teasel 7 barreta, gentian, lobelia, pavonia, petunia, rhodora, spiraea, tamarix, torenia, waratah 8 acanthus, ageratum, damewort, geranium, gerardia, valerian 9 candytuft, coreopsis, gloxinias, goldenrod, hollyhock, monkshood 10 pulsatilla, snapdragon
flowerless plant: 4 fern, moss 6 lichen 7 acrogen
flowerlike: 7 anthoid
flowerpot: 10 jardiniere
flowery: 6 florid 7 florent 9 flowering 10 figurative, flosculous
flowing: 4 flux 5 fluid, fluor, tidal 6 afflux, fluent 7 copious, current, cursive, emanent, fluxing 9 affluxion, emanation 10 transitive
together: 9 confluent
flu: 6 grippe
flub: 4 muff 5 boner, botch, error 6 bollix, bungle, goof up 7 blunder
fluctuate: 4 sway, vary, veer, wave 5 waver 7 vibrate 8 undulate, unsteady 9 oscillate, vacillate 10 irresolute 12 undetermined
fluctuating: 8 unstable, unsteady
flue: net 4 barb, down, open, pipe, thin 5 flare, fluff, fluke, stack 6 expand, feeble, funnel, sickly, tunnel 7 chimney, flaring, passage, shallow
fluency: 9 eloquence, profusion 10 smoothness
fluent: 4 glib 5 fluid, ready 6 facile, liquid, smooth, stream 7 copious, flowing, fluidic, renable, verbose, voluble 8 eloquent, flippant 9 talkative 12 smoothspoken 13 talkativeness
fluff: nap 4 down, flue, lint, puff 5 flash, floss, whiff
fluffy: 4 soft 5 downy, drunk, fluey, fuzzy 6 linten 8 feathery, unsteady 12 undependable
fluid: ink 5 rasa 6 water 6 fluent, liquid, watery 7 flowing, fluible, fluxile, gaseous 8 floating, fluxible
kind of: gas, ink, oil, sap, tar 4 bile, icor, milk 5 blood, ether, grume, ichor, latex, nerol, plasm, serum 7 acetone, coal oil, naphtha, tearlet 8 gasoline, kerosene
measure: rhe
pert to: 7 humoral
without: 7 aneroid
fluidity unit: rhe
fluke: 4 fish, flue 5 blade 8 flounder
fluky: 8 unsteady 9 uncertain 10 capricious
flume: 4 leat 5 chute, gorge, water 6 ravine, sluice, stream 7 channel

flummox: 4 fail 7 confuse, perplex 8 confound 9 embarrass 10 disconcert

flunk: 4 bust, fail 7 flicker

flunky, flunkey: 4 snob 5 toady 6 cookee 7 footman, servant, steward

flurry: ado 4 gust, stir 5 haste, skirl 6 bother, bustle, scurry, squall 7 confuse, flusker, fluster, flutter, fooster 9 agitation, carfuffle 10 discompose

flush: 4 even, glow, pool, rose 5 blush, elate, rouge, vigor 6 aflush, excite, lavish, mantle, morass, redden, thrill 7 animate 8 abundant, affluent, prodigal, rosiness 9 abounding, encourage 10 prosperous

flushed: red 4 ruby 5 aglow 6 florid 7 scarlet 8 vigorous 10 prosperous

flushing: 8 blushing 9 rubescent

fluster: 5 shake 6 flurry, fuddle, muddle, pother, rattle 7 confuse, flusker, fooster 8 befuddle, flustrum 10 discompose

flute: nay 4 fife 5 crimp 6 flauto, goffer, zufolo 7 chamfer, channel, gauffer, magadis, piccolo, zuffolo 8 flautino

ancient: 5 tibia

Hindu: bin 5 pungi

player: 5 piper 6 aulete 7 flutist, tootler 8 auletris, flautist

stop: 7 ventage

wood for: 5 kokra

fluting: 5 strix 7 gadroon, godroon, strigil 10 gadroonage, godroonage

flux: 4 flow, fuse, melt 5 float, flood, resin, rosin, smear, smelt 6 fusion, stream 7 euripus, flowing, outflow

fly: bee, hop 4 flee, fleg, flit, leap, melt, scud, soar, solo, whir, whiz, wing 5 agile, alert, float, midge, pilot, quick, sharp, whirr 6 aviate, insect, nimble, spring, vanish 7 avigate, avolate, knowing 8 coachman 9 disappear

African: 4 zimb 5 zebub 6 tsetse

enemy: 6 spider

fishing: bee 4 lure 5 nymph, sedge 6 Cahill 7 Babcock, grannom, huzard 8 coachman, Ferguson, hare's ear 9 alexandra 10 Barrington

genus: 5 Dacus

kind of: bee, bot, fag, mau, plu 4 gnat, kivu, zimb 5 alder, cadew, horse, midge, whame 6 breeze, gadfly, seroot, tsetse 7 butcher, collier, tachina 8 housefly 9 shoemaker 10 bluebottle 11 caterpillar, trichoptera

small: 4 gnat 5 midge

two-winged: 8 dipteron

flyaway: 5 giddy 7 flighty 8 restless 12 unrestrained

flybane: 12 cinnamonroot

flyblow: 5 larva

fly-by-night: 6 unsure 7 dubious 10 unreliable 12 undependable 13 untrustworthy

flycatcher: 4 tody 5 pewee 6 phoebe, yetapa 7 fielder, grignet, grinder

flyer: ace 5 pilot 7 Pegasus 8 aeronaut, operator

flying: 5 awing 6 flight, volant, waving 8 aviation, floating 9 fugacious

pert to: 7 aviatic

flying adder: 9 dragonfly

flying boat: 8 seaplane 9 amphibian

flying body: 6 meteor

flying device: 4 kite 6 glider

Flying Dutchman heroine: 5 Senta

flying expert: ace

flying fish: 5 saury 7 gurnard

flying machine: 5 plane 8 aerostat 9 gyroplane 10 helicopter

flying mammal: bat

flying ship: 5 blimp 7 aeronat, biplane 8 airplane 9 amphibian, dirigible, monoplane 10 helicopter

Fo: 6 Buddha

foal: 4 colt 5 filly

foam: fob, sud 4 fume, head, scud, scum 5 frost, froth, spume, yeast 6 bubble, freath, lather 7 blubber

foaming: 4 nappy 6 yeasty 7 spumous

foamy: 5 barmy, spumy, sudsy 6 frothy

fob: 4 buck, foam 5 cheat, froth, trick 6 impose, pocket 8 flimflam, imposter, ornament, swindler

focal: 7 central, centric, nuclear, nucleus 13 concentrative

focus: 4 foci(pl.) 5 point, train 6 center, hearth 8 converge, polestar 9 fireplace 11 concentrate, nerve center

fodder: hay 4 feed, food, vert 5 mange 6 forage, silage 9 provender

kind of: ers, oat, rye 4 corn, rape 5 batad, maize, vetch, wheat 6 barley, clover, millet 7 alfalfa 8 deerweed 11 bitter vetch

storing place: 4 silo 5 bakie 6 haymow, silage 8 ensilage

trough for: 6 manger

foe: 5 enemy, fiend, rival 7 adverse, hostile, opposer, saracen 8 opponent 9 adversary, ill-wisher 10 antagonist

fog: dag, rag 4 damp, daze, haar, haze, mist, moke, moss, murk, prig, roke, smog 5 bedim, brume, cloud, grass, vapor 6 nebula, salmon, stupor 7 obscure, pogonip 8 bewilder, moisture 10 aftergrass 12 bewilderment

foggy: dim 4 dull, hazy, moky, roky 5 dense, dirty, misky, misty, murky, rooky 6 cloudy, marshy 7 brumous, muddled, obscure 8 confused, nubilous 9 beclouded

foghorn: 5 siren

fogy: 6 foozle

foible: fad 4 weak 5 fault, ferly 6 feeble 7 frailty 8 weakness 9 infirmity 11 shortcoming 12 imperfection

foil: 4 balk, soil, tain 5 blade, blunt, elude, evade, stain, stump, sword, track, trail 6 baffle, blench, boggle, defeat, defile, outwit, stigma, stooge, thwart 7 beguile, failure, pollute, repulse, impede 8 disgrace 9 frustrate, overthrow 11 frustration

foist: 4 cask, dupe, gull 5 barge, cheat, fudge, fusty 6 galley, suborn 7 palm off, swindle 8 brackish, hoodwink 9 rascality 11 interpolate

fold: bow, lap, pen, ply, wap 4 bend, cote, fail, flap, furl, loop, plie, ruga, tuck 5 clasp, crimp, drape, flipe, flock, layer, plait, pleat, plica, prank, sinus, yield 6 bought, crease, double, hurdle, infold, plight, pucker, rimple 7 crumple, embrace, flexure, placate, plicate 8 surround 9 enclosure, overthrow, plicature
kind of: 4 loop 5 bight, lapel, plica, quire 6 bought, dewlap, octavo 7 plicate 9 replicate
of skin: 4 ruga 5 plica

folded: 4 shut 6 closed 7 plicate

folder: 5 cover, folio 6 binder 7 leaflet 8 pamphlet

folderol, falderal: 8 nonsense

foliage: 6 leaves 7 leafage

foliated: 5 lobed 7 spathic

folio: fo 4 case, leaf, page

folk: 6 daoine, people 7 friends 9 intimates, relatives

folklore: 4 myth 6 custom, history, legend 9 tradition 12 superstition
genie of: 7 sandman

folks: 6 people

folkway: mos 5 mores(pl.) 6 custom 7 pattern

folletto: imp 5 fairy 6 goblin, spirit

follicle: sac, 5 crypt

follow: ape, dog, see, tag 4 copy, hunt, next, seek, shag, tail 5 adopt, after, chase, ensue, snake, spoor, trace, track, trail 6 attend, pursue, result, shadow 7 imitate, observe, replace, succeed 8 practice, supplant 9 accompany, alternate, supervene 10 comprehend, understand

follow behind: dog, lag, tag 4 heel, hunt, nose, tail 5 hound, trace 6 shadow, trail 7 draggle 9 supervene

follower: fan, ist, ite, son 4 aper, beau, zany 5 gilly 6 bildar, ensuer, gillie, gudget, sequel, sulter, votary 7 devotee, grifter, pursuer, retinue, spaniel 8 adherent, disciple, henchman, partisan, retainer, servitor 9 attendant, caudatory, cuadrilla, dependent, satellite, successor 10 aficionado, sweetheart 11 cuadrillero

following: 4 next, sect 5 after, below, suant, train 6 sequel 7 devotee, ensuing, sequent 8 business, trailing, voca-

tion 9 clientele, supporter 10 posthumous, profession, sequential, subsequent, succeeding, successive 12 subsequent to
exact words: 6 literal
laws of arithmetical algebra: 6 scalor

follow-up: 6 sequel

folly: sin 4 whim 6 betise, dotage, lunacy 7 daffery, daffing, foolery, foppery, madness, mistake 8 fondness, idleness, lewdness, morology, nonsense, rashness 9 silliness 10 imprudence, wantonness 11 foolishness, witlessness 12 indiscretion

foment: 4 abet, brew, spur 5 rouse, stupe 6 arouse, excite, incite 7 agitate, ferment, provoke 9 encourage, instigate

fond: tid 4 dear, dote, fain, fool, fund, warm, weak 5 silly, stock, store 6 ardent, befool, caress, dearly, doting, loving, simple, tender 7 amatory, amorous, beguile, browden, devoted, foolish, insipid 8 desirous, enamored, sanguine, trifling, uxorious 9 credulous, enamoured, indulgent, savorless 10 curcuddoch, infatuated, passionate 12 affectionate
of dainties: 6 friand 9 friandise
of drink: 8 bibulous
of hunting: 7 venatic

fonda: inn 5 hotel

fondle: hug, pet 4 baby, coax, love, neck, waly 5 clasp, daunt, wally 6 caress, cocker, coddle, cosset, dandle, pamper, stroke 7 cherish, embrace 8 blandish, canoodle

fondly: 6 dearly 7 foolish 8 tenderly 9 foolishly 14 affectionately

fondness: gra 4 love 5 folly, taste 8 dearness, weakness 9 affection 10 attachment, tenderness 11 affectation, foolishness 12 predilection 15 Philotherianism

fondu: 6 cheese 7 souffle

fons: 6 origin, source 8 fountain

font: 4 pila 5 basin 6 source, spring 7 piscina 8 delubrum, fountain 10 aspersoria (pl.) 11 aspersorium

fontal: 6 source 8 original 9 baptismal

food: bit, pap 4 bite, cate, chow, diet, eats, fare, farm, gear, grub, meat, peck, prog 5 bread, broma, cheer, foray, scaff, tripe 6 fodder, foster, morsel, viands, wraith 7 aliment, edibles, handout, pabulum, vittles 8 flummery, grubbery, victuals 9 nutriment, provender 10 provisions, sustenance 11 comestibles, nourishment
animal: 4 feed 5 grain, grass 6 fodder, forage 9 provender
choice: 4 cake 6 pastry
container: jar 4 bowl, dish, olla 5 crock, plate 6 saucer

craving for: 4 pica 7 bulimia

devotee: 7 epicure, gourmet

dislike of: 6 asitia 9 sitomania 10 cibophobia

dressing: 5 sauce

element: 6 gluten 7 protein, vitamin

farinaceous: 4 sago

garnish: 5 sauce

heavenly: 5 manna

invalid: pap 5 broth

kind of: pap, poi, sop 4 ants, chum, crum, mess, mush, sago 5 acate, balut, bread, broma, cates, gruel, jelly, manna, puree, salep, scaff, souse, tripe 6 cagmag, cereal, farina, forage, hominy, vivres 7 abalone, boscage, pemican, tapioca 8 ambrosia, aperient, beebread, pemmican 9 aperitive, rechauffe 10 rechauffee

list: 4 diet, menu 5 carte

of gods: 6 amrita 7 amreeta 8 ambrosia

pert. to: 8 cibarial 9 cibarious

protein: 4 fish, meat 6 cheese

provision of: 4 mess 6 ration 8 catering

scarcity: 6 famine

seller: 6 grocer 7 viander

semidigested: 5 chyme

soft: pap

storage pit: 4 cist

southern: 4 okra, pone 5 gumbo 6 hominy 7 hoecake 11 chitterling

special dish: 4 hogo, olla, stew 5 bredi, pilaf, pilau, pilaw, pizza 6 haslet, hominy, majoon, omelet, panada, pilaff, ragout, salmis, scouse, sundae, zimmis 7 chowder, custard, rarebit, ravioli, souffle 8 cabeliau, hautgout, omelette, sillabub, sukiyaki 9 cabilliau, colcannon, galantine, succotash 10 salmagundi, shishkebab

fool: ass, cod, cow, fop, fox, kid, mug, oaf, sap 4 boob, butt, dolt, dupe, gowk, gull, hoax, jape, jest, joke, simp, zany 5 bluff, clown, dunce, goose, idiot, moron, ninny, noddy, silly, spoof, trick 6 cuckoo, delude, dotard, gammon, jester, motley, nitwit, outwit, take in, tamper 7 buffoon, coxcomb, deceive, mislead, witling 8 hoodwink, imbecile, surprise 9 blockhead, simpleton 10 nincompoop

around: 4 play 5 cut up, dally 6 trifle 7 have fun, toy with, skylark 8 lallygag 9 philander, waste time

foolable: 5 naive 8 gullible

foolhardy: 4 rash 8 headlong, reckless 11 adventurous 12 presumptuous

foolish: mad 4 daft, rash, zany 5 anile, barmy, batty, buggy, crazy, dizzy, goofy, goosy, inane, inept, silly 6 absurd, harish, simple, stupid, unwise 7 asinine, fatuous, flighty, foppish, gullish, idiotic, puerile, witless 8 anserine, cockeyed, heedless 9 brainless, childlike, desipient, doddering, imprudent, insensate, ludicrous, senseless 10 half-witted, indiscreet, irrational 11 nonsensical 12 preposterous

foolishness: 5 folly 6 levity 9 absurdity, horseplay, stupidity 10 insipience

foolproof: 4 sure 7 certain 8 risk free 10 infallible

fool's gold: 6 pyrite

fool's paradise: 7 chimera 8 illusion

fool's stitch: 6 tricot

foot: dog, pes 4 base 5 meter, speed 6 bottom, pay for, tootsy, trilby 7 measure 9 extremity

animal: pad, paw 4 hoof 7 fetlock, pastern

armor: 8 solleret

lever: 5 pedal 7 treadle

metric: 4 iamb 5 arsis, paeon 6 dactyl, iambus 7 anapest, pyrrhic, spondee, triseme, trochee 8 bacchius, epitrite, molossus, tribrach

pain 8 talalgia

part: toe 4 arch, heel, sole 6 instep, thenar

pert. to: 5 pedal, podal 6 pedate

foot bone: 6 cuboid, tarsus 7 phalanx 8 scaphoid 10 astragulus, metatarsus

foot doctor: 10 podiatrist 11 chiropodist

foot soldier: 4 kern(Sc.), peon 6 Zouave 7 dogface 8 doughboy 11 infantryman

football: 5 rugby 6 rugger, soccer 7 pigskin

famous coach: 4 Yost 5 Brown, Halas, Jones, Leahy, Hayes, Stagg 6 Bryant, Devine, Ewbank, Layden, Rockne 8 Lombardi 10 Parseghian

field: 8 gridiron

kick: 4 drop, place, punt 6 spiral

pass: 4 flare 6 shovel 7 forward, lateral 9 square out

position: end 5 guard 6 center, tackle 8 fullback, halfback, split end, tailback, tight end 10 cornerback, linebacker 11 quarterback, running back

pro teams (NFL): 4 Jets (New York), Rams (Los Angeles) 5 Bears (Chicago), Bills (Buffalo), Colts (Baltimore), Lions (Detroit) 6 Browns (Cleveland), Chiefs (Kansas City), Eagles (Philadelphia), Giants (New York), Saints (New Orleans) 7 Bengals (Cincinnati), Broncos (Denver), Cowboys (Dallas), Falcons (Atlanta), Oilers (Houston), Packers (Green Bay), Raiders (Oakland), Vikings (Minnesota) 8 Chargers (San Diego), Dolphins (Miami), Patriots (New England), Redskins (Washington, D.C.), Seahawks (Seattle), Steelers (Pittsburgh) 9 Cardinals (St. Louis) 10 Buccaneers (Tampa Bay) 11 Forty-Niners (San Francisco)

pro teams (USFL): 4 Gold (Denver) 5

Blitz (Chicago), Stars (Philadelphia) **7** Bandits (Tampa Bay), Express (Los Angeles) **8** Breakers (Boston), Federals (Washington), Generals (New Jersey), Invaders (Oakland), Panthers (Michigan) **9** Stallions (Birmingham), Wranglers (Arizona)

score: 4 goal 6 safety 9 field goal, touchback, touchdown 10 conversion

team: 6 eleven (see *pro teams* above)

term: 4 down, sack, yard 5 block, flank, drive 6 fumble, huddle 7 defense, end zone, holding, kick-off, offense, offside, rushing 8 clipping, uprights 9 scrimmage, secondary 12 interception, interference

trophy: 7 Heisman (college)

footer: 6 walker 10 pedestrian

footfall: pad 4 step 5 tread 7 vestige

footing: 4 base, lace, rank 5 basis, track 6 status 7 balance, support, surface, toehold 8 standing 9 condition 12 relationship

footless: 5 inept 6 apodal, clumsy, futile, stupid 9 useless 13 unsubstantial

footloose: 4 free 7 nomadic 9 wandering 10 unattached

footman: 6 flunky, lackey, menial 7 servant 8 chasseur 9 attendant

footnote: 9 reference 11 explanation

footpad: 4 thug 5 thief 6 mugger, robber 9 holdup man 10 stickup man

footpath: 4 lane 5 trail 8 trottoir, sidewalk 9 banquette

footprint: 5 trace, track, tread

fossil: 9 ichnolite

rabbit: 5 prick

footrest: 4 pouf, rail 5 stool 7 cricket, hassock, ottoman

footstalk: 7 pedicel, petiole 8 peduncle

footwear (see also *shoe*): pac 4 boot, hose, pack, shoe, sock 5 kamik, sabot 6 arctic, galosh, kamika(pl.), patten, rubber 8 stocking

fop: 4 buck, dude, dupe, fool 5 dandy 7 coxcomb, jessamy 8 gimcrack, popinjay 9 exquisite 11 Beau Brummel 12 fashion plate, lounge lizard, man-about-town

foppery: 9 absurdity

foppish: 5 apish, dandy, silly 6 dapper, spruce, stupid 7 fangled, finical, foolish 8 dandyish

foppishness: 13 dandification

for: 7 because 8 favoring 9 favouring 10 concerning

for all voices: 5 tutti

for cash: 9 al contado(Sp.)

for each: per

for fear that: 4 lest

for nothing: 6 gratis, lanyap 8 gratuity 9 lagniappe

for shame: fie

for temporary use: 4 jury

for that reason: 4 ergo(L.) 9 therefore

for which reason: 6 whence

forage: ers, oat, rye 4 corn, mast, raid, rape 5 grass, maize, raven, spoil, wheat 6 barley, browse, clover, fodder, millet, ravage, russud 7 alfalfa 8 deerweed 9 pasturage 10 provisions 11 bitter vetch

foramen: 4 pore

foray: 4 rade, raid 5 melee 6 ravage, sortie 7 chappow, hership, pillage 9 incursion

forbear, forebear: 4 bear, help, shun, sire 5 avoid, forgo, spare 6 desist, endure, forego, parent 7 abstain, decline, refrain 8 ancestor 10 ancestress, forefather, foreparent

forbearance: 5 mercy 6 lenity 8 mildness, patience 9 tolerance 10 abstinence, self-denial 13 self-restraint

forbearing: 4 easy, mild 7 lenient, patient 8 tolerant 9 desisting, restraint

forbid: ban 4 defy, deny, fend, tabu, veto 5 debar, taboo 6 defend, enjoin, impede, refuse 7 forfend, forwarn, gainsay, inhibit 8 disallow, forefend, forspeak, preclude, prohibit 9 challenge, interdict, proscribe 10 contradict 11 countermand

forbiddance: ban 4 veto 12 interdiction, proscription

forbidden: 4 tabu 5 taboo 6 banned, denied 8 verboten 10 prohibited

Jewish law: 4 tref

Forbidden City: 5 Lhasa

forbidding: 4 grim 5 black, gaunt, stern 6 fierce, odious, strict 9 offensive, repellent 10 unpleasant 11 displeasing, prohibiting 2 disagreeable, interdicting

force: gar, gut, vim, vis 4 bang, birr, clip, cram, dint, feck, make 5 coact, drive, exert, farce, impel, might, peise, poach, power, press, repel, shear, stuff, wrest 6 coerce, compel, cudgel, energy, extort, oblige, ravish, stithy 7 ability, afforce, cascade, impetus, impulse, require, violate 8 coaction, coercion, efficacy, momentum, pressure, strength, validity, violence, virility 9 constrain, influence, puissance, restraint, waterfall 10 compulsion, constraint, constringe 11 necessitate

air upon: 4 blow

down: 4 tamp 5 stuff

into smaller space: 8 compress

kind of: 4 army, birr, dyne, elod, soul, task 5 agent, cadre, dynam, enemy, fohat, nerve, posse, steam, tonal 6 nature 7 voltage 8 battalia, sanction 9 bioenergy 13 reinforcement

onward: 4 urge 6 propel

out: 5 evict 6 banish, unseat
producing rotation: 6 torque
to do without: 7 deprive
with full: 5 amain

forced: 5 rigid, stiff 7 labored 8 spurious, strained 9 reluctant 10 artificial, compulsory, farfetched 11 constrained, involuntary, spontaneous 12 artificially
contribution: tax 4 duty, levy, toll 6 demand, excise, impost 7 tribute 8 exaction 10 assessment
feeding: 6 gavage

forceful: 6 mighty, strong, virile 7 dynamic, violent 8 eloquent, enfatico, forcible, vigorous 9 effective, energetic

forcemeat: 5 farce

forceps: 7 pincers 8 dentagra

forces: 4 army 6 troops

forcible: 5 stout, valid 6 cogent, mighty, potent 7 intense, violent, weighty 8 emphatic, forceful, powerful, puissant, vigorous 9 energetic, impetuous, necessary 10 compulsory, convincing, impressive, obligatory 11 efficacious, influential

forcibly: 5 amain 6 hardly 9 violently 10 vigorously

ford: 4 wade, wath 5 drift 6 stream 7 current 8 crossing 9 wathstead

Fordham's team: 4 Rams

fore: van, way 5 afore, ahead, front, prior, track 6 former 7 earlier, further, journey 8 advanced, formerly 10 antecedent, previously

forearm: arm
bone: 4 ulna
pert. to: 7 cubital

forebear: See **forbear**

forebode, forbode: 4 bode, omen 5 augur, croak 6 divine 7 betoken, portend, predict, presage 8 foretell 13 prognosticate 15 prognostication

foreboding, forboding: 4 omen 5 black 6 augury, boding, gloomy 7 anxiety 8 bodement, sinister 10 prediction 11 pessimistic, presagement 12 apprehension, presentiment

forecast: 4 bode 5 guess, infer 6 scheme 7 caution, foresee, fortune, predict, surmise 8 foredeem, foretell, prophesy 9 calculate, foregleam, forepoint, forescent, foretoken, prognosis 10 conjecture, foreordain, prediction, prognostic 11 calculation, foredestiny 12 predetermine 15 prognostication

forecaster: 4 seer 6 oracle 7 prophet 8 dopester 11 nostradamus 13 meteorologist

foreclose: 5 debar 6 hinder 7 prevent 8 preclude

foredoom: 7 destiny 10 predestine

forefather: 4 sire 5 elder 6 parent 7 forbear 8 ancestor 9 grandsire 10 forerunner, progenitor

forefinger: 5 index

forefoot: paw, pud

forefront: van 5 front

foregather: 4 meet 7 consort, convene 8 assemble 9 encounter 10 fraternize

forego, forgo: 5 waive 7 abstain, neglect, precede, refrain 8 dispense, renounce

foregoer: 7 example 8 ancestor 10 forerunner 11 predecessor

foregoing: 4 past 5 above 8 anterior, previous 9 preceding 10 antecedent

foregone: 4 past 8 previous
conclusion: 9 certainty

forehanded: 5 early 6 timely 7 prudent, thrifty

forehead: 4 brow 5 frons, front 7 frontes 8 sinciput
pert. to: 7 metopic
prominence: 8 glabella
strap: 4 tump

foreign: 5 alien, fremd 6 exiled, exotic, forane, remote 7 distant, ecdemic, exclude, strange 8 barbaric, peregrin 9 barbarous, extrinsic, peregrine 10 extraneous, irrelevant, outlandish, tramontane 12 adventitious, exallotriote, exterraneous, incompatible, inconsistent
geology: 7 epigene

foreign quarter: 6 barrio, ghetto 7 enclave

foreign service: *official:* 6 consul 7 attache 8 diplomat 10 ambassador
residence: 9 consulate

foreign to: 6 dehors

foreigner: 5 alien, haole 6 gringo, pakeha 7 greener, pardesi 8 outsider, stranger 9 barbarian, estranger, outlander 10 tramontane 12 ultramontane

foreknow: 5 infer 6 divine 7 foresee 8 conclude 9 prescient 11 preconceive

foreknowledge: 10 prescience

forel: 4 case 6 border, sheath 7 selvage 8 slipcase

foreland: 8 headland 10 promontory

forelock: 4 bang 6 cotter 8 linchpin

foreman: 4 boss 5 chief 6 gaffer, ganger, leader 7 capataz, captain, headman, manager, steward 8 overseer 9 chargeman 10 supervisor

foremost: 4 head, high, main 5 chief, first, forme, front, grand 6 banner 7 leading, supreme 9 principal
part: van 5 front

forenoon: 7 morning

forensic: 6 debate 11 disputation 13 argumentative

foreordain: 7 destine, foresay, predoom 8 forecast 9 preordain 10 predestine 12 predestinate, predetermine

forepart: 5 front 9 stomacher
of horse's hoof: toe

forerun: 6 herald, outrun 7 precede, prelude 8 announce 9 forestall, introduce, precourse, prefigure 10 anticipate, foreshadow

forerunner: 4 omen, sign 5 usher 6 augury, herald 8 ancestor, foregoer, fourrier 9 harbinger, messenger, precedent, precursor 10 forefather, foreganger, progenitor, prognostic 11 predecessor

foresee: 4 read 6 divine 8 forecast, foreknow 10 anticipate

foreshadow: 7 forerun 9 adumbrate, prefigure

foreshank: 4 shin

foreshow: 4 bode 5 abode, augur 7 betoken 8 foretell, prophesy 9 auspicate, foretoken 13 prognosticate

foresight: 6 vision 8 prudence 9 prevision 10 prescience, prevoyance, providence 11 forethought 12 anticipation 14 farsightedness

foresighted: 9 prescient, provident 10 farsighted

forest: 4 gapo, wood 5 Arden, glade, gubat, sylva(L.), taiga, waste 6 jungle, timber 7 boscage 8 caatinga, woodland 10 wilderness
deity: 4 faun 5 satyr 7 Aegipan
glade: 5 camas 6 camass, cammas 7 quamash
god: Pan 5 Tapio
love of: 9 hemophily
open place: 5 drive
pert. to: 6 sylvan 7 nemoral 9 forestral
road: 4 ride 5 trail
subarctic: 5 taiga
treeless: 4 wold
warden: 6 ranger

Forest City: 8 Portland, Savannah 9 Cleveland

forest fire locator: 7 alidade

forestall: 5 avert, deter 7 rule out 8 preclude, stave off

forester: 7 montero, treeman, woodman 8 woodsman

foretaste: 4 gust 6 teaser 8 prospect 12 anticipation

foretell: 4 bode, erst, read, spae 5 augur, insee, weird 6 divine 7 bespeak, foresay, portend, predict, presage 8 forebode, forecast, foreshow, prophesy, soothsay 9 predicate, prefigure, prophetic 10 vaticinate 13 prognosticate

foretelling: 9 fatidical, prophetic

forethought: 7 caution 8 prepense, prudence 9 foresight, provident 12 aforethought, anticipation 13 premeditation

foretoken: 4 omen 7 promise 8 forecast, foreshow, foresign 9 auspicate 10 presignify 13 prognosticate

foretold: 10 annunciate

foretooth: 5 biter 6 cutter 7 incisor

forever: aye 4 ever 5 etern 6 always, eterne 7 endless 8 eternity 9 endlessly, eternally, perpetual 10 constantly, invariably 11 ceaselessly, continually, everlasting, incessantly, perpetually, unceasingly 12 interminably, unchangeably 13 everlastingly

forewarn: 5 augur

forewarning: 4 hint 7 portent 11 premonition

foreword: 5 proem 7 preface 8 preamble 12 introduction

for example: 6 such as

forfeit: 4 fine, lose 5 crime, dedit, forgo 6 forego 7 escheat, misdeed, penalty 8 forfault
law: 7 abandum

forfeiture: 4 fine 5 mulct 7 penalty 9 decheance 10 amercement

forfend, forefend: 5 avert 6 secure 7 prevent, protect 8 preserve

forge: 4 mint 5 feign 6 smithy, swinge 7 falsify, fashion 8 bloomery 9 fabricate 11 counterfeit, fabrication, manufacture
nozzle: tew 5 tewel
on: 5 drive
tongs: tew
waste: 5 dross, sprue
wrought iron: 8 bloomery

forged: 10 artificial 11 counterfeit

forger: 5 smith 9 falsifier 10 coachsmith, fabricator

forgery: 4 sham 7 fiction 8 bloomery 11 counterfeit, fabrication 13 falsification

forget: 4 omit 5 fluff 6 ignore 7 neglect 8 overlook 9 disregard 10 draw a blank 11 disremember
one's lines: 5 fluff

forgetful: 6 remiss 7 bemused 8 careless, heedless 9 negligent, oblivious 10 neglectful 11 inattentive

forgetfulness: 7 amnesia, amnesty 8 oblivion
fruit of: 5 lotus
river of: 5 Lethe

forgivable: 6 venial

forgive: 5 remit, spare 6 excuse, pardon 7 absolve, condone 8 overlook 9 exculpate

forgiven: 7 excused

forgiveness: 6 pardon 9 remission 10 absolution 11 condonation

forgiving: 6 humane 7 clement 8 merciful, placable 9 remissive 10 charitable

forgo, forego: 4 quit 5 leave, waive 7 abstain, forbear, forfeit, forsake, neglect, refrain 8 abnegate, forebear, overlook, renounce 9 sacrifice, surrender 10 relinquish

forgoing: 5 above

fork: 4 tine 5 prong 6 bisect, branch, crotch, divide 7 fourche 10 divaricate, fourchette

kind of: 4 croc, evil 5 graip, pikle, glack 7 biprong 9 tormentor

forked: 5 bifid 6 furcal 7 divided, furcate 8 branched 9 furciform 10 bifurcated 11 forficulate

forlorn: 4 lorn, lost, reft 5 alone, stray 6 abject, bereft, ruined 7 forfare 8 deserted, desolate, forsaken, helpless, hopeless, pitiable, wretched 9 abandoned cheerless, desperate, destitute, miserable 10 friendless 11 comfortless 12 disconsolate

form: 4 ame 4 blee, body, make, mode, mold, plan, rite, thew 5 bench, build, frame, guise, image, model, shape 6 adjust, create, figure, invent, manner, ritual, schema, sponge 7 arrange, compose, confect, contour, develop, fashion, outline, pattern, portray, produce, profile 8 ceremony, conceive, likeness, organize, schemata(pl.) 9 construct, etiquette, fabricate, formation, structure 10 appearance, constitute, expression, figuration, observance, similitude 12 conformation 13 configuration, questionnaire

carved: 8 statuary

display: 4 rack 7 manikin 9 mannequin

geometrical: See **figure:** *geometrical*

into arc: 5 embow

into ball: 8 conglobe

into chain: 8 catenate

into fabric: 4 knit

into network: 10 reticulate

literary: ode 5 novel, poesy 6 satire, sonnet 7 romance

liturgical: 6 litany 7 service

lyrical: 6 rondel 7 sestina, sestine(pl.)

of government: 6 polity

of greeting: bow 5 hello, salam 6 salaam, salute 7 curtsey

pert. to: 5 modal

formal: set 4 prim 5 exact, stiff 6 solemn 7 nominal, orderly, precise, regular, solward, starchy, stilted 8 academic, affected, formular, starched 9 essential, officious, reserved 10 ceremonial, methodical, systematic 11 ceremonious, punctilious, superficial 12 conventional

formality: 4 form, rite 8 ceremony 15 conventionality

format: 4 size 5 shape, style 6 makeup 7 pattern

formation: 4 form, rank 5 spread 9 structure 10 procession 11 composition, development 12 construction

bone: 7 ostosis 10 parostosis

cell: 6 tissue

ecological: 5 biome

flesh: 8 sarcosis

geological: lia 4 ione 5 atoll, ledge 6 schist 7 tapeats, terrain, terrane

military: 4 line 5 herse, snail 6 flight 7 echelon

sand: 4 dene, dune

formative: 7 plastic

formed: 5 built 7 decided, matured, settled, wrought 10 constitute

at foot of mountain: 8 piedmont

by law: 9 corporate

crudely: 9 roughhewn

from above: 8 catogene

ingeniously: 5 dedal 6 daedal

of clustered grains (bot.): 7 grumose

on earth's surface: 7 epigene

former: die, old 4 erst, fore, late, once, past 5 forme, gauge, guide, maker, prior 6 whilom 7 ancient, creator, earlier, further, pattern, quondam, templet 8 previous, sometime 9 aforetime, erstwhile 10 antecedent

formerly: ere, nee 4 erst, fore, once, then 5 grave 6 before 7 onetime 8 sometime 9 aforetime, anciently, erstwhile 10 heretofore

formicary: ant 7 anthill, dweller

formicid: ant

formidable: 5 awful, tough 7 fearful 8 alarming, dreadful, menacing, terrible 11 redoubtable, threatening

formless: raw 5 arupa 7 anidian, chaotic 8 deformed, unshaped 9 amorphous, shapeless 13 indeterminate

Formosa: See **Taiwan**

formula: law 4 rule 6 method, recipe, theory 7 receipt

formular: 5 model 6 formal, proper 7 regular

formulate: put 5 draft, frame 6 cook up, devise, draw up, make up 7 dream up, hatch up

formulated: 6 stated 7 written

forsake: 4 deny, drop, flee, quit, shun 5 avoid, forgo, leave, waive 6 believe, defect, depart, desert, forego, refuse, reject 7 abandon, beleave, discard 8 renounce, withdraw 9 surrender, throw over 10 relinquish

forsaken: 4 lorn 7 forlorn 8 deserted, desolate 9 abandoned, destitute

forswear: 4 deny 6 abjure, reject 7 abandon, perjure 8 abnegate, renounce, take back

forsworn: 8 perjured 11 disaffected

fort: dun, lis, pah 4 liss, shee 5 gotta, redan, sidhe 6 castle, strong 7 bastile, bastion, bulwark, citadel, fortify 8 bastille, castillo, fastness, fortress 10 blockhouse, protection, stronghold

sloping bank of: 6 glacis

forte: bag 5 skill, thing 6 metier 7 calling

8 long suit, strength 9 specialty 11 strong point

forth: out 4 away 6 abroad, manage, onward 7 forward 8 outdoors 10 accomplish

forthright: 7 frankly 9 downright 11 straightway 13 straightforth 5 straightforward

forthwith: now 6 bedene, believe, direct 7 betimes 8 directly 9 extempore, presently, therewith 11 immediately

fortification (see also **defense**): 4 boma, moat, wall 5 redan, tower 6 abatis, castle, glacis, shield 7 bastion, bulwark, citadel, parapet, rampart, ravelin, redoubt 8 fortress 9 barricade 10 stronghold 12 machiolation

kind of: 4 fort 5 redan 6 abatis, sconce 7 lunette, ravelin, redoubt, parados 8 ceinture, demilune, estacade 9 fortalice, bastionet

part: 5 redan 7 bastion, ravelin 8 barbette

fortify: arm, man 4 fort 5 spike 6 abatis, picket 7 bastile, confirm 8 bastille, embattle, fortress, palisade 9 barricade 10 invigorate, strengthen, stronghold

fortitude: 6 mettle 7 bravery, courage, heroism, stamina 8 strength 9 endurance 10 resolution 12 resoluteness 14 impregnability

fortress: 4 fort, keep 5 rocca 6 castle 7 alcazar, barrier, bastile, borough, castlet, castrum, chateau, citadel, fortify 8 alcalzar, alcazava, bastille, chateaux(pl.), fastness 10 stronghold 13 fortification, propugnaculum

outwork of: 6 tenail 8 tenaille

fortuitous: 6 casual, chance, random 9 hazardous 10 accidental, contingent, incidental 12 adventitious

fortuity: 4 luck 6 chance 9 accidence

fortunate: edi, hap, sri 4 good, shri, well 5 faust, happy, lucky, shree 6 dexter 7 favored 8 gracious 9 favorable 10 auspicious, prosperous, successful

fortune: hap, lot 4 bahi, doom, fate, hail, luck 5 weird 6 boodle, bundle, chance, estate, mishap, riches, wealth 7 destiny, success, tidy sum 8 accident, hacienda 9 adventure 10 prosperity 11 king's ransom 13 circumstances

goddess: 5 Tyche

fortune teller: 4 seer 5 gypsy, sibyl, sybil 7 diviner, palmist

forty: 13 quadragesimal

forty days: 4 Lent

forty-five-degree angle: 6 octant

forty-five inches: ell

forty-third asteroid: 4 Eros

43,560 square feet: 4 acre

forty winks: nap 6 snooze

forum: 5 court 8 tribunal

forward: on, to; aid, bog, bug 4 abet, bain, bold, free, help, pert, send, ship, step 5 ahead, along, brash, eager, favor, forth, frack, freck, front, hasty, ready, relay, remit, saucy, serve, spack, ultra 6 afford, ardent, avaunt, before, bright, coming, favour, forthy, hasten, onward, prompt, send on 7 advance, earnest, extreme, further, promote, radical, support 8 adelante, arrogant, champion, immodest, impudent, perverse, petulant, transmit 9 audacious, encourage, forthward, obtrusive, overready 10 accelerate, forritsome, precocious 11 disobedient, progressive

fossa: pit 4 foss, moat 5 canal, ditch, fosse, fovea, graff, grave 6 cavity, trench 10 depression

fossil: 4 fogy 6 dolite 7 antique, lituite 8 calamite, conodont 10 antiquated

egg: 7 ovulite

footprint: 7 ichnite

mollusk: 6 dolite

resin: 5 amber 8 retinite

science: 12 paleontology

shell: 6 dolite

toothlike: 8 conodont

worm track: 7 nereite

fossorial: 9 burrowing

foster: 4 feed, food, help, rear 5 nurse 6 harbor 7 cherish, embosom, gratify, imbosom, indulge, nourish, nursing, nurture, promote, sustain 8 befriend, forester, nursling 9 cultivate, encourage, fosterage, offspring 11 nourishment

foster child: 5 nurry 7 stepson 12 stepdaughter

foudroyant: 8 dazzling, stunning 10 thundering

fougue: 5 ardor 11 impetuosity

foul: 4 base, hory, roil, vile 5 bawdy, black, dirty, grimy, horry, muddy, nasty, sully, weedy 6 clarty, defame, dirten, filthy, impure, malign, odious, putrid, rotten, soiled, unfair 7 abusive, defaced, fulsome, hateful, illegal, noisome, obscene, profane, smeared, squalid, unclean, vicious 8 entangle, indecent, polluted, stinking, wretched 9 dastardly, dishonest, loathsome, nastiness, obnoxious, offensive 10 detestable, disgusting, scurrilous 11 contaminate, unfavorable 12 dishonorable, inauspicious, scatalogical

foulard: tie 11 neckerchief 12 handkerchief

foulmouthed: 7 abusive, obscene, profane 10 scurrilous 11 opprobrious

foulness: 9 feculence

foul play: 5 crime 6 murder 7 killing 8 violence

found: fix, try 4 base, cast, rest 5 board, build, endow, erect 6 attach, depart 8 equipped, practice, provided, supplied 9 establish, institute, originate, supported 10 foundation

foundation: bed 4 base, body, fund, gist, sill 5 basis, bases(pl.), found, stock 6 bottom, legacy, reseau, riprap 7 bedding, bedrock, chantry, roadbed 8 donation, pedestal 9 beginning, endowment 11 corporation 12 substructure

founder: 4 fail 6 author, caster, dismay, dynast 7 stumble 8 miscarry 9 architect, patriarch, supporter, undermine 10 maintainer, originator 11 dumbfounder, establisher

metal: 5 yeter 6 yetter

founding: 8 settling

foundling: oaf 4 waif 6 infant, orphan 8 nursling

fount: 4 fons 6 source 8 fountain 9 reservoir

fountain: jet 4 fond, head, syke, well 5 fount 6 phiale, pirene, source, spring 7 bubbler 8 aganippe 9 reservoir 10 wellspring

god of: 4 Fons

nymph: 5 naiad

Fountain of Youth site: 6 Bimini

fountain pen: 5 stick, stylo

fountainhead: 6 origin, source

four: 6 tetrad 7 quartet

four-footed: 9 quadruped

Four Horsemen: war 5 death 6 famine 8 conquest

four hundred: 5 creme, elect, elite 6 select

four-in-hand: 7 necktie

four inches: 4 hand 7 measure

four-sided: 13 quadrilateral

fourchette: 4 fork 8 wishbone

fourflusher: 9 pretender

fourgon: van 4 cart 5 wagon 7 tumbril

fourpence: 5 groat

fourscore: 6 eighty

foursome: 6 tetrad 7 quartet

foursquare: 7 solidly 8 quadrate 10 forthright

fourth: 5 quart 6 fardel 7 quarter 8 quadrant

fourth estate: 5 press 10 newspapers

foveate: 6 pitted

fowl: hen 4 bird, cock 5 chick, chuck, manoc 7 chicken, rooster 8 volaille

kind of: 4 keel, coot 5 malay, banty, snipe, poult, brant 6 bantam, Houdan, Sussex, rumkin 7 minorca, galeeny

fox: tod 4 fool 5 trick 6 baffle, canine, outwit 7 beguile, confuse, stupefy, vulpine 10 intoxicate, perplexity

foot: pad

hunter's cry: 4 soho 5 yoick

kind of: 4 asse, stag 5 vixen, zorro 6 fennec, corsac 7 reynard, karagan

scent of: 4 drag

young: cub

fox-trot: 5 dance

foxglove: 7 popdock

leaf: 9 digitalis

foxlike: 9 alopecoid

foxtail: 5 brush, grass

foxy: sly 4 wily 5 coony 6 shrewd 7 cunning, vulpine 10 fraudulent

foyer: 5 lobby 6 hearth 8 anteroom, entrance 9 fireplace, greenroom

fra: 4 monk 5 friar 6 priest 7 brother

Fra Diavolo composer: 5 Auber

fracas: 4 bout 5 brawl, melee, set-to 6 rumpus, uproar 7 quarrel 8 fraction 9 commotion 11 disturbance

fraction: bit 4 part 5 break, piece, scrap 6 breach, fracas, little 7 ruction, rupture 8 breaking, fracture, fragment

fractional: 7 partial

fractious: 4 ugly 5 cross 6 unruly 7 crabbed, peevish, waspish 8 perverse, snappish 9 irritable

fracture: 4 flaw, rend 5 break, cleft, crack 6 breach 7 rupture 8 fraction

fragile: 4 fine, frow, weak 5 frail, frowy, light 6 feeble, frough, infirm, slight 7 brickle, brittle, froughy, slender 8 delicate, ethereal 9 frangible

fragility: 8 delicacy 12 delicateness

fragment: bit, ort 4 blad, chip, flaw, grot, part, snip, wisp 5 broke, crumb, flake, groat, piece, relic, scrap, shard, sherd, shred, spall 6 gobbet, morsel, parcel, screed, sheard, sippet, sliver 7 cantlet, flinder, flitter, fritter, oddment, portion, remnant 8 fraction 10 smithereen

biographical: 8 anecdote

diamond: 4 bort

ice afloat: 5 brash

fragmentary: 5 hashy 6 broken

fragments: 5 frush 7 gubbins

literary: ana 7 analect

Fragonard painting: 7 Bathers

fragrance: 4 odor 5 aroma, scent, smell 6 flavor 7 flavour, incense, perfume 9 perfumery, redolence

fragrant: 5 balmy, olent, spicy 7 odorant, odorous, perfumy, scented 8 aromatic, redolent 9 ambrosial 11 odoriferous

fragrant ointment: 4 balm, nard

fragrant wood: 5 aloes, cedar

frail: 4 fine, puny, weak 5 crazy 6 basket, flimsy, infirm, sickly 7 brittle, bruckle, fragile 8 delicate 12 destructible 13 insubstantial

frailty: sin 4 vice 5 fault 6 foible 7 failing 8 weakness 9 frailness, infirmity 10 peccadillo 12 imperfection

fraise: 4 fray, fuss, ream, ruff 6 cajole, defend, praise **7** defense, enlarge, flatter, pancake **8** cajolery **10** strawberry

frame (see also **framework**): bin **4** bunk, form, mold, plan, plot, sill **5** build, cadre, easel, panel, serve, shape, trave **6** abacus, adjust, binder, border, cook up, devise, fabric, invent, manage, profit, redact, resort, tenter **7** arrange, attempt, chassis, fashion, furnish, hatch up, outline, portray, prepare, proceed, prosper **8** contrive, regulate **9** calculate, construct, fabricate, structure

kinds of: ame, mat **4** bier, calm, caum, gill, sash, sess, sime, sley **5** airer, cadar, cader, dekle, easel, grate, herse, knape, trave, scray **6** abacus, deckel, deckle, tenter **7** drosser, hayrack, taboret

frame of mind: 4 bent, mood **5** humor

frame-up: 4 plot **10** conspiracy

framework: 4 rack, sill **5** cadge, cadre, racke **6** replum, stroma **7** chassis, nacelle, trestle **8** skeleton **9** structure

franc: *piece of twenty:* **5** louis

twentieth part of: **7** centime

France: 4 Gaul **6** Gallia

airplane: **5** avion

among: **5** entre

ancient name: **4** Gaul **6** Gallia

and: et

annuity: **5** rente

appellation: nom

architect: **7** LeNotre **9** Corbusier

article: la, le, un; les, une

author: **4** Gide, Hugo, Loti, Sand, Zola **5** Benda, Camus, Dumas, Renan **6** Balzac, Proust, Racine, Sartre **8** Stendhal, Voltaire

axe: **5** hache

baby: **4** bebe **6** enfant

bachelor: **6** garcon

bacteriologist: **7** Pasteur

ball: bal

ballad: lai **7** virelai

bay: **6** Biscay

beach: **5** plage

beast: **4** bete

bed: lit **5** couche

beef: **5** boeuf

billiards: **7** bouchon

bitters: **4** amer

blessed: **4** beni **5** sacre

boat: **6** bateau **8** chaloupe

bond: **5** rente

boxing: **6** savate

boy: **6** garcon

brandy: **8** armagnac, eau de vie

brewery: **9** brasserie

brush: **6** brosse

butcher shop: **11** charcuterie

cafe: **9** estaminet

cape: **5** talma

capital: **5** Paris

card game: **6** ecarte **7** baccara **8** baccarat

cardinal: **7** Mazarin **9** Richelieu

care: **4** soin

cathedral city: **5** Reims, Rouen **6** Nantes, Rheims

chanteuse: **4** Piaf

chaperon: **11** gouvernante

cheese: **4** Brie **9** Camembert, Roquefort

chemist: **5** Curie **7** Pasteur

chestnut: **6** marone, maroon

citizen: **7** citoyen

city: Aix, Pau **4** Caen, Metz, Nice, Vimy **5** Aries, Arles, Arras, Brest, Dijon, Havre, Lille, Lisle, Lyons, Nancy, Nerac, Nesle, Nimes, Paris, Reims, Rouen, Tours, Tulle, Vichy **6** Amiens, Angers, Calais, Lemans, Nantes, Pantin, Perret, Rennes, Rheims, Senlis, Sevres, Tarare, Toulon **7** Limoges, Orleans, Valence **8** Bordeaux, Clermont, Mulhouse, Rochelle, Toulouse **9** Levallois, Marseille

cleric: **4** abbe

cloth: ras **5** toile **8** blancard

cloud: nue

coffeehouse: **9** estaminet

coin: ecu, sol, sou **4** gros **5** agnel, blanc, blank, franc, obole, livre **6** denier, dizain, teston **7** centime, dizaine, testoon **8** cavalier, Louis d'or, Napoleon

commune: Pau **4** Auby, Bron, Dole, Laon, Loos, Orly, Reze, Vimy **5** Ancre, Rodez, Vichy **6** Pessac, Sanvic, Stains, Tarare

composer: **4** Lalo **5** Bizet, Ravel, Thome **6** Gounod, Halevy **7** Debussy

comrade: ami

concrete: **5** beton

conjunction: **4** mais

cordial: **8** anisette

cotton: **7** jasmine

couturier: **4** Dior **5** Patou **6** Chanel **7** Balmain **8** Givenchy **9** Courreges, St. Laurent

cowardly: **5** lache

cowboy: **6** baille **7** gardian

creamcake: **7** dariole

crown: ecu

custom: **9** Gallicism

daffodil: **10** polyanthus

daisy: **10** marguerite

dance: bal **5** gavot **6** branle, canary, cancan **7** bourree, boutade

dash: **4** élan

daughter: **5** fille

dead: **4** mort

dean: **5** doyen

dear: **4** cher

delicatessen: **11** charcuterie

department: Ain, Lot, Var **4** Aube, Aude, Cher, Eure, Gard, Gers, Jura, Nord, Oise, Orne, Tarn **5** Aisne, Corse, Doubs, Drome, Indre, Isere, Loire, Marne, Meuse, Rhone, Seine, Somme,

Yonne **6** Allier, Ariege, Cantal, Creuse, Landes, Loiret, Lozere, Manche, Nievre, Sarthe, Savoie, Vendee, Vienne, Vosges **7** Ardeche, Aveyron, Correze, Dordgne, Gironde, Herault, Mayenne, Meurthe, Moselle

devil: **6** diable
directory: **10** directoire
division: **6** canton **7** commune **10** department **14** arrondissement
division, ancient: **5** Arles **6** Arelas **7** Arelate **9** Aquitaine
doorkeeper: **9** concierge
dramatist: **5** Piron **6** Halevy, Racine, Sardou **7** Moliere
dressmaker: **9** couturier **10** couturiere
duke: duc
dungeon: **6** cachot
dynasty: **5** Capet **6** Valois **7** Bourbon, Orleans
ecclesiastic: **4** abbe
egg: **4** oeuf
empress: **7** Eugenie **15** Marie Antoinette
essayist: **4** Gide **9** Montaigne
evening: **4** soir
exclamation: **4** hein
FBI: **15** Surete Nationale
farmhouse: **5** ferme
father: **4** pere
finally: **5** enfin
friar: **5** frere
friend: ami
gala: **4** fete
game: jeu **4** jeux(pl.)
god: **4** dieu
good: bon
goodbye: **5** adieu
green: **4** vert
hairdresser: **7** friseur **8** coiffeur
hat: **5** beret **7** chapeau **8** chapeaux
health: **5** sante
heaven: **4** ciel
here: ici
high: **5** haute
horse stable: **6** ecurie
husband: **4** mari
income: **5** rente
inn: **5** hotel **7** auberge
island: ile, yeu **4** Elba **6** Hyeres, Oleron, Ushant **7** Corsica **8** Bellelze
judgment: **5** arret
king: roi **5** Louis, Capet
knife: **7** couteau
lace: **10** colberteen, colbertine **12** Valenciennes
lake: **6** Annecy **7** Bourget
language: **7** Catalan **9** Provencal
laugh: ris **4** rire
laundry: **13** blanchisserie
leather: **4** cuir
lenten season: **6** Careme
liqueur: **5** creme **8** anisette **9** Cointreau

lord: **8** seigneur
lover: **5** amant
lyric: **6** rondel **7** descort, rondeau
magistrate: **7** echevin
maidservant: **5** bonne **7** lisette
marshal: Ney **4** Foch, Saxe **5** Murat **6** Petain
mask: **5** loups
mathematician: **5** Borel
me: moi
measure: pot **4** aune, line, mile, mine, muid, pied, sack, velt **5** arpen, carat, lieue, ligne, minot, perch, pinte, point, pouce, toise, velte **6** arpent, hemine, league, perche, quarte, setier **7** chopine, heminee, poisson, septier **8** boisseau, quartaut, roquille **9** decillion, quarteron **12** tonneau de mer
milk: **4** lait
mine: **4** a moi
money: See *coin* above
month: Mai **4** Aout, Juin, Mars, mois **5** Avril **7** Fevrier, Janvier, Juillet, Octobre **8** Decembre, Novembre **9** Septembre
mountain: **4** Alps, Jura **6** Vosges **8** Auvergne, Cevennes, Cote d'Or, Pyrenees **9** Mont Blanc, Puy de Dome, Vignemale **10** Puy de Sancy
museum: **5** musee
nail: **4** clou
name: nom
national anthem: **12** Marseillaise
national flower: **4** lily **10** fleur de lis
no: non
noon: **4** midi
nose: nez
nothing: **4** rien
novelist: **4** Gide, Hugo, Loti, Zola **5** Camus, Dumas, Ohnet, Sagan, Verne **6** Halevy, Proust **7** Merimee **8** Flaubert
nursemaid: **5** bonne
of: de
officer: **7** prefect
old money: **6** besant
one: une
opera: **5** Faust, Lakmé, Manon **6** Carmen, Mignon **7** La Juive
painter: **4** Dore **5** Corot, Degas, Manet, Monet **6** Cormon, Legros, Renoir, Seurat, Vernet **7** Chardin, Deveria, Lorrain, Poussin, Utrillo, Watteau **8** Steinlen **9** Deschamps
palace: **6** palais
pancake: **5** crepe
parish priest: **4** cure
Parliament chamber: **5** senat
party: bal
pastry shop: **10** patisserie
patron saint: **5** Denis, Denys **6** Martin
peer: duc **8** seigneur
philosopher: **4** Caro **5** Camus **6** Pascal,

Sartre 8 Rousseau 9 Descartes

physicist: 5 Arago, Binet 6 Ampere

pocket: 5 poche

poem: dit, lai 7 rondeau

poet: 4 Labe 6 Racine 7 Rimbaud, Rostand 8 Verlaine 9 Deschamps, Desportes 10 Beaudelaire

police: 4 flic 6 Surete 8 gendarme

porcelain: 7 Limoges

port: 4 Caen 6 Calais 7 Le Havre 10 Marseilles

preposition: de

president's residence: 6 elysee

pretty: 4 joli 5 jolie

priest: 4 abbe, cure, pere

pronoun: ils, lui, mes, moi 4 elle, nous, vous 6 tienne

psychologist: 5 Binet

pupil: 5 eleve

queen: 5 reine

rabbit: 5 lapin

race course: 7 Auteuil

railroad: 11 chemin de fer

railroad station: 4 gare

read: 4 lire

rear: 7 arrière

region: 6 Alsace

Republic calendar: 6 Nivose 7 Floreal, Ventose 8 Brumaire, Fervidor, Frimaire, Germinal, Messidor, Pluviose, Prairial 9 Fructidor, Thermidor 11 Vendemiaire

resort: Pau 4 Nice 5 Vichy 6 Cannes, Menton 7 Riviera 8 Biarritz 9 Deauville

rest: 5 repos

restaurant: 6 bistro

Revolutionary hero: 6 Danton

Revolutionary leader: 5 Marat

Revolutionary radical: 7 Jacobin

river: Ain, Lot, Lys 4 Aire, Aude, Cher, Eure, Gard, Gers, Loir, Oise, Orne, Saar, Tarn, Yser 5 Adour, Aisne, Drome, Indre, Isere, Loire, Maine, Marne, Meuse, Rance, Rhone, Saone, Sarre, Seine, Seyre, Somme, Veste, Yonne 6 Allier, Ariege, Escaut, Loiret, Nievre, Sambre, Scarpe, Vienne 7 Ardeche, Durance, Garonne, Gironde, Moselle, Scheldt 8 Charente, Dordogne, Nantaise

roast: 4 roti 5 rotir

room: 5 salle

royal family: 5 Capet 6 Valois

saint: 5 Denis, Denys 6 Martin

savant: 7 Diderot

school: 5 ecole, lycee 8 Barbison, Barbizon

scientist: 5 Curie 7 Pasteur

sculptor: 5 Barye, Rodin 9 Bartholdi

sea: mer

seaport: 4 Caen 5 Brest, Havre 6 Calais,

Toulon 8 Bordeaux 9 Dunkerque

shelter: 4 abri

shield: ecu 5 targe

shoe: 9 chaussure

shopgirl: 9 midinette

sister: 5 soeur

slang: 5 argot

soldier: 5 assis, poilu 6 Zouave 8 chasseur

son: 4 fils

song: 5 caira, chant 6 aubade 7 ballade, chanson, Madelon, virelai, virelay

soul: ame

south: sud 4 Midi

spirit: ame 4 elan 6 esprit

stable: 6 ecurie

star: 6 etoile

state: 4 etat

stock exchange: 6 bourse

store: 8 boutique

story: 5 conte

street: rue

stupid: 4 bete

summer: ete

sun king: 8 Louis XIV

symbol: 4 lily 10 Fleur-de-lis

the: la, le; les(pl.)

theater: 5 odeon

then: 5 alors

ticket window: 7 guichet

title: duc 5 comte

tobacco: 5 tabac

town: 4 Agen, Aire, Caen, Sens, Sete 5 Douai, Ernee, Laval, Nerac, Ornes 6 Longwy, Sarlat, Tarbes, Troyes, Verdun 7 Castres 8 Le Perche, Rochelle

true: 4 vrai

Verdun battle: 4 Vaux

verse: 4 vers

verse form: lai 4 alba 6 rondel 7 ballade, virelay

very: 4 tres

vessel: 7 navette

vinegar: 8 vinaigre

vineyard: cru 5 vigne

waiter: 6 garcon

wall: mur

water: eau 4 eaux(pl.)

weight: 4 gros, marc, once 5 carat, livre, pound, tonne, uckia 7 tonneau 8 esterlin 9 esterling

who: qui

wicket: 7 guichet

wind: 7 mistral

wine: vin 4 Bois 8 sauterne 10 Roussillon

wine district: 5 Medoc 8 Bordeaux, Burgundy, Provence 9 Champagne

wine shop: 6 bistro

woman: 5 femme

world: 5 monde

you: 4 vous

Franciscan: 8 Minorite, Capuchin 9 Cordelier

nun: 5 Clare

franchise: soc 5 grant 6 patent 7 license 8 freelage, suffrage 9 privilege

old English: soc 4 soke

francolin: 4 bird 5 titar 9 partridge

frangible: 7 brittle, fragile 9 breakable

frank: 4 free, open, rank 5 bluff, lusty, naive, plain 6 candid, direct, honest 7 artless, genuine, liberal, profuse, sincere 8 carefree, cavalier, generous, vigorous 9 ingenuous, luxuriant, outspoken 10 licentious, unreserved 15 straightforward, unsophisticated

frankincense: 8 olibanum

Frankish hero: 6 Roland

Franklin: *invention:* 5 stove 8 bifocals

pen name: 11 Poor Richard

frankly: 6 freely, openly 7 plainly 8 candidly 9 artlessly, liberally, sincerely, willingly 10 forthright 11 ingenuously 12 unreservedly 13 undisguisedly

frankness: 6 candor 7 freedom 8 openness 9 telltruth, unreserve

Franks: 7 Salians

hero: 6 Roland

king: 5 Pepin 6 Clovis

law of: 5 Salic

peasant: 4 liti(pl.) 5 litus

vassal: 4 leud

frantic: mad 9 rabid 6 insane 7 furious, lunatic, violent 8 deranged, feverish, frenetic, frenzied 9 delirious, desperate, phrenetic 10 distracted, distraught

frap: 5 brace 6 secure, strike 7 tighten 10 strengthen

frappe: ice 4 iced 5 chill 6 cooled, freeze, frozen 9 milk shake

frat: 11 brotherhood

frater: 7 brother, comrade

fraternal: 9 brotherly

fraternity: 4 club 8 sorority 10 sisterhood 11 brotherhood

fraternize: 6 cotton 9 affiliate, associate, forgather 10 foregather

fraud: 4 dole, fake, gaff, gaud, gull, jape, ruse, sham, wile 5 cheat, craft, faker, guile, hocus, quack, trick 6 brogue, deceit, humbug 7 defraud, knavery, roguery, swindle 8 artifice, impostor, subtlety, trickery, trumpery 9 collusion, deception, imposture, stratagem 10 imposition 11 fraudulency 13 bamboozlement, circumvention

fraudulent: 4 fake, wily 5 snide 6 crafty, quacky 7 abusive, crooked, cunning 8 cheating, covinous, guileful, spurious 9 deceitful, deceiving, deceptive, designing, dishonest, horsefair, insidious, underhand 10 fallacious, misleading 11 clandestine, counterfeit, treacherous

fraught: 4 fill, lade, load 5 cargo, equip, laden 6 burden, supply 7 freight 9 freighted, transport

fraxinus: ash 4 tree

fray: 4 feud, fret, riot 5 alarm, brawl, broil, broom, clash, dread, feaze, fight, melee, panic, ravel 6 affray, assail, attack, battle, bustle, combat, fraise, fridge, fright, inroad, terror, tumult 7 contest, frazzle, ruction, terrify 8 disperse, frighten 9 commotion, dissipate 12 apprehension

frayed: 4 worn 7 raveled 10 threadbare

frazzle: 5 upset 7 exhaust, wear out 9 prostrate

freak: 4 bold, flam, lune, mood, whim 5 braid, fancy, fleck, humor, prank, sport 6 frolic, greedy, humour, megrim, mosaic, streak, vagary, whimsy 7 caprice, checker, chimera, crochet, monster, whimsey 8 capricci(pl.), flimflam 9 capriccio, variegate 10 enthusiast 11 monstrosity 12 whimsicality

freakish: odd 6 screwy 7 curious, flighty 9 arbitrary, fantastic, whimsical 10 capricious

fream: 4 roar

freckle: 4 spot 7 ephelis, frecken, lentigo, speckle

remover: 6 adarce

Frederick I's nickname: 10 Barbarossa

Frederick the Great: 6 Alaric

free: lax, rid 4 liss, open, quit, void 5 broad, clear, enode, frank, lisse, loose, ready, siker, slake, spare, untie 6 acquit, adjust, beyond, degage, devoid, exempt, gratis, immune, lavish, loosen, remove, rescue, sicker, unbind 7 absolve, deliver, forward, grivois, inexact, leisure, liberal, manumit, outside, release, relieve, unbound, willing 8 abundant, detached, dispatch, distinct, expedite, familiar, floating, generous, grivoise, indigent, innocent, liberate, overfree, separate, unfasten, unhamper 9 at liberty, discharge, disengage, exculpate, exonerate, expansive, extricate, footloose, guiltless, ingenuous, outspoken, separated, unbridled, unchecked, unimpeded, unleased 10 autonomous, emancipate, gratuitous, immoderate, licentious, openhanded, self-ruling, unattached, uncombined, unconfined, unfettered, unimpaired, unreserved 11 disencumber, disentangle, independent, magnanimous, spontaneous, untrammeled 12 uncontrolled, unencumbered, unrestrained, unrestricted 13 communicative, self-directing, unconstrained

from bacteria: 7 aseptic, sterile

from blame: 5 clear 6 acquit 7 absolve, relieve 9 exonerate

from bondage: 7 manumit 10 emancipate 11 affranchise

from dirt: 7 apinoid

from discount: net

from moisture: dry 9 dehydrate

from restraint: 5 untie

from suspicion: 5 clear, purge 6 acquit 7 absolve 9 exculpate, exonerate

free-for-all: 4 race 5 fight, melee 6 barney 11 competition

free of charge: 8 buckshee

free time: 4 rest 6 recess 7 leisure

freebooter: 5 rider 6 pirate 7 cateran, corsair 8 pillager 9 buccaneer, plunderer 10 filibuster

freed: 8 absolute 13 disencumbered

freedom: 4 ease 7 abandon, content, leisure, liberty, license, release 8 facility, freelage, immunity, latitude 9 exemption, frankness, readiness 10 generosity, liberality, liberation 11 manumission, willingness 12 emancipation, independence 13 outspokenness 14 unreservedness

from activity: 4 rest 6 recess 7 respite

from fraud: 7 honesty 9 bonafides

from pain: 6 aponia

from strife: 5 peace

of access: 6 entree

freehold: 4 alod 5 allod 6 estate, tenure 7 alodium 8 allodium

freeholder: 6 yeoman

freeing: 8 acquital 11 manumission

freeloader: 5 leech 6 sponge 8 hanger-on, parasite 12 lounge lizard

freely: 4 lief 5 noble, nobly 6 gratis 7 frankly, largely, readily 8 heartily 9 beautiful, bounteous, bountiful, copiously, excellent, liberally, voluntary, willingly 10 abundantly, generously 11 beautifully, bounteously, bountifully, excellently, plenteously, plentifully, voluntarily 12 munificently 13 spontaneously 14 unobstructedly 15 unconditionally

freeman: 4 aire 5 ceorl, churl, thane, thegn 6 yeoman 7 burgess, burgher, citizen

Freestone State: 11 Connecticut

freethinker: 7 infidel, skeptic 8 agnostic 10 espritfort, unbeliever

freeze: ice 4 rime 5 chill 6 frappe, harden 7 chilled, congeal, impound 11 conglaciate, refrigerate

freezer: 4 icer

freezing: icy 4 cold 5 gelid, nippy 6 frigid, frosty

freight: 4 load 5 cargo, laden 6 lading 7 fraught 9 transport 10 freightage

freightage: 5 cargo 6 lading 7 freight

freighted: 5 laden 7 fraught

French: See France

French-Belgian river: Lys 4 Yser

Frenchman: 4 Gaul 6 Picard 8 Parisian

frenetic, phrenetic: mad 4 wild 5 crazy, fresh, rabid 6 insane, madman 7 fanatic, frantic, madness, violent, zealous 9 delirious 10 distracted, ornamental, passionate 12 absentminded

frenzied: 4 amok, mang 5 amoke, amuck, rabid 6 ramage 7 berserk, frantic, furious 8 frenetic, furibund, maddened 9 delirious

frenzy: mad 4 amok, fury, rage 5 amoke, amuck, furor, mania 7 frantic, madness, oestrus 8 delirium, insanity, maniacal 9 amazement 11 distraction

frequency: 5 crowd 6 throng 7 crebity 9 community, concourse 11 familiarity

unit: 7 fresnel

frequent: 5 haunt, howff, often, usual, visit 6 affect, common, effect, hourly, sundry 7 current, enhaunt, prevail 8 familiar, habitual 9 assiduous, crebrouse, habituate 10 persistent

frequented places: 5 dives 6 haunts 7 resorts

frequenter: 7 denizen, habitue

frequently: oft 5 often 6 hourly 8 ofttimes 10 repeatedly

fresco: 5 mural, shade 8 coolness

fresh: new 4 cool, good, pure, racy 5 brisk, green, ruddy, saucy, sound, sweet, vivid 6 breezy, bright, caller, florid, lively, recent, strong, unused 7 unfaded, untried 9 obtrusive, unspoiled 10 additional, meddlesome, refreshing, unimpaired 11 smart-alecky 12 invigorating, presumptuous

and lively: 4 racy

freshen: 5 renew 6 breeze, revive 7 refresh, sweeten

freshet: 5 flood, spate, stream 9 streamlet 10 inundation

freshly: 5 again

freshman: 4 colt, tyro 5 bejan, frosh, plebe 6 bejant, novice, rookie 8 neophyte, newcomer 10 apprentice

freshness: 4 verd 8 verdancy 9 fraicheur

lose: dry 4 fade, wilt 6 wither

fret: nag, rub, vex 4 care, fray, gall, gnaw, pout, rage, stew 5 chafe, grate, pique, tease, worry 6 abrade, devour, harass, murmur, nettle, plague, rankle, ripple, ruffle, strait 7 agitate, consume, disturb, grizzle, roughen 8 diminish, disquiet, irritate, vexation

fretful: 5 angry, cross 6 repine, sullen 7 carking, frecket, gnawing, peevish, pettish 8 captious, corroded, fretsome, petulant, restless 9 corrosive, impatient, irascible, irritable, plaintive, querulous 10 ill-humored, ill-natured

Freudian term: id; ego 8 superego

Frey: *father:* 5 Njord 6 Njorth

sister: 5 Freya 6 Freyja

wife: 4 Gerd

Freya's husband: 4 Oder

friable: 5 crimp, crisp, crump, loamy, mealy

clay: 4 bole

friar: fra 4 fish, monk 5 frere 6 Bhikku, fraile, frater 7 Bhikshu, brother 8 monastic 9 Carmelite 10 Franciscan 11 Augustinian

black: 9 Dominican

mendicant: 7 Servite

friary: 8 cloister 9 monastery 11 brotherhood

fribble: 4 fool 6 falter, totter, trifle 7 stammer 8 trifling 9 frivolity, frivolous

fricassee: 6 potpie 10 blanquette

friction: rub 5 chafe 9 attrition 10 dissension

air: 7 windage

fridge: rub 4 fray 5 chafe 6 fidget 8 irritate

fried: 4 frit 7 sauteed

fried cake: 7 cruller 8 doughnut

friend: ami(F.), amy, eme, pal 4 ally, amie(F.), chum, kith 5 amigo(Sp.), amiga(Sp.), crony 6 bonami(F.), cummer, gimmer, kimmer 7 comrade, gremial, kinsman 8 cockmate, compadre, paramour, relative 9 associate, attendant, bonne amie(F.), broadbrim, companion, confidant 10 confidante 12 acquaintance

Friend: 6 Quaker

church founder: 9 George Fox

friendless: 7 forlorn

friendliness: 5 amity 6 affinity, amicable, goodwill 10 fellowship 13 companionship

friendly: sib 4 cosh, good, kind 5 chief, howdy 6 blithe, chummy, genial, homely, howdie 7 affable, amiable, amicous, cordial 8 amicable, homelike, intimate, sociable 9 favorable 10 favourable, hospitable 11 warmhearted 12 well-disposed

Friendly island: 5 Tonga

friendship: 5 amity 6 accord 8 relation 9 affection 10 attachment

Friendship author: 6 Cicero

frieze: 4 kelt(Sc.) 5 adorn, chase 8 trimming 9 embroider 10 decoration

band: 6 taenia

frigate (see also boat, ship): 5 zabra(Sp.)

frigate bird: iwa 8 alcatras

Frigg: *husband:* 4 Odin

son: 6 Balder

fright: awe, cow 4 fear, fray, funk, gast 5 alarm, gliff, panic, scare, shock 6 affray, dismay, horror, schrik, terror 7 startle 11 trepidation 13 consternation

frighten: awe, cow 4 fray, funk, hare, haze, shoo 5 afear, alarm, appal, gliff, hazen, scare 6 affray, appall, ascare, boggle 7 frecken, startle, terrify 8 affright 10 intimidate

frightened: 4 awed, eery, gast 5 eerie, timid 6 afraid 8 skittish

frightful: 4 grim 5 awful, ferly, scary 6 horrid, ugsome 7 affreux, fearful, gashful, ghastly, hideous 8 alarming, dreadful, fearsome, horrible, horrific, shocking, terrible, terrific 10 horrendous, tremendous

frightfulness: 13 atrociousness 15 schrecklichkeit(Ger.)

frigid: icy 4 cold 5 acold, bleak 6 arctic, frosty 8 freezing

frill: 4 purl 5 jabot, ruche 6 ruffle 7 flounce 8 furbelow 9 balayeuse 11 chitterling

fringe: hem, rim 4 loma 6 border, edging, margin 8 ciliella, trimming

fringed: 9 laciniate 10 frimbriate

frippery: 6 finery 7 regalia 9 full dress 10 Sunday best

frisk: 4 leap, skip, whid 5 brisk, caper, dance, flisk 6 curvet, frisco, frolic, gambol, lively, search 7 disport, friscal 8 caracole 9 shake down 10 frolicsome

frisky: gay 4 pert 6 lively 7 playful 8 frisking, sportive 9 kittenish 10 frolicsome

frisson: 5 chill 6 quiver, shiver, thrill 7 shudder

frith: 4 help 5 firth, hedge 6 hurdle, wattle 7 coppice, estuary, freedom 8 liberate, security 9 brushwood, copsewood, underwood 12 protection

fritter: 5 shred, spend, waste 6 bangle 7 pancake, scatter 8 fragment

frivol: 6 trifle 9 frivolous

frivolity: 6 levity 7 fribble, inanity 8 nonsense 9 lightness

frivolous: gay 5 giddy, inane, petty 6 frivol, futile 7 fatuous, fribble, shallow, trivial 8 gossamer 9 childlike, worthless 11 empty-headed, light-headed 14 featherbrained

frizzed: 5 crepe 6 crispy

fro: 4 away, back, from 5 hence, since 8 backward

frock (see also dress): jam 4 grown, slip, wrap 5 tunic 6 cleric, jersey, mantle 7 workman 9 gaberdine

frog: 4 toad 5 frosh, frosk, jakie 6 peeper 7 paddock, quilkin 8 ferreiro 9 amphibian

order of: see zoological order below.

pert. to: 6 ranine

rearing place: 7 ranaria(pl.) 8 ranarium

zoological order: 5 anura 6 anoura 9 salientia

frogman: 5 diver 7 swimmer

gear: 5 scuba

frohlich: gay 5 happy 6 joyous

frolic: bum, gay 4 blow, game, gell, jink, lark, orgy, play, ramp, romp 5 caper, freak, frisk, merry, prank, randy, sport, spree 6 curvet, gambol, plisky, prance, rollix, shindy, splore 7 disport, gammock, pliskie, scamper, stashie, wassail 8 carousal 9 gilravage 10 masquerade

frolicsome: gay 4 roid 5 gilpy 6 frisky, gilpey 7 jocular, waggish 8 espiegle, friskful, gamesome, sportive

from: fro
  beginning to end: 4 over 7 through
  head to foot: 7 capapie
  here: 5 hence
  that time: 6 thence
  the egg: ab ovo
  the time that: 5 since
  this time: 5 hence

front: bow, van 4 brow, face, fore, head, prow 5 afore 6 before, facade, facing, oppose, sector 7 forward, further, obverse 8 forehead, foremost, forepart, foreside 9 forefront 10 appearance, effrontery 11 countenance
  toward the: 8 anterior

frontal: 6 sindon 7 metopic

frontier: 4 face 5 bound, march 6 border, oppose 7 barrier, defense 8 boundary

frontiersman: 4 Cody 5 Boone, Clark 6 Carson 7 pioneer, settler 8 Crockett

fronton: 7 jai-alai

frore: 4 cold 6 frosty, frozen

frost: ice, nip 4 foam, hoar, rime 7 failure

frosted: 4 iced 5 glace 6 frozen

frostfish: 5 smelt 6 tomcod 9 whitefish

frosting: ice, mat 5 icing

frosty: icy 4 cold, rimy 5 chill, frore, gelid, glary 6 frigid, froren 8 chilling, freezing

froth: fob 4 barm, foam, scum, suds 5 spume 6 freath, lather

frow: 4 frau, froe, wife 5 vrouw, woman

froward: 5 balky, cross 7 adverse, awkward, peevish, wayward 8 contrary, perverse, petulant, untoward 9 obstinate 10 refractory, unyielding 11 disobedient, unfavorable 12 ungovernable

frown: 4 lour, pout, sulk 5 gloom, glout, lower, scowl 6 glower, glunch 7 frounce

frowsy, frowzy: 5 musty 6 blowzy 7 raffish, unkempt 8 slovenly 10 disordered

frozen: 4 hard 5 fixed, frore, gelid, glary 6 chilly, frappe, froren 7 chilled, frosted 8 hardened, immobile 9 congealed 10 unyielding 11 coldhearted 12 refrigerated 13 unsympathetic

fructify: 9 fertilize 10 impregnate

frugal: 4 mild 5 chary, roman, spare 6 saving 7 careful, sparing, thrifty 9 economize, provident 10 economical,

unwasteful 12 parsimonious 13 penny-pinching

frugality: 6 thrift 7 economy 8 prudence 9 chariness

fruit: fig 4 date, lime, pear, plum, pome 5 apple, berry, drupe, grape, issue, lemon, melon, olive, peach, young 6 cherry, orange, result 7 apricot, azarole, product, progeny 8 dewberry 9 blueberry, nectarine, offspring, pineapple, tangerine 10 grapefruit, production
  aggregate: 7 etaerio
  apple-like: 4 pome 6 quince
  astringent: 4 sloe
  baccate: 5 berry
  beverage: ade 4 wine
  blackthorn: 4 sloe
  buttercup: 5 akene 6 achene 7 achenia(pl.) 8 achenium
  citrus: 4 lime 5 grape, lemon 6 orange 7 kumquat, tangelo 8 mandarin 9 tangerine 10 grapefruit
  collective: 7 syncarp 10 syncarpium
  cooked in syrup: 7 compote
  decay: 4 blet
  desert region: 5 terfa 6 terfez
  dish: 7 compote
  dried: 5 prune 6 orejon, raisin
  drink: ade 5 juice, punch
  dry: 5 regma 6 achene, samara
  early maturing: 8 rareripe
  elm tree: 6 samara
  fleshy: 4 pear, plum, pome 5 berry, drupe, melon 6 tomato
  fleshy part: 9 sarcocarp
  goddess of: 6 Pomona
  gourd family: 4 pepo
  horseradish tree: ben
  husk: 5 lemma
  hybrid: 7 tangelo
  imperfect: 6 nubbin
  juicy: 4 lime, pear, plum 5 grape, lemon, peach 6 orange 7 apricot 9 pineapple 10 grapefruit
  layer: 7 epicarp
  less: 8 acarpous
  lime & lemon: 6 citron
  many-seeded: 11 pomegranate
  maple: 6 samara
  mild acid: 5 guava
  multiple: 4 cone
  of cactus: 5 sabra
  of rose: 11 cynorrhodon
  of strawberry: 7 etaerio
  oily: 5 olive
  one-seeded: 5 akene 6 achene, samara 7 achenis(pl.) 8 achenium
  palm tree: 4 date
  peach-like: 7 apricot 9 nectarine
  pear-shaped: fig 7 avocado
  plum-like: 4 sloe 7 carissa
  pome: 4 pear 5 apple 7 azarole

preserving: 6 medlar
pulp: pap
pulpy: uva 4 pome 5 drupe, grape, berry
red: 4 plum 5 apple 6 cherry 9 raspberry 10 strawberry
refuse: 4 marc
rind: 7 epicarp
rosebush: hip
science of: 8 pomology
seed: pip, pit
spore: 6 aecium
stalk: 8 peduncle
stone: 4 paip, plum 5 drupe, peach, prune 6 cherry 7 apricot 9 nectarine
study of: 8 pomology 9 carpology
strawberry-family: 7 etaerio
sugar: 7 glucose 8 fructose
tropical: fig 4 date 5 guava, gourd, mango 6 banana, papaya, pawpaw 9 sapodilla
vine: 5 grape
winged: 6 samara
withered: 6 nubbin
yellowish: 5 papaw 6 quince
fruit basket: 6 pottel, pottle
fruit bats: 8 pteropid 10 pteropidae
fruit dealer: 9 frontsman, fruiterer 11 greengrocer
fruit of Jove: 9 persimmon
fruit of paradise: 6 pomelo 10 grapefruit
fruit stone: pit 4 paip 6 pyrene 7 putamen
fruitful: fat 6 fecund 7 fertile 8 abundant, prolific 9 feracious, plenteous, plentiful, procreant 10 productive
fruitgrower: 8 fruitist 10 orchardist, pomologist 14 horticulturist
fruition: joy 8 pleasure 9 enjoyment 11 achievement, fulfillment, realization
fruitless: dry 4 geld, vain 5 addle, blank 6 barren, futile 7 sterile, useless 8 abortive 10 profitless 11 ineffectual 12 unprofitable, unsuccessful
frump: vex 4 mock, snub, sulk 5 dowdy, flout 6 gossip 7 provoke 8 irritate
frustrate: 4 balk, bilk, dash, foil, null, vain, void 5 baulk, blank, block, check, cross, crush, elude 6 baffle, blight, defeat, delude, outwit, scotch, thwart 7 deceive, nullify, prevent, useless 8 confound, infringe, nugatory 9 cancel out, checkmate, discomfit 10 circumvent, counteract, disappoint, disconcert, neutralize 11 countermand, ineffectual 12 unprofitable
frustration: 4 foil, 6 fiasco 12 discomfiture 15 disillusionment
fry: 4 sile 5 brook, roast, saute, young 6 sizzle 9 offspring
fryer: 6 pullet
frying pan: 6 spider 7 griddle, skillet
fuddle: 5 booze 6 muddle, tipple 7 fluster
fuddled: fap, ree 5 bosky, tipsy 7 muddled

fudge: pad 4 fake 5 candy, foist, hunch 6 devise, humbug 8 contrive, nonsense 9 interlope, makeshift 10 substitute 11 counterfeit
fuel: gas, oil 4 coal, coke, peat, wood 5 argal, argol, argul, stoke 6 acetol, elding, firing, petrol 7 pabulum 8 charcoal, gasoline, kerosene, kerosine 9 petroleum 10 exaggerate 11 combustible
fugacious: 6 flying 8 fleeting, volatile 10 evanescent
fuggy: 6 smelly, stuffy
fugitive: 5 exile, fleme 6 emigre, exiled, outlaw 7 fleeing, refugee, roaming, runaway 8 banished, deserter, fleeting, runagate, unstable, vagabond, volatile 9 fugacious, strolling, transient, uncertain 10 evanescent
fugue: 4 fuga 9 ricercare
exponent: 4 Bach 6 Handel
Führer, der: 6 Hitler
Fukien river: Min
fulcrum: 4 bait, prop 5 thole 7 support
fulfill: 4 fill, full, meet 6 effect, finish, occupy 7 achieve, execute, perform, satisfy 8 complete 9 implement 10 accomplish, effectuate
fulfillment, fulfilment: 6 effect 9 execution 10 completion 11 performance, realization 14 accomplishment
fulgent: 6 bright 7 shining 8 dazzling, luminous 9 effulgent
full: bad, big 4 good 5 ample, round, sated, solid, total 6 entire, fulfil, honest 7 baptize, copious, destroy, diffuse, fulfill, fulsome, orotund, perform, plenary, replete, teeming, trample 8 adequate, bouffant, brimming, complete, resonant 9 bouffante, capacious, plentiful 10 consecrate, exhaustive 13 comprehensive
full-blooded: 5 flush, ruddy 6 florid 8 rubicund 12 thoroughbred
full-blown: 4 lush, ripe 5 adult 6 all-out, mature 7 grown-up
full force: 6 brunt
full-grown: 6 mature 9 developed
full of: *cracks:* 6 rimose
glands: 7 adenose
hollows: 8 lacunose
minute openings: 6 porous
sand: 7 arenose
sap or juice: 7 succous 9 succulent
thorns: 6 briary
twists: 5 kinky 7 winding
wrinkles: 6 rugose
fuller: 7 creaser
fuller's grass: 8 soapwort
fullness, fulness: 5 fulth 6 plenty 7 satiety 8 pleonasm 9 abundance, amplitude, plumpness, repletion 10 fleshiness, perfection 12 completeness

fully: 5 amply 6 wholly 7 clearly, largely, utterly 8 entirely, maturely 9 perfectly 10 abundantly, completely, distinctly 11 plenteously, plentifully

fulmar: 4 bird 5 nelly 7 malduck

fulminate: 7 explode, inveigh 8 detonate

fulsome: fat 4 foul, full 5 gross, plump, suave 6 coarse, wanton 7 copious, lustful, overfed 8 abundant, nauseous 9 offensive, overgrown, repulsive, satiating, sickening 10 disgusting, indelicate, nauseating

fumble: paw 4 boot 5 abase, botch, error, grope 6 bobble, bungle, faffle, haffle, huddle, mumble

fume: 4 emit, foam, odor, rage, rant, reek 5 ewder, fumet, smoke, storm, vapor 6 exhale 7 flatter, fumette 8 fumigate, outburst 10 exhalation

fun: gag, gig 4 game, gell, glee, hoax, jest, joke, play 5 mirth, sport 6 gaiety, gayety 9 amusement, diversion, horseplay, merriment 10 pleasantry

function: act, run, use 4 duty, role, work 5 doing 6 action, office 7 calling, operate, service 8 activity, business, ceremony, occasion 9 festivity, gathering, operating, operation 10 occupation, profession, providence 11 performance 13 entertainment

   social: tea 4 ball 5 party 6 soiree 9 reception

   trigonometrical: 4 sine 6 cosine, secant 7 tangent

fund: 4 fond, pool 5 basis, stock, store 5 endow 6 bottom, ground, supply 7 deposit, reserve 10 foundation, groundwork 12 accumulation

fundamental: 5 basal, basic, vital 7 basilar, organic, primary, radical 8 original, rudiment 9 elemental, essential, important, necessary, paramount, principle 10 elementary

funds: 4 caja, cash 5 money 9 resources

funeral: 6 burial, dismal, exequy 7 cortege, funebre 8 exequial, funereal 9 forthfare, obsequies 10 sepulchral

   bell: 5 knell

   director: 9 mortician

   oration: 5 eloge 6 eulogy 8 encomium 9 panegyric

   pile: 4 pyre

   song: 5 dirge, elegy, elogy, nenia 6 elegie 7 elogium, epicede 8 threnody 9 epicedium

   structure: 10 catafalque

funereal: 5 feral, grave 6 dismal, gloomy, solemn 7 funebre, funeral 8 mournful 9 funebrial, funebrous 10 funebrious

funest: sad 4 dire 5 fatal 7 doleful

fungus: 4 bunt, cepe, mold, rust, smut 5 ergot, fungo, morel, moril, uredo, yeast 6 agaric, fungal, mildew, oidium, telium 7 agarics, amanita, blewits, fungoid, fungous, geaster, truffle 8 amanitin, mushroom, puffball 9 stinkhorn, toadstool 10 fungaceous

   disease: rot 5 tinea

   edible: 4 cepe 5 morel 7 truffle 8 mushroom

   parasitic: 5 ergot

fungus-like: 6 agaric

funk: 4 kick, odor, rage 5 shirk, smell, spark 6 coward, flinch, fright, recoil, shrink 8 frighten 9 cowardice, touchwood

funnel: 4 pipe 6 hopper 7 conduct 8 transmit

funny: odd 5 comic, droll, queer 7 comical, jocular, risible, strange 8 humorous 9 laughable, ludicrous

   funny bone: 9 olecranon

funnyman: wit 8 comedian

fur: 4 flix, pell, pelt 5 budge, stole 6 furrow, pelage

   coat: 6 pelage

   collection of: 5 pelts 6 peltry

   kind of: fox 4 mink, paen, scut, seal, vair, woom 5 budge, civet, coney, fitch, lapin, otter, sable 6 ermine, galyac, galyak, marten, martin, moutin, nutria 7 calabar, calaber, caracul, karakul, miniver, platina, sealine 8 karakule, ragondin 9 silver fox

   piece: 5 stole

   refuse: 4 kemp

fur-bearing animal: fox 4 mink, seal 5 genet, otter, sable 6 marten, martin

furbelow: 4 frill 6 ruffle 7 falbala, falbelo, flounce 8 trimming

furbish: fig, rub 4 fake, vamp 5 clean, scour 6 polish 7 burnish 8 renovate

Furies: 5 Dirae 7 Erinyes

   individual: 6 Alecto, Erinys 7 Erinnys, Erinyes, Megaera 9 Tisiphone

furious: mad 5 angry, brain, irate, rabid 6 fierce, furied, insane, stormy 7 frantic, mankind, rushing, violent 8 frenzied, vehement, wrathful 9 impetuous, turbulent 10 boisterous, tumultuous, uproarious

furl: 4 fold, roll, wrap 5 frese 6 enfold, fardel, furdel

furlana: 5 dance, music

furlong: 4 shot 5 stade 7 stadium 10 quarentene

furlough: 5 leave 6 permit 8 passport

furnace: 4 bosh, dome, kiln, oven 5 stove, tisar 6 calcar, cupola, heater 7 athanor, howells, rotator, smelter 8 bloomery, bruckner 9 scorifier 11 incinerator

   part: 4 bosh, flue 5 grate

furnish: arm 4 feed, give, lend 5 array, endow, equip, frame, indue 6 afford, graith, insure, render, supply **7** apparel, appoint, garnish, provide **8** hand over, minister, palisade **10** accomplish, administer

crew: man

with battlements: **9** crenelate

with meals: **5** board, cater

furnished: 5 boden, garni **8** equipped, provided, supplied **9** garnished

furnishing: 5 stuff **7** fitment **8** fixtures, muniment, ornament **9** adornment, apparatus, furniture **10** enrichment, habiliment

furniture: 6 graith, outfit **7** fitment, tallboy **8** equipage **9** equipment **10** decoration, encoignure, furnishing **13** embellishment

style: **6** Empire **8** Colonial, Sheraton **11** Chippendale, Hepplewhite, Renaissance

furor: ado, cry, fad **4** fury, rage, to-do **5** craze, mania **6** frenzy **7** madness **10** dernier cri

furrow: fur, rut **4** grip, plow, rout **5** chase, drain, drill, field, rigol, score, stria **6** groove, sulcus, trench **7** channel, crumple, windrow, wrinkle

furrowed: 6 rivose rugose **7** sulcate, porcate **8** porcated **10** corrugated

furry: 5 hairy

further: aid, and, new, yet **4** abet, also, fore, help, more **5** again, front, serve **6** afford, beyond, former **7** advance, earlier, forward, promote, remoter **8** moreover **9** advantage **10** accelerate, additional, in addition

furtherance: 6 assist **8** facility, progress **9** promotion **10** assistance **11** advancement

furthermore: and **4** also **7** besides **8** moreover

furthersome: 4 rash **7** helpful **11** venturesome **12** advantageous

furtive: sly **4** wary, wily **6** secret, sneaky **7** hangdog **8** mystical, sneaking, stealthy **10** creepmouse **11** clandestine **13** under-the-table

fury: ire **4** rage **5** anger, breth, furor, rigor, vixen, wrath **6** beldam, choler, frenzy **7** beldame, madness, oestrus **8** delirium, violence **9** furiosity, vehemence **10** fierceness, turbulence **11** indignation

fuse: 4 flux, frit, melt, weld **5** blend, smelt, unite **6** anneal, mingle, solder **7** liquefy **8** dissolve **10** amalgamate **11** incorporate

fusee: 5 flare, torch **6** signal

fusion: 4 flux **6** fusure, merger **8** alliance, blending **9** coalition **11** coalescence

fuss: ado, row, tew, vex **4** busk, fike, rout, spat, stir, to-do **5** bearm, touse, whaup, worry **6** bother, bustle, caddle, fantad, fantod, fettle, fidget, fissle, fistle, fizzle, fraise, fuffle, fustle, pother, potter, tumult **7** dispute, friggle, fussock, quarrel, sputter, trouble **8** business **9** confusion **10** disconcert

fussy: 6 bustle, fidfad, spruce **7** fidgety, finical **8** overnice **10** fastidious, meticulous **14** overparticular

fustanella: 5 skirt **8** petticoat

fustian: 4 rant **5** tumid **7** bombast, pompous **8** claptrap, inflated **9** bombastic, worthless

fustigate: 4 beat, whip **6** strike

futile: 4 idle, vain **5** empty **6** otiose **7** useless **8** hopeless, trifling **9** frivolous, worthless **11** ineffectual

futility: 11 uselessness **13** frivolousness

future: 5 later **6** coming, onward **9** hereafter

fuzz: nap **4** down, lint, pile **5** fluff **8** puffball

fyke: 7 fishnet

fylfot: 5 cross **6** emblem **8** swastika

G

Gaal's father: 4 Ebed

gab: lie, yap 4 talk 5 boast, mouth, prate, scoff 6 gossip 7 chatter, deceive, prattle

Gabael's son: 5 Aduel

gabardine: 5 cloth 6 fabric

gabbard, gabbart: 4 scow 5 barge 6 vessel 7 lighter

gabble: rai(Sc.), yap 4 cank, chat, talk 6 babble, cackle, gossip, habble, jabber, yabble 7 chatter, clatter, twaddle

gabbro: 4 rock 6 norite

gabelle: tax 4 duty 5 excise, impost

gaberdine: 4 coat, gown 5 frock, smock 6 mantle 7 garment 8 pinafore

gabi: 4 taro

gabirit: 4 mold 5 gauge, model

gable: 4 wall 6 dormer, pinion

Gabon: *capital:* 10 Libreville

  city: 4 Oyem 5 Bitam, Kango 10 Port Gentil

  ethnic group: 5 Fangs 8 Bapounon

  monetary unit: 5 franc 7 centime

  mountain: 8 Iboundji

  river: 6 Ogooue

Gabriel's instrument: 4 horn 7 trumpet

gad: 4 band, oath, roam, rope, rove 5 prowl, stray 6 ramble, wander 7 traipse 9 gallivant

Gad: *chieftain:* Ahi

  descendant: Zia

  father: 5 Jacob

  mother: 6 Zilpah

  son: Eri 5 Ezbon

  tribe of: 6 Erites

gadfly: 4 pest 6 bother, critic 7 annoyer 8 busybody

gadget: 4 tool 5 gibbe(Sc.) 6 device, doodad, jigger 9 doohickey 11 contrivance

gadus: 7 codfish

gadwall: 4 duck

gadzooks: 4 egad

Gaea: 6 Tellus

  consort: 6 Uranus

  offspring: 5 Titan 6 Pontus, Titans, Uranus

  parent: 5 Chaos

Gaelic (see also *Irish*): 4 Erse 6 Celtic 8 Highland

  clan: 4 Sept

  hero: 6 Ossian

  John: Ian

  land distribution: 7 rundale

  poem: 4 Duan

  spirit: 5 kelpy 6 kelpie 7 banshee

  warrior: 5 Dagda 6 Fenian

gaff: 4 hoax, hook, pick, spar, spur, talk 5 fraud, laugh, spear, trick 6 clamor, deceit, fleece, outcry 7 prating 8 raillery

gaffe: 4 goof 5 boner 7 blooper, faux pas

gag: 4 hoax, hush, joke 5 choke, heave, retch 6 be sick, muffle, muzzle 7 prevent, silence 8 obstruct, suppress, throttle 9 wisecrack 13 interpolation

gage (see also *gauge*): bet 4 pawn, risk 5 stake, wager 6 pledge 8 appraise, defiance, security 9 challenge

gaiety: fun, joy 4 glee 5 mirth 7 jollity 8 hilarity 9 festivity, good humor, merriment

gain: buy, get, net, win 4 boot, earn, good, pelf, reap 5 clear, lucre, reach 6 attain, effect, income, obtain, profit, secure 7 achieve, acquire, advance, benefit, conquer, prevail, procure, realize 8 increase 9 accretion, advantage, increment 12 appreciation

ill-gotten: 4 pelf 5 graft, lucre 6 payola

gainsay: 4 deny 6 forbid, impugn, negate, oppose, refute, resist 7 dispute 10 contradict, controvert

Gainsborough painting: 7 Blue Boy

gait: run 4 lope, pace, rack, step, trip, trot, walk 5 amble, strut, tread 6 canter, gallop 7 journey, shamble

gaiter: 4 boot, spat 6 puttee 7 cutikin(Sc.), legging 8 overshoe

gala: gay 4 fete 5 merry 6 festal, fiesta 8 festival 9 glamorous 11 celebration

galago: 5 lemur 6 monkey

Galahad: *father:* 8 Lancelot

  mother: 6 Elaine

  quest: 5 grail

Galapagos Islands resident: 8 tortoise

Galatea: *lover:* 4 Acis

  suitor: 10 Polyphemus

galaxy: 6 nebula

gale: 4 blow, gust, wind 5 blast, storm 7 tempest 8 outburst 9 hurricane, windstorm 11 northeaster, northwester, southeaster, southwester

galea: cap 6 helmet

Galen: 9 physician

galilee: 5 porch 7 portico

Galilee: *ruler:* 5 Herod

town: 4 Cana, Nain 8 Nazareth, Tiberias 9 Capernaum

Galileo's birthplace: 4 Pisa

galimatias: 6 jargon 8 nonsense 9 gibberish

galipot, gallipot: sap 5 rosin 6 barras 10 turpentine

gall: vex 4 bile, fell, flaw, fret 5 annoy, chafe, cheek, spite 6 abrade, harass, injure, poison, rancor 7 blemish 8 acerbity, cecidium, irritate, temerity 9 excoriate, impudence 10 bitterness, effrontery, exasperate

Gallagher's partner: 5 Shean

gallant: gay 4 beau, prow 5 blade, brave, bully, lover, noble, showy, swain 6 escort, polite, suitor 7 amatory, conduct, stately 8 cavalier, handsome, polished, splendid 9 attentive, chevalier, courteous 10 chivalrous, courageous 11 fashionable 12 high-spirited

gallantry: 7 bravery, courage, heroism 8 courtesy 9 attention 11 intrepidity

galled: mad, raw 4 sore 6 peeved

galleon: 4 ship 6 carack, vessel 7 carrack *cargo:* oro 4 gold

gallery: 5 porch, salon 6 arcade, loggia, piazza 7 balcony, portico, terrace, veranda 8 audience, catacomb, corridor 9 promenade

galley: 4 boat, ship, tray 5 cuddy, proof 6 bireme, galiot, hearth 7 birling, birlinn, galliot, kitchen, trireme, unireme 8 cookroom, galleass 10 triaconter

galliard: 5 dance

Gallic: 6 French

gallimaufry: 4 hash 6 jumble, medley, ragout 7 melange, mixture 8 pastiche, potpourri 10 hodgepodge

gallinae: 6 grouse, quails 7 rasores, turkeys 8 peafowls 9 curassows, partridge, pheasants

gallinule: hen 4 coot, fowl, rail

gallivant: gad 4 flit, roam 6 travel

galloon: 4 lace 5 braid 7 ribbon 8 trimming

gallop: run 4 gait, pelt 5 chase, speed 6 hasten, sprint 7 mad dash 8 fast clip

galloping dominoes: 4 dice

gallows: 5 bough 6 gibbet 7 potence 8 scaffold

galluses: 10 suspenders

galoot: guy 6 fellow, person 9 screwball, simpleton

galore: 7 profuse 8 abundant 9 plentiful

galosh: 4 boot, 6 arctic, rubber 8 overshoe

galvanize: 4 coat 6 excite 7 startle 9 electrify, stimulate 12 move to action

Galway islands: 4 Aran

galyak: fur

gam: leg 4 chat 5 visit

gamb, gambe: leg 5 shank

gambado: 4 boot 5 antic, caper, prank 6 spring 7 legging

Gambia: *capital:* 6 Banjul
city: 5 Basse 6 Fatoto 7 Kuntaur 10 Georgetown
ethnic group: 4 Fula 5 Wolof 8 Mandinka
monetary unit: 5 butut 6 dalasi
river: 6 Gambia
village in "Roots": 7 Juffure

gambit: 4 move, ploy, ruse 5 trick 7 gimmick, opening 8 maneuver 9 strategem

gamble: bet 4 dice, gaff, game, risk, spec 5 stake, wager 6 chance, hazard, plunge 9 speculate 11 uncertainty

gambler: 5 dicer 6 carrow(Ir.), player 7 plunger, sharper 8 blackleg, gamester 10 speculator
accomplice: 5 shill

gambling (see also **game:** *gambling*):
pert. to: 8 aleatory
place: 4 Reno 6 casino 8 Las Vegas 10 Monte Carlo
stake: pot 4 pool

gambol: hop 4 play 5 caper, frisk, prank 6 cavort, frolic

game: fun, jeu(F.) 4 lame, lark, plan, play, prey 5 brave, dodge, prank, sport, trick 6 course, frolic, gamble, gritty, plucky, quarry, racket, spunky 7 contest, foolery, pastime, project 8 enduring, resolute 9 amusement, diversion 10 courageous
ball: cat, tut 4 golf, polo, pool 5 fives, rugby 6 hockey, pelota, soccer, squash, tennis, tipcat 7 cricket, croquet 8 baseball, football, handball, ping-pong, softball 9 billiards 10 basketball, volleyball
bird: 4 duck 5 quail 6 turkey 7 bustard 8 pheasant 9 partridge
board: 4 keno 5 bingo, chess, Halma, lotto, salta 7 Pachisi 8 checkers, cribbage, Monopoly, Parchesi, Parchisi, Scrabble squails 9 crokinole, Parcheesi 10 backgammon
card: gin, hoc, loo, nap, pam, war 4 bank, brag, faro, hock, jass, ruff, skat, slam, snap, solo, spin, vint 5 beast, chico, cinch, comet, crimp, decoy, gilet, gleek, monte, omber, ombre, pedro, pique, pitch, poker, rummy, stuss, trump, two-up, waist, whist 6 basset, birkie, boston, bridge, casino, commit, ecarte, flinch, hearts, loadum, masset, piquet, rounce, sledge, smudge 7 bezique, canasta, cayenne, Chicago, cooncan, hundred, old maid, primero, reversi, seven-up 8 baccarat(F.), Canfield, commerce, conquian, contract, cribbage, handicap, Michigan, napoleon, patience, penneeck, pinochle 9 cinq-cents, montebank, new market, solitaire, tredrille 11 speculation 14 spite and malice

carnival: 5 darts 6 hoopla

child's: tag 7 marbles 8 leapfrog 9 hop-scotch 13 tiddledy winks

confidence: 4 scam 5 bunco, bunko, sting 6 racket

court: 5 roque 6 pelota, squash, tennis 7 jai alai 8 handball 9 badminton 10 basketball, volleyball

dice: 4 ludo 5 craps 7 pachisi 8 dominoes, trey-trip

gambling: 4 beno, faro, keno, pico 5 beano, bingo, boule, craps, keeno, lotto, monte, pique, pitch, poker, rondo, stuss 6 brelan(F.), fan-tan(Ch.), piquet, policy 7 baccara, barbudi, primero, rondeau(F.) 8 baccarat, crackloo, roulette 9 black-jack, crackaloo, montebank, twenty-one, vingt-et-un(F.) 10 panguingui (Phil. Is.)

goal: run 4 home 5 first, score, spare, tally 6 basket, strike 9 touchdown

kind of: 4 mora(It.) 6 merels, morris, quoits 7 diabolo, loggats, loggets, marbles 9 philopena 10 electronic, jack-straws, spillikins

official: 5 judge, timer 6 umpire 7 referee, starter 8 linesman 10 timekeeper

outdoor: 4 polo 6 tennis 7 cricket, croquet 9 badminton

parlor: 5 jacks 7 matador 8 charades

pin: 7 bowling, kegling, tenpins 8 ninepins, skittles

plan: 8 strategy

racket: 5 bandy 6 squash, tennis 8 lacrosse 9 badminton

rule authority: 5 Hoyle

stewed in wine: 5 salmi 6 ragout

war: 10 kriegspiel

word: 5 ghost, rebus 6 crambo 7 anagram 8 acrostic, scrabble 9 crossword

gamekeeper: 8 warrener

gamester: 5 dicer 6 player 7 gambler

gamete: egg 4 ovum 5 sperm 6 zygote 8 oosphere

gamin: imp, tad 6 urchin

domain: 6 street

gaming cube: die

gammon: leg 4 bosh, dupe, foot, gull 5 bacon, cozen, feign, thigh 6 delude, humbug 7 beguile, deceive, mislead, pretend

gamp: 8 umbrella

gamut: 4 A to Z 5 orbit, range, reach, scale 6 extent, series 7 compass

gamy: 5 spicy 6 smelly 7 lustful 8 spirited 10 malodorous 12 disreputable

ganch: 4 kill 6 impale 7 execute

gander: 4 look 5 goose 6 glance 9 simpleton

Gandhi: *name:* Aba, Abu 4 Abba, Abou, Bapu 7 Mahatma

publication: 7 Harijan

ganef: 5 thief 6 rascal

gang: mob, set 4 band, crew, pack, team 5 group, horde, shift 6 clique, outfit, travel 7 company

member of: 4 b'hoy 5 rowdy, tough

Ganges River city: 7 Benares

gangling: 4 bony 5 lanky 6 skinny 7 awkward 9 spindling

ganglion: 5 tumor

gangplank: 6 bridge 8 platform

gangrene: rot 7 mortify 8 necrosis 9 sphacelus

gangster: 4 goon, hood, thug, yegg 5 rough, thief 6 bandit, gunman 7 mobster, ruffian 8 criminal, hireling

female companion: 4 moll

gangway: 7 couloir 8 corridor 10 passageway

gannet: 4 bird, fowl 5 goose, solan

family: 4 sula

ganoid fish: gar 6 bowfin 8 sturgeon

gaol: 4 brig, jail 6 prison

gaoler: 5 guard 6 warden

gap: col 4 flaw, pass, rent 5 break, breck, chasm, chawn, cleft, clove, meuse, notch, space 6 breach, hiatus, lacuna, ravine 7 fissure, lacunae(pl.), opening 8 aperture, interval, quebrada 10 interstice 12 interruption 13 discontinuity

gape: ope 4 gasp, gawk, gaze, pant, rent, yawn 5 chawn, stare 6 rictus 7 dehisce 8 oscitate 10 rubberneck

gaping: 4 open 7 cracked, yawning 9 cavernous, separated

of plant capsule: 10 dehiscence

garage: 6 hangar, siding 8 building

garb (see also *dress*)**:** 5 array, dress, habit, style 6 attire, bundle, clothe, custom, method 7 apparel, clothes, costume, fashion, raiment, vesture 8 carriage, clothing, vestment 10 appearance, habiliment

garbage: 6 offal, trash, waste 6 debris, litter, refuse, scraps 7 rubbish

garble: 4 sift, 5 twist 6 jumble, mangle, refine, refuse, select 7 distort, pervert 8 disguise, mutilate

garcon: boy, lad 6 waiter

garden: 4 Eden, hall, park, yard 5 arbor, patch, tract 8 outfield 9 cultivate, enclosure 11 commonplace

implement: hoe 4 rake 5 mower, spade 6 scythe, sickle, trowel, weeder

kind of: 4 herb, rock 5 oasis, truck 6 cactus, flower, formal 7 kitchen 8 chinampa 9 botanical, terrarium, vegetable 10 zoological

protector: 7 Priapus

garden plant: See *plant: garden*

Garden State: 9 New Jersey

gardener: 8 yardman 9 topiarist 14 horticulturist

garfish: 8 hornbeak, hornfish

Gargantua's son: 10 Pantagruel

gargantuan: 4 huge, vast 5 giant 7 titanic 8 enormous, gigantic 9 monstrous

gargle: 9 mouthwash 11 collutorium

garish: 4 loud 5 cheap, gaudy, showy 6 bright, tawdry 8 dazzling 9 offensive

garland: 4 lei 4 band 5 crown, glory 6 anadem, corona, crants, diadem, laurel, rosary, wreath 7 chaplet, coronal, festoon 9 anthology

garlic: 4 moly, ramp 5 chive, clove 6 ransom

garment (see also **undergarment**): 4 brat, cape, coat, gear, gown, jupe, rail, robe, sari, vest 5 cloak, dress, habit 6 attire, kimono 7 apparel, leotard, raiment 8 vestment 10 investment

ancient: 4 toga 5 palla, stola 6 chiton 7 chlamys 8 himation

ecclesiastical: see **vestment**

infant's: 6 woolly 7 bunting

Malay: 6 cabaya, kabaya, sarong

medieval: 5 simar 6 kirtle, rochet, tabard 8 chausses

mourning: 5 weeds 9 sackcloth

protective: 4 brat 5 apron, armor, chaps, smock 7 cuculla 8 overalls, pinafore 9 coveralls

rain: 6 poncho 7 oilskin, slicker

sleeveless: aba 4 cape, vest 6 mantle 7 sweater 8 slip-over

South Seas: 5 pareu 8 lavalava

upper: 4 coat, vest 5 jupon, shirt, tunic, waist 6 blouse, jersey, peplos, peplus 7 sweater 8 guernsey, slip-over

garner: 4 reap 5 store 6 gather 7 collect, granary 10 accumulate

garnet: 5 jewel, stone 8 essonite

black: 8 melanite

deep-red: 6 pyrope 9 almandine, almandite

green: 7 olivine

garnish: 4 trim 5 adorn, dress, equip 6 set off 7 furnish 8 decorate, ornament 9 embellish

garret: 4 loft 5 attic, solar 6 soller, turret 7 mansard 8 cockloft 10 upper floor, watchtower

garrote, garrotte: 4 kill 7 execute 8 strangle, throttle

garrulous: 5 talky, wordy 7 gossipy, voluble 8 fanfaron 9 talkative 10 longwinded, loquacious

garter: 4 belt 5 snake 7 elastic 9 supporter

garth: dam 4 weir

garvey: 4 boat, scow

gas: 4 fuel, fume, reek, talk 5 steam, vapor 6 gossip, petrol 7 bombast 10 anesthetic, asphyxiate, illuminant

air: 4 neon 5 argon, ozone, xenon 6 oxygen 7 ammonia, krypton, sulfate 8 nitrogen

balloon: 6 helium

blue: 5 ozone

charcoal: 5 oxane

charge with: 6 aerate

colorless: 5 keten, ozone 6 arsine, ethane 7 ammonia

inert: 5 argon, radon, xenon 6 helium 8 nitrogen

inflammable: 6 butane, ethane 7 methane, propane 8 hydrogen

marsh: 7 methane

mustard: 7 yperite

nitrogen and carbon: 8 cyanogen

oxygen: 5 ozone

poisonous: 6 arsine 7 mustard, stibine

gasbag: 7 balloon

gascon: 7 boaster 8 braggart 10 swaggering 12 swashbuckler

gasconade: 7 bluster, bravado 8 boasting

gaseous: 4 thin 5 fluid, light 7 tenuous 8 aeriform, gasiform, volatile 13 unsubstantial

gash: cut 4 bite, chop, slit 5 cleft, gorge, slash, wound 6 pierce 8 incision

gasket: 4 ring, seal

gasoline: gas 6 petrol

gasp: 4 gulp, huff, pant 5 croak 6 wheeze 9 suck in air 13 inhale sharply

gassy: 5 windy 8 inflated 9 flatulent

gastronome: 7 epicure, gourmet 8 gourmand 11 connoisseur

gastropod: 4 slug 5 harpa, oliva, snail 6 nerita, nerite, volute 7 mollusk 8 pteropod

ear-shaped: 7 abalone

marine: 5 cowry, murex 6 cowrie, limpet, tethys 7 aplysia

gat: gun 6 pistol 7 channel, passage 8 revolver

gata: 5 shark

gate: bar, way 4 door, exit, hole, pass, take 5 hatch, valve 6 defile, escape, method, portal, spigot, wicket 7 barrier, opening, postern 8 entrance, receipts 9 box office, threshold, turnstile

flood: 6 sluice

gate money: fee 5 price 9 admission

Gates of Hercules: 9 Gibraltar

gatehouse: bar 5 lodge

gatekeeper: 6 porter, warden 8 guardian, watchman

gateway: 4 arch 5 pylon, toran, torii (Jap.) 6 portal, torana 8 entrance

gather: 4 bale, brew, cull, furl, herd, mass, meet, pick, rake, reap 5 amass, bunch, flock, glean, group, infer, pleat, pluck, raise, shirr 6 bundle, deduce, derive, garner, muster, scrape, summon 7 collect, compile, convene, convoke, harvest, recruit 8 assemble, colonize, compress, conclude, contract, increase 10 accumulate, congregate 11 agglomerate, concentrate 12 conglomerate

gatherer: 5 miser 7 gleaner 9 collector

gathering: bee, tea 4 bevy, fest, stag 5 crowd, party, troop 6 galaxy, plisse, shivoo, smoker 7 company, meeting, klatsch, turnout 8 assembly, function 9 concourse 10 assemblage, collection, congestion, convention 11 convocation 12 accumulation, congregation

gauche: 5 crude, inept 6 clumsy 7 awkward, uncouth 8 bumbling, plebeian, tactless 10 left-handed

gaucho: 6 cowboy 8 herdsman
lariat: 5 riata
weapon: 4 bola 7 machete

gaud: 4 bead 6 bauble, gewgaw 7 trinket 8 artifice, ornament

gaudy: 4 loud 5 cheap, feast, showy 6 flashy, garish, tawdry, tinsel 7 brankie(Sc.), glaring 8 festival 9 tasteless 11 pretentious 12 meretricious, ostentatious

gaufre: 5 wafer 6 waffle

gauge, gage: 4 size 5 judge, meter, scale 7 measure 8 estimate, standard 9 criterion, indicator, yardstick
pressure: 9 manometer
rain: 8 udometer
wind: 10 anemometer

Gauguin's island: 6 Tahiti
autobiography: 6 Noa Noa

Gaul: 6 France, Gallia(L.)
chariot: 5 esses 6 esseda, essede
god of thunder and rain: 7 Taranis
god of vegetation: 4 Esus
magistrate: 9 vergobret
people: 4 Remi
priest: 5 druid
river goddess: 8 Belisama
seer: 5 vates

gaulding: 4 bird 5 egret, heron

gaunt: 4 bony, grim, lank, lean, slim, thin 5 spare 6 barren, hollow, meager, wasted 7 haggard, scraggy, scrawny, slender 8 desolate, rawboned 9 emaciated 10 attenuated, cadaverous, forbidding

gauntlet: 4 dare, test 5 glove 6 ordeal 9 challenge, cross fire

Gautama: 6 Buddha 10 Siddhartha
wife: 6 Ahalya

gauze: 4 film, leno 5 crepe, lisse, tulle 6 fabric, tissue 7 bandage, chiffon 11 cheesecloth

gavel: 4 maul 6 hammer, mallet 9 grain pile

gavial: 9 crocodile

Gawain: *brother:* 6 Gareth 7 Gaheris
father: Lot
slayer: 8 Lancelot
son: 5 Lovel 8 Florence, Gyngalyn
uncle: 6 Arthur

gawk: 4 gape, gaze, lout 5 stare 7 bump-

kin 9 simpleton 10 rubberneck

gawky: 6 clumsy 7 awkward 8 bumbling, ungainly 9 lumbering

gay: 4 airy, boon, daft, glad, gleg 5 bawdy, bonny, brisk, happy, jolly, loose, merry, riant, showy 6 blithe, bonnie, bright, flashy, frisky, garish, jocund, jovial, joyful, lively, wanton 7 festive, gleeful, jocular 8 cavalier, cheerful, colorful, mirthful, sportive 9 brilliant, convivial, sprightly, vivacious 10 brilliante, frolicsome, homosexual, licentious 12 lighthearted

gazabo: guy 6 fellow, person

gaze: eye 4 gape, gawk, leer, look, moon, ogle, peer, pore, scan, view 5 glare, gloat, sight, stare 6 behold, glower, regard

gazebo: 6 pagoda 8 pavilion 9 belvedere 11 summerhouse

gazelle: ahu, goa 4 admi, cora, dama, kudu, mohr, oryx 5 ariel, mhorr 7 buffalo, chikara, corinne 8 antelope 9 springbok
kin: 6 impala

gazelle hound: 6 saluki

gazette: 7 courant, journal 9 newspaper

gazetteer: 5 atlas, guide 10 dictionary

Ge: See Gaea

gazump: 5 cheat 7 swindle

gean: 6 cherry

gear: 4 cam, cog, rig 4 duds, togs 5 dress, equip, goods, stuff, tools 6 doings, graith(Sc.), outfit, pinion, tackle, things 7 apparel, harness, rigging 8 clothing, cogwheel, garments, materiel, property 9 apparatus, equipment, mechanism, trappings, vestments 10 appliances, belongings, implements 12 appurtenance 13 accoutrements, paraphernalia

Geb: *daughter:* 4 Isis 8 Nephthys
father: Shu
son: Set 6 Osiris
wife: Nut

gecko: 6 lizard 7 tarente

gee: 4 jibe 5 agree 7 command 9 turn right

Gehenna: pit 4 hell 5 hades 7 inferno 10 underworld

geige: 6 fiddle, violin

gel: set 6 harden 7 congeal, thicken 8 solidify 9 coagulate

gelatin, gelatine: 5 jelly 7 sericin 8 agaragar

geld: fix 4 spay 5 alter, prune 6 neuter 8 castrate, multilate 9 expurgate 10 emasculate

gelid: icy 4 cold, iced 6 frozen

gelt: 4 gold 5 money

gem: bud 4 keas, naif, onyx, opal, ruby, sard 5 agate, beryl, cameo, jewel, paste, pearl, stone, topaz 6 amulet, bedeck, garnet, muffin, scarab, spinel **7** diamond, emerald, paragon **8** intaglio, sapphire, tigereye **9** carnelian, germinate **10** aquamarine **11** masterpiece

blue: **8** sapphire **9** turquoise **10** aquamarine

cut: **7** navette **8** baguette, cabachon, marquise **9** brilliant

face: **5** facet

green: **7** emerald, peridot **10** chrysolite

imperfect: **5** loupe

iridescent: **4** opal **5** pearl **7** cat's-eye **8** tigereye **9** moonstone

measure of weight: **5** carat

of fidelity: **5** topaz

of immortality: **7** emerald

of law: **4** ruby

of love: **8** amethyst

of peace: **7** diamond

of purity: **5** pearl

of truth: **8** sapphire

paste: **6** strass

purple: **8** amethyst

rectangular: **6** baguet **8** baguette

red: **4** ruby, sard **5** avena **6** garnet, pyrope **9** carnelian

relief-carved: **5** cameo

setting for: **4** ouch, pave **6** chaton

support: **7** setting

surface: **5** bezel, bezil, facet

Gem State: 5 Idaho

gemel: 4 twin **6** hinged, paired

geminate: 6 binate, double **7** coupled

Gemini: 5 twins **6** Castor, Pollux

gemmule: 4 bud **6** ovule

gemsbok: 4 oryx **8** antelope

gemutlich: 4 cozy **6** genial, kindly **8** cheerful **9** agreeable **11** comfortable, good-natured

gendarme: 7 soldier **9** policeman **10** cavalryman

gender: sex 4 male **5** class, genus **6** female, neuter

genealogy: 7 lineage **8** pedigree **10** family tree **12** descent chart, family record

general: 5 broad, gross **6** common, leader **7** average, officer **8** catholic **9** commander, customary, prevalent, universal **10** prevailing, widespread

Civil War: Lee **5** Grant, Meade **7** Sherman

generalize: 5 widen **6** extend, spread **7** broaden

generate: 4 make **5** beget, breed, steam **6** create **7** develop, produce **8** engender **9** originate, procreate, propagate

generation: age, era 4 kind, race **5** breed, stock **6** family **7** descent, progeny **8** creation **9** genealogy, offspring, posterity **11** descendants, procreation

generative: 8 prolific **10** productive

generator: 6 dynamo, engine **7** creator **8** auto part

generic: 6 common **9** universal **12** encompassing **13** comprehensive

generosity: 7 charity, largess **8** largesse

generous: big 4 free, good, kind, rich **5** ample, frank, noble **6** honest **7** fertile, liberal **8** abundant, gracious, handsome, highborn, spirited **9** bountiful, excellent, honorable, plenteous, unselfish, unstinted **10** altruistic, benevolent, bighearted, charitable, courageous, freehanded, munificent, openhanded **11** magnanimous, stimulating, warmhearted

genesis: 5 birth **6** origin **9** beginning **11** origination

genet: 5 berbe, horse **8** civet fur

genial: 4 bein, bien, warm **5** douce **6** benign, forthy, inborn, jovial, kindly, native **7** cordial, festive **8** cheerful, friendly, pleasant **9** benignant, expansive, gemutlich **10** enlivening

genie: 5 demon, jinni **6** spirit

genitor: 6 parent **7** creator **10** procreator

geniture: 5 birth **8** nativity **9** offspring **10** generation

genius: 5 flair, knack **6** talent, wizard **8** aptitude **9** intellect **10** brilliance

genouillere: 7 kneelet **9** kneepiece

genre: 4 kind, sort, type **5** class, style **7** species **8** category **11** description **14** classification

gens: 4 clan **5** tribe **6** family

genteel: 4 nice **6** polite **7** stylish **8** graceful, lady-like, well-bred **11** fashionable

gentian: 6 flower **7** felwort **9** baldmoney

Gentile: 7 heathen **9** Christian

gentility: 8 breeding **10** refinement

gentle: moy 4 calm, deft, dewy, easy, fair, kind, meek, mild, soft, tame **5** bland, light, milky, quiet, sweet, tamed **6** benign, docile, facile, placid, polite, tender **7** amabile, bonaire, clement, gradual, lenient **8** amenable, dovelike, lenitive, maidenly, mansuete, moderate, peaceful, soothing, tranquil, well-born **9** courteous, excellent, honorable, tractable **10** chivalrous **11** considerate **13** compassionate

gentlemen: don, rye, sir 5 sahib, senor **6** bayard, mister **7** younker **8** cavalier **9** caballero

Gentlemen Prefer Blondes author: 4 Loos

gentlewoman: 4 lady

gentry: 5 elite **7** quality, society **10** gentlefolk, upper class

genty: 5 noble **7** genteel **8** graceful **9** courteous

genu: 4 knee **5** joint

genuflect: 5 kneel **6** kowtow **10** bend the knee

genuine: 4 pure, real, true, vrai(F.) **5** frank, plain, pucka, pukka **6** actual, dinkum, honest **7** germane, gradely, sincere **8** bonafide **9** authentic, heartfelt, intrinsic, simon-pure, true-penny, unalloyed, unfeigned, veridical, veritable **10** legitimate **13** unadulterated **15** unsophisticated

genus: 4 kind, sort **5** class, order **6** gender **8** category **14** classification

pert. to: **7** generic

geode: 5 druse **6** cavity, nodule

geology: 12 earth science

age: **7** Permian **8** Cambrian, cenezoic, Devonian, Jurassic, mesozoic, Silurian, Triassic **9** paleozoic **10** Cretaceous, cryptozoic, Ordovician **13** Mississippian, Pennsylvanian

division: age, era **4** lias, lyas **5** epoch, trias

period: **6** eocene **7** miocene **8** pliocene, tertiary **9** oligocene **10** quaternary **11** pleistocene

remains: **7** fossils

science: **12** paleontology **13** palaeontology

geometric: 8 analytic **9** algebraic **10** arithmetic

geometry: angle: 9 incidence

curve: **6** spiral **7** ellipse, evolute **8** parabola, sinusoid

father: **6** Euclid

figure: **4** cone, lune **5** prism, rhomb **6** circle, gnomon, oblong **7** ellipse, rhombus **8** triangle

proposition: **7** theorem

solid: **4** cube **5** prism **7** pyramid

surface: **5** nappe, torus

geoponic: 5 rural **12** agricultural

Georgia: capital: 7 Atlanta

city: **5** Macon **6** Albany, Athens, Dalton **7** Augusta **8** Columbus **9** Savannah

county: Lee **4** Bibb, Clay, Cobb, Cook, Dade, Hall, Hart, Long, Pike, Polk, Tift, Ware **5** Bacon, Banks, Burke, Butts, Crisp, Dodge, Dooly, Early, Floyd, Grady, Peach, Rabun, Troup **6** Brooks, Clinch, Coffee, Coweta, De Kalb, Echols, Elbert, Oconee, Sumter, Twiggs, Wilkes **7** Appling, Berrien, Catoosa, Decatur, Jenkins, Lumpkin, Quitman, Screven, Telfair

early explorer: **6** de Soto

island: Sea **6** Amelia, Sapelo **7** Ossabaw, St. Simon **10** Cumberland **11** St. Catherine

lake: **7** Eufaula **8** Seminole, Sinclair **12** Sidney Lanier

mountain: **9** Blue Ridge **13** Brasstown Bald

President Carter's birthplace: **6** Plains

river: **5** Flint **6** Oconee **8** Altamaha, Ocmulgee, Savannah **12** Apalachicola **13** Chattahoochee

state bird: **8** thrasher

state flower: **12** Cherokee rose

state motto: **23** Wisdom, justice, moderation

state nicknames: **5** Peach **18** Empire State of South

state tree: **7** live oak

swamp: **10** Okefenokee

Geraint's wife: 4 Enid

germ: bud, bug **4** seed **5** spore, virus **6** embryo, sprout **7** microbe **8** rudiment **9** bacterium, beginning

germ cell: egg **4** ovum **5** sperm

germane: 4 akin, true **6** allied **7** genuine, related **8** relevant **9** pertinent **11** appropriate

German (see also **East Germany, West Germany**): **4** Goth **5** Boche, Saxon **6** Teuton

ancient tribesman: **4** Jute **6** Teuton **9** Ostrogoth

angry: **4** bose

animal: **4** tier

article: das, der, des, die

artist: **5** Durer

bacteriologist: **4** Koch

beautiful: **5** schon

blue: **4** blau

bread: **4** brot

bright: **4** hell

but: **4** aber

cake: **5** torte **9** lebkuchen **11** pfeffernuss

canal: **4** Kiel

castle: **7** schloss

cheese: **4** kase

chicken: **4** huhn

child: **4** kind

Christmas: **11** Weihnachten

clever: **5** klug

clock: uhr

code: **5** Salic

coin: **4** mark **6** kronen, thaler **7** pfennig **8** groschen

cold: **4** kalt

day: tag

dead: **4** tot

dear: **4** lieb

deep: **4** tief

dog: **4** hund

door: tur

early: **4** fruh

earth: **4** erde

evening: **5** abend

eye: **4** auge

field: **4** feld

forest: **4** wald

forest-keeper: **9** waldgrave

gnome: **6** kobold

good: gut

hair: **4** haar

hall: **4** aula, saal **5** diele

happy: **4** froh

head: **4** kopf

heart: **4** herz

highway: **8** autobahn

home: 4 heim
knight: 6 ritter
lancer: 4 ulan
language: 7 Deutsch
leaf: 5 blatt
letter: 5 brief
measles: 7 rubella
measure: aam, imi 4 last, sack, stab 5 carat, eimer, kanne, kette, maass 6 strich 7 klafter 8 scheffel, schoppen, stubchen 9 masskanne
mister: 4 herr
moon: 4 mond
never: nie
nine: 4 neun
no: 4 nein
nobleman: 4 graf 5 adlig 6 junker, ritter 7 younker
overture: 8 vorspiel
philosopher: 4 Kant 5 Hegel
school: 10 realschule, volkschule 14 oberrealschule
shoe: 5 schuh
singing festival: 10 sangerfest 11 saengerfest
society: 4 bund 6 verein 10 turnverein 12 gesellschaft
son: 4 sohn
song: 4 lied
star: 5 stern
stone: 5 stein
teacher: 6 docent, dozent
tooth: 4 zahn
tower: 4 turm
two: 4 zwei
village: 4 dorf
vowel change: 6 umlaut
weight: lot
white: 5 weiss
wine: 4 hock, wein 5 Rhine 7 Moselle
woman: 4 frau, frow 8 fraulein
world: 4 welt
year: 4 jahr
young: 4 jung
germane: 5 ad rem 7 apropos 8 relevant 9 pertinent
germicide: 5 iodin 6 iodine 10 antiseptic 11 bactericide 12 disinfectant
germinate: bud, gem 6 evolve, sprout 7 develop 10 effloresce
geryon 7 monster
gesso: 5 paste 7 plaster
gest, geste: 4 deed, feat, tale 7 exploit, romance 9 adventure
gestation: 7 bearing 8 breeding, carrying 9 pregnancy
gesture: act, nod 4 sign, wave 6 beckon, motion, salute 8 courtesy 9 formality 10 empty offer 11 gesticulate
get: pen, win 4 earn, find, gain, take, trap 5 annoy, beget, catch, fetch, learn, reach, seize 6 appear, attain, baffle, become, corner, derive, induce, obtain, puzzle, secure, suffer 7 achieve, acquire, capture, conquer, possess, prepare, procure, realize, receive, recover 8 contract, irritate, overcome, persuade, retrieve, vanquish 9 ascertain, determine 10 comprehend, conciliate, understand
get along: 4 fare 5 hurry 7 advance, prosper, succeed 8 progress
get away: lam 4 flee, scat, shoo 6 depart, escape
get back: 6 recoup, redeem, regain 7 recover
get on: 5 board 6 embark
get out: 4 exit 5 leave, scram 6 elicit, escape, reveal 7 publish, take off 8 evacuate
get-together: bee 4 stag 6 social 7 meeting
get up: 5 arise, array, dress, style 6 invent 7 arrange, costume, prepare 9 construct
get well: 4 heal 10 recuperate
gewgaw: toy 4 gaud 6 bauble, fangle, fegary, trifle 7 trinket 8 gimcrack 10 knickknack
geyersite: 4 opal
Ghana: *capital:* 5 Accra
  city: 6 Elmina, Kumasi, Tamale 7 Sunyani 9 Cape Coast, Koforidus 10 Bolgatanga
  ethnic group: Ewe 4 Akim 7 Akwapim, Ashanti, Dagomba
  former name: 9 Gold Coast
  monetary unit: 4 cedi 6 pesewa
  mountain: 8 Afadjato
  region: 5 Upper, Volta 7 Ashanti, Central, Eastern, Western 8 Northern 10 Brong-Ahafo
  river: 5 Volta
ghastly: wan 4 grim, pale 5 lurid 6 dismal, grisly, pallid 7 charnel, deathly, fearful, hideous, macabre 8 dreadful, gruesome, horrible, shocking, terrible 9 frightful
ghat: 4 pass 5 range 7 landing 8 mountain
gherkin: 6 pickle 8 cucumber
ghost: hag 4 bhut, hant 5 duppy, shade, spook 6 daemon, spirit, wraith 7 eidolon, haunter, lemures(pl.), phantom, specter 8 guytrash, phantasm, revenant 10 apparition, glimmering 11 poltergeist
ghostly: 4 eery 5 eerie, scary, weird 6 spooky 7 shadowy, spectral, uncanny 9 spiritual
ghoul: 4 ogre 5 fiend 7 monster, vampire 11 grave robber
ghoulish: 9 loathsome
giant: 4 Bara, eten, huge, ogre, rahu, Ymir 5 Argus, Cacus, jumbo, titan, troll 6 ogress 7 Antaeus, Cyclops, Goliath,

monster 8 behemoth, Bellerus, colossus 9 monstrous 10 gargantuan, prodigious, tremendous

gibber: 5 stone 6 pebble 7 boulder, chatter

gibberish: 6 jabber, jargon 7 blather, twaddle 8 claptrap 9 rigmarole 10 double-talk, mumbo jumbo

gibbet: 4 hang 5 noose 7 gallows 8 string up

gibbon: ape, lar 6 monkey, wou-wou 7 hoo-lock, siamang 10 anthropoid

gibbous: 6 convex, humped 7 hunched, rounded 11 hunchbacked, protuberant

gibe 4 gird, jape, jeer, mock, quip, twit 5 fleer, fling, flirt, flout, gleek, scoff, sneer, taunt 6 deride, heckle 7 laugh at, poke fun, sarcasm 8 ridicule

giddy: 4 daft 5 dizzy, faint, silly 6 fickle, volage 7 erratic, flighty, reeling, heedless 9 befuddled, frivolous, 11 harebrained 13 featherheaded

gift: sop 4 bent, boon, dash, dole 5 bonus, bribe, dower, dowry, favor, grant, knack, pilon, power, token 6 bounty, donary, gersum, hansel, legacy, talent 7 aptness, benefit, faculty, handsel, largess, present, subsidy 8 aptitude, bestowal, blessing, donation, gratuity, largesse, offering, pittance, potlatch 9 endowment, gratitude, lagniappe, readiness 10 compliment 11 benefaction, beneficence, serendipity 12 contribution

gifted: 4 deft 5 smart 6 clever 8 talented 9 brilliant, ingenious

gig: job 4 boat, goad, spur 5 rouse, spear, stint 6 chaise 7 demerit, provoke 8 carriage

gigantic: big 4 huge, vast 5 giant, large 7 immense, mammoth, titanic 8 colossal, enormous 9 cyclopean, gigantean, monstrous 10 gargantuan, prodigious

giggle: 5 tehee 6 teehee, titter 7 snicker, snigger

gila: 5 trout 6 lizard 10 woodpecker

Gilbert and Sullivan opera: 7 Thespis 8 Iolanthe, Patience 9 Ruddigore, The Mikado 11 H. M. S. Pinafore

Gilbert island: 5 Makin 6 Tarawa

gild: 5 adorn, tinge 7 overlay 8 brighten, inaurate 9 embellish

Gilda's father: 9 Rigoletto

gilet: 4 vest 6 bodice 9 waistcoat

gill, ghyl: ivy 4 cove, girl, lass 5 brook 6 collar, ravine, stream, tipple, valley, wattle 10 sweetheart

four: 4 pint

gilt: hog, sow 4 gold 5 money 6 gilded, golden

gimcrack: fop, toy 6 bauble, flimsy, gewgaw, trifle 7 trinket, trivial 8 ornament,

trumpery 9 frivolous 10 knickknack 13 unsubstantial

gimlet: 4 tool 8 cocktail

gimme: 6 greedy 11 acquisitive

gimmick: 4 ploy, ruse 5 trick 6 device, gadget 8 maneuver

gimp: vim 4 trim 5 orris 6 spirit 7 cripple 8 lame walk, trimming

gin: net 4 crab, grin, rack, sloe, trap 5 snare, trick 6 device, diddle, liquor, scheme 7 springe 8 artifice, beverage, schnapps 10 intoxicant 11 contrivance

ginger: pep, vim 5 spice, vigor 6 mettle, revive, spirit 8 piquancy, spirited

genus: 8 zingiber

wild: 6 asarum

ginger cookie: 4 snap

ginger root: 4 race

gingerbread: 4 cake 5 money 6 wealth 8 trimming 13 pfefferkuchen(Ger.)

gingerly: 6 warily 7 charily 8 daintily 9 carefully, elegantly, finically, guardedly, mincingly 10 cautiously 12 fastidiously

gingham: 8 chambray

ginseng: 4 herb 5 panax 6 aralia

Gioconda, La: 8 Mona Lisa

painter: 7 da Vinci

giraffe: 5 piano 6 animal, spinet 10 camelopard

girandole: 7 pendant 8 water jet 11 candelabrum

girasol, girasole: 4 opal 5 thorn 9 artichoke

gird, girt: 4 belt, bind, gibe, hasp, hoop, jerk, mock 5 brace, equip, scoff, sneer 6 clothe, fasten, secure 7 besiege, enclose, prepare, provide 8 encircle, surround 9 encompass

girder: 4 beam 6 binder

girdle: obi 4 band, bark, belt, bind, cest, ring, sash, zone 5 girth 6 bodice, cestus, circle, corset, moocha 7 baldric, balteus, environ, equator 8 cincture, cingulum, encircle

girl: gal, sis 4 chit, coed, gill, jill, lass, maid, minx 5 fille, filly, quean(Sc.), skirt, sylph, wench 6 amoret, calico, damsel, female, hoyden, tomboy 7 colleen, flapper, ingenue 9 backfisch, debutante 10 jeune fille, sweetheart 11 maidservant

of song: Amy, Ida, Sue 4 Lucy, Lulu, Mary 5 Daisy, Dinah, Dolly, Laura, Molly, Sally, Susie 6 Louise, Margie 7 Adeline, Jeannie, Mary Lou, Rosalie, Susanna

girlish: 5 sissy 7 artless 8 immature, youthful

girth: 4 band, belt, hoop 5 cinch, cinct, strap, width 6 girdle 7 measure 8 cincture, encircle 13 circumference

gist: nub 4 core, crux, pith 5 heart, point

7 essence, meaning 10 foundation

gitano, gitana: 5 gipsy, gypsy

give: gie(Sc.) 4 cede, dole, emit, hand, mete 5 apply, endow, grant, serve, yield 6 accord, afford, bestow, commit, confer, denote, devote, donate, impart, render, supply 7 consign, dispose, furnish, intrust, present, proffer, propose, provide, stretch 8 bequeath 9 vouchsafe 10 administer, contribute, deliquesce, elasticity

give a hand: aid 4 abet, help

give away: 4 dump 6 betray 7 divulge 8 disclose, get rid of, part with, telltale 9 sacrifice

give back: 4 echo 6 recede, remise, retire, return 7 replace, restore 8 make good

give forth: 4 emit 6 exhale 8 eradiate

give in: 5 bow to, yield 6 relent 7 succumb 8 back down 9 surrender

give off: 4 emit 5 cease, exude, issue 7 publish

give out: 4 deal, emit, mete 5 exude, issue, print 6 weaken 7 publish, release 9 circulate

give rise: 6 gender 7 produce 8 engender, occasion 9 originate

give up: 4 cede, drop, quit, stop 5 cease, demit, forgo, spare, waive, yield 6 devote, forego, resign, retire, reveal, vacate 7 abandon, deliver, despair, present, succumb 8 abdicate, renounce, swear off 9 lose heart, sacrifice, surrender 10 have no idea, relinquish

given: 5 fixed 6 stated 7 donated, granted 8 addicted, disposed, inclined 9 specified

givey: 4 soft

glabrous: 4 bald 6 smooth

glace: ice 6 glazed 8 polished

glacial: icy 4 cold 5 gelid 6 arctic, frigid, frosty, frozen, wintry 7 hostile

glacier: 6 icecap 8 ice sheet

deposit: 4 eskar, esker 6 placer 7 moraine 8 diluvium

direction: 5 stoss

fissure: 8 crevasse

fragment: 5 serac 7 iceberg

hill: 4 paha 7 drumlin

ridge: 4 kame, osar(pl.) 5 eskar, esker

snow: 4 neve

snow field: 4 firn, neve

glacis: 5 slope 7 incline

glad: gay 4 fain 5 eager, happy, merry, sunny 6 blithe, bright, elated, joyous 7 pleased, willing 8 cheerful 9 delighted, gratified, satisfied 11 exhilarated, tickled pink 12 lighthearted

gladden: 5 cheer, elate 6 please 7 delight, gratify, rejoice

glade: 4 vale 5 marsh 8 clearing

gladiator: 5 boxer 6 fencer 7 fighter

competition: 5 ludus

trainer: 7 lanista

gladness: joy 5 bliss, mirth 8 pleasure 9 happiness 12 cheerfulness, exhilaration

glamor, glamour: 5 charm, magic, allure 7 glitter, romance 8 illusion, witchery 9 magnetism 11 enchantment

glamorous, glamourous: 6 exotic 8 alluring, charming, romantic 11 fascinating

glance: 4 peek, peep, scan 5 brush, flash, graze 6 careen, squint 7 glimpse, rebound 9 quick look

gland: 5 liver, lymph 6 carnel, thymus 7 adrenal, parotid, thyroid 8 exocrine 9 endocrine

edible: 5 liver 6 thymus

enlargement: 7 adenoma

secretion: 5 sebum 7 hormone

swelling: 4 bubo

glandular: 7 adenoid

glare: 4 gaze 5 blaze, flame, scowl, stare 6 glower 7 glitter 8 radiance 9 showiness

glaring: 4 rank 5 clear, gaudy, gross, plain, vivid 6 brazen, bright, strong 7 blatant, burning, evident, obvious, staring, visible 8 apparent, flagrant, manifest 9 barefaced 11 conspicuous

glary: 6 frosty, frozen 7 intense, shining 8 slippery

glass: 4 lens, pane 6 beaker, bottle, cloche, cullet, goblet, mirror 7 tumbler 9 barometer, telescope

alcohol: mug 4 pony 5 stein 6 jigger, rummer, seidel 7 snifter 8 schooner

colored: 5 smalt 7 opaline 10 aventurine

container: jar 6 bottle 7 matrass

design: 4 etch

gem: 5 paste 6 strass

molten: 5 metal 7 parison

pert. to: 6 vitric

remove bubbles: 5 plane

glasses: 5 specs 6 shades 7 goggles 8 pince-nez 10 spectacles, binoculars

glassmaking: *device:* 7 ironman

frame: 7 drosser

material: 4 frit

oven: 4 lehr

glassworker: 6 blower, teaser 7 glazier

glasswort: 4 kali 5 plant

glassy: 4 hard 5 sharp 6 shrill 8 strident 9 apathetic 10 forbidding, lackluster, unwavering, unyielding

Glaucus: *father:* 8 Sisyphus

son: 11 Bellerophon

glaze: 4 blur, coat 5 cover, glare 6 enamel, finish, polish, veneer 7 burnish, grow dim, incrust, overlay, vitrify 8 film over

glazier: 11 glassworker

gleam: ray 4 beam, glow 5 blink, blush, flash, glint, sheen, shine 7 glimmer, glitter, shimmer, sparkle 8 radiance, splendor 9 coruscate 10 brightness 11 coruscation, scintillate

gleaming: 6 ablaze, bright

glean: 4 cull, reap 6 garner, gather 7 collect, extract

gleaning: 4 crop

glee: joy 4 song 5 mirth, sport 6 gaiety 7 delight, elation 8 hilarity 9 merriment 10 minstrelsy 12 cheerfulness 13 entertainment

gleeful: gay 5 merry 6 joyous 7 jocular

gleeman: 8 minstrel, musician

glen: 4 dale, dell, vale 5 heuch(Sc.) 6 dingle, valley 10 depression

glib: pat 4 easy, oily 5 quick, ready, slick 6 casual, facile, fluent, smooth 7 offhand, shallow, voluble 8 flippant, slippery, unforced 9 impromptu, talkative, insincere 10 nonchalant, unthinking 11 superficial

glide: 4 flow, sail, sile, skim, slip, soar 5 coast, creep, merge, slide, steal 6 glance 7 slither 8 glissade

gliding over: 6 labile 7 eliding

glim: bit, eye 5 light, watch 12 illumination

glimmer: 4 fire, glow 5 blink, flash, gleam 7 glimpse, glitter, shimmer, sparkle

glimmering: 5 flash, ghost 7 inkling

glimpse: 4 espy, peek, 5 trace 6 glance 7 glimmer 11 view briefly 12 fleeting look

glint: 5 flash, gleam, shine 6 luster 7 glisten, glitter, sparkle 10 brightness

glitch: 5 error 6 mishap 11 malfunction

glitter: 4 fire, glow, pomp, show 5 flash, gleam, sheen, shine 6 glamor, tinsel 7 glamour, glimmer, glisten, spangle, sparkle, twinkle 8 radiance 9 coruscate 10 brilliancy 11 coruscation, scintillate

glittering: 5 gaudy, gemmy 6 bright, fulgid 7 radiant 8 lustrous 9 brilliant, clinquant, sparkling, twinkling

gloaming: eve 4 dusk 8 twilight

gloat: 4 brag 5 exult, vaunt 7 revel in 8 crow over

global: 6 all-out, cosmic 7 general 9 universal, worldwide

globe: orb 4 ball, clew 5 earth, world 6 planet, sphere

half: 10 hemisphere

pert. to: 7 spheric

globular: 5 beady, round 9 orbicular, spherical

globule: 4 bead, blob, drop 6 bubble 7 droplet 8 particle, spherule

glockenspiel: 4 lyra 8 carillon 9 xylophone

glom(sc.): 4 take 5 steal, swipe, watch 10 understand

gloom: 4 dusk, murk 5 cloud, drear, frown 7 despair, dimness, sadness 8 darkness 9 dejection, heaviness, obscurity 10 cloudiness, depression, desolation, melancholy

gloomy: dim, sad, wan 4 blue, dark, dour, eery, glum 5 black, brown, dusky, heavy, moody, murky, stern 6 cloudy, dismal, dreary, morose, somber, sullen 7 clouded, obscure, stygian 8 darkling, darksome, dejected, desolate, downcast, overcast 9 cheerless, darkening, depressed, saturnine, tenebrous 10 depressing, despondent, foreboding, husterless, melancholy, sepulchral, tenebrific 11 pessimistic 12 disconsolate, disheartened

glop: goo 4 guck, muck 11 thick liquid

glorify: 4 hery, laud 5 adore, adorn, bless, boast, exalt, extol, glory, honor, vaunt 6 praise 7 clarify, elevate, ennoble, magnify 8 emblazon, eulogize 9 celebrate 11 apotheosize

gloriole: 4 aura, halo 7 aureole

glorious: 5 grand, noble 6 bright 7 eminent, haughty, radiant 8 boastful, ecstatic, gorgeous, renowned, splendid 9 wonderful 10 celebrated, delightful 11 illustrious, magnificent, resplendent

glory: 4 fame, halo 5 boast, eclat, exult, honor, kudos, pride 6 beauty, praise, renown 7 aureole 8 ambition, splendor 9 greatness 10 admiration, brilliancy, effulgence, reputation 11 distinction 12 magnificence

gloss: 4 glow 5 dodge, gloze, sheen, shine 6 blanch, enamel, excuse, luster, polish, remark, veneer 7 burnish 8 annotate, flourish, palliate, pretense 9 semblance, sleekness 10 brightness, commentary 14 interpretation

glossal: 7 lingual

glossary: 4 list 7 lexicon

glossy: 5 nitid, silky, sleek 6 bright, smooth 7 shining 8 lustrous, polished, specious 9 plausible

glove: 4 cuff, mitt 6 mitten, sheath 7 chevron, dannock, gantlet 8 gauntlet

fabric: 4 silk, wool 5 nylon 6 cotton

leather: kid 4 napa 5 mocha, suede 7 pigskin

shape: 5 trank

glow: 4 beam, halo 5 ardor, blush, flame, flush, gleam, gloss, shine 6 warmth 7 glimmer 13 incandescence

glower: 4 sulk 5 frown, scowl, stare 9 look black

glowing: hot, red 5 fiery, vivid 6 ardent 7 burning, candent, fervent, radiant, shining 10 candescent

Gluck opera: 5 Orfeo 7 Alceste

glucose: 5 sugar 6 starch 7 sucrose 8 dextrose

glue: fix 5 mount, paste, stick 6 adhere,

attach, cement, fasten, gluten, sizing **7**
sericin **8** adhesive, mucilage

glum: 4 dour **5** moody, surly **6** dismal,
gloomy, morose, sullen **8** dejected,
frowning, overcast **10** melancholy **11**
threatening

glume: 4 leaf **5** bract

glut: 4 cloy, fill, gulp, sate **5** draft, gorge **6**
englut, excess, pamper **7** engorge, sa-
tiate, surfeit, swallow **8** overfeed, overload, plethora, saturate

gluten: gum **4** glue **7** fibrin **8** adhesive

glutethimide: 8 sedative **13** phenobarbi-
tol

glutinous: 4 ropy, sizy **5** gluey, gummy **6**
sticky **7** viscous

glutton: hog, pig **8** gourmand **9** overeater,
wolverine

gluttonous: 6 greedy **7** hoggish **9** voracious

glyph: 6 symbol **7** channel

gnar, gnarr: 5 growl, snarl

gnarl: 4 knot **5** growl, knurl, snarl, twist **6**
tangle **7** contort

gnarled: 6 knotty, rugged, sinewy **7**
crabbed, twisted **8** hardened **9** roughened

gnash: 4 bite **5** chomp, grind

gnat: 4 fly **4** pest **5** midge **6** insect

gnaw: eat **4** bite, chew, fret **5** erode **6** harass, nibble **7** corrode, torment **8** wear
away

gnome: elf, saw **5** adage, bogey, dwarf,
elves(pl.), maxim, motto, pigmy, troll **6**
goblin, kobold, sprite **8** aphorism, apothegm

gnomon: 9 indicator **10** sundial pin

gnostic: 4 wise **6** clever, shrewd **7** knowing
12 intellectual

gnu: 5 takin **6** mammal **8** antelope **10** wil-
debeast

go: act, bet, bid, die, gae, mog, run **4** fall,
fare, gang, lead, mosy, move, pass, read,
ride, turn, walk, wane, wend, work **5**
break, elope, leave, occur, set-to, steal,
visit **6** attain, become, belong, betake,
depart, elapse, follow, happen, intend,
resort, result, retire, travel **7** conduce,
operate, proceed, succeed **8** diminish,
traverse, withdraw **9** circulate, harmonize, undertake

aboard: **6** embark **7** entrain

ahead: **7** proceed **8** continue, progress

along: **5** agree **6** concur

around: **5** avoid **6** detour **10** circumvent

ashore: **4** land **6** debark **9** disembark

astray: err **8** aberrate, miscarry

away: **4** exit, scat, shoo **5** leave, scram **6**
begone, depart, retire

back: ebb **6** recede, return, revert **7** regress, retreat **10** retrogress

back on: **6** betray, renege **7** abandon **10**
break faith

before: **4** lead **7** precede **8** antecede

between: **7** mediate **9** interpose

down: sag **4** fall, sink **5** lower **7** decline,
descend, founder **8** decrease **11** deteriorate

forward: **4** fare **7** advance **8** progress

into: **5** audit, delve, enter, probe **7** examine

mad: **4** rage, rave, roar **5** erupt

on: **5** enter **7** proceed **8** continue

over: **5** renew **7** retrace **9** backtrack

swiftly: run **5** scoot, speed

through: **6** endure, suffer **9** penetrate **10**
experience

to and fro: **5** waver **6** totter, wig-wag **7**
stagger **9** fluctuate, vacillate **11** shuttlecock

to pot: die **4** fail **7** decline

up: **4** rise **5** arise, raise **6** ascend

with: fit **4** date, suit **5** agree **6** escort **9**
accompany, harmonize

go-ahead: 4 okay **8** all clear **11** green
light **13** authorization

go-between: 5 agent, envoy **6** broker **7**
arbiter **8** mediator **10** mouthpiece **11**
internuncio **12** intermediary

go-cart: 4 pram **5** wagon **12** perambulator

goa: 6 mugger(Ind.) **7** gazelle

goad: egg, gad, rod **4** brod, dice, edge,
move, prod, spur, urge, yerk **5** ankus,
decoy, impel, pique, prick, sting, thorn
6 incite **7** inflame **8** irritate, stimulus **9**
incentive, instigate, stimulate **10** incitement

goal: aim, end **4** base, butt, dole, hail,
mark, mete **5** bourn, finis, score, **6**
object **7** purpose **8** ambition **9** intention, objective **10** aspiration **11** destination **12** consummation

goat: kid, ram, tur **4** ibex, tahr **5** beden,
billy, goral, nanny **6** alpaca, chamal, pa-
sang, victim **7** fall guy, markhor **8** aega-
grus, ruminant **9** bouquetin, stambecco,
steinbock

constellation: **9** Capricorn

disease: **7** takosis

flesh: **6** chevon

genus: **5** capra

god of: Pan

male: **4** buck **5** billy

pert. to: **6** capric **7** caprine, hircine

wild: **4** ibex **7** markhor

goatee: 5 beard **7** Vandyke

goatherd: 5 Damon

goatish: 4 lewd **6** coarse **7** caprine, hircine, lustful **9** salacious **10** lascivious

goatskin: 9 chevrette

gob: 4 hunk, lump, mass **5** chunk **6** sailor,
seaman **7** mariner **8** quantity

gobbet: 5 gout **5** piece **6** morsel **7**
driblet, portion **8** fragment, mouthful

gobble: 4 gulp **6** snatch **7** swallow

Gobi Desert site: 4 Asia

goblet: cup 5 glass, hanap 6 beaker, vessel 7 chalice 8 standard

goblin: elf, hag, nis 4 bhut 5 bogey, bogle, bucca, gnome, nisse, ouphe, pooka 6 booger, churel, kobold, sprite 7 brownie

gobs: lots 5 heaps, loads, scads 6 oodles, plenty

god (see also **deity, gods**): Ada, Ani, Asa, Bel, Bes, Geb, Keb, Ler, Min, Pan, Ran, Seb, Tiu, Tyr, Ull, Van 4 aitu, Amen, Amon, Aten, Aton, Baal, deus(L.), deva, dieu(F.), Frey, Hler, idol, Kama, Loke, Loki, Nora, Odin, Orra, Ptah, Rama, Surt, Thor, Vali, Yama, Zeus 5 Aeger, Aegir, Asura, Baldr, Brage, Brama, Donar, Freyr, Hades, image, Othin, Pluto, Shiva, Surtr, Woden 6 Apollo, Brahma, Cronus, Elohim, Ganesa, Hermes, Hoenir, Kronus, Marduk, Njorth, Osiris, Saturn, Vulcan, Yahweh 7 Bacchus, creator, Forsete, godhead, Heimdal, Jehovah, Jupiter, Krishna, Mercury, Serapis, Vitharr 8 Almighty, Dionysus 9 Heindallr, Hlorrithi 10 Hephaestus 11 Ramachandra

false: 4 Baal 6 Mammon

love for: 5 piety 6 amadis, bhakti

God be with you: 5 adieu, adios 7 goodbye

god-fearing: 5 pious 6 devout 9 religious

god-horse: 6 mantis

god-like: 5 pious 6 deific, devout, divine 8 immortal 9 religious

goddess (see also **god**): Bau, Dis, Eir, Eos, Hel, Mut, Nut, Uma 4 Anta, Bast, Devi, Gaia, Hela, Hera, Isis, Juno, Kali, Nina, Norn, Saga, Urth, Wyrd 5 Belit, Ceres, Diana, Durga, Freya, Frigg, Gauri, Nanna, Venus 6 Athena, Aurora, Chandi, Freyja, Frigga, Hecate, Hestia, Shakti, Tiamat 7 Artemis, Asynjur, Demeter, Mylitta, Parvati 9 Aphrodite, Haimavati 10 Persephone, Proserpina

godfather: don 7 sponsor

godforsaken: 6 dismal 8 desolate, wretched 9 miserable, neglected

godless: 6 unholy, wicked 7 impious, profane 9 atheistic

godliness: 5 piety 13 righteousness

godly: 5 pious 6 devout 8 gracious 9 religious, righteous

gods: For gods of specific localities, religions, or functions, see under the specific locality, religion, or function. Examples: "hindu god": see **Hindu:** *deity;* "god of war": see **war:** *god of.*

gods' abode: 6 heaven 7 Olympus

godsend: 4 boon 8 blessing 9 life saver

Goethe drama: 5 Faust 6 Egmont, Stella 7 Clavigo

gofer: 9 errand boy, messenger

goffer: 4 iron 5 crimp, pleat

go-getter: 6 dynamo 7 hustler 8 live wire

goggle: bug, eye 4 roll 5 stare 6 squint

goggler: 4 scad 5 akule

goggles: 5 specs 5 glasses 8 blinkers

going: run, way 4 exit, fare, gait, gate, path, road 5 bound 6 access 7 current 8 behavior 9 departure 10 passageway

goiter: 6 struma 7 strumae(pl.)

gola: 4 cyma 7 granary 9 storeroom

gold: oro(Sp.) 4 gelt, gilt 5 aurum, metal 6 riches, wealth 7 bullion 9 clinquant

bar: 5 ingot

black: oil

deposit: 6 placer

fool's: 6 pyrite

imitation: 6 ormolu, oroide

measure of weight: 5 carat

pert. to: 4 dore 6 aurous

thin sheet of: 4 foil 6 latten

uncoined: 7 bullion

yielding: 10 auriferous

gold braid: 5 orris

gold-brick: 7 swindle

Gold Bug author: Poe

gold-plate: 4 gild, gilt

golden: 4 gilt, rich 5 auric, blest, blond 6 blonde, mellow, yellow 7 aureate, halcyon, shining 8 precious 9 favorable, Pactolian, yellowish 10 propitious

golden age: 9 siecle d'or(F.)

golden ager: 7 oldster 13 elderly person, senior citizen

golden apple giver: 5 Paris

golden bough: 9 mistletoe

golden chain: 8 laburnum

Golden Fleece: *keeper of:* 6 Aeetes

land of: 7 Colchis

seeker: 5 Jason 8 Argonaut

ship used: 4 Argo

golden oriole: 5 pirol 6 loriot

Golden State: 10 California

goldeneye: cur 9 merrywing

goldenrod: 8 solidago

goldfinch: 8 graypate, greypate 12 yellow-hammer

goldfish: 4 carp 6 calico 9 garibaldi, shubunkin

goldsmith: 7 artisan 9 artificer

crucible: 6 cruset

golem: 5 robot 9 automaton, blockhead

golf: *assistant:* 5 caddy 6 caddie

club: 4 iron, wood 5 baffy, cleek, mashy, spoon 6 brassy, driver, jigger, mashie, putter 7 brassie, midiron, niblick

conceded putt: 5 gimme

course: 5 links

cry: 4 fore

cup: 5 Ryder 6 Walker

hazard: 4 trap 5 stymy 6 bunker, stymie

mound: tee

mulligan: 9 free drive

score: par 5 bogey, bogie, eagle 6 birdie, Nassau

stroke: 4 hook, loft, putt 5 drive, slice
target: cup 4 flag 5 green
term: lie, tee 4 baff, 5 divot, dormy, green 6 dormie, stroke 7 gallery
golfer: 8 linksman
notable men: 4 Ford (Doug), Pate (Jerry) 5 Boros (Julius), Hagen (Walter), Hogen (Ben), Irwin (Hale), Jones (Bobby), Shute (Denny), Smith (Horton), Snead (Sam) 6 Casper (Billy), Miller (Johnny), Nelson (Byron), Ouimet (Francis), Palmer (Arnold), Player (Gary), Rogers (Bill), Watson (Tom) 7 Sarazen (Gene), Stadler (Craig), Trevino (Lee), 8 Nicklaus (Jack), Weiskopf (Tom) 10 Middlecoff (Cary) 11 Ballesteros (Seve)
notable women: 4 Berg (Patty) 5 Lopez (Nancy), Suggs (Louise) 6 Alcott (Amy), Caponi (Donna), Daniel (Beth), Rankin (Judy), Wright (Mickey) 9 Whitworth (Kathy)
Goliath: 5 giant
home: 4 Gath
place of death: 4 Elah
slayer: 5 David
golly: 4 oath, yell
Gomer: *father:* 7 Japheth
husband: 5 Hosea
gondola: car 4 boat 5 barge, coach
gone: 4 away, left, lost 6 absent 7 missing 8 absorbed, departed, finished, vanished
gone by: ago, o'er 4 over, past
Goneril: *father:* 4 Lear
sister: 5 Regan 8 Cordelia
gonfalon: 4 flag 6 banner, ensign 7 pennant 8 standard
goober: 6 peanut
good: bon(F.), fit 4 able, bein, bien(F.), boon, braw, fine, full, gain, kind, nice, prow 5 ample, brave, bueno(Sp.), bully, moral, nifty, pious, sound, valid 6 benign, devout, expert, profit, proper 7 copious, gradely, helpful, liberal, trained, upright 8 becoming, budgeree, decorous, friendly, gracious, interest, orthodox, pleasant, pleasing, salutary, skillful, suitable, virtuous 9 agreeable, bountiful, competent, dauntless, enjoyable, estimable, excellent, favorable, fortunate, indulgent, reputable, righteous, well-being 10 auspicious, beneficial, benevolent, courageous, gratifying, profitable, sufficient 11 pleasurable, respectable, responsible, well-behaved 12 considerable, satisfactory, stouthearted, well-disposed
good-bye, good-by: 4 tata 5 adieu(F.), adios(Sp.), aloha, ciaou(It.) 6 so-long 7 cheerio 8 farewell
Good Earth author: 4 Buck
good-for-nothing: 4 orra 7 useless, wast-

rel 8 spalpeen(Ir.) 9 worthless 10 ne'er-do-well 11 rapscallion
good health: 5 skoal 6 prosit 7 slainte
good-looking: 4 fair 5 bonny 6 comely, pretty 7 eyesome, winsome 8 handsome 9 beautiful 10 attractive, personable
good luck: 7 fortune
image: 6 alraun
good-natured: 6 genial, jovial 7 amiable 8 cheerful, obliging 9 easy-going, gemutlich
good spirit: 8 eudaemon
goodliness: 5 grace 6 beauty 8 goodness, kindness 10 comeliness, excellence
goodly: 4 kind 5 large 6 comely, portly 8 gracious, handsome 9 capacious, excellent 12 considerable
goodness: 6 bounty, purity, virtue 8 chastity, kindness 10 excellence, generosity, goodliness 11 beneficence, benevolence
goods: 4 gear 5 stock, wares 7 chattel, effects 8 property 11 commodities, merchandise, possessions
cast overboard: 5 lagan, ligan 6 jetsam, lagend
lost in shipwreck: 7 flotsam
smuggled: 10 contraband
stolen: 4 loot, pelf 5 booty 6 spoils
goodwill: 4 love 5 amity, favor 8 kindness, sympathy 9 readiness 10 friendship, heartiness 11 benevolence 12 friendliness
goody: 5 candy 6 bonbon, tidbit 8 goodwife 9 sweetmeat
goof: err 5 gum up, spoil 7 blunder
goofy: 5 silly 6 insane 7 foolish 8 gullible
gook: 4 muck 5 bilge, hooey, trash 6 drival
goon: sap 4 boob, dope, thug 6 mugger 7 hoodlum
gooney bird: 9 albatross
goosander: 9 merganser
goose: 4 bird 5 ninny, solan 7 widgeon 9 screwball, simpleton
cry: 4 honk, yang 5 cronk
flock: 4 raft 6 gaggle
genus: 4 chen 5 anser, brant
mackerel: 9 phalarope
male: 6 gander
pert. to: 8 anserine 9 grossular
snow: 4 chen 5 wavey 9 whitehead
tailor's: 8 flatiron
wild: 5 brant 7 gray-lag 8 barnacle
young: 7 gosling
goose egg: 4 zero 5 zilch 6 cipher, naught 7 nothing
gooseflesh: 5 bumps 7 pimples
goosefoot: 5 blite, plant, shrub
gopher: 4 tuza 6 rodent 8 squirrel, tortoise
Gopher State: 9 Minnesota
Gorboduc's son: 6 Porrex

Gordian: 9 intricate 11 complicated

gore: 4 stab 5 blood, filth, inset, slime 6 gusset, insert, pierce 7 carnage 9 penetrate

gorge: 4 fill, gaum, glut, pass, sate 5 cajon, canon, chasm, flume, gulch, gully, kloof, strid 6 canyon, coulee, defile, englut, nullah, ravine, valley 7 couloir, overeat, pitcher, satiate 8 quebrada 10 gluttonize

gorgeous: 4 vain 5 grand, showy 6 costly 8 dazzling, glorious, splendid 9 beautiful, luxurious 11 magnificent, resplendent

Gorgon: 6 Medusa, Stheno 7 Euryale

watcher for: 4 Enyo 5 Deino 6 Graeae(pl.) 8 Pephredo

gorilla: ape 7 primate 10 anthropoid

gorse: 4 whin 5 furze 7 juniper

gory: 6 bloody 9 murderous 10 sanguinary 12 bloodstained

goshawk: 7 tiercel

keeper: 8 ostreger 10 austringer

gospel: 5 creed 7 tidings 8 doctrine, last word, teaching

harmony of the four: 11 diatessaron

gossamer: 4 airy 5 filmy, gauzy, sheer 10 diaphanous

gossip: gab 4 blab, chat, dirt 5 clack, rumor, snoop 6 babble, gabble, magpie, tattle 7 chatter, hearsay, prattle, scandal 8 busybody, idle talk, informer, quidnunc 9 chatterer 10 newsmonger, talebearer, tattletale 11 scuttlebutt

Goth: 8 Visigoth 9 barbarian, Ostrogoth

hero: 5 Wudga

last: 8 Roderick

Gothamite: 9 New Yorker

Gothic: 4 rude 5 rough 6 fierce 8 barbaric, medieval, Teutonic

Gouda: 6 cheese

kin of: 4 Edam

gouge: 4 tool 5 cheat, fraud 6 cavity, chisel, groove 7 defraud 9 extortion 10 overcharge

goulash: 4 stew 6 jumble 7 mixture 8 mishmash

Gounod opera: 5 Faust

gourd: 4 hole, pepo 5 melon, pepos 6 bottle, vessel 7 anguria 8 calabash, cucurbit 9 colocynth 11 chilacayote

rattle: 6 maraca

sponge: 4 loofa, luffa

gourmand: 7 glutton, gourmet 8 big eater 11 trencherman

gourmet: 7 epicure 8 gourmand 9 bon vivant 10 gastronome 11 connoisseur

gout: 4 clot, drop 5 taste 6 blotch 7 podagra 9 arthritis 11 coagulation, discernment

govern: run 4 curb, rein, rule, sway 5 guide, regle, steer 6 bridle, direct, manage, police 7 command, conduct, control, preside, refrain 8 dominate, regulate, restrain 9 influence, supervise 10 administer, discipline

governance: 7 control 10 government, management

governess: 5 nanny, tutor 6 abbess 8 mistress 9 nursemaid

government: law 4 rule 5 power 6 regime 7 conduct, regency, regimen 8 guidance monarchy, republic 9 authority, autocracy, democracy, hierarchy, oligarchy 10 governance, management, regulation 11 aristocracy

agent: 5 envoy 6 consul 8 diplomat, minister 10 ambassador

art of: 8 politics 13 statesmanship

by a few: 9 oligarchy

by church: 9 hierarchy 10 hierocracy

by one: 8 monarchy 12 dictatorship

by people: 9 democracy

by rich: 10 plutocracy

by three: 8 triarchy 11 triumvirate

by women: 8 gynarchy 11 gynecocracy

head: 4 czar, king 5 queen 7 emperor, empress, premier 8 dictator 9 president 10 presidente

official: 6 syndic 10 bureaucrat

opposition to: 10 antarchism

without: 6 acracy 7 anarchy

governor: bey 4 lord 5 deity, nabob, pilot, ruler 6 rector, regent 7 captain, control, manager, viceroy 8 director 9 president, regulator 10 gubernator, magistrate

castle: 6 alcaid 7 alcaide 9 castellan

gown (see also **dress, garment):** 4 robe, toga 5 frock, habit, manto, toosh 6 clothe, invest, mantua 7 garment 11 formal dress

dressing: 4 robe 6 kimono 8 peignoir

loose: 5 smock 6 banian, camise, chimer 7 cassock, chemise

Moslem: 4 jama 5 jamah

Goya figure: 4 Maja

grab: nab 4 boat, hold, take 5 catch, clasp, grasp, seize 6 arrest, clutch, collar, snatch 7 capture, grapple 11 appropriate

grabble: 5 grope, seize 6 snatch, sprawl 7 grapple 11 appropriate

grace: 4 ease 5 adorn, charm, favor, leave, mercy 6 beauty, become, bedeck, polish, prayer, virtue 7 commend, dignify, gratify 8 beautify, easiness, efficacy, elegance, kindness 9 embellish, privilege 10 comeliness, goodliness, permission, refinement, seemliness 12 dispensation 14 attractiveness

Grace: 6 Aglaia, Charis, Thalia 10 Euphrosyne

mother of: 5 Aegle

graceful: 4 airy, easy 6 comely, gainly,

mignon, seemly **7** elegant, fitting, genteel, tactful **8** charming, debonair, delicate **9** beautiful **11** appropriate

graceless: 4 ugly **5** cruel **7** awkward **8** depraved **9** abandoned, inelegant, merciless **10** ungracious **11** unfortunate

gracenote: 12 appoggiatura

graces: 8 agremens **9** agrements

gracile: 4 thin **6** slight **7** slender **8** graceful

gracious: 4 good, kind, mild **5** civil, godly, happy, lucky, suave **6** benign, godly, kindly **7** affable **8** benedict, debonair, generous, handsome, merciful, pleasing **9** benignant, courteous

grackle: 9 blackbird

gradation: 4 rank, step **5** scale, stage **6** degree, series **8** position **10** difference

grade: peg **4** mark, rank, rate, size, sort **5** class, level, order, stage **6** ascent, assort, degree, rating, select **7** incline, inspect **8** classify, gradient, graduate **14** classification

grader: 9 bulldozer

gradient: 4 ramp **5** grade, slope

gradine, gradin: 5 shelf **7** retable

gradual: 4 easy, slow **6** gentle **9** leisurely **10** step by step

graduate: 6 alumna **7** alumnus **9** calibrate

Graeae, Graiae: 4 Enyo **5** Deino **8** Pephredo
father: **7** Phorcus, Phorcys
sister: **6** Gorgon, Medusa **7** Gorgons

graff: 5 canal, ditch, fosse **6** trench

graft: dig **4** cion, toil, work **5** ditch, gravy, labor, scion, trade **6** boodle, inarch, payola, trench **7** bribery

grafted: 6 united **8** attached
heraldry: **4** ente

grail: ama, cup **4** bowl **6** vessel **7** chalice, platter **8** sangraal, sangreal
knight of: **4** Bors **7** Galahad **8** Percival

grain: jot, rye **4** corn, grit, meal, oats, rice, seed, wale, whit **5** fiber, grist, maize, scrap, spark, speck, trace, wheat **6** barley, cereal, kernel, russud(Russ.) **7** granule, modicum, texture **8** particle **9** granulate
beard: awn
brewing: **4** malt
bundle: **5** sheaf
chaff: **4** bran, grit
coating: **4** bran
disease: **4** smut **5** ergot
dried: **5** straw **6** groats, rissom, rizzom
ear of: **5** spike **6** ressum
foodstuff: **6** cereal
fungus: **5** ergot
funnel: **6** hopper
goddess of: **5** Ceres **7** Demeter
ground: **4** meal **5** flour, grist

line: **5** swath
measure: **6** thrave
mixture: **6** fodder **7** farrage **9** bullimong
outer membrane: **6** extine
parched: **7** graddan
price: **4** fiar(Sc.)
receptacle: bin **8** elevator
refuse: pug **5** chaff
scoop: **5** shaul
spike: ear
stack: **4** rick
tool: **5** flail
warehouse: **8** elevator

grainy: 6 coarse **8** granular, textured

gram: 6 weight
one-tenth: **8** decigram
molecule: mol **4** mole

gramary: 5 magic **10** necromancy **11** enchantment

grammar: 6 syntax **9** accidence **11** linguistics
case: **6** dative **8** ablative, genitive, vocative **9** objective **10** accusative, nominative, possessive
describe: **5** parse
direct address: **8** vocative
example: **8** paradigm
term: **6** phrase, simile **8** metaphor

grampus: orc **4** ocra **5** whale **7** cetacea, dolphin **8** cetacean, scorpion

granada: 11 pomegranate

granary: bin **4** gola **6** garnel, garner, girnal, girnel, grange **8** cornloft **9** cornhouse **10** repository, storehouse

grand: 4 epic, main **5** chief, great, lofty, noble, showy **6** august, epical, famous, superb, swanky **7** exalted, immense, stately, sublime **8** foremost, glorious, gorgeous, majestic, splendid **9** dignified, grandiose, principal, sumptuous **10** impressive, preeminent **11** ceremonious, illustrious, magnificent **13** comprehensive

Grand Canyon state: 7 Arizona

Grand Duke of Hell: 6 Abogor

grand slam: 4 vole **5** homer **7** home run

grandee: 6 bashaw **7** magnate **8** nobleman **10** clarissimo(It.)

grandeur: 4 pomp **5** state **6** parade **7** majesty **8** elegance, splendor, vastness **9** greatness, immensity, loftiness, nobleness, sublimity **10** augustness **12** magnificence

grandfather: 6 atavus **8** grandfer, gudesire(Sc.)
pert to: **4** aval

grandiloquent: 6 heroic, turgid **7** pompous **9** bombastic

grandiose: 4 epic **5** grand **6** turgid **7** pompous **8** imposing **9** bombastic, expansive, flaunting **10** impressive

grandmother: 6 granny, gudame(Sc.) **7**

grannie: 8 babushka(Russ.)

Devil's: 4 Baba

grange: 4 farm 7 granary 9 farmhouse

granger: 6 farmer

granite: 6 aplite 7 haplite, syenite 8 alaskite

Granite State: 12 New Hampshire

granitic: 4 hard 7 austere 10 inflexible

grant: aid 4 boon, cede, gift, give, lend, loan, mise 5 admit, allot, allow, bonus, chart, cowle, spare, yette, yield 6 accede, accord, afford, assent, bestow, betake, beteem, bounty, confer, octroi, patent, permit, remise 7 adjudge, concede, consent, promise, subsidy, tribute 8 bestowal, donation, transfer 9 franchise, undertake 10 concession, permission, relinquish 11 acknowledge

granular: 5 sandy 6 coarse, grainy

granule: 4 pill 5 grain 6 nodule, pellet 8 particle

grape: uva 5 Pinot, Tokay 6 Agawam, Lalang, Malaga, Malage, Muscat 7 Catawba, Concord, Hamburg, Mission, Niagara 8 Delaware, Riesling, Thompson 8 muscadine 11 Scuppernong

acid: 7 racemic

cluster: 10 racemation

conserve: 5 jelly, uvate

cultivation: 11 viniculture, viticulture

dried: 6 raisin

drink: 4 dibs, sapa, wine

fermentation: 6 cuvage(Fr.)

gatherer: 8 vintager

genus of: 5 vitis

juice: 4 dibs, must, sapa, stum

pert. to: 4 uval 10 botryoidal

refuse: 4 marc

residue: 4 marc, rape 6 pomace

seed: 4 acinus

spirit: 4 marc

sugar: 8 dextrose, fructose

grapefruit: 6 pomelo 8 shaddock

Grapes of Wrath: *author:* 9 Steinbeck

family: 4 Joad

people: 5 Okies

grapevine: 4 caro 5 rumor 6 gossip, report

pest: 10 phylloxera

graph: map 5 chart 6 sketch 7 diagram, outline

graphic: 5 lucid, vivid 6 visual 7 precise 8 explicit, incisive 9 pictorial, realistic, well drawn 11 picturesque

graphite: 4 lead 6 carbon

grapnel: 4 drag, hook 6 anchor

grapple: 4 grab, hold 5 grasp 6 clinch, tackle 7 contend, grapnel, seizing, seizure, wrestle 8 struggle

grasp: nap, see 4 clam, fist, grab, grip, hold, take 5 catch, clasp, seize, snare 6 clench, clinch, clutch, snatch 7 control, embrace, grapple 8 handfast 9 apprehend 10 comprehend, understand 13 comprehension

grasping: 4 avid, hard 6 greedy, grippy 7 miserly 8 covetous 10 avaricious 12 apprehension, parsimonious

adapted for: 10 prehensile, prehensive

grass (see also *cereal*): pot 4 lawn, reed, turf 6 darnel 7 hassock, herbage, pasture 9 colieroot, marijuana, vetiveria 10 greensward

blade of: 7 traneen

dried: hay 6 fodder

fiber: 4 flax 5 istle, ramee, ramie 6 bhabar

fodder: 4 dura, gama 6 millet

forage: 7 setaria

genus of: 4 aira, 5 stipa 6 clover, lygeum 7 setaria

kinds of: eel, fog, hay, poa 4 alfa, bent, cane, diss, leaf, reed, 5 avena, grama, sedge, spart, spike, stipa 6 enalid, marram, quitch, redtop, sesame, sorrel 7 esparto, traneen 8 calfkill 9 bouteloua

tuft: 7 tussock

grasshopper: 4 grig 6 locust

relative: 7 katydid

grassland: lea 4 lawn, rakh(Ind.), vale 5 field, range, veldt 6 meadow, pampas 7 pasture, prairie, savanna

grate: jar 4 fret, grid, grit, rasp 5 grill, grind 6 abrade, basket, offend, prison, scrape 7 grating 8 imprison, irritate

grateful: 8 thankful 9 agreeable 12 appreciative

gratification: 4 gust 6 reward 8 delicacy, gratuity, pleasure 9 enjoyment 10 recompense 11 contentment 12 satisfaction

gratified: 4 glad 5 proud 7 pleased 9 delighted

gratify: 4 feed, sate 5 adorn, amuse, feast, grace, humor, wreak 6 arride, foster, pamper, please 7 appease, content, delight, flatter, gladden, indulge, requite, satisfy

grating: 4 grid, rasp 5 grill, harsh, raspy, rough 6 grille, hoarse 8 gridiron, grinding, strident 9 dissonant 11 latticework

gratitude: 6 thanks 7 tribute 12 appreciation, gratefulness, thankfulness

gratuitous: 4 free 6 gratis, wanton 7 unasked 8 baseless, needless 9 voluntary 10 groundless 11 superfluous, unwarranted

gratuity: fee, tip 4 dole, gift 5 bonus, bribe, pilon 6 bounty 7 cumshaw, pension, present 9 baksheesh, lagniappe, pourboire 10 compliment 11 benefaction

grave: 4 tomb 5 carve, sober, staid 6 sedate, solemn, somber 7 austere, earnest, engrave, serious 8 decorous, 9 important, momentous, sepulcher

cloth: 8 cerement

robber: 5 ghoul

gravel: 4 dirt, grit 6 bother 7 perplex 8 alluvium 9 embarrass

gravelly: 5 harsh 6 coarse 7 rasping

graven: 6 etched 8 engraved 10 sculptured

graver: 5 burin 8 engraver, sculptor

gravestone: 5 stela, stele 6 cippus, marker 8 monument 9 tombstone

graveyard: 8 cemetery 10 churchyard

gravid: 8 pregnant

graviers: 4 dice

graving tool: 5 burin

gravity: 7 dignity 8 enormity, sobriety 9 heaviness, influence, solemnity 10 importance 11 earnestness, seriousness, weightiness 12 significance 13 momentousness 17 authoritativeness

law discoverer: 6 Newton

without: 7 agravic

gravy: jus(F.) 5 graft, juice, sauce 8 windfall

gravy dish: 9 sauceboat

gray: dim 4 ashy, dull, gris, hoar 5 ashen, bleak, hoary, slate 6 dismal, leaden 7 grizzly, hueless, neutral 9 cheerless 10 achromatic

bluish: 7 cesious

dark: 5 taupe 6 Oxford 8 charcoal

light: 4 ashy 5 pearl

Quaker: 5 acier

Gray's churchyard opus: 5 Elegy

gray matter: 4 head, mind, obex 5 brain 9 intellect 11 thinking cap

gray whale: 7 ripsack

graylag: 5 goose

grayling: 4 fish 9 butterfly

graze: 4 crop, feed, rase, skim 5 brush, shave, touch 6 browse, scrape 7 pasture

grazing ground: 4 colp 5 range 6 collop, meadow 7 pasture

grease: fat, oil 4 lard, soil 5 bribe, cheat, cozen, smear 6 creesh(Sc.) 7 lanolin 9 lubricate

greaser: 6 stoker

greasewood: 5 chico 6 orache 7 chamiso, hopsage 10 iodine bush

greasy fat 4 oily, rich 5 dirty, fatty, gross, porky 7 smeared 8 indecent, slippery, unctuous 10 indelicate 11 threatening

great: big 4 deep, fell, huge, much, rial, unco, vast 5 ample, chief, grand, large, yeder 6 grande(F.), heroic, mickle 7 capital, eminent, extreme, howling, immense, intense, titanic, violent 8 almighty, viand, enormous, favorite, horrible 9 elaborate, excellent, important, prolonged 10 delightful, omnipotent 11 magnificent

great albacore: 5 tunny 7 bluefin

Great Barrier island: 4 Otea

Great Bear: 9 Big Dipper, Ursa Major

great blue heron: 5 crane

Great Britain: See England, Ireland, Scotland, Wales

great deal: 4 gobs, lots

Great Divide: 7 Rockies

Great Expectations hero: Pip

Great Lake: 4 Erie 5 Huron 7 Ontario 8 Michigan, Superior

great many: lac 4 lakh

greaten: 5 exalt 7 enhance, enlarge, magnify 8 increase

greater: 6 better 8 mightier, superior

greatest: 4 arch, best, most 6 utmost 7 extreme, noblest, supreme

greathearted: 5 brave 7 gallant 8 fearless, generous 9 unselfish 10 courageous

greatly: 4 much 6 vastly 8 markedly 9 immensely 10 infinitely

greatness: 8 grandeur 9 magnitude 11 magnanimity

grebe: 8 dabchick 10 diving bird

Grecia: 6 Greece

Grecian: 5 Greek 9 Hellenist

Greece: (see also Athens, Greek): *capital:* 6 Athens

city: 4 Elis 6 Candia, Delphi, Nikhia, Patras, Sparta 7 Piraeus 8 Salonika 9 Peristeri

department: 4 Arta, Elis 5 Canea, Chios, Corfu, Drama, Evros, Pella, Samos, Zante 6 Achaea, Attica, Euboea, Kilkis, Kozane, Lesbos, Leukas, Phocis, Pieria, Serrai, Xanthe 7 Aetolia, Arcadia, Argolis, Boeotia, Corinth, Florina, Gravena, Kavalla, Laconia, Larissa, Preveza, Rhodope 8 Cyclades, Ioannina, Karditsa, Kastoria, Magnesia, Messenia, Trikkala

gulf: 7 Argolis, Corinth, Laconia, Saronic 8 Messenia, Salonika, Toronaic 9 Strymonic

island: Ios, Kos 4 Keos, Milo 5 Chios, Corfu, Crete, Delos, Melos, Naxos, Paros, Paxos, Psara, Samos, Syros, Thira, Tenos, Zante 6 Andros, Candia, Cerigo, Ikaria, Ithaca, Lemnos, Lesbos, Leukas, Patmos, Rhodes, Skyros 7 Amorgos, Cimolus, Kythnos, Mykonos, Siphnos 10 Cephalonia, Samothrace

island group: 6 Aegean, Ionian 8 Cyclades, Sporades 10 Dodecanese

monetary unit: 6 lepton 7 drachma

mountain: Ida 4 Oeta, Ossa 5 Athos 6 Othrys, Pelion, Pindus 7 Cyllene, Helicon, Olympus 8 Hymettus, Taygetus 9 Cambunian, Cithaeron, Parnassus 10 Erymanthus 11 Hagios Elias

region: 5 Crete 6 Aegean, Athens, Epirus,

Ionian, Thrace **7** Central **8** Thessaly **9** Macedonia **11** Peloponnese

river: **4** Arta **6** Peneus, Struma **7** Alpheus **8** Achelous, Cephisus **9** Arakhthos, Vistritsa

greed: 7 avarice **8** cupidity, voracity **11** selfishness

greedy: 4 avid **5** eager **6** grabby **7** miserly **8** covetous, grasping **9** rapacious **10** avaricious, gluttonous, insatiable

Greek: 7 Hellene

abode of gods: **7** Olympus

administrator: **10** amphodarch

alphabet: (see **letters** below)

altar: **7** eschara

army corps: **6** evzone

assembly: **5** agora, boule

assembly hill: **4** Pnyx

avenging spirit: **4** Fury **6** Erinys

basin: **6** louter

beauty: **4** Lais

bondman: **6** penest

castanet: **8** crotalum

Catholic: **5** Uniat **6** Uniate

chamber: **12** bouleuterion

chariot: **4** biga

church: **8** Orthodox

citadel: **9** Acropolis

clan: **4** obes **5** genos

cloak: **6** abolla **7** chlamys

coin: **4** mine, obol **5** hecte, nomas **6** lepton, phenix, stater **7** diobolo, drachma

column: **5** Doric, Ionic **10** Corinthian

contest: **4** agon

counselor: **6** Nestor

courtesan: **5** Thais **7** Aspasia

cup: **5** depas

dialect: **5** Doric, Elean, Eolic, Ionic **6** Aeolic

dirge: **5** linos

doom: ker

dramatist: **9** Aeschylus, Euripides, Sophocles **12** Aristophanes

drink: **4** ouzo

enchantress: **5** Circe, Medea

epic: **5** Iliad **7** Odyssey

essence: **6** ousia

fabulist: **5** Aesop

Fate: **6** Clotho **7** Atropos **8** Lachesis

festival: **5** delia, haloa **8** Apaturia

flask: **4** olpe

fleet commander: **7** navarch

flute: **7** hemiope

folk dance: **7** romaika

foot-race course: **6** stadia(pl.) **7** diaulos, stadium

foot soldier: **7** hoplite

Fury: **6** Alecto, Erinys **7** Erinyes, Megaera **9** Tisiphone

galley: **6** bireme **7** trireme, unireme

garment: **5** tunic **6** abolla, chiton, peplos, peplus **7** chlamys

giant: **4** Otus **5** Mimas **7** Aloadae **9** Enceladus, Ephialtes

gift: **6** xenium

god: Dis, Pan **4** Ares, Eros, Zeus **5** Hades, Momus, Pluto, satyr **6** Apollo, Cronus, Hermes, Kronos, Nereus, Triton **7** Bacchus **8** Dionysus, Poseidon

god of love: **4** Eros

god of sea: **6** Triton **8** Poseidon

god of war: **4** Ares

god of wind: **6** Aeolus

goddess: Ara, Ate, Eos, Not, Nyx, Ops **4** Alea, Dice, Dike, Enyo, Gaea, Gaia, Hebe, Hera, Leto, Nike **5** Horae, Irene, Metis, Moera, Niobe, Vesta **6** Athena, Eirene, Hecate, Hekate, Hestia, Selena, Selene, Semele **7** Ariadne, Artemis, Astarte, Demeter, Eunomia, Nemesis **9** Aphrodite **10** Persephone

Gorgon: **4** Enyo **5** Deino **6** Graeae, Graiae, Medusa, Stheno **7** Euryale **8** Pephredo

governor: **6** eparch

gymnasium: **4** xyst **9** palaestra

hero: **4** Aias, Ajax, Idas **5** Jason **7** Cecrops, Theseus **8** Heracles

historian: **7** Ctesias **8** Polybius, Xenophon **9** Herodotus **10** Thucydides

hobgoblin: **6** Empusa

hunter: **5** Orion

huntress: **7** Artemis **8** Atalanta

instrument: **5** aulos **8** barbiton

jar: **7** amphora

judge: **6** dikast **7** heliast

jug: **5** ascos

king: **5** Minos **6** Nestor **9** Agamemnon

lawgiver: **5** Draco, Minos, Solon

legislative council: **5** boule

letters: chi, eta, phi, psi, rho, tau **4** beta, iota, zeta **5** alpha, delta, gamma, kappa, omega, sigma, theta **6** lambda **7** epsilon, omicron, upsilon

letter(primitive): san **5** koppa, sampi **7** digamma

lover: **7** Rhoecus

lyre player: **5** Arion

man of brass: **5** Talos

marker: **5** stela, stele

market place: **5** agora

marriage: **5** gamos

mathematician: **6** Euclid **10** Archimedes

measure: pik **4** bema, piki, pous **5** baril, cados, chous, cubit, diote, doron, pekhe, pygon, xylon **6** acaena, bachel, bacile, barile, cotula, dichas, hemina, koilon, lichas, milion, orgyia, palame, pechys, schene, xestes **7** amphora, choemix, cyathos, diaulos, hekteus, metreta, stadion, stadium, stremma **8** condylos, daktylos, dekapode, dolichos, medimnys, palaiste, plethron, spithame, stathmos **9** hemiekton, oxybaphon

monster: 5 Hydra
musical interval: 6 ditone, meseme
musical note: 4 mese, nete
musical system: 5 neume
mustard: 6 sinapi
nymph: 5 Oread 8 Arethusa
old testament: 10 Septuagint
overseer: 5 ephor
paradise: 7 Elysium
patriarch: 5 Arius
patriot: 6 klepht
people: 5 demos 6 Argive, Cretan, Ionian
  7 Hellene, Spartan 8 Athenian
philosopher: 4 Zeno 5 Galen, Plato 6
  Thales 8 Diogenes 9 Aristotle 10 Pythagoras
physician: 5 Galen 11 Hippocrates
pilaster: 4 anta
pillar: 5 stela, stele
pitcher: 4 olla, olpe 8 oenochoe
platform: 4 bema 6 logeum
poem: 5 Iliad 7 Odyssey
poet: Ion 5 Arion, Homer 6 Pindar 9
  Aeschylus, Euripides, Simonides, Sophocles
poetess: 5 Sapho 6 Sappho 7 Corinna
portico: 4 stoa, xyst
precinct: 7 temenos
priest: 4 papa
priestess: 4 Auge, Hero, Iole 8 Caryatid
promontory: 6 Actium
province: 4 nome 5 nomos 7 eparchy
resistance group: Eam 4 Elas
rose 7 glaieul
sacred place: 6 abaton
sage: 5 Solon 6 Thales 8 Socrates
sanctuary: 5 hiera
sculptor: 5 Myron 7 Phidias
senate: 5 boule
serpent: 4 seps
settler: 5 metic
shield: 5 pelta
ship: 4 saic 5 diota
shrine: 5 secos, sekos
skeptic: 5 Timon
slave: 5 helot 6 penest
slave woman: 5 Baubo, Iambe
soldier: 7 hoplite, palikar
song: ode 5 melos, paeon
soothsayer: 7 Calchas
sorceress: 5 Circe, Medea, Siren
speech: 6 rhesis
statesman: 8 Pericles 9 Aristides 12 The-
  mistocles
statue: 6 xoanon
storm wind: 6 lelaps 7 lealaps
subdivision: 5 phyle
temple: 4 naos 5 cella
theater: 5 odeon, odeum
time: 7 chronos
township: 4 deme
tribal division: 7 phratry

underworld: Dis 5 Hades
vase: 5 dinos
verse: 6 Alcaic
village: obe
weight: 4 mna, oka, oke 4 mina 5 litra,
  maneh, minah, obole, pound 6 diobol,
  dramme, kantar, obolos, obolus, stater,
  talent 7 chalcon, chalque, drachma 8
  diobolon, talanton 12 tetradrachma
wine: 7 retsina
wine pitcher: 4 olpe
word: 5 logos
green: new, raw 4 bice, live, verd, vert
  (Fr.) 5 cedre, crude, fresh, mossy, virid,
  young 6 callow, recent, unripe 7 untried, verdant 8 blooming, gullible, ignorant, immature, inexpert 9 malachite, undecayed, unskilled, untrained
  11 flourishing 13 inexperienced 15 unsophisticated
blue: 4 cyan, saxe 7 sistine 9 turquoise
gray: 5 olive
pale: 7 celadon
shade: 4 lime, nile 5 apple, kelly 6 bottle
  7 emerald
woodbine: 7 peridot
yellow: 7 opaline
green light: 4 okay 7 go-ahead 8 approval
Green Mansions author: 6 Hudson
Green Mountain Boys' leader: 10
  Ethan Allen
Green Mountain state: 7 Vermont
green peak: 10 woodpecker
greenback: 8 frogskin 10 paper money
greenery: 7 verdure
greengage: 4 plum
greenhorn: 4 hick, jake, rube, tyro 6 novice 8 beginner 9 cheechaco, cheechako
  10 tenderfoot 12 apple knocker
Greenland: base: 4 Etah
  discoverer: 4 Eric
  Eskimo: Ita
greenlet: 5 vireo
greenroom: 5 foyer 6 lounge
greens: 5 salad
greenstone: 4 jade 7 diorite 8 nephrite 9
  malachite
greensward: 4 turf 5 grass
greet: cry 4 hail 6 accost, salute 7 address, receive, welcome
greeting: ave, bow 4 hail 5 aloha, hello,
  salut (Fr.) 6 salute 7 address, welcome
  9 reception 10 salutation
gregarious: 6 social 8 friendly, outgoing,
  sociable 9 convivial, talkative 11 extroverted
gremlin: imp 5 devil, gnome
Grenada: capital: 9 St. Georges
  Indian: 5 Carib
  Island: 9 Carriacon 16 Petite Martinique
  monetary unit: 4 cent 6 dollar

mountain: 11 St. Catherine
grenade: 4 bomb 5 shell 9 explosive
grenadier: 4 fish 7 rattail, soldier
grenadine: 5 cloth, syrup 6 fabric 9 flavoring
gres: 8 ceramics 9 stoneware
Gretna Green visitor: 6 eloper
Greya's husband: 4 Oder
grid: 5 grate 6 buccan 7 grating, network 8 gridiron
griddle: 5 grill
griddle-cake: 7 crumpet, pancake 8 flapjack
gridiron: 5 field, grill 7 brander, grating, network
grief: woe 4 care, harm, hurt, pain 5 agony, dolor, tears, trial, wrong 6 mishap, regret, sorrow 7 anguish, chagrin, emotion, failure, offense, sadness, trouble 8 disaster, distress, hardship 9 grievance, suffering 10 affliction, desolation, 11 lamentation
Grieg's dancer: 6 Anitra
grievance: 4 beef 5 wrong 6 burden, injury 8 gravamen, hardship 9 complaint, injustice 10 affliction, oppression 11 displeasure
grieve: rue 4 pain, pine, sigh, wail, weep 5 mourn, wound 6 bemoan, lament, sadden, sorrow 7 afflict 8 complain, distress
grievous: sad 4 sore 5 heavy, sorry 6 bitter, severe, tragic, woeful 7 heinous, intense, very bad 8 dolorous, shocking 9 atrocious 10 burdensome, calamitous, deplorable, oppressive 11 distressing
griffon: 7 monster 8 Dutch dog
grifter: 6 con man 8 swindler 12 rip-off artist
henchman: 5 shill 6 come-on
grigri: 5 charm 6 amulet, fetish 8 talisman
grill, grille: 5 broil, grate 7 grating, griddle 8 gridiron, question 11 interrogate, third-degree 12 cross-examine
grilse: 5 trout 6 salmon 7 botcher
grim: 4 dour, sour 5 angry, cruel, gaunt, harsh, stern 6 fierce, grisly, horrid, ragging, savage, sullen 7 furious, ghastly, hideous, ominous 8 horrible, pitiless, ruthless, sinister 9 ferocious, frightful, merciless, repellent 10 forbidding, inexorable, relentless, unyielding
grimace: mop, mow, mug 4 face, mock, moue, 5 fleer, scowl, smirk, sneer 6 glower 9 make a face
grimalkin: cat 6 feline, she-cat
grime: 4 dirt, smut, soil, soot 5 filth, sully
grimp: 5 climb
grimy: 4 foul 5 dingy, dirty 6 grubby, soiled 7 swarthy
grin: 5 fleer, smile

grind: rut 4 chaw, chew, grit, mill, mull, whet 5 chafe, chore, crush, gnash, grate, study 6 abrade, crunch, drudge, harass, polish, powder 7 oppress, sharpen 8 bookworm 9 blackfish, comminute, pulverize, triturate
grinder: 5 molar, tooth 9 submarine 10 flycatcher 12 hero sandwich
grinding: 7 grating, wearing 10 burdensome, oppressive 12 excruciating
grindle: 6 bowfin
grip: bag 4 hold, vise 5 cinch, clamp, clasp, cleat, grasp, rivet, seize 6 clench, clutch, control, handle, valise 7 grapple, handbag, mastery 8 handfast, take hold 9 constrict 12 scene-shifter
gripe: 4 beef, carp, fret, kick, rail 5 annoy 6 grouse, harass, squawk, 7 grumble, protest 8 complain 9 bellyache
grippe, grip: flu 9 influenza
gripper: 6 nipper
gripping device: dog 4 hand, vise 5 tongs 6 pliers
gripsack: 7 handbag
grisly: 4 grim 7 ghastly, hideous 8 dreadful, gruesome, horrible, terrible 10 terrifying
grison: 5 huron 6 weasel
grist: lot 4 malt 5 grain, stint 6 output 8 quantity 9 provision
gristle: 9 cartilage
grit: 4 guts, sand, soil, soot 5 earth, nerve, pluck 6 gravel 7 bravery, courage 8 backbone, decision, tenacity 12 perseverance
gritty: 4 game 5 sandy 6 plucky 7 arenose, arenous 8 resolute, sabulous 10 persistent
grivet: 6 monkey
grivois: 4 bold, free 5 broad 8 indecent
grizzly: 4 bear 7 grayish
groan: 4 moan 5 creak 6 lament 7 whimper
grog: rum 5 drink, 6 liquor 8 beverage
groggery: pub 6 saloon, tavern 7 barroom 8 alehouse
groggy: 5 shaky, tipsy 8 unsteady, wavering 9 tottering
groom: 4 comb, mafu, syce, tend, tidy 5 brush, clean, curry, dress, mafoo, train 7 hostler, marshal, prepare, servant 8 benedict 9 assistant 11 horsekeeper
grooming: 8 toilette
groove: rut 4 dado, rake, slot 5 canal, chase, flute, glyph, regal, rigol, scarf, shaft, stria, sulci(pl.) 6 furrow, gutter, hollow, rabbet, raglet, scrobe, striae(pl.), sulcus 7 channel, striate 10 excavation
groovy: 6 modern 9 excellent, marvelous
grope: 4 feel, poke, test 5 probe 6 fumble, handle 7 examine, fish for, grabble 11 move blindly

grosbeak: 7 warbler 8 hawfinch

gross: big, fat, low, sum 4 bulk, clod, dull, mass, rank, rude 5 amass, broad, brute, bulky, burly, close, crass, dense, heavy, plain, rough, thick, total, whole 6 animal, brutal, coarse, earthy, entire, filthy, greasy, impure, vulgar 7 beastly, brutish, compact, fulsome, general, glaring, massive, obscene, obvious, sensual, swinish, witless 8 cloddish, flagrant, indecent 9 egregious, unlearned, unrefined 10 indefinite, indelicate, scurrilous

grotesque: 5 antic, eerie, weird 7 baroque, bizarre 8 fanciful 9 fantastic, whimsical 11 incongruous 12 preposterous

grotto: den 4 cave, grot, hole 5 crypt, speos, vault 6 cavern, recess

grouch: 4 crab, sulk 5 crank, scold 6 grouse 7 grumble 8 sourpuss 10 crosspatch

ground: 4 base, dirt, fund, land, root, soil 5 earth, field, train 6 bottom, estate, reason 7 country, premise, terrain 8 initiate 9 establish, territory 10 foundation, fundamenta(pl.) 11 fundamentum

break: dig 4 plow 8 excavate 12 start to build

gain: 8 progress 9 move ahead

give: 5 yield 6 retreat

kinds of: bog, lot 4 moor, acre, farm, plat, park 5 arada, glebe, tilth, range, marsh, swale, patch 6 meadow, calade, reseau, maidan 7 pasture, cripple, curragh

raised: 5 ridge 7 hillock, hummock

ground pine: iva

ground squirrel: 6 gopher 8 chipmunk

groundhog: 6 marmot 9 woodchuck

Groundhog Day: 9 Candlemas

groundless: 4 idle 5 false 8 baseless 9 unfounded 10 gratuitous 11 unwarranted

groundnut: 5 chufa, gobbe 6 goober, peanut

grounds: 4 lees 5 basis, dregs, grout 6 bottom 8 sediment 9 settlings

college: 6 campus

military: 4 camp, fort 8 presidio 11 reservation

groundwork: 4 base, root 5 basis 6 bottom, fundus 7 support 8 planning, practice, training 10 foundation 11 preparation 12 underpinning

group: lot, mob, set 4 bevy, gang, herd, mass, ring, sect, team 5 batch, brood, cabal, class, clump, drove, firca, flock, genus, horde, party, squad, suite, tribe 6 bundle, clique, family, galaxy, gather, nation 7 arrange, cluster, collect, company, consort 8 assemble, assembly, classify, division 10 assemblage, assortment, collection, congregate 11 aggregation

pert to: 7 generic

group together: 4 band, meet 7 cluster 8 assemble

grouper: 4 fish, hind, mero 5 guasa

groupies: 4 fans 9 followers, hangers-on

grouse: 5 gripe, quail 6 gorhen, grouch, repine 7 cheeper, gorcock, grumble 8 complain, pheasant, squealer 9 gelinotte, ptarmigan 10 whitebelly 12 capercaillie

grout: 5 dregs 6 mortar 7 grounds, plaster

grouty: 5 cross, sulky 6 sullen

grove: 4 bush, tope, wood 5 copse, hurst, lucus(L.) 6 pinery 7 boscage, boskage, coppice, thicket

pert. to: 7 nemoral

grovel: 4 fawn 5 crawl, toady 6 cringe, kowtow, wallow 7 truckle 9 be servile

groveling: 6 abject 7 hangdog 12 contemptible

grow: age, bud, get, wax 4 come, eche, rise 5 edify, raise, swell 6 accrue, batten, become, expand, extend, thrive 7 augment, develop, distend, enlarge, improve, nourish 8 develope, flourish, increase 9 cultivate 10 accumulate

grow old: age 5 ripen 7 senesce

grower: 6 farmer, raiser 7 rancher 10 orchardist 13 agriculturist 15 arboriculturist

growl: 4 gnar, gurr 5 gnarl, snarl 6 mutter, rumble 7 grumble

grown: 5 adult, risen 6 mature 8 expanded

grownup: man 5 adult

growth: wen 4 rise 5 swell 7 stature 8 increase, swelling 9 accretion, expansion, heterosis 11 development, enlargement 12 augmentation

in clusters: 8 racemose

on another: 8 parasite

on surface: 9 epigenous

organic: 9 accretion

promoting: 8 nutrient 9 nutriment

retarding: 9 paratonic

grub: bob, dig, eat 4 chow, feed, food, moot, plod, root 5 dwarf, larva, stump 6 drudge, larvae(pl.), maggot, search 7 plodder 8 victuals

grubby: 5 dirty, grimy, small 8 dwarfish, slovenly

grudge: 4 envy 5 pique, spite 6 malice, rancor 10 resentment

grue: 6 shiver 7 shudder

gruel: 5 atole 6 burgoo, crowdy 8 porridge

grueling: 4 hard 6 brutal, tiring 7 racking 9 fatiguing, punishing

gruesome: 4 ugly 6 grisly, horrid, sordid

7 fearful, ghastly, hideous, macabre **8** horrible

gruff: 4 curt, rude, sour **5** bluff, harsh, rough, short, surly **6** abrupt, hoarse, morose, severe, sullen **7** brusque, crabbed **8** churlish

grumble: 4 crab, fuss, kick **5** bitch, croak, growl, snarl **6** grouch, grouse, repine, rumble, squawk, yammer **8** begrudge, complain

grumpy: 5 cross, moody, surly

grungy: 5 dirty **10** uncared for

grunt: 4 fish, **5** groan, snork, snort

guacharo: 7 fatbird, oilbird

guaiol: 7 alcohol

Guam: *capital:* **5** Agana
native: **8** Chamorro
port: **4** Apra

guanay: 9 cormorant

guanaco: 5 llama **6** alpaca
relative: **5** camel

guar: 4 bean

guarantee: 4 bail, band, bond, seal **6** assure, avouch, ensure, insure, surety **7** certify, avouch, endorse, hostage, warrant **8** guaranty, security, warranty **9** assurance, vouchsafe

guarantor: 5 angel **6** backer, patron **7** sponsor **11** underwriter

guarapucu: 4 fish, peto **5** wahoo

guard: 4 care, curb, herd, hold, keep, rail, tend, ward **5** bless, fence, hedge, watch **6** bantay, bridle, convey, custos, defend, dragon, escort, fender, gaoler, jailer, jailor, keeper, patrol, police, sentry, shield, warden **7** keeping, lineman, protect **8** conserve, preserve, restrain, security, sentinel, watchman **9** attention, custodian, protector **10** cowcatcher, protection
foil: **6** button
line of: **6** cordon
on: **4** wary **5** alert, ready **8** vigilant, watchful **9** observant

guarded: 4 wary **6** manned **7** careful **8** cautious, defended, discreet **9** protected **11** circumspect

guardhouse: 4 brig **5** clink **6** prison **8** hoosegow

guardian: 6 keeper, parent, pastor, patron, warden **7** curator **8** defender, watchdog **9** custodian, protector
church relics: **10** mystagogue
heavenly: **5** angel
legal: **7** trustee
pert. to: **7** tutelar **8** tutelary
subject of: **4** ward
watchful: **5** Argus **8** Cerberus

guardianship: 4 care **5** trust **7** custody, keeping, tuition **8** tutelage

guasa: 7 grouper, jewfish

Guatemala: *capital:* **13** Guatemala City
city: **5** Coban **6** Flores, Jalapa, Salama, Solola **7** Antigua, Jutiapa **9** Escuintla, Tiquisate
department: **5** Peten **6** Izabal, Jalapa, Quiche, Solola, Zacapa **7** Jutiapa **9** Escuintla, San Marcos, Santa Rosa **10** Chiquimula, El Progreso
Indian: **4** Itza, Ixil, Maya **5** Xinca
lake: **6** Izabal **7** Atitlan **9** Peten Itza
measure: **4** vara **6** fanega **7** manzana
monetary unit: **7** centavo, quetzal
mountain peak: **6** Tacana **9** Tajumulco **10** Acatenango, Santa Maria
mountain range: **11** Sierra Madre
river: **5** Dulce **7** Motagua **8** Polochic, Sarstoon **10** Usumacinta
volcano: **4** Agua **5** Fuego **7** Atitlan

Guaycuruan Indian: **4** Toba

gudgeon: pin **4** bait, fish, lure **5** pivot **6** burbot, socket

Gudrun: *brother:* **6** Gunnar
husband: **4** Atli

guenon: 4 mona **6** grivet, monkey

guerdon: 6 reward **8** requital **10** recompense

guerrilla: 8 partisan **11** bush fighter

guess: aim **4** shot **5** fancy, infer, think **6** assume, deduce, divine **7** believe, imagine, opinion, presume, surmise, suspect **8** estimate **9** speculate **10** conjecture

guest: 6 caller, inmate, lodger, patron, roomer **7** visitor

guesthouse: inn **5** hotel **11** caravansary

guff: lip **4** sass **5** hooey **6** humbug **7** hogwash **8** claptrap, nonsense **10** balderdash

guffaw: 5 howl **6** heehaw **10** horselaugh, belly laugh

guidance: 4 helm, help **6** advice **7** auspice, conduct, counsel **8** steerage **9** direction **10** leadership, management **11** instruction

guide: 4 airt, buoy, clue, lead, pole, rein, rule, show **5** model, pilot, reign, steer, teach, treat, tutor, usher **6** beacon, bridle, convey, convoy, direct, escort, govern, leader, manage **7** conduce, conduct, control, marshal, teacher **8** director, instruct, landmark, polestar, regulate, shepherd, textbook **9** catechism, conductor, itinerary, prescribe, regulator **10** instructor **11** superintend **12** show the way to

guidebook: 8 baedeker **9** itinerary **11** tourist's aid

guided missile: ABM, ATA, SAM, SSM **4** Hawk, ICBM, IRBM, Lark, Loki, Loon, Nike, SLBM, Thor, Zuni **5** Atlas, drone, Snark, Titan **6** Bomarc, Falcon, Redeye, Viking **7** Bullpup, Patriot, Polaris, Terrier, Tiny Tim **8** Hellfire, Redstone, Tomahawk **9** Minuteman **10** Copperhead, Sidewinder

guideway: 4 slot **5** track **7** channel

Guido: *fifth note:* sol
first note: ut
fourth note: fa
high note: la
highest note: E; la
second note: re
third note: mi

guild: 4 club **5** order, union **6** league **7** society **8** alliance, sodality **10** fellowship **11** association, brotherhood

guile: 4 wile **5** cheat, craft, fraud **6** deceit, humbug **7** cunning **9** duplicity, treachery

guileful: 9 deceitful, insidious **10** fallacious, fraudulent **13** Machiavellian

guileless: 5 naive **6** candid, honest **7** artless **8** innocent **9** ingenuous

guillemot: 6 auk **4** loom, quet **5** murre **7** dovekey, dovekie

guillotine: 6 behead **10** decapitate
wagon for: **7** tumbrel, tumbril

guilt: 6 sin **5** culpa, fault **6** piacle **7** offense **8** iniquity **10** wickedness **11** criminality, culpability

guiltless: 4 pure **5** clean **8** innocent **9** blameless, righteous

guilty: 6 nocent, wicked **7** correal **8** culpable

Guinea: *capital:* **7** Conakry
city: **4** Boke, Labe, Pita **5** Fouta **6** Kankan **7** Dubreka
ethnic group: **4** fula **7** Malinke **8** Soussous
island: Los **5** Tombo
monetary unit: **4** kori, syli
mountain: **5** Nimba
river: **4** Milo **5** Niger **6** Bafing, Gambia **7** Senegal **8** Konkoure

Guinea-Bissau: *capital:* **6** Bissau
ethnic group: **4** Fula **7** Balanta **8** Mandyako
island group: **7** Bijagos
monetary unit: **4** peso **7** centavo
river: **4** Geba

guinea fowl: 4 keet

guinea pig: 4 cavy

Guinevere's husband: 6 Arthur

guise: hue **4** form, garb, mask, mien **5** cloak, cover, dress, habit, shape **6** aspect, attire, deceit, manner **7** arrange, fashion **8** behavior, likeness, practice **9** semblance **10** appearance, masquerade

guitar: uke **5** sitar, tiple **6** sancho **7** cittern, ukulele **8** chitarra **10** calascione
guitarlike instrument: **4** lute, rota **6** citole **7** bandore, pandora, samisen **8** mandolin

half step in pitch: **5** dital
key: **5** dital
of India: **4** vina **5** sitar
play: **5** pluck, strum
small: **7** ukelele
style of playing: **10** bottleneck

guitguit: 4 bird **6** pitpit

gula: 4 cyma, ogee **6** gullet, throat **7** molding

gulch: gorge, gully **6** arroyo, canyon, coulee, ravine, valley

gulf: arm, bay, gap **4** cove, eddy **5** abyss, chasm **6** vorago **9** barathrum, whirlpool **10** separation

Gulf States: 5 Texas **7** Alabama, Florida **9** Louisiana **11** Mississippi

gull: mew **4** dupe, fool, tern **5** cheat, larid **6** sucker, teaser, victim **7** cheater, deceive, defraud, fall guy, mislead **8** dotterel, hoodwink **9** bamboozle, kittiwake **10** mountebank
kinds of: cob **4** skua **5** allan, annet, pewit **6** larine, teaser, waggel **11** burgomaster
pert. to: **6** larine, laroid

gullet: maw **6** throat **9** esophagus

gullible: 5 green, naive **9** credulous

Gulliver's Travels: *author:* **5** Swift
flying island: **6** Laputa
human beast: **5** Yahoo
island kingdom: **8** Lilliput

gully: 5 gorge, gulch **6** arroyo, gutter, ravine, valley **7** couloir **11** watercourse

gulp: 4 bolt, glut, swig **5** swill **6** gobble, guzzle **7** swallow

gum: 4 clog, hive, kino **5** cheat, nyssa, stick, trick **6** chicle, gluten, hashab, humbug, impede, tissue, tupelo **7** bilsted, gingiva **8** mucilage **10** eucalyptus **11** masticatory
derivative: **8** bassorin **10** tragacanth, traganthin **12** tragacanthin
kinds of: **5** tuart **6** acacia, acacin, balata, touart **7** acacine, dextrin
resin: **5** elemi, gugal, myrrh **6** salban **9** sagapenum **12** frankincense

gum tree: 5 xylan

gumbo: 4 ocra, okra, soup **7** melange

gumma: 5 tumor

gummy: 6 mastic, sticky **7** viscous **8** adhesive

gumption: 7 courage **8** boldness **10** enterprise, initiative, shrewdness

gums: ula **7** alveoli
pain in: **7** ulalgia
pert. to: **6** uletic **8** gingival

gumshoe: cop, tec **4** dick **5** skulk, sneak **6** sleuth **9** detective, pussyfoot

gun: gat, rod **5** rifle, tommy **6** cannon, heater, pistol, weapon **7** carbine, shotgun **8** revolver **9** matchlock, surfboard **11** blunderbuss *barrel cleaner:* 6 ramrod

kinds of: 4 bore, bren, roer, sten 5 baril 6 ack-ack, archie, barker 7 aerogun, bazooka 8 amusette

mount: 6 turret

part: pin 4 bolt, bore, butt, lock 5 sight, stock 6 barrel, breech, hammer, muzzle, rammer, safety 7 trigger

platform: 11 emplacement

gunfire: 4 rake, shot 5 salvo 6 strafe, volley 7 barrage 8 enfilade 9 fusillade

gunman: 6 killer 7 torpedo 8 assassin

gunner: 7 shooter 8 marksman, rifleman 9 cannoneer 10 bombardier 12 artilleryman

gunny: tat 4 jute 6 burlap

gunpowder: 5 nitro

Gunther's uncle: 5 Hagen

gurgle: 6 plash 6 babble, burble 7 sputter

Gurkha's sword: 5 kukri

gurnard: 4 fish 7 sea robin 8 dragonet

guru: 6 guide 7 teacher

gush: 4 flow, pour, teem 5 issue, smarm, spate, spout, spurt 6 effuse, stream 10 outpouring

gushing: 7 mawkish, prating 8 effusive, unctuous 10 blabbering, flattering

gusset: 4 gore 5 brace 6 insert

gust: 4 puff, scud, waft, wind 5 blast, draft, whiff 6 flurry, squall 8 outburst, paroxysm 9 explosion

gusto: 4 elan, zest 5 taste 6 fervor, liking, relish 7 delight, passion 8 pleasure 9 enjoyment 12 appreciation

gusty: 5 windy 6 savory, stormy 7 squally 8 agitated 11 tempestuous

gut: 5 belly, clean 6 paunch, ravage 7 plunder, stamina, stomach 9 bay window 10 disembowel, eviscerate

gutsy: 4 bold 5 brave, nervy 6 spunky 7 fearless, intrepid 9 audacious 10 courageous

gutta: 8 ornament

gutta-percha: 5 latex 6 balata

gutter: 5 ditch, gully, siver(Sc.) 6 groove, trench, trough, 7 channel, scupper 11 watercourse

guttural: 4 deep 5 burry, harsh, velar 7 rasping, throaty

guy: kid, rod 4 josh, rope, stay twit 5 chain, guide, spoof, tease 6 decamp, fellow, gazabo, gazebo, person 8 ridicule

Guyana: *capital:* 10 Georgetown

city: 6 Enmore, Suddie 7 Bartica, Charity

8 Mackenzie 10 Enterprise 12 New Amsterdam

district: 7 Berbice 8 Demerara, Rupununi 9 Essequiba, North West

monetary unit: 4 cent 6 dollar

mountain: 6 Acarai 7 Roraima 9 Pacaraima

river: 6 Cuyuni, Potaro 7 Berbice 8 Demerara, Mazaruni 9 Essequibo 10 Courantyne

guy rope: 4 stay, vang

guzzle: 4 bolt, gulp, swig 5 quaff, swill 6 devour, tipple 7 toss off

gymnast: 6 turner 7 acrobat, athlete, tumbler 8 balancer

gymnastic: *stunt:* kip 4 flip 5 vault 9 handstand, headstand 10 handspring, headspring

swing: 7 trapeze

gyp: 5 cheat, steal, sting 6 diddle, rip off 7 defraud, sharper, swindle 8 swindler 9 trickster 10 overcharge

gypsum: 4 geso 6 parget 8 selenite 9 alabaster

resembling: 11 alabastrine

gypsy, gipsy: 4 calo 5 caird, nomad 6 Gitana, Gitano, roamer 7 czigany, tzigany, zincala, zincalo, zingana, zingano, zingara, zingaro 8 Bohemian, brunette, wanderer, zigeuner

boy: 4 chal

camp: tan

dance: 10 zingaresca

devil: 4 beng

dialect: 6 Romany 7 Rommany

fortune: 4 bahi

gentleman: rye

girl: chi 4 chai

horse: gri, gry

husband: rom

nongypsy: 4 gajo

paper: lil

Syrian: 5 Aptal

thief: 4 chor

village: gav

wife: 4 romi

gyrate: 4 spin, turn 5 twirl, whirl 6 rotate 7 revolve

gyrator: top

gyre: 4 ring 6 vortex 7 circuit 10 revolution

gyrfalcon: 6 jerkin

gyve: 4 iron 5 chain 6 fetter 7 shackle

H

H: 5 aitch 8 aspirate
sound of: 8 aspirate
H-shaped: 5 zygal
habeas corpus: 4 writ
haberdashery: hat 5 shirt 6 gloves 7 necktie 8 menswear
habile: 4 able 6 adroit, clever, expert 8 skillful
habiliment (see also **dress, gown**): 4 garb 5 habit 6 attire 7 apparel, clothes, costume, raiment 8 billiment, clothing, equipage, fittings, ornament, vestment 9 equipment, faculties 11 furnishings
habilitate: 5 dress, equip, train 6 clothe, outfit 7 educate
habit (see also **dress**): rut, use 4 coat, garb, gown, suit, vice, wont 5 array, guise, haunt, thews, usage 6 attire, clothe, custom, estate, groove 7 bearing, clothes, costume, garment 8 demeanor, practice, tendency 9 addiction 10 consuetude 11 disposition
habitant: 7 dweller
habitat: 4 home 5 abode, range 6 patria 7 station 8 locality 11 environment
habitation: 4 home, tent 5 abode, house, hovel, igloo 6 colony, harbor, warren 7 lodging 8 domicile, dwelling, tenement 9 chaumiere (F.), residence
habitual: 5 usual 6 common, hectic 7 regular 8 familiar, frequent, ordinary 9 customary 10 accustomed, inveterate
habituate: use 5 enure, inure 6 addict, season 8 accustom, frequent 9 acclimate, 11 acclimatize, familiarize
habitude: 5 habit 6 custom 11 familiarity
habitue: 8 customer 10 frequenter
hachure: 4 line, mark 7 shading
hacienda: 4 farm, 5 ranch 6 estate 10 plantation 13 establishment
proprietor: 9 hacendado
hack: cab, cut, hag, hew 4 chop, taxi 5 coach, cough 6 drudge, fiacre, haggle, mangle 7 butcher, chatter, stammer, stutter 8 carriage, mutilate 9 mercenary
hackee: 8 chipmunk
hackle: 4 bait, comb 6 mangle 7 plumage 8 feathers
hackly: 5 rough 6 broken, jagged
hackney: nag 4 hack, pony 5 horse, noddy 8 carriage

hackneyed: old 4 worn 5 banal, stale, trite 6 common 7 worn out 8 outdated 10 threadbare 11 commonplace, stereotyped
Hades: dis, pit 4 hell 5 Orcus, Sheol 7 Gehenna, inferno 8 Tartarus 11 netherworld
god: 5 Pluto
guard: 8 Cerberus
inhabitant of: 7 hellion
lake to: 7 Avernus
mother: 4 Rhea
pert to: 7 sheolic 8 infernal
river: 4 Styx 5 Lethe 7 Acheron
hadj, hajj: 10 pilgrimage
haff: 6 lagoon
haft: 6 handle
hag: bog, cut 4 bogy, hack, wood 5 copse, crone, demon, ghost, marsh, notch, rudas(Sc.), witch 6 beldam, goblin, harass, spirit 7 beldame, fatigue, pasture, terrify 8 harridan, quagmire 9 cailleach, cailliach, enclosure, hobgoblin
Hagar's son: 7 Ishmael
hagdon: 6 fulmar 7 seabird 10 shearwater
hagfish: 5 borer
haggard: 4 bony, lank, lean, pale, thin, wild 5 drawn, gaunt, spare 6 wasted 7 anxious, untamed 8 careworn, harrowed, 9 exhausted, suffering 10 cadaverous
Haggard novel: She
haggle: cut, hew 4 hack, prig 5 cavil 6 badger, barter, chisel, dicker, higgle, huckle, palter, scotch 7 bargain, chaffer, dispute, stickle, wrangle 8 beat down
haggler: 6 dodger 8 huckster
hagioscope: 6 squint 7 opening
hagride: 6 harass, obsess 7 oppress, torment
hail: ave 4 ahoy, call, goal 5 greet, sleet, sound, whole 6 accost, health, salute 7 address, fortune, graupel 8 greeting 10 salutation 13 precipitation
hailer: 8 bullhorn
hair: fax, fur 4 barb, coma, mane, shag 5 crine, tress 6 crinet, nicety, trifle 7 bristle 8 capillus, filament, finespun 9 chevelure
accessory: 8 barrette
Angora goat: 6 mohair

braid: 5 queue 7 pigtail
coarse: 4 kemp, seta, shag 7 bristle
curl: 7 ringlet
disease: 8 dandruff, psilosis
dye: 5 henna
excessive: 7 pilosis
facial: 5 beard 6 goatee 8 whiskers 9
  moustache, sideburns
false: rat, wig 6 peruke, switch, toupee 7
  periwig
fringe: 8 frisette, frizette
grooming aid: 4 comb 5 brush 6 pomade
having: 6 pilose 7 barbate, hirsute, villous
  8 crinated
horse: 4 mane 5 seton 7 fetlock
intestinal: 6 villus
knot: bun 7 chignon
lock: 4 curl 5 tress 7 cowlick
loss: 8 alopecia, baldness
ornament: bow 4 comb 5 tiara 6 ribbon 7
  coronet 8 barrette
pert. to: 6 crinal
plant: 6 villus
remover: 8 epilator 9 depilator, epilatory
  10 depilatory
roll: 4 puff 5 twist 7 chignon 9 pompadour
short: 6 setula, setule
soft: 4 down 6 villus
unruly: mop 6 tousle 7 cowlick
white: 4 snow
hairbrained: 5 giddy 8 heedless, volatile
hairbreadth: ace 5 close 10 very narrow
haircloth: aba 6 cilice
haircut: 7 tonsure
hairdo: bob 4 afro, glib(Ir.) 5 braid 6 bubble, marcel 7 beehive, crew cut, pageboy, pigtail, shingle 8 bouffant, duck-
  tail, ponytail 9 pompadour
hairdresser: 6 barber 7 friseur 8 coiffeur
  9 coiffeuse
hairless: 4 bald 8 depilous
hairnet: 5 snood
hairpin: 4 bend 6 bodkin 8 bobbypin
hair-raising: 4 eery 5 eerie, weird 10 terrifying
hairy: bushy 6 comate, comous, pilose,
  shaggy 7 bristly, crinite, hirsute 9 dangerous, difficult, harrowing
Haiti: *capital:* 12 Port-au-Prince
city: 5 Cayes 8 Gonaives 10 Cap Haitien
discoverer: 8 Columbus
island: 5 Vache 6 Gonave 7 Tortuga
monetary unit: 6 gourde 7 centime
mountain: 7 La Selle
national liberator: 9 Toussaint 10 Dessa-
  lines
original name: 10 Hispaniola
province: Sud 4 Nord 5 Ouest 9 Nord-
  ouest 10 Artibonite
river: 10 Artibonite
hake: 4 fish, idle 5 tramp 6 loiter, trudge

halberd: 6 weapon 8 battle-ax
halcyon: 4 bird, calm 5 happy, quiet 6
  golden 8 peaceful, tranquil, affluent 9
  unruffled 10 kingfisher, prosperous
Halcyone: *father:* 6 Aeolus
husband: 4 Ceyx
hale: 5 sound 6 hearty, robust, strong,
  summon 7 healthy 8 vigorous
Halevy opera: 5 Juive
half: 6 moiety 7 partial, portion
half breed: 5 metis 6 mustee 7 mestizo,
  mestiza, mulatto, mulatta 8 octoroon,
  quadroon
half circumference: 10 semicircle
half diameter: 6 radius
half-man: 4 faun 6 garuda 7 centaur 8
  minotaur
half mask: 4 loup 6 domino
half-month: 9 fortnight
half-moon: 8 crescent 9 semilunar
figure: 4 lune
half-turn: 8 caracole
half-wit: 4 dolt 5 dunce, idiot, moron 8
  imbecile 9 blockhead
half-witted: 4 dull 5 dotty, silly 7 foolish
  9 senseless
halfbeak: ihi 5 balao
halfhearted: 4 tame 5 faint, tepid 8 listless, lukewarm 10 spiritless
halfway: mid 6 almost, nearly, middle 7
  midmost, partial 9 partially 11 equidistant
Halicarnassian: 9 Dionysius, Herodotus
halicore: 4 dugong, sea cow 7 manatee
Halifax citizen: 10 Haligonian
halite: 4 salt 8 rock salt
hall: 4 aula, room, saal(G.) 5 entry, foyer,
  lobby, manor, odeon, odeum, salle 6
  atrium, durbar, saloon 7 chamber, gallery, hallway, passage 8 anteroom, corridor 9 vestibule 10 auditorium, misericord, passageway 11 misericorde
music: 4 gaff 5 odeon, odeum
reception: 5 salon 6 parlor
student residence: 4 dorm 5 bursa 9 dormitory
halloo: 5 shout 6 accost
hallow: 5 bless 8 dedicate 10 consecrate
hallowed: 4 holy
hallowed place: 4 fane 5 altar 6 bethel,
  chapel, church, shrine, temple 9 cathedral, synagogue
hallucination: d.t.'s 6 mirage 7 fantasy 8
  delirium, delusion
hallux: 6 big toe
halo: arc 4 glow, nimb 5 glory 6 areola,
  areole, brough(Sc.), circle, corona, nimbus 7 aureola, aureole 8 cincture, gloriole
halogen: 6 iodine 7 bromine 8 chlorine 8
  cyanogen, fluorine
haloperidal: 10 depressant, 12 tranquilizer

halothane: 10 anesthetic

halt: hop 4 bait, lame, limp, stem, stop 5 cease, hilch, hitch, pause, stand 6 arrest, desist, docked 7 limping 8 lameness, stoppage 9 cessation, mutilated, terminate

halter: 4 rope 5 leash, noose, strap, widdy 6 bridle, hamper 8 cavesson, restrain 9 hackamore

halting: 4 lame 7 limping 8 spavined 9 defective 10 hesitating 11 vacillating

ham: pig 4 hock, pork, 5 actor, thigh 7 amateur, overact

Ham: *brother:* 4 Shem

father: 4 Noah

son: 4 Cush 6 Canaan

son's land: 8 Ethiopia

hamadryad: 5 nymph 6 baboon

hamate: 6 curved, hooked 7 hamular 8 hamiform

Hamilcar: 5 Barca

conquest: 5 Spain

home: 8 Carthage

son: 8 Hannibal

Hamite: *father:* 4 Abel

language: 4 Afar, Agao, Beja 5 Belin, Galla 6 Berber, Kabyle, Shilha, Somali, Zenaga 8 Cushitic, Numidian, Tamashek 9 Ethiopian, Gaetulian 11 Mauretanian

people: 4 Beja, Bogo 5 Fulah 6 Berber, Gallas, Somali

hamlet: 4 dorp 5 aldea(Sp.), casal, hamel, moray, vicus(L.) 6 bustee, casale(It.), thorpe 7 clachan(Sc.), village 10 settlement

Hamlet: *beloved:* 7 Ophelia

castle: 8 Elsinore

character: 7 Laertes, Ophelia 8 Gertrude, Polonius

country: 7 Denmark

dramatist: 11 Shakespeare

friend: 7 Horatio

mother: 8 Gertrude

slayer: 7 Laertes

uncle: 8 Claudius

victim: 7 Laertes 8 Claudius, Polonius

hammer: bit, tup 4 beat, claw, jack, maul, mell, reel, tack, tamp 5 gavel 6 batter, beetle, mallet, martel, pummel, sledge, strike, swinge 7 belabor 8 malleate 11 door-knocker

blacksmith's: 6 fuller, oliver

bricklayer's: 6 scutch

face: 4 trip

firearm: 4 cock 7 doghead

half-round: 4 fuller

head: 4 peen, poll

medical: 6 plexor 7 plessor

stone: 5 kevel, spall

type: air 4 claw 5 sledge 8 ball peen 9 pneumatic

hammerhead: 5 shark 8 numskull 9 hog sucker

hammock: 5 swing 7 machila

hamper: bin, ped 4 beat, clog, curb, load, slow 5 block, cramp, crate, rusky(Sc.), seron(Sp.) 6 basket, burden, fetter, halter, hinder, hopple, impede, panier 7 buffalo, confine, hanaper, manacle, pannier, perplex, shackle, trammel 8 encumber, entangle, obstruct, restrain, restrict 9 container, embarrass

hamstring: hox 4 hock, lame 5 hough 6 hinder, impair 7 cripple, disable

Hananiah: *father:* 4 Azur

son: 8 Zedekiah

hand: fin, paw, pud 4 claw, give, mano, mitt, neif, pass 5 claut(Sc.), grasp, nieve, power, share 6 clunch, daddle, famble, pledge, worker 7 ability, flipper, forepaw, laborer, proffer, workman 8 applause, bestowal, transmit 9 betrothal, craftsman, indicator, operative, signature 11 handwriting

back: 10 opisthenar

by: 8 manually

clenched: 4 fist

covering: 4 mitt, muff 5 glove 6 cestus(L.) 7 gantlet 8 gauntlet

deformity: 11 talipomanus

down: 8 bequeath

hollow: 6 gowpen, gowpin

on hip: 6 akimbo

palm: 6 thenar

part: 4 palm 5 thumb 7 fingers

pert. to: 6 manual

poker: 5 flush 8 straight 9 full house

without: 7 amanous

hand-me-down: 5 cheap 9 ready-made 10 secondhand

hand mill: 5 quern 7 grinder

hand out: 6 donate 7 present 8 give away 10 administer, distribute

hand over: 4 ante, cede 5 yield

hand-picked: 5 elite 8 selected

handbag: bag 4 etui, grip 5 cabas, etwee, purse 6 valise 7 satchel 8 gripsack, pochette, reticule

handball: *game:* 6 pelota 7 jai alai

point: ace

handbarrow: 4 bier

handbill: 5 flyer, libel 6 dodger 13 advertisement

handbook: 6 manual 9 guidebook 11 enchiridion

handcar: 6 gocart 7 go-devil

handcloth: 5 towel 6 napkin 12 handkerchief

handcuff: 4 cuff, iron 5 darby 6 nipper 7 manacle 8 bracelet, handbolt, handlock, restrain

Handel: *composition:* 5 Largo

opera: 4 Nero 6 Almira, Xerxes 7 Rodrigo 8 Berenice 9 Agrippina

oratorio: 4 Saul 6 Esther 7 Messiah

handful: 4 grip, wisp 5 claut, gripe 6 gowpen, gowpin, yaffle 7 maniple 8 quantity

handicap: bar, law 4 edge, lame, lisp, odds 6 burden, hinder, impede 7 stammer, stutter 8 drawback, encumber 9 advantage, embarrass, head start 12 disadvantage

handicapper: 5 rater

handicraft: art 5 trade, metier 8 vocation

handicraft goddess: 7 Minerva

handicraftsman: 7 artisan, workman 9 craftsman

handiwork: tat 7 sampler 10 embroidery

handjar: 5 knife 6 dagger 7 khanjar

handkerchief: 5 clout, fogle 6 madras 7 bandana, belcher, sneezer 9 barcelona, handcloth, muckender, neckcloth 11 neckerchief

handle: ear, fan, lug, nob, paw, ply, use 4 ansa, bail, bool, deal, feel, gaum, grip, haft, hank, hilt, knob, name 5 gripe, grope, helve, lever, shaft, swipe, touch, treat, wield 6 behave, direct, finger, manage 7 act upon, control 8 doorknob, handgrip 10 manipulate

ancient: 4 ansa

bucket: 4 bail, bale

cup: ear

equipped with: 6 ansate

pail: 4 bail

printing press: 6 rounce

pump: 5 brake

scythe: 5 snath, snead, thole 6 snathe

shaped: 6 ansate

sword: 4 haft, hilt

whip: 4 crop

handled: 5 dealt 6 ansate

handling: use 4 care 7 control, running 9 treatment 10 management 11 supervision

handout: aid 4 alms, dole, food, gift, meal, mete 5 snack 7 charity

handreading: 9 palmistry

hands: men 4 crew 8 pointers

hands off: 4 tabu 5 taboo

handsome: 4 braw(Sc.), fair, fine, pert 5 ample, belle, bonny, handy, ready 6 bonnie, clever, comely, goodly, heppen, limber 7 elegant, gallant, liberal 8 becoming, budgeree, generous, gracious, suitable 9 beautiful, dexterous 10 attractive, convenient, manageable 11 appropriate, good-looking 12 considerable

handspring: 6 tumble 9 cartwheel

handwriting: 4 fist, hand 5 ronde 6 script 10 griffonage, manuscript 11 chirography

on the wall: 4 mene 5 tekel 8 graffiti, upharsin

study of: 10 graphology

handy: 4 deft, near 5 adept, ready 6 adroit, clever, heppen 7 close-by 8 adjacent, dextrous, handsome, skillful 9 available, dexterous, versatile 10 accessible, convenient

Handy Andy's catch: 5 Oonah

handyman: 5 fixer 8 factotum, repairer

hang: lag, lop, sag 4 kilt, loll, pend, rest 5 drape, droop, hinge, knack, slope, swing 6 append, dangle, depend, gibbet, talter 7 crucify, execute, stretch, suspend 9 declivity 11 inclination

around: 4 loaf 5 hover 6 loiter 7 frequent

back: lag 6 falter 8 hesitate

down: 5 droop 6 dangle 7 suspend

onto: 5 cling

hang fire: 4 pend 8 hesitate, postpone 13 procrastinate

hangar: 4 shed 6 garage, stable 7 shelter 9 penthouse

hangdog: 4 base 5 cowed 6 shifty 7 ashamed, fawning, furtive 8 cringing, sneaking 9 groveling

hanger-on: bur 5 leech, toady 6 hangby, heeler 7 adjunct, dangler, slinger, sponger 8 bottomer, loiterer, onsetter, parasite 9 appendage, dependent, sycophant 10 blackguard, free-loader

hanging: 5 arras, drape 6 celure, tippet 7 pendent, pensile, valance 8 inclined 9 declivity, execution, suspended 11 inclination

Hanging Gardens site: 7 Babylon

hangman: 6 hangie 9 Jack Ketch 11 executioner

hangout: 5 joint 10 rendezvous

hangover: 8 residuum 11 aftereffect

hang-up: 5 block, 6 phobia 8 fixation 9 obsession

hank: 4 coil, loop 5 skein 6 bundle, handle 7 control 9 influence

hanker: yen 4 ache, long 5 crave, yearn 6 desire, hunger, thirst

Hannibal: 7 general

conqueror: 6 Scipio

father: 8 Hamilcar

home: 8 Carthage

place of victory: 6 Cannae

hansom: cab

hap: lot 4 luck 5 check, occur, seize 6 befall, chance, snatch 7 fortune, venture 9 happening 10 occurrence, prosperity

haphazard: 6 casual, chance, random 8 careless 10 accidental 11 any which way 13 helter-skelter

hapless: 4 poor 7 unlucky 11 star-crossed, unfortunate

happen: 4 come, fall, fare 5 evene, occur 6 arrive, befall, betide, chance, mayhap 7 come off, perhaps, stumble 9 eventuate, transpire

happen again: 5 recur

happening: hap 4 case, fact 5 event, thing 6 chance, faring, 7 episode 8 incident, occasion 10 occurrence

happily: 5 fitly, haply 6 gladly 7 luckily 8 joyously 10 gracefully 11 contendedly, fortunately, opportunely 12 felicitously, peradventure, prosperously, successfully 13 appropriately

happiness: joy 4 sele(Sc.), weal 5 bliss, mirth 6 felice, gaiety 7 delight, ecstasy, felicia, rapture 8 felicity, gladness, hilarity 9 beatitude, enjoyment, eudaemony, transport, well-being 10 exaltation, prosperity 11 blessedness

god: 5 Ebisu

incapacity for: 9 anhedonia

happy: apt, gay 4 cosh, glad, gleg 5 blest, lucky, merry, ready, seely, sonsy, sunny 6 elated, sonsie 7 blessed, content, fitting, halcyon, radiant 8 carefree, frohlich, gracious, mirthful 9 contented, fortunate 10 felicitous, propitious, prosperous

happy-go-lucky: 6 casual 8 carefree 9 easygoing

happy hour: 12 cocktail time

happy hunting ground: 6 heaven 8 paradise

Haran: *brother:* 7 Abraham
daughter: 5 Iscah 6 Milcah
father: 5 Terah
son: Lot

harangue: nag 4 rave 5 orate, spiel 6 screed, sermon, speech, tirade 7 address, declaim, oration 8 diatribe, jeremiad, perorate 10 concionate

harass: fag, hag, nag, try, vex 4 bait, fret, gall, hake, hale, haze, jade, rack, raid, tire 5 annoy, beset, bully, chafe, chase, grind, gripe, harry, herry(Sc.), hurry, pique, tease, weary, worry 6 badger, bother, bucket, cumber, hatter, heckle, impede, molest, obsess, pester, plague, pother, scrape 7 afflict, affront, agitate, disturb, exhaust, fatigue, hagride, oppress, perplex, provoke, scourge, torment, trouble 8 distract, distress, irritate 9 exagitate, persecute, tantalize

harbinger: 4 camp, host, omen, sign 5 usher 6 herald, symbol 7 presage, shelter 8 fourrier, harborer 9 messenger, precursor 10 forerunner

spring: 5 robin 6 crocus

harbor, harbour: bay, inn 4 hold, port 5 basin, bayou, haven 6 billet, breach, bunder, covert, foster, refuge 7 fairway, lodging, quarter, retreat, seaport, shelter 9 harborage

entrance: 4 boca
fee: 7 keelage
harbor master: 7 havener

hard: fit 4 acid, cold, dear, dere, dure, firm, iron, mean, oaky, sour 5 champ, close, cruel, hardy, harsh, horny, rigid, rocky, rough, solid, stern, stiff, stony 6 coarse, frozen, knotty, marble, robust, severe, steely, strict, strong 7 adamant, arduous, austere, callous, compact, earnest, intense, onerous, scleral 8 diligent, granitic, grasping, hardened, obdurate, renitent, rigorous, scleroid, toilsome 9 difficult, energetic, fatiguing, inclement, intricate, laborious, petrified, repelling, reprobate, resistant, strenuous, stringent, unfeeling, wearisome 10 inflexible, oppressive, perplexing, persistent, relentless, ungraceful, unyielding 11 at close hand, complicated, distressing, down-to-earth, impregnable, persevering, unremitting 12 blood-and-guts, disreputable, extortionate, impenetrable, incorrigible, unalleviated 13 unsympathetic

to please: 7 finicky

hard-boiled: 5 rough, tough 7 callous 8 obdurate, seasoned 11 down-to-earth 13 unsympathetic

hard coal: 10 anthracite

hard core: 12 intransigent 13 dyed-in-the-wool

hard corn: rye 5 wheat

hard drawn: 4 taut 5 tense

hard-shell: 9 confirmed, extremist

hard times: 9 recession 10 depression

harden: gel, set 4 bake, cake, salt, sear 5 beath, enure, inure, steel 6 endure, freeze, ossify, temper 7 congeal, petrify, stiffen, thicken, toughen 8 concrete, condense, indurate, solidify 10 habituate 11 acclimatize, strengthen

hardened: 4 hard 5 caked 6 frozen, gelled, inured 7 callous, steeled 8 obdurate 9 abandoned, reprobate 10 impenitent, impervious inveterate, solidified 12 impenetrable

hardhat: 7 builder 12 conservative

hardhead: 4 fish 5 whale 7 ribwort 8 knapweed, mackerel, menhaden 9 blockhead 10 niggerhead

hardheaded: 4 keen 6 shrewd 7 willful 8 stubborn 9 sagacious 10 longheaded 11 down-to-earth, sharp-witted 12 matter-of-fact

hardhearted: 4 mean 5 cruel, stern 7 callous 8 obdurate, pitiless 9 unfeeling 10 marblehearted, unsympathetic

hardihood: 5 pluck, vigor 7 bravery, courage 8 audacity, boldness, temerity 9 hardiness, impudence, stoutness 10 confidence, effrontery, imprudence, resolution, robustness **11** intrepidity **13** audaciousness

hard line: **4** firm **5** fixed **10** determined, inflexible

hardly: **6** barely **7** faintly, hardily, harshly, roughly **8** forcibly, scarcely, severely, unfairly **11** unfavorably

hardness: **6** durity **8** asperity, severity, solidity **9** substance
measuring device: **9** durometer

hardpan: **7** bedrock **8** ortstein

hardship: **5** assay, peril, rigor, trial **6** injury **7** penalty **8** asperity, hardness **9** adversity, endurance, grievance, injustice, privation **10** affliction, difficulty

hardtack: **7** biscuit, galette(F.), pantile

hardwood: ash, oak **4** pelu, teak **5** maple **6** walnut **7** hickory **8** mahogany
genus: **7** quercus

hardy: **4** bold, firm, hard, rash, wiry **5** brave, lusty, manly, stout, tough **6** chisel, daring, robust, rugged, strong, sturdy **7** compact, spartan **8** galliard, intrepid, resolute, stubborn, vigorous **9** audacious, confident **10** courageous

Hardy heroine: **4** Tess

hare: dol **4** bawd(Sc.), pika **5** harry, lepus, tease, worry **6** malkin, rabbit **7** leporid, leveret **8** frighten, leporide **10** jack rabbit
female: doe
genus of: **5** lepus
male: **4** buck
pert. to: **8** leporine
tail: **4** scut
track: **4** file, slot
young: **7** leveret

harem: oda **4** odah **5** serai **6** serail, zenana **8** seraglio
male attendant: **6** eunuch
room: oda
slave: **9** odalisque

haricot: **4** stew **6** ragout

hark: **4** hear, heed, hist **6** attend, listen, notice **7** whisper

harlequin: **5** clown **7** buffoon **9** fantastic **11** masquerader

harlot: low, pug **4** base, doxy, lewd, slut **5** churl, knave, quean, rogue, whore **6** menial, rascal, wanton **7** buffoon, juggler **8** strumpet, vagabond **10** fricatrice, prostitute

harm: hob, ill, mar, sap **4** bale, bane, evil, hurt, pain, teen **5** abuse, annoy, grief, shend, wound, wrong **6** damage, damnum, injure, injury, scathe, sorrow **7** disease, impeach **8** disserve, endamage, nuisance **10** disservice, misfortune, wickedness **11** impeachment

harmful: bad **4** evil **5** nasty, toxic **6** no-

cent **7** baneful, hurtful, malefic, noisome, noxious **8** damaging, sinister **9** injurious **10** pernicious **11** contrarious, deleterious, detrimental, mischievous

harmless: **4** safe **6** dovish **8** innocent, nontoxic **9** innocuous **11** inoffensive

harmonica: **10** mouth organ
relative of: **7** panpipe

Harmonia: *father:* **4** Ares, Mars
husband: **6** Cadmus
mother: **5** Venus **9** Aphrodite

harmonious: **6** cosmic, dulcet **7** cordial, musical, spheral, tuneful **8** amicable, peaceful **9** accordant, agreeable, congruous, consonant, harmonial, melodious, peaceable **10** compatible, concentive, concordant **11** harmoniacal, symmetrical **12** proportional

harmonize: gee, key **4** jibe, tone, tune **5** adapt, agree, blend, chime, hitch, rhyme **6** accord, adjust, attune, cotton **7** consent, concord, consist, consort **9** reconcile **10** correspond, sympathize

harmony: **4** tune **5** amity, music, peace **6** cosmos, melody **7** concert, concord, rapport **9** agreement **10** accordance, atmosphere, conformity, congruence, consonance **11** cooperation **12** togetherness
bring into: **6** attune
lack: **7** discord

harness: **4** gear, yoke **5** heald **6** fettle, tackle **7** enclose, hitch-up **9** equipment, trappings
marker: **7** knacker, lorimer
part: bit, tug **4** hame, rein **5** blind, trace **6** billet, bridle, collar, saddle, terret **7** crouper **9** breeching, circingle, martingal, ridgeband, surcingle **10** breastband, crownpiece, martingale

harp: **4** arpa, koto, lyre **6** trigon **8** bedlamer **10** instrument **11** clairschach

harper: **4** coin **8** minstrel, musician

harpoon: **5** spear **7** javelin

harpsichord: **6** spinet **8** clavecin, virginal **12** clavicembalo

harpy: **5** leech, scold, vixen **6** virago **8** fishwife, swindler **11** extortioner

Harpy: **5** Aello **7** Celaneo, Ocypete, Podarge

harridan: hag **5** crone, horse, vixen, woman **8** strumpet

harrier: dog **4** hawk **5** bully **8** harasser

harrow: vex **4** disk, drag **5** brake, harry, wound **6** spader **7** oppress, torment **8** distress, lacerate **9** cultivate **10** cultivator

harrowed: **6** pained **7** haggard **8** tortured

harry: rob, vex **4** sack **5** annoy, hound, hurry, spoil, steal, worry **6** harass, harrow, hector, plague, ravage **7** agitate, bedevil, despoil, pillage, plunder, torment 9 persecute

harsh: raw 4 grim, hard, hask 5 acerb, acrid, asper, brute, crude, cruel, grill, gruff, raspy, rough, sharp, stern, stiff 6 bitter, brazen, coarse, severe, strict, sullen, unkind 7 austere, braying, drastic, grating, rasping, raucous 8 acerbate, catonian, clashing, croaking, district, guttural, jangling, rigorous, strident, ungentle 9 dissonant, inclement, insensate, repellent, squawking, truculent, unfeeling 10 astringent, discordant, oppressive, relentless 11 acrimonious, disagreeing 12 disagreeable

harshness: 5 rigor 6 duress 7 crudity, raucity 8 acerbity, acrimony, asperity, severity

hart: roe 4 deer, stag 7 red deer, venison
mate: 4 hind

hartebeest: 4 asse, tora 5 caama, kaama 6 lecama 7 bubalis 8 antelope

hartshorn: 6 antler 7 ammonia 11 sal volatile

harum-scarum: 4 rash, wild 7 flighty 8 reckless 11 thoughtless 13 irresponsible

Harun-Al-Rashid's wife: 7 Zobeide

haruspex: 5 augur 7 diviner, prophet 8 foreseer 9 predictor 10 soothsayer 14 prognosticator

harvest: 4 bind, crop, reap 5 amass, cache, hoard 6 foison, gather 8 ingather, stow away
festival: 6 Opalia
fly: 6 cicada
god: 6 Cronus
goddess: Ops 4 Rhea 5 Ceres 7 Demeter

harvest home: 4 kern, kirn(Sc.)

harvester: 8 spalpeen

hash: 4 chop 5 mince, mix-up 6 jumble 7 mixture 9 talk about 11 gallimaufry, olla podrida(Sp.)

hashish: 4 hemp 5 bhang 8 cannabis, narcotic

hashmark: 6 stripe

hasp: 4 gird 5 catch, clasp 7 confine 8 fastener

hassle: row, try 4 talk 6 hustle 7 quarrel, wrestle 8 argument, squabble 9 commotion 10 discussion 11 altercation, controversy

hassock: 4 boss, pess 5 grass, sedge 6 buffet 7 cushion, ottoman, tussock 8 footrest 9 footstool

haste: hie 4 rush 5 hurry, speed 6 bustle, flurry 7 urgency 8 dispatch, rapidity 9 quickness, swiftness 10 expedition, nimbleness 11 festination, impetuosity 12 precipitance 13 impetuousness, precipitation

hasten: hie, run 4 pell, race, rush, trot 5 crowd, drive, fleet, hurry, speed 6 expede, gallop, scurry 7 advance, scamper 8 dispatch, expedite 9 festinate 10 accelerate 11 precipitate

hastily: 6 nimbly 8 speedily 11 impatiently 13 precipitately

hasty: 4 fast, rash 5 brash, fleet, quick, swift 6 abrupt, daring, nimble, speedy, sudden 7 cursory, forward, hurried 8 headlong, pell-mell, succinct 9 hotheaded, hurrisome, impatient, impetuous 10 indiscreet 11 expeditious, precipitate, precipitous

hasty pudding: 4 mush 6 supawn 9 stirabout

hat: cap, dip, fez, lid, nab, tam 4 baku, felt, topi 5 beany, benjy, benny, beret, boxer, cordy, derby, dicer, kelly, terai, topee, toque 6 Alpine, beaver, boater, bonnet, bowler, castor, claque, cloche, fedora, panama, shovel, turban 7 biretta, caubeen, chapeau, homburg, petasus, salacot, shallow 8 capeline, copatain, headgear, sombrero 9 Dunstable, stovepipe, wide-awake 10 belltopper 11 mortarboard
brimless: 7 pillbox
close fitting: 5 toque 6 turban
covering: 8 havelock
crown: 4 poll
ecclesastic: 5 miter 7 biretta
fiber: 4 felt, sola 5 straw
fur used in: 4 mink 5 coney 6 beaver, ermine 8 coonskin
ladies: 5 caddy, cooie 6 Breton, caddie, slouch 7 leghorn 8 duckbill 9 harlequin 12 Gainsborough
maker: 8 milliner
medieval: 6 abacot 7 bycoket
military: 5 shako
oilskin: 5 squam 9 sou'wester
opera: 5 crush, gibus 6 claque, topper
palm-leaf: 7 salacot
pert. to: 9 castorial
pith: 4 topi 5 topee
Quaker: 7 broadbrim
silk: lum(Sc.) 4 tile 5 opera 6 topper 7 catskin 8 gossamer
soft: 6 fedora
straw: 6 boater
tall: 9 stovepipe
three-cornered: 7 tricorn
ventilated: 5 terai
wide-brimmed: 9 sou'wester

hatch: 4 brew, door, gate, sire, vent 5 breed, cleck, clock, cover 6 clutch, wicket 7 concoct 8 contrive, hatchway 9 floodgate
covering: 4 tarp

hatchel: 5 tease, worry 6 heckle 7 torment

hatchet: adz, axe 4 adze, mogo 8 tomahawk

hatchet man: 4 tool 6 critic, killer, stooge 8 assassin, henchman

hatching: 6 cletch 8 breeding

hatchway: 7 scuttle

hate: 4 teen 5 abhor, scorn 6 detest, loathe, rancor, revile 7 contemn, despise, ill will 8 aversion 9 abominate, malignity 11 detestation

hateful: 4 evil, foul 5 black, nasty 6 odious 7 heinous 8 flagrant, infamous 9 abhorrent, invidious, loathsome, malignant, obnoxious, offensive, revolting 10 abominable, detestable, disgusting, malevolent 11 distasteful 12 disagreeable

hatful: 4 lots, many, much 8 quantity

hatred: 5 odium, spite 6 enmity, rancor 8 aversion 9 animosity, hostility, malignity 10 abhorrence, repugnance 11 abomination, detestation, malevolence

of argument: 8 misology

of children: 9 misopedia 10 misopaedia

of mankind: 11 misanthropy

of marriage: 8 misogamy

of strangers: 10 xenophobia

hatter: 8 milliner

haughtiness: 4 airs 5 pride 6 morgue 7 hauteur 9 arrogance, insolence

haughty: 4 airy, bold, high 5 aloof, dorty, lofty, noble, proud 6 snooty 7 distant, exalted, fatuous, hontish, paughty, stately 8 arrogant, cavalier, glorious, scornful 9 egotistic, imperious, masterful 10 disdainful, fastidious 11 domineering, magisterial, overbearing 12 contemptuous, presumptuous, supercilious

haul: lug, tow, tug 4 cart, drag, draw, hurl, move, pull, tote 5 bouse, catch, heave, shift, trice 8 cordelle 9 transport

haulage: 6 towage 7 cartage, drayage

hauler: 7 tractor

haulm: 4 culm, stem 5 straw 6 stalks

haunch: hip 4 huck 5 hance 12 hindquarters

haunt: den 4 dive, howf, lair, nest 5 ghost, habit, howff, skill 6 custom, infest, obsess, resort, spirit, wraith 7 hang out, terrify 8 frequent, practice 9 companion 10 fellowship, hang around

haunted: 6 filled, spooky 8 infested

hautboy, hautbois: 4 oboe 9 organ stop 10 strawberry

hauteur: 5 pride 9 arrogance 11 haughtiness

haut monde: 11 high society

have: hae(Sc.), own 4 hold 5 enjoy, ought 6 retain 7 carry on, contain, possess, undergo 10 experience

on: 4 wear

to do with: 4 deal

haven: bay, lee 4 hope, port 5 hotel, inlet 6 asylum, harbor, recess, refuge 7 retreat, shelter 9 anchorage, roadstead, sanctuary

haversack: bag

havoc: hob 4 loss, ruin 5 waste 6 ravage 7 destroy 9 devastate 10 desolation 11 destruction, devastation

haw: 4 sloe, yard 5 fence, hedge 6 falter 8 hawthorn

Hawaii: *ballad:* 4 mele

beach: 7 Waikiki

beverage: 4 kava 8 kava-kava

breechcloth: 4 malo

bush: See *shrub* below

canoe: 5 waapa

capital: 8 Honolulu

channel: 4 Auau

chant: 4 mele

city: 4 Hilo 5 Lihue 6 Kailua 7 Kanache, Wailuku

cloak: 4 mamo 6 ahuula

cloth: 4 kapa, tapa 5 tappa

cookout: 4 luau

county: 4 Maui 5 Kauai 6 Hawaii 8 Honolulu

cord: aea

crater: 7 Kilauea

dance: 4 hula

discoverer: 4 Cook

district: 4 Puna, Kona

farewell, hello: 5 aloha

feast: 4 luau 7 ahaaina

fern: 4 heii 5 ekaha, uluhi 6 iwaiwa 7 amaumau

fiber: 4 pulu

first settler: 10 Polynesian

fish: ahi 4 ulua 5 akule

fish poison: hola 6 auhuhu

flower: 5 ilima

food: poi 4 kalo, taro

game: hei

garland: lei

garment: 6 holoku, muumuu 7 holomuu

god: 4 Kane 5 Wakea

goddess: 4 Pele

goose: 4 nene

grass: 6 emoloa

greeting: 5 ahola

harbor: 5 Pearl

hawk: io

herb: ape, pia 4 hola 5 awiwi 6 auhuhu

instrument: uke 7 ukalele, ukelele, ukulele

island: 4 Maui, Oahu 5 Kauai, Lanai 6 Hawaii, Niihau 7 Molokai 9 Kahoolawe

lava: aa 8 pahoehoe

loincloth: 4 malo, maro

lomilomi: rub 7 massage, shampoo

love: 5 aloha

massage: 8 lomilomi

morning glory: 5 koali

mountain: 5 Kaala 7 Waianae 8 Mauna Kea, Mauna Loa

native: 6 Kanaka 10 Polynesian
naval base: 11 Pearl Harbor
nickname: 10 Aloha State
octopus: hee
pantheon: 4 Kane
parrot fish: 5 lauia
partnership: hui
pepper: ava
pit for baking: imu
plant: pia 4 akia, hala, taro 5 olona 8 pandanus
poem: 4 mele
porch: 5 lanai
precipice: 4 pali
priest: 6 Kahuna
raven: 5 alala
root: 4 taro
root paste: poi
seaweed: 4 limu
shaman: 6 Kahuna
shrub: pia 4 akia, akala, olona 6 aupaka
song: 4 mele
staple: poi 4 taro
starch plant: pia
starch root: pia 4 taro
state bird: 4 nene 5 goose
state flower: 8 hibiscus
state song: 11 Hawaii Ponoi
state tree: 9 candlenut
temple: 5 heiau
thrush: 4 amao 6 olomao
valley: 5 Manoa
volcano: 7 Kilauea 8 Mauna Kea, Mauna Loa
white man: 5 haole
wind: 4 kona
windstorm: 4 kona
woman: 5 haole
wreath: lei
yam: hoi

hawfinch: 4 kate 8 grosbeak
hawk: io; cry, gos 4 eyas, kite, sell, vend 5 astur, cadge 6 falcon, osprey, peddle, 7 buzzard, harrier, haggard, kestrel, puttock, vulture 8 caracara, jingoist, militant 9 accipiter, swindler, warmonger 11 mortar-board
cage: mew
male: 6 musket, tercel 7 tiercel
leash: 4 jess, lune
nest: 5 aerie
nestling: 4 eyas
pinion feather: 6 sarcel
hawker: 6 badger, cadger, coster, duffer, pedlar, vendor 7 chapman, mercury, packman, peddler 8 falconer, huckster, pitchman 9 colporter 10 colporteur 12 costermonger
hawk-eyed: 12 sharp-sighted
Hawkeye State: 4 Iowa
hawklike: 9 bellicose 11 accipitrine, belligerent
hawser: 4 line, rope

post: 4 bitt 7 bollard
hawthorn: haw, may 5 aglet 6 aiglet 8 cockspur, maybloom, quickset
hay: bed, net 4 park 5 chaff, fence, grass, hedge 9 provender
bundle: mow 4 bale, rick, wisp 5 gavel, stack, truss 7 hayrick
kind of: 6 clover 7 alfalfa, timothy
line: 5 swath 7 windrow
second cutting: 5 rowen
spreader: 6 tedder
storage: mow 4 loft
haycock: 4 coil
hayfork: 4 pike 5 pikel
haymaker: 8 farm hand 10 boxing blow
hayseed: 4 hick 5 yokel 6 farmer, rustic 10 countryman
hazard: die, lay, lot 4 risk 5 peril, stake 6 chance, danger, gamble, menace 7 imperil, venture 8 accident, casualty, endanger, jeopardy 9 adventure 10 jeopardize
hazardous: 5 risky 6 chance, chancy, queasy, unsafe 8 insecure, perilous 9 dangerous, uncertain 10 fortuitous, jeopardous, precarious 11 adventurous
haze: fog 4 beat, film, mist, smog 5 cloud, devil, scold, vapor 6 harass, vapour 7 drizzle, obscure, reverie 8 frighten
hazel: nut 4 bush 6 cobnut 7 filbert 8 noisette 12 reddish brown
Hazor king: 5 Jabin
hazy: dim 5 filmy, foggy, misty, smoky, thick, vague 7 clouded, nebular, obscure, unclear 8 nebulous 9 uncertain 10 indistinct
head: aim, cop, mir, nab, nob, top 4 bean, boro, cape, coco, conk, crop, kopf(G.), lead, mind, pate, poll, tete(F.), turn 5 caput(L.), chief, chump, first, front, froth, start, tibby 6 cabeza(Sp.), cobbra, direct, garret, leader, manage, noggin, noodle, person, sconce, source, spring 7 captain, coconut, costrel, cranium, crumpet, leading, prelate 8 director, foremost, fountain, headland, initiate 9 intercept, president, principal 10 caper-nutie, drug addict, headmaster, promontory 11 caper-noitie 12 intelligence
army camp: 10 commandant
back part: 7 occiput
bald: 9 pilgarlic
boar: 4 hure
bone: 5 skull 7 cranium 8 parietal
crown: 6 cantle
muscle: 11 occipitalis
nautical: 6 toilet 8 lavatory
ornament: hat, wig 4 hair, veil 5 tiara 7 coronet
part: 4 pate 5 scalp 6 earlap, temple 7 cranium

pert. to: 8 cephalic
shaven: 7 tonsure
shrunken: 7 tsantsa
side of: 4 lore 5 lorum 6 temple
skin: 5 scalp
top: 4 pate 5 crown, scalp 7 coxcomb
head cook: 4 chef
head covering (see also **cap, hat**): fez, tam, wig 4 barb, caul, coif, hair, hood 5 beret, scalp, snood, toque 6 bonnet, coiffe, peruke, toupee 7 biretta, chapeau, periwig 8 berretta, kerchief, maharmah, sombrero 9 rigolette 10 fascinator
head-shaped: 8 capitate
head to foot: 7 cap-a-pie
headache: 6 megrim 8 headwork, migraine 10 cephalagia
headband: 5 miter, mitre, vitta 6 diadem, fillet, infula 7 circlet, coronet 8 frontlet 9 sphendone
headcheese: 5 brawn
headdress: 4 caul, coif, pouf 5 ampyx, crown, cupee, miter, mitre, tiara, toque 6 almuce, bonnet, coiffe, faille, hennin, mobcap, pinner, turban 7 bandore, bycoket, coronet, topknot 8 biliment, binnogue, capriole, coiffure, stephane, tressure 9 rigolette
medieval: 5 barbe 6 abacot
military: 5 busby, shako 6 casque, helmet
royal: 5 crown, tiara 6 diadem
sacerdotal: 5 miter 7 biretta
sacred: 6 uraeus
Spanish woman's: 8 mantilla
widow's: 7 bandore
headgear: See **headdress**
headily: 6 rashly 9 violently
heading: 5 title, topic 7 caption 8 headline
topical: 5 trope
headland: ras 4 bill, cape, head, nase, naze, ness, peak 5 Morro, ridge, strip 8 foreland 10 promontory
headless: 4 rash 6 stupid, topless 7 foolish 8 beheaded 10 acephalous, leaderless
headline: 6 banner 7 feature, 8 streamer
headliner: 7 star 11 personality
headlong: 4 rash 5 hasty, steep 6 abrupt, sudden 8 reckless 9 desperate, foolhardy, headfirst, impetuous, impulsive 11 precipitate, precipitous
headman: 4 boss 5 chief 6 ataman, cabeza, hetman 7 capitan, captain, foreman 8 alderman, caboceer, capitano 11 executioner
headmaster: 9 principal 11 gymnasiarch
headpiece: See **headdress**
headquarters: 5 depot, yamen 6 center 8 exchange, precinct 9 battalion
headstone: 8 monument 11 grave marker

headstrong: 4 rash 5 cobby 6 mulish, unruly 7 hotspur, violent, willful 8 stubborn 9 obstinate 10 bullheaded, forthright, hotspurred, self-willed 11 intractable, stiff-necked 12 contumacious, ungovernable
heady: 4 rash 7 huffcap, violent, willful 9 impetuous 11 exhilarated, intoxicated, precipitate 12 intoxicating
heal: 4 cure, hale, knit, mend 5 amend 6 remedy, repair 7 restore 10 recuperate
heal-all: 4 balm 7 figwort, panacea
healer: asa 4 balm 6 doctor 9 naprapath 12 practitioner
healing: 5 balmy 8 covering, curative, remedial, sanative
agent: 6 balsam
goddess: Eir
pert. to: 7 medical 9 medicinal
science: 8 medicine 9 iatrology, latrology
health: 4 hale, hail 5 sante(F.), toast 7 slainte, stamina 8 eucrasia, euphoria, haleness, vitality 11 disposition
goddess: 7 Minerva
poor: 4 sick 7 illness
resort: spa
healthy: fit 4 hale, sane, well 5 bonny, hoddy 6 bonnie, hearty, robust 8 salutary, vigorous 9 wholesome 10 healthsome, salubrious
heap: ahu, cob, cop, mow 4 balk, bing, bulk, deck, dess(Sc.), gobs, hill, lump, mass, much, pile, pyre, raft, rick, ruck 5 amass, cairn, clump, crowd, spire, stack 6 burrow, hipple, jumble, plenty, throng 7 bourock, cumulus, hurrock 9 congeries, multitude 10 accumulate, collection, congestion, cumulation
hear: ear, see 4 feel, hark, heed, obey 5 learn 6 attend, harken, listen 7 hearken 8 perceive 10 adjudicate
hear ye: 4 oyes, oyez
hearer: 7 audient, auditor 8 disciple, listener
hearing: ear 4 test 5 sound, trial 6 assize, report 7 earshot, lecture, meeting 8 audience, audition, scolding 9 attention, audiencia, interview, knowledge 10 attendance, conference, discussion
court: 4 oyer
distance: 7 earshot
judicial: 5 trial 7 retrial
pert. to: 8 acoustic
hearken, harken: 4 hark, hear, heed, wait 6 attend, listen 7 inquire, whisper
hearsay: 4 buzz, fame, talk 5 on-dit, rumor 6 report 9 grapevine 11 scuttlebutt
hearse: 4 bier, bury, tomb 5 dirge, grave 6 coffin 8 monument, threnody
heart: cor, hub 4 core, gist, hati, love 5 cheer, focus 6 center, centre, depths,

middle, ticker 7 courage, emotion, essence, feeling 9 affection, character 10 compassion

cavity: 6 atrium

chamber: 7 auricle 9 ventricle

contraction: 7 systole

covering: 11 pericardium

disease: 7 cardiac

expansion: 8 diastole

record: 17 electrocardiogram

stimulant: 8 thaildin 9 digitalis, thialdine 10 adrenaline, epinephrin 11 epinephrine

heart-shaped: 7 cordate

heartache: rue, woe 4 pang 5 grief 6 sorrow 7 anguish 10 affliction, cardialgia

heartbeat: 5 pulse, throb 7 systole 9 pulsation

irregular: 10 arrhythmia

heartbreak: 5 grief 6 sorrow 7 tragedy

heartbroken: 12 inconsolable 13 grief-stricken

heartburn: 4 envy 6 enmity 7 pyrosis 8 jealousy 10 cardialgia, discontent, heartscald, heartscaud

hearten: 5 cheer 6 arouse, spirit 7 cheer up, refresh 8 embolden, inspirit, reassure 9 encourage

heartfelt: 4 dear, deep, real, true 6 honest 7 earnest, genuine, sincere 8 bona fide, profound

hearth: 5 cupel, focus, fogon, foyer 8 bloomery, fireside

goddess: 5 Vesta 6 Hestia

line: 6 fettle

heartily: 6 dearly, freely, warmly 8 actively, strongly 9 cordially, earnestly, profusely, sincerely, zealously, zestfully 10 abundantly, completely, vigorously 14 wholeheartedly

heartiness: 4 soul 8 goodwill, strength 9 soundness 10 cordiality

heartless: 5 cruel 7 callous 8 hopeless, listless 9 merciless, unfeeling 10 despairing, despondent, hard-boiled, spiritless 13 unsympathetic

heartsease, heartease: 5 pansy, peace 11 peace of mind 12 tranquillity

heartthrob: 4 dunt, love 5 flame, honey, sweet

heartwood: 4 dura 7 duramen

hearty: 4 firm, hale, real, rich, warm, well 5 cobby, heavy, sound 6 active, cheery, devout, robust, sailor, stanch 7 comrade, cordial, earnest, fertile, healthy, sincere, staunch 8 abundant, cheerful, heartful, vigorous 9 energetic, unfeigned, wholesome 10 full-bodied, nourishing 11 substantial, warmhearted 12 enthusiastic

heat: ire 4 fire, mull, rage, warm, zeal 5 ardor, cauma, chafe, fever, roast, tepor

6 anneal, choler, degree, warmth 7 caloric, ferment, hotness, inflame, passion 8 fervency 9 agitation, animation, chauffage, commotion, vehemence 10 excitement, hot weather 11 temperature 12 exasperation 14 passionateness

measure: 5 therm 6 calory, therme 7 calorie 10 centigrade, fahrenheit 11 calorimeter, pyronometer

pert. to: 7 thermic

quantity: 6 degree 11 temperature

unit of: 5 therm 7 calorie

white: 13 incandescence

heated: 6 ardent 7 excited 8 sizzling, vehement 10 phlogistic 11 acrimonious

heater: 4 etna, oven 5 stove 6 boiler 7 choffer(Sc.), furnace 8 radiator

heath: 4 ling, moor 5 besom, erica, plain

scrub: 9 chaparral

tree: 5 briar, brier

heathen: 5 pagan 6 ethnic, paynim 7 saracen 8 paganist 11 irreligious

deity: 4 idol

non-Jewish: 6 ethnic

non-Muslim: 7 infidel

heather: 4 grig, ling 5 erica

family: 9 ericaceae

heatless: 8 athermic

heautarit: 7 mercury 11 quicksilver

heave: gag 4 cast, haul, heft, hurl, keck, lift, pant, pull, push, quap, toss 5 hoist, pitch, raise, retch, scend, throw, vomit 7 elevate, estuate 8 struggle

heaven: sky 4 Zion 5 dyaus, ether, glory 6 Himmel(G.), utopia, welkin, zodiac 7 Elysium, Nirvana, Valhall, Vahalla 8 devaloka, empyrean, paradise 9 firmament 12 promised land

pert. to: 6 uranic 9 celestial

queen: 7 Astarte

heavenly: 4 lush 5 yummy 6 divine, sacred 7 angelic, olympic, sublime, uranian 8 ethereal, supernal 9 angelical, celestial, celestine

heavenly being: 5 angel 6 seraph

heavenly belt: way 6 galaxy, nebula, zodiac

heavenly body: sun 4 luna, moon, star 5 comet 6 planet 8 luminary

heavenly city: 4 Sion, Zion

heavenly twins: 6 Castor, Gemini, Pollux

heaviness: 5 gloom 6 weight 7 gravity, sadness 10 oppression 12 sluggishness

heavy: 4 clit, deep, dull, logy, loud 5 actor, beefy, burly, dense, grave, gross, hefty, hoggy, massy, thick 6 clayey, cloggy, coarse, gloomy, hearty, leaden, stodgy, strong, stupid 7 big shot, doleful, intense, massive, onerous, porcine, serious, villain, violent, weighty 8 burdened, grievous, inactive, lifeless, lowering, overcast, pregnant, profound, sluggish 9 heavisome, laborious, lethargic, ponderous, saturnine 10 afflictive, burdensome, cumbersome, encumbered, oppressive 13 consequential

heavy-headed: 4 dull 5 inept 6 drowsy, gauche, stupid 8 bumbling 9 maladroit, ponderous 10 uninspired

heavy-hearted: sad 10 despondent, melancholy

hebdomad: 4 week 5 seven

hebetate: 4 dull 5 blunt

Hebrew (see also **Israel, Judaism**): Jew 6 Semite 7 Semitic 8 Hebraean 9 Israelite

acrostic: 4 agla

alphabet: Mem, Nun, Sin, Taf, Tav, Tet, Vav, Yod, Yud 4 Alef, Ayin, Beth, Caph, Cheth, Gimel, Lamed, Sadhe, Tsade, Zayin 6 Daleth, Samekh

ancestor: 4 Eber

clean: 6 kosher

dance: 4 hora

day: yom

eternity: 4 olam

gentile: goi, goy 5 goyim(pl.)

God: El 5 Eloah 6 Adonai, Elohim 7 Jehovah

greeting: 6 shalom

high priest: Eli 5 Aaron

infinity: 6 adalam

Jehovah: 5 Jahve, Yahve, Yahwe 6 Jahvah, Jahveh, Yahveh, Yahweh 7 Jahaveh

juniper: 4 ezel

lawbreaking: 6 averah

lesson: 9 Haphtarah

man: rab 5 bahur, hakam

measure: cab, hin, kab, kor 4 epha, ezba, omer, reed, seah 5 cubit, ephah, homer

month: Ab 4 Adar, Elul 5 Iyyar, Nisan, Tebet 6 Kislew, Shebat, Tammuz, Tishri, Veadar 7 Heshwan

name for God: 6 Adonai, Elohim, Yahweh 7 Jehovah

parchment: 6 mezuza 7 mezuzah

school: 5 heder, schul

scriptures: 4 Tora 5 Torah

son: ben

teacher: 5 rabbi

thief: 5 ganef, ganof, gonof 6 gonoph

title: rab 4 abba

unclean: 4 tref

weight: 4 beka, reba

Hebrides island: 4 Mull, Skye 5 Islay

hecatomb: 9 sacrifice, slaughter

heckle: nag 4 bait, gibe 5 chivy, hound, tease 6 badger, hackle, harass, hector, needle 7 torment 8 bullyrag

hectic: 6 fervid 8 exciting, feverish, habitual, restless 11 consumptive 13 constitutional

hector: nag 4 bait 5 bully, harry, worry 6 harass, heckle, plague 7 bluster, dragoon, torment 8 braggart, bludgeon, browbeat, irritate 9 roisterer, swaggerer 10 intimidate

Hector: *companion:* 8 Diomedes

father: 5 Priam

mother: 6 Hecuba

rescuer: 6 Agenor

slayer: 8 Achilles

wife: 10 Andromache

Hecuba: *daughter:* 6 Creusa 8 Polyxena 9 Cassandra

husband: 5 Priam

son: 5 Paris 6 Hector 7 Helenus, Troilus 9 Deiphobus

victim: 11 Polymestor

hedenbergite: 8 pyroxene

hedge: bar, haw, hem 4 boma, cage, coop 5 beard, evade, fence, frith, guard, skulk 6 hinder, hurdle, privet 6 weasel 7 barrier, enclose, protect 8 boundary, obstruct, quickset, separate, sepiment, sidestep, straddle, surround 14 counterbalance

hedgehog: 6 urchin 7 echinus 8 herisson, hurcheon 9 porcupine

hedonic: 8 cyrenaic

hedonist: 4 rake 7 epicure 9 bon vivant 13 pleasure lover

heed: ear 4 care, cark, cure, gaum, hark, hear, mind, note, obey, reck 5 await, watch 6 attend, beware, harken, listen, notice, regard, remark 7 caution, hearken, observe, respect 8 consider 9 attention, diligence 10 cognizance, solicitude 11 observation

heedful: 4 wary 5 alert, chary 6 attent 7 careful, mindful 8 diligent, watchful 9 advertent, attendant, attentive, observant 10 meticulous, respectful 11 considerate

heedless: 4 rash 5 giddy 6 remiss, unwary 7 languid, witless 8 careless, reckless 9 blindfold, forgetful, negligent, oblivious 10 incautious, indiscreet, insouciant, regardless, unthinking 11 hairbrained, inadvertent, inattentive, indifferent lightheaded, thoughtless, unobservant

heehaw: 4 bray 5 laugh 6 giggle, guffaw 10 horselaugh

heel: cad, end, tip 4 calx, cant, knob, lean, list, tilt 5 knave, rogue, slant, talon 6 careen, rascal 7 incline 12 protuberance

bone: 9 calcaneus

heft: 5 heave, hoist, raise 6 strain, weight 8 exertion 9 heaviness, influence 13 ponderousness

hefty: big 5 beefy, burly, heavy, rough 6 rugged 7 massive, weighty 8 powerful, vehement, vigorous

hegemony: 9 authority, dominance, influence 10 leadership

hegira, hejira: 6 exodus, flight 9 migration

heifer: 4 quey 5 stirk 10 colpindach(Sc.)

height: 4 acme, apex, mote 5 crest 6 climax, summit, zenith 7 stature 8 altitude, eminence, pinnacle 9 celsitude, dimension, elevation, procerity, steepness 11 magnanimity
fear of: 10 acrophobia

heighten: 4 lift 5 elate, exalt, raise 6 accent, bolster 7 advance, augment, elevate, enhance 8 increase 9 aggravate, intensify 10 aggrandize

heinous: 6 crying, malign, odious, wicked 7 hateful 8 flagrant, grievous, shocking 9 atrocious, malicious, nefarious 10 abominable, flagitious, outrageous

heir: son 5 heres, scion 7 heritor, legatee 9 firstborn, inheritor, successor 11 beneficiary

heiress: 5 begum 8 heretrix, heritrix

Hejaz city: 5 Mecca

Hel: *dog:* 4 Garm
father: 4 Loki
mother: 9 Angurboda
realm: 7 Niflhel 8 Niflheim

held: See hold

Helen of Troy: *abductor:* 5 Paris
brother-in-law: 9 Agamemnon
daughter: 8 Hermione
half-sister: 12 Clytemnestra 13 Clytaemnestra
husband: 8 Menelaus
mother: 4 Leda

heliacal: 5 solar

helical: 6 spiral

helicon: 4 tuba

helicopter: 4 gyro 7 chopper 8 autogiro 9 eggbeater 10 rotor plane, whirlybird

Helios: 6 Apollo
daughter: 5 Circe 8 Heliadae, Heliades
father: 8 Hyperion
son: 8 Phaethon

heliotrope: 10 bloodstone

heliport: 10 landing pad

helix: 4 coil 6 spiral

hell: 5 hades, limbo 6 prison, tophet 7 dungeon, inferno 9 barathrum

hell-bent: 8 reckless 10 determined

hellebore: 5 plant 7 bugbane

Hellen: *father:* 9 Deucalion
mother: 6 Pyrrha
son: 5 Dorus 6 Aeolus, Xuthus

Hellene: See Greece

Hellenistic school: 9 Pergamene

Hellespont: 11 Dardanelles
swimmer: 7 Leander

hellgrammite: 6 dobson 8 fish bait, sialidae

hellish: 6 wicked 7 avernal, stygian 8 devilish, diabolic, infernal, plutonic 9 malignant 10 detestable, diabolical

hello: 8 greeting 10 salutation

helm: 5 helve, steer, wheel 6 direct, tiller 8 guidance
position: 4 alee 5 aport

helmet: cap 4 sola, topi 5 armet, galea, topee 6 casque, heaume, morion, salade, sallet 7 basinet 8 schapska 9 casquetel, headpiece
part: 4 bell 5 crest 7 ventail 8 aventail

helmet-shaped: 7 galeate

helmsman: 5 pilot 9 steersman

helot: 4 serf 5 slave 6 vassal 7 bondman

help: aid, bot, S.O.S., use 4 abet, boot, bote, cure, lift, mend, rede, tide 5 avail, boost, favor, frith, heeze, serve, speed, stead 6 assist, favour, relief, remedy, repair, succor 7 advance, benefit, forbear, forward, further, improve, promote, relieve, support, sustain 8 befriend, champion, facility 9 adminicle, alleviate, forestall 10 assistance, contribute, facilitate, strengthen 11 cooperation

helper: aid 4 ally 5 aider 6 deputy, server 7 abetter, abettor, ancella, servant, striker 8 adjutant, adjutrix, employee, helpmate 9 adjutrice, assistant, samaritan 10 apprentice, benefactor 11 subordinate

helpful: 6 hermione 6 aidant, useful 8 adjuvant, helpsome, salutary 9 auxiliary 10 beneficial, profitable 11 furthersome, serviceable 12 advantageous, constructive

helpless: 4 numb, weak 6 feeble, futile, unable 7 forlorn 8 impotent, unaiding 9 destitute, powerless 10 bewildered, unsupplied 11 defenseless, incompetent, unprotected 12 irremediable

helpmate: 4 wife 6 helper 8 helpmeet 9 companion

helter-skelter: 6 random 7 flighty, hotfoot, turmoil 8 pellmell 9 hit-or-miss 11 any which way

helve: 4 haft 5 lever 6 handle

Helvetian: 5 Swiss 6 Suisse

hem: 4 edge, seam 5 hedge 6 border, edging, margin, stitch 7 confine, enclose, environ, inclose 8 surround 9 fimbriate

hem in: 5 beset, limit 6 impale 7 enclose, inclose 8 surround

hematite: 7 iron ore 10 bloodstone 12 black diamond

hemeralopia: 6 defect 9 blindness

hemi: 4 half

hemlock: 4 bunk, herb, tree 5 tsuga 6 conium
drinker: 8 Socrates
poison: 6 conium

hemoglobin: 10 sickle cell

hemophiliac: 7 bleeder

hemp: ife, kef, kif, pua, tow 4 bang, carl, flax, harl, jute, rine, sunn 5 abaca, bhang, istle, ramie, sisal, sizal 6 ambary, banana, cabuja, cabuya, fennel, manila 7 hashish 8 cannabis, nepenthe

hen: pea 4 fowl, rail, wife 5 biddy, chuck, woman 6 gorhen, nester, pullet, towdie 7 chicken 9 gallinule
  broody: 6 sitter
  coop: 5 caire
  spayed: 7 poulard
  young: 6 pullet

henbane: 10 nightshade

hence: fro 4 away, ergo(L.), thus 5 since 7 hereout, thither 9 therefore 11 accordingly

henceforth: 9 from now on, hereafter

henchman: 4 page 6 gillie, lackey, minion, squire 7 mobster 8 adherent, disciple, follower 9 attendant, supporter

Hengist: *brother:* 5 Horsa
  daughter: 6 Rowena
  kingdom: 4 Kent
  people: 5 Jutes

henna: dye 6 alcana 7 alcanna

henpeck: Uag 4 carp

Henry II: *adversary:* 6 Becket
  drama about: 15 The Lion in Winter
  surname: 5 Anjou 11 Plantagenet
  wife: 7 Eleanor

Henry V: Hal

Henry VIII:
  daughter: 4 Mary 9 Elizabeth
  first wife: 9 Catherine
  second wife: 4 Anne
  third wife: 4 Jane
  fourth wife: 4 Anne
  fifth wife: 9 Catherine
  sixth wife: 9 Catherine
  son: 6 Edward
  surname: 5 Tudor

hepatitis: 8 jaundice

Hephaestus: 6 Vulcan
  father: 4 Zeus 7 Jupiter
  mother: 4 Hera, Juno
  wife: 5 Venus 6 Charis 8 Charites 9 Aphrodite

heptad: seven 11 septivalent

Hera: 4 Juno
  husband: 4 Zeus
  mother: 4 Rhea
  son: 4 Ares

Heracles: See Hercules

herald: 4 bode 5 crier, greet, usher 6 beadle, Hermes, signal 7 declare, forerun, trumpet 8 announce, blazoner, foretell, outrider, proclaim 9 harbinger, introduce, messenger, precursor 10 forerunner, foreshadow

heraldry: 6 armory 9 pageantry
  band: 4 fess 5 fesse

  bastardy mark: 4 bend 5 baton 7 bendlet 8 sinister
  bearing: 4 orle
  bell: 7 compane 10 campanella
  blood-red: 6 murrey
  chaplet: 4 orle
  charge: vol 7 boterol, saltier, saltire 8 boteroll, tressour, tressure
  circle: 6 bezant
  cross: 4 paty 5 patee, patte 6 ermine, moline, pattee 7 erminee, patonce, saltier, saltire
  device: 4 ente, orle 5 crest 6 altier
  fleur-de-lis: lis, lys
  gold: or
  grafted: 4 ente
  green: 4 vert
  keylike: 4 urde
  knot: 4 Lacy, Wake 5 Bowen, Dacre 7 Heneage 8 Stafford 9 Bourchier 10 Harrington
  leg: 4 gamb, jamb 5 gambe, jambe
  line: 4 unde
  scattered: 4 seme
  shield: 10 escutcheon
  tincture: or 5 tenne 6 argent
  triangle: 5 giron
  winged: 4 aile
  wreath: 4 orle 5 torse

herb: iva 4 anet, balm, dill, leek, mint, moly, sage, wort 5 anise, basil, chive, plant, sedge, thyme 6 annual, borage, catnip, clover, lovage, sesame, yarrow 7 caraway, oregano, parsley 8 marjoram, tarragon
  aromatic: 4 anet, dill, hemp, mint, nard, sage 5 anise, basil, clary, nondo, tansy, thyme 6 catnip, fennel, hyssop 7 chervil, cudweed, mustard, vetiver 8 wormseed 9 basilmint, spearmint 11 everlasting
  bitter: rue 4 aloe, woad 7 aletris, boneset 8 centaury 10 turtlehead
  bog: 5 calla 9 steepweed, steepwort
  climbing: 4 faba 5 vicia
  coarse: 5 tansy 6 eringo, eryngo 7 leafcup 8 pokeweed
  flowering: 7 anemone, dittane 8 stapelia 9 celandine
  genus: iva 4 ruta 5 ajuga, canna, cicer, cruca, galax, gavra, inula, lemna, loasa, rheum 6 aralia, asarum, cassia, dondia, isatis, mentha, nerine 7 alyssum, anemone, cirsium, hedeoma, torenia 8 psoralea 9 grindelia
  medicinal: rue 4 aloe 5 senna, sumac, tansy 6 arnica, lovage, tutsan 7 aconite, boneset
  mythical: 4 moly
  narcotic: 4 hemp
  perennial: pia 4 balm, irid 5 sedum 6 fennel, madder, yarrow 7 bugbane, lopweed

8 sainfoin, soapwort **9** digitalis
poisonous: **4** loco **6** conium **7** hemlock, henbane **9** hellebore
salad: **6** endive **7** chicory **10** watercress
shoot: udo
sweet-scented: **8** woodruff
trinity: **8** hepatica
woody: rue
herbage: 5 grass **7** foliage, pasture
herbicide: 10 weed killer
herculean: 4 huge, vast **5** giant **7** immense, mammoth, titanic **8** colossal, enormous, gigantic **10** superhuman
Hercules: 8 Heracles
captive: **4** Iole
companion: **5** Hylas
friend: **6** Iolaus
lion's home: **5** Nemea
mother: **7** Alcmene
stone: **9** loadstone
sweetheart: **4** Iole
victim: **5** Hydra
wife: **4** Hebe **8** Deianira
herd: mob **4** crew, lead, ruck **5** bunch, crowd, drift, drove, flock, group, guard **6** gather, hirsel, pastor, rabble **7** creaght, shelter **8** guardian **9** associate **10** assemblage, congregate **11** aggregation
herdsman: 5 booly **6** booley, cowboy, drover, gaucho **7** bucolic, vaquero **8** garthman, ranchero(Sp.), wrangler
god: **5** Pales
here: ici(F.), **5** ready **6** hither **7** on earth, present
hereafter: 5 after, later **6** beyond, future
hereditary: 6 inborn, innate, lineal **8** heirship **9** ancestral, descended **10** congenital **11** inheritable, patrimonial
heredity: 4 line **10** inheritance
factor: **4** gene
heresy: 6 schism **7** dissent **9** defection, misbelief **10** infidelity, radicalism **11** unorthodoxy **13** nonconformism
heretic: 6 bugger **7** infidel, Patarin **8** apostate **9** dissenter, miscreant, sectarian **10** schismatic, unbeliever **13** nonconformist
heretofore: 4 erst **6** before **8** erewhile, formerly, hitherto, previous **9** erstwhile
heritage: 6 legacy **9** patrimony, tradition **10** birthright **11** inheritance
heritor: 4 heir **5** donee **9** inheritor
heritrix, heretrix: 7 heiress
herl: fly **4** barb
hermaphrodite: 5 scrat **9** androgyne **10** androgynus
Hermes: 7 Mercury
birthplace: **7** Cyllene
father: **4** Zeus
mother: **4** Maia
son: **7** Evander **9** Autolycus

staff: **8** caduceus
winged cap: **7** petasos, petasus
winged shoes: **7** talaria
hermetic: 6 sealed, secret **8** airtight **9** alchemist, resistant
Hermione: *father:* **8** Menelaus
husband: **7** Orestes **11** Neoptolemus
mother: **5** Helen
hermit: 4 monk **5** clerk, loner **6** anchor **7** ascetic, eremite, incluse, inclusa, recluse, stylite **8** anchoret, beadsman, bedesman, inclusus, marabout **9** anchorite
hut: **4** cell
hermit crab: 8 pagurian
hermitage: 7 ashrama **8** cloister, hideaway **9** monastery, reclusery
hernia: 6 breach **7** rupture **10** protrusion
hero: ace **4** idol **5** darer **6** knight **7** demigod **8** champion **9** conqueror **10** topnotcher **11** protagonist
deified: **7** demigod
legendary: **6** Amadis, Roland **7** Paladin
Hero's lover: 7 Leander
Herodias: *daughter:* **6** Salome
husband: **5** Herod
heroic: 4 bold, epic, huge **5** brave, great, large, noble **6** daring, epical, mighty **7** extreme, gallant, spartan, valiant **8** colossal, enormous, fearless, intrepid, powerful **9** bombastic **10** courageous **11** extravagant, illustrious, magnanimous, outstanding, venturesome **13** grandiloquent
heroin: 4 drug **5** horse, smack **8** narcotic
heroine: 8 lead role **11** demigoddess, leading lady
heroism: 5 valor **6** valour **7** bravery, courage **8** chivalry, nobility **9** fortitude **13** unselfishness
heron: 4 hern, rail, soco **5** crane, egret, herne, quawk, wader **7** bittern, hernser, quabird **8** aigrette, gaulding, heronsew **9** cormorant, herneshaw, heronsewe, heronshaw
genus: **5** ardea
herpes 6 eczema **8** shingles
herring: 4 raun **7** alewife, anchovy **8** scud-dawn
barrel: **4** cade, cran
catch: **4** tack
family: **8** pilchard
female: **4** raun
fry: **4** sile
genus: **6** clupea
head: cob
lake: **5** cisco
young: **4** brit **5** matie, sprat, sprot
Hersey setting: 5 Adano
Hertha: 4 Erda **7** Nerthus
hesitancy: 10 hesitation, indecision, reluctance

hesitant: shy 4 loth 5 chary, loath 6 averse, wobbly 7 halting 8 timorous 9 reluctant

hesitate: 4 wait 5 delay, demur, doubt, pause, stall, waver 6 boggle, falter, loiter, scotch 7 stammer 8 hang back 10 dillydally 12 shilly-shally, wiggle-waggle 13 procrastinate

hesitating: coy 4 hink 7 halting 8 backward, doubtful 9 ambiguous 10 indecisive 11 vacillating

Hesperides: 5 Aegle 6 Hestia 7 Hespera 8 Arethusa, Erytheia, Erytheis

Hesperus: 5 Venus 11 evening star
father: 8 Astraeus
mother: Eos

hessonite: 6 garnet

Hestia: *father:* 6 Cronus
mother: 4 Rhea

hetaera, hetaira: 8 mistress, paramour 9 companion, concubine 12 demimondaine

heterogeneous: 5 mixed 6 motley, unlike 7 diverse 10 dissimilar 13 miscellaneous 14 indiscriminate

Heteroousian: 5 Arian

hetman: 6 ataman 7 Cossack, headman

hew: cut 4 chip, chop, fell, hack 5 carve, wound 6 haggle, strike, stroke

hex: 4 jinx 6 voodoo 7 bewitch

hexad: 6 sextet

hexadecene: 6 cetene

hexastich: 6 sestet, stanza 7 strophe

heyday: joy, May 4 acme 5 prime 6 spring 9 wildness 14 frolicsomeness

Hezekiah: *father:* 4 Ahaz 7 Neariah
kingdom: 7 Judah
mother: Abi
son: 8 Manasseh
wife: 9 Hephzibah

hiatus: gap 5 break, chasm 6 breach, lacuna 7 opening 8 interval 12 interruption

Hiawatha: *author:* 10 Longfellow
grandmother: 7 Nokomis
mother: 7 Wenonah
wife: 9 Minnehaha

Hibernia: 4 Eire, Erin 7 Ireland

hiccup, hiccough: 4 burp 5 spasm 9 singultus

hick: 4 jake, rube 5 yokel 6 hiccup, rustic 7 bumpkin, hayseed 8 cornball

hickey: 6 pimple 7 pustule

hickory: 5 pecan 9 bitternut, shellbark

hidden: 4 lost 5 inner, perdu 6 arcane, buried, cached, closed, covert, innate, latent, masked, occult, secret, veiled 7 arcanum, covered, cryptic, obscure, recluse 8 screened, secluded, secreted 9 concealed, invisible, recondite 10 mysterious 11 clandestine, delitescent, undisclosed 12 subterranean

hide: bar, kip, lie 4 bury, coat, dern, fell, hill, hood, lurk, pelt, skin, stow, veil 5 cache, cloak, cloud, couch, cover, derne(Sc.), skulk 6 huddle, screen, shroud 7 abscond, conceal, cover up, eclipse, leather, secrete, shelter 8 carucate, disguise, ensconce, hoodwink, palliate, suppress, withhold 9 dissemble 10 camouflage, flagellate
cleaning instrument: 6 slater
measured in: 8 hidation
remove hair from: 4 moon
undressed: kip 4 pelt
worker: 6 tanner

hidebound: 6 narrow 7 bigoted, miserly 9 barkbound, bourgeois, illiberal, niggardly 10 restrained 12 conventional

hideous: 4 fell, grim, ugly 5 awful 6 grisly, horrid, odius, ogrish 7 ghastly, ogreish 8 deformed, dreadful, grewsome, gruesome, horrible, shocking, terrible 9 dismaying, frightful, revolting 10 detestable, discordant, terrifying

hideout: den, mew 4 cave, lair 5 cache 7 retreat 8 hideaway

hides: 4 furs 5 skins 6 peltry

hiding: 7 secrecy 8 flogging 9 coverture

hie: 5 haste, hurry, speed 6 betake, hasten, scurry, strive 8 expedite

hiemal: 6 wintry

hierarch: 4 boss, head 5 chief 6 leader, master, satrap, 10 high priest

hieroglyphic: 7 cryptic 9 illegible

hieroglyphics key: 7 Rosetta stone

higgle: 6 haggle 7 bargain, chaffer

high: alt 4 dear, haut(F.), main, much, tall 5 acute, chief, first, lofty, sharp, steep 6 costly, shrill 7 eminent, exalted, haughty, violent 8 elevated, foremost, hopped up, piercing, towering, turned on 9 admirable, expensive, important, principal, turbulent 10 tumultuous, tripped out 11 mountainous

high and dry: 8 marooned

high-and-mighty: 8 arrogant, insolent, superior 9 imperious 11 overbearing

high-brow: 7 egghead 10 doubledome 14 intelligentsia

high-class: 6 classy 10 first-class

high-flying: 7 icarian 11 pretentious

high-handed: 6 lordly 8 arrogant, cavalier, despotic 9 arbitrary 11 dictatorial, domineering, overbearing

high-hat: 4 snub 8 snobbish 12 aristocratic

high-pitched: 6 shrill 7 shrieky, agitated

high-pressure: 8 forceful, pressing 9 insistent 10 aggressive

high-priced: 4 dear 6 costly 9 expensive

high priest: Eli

high-sea: 4 main

high-sounding: 4 arty 7 fustian, pomp-

ous 8 imposing 9 bombastic, overblown 10 altisonant
high-spirited: 5 fiery, jolly, merry 6 lively 7 gallant, gingery, peppery 8 cavalier 10 mettlesome
high-strung: 5 tense 7 nervous, uptight 9 excitable
high-toned: 7 stylish 8 elevated 9 dignified 11 fashionable
highborn: 5 noble 8 generous 12 aristocratic
highbred: 7 genteel, refined
higher: 8 superior
highest: top, 5 first 6 upmost 7 extreme, maximal, supreme 8 bunemost, overmost
highest point: 4 acme 6 zenith
Highland war cry: 6 slogan
Highlander (see also **Scotland**): 4 Celt, Gael, Kelt, Scot 6 Tartan 8 clansman 9 Gluneamie
dance: 4 reel 5 fling
language: 4 Erse
pouch: 6 sporan 7 sporran
weapon: 8 claymore, skeandhu
high-rise: 4 tall 5 lofty 10 multistory
highroad: 7 highway
highway: way 4 bahn(G.), iter(L.), path, pike, road 5 Alcan 6 Appian, artery, causey, course, rumpad, street 7 Lincoln 8 autobahn, causeway, chaussee(F.), highroad, turnpike 9 boulevard 12 thoroughfare
highwayman: pad 5 rider, thief 6 bandit, padder, robber, 7 brigand, footpad, ladrone 8 hightoby 9 bandolero
Highwayman: *author:* 5 Noyes
hijack: rob 6 coerce
hike: 4 jerk, toss, walk 5 march, raise, throw, tramp 6 ramble
hilarious: mad 5 funny, merry, noisy 6 jovial 7 jocular 8 mirthful 9 ludicrous
hilarity: gig, joy 4 glee 5 cheer, mirth 6 gaiety 7 jollity, whoopee 9 happiness, joviality, laughter, merriment 10 joyousness 12 cheerfulness, exhilaration
hill: ben, hoe, kop, pap, tor 4 bank, brae, bult, dagh, dune, fell, heap, hide, knap, knob, loma, mesa, pile 5 bargh, butte, cerro(Sp.), cliff, cover, hurst, morro, mound, mount 6 ascent, barrow, copple, djebel 7 colline, picacho 9 acclivity, elevation, monadnock
D.C.: 7 Capitol
glacial: 4 kame, paha 7 drumlin
Jerusalem: 6 Olivet
range: 5 ridge
sand: 4 dene, dune
top of: tor 4 peak 6 summit
hillbilly: 4 rube 5 yokel 6 rustic 7 bumpkin 12 backwoodsman
hillock: 4 tump 5 croft, hurst, knoll, kop-

je, mound, toman(Sc.) 6 coppet 7 hummock 8 molehill
over grave: 7 tumulus
hillside: 4 brae, cote 5 cleve, cliff, falda(Sp.), slade, slope 6 cleeve
hilly: 5 steep
hilt: 6 handle 8 handgrip
hilum: 4 scar 5 porta 7 nucleus
Himalaya: *animal, bear-like:* 5 panda
antelope: 5 goral, serow
bear: 5 bhalu
bearcat: 5 panda
cedar: 6 deodar
cypress: 6 bhutan
dweller: 8 Nepalese
goat: 4 kras, tahr, tair, thar
oxen: yak
peak: Api 7 Everest
pheasant: 5 monal
sheep: 6 bharal, nahoor
swamp: 5 Terai
tableland: 5 Tibet
Himavat's daughter: 4 Devi
himene, himine: 4 hymn, song
himself: 4 ipse(L.)
Himyarite: 4 Arab 7 Axumite, Sabaean
Hinayana Buddhism: 5 shojo 6 lesser
hind: doe, lad, roe 4 back, chap, stag 5 coney 6 fellow, rustic, worker 7 bailiff, peasant, servant, steward, venison 8 cabrilla, domestic 9 posterior 11 hindquarter
hinder: bar, let 4 slow 5 after, block, cheat, check, choke, cramp, debar, delay, deter, embar, estop, hedge 6 arrest, detain, hamper, harass, impede, impend, injure, retard, scotch 7 bog down, deprive, forelay, impeach, inhibit, prevent 8 encumber, handicap, obstruct, preclude, prohibit 9 embarrass, foreclose, forestall, frustrate, hamstring, interrupt, posterior
hindmost: 4 last, rear 9 aftermost
hindrance: bar, rub 4 clog, curb, snag, stop 5 block, check, delay, hitch 6 arrest 7 barrier 8 drawback, obstacle 9 detention, deterrent, restraint 10 difficulty impediment 11 encumbrance, impeachment, obstruction 12 interruption
Hindu (see also **Indian**): 4 Babu, Koli, Sikh 5 Tamil 6 Gentoo, Hindoo 8 Kolarian
abode of gods: 4 Meru
adherent: Sik 4 Jain, Seik, Sikh 5 Jaina, Seikh
age of world: 4 yuga
alphabet: 6 Sarada
ancestral race: 5 Aryan
apartment: 5 mahal
Aryan race: 4 Swat
ascetic: 4 jogi, sadh, yati, yogi 5 sadhu

atheist: 7 nastika

book: 4 Veda 6 Tantra 11 Yajna-valkya

calendar: Pus 4 Jeth, Asin, Kaur, Magh 5 Asarh, Sawan, Katik, Aghan, Chait 6 Bhadon, Kartik, Phagun 7 Baisakh, Sarawan, Phalgun

call to prayer: 4 azan

caste: Dom, Mal, Meo 4 Dasi, Gola, Koli, Kori, Mali, Pasi, Teli 5 Goala, Palli, Sudra 6 Babhan, Soodra 7 Brahman

caste member: Jat 4 Jain 6 Banian, Banyan, Rajput, Vaisya 7 Rajpoot 9 Kshatriya, Vakkaliga

charm: 6 mantra

chief: mir 6 sirdar

coin: ana, pai, pie 4 anna, pice 5 paisa, rupee

congregation: 5 samaj, somaj

convert to Islam: 6 shaikh

cremation: 4 sati 6 suttee

dancer: 8 devadasi

deity: Dev 4 Deva, Dewa, Maya, Rama, Yama 6 Ganesa, Varuna, Vishnu 7 Ganesha, Krishna 9 Jagannath 10 Jagannatha, Juggernaut 11 Ramachandra

demon: 4 Bali, Bhut, Ketu, Rahu 5 Asura 6 Daitya

devotee: 4 yati

disciple: 4 sikh

divine being: dev 4 deva

doctrine: 5 Karma 6 dharma

drink: 4 soma

duty: 6 dharma

ejaculation: om, um

essence: 4 rasa, rata 5 atman 6 amrita

family: 5 gotra

female energy: 5 Sakti 6 Shakti

festival: 4 Holi, mela 6 Dewali, Hoolee 7 Dashara

flute: bin 5 pungi

garment: 4 sari 5 saree

gentleman: 4 babu 5 baboo, sahib

god (see also deity above): 4 Agni, Deva, Kama, Siva, Vayu, Yama 5 Asura, Shiva, Simia 6 Brahma, Ganesa, Skanda, Varuna 7 Ganesha

goddess: Sri, Uma, Vac 4 Devi, Kali, Shri, Vach 5 Durga, Gauri, Sakti, Shree, Ushas 6 Chandi, Shakti 7 Parvati 8 Haimavati

guitar: 5 sitar

headdress: 5 rumal

heaven: 5 dyaus

hermitage: 7 ashrama

hero: 4 Nala, Rama

holy book: 4 Veda 6 Sastra

holy sage: 4 rishi

hymn: 6 mantra

idol worship: 5 arati

incarnation: 6 avatar

Indra: 5 Sakka, Sakra

king: 4 Nala 5 Sesha 6 Shesha

lady: 4 devi, rani 5 ranee

language: 4 Pali, Urdu 5 Hindi, Tamil 8 Sanskrit 10 Hindustani

lawgiver: 4 Manu

leader: 5 Nehru 6 Ghandi, sirdar

life principle: 4 jiva 5 atman, prana

literature: 4 Veda 5 sruti 6 shruti

loincloth: 5 dhoti

magic: 4 jadu, maya 5 jadoo

magician: 5 fakir 6 fakeer

mantra: om, um

master: 5 sahib

mendicant: 4 naga 7 bairagi, vairagi 8 sannyasi

mental discipline: 4 yoga

monastery: 4 math

monkey god: 7 Hanuman

month: see *calendar* above

mother goddess: 6 matris

mystic: 4 yogi

noble: 5 rajah 8 maharaja

non-violence: 6 ahimsa

offering: 4 bali, lepa 5 pinda

paradise: 7 Nirvana

patriarch: 5 pitri

philosophy: 4 yoga 5 tamas

poem: 8 Ramayana 11 Mahabharata 12 Bhagavad-Gita

poet: 6 Tagore

policeman: 5 sepoy

prayer rug: 4 asan 5 asana

priest: 5 hotar

prince: 4 raja, rana 5 rajah 8 maharaja 9 maharajah

princess: 4 rani 5 ranee

pundit: 5 swami

queen: 4 rani 5 ranee 8 maharani 9 maharanee

religion: 5 Prana 7 Jainism, Sivaism 8 Shivaism

rice: 4 boro

rite: 4 puja 5 achar, pooja

ruler: 5 rajah

scripture: Li; rig 4 Veda 5 Sruti 6 Purana, Sastra, Smriti, Tantra 7 Shastra

sect: 4 Sikh, siva 6 Aghori

social division: 5 caste, varna

soldier: 4 Sikh 5 sepoy

soul: 4 atma 5 atman

spirit: 4 Jiva, Mara 5 Asura, Atman, Prana 7 Muktama

supreme being: 6 Vishnu

teacher: pir 4 guru

temple: 4 deul 6 vimana

term of respect: 5 sahib

title: aya, sri 4 mian, raja, shri, sidi 5 rajah, sahib, shree, swami 7 bahadur

tower: 5 stupa

triad god: 4 Siva

tunic: 4 jama 5 jamah

unknown god: Ka

unorthodox: 4 Jain 5 Jaina

Upanishad: 4 Isha, Veda 7 Vedanta
worship: 4 puja 5 pooja
Hindustan: Ind
  language: 4 Urdu 5 Hindi
  tribesman: 4 toda
hinge: har 4 butt, hang, turn 5 gemel,
  joint, mount, pivot, stand 6 depend
  gimmer, gimmor, hingle, lamina, pintle
Hinnom Valley: 7 Gehenna
hint: cue, tip 4 clew, clue, time, turn 5
  cheep(Sc.), imply, infer, trace 6 allude,
  moment 7 inkling, mention, suggest 8
  allusion, innuendo, intimate, occasion 9
  catchword, insinuate 10 indication, intimation, suggestion 11 insinuation
hip: hop 4 coxa, huck, limp, miss, skip 6
  haunch, huckle
  pert. to: 7 sciatic
hip boots: 6 waders
hipbone: 5 ileum, ilium
hippie: mod 5 rebel 6 copout 8 bohemian,
  longhair
Hippocrates: *birthplace:* kos
  drug: 5 mecon, opium
hippodrome: 5 arena 6 circus 7 contest
Hippolytus: 9 Greek hero
  father: 7 Theseus
  mother: 7 Antiope 9 Hippolyne
  stepmother: 7 Phaedra
hippopotamus: 6 seacow 8 behemoth 9
  pachyderm
hire: buy, fee, let, use 4 rent, sign, wage 5
  bribe, lease, put on, price, wages 6 employ, engage, retain, reward, salary 7
  charter, conduce, recruit, stipend 9 allowance 12 compensation
hireling: 4 esne, grub, hack, serf 5 slave 8
  gangster 9 mercenary
hirsute: 5 hairy, rough 6 coarse, shaggy 7
  pileous
hispid: 5 rough, spiny 7 bristly 8 strigose,
  strigous
hiss: boo 4 hish, sizz, whiz 5 whizz 6
  fissle, fistle 8 goose cry, pooh-pooh 9
  raspberry 10 assibilate
hissing: 6 fizzle 8 sibilant 9 sibilance
hist: 4 hark, hush 7 be quiet
historian: 8 annalist 10 chronicler
history: 4 tale 5 drama, story 6 annals,
  memoir, record 7 account 8 relation 9
  biography, chronicle, genealogy, narrative
  muse: 4 Clio
histrio: 5 actor
histrionics: 6 acting 9 dramatics 11
  theatricals 13 theatricality
hit: bat, lam, lob, ram, rap, tap 4 bump,
  bunt, cast, club, slog, slug, sock, swat,
  wham 5 fizzle, flick, knock, smack,
  smite, smote, throw, touch 6 attain,
  batted, binge, strike 7 collide, success
  8 bludgeon 10 production, succession
  baseball: 4 bunt 5 homer, liner 6 double,

single, triple 7 home run 8 grounder 9
  line drive
  golf: 5 drive, shank, slice
hit-or-miss: 6 casual, chance, habnab,
  random 7 aimless 8 careless 9 haphazard
hitch: hop, tie, tug 4 halt, hook, join, knot,
  limp, pull 5 agree, catch, crick, hotch,
  marry, thumb, unite 6 attach, enlist,
  hobble 8 obstacle, stoppage 9 harmonize, hindrance 10 enlistment, impediment 11 contretemps, obstruction
hither: 4 here 6 nearer 11 to this place
hitherto: ago, yet 5 as yet 6 before 7 thus
  far
Hitler: *aerie:* 13 Berchtesgaden
  chosen race: 5 Aryan
  follower: 4 Nazi
hitter: 6 batter 7 batsman, slugger
Hittite: *ancestor:* 4 Heth
  capital: 6 Pteria
  storm god: 6 Teshub, Teshup
hive: 5 store, swarm 6 apiary 7 store up 9
  multitude
hives: 5 uredo 7 allergy 9 urticaria
hoagie, hoagy: 4 hero 9 submarine 13
  large sandwich
hoar: 4 cold, gray, rime 5 frost, hoary,
  musty, stale 6 biting 7 ancient 9 antiquity, venerable 13 venerableness
hoard: 4 save 5 amass, chest, hutch, lay
  up, stash, stock, store 6 supply 7 husband, reserve 8 quantity, treasure, treasury 10 accumulate, collection
hoarder: 5 miser 6 storer 9 treasurer
hoarfrost: rag 4 rime 5 rind 9 cran-
  reuch(Sc.)
hoarse: dry, raw 5 gruff, harsh, rocky,
  rough 7 grating, raucous 10 discordant
hoarseness: 4 frog 5 croup
hoary: old 4 aged, gray, hoar 5 moldy,
  mossy, musty 7 ancient, hoarish, whitish 9 canescent, venerable
hoax: bam, cod, fun, gyp, hex, kid 4 bilk,
  dupe, fake, gaff, gegg, gunk, joke, ruse,
  sell, sham 5 bluff, cheat, spoof, trick 6
  canard, diddle, humbug, string 7 deceive 8 artifice 9 bamboozle, deception
  11 hornswoggle
hob: elf, peg, pin, tap 4 game, mark, nail,
  nave 5 clown, fairy, ledge 6 ferret, rustic, sprite 7 mandrel 8 mischief 10
  countryman, projection
hobble: tie 4 clog, clop, gimp, limp 5
  bunch, cramp, hitch, leash 6 fetter,
  hamper, hog-tie 7 cramble, perplex,
  shackle, spancel 9 embarrass 10 difficulty, perplexity 13 embarrassment
hobbledehoy: lad 5 youth
hobbler: 5 pilot 7 boatman, hoveler, laborer 8 retainer 12 longshoreman
hobby: fad 5 horse 6 falcon 7 pastime 9
  avocation, diversion

hobgoblin: bug, elf, hag, imp **4** bogy, Puck **5** bogey, bogie, bugan, poker, spook **6** boodie(Sc.), sprite **7** bugaboo **8** bogglebo, worricow(Sc.) **9** coltpixie **10** apparition

hobo: boe, bum **5** tramp **7** drifter, floater, vagrant **8** vagabond

hock: ham, hox **4** pawn **5** ankle, hough, thigh **6** mallow, pledge **8** mortgage **9** hamstring **10** houghsinew

hocket: **6** hiccup **8** obstacle **12** interruption

hockey: **5** bandy **6** shinny
arena: **4** rink
cup: **7** Stanley
disk: **4** puck
goal: net
official: **7** referee **8** linesman
players: Orr (Bobby) **4** Hull (Bobby) **5** Bucyk (John) **6** Mikita (Stan), Parent (Bernie) **7** Ratelle (Jean) **8** Beliveau (Jean), Esposito (Phil) (Tony) **9** Mahovlich (Frank) **10** Delvecchio (Alex)
pro teams (NHL): **4** Jets (Winnipeg) **5** Blues (St. Louis), Kings (Los Angeles) **6** Bruins (Boston), Devils (New Jersey), Flames (Calgary), Flyers (Philadelphia), Oilers (Edmonton), Sabres (Buffalo) **7** Canucks (Vancouver), Rangers (New York), Rockies (Colorado), Whalers (Hartford) **8** Capitals (Washington), Penguins (Pittsburgh), Red Wings (Detroit) **9** Canadiens (Montreal), Islanders (New York), Nordiques (Quebec) **10** Black Hawks (Chicago), Maple Leafs (Toronto), North Stars (Minnesota)
positions: **4** wing **6** center, goalie **7** forward **10** defenseman, goaltender
stick: **6** burley **7** cammock(Sc.)
terms: **7** face-off **8** blue line, empty net **9** backcheck, bodycheck, forecheck, power play **10** center line, penalty box **11** shorthanded **12** box formation **14** penalty killing

hocus: **4** drug **5** cheat, fraud **7** deceive **8** cheating, deceiver, trickery **10** adulterate

hocus-pocus: **5** cheat, trick **6** humbug **7** juggler **8** flimflam, quackery **9** trickster **12** charlatanism

hod: **4** soil, tray **6** barrow **7** scuttle **11** coal scuttle

hodgepodge: ana **4** mess, olio, stew **5** cento **6** medley **7** mixture **8** mishmash **10** hotchpotch, miscellany **11** gallimaufry, olla podrida **12** mingle-mangle

hoe: dig **4** brod, hill, till **5** clean, cliff, paddle, worry **6** sarcle, scrape **7** dogfish, trouble **8** griffaun **9** cultivate **10** promontory

hog (see also **pig**): sow **4** bene, boar, dime, galt, gilt **5** shoat, shote, swine **6** barrow

7 glutton, hogling **8** shilling **9** boschvark **10** backfatter
breed: **5** Essex **9** Hampshire
food: **4** mash **5** slops, swill **6** acorns
genus: sus
young: pig **5** shoat

hog peanut: **8** earthpea

hog plum: **4** amra

hog side: **6** flitch

hog thigh: ham

hogfish: **8** scorpene

hoggish: **5** hoggy **7** selfish, swinish **10** gluttonous

hognut: **5** ouabe **6** pignut **8** earthnut

hogshead: **4** cask **6** barrel, hogget, vessel

hogtie: **4** clog, curb **5** leash **6** fetter, hamper

hogwash: **4** slop **5** draff, swill **7** pigwash

hoi polloi: mob **6** masses, rabble **8** populace, riffraff

hoist: cat, gin **4** jack, lift **5** boost, crane, davit, heave, heeze, horse, lewis, raise, setup, winch **7** derrick, elevate **8** elevator, windlass

hoist sail: **4** swig

hoity-toity: **5** dizzy, giddy, proud **6** snooty **7** flighty, haughty, pompous **8** arrogant **11** harum-scarum, patronizing, thoughtless **13** irresponsible

hokum: **4** blaa, blah, bunk **11** foolishness

hold: own **4** bind, bite, bulk, clip, fill, have, hook, keep, rely, seat, stow, tend **5** avast, carry, catch, grasp, guard, rivet **6** adhere, arrest, behold, cleave, clench, clutch, decree, defend, detain, harbor, occupy, retain **7** adjudge, contain, control, support, sustain **8** consider, interest, maintain, thurrock **9** entertain, mesmerize, spellbind **10** possession, stronghold **11** catch hold of

hold a brief for: **6** defend **8** advocate

hold back: dam **4** curb, stem, stop **5** check, deter **6** detain, retard **7** inhibit, repress **9** restrain **9** hindrance

hold fast: hug **4** hook, nail **5** cling, stick **6** clinch, cohere

hold forth: **5** offer **7** exhibit **8** continue, maintain, propound

hold in custody: **4** jail **6** detain, intern

hold off: **5** avert **7** refrain

hold on: **4** stop, wait **7** forbear **8** continue

hold out: **4** last **6** endure **7** exclude, pretend **8** continue

hold up: rob **4** halt, lift, rein **5** boost, check, delay, raise **7** display, exhibit, robbery, support, sustain **8** stoppage **10** overcharge

hold water: **5** sound **10** consistent

holder: **5** haver **6** tenant **9** container **10** receptacle

holding: **4** land **5** asset **6** estate, tenure **8** property
adapted for: **10** prehensile

hole: bay, den, gap, pit 4 bore, cave, cove, deep, dump, flaw, gate, gulf, inlet, leak, mine, nook, peck, rent, vent 5 abyss, chasm, shaft 6 burrow, cavern, cavity, cranny, crater, defect, eyelet, grotto, hollow, pierce, prison, recess 7 dungeon, mortise, opening, orifice, ostiole 8 aperture, bunghole, peephole 9 perforate 10 excavation 11 perforation, predicament

instrument for making: awl 4 bore 5 drill 8 stiletto

wall: 4 muse 5 meuse, niche

Holi, Hoolee: 8 festival

holia: 4 fish 6 salmon

holiday: 4 fete 5 feria, festa, merry 6 fiesta, jovial, outing 7 festive, playday 8 festival, vacation 9 convivial, Mardi Gras

holiness: 5 piety 7 halidom 8 divinity, halidome, sanctity 9 sanctuary 11 saintliness 12 consecration 13 righteousness

Holland: see Netherlands

holler: 4 yell 5 shout 6 shriek 7 protest

hollow: den, dip 4 boss, cave, cove, deep, dent, doke, glen, hole, holl, howe, huck, lean, thin, vain, void 5 bight, chase, cuppy, empty, false, gaunt, goyal, goyle, heugh, scoop, sinus, stria 6 cavern, cavity, cirque, groove, hungry, socket, sunken, vacant, valley 7 concave, muffled, unsound 8 alveolus, fossette, not solid, specious 9 cavernous, deceitful, deeply set, depressed, faithless, worthless 10 depression, sepulchral 11 treacherous 12 unsatisfying

out: cut, dig 4 bore 6 excise

hollow-eyed: 7 haggard

hollowed: 7 concave, glenoid, spouted

hollowed out: 6 cavate

hollowness: 6 vanity 7 vacuity

holly: 4 assi, holm, ilex 5 shrub, yapon, yupon 6 hulver, yaupon, youpon

pert to: 6 ilicic

holm oak: 4 ilex 5 holly

Holmes' word: 10 elementary

holobaptist: 12 immersionist

holocaust: 7 inferno 9 sacrifice 11 destruction

holster: 4 case 7 housing 8 scabbard 10 pistol case

holt: den 4 grip, hill, hold, lair, wood 5 copse, grasp 7 retreat 10 wooded hill

holy: 5 pious, sacre(F.), saint, santo 6 devout, divine, hallow, sacred 7 blessed, perfect, sainted, saintly, sinless 8 blissful, hallowed 9 inviolate, sanctuary, spiritual 10 sacrosanct 11 consecrated 13 sanctimonious

Holy City: 4 Kiev, Rome, Zion 5 Mecca, Lhasa, Medina, Moscow 7 Benares 9 Allahabad, Jerusalem

Holy Grail: 8 Sangraal, Sangreal

castle: 9 Monsalvat

knight: 7 Galahad

Holy Joe: 9 clergyman

Holy Land: 9 Palestine

pilgrim: 6 palmer

holy oil: 6 chrism

Holy One: God 6 Christ 7 Jehovah 8 Mohammed 12 Supreme Being

Holy Roman emperor: 4 Otho, Otto

Holy Rood: 5 cross 8 crucifix

holy statue: 4 icon, ikon 5 ikono

holy water: *font:* 5 paten

receptacle: 5 stoup

sprinkler: 11 aspergillum

homage: 5 honor 6 eulogy, fealty, regard 7 loyalty, manrent, ovation, respect 9 adoration, deference, obeisance, reverence 10 allegiance

homager: 6 tenant, vassal

homaloidal: 4 even, flat

hombre: guy, man 6 fellow

homburg: hat 4 felt

home: den 4 nest 5 abode, being, domus, house 6 asylum, estate, maison(F.), 7 habitat, hospice, village 8 domestic, domicile, dwelling 9 homestead, orphanage, residence 10 habitation 11 hearthstone

at: 4 chez(F.)

country: 7 cottage 8 bungalow

wheeled: 7 trailer

home base: den 5 plate

homeborn: 6 native 10 indigenous

homelike: 4 cozy 5 homey 6 homely, homish 8 cheerful, friendly, homesome 11 comfortable

homely: 4 rude, ugly 5 plain 6 hameil, hamelt, hamilt, kindly, simple 7 plainly 8 domestic, familiar, friendly, homelike, intimate 9 unsightly 10 intimately 12 unpretending 13 unpretentious

homemade: 5 plain 6 simple 8 domestic

Homer: *birthplace:* 5 Chios

character: 4 Ajax 6 Nestor 8 Achilles, Odysseus

poem: 5 Iliad 7 Odyssey

Homeric: 4 epic 6 epical

homesickness: 9 nostalgia

homespun: 4 kelt(Sc.), rude 5 plain 6 coarse, folksy 13 unpretentious

homestead: 4 toft, tref(W.) 7 onstead

homicide: 6 murder

homilist: 8 preacher

homily: 5 adage 6 sermon 8 assembly 9 communion, discourse 11 exhortation

hominy: 4 bran, corn, samp 5 grits

Homo sapiens: man

homogeneous: 4 like 5 equal, solid 6 entire 7 similar 10 comparable, compatible, consistent

homologous: 9 identical

homonym: 8 namesake 10 soundalike

homunculus: 5 dwarf 7 manikin

honcho: 4 boss 6 leader 8 in charge

Honduras: *capital:* 11 Tegucigalpa
city: 7 Gracias, La Ceiba 8 Yuscaran 9 Choluteca, Comayagua, Juticalpa, Santa Rosa 12 San Pedro Sula
department: 4 Yoro 5 Colon, Copan, La Paz, Valle 6 Cortes 7 Lempira, Olancho 8 Intibuca 9 Atlantida, El Paraiso 11 Ocotepeque
Indian: 4 Maya, Ulua, Ulva 5 Lenca
island: 5 Utila 6 Rostan 7 Guanaja
island group: 5 Bahia
lake: 5 Yojoa
measure: 4 vara 5 milla 6 mecate, tercia 7 cajuela, manzana 10 caballeria
monetary unit: 7 centavo, lempira
river: 4 Coco, Sico, Ulua 5 Aguan 6 Patuca 9 Choluteca 10 Chamelecon
weight: 4 caja

hone: 4 long, pine, whet 5 delay, dress, strop 6 lament 7 grumble, sharpen 8 oilstone 9 whetstone

honest: 4 fair, full, just open, pure 5 frank, roman 6 candid, chaste, decent, dexter, dinkum, proper, rustic, square 7 genuine, sincere, upright 8 bonafide, faithful, rightful, reliable, straight, suitable, truthful, upright, virtuous 9 equitable, guileless, honorable, ingenuous, veracious 10 creditable, forthright 11 trustworthy 13 conscientious, dispassionate, incorruptible, unadulterated 15 straightforward

honestly: 5 truly 6 dinkum, justly 8 directly 9 telltruth

honesty: 5 honor 6 equity 7 decency, justice, probity 8 fairness, fidelity, veracity 9 constancy, integrity 10 generosity, liberality 11 uprightness 12 incorruption, suitableness, truthfulness 13 honorableness 15 trustworthiness 19 straightforwardness

honesty plant: 8 moonwort

honey: mel 4 dear, niel(F.) 5 sweet 6 nectar 7 darling, flatter 8 precious
fermented drink: 4 mead
source: bee 6 nectar

honey badger: 5 ratel

honey bear: 8 kinkajou

honey buzzard: 4 hawk, pern

honey eater: iao 6 manuao

honeybee: 7 deseret 8 angelito
disease: 8 sacbrood

honeyberry: 4 tree 5 genep, genip

honeycomb cell: 7 alveola 8 alveolus

honeycombed: 6 favose, pitted 8 alveolar

honeydew: 5 melon 6 mildew, orange

honeyed: 5 sweet 6 sugary 7 candied 11 mellifluous 10 flattering

honeysuckle: 6 azalea, widbin 9 columbine

Hong Kong: *bay:* 4 Mirs 5 Sheko 7 Repulse
capital: 8 Victoria
coin: 4 cent 6 dollar 13 British dollar 14 Hong Kong dollar
peak: 8 Victoria
peninsula: 7 Kowloon

honor: 4 fame, fete, prow 5 adore, award, exalt, glory, grace, izzat 6 credit, decore, esteem, homage, laurel, praise, regard, repute, revere 7 dignify, dignity, emblaze, ennoble, glorify, honesty, respect, worship 8 accolade 9 celebrate, deference, obeisance, reverence 10 estimation, reputation
pledge: 6 parole

honorable: 4 dear 5 moral, noble, white 6 gentle, honest 7 upright 8 generous, honorary, sterling 9 dearworth, estimable, reputable 10 creditable 11 commendable, illustrious, magnanimous, meritorious, respectable

honorarium: fee, tip 6 reward, salary 7 douceur, payment 8 gratuity

Honshu: *bay:* Ise
port: 4 Kobe

hood: cap 4 coif, cowl, hide, thug 5 amice, blind 6 biggin, bonnet, burlet, camail, canopy, chapel, tippet 7 calotte, capuche, surtout 8 capsheaf, caputium, chaperon, covering
academic: 8 liripipe, liripoop
monk's: 4 atis, cowl 5 atees
saddle: 8 tapadera, tapadero
vehicle: 8 bonnet, capote

hooded: 9 cucullate 10 capistrate

hoodlum: yap 5 rowdy 6 goonda 8 hooligan

hoodoo: 4 jinx 5 Jonah 6 voodoo 7 bewitch, bad luck, unlucky

hoodwink: 4 dupe, fool, hide, wile 5 blear, blind, bluff, cheat, cosen, cover, cozen 6 befool, delude 7 blinder, blinker, deceive, mislead 9 blindfold

hooey: 4 bunk 6 bunkum 7 baloney, bologney, bushwah 8 buncombe, nonsense

hoof: 4 clee, foot, walk 5 cloof, cloot, cluif, dance, tramp 6 ungula

hoofer: 6 dancer, walker

hook: 4 barb, gaff, gore hake, hock, hold, huck, trap 5 catch, cleek, hamus, hitch, larin, seize, snare, steal 6 agrafe, anchor, larree, pilfer, tenter 7 agraffe, capture, grunter, hamulus, hitcher 8 crotchet 10 chatelaine

hooka, hookah: 4 pipe 7 nargile 8 narghile 9 narghileh

hooked: 6 hamate 7 hamular, uncinal 8 addicted, ankyroid, aquiline, uncinate

hooker: 10 prostitute

hooky player: 6 truant
hooligan: 6 loafer 7 hoodlum, ruffian
hoop: 4 bail, band, ring, tire 5 clasp, garth, girth, shout 6 circle, frette 7 circlet, trundle 8 encircle, surround 10 finger ring
hoopskirt: 9 crinoline
hoosegow: jug 4 jail 6 lockup, prison 10 guardhouse
Hoosier State: 7 Indiana
hoot: boo 4 jeer, whoo 5 shout, whoop 6 boohoo 7 ululate
hootch, hooch: 5 house 8 barracks, dwelling 10 thatched hut
Hoover Dam lake: 4 Mead
hop: fly, hip 4 dope, halt, jump, leap, limp, skip 5 bound, dance, hitch 6 flight, gambol, spring 8 jump over 11 supercharge
hop kiln: 4 oast
hop-o'-my-thumb: 5 dwarf, fairy 6 midget
hopbush: 6 akeake
hope: 4 deem, spes(L.), want, wish 5 haven, trust 6 aspire, desire, expect, morale 7 cherish, confide 8 prospect, reliance 9 esperance 10 aspiration 11 expectation 12 anticipation
  goddess of: 4 Spes
  lack of: 7 despair
  symbol of: 4 opal
hopeful: 8 sanguine 9 confident, expectant 10 optimistic
hopeless: 4 gone, vain 6 futile 7 forlorn, useless 8 downcast 9 desperate, heartless, incurable 10 despairing, despondent, desponding, remediless 11 ineffectual 12 disconsolate, irremediable 13 irrecoverable, irretrievable
hophead: 6 addict
Hophni: brother: 8 Phinehas
  father: Eli
Hopi Indian: 4 Moki 5 Moqui
  god: 7 Kachina, Katcina 8 Katchina
  prayer stick: 4 paho
hoplite: 7 soldier
hopped up: 4 high 6 stoned, zonked 7 drugged
hopper: box 4 tank 5 chute 6 dancer, leaper 10 freight car, receptacle
hopple: See hobble
hopscotch: 7 pallall
  stone: 5 potsy 6 peever
Horae: 4 Dike 6 Eirene 7 Euromia
horde: 4 army, camp, clan, pack 5 crowd, group, swarm 6 legion, throng 9 multitude
horehound: 4 mint 6 henbit
Horite chief: 4 Seir
horizon: rim 4 edge, goal 8 prospect
horizontal: 4 flat 5 level
hormigo: 5 quira 7 ant tree

hormone: 8 autacoid 13 cell secretion
  female: 8 estrogen
  male: 8 androgen
horn: 4 scur, tuba 5 brass, bugle, cornu, drone, siren 6 antler, cornet, rhyton 7 antenna, trumpet 8 oliphant 9 alpenhorn 10 cornucopia
  blast: 4 mort, toot 7 fanfare, tantara 9 tantarara
  crescent moon: 4 cusp
  deer: 4 tine 5 prong 6 antler
  drinking: 6 rhyton
  Hebrew: 6 shofar 7 shophar
  player: 6 bugler 9 cornetist, trumpeter
  without: 5 doddy 6 doddie, polled 7 acerous
hornbill: 4 bird, tock 6 homrai
  genus of: 7 buceros
hornet: 4 wasp
hornpipe: 4 tune 5 dance 8 matelote
hornswoggle: 4 hoax 5 trick 7 swindle 9 bamboozle
horny: 4 hard 8 ceratoid 9 calloused, toughened 10 semiopaque 15 sexually aroused
hornyhead: 4 chub
horologe: 4 dial 5 clock, watch 9 hourglass, timepiece
horoscope: 4 dial 7 diagram
horrendous: 7 fearful 8 horrible 9 frightful
horrible: 4 dire, grim, ugly 5 great 6 grisly, horrid 7 fearful, ghastly, hideous, horrent, very bad 8 dreadful, gruesome, horrific, shocking, terrible 9 atrocius, excessive, frightful, horrified, nefarious 10 horrendous, tremendous, unpleasant
horrid: 4 grim, ugly 5 awful, rough, shaggy 6 rugged 7 hideous 8 dreadful, grewsome, gruesome, horrible, shocking, terrible 9 bristling, frightful, obnoxious, offensive, revolting 10 detestable, terrifying, unpleasant 13 objectionable
horrific: 5 awful 7 fearful 8 horrible 9 frightful 10 formidable
horrified: 6 aghast 7 ghastly
horrify: 5 shock 6 appall, dismay
horrifying: 8 horrific 9 execrable
horror: 4 fear 5 dread 6 terror 8 aversion 10 abhorrence, repugnance, shuddering 11 abomination, detestation 13 consternation
hors d'oeuvre: 6 canape, relish 7 zakuska 8 aperitif 9 antipasto, appetizer
Horsa's brother: 7 Hengist
horse: gee, nag, pad 4 barb, mare, plug, prad 5 brock, caple, capul, draft, filly, hobby, hoist, mount, pacer, raise, shier, steed, waler 6 cheval, equine, geegee, ladino, pelter, rouncy 7 caballo(Sp.), cavallo(Sp.), cavalry, charger, clipper, courser, hackney, mustang, saddler,

sheltie, sleeper, stepper, trestle 8 bat-
horse, cartaver(Sc.), footrope, jackstay
10 breastband
Achilles': 7 Xanthus
ankle: 4 hock
breastplate: 7 peytrel, poitrel
breed: 4 Arab, Barb 5 Shire 6 hunter,
Morgan 7 Belgian, harness, Suffolk,
trotter 8 Galloway, Normandy, Shetland 9 Percheron 10 Clydesdale
brown: bay 6 sorrel 8 chestnut
buyer: 5 coper 6 trader 7 knacker
calico: 5 pinto
color: bay 4 pied, roan 5 pinto 6 calico,
sorrel 8 chestnut, palomino, schimmel
command: gee, haw, hup 4 whoa 6 giddap
covering: 9 caparison
cry: nie 5 neigh 6 whinny
dappled: 4 roan 5 pinto 7 piebald
dark: 4 zain
dealer: 7 chanter, scorser
disease: 5 surra 6 heaves, lampas 7 lam-
pers, quittor, spavins 9 distemper
docked-tail: 6 curtal 8 cocktail
draft: 4 aver 5 aiver, hairy
dressage: 15 movement control
driver: 6 jockey 7 sumpter 8 coachman
farm: 6 dobbin
feeding box: 6 manger
female: 4 mare, yaud 5 filly
foot: 4 frog, hoof 7 coronet, fetlock, pastern
forehead: 8 chanfrin
gait: run 4 lope, pace, rack, trot, vott,
walk 6 canter, gallop
genus: 5 equus
goddess of: 5 Epona
golden: 8 palomino
gray: 8 schimmel
guide: 4 rein 5 longe
harness: 5 pacer 7 trotter
hired: 4 hack 7 hackney
hybrid: 4 mule
horned: 7 unicorn 9 monoceros
leg: 6 instep 7 fetlock
lover: 10 hippophile
male: 4 stud 7 entire 8 stallion
measure: 4 hand
menage: 6 school 7 academy
pace: 4 lope, trot 5 amble 6 canter
pack: 5 bidet 7 sumpter
pair: 4 span, team
pert. to: 6 hippic
piebald: 5 pinto
prehistoric: 8 Eohippus
races: 8 claiming
racing: 4 turf
rearing: 6 pesade
relay: 6 remuda
round-up: 5 rodeo
saddle: cob 5 mount 7 palfrey
small: cob, nag, tit 4 pony 5 bidet, genet

6 cayuse, jennet(Sp.) 8 galloway, Shetland
sorrel: 4 roan 8 chestnut
spirited: 4 Arab 5 steed 6 rearer 7 courser
stable of: 6 string
talking: 5 Arion
track slope: 6 calade
trainer: 5 valet
trapping: 6 tackle 7 harness 9 caparison
trotting: 6 Morgan
turn: 7 passade
war: 5 steed 7 charger, courser 8 destrier
white-streaked face: 4 shim 5 blaze, reach
wild: 6 bronco, brumby, tarpan 7 mustang 8 warragal, warrigal
winged: 7 Pegasus
working: 4 aver 5 aiver 6 dobbin
worn-out: nag 4 hack, jade, moke, plug 5
crock, skate 6 garran, garron, gleyde 7
knacker 8 harridan 9 rosinante
horse-and-buggy: rig 12 old-fashioned
horse collar: 7 bargham(Sc.)
horse mackerel: 4 fish, scad, tuna 5
atule, tunny 6 bonita, saurel
horse opera: 7 western
horse tackle: 7 harness
horsefly: 4 cleg 5 clegg 6 botfly, gadfly
horsehair: 4 mane 9 haircloth
horsehide: 8 cordovan
horsekeeper: 5 groom 7 hostler
horselaugh: 5 snort 6 guffaw, heehaw
horseman: 5 rider 6 carter, cowboy 7
centaur, courier, vaquero 8 buckaroo,
chevalier 9 cavalryman, equestrian 12
broncobuster, equestrienne
horseman goad: 4 spur
horsemanship: 5 skill 6 manege, riding
10 equitation
rearing: 6 pesade
sidewalk: 4 volt
turn: 8 caracole
horseradish: 5 plant 6 relish
horseshoe: *point:* 6 sponge
spur: 4 calk
rim: web
horseshoer: 6 smithy 7 farrier 10 blacksmith
horsewhip: 4 flog 5 quirt 7 chabouk
horticulturist: 8 gardener
Horus: 6 Sun God
brother: 6 Anubis
father: 6 Osiris
mother: 4 Isis
hose: 4 sock, tube, vamp 5 water 6 drench
8 stocking
Hosea: 7 prophet
father: 5 Beeri
wife: 5 Gomer
hospice: inn 5 house 6 asylum, imaret
hospitable: 5 douce 6 cheery 7 cordial 8
friendly 9 receptive

hospital: 6 creche, refuge, spital 9 infirmary 10 sanatorium 11 xenodochium 12 ambulatorium

attendant: 5 nurse 6 intern 7 orderly

mobile: 9 ambulance

user: 7 patient

hospitality: 7 welcome 10 cordiality

to strangers: 9 xenodochy

host: inn 4 army, here 5 crowd, guest, swarm 6 housel, legion, myriad, throng 7 company, lodging 8 landlord 9 harbinger, multitude, sacrifice 10 assemblage 11 entertainer

receptacle for: pyx 5 paten 8 ciborium

hostage: 4 pawn 5 token 6 pledge 8 security 9 guarantee

hostel: inn 5 hotel, lodge 6 tavern 11 caravansary 12 lodginghouse

hostile: foe 5 black, enemy, fremd 7 adverse, opposed, warlike 8 contrary, inimical 9 resisting 10 malevolent, unfriendly 11 belligerent 12 antagonistic 13 unsympathetic

hostility: 4 feid, feud 6 animus, enmity, hatred, rancor 7 ill-will, warfare 9 animosity, antipathy 10 antagonism, bitterness, opposition, resistance 12 disaffection 14 unfriendliness, vindictiveness

hostler: 5 groom 6 ostler 9 stableman

hot: 5 acrid, angry, calid, eager, fiery, spicy 6 ardent, biting, fervid, recent, strong, sultry, torrid, urgent 7 burning, excited, fervent, flaming, glowing, intense, lustful, peppery, pungent, thermal 8 sizzling, vehement, very warm 9 excitable, impatient, impetuous 10 passionate

hot cakes: 7 pancake 11 griddle cake

hot dog: 6 wiener 7 sausage, show off 11 frankfurter

hot-tempered: 7 iracund 8 choleric 9 irascible

hot-water bottle: pad, pig

hotbed: 4 nest

hotchpotch: 4 stew 6 jumble 9 tripotage(F.) 10 hodgepodge

hotel: inn 5 fonda, haven, house 6 hostel, imaret, tavern 7 auberge, gasthof, hostage 8 building, dwelling, gasthaus 11 caravansary, public house 12 caravanserai, lodginghouse

airport: 6 airtel

auto: 5 motel

keeper: 4 host 7 padrone 8 boniface, hotelier

hotheaded: 5 fiery, hasty 8 reckless 9 impetuous

hothouse: 6 bagnio 10 greenhouse

hot line: 14 emergency phone

hotspur: 4 rash 6 madcap 7 violent 8 reckless 9 impetuous 10 headstrong

Hottentot: *dialect:* 4 Gona, Kora, Nama

garment: 6 kaross

instrument: 4 gora 5 gorah, goura

tribe: 4 Gona, Kora, Nama 6 Damara, Griqua 7 Sandawe, Sandawi

war club: 10 knobkerrie

hound: dog 4 bait, hunt 5 harry 6 addict, talbot 7 devotee, harrier 9 persecute

tail: 5 stern

hour: *canonical:* 4 none, sext

class: 6 period

lights out: 4 taps 6 curfew

hourly 4 soon 5 brief, horal 6 horary, recent 7 quickly 8 frequent 9 continual 10 frequently 11 continually

hourglass: 5 clock 7 shapely

house: cot, hut 4 casa(It.), cote, dorm, dump, firm, flat, flet, haus(G.), home, live, nest 5 abode, bahay, booth, cabin, cover, dacha, domus(L.), hovel, lodge, manor, shack, villa 6 biggin, billet, bottle, camara, casino, duplex, family, grange, harbor, maison(F.), palace, reside, shanty 7 cabildo, chateau, cottage, enclose, mansion, quarter, shelter, theater 8 ancestry, audience, building, bungalow, domicile, dwelling, tenement 9 dormitory, playhouse, residence 10 enterprise, habitation

cluster: 4 dorp 6 hamlet 7 village

commercial: 4 firm 5 store 8 emporium

dog: 6 kennel

eating: inn 4 cafe 6 tavern 9 chophouse 10 restaurant

English royal: 4 York 5 Tudor 6 Stuart 7 Hanover, Windsor 9 Lancaster

guest: inn 5 hotel 11 caravansary

Newfoundland: 4 tilt

Oriental: 5 serai

pert. to: 5 domal

public: inn 5 hotel 6 hostel, tavern 7 hospice 8 hostelry

religious: 4 kirk 6 chapel, church, priory, temple 9 cathedral, synagogue 10 tabernacle

Russian: 4 isba 5 dacha

summer: 6 gazebo 9 belvedere

Upper: 6 Senate

house organ: 8 magazine 10 periodical

house servant: 4 maid 8 domestic

houseboat: 5 barge 6 wangan, wangun 7 wanigan 8 dahabeah, wannigan

housefly: 4 pest 5 musca 6 insect

household: 5 meiny 6 common, family, housal, menage 8 domestic, familiar, ordinary 9 belonging

gods: 5 Lares 7 Penates

regulation: 6 thrift 7 economy 9 husbandry

housekeeper: 6 matron 7 janitor 8 janitrix 9 caretaker, janitress

houseleek: 8 sengreen

houseplant: ivy 5 aphis, calla 6 coleus 7 begonia, violets 11 asphidistra

housewarming: 6 infare

housewife: 8 hausfrau(G.) 9 sewing kit

housework: 5 chore 8 drudgery

housing: box, pad 4 cowl 5 cover, niche 6 garage 7 lodging, shelter 8 covering 10 protection

Houston college: 4 Rice

hove: See heave

hovel: hut, sty 4 crib, hole, hulk, hull, shed 5 cabin, hutch, lodge 6 cruive, hemmel, pigpen, pigsty, shanty 7 shelter 10 tabernacle

hover: 4 flit 5 float, pause, waver 7 flitter, flutter

howdy, howdie: 7 midwife 10 salutation

however: but, tho, yet 5 still 6 though 8 after all, although 10 all the same, howsomever 12 nevertheless 15 notwithstanding

howitzer: 6 cannon

howl: bay, cry, wow(Sc.) 4 bawl, gowl, gurl, hurl, wail, wawl, yawl, yell, yowl, yowt 5 whewl 6 lament, scream, squeal, steven 7 ululate 9 complaint 12 side-splitter

howling: 4 wild 5 great 6 baying, dreary, savage 7 extreme, ululant 10 pronounced

howling monkey: 5 araba 7 guereba, stentor

howsoever: 8 although

howsomever: 8 although 12 nevertheless

hox: 4 hock 5 annoy, worry 6 harass, pester 7 trample 9 hamstring

hoyden, hoiden: 4 romp, rude 6 blowze, tomboy 7 ill-bred 10 roistering

Hreidmar's son: 5 Otter, Regin 6 Fafnir, Reginn

huaca: 4 holy, idol, tomb 5 fetish, sacred, shrine, temple

hub: 4 core, nave 6 center, centre 10 focal point 11 nerve center

Hub: 6 Boston

hubbub: ado, din 4 stir 5 noise 6 clamor, hubble, racket, rumpus, tumult, uproar 7 bobbery 9 commotion, confusion 11 disturbance

hubristic: 4 vain 7 insolent 8 arrogant 12 contemptuous, supercilious 13 high-and-mighty

huckleberry: 9 blueberry

family: 9 ericaceae

Huckleberry Finn: *author:* 9 Mark Twain 13 Samuel Clemens

character: Jim, Tom

river: 11 Mississippi

huckster: 4 sell, vend 5 adman, cheap 6 badger, broker, cadger, cagier(Fr.), hawker 7 haggler, peddler 8 regrater, retailer 9 middleman

huddle: hug 4 hide, raff 5 crowd, hurry 6 bustle, fumble, jumble, mingle 7 conceal, embrace, meeting, scrunch 8 assemble, disorder 9 confusion 10 conference, discussion 14 conglomeration

Hudibras author: 6 Butler

hue: 4 balk, blee, form, tint 5 color, guise, shade, shout, tinge 6 aspect, clamor, depict, figure, outcry 7 clamour 8 shouting 10 appearance, complexion

hueless: 4 gray 9 colorless

huff: dod, pet 4 blow, brag, puff 5 bully, peeve, swell 6 hector 7 bluster, enlarge 8 boasting, offended 11 take offense

huffy: 4 airy 5 fuffy, puffy, windy 6 touchy 7 pettish 8 arrogant 9 conceited 10 swaggering

hug: hug 4 clip, coll 5 carry, clasp, cling, creem, halse, press 6 cuddle, huddle, huggle 7 cherish, embrace, squeeze 9 hold close

huge: big 4 stor(Sc.), vast 5 enorm, giant, great, jumbo, large 6 heroic 7 banging, bumping, immense, massive, monster 8 colossal, enormous, gigantic, titanic 9 monstrous, pyramidal, very large 10 gargantuan, prodigious, tremendous, unmeasured 11 elephantine

hugger-mugger: sly 6 jumble, muddle, secret 7 secrecy 8 confused, hush-hush, in camera, secretly 9 confusion 10 disorderly 11 clandestine 13 clandestinely

hui: 4 firm 5 guild 7 society 8 assembly 11 partnership

huisache: 4 wabe, wabi 5 aromo, shrub 6 cassie 7 popinac 10 spiny plant

huitain: 6 octave, stanza

huke: 4 cape 5 cloak, dress

hulk: 4 bulk, hull, loom, ship 5 hovel 10 disembowel

hulking: 5 bulky, hulky, husky, large 7 loutish, massive 8 unwieldy

hull: hud, hut, pod 4 bulk, hulk, husk, shed 5 shell, strip 6 casing 8 covering 11 decorticate

grain: 4 bran

hullabaloo: ado, din 5 noise 6 clamor, hubbub, racket, tumult, uproar 7 clamour 9 confusion

hum: 4 blur, buzz, huss, huzz, sing, whiz 5 croon, drink, drone, feign, whizz 6 murmur 7 vibrate 9 bombinate 11 bombilation, bombination

human: 6 humane, mortal, person 7 hominid 9 enigmatic

human being: man 6 mortal, person 7 Adamite 8 creature

humane: 4 kind 6 kindly, tender 8 merciful 9 forgiving 10 charitable, civilising 11 sympathetic 13 compassionate, tenderhearted

humanitarian: 14 philanthropist

humanity: 5 flesh, mercy 6 lenity, people 7 mankind 8 kindness 9 mortality 11 human nature

humanize: 6 refine 8 civilize

humble: low 4 mean, meek, mild, poor 5 abase, abash, lower, lowly, plain, stoop

6 debase, deject, demean, demiss, modest, reduce, simple 7 afflict, conquer, degrade, depress, ignoble, mortify 8 contrite, deferent, disgrace, reverent 9 humiliate 10 submissive, unassuming

humbug: gum, kid, pah 4 bosh, flam, guff, hoax, sham 5 cheat, faker, fraud, fudge, guile, trick 6 barney, blague, bunkum, cafard, cajole, gammon 7 deceive, flummer, mislead 8 flimflam, flummery, huckmuck, nonsense, pretense 9 bamboozle, deception, imposture, strategem 10 flumdiddle 11 flumadiddle

humdinger: 4 oner 5 dandy, doozy, nifty 6 corker 8 jimdandy 11 crackerjack

humdrum: 4 dull 6 boring 7 irksome, prosaic 10 monotonous 11 commonplace, indifferent 13 uninteresting

humerus: 4 bone 8 shoulder, upper arm

humid: wet 4 damp, dank 5 moist 6 sultry 8 humorous, vaporous

humidity: 8 dampness, 9 moistness

humiliate: 5 abase, abash, shame 6 debase, humble 7 degrade, mortify 8 belittle, disgrace

humility: 7 modesty 8 meekness, mildness 9 lowliness 10 diffidence

humming: big 5 brisk, brool 6 lively, strong 7 buzzing, droning 8 frothing, seething 13 extraordinary

hummingbird: ava 5 carib 6 hummer 8 froufrou 9 sheartail

genus of: 6 sappho

hummock: 4 hump 5 knoll 7 hillock

humor, humour: pet, tid, wit 4 baby, mood, whim 5 fancy, fluid, freak, vapor 6 levity, megrim, please, temper 7 caprice, cater to, gratify, indulge 8 drollery, moisture 11 inclination, temperament

humorist: wag, wit 4 card 5 cutup, joker 6 jester

humorous, humourous: 5 comic, droll, funny, humid, moist, witty 6 watery 7 amusive, comical, jocular, playful 8 pleasant 9 facetious, laughable, whimsical 10 capricious

hump: 4 bile, hunk, lump 5 bouge, bulge, bunch, crump, hunch, mound, ridge 6 gibber, gibbus, hummie 7 hummock 12 protuberance

humpback: 5 whale 9 hunchback 10 huckleback

Humperdinck opera: 15 Hansel and Gretel

humus: mor 4 mull, soil

Hun: 6 vandal 9 barbarian

leader: 4 Atli 5 Etzel 6 Attila

Hunan river: 4 Yuan, Yuen

hunch: 4 balk, bend, hump, hunk, lump, push 5 chunk, fudge, shove 6 chilly, frosty, thrust 9 intuition 11 premonition 12 protuberance

Hunchback of Notre Dame: 9 Quasimodo

author: 4 Hugo

hundred: 7 cantred, cantref 11 ten times ten

division into: 12 centuriation

hundred-eyed being: 5 Argus

hundred percent: 6 entire 7 genuine, perfect 9 unalloyed 13 thoroughgoing 14 unquestionable

hundred years: 7 century 9 centenary

hundredfold: 8 centuple 12 centuplicate

hundredweight: cwt 6 cental 7 quintal

hung: See hang

Hung Wu: 4 Ming

Hungary: *army:* 6 Honved 9 Honvedseg

capital: Budapest

cavalryman: 6 Hussar

city: 4 Pecs 5 Erlau 6 Szeged 7 Miskolc 8 Debrecen 9 Debreczin, Kecskemet

coin: 6 filler, forint

commune: Mor

composer: 5 Lehar 6 Bartok

county: Vas 4 Pest, Zala 5 Bekes, Fejer, Heves, Tolna 6 Nograd, Somogy

dance: 7 czardas

dog: 4 puli 6 kuvasz

ethnic group: 4 Slav 5 Croat, gypsy 6 Magyar

gypsy: 7 tzigane

lake: 7 Balaton 9 Blaten See

measure: ako 4 hold, joch, yoke 5 antal, itcze, marok, metze 7 huvelyk, merfold

mountain range: 10 Carpathian

poet: 5 Arany

river: 4 Raab 5 Drave, Maros 6 Danube, Poprad, Theiss 7 Vistula

weight: 7 vamfont 8 vammazsa

wine: 5 tokay

hunger: 4 long, want 5 belly 6 desire, famine, starve 7 craving 8 appetite, need food, voracity 9 esurience 10 starvation

abnormal: 7 bulimia 10 polyphagia

hungry: 4 avid, howe, poor 5 eager 6 barren, hollow, jejune 7 craving, uneaten 8 esurient, hungered 10 avaricious

hunk: dad, gob, wad 4 daud, hump, lump 5 chunk, hunch, piece 6 nugget

hunt: dig 4 drag, seek 5 chase, chevy, chivy, delve, drive, hound, probe, quest, stalk, track, trail 6 chivvy, ferret, follow, forage, hunter, pursue, search, shikar 9 persecute, try to find 11 inquisition

god of: 5 Ninip 6 Apollo

hunted: 4 game, prey

hunter: 5 jager, yager 6 chaser, nimrod 7 stalker 8 chasseur 9 sportsman

assistant: 5 gilly, jager

attendant: 5 gilly(Scot.) 6 gillie

constellation: 5 Orion
mythological: 5 Orion
Golden Fleece: 5 Jason
patron saint: 6 Hubert
hunting: *bird:* 6 falcon
cry: yoi 4 toho 5 chevy, chivy, hoick 6 chivvy, hoicks, yoicks
expedition: 6 safari
game: 6 shikar, venery
horn note: 4 mort
pert. to: 7 venatic
hunting dog: 5 hound 6 basset, beagle, setter 7 pointer, spaniel
huntress: 5 Diana 7 Artemis 8 Atalanta
huntsman: 5 jager 6 jaeger 7 catcher, venerer 8 chasseur
changed into stag: 7 Actaeon
hurdle: pen 4 clew, fold, leap 5 bound, cover, crate, frith, hedge 6 raddle 7 barrier, confine 8 obstacle, surmount 9 enclosure 10 impediment 11 obstruction
hurdy-gurdy: 4 lira, rota
hurl: 4 cast, dash, haul, howl, hurl, pelt, roar, send, toss, turn 5 fling, heave, pitch, sling, smite, throw, twist, whang 6 elance 9 overthrow
hurly-burly: 6 hubbub, tumult, uproar 7 turmoil 8 confused 9 confusion
huron: 6 grison
hurrah: joy 5 cheer, huzza, shout 6 tumult 7 triumph 8 applause 9 commotion 13 encouragement
hurricane: 4 wind 5 storm 7 cyclone, prester, tempest 8 chubasco 9 hurricano, windstorm 13 tropical storm
center of: eye
hurried: See hurry
hurry: ado, hie, run 4 pass, pell, race, rese, rush, scud, stir, trot, urge, whir 5 drive, fight, haste, impel, slide, speed, worry 6 convey, harass, hasten, hustle, scurry, tumult, urge on 7 agitato(It.), dispute, quarrel, quicken 8 dispatch, expedite 9 agitation, commotion 10 expedition 11 disturbance, festination, precipitate
hurst: 4 hill, wood 5 copse, grove, knoll 7 hillock 8 sandbank 11 wooded mound
hurt: 4 harm, maim, pain 5 abuse, blame, grief, sorry, wound 6 damage, grieve, impair, injure, injury, mittle, offend, scathe, strike 7 afflict, collide, hurting 8 be bad for, distress, mischief, nuisance 9 detriment 12 disadvantage
hurtful: bad 4 evil 6 nocent 7 baneful, harmful, malefic, noisome, noxious 10 pernicious 11 deleterious, destructive, detrimental, prejudicial
hurtle: 4 dash 5 clash, fling, whirl 6 assail, jostle 7 collide 8 brandish
husband: eke, man, rom 4 bond, buck, chap, keep, mate, save 5 churl, hoard, marry, store 6 manage, spouse, tiller 7 consort, espouse, partner, plowman, steward 8 conserve, helpmate 9 cultivate, economize, other half 10 cultivator, husbandman
more than one: 9 polyandry
property right: 7 curtesy
husbandman: 4 bond, boor, carl 5 colon 6 farmer, tiller 7 acre-man 8 agricole 10 cultivator
husbandry: 6 thrift 7 economy 8 managery 9 frugality 11 cultivation 12 conservation
god: 6 Faunus
hush: tut 4 calm, clam, hist, lull 5 allay, quiet, still 6 soothe 7 appease, repress, silence
husk: cod, hud 4 bark, bran, coat, hulk, hull, leam, peel, rind, skin 5 lemma, scale, shack, shell, shuck, straw, strip 6 colder 7 envelop, epicarp 8 covering, envelope 11 decorticate
Husky: dog 6 Eskimo
huss: 7 dogfish
hussar: 7 soldier 10 cavalryman
headdress: 5 busby
uniform jacket: 6 dolman
hussy: 4 jade, minx 5 besom(Sc.), gipsy, gypsy, madam, quean 7 drossel 9 housewife 11 housekeeper
hustle: 4 push 5 crowd, hurry, shove 6 bustle, jostle, thrust 8 activity
hustler: 6 peeler 8 go-getter
hut: cot 4 bari, cote, crib, hulk, shed 5 benab, bohio, bothy, cabin, choza, house, hovel, humpy, hutch, kraal, lodge, scale, shack, toldo, wurly 6 bohawn, canaba, chalet, gunyah, gunyeh, lean-to, rancho, shanty 7 balagan, bourock, camalig, cottage, edifice, huddock, wickiup 8 barabara, building, chantier
fisherman's: 4 skeo
hermit's: 4 cell
military: 6 Nissen
mining: coe
shepherd's: 5 bothy
hutch: ark, bin, box, car, hut, pen 4 coop 5 chest, hoard, hotch, hovel 6 coffer, humped, shanty 7 hunched, shelter 9 inclosure
hutzpah: 4 gall 5 nerve
huzza: 5 cheer, shout 6 hurrah
hyacinth: 7 greggle 8 bluebell, harebell
hyalite: 4 opal
hybrid: 4 mule 5 blend, cross 7 mongrel 9 composite 10 crossbreed
bovine: 7 cattalo
dog: 4 mutt 7 mongrel
horse and ass: 4 mule 5 hinny
horse and zebra: 7 zebrula, zebrule 8 zebrinny
zebra and donkey: 7 zebrass
hydrant: 4 plug 6 faucet 8 fireplug

hydraulic engine: ram
hydrazoate: 4 azid 5 azide
hydrocarbon: 6 butane, carane, nonane, retene 7 benzene, methane, olefine, pentane
gaseous: 6 ethane, ethene
liver oil: 8 pristane
tree: 7 terpene
hydrocyanic acid: 7 prussic
hydrogen: gas 5 arsin 6 arsine
hydroid: 5 polyp 6 obelia 7 acaleph
hydromel: 4 mead 5 aloja 10 melicratum
hydrometer: 9 aerometer
hydromica: 4 mica 9 muscovite
hydrophobia: 5 lyssa 6 rabies
hydrophyte: See aquatic plant
hygienic: 4 good 6 healthy 8 sanitary
hymenopteron: ant, bee 4 wasp 6 sawfly 7 gallfly 9 ichneumon
hymn: ode 4 sing, song 5 psalm 6 himene, himine, hirmos, hirmus 7 introit 8 canticle 11 recessional 12 processional
following psalm: 9 sticheron
funeral: 5 dirge
praising: 4 pean 5 paean
ritual: 8 encomium
sung in unison: 6 choral 7 chorale 9 plainsong
tune: 6 choral 7 chorale
victory: 9 epinicion, epinikion
hyoscyamus: 8 narcotic
hype: 5 boost, put on 6 jack up, promote 7 deceive, mislead
hyperbole: 12 exaggeration 13 overstatement

Hyperborean sage: 6 Abaris
hypercritical: 7 carping 8 captious 10 censorious 12 faultfinding, overcritical, supercilious
Hyperion: *daughter:* Eos 6 Selene
father: 6 Uranus
son: 6 Helios
hyphen: 4 band, dash
hypnotic: 6 opiate 8 narcotic 9 soporific 12 somnifacient
hypnotic condition: 4 coma 6 trance 8 lethargy
hypnotize: 5 charm 9 mesmerize, spellbind
hypnum: 4 moss
hypochondria: hyp 6 megrim
hypocrisy: 4 cant 6 deceit 10 simulation
hypocrite: 4 sham 5 faker, phony, quack 6 humbug, poseur 7 Tartufe 9 charlatan, lip server
hypocritical: 5 false 7 bigoted, canting 8 captious, specious 9 deceptive, insincere 11 dissembling, pharisaical 13 sanctimonious, self-righteous
hypostatic: 5 basic 9 elemental
hypotenuse: 5 slant
hypothesis: ism 6 system, theory 9 postulate 10 assumption 11 supposition
hypothetical being: ens 6 entity
hyrax: 5 coney 8 procavia
hyssop: 4 mint 5 plant 11 aspergillum
hysteria: 6 nerves
hysterical: 9 emotional 12 uncontrolled

I

I, Claudius author: 6 Graves
I do not wish to contend: 14 nolo contendere(L.)
I have found it: 6 eureka
I understand: 5 roger
Iago's wife: 6 Emilia
Iasion's father: 4 Zeus
Iberian: 4 Pict
ibex: tur, zac
ibis: 5 guara, stork 9 gourdhead
Ibsen (Henrik): *character:* Ase 4 Gynt, Nora 5 Hedda

native country: 6 Norway
play: 5 Ghosts 8 Peer Gynt, Wild Duck 10 Doll's House 11 Hedda Gabler
Icarian: 4 rash 6 daring 9 foolhardy
Icarius' daughter: 7 Erigone 8 Penelope
Icarus' father: 8 Daedalus
ICBM: 5 Atlas 6 weapon 7 missle
ice: 4 cool, geal, grue(Sc.), rime 5 chill, frost glace(F.). 6 freeze, payola 7 congeal, hauteur 8 diamonds 10 confection 11 refrigerant, refrigerate
crystals: 4 snow 5 frost

floating: 4 berg, floe
fragment: 5 brash
mass: 7 glacier
patch: 4 rone(Sc.)
pendant: 6 icicle
pinnacle of glacier: 5 serac
sea: 6 sludge
sheet: 4 floe
slushy: 4 sish

ice cream dish: 4 soda 6 frappe, sundae 7 parfait
icebox: 6 cooler 12 refrigerator
icecap: 7 calotte
Iceland: *capital:* 9 Reykjavik
city: 8 Akureyri, Keflavik 9 Kopavogur
ethnic group: 4 Celt 5 Norse
measure: fet 4 alin, lina 5 almud, turma 6 almenn, almude, ferfet, pottur 7 fathmur, feralin, fermila, oltunna, sjomila 9 korntunna 10 ferfathmur, kornskeppa, thumlungur
monetary unit: 5 eyrir, krona
notable volcano: 5 Hekla
parliament: 7 Althing
river: 5 Hvita 7 Jokulsa
weight: 4 pund 5 pound 11 tunna smjors
Icelandic epic: 4 Edda 10 Grettisaga
Icelandic Nobel novelist: 7 Laxness (Halldor)
ichneumon: fly 8 mongoose 11 hymenoptera(pl.)
ichnography: map 9 floor plan
ichnolite: 6 fossil 9 footprint
icicle: 10 ice pendent
limestone: 10 stalactite, stalagmite
icing: 7 topping 8 frosting
icky: 6 sticky 7 cloying 10 disgusting 11 distasteful, sentimental
icon, ikon: 5 image 6 eidola(pl.), idolon, symbol 7 eidolon, picture 8 portrait 12 illustration
iconoclast: 5 rebel 7 radical 9 dissenter 13 nonconformist
icterus: 8 jaundice
ictus: fit 4 blow 6 attack, stress, stroke
ICU: 17 intensive care unit
icy: 4 cold 5 gelid 6 arctic, frigid, frosty 8 chilling
Idaho: *capital:* 5 Boise
city: 5 Nampa 6 Burley, Moscow, Rupert 8 Caldwell, Lewiston 9 Blackfoot, Pocatello, Twin Falls
county: Ada, Gem 5 Camas, Latah, Lemhi, Power, Teton 6 Bonner, Cassia, Custer, Oneida, Owyhee 7 Bannock, Benewah, Caribou, Gooding, Payette 8 Kootenai, Minidoka
dam: 8 Brownlee, Dworshak 13 Anderson Ranch
early explorer: 5 Clark (William), Lewis (Meriwether)
gorge: 11 Hell's Canyon
Indian: 7 Bannock 8 Nez Perce, Shosho-

ne 10 Sheepeater
lake: 4 Bear 5 Grays 6 Priest 11 Coeur d'Alene, Pend Oreille
mountain peak: 4 Ryan 5 Borah, Devil, Scott, Waugh 6 Castle, Mormon, Taylor 8 Cape Horn
mountain range: 5 Lemhi 7 Cabinet 8 Sawtooth 9 Lost River 10 Bitterroot
river: 4 Bear 5 Boise, Lemhi, Snake 6 Lochsa, Salmon 7 Big Wood, Payette 10 Clearwater
state bird: 8 bluebird
state flower: 7 syringa
state gem: 10 star garnet
state horse: 9 Appaloosa
state motto: 12 Esto perpetua
state nickname: Gem
state tree: 9 white pine
tourist resort: 9 Sun Valley
Idas' consort: 8 Marpessa
ide: 4 orfe 8 foodfish
idea: 4 idee(F.) 5 fancy, ideal, image 6 design, figure, notion 7 conceit, concept, fantasy, inkling, opinion, project, thought 8 gimcrack 9 archetype 10 appearance, cogitation, conception, impression, reflection
impracticable: 7 chimera 8 chimaera
prompting action: 6 motive
ideal: 5 dream, model 6 mental 7 paragon, perfect, Utopian 8 abstract, fanciful, standard 9 imaginary, visionary 10 aspiration, conceptual
ideal state: 4 Eden 6 Oceana, Utopia
ideate: 5 fancy 7 imagine 8 conceive
idée fixe: 9 fixed idea, obsession
identical: one 4 same, self, twin, very 5 alike, equal, samen(Sc.) 8 selfsame 10 equivalent, tantamount
identify: tag 4 mark, name 5 brand, prove 7 earmark, pick out 9 designate, establish, recognize
identity: 4 name 5 unity 7 oneness 8 sameness 9 exactness 11 homogeneity
crisis: 13 self conflict
false: 5 alias
ideologist: 7 dreamer 8 theorist 9 visionary
ideology: ism 5 credo, dogma 7 beliefs 8 doctrine 10 philosophy
idiasm: 9 mannerism 11 peculiarity 12 idiosyncrasy
idiocy: 7 anoesia, fatuity
idiograph: 9 signature, trademark
idiom: 5 style 6 phrase 7 dialect
idiosyncrasy: way 6 idiasm, manner 11 peculiarity 12 eccentricity
idiot: oaf 4 dolt, fool 5 ament, booby, dunce, moron 6 cretin, hobbil, nidget 7 dullard, omadawn 8 imbecile, omadhuan 9 blockhead, simpleton 10 changeling
idiotic: 4 daft, zany 5 barmy, inane 7 asi-

nine, fatuous, foolish **9** senseless

idle: 4 lazy loaf, sorn(Sc.), vain **5** dally, empty **6** dawdle, futile, loiter, otiose, unused, vacant **7** aimless, loafing, useless **8** baseless, inactive, indolent, slothful, trifling **9** desultory, unfounded, worthless **10** groundless, unemployed, unoccupied **11** ineffectual

idle talk: 5 rumor **6** gossip

idleness: 5 sloth **7** inertia **8** inaction, laziness **9** indolence **10** inactivity

idler: 5 bum **5** drone **6** loafer **8** faineant, loiterer, sluggard **9** do-nothing, goldbrick, lazybones

Idmon: *father:* **6** Apollo
killer: **4** boar
mother: **6** Cyrene
ship: **4** Argo

idol: 4 god **4** Baal, hero, icon **5** image **6** fetish
matinee: **4** star

idolater: 5 pagan **6** adorer **7** Baalite **9** worshiper

idolatrous: 5 pagan

idolize: 5 adore **6** admire, revere **7** worship **8** venerate

idyl, idyll: 4 poem **7** eclogue

idyllic: 7 bucolic **8** pastoral **9** unspoiled

if: 8 granting, provided **9** supposing

i'faith: 5 truly **6** indeed

iffy: 6 chancy **8** doubtful **9** uncertain

igneous rock: 4 lava **5** magma **6** basalt, gabbro, pumice, scoria **8** porphyry

ignis fatuus: 8 delusion **9** pipe dream **12** will-o'-the-wisp

ignite: 4 fire **5** light **6** kindle **7** inflame

ignoble: low **4** base, mean, vile **6** abject, sordid **8** shameful, wretched **11** disgraceful **12** dishonorable

ignominious: 4 base **5** sorry **6** odious **8** infamous, shameful **9** degrading **10** despicable, inglorious, mortifying **11** disgraceful, humiliating **12** contemptible, dishonorable

ignoramus: 4 dolt **5** dunce **6** nitwit

ignorant: 5 green, naive, young **6** stupid **7** artless, unaware, uncouth **8** nescient, untaught **9** in the dark, unlearned, unskilled, untutored **10** illiterate, unlettered **11** unconscious

ignore: cut **4** omit, snub **5** blink, elide **6** slight **7** neglect **8** overlook **9** disregard, eliminate

Igorot, Igorrote: 6 Bontok **7** Nabaloi **8** Kankanai
chief: Apo

iguana: 6 lizard **7** tuatara

Iguvine: 7 Umbrian **8** Eugubine

ihi: 4 fish **7** skipper **8** halfbeak **9** stichbird

Ihlat: 8 Sunnites

ijolite: 7 apatite, calcite **8** titanite

ilex: 5 holly

Iliad: 4 epic, poem
attributed to: **5** Homer
character: **4** Ajax **5** Helen, Paris, Priam **6** Aeneas, Hector **8** Achilles, Diomedes, Menelaus, Odysseus **9** Agamemnon, Cassandra, Patroclus

ilium: 4 bone

Ilium, Ilion: 4 Troy

ilk: 4 kind, sort, type **5** breed, class, **6** family, nature, stripe

ill: bad **4** evil, harm, poor, sick **5** amiss, badly, wrong **6** ailing, faulty, wicked **7** adverse, ailment, baneful, noxious, trouble, unlucky **8** improper **9** adversity, defective **10** indisposed, iniquitous, misfortune **11** unfortunate

ill-advised: 4 rash **5** hasty **6** unwise **8** reckless **9** imprudent **10** indiscreet **11** thoughtless

ill at ease: 7 awkward **13** uncomfortable

ill-boding: 4 dire **7** ominous, unlucky **12** inauspicious

ill-bred: 4 rude **7** boorish, plebian, uncivil **8** churlish, impolite, malapert **9** bourgeois **11** impertinent **12** discourteous

ill-defined: 4 dim **5** faint, fuzzy, vague **7** unclear **10** indistinct

ill-favored: 4 ugly **9** offensive **10** unpleasant **12** disagreeable

ill-humored: 5 cross **6** cranky, morose **7** fretful, grouchy, peevish

ill-natured: 4 dour **5** nasty, surly **6** crabby

ill-suited: 5 inapt, unfit **8** improper **10** unbecoming **13** inappropriate

ill-tempered: 5 cross, moody **6** crusty **7** bilious **8** choleric, snappish **9** dyspeptic, irritable

ill-treat: 5 abuse **6** misuse

ill will: 4 hate **5** spite, venom **6** animus, enmity, malice, rancor **7** dislike **9** hostility **10** bad feeling
showing: **7** hostile **8** choleric **9** bellicose, irascible, litigious, wrangling **10** pugnacious **11** belligerent, contentious, quarrelsome **12** disputatious

illation: 9 deduction, inference

illegitimate: 7 bastard, bootleg **8** improper, spurious, unlawful, wrongful **9** illogical

illiberal: 6 stingy **7** bigoted **8** partisan **9** hidebound **10** intolerant **11** opinionated **12** narrow-minded

illicit: 7 bootleg, illegal **8** criminal, improper, unlawful **10** contraband, prohibited **12** unauthorized

illimitable: 4 vast **8** infinite **9** boundless **11** measureless **12** immeasurable

Illinois: *capital:* **10** Springfield
city: **5** Cairo, Pekin **6** Galena, Geneva, Joliet, Peoria, Urbana **7** Chicago, Decatur, Wheaton **8** Carthage, Kankakee,

Rockford, Waukegan 10 Belleville, Rock Island 11 East St. Louis

county: 4 Bond, Cass, Clay, Cook, Kane, Knox, Ogle, Will 5 Adams, Boone, Coles, Edgar, Piatt, Stark 6 Bureau, De Kalb, De Witt, Du Page, Grundy, Hardin, Massac, Menard, Saline 7 Carroll, Kendall, La Salle 8 Crawford, Gallatin, Macoupin, Moultrie, Sangamon

Indian: Fox 4 Sauk 8 Kickapoo

lake: 8 Michigan

river: 4 Ohio, Rock 6 Wabash 8 Illinois, Kankakee, Mackinaw, Sangamon 9 Kaskaskia, Vermilion 10 Des Plaines

state bird: 8 cardinal

state flower: 6 violet

state insect: 9 butterfly (Monarch)

state mineral: 8 fluorite

state nickname: 7 Prairie

state slogan: 13 Land of Lincoln

state tree: 8 white oak

illiterate: 6 unread 8 ignorant, untaught 9 barbarous, unlearned, untutored 10 unlettered

illness: 5 colic 6 malady, morbus 7 ailment, cachexy, disease 8 cachexia, disorder, sickness 9 complaint, distemper 10 affliction, wickedness 13 indisposition

feign: 8 malinger

mental: See **mental disorder**

illogical: 7 invalid, unsound 8 specious 9 senseless 10 irrational, unreasoned 12 inconsequent

illuminate: 4 fire 5 adorn, flare, light 6 inform, kindle 7 clarify, emblaze, explain 8 brighten, 9 enlighten, irradiate, make clear 10 illustrate

illumination: *device:* 4 lamp 5 torch 7 lantern 10 flashlight

in eclipse: 8 penumbra

measure: 4 phot 5 lumen 6 candle

illusion: 5 fancy 6 mirage 7 chimera, fallacy, mockery, phantom 8 delusion 9 deception 10 appearance

illusive: 4 sham 5 false 6 unreal 7 seeming 8 apparent, illusory 9 deceitful, deceptive, imaginary 10 fallacious, phantasmal

illustrate: 4 show 5 adorn 7 picture, point up, portray 8 elucidate, exemplify, make clear, represent 10 illuminate

illustration: 4 case 7 example 8 instance, vignette 13 demonstration 15 exemplification

illustrator: 6 artist

illustrious: 5 famed, grand, noble, noted 6 bright, candid, heroic 7 eminent, exalted 8 glorious, renowned 9 honorable 10 celebrated 11 conspicuous 13 distinguished

ilvaite: 8 silicate

image: god 4 copy, form, icon, idol, ikon 5 eikon 6 double, effigy, emblem, figure, statue, symbol 7 phantom, picture 8 likeness 9 depiction, semblance 10 conception, impression, reflection, similitude, simulacrum

attacker: 10 iconoclast

rainbowlike: 7 spectra(pl.) 8 spectrum

religious: 4 icon

stone: 5 herma 6 hermae(pl.)

pert. to televised: 5 video

wooden: 4 tiki 6 xoanon

worship: 8 idolatry 10 iconolatry

imaginary: 5 ideal 6 unreal 7 fancied, feigned 8 illusory, mythical, notional 9 dreamed up, fantastic, visionary 10 artificial, chimerical, fictitious 11 make believe

imagination: 5 fancy 7 fantasy, thought 9 ingenuity, invention 10 creativity, enterprise

imaginative: 6 dreamy, poetic 8 fanciful, original 9 fantastic

imagine: 5 dream, fancy, feign, think 6 gather 7 picture, suppose, surmise 8 conceive, envision 9 apprehend 10 comprehend, conjecture

imago: 12 winged insect

imam: 5 ruler 6 caliph

imaret: inn 7 hospice 11 caravansary

imbecile: 4 dolt, jerk 5 anile, daffy, idiot, moron 6 cranky, dotard, nitwit 7 fatuous 8 dumbbell 9 driveling 10 changeling, half-witted

imbed: fix 5 embed, inset 6 cement

imbibe: sip 4 soak 5 drink, imbue, steep 6 absorb 7 swallow 8 saturate 10 assimilate

imbricate: 5 tiled 6 scaled 7 overlap

imbroglio: row 4 spat 7 dispute 8 squabble 9 bickering 11 altercation 12 disagreement 16 misunderstanding

imbrue: wet 4 soak 5 stain 6 drench

imbue: dye 4 soak 5 steep, tinge 6 imbibe, infuse, leaven 7 animate, ingrain, inspire, instill, pervade 8 permeate, saturate 9 inoculate 10 impregnate

imitate: ape 4 copy, echo, mime, mock 5 mimic 6 follow, repeat 7 copycat, emulate 8 resemble, simulate 9 dissemble 11 counterfeit

imitation: 4 copy, echo, fake, sham 5 dummy, phony 6 ersatz 7 replica 8 likeness 9 emulation, facsimile

derisive: 6 parody 7 mockery 9 burlesque

fantastic: 8 travesty

imitation gem: 5 glass, paste

imitation pearl: 6 olivet

immaculate: 4 pure 5 clean 6 candid, chaste 7 correct, perfect 8 innocent, spotless, unsoiled 9 faultless, undefiled, unspotted, unstained, unsullied

immalleable: 5 rigid 10 unyielding

immanent: 8 inherent 9 intrinsic 10 in-dwelling, subjective

immaterial: 6 slight 8 trifling 9 asomatous, spiritual, unearthly 10 impalpable, intangible 11 unimportant 12 not pertinent 13 insignificant, unsubstantial

immature: 5 crude, green, young 6 callow, unripe 7 puerile, untried 8 childish, youthful 10 incomplete, unfinished 11 undeveloped

immaturity: 5 youth 6 nonage

immeasurable: 7 immense 8 infinite 9 boundless, unlimited, 10 indefinite 11 illimitable 12 incalculable

immediate: 4 next 6 direct 7 instant 8 adjacent 9 proximate 10 contiguous, succeeding

immediately: now 4 anon 6 presto 8 directly 9 extempore, forthwith, presently

immemorial: 7 ageless, ancient 8 dateless 11 prehistoric, traditional

immense: 4 huge, vast 5 grand, great, large 7 titanic 8 colossal, enormous, gigantic, infinite 9 extensive, monstrous 10 prodigious, tremendous 12 immeasurable

immerse: dip 4 bury, duck 5 bathe, douse, souse 6 absorb, drench, occupy, plunge 7 baptize, engross 8 submerge

immigrant: 8 newcomer

Israel: 6 halutz 7 chalutz

imminent: 8 expecting 9 impending 10 approaching, threatening

immitigable: 10 implacable

immobile: set 4 firm 5 fixed, inert 6 frozen, laid up, stable 9 immovable 10 motionless, stationary, stock-still

immoderate: 5 undue 7 extreme 9 boundless, excessive, voracious 10 exorbitant, inordinate 11 extravagant, intemperate 12 unreasonable

immodest: 4 bold 6 brazen, coarse 7 forward, obscene 8 indecent, unchaste 9 shameless 10 indecorous

immolation: 8 offering 9 sacrifice

immoral: bad 4 evil 5 loose, wrong 7 corrupt, vicious 8 culpable, depraved, indecent 9 dissolute 10 licentious 11 unwholesome

immortal: 6 divine 7 endless, eternal, godlike, undying 8 enduring 9 ceaseless, deathless 11 amaranthine, everlasting 12 imperishable

immortality: 8 athanasy 9 athanasia 11 endless life

Hindu: 6 amrita

immovable: pat, set 4 fast, firm 5 fixed, rigid 7 adamant 8 constant, immobile, obdurate 9 steadfast 10 adamantine, stationary

immunity: 7 freedom 9 exemption 12 resistance to

immunize: 8 make safe 9 inoculate

immunizer: 5 serum 7 vaccine

immure: 4 wall 7 confine 8 cloister, imprison 11 incarcerate

immutable: 4 firm 7 eternal 10 invariable, unchanging 11 unalterable

Imogen's father: 9 Cymbeline

imp: bud, elf 4 brat, cion, slip 5 child, demor., devil, graft, rogue, scamp, scion 6 sprite, urchin 7 gremlin, progeny 8 devilkin, folletto, folletti(pl.) 9 hobgoblin, offspring 13 mischiefmaker

impact: 4 blow, jolt, pack, slam 5 brunt, crash, force, shock, wedge 6 effect, stroke 7 impulse 9 collision 11 implication

impair: mar 4 harm, hurt 5 spoil, waste 6 damage, debase, hinder, injure, lessen, reduce, sicken, weaken 7 blemish, cripple, vitiate 8 decrease, enfeeble

impaired: 9 afflicted

impala: 7 rooibok 8 rooyebok

impale: 4 spit 5 spear, spike 6 pierce, skewer 8 transfix 10 run through

impalpable: 7 elusive 10 immaterial, intangible

impart: 4 give, lend, tell 5 share, yield 6 bestow, confer, convey, direct, impute, reveal 7 divulge, inspire, instill 8 disclose, discover 10 distribute 11 communicate

impartial: 4 even, fair, just 7 neutral 8 unbiased 9 colorless, equitable, objective 12 unprejudiced 13 disinterested, dispassionate

imparting motion: 7 kinetic

impassable: 5 solid 10 impervious

impasse: box 7 dead end 8 cul-de-sac(F.), deadlock, standoff 9 stalemate 10 blind alley

impassible: 9 impassive, unfeeling 12 invulnerable

impassioned: 5 fiery 6 ardent, fervid 7 fervent 8 eloquent, feverish

impassive: 4 calm 5 stoic 6 serene, stolid 9 apathetic 10 impassible, insensible, phlegmatic 11 emotionless 13 imperturbable

impatient: hot 4 avid, edgy, keen 5 eager, hasty, testy 7 anxious, chafing, fidgety, fretful, peevish 8 choleric, petulant, restless 9 irascible, irritable

impeach: 6 accuse, charge, indict 7 arraign, censure 9 challenge, discredit

impeccable: 5 right 7 correct, perfect 8 flawless 9 exquisite, faultless 11 unblemished

impecunious: 4 poor 5 needy 8 indigent 9 destitute, penniless

impede: 4 clog 5 block, check, choke, delay 6 hamper, harass, hinder, retard, stymie 7 disrupt 8 encumber, handicap, hold back, obstruct

legally: bar 5 debar, estop

impediment: bar, rub 4 clog, flaw, snag 5 hitch 6 defect, malady, remora 8 obstacle 9 detriment, hindrance 10 difficulty

impedimenta: 7 baggage

impel: pat 4 blow, goad, move, send, spur, urge 5 drive, force, hurry 6 compel, excite, incite, induce 7 actuate 8 motivate 9 constrain, encourage, influence, instigate, stimulate

impelling force: 7 impetus 8 momentum

impending: 7 looming 8 imminent, menacing, oncoming 11 approaching, threatening

impenetrable: 4 hard 5 dense 8 airtight 10 impervious, impassable 11 impermeable, inscrutable 12 unfathomable

impenitent: 8 hardened, obdurate 11 remorseless, unrepentant

imperative: 4 duty, rule 5 order, vital 6 urgent 7 crucial 8 pressing, verb form 9 essential, mandatory 10 commanding, compelling, compulsory, peremptory

imperator: 6 leader 7 emperor, general

imperceptible: 10 insensible, intangible 13 inappreciable, indiscernible 17 indistinguishable

imperfect: 4 cull, poor 5 rough 6 faulty, second 7 defective 10 inadequate, incomplete, unfinished

imperfection: 4 flaw, vice 5 fault 6 defect, foible 7 blemish, failing, frailty 8 weakness 10 deficiency 11 shortcoming

imperfectly: 4 half 5 badly

imperial: 5 regal, royal 6 kingly 8 majestic

cap: 5 crown

domain: 6 empery, empire

officer: 8 palatine

imperial woodpecker: 9 ivorybill

imperil: 4 risk 6 expose, hazard 8 endanger 10 jeopardize

imperious: 6 lordly 7 haughty 8 arrogant, despotic, dominant, pressing 10 commanding, imperative, tyrannical 11 dictatorial, domineering, magisterial, overbearing 13 authoritative

imperishable: 7 eternal, undying 8 enduring, immortal 9 continual, deathless 11 everlasting 14 indestructible

impermanent: 8 fleeting 9 ephemeral, temporary, tentative, transient 10 evanescent

impersonal: 4 cold 7 general 8 detached 9 objective 12 matter-of-fact

impersonate: act, ape 4 pose 5 mimic 6 typify

impersonator: 8 imitator, imposter, impostor, 11 entertainer, masquerader

impertinence: 4 sass 8 audacity 9 insolence 10 incivility 11 impropriety, irrelevance

impertinent: 4 rude 5 sassy, saucy 7 ill-bred 8 arrogant, impudent 9 audacious, officious 10 inapposite 12 inconsequent 13 disrespectful

imperturbability: 8 ataraxia, calmness 9 composure, sangfroid 10 equanimity

imperturbable: 4 cool 6 placid, serene, stable 8 tranquil 9 impassive 10 phlegmatic 11 unexcitable

impervious: 5 tight 8 hardened 10 impassable 11 impermeable 12 impenetrable

impetrate: 7 beseech, entreat, procure

impetuous: hot 4 rash 5 eager, fiery, hasty, heady, sharp 6 abrupt, ardent, fervid, fierce, flashy, sudden 7 furious, rushing, violent 8 forcible, headlong, vehement 9 impulsive, hot-headed 11 precipitate

impetus: 4 prod, push, spur 5 drive, force 6 motive 7 impulse 8 momentum, stimulus 9 incentive

imphee: 5 plant 7 sorghum

impi: 8 soldiers, warriors

impiety: 9 blasphemy 10 disrespect 11 irreverence, ungodliness

impinge: 6 strike 7 intrude, touch on 8 encroach, trespass

impious: 7 unholy 7 godless, profane, ungodly 9 atheistic, undutiful 10 irreverent 11 irreligious

impish: 6 elfish 7 naughty 11 mischievous

implacable: 6 deadly 10 relentless 11 immitigable 12 unappeasable 14 irreconcilable

implant: sow 4 root 5 embed, infix, inset 6 enroot, infuse 7 impress, inspire, instill 9 inculcate, inoculate, insinuate, introduce 10 impregnate

implausible: 5 fishy 6 flimsy 7 dubious 8 unlikely 9 illogical 10 improbable 12 unbelievable

implement (see also **tool**)**:** 4 gear 6 device, gadget 7 enforce, fulfill, realize, utensil 8 complete, material 9 apparatus, appliance 10 accomplish, instrument

ancient: 4 celt 6 amgarn, eolith 9 paleolith

baker's: 4 peel

barbed: 7 harpoon

cleaning: mop 4 swab 5 broom, brush 6 vacuum 7 sweeper

cutting: 5 knife, mower, razor 6 reaper, scythe, shears 8 scissors 9 jackknife 11 pocketknife

enlarging: 6 reamer 7 dilator
farm: 4 disc, disk, plow, rake 6 seeder, tiller 7 tractor
furcate: 4 fork
garden: hoe 4 rake 5 mower, spade 6 shovel, sickle, weeder
grasping: 5 tongs 6 pliers 8 tweezers
hand printing: 6 brayer, roller
hide cleaning: 6 slater
kind of: 5 dolly 6 fraise, mortar, pestle, rabble 7 mattock, sadiron, scraper
kitchen: pot, pan 5 corer 6 kettle 7 skillet, spatula
lifting: pry 5 lever, tongs
logging: 6 peavey
nap-raising: 6 teasel
pounding: 4 maul 6 hammer, pestle
printer's: 5 biron, press
shovel-like: 5 scoop, spoon 6 trowel
surgical: 7 scalpel 9 tenaculum
threshing: 5 flail
implicate: 5 imply 7 concern, embroil, involve 11 incriminate
implicit: 5 tacit 8 absolute, complete, inherent 9 suggested 10 unshakable
implied: 5 tacit 6 hinted 10 understood
implore: ask, beg 4 coax, pray 5 crave, plead 6 appeal 7 beseech, entreat, solicit 8 petition 10 supplicate
imply: 4 hint 7 connote, involve, presume, signify, suggest 8 comprise, intimate 9 insinuate, presuppose
impolite: 4 rude 5 bluff, crude, rough 7 ill-bred, uncivil 10 indecorous, ungracious, unmannerly, unpolished 12 discourteous 13 disrespectful
impolitic: 6 unwise 10 indiscreet 11 inexpedient, injudicious 12 undiplomatic
import: 5 sense, value 6 convey, denote 7 betoken, bring in, meaning, signify 8 indicate 9 introduce, substance
tax: 4 duty 6 tariff
importance: 4 rank 5 worth 6 moment, weight 7 account, gravity, stature 8 prestige, standing 9 dimension, influence 11 consequence 13 consideration
to be of: 6 matter
important: 4 dear, high 5 grave, great 6 urgent 7 pompous, serious 8 eventful, material 9 momentous, ponderous 10 noteworthy, preeminent 11 influential, significant 12 considerable 13 consequential
important person: VIP 6 bigwig 7 magnate
importunate: 6 urgent 7 teasing 8 pressing 9 demanding, imploring 10 burdensome, persistent
importune: beg, dun, nag, ply, woo 4 urge 5 plead 6 appeal 7 beseech, entreat, solicit 10 supplicate

impose: 4 levy 5 apply 6 create, slap on 7 command, dictate, inflict, obtrude 8 generate 9 institute
impose upon: 4 dupe 5 cheat 7 exploit, palm off
imposing: big 5 burly, proud 6 august 7 stately 9 grandiose, pyramidal 10 commanding, impressive 11 outstanding
imposition: tax 4 duty, fine, levy 5 fraud, gouge, trick 6 burden 7 penalty 9 deception
impossible: 9 insoluble 12 beyond reason, unattainable 13 impracticable
impost: tax 4 duty, levy task, toll 6 annale, avania, custom, excise, surtax, tariff, weight 7 tribute 8 chaptrel
India: 5 abwab
salt: 7 gabelle
impostor: 4 sham 5 cheat, faker, fraud, phony, quack 8 deceiver 9 charlatan, pretender 10 mountebank
imposture: gag 4 sham 5 cheat, fraud, trick 6 deceit, humbug 8 artifice, delusion, quackery 9 deception, falsehood, imitation 10 imposition, simulacrum 11 counterfeit
impotence: 7 acratia 8 weakness 10 feebleness
impotent: 6 barren 7 sterile 8 helpless 9 powerless 11 ineffective
impound: 5 seize, store 6 freeze 7 collect 11 appropriate
impoverish: 4 ruin 6 beggar, weaken 7 deplete, exhaust
impoverished: 4 poor 5 needy 6 bereft 7 drained 8 bankrupt, indigent 9 destitute
impractical: 9 visionary 10 idealistic, starry-eyed, unfeasible 11 unrealistic
imprecation: 4 oath 5 curse 8 anathema 9 blasphemy, profanity 10 execration 11 deprecation, malediction
impregnable: 4 firm, hard 10 unshakable, unyielding 12 inexpugnable
impregnate: 4 soak 6 charge, infuse, leaven 8 fructify, permeate, saturate 9 fecundate, fertilize
impresario: 7 manager 8 director 9 conductor 12 entrepreneur
impress: fix 4 levy, mark, seal, sway 5 affix, brand, delve, print, stamp 6 affect, enlist 7 engrave, implant, imprint 9 inculcate, influence
impressed: 4 awed 8 affected
impression: 4 dent, dint, idea, mark 5 fancy, print, stamp 6 effect, signet 7 opinion 8 reaction 10 conception
printing: 6 macule
impressionable: 7 plastic 9 sensitive 10 responsive 11 susceptible
impressionist painter: 5 Manet, Monet

6 Renoir 8 Pissarro

impressive: 5 grand 6 august, moving, solemn 8 forcible, imposing, majestic, striking 9 arresting, memorable

imprimatur: 7 license 8 approval, sanction

imprint: fix 4 mark 5 press, stamp 6 effect 7 engrave, impress

imprison: 4 cage, jail 5 limit 6 arrest, commit, detain, immure, intern 7 confine, enclose 8 restrain 11 incarcerate

imprisonment: 6 duress 7 durance 9 captivity 11 confinement

improbable: 5 fishy 8 unlikely

impromptu: 7 offhand 9 extempore 10 off the cuff 11 unrehearsed 14 extemporaneous

improper: ill 4 evil 5 amiss, undue, unfit, wrong 6 unjust, naught 7 illegal, illicit 8 indecent, infra dig, shameful, unseemly 9 incorrect 10 inaccurate, indecorous, indelicate, out of place, unbecoming 12 illegitimate

impropriety: 5 gaffe, shame 7 faux pas 8 solecism 9 barbarism 12 impertinence

improve: 4 grow, help, mend 5 amend, edify, emend 6 better, enrich 7 advance, augment, benefit, correct, enhance, perfect, promote, rectify, retouch 9 cultivate, intensify 10 ameliorate

improvident: 8 prodigal, wasteful 9 negligent 10 thriftless 11 extravagant

improvise: 5 ad-lib 6 devise, invent 7 compose 8 contrive 11 extemporize

music: 4 vamp

imprudent: 4 rash 6 unwary, unwise 7 foolish 8 reckless 10 incautious, indiscreet 11 injudicious 12 shortsighted

impudence: lip 4 gall 5 brass, cheek, folly 8 audacity 9 arrogance, assurance, hardihood, insolence 10 confidence, effrontery 11 presumption 13 shamelessness

impudent: 4 bold, pert, rude 5 brash, sassy, saucy 6 brazen 7 forward 8 insolent 9 barefaced, officious 11 impertinent 13 disrespectful

impugn: 4 deny 5 fight 6 assail, resist 7 gainsay 9 challenge, insinuate 10 contradict

impulse: 4 urge 5 drift, force 6 impact, motive 7 impetus 8 instinct, stimulus 9 incentive 11 instigation

blind: ate

characterized by: 7 sensory

divine: 8 afflatus

traveling: 10 wanderlust

impulsive: 5 quick 6 fitful 8 headlong 9 impellent, impetuous

impure: 4 foul, lewd, vile 5 dirty, gross, mixed 6 coarse, filthy, unholy 7 bastard, defiled, obscene, unclean, vicious 8 indecent, inferior, unchaste 10 unhallowed 11 adulterated, incongruous, unwholesome

impurity: 5 dross, filth, taint 8 foulness 9 pollution 10 corruption 11 contaminant

impute: 4 give 5 count 6 charge, credit, impart, reckon 7 arraign, ascribe 8 consider 9 attribute

in: 4 amid 5 among 6 corner, entree 7 arrived 9 incumbent

a bad way: 4 sick 5 upset 9 on the spot

a row: 4 arow 6 alined, serial 7 aligned

abeyance: 7 pending

abundance: 6 galore, plenty

accordance with: 5 as per 10 pursuant to

addition: too, yet 4 also, more, plus 7 besides, further 8 moreover

advance: 5 ahead 6 before

another direction: 4 away

any case: 8 however 11 nonetheless

any event: 15 notwithstanding

arrears: 5 owing 6 behind 7 overdue

as much: 5 since 7 because

camera: 7 sub rosa 8 secretly 10 furtively

capacity of: qua

case: 4 lest

common: 5 alike

company of: 4 with

concert: 8 together

due course: 4 soon 11 opportunely

Dutch: 9 disgraced 10 out of favor

every way: 5 fully 6 wholly 7 totally 8 entirely 10 completely, thoroughly

excess: too 4 over

existence: 6 extant

fact: 5 truly 6 indeed 7 de facto(L.)

favor of: for, pro

few cases: 6 rarely, seldom

good season: 5 early 6 betime

great need: 7 straits

manner of: ala

name only: 7 nominal 10 supposedly

place of: for 5 stead 7 instead

reality: 8 actually

regard to: 5 anent 10 concerning

same place: 4 ibid

shape: fit 4 neat, trim 5 ready

spite of: 10 regardless

stitches: 6 amused 8 laughing

store: 8 awaiting

that case: 4 then

the case of: 4 in re(L.)

the center of: 4 amid

the interim: 9 meanwhile

the know: hep, hip

the main: 9 generally

the manner of: a la

the mood: 5 eager 7 willing

the raw: 4 nude 10 dishabille

the red: 5 broke 8 bankrupt, strapped

the same period: 15 contemporaneous

the time of: 6 during

this: 6 herein

this way: 4 thus

toto: all 5 whole 8 complete 10 completely

truth: 6 certes, indeed, verily 8 forsooth

what way: how 7 quomodo(L.)

year of: 4 anno

inability: 9 impotence 10 incapacity 12 incompetence

to articulate: 7 anaudia

to chew: 8 amasesis

to comprehend: 11 acatalepsia

to name correctly: 9 paranomia

to read: 6 alexia

to remember: 7 amnesia

to speak: 6 anepia

to stand erect: 7 astasia

to swallow: 7 aphagia

to understand speech: 7 aphasia

inaccessible: 6 closed 11 unreachable 12 unattainable 14 unapproachable

inaccuracy: 5 error 7 mistake

inaccurate: 5 false, wrong 6 faulty 7 inexact 8 specious 9 defective, erroneous, incorrect, off target

Inachus's daughter: Io

inaction: 8 idleness 9 inertness

temporary: 5 pause 6 recess 7 respite

inactive: lax 4 dead, idle, slow 5 heavy, inert, prone, slack, still 6 latent, otiose, supine 7 dormant, passive 8 dilatory, faineant, indolent, sleeping, slothful, sluggish 9 quiescent, recumbent, sedentary 10 unemployed

inadequate: 5 short 6 scanty 7 wanting 8 below par 9 deficient, imperfect 12 insufficient

perilously: 7 Icarian

inadvertence: 10 negligence 12 carelessness, heedlessness 15 thoughtlessness

inadvisable: 4 rash 6 unwise 10 indiscreet

inalienable: 6 sacred 8 absolute, inherent 10 inviolable

inalterable: 9 steadfast 12 unchangeable

inamorata: 8 mistress 10 sweetheart

inane: 5 empty, silly, vapid 6 vacant 7 fatuous, foolish, idiotic, vacuous 8 trifling 9 doddering, frivolous, pointless, senseless, worthless 11 nonsensical 13 characterless

inanimate: 4 dead, dull, flat 5 inert 6 stolid 8 lifeless 10 insensible, spiritless 11 unconscious

inanition: 7 fasting 8 lethargy 9 emptiness

inanity: 7 vacuity 9 emptiness, frivolity, silliness 10 flimsiness, triviality 11 foolishness 13 senselessness

inapposite: 10 irrelevant

inappreciable: 4 thin 7 tenuous 10 impalpable 11 microscopic 13 imperceptible

inappropriate: 5 inapt 8 improper 9 unfitting 10 out of place, unsuitable

inapt: 5 inept 6 clumsy 7 awkward 8 backward 10 amateurish, unsuitable

inarch: 5 graft

inarticulate: shy 4 dumb, mute 7 blurred 10 tongue-tied

inartistic: 9 tasteless

inasmuch as: for 5 since 7 because 11 considering

inattention: 7 neglect 9 disregard 10 negligence

inattentive: lax 6 absent, remiss 8 careless, heedless 9 forgetful, negligent, unheeding, unmindful 10 abstracted, neglectful 11 inadvertent, thoughtless 13 inconsiderate

inaugurate: 4 open 5 begin, start 6 induct, launch 7 install, usher in 8 initiate 9 auspicate, introduce 10 consecrate

inauspicious: bad 4 foul 7 adverse, ominous 8 sinister 12 unpropitious

inauthentic: 5 false 6 mythic, unreal 8 doubtful, spurious 9 uncertain 10 apocryphal, fictitious

inborn desire: 7 conatus

inbreak: 6 inroad 8 invasion 9 incursion

inbred: 6 inborn, innate, native 7 natural 10 congenital

Inca: 9 Atahualpa

clan: 5 ayllu

empire: 4 Peru

god: 4 Inti 5 Choun, Iraya 6 Chasca 9 Uiracocha, Viracocha 10 Pachacamac

king: 9 Atabalipa, Atahualpa

priests: 6 Amauta

ruler's sister-wife: 5 Ccoya

incalculable: 6 untold 8 infinite 9 boundless, countless, uncertain 11 illimitable 12 immeasurable 13 unpredictable

incandescence: 5 glow, heat

incantation: 5 chant, charm, magic, spell 6 carmen(L.) 7 sorcery 11 conjuration, enchantment

incapable: 5 unfit 6 unable 9 untrained 11 inefficient, unqualified

incapacitate: 4 lame 7 cripple, disable 10 disqualify

incarcerate: 4 jail 6 immure, shut up 7 confine 8 imprison

incarnate: 4 embody 8 make real 10 give form to 11 personified

incarnation: 6 avatar, Christ 10 embodiment

of Vishnu: 4 Rama

incase: 5 cover 7 enclose 8 surround

incautious: 4 rash 6 unwary 8 careless,

heedless, reckless 9 impolitic, imprudent, unguarded 10 indiscreet

incendiarism: 5 arson 9 pyromania

incendiary: 7 firebug 8 agitator 10 pyromaniac 12 inflammatory

incense: 5 anger, aroma 6 arouse, enrage, incite 7 perfume, provoke 8 enkindle, irritate

burner: 6 censer 8 thurible

spice: 6 balsam, stacte

incentive: 4 goad, spur 5 spark 6 motive 7 impetus, impulse 8 stimulus 9 influence 10 incitement, inducement 11 provocation 13 consideration, encouragement

inception: 5 start 6 origin 9 beginning 10 initiation 12 commencement

incertitude: 5 doubt 9 suspicion 10 skepticism, insecurity

incessant: 6 steady 7 endless, eternal 8 constant 9 ceaseless, continual 11 everlasting, unremitting

incessantly: 7 forever 11 continually, unceasingly

inch: 5 creep 7 measure 10 move slowly

one-thousandth: mil

three-quarters of: 6 digit

inch along: 9 worm ahead

inches: *forty-five:* ell

four: 4 hand

nine: 4 span

39.37: 5 meter

two and one-quarter: 4 nail

inchmeal: 9 gradually

inchoate: 8 unformed, unshaped 9 incipient 10 disordered, incomplete

incident: 5 event 7 episode 8 accident, casualty, occasion 9 happening 11 contingency

incidental: minor 6 casual 8 episodic 9 accessory, extrinsic, secondary 10 accidental, contingent, fortuitous, occasional 12 adventitious 14 circumstantial

incidentally: 6 obiter 7 apropos 8 by the way

incinerate: 4 burn 7 combust, consume, cremate

incinerator: 7 furnace 9 crematory

incipient: 7 budding, initial, nascent 8 inchoate 9 beginning 10 commencing

incise: cut 4 chop, etch, rase 5 carve 7 engrave

narrowly: 9 laciniate

incision: cut 4 gash, slit 5 notch, slash

incisive: 5 acute, sharp 6 biting 7 cutting, probing 9 sarcastic, trenchant 10 perceptive 11 penetrating

incisor: 6 cutter 9 foretooth

incite: egg, hie 4 abet, fire, goad, move, prod, spur, urge 5 impel 6 arouse, compel, entice, excite, exhort, foment, induce 7 actuate, agitate, animate, com-

move, provoke 8 motivate 9 encourage, instigate, stimulate

incitement: 6 motive 8 stimulus 9 incentive

incivility: 8 rudeness 9 surliness 10 disrespect, effrontery 11 discourtesy 12 churlishness, impertinence 14 unmannerliness

inclemency: 8 asperity

inclement: raw 4 hard, rude 5 harsh, rough 6 severe, stormy 8 rigorous 10 unmerciful

inclination: 4 bent, bias, broo, hang, love, urge, will 5 fancy, slant, slope, taste, tenor, trend 6 affect, animus, ascent, desire, liking 7 descent, leaning 8 fondness, gradient, penchant, tendency 9 acclivity, affection, direction, proneness 10 attachment, proclivity 11 disposition 12 predilection

incline: bow, dip, tip 4 bend, cant, heel, lean, list, ramp, tend, tilt 5 be apt, grade, pitch, shape, slant, slide, slope, trend 6 prefer 7 upgrade

inclined: apt 4 fain, wont 5 alist, atilt, prone 6 biased, likely, minded 7 hanging 8 addicted 11 predisposed

inclose: 5 hem in, pen in 6 encase 7 contain 8 surround

inclosure: ree(Sc.) 4 wall 5 fence 8 sepiment 10 impalement

animal: pen, sty 4 cage, cote, fold 5 hutch, kraal 6 corral

include: 5 cover 6 entail, take in 7 contain, embrace, involve 8 comprise 9 encompass

incognito: 7 unknown 8 disguised 12 unidentified

incoherent: 6 broken 8 rambling 9 illogical 10 disjointed 11 incongruous 12 disconnected, inconsequent, inconsistent

income: 4 gain 5 rente(F.) 6 profit, return 7 produce, revenue 8 interest, proceeds, receipts 9 emolument

incommensurate: 7 unequal 10 dissimilar 12 insufficient, inconsistent 16 disproportionate

incommode: vex 5 annoy 6 molest, plague 7 trouble 8 disquiet 9 disoblige 10 discommode, 13 inconvenience

incomparable: 8 peerless 9 matchless, unequaled, unrivaled 10 surpassing 11 superlative 15 incommeasurable

incompatible: 8 contrary 9 unmixable 10 discordant 11 conflicting, incongruous 12 inharmonious 13 contradictory, unsympathetic 14 irreconcilable

incompetence: 9 inability, unfitness 10 disability

incompetent: 5 inept, unfit 8 helpless 9 incapable, unskilled 10 untalented 11 inefficient, unqualified **12** insufficient

incomplete: **5** rough, short **6** broken, undone **7** divided, lacking, partial, wanting **8** immature, inchoate **9** defective, imperfect **10** unfinished **11** fragmentary

incomprehensible: **8** abstruse **9** graspless **10** fathomless, mysterious, unreadable **11** unthinkable **12** unimaginable **13** inconceivable **14** unintelligible

inconceivable: **7** strange **10** improbable, incredible **11** unthinkable **12** beyond belief

inconclusive: **4** open **9** uncertain, undecided **10** indefinite, up in the air **11** ineffective

incondite: **5** crude **9** unrefined **10** unpolished **11** unorganized

incongruity: **9** inharmony **10** dissonance **11** incoherence **12** disagreement **13** inconsistency **14** unsuitableness

incongruous: **5** alien **6** absurd, impure **8** grotesque **10** discordant, unsuitable **12** disagreeable, inconsistent, inharmonious **13** inappropriate

inconsequential: **5** petty, small **6** paltry **7** trivial **8** picayune, piddling, trifling **10** irrelevant **11** unimportant

inconsiderable: **5** petty **7** trivial **8** careless, unworthy **10** negligible

inconsiderate: **4** rash **6** unkind **8** careless **9** imprudent, negligent **10** incautious, indiscreet, neglectful **11** improvident, injudicious, thoughtless

inconsistent: **6** fickle **8** unstable **9** dissonant **10** capricious, discordant, discrepant, inconstant **11** vacillating **13** contradictory **14** irreconcilable

inconsolable: **11** comfortless, heartbroken **12** disconsolate

inconstant: **6** fickle **7** elusive, erratic **8** disloyal, variable **9** desultory, faithless **10** capricious, changeable **12** inconsistent

incontestable: **4** sure **5** valid **7** certain **10** undeniable **11** indubitable, irrefutable

incontrovertible: **7** certain **10** undeniable

inconvenience: **5** annoy **8** disquiet **9** annoyance **10** discomfort, discommode, uneasiness **11** awkwardness, disturbance **12** discomfiture **13** embarrassment

inconvenient: **7** awkward, unhandy **8** annoying **10** unsuitable **11** troublesome **12** unreasonable

incorporate: mix **4** fuse, join **5** blend, merge, unite **6** absorb, embody **7** combine **9** integrate **10** assimilate

incorporation: **10** absorption **11** combination

incorporeal: **4** airy **8** bodiless **9** asomatous, spiritual, sprightly **10** immaterial **13** unsubstantial

incorrect: bad **5** false, wrong **6** faulty, untrue **9** erroneous

incorrect naming of objects: **9** paranomia

incorrigible: **8** hardened **10** beyond help **11** intractable **12** unmanageable

incorruptible: **4** just, pure **6** honest **7** upright

increase: add, eke, wax **4** eche, gain, grow, rise, rist **5** boost, raise, swell **6** accrue, amount, better, dilate, expand, extend, gather, growth **7** amplify, augment, enhance, enlarge, greaten, inflate, magnify **8** addition, flourish, heighten, multiply **9** accession, advantage, aggravate, expansion, extension, increment, intensify **10** accelerate, accumulate, aggrandize, appreciate **11** aggravation, development, enlargement **12** augmentation **13** amplification **15** intensification

in sound: **9** crescendo

possessions: **5** amass **6** enrich

salary: **5** raise

incredible: **6** absurd **7** awesome **10** astounding, far-fetched, impossible **12** preposterous, unbelievable

incredulous: **7** dubious **8** doubting **9** faithless, skeptical **10** mistrustful, unbelieving

increment: **4** gain **6** growth, income **8** increase **12** augmentation

increscent: **6** waxing **7** growing **9** enlarging **10** increasing

incriminate: **6** accuse **7** impeach, involve **9** implicate

incrust: **4** coat **5** glaze **6** barkle

incubate: **5** brood, hatch **7** develop

incubus: **4** load **5** demon **6** burden, spirit **9** hindrance, nightmare **10** impediment **11** encumbrance

inculcate: **5** infix **6** infuse, instil **7** implant, impress, instill

inculpate: **5** blame **11** incriminate

incumbent: **7** binding **8** occupant **9** overlying **11** leaning upon

incunabula: **7** infancy, origins **10** beginnings **11** first stages

incur: **8** contract **9** encounter

incurable: **8** hopeless **11** irreparable **12** irremediable **13** irretrievable

incurious: **9** apathetic **11** unconcerned, uninquiring **12** uninterested

incursion: **4** rade(Sc.), raid **5** foray **6** inroad **7** assault, descent, hosting **8** invasion **10** dragonnade

incurved: **7** concave

incus: ear **5** ambos, anvil

indebted: **8** beholden **9** obligated

indecency: **8** impurity **9** immodesty, in-

decorum, obscenity 10 indelicacy
indecent: 4 foul 5 gross, nasty 6 coarse, greasy, impure 7 immoral, obscene 8 immodest, improper, unseemly 9 dishonest 10 scurrilous
indecipherable: 9 illegible
indecision: 5 doubt 9 hesitancy 10 hesitation 11 uncertainty, vacillation 12 irresolution
indecorous: 4 rude 6 coarse 7 uncivil 8 immodest, impolite, improper, unseemly 10 unbecoming 11 distasteful
indeed: yea 5 truly 6 really 7 in faith, in truth 8 actually, forsooth, honestly 9 certainly 10 positively
indefatigable: 4 busy 8 tireless, untiring 9 assiduous 10 persistent, unwearying 11 persevering
indefensible: 11 inexcusable 12 unpardonable 13 insupportable
indefinite: 5 loose, vague 7 inexact, neutral 8 aoristic 9 ambiguous, equivocal, uncertain, unlimited 10 inexplicit 12 inconclusive
pronoun: any, one 4 some
indehiscent fruit: uva 5 grape, melon
indelible: 4 fast 5 fixed 9 permanent 10 inerasable 12 ineffaceable, ineradicable, inexpungible
indelicate: raw 5 broad, gross 6 coarse, greasy 7 fulsome 8 impolite, improper, unseemly 9 offensive, unrefined 10 indecorous, unbecoming
indemnification: 10 reparation 11 restitution
indemnify: pay 6 recoup 9 reimburse 10 compensate, recompense
indemnity: 7 amnesty 9 exemption 10 protection 12 compensation
indent: jag 4 dent, gimp 5 chase, delve, inlay, notch, press, stamp, tooth 6 bruise, emboss 7 depress
indentation: bay 4 dent, nick 5 notch 6 dimple, recess 10 impression
indenture: 8 contract 9 agreement, inventory
independence: 7 freedom 10 competency
independent: 4 free 5 proud 9 sovereign, uncoerced 11 self-reliant 12 self-centered, uncontrolled, unrestricted 13 self-governing
independently: 5 apart 10 absolutely
indestructible: 7 durable, lasting 9 permanent 10 inviolable 12 imperishable
indeterminate: 5 vague 7 obscure 8 formless 9 uncertain, unlimited
index: 4 file, list 5 table 7 catalog 9 catalogue, repertory
India: *capital:* 8 New Delhi
  city: 4 Agra 5 Delhi, Patna, Poona, Simla 6 Baroda, Bombay, Guntur, Howrah, Imphal, Indore, Jaipur, Kanpur, Madras, Nagpur, Ranchi 7 Lucknow 8 Calcutta, Shillong, Sholapur 9 Ahmadabad, Allahabad, Bangalore, Hyderabad
  desert: 4 Thar
  ethnic stock: 5 Aryan, Munda 6 Mongol 9 Dravidian
  founder of Mogul dynasty: 5 Baber
  island group: 7 Andaman, Minicoy, Nicobar 8 Amindivi 9 Laccadive
  language: 4 Urdu 5 Hindi, Oriya, Tamil 6 Sindhi, Telugu 7 Bengali, Kannada, Marathi, Punjabi 8 Assamese, Gujarati, Kashmiri 9 Kannarese, Malayalam
  monetary unit: 5 paisa, rupee
  mountain range: 5 Ghats 6 Zaskar 7 Satpura, Siwalik 8 Aravalli, Himalaya 9 Hindu Kush
  mountain pass: 5 Bolan, Gumal 6 Khyber
  native: 5 Hindu
  plateau: 6 Deccan 8 Nilgiris
  port: 6 Bombay, Cochin, Madras, Mandvi, Panaji 8 Calcutta 10 Trivandrum
  river: 4 Beas, Luni, Kosi, Ravi, Sind 5 Bhima, Indus, Rapti, Tapti, Tista 6 Chenab, Ganges, Gomati, Jhelum, Sutlej, Yamuna 7 Cauvery, Krishna, Narmada 8 Ghaghara, Godavari, Mahanadi 9 Indravati 11 Brahmaputra
  state: 5 Assam, Bihar, Delhi 6 Kerala, Orissa, Punjab, Sikkim 7 Gujarat, Haryana, Manipur, Tripura 8 Nagaland 9 Karnataka, Meghalaya, Rajasthan, Tamil Nadu 10 West Bengal
  statesman establishing British control: 5 Clive
Indian (see also **Hindu**): *abuse:* 4 gali 5 galee
  acrobat: nat
  agent: 4 amin 5 ameen
  alphabet: 10 Devanagari
  ambassador: 5 vakil 6 vakeel
  ancestor: 4 Manu 5 Pitri
  animal, ox-like: 4 zebu
  antelope: 6 nilgai, nilgau 7 chikara, nilghai
  apartment: 6 zenana
  army officer: 4 naig, naik 6 naique 7 jemadar, jemidar
  astrologer: 5 joshi
  attorney: 6 muktar
  awning: 9 shamianah
  baby: 4 baba
  bandit: 6 dacoit
  bard: 4 bhat
  bathing place: 4 ghat 5 ghaut
  bazaar: 5 chawk, chowk
  bean: urd
  bear: 4 balu 5 baloo
  bearer: 6 sirdar
  bed: 7 charpai, charpoy
  bed cover: 9 palampore

bill of exchange: 5 hundi
bird: 5 shama 8 avadavat
blight: 4 soka
boat: 7 masoola
bodice: 5 choli
body servant: 6 sirdar
boy: 6 chokra, Mowgli
bracelet: 6 sankha
bread: 7 chapati 8 chapatti
breakfast: 5 hazri
brick: 6 soorki, soorky 7 soorkee
buck: 5 sasin
buffalo: 4 arna 5 arnee
bulbul: 4 kala
butter: ghi 4 ghee
buzzard: 4 tesa
cabinet: 7 almirah
calico: 5 saloo 6 salloo
cannabis: 5 ganja
canoe: 5 tanee
cape: 4 divi
carpet: 4 agra
carriage: 4 ekka 5 bandy, tonga 6 gharri, gharry
cashmere: 5 ulwan
caste: 4 Ahir, Mali 5 Dhobi, Lohar, Singh, Sudra 6 Vaisya 7 Agarwal, Brahmin, Harijan 9 Kshatriya
cavalryman: 5 sowar 6 risala
cedar: 6 deodar
chamber: 4 Kiva 8 Tahkhana
charm: 6 mantra
chief: mir 4 raja, rana 5 rajah 6 sirdar
church: 5 samaj
cigarette: 4 biri
civet: 5 rasse, zibet 6 zibeth
clarinet: 4 been
clerk: 4 babu 5 baboo
cloak: 5 choga
cloth: 7 dhurrie
coin: lac, pie 4 anna, dawm, fels, hoon, lakh, pice, tara 5 abidi, crore, paisa, rupee
college: Tol
colonialist: 5 Clive
cook: 8 bawarchi
corn: zea
coronation: 8 abhiseka
court official: 5 nazir
cowrie: 5 zimbi
crane: 5 sarus
crocodile: 6 gavial, mugger
crop: 4 rabi
cymbal: tal
dagger: 5 katar
dais: 8 chabutra
dance: 6 nautch 7 cantico
dancer: nat 8 bayadere
deer: 4 axis 6 chital, chitra, sambar, sambur
demon: 4 bhut 5 asura
deputy: 5 nabob, nawab

devil tree: 4 dita
dignitary: 5 rajah
dill: 4 soya
disease: 5 agrom
dog: 5 dhole 6 pariah
drama: 6 nataka
drink: 4 soma 6 arrack
drinking pot: 5 lotah
drought: 4 soka
drug: 5 bhang
dust storm: 7 shaitan, sheitan
earth: 5 regur
educated man: 4 babu 6 pundit
educated woman: 7 pundita
elephant: 5 hathi
elephant driver: 6 mahout
epic: 8 Ramayana 11 Mahabharata
falcon: 6 shahin 7 shaheen
fan: 5 punka 6 punkah
father: 4 babu
festival: 4 Holi, mela
fiber: 5 ambary
fig tree: 5 pipal 6 peepul
fish: 5 dorab
flower: 5 lotus
fruit: bel
garment: 4 sari 5 burqa, saree
god: 4 Deva, Yama 5 Shiva
goddess: 4 Amma 5 Amman
gossip: gup
government: 6 sircar
governor: 5 nazim
grass: 4 kusa 5 kusha 6 bhabar, darbha
grinding stone: 4 mano 6 metate
grove: 5 Sarna
guard: 7 daloyet
guide: 7 shikari 8 shikaree
hall: 6 durbar
handkerchief: 7 malabar
harem: 6 zenana
harvest: 4 rabi
hemp: 4 bang 5 bhang, ramie
herb: 6 sesame 7 curcuma, tumeric
hero: 4 Rama
holy: sri 4 shri 5 shree
holy man: 5 fakir, sadhu 6 saddhu
house: 5 mahal 8 bungalow
impost: 5 abwab
instrument: 4 vina 5 sarod, sitar 7 sarinda
intoxicant: 4 soma
jungle: 5 shola
justice: 7 adawlut
knife: dah
laborer: 4 toty 7 totyman
lady: 7 sahibah
law opinion: 5 futwa
leader: 5 Nehru 6 Gandhi
legal claim: hak 4 hakh
leopard, hunting: 7 cheetah
loincloth: 5 dhoti
lord: 4 mian

mahogany: 4 toon 5 toona
mail: dak 4 dawk
mangrove: 5 goran
master: 5 saheb, sahib
matting: 5 tatta
meal: ata 4 atta
measure: ady, dha, gaz, gez, guz, jow, kos, lan, ser 4 byee, coss, dain, dhan, hath, jaob, koss, kunk, moot, para, rati, raik, seit, taun, teng, tola 5 bigha, cahar, covid, crosa, danda, denda, drona, garce, gireh, hasta, krosa, pally, parah, ratti, salay, yojan 6 adhaka, amunam, angula, covido, cudava, cumbha, geerah, lamany, moolum, mushti, palgat, parrah, ropani, tipree, unglee, yojana 7 adoulie, dhanush, gavyuti, khahoon, niranga, prastha, vitasti 8 okthabah
merchant: 5 banya 6 banian 8 soudagur 9 brinjaree
millet: 4 joar
mulberry: 6 alroot
muslin: 5 doria 6 gurrah
narcotic: 4 bang 5 bhang 7 hashish
nonviolence: 6 ahimsa
nurse: 4 amah, ayah, dhai
old money: 5 mohur
ox: 4 zebu
peasant: 4 ryot
pheasant: 5 monal 6 monaul, moonal
pipe: 6 hookah
policeman: 4 peon 5 sepoy
priest: 5 mobed, mulla 6 mullah
prince: 4 bana, rana 5 rajah
princess: 4 rani 5 begum, ranee
property: 4 dhan
queen: 4 rani 5 begum, ranee 8 maharani
rainy season: 6 varsha 7 monsoon
religion: 5 Islam 8 Buddhism, Hinduism
religious sect: 4 Sikh
rice: 4 boro
rubber: 10 caoutchouc
rule: raj
sacred grove: 5 Sarna
saffron: 7 zedoary 8 turmeric
sage: 6 pandit, pundit
servant: 4 maty 6 bearer 10 mussalchee
sheep: 5 urial 6 oorial
shirt: 6 banian
shrine: 6 dagaba, dagoba
silk: 4 muga 6 cabeca
silkworm: eri
snake: 5 krait
soldier: 4 peon 5 sepoy
song: 4 raga
spinning wheel: 6 charka 7 charkha
storm: 5 tufan
sun worshiper: 5 parsi 6 parsee
supreme court: 5 Sudder
Taj Mahal site: 4 Agra
tapir: 8 saladang
tariff: 6 zabeta

tax: 10 chaukidari
teacher: 4 guru 5 akhun, mulla 6 akhund, mullah, pandit, pundit 7 akhoond
tenant: 4 ryot
title: sri 5 sahib 6 sirdar 7 sahibah
tower: 5 minar
tree: bel, dar, lin, sal 4 dita, myxa, shoq, teak 5 anjan, pipal, salai 6 banyan, deodar 7 majagua
tribe: Gor, Jat 4 Bhil 6 Badaga 7 Sherani, Shirani
turban: 8 seerband
vessel: 4 doni 6 shibar
viceroy: 5 nabob, nawab
village: 5 abadi 6 mouzah
weight: moo, pai, ser, vis 4 bhar, dhan, drum, kona, myat, pala, pank, pice, raik, rati, ruay, seer, tank, tola, yava 5 adpao, bahar, candy, catty, hubba, masha, maund, pally, pouah, ratti, retti, tical, ticul, tikal 6 abucco, dhurra, karsha, ruttee 7 chittak, peiktha 8 chittack
wheat: 4 suji 5 sujee
wife's cremation: 6 suttee
wild ox: 4 gaur
wine: 5 shrab
wood: eng, sal 4 toon 5 kokra
Indian (Americas): 6 red man 7 Amerind
American: Aht, Kaw, Oto, Sac, Ute 4 Cree, Dene, Erie, Hopi, Ioni, Iowa, Otoe, Pima, Sauk, Tana, Taos, Yuma, Zuni 5 Banak, Caddo, Coree, Creek, Huron, Kania, Kansa, Keres, Kiowa, Miami, Omaha, Osage, Piute, Sioux, Tinne 6 Abnaki, Apache, Dakota, Kansas, Lenape, Mohave, Mojave, Navaho, Navajo, Nootka, Ojibwa, Oneida, Ottawa, Paiute, Pawnee, Sambos, Seneca, Siwash 7 Abenaki, Arikara, Arapaho, Choctaw, Keresan, Mohegan, Shawnee 8 Apalachi, Cherokee, Cheyenne, Chippewa, Comanche, Delaware, Hitchiti, Illinois, Iroquois, Kickapoo, Onondaga, Pokonchi, Sagamore, Seminole, Shoshone 9 Algonquin, Apalachee, Blackfoot, Chickasaw, Tuscarora, Winnebago 10 Muskhogean 12 Narragansett
blanket: 6 stroud 9 strouding
Bolivia: Uro 4 Iten, Moxo 6 Aymara 10 Chiriguano
Brazil: 5 Bravo 7 Tariana
Canadian: 4 Cree, Dene 5 Tinne 6 Micmac, Tinneh 7 Sanetch 9 Athabasca 10 Athabascan
Caribbean: 4 Yaos 5 Arara, Trios 6 Caribs, Oyanas 7 Akawais, Aparais, Chaymas, Macusis 8 Arawakan
ceremonial chamber: 4 kiva
chief: 6 sachem 8 sagamore
child: 7 papoose

corn: zea 4 samp 5 maize
council: 6 powwow
craft: 5 canoe, kayak 6 dugout
female: 5 squaw 6 mahala, mahaly
festival: 8 potlach
fighter: 5 Boone, Miles 6 Custer
flathead: 7 Chinook
game: 6 canute
Great Spirit: 6 manito
guardian spirit: 5 totem
hatchet: 8 tomahawk
headdress: 7 topknot
hut: 5 hogan, toldo 6 wikiup 7 wickiup
leader: 7 Cochise, Pontiac 8 Geronimo, Powhatan, Tecumseh 10 Crazy Horse, Sitting Bull
lodge: 5 tepee
man: 4 buck 5 brave, chief 6 sannup
meal bread: 8 corncake
memorial post: xat 5 totem
moccasin: pac
money: 6 seawan, wampum 7 seawant
Paraguay: 7 Guarani
peace pipe: 7 calumet
Peru: 4 Ande, Cana, Inca, Inka, Peba, Yutu 5 Boros, Campa, Carib, Panos 6 Aymara, Jibaro, Jiyaro, Kechua, Lamano 7 Quechua
pillar: lat, xat
pony: 6 cayuse
porridge: 4 samp
potato: 4 yamp 9 breadroot
prayer stick: 4 paho
Quechuan: 4 Inca
Rio Grande: Tao
Seminole chief: 7 Osceola
snake dancer: 4 Hopi
sorcery: ob; obe, obi
spirit: 5 totem 7 Manitou
tent: 5 tepee 6 wigwam
Tierra del Fuego: Ona 4 Agni
village: 6 pueblo
wampum: 4 peag 5 peage
warrior: 5 brave
weapon: 8 tomahawk
wigwam: 5 tepee
woman: 5 squaw
Indiana: *capital:* 12 Indianapolis
city: 4 Gary, Peru 5 Paoli 6 Brazil, Delphi, Goshen, Kokomo, Marion, Muncie, Warsaw 7 Hammond, La Porte 8 Danville 9 Fort Wayne, Lafayette, South Bend 10 Evansville, Huntington, Terre Haute, Valparaiso
county: Jay 4 Clay, Knox, Lake, Owen, Rush, Vigo 5 Miami, Posey, Wayne 6 Dubois, Fulton, Ripley, Tipton 7 Daviess, Decatur, Hancock, Spencer, Steuben, Warrick, Whitley
Indian: 5 Miami 7 Shawnee
lake: 7 Wawasee 8 Michigan

river: Eel 4 Ohio 5 White 6 Maumee, Pigeon, Wabash 7 Big Blue, St. Marys 8 Kankakee, St. Joseph 10 Tippecanoe
spa: 9 West Baden 10 French Lick
state bird: 8 cardinal
state flower: 5 peony
state motto: 22 the crossroads of America
state nickname: 7 Hoosier
state tree: 5 tulip
indicate: say 4 bode, cite, mark, read, show 5 argue, augur, point 6 allude, denote, evince, import, reveal 7 bespeak, betoken, connote, declare, display, signify, specify 8 decipher, disclose, evidence, manifest, register 9 designate 10 denominate 12 characterize
indicating: *chemical group:* azo
literal transcript: sic
succession: 7 ordinal
indication: 4 clue, hint, mark, note, omen, sign 5 proof, token, trace 6 augury, signal 7 auspice, symptom 8 argument, evidence 10 intimation 11 designation 13 manifestation
indicative: 10 expressive, suggestive
indicator: 4 dial, hand, sign, vane 5 arrow, clock, gauge, index 6 gnomon, marker 7 indices(pl.), pointer 11 annunciator
indict: 6 accuse, charge 7 impeach
indifference: 6 apathy 8 coldness, lethargy 9 aloofness, disregard 10 negligence 11 disinterest 12 carelessness, heedlessness 13 insensibility
indifferent: 4 cold, cool, soso 5 aloof, blase, stoic 6 casual 7 neutral, uneager 8 careless, listless, lukewarm, mediocre 9 apathetic, Laodicean 10 nonchalant 11 adiaphorous, unconcerned, pococurante 12 nonessential
indigene: 6 native
indigenous: 5 natal 6 inborn, innate, native 7 endemic, natural 8 homeborn, inherent 10 aboriginal 13 autochthonous
indigent: 4 free, poor, void 5 needy 7 lacking, wanting 8 beggarly 9 destitute, penniless 11 impecunious, necessitous
indigestion: 9 dyspepsia
indignant: 5 angry, irate, worth 7 annoyed 8 incensed, wrathful, 11 exasperated
indignation: ire 4 fury 5 anger, wrath 7 disdain 8 contempt 11 displeasure
indignity: cut 5 abuse, wrong 6 insult, slight 7 affront, outrage, 9 injustice 13 disparagement
indigo: 4 anil, blue
artificial source: 6 isatin
bale of: 6 seroon
derivative: 5 indol 6 indole

natural source: 4 anil 7 indican
wild genus: 8 baptisia
indigo bunting: 4 bird 5 finch
indirect: 4 side 5 vague 6 shifty, zigzag 7 devious, evasive, oblique 8 circular, rambling 9 dishonest 10 circuitous, collateral, meandering, misleading, roundabout
expense: 8 overhead
indiscernible: 13 imperceptible 17 indistinguishable
indiscreet: 4 rash 5 hasty, silly 6 unwise 7 foolish, witless 8 careless, heedless 9 impolitic, imprudent 10 ill-advised, incautious 11 injudicious 12 undiscerning 13 inconsiderate
indiscretion: 4 slip 5 folly 10 imprudence
indiscriminate: 5 mixed 6 motley, random 7 jumbled, mingled 8 confused, slap-dash 9 haphazard, hit-or-miss, wholesale 13 heterogeneous
indispensable: 5 basic, vital 7 exigent 9 essential, requisite 10 imperative
indisposed: ill 4 sick 6 ailing, averse, unwell 7 opposed 8 hesitant 9 reluctant 11 disinclined
indisposition: 6 malady 7 ailment, illness, malaise 8 disorder, sickness 9 distemper 10 discomfort, reluctance 12 disaffection 13 unwillingness
indisputable: 4 sure 7 certain, evident 8 positive 10 undeniable 11 indubitable 12 irrefragable 13 incontestable 14 unquestionable 16 incontrovertible
indissoluble: 4 firm 6 stable 7 lasting
indistinct: dim 4 dark, hazy 5 faint, misty, vague 6 cloudy, feeble 7 blurred, obscure, shadowy 9 ambiguous, unrefined 10 indefinite 17 indistinguishable
indite: pen 5 write 7 compose 8 inscribe
individual (see also *person*): one 4 oner, self, sole, unit 6 person, single, unique 7 private, special 8 distinct, selfsame, solitary 9 identical 11 inseparable
of compound animal: 4 zoon 5 zooid
selfish: 6 egoist
smug: 4 prig
individuality: 5 seity 7 oneness 9 character 10 uniqueness 11 distinction, personality 14 indivisibility, inseparability
individually: 9 severally 10 personally 14 distributively
Indo-Aryan: Jat 6 khatri, Rajput
deity: 5 Indra
Indo-European: 4 Lett, Serb, Slav 5 Aryan, Croat, Czech
language: 5 Greek, Indic 6 Baltic, Celtic, Italic, Slavic 7 Iranian 8 Albanian, Germanic, Hellenic

indoctrinate: 5 imbue, teach, tutor 7 educate 8 instruct
indolence: 5 scorn, sloth 7 inertia, languor
indolent: 4 idle, lazy 5 inert 6 otiose, supine 7 dronish 8 inactive, slothful, sluggish
indomitable: 6 dogged 8 resolute 9 steadfast 10 invincible 11 intractable 13 unconquerable
Indonesia: *capital:* 7 Jakarta
city: 5 Medan 6 Kupang, Malang, Manado, Padang 7 Bandung 8 Semarang, Surabaja 9 Palembang, Pontianak, Samarinda, Surakarta
ethnic group: 4 Dyak 5 Malay 6 Papuan 7 Chinese 8 Balinese, Javanese 9 Sundanese
island, island group: Aru, Kai, Obi 4 Bali, Batu, Buru, Leti, Nias, Java, Sawu, Sula 5 Ambon, Babar, Ceram, Dolak, Sumba, Timor, Wetar 6 Bangka, Banjak, Batjan, Borneo, Flores, Lombok, Komodo, Tidore 7 Celebes, Sangihe, Sumatra, Sumbawa, Ternate 8 Moluccas, Tanimbar 9 Halmahera 11 Lesser Sunda
lake: 4 Toba 8 Kerintji
monetary unit: sen 6 rupiah
mountain peak: 4 Lawu, Raja 5 Djaja, Raung 6 Leuser, Slamet
mountain range: 4 Iran 5 Maoke 7 Barisan, Tengger
province: 4 Bali, Java, Riau 5 Atjeh 6 Djambi, Maluku 7 Jakarta, Lampung, Sumatra 8 Bengkulu, Sulawesi (Celebes) 10 Irian Barat, Jogiakarta, Kalimantan (Borneo)
river: 4 Deli, Hari, Musi, Solo 6 Asahan, Barito, Kampar, Kapuas, Liwung 7 Brantas, Kahajan, Kali Mas, Mahakam 9 Indragiri
sea: 4 Bali, Java, Savu 5 Banda, Ceram, Timor 6 Flores 7 Arafura, Celebes, Molucca
strait: 4 Sape 5 Sunda 6 Bangka 7 Berhala, Malacca 8 Karimata, Makassar
volcano: Awu 4 Gede 6 Agung, Semeru 7 Sumbing, Tambora 8 Kerintji
volcanic plateau: 5 Idjen
indorse: See **endorse**
Indra: 5 Sakka, Sakra
dragon: 6 Vritra
elephant: 8 Airavata
father: 8 Tvashtri
food: 4 soma
heaven capital: 9 Amaravati
indubitable: 4 sure 7 assured, certain, evident 8 apparent 10 infallible, undeniable 12 irrefragable 13 incontestable 16 incontrovertible

induce: get 4 draw, lure, urge 5 infer, tempt 6 advise, elicit, persuade 7 actuate 8 conclude, convince, persuade 9 encourage, influence

inducement: 4 bait, lure 5 prize 6 motive, reason 7 incentive, influence 10 enticement 13 consideration

induct: 5 enrol 6 enlist, enroll 7 install 8 initiate 9 introduce 10 inaugurate

inductance unit: 5 henry

inductile: 10 inflexible, unyielding

induction: 8 entrance 9 accession, deduction 10 initiation 12 commencement, introduction

indue: 5 endow 6 assume, clothe, invest 7 furnish

indulge: pet 4 baby, feed 5 favor, humor, spoil 6 coddle, cosset, foster, pamper, please 7 cherish, gratify

in antics: 7 skylark

in fault finding: 5 cavil

in recreation: 4 play

to excess: 7 debauch

indulgence: 5 favor, spree 8 clemency, humoring, lenience 9 tolerance 12 dispensation 13 gratification

indulgent: 4 easy, fond, good, kind, mild 7 lenient 8 tolerant 9 compliant 10 charitable

indurate: 5 inure 6 harden 7 callous, scleral 8 obdurate, stubborn

Indus tribesman: Gor

industrial magnate: 6 tycoon

industrious: 4 busy 6 active 7 zealous 8 diligent, sedulous 9 assiduous 11 painstaking 13 indefatigable

industry: 4 toil, zeal 5 labor, skill 6 energy 8 business, hard work 9 assiduity, diligence, ingenuity 10 occupation

indwell: 6 inhere 9 be present

indwelling: 8 immanent, inherent 9 intrinsic

inebriacy: 11 drunkenness 12 intemperance

inebriate: sot 4 lush, soak 6 boozer 7 tippler, tosspot 8 drunkard 11 intoxicated

ineffable: 11 unspeakable, unutterable 13 indescribable, inexpressible 15 unpronounceable

ineffaceable: 9 indelible 12 ineradicable

ineffectively: 6 feebly 9 uselessly

ineffectual: 4 dead, idle, vain, weak 6 futile 7 useless 8 hopeless, impotent, nugatory 9 fruitless 10 inadequate, unavailing 11 inefficient 13 inefficacious

inefficient: 4 poor 5 inept 8 slipshod 9 unskilled 11 incompetent

inelastic: 5 rigid, stiff 9 unbending 10 inflexible, unyielding

inelegant: 5 crass, crude, rough, 6 coarse, vulgar 7 awkward, blatant 9 graceless

ineluctable: 4 sure 5 fated 6 doomed 7 certain 10 inevitable 11 inescapable

inept: 4 dull, slow 5 unfit 6 absurd, clumsy 7 awkward, foolish 8 backward, unsuited 10 unbecoming, unsuitable 11 incompetent 13 inappropriate

inequal: 5 rough 6 uneven

inequality: 4 odds 5 disparity, diversity 10 unevenness 13 disproportion

inequity: 9 injustice 10 unfairness

ineradicable: 7 lasting 9 indelible, permanent 12 ineffaceable

inerrant: 8 unerring 10 infallible

inerratic: 5 fixed 7 settled 11 established

inert: 4 dead, dull, lazy, slow 5 still 6 stupid, supine, torpid 7 passive 8 immobile, inactive, indolent, lifeless, slothful, sluggish 9 apathetic, lethargic 10 motionless, phlegmatic

inertia: 5 sloth 8 idleness 9 indolence

inesculant: 8 inedible

in essence: 9 basically 11 practically 13 fundamentally

inessential: 9 extrinsic 11 unimportant

inestimable: 9 priceless 10 invaluable 12 incalculable

inevitable: due 5 fated 7 certain, fateful 11 ineluctable, inescapable, unavoidable

inexact: 4 free 5 rough 10 inaccurate

inexhaustible: 8 tireless 9 unfailing, unlimited 13 indefatigable

inexorable: 4 grim 5 stony 6 strict 7 ominous 8 rigorous 9 unbending 10 inflexible, relentless, unyielding 11 unrelenting

inexpedient: 6 unwise 9 impolitic, imprudent 10 indiscreet 11 inadvisable, injudicious 12 unprofitable 15 disadvantageous

inexpensive: 5 cheap 6 frugal 9 low-priced 10 reasonable

inexperienced: raw 5 crude, green, naive, young 6 callow 7 untried 8 inexpert 10 amateurish

inexpert: 5 green 9 unskilled

inexplicable: odd 7 uncanny 8 abstruse, peculiar, puzzling 9 ambiguous, enigmatic 10 mysterious 12 supernatural

inexpressible: 8 nameless 9 ineffable 11 unutterable

inexpressive: 4 dull, dumb 13 unintelligent

infallible: 4 sure 7 certain 8 inerrant, unerring 9 faultless, foolproof, unfailing 11 indubitable

infamous: 4 base 6 bloody, odious 8 shameful 9 nefarious 10 detestable 11 ignominious 12 contemptible

infamy: 5 odium, shame, stain 8 disgrace, dishonor, reproach 10 opprobrium

infancy: 8 babyhood 10 immaturity 11 incunabulum

infant: 4 baby 5 child, minor 7 bambino, chrisom 8 bantling 9 foundling

in law: 5 minor

Indian: 7 papoose

murder: 11 infanticide

infantile 7 babyish, puerile 8 childish 10 sophomoric

infantryman: 6 doggie 7 dogface 8 doughboy

infatuated: mad 4 fond 6 engoue 7 engouee, fatuous 8 enamored, obsessed 9 enamoured 10 captivated 12 enthusiastic

infeasible: 13 impracticable

infect: 5 taint 6 canker, defile, poison 7 pollute 11 contaminate

infection: 6 malady, plague 7 disease, illness

freedom from: 7 asepsis

infectious: 8 catching 9 vitiating 12 demoralizing, pestilential

infelicitous: 7 unhappy 11 unfortunate

infelicity: 6 misery 10 misfortune 11 unhappiness 12 wretchedness

infer: 4 hint 5 drive, educe, guess 6 adduce, deduce, derive, gather 7 surmise 8 conclude, construe

inference: 9 corollary, deduction 10 assumption, conclusion, derivation 11 consequence

inferential: 7 implied 8 illative 9 deductive

inferior: bad 4 base, cull, less, poor 5 baser, below, lower, minor, petit, petty, snide, worst 6 cagmag, common, feeble, impure, lesser, nether 7 cheaper, humbler, unequal 8 mediocre 9 underling 10 inadequate 11 subordinate 12 contemptible 13 insignificant

infernal: 7 avernal, hellish, satanic, stygian 8 all-fired, damnable, devilish, diabolic 9 tartarean 10 acherontic, demoniacal, diabolical

inferno: 4 fire, hell 9 holocaust

infertile: 4 poor 6 barren 7 sterile

infest: 5 beset, haunt 6 plague 7 overrun, 9 swarm over

infidel: 5 pagan 7 atheist, heathen 8 agnostic 10 unbeliever

infiltrate: 4 leak, seep

infinite: 6 Ananta 7 endless, immense 9 boundless, countless, limitless, unlimited 11 everlasting, illimitable, measureless 12 immeasurable, interminable

absorption into: 7 nirvana

infinitesimal: 4 tiny 5 small 6 minute 10 negligible 11 microscopic

infirm: old 4 lame, weak 5 anile, frail 6 cranky, feeble, senile, sickly 7 brittle, failing, fragile 8 decrepit, disabled 9 doddering 10 irresolute 11 debilitated, vacillating

infirmary: 8 hospital

infirmity: 4 vice 7 ailment, disease, failing, frailty 8 debility, sickness, weakness 10 feebleness

infix: 5 inset 6 insert 7 engrave, implant, impress, ingrain, instill 9 inculcate

inflame: 4 boil, fire, goad, heat, stir 5 anger, chafe 6 anneal, arouse, enrage, excite, rankle, redden 7 incense, provoke 8 enkindle, irritate 10 exasperate

with love: 6 enamor

with rage: 6 madden

inflamed: red 5 angry, fiery 6 ablaze

inflammable: 5 fiery 6 ardent, tinder 7 bitumen, piceous 9 excitable, irascible, irritable 10 accendible 11 combustible

inflammation: 4 fire 10 combustion, phlegmasia 13 conflagration

inflate: 4 blow, fill 5 bloat, elate, swell 6 aerify, dilate, emboss, expand, tumefy 7 amplify, distend 8 increase

inflated: 5 wordy 6 turgid 7 bloated, fustian, pompous, swollen 8 expanded 9 bombastic, distended, flatulent, plethoric

inflect: bow 4 bend 5 curve 8 modulate

inflection: 4 tone 6 accent, timbre

of words: 8 paradigm

inflexibility: 8 acampsia

inflexible: 4 dour, hard 5 eager, rigid, stiff, stony 6 strict 7 adamant 8 granitic, obdurate, rigorous 9 immovable, inelastic, unbending 10 implacable, inexorable, relentless 14 uncompromising

inflict: 4 dump 5 wreak 6 impose, unload 7 put upon 10 make suffer, perpetrate

infliction: 7 scourge

inflorescence: 6 raceme

axial circle of: 5 whorl

inflow: 6 influx, inrush

influence: 4 egis, hank, heft, lead, move, pull, rule, sway 5 clout, force, impel 6 affect, aspect, compel, effect, govern, induce, infuse, leaven, motive, weight 7 attract, bearing, command, control, gravity, impress, inspire, mastery 8 hegemony, persuade, pressure, prestige, reaction 9 authority 10 ascendancy, attraction, inducement 13 consideration

by fixed idea: 6 obsess

by reward: 5 bribe

region of: 5 orbit 6 sphere

influence peddling: 8 intrigue, lobbying

influenced: 6 biased 8 affected

easily: 7 pliable

influential: 5 grave 6 potent 8 powerful 9 effective, important, momentous

influenza: flu 5 virus 10 coqueluche

influx: 4 tide 6 inflow 7 arrival, illapse 8 increase 9 inpouring

infold See **enfold**

inform: 4 post, tell 5 train 6 advise, noti-

fy, preach **7** apprise, apprize, educate,
lighten **8** acquaint, instruct **9** advertise
11 communicate

informal: 6 casual, simple **7** relaxed **8** sociable **9** easygoing **10** colloquial **13** unceremonious **14** unconventional

conversation: rap **4** chat

information: 4 data(pl.), dope, news,
word **5** aviso, datum **6** notice **7** tidings
9 direction, knowledge **11** instruction

condensed: **6** digest, precis **7** summary

detailed: **7** dossier

informative: 11 instructive **12** enlight-
ening

informed: hep, hip **4** told, wise **5** aware **6**
posted **7** knowing **8** apprised, notified
11 enlightened

informer: 4 fink, tout **6** canary, gossip,
pigeon, snitch, teller **7** stoolie, tipster **8**
observer, squealer, telltale **9** informant
10 discoverer, talebearer **11** stool-
pigeon

military: spy **5** agent

infraction: 6 breach **8** trespass **9** violation **12** encroachment, infringement
13 transgression

infrequent: 4 rare **6** scarce, seldom,
sparse **8** sporadic, uncommon, unwonted **10** occasional

infringe: 6 refute **7** impinge, intrude **8**
encroach, overstep, trespass **10** contravene

upon: **6** butt in **7** violate

infringement: 6 breach **8** trespass **9** violation **10** infraction **13** transgression
14 nonfulfillment

infuriate: vex **6** enrage, madden **7** outrage

infuscate: 6 darken **7** obscure

infuse: 4 soak **5** imbue, steep **6** aerify **7**
engrain, implant, inspire, instill **9** inculcate, influence, insinuate, introduce

infusion: 7 extract **8** tincture **9** admixture, decoction

malt: **4** wort

Inge play: 6 Picnic **7** Bus Stop

ingeminate: 6 repeat **9** reiterate

ingenious: 4 cute, fine **5** acute, sharp,
smart, witty **6** adroit, clever, crafty,
daedal, gifted, subtle **7** artless, cunning
8 original, skillful, talented **9** daedalian,
deviceful, inventive **11** intelligent, resourceful

ingenuity: art **7** address, cunning **8** artifice **10** adroitness, cleverness **11** origi-
nality **13** inventiveness

ingenuous: 4 naif **5** frank, naive, noble,
plain **6** candid, honest, simple **7** artless,
sincere **8** innocent **9** childlike, guileless
10 unaffected, unreserved **5** unsophisticated

ingenuousness: 7 naivete **9** innocence

ingest: eat **6** absorb **7** consume, swallow

inglorious: 6 shoddy **8** shameful **11** disgraceful, ignominious **12** dishonorable

ingoing: 8 entering

ingot: bar, pig **4** mold

ingrained: 6 imbued, inborn, inbred, innate, native **7** built-in, chronic **8** inherent **9** confirmed **10** congenital, deep-
seated, inveterate

ingratiating: 4 oily **5** sweet **6** genial,
smarmy **7** gushing, likable **8** unctuous
9 appealing **10** flattering, personable
11 sycophantic

ingredient: 7 element **9** component **11**
constituent

baking: **4** alum, soda **5** yeast

cough-syrup: **8** glycerin

facial: **5** cream, rouge **6** powder **7** lanolin
8 lanoline

incense: **6** stacte

ink: **6** tannin

varnish: lax **5** drier, resin, rosin

ingress: 4 adit **5** entry **8** entrance

inhabit: 6 live in, occupy, people, settle **7**
dwell in, possess **8** populate

inhabitant: 6 inmate, native, tenant **7**
citizen, denizen, dweller **8** resident

inhale: 5 sniff **7** respire **9** breathe in

inharmonious: 6 absurd, atonal **7** jarring
9 dissonant, unmusical **10** discordant
11 conflicting **12** antagonistic

inherent: 5 basic **6** inborn, innate **7** in-
fixed **8** immanent **9** essential, ingrained, intrinsic **10** congenital, deep-
rooted, indwelling

inheritable: 10 hereditary

inheritance: 6 estate, legacy **7** bequest **8**
heredity, heritage **9** patrimony **10**
birthright

by first-born: **13** primogeniture

portion: **8** legitime

restricted: **10** entailment

Scotch law: **5** annat

seizer: **6** abator

inherited: 6 inborn, native **7** connate,
natural **10** handed down

inheritor: 4 heir **7** heiress, legatee

inhibit: ban, bar **4** curb **5** check **6** forbid,
hinder **8** prohibit, restrain **9** interdict

inhuman: 4 fell **5** cruel **6** brutal, savage **7**
beastly, bestial, brutish **8** devilish **9**
barbarous, bloodless, ferocious **10** diabolical

inhumanity: 7 cruelty **9** barbarity

inhume: 4 bury **5** inter **6** entomb **7** deposit

inimical: 6 averse, frosty **7** hostile **8** contrary **9** repugnant **10** unfriendly **11** unfavorable

iniquitous: bad, ill **5** wrong **6** sinful, unjust, wicked **9** nefarious

iniquity: sin **4** evil, vice **5** crime, guilt **8**

darkness 9 injustice 10 wickedness
initial: 5 first 6 letter, maiden 7 opening 8 earliest, monogram, original 9 beginning, incipient 10 commencing, elementary
initial payment: 4 ante 7 deposit
initiate: 4 head, open 5 admit, begin, enrol, found, start 6 enroll, induct, launch 7 install, kick off 8 commence 9 introduce, originate 10 inaugurate
initiation: 7 baptism 8 entrance 9 admission, beginning, induction 10 admittance, 12 commencement
initiative: 6 energy 8 aptitude, gumption 9 first move 10 creativity, enterprise, get-up-and-go, leadership
inject: put 4 pump 5 force 6 insert, instill 11 interpolate
injection: 4 hypo 5 enema
injudicious: 6 unwise 9 impolitic, imprudent 10 indiscreet 11 inexpedient
injunction: 4 hest, writ 5 order 6 behest, charge 7 mandate, precept, process 9 direction
injure: mar 4 harm, hurt, maim 5 abuse, spoil, sully, wound, wrong 6 impair, insult 7 affront, cripple 8 aggrieve, maltreat 9 disfigure
　by bruising: 7 contuse
　by scorching: 4 burn, char 5 singe
injury: cut, ill, 4 bane, blow, evil, harm, hurt, loss, risk, stab 5 wound, wrong 6 damage, lesion, trauma 7 scratch 8 hardship 9 contusion, detriment, injustice 10 affliction, aggression, disservice, impairment, laceration, mutilation
　causing: 7 malefic 9 traumatic
　sense of: 7 umbrage
injustice: 5 wrong 6 injury 8 hardship, inequity, iniquity 9 grievance 10 imposition, unfairness
ink: 4 sign 9 autograph 13 fish secretion
ink fish: 5 squid 6 cuttle
inkling: 4 hint, idea 5 rumor, scent 6 desire, report 7 glimpse 10 glimmering, intimation 11 inclination
inky: 4 dark 5 black 9 cimmerian
inland: 8 domestic, interior
　sea: 4 Aral 5 Black
inlay: 5 adorn, couch, set in 6 insert 7 enchase 8 ornament 9 marquetry
　work: 6 mosaic 9 certosina, certosino, champleve
inlet: arm, bay, cay, ria 4 cove, gulf, rias(pl.), slew, sloo, slue 5 admit, bayou, bight, creek, fiord, firth, fjord, inlay, sound 6 estero, slough, strait 7 estuary, narrows, orifice, passage 8 entrance
　coastline: 5 bight 6 strait
in loco parentis: 8 guardian
inmate: 5 guest, lifer 6 termer 8 domestic,

occupant, prisoner 10 inhabitant
harem: oda
inmost: 8 intimate 10 most secret
inn: pub 4 host, khan 5 fonda, hotel, lodge, serai, tambo, venta 6 fonduk, hostel, imaret, tavern 7 albergo, auberge, boliche, fondaca, fondouk, fonduck, hospice 8 choultry, gasthaus, hostelry, wayhouse 11 caravansary
innamorato(It.): 5 lover 10 sweetheart
innards: 4 guts 7 viscera 8 entrails
innate: 4 born 6 inborn, inbred, native 7 connate, natural 8 inherent 9 ingrained, intrinsic 10 congenital, hereditary 11 instinctive 14 constitutional
inner: ben 5 ental 6 inside, inward 8 esoteric, interior, internal
Innisfail: 4 Eire, Erin 7 Ireland
innkeeper: 4 host 8 boniface, hosteler, publican
innocence: 6 purity 7 naivete 9 ignorance 11 sinlessness 13 guiltlessness
　symbol of: 7 diamond
innocent: 4 free, naif 5 naive 6 chaste, dovish, simple 7 artless, upright 9 blameless, childlike, guileless, guiltless, ingenuous, stainless 10 immaculate, unblamable 12 simpleminded 15 unsophisticated
　Hebrew: 8 zaccheus 9 zacchaeus
innocent one: 4 babe, lamb 5 child 6 infant
innocuous: 8 harmless, innocent 9 innoxious 11 inoffensive, unoffending
innominate: 7 unnamed 9 anonymous
innovation: 6 change 7 novelty 9 departure 10 new wrinkle
innuendo: 4 clue, hint, slur 8 allusion 10 intimation 11 implication, insinuation
innumerable: 4 many 6 legion, myriad
Ino's grandfather: 6 Agenor
inoculate: 5 imbue 6 infect 7 implant 9 immunize
inoffensive: 8 harmless 9 innocuous
inoperative: 4 dead, idle 10 out of order, unworkable
inopportune: bad 8 ill-timed, untimely 10 malapropos 11 importunate 12 unseasonable, inconvenient
inorb: 8 encircle
inordinate: 5 undue 6 wanton 7 extreme, surplus 8 needless, overmuch 9 excessive 10 disorderly, immoderate 11 unregulated 12 unrestrained
inorganic: 7 mineral
in perpetuum: 4 ever 6 always 7 forever 9 eternally
inquest: 6 search 7 inquiry 11 examination 13 investigation
　official: 7 coroner
inquire: ask, esk(Sc.) 4 quiz, seek 5 query 6 demand, search 7 dig into 8 question

11 interrogate, investigate

inquiring: 7 curious

inquiry: 4 hunt 5 audit, check, probe, query 7 inquest 8 question, research, scrutiny 11 examination 13 investigation

for lost goods: 6 tracer

inquisition: 5 trial 8 grilling, tribunal 11 third-degree

inquisitive: 4 nosy 5 nosey 6 prying 7 curious 8 meddling 10 meddlesome

in re(L.): 5 about 9 regarding 10 concerning

inroad: 4 raid 5 foray 6 breach 8 invasion 9 incursion, irruption 12 encroachment

ins and outs: 5 ropes 7 details 11 particulars

insane: mad 4 daft, luny 5 balmy, crazy, daffy, loony, manic 6 cranky, crazed 7 frantic, furious 8 bughouse, demented, deranged, distract, frenetic 9 delirious, phrenetic, psychotic

house for: 6 asylum, bedlam 10 booby hatch, sanitarium

to make: 6 dement 7 derange

insanity: 5 folie, mania 6 frenzy, lunacy 7 madness, vesania 8 delirium, dementia 9 psychosis 10 aberration, alienation 11 derangement

temporary: 7 amentia

insatiable: 6 greedy 9 voracious 11 unsatisfied

inscribe, enscribe: 4 etch 5 delve, enter, stamp, write 6 blazon, enroll, indite, scroll 7 ascribe, engrave 8 dedicate, describe 9 character 12 characterize

inscribed: 8 lettered 9 dedicated

on stone: 10 lapidarian

with Teutonic characters: 5 runed

inscription: 6 legend 7 epigram, writing 8 epigraph

appropriate: 5 motto

end of book: 8 colophon

explanatory: 6 tituli(pl.) 7 titulus

on coins: 5 sigla

tomb: 7 epitaph

inscrutable: 6 secret 10 mysterious 12 impenetrable, inexplorable, unfathomable 16 incomprehensible

insect: ant, bee, bug, fly 4 flea, gnat, lice, mite, moth, tick, wasp 5 emmet, roach 6 beetle, earwig, mantis, spider, weevil 7 cricket, katydid, termite 9 bumblebee, centipede

adult: 6 imago

antenna: 4 palp 6 feeler

back surface: 5 notum

chirping: 7 cricket

destructive: 5 scale 7 termite 8 predator

dipterous: 8 mosquito

eating bird: 5 pewee, vireo 8 redstart 10 flycatcher

eye: 6 ocelli(pl.), stemma 7 ocellus

female: 4 gyne

genus of: 4 nepa 5 emesa 6 acarus, cicada, cicala, mantis, termes

hard covering: 6 chitin

hymenopterous: ant, bee 4 wasp 6 sawfly 7 gallfly 10 ichneumons

immature: 4 grub, pupa 5 larva 6 larvae(pl.) 9 chrysalis 11 caterpillar

long-legged: 5 emesa

molting of: 7 ecdysis

order: 7 diptera

organ: 8 plantula 9 plantulae(pl.)

parasitic: 4 lice 5 louse

part of: 5 chirr, media, palps 7 antenna 8 pronotum, tentacle

pert. to: 11 entomologic

plate: 6 scutum

repellant: 4 deet

resin: lac

science: 10 entomology

secretion: lac

small: 4 flea, gnat, mite 5 aphid, aphis, micro, midge 6 garfly 8 bullhead

social: ant, bee 5 emmet

stage: 4 pupa 5 imago, larva 6 instar 9 chrysalis

stinging: ant, bee 4 wasp 6 hornet 7 sciniph 12 yellowjacket

trap: web

winged: bee 4 wasp 6 hornet 7 termite 8 mosquito 12 yellowjacket

wingless: 4 flea 6 aptera(pl.)

insecticide: DDT 6 endrin, ethion 9 hellebore, Malathion, parathion 10 endosulfan

insecure: 5 loose, risky, shaky 6 infirm, unsafe, unsure 7 rickety, unsound 8 doubtful, perilous, unstable 9 dangerous, hazardous 10 precarious

inseminate: sow 7 implant, instill 9 fertilize 10 impregnate

insensate: 4 surd 5 blind, harsh 6 brutal, stupid 7 brutish, fatuous, foolish 9 senseless, unfeeling, untouched 10 insensible

insensibility: 4 coma 9 apathy, torpor, trance 8 lethargy 9 analgesia 10 anesthesia 11 insentience

insensible: 4 dull 7 unaware 8 obdurate 9 inanimate, insensate, unfeeling 10 insentient 11 indifferent, unconscious 13 imperceptible

insensitive: 4 cold, dead, numb 5 blase 7 callous 11 unconcerned

insert: 5 foist, infix, inlay, inset 9 interpose 11 intercalate, interpolate

for growth: 5 graft 7 engraft

triangular: 4 gore 5 wedge

insertion: 5 inset

kind of: 5 shinn 11 parenthesis 13 interpolation, intercalation

of sound in word: 10 epenthesis

inset: 4 gore 5 imbed, infix, panel 6 gusset, insert 7 appoint, engraft, implant 9 insertion

inside: 5 inner 6 lining, within 7 private 8 interior

toward: 5 entad 6 inward

track: 9 advantage

inside out: 6 everted 8 reversed 10 completely, thoroughly

insidious: 4 deep 6 covert 7 cunning 8 guileful 9 concealed, deceitful 10 fallacious, fraudulent 11 disaffected, treacherous

insight: ken 6 acumen, wisdom 9 intuition 10 perception 11 discernment 12 clairvoyance

insignia: 4 mark 5 badge 6 emblem

kind of: tie 7 caducei(pl.), regalia 8 caduceus

insignificance: 10 effacement

insignificant: 4 puny 5 dinky, petit, petty 6 paltry 7 trivial 8 inferior, smallfry, trifling 9 minuscule, senseless 10 immaterial 11 minor-league 12 unimportant

part: bit 4 iota 5 tithe 8 molehill

insincere: 5 false 7 feigned 8 two-faced 9 deceitful, deceptive 12 hypocritical

insinuate: 4 hint 5 imply 6 allude, infuse 7 implant, instill 9 introduce, penetrate 10 ingratiate, serpentine

insinuation: 4 hint 8 innuendo

insipid: dry 4 dead, dull, flat, pale, tame 5 bland, prosy, stale, tepid, vapid, waugh 6 jejune 7 prosaic 8 lifeless 9 pointless, tasteless 10 monotonous, spiritless, unanimated 13 uninteresting

insist: 4 aver 5 claim 6 assert, demand 7 contend 8 maintain 9 reiterate

insistence: 7 command, urgency

insolence: 4 gall 5 nerve 6 insult 8 audacity, contempt 9 arrogance, contumely, impudence 10 effrontery 11 haughtiness, presumption 12 impertinence

insolent: 4 pert, rude 5 saucy 6 brazen 7 abusive, defiant 8 arrogant, impudent 9 audacious, hubristic 11 overbearing 12 contemptuous, contumelious

insolvency: 7 failure 10 bankruptcy

insolvent: 5 broke 6 busted, ruined 8 bankrupt 9 destitute 12 impoverished

insomnia: 7 ahypnia 8 agrypnia

insouciant: 4 calm 8 carefree, heedless 10 unbothered 11 indifferent, unconcerned

inspect: 4 scan, view 5 check, study, 6 peruse 7 examine, observe 8 consider, look over 9 supervise 10 scrutinize

inspection: 4 oyer 6 parade, review 8 scrutiny 11 examination

inspiration: 4 spur 5 flash 6 motive, vision 7 impulse 8 afflatus, stimulus 9 incentive, influence 10 brainstorm

poetic: 7 pierian

pretender to: 6 eolist

inspire: 4 fire, move, stir 5 exalt, imbue 6 arouse, excite, inhale, prompt 7 actuate, animate, enliven, implant 8 motivate 9 encourage, influence, stimulate

inspirit (see also **inspire**): 4 stir 5 cheer, elate, rouse 7 animate, cherish, comfort, hearten, quicken 10 invigorate

inspissate: 7 thicken 8 condense 10 incrassate

instability: 8 fluidity 9 shakiness 10 insecurity 12 irresolution, unsteadiness 13 changeability

install: lay 4 seat, vest 6 induct, invest, locate 7 instate 8 initiate 9 establish 10 inaugurate, set in place

installation: 11 investiture

instance: 4 case, cite, time 7 example, request, symptom 8 occasion 9 exemplify 10 suggestion 12 illustration

instancy: 7 urgency 8 pressure 9 imminence 10 insistence

instant: 4 urge 5 clink, flash, gliff, glisk, trice 6 breath, minute, moment, second, urgent 7 solicit 8 pressing 9 handwhile, immediate 11 importunate

instantly: now 4 just 8 directly

instate: set 6 bestow, confer, 7 install 8 initiate 9 establish 10 inaugurate

instead: 4 else 6 in lieu 10 equivalent, substitute

of: for

instigate: egg 4 abet, goad, move, prod, sick, spur, urge 5 impel 6 compel, excite, foment, incite, prompt, suborn 7 provoke 8 motivate 9 encourage, stimulate

instigator: 6 author 10 ringleader

instill: 5 imbue, infix 6 impart, infuse 7 implant, pervade 9 inculcate, insinuate

instinct: 4 bent, gift, urge 5 knack 7 impulse 8 aptitude

instinctive: 6 innate 7 natural 8 inherent, original 9 automatic, intuitive 11 involuntary, spontaneous

institute: 5 begin, erect, found 6 asylum, ordain 7 academy 8 initiate, organize 9 establish, originate 10 inaugurate

institution: 6 clinic, school 7 academy, college 8 hospital, seminary 10 university 12 constitution

instruct: 4 lead, show 5 breed, coach, drill, edify, guide, teach, train, tutor 6 direct, inform, preach 7 counsel, educate 8 document 9 enlighten 10 discipline 12 indoctrinate

instruction: 6 advice, charge, lesson 7 precept 8 teaching, training, tutelage 9 education, knowledge, schooling 10 directions

art of: 8 pedagogy

period: 4 term, year 7 quarter, session 8

semester 9 trimester

instructive: 8 didactic, sermonic

instructor: don 5 coach, tutor 6 docent, mentor 7 acharya, teacher, trainer 9 preceptor, professor

instrument (see also **apparatus, device, tool**): 4 deed, writ 5 agent, means 6 medium 7 utensil, writing 9 appliance, implement 11 contrivance

altitude: aba 9 altimeter 10 altazimuth

board: 5 panel

calculating: 6 abacus 8 computer 9 slide rule

copying: 10 hectograph

cutting: 5 knife, razor 6 scythe, shears, sickle 8 scissors

for studying motion: 11 stroboscope

musical: See **musical instrument**

percussion: 12 Glockenspiel

sacred: 4 urim

sealed: 4 deed 5 crypt, vault 6 escrow

surveying: 7 transit 10 theodolite

instrumental: useful 7 helpful 9 conducive, effective 12 of assistance

instrumentalist: 6 oboist 7 flutist, harpist, pianist 8 flautist, minstrel 9 cornetist, violinist 10 trombonist

instrumentality: 5 means 6 agency, medium

insubordinate: 6 unruly 7 defiant, riotous 8 mutinous, perverse 9 fractious, seditious 10 headstrong, rebellious, refractory, unyielding 11 disobedient, intractable 12 contumacious, recalcitrant

insubstantial: 4 airy, thin 5 frail 6 flimsy 10 intangible 12 apparitional

insufferable: 7 hateful, painful 10 unbearable 11 intolerable

insufficient: 4 bare, poor 5 short 6 feeble, scanty, scarce 7 unequal, wanting 9 deficient 10 inadequate 14 incommensurate

insular: 6 biased, narrow 8 isolated 9 parochial, separated 10 provincial

insulate: 6 enisle 7 isolate 9 segregate 10 quarantine

material to: 4 cork 6 Kerite, rubber

insulator: 4 tape 5 cleat 12 nonconductor

insult: 4 slap, slur 5 abuse, flout, scorn, shame 6 offend, revile 7 affront, offense, outrage 9 contumely, indignity, insolence

insulting: 4 rude 8 arrogant, derisive 9 offensive 10 scurrilous 11 opprobrious 12 contumelious, vituperative

insurance: 8 guaranty, warranty 9 assurance 10 protection

computer: 7 actuary 8 adjuster

payee: 11 beneficiary

system: 7 tontine

insurgent (see also **insubordinate**): 5 rebel 8 maverick, mutinous, revolter 9 dissident 10 rebellious

insurmountable: 8 hopeless, too great 10 impassable, invincible 11 insuperable 13 unconquerable

insurrection: 6 mutiny, revolt 8 outbreak, uprising 9 rebellion

insusceptible: 6 immune 9 unfeeling

intact: 5 sound, whole 8 complete, unbroken 9 undefiled, undivided, uninjured, untouched 10 unimpaired

intaglio: cut, gem 9 engraving

intake: net 4 gain, gate 6 profit 8 receipts 11 contraction

intangible: 5 vague 10 immaterial, impalpable 13 imperceptible, unsubstantial

integer: 5 digit 6 figure, number 7 numeral

integral: 4 full 5 basic, total, whole 8 complete 9 component, essential, requisite

integrate: mix 4 join 5 unite 7 combine

integrity: 7 honesty, probity 9 chariness, constancy

integument: 4 aril, coat, skin 5 shell, testa 7 cuticle 8 covering, envelope

intellect: wit 4 mind 5 brain 6 genius, reason 9 mentality 12 intelligence

limited in: 8 retarded

intellection: 6 notion 9 cognition, knowledge 12 apprehension 13 comprehension, understanding

intellectual: 5 ideal 6 brainy, mental, noetic 7 egghead, learned 8 highbrow 9 scholarly

intelligence: 4 chit, mind, news, word 5 sense 6 esprit, notice, wisdom 8 learning 13 understanding

used alone: 6 noesis

without: 4 dull 5 inane 6 stupid

intelligence test deviser: 5 Binet, Simon

intelligencer: spy 9 informant, messenger 10 newsmonger

intelligent: 5 acute, aware, smart 6 bright, mental 7 knowing 8 rational, sensible 9 cognizant 13 understanding

intelligentsia: 8 thinkers 13 intellectuals

intelligible: 5 clear, lucid, plain 10 conceptual 11 perspicuous 14 comprehensible

intemperate: 6 severe 7 extreme, violent 9 excessive, inclement 10 immoderate, inordinate 12 ungovernable, unrestrained

intend: aim 4 mean, plan 6 design 7 destine, propose 9 calculate 10 have in mind 11 contemplate

intended: 5 meant 6 fiance 7 fiancee

intense: hot 4 deep, hard, keen 5 acute, great, heavy, vivid 6 ardent, severe, strong 7 chronic, earnest, extreme, fervent, violent, zealous 8 grievous, powerful, strained, vehement 9 assiduous, excessive, strenuous 11 far-reaching

intensify: 5 exalt 6 deepen 7 enhance, magnify, quicken, sharpen 8 condense, heighten, increase 9 aggravate 10 accentuate 11 concentrate

intensity: 5 depth, force, power, vigor 6 energy, fervor 7 potency 8 severity, strength

of color: 6 chroma

intent: aim 4 rapt 5 eager, fixed, tense 6 design, effect 7 earnest, meaning, purpose 8 absorbed, diligent, sedulous 9 attentive, engrossed, steadfast 10 determined

intention: aim, end 4 goal, plan, will 6 animus, design, motive, object 7 meaning, purpose 11 designation 13 contemplation

intentional: 5 meant 7 planned 8 designed 9 voluntary 10 deliberate 12 premeditated

inter: 4 bury 6 entomb, inhume

interagent: 6 medium 12 intermediary

intercalary month: 4 Adar 6 Veadar

intercalate: 7 insert 9 insinuate, interpose 11 interpolate

intercede: 6 step in 7 mediate 9 arbitrate, interpose, intervene

intercept: nab 4 grab, stop 5 block, catch, seize 7 head off 9 forestall, interrupt

intercessor: 8 advocate, mediator

interchange: 4 vary 7 commute, permute 8 converse, exchange 9 alternate 10 transposal 11 reciprocate 12 conversation

interchangeable: 10 reversible 11 convertible

interconnection: 5 nexus 8 junction

intercourse: 7 dealing 8 business, commerce, converse 9 communion, 10 connection, fellowship 12 conversation 13 communication

interdict: ban 4 veto 5 debar, fence 6 forbid 7 inhibit 8 prohibit 9 proscribe

interdiction: 4 tabu 5 taboo

interest: 4 good, part 5 hobby, share, stake 6 behalf, engage, excite, notice 7 benefit, concern, involve, service, welfare 8 sympathy 9 advantage, attention, fascinate

exorbitant: 5 usury

in law: 5 right, title

lose: 4 tire

rate: 5 yield

without: 6 jejune 9 apathetic

interested: 4 rapt 6 caring

interfere: 5 barge, clash 6 meddle, tamper 7 collide, disturb, intrude 8 obstruct, sabotage 9 interpose, intervene

interference: 6 static

interim: 5 break 6 hiatus 7 stopgap 8 interval, meantime 9 interlude 10 pro tempore 11 provisional

interior: ben 5 ental, inner 6 inland, inside 8 midlands 9 heartland

interject: 5 put in 6 insert, slip in 9 introduce

interjection: boo, hic, rah 4 ahem, alas, amen, egad, ouch, well 6 aroint 7 criminy 11 exclamation

interlace: mat 5 braid, twine, weave 7 entwine 9 interfret, interlink 10 intertwine, interweave 11 interpolate

interlaced: 7 complex

interlock: 4 knit 5 unite 6 clench, engage 9 interlace 11 interrelate

interlocution: 12 conversation 13 communication

interlocutory: 9 mediatory 12 intermediate 14 conversational

interlope: 6 horn in, meddle 7 intrude 8 trespass 9 interfere

interlude: 4 lull 5 let up, pause 6 recess 7 respite 8 breather, entr'acte, interval

intermediary: 5 agent 6 medium 7 referee 8 mediator 9 go-between, middleman 10 ambassador, interagent

intermediate: 5 mense 6 median, middle 7 average, between 8 middling, moderate 10 interposed 11 intervening

interminable: 7 endless, eternal 8 infinite, timeless, unending 9 boundless, limitless, unlimited 10 long-winded

interminably: 7 forever

intermingle: 8 intermix 9 socialize 10 infiltrate

intermission: 4 rest, stop 5 dwell, pause 6 recess 7 respite 8 entr'acte, vacation 9 cessation 10 suspension 13 interposition 14 discontinuance

intermittent: 6 broken, fitful 8 on and off, periodic, sporadic 9 recurrent, spasmodic 10 occasional 11 alternating, interrupted

intermix: 6 mingle 10 interweave

intern: 6 detain, doctor 7 confine, impound, trainee 8 imprison

internal: 5 inner 6 inward, mental 8 domestic, enclosed 9 spiritual

combustion engine part: 5 timer

international: 9 universal, world-wide

international organization: OAS, WHO 4 NATO 5 SEATO 6 UNESCO, UNICEF

internecine: 6 deadly

interpolate: 5 alter 6 insert 9 introduce 11 intercalate

interpose: 6 thrust 7 intrude, mediate 9 intercede, interfere, intervene

interpret: 4 read 6 decode, define, render 7 explain, expound 8 construe 9 elucidate, explicate, make clear, translate 10 blackmail, paraphrase

interpretation: 5 sense 7 meaning, version 8 exegesis 9 rendering 10 conception 11 translation 12 construction

mystical: 7 anagoge

science of: 12 hermeneutics

interpretive: 10 expository 11 explanatory, hermeneutic 12 constructive

interrogate: ask 4 quiz 5 grill, query 7 examine, inquire 8 question

interrogation: 5 probe 7 inquest 9 catechism

interrogation mark: 7 eroteme

interrogative: how, who, why 4 what, when 5 where 8 question

interrupt: 4 stop 5 break, burst, cease, check, cut in 6 arrest, hinder, thwart 7 disturb, suspend 8 obstruct 9 intercept 11 discontinue

interruption: gap 5 pause 6 breach, hiatus 7 caesura 9 cessation 12 intermission

intersect: cut 4 meet 5 cross 6 divide, pierce 9 decussate

intersection: 6 corner 7 crossing, junction 10 crossroads

interstice: 4 mesh, pore, seam 5 chink, crack, space 6 areola, areole, cranny 7 crevice 8 interval

pert. to: 7 areolar

intertwine: 4 knit, lace 5 twist 9 interlace 10 intertwist

interval: gap 4 rest, span 5 break, space 6 breach, hiatus, recess 7 caesura, respite 8 entracte 9 cessation 12 intermission

at irregular: 12 sporadically

musical: 5 fifth, ninth, sixth, tenth, third 6 fourth, octave, second 7 seventh

intervene: 7 mediate 9 intercede, interpose

intervening: 5 mesne(law) 12 intermediate

interview: see 7 consult, hearing 8 audience, question 9 encounter 10 conference 12 consultation

intervolve: 4 coil, roll, wind 5 twist

interweave: mat 5 braid, plait 6 splice 8 intermix 9 interlace

intestinal fortitude: 4 grit, guts 5 nerve, pluck, spunk 7 courage 8 backbone

intimate: pal 4 boon, chum, dear, hint, homy, near 5 bosom, buddy, close, crony, homey, imply 6 allude, chummy, homely, inmost, secret 7 signify, suggest 8 announce, domestic, familiar, friendly, informal, personal 9 associate, confidant 11 contubernal 12 acquaintance, confidential

intimation: cue 4 clue, hint, wind 5 scent 6 notice 7 inkling 10 suggestion 11 declaration

intimidate: awe, cow 5 abash, bully, daunt, deter, scare 6 hector 7 overawe, terrify 8 browbeat, dispirit, frighten 9 blackmail, terrorize

into: 4 unto 5 among, until 6 inside

intolerance: 4 bias 6 racism 9 misoneism 10 chauvinism

intolerant: 6 narrow, stuffy 7 bigoted 8 dogmatic 9 hidebound, illiberal, impatient 10 prejudiced

intonation: 5 pitch, sound 7 sonance

intonational: 7 tonetic

intone: 4 cant, sing 5 chant 8 modulate 10 cantillate

in toto: 8 as a whole 10 altogether

intoxicant: (see also **alcoholic drink, liquor):** gin, rum 4 wine 5 booze, drink 6 liquor 7 alcohol, whiskey

intoxicated: 4 high 5 drunk, tight, tipsy 6 boiled, soused, stewed, stoned, zonked 7 excited 8 besotted, glorious, polluted, squiffed 9 crapulous 10 inebriated

intoxicating: 5 heady 12 exhilarating

intracellular: 8 histonal

intractable: 6 mulish, unruly 7 willful 8 indocile, mutinous, obdurate, perverse, stubborn 9 obstinate 10 headstrong, refractory 11 disobedient, unteachable 12 contumacious, ungovernable 14 uncontrollable

intrada: 7 prelude 12 introduction

intranquillity: ado 12 restlessness

intransigent: 8 obdurate 9 unmovable 10 iron-willed, unyielding 14 irreconcilable, uncompromising

intrepid: 4 bold 5 brave, hardy, nervy 6 daring, heroic 7 assured, doughty, gallant, valiant 8 fearless, resolute, valorous 9 dauntless, dreadless, nerveless 10 courageous

intricate: 4 hard 5 dedal 6 daedal, knotty 7 complex, Gordian, sinuous 8 involved 9 Daedalian, difficult, involuted 10 perplexing 11 complicated 12 labyrinthine

intrigue: 4 plot 5 cabal, charm 6 brigue, deceit, design, scheme 7 faction 8 artifice, collogue 9 fascinate 10 concoction, conspiracy 11 machination

intrinsic: 4 real, true 6 inborn, inbred, innate, native 7 genuine, natural 8 immanent, inherent, intimate 9 essential, necessary 11 inseparable 13 indispensable

intrinsically: 5 per se 6 as such

introduce: 5 begin, enter, start, usher 6 broach, herald, infuse, insert 7 forerun, implant, precede, preface, present, sponsor 8 approach, initiate 9 insinuate, institute, originate

introduction: cue 5 debut, proem 7 intrada, introit, isagoge, preface, prelude 8 entrance, exordium, foreword, overture, preamble, prologue, protasis 11 preparation

of new word: **7** neology
to treatise: **7** isagoge

introductory: 7 initial **8** exordial **9** prefatory, prelusive **11** preliminary

introductory cry: 4 hear, oyes, oyez

introit: 4 hymn **5** psalm **12** introduction

introverted: 8 brooding **9** withdrawn **13** contemplative

intrude: 6 invade, meddle **8** encroach, infringe, muscle in, trespass **9** interfere, interlope, interpose

intruder: 8 outsider **11** gate crasher

intrusion: 10 aggression, infraction

intrusive: 7 curious

intrust: See **entrust**

intuit: 4 feel **5** sense **8** perceive **9** apprehend

intuition: 5 hunch **7** feeling, insight **8** instinct **10** perception, sixth sense

inulase: 6 enzyme

inunction: 7 unguent **8** ointment **9** anointing
pert. to: **7** aliptic

inundate: 4 flow **5** drown, flood **6** deluge **8** overflow, submerge **9** overwhelm **10** overspread

inundation: 8 alluvion

inure, enure: 5 steel **6** harden, season **7** toughen **8** accustom **9** habituate **10** discipline **11** acclimatize

inurn: 4 bury **6** entomb

inutile: bad **7** useless **8** unusable **9** worthless **12** unprofitable

inutterable: See **unutterable**

invade: 4 raid **6** attack, engulf, infest **7** assault, intrude, overrun **8** encroach, trespass **9** march into, penetrate

invalid: 4 null **6** feeble, infirm, sickly **8** nugatory **11** ineffective **14** valetudinarian

invalidate: 4 undo **5** annul, break **7** abolish

invaluable: 8 precious **9** priceless **11** inestimable **13** inappreciable

invariable: 4 same **6** steady **7** uniform **8** constant **9** continual, immutable **10** unchanging **11** determinate **12** unchangeable

invariably: 6 always **7** forever **9** regularly **11** without fail

invasion (see also **invade**): inroad **9** incursion **10** aggression

invective: 5 abuse, venom **6** tirade **7** railing **8** diatribe, reproach **12** vituperation

inveigh: 9 fulminate

inveigle: 4 coax, lure **5** snare **6** allure, entice, entrap **8** persuade

invent: 4 coin, form, make, vamp **5** feign, forge, frame **6** create, design, devise, patent **7** concoct, fashion **8** contrive, discover, engineer **9** fabricate, improvise, originate **11** manufacture

invention: 7 fiction, figment

inventive: 6 adroit **7** fertile **9** ingenious

inventor: 6 author, coiner **7** creator **8** engineer **10** discoverer, originator
airplane: **6** Fokker, Wright
baseball: **9** Doubleday
condensing steam engine: **4** Watt
cotton gin: **7** Whitney
dynamite: **5** Nobel
electric light: **6** Edison
electric motor: **9** Davenport
elevator: **4** Otis
gun: **4** Colt **9** Remington
internal combustion engine: **6** Lenoir **7** Daimler
logarithm: **6** Napier
phonograph: **6** Edison
photography: **6** Niepce, Talbot
power loom: **10** Cartwright
printing: **9** Gutenberg
printing press: Hoe
radio: **7** Marconi **8** de Forest
safety lamp: **4** Davy
sewing machine: **4** Howe **6** Lester
steam locomotive: **10** Stephenson
steamboat: **5** Fitch **6** Fulton, Rumsey
telegraph: **5** Morse
telephone: **4** Bell
television: **6** Nipkow
wireless: **7** Marconi

inventor's right: 6 patent

inventory: 4 list **5** stock, store, tally **7** account, backlog, reserve **8** register, schedule **9** catalogue, stockpile

inveracity: fib, lie **9** falsehood, falseness

inverse: 8 backward, contrary, opposite **11** bottom-to-top

invert: 4 turn **7** reverse

invertebrate: 4 worm **5** polyp **6** insect, sponge **7** mollusk **8** arachnid **12** coelenterate
group: **7** radiata

invest: don **4** belt, gird, gown, robe, vest, wrap **5** allot, array, crown, dress, endow, endue, imbue **6** clothe, confer, embark, ordain **7** envelop, install, instate **8** accredit, enthrone, surround

investigate: pry **4** nose **5** probe, study, trace **6** search **7** examine, explore, inquire **8** research **10** scrutinize

investigator: 6 prober, tracer **9** detective
body: **4** jury **5** panel **9** committee

investiture: 8 clothing **9** induction **10** initiation **12** installation

investment: 4 ante **5** share, stake **6** venture **12** contribution
list: **9** portfolio

investor: 10 capitalist, shareowner **11** stockholder

inveterate: 6 rooted **7** chronic **8** habitual, hardened **9** confirmed, ingrained

invidious: 6 odious **7** envious, hateful **8** spiteful **9** malignant **12** disagreeable invigorate: 5 cheer, pep up, renew 6 vivify 7 animate, enliven, fortify, refresh 9 stimulate 10 exhilarate, strengthen

invigorating: 7 bracing 9 healthful 10 energizing 12 rejuvenating

invincible: 10 unbeatable 11 indomitable

inviolate: 4 holy 6 sacred 9 undefiled, unstained 10 sacrosanct 13 incorruptible

invisible: hid 6 unseen 10 indistinct, unapparent 13 undiscernible

Invisible Empire: 4 Klan

invitation: bid 4 call, lure 7 request, summons 8 entreaty 9 challenge
 initials: 4 RSVP

invite: ask, bid 4 call 5 court 6 allure, entice 7 attract, provoke, request, solicit

invocation: 4 plea 6 prayer, sermon 7 benison 8 entreaty 11 benediction

invoice: 4 bill 5 brief 7 account 8 manifest 9 statement

invoke: 4 call, pray 6 appeal, attest 7 conjure, entreat, provoke, solicit 9 imprecate 10 supplicate

involuntary: 6 forced 9 automatic, unwitting 10 compulsory 11 inadvertent, instinctive, spontaneous

involute: 6 curled, rolled 8 involved 9 intricate

involve: 4 wrap 5 imply, snare 6 bemist, employ, enmesh, engage, entail 7 concern, embrace, embroil, ensnare, include 8 comprise, encumber, entangle 9 implicate 10 complicate, comprehend

involved: 7 complex 12 labyrinthine

inward: 5 entad, inner 6 inside 8 interior 10 internally

Io: *father:* 7 Inachus
 guard: 5 Argus
 son: 7 Epaphus

iodine: *compound:* 6 iodide
 salt: 6 iodate
 source: 4 kelp
 substitute: 7 aristal
 treat with: 6 iodate

Iolcus king: 6 Pelias

ion: *negative:* 5 anion
 positive: 6 cation, kation

Ion: *father:* 6 Apollo
 mother: 6 Creusa

iota: bit, jot 4 atom, whit 6 tittle 8 particle

Iowa: *capital:* 9 Des Moines
 city: 4 Ames 5 Anita 7 Dubuque, Ottumwa 8 Iowa City, Waterloo 9 Davenport, Oskaloosa, Sioux City 11 Cedar Rapids
 county: Ida, Lee, Sac 4 Linn, Lyon, Page, Tama 5 Adair, Emmet, Floyd, Lucas, Mills, Onawa, Story, Worth 6 Bremer, Butler, Hardin, Keokuk, Warren 7 Audubon, Guthrie, Kossuth, Wapello
 Indian: Fox 4 Iowa, Sauk 5 Sioux
 lake: 5 Storm 6 Spirit 7 Okoboji, Red Rock

President Hoover's birthplace: 10 West Branch
 river: 4 Iowa, Rock 5 Boyer, Cedar, Skunk 6 Turkey 7 Nodaway 8 Big Sioux 9 Des Moines 11 Mississippi
 state bird: 9 goldfinch
 state flower: 8 wild rose
 state nickname: 7 Hawkeye
 state tree: oak

ipecac: 4 evea
 substance: 7 emetine

Iphicles: *brother:* 8 Heracles, Hercules
 mother: 7 Alcmene
 son: 6 Iolaus

Iphis' daughter: 6 Evadne

ipso facto: 11 by the fact of

irade: 5 edict 6 decree

Iran: (see also **Persia**) *capital:* 7 Teheran
 city: Qom 5 Ahvaz 6 Abadan, Kashan, Shiraz, Tabriz 7 Esfahan, Hamadan, Mashhad
 ethnic group: 4 Arab, Kurd, Turk 5 Farsi
 former name: 6 Persia
 governorship: 4 Ilam, Yazd 6 Semnan, Zanjan 7 Hamadan 8 Lorestan
 gulf: 4 Oman 7 Persian
 island: 5 Kharg, Qeshm 6 Abadan
 lake: 5 Niriz, Tashk, Urmia 7 Shahpur
 monetary unit: 4 rial 5 dinar
 mountain peak: 6 Alwand, Bazman, Sahand, Taftan 8 Damavand, Lalehzar
 mountain range: 6 Elburz, Zagros 8 Poshtkuh 9 Hindu Kush
 oil center: 6 Abadan
 port: 7 Bushire 11 Bandar Abbas
 province: 4 Fars 5 Gilan 6 Kerman 7 Esfahan, Teheran 8 Khorasan 9 Khuzestan, Kordestan 10 Azerbaijan
 river: 4 Mand 5 Atrek, Karun, Safid 7 Karkheh 9 Kizil Uzen
 salt desert: 9 Dasht-e-lut 11 Dasht-e-Kavir
 sea: 7 Caspian
 strait: 6 Hormuz

Irani, Iranian: 7 Persian
 almond: 5 badam
 angel: Mah
 bazaar: 9 bezooteen
 bird: 6 bulbul
 cap: taj
 coin: pul 4 asar, cran, kran, lari, rial 5 bisti, daric, dinar, larin, shahi, toman 6 shahee, stater 7 ashrafi, kasbeke, pahlavi
 comedy: 7 temacha
 dynasty: 5 Kajar, Seljuk 7 Pahlavi, Safavid, Safawid 10 Sassanidae
 founder of ancient empire: 5 Cyrus
 god: 6 Ormazd 7 Mithras
 hat: fez 6 turban
 javelin: 6 jereed
 king: 6 Darius, Xerxes 7 Jamshid, Jamshyd 9 Giamschid 10 Artaxerxes

Koran student: 5 hafiz
language: 5 Farsi 7 Kurdish, Pahlavi
measure: guz, mou, zar, zer 4 cane, foot 5
  gareh, jerib, kafiz, makuk, qasab 6 artaba, charac, chebel, gariba, ghalva, our-
  oub 7 capicha, chenica, farsakh, farsang, mansion, mishara 8 parasang,
  piamaneh, sabbitha, stathmos 9 col-
  lothun, colluthun
moon: 4 Mahi
news agency: 4 IRNA
New Year's Day: 7 Nowroze
people: 4 Kurd, Mede 5 Kajar, Mukri,
  Tajik 6 Tadjik 7 Hadjemi, Persian
poet: 4 Omar 6 Saadi
religion founder: 9 Zoroaster 11 Zarathu-
  stra
religious doctrine: 6 babism
revenue officer: 9 tahsildar 10 tahseeldar
ruler: 4 khan, shah 6 atabeg, atabek, satrap, sultan
screen: 6 purdah
sect: 5 Shiah, Sunni 6 Shiite
tapestry: 7 susanee
tax collector: 9 tahsildar 10 tahseeldar
tent-maker: 4 Omar
throne room: 5 aiwan
tiara: 7 cidaris
title: mir 4 azam 5 mirza
tobacco: 6 tumbak, tumbek 7 tumbaki,
  tumbeki
traders: 4 sart
trumpet: 6 kerana 7 kerrana
vessel: 6 aftaba
water-pipe: 5 hooka 6 calean, hookah 8
  narghile 12 hubble-bubble
water wheel: 5 noria
weight: ser 4 dram, dung, rotl, sang, seer
  5 abbas, artal, artel, maund, pinar, ratel
  6 batman, dirhem, gandum, karwar,
  miscal, miskal, nakhod 7 abbassi 8
  tcheirek 9 saddirham
Iraq: *capital:* 7 Baghdad
  city: 5 Basra, Erbil, Mosul 6 Kirkuk 7 An
    Najaf, Karbala
  desert: 6 Syrian 8 Al Hajara
  ethnic group: 4 Arab, Kurd
  gulf: 7 Persian
  historic site of: 7 Assyria 9 Babylonia
  lake: 6 Dalmaj, Sadiya 8 Al Hammar 9
    Habbaniya
  monetary unit: 4 fils 5 dinar
  mountain range: 8 Poshtkuh
  port: 5 Basra
  river: Zab 6 Diyala, Tigris 7 Hindiya 9
    Euphrates 11 Shatt-al-Arab
irascible: 5 irate, testy 6 snappy, touchy
  7 fretful, peevish 8 captious, choleric,
  petulant, snappish 9 impatient, splenetic 10 passionate 11 bad-tempered,
  belligerent, hot-tempered 13 quick-
  tempered
irate: mad 5 angry, het up, wroth 6 bitter

  7 angered, enraged, furious, teed off 8
  incensed, provoked, up in arms, wrathful 9 indignant, irascible
ire: vex 4 fury, heat, rage 5 anger, annoy,
  wrath 6 choler, dander, temper 8 asperity, vexation 9 vehemence 10 exasperate, resentment 11 displeasure 12 exasperation
Ireland (see also **Irish**): 4 Eire, Erin 5
  Ierne 8 Hibernia 9 Innisfail
  bay: 4 Clew 5 Sligo 6 Bantry, Dingle,
    Galway, Mannin, Tralee 7 Donegal,
    Killala, Youghal 8 Blacksod, Drogheda
  capital: 6 Dublin
  city: 4 Cobh, Cork 5 Ennis 6 Galway 7
    Dundalk 8 Limerick 9 Killarney, Tip-
    perary, Waterford 12 Dun Laoghaire
  county: 4 Cork, Mayo 5 Cavan, Clare,
    Kerry, Louth, Meath, Sligo 6 Carlow,
    Dublin, Galway, Offaly 7 Donegal, Kil-
    dare, Leitrim, Wexford, Wicklow 8 Kil-
    kenny, Laoighis, Limerick, Longford,
    Monaghan 9 Tipperary, Roscommon,
    Waterford, Westmeath
  early inhabitant: 4 Celt, Pict
  island: 4 Aran 5 Clare, Clear, Great 6
    Achill, Dursey, Saltee 7 Elasket 8 Scar-
    riff, Valentia
  lake: Ree 4 Conn, Derg, Gara, Mask 5 Al-
    len, Foyle, Leane 6 Corrib, Melvin 9
    Killarney
  monetary unit: 5 penny, pound
  port: 4 Bray, Cobh, Cork 6 Arklow, Dub-
    lin, Tralee 7 Dundalk, Wexford, Wick-
    low 8 Drogheda 12 Dun Laoghaire
  province: 6 Ulster 7 Munster 8 Con-
    nacht, Leinster
  river: Lee 4 Erne, Nore, Suir 5 Avoca,
    Boyne, Foyle 6 Barrow, Liffey, Slaney
    7 Shannon 10 Blackwater
irenic: 4 calm 8 pacifist, peaceful 10 nonviolent 12 conciliatory
iridescent: 8 colorful 9 prismatic 10
  opalescent 11 rainbow-like
iris: 4 flag 5 orris 7 eye part, rainbow 9
  perennial
  family: 4 irid, ixia 6 crocus 9 gladiolus
  inflammation of: 6 iritis
Irish: 4 Erse 6 Celtic, Gaelic
  accent: 6 brogue
  ancestor: Mil 6 Miledh 8 Milesius
  assembly: 6 aenach, aonach
  basket: 7 skeough
  battle cry: abu
  boat: 7 pookaun 8 pookhaun
  cabstand: 6 hazard
  cap: 6 barrad
  cattle: 5 Kerry
  chamber of deputies: 4 Dail
  chemist: 5 Boyle
  chieftan: 6 Tanist
  church: kil
  church steward: 7 erenach

clan: 4 sept 5 Cinel
club: 8 shillala 9 shillalah, shillelah 10 shillelagh
coin: rap 4 real
cordial: 10 usquebaugh
coronation stone: 7 Lia Fail
dagger: 5 skean
dance: 10 rinkafadda, rinncefada
dirge: 4 keen
dish: 4 stew
dramatist: see *playwright* below
epic tales: 4 tain, tana(pl.)
exclamation: och 4 arra 5 arrah, ohone
fair: 6 aenach, aonach
fairy: 4 shee 5 sidhe 7 banshee, banshie 10 leprechaun
festival: 4 feis
fort: Lis 4 rath
freebooter: 8 rapparee
freeman: 4 aire
fuel: 4 peat
garment: 4 inar
goblin: 5 pooka
god's mother: Ana, Anu
god of love: 5 Dagda 6 Aengus, Oengus
god of sea: Ler
goddess: 4 Badb, Bodb, Dana
good-for-nothing: 8 spalpeen
groggery: 7 shebeen
harvester: 8 spalpeen
herring: 8 scud-dawn
holiday: 10 Whitmonday
infantryman: 4 kern
king: Rig 5 Ardri
king's home: 4 Tara
lamentation: 6 ochone
landholding system: 7 rundale
lawyer: 6 brehon
legislature: 10 Oireachtas
liquor: 6 poteen 7 potheen
lord: 6 tanist
luck: 4 cess
measure: 4 mile 6 bandle
melody: 7 planxty
militant group: IRA
moccasin: 9 pampootee, pampootie
monk: 6 culdee
monk's cell: kil 4 kill
musical festival: 4 feis
musical instrument: 4 harp, lyre
national emblem: 8 shamrock
nationalist society: 8 Sinn Fein
negative: 5 sorra
novelist: 4 Shaw
oath: 5 bedad
patriot: 5 Emmet 6 Oakboy 7 Parnell
patron saint: 7 Patrick
peasant: 4 kern 5 kerne
peat: gor
person: 4 aire, kern 5 kerne, paddy 7 shoneen 8 spalpeen 10 Eireannach
pig: 5 bonav

playwright: 4 Shaw 5 Synge, Wilde, Yeats 6 O'Casey
poem: 6 amhran
poet: 5 Moore, Wilde, Yeats
priest: 5 druid
princess: 6 Iseult
proprietor: 6 tanist
Protestant: 9 Sassenach
republicanism: 9 Fenianism
revolutionist: 6 Fenian
robber: 8 woodkern
saint: 5 Aidan 7 Patrick
salutation: 6 a chara
servant: 5 biddy 7 gossoon
society: 4 aire
soldier: 6 bonagh 8 rapparee
soldiers' quartering: 7 bonaght 8 bonaught
song: 4 rann
spirit: see *fairy* above
steward: 7 erenach 8 herenach
stock: 4 daer
straw load: 5 barth
surgeon: 6 Colles
sweetheart: gra
symbol: 4 harp 8 shamrock
tax: 7 bonaght 8 bonaught
tenant: 4 saer
tenure: 6 sorren 7 sorehon
term of endearment: 5 aroon, aruin 7 acushla, alannah, asthore 9 avourneen 10 mavoureen
theatre: 5 Abbey
trout: 7 gilaroo
verse: 4 rann
whiskey: 6 poteen 10 usquebaugh
white: 4 bawn
womanhood: 4 emer
writing system: 4 ogam 5 ogham

irk (see also **ire**): vex 4 bore 5 anger, annoy, chafe, peeve, tease, upset, weary 6 nettle 7 trouble 8 irritate 10 exasperate

irksome: 4 dull 7 humdrum, painful, tedious 8 tiresome 9 fatiguing, wearisome 10 burdensome, monotonous, unpleasant 11 displeasing

iron: fer(F.) 4 gyve, hard 5 metal, power, press 6 fetter, smooth, robust, strong 7 manacle, shackle 8 firmness, handcuff, hematite, siderite 10 unyielding
compound: 5 steel
curtain: 7 barrier 8 frontier
dross: 6 sinter
magnet: 8 armature
lump: pig
lung: 10 respirator
marking: 7 brander
meteoric: 8 siderite
pert. to: 6 ferric
sulphate: 7 ilesite
tailor's: 5 goose

Iron City: 10 Pittsburgh

ironclad: 6 strict 7 armored, 9 immutable

ironer: 6 mangle 7 presser

ironhanded: 4 firm 6 strict 8 despotic 11 dictatorial

ironic: 7 satiric 9 sarcastic

iron out: 10 smooth over 11 come to terms

irons: 6 chains 7 fetters 8 shackles

irony: 6 satire 7 asteism, sarcasm 8 ridicule 13 dissimulation

Iroquois tribes: 6 Cayuga, Mohawk, Oneida, Seneca 8 Onondaga 9 Tuscarora

irradiate: ray 4 beam, emit 6 bright 7 diffuse 8 brighten 9 enlighten 10 illuminate

irrational: 4 surd 5 brute 6 absurd, insane, stupid, unwise 7 bestial, brutish, foolish 9 fanatical, illogical, senseless 10 ridiculous 12 preposterous, unreasonable 13 unintelligent

irreclaimable: 4 lost 8 hopeless 9 abandoned 11 irrevocable 12 irredeemable

irreconcilable: 11 conflicting 12 incompatible, inconsistent, intransigent

irrefutable: 11 conclusive, undeniable

irregular: 4 wild 5 erose, false 6 ataxic, fitful, rugged, spotty, uneven, unlike 7 atactic, crabbed, crooked, cursory, devious, erratic, snatchy, unequal, wayward 8 abnormal, atypical, sporadic, unlawful, unstable, unsteady, variable 9 anomalous, desultory, eccentric, unsettled 10 changeable, disorderly, immoderate 11 intemperate 12 uncontrolled, unsystematic 13 extraordinary

irregularity: 4 flaw 5 error 7 anomaly 8 disorder 9 variation 10 unevenness 11 derangement 12 imperfection

irrelevant: 9 unrelated 10 extraneous, immaterial, inapposite 11 unessential 12 inconsequent

irreligious: 5 pagan 6 wicked 7 godless, heathen, impious, profane

irremediable: 6 ruined 8 helpless, hopeless 9 desperate, incurable 11 irreparable 13 irretrievable

irreproachable: 8 spotless 9 blameless, exemplary, faultless 10 impeccable

irresistible: 10 superhuman 11 fascinating, unopposable 12 overpowering, spellbinding

irresolute: 6 fickle, infirm, unsure 8 doubtful, unstable, wavering 9 uncertain, undecided 10 changeable, inconstant 11 fluctuating 12 undetermined

irresponsible: 8 carefree 10 fly-by-night 11 harum-scarum 12 undependable 13 unaccountable

irreverence: 7 impiety 8 dishonor 9 blasphemy, impudence, profanity

irrevocable: 4 firm 5 final 9 immutable 10 conclusive 11 unalterable

irrigate: wet 5 water 6 sluice 7 moisten

irritable: 4 edgy 5 cross, fiery, testy 6 cranky, ornery, tetchy, touchy 7 fretful, peevish, pettish 8 snappish 9 excitable, fractious, impatient, querulent 12 disagreeable

irritate: irk, nag, rub, vex 4 gall, goad, rile, roil 5 anger, annoy, chafe, cross, grate, peeve, pique, spite, sting, tease 6 abrade, badger, bother, burn up, enrage, excite, harass, hector, madden, needle, nettle, put out, ruffle 7 affront, incense, inflame, provoke 8 acerbate, make sore 9 aggravate, displease, stimulate 10 exacerbate, exasperate

irritating: 5 acrid 8 rankling, stinging

irritation: 4 itch, rash, sore 12 inflammation

Isaac's kin: 4 Esau 5 Jacob 7 Abraham

isagoge: 12 introduction

Iseult: *beloved:* 7 Tristan

husband: 4 Mark

Ishmael: 5 rover 6 pariah 7 outcast

kin: 5 Hagar 7 Abraham 8 Nebaioth

Ishtar's lover: 6 Tammuz

isinglass: 4 mica

Isis: *kin:* 5 Horus 6 Osiris

mother: Nut

shrine: 5 Iseum 6 Iseium

son: Set 4 Seth

Islam: *adherent:* 6 Moslem, Muslim

festival: Eed

founder: 7 Mahomet 8 Mohammed, Muhammad

god: 5 Allah

holy city: 5 Mecca 6 Medina

law: 4 adat 5 sheri 6 sharia, sheria

paradise: 5 jenna

pert. to shrine at Mecca: 5 Kaaba

priest: 4 imam

scriptures: 5 Koran

Isle of Man: *capital:* 7 Douglas

legislature: 7 tynwald

lighthouse point: 4 Ayre

measure: 6 kishen, kishon

mountain: 8 Snaefell

tailless cat: 4 Manx

watering place: 4 Ryde

ism: 5 ology, tenet 6 belief 8 doctrine 10 hypothesis

isolate: 6 detach, enisle, island 7 seclude 8 insulate, separate 9 segregate, sequester 10 quarantine

isolated: 4 sole 5 alone 6 lonely 7 insular 8 singluar, solitary

Isolde's lover: 7 Tristan
isopod: 6 slater 9 wood louse
Israel (see also **Hebrew, Judaism**):
  capital: 9 Jerusalem
  city: Lod 4 Gaza 5 Haifa, Holon, Ramla
    6 Bat Yam 7 Natanya, Rehovot, Tel
    Aviv 8 Ashkelon, Nazareth, Ramat
    Gan 9 Beersheba
  desert: 5 Negev
  district: 5 Haifa 7 Central, Tel Aviv 8
    Northern, Southern 9 Jerusalem
  early name: 5 Judea 9 Palestine
  ethnic group: Jew 4 Arab 5 Druze
  gulf: 5 Aqaba
  lake: 4 Hule 7 Dead Sea 8 Kinneret
  monetary unit: 5 agora 6 shekel
  mountain: 5 Meron, Ramon 6 Carmel,
    Gilboa
  nationalist movement: 7 Zionism
  nationalist pioneer: 5 Herzl (Theodor)
  parliament: 7 Knesset
  plain: 9 Esdraelon
  port: 4 Acre, Gaza 5 Eilat, Haifa 6 Ash-
    dod 7 Tel Aviv
  settlement: 6 moshav 7 kibbutz
  statesman: 4 Meir (Golda) 8 Weizmann
    (Chaim) 9 Ben-Gurion (David)
issuance: 5 issue 6 sortie 7 issuing 9 em-
    anation 12 distribution
issue: 4 emit, flow, gush, pour, send 5
    arise, child, sally, spout, topic, yield 6
    accrue, emerge, source, upshot 7 de-
    scent, dispute, edition, emanate, for-
    tune, outcome, problem, proceed, proge-
    ny 8 question 9 effluence, offspring 10
    distribute
Istanbul: 9 Byzantium 14 Constantinople
  business area: 6 Galata
  foreign quarter: 7 Beyoglu
  patriarch: 9 Nestorius
  suburb: 7 Uskudar
isthmus: 4 neck 6 strait 9 peninsula
istle fiber: 4 pita, pito
it may be: 5 haply 8 possibly
Ita: Ata 4 Aeta 7 Negrito
Italian (see also **Italy**): *actress:* 4 Duse
  astronomer: 6 Secchi 7 Galileo
  bell town: 5 Adano
  bowling game: 5 bocce
  carriage: 7 vettura
  cathedral: 5 duomo
  cereal: 5 arzun
  cheese: 6 Romano 7 riccota 8 Bel paese,
    Parmesan 10 gorgonzola
  chest: 7 cassone
  coin: 4 lira, sudo tari 5 grano, paoli, soldo
    6 ducato, sequin, teston, zequin 8 zec-
    chino 9 centesimo
  composer: 5 Verdi 7 Bellini, Puccini,
    Rossini, Vivaldi 8 Mascagni 9 Donizet-
    ti, Scarlatti

  dance: 5 volta 8 courante 9 rigoletto 10
    tarantella
  dictator: 9 Mussolini
  dough: 5 pasta
  engraver: 8 Raimondi
  entertainment: 5 festa
  family: 4 Asti, Este 5 Amati, Cenci, Sa-
    voy 6 Borgia, Medici, Sforza
  food: 5 pizza 6 scampi 7 lasagna, ravioli,
    tortoni, spumoni 8 linguine 9 manicotti
  gentleman: ser 6 signor 7 signore
  goldsmith: 7 Cellini
  grape: uva 6 verdea
  guessing game: 4 mora
  guitar: 8 chitarra
  hamlet: 5 casal 6 casale
  hello: 4 ciao
  holiday: 5 festa
  house: 4 casa 6 casino
  ice cream: 6 gelato
  infant cupids: 8 amoretti
  inlay work: 6 tarsia
  inn: 7 albergo, locanda, osteria
  innkeeper: 4 oste 7 padrone
  lady: 5 donna 7 signora
  land: 5 paese, terra
  landlord: 7 padrone
  leader: 4 duce
  lover: 6 amante 7 amoroso
  magistrate: 7 podesta
  marble: 7 carrara
  master: 7 padrone
  mayor: 7 sindaco
  measure: pie 4 orna 5 canna, carat, pal-
    ma, piede, punto, salma, staio, stero 6
    barile, miglio, moggio, rubbio, tavola,
    tomolo 7 boccale, braccio, secchio 8
    giornata, polonick, quadrato
  medieval faction: 4 Neri
  millet: 4 buda, moha 5 mohar, tenai
  monk: 5 padre 6 abbate
  month: 4 mese 5 Marzo 6 Agosto, Aprile,
    Giugno, Luglio, Maggio 7 Gennaio, Ot-
    tobre 8 Dicembre, Febbraio, Novembre
    9 Settembre
  musician: 5 Guido
  needlework: 6 ricamo 8 trapunto
  noblewoman: 8 contessa, marchesa
  omelet: 8 frittata
  opera house: 5 Scala
  organization: 7 Balilla
  painter: 4 Reni, Tisi 5 Colle, Lippi, Lot-
    to, Vinci 6 Crespi, Giotto, Guardi,
    Monaco, Sacchi, Titian 7 Amigoni, da
    Vinci, di Credi, di Paolo, Raphael, Ro-
    busti, Strozzi, Tiepolo 8 Angelico,
    Bronzino, Cagliari, Mainardi, Sassetta
    9 Correggio, del Piombo, Giorgione,
    Veneziano 10 Botticelli, Caracciolo,
    Tintoretto
  painting: 9 tenebrosi

patriot: 6 Cavour, Rienzi 7 Mazzini 9 Garibaldi

patron saint: 7 Francis

peasant: 7 paesano 9 contadino

people: 5 Latin, Oscan, Roman 6 Sabine, Tuscan 8 Etruscan, Venetian

philosopher: 5 Croce 7 Aquinas, Rosmini

physicist: see *scientist* below

pie: 5 pizza

plays: 7 Vangeli

poet: 4 Redi, Rota 5 Boito, Dante, Tasso 7 Ariosto, Guarini 8 Petrarch

poetic name: 7 Ausonia

police officer: 6 sbirri, sbirro

policeman: 11 carabiniere, carabinieri

porridge: 7 polenta

pottery: 8 majolica

priest: 5 prete

printer: 6 Bodoni

procession: 5 corso 7 trionfi, trionfo

pronoun: che, chi, lei, mia 4 egli, ella, essa, esse, essi, esso, loro

resort: 4 Como, Lido 5 Capri 6 Ischia, Stresa 7 San Remo 8 Positano, Sorrento, Taormina

rice: 7 risotto

road: 6 strada

rock: 7 scaglia

sausage: 6 salami

scientist: 5 Fermi, Volta 7 Galileo, Galvani, Marconi

sculptor: 6 Pisano 7 Bernini, da Vinci 8 Ghiberti 9 Donatello 12 Michelangelo

secret society: 5 Mafia 7 Camorra 9 Carbonari

shore: 4 riva

soldier: 7 soldato 11 bersagliere

song: 5 canto 7 canzone

soup: 8 minestra 10 minestrone

stream: 4 rivo

summer house: 6 casino

theme: 4 tema

theologian: 7 Aquinas, Peronne

vessel: 7 trabacolo 10 trabascolo

violin maker: 5 Amati 7 Guarner 10 Stradivari

violinist: 7 Corelli, Tartini 8 Paganini

weight: 5 carat, libra, oncia, pound 6 denaro, libbra, ottava 11 chilogrammo

wind: 7 sirocco

wine: 4 Asti 5 Corvo, Soave 6 Barolo, Massic 7 Barbera, Chianti, Marsala 9 Bardolino, Vernaccia

italicize: 6 set off 9 emphasize, underline 10 underscore

Italy: capital: 4 Rome

   city: 4 Bari, Pisa 5 Genoa, Milan, Parma, Siena 6 Ancona, Foggia, Modena, Naples, Venice 7 Bologna, Catania, Ferrara, Leghorn, Messina, Palermo, Perugia, Ravenna, Trieste 8 Brindisi, Cagliari, Florence

   gulf: 5 Gaeta, Genoa 6 Venice 7 Salerno, Taranto

   island: 4 Elba 5 Capri, Egadi, Ponza 6 Giglio, Ischia, Lipari, Salina, Sicily, Ustica 7 Capraia 8 Sardinia 9 Stromboli

   lake: 4 Como 5 Garda 6 Albano, Lugano 7 Bolsena 8 Maggiore 9 Bracciano, Trasimeno

   monetary unit: 4 lira 9 centesimo

   mountain pass, tunnel: 4 Cisa, Futa 5 Cenis, Giovi 7 Brenner, Pescara, Simplon 8 Scheggia 9 Bocchetta

   mountain peak: Bue 4 Etna, Rosa 5 Corno 6 Gimone, Nerone 7 Miletto, Pollino, Vettore

   mountain range: 4 Alps 9 Apennines

   port: 4 Bari 5 Genoa 6 Ancona, Naples, Pesaro, Reggio, Rimini, Venice 7 Leghorn, Marsala, Messina, Pescara, Salerno, Taranto, Trieste 8 Brindisi, Cagliari, La Spezia, Syracuse

   pre-Roman nation: 7 Etruria

   province: 4 Asti, Como, Enna 5 Aosta, Cuneo, Forli, Lecce, Lucca, Nuoro, Parma, Pavia, Rieti, Terni, Udine 6 Aquila, Arezzo, Chieti, Latina, Matera, Modena, Novara, Padova, Ragusa, Rovigo, Savona, Teramo, Varese, Verona 7 Belluno, Bergamo, Bolzano, Brescia, Caserta, Cosenza, Cremona, Gorizia, Imperia, Isernia, Mantova, Pistoia, Potenza, Sassari, Sondrio, Trapani, Treviso, Vicenza, Viterbo

   region: 6 Apulia, Latium, Molise, Sicily, Umbria, Veneto 7 Abruzzi, Campania, Liguria, Marches, Tuscany 8 Calabria, Lombardy, Piedmont, Sardinia

   region forming "heel": 6 Apulia

   region forming "toe": 8 Calabria

   river: 4 Adda, Arno, Liri 5 Adige, Oglio, Piave, Tiber 6 Aterno, Isonzo, Mincio, Panaro, Ticino 7 Pescara 8 Volturno

   sea: 6 Ionian 8 Adriatic, Ligurian

   volcano: 4 Etna 8 Vesuvius 9 Stromboli

itch: 4 reef, yeuk(Sc.) 6 desire 9 cacoethes, hankering 10 irritation

item (see also **object**): bit 5 entry, scrap, thing, topic 6 detail 7 account, article, product 8 personal 9 paragraph 10 particular 12 circumstance

itemize: 4 list 9 enumerate

Ithaca king: 8 Odysseus

Ithunn's husband: 5 Brage, Bragi

itinerant: 6 errant, roving 7 migrant, nomadic 8 traveler, wanderer 9 migratory, transient, traveling, unsettled, wandering 11 peripatetic

itinerary: 4 plan, tour 5 guide, route 6 record 8 roadbook 9 guidebook

Ivan the Terrible: 4 Tsar
  wife: 9 Anastasia
Ivanhoe: *author:* 5 Scott
  character: 4 Tuck 5 Isaac 6 Cedric, Rowena 7 Rebecca, Wilfred 9 Robin Hood
ivory: die 4 tusk 5 tooth 6 creamy 7 dentine
Ivory Coast: *capital:* 7 Abidjan
  city: Man 5 Daloa 6 Bouake 7 Korhogo
  monetary unit: 5 franc 7 centime
  native: 5 Baule 6 Senufo 7 Malinke

  peak: 5 Nimba
  port: 6 Bassam 9 Sassandra
  river: 7 Bandama 9 Sassandra
ivory tower: 6 dreamy, unreal 7 retreat 8 escapist 9 visionary 11 impractical
ivy: 4 vine 6 hedera
  poison: 5 sumac
Ixion's descendants: 8 Centaurs
ixtle: 4 pita 5 fiber, istle
izzat: 5 honor 6 credit 8 prestige 10 reputation

J

jaal: 4 goat, ibex 5 beden
jab: hit, jag 4 poke, prod, stab 5 nudge, prick, punch 6 thrust
Jabal's father: 6 Lamech
jabber: 4 chat 6 burble, gabble 7 chatter 9 gibberish
jabberwocky: 8 nonsense 9 gibberish, rigmarole
jabiru: 4 ibis 5 stork
jabot: 5 frill 6 ruffle
jacare: 6 caiman 9 crocodile
jack: nob 4 card, lift 5 knave, money 6 sailor
  group of 4: 8 quatorze
jack-in-the-pulpit: 4 herb 5 plant 7 figwort
jack-of-all-trades: 6 tinker 8 handyman
jack tree: 4 jaca
jackal: 5 diebs
jackanapes: ape, fop 4 beau 5 dandy 6 monkey 7 coxcomb
jackass: 4 dolt, fool 5 dunce 6 donkey, nitwit 9 blockhead
jackdaw: coe 6 caddow 9 blackbird
jacket: 4 bajo, coat, Eton 5 acton, grego, wamus 6 anorak, banian(Ind.), bietle, blazer, bolero, dolman, reefer, sliver, wammus, wampus 7 cassock, doublet, pea coat, ristori, spencer 8 camisole, chaqueta, hanselin 9 habergeon 10 carmagnole(F.), roundabout 11 nightingale
  knitted: 5 gansy 6 gansey, sontag 7 sweater 8 cardigan, penelope
  sleeveless: 4 vest 6 bolero, jerkin

jackknife: 4 dive 6 barlow
Jack of clubs: pam
jackpot: all 4 pool 5 award 8 windfall
jackrabbit: 4 hare
jackstay: 4 rope 5 staff
jackstones: 4 dibs
Jacob: *brother:* 4 Edom, Esau
  daughters: 5 Dinah
  descendant: 6 Levite 9 Israelite
  father-in-law: 5 Laban
  new name: 6 Israel
  parent: 5 Issac 7 Rebekah
  retreat: 5 Haran
  son: Dan, Gad 4 Aser, Levi 5 Asher, Judah 6 Bononi, Joseph, Reuben, Simeon 7 Gershon, Zebulun 8 Benjamin, Issachar, Naphtali
  vision(scene): 6 Bethel
  wife: 4 Leah 6 Rachel
jade: fag, nag 4 hack, minx, plug, tire 5 hussy, weary, wench 6 harass 7 exhaust, fatigue, hilding, pounamu 8 nephrite 10 greenstone
jaded: 4 worn 5 blase, tired, weary 6 dulled 7 wearied 9 exhausted, forjaskit, forjesket
jaeger: 4 bird, gull, skua 6 hunter 7 diamond 8 huntsman
jag: dag, jab, rag 4 barb, hair, load, mess, stab 5 carry, notch, prick, scrap, shred, slash, souse, spree, tooth 6 indent, tatter 7 bristle, pendant, portion 8 quantity 13 denticulation
jagged: 5 erose, rough, sharp 6 hackly, ragged 7 cutting

jaguar: 5 ounce 8 large cat

jai alai: 4 game 6 pelota
  court: 6 cancha 7 fronton
  racket: 5 cesta

jail: can, jug 4 brig, dump, gaol, keep, stir
  5 clink, pokey 6 asylum, carcel, cooler,
  lockup, prison 7 hoosgow 8 bastille,
  hoosegaw, hoosegow, imprison 9 calaboose 11 incarcerate

jailer, jailor: 4 caid 5 guard 6 gaoler,
  keeper, warden 7 alcaide, turnkey

Jairite: Ira

jake: 4 fine, hick, rube 5 dandy 6 rustic 9
  first-rate, greenhorn

jako: 6 parrot

jalousie: 5 blind 7 shutter

jam: 4 bind 5 crowd, crush 6 spread 7
  squeeze 9 marmalade 10 congestion

Jamaica dogwood: 8 barbasco
  ginger alcohol: 4 jake

James' father: 7 Zebedee

jangle: 4 ring 5 clang, upset 6 bicker,
  racket 7 quarrel, wrangle 8 irritate 11
  altercation

jangling: 5 harsh 7 grating 9 dissonant
  10 discordant 11 cacophonous

janitor: 6 porter 9 caretaker, custodian
  10 doorkeeper 11 housekeeper

japan: 7 lacquer, varnish

Japan: 6 Nippon
  bay: Ise 5 Mutzu, Osaka 6 Suruga, Toyama, Wakasa 8 Ishikari 9 Kagoshima,
  Shimabara
  capital: 5 Tokyo
  city: Ome, Usa 4 Kobe, Nara, Ueda 5
  Kyoto, Osaka, Otaru, Sakai 6 Nagoya,
  Sendai 7 Okayama, Okazaki, Sapporo 8
  Kawasaki, Nagasaki, Yokohama, Yoko-
  suka 9 Hiroshima
  island: 6 Honshu (mainland), Kyushu 7
  Shikoku 8 Hokkaido
  island group: Oki 4 Goto 5 Bonin 6 Mar-
  cus, Ryukyu 7 Okinawa, Volcano
  lake: 4 Biwa 8 Chuzenji 10 Inawashiro
  monetary unit: sen, yen
  mountain peak: 4 Kuju 5 Iwaki 6 Ontake
  7 Shirane 9 Asahi Dake
  mountain range: 5 Nikko 8 Sakhalin 9
  Kirishima
  opened by: 5 Peary
  port: 4 Kobe 5 Chiba, Nanao, Osaka,
  Tokyo 6 Nagoya, Sasebo 7 Fukuoka,
  Shimizu, Shimoda 8 Hakodate, Kawasaki, Yokohama
  prefecture: Mie 4 Gifu, Nara, Oita, Saga
  5 Aichi, Akita, Chiba, Ehime, Fukui,
  Gumma, Hyogo, Iwate, Kochi, Kyoto,
  Osaka, Shiga, Tokyo 6 Aomori, Miyagi,
  Nagano, Toyama 7 Ibaraki, Okayama,
  Shimane
  river: 4 Kiso, Tone 5 Iwaki, Shira 6 Su-
  mida, Tashio 7 Shinano

  sea: Suo 6 Harima, Inland, Kumano, Sa-
  gami 7 Okhotsk 9 East China
  strait: 5 Bungo, Korea 7 Tsugaru
  volcano: Aso 4 Fuji 5 Asama, Iwate 6
  Daisen, On-take

Japanese: *abacus:* 7 soroban
  abalone: 5 awabi
  aborigine: 4 Ainu
  alcoholic beverage: 4 sake, saki
  alloy: 5 mokum
  allspice: 12 chimonanthus
  apricot: ume 4 ansu
  art design: 5 notan
  baron: 6 daimio, daimyo
  battle cry: 6 banzai
  biwa: 6 loquat
  boxes: 4 inro
  brake: 6 warabi
  brazier: 7 hibachi
  brocade: 7 nishiki
  Buddha: 5 Amida
  Buddhist festival: Bon
  Buddhist sect: Zen 4 Jodo, Shin
  bush clover: 4 hagi
  button: 7 netsuke
  calculator: 6 abacus 7 soroban
  calisthenics: 4 judo
  cape: 4 mino
  cherry: 4 fuji
  chess: 5 shogi
  chevrotain: 4 napu
  church: 4 tera
  circle: 4 maru
  clan: 7 Satsuma
  class: eta, roi 6 heimin 7 kwazoku, samurai, shizoku
  clogs: 4 geta
  clover: 4 hagi
  coin: bu; rin, sen, yen 4 oban 5 koban,
  obang, tempo 6 cobang, ichebu, ichibu,
  itzebu, itzibu, kobang 7 itzeboo, itziboo
  combine: 8 zaibatsu
  composition: 6 haikai
  costume: 7 netsuke
  court: 5 dairi
  crepe: 8 chirimen
  crest: mon 7 kikumon
  dancing girl: 6 geisha
  deer: 4 sika
  deity: 9 Amaterasu
  dextrose: ame
  dish: 7 sashimi, tempura 8 sukiyaki, teri-
  yaki
  dog: 6 tanate
  door: 6 fusuma
  drama: noh 6 kabuki
  drink: 4 mate, sake, saki
  drum: 5 tarko
  dwarf tree: 6 bonsai
  dye process: 5 yuzen
  earthenware: 5 banko 7 Satsuma 8
  rakuware

emperor: 8 Hirohito
emperor's title of old: 6 mikado
ethics: 7 Bushido
explosive: 7 shimose
fabric: 6 birodi 7 habutai, nishiki 8 chirimen, habutaye
family concern: 8 zaibatsu
fan: ogi
festival: Bon 7 Matsuri
fish: ayu, tai, tho 4 fugu, funa
flag: 7 sunflag
flower: 9 nelumbium
flute: 4 fuye
founder of imperial line: 10 Jimmu Tenno
game: 5 goban 6 gobang
garment: 5 haori 6 kimono, mompei
gateway: 5 torii
girdle: obi
girdle receptacle: 4 inro
god: 5 Ebisu, Hotei 6 Benten 7 Daikoku, Jurojin 8 Bishamon 10 Fukurokuju
goddess: 9 Amaterasu
governor's title: 6 shogun, taikun, tycoon
hanging: 8 kakemono
harp: 4 koto
herb: udo
kelp: 4 kome
lacquer: 6 urushi
legislature: 4 Diet
litter: see *palanquin* below
loquat: 4 biwa
lyric: 5 haiku, hokku
magnolia: 5 yulan
measure: bu, jo; boo, cho 4 hiro 5 tsubo 11 kujira-shaku
measure of distance: ri
measure of land: se; tan
measure of weight: mo; fun, kin, kon, rin, shi 4 kati, kwan, niyo 5 carat, catty, momme, picul 6 kwamme 8 hiyak-kin 11 komma-ichida
metalwork: 5 zogan
military ruler: 6 shogun
monastery: 4 tera
music and dancing: 7 san-gaku 8 sarugaku
musical instrument: 4 fuye, koto 5 tarko 7 samisen, truyume
nautical mile: 5 kairi
news service: 5 Domei
nobility: 7 kwazoku
ornament: 4 inro
outcast: eta 5 ronin
overcoat: 4 mino
pagoda: taa
painting style: 4 kano 7 ukiyoye
palanquin: 4 kago 5 cango 7 norimon
paper-folding art: 7 origami
paper mulberry: 4 kozo
persimmon: 4 kaki 7 Hyakume
pine: 5 matsu

plant: udo 5 kùdzu 6 sugamo
plum: 6 kelsey
porcelain: 5 Hizen, Imari 6 Hirado 9 Nabeshima, Sanda ware
porter: 5 akabo
potato: imo
quince: 8 japonica
radish: 6 daikon
receptacle: 4 inro
religion: 6 Shinto 8 Buddhism 9 Shintoism
rice cake: ame
rice wine: 4 sake
robe: 6 kimono
salad plant: udo
salmon: 4 masu
sash: obi
screen: 5 shoji
seaweed: 4 nori
self-defense: 4 judo 6 karate 7 jujitsu, jujutsu
Shinto temple: Sha 5 Jinja 6 Jinsha 7 Yashiro
ship: 4 maro, maru
shoe: 4 geta, zori
shrub: 4 fuji 5 goumi 8 japonica
silk: 7 habutai 8 chirimen, habutaye
silkworm: 7 yamamai
silkworm disease: uji
sock: 4 tabi
song: uta
storm: 7 tsunami
suicide: 7 seppuku 8 hara-kari, hara-kiri, hari-kari, kamikaze
suntree: 7 hinokis
sword: 5 catan 6 cattan 8 wacadash
sword guard: 5 tsuba
tea ceremony: 7 chanoyu
tea girl: 6 mousme 7 mousmee
temple: 4 tera
throne: 6 shinza
title: 4 kami 6 shogun
tortoise shell: 5 bekko
tree: 4 kozo, sugi 5 akeki, kiaki, yeddo 6 urushi 7 camphor 8 akamatsu 10 shirakashi
untouchable: eta
vehicle: 7 ricksha 8 rickshaw 10 jinricksha, jinrikisha
velvet: 6 birodi
verse: 5 tanka
vine: 5 kudzu
wall: 5 shoji
warrior: 7 samurai
windstorm: 5 taifu
winged being: 5 tengu
wrestling: 4 Sumo
writing: 4 kana
zitherharp: 4 koto
Japanese-American: 5 Issei, Kibei, Nisei 6 Sansei
jape: 4 fool, gibe, jeer, jest, joke, mock 5

fraud, trick 6 deride
japery: 10 buffoonery
Japheth: *father:* 4 Noah
  son: 5 Magog, Tubal 7 Meshech
japonica: 4 bush 5 shrub 8 camellia
jar: jug, ola, urn 4 jolt, olla, vase 5 banga,
  clash, cruse, shake, shock 6 croppa, hy-
  dria, krater, tinaja 7 agitate, amphora,
  clatter, concuss, discord 10 jardiniere
  fruit: 5 mason
  rubber: 4 lute
  top: lid
  two-handled: 7 amphora
  wide-mouthed: 4 ewer
jardiniere: jar, jug, urn 4 vase 5 stand 7
  garnish 9 flowerpot
jargon: 4 cant 5 argot, idiom, lingo, slang
  6 pidgin 9 baragouin, gibberish 10 balderdash, vernacular 12 gobbledygook •
  lawyer's: 8 legalese
  scholar's: 9 academese
jarl: 4 earl 7 headman 9 chieftain
jarring: 5 rough 9 dissonant 10 discordant
jasmine: 4 vine 6 flower 7 perfume
Jason: *father:* 5 Aeson
  love: 6 Creusa
  men: 9 Argonauts
  ship: 4 Argo
  teacher: 7 Cheiron
  uncle: 6 Pelias
  wife: 5 Medea
jasper: 6 morlop, quartz 10 bloodstone,
  chalcedony
jaundice: 4 bias, envy 7 gulsach, icterus 8
  jealousy 9 prejudice
jaunt: 4 ride, trip 5 sally, tramp 6 ramble
  7 journey 9 excursion
jaunty: 4 airy 5 cocky, perky, showy,
  smart 7 finical, stylish 8 debonair 9 debonaire, sprightly
java: 6 coffee
Java: see **Indonesia**
Javanese: *almond:* 7 talisay
  arrow poison: 4 upas
  badger: 5 ratel 6 teledu
  berry: 5 cubeb
  carriage: 4 sado 5 sadoo
  civet: 5 rasse
  cotton: 5 kapok
  dancers: 6 bedoyo
  drama: 6 topeng
  Dutchman: 6 blanda
  fabric: 4 ikat
  fig tree: 7 gondang
  grackle: beo
  measure: 4 paal 5 palen
  musical instrument: 5 saron 6 bonang,
    gender 7 gambang, gamelan 8 gamelang
  orchestra: 7 gamelan 8 gamelang
  ox: 7 bantens
  pepper: 5 cubeb

  plum: 5 duhal 6 jambul, lomboy 7 jam-
    bool
  puppet show: 6 wajang, wayang
  rice field: 5 sawah
  skunk: 6 teledu
  speech: 5 krama, ngoko
  squirrel: 8 jelerang
  straw: 6 peanit
  sumac: 6 fuyang
  temple: 5 candi 6 chandi, tjandi
  tree: 4 upas 6 antiar 7 gondang
  village: 5 dessa
  weight: 4 amat, pond, tali 5 pound
  wild dog: 5 adjag
javelin: 4 dart 5 lance, spear 7 assagai,
  assegai, harpoon
  cord: 7 amentum
jaw: maw 4 chaw, chop, talk 5 scold 6 berate, jabber 7 chatter 8 prattle
  lumpy: 13 actinomycosis
  muscle: 8 masseter
  part: 4 chin
  pert. to: 5 malar 7 gnathic
jawbone: 7 maxilla 8 mandible 13 apply
  pressure
Jayhawker: 6 Kansan
jazz: hot 4 cool, scat 5 funky, swing 6
  modern 7 ragtime 11 barrelhouse, progressive
jealous: 7 envious 8 watchful 9 green-
  eyed 10 suspicious 11 mistrustful
jeer: bob, boo 4 gibe, hoot, jape, mock 5
  fleer, flout, scoff, scout, sneer, taunt 6
  deride 8 ridicule
Jeffersonian: 7 liberal 10 democratic
Jefferson's home: 10 Monticello
Jehiada's wife: 9 Jehosheba 12 Jeho-
  shabeath
Jehoahaz's mother: 7 Hamutal
Jehoiachin's successor: 9 Salathiel
Jehoshaphat: *father:* Asa
  son: 4 Jehu
Jehovah: God 5 Jahve, Yahwe 6 Elohim,
  Jahveh, Yahweh
jehu: 6 driver
jejune: dry 4 arid, dull, flat 5 empty,
  inane, prosy, trite, vapid 6 barren,
  hungry, meager 7 insipid, sterile 8
  foodless, lifeless 9 innocuous
jell: 7 thicken 9 coagulate 11 crystallize
jelly: gel 6 spread 7 gelatin 8 gelatine
  meat: 5 aspic
  vegetable: 6 pectin
jellyfish: 6 medusa 7 acaleph, milksop 8
  weakling
  group: 10 discophora
  part: 10 exumbrella
jellylike: 10 gelatinous
je ne sais quoi: 13 I don't know what 14
  elusive quality
jennet: ass 5 horse 6 donkey
jeopardize: 6 expose 7 imperil 8 endan-

ger 10 compromise

jeopardy: 4 risk 5 peril 6 danger, hazard, menace

Jerahmeel's son: 4 Oren 5 Achia

jeremiad: 6 lament, tirade 9 complaint

jerez: 6 sherry

Jericho: *publican:* 8 Zaccheus 9 Zacchaeus

   woman: 5 Rahab

jerk: ass, bob, tic, 4 fool, yank 5 idiot, pluck, twist 6 twitch, wrench

jerkin: 4 coat 6 jacket, salmon 9 blackjack, waistcoat

jerky: 4 meat 5 wagon 7 charqui 8 saccadic, staccato 9 irregular, twitching 10 paroxysmal

jeroboam: 4 bowl 6 bottle, goblet

jerry-built: 5 tacky 6 sleazy 13 unsubstantial

jersey: 6 gansey 7 sweater

Jersey tea: 11 wintergreen 12 checkerberry

Jerusalem: 4 Sion, Zion 5 Salem

   captor: 4 Omar

   garden: 10 Gethsemane

   mosque: 4 Omar

   mountain: 4 Sion, Zion 6 Moriah, Olivet

   oak: 7 ambrose

   pool: 6 Siloam 8 Bethesda

   priest: 5 Zadoc, Zadok

   prophetess: 4 Anna, Anne

   region: 5 Perea

   spring: 5 Gihon 6 Siloam

   temple treasury: 6 Corban

   thorn: 6 retama

Jerusalem artichoke: 5 tuber 7 girasol 8 girasole 10 topinambou

Jerusalem corn: 5 durra

Jerusalem haddock: 4 opah

jess: 5 strap, thong 7 binding

jessamy: fop 5 dandy

Jesse: *father:* 4 Obed

   son: 5 David

jest: fun, gag, kid 4 bull, fool, jape, joke, mime, quip 5 chaff, prank, sport, tease 6 banter, japery, trifle 8 drollery 9 burlesque 10 jocularity

jester: 4 fool, mime, zany 5 clown, droll 6 motley 7 buffoon, 8 comedian, humorist 11 merry-andrew

Jesuit: *founder:* 6 Loyola (Ignatius)

   motto: 4 A.M.D.G.

   saint: 5 Regis

Jesuits' bark: 8 cinchona

jet: 4 ebon, gush 5 black, raven, spout, spurt 6 nozzle 7 lignite 8 aircraft

   lag: 7 fatigue

   set: 11 social group

jet-assisted takeoff: 4 JATO

Jethro's daughter: 8 Zipporah

jettison: 5 eject, scrap 6 discard 7 abandon 9 throw away

jetty: 4 mole, pier 5 groin, wharf 6 groyne

jeu: 4 game, play 9 diversion

jeune fille: 4 girl, miss

Jew: (see also **Hebrew, Judaism**): 6 Essene, Hebrew, Semite 9 Israelite

jewel: (see also **gem**): gem 5 bijou(F.), ideal, stone 7 paragon 8 ornament

   box: 6 casket 7 casquet

   case: tye

   connoisseur: 10 lapidarist

   magnifying lens: 5 loupe

   set: 6 parure

   weight: 5 carat

jewelry: 10 bijouterie

   alloy: 6 oreide, oroide

   artificial: 5 paste 6 strass 7 costume

   cutting device: dop

   piece: pin 4 ring 6 brooch 7 earring 8 bracelet, lavalier, necklace

   setting: 4 pave

jezebel: 4 slut 5 hussy, wench 6 virago 7 trollop 8 strumpet

Jezebel: *father:* 7 Ethbaal

   husband: 4 Ahab

   slayer: 4 Jehu

   victim: 6 Naboth

jib: 4 balk, boom, sail 8 crane arm

jibe: 5 agree, shift 6 accord

jiffy: 5 flash, hurry, trice 6 moment, second 7 instant

jig: 4 tool 5 dance, drill 8 fishhook

jigger: cup 4 boat 5 glass 6 gadget

jiggle: jar 5 dance, shake 6 fidget, diddle, teeter 7 agitate

jihad, jehad: war 6 strife 7 contest, crusade 8 campaign

jill: 4 girl 5 woman 10 sweetheart

jilt: 5 leave 6 betray, desert, reject 7 abandon, discard, forsake, let down

jimmy: bar, pry 5 lever 7 crowbar, pry open

Jimsonweed: 6 datura

jingle: 4 ring 5 clank, clink, rhyme, verse 6 tinkle 7 chinkle

jingoist: 10 chauvinist

jinni: 5 genie 6 afreet, Alukah, jinnee, Yaksha, Yakshi(fem.)

jinx: hex 5 jonah 6 hoodoo, whammy 7 evil eye, nemesis

jitters: 5 panic 6 dither, shakes 7 willies

jittery: 5 jumpy 7 fidgety, nervous

jive: kid 5 dance, swing 6 jargon, phoney 7 hot jazz 9 deceitful, jitterbug

Joan of Arc: 7 Pucelle

   birthplace: 7 Domremy

   counselors: 6 voices

   victory: 7 Orleans

Joan's spouse: 5 Darby

job: 4 duty, task 5 chare, cheat, chore, stint, trick 7 farm out 8 position, vocation 10 employment

Job: *daughter:* 5 Kezia 6 Jemima

friend: 5 Elihu 6 Bildad, Zophar 7 Eliphaz

Job's tears: 4 coix 4 adlai, adlay, grass, plant

jobber: 6 dealer 10 wholesaler

Jocasta: *daughter* 6 Ismene 8 Antigone
husband: 5 Laius 7 Oedipus
son: 7 Oedipus 8 Eteocles 9 Polynices 10 Polyneices

jock: 7 athlete

jockey: 4 gull 5 rider, trick 6 driver, outwit 8 maneuver, operator 10 manipulate
kind of: 4 disc

jocose: dry 6 joking 7 playful 9 full of fun

jocular: gay 4 airy 5 droll, funny, jolly, merry, silly, witty 6 blithe, elated, jovial, joyous, lively, ribald 7 comical, festive, gleeful, jesting, playful, waggish 8 animated, cheerful, gladsome, humorous, mirthful, sportive 9 burlesque, convivial, facetious, hilarious, vivacious 10 frolicsome

joculator: 4 mime 6 jester 7 juggler 8 conjurer, jongleur, minstrel 11 entertainer

jocund: gay 6 genial 8 cheerful

jog: run 4 jerk, lope, poke, prod, trot 5 nudge 6 canter 7 refresh 9 stimulate

John: Ian 4 Ivan, Juan, Sean

John Brown's Body author: 5 Benet

John of Gaunt: 9 Lancaster

John the Baptist: *father* 7 Zachary 9 Zachariah, Zacharias
mother: 9 Elizabeth

johnnycake: 4 pone 7 corn bread

Johnson grass: 7 sorghum

join: add, mix, tie, wed 4 ally, fuse, knit, knot, link, mate, meet, seam, team, weld, yoke 5 annex, blend, enrol, enter, graft, hitch, marry, merge, miter, piece, unite 6 attach, cantle, cement, cocket, concur, couple, engage, enlist, enroll, mingle, solder, splice, suture 7 combine, connect, consort, mortise 8 coalesce 9 associate 10 amalgamate 11 consolidate, participate

joint: ell, hip, tee 4 butt, dive, knee, node, seam 5 ankle, cross, elbow, hinge, scarf, wrist 6 arthra(pl.), mutual, rabbet, resort 7 arthron, brothel, calepin, hangout, knuckle, pastern 8 coupling 12 articulation
pert. to: 5 nodal 9 articular
plant stem: 6 phyton 8 phytomer
put out of: 5 upset 9 dislocate
right angle: ell, tee
turned outward: 6 valgus
without: 10 acondylose, acondylous
wooden: 5 tenon

joist: 4 beam 7 sleeper 8 studding

joke: fun, gag, kid, pun 4 fool, gibe, hoax,

jape, jest, quip 5 flirt, prank, sally, sport, tease 6 banter 9 wisecrack
old: 6 wheeze 8 chestnut

joker: wag, wit 4 card 5 clown, cutup 6 gagman, jester 7 farceur 11 hidden catch

jollity: fun 5 cheer, mirth, revel 6 gaiety, gayety 7 revelry 8 hilarity 9 amusement, festivity, joviality, merriment 11 merrymaking 12 cheerfulness, exhilaration

jolly: 5 buxom, rally 6 cajole, jovial, mellow 7 jocular 9 convivial 11 intoxicated

jolly boat: 4 yawl

jolt: jar 4 blow, bump, butt 5 knock, shake, shock 6 jostle, jounce 7 startle

Jonah: 4 jinx 7 prophet
deliverer: 5 whale

jonquil: 8 daffodil 9 narcissus

Johnson comedy: Fox 7 Epicene, Volpone 9 Alchemist

Jordan: *capital:* 5 Amman
city: 5 Irbid, Zarqa 6 Nablus
ethnic group: 4 Arab, Kurd 8 Armenian
monetary unit: 4 fils 5 dinar
port: 5 Aqaba
river: 6 Jordan

Joseph: *brother:* Dan, Gad 4 Levi 5 Asher, Judah 6 Reuben, Simeon 7 Zebulun 8 Benjamin, Issachar, Naphtali
buyer: 8 Potiphar
father: 5 Jacob
mother: 6 Rachel
son: 4 Igal 7 Ephraim

josh: guy, kid, rib 4 joke 5 chaff, spoof, tease 6 banter 9 poke fun at

Joshua: *associate:* 5 Caleb
burial place: 5 Gaash
father: Nun
place of importance: 7 Aijalon

Joshua tree: 5 yucca

Josiah: *father:* 4 Amon
mother: 7 Jedidah
son: 8 Jehoahaz 9 Jehoiakim

joss: 4 idol 5 image 8 divinity

jostle: jar, jog 4 jolt, push 5 crowd, elbow, shove 6 hurtle, hustle

jot: ace, bit 4 atom, iota, whit 5 grain, minim, point 6 tittle 7 smidgen 8 particle

jotting: 4 memo 9 short note

jounce: 4 jolt 5 shake 6 bounce

journal: log 5 diary, paper 6 record 7 daybook, gazette, logbook 8 magazine 10 periodical
keeper: 7 diarist

journalist: 6 editor 8 reporter 9 columnist

journey: run 4 eyre, fare, iter(L.), ride,

sail, tour, trek, trip **5** jaunt, route **6** junket, safari, travel, voyage **7** circuit, odyssey, passage **8** navigate **9** excursion **10** expedition, pilgrimage **13** peregrination

course of: **9** itinerary

division of: lap, leg

pert. to: **6** viatic **11** peripatetic

joust: 4 tilt **6** combat **7** tourney **10** tournament

field: **4** list

ready to: **5** atilt

jovial: gay **5** bully, jolly, merry **6** elated, genial, jocose, jocund, joyous **7** jocular **9** convivial, hilarious

jowl: jaw **4** chop **5** cheek **6** dewlap, wattle **7** jawbone

joy: 4 glee **5** bliss, mirth **6** gaiety, gayety **7** delight, ecstasy, elation, rapture, revelry **8** felicity, gladness, hilarity, pleasure **9** beatitude, festivity, happiness, rejoicing **10** exultation **12** cheerfulness, exhilaration

Muse: **4** Tara

Joyce (James): *character:* **5** Bloom, Rowan **7** Dedalus **9** Earwicker

work: **6** Exiles **7** Ulysses **9** Dubliners **12** Chamber Music **13** Finnegan's Wake, Pomes Penyeach

joyless: 6 dismal **9** cheerless

joyous: gay **4** glad **5** merry **6** blithe, festal **7** blessed, festive, gleeful, jocular **8** cheerful, mirthful **9** blitheful, delighted

Jubal's father: 6 Lamech

jubilant: 6 elated **9** exulting **9** rejoicing **10** triumphant

Judah: *brother:* **4** Levi **6** Joseph, Reuben, Simeon

daughter-in-law: **5** Tamar

descendant: **4** Anub, Boaz **5** David, Jesse **9** Jerahmeel

father: **5** Jacob

mother: **4** Leah

queen: **8** Athaliah

son: Er **4** Onan

Judaism (see also **Hebrew, Israel**): *abode of the dead:* **5** Sheol

ascetic: **6** Essene

Bible: **4** Tora **5** Torah

Bible text: **5** miqra

Book of Psalms: **8** Tehillim

bread: **5** echem, matzo **6** hallah, matzos **7** challah, matzoth **8** afikomen

butcher: **6** shohet **8** shochtim

cabalistic book: **5** Zohar

calendar: see *month* below

ceremony: **8** habdalah

community: **6** aljama **8** kehillah

confession of sins: **5** Alhet **7** Ashamnu

convert: ger

Day of Atonement: **9** Yom Kippur

devil: **6** Belial

dietary regulations: **7** kashrut

dispersion: **5** golah **8** diaspora

doctor of law: **6** scribe

doctrine: **6** Mishna **7** Mishnah **8** Kodashim

drum: **4** toph

festival: see *holiday* below

garment: **5** shawl, talis **7** tallith

harp: **5** nebel

healer: Asa

heretical doctrine: **7** Karaism

holiday: **5** Pesah, Purim **6** Pesach, Succos, Sukkos, Yom Tov **7** Sukkoth **8** Chanukah, Hanukkah, Lagbomer, Shabouth **9** Tishahbab, Yom Kippur **11** Rosh Hashana **12** Simhath Torah

horn: **6** shofar **7** shophar

immigrant: **4** oleh **6** halutz **7** chalutz

instrument: **4** asor **5** nebel

instrument player: **9** psalterer, psaltress

judge: **7** shophet

land: **4** Zion

law: **4** Chok, Tora **5** Torah **6** Chukah, Talmud **7** Halacha, Halakah **8** Kashruth

lawgiver: **5** Moses

liturgy: **6** Maarib, Minhah **9** Shaharith

lyre: **4** asor

marriage broker: **8** shadchen

marriage custom: **8** levirate

meat inspection: **7** bedikah

miter: **7** petalon

month: **4** Adar, Iyar, Elul **5** Tebet, Nisan, Sivan **6** Tishri, Kislev, Shebat, Beadar, Tammuz **7** Heshvan

mourning period: **6** Shivah

New Year: **11** Rosh Hashana

Old Testament division **11** Hagiographa

patriarch: **5** Isaac, Jacob **7** Abraham

patriot family: **8** Maccabee

pioneer: **6** halutz **7** chalutz

poems: **6** yigdal **8** Azharoth

prayer: **5** Alenu, Shema **7** Geullah

prayer book: **6** mahzor, siddur

priest: **4** Ezra **5** Aaron, Cohen **6** Levite

priestly caste: **7** Cohanim, Levites

prophet: **4** Amos, Ezra **5** Elias, Hosea, Jonah, Micah, Nahum **6** Daniel, Elijah, Elisha, Haggai **8** Habakkuk, Jeremiah **9** Zechariah

prophetess: **6** Huldah

proselyte: ger

psalm of praise: **6** hallel

redeemer: **4** goel

revelation: **5** Torah

ritual: see *ceremony* above

sabbath: **8** Saturday

sacred objects: **4** urim

sage: **4** Agur

scarf: **5** abnet **7** tallith

scroll: **11** Sepher Torah

sect member: **6** Essene, Hassid

skullcap: 6 kippah 7 yamilke 8 yarmulka

song: 8 hatikvah 9 hattikvah

spirit: 8 Asmodeus

synagogue: 5 schul

tassel: 6 zizith

teacher: 5 amora, rabbi, tanna

temple precentor: 6 cantor

trumpet: 6 shofar 7 shophar

vestment: 5 ephod

women's organization: 8 Hadassah

Judas: 7 traitor 8 betrayer

place of suicide: 8 Aceldama, Akeldama

Judea: *ancient name:* 5 Judah

governor: 6 Pilate

king: Asa 4 Ahaz, Amon 5 Herod 7 Jehoram 8 Manesseh 10 Jehoiachin 11 Jehoshaphat

place: 5 Berea

judge: try 4 deem, gage, rank, rate 5 court, gauge, opine 6 assess, critic, decide, reckon, umpire 7 arbiter, believe, justice, referee, suppose 8 consider, estimate, mediator, sentence 9 criticize, determine 10 adjudicate, arbitrator, chancellor, magistrate

bench: 4 banc 6 bancus

chamber: 6 camera

circuit: 4 iter

entry of, after verdict: 6 postea

group: 5 bench

junior or subordinate: 6 puisne

mallet: 5 gavel

of Hades: 5 Minos

of the dead: 6 Osiris

robe: 4 toga

judgment: 5 arret, award, sense, taste 6 insight, 7 censure, insight, opinion, verdict 8 decision, sentence 9 criticism 10 astuteness, discretion, horse sense 11 sensibility

left to one's: 13 discretionary

judicable: 12 determinable

judicial assembly: 5 court

judiciary: 5 bench

document: 4 writ 8 decision

judicious: 4 wise 7 prudent 8 rational, sensible 9 sagacious 10 discerning

Judith: *husband:* Manasses

victim: 10 Holofernes

judo: 7 jujitsu 10 martial art

rel. of: 9 wrestling

jug: jar 4 ewer, jail, olla 5 crock, cruse 6 carafe, flagon, lockup, prison, tinaja, urceus 7 pitcher 9 container 10 bellarmine, jardiniere

shaped like a man: 4 Toby

Juggernaut: 6 Vishnu

juggle: 7 falsify, shuffle 10 manipulate

jugglery: 8 trickery 9 deception 10 escamotage(F.), hanky-panky 11 legerdemain 13 sleight-of-hand

juice: jus(F.), oil, sap 4 broo 6 cremor 8 gasoline 10 succulence 11 electricity

apple: 6 cider

fruit: rob 4 must, stum, wine 5 cider 6 casiri 7 vinegar

plant: sap 4 milk 5 latex 6 achete

juicy: 4 frim, racy 5 spicy 6 lively 7 piquant 9 succulent

juju: 5 charm 6 amulet, fetish

juke: 4 fake 5 cheat 7 deceive

julep: 5 drink 8 beverage

Juliet: *betrothed:* 5 Paris

father: 7 Capulet

lover: 5 Romeo

jumble: 4 hash, heap, mess 5 mix up 6 huddle, medley, muddle 7 clutter, mixture 8 disorder, mishmash 9 confusion 10 hodgepodge

jump: hop 4 leap 5 bound, caper, vault 6 hurdle, prance, spring 7 saltate 8 increase

stick for: 4 pogo, pole

jumper: 5 dress, smock 6 blouse, jacket

jumpsuit: 8 coverall

jumpy: 7 jittery, nervous 12 apprehensive

junco: 5 finch 8 snowbird

junction: 4 axil, seam 5 joint, union 6 suture 7 contact, meeting 8 crossing 10 confluence, connection

juncture: 4 pass 5 union 6 choice, crisis 8 exigency 9 emergency 10 crossroads 12 turning point

June bug: 6 beetle 8 figeater

June grass: poa

Jungfrau: 4 peak 8 mountain

site of: 4 Alps

jungle: 4 maze 6 tangle 9 labyrinth 10 wilderness

junior: 7 student, younger 8 namesake 11 subordinate

juniper: 4 cade, ezel 5 grose, retem, savin 6 sabine, savine

junk: 4 boat, dope, drug 5 scrap, trash, waste 6 heroin, refuse 7 discard, rubbish 8 jettison 9 narcotics

junker: 5 crate, noble, wreck 6 German 10 aristocrat

junket: 4 trip 5 feast 6 picnic 9 excursion 13 entertainment

Juno: 4 Hera

consort: 7 Jupiter

special messenger: 4 Iris

junta: 7 council 8 tribunal 9 committee 10 government

junto: 5 cabal 6 clique 7 coterie, faction

Jupiter: 4 Jove, Zeus

angel: 7 Zadkiel

consort: 4 Juno

daughter: 4 Bura 7 Minerva

epithet: 6 Stator

Roman temple: 7 Capitol

satellite: Pan 4 Hera, Leda 5 Hades 6 Europa, Hestia 7 Demeter 8 Adrastea,

Amalthea, Callisto, Ganymede, Poseidon
son: Castor, Pollux
Jupiter Pluvius: 4 rain
jural: 5 legal 8 juristic
Jurassic division: 4 Lias
jurisdiction: law 5 venue 6 county, domain, sphere 8 dominion, province 9 authority, bailiwick, territory
ecclesiastical: see 6 parish 7 deanery, diocese
jurisprudence: law 14 court decisions
juror: 7 assizer, juryman 8 talesman
group: 4 jury 5 panel
selection list: 6 venire
just: due, fit 4 even, fair, only, true 5 equal, exact, legal, valid 6 candid, honest, merely, normal, purely, simply 7 correct, equable, upright 8 accurate, unbiased 9 equitable, impartial 10 legitimate
justice: law 5 judge 6 equity 7 honesty

god: 7 Forsete, Forseti, Forsite
goddess: 4 Maat
justification: 6 excuse, reason 7 apology, defense 9 authority, rationale
justify: 4 avow 6 adjust, defend, excuse 7 support, warrant 8 maintain, sanction 9 authorize, exculpate, vindicate
jut: 4 butt 5 bulge 6 beetle 7 project 8 overhang, protrude, stick out 10 projection
jute: 4 desi 5 gunny 6 burlap 7 sacking
Jutlander: 4 Dane
jutting: 7 salient 10 protruding 11 overhanging
juvenile: 5 actor, young 6 callow 8 immature, youthful 10 adolescent 11 undeveloped
Juventas: 4 Hebe
juxtaposition: 7 contact 8 nearness 9 adjacence, adjacency, proximity 10 contiguity

K

kaama: 10 hartebeest
kaddish: 6 prayer 8 doxology
kae: 7 jackdaw
kaffeeklatsch: 6 social 9 gathering 11 get-together
Kaffir, Kafir: 5 Bantu
language: 4 Xosa
warriors: 4 Impi
Kafka character: 4 Olga
kaiser: 5 ruler 7 emperor
kaka: 6 parrot
genus: 6 nestor
kakapo: 6 parrot
kaki: 4 bird 5 stilt 9 persimmon
kakkak: 7 bittern
kale: 4 cole 5 green 7 cabbage, collard 8 colewort
kali: 5 plant 6 carpet 8 saltwort
Kali's husband: 4 Siva 5 Shiva
kalinite: 4 alum 7 mineral
Kalmuck, Kalmuk: 6 Mongol
kamias: 7 bilimbi
Kanaka: 8 Hawaiian 10 Melanesian, Polynesian 11 Micronesian
kanari: 6 almond

kangaroo: 'roo 4 euro 5 bilbi, bilby 6 turatt 7 bettong, wallaby 8 bettonga, boongary, forester 11 macropodian
female: doe, gin, roo
male: 6 boomer
young: 4 joey
kangaroo rat: 7 potoroo
Kansas: *capital:* 6 Topeka
city: 4 Iola 5 Lyons, Paola 6 Salina 7 Abilene, Wichita 8 Lawrence 9 Dodge City 10 Hutchinson, Kansas City
county: Elk 4 Gove, Lane, Ness, Reno, Rice 5 Chase, Cloud, Ellis, Geary, Kiowa, Pratt, Riley, Rooks, Trego 6 Barber, Coffey, Finney, Harper, Harvey, Jewell, Kearny, Nemaha, Neosho, Seward, Sumner 7 Bourbon, Greeley, Labette, Rawlins, Stanton
early explorer: 8 Coronado
fort: 5 Riley 6 Larned 11 Leavenworth
Indian: 5 Kiowa 6 Pawnee 7 Wichita 8 Comanche, Kickapoo
President Eisenhower's Library: 7 Abilene
river: 5 Osage 6 Kansas (Kaw), Saline 7

Solomon 8 Arkansas, Cimarron 9 Smoky Hill 10 Republican

state animal: 7 buffalo

state bird: 10 meadow lark

state flower: 9 sunflower

state motto: 16 Ad astra per aspera

state nickname: 9 Sunflower

state song: 14 "Home on the Range"

state tree: 10 cottonwood

Kant's category: 7 quality 8 modality, quantity, relation

kaolin: 4 clay

kaput: 6 broken, ruined 8 defeated 9 destroyed

karakul: 5 sheep

karate: 10 martial art 14 self-defense art

karma: 4 fate 7 destiny 10 vibrations

karyotin: 9 chromatin

kasha: 4 mush 5 grain 6 cereal

katchung: 6 peanut

kava: ava, awa 6 pepper

bowl: 5 tanoa

kayak: 5 canoe

kayo: 8 knockout

Kazantzakis hero: 5 Zorba

kea: parrot

Keats poem: 5 Lamia

kebbie: 4 club 5 stick 6 cudgel

ked: 4 tick

kedge: 6 anchor

keel: vat 4 ship 5 upset 6 careen, carina 7 capsize, carinae(pl.) 8 flounder, navigate

part: 4 skag, skeg

right angle to: 5 abeam

without: 9 ecarinate

keel over: 5 faint, upset 7 capsize

keel-shaped: 8 carinate

keelbill: ani

keeling: 7 codfish

keen: 4 avid, fell(Sc.), nice, wide 5 acute, awake, eager, sharp 6 ardent, astute, bewail, biting, clever, hearty, lament, severe, shrewd 7 cunning, fervent, intense, parlous, pungent 9 trenchant 10 hardheaded 12 enthusiastic 13 perspicacious

keenly: 6 dearly

keenness: 4 edge 6 acumen, genius, talent

keep: 4 fend, hold 5 board, guard, lodge, place 6 arrest, behold, living, stable 7 confine, contain, husband 8 fortress, maintain, preserve, restrain, withhold 9 celebrate 10 livelihood

going: 7 sustain

keep back: bar, dam 4 save 6 detain 7 reserve 8 withhold 10 stay behind

keep in: 6 retain

keep on: 7 persist 8 continue 9 persevere

keep out: 4 save 5 debar 7 exclude, reserve 8 hold back

keeper: 5 guard 6 pastor, warden 7 curator, janitor 8 guardian, watchdog 9 caretaker, constable, custodian 10 maintainer

of golden apple: 5 Ithun

of marches: 8 margrave

of park: 6 ranger

keeping: 4 care 5 award, guard, trust 6 charge 7 custody 10 caretaking, possession 11 maintenance 12 guardianship

keepsake: 5 token 7 memento 8 giftbook, souvenir

keest: sap 6 marrow 9 substance

keeve: tub, vat 5 basin

kef: 7 languor, tobacco 8 euphoria 10 dreaminess 12 tranquillity

keg: cag 4 cade, cask 6 barrel 7 barrico

open: 6 unhead

kegler: 6 bowler

keister, keester: 4 rump 7 satchel 8 suitcase

keitloa: 5 rhino

kelly: hat 5 color, derby, green

kelp: 5 algae, varec 6 varech 7 seaweed 8 bellware(Sc.)

kempt: 4 neat, tidy 11 well-groomed

ken: 4 know(Sc.), view 5 admit, sight 7 discern, insight 9 knowledge 10 cognizance, 11 recognition 13 understanding

Kenilworth author: 5 Scott

kennel: 5 drain, sewer 6 cannel, gutter, stable 7 shelter 8 doghouse 9 enclosure

kentledge: 5 metal 7 ballast, pig iron

Kentucky: *capital:* 9 Frankfort

city: 5 Paris 6 Hazard 7 Paducah 8 Richmond 9 Covington, Lexington, Owensboro 10 Louisville

county: 4 Bath, Bell, Boyd, Hart, Pike, Todd 5 Adair, Boone, Boyle, Casey, Floyd, Grant, Knott, Larue, Mason, Rowan, Trigg, Wolfe 6 Estill, Graves, Harlan, Kenton, Laurel, Leslie, Mercer, Oldham, Owsley 7 Bourbon, Bracken, Bullitt, Daviess, Garrard, Greenup, Letcher, Menifee, Trimble, Whitley

gold depository: 8 Fort Knox

horse race: 5 Derby

Indian: 7 Shawnee 8 Cherokee, Iroquois

lake: 5 Dewey 7 Barkley 10 Dale Hollow

mountain peak: 5 Black

plateau: 10 Cumberland

President Lincoln's birthplace: 11 Hodgenville

river: 4 Ohio, Salt 5 Green, Rough 6 Barren 7 Licking, Rolling 8 Big Sandy 10 Cumberland, Tradewater

state bird: 8 cardinal

state flower: 9 goldenrod

state nickname: 9 Bluegrass

state tree: 10 coffee tree

trailblazer: 11 Daniel Boone

Kentucky bluegrass: poa

Kentucky coffee tree: 6 bonduc, chicot

Kenya: *capital:* 7 Nairobi
  city: 5 Nyeri 6 Kisumu, Nakuru 7 Mombasa 8 Kakamega
  desert: 5 Nyiri
  lake: 6 Rudolf 8 Victoria
  monetary unit: 4 cent 8 shilling
  mountain peak: 5 Elgon, Kenya
  native group: Luo 5 Bantu, Kamba, Kisii, Masai, Nandi 6 Kikuyu 7 Swahili, Turkana 8 Kipsigis
  province: 5 Coast 6 Nyanza 7 Central, Eastern, Nairobi, Western 10 Rift Valley 12 Northeastern
  river: 4 Athi, Tana 5 Ewaso, Tsavo 6 Galana, Sabaki
  secret society: 6 Mau Mau
  valley: 9 Great Rift

kepi: cap

keratosis: 4 wart

kerchief: 5 curch(Sc.) 6 hankie 7 panuelo 8 bandanna, headrail

kerchoo: 6 sneeze
  answer to: 10 gesundheit 11 God bless you

Keresan Indian: Sia

kerf: cut 4 slit 5 notch 6 groove 7 cutting

kermis, kermess: 4 fair 8 carnival 11 celebration

kernel: nut 4 bunt, core, meat, pith, seed 5 acini(pl.), grain 6 acinus, nuclei(pl.) 7 nucleus

kersenneh: ers 5 vetch

kestrel: 6 falcon, fanner 7 stannel 9 windhover

ketch: 4 boat 8 sailboat

ketone: 5 irone 7 acetone, camphor, muscone-shogaol 8 acridone, civetone, deguelin 9 heptanone 14 cyclopentanone

kettle: pot, vat 4 cazo(Sp.) 5 lebes 6 hollow 7 caldron 8 cauldron, flambeau 9 teakettle 10 kettledrum
  nose: 5 spout

kettledrum: 5 naker, tabor 6 atabal, nagara(Ind.), timbal 7 attabal, timbale, timpano, timpani(pl.), tympani(pl.)

kevel: bar, bit, peg 4 bolt 5 cleat, staff 6 cudgel 7 bollard

key: cay, fin 4 clef, isle, quay, reef 5 dital, islet, pitch 6 claves(pl.), clavis, island, opener, spline, tapper 7 digital 8 clavecin, solution, tonality 11 explanation
  notch: 4 ward
  part: bit
  pert. to: 5 tonal, tonic
  skeleton: 4 gilt 5 screw 7 twirler

key chain: 10 chatelaine

keyboard: 6 manual 7 clavier 8 pedalier 10 claviature

keyed up: 4 agog 5 eager 7 excited 10 stimulated

keynote: 5 theme, tonic, topic 7 feature

keynoter: 6 orator 11 main speaker

keystone: 7 support 8 main part 9 principle

Keystone State: 12 Pennsylvania

khan: inn 5 ruler 9 sovereign 11 caravansary

khedive's estate: 5 daira

Khnemu's consort: 6 Anukit

kiang: ass

kibbutz: 4 farm 7 commune 10 collective, settlement

kibble: 5 grind 10 coarse bits

kibitzer: 7 adviser, meddler 9 spectator

kick: 4 boot, funk(Sc.), punt 5 gripe, growl 6 fitter(Sc.), object, recoil, thrill 7 grumble 8 complain 10 calcitrate, enthusiasm

kick off: 5 begin, start 6 launch 8 commence

kick out: 4 fire, sack 5 evict 6 bounce 7 dismiss 9 discharge

kicker: 8 odd twist, surprise 11 hidden point

kickshaw: toy 6 bauble, gewgaw, trifle, tidbit 7 trinket 8 delicacy

kid: guy 4 goat, hoax, joke 5 child, suede, tease 6 banter 7 fatling, leather 8 cheverel, cheveril 9 youngster

kidcote: 6 prison

kidnap: 6 abduct 8 shanghai 10 spirit away

kidney: 4 neer (Sc.) 5 organ
  pert. to: 5 renal

kidney-shaped: 8 reniform

kidney stone: 4 jade 8 calculus, nephrite 10 nephrolith

Kilauea goddess: 4 Pele

kilderkin: 4 cask 6 barrel 7 measure

Kilimanjaro peak: 4 Kibo 7 Mawenzi

kill: 4 hang, slay, veto 5 croak, 6 deaden, murder 7 achieve, destroy, execute, 8 dispatch, lapidate 9 finish off, slaughter 11 assassinate
  by stoning: 8 lapidate
  by strangling: 7 garotte, garrote

killed: 4 slew 5 slain 9 immolated

killer: 6 gunman, hit man, slayer 7 torpedo 8 assassin, murderer 10 triggerman

killer whale: orc 4 orca 7 grampus

killing: 6 murder 7 slaying 8 homicide 9 martyrdom, slaughter 10 euthanasia
  of brother or sister: 10 fratricide
  of father: 9 patricide
  of king: 8 regicide
  of mother: 9 matricide
  of race: 8 genocide
  of self: 7 suicide
  of small child: 11 infanticide

killjoy: 8 hinderer, 9 pessimist 10 spoilsport

Kilmer poem: 5 Trees

kiln: 4 oast, oven 5 clamp, stove, tiler

6 cockle 7 furnace

kiloliter: 5 stere

kilt: 4 hang 5 pleat 6 fasten 7 filibeg

pouch for: 7 sporran

kilter: 5 order 9 condition

kimono sash: obi

kin: (see also **kinship**): 4 clan, folk, race, sept 5 flesh, tribe 6 family 7 related 8 affinity, cousinry, relation, relative 12 relationship

kind: ilk, 4 boon, gest, good, kith, mild, soft, sort, type 5 breed, class, genre, genus, geste, order 6 benign, blithe, gender, genera(pl.), genial, gentle, goodly, humane, tender 7 amiable, clement, species, variety 8 amicable, benedict, friendly, generous, gracious, merciful 9 benignant, brotherly, favorable, indulgent, 10 benevolent, charitable, 11 considerate, description, kindhearted, sympathetic 13 compassionate

same: 10 homogeneal

kindle: 4 fire, move 5 brood, light, young 6 arouse, decoct, excite, ignite, illume, incite 7 animate, emblaze, inflame, inspire, provoke

kindling: 5 fagot 6 faggot, sticks, tinder

kindness: 5 aloha 6 bounty 8 benefice 9 benignity 11 beneficence

kindred: kin, sib 5 blood, flesh 6 allied, family 7 cognate, kinsmen 8 affinity, kinsfolk 9 congenial 12 relationship

kine: 4 cows 6 cattle

kinetic: 6 active 7 dynamic 9 energetic

king: rex(L.), rey(Sp.), roi(F.) 4 czar, tzar 5 ruler 7 monarch 9 sovereign

title of address: Sir 4 Sire 7 Majesty 8 Highness

King Arthur: *abode:* 6 Avalon

birthplace: 8 Tintagel

court site: 7 Camelot 8 Caerleon

crowner: 6 Dubric

death place: 6 Camlan

father: 5 Uther

fool: 7 Dagonet

forest: 7 Calydon

foster brother: Kay

hound: 6 Cavall

jester: 7 Dagonet

knight: Kay 6 Gareth, Gawain 7 Galahad, Mordred 8 Lancelot, Tristram 9 Percivale

lady: 4 Enid

lance: Ron

magician: 6 Merlin

mother: 7 Igraine

nephew: 6 Gareth 7 Mordred

queen: 8 Guinever 9 Guinevere

shield: 7 Pridwin

sister: 7 Morgain 11 Morgan le Fay

sword: 9 Excalibur

King Canute's consort: 4 Emma

king clover: 7 melilot

king crab: 7 limulus

King Henry IV character: Hal 5 Blunt, Henry, Percy, Poins 6 Scroop

King Lear: See **Lear**

king of beasts: 4 lion

king's evil: scrofula

king's yellow: orpiment

kingdom: 5 realm 6 domain, empire 8 dominion

kingfish: 4 barb, haku, opah 6 bagara

kingfisher: 7 halcyon

kingly: 5 regal, royal 6 regnal 7 basilic, leonine 8 imperial, majestic

kinin: 7 adenine, hormone

kink: 4 bend, curl, loop 5 bunch, chink, cramp, quirk, snarl, twist 6 buckle, tangle 7 caprice 11 peculiarity

kinkajou: 5 potto 6 mammal

kinky: odd 6 far-out 7 bizarre, strange 10 outlandish

kinship (see also **kin**): 5 blood, nasab 6 nearness 9 cognation 10 connection 11 propinquity 13 consanguinity

father's side: 8 agnation

mother's side: 7 enation

kinsman (see also **kin, kindred**): 4 ally 6 friend 8 bandhava 9 rishtadar

kiosk: 5 booth 8 pavilion 9 newsstand

kip: 4 hide, pelt, skin 5 sleep

Kipling: *poem:* 6 L'Envoi

tale: Kim

Kiribati: *capital:* 6 Tarawa

ethnic group: 11 Micronesian

island groups: 4 Line 7 Gilbert, Phoenix

monetary unit: 6 dollar

kirtle: 4 coat, gown 5 dress, skirt, tunic 7 garment 9 petticoat

Kish: *father:* Ner

son: 4 Saul

kismet: 4 fate 7 destiny

kiss: 4 bass, buss 5 smack 6 caress 8 osculate

kiss-me-quick: 6 bonnet

kiss of peace: pax

Kiss sculptor: 5 Rodin

kist: box 4 cist 5 chest 6 locker

kit: bag, box, lot, set 6 outfit 9 container 10 collection

and caboodle: all 10 everything

kitchen: ben(Sc.) 4 chil(Ind.) 5 calan(P.I.) 6 chilla(Ind.) 7 cuisine 8 scullery

pert. to: 8 culinary

ship's: galley

tool or utensil: 5 corer, ricer 6 beater, grater, opener, sifter 7 spatula 8 colander, strainer

kite: 4 bird, hawk, sail, soar 6 decamp 10 check, fraud

kith: 6 friend 10 associates 12 acquaintance

kittenish: coy 6 frisky 7 playful 8 childish

kittiwake: 4 gull 5 annet

kitty: 4 bowl, pool 6 stakes

kiwi: 5 fruit 7 Apteryx 14 flightless bird

kleptomaniac: 5 thief 7 filcher 8 pilferer 10 shoplifter

kloof: 4 glen 5 gorge 6 ravine, valley

klutz: oaf 4 lout 6 lummox 9 schlemiel

knack: art 4 ease, gift, hang 5 catch, skill, trick 8 facility 9 dexterity 10 adroitness

knap: cut, rap, top 4 bite, blow, chip, crop, hill, snap 5 break, crest, knock, knoll 6 nibble, strike, summit 7 hilltop, hillock

knapsack: bag 4 case, pack

knarred: 6 knotty 7 gnarled

knave: boy, nob, pam 4 fool, jack 5 cheat, churl, losel, rogue, scamp 6 harlot, rascal, varlet 7 villain 9 miscreant, scoundrel, trickster

knavery: 5 fraud 8 mischief 10 dishonesty 12 sportiveness

knead: elt(Sc.), mix 5 malax 7 massage 8 malaxate 9 masticate 10 manipulate 11 incorporate

knee: bow 5 joint 10 supplicate
armor: 11 genouillere
bend: 5 kneel 6 curtsy 9 genuflect

knee breeches: 8 knickers 12 smallclothes

kneecap: 7 patella

knee-jerk: 9 automatic 11 predictable

kneeling desk: 8 prie-dieu

knell: 4 bell, omen, ring, toll 6 stroke, summon 7 warning 8 proclaim

knickers: 7 panties 8 bloomers 9 plus fours

knickknack: toy 6 bauble, bawble, gadget, gewgaw, trifle 7 novelty, trinket 8 gimcrack, kickshaw

knife: cut 4 bolo, dirk, shiv, snee, stab 5 bowie, gully, slash, sword 6 barong, colter, coutel, dagger, worker 7 carving, machete, spatula, whittle, stiletto, yataghan 11 cutting tool, switchblade
case: 6 sheath
maker: 6 cutler
one-bladed: 6 barlow
plaster and paint: 7 spatula
sharpener: 4 hone 5 steel, stone
surgical: 6 catlin 7 catling, scalpel

knight: dub, sir 5 eques 6 equite, Ritter 8 banneret, cavalier 9 caballero, chevalier
attendant: 9 squire
banner: 8 gonfanon
cloak: 6 tabard
famous: 7 Caradoc, Cradock, Galahad 9 Lohengrin
fight: 5 joust
horse: 7 charger, palfrey
rank above: 7 baronet

servant: 4 page 6 varlet
title: sir
wife: 4 lady
wreath: 4 orle

knight-errant: 7 paladin

knight of the road: 4 hobo 5 tramp 8 vagabond

knighthood: 8 chivalry
confer: dub

knightly: 5 brave 9 courteous 10 chivalrous

knit: 4 bind, heal, join, mend, purl 5 plait, unite, woven 6 cement, fasten 7 conjoin, connect, crochet, wrinkle 8 contract, entangle 10 intertwine 11 compaginate, consolidate

knitted blanket: 6 afghan

knitter: 6 legger

knitting: 5 craft 9 handiwork
rod: 6 needle
term: 4 purl 7 castoff

knob: bob, bur, nub 4 boss, buhr, burr, club, heel, lump, node, tore, umbo 5 bulge 6 button, croche, emboss, handle, pommel 12 protuberance
pointed: 6 finial

knobby: 5 gouty, hilly 6 knotty

knobkerrie: 4 club 5 stick

knobstick: 4 cane, club 5 stick 8 blackleg

knock: hit, rap, tap 4 beat, blow, bolt, bump, chop, dash, jolt, rout, slay 5 abuse, pound, thump 6 bounce 7 hillock(Sc.) 8 belittle 9 criticize 12 faultfinding

knock down: 4 fell 5 floor 9 prostrate

knock-kneed: 6 valgus

knock off: rob 4 copy, kill, stop 6 deduct 8 overcome 11 assassinate, discontinue

knock out: 4 daze, stun 6 defeat 7 exhaust 8 paralyze

knockabout: 5 actor, sloop, yacht

knockout: 4 kayo 5 facer 6 eyeful, looker 7 stunner
blow: 8 haymaker

knoll: 4 knap, knob, lump 5 mound 7 hillock

knop: 5 knosp 6 button 8 ornament

knot: bow, nep, tie 4 bond, burl, burr, harl, knag, knar, knob, knur, loop, lump, node, snag 5 gnarl, hitch, knurl, nodus, snarl 6 finial, granny, nodule, puzzle, tangle 7 bowline, chignon, cockade, laniard, lanyard, rosette 8 entangle 12 entanglement, protuberance
running: 4 slip 5 noose
pert. to: 5 nodal

knotted: 5 noded 7 crabbed, nodated 9 intricate

knotted lace: 7 tatting

knotty: 4 hard 5 bumpy, gouty 6 craggy 7 complex, gnarled 9 difficult, intricate 10 perplexing

knout: 4 flog, lash, whip

know: can, con, ken(Sc.), 7 realize 8 perceive 9 recognize 10 comprehend, experience, understand

know-how: 5 knack, skill 7 ability 9 expertise

know-it-all: 6 smarty 8 wiseacre

know-nothing: 8 agnostic 9 ignoramus 11 scissorbill

knowing: 4 able, gash, wise 5 cagey, downy, leery, smart, witty 6 scient, shrewd 7 gnostic, sapient, stylish 8 informed 9 cognitive, conscious, gnostical, wide-awake 10 experience, perceptive 11 intelligent 13 comprehension

knowledge: ken 4 lore 6 wisdom 7 cunning, hearing, science 8 learning, sapience 9 cognition, erudition 10 cognizance, experience 11 information, instruction 12 acquaintance 13 enlightenment, understanding

  instrument: 7 organon

  lack of: 9 ignorance, nescience

  object of: 7 cognita(pl.), scibile 8 cognitum

  pert. to: 7 gnostic

  seeker: 10 philonoist

  slight: 7 inkling, smatter 8 sciolism 10 smattering

  summary: 13 encyclopaedia

  systematized: 7 science

  universal: 9 pantology

known: 5 couth, famed 6 famous 7 notable 8 familiar, renowned 9 notorious

knuckle: 5 joint

  head: 5 dunce 8 numbskull

knuckle under: bow 4 cave 5 defer, yield 6 submit 7 succumb 10 capitulate

kobird: 6 cuckoo

kobold: nis 5 gnome 6 goblin 7 Hodeken(G.) 10 nissespire

koel: 4 bird 6 cuckoo

kohl: 8 antimony

kohlrabi: 6 turnip

kokoon: gnu

kokopu: 4 fish, para 5 trout 10 galaxiidae

kola: nut 6 jackal

kooky: 5 crazy 6 far out, insane 7 offbeat 9 fantastic

kopecks (100): 5 ruble

kopje: 4 hill 5 mound 7 hillock

Koran: 10 Islam Bible

  division: 4 Sura

  interpreter: 5 ulema 7 alfaqui 8 alfaquin

  register: 5 sijil 6 sijill

Korea: See **North Korea, South Korea**

kosher: fit 4 pure 5 clean 6 proper 8 Kashruth 9 undefiled

  meat maker: 6 porger

  opposite of: 4 tref

kowtow: 4 fawn 5 cower, toady 6 tringe, grovel 8 butter up 11 apple polish

kra: ape 7 macaque

kraal: pen 5 crawl 6 corral 9 enclosure

krimmer: fur 4 skin 8 lambskin

Krishna: 6 Vishnu 10 Juggernaut

  grandson: 9 Aniruddha

  mother: 6 Devaki

  paradise: 6 Goloka

kudos: 4 fame 5 award, glory, honor 6 praise, renown 8 prestige 9 extolling

kudu: 8 antelope

kulak: 6 farmer 7 peasant

kumiss: 4 milk 5 drink 8 beverage

kumquat: 5 fruit

  relative: 6 orange

kung fu: 10 martial art 14 Chinese defense

  kin of: 6 karate

Kurile island: 7 Iturup

Kurland Peninsula inhabitant: 4 Lett

kurrajong: 4 tree 5 shrub 6 calool

kurtosis: arc 9 curvature

Kuwait: *capital:* 8 Al-Kuwait

  city: 5 Magwa 7 Hawalli 8 Al Bahrah

  dynasty: 7 Al Sabah

  island: 7 Bubiyan, Failaka

  monetary unit: 4 fils 5 dinar

kvetch (Yid.): 5 gripe, whine 8 complain

kyphosis: 8 humpback 9 curvature, hunchback

L

L: 5 fifty
La Boheme: *composer:* 7 Puccini
   heroine: 4 Mimi
laagte: 6 bottom, valley
Laban's daughter: 4 Leah 6 Rachel
label: tab, tag 4 band, call 5 brand 6 docket, lappet, tassel 8 classify 9 designate, dripstone 10 definition
labellum: lip 5 petal
labile: 8 shifting, unstable 9 adaptable 10 changeable
labium: lip
labor: 4 moil, task, toil, work 5 sweat, yakka 6 effort, labour, stress, strive 7 travail 8 business, drudgery, exertion, industry, struggle 11 lucubration, parturition
labor organization: AFL, CIO, UMW 5 ILGWU, union
labored: 8 heavy 6 forced 8 strained 9 difficult, elaborate
laborer: man, 4 hand, hind, peon, prol 5 cooly, plebe 6 coolie, toiler, worker 7 bracero, dvornik, hobbler, wetback, workman 10 bluecollar
laborious: 4 hard 5 heavy 6 uphill 7 arduous, operose, tedious 8 diligent 9 assiduous, difficult 11 displeasing, hardworking, painstaking
Labrador retriever: 12 Newfoundland
Labrador tea: 5 ledum 8 gowiddie 9 evergreen
labyrinth: web 4 knot, maze, mesh 6 jungle, morass, tangle
   builder: 8 Daedalus
   monster: 8 Minotaur
labyrinthine: 7 complex 8 involved, puzzling, tortuous 9 intricate 10 perplexing 11 complicated
lac: 4 milk 5 resin 6 veneer 10 sealing wax
lace: gin, net, tat 4 band, beat, cord, lash, line 5 braid, lairs, noose, plait, snare, twine, unite 6 fasten, ribbon, string 7 ensnare, entwine, laniard, lanyard 8 biliment, openwork 9 embroider, interlace 10 embroidery, intertwine, shoestring
   barred: 6 grille
   edge: 5 picot
   frilled: 5 jabot, ruche
   front: 5 jabot
   into: 5 abuse 6 attack 7 condemn

   kind: 5 lisle, orris, tulle 7 alencon, allover, guipure, macrame, potlace 9 Alostlace 10 colberteen, colbertine 12 Valenciennes
   knotted: 7 tatting
   loop in: 5 picot
   make: tat
   opening: 6 eyelet
lacerate: cut, rip 4 bite, rend, rive, tear 6 harrow, mangle 8 distress
laceration: rip 4 tear 5 wound
lacework: See lace
lachrymose: sad 5 teary, weepy 7 tearful
lack: 4 need, void, want 5 fault, minus 6 dearth 7 absence, failure, in need, paucity, poverty 8 scarcity, shortage 9 indigence 10 deficiency 11 destitution
lackadaisical: 4 blah 7 languid 8 listless 10 spiritless 11 sentimental
lackaday: 4 alas
lackey: 5 toady, valet 7 footman, servant
lacking: shy 5 short 6 absent, barren 7 wanting 8 desolate 9 deficient, destitute
lackluster: 4 dull 6 cloudy 8 dullness
Laconia: *capital:* 6 Sparta
   people: Obe
laconic: 5 brief, pithy, short, terse 7 concise, pointed, summary 8 succinct
lacquer: 5 gloss 7 shellac, varnish
lactate: 4 salt 5 actol, ester
lacteal: 5 milky
lacuna: gap 4 hole 5 break 7 opening 8 interval 10 depression
lacy: 7 weblike 8 delicate
lad: boy, tad 4 carl, dick, hind 5 caddy, youth 6 caddie, shaver 9 stripling 10 adolescent
   on call: 4 page 7 bellboy 9 messenger
   serving: 7 gossoon 8 coistrel, coistril
ladder: run, sty 4 stee 5 scale 6 series 7 scalade
   on fortification: 8 escalade
   step: 7 ratline
ladderlike: 6 scalar
lade: dip 4 bail, draw, lave, load, ship 5 drain, scoop 6 burden, charge, weight 7 fraught, freight
ladies' man: 4 beau 5 dandy 11 philanderer
lading: 4 load 5 cargo 6 burden 7 freight 10 freightage

ladle: dip 4 bail 5 scoop, serve, spoon 6 dipper

ladrone: 5 thief 6 bandit, robber 7 brigand 9 mercenary 10 highwayman

Ladrone island: 4 Guam 6 Saipan 8 Marianas

lady (see also **woman**): 4 burd, dame, dona(Sp.), rani(Ind.) 5 begum(Ind.), donna(It.), madam, ranee(Ind.) 6 domina(L.), female, senora(Sp.) 7 signora (It.) 11 gentlewoman
  noble: 5 queen 7 duchess 8 countess, princess
  young: 7 damozel 10 demoiselle, jeune fille(F.)

lady-killer: 4 wolf 5 sheik 7 Don Juan 8 Casanova

Lady of the Lake: 5 Ellen, Nimue 6 Vivien
  author: 5 Scott

lady's thumb: 5 plant 9 peachwort, persicary

ladybird: bug 6 beetle
  genus: 9 epilachna

ladyfish: oio 6 tarpon, wrasse

ladylike: 6 female, polite 7 genteel 8 feminine, mannerly

ladylove: 5 amour, lover 8 mistress 10 sweetheart

Laertes: *father:* 8 Acrisius, Polonius
  sister: 7 Ophelia
  son: 7 Ulysses, 8 Odysseus
  wife: 8 Anticlea

lag: 4 flag, rift, tire 5 delay, stave, tarry, trail, weary 6 dawdle, linger, loiter 8 fall back 9 drawlatch 10 dillydally 11 retardation

lager: ale 4 beer 5 drink 8 beverage

laggard: 4 slow 6 remiss 8 backward, loiterer, sluggish 9 straggler 10 slow person

lagging: 5 tardy 8 backward

lagniappe: tip 4 gift 5 bonus, pilon 7 present 8 gratuity

lagomorph: 4 hare, pika 5 coney 6 rabbit

lagoon: 4 cove, haff, pond, pool 5 liman 6 laguna(Sp.)

Lagoon Islands: 6 Ellice

laic: 6 layman 7 secular 15 nonprofessional

laid-down: 5 posed 6 thetic 8 academic 10 prescribed 11 traditional

lair: den, lie 4 holt, nest 5 haunt 6 cavern 7 hideout, retreat 8 quagmire

Lais: 7 Burmese

laissez-faire: 8 inactive, tolerant 9 donothing, unconcern 11 philosophic 12 indifference, mercantilism 15 individualistic, noninterference

laity: 6 laymen

Laius' son: 7 Oedipus

lake: dye 4 loch, mere, pond, pool, shat, shot, tarn 5 bayou, chott, color, lough, shott 6 lagoon 7 pigment
  deposit: 5 trona
  highest: 8 Titicaca
  Indian: 4 Erie
  marshy: 5 liman

Lake State: 8 Michigan

lam: hit 4 bash, beat, flog 6 thrash 7 getaway

Lamaism: *dignitary:* 8 hutukhtu
  priest: 6 Getsul
  stupa: 7 Chorten

lamasery: 9 monastery

lamb: ean 4 yean 5 agnus(L.) 6 agneau(F.), cosset 7 chilver, fatling, hogling
  hand-raised: hob
  leg of: 5 gigot
  pert. to: 5 ovine
  pet: 4 cade 6 cosset

Lamb of God: 8 Agnus Dei

lambaste: 4 drub, flay 5 paste, poynd 6 thrash 7 clobber 8 lash into 10 tonguelash

Lamb's penname: 4 Elia

lambskin: 4 case 5 suede 6 bagdad 7 bághdad

lambent: 7 glowing, radiant 8 wavering 9 brilliant 10 flickering

lame: 4 game, halt 5 gammy 6 feeble 7 halting 8 crippled, decrepit, disabled 9 defective, hamstring 11 handicapped 12 incapacitate

Lamech: *father:* 10 Methuselah
  son: 4 Noah 5 Jabal, Jubal 9 Tubalcain
  wife: 4 Adah 6 Zillah

lament: cry, rue 4 care, howl, keen, moan, pine, sigh, wail, weep 5 croon, dolor, dirge, elegy, greet, grief, mourn 6 bemoan, bewail, beweep, dolour, grieve, lament, ochone, outcry, plaint, regret, repent, repine, yammer 7 condole, deplore, elegize, wailing 8 jeremiad, mourn for, mourning 9 complaint

lamentable: sad 8 grievous, wretched 10 deplorable 11 distressing

lamia: hag, hex 5 witch 7 vampire 9 sorceress

lamina: 5 blade, flake, hinge, layer

laminated: 5 flaky 6 scaled 7 fissile, spathic, tabular 8 foliated, lamellar

lamp: arc, eye, orb 4 davy, etna 5 light, torch 7 lantern 8 lanthorn 9 veilleuse
  hanging: 10 chandelier
  safety: 4 davy

lampblack: 4 soot

lamplighter: 5 match, spill, torch

lampoon: 5 squib 6 satire 8 ridicule, satirize 10 caricature, pasquinade

lamprey: eel 6 ramper
  migration: 7 eelfare

lanai: 5 patio, porch 7 terrace, veranda

lanate: 5 hairy, wooly 6 woolly
Lancashire section: 6 Eccles
lance: cut 4 dart, hurl 5 joust, spear 6 faucre, lancet, launch, pierce, weapon 7 javelin
head: 5 morne
Lancelot: *lover:* 6 Elaine 9 Guinevere
son: 7 Galahad
victim: 6 Gawain
lancer: 4 ulan 5 uhlan 7 soldier, spearer 10 cavalryman
lancet: 5 fleam, knife
lancinate: 4 stab, tear 5 gouge 6 pierce 8 lacerate
land: erd 4 ager(L.), soil 5 catch, earth, end up, glebe, realm, shore, terra(L.) 6 alight, arrive, debark, estate, ground 7 acreage, capture, country, terrene 9 disembark, territory
alluvial: 5 delta
ancestral: 5 ethel
arid: See *desert*
barren: See **wasteland**
body: 9 continent
church: 5 glebe 8 abadengo
cultivated: 4 farm 5 arada, arado, ranch, tilth 7 orchard, tillage
dealer: 7 realtor
depressed: 6 graben
elevated: alp 4 hill, mesa 5 mound, ridge 7 plateau 8 mountain
grazing: 5 field, plain, range 6 meadow 7 pasture
heritable: 4 alod, fief, odal 5 allod 7 alodium 8 allodium
hilly: 4 down
householder's: 6 barton, casate 7 demesne
in foreign territory: 7 enclave
living on: 11 terrestrial
low: 4 vale 5 carse(Sc.) 6 polder, valley 7 intervale
measure: are, rod 4 acre, mile, rood 5 meter, perch 6 decare
mythical: 4 Eden 6 Utopia 7 Erewhon, Lemuria 9 Shangri-La
narrow: 4 neck 6 strake 7 isthmus 9 peninsula
open: 4 moor, vega, wold 5 field, heath, slash, weald
owned: see *heritable* above
pasture: ham 5 grass 6 meadow
pert. to: 11 continental
piece: lot 4 acre, farm 5 laine, ranch, range, solum (law) spong 6 estate, parcel
plowed: 5 arada, arado, field 6 arable, fallow, furrow 7 thwaite
point of: 4 cape, ness, spit
profit: 4 crop, rent 7 esplees
public: 4 parc, park
reclaimed: 6 polder 7 novalia(Sc.)
river drained: 5 basin

sandy: 4 dene
tilled: see *plowed* above
treeless: 5 llano 6 steppe 7 prairie, savanna 8 savannah
triangular: 4 gore
uncultivated: 5 heath, waste 6 desert, forest
uplifted: 5 horst
waste: See **wasteland**
waterlocked: ile(F.) 4 isle 6 island
watery: bog 4 flow, moor 5 marsh, swamp 6 morass 7 maremma(It.)
Land of Cakes: 8 Scotland
Land of the Midnight Sun: 6 Norway
Land of Nod: 5 sleep
Land of Plenty: 6 Goshen
Land of Promise: 7 Canaan 9 Palestine
Land of Rising Sun: 5 Japan
land's end guardian: 8 Bellerus
landed: See *estate, land*
landholder: 5 laird 6 coscet, yeoman
landholding: 6 tenure
landing: 7 arrival
kind: 5 crash 10 three-point
place: 4 dock, pier 5 wharf 6 runway, stairs 7 airport
landlady: 5 duena 7 hostess 8 mistress 9 concierge
landlord: 4 host 5 laird(Sc.) 6 lessor
landmark: 8 monument 9 milestone 10 guide point 11 classic case
landscape: 4 plan 5 plant, scene 7 scenery, paysage, picture 8 decorate, painting
landslide: 9 avalanche 10 eboulement
debris: 5 scree, talus
landsman: 6 lubber, sailor 10 compatriot
lane: way 4 char, path, race 5 aisle, alley, byway, chare, tewer 6 boreen, bypath, gullet, street, throat, vennel 7 pathway 8 footpath 10 passageway
language: 4 chib 5 argot, idiom, lingo, slang 6 jargon, speech, tongue 7 dialect, diction
ancient: 4 Pali 5 Aryan, Greek, Latin 6 Hebrew 7 Chinese 8 Sanskrit 10 vernacular, vocabulary
artificial: 9 Esperanto
change: 8 misquote 9 interpret, translate 10 paraphrase
classical: 5 Greek, Latin
common: 6 French, German 7 Chinese, English, Italian, Russian, Spanish
Cretan: 6 Minoan
dead: 5 Latin
expert: 8 linguist
figurative: 7 imagery
international: od, ro; ido 7 volapuk 9 esperanto
meaningless: 9 gibberish
nonmetrical: 5 prose
pert. to: 8 semantic

pompous: 4 bull, wind 6 hot air 7 bombast, oratory 8 rhetoric

principles: 7 grammar

Romance: 5 Latin 6 French 7 Catalan, Italian, Spanish 8 Rumanian 10 Portuguese

sacred: 4 Pali

secret: 4 cant, code 5 argot

Semitic: 6 Arabic, Hebrew

spoken: 7 diction 13 pronunciation

unintelligible: 9 gibberish

languid: 4 dull, slow, weak 6 dreamy, tender 8 drooping, indolent, listless, lovesick, sluggish 9 lethargic 11 indifferent

languish: 4 fade, fail, flag, long, pine, wilt 5 droop, dwine, faint, swoon 6 linger, repine 7 decline 12 fail in health

languor: kef 4 kaif, keef, kief 5 ennui 7 boredom 8 debility 9 lassitude 10 stagnation

langur: 6 monkey 8 wanderoo

lanky: 4 lean, slim, tall, thin 5 gaunt, rangy, spare 6 gangly, meager, meagre, skinny 7 haggard, slender 8 gangling, ungainly 9 elongated 12 loose-jointed

lantern: 4 lamp 5 bouet

lanyard: 4 cord, knot, line, rope

Laocoon: 11 Trojan priest

killer: 7 serpent

Laodamia's father: 7 Acastus

Laodicean: 8 lukewarm 9 apathetic 10 uninvolved 11 indifferent

Laomedon: *father:* 4 Ilus

kingdom: 4 Troy

mother: 8 Eurydice

slayer: 8 Hercules

son: 5 Priam

Laos: *capital:* 9 Vientiane

Communist group: 9 Pathet Lao

language: Lao

monetary unit: kip

religion: 8 Buddhist

river: 6 Mekong, Sabang

supply line: 14 Ho Chi Minh Trail

town: 5 Khong, Pakse 12 Luang Prabang

lap: sip 4 fold, lick, wash 5 bathe, drink, slurp 6 circle, cuddle, enfold, infold 7 circuit

lap robe: rug 5 throw 6 afghan 7 blanket

lapactic: 8 laxative 9 cathartic

lapel: 5 rever 6 revers

lapidary: 7 jeweler 8 engraver 9 gem cutter

instrument: 4 dop 5 dial

lapidate: 4 pelt 5 stone

lapin: 6 rabbit

Lapland: *animal:* 8 reindeer

city or town: 4 Kola 6 Kiruna

sled: 4 pulk 5 pulka

lappet: 4 flap, fold, lobe, moth 5 lapel 6 fabric, revers

lapse: err 5 break, error, fault 6 expire 7

delapse, escheat, failure, relapse 8 caducity, slipping 9 backslide

lapsed: 4 dead, null, void

laputan: 6 absurd, dreamy 7 utopian 9 visionary 10 unfeasible 11 impractical

lapwing: 5 pewit 6 plover

Lar: god 6 gibbon, spirit

larboard: 4 left, port

larceny: 5 theft 7 looting, robbery 8 burglary, stealage

kind: 5 grand, petty

lard: fat, oil 4 mort 5 add to, adeps(L.), baste, enarm, inarm 6 enrich, fatten, grease 7 garnish 9 embellish

larder: 4 cave 6 pantry, spence, spense 8 cupboard

large: big 4 bold, free, huge, main, vast, waly 5 ample, broad, bulky, burly, enorm, giant, great, hulky, massy, wally 6 goodly, heroic 7 copious, immense, liberal, massive, pompous, titanic, weighty 8 colossal, enormous, generous, gigantic 9 capacious, extensive, plentiful 11 exaggerated, far-reaching 12 considerable 13 comprehensive

largess, largesse: 4 gift 6 bounty 7 charity, present 10 generosity, liberality 11 beneficence

lariat: 4 rope 5 lasso, noose, reata(Sp.), riata(Sp.)

loop: 5 honda, hondo 6 hondoo, hondou

lark: 4 bird, dido 5 spree, pipit 6 frolic 8 carousal 9 make merry

larkspur: 10 delphinium

larrigan: 8 moccasin

larrup: 4 beat, blow, flog, whip

larry: hoe 5 grout, noise 6 mortar 7 mine car 9 confusion 10 excitement

larva: bot, fly, loa 4 bott, grub, worm 5 eruca 6 botfly, woubit 7 atrocha, oestrid 8 cercaria, horsefly 11 caterpillar

aquatic: 12 hellgrammite

beetle: 4 grub

larvate: 6 masked 7 covered 9 concealed

lascar: 6 sailor 12 artilleryman

lascivious: 6 wanton 7 blissom 9 lecherous, salacious, seductive 10 libidinous, licentious

lash: 4 beat, bind, blow, flog, lace, whip, yerk 5 slash 6 berate, fasten, strike, stroke, swinge 7 belabor, eyelash, scourge

lasket: 8 latching

lass: gal 4 gill, girl, maid, miss 5 trull, woman 6 cummer, kimmer, lassie, maiden 7 colleen 10 sweetheart 11 maidservant

lassitude: 5 ennui 7 languor 8 debility, lethargy 10 exhaustion

lasso: See **lariat**

last: 4 dure, tail 5 abide, final, omega 6 endure, latest, newest, utmost 7 der-

nier, extreme, tail-end 8 at the end,
continue, eventual, hindmost, rearmost,
ultimate 9 aftermost 10 concluding,
most recent
but one: 6 penult
long: 7 outwear 9 perendure
word: 8 up-to-date
Last of the Mohicans: 5 Uncas
author: 6 Cooper
Last Supper: *painter:* 7 da Vinci
representation: 4 cena
room: 7 cenacle
lasting (see also **last**): 6 stable 7 chronic,
lasting, eternal 8 constant, enduring 9
perennial, permanent, steadfast 11 everlasting
briefly: 9 ephemeral, temporary
latch: 5 catch, sneck 6 fasten 8 fastener
latchet: tab 4 lace 5 thong
late: new 4 dead, sere 5 tardy 6 former,
recent 7 belated, overdue 8 neoteric,
serotine 10 behindhand
latent: 6 hidden 7 dormant 9 concealed,
potential, quiescent, suspended 11 undeveloped
later: 4 anon, soon 5 after, newer 6 behind, future, puisne 7 elderly, neozoic 9
hereafter, posterior, presently 10 subsequent 12 subsequently
lateral: 4 pass, side 8 indirect, sideward,
sideways
latest: 4 last 6 newest
latex: 5 juice 6 rubber 9 secretion
lath: 4 slat 5 spale, stave, stick 8 forepole
attachment: 7 setover
operator: 6 turner
part: 7 mandrel
lather: 4 flog, foam, soap, suds 5 froth 6
bustle, freath 10 foamy sweat
Latin (see also **Rome**): 5 Roman 7 Italian, Romanic
always: 6 semper
barracks: 6 canaba
bath, bathhouse: 7 balneum
booth: 7 taberna
bowl: 6 patina
boxing glove: 6 cestus, ceston
boy: 4 puer
breath: 7 halitus
bronze: aes
building: 5 aedes
cape: 5 sagum 6 byrrus
cistern: 9 impluvium
connective: et
contract: 5 nexum
couch: 9 accubitum
deity: 4 deus
dish: 4 lanx 6 lances, pateral, patina
food: 5 cibus
foot: pes
for example: 4 vide
force: vis

friend: 6 amicus
garland: 6 corona
ghosts: 7 lemures
grammar: 5 donat, donet
grammatical case: 6 dative 8 ablative,
genitive, vocative 10 accusative, nominative
hope: 4 spes
hour: 4 hora
javelin: 4 pile 5 aclys, pilum
life: 4 vita
ornament: 5 bulla
post: 4 meta
pronoun: tu; ego, hic 4 ille, ipse, iste
ram: 5 aries
rite: 4 orgy 5 sacra
roof opening: 10 compluvium
seat: 5 sella
shelter: 7 taberna
towel: 5 mappa
trumpet: 4 tuba 6 buccin 7 buccina
Latin America: See **Central America,
South America**
Latinus's daughter: 7 Lavinia
latite: 4 lava
latitude: 4 room 5 scope, width 6 extent,
leeway, margin 7 breadth, freedom 8
distance 9 elbowroom
complement: 10 colatitude
measure: 6 degree 8 parallel
zero degrees: 7 equator
latke: 7 pancake 11 griddle cake
latrant: 7 barking 8 snarling 11 complaining
latrine: 5 privy 6 toilet
latter: 4 last 5 final 6 latest 10 more recent
Latter Day Saints: 7 Mormons
latterly: 4 anew 6 lately 8 recently
lattice: 4 door, gate 6 pinjra(Ind.) 7 trellis
8 espalier
latticework: 5 arbor, grate 6 arbour 7
grating, tracery
Latvia: *city:* 4 Riga(c.) 5 Libau 6 Dvinsk,
Libava 8 Dunaburg 10 Daugavpils
coin: lat 6 rublis 7 kapeika 8 santimas
measure: 4 stof 5 kanne, stoff, verst 6
kulmet, sagene, versta, verste 7 verchoc, verchok 8 krouchka, kroushka,
pourvete 9 deciatine, lofstelle 10 tonn-
stelle
parliament: 6 Saeima
people: 5 Letts
river: 4 Ogre 5 Gauga 6 Salaca
university site: 4 Riga
weight: 9 liespfund
laud: 4 lute 5 extol 6 extoll, praise 7 adulate, applaud, cittern, commend, glorify,
magnify 8 emblazon, eulogize 9 panegyric 10 compliment
laudable: 9 allowable, exemplary 11 commendable 12 praiseworthy

laugh: 4 gaff, haha 5 fleer, snort 6 cackle, giggle, guffaw, hawhaw, nicker, titter 7 chortle, grizzle, snicker 9 cachinate
disposed to: 7 risible
incipient: 4 grin 5 smile
pert. to: 8 gelastic

laughable: odd 5 comic, droll, funny, merry, queer, witty 7 amusing, comical, risible, strange, waggish 8 gelastic, humorous, sportive 9 burlesque, diverting, facetious, grotesque, ludicrous 10 ridiculous

laughing: 5 riant

laughing bird: 4 gull, loon 5 pewit 10 woodpecker

laughing owl: 5 wekau

laughing stock: 4 butt, jest, joke 5 sport 7 mockery 8 derision, ridicule

laughter: 5 mirth, risus(L.)
pert. to: 7 risible

launch: 4 open, toss 5 begin, fling, leave, set up, start, throw 6 get off 7 propose 9 motorboat 10 inaugurate

launder: tye 4 wash

laundry: 4 wash 10 laundromat 13 blanchisserie(F.)

laureate: 13 distinguished

laurel: bay 4 fame 5 honor 6 daphne, myrtle, tarata, trophy 7 cajuput, garland, taratah 9 spoonwood 11 distinction
fragment of: 8 lapillus
sheet of: 6 coulee

lava: 4 slag 5 ashes 6 coulee, latite, scoria, verite 7 clinker 8 pahoehoe

lavabo: 5 basin 8 washbowl 9 cleansing 11 wall planter

lavaliere, lavalier: 7 pendant 8 necklace

lavation: 4 bath 6 lavage 7 washing 9 cleansing

lavatory: 5 basin 6 toilet 8 washbowl, washroom

lave: 4 bail, lade, pour, soak, wash 5 bathe, rinse

lavender: 6 pastel, purple, violet

laver: 5 basin 6 trough, vessel 7 cistern, seaweed

Lavinia: *father:* 7 Latinus
husband: 6 Aeneas
mother: 5 Amata

lavish: 4 free, lash, rank, wild 5 flush, spend, waste 7 opulent, profuse 8 prodigal, reckless, splendid, squander 9 bountiful, expensive, exuberant, impetuous, luxuriant, sumptuous, unstinted 10 immoderate 11 extravagant, magnificent 12 unrestrained 13 superabundant

law: act, bar, ius(L.), jus(L.), lex(L.) 4 code, doom, rule, Tora 5 canon, edict, mesne, sutra, Torah 6 custom, decree, equity, noetic, sutrah, suttah 7 derecho,

justice, precept, statute 8 handicap 9 enactment, ordinance, principle, regulation 11 commandment, legislation 12 constitution, jurisdiction 13 jurisprudence
action: res 4 suit 5 actus 8 replevin 9 gravamina
body of: 4 code 12 constitution
breaker of: 5 felon 6 sinner 8 criminal
claim of: 4 lien
contrary to: 7 illegal, illicit 8 unlawful 16 unconstitutional
decree: 4 nisi 5 edict
degree: LLB, LLD
delay: 4 mora
document: 4 deed, writ 6 capias, elegit
expounder of: 6 jurist
goddess: 4 Maat
male succession: 5 Salic
man of: 5 judge 6 jurist, lawyer 7 counsel, justice 8 attorney 9 barrister
Manu: 5 sutra, sutta
offender: 8 criminal 9 desperado, wrongdoer
offense: 4 tort 5 crime, malum 6 delict
oral: 5 parol 11 nuncupative
order: 4 writ
permitted by: See **lawful**
pert. to: 5 legal 7 canonic 9 canonical, judiciary 11 legislative
philosophy of: 13 jurisprudence
prevent by: 5 estop
violation of: sin 4 tort 5 crime, malum 6 felony
warning: 6 caveat

lawful: due 5 legal, licit, valid 7 canonic, ennomic 10 legitimate

lawgiver: 5 Moses, solon 10 legislator

lawless: 4 lewd 6 unruly 7 illegal 8 anarchic 9 dissolute 10 anarchical, disorderly, tumultuous

lawlessness: 4 riot 5 chaos 6 mutiny, strife 7 anarchy, license 9 mobocracy 10 illegality

lawmaker: 5 solon 7 senator 10 legislator

lawn: 5 arbor, glade, grass, sward 6 arbour 7 batiste 8 grassland, grassplot, grasswork

lawsuit: 4 case 6 action 10 litigation
one engaged in: 8 litigant
subject: res

lawyer: 6 avocat(F.) 7 counsel 8 attorney, commoner 9 barrister, counselor, solicitor 10 counsellor
bad: 7 shyster 11 pettifogger

lax: 4 dull, free, limp, open, pave, slow 5 loose, slack, tardy 6 remiss 7 lenient 8 backward, careless, inactive 9 dissolute, negligent 10 unconfined 11 inattentive 12 unrestrained

lay: bet, put, set 4 bury, cast, cite, hymn,

poem, rest, song 5 allay, carol, ditty, place, quiet, stake, still, wager 6 ballad, entomb, hazard, impose, impute, melody 7 appease, ascribe, deposit, secular, work out 8 suppress 9 knock down, short poem 14 unprofessional 15 nonprofessional

lay aside: 5 table 6 shelve 7 abandon, discard, neglect

lay away: See **lay by**

lay bare: 4 show 5 strip 6 denude, expose, reveal 7 uncover

lay by: 4 hive, save 5 amass, cache, hoard, store 7 deposit, husband, reposit 8 salt away, treasure 10 accumulate

lay down: set 5 posit 6 affirm, give up 9 establish, surrender

lay hold of: 4 grab, grip 5 grasp, gripe, seize 9 apprehend

lay out: 4 plan 5 set up, spend 6 design, expend, extend, invest, make-up 7 arrange 9 residence

lay up: See **lay by**

lay waste: 4 ruin 6 harass, ravage 7 destroy 8 desolate 9 depredate, devastate

layer: bed, hen, ply 4 coat, film, fold, seam, tier, zona 5 paver 6 folium, lamina, veneer 7 bedding, provine, stratum 8 laminate 10 substratum
of coal: 4 seam
of stones: 4 dess
of wood: 4 core 6 veneer
pert. to: 7 stratal

layered: 7 laminal, laminar 8 tunicate

laymen: 4 laic 5 laity

lazar: 5 leper

lazy: 4 idle, laze 5 inert 8 indolent, slothful, sluggard

lea: 6 meadow 7 pasture 9 grassland

leach: wet, 4 soak 7 draw out, moisten 9 lixiviate, percolate 11 bloodsucker

lead: con, van, wad 4 head, lode, star, wadd 5 carry, first, guide, krems, metal, pilot, steer, usher 6 bullet, ceruse, convey, deduce, direct, escort, induce, manage 7 command, conduct, pioneer, plumbum, precede 8 graphite, instruct, outstrip 9 influence 10 show the way
astray: 4 lure 6 allure, delude, entice, seduce 7 deceive, mislead, pervert 8 inveigle
color: 4 dull, gray 5 livid, olive
ore: 6 galena 9 anglesite, cerrusite
paste: 6 strass
pig: 6 fother
sounding: 7 plummet
sulfide: 6 galena

leaden: 4 dull, gray 5 heavy, inert 7 languid, stilted 8 sluggish 9 colorless, plumbous

leader: bo; boh, cob, dux 4 cock, duce, duke, head, line, wire 5 chief, coach, pilot, sinew, snell 6 cantor, Fuhrer(G.), tendon 7 captain, demagog, foreman, Fuehrer(G.) 8 caudillo, choragus, headsman, preceder 9 chieftain, demagogue, drainpipe, principal 10 bellwether 11 condottiere, gymnasiarch
ecclesiastical: fra 4 pope 5 rabbi 6 bishop, father, priest 8 cardinal, minister, preacher 10 evangelist

leadership: 8 guidance, hegemony 9 authority

leading: big 4 duct, head, main 5 ahead, chief, first 6 banner 7 capital, central, guiding, premier, stellar 8 foremost 9 conducive, directing, governing, hegemonic, inductive, principal 11 controlling

leaf: ola, ole, pan 4 foil, olay, olla, page 5 blade, bract, folio, frond, palet, scale, sepal 6 areola, insert, spathe 7 tendril
angle with branch: 4 axil
aperture: 5 stoma
appendage: 6 ligula, stipel 7 stipule
aromatic: See **herb**
circle: 7 corolla
division: 4 lobe
edge: 9 crenation
fern: 5 frond
floating:
    pad
kind: 5 calxy, petal, sepal 7 corolla
part: pen 4 axil 5 costa, stoma 6 pagina 7 petiole, stomate
secretion on: 4 lerp
set: 5 calxy 7 corolla
vein: rib 5 costa

leafage: 7 foliage, umbrage, verdure

leaflet: 5 pinna, tract 6 folder 7 booklet 8 pamphlet

leafy: 4 lush, 5 green, shady 6 foliar 7 layered, sepaled

league: 4 bond 5 union 7 compact 8 alliance, covenant 9 coalition 10 federation 11 association, combination, confederacy 13 confederation

Leah: *father:* 5 Laban
husband: 5 Jacob
sister: 6 Rachel
son: 6 Simeon

leak: 4 drip, hole, loss, ooze, seep 5 crack 6 escape 7 channel, crevice, fissure

leaky: 6 porous

leal: 4 just, real, true 5 legal, loyal 6 lawful 7 correct, genuine 8 accurate, faithful

leam: 4 husk

lean: 4 bend, cant, lank, mean, poor, rely, slim, tend, thin, tilt 5 gaunt, lanky, scant, spare 6 depend, hollow, meager, meagre, skinny 7 conform, deviate, haggard, incline, recline, scrawny, slender 8 rawboned, scragged 9 deficient, emaciated 10 inadequate 12 unproductive

lean-to: hut 4 shed 5 shack

Leander's sweetheart: 4 Hera, Hero

leaning: 6 desire, 7 pronate 8 aptitude, penchant, tendency, 9 accumbent, prejudice 10 preference

leap: fly, hop 4 dart, dive, jump, loup, skip 5 bound, caper, exult, frisk, lunge, salto, vault 6 bounce, breach, cavort, curvet, gallop, gambol, hurdle, hurtle, spring 7 saltate 8 capriole 9 ballotade, entrechat

leap year: 10 bissextile

leaping: 7 jumping, salient, saltant 9 caprizant, saltation

lear: 4 lore 6 lesson 8 learning

Lear: *daughter:* 5 Regan 7 Goneril 8 Cordelia

dog: 4 Tray

follower: 4 Kent

learn: con, get 4 find, here, lere 6 master, pick up 7 acquire, apprise, apprize, realize 8 memorize 9 ascertain

learned: wot 4 blue, read, sage, wise 6 astute, doctus 7 clerkly, cunning, erudite 8 lettered, literary, literose 9 scholarly 10 well-informed

learner: 5 pupil 7 scholar, trainee 8 disciple, opsimath 10 apprentice

learning: art 4 lear, lore 6 wisdom 7 cunning 8 pedantry 9 education, erudition, knowledge 10 discipline, experience 11 information, scholarship

display of: 8 pedantry

love of: 8 philology

man of: 4 sage 6 pundit, savant 7 scholar, teacher 9 philomath, professor 12 intellectual

lease: let 4 hire, rent 6 demise, engage, rental, tenure 7 charter 8 contract 10 concession

leash: 4 bind, cord, curb, harl, jess, lune 5 strap 6 couple, tether 7 control 8 restrain

least: 6 fewest, little, lowest 7 minimal, minimum 8 shortest, smallest 9 slightest

leather: tan 4 napa, whip, yuft(Russ.) 5 balat, leder, strap 6 thrash

artificial: 7 keratol

drying: sam 4 samm 5 sammy

fine: kid 6 vellum

finish: 4 buff

inspector: 6 sealer

kind: elk, kid, kip 4 bock, buff, calf, doze, napa, roan, seal, vici 5 aluta, basil, mocha, suede, trank 6 castor, levant, oxhide, skiver 7 buffalo, canepin, chamois, morocco, saffian 8 cheverel, cheveril, Cordovan

napped: 5 suede

pare: 5 skive

piece of: 4 rand, welt 5 clout, strap, thong 6 latigo

prepare: tan, taw 4 mull 5 curry, sammy

sheepskin: 4 roan 6 skiver

soft: 5 aluta, mocha, suede 8 cabretta

tool: 6 skiver

waste: 6 tanite

worker: 6 chamar, tanner 8 chuckler

leatherback: 6 turtle

leatherneck: 6 marine

leave: go; let 4 bunk, exit, quit 5 favor, forgo, grace, scram 6 beleve, decamp, depart, desert, entail, favour, forego, forlet, go away, permit, retire, vacate 7 abandon, beleave, forsake, getaway, liberty, license 8 bequeath, emigrate, furlough, vacation 9 allowance 10 permission, relinquish

behind: 11 outdistance

in the lurch: 6 desert, maroon, strand

off: 4 halt, quit, stop 6 desist 8 knock off

out: 4 omit, skip 5 elide 7 exclude

leave of absence: 5 exeat 8 furlough

leave-taking: 5 adieu, conge 6 congee 7 parting 8 farewell 9 departure

leaven: 5 imbue, yeast 7 lighten 10 impregnate

leaves (see also **leaf, leave):** 7 foliage

having: see **leafy**

medicinal: 5 senna

leavings: See **lees, rubbish**

Lebanon: *capital:* 6 Beirut

dance: 6 dabkeh

fort: 6 Byblos

language: 6 Arabic

monetary unit: 5 pound 7 piaster

mountain: 4 Mzar 5 Aruba 6 Hermon 7 Sannine

mountain range: 7 Lebanon 11 Anti-Lebanon

river: 5 Kebir 6 Litani 7 Orontes

town: 4 Tyre 5 Sidon, Zahle 7 Tripoli

valley: 6 El Bika

lech: 4 slab 8 capstone, monument

lecher: 4 rake, roué 7 glutton 8 gourmand, parasite 9 debauchee, libertine

lecherous: 4 lewd 7 boarish, goatish, lustful 9 salacious

lectern: 4 ambo, desk 5 stand 6 podium 10 escritoire

lecture: 5 scold 6 lesson, preach, rebuke, sermon, speech 7 address, hearing, lection, oration, prelect 8 scolding 9 discourse, sermonize 12 dissertation

lecturer: 6 docent, reader 9 prelector, professor

led: See **lead**

Leda: *daughter:* 5 Helen 12 Clytemnestra

lover: 4 swan, Zeus

son: 6 Castor, Pollux

ledge: 4 berm, sill 5 bench, berme, shelf 7 retable

ledger: 4 book, tome 6 record

lee: 5 haven 7 shelter 10 protection

oposite of: 5 stoss 8 windward

leech: 8 parasite 9 blackmail 11 blood-sucker

leer: 4 face, lear, lehr, loin, look, lust, ogle, void 5 empty, flank, fleer, smirk 6 entice, unlade 7 grimace

leery, leary: 4 wary 7 knowing 10 suspicious 11 distrustful 12 on one's guard

lees: 5 draff, dregs, dross, grout 6 bottom, dunder, refuse, ullage 7 ground° 8 leavings, sediment, settling 9 emptyings, excrement, left-overs

leeward: 4 alee
drift: 4 crab

Leeward group island: 5 Nevis 7 Antigua, Barbuda, St. Kitts 8 Anguilla, Dominica, Windward 10 Montserrat

leeway: 4 room 5 space 9 elbowroom

left: 4 port 8 larboard
toward: haw 5 aport 9 sinistrad

left-handed: car 6 clumsy, gauche 7 awkward 8 southpaw 9 portsided

leftist: red 7 liberal, radical 13 revolutionary

leg: gam, run 4 gamb, hoof, limb, prop, walk 5 bough, brace, gambe, shank 6 bender, gammon 8 cabriole
armor: 4 jamb 6 greave
bone: 4 shin 5 femur, ilium, tibia 6 fibula
in heraldry: 6 gamb
muscle: 8 peroneus 9 peronaeus
ornament: 6 anklet
part: 4 calf, crus, knee, shin 5 ankle, thigh 11 anticnemion
pert. to: 6 crural

legacy: 4 gift 6 legate 7 bequest 8 windfall 10 foundation
inheritor: 4 heir 7 legatee

legal (see also law): 5 licit, valid 6 lawful 7 juridic 9 juridical 10 authorized, legitimate

legal matter: res

legal right, by: 6 ex jure

legal tender: 4 cash, coin 5 money 6 dollar, specie

legalize: 9 authorize

legate: 5 envoy 6 deputy, legacy, nuncio 7 bequeath, delegate 9 messenger 10 ambassador 14 representative

legatee: 4 heir
joint: 6 coheir

legend: 4 edda, lore, myth, saga, tale 5 fable, story 6 record 7 fiction, proverb 9 tradition

legerdemain: 5 magic 6 deceit 8 trickery 9 conjuring 13 sleight of hand

legging: 4 spat 5 chaps 6 cnemis, cocker, puttie 7 bottine, gambado 8 bootikin, chivarra, chivarro, gamashes 11 galligaskin, spatterdash 12 antigropelos

legible: 8 distinct, readable 14 understandable

legion: 4 army, host 9 multitude

legislate: act 5 elect, enact

legislation: act, law 4 bill 7 statute

legislative body: 4 Dail, diet, rada 5 house, junta 6 senate 7 althing 8 assembly, congress 9 Reichstag 10 parliament

legislator: 5 solon 7 enactor, senator 8 lawmaker 9 statesman 14 representative

legitimate: 4 fair, just, real, true 5 legal, licit, valid 6 cogent, lawful 7 genuine 11 efficacious

legman: 8 reporter

legume: pea, pod, uva 4 bean, soya 5 pulse 6 lentil, loment 9 vegetable

lei: 6 wreath 7 flowers, garland

leisure: 4 case, free, idle, time 5 otium(L.), spare 6 otiose 7 freedom 10 relaxation, unemployed, unoccupied 11 convenience, opportunity 12 unproductive

leisurely: 4 slow 7 gradual 12 deliberately

leitmotiv: 5 theme 6 motive 7 pattern

leman: 5 lover 8 mistress, paramour 10 sweetheart

lemma: 5 bract, theme 7 premise, theorem 8 membrane

lemon: dud 5 fruit 7 failure 9 sour thing

lemonade: 5 drink 6 cooler 8 beverage

lemur: 4 maki, vari 5 avahi, indri, loris, potto 6 aye-aye, colugo, galago, macaco, maholi 7 half-ape, semiape, tarsier 8 kinkajou 9 babacoote 10 angwantibo

lend: 4 give, loan 5 grant, prest 6 afford, impart, settle 7 advance, furnish 11 accommodate

length: 4 pace, term 7 yardage 8 duration 9 dimension
measure: mil 4 foot, inch, yard

lengthen: eke 6 dilate, expand, extend 7 amplify, produce, prolong, stretch 8 elongate, increase, protract

lengthwise: 4 along 7 endlong, endways 14 longitudinally

lengthy: 4 long 8 drawn-out, extended 10 protracted

lenient: lax 4 easy, kind, mild 6 facile, gentle, humane 7 clement 8 lenitive, merciful, mitigant, relaxing, soothing, tolerant 9 assuasive, emollient, softening 10 charitable, forbearing, palliative

Leningrad: 9 Petrograd

lens: 5 glass, optic 7 bifocal 8 meniscus 10 anastigmat

Lent: 6 Careme(F.)

Lenten: 5 plain 6 meager, meagre, somber, sombre 8 meatless 9 cheerless 14 unostentatious

lentigo: 7 freckle

lentil: 6 legume

Leo star: 7 Regulus

leonine: 8 lionlike, powerful

leopard: cat 4 pard 5 ounce 7 cheetah, panther

lepidopter: 4 moth 9 butterfly

leprechaun: elf 5 fairy

leprosy: 5 lepra

lerot: 8 dormouse

lese majesty: 7 treason

Les Miserables author: 4 Hugo

lesion: cut 4 sore 5 ulcer, wound 6 injury 7 fissure

Lesotho: *capital:* 6 Maseru
former name: 10 Basutoland
language: 7 Sesotho
monetary unit: 4 rand
mountain range: 11 Drakensburg
people: 7 Basotho
river: 6 Orange 7 Caledon
town: 4 Hoek 7 Mohales 8 Mafeteng

less: 5 fewer, minus, under 7 smaller 8 inferior

lessee: 6 leaser, renter, tenant 7 huurder(D.)

lessen: 4 bate, ease, wane 5 abase, abate, decry, lower, peter 6 impair, reduce, soften, shrink, weaken 7 amenuse, assuage, curtail, depress, relieve 8 belittle, condense, contract, decrease, derogate, diminish, minimize, mitigate, palliate, retrench, truncate 9 alleviate, attenuate, disparage, extenuate 10 depreciate 11 deteriorate

lesser: 5 minor 7 reduced 8 inferior 9 small-time 11 minor-league

lesson: 4 lear, task 5 moral, study 6 rebuke 7 example, lecture, precept, reading, reproof, warning 8 exercise 10 assignment 11 composition, instruction

lessor: 8 landlord

lest: 6 in case 11 for fear that

let: 4 hire, rent 5 allow, lease, leave 6 hinder, impede, permit, suffer 7 prevent 8 obstacle 9 hindrance
fall: 4 drop, slip 5 lower, spill 7 mention
forth: 4 emit
in: 5 admit, enter 6 insert

let it stand: sta 4 stet

letdown: 5 slump 8 comedown, drawback 10 anticlimax, relaxation, slackening

lethal: 5 fatal 6 deadly, mortal, poison 9 poisonous 12 death-dealing

lethargic: 4 dull 5 heavy, inert 6 drowsy, sleepy, torpid 8 comatose, sluggish 9 apathetic

lethargy: 5 sopor 6 stupor, torpor 8 hebetude

Lethe: 8 oblivion 13 forgetfulness

Leto: 6 Latona
daughter: 7 Artemis
father: 6 Coeus
mother: 6 Phoebe
son: 6 Apollo

Lett: 4 Balt 7 Latvian

letter: 4 bull, chit, line, note 5 breve, brief, chain, favor, vowel 6 billet, cartel, charta, favour, screed, symbol 7 collins, courant, epistle, message, missile, missive 9 consonant, precisely, semivowel 12 exact wording 13 communication, semiconsonant
Anglo-Saxon: edh, eth, wen, wyn 4 wynn
decorated: fac
large: 7 capital 9 majuscule, upper case
sloping: 6 italic
small: 9 lower case, miniscule

letter carrier: 6 correo(Sp.) 7 mailman, postman 9 messenger

lettered: 7 learned, stamped 8 educated, literate 9 instructed

lettuce: *kind of:* cos 4 head, leaf 6 butter 7 romaine, simpson
sea: 4 alga 5 laver

letup: 7 respite 9 abatement, cessation

leucite: 5 lenad 9 amphigene

levant: 5 waver 6 decamp 7 abscond

Levant: 4 East 6 Orient 13 Mediterranean
garment: 6 caftan
river: 4 wadi, wady
ship: 4 jerm, saic
valley: 4 wady

levee: 4 bank, dike, dyke, pier, quay 6 durbar 9 reception 10 embankment

level: aim, par 4 even, flat, raze, true 5 equal, flush, grade, peavy, plane, point, scalp 6 evenly, peavey, peavie, smooth 7 flatten, mow down, planate, uniform 8 demolish 10 horizontal 12 standardized
social: 5 caste, class
tool: 5 plane 6 gimbal

level-headed: 8 sensible

lever: bar, lam, pry 5 helve, jemmy, jimmy, peavy, pedal, prise, swipe 6 binder, garrot, peavey, peavie, tappet, tiller 7 crowbar, treadle 9 rockshaft
part: 7 fulcrum

leverage: 5 power 9 influence

leveret: 4 hare 8 mistress

Levi: *descendant:* 6 Levite 7 Gershon
father: 5 Jacob
son: 6 Kohath

leviathan: 4 ship 5 titan, whale 6 dragon

levigate: 5 grind 6 polish, smooth 9 pulverize

levin: 9 lightning

levitate: 4 rise 5 float

levity: 5 humor 6 gaiety, humour 8 buoyancy 9 frivolity, lightness, silliness 10 fickleness 11 foolishness, instability

levy: tax 4 cess, duty, fine, wage 5 exact, stent 6 assess, extent, impose, impost 7 collect 10 assessment, imposition

lewd: 4 base, rude 5 bawdy 6 carnal,

coarse 7 lustful, obscene, rammish, sensual 8 unchaste 9 debauched, dissolute, lecherous, salacious 10 lascivious, libidinous, licentious 12 pornographic

lexicographer: 6 author 8 compiler 9 onomastic

lexicon: 7 calepin 10 dictionary 11 onomasticon

Leyte capital: 8 Tacloban

liability: 4 debt, loan 5 debit 6 burden 10 obligation

liable: apt 6 likely 8 amenable 10 answerable 11 accountable, responsible 12 legally bound

liaison: 4 bond 6 affair 8 intimacy, intrigue 12 relationship

liana: 4 cipo, vine 5 plant

liang: 4 tael

liar: 5 cheat 6 fibber 7 Ananias, cracker 8 deceiver, fabulist 10 fabricator 11 pseudologue 12 prevaricator, pseudologist 14 misrepresenter

lias: 4 rock 9 limestone

libation: 5 drink 8 potation

libel: 4 bill 6 defame, malign, vilify 7 calumny, lampoon, request, scandal, slander 8 circular, handbill, roorback 10 calumniate, defamation 11 certificate, declaration 12 supplication

libelant: 7 accuser

liberal: 4 free, good, open 5 ample, broad, frank, noble 6 honest 7 electic, profuse 8 abundant, eclectic, generous, handsome 9 benignant, bounteous, bountiful, expansive, expensive, plenteous, plentiful 10 benevolent, charitable, ecumenical, munificent 11 broad-minded, progressive

Liberal: 4 Whig

liberate: rid 4 flee, free 5 clear, loose, remit 6 acquit, redeem, rescue 7 deliver, manumit, release 8 unfetter 9 discharge, disengage, extricate 10 emancipate

Liberia: *boatman:* Kru
capital: 8 Monrovia
city: 8 Buchanan, Marshall 10 Greenville
language: Kwa
measure: 4 kuba
monetary unit: 6 dollar
people: Kru, Kwa, Vai, Vei 4 Kroo, Toma 5 Bassa, Gibbi, Greba 6 Krooby, Kruman 7 Krooboy, Krooman
river: 5 Manna 8 San Pedro

libertine: 4 rake, roue 7 sceptic 9 debauchee, dissolute 10 lascivious, licentious

liberty: may 4 ease, play 5 leave, right 7 freedom, license 9 privilege 11 presumption 12 emancipation

library: 7 archive, bhander 8 atheneum 9 athenaeum 11 bibliotecha, reading room

libretto: 4 book 5 words

Libya: *capital:* 7 Tripoli
chief export: oil
city: 8 Benghasi
gulf: 5 Sidra
language: 6 Arabic
measure: 4 drah 5 bozze, donum, jabia, teman 6 barile 7 mattaro
monetary unit: 5 dinar
mountain: 5 Bette
oasis: 6 Fezzan, Giofra 8 Al-Kufrah, Giarabub
religion: 5 Islam
weight: 4 kele 5 uckia 6 gorraf 7 termino 8 kharouba
wind: 7 sirocco

Libya's child: 5 Belus 6 Agenor

lice: See louse

license: tax 5 exeat, leave 6 patent, permit 7 dismiss, freedom, liberty 8 escambio, passport, sanction 9 approbate, authority, authorize, franchise 10 permission 11 imprimateur, unrestraint

licentious: gay, lax 4 free, lewd 5 frank, loose 6 unruly 7 immoral, obscene 9 dissolute 10 lascivious, profligate 12 pornographic, uncontrolled, unrestrained

lichen: 4 moss
derivative: 6 archil, litmus
genus: 5 usnea 7 evernia 10 pertusaria

lich-house: 8 mortuary

licit: 5 legal 6 lawful 9 permitted

lick: bit, dab, lap, win 4 flog 5 slake, taste 6 defeat, thrash 7 clobber, conquer, shellac 8 overcome, vanquish

lickety-split: 4 fast 5 apace 7 quickly, rapidly, swiftly 9 posthaste

licorice: 5 abrin, anise 8 absinthe 9 jequirity
pill: 6 cachou
seed: 9 jequirity

lid: cap, hat, top 4 curb 5 cover 7 shutter 9 operculum, restraint

lie: cog, fib, gab 4 bask, cram, flaw, hide, loll, rest 5 exist 6 covet, extend, grovel, patter, remain, repose 7 cracker, crammer, deceive, falsify, falsity, pronate, untruth 8 position, roorback 9 deception, fabricate, falsehood, fish story, mendacity, prostrate 10 equivocate, inveracity, taradiddle 11 fabrication, prevaricate, tarradiddle 12 song and dance
in ambush: 4 lurk 6 hugger 9 insidiate

Liebestraum composer: 5 Liszt

Liechtenstein: *capital:* 5 Vaduz
monetary unit: 5 rappe

lief: 4 fain, soon 5 leave 6 freely, gladly 7 happily 9 willingly 10 permission

liege: 5 loyal 6 vassal 7 devoted, subject 8 faithful, overlord 9 sovereign

lien: 5 claim 6 charge 8 mortgage 9 trust deed 11 encumbrance, garnishment

lieu: 5 place, stead 7 instead
lieutenant: 7 officer 10 aide-de-camp
life: vie 5 blood, vigor 6 biosis, energy,
    spirit 8 vitality, vivacity 9 animation,
    biography, existence 11 anilopyrine
    animal: 4 bios 5 biota, fauna
    god of: 6 Faunus
    pert. to: 5 vital 6 biotic, mortal 8 biotical
    plant: 4 bios 5 flora, flora
    principle: 5 atman, prana, tenet
    professional: 6 career
    science: 7 anatomy, biology, zoology 12
        paleontology
    sea: 5 coral 8 halibios, plankton
    simple form: 5 ameba 6 amebic, amoeba
        7 amoebic, examinate
        without: 4 dead 5 azoic 9 inanimate
life jacket: 7 Mae West
life-like: 9 realistic
lifeless: 4 arid, dead, dull, flat 5 amort,
    heavy, inert, vapid 6 anemic, jejune,
    torpid 7 anaemic 8 inactive, listless 9
    bloodless, examinate, inanimate, power-
    less, tasteless 10 spiritless, unanimated
lifer: 7 convict 13 career soldier
lifetime: age, day, eon 4 aeon 5 being 8
    duration
lift: pry 4 help, jack, perk, rear 5 boost,
    crane, exalt, heave, hoick, hoist, hoosh,
    raise, scend 6 cleach, cleech 7 derrick,
    elevate, enhance 8 elevator, heighten
ligament: 4 band, bind, bond 6 artery 7
    bandage
ligan, lagan: 6 debris
ligate: 4 bind 5 tie up 7 bandage
ligature: tie 4 band, bond 6 taenia 7 ban-
    dage
light: dey, gay 4 airy, deft, easy, fair, fire,
    glim, lamp, mild, moon, neon, soft 5 ag-
    ile, blond, fanal, filmy, flaky, flame,
    flare, happy, merry, torch 6 alight, bea-
    con, bright, candle, floaty, gentle, ignite,
    kindle, lively, lumine, nimble, pastel,
    volant 7 animate, buoyant, cresset, fly-
    away, fragile, trivial, whitish 8 bright-
    en, cheerful, delicate, ethereal, gossa-
    mer, graceful, illumine, luminary,
    luminous, trifling 9 frivolous, knowl-
    edge, touch down 10 capricious, illumi-
    nate
    circle: 4 halo 7 aureola, aureole
    cloud: 6 nimbus
    faint: 7 glimmer, shimmer 9 starlight 10
        glimmering, shimmering
    globe: 4 bulb
    god: 5 Baldr 6 Balder
    kind of: arc 4 lamp 5 klieg, torch 7 lan-
        tern 9 headlight 10 flashlight 12 in-
        candescent
    measure: lux, pyr, rad 5 lumen 6 Hefner
    overpower with: 6 dazzle
    portable: 4 lamp 5 flare, taper, torch 6

    candle 7 lantern 10 flashlight
    reflector: 4 lens 6 mirror
    refractor: 5 prism
    science: 6 optics
    source: sun
    unit: lux, pyr 4 phot 5 lumen
    without: 4 dark 5 blind 7 aphotic
lighten: 4 ease, fade 5 allay, clear 6 alight,
    allege, bleach, illume, leaven 7 gladden,
    relieve 8 brighten 9 alleviate 10 illumi-
    nate
lighter (see also light): 5 barge, spill 7
    pontoon 8 chopboat
lightheaded: 5 dizzy, giddy 6 fickle 7
    flighty, glaiket, glaikit 8 flippant, heed-
    less, unstable, unsteady 9 delirious,
    frivolous 10 disordered, inconstant 11
    thoughtless
lighthearted: gay 4 glad 5 merry 7 buoy-
    ant 8 carefree, cheerful, gleesome, vola-
    tile 9 vivacious 12 free from care
lighthouse: 5 phare 6 beacon, pharos 7
    seamark, warning
lightness: 6 levity 8 delicacy, mildness
    12 cheerfulness
lightning: 4 bolt 5 levin
    defier of: 4 Ajax
    pert. to: 8 fulgural
    protective device: rod 8 arrester
lightning bug: 6 beetle 7 firefly
lightning stone: 9 fulgurite
lights out: 4 taps
ligneous: 5 woody
lignite: 4 coal
ligulate: 11 strap-shaped
likable: 6 genial 7 winning 8 charming,
    pleasant 10 attractive
like: 4 love, same 5 alike, enjoy, equal 6
    admire, prefer, relish 7 similar 9 analo-
    gous, semblance 10 preference, synony-
    mous 11 counterpart, homogeneous
like a: For definitions beginning with
    these words, see following important
    words. EXAMPLES: "like a cat": see cat-
    like; "like a house": see house: *pert.
    to.*
likelihood: 10 appearance 11 probability
    14 verisimilitude
likely: apt 5 prone 6 liable 7 tending 8
    credible, feasible, probable, suitable 9
    promising 11 verisimilar
liken: 5 apply 7 compare 10 assimilate
likeness: 4 copy, form, twin 5 guise, im-
    age 6 effigy, figure, statue 7 analogy,
    parable, picture, replica 8 parallel, por-
    trait 9 duplicate, facsimile, imitation,
    semblance, simulacre 10 comparison,
    photograph, similarity, similitude, sim-
    ulacrum 11 counterfeit 12 reproduc-
    tion 14 representation
likewise: and, nor, not, too 4 also 5 ditto
    7 besides 8 moreover
liking: goo 4 gust, lust 5 fancy, gusto,

taste 6 comely 7 delight 8 affinity, appetite, fondness, penchant, pleasing, pleasure 9 affection 10 preference, sensuality 12 predilection

lilac: 5 mauve, shrub 6 flower 7 syringa

Lilith's successor: Eve

lilliputian: 4 tiny 5 pretty, small 6 midget 7 dwarfed 10 diminutive, teeny-weeny

lilt: air 4 sing, song, tune 7 cadence

lily (see also **water lily**): 4 aloe, ixia, sego 5 calla, niobe, tiger, water, yucca 6 titree 8 mariposa
family: 9 liliaceae
genus: 7 bessera
sea: 7 crinoid

lily iron: 7 harpoon

lily-livered: 5 timid 6 coward 7 gutless 9 spunkless

Lily Maid of Astolat: 6 Elaine

lily of France: 10 fleur-de-lis

lily of the valley: 6 mugget, mugwet 10 convallily
family: 15 convallariaceae

lima: 4 bean, seed 7 mollusk

liman: bay 5 marsh 6 lagoon 7 estuary

limation: 6 filing 9 polishing

limb: arm, fin, leg 4 edge, wing 5 bough 6 branch, member, rascal, switch 7 flipper, pleopod, support 9 appendage
adapted for swimming: 8 nectopod
flexion: 9 anaclasis

limber: 4 bain, flip, limp 5 lithe 6 pliant, supple, swanky 8 flexible, flippant, handsome, yielding

limbo (see **hell**): 4 hell 5 dance 9 purgatory

lime: 5 color, fruit, green 6 cement, citrus
pendent: 10 stalactite
phosphate: 7 apatite
tree: 4 teil 6 linden, tupelo

limen: 9 threshold

limestone: 4 calp, cauk, malm 5 chalk, ganil, poros(Gr.) 6 clunch, marble, oolite 7 hurlock 8 peastone, pisolite

limey: 6 sailor 7 soldier 10 Engishman

limit: end, fix 4 curb, mete 5 ambit, bound, bourn, check, fence, hedge, scant, stint, verge 6 border, bourne, curfew, define, extent, finish 7 astrict, barrier, closure, confine, environ, extreme 8 boundary, conclude, contract, deadline, restrain, restrict, terminal, terminus 9 condition, constrain, extremity 10 limitation 11 restriction, termination 12 boundary line, circumscribe 13 determination, qualification

limited: few, ltd 5 local, scant 6 finite, narrow, scanty, strait 8 reserved 9 parochial 10 restricted 11 topopolitan

limiting: 5 final 9 bordering, enclosing 10 qualifying, relational

limitless: 4 vast 8 infinite 9 boundless,

unbounded, unlimited 11 measureless

limn: 4 draw 5 paint 6 depict, sketch 7 portray 8 describe 9 delineate

limp: hop, lax 4 himp, soft, then 5 hilch, hitch, loose 6 flabby, flimsy, hirple, hobble, limber, wilted 7 flaccid 8 drooping, flexible, hang down 9 inelastic 13 unsubstantial

limpid: 4 pure 5 clear, lucid 6 bright 7 crystal 8 pellucid 11 translucent, transparent

limping: 4 halt 10 claudicant

limy: 6 sticky 7 viscous

Lincoln:
assassin: 5 Booth
debater: 7 Douglas
nickname: 9 Honest Abe 12 Railsplitter
secretary of state: 6 Seward
secretary of war: 7 Stanton
son: Tad
wife: 8 Mary Todd

linden: lin 4 lime, teil 8 basswood
genus of: 5 tilia

line: job, pad, ray, row, wad 4 axis, ceil, cord, dash, etch, face, file, mark, mere, race, rein, rope, rule, seam, wire 5 curve, front, leger, queue, route, serif, snell, steen, stich, stria, swath 6 border, ceriph, cordon, fettle, hawser, isobar, metier, nettle, streak, string, stripe, suture 7 barrier, carrier, contour, outline, radiant, scratch 8 boundary, crossbar, isotherm, wainscot 9 delineate
bottom: 7 net loss 9 net profit
conceptual: 6 agonic, tropic 7 equator, isother 8 latitude, meridian 9 longitude
curved: arc
diagonal: 4 bias
geometrical: arc, ess 4 cant, sine 6 secant 7 tangent 8 parallel 9 asymptote
mathematical: 6 vector
nautical: 6 earing, hawser, ratlin 7 marline, painter, ratline
of soldiers: 4 file, rank 6 column
pert. to: 5 filar 6 linear
raised: 4 weal, welt 5 ridge
with boards: 8 wainscot

lineage: 4 race 5 birth, blood, caste, tribe 6 family, havage, stirps 7 descent, stirpes(pl.) 8 ancestry, heredity, pedigree 9 genealogy 10 progenitor

lineal: 6 direct, racial 9 ancestral 10 hereditary

lineament: 7 feature 14 characteristic

linear: 9 elongated

lineate: 7 striped 8 streaked

lined: 5 ruled 6 notate 7 striate 8 careworn 9 lineolate

lineman: end 5 guard 6 center, tackle 7 wireman

linen: 4 brin, crea(Sp.), lawn 5 toile 6 barras, damask, dowlas, forfar 7 bra-

bant, cambric, dornick 13 linsey-wool-
sey
fabric: 7 taffeta
household: 6 napery, sheets 10 tablecloth
source: 4 flax
yarn: lea
liner: 4 boat, ship 6 facing, vessel 7 backing, steamer 9 steamship
wrecked: 7 Titanic
lines: net 5 looks 7 harness, network, reticule
ling: 4 fish, hake 5 heath 6 burbot 7
heather 8 chestnut
linger: lag 4 drag, stay, wait 5 dally, delay, dwell, hover, tarry 6 dawdle, loiter,
remain, stay on
lingerie: 9 underwear 11 underthings
lingering: 4 slow 7 chronic
lingo: 4 cant 5 argot 6 jargon, patter,
tongue 7 dialect 8 language 10 vernacular
lingual: 7 glossal 10 linguistic, tonguelike
linguist: 8 polyglot 9 pantoglot 10 vocabulist 11 interpreter, philologist
linguistics: 7 grammar 9 philology
lingy: 5 agile 6 active, healthy, limber,
nimble 8 heathery
liniment: oil 6 lotion 8 ointment 11 embrocation
lining: 5 steen 6 facing, insert 7 backing,
ceiling 8 wainscot
link: tie 4 join, joke 5 cleek, nexus, torch,
unite 6 braced, catena, copula, couple,
course, faster 7 conjoin, connect 8 catenate 10 connection, golf course 11 concatenate
series: 9 chain 13 concatenation
linn, lin: 4 pool 6 linden, ravine 8 cataract 9 precipice, waterfall
linnet: 5 finch, twite 9 gorsebird
linseed: 4 flax
lint: 4 fuzz, pile 5 fluff 7 charpie 8 raveling
lintel: 5 hance 6 clavel 7 transom
lion: 4 puma, star 5 simba 6 cougar, roarer 9 carnivore, celebrity
group: 5 pride
hair: 4 mane
winged, with woman's head: 6 sphinx
young: cub 6 lionet
Lion of God: Ali
lionlike: 7 leonine
lion's share: 8 best part 10 whole thing
lip: rim 4 brim, edge, kiss 5 brink, la-
bia(pl.) 6 labium, margin, 7 labella 8
labellum
ornament: 6 labret
part: 8 philtrum
pert. to: 6 labial 11 labiodental
lipoma: 5 tumor
lipid: fat, wax
liquefy: 4 fuse, melt 6 fusile 7 liquate 8

dissolve, eliquate 10 colliquate, deliquesce, make molten
liqueur: 5 creme, noyau 6 genepi 7 cordial, ratafee 8 anisette, beverage 9 cointreau 10 pousse cafe 11 benedictine
liquid: 5 fluid 6 fluent, watery 8 beverage
colorless: 5 water, 7 alcohol
container: cup, jar, jug, mug, pan, pot 4
etna, ewer, vase, vial 5 cruse, glass, phial 6 boiler, bottle, bucket, goblet, kettle
7 creamer, pitcher, tumbler 8 decanter,
demijohn
gasified: 5 steam, vapor
inflammable: see *volatile* below
measure: 4 pint 5 liter, ounce 6 gallon,
tierce
oily: 6 cresol, octane 7 aniline, picamar
particle form: 4 mist 5 spray
sweet: 5 sirup, syrup 7 treacle 8 molasses
volatile: gas 5 ether 6 butane 7 alcohol,
ligroin 8 gasolene, gasoline, ligroine
liquidate: 5 pay up 6 murder, settle 8 amortize 9 discharge
liquor (see also **liqueur**): ale, bub, dew,
gin, rum, rye 4 arak, bang, beer, beno,
brew, grog, nipa, raki, sake, saki, soma
5 bhang, booze, budge, drink, hooch, lager, pisco, stout 6 arrack, brandy, porter, pottle, scotch, stingo, strunt, tipple
7 bitters, whiskey 8 beverage 9 aqua vi-
tae, moonshine 10 intoxicant
bad: 5 smoke 6 rotgut 10 balderdash
cabinet: 8 cellaret
crude: 5 hooch, 6 rotgut 9 hoochinoo,
moonshine
drugged: 5 hocus 6 mickey 10 mickey-
finn
manufacturer: 6 abkari 9 distiller
measure: 4 dram 5 rouse 7 snifter
mix with: 4 lace
mixture: 5 bogus 7 bragget
residue: 4 must 5 dregs 8 heeltaps
server: 6 barman 7 barmaid, skinker, tapster 9 barkeeper, bartender
shop: bar 6 saloon, tavern 7 shebeen
vessel: ama, keg 4 bowl 5 amula, flask 6
barrel, bottle, flagon 7 bombard,
psykter, stamnos 8 cruisken, decanter 9
cruiskeen
lira (one-twentieth): 5 soldo
liripipe, liripoop: 4 hood 5 scarf 6 tippet
lirk: 6 crease 7 wrinkle
lish: 5 agile, quick 6 active, nimble
lisk: 4 loin 5 flank, groin
lisp: 7 prattle
lissome, lissom: 5 agile, lithe 6 limber,
nimble, supple 8 flexible
list: tip 4 bill, cant, cast, file, item, keel,
leet, memo, ordo, roll, rota, rote, tilt 5
brief, canon, index, panel, scrip, slate 6
careen, docket, roster 7 catalog, incline
8 manifest, register, schedule, tabulate

9 catalogue, inventory, portfolio, repertory 10 repertoire 11 enumeration

listen: ear 4 hark, hear, heed, note 5 audit 6 attend, harken 7 hearken 8 give heed, overhear 9 eavesdrop 10 auscultate, take advice

lister: 4 plow 8 assessor 9 appraiser 10 cataloguer

listing: 5 atilt 7 tilting, tipping 8 register 10 enlistment, enrollment

individual: 4 item 5 entry

listless: 4 dull 5 faint, inert 6 abject, drowsy, supine 7 languid 8 careless, heedless, prosaic 8 accurate, verbatim sluggish 9 apathetic, heartless 10 spiritless 11 indifferent 13 uninteresting

listlessness: 8 doldrums

litany: 6 ectene, ektene, prayer 8 rogation 11 orapronobis

liter: kan(D.) 7 measure

literal: 4 bald, dull, real 5 exact 7 factual, precise, prosaic 8 accurate, verbatim 11 word for word 13 unimaginative

literary: 6 versed 7 bookish, erudite, learned 8 lettered 9 scholarly

literate: 6 reader, writer 8 educated, lettered

literati: 12 men of letters 14 intelligentsia

literator: 6 critic

literature: 7 letters

extracts: 9 anthology

form: 5 novel, prose 6 poetry 7 fiction 9 technical 10 nonfiction, scientific 11 pornography

lithe: 4 bain, slim 6 clever, limber, lissom, pliant, supple, svelte 7 lissome, slender 8 flexible

lithograph: 5 print 6 chromo

Lithuania: *capital:* 7 Vilnius

city: 6 Kaunas 8 Klaipeda

coin: lit 5 litas, marka 6 centas, fennig 7 ostmark 8 auksinas, skatikas

dialect: 5 Zmudz

lowlander: 5 Zhmud 10 Samogitian

people: 4 Balt, Lett 5 Zhmud 6 Litvak 7 Yatvyag

railroad junction: 5 Vilna

litigant: 4 suer 6 suitor 7 accuser

litigation: 4 case, moot, suit 6 action 7 contest, dispute, lawsuit 10 contention, discussion

one involved in: 8 barrater, barrator, litigant

litigious: 10 disputable 11 belligerent, contentious, quarrelsome 14 controvertible

litter: bed, hay 4 bier, mess, raff 5 cabin, couch, dooly, mulch, straw, trash, young 6 doolie, refuse 7 cacolet, clutter, mullock, rubbish, rummage 8 brancard(F.), disorder 9 offspring, stretcher 10 untidiness

litterateur: 7 bookman

little: sma(Sc.), wee 4 poco(It.), puny, tiny 5 crumb, petit, small 6 petite 8 fraction 10 diminutive

by little: 8 inchmeal 9 gradually, piecemeal

Little Dipper: 7 Polaris 9 North Star 13 constellation

little finger: 5 pinky 6 pinkie 7 minimus

little toe: 7 minimus

Little Women: Amy, Meg 4 Beth

author: 6 Alcott

surname: 5 March

littoral: 7 coastal

lituite: 6 fossil

liturate: 7 spotted

liturgy: 4 rite 6 ritual 7 service

livable: 8 bearable 9 endurable, habitable, tolerable

live: 4 fare, room 5 abide, alive, dwell, exist, green, vital, vivid 6 active, reside 7 animate, blazing, breathe, dynamic, subsist 8 animated, continue, converse 9 energetic 10 experience, unexploded

in: 7 inhabit

in the country: 9 rusticate

passively: 8 vegetate

permit to: 5 spare 8 reprieve

with: 7 cohabit

livelihood: 4 keep 5 being 6 living 11 subsistence

liveliness: 6 spirit 8 vitality

lively: gay, vif(F.) 4 airy, cant, fast, pert, racy, vive, yare 5 agile, alert, alive, brisk, canty, chirk, cobby, desto(It.), fresh, peart, peppy 6 active, blithe, bright, cheery, chirpy, cocket, crouse, dapper, frisky, nimble, snappy 7 allegro(It.), animate, animato(It.), buoyant, chipper 8 animated, galliard, spirited, vigorous 9 energetic, sprightly, vivacious

liven: 5 cheer, pep up 7 animate 8 brighten

liver: 4 foie 5 hepar 8 tomalley

disease: 9 cirrhosis, hepatitis

fluid: 4 bile

pert. to: 7 hepatic

liverwort: 4 moss 8 agrimony, hepatica 9 bryophyte

genus: 6 riccia

livery: 7 uniform 8 clothing

livestock: 6 cattle 7 chattel

livid: 4 gray 5 bleak 6 purple 7 deathly 9 colorless 10 discolored 12 black and blue

living: 4 keep 5 alive, being, bread, vivid 6 extant 7 animate 8 animated, benefice 10 livelihood, sustenance 11 subsistence

again: 6 reburn 9 redivivus

correct: 7 regimen 11 orthobiosis

off others: 8 entozoic 9 parasitic, raptorial

together: 11 contubernal

lixiviate: 5 leach

lixivium: lye

lizard: dab, eft 4 adda, dabb, dhab, evet, gila, ibid, newt, seps, uran 5 agama, anole, dhabb, gecko, gekko, goana, scink, skink, varan, waran 6 ameiva, anolis, dragon, goanna, iguana, komodo, lacert, moloch, worral, worrel 7 cheecha, geitjie, monitor, saurian, tuatera 8 basilisk 9 chameleon, galliwasp 10 chuckwalla, horned toad 12 scheltopusik
  family: 12 xenosauridae
  genus: uta 5 agama 6 ameiva, anolis
  mammal similar to: 10 salamander

lizard like: 8 iguanoid

llama: 4 alpaca, vicuna 7 guanaco
  habitat: 5 Andes

llanero: 6 cowboy 8 herdsman

llano: 5 plain 7 lowland, prairie

Llyr's son: 4 Bran 7 Branwen

load: jag 4 clog, jagg, lade, onus, pack, tote, stow 5 cargo, weigh 6 burden, charge, hamper, lading, steeve, weight 7 fraught, freight, oppress 8 carriage, encumber 9 aggravate, exonerate 10 adulterate 11 encumbrance
  small: jag 4 jagg 5 hurry

loader: 9 stevedore

loadstone: See **lodestone**

loaf: 4 idle, laze 5 bread 6 dawdle, loiter, lounge 10 dilly-dally

loafer: bum 4 hood, shoe 5 idler 7 flaneur, hoodlum, lounger, vagrant 8 hooligan, larrikin, vagabond 11 chairwarmer

loam: rab 4 silt 5 loess, regur(Ind.) 6 cledge 8 dark soil
  constituent: 4 clay, lime 5 chalk
  deposit: 4 silt 5 loess

loan: 4 dhan(Ind.), lend 5 prest 6 borrow 7 advance 10 obligation, provisions 13 accommodation

loan shark: 6 usurer 11 money-lender

loath, loth: 6 averse, odious 7 hateful 8 backward 9 reluctant, repulsive, unwilling

loathe: 4 hate 5 abhor 6 detest 7 adverse, condemn, despise, dislike 9 abominate

loathsome: 4 foul, ugly, vile 7 carrion, cloying, hateful 8 abhorrent, deformed 9 offensive, repellent, repugnant 10 abominable, detestable, disgusting 11 distasteful

lob: hit 4 bowl, lots, lout, lump, step, till, toss, vein 5 droop, stair, throw 6 propel 7 pollack 9 chandelle

lobby: 4 hall, room 5 foyer 8 anteroom, coulisse 9 enclosure, vestibule

lobbyist: 8 promoter 12 propagandist

lobe: 4 flap 5 alula 6 alular, earlap, lappet, lobule

lobelike: 6 lobate

loblolly: 4 mush, pine, tree 5 gruel 6 puddle 7 mudhole

lobo: 4 wolf 10 timber wolf

lobster: *claw:* 5 chela 6 nipper 10 crustacean
  female: hen
  part: 4 claw 6 pincer, telson, thorax
  roe: 5 coral
  trap: pot 5 creel 6 bownet

local: 6 narrow, native 7 bucolic, endemic, limited, topical 8 regional, specific 10 restricted

locale: 4 loci(pl.), site 5 locus(L.), place, scene 6 region 9 situation

locality: 4 loci(pl.), seat, site, spot 5 locus, place, situs 6 region 7 habitat 8 district, position 12 neighborhood

localize: 7 situate 9 pinpoint

locate (see also **place**)**:** sat 4 espy, find, seat, show, site, spot 5 stand, trace 6 settle 7 situate, station 8 discover, pinpoint 9 establish

locatio: 7 leasing, letting

locating device: 5 lidar, radar, sonar

location: 4 area, seat, site, spot 5 place, scene, situs 6 ubiety 7 habitat 9 situation

loch: bay 4 lake, pond, pool 5 lough

loci: See **locus**

lock: 4 bolt, curl, frib, hank, hasp, wisp 5 latch, sasse, tress 6 fasten 7 confine, cowlick, ringlet 8 fastener
  part: 4 bolt 5 stump 8 cylinder

locker: 5 hutch 6 ascham

locket: 7 jewelry 8 ornament

lockjaw: 7 tetanus, trismus 11 ankylostoma
  remedy: 11 antitetanic, antitetanus

lockman: 11 executioner

lockup: jug 4 jail 5 clink 6 cooler 7 hoosgow 8 hoosegaw, hoosegow 9 calaboose

loco: mad 5 crazy 6 insane 8 demented

locomotive: 5 dolly, mogul 6 diesel, dinkey, engine, mallet 8 electric
  part: cab 5 pilot
  service car: 6 tender 7 coalcar
  type: 5 steam 6 diesel 8 electric

Locrine: *daughter:* 7 Sabrina
  father: 4 Brut

locus: 4 area, site 5 place 8 locality

locust: 5 bruke, cicad, carob 6 cicada, cicala, cigala, insect 11 grasshopper
  wingless: 4 weta

locust bird: 7 grackle 8 starling

locust plant: 5 senna

locust tree: 5 carob 6 acacia

locustberry: 5 drupe, nance 9 glamberry

lode: 4 path, road, vein 5 canal, drain, ledge 6 course 7 deposit, fissure 8 waterway
  cavity: vug 4 vugg, vugh

lodestone, loadstone: 6 magnet 7 adamant 8 terrella 9 magnetite

lodge: dig, lie **4** club **5** board, couch, dwell, hogan, motel **6** alight, bestow, encamp, hostel **7** deposit **8** harbinge, domicile **11** brotherhood

lodger: 5 guest **6** roomer, tenant

lodging: bed, hut, inn **4** camp, gite(F.), host, howf, nest, room, tent **5** cabin, hotel, house, hovel, howff **6** billet, tavern, teepee, wigwam **7** mansion **8** barracks, dwelling, hostelry, quarters **9** dormitory, harborage, residence **10** habitation, harbourage

cost: **4** rent **11** maintenance

loess: 4 loam, silt **7** deposit

loft: 4 bin **4** balk **5** attic, raise **6** garret

lofty: 4 aery, epic, high, tall **5** aerie, elate, grand, noble, proud, steep **6** aerial, Andean, andine **7** Andesic, arduous, eminent, haughty, sublime **8** arrogant, assuming, elevated, eloquent, majestic **9** cockhorse, dignified, overproud **11** magisterial, mountainous

log: 4 clog, wood **5** diary **6** billet, loggat, logget, record, timber **7** journal

kind: **4** slab **5** splat **8** puncheon

mass: **5** drive

revolve: **4** birl **7** logroll

log gin: 6 jammer

logarithm: *unit:* bel

inventor: **6** Napier

loge: box **4** room **5** booth, stall

logger: 6 sniper **9** lumberman **10** lumberjack, woodcutter **11** woodchopper

boot: pac **4** pack

loggerhead: 4 turtle **9** blockhead

loggerheads: 4 odds, outs **10** quarreling

loggia: 6 arcade **7** balcony, gallery

logging: *sled:* **4** tode **7** travois **8** travoise

tool: **4** pevy **5** peavy, peevy **6** nigger, peavey

logic: 9 reasoning

inductive: **7** epagoge

specious: **7** sophism

term: **5** ferio, lemma **7** ferison

logical: 4 sane **5** sound, valid **8** coherent, rational **10** consistent, reasonable

logion: 5 maxim, motto **6** saying **11** observation

logogriph: 5 rebus **6** puzzle, riddle **7** anagram

logotype: 8 colophon **9** nameplate, signature, trademark

logroll: 4 birl

logy: 4 dull **5** heavy **6** drowsy, groggy **8** sluggish

Lohengrin: *character:* **4** Elsa **8** Parsifal

composer: **6** Wagner

loincloth: 5 pagne

loir: 8 dormouse

loiter: lag **4** idle, loaf **5** dally, delay, drawl, shool, tarry **6** cooter, dawdle, linger **7** saunter **8** hesitate

loiterer: 4 slug **5** drone, idler **7** laggard **8** sluggard

Loki: *child:* Hel **4** Hela, Nare, Nari

mother: **9** Angrbodha

victim: **6** Balder

wife: **5** Sigyn

loll: 4 hang **5** droop, tarry **6** dangle, froust, frowst, lounge, sprawl **7** recline

loma, 4 hill

lombard: 6 cannon

Lombardy: *king:* **6** Alboin

lake: **4** Como

lomilomi: rub **7** massage, shampoo

lomita: 4 hill

London: *bus conductor:* **6** clippy

district: **4** Soho **5** Acton **7** Adelphi, Alsatia, Mayfair

fish market: **12** Billingsgate

monument: Gog **5** Magog **6** Nelson **8** Cenotaph, Victoria

museums and galleries: **4** Tate **8** National **13** Madame Tussaud **17** Victoria and Albert

parks: **4** Hyde **7** Holland, Regent's, St. James **9** Battersea **10** Kew Gardens

promenade: **4** Mall

river: **6** Thames

roisterer: mun

society: **7** Mayfair

square: **9** Leicester **9** Trafalgar

stables: **4** mews

street: **4** Bond **5** Fleet **6** Savile, Strand **7** Downing, Wardour **9** Cheapside, Haymarket, Whitehall **10** Piccadilly

suburb: Kew **8** Finchley

subway: **4** tube **11** underground

timepiece: **6** Big Ben

Londoner: 7 Cockney

Lone Ranger's companion: 5 Tonto

Lone Star State: 5 Texas

loneliness: 8 solitude **9** dejection, isolation **10** depression, desolation **12** lonesomeness

lonely: 4 lorn, sole **5** alone, apart **6** dismal, dreary **7** deavely, forlorn **8** deserted, desolate, lonesome, secluded, solitary **11** sequestered **12** unfrequented

long: far **4** hone, hope, pine **5** yearn **6** aspire, hanker, hunger, prolix, thirst **7** lengthy, tedious **8** drawn-out, extended, tiresome **9** elongated, prolonged, wearisome **10** protracted

and slender: **5** lathy, reedy **6** linear **9** elongated

for: **4** miss, want, wish **5** covet, crave **6** aspire, desire

long ago: 4 yore

long dozen: 8 thirteen

long-suffering: 4 meek **7** patient **8** pa-

tience 9 endurance 10 forbearing
long-winded: 6 prolix 7 prosaic 9 garrulous
Longfellow hero: 8 Hiawatha
longheaded: 4 wise 6 shrewd 9 sagacious 10 hardheaded 11 foresighted
longing: yen 4 envy, itch 6 desire 7 athirst, craving, wistful 8 appetite, cupidity, homesick, prurient, yearning 9 nostalgia 10 desiderium
longitudinally: 7 endlong 10 lengthwise
longshoreman: 8 dockhand 9 stevedore
loo: pam 6 toilet 8 card game
look: con, pry, see 4 gaze, leer, ogle, peek, peep, peer, pore, scan, seem, skew 5 blush, dekko, fleer, glare, gliff, glime, gloat, gloom, glower, glunch, notice, regard, search, squint, visage 7 observe 8 demeanor 10 appearance, get a load of
look after: 4 tend 6 attend 7 care for
look at: eye, see 4 glom, ogle, view 6 behold, regard 7 examine, observe
look back: 6 recall, relive, review 7 rethink 8 remember 10 retrospect
look down on: 7 despise
look for: 4 seek 5 await 6 expect 10 anticipate
look forward to: 5 await 6 expect 10 anticipate
look into: 5 study 6 search 7 examine, inspect 8 sound out 11 investigate
look like: 8 resemble
look over: 4 scan 6 ignore, survey 7 examine 8 overlook 9 disregard 11 reconnoiter, reconnoitre
look toward: 4 face
looker-on: 8 audience, beholder 9 bystander, spectator
lookout: 5 scout, watch, worry 6 conner, sentry 7 concern, palaver 8 observer 9 crow's nest 10 watchtower, widow's walk
looks (see also **look**): 4 face 8 features 10 attraction
loom: auk 4 brew, hulk, loon, tool 5 dobby, weave 6 appear, emerge, gather, gentle, impend, puffin, vessel 7 machine 9 guillemot, implement 10 receptacle
part: bar, lam 4 caam, leaf, reed, sley 5 easer, lathe 6 hanger, heddle 7 harness, shuttle, treadle
loon: nut, sap 4 bird, dolt, lout 5 diver, rogue, scamp, wabby 6 cobble, rascal
loony: 5 crazy 8 demented 11 harebrained
loop: eye, tab 4 ansa, coil, fold, hank, kink, knot, oese, ring 5 bight, bride, coque, curve, honda, hondo, noose, picot, terry 6 becket, billet, circle 7 circuit, curette, folding 8 doubling 11 aiguillette
loophole: out 4 muse 5 meuse, oilet 6 escape, eyelet, outlet 7 opening 8 aperture, weakness
loose: gay, lax 4 fast, floa, free, open 5 baggy, bulgy, crank, let up, loose, relax, slack, vague 6 coarse, dangly, random, unlash, wobbly 7 ease off, immoral, movable, relaxed, unbound, unleash 8 insecure, unstable, withdraw 9 desultory, dissolute, unbridled, unchecked 10 incoherent, indefinite, licentious, unattached, unconfined, unfastened 11 untrammeled 12 disconnected, uncontrolled, unrestrained 14 unconventional
loose ends: 4 dags 5 bored 7 details, tagrags 8 restless 9 fragments
loose-jointed: 5 lanky, rangy 6 clumsy, wobbly 7 rickety 10 ramshackle
loosen: pry 4 ease, free, undo 5 relax, untie 7 slacken 8 liberate, unfasten 9 disengage, extricate 10 talk freely 11 disentangle
loot: rob, sum 4 sack, swag 5 booty, money, spoil, strip 6 pilfer, ravage, spoils 7 pillage, plunder
receipt of: 9 theftbote
lop: bob, cut, dod 4 clip, flop, hang, sned(Sc.), snip, trim 5 droop, prune, slice 6 dangle 7 pendant, pendent 8 truncate
lope: job 4 gait 6 canter 7 dogtrot
lopper: 4 clot 6 curdle 7 clabber 9 coagulate
lopsided: 4 alop 6 uneven 7 crooked 9 unbalanced
loquacious: 5 gabby 6 verbal 7 prating 8 cackling 9 garrulous, talkative 10 babblative, chattering
loquacity: 9 garrulity 13 talkativeness
lord: aga 4 agha, earl, peer, rule, tsar 5 liege, ruler 6 domine, master, prince 7 marquis, vavasor 8 domineer, governor, nobleman, seigneur, suzerain, vavasour, viscount 9 dominator
attendant: 5 thane
Lord have mercy upon us: 8 response 10 invocation 12 Kyrie eleison
Lord High Executioner: 4 Koko
Lord Jim author: 6 Conrad
Lord's Prayer: 11 Paternoster
lordly: 5 grand, noble, proud 6 uppish 7 haughty 8 arrogant, despotic 9 imperious, masterful 10 tyrannical 11 dictatorial, domineering, magisterial, overbearing
lordship: 4 rule 7 dynasty 8 dominion 10 allegiance
lore: 4 lear, myth 6 advice, wisdom 7 counsel 8 learning 9 erudition, knowledge, tradition 11 instruction

Lorelei: 5 siren 9 temptress 11 femme fatale
  poet: 5 Heine
lorgnette: 8 eyeglass 10 opera glass
lorica: 5 shell 7 cuirass 8 corselet
lorikeet: 6 parrot
loriot: 6 oriole
loris: 5 lemur
lorn: 5 alone 6 bereft 7 forlorn 8 desolate, forsaken, lonesome 9 abandoned
Lorna Doone: 5 novel
  author: 9 Blackmore
Lorraine: *capital:* 4 Metz
  river: 4 Saar
lose: 4 amit, fail, miss 5 waste 6 defeat, mislay 7 forfeit 9 dissipate, fail to win
losel: bum 6 loafer 10 ne'er-do-well
loss: 4 cost, leak, ruin, toll 5 price, waste 6 damage, damnum, defeat, injury, ullage 7 expense, failure 8 amission, decrease 9 decrement, detriment, privation 10 affliction, bankruptcy 11 bereavement, deperdition, deprivation, destruction
lost: 4 gone, lorn 5 perdu(F.) 6 absent, hidden, ruined, wasted 7 forlorn, mislaid, strayed 8 absorbed, confused, defeated, estrayed, obscured, prodigal 9 abandoned, forfeited, perplexed, reprobate, subverted 10 abstracted, bewildered, dissipated, overthrown 11 preoccupied 13 irreclaimable
Lost Horizon: *author:* 6 Hilton
  land: 9 Shangri-La
lot: hap 4 dole, doom, fate, land, luck, much, plat, plot 5 batch, field, grist, group, share, weird 6 amount, bundle, chance, divide, hazard, parcel 7 destiny, fortune, portion 8 caboodle, quantity 9 allotment, apportion, great deal 13 apportionment
  appointment by: 9 sortition
  miscellaneous: 6 fardel, job lot
Lot: *father:* 5 Haran
  grandson: 7 Moabite
  nephew: 7 Abraham
  place of flight: 5 Sodom
  sister: 6 Milcah
  son: 4 Moab 5 Ammon
lotion: 4 balm, wash 8 ablution, linament
lots: 4 gobs 5 scads 6 plenty
lottery: 6 raffle 7 drawing 10 sweepstake
lotto: 4 keno 5 bingo, keeno
lotus, lotos: 7 nelumbo 10 chinquapin
lotus bird: 6 jacana
lotus-eater: 7 dreamer
lotus tree: 4 sadr 9 persimmon
loud: 5 gaudy, heavy, noisy, showy, vivid 6 coarse, flashy, vulgar 7 blatant, clamant, obvious, raucous 8 emphatic, strepent, vehement 9 clamorous, insistent, turbulent, unrefined 10 blustering, boisterous, stentorian, tumultuous,

vociferous 11 ear-piercing, thersitical 12 obstreperous
lough: sea 4 lake, loch, pool 5 water
Louisiana:
  bird: 7 pelican
  capital: 10 Baton Rouge
  city: 7 Augusta 9 Biddeford 10 New Orleans, Shreveport
  dialect: 6 creole
  festival: 9 Mardi Gras
  flower: 8 magnolia
  mountain: 8 Driskill
  native: 5 Cajun 6 Creole 7 Acadian
  nickname: 6 Creole 7 Pelican
  parish: 4 Winn 5 Allen, Caddo, Union 6 Acadia, De Soto, Iberia, Sabine, Tensas, Vernon
  tree: 11 bald cypress
  university: LSU 6 Tulane
lounge: 4 idle, loaf, loll, sofa 5 bange, couch, divan, relax 6 froust, frowst, loiter
loup: 4 flee, jump, leap
louse: nit 5 aphid, aphis 6 cootie, slater
lousy: 5 dirty 9 pedicular 10 pediculous
lout: bow, oaf 4 bend, boor, clod, coof, dolt, fool, gaum, gawk, hulk 5 clown, cuddy, stoop, yahoo, yokel 6 curtsy, lubber 7 bumpkin, grobian, palooka 10 clodhopper
loutish: 4 rude 5 crude 6 clumsy, gauche(F.), stupid 7 awkward
lovable, loveable: 4 dear 7 amative, amiable 8 adorable, dovelike 9 endearing 11 captivating, enthralling
love: gra(Ir.), loe(Sc.), 4 dear, dote, like 5 adore, aloha, amore(It.), amour(F.), Cupid, fancy, liebe(G.), lover 6 enamor 7 charity, embrace, idolize 8 fondness, goodwill, idolatry 9 adoration, affection 10 attachment, sweetheart 11 inclination
  god of: 4 Amor, Ares, Eros, Frey, Kama 5 Bhaga, Cupid
  goddess of: 5 Athor, Freya, Venus 6 Freyja, Hathor, Ishtar 9 Aphrodite
  science of: 9 erotology
  token of: 6 amoret
love apple: 6 tomato
love feast: 5 agape 7 banquet 9 gathering
love knot: 6 amoret
love potion: 5 charm 7 philter, philtre 11 aphrodisiac
love story: 7 romance
lovebird: 7 parrot
loveliness: 6 beauty 11 pulchritude
lovelock: 4 curl 5 tress 12 heartbreaker
lovely: 5 sweet 6 loving, tender 7 amiable, amorous, angelic 8 adorable, angelina, charming, graceful 9 beautiful 10 attractive
lover: ami(F.), gra(Ir.) 4 beau, chap 5

amant(F.), leman, Romeo 6 adorer, amadis, amante(F.), bon ami(F.) 7 admirer,
amateur(F.), amorist, amoroso(It.), Don
Juan, gallant 8 belamour, Lothario 9
bonne amie(F.), enamorata (It.) 10 dilettante, innamorata(It.), innamora-
to(It.), sweetheart 11 philanderer
meeting place: 5 tryst
patron saint: 9 Valentine
rustic: 7 Celadon
lovesick: 6 pining 7 longing 11 languish-
ing
loving: 4 fond 6 erotic, lovely 7 adorant,
amative, amatory, amorous, devoted 9
affecting 12 affectionate
loving cup: tyg 5 prize 6 trophy
low: bas(F.), moo 4 base, bass, blue, deep,
hill, mean, neap, weak 5 dirty, gross,
snide 6 bellow, coarse, common, earthy,
feeble, filthy, humble, humbly, slight,
sordid, vulgar 7 bestial, cut-rate, ignoble, plebian, shallow, slavish 8 dejected,
off-color 9 depressed, earthbred 10
melancholy 11 undignified, unfavorable
12 contemptible, disreputable
lowan: 4 bird 6 leipoa, mallee
Low Country: 7 Belgium, Holland 10
Luxembourg 11 Netherlands
low-lived: 4 mean 10 despicable 12 contemptible
low-necked: 9 decollete
low tide: ebb 4 neap
lowbred: 5 crude 6 coarse, vulgar 11 ill-
mannered
lower: dip 4 alow, bate, drop, sink, vail 5
abase, abate, baser, below, decry, demit,
frown, glare, scowl, under 6 bemean,
debase, deepen, demean, derate, glower,
humble, lessen, meaner, nether, reduce
7 beneath, degrade, depress, descend,
subside 8 diminish, downward, inferior,
mark down 9 disparage 10 depreciate,
nethermore
lowering: 4 dark 5 heavy 6 beetle,
cloudy, gloomy, lowery, sullen 8 overcast 11 threatening
lowest: 5 least, nadir 6 bottom 7 bedrock
10 nethermost
lowing (see also **low**): 7 mugient 9 bellowing
lowland: 4 flat, holm, spit, vale 5 ter-
ai(Ind.) 6 valley 7 bottoms
Lowlander (see also **Scotland**): 4 Scot 9
Sassenach
language: 6 Lallan 7 Lalland
lowly: 4 base, mean, meek 6 humble,
modest 7 ignoble 8 ordinary 11 commonplace 12 unpretending 13 unpretentious
lox: 6 salmon
loy: 4 tool 5 slick, spade
loyal: 4 feal, firm, leal, true 5 liege, pious

6 stanch 7 devoted, staunch 8 constant, faithful
loyalty: 6 homage 10 allegiance 12 faithfulness
Loyalty island: Uea 4 Lifu, Uvea
Loyolite: 6 Jesuit
lozenge: 4 pill 5 candy 6 jujube, pastil,
tablet, troche 7 diamond 8 pastille 9
cough drop
lubber: oaf 4 boor, gawk, lout 5 churl,
drone, idler 6 sailor 8 landsman
lubricate: oil 4 dope 6 grease 7 moisten
lubricious: 4 lewd 6 shifty, tricky, wanton 7 elusive 8 slippery, unstable 9
lecherous, salacious 10 lascivious
luce: 4 pike
lucent: 5 clear, lucid 6 bright 7 shining
11 translucent, transparent
lucerne, lucern: 7 alfalfa
lucid: 4 sane 5 clear 6 bright, lucent 7
crystal, shining 8 luminous, pellucid,
rational 11 clear-headed, resplendent,
translucent
lucidity: 6 sanity 7 clarity
Lucifer: 5 devil, Satan
luck: hap, lot, ure 4 cess, eure, fate 5
deuce 6 chance, hansel 7 ambsace, fortune, handsel, success 8 fortuity 9 mischance, advantage 11 good fortune,
prosperity
bringer: 5 Jonah 6 clover, mascot 9
horseshoe 10 rabbit-foot
stroke of: 5 fluke
token for: 5 charm 6 amulet, mascot 7
periapt 8 talisman 9 horseshoe
lucky: 5 canny, happy, sonsy 6 sonsie 8
gracious 9 fortunate 10 propitious,
prosperous, successful 12 providential
lucrative: 6 paying 7 gainful 10 beneficial, productive, profitable 12 remunerative
lucre: 4 gain, loot, pelf 5 booty, money 6
profit, riches, wealth
ludicrous: 5 antic, awful, comic, droll,
funny 6 absurd 7 comical, foolish, risible 8 farcical 9 burlesque, laughable 10
ridiculous
lug: box, ear 4 drag, draw, pull, tote,
worm, haul 5 carry 10 projection
luggage: 4 bags 7 baggage 9 suitcases
lugubrious: sad 6 dismal 7 doleful 8
mournful
lukewarm: 5 tepid
lull: 4 calm, hush, rock 5 allay, quiet, still
6 pacify, soothe 7 compose 8 calmness,
mitigate 9 cessation 11 tranquilize
lullaby: 4 song 5 baloo, balow(Sc.) 10
cradlesong
lumber: 4 raff, wood 6 refuse, timber
lumbering: 7 awkward 11 heavy footed
lumberman: 6 logger, sawyer, scorer 10
lumberjack

boot: pac

hook: 5 peavy 6 peavey

sled: 4 tode 7 travois 8 travoise

luminary: sun, VIP 4 lion, name, star 5 light 7 notable 12 illumination, intellectual

luminous: 5 clear, lucid 6 bright 7 shining 9 brilliant 11 illuminated, transparent 14 phosphorescent

lummox: 4 boor, lout 5 yahoo 7 bumpkin, bungler

lump: bat, cob, dab, dad, dot, gob, nub, wad 4 beat, blob, burl, cake, clog, clot, daud, heap, hump, hunk, knob, knot, mass 5 bulge, claut, clump, clunk, hunch, wedge 6 dollop, gobbet, nodule, nugget 8 swelling 12 protuberance

lumpfish: 6 paddle

lumpish: 4 dull 5 heavy, inert 6 stodgy, stupid 8 sluggish 9 shapeless

lumpy: 5 heavy, rough 6 choppy, clumsy

lunacy: 5 folly, mania 7 madness 8 delirium, insanity 9 craziness 11 derangement

lunar (see also **moon**): 6 lunate 8 crescent 9 satellite

lunatic: mad 6 insane, madman 7 frantic 8 demoniac 9 bedlamite 10 moonstruck

lune: 5 leash 8 crescent

lung: 5 organ

disease: 11 anthracosis

having: 9 pulmonate

sound: 4 rale

lunge: jab 4 foin, leap, stab 5 barge, longe, lurch, pitch 6 plunge, thrust

lupine: 6 fierce 7 wolfish 8 ravenous, wolflike

lurch: rob 4 jolt, reel, roll 5 barge, cheat, fraud, lunge, pitch, steal, trick 6 careen, career, swerve 7 stagger, stumble

lure: 4 bait, draw, trap 5 decoy, snare, tempt 6 allure, entice, seduce 7 attract, beguile, pitfall 8 inveigle 10 allurement, attraction, enticement

lurer: 4 bait 5 siren 7 trapper

lurid: wan 4 pale 5 gaudy, livid 6 dismal, gloomy 7 ghastly, hideous 8 gruesome, shocking, terrible 9 startling 11 sensational

lurk: 4 hide 5 skulk, slink, sneak 6 ambush 9 lie in wait

luscious: 4 rich, ripe 5 sweet 6 creamy 7 cloying 8 delicate 9 delicious 10 voluptuous

lush: sot 4 rich, soft 5 drunk 6 limber, mellow 7 profuse 9 alcoholic, luxuriant, succulent 11 intoxicated

lusory: 7 playful 8 sportive

lust: 6 desire, liking 7 passion 8 appetite, cupidity 11 inclination 12 sexual desire

luster, lustre: 4 cave, naif 5 sheen, shine, water 6 polish 7 glister 8 radiance, schiller, splendor 10 brightness, brilliance 11 distinction, iridescence

lusterless: mat, wan 4 dead, dull 5 faded, fishy 6 gloomy 9 tarnished

lustful: hot 4 gamy lewd 5 cadgy 7 fulsome, rammish 9 lecherous, salacious

lustrous: 5 nitid 6 bright, glossy, orient 7 radiant 8 nitidous 9 brilliant 11 illustrious, transparent

lusty: 4 cant 5 crank, frack, frank, freck, hardy 6 cranky, gawsie, hearty, robust, strong, sturdy 8 bouncing, vigorous

lute: tar 4 clay, ring 6 cement 7 dyphone 10 instrument

relative of: 8 mandolin

luxe: 8 elegance, richness

Luxembourg: *capital:* 10 Luxembourg

measure: 5 fuder

monetary unit: 5 franc

river: 7 Moselle

luxuriant: 4 lush, rank, rich 5 frank 6 lavish 7 fertile, opulent, profuse, teeming 8 prolific 9 exuberant 10 voluptuous

luxuriate: 4 bask, riot 5 revel 6 wallow

luxurious: 4 posh, rich 5 gaudy 6 costly 7 elegant, opulent 8 gorgeous, sensuous 9 sumptuous 11 comfortable, extravagant

luxury: 6 frills 7 amenity, comfort 8 delicacy, grandeur

lover of: 8 Sybarite

Luzon: *city:* 5 Gapan 6 Ilagan, Manila 10 Cabanatuan

dialect: 6 Itaves

mountain: Iba

people: Ata, Ita 4 Aeta, Atta 5 Tagal 6 Aripas, Arupas, Igorot, Isinay, Itaneg 7 Igorote, Italone, Kalinga, Kankana, Tagalog

seaport: 6 Aparri, Manila

volcano: 5 Mayon

lyam: 5 leash 10 bloodhound

lycanthrope: 8 werewolf

lycee: 6 lyceum, school

lyceum: 11 meeting hall

Lydia: *capital:* 6 Sardis

king: 5 Gyges 7 Croesus

river: 8 Pactolus

lye: 6 potash 7 caustic 8 lixivium

lying: 4 flat 5 awald, awalt, false, prone 6 supine 8 couchant 9 dishonest, mendacity 10 pseudology

lying-in: 11 confinement 12 accouchement

lymph: sap 5 chyle, water 6 plasma, spring

lynch: 4 hang 6 murder 7 execute

Lynette's knight: 6 Gareth

lynx: cat 5 pishu 6 bobcat, lucern 7 cara-

cal 8 carcajou 9 catamount
Lyra star: 4 Vega
lyrate: 9 spatulate
lyre: 4 asor, harp 6 kissar, trigon 7 cithara, kithara, testudo
lye turtle: 11 leatherback
lyric: lai, lay, ode 4 alba, odic, poem 5 epode, gazel, melic, verse 6 ghazel, poetic,

rondel 7 cancion, canzone(It.), descort, madrigal, rondeau 9 dithyramb
Muse: 5 Erato 8 Polymnia 10 Polyhymnia
lyrical: 6 epodic 7 sestina
lyrichord: 11 harpsichord
lysogenic: 9 temperate 11 not virulent
lyssa: 6 rabies 11 hydrophobia

M

Maacah: *father:* 6 Talmai 7 Absalom
  husband: 5 David 8 Rehoboam
  son: Asa 5 Hanan 6 Abijah 7 Absalom
mabolo: 4 plum 7 camagon
macabre: 4 eery, grim 5 eerie 7 ghastly 8 grewsome, gruesome, horrible 9 deathlike
macaca: 5 lemur 6 monkey
macadam: tar 8 pavement
macaque: 4 bruh 6 monkey, rhesus
macaw: ara 4 arra, bird 5 arara 6 parrot 7 maracan 8 aracanga, ararauna, cockatoo
Macbeth: *character:* 5 Angus 6 Banquo
  slayer: 7 Macduff
  title: 5 Thane
  victim: 6 Banquo, Duncan
maccaboy: 5 snuff
mace: dod, rod 4 club, maul, rush 5 spice, staff 6 mallet 7 swindle
  bearer: 6 beadle
  royal: 7 scepter, sceptre
Macedonia:
  capital: 6 Skopje
  king: 6 Philip 9 Alexander
  last king: 7 Perseus
  mountain: 5 Athos 7 Olympus 8 Olympiad
  people: 6 Greeks 8 Serbians 9 Albanians 10 Bulgarians
  statesman: 9 Antipater
macerate: ret 4 soak 5 steep 8 grow thin
machete: 4 bolo, fish 5 blade, knife 6 guitar, tarpon
Machiavellian: 4 wily 6 crafty 7 cunning 8 guileful 9 deceitful 11 treacherous
Machiavelli's book: 6 Prince 8 Mandrake

machila: 7 hammock
machination: 4 plan, plot 5 cabal 6 scheme 8 artifice, intrigue 10 conspiracy 11 contrivance
machine: car 4 auto 5 robot 6 device, engine 7 vehicle 9 apparatus, appliance, automatic, automaton, mechanism 10 automobile 11 contrivance, machination, stereotyped 12 organization, standardized
  hydraulic: 9 telemotor
  part: cam 5 rotor, wheel 6 piston, stator, tappet
machine gun: 4 Sten 5 Maxim 7 Gatling 9 Hotchkiss 10 chatterbox
  place: 4 nest
machismo: 7 manhood, 14 masculine pride
macilent: 4 lean, thin 9 emaciated
mackerel: 4 scad 5 akule, atule, tunny 7 escolar, tassard 8 hardhead
  genus: 7 scomber
  net: 7 spiller
  young: 5 spike 6 tinker 7 blinker
mackerel bird: 7 wryneck 9 kittiwake
mackle: See macula
macle: 7 crystal 11 chiastolite
macrobiotic: 4 diet
macula: 4 blot, blur, spot 5 stain 6 blotch, mackle, macule 7 blemish
maculate: 6 impure 7 defiled 8 speckled, unchaste 10 besmirched
mad: 4 gite, gyte, hute(Sc.) 5 angry, crazy, folle, irate, rabid, vexed 6 frenzy, insane, unwise 7 enraged, foolish, frantic, furious 8 demented, frenetic, incensed, maniacal 9 desperate, fanatical, hilarious, phrenetic, psychotic 10 distracted,

distraught, infatuated, infuriated 11 fantastical, mentally ill 12 arreptitious, unreasonable

Madagascar: *animal:* 6 aye-aye, tanrec, tenrec, 7 tendrac

capital: 12 Antananarivo

city: 7 Mojanga 8 Tamatave 10 Tananarive, Tananarivo

civet: 7 fossane

garment: 5 lamba

island group: 7 Aldabra

language: 8 Malagasy

lemur: 5 avahi, indri 6 aye-aye 9 babacoote

measure: 7 gantang

monetary unit: 5 franc

native: 4 Hova 6 Merina 8 Sakalava

palm: 6 riffia

people: 4 Hova

tree: 11 antankarana

tribe: 4 Bara 5 Hovas 8 Betsileo, Malagasy, Sakalava 13 Betsimasaraka

madam, madame: Mme., Mrs. 4 bawd, lady 5 donna, hussy, woman, title, wench 6 senora 8 mistress 9 courtesan

madcap: 4 wild 7 hotspur 8 reckless 9 impulsive

madder: aal 7 munjeet 8 dyestuff

family: 9 rubiaceae

made: 10 artificial

to-order: 6 custom 11 custom built

up: 8 invented 10 fabricated

Madeira: *capital:* 7 Funchal

wine: 4 bual 5 tinta, tinto 7 malmsey, sercial 8 verdelho

mademoiselle: 4 miss

madhouse: 5 chaos 6 asylum, bedlam 8 bughouse 11 insane asylum

madid: wet 6 moist

madman: 6 maniac 7 furioso, lunatic 8 frenetic 9 phrenetic, psychotic

madness: ire 4 fury 5 folly, furor, mania 6 bedlam, frenzy, lunacy, rabies 7 dewanee, ecstasy, widdrim 8 delirium, dementia, insanity 9 amazement, furiosity, nonsomania, phrenetic 10 great folly 11 derangement

Madras: *present name:* 9 Tamil Nadu

madrepore: 5 coral 6 fossil

Madrid promenade: 5 Prado

madrigal: ode 4 glee, poem 5 lyric 6 verses 8 part-song

Maecenas: 6 patron 10 benefactor

maelstrom: 4 eddy 5 swirl 7 current, turmoil 9 whirlpool

maenad: 9 bacchante

maestro: 6 master 7 teacher 8 composer 9 conductor 10 bandleader 11 choirmaster 13 kapellmeister

di-cappela: 11 choirmaster 13 kapellmeister

maffle: 6 muddle, mumble 7 confuse, stammer, 8 bewilder, squander

mafia: 8 brigands 10 underworld

Magadha king: 9 Bimbisara 10 Ajatasatru

magadis: 5 flute 9 monochord

magazine: 4 pulp 5 depot 7 almacen, arsenal, chamber, journal 9 ephemeris, reservoir, warehouse 10 periodical, repository, storehouse 11 armamentary

magenta: dye 7 fuchsia

maggot: 4 bug 4 grub, mawk, whim 5 larva, mathe 6 gentle, notion 7 caprice 12 eccentricity

magi: 5 Sages 6 Gaspar 8 Melchior 9 Balthasar

gift of: 4 gold 5 myrrh 12 frankincense

magic: art 4 rune 5 fairy, obeah, spell, turgy 6 glamor, voodoo 7 glamour, gramary, sorcery, theurgy 8 brujeria(Sp.), gramaryе, wizardry 9 deception, diablerie 10 necromancy, witchcraft 11 conjuration, enchantment, legerdemain, thaumaturgy 12 invultuation

act of: 11 conjuration

lantern: 11 epidiascope 12 stereopticon

perform: hex 6 sorcer 7 conjure

pert. to: 6 goetic

staff: 4 wand 7 rhabdos 8 caduceus

symbol: 5 charm 6 caract 8 pentacle

tree: 13 polemoniaceae

word: 5 selah 6 presto, sesame, shelah 11 abracadabra

Magic Mountain: *author:* 4 Mann

character: 7 Castorp

magical: 6 occult 8 charming 10 bewitching 11 necromantic

magician: 4 mage, magi 5 magus 6 Merlin, wabeno, wizard 7 juggler 8 conjurer, conjuror, mandrake, sorcerer 9 archimage, charlatan, enchanter 11 entertainer, medicine man, necromancer, thaumaturge 13 thaumaturgist 15 prestidigitator

assistant: 6 famuli(pl.) 7 famulus

manual: 8 grimoire

motion: 4 pass

magirist: 4 cook

magisterial: 5 lofty, proud 6 august, lordly 7 haughty, stately 8 arrogant, dogmatic 9 dignified, imperious, masterful 11 dictatorial, domineering, overbearing 13 authoritative

magistrate: 4 beak, doge 5 edile, judge 6 alcade, alcaid, archon, bailie, bailli, syndic 7 alcaide, alcalde, bailiff, burgess, podesta(It.) 8 alderman, governor, mittimus, official 11 burgomaster

orders: 4 acta(pl.) 5 actum

magma: 5 dregs 8 sediment

basalt: 10 limburgite, molten rock

magnanimous: big 4 free 5 lofty, noble 6 heroic 7 exalted, liberal 8 generous 9 honorable, unselfish, unstinted 10 high-minded, high-souled 13 disinterested

magnate: 4 lord 5 baron, mogul, noble 6 bashaw, tycoon 7 grandee, rich man 10 clarissimo 11 millionaire

magnesian limestone: 8 dolomite

magnesium: *silicate:* 4 talc
sulfate: 7 loweite

magnet: 7 terella 8 solenoid, terrella 9 loadstone, lodestone
end: 4 pole
pole: red
type of: bar 9 horseshoe

magnetic: 5 polar 10 attractive, electrical
unit: 5 weber

magnetize: 4 lure 5 charm 7 attract 9 captivate

magnificence: 4 pomp 8 grandeur, splendor 13 sumptuousness

magnificent: 4 rial, rich 5 grand, great, noble, regal 6 august, lavish 7 exalted, stately, sublime 8 glorious, gorgeous, palatial, splendid, striking 9 beautiful, excellent, sumptuous 10 munificent

magnify: 4 laud 5 exalt 7 enhance, enlarge greaten 8 increase 9 aggravate, overstate 10 exaggerate

magniloquent: 6 turgid 8 boastful 9 bombastic 12 ostentatious 13 grandiloquent

magnitude: 4 bulk, mass, size 6 extent 7 bigness 9 dimension, greatness

magnolia: 5 yulan

Magnolia State: 11 Mississippi

magnum: 6 bottle

magnum opus: 4 work 11 achievement

magot: ape 6 figure

magpie: 4 bird, pica, piet, piot, pyat 6 gabber, prater 9 chatterer, haggister
diver: 4 smew
shrike: 7 tanager

magsman: 8 swindler

maguari: 8 stork

maguey: 4 aloe 5 agave, fiber, plant 7 cantala

magus: 4 magi 6 wizard 7 charmer 8 magician

Magyar: 6 Ugrian 9 Hungarian

maha: 4 deer 6 langur, sambar

mahajan: 11 moneylender

mahala: 5 squaw

mahogany: 4 toon 6 acajou, totara 7 albarco, gunnung 8 bangalay 9 cailcedra 11 reddish brown

maholi: 5 lemur

Mahomet: See **Mohammed**

Mahometan: See **Muslim**

Mahound: 5 devil

mahout: 6 driver, keeper 14 elephant driver

Maia: 12 Earth Goddess
father: 5 Atlas
sisters: 8 Pleiades
son: 6 Hermes 7 Mercury

maid: 4 ayah, girl, help, lass 5 bonne, woman 6 damsel, maiden, slavey, virgin 7 Abigail, ancilla, colleen, servant 8 domestic, suivante 9 attendant, cameriera, tirewoman
changed to spider: 7 Arachne
mythical: 5 nymph

Maid of Astolat: 6 Elaine

Maid of Orleans: 7 Pucelle 9 Joan of Arc

maiden: deb, new 4 girl, jill, lass 5 nymph, sylph 6 damsel 7 damosel, damozel, untried 8 damozell 9 damosella, damoysell, debutante

maiden name: nee

maidenhair: 4 fern 8 adiantum
tree: 6 ginkgo

maidenly: 6 gentle, modest, virgin

mail: bag 4 post, send, ship 5 armor 6 wallet 8 dispatch
boat: 6 packet

maim: 4 hurt 6 mangle 7 cripple, disable 8 mutilate 9 dismember

main: sea 4 duct, high, pipe 5 chief, first, grand, ocean, prime 7 capital, conduct, conduit, leading, purpose 8 foremost 9 principal

Main Street author: 5 Lewis

Maine: *capital:* 7 Augusta
city: 4 Bath 6 Bangor 8 Lewiston, Portland 9 Biddeford, Skowhegan
county: 5 Waldo 9 Penobscot 10 Cumberland
lake: 5 Moose 6 Sebago 8 Rangeley 9 Moosehead
motto: 6 Dirigo (I direct)
mountain: 5 Kineo 7 Bigelow 8 Cadillac, Katahdin
nickname: 6 Lumber 8 Pine Tree
port: 6 Bangor 8 Portland
river: 4 Saco 8 Kennebec
state bird: 9 chicadee
state flower: 8 pinecone
state tree: 4 pine

mainland: 8 fastland 9 continent

mainsheet: 4 rope

mainstay: key 7 support

maintain: 4 avow, bear, fend, hold, keep 5 argue, claim 6 affirm, allege, assert, avouch, defend, retain, uphold 7 bolster, contend, declare, espouse, justify, support, sustain 8 conserve, preserve 9 vindicate 10 provide for
again: 8 reassert

maintainable: 7 tenable

maintenance: 5 batta 6 upkeep 7 alimony, prebend 10 livelihood

maison: 5 house
de sante: 6 asylum 8 hospital 10 sanatorium

maize: 4 corn, samp 5 grain 7 mealies
bread: 4 piki
genus: Zea

majestic: 5 grand, lofty, noble, regal, royal 6 august, kingly 7 leonine, stately, sublime 8 elevated, imperial, splendid 9 dignified, sovereign 11 magnificent

major: big 5 chief 7 capital, greater, officer 8 superior 9 principal
music: dur

majordomo: 6 butler 7 bailiff, manager, servant, steward 9 seneschal

Majorca city: 5 Palma

majority: age 4 body, more, most 6 quorum 7 greater

make: cut, gar(Sc.) 4 coin, form 5 build, force, frame, shape 6 compel, create, invent, render 7 compose, confect, fashion, prepare, produce 8 contrive, generate 9 construct, fabricate 11 manufacture

make-believe: 4 sham 5 feign, magic 7 charade, feigned, fiction, pretend 8 pretense

make do: eke 9 improvise

make fun of: rib 5 scoff 8 ridicule

make known: 6 impart, reveal 7 divulge, publish, uncover 8 disclose, discover, proclaim 9 advertise, publicize

make off: fly, run 4 bolt, flee 7 abscond, run away

make out: see 4 fare 7 succeed 8 copulate

make over: 4 redo 6 revamp 9 refashion

make up: 6 create, devise 7 arrange, compose, typeset 8 assemble, complete, cosmetic 9 fabricate, improvise

make up for: 5 atone 10 compensate

maker: 4 doer 6 author, factor 7 creator 8 declarer, inventor 9 architect 10 originator 12 manufacturer

makeshift: 4 rude 8 resource 9 temporary

mal: bad 4 evil
de mar: 11 seasickness
du pays: 12 homesickness

Malabar: *black:* 5 ochna
canoe: 5 tonee
monkey: 8 wanderoo
palm: 7 talipot
people: 4 Nair

malacca: 4 cane 5 stick

malachite: 4 bice 7 azurite, mineral

maladive: ill 4 sick 6 feeble, sickly, unwell 9 unhealthy

maladroit: 6 clumsy 7 awkward, unhandy 8 bungling, inexpert

malady (see also **disease**)**:** 7 ailment, illness 8 disorder, sickness 9 affection, complaint, distemper 10 affliction 13 indisposition

malanders: 6 eczema

malapropism: 8 solecism, word play 11 error in speech

malapropos: 8 untimely, 10 irrelevant 11 inexpedient, inopportune

malar: 6 zygoma 9 cheek-bone

malaria: 4 agie, ague 5 chill, fever, miasm 6 miasma
antidote: 7 quinine
carrier: 8 mosquito 9 anopheles

malarkey: 6 drivel 8 nonsense

Malawi: *capital:* 8 Lilongwe
export: tea 7 tobacco
former name: 9 Nyasaland
monetary unit: 6 kwacha

malaxate: 5 knead

Malaysia: *almond:* 6 kanari
ape: lar
archipelago: See *island* below
boat: 4 proa 5 praam, prahu 6 praham 7 cougnar
buffalo: 7 carabao 8 seladang
capital: 11 Kuala Lumpur
Christian: 7 Ilokano
condiment: 6 sambal, sambei 7 semball
crane: 5 sarus
disease: 4 amok, lata 5 amuck, latah
export: tin 6 rubber, timber 7 palm oil
form of address: 4 tuan
fruit: 8 rambutan
garment: 6 sarong
island: Aru, Goa, Kei, Oma 4 Bali, Buru, Gaga, Java, Sulu 5 Ambon, Arroe, Arrou, Banca, Banda, Buton, Ceram, Misol, Sangi, Sumba, Timor 6 Boefon, Boeroe, Borneo, Flores, Jilolo, Lombik, Madura, Musool, Sangir, Soemba, Talaur, Waigeu
isthmus: Kra
jacket: 4 baju
knife: 4 cris, kris 5 crise 6 crease, creese, kreese, parang
language: 5 Malay 7 Chinese, English, Tagalog
mammal: 10 chevrotain
measure: 4 tael, wang
monetary unit: 7 ringgit
mountain: 6 Gunong, Gunung
musical instrument: 7 anklong
ox: 5 tsine 7 banteng
palm: 4 ejoo, sago 5 areng 6 arenga, gebang, gomuti, nibong, nibung 7 talipot
parrot: 4 lory 6 lories
people: Ata 5 Bajau, Tagal 6 Aripas, Semang 7 Bisayan, Tagalog, Visayan
pepper: 4 siri 5 sirih
pewter: 4 trah
rice field: 5 sawah
state: 5 Kedah, Perak 6 Johore 7 Malacca

title: 4 tuan

town: 7 Malacca

tree (see also *palm* above): 4 upas 5 kapur, niepa, terap 6 durian, durion

ungulate: 5 tapir

malconformation: 9 imperfect 16 disproportionate

malcontent: reb 5 rebel 6 uneasy 8 agitator, Frondeur 10 discontent, rebellious 12 discontented, dissatisfied

Maldives: 13 Pacific atolls

capital: 4 Male

former name: 14 Maldive Islands

language: 6 Divehi

monetary unit: 5 rupee

people: 7 Islamic

religion: 5 Islam

male: man, mas 4 gent 5 manly 7 mankind, manlike, mannish 9 masculine

animal: tom 4 buck, bull, hart, jack, stag, stud 8 stallion

figure: 7 telamon

gelded: 4 galt 5 steer 6 eunuch 7 gelding

malediction: ban 5 curse 7 malison, slander 8 anathema, evil talk 9 blasphemy 11 imprecation 12 denunciation

malefactor: 5 felon 7 convict, culprit 8 criminal, evildoer, offender 9 wrongdoer

malefic: 4 evil 7 harmful, hurtful 11 mischievous

malevolence: 4 evil, hate 5 pique, spite 6 enmity, hatred, malice, rancor 8 ferocity 9 animosity, hostility, malicious, malignity 10 bitterness

malfeasance: 5 crime, wrong 8 trespass 11 delinquency

malheur: 10 misfortune

Mali: *ancient city:* 8 Timbuktu

capital: 6 Bamako

monetary unit: 5 franc

malice: 5 pique, spite 6 enmity 7 ill will 9 animosity 12 maliciousness

malicious: 4 evil 5 catty, depit 6 bitter 7 heinous 8 sinister, spiteful 9 felonious, green-eyed, malignant, rancorous, resentful 10 calumnious, despiteful, despiteous, malevolent 11 ill-disposed 12 cantankerous, unpropitious

action: 5 arson 8 sabotage 9 vandalism

intention: 6 animus

malign: 4 evil, foul 5 abuse, curse, libel, smear 6 bewray, defame, revile, vilify 7 asperse, baleful, blacken, deprave, hurtful, slander 8 sinister, virulent 10 calumniate, pernicious

malignant: 4 evil 6 wicked 7 hateful, heinous, hellish, noxious, vicious 8 spiteful, venomous, virulent 9 cancerous, felonious, ferocious, invidious, malicious, poisonous, rancorous 10 rebellious 11 deleterious

malikana: fee 4 duty 7 payment

maline: net 4 lace

malinger: 5 dodge, shirk, skulk

malkin: cat, mop 4 drab, hare 6 sponge 8 slattern 9 scarecrow

mall: 4 walk 5 allee, alley 6 arcade, mallet 7 meeting 9 promenade

mallard: 4 duck

genus: 4 anas

malleable: 4 soft 7 ductile, pliable

mallemuck: 6 fulmar, petrel 9 albatross

mallet: tup 4 club, mace, mall, maul, mell(Sc.) 5 gavel, madge 6 beater, beetle, driver, hammer

hatter's: 6 beater

presiding officer's: 5 gavel

wooden: 4 maul 6 beetle

mallow: 4 okra 5 plant 6 escoba 9 hollyhock

malm: 4 loam 5 brick 9 limestone

malmsey: 4 wine 5 grape 7 madeira

malnutrition: 7 cachexy, wasting 8 cachexia

malodorous: 4 rank 5 fetid 6 putrid, smelly 7 noisome 8 stinking 9 odiferous

malt: 8 diastase

beverage: ale 4 beer, brew 5 lager, stout 6 zythem

froth: 4 barm

ground: 5 grist

infusion: 4 wort

vinegar: 6 alegar

worm: 5 toper 7 tippler

Malta: *capital:* 7 Valetta 8 Valletta

hamlet: 5 casal 6 casale

island: 4 Gozo 6 Comino

measure: 4 salm 5 canna, salma 7 caffiso

monetary unit: 5 pound

weight: 4 rotl, salm 5 artal, artel, parto, ratel, salma 6 kantar

wind: 7 gregale 8 levanter

maltreat: 5 abuse 6 defile, defoul, demean, misuse, 9 humiliate

malum: 4 evil 5 wrong 7 offense

malvaceous plant: 4 okra 6 cotton, escoba, mallow 8 althaea

malvasia: 5 grape

mameluke: 5 slave 7 servant

mammal (see also **animal**): cat 5 beast, ovine, swine 6 bovine, equine, feline, monkey, rodent 7 primate 8 edentate, ruminant, ungulant 9 carnivore, marsupial

amphibious: 5 otter

antlered: elk 4 deer 5 moose 7 caribou 8 reindeer

aquatic: 4 seal 5 otter, shark, whale 6 desman, dugong, manati, rytina, walrus 7 dolphin, manatee, sea lion 8 sirenian 12 hippopotamus

aquatic order: 4 cete 7 cetacea

arboreal: ai 5 lemur, sloth 6 fisher, monkey 7 glutton, opossum, raccoon 8 banxring, kinkajou 9 orangutan
armored: 9 armadillo
badgerlike: 5 ratel 8 balisaur
bearlike: 5 panda
bovine: ox; bos, cow 4 bull, calf, zebu 5 bison, steer 7 taurine 8 longhorn
burrowing: 4 mole 6 badger, gopher, wombat 8 squirrel 9 armadillo
camellike: 7 guanaco
caprine: 4 goat
carnivorous: 9 carnivore
cetacean: see *aquatic* above
civetlike: 5 genet
coat: fur 4 hide, skin 6 pelage
cud-chewing: 8 ruminant
deerlike: 10 chevrotain
desert: 5 camel
doglike: 6 jackal
dolphinlike: 4 inia
domestic: cat, cow, dog 5 horse, sheep 6 cattle
edentate: 7 ant bear 8 anteater, pangolin, tamadau
equine: 4 colt, foal, mare 5 filly, horse, zebra 8 stallion
extinct: 6 rytina 8 mastodon
feline: cat 4 lion, lynx, puma 5 ounce, tiger 6 bobcat, cougar, jaguar, ocelot, serval 7 leopard, panther
fish-eating: 5 otter
fleet: 4 deer, hare 8 antelope
flying: bat
fur-bearing: 4 coon, mink 5 coypu, otter, sheep, skunk 6 badger, ermine, marten, martin, nutria, rabbit 7 genette, raccoon 8 squirrel
giraffelike: 5 okapi
gnawing: 6 rodent
hands different from feet: 6 bimana
hedgehog-like: 6 tenrec
herbivorous: 5 daman, tapir 6 bovine, dugong, equine 7 manatee 8 ruminant 9 orangutan 10 rhinoceros 12 hippopotamus
highest order: 7 primate
horned: ox; cow 4 gaur, goat, reem 5 bison 7 buffalo, unicorn 8 antelope, reindeer, seladang 10 rhinoceros
insectivorous: bat 4 mole 6 tenrec 7 tendrac 8 hedgehog
large: 5 whale 7 mammoth 8 behemoth, elephant, mastodon 10 rhinoceros 12 hippopotamus
largest: 5 whale
lemurine: 5 potto
leopardlike: 4 lion, lynx, pard, puma 5 tiger 6 cougar, jaguar, ocelot 7 polecat, wildcat
llamalike: 6 vicuna
lowest order: 9 marsupial 11 marsupialia

marine: see *aquatic* above
marsupial: 4 tait 5 koala 7 opossum 8 kangaroo 9 bandicoot
meat-eating: 9 carnivore
molelike: 6 desman
monkey-like: 5 lemur, loris
mouselike: 5 shrew
musteline: 5 otter, ratel
nocturnal: bat 5 hyena, lemur, ratel, tapir 6 macaco, racoon 7 raccoon, tarsier 8 kinkajou, platypus
omnivorous: hog, pig 5 swine
ovine: 5 sheep
plantigrade: 6 racoon 7 raccoon
porcine: hog, pig 4 boar 5 swine 7 peccary
pouched: 9 marsupial
raccoon-like: 5 coati
retentive: 8 elephant
rhinoceros-like: 5 tapir 14 baluchitherium
ring-tailed: 4 coon 5 lemur
ruminant: ox; yak 4 deer, goat 5 bison, camel, llama, moose, okapi, sheep, steer 6 alpaca, cattle, chewer, vicuna 7 buffalo, giraffe 8 antelope
scaled: 8 pangolin
shelled: 7 armadillo
short-tailed: 7 bobtail
skunk-like: 5 zoril
slow-moving: 5 loris, sloth
smallest: 5 shrew
snake-eating: 8 mongoose
spiny: 6 tenrec 9 porcupine
thick-skinned: 8 elephant 9 pachyderm 10 rhinoceros
toothless: 8 edentate
tropical: 5 coati, rhino 7 peccary 9 coatimodi 10 coati-mundi, rhinoceros
tusked: 6 walrus 7 mammoth 8 elephant, mastodon
ursine: 4 bear 5 panda
viverrine: 8 falanaka
vulpine: fox 4 wolf
web-footed: 5 otter
wing-footed: 6 aliped
winged: bat
zebra-like: 9 quagga
mammock: 4 tear 5 break, scrap 6 mangle
mammogram: 10 breast X ray
mammon: 6 riches, wealth
mammoth: 4 huge 5 large 8 gigantic 10 gargantuan 11 elephantine
man (see also **fellow, person**): guy, vir(L.) 4 aner(Gr.), chal, chap, homo(L.), male, mann(G.), uomo(It.), work 5 bloke, chiel, guard, homme(F.), human, valet 6 andros(Gr.), chield, hombre(Sp.), mensch(Yid.) 7 counter, fortify, homines(L.pl.), husband, laborer, mankind, operate 8 creature 9 anthropos(Gr.)

aged: vet 4 cuff, sire 5 elder, senex(L.), uncle 6 gaffer, geezer, stager 7 grandpa, starets(Russ.) 8 grandpop, old-timer 9 grandsire, graybeard, patriarch 10 golden-ager, Methuselah 11 grandfather 12 octogenarian

bad-tempered: 6 bodach 10 curmudgeon

bald: 9 pilgarlic 10 pillgarlic

big: cob

brass: 5 Talos

brave: 4 hero, lion

castrated: 6 eunuch

coarse: 5 churl, knave 7 ruffian

conceited: 7 coxcomb

cruel: 4 ogre 7 monster, ruffian, villain

cunning: 5 rogue 7 shyster 9 trickster 10 mountebank

dissolute: 4 roue

eccentric: 6 codger

effeminate: 5 fairy, sissy 9 androgyne

elderly: see *aged* above

enlisted: 6 rating, sailor 7 private, soldier 8 sargeant

fashionable: fop 4 dude 5 dandy 10 Corinthian 11 Beau Brummel 12 boulevardier

handsome: 6 Adonis

hard-pressed: Job

hardheaded: 7 boche

henpecked: 10 hoddy-doddy 11 milquetoast

impetuous: 7 hotspur

important: VIP 4 hero, name 5 nabob 7 grandee

ladies': 4 beau 5 beaux(pl.)

learned: PhD 4 bhat 6 doctor, pundit savant 7 erudite, scholar, teacher 8 literati 9 literatus, professor 11 philologist

little: 6 mankin, shrimp, squirt 8 homuncio 10 homunculus

mechanical: 5 robot 9 automaton

medicine: 6 priest, shaman

money: 9 paymaster

mother of: Eve 6 Cybele

newspaper: 6 editor 8 reporter 9 columnist 10 journalist

objectionable: oaf 4 boor 5 bully 8 wiseacre

of all work: 4 joey, mozo 8 factotum, handyman

of letters: 6 savant 11 litterateur

of straw: 6 figure 9 nonentity

of the world: 6 layman 10 secularist 11 cosmopolite 12 sophisticate

old: see *elderly* above

old-clothes: 4 poco

outdoor: 6 camper, hunter 7 athlete 9 fisherman

personifying: 15 anthropomorphic

pert. to: 5 human 6 humane, mortal

political: 7 senator 8 diplomat 9 statesman 10 ambassador 11 assemblyman 14 representative

poor: 6 pauper 7 peasant 8 beadsman, bedesman

primitive: 6 savage 8 urmensch(Yid.)

resembling: 7 android 10 anthropoid

rich: 5 Midas, nabob 6 tycoon 7 Croesus, magnate 9 plutocrat 10 capitalist 11 billionaire, millionaire

science: 9 ethnology 12 anthropology

self-important: 10 cockalorum

shadowless: 6 ascian

single: 4 stag 7 widower 8 bachelor, celibate

unattractive: 4 clod, goon, jerk, lout, rube, slob 5 yokel 6 lummox 7 fathead 10 clodhoppper

undercover: spy 5 agent 9 detective 12 investigator

unemployed: 6 batlan, batlon(Yid.)

unmarried: see *single* above

white: 6 buckra 7 cachila(P.I.) 8 paleface

wicked: 7 villain

wise: 4 sage, seer 5 solon 6 nestor 7 Solomon

worthless: bum 4 hobo 5 idler, tramp

young: boy 5 youth 6 varlet

Man of Destiny: 17 Napoleon Bonaparte

Man of Galilee: 11 Jesus Christ

man of God: 5 rabbi, saint 6 pastor, priest 7 ascetic, prelate 8 minister 12 ecclesiastic

man-of-war: 7 frigate, soldier, warrior

deck: 5 orlop

Man O'War: 5 horse 6 winner

Man Without a Country: *author:* 4 Hale

character: 5 Nolan

manacle: 4 bond, cuff, iron 5 chain, darby 6 fetter, hamper 7 confine, shackle 8 handcuff 9 restraint

manada: 4 herd 5 drove, flock

manage: man, run 4 boss, head, lead, rule 5 dight, frame, get by, guide, order, steer, wield 6 convoy, demean, direct, govern, handle 7 conduct, control, dispose, execute, husband, operate, oversee 8 contrive, dispense, engineer, maneuver 9 supervise 10 accomplish, administer, manipulate

frugally: 6 eke out 7 husband 9 economize

hard to: 6 ornery

manageable: 4 easy, tame, yare 6 docile, wieldy 7 ductile, pliable 8 flexible, maniable, workable 9 compliant, tractable 10 governable

management: 4 care 6 agency, charge, menage 7 address, economy, gestion 8 carriage, demeanor 9 demeanour, governail, ordinance 10 enterprise, governance 11 generalship

good: 6 eutaxy

manager: 4 doer 6 gerent 7 captain, cura-

tor, foreman, handler, steward 8 director, governor 12 entrepreneur

Manasseh: *father:* 6 Joseph
grandfather: 5 Jacob
son: 4 Amon, Jair 6 Machir

manatee: 6 seacow 8 sirenian

Manchuria: *city:* 5 Hulan, Kirin 6 Harbin, Mukden 8 Shenyang 9 Niuchwang
province: 5 Jehol
river: 4 Amur, Liao, Yalu

manciple: 7 steward 8 purveyor

mandarin: 4 duck, tree 6 orange 7 Chinese 8 official 9 tangerine·
residence: 5 yamen

mandate: 4 writ 5 brief, order 6 behest,
charge, decree, demand, firman 7 bidding, command, precept 8 warranty 9
direction 10 commission, injunction,
referendum

mandatory: 10 imperative, obligatory

mandible: jaw 4 beak 9 chelicera
part: 5 molar

mandrel: bar, rod 4 axle, ball, beam, pick
5 arbor, winch 7 spindle

mandrill: 6 baboon

manducate: eat 4 chew 9 masticate

mane: 4 hair 5 brush 6 grivna 8 encoiure

manege: 4 lope, trot 13 riding academy

maneuver: 4 ploy 5 trick 6 deploy, jockey, scheme, tactic 7 echelon 8 artifice,
contrive, engineer 9 evolution, stratagem 10 manipulate
aviation: 4 loop, spin 7 echelon, flathat 9
chandelle, Immelmann
military: 6 tactic

manful: See manly

mange: eat 4 itch, meal, scab 6 fodder,
scurvy
cause of: 4 mite 6 acarid

manger: bin, box 4 crib, meal 5 stall 6
trough 7 banquet

mangle: cut, mar 4 hack, maim 5 botch,
spoil 6 bruise, garble, ironer, smooth 8
calender, lacerate, mutilate 9 dismember

mango: 4 tree 5 bauno, fruit
bird: 6 oriole 11 hummingbird
fish: 9 threadfin
tree: 4 tope

mangrove: 4 tree 5 goran, shrub

mangy: 4 mean 5 seedy 6 scurvy, shabby
7 squalid 10 despicable 12 contemptible

manhandle: 4 maul 7 rough up 10 knock
about, slap around

mani: 6 peanut

mania: 4 rage 5 craze, furor 6 frenzy, furore, hangup 7 madness, passion 8 delirium, idée fixe(F.) 9 cacoethes, obsession 11 derangement
buying: 9 oniomania
stealing: 11 kleptomania

maniac: 6 crazed, insane madman 7 lunatic 8 demented, deranged 9 psychotic
10 hysterical

manicure: cut 4 clip, pare, trim 6 polish

manifest: 4 open, show 5 argue, clear, index, overt 6 attest, evince, extant,
graith, patent, reveal 7 approve, confess, declare, develop, display, evident,
exhibit, explain, express, glaring,
invoice, obvious, signify, visible 8
apparent, develope, disclose, discover,
evidence, indicate, palpable 11 conspicuous, demonstrate, discernible, indubitable, perspicuous 12 indisputable, unmistakable

manifestation: 4 sign 5 phase 6 effect,
ostent 7 display 8 epiphany 10 revelation

manifesto: 5 edict 7 placard 8 evidence 9
statement 11 declaration 13 demonstration

manifold: 4 many 7 various 8 multiple,
numerous 9 different, multifold, multi-
plex, replicate 12 multifarious

manikin: 4 puny 5 dwarf, model, pygmy
7 phantom 9 mannequin 10 diminutive, homunculus

Manila: *airfield:* 5 Clark
creek: 6 estero
hemp: 5 abaca, abaka 6 banana
hero: 5 Dewey
nut: 6 peanut
river: 5 Pasig

Manila Bay boat: 6 bilalo

manioc: 7 cassava, tapioca

manipulate: rig, use 4 work 5 treat, wield
6 handle, manage 7 control, operate

manipulator: 9 osteopath

Manitoba: *capital:* 8 Winnipeg
city: 7 Brandon, Portage, St. James 10
St. Boniface
lake: 8 Manitoba, Winnipeg 12 Winnipe-
gosis
national park: 14 Ricing Mountain
province of: 6 Canada
provincial flower: 6 crocus
river: Red 8 Winnipeg 9 Churchill 12
Saskatchewan

mankind: man 4 Adam, male 5 flesh,
world 6 humans, people 8 humanity
division: 4 race 5 tribe 6 people
hater: 11 misanthrope

manly: 4 bold, male 5 brave, hardy, noble
6 daring, strong, virile 7 manlike, mannish 8 resolute 9 dignified, honorable,
masculine, undaunted 10 courageous

Mann character: 7 Castorp

manna: 4 gift 7 Godsend, support 8 delicacy

mannequin: See manikin

manner: air, way 4 cost, form, mien,
mode, more, thew 5 guise, trick 6 as-

pect, course, method **7** address, bearing, fashion, quomo1o **8** attitude, behavior **9** behaviour, technique **10** appearance, deportment
law: **4** modi(pl.) **5** modus
mannered: 8 affected, stylized **10** artificial **13** self-conscious
mannerism: 4 mode, pose **5** trait **7** bearing **11** affectation, peculiarity
mannerly: 4 nice **5** civil, moral **6** decent, polite, seemly **8** courteous, decorous **11** well-behaved
manners: 5 lates **8** courtesy **9** amenities, etiquette
Mannus' father: 6 Tuisto
manor: 4 hall **5** abode, house **6** estate **7** mansion
land: **6** barton **7** demesne
manse: 7 rectory
manservant: 4 help, mozo, syce **5** gilly(Sc.), groom, valet **6** Andrew, butler, garcon, gillie **8** factotum
manship: 5 honor **6** homage **7** courage, manhood **8** courtesy, humanity **9** manliness
mansion: 4 hall, home **5** abode, house, manor, siege **7** chateau, lodging **8** chateaux(pl.), dwelling **9** residence
papal: **7** Lateran
manslaughter: 6 murder **7** killing, slaying **8** butchery, homicide
mansuete: 4 kind, tame **6** gentle
manta: 4 wrap **5** cloak, cloth **7** blanket, bulwark, shelter **8** mantelet **9** devilfish
mantegar: ape
mantel: 4 arch, beam **5** brace(Sc.), ledge, shelf, stone **6** clavel, lintel **10** manteltree
mantilla: 4 cape **5** cloak, scarf
mantle: 4 brat, capa, cape, coat, cope, hood, mant, robe **5** blush, brain, cover **6** capote, pinken, redden **7** encloak, envelop **8** insignia, mantilla, vestment
mantra: 4 hymn **5** charm, spell
mantua: 4 gown, robe **5** cloak **9** overdress
manual: 4 book, text **7** clavier, didache **8** grimoire, handbook **9** catechism **11** enchiridion
art: **5** craft
religious: **9** catechism
manufacture: 4 fake, make **5** forge **6** invent, make up **7** confect, produce **9** fabricate
manufacturer: 8 employer **9** fabricant, operative **10** fabricator **12** entrepreneur **13** industrialist
manumission: 7 freedom, freeing, release **10** liberation **11** deliverance **12** emancipation
manure: 4 dung **5** addle **7** compost **10** composture
manuscript: 4 copy **5** codex **7** papyrus,

writing **8** document **9** archetype, minuscule **11** composition, handwriting
back: **5** dorso
space: **6** lacuna
copier: **6** scribe
mark: **5** obeli(pl.) **6** obelus
many: 4 fele, raff **6** legion, myriad **7** diverse, several, various **8** manifold, multiple, numerous **9** multifold, multitude, plurality **10** multiplied **11** large number
many-footed: 8 multiped
many-sided: 9 versatile **12** multilateral
mao: 7 peacock
Maori: *bird:* poe, tue, tui
canoe: **4** waka
charm: **7** heitiki
chief: **5** ariki
clan: ati **4** hapu
club: **4** mere, patu, rata
compensation: utu
dance: **4** haka
food: kai
fort: pa; pah
god: **4** tiki
hen: **4** weka
hero: **4** Maui
house: **5** whare **8** wharekai **9** wherekura **12** wharewananga
over: umu
priest: **7** tuhunga
raft: **4** moki **6** moguey
sect: **7** Ringatu
store: **6** pataka
tatooing: **4** moko
tree: **5** mapau **6** manuka **9** tanehakas
tribe: Ati **4** Hapu
village: pah **4** kaik **5** kaika **6** kainga
wages: utu
weapon: **4** mere, patu, rata
map: 4 card, plan **5** carte, chard, chart, image **6** design, set out, sketch, survey **7** diagram, epitome, explore, outline, picture **8** roadbook **9** delineate **10** cartograph, embodiment **14** representation
book: **5** atlas
copier: **10** pantograph
maker: **7** charter **8** Mercator **12** cartographer
townsite: **4** plat
weather line: **6** isobar
maple: 4 acer **5** mazer **7** dogwood **8** sycamore
cup: **5** mazer
derived from: **6** aceric
family: **9** aceraceae
sap: **5** humbo
scale: **10** pulvinaria
seed: **6** samara
spout: **5** spile
mar: 4 amar, blot, scar **5** botch, spoil **6**

damage, deface, deform, impair, injure, mangle 7 blemish 8 obstruct 9 disfigure
marabou: 4 bird, silk 5 stork 6 argala, fabric 8 adjutant 11 feather trim
maral: 4 deer
marasca: 6 cherry 10 maraschino
marasmus: 5 waste 10 emaciation 13 contabescence
marathon: 4 race 7 therapy 10 protracted 13 endurance test
maraud: 4 loot, raid, rove 7 pillage, plunder
marauder: 6 bandit, pirate 7 cateran(Sc.)
marble: 4 cold, hard 5 agate, rance, stone 6 basalt 7 cipolin 8 brocatel, dolomite 9 unfeeling 10 brocatelle
  game: taw
  mosaic: 7 tessera
  playing: mib, pea, taw 4 doby 5 alley, dobie 6 glassy 7 shooter
  slab: 5 dalle(F.)
marbled: 7 striped 10 variegated
Marble Faun: *author:* 9 Hawthorne
  character: 5 Hilda 6 Kenyon, Miriam 9 Donatello
marc: 6 pomace, refuse 7 residue
march: 4 hike, slog, trek 5 route, troop 6 border, defile, parade 8 boundary, frontier, smallage 9 cavalcade 10 procession
  day's: 5 etape
  horsemen: 9 cavalcade
  spirited: 9 quickstep
March 15: 4 ides
March King: 5 Sousa
March sisters: Jo; Amy, Meg 4 Beth
marchland: 8 frontier 10 borderland
marcid: 4 weak 7 decayed, tabetic 8 withered 9 exhausted 10 emaciating
marcor: 5 decay 7 maramus
Mardi Gras: 8 carnival
  king: Rex
mare: yad 4 jade, yade, yaud(Sc.) 5 gilot, horse, meare 6 dobbin, equine, grasni
  young: 5 filly
mare's nest: 4 hoax, mess 5 trick 8 disorder 9 confusion
mare's tail: 5 cloud 6 cirrus
margarine: 4 oleo
margin: hem, lip, ori, rim 4 bank, brim, edge, orae(L.), rand, side 5 brink, shore, verge 6 border, fringe, leeway 7 minimum 8 latitude
  narrow: 4 hair
  note: 7 apostil 8 scholium 10 annotation
  set in: 6 indent
marginal: 9 bordering 11 unimportant
Marianas: 4 Guam 6 Saipan
marigold: 5 boots, caper, gools 6 buddle 7 cowslip, elkslip, golland
  genus: 7 tagetes
marijuana: boo, hay, pot, tea 4 hemp, weed 5 grass
  cigarette: 5 joint, stick 6 greefa, griffo, moocah, reefer 7 mohasky 8 joy-smoke, loco weed, Mary Jane 9 Indian hay 10 bambalacha, Mary Warner, Mary Weaver 11 giggle-smoke
  cigarette holder: 6 crutch
  user: 7 pothead
marina: 4 dock 5 basin 9 esplanade, promenade
marinade: 5 brine 6 pickle 8 marinate
marinal: 6 marine, sailor, saline 7 mariner 8 nautical
marinara: 11 garlic sauce
marine: tar 5 jolly, naval, water 7 aquatic, marinal, mariner, oceanic, pelagic 8 halimous, maritime, nautical 9 aequoreal 11 leatherneck
  crustacean: 8 barnacle
  instrument: aba 5 radar 7 pelorus, sextant
  plant: 4 alga 5 algae 6 enalid 7 seaweed
  science: 10 oceanology 12 oceanography
  skeleton: 5 coral
  slogan: 6 gung ho
marine animal: orc 4 salp 5 coral, polyp 9 jellyfish
marine fish: 8 menhaden
mariner: gob, tar 5 Jacky 6 galoot, sailor, seaman 7 buscarl 8 buscarle, seafarer, waterman 9 aequoreal
  card: 5 chart
  compass card: 4 rose
  compass points: 6 rhumbs
marionette: 6 puppet 10 bufflehead
marital: 9 connubial 11 matrimonial
maritime: See marine
marjoram: 4 herb, mint 6 origan
mark: dot, hob, tag, tee 4 belt, goal, heed, line, note, rate, rist, scar, wale 5 badge, brand, grade, label, score, sign, stamp, track, watch 6 accent, beacon, caract, denote, notice, target 7 betoken, blemish, earmark, impress, imprint, insigne, manifest, observe 8 identify, insignia(pl.), standard 9 character, designate, influence 10 impression, indication 11 distinguish 14 characteristic
  bad: 7 demerit
  diacritical: 5 breve, tilde 6 macron, umlaut 7 cedilla(F.)
  down: 5 lower
  out: 6 cancel, define 7 measure 10 obliterate
  possessive: 10 apostrophe
  printer's: 4 dele, fist, stet 5 caret, obeli 6 dagger, diesis, obelus 7 obelisk
  pronunciation: see *diacritical* above
  punctuation: 4 dash 5 colon, comma 6 period 8 dieresis 9 diaeresis, semicolon 11 parenthesis, parentheses(pl.)
  question: 7 erotema, eroteme
  reference: 4 star 6 dagger 8 asterisk
  tiny: dot

under letter: 7 cedilla
white: 5 rache, ratch
with critical notes: 8 annotate
Mark Antony's wife: 7 Octavia
Mark Twain's name: 22 Samuel Langhorne Clemens
markaz: 8 district 11 subdivision
marked: 5 fated, noted 7 eminent 9 prominent 10 emphasized 11 conspicuous, outstanding
with lines: 5 ruled 6 gyrose, linear, notate
marker: peg 5 arrow 6 scorer, signal 7 brander, counter, monitor 8 bookmark, recorder 9 indicator, milestone, tombstone 10 gravestone
air course: 5 pylon
floating: 4 buoy
market: 4 gunj(Ind.), mall, mart, sale, sell, shop, sook, vend 5 agora(Gr.), bazar, gunge, halle, plaza, store, tryst(Sc.) 6 bazaar, outlet, rialto, shoppe 8 boutique, debouche(F.), emporium
marketable: 7 salable 8 vendible 10 commercial
markhor: 4 goat
marksman: 4 shot 6 sniper
marl: 4 clay, loam, malm, sand, silt 5 earth 6 manure 10 fertilizer, overspread
marli: 4 lace 5 gauze, tulle
marlin: 6 curlew, godwit 9 spearfish
marlinspike: fid 4 skua, tool 6 Jaeger
marmalade: jam 5 jelly 6 sapote 8 preserve
tree: 6 mammee
marmite: pot 4 soup 6 kettle 9 casserole
marmoset: 4 mico 6 monkey, pinche, sagoin, wistit 7 tamarin, wistiti
marmot: 5 bobac 6 rodent 8 burrower, whistler 9 groundhog, woodchuck
maroon: 6 enisle, strand 7 abandon, cast off, forsake, isolate, reddish 8 cimarron, purplish
marooner: 6 pirate 9 buccaneer
Marapessa's abductor: 4 Idas
marplot: 7 meddler, snooper 8 busybody
Marquand character: 4 Moto 5 Apley, Wayde 6 Pulham 7 Goodwin
marquee: 4 tent 6 awning, canopy
marquetry: 5 inlay
kind of: 8 intarsia
marriage: 5 match, union 6 splice 7 wedding, wedlock 8 nuptials 9 matrimony
absence of: 5 agamy
broker: 9 schatchen(Yid.)
forswearer: 8 celibate
fourth: 9 tetragamy
god: 5 Hymen
goddess: 4 Hera
hater of: 10 misogamist
more than one husband: 9 polyandry
more than one wife: 6 bigamy 8 polygamy
notice: 5 banns

of aged: 8 opsigamy
of gods: 8 theogamy
outside tribe: 7 exogamy
pert. to: 7 marital, nuptial, spousal 8 conjugal, hymeneal 9 connubial, endogamic
portion: dot 5 dowry
second: 6 digamy
secret: 9 elopement
single: 8 monogamy
to promise: 7 betroth 8 affiance
to two people: 6 bigamy
marriageable: 6 nubile
married person: 4 wife 6 spouse 7 husband 8 benedict
marrow: 4 best, pith 5 reest(Sc.) 6 inmost 7 essence, medulla
bones: 5 knees
marry: wed 4 join, mate, wive, yoke 5 cleek, hitch, unite 6 buckle, couple 7 espouse, husband 10 tie the knot
Mars: 4 Ares 6 planet, war god
consort: 10 Rhea Silvia
day: 7 Tuesday
discoverer of satellites: 4 Hall
pert. to: 5 Arean 7 Martian
planet belt: 5 Libya
planet spot: 5 oasis, oases(pl.)
priests of: 5 Salii
region (dark): 4 mare
satellites: 6 Deimos, Phobos
space-craft: 6 Viking 7 Mariner
twin sons: 5 Remus 7 Romulus
Marseillaise author: 13 Rouget de Lisle
marsh: bog, fen, hag 4 jeel, mire, moor, slew, sloo, slue 5 flash, liman, slash, swale, swamp 6 morass, palude, slough 7 cienaga, maremma(It.) 8 quagmire 9 everglade
bird: 4 rail, sora 5 snipe, stilt 7 bittern
crocodile: goa 6 mugger
elder: iva
fever: 7 helodes 8 malaria
gas: 7 methane 8 firedamp
grass: 4 tule 5 sedge, spart
hawk: 7 harrier
marigold: 5 boots 7 cowslip
salt: 5 salina 7 corcass
shrub: 4 reed 7 bulrush, cattail 8 buckbean, moorwort
marsh plant genus: 4 sium 5 calla 6 caltha 7 elatine
marshal: 4 lead 5 align, aline, array, guide, usher 6 direct, parade 7 arrange, officer 8 official
marshwort: 9 cranberry
marshy: wet 5 fenny 6 callow, quaggy 7 helodes, paludal 8 paludous
lake: 5 liman
marsupial: 4 tait 5 coala, koala, tapoa 6 possum, wombat 7 dasyure, opossum 9 bandicoot
Australian: 4 tait 6 cuscus 7 dasyure, wallaby 8 kangaroo 9 phalanger

bearlike: 5 coala, koala 6 wombat
feature: 5 pouch
mart: 4 fair 5 bazar 6 bazaar, market, *rialto* 8 emporium
martel: 6 hammer
marten: fur 5 sable 6 animal, fisher
beech: 4 foin
genus: 7 mustela
stone: 4 foin
martial: 7 warlike 8 military
martial art: 4 judo 6 karate, kung fu
Martial's writing: 7 epigram
Martian: 5 Arean
martin: 7 swallow
martinet: 6 tyrant 14 disciplinarian
Martinique: *capital:* 12 Fort-de-France
garment: 4 jupe
volcano: 5 Pelee
martyr: 5 saint 8 sufferer 10 sacrificer
first Christian: 7 Stephen
royal: 7 Charles
martyrdom: 7 killing, passion, torment, torture 8 butchery, distress 10 affliction
place of: 8 Golgotha
marvel: 5 ferly 6 admire, wonder 7 miracle, portent 8 astonish 9 horehound 12 astonishment
marvelous: 7 strange 8 splendid, wondrous 9 excellent 10 improbable, incredible
Mary Jane: 9 marijuana
Maryland: *bay:* 10 Chesapeake
capital: 9 Annapolis
city: 5 Bowie 8 Baltimore, Frederick 10 Hagerstown
county: 5 Cecil 7 Hartford 10 Montgomery 12 Prince George
fort: 7 McHenry
founder: 7 Calvert
island: 4 Kent 5 Smith 10 South Marsh
mountain: 8 Backbone, Catoctin 11 Appalachian
nickname: 4 Free 7 Cockade, Old Line
racetrack: 5 Bowie
river: 7 Potomac 8 Patuxent
state bird: 6 oriole
state flower: 14 black-eyed Susan
state tree: oak
masa: 8 cornmeal
Masada: 8 fortress
builder: 5 Herod
defender: 6 zealot
enemy: 4 Rome
historian: 8 Josephus
masculine: 4 male 5 manly 6 strong, virile 7 manlike, mannish
mash: 4 chap, mess, ogle 5 champ, cream, crush, flirt, smash 6 muddle 7 farrago, mixture, touble
marshal: 7 parable, proverb
masher: 4 chap 5 flirt, ricer

masjid: 6 mosque
mask: 4 hide, veil 5 cloak, cover, guise, visor 6 screen 7 conceal, curtain 8 defilade, disguise 9 dissemble
half: 4 loup(Fr.) 6 domino(Fr.)
top knot on: 5 onkos
masked: 6 covert 7 larvate, obscure 8 larvated 9 concealed, disguised
masker: 6 domino, mummer
maslin: 5 brass 7 mixture 9 potpourri
mason: 7 builder 11 stoneworker
mixing rod: rab
masonry: 6 ashlar 7 backing, blocage 9 stonework
masquerade: 5 guise 7 pass for 8 disguise
mass: bat, gob 4 blob, body, bulk, clot, heap, lump, size, swad 5 amass, batch, gross, group, store 6 gather, gobbet, prayer 7 phalanx, service 8 assemble, majority 9 aggregate, magnitude 10 accumulate, assemblage, congregate, large-scale 11 agglomerate, composition, compositure, concentrate, consolidate 12 congregation
book: 6 missal
cloudlike: 6 nebula 7 nebulae(pl.)
confused: cot 5 chaos 6 welter 9 imbroglio 10 hotchpotch
directory: 4 ordo
for dead: 7 requiem
musical number: 5 Credo, Kyrie 6 Gloria 7 Sanctus
of particulars: 9 aggregate
pert. to: 5 molar
small: dab, pat, wad 4 floc
tangled: mop 4 shag
mass meeting: 5 rally
Massachusetts: *cape:* Ann, Cod
capital: 6 Boston
city: 8 Brockton 9 Cambridge, Fall River, Worcester 10 New Bedford 11 Springfield
county: 5 Dukes, Essex 9 Berkshire, Middlesex, Nantucket 10 Barnstable
island: 9 Nantucket 15 Martha's Vineyard
mountain: Tom 6 Brodie 8 Greylock
mountain range: 9 Berkshire
nickname: Bay 6 Old Bay 9 Old Colony
pond: 6 Walden
river: 6 Nashua 7 Charles, Concord 9 Merrimack 11 Connecticut
state bird: 9 chickadee
state fish: cod
state flower: 9 mayflower
state tree: elm
massacre: 6 pogrom 7 carnage 8 butchery 9 slaughter
massage: rub 5 knead
massager: 7 masseur 8 masseuse
massed: 7 serried
Massenet's opera: 5 Manon, Thais

massive: big 4 bold, huge 5 beamy, bulky, gross, heavy, large, massy 7 hulking, weighty 9 cyclopean, ponderous 10 boisterous

mast: cue 4 spar 5 stick 6 forage 8 beechnut
against: 5 aback
crosspiece: fid
inclination from perpendicular: 4 rake
middle: 8 mainmast
wood for: ash 4 poon

mastaba: 4 tomb 8 platform

master: get, man, rab 4 baas, boss, lord, mian, rule, sire 5 chief, rabbi, sahib(Ind.), tutor 6 artist, bridle, buckra, defeat, doctor, domine, govern, humble, subdue 7 captain, conquer, maestro, padrone(It.) 8 educator, overcome, regulate, surmount, vanquish 9 commander, overpower, preceptor, subjugate 10 proprietor
Eton: 4 beak
fencing: 7 lanista
harbor: 7 havener, havenor
hard: 6 despot, Legree
of house: 13 paterfamilias
pert. to: 6 herile
ship's: 7 captain, skipper

master of ceremonies: 5 emcee

master stroke: 4 coup

masterful: 6 lordly 7 haughty 8 arrogant, masterly 9 arbitrary, imperious 10 commanding 11 dictatorial, domineering, magisterial, overbearing 13 authoritative

mastermind: 4 plan 6 expert 8 wiseacre

masterpiece: 4 coup 6 classic 7 triumph 9 objet d'art 10 masterwork 11 chef d'oeuvre

mastery: 4 gree 5 gripe, skill 7 control, victory 8 conquest, facility 9 influence, supremacy 13 understanding

mastic: 4 tree 5 gummy, resin 8 adhesive

masticate: 4 chaw, chew 5 crush, gnash, grind 6 crunch 8 manducate

mastiff: dog 5 burly 7 massive

mastodon: 5 giant 7 mammoth 9 pachyderm

mat: cot, rug 4 felt 5 doily, platt, snarl 6 carpet, cotter, petate(Sp.), tangle 7 cushion, drugget, gardnap 8 entangle 10 interweave, lusterless

mat grass: 4 nard

Mata Hari: spy 5 agent

Mataco: 4 apar 6 Indian 9 armadillo

matador: 6 torero 8 toreador 11 bullfighter
adversary: 4 bull, toro
garment: 4 cape
staff: 6 muleta
sword: 7 estoque 8 estocada

matagasse: 11 butcherbird

match: go; cap, pit, tir(F.) 4 bout, cope, even, game, mate, pair, peer, side, spar, suit, team, wife 5 amate, equal, fusee(F.), marry, rival, tally, torch, vesta 6 fellow, spouse 7 compare, compeer, contest, husband, lucifer(Eng.) 8 equalize, lampwick, marriage 9 allumette(F.) 10 candlewick, correspond 11 counterpart, countervail, parallelize

matched: 6 paired, teamed

matchless: 5 alone 6 unlike 8 peerless 9 exquisite, unequaled 10 inimitable 12 incomparable

mate: cap, pal, wed 4 fear, fere, join, pair, peer, wife 5 billy, buddy, bully, cully, feere, marry, match 6 bunkle, cobber, couple, fellow, spouse 7 brother, compeer, comrade, consort, espouse, husband, partner 9 associate, companion 10 yokefellow

matelot: 6 sailor

mater: mom 4 mama 6 mother

material (see also **cloth, fabric, substance**): 4 data, gear 5 goods, stuff 6 bodily, carnal, matter 7 apropos, weighty 8 physical, tangible 9 corporeal, essential, important 12 nonspiritual
discard: 4 junk, slag 5 scrap, trash, waste 6 refuse 7 rubbish
raw: ore 6 staple

materialism: 9 carnality, physicism

materialize: 4 loom, rise 6 appear, embody, emerge, show up 8 manifest

materiel: 8 supplies 9 apparatus, equipment

maternal: 8 motherly
relation: 7 enation

matey: 6 chummy 13 companionable

matezite: 7 pinitol 10 caoutchouc

matgrass: 4 nard 8 fogfruit

mathe: 4 grub 6 maggot

mathematician: 5 adder 7 figurer

mathematics: *abbreviation:* Q.E.D.
branch: 7 algebra, geodesy 8 calculus, geometry 9 logarithm 10 arithmetic 12 trigonometry
constant (arbitrary): 9 parameter
deduction: 8 analysis
diagram: 5 graph
equation: 4 surd
exercise: 7 problem
factor: 10 quaternion
function: 4 sine 6 cosine
instrument: 6 sector 7 compass 8 arbalest
irrational number: 4 surd
line: 6 vector
number: 5 digit 12 multiplicand
operation: 7 operand
operator: 5 nabla 10 quaternion
proposition: 7 theorem
quantity: 6 scalar
ratio: pi 4 sine 8 derivate

symbol: **7** faciend, operand **12** multiplicand

term: **4** root, sine **6** cosine

mathemeg: 7 catfish

matie: 7 herring

matin: 4 call, song **6** prayer **9** matutinal

song: **6** aubade

matinee: 5 party **6** soiree **8** negligee **9** reception **13** entertainment

matinee idol: 4 lion, star **5** actor

matka: 4 seal

matrass: 4 tube **5** flask **6** bottle **8** bolthead

matriculate: 5 adopt, enter **6** enroll **8** register **10** naturalize **13** immatriculate

matrimonial: 7 nuptial, spousal **8** conjugal, hymeneal **9** connubial

matrimony: 7 wedlock, **8** marriage

matrix: bed, die, mat **4** form, mold, womb **5** plasm **6** gangue **7** pattern

plate: **6** stereo

matron: 4 dame, wife **5** widow **11** housekeeper

matte: 10 dull finish

matter: pus **4** gear, malm, mass **5** solid, topic **6** affair, behalf **7** article, concern, problem, signify, trouble **8** business, material **11** constituent

law: res

particle: **4** atom

pert. to: **5** hylic

property: **4** mass **7** inertia

rarefied: fog, gas **4** mist **5** vapor **6** miasma

matter of fact: 4 dull **7** literal, prosaic **9** practical, pragmatic **11** utilitarian **12** in plain style

mattock: axe, hoe **4** bill **5** tubal **6** twibil **7** twibill

mattress: pad **4** sack **6** pallet

cover: **4** tick **7** ticking

mature: age, old **4** aged, form, gray, grow, ripe **5** adult, grown, ripen **6** accrue, autumn, decoct, digest, mellow, season **7** develop **8** complete **9** come of age

matutinal: 5 early, matin **10** before noon

Mau Mau land: 5 Kenya

maud: 5 plaid, shawl **7** blanket

maudlin: 5 beery, corny, tipsy **7** tearful, weeping **10** lachrymose **11** sentimental

mauger: 5 spite **7** ill-will **9** unwilling **15** notwithstanding

Maugham: *heroine:* **5** Sadie

play: **4** Rain

maul: paw **4** beat, bung, club, mace, mall, mell, moth **5** abuse, gavel, staff **6** beater, beetle, bruise, hammer, mallet **7** rough up **9** manhandle

maumet: god, guy **4** doll, idol **5** image **6** puppet

maud: beg **6** basket, hamper

maunder: 5 growl, haver **6** beggar, drivel, ramble **7** grumble

Maupassant character: 4 Fifi

Mauritania: *capital:* **10** Novakchott

ethnic group: **5** Arabs, Moors **6** Wolofs **7** Berbers, Poulars **8** Sonunkes

monetary unit: **6** ougiya

language: **6** Arabic, French

neighbor: **4** Mali **7** Algeria, Morocco, Senegal

religion: **5** Islam

river: **7** Senegal

town: **4** Atar **5** Kaldi

Maurois subject: 4 Hugo, Sand **5** Byron, Dumas **6** Proust **8** Disraeli

Mauser: arm, gun **5** rifle **6** weapon **7** firearm

mausoleum: 4 tomb **8** baradari(Ind.)

mauve: 5 lilac **6** purple, violet

maux: 8 slattern, slipshod **10** prostitute

maven: 6 expert **11** connoisseur

mavis: 6 thrush **8** thrasher

maw: 4 craw, crop **6** gullet, mallow **7** stomach

mawk: 6 maggot

mawkish: 5 vapid **6** sickly **8** nauseous **9** squeamish **10** disgusting **11** sentimental

maxilla: jaw **4** bone

maxim: saw **4** dict, rule, word **5** adage, axiom, gnome, logia(pl.), moral, motto **6** logion, saying **7** brocard, precept, proverb **8** aphorism, apothegm, doctrine, moralism **9** erudition, principle **10** apophthegm

maximum: 4 most, peak **5** limit **7** highest, largest **8** greatest

may: can **4** mote **5** might, shall, shrub **6** hawthorn, possible

May: *festival:* **7** Beltane

goddess: **4** Maia

Maya: *day:* **5** uayeb

month: **5** uinal

people: **4** Mam **8** Pokonchi

year: **4** haab

maybe: 6 mayhap **7** perhaps **8** possibly **9** not surely **10** indecision **11** possibility, uncertainty

maybird: 4 knot **6** thrush **8** bobolink

maycock: 5 melon **6** maypop, plover

mayfish: 9 killifish

mayflower: 7 arbutus **8** hawthorn, marigold **10** stitchwort **12** cuckooflower

Mayflower's sister ship: 9 Speedwell

mayfly: dun **6** insect

mayor: 5 maire(F.) **7** alcalde(Sp.) **8** official **10** magistrate **12** burgomeister(G.)

maze: 4 daze **5** amaze, fancy **7** confuse, perplex, stupefy **8** bewilder, confound, delirium, delusion **9** amazement, deception, labyrinth **10** hodgepodge **12** bewilderment

mazer: 4 bowl **6** goblet

mazy: 7 complex **9** intricate **10** circuitous, perplexing **11** bewildering

mea culpa: 10 I am to blame

mead: 5 drink 6 meadow 8 hydromel 9 metheglin

meadow: lea 4 mead, vega, wish, wong 5 field, haugh, marsh 6 saeter 7 pasture 9 grassland, grassplot

piece of: 5 swale

meadowlark: 5 acorn 6 medlar

meadowmouse: 4 vole

meadowsweet: 4 rose 7 spiraea

meager: 4 arid, bare, lank, lean, poor, slim, thin 5 gaunt, scant, spare 6 barren, jejune, lenten, meagre, narrow, pilled, scanty, scarce, sparse 7 scranny, starved, sterile, tenuous 9 emaciated 10 inadequate

meal: tub 4 bite, dune, feed, menu 5 feast, flour, grain, lunch, padar, salep, snack 6 bucket, dinner, morsel, nocake, powder, repast, supper 7 banquet, blowout, potluck, rations 8 sandbank 9 breakfast, collation, pulverize

army: 4 chow, mess

coarse: 5 grout 7 cribble 8 gurgeons

last course: 7 dessert

light: tea 5 lunch, snack 6 tiffin

main dish: 6 entree

wheat: 4 atta(Ind.)

meals: 5 board

mealy: 4 pale 6 floury, spotty, uneven 7 friable, powdery, starchy 8 farinose 9 colorless, personate 11 farinaceous

mean: low 4 base, clam, hard, lean, norm, poor, show 5 argue, augur, footy, nasty, petty, ratty, snide, snivy, sorry 6 abject, chetif, coarse, common, denote, design, dirten, feeble, humble, intend, medial, median, medium, middle, narrow, paltry, pilled, snivey, sordid 7 average, caitiff, ignoble, pitiful, purport, purpose, signify 8 baseborn, beggarly, churlish, recreant, shameful 9 irascible, malicious, niggardly, penurious, truculent 11 disgraceful, hardhearted 12 contemptible, dishonorable, intermediate, narrow-minded, parsimonious

mean line: 9 bisectrix

meander: 4 roam, turn, wind 5 amble, curve, stray, twist 6 wander 7 complex 8 straggle 9 labyrinth

meaning: 5 sense 6 import, intent, spirit 7 anagoge, bearing, purport, purpose 9 intending, intention, knowledge 10 definition, indication 11 designation, implication 12 apprehension, significance 13 signification, understanding

without: 4 null

meanly: 6 humbly, poorly 8 beggarly, shabbily

means: 4 cost, tool 5 agent, funds 6 agency, assets, method 7 quomodo 8 averages, resources 10 instrument 11 wherewithal 12 intermediary

of livelihood: 4 work 5 labor, trade 8 vocation 10 profession

support: 4 hold 6 income 7 aliment 11 maintenance

meantime: 7 interim 8 interval

meanwhile: 9 adinterim

mear: 8 boundary

measles: 7 rubeola

measly: 4 mean 6 skimpy, slight 9 worthless 12 contemptible

measure (see also **measuring instrument**): act, law 4 area, gage, mete, rule, span, tape, time 5 clock, gauge, girth, meter, ruler, scale 6 amount, assize, degree, length, stadia 7 battuta, caliper 8 odometer, tapeline 9 admeasure, calculate, criterion, rotameter

area: are, rod 4 acre 6 decare 7 hectare

astronomical: 7 azimuth

Biblical: cab, hin, kor, log 4 epha 5 cubit, aphah, homer

cable: 4 naut

capacity: 4 cask, gill, orna, peck, pint 5 liter, quart 6 barrel, bushel, gallon

cloth: ell 4 yard

cubic: 4 cord 5 stere 10 hectostere

cut wood: 4 cord

distance: see *length* below

degree of angle: arc

dry: 4 bale, peck 6 bushel

energy: erg 5 ergon, joule

established: 8 standard

fish: vog 4 cran(Sc.) 5 crane, crans

flexible: 4 tape 8 tapeline

heat: 5 term 6 calory, therme 7 calorie 10 centigrade, Fahrenheit

horse: 4 hand

land: ar; are, rod 4 acre, area, mile, rood 6 decare 7 hectare, stadia

length: dra, ell, pik, rod 4 foot, inch, knot, mile, nail, pace, pole, yard 5 cubit, digit, meter, metre, perch, toise(F.) 6 league, micron, mikron 9 decimeter, kilometer 10 centimeter, hectometer, millimeter

liquid: aam, keg 4 gill, pint 5 lagen, liter, quart 6 barrel, gallon, magnum, minims, runlet, tierce 7 rundlet 8 hogshead 9 hectolite, kiloliter

loudness: 4 phon

medicinal: 4 dram 5 minim, ounce 7 scruple

nautical: 4 knot 6 fathom

paper: 4 page, ream 5 quire, sheet

printer's: 4 pica 5 agate, empen

short: 4 ullage

sound: bel

space: 6 parsec

time: day 4 hour, week, year 5 month 6 decade, minute, moment, second

water depth: 5 sound

weight: ton 4 bale 5 carat, liter, ounce, pound 9 kiloliter 10 hectoliter

wheat: 4 trug
wine: tun 4 butt, pipe
wire: mil 5 stone
work: erg 5 ergon
yarn: lea 4 heer, typp 6 denier 7 spindle
Measure for Measure character: 5 Elbow, Froth, Lucio 6 Angelo, Juliet
measured: 7 careful, guarded, regular,
uniform 10 deliberate
measureless: 4 vast 7 endless, immense 8
infinite 9 boundless, limitless, unbounded, unlimited 11 illimitable 12
immeasurable
measurement: 9 dimension 11 mensura-
tion
pert. to: 6 metric 11 dimensional
measuring instrument: 4 gage, tape 5
chain, gauge, meter, ruler 7 alidade 8
measurer, tapeline 9 container, yardstick 13 saccharimeter
acidity: 10 acidimeter
heat: 11 calorimeter
lumber: 6 scaler
surveying: 11 stratameter
thickness: 7 caliper
measuring wheel: 8 odometer 12 perambulator
meat: 4 beef, food, gist, lamb, pork, veal 5
flesh 6 chevon, mutton 7 chilver, venison 9 nutriment
and-potatoes: 5 basic
ball: 7 rissole 9 croquette, fricandel 11
fricandelle
bony: 5 scrag 9 spareribs
cured: ham 5 bacon 6 flitch, salame, salami 7 biltong, bultong, sausage 8 pastrami, pastroma 9 biltongue
cut: ham, rib 4 chop, loin, rump 5 flank,
roast, steak 6 cutlet, rasher 7 icebone,
sirloin 9 aitchbone, club steak, rump
roast, short ribs
dish: 5 pasty 6 potpie, ragout 7 goulash,
haricot, ravioli 8 fricando 10 fricandeau
dish with vegetables: 4 olla, stew 8 mulligan 9 lobscouse 10 lobscourse
dried: 5 jerky 7 biltong, bultong, pemican
8 pemmican 9 biltongue
frozen: 5 frigo
ground: 7 rissole, sausage 9 hamburger
jelly: 5 aspic
pie: 5 pasty 7 rissole
pin: 6 skewer
potted: 7 rillett 8 rillette
roasted: 5 brede, cabob, kabob
sauce: 4 A-one 5 caper, gravy 14 Worces-
tershire
slice: 6 collop
smoking place: 5 bucan
unwholesome: 6 cagmag
meatless: 6 lenten, maigre
meatus: 4 butt, duct 5 canal 7 foramen,
passage

meatworks: 8 abattoir 14 slaughterhouse
meaty: 5 heavy, pithy, solid 11 substantial
Mecca (see also **Muslim**): *deity:* 5 Hobal,
Hubal
mosque: 5 Caaba, Kaaba 6 Kaabeh
pilgrim's dress: 5 ihram
pilgrimage: 4 hadj
mechanic: erk(F.) 7 artisan, workman 8
operator 9 artificer, craftsman, operative
mechanical: 9 automatic 10 uninspired
11 automatical, involuntary, perfunctory, stereotyped
mechanical man: 5 robot 9 automaton
mechanical part: 5 rotor 6 stator, tappet
mechanics branch: 7 statics 8 dynamics
mechanism: 4 gear, tool 5 apron, catch,
slide 7 ratchet, tripper 8 selector, sig-
naler 9 apparatus, machinery
driving: 9 propeller
eccentric: cam
self-moving: 8 antomata(pl.) 9 automaton
medal: 4 disk 5 badge 6 plaque 7 medalet
10 decoration
medallion: 4 coin 8 ornament 11 contor-
niate, contorniato
Medb's consort: 6 Ailill
meddle: 4 nose 5 snoop 6 dabble, finger,
monkey, potter, tamper 7 intrude 9 interfere
meddler: 5 snoop 7 marplot 8 busybody
meddlesome: 4 busy 5 fresh 6 prying 7
curious 9 intrusive, officious
Mede: 5 Aryan, Mesne 6 Median
caste: 4 magi
king: Evi
Medea: *father:* 6 Aeetes
husband: 5 Jason
rival: 6 Creusa
son: 6 Medeus
media: See **medium**
medial: 6 middle 8 ordinary
median: 4 mean 6 medial, middle 7 average, central 12 intermediate
mediate: 7 referee 8 ruminate 9 arbitrate,
intercede, interpose
mediator: 5 judge 6 broker 7 daysman 9
go-between, middleman 10 ambocepter,
interagent 12 intermediary
medic: 6 clover, doctor, intern, medico 7
alfalfa, luterne, student, surgeon 8 resident 9 physician
false: 5 quack 9 charlatan 10 medicaster
medical: 6 iatric 11 aesculapian
medical officer: 7 coroner
medical student: 6 extern, intern 7 ex-
terne, interne 8 resident
medicinal: 6 curing 7 healing 8 salutary
9 relieving 11 aesculapian 12 pharma-
ceutic
bark: 6 cartex
berry: 5 cubeb

capsule: 6 cachet
compound: 4 pill, sera 5 hepar, iodin, se-
    rum 6 iodine 7 turpeth
nut: 4 cola
plant (see also *root* below): rue 4 aloe 5
    ergot, senna, tansy 6 arnica, cohosh, ip-
    ecac 7 chirata 8 valerian
remedy: 8 antidote
root (see also *plant* above): 5 artar, jalap,
    orris 6 seneca, senega 8 licorice
solution: 8 tincture
tablet: 4 pill 6 troche 7 lozenge
medicine: 4 cure, drug 5 tonic 6 physic,
    remedy 7 anodyne, nostrum, placebo
    10 abirritant, alterative
amount: 4 dose 6 dosage
god of: 11 Aesculapius
institution: 6 clinic 8 hospital
instrument: See **surgery:** *instrument*
mild: 6 tisane
noncuring: 6 ptisan
patent: 7 nostrum
vessel: 4 vial 5 ampul, phial 6 ampule 7
    ampoule 8 gallipot
medicine dropper: 7 pipette
medicine man: 4 piay 6 doctor, shaman
    8 magician, sorcerer 9 physician
mediety: 4 half, part 6 moiety
medieval: old 6 Gothic
battle: 4 Acre
coin: 9 bracteate
dagger: 6 anlace
fiddle: 4 giga
fort: 11 Carcassonne
gown: 6 cyclas
guild: 5 Hanse
helmet: 5 armet 6 heaume
lyric: 4 alba
prayer book: 7 portass
shield: ecu
weapon: 5 lance, oncin 7 gisarme 8 cross-
    bow
Medina (see also **Muslim**): 8 holy city
citizen: 5 Ansar
mediocre: 4 mean, so-so 6 common, me-
    dium 7 average 8 inferior, middling,
    not so hot, ordinary, passable 11 com-
    monplace, indifferent
meditate: 4 chew, mull, muse, pore 5
    brook, study, think, watch, weigh 6
    ponder, reason 7 reflect, revolve 8 cogi-
    tate, consider, ruminate 10 deliberate
    11 contemplate
meditation: 4 yoga 6 prayer 8 inaction
    11 engrossment 13 consideration 14
    omphaloskepsis
meditative: 7 pensive
mediterranean: 6 inland 7 midland 10
    landlocked
Mediterranean: sea 11 mare nostrum
boat: nef 4 saic 5 setee, xebec, zebec 6
    galiot, mistic, settee, tartan, zebeck 7
    felucca, mistico, polacre

coast: 7 Riviera
country: 5 Italy 6 France, Greece 7 Alge-
    ria
Eastern: 6 Levant
falcon: 6 lanner
fish: aco 6 remora
fruit: 5 olive 7 azarole
galley: 6 galiot
grass: 4 diss
gulf: 5 Tunis
island: 4 Elba 5 Capri, Crete, Ibiza, Iviza,
    Malta 6 Candia, Cyprus, Ebusus, Les-
    bos, Lipari, Rhodes, Sicily 7 Corsica,
    Majorca, Panaria 8 Cyclades, Sardinia,
    Sporades 9 Stromboli 10 Dodecanese
pert. to: 9 Levantine
port: 5 Tunis 7 Tunisia
resort: 4 Nice 6 Menton 7 Mentone
shrub: 7 azarole
storm: 7 borasca, borasco
tree: 5 carob 6 mastic 7 azarole
wind: 6 otesan, solano 7 gregale, mistral,
    sirocco 8 levanter 10 euroclydon
medium: 4 mean 5 media(pl.), midst, or-
    gan 6 degree, medial 7 average, chan-
    nel, psychic 8 mediator 10 instrument,
    interagent 11 environment 12 `inter-
    mediary, intermediate
communication: 4 note 5 cable, pho.
    radio 6 letter 9 telegraph, telephone 1.
    television
culture: 4 agar
news: 5 radio 7 journal 8 magazine 9
    newspaper 10 periodical, television
medlar: 4 lark, tree 5 fruit 6 loquat
medley: 4 olio 6 jumble 7 farrago, me-
    lange, mixture 8 mingling 9 patchwork,
    potpourri 10 hodgepodge, miscellany,
    variagated 11 gallimaufry 12 mingle-
    mangle
musical: 8 fantasia
medrick: 4 gull, tern
medulla: 4 pith 6 marrow 7 essence, sum-
    mary 10 compendium 12 adrenal gland
Medusa: 6 Gorgon 7 blubber 9 jellyfish
offspring: 9 Pegasus 8 Chrysaor
representation: 9 Gorgoneum
sister: 6 Stheno 7 Euryale
slayer: 7 Perseus
meed: due 4 gift 5 award, bribe, merit, re-
    pay, worth 6 desert, reward 7 bribery
    10 excellence, recompense
meek: 4 deft, kind, mild 5 lowly 6 docile,
    gentle, humble, modest 7 pacific, pa-
    tient 8 moderate, resigned, sheepish,
    yielding 9 childlike, spineless 10 spirit-
    less, submissive
meerkat: 6 monkey 8 mongoose, suricate
meerschaum: 4 pipe 7 seafoam 8 sepio-
    lite
meet: fit, kep(Sc.), sit 4 duel, face, join,
    tidy 5 equal, occur, touch, tryst 6 bat-
    tle, combat, confer, gather, proper 7

contact, contend, convene, fitting, fulfill, satisfy 8 assemble, assembly, confront, deal with, moderate, suitable 9 encounter, forgather, gathering, intersect 10 congregate, experience, foregather 11 appropriate, contend with

athletic: 8 gymkhana 10 tournament

meeting: 4 mall, moot 5 gemot, rally, union 6 caucus, gemote, huddle, parley 7 coition, consult, session 8 adjacent, assembly, conclave, congress, junction 10 concurrent, conference, confluence, rendezvous 11 convocation

place: 5 forum

meg: 6 guinea 9 halfpenny

Meg's sisters: Jo; Amy 4 Beth

megalithic chamber: 6 dolmen

megaphone: 8 bullhorn, vamphorn

megapod: 4 bird 5 maleo 6 leipoa 11 large-footed

Megara king: 5 Nisus

megrim: 4 whim 5 blues, fancy, freak, humor, whiff 7 stagger, vertigo 8 flounder, headache 9 dizziness 10 low spirits 12 hypochondria

Mehitabel: cat

companion: 6 Archie 9 cockroach

creator: 7 Marquis

Mekong River: *site:* 4 Asia 7 Vietnam

tribe: Moi

mel: 5 honey

melancholia: 6 athymy 7 athymia

melancholy: sad 4 blue, dram, dull, dump, glum 5 dolar(L.), drear, dusky, gloom 6 dismal, somber, sombre, sorrow, yellow 7 chagrin, doleful, pensive, sadness, unhappy 8 atrabile, downcast, tristful 9 cheerless, dejection, plaintive 10 allicholly, depression, desolation 11 despondency, downhearted 12 disconsolate, heavy-hearted, hypochondria, mournfulness

Melanesia: *language:* 6 Santo

people: 4 Fiji

melange: 4 olio 6 medley 7 mixture 10 hodgepodge

melanic: 5 black

melanous: 4 dark 6 brunet 8 brunette

meld: 4 play 5 blend, merge, unite

mele: 4 poem, song 5 chant, lyric 6 ballad

melee: row 4 fray, riot 5 brawl, fight, foray, mix-up 6 affray, fracas, ruckus 7 ruction, scuffle 8 dogfight, skirmish 9 commotion 10 free-for-all

melilotus: 6 clover

meliorate: 6 better, change, soften 7 improve, get better 10 ameliorate

Melkarth: 4 Baal 6 Moloch

mell: mix 4 maul 5 fight, honey 6 beetle, hammer, mallet, meddle, mingle

mellifluous: 6 sweet 7 honeyed, sugared 8 pleasant 9 melodious

mellow: age 4 aged, rich, ripe, soft 5 loamy, ripen 6 mature, tender 7 matured 8 patinate

melodeon: 6 organ 9 seraphine

melodious: 6 ariose, arioso, dulcet 7 lyrical, melodic, musical, tunable, tuneful 8 canorous 10 harmonious

melodist: 6 singer 8 composer 9 harmonist

melodramatic: 8 dramatic 9 emotional 10 theatrical 11 sensational

melody: air, lay 4 aria, lilt, note, raga (Ind.), solo, song, tune 5 charm, dirge, music, theme 6 strain 7 arietta, harmony, rosalia, sortita 9 cantilena 11 tunefulness

characterization: 6 ariose, arioso

counter: 7 descant

outline: 5 melos

pert. to: 6 plagal

unaccompanied: 4 solo 6 monody

meloid: 6 beetle 9 oil beetle

melon: 4 musk, pepo 5 gourd, water 6 casaba, papaya, spoils 7 Persian 8 honeydew 10 cantaloupe, paddymelon

melon pear: 6 pepino

melongena: 7 mollusk 8 eggplant

melos: 4 song 6 melody

melt: rin(Sc.), run 4 flow, flux, fuse, thaw 5 blend, smelt, sweal 6 render, soften 7 dwindle, liquefy 8 discandy, dissolve, eliquate 10 colliquate, deliquesce 12 disintegrate

down: 6 render 7 liquefy

partly: 4 frit

Melville: *character:* Pip 4 Ahab 5 whale 8 Queequeg, Starbuck

novel: 4 Omoo 5 Typee 8 Moby Dick

member: 4 limb, part 5 organ 6 branch, fellow 7 section 8 district 11 communicant

new: 6 novice 7 entrant 8 neophyte 10 apprentice

oldest: 4 dean

membership: 4 seat 10 fellowship

membrane: web 4 caul, coat, skin, tela 5 layer 6 amnion, amnios, retina, tissue 7 cuticle, eardrum, velamen 8 stiffen

diffusion through: 7 osmosis

fold of: 5 plica

fringe: 4 loma

of bird: 4 cere

spore: 6 intine

weblike: 4 tela

memento: 5 relic, token 6 trophy 8 keepsake, memorial, reminder, souvenir 11 remembrance

memo: 4 chit 8 reminder

memoir: 4 note 5 eloge 6 record, report 7 history 8 memorial 9 biography, narrative 10 commentary

memorabilia: ana 7 history 8 archives

memorable: 7 namable, notable, special 9 reminding 10 remarkable 11 reminiscent 13 distinguished, extraordinary

memorandum: 4 bill, note, stub 5 brief 6 agenda(pl.) 7 agendum, memento, minutes, notanda(pl.), proctol 8 notandum, notation, reminder 9 directive

book: 5 diary 6 agenda 7 tickler 8 calendar

legal: 5 jurat

memorial: ahu 5 facta(pl.), relic 6 factum, memoir, record, trophy 7 memento 8 mnemonic, monument 11 remembrance 12 recollection 13 commemorative

carved: 5 totem

stone: 5 cairn 6 statue 9 mausoleum

memorist: 8 prompter

memory: 4 mind, rote 8 memorial, mind's eye, 9 retention 11 remembrance 12 recollection, reminiscence 13 retrospection

aid: 8 mnemonic, reminder 10 anamnestic

goddess: 9 Mnemosyne

loss: 5 blank, lethe 7 amnesia, aphasia 13 forgetfulness

pattern: 6 engram

pert. to: 6 mnesic 7 mnestic 8 mnemonic

vivid: 7 eidetic

memory book: 5 album, diary 9 scrapbook

Memphis (see also **Egypt**): *chief:* Evi

god: Ra 4 Ptah

men: 4 crew 6 people, troops 9 work force

armed body: 4 army 5 posse

party: 4 stag 6 smoker

section of Greek church: 6 andron

wise: 4 Magi 6 Gaspar 8 Melchior 9 Balthasar, Balthazar

menace: 5 boast, peril 6 danger, impend, threat 8 denounce, forebode, jeopardy, threaten, work evil 9 fulminate

menacing: 10 formidable

menage: 4 club, home 6 family 7 society 8 domicile 9 household 10 management 12 housekeeping

menagerie: zoo 10 collection

mend: fix, sew 4 beet, darn, heal, help, knit 5 amend, botch, clout, emend, moise, patch 6 better, cobble, repair, solder 7 improve, restore 9 get better 10 ameliorate, convalesce

mendacity: lie 5 lying 6 deceit 7 falsity, untruth 9 falsehood

mender: 6 tinker 7 cobbler 9 repairman

mendicant: 4 monk 5 fakir 6 beggar, fakeer, frater

Menelaus: 12 king of Sparta

brother: 9 Agamemnon

daughter: 8 Hermione

father: 6 Atreus

steersman: 7 Canopus

wife: 5 Helen

meng: mix 5 blend 6 mingle

menhaden: 4 fish, pogy 5 pogie, porgy 8 bonyfish 10 mossbunker

young: 7 sardine

menial: fag, low 4 base, mean 6 drivel, harlot, sordid, stocah, varlet 7 servant, servile, slavish 8 coistrel, coistril, servitor 9 degrading underling

meniscus: 4 lens 8 crescent 12 crescent moon

Mennonite: 5 Amish

meno: 4 less

menopause: 12 change of life

Menotti character: 5 Amahl

mental: 5 ideal 6 insane 7 phrenic 9 cognitive 11 intelligent 12 intellectual 13 temperamental

mental aberration: fog 4 daze, haze 5 lapse 6 stupor 7 doldrum, madness 8 insanity

mental defective: 5 idiot, moron 8 imbecile 9 retardate

mental disorder: 6 ataxia 7 aphasia 8 neuritis, neurosis, paranoia 9 melomania, paranomia, psychosis 11 megalomania 12 hypochondria 13 schizophrenia

specialist: 12 psychiatrist

mental faculties: 4 mind, wits

mental image: 4 idea 5 dream 6 idolum 7 fantasy 8 phantasm 10 conception

mental state: 5 blues 6 morale 7 doldrum 8 euphoria

mentality: 4 mind 5 sense 6 acumen, reason 9 endowment, intellect 11 rationality 12 intelligence

mention: 4 cite, hint, mind, name 5 clepe, honor, refer, speak, trace 6 allude, denote, inform, notice, record, remark 7 specify, vestige 8 allusion, citation 9 statement 10 indication

implied: 11 connotation

mentor: 4 guru 7 monitor, teacher 9 counselor 10 instructor

menu: 4 card, meal 5 carte 10 bill of fare

part of: 4 soup 5 salad 6 entree 7 dessert, special 9 appetizer

Mephistophelean: sly 4 evil 6 crafty 7 satanic 8 devilish

mephitic: 4 foul 6 deadly, smelly 7 noxious 8 stinking

mercantile: 7 trading 10 commercial

mercenary: 4 hack 5 venal 6 greedy, sordid 7 Hessian, soldier 8 covetous, hireling, vendible 10 galloglass(Sc.) 11 corruptible, gallowglass 13 stipendiarian

merchandise: 4 sell, ware 5 goods, wares 6 deal in 7 chaffer

cheap: 5 borax 7 camelot, schlock

pert. to: 10 emporeutic

merchant: 4 Seth(Ind.) 5 buyer 6 dealer, seller, sutler, trader, vendor 7 chapman, goladar, howadji, vintner 8 purveyor 9 tradesman 10 shopkeeper 11 store-keeper

group: 5 guild, hansa 6 cartel

ship: 5 oiler 6 argosy, coaler, packet, tanker, trader 7 collier, steamer 8 bilander, Indiaman 9 freighter

wholesale: 6 packer

Merchant of Venice: 7 Antonio

character: 5 Tubal 6 Portia 7 Jessica, Lorenzo, Nerissa, Shylock 8 Bassanio

merciful: 6 benign 7 clement, lenient, sparing 9 benignant, forgiving 10 charitable 13 compassionate

merciless: 4 grim 5 cruel 6 savage 8 pitiless 9 ferocious, graceless, heartless 10 despiteous, implacable, relentless

mercurial: 6 clever, lively, shrewd 8 changing, thievish 9 faithless 10 inconstant

mercury: 5 azoth, guide, thief 6 hawker 9 messenger 11 quicksilver

derivative: 11 quicksilver

Mercury: 6 Hermes, planet

son: 5 Cupid

staff: 8 caduceus

winged cap: 7 petasos, petasus

winged shoes: 7 talaria

mercury chloride: 7 calomel

mercy: law 4 pity, ruth 5 grace, grith 6 lenity 7 charity 8 clemency, humanity, kindness, lenience, leniency, mildness 9 tolerance 10 compassion, indulgence, tenderness 11 forbearance, forgiveness

show: 5 spare 6 pardon 7 forgive 8 reprieve

mercy killing: 10 euthanasia

mere: but, sea 4 bare, club, lake, mear, only, pool, pond, pure, sole 5 bound, limit, plain, sheer, utter 6 divide, entire, famous, scarce, simple 7 unmixed 8 absolute, boundary, glorious, landmark, trifling 9 beautiful, undiluted 11 unqualified

merely: 4 also, just only 5 quite 6 anerly

meretricious: 5 gaudy 6 paltry, vulgar 9 deceptive 10 misleading

merganser: 4 smee, smew 5 harle, robin 7 becscie, bracket, garbill 9 goosander

merge: mix 4 fuse, join, meld 5 blend, unify, unite 6 absorb, mingle 7 combine, conjoin 8 coalesce 9 commingle 10 amalgamate 11 consolidate, incorporate

merger: 5 union 9 coalition 12 amalgamation

mericarp: 8 hemicarp

meridian: 4 apex, noon 6 midday 11 culmination

meringue: 5 icing

merino: 4 wool 5 sheep 6 fabric 7 Delaine

merit: 4 earn, meed 5 worth 6 desert, reward 7 deserve, warrant 10 condignity, excellence

merited: due, fit 7 fitting 8 adequate, suitable

meritorious: 6 worthy 8 laudable, valorous 9 honorable

merkin: mop

merlin: 6 falcon 10 pigeon hawk

Merlin: 4 poem, seer 8 magician 9 alchemist

Merlin's grass: 9 quillwort

mermaid: 5 nymph, siren 6 merrow

meropia: 9 blindness

meros: 5 thigh

merriment: fun 5 deray 9 amusement, diversion, rejoicing, wittiness 11 galliardise 12 cheerfulness, conviviality

merrow: 7 mermaid

merry: gai(F.), gay 4 agog, airy, boon, cant, glad 5 bonny, droll, happy, jolly, sunny 6 blithe, bonnie, cocket, hilary, jocose, jocund, jovial, joyous, lively 7 festive, gleeful, jocular 8 cheerful, chirping, gamesome, gleesome, mirthful, pleasant, sportive 9 hilarious, sprightly 10 blithesome, frolicsome 11 exhilarated 12 lighthearted

merry andrew: 4 zany 5 antic, clown, joker 6 jester 7 buffoon 8 merryman 10 mountebank

merry-go-round: 8 carousel 9 carrousel

Merry Widow composer: 5 Lehar

Merry Wives of Windsor character: Nym 4 Ford 5 Robin 6 Fenton, Pistol 8 Falstaff

merrymaking: 5 jolly, revel 6 splore 7 festive, revelry, wassail 8 carnival 9 festivity, merriment 12 conviviality

merrythought: 8 wishbone

merrywing: 4 duck 5 goldeneye 10 bufflehead

merse: dip 5 marsh 6 plunge 7 immerse

merycism: 10 rumination

mesa: 7 plateau 8 plateaux(pl.) 9 tableland

mescal: 5 cacti(pl.), drink 6 cactus, maguey, peyote, peyotl

mesel: 5 leper 7 leprosy

mesh: net 4 moke 5 snare 6 areola, engage, macula, tangle 7 areolae, ensnare, maculae(pl.), netting, network 8 entangle 9 interlock 10 reticulate

mesial: 6 median, middle

mesmerize: 9 fascinate, hypnotize, spellbind

mesne: 6 middle 11 intervening 12 intermediate

Mesopotamia: 4 Irak, Iraq

ancient city or town: 6 Nippur 7 Babylon

Biblical name: 10 Paddan Aram

capital: 6 Bagdad 7 Baghdad
captives' place: 5 Halah
city: 5 Mosul 7 Edessan, Kerbela
people: 5 Iraki, Iraqi 7 Aramean
river: 6 Tigris 9 Euphrates
wind: 6 shamal

mesquite: 4 tree 5 plant, shrub 9 algarroba
genus: 8 prosopis

mess: jag, row 4 clat, jagg, meal, mull,
much, muss, soil 5 batch, botch, cauch,
dirty, lelee 6 bungle, dabble, jumble, litter, muddle, rumple, tousle 7 crumple,
mixture, rations, wrinkle 6 disarray, dishevel, disorder, scramble, slaister,
squabble 9 commotion, confusion,
mares nest, ugly thing 10 hodgepodge,
picklement

message: 4 bode, line, memo, news, note,
wire, word 5 cable 6 brevet, letter 7
bodword, depeche, epistle, mission, missive, tidings 9 memoranda 10 communique, memorandum 13 communication
coded: 10 cryptogram
good news: 7 evangel

Messalina: 6 wanton 10 prostitute
husband: 8 Claudius

messenger: 4 bode, page, sand, toty 5 angel, envoy, miler 6 beadle, chiaus, herald, legate, nuncio 7 apostle, carrier,
courant, courier, hi-carra, mercury,
prophet, totyman 8 hi-carrah, minister,
nunciate, portator 9 harbinger 10 ambassador, evangelist, forerunner 11 internuncio
mounted: 6 cossid(Ind.) 7 courier, estafet
9 estafette
of the gods: 6 Hermes 7 Mercury

Messiah: 6 Christ, Savior 7 prophet, Saviour

Messina Strait rock: 6 Scilla, Scylla
messy: 5 dirty 6 sloppy, sticky, untidy
mestizo: 5 cross, metis 7 mixture 9 half-
breed
metad: rat
metagnomy: 10 divination
metagnostic: 10 unknowable
metal: ore, tin 4 gold, iron, lead, zinc 6
cobalt, copper, oroide, pewter, radium,
silver, sodium, spirit 7 bullion, gallium,
mercury 9 potassium, substance
alloy: 5 brass, steel
bar: gad 5 ingot
base: 5 dross, sprue
box: 8 canister
cake: 4 slag
clippings: 7 scissel
containing: 13 metalliferous
crude: 5 matte
decorate: 4 etch 6 emboss 9 damascene,
damaskeen

decorative: 6 chrome, niello
deposit: 4 lode
disc: 5 paten 6 patten
fastener: pin 4 bold, brad, nail 5 rivet,
screw 6 cotter, solder
filings: 5 lemel
heavy: 6 osmium 7 uranium
impure mass: 7 regulus
layer: 4 seam 5 stope
leaf: 4 foil
lightest known: 7 lithium
lump: pig 4 slug 6 nugget
magnetized: 13 electromagnet
mixture: 5 alloy
nonexpanding: 5 invar
oblong piece: sow
patch: 6 solder
plate: gib
rare: 4 zinc 6 cerium, erbium 7 iridium,
terbium, uranium, yttrium 8 lutecium,
platinum
refuse: 4 slag 5 dross 6 scoria
scrap: 6 filing
shaper: 5 swage
sheet: 4 foil 5 lames, plate 6 lamina, latten, tagger
spike: gad
stannic: tin
strip: 6 spline
suit: 4 mail 5 armor
test: 5 assay
tin-like: 7 cadmium
unrefined: ore
vein: 4 lode
waste: 4 slag 5 dross 6 scoria 9 recrement
worker: 5 smith 6 barman 7 riveter 8 tinsmith 9 goldsmith 11 coppersmith, silversmith

metallic: 4 hard 5 tinny 6 brazen 13
metalliferous
content: ory

metamere: 6 somite 8 somatome
metamerism: 12 segmentation
metamorphose: 6 change 9 transform,
transmute 16 transubstantiate
metamorphosis: 4 pupa 6 change 8 mutation
metaphor: 5 image, trope 6 figure, simile
8 allegory 10 comparison 11 tralati-
tion
faulty or mixed use of: 11 catachresis
metaphorical: 10 figurative
metaphysical: 10 immaterial 12 supernatural, transcendent
metastrophe: 11 interchange
metayer: 6 farmer
mete: 4 dole, give, goal, post 5 allot,
award, bound, limit, stake 7 measure 8
allocate, boundary 9 apportion 10 distribute
meteor: 5 bolis, Cetid, comet, Lyrid 6
Antlid, bolide, Lyraid 8 aerolite, fireball

9 Andromede 10 Andromedid 12 heavenly body

August: 8 Perseids

November: 6 Leonid

meteoric: 8 flashing 9 celestial, transient

meteorite: 8 aerolite, aerolith, siderite

meteorological instrument: 6 bolide 9 barometer 11 thermometer

meteorologist: 10 forecaster

meteorology: 14 study of weather

meter: 4 beat, time 5 metre, swing, verse 6 rhythm 7 cadence, measure 8 measurer

cubic: 5 liter, litre, stere

one-hundredth: 10 centimeter

one-millionth: 6 micron

one-tenth: 9 decimeter

one-thousandth: 10 millimeter

square: 7 centare

unit: 4 mora 5 morae(pl.)

meterist: 10 verse-maker

meters: *10:* 9 decameter

100: 10 hectometer

100 square: ar; are

1,000: 9 kilometer

10,000: 10 myriameter

methane hydrocarbon: 8 paraffin 9 paraffine

metheglin: 4 mead 8 beverage

method: way 4 dart, form, garb, mode, rule 5 means, order, style, usage 6 course, manner, system 7 fashion, formula, process 9 procedure, technique 11 orderliness

customary: rut 5 habit 7 routine

methodical: 5 exact 6 severe 7 orderly, precise

methodize: 8 regulate 11 systematize

Methuselah: *father:* 5 Enoch

grandson: 4 Noah

son: 6 Lamech

methyl: *cyanide:* 7 nitrile

ethyl ketone: 8 butanone

ketol: 6 acetol

meticulous: 4 neat, nice, prim 5 fussy, timid 7 careful, fearful, finical 10 fastidious, scrupulous

metier: 4 line 5 trade 7 calling 8 business 10 occupation, profession

metis: 8 octoroon 9 halfbreed

metric: 8 criteria(pl.) 9 criterion

measure: are 5 carat, liter, litre, meter, stere, tonne 6 decare, hectar, micron, miglio 7 centare, deciare, dekiare, hectare, kiliare, manzana, myriare 8 centiare, dekagram, milliare 9 decaliter, decameter, decastere, deciliter, decimeter, decistere, dekaliter, dekameter, dekistere, kiloliter, kilometer, kilostere, megameter 10 centiliter, centimeter, centistere, dekadrachm, hectoliter, hectometer, hectostere, microliter, milliliter,

millimeter, millistere, myrialiter, myriameter 15 micromillimeter

metrical beat: 5 ictus

metrical foot: 4 iamb 6 iambic, iambus 7 anapest

accented syllable: 5 arsis

four syllables: 6 syzygy

three short syllables: 8 tribrach

two syllables: 7 spondee, trochee

two together: 6 dipody

metrist: 4 poet 9 metrician

metronome: 5 timer

metropolis: see 4 city, seat 6 center

metropolitan: cit 5 chief, urban 7 bishops, leading 9 principal 10 archbishop

mettle: 4 fire 5 ardor, nerve, pluck, spunk 6 ginger, spirit 7 bravery, courage 9 fortitude

mettlesome: 5 brave, fiery, proud 6 ardent 8 skittish, spirited

Metz's river: 7 Moselle

meuse: gap 4 hole, lurk 7 conceal, opening 8 loophole

mew: den 4 cage, cast, coop, gull, maas(Sp.), molt, shed 5 miaow, miaul 6 change 7 conceal, confine, enclose, garages, stables 8 spicknel 9 enclosure 11 concealment, confinement

mewl: cry 5 whine 6 squall 7 whimper

Mexico: *agave:* 5 datil 6 zapupe

alcoholic beverage: 6 mescal, pulque 7 tepache, tequila

American: 6 gringo

annuity: 5 censo

antelope: 9 pronghorn

bean: 6 fejol, frijol 7 frijole

bedbug: 8 conenose

beverage: 4 chia

bird: 6 jacana, towhee 7 jacamar, tinamou 8 zopilote

blanket: 6 serape

bread: 6 tamale

brigand: 7 ladrone

bull: 4 toro

cactus: 6 bavoso, chaute, chende, mescal 8 alicoche, chichipe 11 alfilerillo

candlewood: 8 ocotillo

capital: 10 Mexico City

cat: 6 margay

chaps(leather): 10 chaparajos, chaparejos

city: 4 Leon, Tula 5 Tepic 6 Colima, Jalapa, Juarez, Merida, Oaxaca, Puebla, Potosi 7 Durango, Orizaba, San Luis, Tampico, Tijuana, Torreon 8 Culiacan, Mazatlan, Mexicali, Saltillo, Vera Cruz, Victoria 9 Chihuahua, Monterrey 10 Hermosillo 11 Guadalajara

cloak: 5 manta 6 serape

cockroach: 9 cucaracha

coin: 4 peso 5 adobe 6 azteca 7 centavo, piaster

conqueror: 6 Cortes, Cortez

cottonwood: 5 alamo
dish: 4 taco 5 atole, tamal 6 tamale 8 tortilla 9 enchilada, guacamole
dollar 4 peso
drug: 7 damiana
early dweller: 4 Maya 5 Aztec
export: 6 coffee, cotton, sulfur 9 petroleum
fiber: 4 pita 5 istle, sisal 6 catena
fish: 6 salema 7 totuava
garment: 5 manga 6 serape 7 chiripa
gopher: 4 tuza 7 quachil
grapefruit: 7 toronja
grass: 5 otate 7 sacaton, zacaton 8 hanequen, hanequin
guardian spirit: 6 nagual
hero: 4 Diaz 6 Juarez
hog: 7 peccary
house: 5 jacal
Indian: see *people* below
ivy: 6 cobaea
laborer: 4 peon 7 bracero, wetback
lake: 7 Chapala
land owner: 8 ranchero
language: 7 Nahuatl, Spanish
laurel: 7 madrona
masonry: 5 adobe
mat: 6 petate
measure: pie 4 alma, vara 5 almud, baril, jarra, legua, linea, sitio 6 almude, fanega 7 pulgada 8 curtillo 9 cuarteron 10 caballeria
measure of weight: bag 4 onza 5 carga, libra, marco 6 adarme, arroba, ochava, tercio 7 quintal
mixed blood: 7 mestizo
mountain: 7 Orizaba 12 Citlaltepetl, Ixtaccihuatl, Popocatepetl
musical instrument: 6 clarin, guiros 7 cabacas, maracas 11 chiapanecas
onyx: 6 tecali
orange: 7 choisya
painter: 6 Orozco, Rivera
pancake: 5 arepa
peasant: 4 peon
peninsula: 7 Yucatan 14 Baja California
people: Mam 4 Cora, Maya, Seri, Xova 5 Aztec, Hauve, Lipan, Nahau, Opata, Otomi, Yaqui, Zoque 6 Indian, Mixtec, Otonia, Toltec 7 Haustec, Nahuatl, Tepanec, Zacatec, Zapotec 8 Totonaco, Zaceteco 9 Campesino 10 Cuitlateca, Cuitlateco
plant: 4 chia 5 agave, amole, datil, jalap, sotol 6 chaute, maguey, slavia 7 tequila 8 acapulco 9 sabadilla
plantation: 8 hacienda
porridge: 5 atole
porter: 5 tamen
ranch: 8 hacienda
resort: 8 Acapulco
river: 6 Penuco 7 Tabasco 9 Rio Grande

rubber tree: ule
sandal: 8 gauracha, guarache, guaracho, huarache, huaracho
sandwich: 4 taco
sauce: 7 tabasco
scarf: 6 rebozo, tapalo
shawl: 6 serape
shrub: 6 anagua, anaqua, colima 7 choisya
state: 6 Colima, Sonora 7 Durango, Hidalgo, Sinaloa, Tabasco, Yucatan 9 Michoacan
sugar: 7 panocha
tea: 6 basote 7 apasote 9 alpasotes
thong: 5 romal
tree: ule 4 sero 5 abeto, amapa, ebano, ocote 6 chacte, colima, mezcal, sabino 7 capulin, colorin 8 chaparro, ulmaceae 9 ahuehuete, canadulce 10 anacahuita
village: 6 ejidos, tecali
volcano: 6 Colima 7 Jorullo 9 Paricutin 12 Popocatepetl
weight: 4 onza
yucca: 5 isote

mezereum: 5 shrub 6 daphne 8 camillia
mezzanine: 5 story 7 balcony 8 entresol
mias: 9 orangutan
miasma: 7 malaria
miaul: mew 4 meow, wraw 5 miaou, miaow 7 caterwaul
mib: 6 marble
mica: 4 talc 5 glist 7 biotite 8 silicate 9 damourite, hydromica, isinglass, muscovite 10 lepidolite
micaceous: 7 talcose
Micah: 7 prophet
  son: 5 Abdon
miche: 4 lurk 5 skulk, sneak 6 pilfer 7 conceal, spy upon
Michelangelo work: 5 David, Pieta 12 Last Judgment 13 Sistine Chapel
micher: 5 cheat, thief 6 truant 8 panderer
Michigan: *capital:* 7 Lansing
  city: 5 Flint, Ionia 7 Detroit, Pontiac 8 Ann Arbor, Muskegon 9 Marquette 11 Grand Rapids
  county: Bay 4 Kent 6 Inghum 7 Berrien, Calhoun, Genesee 9 Kalamazoo
  early explorer: 7 La Salle 9 Marquette
  Indian: 6 Ottawa
  island: 8 Mackinaw
  lake: 4 Burt, Erie 5 Huron, Torch 8 Houghton, Michigan
  mountain peak: 7 Curwood
  nickname: 9 Wolverine
  river: 5 Huron 7 Au Sable 8 Manistee, Muskegan 9 Menominee
  state bird: 5 robin
  state fish: 10 brook trout
  state flower: 12 apple blossom
  state tree: 9 white pine
mickle: 4 much 5 great

mico: 8 marmoset
micraner: ant
micro: 4 moth
microbe: 4 germ 8 bacillus, organism
microcosm: 5 world 7 village 8 universe 9 community
microfilm sheet: 5 fiche
Micronesia island: 4 Guam, Wake 5 Palau 6 Bikini, Ellice, Saipan
microorganism: 4 germ 5 virus 6 aerobe 7 aerobia 8 aerobium 9 autoblast, spirillum 10 spirochete 11 spirochaete
microphone: bug, 4 mike 8 parabola
microscope: 5 glass 9 magnifier
microscopic: 5 small 6 minute 9 engyscope
microspore: 8 pollen
microsporophyll: 8 stamen
mid: See midst
midday: 4 noon 8 noontide
  intermission: 5 lunch 7 nooning 8 noon hour
  nap: 6 siesta
middle: 4 mean, part 5 mesne, midst, waist 6 center, centre, centry, median, mesial 7 average, central, centric 9 in between 11 intervening 12 intermediate 13 intermediator
  combining form: mes 4 medi, meso
  way: 6 midway 7 halfway 10 moderation
Middle Ages: See medieval
Middle East: 6 Levant
  country: 4 Iran, Iraq, Oman 5 Egypt, Qatar, Sudan, Syria, Yemen 6 Israel, Jordan, Kuwait 7 Bahrain, Lebanon 11 Saudi Arabia
middleman: 5 agent, butty 6 dealer, trader 8 huckster, retailer 9 go-between 12 interlocutor, intermediary
middling: 4 fair, so-so 6 fairly, medium 7 average 8 mediocre, moderate, ordinary, somewhat 10 moderately 11 indifferent
midge: fly 4 fish, gnat, runt 5 dwarf, stout 6 insect, midget, punkie 7 carriage
midget: 5 dwarf, small 9 miniature
midi: (see also mini) 11 skirt length
Midianite: *king:* Hur 4 Reba
  prince: Evi, Zur
midshipman: 5 cadet 6 reefer
midst: 4 amid, mean 5 among, depth 6 amidst, center, centre, medium, middle, mongst 7 between, halfway, setting 11 surrounding
midwife: 4 baba, dhai(Ind.) 6 cummer, kimmer 9 gracewife 10 accoucheur(F.) 11 accoucheuse(F.), finger-smith
mien: air, eye 4 brow, vult 5 guise 6 aspect, manner, ostent 7 bearing, conduct 8 attitude, behavior, carriage, demeanor 9 behaviour, demeanour 10 appearance, deportment 11 countenance
miffed: 5 sulky, vexed 8 offended 10 displeased
mig: 6 marble 11 sitting duck
migale: 5 mouse, shrew
migeloid fish: 4 bobo
might: arm 4 mote 7 ability 8 strength
mighty: big 4 bulk, fell, vast, very 5 felon, great 6 potent, strong 7 violent 8 enormous, forceful, forcible, powerful, puissant, vigorous 9 extensive, extremely, gigantean 10 omnipotent 11 efficacious
migniard: 6 dainty, minion 7 mincing 8 delicate, mistress
mignon: 5 small 6 dainty, petite 8 delicate, graceful
mignonette: 4 herb 6 reseda
  vine: 7 Madeira, tarweed
migraine: 4 whim 8 headache 10 hemicrania
migrant: See migratory
migrate: 4 flee, flit, move, pass, trek 8 colonize, transfer
migration: 5 exode 6 exodus, flight 8 diaspora, movement
  of top experts: 10 brain drain
migratory: 6 roving 7 nomadic 9 peregrine, wandering
  bird: 4 duck 5 goose, robin
  farm worker: 4 Okie
Mikado: 8 operetta 9 sovereign
  court: 5 dairi
  office 9 mikadoate
milke: 10 microphone
milady: 4 dame 5 madam 10 noblewoman 11 gentlewoman
Milan opera house: 5 Scala
milarite: 8 silicate
mild: moy 4 calm, easy, kind, meek, soft, tame 5 balmy, bland, claro 6 benign, gentle, humble 7 clement, lenient 8 benedict, favonian, gracious, lenitive, merciful, moderate, soothing, tranquil 9 assuasive, forgiving, indulgent, temperate 10 forbearing, mollifying 11 considerate
mildew: 4 mold, rust 5 mould 6 blight, fungus 8 honeydew
  genus of: 7 erysibe 8 erysiphe
mildness: 6 comity 8 leniency, meekness 10 good nature, moderation
mile: *nautical:* 4 knot, naut
  one-eighth: 7 furlong
mileage: 8 distance
milepost: 4 mark 5 stela, stele 6 marker, stelae
miler: 6 runner
milestone: 5 event 8 landmark, occasion
milfoil: 6 yarrow 9 ahartalav
milieu: 11 environment 12 surroundings

militant: 7 martia!, soldier, warlike 8
    fighting 9 combating, combative 10 ag-
    gressive
military (see also **army, troop**)**:** 7 mar-
    tial, warlike
advance: 5 drive 8 anabasis 11 penetra-
    tion 12 breakthrough
adventurer: 10 filibuster
area: 6 sector
assistant: 4 aide 8 adjutant
base: 4 camp 5 depot, field 7 billets 8
    barracks, quarters 10 encampment
call: 6 tattoo
chest: 5 funds
cloak: 5 sagum
command: 4 halt 6 at ease 9 attention
commander: 7 marshal
commission: 6 brevet
engine: ram 6 cannon, onager 7 robinet 8
    catapult, mangonel
force: 5 guard 6 legion, troops 7 reserve
formation: 4 file, line 7 echelon
front: 5 lines 6 sector
guard: 6 patrol
hat: 4 kepi 5 shako 6 helmet
hat covering: 8 havelock
horsemen: 7 cavalry, Hussars
informer: spy
inspection: 5 drill 6 parade, review
landing point: 9 beachhead
machine: 4 jeep, tank
maneuver: 6 tactic
messenger: 7 estafet
obstruction: 6 abatis 7 abattis
officer: 5 major 7 captain, colonel, general
    9 brigadier, subaltern 10 lieutenant
operations: 8 campaign, strategy
order: 7 command
organization: 5 cadre
pit: 10 trou-de-loup
police: M.P. 9 gendarmes 12 constabu-
    lary
prisoner: POW
punishment: 9 strappado
quarters: 4 camp 7 billets 8 barracks
rank: 6 brevet 8 banneret
salute: 5 salvo
signal: 7 chamade
special forces: 10 Green Beret
staff officer: 4 aide
storage place: 5 depot, étape 6 armory 7
    arsenal
supplies: 8 materiel, ordnance
survey: 11 reconnoiter
unit: van 4 rear 5 cadre, corps, squad,
    troop 7 company, platoon 8 division,
    regiment 9 battalion
vehicle: 4 jeep, tank 6 camion 7 caisson 9
    half-track
weapon: 4 croc 6 onager 7 robinet 8 bal-
    lista 9 catapult

work: 4 fort
militate: 5 fight, weigh 6 debate 7 con-
    tend 8 conflict
milk: lac 4 draw, lait(F.) 5 drain, nurse 6
    elicit, suckle 7 exploit
coagulator: 6 rennet
curdled: 6 yogurt 7 clabber, yoghurt, yo-
    gourt 8 yoghourt
curdler: 4 ruen 6 rennet
deodorizer: 7 aerator
derived from: 6 lactic
fermented: 5 kefir, kumys 6 koumis,
    koumys, kumiss 7 koumiss, matzoon
first after delivery: 9 beestings, biestings,
    colostrum
food: 10 lacticinia
mouse: 6 spurge
pail: soa, soe 5 bowie
pert. to: 6 lactic 7 lactary, lacteal
preparation: 9 lactarene, lactarine
protein: 6 casein
sap: 5 latex
selling place: 5 dairy 9 lactarium
separator: 7 creamer
sour: 4 whig 6 blinky
sugar: 7 lactose
thickened part: 4 curd
watery: 8 blue John
watery part: 4 whey
with: 6 aulait(F.)
milk and honey: 10 prosperity
milk-and-water: 4 weak 7 insipid 10
    mamby-pamby, wishy-washy
milk leg: 9 phlebitis
milkfish: awa 6 sabolo
milksop: 4 fool 5 sissy 6 coward 7 cock-
    ney 8 weakling 11 mollycoddle
milkweed: *down:* 4 silk
family: 14 asclepiadaceae
fluid: 5 latex
milkwood: 4 tree 5 shrub 9 paperbark
milky: 4 meek, milk, tame 5 timid, white
    6 chalky, gentle 7 lacteal, opaline 8
    timorous 10 effeminate
Milky Way: 6 galaxy
black spaces in: 9 coalsacks
mill: box 4 beat, nurl 5 crush, dress, fight,
    grind, knurl, shape, thief 6 finish, pow-
    der, thrash 7 factory, machine 8 snuff-
    box, vanquish 9 comminute, transform
    12 housebreaker
end: 7 remnant
run of the: 7 average 8 ordinary
millennium: 6 utopia 8 paradise
millepore: 5 coral
miller: ray 4 moth 5 boxer 7 harrier 8 pu-
    gilist 10 flycatcher
miller's thumb: 4 bird, fish 7 warbler 8
    cottidae, titmouse 9 goldcrest
millerite: 7 sulfide
millesimal: 10 thousandth

millet: 5 grain 6 cereal
millimeter: *one millionth:* 15 micromillimeter
one thousandth: 6 micron
milliner: 6 hatter
millions of millions: 9 trillions
millpond: dam
millrace: 4 lade(Sc.) 10 millcourse
below wheel: 8 tailrace
millrind: 6 moline
millstone: 6 burden 7 grinder 9 albatross
10 affliction, deadweight
support: 4 rind, rynd
millstream: 5 fleam
milo: 5 grain 7 sorghum
milpa: 5 field 6 chacra 8 clearing
milt: 6 spleen
mim: shy 4 prim 5 quiet 6 demure, modest
mime: ape 4 aper, copy, jest 5 actor, clown, drama, farce, mimer,¹ mimic 6 comedy, jester 7 buffoon, gesture, imitate 9 represent 11 impersonate
chief: 9 archi-mime
mimeograph: 4 copy 7 stencil
mimesis: 7 mimicry 9 imitation
mimic (see also **mime**): 4 mima, mimo(G.), mock 6 parrot 7 copy-cat, copying, mimetic 9 burlesque 11 counterfeit
mimic thrush: 11 mockingbird
mimicry: 4 echo 5 apery, apism 7 mimesis 8 parrotry 9 imitation 10 camouflage
mimidae: 7 catbird 8 thrasher 11 mockingbird
mimmock: 6 dainty 10 fastidious
mimosa: 4 tree 6 acadia 8 turmeric
mimsey: 4 prim 7 prudish
minaret: 5 tower
minatory: 8 menacing 11 threatening
minaway: 7 minuet
mince: cut 4 chop, gait, hash, meat 5 grind 6 affect 7 finnick 9 subdivide 11 affectation
mincemeat: 5 gigot 10 pie filling
minchiate: 5 tarot
mincing: 5 fussy 6 la-di-da, too-too 7 finical 8 affected 11 persnickety
mincingly: 8 gingerly
mind: min(Sc.) 4 care, chit, heed, obey, reck, tend, will 5 besee, brain, manas (Ind.), watch 6 animus, burrow, memory, notice, psyche, regard 7 dislike, dispose 9 intellect, mentality 11 inclination, remembrance 12 intelligence, recollection
keep in: 9 entertain
origin and development: 13 psychogenesis
pert. to: 6 mental, noetic 7 phrenic 13 psychological
split: 13 schizophrenic

state of: 4 mood, tune
Mindanao: *gulf:* 5 Davao
island: 5 Samal
language: Ata
people: Ata 5 Lutao 6 Bagobo, Illano, Lutayo
town: 4 Dapa
volcano: Apo
mind-blowing: 11 psychedelic 12 overwhelming
mindful: 5 aware 7 heedful 9 attentive, observant, regardful
mine: bal, dig, pit, sap 4 delf, hole, meum (It.) 5 bargh, delft, delve 6 cavity, gopher, threat 7 gallery, passage 8 colliery 10 excavation 13 treasure trove
basket: 4 corf
ceiling: 5 astel
chisel: gad
coal: rob
deposit: 4 lode, vein
entrance: 4 adit 5 stulm
excavation: 5 stope
extraction: ore, tin 4 gold, lead 6 silver 8 diamonds
partition: 8 brattice
passage: 4 sill 5 stope
platform: 6 sollar, soller
product: ore 4 coal, iron
prop: 5 sprag
refuse: 4 dead 5 attle
reservoir: 4 sump 8 standage
rich: 4 lode 6 bonanza 8 golconda
roof support: nog
shaft: 4 sump
surface: 6 placer
sweeping device: 8 paravane
tunnel: 4 adit 5 stulm
vein: 4 lode
wagon: 4 tram
waste: gob 4 goaf 5 attle 7 rubbish
worker: 5 cager, miner 6 canary 7 cageman, trapper 10 onsetter
mine run: 6 common 7 average 11 unsorted ore
miner: 6 dammer(Sc.), digger, sapper 7 collier
miner's consumption: 8 phthisis 9 black lung
mineral (see also **ore**, **metal**): cal, tin 5 irite 6 barite, iolite 7 alumite, ataxite, uralite 9 celestite, galactite, inorganic, uraninite 10 gadolinite, retinalite
amorphous: 6 pinite
black: jet 4 coal 5 irite 6 cerine, yenite 7 knopite, niobite 8 graphite 10 minguetite
blue-green: 5 beryl
brittle: euclase
brown: 6 cerine, egeran, rutile 8 lederite 9 elaterite
calcium and magnesium: 8 diopside

calcium carbonate: **7** calcite **8** calcspar

crystalline: **4** spar **6** yenite **7** apatite, felsite, felspar, knopite **8** boracite, elaterin, felspath

deposit: **4** lode, nest, vein **6** placer

deposit cavity: vug **4** voog, vugg, vugh

earth like: **5** glebe

fibrous: **8** asbestos, oakenite

flaky: **4** mica

gray-green: **7** edenite

gray-white: **5** trona **14** chromiumptrona

green: **7** alalite, apatite, epidote, erinite, prasine, uralian **9** demantoid

gunpowder: **5** niter

hard: **6** spinel **7** adamant **8** corundum, spinelle

lustrous: **4** spar **7** blendes **8** smaltine, smaltite

magnetic: **9** lodestone

mixture: **5** magma

native: ore

non-combustible: **8** asbestos

non-metallic: **4** spar **5** boron **6** gangue, iodine

plaster of paris: **6** gypsum

potash: **4** alum

potassium sulfate: **8** misenite

quartz-like: **4** opal

rare: **7** euclase, thorite

red: **5** balas **6** garnet, rutile

salt: **4** alum

seam: **4** vein

silicate: **4** mica

smelting: ore

soft: **4** talc **6** gypsum

spot: **5** macle

tallow: **11** hatchettine

tar: **4** brea **6** maltha

transparent: **4** mica **5** fluor

vitreous: **4** spar **7** apatite

wax-like: **9** ozocerite

white: **6** barite **8** smaltine, smaltite

yellow: **4** iron **5** topaz **6** pyrite

yellowish green: **7** apidote

mineral jelly: **8** Vaseline

mineral oil: **5** colza **9** petroleum

mineral spring: spa **4** well

mineral water: **6** selter **7** seltzer

Minerva: **6** Athena, Athene

shield: **5** aegis

minestrone: **4** soup

ming: **6** remind **7** mention, recount **8** remember

minge: **5** midge

mingle: mix **4** amix, fuse, join, meng, mool **5** admix, blend, merge, unite **6** huddle **7** blender, combine, compost **8** coalesce, compound, intermix **9** associate, commingle **10** amalgamate, be sociable **11** consolidate

mingle-mangle: **6** medley **7** mixture **10** hodgepodge

mingwort: **8** wormwood

mingy: **4** mean **6** stingy

mini: **8** small car, **9** miniature, **10** short skirt

miniate: **8** decorate, luminate, paint red **9** rubricate

miniature: **4** copy, tiny **5** small, teeny **6** little, minute **8** painting, portrait **9** lineament, miniating **10** diminutive **11** little thing, rubication **12** illumination **14** representation

minikin: **6** dainty **7** darling, elegant, mincing **8** affected, delicate **10** diminutive

minim: jot **4** drop, fish **6** minnow, minute **7** tiniest **8** smallest **9** miniature **10** diminutive

minimize: **6** reduce **7** detract **8** belittle **9** disparage **10** depreciate

minimum: **5** least **6** lowest

minion: **4** idol, neat **5** lover **6** dainty, pretty **7** darling, elegant **8** creature, delicate, favorite, ladylove, mistress, paramour **9** underling

minister: **4** tend **5** angel, serve **6** afford, attend, cleric, curate, divine, pander, parson, pastor, supply **7** furnish, provide, servant **8** executor, preacher, reverend **9** attendant, clergyman, upstander **10** administer, ambassador

home: **5** manse **9** parsonage

minitant: **11** threatening

Minnesota: *capital:* **6** St. Paul

city: Ely **5** Edina **6** Duluth, Winona **7** St. Cloud **9** Rochester **11** Bloomington, Minneapolis

county: **4** Cass, Clay, Cook, Lake, Pine, Polk, Pope, Rice, Todd **5** Dodge, Swift **6** Atkin, Benton, Carver, Dakota, Ramsey, Roseau, Sibley, Wadena, Wilkin **7** Kanabee, Stearns **8** Hennepin

early explorer: **4** Pike **7** La Salle **8** Hennepin

Indian: **5** Sioux **6** Ojibwa **8** Chippewa

lake: Red **7** Bemidji **8** Superior

motto: **9** North Star

mountain peak: **5** Eagle **7** Misquah

mountain range: **6** Cuyuna, Mesabi **10** Vermillion

nickname: **6** Gopher **9** North Star

river: **5** Rainy **7** St. Croix

state bird: **4** loon

state flower: **11** lady slipper

state tree: **7** red pine

minnow: **5** guppy **6** baggie

minor: **4** less **5** petit, petty, youth **6** infant, lesser, slight **7** smaller **8** inferior **11** subordinate **15** inconsequential

minorate: **7** curtail **8** diminish

minority: few **6** nonage **10** immaturity **11** inferiority

Minos: *child:* **7** Ariadne, Phaedra **9** Androgeus

country: 5 Crete
father: 4 Zeus
lover: 6 Scylla
monster: 8 Minotaur
mother: 6 Europa
slayer: 7 Cocalus
wife: 8 Pasiphae

Minotaur: *father:* 4 bull
home: 9 labyrinth
mother: 8 Pasiphae
owner: 5 Minos
slayer: 7 Theseus

minster: 6 church 9 cathedral, monastery

minstrel: 4 bard, bhat(Ind.), moke, poet 6 harper, jockey, singer 7 gleeman, goliard. Pierrot 8 jongleur, musician 9 blackface, troubador 10 gleemaiden, mountebank, troubadour 11 entertainer

accompanist: 7 harpist

minstrel show: *endman:* 7 Mr. Bones, Mr. Tambo
middleman: 12 interlocutor
part: 4 olio

mint: aim, iva 4 blow, coin, sage 5 basil, feint, money, thyme 6 catnip, hyssop, intend, mentha, ramona 7 attempt, dittany, potherb, purpose, venture 8 bergamot, brand-new, calamint, endeavor, lavender, marjoram 9 fabricate, horehound 12 spick-and-span

charge: see *levy* below
family: 9 lamiaceae
genus of: 7 melissa 10 moluccella
geranium: 8 costmary
herb family: 4 balm 5 basil 6 hyssop
levy: 8 brassage 11 seigniorage

mintage: 5 stamp 7 coinage

minuet: 5 dance

movement: 7 scherzo

minus: 4 lack, less 6 defect, devoid 7 lacking, without 8 negative, subtract 10 deficiency

minuscule: 4 tiny 5 petty, small 6 minute 9 very small 10 diminutive, manuscript 13 insignificant

minute: jot, wee 4 mite, nice, note, time, tiny 5 draft, exact, petty, small 6 atomic, little, moment, record, slight, tittle 7 instant, minutia, precise 8 detailed, trifling 9 memoranda(pl.) 10 blow-by-blow, memorandum 13 imperceptible 14 circumstantial

glass: 9 hourglass

minutely: 7 exactly 9 continual, unceasing

minutes: 4 acta 5 actum 6 record

minutiae: 7 details, trifles 11 particulars

minx: dog 4 girl, jade 5 woman

Minyae king: 7 Athamas

minyan: 6 quorum

mir: 4 head 5 chief 6 leader 9 community

Mira: 4 star

constellation: 5 Cetus

mirabile dictu: 9 wonderful

mirabilia: 7 marvels, wonders 8 miracles

miracle: 4 feat 5 anomy 6 marvel, wonder 8 act of God 10 occurrence, phenomenon

scene of: 4 Cana

worker of: 8 magician 11 thaumaturge

miraculous: 9 marvelous, unnatural, wonderful 12 supernatural

mirador: 5 oriel 6 loggia, turret 7 balcony 10 watchtower

mirage: 5 serab 7 chimera 8 delusion, illusion 10 phenomenon, refraction

Miranda's father: 8 Prospero

mire: bog, mud, wet 4 glar, moil, ooze, slew, slob, sloo, slud, slue 5 addle, embog, glaur(Sc.), marsh, sluig, slush, stall, swamp 6 defile, slough, sludge 7 clabber, sludder 8 entangle, slow down

mire duck: 7 mallard

Miriam: *brother:* 5 Aaron, Moses
father: 5 Amram
mother: 8 Jochebed

mirific: 9 marvelous, wonderful

mirror: 5 glass, model 7 reflect 8 speculum 9 girandole 12 looking glass

pert. to: 9 catoptric 11 catoptrical

mirth: fun, joy 4 glee 5 cheer 6 bawdry, gaiety, levity, spleen 7 delight, jollity 8 gladness, hilarity, laughter 9 festivity, happiness, merriment 10 jocularity, joyousness 12 cheerfulness

god: 5 Comus

mirthful: 5 cadgy, merry

miry: 5 boggy, muddy 6 filthy, swampy 7 guttery

misadventure: 4 slip 5 boner, lapse 6 mishap 7 faux pas 8 accident 9 cataclysm 11 catastrophe

misanthrope: 5 cynic, hater, loner, Timon

misanthropic: 7 cynical 10 antisocial

misapplication: 5 abuse 6 disuse 10 perversion

misappropriate: 5 steal 8 embezzle

misbegotten: 7 bastard 8 spurious 10 fatherless 12 illegitimate

misbehave: 7 disobey, misbear, mislead

misbeliever: 7 heretic, infidel 9 miscreant

misbirth: 8 abortion

miscalculate: err 9 overshoot

miscall: 5 abuse 6 revile 7 misname, slander

miscarriage: 5 lapse 6 mishap 7 failure, misdeed, mistake 8 abortion 9 mischance 11 misdemeanor 13 mismanagement

miscarry: err 4 fail 5 misgo 7 founder 9 fall short

miscegenation: 13 interbreeding

miscellaneous: 5 mixed 6 sundry, varied

8 assorted 13 heterogeneous 14 indiscriminate

miscellany: 4 olio 10 adversaria, hodgepodge

mischance: See **misfortune**

mischief: ate, hob, ill 4 bane, evil, harm, hurt 5 prank, wrack 6 damage, injury 7 cantip, devilry 8 deviltry 9 devilment, diablerie 10 disservice

god: 4 Loki

goddess: Ate 4 Eris

mischiefmaker: elf, imp, wag 5 knave, rogue

mischievous: sly 4 arch, impy 5 elfin, hempy 6 elfish, elvish, impish 7 harmful, knavish, malefic, mocking, naughty, parlous, roguish, teasing, waggish 8 prankish, sportive, venomous 9 injurious

mischievous child: imp 4 brat, limb 5 devil, scamp 6 monkey 7 hellion

miscible: 7 mixable

misconception: 8 abortion 16 misunderstanding

misconduct: 7 offense 8 disorder 9 mismanage 11 delinquency, malfeasance, misbehavior, misdemeanor

mark of: 7 demerit

miscreant: 5 knave 6 rascal, wretch 7 heretic, infidel, villain 8 criminal 9 hereticl, scoundrel 10 unbeliever 11 misbeliever, unbelieving 12 unscrupulous

miscue: 4 miss, slip 5 error 7 mistake

misdeed: sin 4 slip 5 crime, wrong 7 forfeit, offense 8 disorder 11 delinquency 13 transgression

misdemeanor: sin 5 crime, fault, wrong 6 delict 7 misdeed, offense 8 disorder 11 delinquency 12 misdemeanant 13 transgression

misdirect: 7 distort, pervert

mise: 4 levy, pact 5 grant 6 layout, treaty 8 immunity 9 agreement, privilege

misease: 7 poverty 8 distress 10 discomfort

mise-en-scène: set 4 site 7 setting 12 stage setting

miser: 4 cuff 5 churl, flint, hayne, hunks, Nabal 6 codger, huddle, nipper, snudge, wretch 7 hoarder, niggard 8 holdfast 9 collector, skinflint 10 curmudgeon

miserable: bad 4 dawy 6 abject, chetif, elenge, feeble 7 forlorn, pitiful 8 pitiable10 despicable, discomfort, inadequate 12 disconsolate 13 commiserative

misericord: 4 hall 6 dagger 9 refectory 10 compassion

miserly: 4 mean 5 close, gnede 6 greedy, grippy, stingy 8 covetous, grasping 9 penurious, scrimping 10 avaricious 12 parsimonious

misery: woe 4 ache, pain, ruth 5 agony 6 sorrow 7 anguish, avarice, poverty, sadness, squalor 8 calamity, distress 9 adversity, privation, suffering 10 affliction, depression, misfortune 11 despondency, unhappiness 12 covetousness, wretchedness 13 niggardliness 14 unpleasantness

misfeasance: See **malfeasance**

misfortune: woe 4 dole, evil, harm, slip 5 grief 6 misery, mishap, scathe 7 illluck, misfare, reverse, trouble 8 accident, calamity, casualty, disaster 9 adversity, holocaust, infortune, mischance 10 affliction, ill-fortune 11 catastrophe, contretemps, miscarriage 12 misadventure

misgiving: 5 doubt, qualm 7 anxiety 12 apprehension

misguide: 5 abuse 6 injure 7 mislead 8 misteach 9 misbehave, misdirect, misgovern, mismanage

mishandle: 6 bungle 7 rough up

mishap: See **misfortune**

mishmash: 4 olio 6 jumble 10 hodgepodge

Mishnah: 6 Talmud 9 scripture

pert. to: 7 tannaic 8 Mishnaic

section: 4 Moed 5 Aboth

supplement: 8 Toseftas

misinterpret: err 4 warp 7 misread

misjudge: err 12 miscalculate, misinterpret

misky: 5 foggy, misty

mislay: 4 lose 8 misplace

mislead: 4 dupe, fool 5 blear, cheat 6 betray, delude, humbug 7 beguile, debauch, deceive 8 hoodwink, inveigle, misguide 9 duplicate, mismanage

misleading: 5 false 7 crooked 10 fallacious, fraudulent

mismanage: 5 blunk 6 bungle

misplace: 4 lose 6 mislay

misplay: err 5 error 6 renege

mispronunciation: 8 cacology 12 speech defect 13 error in speech

misrepresent: lie 5 belie 6 garble 7 deceive

miss: err, fau, hip 4 balk, chit, fail, girl, lack, lass, lose, muff, omit, skip, slip, snab, want 5 lapse, title 6 escape, lassie, miscue 7 deviate, failure, neglect 8 fraulein(G.), miscarry, mistress, overlook, senorita(Sp.), spinster 9 signorina(It.) 10 desiderate, jeune fille, prostitute 12 mademoiselle(F.) 13 misunderstand

missay: 5 abuse 6 vilify 7 slander

misshapen: 4 ugly 6 clumsy 8 deformed 9 distorted, misformed, monstrous 11 counterfeit

missile: (see also **guided missile**) 4 bola, bolt, dart, shot 5 arrow, shaft, spear 6 bullet, rocket, weapon 7 missive, outcast 8 brickbat 9 boomerang 10 projectile

pert. to: 9 ballistic

missing: out 4 lost 6 absent

mission: 6 charge, errand 7 calling, embassy, message 10 commission, delegation, deputation

missionary: 6 Marist 7 apostle

Mississippi: *capital:* 7 Jackson

city: 6 Biloxi 8 Gulfport, Meridian 10 Greenville

chief product: 6 cotton 8 soybeans

county: 5 Hinds, Jones, Yazoo 7 Neshoba 8 Harrison, Itawamba

early explorer: 6 De Soto

highest point: 9 Woodall Mt.

Indian: 5 Osage 9 Merrimack

lake: 6 Ozarks 9 Tablerock

motto: 14 Virtute et armis (By valor and arms)

nickname: 5 Bayou 8 Magnolia

state bird: 11 mockingbird

state flower: 8 magnolia

Mississippi River: *mouth:* 4 pass

source: 6 Itasca

Mississippian: 15 Eocarboniferous

missive: 4 note 6 billet, letter 7 epistle, message, missile 8 document

love: 9 valentine

Missouri: *capital:* 13 Jefferson City

city: 7 St. Louis 10 Kansas City 11 Springfield 12 Independence

county: 4 Cass, Clay, Cole 5 Adair, Bates, Boone, Lewis, Scott, Taney 6 Pettis 7 Jackson, Pulaski 8 Buchanan 9 Jefferson

dam: 7 Bagnell

early explorer: 6 De Soto 7 La Salle

highest point: 10 Taum Sauk Mt.

Indian: 5 Osage

native: 5 Piker

nickname: 6 Show Me 7 Bullion

plateau: 5 Ozark

river: 5 Osage 9 Merrimack

state bird: 8 bluebird

state flower: 8 hawthorn

state tree: 7 dogwood

Truman library and museum: 12 Independence

misspelling: 10 cacography

misspend: 4 lose 8 squander

misstep: 4 slip, trip 5 error 7 faux pas

miss the mark: 4 fail 9 fall short

mist: dag, dim, fog, hag, rag 4 blur, damp, drow(Sc.), film, haze, scud, smog, soup 5 bedim, brume, cloud, smurr, vapor 6 mizzle, shadow, spirit 7 mystery 9 confusion, obscurity 13 precipitation

mistake: err 4 balk, bull, slip 5 amiss, boner, error, fault, folly 6 astray, erring, escape, miscue, renege 7 blunder, default, erratum, rhubarb 10 inaccuracy 12 inadvertence 13 misconception 15 misapprehension

mistaken: 5 wrong 9 erroneous, incorrect 13 misunderstood

mister: don, sir 4 herr(G.) 5 senor(Sp.), title 6 signor(It.) 8 monsieur(F.)

mistletoe: 7 allheal, gadbush

family: 12 loranthaceae

mistreat: 5 abuse 6 ill-use 7 violate

mistress: 4 amie, doll, dozy 5 amiga, dolly, donna, duena, leman 7 hostess 8 gudewife(Sc.), ladylove 9 chamberer, concubine, courtesan, courtezan, governess, kept woman 10 chatelaine, proprietor, sweetheart

mistrust: 5 doubt 8 distrust 12 apprehension

misty: dim 5 foggy, musky, vague 6 vapory 7 obscure 10 indistinct 13 unilluminated 14 unintelligible

misunderstanding: 6 breach 7 quarrel 9 imbroglio 12 disagreement

misuse: 5 abuse 6 disuse 7 abusion, pervert 8 maltreat, mistreat 9 misemploy

mite: bit 4 atom, dite, dram, tick 5 acari (pl.), atomy, speck 6 acarid, acarus, minute, smidge 7 acarina, chigger, smidgen, smidgin 8 acaridan, arachnid, particle, smidgeon, smitchin

miter: 4 belt 5 frank, mitre, tiara 6 fillet, girdle, gusset, tavern 7 tall hat 8 headband 9 headdress

flower: 8 cyclamen

Jewish part: 7 Petalon

mithridate: 8 antidote 9 electuary 12 alexipharmic

mitigate: 4 balm, bate, cool, ease, tone 5 abate, allay, delay, mease(Sc.), relax, remit, slake 6 lessen, pacify, soften, temper 7 appease, assuage, mollify, qualify, relieve, sweeten 8 diminish, lenitive, moderate, palliate 9 alleviate, meliorate

mitten: 4 cuff, jilt, mitt 5 glove, hands

mittimus: 4 writ 6 notice 7 quietus, warrant 9 discharge, dismissal 10 magistrate

mittle: 4 hurt 8 mutilate

mix: pug 4 amix, fuse, join, link, meng, stir 5 admix, alloy, blend, cross, knead, merge, unite 6 jumble, mingle, muddle, wuzzle 7 blunder, combine, confect, confuse, shuffle 8 coalesce, compound, confound 9 associate, commingle, hybridize 10 amalgamate 11 incorporate, intermingle

up: 7 confuse, mistake 8 disorder

with water: 5 slake 6 dilute, weaken

mixable: 8 miscible

mixed: 6 impure, motley 7 piebald 11 farraginous 13 heterogeneous 14 indiscriminate

mixed blood: See hybrid

person of: 5 metis 6 Baluga, Ladino, mestee, mustee 7 mestizo, metisse, mulatto

mixed metaphor: 11 catachresis

mixed-up: 7 complex, tangled 8 confused 10 disordered

mixer: 5 party, paver 9 bartender

mixture: 4 hash, mash, olio 6 batch, blend 6 medley 7 amalgam, compost, farrage, farrago, melange 8 blendure 9 admixture, potpourri 10 concoction, hodgepodge 11 composition 12 mingle-mangle

mizmaze: web 4 knot, mesh 5 skein 6 tangle 9 confusion 12 bewilderment

mizzle: 4 mist, rain 5 misle 6 decamp 7 confuse, drizzle, speckle 9 disappear, misinform

mnemonic: 12 recollective 14 memory training

Mnemosyne: 6 Memory
daughters: 5 Muses
father: 6 Uranus
lover: 4 Zeus
mother: 4 Gaea

moa: 4 bird 6 ratite 8 dinornis

Moab: *city:* Kir
descendant: 7 Moabite
famous woman: 4 Ruth
god: 7 Chemosh
king: 5 Eglon, Mesha
mountain: 4 Nebo
people: 5 Emims

moan: cry 4 sigh, wail 5 groan 6 bemoan, bewail, grieve, lament 7 deplore, whimper 8 complain 9 complaint 11 lamentation
as the wind: 5 sough

moat: gap 4 foss, lake, pond 5 ditch, fossa, fosse 6 trench 7 barrier

mob: set 4 crew, gang, herd, rout 5 cohue, crowd, drove, flock, group, volge 6 clique, masses, rabble 9 multitude 10 prostitute
member: 6 rioter 8 gangster
rule: 7 anarchy 8 violence
worship: 9 mobolatry

mobbish: 7 lawless 10 disorderly

mobile: 5 fluid 6 fickle, vision 7 movable 8 populace 9 wandering 10 changeable

mobsman: 10 pickpocket

mobster: 7 hoodlum 8 gangster

Moby Dick: 5 whale
author: 8 Melville
character: Pip 6 Daggoo, Parsee 7 Ishmael
pursuer: 4 Ahab
ship: 6 Pequod

moccasin: pac 4 pack, shoe 5 snake, tegua 6 loafer 7 slipper 8 larrigan 11 cottonmouth

moch: 4 moth

mocha: 6 coffee 7 leather
stone: 5 agate

mochy: 4 damp 5 misty, moist, muggy

mock: ape, bob, dor, gab 4 gibe, gird, jape, jeer, jibe, leer, sham 5 bourd, elude, false, fleer, flirt, flout, frump, hoker, mimic, scoff, sneer, taunt 6 banter, deride 7 deceive, grimace, imitate 8 ridicule 9 burlesque, imitation 10 disappoint 11 counterfeit

brawn: 10 headcheese

cucumber: 5 apple

nightingale: 7 warbler 8 blackcap

orange: 7 seringa, syringa, syringe

ore: 10 sphalerite

plane: 8 sycamore

mocker: 4 bird 7 flauter 11 mockingbird
nut: 7 hickory

mockery: 5 bourd, farce, glaik, irony 6 satire, trifle 7 hething, sarcasm 8 futility, illusion, ridicule, travesty 9 burlesque, imitation, indignity 11 insincerity 13 laughingstock

mocking: 8 fleering

mockingbird: 8 imitator, songster
genus: 5 mimus

mod: 4 bold, free 6 modern 7 offbeat 11 fashionable

mode: cut, fad 4 form, thew 5 modus, order, state, style, vogue 6 course, custom, fangle, manner, method, regime, system 7 fashion 10 convention

model: act, sit 4 form, mold, norm, plan, plot, pose, type 5 canon, ideal, shape 6 design, sitter 7 example, fashion, manikin, paragon, pattern, perfect, templet, typical 8 ensample, exemplar, formular, fugleman, mannikin, paradigm, pattern, specimen, standard, template 9 archetype, construct, exemplary, facsimile, flugelman, mannequin, miniature, precedent, prototype

moderate: 4 bate, calm, ease, easy, even, meek, mild, soft 5 abate, bland, lower, slake, sober 6 ease up, frugal, gentle, lessen, slight, soften, temper 7 average, control 8 attemper, decrease, diminish, tone down 9 abstinent, alleviate, temperate 10 abstemious, reasonable 12 conservative 13 dispassionate

moderating: 9 remissive

moderation: 7 control 9 restraint 10 abstinence, diminution, governance, limitation, mitigation, sedateness 11 restriction 12 middle course 13 temperateness

moderator: 6 umpire 7 arbiter 8 mediator 9 anchorman 10 arbitrator, negotiator

modern: new 4 late 6 latter, recent 8 neoteric

modernize: 8 renovate

modest: coy, mim(Sc.), shy 4 deft, prim 5 douce, lowly, plain 6 chaste, decent, demure, humble 7 bashful 8 decorous, maidenly, moderate, reserved, retiring, verecund, virtuous 9 diffident 10 unassuming 13 unpretentious

modicum: bit 6 amount 7 portion, soupcon

modify: 4 edit, tone, vary 5 alter, limit 6 change, master, temper 7 assuage, qualify 8 attemper, mitigate, moderate, modulate 9 influence

modish: 4 chic 7 stylish

modiste: 7 stylist 8 milliner 9 couturier 10 dressmaker

modulated: 5 toned 7 changed, intoned 8 softened, tempered 9 inflected, moderated, regulated

modulation: 9 inflexion 10 inflection

modus: way 5 means 6 manner, method

modus operandi: 12 way of working

mog: jog 4 move, plod, walk 6 depart

moggan: leg 6 sleeve 9 stocking

moggy: cat, cow 4 calf 8 slattern 9 scarecrow

moguey: 4 moki, raft 5 mokhi

mogul: 4 lord, snow 5 nabob, ruler, Tatar 6 Tartar 7 magnate 8 autocrat 9 Mongolian, personage 10 locomotive

Mohammed, Muhammed: 7 Mahomet, Mahound

birthplace: 5 Mecca

daughter: 6 Fatima

descendant: Ali 5 Hasan 6 Hosein, Husain, She-rif 7 Ibrahim, She-reef

father: 8 Abdallah

flight from Mecca: 6 hegira, hejira

follower: 6 Moslem, Muslim, Wahabi 7 Wahabee, Wahabit, Wahhabi 8 Wahabite

horse: 5 Buraq 7 Alborak

nephew: Ali

religion: 5 Islam

son-in-law: Ali

successor: 5 Calif 6 Caliph 7 Abu Bakr

title: 4 Iman

tomb: 6 Medina

uncle: 8 Abu-Talib

wife: 5 Aisha 6 Avesha, Ayesha 7 Khadija

Mohammedan: See **Muslim**

moho: 4 bird, rail 9 gallinule

mohock: 6 attack 8 maltreat

mohr: 7 gazelle

moider: 4 toil 5 worry 6 bother, wander 7 perplex, smother 8 distract, encumber

moiety: 4 half, part 5 piece, share 7 portion 9 community

moil: bar 4 mire, soil, spot, tire, toil, work 5 labor, taint, weary 6 defile, drudge 7 torment, trouble, turmoil 8 drudgery, vexation 9 agitation, confusion 10 defilement

moira: 4 fate 7 destiny

moire: 7 watered

moist: 4 damp, dank 5 humid, rainy 6 clammy 7 maudlin 8 humorous

moisten: dew, dip, ret, wet 4 moil 5 bedew, leach 6 anoint, dabble, dampen, humect, humify, imbrue, sparge 8 irrigate, sprinkle 9 humectate

moisture: fog 4 bree(Sc.), drip, drop 5 humor, vapor, water 6 humour, liquid 8 aquosity, humidity 13 precipitation

excess: 5 edema

remove: dry 4 wipe 5 wring 9 dehydrate

moisture-laden: 6 sodden

moistureless: dry 4 arid, sere 6 burned 7 parched 8 scorched 10 desiccated

mojo: 4 Moxo 5 charm, spell 6 amulet 7 majagua

mokaddam: 5 chief 7 headman

moke: fog, net 4 dolt, mesh, mist 5 horse 6 donkey 7 network 8 minstrel 9 performer

moki: 4 fish, raft 9 trumpeter

moko: 9 tattooing

moko-moko: 6 lizard

mokum: 5 alloy

molar: 5 tooth 7 chopper, grinder

molarimeter: 11 thermometer

molasses: 5 syrup 7 claggum, treacle 8 adherent, theriaca 10 blackstrap, sweetening

molave: 4 tree, wood 5 vitex

mold: die, fen 4 calm, cast, copy, core, form, mull, must, soil 5 decay, frame, humus, knead, model, shape 6 blight, matrix, moulage, pattern 9 ceroplast, character, sculpture

opening: 6 ingate

part: 5 nowel, sprue

pert. to: 5 humic

pouring hole: 5 sprue

moldable: 7 fictile

Moldavia: *Rumania capital:* 4 Iasi

department: 4 Iasi 5 Jassy

measure: 7 faltche

molder: rot 5 decay 7 crumble 8 sculptor 9 become old, waste away 12 disintegrate

molding: ess 4 bead, beak, cima, cove, cyma, gula, ogee, reed, tore 5 angle, arris, conge, ogive, ovolo, splay, talon, thumb, torus 6 baguet, baston, fascia, fillet, listel, nebule, reglet, scotia 7 annulet, beading, cavetto, cornice, fingent, reeding, shaping 8 astragal, bageette, bezantee 9 trochilus

case: 5 chape

combination: 9 ledgement

concave: 4 gula 5 oxeye 7 cavetto

convex: 5 torus

curved: 4 ogee 6 nebule

flat: 6 fillet

ogee: 5 talon

pedestal: 7 surbase

rounded: 5 ovolo, torus 6 billet

rule for: 6 screed

moldy: 5 fusty, hoary, mucid, musty, stale 7 foughty 8 mildewed 12 old-fashioned

mole: cob 4 cobb, pier, pile, quay 5 fault, jetty 6 anicut, burrow, rodent 7 annicut, barrier 8 excavate, starnose, tunneler 9 birthmark 10 breakwater 12 imperfection

cricket: 9 churrworm

genus: 5 talpa

mole-like animal: 4 tape 6 desman

molecule: 4 iota 5 speck 7 modicum 8 particle

component: 4 atom

gram: mol 4 mole

moleskin: fur 6 fabric

color: 5 taupe

molest: vex 5 annoy, tease 6 assail, bother, harass, heckle, pester 7 disturb, torment, trouble 9 incommode, interfere 10 discommode

moliminous: 7 massive, weighty 9 laborious, momentous 10 cumbersome

moline: 8 millrind

moll: gal 5 wench 8 mistress 9 companion 10 prostitute

mollescent: 9 softening

mollify: 4 bate, calm, ease 5 abate, allay, relax, sleek 6 lessen, pacify, relent, soften, soothe, temper 7 amolish, appease, placate, relieve, sweeten 8 mitigate 9 attemper 10 conciliate 11 tranquilize

mollusk: 5 snail, whelk 6 chiton, limpet 7 abalone 10 cuttlefish

bivalve: 4 clam, leda, spat 5 chama 6 cockle, mussel, oyster 7 scallop

cephalopod: 8 argonaut

conical-shaped: 6 limpet

eight-armed: 7 octopus

fresh water: 7 etheria

gastropod: 4 slug 5 snail, whelk 7 abalone 12 taenioglossa

genus: 4 arca, leda(pl.) 5 eolis, ledum

group: 8 pteropod

large: 5 chama

larval: 7 veliger

marine: asi 4 welk 5 murex 7 abalone, scallop 8 nautilus

one shell: 5 snail 8 univalve

shell: 4 test 5 cowry, testa 6 cowrie, testae

shell concretion: 5 pearl

shell-less: 4 slug

teeth: 6 radula

ten-armed: 5 squid

used for bait: 5 squid 6 limpet

wrinkled shell: 6 cockle

young: 4 spat

mollycoddle: 6 coddle, pamper 7 indulge 8 weakling 12 spoiled child

moloch: 6 lizard

molt: mew 4 cast, mute, shed 8 exuviate

molten rock: 4 lava 5 magma

molting: 7 ecdysis

Molucca islands: Aru, Kai, Obi 4 Buru 5 Banda, Ceram 6 Maluku 7 Amboina 9 Halmahera

moly: 4 herb 6 garlic

momble: 6 jumble, tangle

moment: sec, use 4 gird, hint, tick, tide, time 5 avail, braid, clink, filip, gliff, point, stage, trice, value 6 fillip, import, minute, second, weight 7 instant 8 occasion 9 short time, twinkling 10 importance 11 consequence

critical: 4 inch, nick 6 crisis, crises

particular: 4 then, when

momentary: 5 brief, quick, short 9 ephemeral, impulsive, transient 10 transitory 13 instantaneous

momentous: 4 fell 5 grave 7 epochal, fateful, serious, weighty 8 eventful 9 important, ponderous 10 chargeable 11 influential

momentum: 5 force, power 7 impetus

mommy: mom 4 duck 5 mammy 6 mother

momus: 6 critic 11 fault-finder

Monaco: *casino:* 10 Monte Carlo

dynasty: 8 Grimaldi

people: 11 Monegasques

prince: 6 Albert 7 Rainier

princess: 8 Caroline

monad: one 4 atom, unit 5 deity, henad 6 person 7 element 8 particle, zoospore

monarch: 4 csar, czar, tsar, tzar 5 ruler 6 despot, prince 7 dynasty, emperor 8 autocrat 9 butterfly, potentate, sovereign

monarchal: 5 regal, royal 6 kingly 8 imperial

monarda: tea 4 mint 5 plant 8 bergamot

monastery: 5 abb, badia 6 friary, mandra, priory 7 convent, hospice, minster, nunnery 8 cloister, lamasery 9 sanctuary

Carthusian: 7 certosa

haircut: tonsure

head: 5 abbot, prior 7 hegumen

Hindu: 4 math

officer: 5 prior

room: 4 cell

superior: 5 prior

title: dom

monastic: 4 monk 5 friar 6 oblate 7 ascetic, monkish, recluse 8 abbatial, cenobite 9 cenobitic 10 conventual

monde: 5 globe, mound, world 6 circle 7 coterie, society

monetary: 9 financial, pecuniary

money (see also **bill, coin**): oof, tin, wad 4 bill, cash, coin, cush, dubs, dump, gelt, gilt, grig, jack, jake, kale, loot, lour, mina, moss, pelf 5 blunt, brass, bread, bunce, chink, clink, dough, funds, livre, lucre, maneh, rhino 6 argent, 'boodle, change, flimsy, hansel, mazuma, moolah, siller(Sc.), spense, steven, tender, wampum, wealth 7 chattel, handsel, lettuce, ooftish 8 currency 9 spondulix 10 greenbacks, spondulics

ancient: aes

blood: cro 7 breaghe

bag: 4 fels 6 follis, wealth 8 follicle

box: 4 arca, safe, till 5 chest 6 drawer 8 register

bribe: 4 soap 6 boodle

broker: 7 changer

certificate: 5 scrip

changer: 5 saraf, seraf 6 shroff

chest for: 7 brazier

coinage: 4 mint

coined: 6 specie

counterfeit: 5 bogus, queer 6 boodle

cowrie: 6 shells

dealer: 6 broker

depreciation: 4 agio 9 inflation

earnest: 5 arles(Sc.), arrha 6 hansel 7 deposit, handsel 8 handgeld

gambler's: 6 barato

gate: 9 admission

gift: 4 alms 7 bequest, charity 9 endowment

given to lord: 6 farleu, farley

found: 6 trove 8 treasure

hearth: 6 fumage

held: 6 escrow

hole for: 4 slot

hood: 4 lari 5 larin 6 larree

lender: 6 banker, usurer 7 shylock 9 loanshark 10 pawnbroker

lots of: pot 4 heap, mint, pile

maker: 4 mint 7 moneyer

manual of exchange values: 7 cambist

metal: 4 coin 6 change, specie 7 coinage

on the: 12 exactly right

overdue: 7 arrears

oversupply: 9 inflation

paid down: 4 cash 7 deposit 11 downpayment

paper: 4 bill, kale 5 green 6 flimsy 7 cabbage, lettuce

premium: 4 agio

ready: 4 cash 5 asset, darby 9 alcontado(Sp.)

roll of coin: 7 rouleau

sent: 10 remittance

shell: 4 peag 5 cowry, peage, sewan, uhllo 6 cowrie, seawan

small amount: 4 mite 7 peanuts 11 chickenfeed

sorter: 6 teller 7 cashier

standard bank: 5 banco

transactions: 7 banking, finance

unit: ora, yen 4 lira, mark, mina, peso, real, tael 5 franc, krona, krone, maneh, pound, ruble, rupee 6 dollar, piatre, talent 7 drachma, guilder, milreis, piaster 8 cruzeiro

without: 4 poor 5 broke 11 impecunious

money of account: ora

moneyed: 4 rich 6 heeled 7 opulent, wealthy 8 affluent 10 well-heeled

moneylender: 6 usurer 10 pawnbroker

mong: mix 5 crowd 6 barter, mingle 7 mixture, traffic 8 mingling 11 intercourse

monger: 6 dealer, hawker, trader 7 peddler 8 huckster

Mongolia: *ass:* 8 chigetai

capital: 9 Ulan Bator

caravan leader: 5 bashi

city: 4 Urga 5 Kobdo 7 Kirghiz

conjurer: 6 shaman

conqueror: 9 Tamerland 10 Kublai Khan 11 Genghis Khan

desert: 4 Gobi

dynasty: 4 Yuan

fuel: 5 argal, argol, argul

measure: lan

monetary unit: 5 mungo 6 tugrik

monk: 4 lama

mountain: 5 Altai 8 Tannu-Ola

people: Lai, Rai 4 Garo, Lapp, Shan 5 Asian, Eleut, Tatar 6 Buriat, Tartar 7 Asiatic, Kalmuck, Khalkha 8 Annamese, Oriental 9 Mongoloid

priest: 6 shaman

province: 6 Chahar 7 Suiyuan

religion: 9 Shamanism, Shintoism 12 Confucianism

river: Pei 4 Onon 5 Peiho 7 Kerulen, Selenga 8 Hobdo Gol

tent: 4 yurt

weight: lan

Mongoloid: See **Mongolia:** *people*

mongoose: 4 urva 5 lemur 7 meerkat 9 ichneumon

Kipling's jungle book: 14 Rikki-Tikki-Tavi

mongrel: cur, dog, mut 4 mutt 6 hybrid 7 bastard, piebald 9 crossbred, half-breed, sandpiper

whitefish: 8 tullibee

monial: nun

moniker: 4 name 5 alias 8 nickname

monition: 5 order 6 advice, caveat, notice 7 caution, summons, warning 8 citation 10 admonition, indication, intimation 11 forewarning, instruction 13 animadversion

monitor: 6 mentor, nozzle 7 inciter 8 ironclad, reminder 9 catamaran 10 instigator

bug: 8 conenose

lizard: 4 ibid, uran 5 varan

monk: dom, fra 4 saki 5 clerk, friar, padre(Sp.) 7 devotee 8 anchoret, ceno-

bite, monastic **9** anchorite, baldicoot,
   bullfinch, hieronach
Buddhist: **4** lama **5** arhat, bonze, goyim,
   yahan **6** bhikku **7** bhikshu, poongee **8**
   poonghee, poonghie, talapoin
cap: **5** kulah **6** kullah
Eastern Church: **7** caloyer, starets
haircut: **7** tonsure
hood: **4** cowl
Muslim: **7** dervish
Roman Catholic: **6** Culdee **8** Capuchin,
   Trappist
room: **4** cell
time in monastery: **9** monachate
monkey (see also **ape**): lar **4** fool, sime **5**
   burro **6** howler, meddle, nisnas, simian,
   tamper, trifle, urchin **7** colobin **9** catarrhina, catarhine **10** catarrhina, catarrhine
African: **4** waag **5** jocko, patas, potto **6**
   grivet, vervet
American: **4** saki **5** acari **6** grison, miriki
   7 ouakari **8** marmoset, orabassu **9** beelzebub
Asiatic: **4** douc **5** toque **6** langur **7** macaque
bearded: **8** entellus
beautiful: **7** guereza
bonnet: **4** zati
Callicebus: **5** yapok **6** yapock
capuchin: sai **7** sapajou
cebine: sai
Diana: **7** roloway
entellus: **7** hanuman **10** hoonoo-maun
genus of: **5** cebus **8** alouatta
god: **7** Hanuman
grivet: **9** tota
handsome: **4** mona
howling: **4** mono **5** araba **7** gauriba, stentor **8** alouatta
large: **5** sajou
long-tailed: sai **4** maha **5** patas **6** guenon,
   langur **7** hanuman, kalasie **8** entellus,
   telapoin, wanderoo
macaque: **6** rhesus
proboscis: **4** kaha **7** noseape
purple-faced: **8** wanderoo
rhesus: **6** bandar
saki: **6** couxia, couxio
small: **4** titi **6** apelet, teetee **7** apeling **8**
   marmoset
spider: **6** ateles, coaita **9** belzebuth
squirrel: **6** samiri
tailless: ape
monkey bear: **5** koala
monkey bread: **6** baobab
monkey business: **7** foolish **11** mischievous
monkey flower: **7** figwort, mimulus **8**
   toadflax
monkey-nut: **6** peanut
monkey pot: **5** fruit

monkey with: **6** meddle **9** interfere
monkey wrench: **7** spanner
monkeyshines: **6** antics, pranks, tricks **7**
   aperies **12** clownishness
monkish: **7** ascetic **8** monastic
monkshood: **4** atis **5** atees **7** aconite **8**
   napellus
monoceros: **7** sawfish, unicorn **9** swordfish
monocle: **8** eyeglass
monocleid: **4** desk **7** cabinet
monocracy: **9** autocracy
monodist: **6** singer, writer **8** composer
monody: ode **4** poem, song **5** dirge **7** oration
monogram: **6** cipher, sketch **7** outline **8**
   initials **9** character
monolith: **6** column, menhir, pillar, statue
   7 obelisk **8** colossus, monument
monologue: **9** soliloquy
monomachy: **4** duel **6** combat
monomaniac: **5** crank **12** single-minded
monophone: **9** homophone
Monophysite: **4** Copt **8** Jacobite
monoplane: **5** Taube
monopolize: **5** sew up **6** absorb **7** consume, engross
monopoly: **5** grant, right, trust **6** cartel,
   corner **7** appalto, charter, control **8**
   privilege, syndicate **10** consortium
monosaccharide: ose **5** sugar
monostele: **4** root, stem
monotonous: **4** dead, drab, dull, flat, same
   6 dreary **7** humdrum, jogtrot, tedious,
   uniform **8** unvaried **9** wearisome **10** re-
   petitive
monotony: **4** drab **6** tedium **9** treadmill
   10 continuity, regularity
monoxylon: **4** boat **5** canoe
monster (see also **beast**): **4** gowl, huge,
   ogre **5** bilsh, demon, devil, fiend, freak,
   giant, teras **6** geryon, sphinx **7** centaur,
   chimera, warlock **12** bandersnatch
fabled: **5** Argus, harpy **6** gorgon, sphinx **8**
   basilisk, Minotaur **9** bucentaur
female: **5** harpy **6** gorgon, scylla
fire-breathing: **6** dragon **7** chimera
handless: **8** acheirus
headless: **9** acephalus
human: **5** teras **6** terata
medical: **5** teras
nine-headed: **5** hydra
short-limbed: **9** nanomelus
study of: **10** teratology
two-bodied: **7** disomus
two-headed: **10** dicephalus
winged: **5** harpy
without hind limbs: api **4** apus
monster like: **8** teratoid
monstrous: **4** huge, vast **5** enorm, large **6**
   mortal **7** hideous, immense, massive,
   strange, titanic **8** colossal, cracking, de-

formed, enormous, flagrant, gigantic, horrible, shocking 9 atrocious, fantastic, unnatural 10 outrageous, prodigious, stupendous, tremendous 12 overpowering, overwhelming, stupendous 13 extraordinary

Montana: *capital:* 6 Helena
city: 5 Butte 8 Billings, Missoula 10 Great Falls
county: 4 Hill 5 Teton 6 Fergus, Wibaux 7 Big Horn, Cascade, Pondera 8 Missoula
highest point: 11 Granite Peak
Indian: 4 Crow 6 Atsina, Salish 8 Shoshone
lake: 8 Flathead
motto: 9 Oro y Plata (Gold and Silver)
mountain range: 5 Rocky 10 Bittersweet
national park: 7 Glacier 11 Yellowstone
nickname: 6 Big Sky 8 Mountain, Treasure
river: 8 Missouri 11 Yellowstone
state bird: 10 meadowlark
state fish: 5 trout
state flower: 10 bittersweet
state tree: 4 pine

Monte Cristo: *author:* 5 Dumas
hero: 6 Dantes

monteith: 9 punch bowl
montero: cap 6 ranger 8 forester, huntsman
Montezuma's revenge: 8 diarrhea
month: *excess of calendar over lunar:* 5 epact
following: 7 proximo
half: 9 fortnight
preceding: 6 ultimo
present: 7 instant
monticule: 4 hill, rise 5 mount 7 hillock
montilla: 6 sherry
Montmorency: 6 sherry
Montrachet: 8 Burgundy
monument: 4 tomb 5 cairn, relic, vault 6 effigy, record, shrine, statue, trophy 8 cenotaph, cromlech, memorial, reminder 9 antiquity, sepulcher 10 gravestone, testament 11 remembrance
pillar-like: 5 stela, stele 6 stelae
monumental: 4 huge, fatal, heavy 7 epochal, massive 8 enduring, historic
moo: low 6 bellow
mooch: beg, bum 4 loaf 5 cadge, skulk, sneak, steal 6 loiter, pilfer, sponge
moocha: 9 loincloth
mood: tid(Sc.) 4 tune, vein, whim 5 freak, humor 6 strain, temper 7 caprice, feeling 10 atmosphere 11 disposition
assumed: 4 pose
recollection of past: 13 retrospection
moody: sad 4 glum 6 gloomy, grumpy, sullen 7 pensive 8 brooding 9 depressed 10 capricious 11 ill-tempered

mools: 10 chilblains
moon: orb 4 Dian, Luna, lune(F.) 5 Diana, lunar 6 Phoebe 7 Cynthia, selenic 8 satelles, selenian 9 satellite
above: 10 superlunar
age at beginning of calendar year: 5 epact
apogee: 5 apsis
area on: 4 mare
aspect: 5 phase
astronaut: 6 Aldrin 9 Armstrong
crescent: 7 menisci 8 meniscus
crescent point: 4 cusp, horn 6 apogee 7 perigee
distance between apogee and perigee: 5 apsis
festival: 8 neomenia
first quarter: 8 crescent
geographer: 13 selenographer
god: Sin 6 Nannar
goddess: 4 Luna 5 Diana, Tanit 6 Hecate, Hekate, Salena, Selene, Tanith 7 Artemis, Astarte
inhabitant: 8 Selenite
instrument: 11 selenoscope
mock: 10 paraselene
new: 6 phasis
perigee: 5 apsis
pert. to: 5 lunar 7 selenic
phase: new 4 full 11 last quarter 12 first quarter
picture: 11 selenograph
position: 6 octant
spacecraft: 6 Apollo
Uranus's: 6 Ariel
valley: 4 rill 5 cleft, rille
vehicle: LEM
moon-mad: 7 lunatic
moon-shaped: 6 lunate
half: 9 semilunate
moon valley: 5 rille
moonack: 9 woodchuck
moonbeam: ray
moonbill: 4 duck
mooncalf: 4 dolt, mole 7 lunatic, monster 11 monstrosity
mooned: 8 crescent
moonery: 7 madness
moonfish: 4 opah 7 sunfish 9 spadefish
moonflower: 5 daisy, oxeye 6 achete
moonglow: 9 moonlight
moonish: 7 flighty 10 capricious
moonlighting: 4 raid 9 adventure 10 expedition 11 moonshining
moonman: 5 gipsy 6 robber
moonraking: 13 woolgathering
moonshine: 4 idle 5 empty, month, sauce 6 liquor 7 bootleg, eyewash, trivial, whiskey 8 nonsense 10 balsamweed, bathtub gin
moonsick: 7 lunatic
moony: 5 round, silly 6 dreamy 8 listless
moor: bog, fen, fix 4 fell 5 heath, lande,

marsh, swale, swamp 6 anchor, fasten, secure

Moor: 6 Berber, Moslem, Muslim 7 Bedouin, Othello, Saracen 8 Moroccan

moor game: 6 grouse

moor hawk: 7 harrier

moorage: 8 berthage 9 anchorage

moorburn: 7 quarrel 9 ill temper

moorcock: 6 grouse 9 blackcock

moorhen: 4 coot 9 gallinule

Moorish: 8 Moresque
alcazar: 4 Alhambra
garment: 5 jupon 7 burnous 8 albornoz, burnoose
horse: 4 barb
judge: 4 cadi
kettledrum: 5 tabor 6 atabal
opiate: 4 kief
palace: 8 Alhambra

moose: elk 4 alce 5 eland
genus: 5 alces
female: cow

mooseberry: 10 hobblebush 13 cranberry bush

moot: dig 4 grub, plea, root, tell 5 argue, plead, speak 6 debate 7 discuss, meeting 8 argument, assembly, complain, disputed 9 debatable, encounter, gathering, uncertain, undecided 10 discussion, litigation

mop: 4 pout, swab, wash, wipe 5 bunch, clean 6 merkin, moppet, scovel 7 cleanse, grimace

mope: 4 pout, sulk 5 brood, idler 9 sad person

moped: 9 motorbike

moppet: tot 4 baby, doll, tike 5 child 7 darling, toddler 9 youngster

mopsy: son 6 moppet 8 slattern

moquette: 6 carpet, fabric 10 upholstery

mora: 5 delay, stool 7 default 9 footstool 12 postponement

moral: 4 good, pure 5 ethic, noble 6 chaste, decent 7 dutiful, epimyth, ethical, upright 8 priggish, virtuous 9 honorable, righteous 10 principled 11 rightminded
fable: 8 apologue
failure: sin
law: 9 Decalogue
teaching: 5 maxim 7 precept 8 apologue 9 preaching 10 preachment 11 edification

morale: 4 hope, mood, zeal 6 spirit 8 morality 9 condition 10 confidence 13 esprit de corps

morals: 6 ethics 9 standards

morass: bog, fen 4 flow, maze, quag 5 flush, marsh, swamp 8 quagmire

morass weed: 8 hornwort

moratorium: ban 5 delay 10 suspension

Moravian city: 4 Brno, Zlin 5 Brunn

moray: eel 6 conger, hamlet 7 muraena

morbid: 4 sick 6 grisly, morose, sullen 8 diseased, gruesome, horrible 9 debatable, saturnine, unhealthy 11 unwholesome 12 apprehensive, pathological

morbilli: 7 measles

morbus: 7 disease, illness

mordant: 4 keen 5 sharp 6 biting 7 burning, caustic, pungent 8 scathing 9 corrosive, sarcastic

more: piu 4 also, mair, plus 5 again, extra 6 better, custom, manner 7 folkway, further, greater 10 additional, convention
or less: 4 some 6 nearly
than: 4 over 5 above
than enough: too 9 excessive
than one: few 4 many 6 couple, plural 7 several

More opus: 6 Utopia

morel: 8 mushroom 10 nightshade

moreover: and 4 also, then 5 again 7 besides, further 8 likewise 11 furthermore

morepork: 4 peho, ruru 7 boobook, frogmouth

mores: 6 ethics 7 manners 9 amenities 10 civilities

morgue: 7 library 8 mortuary 9 deadhouse, stolidity 11 haughtiness, impassivity

moribund: 5 dying 6 effete 8 decadent, decaying 10 acherontic, terminated 12 at death's door 13 deteriorating

morion: 6 helmet, quartz 8 cabasset

Mormon: 6 Danite
emblem: bee
founder: 5 Smith
officer: 5 elder
priesthood: 7 Aaronic 11 Melchizedek
prophet: 6 Moroni
state: 4 Utah

Mormonweed: 6 flower, mallow

morning: 4 dawn, morn 5 matin 6 aurora 7 sunrise 8 forenoon
concert: 6 aubade
coat: 7 cutaway
moisture: dew
pert. to: 5 matin, wight 7 matinal 9 matutinal
prayer: 5 matin 6 matins
reception: 5 levee

morning glory: nil 7 gaybine, ipomoea
family: 14 convolvulaceae

morning star: 4 Mars 5 Venus 6 Saturn 7 Daystar, Jupiter, Lucifer, Mercury 8 Bartonia

moro: 5 finch

Moro: *chief:* 4 Dato 5 Datto
dialect: 4 Sulu
island: 8 Mindanao
knife: 6 barong
people: 4 Sulu 5 Lanao, Yakan

priest: 4 atli 5 sarip
sailboat: 5 sapit
morocco: 7 leather
imitation: 4 roan
Morocco: *cape:* Nun
capital: 5 Rabat
city (see also *port* below): Fez 4 Assa 5 Oujda 9 Marrakech 10 Casablanca
district: Sus 4 Riff
emperor: 9 Miramolin 11 Miramomolin
government: 7 Maghzen, Makhzan, Machzen
hat: fez
island: 7 Madeira
Jews' quarter: 8 El Millah
measure: 4 sahh 6 fanega, tomini
military expedition: 5 harka
monetary unit: 6 dirham
mountain: Rif 5 Atlas
people: 4 Moor 6 Berber, Kabyle, Moslem, Muslim 7 Maghzen, Makhzan, Makhzan
port: 5 Ceuta, Rabat 6 Agadir, Tetuan 7 Mogador, Tangier 8 El Araish, Laraiche 10 Casablanca
ruler: 6 Hassan, she-rif, sultan 7 she-reef
soldier: 5 askar
tree: 4 arar 5 argan 6 alerse 8 sandarac
weight: 4 rotl 5 artal, artel, gerbe, ratel 6 kintar 7 quintal
morology: 5 folly 8 nonsense
moron: 4 dull, fool 5 ament, idiot 6 stupid 7 dullard 8 imbecile, sluggish
moronic: 4 dull, slow 6 stupid 7 idiotic 8 retarded, sluggish
morose: 4 dour, glum, grum, sour 5 gruff, moody, sulky, surly 6 crusty, gloomy, sullen 7 crabbed, clumpse, clumpst, crooked, unhappy 8 choleric, strounge 9 splenetic 10 embittered, ill-humored
moroseness: 8 asperity
morphine derivative: 6 heroin
morro: 4 hill 5 bluff, point 6 castle 8 headland
Morse code signal: dah, dit
morsel: bit, ort 4 bite, snap 5 crumb, piece, scrap, snack 6 tidbit, titbit 7 morceau, rarebit 8 delicacy, fragment, mouthful
mort: 4 dead, lard 5 death, fatal 6 deadly, grease, salmon
mortacious: 4 very 9 extremely
mortal: 4 dire, grim 5 being, fatal, human 6 deadly, lethal 7 capital, deathly, fleshly 8 grievous 9 extremely 10 implacable 11 destructive
mortality: 5 flesh 8 fatality
mortar: 5 compo, putty 6 cannon, cement, holmos, petard 7 perrier
carrier: hod
mixer: rab
tray: hod

mortarboard: cap 4 hawk
Morte d'Arthur author: 6 Malory
mortgage: 4 bond, deed, hock, lien, pawn 5 trust 6 pledge, wadset(Sc.) 11 encumbrance
giver: 6 lienee
receiver: 6 lienor
mortician: 10 undertaker
mortification: 5 shame 7 chagrin 8 gangrene, necrosis, vexation 11 humiliation 13 embarrassment
mortified: 7 ashamed, decayed 10 distressed, humiliated
mortify: 5 abase, abash, spite 6 humble, offend 7 crucify
mortifying: 8 humbling 11 humiliating, ignominious
mortise: 5 joint 6 cocket
complement of: 5 tenon
law: 8 amortize
machine: 7 slotter
mortuary: 6 morgue 9 dead-house, lichhouse, sepulcher 11 funeral home
car: 6 hearse
mosaic: 5 inlay 7 chimera, picture
formed like a: 10 tesselated
tile: 8 abaculus
mosaic gold: 6 ormolu
piece: 7 tessera
Moscow citadel: 7 Kremlin
Moses: 6 leader 8 lawgiver
brother: 5 Aaron
emissary: 5 Caleb
father: 5 Amram
father-in-law: 6 Jethro
law: 4 Tora 5 Torah 10 Pentateuch
mother: 8 Jochebed
mountain: 4 Nebo
sister: 6 Miriam
son: 7 Eliezer, Gershom
successor: 6 Zipporah
Moslem (see also **Muslim):** 7 Islamic, Saracen 9 Moslemite, Mussulman 10 Mohammedan
mosque: 4 jami, mosk 5 Caaba, Kaaba 6 church, dargah, durgah, Kaabeh, Kiblah, masjid, shrine, temple
niche: 4 slab 5 mihrab, 7 chamber
official: 4 imam 5 imaum
student: 5 softa
tower: 7 manarat, minaret 8 minarete
warden: 5 nazir
mosquito: 5 aedes 7 culicid 11 gallinipper
genus of: 5 aedes, Culex 9 Anopheles
killer: 8 culicide
larvae: 8 wigglers
mosquito bee: 5 karbi 8 angelito
mosquito fish: 8 gambusia
mosquito hawk: 9 dragonfly, nighthawk
mosquito plant: 4 mint 10 pennyroyal

Mosquito State: 6 Jersey
moss: bog, fog, rag 5 swamp, usnea 6 lichen, morass 9 bryophyte, treebeard
club: 7 lycoped
edible: 4 agar 8 agaragar
kind: 8 sphagnum
moss cheeper: 5 pipit
moss coral: 8 bryozoan
moss duck: 7 mallard
moss fruit: 11 sporogonium
moss-grown: 10 antiquated 12 old-fashioned
moss hammer: 7 bittern
moss polyp: 8 bryozoan
moss-trouper: 6 raider 8 marauder
mossback: 4 fogy 5 fogey 6 rustic 13 stick-in-the-mud
mossberry: 9 cranberry
mossbunker: 8 menhaden
mosshead: 9 merganser
mosswort: 9 bryophyte
mossy: 4 dull 5 boggy, downy, green, hoary 6 marshy, stupid 7 covered 9 abounding, overgrown
most: 4 best 5 chief 6 utmost 7 maximum 8 majority 9 principal
mostly: 7 chiefly 8 normally 9 generally 10 on the whole
mot: 5 maxim 10 witticism
mote: dot, may 4 atom, hill, iota 5 atomy, match, might, speck, squib, straw 6 barrow, fescue, height, trifle 7 tumulus 8 eminence, impurity, particle 9 lightness 10 stronghold 11 small amount
motel: inn 5 hotel
motet: 4 song 6 anthem 11 composition
moth: 5 tinea 6 bogong, lappet, mallet, miller, tineah, tinean, tineid 7 tineina 8 chloasma, forester 11 yellowshell
clothes: 6 tineid
family: 7 tineina 9 arctiidae
genus of: 5 sesia
larva: 11 caterpillar
spot: 8 chloasma, fenestra
suborder: 10 heterocera
moth-eaten: 4 worn 7 decayed, worn-out 8 decrepit, out-dated
moth hawk: 10 goatsucker
moth hunter: 10 goatsucker
mother: dam 4 dame, womb 5 adopt, dregs, mamma, mater(L.), nurse 6 foster, matron, native, origin, parent, patron 7 nurture, old lady 8 genetrix 10 ancestress, wellspring
of believers: 5 Aisha 6 Ayesha
of gods: 4 Rhea 9 Brigantia
of Gracchi: 8 Cornelia
of Graces: 5 Aegle
of man: 6 Cybele
of months: 4 moon
of presidents: 8 Virginia
of sorrows: 4 Mary 6 Virgin

of states: 8 Virginia
one delivery: 7 unipara
related on side of: 6 enatic
spiritual: 4 amma
three deliveries: 7 tripara
two deliveries: 6 bipara
Mother Carey's chicken: 6 petrel
Mother Hubbard: 4 gown 5 dress
mother-of-pearl: 5 nacre
mother superior: 6 abbess
mother's mark: 9 birthmark
motherland: 4 home 7 country 10 fatherland
motherly: 8 maternal
motion (see also **bodily motion**)**:** 4 fard, idea, move, stir 5 faird 6 signal, unrest 7 gesture, impulse, propose, request, suggest 8 movement, petition, proposal 9 agitation 10 suggestion 11 application, inclination 13 gesticulation
circular: 4 gyre 10 revolution
convulsive: 11 vellication
due to: 7 kinetic
expressive: 7 gesture
impetuous: 6 bensel, bensil 7 bensail, bensall, bensell
pert. to: 7 kinetic 9 kinematic 11 kinematical
producing: 6 motile
quality: 8 momentum
quivering: 6 tremor
rate: R.P.M. 4 time 5 speed, tempo 11 steerageway
science: 10 ballistics, kinematics
transmitter: cog 4 belt, gear
upward: 5 scend 8 upthrust
motion picture: 4 film, show 5 flick, movie, talki 6 cinema 7 flicker 9 photoplay 11 documentary
arc lamp: 5 kleig, klieg
award: 5 Oscar
cowboy and Indian: 5 oater 7 Western
machine: 9 projector 11 kinetoscope 12 animatograph, theatrograph 13 cinematograph 14 cinematographe
outline: 6 script 8 scenario
pert. to: 9 cinematic
prize: 5 Oscar
short: 4 clip 8 newsreel
term: pan 4 shot, take 6 retake 7 reverse
motionless: 4 dead 5 inert, rigid, still 6 asleep 8 becalmed, immobile, stagnant, stagnate, stirless 9 quiescent, sedentary 10 breathless, stock-still
motivate: 4 move 5 impel 6 incite, induce 7 inspire, provoke 9 influence, instigate, stimulate
motive: 4 sake, spur 5 cause 6 object, reason, spring 7 impulse, purpose 8 pressure, stimulus 9 incentive, objective 13 consideration
ostensible: 7 pretext

motley: 4 fool 5 mixed 6 jester 7 diverse, mottled, piebald 9 checkered 10 variegated 11 incongruous 13 heterogeneous, miscellaneous

motmot: 4 bird

motor: car 4 auto, ride 5 drive 6 engine 7 kinetic, machine 8 motorcar 10 automobile

electric: 6 dynamo

hand-powered: 9 baromotor

part: cam 4 coil 5 rotor 6 piston, stator 9 capacitor 10 carburetor

rotary: 7 turbine

motorbike: 5 moped 7 chopper 10 motorcycle

motorboat: 7 cruiser 8 palander, runabout

motor court: inn 5 motel

motor speed control: 8 rheocrat

motorman: 8 engineer, operator

motte: 5 copse, grove

mottled: 4 pied, roed 5 pinto 6 motley 7 brocked, clouded, dappled, piebald, spotted 8 blotched 9 splotched 10 variegated 11 varicolored

motto: mot 4 word 5 adage, axiom, gnome, maxim 6 device, saying, slogan 7 empresa, precept 8 aphorism 9 battle cry 10 shibboleth

mouche: 5 patch

mouchoir: 12 handkerchief

moue: 4 face, pout 7 grimace

mouflon, moufflon: 4 wool 5 sheep

mould: See mold

moulding: See molding

moult: See molt

moulting: See molting

mound: ahu, cop, dam, tee 4 balk, bank, butt, dene, dher, doon, dune, heap, hill, hump, pile, terp 5 agger, berry, cairn, dheri, globe, huaca, knoll, stack, toman(Scot.) 6 barrow, bounds, burrow, causey 8 bourock, bulwark, hornito, rampart, tumulus 8 boundary 9 elevation 10 embankment

of sand: 4 dune

of stones: 5 cairn

pert. to: 7 tumular

prehistoric: 4 terp

mound bird: 8 megapode

Mound City: 7 St. Louis

mound of light: 8 kohinoor

mount: 4 glue, hill, pony, rise, seat 5 arise, climb, horse, paste, stage, steed 6 ascend, aspire 8 escalate, increase, mountain 9 intensify 10 promontory 13 fortification

by ladder: 8 escalade

horizontal bar: kip

two-legged: 5 bipod

Mount Etna city: 7 Catania

Mount Everest peak: 6 Lhotse

Mount Helicon fountain: 8 Aganippe

Mount Ida nymph: 6 Oenone

Mount of Olives: 6 Olivet

Mount Parnassus fountain: 8 Castalia

Mount Rainier: 6 Tacoma

mountain: (see also **peak**): alp, ben (Sc.), kop 4 berg, dagh, fell, mesa, mont(F.) 5 onlay 6 barrow, bundoc, sierra 8 bundocks

base of: 8 piedmont

beyond: 10 tramontane 11 transalpine

Biblical: See Bible: *mountain*

burning: 7 volcano

crest: tor

depression: col

formation: 7 orogeny 9 orogenesy 10 orogenesis

highest: 7 Everest

lake: 4 tarn

low: 5 butte

mythical: Kaf, Qaf 4 Meru 5 candy, glass 7 Helicon 9 Parnassus

nymph: 5 dryad, oread

pass: col, gap 4 cove, duar, gate, ghat 5 ghaut, gorge, kotal 6 defile

pasture: alp 6 saeter

pert. to: 10 orological

range: 4 Alps, Ghat, Ural 5 Andes, chain, Coast, ridge, Rocky, Teton, White 6 Alatau 7 Rockies, Sierras 8 Cascades, Catskill, Pyrenees 9 Allegheny, Blue Ridge, Himalayas 10 San Jacinto 11 Appalachian, San Gorgonio

ridge: 4 aret, peak, spur 5 arete, crest 6 sierra, summit 7 sawbuck

rocky: 7 nunatak

science: 7 orology

sickness: 4 veta 7 soroche

snow: 5 jokul

study: 7 orology 9 orography

sunset reflection: 9 alpenglow

trail marker: 5 cairn

mountain andromeda: 10 fetterbush

mountain ash: 4 sorb 5 rowan, rowen 8 dogberry, winetree

mountain badger: 6 marmot

mountain balsam: fir

mountain banana: fei

mountain barometer: 8 orometer

mountain beaver: 8 sewellel

mountain bluet: 8 centaury

mountain cat: 4 lynx 6 bobcat, cougar 10 cacomistle

mountain climber: 10 alpestrian

equipment: 4 rope 5 piton 10 alpenstock

mountain climbing: 8 alpinism

equipment: axe 5 piton 7 crampon

mountain cock: 12 capercaillie

mountain curassow: 10 oreophasis

mountain dew: 7 bootleg, whiskey 9 moonshine

mountain duck: 9 harlequin, sheldrake

mountain finch: 9 brambling

mountain flax: 8 centaury

mountain fringe: 8 fumitory, wormwood

mountain goat: 4 ibex 6 mazame

mountain ivy: 6 laurel

mountain leather: 12 palygorskite

mountain lion: 4 puma 6 cougar

mountain magpie: 10 woodpecker 11 butcher-bird

mountain mint: 5 basil 8 calamint

mountain oak: 8 chestnut

mountain panther: 5 ounce 6 cougar 7 leopard

mountain parrot: kea

mountain partridge: 4 dove 5 quail

mountain pheasant: 6 grouse

mountain raspberry: 10 cloudberry

mountain rose: 6 laurel

mountain snow: 4 neve 6 jokul

mountain spinach: 5 orach 6 orache

Mountain State: 7 Montana

Mountain States: 4 Utah 5 Idaho 6 Nevada 7 Arizona, Montana, Wyoming 8 Colorado 9 New Mexico

mountain tea: 11 wintergreen

mountaineer: 5 Aaron 6 rustic 7 climber, hillman 9 hillbilly

   song: 5 yodel

mountainlike: 7 etiolin

mountainous: 4 high, huge 5 alpen 6 alpine, rugged 8 elevated 10 alpestrine, monumental, prodigious

mountaintop: 4 cone, peak 6 summit

mountebank: 4 gull 5 cheat, quack 7 empiric 8 impostor, minstrel, swindler 9 charlatan, pretender

   aid: 4 zany

mounting: 7 setting 9 equipment 13 embellishment

moup: 6 nibble 9 associate

mourn: rue 4 dole, erme, long, sigh, wail, weep 6 bemoan, bewail, grieve, lament, murmur, sorrow 7 deplore 8 mourning

mournful: sad 5 black 6 rueful, woeful 7 doleful, elegiac, pitiful 8 dejected, dirgeful, funereal 9 elegiacal, plaintive, sorrowful, threnodic, woebegone 10 deplorable, lamentable, lugubrious, melancholy 11 distressing 12 heavyhearted

mourning: 4 garb 5 dolor 6 dolour 7 drapery

   bride: 5 plant 8 scabious

   dress: 5 black, crape, crepe, weeds 6 sables

   group: 7 cortege

   song: 5 dirge

mouse: erd, pry 4 girl, hunt, knot 5 snoop, steal 6 rodent 8 black-eye

   field: 4 vole 7 harvest

   leaping: 6 jerboa

   male: 4 buck

   milk: 6 spurge

   pert. to: 6 murine

mouse deer: 7 plandok 10 chevrotain

mouse-ear: 8 hawkweed 9 chickweed

mouse hare: 4 pika

mousebird: 4 coly 6 shrike

mouselike: shy 4 drab 5 quiet, timid 6 murine 8 retiring

mouser: cat 8 detective

mouseweb: 6 cobweb 8 gossamer

mousing: 6 prying 7 binding 8 prowling 9 rapacious 11 inquisitive

mousle: 6 rumple

mousse: 7 dessert, messboy

mousy: 4 drab 5 quiet, timid

moutan: 5 peony, plant 6 flower

mouth: gab, gan, gob, mow, mug, mun, ora 4 boca(Sp.), dupe 5 boast, front, orate, stoma 6 cavity, gebbie(Sc.), mumble, rictus 7 flummer, grimace, opening, stomata 8 back talk, entrance 9 impudence, spokesman

   away from: 6 aborad, aboral

   deformity: 7 harelip

   disease: 4 noma 6 canker 10 stomatitis

   muscle: 7 caninus

   of furnace: 6 bocca

   of river: 5 delta, firth

   part: lip 5 uvula 6 palate 7 pharynx

   pert. to: 4 oral 6 rictal 7 oscular, palatal 8 stomatic

   projecting: 5 spout

   roof: 6 palate

   tissue: gum

   toward: 4 orad

   with open: 5 agape

mouth organ: 9 harmonica

mouth-watering: 8 alluring 9 delicious, palatable

mouthful: lot, sup 4 bite, gulp 6 gobbet

mouthpiece: 5 bocal 6 lawyer 8 attorney

mouthwash: 9 collutory 10 antiseptic 11 collutorium

mouthy: 5 talky 9 bombastic, talkative

mouton: fur, spy 4 wool 6 lambskin 9 sheepskin

movable: 5 loose 6 fickle, mobile, motile 8 exorable, floating, unstable, unsteady 10 changeable, inconstant 11 ephelcystic 12 figuratively

move (see also go): go; act, gee, mog 4 goad, pass, play, spur, stir 5 budge, cause, clink, impel, rouse, shift, start, sweep 6 affect, arouse, behave, bestir, betake, excite, incite, induce, kindle, motion, prompt, quetch, remble, remove 7 actuate, advance, agitate, animate, attempt, inspire, migrate, propose, provoke, suggest 8 converse, emigrate, maneuver, motivate, transfer 9 influence, instigate, stimulate, stratagem *along:* mog 5 mosey, scram 7 maunder

away: shy 8 emigrate

back: ebb 6 recede 7 retreat

back and forth: wag 4 flap, rock, tack 5 dodge, weave 6 falter, teeter, wabble, wiggle, wigwag, zigzag 7 shuttle 9 oscillate

false: 4 balk 5 feint 7 misstep

first: 10 initiative

forward: 4 edge 5 drive, forge, surge 7 advance 8 progress

furtively: 5 skulk, slink, sneak

heaven and earth: try 6 strive

heavily: lug 6 lumber, trudge

in: 6 occupy 7 inhabit

in water: 4 swim, wade

noiselessly: 4 slip 5 creep, glide, skulk, slink, sneak, steal 6 tiptoe 9 pussyfoot

noisily: 6 bustle 7 clatter, rollick

obliquely: 4 edge, joll, skew, slue 5 sidle

on wheels: 4 roll 7 trundle

quickly: fly 4 dart, dash, flit, jump, leap, race, scud, scur, whir 5 bound, hurry, scoot, skirr, spank, start, sweep 6 career, gallop, hurtle, scurry, spring

restlessly: 6 kelter, twitch

rhythmically: bob, jig, jog 5 dance, march

round and round: 4 eddy 5 swirl, twirl

sinuously: 5 snake 6 writhe

slowly: lag, mog 5 edge, inch, worm 5 crawl 6 trudge 7 crowhop

smoothly: 4 slip 5 glide, skate, slide

together: 5 unite 8 converge

movement: act 5 tempo, trend 6 rhythm 7 gesture 8 activity 9 mechanism

biological: 5 taxis

capable of: 6 mobile, motile

music: 6 moto

surface: 6 seiche

movie: See motion picture

moving: 7 current 8 ambulant, pathetic, poignant, touching 9 affecting, transient 10 ambulatory, impressive

moving about: 8 ambulant 10 ambulatory

moving part: cam, cog 5 rotor, wheel

moving picture: See motion picture

moving staircase: 9 escalator

mow: bin, cut, lay, mew 4 barb, clip, heap, mass, pile 5 mouth, scowl, stack 6 scythe, sickle 7 grimace, shorten 8 haystack 9 cornfield

mowana: 6 baobab

Mowgli: *elephant:* 5 Hathi

friend: 5 Akela, Baloo

Mozart opera: 6 Figaro 10 Magic Flute 11 Don Giovanni 12 Cosi fan Tutte

much: 4 fele, high, lots, many 5 great, heaps, scads 6 mickle 7 gaylies, geylies, greatly 8 abundant, uncommon 9 great deal, multitude 10 all kinds of

music: 5 molto

Much Ado About Nothing character: 4 Hero 6 Ursula 7 Antonio, Claudio, Leonato

mucid: 5 moldy, musty, slimy 6 mucous

mucilage: gum 5 paste 6 arabin, mucago 8 adhesive

mucilaginous: 5 gluey, slimy 6 sticky, viscid 8 adhesive

muck: goo 4 dirt, dung, mess 5 botch, filth, money, slime, waste 6 manure, refuse, wealth 7 saunter 10 complicate

mucous: 5 moist, slimy 7 viscous 8 blennoid

mud fen 4 dirt, gore, mire, ooze, roil 5 slime, slush 6 sludge 7 clabber

deposit: 4 silt

hole: pan 6 puddle, wallow 8 quagmire

living in: 10 limicolous

pert to: 7 luteous

mud dab: 8 flounder

mud dabbler: 9 killfish

mud dauber: 4 wasp

mud devil: 10 hellbender

mud eel: 5 siren

mud lark: 5 gamin 6 magpie, urchin

mud mark: 7 mudflow

mud peep: 9 sandpiper

mud puppy: 7 dogfish 10 hellbender, salamander

mud snipe: 8 woodcock

mud sunfish: 4 bass

Mudcat State: 11 Mississippi

muddle: mix 4 ball, daze, doze, mess, roil 5 addle, besot, snafu 6 bemuse, burble, fuddle, jumble, pother 7 bedevil, blunder, confuse, fluster, mystify, perplex, stumble, stupefy 8 befuddle, bemuddle, bewilder, confound, disorder, flounder 9 confusion 10 complicate, intoxicate 12 hugger-mugger

muddled: ree 4 asea 5 beery, crazy, drunk, foggy, tipsy 10 incoherent

muddy: 4 miry, roil, soil 5 dirty, drovy, druvy, slaky, vague 6 claggy, clarty, clashy, cloudy, drubly, lutose, sludgy, slushy, turbid 7 clouded, guttery, obscure, sensual, squalid 8 confused, feculent 9 besmeared, spattered 11 bespattered

mudfish: 6 bowfin 9 killfish

mudhold: 4 slew, sloo, slue 6 slough

mudworm: ipo 9 earthworm

mudwort: 7 mudweed

muezzin's call to prayer: 4 adan, azan

muff: fur, vex 4 flub 5 crest, error 6 bungle, goof up, warmer 8 irritate

muffin: cob, gem 5 bread, scone 7 crumpet, popover

muffle: gag 4 damp, dull, mute, wrap 6 bumble, dampen, deaden, shroud, stifle 7 silence 8 envelope, suppress 10 camouflage

muffled: 6 hollow

muffler: 4 mask, mute 5 scarf 6 tippet 8 silencer

mufflin: 8 titmouse

mufti: 4 alim 8 assessor, civilian, clothing, official 9 expounder

mug: cup 4 cram, dupe, face, fool, toby 5 mouth, mungo, pulse, sheep, stein, study 6 noggin, seidel 7 assault, canette, drizzle, goddard, grimace, tankard 8 schooner 10 photograph

muga: 4 silk 11 caterpillar

mugger: ham 4 thug 6 emoter 7 puncher 9 assailant, crocodile

muggy: 4 damp 5 humid, moist, moldy

mugwet: 4 rose 8 woodruff

muir: 4 moor

mulatto: 5 metis 10 crossbreed, high yellow

mulberry bird: 8 starling

mulberry fig: 8 sycamore

mulch: 5 cover, straw 6 litter 7 compost, sawdust

mulct: 4 balk, fine, scot 5 cheat 6 amerce, defect, fleece, punish 7 blemish, deceive, defraud, forfeit, penalize 8 penalize 10 amercement, forfeiture

mule: 4 mewl, mool, mute 5 coble, hinny 6 hybrid 7 bat-mule, slipper, spinner, tractor 9 chilblain 10 locomotive

cry: 4 bray 6 heehaw

group: 5 atajo, drove

leader in pack train: 8 cencerro

male: 4 jack

spinning: 7 ironman

untrained: 9 shavetail

mule killer: 4 wasp 6 mantis 8 scorpion

muleteer: 4 peon 6 driver 7 arriero(Sp.), skinner 9 almocrebe

mulga: 6 acacia

mulish: 5 balky 6 hybrid, sullen 7 sterile 8 perverse, stubborn 9 obstinate, pigheaded 10 determined

mull: cow 4 crag, dust, heat, mess, mold, muse 5 cloth, crush, grind, snout, spice, think 6 fettle, muslin, muzzle, ponder, powder 7 crumble, failure, rubbish, squeeze, sweeten 8 cogitate, consider, ointment, snuffbox 9 pulverize 10 promontory

mullet: 8 food fish

mulligan: 4 stew

mulligatawny: 4 soup

mulligrubs: 5 blahs, blues, colic, sulks

mulloway: 6 maigre 7 jewfish

multicolored: 4 pied 6 calico 7 dappled, spotted

multifarious: 7 diverse 8 manifold

multifold: 4 many 8 manifold, numerous

multiform: 7 diverse

multiple: 4 many 6 plural 8 numerous

multiplier: 7 facient

multiply: 5 breed 6 spread 7 amplify, augment, magnify 8 increase 9 procreate, reproduce

by eight: 11 octuplicate

by ten: 7 decuple

multitude: mob 4 army, heap, hive, host, many, mass, much, ruck 5 cloud, crowd, drove, flock, horde, shoal, swarm 6 legion, myriad, nation, throng

multitudinous: 4 many 8 manifold, numerous 9 countless 10 numberless

mum: ale 4 beer, dark 5 still 6 mother, silent 7 silence 9 voiceless 10 speechless 13 chrysanthemum

mumble 4 chew, mump 5 mouth 6 chavel, chavle, faffle, fumble, haffle, murmur, mutter, palter, patter 7 flummer, grumble

mumbo-jumbo: 4 idol 6 fetich, fetish 7 bugaboo 9 gibberish

mummer: 4 mime 5 actor 6 guiser, player 7 buffoon 9 performer, puppeteer

mummery: 6 acting 8 puppetry 9 hypocrisy 10 hocus pocus 11 abracadabra

mummy: 5 relic 6 corpse 7 cadaver, carcass

mummy apple: 6 papaya

mump: 5 cheat, sulks 6 mumble, mutter 7 grimace 10 sullenness 11 displeasure

mumper: 6 beggar 8 impostor

mumps: 9 parotitis

munch: eat 4 chew 5 champ 6 growse, growze

mundane: 6 cosmic 7 earthly, prosaic, secular, terrene, worldly 8 temporal 11 terrestrial

municipality: 4 city, town 7 cabildo

pert. to: 5 civic

munificent: 4 free 5 ample 6 lavish 7 liberal 8 generous 9 bounteous, bountiful 10 benevolent

munitions: 7 baggage, weapons 8 armament 10 ammunition

munity: 9 privilege

Munro's penname: 4 Saki

muntjac, muntjak: 4 deer 6 kidang

muraena: 5 moray

mural: 6 fresco 12 wall painting

murder: 4 bane, kill, slay 5 death 7 bump-off, butcher, carnage, killing, murther 8 foul play, homicide 9 slaughter 11 assassinate 12 manslaughter

brother: 10 fratricide

father: 9 patricide

fine: cro 7 wergild 9 bloodfine

infant: 11 infanticide

king: 8 regicide

mother: 9 matricide

own child: 9 prolicide

parent: 9 parricide

prophet: 8 vaticide

sister: 10 sororicide

son or daughter: 8 filicide
spouse: 10 mariticide
wife: 9 uxoricide
woman: 8 femicide
murderous: 4 gory 5 felon 6 bloody, brutal, deadly 7 ruinous 9 ferocious, homicidal 10 sanguinary 12 bloodthirsty
mure: 6 shut up, thrust 7 squeeze 8 imprison
murid: rat 5 mouse 6 rodent
murky: dim 4 dark 5 black, dense, foggy, mirky, misty, mucky, thick 6 cloudy, gloomy 7 obscure 12 impenetrable
murmur: coo, hum, pur 4 curr, fret, huzz, purl, purr, sugh 5 brool, drone, grank, sough 6 babble, grutch, hummer, mumble, mutter, repine, report 7 grumble, whisper 8 complain 9 grumbling
nasal: hum
murphy: 6 potato
Musa: 6 banana
muscadine: 5 grape
muscle: 4 beef, thew 5 brawn, flesh, force, power, sinew, teres 6 lacert 8 strength
affliction: 5 crick 6 abasia, ataxia
bound: 6 rigid, stiff
column: 10 sarcostyle
contracting: 7 agonist
curve: 7 myogram
expansion: 7 dilator
lifting: 7 levator
limb-straightening: 8 extensor
round: 5 teres
segment: 8 myocomma
spasm: 5 tonus
straight: 6 rectus
stretching: 6 tensor
sugar: 7 inosite 8 inositol
trapezius: 10 cucullaris
triangular: 7 deltoid
turning: 7 evertor, rotator
two-headed: 6 biceps
muscovado: 7 raw sugar
Muscovite: Red 4 mica, Russ 7 Russian
mica: 4 talc
prince: 4 Ivan
muscular: 4 ropy, wiry 5 thewy 6 brawny, robust, sinewy, strong, torose, torous 7 fibrous, stringy 8 athletic, vigorous
muse: 4 dump, mull, poet, 5 dream, think 6 loiter, ponder, trifle 7 reflect, reverie 8 cogitate, consider, meditate, ruminate 9 amusement 10 meditation 11 contemplate
Muse: 4 Clio 5 Erato 6 Thalia, Urania 7 Euterpe 8 Calliope, Pierides, Polymnia 9 Melpomene 10 Polyhymnia 11 Terpsichore
birthplace: 6 Pieria
epithet: 7 Pierian
father: 4 Zeus

fountain: 8 Aganippe
home: 5 Aonia 7 Helicon
mother: 9 Mnemosyne
mountain: 9 Parnassus
of astronomy: 6 Urania
of comedy: 6 Thalia
of dancing: 11 Terpsichore
of eloquence: 8 Calliope
of epic poetry: 8 Calliope
of history 4 Clio
of love poetry: 5 Erato
of lyric poetry: 5 Erato
of music: 7 Euterpe
of pastoral poetry: 6 Thalia
of sacred poetry: 8 Polymnia 10 Polyhymnia
of tragedy: 9 Melpomene
seat of worship: 6 Pieria
museful: 6 silent 10 meditative, thoughtful
musery: 4 play 9 amusement
musette: air 4 oboe 7 bagpipe, gavotte
museum: 7 gallery, preserve 10 collection repository
custodian: 7 curator
director: 7 curator
mush: cut 5 atole, crush, gruel, march, notch, sepon 6 indent, sepawn, supawn, travel 7 confuse, journey, pudding, suppawn 8 flattery, porridge, sagamite, umbrella 14 sentimentality
mushroom: 4 grow 6 agaric, spread 7 explode, parvenu, upstart
cap: 6 pileus
disease: 5 flock
edible: 5 morel 10 champignon 11 chanterelle
like: 7 fungous
part of: 4 gill 5 stipe, trama 6 pileus 7 annulus 8 basidium, hymenium, sterigma 12 basidiospore
poisoning: 8 mycetism
poisonous: 7 amanita 9 toadstool
stem: 5 stipe
mushy: 4 hazy, soft, weak 5 gushy, thick 8 effusive, yielding 11 sentimental
music (see also **melody, song,** and entries under **musical**): air, art 4 tune 7 harmony
aftersong: 5 epode
beat: 5 ictus, pulse, tempo 6 rhythm
change to another key: 10 modulation 13 transposition
chord: 5 triad
flourish: 7 roulade
for eight: 5 octet
for five: 7 quintet
for four: 7 quartet
for nine: 5 nonet
for one: 4 soli, solo
for seven: 6 septet
for six: 6 sextet 7 sestole 8 sestolet

for three: 4 trio
for two: duo 4 duet
god: 6 Apollo
half tone: 8 semitone
machine for: 5 radio 7 juke-box, pianola 8 musicbox 10 gramophone, phonograph
major scale: 5 gamut
major third: 6 ditone
mania for: 9 melomania
melodic phrase: 9 leitmotif, leitmotiv
morning song: 6 aubade
muse: 7 Euterpe
notation system: 5 neume
outdoor: 6 aubade 8 serenade
patron saint: 7 Cecilia
pert. to chance elements: 9 aleatoric
simple song: air, lay 4 tune
symbol: bar, key, tie 4 clef, flat, note, rest, slur 5 brace, sharp, staff
syncopated: 4 jazz
theme: 4 tema
timing device: 4 metronome
music hall: 4 gaff, odea(pl.) 5 odeum, odeon
musical: 4 show 5 lyric, revue 7 lyrical, melodic 8 harmonic, rhythmic 9 melodious 10 harmonious
musical composition: 4 glee, opus 5 cento, fugue, opera, rondo 6 ballad, sonata 7 ballade, boutade, cantata, chanson, prelude, scherzo, virelai 8 berceuse, concerto, nocturne, operetta, oratorio, serenata, serenade, sonatina, symphony 9 cabaletta, interlude 10 intermezzo
aria-like: 6 arioso
choral: 5 motet 7 chorale 9 plainsong
dancer's: 10 gymnopedie
dawn: 6 aubade
declamatory: 10 recitative
ending: 4 coda, fine 6 finale
exercise: 5 etude, study
feature: 5 motif, theme
folk song: 4 lied
interlude: 6 verset
jazz: rag 4 jive 5 bebop, blues, swing 7 ragtime 11 rock-and-roll 12 boogie-woogie
opera: 5 scena
poetic: ode
prelude: 6 verset
religious: 4 mass 5 motet, psalm 6 anthem 7 cantata 8 oratorio
round: 5 canon, fugue, troll
suite: 7 partita
musical direction: *above:* 5 sopra
accented: 7 marcato 8 sforzato 9 sforzando
again: DC, DS; bis 6 da capo 8 dal segno
all: 5 tutti
always: 6 sempre
animated: 7 animato 9 spiritoso

ardent: 7 ardente 12 appassionato
as written: sta
begin now: 7 attacca
below: 5 sotto
bold: 6 audace
bowed: 4 arco
bright: 5 anime
cold: 6 freddo
continue: va
devout: 6 divoto
dignified: 8 maestoso
disconnected: 8 staccato
dying away: 7 calando
emotional: 12 appassionato
evenly: 10 eugalmente
everyone's: 5 tutti
excited: 7 agitato 9 spiritoso
fast: 4 vivo 5 tosto 6 presto, veloce, vivace 7 allegro 10 tostamente
faster: 7 stretto
freely: 9 ad libitum
furious: 7 furioso
gay: 7 giocoso
gentle: 5 dolce
half: 5 mezzo
heavy: 7 pesante
held: 6 tenuto
hurried: 7 agitato
in the style of: 4 alla
joyous: 7 giocoso
leap: 5 salto
less: 4 meno
little: 4 poco
little by little: 9 poco a poco
lively: 6 vivace 7 allegro, animato, giocoso
loud: 5 forte 10 fortissimo
louder: 9 crescendo
lovingly: 7 amabile, amoroso
lyric: 5 erato
majestic: 8 maestoso
marked: 7 marcato
moderate: 7 andante 8 moderato
more: piu
more rapid: 7 stretta, stretto
much: 5 molto
muted: 5 sorda
passionless: 6 freddo
plaintive: 7 dolente
playful: 7 giocoso 10 scherzando
plucked: 9 pizzicato
proceed: va
quick: 4 vite 5 tosto 6 presto 7 schnell
quick time: 9 alla breve
quickening: 11 affrettando
repeat: bis 6 ancoro 7 ripresa
sadly: 7 dolente 8 doloroso
sharp: 8 staccato 9 sforzando
silent: 5 tacet
singing: 9 cantabile
sliding: 9 glissando
slow: 5 grave, largo, lento, tardo 6 adagio 7 andante 9 larghetto

slower: rit 6 ritard 10 ritardando
slowing: 11 rallentando
smooth: 6 legato 8 grazioso
so much: 5 tanto
soft: 5 dolce, piano 10 pianissimo
softer: 10 diminuendo 11 decrescendo
solemn: 5 grave
somewhat: 4 poco
spirited: 7 animato 9 spiritoso
stately: 7 pomposo 8 maestoso
strong: 5 forte 10 fortissimo
sustained: 6 tenuto 9 sostenuto, susten-
uto
sweet: 5 dolce
tempo irregular: 6 rubato
tender: 7 amabile
thrice: ter
throughout: 6 sempre
together: 8 ensemble
too much: 6 troppo
tranquil: 7 calmato
turn: 9 gruppetto
twice: bis
very: tre 4 tres 5 assai, molto 7 dimolto
with: con
musical disc: 6 cymbal, record 9 recording
musical drama: 5 opera 8 operetta, oratorio 9 singspiel
musical event: 5 opera 6 ballet 7 concert, recital 8 musicale, oratorio
musical instrument: 4 drum, fife, gong,
harp, horn, lute, lyre, oboe, reed, tuba 5
banjo, flute, organ, piano, viola 6 cornet, guitar, spinet, violin 7 bassoon, ocarina, piccolo, saxhorn, trumpet, ukelele
8 castanet, clarinet, dulcimer, mandolin, trombone 9 euphonium, flageolet,
saxophone 11 violoncello
aid: 4 pick 8 diapason, plectrum 9 metronome, pitch pipe
ancient: 4 asor 5 rocta 6 rappel, sebaca 7
cithara, serpent 9 pantaleon
bass: 5 cello 11 violoncello
brass: 4 horn, tuba 5 bugle 6 tromba 7
althorn, helicon, saxhorn, trumpet 8 altohorn, trombone 10 French horn
China: kin
East Indies: 4 bina
Egypt: 7 sistrum
helicon: 4 tuba
Java: 7 gamelon 8 gamelang
keyboard: 5 organ, piano 6 spinet 7 celesta, clavier 8 melodeon 9 accordion 10
clavichord, concertina, pianoforte 11
harpsichord
lute-like: 7 angelot, bandore, cithern, cittern 9 bandurria 10 colascione
lyre-like: 4 asor 6 cither, zither, 7 cithara,
kithara
medieval: 5 rebab, rocta 7 chrotta 10
clavichord, hurdy-gurdy

Mexico: 5 guiro 6 clarin 7 cabacas, maracas 11 chiapanecas
mouthpiece: 4 reed 6 fipple
oboe-like: 5 shawm 7 musette
old: 5 rebec 7 cittern, gittern
percussion: 4 drum, gong 5 bells, traps 6
maraca 7 cymbals, marimba timpani,
tympani 8 bass drum, castanet, triangle
9 snare drum, xylophone 10 kettledrum, tambourine 12 glockenspiel
piano-like: see *keyboard* above
reed: 4 oboe 7 bassoon 8 clarinet 9 harmonica, saxophone 11 English horn
six-stringed: 6 guitar
stringed: oud, uke 4 asor, bass, harp, lute,
lyre, viol, vina 5 banjo, cello, rebec,
ruana, viola 6 citole, fiddle, guitar, rebeck, violin, zither 7 bandore, cythara,
gittern, pandura, samisen, theorbo, ukelele 8 autoharp, dulcimer, mandolin 11
harpsichord, violoncello
supplementary: 7 theorbo
two-necked: 7 ripieno
viol-like: 5 rebec, ruana 6 rebeck 7 claviol
8 claviole
wind: jub, sax 4 fife, horn, oboe, reed,
tuba 5 brass, bugle, flute, organ 6 cornet 7 althorn, bagpipe, bassoon, clarion,
ocarina, panpipe, piccolo, saxhorn, serpent, trumpet 8 altohorn, clarinet, recorder, trombone, zampogna 9 flageolet,
harmonica, saxophone 10 French horn
11 sarrusphone
xylophone-like: 7 marimba
without electronic sound: 8 acoustic
musical interval: 5 fifth, major, minor,
sixth, third 6 ditone, fourth, octave,
second, unison 7 perfect, seventh, tri-
tone 9 augmented 10 diminished
musical medley: 4 olio 5 cento
musical note (see also **musical syllable**):
5 breve, minim, neume 6 quaver 9
semibreve
musical piece: See **musical composition, song**
musical program: 5 opera 7 concert, recital 8 musicale
musical rhythm: 4 beat, time 5 ictus,
meter, pulse, swing, tempo
measuring device: 9 metronome
musical scale (see also **musical syllable**): 5 gamut
musical sign: 5 segno
entrance: 5 presa
hold: 7 fermata, formata
key: 4 flat 5 sharp 7 natural
pitch level: 4 clef
silence: 4 rest
slur: 8 ligature
smooth: 4 slur
staff: bar
musical syllable: Ela, sol 7 alamire

musical term: *arrangement:* **7** ridotto
ballad style: **8** a ballata
between acts: **8** entracte
cadence: **4** half **6** plagal **7** perfect **9** deceptive, imperfect
chapel-style: **9** a cappella
dance-style: **7** da ballo
embellishment: **8** ornament **9** fioritura **12** appoggiatura
ending: **4** coda
florid: **7** bravura
flourish: **7** cadenza
half note: **5** minim
half tone: **8** semitone
major key: dur
melodic phrase: **5** motif **9** leitmotif, leitmotiv
melos: **4** song **6** melody
minor key: **4** moll
movement: **4** moto
note: **5** breve, neume
refrain: **5** epode **8** repetend
repeat: **5** rondo **7** reprise
run: **6** volata **9** glissando
shake: **5** trill **7** tremolo
soft pedal: VC **7** celeste
third: **6** tierce
thirty-second note: **14** demisemiquaver
three-note chord: **5** triad
time: See **musical rhythm**
tones: **5** chord
tremble: **5** trill **7** tremolo, vibrato
triplet: **6** tercet, triole
two notes: **5** duole
unaccompanied: **9** a cappella
upbeat: **5** arsis
vocal part: **5** canto
musical theme: **4** tema **5** motif **9** leitmotif, leitmotiv
musician: **4** bard **5** piper **6** player, singer **7** drummer, flutist, gleeman, pianist **8** bandsman, composer, flautist, minstrel, organist, virtuoso **9** cornetist, performer, serenader, violinist **10** trombonist **11** clarinetist, saxophonist
group: **4** band, duet, trio **5** choir, nonet **6** chorus, septet, sextet **7** nonetto, quartet **8** ensemble, septette, sextette **9** orchestra, quartette
patron saint: **7** Cecelia
musing: **7** reverie **10** meditation, meditative **13** contemplation
musk: **4** deer **7** perfume
musk beaver: **7** muskrat
musk cat: **5** civet
musk cavy: **5** hutia
musk cucumber: **11** cassabanana
musk deer: **6** cervid **10** chevrotain
musk mallow: **8** abelmosk
musk shrew: **6** desman
muskeg: bog **5** marsh
muskellunge: **4** pike

musket: **4** hawk **5** fusil **6** falcon **7** bundock, bundook, dragoon, firearm **8** biscayen **9** flintlock
Musketeers: See **Three Musketeers**
muskmelon: **6** atimon, casaba **10** cantaloupe
muskrat: **5** shrew **6** desman
Muslim, Moslem (see also **Islam, Mohammed**): **4** Moro **6** Paynim **7** abadite, Islamic, Saracen **9** Mahometan, Mussulman **10** Mohammedan
ablution: **4** widu, wudu, wuzu
Alexandria sect: **6** Senusi
angel: **6** Azrael **7** isrefel, israfil **8** israfeel
annual fast: **7** Ramadan
antenuptial settlement: **4** mahr
ascetic: **4** sufi **5** fakir **6** fakeer
bazaar: **4** sook
beads: **6** tasbih
belt: **5** zonar **6** zonnar
Berber dynasty: **6** Hafsid **7** Hafsite
Bible: **5** Coran, Koran **7** Alcoran
bier: **5** tabut
blood relationship: **5** nasab
calendar: **5** Rabia, Rajab, Safar **6** Jumada, Shaban **7** Ramadan, Shawwal **8** Zu'lhijah, Zu'lkadah **9** Mulharram
call to prayer: **4** adan, azan
cap: taj **5** kulah **6** kullah
caravansary: **6** imaret
caste: **5** mopla **6** moplah
chief: **4** rais, sidi **5** datto, syid, sheik
city (sacred): **5** Mecca **6** Medina
coin: **5** dinar
convert: **5** ansar
council: **5** Ulema
creed: **5** Sunna
crusade: **5** jehad, jihad
decree: **5** irade
deity: **5** Allah, Eblis
demon: **5** afrit, eblis, jinni **6** jinnee
dervish: **6** Sadite, Santon
divorce: **5** ahsan, talak **7** mubarat
fast days: **7** Ramadan
festival: Eed **6** Bairam
freethinker: **7** Saracen **9** Aladinist
garment: **4** izar **6** jubbah
god: **5** Allah
guide (spiritual): pir
headdress: fez, taj **5** kulah **6** kullah, turban
hermit: **8** marabout
holy book: **5** Koran
holy city: **5** Mecca **6** Medina
holy war: **5** jehad, jihad
infidel: **5** kafir **6** kaffir
judge: **4** cadi, cazi, imam, kazi **5** hakim, imaum
kinship: **5** nasab
lady: **5** begum
law: **5** halal **7** sheriat
lawyer: **5** mufti

leader: 4 amir, emir 5 ameer, emeer
men's quarters: 8 selamlik
messiah: 5 Mahdi
minaret crier: 7 muezzin
minister of state: 6 vizier
monastery: 5 tekke
month: see *calendar* above
mosque: 6 masjid
mystic: 4 Sufi
mysticism: 6 Sufism
name: Ali
nymph: 5 houri
officer: aga
official: 6 hajib, mufti
orthodox: 5 hanif 7 Sunnite
people: Laz 4 Lazi, Moro, Sufi, Swat 5
    Hanif, Isawa, Salar, Samal, Sunni,
    Swati 6 Dehgan, Senusi 7 Bazigar,
    Senousi, Senussi 8 Senusite 9 Senus-
    sian
physician: 5 hakim 6 hakeem
pilgrim: 4 haji 5 hadji, hajji
pilgrimage: 4 hadj
pilgrim's dress: 5 ihram
prayer: 5 namaz, salat
prayer call: 4 adan, azan
priest: 4 imam 5 imaum 6 wahabi
priests (body): 5 ulema
prince: 4 amir, emir, seid 5 ameer, emeer,
    nawab, sayid
princess: 4 tola 5 begum
religion: 5 Islam
ruler: aga 4 amir, emir 5 ameer, emeer,
    hakim, nawah 6 hakeem, sultan
saber: 7 yatagan 8 scimitar, scimiter, yat-
    aghan
sacred book: see *Bible* above
saint: Pir 5 Abdal 6 Santon 8 Marabout
salutation: 5 salam 6 salaam
sect: 5 Isawa 6 Wahabi 7 Abadite, der-
    vish, Sunnite 8 Ahmadiya, Sifatite
shrine: 5 Kaaba 6 Kaabeh
spirit: 4 jinn(pl.), 5 genie, jinni 7 jinnyeh
spiritual adviser: pir
student: 5 softa
supreme being: 5 Allah
teacher: 4 alim, imam 8 mujtahid
title: sid 4 said, sidi 5 nawab, sayid 6 say-
    yid
tomb: 5 tabut
warrior: 7 Saracen
washing: 4 widu, wudu, wuzu
women's quarters: 5 harem
muslin: 4 mull 6 cotton 7 organdy 8
    nainsook, seerhand, sheeting
muss: See **mess**
mussel: 4 unio 5 naiad 6 mucket, nerita 8
    deerhorn
    genus of: 8 modiolus
    larva: 9 blackhead
    part: 6 byssus
mussitate: 6 mutter

Mussolini: 7 Fascist 8 dictator
    son-in-law: 5 Ciano
    title: 6 Il Duce
Mussulman: See **Muslim**
must: 4 bood, mold, musk, sapa, stum,
    want 5 juice, ought, shall 6 refuse 9
    have got to 10 obligation
mustang: 5 horse, pinto 6 bronco 7 bron-
    cho
mustard: 5 nigra, senvy 6 senapi 7 cad-
    lock 8 charlock
    chemical: 5 allyl
    family: 12 brassicaceae
    genus of: 7 sinapis
    pod: 7 silicle
mustard plaster: 8 poultice, sinapism
musteline animal: 6 weasel
muster: 4 call 5 erect 6 gather, roster,
    sample, summon 7 collect, marshal,
    pattern 8 assemble, generate, mobilize
    10 accumulate, congregate
    out: 7 disband, release 9 discharge
mustiness: 4 fust, mold
musty: 4 dull, sour 5 dirty, fusty, hoary,
    moldy, rafty, stale, trite 6 filthy, rancid
    7 foughty, spoiled, squalid 10 antiquat-
    ed
Mut: *child of:* 5 Chons
    husband: 4 Amen, Amon
mutable: 6 fickle 8 unstable, variable 9
    alterable 10 changeable, inconstant 11
    fluctuating, vacillating
mutate: 4 vary 5 alter 6 change, modify 9
    transform
mutation: 6 change, revolt 9 posthouse
    10 revolution, succession 11 vicissi-
    tude
mute: mum 4 dumb, lene, surd 6 deaden,
    muffle, silent 7 mourner, muffler 8
    deadener, silencer 9 voiceless 10
    speechless 12 inarticulate
mutilate: mar 4 hack, hurt, maim 6 dam-
    age, deface, garble, injure, mangle, mitt-
    le(Sc.) 7 cripple, destroy 9 disfigure,
    dismember, sterilize
mutinous: 6 unruly 9 alienated, seditious,
    turbulent 10 rebellious, refractory, tu-
    multuous 11 disaffected, disobedient,
    intractable 12 contumacious 13 insub-
    ordinate
mutiny: 6 revolt, strife 9 commotion 12
    insurrection
mutt: cur, dog 5 dunce 7 mongrel 9 block-
    head
mutter: 5 growl, rumor 6 mumble, mur-
    mur, patter 7 channer, grumble, maun-
    der 9 mussitate
mutton: 4 meat 5 sheep 6 candle 10 pros-
    titute
    dried: 5 vifda, vivda
    leg: 5 cabob, gigot 7 wabbler, wobbler
muttonbird: oii 6 petrel 10 shearwater

muttonchop: 7 whisker 8 burnside, sideburn

muttonfish: 4 sama 5 pargo, porgy 7 eelpout, mojarra

muttonhead: 5 dunce 9 blockhead, screwball

mutual: 6 common 7 related 10 associated, reciprocal, responsive

mutuality: 13 interrelation

mux: 4 mess 5 botch

muzhik: 7 peasant

muzzle: gag 4 face, grub, nose, root 5 snout 6 clevis, muffle 7 sheathe 8 restrain 10 respirator

muzzy: 4 dull 5 fuzzy 7 blurred, muddled 8 confused 9 befuddled 10 depressive

My Last Duchess author: 8 Browning

mycoid: 7 fungoid

myna: 4 bird 7 grackle

myomorph: rat 5 mouse 6 rodent

myopic: 8 purblind 10 astigmatic 11 nearsighted 12 shortsighted

myriad: 4 host 9 countless 11 innumerable 13 multitudinous

myriapod: 9 centipede

myrmicid: ant

myrmidon: 8 adherent, follower, henchman 9 attendant, underling

myrrh: gum 4 tree 5 resin

myrtle: 6 laurel 8 ramarama 10 periwinkle 11 candleberry

myself: 5 masel(Sc.)

mysterious: dim 4 dark 5 runic 6 arcane, mystic, occult, secret 7 cryptic, strange, uncanny 8 abstruse 9 enigmatic, equivocal, recondite, sphinxine 12 inexplicable, unfathomable

mystery: 4 rune 5 craft, trade 6 cabala, enigma, puzzle, riddle, secret 7 arcanum, esotery, stumper 8 thriller, whodunit 10 closed book 11 brain twister

mystery novel award: 5 Edgar

mystic: 4 seer 5 epopt, magic, runic 6 occult, orphic, secret 7 cryptic, epoptic, obscure 8 anagogic, esoteric, symbolic 9 enigmatic, recondite 10 cabalistic, mysterious

art: 6 cabala

initiate: 5 epopt

Moslem: 4 Sufi

secret sect: 5 cabal

word: 4 evoe 7 abraxas 10 hocus pocus, open sesame 11 abracadabra

mystical: 4 dark 6 occult, secret 8 anagogic, hush-hush, symbolic, telestic 9 spiritual

significance: 7 anagoge

mysticism: 6 cabala 8 cabalism

mystify: 5 befog 6 muddle, puzzle 7 becloud, confuse, perplex 8 befuddle, bewilder 9 bamboozle, obfuscate

myth: 4 saga, tale 5 fable, fancy, story 6 legend 7 parable 9 apocrypha

mythical: 6 famous, unreal 9 imaginary, fabricated 10 fictitious

N

nab: 4 grab 5 catch, seize 6 arrest, clutch, snatch 7 capture 9 apprehend

Nabal: *home:* 4 Maon

wife: 7 Abigail

nabob: 5 nawab 6 bigwig, deputy 7 rich man, viceroy 8 governor 9 personage, plutocrat 10 viceregent 11 billionaire

Nabokov novel: Ada 4 Pnin 6 Lolita

nacelle: 7 shelter 11 compartment

nacket: boy 4 cake 5 lunch

nacre: 8 lustrous 9 shellfish 10 conchiolin, iridescent 13 mother-of-pearl

nadir's opposite: 6 zenith

nag: tit 4 frab, fret, gnaw, jade, plug, pony, twit 5 annoy, cobra, hobby, horse, scold, snake, tease 6 badger, berate, bother, carp at, harass, heckle, hector, padnag, pester, wanton 7 hackney, henpeck 8 harangue, irritate 9 aggravate

naga, nag: 5 cobra, snake

nagor: 8 antelope, reedbuck

Nahor: *father:* 5 Serug

grandson: 7 Abraham

son: 5 Terah

wife: 6 Milcah

Nahuatlan: 5 Aztec

naiad: 5 nymph 6 mussel

naif: See **naive**

nail: cut, fix, hob 4 brad, brag, brod, claw, cloy, dump, spad, stub, stud, tack, trap 5 affix, catch, clout, grope, seize, spike, sprig, steal 6 clinch, detain, fasten, hammer, secure, strike, unguis, ungula 7 capture 8 fastener, sparable, spikelet 9 finishing, intercept

drive at a slant: toe

headless: 5 sprig

ingrowing: 7 acronyx

marking on: 6 lunule

perforated: 4 spad

shoemaker's: 4 brad 8 sparable

nais: 5 naiad, nymph

naissance: 5 birth

naive: 6 candid, simple 7 artless, natural 8 childish, foolish, gullible, innocent, trusting, untaught 9 childlike, guileless, ingenuous, untutored, unworldly 10 unaffected 13 inexperienced, unphilosophic 15 unsophisticated

naked: 4 bare, nude, open 6 cuerpo 7 evident, exposed, obvious 8 manifest 9 au naturel, disclosed, unadorned, unclothed, uncovered, discovered 11 defenseless, unprotected

namaycush: 5 lunge, togue, trout

namby-pamby: 7 insipid 8 weakling 10 wishy-washy 11 sentimental

name: dub, nom(F.) 4 call, idol, term 5 claim, clepe, count, nemme, nemne, neven, nomen, style, title 6 adduce, appeal, monica, select 7 appoint, baptize, entitle, epithet, mention, moniker 8 christen, delegate, identify, identity, nominate 9 designate, personage 10 denominate, denotation, reputation 11 appellation, designation, give a handle 12 denomination, nomenclature

added: 6 agname 7 agnomen

assumed: 5 alias 6 anonym 9 incognito, pseudonym, sobriquet 10 nom de plume, soubriquet

backwards: 6 ananym

based on location: 7 toponym

Biblical: See **Bible:** *name*

derivation: 7 eponymy

family: 7 eponymy, sirname, surname 8 cognomen

fictitious: 9 pseudonym

first: 9 praenomen

list: 11 onomasticon

maiden: nee

objectionable: 7 caconym

pet: 8 nickname 9 sobriquet

tablet: 5 facia

nameable: 6 famous 7 notable 9 memorable 10 noteworthy

named: 6 yclept

nameless: 7 bastard, obscure 9 anony-

mous, unnamable 12 illegitimate 13 indescribable, unmentionable

namely: viz 5 id est, noted, to wit 6 famous 8 scilicet 9 expressly, videlicet 10 especially 12 specifically

namesake: 6 junior

Namibia: 15 Southwest Africa

nandu: nandow 4 rhea

nanism: 12 dwarfishness

nanny: 4 goat 5 nurse

nanny plum: 10 sheepberry

Naomi: 4 Mara

daughter-in law: 4 Ruth 5 Orpah

husband: 9 Elimelech

son: 6 Mahlon 7 Chilion

naos: 5 cella 6 shrine, temple

nap: nod 4 calk, doze, fuzz, lint, pile, rest, shag, wink 5 fluff, grasp, let up, seize, sleep, steal 6 siesta, snooze 7 respite 10 forty winks

nape: nod 5 nucha, nuque 6 scruff 7 niddick

napery: 5 linen

Naphtali: *census taker:* 4 Enan

mother: 6 Bilhah

son: 4 Guni 5 Jezer 7 Jahziel, Shallum

naphtha: 9 petroleum

napkin: 5 cloth, doily, towel 6 diaper 8 kerchief 9 handcloth, serviette 11 neckerchief 12 handkerchief

Naples: *biscuit:* 10 ladyfinger

coin: 6 carlin 7 carline

king: 5 Murat

secret society: 7 Camorra

napless: 10 threadbare

napoleon: 4 coin 6 pastry

Napoleon: *battle:* Ulm 4 Acre, Jena, Lodi 7 Dresden, Marengo 8 Borodino, Waterloo 10 Austerlitz

birthplace: 7 Corsica

brother: 5 Louis 6 Jerome, Joseph, Lucien

brother-in-law: 5 Murat

island of exile: 4 Elba

marshal: Ney 5 Murat, Soult 6 Suchet

nickname: 5 Boney

place of victory: 5 Ligny 10 Austerlitz

sister: 5 Elisa, Maria 8 Carlotta, Carolina

wife: 9 Josephine

nappy: ale 4 dish 5 downy, heady, wooly 6 liquor, strong 7 foaming 8 textured 11 intoxicated

napu: 7 deerlet 10 chevrotain

narcissistic: 4 vain 9 stuck-up 9 conceited 12 vainglorious

narcotic (see also **marijuana**)**:** kat 4 bang, dope, junk 5 bhang, dagga, ether, opium 6 heroin, opiate 7 anodyne, cocaine, hashish 8 hasheesh, hypnotic, morphine, takrouri 9 soporific 10 belladonna, hyoscyamus, stramonium

agent: 4 narc

dose: 5 locus
package: 4 deck 6 bindle
plant: kat 4 coca, cuca, hemp, kaat, khat 5 dutra, poppy
seller: 6 pusher 7 peddler
nard: 5 spice 6 anoint 7 rhizome 9 spikenard
nardoo: 5 plant 6 clover
nargileh: 4 pipe 5 hooka 6 hookah
nark: spy, vex 5 annoy 8 informer, irritate 10 spoilsport 11 stool pigeon
narrate: 4 tell 5 state 6 detail, recite, relate, report 7 descant, discuss, recount 8 describe, rehearse 9 chronicle, discourse, expatiate
narrative: 4 epic, myth, saga, tale, yarn 5 conte, drama, fable, story 6 legend 7 account, episode, history, parable 8 allegory, anecdote 9 narration
narrator: 9 reconteur
narrow: 4 mean 5 close, scant, sound, taper 6 biased, linear, little, meager, meagre, strait, strict 7 bigoted, limited 8 condense, contract 9 constrict, hidebound, illiberal, niggardly, parochial 10 inexorable, inflexible, prejudiced, restricted, straighten, ungenerous 11 reactionary 12 parsimonious 13 circumscribed
narrowminded: 6 biased 7 bigoted
narsinga: 7 trumpet
narthex: 5 porch 7 portico 9 vestibule 10 antetemple
nary: 5 never 6 not any
nasal: 6 narine, rhinal, twangy
nascency: 5 birth 6 origin 7 genesis 9 beginning
naseberry: 9 sapodilla
nasi: 9 patriarch
nasicorn: 10 rhinoceros
nasty: bad 4 foul, mean, ugly 5 dirty 6 filthy 7 harmful, obscene, squalid 8 indecent 9 dangerous, malicious, offensive 10 disgusting, ill-natured, malicious, nauseating, unpleasant 12 disagreeable, dishonorable 13 objectionable
natal: 6 inborn, innate, native 7 gluteal 13 congenital
natant: 6 afloat 8 floating, swimming
natator: 7 swimmer
natatorium: 4 bath, pool
natchbone: 7 hipbone 9 aitchbone
nation: 4 host, race 5 caste, class, state 6 people 7 country 8 community, multitude
symbol: 4 flag 5 crest
national: 7 citizen, federal, subject 11 gentiliation
National Guard member: 10 militiaman
native: 5 natal 6 genial, inborn, innate,

normal 7 citizen, endemic, natural 8 domestic, inherent, original, resident 9 aborigine, congenial, ingrained, unbranded, unrefined 10 congenital, indigenous, inhabitant
nativity: 5 birth 8 geniture 9 horoscope
natrium: 6 sodium
natty: 4 chic, neat, tidy, trig, trim 5 smart 6 spruce 10 fastidious
natural: 4 born, easy, open, fool, wild 5 usual 6 candid, common, cretin, inborn, inbred, innate, native, normal 7 general, regular 8 inherent, ordinary, physical 9 primitive, unassumed, unfeigned 10 congenital 13 unenlightened
dice: 5 seven
naturalize: 5 adopt 8 accustom 9 acclimate 11 acclimatize, domesticate, familiarize
nature: 4 kind, sort, type 5 shape 6 figure 7 essence 8 universe 9 character, framework, structure 11 disposition, temperament
divinity: 5 nymph
god: Pan
goddess: 6 Cybele 7 Artemis
same: 10 homogeneal
naught: 4 evil, zero 5 aught, ought 6 cipher, nought, wicked 7 nothing, useless 9 worthless
naughty: bad 4 evil 5 wrong 6 unruly, wicked 7 obscene, wayward, willful 8 improper 10 indelicate 11 disobedient, mischievous
naupathia: 11 seasickness
Nauru: 13 Pacific island
bay: 7 Anibare
capital: 5 Yaren
former name: 15 Pleasant Island
monetary unit: 6 dollar
nausea: 4 pall 7 disgust 8 loathing, sickness 10 queasiness
nauseating: 5 nasty, waugh 7 fulsome 8 brackish 9 loathsome, offensive, sickening 10 disgusting 11 distasteful
nautical (see also **navigation**)**:** 5 naval 6 marine 7 oceanic 8 maritime
cry: 4 ahoy
flag: 6 cornet, pennon
instrument: aba 7 compass, sextant
mile: 4 knot
term: 4 atry 5 abaft, abeam, alist, avast
nautilus: 7 mollusk 9 argonauta
Navaho hut: 5 hogan
naval stores: tar 5 pitch 8 supplies 10 turpentine
nave: hob, hub, nef 4 apse, axle, body, fist 5 aisle, nieve 6 center 10 church part
navel: 6 orange 9 umbilicus 11 belly button
navigate: 4 keel, sail 5 steer 6 direct, manage 7 journey, operate

navigation: 7 nautics, voyage 8 cabotage 10 seamanship
call: 4 ahoy 5 avast, belay
hazard: fog, sub 4 mine 9 submarine
instrument: aba 7 compass, pelorus, sextant
measure: ton 4 knot, seam 6 fathom 7 renning, sea mile 12 cable's length
signal: 4 bell, flag
term: 4 atry 5 abeam, atrip
navigator: 5 flyer, pilot 6 airman 7 aviator, copilot, laborer 8 aeronaut, seafarer, spaceman
navite: 6 basalt
navvy: 4 hand 6 worker 7 laborer 9 navigator
navy: 5 fleet
board: 9 admiralty
depot: 4 base
force: 5 fleet 6 armada 8 squadron
jail: 4 brig
officer: 4 aide, bosh, mate 5 bosun 6 ensign 7 admiral, armorer, captain 8 armourer 9 commander, commodore 10 lieutenant
vessel: PT; sub 7 carrier, cruiser, flattop, gun boat 9 destroyer, submarine, transport 10 battleship
wireless operator: 6 sparks
nawab: 5 nabob, ruler 7 viceroy
nay: nai, not 4 deny, nyet(Russ.) 5 flute, never 6 denial, refuse 7 refusal 8 negative 11 prohibition
naysay: 6 denial 7 refusal
nayword: 6 signal 9 watchword
naze: 8 headland 10 promontory
Nazi: 9 Hitlerite 10 brownshirt
air force: 9 Luftwaffe
armed forces: 9 Wehrmacht
concentration camp: 6 Belsen, Dachau 9 Auschwitz 10 Buchenwald
police: 7 Gestapo
symbol: 6 fylfot 8 swastika
nazim: 7 viceroy 8 governor
neal: 6 anneal, temper
neanic: 8 immature, youthful
neap: 4 tide
near: gin, kin, nar(Sc.) 4 bain, dear, hend, nigh 5 anear, anent, aside, close, equal, handy, hende, match, rival, touch 6 almost, around, beside, climax, narrow, stingy 7 advance, similar, thrifty, vicinal 8 adjacent, approach, intimate 9 niggardly, thriftily 10 contiguous, juxtaposed 11 approximate, closefisted 12 parsimonious 13 propinquitous
nearest: 4 next 5 ewest(Sc.) 7 closest 9 proximate
nearsighted: 6 myopic 12 shortsighted
neat: gim 4 cosh(Sc.), deft, dink, feil(Sc.), nice, prim, pure, snod(Sc.), snug, tidy, tosh, trig, trim 5 clean, compt, dinky,

douce, natty 6 adroit, cattle, clever, dapper 7 concise, orderly, precise, refined, unmixed 8 skillful, tasteful 9 dexterous, ship-shape, undiluted 10 concinnous, meticulous
neath: 5 below 7 beneath
neatherd: 7 cowherd 8 herdsman
neb: nib, tip 4 beak, bill, nose 5 snout
Nebraska: *capital:* 7 Lincoln
city: 5 Omaha 8 Bellevue, Hastings 11 Grand Island
county: 4 Hall, Loup, Otoe 5 Deuel, Sarpy 6 Colfax, Nemalia 7 Douglas, Madison 9 Lancaster
dune: 9 Sand Hills
Indian: 4 Otoe 5 Omaha, Ponca 6 Pawnee
nickname: 4 Beef 10 Blackwater, Cornhusker 12 Tree Planters
river: 6 Platte 8 Missouri, Niobrara 10 Republican
state bird: 10 meadowlark
state flower: 9 goldenrod
state tree: 10 cottonwood
nebbish: 4 meek 5 timid 11 ineffectual
nebris: 8 fawnskin
nebula: sky 5 vapor 6 galaxy 10 atmosphere
nebulize: 7 atomize
nebulous: 4 hazy 5 foggy, misty, vague 6 cloudy 7 obscure, unclear 9 celestial 10 indefinite, indistinct
necessarily: 8 perforce 10 inevitably 12 consequently
necessary: 5 privy, vital 7 needful 8 forcible, integral 9 essential, mandatory, requisite 10 inevitable, undeniable 11 unavoidable, water-closet 13 indispensable
necessitate: 5 force, impel 6 compel, entail, oblige 7 require 9 constrain
necessity: 4 food, must, need, want 5 drink 7 ailment, poverty, urgency 8 distress 9 emergency, essential 11 destitution
neck: pet 4 cape, crag, crop, hals, kiss 5 halse 6 caress, cervix, collum, fondle, strait 7 channel, embrace, isthmus
armor: 6 gorget
artery: 7 carotid
back of: 4 nape 5 nucha, nuque 6 scruff
muscle: 8 scalenus
part: 4 gula 7 withers
pert. to: 7 jugular 8 cervical
piece: bib, boa 5 amice, rabat, scarf, stole 6 collar 8 kerchief
neck and neck: tie 4 even 5 close
neckband: 6 collar, collet 10 collar-band
neckerchief: 4 gimp 7 belcher 8 kerchief, neckatee 12 handkerchief
necklace: 4 rope, torc 5 beads, chain, noose 6 collar, grivna, locket, torque 7

baldric, chaplet, haltern, necktie, riviere 8 baldrick, carcanet, lavalier 9 esclavage, lavaliere 10 lavalliere

neckpiece: bib, boa 4 ruff 5 amice, choke, jabot, ruche, scarf, stole 6 choker, collar, cravat, dickie 8 kerchief

necktie: bow, tie 4 band 5 ascot, scarf 6 cravat 10 four-in-hand

necktie party: 7 hanging 8 lynching

necrology: 8 obituary

necromancy: art 5 goety, magic 7 grammary, sorcery 8 gramarye, wizardry 11 conjuration, enchantment

necropolis: 8 cemetery

necropsy: 7 autopsy

nectar: 5 honey 8 ambrosia

nee: 4 born 5 named 8 formerly

need: 4 lack, must, want 5 crave 6 behove, demand, desire, hanker, hunger 7 behoove, poverty, require, urgency 8 distress, exigency 9 emergency, extremity, indigence, necessity, requisite 10 compulsion, dependence, obligation, retirement 11 destitution, requirement

needful: 5 vital 8 integral, required 9 essential 13 indispensable

needle: sew 4 acus(L.), darn 5 annoy 6 worry 7 acicula, provoke, spicule 10 strengthen

hole: eye

treatment with: 11 acupuncture

type: 4 sail 5 blunt, style 6 bodkin, stylus 7 darning, obelisk 8 knitting 10 hypodermic, phonograph, upholstery

needlefish: gar 8 pipefish

needlelike: 6 acuate 7 acerate, acerose, acerous, aciform 8 acicular, belonoid

needless: 10 gratuitous 11 superfluous, unnecessary

needlework: 6 sewing 7 sampler, seaming, tatting 8 knitting 9 hemstitch 10 embroidery, crocheting

needy: 4 poor 9 penniless

neep: 6 turnip

ne'er-do-well: bum 5 losel, loser 9 no account, schlemiel, shiftless, worthless 11 incompetent

nef: 6 clock

nefarious: 4 rank 5 gross 6 wicked 7 heinous, impious, vicious 8 flagrant, horrible, infamous 9 atrocious 10 detestable, iniquitous, villainous

nefast: 6 wicked

negate: 4 deny 5 annul 6 refute 7 abolish, nullify 10 neutralize

negation: not 5 empty 6 denial 7 refusal 9 annulment, blankness, nonentity 10 refutation 13 contradiction, nullification

negative: nae(Sc.), nay, non(F.), nor, not 4 film, veto 5 minus, never 7 neutral

neglect: 4 fail, omit, slip 5 fault, forgo, shirk 6 forego, forget, ignore, slight 7 blink at, default, failure 8 omission 9 disregard, oversight, pay no heed, pretermit 10 negligence 11 inattention 12 inadvertence, indifference

neglectful: lax 6 remiss 8 careless, derelict, heedless 9 dissolute, negligent

negligee: 4 robe 7 undress 8 peignoir 9 nightgown 10 dishabille

negligence: 7 laxness 9 disregard, oversight

negligent: lax 5 slack 6 remiss 8 careless, heedless, slipshod 10 delinquent 11 thoughtless, unconcerned 12 indifferent

negotiable: 12 transferable

negotiate: 4 deal 5 treat 6 dicker, settle 7 arrange, bargain, chaffer, discuss 8 transact 10 accomplish

negotiation: 6 treaty 8 entreaty

negus: 4 king 8 beverage

neigh: 6 whinny

neighbor: 4 abut, line 5 touch, verge 6 adjoin, border 8 border on

neighborhood: 4 area 5 venue 6 locale, region 7 section 8 district, locality, vicinage, vicinity 9 community, proximity, territory 11 propinquity

neighboring: 4 nigh 5 close 6 near-by 7 vicinal 8 adjacent 10 contiguous 11 close-at-hand

neither: not

nema: 7 eelworm 9 roundworm

nemesis: 4 bane 7 avenger

nemoral: 6 sylvan, wooded

neophyte: 4 tyro 5 epopt 6 novice 7 amateur, convert 8 beginner 9 proselyte 10 catechumen

neoteric: new 4 late 6 modern, recent

Nepal: *capital:* 8 Katmandu

city: 5 Palan 8 Bhatgaon 9 Bhaktapur

dynasty: 6 Rajput

language: 6 Bhutia, Nepali, Newari

monetary unit: 4 pice 5 rupee

mountain: 7 Everest

mountain climber: 7 Hillary, Tenzing

mountain range: 8 Himalaya

people: Rai 4 Aoul 5 Bokra, Hindu, Limbu, Murmi, Newar, Tharu 6 Bhotia, Gurkha, Lepcha 7 Kiranti 8 Gorkhall

religion: 5 Hindu 8 Buddhist

river: 4 Kusi 5 Bheri, Tamur 6 Gandak 7 Karnali

sheep: 6 bharal, nahoor, nayaur

tree: sal 4 toon 5 sisoo

nepenthe: 6 opiate 7 anodyne 8 narcotic

nephew: 6 nepote(Sc.)

nephrite: 4 jade 6 pounam 10 greenstone

ne plus ultra: 4 acme 6 summit 9 nth degree

nepotism: 9 patronage 10 favoritism

Neptune: sea 5 ocean 6 seagod
consort: 7 Salacia
emblem: 7 trident
Ner's son: 5 Abner
Nereides: *father:* 6 Nereus
mother: 5 Doris
steed: 8 seahorse
Nero: 6 tyrant 7 emperor, fiddler
mother: 9 Agrippina
successor: 5 Galba
victim: 5 Lucan 6 Seneca
wife: 7 Octavia, Poppaea
Nero Wolfe creator: 5 Stout
nerve: 4 grit 5 cheek, phuck, sinew, spunk,
vigor 6 aplomb, daring, energy, tendon
7 courage 8 audacity, boldness, coolness, embolden, strength, temerity 9
encourage, fortitude 10 brazenness, effrontery, invigorate, resolution
apparatus: 6 sensor
cell: 6 neuron
center: 5 brain 8 ganglion
cranial: 5 optic, vagus
inflammation: 8 neuritis
malady: tic 8 neuritis
network: 4 rete 6 plexus
operation: 10 neurolysis
pathway: 4 rete 5 hilum 8 ganglion
pert. to: 5 neuro 6 neural
root: 5 radix
sensory: 6 afferent
tissue: 8 cinerea
tumor: 7 neuroma 9 neurinoma 11 neur-
ocytoma 12 neuromatosis
nerveless: 4 dead, weak 5 brave, inert 8
unnerved 9 foolhardy, powerless 10
courageous
nervous: 4 edgy 5 jumpy, timid 6 fidget,
on edge, sinewy, touchy 7 fearful, fretful, jittery, waspish 8 neurotic, timorous 9 excitable, querulous, sensitive
10 highstrung 12 apprehensive
nervous disorder: See mental disorder
nervous system: *center:* 5 brain
description of: 11 neurography
nomenclature: 9 neuronymy
science: 9 neurology
nervy: 4 bold 5 jerky, tense 6 brazen, sinewy, strong 7 jittery, nervous 8 impudent, vigorous 9 excitable
nescient: 7 infidel 8 agnostic, ignorant
ness: 4 cape 8 headland 10 promontory
nest: den, web 4 aery, bike, dray, drey,
eyry, home 5 abode, aerie, eyrie, haunt,
nidus, swarm 6 cuddle, hotbed 7 lodging, retreat 9 residence 10 nidificate
builder of: ant, bee 4 bird, wasp
eagle's: 4 aery 5 aerie
insect's: 5 nidus
nest egg: 5 hoard, stock 7 reserve 9 reservoir
squirrel's: 4 drey

nester: 7 settler 8 squatter 11 home-
steader
nestle: pet 4 nest 6 cuddle, pettle(Sc.) 7
cherish, shelter, snuggle
nestling: 4 baby, bird, eyas 9 fledgling
nestor: 4 sage 6 parrot 7 adviser, advisor
9 counselor 10 counsellor
net: bag, gin, web 4 caul, flan, gain, lace,
lawn, mesh, moke, neat, pure, rete, toil,
trap, trim, weir 5 clean, clear, gauze, la-
cis, seize, snare, tulle, yield 6 bright,
cobweb, entrap, maline, profit 7 dragnet, ensnare, network, protect, rinsing,
shelter 8 meshwork 9 reticulum 10 reticulate 13 unadulterated
fishing: lam 4 flew, flue, fyke 5 seine,
trawl 6 sagene 7 trammel
hair: 5 snood
interstice: 4 hole, mesh
nether: 5 lower, under 8 downward, inferior
Netherlands: 7 Holland
bailiff: 6 schout
capital: 9 Amsterdam
cheese: 4 Edam 5 Gouda 6 Leyden 7 cottage
city: Ede 5 Asten, Breda, Hague 6 Aalten,
Arnhem, Leiden 7 Commune, Haarlem,
Utrecht 8 Aalsmeer, The Hague 9 Groningen, Rotterdam 10 Gravenhage
commune: Ede, Epe 4 Echt 5 Breda,
Doorn, Hague 6 Dongen, Leyden 9
Amsterdam, Rotterdam 11 Doniawes-
tal
council: 7 heemrad 8 heemraad, heemraat
fishing boat: 4 tode 6 hooker
former colony: 4 Java 6 Borneo 7 Celebes, Sumatra, Surinam 9 New Guinea,
10 East Indies
gin: 8 schnapps
inlet: 9 Zuider Zee
island: 5 Texel 7 Ameland 8 Vlieland 9
Schelling
island group: Aru 5 Arroe, Arrou
lake: 7 Haarlem
legislative assembly: 4 Raad
measure: aam, ahm, aum, ell, kan,
kop(pl.), mud, vat, zak 4 duim, lood,
mijl, rood, rope, voet 5 anker, carat,
roede, stoop, wisse 6 bunder, koppen,
legger, maatje, muddle, mutsje, streep 7
leaguer, schepel 8 mimgelen, okshoofd,
steekkan 10 vingerhoed
monetary unit: 4 cent, doit, raps 5 ryder
6 florin, gulden, stiver 7 ducaton, esca-
lan, escalin, guilder, stooter 8 ducatoon
9 dubbeltje 12 rijksdaalder
native: 5 Dutch 8 Dutchman
painter: Lis 4 Hals, Kalf, Neer 5 Helst,
Steen 6 Leyden 7 De Hoogh, Hobbe-
ma, Seghers, van Gogh, Vermeer 8
'roninck, Mondrian, Mostaert, Ruys-

dael, Ter Borch 9 Rembrandt 10 Van de Velde 11 Van Ruisdael 19 Geertgen Tot Sint Jans

people: 5 Dutch 7 Flemish, Frisian

possessions: 4 Saba 7 Curacao

pottery: 4 delf 5 delft 11 Dutch Guiana, St. Eustacius

province: Epe 7 Brabant, Drenthe, Holland, Limburg, Utrecht, Zeeland 9 Friesland, Groningen 10 Gelderland, Overijssel

reclaimed land: 6 polder

river: Eem 4 Leck, Maas, Rijn, Waal, Ysel 5 Meuse, Rhine, Yssel 6 Ijssel, Kromme 7 Scheldt

scholar: 7 Erasmus

sheriff: 6 schout

town hall: 9 stadhouse

uncle: eme, oom

vessel: 4 koff 5 yanky 6 schuit, schuyt

weight: ons 4 last, lood, pond 5 bahar, grein, pound 6 korrel 7 wichtje 8 esterlin, 9 esterling

woman: 4 frau, frow

netlike: 9 reticular

netop: 5 crony 6 friend 9 companion

netting: 4 lint, mesh 7 network

nettle: vex 4 fret, line 5 annoy, cnida, peeve, pique, sting 6 arouse, henbit, ruffle, splice, stir up 7 affront, blubber, provoke 8 irritant, irritate 9 Urticacea 10 exasperate

nettle cell: 10 nematocyst

family: 10 Urticaceae

genus of: 10 parietaria

network(see also **net**): 4 mesh, rete 5 retia 6 plexus, reseau

neural: 6 dorsal

neurite: 4 axon 5 axone

neurotic: 6 phobic 7 nervous 8 unstable 10 compulsive

neuter: 6 gender 7 neither, neutral, sexless 9 impartial, sterilize

neutral: 4 gray 8 middling, negative 9 colorless 10 achromatic, indefinite, poker-faced 11 adiaphorous, indifferent 12 noncombatant

neutralize: 5 annul 7 abolish, balance, destroy, nullify, vitiate 9 cancel out, frustrate 10 counteract 11 countervail 14 counterbalance

neutralizer: 6 alkali

Nevada: *capital:* 10 Carson City

city: 4 Reno 8 Las Vegas

county: Nye 4 Elko 5 Clark 6 Storey, Washoe

highest point: 12 Boundary Peak

historic site: 9 Hoover Dam 12 Virginia City

industry: 7 divorce 8 gambling

lake: Mud 4 Mead 5 Tahoe 6 Walker 7 Pyramid

mountain range: 4 Ruby 6 Carson 7 Toiyabe

nickname: 6 Silver 9 Sagebrush

plateau: 10 Great Basin

river: 6 Carson 7 Truckee 8 Colorado, Humboldt

state bird: 8 bluebird

state flower: 9 sagebrush

state tree: 5 pinon

neve: 4 firn, snow 7 glacier

never: nay, nie(G.), not 4 nary, ne'er

nevertheless: but, yet 5 still 6 even so 7 how-be-it, however 9 howsoever, natheless 10 howsomever

nevus: 4 mole 5 tumor 7 spiloma 9 birthmark

new: neu(G.) 4 late, nova(L.) 5 fresh, green, novel 6 modern, recent, unused 7 foreign, strange, untried 8 neoteric, original, untested 9 first-hand 10 additional, promethean, unfamiliar 11 fashionable, modernistic 12 unaccustomed 13 inexperienced

New Brunswick: *capital:* 11 Fredericton

city: 6 St. John 7 Moncton

former name: 6 Acadia

island: 10 Campobello

motto: 11 Spem Reduxit

national park: 5 Fundy

province of: 6 Canada

provincial flower: 6 violet

river: 6 St. John 7 St. Croix 9 Miramicki

New Caledonia: *bird:* 4 kagu

capital: 6 Noumea

New Deal agency: CCC, NRA, TVA

New England: *aristocrat:* 7 Brahmin

chair: 6 Carver

inhabitant: 6 Yankee

of the West: 9 Minnesota

settler: 7 Pilgrim, Puritan

New Guinea: *bay:* Oro

capital: 11 Port Moresby

city: Lae 4 Daru 5 Soron 6 Rabaul

export: 5 copra

gulf: 4 Huon 5 Papua

hog: 4 bene

island: Aru 4 Buka 5 Ceram, Papua 6 Mussau

island group: 7 Solomon

mountain: 6 Albert 8 Victoria 9 Carstensz 10 Wilhelmina

parrot: 4 lory

people: 5 Karon 6 Papuan

port: Lae 4 Daru 5 Wewak 6 Madang

river: Fly 5 Sepik 7 Amberno 10 Strickland 15 Kaiserin Augusta

section: 8 Bunagona

New Hampshire: *capital:* 7 Concord

city: 5 Dover, Keene 6 Nashua 10 Manchester, Portsmouth

county: 4 Coos 7 Belknap

explorer: 5 Pring

highest peak: 12 Mt. Washington
lake: 7 Ossipee, Sunapee
motto: 13 Live free or die
mountain: 5 White
nickname: 7 Granite
river: 4 Saco 9 Merrimack 10 Piscataqua
state bird: 5 finch
state flower: 5 lilac
state tree: 5 birch

New Jersey: *capital:* 7 Trenton
city: 6 Camden, Newark 7 Clifton 8 Paterson 9 Elizabeth 12 Atlantic City
county: 5 Essex, Union 6 Bergen, Camden, Mercer, Morris 7 Passaic 8 Monmouth
highest peak: 9 High Point
Indian: 8 Delaware
mountain: 6 Ramapo
nickname: 6 Garden 8 Mosquito
peninsula: 9 Sandy Hook
river: 6 Ramapo 7 Raritan 8 Delaware, Tuckahoe
state bird: 9 goldfinch
state flower: 6 violet
state tree: oak

New Mexico: *capital:* 7 Santa Fe
city: 5 Hobbs 6 Clovis 7 Roswell 9 Las Cruces 10 Farmington 11 Albuquerque
county: 4 Luna, Mora, Quay, Taos, 5 Curry, Otero 6 Catron, Chaves 7 Dona Ana, Hidalgo
highest peak: 7 Wheeler
motto: 12 Crescit eundo (It grows as it goes)
mountain: 14 Sangre de Cresto
mountain range: 6 Chuska 7 Caballo 8 San Mateo 9 San Andres
national park: 15 Carlsbad Caverns
nickname: 8 Sunshine
resort: 4 Taos
river: 4 Gila 5 Pecos 7 San Juan 9 Rio Grande
state bird: 10 roadrunner
state flower: 5 yucca
state tree: 5 pinon

New Testament (see also **Bible**): *book:* 4 Acts, John, Jude, Luke, Mark 5 James, Peter, Titus 6 Romans 7 Hebrews, Matthew, Timothy 8 Philemon 9 Ephesians, Galatians 10 Colossians, Revelation 11 Corinthians, Philippians 13 Thessalonians
gospel: 4 John, Luke, Mark 7 Matthew
letter: 7 epistle

New York: *canal:* 4 Erie
capital: 6 Albany
city: Rye 4 Erie, Rome, Troy 5 Utica 6 Elmira, Ithaca, Malone 7 Buffalo, Yonkers 8 Saratoga, Syracuse 9 Rochester 10 Binghamton
county: 4 Erie 5 Tioga, Wayne, Yates 6 Cayuga, Monroe, Oneida, Oswego, Put-

nam, Seneca 7 Chemung, Genesee, Niagara, Ontario, Orleans, Steuben, Tompkin, Wyoming 8 Allegheny, Dutchess, Schuyler 11 Westchester
explorer: 6 Hudson 9 Champlain, Verrazano
harbor entrance: 14 Ambrose Channel
island (see also **New York City**): 4 Fire, Long, 7 Fishers, Shelter
Indian: 4 Erie 6 Cayuga, Mohawk, Oneida, Seneca
lake: 5 Keuka 6 Cayuga, Croton, Geneva, Oneida, Seneca 7 Ontario, Saranac 8 Onondago 9 Champlain 11 Canandaigua, Skaneateles
motto: 9 Excelsior (Ever Upward)
mountain: 9 Catskills 11 Adirondacks
nickname: 6 Empire
racetrack: 7 Belmont, Yonkers 8 Aqueduct, Saratoga
river: 5 Tioga 6 Harlem, Hudson 7 Genesee, Niagara 8 Delaware 10 St. Lawrence
state bird: 8 bluebird
state flower: 4 rose
state tree: 5 maple
tourist attraction: 12 Niagara Falls

New York City: 6 Gotham
airports: JFK 7 Kennedy 9 La Guardia
boroughs: 5 Bronx 6 Queens 9 Brooklyn, Richmond 11 Manhattan
island: 5 Ellis 6 Staten 7 Bedloes, Liberty, Welfare 9 Governors, Manhattan 10 Blackwells
nickname: 8 Big Apple
prison: 5 Tombs
river: 4 East 6 Hudson
subway: BMT, IND, IRT

New Zealand: *anteater:* 7 echidna
bird: kea, moa, oii, poe, roa 4 kaka, kiwi, koko, kulu, ruru, titi, weka 6 kakapo 7 apteryx, wrybill 8 morepork, notornis
capital: 10 Wellington
city: see *town* below
clay: 4 papa
dance: 4 haka
fern: 4 weki 5 pitau, wheki
fish: ihi 5 hikus
flax: 8 harakeke
flightless bird: 4 weka 7 apteryx
fort: pa; pah, pau
grass: 6 toetoe
gun: 6 tupara
heron: 6 kotuku
hut: 5 whare
island: 5 North, South 7 Chatham, Stewart
kiwi: moa, roa 7 apteryx
lake: Ada 4 Gunn, Ohau, Rere 5 Hawea, Okaro, Taupo 6 Fergus, Pukaki, Rotoma, Sylvan, Teanau, Tekapo, Wanaka 7 Brunner, Diamond, Kanieri,

Okareka, Rotoiti, Rotoroa, Rotorua 8
Okataina, Paradise, Rotoaira,
Tarawera, Wakatipu
mahogany: 6 totara
monetary unit: 6 dollar
mountain: 4 Cook 5 Ohope 6 Egmont 7
Aorangi, Pihanga, Raupehu, Ruapehu,
Tauhara, Tauhera 8 Aspiring, Tarawera, Tauranga
national bird: 4 kiwi
ostrich: moa
outlying island: 8 Auckland, Campbell,
Kermadec 9 Antipodes
owl: 4 ruru
palm: 5 nikau
parrot: kea 4 kaka 6 kakapo
people: Ati 5 Arawa, Maori 7 Ringatu
pine: 4 rima 6 totara 9 kahikatea
port: Lae 7 Aukland, Dunedin 10 Wellington
reptile: 7 tuatara, tuatera
river: 7 Waikato 8 Wanganui
settlement: pah, pau
shark: 4 mako
shrub: 4 tutu
song: 6 waiata
spa: 5 Aroha 7 Rotorua, Tearoha
storehouse: 5 whata
town: 5 Levin, Otaki, Taupo 6 Foxton,
Napier, Nelson, Oamaru Picton, Ti-
maru 7 Dunedin, Raetihi, Rotorua 8
Auckland, Gisborne, Hamilton, Hastings, Tauranga, Wanganui 9 Ashbur-
ton, Greymouth, Masterton, Whangarei
10 Dannenirke, Palmerston, Queens-
town, Wellington(c.) 12 Christchurch,
Invercargill
tree: ake 4 hino, kopi, mako, miro, pelu,
puka, rata, rimu, tawa, toro, toru, whau
5 hinau, hinou, karui, mahoe, maire,
mapau, ngaio 6 ake-ake, karaka, ko-
whai, manuka, puriri, tarata, titoki 7
akepiro, taratah, wahahen 8 hiropito,
makomako
vine: aka
volcano: 6 Egmont 7 Ruapehu 9 Ngauru-
hoe
wages: utu
welcome: 8 haeremai
newcomer: 7 settler 8 comeling 9 immigrant
newel: 4 post 6 pillar 7 upright
newfangled: 5 novel 6 latest, modern
Newfoundland: 6 island
airport: 6 Gander
cape: Ray 4 Race 5 Bauld
capital: 8 St. John's
city: 10 Mount Pearl 11 Corner Brook
12 Stephenville
discoverer: 5 Cabot (John)
Indian: 6 Micmac
island: 4 Bell, Fogo

mainland part: 8 Labrador
province of: 6 Canada
provincial flower: 12 pitcher plant
river: 6 Gander, Humber 8 Exploits
newly: 4 anew 5 again 6 afresh, lately 8
recently
news: 4 word 6 notice 7 tidings 11 information, instruction 12 intelligence
agency: DNB, PAP(Pol.), UPI 4 Tass
(Russ.) 5 Domei 6 Xinhua(Ch.) 7 Reuters 13 International
gatherer: 8 reporter 13 correspondent
media: 5 radio 7 journal 8 magazine 9
newspaper 10 periodical, television
statement: 8 bulletin
newsboy: 7 carrier
newsmonger: 6 gossip 7 tattler 8 reporter
newspaper: 5 daily, organ 7 gazette, journal, tabloid 10 periodical 11 publication
article: 4 item
collectively: 5 press
employee: 6 editor 7 printer 8 engraver,
pressman, reporter 9 columnist, linotyper 10 cartoonist, compositor, journalist, plate maker 12 photographer 13
correspondent
file: 6 morgue
hoax: 6 canard
part of: ear 6 banner 8 obituary 9 editori-
al
newsstand: 5 booth, kiosk, stall
newt: 4 ask, eft 4 evet 6 lizard, triton 7 axolotl 10 salamander
next: 4 then 5 after, ewest(Sc.), neist(Sc.)
6 coming 7 closest, ensuing, nearest 9
adjoining, following, immediate, proximate 10 contiguous, succeeding 12
conterminous
next to: 6 almost, beside, nearly 8 adjacent
nexus: tie 4 bond, link 10 connection 15
interconnection
nib: pen 4 beak, bill 5 point, prong 8 pen
point
nibble: eat, nab 4 bite, gnaw, knap, peck,
pick 6 browse 7 chimble, gnabble, gnatter
Nicaragua: *capital:* 7 Managua
city: 4 Leon 6 Massaya 7 Granada 9 Ma-
tagalpa
lake: 7 Managua 9 Nicaragua
language: 7 Spanish
measure: 4 vara 5 cahiz, milla 6 suerte,
tercia 7 cajuela, estadal, manzana
monetary unit: 7 centavo, cordoba
mountain peak: 6 Madera 9 Momotombo
neighbors: 8 Honduras 9 Costa Rica
river: 4 Coco 7 San Juan 8 Tipitapa
weight: bag 4 caja 8 tonelada
nice: 4 fine, good 5 exact, picky 6 bonita,

dainty, minute, peachy, queasy, subtle 7 correct, elegant, finical, genteel, precise, prudish, refined 8 decorous, delicate, exacting, pleasant, pleasing 9 agreeable, appealing, exquisite, squeamish 10 appetizing, delightful, discerning, fastidious, old-maidish, particular, scrupulous 11 considerate, puntilious, scrumptious 13 hypercritical 14 discriminating

niche: 4 apse, nook 6 alcove, covert, recess 7 edicule, retreat 9 habitacle

nick: cut. nob 4 chip, slit 5 cheat, notch, tally, trick 6 arrest, record 7 defraud 9 indenture

nickle compound: 4 zinc 6 copper

nickelodeon: 7 jukebox

nickname (see also **pen name, pseudonym**): tag 6 agname, byword 7 misname, moniker 8 cognomen, monicker 9 sobriquet 10 soubriquet

James Boswell: 5 Bozzy

Winston Churchill: 6 Winnie

Georges Clemenceau: 5 Tiger

Benjamin Disraeli: 5 Dizzy

Thomas Edison: 17 Wizard of Menlo Park

Dwight Eisenhower: Ike

Elizabeth I: 11 Virgin Queen

Frederick I: 10 Barbarossa

Ernest Hemingway: 4 Papa

Andrew Jackson: 10 Old Hickory

Abraham Lincoln: 9 Honest Abe

Louis XIV: 7 Sun King

Joe Louis: 11 Brown Bomber

Mary I: 10 Bloody Mary

Napoleon I: 14 Little Corporal

Napoleon II: 7 L'Aiglon

Richard Nixon: 10 Tricky Dick

Henry Percy: 7 Hotspur

William Pitt: 13 Great Commoner

Richard I: 11 Lion-Hearted

Richard III: 10 Crouchback

Babe Ruth: 7 Bambino 12 Sultan of Swat

Joseph Stilwell: 10 Vinegar Joe

Charles Stratton: 8 Tom Thumb

nicknaming: 12 prosonomasia

nictate: 4 wink 5 blink 7 twinkle

nide: 5 brood

nidge: 5 shake 6 quiver

nidget: 4 fool 5 idiot

nidification: 7 nesting

nidor: 4 reek 5 aroma, savor, scent, smell

nidus: 4 nest

nifty: 4 good 5 smart 7 stylish

Niger: *capital:* 6 Niamey

monetary unit: 5 franc

people: 4 Peul 5 Hausa 6 Djerma 7 Songhai

Nigeria: *capital:* 5 Lagos

city: 4 Kano 6 Ibadan 8 Ogbomosho

monetary unit: 5 naira

people: Ibo 5 Hausa 6 Fulania, Yoruba

port: 5 Lagos 7 Calabar

province: Isa 4 Nupe, Ondo 5 Warri

river: Oli

tree: 5 afara

walled city: 4 Kano

niggard: 5 miser 8 scrimper 9 skinflint 10 curmudgeon

niggardly: 4 mean 5 close 6 narrow, scanty, stingy 7 miserly 8 churlish, wretched 10 avaricious 11 closefisted 12 parsimonious

niggle: 6 potter, putter, trifle

nigh: 4 near 5 about, close 6 almost, nearly 8 adjacent, approach 10 contiguous 11 neighboring

night: 4 nuit(F.) 8 darkness

goddess: Nox, Nyx

goddess of: Nyx 6 Hecate

pert. to: 9 nocturnal

night bird: 10 shearwater 11 nightingale

night blindness: 10 nyctalopia

night-wandering: 11 noctivagant

nightcap: 6 biggin

nightchurr: 10 goatsucker

nightclub: 5 boite 7 cabaret

nightfall: eve 4 dusk, even 6 sunset 7 evening 8 twilight

nightingale: 6 thrush 8 philomel 9 philomela

nightjar: 5 potoo 9 nighthawk 10 goatsucker

nightmare: 5 dream, fancy, fiend 7 incubus 9 cauchemar(F.), ephialtes 12 apprehension

nightshade: 5 morel 7 henbane, morelle 10 belladonna 11 bittersweet

nightstick: bat 4 club 5 baton, billy 6 cudgel 8 bludgeon

nihil: 7 nothing

nihilist: 8 nihilist 9 anarchist

nil: 4 zero 7 nothing

Nile: 6 Al-Bahr

bird: 4 ibis 7 wryneck

boat: 5 baris 6 nuggar 8 dahabeah

captain: 4 rais, reis

dam: 6 Makwar 9 Aswan High 10 Gebel Aulia

falls: 5 Ripon

fish: 5 saide 8 mormyrid 9 mormyroid

historic ruins: 4 Giza 5 Luxor 6 Karnak 7 Memphis

houseboat: 8 dahabeah

island: 4 Roda

people: 4 Madi 5 Nilot

plant: 4 sudd 5 lotus

reptile: 9 crocodile

river gauge: 9 nilometer

town: 5 Cairo, Rejaf 7 Rosetta

tributary: 6 Atbara, Kagera

nilgai: 8 antelope, blue bull

nimb: 4 halo

nimble: 4 deft, lish, spry 5 agile, alert, fleet, quick 6 active, adroit, clever, feirie, lissom, lively, prompt, volant 9 dexterous, wide-awake 11 quick-witted

nimbose: 6 cloudy, stormy

nimbus: 4 halo 5 cloud, vapor 6 gloria 7 aureole 10 atmosphere

nimiety: 4 glut 6 excess 10 redundancy

nimmer: 5 thief

nimrod: 5 ruler 6 hunter, tyrant

nincompoop: 4 dolt, fool 5 moron, ninny 9 simpleton

nine: 6 ennead 8 ninefold
  based on: 8 novenary
  days' devotion: 6 novena
  group of: 5 nonet 6 ennead
  inches: 4 span

nine-eyes: 7 lamprey

nine-headed monster: 5 Hydra

nine-killer: 6 shrike

ninepins: 6 kayles 7 bowling, skittle 8 skittles

ninth: 5 nonus(L.)

Niobe: *brother:* 6 Pelops
  father: 8 Tantalus
  husband: 7 Amphion
  sister-in-law: 5 Aedon

nip: cut, sip 4 bite, clip, dram, tang 5 blast, check, clamp, draft, drink, frost, hurry, pinch, seize, sever, steal, sting 6 blight, catnip, snatch, tipple, twitch 7 squeeze 8 compress 10 pickpocket

nipa: 4 atap, palm 5 attap, drink 6 liquor

nipcheese: 5 miser 6 purser

nipper: boy, lad 4 claw, grab 5 biter, child 6 cunner, pliers, urchin 7 forceps, incisor, pincers 8 pincenez 9 handcuffs 10 eyeglasses

Nippon: See **Japan**

nippy: 4 cold 5 brisk, quick, sharp 6 active, biting, chilly, nimble, snappy 7 caustic, pungent 8 vigorous

nisse: 6 goblin, kobold, sprite 7 brownie

nisus: 6 effort 7 impulse 8 endeavor, striving 11 inclination

Nisus' daughter: 6 Scylla

nit: egg, nut 5 speck 6 insect 8 hazelnut

niter, nitre: 5 peter, petre 6 potash 9 saltpeter

nither: 5 blast 6 debase, shiver 7 tremble 9 humiliate

nitid: 6 bright, glossy 7 glowing, radiant 8 lustrous, nitidous

nitpick: 6 niggle

nitrate: 4 salt 5 ester
  sodium: 5 niter, nitre

nitrocotton: 9 guncotton

nitrogen: 5 azote 9 quinoline
  compound: 7 ammonia

nitty-gritty: 10 basic facts

niveau: 5 level 7 plateau

nivenite: 9 uranite

niveous: 5 snowy 8 snowlike

nix: 6 goblin, nobody, sprite 7 nothing, refusal 8 negation

Njorth: *daughter:* 5 Freya 6 Freyja
  son: 4 Frey 5 Freyr
  wife: 6 Skathi

no: nae(Sc.), naw, nay, nea(Sc.), nit, nix, non(F.) 4 nein(G.), nyet(Russ.), play 5 drama 6 denial 7 refusal 8 by no means 12 nothing doing

no-account: 9 worthless

Noah: *dove:* 7 Columba
  father: 6 Lamech
  grandson: 4 Aram
  great-grandson: Hul
  place of debarkation: 6 Ararat
  raven: 6 Corvus
  son: Ham, Sem 4 Shem 7 Japheth
  wine cup: 6 Crater

nob: 4 head, jack, toff 5 swell

nobby: 4 chic 5 swell 7 stylish 9 excellent, first-rate 11 fashionable

noble: 4 epic, fine, free, gent, good, pure, rial 5 burly, ducal, grand, ideal, lofty, manly, moral, proud 6 august, epical, famous, heroic 7 eminent, exalted, gallant, liberal, soulful, stately, sublime 8 elevated, generous, glorious, nobleman, precious, renowned, splendid 9 chevalier, dignified, excellent, honorable 10 idealistic, noblewoman 11 illustrious, magnanimous, magnificent

noble pine: 10 pipsissewa

nobleman: don 4 duke, earl, lord, peer 5 barin(Russ.), baron, count 6 knight, prince, varlet 7 baronet, grandee(Sp.), hidalgo, marquis 8 marquess 10 aristocrat
  pert. to: 5 ducal 6 lordly

noblewoman: 4 lady 7 duchess, peeress 8 baroness, countess, marquise, princess 10 marquisess 11 marchioness

nobody: 4 none 9 nonentity

nocent: 6 guilty 7 harmful, hurtful, noxious 8 criminal

noctambulism: 11 sleep walker 12 somnambulism

noctuad: 4 moth, worm

noctule: bat, owl 9 pipistrel 11 pipistrelle

nocturnal: 5 night 7 nightly 11 nightwalker

nocturnal mammal: bat 5 lemur

nocturne: 7 lullaby 8 serenade

nocuous: 7 harmful 8 damaging

nod: bow 4 beck, bend, doze, wink 5 droop 6 assent, beckon, drowse, nutate, salute 7 signify 8 approval, nutation

nodding: 6 drowsy, nutant, sleepy 8 cernuous 9 pendulous

noddy: auk 4 fool 5 dunce, ninny 7 hackney 9 simpleton

node: bow 4 bump, knob, knot, lump 5 joint, nodus 6 nodule 7 dilemma, granule 8 swelling, tubercle 10 difficulty 12 complication, protuberance

noel: 5 carol 9 Christmas

noetic: 8 abstract 12 intellectual

nog: ale, peg, pin 5 block 6 eggnog, noggin 8 beverage, treenail

no-good: 6 wretch 7 wastrel

noggin: cup, mug, nog 4 head, pate

noir: 5 black

noise: air, din 5 bruit, rumor, sound 6 gossip, norate, report 11 pandemonium

noiseless: 5 quiet, still, tacit 6 silent 7 catlike

noisemaker: 4 bell, horn 6 rattle 7 clapper

noisette: 5 hazel

noisome (see also **noxious**): bad 4 foul 5 fetid 7 harmful, hurtful 8 stinking, unsavory 9 offensive 10 disgusting, malodorous, pernicious 11 destructive, unwholesome

noisy: 4 loud 6 clashy 7 blatant, rackety 8 brawling, clattery, strepent 9 clamorous, hilarious, turbulent 10 boisterous, tumultuous, vociferous 12 obstreperous

nom de plume: 7 pen name 9 pseudonym

noma: 5 ulcer

nomad: 4 Arab, Luri, Moor 5 Alani, gypsy, rover 6 roamer, roving 7 Bedouin, Saracen, scenite 8 wandered

nomadic: 9 itinerant

nomadism: 8 vagrancy 10 wanderlust

nome: 4 Elis 5 nomos 8 nomarchy, province 10 department, prefecture

nomen: 4 gens, name

nomenclature: 4 list, name 8 glossary, register 9 catalogue, designate, recounter 10 dictionary, vocabulary 11 appellation, designation, terminology

nomic: 5 valid 8 ordinary 9 customary 12 conventional

nominal: 4 noun 5 cheap, 6 slight, unreal 7 titular, trivial 8 platonic, so-called 11 theoretical 13 unsubstantial

nominate: tap 4 call, leet(Sc.), name 5 enter, put up, slate 7 appoint, entitle, propose, specify 9 designate 10 denominate

nominee: 9 candidate

non-kosher: 4 tref

non-Mahometan: 5 Kafir

nonage: 7 infancy 10 immaturity 12 youthfulness

nonaspirate: 4 lene

nonbeliever: 5 pagan 7 atheist 8 agnostic

nonce: 7 present 8 occasion

nonchalant: 4 cool, easy 6 casual 8 careless 10 insouciant 11 indifferent 12 lighthearted 13 imperturbable

noncleric: lay 4 laic

noncombatant: 8 chaplain, civilian, observer

noncommittal: 7 neutral 8 reserved

noncompliance: 7 refusal 10 obstinance 13 recalcitrance

non compos mentis: 6 insane 14 not of sound mind

nonconcurrence: 7 dissent

nonconductor: 5 resin

nonconforming: 9 anomalous

nonconformist: 5 rebel 6 hippie 7 beatnik, heretic 8 bohemian 9 dissenter

nonconformity: 6 heresy 7 dissent 9 recusance, recusancy 10 dissidence 13 individualism

nondescript: 13 indescribable 14 indeterminable

none: nane 4 nane(Sc.), neen

nonentity: 4 zero 5 zilch 6 cipher 7 nothing, sad sack 9 small beer

nonessential: 9 extrinsic 10 adiaphoron 11 dispensable, unnecessary 12 adventitious 14 circumstantial

nonesuch: 5 apple, model 7 paragon 8 paradigm 9 matchless, nonpareil, unequaled, unrivaled 13 one in a million

nonexistent: 4 null 8 nonbeing

nonfestal: 6 ferial

nonfulfillment: 6 breach 12 infringement

nongrata: 9 unwelcome

nongypsy: 4 gajo

no-no: 9 forbidden 12 unacceptable

nonobjective: 8 abstract

nonobservance: 9 violation

nonpareil: 4 best 5 ideal 7 paragon, perfect, unequal 8 nonesuch, peerless 9 unrivaled

nonpartisan: 4 fair, just 9 impartial, objective

nonpasserine bird: 4 tody 6 hoopoe, motmot 8 hornbill 10 kingfisher

nonphysical: 7 psychic 9 psychical

nonplus: 5 blank, stump, trump 6 baffle, puzzle 7 perplex, stagger 9 embarrass

nonpositive: 8 negative 9 private

nonproductive: 6 barren 7 sterile 10 unfruitful

nonprofessional: lay 4 laic 7 amateur

nonsense: bah, pah, rot 4 blah, bosh, buff, bunk, flam, tosh 5 blash, folly, fudge, haver, hooey, stite(Sc.) 6 bunkum, drivel, faddle, folder 7 blarney, blather, buncome, inanity, twaddle 8 blahblah, blathery, falderal, folderol, flimflam, trumpery 9 absurdity, fandangle, frivolity, gibberish, moonshine, poppycock, silliness 10 balderdash, flapdoodle, flumdiddle, galimatias, triviality 11 flumadiddle, foolishness, monkeyshine 12 fiddle-dee-dee, flummadiddle, flummydiddle 16 preposterousness

non sequitur: 15 it does not follow

nonsolid: 5 fluid 6 liquid

noodle: 4 bean, fool, head, nizy, noll, pate 5 brain, ninny, nizey, noddy 6 boodle, noddle, noggin 9 blockhead, simpleton

nook: out, wro 4 cant, cove, glen, hole 5 angle, herne, niche 6 cantle, corner, cranny, recess 7 byplace, crevice, retreat

noon: 4 apex 6 midday 8 meridian 11 culmination

noose: tie 4 bond, dull, grin, hang, loop, trap 5 bight, grane, honda, snare, widdy 6 entrap, halter, lariat 7 ensnare, execute, laniard, lanyard, springe 8 slipknot
  armed with: 10 laquearian

nor: ner 7 neither 8 negative 10 connective

nori: 4 alga 7 amanori, seaweed

noria: 5 wheel

norite: 4 rock 6 gabbro

norm: 4 rule, type 5 gauge, model, norma 7 average, pattern 8 standard, template

normal: 4 sane 5 usual 6 general 7 natural, regular, typical 11 commonplace 12 compos mentis

Normandy: *beach:* 5 Omaha
  capital: 5 Rollo
  conqueror: 5 Rollo
  department: 4 Eure, Orne 6 Manche 8 Calvados
  duke: 5 Rollo
  town: 7 Saint-Lo

Norn: 4 fate, Urth, Wyrd 5 Skuld 9 Verthandi

Norse (see also **Scandinavian**): 4 mink 8 Teutonic 9 Icelandic, Norwegian 12 Scandinavian
  abode of gods: 6 Asgard
  alphabet: 5 runic
  bard: 5 scald, skald 7 sagaman
  chieftain: 4 jarl, Rolf 5 Rollo
  demigoddess of destiny: 5 Urd
  demon: 4 Mara, Surt 5 Surtr
  epic: 4 Edda
  explorer: 4 Eric 7 Ericson
  fate: 4 Norn
  first man: 4 Askr
  first woman: 5 Embla
  giant: 4 Atli, Loke, Loki, Natt, Norn, Nótt, Wate, Ymer, Ymir 5 Jotun, Mimer, Mimir, Thrym 6 Fafnir, Jotunn
  god (see also *giant* above): Asa, Ase, Ran, Tiu, Tyr, Ull, Zio 4 Frey, Hler, Hoth, Loke, Loki, Odin, Surt, Thor, Vali 5 Aeger, Aegir, Aesir(pl.), Baldr, Brage, Bragi, Donar, Freyr, Gymir, Othin, Surtr, Vanir(pl.), Wodan, Woden, Wotan 6 Balder, Hoenir, Njorth 7 Forsete, Forseti, Heimdal, Vitharr 9 Heimdallr, Hlorrithi

goddess: Dis, Eir, Hel 4 Frea, Hela, Nora, Saga, Urth, Wyrd 5 Freya, Frigg, Nanna 6 Freyja, Frigga 7 Asynjur

goddess of earth: 4 Erda

hall of heroes: 8 Valhalla

king: 4 Atli, Olaf

mythological wolf: 6 Fenrir

night: 4 Natt, Nott

nobleman: 4 yarl

poem: 4 rune

poet: 5 scald, skald

saint: 4 Olaf 5 Olaus

sea serpent: 6 Kraken 7 Midgard

tale: 4 saga

toast: 5 skoal

viking: 5 Rollo

watchdog: 4 Garm 5 Garmr

world tree: 8 Ygdrasil

North Africa: *antelope:* 5 addax 7 gazelle
  country: 5 Libya 7 Algeria, Morocco, Tunisia
  fruit: fig 4 date
  language: 6 Arabic, Berber
  lyre: 6 kissar
  measure: 4 rotl
  native quarter: 6 casbah, kasbah
  oasis: 4 wadi, wady
  people: 4 Moor 5 Nilot 6 Hamite
  port: 4 Oran, Sfax 6 Annaba 7 Tangier 10 Casablanca
  sheep: 4 drui 6 aoudad
  valley: 4 wadi, wady

North America: *bird:* 6 fulmar 7 grackle 8 cardinal, killdeer, kingrail 10 bufflehead
  country: 6 Canada, Mexico 9 Greenland 12 United States
  discoverer: 5 Cabot
  herb: 4 sego
  Indian: see **Indian (Americas)**
  marmoset: 7 tamarin
  orchids: 9 arethusas
  owl: 7 wapacut
  people: 7 Mexican 8 American, Canadian
  reindeer: 7 caribou
  thrush: 5 robin
  tree: lin 4 mabi, sorb, titi 5 balsa, papaw 6 balsam, pawpaw, redbud, tupelo 7 catalpa, hickory 8 basswood, oneberry, sweetsop 9 sassafras

North Atlantic: *island:* 7 Britain, Iceland, Ireland 9 Manhattan
  seagull: 4 skua

North Britain: 8 Scotland 9 Caledonia

North Carolina: *cape:* 4 Fear 7 Lookout 8 Hatteras
  capital: 7 Raleigh
  city: 6 Durham 9 Charlotte 10 Greensboro 12 Winston-Salem
  county: 4 Ashe, Dare, Hoke, Wake 5 Anson, Avery 6 Lenoir, Onslow 8 Buncombe, Guilford 10 Cumberland

island: 10 Outer Banks
lake: 6 Phelps 8 Waccamaw
mountain: 9 Blue Ridge 10 Great Smoky
mountain range: 11 Appalachian
nickname: 7 Tar Heel 8 Old North 10 Turpentine
river: Haw, Tar 5 Neuse 6 Pee Dee, Yadkin 7 Roanoke
state bird: 8 cardinal
state flower: 7 dogwood
state tree: 4 pine
North Dakota: *capital:* 8 Bismarck
city: 5 Fargo, Minot 9 Jamestown 10 Grand Forks
county: 4 Cass, Ward 6 Morton, Traill 8 Burleigh
Indian: 6 Mandan 7 Arikara
highest peak: 10 White Butte
nickname: 5 Sioux 11 Flickertail
river: Red 8 Missouri
state bird: 10 meadowlark
state flower: 11 prairie rose
state tree: elm
North Korea: *capital:* 9 Pyongyang
monetary unit: won 4 hwan
river: Nam 4 Yalu
North Pole discoverer: 5 Peary
North Sea: *arm:* 9 Skagerrak
canal: 4 Kiel
river: 5 Weser
North Star: 7 polaris 8 loadstar, lodestar, polestar 10 tramontane
North Vietnam (see also **Vietnam**)**:** *capital:* 5 Hanoi
city: 8 Haiphong
gulf: 6 Tonkin
monetary unit: 4 dong
Northwest Territories: *bay:* 5 James 6 Baffin, Hudson, Ungava
capital: 11 Yellowknife
district: 8 Franklin, Keewatin 9 Mackenzie
explorer: 7 Simpson 8 Franklin 9 Frobisher
flower: 13 mountain avens
gulf: 7 Brothia 8 Amundsen 9 Queen Maud 10 Coronation
Indian: 10 Athabascan
industry: 6 mining 7 whaling 8 fur trade
island: 6 Baffin
lake: 9 Great Bear 10 Great Slave
people: 5 Inuit 6 Eskimo
river: 9 Mackenzie 10 Coppermine
territory of: 6 Canada
north wind: 6 boreas
northeaster: 4 blow, gale, wind 5 storm
northern: 6 boreal 13 septentrional
Northern Bear: 6 Russia
Norway: *bird:* 4 rype
boat: 4 pram 5 praam 6 praham
capital: 4 Oslo (formerly Christiania)
cart: 11 stolkjaerre

chieftain: 4 jarl
city: see *town* below
coin: ore 5 krone
counties: 5 amter
county: amt 5 fylke 6 fylker(pl.), Tromso 7 Finmark
dance: 7 halling
embroidery: 9 hardanger
goblin: 5 nisse 6 kobold
governor: 6 amtman
haddock: 8 rosefish
inlet: 5 fiord, fjord
language: 5 Norse 9 Norwegian
measure: fot, mal, pot 4 alen, maal 5 kande 6 fathom 7 skieppe 9 korntonde
mountain: 5 Sogne 6 Kjolen 7 Numedal 8 Telemark, Ustetind 9 Blodfjell, Harteigen, Ramnanosi
parliament: 8 Storting 9 Storthing
plateau: 5 Dovre, velde 6 fjells 9 Hardanger
river: Ena 4 Tana 6 Lougen, Glomma
ruler: 6 hersir
saint: 4 Olaf 5 Olaus
town: Nes 4 Oslo(c.), Voss 5 Bjort, Hamar, Skein, Skjak 6 Horten, Larvik, Narvik 7 Alesund, Drammen 9 Stavanger, Trondhjem
traitor: 8 Quisling
weight: lod 4 mark, pund 9 skaalpund 10 bismerpund
nose: neb, nez(F.), pry, spy 4 beak, conk, gift, lora(pl.) 5 lorum, scent, smell, sniff, snoop, snout 6 detect, muffle, muzzle, nozzle, search, socket 7 advance, perfume 8 busybody, discover, informer, perceive 9 proboscis 11 investigate
cartilage: 6 septum
inflammation: 6 coryza 8 rhinitis
kind: pug 5 Roman 8 aquiline
large: 6 nasute
medicine: 7 errhine
muscle: 7 nasalio
opening: 4 nare 7 nostril
partition: 5 vomer
pert to: 5 nasal 6 narial, rhinal
snub: 6 simous
nosebleed: 9 epistaxis
nose-dive: dip 6 plunge 7 plummet
nosegay: 4 posy 7 bouquet, perfume
nosegay tree: 10 frangipani
nosepiece: 5 nasal 6 nozzle
nosh: 4 chew 5 munch, snack
nostalgia: 7 longing 10 melancholy 12 homesickness
Nostradamus: 4 seer 7 prophet 10 forecaster
nostril: 4 nare 5 nares(pl.), naris(pl.) 6 thrill
pert to: 5 naric 6 narial, narine
nostril-shaped: 8 nariform

nosy, nosey: 6 prying 7 curious 8 fragrant 10 malodorous 11 inquisitive

not: nae(Sc.), nay, nor 4 baal, bail, bale, nott 5 shorn 6 nought, polled, shaven 7 neither 8 hornless, negation, negative 11 nothingness

all there: 6 insane

any: nul 4 nane(Sc.), nary, none

at all: 5 never 6 noways, nowise

either: 7 neither

final: 13 interlocutory

otherwise than: 6 merely

the same: 5 other 7 another 9 different

notable: V.I.P. 6 fabled, famous, fat cat 7 eminent, storied 8 big wheel, eventful, historic 9 memorable, notorious 10 noteworthy, remarkable 12 considerable 13 distinguished, extraordinary

notal: 6 dorsal

notandum: 4 note 5 entry 9 memoranda(pl.) 10 memorandum

notarize: 6 attest 7 certify

notary: 5 clerk 8 endorser, observer, official, recorder 9 notorious, scrivener

chief: 11 protonotary 12 prothonotary

notation: 4 memo, note 7 marking 10 annotation 14 representation

phonetic: 5 Romic

notator: 5 noter 8 recorder 9 annotator

notch: cut, dag, gap, hag, jag 4 cope, dent, dint, gash, gimp, hila(pl.), kerf, nick, step 5 crena, grade, hilum, score, tally 6 crenae(pl.), crotch, defile, degree, indent, record, scotch 7 crenate, serrate 8 undercut 9 indenture 10 depression 11 indentation

notched: 5 erose 7 crenate, serrate 8 crenated, serrated

irregularly: 5 erose

note: I.O.U., jot, see 4 bill, call, chit, fame, heed, line, mark, memo, name, sign, sole, song, tone, tune 5 label, sound, token 6 billet, letter, minute, notice, record, regard, remark, renown, report 7 betoken, comment, message, missive, notanda(pl.), observe 8 annotate, breviate, dispatch, eminence, notandum, perceive, reminder 9 character 10 indication, memorandum, prominence, reputation 11 distinction, observation

accompanying: 8 overtone

bank: 6 finnip, flimsy 8 frogskin

bugle: mot

explanatory: 8 scholium 10 annotation

highest: ela

marginal: 6 postil 7 apostil 9 apostille

middle: 4 mese

musical: 4 half 5 breve, gamut, sharp, whole 6 eighth 7 punctus, quarter 8 paramese 9 semibreve

prisoner's: 4 kite

promissory: 11 pledge to pay

writer: 9 annotator

note well: 8 nota bene(L.)

notebook: log 5 diary 6 street 7 journal 10 adversaria

notecase: 10 pocketbook

noted: 9 distingue, well-known 10 celebrated 11 illustrious

notes: *literary:* ana

miscellaneous: 10 adversaria

noteworthy: 6 rubric 7 eminent, notable 9 memorable, red-letter 10 remarkable 11 outstanding 12 considerable

nothing: nil 4 free, luke, nill, zero 5 aught, nihil 6 naught, nought, trifle 7 useless 10 triviality 12 nonexistence, unimportance 14 insignificance

nothing but: all 4 mere, only

notice: ban, see 4 espy, heed, idea, mark, mind, news, note, sign 5 await, quote 6 advice, billet, espial, notion, regard, remark 7 affiche, article, discern, mention, observe, warning 8 apprisal, citation, civility 9 attention, criticism 10 cognizance, intimation, memorandum 11 garnishment 12 announcement, intelligence, notification 13 consideration

advance: 8 heraldry

book: 5 blurb

death: 4 obit 8 obituary

favorable: 4 rave

honorable: 8 citation

leave of: 8 mittimus

legal: 6 caveat

marriage: ban 4 bans 5 banns

official: 5 edict 8 bulletin 12 proclamation

paid: 13 advertisement

Patent Office: 6 caveat

public: 5 edict 8 bulletin

refuse: 6 ignore

noticeable: 7 evident, notable, salient 8 striking 9 prominent 10 noteworthy, remarkable 11 conspicuous, eye-catching, outstanding, significant

notification: 6 notice

notify: bid 4 cite, page, tell, warn 6 inform 7 apprise, declare, frutify, publish 8 acquaint 9 broadcast 10 promulgate

notion: bee 4 buzz, hint, idea, idee, view, whim 5 fancy, image 6 belief, desire, maggot, notice, theory, vagary 7 caprice, conceit, inkling, opinion, thought 9 intention 10 conception 11 inclination

notoriety: 5 eclat 9 publicity

notorious: bad, big 5 known 6 arrant, famous 7 evident 8 apparent, flagrant, infamous 9 acclaimed, well-known 11 conspicuous

notwithstanding: yet 4 even 6 algate, mauger, maugre 7 against, algates, despite, however 8 although 12 nevertheless

nougat: 5 candy 8 nut shell 10 confection
nought: bad, nil 4 zero 5 wrong 7 nothing, useless 9 worthless 10 wickedness
noun: 4 name, word 11 substantive
form: 4 case 6 gender
indeclinable: 6 aptote
kind of: 6 common, proper
verbal: 6 gerund
nourish: 4 feed, grow, rear 5 breed, nurse 6 foison, foster, suckle, supply 7 cherish, support, sustain, develop 9 cultivate, stimulate
nourishing: 4 alma 6 alible, hearty 8 nutrient 9 alimental, nutritive 10 alimentary, nutritious
nourishment: 4 food, keep, meat 5 manna 6 foison, living 7 aliment, pabulum, support 9 nutriment 10 sustenance 13 nutritiveness 14 nutritiousness
nous: 4 mind 6 reason 9 intellect
nova: new 4 star
Nova Scotia: *bay:* 5 Fundy
cape: 5 Canso, Sable 6 Breton, George
capital: 7 Halifax
city: 6 Sydney 8 Glace Bay 9 Dartmouth
county: 10 Cape Breton, Colchester, Cumberland
national park: 7 Fort Ann
native name: 6 Acadia
people: 7 Acadian 8 bluenose
port: 5 Truro
province of: 6 Canada
provincial flower: 7 arbutus 9 mayflower
settler: 10 Highlander, U.S. Loyalist
novel: new, odd 4 book 5 fresh, story 6 recent, unique 7 fiction, romance, strange, unusual 8 original, uncommon 10 newfangled
cut: 11 abridgement 12 condensation
novelette: 5 conte
novelty: fad 6 change 10 innovation, knickknack
novice: cub 4 boot, punk, tyro 5 rooky 6 rookie, tyrone 7 amateur, convert, learner 8 beginner, freshman, neophyte 9 greenhorn 10 apprentice 11 abecedarian
novitiate: 9 probation 14 apprenticeship
now: noo(Sc.) 4 here 5 today 7 because, present 9 forthwith 11 immediately
nowise: 5 navis
noxious: ill 4 evil 5 fetid 6 nocent, putrid 7 baneful, harmful, hurtful, nocuous, noisome, vicious 8 stinking, virulent 9 injurious, miasmatic, poisonous 10 pernicious 11 deleterious, destructive, unwholesome 12 insalubrious
nozzle: 4 nose, vent 5 snout
nuance: 5 shade 7 shading, soupcon 8 subtlety 10 difference, suggestion
nub: 4 core, crux, gist, hang, knob, knot,

knub, lump, neck, snag 9 substance 12 protuberance
nubia: 4 wrap 5 cloud, scarf
nubile: 12 marriageable
nubilous: 5 foggy, misty, vague 6 cloudy 7 obscure 8 overcast 10 indefinite
nuclear particle: 6 proton 7 neutron
nucleus: 4 core, seed 5 focus, umbra 6 kernel, fusion 7 fission
pert. to: 8 nucleate
starch: 4 hila(pl.) 5 hilum
nude: 4 bare 5 model, naked 6 statue 7 denuded, picture 8 buff-bare, painting, stripped 9 au naturel, unclothed, uncovered, undressed
nudge: jog, nog 4 knub, lump, poke, push 5 block, elbow
nudibranch: 7 mollusk
nudie: 9 skin flick
nudist: 7 Adamite 12 gymnosophist
nugatory: 4 vain 7 invalid, trivial 8 trifling 9 frustrate, worthless 11 ineffectual
nugget: 4 hunk, lump, mass, slug
nuisance: 4 harm, hurt, pest 6 injury 9 annoyance 12 exasperation 13 inconvenience
null: nil 6 devoid 7 nullify 11 nonexistent 13 insignificant
nullah: 5 gorge, gully 6 ravine
nullifidian: 7 skeptic 10 unbeliever
nullify: 4 flaw, null, undo, void 5 abate, annul, elide 6 cancel, negate, offset, repeal 7 abolish, destroy 8 abrogate, evacuate 9 frustrate 10 counteract, disappoint, invalidate, neutralize
numb: 4 dead, drug, dull 6 asleep, benumb, deaden, stupid, torpid 7 stupefy 8 enfeeble, helpless 9 incapable 10 indifferent, insensible
number: sum 4 curn(Sc.), data(pl.), many, mort, slew, herd, host 5 count, datum, digit, scads, score, total 6 amount, bundle, encore, figure, myriad, reckon, hirsel 7 chiffer, compute, decimal, several 8 numerate, quantity, fraction 9 aggregate, calculate, enumerate, multitude 10 collection, complement, percentage
cardinal: one, two 4 four 5 three
dice: 4 sise
indeterminate: 7 umpteen, zillion
irrational: 4 surd
ordinal: 5 first, third 6 second
prime: one, two 4 five 5 seven, three 6 eleven 8 thirteen
pure: 6 scalar
third power: 4 cube
under ten: 5 digit
whole: 7 integer
numbles: 7 giblets, innards 8 entrails
numen: 5 deity 6 genius, spirit 8 divinity

numerable: 11 enumerative

numeral: 4 word 5 digit 6 figure, letter
style: 5 Roman 6 Arabic

numerate: 4 list, tell 5 count, tally 7 tick
off

numerical group: duo 4 trio 5 octet 6
septet, sextet 7 octette, quartet, quintet, twosome 8 foursome, sextette 9
threesome

numerous: 4 lots, many 7 copious, crowded 8 abundant, multiple, thronged 9
multifold, plentiful

Numidia: *bird:* 10 demoiselle
city: 5 Hippo
king: 8 Jugurtha

numskull: 4 dolt 5 dunce 9 blockhead

nun: 4 bird, snew 5 clerk 6 pigeon, sister,
vestal 7 confine, devotee 8 titmouse,
votaress 9 priestess 10 cloistress
chief: 6 abbess
Franciscan: 5 Clare
headdress: 6 wimple
Latin: 5 Vesta
order: 6 Marist 8 Trappist 9 Dominican,
Lorettine

Nun's son: 6 Joshua

nun moth: 7 tussock

nunbird: 6 monase

nuncio: 6 legate 8 delegate 9 messenger
14 representative

nuncupate: 7 declare 8 dedicate, inscribe,
proclaim 9 designate

nuncupative: 4 oral 9 unwritten

nunnery: 5 abbey 7 convent 8 cloister 10
sisterhood
head: 6 abbess

nunni: 7 blesbok 8 antelope

nuphar: 9 water lily

nuptial: 6 bridal, genial 7 marital, wedding 11 matrimonial

nurse: 4 amah, ayah, baba, care, feed,
rear, tend 5 bonne(F.), mammy, nanny
6 attend, cradle, foster, norice, suckle 7
cherish, nourice, nourish, nurture, promote 10 breast-feed, minister to

nurse shark: 4 gata

nursery: 6 creche 7 brooder

nursling: 4 baby 9 foundling

nurture: 4 diet, feed, food, rear 5 nurse,
raise, train 6 cocker, foster 7 bring up,
cherish, educate 8 breeding, training 9
education, nutriment

nut: bur, guy, nit 4 burr, cola, core, head,
kola, nute, pili, task 5 acorn, betel,
crank, hazel, pecan 6 almond, Brazil,
cashew, fellow, peanut, pyrene 7 filbert,
hickory, lunatic, problem 8 beechnut,
chestnut, crackpot 9 eccentric 10
crackbrain, enthusiast 11 undertaking
collective: 4 mast 5 shack
edible part: 6 kernel

ivory: 4 anta

kola: 5 bichy 9 gourou-nut

medicinal: 4 cola, kola

palm: 5 betel, lichi 8 cocoanut

pert. to: 5 nucal

tropical: ben 4 cola, kola

nut-brown: 5 hazel 6 walnut 8 chestnut

nut coal: 10 anthracite

nut grass: 5 sedge

nutant: 7 nodding 8 drooping

nutmeg: *covering:* 4 mace

Nutmeg State: 11 Connecticut

nutramin: 7 vitamin

nutria: fur 5 coypu

nutriment: pap 10 sustenance 11 nourishment

nutrition: 11 nourishment 12 alimentation

nutritious: 9 healthful, wholesome 10 salubrious, nourishing

nutritive: 10 nourishing

nuts-and-bolts: 7 details 12 working
parts

nutty: 4 gaga 5 buggy, queer, spicy 7 amorous, piquant 8 demented, pleasant 10
unbalanced 12 crackbrained, enthusiastic

nuzzle: 5 nurse 6 foster, nestle 7 snuggle

nye: 4 eyas, nest, nide 5 brood

nylon: 5 crepe, fiber, ninon, tulle 6 fabric

nymph: 4 doxy 5 Aegle, naiad, siren, oread, sylph 6 nereid 7 Corycia 9 hamadryad
Arcadian: 6 Syrinx
beloved of Narcissus: 4 Echo
Cretan: 8 Cynosura
hills: 5 Oread
laurel tree: 6 Daphne
Messina Strait: 6 Scylla
Mount Ida: 6 Oenone
mountain: 5 Oread
Muslim: 5 houri
ocean: 5 siren 6 Nereid 7 Galatea, Oceanid 10 Callirrhoe
pursued by Apollo: 6 Daphne, Syrinx 8
Arethusa
queen: Mab
sea: 6 Nereid 7 Calypso
water: 4 Nais 5 Naiad 6 Egeria, Lurlei,
Undine 7 Apsaras, Hydriad, Lorelei 8
Arethusa
wood: 5 Dryad 6 Nereid 9 Hamadryad

nymphaea: 8 Castalia 9 water lily

nyssa: 6 tupelo 8 black gum

Nyx, Nox: 5 night
brother: 6 Erebus
daughter: Day 4 Eris 5 Light 10 Hesperides
father: 5 Chaos
husband: 5 Chaos 6 Erebus
son: 6 Charon, Hypnos

O

O. Henry: 6 Porter

oaf: 4 boor, dolt, fool, lout 5 clown, dunce, idiot, yoke 6 lummox 8 dumbbell 9 blockhead, foundling, schlemiel, schlemihl, simpleton 10 changeling

oafish: 6 stupid 7 loutish

oak: 5 roble 6 barren, cerris, encina 7 ambrose, durmast, turtosa 8 chaparro 9 blackjack
bark: 4 crut
bitter: 6 cerris
black: 10 quercitron
blight: 5 louse
evergreen: 4 holm
family: 8 fagaceae
fruit: 5 acron 6 camata
fungus: 10 armillaria
gall: 8 oakapple
holm: 4 ilex 5 holly
immature fruit: 6 camata
seed: 5 acorn
tannin: 6 queric 9 quercinic
white: 5 roble
young: 8 flittern

oak beauty: 4 moth

oak fern: 8 polypody

oam: 5 steam

oar: row 4 pole, pull 5 aloof, rower, scull 6 paddle, propel 7 oarsman 9 propeller
blade: 4 palm, peel
collective: 6 oarage
fulcrum: 7 oarlock
part: 4 loom
short: 5 scull
steering: 5 swape, swipe

oarlock: 5 thole 7 rowlock

oarsman: 5 rower 6 stroke 7 sculler

oasis: ojo, spa 4 merv, wadi, wady 6 refuge, relief

oast: 4 kiln, oven 6 cockle

oat: ait(Sc.) 5 grain 6 angora 7 cereal, egilops
genus: 5 avena
head: 7 panicle

oater: 7 western 10 horse opera

oath: vow 4 aith 5 aithe, curse, haith 6 appeal, pledge 7 serment 8 anathema 9 affidavit, expletive, profanity, swearword 10 adjuration, obligation 11 affirmation, imprecation
mild: 4 darn, drat, ecod, egad, gosh 5 golly 7 gee-wizz

take: 5 swear

oatmeal: 6 cereal 7 granola 8 porridge

obclude: 4 hide, 7 conceal

obdurate: 4 firm, hard 5 rough, stony 6 inured, rugged 7 adamant 8 hardened, stubborn 9 calloused, immovable, obstinate, unbending, unfeeling 10 impenitent, inflexible, insensible, persistent, unyielding 11 hardhearted, intractable, stiff-necked, unrepenting 13 unsusceptible

obeah: obi 5 charm 6 fetish, voodoo

Obed: *father:* 4 Boaz
grandson: 5 David
mother: 4 Ruth
son: 4 Jehu 5 Jesse 7 Azariah

obedience: 5 order 7 control 8 docility 10 compliance, conformity, submission 12 jurisdiction

obedient: 7 duteous, dutiful, heedful, mindful, obeying, slavish 8 amenable, biddable, yielding 9 attentive, observing, tractable

obedient plant: 10 dragonhead

obeisance: bow 5 binge, conge, honor, salam 6 congee, curtsy, fealty, homage, salaam 7 curtsey, loyalty 9 abaisance, deference, reference 10 submission 14 respectfulness

obelisk: 4 mark 5 pylon, shaft 6 dagger, guglia, guglio, needle, obelus, pillar 8 monument

Oberon: 4 king, poem 5 fairy, opera
wife: 7 Titania

obese: fat 5 plump, pudgy, pursy, stout 6 fleshy, pyknic, rotund 8 blubbery, liparous

obesity: 7 fatness 10 corpulence 11 avoirdupois
science of: 10 bariatrics

obey: ear 4 hear, mind 6 accept, submit 7 execute

obfuscate: dim 6 darken 7 becloud, confuse, mystify, obscure, perplex, stupefy 8 bewilder 9 obfuscous

obi: 4 sash 6 girdle

obiter dictum: 6 remark 7 comment 11 observation

obituary: 9 necrology 11 death notice

object: aim, end 4 goal, item 5 argue, cavil, demur, thing 6 design, entity, motive, oppose, target 7 dislike, protest, purpose, quarrel 9 challenge, intention, interpose 10 disapprove 11 expostulate, remonstrate

rare: 5 curio 7 antique

sacred: 4 urim

object lesson: 7 example

object to: 4 mind

objection: but 7 defense, protest 8 demurral 9 challenge, exception

legal: 5 demur

objectionable: 4 vile 6 horrid 9 obnoxious, offensive 11 exceptional 12 disagreeable

objective: aim, end 4 goal 6 motive, realty, target 7 purpose 8 detached 9 intention 10 impersonal

objet d'art: 4 vase 5 curio, virtu 6 bauble, gewgaw 7 bibelot 8 figurine

objurgate: 5 abuse, chide, decry 6 berate, rebuke 7 reprove, upbraid 8 execrate 9 castigate

oblate: 4 monk 8 dedicate, monastic

opposite of: 7 prolate

oblation: 4 gift 6 corban 7 charity 8 devotion, offering 9 sacrifice

obligate: 4 bind 6 fasten 7 promise

obligation: vow 4 band, bond, debt, duty, loan, must, oath, onus 6 devoir, pledge 7 promise 8 contract 9 agreement, liability 10 allegiance, commitment, compulsion 11 obstruction 12 indebtedness 14 responsibility

obligato: 13 accompaniment

obligatory: 7 binding, bounden 8 forcible, imposing 9 mandatory

oblige: 4 pawn 5 favor, force 6 engage, please 7 gratify, require 8 mortgage, obligate 9 constrain 11 necessitate

obliged: 8 beholden, grateful, indebted

obliging: 4 kind 5 buxom, civil 6 clever 7 amiable 9 agreeable, courteous 11 complaisant 13 accommodating

oblique: 4 awry, bias, skew 5 askew, bevel, cross, slant 6 aslant, awash 7 askance, crooked, evasive, scalene 8 inclined, indirect, sidelong, sideways, sidewise, slanting 9 slantways, slantwise, underhand 10 circuitous 12 disingenuous

render: 5 splay

obliterate: 4 blot, dele, rase, raze 5 annul, erase 6 cancel, delete, efface, sponge 7 expunge 10 annihilate, extinguish

obliteration: 7 erasure, removal 10 extinction

oblivion: 5 Lethe, limbo 6 pardon 7 amnesty, nirvana 13 forgetfulness

producer of: 8 nepenthe

oblong: 8 avelonge 9 elongated 11 rectangular

rounded: 7 ellipse

obloquy: 5 abuse, odium 6 infamy 7 calumny, censure 8 disgrace, dishonor 12 reprehension, vituperation 13 animadversion

obnoxious: 4 foul, vile 6 horrid, liable, odious, rancid 7 hateful 9 offensive, repugnant, verminous 13 objectionable

oboe: 4 reed 5 shawm 6 surnai, surnay 7 hautboy, musette 8 szopelka

early relative: 5 shawm

obscene: 4 foul, lewd, nast 5 bawdy, gross, nasty 6 coarse, filthy, impure, vulgar 7 profane 8 immodest, indecent 9 loathsome, offensive, repulsive 10 disgusting, fescennine, licentious 11 foulmouthed 12 pornographic

obscure: dim 4 blot, blur, dark, hazy, hide 5 bedim, befog, blind, faint, foggy, inner, murky, vague 6 bemist, cloudy, darken, darkle, gloomy, mystic, remote 7 becloud, conceal, confuse, cryptic, eclipse, shadowy, unknown, unnoted 8 abstruse, darkling, disguise, mystical, nameless, obstruse, oversile 9 ambiguous, blindfold, difficult, enigmatic, equivocal, mystical, recondite, undefined 10 caliginous, extinguish, indistinct, overshadow 14 uncomprehended

obsecrate: 4 pray 7 beseech, entreat 8 petition 10 supplicate

obsequious: 5 slick 7 devoted, dutiful, fawning, servile, slavish 8 obedient, toadying, toadyish 9 attentive, compliant, parasitic 10 submissive 11 deferential, subservient

obsequy: 4 rite 6 exequy, ritual 7 funeral 8 ceremony 10 compliance

observance: act 4 form, rite, rule 6 custom, notice, regard 8 ceremony, practice 9 attention, deference 11 observation 12 constitution

religious: 6 Novena 9 sacrament

observant: 5 alert 7 careful, mindful 8 watchful 9 attentive 10 perceptive 11 considerate

observation: 4 heed, note 6 notice, remark 7 auspice, autopsy, descant

preliminary: 5 proem

observatory: 4 Lick 5 tower 7 lookout, Palomar 9 astronomy 11 Mount Wilson

observe: eye, see, spy 4 espy, heed, keep, look, nark, note, obey, tout, wait, yeme 5 study, watch 6 behold, descry, follow, notice, regard, remark 7 comment, discern, respect, witness 8 perceive, preserve 9 advertise, celebrate, solemnize 10 animadvert, scrutinize

observer: 8 audience, informer, onlooker 9 bystander, spectator

obsess: 5 beset, haunt 6 harass 9 preoccupy

obsession: 5 craze, mania 6 fetish, hang-up 7 passion 8 idee fixe(F.) 13 preoccupation

obsidian: 5 lapis

obsolescence: 9 desuetude

obsolete: old 4 dead 5 passe 7 ancient, archaic, extinct, outworn 8 out-dated, outmoded 9 discarded, out-of-date 10 antiquated 12 old-fashioned

obstacle: bar, dam, let 4 snag 5 block, hitch 6 bunker, hocket, hurdle 7 barrier 9 hindrance 10 difficulty, impediment 11 Chinese wall, obstruction 12 entanglement

insurmountable: 7 impasse

military: 6 abates

obstetrician: 7 midwife 10 accoucheur

obstetrics: 8 tocology 9 maieutics

obstinate: set 4 dour 5 balky, sulky, tough 6 assish, dogged, mulish, sullen, unruly 7 froward, willful 8 crotched, obdurate, perverse, stubborn 9 foreright, pigheaded 10 bullheaded, determined, headstrong, inflexible, persistent, refractory, selfwilled 11 intractable, opinionated 12 closed-minded, contumacious, pertinacious, recalcitrant

obstreperous: 5 noisy 6 unruly 9 clamorous 10 boisterous, vociferous 11 disobedient

obstruct: bar, dam, dit, gag, mar 4 clog, ditt, fell, stop 5 beset, block, check, choke, delay, hedge 6 arrest, cumber, forbar, hamper, hinder, impede, oppose, retard, screen 7 barrier, forelay, occlude 8 blockade, encumber, incumber 9 barricade, embarrass, interfere, interrupt 10 filibuster 11 fillibuster

obstruction: 4 snag 5 gorce, hitch 7 barrace, barrage, barrier, blinder 8 embolism, obstacle 10 difficulty, impediment 11 impeachment

obtain: beg, bum, eke, get, win 4 earn, fang, gain, hent, reap 5 cadge, ettle, reach 6 attain, derive, secure, sponge 7 achieve, acquire, capture, chevise, prevail, procure, receive, succeed

by threat: 6 extort 9 blackmail

obtainable: 9 available

obtest: 6 beg for 7 beseech 10 supplicate

obtrude: 5 eject, expel 6 butt in, impose

obtruncate: lop 6 behead 7 shorten 8 retrench 10 decapitate

obtrusive: 5 fresh, pushy 7 blatant, forward, pushing 9 intrusive 10 aggressive 11 impertinent 12 presumptuous

obtund: 4 dull 5 blunt, quell 6 deaden

obtuse: dim 4 dull 5 blink, blunt, crass, dense 6 stupid 8 boeotian, hebetate, purblind 11 insensitive

obvelation: 7 veiling 10 concealing

obverse: 4 face 5 front 8 converse 10 complement 11 counterpart

obviate: 7 prevent, ward off 8 preclude 9 forestall, interfere, intervene

obvious: 4 open 5 broad, clear, gross, overt, plain 6 patent 7 evident, glaring, visible 8 apparent, distinct, manifest, palpable 11 conspicuous

obvolute: 9 contorted, convolute 11 overlapping

oca, oka: 5 tuber 6 oxalis, sorrel

occasion: 4 hint, sele, time 5 casus, cause, event, nonce, slant 6 excuse, moment 7 instant, pretext 8 ceremony, engender, exigency, function, incident 9 condition, happening 11 opportunity, point in time

festive: 7 holiday

occasional: odd 4 orra 5 stray 6 daimen, random 8 sporadic 10 infrequent

occasionally: 7 betimes 9 sometimes 10 now and then

Occidental: 4 West 6 ponent 7 Western 9 Hesperian, Westerner

occlude: 5 close 6 absorb 7 shut out, take in 8 obstruct

occult: 4 hide 5 eerie, magic 6 hidden, mystic, secret, voodoo 7 alchemy, cryptic 8 esoteric, mystical 9 concealed, recondite 10 mysterious, necromancy 11 supernormal 12 supernatural 13 imperceptible

science: 9 esoterics

occultation: 7 eclipse 13 disappearance

occultism: 5 magic 6 cabala 7 mystery

occupant: 6 inmate, tenant 7 citizen, dweller 10 inhabitant

occupation: job 4 note, toil, work 5 graft, trade 6 career, metier, tenure 7 calling, pursuit 8 business, function, industry, vocation 10 employment, habitation, profession

transient: 5 hobby 9 avocation

occupied: 4 busy, rapt 9 engrossed, inhabited

occupy: sit, use 4 busy, fill, hold, take 6 absorb, employ, engage, expend, fulfil, tenant 7 cohabit, engross, fulfill, inhabit, oversit, pervade, possess 8 interest

occur: be 4 come, meet, pass 5 clash, exist 6 appear, arrive, befall, betide, happen, strike 9 take place

again: 5 recur 6 repeat

occurrence: hap 4 case 5 event, thing 7 episode 8 incident, occasion 9 encounter, happening 12 circumstance

supernatural: 7 miracle

unusual: 6 oddity

ocean (see also **sea**): 4 brim, deep, main 5 brine 6 Arctic, Indian 7 expanse, Pacific 8 Atlantic 9 Antarctic, vastness

approach: 7 seagate

floating matter: 5 algae, lagan 7 flotsam

mammal: 5 whale

periodic motion: 4 tide
swell: sea 4 wave 6 roller
Oceania: 6 Malaya 9 Australia, Melanesia, Polynesia 10 Micronesia, New Zealand 11 archipelago
Oceanid: 5 nymph
Oceanus: *daughter:* 5 Doris 7 Oceanid 8 Eurynome
father: 6 Uranus
mother: 4 Gaea
sister: 6 Tethys
wife: 6 Tethys
ocellus: 6 stemma 7 eyespot
ocelot: cat 7 leopard
ocher: 5 color 7 pigment
ocrea: 6 greave, sheath 7 legging
octave: 4 cask, note, utas 5 eight 8 interval 9 harmonics, organ stop
Octavia: *brother:* 7 Augustus
husband: 6 Antony
octet: 5 group 7 huitain 8 electron
octopus: 5 polyp, poulp 6 poulpe 7 mollusk, polypus 9 devilfish 10 cephalopod
arm: 8 tentacle
kin: 5 squid 10 cuttlefish
secretion: ink
ten arms: 7 decapod
octoroon: 5 metis 7 metisse, mulatto
octose: 5 sugar
octroi: tax 5 grant 9 privilege 10 concession
octuple: 9 eightfold
ocular: eye 5 optic 6 visual
odd: awk 4 fell, left, lone, orra(Sc.), rare 5 droll, extra, funny, impar, outre(F.), queer, weird 6 quaint, uneven 7 azygous, bizarre, curious, strange, unusual 8 fanciful, freakish, peculiar, singular, unpaired 9 burlesque, eccentric, fantastic, grotesque, unmatched, whimsical 10 accidental, occasional 13 extraordinary
oddity: 5 quirk 8 crotchet, quiddity 9 curiosity 12 eccentricity, idiosyncrasy
oddment: ort 5 scrap 7 remnant 8 fragment, leftover
odds: 7 dispute, quarrel 8 variance 9 advantage 10 dissension 13 probabilities
odds and ends: 4 orts 5 refuse, scraps 7 mixture, seconds 8 remnants, sundries 9 leftovers 10 miscellany, remainders
ode: 4 hymn, poem 5 lyric, paean, psalm, verse 7 epicede 8 canticle 9 epicedium
birthday: 12 genethliacon
kind of: 8 pindaric
part: 5 epode 6 strophe
victory: 9 epinicion, epinikion
odeon: 4 hall 5 odeum 7 gallery, theater
Oder tributary: 6 Neisse
odic: 5 lyric

daughter-in-law: 5 Nanna
descendant: 5 Scyld
father: Bor
hall: 7 Valhall 8 Valhalla
horse: 8 Sleipner
maiden: 8 Valkyrie
mother: 6 Bestla
raven: 5 Hugin, Munin
ring: 8 Draupnir
ship: 7 Naglfar 11 Skidbladnir
son: Tyr 4 Thor, Vali 5 Baldr 6 Balder
spear: 7 Gungnir
sword: 4 Gram
throne: 10 Hlidskjalf
wife: 4 Fria, Rind 5 Frigg, Rindr 6 Frigga
wolf: 4 Gere, Geri 5 Freki
odious: 4 foul, loth, vile 5 loath 7 hateful, heinous, hideous 8 damnable, flagrant, infamous 9 abhorrent, invidious, obnoxious, offensive, repugnant 10 abominable, detestable, disgusting, forbidding 11 ignominious, opprobrious
odium: 6 stigma 8 aversion, disfavor, disgrace 9 antipathy 14 disapprobation
odograph: 9 pedometer
odontalgia: 9 toothache
odor: 4 fume, funk, nose, olid, tang 5 aroma, ewder, fetor, flair, fumet, nidor, scent, smell, stink 6 breath, flavor, foetor, repute, stench 7 bouquet, essence, flavour, fumette, perfume 9 fragrance, redolence 10 estimation, reputation
odoriferous: 4 gamy 5 balmy 6 smelly 8 fragrant 9 odiferous
Odysseus: See Ulysses
Odyssey author: 5 Homer
oeconomus: 7 manager, steward 9 majordomo
Oedipus: *brother-in-law:* 5 Creon
complex: 6 momism
daughter: 6 Ismene 8 Antigone
father: 5 Laius
foster parent: 7 Polybus 8 Periboea
mother: 7 Jocasta
refuge: 7 Colonus
son: 8 Eteocles 9 Polynices 10 Polyneices
victim: 5 Laius 6 Sphinx
wife: 7 Jocasta
oeillade: 4 ogle 6 glance
Oeneus: *father:* 8 Porthaon
kingdom: 7 Claydon, Pleuron
mother: 6 Euryte
wife: 7 Althaea
Oenomaus: *charioteer:* 8 Myrtilus
daughter: 10 Hippodamia
father: 4 Ares
kingdom: 4 Pisa
slayer: 6 Pelops
oeuvre: 4 opus, work
of: 4 from 5 about 10 concerning
off: 4 away, doff, gone 5 aside, wrong 6 absent, cuckoo, remote 7 distant, fur-

ther, removed **8** launched, postpone
and on: **8** fitfully **10** in snatches **11** irregularly

base: bad **5** wrong **7** illegal **9** incorrect, out-of-line **10** unsuitable

beat: odd **5** kinky **6** far out **7** unusual **9** different **11** unorthodox

camera: **9** privately **13** in private life

chance: **10** likelihood **11** possibility

color: **4** blue, racy **5** spicy **6** risque, unwell **10** discordant, out-of-sorts, suggestive

key: **10** discordant

offal: **5** gurry, waste **6** refuse **7** carrion, garbage, hogwash, leaving, rubbish **8** gralloch

offend: sin, vex **4** hurt, miff **5** abuse, anger, annoy, grate, grill, pique, shock, wrong **6** attack, grieve, insult, revolt **7** affront, default, mortify, outrage, violate **8** trespass **9** disoblige, displease **10** transgress

offended: **5** sore **7** injured **8** insulted

offender: **7** culprit **8** criminal

offense: **5** crime, error, fault, guilt, malum **6** attack, felony, pritch **7** misdeed, umbrage **8** peccancy, trespass **9** indignity **10** aggression, peccadillo, resentment **11** delinquency, misdemeanor

civil: **4** tort **11** stellionate

law: **5** delit **6** delict **8** delictum

moral: **4** evil

offensive: bad **4** foul **5** fetid **6** attack, coarse, horrid **7** beastly, fulsome, hateful, noisome **8** invading **9** loathsome, obnoxious, repugnant **10** aggressive, disgusting, forbidding, ill-favored, scurrilous, ungracious, unpleasant **11** distasteful **12** disagreeable **13** objectionable

offer: bid, try **4** bode, show **6** adduce, allege, tender **7** advance, commend, hold out, present, proffer, propine, propose, suggest **8** bequeath, overture, proposal **9** avertment, volunteer

last: **9** ultimatum

solemn: **6** pledge

offering: **4** gift **6** corban, victim **7** present **9** sacrifice

religious: **5** tithe **7** deodate **8** anathema, oblation **12** contribution

sacrificial: **5** hiera **7** sphagia(pl.) **8** sphagion

offhand: **4** curt **6** casual **7** brusque **8** cavalier, informal **9** impromptu **10** improvised **11** extemporary **14** extemporaneous, unpremeditated **15** autoschediastic **16** extemporaneously

office: job **4** post, wike **5** place, wiken **6** bureau **7** camarin, station **8** function, high sign, position **9** bailiwick, situation **10** commission **11** appointment **13** collectorship

chief: **4** boss **7** manager

deprive of: **6** depose **7** impeach

divine: **9** akoluthia

help: **5** clerk **6** typist **9** secretary **12** stenographer

machine: **5** Xerox **6** copier **8** computer **9** stenotype **10** calculator, mimeograph, typewriter **11** comptometer

paid without work: **8** sinecure

purchase or sale: **8** barratry

put in again: **7** re-elect **9** re-instate

seeker of: **7** nominee **9** candidate **10** politician

officeholder: **6** winner **8** official, placeman **9** incumbent **10** bureaucrat

officer: **4** aide **5** usher **6** direct, ensign, manage, tindal **7** command, conduct, general **8** adjutant **9** executive

army: **5** major **7** captain, colonel, general **10** lieutenant

assistant: **4** aide

college: **4** dean **6** bursar **10** chancellor

future: **5** cadet **10** midshipman

law: cop **7** bailiff, marshal, sheriff **9** constable, detective, patrolman, policeman

naval: **4** mate **5** bosun **6** ensign, yeoman **7** admiral, captain, striper **9** boatswain, commander, commodore **10** lieutenant

noncommissioned: **4** mate **5** chief **8** corporal, sergeant

presiding: **6** archon **7** speaker **8** chairman **9** moderator, president

prison: **5** guard **6** warden

warrant: **5** bosun **9** boatswain

officers: **5** staff

official: **6** formal **9** escribano(Sp.), executive, ex officio **10** authorized, bureaucrat, ex cathedra, magistrate **11** ceremonious **13** authoritative

administrative: **5** reeve **9** executive

assistant: **4** aide

city or town: **5** mayor **7** manager, marshal **8** alderman **9** selectman **10** councilman

civil: **5** judge, mayor **7** bailiff, marshal, sheriff **8** governor **9** constable, patrolman, policeman, president **10** magistrate

corrupt: **7** grafter

despotic: **6** satrap

government: **6** syndic

judicial: **8** assessor, recorder **9** treasurer **11** comptroller

local: **6** bailie(Sc.), grieve **7** burgess

public: **6** notary

state: **8** minister **9** secretary

officiate: act **6** supply, umpire **7** perform, referee **9** celebrate

officious: **4** busy, cool, pert **6** formal **8** arrogant, impudent, informal, official **10** impersonal, meddlesome **11** efficacious, impertinent, pragmatical **12** contemptuous **14** supererogatory **16** superserviceable

offing: 6 future 7 by-and-by, picture 10 background

offset: 6 contra 7 balance 10 compensate, complement 11 counterpoise

offshoot: rod 5 bough, scion 6 branch, sprout 7 spin-off 9 by-product, outgrowth 10 descendant

offspring: fry, imp, kid, son 4 brat, chit, seed 5 brood, child, fruit, issue, scion 6 foster, result 7 outcome, produce, product, progeny 8 children, daughter, geniture 9 genealogy, youngster 10 descendant, generation

off the rack: 9 ready-made 11 ready-to-wear

oficina(Sp.): 5 works 6 office 7 factory 10 laboratory

oflete: 5 wafer 8 oblation, offering

often: 4 much 6 common 8 frequent, repeated 10 frequently 11 continually, over and over

ogdoad: 5 eight

ogee: See **molding**

Ogier: 4 Dane, hero 6 prince 8 Norseman

ogle: eye 4 gaze, leer, look 5 stare 7 examine 10 rubberneck

ogre: 5 demon, giant 6 tyrant, yaksha, yakshi 7 bugaboo, monster

ogress: 5 harpy, vixen 6 virago

ogygian: 7 ancient 8 primeval

oh: ach(G.) 4 ouch

Ohio: *capital:* 8 Columbus
  city: Ada 5 Akron, Berea, Cadiz, Niles, Xenia 6 Canton, Dayton, Lorain, Toledo 9 Sandusky 9 Cleveland 10 Cincinnati, Youngstown 11 Chillicothe 13 Yellow Springs
  county: 4 Lake 5 Allen, Clark 6 Butler, Lorain, Summit 8 Cuyahoga, Franklin, Hamilton
  Indian: 4 Erie 7 Wyandot
  lake: 4 Erie
  mountain range: 9 Allegheny
  nickname: 7 Buckeye
  river: 4 Ohio 5 Miami 6 Maumee, Scioto 7 Portage
  state bird: 8 cardinal
  state flower: 9 carnation
  state tree: 7 buckeye

oil: ben, fat ile 4 balm, fuel 5 bribe, oleum 6 aceite, anoint, chrism, grease 7 lanolin 8 flattery, soft soap 9 lubricate, petroleum
  blasting: 14 nitroglycerine
  bone: 6 olanin
  butter: 4 ghee, oleo
  cedar and juniper: 8 alkitran 9 alchitran
  coal: 8 photogen
  derived from: 5 elaic, oleic
  exporting group: 4 Opec
  in skin: 5 sebum
  linseed: 6 carron

liquid compound: 5 olein
mineral: 7 naphtha
orange-blossom: 6 neroli
pert. to: 5 oleic
plant: 6 sesame
prospector: 10 wildcatter
salt: 7 bittern
ship: 6 tanker
torch: 7 lucigen
vegetable: 8 macassar
vessel: 4 drum, olpe 5 cruet, cruse 6 tanker 7 cresset
well: 6 gusher
whale: 5 sperm

oil beetle: 5 meloe

oilbird: 8 guacharo

oil bottle: 5 cruet

oil fish: 7 escolar

oil lamp: 7 coal-oil 8 kerosene

oil plant: 6 sesame

oil rock: 5 shale 9 limestone

oil tree: 4 eboe, tung 5 mahwa

oil well: 6 gusher

oilcan: 5 oiler

oilcloth: 8 linoleum

oiler: 6 oilcan, tanker

oilseed: til 4 teel 6 sesame 7 linseed 8 rapeseed 10 castorbean, cottonseed

oilskin: 5 squam 7 slicker 8 raincoat

oilstone: 4 hone 5 shale 9 whetstone

oily: fat 4 glib 5 bland, fatty, soapy, suave 6 greasy, oleose, supple 7 fulsome, pinguid 8 slippery, unctuous 9 compliant, plausible 10 oleaginous 11 subservient

ointment: 4 balm, mull, nard 5 cream, salve 6 balsam, cerate 7 unguent 9 spikenard
  application: 11 embrocation
  Biblical: 9 spikenard
  dry: 9 xeromyron, xeromyrum
  hair: 6 pomade 7 pomatum
  oil: 6 carron, cerate 7 oleamen
  veterinary: 8 remolade 9 remoulade
  wax: 6 cerate

Oise tributary: 5 Aisne

Oisin's father: 4 Finn

ojo: 5 oasis

okay: yes 6 ratify 7 approve, consent, correct 10 acceptable

Okie: 7 migrant

Okinawa capital: 4 Naha

Oklahoma: *capital:* 12 Oklahoma City
  city: Ada 4 Enid 5 Tulsa 6 Lawton, Norman 8 Muskegee
  county: Kay 5 Atoka, Caddo 6 Carter 8 Comanche
  highest point: 9 Black Mesa
  Indian: 4 Otoe, Waco 7 Wichita 8 Tawkoni
  lake: 7 Eufaula
  mountain: 5 Ozark 6 Boston 7 Wichita 8 Ouachita

nickname: 6 Sooner
river: Red 4 Blue 5 Grand 7 Washita 8 Arkansas, Cimarron, Salt Fork 9 Verdigris
state bird: 10 flycatcher
state flower: 9 mistletoe
state tree: 6 redbud
okra: 4 soup 5 bendy, gumbo 8 hibiscus
old: agy, ald, eld 4 aged, auld 5 anile, hoary, stale 6 former, infirm, mature, senile, shabby 7 ancient, antique, archaic 8 lifelong, medieval, obsolete 9 doddering, hackneyed, long-lived, senescent, venerable 10 antiquated 11 experienced 12 antediluvian
old age: 10 senescence 11 senectitude
science of: 10 geriatrics
Old Bailey: 4 gaol, jail 6 prison
Old Bay State: 13 Massachusetts
old boy: man 6 alumni(pl.) 7 alumnus
Old Dominion State: 8 Virginia
Old Faithful: 6 geyser
old-fashioned: 5 glass, passe 6 drink, fogram, fogrum, quaint 7 ancient, antique, archaic 8 cocktail, obsolete 9 primitive 10 antiquated 13 horse-and-buggy
Old Franklin State: 9 Tennessee
Old Guard: 13 establishment
old hat: 5 dated, stale, trite 6 cliché 7 vintage 8 shopworn 9 hackneyed, out-of-date
Old Hickory: 13 Andrew Jackson
Old Line State: 8 Maryland
old maid: 8 cardgame, spinster
Old Noll: 14 Oliver Cromwell
Old Rough and Ready: 6 Taylor
Old Sod: 4 Erin 7 Ireland
Old Testament: See Bible
old-womanish: 5 anile
Old World: 6 Europe
ape: 6 baboon 10 catarrhina, catarrhine
carnivore: 5 genet
dish: 5 tansy
falcon: 5 saker
goat: 4 ibex
lizard: 5 agama 9 chameleon
mouse: 6 jerboa
olden: 6 bygone 7 ancient
older: 5 elder 6 senior 8 ancestor 11 forefathers 12 predecessors
oldest: 4 dean 6 eldest
olea: 5 olive
oleaginous: 4 oily 5 fatty 7 fulsome
oleander: 5 shrub 9 evergreen 12 rhododendron
olecranon: 5 ancon 9 funny bone
oleo: 9 margarine
oleoresin: 5 anime, elemi, tolus 7 copaiba 10 turpentine
oleum: oil
olfaction: 7 osmesis 8 smelling
olid: 4 gamy 5 fetid

olinda bug: 6 weevil
olio: 4 stew 6 medley 7 melange, mixture 8 mishmash 9 potpourri 10 collection, hodgepodge, miscellany 11 variety show
oliphant: 4 horn 8 elephant
olive: 4 olea 9 appetizer
enzyme: 6 olease
overripe: 5 drupe
pert. to: 9 oleaceous
stuffed: 6 pimola
wild: 8 oleaster
oliver: 6 hammer
olivet: 5 pearl
olla: jar, jug, pot
olivine: 10 chrysolite
ollapodrida: 4 hash, olio, olla, stew 6 medley 9 potpourri
olm: 7 proteus 10 salamander
ology: ism 7 science
oloroso: 6 sherry
olpe: 5 flask 6 vessel 7 pitcher
Olympic cupbearer: 4 Hebe 8 Ganymede
Olympus: *deity:* See Greek: *god*
pert. to: 7 exalted, godlike, Olympic 8 heavenly, majestic 9 celestial
Oman: *capital:* Muscat
monetary unit: rial
Omar Khayyam's country: 4 Iran 6 Persia
omber: 8 cardgame
ombudsman: 3 judge 8 mediator
omega: end 4 last 6 letter
omelet: 4 eggs 8 fooyung
omen: 4 bode, omen, sign 5 augur, boder, freet, freit, token 6 augury, handel, hansel 7 auspice, portent, presage, warning 8 bodement, forebode, foresign 9 foretoken 10 foreboding, forerunner, indication, prediction 11 premonition
ominous: 4 dour, grim 5 fatal 6 dismal 7 fateful, fearful 8 menacing, sinister 9 prophetic 10 inexorable, portentous 11 threatening
omission: cut 5 blank, chasm, error 7 default, failure 9 exclusion, oversight
mark of: 5 caret 7 ellipse 10 apostrophe
of vowel: 7 elision
tacit: 7 silence
omit: cut 4 balk, dele, drop, miss, skip, slip 5 abate, elide, spare 6 beleve, cancel, delete, except, forget, ignore 7 beleave, discard, neglect 8 overlook 9 disregard, pretermit
omneity: 7 allness 13 comprehensive
omnibus: 5 barge, whole 11 compilation
omnipotent: God 4 able 5 deity, great 6 arrant, mighty 8 almighty, powerful 9 unequaled, unlimited 11 all-powerful
omnipresent: 7 allover 10 everywhere, ubiquitous
omniscient: 4 wise 7 learned 8 powerful

10 all-knowing, allwitting 11 everpresent

omnitude: 7 allness 8 totality 12 universality

omoplate: 7 scapula

omphalos: hub 4 boss, knob 5 navel, novel 6 center 9 umbilical 10 focal point

Omri: *daughter:* 8 Athaliah
successor: 4 Ahab

on: 4 atop, upon 5 about, above, ahead, along, anent 6 anenst, within 7 forward 10 concerning
account of: for
all sides: 5 about 6 around
and on: 4 ever 7 endless, forever, tedious
behalf: for
other side: 4 over 6 across

on the contrary: 6 rather

on the other hand: but 7 however 8 although 11 nonetheless 12 contrariwise, nevertheless

on time: 6 prompt

on what account: why

Ona: 7 Fuegian

onager: ass 5 kiang 6 catapult

Onam's son: 4 Jada 7 Shammai

once: ane(Sc.) 4 erst, past 5 aince(Sc.) 6 former 7 quondam 8 formerly, one time, whenever
in a while: 9 sometimes 12 occasionally
more: 4 anew, echo 5 again 6 encore, repeat
over: 6 glance, survey 10 inspection
upon a time: 7 formerly

oncorhynchus: 6 salmon

one: ain(Sc.), ein(G.), tae(Sc.), una, une(F.), yae(Sc.) 4 same, sole, some, unal, unit 5 alone, unity 6 person, single, unique, united 7 numeral, pronoun 8 unbroken 9 singleton, undivided, unmarried 10 individual
after another: 8 serially, seriatim 11 consecutive 12 successively
by one: 6 apiece, singly 10 separately

one-chambered: 10 unicameral

one-colored: 13 monochromatic

one-footed: 6 uniped

one-sided: 6 biased, uneven, unfair, unjust 7 bigoted, partial 10 prejudiced, unilateral

one-spot: 4 buck 6 dollar

one tenth: 5 tithe

one thousand: mil

one twenty-fourth: 5 carat

onegite: 8 amethyst

one-horse: 5 petty 6 little

O'Neill, Eugene: 9 dramatist
character: 4 Anna, Nina, Orin, Yank 5 Brant 7 Christine, Lavinia
play: Ile 11 The Hairy Ape 12 Ah, Wilderness, Anna Christie, Emperor Jones 15 The Iceman Cometh

oneism: 6 egoism, monism

oneness: 7 concord 8 identity, sameness 9 agreement 11 singularity

onerous: 4 hard 5 heavy 7 arduous, onerose 8 exacting 9 laborious 10 burdensome, cumbersome, oppressive

onetime: 7 quondam 8 formerly

one-upmanship: 7 cunning, 11 competition, superiority

onfall: 5 onset 6 attack

ongoing: 6 course 9 improving, operating 10 progressive

onion: 4 boll, cepa, leek 5 cibol, peral 7 Bermuda, onionet, shallot 8 eschalot, rareripe, scallion
genus: 6 allium

onlooker: 5 gazer 7 witness 8 audience, beholder 9 bystander, spectator 10 rubberneck

only: 4 just, lone, mere, sole 5 afald 6 anerly, barely, merely, simple, single, singly, solely 9 allenarly, excepting 11 exclusively

onomasticon: 7 lexicon 10 dictionary

onomatopoeic: 5 mimic 6 echoic 9 imitative

onset: 4 dash, dint, fard, rese, rush 5 braid, brunt, faird, frush, start 6 attack, charge 7 assault, attempt, brattle 9 beginning, encounter, onslaught 12 commencement

onslaught: 5 onset 6 attack 7 assault, descent

Ontario: *bay:* 8 Georgian
capital: 7 Toronto
city: 6 London, Ottawa 7 Windsor 8 Hamilton 9 Kitchener
fort: 5 George, Henry
highest point: 9 Ogidaki Mt.
lake: 4 Erie, Seul 5 Eagle, Rainy 7 Ontario 8 St. Joseph
province of: 6 Canada
provincial flower: 8 trillium
river: 5 Grand, Moose, Trent 6 Thames

onto: 4 atop 6 aboard

onus: 4 duty, load 6 burden, charge, stigma 10 obligation

onward: 4 away 5 ahead, along, forth 7 forward

onyx: 5 black 10 chalcedony

oodles: 4 heap 5 scads 8 lashings 9 abundance

oolong: tea

oomph: vim 5 drive, verve, vigor 6 energy pizazz, spirit 8 strength, vitality

oopak: tea

oorial: sha 5 sheep

ooze: bog, mud 4 drip, leak, mire, seep, slob 5 exude, gleet, marsh, slime, weeze 6 sludge 8 transude 9 percolate

opah: 4 fish 5 cravo

opal: gem 5 noble, resin 7 girasol, hyalite 8 girasole 10 chalcedony
girasole: 10 chalcedony

variety: 8 menilite 9 cacholong

opalescent: 7 opaline 8 irisated 10 iridescent

opaque: 4 dark, dull 5 dense 6 obtuse, stupid 7 obscure 8 eyeshade 10 lightproof 14 unintelligible

open: dup, ope 4 ajar, flue, free, undo 5 agape, apert, begin, clear, frank, lance, overt, naked, plain, start, untie 6 candid, direct, expand, expose, honest, liable, patent, unbolt, unfold, unfurl, unlock, unseal, unstop 7 artless, dispart, obvious, sincere, unclose 8 apparent, commence, disclose, dispread, explicit, extended, initiate, manifest, patulous, unfasten 9 dispread, originate, uncovered 10 accessible, forthright, inaugurate, unreserved 11 susceptible, unconcealed, within reach 13 undissembling 15 straightforward

bursting: 10 dehiscence

fully: 4 wide 5 agape 7 yawning 9 dehiscent, full-blown

partly: mid 4 ajar

open-and-shut: 7 evident 10 guaranteed

open air: 8 al fresco

open bar: 10 free drinks

open door: 6 entree 11 hospitality

open-eyed: 5 awake 8 vigilant, watchful 9 receptive 10 astonished, discerning

opener: key 4 knob 5 latch 6 sesame 8 aperient

openhanded: 4 free 7 liberal 8 generous 9 receptive 10 munificent

opening: os; gap, ora(pl.) 4 bore, door, fent, gate, hole, pass, rift, rima, slit, slot, span, vent 5 brack, cleft, debut, mouth, start, width 6 avenue, breach, hiatus, lacuna, outlet, portal, spread 7 crevice, fissure, orifice 8 aperture, overture 11 opportunity

enlarge: 4 ream

escape: 4 muse 5 batch, meuse

having: 10 fenestrate

in chess: 6 gambit

mouth-like: 5 stoma 7 stomata(pl.)

slitlike: 4 rima

small: 4 pore 5 chink 6 cranny, eyelet 7 foramen, pinhole 8 foramina(pl.)

openmouthed: 6 amazed, gaping, greedy 8 ravenous 9 clamorous 10 vociferous

openwork: 7 tracery

opera: 4 Aida 5 Faust 6 Boheme, Carmen, Otello 7 Fidelio 8 Falstaff, Parsifal, Traviata, Walkyrie 9 Lohengrin, Pagliacci, Rheingold, Rigoletto, Trovatore 10 Magic Flute, Tannhauser 11 Don Giovanni 16 Marriage of Figaro

comic: 5 buffa

division: 5 scena

glasses: 9 lorgnette 10 binoculars

horse: 7 Western

kind: 4 soap 5 comic, horse 8 burletta

part: 4 aria

singer: 4 Bori, Pons 5 Eames, Gigli, Melba, Patti, Sills 6 Callas, Caruso, Farrar 8 Flagstad 9 Pavarotti 10 Sutherland

soap: 6 serial 9 melodrama

solo: 4 aria

song: 4 aria 7 sortita 8 cavatina 9 cabaletta

star: 4 diva

opera house: 7 theater

operate: act, man, run, use 4 work 6 affect, effect, manage, open up 7 conduct 10 accomplish

by hand: 10 manipulate

operation: use 4 deed 6 agency 7 process, surgery 8 creation, exercise, function 9 actuation, influence, procedure 10 production 11 maintenance, transaction

operative: 4 hand, open 6 active, artist 7 artisan 8 mechanic 9 detective

beyond itself: 9 transeunt

for past: 11 retroactive

operator: 5 agent, quack 6 dealer, driver 7 manager, operant, surgeon 8 motorist 9 conductor, operative 10 mountebank

operculum: lid 4 flap 8 covering

operose: 4 busy, hard 8 diligent 9 assiduous, laborious 11 industrious

ophidian: asp, eel 5 snake 6 conger 7 reptile, serpent

ophthalmic: 6 ocular

opiate: 4 dope, drug, hemp 5 dwale, opium 6 deaden 7 anodine, anodyne 8 hypnotic, narcotic 9 paregoric

opificer: 7 workman 9 artificer

opine: 4 deem, hold 5 judge, think 6 ponder 7 suppose

opinion: 4 idea, view, ween 5 dicta(pl.), guess, tenet 6 advice, belief, dictum, esteem, notion, repute 7 concept, feeling, thought 8 decision, doctrine, estimate, judgment 9 sentiment 10 conjecture, conviction, deposition, estimation, expression, evaluation, impression, persuasion, point of view 12 apprehension

erroneous: 13 misconception

expression: 4 vote

preconceived: 9 prejudice

united: 9 unanimous

unorthodox: 6 heresy

opinionated: 6 biased 8 dogmatic 9 conceited, obstinate 11 dictatorial

opinions: *collected:* 9 anthology, symposium

professed: 5 credo

opium: 4 dope, drug 10 intoxicant

addiction: 8 thebaism

alkaloid: 6 codein 7 codeine 8 morphine, narcotin 9 narcotine, papaverin 10 papaverine

camphorate tincture: 9 paregoric

concentrated form: 6 heroin
derivative: 7 meconic
Egyptian: 8 thebaine
poppy seed: maw
prepared: 6 chandu 7 chandoo
source: 5 poppy
opossum: 9 marsupial
kin: 8 kangaroo
water: 5 yapok 6 yapock
oppidan: 5 civic, urban 8 townsman
opponent: foe 5 enemy, rival 7 opposer 9 adversary, assailant 10 antagonist
opportune: fit, pat 5 ready 6 timely 8 suitable 9 favorable, well-timed 10 auspicious, convenient, favourable, seasonable 11 appropriate
opportunely: 7 apropos, happily
opportunity: 4 hent, turn 5 break, slant 6 chance, look-in 7 opening 8 occasion 9 advantage 12 circumstance
oppose: pit, vie 4 buck, cope, face, meet, stem, wear 5 argue, block, check, cross, fight, front, match, rebel, rebut, repel 6 breast, combat, object, oppugn, resist 7 contest, counter, gainsay 8 conflict, confront, contrast, frontier, obstruct 9 encounter, withstand 10 calcitrate, contradict, contravene, controvert
opposed: 4 anti 5 alien 6 averse 7 adverse, against, counter, hostile 8 contrary 11 contrariant
opposite: 5 anent, polar 6 across, anenst, averse, contra, facing 7 adverse, counter, inverse, reverse 8 antipode, antipole, contrary, contrast, converse 9 antipodal, repugnant 10 antipodean 12 antagonistic 13 contradictory
opposite to: 7 abreast, subtend
opposition: 5 enemy, atilt 9 animosity, collision, hostility, renitency 10 antagonism, resistance 11 contrariety
oppress 4 load, rape, thew 5 crush, grind, weigh, wrong 6 burden, defoil, defoul, extort, harass, harrow, ravish, subdue 7 afflict, depress, overlay, repress, trample 8 distress, encumber, pressure, suppress 9 constrain, overpower, overthrow, overwhelm, subjugate, weigh down 10 extinguish
oppressed: 5 laden 7 servile 9 debruised 10 heavy-laden 11 downtrodden
oppression: 8 dullness 9 grievance, lassitude 10 affliction 11 obscuration
oppressive: 4 dire, hard 5 close, harsh, heavy 6 gloomy, severe 7 onerous 8 rigorous 10 hardhanded 11 gravaminous, heavyhanded, overbearing 12 extortionate
oppressor: 4 csar, czar, Nero, tsar, tzar 6 tyrant
opprobrium: 5 abuse, odium, scorn 6 infamy, insult 7 calumny, contempt, of-

fense, scandal 8 disgrace, dishonor, reproach 9 contumely 10 disrespect, scurrility
oppugn: 6 oppose 7 contend 10 contradict
oppugnacy: 9 hostility 10 antagonism
Ops (see also **Rhea**): *associate:* 6 Consus
consort: 6 Saturn
daughter: 5 Ceres
festival: 6 opalia
son: 4 Zeus 8 Poseidon
opt: 4 cull, pick 5 elect 6 choose, decide, select
optical: 6 ocular, visual
instrument: 4 lens 7 alidade 9 eriometer, magnifier, optometer, periscope, telescope 10 microscope 11 stereoscope 15 ultramicroscope
organ: eye
optimist: 5 hoper 7 dreamer 8 idealist 9 Pollyanna 10 positivist
optimistic: 4 rosy 6 joyous 7 hopeful, roseate 8 sanguine
option: 5 right 6 choice 9 privilege 10 free choice 11 alternative
optional: 4 free 8 elective 9 voluntary 10 permissive 13 discretionary
opulent: fat 4 rich 5 ample 6 lavish 7 profuse, wealthy 8 abundant, affluent 9 luxuriant, plentiful 11 extravagant
opus: 4 book, work 5 etude, study 11 composition
overlabored: 11 lucubration
oquassa: 5 trout
or: aut(L.), ere 6 either 11 alternative
heraldry: 4 gold 6 yellow
oracle: 4 seer 5 maxim, sibyl 7 prophet, wise man
pert. to: 8 pythonic 9 prophetic
oracular: 4 otic 5 vatic 7 vatical 9 prophetic 10 mysterious 11 dictatorial 13 authoritative
orage: 5 storm 7 tempest
oral: 4 exam 5 aloud, parol, vocal 6 sonant, spoken, verbal 7 uttered 9 unwritten 10 acroamatic 11 word-of-mouth
orange: 4 mock 5 chino, color, hedge, Jaffa, navel, Osage 6 bodock, Temple 7 Seville 8 bergamot, chinotti, mandarin, Valencia 9 tangerine
genus: 6 citrus
heraldry: 5 tenne
membrane: 4 zest
mock: 7 seringa, syringa, syringe
piece: 4 lith(Sc.) 7 segment
red: 7 saffron
seed: pip
seedless: 5 navel
variety: 5 blood, navel, osage 7 Seville
Orange Bowl site: 5 Miami
orange-flower oil: 6 neroli

orange-shaped: 6 oblate
orangeberry: 9 cranberry
orangebird: 7 tanager
orangelike fruit: bel 9 tangerine
orangutan: ape 4 mias 5 pongo, satyr 7 primate
orate: 5 plead, speak, spiel, spout 7 address, declaim, lecture 8 bloviate, harangue 9 discourse, speechify 10 filibuster 11 expostulate
oration: 6 sermon 7 address, concion 9 discourse, panegyric
funeral: 5 eloge 6 eulogy 7 elogium, encomia(pl.) 8 encomium
orator: 6 rhetor 7 demagog, speaker 8 cicerone, ciceroni(pl.) 9 demagogue, plaintiff 10 petitioner 11 rhetorician, spellbinder
oratorian: 6 priest
oratorical: 8 eloquent 10 articulate, rhetorical
oratorio: 7 Messiah, Seasons
coda in: 7 stretto
oratory: 6 chapel 8 rhetoric 9 elocution, eloquence
orb: eye, sun 4 ball, moon, star 5 earth, globe 6 circle, planet, sphere 7 circuit, enclose
orbed: 5 lunar, round
orbit: 4 path 5 range, scope, track 6 circle, domain, socket 7 circuit, ellipse, revolve
point: 5 apsis, syzgy 6 apogee, epigee 7 perigee
orc: 4 orca 5 whale 6 dragon 7 grampus
orchard: 4 farm 5 arbor, grove 6 garden, huerta 8 arbustum 9 enclosure 10 plantation
orchestra: 4 band 5 group 8 ensemble, symphony
section: 4 wind, wood 5 brass 6 string 7 timpany 8 woodwind 10 percussion
orchestra bells: 12 glockenspiel
orchestra circle: 7 parquet 8 parterre
orchestrate: 5 score 7 arrange, compose 9 harmonize
orchid: 5 faham, petal, vanda 6 flower, praise, purple 7 aerides, calypso, lycaste, pogonia, vanilla 8 arethusa, labellum 10 compliment
appendage: 8 caudicle
dried tubers: 5 salep
genus of: 5 vanda 6 laelia 10 gymnadenia 14 gymnadeniopsis
leaves: 5 faham
meal: 5 salep
petal: lip 8 labellum
tuber: 5 salep 7 cullion
Orcus: See Hades
ordain: 4 deem 5 allot, enact, order 6 decree 8 adjudge, appoint, arrange, behight, command 7 conduct, destine, in-

stall, prepare 9 establish, prescribe 10 adjudicate, commission, constitute
ordeal: 4 gaff, test 5 trial 10 experience 11 tribulation
order: ban, bid 4 boon, fiat, form, ordo, rank, rule, sect, type, will 5 align, array, class, dight, edict, genus, grade, guide 6 billet, charge, cosmos, decree, degree, demand, direct, enjoin, extent, genera(pl.), graith, kilter, manage, method, ordain, police, series, system 7 adjudge, arrange, bespeak, bidding, command, compose, dispose, embargo, mandate, ordines(pl.), precept, process, society 8 decision, neatness, organize, regulate 9 direction, directive, magnitude, procedure 10 injunction, put in shape, succession 11 appointment, arrangement, association, instruction
back: 6 remand 8 recommit
connected: 8 seriatim
cosmic: tao 4 rita
good: 6 eutaxy 7 eutaxie
grammar: 5 taxis
lacking: 5 amiss, chaos, messy, mussy 7 anarchy, chaotic, clutter, unkempt 8 confused 10 disarrayed
law: 4 writ 7 summons 8 subpoena
of business: 6 agenda, docket
of preference: 8 priority
parliamentary: 9 procedure
writ: 7 precipe
orderly: 4 aide, neat, tidy, trim 6 batman 7 regular 8 decorous, obedient 9 peaceable, regulated, shipshape 10 law-abiding, methodical, systematic 11 well-behaved
ordinal: 4 book 6 number 7 regular
ordinance: law 4 doom, fiat, rite 5 bylaw, edict 6 assize, decree 7 control, decreta(pl.), statute 8 decretum 9 direction, prescript, sacrament 10 management, regulation 11 appointment
ordinary: 4 lala, ruck, so-so 5 nomic, plain, prose, usual 6 common, normal 7 average, natural, prosaic, trivial, vulgate 8 everyday, familiar, frequent, habitual, mediocre 9 customary, plain Jane 11 commonplace
ordnance: 4 guns 5 armor, orgue 6 petard 7 weapons 8 basilisk, supplies 9 artillery, torpedoes 10 ammunition, serpentine
ordo: 7 almanac
ore (see also **mineral**): tin 4 gold, iron, lead 5 metal 6 copper, silver 7 mineral 8 platinum
crusher: 5 dolly
deposit: 4 lode, vein 5 scrin 7 bonanza
fusing: 8 smelting
horizontal layer: 5 stope
impure: 6 speiss 7 halvana

iron: 5 ocher, ochre 8 hematite 9 magnetite
layer: 4 seam 5 stope
lead: 6 galena
loading platform: 4 plat
mercury: 8 cinnabar
refuse: 4 slag 5 dross 6 scoria 8 tailings
separator: 6 vanner
silver: 10 stephanite
sluice: 5 trunk
tin: 5 scove
tungsten: 4 cals
washing trough: 6 strake
worthless: 5 matte
oread: 4 peri 5 nymph
Oregon: *capital:* 5 Salem
  city: 6 Eugene 8 Portland
  county: 4 Coos 5 Cutty 7 Gilliam, Klamath, Hamhill 8 Umatilla
  early explorer: 8 Coronado
  highest peak: 6 Mt. Hood
  Indian: 4 Coos 8 Cherokee
  motto: 8 The Union
  mountain range: 4 Blue 5 Coast 7 Cascade, Wallowa
  nickname: 6 Beaver
  river: 5 Snake 8 Columbia 9 Deschutes
  state bird: 10 meadowlark
  state flower: 5 grape
  state tree: fir
oreortyx: 5 quail
Orestes: *father:* 9 Agamemnon
  friend: 7 Pylades
  mother: 12 Clytemnestra
  sister: 7 Electra 9 Iphigenia
  victim: 9 Aegisthus 12 Clytemnestra
  wife: 8 Hermione
orfe: ide 4 fish 5 dusky
orfevrerie: 7 jewelry
organ: 6 medium 7 journal, vehicle 8 magazine 9 equipment 10 instrument, periodical
  auricular: ear
  barrel: 8 autophon 10 hurdy-gurdy
  bristle-like: 4 seta
  cactus: 7 saguaro
  desk: 7 console
  elongated: 8 tentacle
  essential: 5 brain, heart, liver, lungs 6 viscus 7 viscera(pl.)
  fish: 8 drumfish
  flutter device: 7 tremolo
  footlike: pes
  gallery: 4 loft
  interlude: 6 verset
  lymphoid: 6 tonsil
  mouth: 9 harmonica
  note: 9 tremolant
  of insect: 7 stinger
  of living bodies: 8 organism
  of motion: 6 muscle
  of volition: 5 manas

olfactory: 4 nare, nose
opening: os; ora(pl.)
optical: eye
  part: 4 reed, stop
piano: 9 melopiano
pipe: 4 reed 5 flute 7 mixture
portable: 5 regal
prelude: 6 verset
reed: 9 harmonium
respiratory: 4 lung
sawlike: 5 serra
secreting: 5 gland
sensory: ear, eye 4 nose
speech: lip 6 throat, tongue
tactile: 6 feeler
organ stop: 5 quint, viola 7 aeoline, celesta, tertian 8 diapason, dulciana, gemshorn, register 9 philomela, rohrflute 10 quindecima
  adjust: 10 registrate
  bell-like: 8 carillon
  labial: 7 melodia
  reed: 4 oboe 7 bassoon 8 possaune
  storm-imitating: 5 orage
  string: 5 gamba
  two banks of pipes: 7 tertian
organbird: 4 wren 6 magpie
organdy: 6 muslin
organic: 5 vital 6 inborn 7 natural 8 inherent 9 organlike 11 fundamental 14 constitutional
  body: 5 zooid
  compound: 5 amine, ketol
  radical: 5 ethyl
organism: 5 plant 6 aerobe, animal, entity
  bacterial: 4 germ 7 microbe
  body: 4 soma 6 somata(pl.)
  elementary: 5 monad
  minute: 5 ameba, monad, spore
  pelagic: 6 nekton
  process: 6 miosis 7 meiosis
  vegetable: 4 tree 5 plant
organization: 5 setup 11 association, disposition 12 constitution
  business: 4 firm 5 guild 11 cooperative, corporation, partnership 13 establishment
  college: 4 frat 5 alumna, alumni(pl.) 7 alumnus 8 sorority 10 fraternity
  lack of: 5 chaos
  political: 4 bloc 5 party 7 machine
  secret: K.O.P., P.E.O., W.O.W. 4 B.P.O.E., Elks, frat 5 lodge, mafia, Moose 6 apache, maffia, Masons 8 sorority 9 Foresters, Maccabees 10 fraternity, Freemasons 11 underground
  skeleton: 5 cadre
  social: 4 club 5 forum
  veterans: A.V.C., D.A.V., G.A.R., S.A.R., V.F.W. 5 Fidac 6 AMVETS 14 American Legion 21 Veterans of Foreign Wars

women's: D.A.R., W.A.F., W.R.C. 8 sorority

organize: 4 form, plan 5 edify, set up 6 embody 7 arrange 8 regiment

organized: 7 planned 8 arranged 10 systematic

orgy: 4 lark, romp 5 binge, revel, spree 6 frolic, shindy 7 rampage, revelry, wassail 8 carousal, ceremony 9 bacchanal 10 observance 11 celebration, merrymaking

Oriana: *father:* 8 Lisuarte
lover: 6 Amadis

oribi: 8 antelope, bleekbok

oriel: bay 6 recess, window 7 balcony, gallery, portico 8 corridor

orient: 4 dawn 5 adapt, place 6 adjust, locate 7 sunrise 11 accommodate

Orient: 4 Asia, East 6 Levant 7 Far East 8 Near East

Oriental: *animal:* 4 zebu
archangel: 5 Uriel
bearer: 5 hamal
beverage: 4 arrack
bow: 6 salaam
calculator: 6 abacus
cap: 7 calpack
caravansary: 4 khan 5 serai 6 imaret
carriage: 4 sado 10 jinricksha 11 jinrickshaw
cart: 5 araba
chief: 4 khan
Christian: 4 Uniat
coin: sen, yen 4 para, yuan 5 dinar, sapek
commander: ras 4 amir, emir, rais, reis 5 ameer, emeer
corn: 4 para
cosmetic: 4 kohl
council: 5 Divan
cymbal: tal, zel
deity: Bel
destiny: 6 Kismet
disease: 8 beri-beri
dish: 5 pilaf, pilau, pilaw
drug: 4 hemp 6 heroin, opium 7 hashish
drum: 7 anacara
dulcimer: 6 santir
dwelling: dar
emperor: 6 sultan
exercise: 4 judo, yoga 8 jiujitsu
fan: ogi 5 punka
fish: koi, tai
food: 4 rice 5 salep 8 beancurd
garment: aba
gate: dar
guitar: 5 sitar
inn: 5 serai 11 caravansary
liquor: 4 sake, saki
litter: 5 dooli, dooly 6 dooley, doolie
lute: tar
manservant: 5 hamal
mansion: 5 yamen

market: 5 bazar 6 bazaar
measure: dra, mao
measure of weight: 4 kati, rotl, tael 5 abbas, bhaar, catty, picul 6 cantar, kantar, miskal
money of account: rin
monkey: 7 macaque
musical instrument: tar 5 sitar, surna, suray 6 santir 7 anacara, samisen
name: Ali
nomad: 5 Tatar 6 Tartar
nurse: 4 amah, ayah
oboe: 5 surna, suray
pagoda: tea
people: Tai, Tho 4 Sere 5 Asian, Tatar 6 Indian, Korean, Muslim, Tartar 7 Chinese, Eastern 8 Japanese 9 Easterner, Levantine 10 Mohammedan
pine: 5 matsu
pipe: 7 nargile 8 harghile, nargileh
plane-tree: 7 cheenar
porter: 5 hamal
rest house: 4 khan 5 serai
rice dish: 5 pilaf, pilau, pilaw
rice paste: ame
ruler: 4 amir, emir, khan, shah 5 ameer, calif, emeer 6 caliph, sultan
saber: 6 tulwar 7 tulwaar 8 scimitar
sailor: 6 calash, lascar
salutation: 5 saheb, salam 6 kowtow, salaam
sash: obi
sauce: soy
sea captain: ras 4 rais, reis
shoe: 6 sandal
shrub: tea 5 henna 9 wineberry
silkworm: 6 tussah, tusseh, tusser 7 tussore
slipper: 7 baboosh 8 babouche
smoking apparatus: 7 nargile 8 narghile, nargileh
sword: 8 scimitar
tale: 7 Ali Baba 13 Arabian Nights
tamarisk: 4 atle 5 atlee
tambourine: 5 daira
taxi: 7 ricksha 8 rickshaw
tea: cha
title: aga 4 amir, baba 5 pasha 6 huzoor
tower: 6 pagoda
tree: 4 atle 5 atlee
vessel: 4 dhow, saic
wagon: 5 araba
weight: 4 mann, tael 5 artal(pl.), catty, liang
whip: 6 chabuk 7 chabouk
wind: 7 monsoon
worker: 5 cooly 6 coolie

oriental: 5 pearl 6 bright, ortive, rising 7 eastern, shining 8 lustrous, pellucid, precious 9 ascending, brilliant 11 resplendent

Oriental rug: 4 Baku, Kali 5 Herez, Mahal, Saruk, Senna, Sumak 6 Kashan, Kerman, Kirman, Meshed, Pamiri, Sarouk, Shiraz, Soumak, Tabriz 7 Bokhara, Bukhara, Chinese, Hamadan, Isfahan, Ispahan, Karajas, Meshhed 8 Lerestan, Sedjadeh 9 Kurdistan 10 Kermanshah

pattern: 7 ainaleh

variation: 6 abrash

orifice: 4 hole, vent 5 inlet, mouth 6 cavity, outlet 7 chimney, opening, ostiole 8 aperture

in brain: 4 lura

origin: nee 4 rise, root, seed 5 birth, cause, start 6 nature, parent, source 7 genesis, lineage 8 ancestry, nascence, nascency 9 beginning, inception, naissance, parentage, paternity 10 extraction, incunabula(pl.) 11 incunabulum, provenience 12 commencement, fountainhead

foreign: 7 ecdemic

of words: 9 etymology

on earth: 7 epigene

original: new 5 first, model, novel 6 fontal, native, primal, primer 7 primary 8 pristine 9 authentic, eccentric, inventive, primitive, prototype 10 aboriginal, innovative 11 fundamental, primigenial

originally: 5 first 9 initially, primarily 10 inherently

originate: 4 coin, make, open, rise 5 arise, begin, breed, cause, found, start 6 create, derive, devise, invent, spring 7 causate, emanate, produce 8 come from, commence, contrive, discover, generate, initiate 9 construct, establish, institute, introduce

originator: 6 author 7 creator 8 inventor 9 architect, innovator

oriole: *golden:* 5 pirol 6 loriot

Orion: 5 Rigel 13 constellation

hound: 6 Aratus

slayer: 5 Diana 7 Artemis

orison: 7 prayer

Orkney Island: *bay:* 9 Scapa Flow

capital: 8 Kirkwall

fishing ground: 4 haaf

hut: 4 skio

inlet: voe

island: Hoy 6 Pomona, Rousay, Sanday 8 Stronsay

land: 4 odal, udal 6 udaler 7 udalman 8 udalborn

largest: 6 Pomona

tower: 5 broch

orle: 6 border, fillet, wreath 7 bearing, chaplet

orlean: 7 annatto

orlop: 4 deck

ormer: 7 abalone

ormolu: 4 gilt, gold 5 alloy 6 mosaic 7 varnish

ornament (see also **decoration**): dub, fob, pin 4 etch, gaud, gear, tool, trim, waly 5 adorn, braid, chase, decor, gutta, inlay, wally 6 amulet, attire, bedaub, bedeck, billet, brooch, edging, emboss, enrich, finery, flower 7 agremen, engrave, enrich, garnish, spangle, trinket 8 agrement, applique, decorate, flourish, lavalier 9 arabesque, billiment, embellish, embroider, lavaliere 10 decorament, furnishing, habiliment, lavalliere

apex: 6 finial

bell-shaped: 9 clochette

Biblical: 4 Urim

boat-shaped: nef

claw-like: 6 griffe

crescent-shaped: 6 lunula 7 lunette, lunulae(pl.)

delicate: 7 tracery

dress: 4 frog, lace 5 jabot 6 bar-pin, sequin, zequin 7 spangle 8 chequeen, zecchino 10 embroidery

flower-like: 6 anadem 7 rosette

hanging: 6 bangle, fringe, tassel 7 earring, pendant

magical: 6 amulet

mantel: 7 bibelot

neck: 5 chain 6 choker, gorget 8 necklace 9 lavaliere

pagoda: tee

protuberant: 4 boss

scroll-like: 6 volute

shoulder: 7 epaulet

silver: 6 tinsel

spiral: 5 helix 7 helices(pl.)

tufted: 6 pompon, tassel 7 rosette

ornamental: 5 fancy 6 chichi, frilly 7 elegant 8 fanciful 10 decorative

ornamented: 6 figury, ornate, tawdry 9 elaborate

ornate: gay 4 fine 5 fancy, showy 6 florid, rococo 7 aureate, baroque, flowery 8 overdone 9 elaborate, unnatural 10 flamboyant 11 overadorned

ornery: 4 mean 7 crabbed 8 contrary, stubborn 9 irritable 12 cantankerous

ornithologist: 7 Audubon, birdman

ornithon: 6 aviary

orogeny: 8 upheaval

orotund: 4 full, loud 5 clear, showy 6 mellow, strong 7 pompous 8 resonant 9 bombastic 10 stentorian

Orozco specialty: 5 mural

orp: 4 fret, weep

orphan: 4 waif 5 Annie 7 cast-off 9 foundling

orpheum: 7 theater

Orpheus: *birthplace:* 6 Pieria

father: 6 Apollo

instrument: 4 lyre

mother: 8 Calliope

wife: 8 Eurydice

orphrey: 4 band 6 border 10 embroidery

orpiment: 7 arsenic

orpit: 7 fretful

orris: 4 gimp, iris, lace 5 braid 7 galloon

ort: bit 5 crumb, scrap 6 morsel, refuse 7 leaving, remnant 8 fragment, leftover

orthodox: 4 good 6 proper 7 canonic, correct 8 accepted, approved, standard 9 canonical, customary 12 conservative, conventional

orthographer: 7 speller

ortolan: 4 bird, rail 7 bunting 8 bobolink, wheatear

ortstein: 7 bedrock, hardpan

oryx: 7 gazelle, gemsbok 8 antelope

os: 4 bone 5 eskar, esker, mouth 7 opening, orifice

Osaka Bay port: 4 Kobe

oscillate: wag 4 rock, sway, vary 5 swing, waver, weave 7 vibrate 9 fluctuate, vacillate

oscitant: 4 dull 6 drowsy, gaping, sleepy, stupid 7 yawning 8 careless, sluggish 9 apathetic

osculate: 4 buss, kiss

osier: rod 4 wand 5 skein 6 basket, sallow, willow 7 dogwood, wilgers

Osiris: *brother:* Set 4 Seth

crown: 4 atef

enemy: Set 4 Seth 7 brother

father: Geb, Keb, Seb

mother: Nut

recorder: 5 Thoth

sister: 4 Isis

son: 5 Horus 6 Anubis

wife: 4 Isis

Osmanli: 4 Turk

osmesis: 8 smelling 9 olfaction

osmosis: 9 diffusion 10 absorption 12 assimilation

osprey: 4 hawk 9 ossifrage 11 feather trim

osseous: 4 bony 6 osteal, spring

ossicle: 4 bone 5 incus 6 stapes 7 bonelet, malleus

ossify: set 6 harden

osso buco: 10 veal shanks

ossuary: urn 4 tomb 5 vault 10 depository, receptacle

ostend: 4 show 6 reveal 7 exhibit 8 manifest 11 demonstrate

ostensible: 7 alleged, seeming 8 apparent, specious 9 pretended, professed

ostensorium: pix, pyx 10 monstrance

ostentation: 4 show 5 eclat, flare 6 parade 7 display, flutter, pageant, portent, presage 8 flourish, pretense 9 showiness, spectacle 10 exhibition 11 fanfaronade

ostentatious: 4 arty, loud 5 gaudy, showy

6 sporty 7 obvious, pompous, splashy 8 fastuous 9 elaborate, flaunting 10 flamboyant 11 pretentious

osteoma: 5 tumor

osteria: inn 6 tavern 10 restaurant

ostiole: 4 pore 5 stoma 7 opening, orifice 8 aperture

ostracize: bar, cut 4 snub 5 exile 6 banish, reject 7 exclude 9 blackball, proscribe 10 expatriate

ostracon: 5 shell 8 fragment, potsherd

ostrich: 4 rhea 5 nandu

extinct: moa

feather: boa, boo 5 plume

ostrichlike bird: emu 4 emeu

otalgia: 7 earache

otary: 4 seal

Othello: 4 Moor

character in play: 6 Bianca, Cassio, Emilia

friend: 4 Iago

wife: 9 Desdemona

other: 4 else, more 5 ither(Sc.) 6 former, second 7 further 8 distinct 9 different, remaining 10 additional

other-worldly: fey 9 imaginary, spiritual 12 supernatural, transmundane

otherness: 8 alterity 9 diversity 13 dissimilarity

others: 4 rest

and: 4 et al 6 et alii

otherwise: 4 else 5 alias 6 aliter 11 differently

otic: 5 aural 8 auditory 9 auricular

otiose: 4 idle, lazy, vain 6 futile, otiant 7 sterile, surplus, useless 8 inactive, indolent, reposing 10 unemployed 11 ineffective, inexcusable, superfluous

otologist: 6 aurist

ottavino: 7 piccolo

otter: fur 4 fish 6 tackle 7 annatto 8 paravane

genus: 5 lutra

sea: 5 kalan

ottoman: 4 pouf, seat 5 couch, divan, stool 6 fabric 9 footstool

Ottoman (see also Turkey): 4 Turk 5 Osman 6 Othman

court: 5 porte

governor: 5 pasha

imperial standard: 4 alem

leader of: 5 Osman

poetry couplet: 4 beyt

province: 7 Vilayet

subject: 4 Raia 5 Rayah

ouakari: 6 monkey

relative: 4 saki

oubliette: 7 dungeon

ouch: 5 adorn, bezel, clasp 6 brooch, fibula 7 fibulae(pl.) 8 ornament 11 exclamation

ought: 4 bood, must, want, zero 6 cipher,

naught, nought, should **7** behoove **10** obligation

ouija board part: 10 planchette

ounce: ure **6** weight **7** measure
sixteenth of: **4** dram

ouph, ouphe: elf **6** goblin

our: wir(Sc.) **5** notre(F.) **7** pronoun **10** possessive

ousia 6 entity, nature **7** essence **9** substance

oust: bar **5** eject, evict, expel **6** banish, remove **7** deprive, dismiss **9** forejudge **10** dispossess

out: 4 away **5** forth **6** absent, begone, issued **8** external **9** published **10** extinguish **12** disadvantage
at elbows: **5** seedy
of control: **4** amok, wild **7** chaotic
of date: old **5** passe **10** antiquated
of kilter: **4** alop, awry **6** broken
of line: **4** awry **5** askew, fresh, wrong **8** improper
of order: **5** amiss, kaput **6** faulty **9** deficient
of place: **5** inept **13** inappropriate
of play: **4** dead, foul
of sight: **5** great **6** hidden **7** extreme
of sorts: **5** cross **7** peevish **9** irritable
of the ordinary: odd **5** novel **6** unique **7** strange, unusual **8** peculiar, uncommon **9** different
of the way: **5** aside **6** afield, remote **10** farfetched
of this world: **4** fine **6** superb
on a limb: **6** in a fix **7** stumped, up a tree **10** vulnerable

out-and-out: 5 sheer, utter **6** arrant, wholly **8** absolute, complete

outage: 4 vent **6** outlet **7** failure **8** blackout **10** suspension **12** interruption

outback: 4 bush **7** country **10** wilderness

outbreak: fit **4** riot **5** burst **6** bust-up, emeute(F.), revolt, ruckus, tumult **7** boutade, ruction **8** eruption, uprising **12** insurrection
new: **13** recrudescence
widespread: **8** epidemic

outbreeding: 7 exogamy

outbuilding: 4 barn, shed **5** privy **6** barton, garage, hemmel **8** outhouse **9** backhouse

outburst: 4 fume, gale, gust, rage, tiff **5** blast, brunt, flare **6** blower, blow-up, tirade **7** tantrum, torrent **8** eruption **9** explosion **10** ebullition

outcast: 5 exile, leper, ronin **6** outlet, pariah **7** refugee **8** banished, castaway, derelict, rejected, vagabond **10** expatriate

outclass: 4 best **5** excel **6** outwit **7** surpass

outcome: 4 fate **5** issue **6** effect, exitus, payoff, result, sequel, upshot **9** after-

math **10** conclusion, denouement **11** consequence

outcrop: 5 ledge **10** break forth

outcry: hue, yip **4** bawl, bray, yell **5** alarm, noise, shout **6** clamor, hubbub, racket, shriek **7** protest, screech, shilloo **9** objection **11** lamentation **12** vociferation

outdate: 7 outmode **9** antiquate, obsolete

outdistance: 7 surpass **11** leave behind, pull ahead of

outdo: cap, cow, top **5** excel **6** defeat, exceed **7** nonplus, surpass **8** overcome **13** steal a march on

outdoors: 8 al fresco **9** in the open

outer: 5 alien, ectad, ectal **6** remote **7** farther, foreign **8** exterior, external **10** extraneous

outermost: 4 last **5** final, utter **6** utmost **7** extreme **8** farthest, remotest

outface: 4 defy **6** resist, subdue **8** overcome **9** stare down

outfit: kit, rig **4** gang, gear, suit, team, unit **5** equip **6** attire **7** furnish **8** equipage **9** equipment, furniture, grubstake **10** enterprise **12** organization **13** paraphernalia

outflow: 4 flux **6** efflux, run-off **8** drainage

outgoing: 4 warm **6** genial **7** exiting, leaving **8** friendly, sociable **9** departing

outgrowth: 4 node **5** issue, shoot **6** result, sequel, sprout **8** offshoot **9** emergence **11** excrescence

outhouse: 4 shed **5** privy **6** biggin **7** latrine

outing: 4 stay, trip **6** junket, picnic **7** holiday **8** vacation **9** excursion

outlandish: 5 alien, queer, weird **6** exotic, remote **7** bizarre, foreign, strange, uncouth **8** peculiar **9** barbarous, fantastic, grotesque, tasteless **10** unorthodox

outlaw: ban **5** exile **6** bandit, banish, forbid **8** criminal, fugitive, prohibit, renegade **9** desperado, proscribe **10** disqualify

outlawed: 7 illegal, illicit

outlay: 4 cost **5** spend **7** expense **11** expenditure **12** disbursement

outlet: 4 exit, vent **5** store **6** egress, escape, exitus **7** opening, release **8** aperture

outline: map **4** form, plan **5** brief, chart, draft, frame, shape, trace **6** border, design, figure, sketch **7** contour, profile, summary **8** describe, skeleton, synopsis **9** delineate, perimeter **10** compendium, silhouette **13** configuration

outlive: 7 survive

outlook: 4 view **5** vista **6** aspect **7** purview **8** frontage, prospect **9** viewpoint **10** perception **11** expectation *medical:* 9 prognosis

outlying district: 6 suburb 7 purlieu 8 environs

outmoded: 5 dated, passe 6 demode 7 antique 8 obsolete, outdated

outpost: 7 station 8 frontier 10 settlement 11 advance base

outpouring: 4 gale, gush 5 flood 6 stream 9 fusillade

output: 5 power, yield 6 energy 7 harvest 10 production 16 computer feedback

outrage: 4 evil, rape 5 abuse 6 insult, offend, ravish 7 affront, offense, violate

outrageous: 4 base, vile 5 gross 6 brutal, far-out 8 heinous, obscene, ungodly 9 flagrant, shocking 9 atrocious, desperate, execrable, fantastic, monstrous 10 exorbitant

outre: 7 bizarre, strange 9 eccentric 11 exaggerated, extravagant

outreach: 6 exceed, extend, 7 project, surpass 8 protrude

outright: 5 total, whole, utter 6 direct, openly, wholly 8 complete, entirely 9 forthwith, instantly 10 thoroughly 15 straightforward

outrival: 5 excel 7 eclipse

outroot: 9 eradicate, extirpate

outrun: 4 beat 6 exceed 7 ski area 10 escape from

outset: 7 start 9 beginning

outside: 5 faint 6 facade, remote, slight 7 surface 8 exterior, external, al fresco 9 apart from 10 unfamiliar

outsider: 5 alien, loner 8 stranger 9 foreigner

outspoken: 4 bold, free 5 bluff, blunt, broad, frank 6 candid, direct 7 artless 8 explicit 10 unreserved 12 unrestrained

outstanding: big 4 arch, rare 5 famed, noted 6 famous, heroic, marked, unpaid 7 eminent 9 principal, prominent, unsettled 10 noticeable, pre-eminent, projecting 11 conspicuous, exceptional, uncollected, unfulfilled 13 distinguished

outstretched: 5 stent(Sc.) 8 extended

outstrip: cap, top, win 4 best, lead, pass 5 excel, 6 exceed 7 surpass 8 distance 9 transcend

outward: 5 ectad, overt 6 exodic, formal 7 extreme, visible 8 apparent, exterior, external, 9 extrinsic 10 ostensible 11 superficial

outweighing: 8 dominant 12 preponderant

outwit: fox 4 balk, best, foil 5 block, check, cross 6 baffle, jockey, thwart 9 checkmate, frustrate 10 circumvent, disappoint

ouzel: 4 piet 5 colly 6 thrush 8 whistler 9 blackbird

ouzo: 7 cordial `

flavoring: 7 aniseed

oval: 7 ellipse, stadium 8 avelonge 10 elliptical 11 ellipsoidal

ovate: 9 egg-shaped

inversely: 7 obovate

ovation: 7 acclaim, tribute 8 applause

oven: 4 kiln, oast 5 baker, range, stove 6 calcar 7 furnace

annealing glass: 4 leer, lehr

goddess of: 6 Fornax

over: oer, sur(F.), too 4 also, anew, done, uber(G.), upon 5 above, again, clear, ended, extra, vault 6 across, beyond, excess, on high 7 surplus, through 8 finished 9 completed, excessive 10 terminated 11 consummated, superfluous

and above: 7 besides 8 as well as 11 therewithal

overabundance: 4 glut 6 excess 7 surfeit, surplus 8 plethora

overact: 6 emote 7 ham it up 9 burlesque 10 exaggerate

overage: 6 excess 7 surplus

overall: 6 mostly 9 generally 10 throughout 13 comprehensive

overbalance: 7 outweigh 8 dominate

overbearing: 5 proud 6 lordly 7 haughty 8 arrogant, bullying, insolent, snobbish, subduing 9 imperious 10 disdainful, high-handed 11 dictatorial, domineering, magisterial 12 overpowering, supercilious

overburden: 7 oppress 8 encumber, overload 9 surcharge

overcast: dim, sew 4 bind, dark, dull 5 cloud, heavy 6 cloudy, darken, gloomy, lowery 7 accloud, becloud, clouded, obscure

overcharge: gyp, pad 6 excise, fleece 9 extortion

overcoat: 5 benny 6 capote, raglan, slipon(Sc.), ulster 7 paletot(F.), surtout, topcoat 9 balmacaan, greatcoat, inverness 12 chesterfield

close fitting: 7 surtout

loose: 6 raglan 7 paletot

sleeveless: 9 inverness

overcome: awe, get, win 4 beat, best, lick 5 charm, crush, daunt, fordo 6 appall, beaten, craven, defeat, exceed, foredo, master 8 confute, conquer 8 convince, encumber, outstrip, overbear, overturn, suppress, surmount, vanquish 9 overpower, overthrow, overwhelm, prostrate

overcrowded: 6 jammed 9 congested

overdo: 6 exceed 7 exhaust, fatigue 8 go too far, overcook, overwork 9 burlesque 10 caricature, exaggerate

overdue: 4 late 5 tardy 6 behind 7 arrears, belated, delayed 8 expected 10 unpunctual

overeager: 8 feverish

overeat: 5 gorge 7 satiate 8 gourmand 10 gluttonize

overfed: 7 fulsome

overflow: 4 slop, swim, teem, vent 5 excess, float, flood, spate, spill 6 abound, debord, deluge, outlet 7 overrun, surplus 8 alluvion, inundate 9 abundance, cataclysm, ebullient, exuberant

overflowing: 5 awash 7 copious, profuse, teeming

overgrown: 4 lush, rank, 6 jungly 7 fulsome

overhang: jut 5 jetty 6 beetle 7 project, suspend 8 threaten

overhasty: 4 rash 6 daring 8 headlong 11 precipitate

overhaul: 7 examine 8 renovate 9 forereach

overhead: 5 above, aloft 7 expense

overjoyed: 6 elated 8 jubilant 9 delighted

overkill: 9 excessive

overlapping: 5 cover 8 obvolute 9 imbricate

overlay: cap, lap 4 ceil, coat 5 couch, cover, glaze, plate 6 cravat, spread, veneer 7 encrust, oppress, overlie 8 covering 10 overburden 11 superimpose

overload: 4 glut 6 charge 8 encumber

overloaded: 9 plethoric

overlook: 4 balk, miss, omit, skip 5 forgo 6 acquit, excuse, forego, forget, ignore, manage 7 absolve, condone, inspect, neglect 9 disregard, supervise

overlord: 5 liege, ruler 6 despot, satrap, tyrant 8 suzerain

overlying: 8 brochant, superior 9 incumbent

overmatch: 4 best 6 defeat, exceed 7 surpass 8 vanquish

overmodest: 4 prim 7 prudish

overmuch: too 6 excess 7 surplus 9 excessive

overnice: 5 fussy 7 precise 8 dentical, precious 10 fastidious

overpower: awe 4 rout 5 crush, whelm 6 compel, defeat, deluge, master, subdue 7 conquer 8 convince, entrance, overbear, overcome, vanquish 9 enrapture, overthrow, overwhelm

overpowering: 4 dire 6 fierce 8 dazzling, stunning

overreach: do 5 cheat 6 grease, nobble, outwit 8 go too far 10 circumvent

override: 4 veto 6 defeat 7 nullify 8 vanquish

overrule: 4 veto 7 reverse 8 abrogate

overrun: 5 crush 6 infest, invade, ravage, spread 7 destroy 9 overwhelm

overs: 5 boots

overseas: 5 alien 6 exotic 7 foreign, strange 11 ultramarine

oversee: 5 watch 6 survey 7 examine, inspect 9 supervise 11 superintend

overseer: 4 boss 5 chief, ephor(Gk.), grave, reeve 6 bishop, censor, driver, gaffer, grieve 7 baliff, caporal, curator, foreman, manager 8 banksman, martinet 9 inspector 10 acequiador, supervisor 14 superintendent

agricultural: 8 agronome

spiritual: 6 pastor, priest

overshadow: dim 5 cover, dwarf 6 darken 7 eclipse, obscure 8 dominate 9 adumbrate

overshoe: gum 4 boot 6 arctic, galosh, golosh, patten, rubber 7 flapper

overshoot: 6 exceed 8 go beyond

oversight: 4 care 5 error, lapse, watch 6 charge 7 blunder, control, custody, mistake 8 omission 9 direction 10 inspection, management, negligence 11 supervision 12 surveillance 15 superintendence

overskirt: 6 peplum 7 pannier

oversleeve: 6 armlet

overspread: 4 deck, pall 5 brede, cloud, cover 6 deluge, infest

overstate: 7 magnify 10 exaggerate

overstep: 6 exceed 8 trespass 10 transgress

overt: 4 open 6 patent, public 7 obvious 8 apparent, manifest

overtake: 5 catch 9 attain, detect 7 ensnare 9 apprehend, captivate

overtax: 6 exceed, strain 8 overload

overthrow: tip 4 dash, down, fell, foil, fold, hurl, raze, rout, ruin, rush 5 allay, evert, fling, upset, worst, wrack 6 defeat, topple, tumble, unseat 7 afflict, conquer, destroy, dismiss, ruinate, unhorse 8 confound, demolish, overcome, overturn, reversal, supplant, vanquish 9 discomfit, overpower, overwhelm, prostrate 10 defeasance 11 destruction 12 discomfiture

overtone: 4 hint 7 meaning 9 harmonics 11 implication

overture: 5 offer, proem 7 opening, prelude 8 aperture, proposal 11 proposition 12 introduction

opera: 8 sinfonia

overturn: tip 4 cave, coup, tilt 5 throw, upset 6 topple 7 capsize, destroy, pervert, reverse, subvert 8 overcome 9 overthrow, overwhelm

overweening: 4 rash, vain 8 arrogant, insolent 9 confident, excessive

overwhelm: 4 bury, whip 5 amaze, cover, crush, drouk, swamp 6 defeat, deluge, engulf, quench 7 confute, conquer, engross, oppress 8 astonish, inundate, overturn, submerge 9 overpower, overthrow

overword: 7 refrain
Ovid: *birthplace:* 5 Sulmo
 burial place: 4 Tomi 5 Tomis
 work: 5 Fasti 7 Tristia 13 Metamorphoses
ovine: 5 sheep 9 sheeplike
 female: ewe
ovoid: 5 ovate 7 egglike 8 globular
ovule: egg 4 seed 6 embryo, gamete 7 seedlet
 integument: 7 primine
ovum: egg 4 seed 5 spore
owala tree: 4 bobo
owe: due 7 possess 9 attribute
ower: 6 debtor
owl: ule 4 bubo, lulu, momo 5 wekau 7 boobook, harfang, woolert 8 billy-wix, moreport 10 gillhooter, hob-houchin
 barn: 5 madge
 call: 4 hoot
 genus of: 5 ninox
 light: 7 evening
 pert. to: 8 strigine
 plumed eye area of: 4 disk
 short-eared: 4 momo
 small: 4 utum 6 howlet
 young: 4 utum 5 owlet
Owl and Pussycat author: 4 Lear
own: ain(Sc.), owe 4 avow, have, hold, nain(Sc.) 5 admit 7 concede, confess, possess 9 recognize 11 acknowledge
ownership: 5 title 7 tenancy 8 dominium 11 condominium, lawful claim 14 proprietorship
own up: 11 acknowledge
ox: yak 4 anoa, aver, beef, buff, gaur, musk, reem, zebu 5 bison, bugle, gayal, steer, tsine 6 bovine 7 banteng, buffalo 8 seladang 9 quadruped
 extinct: 4 urus
 harness: 4 yoke
 pert. to: 5 bovid 6 bovine 7 taurine
 small: 4 runt
 stall: 5 boose
 wild: 4 gaur 8 seladang
oxalis: oca 5 plant 6 sorrel
oxen: 6 cattle
 yoke: 4 span
oxeye: 5 daisy 14 black-eyed susan

oxford: 4 shoe 5 cloth 10 saddleshoe
Oxford: 10 university
 Earl of: 6 Harley 7 Asquith
 examination: 6 greats
 library: 8 Bodleian
 officer: 5 bedel 6 beadle
 scholar: 4 demy
 scholarship: 6 Rhodes
oxhead: 4 dolt 9 blockhead
oxidation: 4 rust
oxide: *aluminum:* 7 alumina
 barium: 6 baryta
 calcium: 4 lime
 hydrocarbon radical: 5 ether
 iron: 4 rust
 sodium: 4 soda
 strontium: 8 strontia
oxidize: 4 heat, rust 7 calcine, corrode
oxlip: 8 primrose
oxtongue: 7 alkanet, bugloss
oxyacantha: 8 hawthorn
oxygen: gas
 acid: 7 chloric 9 sulphuric
 allotropic: 5 ozone
 binary: 5 oxide
oxygenate: 6 aerate
oyez: 4 hear 6 attend 9 attention
oyster: 5 porte 6 huitre 7 bivalve, mollusk
 bed: 4 park, stew 5 layer 6 clair 9 oyster-age
 eggs: 5 spawn
 fossil: 9 ostracite
 gatherer: 7 tongman
 genus: 6 ostrea
 kind of: 6 native 9 bluepoint
 phylum: 8 mollusca
 rake: 5 tongs
 shell: 4 husk, test 5 shuck
 spawn: 5 culch 6 cultch
 tree: 8 mangrove
 young: 4 spat
oyster catcher: 4 bird 5 tirma
oyster grass: 4 kelp 10 sea lettuce
oyster plant: 7 salsify
oysterfish: 6 tautog 8 toadfish
Oz books author: 4 Baum
Ozark State: 8 Missouri
ozone: air

P

pa, pah: dad, paw 4 fort, papa 5 daddy 6 father 7 village 8 stockade 10 settlement

pabulum: 4 food 6 cereal 7 aliment, support 9 nutriment 10 sustenance 11 nourishment

pac, pack: 4 boot 8 moccasin

paca: 4 cavy, lava 5 agout, labba 6 rodent

pace: way 4 clip, gait, lope, pass, rack, rate, step, trot, walk 5 amble, canto, speed, tempo, tread 6 canter, gallop, strait 7 channel, chapter, dogtrot, measure, passage 8 platform 10 passageway

pacer: 5 horse 9 pacemaker

pachisi: 4 game, ludo

pachyderm: 8 elephant 10 rhinoceros 12 hippopotamus

pacific: 4 calm, meek, mild 5 irene 6 irenic, placid, serene 7 amiable 8 peaceful, tranquil 9 appeasing, peaceable 12 conciliatory

Pacific coast state: 6 Oregon 10 California, Washington

Pacific Islands (see also **Oceania**): *archipelago:* Aru 4 Sulu 5 Malay, Samoa 6 Tulagi
bird: 4 kagu 8 whistler
cloth: 4 tapa
collective name: 7 Oceania
grass: 4 neti
military base: 4 Guam
tree: kou 4 ipil, taro 7 dasheen, madrona, madrono 8 eddyroot

Pacific Ocean: *archipelago:* 4 Sulu 5 Malay, Samoa
discoverer: 6 Balboa
fish: 5 skate 6 bonito, marlin 7 dolphin 8 albacore 9 barracuda, swordfish 10 yellowtail
island: Lae, Yap 4 Guam, Truk, Wake 5 Leyte, Samoa 6 Tahiti 8 Tasmania 9 Carolines, Marquesas
shark: 4 mako
"stepping stones": 9 Aleutians

pacifier: sop 4 ring 6 nipple 8 sugartit 9 comforter 11 tranquilizer

pacifist: 4 dove 8 appeaser, peacenik

pacify: 4 calm, ease, lull 5 abate, allay, quiet, still 6 serene, soften, soothe 7 appease, assuage, mollify, placate, sweeten 8 mitigate 9 alleviate, reconcile 10

conciliate, propitiate 11 tranquilize

pack: jam, wad 4 bale, cram, gang, load, stow, tamp 5 carry, crowd, flock, horde, steve, store, truss 6 barrel, bundle, duffle, embale, encase, fardel, impact, wallet 8 knapsack
back: 8 knapsack
of cards: 4 deck

pack animal: ass 4 mule 5 burro, camel, horse, llama 6 donkey

package: pad 4 bale 6 bundle, packet, parcel

packer: 5 baler, roper 6 canner

packet: 4 boat 6 bundle, parcel 7 fortune

packing: 4 rags 5 gauze, paper, straw, waste 7 stowage
box: 5 crate
clay: 4 lute
material: 6 gasket, baline 9 excelsior
water-tight: 6 gasket

packing plant: 7 cannery

Pacolet: 5 dwarf, horse

pact: 6 cartel, treaty 7 bargain, compact 8 alliance, contract, covenant 9 agreement 10 settlement

Pactolian: 6 golden

pad: mat, wad, way 4 boss, path, road, walk 5 quilt, stuff, tramp 6 basket, buffer, jockey, pillow, tablet, trudge 7 bolster, bombast, cushion 8 footfall 9 embroider 10 highwayman, protection

padding: 7 packing, robbery, wadding 8 stuffing

paddle: oar, row 4 spud, wade 5 aloof 6 dabble, toddle 8 lumpfish

paddock: lot 4 frog, park 5 field 6 sledge 9 enclosure 10 saddle area

Paddy: 8 Irishman

paddywhack: 4 beat, blow 5 spank 9 thrashing

Paderewski opera: 5 Manru

padlock: 4 lock 6 fasten 7 closing 8 fastener

padre: 4 monk 6 cleric, father, priest 8 chaplain

padrona: 8 landlady, mistress

padrone: 4 boss 5 chief 6 master, patron 8 landlord 9 innkeeper

paean, pean: ode 4 hymn, song 6 praise

pagan: 6 ethnic, paynim 7 heathen, infidel 8 idolator 10 idolatrous, unbeliever 11 nonbeliever *god:* 4 Baal, idol

page: boy 4 call, leaf 5 child, folio, sheet 6 donzel, summon, varlet 7 footboy, servant 8 henchboy, henchman 9 attendant, messenger

beginning: 4 leaf 7 flyleaf

book: 5 folio 6 cahier

lady: 8 escudero

left-hand: 5 verso

number: 5 folio 10 pagination

paper: 5 sheet

reverse: 5 verso

right-hand: 5 recto

title: 5 unwan 6 rubric

pageant: 4 pomp, show 6 parade 7 tableau 8 aquacade, pretense 9 spectacle 10 exhibition, procession

pageantry: 7 display 8 splendor 11 ostentation

Pagliacci: *character:* 5 Nedda, Tonio

composer: 11 Leoncavallo

pagoda: taa 6 alcove, gazebo, temple 10 kryailteyo 11 summerhouse

finial or ornament: tee

pagurian: 4 crab

pah: 5 nasty 6 humbug 8 improper

paha: 4 hill 5 ridge

paideutics: 8 pedagogy

pail: can, cog(Sc.), pan, soa, soe 4 beat, bowk, gawn, meal, trug 5 bowie, cogue (Sc.), eshin, skeel 6 bucket, coggie(Sc.), harass, piggin, situla(L.), thrash, vessel 7 collock, situlae(pl.) 8 cannikin

paillette: 7 spangle 8 ornament

pain: try 4 ache, agra, care, cark, harm, hurt, pang 5 agony, cramp, grief, sting, thraw(Sc.), throe, upset, wound 6 grieve, twinge 7 afflict, algesis, anguish, penalty, torture, travail, trouble 8 disquiet, distress 9 suffering 10 affliction, algophilia, discomfort, punishment

abdominal: 5 colic

back: 7 lumbago

darting: 6 twinge

dull: 4 ache

pert. to: 6 asonal 7 algetic

relayer: 5 nerve

sensitiveness to: 7 algesia

painful: raw 4 sore 5 angry 6 bitter 7 algetic, hurting, irksome 8 exacting 9 difficult, laborious

painkiller: 4 drug 6 opiate 7 anodyne, aspirin 8 morphine, reliever 9 analgesic, paregoric

pains: 4 care, work 5 labor 6 effort 7 trouble 8 exertion

painstaking: 6 loving 7 careful 8 diligent, exacting 9 assiduous, elaborate, laborious 10 meticulous, scrupulous

paint: 4 coat, daub, gaud, limn 5 color, feign, fucus, rouge, stain 6 bedaub, depict, enamel, makeup 7 besmear, portray, pretend 8 decorate, disguise

glossy: 6 enamel

painted: 5 pinto 6 fucate 10 artificial, variegated

painter: 6 artist 7 artiste, workman 9 decorator

painting: oil 5 mural 6 canvas 7 acrylic, picture 10 watercolor

equipment: 5 brush, easel, paint 6 canvas, pallet 7 palette

medium: oil 7 gouache, tempera 10 watercolor

one-color: 8 monotint 10 monochrome

plaster: 5 secco 6 fresco

sacred: 5 pieta

scenic: 5 scape 8 seascape 9 cityscape, landscape

small: 9 miniature

studio: 7 atelier

style: 5 genre

three panels: 8 triptych

wall: 5 mural, panel 6 fresco

pair: duo, two 4 case, diad, duad, dyad, mate, span, team, yoke 5 brace, match, unite 6 couple

paisano: pal 7 comrade, peasant 10 countryman

Paisley: 5 shawl 6 design, fabric 7 pattern

Pakistan: *capital:* 9 Islamabad

city or town: Dir 6 Lahore, Multan, Quetta 7 Karachi 9 Hyderabad 10 Rawalpindi

language: 4 Urdu 6 Sindhi 7 Bengali, Punjabi

leader: Zia 4 Ayub 5 Yahya 6 Bhutto

monetary unit: 5 rupee

mountain: 9 Tirich Mir

mountain range: 8 Himalaya

native: 6 Bengal, Pathan, Sindhi 7 Baluchi, Punjabi

province: 4 Sind, Swat 5 Kalat, Sindh 6 Khelat, Punjab 11 Baluchistan

religion: 5 Hindu, Islam

river: 4 Swat 5 Indus 6 Kundar

weight: 4 seer, tola 5 maund

pal: 4 ally, chum, pard 5 buddy, crony 6 cobber, cohort, digger, friend 7 comrade, partner 9 associate, companion 10 accomplice 11 confederate

palace: 5 court, serai 6 castle, palais(F.) 7 alcazar, edifice, mansion 8 Alcazar 9 luxurious, pretorium 10 praetorium

officer: 7 paladin 8 palatine

papal: 7 Lateran, Vatican

paladin: 4 hero, peer 6 knight 8 champion, douzeper 11 protagonist

palaestra: 6 school 9 gymnasium

palamate: 9 web-footed

Palamedes: *enemy:* 7 Ulysses

father: 8 Nauplius

mother: 7 Clymene

war: 6 Trojan

Palamon: *rival:* 6 Arcite

wife: 6 Emelye

palanquin, palankeen: 4 kago 5 dooli, dooly, palki, sedan 6 doolee, dooley, doolie, litter, palkee 10 conveyance

palatable: 5 sapid, tasty 6 savory 8 delicate, pleasing 9 agreeable, delicious, toothsome 10 acceptable, appetizing
render: 4 salt 5 spice 6 season

palatal: 5 front, velar 8 gutteral 9 consonant

palate: 5 taste 6 relish 7 gourmet
hard: 11 roof of mouth
pert. to: 6 uranic
soft: 4 cion, vela(pl.) 5 uvula, velum

palatial: 5 large, regal 6 ornate 7 stately 9 luxurious 11 magnificent

palaver: 4 talk 5 debate, glaver, parley 7 chatter, flatter, wheedle 8 business, cajolery, flattery 10 conference 11 terminology 12 conversation

pale: dim, wan 4 ashy, fade, grey, gull, lily, pall, sick 5 ashen, blake, blate, bleak, faint, fence, livid, lurid, stake, stick, white 6 anemic, blanch, chalky, feeble, pallid, pastel, picket, region, sallow, sickly, whiten 7 anaemic, enclose, ghastly, haggard, insipid, obscure, whitish 8 encircle, etiolate 9 colorless 11 pasty-faced

paleness: 6 pallor

Palestinian (see also **Israel**): *guerrillas:* 7 Al Fatah 8 Fedayeen
leader: 6 Arafat

paletot: 8 overcoat 9 greatcoat

palfrey: 5 horse

palimpsest: 6 tablet 9 parchment

palindrome: 5 verse 7 sotadic

paling: 4 pale 5 fence, flake, limit, stake 6 picket 7 fencing 8 enclosure

palinode: 6 abjure 8 take back 10 retraction 11 recantation

Palinurus: 9 steersman

palisade: 5 cliff, fence, stake 6 picket 7 barrier, enclose, fortify, furnish 8 espalier, stockade, surround 9 enclosure, implement

pall: 4 bore, cloy, pale, sate 5 cloak, cloth, faint, stale, weary 6 mantle, 7 disgust, satiate 8 animetta, covering 11 counterpane

Pall Mall site: 7 West End

pallet: bed, cot, pad 5 couch, quilt 7 blanket 8 mattress, plancher 9 headpiece

palliasse: 6 pallet 8 mattress

palliate: 4 ease, hide 5 cloak, cover, gloss, gloze 6 lessen, soften 7 conceal, shelter 8 disguise, mitigate 9 alleviate, exculpate, extenuate, gloss over, sugarcoat, whitewash

pallid: wan 4 ashy, dull, pale, paly 5 bleak, white 7 ghastly 9 colorless

pallion: bit 5 piece 7 pellet

pallium: 4 band 5 cloak 6 mantle 8 himation

palm: 4 hide, tree 5 shrub 6 palmus(L.), thenar, trophy 7 conceal
betel nut: 5 areca, bonga
beverage: 5 assai
cabbage: 8 palmetto
climbing: 6 rattan
coconut: 4 coco
fan-leafed: 7 talipat, talipot, taliput 8 palmetto
feather: 5 howea 6 gomuti 7 urucuri, urucury
fiber: tal 4 buri 6 raffia
food: nut 4 sago 5 fruit
juice: 4 nipa, sura 5 taree, toddy
kind: ti 4 jara 5 assai, royal, tucum 6 bacaba, tucuma 7 babassu, jaggery, tokopat 8 bangalow
leaf: ola, ole 4 olay, olla 5 frond
low: 5 bussu 6 trooly, trouie, ubussu
palmyra: ola, ole, tal 4 brab, olla 6 ronier
pert. to: 6 palmar 8 frondous 10 palmaceous
pith: 4 sago
reader: 7 palmist
sap: 5 toddy
seeds: 4 nipa
spiny: 6 grigri, grugru
starch: 4 sago
stem: 4 cane 5 ratan 6 rattan
stemless: 5 curua
thatch: 4 nipa 9 barriguda
wing-leaved: 6 cohune

palm-leaf mat: 4 yapa

palm off: 5 foist

palma: 5 fiber, yucca

palmary: 5 chief, palmy 6 palmar 8 superior 9 principal 10 pre-eminent, victorious

palmate: 4 flat 5 broad, lobed 6 palmed, webbed 10 hand-shaped

palmer: 5 louse 6 stroll, travel, votary 7 pilgrim 8 wanderer 15 prestidigitator

Palmetto State: 13 South Carolina

palmistry: 10 chirognomy, chiromancy
practicer: 11 chiromancer

palmodic: 5 jerky

palms down: 7 pronate

palmy: 10 prosperous, triumphant 11 flourishing

Palmyra's queen: 7 Zenobia

palmyra tree: 4 brab 7 talipot

palooka: oaf 4 fool

palp: 6 feeler 7 flatter 8 tentacle

palpable: 4 rank 5 plain 6 patent 7 audible, evident, obvious, tactile 8 apparent, distinct, manifest, tangible 10 noticeable 11 perceptible 12 recognizable

palpebra: 6 eyelid

palpebrate: 4 wink

palpitation: 4 beat, pant 7 flicker, flutter 9 pulsation, quivering, throbbing, trembling

palsied: 5 shaky 7 shaking 9 paralyzed,

tottering, trembling

palsy-walsy: 8 intimate

palter: fib, lie 5 trick 6 babble, haggle, mumble, trifle 7 chatter, deceive, quibble 10 equivocate 11 prevaricate

paltock: 5 tunic 6 jacket 7 doublet

paltry: 4 bald, bare, base, mean, puny, vile 5 footy, petty, trash 6 chetif, flimsy, trashy 7 low-down, pitiful, rubbish, trivial 8 picayune, trifling 9 worthless 10 despicable 11 unimportant 12 contemptible 13 insignificant

paludal: 6 marshy

pampas: 6 plains

cat: 6 kodkod, pajero

pamper: pet 4 baby, cram, delt(Sc.), glut 5 humor, spoil 6 caress, cocker, coddle, cosher, cosset, cuddle, dandle, fondle, posset 7 cherish, cockney, gratify, indulge, satiate, forwean

pamphagous: 10 omnivorous

pamphlet: 5 flyer, tract 6 folder 7 booklet, catalog, leaflet 8 brochure 9 catalogue

pan: ape, rap, tab 4 face, part, wash 5 basin 6 frache(F.), lappet, vessel 7 portion, subsoil, utensil 8 ridicule 9 container, criticize 10 acetabulum, receptacle

coal burner: 5 grill 7 brazier

frying: 6 spider 7 skillet

gold-washing: 4 tina 5 batea

Pan: 6 Faunus

father: 6 Hermes

instrument: 4 pipe, reed

place of worship: 7 Arcadia

son: 7 Silenus 8 Seilenos

pan fry: 5 saute

panacea: 4 cure 6 elixir, remedy 7 allheal, cure-all, heal-all, nostrum 8 nepenthe 10 catholicon 11 panchreston

panache: 5 flare, plume, style, verve

panachure: 6 mottling

Panama: hat

capital: 6 Panama

city: 5 Colon, David 8 Santiago 9 Aspinwall, Cristobal

explorer: 6 Balboa

gulf: 6 Darien

island: Rey

highest point: 8 Chiriqui

lake: 5 Gatum

measure: 7 celemin

monetary unit: 6 balboa

port: 5 Colon 6 Balboa 9 Cristobal 10 Portobello

province: 5 Cocle, Colon 6 Panama 8 Chiriqui, Veraguas

river: 5 Chepo, Sambu, Tuira 7 Chagres

tree: 4 yaya 6 alfaje, cativo

Panama Canal: *dam and locks:* 5 Gatun 10 Miraflores

engineer: 9 de Lesseps

lake: 5 Gatun

nickname: 8 Big Ditch

panatela: 5 cigar

panax: 4 herb 7 ginseng

pancake: 5 arepa(Sp.), flawn 6 blintz, fraise, froise 7 blintze, fritter, hotcake 8 flapjack 11 griddlecake

delicate: 5 crepe

panda: wah 6 animal 7 bearcat

pandemonium: din 4 hell, sink 5 noise 6 tumult, uproar 8 disorder 9 confusion

pander: 4 bawd, pimp 5 cater 7 whiskin 8 procurer 9 go-between, procuress

Pandora: *brother:* 10 Prometheus

daughter: 6 Pyrrha

husband: 10 Epimetheus

pandurina: 4 lute

pane: 5 glass 7 section

panegyric: 5 eloge, elogy 6 eulogy, praise 7 encomia(pl.), oration, tribute, writing 8 encomium 9 discourse, laudation

panel: 4 jury 5 group 6 tympan 8 decorate

paneling: 4 wall 7 ceiling 8 covering

panfish: 4 crab, king 9 horseshoe

pang: 4 ache, gird, pain, stab, tang 5 agony, cramp, spasm, throe 6 twinge, twitch, wrench 7 anguish, travail 8 paroxysm 9 heartache

Pangim native: 4 Goan

pangolin: 5 manis 8 anteater, edentate

order: 9 pholidota

panhandle: beg 5 cadge

Panhandle State: 12 West Virginia

panic: 4 fear, fray, funk, wild 5 alarm, chaos, scare 6 frenzy, fright, terror 8 stampede 13 consternation

panjandrum: 7 magnate 9 personage

pannier, panier: bag, ped 5 seron 6 basket, dorsel, dorser, dosser, pantry 7 overskirt

panoply: 4 pomp 5 armor, array 6 armour 7 display

panorama: 4 view 5 range, scene, sweep, vista 7 picture, scenery 9 cyclorama

pan out: 7 succeed

panpipe: 6 syrinx 8 zampogna 10 mouth organ

pansy: 7 heartease 10 heartsease

pant: 4 ache, beat, blow, gasp, puff 5 heave, throb, yearn 7 pulsate 9 palpitate 11 palpitation

Pantagruel: 5 giant

companion: 7 Panurge

father: 9 Gargantua

mother: 7 Badebec

Panthea's husband: 9 Abradatus

pantheon: 6 temple

panther: cat 4 pard, puma 6 cougar, jaguar 7 leopard, painter

pantile: 7 biscuit 8 hardtack

pantomimist: 4 mime 5 actor 7 Marceau

pantry: 4 cave 5 ambry 6 closet, larder 7 buttery, pannier, pantler 8 cupboard

pants: 5 jeans, Levis 6 slacks 7 drawers 8 trousers
> *leather:* 5 chaps 10 chaparajos, chapareras, chaperejos, lederhosen(G.) 11 chaparreras

pantywaist: 8 weakling 13 characterless

panuelo: 6 collar, ruffle 8 kerchief 9 neckcloth

pap: 4 teat 5 trash 6 nipple 7 garbage, rubbish 8 emulsion, mammilla

papa: dad, paw, pop 6 baboon, father, potato, priest 7 vulture

papal (see also **pope**): 9 apostolic 10 pontifical

papal court: 5 curia

papaya: 5 melon, papaw 6 pawpaw

paper: 5 essay, theme, tract 6 cartel, report 7 journal, writing 8 document, treatise 9 monograph, newspaper, wallpaper 10 periodical 11 credentials, examination 12 dissertation 13 unsubstantial
> *absorbent:* 7 blotter 9 towelling
> *case:* 4 file 5 folio 6 binder
> *collection:* 7 dossier
> *currency:* 5 scrip
> *damaged:* 5 broke, casse, salle 6 cassie
> *design:* 9 watermark
> *detachable:* tab 4 stub 6 coupon
> *fine:* 5 linen 6 vellum
> *folded once:* 5 folio
> *gummed:* 5 label, stamp 6 paster 7 sticker
> *hard:* 6 pelure
> *large-size:* 5 atlas
> *legal:* 4 writ
> *medicinal:* 6 charta
> *official:* 5 targe 8 document
> *pad:* 5 block 6 tablet
> *piece:* 5 scrip, scrap, sheet
> *postage-stamp:* 6 pelure
> *pulp:* 4 ulla 9 waterleaf
> *quantity:* 4 page, ream 5 quire, sheet 6 bundle
> *scroll:* 9 parchment
> *size:* cap 4 copy, demi, demy, pott 5 atlas, crown, folio, legal 7 bastard, emperor 8 foolscap, imperial 9 colombier
> *thin:* 6 pelure, tissue 9 onionskin
> *untrimmed edge:* 6 deckle
> *writing-size:* cap 8 foolscap

paper money: 4 bill, cash 7 lettuce 8 frogskin 9 greenback

papier-mache: 7 collage

papilla: bud 6 pimple

papist: 8 Catholic

papoose: 4 baby

pappy: dad, paw 4 papa, soft 5 mushy 6 father 6 spongy 7 squishy 8 yielding 9 succulent

papule: 6 pimple

papyrus: 4 reed 5 sedge 6 biblos, biblus, scroll 7 bulrush 9 parchment
> *respository:* 5 capsa

par: by 5 equal 6 normal 7 average 8 equality, standard 9 enclosure 11 equivalence

par value: 4 face 7 nominal

parable: 4 myth, tale 5 fable, story 6 apolog, byword 7 byspell 8 allegory, apologue, forbysen 10 comparison, similitude

parabola: arc 5 curve 7 antenna

parachute: *material:* 4 silk 5 nylon
> *part:* 4 pack 6 canopy 7 harness, ripcord

paraclete: 5 aider 6 helper 7 pleader 8 advocate, consoler 9 comforter 9 supporter 11 intercessor

parade: 4 pomp, show, walk 5 march, strut 6 flaunt, review, stroll 7 cortege, display, exhibit, marshal 8 ceremony, flourish, grandeur, splendor 9 advertise, pageantry, promenade, strollers 10 callithump, exhibition, pretension, procession 12 magnificence

paradigm: 5 model 7 example, pattern

Paradise: 4 Eden 5 bliss 6 Aidenn, heaven, Utopia 7 Elysium, Nirvana 12 promised land
> *Buddhist:* 4 Jodo
> *fool's:* 5 limbo
> *Muslim:* 5 Jenna
> *river:* 5 Gihon

Paradise Lost angel: 5 Ariel, Uriel

paraffin: 6 alkane 8 kerosene

paragon: gem 4 type 5 ideal, jewel, model 7 pattern 8 last word 9 nonpariel

paragram: pun

paragraph: 4 item, note, sign 5 caput 8 material

Paraguay: *capital:* 8 Asuncion
> *city:* Ita 9 Paraguari, Villa Rica 10 Concepcion, Encarnacion
> *ethnic group:* 8 Mestizos
> *Indian:* 7 Guarani
> *lake:* 4 Ypoa
> *language:* 7 Guarani, Spanish
> *measure:* pie 4 line, lino, vara 5 legua, linea 6 cordel, cuadra, cuarta, fanega, league
> *money:* 7 guarani
> *river:* Apa 6 Parana 8 Paraguay 9 Tibiquare
> *tea:* 4 mate 5 yerba
> *weight:* 7 quintal

parakeet: 6 parrot, wellat 8 lovebird, paraquet, popinjay 10 budgerygay 11 budgereegah

parallel: 4 even 5 along, equal, match 6 equate, line up 8 analogue 10 collateral 11 counterpart
> *render:* 9 collimate

parallelism: 6 simile 10 similarity 11 resemblance 14 correspondence

parallelogram: 5 rhomb 6 oblong, square 9 rectangle

paralogist: 7 sophist

paralysis: 5 cramp, palsy 7 paresis 9 impotence 10 holoplexia 11 monoparesis
with: 7 paretic 9 paralytic

paralyzed: 4 numb 7 palsied 8 benumbed, crippled, immobile

paramnesia: 6 déjàvu

paramount: 5 above, chief, ruler 7 capital, supreme 8 crowning, dominant, superior, suzerain 10 pre-eminent
lord: 5 liege

paramour: 5 leman, lover, wooer 6 amoret, friend, suitor 7 gallant, hetaera 8 mistress 9 concubine, kept woman 10 sweetheart

paranymph: 7 best man 8 advocate 10 bridesmaid

parapet: 4 butt, wall 5 redan 7 bulwark, railing, rampart 10 breastwork 12 embattlement 13 fortification
part of: 5 crete
V-shaped: 5 redan

paraphernalia: 4 gear 9 apparatus, equipment, trappings 10 belongings 11 furnishings 13 appurtenances

paraphrase: 6 reword 7 version 9 interpret, translate 10 transcribe 11 translation

parasite: bug, bur 4 burr, moss 5 leech, toady, virus 6 fungus, sponge 7 sponger 8 hanger-on 9 dependent, mistletoe, sycophant 10 freeloader
animal: 4 flea, mite, tick 8 entozoan
blood: 4 tryp
disease: 7 malaria 11 trichinosis
marine: 6 remora, sponge
plant: 9 entophyte
trout: sug

parasol: 8 sunshade, umbrella 11 bumbershoot

paratrooper cry: 8 Geronimo

paravane: 5 otter

Parcae: See Fates

parcel: lot 4 deal, mete, pack, part, wrap 5 bulse, bunch, group, piece 6 bundle, divide, packet 7 package, portion 8 fragment 9 apportion 10 collection, distribute

parch: dry 4 burn, sear 5 roast, toast 6 dry out, scorch 7 bristle, brustle, graddan, shrivel

parched: 4 arid, sere 5 fiery 6 gizzen, torrid

parchment (see also **paper, scroll**): 6 charta 7 diploma
book cover: 5 forel 6 forrel
fine: vel 6 vellum
manuscript: 10 palimpsest
piece: 8 membrane
roll: 4 pell 6 scroll

pard: pal 4 chum 7 partner 9 companion

pardesi: 9 foreigner, outlander

pardo: 7 mulatto

pardon: 4 free 5 mercy, remit, spare 6 assoil, excuse 7 absolve, amnesty, condone, forgive 8 liberate, reprieve, tolerate 9 exculpate, remission 10 absolution, indulgence 11 forgiveness
general: 7 amnesty
stall: 12 confessional

pardonable: 6 venial 9 excusable

pare: cut 4 chip, peel, skin 5 shave 6 reduce, remove, resect 7 curtail, cut back, cut down, whittle 8 diminish, trim back 11 decorticate

paregoric: 7 anodyne 8 sedative

parella, parelle: 6 lichen

parent: dad, dam 4 mama, papa, sire 5 cause, daddy, mater(L.), pater 6 author, father, mother, origin 7 forbear, genitor 8 ancestor, begetter, forebear, generate, guardian, producer 10 forefather, progenitor

parentage: 5 birth 6 family, origin 7 lineage, progeny 8 ancestry 10 extraction, parenthood

parget: 4 coat 6 gypsum 7 plaster 8 decorate 9 whitewash

pariah: 7 Ishmael, outcast

parian: 5 china 6 marble, market 9 porcelain

Paris (Greek god)
beloved: 5 Helen
father: 5 Priam
kin: 7 Troilus 9 Cassandra
mother: 6 Hecuba
slayer: 11 Philoctetes
wife: 6 Oenone

Paris (French capital)
airport: 4 Orly 5 Roissy 8 DeGaulle 9 Le Bourget
bishop: 5 Denis 7 Lombard
boulevard: 8 Rue Royal, St. Honore 11 Rue de la Paix, Rue de Rivoli 13 Champs Elysees
cathedral: 9 Notre Dame
cemetery: 12 Pere-Lachaise
city planner: 9 Hausmann
museum: 5 Cluny 6 Louvre 10 Luxembourg
palace: 6 Elysee, Louvre 9 Tuileries 10 Luxembourg
park: 10 Luxembourg 13 Bois de Boulogne
river: 5 Seine
Roman name: 7 Lutetia
section: 8 Left Bank 9 Right Bank 10 Montmartre, Rive Gauche 12 Montparnasse 15 St. Germain-des-Pres
subway: 5 metro
tower: 6 Eiffel
university: 8 Sorbonne

parish: 4 fold 5 flock 8 diocese 12 congregation
head: 5 vicar 6 pastor, priest 8 minister
official: 9 vestryman 10 borsholder

paristhmion: 6 tonsil

parity: 7 analogy 8 equality 10 similarity 11 resemblance

park: 4 stop 6 refuge 7 commons, paddock, preserve 10 playground

parlance: 4 talk 5 idiom 6 speech 7 diction 9 discourse 11 phraseology 12 conversation

parlay: 5 wager 6 double, paroli 7 build up 8 increase

parley: 5 speak, treat, utter 6 confer 7 discuss, palaver 9 discourse 10 conference, discussion 12 conversation

parliament: 4 diet 5 senat(F.) 7 council 8 assembly, congress 9 gathering 10 conference 11 legislature

member: 4 lord

parlous: 4 keen 5 risky 6 clever, shrewd 7 cunning 8 critical, perilous 9 dangerous, hazardous 11 exceedingly, excessively, mischievous 13 disconcerting

parnassian: 4 poet

parochial: 5 petty 6 narrow 7 bigoted 9 small-town 10 provincial

parody: 4 skit 6 satire 8 travesty 9 burlesque, imitation 10 caricature

paroemia: 7 proverb

parole: 6 pledge 7 promise

paronomasia: pun 8 word play 12 agnomination

paroxysm: fit 4 pang 5 agony, spasm, throe 6 access, attack, orgasm 8 epitasis, outburst 9 agitation 10 convulsion 12 exacerbation

parrot: ape, ara 4 copy, echo, jako, kaka, lory 5 arara, mimic, polly 6 repeat, tiriba 7 corella, imitate 8 cockatoo, lorikeet, lovebird, parakeet 9 cockateel, cockatiel

disease: 11 psittacosis

genus: 9 psittacus

gray: 4 jako

green: 5 cagit

hawk: hia

like: 5 arine 11 psittaceous

long-tailed: 5 macaw

monk: 4 loro

owl: 4 kaka 6 kakapo

part of bill: 4 cere

sheep-killing: kea

small: 8 lovebird, parakeet

parrot fish: 4 scar 5 lania 6 scarus 8 bluefish 9 labroidea

parry: 4 fend, ward 5 avoid, block, evade 6 thwart 7 deflect, evasion

parse: 7 analyse, analyze, diagram, dissect 8 construe 9 anatomize

Parsee: See Parsi

Parsi: 11 Zoroastrian

holy book: 6 Avesta

priest: 5 mobed 6 dastur 7 destour, dustoor

parsimonious: 4 mean, near 5 close, scant, spare 6 frugal, meager, narrow,

skimpy, sordid, stingy 7 miserly, sparing 8 covetous, grasping, wretched 9 illiberal, mercenary, niggardly, penurious 10 avaricious, economical, ungenerous 13 penny-pinching 17 narrowheartedness

parsley: herb 5 cumin, garnish 6 eltrot

derivative: 5 apiol 6 apiole

genus: 12 petroselinum

relative: 6 celery

parsley camphor: 6 apiole

parson: 6 pastor, rector 8 minister, preacher 9 clergyman, guidepost

parson bird: poe, tui 4 rook

parson-in-the-pulpit: 10 cuckoopint

parsonage: 5 manse 6 parish 7 rectory 9 pastorium

part (see also **parts**): 4 deal, dole, half, role, rove, side, some, twin 5 chunk, piece, quota, sever, share 6 behalf, canton, cleave, depart, detail, divide, member, parcel, ration, sunder 7 disjoin, element, portion, section, segment 8 alienate, disperse, dissever, disunite, division, estrange, fraction, fragment, separate 9 abteilung(G.), apportion, dismember 10 department, incomplete 11 constituent

baglike: sac

basic: 4 core, pith 7 essence

central: 4 core 5 focus, solar 6 nuclei(pl.) 7 nucleus

choice: 5 cream, elite 6 marrow 7 essence

coarse: 5 dregs

distinct: 4 unit 7 article

essential: 4 core, gist, pith 6 factor

final: 5 shank 6 epilog

hardest: 5 brunt

highest: top 4 apex 5 crest 6 summit

inmost: 4 core 5 heart 6 center

main: 4 body 5 trunk

minor: bit, cog

missing: 6 lacuna

moving: 5 rotor

narrow: 4 neck

revolving: 5 rotor 7 rotator

root-like: 7 radicle

rounded: 4 bulb

small: bit, jot 4 atom, iota, mite 5 tithe 6 detail, moiety 7 snippet

suddenly: 4 rend, snap

uppermost: top 4 peak 6 upside 7 topside

part with: 4 give, lose, sell 5 leave 6 donate 7 abandon

partage: 4 part 5 share 7 portion 8 division

partake: 4 bite 5 eat of, share 6 divide, join in 11 participate

of: use

partan: 4 crab

parted: 5 cleft 7 divided, partite 9 separated

Parthian ruler: 7 Arsaces

parti-colored: 4 pied 7 piebald 9 checkered 10 variegated

partial: 4 half, part 6 biased, unfair 7 colored, halfway 8 coloured, inclined, one-sided, partisan 10 fractional, incomplete, prejudiced 11 predilected, predisposed

participant: 8 partisan 10 accomplice

participate: 4 join, side 5 enter, share 6 be in on 7 compete, partake 9 cooperate 11 get in the act

particle: ace, bit, dot, gru, jot 4 atom, grue, iota, mite, mote, whit 5 fleck, grain, shred, speck 6 morsel, smidge, tittle 7 driblet, smidgen, smidgin 8 smidgeon, smitchin

affirmative: yes

burnt: 6 cinder

coordinating: or

cosmic: 5 meson

electrified: ion 5 anion 6 cation, proton 7 neutron

icy: 5 sheet

incandescent: 5 spark

minute: jot, ort, ray 4 atom, iota, mite, mote 5 grain, speck 7 granule, ramenta(pl.) 8 molecule, ramentum 9 scintilla

negative: nor, not

negative-charged: ion 8 electron

pluvial: 4 drop

positive-charged: ion 6 proton 8 positron

particular: 4 item, nice 5 fussy, point, thing 6 detail, minute 7 article, careful, correct, precise, special, unusual 8 accurate, concrete, detailed, especial, exacting, itemized, specific 10 fastidious, individual, noteworthy, scrupulous 11 scrumptious 12 circumstance 13 extraordinary 14 circumstantial

opposite: 7 general

particularly: 9 expressly 10 especially

parting: 5 death 8 farewell 11 leavetaking

parting shot: 5 taunt

partisan: 4 pike 5 staff 6 biased, fautor 7 devotee 8 adherent, follower 9 truncheon 10 factionary, factioneer, interested

unwavering: 6 zealot 8 stalwart

partite: 6 parted 7 divided 9 separated

partition: 4 wall 5 septa(pl.) 6 divide, screen, septum 7 enclose, portion, scantle 8 cleavage, close off, division 9 severance 10 distribute, enterclose, separation 11 compartment 13 apportionment

partitioned: 7 septate

partlet: hen 5 woman

partner: pal 4 ally, half, mate, wife 5 butty, crony 6 cohort, fellow, sharer 7 comrade, consort, husband 8 camarada, sidekick 9 associate, coadjutor, colleague, companion 10 accomplice 11 confederate, participant

comedian's: 6 stooge

paid: 6 escort, gigolo

partnership: hui 4 firm 5 tie-up 7 cahoots, company 11 association 14 compagnieschap(D.)

partridge: 4 yutu 5 titar 6 chukar, chukor, seesee 7 tinamou 9 francolin

flock: 5 covey

young: 7 cheeper 8 squealer

parts(see also **part**): 9 genitalia

innermost: 10 penetralia

together: 9 adhesions

totality: 5 unity

two: 6 binary

parturition: 5 birth, labor 7 travail 8 delivery 10 childbirth

party (see also **political party**): bal(F.) 4 clan, drum, orgy, sect, side 5 cabal, group 6 comite, fiesta, person 7 company, faction 9 gathering 10 detachment 11 association, combination 12 participator

afternoon: tea 9 reception

evening: 4 ball 6 soiree

gift: 5 favor

guilty: 7 culprit

men's: 4 stag 6 smoker

reconnaissance: 6 patrol

seashore: 6 picnic 8 clambake

party girl: 4 doxy 10 prostitute

party man: 8 partisan

parure: 6 adorn 6 paring 7 apparel, peeling 8 ornament

parvenu: 4 snob 6 arrive 7 upstart 9 arriviste 11 pig in clover 12 nouveau riche

Pascal work: 7 Pensees

Pasch, Pascha: 6 Easter 8 Passover 10 Good Friday

paschal: 4 lamb 6 supper 8 Passover 11 celebration

pasear: 4 walk 6 airing 9 excursion, promenade

pasha: dey 4 emir

territory: 8 pachalic, pashalic, pashalik

Pashur: *father:* 5 Immer 8 Malchiah

son: 8 Gedaliah

Pasiphae: *children:* 7 Ariadne, Phaedra

husband: 5 Minos

pasqueflower: 6 badger 8 gosling 9 aprilfool 10 badgerweed

pasquinade: 5 squib 6 satire 7 lampoon, pasquil

pass: col, end, gap 4 abra, beal(Sc.), comp, cove, fare, ghat, hand, lane, pace, step, wend 5 canto, enact, ghaut, gorge, hurry, kotal, lapse, lunge, occur, relay, smite, spend, utter, yodel 6 billet, convey, defile, elapse, exceed, expire, happen, passus, permit, ticket, twofer 7 allonge, approve, devolve, passage, surpass, undergo 8 beallach, hand down, surmount 10 abjudicate, permis-

sion 11 Annie Oakley, leave behind 13
complimentary

slowly: 4 drag

without touching: 5 clear

pass around: 5 skirt 6 detour

pass away: 4 die 6 expire, perish, vanish 8
transfer 9 disappear, surrender

pass by: 4 cote, omit, skip 6 forego, forget, ignore 8 overlook 9 disregard

pass off: con 4 pose 5 foist

pass on: die 5 leak 6 convey, impart 7 decease 8 transmit 11 communicate

pass over: die 4 omit, skip 5 cross 6
elapse, expire, excuse, ignore 7 neglect
8 overlook, permeate, transfer, traverse
9 disregard

lightly: 4 skim

quickly: 4 scan, scud

smoothly: 5 elide

pass through: 5 cross 6 divide, pierce 7
pervade 8 permeate, traverse 9 penetrate

pass up: 6 reject 7 decline 9 disregard

passable: fit 4 fair, soso 7 genuine 8 adequate, mediocre, moderate 9 navigable,
tolerable 10 admissable, negotiable 11
traversable

passage: gat, gut, wro 4 adit, belt, door,
duct, exit, fare, flue, ford, gang, gate,
hall, iter, lane, pass, path, pawn, race,
ramp, road, slip 5 aisle, allee, alley,
alure, atria(pl.), entry, going, gorge,
meuse 6 access, arcade, atrium, avenue,
burrow, course, defile, egress, strait,
travel, tunnel, voyage 7 channel, couloir, estuary, gangway, itinera(pl.), journey, transit 8 aqueduct, corridor, crossing 9 enactment, ventiduct 10
bottleneck, transition 12 thoroughfare
13 accommodation

air: 4 flue 9 ventiduct

between two walls: 5 slype

covered: 6 arcade

literary: 4 text 7 excerpt 9 quotation

mine: 5 stope

musical: bar, cue 4 link 5 break, stave 7
cadenza 8 flourish, spicatto

one outlet: 7 impasse 8 cul-de-sac

roofed: 6 arcade 9 breezeway

scripture: 4 text

subterranean: 4 mine 6 tunnel 8 cunicu-
li(pl.) 9 cuniculus

passant: 4 past 7 current, cursory, walking 9 ephemeral, excelling 10 proceeding, surpassing, transitory

passe: 4 aged, past, worn 5 faded 7 de-
moded 10 obsolete, outmoded 9 out-of-
date 10 antiquated 12 old-fashioned
13 superannuated

passel: 4 body 5 bunch, group 6 bundle 7
cluster

passementerie: 6 edging 8 trimming

passenger: 4 fare 7 standby 8 ferryman,

traveler, wayfarer

passerby: 9 saunterer

passerine bird: 7 sparrow 8 starling

passing: 5 death 7 cursory 8 elapsing,
fleeting 9 departing, ephemeral, exceeding 10 pre-eminent, transitory, surpassing

passion (see also **mania**)**:** ire 4 fire, fury,
heat, love, lust, raga, rage, zeal 5 anger,
ardor 6 affect, choler, desire, fervor,
temper 7 emotion, feeling, fervour 8
appetite, distress 9 calenture, martyrdom 10 affliction, enthusiasm, heartthrob

passion flower: 6 maypop 8 bullhoof

family: 10 passifloraceae

passionate: 4 fond 6 fervid, fierce 7 amorous, flaming, peppery 8 frenetic 9 hotheaded, irascible, phrenetic 11 hot-
tempered, impassioned 12 affectionate,
concupiscent 13 quick-tempered

passionless: 4 calm, cold 6 freddo(It.) 8
detached

passive: 5 inert, stoic 6 latent, stolid 7
patient 8 inactive, yielding 9 apathetic,
impassive, lethargic, quiescent 10
phlegmatic, submissive

Passover: 5 Pesah 6 Pesach

bread: 5 matzo 6 matzos 7 matzoth 8 afikomen

festival: 5 Sedar

pert. to: 7 paschal

songs of praise: 6 hallel

story: 7 haggada 8 haggadah

passport: key 5 conge 6 dustuk 7 dustuck, ticket 8 furlough 9 safeguard 10
open sesame

endorsement: 4 visa

passus: 4 pace, part, step 5 canto 8 division

password: 11 countersign

past: ago 4 gone, yore 5 after, agone, ended, since 6 behind, beyond, bygone 8
foregone 9 completed, foregoing 11 antecedents

immediate: 9 yesterday

pert to: 8 historic

tense: 11 perteritive

pasta: 4 orzo 7 ravioli 8 linguine, macaroni 9 fettucini, spaghetti 10 vermicelli

paste: hit, pap 4 beat, blow, cuff, duff,
glue, pate 5 cream, dough, false, punch,
stick 6 attach, batter, fasten, strass 7
filling 8 adhesive, mucilage 9 imitation

aromatic: 6 pastil 7 pastile 8 pastille

dried: 7 guarana

pasteboard: 4 card, sham 6 flimsy

pastel: 4 pale 6 crayon 7 picture

pastern: 6 hobble, hopple, tether 7 shackle

Pasternak novel: 7 Zhivago

heroine: 4 Lara

pastiche: 4 olio 6 jumble, medley 9 patchwork, potpourri 10 hodgepodge

pastime: 4 game 5 hobby, sport 9 amusement, diversion 10 recreation 13 entertainment

past master: 6 expert

pastor: 4 herd 5 angel, rabbi 6 curate, keeper, priest, rector 7 dominie 8 guardian, minister, shepherd 9 clergyman

pastoral: 4 poem 5 drama, rural 7 bucolic, idyllic, romance 8 agrarian

god: Pan

pert. to: 8 agrestic, geoponic

pipe: 4 reed

place: 7 Arcadia

poem: 4 idyl 5 idyll 7 eclogue, georgic

pastry (see also **cake, pie**): pie 4 baba, cake, flan, huff, tart 5 torte 6 eclair 7 carcake(Sc.), strudel 8 napoleon, turnover 9 cream puff, vol-au-vent 11 petits fours

garnish: 5 cream, fruit 8 meringue

shell: 7 dariole, timbale

pasturage: 4 gang 6 eatage, forage 7 herbage

pasture: lea 5 agist, drift, grass, graze, veldt 6 meadow, saeter 7 grazing, vaccary 9 grassland 10 agostadero

god: Pan

pasty: pie 6 doughy, pallid, sickly 9 unhealthy

pat: apt, dab, tap 4 blow, glib 5 fitly, fixed, impel, throw 6 caress, soothe, strike, stroke, timely 7 apropos, fitting, readily 8 suitable 9 immovable, opportune, pertinent 10 seasonable 12 commendation

Patagonia: *deity:* 7 Setebos

rodent: 4 cavy, mara

tree: 6 alerce, alerse

patch: bit 4 mend, vamp 5 bodge, clout, clump, cover, piece, scrap 6 blotch, cobble, dollop, emblem, parcel, repair, revamp, solder 7 clobber, overlay, remnant

of woods: 5 motte

up: 4 heal, mend

patchwork: 5 cento 6 jumble, scraps 9 fragments 10 hodgepodge, miscellany

pate: pie, top 4 head 5 crown, paste, pasty, patty 6 badger, noggin, spread

patella: pan 4 dish, vase 6 limpet 7 kneecap, kneepan

paten: 4 arca, disc, dish, disk 5 plate 6 vessel

patent: 4 arca, open 5 clear, gross, overt, plain 7 evident, license, obvious 8 apparent, archives, enduring, flagrant, manifest 9 available, franchise 12 unobstructed

medicine: 7 nostrum

notice: 6 caveat

pater: 6 father, priest

paternal: 8 fatherly

kinsman: 6 agnate

paternity: 6 father, origin 10 authorship, fatherhood 12 fatherliness

path: pad, rut, way 4 fare, lane, line, road, walk 5 alley, byway, going, piste, route, track, trail 6 camino, casaun, comino, course, groove 7 footway, highway, towpath

hill: 4 berm 5 berme 6 roddin 7 rodding(Sc.)

math: 5 locus

pathetic: sad 5 sorry, teary 6 moving 7 pitiful 8 stirring 9 affecting

pathic: 6 victim 7 passive, subject 8 catamite 9 suffering

pathological: 4 sick 6 morbid

pathos: 4 pity 9 poignancy

patience: 4 calm 8 stoicism 9 composure, endurance, fortitude 10 submission 11 forbearance, resignation, self-control 12 acquiescence 13 long-suffering

patient: 4 case, meek 6 bovine 13 longsuffering

patina: 5 gloss 6 finish, polish

patio: 5 court 7 terrace 9 courtyard

patisserie: 4 shop 6 pastry

patois: 4 cant 6 Creole, jargon 7 dialect

patriarch: 4 Enos, Levi, Nasi, Noah 5 elder 7 ancient, veteran 9 venerable

patrician: 5 noble 9 gentleman 10 aristocrat 12 aristocratic

patrimony: 6 legacy 8 ancestry, heritage 10 birthright 11 inheritance

patriot: 8 loyalist, partisan 9 flag-waver 10 chauvinist, countryman 11 compatriate, nationalist

song: 6 anthem 7 America

patrol: 5 guard, scout, watch 7 protect 10 detachment

patrolman: cop 5 guard 9 inspector, policeman

patron: 5 buyer, guest 6 client, fautor 7 sponsor 8 advocate, champion, customer, defender, guardian 9 protector, supporter 10 benefactor

stock exchange: 5 buyer 6 seller, trader

patron saint: *of beggars:* 5 Giles

of children: 8 Nicholas

of cripples: 5 Giles

of England: 6 George

of fishermen: 5 Peter

of Ireland: 7 Patrick

of lawyers: 4 Ives, Yves

of musicians: 7 Cecilia

of Norway: 4 Olaf

of sailors: 4 Elmo 8 Nicholas

of Scotland: 6 Andrew

of shoemakers: 7 Crispin

of winegrowers: 7 Vincent

of workers: 6 Joseph

patronage: 5 aegis, favor 6 custom, favour 7 auspice, fomento 8 business 10 assistance 13 encouragement

patronize: use 5 deign 8 frequent 10 condescend

patsy: sap 4 dupe, fool 5 chump 6 sucker, victim 7 fall guy 9 scapegoat

patten: 4 base, clog, foot, shoe 5 skate, stand, stilt 6 sandal 7 support 8 overshoe, snowshoe

patter: 4 cant, talk 5 lingo 6 jargon 7 blatter, chatter

pattern: 4 form, norm, plan 5 bysen, draft, epure, guide, ideal, model, order, plaid 6 checks, design, figure, format, former, sample, stripe 7 example, project, stencil, templet 8 exemplar, forbysen, paradigm, specimen, template 9 archetype, ensampler, precedent 11 arrangement

patulous: 4 open 8 expanded 9 distended, spreading

paucity: 4 lack 6 dearth 7 fewness 8 exiguity, scarcity 13 insufficiency

Paul: 7 apostle
birthplace: 6 Tarsus
companion: 5 Silas, Titus 7 Artemas, Timothy 8 Barnabas
original name: 4 Saul
place of conversion: 8 Damascus
prosecutor: 9 Tertullus
teacher: 8 Gamaliel
tribe: 8 Benjamin

pauldron: 6 armor 6 splint

paunch: 5 belly, rumen 7 abdomen, stomach 8 potbelly 10 disembowel, eviscerate

pauper: 6 beggar 8 indigent 10 down-and-out

pause: 4 halt, lull, rest, stop, wait 5 abide, break, cease, comma, delay, demur, dwell, hover, letup, selah, tarry 6 breach, breath, falter, stance 7 caesura, respite 8 breather, caesurae(pl.), hesitate, intermit 9 cessation 10 hesitation 12 intermission, interruption

paut: paw 4 poke 5 stamp 6 finger

pavane: 5 dance

pave: lay 4 path, stud, tile 5 cover, floor 6 causey, cobble, smooth 7 overlay, prepare 10 facilitate, macadamize

pavid: 5 timid 6 afraid 7 fearful

pavilion: 4 flag, tent 5 kiosk 6 canopy, ensign, litter 8 covering 9 gloriette

paving: 4 flag, sett 5 block, brick, dalle, paver, stone 6 cobble, Tarmac 7 asphalt 9 flagstone

pavis: 5 cover 6 screen, shield 10 protection

pavo: 7 peacock 13 constellation

paw: pud, toe 4 foot, gaum, hand, maul, paty 5 patte, touch 6 fumble, handle, pattee 7 crubeen, flipper 8 forefoot

pawky: sly 4 arch, bold 5 canny, saucy 6 crafty, lively, shrewd 7 cunning, forward, squeamish

pawl: cog, dog 4 bolt, sear, tent, trip 5 catch, click 6 detent, pallet, tongue 7 ratchet

pawn: 4 gage, hock, soak, tool 6 lumber, pledge 7 counter, hostage 8 chessman, guaranty 11 impignorate

pawnbroker: 11 moneylender

Pawnee: 6 Indian
rite: 4 hako

pawpaw: 5 fruit, papaw 6 papaya 7 immoral, naughty 8 indecent 11 bushwhacker

pax: 5 board, peace 6 friend, tablet 10 friendship, osculatory

pay: fee, tip 4 ante, foot, meet, rent, wage 5 clear, repay, spend, yield 6 defray, pony up, reward, salary, satisfy 7 imburse, requite, satisfy, stipend, tribute 9 indemnify, make up for, reimburse 10 compensate, recompense, remunerate 11 retribution 12 compensation
attention: 4 heed 6 listen
back: 6 rebate, refund 9 reimburse, retaliate
extra: 5 batta, bonus 8 kickback
for: buy 4 rent 8 purchase
homage: 5 adore, honor 6 salaam
out: 5 spend 6 expend 8 disburse 10 distribute
up: 4 ante, quit 6 settle 9 liquidate

payable: due 5 owing 11 outstanding

paying: 5 sound 7 solvent 10 profitable 12 advantageous

paymaster: 6 bakshi, bukshi, purser 7 bukshee(Ind.) 8 buckshee 9 treasurer

payment: cro, fee, tax 4 bill, dole, dues, duty, feal, fine, gale, levy, toll 5 gavel, price 6 pledge, rebate, return, reward, tariff 7 alimony, annuity, customs, pension, stipend, trewage, tuition 8 defrayal, requital 9 acquittal, allowance, discharge, honoraria(pl.) 10 honorarium, recompense, remittance 12 compensation, contribution
demand: dun 4 bill
evade: 4 bilk 7 default
failure: 13 nonredemption
illegal: 5 bribe 6 payola 8 kickback
immediate: 4 cash 9 alcontado(Sp.)
on delivery: COD
press for: dun
without: 4 free 6 gratis

payoff: fix 5 bribe 6 climax, profit, return, reward 9 reckoning 10 settlement

payola: 5 bribe

payong: 8 umbrella

paysage: 7 picture 9 landscape

pea: dal 4 gram, seed 5 arhar, chick, cicer, pease 6 gandul, legume, pigeon 7 carmele, catjang 8 garvanro 12 peavetchling
dove: 7 zenaida
early: 8 hastings

family 8 fabaceae

finch: 9 chaffinch

flour: 9 Erbswurst

pod: 5 quash

sausage: 9 Erbswurst

seeds: 5 pulse

shaped: 8 pisiform

peabird: 6 oriole 7 wryneck

peace: pax(L.), paz(Sp.) 4 calm, ease, liss, rest 5 amity, grith, lisse, quiet 6 repose, shalom 7 concord, harmony, requiem 8 ataraxia, security, serenity 9 armistice, heartease 10 heartsease 11 tranquility

goddess: 5 Irene

symbol: 4 dove, toga 5 olive

peace pipe: 7 calumet

peaceable: 6 gentle 7 amiable, pacific, solomon 8 amicable 11 undisturbed

peaceful: 4 calm 5 still 6 irenic, placid, steady 7 halcyon 8 irenical 9 unruffled 11 undisturbed

peach: 4 blab 5 dilly 6 accuse, betray, indict, inform 7 impeach, whittle 8 jimdandy 11 crackerjack

grafted on quince: 9 melocoton

kind: 6 Carman, Crosby, Salwey 7 Elberta 8 Crawford, quandang, quandong, quantong 9 freestone, nectarine 10 clingstone

origin: 5 China

stone: 7 putamen

peachwort: 9 persicary

Peach State: 7 Georgia

peachy: 4 fine, nice 5 dandy 9 beautiful, excellent

peacock: mao 4 pavo, pawn 5 strut 7 swagger

fan: 9 flabellum

feather fiber: 4 marl

female: 6 peahen

pert. to: 8 pavonine

tail spot: eye

peacock bittern: sun

peacock fish: 6 wrasse

peacock flower: 8 flambeau 9 poinciana

peacock heron: 7 bittern

peacock ore: 7 bornite 12 chalcopyrite

peag, peage: tax 4 toll 5 beads 6 pedage, wampum

pea jacket: 11 seaman's coat 13 hip-length coat

peak: Alp, ben, pic(F.), top, tor 4 acme, apex, cima, cusp, dent, dolt, pico(Sp.) 5 crest, crown, point, slink, sneak, steal, visor 6 shrink, summit 7 epitome, maximum 8 aiguille, headland, mountain, pinnacle 9 ascendant, ascendent, simpleton 10 promontory

ice: 4 berg 5 serac

ornament: epi 6 finial

rock: alp 4 crag

snow-capped: 7 calotte

peaked: wan 4 pale, thin 5 drawn, sharp

6 picked, sickly 7 pointed 9 emaciated

peal: 4 clap, ring, toll 5 chime 6 appeal, shovel 7 resound, summons, thunder 8 carillon

Peale Island: 4 Habe

peanut: 4 mani, mean 5 petty, pinda 6 goober, pindal 7 beennut 8 earthnut, earthpea, grassnut, katchung

peanuts: 8 trifling 15 inconsequential

pear: 4 bosc 5 melon 6 beurre, burrel, warden, winter 7 kieffer, prickly 8 ambrette, Bartlett, bergamot 9 alligator 10 chaumontel

squash: 5 perry 7 chayote

pear-shaped: 6 bulbous, rounded 8 pyriform

pearl: gem 4 seed, tear 5 nacre, onion 6 bouton, orient 9 margarite

artificial: 4 blay 6 olivet

of great luster: 8 oriental

seed: 7 aliofar

pearl blush: 7 rosetan

pearl moss: 9 carrageen

Pearl of Antilles: 4 Cuba

pearl opal: 9 cacholong

pearlbird: 6 barbet 11 guinea-fowl

pearlweed: 6 sagina 8 sealwort

pearlwort: 6 sagina 7 poverty

pearly: 8 nacreous, precious

peasant: 4 bond, boor, hind, kopi, peon, ryot, serf 5 churl, knave, kulak, swain 6 cotman, cottar, cotter, farmer, fellah, rascal, rustic 7 bondman, laborer, paisano(Sp.) 9 chopstick, contadino(It.) 10 countryman

Arab: 6 fellah

class: 9 jacquerie

crop sharing: 7 metayer

dress: 7 dirndle

Irish: 4 kern 5 kerne

Russian: 5 kulak 6 muzhik

peashooter: 6 blower, pistol 7 blowgun 9 slingshot 11 beanshooter

peat: gor(Ir.), pet 4 fuel, turf 6 lawyer, minion 7 darling 8 favorite 11 combustible

bog: 4 cess, moss 6 yarpha

cutter: 5 piner(Sc.)

spade: 5 slane 6 tuscar

peatwood: 11 loosestrife

peau d'ange: 6 fabric, finish 9 angelskin

peavey, peavy: 4 hook 5 lever

peba: 9 armadillo

pebble: 5 scree, stone 6 gravel, quartz, sycite 7 chuckie, crystal 10 chuckstone

pebble-shaped: 9 calciform 11 calculiform

peccadillo: 5 fault 7 offense 8 mischief

peccant: 6 morbid 7 corrupt, sinning 8 diseased 9 incorrect, unhealthy

peccary: 6 warree 7 musk-hog, tagassu, tayassu 8 javelina

pech: 4 pant, sigh 6 breath 7 breathe

pecht: 4 pict 5 fairy, gnome, pygmy

peck: dab, dot, nag, nip 4 beak, bill, carp, food, hole, jerk, kiss, nose 5 pitch, prick, throw 6 nibble, stroke 7 chimble, measure 9 great deal

at: nag 4 twit 5 tease 6 attack, harass

four: 6 bushel

pectase: 6 enzyme

peculate: 5 steal 6 misuse 8 embezzle 11 appropriate

peculiar: odd 5 queer 6 unique 7 curious, special, strange, unusual 8 especial, singular 9 eccentric, exclusive 10 particular 11 distinctive 14 characteristic

peculiarity: 4 kink 5 quirk, trait, twist 6 idiasm, oddity 9 attribute 12 idiosyncracy

of expression: 5 idiom 6 idioma, idiome

pecuniary: 8 monetary 9 financial

ped: 6 basket, hamper, panier 7 pannier

pedagogue: 5 tutor 6 pedant 7 dominie, teacher 12 schoolmaster

pedal: 5 lever 7 treadle

coupler: 7 tirasse

piano: 7 celeste

pedant: 4 prig 5 dunce, tutor 6 dorbel, purist, tassel 9 pedagogue 12 bluestocking, schoolmaster

pedantic: 7 bookish 8 teaching 10 didascalic, moralistic

writing: 9 academese

peddle: 4 hawk, sell 5 cadge, cycle, trant 6 higgle, meddle, piddle, retail 7 colport

peddler: 5 faker 6 broker, coster, duffer, hawker, seller, vendor 7 camelot, chapman 8 huckster, pitchman 12 carpetbagger, costermonger

pedestal: 4 anta, base 5 stand 6 pillar, podium 7 support 10 foundation

part: die 4 dado 5 socle 6 plinth, quadra

put on: 7 idolize 8 enshrine

pedestrian: ped 4 dull, slow 6 hoofer, walker 7 footman, plodder, prosaic 8 ordinary 11 commonplace 13 unimaginative

pedicel: ray 4 stem 5 scape, stalk 8 peduncle 9 footstalk

umbel: ray

pedigree: 6 stemma 7 descent, lineage 8 ancestry, purebred, stemmata 9 genealogy

pedometer: 8 odograph, waywiser 12 perambulator

pedum: 5 crook, staff

peek: 4 peep 6 glance 7 glimpse

peekaboo: 4 game 6 bopeep, peep-bo 7 peepeye

peel: 4 bark, harl, hull, pare, rind, skin 5 flipe, scale, slipe, stake, strip 6 shovel 7 undress 8 palisade, stockade 11 decorticate

peeler: 4 crab 5 bobby, corer 7 hustler 8 pillager 9 policeman 11 stripteaser

peeling: 4 rind, skin 6 paring

peep: pry, spy 4 peek, peer, pule, skeg 5 cheep, chirp, dekko, glint, snoop, tweet 6 glance, squeak 9 sandpiper

hawk: 7 kestrel

show: 5 raree

peeper: eye, Tom 4 frog 6 voyeur

peepeye: 8 peekaboo

peephole: 4 hole 6 eyelet 7 crevice, eyehole, opening

peeping: 4 nosy 5 nosey 11 inquisitive

peer: pry 4 duke, earl, fear, fere, gaze, look, lord, mate, peep 5 baron, equal, feere, gloze, noble, snoop, stare, stime(Sc.), styme(Sc.), thane(Sc.) 7 comrade, marquis 8 nobleman, superior, viscount 9 associate, rubberneck 12 contemporary

residence: 6 barony

Peer Gynt: *author:* 5 Ibsen

character: 4 King 6 Anitra

composer: 5 Grieg

mother: Ase

peerage: 4 rank 7 dignity 8 nobility

peerdom: 8 equality

peerless: 9 matchless, nonpareil, unrivaled 11 superlative

peetweet: 9 sandpiper

peeve: irk 6 grudge, nettle 8 irritate 9 annoyance

peevish: 5 cross, techy, testy, wemod 6 crusty, hipped, snarly, sullen, touchy 7 carping, crabbed, frecket, fretful, forward, pettish, spleeny, waspish 8 captious, choleric, contrary, critical, crotched, frampold, petulant, sawshach, snappish 9 fractious, impatient, irascible, irritable, plaintive, splenetic 10 ill-humored 11 caper-noited, contentious, disgruntled

peewee: 4 bird, lark, tiny 5 dwarf 7 lapwing

peg: fix, hob, nob, nog, pin 4 plug, scob, step 5 cleat, dowel, drink, perch, piton, prong, spill, stake, throw, tooth 6 degree, dowell, marker, reason 7 pretext, support 8 fastener

pega, pegador: 6 remora

pegall: 6 basket

Pegasus: 11 winged horse

rider: 11 Bellerophon

source: 6 Medusa 13 constellation

Peggotty's niece: 5 Emily

peho: 8 morepork

peignoir: 4 gown 5 dress 6 kimono 7 wrapper 8 negligee 9 housecoat 12 dressing-gown

pejorative: 10 derogatory 11 disparaging

pelage: fur 4 hair, pelt

pelagic: 6 marine 7 aquatic, oceanic 9 thalassic

Peleg: *father:* 4 Eber

son: Reu

Peleus: *brother:* **7** Telamon
father: **6** Aeacus
son: **7** Pelides **8** Achilles
wife: **6** Thetis

pelf: rob **4** gain **5** booty, lucre, money, spoil, trash **6** pilfer, refuse, riches, spoils, wealth **7** despoil, rubbish

Pelican State: 9 Louisiana

pelike: jar **4** vase **7** amphora **8** amphorae

pellet: wad **4** ball, pill, shot **5** bolus, stone **6** bullet, pilule **7** granule

pellicle: 4 film, scum, skin **5** crust **7** coating, cuticle **8** membrane

pell-mell 8 confusion, disorder, headlong, stampede **11** impetuously **13** helter skelter

pellock: 8 porpoise

pellucid: 5 clear, sheer **6** bright, limpid **7** crystal **11** crystalline, translucent, transparent

pelmet: 7 cornice, valance

Peloponnesus: *city:* **6** Sparta
people: **7** Moreote
river god: **7** Alpheus

Pelops: *father:* **8** Tantalus
son: **6** Atreus **8** Pittheus, Thyestes
wife: **10** Hippodamia

pelota: 7 jai-alai

pelt: fur **4** beat, blow, cast, dash, fell, hide, hurl, push, skin **5** fitch, flung, hurry, stone **6** gallop, hasten, pelage, refuse, strike, thrust **7** rawhide, rubbish **8** woolfell
dealer: **7** furrier

peludo: 9 armadillo

pelvis: *bone:* **4** ilia **5** ilium, pubes **7** ischium
pert. to: **5** iliac

pen: cot, cub, get, mew, pin, sty **4** bolt, cage, coop, fold, jail, yard **5** bught, crawl, hutch, kraal, quill, write **6** bought, corral, cruive, fasten, hurdle, indite, record, stylus, zareba **7** calamus, compose, confine, enclose, zareeba **9** enclosure **12** penitentiary
kind: ink **8** fountain **9** ball-point **12** stylographic
point: neb, nib **4** stub
seller: **9** stationer

pen-like: 7 styloid

pen name (see also **nickname, pseudonym**)**: 5** alias **6** anonym **9** pseudonym **10** nom de plume
François Arouet: **8** Voltaire
Isaac Bickerstaff: **9** Dean Swift
Henri Beyle: **8** Stendhal
Eric Blair: **6** Orwell
Charlotte Bronte: **10** Currer Bell
Emily Bronte: **9** Ellis Bell
Samuel Clemens: **9** Mark Twain
Charles Dickens: Boz
Charles Dodgson: **12** Lewis Carroll
Amantine Dupin: **10** George Sand

Mary Ann Evans: **11** George Eliot
Benjamin Franklin: **11** Poor Richard
Charles Lamb: **4** Elia
H. H. Munro: **4** Saki
Alexei Peshkov: **10** Maxim Gorky
Jean Baptiste Poquelin: **7** Moliere
William S. Porter: **6** O. Henry
Jacques Thibault: **13** Anatole France
Louis Viaud: **10** Pierre Loti

penal: 8 punitive, punitory

penalize: 4 fine **5** mulct **6** amerce, punish

penalty: 4 fine, loss, pain **5** mulct **6** amende, amerce **7** forfeit **8** hardship **10** forfeiture, punishment **12** disadvantage
pay: aby **4** abye

penance: 6 sorrow **7** remorse **9** atonement, penitence, suffering **10** contrition, repentance **13** mortification

pencel: 4 flag **6** pennon **8** streamer **9** pennoncel

penchant: 4 bent **5** taste **6** liking **7** leaning **8** fondness **10** attraction **11** inclination

pencil: red, wad **4** blue, lead, wadd **8** charcoal **9** eversharp **10** mechanical
pert. to: **6** desmic
worn-down: **4** stub

pendant: bob, jab **4** flag, jagg, pend, tail **5** aglet **6** aiglet, tassel **7** pensile, support **8** gamaliel, lavalier **9** lavaliere, pendulous, suspended, undecided **11** counterpart

pending: 6 during

pendulous: lop **6** droopy **7** hanging **8** swinging

Penelope: *father:* **7** Icarius
father-in-law: **7** Laertes
husband: **7** Ulysses **8** Odysseus
suitor: **7** Agelaus

penetralia: 7 privacy **9** sanctuary

penetrate: 4 bore, dive, gore, stab **5** break, enter, imbue, steep **6** fathom, ficche, pierce **7** discern, pervade **8** permeate **9** insinuate, perforate **10** infiltrate, understand

penetrating: 5 acute, sharp **6** astute, shrewd, shrill, subtle **7** knowing **8** incisive **9** sagacious **10** insightful **11** clairvoyant **14** discriminating

penetration: wit **6** acumen **13** understanding

penguin: auk **6** Johnny
genus: **9** eudyptula
home: **4** pole **7** rookery **10** penguinery
large: **7** emperor
small: **6** Adelie

peninsula: 4 neck **6** penile **10** chersonese

penitence: rue **5** qualm **6** regret, sorrow **7** remorse, sadness, scruple **8** distress, humbling **10** contrition, repentance **11** compunction
season of: **4** Lent

penitent: 4 ruer 5 sorry 6 humble 10 remorseful

penitentiary: jug, pen 4 jail, stir 5 tench 6 prison 8 big-house

penman: 6 author, scribe, writer 10 amanuenses, amanuensis 12 calligrapher

penmanship: 4 hand 6 script 7 writing 11 calligraphy, handwriting

pennant: 4 fane, flag, whip 5 roger 6 cornet, banner, pennon, pinion 8 streamer 9 banderole
  yacht: 6 burgee

pennate: 6 winged 9 feathered, penniform

penniless: 4 poor 5 broke, needy 8 bankrupt 9 insolvent 11 impecunious

pennon: 4 flag, wing 6 banner, pinion 7 feather, pennant

Pennsylvania: *battlefield:* 10 Gettysburg
  capital: 10 Harrisburg
  city: 4 Erie 7 Reading, Scranton 9 Allentown 10 Pittsburgh 12 Philadelphia
  county: 5 Berks, Bucks 7 Cambria, Chester, Venango, Wyoming
  flood: 9 Johnstown
  mountain range: 6 Pocono 9 Allegheny
  native: 5 Amish 9 Mennonite
  nickname: 8 Keystone
  river: 4 Ohio 8 Delaware 10 Schuylkill 11 Monongahela, Susquehanna
  state bird: 6 grouse
  state flower: 14 mountain laurel
  state tree: 7 hemlock
  valley: 6 Lehigh 7 Lebanon 10 Cumberland

penny: 4 cent 5 brown, pence 6 copper, saltee, stiver

penny-pinching: 6 stingy 7 miserly

penology: 11 criminology

Pensees author: 6 Pascal

pensile: 7 pendent 9 suspended 11 overhanging

pension: 6 retire 7 annuity, payment, stipend, subsidy, tribute 8 gratuity 9 allowance 10 exhibition

pensive: 4 blue 5 sober 6 dreamy, musing 7 wistful 10 meditative, melancholy, reflective, ruminating, thoughtful 13 contemplative

pent: 5 caged 6 shut up 8 confined, enclosed

pentacle: 4 star 8 hexagram

pentastitch: 4 poem 6 stanza 7 strophe

Pentateuch: law 4 tora 5 Bible, torah
  first book: 7 Genesis

Pentheus: *grandfather:* 6 Cadmus
  mother: 5 Agave

penthouse: 4 roof, shed 5 aerie 6 hangar 7 pentice 8 dwelling 9 apartment, treehouse

pentyl: 4 amyl

penumbra: 5 shade 6 shadow 7 umbrage

penurious: 4 mean, poor 6 barren, frugal, scanty, stingy 7 miserly, wanting 8 indigent 9 destitute 10 avaricious 12 parsimonious

penury: 7 beggary, poverty 9 privation

peon: 4 hand, pawn, serf 5 slave 6 thrall 7 footman, laborer, peasant, soldier 9 attendant, constable, messenger, policeman
  state of: 7 peonage

peony: 4 piny 5 plant 6 flower, mouton

people (see also **person**): kin, men 4 folk, gens, herd, pais(law) 5 demos, gentée(Sp.), laity, stock 6 daoine, gentry, settle 7 inhabit, society, tilikum(Ind.) 8 canaglia(It.), canaille(F.), populate, tillicum(Ind.) 11 inhabitants, rank and file
  aggregation: 5 tribe
  ancient: 4 Seba 5 Itali, Medes 6 Greeks, Romans 7 Sabines 8 Grecians 9 Assyrians, Egyptians, Etruscans
  ape-shaped skull: 9 proghathi
  body: 4 race 5 tribe 6 nation 7 society 8 assembly, populace 9 citizenry, community 10 electorate, public Rais
  group: mob 4 army, band, team 5 corps, crowd, posse 6 chorus, troupe, throng 7 company, coterie 8 assembly 9 orchestra 11 association
  headless: 8 Acephali
  pert. to: 6 ethnic 7 demotic
  present: 5 class, crowd 10 assemblage, attendance 12 congregation
  well-bred: 9 gentility

pep: vim 4 dash 5 verve, vigor 6 energy, ginger 7 animate, quicken 9 animation, briskness, encourage, stimulate 10 initiative, invigorate, liveliness

peplos: 5 scarf, shawl

peplum: 9 overskirt

pepo: 5 gourd, melon 6 squash 7 pumpkin 8 cucumber

pepper: ava, hot, red 4 kava, siri 5 betel, green, sirih, sweet 6 speckle 7 paprika, paprika 8 capsicum, kavakava, pimiento
  beverage: 4 kava 8 kavakava
  grass: 5 cress
  hot: 5 chili 7 cayenne, tabasco
  package: 6 robin
  shrub: 4 cava, kava
  species: 5 betel 7 cayenne

pepper-and-salt: 4 gray 7 mottled

pepper picker: 5 Peter, Piper

pepper plant: ava 5 chile, chili 6 chilli

peppermint camphor: 7 menthol

peppery: hot 4 keen 5 alert, fiery 6 lively 7 piquant, pungent 8 choleric, spirited, stinging 9 irascible, irritable 10 passionate

peppy: 4 keen 5 alert 6 lively 8 spirited 9 vivacious

Pequod's captain: 4 Ahab

per: 4 each 6 apiece 7 through

per se: 6 as such, itself 8 directly 11 essentially 13 intrinsically

peradventure: hap 5 doubt, maybe 6 chance, mayhap 7 happily, perhaps 8 possibly 11 uncertainty

perambulate: 4 walk 6 ramble, stroll 8 traverse 9 promenade

perambulator: 5 buggy 12 baby-carriage, pushwainling

per capita: all 4 each 6 apiece

perceive: see 4 feel, hear, know, note, take 5 grasp, scent, sense, smell, taste, touch 6 behold, descry, divine, notice 7 discern, observe, realize, sensate 8 comprise, comprize, identify 9 apprehend, recognize 10 articulate, comprehend, understand 11 distinguish 12 discriminate

perceivable: 11 perceptible

perceiving: 5 acute

percentage: 4 agio, odds, part 5 share 6 profit 7 portion, rake-off 9 advantage 11 probability

perceptible: 5 clear, lucid 7 tactile, visible 8 palpable, sensible, tangible 10 cognizable 11 appreciable, discernible, perceivable 12 intelligible, recognizable

perception: 4 idea 6 acumen 7 insight 9 sensation 13 animadversion, consciousness

capable of: 8 sentient

impaired: 13 acatamathesia

perch: bar, peg, rod, sit 4 fish, jook, mado, okow, pike, pole, pope 5 barse, light, roost, ruffe, staff 6 alight, sauger, settle, weapon, zingel 9 trumpeter

perchance: 5 haply, maybe 7 perhaps 8 possibly

Percheron: 5 horse

percolate: 4 ooze, seep, sift, silt 5 exude, leach 6 filter, strain 7 pervade 8 permeate

percolator: 6 biggin 9 coffeepot

percussion: 5 shock 6 impact 9 collision 10 detonation

percussion instrument: 4 drum, gong, trap 6 cymbal 7 marimba 8 triangle 9 xylophone 10 tambourine 12 glockenspiel

percylite: 7 boleite

perdition: 4 hell, loss, ruin 9 damnation 11 destruction

perdue, perdu: 6 hidden 9 concealed

perdurable: 7 durable, eternal, lasting 8 enduring 9 permanent 11 everlasting

Pere Goriot author: 6 Balzac

peregrinate: 4 roam, walk 6 travel, wander 7 journey, sojourn 8 traverse

peregrine: 4 hawk 5 alien 6 exotic, falcon 7 foreign, pilgrim, strange

peremptory: 5 final, utter 7 decided, express 8 absolute, decisive, dogmatic, positive 9 arbitrary, imperious, masterful 10 conclusive, imperative 11 dictatorial 13 authoritative

perennial: old, rue 4 tree 5 carex, liana, liane, peony, plant, sedum 6 annual, banana 7 durable 8 enduring, geophyte, toadflax 9 continual, permanent, perpetual, recurrent, unceasing 12 never-failing

perfect: all 4 fill, fine, holy, pure 5 exact, ideal, right, ripen, sheer, sound, utter, whole 6 entire, expert, finish 7 concoct, correct, improve, plenary, precise, sinless, spheral 8 absolute, accurate, circular, complete, finished, flawless, masterly, thorough 9 blameless, elaborate, exquisite, faultless, righteous 10 accomplish, consummate, immaculate, satisfying

perfecta: 11 betting pool

perfection: 4 acme, pink 5 ideal 7 fulness, paragon 8 fullness, maturity 9 integrity 10 excellence

realm of: 6 Utopia 8 Paradise

perfectly: 4 well 5 quite 10 altogether

perfecto: 5 cigar

perfervid: 6 ardent 7 zealous 11 impassioned

perfidious: 5 false, snaky, venal 8 disloyal, spiteful 9 dishonest, faithless, felonious 10 traitorous 11 dissaffected, treacherous

perfidy: 7 treason 8 apostasy, foul play 9 defection, Judas' kiss, treachery 10 disloyalty, infidelity 13 faithlessness

perforate: eat 4 bore, dock 5 drill, prick, punch 6 pierce, pounce, riddle 8 puncture 9 penetrate, torebrate 10 foraminate

perforation: 4 bore, hole 6 broach, eyelet, tresis 7 stencil 8 aperture

perform: act 4 char, fill, full, play 5 chare, dight, enact, exert 6 effect, fulfil, render, wind up 7 achieve, execute, exhibit, exploit, fulfill, furnish, gesture 8 bring off, transact 9 do up brown 10 accomplish, perpetrate

again: 7 re-enact

inadequately: 5 botch 6 bungle, mess up

while moving about: 11 peripatetic

with ceremony: 9 solemnise, solemnize

performance: act 4 deed, feat, show, test, work 5 stunt 6 acting, action, effect 7 benefit, concert, exploit, matinee 8 feasance, function 9 discharge, execution, rendition 10 completion, efficiency, fulfilment 11 fulfillment 12 consummation 14 accomplishment

daytime: 7 matinee

first: 5 debut 8 premiere

individual: 4 soli, solo

standard: 5 bogey

performer: 4 doer, moke 5 actor, shine 6 artist, worker 7 artiste 8 executor, thespian

company: 6 troupe

diligent: 5 plier 6 drudge 7 plugger 10 workaholic

low-grade: 9 hamfatter

supplementary: 7 ripieno

top-notch: ace 4 star

perfume: 4 atar, aura, balm, nose, otto 5 aroma, attar, cense, irone, myrrh, ottar, scent, smell 6 chypre, flavor, sachet 7 essence, flavour, incense, odorize, sweeten 8 bergamot, fumigate 9 fragrance

base: 4 musk 5 civet 6 neroli 8 bergamot 9 ambergris

container: 4 vial 5 phial 6 censer

medicated: 6 pastil, troche 7 pastile 8 pastille

oriental: 5 myrrh

pad: 6 sachet

powdery: 6 pulvil

shrub source: 8 abelmosk

with burning spice: 5 cense

perfumed cherry: 7 mahaleb

perfumer: 6 censer, sachet 8 atomizer, pomander, thurible

perfunctory: 5 usual 7 routine 8 careless 9 automatic 10 mechanical 11 indifferent, superficial

pergola: 5 arbor, bower 6 arbour 7 balcony, trellis 9 colonnade

perhaps: 5 maybe 6 ablins, belike, theory 7 ablings 8 doubtful, possibly, probably 9 perchance 11 conceivably

peri: elf 5 dwarf, fairy, houri 6 sprite

periapt: 5 charm 6 amulet

pericarp: pod 4 boll 5 berry, shell

Pericles: *consort:* 7 Aspasia

daughter: 6 Marina

disciple: 10 Alcibiades

father: 10 Xanthippus

rival: 10 Thucydides

ward: 10 Alcibiades

periculum: 4 risk 5 peril 6 danger

peril: hap 4 risk 6 crises, crisis, danger, hazard, menace 7 apperil, imperil 8 endanger, exposure, jeopardy 9 adventure 10 insecurity, subjection

perilous: 6 touchy 7 tottery 8 doubtful, unstable, unsteady 9 dangerous, desperate

perimeter: rim 6 border 7 outline 8 boundary 9 periphery 13 circumference

period: age, dot, end, eon, era 4 aeon, span, stop, term, time 5 avail, close, cycle, epact, epoch, spell, stage 6 season 8 duration, semester 10 conclusion 11 termination

critical: 6 crises, crisis

festive: 7 holiday 8 vacation

holding: 6 tenure

infinite: 8 eternity

penitential: 4 Lent

playing: 4 half, hand 5 frame, round 6 inning 7 chukkar, chukker, quarter

sleep: 6 godown 11 hibernation

tertiary: 6 eocene 7 neocene

time: day 4 hour, week, year 5 month 6 decade, minute, second 7 century 9 fortnight

periodic: 4 eral 6 annual 7 etesian, regular 8 frequent, seasonal 9 recurrent 12 intermittent

periodical: 5 daily, paper 6 annual, review, 7 etesian, journal, tabloid 8 bulletin, magazine 9 ephemeris, newspaper

peripatetic: 8 rambling 9 itinerant, wandering

peripheral: 5 outer 6 distal 7 distant 8 confined, external, marginal

periphery: lip, rim 4 brim, edge 5 ambit, limit 6 areola, areole, border 7 areolae, outside 8 confines, environs 9 perimeter 13 circumference

periphrastic: 14 circumlocutory

perique: 7 tobacco

perish: die 4 fade, fall, ruin 5 decay 6 depart, expire 7 consume, crumble, forfare, go under, succumb 8 pass away

perishable: 6 caduke 7 brittle 9 ephemeral 10 transitory

peristyle: 6 arcade 7 portico 9 colonnade 10 peripteral

perite: 7 skilled

peritomy: 12 circumcision

peritoneum: 8 covering, membrane

fold of: 7 omentum

peritroch: 5 larva 6 embryo

periwig: 6 peruke, toupee

periwinkle: 5 color, snail 6 mussel, myrtle 10 bluebutton

perjink: 4 neat, nice, trim 7 precise

perjure: lie 8 forswear 10 equivocate 11 prevaricate

perk: 5 preen, prink 7 improve, smarten 8 animated, gratuity 9 percolate 10 perquisite

permanent: 5 fixed 6 stable 7 abiding, durable, lasting 8 constant, enduring 9 continual, headdress, perennial 10 continuing, invariable 12 imperishable

permeable: 6 porous

permeate: 4 fill, seep 5 bathe, imbue 6 drench 7 pervade 8 saturate 9 penetrate

permission: 5 leave 7 consent, license 13 authorization

to use: 4 loan

permit: let 4 leve, pass 5 admit, allow, conge, favor, grace, grant, leave 6 accord, beteem, dustuk, entree, favour, suffer 7 consent, dustuck, license, pompano, warrant 8 furlough, tolerate 9 authorize 10 permission

travel: 8 passport

permutation: 6 change 10 alteration 11 interchange 12 modification 13 rearrangement

pern: 7 buzzard

pernicious: bad 4 evil 5 fatal, toxic 6 deadly, malign, mortal, wicked 7 baleful, baneful, harmful, hurtful, malefic, noisome, noxious, ruinous 10 villainous 11 deleterious, destructive, detrimental

pernio: 9 chilblain

peronate: 5 mealy, wooly

perorate: 5 orate 7 address, declaim 8 harangue

perpendicular: 4 sine 5 erect, plumb, sheer 6 abrupt 7 apothem, stand-up, straight, upright 8 binormal, vertical 9 downright

perpetrate: 5 wreak 6 commit, effect 7 perform

perpetual: 7 endless, eternal 8 constant, unending 9 continual, incessant, perennial, permanent, unceasing 10 continuous 11 everlasting

perpetually: 4 ever 6 always 7 forever 11 ad infinitum

perpetuate: 4 keep 8 continue, eternize, maintain, preserve

perplex: cap 4 clog, doze 5 amaze, beset 6 baffle, boggle, bother, cumber, darken, gravel, hamper, harass, hobble, muddle, pother, puzzle, thwart, twitch 7 bedevil, confuse, diffuse, embroil, mystify, nonplus 8 astonish, babulyie, bewilder, confound, distract, distress, entangle 9 bamboozle, obfuscate 10 complicate

perplexed: 4 asea 5 upset 7 anxious 8 confused, troubled 9 intricate 10 distraught

perplexing: 4 hard, mazy 6 crabby 7 carking, complex, crabbed 9 equivocal 11 complicated

perplexity: fox 4 knot 6 tangle 7 anxiety, trouble 9 intricacy 11 encumbrance 13 embarrassment

perquisite: fee, tip 5 right 6 income 7 adjunct, apanage 8 appanage, appenage, gratuity 9 accessory 11 appointment, prerogative 12 appurtenance 13 accompaniment

presidential: 4 veto

perquod: 7 whereby

Perry Mason creator: 7 Gardner

per se: 5 alone 6 as such, solely 8 in itself

Perse: *daughter:* 5 Circe 8 Pasiphae

father: 4 Oceanus

husband: 6 Helios

son: 6 Aeetes, Perses

persecute: vex 4 bait 5 annoy, harry, hound, worry, wrack, wrong 6 harass,

pester 7 afflict, oppress, torment, torture

Persephone: 4 Kore 8 Despoina

daughter: 4 Cora, Kore

father: 4 Zeus

husband: 5 Hades, Pluto

mother: 7 Demeter

Perseus: *father:* 4 Zeus

grandfather: 8 Acrisius

mother: 5 Danae

star of: 4 Atik 5 Algol

victim: 8 Acrisius

wife: 9 Andromeda

perseverance: 4 grit 7 stamina 8 patience, tenacity 9 assiduity, constancy, diligence, endurance 10 insistence, steadiness 11 continuance, persistence, pertinacity 12 continuation 13 indefatigable, steadfastness

persevere: 4 go on 5 abide, stick 7 persist 8 keep at it

persevering: 4 busy 10 persistent 11 unremitting

Persia (see also **Iran**): *ancient inhabitant:* 4 Mede

apple: 6 citron

assembly: 6 majlis, meklis

bug: 5 miana

carpet: see *rug* below

cat: 6 Angora

chief officer: 5 dewan, diwan

deer: 5 maral 6 fallow

elf or fairy: 4 peri

founder: 5 Cyrus

gate: bab

gazelle: 4 cora

goddess: 7 Anahita

lamb: 7 karakul 9 astrakhan

lynx: 7 caracal

measure: gaz, guz, zer

nightingale: 6 bulbul

oil center: 6 Abadan

old coin: 5 daric

poet: 4 Omar, Sadi 5 Hafiz

prophet: 9 Zoroaster

rug: 4 Kali 5 Saruk, Senna 6 Sarouk 7 Isfahan, Ispahan, Teheran 8 Serabend

ruler: 4 shah

scriptures: 5 Koran

sungod: 7 Mithras

tick: 8 miana bug

wheel: 5 noria 7 tympana 8 tympanum

Persian Gulf: *kingdom:* 7 Chaldea

port: 7 Bushire

province: 4 Fars

wind: 6 shamal, sharki 7 shurgee

persiennes: 6 blinds

persiflage: 6 banter 7 mockery 8 chaffing, raillery

persimmon: 7 chapote

family: 5 ebony 9 ebenaceae

persist: 4 go on, last 6 endure, insist, remain **7** carry on, prevail **8** continue **9** persevere

persistent: 4 dree, hard **6** dogged, gritty **7** durable **8** constant, enduring, frequent, holdfast, obdurate, resolute, stubborn **9** assiduous, continued, steadfast, tenacious **10** consistent, continuing, determined, relentless **11** persevering **13** indefatigable

person (see also **people**): guy, man, one, urf **4** body, chap, coot, self, soul **5** being, child, human, wight, woman **6** entity, fellow, galoot **10** individual

admirable: **6** mensch

amusing: **8** comedian, comedien **10** comedienne

bad-luck carrier: **4** jinx **5** jonah

baptized: **10** illuminato **11** illuminatus

base: **7** caitiff, hangdog

bearing the blame: **4** goat

beatified: **6** beatus

betrothed: **6** fiance **7** fiancee

blamed for others: **4** butt, goat **9** scapegoat

brilliant: **6** genius **10** mastermind

callow: **6** gorlin, smarty **7** gosling

canonized: **5** saint

careless: **6** tassel **11** pococurante

charitable: **5** samaritan

cheery: **8** optimist

clumsy: **5** klutz

contemptible: cad, yap **4** heel, toad **7** bauchle

cunning: **8** slyboots

deranged: nut **7** lunatic **10** monomaniac, psychopath

despicable: **5** hound **6** rotter **10** blackguard

detested: **8** anathema

disgruntled: **8** sorehead

dull: **5** dunce, moron **8** imbecile **9** blockhead, defective

eighty-year-old: **12** octogenarian

energetic: **10** ball of fire

enterprising: **8** go-getter

fearless: **10** fearnaught, fearnought **11** dreadnaught, dreadnought

fifty-year-old: **15** quinquagenarian

foolish: sop **4** zany **5** clown **6** dotard **7** halfwit **9** simpleton

forty-year-old: **14** quadragenarian

good-luck carrier: **6** mascot

gray-headed: **7** grisard

guilty: **7** culprit

half-grown: **6** haflin **8** halfling **9** stripling

held as pledge: **7** hostage

holy: ste.(F.) **5** saint

horned: **7** cornute

ill: **7** invalid, patient

indefinite: one **6** anyone **7** anybody, so and so, someone **8** somebody

indifferent to pleasure or pain: **5** stoic

injured: **6** victim **8** casualty

learned: **6** pundit, savant **7** scholar **9** professor **12** intellectual

left-handed: **9** portsider

loud-voiced: **7** stentor

married: **4** wife **6** spouse **7** husband

middle-class: **9** bourgeois **11** bourgeoisie

mischievous: imp **4** pest

named after another: **8** namesake

ninety-year-old: **12** nonagenarian

non-Jewish: **7** gentile

of distinction: VIP **4** star **7** notable

of mixed blood: **7** mestizo, mulatto **8** octoroon **9** half-breed

one-hundred-year-old: **11** centenarian

overnice: **4** prig

perfidious: **5** snake **7** serpent, traitor

proposed for office: **7** nominee

rapacious: **4** wolf **5** harpy, shark

representing another: **5** mimic, proxy **9** alternate

rude: **4** boor **7** caveman

scolding: **9** catamaran

second: you **4** thou

seventy-year-old: **14** septuagenarian

shiftless: bum **7** drifter

sick: **5** ailer **7** invalid, patient **9** aegrotant

sixty-year-old: **12** sexagenarian

skilled: **5** adept **6** artist, master, talent **7** artisan **8** mechanic

small: **4** runt **5** dwarf, sprat **6** midget, poppet

sponsored by another: **7** protege

studious: **5** grind, porer

stupid: ass **4** boob, clod, coot, dolt, fool, gump, moke **5** bucca, clout, moron, stirk, stock, stupe, sumph **6** boodle, duffer, gander, nitwit **7** dullard **8** bonehead, dumbbell, gamphrel **9** boeoetian, simpleton

timid: **11** milquetoast

trustworthy: **7** standby

unmarried: **6** maiden **8** bachelor, celibate, spinster

unusual: **4** oner

wealthy: **5** nabob **9** plutocrat **10** capitalist **11** millionaire **12** millionnaire

white: fay **4** ofay **5** haole **6** albino **7** abiculi, redneck

young: **8** chipling **9** stripling **14** whippersnapper

persona non grata: 12 unacceptable

personable: 6 comely **7** shapely **8** handsome **10** attractive **11** good-looking, well-favored

personage: 6 shogun, tycoon **7** magnate, notable

personal: own **7** private **8** intimate, news item

personality: ego **4** self **8** selfhood **11** disposition **13** individuality

dual: **13** Jekyll and Hyde

split: 13 schizophrenia

personification: 10 embodiment 11 incarnation 14 representation

of rumor: 4 Fama

of truth: Una

personify: 6 embody 9 incarnate, represent 11 impersonate

personnel: 5 staff 9 employees

perspective: 5 vista 7 outlook 9 viewpoint

perspicacious: 4 keen 5 acute 6 shrewd 10 discerning, perceptive 11 penetrating, sharp-witted

perspicacity: wit 6 acumen

perspicuous: 5 clear, lucid, plain 8 manifest 11 conspicuous, translucent, transparent 12 intelligible

perspiration: 5 sudor, sweat 9 exudation 10 ephidrosis

abnormal: 8 hidrosis

pert. to: 7 sudoric

sheep: 5 suint

persuade: get, win 4 coax, gain, sway, urge 5 argue 6 allure, assure, engage, entice, induce 7 convert, entreat, win over 8 convince, inveigle 9 influence

persuaded: 7 pliable 8 gullible 9 credulous

persuasion: 4 cult, mind, view 6 belief 8 judgment, religion

persuasive: 6 cogent 8 eloquent 9 impelling, inductive

pert: 4 bold 5 alert, alive, bardy, brisk, cocky, quick, sassy, saucy, smart 6 active, brazen, clever, cocket, comely, dapper, frisky, lively 7 forward, naughty 8 handsome, impudent, insolent, petulant 9 exquisite, officious, sprightly 11 flourishing

pert girl: 4 minx

pertain: 5 belie 6 bear on, befall, belong, relate 7 concern 9 accessory, associate

pertaining to: For all definitions beginning with this phrase, see under following main word or phrase, EXAMPLES: "pertaining to gold": see **gold:** *pert. to;* "pertaining to the sun": see **sun:** *pert. to.*

pertinacious: 4 firm 6 dogged 8 adhering, stubborn 9 obstinate, tenacious 10 determined, inflexible, persistent, unshakable, unyielding

pertinent: apt, fit, pat 6 proper, timely 7 adapted, apropos, germane, telling 8 apposite, relative, relevant 10 applicable, felicitous 11 appropriate 12 appurtenance

perturb: 5 upset, worry 7 agitate, confuse, derange, disturb, trouble 8 disorder, unsettle 10 discompose, disconcert

perturbation: 6 flight, pother 7 trouble, turmoil 9 agitation, commotion 10 un-

easiness 12 irregularity

pertussis: 5 cough 13 whooping cough

Peru: *animal:* 5 llama 6 alpaca

bark: 8 cinchona

capital: 4 Lima

city: Ica 5 Cuzco, Paita 6 Callao 7 Iquitos 8 Arequipa

conqueror: 7 Pizarro

cormorant: 6 Guanay

dance: 5 cueca

department: Ica, Yca 4 Lima 5 Cusco, Cuzco, Piura, Tacna, Tagna

emblem of nobility: 6 llautu

empire: 4 Inca, Ynca

fog: 5 garua

goddess: 4 Mama

hillock: 4 loma

inn: 5 tambo

king: 7 cacique

lake: 8 Titicaca

liberator: 7 Bolivar

liquor: 5 pisco

llama: 4 paco 6 alpaca

mark of nobility: 6 llautu

measure: 4 topo, vara 5 galon 7 celemin 8 fanegada

monetary unit: sol 5 libra 6 dinero, peseta 7 centavo

partridge: 4 yutu

people: 4 Ande, Cana, Inca, Inka, Peba, Yutu 5 Boros, Campa, Carib, Panos 6 Aymara, Jibaro, Jiyaro, Kechua, Lamano 7 Quechau

plant: oca 6 ulluco 7 rhatany

relic: 5 huaco

river: Ica 5 Rimac, Santa 7 Maranon, Ucayale 8 Apurimac, Huallaga, Urubamba 11 Paucartambo

rodent: 10 chinchilla

ruler: 4 Inca, Inka

shrub: 6 chilca, matico, shansa

skin disease: uta

tableland: 4 puna

tavern: 5 tambo

tinamou: 4 yutu

tree: 6 bucare 8 cinchona

tuber: oca

volcano: 5 Misti

weight: 5 libra 7 quintal

wind: 4 puna 5 sures

peruke: wig 6 toupee 7 periwig

peruse: con 4 read, scan 5 study 6 handle, search, survey 7 examine, inspect 9 supervise

pervade: 4 fill 5 bathe, imbue 6 occupy 8 permeate, traverse 9 penetrate

pervading: 8 profound 9 prevalent, universal 10 widespread

perverse: awk 4 awry, wogh, wraw 6 cranky, divers, wicked, wilful 7 awkward, distort, diverse, forward, froward, vicious, wayward 8 backward, camshach, contrary, crotched, petulant 9 camsteary, camsteery, difficult, fractious, obstinate 10 determined 11 contentious, contrarious, disobedient, intractable 12 cantankerous, contumacious

perversely: auk, awk 7 athwart 8 overwart

pervert: 4 ruin, skew 5 abuse, twist, upset 6 debase, divert, garble, invert, misuse, poison 7 contort, corrupt, deprave, distort, outrage, vitiate 8 apostate, misapply, overturn, renegade 9 misdirect 10 demoralize 12 misinterpret, misrepresent

perverted: bad 6 wicked 7 corrupt, twisted, vicious

pervious: 4 open 6 leachy 9 permeable 10 accessible 11 transparent

pervulgate: 7 publish

Pescadores: *island:* 4 Hoko

town: 4 Mako

peshkar: 5 agent 7 steward 8 minister 10 accountant

peshkash: tax 7 present, tribute 8 offering

pesky: 6 plaguy 8 annoying 9 pestering, vexatious 11 troublesome 12 disagreeable

peso: 4 coin

silver: 4 duro

pessimism: 5 gloom 7 despair 8 cynicism

pessimistic: 6 gloomy 7 alarmed, cynical

pest: 4 bane, weed 5 hound, mouse, worry 6 insect, plague, vermin 7 trouble 8 epidemic, nuisance 9 annoyance 10 pestilence

pester: dun, nag, rib 4 ride 5 annoy, devil, tease, worry 6 badger, bother, harass, molest 7 torment, trouble 9 aggravate 10 drive crazy

pestiferous: 4 evil 10 pernicious 11 mischievous

pestilence: 4 pest 5 death 6 plague 7 disease, scourge 8 epidemic

pestilent: 6 deadly 7 noxious 9 poisonous 10 contagious, infectious

pestle: 4 bray 5 grind 6 beetle, muller

vessel: 6 mortar 10 pulverizer

pet: cat, dog, hug 4 coax, daut(Sc.), dawt(Sc.), dear, duck, huff, neck, sulk, tiff 5 drunt, humor, quiet, spoil 6 caress, coddle, cosher, cuddle, dautie(Sc.), dawtie(Sc.), faddle, fantad, fantod, fondle, pamper, stroke 7 cherish, darling, embrace, indulge, tantrum 8 favorite, fondling 9 cherished, favourite

petal: ala 4 leaf 5 sepal 8 labellum

petals: 7 corolla

without: 9 apetalous

petard: 8 firework 11 firecracker

peteman: 5 thief 7 burglar 9 cracksman 10 safeblower

peter: 4 fade, fail, wane 5 cease 7 dwindle, exhaust 8 decrease, diminish

out: 6 fizzle

Peter: 4 czar, rock 5 saint, Simon

father: 5 Jonas

Peter Pan: *author:* 6 Barrie

character: 4 John 5 Wendy 7 Michael 9 Tiger Lily 10 Tinker Bell

dog: 4 Nana

pirate: 4 Smee

petiole: 4 stem 5 stalk 8 peduncle 9 leafstalk 10 mesopodium

petite: 4 size, trim 5 small 6 demure, little 10 diminutive

petition: ask, beg, sue 4 bill, boon, plea, pray, suit, wish 5 apply, orate, plead 6 appeal, entreat, implore, oration, request, solicit 8 entreaty 10 supplicate 11 application, deprecation 12 supplication 13 contemplation

petitioner: 5 asker 6 beggar, seeker 8 appealer, beadsman, bedesman 9 applicant, suppliant

chancery: 7 relator

peto: 5 wahoo

Petrarch's love: 5 Laura

petrel: 4 titi 5 mitty 7 assilag 8 allamoth 9 albatross, allamonti, allamotti, mallemuck

petrify: 4 daze, numb 6 appall 7 horrify, startle 11 turn to stone

petrifying: 7 numbing 9 deadening, hardening 10 petrescent, terrifying 11 fossilizing

Petrograd: 9 Leningrad

petrol: gas 8 gasoline

petroleum: oil 6 octane 7 naphtha 10 illuminant

by-product: 6 butane, diesel 7 propane 9 propylene

product: wax 4 coke 5 ethyl 6 petrol 7 alcohol, asphalt, canadol, naphtha 8 gasoline, kerosene, paraffin 9 righolene

petrosal: 4 hard 5 stony

petticoat: 4 kilt, slip 5 jupon, pagne 6 kirtle 7 placket, whittle 8 basquine, halfslip, vasquine 9 undercoat, waistcoat 10 fustanella, underskirt 11 farthingale

tails: 7 teacake 9 shortcake

pettifogger: 6 lawyer 7 shyster 8 attorney 10 bush lawyer

pettle: 4 spud 5 spade 6 cuddle, nestle, potter 7 cherish, indulge

petty: 4 base, mean, orra, puny 5 minor, small 6 little, paltry, puisne 7 trivial 8 childish, inferior, nugatory, trifling 9 frivolous, jerkwater, minuscule 10 diminutive 11 Mickey Mouse, subordinate, unimportant 12 contemptible 13 insignificant 14 inconsiderable

fault: 10 peccadillo
matter: 6 fidfad
morel: 9 spikenard 10 nightshade
whin: 10 restharrow

petulant: 4 pert 5 cross, huffy, saucy, short, sulky, testy 6 sullen, wanton, wilful 7 forward, fretful, grouchy, peevish, pettish, wayward 8 contrary, immodest, insolent, perverse 9 impatient, irascible, irritable, plaintive, querulous 10 illhumored

pew: 4 desk, seat, slip 5 bench, bught, stall 6 bought(Sc.) 10 amen corner

pewee: 10 flycatcher

pewter: tra 5 bidri, bidry 6 bidery, bidree 7 biddery

peyote: 5 plant 6 cactus, mescal, peyotl

Phaedo's school: 5 Elian

Phaedra: *father:* 5 Minos
husband: 7 Theseus
stepson: 10 Hippolytus

phaeton: 8 carriage 10 towing car

phalacrocorax: 4 coot 9 cormorant

phalanger: 5 ariel, tapoa 6 animal 7 opossum 8 squirrel 9 marsupial

phalera: 4 boss, disk, moth, stud 5 cameo

phantasm: 5 dream, fancy, vapor 6 mirage, shadow 7 phantom 8 delusion

phantasmal: 6 unreal 10 transitory

phantom: 4 idol 5 bogie, idola, image, shade, umbra 6 eidola(pl.), idolon, idolum, shadow, spirit 7 bugbear, eidolon, fantasy, specter, spectre 8 illusion, 10 apparition

Phaon's consort: 6 Sappho

Pharaoh: 4 king 5 ruler 6 tyrant

Pharaoh's chicken: 7 vulture

Pharaoh's fig: 8 sycamore

Pharaoh's mouse: 9 ichneumon

phare: 6 strait 10 lighthouse

pharisaical: 12 hypocritical

pharmaceutical: dia 7 mellite 9 medicinal

pharmacist: 8 druggist 9 dispenser 10 apothecary

pharmacy weight: 5 obole 6 obolus

pharos: 5 cloak 6 beacon 7 lantern 10 chandelier, lighthouse

phase: 4 hand, side 5 angle, facet, stage 6 aspect 8 passover 13 manifestation

pheasant: 5 argus, cheer, monal 6 monaul, moonal, pukras 7 kallege 8 fireback, tragopan
breeding-place: 4 stew
brood: nid, nye 4 nide
nest: 4 nide

pheasant cuckoo: 6 coucal

pheasant duck: 7 pintail 9 merganser

pheasant finch: 7 waxbill

phenol: 6 orcine, thymol 9 germicide
derivative: 4 anol 5 orcin 6 iresol, thymol

phenomenal: 7 unusual 11 exceptional 13 extraordinary

phenomenon: 4 fact 7 miracle, reality, stunner 9 actuality 10 experience

phenyl salicylate: 5 salol

phial: cup 4 bowl, vial 6 bottle, vessel

philander: 5 dally, flirt 7 opossum 10 flirtation, play around

philanthropic: 6 humane 10 altruistic, benevolent, charitable 11 civic-minded 12 humanitarian

philanthropist: 5 donor 10 benefactor 12 humanitarian

philanthropy: 4 alms 10 almsgiving
universal: 15 omnibenevolence

philippic: 6 screed, tirade 8 diatribe

Philippines: *animal:* 5 civet, lemur
ant: 4 anai, anay
archipelago: 4 Sulu
attendant: 5 alila
banana: 7 lacatan, saguing
barracks: 7 cuartel
beer: 7 pangasi
bird: 4 maya 6 abacay
boat: 5 balsa, banca 8 balangay, barangay
breadfruit: 4 rima 8 casmansi
brigand: 7 ladrone
buffalo: 7 carabao, timarau, timerau
canoe: 5 banca, vinta 6 baroto
capital: 10 Quezon City
carriage: 9 carretela, carromata
chief: 4 dato 5 datto, Iloco 7 Ilocano, Ilokano
Christianized tribe: 5 Bicol, Bikol, Tagal, Vicol 7 Bisayan, Tagalog, Visayan
city: Iba 4 Agoa, Cebu, Naga 5 Albay, Davao 6 Aparri, Baguio, Cavite, Ilagan, Manila 7 Dagupan
coconut meat: 5 copra
cyclone: 6 baguio
dagger: 4 itac 7 balarao
deity: 5 Dagon
discoverer: 8 Magellan
drink: 4 beno, vino 5 bubud 7 pangasi
farmer: lao, tao
fern: 4 nito
fetish: 5 anito
fiber: 4 eruc 6 buntal 9 pineapple
fish: 8 langaray
food: poi 4 baha, taro
forest: 5 gubat
fort: 4 Gota 10 Corregidor
garment: 4 saya
grass: 5 cogon
guerrilla: Huk
gulf: 5 Davao, Ragay
hardwood: 4 ipil 5 narra
hat: 7 salacot
hemp: 5 abaca 6 manila
hero: 5 Rizal
house: 5 bahay
idol: 5 anito

island: 4 Cebu 5 Batan, Bohol, Leyte, Luzon, Panay, Samal, Samar 6 Negros 7 Masbate, Mindora, Palawan, Paragua 8 Mindanao

kitchen: 5 calan

knife: 4 bolo, itac 7 balarao, machete

lake: 4 Taal 5 Lanao

language: 4 Moro 5 Bicol, Tagal 6 Ibanag 7 Ilocano, Tagalog, Visayan

liberator: 9 MacArthur

lighthouse: 4 faro

liquor: 4 beno 7 pangasi

litter: 7 talabon

lizard: 4 ibid

mammal: 7 tarsier

mango: 5 bauno 7 pahutan

market-day: 7 tiangue

measure: 4 loan 5 braza, caban, cavan, chupa, ganta 6 apatan, balita, quinon

measure of weight: 5 catty, fardo, picul, punto 6 lachsa 7 quilate 8 chinanta

monetary unit: peso

mother: ina

mountain: Apo, Iba 5 Mayon, Pulog 7 Banahao

mountaineer: 8 mentesco

mudfish: 5 dalag

muskmelon: 6 atimon

Muslim: 4 Moro

native: see *people* below

nut: 4 pili

oil: 5 cebur

pagan: 6 Italon

palm: 4 nipa 6 anahao, anahau

parrot: 5 cagit

peasant: tao

people: Ata, Ati, Ita, Tao 4 Aeta, Atta, Etas, Moro, Sulu 5 Bicol, Bikol, Tagal, Vicol 6 Igorot, Timaua, Timawa 7 Bisayan, Tagalog, Visayan 8 Filipino, Igorrote 10 Philippino

plant: aga 4 alem 5 abaca, baroi, batad 6 agamid

plum: 6 sapote

port: 4 Cebu 6 Cavite, Iloilo

president: 6 Marcos

priest: 7 pandita

province: 4 Abra 5 Albay, Davao 6 Iloilo, Tarlac

raft: 5 balsa

reptile: 6 python

rice: 4 paga 5 barit, bigas, macan

river: 4 Abra, Agno 5 Pasig 7 Cagayan 8 Mindanao, Pampanga

road: 4 daan

rope tree: 4 nabo 5 anabo

sapodilla: 5 chico

sarong: 8 padadion

sea: 4 Sulu

sentinel: 6 bantay

servant: 4 bata 5 alila

shirt: 4 baro

shrub: 4 alem, nabo 6 anilao

silk: 10 alcaiceria

skirt: 4 saya

slave: 6 alipin

slipper: 7 chinela

soap vine: 4 gogo

spirit: 5 anito

stream: 4 ilog

sword: 6 barong 8 campilan

termite: 4 anai, anay

textile: 4 pina, saba 7 sina-may

thatch: 4 nipa

timber: 5 cahuy

town: 4 Agoa, Cebu 5 Bayan, Pasay, Vigan 6 Iloilo

tree: dao, iba, tua, tui 4 acle, anam, ates, bogo, dita, ifil, ipil, supa 5 almon, amaga, anabo, balao, balau, bayok, betis, bulak, guijo, ligas, tabog, yacal 6 alagao, alagau, alupag, amuyon, anagap, aranga, bancal, banuyo, bataan, batino, botong, dungon, lanete, marang, molave 7 amuguis, amuyong, amabong, apitong, banilad, binukau, hapiton, mambong, tinadalo 8 almaciga, bitanhol, macaasim, malapaho, tanguile 9 alintatad, batikulin, batitinan 10 batikuling 11 alibangbang, balinghasay

tree bark: aga 6 agamid

vine: iyo

volcano: Apo 4 Mayo 7 Canlaon

watchtower: 7 atalaya 8 bantayan

water buffalo: 7 carabao

water-jar: 5 bango

weapon: 4 bolo

weight: 5 catty, fardo, piail, punto 7 quilate

white man: 7 cachila

wine: 4 beno

wood: 4 teak 5 ebony, narra 6 sandal

yam: ubi, uve

Philistine: 6 cretan 7 Babbitt 8 outsider 9 barbarian, bourgeois, hypocrite

city: 4 Gath, Gaza 5 Ekron 8 Ashkelon

foe: 5 David 6 Samson

giant: 7 Goliath

god: 4 Baal 5 Dagan, Dagon

Philomela: 11 nightingale

father: 7 Pandion

ravisher: 6 Tereus

sister: 6 Procne

philosopher: wit 4 sage 5 cynic, stoic 7 scholar, thinker

disciples: 4 sect 6 school

famous: 4 Kant 5 Plato, Renan, Solon 6 Nestor, Seneca 7 Emerson 8 Socrates, Voltaire 9 Epictetus

of Syracuse: 4 Dion

philosophical: 4 wise 8 composed, rational 9 temperate, unruffled 11 level-headed

philosophy: 4 yoga 7 dualism 8 stoicism

philter 520

9 esoterics 10 empiricism, esthetics, pragmatism 17 transcendentalism

philter, philtre: 4 drug 5 charm 6 potion 7 amatory 9 fascinate

phlebotomize: 5 bleed 8 venesect

phlegm: 6 apathy 10 equanimity 12 indifference

phlegmasia: 12 inflammation

phlegmatic: 4 calm, cool, dull, slow 5 inert 6 watery 7 viscous 8 composed, sluggish 9 apathetic, impassive, lethargic 11 indifferent 13 imperturbable

phloem: 4 bast, flax 6 tissue

phobia: 4 fear 5 dread 12 apprehension

phoca: 4 seal

Phoebad: 7 seeress 9 priestess 10 prophetess

phoebe: 4 bird 5 pewee, pewit 6 peewee 10 flycatcher

Phoebe: 5 Diane 6 Selene 7 Artemis

Phoebus: Sol, sun 6 Apollo

Phoenicia: *city:* 4 Tyre 5 Sidon
colony: 8 Carthage
dialect: 5 Punic
god: 4 Baal 6 Eshmun
goddess: 5 Tanit 6 Baltis, Tanith 7 Astarte
goddess of love: 7 Astarte
king: 6 Agenor
seaport: 5 Sidon

phoenix: 4 bird 7 paragon 8 rara avis

phonetic: 4 oral 5 vocal
notation system: 5 romic
sound: 7 palatal

phonograph: 6 stereo 8 victrola 9 turntable 10 gramophone
inventor: 6 Edison
record: 4 disc, disk 7 platter

phony: 4 fake, sham 5 bogus, false 8 impostor, spurious 9 charlatan 10 fictitious 11 counterfeit

Phorcys: *child:* 5 Ladon 6 Gorgon, Graeae(pl.)
father: 6 Pontus
mother: 4 Gaea

phosphate: 6 ehlite 7 apatite, uranite 9 wavellite

photocopy: 4 stat 5 print

photoengraving: 8 halftone 15 heliotypography

photograph: mug 4 film, snap, X ray 7 picture, tintype 8 likeness, portrait, snapshot 9 ferrotype, pictorial 10 cheesecake, heliograph 13 daguerreotype
bath: 5 fixer, toner 7 reducer 9 developer
book: 5 album
colored: 10 kodachrome
developer: 4 ortol 6 amidol 9 revelator
fixing agent: 4 hypo
instrument: 8 enlarger
inventor: 6 Niepce, Talbot 8 Daguerre
kind: 5 panel, still 6 motion 7 boudoir,

cabinet, diamond 8 imperial, passport, portrait 9 pictorial 10 commercial, scientific 12 composograph 13 carte de visite
negative: 4 film
old-fashioned: 7 tintype 13 daguerreotype
printing: 7 ozotype

photographer: 9 cameraman 10 shutterbug

photology: 6 optics 7 photics

photometric unit: pyr, rad 5 lumen

phrase: mot 4 term, word 5 idiom, state 6 clause, cliche, saving, slogan 7 adjunct, diction, epigram, epithet, thought 8 acrostic, locution 9 catchword, leitmotif 10 expression

phraseology: 7 dialect, diction, wording 8 parlance

phratry: 4 clan 5 curia, tribe

phrenic: 6 mental

Phrixos: *father:* 7 Athamus
mother: 7 Nephele
sister: 5 Helle

Phrygia: *enthusiast:* 9 Montanist
god: 4 Atys 5 Attis 8 Sabazios
king: 5 Midas 7 Gordius
river: 7 Meander
town: 5 Ipsus

phylactery: 5 charm 6 amulet, scroll 8 talisman

phyletic: 6 lineal, racial

phyma: 5 tumor 6 nodule

physic: 5 purge 6 remedy 9 cathartic

physical: 5 lusty 6 bodily, carnal 7 check up, natural, somatic 8 material 9 corporeal, somatical

physician: asa, doc 5 curer, medic, quack 6 doctor, intern, healer, medico 7 interne 8 restorer, sawbones 10 consultant, medicaster 11 aesculapian, philosopher 12 practitioner
association: AMA
group: AMA 5 panel, staff
symbol: 8 caduceus

physicist: 9 hylozoist 10 naturalist

physiognomy: mug 4 face, mien 5 looks 7 feature 8 portrait 10 expression 11 countenance

physique: 4 body 5 build, frame, shape 6 figure 7 anatomy 8 strength 10 appearance 12 constitution

physostigmine: 5 esere 6 eserin 7 eserine

pian: 4 yaws 5 tumor 9 frambesia 10 framboesia

piano: 6 grand 6 softly, spinet 7 clavial, quietly, upright 8 pianette 10 anemochord, pianoforte
dumb keyboard: 9 digitoria 10 digitorium 11 finger board
early: 6 spinet
key: 7 digital

keyboard: **7** clavier
notes: **6** octave
pedal: **7** celeste
pedal keyboard: **8** pedalier

piatti: 7 cymbals

piazza: 5 porch, square **7** balcony, gallery, portico, veranda

pic: 4 peak **5** lance **8** picayune

picacho: 4 hill **5** butte

picador: wit **6** jester **7** debater **11** bullfighter

picadura: 7 tobacco

picaro, picaroon: 5 knave, rogue, tramp **6** bandit, pirate, rascal **7** sharper **8** vagabond **9** hooka-roon **10** adventurer, freebooter

picayune: 4 mean **5** small **6** little, measly, paltry

pichiciago: 9 armadillo

pick: 4 best, gaff, pike, wale **5** adorn, beele, cavil, elect, elite, pluck **6** choice, choose, gather, pickax, select, twitch **7** bargain, diamond **8** plectrum

on: **5** abuse, annoy, tease **9** criticize

out: **4** cull, sort **5** glean **6** assort, choose, select

pickax: 4 bill, pick **6** tubber, twibil **7** mattock, twibill

picked: 5 spiny **8** selected, stripped **10** fastidious

picket: peg **4** pale, post **5** fence, guard, stake **6** fasten, paling, tether **7** enclose, fortify, postern

pickle: 4 alec, dill, mess, peck **5** achar, brine **6** capers, dawdle(Sc.), muddle, nibble, piddle, pilfer(Sc.), trifle(Sc.) **7** chutney, condite, confect, gherkin, vitriol **8** marinate **9** tight spot **11** predicament

mixed: **6** higdon

pickled: 5 drunk, soust **6** soused **9** preserved **11** intoxicated

pickling herb: **4** dill

pickpocket: dip **4** bung, hook, wire **5** diver, filer, ganef, thief **6** buzzer, cannon, dipper, figboy, hooker, ratero(Sp.), robber **7** foister, mobsman, stealer **8** clyfaker **11** fingersmith

helper: **4** duke **5** shill, stall **6** bulker

pickup: 5 tonic, truck **6** arrest, bracer, chippy **9** recovery **9** stimulant **10** hitchhiker **11** improvement, stimulation **12** acquaintance

again: **6** resume

Pickwick Papers author: **7** Dickens

picky: 4 nice **5** fussy **6** choosy **7** finicky

picnic: 4 snap **6** junket, outing

picot: 4 loop **6** edging **8** notching

picotee: 9 carnation

pictograph: 5 glyph

picture (see also **motion picture**): oil **4** copy, draw, icon, idea, ikon **5** ikono,

image, photo, print, scene, vinet **6** chromo, crayon, depict, marine, pastel **7** diorama, etching, explain, imagine, paysage(F.), portray, porture, reflect, tableau **8** describe, likeness, makimono, painting, panorama, portrait, seascape, triptych, vignette **9** delineate, landscape, miniature, represent **10** illustrate, impression, photograph, watercolor **16** chromolithograph

border: mat **5** frame

composite: **7** montage

drawn with heated instrument: **11** pyrogravure

gallery: **5** salon **6** museum

painted on wall: **5** mural

section: **7** gravure

small: **5** cameo **9** miniature **15** microphotograph

stand: **5** easel

viewer: **9** projector **11** alethoscope, stereoscope

Picture of Dorian Gray author: **5** Wilde

picture puzzle: 5 rebus **6** jigsaw

pictured: 11 counterfeit

picturesque: 5 vivid **6** quaint, scenic **7** graphic **8** informal, scenical, striking

picuda: 9 barracuda

piddle: toy **4** pick, play **6** dawdle, putter, trifle

piddling: 5 petty **6** paltry **7** trivial, useless **13** insignificant

pie: 4 mess, snap, tart **5** chaos, flawn, graft, pasty, patty **6** jumble, pastry, tourte **7** cobbler, dessert, mixture **8** crustade, turnover **9** blackbird, confusion

meat: **5** pasty **7** rissole

with ice cream: **7** a la mode

piebald: 4 pied, piet, pyot **5** mixed, motly, pinto **6** bauson, calico **7** mongrel, mottled, dappled **10** variegated **12** multicolored **13** heterogeneous

piece: bat, bit, cob, eke **4** chip, gare, hunk, join, mend, part, slab, slat, snip, stub, tate(Sc.) **5** crumb, flake, patch, pezzo(It.), scrap, sheet, shred, slice, snack, strip **6** cantle, gobbet, morsel, parcel, sliver **7** cantlet, driblet, flinder, flitter, morceau(F.), oddment, portion, section, segment, snippet **8** assemble, dribblet, fraction

tapering: **4** gore, shim **6** gusset

piece de resistance: 8 main dish **9** showpiece **11** centerpiece, chef d'oeuvre, masterpiece

piecemeal: 7 gradual **8** bit by bit **10** in snatches, step-by-step

piece of eight: 4 peso(Sp.) **6** escudo(Sp.)

piece out: eke **8** assemble, complete **10** supplement

piece together: 4 form, make 5 unite

pied: 7 blotchy, mottled, piebald 10 variegated

pied antelope: 8 bontebok

pieplant: 7 rhubarb

pier: cob 4 cobb, dock, mole, pile, quai, quay 5 groin, stilt, wharf 6 bunder, pillar 7 landing, support 8 buttress, pilaster 10 breakwater
 architectural: 4 anta
 base: 5 socle

pierce: cut, dag, rit 4 bear, bite, bore, brod, cloy, dirl, gore, hole, stab, tang 5 break, drill, enter, gride, lance, probe, smite, spear, spike, stick, sting 6 broach, cleave, empale, ficche, impale, riddle, tunnel 7 discern, poniard 8 puncture 9 intersect, lancinate, penetrate, perforate 10 comprehend, run through
 with horn: 4 gore
 with stake: fix 6 impale

pierced: 5 ajour 8 cribrose

piercer: awl 6 gimlet

piercing: 4 fell, high, keen, loud, tart 5 acute, clear, sharp 6 shrill 7 cutting, pungent 8 poignant 9 searching 10 foraminate

Pierus: *consort:* 4 Clio
 son: 10 Hyacinthus

piety: 4 zeal 7 loyalty 8 devotion, fidelity, holiness, religion 9 godliness, reverence 10 compassion, devoutness

pig (see also **hog**): far, ham, hog, sow 4 boar, pork 5 bacon, chuck, crock(Sc.), ingot, shoat, shote, swine 6 farrow, gussie, porker 7 casting, dogboat, glutton, grumphy(Sc.) 8 grumphie(Sc.), pressman, sixpence
 female: sow 4 gilt
 lead: 6 fother
 litter: far 6 farrow
 male: hog 4 boar 6 barrow
 metal: bar 5 ingot
 pert. to: 7 porcine
 pickled feet of: 5 souse
 red variety: 5 Duroc
 tender: 9 swineherd
 young: elt 4 gilt, runt 5 grice(Sc.), piggy, shoat, shote, snork 6 bonham, farrow, piggie, piglet 7 teatman 9 gruntling

pig bed: sty 4 sand

pig deer: 8 babirusa 9 babirussa 10 babiroussa

pig latin: 5 argot

pig potato: 7 cowbane

pig rat: 9 bandicoot

pigboat: sub 9 submarine

piggy bank: 6 pishke 7 knippel, pushkeh

pigeon: 4 barb, bird, dodo, dove, dupe, fool, gull 5 decoy, pluck, squab, wonga 6 coward, culver, cushat, dodlet, fleece, isabel, pouter, turbit 7 cropper, fantail, jacobin, namaqua, pintado, swallow, tumbler 8 squealer 9 frillback, harlequin 10 sweetheart, turbitteen, turtle-dove, wongawonga
 call: coo
 carrier: 5 homer 6 homing 8 horseman 10 scandaroon
 clay: 5 skeet 6 target
 domestic: nun 4 barb, ruff, runt, spot 6 pouter 9 satinette, trumpeter
 extinct: 4 dodo 9 passenger
 feed: 7 saltcat
 genus of: 5 goura 7 columba
 hawk: 6 falcon, merlin
 pert. to: 9 columboid 12 peristeronic
 short-beaked: 4 barb
 tooth-billed: 6 dodlet
 young: 5 piper 8 squealer

pigeon blood: red 6 garnet

pigeon grass: 7 foxtail 9 crabgrass 12 bristlegrass

pigeon hawk: 6 merlin

pigeon house: 7 dovecot 9 columbary

pigeon-livered: 4 meek, mild 6 gentle

pigeon pea: dal, tur 4 herb, seed 5 arhar 6 gandul 7 cajanus, catjang

pigeon woodpecker: 7 flicker

pigeonberry: 8 pokeweed 9 Juneberry 11 coffeeberry

pigeonhearted: 5 timid 8 cowardly 14 chickenhearted

pigeonhole: 5 label 6 assort, shelve 7 arrange, catalog, cubicle 8 classify 9 cubbyhole

pigeonry: 7 dovecot 8 dovecote

piggery: 6 pigsty 8 crockery(Sc.)

piggish: 4 mean 6 filthy, greedy 7 selfish 8 stubborn 10 gluttonous

pigheaded: 7 willful 8 perverse, stubborn 9 obstinate 10 determined

piglike animal: 7 peccary

pigment: 5 color, paint 8 colorant
 absence of: 8 achromia, alphosis 9 tacheture
 applied to canvas: 7 impasto
 black: tar 5 sepia 7 melanin 8 india ink
 blood: 10 hemoglobin
 blue: 4 bice 5 azure, smalt 7 cyanine 8 cerulean, verditer
 blue-gray: 4 bice
 blue-white: 4 zinc
 brown: 5 sepia, umber 6 bister, bistre, sienna 7 melanin
 green: 4 bice 7 veriter
 kind: 7 aniline, rubiate 8 alizarin, massicot 9 alizarine
 red: 7 amatito, realgar, turacin
 toxic: 8 gassypol
 yellow: 5 ocher, ochre 7 etiolin 8 orpiment

pigmy: See **pygmy**

pignus: 4 lien, pawn 6 pledge
pigpen: sty
pigskin: 5 glove 6 saddle 8 football
pigsney: eye 4 dear 7 darling 10 sweetheart
pigsticker: 4 sled 5 sword 7 butcher 11 pocketknife
pigtail: 5 braid, pleat, queue
pika: 4 hare 5 mouse 6 rodent
pike: gen(Sc.) 4 dore, fish, gedd(Sc.), luce, pick, road 5 cairn, point, spike, tower 6 beacon, pickax, summit 7 highway 8 poulaine 9 spearhead 11 muskallonge, muskallunge, muskellunge
pike perch: 4 dory 6 sander sauger
pikel, pikle: 7 hayfork 9 pitchfork
pikelet: 7 crumpet
piker: 5 thief, tramp 6 coward 7 gambler, quitter, shirker, vagrant 8 pilferer, tightwad 10 speculator
pilar: 5 downy, hairy
pilaster: 4 anta 5 antae 6 column, pillar
Pilate: 10 procurator
 prisoner: 8 Barabbas
 tribunal: 8 Gabbatha
 wife: 7 Claudia
pilchard: 7 herring, sardine
 smoked: 6 fumado
pile: cop, mow, nap 4 bank, bing, cock, dass(Sc.), dess(Sc.), heap, mass, mole, much, pier, rick, sess, shag 5 amass, crowd, spile, stack, stake 6 boodle, bundle, pillar 7 edifice, fortune 8 buttress 10 accumulate, breakwater, coacervate
 funeral: 4 pyre 5 mound
 hay: 4 cock, rick 5 stack 6 doodle
 rubbish: 4 dump
 stone: 5 cairn, scree
pile driver: 6 beetle
 weight: tup
pileup: 4 heap, mass 5 amass, stack 8 accident 9 collision
pilewort: 4 herb 6 ficary 8 fireweed
pilfer: rob 4 hook, loot, pelf, take 5 filch, sneak, steal, swipe 6 finger, snitch 7 purloin 9 scrounge
pilgrim: 5 ihram 6 palmer 8 crusader, traveler, wanderer, wayfarer 9 sojourner 12 peregrinator
 bottle: 7 ampulla, costrel
 garb at Mecca: 5 ihram
 ship: 9 Mayflower, Speedwell
 to Holy Land: 6 palmer
Pilgrim's Progress: 8 allegory
 author: 6 Bunyan
 character: 5 Demas 9 Christian
pilgrimage: 4 hadj, trip 7 journey
pill: 4 ball, goli, pare, peel, pool 5 bolus, creek, strip 6 pellet, pilule 7 capsule, granule, pitcher, placebo 11 decorticate
pill bug: 5 louse 6 isopod, slater
pillage: 4 flay, loot, prey, sack 5 booty, foray, harry, rifle, spoil, steal, strip 6 maraud, rapine, ravage 7 despoil, plunder 8 expilate, spoliate, trespass 9 depredate, devastate 10 confiscate 11 appropriate
pillager: 6 peeler 8 marauder 10 freebooter
 of Rome: 6 Alaric
pillaging: 9 predatory
pillar: lat 4 pile, post, prop 5 cippi(pl.), pylon, shaft, stela, stele 6 cippus, column, stelae(pl.), steles 7 obelisk, osiride, support 8 pedestal, mainstay, pilaster, pillaret 9 stanchion, totem pole
 capital: 7 chapter
 pert. to: 6 stelar
 resembling: 8 stelar
 series of: 9 colonnade
 without: 7 astylar
pillar saint: 7 stylite
pillar-stone: 8 monument 11 cornerstone
Pillars of Hercules: 5 Abila, Calpe 9 Gibraltar
pillbox: cap, hat 7 shelter 8 brougham 11 emplacement 13 fortification
pilled: 4 bald, bare 6 barked, peeled, shaven 8 tonsured 12 decorticated
pillion: pad 6 saddle 7 cushion
pillory: 4 joug(Sc.) 5 stock, trone 6 cangue, punish
pillow: cod, pad 5 block 7 bolster, cushion, support
 stuffing: 5 eider, kapok 6 dacron
pillowcase: 4 sham, slip 5 cover, linen 8 flanerie
pilm: 4 dust
pilon: 4 gift 5 bonus 7 present 8 gratuity, lagnappe 9 lagniappe
pilose: 5 hairy
pilot: ace, fly 4 lead 5 flyer, guide, steer 6 airman, leader 7 aviator, conduct, hobbler 8 chaplain, coxswain, director, governor, helmsman, preacher 9 clergyman, cockswain, steersman 10 cowcatcher
 test for: 4 solo
pilot bird: 8 plover
pilot fish: 6 remora, romero 9 whitefish
pilot snake: 4 bull 10 copperhead
pilot whale: 9 blackfish
pilum: 6 pestle 7 javelin
Piman Indian: 5 Opata
pimento: 7 paprika 8 allspice
pimple: 4 blob, burl, flaw 6 burble, papule 7 abscess, bubukle
pin: fed, fix, hob, nog, peg, pen, tit 4 axle, bolt, coak, dart, join, lill, scob 5 affix, arrow, badge, dowel, preen, rivet, spile, stake, style 6 bobbin, broach, brooch, cotter, fasten, pintle, secure, skewer 7 confine, enclose, eyebolt, gudgeon, jewelry, skittle, spindle, trenail 8 fastener,

kingbolt, linchpin, ornament, spilikin, transfix 9 spillikin 10 chatelaine
for fastening meat: 6 skewer
machine: 6 cotter
money: 4 cash 9 allowance
oar: 5 thole
rifle: 4 tige
wooden: fid, peg 5 dowel, thole
pin grass: 7 erodium 9 alfilaria
pin point: 5 tacca
pin-wing: 6 pinion
pinafore: 4 slip 5 apron, dress, smock 6 daidly(Sc.) 8 sundress 9 gaberdine
Pinafore author: 7 Gilbert 8 Sullivan
pince-nez: 5 specs 7 glasses, lorgnon 10 eyeglasses, lorgnette, spectacles
pincers: tew 5 chela, tongs 6 pliers, tenail 7 forceps 8 tenaille
pinch: nip, rob, wry 4 bite, raid 5 cramp, gripe, hinch, steal, stint, theft, tweak 6 arrest, crisis, extort, snatch, snitch, twince 7 confine, squeeze 8 contract, juncture, straiten 9 emergency, vellicate
pinch bar: pry 5 lever
pinchbeck: 4 sham 5 alloy, cheap 8 spurious 11 counterfeit
pinched: 6 wasted 7 haggard
pinch-hitter: sub 6 fill-in 7 stand-in 9 alternate 10 substitute, understudy
pinchpenny: 4 carl 5 miser, stint 9 niggardly
Pindaric: ode
pine: ara, fir, iva, lim 4 ache, flag, fret, hone, mope, tree 5 cedar, droop, dwine, kauri, kaury, larch, mourn, pinon, vacoa, waste, white, yearn 6 balsam, grieve, lament, pandan, repine, spruce, totara, vacona, vacoua, wither 7 agonize, dwindle 8 galagala, languish, Northern 9 evergreen, Norwegian
acid: 5 pinic
exudation: 5 resin, rosin
fruit: 4 cone
grove: 7 pinetum
leaf: 6 needle
mahogany: 8 totara
product: tar 5 resin 10 turpentine
pine bark aphid: 10 phylloxera
pine family: 8 pinaceae
pine gum: 8 sandarac 9 oleoresin
pine knot: 7 dovekie
pine siskin: 5 finch
pine tar: 6 retene
Pine Tree State: 5 Maine
pine tulip: 10 pipsissewa
pineapple: 4 bomb, nana, pina(Sp.) 5 anana(It.) 7 grenade 8 ornament 10 decoration
family: 12 bromeliaceae
genus of: 6 ananas
segment: pip
pineapple weed: 8 marigold

pinecone: 4 clog 8 strobile
pinfold: 4 jail 5 pound 7 confine
ping: 4 push, urge 5 prick
pinguid: fat 5 fatty
pinguin: 7 aguamas
pinguitude: 7 fatness, obesity 8 oiliness 10 greasiness
pinhead: 4 fool 5 clown 6 minnow
pinion: pin, tie 4 bind, gear, wing 5 quill 7 confine, disable, feather, pennant, shackle, trundle 8 cogwheel, restrain
pink: cut 4 deck, rose, rosy, stab, tint 5 adorn, blush, color, coral, prick 6 flower, minnow, pastel, pierce, salmon 7 blossom, radical 8 decorate, grayling 9 carnation, embellish
eye: 14 conjunctivitis
family: 15 caryophyllaceae
genus of: 6 silence
pink needle: 9 alfilaria
pink pill: 7 cure-all
pinkeen: 6 minnow
pinkeye: 14 conjunctivitis
pinnace: 4 boat, ship 5 woman 6 tender 8 mistress
pinnacle: epi, tee, top, tor 4 acme, apex, peak 5 crest, crown, serac 6 finial, needle, summit, 7 gendarme
glacial: 5 serac
rocky: tor 8 aiguille
pinnate: 6 winged 9 feathered 11 featherlike
pinniped: 4 seal 6 walrus
Pinocchio author: 7 Collodi 9 Lorenzini
pinochle: 8 card game
term: 4 meld 5 widow 7 auction
two-handed: 7 goulash
pinpoint: aim, dot, fix 5 exact, point 6 trifle 7 precise 8 identify
pintado: 4 cero, fish, sier 6 chintz, pigeon, sierra 7 siering, spotted
pintail: 4 duck, smee 6 grouse
pintle: 4 bolt 5 hinge, dowel
pinto: 4 pied, pony 5 horse 6 calico 7 mottled, painted, piebald
pinxter flower: 6 azalea 11 honeysuckle
pioneer: 5 first, miner 6 digger, open up 7 settler 8 colonist, explorer 9 excavator
pious: 4 good, holy 5 froom, godly, loyal 6 devout, devine, pietic 7 canting, goddard, godlike, piteous 8 faithful, priestly 9 religious 11 reverential 13 sanctimonious
pip: dot 4 lulu, paip, peep, seed, spot 5 cheep, chirp, speck 8 insignia
pipe: oat 4 cask, duct, flue, lead, main, reed, snap, tube 5 briar, canal, drain, spout, stack 6 dudeen, leader, outlet, tubule 7 calumet, conduit, fistula, larigot 8 mirliton(F.)
angle: 5 elbow
bender: 6 hickey

ceremonial: 7 calumet
clay: 4 tile 5 straw 12 churchwarden
closer: 5 valve
connection: ell, tee 5 cross, elbow
end: 4 taft 6 nozzle
joint: ell, tee, wye 5 cross, elbow 7 calepin
  8 coupling
Oriental: 5 hooka 6 hookah 7 nargile 8
  narghile, nargileh 12 hubble-bubble
part: 4 bowl, stem
pastoral: oat 4 reed
pert. to: 6 tubaté
player: 5 fifer 8 shepherd
smoke: 5 tewel
steam: 5 riser
stove: 4 flue 5 tewel 7 chimney
pipe dream: 4 hope 6 bubble 7 chimera,
  fantasy 8 illusion
pipe wrench: 8 Stillson
pipeline: 7 channel, conduit 9 grapevine
Piper's son: Tom
piperly: 7 trivial 9 worthless
pipette: 4 tube 6 baster, taster 7 burette,
  dropper
measuring: 11 stactometer
piping: 6 edging, tubing
pipistrel, pipistrelle: bat
pipit: 6 wekeen 7 titlark
pippin: 4 seed 5 apple
pipsqueak: 5 twerp 6 nobody 7 upstart
piquancy: 4 salt 6 flavor, ginger 7 flavour
piquant: 4 racy, tart 5 salty, sharp, spicy,
  tasty, zesty 6 biting, bitter 7 peppery,
  pungent, zestful 8 poignant, stinging
  11 provocative, stimulating
pique: 4 fret, goad, tick 5 annoy, pride,
  spite, sting 6 arouse, excite, fabric,
  grudge, harass, malice, nettle, offend,
  pritch, strunt 7 chigger, dudgeon, offense, provoke, umbrage 8 irritate, vexation 9 annoyance, displease 10 irritation, resentment 11 displeasure
piqued: 5 pouty
piquet: 8 card game
score: pic
tricks: 5 capot
pirate: 4 Hook, Kidd 5 rover 6 robber,
  seadog 7 brigand, corsair, omnibus, sea
  wolf 8 algerine, marauder, picaroon,
  predator 9 buccaneer, privateer 10
  Blackbeard, freebooter, plagiarize
flag: 10 Jolly Roger
gallows: 7 yardarm
piripiri: 4 weed 5 birch, mapau
pirl: 4 spin 5 twine, twist
pirn: 4 reel 5 spool 6 bobbin 7 spindle
pirogue: 5 canoe
pirol: 6 oriole
piscation: 7 fishery, fishing
piscator: 6 angler 9 fisherman
piscina: 4 pool, tank 5 basin 8 fishpond,
  lavatory 9 reservoir

Pisgah summit: 4 Nebo
pishogue, pishoge: 5 charm, spell 7 sorcery 10 witchcraft
pismire: ant 5 emmet, twerp 9 nonentity
pismo: 4 clam
piste: 4 path 5 spoor, track, trail 8 ski
  trail
pistil: 6 carpel, umbone
pistle: 4 tale 5 story 7 epistle
pistol: dag, gat, gun, rod 6 barker, buffer 7
  dungeon, hand gun 8 bulldoze, revolver
  9 automatic, derringer
case: 7 holster
lock: 5 rowet
piston: 4 disk, knob, plug 5 valve 6 roller
  7 plunger
pit: 4 butt, delf, foss, hell, hole, mine, pool,
  seed, sump, trap, weem, well 5 abyss,
  chasm, delft, delve, fossa, fosse, fovea,
  grave, shaft, snare, stone 6 cavern, cavity, fossae, hollow, oppose 7 abaddon,
  cockpit 8 downfall 9 barathron, water-
  hole 10 depression, excavation 11 inden-
  dentation
bottomless: 5 abyss 7 Abaddon
of peach: 4 seed 7 putamen
of theater: 7 parquet
small: 6 areole, lacuna 7 foveola 8 alveolus
pit viper: 4 habu 8 lachesis 10 bushmaster, copperhead, fer-de-lance 11 rattlesnake
pitch: dip, key, tar 4 cant, cast, fall, hurl,
  line, roll, send, tone, toss 5 fling, heave,
  lunge, lurch, resin, rosin, spiel, throw 6
  accent, encamp, patter, plunge, seesaw,
  totter 7 asphalt, bitumen 8 alkitran 9
  alchitran
above: 5 sharp
apple: 5 copei, cupay
baseball: 5 curve 8 knuckler, spitball
below: 4 flat
high in: alt
in: 5 set to 7 get busy 8 get going 10 contribute
pipe: 9 epitonion
relating to: 7 piceous
pitchblende: 6 radium 7 uranium
pitcher: jar 4 ewer, olla, olpe, toby 5
  buire, gorge, gotch, ollae, olpae 6 carafe,
  heaver, hurler, tosser, urceus 7 canette,
  creamer 8 cruisken, oenochoe 9 container, cruisken 10 ballplayer
false move: 4 balk
handle: ear 4 ansa
left-handed: 8 southpaw
motions: 6 windup
place: 5 mound
relief: 7 fireman
pitchfork: 4 evil 5 pikel, pikle 8 shep-
  peck, sheppick
piteous: 5 pious 6 devout, moving, ruined,
  tender 7 pitiful, pitying 8 pitiable,

touching **9** imploring **10** beseeching, entreating **13** compassionate

pitfall: **4** lure, trap **5** snare **6** danger **9** booby trap **10** difficulty

pith: jet, nub **4** core, crux, gist, meat, pulp **5** force, vigor **6** center, kernel, marrow **7** essence, medulla, nucleus **8** strength **9** substance

full of: **5** heady, meaty, terse **7** concise

pith helmet: **4** topi **5** topee

pith tree: **7** ambatch

pithy: **5** crisp, meaty, terse **7** compact, concise, laconic **11** sententious **12** apothegmatic **13** short and sweet

plant: **4** sola

saying: mot **5** maxim **9** witticism

pitiful: sad **4** mean **6** rueful, woeful **7** forlorn, piteous **8** pathetic, pitiable **9** miserable, sorrowful **10** despicable, lamentable **12** contemptible

pitiless: **4** grim **5** cruel, stony **6** savage **8** ruthless **9** ferocious, merciless, unfeeling **10** despiteous, dispiteous, relentless **11** hardhearted

pitpit: **8** guitguit

pittance: bit **4** alms, dole, gift, mite, song **5** trace **6** trifle **7** peanuts

pitted: **6** etched **7** foveate, opposed, scarred **9** alveolate **10** pockmarked **11** honeycombed

pity: **4** ruth **5** mercy, piety **6** pathos **8** clemency, sympathy **10** compassion, condolence, tenderness **11** commiserate **13** commiseration

Pius: **4** Pope

pivot: toe **4** slew, slue, turn **5** hinge, swing **6** evener, swivel **7** gudgeon

pivot pin: **6** pintle **8** kingbolt

pivotal: **5** polar, vital **7** central, crucial **8** cardinal

pixie, pixy: elf **5** fairy **6** sprite **9** prankster

pixilated: **5** dotty, drunk **9** whimsical **11** intoxicated

placable: **4** calm **8** tolerant **9** agreeable, peaceable, tractable

placard: **4** bill, post, sign **6** poster **7** affiche **9** manifesto **12** proclamation **13** advertisement

placate: **4** calm **5** quiet, sooth **6** pacify, please, soothe **7** appease, comfort **10** conciliate, lay the dust **11** tranquilize

place: lay, put, set **4** area, calm, city, lieu, loci, post, room, seat, site, spot, town **5** being, court, estre, locus, plant, point, posit, siege, situs, space, stead, where **6** bestow, locale, region, repose, square, status **7** allodge, bestead, demesne, deposit, dispose, situate, village **8** dwelling, estimate, identify, location, locality, position **9** collocate, residence, situation

again: **6** reseat **7** restore

apart: **6** enisle **7** isolate **8** separate

before: **6** appose, prefix

beneath: **9** infrapose

between: **6** insert **9** interpose

business: **5** plant, store **6** office

by itself: **7** isolate

camping: **5** etape

end for end: **7** reverse

frequented: **4** dive **5** haunt **6** resort **7** hangout

hiding: mew **4** cave

holy: **6** shrine

in a row: **5** align, aline

in the sun: **5** glory **11** recognition

intermediate: **5** limbo

little hiding: **5** niche

market: **4** mart **5** agora

meeting: **5** tryst **10** rendezvous

one inside another: **4** nest

perfect: **6** heaven, utopia **8** paradise

side by side: **9** collocate, juxtapose

trial: **5** venue

placebo: **5** toady **7** vespers **8** medicine **11** preparation

placid: **4** calm, even, mild **5** downy, quiet, suant **6** gentle, irenic, serene **8** peaceful, tranquil **9** unruffled **11** undisturbed **13** imperturbable

placket: **4** slit **6** pocket **7** opening

plage: **4** zone **5** beach **6** region **7** country **8** transept

plagiarize: rob **4** crib, lift **5** steal **6** borrow, pirate, thieve **7** purloin

plague: dun, pox, vex **4** fret, gall, pest, twit **5** annoy, chafe, harry, tease, worry **6** badger, harass, hector, pester, wanion **7** scourge, torment, trouble **8** calamity, epidemic, irritate, nuisance **9** annoyance **10** affliction, pestilence **11** infestation

carrier: fly, rat

pert. to: **6** loimic

plaice: **5** fluke **8** flatfish, flounder

plaid: **4** maud **5** cloth **6** design, tartan **7** bracken, garment, pattern **9** checkered **11** crossbarred

plain: dry, lea **4** bald, bare, chol, down, even, fair, mead, mere, mesa, moor, open, vega, wold **5** blair, blunt, broad, camas, campo, clear, corah, frank, gross, heath, homey, llano, veldt **6** coarse, graith, homely, humble, lenten, meadow, pampas, simple, steppe, tundra, undyed **7** artless, certain, evident, genuine, glaring, legible, obvious, prairie, quamash, savanna **8** apparent, campagna(It.), campaign, distinct, explicit, flatland, homemade, homespun, ordinary, straight, tailored **9** champaign, downright, outspoken, primitive, unadorned, unfigured, untwilled **10** unaffected 11 perspicuous, transparent, undisguised 12 short on looks, unattractive 13 unembellished 15 straightforward

depression: 5 swale

elevated: 4 mesa 7 plateau

Indian: Ute 5 Caddo, Kiowa, Omaha, Sioux 6 Oneida, Pawnee 9 Algonquin 10 Athapascan

Olympic games: 4 Elis

salt-covered: 5 flats 6 salada

treeless: 5 llano, pampa, veldt 6 tundra 7 prairie, savanna 8 savannah

upland: 4 wold 5 weald

plaint: 6 lament 7 protest 9 complaint 11 lamentation

plaintiff: 4 suer 7 accuser 8 litigant 9 recoverer 10 prosecutor 11 complainant

opposite: 9 defendant

plaintive: sad 5 cross 7 elegiac, fretful, peevish, pettish 7 piteous, pitiful, wailing 8 dolorous, mournful, petulant, repining 9 lamenting, sorrowful 10 melancholy 11 complaining 12 discontented

plait: cue 4 fold, knit 5 braid, crimp, pleat, weave 6 border, gather, goffer, pleach 7 gauffer, pigtail 9 gathering 10 interweave

plaited: 7 browden 10 corrugated

plan: aim, map 4 card, dart, form, game, idea, plat, plot 5 draft, epure, ettle, frame 6 budget, decoct, design, devise, intend, layout, method, policy, scheme, sketch, system 7 arrange, concert, diagram, draught, drawing, outline, program, project, purpose 8 conspire, contrive, engineer, platform, prepense, schedule, strategy 9 blueprint, calculate, machinate, stratagem 10 concoction 11 arrangement, contemplate, contrivance, preconceive, precontrive, premeditate

planate: 5 level 9 flattened

plancher: bed 4 slab 5 board, floor, plank 6 pallet 7 ceiling 8 planking, platform

plane: 4 even, flat, soar 5 glide, level 6 aequor, chinar, smooth 7 surface 8 sycamore

block: 5 stock

handle: 4 toat, tote

inclined: 4 ramp 5 chute, shute

kind of: 4 iron, jack 5 block 6 router 8 grooving, tounging

on same: 8 coplanar

plane figure: *boundary:* 9 perimeter

four angles: 8 tetragon

nine-sided: 7 nonagon

plane iron: bit 5 blade, knife

plane-tree: 8 plantain, sycamore

planer: 4 tool 6 shaper 8 surfacer

planet: orb 4 Mars, moon, star 5 Earth, Pluto, Venus 6 Saturn, sphere, Uranus

7 Jupiter, Mercury, Neptune 8 asteroid, terrella, wanderer 9 satellite

brightest: 5 Venus

cone: 8 strobile

course: 5 orbit

nearest sun: 7 Mercury

newest: 5 Pluto

orbit: 7 ellipse

orbit point: 5 apsis, nadir 6 apogee, zenith 8 parigree

path: 5 orbit

period: 9 alfridary

red: 4 Mars

relation to another: 5 trine 7 sextile 10 opposition 11 conjunction

ringed: 6 Saturn

ruling: 9 dominator

satellite: 4 moon

shadow: 5 umbra

planeta: 5 cloak

planetarian: 10 astrologer

planetarium: 6 orrery 11 observatory

planetary: 4 huge 7 erratic 9 universal, wandering, worldwide 10 astrologer 11 terrestrial

planisphere: 9 astrolabe 11 meteorscope

plank: 4 deal, slab 5 board, slate, stone 6 lumber, timber 8 plancher 9 two-by-four 10 gravestone

breadth: 6 strake

increasing bearing surface: 5 shole

lengthwise: 8 stringer

plank down: pay 7 advance, deposit

planking: 8 flooring

plankton: 4 alga 5 krill 8 organism, protozoa

planner: 9 architect

plant: fix, set, sow, spy 4 arum, bury, bush, fern, herb, hide, rape, root, seed, trap, tree, vine, weed, wort 5 berry, decoy, found, fruit, grain, place, put in, shoot, shrub, sotol, spice, trick, works 6 annual, clover, flower, legume, scheme, settle 7 conceal, creeper, factory, furnish, pungent, sapling 8 building, business, geophyte, radicate 9 detective, equipment, establish, perennial, seasoning, succulent, swindling, vegetable 10 prearrange 13 establishment

acid-juice: 5 ribes 6 nettle 8 knotweed 9 smartweed

aconite: 4 bikh

amaryllis family: 5 agave

ambrosia genus: 7 ragweed

ammoniac: 5 oshac

apiaceous: 4 ache

apoplexy: 4 esca

appendage: 7 stipule

aquatic: See **aquatic plant**

arboreal: 4 tree

aromatic: See **aromatic**

arrowroot-yielding: 7 curcuma

arum family: 4 arad, taro 5 aroid, calla
aster family: 5 oxeye, tansy 8 fleabane
asteraceous: 5 daisy
bayonet: 5 datil
bean family: 6 lupine 8 licorice 9 liquorice
benthonic: 6 enalid
bitter: ers, rue 9 colicroot
blue-blossomed: 6 lupine 8 ageratum
body: 6 cormus
bog genus: 5 abama 10 narthecium
bramble: 5 briar, furze, gorse, thorn
branched: 4 bush, tree 5 shrub
breathing organ: 5 stoma 7 stomata(pl.)
bulbous: 4 lily 5 camas, onion, tulip 7 jonquil, quamash 8 hyacinth 9 narcissus
cabbage family: 4 rape
cactus family: 5 dildo 6 cereus, mescal 7 saguaro 11 prickly pear
cactus-like: 8 stapelia 9 xerophyte
capsule: pod
carrot-like: 7 parsnip
cassia genus: 5 senna
catnip family: nep 6 nepeta
celery family: 5 anise
celery-like: udo
cell: 6 gamete
chlorophyll-rich: 4 alga 5 algae(pl.)
chromatophore-lacking: 6 albino
class: 4 alga 5 algae(pl.)
climbing: ive, ivy 4 bine, vine 5 betel, liana, vetch 6 byrony, smilax 7 creeper, jasmine 8 wisteria 12 morning glory, philodendron
clover-like: 5 medic 7 calomba
coloring matter: 8 clorofil 10 endochrome 11 chlorophyll
corn lily: 4 ixia
crocus family: 4 irid
crossbred: 6 hybrid
crowfoot family: 5 peony 8 clematis
cruciferous: 5 cress 7 alyssum
cryptogamous: 4 moss
cuticle: 5 cutin
cyperaceous: 5 sedge
decorative: ivy 4 bush, fern 6 flower
desert: 5 agave 6 alhagi, cactus 8 mesquite 11 brittlebush
dipsacus genus: 6 teasel
disease: 4 gall, mold, rust, scab, smut 5 ergot 6 blight, mildew 7 blister
division: 15 archichlamydeae
dock-like: 6 sorrel
dry-climate: 5 xerad 9 xerophyte 10 ombrophobe
dwarf: 5 cumin, stunt
dye: 4 anil, weld, woad, wold 5 henna, woald, would 6 kamala, madder, wurras, wurrus 8 alhenna, orselle
dye-yielding: 4 anil, woad 5 henna, sumac 6 madder 7 alkanet

ebony family: 6 ebenad
embryo: 8 plantule
environmentally modified: 4 ecad
erica genus: 5 heath 7 heather
Euphorbia genus: 6 spurge
exudation: gum, sap 4 milk 5 latex, resin, rosin
fabaceous: pea 5 vetch 9 coronippa
family: 7 araceae
fernlike: 8 filicoid
fiber: See **fiber**
flag-family: 4 irid
floating: 5 lotus 7 frogbit 9 water lily
flowering: See **flowering plant**
flowerless: 4 fern, moss 6 fungus, lichen 7 seaweed
forgetfulness-causing: 5 lotus
fragrant: 5 orris 8 angelica
garden: 4 geum, iris, ixia, rose 5 aster, calla, canna, daisy, pansy, phlox, poppy, stock, viola 6 bellis, bletia, celery, clivia, cosmos, crocus, lupine, oxalis, zinnia 7 agathea, alyssum, anchusa, anemone, begonia, celosia, clarkia, gazania, gerbera, godetia, lettuce, lobelia, muscari, petunia, primula, statice, verbena 8 ageratum, arctotis, cyclamen, daffodil, dianthus, herebell, hyacinth, larkspur, marigold, myosotis, scabiosa, sparaxis, sweet pea, tithonia, watsonia 9 amaryllis, calendula, campanula, candytuft, carnation, centaurea, cinararia, coreopsis, digitalis, gladiolus, hollyhock, linararia, narcissus, nicotiana, pensemon, portulaca 10 delphinium, gaillardia, gypsophila, marguerite, ranunculus, snapdragon, sweet basil, wallflower 11 dusty miller, forget-me-not, helichrysum, hunnemannia, Madonna Lily, shasta daisy 12 nierembergia, rhododendron, salpiglossis, sweet William 13 chrysanthemum, dimorphotheca, glory of the sun 14 canterbury bell 15 Star of Bethlehem 16 spring snowflakes
genus: 4 dion
geography: 14 phytogeography
gourd family: 5 melon
grain: oat, rye 4 corn, teff 5 wheat 6 barley
grass: 5 avena
grass cloth: 5 ramee, ramie
grass-like: 5 sedge
grassland: 6 baccar 7 bacchar
growing from inside: 7 endogen 9 endogenae(pl.)
growing from outside: 6 exogen
growth layer: 7 cambium
growth on: 4 gall
habitat: 4 ecad
hawthorn: 7 azarole 9 mayflower
head: bud, bur 4 burr 5 fruit 6 flower
healing: 7 sanicle

heather family: 4 ling 5 erica
hedge: 6 espino
herbaceous: See **herb**
honey-secreting organ: 7 nectary
house: See **houseplant**
interior chaff: 5 palea, palet
iridaceae: 4 irid
iris family: 4 irid, ixia 7 freesia
joined to another: 5 graft
joint: 4 node
juice: see *exudation* above
leafless: 4 ulex 6 dodder 7 restiad, triurid
leguminous: See **legume**
liliaceous: 4 aloe, leek 5 onion 9 birthroot
lily family: 4 aloe, sego 5 lotos, lotus, yucca 6 camass
linen-producing: 4 flax
main axis: 4 stem 5 stalk, trunk
male: 3 mas 16 androgametophore
mallow family: 5 altea 6 escoba
manufacturing: 4 mill
marine: See **aquatic plant**
marsh: 4 fern, reed 6 juncus 7 bulrush, cattail
masculine: see *male* above
medicinal: hop, oak 4 aloe, dill, flax, herb, lime, sage 5 buchu, elder, erica, guaco, jalap, peony, poppy, senna, tansy 6 arnica, carrot, catnep, catnip, fennel, garlic, ipecac, kousso, laurel, nettle, simple 7 aconite, boneset, calamus, camphor, caraway, catechu, copaiba, ephedra, gentian, hemlock, henbane, juniper, lobelia, mullein, mustard, parsley, rhubarb, saffron 8 barberry, camomile, crowfoot, foxglove, licorice, plantain, rosemary, valerian, wormwood 9 asparagus, bearberry, buckthorn, chamomile, colchicum, coltsfoot, dandelion, liquorice, monkshead 10 assafetida, pennyroyal, peppermint, stavesacre 11 assafoetida, bittersweet
microscopic: 5 spore 10 microphyte
millet: 5 hirse
mock orange: 7 syringa
modified by environment: 4 ecad
moss-like: 6 orpine 7 hepatic
mottled leaf: 8 ratsbane
multicellular: 9 metaphyte
mushroom-type: 6 fungus
mustard family: 4 woad 5 cress 6 radish 7 alyssum
native: 8 indigene
nettle family: 4 hemp
nightshade family: 6 tomato
nursery: 8 seedling
oil-yielding: 4 odal 6 sesame
old-world: 5 lotus
one-seeded fruit: 9 olacaceae
onion family: 4 leek
onion-like: 5 chive 7 shallot
opening: 5 stoma 7 stomata(pl.)

packing: 7 cannery
painful to touch: 5 briar, thorn 6 nettle 8 knotweed 9 smartweed
parsley family: 4 dill 5 anise
part: 6 stamen, stipel 7 tendril
pepper: ara
pert. to: 6 agamic 7 botanic, vegetal 9 botanical 10 vegetative
pigment-lacking: 6 albino
poaceae: 5 grass
pod: 4 boll
poisonous: 4 atis 6 datura 7 amanita, cowbane 8 oleander 10 belladonna
poisonous to cattle: 4 loco 8 calfkill, locoweed
poisonous to fowls: 7 henbane
poppy family: 9 celandine
pore: 8 lenticel
potato-like: oca
potted: 6 bonsai
preserving: 4 dill 7 cannery
prickly: 4 rose 5 briar, brier, cacti(pl.), thorn 6 cactus, nettle, teasel 7 thistle 9 tearthumb
rat poison: 8 oleander, ratsbane
reproductive organ: 5 spore
root: 5 radix
rope: 4 hemp
rose family: 5 avens
round-leaved: 9 pennywort
salad: 5 cress 6 celery, endive, greens 7 lettuce, romaine 8 purslane 10 watercress
scented: 4 mint 6 catnip 7 catmint
science: 6 botany
seasoning: 8 tarragon
sedge family: 5 carex
seed: nut, pip 4 bulb 5 grain 6 button 7 putamen
seedless: 4 fern
seller: 7 florist
shoot: rod 4 cion 5 scion, sprig 6 stolon
silk: 5 floss
soap: 5 amole
solanaceous: 7 tobacco
sour-juice: 6 sorrel
starch: pia 4 arum, taro 7 cassava
stem: 4 bine 5 shaft 6 caulis
stem joint: 4 node
stem tissue: 4 pith 6 phloem
submerged: 6 enalid
succulent: 4 aloe, herb 8 gasteria 9 houseleek
tanning: 5 sumac
tapioca-yielding: 6 casava, casave, casavi 7 cassava
tequila-yielding: 5 agave
thistle family: 5 aster
thorny: see *prickly* above
three-leaved: 9 trifolium
tissue: 4 pith 5 xylem 6 phloem 7 cambium

trailing: 7 arbutus
tropical: 4 arum, palm, taro 5 agave, altea, canna, liana, liane, yucca, zamia 6 pepino 7 dasheen, hamelia 8 mangrove, redwithe
tufted: 4 moss 5 dryas
twining: see *climbing* above
type: 6 exogen
urticaceous: 6 nettle
valerian genus: 4 nard
verbenaceous: 7 lantana
vetch family: ers
vine: ivy 5 liana
wall: ivy
waterside: 5 sedge
wild-growing: 9 agrestial
woody: 4 bush, tree, vine 5 shrub
woody-vine genus: 5 vitis
xyloid: 4 tree
young: 4 cion 5 scion, shoot 6 sprout 7 vinelet 8 seedling
yucca-like: 5 sotol
plant life: 5 flora 10 vegetation
plant louse: 5 aphid
secretion: 4 laap, lerp 5 laarp
plant raising: *pert. to:* 13 floricultural
Plantagenets: 7 Angevin
plantain: 4 weed 6 banana, wabron 8 balisier
plantain eater: 7 touraco 9 splitbeak
plantation: 4 farm 6 estate 8 hacienda
cacti: 7 nopalry
coffee: 5 finca 7 cafetal, fazenda
coniferous tree: 7 pinetum
fictional: 4 Tara
oak tree: 9 quercetum
sugar: 8 trapiche
trees: 5 grove 6 forest 7 orchard
willow: 4 holt 6 osiery
planter: 5 sower 6 farmer, grower, seeder 7 pioneer, settler 8 colonist 13 agriculturist
government by: 11 plantocracy
wall: 6 lavabo
planting stick: 6 dibble
plaque: pin 5 medal 6 broach, brooch 9 nameplate
plash: 4 pool 5 blash, hedge 6 pleach, puddle, splash 9 bespatter
plashy: wet 6 marshy
plasm: 4 mold 6 matrix
plasma: 5 lymph 11 trophoplasm
plaster: 4 coat, daub, harl 5 affix, cover, gatch, gesso, grout, salve, smear 6 cement, mortar, parget 9 slick down
adhesive: 4 tape 7 bandage 8 dressing
artist's: 5 gesso
coarse: 5 grout 6 parget, stucco
of paris: 5 gesso 6 gypsum
patch: 7 spackle
stone: 6 gypsum
support: 4 lath

tool: 7 spatula
wax: 6 cerate
plastered: 5 drunk 6 soused 11 intoxicated
platerer: 5 mason 6 dauber
plastic: 4 soft 7 ductile, fictile, flexile, pliable 8 flexible, unctuous 9 adaptable, formative 14 impressionable
cotton-sizing: 7 viscose
dentist's: 6 cement
plastron: 6 dickey 7 calipee 8 trimming 11 breastplate
plat: lot, map 4 boat, plan 5 braid, chart, plait 6 buffet 7 plateau 9 tableland 10 interweave
plate: cut, gib 4 coat, disc, dish, disk, lame, tile 5 aglet, armor, facia, layer, scute, stove 6 aiglet, discus, lamina, platen, tagger, veneer 7 denture, lamella, laminae, overlay 8 assiette, lamellae, laminate 9 silverize
communion: 5 paten 6 patina
cooking: 4 grid
for throwing: 6 discus
from matrix: 6 stereo 10 stereotype
glass: 4 pane 5 slide
horny: 5 scale, scute
perforated: dog 4 grid 7 stencil 8 hallmark 14 identification
pitcher's: 4 slab 5 mound
ship-shaped: nef
stereotype: 6 cliche
thin: 6 lamina 7 lamella
plateau: 4 dish, mesa, puna, seir 5 fjeld 6 hamada, plaque, salver 7 uplands 9 altiplano, tableland 12 altiplanicie
plateholder: 8 cassette
platen: 6 roller
platform: map 4 bank, bema, dais, deck, plan 5 bench, chart, floor, stage, stand 6 bemata(pl.), podium, pulpit 7 estrade, program, rostrum, tribune 8 chabutra, plancher 9 banquette, gangplank, vestibule
church: 5 solea 6 pulpit
fort: 8 barbette
mining: 6 sollar, soller
nautical: 7 maintop
reloading: 6 staith
salt-manufacturing: 6 hurdle
ship: 7 foretop, maintop 9 gangplank
sleeping: 4 kang
temple: 5 dukan
temporary: 8 scaffold
theater: 7 logeion
wheeled: 5 dolly, float
wooden: 9 boardwalk
platinum: *blond:* 7 towhead
crude: 7 platina
wire: 4 oese
platitude: 6 cliche, truism 7 bromide 8 banality, chestnut, dullness, flatness 9

rechauffé, staleness, triteness 10 triviality 11 commonplace 15 commonplaceness

Plato: *idea:* 5 eidos
knowledge: 6 noesis
literary form: 8 dialogue
pupil: 9 Aristotle
school: 7 Academe
teacher: 8 Socrates
work: 4 Meno 5 Crito 6 Phaedo 7 Apology, Gorgias, Sophist, Timaeus 8 Republic

platoid: 4 flat 5 broad

platonic: 9 spiritual, visionary 10 idealistic 11 impractical, theoretical
body: 4 cube 10 hexahedron, octahedron 11 icosahedron, tetrahedron 12 dodecahedron
philosophy follower: 9 academist

platoon: set 4 team, unit 5 group, squad 6 volley 7 coterie 8 division 9 formation

platter: 4 dish, lanx(L.) 5 ashet(Sc.), grail, plate 7 charger

platter-shaped: 10 scutellate

platyfish: 8 moonfish

platypus: 8 duckbill 9 mallagong

plaudit: 4 clap, kudo 6 praise 8 applause, approval, encomium 11 acclamation, approbation

plausible: 4 oily 6 glossy 7 colored 8 coloured, credible, specious 10 applausive, believable, creditable ostensible, plauditory

Plautus: 10 playwright
forte: 6 comedy
language: 5 Latin

play: act, fun, jeu(F.), hit, toy 4 game, jeux(F.), move, romp 5 amuse, charm, dally, drama, enact, flirt, sport 6 cavort, divert, engage, fiddle, frolic, gamble, gambol, rollix 7 disport, execute, perform 8 amusement, dalliance, diversion, pantomime 10 manipulate, recreation 13 entertainment
around: 9 philander
badly: err 4 miff 6 bobble
ball: 5 begin 6 resume 9 cooperate
complication: 4 node
down: 10 soft-pedal
festival: 9 festspiel
kind: 4 auto 5 farce 6 comedy, one-act 7 musical, tragedy 8 burletta 9 melodrama, pantomime 13 curtain-raiser
musical: 5 opera 8 burletta, operetta
off: 4 game 6 oppose 8 showdown
on words: pun
outline: 8 scenario
part: act, bit 4 acte(F.), role 5 exode, scene 7 prelude 8 epilogue, epitasis, prologue
possum: 4 sham 5 feign 7 pretend
put on: 5 stage 7 produce

silent: 9 pantomime
up: 6 stress 9 emphasize

playa: 4 lake 5 basin, beach 6 salina

playboy: 4 fool 5 clown, idler 6 madcap 7 buffoon

played out: 5 all in, ended, spent, tired 8 finished, unreeled 9 exhausted

player: man 4 cast, star 5 actor 6 leader 7 enactor, gambler 8 gamester, thespian 9 performer 10 competitor, contestant
card: 4 pone 6 dealer, eldest
leading: 4 star
poor: dub, dud, ham, sub 5 scrub 12 second-string
strolling: 9 serenader, troubador 10 troubadour 11 barnstormer

playful: 5 elfin, merry 6 blithe, frisky, joking, lusory, wanton 7 jocular, larkish, puckish 8 gamesome, humorous, playsome, sportive 10 frolicsome

playground: 4 grid, park, yard 5 field 7 diamond

playhouse: 5 movie 6 casino, cinema 7 theater

playing cards: 4 deck 6 tarots
hand: cat 4 deal

playlet: 4 skit

playmate: pal 6 friend

playroom: bar, den, gym 7 nursery

plaything: die, toy 4 hoop 6 bauble, trifle

playtime: 6 recess

playwright: 6 author 9 dramatist

plaza: 4 park, 5 green 6 common, square 9 carrefour 11 marketplace

plea: sue 4 suit 6 abater, answer, appeal, excuse, prayer 7 apology, pretext, request, solicit 8 argument, entreaty, petition, pretense 12 supplication 14 nolo contendere
defendant's: 4 nolo 6 guilty 9 not guilty

pleach: 5 plait 9 interlace 10 interweave

plead: beg, sue 5 orate 6 allege, assert 7 beseech, entreat, implore, solicit 8 advocate, appealed, petition 9 importune, intercede 10 supplicate

pleading: 4 oyer 6 answer 8 argument, demurrer 9 suppliant 10 litigation 12 supplication

pleasant: gay 4 bien(F.), fair, fine, good, hend, joli, nice, waly 5 bigly, cushy, douce(F.), hende, hoddy, jolie, lepid, merry, sweet, wally 6 genial 7 amiable, amusing, farrand, farrant, jesting, jocular, leesome(Sc.), playful, welcome, winsome 8 delicate, gracious, grateful, humorous, pleasing, sportive 9 agreeable, appealing, congenial, diverting, enjoyable, laughable, sprightly 10 acceptable, delightful, gratifying

pleasantness: 7 amenity 8 goodness, niceness

pleasantry: fun 4 jest, joke 6 banter 7 jesting 10 jocularity 11 gauloiserie 13 facetiousness

please: 4 suit, will 5 agree, amuse, elate, humor 6 arride, humour, tickle 7 aggrate, appease, content, delight, gladden, gratify, indulge, placate, satisfy 9 delectate, titillate

pleased: happy 8 gladsome

pleasing: 4 glad, lief 5 amene, sooth 6 comely, eesome(Sc.), liking 7 roseate 8 fetching, pleasant 9 desirable, favorable, palatable 10 attractive, delectable, delightful, enchanting, favourable

pleasure: fun, joy 4 ease, este, gree, will 5 bliss, mirth, sport, treat 6 gaiety, liking, relish 7 delight, jollity 8 delicacy, fruition, gladness, hilarity 9 amusement, diversion, enjoyment, happiness, merriment 10 beneplacit 11 beneplacity, contentment, delectation 12 cheerfulness 13 gratification

  god: Bes

  ground: 4 park 9 pleasance

  insensitiveness to: 9 anhedonia

  pert. to: 7 hedonic

  philosophy of: 8 hedonism

  seeker: 5 sport 7 epicure, playboy 8 hedonist

pleat: 4 fold, kilt, shir 5 braid, prank 7 plicate

plebe: 5 cadet, 8 commoner, freshman 10 midshipman

plebeian: 5 crude 6 coarse, common, homely, vulgar 7 ignoble, illbred, lowborn 8 baseborn, everyday, ordinary

plebiscite: 4 vote 6 decree 7 mandate 10 referendum

plectrum: 4 pick 5 uvula 6 fescue, tongue 7 malleus

pledge: bet, vas(L.), vow 4 adhi, band, bond, gage, hand, hest, hock, oath, pawn, seal, wage, word 5 siker, skoal, toast, troth 6 arrest, assure, borrow, commit, engage, lumber, parole, plight 7 betroth, earnest, espouse, hostage, promise, warrant 8 affiance, contract, guaranty, mortgage, security 9 assurance, certainty, sacrament 11 association, impignorate

  security for: IOU 4 bond, gage 6 marker

pledget: 4 swab 5 oakum 8 compress

Pleiad of Alexandria: 5 Homer 6 Aratus 8 Nicander 9 Lycophron 10 Apollonius, Theocritus 11 Callimachus

Pleiades: 4 Maia 6 Merope 7 Alcyone, Celaeno, Electra, Sterope, Taygeta, 8 Asterope

  constellation: 6 Taurus

  father: 5 Atlas

  mother: 7 Pleione

Pleione's offspring: 8 Pleiades

plenary: 4 full 6 entire 7 perfect 8 absolute

  opposite: 7 summary, complete 11 unqualified

plenipotentiary: 5 agent, envoy 8 minister 10 ambassador

plentiful: 4 full, rich, rife 5 ample, sonsy 6 galore, sonsie 7 copious, fertile, liberal, opulent, profuse 8 abundant, affluent, fruitful, generous, prolific 9 abounding, bounteous, bountiful, exuberant, plenteous 10 productive

plenty: 4 enow, heap, much, raff 5 ample, cheap, fouth 6 enough, foison, scouth 7 copious 8 fullness, opulence 9 abundance, affluence, plenitude 10 exuberance, luxuriance, perfection, sufficient 11 copiousness, sufficiency 12 completeness

  goddess: Ops

  horn of: 10 cornucopia

plenum: 5 space 8 assembly, fullness, plethora

pleonasm: 7 verbiage 8 fullness 9 tautology 10 redundancy 11 superfluity

plethora: 4 glut 6 excess 8 fullness 9 profusion, repletion 13 overabundance 14 superabundance

plethoric: 6 turgid 7 swollen 8 inflated, overfull 9 bombastic 10 overloaded

pleurapophysis: rib

plexiform: 7 complex, netlike 9 intricate 11 complicated

plexus: 4 rete 5 retia(pl.) 6 tangle 7 network

pliable: 4 easy, limp, soft, waxy 5 lithe 6 docile, limber, pliant, supple 7 bending, ductile, flaccid, flexile, plastic, tensile, willowy 8 amenable, flexible, fluxible, informal, suitable, tractile, workable, yielding 9 adaptable, compliant, malleable, tractable 10 applicable 13 unconstrained

plicate: 4 fold 5 pleat

plight: fix, jam 4 fold, risk 5 array, braid, plait, state 6 engage, pickle, pledge, status 7 betroth, embrace, promise 8 position, quandary 9 betrothal, condition 10 difficulty 11 predicament

plinth: 4 base, orlo 5 block, couch, stone, table 6 course 7 subbase 8 skirting 9 baseboard

  flat: 4 orlo

plod: dig, mog, peg 4 grub, plow, slog, toil, tore, vamp, work 5 tramp 6 drudge, trudge

plop: 4 fall 5 plump 8 drop down 10 sit heavily

plot: lot, map 4 land, plan, plat 5 cabal, chart, draft, story, tract 6 design, devise, scheme, secret 7 compact, connive, diagram, outline 8 conspire, con-

trive, engineer, intrigue, scenario 9
insidiate, machinate 10 conspiracy 11
machination

garden: bed 5 patch 8 parterre

ground: lot 5 grave 7 terrain

inventor: 8 schemist

play: 4 node

plover: 4 bird, crab, dupe 5 drome, kolea,
oxeye, sandy 6 kildee, piping 7 collier,
killdee, lapwing, maycock, Wilson's 8
dotterel, killdeer, squealer, toadhead 9
courtesan, turnstone 10 beetle-head,
blacksmith

relative: 7 wrybill 9 sandpiper

plow, plough: dig, ear 4 farm, mole, rove,
till 5 break 6 cleave, digger, furrow 9
cultivate 10 cut through

handle: 5 stilt

kind of: 4 snow 5 sulky 6 gopher, lister,
rotary, shovel 7 breaker 8 stirring,
turnplow 9 moldboard 14 prairie-
breaker

knife: 6 colter 7 coulter

part: 4 beam, frog, hale 5 sheth, slade,
stilt 6 sheath 7 pinhead 9 plowshare,
sharebeam

plowhead: 4 beam 5 frame 6 clevis

plowing: 8 aeration

plowshare, ploughshare: lay 5 laver 6
colter 7 coulter

bone: 5 vomer

ploy: 4 joke 5 sport, trick 6 frolic, gambit,
tactic 7 pastime 8 escapade 11 merrymaking

pluck: rob, tug 4 grit, guts, jerk, pick, pull,
sand, tear 5 cheek, nerve, spunk, strip,
strum, twang 6 daring, finger, fleece,
gather, snatch, spirit, twitch 7 bravery,
courage, deplume, plunder 8 decision,
gameness 9 endurance, fortitude, hardihood 10 resolution

plug: peg, tap, tit 4 blow, bung, calk, cork,
puff, push, slog 5 boost, caulk, estop,
knock, punch, shoot, spile, spill 6 dottle, tampon 7 bouchon, pledget, promote, stopper, stopple 9 advertise, persevere

cannon muzzle: 7 tampion

clay: bod 4 bott

fire: 7 hydrant

medical: 4 clot 7 embolus

wall: 6 outlet

water: 7 hydrant

plug bib: 6 faucet, spigot

plug cock: 6 spigot

plug hat: 4 tile 5 gibus 6 topper

plug-in: 4 jack

plug-ugly: 4 thug 5 rowdy, tough 7 ruffian 8 gangster 9 roughneck

plugboard: 11 switchboard 12 control-
panel

plum: hog 4 amra, coco, find, gage, sloe 5

catch, drupe, duhat, icaco, prune 6
damson, jambul, reward, sapote 7 bul-
lace, jambool 8 dividend, windfall 9
greengage 10 amatungula

dried: 5 prune

seed: pit 7 putamen

wild: 4 skeg, sloe 5 islay

plum-colored: 4 puce 5 mauve 6 purple

plum duff: 7 pudding

plum weevil: 8 curculio

plumage: 4 down 5 dress 6 hackle 7 floc-
cus 8 feathers 9 adornment

plumb: 4 bung, well 5 delve, probe, solve,
sound 6 chunky, fathom, plunge 7 explore, plummet 8 absolute, complete,
entirely, vertical 9 downright 10 absolutely, straighten, understand 13 perpendicular

plumbeous: 6 leaden

plume: 4 tuft 5 crest, egret, preen, pride,
prize, prune 6 aigret, plumet 7 feather,
panache 8 aigrette 9 plumicorn

plummet: dip 4 drop, fall, lead 5 plumb 6
plunge, tumble, weight 8 nose-dive

plump: fat 4 back, drop, fall, plop, sink,
tidy 5 bonny, buxom, obese, plunk,
stout 6 bonnie, chubby, dilate, flatly,
fleshy, portly, rotund 7 bluntly, distend,
fulsome, support 9 downright

plunder: gut, rob 4 boot, loot, pelf, prey,
raid, sack, swag 5 booty, cheat, harry,
pluck, poach, raven, reave, rifle, spoil,
steal, strip 6 bezzle, boodle, creach(Sc.),
creagh(Sc.), dacoit, maraud, pilfer, pirate, rapine, ravage, ravish, spoils 7 despoil, pillage, ransack 8 spoliate 9 depredate, devastate

plunderer: 5 thief 6 bandit, vandal 8 marauder, predator 10 freebooter

plunge: bet, dig, dip 4 cave, dive, duck,
dump, pool, rush, sink 5 douse, dowse,
drive, fling, lunge, merse, pitch, plumb,
souse 6 absorb, emerge, footer, gamble,
thrust 7 immerge, immerse 8 submerge

plunger: ram 6 risker 10 speculator

plunk: 4 drop, flop, pull, push, sink, toss 5
drive, pluck, plump, sound, throw 6 dollar, strike

plunther: 4 plod 8 flounder

plurality: 4 most 8 majority 9 multitude

plus: add 4 more, over 5 extra 6 excess 8
addition, increase, positive

plush: 4 posh 6 deluxe 7 opulent 8 palatial 9 luxurious 11 upholstered

Plutarch work: 5 Lives

Pluto: Dis 5 Hades

kingdom: 5 Hades

wife: 10 Persephone, Proserpina

plutocracy: 13 establishment

plutocrat: 5 nabob 6 fat cat 7 Croesus,
rich man 9 moneybags 10 capitalist

Plutus: *father:* 6 Iasion

mother: 7 Demeter

ply: web 4 bend, fold, mold, sail, urge, work 5 beset, exert, layer, plait, wield 6 double, handle, travel 7 belabor, shuttle 8 belabour, exercise, function 9 importune, thickness

with drink: 5 birle

pneuma: 4 soul 5 neume 6 breath, spirit, 8 ligature 9 breathing, life force

pneumonia: *kind:* 5 lobar, viral 9 bronchial

Po tributary: 4 Adda 5 Oglia 7 Trebba 9 Cispadane

poach: 4 boil, cook 5 shirr, spear, steal, steam 6 pierce, thrust 7 trample 8 encroach, trespass

poacher: pan 5 thief 7 lurcher, stalker, widgeon 8 baldpate

salmon: 7 rebecca, rebekah

Pocahontas: *father:* 8 Powhatan

husband: 5 Rolfe

pochard: 4 duck, 5 scaup 6 dunker

pochette: 6 violin 7 handbag 8 envelope

pock: pit 4 hole, scar 6 hollow 7 pustule

pocket: bin, cly, fob 5 poke, prat, sack 7 cantina, conceal, confine, enclose, isolate, put away 8 cul-de-sac 9 miniature, small area 10 blind alley 11 appropriate

ore: 4 lode 7 bonanza

water: 6 tinaja

pocketbook: bag, fob, lil 4 poke 5 burse, pouch, purse 6 clutch, wallet 8 billfold 12 portemonnaie

poco: 6 little 8 slightly, somewhat

pococurante: 9 apathetic 10 nonchalant 11 indifferent

pocosin, pocoson, pocosen: 5 marsh, swamp

pod: bag, bur, cod, kid, sac 4 aril, boll, hull, swad 5 belly, carob, pouch, shell, shuck 6 legume, loment 7 silicle 8 potbelly

podesta: 5 judge, mayor 8 executor, governor, official 10 magistrate

podgy: fat 5 pudgy, squat

podium: 4 base, dais, wall 7 lectern 8 pedestal, platform 12 substructure

Poe: *bird* 5 raven

house: 5 Usher

poem: 5 Raven 6 Lenore 7 Ulalume

poem: ode 4 duan, epic, raff, rann(Ir.), rime, rune, song, vers(F.) 5 canto, ditty, elegy, ionic, lyric, poesy, raffe, rhyme, stave, verse 6 ballad, carmen, epopee, eulogy, iambic, jingle, poetry, screed, sonnet, tercet 7 ballade, dimeter, sestina, triolet, virelay 8 acrostic, doggerel, hexapody, limerick, madrigal, senarius, trimeter 9 hexameter, hexastich, monometer, octameter, soliloquy 10 tetrameter 11 acatalectic

break in rhythm: 6 cesura 7 caesura

bucolic: 8 pastoral

closing: 5 envoi, envoy

collection: 5 sylva

division of: see *part* below

eight-line: 7 triolet

foot: 4 iamb 6 iambus 7 anapest, spondee

four-line: 8 quatrain

heroic: 4 epic

line: 8 trimeter 9 hexameter 12 decasyllabic

love: 6 erotic 8 madrigal

lyric: lay 4 alba 6 roundel

medieval: lai 4 alba

melodic: 5 lyric

moral: dit

mournful: 5 elegy

narrative: 4 epos

node: 4 plot

nonsensical: 8 doggerel, limerick

part: fit 4 feet, foot, line 5 canto, epode, stich, verse 6 epilog, prolog, stanza 7 refrain 8 epilogue, prologue

pastoral: 4 idyl 7 bucolic, eclogue, georgic

pert. to: 4 odic

religious: 4 hymn 5 psalm

rural: 7 eclogue, georgic

satirical: dit(F.) 6 iambic, kasada, parody

seven-line: 10 heptastich

sort: dit(F.) 5 ditty 6 sonnet 7 epigram 8 rondelet

six-line: 9 hexastich

six-stanza: 7 sestina

ten-line: 6 dizain 7 dizaine 9 decastich

poesy: 4 poem 5 motto, verse 7 nosegay

poet: 4 bard, fili, muse, scop 5 odist, rishi 6 lyrist 7 dreamer, imagist, metrist 8 idyllist, minstrel 9 bucoliast 10 Parnassian 13 cinque-centist

humorous: 4 Lear, Nash

inferior: 5 rimer 6 rhymer 8 rimester 9 poetaster, poeticule, rhymester, versifier

inspiration: 4 Muse

poetic: 4 odic 5 lyric 6 dreamy 8 romantic 9 beautiful, visionary 11 imaginative

poetical: 8 sonnetic

poetry: *accented foot:* 5 arsis

god: 5 Bragi

inspiring to: 7 helicon

muse: 5 Erato 6 Thalia 7 Euterpe 8 Calliope

pogonip: fog

pogrom: 6 attack 7 pillage 8 genocide, massacre 9 slaughter

pogy: 5 perch, trout 8 menhaden

poi: 4 food 5 paste

source: 4 taro

poietic: 8 creative

poignant: 4 keen, tart 5 acute, sharp 6 biting, bitter, moving 7 cutting, piquant, pointed, pungent **8** piercing, pricking, touching

poind: 4 sell **5** seize **7** impound

point: aim, dot, jag, jet, jot, neb, nib, tip **4** apex, barb, cape, crux, cusp, gist, horn, item, peak, pith, pole, show, spit, spot **5** angle, focus, issue, level, prong, punch, refer, sense, taper **6** allude, degree, detail, direct, tip-off, tittle **7** apicula(L.), apiculi(L.), article, element, feature, meaning **8** apiculus(L.), emphasis, indicate, salience, validity **10** particular, promontory

cardinal: 4 east, west **5** north, south

final: dot, end **6** period **7** outcome

finishing: 4 tape

highest: tip 4 acme, apex, noon, peak **6** apices, apogee, maxima, summit, zenith **7** maximum **8** meridian, pinnacle **11** ne plus ultra

land: 4 hook, spit

law: res

lowest: 4 zero **5** nadir **6** bottom, pergee **7** bedrock

pert. to: **6** apical

scoring: ace, run **5** punto **6** sponge

spear: grad

strong: **5** forte

supporting: **5** pivot **7** fulcrum

to the: **6** cogent **8** relevant **9** pertinent

turning: 4 tide **5** cardo, epoch **6** crisis, crises

utmost: **7** extreme, sublime

vibration: 4 node

weak: 4 blot, flaw **5** fault **6** foible

point-blank: 6 direct, wholly **7** bluntly, exactly **8** directly **9** perfectly, precisely **10** completely **13** unqualifiedly

point of view: eye **4** bras **5** angle, sight, slant **7** opinion, outlook **8** attitude

pointed: **5** acute, sharp, tangy, terse **6** acuate, marked, picked **7** actuate, capapie, concise **8** aculeate, piercing, poignant, spicated, stinging **9** acuminate, apiculate, fastigiate **10** noticeable **11** conspicuous

pointer: arm, dog, tip **4** clue, hand, hint **5** index **6** fescue, gnomon **7** indices **9** indicator

pointless: 4 dull **5** blunt, inane, silly, vapid **6** stupid **7** insipid **9** senseless

pointsman: **7** flanker, trapper **9** switchman

poise: tee **4** tact **5** carry, grace, weigh **6** aplomb **7** balance, ballast, bearing, support, suspend **8** calmness, carriage, liberate, maintain **9** assurance, elegance, equipoise, stability **10** confidence, equanimity **11** equilibrium **12** counterpoise **14** counterbalance

poison: fig **4** bane, drab, gall **5** atter, taint, venin, venom, virus **6** amarin, debase,

infect, miasma **7** amarine, arsenic, botulin, corrupt, pervert, vitiate **8** empoison, ptomaine **11** contaminate

ant: **10** formmicide **11** formicicide

arrow: 4 haya, inee, upas **5** urali, urare, urari **6** antiar, curare, curari **7** ouabain, woorlai

hexapod: **11** insecticide

kind: 4 bikh **5** abrin, nabee, ricin **6** antiar **7** arsenic, tanghin

pert. to: **9** arsenious

tree: 4 upas

poison ash: **5** sumac **6** sumach **9** torchwood

poison fish: 4 fugu **6** weever **8** scorpion, toadfish

poison flag: 4 iris

poison flower: **11** bittersweet

poison ivy: **5** sumac **6** laurel

poison tobacco: **7** henbane

poisoned: **6** sepsis

poisoning: **6** pyemia **7** jimmies **9** ichthyism, lathyrism

food: **8** botulism

lead: **8** plumbism

poisonous: **5** toxic **6** virose **7** baneful, noxious **8** mephatic, venomous, virulent **9** malignant **11** destructive

fish: 4 fugu

fungus: **7** amanita

gas: **6** arsine **8** phosgene

herb: **8** aconitum

lizard: 4 gila

plant: **8** mandrake **10** nightshade

weed: 4 loco

poisonwood: **5** sumac **8** metopium **10** manchineel

poisson bleu: **7** blue cat, catfish **8** grayling

poitrel: **5** armor, plate **7** pectron **9** stomacher **11** breastplate

poke: bag, dig, hat, jab, jog **4** blow, bore, brod, cuff, prod, root, sack **5** bulge, delay, dunce, nudge, probe, punch, purse, snoop **6** bonnet, dawdle, loiter, meddle, pocket, potter, putter, sleeve, thrust, wallet **7** dawdler, intrude, tobacco

poker: rod **4** dart, game

drawing by: **10** pyrography

forerunner: **7** primero

form: **7** draw, stud

stake: pot **4** ante **5** chips, kitty

poker-faced: **7** neutral, serious

pokeweed: **5** pocan **6** garget **8** inkberry

family: **14** phytolaccaceae

pokey, poky: 4 dull, jail, mean, slow **5** dowdy **6** narrow, shabby, stuffy **7** tedious **8** trifling

Poland: **6** Polska **7** Polonia **8** Sarmatia

astronomer: **10** Copernicus

cake: 4 baba

capital: **6** Warsaw

carriage: 7 britska
city: 4 Lodz 5 Brest, Posen, Vilna 6 Cracow, Gdansk, Gdynia, Grodno, Krakow, Lublin, Poznan, Tarnow 7 Beuthen, Lemberg, Litovsk, Wroclaw 8 Gleiwitz, Katowice, Szczecin, Tarnopol 9 Bialystok, Bielostok, Byelostok
commune: 4 Ruda 5 Plock, Radom
composer: 6 Chopin 10 Paderewski
dance: 5 polka 7 mazurka 9 krakowiak, polonaise 11 cracovienne
dollar: 5 dalar
dynasty: 5 Piast
island: 5 Wolin
labor leader: 6 Walesa
labor union: 10 Solidarity
measure: cal 4 mila, morg, pret 5 linja, morga, sazen, stopa, vloka, wloka 6 cwierc, korzec, kwarta, lokiec 7 garniec 9 kwarterka
monetary unit: 5 ducat, grosz, marka, zloty 6 fennig, halerz, korona
nobleman: 7 starost
parliament: 4 Seim, Sejm, Seym 5 Senat
people: 4 Slav 5 Marur 8 Silesian
premier: 10 Jaruzelski
river: Bug, San 4 Oder, Styr 5 Dwina, Seret 6 Neisse, Niemen, Pripet, Strypa 7 Vistula
scientist: 5 Curie
szlachta: 6 gentry 8 nobility 9 landowner
title of address: 4 Pani
weight: lut 4 funt 5 uncya 6 kamian 7 centner, skrupul
polar: 6 Arctic 7 pivotal 8 opposite
polar explorer: 4 Byrd 5 Peary 6 Wilkes 8 Amundsen
Polaris: 7 missile 9 North Star
pole: bar, pew, poy, rod, xat 4 axis, boom, brog, mast, palo(Sp.), pike, prop, punt, spar, wand 5 caber, guide, nader, perch, sprit, staff, stake, stick, stool, sweep, totem 6 crotch 7 barling
circle: 11 circumpolar
electric: 5 anode 7 cathode, kathode 9 electrode
fishing: rod
tribal: xat 5 totem
vehicle: 4 cope, neap 5 thill
pole fluke: 8 flounder
pole horse: 7 wheeler
pole strip: 8 template
polecat: 5 fitch, skunk, zoril 6 ferret, musang 7 fitchet, fitchew, foumart
polehead: 7 tadpole
polemic: 8 argument 9 disputant 10 discussion 11 disputation 12 disputatious 13 argumentative, controversial
polenta: 4 mush 8 cornmeal, porridge
polestar: 5 guide 8 lodestar 10 tramontane
police: 5 guard, watch 6 govern, patrol 7

protect, rurales 8 officers 11 carabinieri(It.) 12 constabulary
headquarters: 4 tana 7 station 8 bargello, barracks 9 marshalcy
line: 6 cordon
officer: 6 kotwal 8 bargello 10 prefecture
organization: PAL
trap: 7 dragnet
vehicle: car, van 7 cruiser 8 prowl car, squad car
policeman: cop 4 bull 5 bobby, bulky, burly, rural, sepoy 6 bobbie, copper, peeler 7 crusher, gumshoe, officer, trooper 8 flatfoot, gendarme(F.) 9 burkundaz, constable, patrolman 11 burkundauze, carabiniere(It.)
badge: 6 buzzer, shield
club: 5 billy 9 espantoon, truncheon 10 nightstick
policy: wit 4 plan 6 course, wisdom 8 contract, prudence, sagacity 9 diplomacy, principle, procedure 10 artfulness, management, shrewdness 14 administration
polish: rub 4 buff 5 frush, glaze, gloss, grind, rabat, scour, scrub, sheen, shine, slick 6 finish, glance, luster, lustre, rabbat, refine, smooth 7 brush up, burnish, culture, furbish, perfect 8 brighten, civilize, elegance, lapidate, levigate, urbanity 10 refinement
polish off: end 4 kill 5 eat up 6 consume, finish
polished: 4 fine 5 compt, suave 6 polite 7 gallant
polisher: 5 brush, emery, rabat(F.) 6 glazer, pumice 8 abrasive
polishing: 7 sanding 8 frottage, limation
polite: 5 civil, suave 6 gentle, smooth, urbane 7 correct, courtly, cunning, gallant, genteel, refined 8 cultured, debonair, decorous, discreet, polished 9 attentive, courteous, debonaire 10 cultivated, debonnaire, thoughtful 11 complaisant, considerate
politesse: 8 courtesy 12 decorousness
politic: 4 wary, wise 5 suave 6 artful, astute, crafty, shrewd 7 prudent 8 discreet 9 expedient, politique, provident, sagacious 10 diplomatic 12 unscrupulous
political: *division:* 4 city, town, ward 5 shire, state 6 county 8 province 9 community
gathering: 5 rally 6 caucus 10 convention
group: 4 bloc, cell, ring 5 cadre, junta, party 6 caucus 7 faction, machine
hanger-on: 10 ward heeler
incumbents: ins
influence: 5 lobby
list: 5 slate
political party: G.O.P. 4 Tory, Whig 5

Labor **9** Communist, Socialist **10** Democratic, Republican **12** Conservative
principles: **8** platform
program article: **5** plank
unit: **4** city, East, ward, West **5** state **6** county, parish **7** borough, hundred, kingdom **8** district **9** sultanate
politician: pol **4** boss **7** schemer, senator, statist **8** lawmaker **9** intriguer, president, statesman **10** wirepuller **16** congressionalist
polka dot: **4** spot **6** circle
poll: cow **4** clip, coll, head, list, trim **5** count, shave, shear **6** ballot, cut off, fleece, survey **7** canvass, despoil, listing **8** counting, register **9** enumerate
pollack: **4** fish, pool **6** billet, saithe **7** baddock(Sc.) **8** bluefish, coalfish
pollan: **9** whitefish
pollard: cow **4** bran, deer, goat, stag, tree **5** prune, sheep **8** truncate
polled: **8** hornless
pollen: **4** dust, meal **5** flour **6** powder
pollen brush: **5** scopa **6** scopae
pollen grain: *mass:* **8** pollinia **9** pollinium
pollenization: **5** xenia
pollex: **4** inch **5** digit, thumb **6** finger **7** phlange
pollicitation: **7** promise **8** proposal
pollinate: **9** fecundate, fertilize
pollinosis: **8** hay fever
polliwog: **7** tadpole
pollute: **4** foul, soil **5** dirty, smear, stain, sully, taint **6** befoul, defile, ravish **7** corrupt, debauch, profane, violate, vitiate **9** desecrate **11** contaminate
pollution: **4** smog **5** filth **8** impurity **11** desecration, uncleanness
Pollux: *brother:* **6** Castor
father: **4** Zeus
mother: **4** Leda
polo: *division:* **7** chucker, chukker
mount: **4** pony **5** horse
stick: **6** mallet
team: **4** four
Polonius: *daughter:* **7** Ophelia
son: **7** Laertes
Polony: **6** Polish **7** sausage **9** polonaise
polt: **4** blow, club **5** knock, thump
poltergeist: **5** ghost **6** spirit, spook
poltfoot: **8** clubfoot
poltroon: cad **4** idle, lazy **6** coward, craven, wretch **7** dastard **8** cowardly, sluggard **9** dastardly
polverine: **6** potash **8** pearlash
polyandrium: **4** cemetery
polychromatic: **10** variegated **12** multicolored
polygamy: **6** bigamy
polygon: **4** ngon **6** square **7** decagon, hexagon, nonagon, octagon **8** pentagon, triangle

equal sides: **6** isagon
nine sides: **7** nonagon
twelve sides: **9** dodecagon
Polynesia: *apple:* **4** hevi
baking pit: umu
banana: fei
beverage: **4** kava, kawa
breech cloth: **4** malo
burial place: ahu
butterfly: io
chestnut: **4** rata
cloth: **4** tapa
dance: **4** siva
dragon: ati
fern: **4** tara
garment: **5** pareu
god: Oro **4** Tane, Tiki
goddess: **4** Pele
herb: pia
homeland: **7** Havaiki
image: **4** Tiki
island: **4** Cook, Fiji, Line **5** Samoa, Tonga **6** Easter, Ellice **7** Phoenix, Tokelau
language: **7** Tagalog
magical power: **4** mana
memorial: ahu
oven: umu
people: Ati **5** Malay, Maori **6** Kanaka, Samoan, Tongan **8** Hawaiian, Tahitian **9** Marquesan
pepper plant: **4** avas
pigeon: **4** lupe
pine: ara **4** hala
plant: **4** taro
ruler: **7** faipule
sky: **5** langi
sling: ma
spirit: **4** Atua
statue: **4** Tiki
tree: ti **4** ahia, rata
wages: utu
woman: **6** vahine
yam: ube, ubi, uve, uvi
polyp: **5** hydra, tumor **6** seapen **7** anemone, hydroid, octopod
skeleton: **5** coral
polytrophic: **9** versatile
Polyxena: *father:* **5** Priam
lover: **8** Achilles
mother: **6** Hecuba
pomade: **4** balm **5** salve **7** pomatum, unguent **8** cosmetic, ointment
pomander: **4** case **7** pouncet
pome: **4** ball, pear **5** apple, fruit, globe **6** quince, sphere **9** juneberry
pomegranate: **6** granet **7** grenade **8** balausta
syrup: **9** grenadine
pomelo: **8** shaddock **10** grapefruit
Pomerania: *capital:* **5** Stettin
city: **5** Thorn, Torun **6** Anklam
island: **5** Rugen **6** Usedom

province: 7 Pomorze

river: 4 Oder

Pomeranian: dog

pomme de terre: 6 potato

pommel: bat 4 beat, knob 6 finial, handle 12 protuberance

bag: 7 cantina

pomp: 4 fare, form 5 boast, pride, state 6 estate, parade, ritual 7 cortege, display liturgy, pageant 8 ceremony, grandeur, splendor 9 pageantry, spectacle 10 ceremonial 11 ostentation 12 magnificence

Pomp and Circumstance composer: 5 Elgar

pompano: 4 fish 7 alewife, cobbler 8 mackerel 9 poppy fish

Pompeii: *archeologist:* Mau

heroine: 4 Ione

mountain: 8 Vesuvius

pom-pom: gun 6 cannon

pompon: 4 ball, tuft 6 dahlia 8 ornament 13 chrysanthemum

pompous: big 7 bloated, fustian, orotund, stately, stilted 8 arrogant 9 bombastic, flatulent, grandiose 10 altisonant, pontifical, rhetorical 11 altiloquent, dictatorial, magnificent, pretentious, stateliness 12 ostentatious 13 grandiloquent, self-important

Ponchielli opera: 8 Gioconda

pond: dam, lum 4 delf, dike, lake, mere, pool, tarn 5 lagoon, stalina 7 lakelet

fish: 7 pisoina 8 aquarium

frog: 8 ranarium

oyster: 6 claire

pond dogwood: 10 buttonbush

pond duck: 7 mallard

pond hen: 4 coot 6 fulica

ponder: 4 chaw, mull, muse, pore 5 brood, opine, study, think, weigh 6 reason 7 mediate, reflect, revolve 8 appraise, cogitate, consider, evaluate, meditate, ruminate, turn over 10 deliberate 11 contemplate

ponderous: dry 4 dull 5 bulky, grave, heavy, hefty, massy 7 awkward, massive, weighty 8 unwieldy 9 important, momentous 11 elephantine, heavy-footed

pondfish: 7 sunfish

pondokkie: hut 5 hovel

pone: 4 lump, turf 8 swelling 10 johnny-cake

pongee: 4 silk 5 cloth 6 fabric 7 paunche 8 shantung

pongy: 4 monk 6 priest 8 Buddhist

poniard: 4 dirk, kill, stab 6 bodkin, dagger, pierce, stylet 8 stiletto

pont: 5 ferry, float 6 bridge 7 caisson 9 ferryboat

pontiff: 4 pope 6 bishop

pert. to: 5 papal 7 sistine

pontifical: 5 papal 7 pompous 8 dogmatic

pontoon: 4 boat 5 barge, float 6 bridge, vessel 7 caisson

plank: 5 chess

pony: 4 cab, cob, nag 4 crib, trot 5 glass, horse 6 garran, liquor 7 hackney, measure

kind: 5 pinto, tatoo 6 cayuse, Exmoor 8 Shetland

student's: 4 crib, trot

pooch: dog 6 barbet 7 mongrel

pooh-pooh: 7 dismiss, kiss off 8 ridicule 9 denigrate, raspberry

pook: 4 heap, pile, pull 5 pluck, stack

pooka: 6 goblin 7 specter

pool: car, dib(Sc.), dub(Sc.), lin, pit, pot 4 carr, dike, game, jeel, linn, loch, mear, meer, mere, pond, tank, tarn 5 flash, flush, funds, kitty, lough, plash, stake, trunk, trust 6 cartel, charco, flodge, lagoon, plunge, puddle, salina 7 alberca, carline, combine, jackpot, plashet 8 monopoly 9 billabong, billiards, reservoir, resources, syndicate 10 natatorium 11 combination

ball: cue 4 spot 6 ringer

poon: 4 dilo, tree 5 domba, keena 8 mastwood

poonghie: See pongy

poop: 4 deck, fool, gulp, seat 5 cheat, cozen, stern 7 exhaust 8 hinddeck 10 nincompoop 11 information

poor: bad, ill 4 bare, base, lean, mean 5 broke, cheap, dinky, naked, needy, seedy 6 abject, barren, feeble, hard up, humble, hungry, in need, paltry, pilled, scanty, shabby 7 hapless, sterile, unlucky 8 dirt poor, indigent, inferior 9 defective, destitute, emaciated, imperfect, infertile, penurious 10 inadequate, ungenerous 11 impecunious, inefficient, unfortunate 12 contemptible, impoverished, insufficient 13 insignificant 14 unsatisfactory

Poor Clare: nun 6 sister

poor joe: 4 bird 5 heron

poor John: cod 4 fish, food, hake

poor man's pepper: 9 stonecrop 11 peppergrass

poor man's soap: 7 spiraea 8 hardhack

poor man's weatherglass: 9 pimpernel

poor soldier: 9 friarbird

poor-spirited: 4 base, mean 8 cowardly

poorer: 5 worse 8 inferior

poorhouse: 6 asylum 9 almshouse, measondue, workhouse

poorly: low 4 mean 6 ailing, sickly, unwell 10 indisposed 13 disparagingly

pop: 4 dart, pawn 5 fling 6 father, strike 8 beverage 9 explosion

popadam: 4 cake 5 wafer 6 cookie
popdock: 8 foxglove
pope: 4 ruff 6 bishop, priest, puffin, shrike 7 pontiff 9 bullfinch, patriarch 10 holy father
cape: 5 fanon, orale 7 mozetta 8 mozzetta
court: 8 Curia
court office: 6 datary 7 dataria
court officer: 6 datary
crown: 5 tiara 9 triregnum
decree: 8 rescript
envoy: 6 legate 7 nuntius 8 ablegate
epistle: 8 decretal
headdress: 5 miter, mitre, tiara
letter: 4 bull
line: 6 papacy
name: Leo 4 John, Pius 5 Peter, Ratti, Urban 6 Adrian 7 Gregory, Zachary 8 Benedict, Innocent
palace: 7 Lateran, Vatican
pert. to: 5 papal
seal: 5 bulla
secretary: 11 apocrisiary
veil: 5 orale 6 fannel
Popeye: *baby:* 7 Swee'Pea
creator: 5 Segar
girl: 8 Olive Oyl
occupation: 6 sailor
rival: 5 Bluto
popinac: 8 huisache
popinjay: 6 parrot 7 papingo 8 parakeet 10 woodpecker
poplar: 4 liar 5 abele, alamo, aspen, bahan, bolle, garab 6 balsam 7 populus 9 tacamahac 10 cottonwood
white: 4 abele, aspen
Poppaea's husband: 4 Nero
poppy: 5 plant 6 blaver, canker, flower 7 coprose, papaver, ponceau 8 foxglove 10 coquelicot
herb family: 9 celandine
seed: maw
poppycock: rot 4 bosh, dung 8 nonsense
populace: mob 4 mass 5 demos, plebs 6 people 10 commonality 11 rank and file, third estate
popular: lay, pop 6 common, simple 7 demotic, favored 8 accepted, favorite 9 prevalent, well-liked 10 democratic, prevailing 11 proletarian 12 nontechnical
popularity: 5 vogue 8 claptrap
populate: 6 occupy, people 7 inhabit
population: 8 universe 9 habitancy 11 inhabitants
count: 6 census
study: 10 demography, larithmics
populous: 7 crowded 9 abounding
porbeagle: 5 shark 7 lamnoid
porcelain: 4 frit 5 china 7 biscuit
ancient: 5 murra
clay: 6 kaolin 7 kaoline

furnace: 5 hovel
kind of: 5 Lenox, Spode 6 Sevres 7 Celadon, Dresden, Limoges, Meissen 8 Haviland 9 Wedgwood
porch: 4 door, stoa 5 lanai, plaza, stoae(pl.), stoop 6 harbor, loggia, piazza 7 balcony, galilee, gallery, portico, terrace, veranda 8 entrance 9 colonnade
church: 7 galilee, martliex
sun: 7 solaria(pl.) 8 solarium
swing: 6 glider
porcine: fat 7 piglike
porcupine: 5 urson 7 cawquaw 8 hedgehog
disease: 10 ichthyosis
genus of: 7 hystrix
spine: 5 quill
porcupine anteater: 7 echidna
porcupine fish: 6 atinga, diodon
porcupine grass: 5 stipa 8 spinefex
quill: pen
pore: con 4 gaze 5 gloze, stare, stoma, study 6 ponder 7 foramen, opening, orifice, ostiole, stomata(pl.) 8 lenticel, meditate
plant: 7 ostiole 8 lenticel
porgy: tai(Jap.) 4 fish, scup 6 besugo, pagrus 7 margate, pinfish 8 menhaden 9 spadefish
pork: ham, pig 5 bacon, money, swine 6 hamhog 7 griskin, sausage 8 position
pork-barrelling: 9 patronage
porker: hog, pig 5 swine
porkfish: 4 sisi
porky: fat, pig 6 greasy
pornographic: 4 lewd 7 obscene 10 licentious
porous: 4 open 5 leaky, light 6 leachy 9 permeable 10 penetrable 13 insubstantial
porphyry: 4 rock
porpoise: 4 inia 6 seahog 7 dolphin, pellock(Sc.) 8 cetacean, gairfish
porrect: 6 extend, tender 7 present
porret: 4 leek 5 onion 6 garlic 8 scallion
porridge: 4 samp 5 atole, brose(Sc.), grout, gruel 6 burgoo 7 brochan, burgout, oatmeal, polenta, pottage 9 stirabout 10 miscellany 11 skilligalee
container: 6 bicker
port: 4 gate, toal, left, wine 5 carry, haven 6 apport, harbor, market, portal, refuge 7 bearing, harbour, meaning, purport, shelter 8 carriage, demeanor, larboard 9 demeanour, transport 10 deportment 11 destination
portable: 5 handy 6 mobile 7 movable 8 bearable 10 convenient, manageable
bathtub: 4 tosh
bed: cot 8 rollaway
chair: 5 sedan
lamp: 7 lantern

stove: 4 etna

portal: 4 arch, door, gate 7 gateway 8 entrance

portance: 7 bearing, conduct 8 carriage, demeanor

portcullis: bar 4 door, gate, shut 5 grate, herse 7 grating, lattice

porte-monnaie: 5 purse 10 pocketbook

portefeuille: 9 portfolio

portend: 4 bode 5 augur 6 divine 7 betoken, forbode, predict, presage 8 forebode, foretell, prophesy 10 foreshadow

portent: 4 omen, sign 5 event 6 marvel, ostent, wonder 7 meaning, prodigy 8 ceremony 9 foretoken 10 foreboding, prognostic 11 forewarning

portentous: 4 dire 5 fatal, grave 6 solemn 7 fateful, ominous, pompous, weighty 10 impressive 11 significant

porter: ale 4 beer 5 carry, hamal, stout 6 bearer, durwan, hamaul, hammal, khamal, redcap, suisse 7 bailiff, carrier, durwaun, dvornik(Russ.), gateman, hummaul, janitor 8 beverage, cargador, janitrix 9 attendant, concierge, janitress, transport 10 doorkeeper

Portia: *alias:* 9 Balthazar
husband: 6 Brutus
lover: 8 Bassanio
maid: 7 Nerissa

portia tree: 4 maho 5 bendy

portico: 4 stoa(Gr.), xyst 5 porch, stoae(Gr., pl.) 6 atrium, piazza, xystus 7 narthex, pteroma, terrace, veranda 9 colonnade, pteromata(pl.) 10 ambulatory, antetemple
enclosed: 9 peridrome
long: 6 xystus 7 veranda

portiere: 5 drape 7 curtain

portion: bit, cut, dab, dot, jag, lot, nip 4 chaw, deal, dole, dunt, fate, jagg, part, some 5 allot, allow, divvy, dower, dowry, endow, piece, quota, ratio, share 6 canton, divide, dowery, gobbet, moiety, parcel, rasher, ration 7 destiny, helping, scruple, section, segment, serving 8 legitime, quantity 9 allotment, allowance, apportion 10 distribute 13 apportionment

portly: fat 5 ample, obese, stout 6 chubby, chunky 7 stately 8 imposing, majestic 9 corpulent, dignified

portmanteau: bag 4 case 6 valise 8 suitcase 9 carpetbag, gladstone

Porto Rico: See **Puerto Rico**

portrait: 4 copy, icon, ikon 5 image 6 effigy 7 picture 8 likeness 10 similitude
pert. to: 6 iconic
sitting: 6 model

portray: act 4 copy, draw, form, limn, mime, show 5 enact, frame, graph, image, paint 6 depict 7 fashion, picture 8

describe 9 delineate, duplicate, pantomime, represent, reproduce 11 demonstrate

portreeve: 5 mayor 7 bailiff, officer

portress, porteress: 6 porter 9 charwoman 10 doorkeeper

Portugal: *brandy:* 10 aguardente
capital: Lisbon
city: 4 Ovar 5 Braga, Evora 6 Guarda 7 Coimbra, Opporto 8 Braganca
commune: 5 Braga
district: 4 Tete 5 Evora
explorer: Cao 4 Diaz
festival: 9 chamarita
former colony: Diu, Goa 5 Damao, Timor 6 Angola, Guinea 7 Sao Tome 8 Principe 9 Cape Verde 10 Mozambique
former money: 5 dobra
guitar: 7 machete
harbor: 4 Faro, Ovar 5 Macao 6 Aveiro, Lisbon, Oporto, Vianna 7 Setubal 8 Figueira
island: 6 Angola, Azores 7 Madeira 8 Principe, Sao Thome
legislature: 6 cortes
liquid measure: 6 canada
measure: pe 4 alma, bota, meio, moio, pipa, vara 5 almud, braca, fanga, geira, legoa, linha, milha, palmo 6 almude, covado, quarto 7 alquier, estadio, ferrado, selamin 8 alqueire, tonelada
monetary unit: 6 escudo 7 centavo
mountain: 15 Serra d'Estrella
navigator: 4 Gama 8 Magellan
news agency: 4 ANOP
overseas territory: 5 Macao
people: 7 Iberian
poet: 7 Camoens
province: 4 Ovar 5 Beira, Minho 6 Azores 7 Algarve, Madeira 8 Alentejo
river: 4 Sado 5 Douro, Duero, Minho, Tagus 7 Mondego 8 Guadiana
saint: Sao
song: 4 fado
title: dom 4 dona 6 senhor 7 fidalgo, senhora 9 senhorita
vessel: 7 caravel
weight: 4 grao, onca, once 5 libra, marco 6 arroba, oitava 7 arratel, quintal

porwigle: 7 tadpole

posada: inn 5 hotel

posaune: 8 trombone

pose: set, sit 4 airs 5 model, offer, place, strut 6 baffle, puzzle, stance 7 nonplus, posture 8 attitude, confound, position, propound, question 9 mannerism 10 disconcert, expression 11 affectation, impersonate 12 attitudinize

Poseidon: 7 Neptune(L.) 11 earthshaker
brother: 4 Zeus 5 Hades, Pluto
father: 6 Cronus
mother: 4 Rhea

scepter: **7** trident

servant: **7** Proteus

son: **6** Albion, Triton **7** Alebion, Antaeus, Antaios

wife: **10** Amphitrite

poser: **5** facer **6** puzzle **7** problem **8** question

posh: **5** smart **6** spruce, swanky **7** elegant, stylish **9** luxurious

posit: **6** affirm, assert, assume **9** postulate **10** presuppose

position (see also **place**): job, lie, set **4** loci(pl.), pose, post, rank, side, site, view **5** cense, coign, locus, place, situs, stand **6** billet, coigne, estate, locale, office, plight, stance, status **7** calling, posture **8** attitude, doctrine, location, sinecure, statuses(pl.) **9** condition, gradation, situation **10** standpoint **11** affirmation, appointment, disposition **12** circumstance

change: **4** move

correct: **8** oriented

defensive: **4** fort **10** bridgehead

relative: **5** grade **8** standing

troops: **6** deploy

with little work: **8** sinecure

positional: **6** situal

positive: set **4** plus, sure **6** actual, thetic **7** assured, certain, decided **8** absolute, complete, constant, definite, dogmatic, emphatic, explicit **9** assertive, confident, downright, empirical, practical **10** peremptory **11** affirmative, categorical, dictatorial, opinionated, right-handed, unqualified **13** authoritative, overconfident

positively: **5** truly **6** easily, really **8** actually **9** certainly, obviously **11** indubitably

positivism: **7** Comtism **9** certainty, dogmatism **11** materialism

founder: **5** Comte

positure: **7** posture **11** arrangement, disposition **13** configuration

poss: **4** beat, dash, push **5** drive, knock, pound, stamp **6** thrust

posse: **4** band **6** throng

possess: get, owe, own **4** bear, have **5** reach **6** occupy **7** inhabit **8** dominate, maintain

possessed: mad **4** calm **8** demoniac

possession: **4** aver, hold **5** asset, aught **6** havior, seisin, wealth **7** control, dewanee, haviour, mastery **8** property **9** ownership

family: **8** heirloom

legal: **5** title **6** estate

of goods by finding: **6** trover

take: **5** seise

time: **5** lease

possessions: **5** goods **6** graith **8** chattels

possessor: **5** owner **10** proprietor

posset: **4** turn **6** curdle, pamper **8** beverage **9** balductum, coagulate

possibility: **11** contingency, eventuality

possible: may **6** likely **8** feasible, probable **9** expedient, potential **10** contingent **11** practicable

possibly: may **5** maybe **7** perhaps

possum: **4** coon, tait **9** marsupial, phalanger

comic strip: **4** Pogo

play: **4** sham **5** feign **7** pretend

post: set **4** dole, dool, fort, mail, pole, ride, send **5** cippi(pl.), newel, place, stake, stock **6** assign, cippus, column, inform, office, pillar, poster, travel **7** courier, placard, station **8** announce, dispatch, garrison, position **9** advertise, situation

airplane race: **5** pylon

boat rope: **7** bollard, capstan

easy: **4** pipe, snap **8** sinecure

middle: **8** kingpost

post chaise: **4** jack **5** coach **8** carriage

post office: **6** correo(Sp.)

letter box: **8** apartado(Sp.)

postage: **5** stamp

stamp design: **6** burele **8** burelage, spandred

postbox: **7** mailbox

postboy: **7** courier, yamshik(Russ.) **8** horseman yemschik **9** messenger, postilion, yamstchik(Russ.)

postdate: **9** afterdate

poster: **4** bill, clap, sign **6** banner **7** affiche, courier, placard, sticker **9** broadside **10** billposter **12** announcement **13** advertisement

posterior: **4** back, hind, rear **6** behind, caudal, dorsal, hinder **7** adaxial **8** buttocks **10** subsequent

posterity: **6** sequel **9** offspring **10** generation **11** descendants

postern: **4** door, exit, gate, side **7** clocket, private **8** entrance **10** undercover

postfix: add **5** annex **6** append **7** suffix

postiche: wig **4** sham **5** switch, toupee **8** pretense, spurious **9** imitation **14** counterfeiting

postil: **6** homily **7** comment **10** commentary

postilion: **7** courier, postboy

postpone: **4** stay, wait **5** defer, delay, remit, table **6** remand, retard, shelve **7** adjourn, prolong **8** reprieve **10** pigeonhole **11** subordinate **13** procrastinate

postponement: **4** mora, stay **5** delay, morae(pl.) **7** respite **8** reprieve **10** ampliation

postprandial: **11** after-dinner

postscript: **6** sequel **8** footnote

postulant: **9** applicant, candidate **10** petitioner

postulate: **5** claim, posit **6** assume, demand 7 premise, require 10 assumption, hypotheses(pl.), hypothesis, presuppose 11 proposition 12 prerequisite

posture: 4 pose 5 state 6 stance 7 bearing, gesture 8 attitude, carriage, position 9 composure

erect: 11 orthostatic

posy: 5 motto, verse 6 flower, legend 7 bouquet, nosegay 9 anthology, sentiment 11 composition

pot: bag, pan, win 4 dixy, pool 5 abyss, crewe, dixie, drink, kitty, shoot 6 aludel, basket, cruset, posnet, secure, toilet, vessel 7 caldron, capture, cuvette, fortune, notable 8 cauldron, crucible, potation 9 marijuana 11 deteriorate

arch: 4 kiln

earthen: 4 olla 5 crock, cruse 6 chytra

handle: 4 bool

hat: 5 derby 6 bowler

lead: 8 graphite

wheel: 5 noria

pot-au-feu: 4 soup, stew

pot liquid: 6 brewis

pot-rustler: 4 cook

potable: 4 pure 5 clean, drink 8 beverage 9 drinkable

potage: 4 soup 5 broth

potash: 4 kali 5 niter, nitre, salin 6 alkali, saline 6 pearlash

potassium: 6 kalium

compound: 4 alum 6 chrome, potash

sulphate: 4 alum 8 misenite

potation: 4 bout, dram 5 draft, drink 6 liquid, liquor 7 spirits 8 beverage, drinking, libation

potato: ima, oca, yam 4 chat, papa, spud 5 rural, tuber 6 murphy 7 manroot 12 pomme de terre(F.)

beetle: 8 hardback

bud: eye

disease: pox 4 curl

dish: 8 au gratin 9 lyonnaise, scalloped

family: 10 solanaceae

planting ridge: 4 ruck

seed part: eye

starch: 6 farina

state: 5 Idaho, Maine

sweet: yam 6 batata, comote, patata 7 batatas, ocarina

potbank: 7 pottery

potbelly: 5 stove 6 paunch 9 bay window

potboiler: 4 book 8 painting 9 potwaller 10 manuscript

potboy: 8 Ganymede 9 cupbearer

pote: 4 kick, poke, push 5 nudge, shove 6 thrust

poteen, potheen: 6 whisky

potence: 5 cross 6 gibbet 7 gallows

potency: vis 5 force, might, power, vigor 6 energy 8 efficacy, strength, vitality 9 fertility

potent: 4 able 6 cogent, mighty, strong 7 dynamic 8 powerful, puissant, vigorous, virulent 9 effective, efficient 10 convincing 11 influential

potentate: 4 amir, emir, king 5 ameer, emeer, mogul, ruler 6 moghul, prince 7 monarch 9 sovereign

potential: 6 latent, mighty 8 inchoate, possible 10 unrealized 11 influential, possibility, undeveloped

potentiality: 5 power 8 capacity 9 pregnancy

potgun: 6 pistol, popgun 8 braggart

pothead: 9 blackfish

pother: ado, row, vex 4 fuss, stir 5 worry 6 bother, bustle, harass, muddle, uproar 7 fluster, perplex, trouble 9 annoyance, commotion, confusion 11 disturbance 12 perturbation

potherb: 4 kale, mint, wort 5 chard 6 greens 7 mustard, quelite, spinach

pert. to: 7 olitory

pothole: 5 cahot 6 kettle, tinaja

pothook: rod 4 hake, nine 5 crook 6 collar, scrawl

pothouse: bar 6 tavern 8 alehouse

potiche: jar 4 vase

potion: 4 brew, dose, drug 5 draft, drink 6 drench 7 draught, philter, philtre 8 nepenthe

sleeping: 5 dwale 6 opiate 8 narcotic 9 soporific 10 belladonna

potlatch: 4 gift 5 feast

potomania: 10 dipsomania

potpie: 4 stew 9 fricassee

potpourri: jar 4 olio, stew 5 medley 7 mixture 9 anthology 10 miscellany 11 salamagundi

potrero: 6 meadow 7 pasture

potsherd: bit 4 chip 5 shard 8 fragment

potshot: 4 jibe, jeer 5 shoot 6 assail, attack, insult 9 aspersion, sideswipe

potstone: 8 steatite

pottage: 4 soup, stew 6 brewis 8 porridge

potah: 4 deed 5 lease 11 certificate

potted: 5 drunk 9 condensed 11 intoxicated

potter: fad, pry 4 fuss, mess, poke, push 6 cotter, dabble, dacker, daiker, dawdle, dodder, fiddle, footer, footle, loiter, meddle, putter, tamper, tinker, trifle 7 cloamer, fossick, saunter 8 ceramist 10 ceramicist, mess around

potter's clay: 5 argil

potter's field: 8 Aceldama, cemetery

potter's wheel: 4 disk 5 lathe, palet, throw 6 jigger, pallet

pottery: 4 bank, ware 5 china, delft 7 Keramos(F.) 8 ceramics 9 delftware, Keramikos(Gr.), stoneware 11 earthenware

civilization: 6 Minyan

decorating paste: 9 barbotine

dish: 7 ramekin

enameled: 8 majolica

firing box: 6 saggar, sagger 7 saggard

fragment: 5 shard, sherd

kind: uda(Ind.) 4 delf 5 delft 6 basalt 7 aretine, bocraro 8 bucchero, Majolica, vitreous 9 delftware, sigillate 12 buccheronero

maker: 6 potter 8 ceramist

mineral: 8 feldspar

pert. to: 7 ceramic

pottle: 6 liquor 7 tankard 10 half-gallon

potty: 5 crazy, dotty, petty 6 little 7 foolish, haughty, trivial 8 snobbish 9 eccentric 12 supercilious

pouch: bag, cod, pod, sac 4 cyst, sack 5 bulge, bursa, purse 6 budget, gipser, pocket, sporan 7 alforja, gipsire, mailbag, saccule, silicle, sporran 9 spleuchan 10 pocketbook

abdominal: 9 marsupium

Highlander's: 7 sporran

pouch bone: 9 marsupial

pouched: 9 sacculate

dog: 4 wolf

marmot: 8 squirrel 11 spermophile

pouf: 4 bang, puff 5 quilt 7 ottoman 9 hairdress

poule: 6 wanton 10 prostitute

poulp, poulpe: 7 octopus

poultice: 7 plaster 8 compress, dressing 9 cataplasm

poultry: 4 fowl 5 ducks, geese, quail 7 pigeons, turkeys 8 chickens 9 partridge, pheasants 10 guinea fowl

breed: 6 Ancona 7 Dorking, Leghorn 12 Plymouth Rock 14 Rhode-Island Red

dealer: 6 eggler

disease: pip 4 roup

dish: 9 galantine

farm: 7 hennery

yard: 6 barton

pounamu: 4 jade 8 nephrite 10 greenstone

pounce: nab 4 leap, pink, poke, stab 5 pound, prick, punch, stamp, swoop, talon 6 emboss, spring, thrust 8 ornament 9 comminute, perforate

pound: 4 bang, bash, beat, bray, ding, maul, pond, tamp, unit 5 knock, thump 6 bruise, buffet, hammer, powder, wallop, weight 7 contuse 8 malleate 9 enclosure, pulverize

poundage: 6 charge, weight 8 distrain 9 constrain, enclosure 11 confinement

pour: 4 emit, flow, gush, hale, lash, lave, pass, rain, teem, tide, toom(Sc.), vent, well 5 birle, drain, empty, flood, heald, hield, issue, spout, utter 6 affuse, decant, deluge, effuse, libate, sluice, stream 8 downpour 9 discharge

pourboire: fee, tip 7 douceur 8 gratuity 9 buona-mani(pl.), buona-mano

pout: bib, mop 4 moue, sulk 5 boody, bulge, pique 7 catfish, eelpout 8 bullhead 9 sulkiness

poverty: 4 lack, need, want 6 dearth, penury 7 paucity, tenuity 8 scarcity 9 indigence 10 inadequacy, scantiness 11 destitution, inferiority

program: 5 Vista

stricken: 9 penurious

powder: 4 abir(Ind.), dust, kish, mull, talc 5 boral, boron, flour, grind 6 empasm, pollen, pounce, yttria 7 araroba, aristol, malarin, saponin, tripoli 8 cosmetic, sprinkle, tannigen 9 pulverize 10 epiplastic

abrasive: 5 emery

case: 9 bandolier

container: 4 horn 7 arsenal 8 magazine

make: 4 bray 5 grind 7 calcine 9 pulverize

poisonous: 4 antu 5 robin

sachet: 6 pulvil

smokeless: 6 filite, poudre 7 cordite 8 amberite

powdered: 4 seme 5 semee 6 floury

power: arm, art, vis 4 bulk, dint, gift, hand, iron, rial, sway, thew 5 force, might, state, steam, vigor, vires(pl.), wield 6 agency, effort, empire, energy, foison, throne, weight 7 ability, command, control, mastery, potence, potency, stamina 8 capacity, efficacy, function, momentum, strength, virility 9 authority, dominator, influence, intensity, puissance 10 domination, efficiency 11 sovereignty 12 jurisdiction, potentiality

deprive of: 4 maim 7 impeach 8 dethrone 12 depariliament

intellectual: wit 5 brain 6 genius

lack: 5 atony

natural: 4 odyl 5 odyle

partnership: 9 champerty

provide with: 5 endue, endow

reduction: 8 brownout

superior: 10 prepotency 12 predominance

symbol: 5 sword 7 scepter, sceptre

third: 4 cube

unit of: RPM 4 watt

unlimited: 11 omnipotence

power of attorney: 5 agent 10 procurator

powerboat: 5 yacht 9 motorboat

powerful: 4 able, bold, deep 5 stout 6 brawny, cogent, heroic, strong 7 feckful, leonine, weighty 8 puissant 9 effective, effectual 10 dominating 11 efficacious

powerless: 4 weak 6 feeble, supine, unable 7 passive 8 helpless, impotent, inactive, lifeless

Powhatan: *daughter:* 10 Pocahontas

powwow: 4 talk 6 confer, priest 7 meeting 8 assembly, ceremony, congress, conjurer 10 conference

poyou: 6 peludo 9 armadillo

prabble: 7 chatter, quarrel 8 squabble

prabhu: 4 lord 5 chief 6 writer

practic: 6 artful, shrewd 7 cunning, skilled 8 decision(Sc.) 9 practical, practiced

practical: 5 handy, utile 6 actual, beaten, usable, useful 7 practic, working 8 feasible, possible, workable 9 available, pragmatic, realistic 11 pragmatical, utilitarian

example: 6 praxis

joke: 4 hoax 5 prank, trick 7 waggery

practically: 6 almost, nearly 9 virtually 13 substantially

practice: do; ply, rut, try, use 4 mode, plot, rote 5 apply, canon, cause, drill, habit, trade, train, usage 6 custom, follow, praxic, system 7 perform, process 8 exercise, intrigue, rehearse 9 construct, negotiate, procedure 10 experience

pert. to: 9 pragmatic

sharp: 4 game 5 dodge, fraud, usury 6 deceit 9 chicanery

practiced: 7 skilled, veteran 10 conversant

practitioner: 5 agent 6 artist, doctor, healer, lawyer, novice 7 learner, plotter, schemer 8 civilian 9 assistant

prad: 5 horse

praenomen: 4 name 5 Caius, Gaius, Titus 9 first-name

pragmatic: 7 skilled 8 busybody, dogmatic, meddling 9 conceited, empirical, officious, practical, realistic 10 meddlesome, systematic 11 dictatorial, opinionated, pragmatical

Prague: 4 Prag 5 Praha

river: 6 Moldau, Vltava

prairie: bay 5 camas, llano, plain 6 camass, steppe 7 quamash 9 grassland

clump of trees in: 5 motte

mud: 5 gumbo

plant: 5 camas 6 camass

prairie anemone: 12 pasqueflower

prairie antelope: 9 pronghorn

prairie apple: 9 breadroot

prairie berry: 9 trompillo 10 nightshade

prairie breaker: 4 plow

prairie chicken: 6 grouse

prairie crocus: 12 pasqueflower

prairie dog: 5 gopher, marmot 11 wishton-wish

prairie dog weed: 8 marigold

prairie pigeon: 6 plover 9 sandpiper

prairie potato: 9 breadroot

prairie schooner: ark 12 covered wagon

Prairie State: 8 Illinois

prairie wolf: 6 coyote

prairieweed: 10 cinquefoil

praise: 4 hery, laud, tout 5 adore, allow, alose, bless, cry up, extol, glory, honor, kudos, roosa, roose 6 eulogy, extoll, kudize 7 acclaim, adulate, applaud, commend, encomia(pl.), glorify, hosanna, magnify, plaudit, tribute 8 applause, appraise, blessing, encomium, eulogize, macarism 9 adulation, celebrate, intensify, panegyric 10 compliment, panegyrize 11 approbation 12 commendation 13 glorification

ascription of: 6 Gloria

praiseworthy: 9 exemplary, meritorious 13 complimentary

Prakrit: 4 Pali 7 Bahlika 8 language 11 Dakshinatya

praline: 5 candy 10 confection

pram: 4 cart 5 barge 8 carriage, pushcart, stroller 12 baby carriage, perambulator

prance: 5 brank, caper, dance, strut 6 cavort, frolic, sashay 7 swagger

prank: jig 4 dido, fold, lark, prat, whim 5 adorn, antic, caper, freak, pleat, shine, trick 6 curvet, fegary, frolic, gambol, caprice, dress up 8 capricci(pl.), escapade, mischief 9 capriccio 11 monkeyshine

prase: 6 quartz 10 chalcedony

prat: 4 push 5 nudge, prank, trick 8 buttocks

prate: gab 4 blab, buck, bukh, carp, chat, talk 5 blate, boast, clack, clash 6 babble, claver, tattle, tongue 7 blatter, chatter, deblate, prattle, twaddle 8 harangue 11 deblaterate

prattle: 4 gaff, lisp 5 prate 6 cackle 7 blather, blether, clatter 9 bavardage 11 confabulate

prawn: 6 shrimp 10 crustacean

praxis: 5 habit 6 action, custom 8 practice

pray: ask, beg, bid, sue 5 daven(Heb.) 6 appeal, invite, invoke 7 beseech, conjure, entreat, implore, request 8 petition 10 supplicate

praya: 4 road 5 beach 6 strand 9 esplanade 10 waterfront

prayer: ave 4 bead, bede, bene, boon, plea, suit 5 grace, matin 6 appeal, ectene, ektene, errand, orison 7 Angelus, bidding, collect, complin, gayatri, oration, request, savitri 8 compline, entreaty, petition 9 competory, precation, suppliant 10 paratheses(pl.), parathesis, requiescat 11 application, benediction, paternoster 12 intercession, supplication

beads: 6 rosary

call: 4 adan, azan, bell 5 chime 6 oremus

chancery: 7 relator

day's last: **7** complin **8** compline

for the dead: **7** kaddish, requiem

form of: **5** chant **6** litany

group: **12** comprecation

nine-day: **6** novena

set: **9** akoluthia

short: **5** grace **11** benediction

prayer book: 6 missal, portas, ritual **7** brevary, portass **9** porthouse

prayer desk: 8 prie-dieu

prayer rug: 5 asana

prayer shawl: 5 orale **7** tallith

prayer tower: 5 minaret

praying figure: 5 orant

preach: 4 sugh **5** sough, teach **6** exhort, inform **8** advocate, homilize, instruct, moralize, proclaim **9** discourse, predicate, sermonize **10** concionate, evangelize

preacher: 6 parson, rector **8** minister **9** clergyman, predicant, pulpiteer

preachment: 6 sermon **7** lecture **9** discourse **11** exhortation

preachy: 8 didactic **10** moralistic

preamble: 7 preface **12** introduction

prebend: 4 land **5** tithe **7** stipend **8** benefice **9** allowance

prebendary: 5 canon

precarious: 5 risky **7** assumed, dubious **8** delicate, doubtful, insecure, perilous, unstable **9** dangerous, hazardous, uncertain, unsettled **10** touch-and-go **11** unwarranted

precative: 10 beseeching **12** supplicating

precaution: 4 care **6** cautel **7** caution **8** prudence

precede: 4 lead, pace, rank **5** usher **6** forego **7** forerun, outrank, predate, preface **8** antecede, antedate **9** introduce **10** foreshadow

precedence: pas **8** priority

right: pas

precedent: 5 model, usage **7** example **8** decision, standard

preceding: 5 first **6** before **8** anterior

precentor: 6 cantor

precept: law **4** hest, rule, tora, writ **5** adage, axiom, breve, brief, dogma, maxim, order, sutra, tenet, torah **6** behest, lesson **7** caution, command, mandate **8** doctrine, document, teaching **9** direction, principle **10** injunction **11** commandment, fundamental, instruction

perceptive: 8 didactic **9** mandatory **11** instructive

preceptor: 5 tutor **6** master

precinct: 4 beat **5** ambit, bound **6** hieron **7** temenos **8** boundary, district, environs **9** enclosure

precious: 4 dear, nice, rare, very **5** chere(F.), loved **6** costly, valued **7** beloved, genteel **8** affected, esteemed, favorite, valuable **9** extremely **10** fastidious **11** inestimable, overrefined

precious stone: See gem

precipice: lin **4** crag, drop, linn, pali, scar **5** bluff, brink, cliff, steep **7** clogwyn **8** downfall **9** declivity

precipitate: 4 fall, floc, hurl, rash **5** hasty, heady, hurry, speed, steep, throw **6** abrupt, effect, hasten, madcap, sudden, tumble, unwary **7** hurried, willful **8** headlong, sediment, settling, slapdash **9** desperate, impetuous, impulsive **11** precipitous

precipitation: 4 dew **4** hail, mist, rain, snow **5** haste, sleet **7** downpour **9** hastening **10** deposition **11** impetuosity **12** acceleration

precipitous: 5 sheer, steep **6** steepy **7** prerupt

rock: **4** crag, scar **5** steep

precis: 7 epitome, summary **8** abstract **10** compendium **11** abridgement

precise: 4 even, nice, prim, very **5** exact, rigid, stiff **6** formal, minute, strict **7** buckram, certain, correct, finicky, literal, starchy **8** accurate, definite, delicate, explicit, overnice, priggish, specific **9** faultless, stringent, veracious **10** ceremonial, fastidious, particular, scrupulous **11** ceremonious, on the button, painstaking, punctilious **14** circumstantial

preclude: bar **4** quit, stop **5** avert, close, debar, estop **6** forbid, hinder, impede **7** obviate, prevent **9** foreclose **11** discontinue

precocious: 5 early **6** unripe **7** forward **8** advanced **9** premature

preconceive: 5 dream **6** ideate, scheme **7** foreknow

precursor: 5 usher **6** herald **8** ancestor, foregoer **9** harbinger, messenger **10** forefather, forerunner **11** predecessor

precursory: 11 preliminary, premonitory **12** introductory

predatory: 7 harmful, robbing **8** ravenous **9** pillaging, piratical, rapacious, raptorial **10** plundering, predacious

bird: owl **4** hawk **5** eagle

insect: **6** mantis

predestine: 4 doom, fate **6** decree, ordain **7** destine, predoom **8** foredoom **9** determine, forepoint, preordain **10** foreordain **12** predetermine

predetermine: 4 bias **6** decree **7** destine, predict **8** forecast **9** prejudice **10** prepossess

predicament: box, fix **4** hole, stew **5** state **6** pickle, plight, scrape **7** dilemma, in a bind **8** quandary **9** condition, situation

predicant: 5 friar **8** preacher **9** dominican

predicate: cry 4 aver, base 5 imply 6 affirm, assert, preach 7 commend, declare, foresee, involve, predict 8 foretell, proclaim

predict: 4 bode, call, dope, omen 5 augur, guess, weird 6 divine, halsen 7 forbode, presage, presume, suppose 8 forebode, forecast, prophesy, soothsay 9 auspicate, predicate 13 prognosticate

prediction: 5 weird 7 bodword 12 forespeaking, vaticination

predictor: 4 seer 7 prophet

predilection: 4 bent, bias 7 leaning 8 fondness, tendency 9 prejudice 10 partiality, preference, propensity 11 inclination 14 predisposition, susceptibility

predisposed: 5 prone 6 biased 7 partial, willing

predisposition: 7 leaning 12 predilection

predominant: 5 chief 6 ruling 8 dominant, reigning, superior 9 ascendant, ascendent, hegemonic, prevalent 10 dominating, noticeable, prevailing 11 controlling, outstanding 12 preponderant

predominate: 4 rule 6 domine, exceed 8 domineer

preeminent: big 4 star 5 chief, grand 7 capital, palmary, ranking, supreme 8 dominant, superior 9 excellent, prominent 10 surpassing 11 outstanding

preempt: 5 usurp 8 arrogate 9 establish 10 monopolize 11 appropriate

preen: pin, sew 4 perk, trim 5 adorn, clasp, dress, plume, press, pride, primp, prink, prune 6 bodkin, brooch, smooth, spruce, stitch

preface: 5 front, proem 6 herald 7 forerun, precede, prelude 8 exordium, foreword, preamble, prologue 9 introduce 11 preliminary 12 forespeaking, introduction, introductory

prefect, praefect: 4 dean 7 monitor, officer 8 director, minister, official 9 president 10 magistrate

prefecture: 7 eparchy(Gr.) 8 district

prefer: opt 4 like 5 elect, favor 6 choose, desire, favour, rather, select 7 advance, propose

preferable: 6 better

preference: 6 choice 8 appetite, priority 10 partiality 11 advancement, alternative 12 predilection

prefigure: 4 type 6 ideate, typify 7 forerun 8 foretell 9 adumbrate 10 foreshadow

prefix: See list page 825

pregnable: 10 assailable, expugnable, vulnerable 11 conquerable

pregnancy: 6 cyesis 9 fertility, gestation

pregnant: big 5 heavy 6 gravid 7 fertile, teeming, weighty 8 enceinte, fruitful, prolific 9 abounding, gestating, potential, with child 10 expressive, germinable

prehend: 5 catch, seize

prehistoric: 10 immemorial

preindicate: 7 presage 8 announce, prophesy

prejudice: 4 bent, bias, harm, hurt 6 damage, hatred, impair 7 bigotry, leaning 9 suspicion 10 partiality, prepossess 11 inclination, intolerance 12 disadvantage, jaundiced eye, predetermine, predilection, prejudgement 13 prejudication

prejudicial: 7 harmful 8 contrary 9 injurious 11 contrarious, detrimental 14 discriminatory

prelate: 4 head 5 chief 6 abbess, bishop, priest 7 primate 8 ordinary, superior 9 dignitary 10 archbishop 12 ecclesiastic

prelector: 6 reader 8 lecturer 9 professor 10 discourser

preliminary: 5 basic, prior 7 preface 8 entrance, previous, proemial 9 elemental, inductive, prefatory, threshold 10 antecedent 11 fundamental, preparatory

prelude: 6 verset 7 descant, intrada, opening, preface 8 overture, ritornel 10 ritornelle 12 introduction

premature: 5 early 6 unripe 8 immature, untimely 10 precocious 12 unseasonable

premeditate: See meditate

premeditation: 11 forethought 12 aforethought

premier: 5 chief, first 7 leading 8 earliest, foremost 9 principal

premise: 6 ground 9 postulate 10 assumption 11 proposition, supposition

premium: 4 agio 5 bonus, prize, spiff 6 bounty, deport, reward 8 lagnappe, superior 9 lagniappe 10 recompense

premonition: 4 omen 5 hunch 6 notice 7 bodword, warning 9 forescent 10 foreboding 11 forewarning, information 12 apprehension, presentiment

preoccupied: 4 lost, rapt 6 absent, filled 8 absorbed 9 engrossed

preordain: 10 predestine

preparation: 5 array 7 extract, product 8 cosmetic, training 9 condiment, decoction 9 makeready, rehearsal 10 confection 11 arrangement 12 introduction

place of: 10 laboratory, paratorium

without: 5 ad lib 8 careless 9 extempore, impromptu

prepare: arm, fit, fix, get, set 4 bush, busk, gibe, gird, make, pave, suit, tibe 5 adapt, alert, coach, curry, dight, dower, equip, ettle, frame, groom, prime, ready, train 6 adjust, devise, graith, make up 7 address, affaite(F.), apparel, arrange, concoct, confect, dispose, furnish, provide, qualify **8** accustom, compound, instruct, rehearse **9** calculate, condition, construct **10** concinnate **11** set the stage

for the press: **4** edit **6** redact, revise

prepared: apt **4** yare **5** ready

prepaschal period: **4** Lent

prepense: **8** designed **11** forethought **12** aforethought, premeditated

preponderance: **6** weight **8** majority **9** dominance, supremacy **10** ascendancy, ascendency, prevalence **12** predominance

preponderate: **4** rule, sink **7** incline, surpass

prepossess: **4** bias **7** prevent **12** predetermine

prepossessing: **10** attractive

prepossession: **4** bent, bias **9** prejudice **10** absorption **11** inclination **12** predilection **14** predisposition

preposterous: **6** absurd, screwy **7** foolish **9** grotesque, senseless **10** irrational, ridiculous **11** extravagant, nonsensical

preppy: **6** trendy **7** current **9** the latest

prerequisite: **8** essential, postulate

prerogative: **5** right **8** appanage, immunity, priority **9** exemption, privilege **10** precedence

eldest son's: **6** esnecy

prerupt: **5** steep **11** precipitous

presage: **4** bode, omen, osse, sign **5** augur, token **6** augury, betide, divine, import **7** bespeak, betoken, forbode, meaning, portend, portent, predict, warning **8** announce, forebode, foretell, indicate, prophecy, prophesy **9** foretoken, harbinger **10** foreboding, prediction, prognostic **11** foreknowing, preindicate **12** apprehension, presentiment **13** prognosticate

presbyter: **5** elder **6** priest **7** prester **8** minister **9** clergyman

presbytery: **5** court **7** council, rectory **9** residence

prescience: **9** foresight **11** omniscience **13** foreknowledge

prescind: **6** detach **7** isolate **8** abstract, separate

prescribe: fix, set **5** allot, guide, limit, order **6** assign, define, direct, ordain, outlaw **7** appoint, command, control, dictate, lay down **9** prescript **10** invalidate

prescribed: set **5** basic **6** thetic **9** formulary

prescript: law **7** command, mandate

prescription: **6** recipe **7** formula

presence: **4** mien **5** being **6** aspect, spirit **7** bearing, company, dignity, seeming, spectre **8** assembly **9** influence **10** apparition, appearance, attendance, deportment

present: now **4** boon, gift, give, here **5** adsum(L.), being, bonus, cuddy, grant, nonce, offer, ready, today **6** adduce, allege, bestow, bounty, confer, donate, render, tender **7** cumshaw, display, exhibit, largess, perform **8** donation, gratuity, lagnappe **9** collected, introduce, lagniappe, personate **10** exhibition, here and now **11** benefaction, efficacious

again: **5** rerun

pert. to: **6** modern **7** current **12** contemporary

to guest or stranger: **6** xenium

with another: **8** collocal

presentable: fit **6** decent, proper **11** appropriate, respectable

present-day: **7** current **12** contemporary

presentiment: **10** foreboding **11** disquietude, premonition **12** apprehension

presently: **4** anon, enow, soon **6** by and by **7** shortly **8** directly **9** forthwith **11** immediately

preservation: **6** saving **7** defense **11** safekeeping

preservative: **4** salt **5** borax, brine, spice, sugar **7** alcohol, vinegar **8** creosote **12** conservative

preserve: can, dry, jam, tin **4** corn, cure, keep, salt, save **5** bless, guard, jelly, spare, store, uvate **6** athold, comfit, defend, govern, keep up, retain, secure, shield, uphold **7** compote, condite, confect, forfend, protect, succade, sustain **8** conserve, forefend, maintain **9** confiture, safeguard

preside: run **5** chair **6** direct **7** control, oversee **8** moderate, regulate **9** supervise

president: mir **4** head **5** ruler **8** governor **9** sovereign

successor: **9** designado(Mex.)

President (U.S.): (1, 1789-97) George Washington; (2, 1797-1801) John Adams; (3, 1801-09) Thomas Jefferson; (4, 1809-17) James Madison; (5, 1817-25) James Monroe; (6, 1825-29) John Quincy Adams; (7, 1829-37) Andrew Jackson; (8, 1837-41) Martin Van Buren; (9, 1841) William Henry Harrison; (10, 1841-45) John Tyler; (11, 1845-49) James K. Polk; (12, 1849-50) Zachary Taylor; (13, 1850-53) Millard Fillmore; (14, 1853-57) Franklin Pierce; (15, 1857-61) James Buchanan; (16, 1861-65) Abraham Lincoln, (17, 1865-69) Andrew Johnson; (18, 1869-77) Ulysses S. Grant; (19, 1877-81) Rutherford B. Hayes; (20, 1881) James A. Garfield; (21, 1881-85) Chester A. Arthur; (22, 1885-89) Grover Cleveland; (23, 1889-93) Benjamin Harrison; (24, 1893-97)

Grover Cleveland; (25, 1897-1901) William McKinley; (26, 1901-09) Theodore Roosevelt; (27, 1909-13) William H. Taft; (28, 1913-21) Woodrow Wilson; (29, 1921-23) Warren G. Harding; (30, 1923-29) Calvin Coolidge; (31, 1929-33) Herbert Hoover; (32, 1933-45) Franklin D. Roosevelt; (33, 1945-53) Harry S Truman; (34, 1953-61) Dwight D. Eisenhower; (35, 1961-63) John F. Kennedy; (36, 1963-69) Lyndon B. Johnson; (37, 1969-74) Richard M. Nixon; (38, 1974-77) Gerald R. Ford; (39, 1977-81) Jimmy Carter; (40, 1981-) Ronald Reagan

last name: 4 Ford, Polk, Taft 5 Adams, Grant, Hayes, Nixon, Tyler 6 Arthur, Carter, Hoover, Monroe, Pierce, Reagan, Taylor, Truman, Wilson 7 Harding, Jackson, Johnson, Kennedy, Lincoln, Madison 8 Buchanan, Coolidge, Fillmore, Garfield, Harrison, McKinley, Van Buren 9 Cleveland, Jefferson, Roosevelt 10 Eisenhower, Washington

nickname: Abe, Cal, FDR, Ike 5 Teddy

presignify: 7 presage 8 intimate 9 foretoken

press: hug, jam 4 bale, bear, bind, cram, dint, iron, mash, push, spur, thew, urge 5 brize, brizz, chest, chirt, crowd, crush, drive, force, knead, preen, serry, wring 6 compel, crunch, impact, squash, roller, smooth, throng 7 armoire, embrace, entreat, express, flatten, impress, imprint, scrunge, smasher, squeeze 8 calender, compress, pressure, straiten, wardrobe 9 constrain, embarrass, emphasize, importune 10 constipate, newspapers

corrector: 11 proofreader

critic: 6 censor

press agent: 5 flack

press down: 4 quat, tamp

pressed: 5 dense 7 compact, serried

presser: 5 baler 6 ironer, mangle

of skins: 7 sammier

pressing: 4 dire 5 acute 6 urgent 7 burning, crucial, exigent 8 exacting 9 imperious 10 imperative 11 importunate

pressman: pig 7 printer

pressure: 4 heat, push 5 force 6 duress, stress 7 bearing, squeeze 8 exigency, instancy 10 affliction, constraint, impression, oppression 11 compression

equal: 8 isobaric

gauge: 9 barometer, manometer, manoscope

unit: 4 atmo, dyne 5 barad 7 mesobar

using: 11 arm-twisting

pressure group: 5 lobby

pressure measuring instrument: 10 piezometer

prester: 4 vein 5 snake 6 priest 7 serpent 9 hurricane, presbyter, whirlwind

prestidigitator: 6 palmer 7 juggler 8 conjurer, magician, pythonic

prestige: 4 sway 6 renown, status 7 sorcery 8 eminence, illusion 9 deception, influence 10 importance, prominence

presto: 4 fast 7 passing, quickly 8 suddenly 11 immediately 13 instantaneous

presumably: 6 likely 8 probably 9 assumably 10 ostensibly, supposedly

presume: 5 guess 6 impose 7 daresay, suppose, venture 8 arrogate 9 postulate 10 conjecture, presuppose

presumptuous: 4 bold, smug 5 brash, fresh, pushy 6 uppity 7 forward, haughty, icarian 8 arrogant, assuming, familiar, impudent, insolent 9 audacious, confident, foolhardy 11 adventurous, venturesome

presuppose: 5 posit 6 assume

pretend: act 4 pose, seem, sham 5 claim, feign 6 affect, allege, assume, gammon 7 profess 8 disguise, simulate 10 conjecture 11 dissimulate, make-believe

pretended: 4 fake 5 false 7 alleged, colored, reputed 8 coloured, intended, proposed 10 fictitious, ostensible

pretender: fop 4 fake, idol, snob 5 cowan(Sc.), faker, quack 6 poseur, seemer 8 aspirant, claimant, deceiver, impostor 9 charlatan 10 mountebank 11 fourflusher 12 dissimulator

pretense, pretence: act, peg 4 brag, cant, flam, mask, plea, ruse, sham, show 5 claim, cloak, cover, feint, gloze, study, trick 6 excuse, humbug, tinsel 7 charade, fiction, grimace, pageant, potiche, pretext 8 artifice, disguise, occasion 9 deception, moonshine, semblance 10 appearance, assumption, pretension, subterfuge 11 affectation, fabrication, make-believe, ostentation 13 stalkinghorse

pretentious: big 4 arty 5 gaudy, showy 6 turgid 7 pompous 8 affected, assuming 10 flamboyant 12 highfaluting, ostentatious

pretermit: 4 omit 6 ignore 7 neglect, suspend 8 intermit 9 disregard, interrupt

preternatural: 6 gousty 7 goustie 8 abnormal, uncommon 9 irregular 12 supernatural

pretext: 4 mask 6 excuse 8 pretense

pretty: gay, toy 4 cute, deft, fair, gent, joli 5 bonny, jolie, lindo(Sp.) 6 bonita, bonnie, clever, comely 7 cunning, dollish 8 betcheri, budgeree, handsome, skillful, somewhat 9 beautiful, ingenious 10 attractive, knickknack, moderately

prevail: win 4 rule 5 reign 6 induce, ob-

tain 7 conquer, persist, succeed, triumph 8 dominate 11 predominate
upon: 4 urge 6 allure, induce 7 entreat 8 persuade 9 influence

prevalent: 4 rife 6 common, potent, wonted 7 current, general 8 dominant, powerful 9 extensive 10 prevailing, successful, victorious, widespread 11 efficacious, influential

prevaricate: fib, lie 5 evade 6 garble 7 quibble, shuffle 10 equivocate 12 misrepresent

prevarication: lie 10 subterfuge

prevent: bar, gag, let 4 balk, bind, save, stop, ward, warn 5 avert, debar, deter, estop 6 defend, forlet, hinder, impede, resist, thwart 7 forfend, impeach, obviate, prevent, rule out 8 antevert, forefend, preclude, prohibit, restrain, stave off 9 foreclose, forestall, frustrate 10 anticipate, circumvent
by law: 5 estop

preventive: 12 prophylactic 13 precautionary

previous: ere 4 erst, fore, past 5 early, prior, supra 6 before, bygone, former 7 earlier 8 anterior, foregone, untimely 9 foregoing, preceding, premature 10 antecedent, beforehand, heretofore 11 unwarranted

prevision: 8 forecast 9 foresight 10 prediction, prescience, prevoyance 13 foreknowledge 15 prognostication

prewar: 10 antebellum

prey: 4 feed, game 5 booty, raven, ravin, seize, spoil 6 quarry, ravage, ravine, victim 7 capture, plunder 8 underdog 9 victimize
living on: 9 predatory

prey upon: 4 feed 5 seize 6 devour 9 victimize, deprecate

Priam: 10 King of Troy
daughter: 6 Creusa 8 Polyxena 9 Cassandra
grandfather: 4 Ilus
servant: 7 Agelaus
son: 5 Paris 6 Hector 7 Helenus, Troilus
slayer: 7 Pyrrhus
wife: 6 Hecuba

price: fee, tab 4 cost, fare, fiar(Sc.), fier(Sc.), hire, rate 5 cheap, value, worth 6 charge, ransom, reward 7 expense 8 appraise, evaluate 10 estimation, excellence 12 preciousness 13 consideration
maintain: peg
reduced: 4 sale 7 bargain
rising: 4 boom 9 inflation

priceless: 4 rare 6 absurd, costly, unique 7 amusing 8 valuable 9 unsalable 10 invaluable 11 inestimable

prick: dot, jag 4 brod, brog, cloy, drob,

goad, jagg, ping, pink, prod, stab, tang, urge 5 briar, point, smart, spine, sting, thorn 6 broach, cactus, incite, nettle, pierce, skewer, tingle 7 bramble, pricker, prickle 8 puncture 9 perforate, stimulate

prick song: 7 descant

pricket: 4 buck 5 spike 11 candlestick

pricking: 8 poignant

prickle: 4 barb, seta 5 setae(pl.) 6 basket 7 acantha, aculeus, spicula(pl.) 8 spiculum

prickly: 5 burry 8 echinate
animal: 8 hedgehog 9 porcupine
plant: 6 cactus, nettle
seed coat: 4 bur 4 burr
shrub: 4 rose 5 briar

prickly heat: 4 rash 6 lichen 8 eruption

prickly pear: 4 tuna 5 nopal 6 cactus 7 opuntia

pride: 5 glory, pique, plume, valor 6 egoism, esteem, spirit, vanity 7 conceit, dignity, disdain, egotism, elation, hauteur, respect 8 nobility, splendor, valiancy 9 arrogance, cockiness, insolence, loftiness 10 lordliness, self-esteem 11 amour propre, haughtiness, self-conceit, self-respect 12 independence 13 selfassurance 15 self-approbation 16 superciliousness

Pride and Prejudice: *author:* 6 Austen
character: 5 Darcy 9 Elizabeth

prier, pryer: 8 busybody 10 inquisitor

priest: fra 4 abbe, club, cura, cure(F.), imam, lama, papa(It.), pere(F.) 5 clerk, druid, hotar(Ind.), imaum, mulla, padre(Sp.), rabbi, sarip, vicar 6 bhikku, bishop, cleric, dastur, divine, father, gallah(Heb.), mullah, oblate, rector, shaman, vestal, wahabi 7 cassock, destour, dustoor, prester, tuhunga, wahhabi 8 minister 9 clergyman, dignitary, oratorian, priesteen 10 chancellor, hierophant, priestling 12 ecclesiastic
army: 5 padre 8 chaplain
assistant: 7 acolyte
cap: 7 biretta
garment: alb 4 cope, robe 5 ephod, habit 8 scapular 9 vestments
habit ornament: 4 urim
headdress: 9 saghavart
high: Eli 5 Aaron 7 pontiff, prelate
neckpiece: 5 amice, stole
pert. to: 10 sacerdotal
scarf: 5 rabat 7 maniple
server: 7 acolyte
surplice: 5 ephod
voodoo: 5 mambu 6 hungan 7 gangang

priestly: 8 hieratic 10 sacerdotal

prig: beg, fop, pan 4 buck, prim 5 dandy, filch, plead, prink, prude, steal, thief 6 haggle, pilfer, purist, tinker 7 bargain, entreat, pitcher 8 pilferer 9 precision 10 pickpocket

priggish: 4 prim, smug 8 thievish 10 complacent 11 overprecise

prill: 4 rill 6 button, nugget, pellet, stream

prim: mim, set 4 neat, nice 5 stiff 6 demure, formal, proper, wooden 7 correct, genteel, precise, prudish 8 accurate, decorous 9 bluenosed 10 ceremonial

prima donna: 4 diva, lead, star 6 singer 7 actress

prima facie: 11 self-evident

primary: 4 main 5 chief, first, prime 6 primal 7 capital, central, initial 8 earliest, original, primeval, pristine 9 elemental, primitive, principal 10 elementary, pre-eminent, primordial 11 fundamental

primate: ape, man 5 lemur, orang 6 bishop, monkey 8 marmoset 9 orangutan 10 anthropoid, archbishop 11 orangutang

prime: 4 best, size 5 coach 7 morning, prepare, primary, provoke 9 copacetic, excellent, undercoat
of life: 5 bloom 6 heyday

prime minister: 7 premier

primer: 8 hornbook, textbook 11 abecedarium

primeval: 6 primal 7 ancient, ogygian 8 original, pristine 9 primitive

primitive: 5 basic, crude, first, rough 6 simple 7 ancient, archaic, primary, priscan, radical 8 barbaric, original, pristine 9 elemental, underived 10 aboriginal, antiquated 11 uncivilized 12 old-fashioned

primordial: 5 early, first 7 primary 9 elemental 11 fundamental

primordium: bud 6 embryo, origin 8 rudiment

primp: 5 adorn, preen, prink, 7 dress up

primrose: 4 best 5 oxlip, spink(Sc.) 7 cowslip, primula 8 auricula
family: 11 primulaceae

primus: 5 first, stove

prince: bey, ras 4 amir, emir, raja, rial 5 alder, ameer, emeer, ruler 6 despot, dynast, satrap 7 dynasty, monarch 8 archduke 9 potentate, princekin, princelet, sovereign 10 princeling
allowance: 8 appanage
petty: 6 satrap 9 vergobret
pine: 10 pipsissewa
title: 6 serene

Prince Edward Island: *capital:* 13 Charlottetown
city: 8 Sherwood 10 Summerside
discoverer: 7 Cartier
former name: 9 Ile St. John
province of: 6 Canada
provincial flower: 12 lady's slipper

Prince of: *Apostles:* 8 St. Peter
Darkness: 5 devil, Satan 7 Ahriman 9 Beelzebub
Destruction: 6 Timour 9 Tamerlane
Evil Spirits: 7 Sammael
Liars: 5 Pinto
Peace: 7 Messiah
the Ode: 7 Ronsard
the Sonnet: 15 Joachim du Bellay

princedom: 4 rank 11 sovereignty 12 jurisdiction

princely: 5 grand, noble, regal, royal 6 kingly 7 stately 9 sovereign 10 munificent 11 magnificent

princeps: 4 head 5 first 7 headman 8 original

princess: 5 begum(Muslim), ranee(Muslim)
loved by Cupid: 6 Psyche
loved by Zeus: 6 Europa
mythological: 8 Atalanta

Princeton symbol: 5 tiger

principal: top 4 arch, head, high, main, star 5 chief, first grand, major, prime 6 leader, staple 7 capital, captain, chattel, leading, palmary, primary, stellar 8 cardinal, dominant, foremost 9 important, preceptor 10 headmaster 11 outstanding

principle: law 4 rule 5 axiom, canon, dicta(pl.), maxim, prana, tenet 6 dictum 7 brocard, essence, precept, theorum 8 doctrine 9 integrity 11 fundamental, uprightness
accepted: 5 axiom
embodiment: 6 avatar
first: ABC 4 base, seed 5 basis 8 rudiment
general: 9 generalia 12 generalities
statement: 5 credo, creed, motto
vital: 4 soul 5 anima
without: 6 amoral

principles: 5 creed 6 ethics 8 alphabet

princox: fop 7 coxcomb

prink: 4 deck, perk, wink 5 adorn, dress, preen, primp, prune 6 bedeck, glance, sashay

print: 4 copy, film 5 issue, stamp 6 fabric 7 edition, engrave, impress, publish 8 negative 9 engraving, newspaper 10 impression

printer: 4 type 8 letterer, pressman 9 linotyper 10 compositor 11 typographer 12 lithographer
aid: fly 5 devil
cross stroke: 5 serif
direction: cut 6 delete
emblem: 8 colophon

printing: *block:* 4 wood 7 edition 8 linoleum
blurred appearance: 5 macul
color: 17 chromolithography

error: pie 6 errata(pl.) 7 erratum

form: cut, die, mat 5 frame 6 matrix 7 matrice

implement: 5 burin 6 brayer, dabber, dauber

ink spreader: 6 brayer

mark: 4 dash, dele, list, stet 5 caret, obeli, tilde 6 dagger, diesis, obelus 7 obelisk 8 ellipses

measure: 4 pica 5 agate, empen

metal block: 4 quad

plate: 6 stereo 10 stereotype

press part: 6 platen, roller, rounce 7 frisket

process: 6 offset 7 braille, typeset 8 cerotype 10 photolitho 11 letterpress, lithography, rotogravure 14 photoengraving

second: 7 reissue

space block: 4 quad

system for the blind: 7 braille

type for spacing: 4 quad, slug

prion: 6 petrel

prionid: 6 beetle

prior: ere 4 fore, past 5 ahead, elder, until 6 before, former 7 earlier, forward 8 anterior, previous 9 preceding 10 antecedent 11 retroactive

priority: 5 order 8 position 9 privilege 10 ascendancy, precedence, preference 11 superiority

priory: 5 abbey 7 nunnery 8 cloister 9 monastery, sanctuary

priscan: 4 rare 7 ancient 9 primitive

prism: 5 block, nicol 8 cylinder, spectrum, wernicke

prism device: 8 iriscope

prismatic: 5 showy 9 brilliant 10 iridescent 12 orthorhombic

prison: gib, jug 4 brig, cell, gaol, hell, hole, jail, keep, quod, rock, stir 5 bagne, clink, grate 6 bagnio, carcel, carcer, cooler, lockup 7 Atlanta, Bocardo, college, dungeon, Gehenna, hoosgow, kidcote, Ludgate, Newgate, Spandau 8 Alcatraz, Bastille, Dartmoor, hoosegaw, hoosegow, Sing Sing 9 Bridewell, calaboose, enclosure, Old Bailey 10 guardhouse, panopticon, San Quentin 11 Leavenworth 12 penitentiary

guard: 5 screw

keeper: 5 guard 6 gaoler, jailer, jailor, keeper, warden 7 turnkey

naval or ship: 4 brig

room: 4 cell, hole, tank 7 dungeon 8 solitary

sentence: rap

spy: 6 mouton

prisoner: con 5 lifer 6 detenu(F.), inmate 7 caitiff, captive, convict, detenue(F.), parolee 9 collegian 10 emancipist 11 probationer

exchange agreement: 6 cartel

Prisoner of the Vatican: 4 Pope

prisoner of war: PW; P.O.W. 7 kriegie

prissy: 4 prim 5 fussy 7 finicky, precise, prudish 9 sissified 10 effeminate 11 over-refined

pristine: new 4 pure 5 early, fresh 7 ancient, primary 8 original 9 primitive, unspoiled, untouched 11 uncorrupted

pritch: 5 prick, spike, staff 6 pierce 9 perforate

privacy: 7 privity, retreat, secrecy 8 darkness, solitude 9 seclusion 10 penetralia 12 hugger-mugger

privado: 6 friend 8 intimate 9 confidant

private: 5 privy 6 closet, covert, hushed, inside, secret 7 soldier 8 esoteric, homefelt, intimate, personal, secluded, singular, solitary 10 unofficial 12 confidential, unpublicized

private eye: 6 tailer 7 gumshoe 9 detective, operative 12 investigator

privateer: 4 Kidd 5 caper 6 pirate 7 corsair, drumler 8 drumbler

privately: 5 aside 8 inwardly, secretly

privation: 4 loss, want 6 misery 7 absence, poverty 8 hardship 9 suffering 11 deprivation, destitution

privet: 5 hedge, ibota, shrub 7 alatern, ibolium 9 houseleek

privilege: law, soc, use 4 boon, soke 5 favor, grace, grant, right 6 favour, patent 7 charter, liberty 8 easement, immunity 9 advantage, allowance, exemption, franchise, vouchsafe 10 concession 11 prerogative

privy: 4 gong 5 biffy, jakes 6 cloaca, closet, hidden, secret, toilet 7 cloacae(pl.), furtive, private 8 familiar, intimate, out-house 9 backhouse, confidant, necessary 11 clandestine, water-closet 12 confidential 13 surreptitious

prix: 5 prize

prize: cup, pry 4 best, gree(Sc.), prix(F.), tern 5 award, bacon, booty, lever, medal, plate, purse, spoil, stake, value 6 esteem, glaive, reward, trophy 7 capture, premium, seizure 8 estimate, leverage, purchase, treasure 10 appreciate

prizefight: 4 bout, mill 5 match, scrap 7 contest 11 boxing match

ring: 5 arena

prized: 4 dear 5 chary 9 treasured

pro: for 4 with, whiz 6 expert 8 advocate, favoring 9 favouring, in favor of 12 professional

probability: 4 odds 6 chance 8 prospect 10 appearance, likelihood, likeliness 11 credibility

probable: 5 maybe 6 likely 8 apparent, credible, feasible

probably: 6 belike, likely 10 presumably

probation: 4 test 5 trial 6 parole 9 novitiate 11 examination

probe: 4 acus, tent, test 5 grope, query, sound 6 pierce, search seeker, stylet, tracer 7 examine, explore, feel out, inquiry 9 catechize, delve into, penetrate 10 ankylomele, instrument, scrutinize 11 exploration, investigate 13 investigation

probity: 7 honesty 8 goodness 9 integrity, rectitude 11 uprightness

problem: not, sum 4 crux, knot 5 hydra, issue, poser 6 enigma, puzzle, riddle 8 question 9 situation

problematical: 4 moot, open 8 doubtful 9 ambiguous, equivocal, uncertain, unsettled 12 questionable

proboscis: 4 nose 5 snout, trunk

proboscis monkey: 4 kaha

procacious: 4 pert, wise 8 impudent, insolent, petulant

Procas' son: 7 Amulius, Numitor

procavia: 5 hyrax 10 hyracoidea

procedure: 6 course, tactic 7 measure, process, program, routine

proceed: 4 fand, fare, move, pass, wend 5 arise, frame, issue 6 derive, spring 7 advance, emanate, forthgo 8 continue, progress 9 originate
    laboriously: mog 4 plod, plow, slog, wade 6 trudge
    rapidly: run 5 speed 6 gallop

proceeding: 4 acta(pl.), step 5 actum, doing 6 affair, afflux, course 7 conduct, measure, process 9 affluxion, procedure 11 transaction

proceeds: 4 loot 5 booty 6 income, profit, return 8 stealage

procerity: 6 height 8 tallness

process: 4 cook, writ 5 lapse, order 6 capias, course, manner, method, notice, system 7 advance, mandate, routine, summons 8 progress 9 operation, outgrowth, procedure, sterilize, technique 10 injunction

procession: 4 file 5 march, order 6 course, exequy, litany, parade 7 cortege, pageant 9 cavalcade, formation, recession

prochein: 4 next 7 nearest

proclaim: bid, cry 4 call, deem, show, toot, tout 5 blare, blast, blaze, claim, grede, knell, utter, voice 6 blazon, bounce, defame, herald, indict, outcry, preach 7 declare, divulge, enounce, publish 8 announce, denounce, forspeak 9 advertise, celebrate, enunciate, forespeak, ventilate 10 promulgate

proclamation: ban 4 bans, fiat 5 bando(Sp.), banns, blaze, edict, ukase 6 notice 7 bidding, placard 9 manifesto 11 declaration, publication 12 announce-

ment, annunciation, denunciation, notification, promulgation

proclivity: 4 bent 6 talent 7 leaning 10 propensity 11 disposition, inclination

Procne: *father:* 7 Pandion
    husband: 6 Tereus
    sister: 9 Philomela
    son: 4 Itys

procrastination: 5 delay, stall 9 deferment 10 cunctation, inactivity 12 dilatoriness, postponement

procreant: 8 fruitful 9 producing 10 generating

procreate: 4 sire 5 beget 6 father 7 produce 8 engender, generate 11 give birth to

procreation: 8 virility 9 offspring 10 generation, production

Procris: *father:* 10 Erechtheus
    husband and slayer: 8 Cephalus

proctor: 5 agent, proxy 7 monitor 8 advocate, attorney 9 supervise 10 supervisor

procumbent: 5 prone 8 prostate

procurable: 7 parable 10 accessible

procure: get 4 fang, find, gain 5 bring 6 effect, induce, obtain, secure, suborn 7 acquire, chevise, receive 8 contrive 9 impetrate

procurer: 4 bawd, pimp 8 purveyor

procuress: 4 bawd, hack 7 commode

prod: egg, jab 4 brog, goad poke, urge 5 pique 6 excite, incite, thrust 9 instigate, stimulate

prodigal: 5 flush 6 lavish 7 liberal, profuse, spender, wastrel 8 abundant, generous, wasteful 10 profligate, squanderer 11 extravagant, spendthrift, squandering

prodigious: 4 huge 5 giant 7 amazing, immense 8 enormous, gigantic 9 marvelous, monstrous, wonderful 10 portentous, tremendous 11 astonishing 13 extraordinary

prodigy: 4 omen, sign 6 marvel, ostent, wonder 7 miracle, portent 8 ceremony

prodition: 7 treason 8 betrayal 15 treacherousness

prodrome: 7 symptom

produce: 4 bear, form, give, grow, make, show 5 breed, carry, cause, shape, stage, yield 6 create, effect, fruits 7 exhibit, product 8 engender, generate 9 fabricate, offspring, procreate 10 bring about, production, vegetables 11 manufacture
    new: 6 create, invent 9 originate

producer: 6 author, farmer, grower, parent 7 creator 8 director 12 manufacturer

product: 4 item 5 fruit, yield 6 number, result 9 offspring, outgrowth

production: 4 work 5 fruit 6 output 11 performance

productive: 4 rich 6 active, parous 7 fertile 8 creative, fruitful, sonorous 10 generative 11 originative

proem: 7 preface, prelude 8 foreword, overture, preamble, prologue 12 introduction

profanation: 9 blasphemy, sacrilege, violation 10 desecration

profane: lay 4 foul 5 abuse 6 debase, defile, defoil, defoul, unholy, vulgar, wicked 7 godless, heathen, impious, obscene, secular, ungodly, violate, worldly 8 temporal 9 desecrate, vulgarize 10 irreverent, unhallowed 11 blasphemous 12 sacrilegious, unsanctified

profanity: 4 oath 5 curse 9 blasphemy

profess: own 4 avow 5 admit, claim 6 affect, affirm, allege, assert 7 confess, declare, pretend, protest 8 proclaim 11 acknowledge

profession: art, job 5 craft, faith, forte, trade 6 avowal, career, metier(F.) 7 calling 8 function, vocation 9 following 10 employment, occupation

professional: pro 4 paid 5 hired 6 expert 7 artiste, skilled, trained 8 finished

professor: don, fly 5 tutor 7 teacher 10 instructor

proffer: bid 4 give, hand 5 offer 6 extend, tender 8 proposal 11 countenance

proficiency: 5 skill 7 ability, advance, aptness 9 adeptness 10 capability, competence, efficiency, expertness 14 accomplishment

proficient: 6 actual, expert, master, versed 8 skillful 9 effective, effectual 10 conversant 11 crackerjack, experienced

profile: 4 form 6 figure 7 contour, drawing, outline 10 silhouette 14 representation

profit: net, pay, use 4 boot, gain, good, help, mend, nett 5 avail, frame, lucre, melon 6 behoof, return 7 account, benefit, bestead, revenue, utility 8 earnings, increase, interest, proceeds 9 advantage, emolument 12 remuneration

receiver of: 6 pernor

undercover: 4 loot 5 booty 6 payola

profitable: fat 8 repaying 9 expedient 12 advantageous

profitless: 9 fruitless 12 unprofitable

profligate: 6 rioter 7 corrupt, riotous, spender, vicious, wastrel 8 depraved, flagrant, prodigal, rakehell, wasteful 9 abandoned, dissolute, reprobate 10 licentious 11 extravagant, spendthrift

profound: low 4 deep, sage, wise 5 heavy 7 abysmal, intense 8 abstruse, unbroken 9 intensive, recondite, sagacious

10 acroamatic, exhaustive 11 far-reaching 12 unfathomable

profuse: 4 lush 5 frank 6 galore, hearty, lavish 7 copious, liberal, opulent, riotous 8 abundant, generous, prodigal, wasteful 9 bountiful, excessive, exuberant, luxuriant, plentiful 10 munificent 11 extravagant, overflowing

prog: 4 food 5 prick, prowl, tramp 6 forage 7 vagrant 8 supplies 9 provender

progenitor: 4 sire 6 parent 8 ancestor 10 forefather, foreparent, forerunner

progeny: imp, son 4 race, seed 5 breed, brood, brook, child, issue, scion, shoot 6 family, strain 8 children, daughter 9 genealogy, offspring 10 generation 11 descendants

prognostic: 4 omen, sign 5 token 8 forecast 10 prediction

prognosticate: 4 bode 5 augur 6 divine 7 betoken, forbode, forerun, portend, predict, presage 8 forebode, forecast, foreshow, foretell, prophesy 9 foretoken, hariolate

prognosticator: 4 seer 5 augur 6 divine 7 augurer, diviner, prophet 9 predictor 10 soothsayer

program: 4 card, list, show, sked 5 draft, edict 6 agenda, course, notice 7 agendum, catalog, outline 8 bulletin, calendar, schedule, syllabus 9 broadcast 10 prospectus 12 proclamation

theater: 8 playbill

programma: 5 edict 6 decree 7 preface 12 prolegomenon

progress: 4 fare, flow, grow, tour, wend 5 march 6 course, growth, motion 7 advance, circuit, develop, headway, improve, journey, passage, proceed 10 betterment, expedition 11 development, furtherance, improvement

planned: 7 telesia, telesis

progression: 5 stage 8 sequence 9 unfolding 10 succession 11 development

progressive: 6 active, onward 7 forward, liberal 9 advancing, ascensive 12 enterprising

prohibit: ban, bar, bid 4 stop, veto 5 debar, estop, fence 6 defend, enjoin, forbid, hinder, outlaw 7 forfend, forwarn, prevent 8 disallow, forefend 9 interdict, proscribe 11 countermand

prohibited: hot 4 tabu 5 taboo 7 illegal, illicit 8 unlawful, verboten(G.)

prohibiting: 8 vetitive

prohibitionist: dry

project: jet, jut, lap 4 abut, apse, barb, butt, game, idea, plan, send, task 5 bulge, filip, shoot, think 6 beetle, design, device, extend, fillip, scheme, wander 7 extrude, imagine, pattern, problem, prolong 8 contrive, lengthen, proposal, protrude 9 intention 10 enterprise 11 contrivance, proposition, undertaking

projectile: 4 bomb, dart, rock, shot 5 arrow, shell 6 bullet, rocket 7 missile, torpedo 8 shrapnel 9 cartridge
curve: 8 parabola
explosive part: 7 warhead, warnose
pert. to: 9 ballistic
submarine: 7 torpedo

projecting: 6 beetle 7 salient

projection: arm, cam, ell, hob, hub, jag, lee, lug, toe 4 apse, barb, croc, fang, lobe 5 bulge, crena, redan, socle, tenon, tooth 6 corbel, crenae(pl.), dormer, lobule, tappet 7 cornice, empathy 8 abutment, ejection, eminence 9 crenation 10 protrusion 12 protuberance

projector: 4 kino 8 bioscope 9 vitascope 12 stereopticon 13 cinematograph, kinematograph

projet: 4 plan 5 draft

prolapse: 7 falling

prolate: 9 elongated
opposite of: 6 oblate

proletarian: 4 mean, rude 6 coarse, vulgar, worker 7 laborer

proletariat: mob 4 mass 6 rabble 11 rank and file 12 working class

prolific: 6 birthy, fecund 7 fertile, teeming 8 fruitful, spawning, swarming 9 abounding, plentiful 10 generative 11 propagative 12 reproductive

prolix: 7 wordy 7 diffuse, irksome, prosaic, tedious, verbose 8 tiresome 9 prolonged, wearisome 10 longwinded, protracted 11 displeasing 13 uninteresting

prolocutor: 6 orator 7 speaker 8 advocate, chairman 9 spokesman 10 mouthpiece

prologue: 7 preface 12 introduction

prolong: 5 defer 6 endure, extend 7 persist 8 continue, lengthen

prolonged: 4 long 5 great 6 prolix 7 chronic, delayed, dilated 8 extended 9 continued, postponed, sostenuto, sustained 10 lengthened, protracted

prom: 4 ball 5 dance

promenade: 4 deck, hall, mall, walf 5 prado(Sp.) 6 avenue, marina, parade, pasear(Sp.) 7 alameda, gallery 9 boardwalk, esplanade

Prometheus: *father:* 7 Iapetus
gift to man: 4 fire
mother: 7 Clymene

prominence: 4 cusp 5 agger 8 eminence, prestige, salience 10 colliculus, promontory 11 distinction

prominent: 5 chief 6 famous, marked, signal 7 capital, eminent, notable, obvious, salient 8 aquiline, manifest 9 egregious, well-known 10 celebrated, noticeable, projecting 11 conspicuous, distinctive 13 distinguished

promiscuous: 6 random, wanton 7 immoral 8 careless 9 haphazard

promise: vow 4 band, hest, hote, oath, pawn, word 5 agree, grant 6 assure, behest, engage, parole, pledge, plight 7 behight, betroth, fianced 8 affiance, contract, covenant 9 assurance, betrothal, foretoken 10 convenable, engagement, obligation 11 declaration, word of honor

Promised Land: 6 Canaan

promissory note: I.O.U. 5 check 6 pledge, ticket

promontory: hoe 4 bill, cape, head, mull, nase, naze, ness, peak, scaw, skaw, spit 5 mount, point 8 headland 10 projection, prominence

promote: aid 4 help, plug, push 5 boost, exalt, nurse, raise, speed 6 better, foster, prefer 7 advance, build up, dignify, elevate, forward, further 9 advantage, encourage, patronize, publicize 10 aggrandize, make much of

promoter: 5 agent 7 abetter, abettor, booster, hustler 8 broacher, lobbyist

promotion: 6 brevet 7 advance 9 publicity 10 graduation, preferment 11 advancement, furtherance

prompt: apt, cue 4 move, urge, yare(Sc.) 5 alert, quick, ready, yeder 6 active, assist, excite, induce, nimble, remind 7 animate, forward 8 punctual, vigilant, watchful 11 expeditious

prompter: aid 4 cuer 7 readier

promptly: 4 soon, tite(Sc.) 8 directly

promptness: 8 alacrity, dispatch

promulgate: 7 declare, publish 8 announce, proclaim 9 advertise

prone: apt 4 bent, flat 5 buxom 6 agroof, agrufe, agruif, liable, supine 7 passive, willing 8 addicted, disposed, inclined, pronated 9 declivous, groveling, lying down, prostrate, reclining, recumbent 10 decubitous

prong: nib, peg 4 fang, fork, horn, tine 5 point, tooth 6 branch

prongbuck: 9 pronghorn, springbok

prong key: 7 spanner

pronghorn: 4 deer 6 cabree 8 antelope, berrendo

pronoun: any, her, him, his, its, one, our she, thy, you 4 mine, ours, that, thee, them, they, this, thou, your 5 their, these, thine, those 6 itself, myself 7 herself, himself, oneself, ourself 8 yourself 9 ourselves 10 themselves, yourselves
demonstrative: 4 that, this 5 these, those
interrogative: who 4 whom 5 whose
substantive: who 7 whoever 9 whosoever

pronounce: 4 pass 5 speak, utter 6 affirm 7 behight, declare, deliver, enounce 8 announce 9 enunciate 10 articulate

free: 7 absolve

guilty: 7 condemn

indistinctly: 4 slur

pronounced: 6 marked 7 decided, howling 12 unmistakable

pronouncement: 4 fiat 5 dicta(pl.) 6 dictum 9 manifesto, statement 11 declaration 12 announcement, proclamation, promulgation

pronto: 4 fast 5 quick 6 at once 7 quickly 8 promptly 11 immediately

pronunciation: 4 burr, lisp, slur 5 drawl, twang

correct: 8 orthoepy 9 phonology

incorrect: 7 cacoepy 8 psellism 9 psellisum

pronunciation mark: 5 tilde 8 dieresis 9 diacritic

proof: 4 test 5 trial 6 reason, result 7 approof, probate, exhibit, outcome 8 argument, evidence 9 testimony 10 indication 11 approbation 12 confirmation, impenetrable, verification 13 certification, demonstration

proofreader mark: cap 4 dele, ital, stet 5 caret, space

prop: leg, nog 4 stay 5 appui, brace, shore, sprag, staff, stell(Sc.), stilt 6 scotch, shorer 7 fulcrum, shore up, support, sustain 8 buttress 10 strengthen

propaganda: 4 hype, plan 5 ideas 6 scheme, system 8 agitprop, doctrine 12 brainwashing

propagation: 12 continuation

propagate: 4 grow 5 breed 6 spread 7 diffuse 8 engender, generate, increase, multiply 9 circulate, procreate 11 disseminate

propel: gun, row 4 flip, move, pole, push, send, urge 5 drive, egg on, flick, force, impel, shove 7 project

propeller: fan, fin, oar 4 vane 5 screw 6 driver, paddle 8 windmill

arm: 4 vane

propensity: yen 4 bent, bias 6 liking 7 aptness, avidity, leaning 8 appetite, tendency 9 affection, proneness 10 proclivity, propension 11 disposition, inclination 12 predilection

proper: due, fit 4 able, fair, fine, good, meet, prim, true 5 right, stiff, utter 6 behove, chaste, comely, decent, honest, modest, sedate, seemly, strict 7 behoove, correct, fitting, seeming 8 accurate, decorous, formular, suitable 9 advisable, allowable, befitting, beseeming, excellent 10 commodious, convenient, scrupulous 11 appropriate, respectable

properly: 6 featly, gladly 8 by rights

property: lot, res 4 acre, alod, aver, bona, dhan(Ind.), gear 5 addle, allod, asset, aught, glebe, goods, manor 6 domain, estate, havier, realty, wealth 7 acquest, alodium, chattel, haviour, holding, quality 8 allodium 9 acensuada, attribute, homestead, ownership 11 appropriate, possessions 14 characteristic

act to regain: 8 replevin

bride's gift to husband: dos 5 dowry

charge against: 4 lien 8 mortgage

conveyor of: 7 alienor, grantor

deceased wife's gift to husband: 8 courtesy

destruction of: 5 arson 8 sabotage 9 vandalism

found on the thief: 6 mainor

personal: 5 goods 7 chattel

real: 4 land 7 acreage

receiver: 7 alienee

seller: 7 realtor

settle: 6 entail

stolen: 4 loot, pelf 5 booty, lucre, spoil

suit for: 6 trover

transferring party: 7 alienor

property right: 4 lien 5 title 8 easement

prophecy: 5 weird 6 oracle 8 bodement 9 utterance 10 prediction, revelation 11 declaration, foretelling 12 vaticination

pert. to: 9 vaticinal

prophesy: 4 dope, osse, spae 5 aread, areed, augur 6 divine 7 predict, presage 8 ariolate, forecast, foreshow, foretell 10 vaticinate 11 preindicate 13 prognosticate

prophet: 4 Amos, John, seer 5 augur, Elias, fatal, Hosea, Syrus 6 divine, Elijah, Elisha, leader, mantis, oracle 7 augurer, diviner, Malachi, teacher 8 Mohammed, Muhammed, presager 9 John Smith, predictor 10 soothsayer 11 Nostradamus, vaticinator

prophetess: 5 Sibyl 6 Miriam 7 Deborah, Pythian, seeress 9 Cassandra

prophetic: 5 vatic 6 mantic 7 fateful, fatidic, vatical 8 foretell, oracular 9 prescient, sibylline 10 divinatory, mysterious, predictive, presageful, signifying 11 apocalyptic, fatiloquent, foretelling, nostradamic 12 vaticinatory 14 interpretative

propine: 5 offer 6 pledge 7 present, propose

propinquity: 7 kinship 8 affinity, nearness, vicinity 9 proximity 12 neighborhood, relationship

propitiate: 5 adapt, atone 6 adjust, pacify 7 appease, conform, expiate, satisfy 9 reconcile 10 conciliate

propitious: 4 good, rosy 5 happy, lucky 6 benign, timely 8 benedict 9 benignant, favorable, opportune, promising 10 auspicious, benevolent, prosperous 12 advantageous

proponent: 6 backer 8 advocate 9 supporter

proportion: 4 part, rate, size 5 quota, ratio, share 6 degree 7 analogy, portion, prorate 8 relation, symmetry 9 dimension

proportional: 5 equal 7 ratable 8 adequate, relative 10 answerable, equivalent, reciprocal 11 symmetrical 12 commensurate

proportionately: 6 fairly 7 prorata 10 adequately

proposal: 4 idea, plan 5 offer 6 design, feeler, motion, scheme 7 project 8 overture 10 invitation, nomination, suggestion 11 proposition

propose: ask, put 4 give, moot, move 5 offer, state 6 allege, design, submit, tender 7 suggest 8 propound 11 contemplate

proposition: 5 axiom, offer, point 6 affair, porism 7 premise, project, theorem 8 offering, overture, proposal, question 9 corollary, postulate, situation, statement 11 affirmation, undertaking
antecedent: 6 premise
preliminary: 7 lemma 7 lemmata(pl.)

propound: 4 pose 5 posit, state 7 propose

proprietor: 5 owner 6 master, tanist 7 lairdie

propriety (see also **proper**): 4 code, rule 7 customs, manners, quality 8 behavior, elegance, standard 9 attribute, etiquette 13 possessorship

propugnator: 8 defender 10 vindicator

propulsion: jet 5 drift 8 ejection 9 expulsion

prorate: 5 allot 6 assess, divide 9 apportion 10 distribute, proportion

prorogue: 5 defer 6 extend 7 adjourn, prolong 8 postpone, protract

prosaic: 4 drab, dull, flat 5 prosy 6 common, prolix, stolid, stupid 7 humdrum, insipid, tedious 8 everyday, tiresome, unpoetic 9 colorless 10 unexciting 11 commonplace 12 matter-of-fact 13 unimaginative, uninteresting

proscenium: 5 stage
front area: 5 apron

proscribe: ban 4 tabu 5 exile, taboo 6 banish, forbid, outlaw 8 prohibit, sentence 9 interdict, ostracize

prose form: 5 essay, novel, story, tract 7 fiction, romance 8 treatise 9 biography 10 nonfiction

prosecute: sue 4 urge 5 carry, chase, hound, press 6 accuse, charge, follow, indict, pursue 7 enforce 8 continue

prosecutor: 7 accuser, relator 8 quaestor

proselyte: 5 alien 7 convert 8 neophyte, newcomer
to Judaism: ger

Proserpine: See **Persephone**

perseuche: 7 oratory 9 synagogue

prosit: 5 toast 10 salutation

prosody: 5 meter

prospect: 4 hope, mine, view 5 buyer, scene, vista 6 aspect 7 explore, outlook 8 customer, exposure 9 applicant, candidate, foretaste 10 contestant

prospective: 5 lofty 6 future, likely 7 eminent 8 expected, prospect 9 provident 11 anticipated, perspective

prospector: 9 sourdough

prosper: dow, hie, wax 4 fare 5 cheve, edify, frame, speed 6 thrive 7 augment, blossom, succeed, turn out 8 flourish, increase

prosperity: hap, ups 4 boom, weal 5 ikbal 6 thrift, wealth 7 fortune, success, welfare 9 abundance, happiness, well-being
god: 4 Frey
goddess: 5 Salus
symbol: 9 turquoise

Prospero: *daughter:* 7 Miranda
servant: 5 Ariel
slave: 7 Caliban

prosperous: 4 bein, bien, boon, rich 5 flush, happy, lucky, palmy, sonsy 6 sonsie, timely 7 halcyon, well-off 8 thriving 9 favorable, fortunate 10 auspicious, propitious, successful, well-heeled 11 flourishing

prostitute: bat, cat 4 aunt, drab, doxy, hack, trug 5 abuse, broad, venal, whore 6 callet, debase, harlot, hooker 7 baggage, brothel, corrupt, Cyprian, hackney 8 berdache, call girl, commoner, customer, infamous, occupant 9 courtesan, courtezan 10 crosha-bell, hobby-horse, licentious 12 camp follower, streetwalker 13 commercialize
customer: 4 john
reformed: 8 Magdalen

prostitution, house of: 6 bordel 7 brothel 8 bordello

prostrate: bow 4 fell, flat 5 prone 6 fallen, supine 7 exhaust 8 dejected, helpless, overcome, paralyze 9 collapsed, flattened, overthrow, overwhelm, recumbent 10 subjugated, submissive

prosy: dry 4 dull 6 jejune 7 humdrum, prosaic, tedious 9 colorless 11 commonplace, displeasing 13 unimaginative

protagonist: foe 4 hero, star 5 actor, agent, enemy 6 leader 7 heroine 8 advocate, champion, defender 9 contender, principal, spokesman

protasis: 8 foreword 11 conditional, proposition 12 introduction

protean: 9 many-sided 10 changeable

protect: arm 4 bind, hill, save, wear 5 bield, bless, guard, hedge, shade 6 assert, defend, harbor, insure, patent, police, screen, shield **7** bulwark, cherish, forfend, shelter, tuition **8** champion, conserve, forefend, preserve **9** copyright

protecting: 7 tutelar **8** tutelary

protection: bib, lee, pad **4** egis, fort, moat, pass **5** aegis, apron, armor, bribe, frith, graft, guard, shell, smock **6** amulet, armour, patent, safety **7** auspice, defense, parapet, shelter, squeeze, tuition, umbrage **8** passport, security **9** shakedown **12** preservation

protector: 5 guard **6** fautor, patron, shield **8** defender, guardian **9** custodian

name meaning: **5** Edgar **9** Alexander

protectorate: 6 colony **9** territory **10** dependency, possession **11** condominium

protege: 4 ward

proteid: 6 alexin **7** albumin **9** legumelin

Proteida family: olm **7** proteus **8** necturus **11** salamanders, typhlomolge

protein: 6 avidin, casein, fibrin **7** albumin, edestin, mucedin **8** aleurone, creatine, prolamin

group: **8** globulin

poison: **5** abrin, ricin **6** ricine

source of: egg **4** bean, meat, milk **6** cheese, lentil

pro tem: 6 acting **7** interim **9** temporary

protest: 4 aver, beef, deny, kick **5** demur, fight **6** affirm, assert, assure, holler, object, oppose, plaint **7** contest, declare, dissent, testify **8** complain **9** complaint, objection, stipulate **10** asseverate **11** expostulate, remonstrate **12** remonstrance

Protestant: 7 Baptist **8** Anglican, Lutheran **9** Calvinist, dissenter, Methodist **10** Anabaptist **12** Presbyterian

proteus: olm **5** ameba **6** amoeba

Proteus: 6 sea god

friend: **9** Valentine

love: **6** Silvia

wife: **9** Julia

protograph: 7 writing **9** holograph **12** illustration

protoplasm: 5 ameba, spore **6** amoeba **7** sarcode

outer layer: **9** ectoplasm

substance: gel

prototype: 5 model **6** emblem **7** pattern **8** antetype, original **9** archetype **10** forerunner

protozoan: 5 ameba **6** amoeba **7** stentor **8** rhizopod

genus of: **7** arcella

order: **6** lobosa

parasitic: **5** ameba **6** amoeba **8** amoebida

protract: 4 spin **5** defer, delay **6** dilate, extend **7** detract, prolong **8** continue, elongate, lengthen, protrude

protrude: jut **5** blear, bulge **7** extrude,

project **8** stick out **9** interfere

protuberance: nub, wen **4** boll, boss, bulb, bump, heel, hump, knob, knot, lobe, lump, node, snag, umbo **5** bulge, bunch, caput, hunch, torus **8** eminence, swelling **9** gibbosity **10** projection, prominence, protrusion

rounded: **4** hump, umbo

protuberant: 6 convex, extant **7** bottled, gibbous **8** blubbery **9** prominent

proud (see also **pride**): **4** ikey, vain **5** brant, chuff **7** haughty, pompous, stately, valiant **8** imposing, splendid **9** cockhorse, hubristic **10** impressive **11** magisterial, overbearing **12** presumptuous, supercilious

prove: try **4** aver, fand, pree, test **5** argue, essay, nurse, prive(Sc.) **6** argify, argufy, attest, evince, verify **7** confirm, justify, probate **8** identify, indicate, manifest **9** ascertain, establish **11** corroborate, demonstrate

provenance: 6 origin, source **10** derivation

provender: hay **4** corn, feed, food, oats, prog **5** grain, straw **6** fodder, forage **7** prebend **10** provisions

proverb: saw **4** word **5** adage, axiom, maxim, motto **6** ballad, byword, enigma, saying **7** byspell, parable **8** allegory, aphorism, forbysen

proverbial: 6 common **9** well-known **11** sententious

provide: 4 give **5** cater, equip, stock, store, yield **6** afford, foison, purvey, ration, render, supply **7** chevise, furnish, support **8** accouter, accoutre **9** stipulate **10** contribute

provided: but **5** boden, found **6** if only, sobeit **8** afforded, equipped, supplied **9** furnished

providence: 6 thrift **7** economy **8** function, guidance, prudence

provident: 4 wise **6** frugal, saving **7** careful, prudent, sparing, thrifty **8** cautious, discreet **9** farseeing **10** economical, farsighted **11** foresighted

providential: 4 kind **5** happy, lucky **9** fortunate **10** auspicious

province: 4 area, nome, work **5** arena, range, realm, shire, tract **6** colony, domain, eparch, region, sphere **7** country, emirate, pursuit **8** district, division, function **9** bailiwick, territory **10** department, palatinate **12** jurisdiction

pert. to: **5** nomic

provincial: 4 rude **5** crude, local, rural **6** narrow, rustic **7** bigoted, insular, limited **9** hidebound, parochial **10** uncultured **11** countrified **15** unsophisticated

provision: 4 fare, food **5** board, cater, grist, stock, store **6** clause, supply, wraith **7** proviso **9** condition

provisional: 4 iffy **7** aeolian **9** makeshift, provisory, temporary, tentative **10** contingent **11** conditional

provisions: 4 cate, chow, fare, food **5** board, bouge, terms **6** forage, stocks, stores, viands **7** rations **9** provender **10** chevisance

search for: **6** forage

stock of: **6** larder **8** magazine

proviso: 5 salvo **6** clause **7** article, caution **9** condition **11** stipulation

provisory: 11 provisional

provocation: 6 appeal **9** annoyance, incentive

provocative: 7 agacant **8** agacante, stimulus **9** provoking **10** aggressive **11** stimulating

provoke: ire, vex **4** bait, move, spur, stir **5** anger, annoy, cause, eager, evoke, frump, pique, start, tease **6** arouse, excite, harass, incite, insult, invite, invoke, madden, nettle, summon **7** affront, incense, outrage, perturb, quicken **8** generate, irritate **9** aggravate, challenge, displease, forthcall, stimulate **10** exasperate

provost: 4 head **5** chief **6** jailer, keeper **7** prefect **8** director, official **10** magistrate **13** administrator **14** superintendent

prow: bow **4** beak, nose, stem **5** brave, prore **6** steven **7** gallant, rostrum, valiant **9** honorable **10** courageous

prowess: 5 skill, valor **6** valour **7** address, bravery, courage, heroism **9** ingenuity **10** excellence

prowl: 4 lurk, roam **6** brevit, ramble, wander

proximate: 4 next **6** direct, nearby **8** imminent **9** immediate **10** near-at-hand

proximity: 8 nearness, nighness, vicinage, vicinity **9** adjacence, closeness, immediacy **10** contiguity **11** propinquity **13** approximation, juxtaposition

proxy: 5 agent, power, vicar **6** agency, deputy **7** proctor **8** assignee, function **9** authority **10** procurator, substitute

prudence: wit **6** acumen **7** economy **10** management **11** calculation

prudent: 4 sage, wary, wise **5** canny, chary, douce, siker **6** frugal, sicker **7** careful, politic **8** cautious, discreet, sensible **9** advisable, cautelous, expedient, provident, sagacious **10** economical, forehanded **11** circumspect, considerate, foresighted **14** forethoughtful

prudish: 4 nice, prim **5** stern **6** severe, stern **7** austere **8** priggish **10** overmodest

prune: cow, cut, lop **4** clip, coll, frog, geld, plum, sned(Sc.), thin, trim **5** brake,

dress, dunce, fruit, plume, preen, purge, rasee, razee, shave **6** anoint **7** exclude, tonsure **8** castrate **9** eliminate, simpleton

pruning knife: 8 serpette

prurient: 4 lewd **5** bawdy **6** erotic **7** itching, longing, lustful **10** lascivious

pruritis: 4 itch

Prussia: 11 German state (former)

bay: **4** Kiel **6** Danzig **10** Pomeranian

city: **4** Kiel **5** Essen **6** Aachen, Altena, Berlin, Tilsit **7** Breslau, Hanover, Munster, Stettin **9** Frankfurt, Magdeburg **10** Dusseldorf, Konigsberg **14** Charlottenburg

district: **7** Stettin

island: **5** Rugen **6** Usedom, Wollin **7** Frisian

lagoon: **4** haff **7** Frische **8** Kurische **11** Pommerische

lancer: **4** Ulan **5** Uhlan

land-holding aristocracy: **6** Junker

legislature, upper house: **10** Herrenhaus

measure: **4** fuss, rute, zoll **5** fuder, meile **6** morgen, oxhoft **8** scheffel

mountain: **4** Harz **7** Sudeten **11** Schneekoppe **13** Riesengebirge

province: **5** Posen **6** Berlin, Saxony **7** Hanover, Prussia, Silesia **9** Pomerania, Rhineland **10** Westphalia **11** Brandenburg, East-Prussia, Hesse-Nassau, West-Prussia **12** Hohenzollern **17** Schleswig-Holstein

river: Ems **4** Alle, Eder, Elbe, Oder, Saar **5** Memel **6** Niemen, Pregel **7** Vistula **8** Passarge, Weichsel

seaport: **4** Kiel **5** Emden

spa: Ems

university town: **5** Halle

weight: **4** mark **9** quentchen

prussiate: 4 salt **7** cyanide **12** ferricyanide, ferrocyanide

pry: spy **4** gaze, lift, move, nose, peek, peep, peer **5** jemmy, jimmy, lever, mouse, prize, raise, snoop, twist **6** pick up, potter **7** crowbar **8** leverage, scrounge, separate **10** scrutinize

prying: 4 nosy **5** nosey **7** curious **9** obtrusive, officious **11** inquisitive

psalm: ode **4** hymn, poem, song **6** praise **11** composition

collection: **6** hallel **7** psalter

kind: **4** laud **6** hallel, Venite **7** Cantate, introit **8** Miserere

opening communion: **7** introit

sign: **5** selah

word of punctuation: **5** selah

psalmist: 4 poet **5** David **6** cantor, writer **8** composer **9** precentor

psalterium: 4 bouk, lyra **6** omasum **7** stomach **9** manyplies

psammite: 9 sandstone

pseudo: 4 fake, mock, sham 5 bogus, false, wrong 7 feigned 8 spurious 9 pretended, simulated 11 counterfeit
pseudologist: 4 liar
pseudonym (see also **nickname, pen name**): 5 alias 6 anonym 7 anonyme
Lev Bronstein: 11 Leon Trotsky
Josip Broz: 4 Tito
Iosif Dzhugashvili: 12 Joseph Stalin
Adolf Schicklgruber: 11 Adolf Hitler
Vladimir Ulyanov: 13 Vladimir Lenin
Ehrich Weiss: 7 Houdini
psittaceous: 10 parrotlike
psyche: 4 mind, soul 6 spirit
psychiatrist: 4 Jung 5 Adler, Freud 6 shrink 7 analyst 8 alienist
psychic: 6 mental 7 sensile 9 animistic, spiritual 10 responsive, telepathic 11 impressible
psychic power: ESP
psychotic: mad 5 crazy 6 insane 8 schizoid 10 disordered 12 unreasonable
Ptah's wife: 6 Sekhet
ptarmica: 10 sneezewort
ptarmigan: 4 bird, ripa, rype 6 grouse
PT boat: 11 torpedo boat
pteric: 4 alar 8 winglike
pteroid: 8 fernlike, winglike
ptisan: tea 5 drink 6 coddle, tisane 9 decoction
Ptolemy: *astronomy work:* 8 almagest
wife: 12 Philadelphia
ptomaine: 6 poison
pub: bar, inn 5 hotel 6 tavern
pubble: fat 5 plump
public: 4 open 5 civic, civil, overt, state 6 common, vulgar 7 general, popular, society 8 national, open-door 9 community, following 10 widespread
discussion: 7 forum
record office: 7 archion 8 archives
service: 7 railway, utility 9 telegraph, telephone 10 waterworks
way: 4 road 5 alley 6 bridge, tunnel 7 highway 9 turnpike 9 boulevard
publican: 6 farmer, keeper 9 catchpole, catchpoll, collector 12 saloon keeper, tax collector
publication: 4 book 5 paper 6 annals, blazon, digest 7 booklet 8 pamphlet 9 ephemeris 10 periodical 11 declaration 12 notification, proclamation, promulgation
examiner: 6 censor
list: 12 bibliography
make-up: 6 format
permit: 7 release
preliminary: 9 prodromus
prepare for: 4 edit
regular: 10 periodical
publicist: 5 agent, solon 6 writer 10 journalist

publicity: air 7 buildup, puffery, reclame, write-up 8 ballyhoo 9 promotion 11 advertising, information
publicize: 4 tout 5 extol 7 promote 9 advertise
publish: air 4 blow, edit, vent 5 issue, print 6 blazon, defame, delate, expose, get out, put out 7 declare, diffuse, divulge, release 8 announce, evulgate, forspeak, proclaim, promulge 9 advertise, forespeak 10 promulgate 11 disseminate
without authority: 6 pirated 10 plagiarize
publisher: 6 editor, issuer 7 printer 8 broacher 10 journalist
copy: 5 blurb 8 colophon 12 announcement
Puccini: *heroine:* 4 Mimi
opera: 7 La Tosca 8 La Boheme 12 Manon
puck: elf, imp 4 disk 5 fairy 6 roller, sprite, strike 9 hobgoblin, prankster 10 goatsucker
pucker: 4 fold 5 bulge, purse, reeve, smock 6 cockle, cotter, lucken 7 wrinkle 8 contract
puckered: 7 bullate
puckfist: 8 braggart, puffball
puckish: 7 playful 8 annoying 10 mysterious 11 mischievous
pud: paw 4 hand 7 pudding 8 forefoot
pudding: 4 duff, mush, sago 6 burgoo, hackin, haggis(Sc.), panada 7 burgout, custard, dessert, hacking, sausage, tapioca 8 roly-poly 9 stir-about
puddle: dub 4 plud, pond, pool 5 plash, swamp 6 charco, fiddle, flodge 7 plashet 8 quagmire
pudency: 7 modesty 8 delicacy 11 bashfulness, prudishness 13 embarrassment 14 shamefacedness
pudgy: fat 5 dumpy, plump, squab, squat 6 rotund 7 bulging 8 roly-poly
pueblo: 4 town 7 village 8 dwelling
Pueblo: 4 Hopi, Zuni 6 Indian
assembly hall: 6 estufa
ceremonial chamber: 4 kiva
village: 4 Taos
puerile: 4 weak 5 silly, young 6 jejune 7 babyish, foolish, trivial 8 childish, immature, juvenile, unworthy, youthful 10 unthinking
Puerto Principe: 8 Camaguey
Puerto Rico: *capital:* 7 San Juan
bark: 4 mavi
beverage: 4 mavi
bird: 4 rola 7 yeguita
breadfruit: 7 castana
city: 5 Ponce 6 Dorado 7 Arecibo 8 Mayaguez
conqueror of: 5 Miles
discoverer: 8 Columbus

fish: 4 sama, sisi
island: 4 Mona
measure: 6 cuerda 10 caballeria
person of mixed blood: 6 jibaro
tree: 4 mora 5 yagua, yaray 8 guayroto 9 guaraguao

puff: 4 blow, chug, flam(Sc.), flan, fuff, gust, pant, pegh(Sc.), plug, pouf, waff, waft 5 fluff, quilt, whiff 6 praise

puff up: 5 bloat, swell 6 tumefy 7 distend, inflate

puffball: 4 fist, fuzz 5 smoke 8 fuzzball, snuffbox

puffbird: 6 barbet 8 barbacou
genus: 6 monasa

puffed up: 5 large 6 astrut 7 souffle 8 bouffant, imposing, inflated 9 bombastic, bouffante 11 pretentious

puffer: 6 blower 8 blowfish 9 globefish

puffin: auk 4 bird 9 sea parrot

puffy: 4 soft 5 pursy 6 flabby 7 pompous

pug: dog, elf 4 clay, plug, poke, puck 5 boxer, chaff, churn, dwarf, knead, track 6 harlot, refuse, sprite, thrust 7 trample 8 mistress, pugilist 9 footprint, hobgoblin

pug-nosed: 5 camus

puggy: 6 monkey(Sc.), sweaty 10 sweetheart

pugilist: lug 5 boxer 7 battler, bruiser, fighter
assistant: 6 second 7 handler

pugnacious: 7 defiant, warlike 8 brawling, fighting 9 bellicose, combative 10 aggressive 11 belligerent, contentious, quarrelsome

puisne: 4 puny 5 judge, later, petty 6 feeble, junior 9 associate 10 subsequent 11 subordinate 13 insignificant

puissance: 4 army, host, sway 5 clout, force, might, power, vigor 7 potency 8 strength 9 influence 12 forcefulness

puissant: 6 mighty, strong 8 powerful 10 commanding

puke: 4 snot, wool 5 vomit

pukka, pucka: 4 good, real 7 genuine 8 complete 9 authentic 11 substantial 13 thoroughgoing

pulchritude: 5 grace 6 beauty 10 comeliness, excellence, loveliness

pule: cry 4 peep 5 cheep, whine 6 repine, snivel 7 whimper 8 complain

pull: lug, row, tew, tit, tow, tug, wap 4 claw, drag, draw, duct, hale, haul, jerk, yank, yerk 5 bouse(naut.), heave(naut.), hitch, pluck, tweak 6 arrest, twitch 7 attract, revulse, stretch 9 influence 10 persuasion 12 drawing power
apart: rip 4 rend, tear 8 separate 9 criticize
away: 5 wrest 6 remove 8 withdraw
down: 4 raze 5 wreck 7 destroy 8 demolish

off: pug 6 avulse, manage 7 achieve, succeed 10 accomplish
one's freight: 5 leave 6 depart
one's leg: 4 hoax, joke 7 deceive 8 hoodwink
out: 7 extract 9 extirpate 10 deracinate
through: 7 recover, succeed, survive
up: 4 halt, stop 5 elate, trice

pullet: hen 4 fowl 5 frier 6 earock(Sc.) 7 pollard 8 poullard

pulley: 4 ring 5 fusee, fuzee, wheel 6 sheave
part: 4 arse, drum 6 rigger

Pullman: car 5 coach 7 sleeper

pullulate: bud 4 teem 5 swarm 7 germinate

pulp: pap 4 marc, mash, mass, pith 5 chyme, crush, magma 6 pomace 7 bagasse
machine: 9 macerater

pulpit: 4 ambo, bema, desk 5 chair, stage 7 lectern, rostrum 8 ministry, platform, scaffold

pulpy: 6 flabby, fleshy

pulque: 5 drink 6 liquor, mescal 9 stimulant

pulsate: 4 beat, move, pant 5 pound, throb 6 quiver, strike, thrill 7 vibrate

pulsatory: 8 rhythmic 9 systaltic, throbbing

pulse: mug 7 battuta 8 sphygmus

pulverize: 4 bray, meal, mull, ruin 5 crush, grind 6 bruise 7 atomize, destroy, shatter 8 demolish, levigate 9 comminute, triturate 12 contriturate

pulverized: 4 fine 5 dusty

pulverizer: 7 blender, grinder 13 disintegrator

pulverulent: 5 dusty 7 crumbly, powdery 8 powdered

puma: cat 6 cougar 7 panther 9 carnivore

pumice: 5 stone 8 abrasive
powdered: 4 talc

pummel: fib 4 beat, maul 5 thump 6 batter, hammer

pump: gin, ram 4 jack 5 drain 6 racker 7 draw off, stirrup, syringe 10 pulsometer
handle: 5 sweep, swipe

pumpernickel: 5 bread

pumpkin: 4 pepo 5 clump, gourd 6 citrul, squash
head: 4 dolt 5 dunce 7 Puritan 9 blockhead

pumpkinseed: 7 sunfish 8 bluegill, flatfish, flounder 10 butterfish

pun: mot 4 beat, joke 5 knock, pound 7 quibble 8 paragram 9 calembour, conundrum 11 paronomasia, play on words

punch: ade, jab 4 cuff, glog, poke, prod 5 douse, dowse, drink, negus, paste, point, vigor 6 pierce, strike 7 mattoir 8 beverage, puncture 9 perforate

Punch: 5 clown 7 buffoon, journal 8 magazine 10 periodical

first editor of: 5 Lemon

puncheon: die 4 cask, post, snap, stud, tool 5 punch, stamp 6 timber

puncher: 6 cowboy 7 cowpoke 10 cowpuncher, perforator

Punchinello: 5 clown 7 buffoon

punctilious: 4 nice 5 exact 6 formal, proper 7 careful, correct, precise 8 exacting 9 observant 10 ceremonial, scrupulous 11 ceremonious 13 conscientious

punctual: 6 on time, prompt, timely 7 careful

punctuate: 4 mark 5 point 6 divide 8 separate 9 emphasize 11 distinguish

punctuation mark: dot 4 dash, stop 5 colon, comma, quote, slash 6 hyphen, period 7 bracket 8 ellipsis 9 semicolon 10 apostrophe 11 parenthesis

puncture: 4 bite, hole, stab, vent 5 prick, wound 6 pierce, riddle 9 perforate 11 perforation

pundit: 4 sage 5 swami 6 nestor 7 Brahman, scholar, teacher

pung: 4 sled 6 sleigh

pungent: hot 4 fell, keen, racy, rich, tart 5 acrid, acute, cress, minty, salty, sharp, smart, spicy, tangy 6 biting, bitter, pepper, snappy 7 caustic, cutting, peppery, piquant 8 aromatic, incisive, piercing, poignant, stinging 9 trenchant 10 expressive, irritating 11 acrimonious, stimulating

pungi: bin 4 pipe 5 flute

pungled: 8 shrunken 9 shriveled

Punic: 9 faithless 11 treacherous 12 Carthaginian

punish: 4 beat, fine, whip 5 abuse, mulct, scold, slate, smite, spank, strap, wreak 6 amerce, strike 7 chasten, consume, correct, corrige, revenge, scourge 8 chastise, penalize 9 castigate 10 discipline 13 excommunicate

punishing: 8 grueling

punishment: 4 loss, pain 5 peine(law), wrack 6 desert, dirdum, ferule 9 suffering 10 correction, discipline 11 castigation 12 chastisement 13 animadversion

device: rod 6 stocks

freedom from: 8 impunity

spare: 6 acquit 7 absolve 9 exculpate, exonerate

punitive: 5 penal 9 punishing 10 vindictive

Punjab: *East:* 5 India

West: 8 Pakistan

punk: bad 4 fuel, poor b conch, tough, tramp 6 amadou, novice, rookie, tinder 8 beginner, elephant, inferior, non-

sense, strumpet 9 beginning, miserable, touchwood, worthless 10 prostitute

punt: 4 boat, kick 6 gamble

punter: 5 poler 6 bettor 7 scalper

puny: 4 weak 5 dawny, frail, petty, small 6 feeble, puisne, sickly, slight 8 droghlin, inferior 9 unskilled 13 inexperienced, insignificant

pupa: 9 chrysalis

case: 5 theca

pupil: 4 tyro 5 cadet, eleve(F.), minor, plebe, youth 6 junior, senior 7 ecolier(F.), learner, scholar, student 8 disciple, neophyte, freshman 9 sophomore

pupilage: 6 nonage 10 immaturity

puppet: 4 baby, doll, dupe, tool 5 image, slave 8 drollery 9 neuropast 10 marionette

show: 6 wajang, wayang 10 shadow-play

puppy: fop 5 twerp, whelp

purblind: 5 blind 6 bisson, myopic, obtuse 12 shortsighted

purchasable: 5 venal 7 corrupt, salable, to be had 9 available 10 marketable

purchase: buy 5 cheap, yield 6 emptio, income, obtain, return 7 acquire, bargain, emption 11 acquisition

back: 6 redeem, regain

purchaser: 4 user 5 buyer 6 emptor, patron, vendee 8 co-emptor, customer 9 acquereur 13 adjudicataire

purdah: 6 screen 7 curtain 9 seclusion

pure: 4 fine, good, mear, meer, mere, neat, nice, pute, true 5 clean, clear, fresh, moral, sheer, utter 6 candid, chaste, simple, vestal, virgin 7 cleanly, genuine, perfect, refined, sincere, sinless, unmixed 8 absolute, complete, dovelike, filtered, innocent, straight, virtuous, zaccheus(Heb.) 9 authentic, blameless, downright, elemental, faultless, guiltless, out-and-out, stainless, unalloyed, undefiled, unsullied 10 immaculate 11 crystalline, unblemished, uncorrupted, unqualified 13 unadulterated 15 unsophisticated

puree: 4 mush, soup 8 porridge

purely: all 4 just 5 quite 6 solely, wholly

purfle: hem 6 border 7 outline 8 decorate, ornament, trimming

purgative: 5 jalap 6 physic 8 cleanser, evacuant 9 cathartic 10 alviducous

purgatory: 5 limbo, swamp

purge: rid 5 diet 6 physic, purify, remove, seethe 7 cleanse, deterge, shut out 8 absterge 9 exculpate, expurgate, liquidate 11 exterminate

purification: 7 baptism 9 catharsis

purify: 5 clean, clear, purge 6 bleach, filter, refine 7 baptize, clarify, cleanse, distill, epurate 8 depurate, lustrate, renovate 9 elutriate

Puritan: 9 Roundhead

puritanical: 4 prim 6 strict 7 genteel, prudish 8 rigorous 9 blue-nosed

purl: rib 4 eddy, knit, spin 5 frill, swirl 6 murmur, purfle, stitch

purlieu: 5 haunt 6 resort 7 environ 12 neighborhood

purloin: 4 crib 5 filch, steal, swipe 6 finger, pilfer, pirate 7 cabbage 8 abstract 10 plagiarize 11 appropriate

purple: 4 plum 5 grape, lilac, mauve, royal 6 blatta, emblem, maroon, ornate, risqué, tyrian, violet 7 cassius 8 amaranth, imperial, lavender 9 cathedral, elaborate 10 rhetorical

delicate: 5 mauve

dye: 7 cassius

purple copper ore: 7 bornite

Purple Heart: 5 award, medal, order

purple ragwort: 4 herb 6 jacoby

purport: 4 feck, gist, mean 5 drift, sense, tenor 6 effect, import, object 7 bearing, meaning 9 intention, substance 11 connotation, implication

purpose: aim, end, use 4 bent, goal, main, mean, plan, sake 5 avail, point 6 design, intend, intent, motive 7 mission 8 ambition, proposal 9 intention, objective, predesign 10 aspiration, cogitation, conception, employment, resolution 13 determination

alleged: 6 excuse 7 pretext

lacking: 9 driftless

purposive: 5 telic, 6 hormic 12 teleological

purpure: 6 purple 7 mercury

purr: hum 5 noise, sound, thrum, whurl 6 murmur

purse: bag, cly 4 bung, poke 5 bulse, burse, money, pouch 6 pucker, wallet 7 almoner, handbag 8 coco-wort, finances, treasury 9 exchequer 10 pocketbook 12 portemonnaie

purse crab: 5 ayuyu 7 pagurid

purser: 6 bursar 7 boucher, cashier 8 pinchgut 9 paymaster, treasurer

pursue: run 4 bait, hunt, seek 5 chase, chevy, chivy, hound, stalk 6 badger, follow, gallop 7 address, persist, proceed 8 continue 9 prosecute

pursuer: 5 lover 6 hunter 8 huntress 9 plaintiff

pursuit: 4 work 5 quest, scent 7 calling 10 occupation

means: 7 dragnet

pursy: fat 5 obese, puffy 7 swollen, wealthy 9 asthmatic

purulent: 4 foul, pyic 5 pussy

purvey: tax 5 cater 6 supply 7 foresee, furnish, procure, provide 10 assessment

purveyor: 6 seller, sutler 7 caterer 9 victualer

push: go; pop, por, ram 4 birr, bore, bunt, butt, ding, dush, pelt, ping, pole, porr, poss, prod, urge 5 bevel(Sc.), boost, crowd, drive, elbow, force, heave, hunch, impel, nudge, press, shove, vigor 6 clique, effort, energy, expand, extend, hustle, jostle, launch, potter, propel, thrust 7 advance, promote 8 bulldoze, increase, pressure, stimulus 10 enterprise 14 aggressiveness

along: 4 prod 5 nudge

around: 4 bait 5 bully 6 heckle

down: 7 detrude

in: 5 stove

pushy: 5 bossy 7 forward 9 officious 10 aggressive 11 presumptuous

pusillanimous: 4 tame 5 timid 6 afraid 8 cowardly 10 irresolute 12 fainthearted

puss: cat 4 face, girl, hare 5 child, mouth, woman 8 baudrons(Sc.)

pustule: 4 blob, burl 5 achor, blain 6 blotch, pimple 7 abscess, blister 8 eruption, swelling 9 carbuncle

put (see also **place**): lay, set 4 cast, push, urge, word 5 clink, drive, fixed, force, impel, place, state, throw 6 appose, attach, bestow, fasten, incite, thrust 7 deposit, express, propose 8 estimate 9 attribute, constrain, translate

away: 4 kill 5 store 6 murder 7 consume

back: 6 demote 7 replace, restore

before: 7 apposed, present

by: 4 save 5 store 6 reject

down: 6 humble, record 7 degrade, depress 8 suppress 9 deposited

forth: 4 show 5 exert, offer 7 extrude, propose, publish 9 circulate

forward: 7 prepose, propone

in: 4 ante 5 defer, delay, elude, plant 6 baffle, divert, insert 7 discard, enclose 8 postpone 9 frustrate

off: fob 4 doff, haft 5 defer, delay, evade, table 6 divert, remove, shelve 7 discard 8 deferred, postpone

on: act, don 5 apply, endue, indue, stage 6 employ 7 assumed, feigned, pretend 10 exaggerate

out: irk, vex 4 oust 5 anger, annoy, eject, evict, exert, exile, expel 6 banish, deport, retire 7 publish 8 displace, distress, irritate 9 ostracize 10 discompose, disconcert, expatriate, extinguish 14 discountenance

over: 4 bilk, hoax 5 cheat, defer, trick 7 deceive

together: add 5 piece, unite 6 gather, muster 7 collect 8 assemble 9 construct 10 congregate

up: can 4 post 5 build, erect

up with: 4 bear, take 5 brook, stand 6 endure 7 stomach 8 tolerate

putrefy: rot 5 decay 6 fester 7 corrupt 9

decompose 12 disintegrate

putrid: bad 4 foul 7 friable, noisome, vicious 8 depraved 10 malodorous, putrescent 11 displeasing 12 disagreeable

puttee: 4 spat 6 gaiter 7 legging

putter: 6 dawdle, fiddle 8 golf club 10 boondoggle

putting area: 5 green

putty: 6 cement

puxy: 5 swamp 8 quagmire

puzzle: cap, get 5 addle, amaze, glaik, griph, pinon, poser, rebus, stick 6 baffle, enigma, fickle, riddle 7 anagram, charade, confuse, foitter, griphus, mystery, mystify, nonplus, paradox, perplex 8 acrostic, bewilder, distract, entangle, intrigue 9 conundrum, dumbfound 10 difficulty, disconcert, palindrome

puzzled: 4 asea

puzzling: 6 knotty 7 knotted 9 difficult, equivocal

pygarg: 5 addax 6 osprey

Pygmalion: *sister:* 4 Dido
  offspring: 6 Paphos, Paphus
  sister's husband: 8 Sichaeus
  statue: 7 Galatea
  victim of: 8 Sichaeus

pygmy, pigmy: elf 4 pixy, runt, tiny 5 atomy, dwarf, gnome, minim, short 8 dwarfish 9 dandiprat 10 chimpanzee

pygmy musk deer: 10 chevrotain

pygostyle: 4 bone 5 vomer

pyknic: 5 solid, squat 6 stocky, sturdy 8 muscular 9 endomorph, squatness 11 endomorphic

pylon: 4 post 5 tower 6 marker 7 gateway 8 monument

Pylo's king: 6 Nestor

pyramid: 4 heap, pile, tomb 6 accrue 8 increase
  builder of largest: 6 Cheops
  inhabitant: 5 Khufu 6 Cheops
  site: 4 Giza 7 Cholula

pyramidal: 4 huge 8 enormous, imposing

pyre: 4 bale, bier 6 suttee 7 bonfire

pyrene: pip 4 seed 5 stone

Pyrenees: *bandit:* 8 miquelet
  chamois: 5 izard
  mountain peak: 5 Aneto
  people: 6 Basque
  republic: 7 Andorra
  resort: Pau

pyriform: 10 pear-shaped

pyromaniac: 7 firebug 8 arsonist

pyrosis: 9 heartburn

pyrotechnics: 9 fireworks

pyrotechnical device: 8 pinwheel

pyroxene: 6 augite 8 diopside 11 schefferite 12 hedenbergite

Pythagoras' birthplace: 5 Samos

Pythias' friend: 5 Damon

python: boa 5 snake 7 serpent
  slayer: 6 Apollo

pythonic: 4 huge 8 inspired, oracular 9 monstrous

pyx, pix: box 4 case, test, vase 5 assay, capsa, carry, chest 6 casket, coffer, vessel 8 binnacle, ciborium, preserve 10 tabernacle

Q

Q: cue 5 queue

Qatar's capital: 4 Doha

q.e.d.: 21 quod erat demonstrandum

quaalude: 8 hypnotic, sedative

quabird: 5 heron

quack: cry 4 duck 5 couch, faker, fraud 6 crocus 7 shammer 8 impostor 9 charlatan, pretender 10 mountebank, stimulator 13 counterfeiter

quad: 4 quod, yard 5 block, court 6 campus, person 7 sibling

quadra: 6 fillet, listel, plinth

quadragenarian: 8 fortyish

quadragesimal: 5 forty 6 Lenten

quadrangle: 5 court 6 square 8 tetragon

quadrant: arc, bow 4 gill 6 fourth, radial 8 farthing 9 antimeter 10 instrument

quadrate: 4 suit 5 adapt, agree, ideal 6 square 7 perfect, squared 8 balanced 9 rectangle 10 correspond 13 correspondent

quadriga: 4 cart 6 horses 7 chariot

quadrille: 5 cards, dance 9 cotillion

quadroon: 6 hybrid 7 mixture, mulatto 8 terceron

quadrumane: ape 6 monkey 7 gorilla 10 chimpanzee

quadruped: 6 mammal 10 four-legged

quaff: sip 5 draft, drink 6 tipple, waught

quag: 5 quake 6 quiver 8 quagmire

quagga: 7 wild ass
relative: 5 zebra

quaggy: 4 miry, soft 5 boggy 6 flabby, spongy 7 queachy 8 yielding

quagmire: bog, gog, hag 5 marsh, swamp 6 morass

quahog: 4 clam 10 little neck 11 cherry stone

quail: cow 4 bird 5 colin, cower, quake, shake 6 blench, cringe, curdle, flinch, recoil, shrink, tremor, turnix 7 massena, tremble 8 bobwhite 9 partridge
flock of: 4 bevy 5 covey
young: 7 cheeper 8 squealer

quail snipe: 9 dowitcher

quaint: odd 4 nice 6 crafty 7 antique, curious, strange, unusual 8 fanciful, graceful, peculiar, singular 9 whimsical

quake: 5 quail, shake, waver 6 quiver, shiver, tremor 7 shudder, tremble, vibrate 10 earthquake

Quaker: Fox 4 Penn 6 Friend 9 broadbrim

Quaker City: 12 Philadelphia

Quaker gray: 5 acier

Quaker-ladies: 5 bluet 11 meadowsweet

Quaker State: 12 Pennsylvania

Quaker's founder: 9 George Fox

quaking: 4 aspen, quaky 6 trepid 8 timorous 9 trembling, trepidity

qualification: 7 ability 8 aptitude 9 condition, endowment, knowledge, requisite 10 adaptation, capability, competence, experience 11 acquirement, designation, restriction 12 capacitation, modification

qualified: 4 able 5 ready 8 eligible

qualify: fit 5 abate, adapt, equip, limit 6 enable, modify, soften, temper 7 ascribe, assuage, entitle, prepare 8 diminish, mitigate, moderate, restrain, restrict 9 predicate 10 habilitate 11 characterize

quality: 4 cost, kind, rank, rate, sort, thew, tone 5 class, grade, power, quale, taste, trait 6 nature, status, strain, virtue 7 caliber, calibre, element, feature, stature 8 capacity, nobility, property 9 attribute, character 10 excellence 11 superiority 14 accomplishment, characteristic
of tone: 6 timbre 9 resonance

qualm: 4 drow, pall 5 doubt, spasm 6 attack, nausea, plight, puzzle, regret, twinge 7 scruple 8 sickness 9 faintness, misgiving 10 perplexity 11 compunction 12 apprehension

quandary: fix, jam 4 pass 6 pickle, plight, scrape 7 dilemma, nonplus 11 predicament 12 bewilderment

quantity (see also **amount**)**:** ace, any, bit, jag, jot, lot, sea, sum 4 atom, body, bulk, dash, dose, dram, drop, feck, iota, lick, lots, mass, mort, much, raff, raft, slew, unit 5 batch, bunch, grist, hoard, scads, stack, store 6 amount, capful, degree, extent, hirsel, morsel, number, weight 7 average, driblet, handful, modicum, portion, slather 9 allowance
excessive: 4 glut 5 spate
fixed: 8 constant
full: 10 complement
irrational: 4 surd
per unit: 4 rate
prescribed: 4 dose 6 dosage
small: 4 dram, drop, iota 5 scrap, shred 7 dribble, smidgen
without direction: 6 scalar

Quantrill's men: 7 raiders

quantum: 4 unit 6 amount 7 portion 8 quantity 9 aggregate

quarantine: ban 7 exclude, isolate 8 restrain, sanction 9 interdict, segregate

quaranty: 5 court

quarantene: 4 rood 7 furlong

quark: caw 5 croak, quawk

quarl, quarle: 4 tile 5 brick

quarrel: row 4 feud, fuss, spat, tiff 5 brawl, broil, cavil, flite, flyte, scene, scrap, set to 6 affray, barney, bicker, breach, breeze, fracas, hassle, jangle, ruckus, strife 7 brabble, contend, dispute, faction, rhubarb, wrangle 8 argument, disagree, squabble 9 upscuddle 10 contention 11 altercation, controversy 12 disagreement 16 misunderstanding

quarrelsome: 7 hostile, scrappy 8 brawling, choleric, petulant 9 bellicose, irascible, irritable, litigious 10 discordant, pugnacious 11 belligerent, contentious 12 disputatious 13 argumentative

quarry: pit 4 game, mine, prey 6 object, ravine, victim

quart: 6 fourth 7 measure
four: 6 gallon
metric: 5 liter, litre
one-eighth: 4 gill
two: 6 flagon

quartan: 5 fever 7 malaria

quarter: 4 coin, digs 5 house, lodge, mercy, put up, tract 6 bestow, billet, canton, fourth, harbor, region, supply 7 furnish, harbour, housing, shelter 8 clemency, district, division 9 direction, dismember 11 forbearance

quarters: 4 camp, room 7 billets, lodging, shelter 8 barracks 9 dormitory
nautical: 6 fo'c'sle 7 gunroom 8 steerage, wardroom 10 forecastle
sleeping: 9 dormitory
winter: 10 hibernacle
women's: 5 harem
quarter note: 8 crotchet
quartz: 4 onyx, sand, sard 5 agate, flint, prase, silex, topaz 6 jasper, silica 7 citrine, crystal, rubasse, sinople 8 amethyst 9 carnelian 10 calchedony
quartzite: 9 itabarite, sandstone
quash: 4 cass, drop, void 5 abate, annul, crush, quell 6 cancel, subdue 7 abolish, destroy, shatter 8 abrogate, suppress 9 overthrow
Quasimodo: 9 hunchback
creator: 4 Hugo
occupation: 10 bell ringer
residence: 9 Notre Dame
quaternion: 6 tetrad 7 quartet 8 quatrain
turning factor: 6 versor
quaver: 5 shake, trill, waver 6 falter, quiver 7 tremble, tremolo, vibrate 9 vacillate, vibration
quawk: caw 5 heron 6 squall 7 screech
quay: key 4 bund, dock, mole, pier, wall 5 levee, wharf 7 landing 10 embankment
quean: 4 jade 5 hussy, wench 6 harlot 10 prostitute
queasy: 5 timid 8 delicate, doubtful, qualmish, ticklish, troubled 9 hazardous, nauseated, squeamish, uncertain, unsettled 10 fastidious 11 embarrassed 13 uncomfortable
Quebec: *bay:* 6 Hudson, Ungava
capital: 11 Quebec City
city: 4 Hull 5 Laval 6 Quebec, Verdun 8 Montreal
founder: 9 Champlain
land measure: 6 arpent
patron saint: 4 Anne
peninsula: 5 Gaspe
province of: 6 Canada
provincial flower: 4 lily
river: 10 St. Lawrence
quebrada: gap 5 brook, creek, gorge 6 ravine, stream 7 fissure 8 brooklet
Quechua: 4 Inca 6 Indian
queen: ant, bee 4 card, fers, rani(Ind.) 5 ranee(Ind.), reine(F.) 6 regina 7 monarch 9 sovereign 10 chess piece
fairy: Mab 7 Argante, Titania
widowed: 7 dowager
queen it: 8 domineer 9 put on airs, tyrannize
queen of fairies: Mab, Pam, Una 7 Titania 8 Gloriand
Queen Anne's lace: 10 wild carrot
Queen City: 10 Cincinnati
Queen of the Adriatic: 6 Venice

Queen of the Antilles: 4 Cuba
Queen of the East: 7 Zenobia
queen of gods: 4 Hera, Juno, Sati
Queen of Hearts: 9 Elizabeth
Queen of Heaven: 4 Hera, Mary, moon 7 Astarte
Queen of Isles: 6 Albion
Queen of Palmyra: 7 Zenobia
Queen of Sheba: 6 Balkis
queen of spades: 5 basta
Queen of Thebes: 5 Dirce
queen of underworld: Hel 4 Hela
queen's arm: 6 musket
queen's-delight: oil 4 herb 9 perennial, queenroot
queen's-flower: 6 myrtle 9 bloodwood
queenly: 5 noble, regal, royal 7 haughty, reginal 8 majestic
Queensland: *river:* 8 Brisbane
seaport: 8 Brisbane
queer: odd, rum 4 harm, sham 5 drunk, faint, funny, giddy, rally, spoil 6 banter, insane 7 curious, disrupt, erratic, strange, touched, unusual 8 abnormal, doubtful, fanciful, obsessed, peculiar, qualmish, singular, spurious 9 dishonest, eccentric, fantastic, squeamish 10 homosexual, jeopardize, suspicious 11 counterfeit, intoxicated 12 questionable
queest: 8 ringdove
queet: 4 coot
quell: end 4 calm, cool, dash, kill, quay, sate 5 allay, check, crush, quash, quiet, still 6 obtund, pacify, reduce, soothe, spring, stanch, stifle, subdue 7 assuage, destroy, put down, repress, satisfy 8 fountain, overcome, suppress 9 overpower, overwhelm, subjugate 10 extinguish
quelque-chose: 6 trifle
quench: 5 allay, douse, slake 6 put out 7 satisfy 8 mitigate 10 extinguish
quenelle: 8 meatball 9 forcemeat
quercus: oak 4 tree 9 evergreen
querent: 8 inquirer 9 plaintiff 11 complainant
querist: 8 inquirer 10 questioner
quern: 4 mill 7 grinder 9 millstone
querulous: 7 fretful, peevish, whining 9 irritable, plaintive 11 complaining 12 querimonious
query: ask 5 doubt 6 demand 7 examine, inquire, inquiry 8 question 9 challenge 11 interrogate, uncertainty
quest: ask, bay 4 hunt, seek 6 search 7 examine, inquest, journey, pursuit, seeking 9 adventure 10 enterprise, expedition 13 investigation
question: ask 4 crux, pump, quiz 5 demur, doubt, grill, poser, query, scout, targe(Sc.) 6 appose, cruces(pl.), debate, de-

mand, quaere, riddle, shrive **7** dispute, inquire, inquiry, problem, scruple, stumper **9** catechise, catechize, challenge, interview **10** discussion **11** examination, interrogate, proposition **12** interpellate **13** interrogation, interrogative, investigation

denoting: **15** interrogational

rhetorical: **10** eperotesis

question mark: 7 erotema, eroteme

questionable: 4 moot **7** dubious, suspect **9** ambiguous, equivocal, uncertain **10** improbable, unreliable

questionnaire: 4 form, poll **7** canvass

quetzal: 4 bird, coin **5** dance **6** trogon

queue: cue **4** line **5** braid **7** pigtail

quiaquia: 4 scad **9** cigarfish

quibble: 4 carp **5** cavil, cheat, dodge, evade, hedge **6** bicker **7** evasion, shuffle **8** pettifog **9** find fault **10** equivocate, split hairs **12** equivocation

quica: **7** opossum

quick: apt, yap **4** deft, fast, flit, lish, live, spry, vite(F.), yare **5** acute, agile, alert, alive, apace, brisk, fiery, fleet, hasty, rapid, ready, sharp, swift, tosto(It.), yeder **6** abrupt, active, lively, moving, nimble, prompt, speedy, sudden, volant **7** intense **8** animated, dextrous, shifting, vigorous **9** dexterous, impatient, sensitive, sprightly **10** celeritous, perceptive **11** expeditious **12** invigorating

quick bread: 6 scones **7** muffins, popover **8** biscuits **9** cornbread

quicken: 4 whet **5** hurry, speed **6** arouse, excite, hasten, incite, revive, vivify **7** animate, enliven, provoke, refresh, sharpen **8** expedite, inspirit **9** reanimate, stimulate **10** accelerate **11** resuscitate **12** reinvigorate

quicker than: ere

quick kick: 12 football punt

quicklime: 5 rusma

quickly: 4 fast, rath, soon, vite(F.) **5** alive, apace **6** belive, hourly, presto, pronto **7** rapidly **8** promptly, speedily, vigorous

quickness: 5 speed **6** acumen **7** acidity **8** dispatch, progress, pungency, sagacity **9** acuteness **10** expedition

quicksand: 4 flow, syrt, trap **6** danger, syrtis

quickset: 5 hedge **7** thicket **8** hawthorn

quicksilver: 7 mercury **9** heautarit

quid: cud, fid **4** chaw, chew **5** pound, trade **6** barter, return **8** exchange, quiddity **9** sovereign

quidnunc: 5 frump **6** gossip, tatler **8** busybody

quiescent: 5 quiet, still **6** latent, static **7** dormant, resting **8** inactive, sleeping **10** motionless

quid pro quo: 9 tit-for-tat **10** equivalent **11** interchange

quiet: coy, pet **4** calm, cosh, dead, ease, fair, hush, lull, mild, rest, tame **5** allay, downy, inert, peace, privy, sober, still, tasty **6** gentle, hushed, merely, modest, placid, repose, secret, sedate, serene, settle, silent, smooth, soothe, static, stilly **7** appease, compose, halcyon, restful, retired, silence, subdued, tasteful **8** composed, decorous, inactive, peaceful, secluded, tranquil **9** alleviate, contented, noiseless, peaceable, placidity, quiescent, reposeful, unruffled **10** motionless, silentness, unmolested **11** clandestine, tranquilize, undisturbed

quietus: 5 death **6** repose **8** mittimus **11** acquittance

quiff: 4 girl, puff **5** whiff **8** forelock

quill: cop, pen **5** remex, spina **6** bobbin, pinion **7** remiges(pl.), spindle

porcupine: pen **5** spine

quilt: pad, sew **4** gulp **5** eider **6** caddow, pallet, stitch **7** blanket, comfort, swallow **8** coverlet **9** comforter **11** counterpane

quink: 5 brant

quinoa: 5 seeds **7** pigweed

quinoline derivative: 7 analgen

quintuplets: 6 Dionne **7** Fischer

quip: mot, pun **4** gibe, jest, joke **5** sally, taunt **6** saying **7** quibble

quire: 4 fold **5** choir, paper

quirk: 4 bend, kink, quip, turn **5** clock, crook, knack, sally, trait, twist **6** groove, strike **7** caprice, evasion **8** flourish **9** deviation, mannerism **10** subterfuge **11** peculiarity **12** equivocation

quirquincho: 5 pichi **6** peludo **9** armadillo

quirt: 4 whip **5** romal

quis: 8 woodcock

quisling: rat **7** traitor **8** turncoat

quit: rid **4** free, stop **5** avoid, cease, clear, forgo, leave, repay **6** acquit, depart, desist, forego, resign, vacate **7** abandon, forsake, release, relieve **8** abdicate, absolved, liberate, renounce **9** surrender **10** relinquish **11** discontinue

quitclaim: 5 grant **7** release **12** convey by deed **14** relinquishment

quite: all **4** very, well **5** stark, truly **6** really, wholly **7** totally, utterly **8** entirely **10** altogether, completely, positively **12** considerably

quite so: 7 exactly **9** precisely

quittance: 5 repay **6** return **8** requital **9** discharge, repayment **10** recompense, reparation

quitter: 4 seal, slag **5** piker **6** coward **7** shirker

quiver: 4 beat, case, quag, tirl(Sc.) 5 bever, quake, quick, shake, thirl(Sc.), throb, trill 6 active, arrows, bicker, cocker, dindle, lively, nimble, quaver, sheath, shiver, tremor 7 frisson, pulsate, tremble, vibrate 8 flichter 9 palpitate, vibration

quivering: 5 aspen 6 ashake, didder 7 aquiver 8 blubbery 9 tremulous

quiverleaf: 5 aspen

quixotic: 6 unreal 7 utopian 9 imaginary, visionary 10 chivalrous, idealistic 11 impractical, in the clouds 13 impracticable

quiz: ask 4 exam, hiss, hoax, jest, joke, mock, test, whiz 5 chaff, probe 7 examine 8 instruct, question, ridicule 11 examination, questioning

quizzical: odd 7 amusing, comical, curious, probing, teasing 9 bantering, eccentric, perplexed 11 incredulous

quizzing glass: 7 monocle

quod: jug 4 jail 8 imprison

quodlibet: 6 debate, medley 8 fantasia, question, subtlety

quod vide: 8 which see

quoin: 4 coin 5 angle, wedge 6 corner 8 keystone, voussoir

quoit: 4 disc, ring 5 throw 6 discus 8 cromlech

mark aimed at: tee

pin: hob

quomodo: 5 means 6 manner

quondam: 4 once 6 former 7 onetime 8 sometime

quonset hut: 6 prefab

British type: 6 Nissen

quorum: 5 group 7 council 8 majority

quota: 4 part 5 share 6 divide, ration 8 dividend 9 apportion 10 contingent, proportion

quotation: 5 price, quote

quotation mark: 9 guillemet(F.)

quote: 4 cite, cote, name, note 5 motto, refer 6 adduce, allege, allude, notice, repeat, select 7 excerpt, extract, passage 9 reference, selection 10 memorandum

quoth: 4 said 5 spoke

quotidian: 5 daily 7 trivial 8 everyday, ordinary 9 recurring 11 commonplace

quotient: 5 ratio 6 result 8 fraction

quotity: 5 group 10 collection

R

R: rho 6 letter

Ra: Shu, Tem, Tum 4 Aten 5 Horus 7 Chepera, Khepera, Sokaris 9 Harmachis

bull form: 5 Bacis

child: Mat, Shu 4 Maat 5 Athor

parent: Geb, Keb, Nut, Seb 5 Neith

wife: 4 Mout

raad: 7 catfish

rab: 6 beater

rabato, rebato: 4 ruff 6 collar

rabban: 6 master 7 teacher

rabbet: 4 plow 5 check 6 groove, recess 7 channel 9 fillister

rabbi: 4 lord 5 amora 6 master, rabbin 7 amoraim, tannaim, teacher 8 sabaraim, saboraim 9 clergyman

assistant: 6 cantor

school: 7 yeshiva 8 yeshibah, yeshivah 9 yeshiboth(pl.)

wife: 9 rebbetzin

rabbit: bun, doe 4 buck, cony, hare, tyro 5 bunny, capon, coney, lapin(F.) 6 coward, novice, rodent, tapeti

fictional: 5 Mopsy, Peter 6 Harvey 9 Bugs Bunny

fur: 4 cony, rack, scut 5 coney, lapin

genus: 5 lepus

relative: 4 pika

shelter: 5 hutch 6 burrow, warren 7 clapper

tail: fud(Sc.) 4 scut

young: 4 rack 6 gazabo, gazebo 7 starter

rabbit-ear: 6 aerial, cactus 8 antenna, toadflax

rabbit fever: 9 tularemia

rabbit flower: 8 foxglove, toadflax

rabbit-foot: 5 charm 8 talisman

rabbit-meat: 5 lapin 9 archangel

rabbit tobacco: 10 balsamweed

rabbit vine: 9 groundnut
rabbitfish: 8 chimaera
rabbitmouth: 10 harelipped, snapdragon
rabbitry: 5 hutch 6 warren
rabbit's-root: 12 sarsaparilla
rabble: mob 4 herd, raff, rout, scum 5 crowd 6 polloi, ragtag 7 bobtail 8 canaglia, canaille, riffraff 9 confusion, tag and rag 10 clamjamfry, hubble-shoo, hubble-show 11 commonality, rank and file
rabble-rouser: 6 ragtag 8 agitator 9 demagogue
Rabelaisian: 5 bawdy 6 earthy
rabid: mad 6 raging 7 extreme, frantic, furious, violent, zealous 8 demented, deranged, frenzied, virulent 9 fanatical 12 enthusiastic
rabies: 5 lyssa, lytta 7 madness 11 hydrophobia
raccoon: 5 guara, tejon 6 mapach 7 mapache 9 crabeater
related animal: 5 coati, panda
race: cut, ilk, run 4 dash, gest, herd, kind, lane, line, root, rush, slit, sort, stem, stud, type 5 blood, breed, brood, caste, chevy, chivy, class, corso, creek, flesh, geste, hurry, relay, speed, stock, track, tribe 6 arroyo, bicker, broose, chivvy, course, family, groove, hasten, hurdle, nation, people, slalom, sprint, stirps, strain 7 bombast, channel, contend, contest, dynasty, lineage, regatta, running, scamper, scratch, species 8 marathon 9 holethnos 10 freeforall, generation, passageway 11 competition, descendants, nationality, watercourse
division: 7 Negroid 9 Caucasian, Mongolian
human: man 7 mankind 9 mortality
mixed: See **person:** *of mixed blood*
murder: 8 genocide
pert. to: 6 ethnic
series: 7 regatta
science: 9 athletics, ethnology
starting line: 7 scratch
race board: 9 gangplank
raceabout: 5 sloop 8 roadster
racecourse: 4 heat, oval, ring, turf 6 career, circus, course 8 gymkhana 10 hippodrome
marker: 4 meta 5 pylon
racehorse: 5 pacer 6 maiden, mantis, plater 7 sleeper, trotter
racer: 4 crab 5 miler, snake 6 runner 7 courser, serpent 8 sprinter 9 turntable 10 blacksnake
racetrack: 5 Ascot 7 Belmont, Hialeah 10 Epsom Downs, Gulf Stream, Santa Anita
raceway: 5 canal 7 channel, fishway 8 millrace

Rachel: *children:* 6 Joseph 8 Benjamin
father: 5 Laban
husband: 5 Jacob
sister: 4 Leah
rachis: 4 stem 5 spine 7 spindle 8 backbone
rachitis: 7 rickets
racist: 5 bigot 9 sectarian
rack: bar, fly, gin, jib 4 bink, crib, gait, pace, path, scud, skin, tree 5 airer, brake, creel, flake, horse, stand, touse, trace, track, vapor 6 course, cratch, gantry, harass, strain, wrench 7 afflict, agonize, grating, oppress, pathway, stretch, torment, torture, vestige 9 framework, persecute 10 excruciate, foresaddle
racket: bat, din 4 shoe 5 bandy, dodge, noise, trick, work 6 bustle, clamor, crosse, hubbub, outcry, scheme, strike 7 clangor, clatter, pattern, revelry 8 business, snowshoe 10 battledore, turbulence 11 merrymaking
jai alai: 5 cesta
rack up: 4 gain 5 score 7 achieve 10 accomplish
rackle: 5 clank 6 rattle 7 clatter 8 reckless 9 impetuous 10 headstrong
raconteur: 8 narrator 11 storyteller
racy: 5 brisk, fiery, fresh, smart, spicy, swift 6 lively, risque 7 piquant, pungent, zestful 8 indecent, spirited, stirring, vigorous 10 suggestive 12 exhilarating
rad: 5 eager, quick, ready 6 afraid, elated 11 exhilarated
Radames' love: 4 Aida
radar: 15 detection system
image: 4 blip
screen: 5 scope
raddle: rod 4 beat 5 color, ocher, twist 6 branch, cudgel, thrash 9 separator 10 interweave
radial: ray 8 quadrant
radiance: 4 beam, glow 5 glare, gleam, glory, nitor, sheen, shine 6 luster 7 glitter, glowing, shining 8 lambency, splendor 9 brilliant 10 brightness, brilliancy, effulgence, refulgence
radiant: 6 bright 7 auroral 11 resplendent
radiate: 4 beam, emit 5 shine 6 spread 7 diffuse, emanate 9 coruscate 10 illuminate
radiating: 6 radial 8 stellate 11 centrifugal
radiation detector: 6 geiger
radiator: 6 heater
radical: red 4 root, surd 5 basal, basic, rebel, ultra 7 capital, drastic, extreme, forward, leftist, liberal, organic, support 8 cardinal, complete 9 extremist 10

foundation, iconoclast **11** fundamental **12** intransigent **13** revolutionary

chemical: ion **4** amyl, aryl **6** acetyl, adenyl, adipyl **7** nitrate, nitrite, sulfate, tartryl **8** aluminyl

political: **9** anarchist, extremist **13** revolutionary

radicate: fix **4** root **5** plant **9** establish

radicle: **7** rootlet **9** hypocotyl

radio: set **8** portable, wireless **9** broadcast, radiogram **10** transistor **12** walkie-talkie

detector: **5** radar

frequency: **5** audio

interference: **6** static

operator: ham **6** sparks **11** broadcaster

part: **5** diode **8** detector, selector

rating: **6** Hooper

signal check: **7** monitor

wave: **5** micro, short

radish: **5** radis(F.) **7** cadlock **9** crossweed

radium: *discoverer:* **5** Curie

emanation: **5** niton, radon

source: **7** uranite

radius: ken **5** orbit, range, spoke, sweep **6** extent, length

pert. to: **6** radial

radix: **4** root **6** etymon **7** radical

raffish: low **4** wild **5** cheap **6** flashy, frowsy, tawdry **7** unkempt **9** worthless **11** disgraceful **12** disreputable

raffle: **4** raff **6** jumble, rabble, refuse, tangle **7** drawing, lottery, rubbish, serrate **8** entangle, riffraff

raft: cow, lot, mat **4** crib, floe, heap, moki, raff, slew, spar **5** balsa, barge, float **6** dinghy, jangar **9** catamaran, transport **10** collection

part: **6** brail

rider: **8** Huck Finn

raft duck: **5** scaup **7** redhead **8** bluebill

rafter: **4** balk, beam, firm, viga **7** carline, chevron

rag: jag, kid, rib **4** mock, rail, rate, tune **5** annoy, dance, scold, scrap, shred, tease **6** banter, harass, rumpus, tatter, uproar **7** quarrel, remnant, wrangle **9** newspaper

ragamuffin: bum **4** hobo, waif **5** tramp **6** loafer, orphan **9** scarecrow **14** tatterdemalion

rage: fad, ire **4** beef, fret, fume, funk, fury, heat, rant, rave, tear **5** anger, chafe, craze, furor, mania, storm, wrath **6** choler, fervor, frenzy, furore, temper **7** amentia, bluster, bombast, emotion, fashion, fervour, passion, thunder **8** acerbity, acrimony, insanity, violence **9** vehemence **10** enthusiasm

ragged: **5** harsh, rough, seedy **6** jagged, shaggy, uneven **7** shreddy, unkempt, worn out **8** strident, tattered **9** defec-

tive, dissonant, imperfect, irregular **10** straggling, threadbare, unfinished **11** dilapidated

ragged jacket: **4** seal

ragged lady: **5** guara **11** love-in-a-mist

ragged sailor: **10** bluebottle, cornflower

raggedy doll: Ann **4** Andy, Anne

raging: **4** grim, wild **5** rabid **6** fierce **7** fervent, furious **8** furibund **9** ferocious

raglan: **6** sleeve **8** overcoat

ragout: **4** hash, stew **5** salmi **6** salmis **7** goulash, haricot, terrine **8** salpicon **10** capilotade **11** gallimaufry

ragpicker: **6** bunter **10** chiffonier **11** chiffonnier(F.)

rags: **4** duds **6** shreds **7** clothes, tatters

ragshag: **10** ragamuffin **11** masquerader

ragwort: **5** plant **8** ambrosia **9** groundsel **10** butterweed

rah: **5** cheer **6** hurrah

raid: **4** bust, tala **5** foray **6** attack, creach(Sc.), creagh(Sc.), forage, harass, inroad, invade, maraud, piracy **7** assault, chappow, despoil, hership **8** invasion **9** chevachie, incursion, onslaught, roadstead, cavalcade

rail: bar, jaw **4** coot, flow, gush, jest, rant, rate, slat, sora **5** abuse, array, chide, cloak, crake, dress, guard, heron, plank, scoff, scold, soree, track **6** banter, berate, callet, revile, septum **7** arrange, bidcock, bilcock, clocker, footrest, garment, inveigh **8** decorate, Rallidae(pl.), reproach **9** spectator

genus of: **4** sora **6** rallus

railing: bar **5** fence **7** barrier, parapet **8** balconet, banister, espalier, rabulous **9** bannister, guardrail **10** balconette, balustrade **12** vituperation

raillery: **4** gaff **5** chaff, sport **6** banter, blague, satire **8** badinage, ridicule **10** persiflage

railroad: **4** herd, line, push, rush **5** hurry, track **8** ceinture, monorail **9** transport

branch: **4** spur, stub **6** feeder

bridge: **7** trestle, viaduct

car: **5** coach, diner **6** parlor **7** caboose, coal-car, parlour, Pullman, sleeper

center: **7** station **8** terminal, terminus **10** roundhouse

cross rail: **4** frog

flare: **5** fusee

signal: **5** fusee **9** semaphore

station: **4** gare(F.) **5** depot

switch: **4** frog

tie: **6** timber **7** sleeper

worker: **6** boomer, porter **7** fireman **8** brakeman, engineer, strapper **9** conductor

railway: **5** train **6** subway **8** elevated, jackstay, monorail **9** funicular

raiment: See **dress**

rain: dag, fog 4 mist, pour 5 blizz, blout, misle, plash, spate, storm 6 deluge, mizzle, serein, shower 7 drizzle 8 downpour, sprinkle 10 cloudburst 13 precipitation

check: 4 stub 12 postponement
fine: 4 mist 6 serein 7 drizzle
god: 8 Parjanya
icy: 4 hail, snow 5 sleet
pert. to: 7 pluvial
unit of measure: 4 inch

rain bird: 6 plover 7 tomfool
rain cloud: 5 nimbi(pl.) 6 nimbus
rain forest: 5 selva
rain gauge: 8 udometer 10 hyetometer 11 pluviograph, pluviometer 15 hyetometrograph
rain glass: 6 barometer
rain leader: 9 downspout
rain tree: 5 saman, zaman 6 zamang 8 genisaro 9 monkeypod
rainbow: arc, bow 4 iris
goddess: 4 Iris
measuring device: 12 spectrometer
pert. to: 6 iridal
rainbow chaser: 8 idealist 9 visionary 11 doctrinaire
rainbow-like: 6 iridal 10 iridescent
raincoat: mac 4 mino 6 poncho, ulster 7 slicker 10 mackintosh, trenchcoat
rainfall: *pert. to:* 6 hyetal
rainfowl: 6 cuckoo 10 woodpecker 11 channelbill
rainspout: 4 rone(Sc.)
rainy: wet 4 damp 5 moist 7 flooded 8 cluttery
season: 7 monsoon

raise: end 4 buoy, grow, hain, heft, hike, levy, lift, rear, rise, stir 5 arear, boost, breed, build, crane, dight, elate, erect, exalt, hance, heave, heeze, hoist, horse, rouse, set-up, start, trice 6 arouse, ascend, assume, awaken, cantle, create, emboss, excite, gather, incite, leaven, muster, obtain, remove, uplift 7 address, advance, bring up, chevise, collect, elevate, enhance, ennoble, lighten, present, procure, produce, promote 8 addition, heighten, increase 9 cultivate, establish, institute, intensify, originate, propagate, resurrect 10 aggrandize, appreciate, invigorate

raised: 4 hove 6 arrect, enleve(F.) 8 elevated
raisin: 5 lexia, zibeb 7 currant, sultana 8 muscatel
raison d'être: 14 reason for being
raj: 4 rule 5 reign 11 sovereignty
rajah: 4 king 5 chief 6 prince 9 dignitary
wife: 4 rani 5 ranee
Rajmahal creeper: 4 jiti, vine

rake: gad, rue, rut 4 path, raff, roue, rove, trip 5 claut, glean, scour, track 6 gather, groove 7 collect, gleaner, scratch 8 enfilade, rakehell 9 debauchee 11 inclination
with gunfire: 8 enfilade
rakehell: 4 wild 7 immoral 9 debauched, debauchee, dissolute 10 profligate
rake-off: 4 take 6 profit, rebate 10 commission, percentage
rakish: 4 lewd, pert 7 roguish 9 dissolute
rale: 6 rattle
rally: 4 drag, mock, stir 5 chaff, noise, rouse 6 arouse, attack, banter, deride, revive 7 recover, restore, reunite 8 assemble, mobilize, raillery, ridicule 10 recuperate, strengthen 11 concentrate
rallying cry: 5 motto 6 slogan 9 battle cry
ram: hit, pun, tup, wad 4 buck, butt, cram, tamp, teap 5 Aries, crash, sheep, stuff 6 batter, beetle, chaser, rancid, strike, thrust, wether 7 collide, plunger 8 bulldoze
ram cat: tom 4 male
ramage: 4 wild 5 bough, rough 6 unruly 7 untamed 8 branches, frenzied, wildness
ramage hawk: 8 brancher
Rama's bride: 4 Sita
ramate: 8 branched
ramble: gad 4 roam, rove, walk 5 jaunt, prowl, range 6 sprawl, stroll, travel, wander 7 digress, saunter 8 straggle 9 excursion
rambling: 7 cursory, devious 9 desultory, scattered, wandering 10 circuitous, discursive 11 peripatetic 12 disconnected
rambunctious: 4 wild 5 rough 6 unruly 9 turbulent 10 boisterous, disorderly, rampageous 12 obstreperous 14 uncontrollable
ramekin: pan 4 dish 9 casserole
ramentum: 5 palea, palet 6 paleae(pl.), scales 7 shaving 8 particle
ramie, ramee: 4 hemp, rhea 5 fiber 6 ortiga
ramification: arm 4 rami(pl.) 5 ramus 6 branch, spread 8 division, offshoot 9 branching 10 divergence 12 embranchment
rammish: 4 lewd, rank 7 violent
Ramona author: 7 Jackson
ramose: 7 cladose 8 branched 9 branching
ramp: rob 4 bank, rage, walk 5 apron, crawl, creep, slope, storm 6 dupery, unruly 7 incline, swindle 8 gradient, platform 9 helicline 10 cuckoopint
rampage: 5 binge, spree, storm 6 uproar 7 turmoil
rampageous: 4 wild 6 unruly 7 riotous 10 boisterous

rampant: 4 rife 6 fierce 7 violent 9 excessive, unchecked 10 immoderate, prevailing, rampageous, widespread 11 extravagant, flourishing, threatening, 12 unrestrained 14 uncontrollable

rampart: 4 wall 5 agger, mound, redan 6 vallum 7 barrier, bastion, bulwark, parapet, ravelin 10 embankment 13 fortification

part: 4 spur

ramper: 7 lamprey

rampire: dam 7 fortify, rampart 10 embankment, strengthen

Ramses' goddess: 4 Anta

ramshackle: 4 rude 5 loose, shaky 7 rickety 10 disorderly, dissipated, tumbledown

ramus: 6 branch 10 branchlike

rancel: 6 search 7 ransack

ranch: 4 casa, farm, tear 5 finca, pluck 7 acreage, scratch 8 estancia, hacienda 9 estantion

worker: 4 hand 5 owner 6 cowboy, farmer, gaucho 7 cowpoke, rancher 8 herdsman, ranchero(Sp.), ranchman

rancid: 4 rank, sour 5 musty, stale 6 frowsy, putrid 7 spoiled 8 stinking 9 obnoxious, offensive, repulsive 10 malodorous, unpleasant

rancor, rancour: ire 4 gall, hate 5 spite 6 enmity, grudge, hatred, malice 8 rankling 9 animosity, antipathy, hostility, virulence 10 bitterness

randan: row 4 boat 5 spree 6 uproar 7 rampage

random: 5 loose, stray 6 casual, chance 7 aimless 9 desultory, haphazard, hit-or-miss 10 accidental, fortuitous 11 purposeless

randy: 5 crude, revel, shrew 6 beggar, coarse, frolic, virago, vulgar 7 canvass 8 carousal 9 festivity 10 disorderly, licentious 12 unmanageable

range: ken, row 4 ally, area, farm, line, rank, roam, rove 5 align, aline, ambit, blank, class, field, gamut, orbit, order, reach, ridge, scope, space, stove, stray, sweep 6 extent, ramble, series, sphere, stroll, tether, wander 7 arrange, compass, explore, habitat, saunter 8 classify, distance 9 cookstove, grassland 11 systematize

range-finder: 6 stadia 9 mekometer, telemeter 10 trekometer

ranger: 4 seal 5 rover, sieve 6 keeper, warden 8 commando, wanderer

rangy: 8 gangling, spacious

rank: row 4 army, file, foul, line, rate, sort, tier 5 array, caste, cense, class, fetid, frank, genus, grade, gross, order, proud, range, space, utter 6 barony, coarse, degree, estate, gentry, mighty, rancid, rating, series, status, strong 7 caliber, calibre, calling, compeer, copious, corrupt, dignity, extreme, fertile, froward, glaring, haughty, noisome, obscene, overfed, peerage, precede, quality, rammish, rampant, station, stratum, swollen, violent 8 absolute, abundant, classify, division, eminence, estimate, flagrant, gentrice, headlong, indecent, palpable, position, powerful, vigorous 9 condition, downright, egregious, excessive, exuberant, formation, gradation, hierarchy, luxuriant, offensive, overgrown, plentiful 10 coordinate, malodorous 11 arrangement, distinction 14 classification

deprive of: 4 bust 5 break 6 depose 7 cashier

mark of: 6 stripe

military: PFC 5 major 7 captain, colonel, general, private 8 banneret, corporal, sergeant 10 lieutenant

rank and file: 6 member, plebes 9 common man 11 commonality

rankle: irk, vex 4 fret, gall 6 fester, obsess, plague 7 inflame 8 irritate, ulcerate

rann: 5 verse 6 stanza, strain

ransack: 4 loot, rake, sack 5 rifle, steal 6 search 7 pillage, rummage

ransom: buy, fee 5 atone, price 6 redeem, rescue 7 deliver, expiate, release 8 liberate, retrieve 13 consideration

money: 10 redemptory

rant: 4 fume, huff, rage, rail, rand, rave, riot, song, tune 5 dance, orate, revel, scold, spout 6 frolic, speech, steven 7 bluster, bombast, carouse, declaim, fustian 9 discourse 11 merrymaking, rodomontade 13 jollification

rantipole: 4 wild 6 rakish, unruly 9 termagant

ranula: 4 cyst 8 swelling

rap: bob, box, con, hit, tap 4 blow, chap, chat, grab, knap, talk, tirl 5 blame, clink, clout, knock, seize, smite, steal, utter 6 rebuke, snatch, strike, thwack 7 deliver 8 sentence 9 criticize, criticism, enrapture, transport 10 conference, punishment

rapacious: 6 fierce, greedy 8 covetous, grasping, ravening, ravenous 9 ferocious, voracious 10 avaricious, predacious

rapacity: 5 claim, ravin 7 edacity 8 appetite, cupidity, exaction 9 extortion

rape: 4 file, rasp 5 abuse, haste, hasty, hurry, quick, seize, spoil 6 defile, pomace, ravish, turnip 7 despoil, hastily, outrage, pillage, plunder, robbery, scratch, violate 9 violation 10 plundering, spoliation

rapeseed: 5 colza 7 ravison

Raphael: 5 angel 7 painter 9 archangel

raphe: 4 line, seam 5 joint 6 suture

rapid: 4 fast 5 agile, brisk, chute, fleet, quick, steep, swift 6 abrupt, moving, nimble, speedy 10 fastmoving 11 expeditions

rapidity: 5 haste, speed 8 celerity, velocity 9 quickness

rapidly: 4 fast 5 apace

rapier: 5 bilbo, sword 6 verdun 7 ricasso
blade heel: 7 ricasso
part of: 5 forte 6 foible

rapine: 7 pillage, plunder 10 spoliation

rapparee: 6 robber 8 vagabond 9 plunderer 10 freebooter

rappee: 5 snuff

rapport: 6 accord 7 harmony 8 affinity, relation 9 agreement 12 relationship

rapscallion: 5 rogue, scamp 6 rascal, wretch 7 villain 8 vagabond 11 ne'er-do-well 14 good-for-nothing

rapt: 4 deep 5 tense 6 intent 8 absorbed, ecstatic 9 comprised, enchanted, engrossed, entranced, transport 10 enraptured, unthinking 11 preoccupied, transported

raptorial: 9 rapacious 11 accipitrine

raptorial bird: owl 4 hawk 5 eagle 7 vulture

rapture: 5 bliss 6 trance 7 delight, ecstasy 8 rhapsody 9 enrapture, happiness, transport 10 exultation

rara avis: 6 rarity, wonder 7 phoenix

rare: odd, raw 4 fine, good, nice, thin 6 choice, dainty, geason, scarce, seldom, unique 7 antique, capital, curious, extreme, special, tenuous, unusual 8 precious, uncommon, unwonted 9 beautiful, excellent, exclusive, exquisite, scattered, underdone 10 infrequent 11 distinctive, exceptional 13 distinguished, extraordinary

rarefied: 4 thin 7 diluted, ethered, gaseous, refined 8 aethered 10 attenuated

rarely: 5 extra 6 seldom 10 hardly ever

rarity: 5 curio, relic 6 geason, oddity 7 antique

ras: 4 cape 6 fabric, prince 7 fascist 8 headland 9 commander

rascal: boy, cad, imp 4 file, loon 5 foist, gipsy, gypsy, knave, rogue, scamp 6 ablach, budzat, coquin, harlot 7 budzart, glutton, villain 8 hosebird, scalawag, sealpeen, widdifow 9 miscreant, reprobate, scallawag, scoundrel, trickster 11 rapscallion

rascally: 4 base, mean 6 arrant 9 dishonest, worthless 11 furciferous, mischievous

rash: cut, mad 4 bold 5 brash, erase, hardy, hasty, heady, hives, scamp, shave, slash, uredo 6 daring, eczema, scrape,

unwary 7 foolish, hotspur, icarian, scratch 8 careless, epidemic, eruption, headlong, heedless, reckless, temerous 9 desperate, exanthema, foolhardy, foreright, hotheaded, impetuous, imprudent, overhasty, urticaria, venturous 10 headstrong, hotspurred, incautious, indiscreet, unthinking 11 adventurous, furthersome, harum-scarum, precipitate, precipitous, temerarious, thoughtless, venturesome 13 adventuresome, efflorescence

rasher: 5 slice 6 collop 7 portion 8 rockfish

rashness: 4 rage, rese 5 folly 6 acrisy 8 temerity 9 headiness

rasorial: 7 gnawing 10 scratching

rasp: rub 4 file 5 belch, eruct, grate 6 scrape 8 irritate

rasping: 5 harsh, raspy, rough 6 hoarse, rasion 7 raspish, raucous 8 guttural 9 offensive

rasse: 5 civet 6 weasel

rat: pad 4 scab, snot 6 defect, inform, rodent, vermin 8 betrayer, deserter, informer, renegade, squealer 9 councilor, counselor 11 stool-pigeon 13 double-crosser
catcher: 9 pied piper
genus: 6 spalax
kind: kok 5 metad, zemmi, zemni 6 tosher 7 hamster
poison: 7 arsenic 8 ratsbane

ratafia: 4 noyau 7 biscuit, cordial, liqueur 8 macaroon

rataplan: 8 drumbeat

ratch: bar 4 rend 7 stretch 8 distance

ratchet: 4 pawl 5 click 6 bobbin, detent

rate: fee, tax 4 earn, fare, file, pace, rank 5 abuse, blame, chide, class, grade, price, scold, score, tempo, value 6 assess, assize, charge, degree, reckon, regard, tariff 7 account, censure, chasten, despise, quality, reprove 8 appraise, classify, consider, estimate, evaluate 10 proportion 14 classification

rate of exchange: 4 agio 5 batta

ratel: 6 badger, burier

ratfish: 8 chimaera

rathe, rath: 4 soon 5 eager, early, quick 6 prompt, speedy 7 betimes 8 promptly, speedily

rather: 5 prior 6 before, choice, enough, in lieu, pretty, sooner 7 earlier, instead, quickly 8 somewhat 10 preferably, preference 11 immediately

rather than: ere 6 before

ratify: 4 amen, pass, seal 6 affirm, enseal, verify 7 approve, confirm, endorse, license 8 roborate, sanction 9 authorize, establish

rating: 4 rank 5 cense, class, grade 6 rebuke 8 estimate, scolding, standing 9 reprimand 10 evaluation 14 classification

ratio: cos 4 rate, sine 5 quota, share 6 cosine, degree, ration 7 average, portion 8 relation 10 percentage, proportion 11 capacitance

ratiocination: 5 logic 7 thought 8 argument 9 inference, reasoning

ration: 4 dole, food, meed, mete 5 allot, quota, ratio, share 6 divide 7 portion 8 relation 9 allotment, allowance, apportion 10 distribute 11 calculation

rational: 4 sane 5 sober, sound 7 logical, prudent 8 sensible 10 reasonable 11 intelligent, level-headed 13 philosophical

rational integer: 4 norm

rational principle: 5 logos

rationale: 6 reason 11 explanation

rations: 8 buckshee 10 provisions

ratite: emu, moa 4 bird, emeu 7 ostrich 9 cassowary
genus: 7 apteryx 8 dinornis

ratoon: 5 shoot, stalk 6 spring, sprout

rattail: 4 file 5 braid 7 pigtail

rattan: 4 cane, lash, palm, sega, whip 5 noose, thong 6 punish, switch, wicker

ratter: cat, dog 8 betrayer

rattle: din 4 birl, chat, rick, stun, tirl 5 addle, annoy, clack, rouse, scold, upset 6 assail, bicker, maraca, racket, uproar 7 agitate, chatter, clapper, clatter, clitter, confuse, fluster, gnatter, shatter 9 crepitate, embarrass 10 disconcert

rattlebrained: 5 dizzy, giddy, silly 7 flighty 9 frivolous 11 empty-headed, harebrained

rattlepate: ass 4 dolt 9 chatterer

rattleroot: 7 bugbane

rattlesnake: 8 cascavel, crotalus 9 sistrurus 10 massasauga

rattlesnake fern: 9 sporangia

rattlesnake herb: 9 baneberry

rattlesnake pilot: 10 copperhead

rattle-top: 7 bugbane

rattletrap: 5 ratty 7 gewgaws, rickety 10 ramshackle 11 knickknacks

ratty: 4 mean 6 shabby 7 unkempt 11 dilapidated

ratwa: 7 muntjac

raucous: dry 4 loud 5 gruff, harsh, noisy, rough 6 coarse, hoarse 7 braying, brusque, rasping 8 strident 9 turbulent 11 cacophonous

raun: roe 5 spawn

raupo: 7 cattail

ravage: eat 4 loot, prey, ruin, sack 5 foray, harry, havoc, spoil, waste 6 forage 7 despoil, destroy, overrun, pillage, plunder, scourge, violate 8 deflower, desolate, lay waste 9 devastate 10 depopulate, desolation 11 despoilment, devastation

rave: 4 rage, rant 5 blurb, crush, orate, storm 7 bluster, bombast, declaim, enthuse 8 harangue 11 infatuation 12 commendation

ravel: run 4 comb, fray, rail 5 snarl 6 runner, sleave, tangle, unwind 7 crumble, involve, perplex, railing, untwist, unweave 8 entangle, separate 10 complicate 11 disentangle

ravelin: 8 demilune 13 fortification

raveling: 4 lint 6 thread

raven: 4 crow 5 black 9 blackbird
genus: 5 corvus
of Odin: 5 Hugin

Raven: *author:* Poe
character: 6 Lenore
refrain: 9 Nevermore

ravenous: 6 greedy, hungry, lupine, toothy 7 starved 8 edacious, famished 9 cormorant, ferocious, rapacious, voracious 10 catawampus, gluttonous

ravine: cut, den, gap, lin 4 dell, ghyl, gill, linn, sike, wadi, wady 5 abyss, canon, chasm, chine, clove, ditch, flume, glack, gorge, goyal, goyle, griff, grike, gulch, gully, kloof, notch, strid 6 arroyo, canyon, cleuch, clough, coulee, gulley, hollow, nullah 7 crevice, dry wash 8 barranca, barranco, quebrado 10 depression

raving: 8 frenzied 9 delirious 10 incoherent, irrational 12 arreptitious

ravish: rob 4 rape 5 abuse, charm, force, harry, seize 6 defile, snatch 7 afforce, corrupt, delight, despoil, enchant, plunder, violate 8 deflower, entrance 9 captivate, constrain, enrapture, transport

ravishment: 7 ecstasy, rapture 9 transport

raw: 4 cold, damp, dazy(Sc.), lash, nude, rare, rude 5 bawdy, bleak, chill, crude, green, harsh, naked 6 abrade, chilly, coarse, unfair 7 cutting, natural, obscene 8 immature, indecent, uncooked 9 inclement, unexposed, unrefined, unskilled, untrained 10 indelicate, unfinished, unprepared, unseasoned 11 uncivilized, unpracticed, unprocessed 12 uncultivated 13 inexperienced

rawboned: 4 lean 5 gaunt 7 angular, scrawny

rawhide: 4 pelt, whip 5 knout, quirt, thong

ray: 4 beam, beta, dorn, soil 5 array, dress, flair, gleam, gleed, light, manta, order, shaft, shine, sight, skate 6 defile, glance, obispo, radial, streak, stripe, vision 7 besmear, homelyn, radiate, raiment 9 irradiate, selachian 10 perception, vertebrate 11 arrangement, irradiation

fish: 4 dorn 5 skate
penetrating: 5 gamma
rayon: 5 moire, ninon, tulle 6 faille, pongee 7 taffeta
yarn size: 6 denier
raze, rase: cut, rub 4 rage, ruin, tear 5 erase, graze, growl, level, shave, wreck 6 efface, incise, scrape 7 destroy, scratch, subvert 8 demolish, dismantle 9 deprecate, overthrow, prostrate 10 obliterate
razee: cut 5 prune 6 reduce 7 abridge
razor: 4 clam 6 shaver
kind: 7 rattler 8 electric
sharpen: 4 hone 5 strop
razorback: hog 5 ridge 10 roustabout
razorbill: auk 7 skimmer
razor stone: 10 novaculite
razz: 5 chaff, tease 6 banter, deride, heckle 8 ridicule
razzle-dazzle: 5 spree 7 confuse 8 hilarity 9 confusion
re: anent 9 regarding 10 concerning
Re: See Ra
reach: ken, run, toe 4 come, gain, hawk, hent, ryke(Sc.), seek, span, spit 5 get to, grasp, retch, scope, vomit 6 advene, affect, amount, arrive, attain, extend, extent, strive 7 achieve, contact, expanse, possess, stretch 8 approach, make up to 9 culminate, penetrate 10 accomplish
under: 7 subtend
reachable: 10 accessible
reaching: 6 effort 8 profound
reaction: 4 kick 5 start 6 answer 7 tropism 8 response 9 influence 10 impression, opposition
adverse: 8 backlash
read: con 4 lire(F.), pore, scan, show, skim, tell 5 aread, areed, drone, guess, solve, study 6 advise, browse, peruse, relate 7 counsel, declare, discern, foresee, learned 8 decipher, describe, foretell, indicate 9 interpret, supervise
ability to: 8 literacy
inability to: 6 alexia 8 dyslexia
metrically: 4 scan
superficially: 4 skim
readable: 7 legible
reader: 6 lector, lister, primer 7 reciter 8 bookworm, lectrice, lecturer 9 anthology, 10 instructor 11 proofreader 12 elocutionist
readily: 4 well 6 easily, freely 7 lightly
readiness: art 4 ease, gift 6 graith 7 address, freedom 8 alacrity, facility, goodwill, volition 9 dexterity, eagerness, quickness 10 promptness, volubility 12 preparedness
reading: 6 lesson 7 lection, lecture, perusal, recital, version 9 collation, rendition 10 prelection

ready; apt, fit 4 free, gird, glib, here, pret(F.), ripe 5 alert, apert, bound, eager, handy, happy, point, quick 6 active, adroit, facile, fluent, prompt 7 forward, prepare, willing 8 cheerful, dextrous, handsome, prepared, skillful 9 agreeable, schedule, dexterous 10 convenient 11 expeditious 12 unhesitating
real: 4 very, true, vrai(F.) 5 being, loyal 6 actual, hearty 7 certain, cordial, factual, genuine, gradely, literal, sincere 8 existent, faithful, tangible 9 authentic, effective, heartfelt, intrinsic, unfeigned, veritable 10 unaffected
real estate: 4 alod 5 allod, lands 6 realty 8 allodium, freehold, premises, property 13 hereditaments
claim: tax 4 lien 8 mortgage 9 trust deed 11 encumbrance
pert. to: 7 predial
realistic: 5 vivid 6 shrewd 7 prudent 8 lifelike 11 down-to-earth 12 matter-of-fact
realization: 8 fruition 9 awakening
realize: get 4 gain, know 5 sense, think 6 effect, obtain 7 achieve, acquire, convert, fulfill 8 complete, conceive 9 apprehend 10 accomplish, appreciate, understand
really: aru 4 very, well 5 quite, sooth 6 indeed 8 actually
realm: 4 land 5 bourn, clime, range 6 bourne, circle, domain, empire, region, sphere 7 country, demesne, dynasty, kingdom, terrene 8 division, dominion, province 9 territory 10 department 11 sovereignty 12 jurisdiction
realty: 7 honesty, loyalty, royalty 8 fidelity, property 10 possession
ream: 4 bore, draw, foam, scum 5 bevel, cheat, cream, froth, widen 7 enlarge, stretch 8 quantity 11 countersink
reamer: 4 tool 5 borer, drift 6 broach
reanimate: 5 rally, renew 6 revive 11 resuscitate 12 reinvigorate
reap: cut 4 crop, rake 5 glean 6 garner, gather 7 acquire, collect, harvest
rear: aft, end, fix 4 back, buck, cave, grow, last, lift, rere, tail 5 abaft, breed, build, erect, nurse, raise, stern, train 6 astern, behind, foster, nursle 7 arriere(F.), bring up, buttocks, educate, elevate, nurture 9 construct, establish, posterior 10 background, forthbring
toward: aft 5 abaft 6 astern
rearing by horse: 5 stend 6 pesade
rearhorse: 6 insect, mantis
rearward: 8 backward 9 posterior 10 retrograde
reason: peg, why, wit 4 mind, nous 5 argue, brain, cause, logic, sense, think 6 debate, ground, motive, ponder, sanity

7 meaning **8** argument, converse **9** discourse, intellect, rationale, wherefore **10** moderation, understand **11** explanation, expostulate, ratiocinate, rationality, rationalize **12** plausibility **13** consideration, understanding

alleged: **7** pretext

deprived of: **8** demented

pert. to: **6** noetic

want of: **5** folie **7** amentia, madness **8** insanity

reasonable: 4 fair, just **5** cheap **8** feasible, moderate, rational **9** equitable **11** inexpensive

reasoning: 5 logic **8** argument **10** conclusion **13** argumentation

basis of: **7** premise

reassure: 5 cheer **7** comfort, hearten **9** encourage

reata, riata: 4 rope **5** lasso **6** lariat

reave: rob **4** tear **5** burst, seize, split **7** bereave, pillage, plunder, unravel

rebato: See rabato

rebate: 5 check **6** lessen, reduce, refund, weaken **8** diminish, discount, kickback **9** abatement, deduction, reduction, remission

rebec: 4 lyre **5** sarod, rebab **6** fiddle, violin

Rebekah: *brother:* **5** Laban

father: **7** Bethuel

husband: **5** Isaac

mother: **6** Milcah

son: **4** Esau **5** Jacob

rebel: 4 rise **6** oppose, revolt, rise up **8** renegade **9** adversary, insurgent **10** antagonist

rebellion: 6 mutiny, putsch, revolt **8** defiance, sedition, uprising **10** resistance, revolution **12** disobedience, insurrection, renunciation **15** insubordination

rebellious: 9 estranged **10** refractory **12** contumacious, recalcitrant **13** insubordinate

rebirth: 7 revival **10** conversion, renascence **11** renaissance **13** reincarnation

reboant: 7 echoing **13** reverberating

rebound: dap **4** echo, stot **5** bound, carom **6** bounce, carrom, recoil, re-echo, resile, return, spring **7** recover, reflect, resound **8** ricochet, snap back **9** boomerang **11** reverberate

rebuff: cow **4** scat, slap, snub **5** check, chide, fling, repel, scold, spurn **6** lesson **7** censure, fend off, refusal, reprove, repulse **9** rejection, reprimand

rebuke: nip, rap, tsk, tut, wig **4** beat, snub, tush **5** barge, blame, check, chide, scold **6** berate, dirdum, lesson, rating **7** downset, lecture, repress, reproof, reprove **8** admonish, chastise, reproach, restrain **9** criticism, criticize, reprehend, reprimand, talking-to **10** correction **11** comeuppance, reprobation

rebus: 6 enigma, puzzle, riddle

rebut: 5 reply **6** oppose, rebuff, refute, revile **7** fend off, repulse **8** disprove **10** contradict

recalcitrant: 5 rebel **6** unruly **7** defiant **8** stubborn **9** obstinate, resisting **10** rebellious, refractory

recall: 5 annul **6** abjure, cancel, encore, memory, remind, repeal, revoke **7** abolish, bethink, rescind, restore, retrace, retract, summons **8** remember, withdraw **9** recollect, reminisce **11** countermand

recant: 6 abjure, revoke **7** abandon, disavow, retract **8** renounce, take back, withdraw **9** repudiate **10** contradict

recapitulate: sum **5** essay **6** repeat, review **7** restate **8** argument **9** enumerate, reiterate, summarize

recapture: 6 recall, regain, retake **7** recover **9** reacquire

recede: ebb **6** depart, retire **7** deviate, regress, retreat **8** decrease, fall back, withdraw **10** retrograde

receipt: 4 chit, stub, take **6** acquit, apocha, binder, recipe **7** formula **11** acquittance **14** acknowledgment **15** acknowledgement

receipts: 6 income **7** revenue **8** payments

receive: get **4** take **5** admit, adopt, greet, **6** accept, assume, derive, obtain, take in **7** acquire, procure

receiver: 4 host **5** donee, fence **6** pernor, porter **7** breaker, catcher, hostess, rentier **8** cymaphen, receptor **9** collector, condenser, treasurer **12** receptionist

of property in trust: **6** bailee **7** trustee

of stolen goods: **5** fence

recension: 6 review **8** revision **9** reviewing **11** enumeration, examination

recent: new **4** late **5** fresh **6** modern **7** current **8** neoteric

recently: 4 anew **8** latterly

receptacle: bin, box, can, cup, fat, pan, pot, tub, urn, vat **4** case, cell, cist, crib, font, pail, tray, vase, well, tank **5** basin, chest, torus **6** basket, bottle, bucket, carton, holder, hopper, trough **7** cistern, humidor, pitcher **8** canister, receiver **9** container, reservoir

reception: tea **5** levee, party **6** accoil, durbar, soiree **7** accueil, ovation, receipt, welcome **8** greeting **9** admission, collation **10** admittance **13** entertainment

morning: **5** levee

place: **4** hall **5** atria(pl.), foyer, salon **6** atrium, parlor **7** parlour **9** vestibule

receptive: 8 amenable **9** acceptant **10** hospitable, open-minded **11** sympathetic

receptor: 5 basin 8 receiver 10 dispositor, sense organ 11 nerve ending

recess: ala, bay 4 apse, cave, cove, grot, hole, nook 5 ambry, cleft, crypt, niche, sinus 6 alcove, closet, grotto, rabbet, retire 7 adjourn, conceal, retreat, seclude 8 dissolve, interval, vacation 9 cessation, embrasure, suspension

recessive: 8 backward, receding

Rechab's son: 7 Jonadab

recherché: new 4 rare 5 fresh, novel 6 choice, exotic 7 unusual 8 uncommon 9 exquisite 10 farfetched

recidivation: 7 relapse 8 apostasy 11 backsliding

recipe: 7 formula, pattern, receipt 12 prescription

recipient: 4 heir 5 donee 7 alienee, devisee, legatee 8 receiver 9 receiving, receptive

reciprocal: 4 mate, twin 6 mutual 9 alternate 11 convertible, correlative

reciprocate: 5 bandy, repay 6 return 7 requite 8 exchange, give back 9 alternate 10 recompense 11 countervail, interchange

recital: 4 saga, tale 5 story 6 report 7 account, concert, program 8 relation 9 narration, narrative, rehearsal, statement 10 recitation, repetition 11 declamation, description, enumeration

recitation: 7 reading

recitative: 5 scena 9 narrative

recite: say 4 carp, scan, tell 5 chant, spout 6 intone, relate 7 recount 9 enumerate 10 cantilate 12 recapitulate

reciter: 6 anteri, diseur(F.) 7 diseuse(F.) 8 narrator 12 elocutionist

reck: 4 care, deem, heed, mind 7 concern 8 consider, estimate

reckless: 4 bold, rash 5 blind, folle, perdu 6 madcap, perdue 7 hotspur 8 careless, headlong, heedless 9 blindfold, bodacious, daredevil, desperate, dissolute, hotheaded, imprudent 10 neglectful, regardless 11 adventurous, extravagant, harum-scarum, indifferent, thoughtless 13 inconsiderate, irresponsible

reckon: 4 aret, date, deem, rate, rely, tell 5 audit, count, guess, think 6 arette, impute, number, regard, repute 7 account, ascribe, compute, include, suppose, surmise 8 consider, estimate, numerate 9 calculate, enumerate 10 adjudicate, understand 11 connumerate

reckoner: 5 abaci, brain 6 abacus 9 tabulator 10 calculator 11 comptometer

reckoning: 4 bill, rate, scot, shot 5 chalk, score 6 compot, esteem 11 computation

machine: I.B.M. 5 adder, brain 6 abacus 9 tabulator 10 calculator

reclaim: 4 save, tame 5 train 6 ransom, recall, redeem, reform, repair, rescue, revoke 7 recover, restore, salvage 8 civilize, empolder 10 regenerate 11 domesticate

reclaimed land: 6 polder

recline: lay, lie, sit 4 lean, loll, rest 5 slant 6 repose 7 incline

reclining: 5 lying, prone 6 supine 7 leaning, lolling, passive, resting 8 reposing 9 accumbent, recumbent

recluse: nun 4 monk 6 hermit, hidden, secret 7 eremite 8 anchoret, secluded, solitary 9 anchoress, anchorite, cloistral 10 cloistered 11 sequestered

recognition: 4 fame 6 credit 9 awareness

recognize: ken, own, see 4 avow, know, note, spot 5 admit, greet 6 accept, acknow, agnize, beknow, notice, recall, remark, review, revise, salute 7 consent, correct, recover 8 identify, perceive 9 apprehend 10 appreciate 11 acknowledge, distinguish

recoil: shy 4 kick 5 quail, wince 6 blanch, flinch, shrink 7 rebound, retreat, reverse, squinch 8 withdraw

recollect: 4 cite 5 waken 6 recall 7 bethink 8 remember 9 remininisce

recollection: 4 mind 6 memory 8 memorial 9 anamnesis 11 remembrance 12 reminiscence

recommence: 5 renew 6 resume 7 reprise

recommend: 4 tout 5 refer 6 advise, commit, denote 7 commend, consign, counsel, entrust 8 advocate

recommit: 6 remand

recompense: fee, pay 5 repay 6 amends, bounty, reward, salary 7 premium, requite 8 requital 9 gratulate, indemnify, reimburse, repayment 10 compensate, remunerate, reparation 11 reciprocate, restitution, retribution 12 compensation, remuneration 13 consideration, gratification

without: 4 free 6 gratis

reconcile: 4 wean 5 adapt, agree, atone 6 accord, adjust, pacify, regain, settle, shrive, square 7 absolve, conform, expiate, explain, restore, reunite, satisfy 9 harmonize, make peace 10 conciliate, propitiate

recondite: 4 dark, deep 6 heavy, hidden, mystic, occult, secret 7 cryptic, obscure 8 abstract, abstruse, esoteric, profound 9 concealed

reconnaissance: 5 recce 6 survey

reconnoiter: spy 5 scout 6 recall, survey 7 examine, explore, inquire 8 discover

record: log, tab 4 acta(pl.), book, dope, file, memo, note, past, roll, show 5 actum, album, annal, chart, diary, enrol, enter, entry, graph, score 6 agenda, enroll, legend, memoir, postea, report **7** account, archive, blotter, calends, catalog, dossier, estreat, history, journal, kalends, rotulet **8** calendar, document, memorial, register **9** catalogue, chronicle, itinerary, narration **10** background, chronology, memorandum, transcribe, transcript

historical: **6** annals

holder: **4** file **6** binder **7** cabinet

keeper: **8** recorder **9** registrar

of arrest: **7** blotter

of meeting: **7** minutes

of proceedings: **4** acta(pl.) **7** minutes

of ship: log

of travel: **9** itinerary

official: **4** acta(pl.) **5** actum

personal: **5** diary **7** journal

recorder: **5** flute, judge **8** greffier, register **9** cartulary, registrar **10** chartulary

recording: **5** album, label **7** cutting

recording device: **4** tape **5** meter

recount: **4** deem, tell **5** count **6** recite, reckon, relate, repeat, retail **7** account, include, narrate **8** describe, rehearse **9** enumerate

recoup: **7** recover **9** indemnify, reimburse **10** compensate, recuperate

recover: get **5** amend, rally, upset **6** obtain, recoup, reform, regain, rescue, resume, retake **7** balance, get back, reclaim, recruit, restore, salvage **8** overcome, retrieve, snap back **9** repossess **10** bounce back, compensate, convalesce, recuperate

recovery: **4** cure **8** comeback **13** convalescence

law: **6** trover

recreant: **5** false **6** coward, craven, crying, wretch, yellow **7** traitor **8** apostate, betrayer, cowardly, deserter, disloyal, renegade, yielding **9** faithless **10** traitorous, unfaithful **11** disaffected **12** mean-spirited

recreation: **4** meal, play **5** dance, hobby, sport **6** picnic **7** renewal **9** amusement, avocation, diversion **10** relaxation **11** delassement, refreshment **12** regeneration **13** divertisement, entertainment

time: **6** recess **7** holiday **8** vacation

recrement: **4** scum, slag **5** dregs, dross, spume **6** refuse, scoria

recruit: **4** bleu(F.), boot **5** raise, renew, rooky **6** gather, muster, novice, revive, rookie, supply **7** draftee, private, recover, refresh, restore, soldier **8** assemble, bezonian, inductee, renovate **9** reinforce, replenish **10** recuperate, strengthen

rectangle: **6** oblong, square

rectifier: **5** diode

rectify: **5** amend, emend, right **6** adjust,

better, purify, refine, reform, remedy, repair **7** correct, distill, rebuild **8** emendate, regulate **10** straighten

rectitude: **6** equity, virtue **7** fitness, honesty **8** goodness **10** straitness **11** uprightness **12** straightness

rector: **4** head **5** chief, ruler **6** leader, priest **7** proctor **8** director, governor, minister **9** clergyman, connector **10** headmaster, proprector

rectory: **5** manse **8** benefice **9** parsonage

recumbent: **4** idle **5** lying, prone **7** leaning, resting **8** inactive, reposing **9** reclining

recuperate: **4** heal, rest **5** rally **6** perk up, regain **7** improve, recover **10** convalesce

recur: **6** advert, repeat, resort, return **7** iterate, rearise, **8** reappear

recurrent, recurring: **6** cyclic **7** chronic **9** returning **10** isochronal **11** reappearing **12** intermittent

recusant: **9** dissenter **11** dissentient **12** non-conformer

red: **4** lake, puce, rosy, ruby **5** canna, color, coral, fiery, gules, peony, roset, ruddy **6** cerise, cherry, claret, garnet, maroon, rubric, sienna, titian **7** carmine, crimson, glowing, leftist, magenta, nacarat, radical, roseate, Russian, scarlet **8** amaranth, blushing, inflamed, rubicund **9** anarchist, bloodshot, Bolshevik, communist, Muscovite, vermilion **10** erubescent **11** incarnadine **12** bloodstained

antique: **5** canna

brown: **5** sepia **6** russet, sorrel

dye: aal, lac **4** chay, choy **5** aurin, eosin **6** aurine **8** morindin

marked with: **6** rubric

purplish: **4** lake **6** claret

Venetian: **5** siena **6** sienna

yellow: **4** lama **5** aloma, brass, ochre, tenne **6** alesan, orange **7** saffron **9** alabaster, peachblow

red ape: **9** orangutan

red arsenic: **7** realgar

red-backed sandpiper: **6** dunlin

red bell: **9** columbine

red-bellied snipe: **9** dowitcher

red benjamin: **9** birthroot

red-blooded: **8** vigorous

red blotch: **10** adustiosis

red box: **8** official **12** bureaucratic

red bug: **7** chigger

red cedar: **5** savin **6** sabine, savine **7** juniper **8** flindosa

red cell: **11** erythrocyte

red chalk: **4** bole **6** ruddle

red cobalt: **9** erythrite

red copper ore: **7** cuprite

red corpuscle deficiency: **6** anemia

Red Cross founder: 6 Barton
Red Cross Knight: 6 George
wife: Una
red deer: roe 4 hart, hind, spay, stag
red-faced: 7 blowzed, flushed 8 blushing
red fever: 10 erysipelas
red fir: 4 pine 6 spruce 7 Douglas
red gum: 10 eucalyptus, strophulus
red-handed: 6 openly
red honeysuckle: 5 sulla
red-hot: 8 up-to-date
red lead ore: 8 corcoite
red-letter: 10 noteworthy
red man: 6 Indian
red-neck: 4 hick, rube 5 yokel 6 rustic
red pepper: 5 chile, chili 6 chilli
red perch: 8 rosefish
Red Planet: 4 Mars
Red Sea: 9 Erythrean
gulf: 4 Suez 5 Aqaba
island: 5 Perim
peninsula: 5 Sinai
red viper: 10 copperhead
red willow: 5 osier 6 cornel
redact: 4 edit 5 draft, frame 6 reduce, revise
redan: 7 rampart 8 fortress 10 breastwork 13 fortification
redbelly: 4 char 7 grouper 8 terrapin
redbird: 7 tanager 8 cardinal 9 bullfinch
redbird cactus: 7 jewbush
redbreast: 5 robin
redbud tree: 5 judas
redcap: 6 porter 7 carrier, specter, spectre 8 tarboosh 9 goldfinch, policeman
redden: 5 blush, flush, rouge
redeem: buy 4 free, save 6 ransom, regain, rescue 7 deliver, fulfill, reclaim, recover, release, restore 8 liberate 10 compensate, repurchase
redeye: 4 rudd 5 vireo 6 whisky 7 sunfish, whiskey 8 rock bass 10 copperhead
redhead: 5 finch 7 pochard 10 woodpecker
redmouth: 4 fish 5 grunt
redolence: 4 balm, odor 5 aroma, odour, scent, smell, 7 bouquet, perfume 9 fragrance, sweetness
redouble: 6 reecho, repeat 7 reprise, retrace 9 intensify 10 ingeminate
redoubt: 4 fort 6 schanz 10 breastwork, stronghold 13 fortification
redoubtable: 5 dread 6 famous 7 fearful 8 fearsome 10 formidable
redound: 5 react 6 accrue, recoil 7 conduce, resound 10 contribute 11 reverberate
redress: 5 amend, emend 6 adjust, relief, remedy 7 correct, relieve 10 compensate, reparation 12 compensation, satisfaction

redshank: 4 bird, clee 9 sandpiper
redshirt: 9 anarchist 11 Garibaldian 13 revolutionist
reduce: cut 4 bant, bate, bust, diet, ease, pare, raze, thin 5 abase, abate, annul, break, level, lower, scale, slash, smelt 6 appall, change, debase, demote, depose, derate, dilute, equate, humble, impair, lessen, rebate, refine, subdue, weaken 7 abridge, assuage, commute, conquer, curtail, cut back, degrade, deplete, whittle 8 attemper, condense, contract, decrease, diminish, discount, emaciate, minimize, retrench, slim down 9 subjugate 10 annihilate, bantingize, depreciate
to half: 9 dimidiate
sail: 4 reef
reduction: cut 5 slice 6 rebate 7 cut back, cutting, meiosis 8 analysis, discount 9 attrition 11 contraction, degradation 12 annihilation
redundancy: 7 nimiety 8 pleonasm, verbiage 8 plethora 9 verbosity 10 flatulence 11 periphrasis, superfluity
redundant: 5 wordy 6 lavish, prolix 7 copious, diffuse, verbose 9 excessive, exuberant 10 pleonastic 11 overflowing, superfluous 12 overabundant, tautological 13 superabundant 17 circumlocutionary
redwing: 6 thrush 7 gadwall 9 blackbird, francolin
redwood: 4 tree 7 Sequoia 9 evergreen
Ree: 7 Arikara
re-echo: rebound, resound 8 resonate 11 reverberate
reed: sag 4 dart, junk, pipe, sley, stem 5 arrow, grass, spear, stalk 7 bulrush, calamus, fistula
loom: 4 sley
reed organ: 8 melodeon 9 harmonium
reedbird: 7 warbler 8 bobolink
reedbuck: kob 4 koba 5 bohor, nagor 7 reitbok 8 antelope 9 waterbuck
reeder: 8 thatcher
reedy: 4 thin, weak 11 arundineous
reef: bar, cay, key 4 cayo, itch, lode, vein 5 atoll, mange, shoal 6 boiler 7 bioherm, shorten 8 eruption
mining: 4 lode, vein
sail: 4 furl 7 shorten
reefer: 4 coat, eton 5 miner 6 jacket, oyster 9 cigarette 10 midshipman
reek: rig 4 emit, fume, heap, pile, vent 5 equip, exude, smell, smoke, steam, vapor 6 exhale, stench 7 seaweed 8 mountain 10 exhalation
reel: 4 drum, pirn(Sc.), roll, spin, sway, swim, wind 5 dance, lurch, spool, swift, swing, waver, whirl, wince 6 bobbin, careen, hammer, teeter, totter, wintle 7

stagger, stumble 8 titubate, windlass
fishing: 4 pirn
reem: 4 moan, uris 7 unicorn
reeve: pen 4 pass, wind 5 twist 6 pucker,
thread 7 bailiff, provost, steward, wrinkle 8 overseer 9 enclosure, sheepfold
refection: 4 food, meal 5 drink, lunch 6
repast 11 refreshment
refectory: 4 mess 10 dining hall
monastery: 6 frater
refer: 4 cite, harp, send 5 recur 6 advert,
allude, appeal, assign, charge, commit,
direct, impute, regard, relate, return,
submit 7 ascribe, bring up, consult,
mention, specify 8 identify 9 affiliate,
appertain, attribute
referee: 5 judge 6 decide, umpire 7 arbiter 8 mediator 10 arbitrator
decision: nod
reference: 5 quote 6 aspect 7 respect 9
relevance 10 connection, pertinence 11
credentials 12 relationship 13 recom-
mendance 14 recommendation
mark: 4 star 6 dagger 8 asterisk
reference book: 5 atlas 7 almanac 8
handbook, syllabus 9 thesaurus 10 dictionary 12 encyclopedia
referendum: 4 poll, vote 7 mandate 10
plebiscite
refine: 4 edit 5 exalt, smelt 6 decoct, filter, finish, polish 7 clarify,
cleanse, concoct, elevate, improve, perfect 8 chastise, separate 9 cultivate,
elaborate, subtilize 12 spiritualize
refined: 4 nice 5 civil 6 artful, chaste, polite, urbane 7 courtly, elegant, genteel 8
delicate, graceful, highbred 9 courteous,
exquisite 10 fastidious
refinement: 5 grace 6 polish 7 culture,
dignity, finesse
refining cup: 5 cupel
reflect: 4 echo, muse, pore 5 glass, image,
study, think, weigh 6 divert, mirror,
ponder 7 bethink, deflect 8 cogitate,
consider, meditate, ruminate 9 reproduce 10 deliberate 11 contemplate, reverberate
reflected: 7 derived 8 mirrored, specular
reflection: 4 idea 5 image 6 musing 7
thought 8 likeness 10 cogitation, meditation, rumination 12 deliberation 13
consideration, contemplation
measuring device: 11 albedograph
reflective: 7 pensive 11 thoughtful
reflex: 4 bend, fold, turn 11 involuntary
reflux: ebb 6 ebbing, euripi(pl.), reflow 7
euripus 9 refluence, returning
reform: 4 mend, trim 5 amend, emend,
prune, renew 6 better, direct, punish,
remass, repair, revise 7 censure, correct,
improve, rebuild, reclaim, rectify, redress, reprove, reshape, restore 8 in-

struct 10 regenerate 11 reformation
refract: 6 impair 7 deflect, reflect 8 diminish 9 break down
refraction: device: 4 lens 5 prism 9 telescope
pert. to: 10 anaclastic
refractory: 6 immune, unruly 7 froward,
restive 8 contrary, perverse, stubborn 9
camsteary, camsteery, obstinate 10
headstrong rebellious, unyielding 11
contrarious, disobedient, intractable,
stiff-necked 12 contumacious, ungovernable, unmanageable, unresponsive
13 insusceptible
refrain: bob 4 curb, deny, shun 5 avoid,
cease, check, epode, forgo 6 chorus,
forego, govern 7 abstain, forbear, inhibit 8 response, restrain, withhold
music: 4 aria, song 5 ditty
refresh: 4 rest 5 bathe, cheer, renew,
slake 6 caudle, revise, revive, vivify 7
comfort, enliven, freshen, hearten,
quicken, restore 8 recreate, renovate 9
reanimate, replenish 10 invigorate, rejuvenate, strengthen 12 reinvigorate
refreshing: 4 dewy 5 balmy, tonic 11 re-
fectorial, refrigerant
refreshment: 8 refresco 9 collation
refrigerant: ice 5 freon 6 cooler 7 ammonia, coolant, cooling 13 carbon dioxide
refrigerate: ice 4 cool 5 chill 6 freeze
refuge: ark 4 home, port, rock 5 haven 6
asylum, bilbie, covert, harbor, resort,
shield 7 crannog(Sc.), harbour, retreat,
shelter 8 crannoge(Sc.), hospital, immunity, resource 9 sanctuary 10 protection, rendezvous, subterfuge
refugee: 5 exile, 6 emigre 8 fugitive
refulgent: 6 bright 7 glowing, radiant,
shining 8 splendid 9 brilliant 11 resplendent
refund: 5 repay 6 rebate 8 kickback 9 reimburse, repayment
refurbish: 5 renew, 6 polish, revamp 7
freshen 8 brighten, renovate
refusal: nay 6 denial
refuse: nay, ort 4 balk, coom, culm, deny,
dirt, dreg, junk, marc, nite, pelf, pelt,
veto 5 chaff, coomb, crawm, debar,
drast, drest, dross, grith, offal, renig, repel, scrap, trash, waste, wrack 6 debris,
forbid, garble, litter, lumber, reject, renege 7 backing, baggage, decline, disavow, forsake, garbage, gubbins, leaving, mullock, rubbish, repulse 8
disclaim, renounce, withhold 9 excrement, repudiate
coffee beans: 6 triage
grape: 4 marc
metal: 4 slag 5 dross 6 scoria
table: ort 5 scrap

wine: 4 lees

refute: 4 deny, meet 5 avoid, rebut, refel 6 assoil 7 confute 8 disprove, infringe, redargue 9 overthrow 10 contradict

serving to: 8 elenctic 10 elenctical

regain: 4 save 6 recoup 7 get back, recover 8 retrieve

regal: 5 jewel, royal 6 august, kingly 7 channel, stately 8 imperial, imposing, majestic, splendid

regale: 4 dine, fete 5 feast, treat, 6 dinner, spread 7 delight, gratify 9 entertain

regalia: kit 5 crown, dress 6 finery 7 emblems, ensigns, scepter, symbols 8 costumes, insignia 9 full dress 11 decorations 13 paraphernalia

Regan: *father:* 4 Lear
sister: 7 Goneril 8 Cordelia

regard: air, awe, con, eye 4 care, deem, gaze, heed, hold, look, mind, note, rate, sake, view, yeme 5 assay, honor, think, treat, value, watch 6 admire, aspect, assess, attend, behold, esteem, glance, homage, notice, remark, repute, revere, 7 adjudge, concern, observe, respect 8 consider, estimate, interest, relation 9 adoration, affection, attention, deference, reference 10 admiration, appearance, attendance, estimation, veneration 11 contemplate 13 consideration, contemplation

regarding: 4 as to, in re 5 about, anent 6 anent 7 apropos

regardless: 9 negligent 10 neglectful

regatta: 4 race 8 boat race

regency: 4 rule 8 dominion 10 government

regenerate: 5 renew 6 reborn, redeem, reform, revive 7 convert, newborn, reclaim, refresh, restore 8 gracious, recreate, renovate 9 reproduce

regent: 5 ruler 6 ruling 7 regnant, teacher 8 governor 9 governing
of sun: 5 Uriel

regimen: 4 diet, rule 6 system 7 control, hygiene 10 government, regulation 14 administration

regiment: 4 alai 5 cadre, order 11 systematize 12 military unit
flag: 6 pennon
member: 9 grenadier
nucleus: 5 cadre
officer: 5 boots 7 colonel

regina: 5 queen

region: des, erd, gay 4 area, belt, part, zone 5 clime, field, place, realm, space, tract 6 locale, sector, sphere 7 climate, country, demesne, kingdom 8 district, division, latitude, province, vicinity 9 territory 12 neighborhood 13 neighbourhood
elevated: 8 highland

infernal: 5 Hades 7 Avernus 8 Tartarus 10 underworld

pert. to: 5 areal

surrounded by alien power: 7 enclave

upper: 5 ether

warm: 7 tropics

wooded: 5 taiga 6 forest

woodless: 4 wold 5 llano, plain, weald 6 desert, meadow, steppe 7 pasture, savanna 8 savannah

regional: 5 local 9 sectional 10 provincial

register: lid 4 book, list, roll, rota, show 5 album, annal, diary, enter, entry, slate 6 agenda, docket, enlist, enroll, record, roster 7 ascribe, calends, catalog, certify, coucher, kalends, license, stopper 8 archives, bookmark, calendar, indicate, recorder, registry, schedule 9 catalogue, chronical, inventory, registrar
cash: 6 damper
legal: 6 docket
of deaths: 9 necrology

registrar: 5 clerk 7 actuary 8 greffier, recorder, register

reglet: 5 strip 7 molding

regnal: 5 royal 6 kingly

regnant: 6 regent, ruling 8 dominant, reigning 9 prevalent 10 widespread 11 predominant

regorge: 5 vomit 8 disgorge

regress: 6 egress, return, revert 9 backslide, throwback 10 retrograde, withdrawal

regret: rew, rue 4 miss, ruth 5 demur, grief, mourn, qualm, sorry, spurn 6 lament, repent, repine, sorrow 7 bethink, deplore, dislike, remorse, scruple 8 aversion, distress, forthink 9 penitence 10 misgivings, repentance 11 compunction, lamentation 14 disappointment

regular: 4 even 5 exact, sober, usual, utter 6 formal, normal, proper, serial, stated, steady 7 amiable, correct, general, habitue, ordered, orderly, typical, uniform 8 complete, constant, decorous, formular, habitual, ordinary, ordinate, periodic, pleasant, rhythmic, rotative, standard, thorough 9 continual, customary, isometric 10 consistent, dependable, methodical, systematic 11 symmetrical

regulate: set 4 pace, rule, time 5 frame, guide, order 6 adjust, behave, direct, govern, police, settle 7 arrange, compose, conduct, control, correct, dispose, rectify 8 attemper, modulate 9 establish 10 discipline 11 standardize

regulation: law 5 bylaw, canon, regle 6 assize, normal 7 precept, regimen, repulse, statute 8 ordinary 9 ordinance 14 administration

regulator: 5 valve

electricity: 9 rheometer

regulus: 4 king, star 5 matte, ruler

rehabilitate: 7 reclaim, recover, restore 9 reinstate

rehash: 7 restate 9 rechauffe

rehearse: say 4 cite, tell 5 drill, quote, speak, train 6 detail, recite, relate, repeat 7 mention, narrate, prepare, recount 8 describe, instruct, practice 9 enumerate 12 recapitulate

Rehoboam: *father:* 7 Solomon
kingdom: 5 Judah 6 Israel
son: 6 Abijah

reign: raj 4 rule, sway 5 guide, power, realm 6 empire, govern 7 kingdom, prevail 8 dominate 9 authority, dominance 10 prevalence 11 predominate
pert. to: 6 regnal

reimburse: pay 5 repay 6 defray, offset, recoup, refund 7 recover, replace 9 indemnify 10 compensate, recompense, remunerate

rein: 4 curb, slow, stop, turn 5 check, guide, leash, strap 6 bridle, direct, govern, haunch, kidney 7 compose, control, repress 8 restrain 9 hindrance

reindeer: 6 tarand 7 caribou, cervine
genus: 8 rangifer
Santa's: See Santa Claus's reindeer

reinforce: 4 back 5 brace, reman 6 second 7 afforce, augment, support 8 buttress, multiply 10 strengthen

reinforcement: 4 sput 9 accession

reinstate: 6 recall, revest 7 put back

reinvigorate: 7 quicken, refresh

reiterate: 4 drum, harp 6 repeat, resume 8 rehearse 10 ingeminate 12 recapitulate

reject: 4 defy, snub 5 eject, repel, scorn, scout, spurn, vomit 6 abjure, disown, rebuff, recuse, refuse 7 cashier, decline, discard, dismiss, disobey, forsake, shut out 8 abnegate, castaway, disallow, forswear, relegate, renounce 9 blackball, eliminate, ostracize, reprobate, repudiate 10 disapprove, disbelieve 13 excommunicate

rejoice: 5 cheer, elate, exult, glory 6 please 7 delight, gladden 8 jubilate 10 exhilarate, tripudiate

rejoin: 5 reply 6 answer 7 respond, reunite

rekindle: 6 revive 7 relight

relapse: 4 fall, sink, slip 7 setback, subside 9 backslide 10 recurrence 12 recidivation

relate: 4 ally, tell 5 apply, refer, state 6 allude, detail, recite, report 7 connect, declare, narrate, pertain, recount, restore 8 describe, rehearse 9 appertain, associate, correlate, enumerate 10 make public

related: kin 4 akin 7 cognate, connate,

germane, kindred 9 affiliate, connected 10 becousined 11 appropriate
on father's side: 6 agnate
on mother's side: 5 enate 6 enatic 7 cognate

relation: sib 5 blood, ratio 6 degree, family, status 7 account, bearing, history, kinship 8 affinity, standing 10 connection, friendship 12 relationship 13 consanguinity
mutual: 11 correlation
on father's side: 6 agnate
on mother's side: 5 enate

relative: eme, kin, sib 4 aunt, mama, papa 5 aunty, niece, uncle 6 auntie, cousin, father, friend, mother, nephew, sister 7 brother, kindred, kinsman, sibling 8 ancestor, apposite, relation, relevant 9 connected, kinswoman, pertinent 10 pertaining 11 comparative 13 corresponding, proportionate
maternal: 5 enate

relative amount: 5 ratio 6 ration

relatives: 7 kinfolk 8 cousinry, kinsfolk
favoritism to: 8 nepotism

relax: 4 ease, open, rest 5 abate, loose, remit 6 divert, lessen, loosen, reduce, soften, unbend 7 cool off, mollify, release, relieve, slacken 8 be at ease, calm down, mitigate 10 feel at home

relaxation: 4 ease, rest 6 repose 7 detente(F.), relache 9 amusement, diversion 10 recreation 11 delassement

relaxed: 4 lash 7 lenient 8 flexuous

relay: 4 post, race 5 spell 6 remuda(Sp.), supply 7 forward, relieve, station 8 avantlay, transmit

release: 4 bail, drop, emit, free, liss, trip, undo, vent 5 let go, lisse, relay, remit, slake, untie, yield 6 acquit, assoil, demise, exempt, loosen, parole, remise, rescue, spring 7 absolve, deliver, disband, freedom, manumit, publish, relieve, unleash, unloose 8 cut loose, liberate, mitigate, unfasten 9 acquittal, discharge, disengage, eliminate, exculpate, extricate 10 emancipate, liberation, relinquish 11 acquittance, deliverance 12 emancipation

relegate: 5 exile, refer 6 banish, charge, commit, deport, remove 7 consign, dismiss 8 accredit, turn over

relent: 4 melt 5 abate, let up, yield 6 soften 7 abandon, liquefy, mollify, slacken 8 dissolve, moderate 10 deliquesce

relentless: 4 grim, hard 5 harsh, stern, stony 6 fierce, strict 8 pitiless, rigorous 9 ferocious, immovable, merciless 10 inexorable, inflexible, persistent 11 unremitting

relevant: apt 5 ad rem 6 timely 7 apropos, germain, germane 8 apposite 9 connected, pertinent 10 applicable, to the point 11 appropriate, referential

reliable: 4 safe, true 5 tried 6 dinkum, honest, secure, steady, trusty 7 certain 9 authentic 10 dependable 11 trustworthy

reliance: 4 hope 5 faith, trust 6 belief 8 affiance 10 confidence, dependence

relic: 5 curio, mummy 6 corpse, hallow, remain 7 antique, leaving, memento, remnant, residue, vestige 8 memorial, souvenir 11 remembrance

pert. to: 9 reliquary

relic cabinet: 6 etager 7 etagere, whatnot

relict: 5 widow 7 widower 8 residual, survivor

relief: bot 4 alms, boot, bote, dole, ease, help 15 indemnification

ornamental: 4 fret 7 relievo

relieve: aid 4 beet, ease, free, help, liss 5 abate, allay, beete, erase, lisse, raise, relay, slake, spare, spell 6 assist, lessen, remedy, remove, succor 7 assuage, comfort, console, deliver, lighten, redress, release, support, sustain, unloose 8 diminish, mitigate 9 alleviate, debarrass, disburden, discharge, exonerate

religieuse: nun 6 sister

religieux: 4 monk 5 pious 9 religious

religion (see also next entry): 4 cult, sect 5 faith, piety 6 voodoo 7 service, worship 8 devotion, doctrine, fidelity 9 adoration, voodooism 10 conformity, observance, persuasion 17 conscientiousness

sect: 5 alogi

study of: 8 theology

system of: 5 faith

religion: See also under specific religions. EXAMPLE: "Islamic priest," see **Islam:** *priest*

religious: 4 holy 5 exact, godly, pious 6 devout, divine 7 fervent, godlike, zealous 8 faithful, monastic 9 pietistic, spiritual 10 devotional, scrupulous 13 conscientious

belief: 5 credo, creed

brotherhood: 8 sodality

denomination: 4 sect

devotion: 6 novena

directory: 4 ordo 7 ordines(pl.)

festival: 5 Purim 6 Easter 8 Passover

formally: 5 rigid 6 strict 8 orthodox 9 pharisaic

image: 4 icon

military order member: 7 Templar

observance: 4 fast, Lent

offering: 5 tithe 7 deodand 8 oblation

reformer: Hus 4 Huss, Knox 6 Luther

sayings: 5 logia

relinquish: 4 cede, drop, quit 5 demit, forgo, grant, leave, waive, yield 6 desert, forego, give up, remise, resign 7 abandon, dispose, forsake, lay down 8 abdicate, abnegate, disgorge, renounce 9 surrender

reliquary: box 4 apse, arca 5 apsis, chest 6 casket, chasse, shrine 7 chorten

reliquiae: 6 relics 7 remains

relish: 4 dash, gust, like, tang, zest 5 achar, enjoy, gusto, sauce, savor, taste 6 admire, canape, degust, flavor, palate, savour 7 delight, flavour 8 appetite, hautgout 9 appetizer, degustate, enjoyment, seasoning 11 inclination

kind: 5 achar, curry 6 catsup, caviar 7 botargo, chutney, mustard

relucent: 6 bright 7 radiant, shining 9 refulgent

reluct: 5 fight 6 revolt 8 struggle

reluctance: 6 revolt 8 aversion 9 adversion, antipathy, hesitancy 10 opposition, repugnance, resistance 13 indisposition, unwillingness 14 disinclination

reluctant: 4 loth 5 loath 6 averse, forced 7 adverse 8 backward, grudging, hesitant, opposing 9 resisting, unwilling 11 disinclined

rely: 4 bank, base, hold, hope, lean, rest 5 count, rally, trust 6 belong, cleave, depend, expect, lippen, reckon, repose 7 believe, confide, count on

Remagen's river: 5 Rhine

remain: lie 4 bide, last, rest, stay, wait 5 abide, dwell, hover, stand, tarry, thole 6 endure, linger, reside 7 persist, survive 8 continue 11 stick around

remainder: 4 rest, stub 5 stump 6 excess 7 balance, remanet, remnant, residue, surplus 8 leavings, residual, residuum 9 leftovers

remains: 4 dust 5 ashes, relic, ruins, trace 6 corpse, fossil 7 vestige

remand: 6 commit 7 consign 8 recommit, send back

remanent: 7 further 8 enduring 10 additional 13 supplementary

remark: say, see 4 barb, heed, note, word 5 aside, gloss, state, write 6 notice, postil, regard 7 comment, descant, express, observe 8 indicate, perceive 9 aspersion, platitude 10 animadvert, annotation, commentary, expression 11 distinguish, observation

embarrassing: 5 boner, break 7 blooper, faux pas

incidental: 12 obiter dictum

witty: gag, mot 4 quip 5 sally 7 sarcasm 9 witticism

remarkable: 7 notable, strange, unusual 8 uncommon 9 egregious, wonderful 10 noticeable 11 exceptional 12 considerable 13 extraordinary

remble: 4 move, stir

remedy: aid, bot 4 balm, boot, bote, cure, drug, gain, hale, heal, help 5 amend, salve, topic 6 arcana(pl.), elixir, physic, relief, repair 7 arcanum, correct, cure-all, nostrum, panacea, placebo, rectify, redress, relieve 8 antidote, curative, medicine 9 treatment 10 assistance, catholicon, chevisance, corrective, reparation 13 counteractive

imaginary: 6 elixir 7 panacea

quack: 7 nostrum, placebo

soothing: 4 balm 6 balsam

remember: 4 cite 6 ideate, recall, record, remind, reward 7 bethink, mention 9 recollect, reminisce 10 look back on 11 commemorate

remembrance: 4 gift, mind 5 relic, token 6 memory, minnie, notice, trophy 7 memento, mention 8 allusion, keepsake, memorial, souvenir 9 discourse, reference 10 impression 11 inscription 12 recollecting, recollection

remex: 5 quill 7 feather

remind: 4 hint 6 recall 7 suggest

reminder: cue 4 hint, memo, note, prod, twit 7 memento, monitor 10 admonition, expression

reminiscence: act 4 fact 5 power 6 memory 7 anamnesis, recalling 10 experience 11 memorabilia, remembering, remembrance 12 recollection

remiss: lax 4 lazy, mild, pale 5 slack, tardy 6 gentle 7 diluted, languid, lenient, relaxed 8 careless, derelict, dilatory, faineant, heedless, indolent, moderate, slothful 9 dissolved, liquefied, negligent 10 neglectful, 11 inattentive, thoughtless 13 irresponsible

remission: 6 rebate 9 abolition, cessation, lessening 10 diminution

remit: pay 4 bate, send 5 abate, defer, enter, refer, relax, spend 6 cancel, excuse, insert, pardon, resign, return, submit 7 abandon, absolve, forgive, forward, readmit, release, restore, slacken, suspend 8 abrogate, liberate, mitigate, moderate, postpone, recommit, transmit 9 exculpate, surrender

remittance: 9 allowance

remnant: bit, end, ort, rag 4 dreg, fent, left, part, rest, stub 5 crumb, piece, relic, scrap, trace, wrack 7 leaving, portion, remains, residue 8 fragment 9 remainder 10 suggestion

remodel: 6 change, recast 7 rebuild 11 reconstruct

remolade, remoulade: 5 sauce 8 dressing, ointment

remonstrance: 5 demur 7 protest 10 benedicite 13 expostulation

remonstrate: 5 fight, argue 6 combat, object 7 declare, profess, protest 8 complain 11 demonstrate, expostulate

remora: 4 clog, drag, fish, pega 5 delay 7

pegador 9 hindrance 10 impediment 11 sucking fish

remorse: rue 4 pity, ruth 5 grief, qualm 6 regret, sorrow 7 penance 8 distress 9 penitence 10 compassion, contrition, repentance 11 compunction

remote: far, off 4 afar, back, cool 5 alien, aloof, faint, vague 6 forane, slight 7 distant, faraway, foreign, obscure, removed 8 secluded, separate 10 abstracted, impersonal, unfriendly 11 indifferent 12 inaccessible

goal or end: 5 Thule

more: 7 endmost, further 8 ulterior

most: 6 ultima 9 diametric 11 ultima Thule

place: 9 backwoods, boondocks

remove: rid 4 bate, dele, doff, fire, free, kill, move, oust, pare, raze, rend, sack, void, weed 5 amove, apart, avoid, elide, eloin, erase, evict, expel, strip 6 betake, cancel, change, convey, deduct, delete, depose, disbar, distal, eloign, recall, remble, retire, uproot 7 cast off, deprive, despoil, dismiss, extract, take off, uncover, whittle 8 abstract, disclose, discover, dislodge, displace, relegate, separate, supplant, transfer 9 clear away, eliminate, eradicate, translate 10 disconnect 11 assassinate

by surgery: 6 ablate

clothing: 5 strip 7 disrobe, undress

from office: 4 oust 6 depose, recall 7 dismiss

hair: 5 shave 8 depilate

ice: 7 defrost

impurities: 5 smelt 6 filter, refine

legally: 4 oust 6 disbar

seeds: 5 stone

skin: 4 hull, husk

to another place: 8 transfer

removed: off 4 away, move 5 alone, aloof, apart 6 remote 7 distant, obscure 10 abstracted

remuneration: pay 5 wages 6 reward 7 payment, stipend 8 requital 9 emolument, repayment 10 recompense 12 compensation, satisfaction 13 consideration, gratification, reimbursement

remunerative: 10 beneficial, profitable 12 advantageous

Remus: *father:* 4 Mars

foster mother: 4 wolf

mother: 4 Rhea

slayer: 7 Romulus

twin brother: 7 Romulus

renaissance: 7 rebirth, revival

renal: 7 nephric 9 nephritic

Renard: See Reynard

rend: cut, rip 4 pull, rent, rive, slit, tear 5 break, burst, sever, split, wrest 6 breach, cleave, divide, enrive, pierce, remove, screed, sunder 7 abscind, dispart, disrupt, rupture 8 fracture, lacerate, separate 9 dismember 12 disintegrate

render: pay, put, try 4 emit, give, make, melt 5 treat, yield 6 depict, recite, repeat, return, submit 7 clarify, deliver, exhibit, extract, furnish, inflict, payment, perform, present, requite, restore 8 transmit 9 interpret, represent, surrender, translate 10 administer, contribute

rendezvous: 4 date, meet 5 place, tryst 6 gather, refuge 7 hangout, meeting, retreat 8 assemble, mobilize 9 agreement, gathering 11 appointment

rendition: 8 delivery 9 surrender 11 deliverance, performance, translation 14 interpretation

renegade: rat 5 rebel 6 bolter 7 traitor 8 apostate, deserter, fugitive, renegado, turncoat 9 changeling

renege, renig: 4 deny 5 welsh 6 desert, refuse, revoke 7 decline 8 back down, renounce

renew: 4 beet 5 beete 6 extend, refill, repair, repeat, resume, revamp, revive 7 freshen, rebuild, refresh, replace, restore 8 make over, reassume, re-create, renovate 9 modernize, replenish 10 invigorate, recommence, regenerate, rejuvenate 11 re-establish, resuscitate 12 redintegrate

renitent: 7 opposed 8 opposing 9 obstinate, resistant 12 recalcitrant

rennet: lab 5 apple 6 curdle, keslop 7 earning(Sc.) 8 earnings(Sc.), membrane 9 cheeselip, coagulate

ferment: 6 enzyme, rennin

renounce: 4 cede, defy, deny 5 cease, forgo, renay, renig, waive 6 abjure, defect, desert, disown, forego, forlet, forsay, recant, reject, renege, repeal, resign 7 abandon, disavow, forsake, retract 8 abdicate, abnegate, disclaim, forspeak, forswear, renounce 9 repudiate, surrender 10 abrenounce, relinquish 12 abrenunciate

renovate: 4 redo 5 alter, clean, renew 6 purify, repair, resume, revive 7 cleanse, furbish, refresh, replace, restore 10 invigorate, regenerate

renown: rap 4 fame, note 5 eclat, glory, kudos, rumor 6 report 7 acclaim 8 eminence 9 celebrity 10 reputation 11 celebration, distinction

renowned: 5 known 6 famous 11 illustrious

rent: (see also **rend**): let, pay 4 gape, hire, hole, rime, toll 5 censo, chink, cleft, crack, cuddy, gavel, gorge, lease, share, split, yield 6 breach, engage, income, profit, return, reward, schism 7 fissure,

opening, revenue, rupture, tribute 9 lacerated

high: 8 rackrent

transfer: 6 attorn

rental: 4 cost, flat, list 5 house 8 lodgings, schedule 9 apartment

rente: 6 income(Fr.) 7 annuity, revenue

renter: 6 lessee, tenant 8 occupant

reopen: 6 resume 10 recommence

rep: 4 fame 5 cloth 6 fabric, 10 reputation

repair: fix 4 darn, heal, help, mend 5 amend, order, patch, piece, refit, renew 6 remedy, return, revamp, revive 7 correct, rebuild 8 overhaul, renovate

repairman: 6 tinker 7 cobbler 8 mechanic

repand: 4 bent, wavy 6 uneven

reparation: 4 bote 6 amende, amends, reward 7 damages, redress 8 requital 9 amendment, atonement, indemnity, quittance, repairing 10 recompense 11 restitution 12 compensation, distribution, partitioning 14 redistribution

repartee: wit 5 reply 6 banter, retort 7 riposte, sarcasm 8 badinage

repast: tea 4 bait, feed, food, meal 5 bever, feast, snack, treat 6 dinner 7 banquet 9 collation, refection 11 refreshment

pert. to: 8 prandial

repatriation: 6 return 11 restoration

repay: pay 4 meed 5 appay, award 6 avenge, offset, profit, punish, refund, return, reward 7 balance, deserve, requite, restore 9 gratulate, reimburse, retaliate 10 compensate, recompense, remunerate 12 reciprocate

repeal: 4 lift, void 5 amend, annul, emend 6 appeal, cancel, recall, revoke 7 abolish, rescind, retract, reverse 8 abrogate, derogate, renounce, withdraw

repeat: bis(It.), din 4 cite, echo, rame 5 ditto, quote, recap, recur 6 encore, parrot, resume, retell 7 iterate, recount, reprise, restate 8 redouble 9 duplicate, reiterate 10 ingeminate, repetition 11 battologize 12 recapitulate

music: bis

performance: 6 encore

sign in music: 5 segno

repeatedly: oft 5 often 10 frequently 11 continually, day after day 12 continuously

repeater: gun 5 rifle, watch 6 pistol 7 firearm 8 holdover 10 recidivist

repel: 4 beat, stop 5 check, debar, force 6 combat, defend, oppose, rebuff, refuse, reject, remove, resist 7 decline, disgust, fend off, repulse 8 vanquish 10 extinguish

repellent: 4 grim 5 harsh 9 offensive, repugnant 10 forbidding 12 antipathetic

repent: rue 5 atone 6 grieve, lament, regret 7 reptant 8 crawling, creeping, forthink, penitent

repentance: 4 pity, ruth 5 shame 7 penance, remorse 9 attrition, penitence 10 contrition 11 compunction

repentant: 9 regretful 10 remorseful 11 penitential

repercussion: 4 blow, echo 5 tenor 6 impact, recoil 7 rebound 8 backwash, reaction 10 reflection 11 reiteration 12 ballottement 13 reverberation

repertory: 4 list 5 index 7 theater, theatre 8 calendar, magazine, treasury 9 catalogue 10 collection, storehouse

repetition: bis 4 copy, echo, rote 5 rondo 6 dilogy, encore 7 replica, tremolo 8 iterance 9 iteration, rehearsal 10 redundancy 12 reproduction

mechanical: 4 rote 8 anaphora

of homologous parts: 6 merism

of idea: 8 pleonasm 9 tautology

of others: 7 echolia, mimicry 9 echolalia

of sound: 4 echo

repine: 4 fail, fret, wane 5 mourn 6 grouse, lament, regret, weaken 7 grumble, whimper 8 complain, languish

replace: 5 alter, change, reset, stead 6 follow 7 relieve, restore, succeed 8 supplant 9 reimburse, supersede 10 substitute

replacement: 6 ersatz 9 successor 10 substitute

replenish: 4 feed, fill 5 renew, stock 7 restore

replete: fat 4 full, rife 5 alive, sated, stout 6 filled, gorged 7 bloated, implete, stocked, stuffed 8 complete 9 abounding, surfeited

replica: 4 copy 5 image 6 carbon, ectype 8 likeness 9 facsimile 10 repetition 12 reproduction

replicate: 4 bend, copy, fold 5 reply 6 repeat 8 manifold, repeated 9 duplicate, multifold

reply: 4 echo, fold, sass 5 rebut 6 answer, oracle, re-echo, rejoin, repeat, retort, return 7 respond, retract, riposte 8 repartee, response 9 rejoinder 11 replication

report: pop 4 fame, tell, word 5 bruit, noise, rumor, state, story 6 breeze, cahier(F.), delate, digest, recite, relate, repeat, return, rumour 7 account, crackle, hansard, hearing, hearsay, inkling, narrate, recital, summary 8 announce, describe 9 circulate, grapevine, narration, narrative 10 reputation

false: fib, lie 6 canard 7 slander 8 tall-tale 12 misstatement

reporter: cub 6 legman, writer 7 newsman 9 columnist 10 journalist

symbol: 6 thirty

young: cub

repose: lie, set, sit 4 calm, ease, rely, rest, seat 5 peace, place, quiet, sleep 6 relief 7 compose, confide, deposit, dignity, recline, replace, restore, support 8 calmness, serenity 9 composure, quietness 10 relaxation, stretch out 12 requiescence, tranquillity

repository: ark, box 4 bank, file, safe, shop 5 ambry, capsa, chest, depot, vault 6 closet, museum 7 arsenal, capsule, granary, storage 8 magazine, treasury 9 confidant, reliquary, sepulcher, warehouse 10 depository, storehouse

reposoir: 5 altar

repossess: 6 regain 7 recover, retrieve, take back

reprehend: 4 warn 5 blame, chide, scold 6 rebuke 7 censure, reprove, upbraid 8 admonish, disprove 9 criticize, reprimand

reprehensible: 8 criminal, culpable 11 blameworthy

represent: act 4 show 5 enact, image 6 clothe, denote, depict, embody, typify 7 exhibit, express, picture, portray, produce, profess 8 describe, simulate 9 delineate, designate, exemplify, reproduce, symbolize 10 illustrate, substitute 11 impersonate 12 characterize

representation: map 4 icon, idol, ikon 5 chart, graph, image, model 6 avowal, blazon, sample 7 account, diagram, picture 8 likeness, notation 9 portrayal, statement 10 similitude 11 histrionics, performance, portraiture

favorable: 14 recommendation

graphic: 5 chart 6 bisect

representative: 4 heir 5 agent, envoy 6 consul, deputy, legate 7 tribune, typical 8 delegate, executor, exponent, instance, salesman 10 ambassador 12 illustrating, illustrative 13 administrator

repress: 4 bury, curb, hush, rein, stop 5 check, choke, crush, daunt, press, quell 6 bridle, deaden, reduce, stifle, subdue 7 compose, depress 8 compress, restrain, suppress, withhold 9 constrain, overpower

reprieve: 5 defer, delay, grace 6 escape 7 respite, suspend 8 postpone 12 postponement

reprimand: rap, wig 4 call 5 check, chide, slate 6 rebuff, rebuke 7 censure, chapter, chasten, repress, reproof, reprove 8 admonish, call down 9 reprehend 12 reprehension

reprint: 4 copy

reprisal: 8 requital 9 tit for tat 11 retaliation

reprise: 6 repeat 8 reassume 10 compensate, recommence, repetition

reproach: 4 blot, slur, twit 5 abuse, blame, braid, chide, shame, shend, sully, taunt 6 accuse, infamy, rebuke, revile, stigma, vilify 7 censure, condemn, reprove, traduce, upbraid 8 besmirch, disgrace, dishonor 9 bespatter, challenge, contumely, discredit, disrepute, invective 10 correction, exprobrate, opprobrium, scurrility 11 impeachment 12 vilification 13 animadversion 15 discommendation

old word of: 4 raca

reprobate: 4 hard 5 Satan, scamp, wrong 6 disown, rascal, reject 7 abandon, condemn, corrupt, decline, vicious 8 blamable, castaway, denounce, hardened 9 abandoned, blameable, criticize, reprehend, scoundrel 10 censurable, condemned, disallowed 11 blameworthy, disapproved 12 unprincipled 13 reprehensible

reproduce: 4 copy, draw 6 repeat 7 imitate 8 multiply 9 duplicate, procreate, propagate, represent 11 reconstruct

asexually: 5 clone

reproduction: 6 ectype 7 fission, replica 8 likeness 9 facsimile, photostat 10 carbon copy 11 counterpart 13 proliferation

reproductive: 8 prolific

reproductive cell: 6 gamete

reprove: 4 flay, rate, slam 5 blame, check, chide, roast, scold, shame 6 berate, rebuff, rebuke, refute, reject 7 censure, confute, correct, lecture, upbraid 8 admonish, carritch, chastise, disgrace, disprove, lambaste, redargue, reproach 9 castigate, challenge, criticize, objurgate, reprehend, reprimand, reprobate 10 administer, animadvert, carritches, take to task 11 expostulate

reptant: 8 crawling, creeping

reptile: 4 croc, worm 5 snake 6 turtle 8 dinosaur, tortoise 9 alligator, crocodile, pterosaur 11 pterodactyl

age: 8 Mesozoic

edible: 6 iguana, turtle

group: 6 sauria

legless: 4 apod 5 snake

pert. to: 7 saurian 8 ophidian

scale: 5 scute

study of: 11 herpetology

reptilian: low 4 mean 5 snaky 6 lizard, sneaky 7 reptant, saurian, serpent 8 crawling, creeping, ophidian 9 groveling, malignant 10 despicable

republic: 5 state 6 nation 9 democracy 10 commonweal, government 12 commonwealth

imaginary: 7 Oceania

world's smallest: 5 Nauru

Republic author: 5 Plato

repudiate: 4 defy, deny 6 abjure, defect, disown, recant, refuse, reject 7 abandon, decline, disavow, discard, divorce, forsake, retract 8 abrogate, disclaim, renounce 9 disaffirm

repugn: 6 oppose, resist

repugnance: 5 odium 6 enmity, hatred 7 disgust, dislike 8 aversion, distaste, loathing 9 antipathy, hostility, repulsion 10 abhorrence, antagonism, opposition, reluctance 11 abomination, contrariety, incongruity 13 inconsistency

repugnant: 4 foul, vile 8 inimical 9 offensive, repellent 10 refractory 12 disagreeable

repulse: 4 deny, foil, rout 5 check, fling, rebut, refel, repel 6 defeat, denial, rebuff, refuse, reject 7 disgust, exclude, refusal 8 fend off 9 rejection

repulsive: 4 dain, evil, loth, ugly, vile 5 loath, toady 6 odious 7 fulsome, hateful, loathly 9 offensive, repellent, repugnant 10 abhorrent, forbidding 11 distasteful, gorgonesque

repurchase: 6 redeem

reputable: 4 good 8 credible 10 creditable 11 respectable, responsible

reputation: 4 fame, name, note, odor 5 eclat, glory, honor, izzat, odour, stamp 6 credit, honour, renown, repute 7 respect 8 standing 9 attribute, character 11 distinction 13 consideration

loss of: 7 scandal

reputed: dit 8 putative, supposed 11 conjectural 12 hypothetical

request: ask, beg, sue 4 plea, pray, suit, wish 5 apply, crave, order 6 appeal, behest, demand, invite 7 entreat, prithee, solicit 8 entreaty, petition, rogation 11 application 12 solicitation, supplication

for help: SOS

formal: 8 rogation

requiem: 4 hymn, mass, rest, song 5 chant, dirge, peace, quiet 7 service

requiescat: 4 wish 6 prayer

in pace: 11 rest in peace

requiescence: 4 rest 6 repose

requin: 5 shark 8 man-eater

require: ask 4 lack, need 5 claim, crave, exact, force 6 behove, compel, demand, enjoin, entail, expect, oblige 7 behoove 9 postulate 11 necessitate

requirement: 4 duty 9 essential, formality, requisite

requisite: 4 just, need 7 needful 9 condition, essential 11 requirement 13 indispensable

requisition: 5 order 6 billet, demand 9 embargo, request 11 application, requirement

requital: 7 guerdon 8 reprisal 9 vengeance 11 retaliation, retribution

requite: pay 5 atone, repay 6 acquit, avenge, defray, return, reward 7 content, deserve, gratify, revenge, satisfy 9 retaliate 10 compensate, recompense, 11 reciprocate

reredos: 4 wall 6 screen 7 brazier, drapery 9 backplate, partition

rerun: 6 replay, reshow

res: 5 point, thing 6 matter 7 subject

rescind: 4 lift, void 5 annul 6 cancel, repeal, revoke 7 abolish, retract, reverse 8 abrogate 11 countermand

rescript: 5 edict, order 6 answer, decree, letter 9 rewriting 11 counterpart

rescue: 4 free, save 6 ransom, redeem, succor 7 deliver, reclaim, recover, release, salvage 8 delivery, liberate 9 extricate 11 deliverance

research: 7 inquiry 11 examination 13 investigation 5 experimentation

reseau: net 6 ground 7 network 10 foundation 11 filter screen

reseda: 5 plant 10 mignonette

resemblance: 5 image 6 simile, symbol 7 analogy 8 affinity, likeness, parallel, vicinity 9 agreement, imitation, semblance 10 comparison, similarity, similitude 12 assimilation 14 representation

one bearing: 6 ringer, 9 lookalike

resemble: 5 favor 8 look like 9 take after

resentment: ire 4 gall 5 anger, depit, pique, spite 6 animus, choler, enmity, grudge, hatred, malice, rancor, spleen 7 dudgeon, ill will, offense, umbrage 8 acrimony 9 animosity, annoyance, hostility, malignity 10 irritation 11 displeasure, indignation

reserve: 4 book, cash, cave, fund, keep, save 5 spare, stock, store 6 assets, retain, supply 7 backlog, bespeak, caution, modesty, shyness, silence, surplus 8 coldness, distance, forprise, nest egg, preserve, withhold 9 exception, reservoir, restraint, retention, reticence 10 constraint, diffidence, discretion, limitation, substitute 11 reservation, taciturnity

reserved: coy, shy 4 cold 5 aloof, staid, taken 6 sedate 7 bashful, distant 8 backward, cautious 9 qualified 10 unsociable 15 incommunicative, uncommunicative

reservoir: vat 4 font, pond, pool, sump, tank 5 basin, fount, stope, store 6 cenote, supply 7 cistern, favissa, forebay, piscina, reserve 8 favissae(pl.), fountain

reset: 4 help 5 abode, alter 6 harbor, refuge, resort, succor 7 receipt, receive, replace, secrete, shelter 9 receiving 10 receptacle

reside: lie 4 bigg, live, room, stay 5 abide, dwell, habit, lodge 6 remain, settle 7 consist, hang out, inhabit, sojourn, subside 8 habitate

residence: 4 digs, home, seat, shed 5 abode, house, villa 6 biding, castle, palace 7 habitat, mansion 8 domicile, residuum, sediment 9 apartment 10 habitation, villanette 13 collectorship

resident: cit 6 lessee, tenant 7 burgess, citizen 8 inherent, occupant 10 inhabitant

residue: ask 4 dreg, lees, marc, orts, rest, silt, slag 5 ashes, dregs 6 cinder, excess, relics, sludge, sordes 7 balance, remains, remnant 8 leavings, remanent, residuum, sediment 9 remainder

residuum: 7 deposit 8 hangover 9 remainder

resign: 4 cede, quit 5 demit, remit, yield 6 devote, submit 7 abandon, consign, deliver 8 abdicate, renounce 9 surrender 10 relinquish

resignation: 7 modesty 8 meekness, patience 9 endurance 12 acquiescence

resile: 6 recede, return 7 rebound, retract, retreat 8 back down, withdraw

resilient: 5 toned 6 buoyant, elastic, springy 8 bouncing, flexible, stretchy, volatile 9 recoiling 10 rebounding

resin, rosin: alk, gum, lac, tar 4 aloe, balm, tolu 5 amber, anime, animi, copal, damar, elemi, gugal, gugul, loban, myrrh, pitch, roset, syrup 6 balsam, charas, dammar, derrid, elemin, googul, salban, storax 7 acouchi, acrylic, ambrite, arioera, copaiba, copaiva, derride, exudate, fluavil, galipot, hartite, ladanum, retinol 8 alkitran, bdellium, fluavile, gedanite, glessite, guaiacum, labdanum, retinite, sandarac 9 alchitran, colophony, elaterite 11 colophonium 12 frankincense

fossil: 5 amber 8 glessite, retinite

gum: 5 gugal, myrrh 6 mastic 8 bdellium

incense: 8 sandarac

purified: 7 shellac

varnish: 5 anime, copal

resinous tree: fir 4 pine 6 balsam

resist: 4 buck, fend 5 rebel, repel 6 baffle, combat, defeat, defend, impugn, oppose, wither 7 contest, counter, dispute, prevent 8 obstruct, traverse 9 frustrate, gainstand, withstand

resistance: 6 rebuff 7 defense 9 hostility, renitence 10 antagonism, oppugnance 13 recalcitrance

resistance box: 8 rheostat

resistant: 4 hard 8 obdurate, renitent, stubborn

resolute: 4 bold 5 fixed 7 animose, animous 8 faithful, positive, resolved, stalwart, stubborn, unshaken 9 unbending 10 unwavering

resolution: vow 4 grit, thew 5 heart, nerve 7 courage, purpose, resolve, verdict 8 analysis, backbone, decision, firmness, proposal, strength 9 assurance, certainty, constancy, fortitude, hardihood, statement, sternness, stoutness 10 conviction, separation, steadiness 11 intrepidity, persevering 12 deliberation, faithfulness, perseverance, resoluteness 13 determination, inflexibility, steadfastness 14 simplification 15 disentanglement

resolve: 4 free, melt 5 relax, solve, untie 6 answer, assoil, decide, dispel, inform, loosen, reduce, remove, settle 7 analyze, appoint, dispose, explain, liquefy, scatter, unravel 8 conclude, decision, dissolve, enfeeble, persuade, separate

resonant: 4 deep, full, rich 5 round 6 mellow, rotund 7 ringing, vibrant 8 sonorous, sounding 10 resounding 11 reverberant

resort: spa, use 4 howf 5 crowd, haunt, howff, joint, place, visit 6 betake, casino, refuge, return, revert, throng 7 company 8 frequent, habitual, recourse 10 assemblage, fall back on
health: spa 10 sanatorium
place of: 5 haunt 7 purlieu

resound: 4 echo, peal, ring 5 clang 6 re-echo 11 reverberate

resounding: 7 vibrant 8 emphatic, plangent

resource: 5 shift 6 device 7 stopgap

resourceful: apt 5 sharp 6 clever, facile 7 fertile

resources: 5 funds, means, money 6 assets, riches, stocks, stores 7 capital, fortune, resorts 8 property, reserves, supplies, supports 10 expedients 12 contrivances
guardian: 15 conservationist

respect: awe 4 heed 5 defer, honor, value 6 admire, esteem, homage, regard, revere 7 concern, observe, respite, tribute, worship 8 postpone, venerate 9 attention, deference, reference, reverence 10 admiration
act of: 6 devoir
pay: 5 greet, kneel, toast 6 salute 9 genuflect

respectable: 4 good 6 decent, honest, proper 7 fausant 8 decorous 9 estimable, honorable, reputable 10 creditable 11 presentable

respectful: 5 civil 6 polite 7 careful, duteous 8 gracious 9 courteous 11 ceremonious

respective: 4 each 6 sundry 7 partial, several 9 regardful 10 individual, particular

respiration: 6 breath 7 eupnoea 9 breathing
difficulty: 4 rale 5 cough 7 dyspnea 8 dyspnoea
normal: 7 eupnoea

respire: 4 live, sigh 6 exhale, inhale 7 breathe

respite: 4 lull, rest 5 break, delay, pause 6 recess 7 leisure 8 interval, reprieve, surcease 9 cessation 10 suspension 12 intermission, postponement

resplendent: 6 bright 7 aureate, blazing, flaming, glowing, radiant, shining 8 dazzling, glorious, gorgeous, lustrous, splendid 9 brilliant, refulgent 10 epiphanous, flamboyant

respond: 4 echo, feel 5 react, reply, write 6 accord, answer, pillar, rejoin, retort return 8 response 10 correspond

response: 4 word 5 verse 6 anthem, chorus, phrase 7 introit, refrain 8 sentence
involuntary: 6 reflex 7 tropism

responsibility: 4 care, duty, onus 6 burden, charge 9 liability 10 obligation 11 reliability 14 accountability 15 trustworthiness

responsible: 6 liable 8 amenable 9 accordant, reputable 10 answerable, dependable, sufficient 13 correspondent

responsive: 6 mutual, tender 8 amenable, sentient 9 sensitive 11 sympathetic

res publica: 5 state 8 republic 10 commonweal 12 commonwealth

rest: lay, lie, set, sit 4 clam, ease, hang, lair, lean, liss, prop, rely, seat, slip, stay, stop 5 abide, cease, found, let up, lie down, lisse, pause, peace, quiet, relax, renew, repos(F.), sleep, stand 6 alight, cesura, depend, desist, ease up, remain, repose, settle 7 balance, caesura, comfort, leisure, refresh, remains, remnant, reposal, residue, respite, shelter, support, surplus 8 breather, interval, slack off, vacation 9 cessation, establish, quietness, remainder, stillness 10 immobility, inactivity, relaxation 11 refreshment 12 intermission, peacefulness, tranquillity
noonday: nap 6 siesta
poetic: 7 caesura

rest house: inn 4 chan, khan 5 hotel, serai 6 abalam, hostel, tavern 7 chhatri

restate: 6 reword 8 reassert 10 paraphrase

restaurant: inn 4 cafe 5 diner, grill, hotel 6 bistro, tavern 7 automat, beanery, cabaret, tearoom 9 brasserie, cafeteria, chophouse, hashhouse, trattoria 10 rotisserie, steakhouse 11 rathskeller(G).

restful: 5 quiet 6 placid 8 peaceful, tranquil

resting: 4 abed 6 asleep, latent 7 dormant

restitution: 6 amends, return 8 recovery

10 recompense, reparation 11 restoration 12 compensation 13 reimbursement

restive: 5 balky, tense 6 uneasy, unruly 7 fidgety, nervous 8 contrary, perverse, restless, stubborn 9 impatient 10 refractory 12 unmanageable

restless: 5 itchy, jumpy 6 fidget, fitful, haunty, hectic, roving, uneasy 7 agitato(It.), fidgety, fretful, inquiet, jittery, nervous, restive, unquiet 8 agitated, feverish, stirring 9 disturbed, impatient, sleepless, unsettled, wandering 10 disquieted, reposeless 12 discontented

restoration: 7 renewal 10 reparation 11 restitution

restorative: 5 tonic 7 anodyne 8 salutary 9 analeptic

restore: 4 cure, heal, mend 5 amend, atone, renew, repay, right 6 redeem, refund, repair, return, revive 7 convert, get back, put back, rebuild, recover, replace 8 renovate 9 reinstate, resurrect 10 regenerate 11 reconstruct, re-establish, resuscitate 12 redintegrate, rehabilitate

printer's mark: 4 stet

restrain: bar, dam, gag 4 bate, bind, calm, clog, curb, hold, rein, rule, stay, stop 5 chain, check, cramp, deter, guard, limit, still, stint 6 arrest, behave, bridle, coerce, detain, fetter, forbid, govern, halter, hamper, hinder, pinion, tether 7 abridge, abstain, chasten, command, compose, confine, contain, control, deprive, forbear, inhibit, prevent, repress, shackle, trammel 8 attemper, compesce, compress, conclude, imprison, moderate, prohibit, restrict, suppress, withhold 9 constrain 12 circumscribe

restrained: 5 quiet 6 severe 8 reserved 9 hidebound 11 disciplined

restraint: bit 5 force 7 barrier, durance, reserve 9 avoidance, reticence 10 internment

legal: 5 estop

of trade: 7 embargo

restrict: bar, tie 4 curb 5 bound, cramp, limit, scant, shrink, stint 6 censor, coerce, hamper, modify, ration 7 confine, repress, tighten 8 contract, derogate, prohibit, restrain, straiten 9 constrict 12 circumscribe

restricted: 5 local 6 closed, finite, narrow, strait 9 parochial 10 provincial

restriction: 5 cramp 9 restraint 10 regulation 11 reservation 12 ball and chain 13 qualification

restrictive: 7 binding 8 limiting 9 confining, stringent

result: end, sum 4 leap, rise 5 close, ensue, event, fruit, issue, score, total 6 accrue, answer, effect, finish, follow, sequel,

spring, upshot 7 outcome, proceed, redound 8 aftering, decision 9 aftermath, eventuate, terminate 10 conclusion 11 achievement, consequence, termination

result in: 5 cause

resume: 4 go on 5 renew 6 pick up, reopen, repeat, review 7 epitome, summary 8 continue, reoccupy, return to, synopsis 9 epitomize, reiterate, summarize 10 abridgment, recommence 12 recapitulate 14 recapitulation

resurrection: 7 rebirth, revival 11 restoration

resuscitate: 6 revive 7 quicken, restore 8 revivify

ret: rot, sop 4 soak 5 steep 6 dampen

retable: 5 ledge, shelf 6 gradin 9 framework

retail: 4 hawk, sell, vent 5 trade 6 barter, peddle, relate, repeat

retailer: 6 dealer 8 clothier, huckster, merchant

retain: 4 have, hire, hold, keep, save 6 adhere, athold, behold, employ 7 contain, prevent, reserve 8 maintain, preserve, remember, restrain, withhold 9 entertain, recollect

retainer: fee 4 cage, hewe 5 frame 6 menial, minion, vassal 7 hobbler 8 follower 9 burkundaz

retaining: 9 retentive

retaliate: 5 repay 6 avenge, punish, retort 7 requite, revenge

retaliation: 6 talion 8 reprisal, requital 11 retribution

retard: 4 slow 5 brake, catch, defer, delay, deter, trash 6 belate, deaden, detain, fetter, hamper, hinder, impede 8 encumber, obstruct, postpone, restrain 10 decelerate

retardation: lag 4 drag 5 delay

retch: gag 4 hawk, keck, spit 5 heave, reach, vomit 6 expand, extend, strain 7 stretch

rete: 6 plexus 7 network

retem: 7 juniper

retention: 6 memory 7 holding, keeping, storage 11 maintenance, remembering

retiarius: 9 gladiator

retiary: 6 meshed, telary 7 netlike

reticent: 4 dark 6 silent 7 sparing 8 discreet, reserved, retiring, taciturn 9 secretive 10 mysterious 15 uncommunicative

reticule: bag 4 etui 5 cabas, etwee 6 pocket, sachet 7 handbag, reticle, workbag 8 carryall

reticulum: net 7 network, stomach 8 meshwork

retinaculum: 6 frenum

retinue: 4 band, crew, ging, rout, suit, tail 5 harem, meiny, suite, train 6 attend, escort 7 cortege, service 8 equipage 9 entourage, following, retainers 10 attendants

retire: ebb 5 leave 6 depart, recede, recess, remove, vanish 7 pension, retreat 8 withdraw 9 disappear, sequester 10 hit the sack

retired: 4 abed, lone 5 quiet 6 secret 7 obscure, private, recluse 8 abstruse, emeritus, reserved, secluded, solitary 9 recondite

retiring: shy 5 timid 6 modest 7 bashful, fugient 8 reserved 9 diffident 11 unobtrusive

retort: mot 4 quip, turn 5 facer, repay, reply, sally 6 answer, recoil, return 7 alembic, cornute, respond, riposte 8 blizzard, repartee, take back 9 retaliate

retortion, retorsion: 7 bending 8 reprisal, twisting 10 reflection

retract: 4 bend 6 abjure, cancel, disown, recall, recant, remove, repeal, retire, revoke 7 disavow, prevent, rescind, retreat 8 restrain, withdraw 9 repudiate

retraction: 8 palinode

retral: 8 backward 9 posterior 10 retrograde

retreat: den 4 abri, cave, holt, lair, nest, nook, rout 5 arbor, bower 6 arbour, asylum, harbor, recede, recess, refuge, retire 7 harbour, privacy, pull out, retiral, shelter 8 fall back, solitude, withdraw 9 departure, hibernate, sanctuary, seclusion 10 rendezvous, retirement, sanitarium, withdrawal

religious: 5 asram

underground: 4 abri, cave

retrench: cut 4 bate, omit, pare 6 delete, excise, lessen, reduce, remove 7 abridge, curtail, cut back, repress, shorten 8 decrease, diminish 9 economize, intercept

retrenchment: 5 ditch 7 parapet, rampart 8 traverse 10 breastwork 12 entrenchment

retribution: pay 6 return, reward 7 nemesis, revenge, tribute 8 requital 9 vengeance 10 punishment, recompense 11 retaliation

goddess of: Ate 4 Fury 7 Nemesis

retrieve: 6 recall, regain, revive 7 recover, restore 8 discover 10 recuperate

retrograde: 4 slow 5 lapse 6 recede, retral, worsen 7 decline, inverse, opposed, regress 8 backward, contrary, decadent, inverted, rearward, withdraw 9 backslide, catabolic, reversely 10 degenerate, retrogress 11 deteriorate

retrogress: 4 sink 6 revert, 9 backslide 10 degenerate

retrospective: 6 review 8 backward 11 retroactive 13 contemplative

return: lob 4 bend, turn 5 recur, remit, repay, yield 6 advert, answer, come in,

profit, render, report, retort, revert 7 put back, regress, replace, reprise, requite, respond, restore, revenue, reverse 8 give back, requital, response, take back 9 repayment, repercuss, retaliate, reversion 10 recompense, recurrence 11 reciprocate, replacement, restoration 12 reappearance 13 reciprocation

Return of the Native author: 5 Hardy

Reuben: *brother:* 6 Joseph

father: 5 Jacob

mother: 4 Leah

Reuel's father: 4 Esau

reunite: 6 rejoin 9 reconcile

reus: 9 defendant

rev: 10 accelerate, give the gun, race a motor

revamp: 5 renew 7 restyle, rewrite

reveal: bid 4 bare, blab, jamb, open, show, tell, wray 5 exert 6 betray, bewray, descry, detect, expose, impart, unveil 7 confide, develop, display, divulge, exhibit, give out, let slip, publish, uncover 8 announce, decipher, develope, disclose, discover, evidence, manifest, revelate 11 communicate

reveille: 4 call, dian 5 diana, levet, rouse 6 signal

revel: joy 4 orgy, riot, wake 5 feast, let go, randy, spree, watch 6 bezzle, gavall, high-go 7 carouse, delight, revelry, roister 8 carnival, carousal, cut loose, domineer, festival 9 celebrate, festivity 11 celebration, merrymaking 12 conviviality

revelation: 4 tora 5 torah 6 vision 8 epiphany, prophecy 9 discovery 10 apocalypse, disclosure 13 manifestation

reveler, reveller: 6 ranter, rioter 8 bacchant 9 bacchanal, roisterer 10 merrymaker

cry: 4 evoe

revenant: 5 ghost 7 specter 9 recurring 10 apparition

revenge: 6 avenge, defend 7 requite 8 requital 9 retaliate 11 retaliation, retribution

revenue: 4 rent 5 yield 6 income, profit, rental, return, salary 7 finance 8 earnings, interest

reverberate: 4 echo, ring 6 return 7 reflect, resound

reverberating: 7 reboant 8 resonant 12 repercussive

revere: 4 love 5 adore, honor, prize, value 6 admire, esteem, regard, repute 7 respect, worship 8 venerate

reverence: awe 4 fear 5 dread, honor, piety 6 homage 8 devotion 9 deference, obeisance, solemnity

gesture of: 8 kneeling 11 genuflexion 12 genuflection

reverend: sri 4 holy 5 abbot 6 clergy, sacred 9 clergyman, monsignor, venerable

reverent: 6 devout, humble 7 awesome, dutiful

reverie: 5 dream 6 musing, trance, vision 7 fantasy 8 daydream

revers: 5 lapel

reverse: 5 annul, upset 6 defeat, invert, regard, repeal, revoke 7 abolish, backset, convert, subvert 8 backward, contrary, converse, disaster, opposite, overturn 9 about face, disaffirm, overthrow, transpose 10 misfortune 11 countermand

reversion: 6 return 7 relapse 9 throwback, volte-face

to state: 7 escheat

to type: 7 atavism

revert: 5 lapse, react 6 advert, return, revive 7 escheat, recover, reverse 9 backslide, throw back 11 antistrophe

review: 4 edit 5 recap 6 parade, resume, survey 7 account, journal 8 ceremony, critique, revision 9 criticise, criticism, criticize, re-examine 10 certiorari, inspection, periodical, reconsider, retrospect 11 examination

revile: 4 hate, rail 5 abuse, blame, brawl, libel, scold 6 debase, malign, vilify 7 chew out, slander 8 reproach 9 blaspheme 10 calumniate

revise: 4 edit 5 alter, amend, emend 6 change, polish, redact 7 correct, improve, recense, rewrite 8 readjust, work over 9 castigate, reexamine, supervise

reviser, revisor: 8 redactor, reformer

revival: 7 recall 7 rebirth 8 wakening 11 renaissance 12 reproduction 13 recrudescence

revive: daw 4 gain, wake 5 rally, renew, rouse 6 return 7 enliven, freshen, quicken, recover, refresh, restore 8 reawaken, recreate, rekindle, remember, revivify 9 reanimate, refreshen, resurrect 10 recuperate, regenerate, rejuvenate 11 resuscitate 12 reinvigorate

revoice: 4 echo 5 refit 7 restore

revoke: 4 lift, void 5 adeem, annul, check, renig 6 cancel, recall, recant, renege, repeal 7 abolish, fenagle, finagle, prevent, repress, rescind, retract, reverse 8 abrogate, remember, restrain, withdraw 9 fainaigue 11 countermand

revolt: 5 rebel, repel 6 mutiny, offend 7 disgust, retreat 8 renounce, sedition, uprising 9 rebellion 11 rise against 12 insurrection, renunciation

revolting: 4 ugly 6 horrid 7 hateful, hideous 8 shocking 9 loathsome, offensive, repellent, repulsive 10 disgusting, nauseating

revolution: 4 gyre, turn 5 cycle 7 circuit,

shake-up 8 disorder, rotation, uprising 9 overthrow, rebellion 12 renunciation

revolutions per minute: RPM 4 revs

revolve: con 4 birl, roll, spin, turn, whir 5 recur, swing, trend, twirl, wheel, whirl, whirr 6 circle, gyrate, ponder, rotate 7 agitate, reflect, trundle 8 consider, meditate 10 deliberate

revolver: gat, gun 6 pistol 7 firearm

revolving: 4 orby 6 rotary

part: 5 rotor 7 rotator

revue: 4 show 6 follies 9 burlesque 13 entertainment

revulsion: 4 fear 6 change 8 reaction 9 reversion 10 withdrawal 11 abomination

reward: fee, pay, utu 4 heed, hire, meed, plum, rent 5 ameed, award, bonus, check, crown, merit, medal, prize, repay, wages, yield 6 bounty, carrot, gersum, notice, profit, regard, return, salary, trophy 7 guerdon, premium, success 8 requital 9 honoraria(pl.) 10 compensate, honorarium, recompense, remunerate 11 retribution 12 compensation, remuneration 13 gratification

rewarding: 7 helpful 10 beneficial

rewrite: See revise

rex: 4 king

Reynard: fox

rezai: 8 coverlet, mattress

rhamn: 9 buckthorn

rhapsodic: 8 ecstatic, effusive 9 emotional

rhea: emu 4 emeu 5 nandu 6 ratite 7 ostrich 8 avestruz(Sp.)

Rhea: Ops

child: 4 Hera, Zeus 5 Hades 6 Hestia 7 Demeter 8 Poseidon

father: 6 Uranus

husband: 6 Cronus, Saturn

rhema: 4 term, verb, word

rheoscope: 12 galvanoscope

rheostat: 6 dimmer 8 resistor 9 regulator

rheotome: 11 interrupter

rhesus: 6 monkey 7 macaque

rhetor: 6 master, orator 7 teacher

rhetoric: 6 speech 7 bombast 9 eloquence

rhetorical: 6 florid 8 forensic 9 highflown 10 figurative, oratorical

rhetorician: 6 master, orator, writer 7 speaker, teacher

rhetorics: *digression:* 6 ecbole

diminution: 7 litotes

figure of speech: 6 aporia, simile 7 epandos 8 metaphor 10 apostrophe 12 alliteration, onomatopoeia 15 personification

rheum: 4 cold 7 catarrh 8 rhinitis

rhexis: 7 rupture

rhinal: 5 nasal 6 narial

Rhine: 5 river

city: 4 Bonn, Koln 5 Mainz 7 Cologne 8 Mannheim 9 Wiesbaden
magic hoard: 9 Rheingold, Rhinegold
nymph: 7 Lorelei
pert. to: 7 Rhenish
tributary: 7 Aar, Ill 4 Aare, Lahn, Main, Ruhr, Waal
wine: 7 Moselle

rhino: 4 cash 5 money 10 rhinoceros

rhinoceros: 5 abada, topan 6 borele, umhofo 7 keitloa, upeygan
black: 6 borele
cousin of: 5 tapir
feature: 4 horn

rhinoceros beetle: 4 uang

rhinoceros bird: 9 beefeater

rhizoid: 7 rootlet 8 rootcell

rhoda: 4 rose

Rhode Island: *bay:* 12 Narragansett
capital: 10 Providence
city: 7 Warwick 8 Cranston 9 Pawtucket 10 Woonsocket
founder: 13 Roger Williams
island: 5 Block 8 Prudence 9 Aquidneck
motto: 4 Hope
nickname: 5 Ocean 11 Little Rhody
resort: 7 Newport
river: 9 Pawcaduck 10 Woonsocket
state flower: 6 violet
state tree: 5 maple

Rhodes: *ancient wonder:* 8 Colossus
festival: 10 Chelidonia

Rhodesia: See Zimbabwe

rhoeadales: 5 poppy

rhomboid: 13 parallelogram

rhonchus: 4 rale 7 snoring 8 croaking 9 whistling

Rhone: *town:* 5 Arles
tributary: 5 Isere, Saone

rhubarb: 5 error 6 hassle 7 mistake, quarrel, yaw-weed 8 argument, pieplant 9 butterbur, rhapontic 10 discussion
derived from: 5 rheic
genus: 5 rheum

rhus tree: 5 sumac 6 sumach

rhyme: 5 agree, verse 6 poetry 9 harmonize

rhymester: 4 poet 6 rhymer 8 rimester 9 poetaster

rhythm: 4 beat, lilt, time 5 clink, meter, pulse, swing, tempo 7 cadence, measure
break in: 7 caesura 8 caesurae(pl.)
instrument: 4 drum 7 cymbals 8 triangle 10 tambourine
monotonous: 8 singsong

rhythmic: 6 poetic 8 metrical 9 recurrent

ria: bay 5 creek, inlet

rialto: 4 mart 6 bridge, market 8 district, exchange

riant: gay 6 bright, merry 8 cheerful, laughing, smiling

riata: See **reata**

rib: 4 bone, hair, purl, stay, wale, wife 5 costa, ridge, tease 6 banter, costae(pl.), lierne 7 bristle, support 9 cotelette, tierceron
pert. to: 6 costal 7 costate

ribald: low 5 rogue, scamp 6 coarse, rascal, vulgar 7 obscene 9 offensive 10 irreverent, scurrilous 11 blasphemous

ribband: bar 4 spar 5 plank, strip 6 bridge, timber 9 scantling

ribbed: 6 barred, corded 7 costate
fabric: rep 5 twill 6 faille

ribbon: bow 4 tape 5 braid, corse, padou, reins, shred, snood, strip, taste 6 cordon, fillet, riband, silver, taenia, tatter 7 bandeau, binding, taeniae(pl.) 8 banderol, decorate, tressour, tressure 9 banderole
badge: 6 cordon
binding: 6 lisere

ribbon-fish: 7 cutlass, oarfish 8 bandfish, dealfish

ribbon gum: 8 eucalypt

ribbon-like: 8 taeniate, taenioid

ribbon worm: 9 nemertean

ribless: 8 ecostate 9 decostate

ribwort: 8 hardhead, plantain

rice: 4 boro, chit, paga, twig 5 arroz(Sp.), bigas, canin, macan, pilaf, pilau, stick 6 branch 7 risotto 9 brushwood
boiled with meat: 5 pilaf, pilau
drink: 4 sake 5 bubud 7 pangasi
field: 4 padi 5 paddy
husk: 4 shud 5 shood
inferior: 4 chit
long-stemmed: 4 aman
milk: 5 gruel 7 pudding 8 porridge
paste: ame
polishings: 5 darac

rice rail: 4 sora

ricebird: 7 bunting, sparrow 8 bobolink 9 gallinule

rich: fat 4 dear, oofy 5 ample, heavy, opime 6 absurd, costly, creamy, daedal, fruity, greasy, hearty, mellow, mighty, oofier, ornate, potent 7 copious, fertile, moneyed, opulent, orotund, pinguid, wealthy 8 abundant, affluent, generous, luscious, powerful, valuable, well-to-do 9 abounding, bountiful, elaborate, laughable, luxuriant, plentiful, sumptuous 10 in the money, productive 12 concentrated, preposterous
man: 5 Midas, nabob 7 Croesus 9 plutocrat

Richelieu's successor: 7 Mazarin

riches: 4 gold, pelf, weal 5 lucre, worth 6 wealth 7 fortune 8 treasure
demon of: 6 Mammon
region of: 8 Eldorado
worship of: 10 plutomania

rick: 4 goaf, heap, pile 5 noise, scold,

stack, twist 6 jingle, rattle, sprain, wrench 7 chatter

rickety: 4 weak 5 crazy, shaky 6 feeble, senile 7 unsound 8 unstable 9 tottering 10 ramshackle

ricksha, rickshaw: 6 samlor 8 carriage

ricochet: 4 skip 5 carom 6 bounce, glance 7 rebound

rictus: 4 gape, grin, mask 7 grimace

rid: 4 free 5 clear, empty 6 assoil, remove, rescue 7 deliver, relieve 8 dispatch, liberate, throw off 9 eradicate 11 disencumber

ridder: 4 sift 5 sieve

riddle: ree 4 crux, sift 5 aread, areed, griph, rebus, sieve 6 enigma, pierce, puzzle 7 griphus, mystery, perplex 8 disprove, separate 9 conundrum, criticize, perforate

ride: 4 bait, dosa 5 drift, drive, float, motor, tease 6 harass 7 hagride, journey, torment 8 ridicule 9 carrousel, cavalcade, excursion 10 go for a spin 12 merry-go-round

to hounds: 4 hunt

without power: 5 coast, glide

rider: 6 clause, cowboy, jockey, knight 7 allonge 8 addition, appendix, bucaayro, buckaroo, cavalier, desultor, horseman 9 amendment, performer, straddler 10 equestrian, freebooter, highwayman, horsewoman 11 endorsement, mosstrooper 12 bronco-buster, equestrienne(fem.)

ridge: aas, rib, top 4 aret, asar, back, balk, bank, barb, bult, dene, dune, gold, kame, lira, loma, osar(pl.), rand, reef, ring, ruck, ruga, seam, spur, wale, wave, weal, welt 5 arete, arris, bargh, chine, costa, crest, eskar, esker, hause, oesar(pl.), rugae(pl.), serac, spine, stria, varix, wheal, whelk 6 costae(pl.), crista, rideau, striae(pl.) 7 annulet, costula, cristae(pl.), hogback, porcate, varices(pl.), wrinkle, yardang 8 costulae(pl.), headland, sastrugi, shoulder, zastrugi 9 elevation, razorback

anatomical: 5 spine, stria

cloth: 4 wale

glacial: 5 esker

pert. to: 7 cardinal

shell: 5 varix 7 varices(pl.)

skin: 4 wale, welt

ridge oak: 9 blackjack

ridged and furrowed: 7 porcate

ridicule: guy, pan 4 gibe, jeer, lout, mock, quiz, razz, twit 5 borak, chaff, irony, roast, scout, sneer, taunt 6 banter, deride, expose, satire 7 asteism, buffoon, lampoon, mockery, pillory, sarcasm 8 derision, raillery, satirize 9 burlesque, make fun of, poke fun at

deity: 5 Momus

object of: 4 butt 13 laughingstock

ridiculous: 5 droll 6 absurd 7 amusing, foolish 8 farcical 9 laughable, ludicrous 10 indecorous, irrational, outrageous 12 preposterous

riding: 8 shivaree 9 chevachie 10 equitation

costume: 5 habit

pants: 8 jodhpurs

shoe: 8 solleret

riding school: 6 manege

riding whip: 4 crop 5 quirt

ridotto: 6 resort 7 redoubt, retreat 8 festival 9 gathering 10 masquerade 11 abridgement, arrangement 12 entertainment

riem: 5 strap, strip, thong

Rienzi composer: 6 Wagner

rife: 5 alive, brief 7 current, replete 8 abundant, numerous 9 abounding, plentiful, prevalent 10 prevailing, widespread

riff: 4 scan, skim 6 browse, riffle, ripple 7 midriff 9 diaphragm

Riff: 6 Berber

riffle: 4 plow, reef 5 rapid, shoal 6 rattle, ripple 7 shallow, shuffle 11 obstruction

riffraff: mob 4 raff, scum 5 trash 6 rabble, refuse 7 rubbish 9 sweepings

rifle: arm, gun, rob 4 tige 5 reeve, steal 6 furrow, groove, weapon 7 bundock, carbine, despoil, escopet, firearm, pillage, plunder, ransack 8 bandhook 9 chassepot, escopette

accessory: 6 ramrod

ball: 5 minie

instrument: 7 bayonet

kind of: 6 Garand, Mauser 7 Enfield 9 Remington 10 Winchester 11 Springfield

magazine: 6 Mauser

pin: 4 tige

rifleman: 5 jager, yager

rift: lag 4 flaw, rive 5 belch, break, chasm, cleft, crack, rapid, split 6 breach, cleave, divide 7 blemish, fissure, opening, shallow 8 crevasse, division

rig: fig, fit, fix 4 dupe, fool, gear, hoax, wind 5 dress, equip, prank, rifle, storm, trick 6 lateen, outfit, square, tackle 7 arrange, costume, derrick, furnish, ransack, swindle, turnout 8 accouter, accoutre, carriage, equipage 9 apparatus, equipment, imposture 10 manipulate 11 contraption

riga: 6 balsam

Riga Gulf island: 5 Oesel

Riga native: 4 Lett 7 Latvian

rigadoon: 5 dance

rigescence: 8 numbness 9 stiffness

rigging: 4 gear, spar 5 ropes 6 tackle 7 clothes

right: due, fit, gee, hak 4 mend, fair, good, real, sane, soke, true 5 droit, sound 6 angry, dexter, equity, excuse, lawful, normal, patent, proper 7 correct, diehard, fitting, genuine, liberty, rectify, redress 8 appanage, becoming, courtesy, directly, easement, interest, straight, suitable, usufruct, virtuous 9 authority, equitable, faultless, franchise, privilege 10 obligation, perquisite 11 appropriate, certificate, prerogative

exclusive: 7 patents 10 concession

law: ius, jus 5 droit

of way: 8 easement

proprietary: 8 interest

royal: 7 regalia

widow's: 5 terce

right-angled: 10 orthogonal, rectangled 11 rectangular

right hand: 6 dextra 7 dextera

right-hand page: 5 recto

right-handed: 7 dextral 8 dextrous, positive 9 clockwise dexterous

right-minded: 5 moral 7 ethical 10 principled

right-winger: 7 diehard 11 bitter-ender 12 conservative

righteous: 4 good, holy, just 5 godly, moral, pious, zadoc, zadok 6 devout, worthy 7 perfect, sinless, upright 8 virtuous 9 blameless, equitable, guiltless

righteousness: 6 dharma 9 rectitude

rightful: due, fit 4 fair, just, true 5 legal 6 honest, lawful, proper 7 fitting, upright 9 equitable 11 appropriate

rightist: 4 Tory 11 reactionary 12 conservative

rigid: set 4 firm, hard, taut 5 fixed, stark, stern, stiff, stony, tense 6 marbly, severe, strait, strict 7 austere 8 hard-line, rigorous 9 immovable, stringent, unbending 10 inflexible, ironhanded, motionless, unyielding

rigmaree: 4 coin 6 trifle

rigmarole: 8 nonsense 10 balderdash

Rigoletto: *composer:* 5 Verdi

role: 5 Gilda

rigor, rigour: 4 fury 5 trial 7 cruelty 8 asperity, hardship, rigidity, severity, violence 9 austerity, harshness, rigidness, sharpness, stiffness 10 difficulty, exactitude, puritanism, strictness, visitation 13 inflexibility

rigorous: 5 angry, rigid, stern, stiff 6 severe, strait, strict 7 ascetic, correct, drastic, onerous, precise 8 accurate 9 inclement 10 inexorable, oppressive, relentless

rikk: 10 tambourine

rile: vex 4 roil 5 anger, annoy, upset 7 agitate, disturb 8 irritate 9 turbidity

rill: 5 brook, creek, crick, ditch 6 course, furrow, groove, runnel, trench 7 rillock, rivulet 8 brooklet 9 arroyuelo(Sp.), streamlet

rim: lip 4 bank, brim, edge, orle, ring, tire 5 basil, bezel, bezil, brink, somma, verge 6 border, flange, margin, shield 7 enclose, horizon 8 boundary 9 perimeter

external: 6 flange

horseshoe: web

wheel: 4 tire 5 felly 6 felloe

rima: 5 cleft, crack 7 fissure 8 aperture 10 breadfruit

rimate: 7 cracked 8 fissured

rime: ice 4 hoar, poem, rent, rung, step 5 chink, crack, frost, rhyme, verse 6 freeze 7 fissure, versify 8 aperture 9 cranreuch(Sc.), hoarfrost 10 incrustate

rimple: 4 fold 6 crease, ripple, rumple 7 wrinkle

rimption: lot 4 scad 9 abundance

Rinaldo's steed: 6 Bayard 7 Bajardo

rind: 4 bark, husk, melt, peel, skin 5 crust, waste 6 cortex 7 clarify, epicarp, peeling 8 cortices(pl.)

rindle: 5 brook, creek 6 runnel 7 rivulet

ring: bee, cut, rim, set 4 bail, band, cric, ding, dirl, echo, gyre, halo, hank, hoop, link, lute, peal, toll, tore 5 anlet, arena, bague, bezel, chime, clang, group, knell, longe, ridge, rigol 6 arenae, border, boxing, brough(Sc.), chaton, circle, circus, clique, collar, collet, corona, dindle, dingle, famble, gasket, girdle, terret, tingle, tinkle, toroid 7 annulet, annulus, circlet, coterie, curette, ferrule, grommet, resound, ringlet, tanbark, vibrate 8 bracelet, cincture, encircle, surround 9 archivolt, enclosure, encompass, telephone 10 racecourse 11 combination, reverberate 14 tintinnabulate

carrier: 9 go-between

gem setting: 5 bezel 6 chaton

of chain: 4 link

of rope: 7 grommet

pert. to: 7 annular

stone: gem

to hold reins: 6 terret

to tighten joint: 6 washer

wedding: 4 band

ring finger: 5 third

ring ouzel: 5 amsel 6 thrush 8 whistler

ring plover: 5 sandy

ring-shaped: 7 annular 8 annulate, circular 9 annulated

ring-worm: 5 tinea 6 kerion, tetter 7 serpigo 8 millepod 9 millepede

ringdove: 6 cushat, pigeon

ringed: 6 wedded 7 engaged, married 8 annulate, circular 9 annulated, decorated, encircled **10** surrounded

ringed worm: 7 annelid

ringent: 6 gaping

ringing: 4 clam 6 bright 7 orotund 8 resonant

ringleader: **10** instigator

ringlet: 4 curl, lock, ring 5 tress

rings: *interlocking:* 6 gimmal
series: 4 coil

rink: man 4 hero, race, ring 9 encounter

rinse: 4 lave, sind(Sc.), wash 5 douse, swill 6 douche, gargle, sluice 7 cleanse

riot: din, wow 4 clem, howl 5 brawl, feast, melee, revel 6 affray, bedlam, clamor, excess, pogrom(Russ.), tumult, uproar 7 dispute, quarrel, revelry 8 carousal, debauche, disorder, outburst, sedition, uprising 9 commotion, confusion, luxuriate **10** donnybrook **11** dissolution, disturbance

riotous: 4 loud, wild 5 loose 6 wanton 7 profuse **10** boisterous, profligate **11** saturnalian **12** contumacious, unrestrained

rip: hag, rit 4 rend, rent, rive, tear 6 sunder 7 sputter 8 disunite, harridan, lacerate 9 debauchee **10** laceration
roaring: 5 noisy 6 lively 8 exciting 9 hilarious **10** boisterous, uproarious

ripa: 4 bank 5 beach, shore 6 strand

ripe: fit, rob 4 aged, bank, rife 5 adult, ready 6 addled, august, mature, mellow 7 grown-up, matured, plunder 8 complete, finished, seashore 9 developed, full-grown, perfected, riverbank **10** consummate, seasonable **11** intoxicated
early: 8 rareripe

ripen: age 4 grow 6 mature, mellow, season 7 develop, enhance, improve, perfect, prepare 8 heighten

ripost, riposte: 5 reply 6 retort, return, thrust 8 repartee

ripper: 5 dilly 6 corker 7 bobsled 8 jimdandy 9 humdinger **10** crackerjack

rippet: 4 fuss, romp 6 uproar 7 quarrel

ripping: 4 fine 8 splendid 9 admirable, excellent, marvelous **10** remarkable

rippit: 5 fight

ripple: cut, lap 4 curl, fret, purl, riff, tear, wave 5 acker, graze 6 cockle, dimple, riffle, rimple 7 crinkle, scratch, wavelet, wrinkle 8 undulate

ripple grass: 7 ribwort

rise: 4 flow, grow, hulk, loom, rare, rear, soar, stem, well 5 arise, begin, climb, get up, issue, mount, reach, rebel, stand, start, surge, swell, tower 6 amount, appear, ascend, ascent, aspire, assume, attain, derive, emerge, growth, mature, revolt, spring, thrive 7 adjourn, advance, elevate, emanate, prosper, roll out, stand up, succeed 8 addition, eminence,

flourish, increase, levitate 9 ascension, beginning, elevation, originate
above: 8 surmount
again: 7 resurge 9 resurrect
against: 5 rebel 6 mutiny 9 insurrect
and fall: 4 tide 5 heave 6 welter
up: 4 fume 5 tower 6 ascend

riser: 4 pipe, step

risible: 5 funny 7 amusing 9 laughable, ludicrous

rising: 5 arise 6 orient, ortive, revolt 7 montant, nearing 8 gradient, uprising 9 ascendant, ascension **11** approaching **12** extumescence, insurrection

risk: 4 dare, defy, face, gage, wage 5 peril, stake 6 chance, danger, expose, gamble, hazard, injury, plight, plunge 7 imperil, venture 8 endanger, exposure, jeopardy 9 adventure, liability **12** disadvantage

risky: 5 hairy 6 chancy 7 parlous 8 ticklish 9 hazardous

risqué: 4 racy 5 salty, spicy 6 daring 8 off-color 9 audacious, hazardous, salacious **10** suggestive

rissle: 4 pole 5 staff, stick

rist: 4 mark 5 wound 6 ascent 7 engrave, scratch

risus: 5 laugh 8 laughter

ritardando: 9 retarding **11** rallentando

rite: 4 cult, form, orgy 5 sacra 6 augury, exequy, novena, prayer, ritual 7 liturgy, obsequy 8 accolade, ceremony, occasion 9 formality, ordinance, procedure, sacrament, solemnity **10** ceremonial, initiation, observance

Ritter: 6 knight

ritual: 4 cult, form, rite 7 liturgy, obsequy 8 ceremony 9 obsequies(pl.) **10** ceremonial

ritus: 5 usage 6 custom

ritzy: 6 modish 7 elegant, haughty 9 expensive, luxurious **11** fashionable

rivage: 4 bank, duty 5 coast, shore

rival: try, vie 4 even, peer 5 equal, match 6 amount 7 compete, emulate, feuding 8 corrival, emulator, opponent, struggle 9 adversary, competing **10** antagonist, competitor, contending **11** comparative

rivalry: 7 contest 8 tug-of-war **11** competition

rive: rip, rob 4 bank, chop, plow, pull, rend, rent, rift, tear 5 break, cleft, shore, split, steal 6 arrive, cleave, pierce, sunder, thieve, thrust 7 dispart, shatter 8 lacerate 9 disembark

rivel: 6 shrink 7 shrivel, wrinkle

river: ree, ria(Sp.), rio(Sp.), run 4 wadi, wady 5 bayou, waddy 6 stream 7 channel 8 effluent 9 abundance **11** watercourse
arm: 4 fork 7 estuary 9 tributary
bank: 4 rand, ripa 5 levee

channel: bed 6 alveus
current: 4 eddy 6 rapids
dam: 4 weir
gauge: 9 nilometer
god: 7 Alpheus, Inachus 8 Achelous
horse: 5 hippo, rhino 12 hippopotamus
ice: 7 glacier
inlet: 5 bayou 6 slough
island: ait 4 holm
Kubla Khan's: 4 Alph
land: 5 carse(Sc.), flats 7 bottoms
living in: 9 amphibian, rheophile
long run: 9 sluiceway
longest: 4 Nile
mouth: 4 beal(Sc.), lade 5 delta 7 estuary
mythical: 4 Styx
nymph: 4 nais 5 naiad
obstruction: 4 snag 5 gorce
of oblivion: 5 Lethe
passage: 4 ford 7 estuary
pert. to: 5 amnic 7 fluvial, potamic 8 riverine 9 fluminose, fluminous
sacred: 5 Ganga 6 Ganges
siren: 7 Lorelei
small: 5 brook, creek, tchai 6 stream 7 rivulet 8 riverlet 9 streamlet
thief: 6 ackman
underworld: 4 Styx 5 Lethe 7 Acheron, Cocytus
winding part: ess
river dog: 10 hellbender
river duck: 4 teal 7 mallard, widgeon
river mussel: 4 unio
River of Forgetfulness: 5 Lethe
River of Hate: 4 Styx
River of Sorrows: 7 Acheron
riverbed: 4 wadi, wady 5 waddy 7 batture
riverboat: ark 5 barge 6 pulwar 7 rowboat, towboat 8 flatboat
riverside: 4 bank 5 shore
riverweed family: 13 podostemaceae
rivet: fix 4 bolt, brad 6 clinch, fasten 8 fastener
riviere: 8 necklace
rivulet: 4 burn, rill 5 bache, bayou, bourn, brook, creek 6 bourne, rindle(Sc.), runlet, runnel, stream 7 channel 9 streamlet
rixatrix: 5 scold 6 virago
rixy: 4 tern
roach: bug, cut 4 fish, hill, rock, roll, soil, spot 6 braise 7 sunfish 9 cockroach
road: way 4 fare, gang, iter, path, raid, ride 5 agger, bargh, going, itero(pl.), route 6 avenue, camino, career, causey, chemin, course, street 7 calzada(Sp.), estrada, gangway, highway, itinera(pl.), journey, passage, railway 8 beallach, causeway, chaussee(F.), cul-de-sac, pavement, railroad 9 direction, incursion, roadstead 10 expedition

bend: 7 hairpin
character: 4 hobo 5 tramp 10 hitchhiker
country: 4 lane 6 boreen (Ir.)
edge: 4 berm 8 shoulder
machine: 4 harl 5 paver 6 grader 9 bulldozer
menace: 7 speeder
military: 5 agger
surface: tar 6 bricks, gravel, stones 7 macadam 8 concrete, pavement
roadblock: bar 7 barrier 8 blockade
road book: map 9 gazetteer, itinerary
roadhouse: inn 5 hotel, lodge 6 tavern
roadman: 7 drummer, peddler 8 salesman 9 canvasser
road runner: 6 cuckoo 7 paisano(Sp.)
roadster: 5 horse 7 bicycle 8 runabout
roam: err, gad 4 roil, rove 5 prowl, range, stray 6 bangle, ramble, stroll, travel, wander 7 meander 8 straggle 9 gallivant
roamer: 5 gipsy, gypsy, nomad, rover 8 fugitive 12 peregrinator
roan: bay 5 color, horse 9 sheepskin
Roanoke bell: 7 cowslip
roar: cry, din 4 bawl, beal, bell, bere, boom, bray, clap, hurl, rote, rout, yell 5 blart, brool, fream, laugh, shout 6 bellow, buller, clamor, outcry, steven 7 bluster, thunder 8 shouting
roaring: 4 loud 5 aroar, brisk, noisy 7 riotous 10 boisterous, disorderly, stentorian 11 flourishing
roaring game: 7 curling
roaring Meg: 6 cannon
roast: fry 4 bake, burn, cook, razz, roti(F.) 5 asado(Sp.), brede, grill, parch 6 assate, banter 7 torrefy, torrify 8 lambaste, ridicule 9 criticize
meat on stick: 5 cabob, kabob
prepare: 5 truss
roasting stick: 4 spit 6 skewer
rob: cop 4 fake, flap, loot, pelf, take 5 bribe, filch, harry, heist, pilch, pinch, pluck, raven, reave, rifle, spoil, steal, strip, touch 6 burgle, hold up, pilfer, pirate, ravish, shrive, snatch, snitch, thieve 7 bereave, defraud, deprive, despoil, pillage, plunder, purloin 10 burglarize, housebreak, plagiarize
Rob Roy: 5 canoe
robber: 4 goul, yegg 5 ghoul, thief 6 arrant, bandit, cat-man, dacoit, pirate 7 brigand, corsair, footpad, ladrone, yeggman 8 marauder 9 bandolero, buccaneer, privateer 10 depredator, highwayman
robe (see also **dress, gown**): aba 4 skin, vest, wrap 5 array, camis, camus, cloak, cover, cymar, habit, simar, talar, tunic 6 caftan, chimer, clothe, dolman, invest, kimono, mantle, revest 7 chimere,

costume, garment, manteau, vesture 8
clothing, covering, vestment 10 sticharion
robin: 4 lout, tody 6 oriole, thrush 7
bumpkin, chewink, warbler 8 trimming
10 cuckoopint, toxalbumin
Robin Goodfellow: elf 4 Puck 5 fairy 6
sprite 9 hobgoblin
Robin Hood: *chaplain:* 9 Friar Tuck
follower: 4 John 9 Friar Tuck
sweetheart: 6 Marian 10 Maid Marian
robin sandpiper: 4 knot 9 dowitcher
robinet: 6 cannon 9 chaffinch
Robinson Crusoe: *author:* 5 Defoe
companion: 9 Man Friday
roborant: 4 drug 5 tonic 13 strengthening
roborean: 5 oaken, stout 6 strong
robot: 5 droid, golem 7 android 9 an-
droides, automaton
drama about: RUR
robust: 4 hale, hard, iron, rude 5 hardy,
lusty, rough, sound, stout, wally 6
brawny, coarse, hearty, rugged, sinewy,
strong, sturdy 7 healthy 8 athletic,
muscular, vigorous 10 boisterous, flourishing
roc: 4 bird 6 simurg 7 simurgh, soldier
rocca: 4 hold, keep 6 donjon 8 fortress
rochet: 5 cloak, frock 7 camisia, garment,
gurnard 8 vestment
relative: alb
rock: dag, ore, tor 4 clay, crag, lull, peak,
reef, reel, roll, scar, shog, spar, sway,
toss, trap, tufa, tuff, wash 5 agate,
brack, candy, chert, cliff, earth, flint,
geest, hurry, lytta, prase, scree, shake,
shale, shaul, slate, stane(Sc.), stone,
swing, wacke 6 aplite, basalt, dacite,
egeran, gneiss, gravel, issite, oolite, pebble, refuge, rognon, schist, silica, sinter,
teeter, totter 7 adinole, akerite, alunite,
defense, diamond, gondite, granite, grie-
sen, support, tremble, vibrate 8 andes-
ite, banakite, dolomite, laterite, obsidian, porphyry, psephite, rhyolite,
undulate 9 epidosite, flagstone, oscillate, phanerite 10 greenstone, promontory 11 petrography
boring tool: 6 trepan
cavity: vug 4 vugg 5 vugg, druse, geode
clay: 8 ganister
debris: 5 talus 8 detritus, xenolith
decomposed: 6 gossan
discarded: 5 attle
finely broken: 4 sand
fissile: 5 shale
flintlike: 5 chert 6 quartz
fold: 8 syncline 9 anticline
fragments: see *debris* above
glacier deposit: 7 moraine
glacier-transported: 7 erratic

igneous: 4 boss, sial, sima, trap, tufa 5
trass 6 basalt, domite, latite 7 diabase,
diorite, felsite, ijolite, peridot 8 extax-
ite, ijussite, porphyry 11 agglomerate
laminated: 4 mica 5 shale, slate
liquid: 4 lava
mythical: 6 Scylla
nodule: 5 geode
pert. to: 6 petric 7 petrean
point: 4 crag, peak
science: 9 petrology
strata: see *fold* above
volcanic: 4 lava, tufa, tuff
rockabilly: 12 country music
rock badger: 4 cony 5 hyrax
rock bass: 6 red-eye 8 cabrilla
rock bottom: 6 lowest 7 essence 8 cheap-
est
rock dove: 6 pigeon 9 guillemot
rock eel: 6 gunnel
rock falcon: 6 merlin
rock geranium: 8 alumroot
rock goat: 4 ibex
rock grouse: 9 ptarmigan
rock hind: 7 grouper
rock hopper: 7 penguin
rock kangaroo: 7 wallaby
rock oak: 8 chestnut 10 California, chinquapin
rock oil: 9 petroleum
rock plant: 4 moss 6 lichen
rock rabbit: 5 hyrax
rock snake: 5 krait 6 python
rock starling: 5 ouzel
rock tar: 9 petroleum
rock tripe: 6 lichen
rock wren: 4 bird
rockaway: 8 carriage
rockbell: 9 columbine
rockbird: 5 murre 9 sandpiper
rocker: 5 chair, skate 6 cradle 7 shoofly
rocket: 4 weld, wold 5 slate, woald, would
9 satellite 11 firecracker
end of combustion: 7 burnout
landing: 7 reentry 10 splashdown
launcher: 7 bazooka
launching: 4 shot 8 blastoff
launching postponement: 5 abort
rockfish: 4 bass, rena 5 perch, reina,
viuva 6 gopher, tambor 7 grouper 9 killifish 10 priestfish
rockling: 4 fish, gade
rockrose: 6 cistus
rocky: 4 hard, weak 5 dizzy, shaky, stony
6 cliffy 7 obscene, petrean 8 obdurate,
unsteady 9 unfeeling 10 insensible
Rocky Mountain: *goat:* 6 mazame 8 antelope
park: 5 Estes
peak: 5 Logan, Pikes
range: 5 Teton 7 Wasatch
sheep: 7 bighorn

wind: 7 chinook

rococo: 4 arty 6 ornate 9 fantastic 10 fiamboyant

rod: bar, gad, guy, rab, rib 4 axle, bolt, came, cane, crop, goad, I-bar, lath, pole, prod, race, scob, spit, wand, wire 5 arrow, baton, board, lytta, osier, perch, power, scion, spoke, staff, stick, stock, strip, tribe 6 baculi(pl.), batten, broach, carbon, etalon, eyebar, ferule, needle, pistol, piston, pontil, raddle, skewer, switch, toggle 7 baculus, caliper, crowbar, distaff, measure, scepter, sceptre, spindle, stemmer, support, tringle, tyranny 8 arrester, offshoot, revolver 9 authority 10 oppression, punishment 12 chastisement

bundle: 6 fasces

divination by: 7 dowsing 11 rhabdomancy

movable: 6 piston

square: 5 perch

rod-like: 6 rhabdo 7 virgate

rodd: 8 crossbow, stonebow

rodent: jap, rat 4 cavy, cony, cypu, degu, hare, mole, paca, pica, pika, utia, vole 5 aguti, hutia, jutia, lerot, mouse, ratel, zokor 6 agouti, agouty, beaver, biting, cururo, gerbil, gopher, gundie, jerboa, marmot, murine, rabbit, weasel 7 chincha, hamster, leveret, muskrat, pack rat 8 capibara, capybara, dormouse, gerbille, leporide, sewellel, squirrel, viscacha, vizcacha 9 porcupine 10 chinchilla

aquatic: 6 beaver 7 muskrat

genus: Mus 5 Lepus

jumping: 6 jerboa

pert. to: 8 rosorial

rodeo: 7 roundup 9 enclosure 10 exhibition

rodge: 7 gadwall

rodman: 4 thug 10 highwaymen

rodomontade: 4 brag, rant 5 boast, empty, pride 6 vanity 7 bluster, bombast 8 boastful, boasting, braggart

roe: ova, pea 4 deer, eggs, hart, hind 5 coral, spawn 6 caviar

roebuck: 4 girl 9 chevreuil

Roentgen's discovery: 4 X ray

roestone: 6 oolite

rogation: law 6 decree, litany, prayer 7 inquiry 12 supplication

rogue: boy, gue, imp, wag 4 hemp, kite 5 catso, cheat, crank, decry, gipsy, gypsy, hempy, knave, scamp, shark, tramp 6 beggar, canter, coquin, harlot, pirate, rascal, wander 7 corsair, culprit, erratic, hellion, sharper, vagrant, villain, waggish 8 picaroon, swindler, vagabond 9 scoundrel, trickster 10 delinquent, frolicsome, stigmatize 11 rapscallion

pert. to: 10 picaresque

roguery: 5 fraud 8 mischief, trickery 15 mischievousness

roguish: coy, sly 4 arch 5 pawky 6 wanton 7 playful, puckish 8 espiegle, sportive 9 dishonest, fun-loving 12 unscrupulous

roid: 5 rough 6 severe 7 riotous, roguish 10 frolicsome 12 unmanageable

roil: mud, vex 4 foul, rile, roam, romp, rust, stir 5 anger, annoy, muddy, rouse 6 cloudy, fidget, ruffle, wander 7 blunder, disturb, pollute 8 irritate 9 displease, unsettled 10 exasperate 11 contaminate

roily: 6 turbid

roister: 4 brag, rude 5 bully, revel, spree 7 bluster, boorish, carouse, reveler, swagger, violent 9 gilravage

roistering: 6 hoiden, hoyden

rojo: 6 Indian 7 redskin

roke: fog 4 mist, stir 5 smoke, steam, vapor 8 moisture

roker: ray 8 rockling 9 thornback

roky: 4 damp 5 foggy, misty, smoky 6 hoarse

Roland: 7 Orlando

beloved: 4 Aude

emperor: 11 Charlemagne

enemy: 4 Gano 7 Ganelon

friend: 6 Oliver

horn: 7 Olivant

horse: 10 Veillantif

sword: 8 Durendal

uncle: 11 Charlemagne

role: bit 4 cast, duty, part 5 cameo, heavy 6 office 8 business, function 9 character, soubrette 13 impersonation 16 characterization

leading: 4 star

roll: bun, gad, rob 4 bolt, coil, file, flow, furl, list, pell, pour, roam, rota, seel, sway, toss, turn, wind, wrap 5 bagel, cadre, frisk, lurch, shift, surge, swing, trill, troll, wheel 6 bundle, enroll, enwrap, goggle, grovel, ponder, roster, rotate, rumble, scroll, spiral, swathe, tumble, wallow, wander, welter, whelve, wintle 7 biscuit, brioche, fortune, revolve, rissole, stagger, swagger, trundle 8 cylinder, flounder, register, undulate

of hair: bun 7 chignon

sweet: 6 danish 9 schnecken

roll back: 5 lower 6 reduce 7 repulse

roll in: 4 flow 6 arrive, wallow, welter

roll up: 4 furl 5 amass 6 arrive, gather 10 accumulate

roller: 4 band, wave 5 finer, inker, swath 6 canary, caster, fascia, fillet, pigeon, platen, rowlet, sponge 7 bandage, breaker, presser, sirgang, tumbler 8 cylinder 9 surcingle

rolleyway: 4 road 5 track 7 gangway, tramway

rollick: 4 romp 5 sport 6 frolic, gambol, wallow 8 escapade

rollicking: gay 5 antic, happy 6 jovial, lively 8 careless 9 hilarious 12 lighthearted

rolling stock: 4 cars 6 trucks 7 coaches, engines 8 cabooses, Pullmans, sleepers, trailers 11 locomotives

rolling stone: 5 rover 7 drifter 8 wanderer

rolling weed: 10 tumbleweed

rolltop: 4 desk

roly-poly: 5 dumpy, pudgy, round 6 portly, rotund 7 pudding

rom: 5 gipsy, gypsy

romaine: cos 5 plant 7 lettuce

romal: 5 thong

Roman: 5 brave, Latin 6 frugal, honest, simple 7 Italian

Roman Catholic: *cassock:* 7 soutane, zimarra

church: 7 lateran

ecclesiastic: 7 Rosmini

priest: 4 abbe(F.) 6 father 8 sacerdos 9 monsignor

skullcap: 9 zucchetto

society: 7 Jesuits

romance: woo 4 gest, tale 5 court, dream, fable, fancy, feign, geste, novel, story 6 affair 7 chimera, fantasy, fiction, romanza 9 falsehood, sentiment 10 exaggerate, love affair 12 exaggeration

Romance language: 6 French 7 Catalan, Italian, Spanish 8 Rumanian 9 Provencal 10 Portuguese

Romania: See **Rumania**

romantic: 6 exotic, poetic, unreal 8 quixotic 9 imaginary, visionary 10 idealistic 11 extravagant, sentimental

Romany, Rommany: 5 gipsy, gypsy

tongue: 7 Romanes

romanza: 7 fiction, romance

Rome (see also **Latin**): 4 Roma

abode of gods: 7 Olympus

adviser to king: 6 Egeria

airport: 8 Ciampino 9 Fiumicino 15 Leonardo da Vinci

amphitheater: 9 colosseum

apostle: 4 Neri, Paul

army unit: 6 cohort

army wing: ala

assembly: 5 forum 6 senate 7 comitia

attendant: 7 aliptes 8 aleiptes

augur: 6 auspex

author (see also *biographer, historian, poet,* below): 5 Pliny, Varro

authority symbol: 6 fasces

basilica: 7 lateran

battle array: 5 acies

biographer: 5 Nepos 9 Suetonius

brothers: 5 Remus 7 Romulus

burial site: 9 Catacombs

Caesar's title: 9 imperator

captain: 9 centurion

carriage: 5 essed

chapel: 7 Sistine

chief god: 4 Jove 7 Jupiter

citadel: arx

clans: 4 gens

cloak: 4 toga

coin: aes 5 assis(pl.), aurei(pl.), semis 6 aureus, dinder, solidu, triens 7 denarii(pl.), siliqua decussis, denarius, sesterce, sesteria(pl.) 9 sesterium 10 sestertius, victoriate 11 victoriatus

comedy: 5 exode

comedy writer: 6 Cicero 7 Plautus, Terence

concert hall: 5 odeum

conqueror: 6 Alaric

conspirator: 8 Catiline

court: 5 atria(pl.) 6 atrium

custodian: 10 neocorates

date: 4 Ides 5 Nones

district: 5 Pagus 7 Pontine 8 Pomptine

diviner: 5 augur 6 auspex

division: 5 curia

earthwork: 5 agger

emperor: 4 Nero, Otho, Otto 5 Galba, Nerva, Titus 6 Caesar, Julian, Trajan 7 Hadrian 8 Augustus, Claudius, Domitian, Tiberius 9 Vespasian 10 Elagabalus 11 Constantine

empress: 7 Eudocia

encampment: 7 castrum

entrance hall: 5 atria(pl.) 6 atrium

epic: 6 Aeneid

family: 7 familia

farmer: 7 colonus 8 agricola

Fate: 4 Nona 5 Morta, Parca 6 Decuma, Parcae(pl.)

fighter: 9 gladiator

fortress: 7 castrum

founder: 5 Remus 7 Romulus

fountain: 5 Trevi

galley: 6 bireme 7 trireme

garment: 4 toga 5 palla, sagum, stola, stole, togae(pl.), tunic

general: 5 Sulla, Titus 6 Antony, Marius, Scipio 8 Agricola

god: Dis, Lar, Sol 4 Amor, Jove, Mars 5 Comus, Cupid, Fauns, Janus, Lares, manes, Orcus, Pluto 6 Faunus, Vulcan 7 Jupiter, lemures, Neptune, penates, Phoebus, Vatican 8 Dispater, Morpheus, Quirinus 11 Aesculapius

god of dead: 5 Orcus

god of death: 4 Mors

god of fire: 6 Vulcan

god of love: 4 Amor

god of mirth: 5 Comus

god of sea: 7 Neptune

god of sleep: 8 Morpheus

god of sun: Sol
god of underworld: Dis 5 Pluto
god of war: 4 Mars
god of wind: 5 Eurus 6 Boreas
god of wine: 7 Bacchus
goddess: dea(L.), Lua, Nox, Ops, Pax 4
  Caca, Juno, Luna, Maia, Paca 5 Ceres,
  Diana, Epona, Terra, Venus, Vesta 6
  Aestas, Annona, Aurora, Lucina, Rumi-
  na, Tellus, Vacuna 7 Bellona, Fortuna,
  Minerva 8 Libitina 9 Abudantia, Discordia, Felicitas
goddess of agriculture: Ops 5 Ceres
goddess of beauty: 5 Venus
goddess of flowers: 5 Flora
goddess of hearth: 5 Vesta 6 Hestia
goddess of hope: 4 Spes
goddess of hunting: 5 Diana
goddess of love: 5 Venus
goddess of marriage: 4 Juno
goddess of moon: 4 Luna
goddess of night: Nox
goddess of peace: Pax 5 Irene
goddess of plenty: Ops
goddess of underworld: 10 Proserpina
goddess of vegetation: 5 Ceres
goddess of victory: 6 Vacuna
goddess of war: 7 Bellona, Minerva
goddess of wisdom: 7 Minerva
greeting: ave
guard: 6 lictor
hall: 5 atria(pl.) 6 atrium
hat: 7 petasos, petasus
helmet: 5 galea 6 galeae(pl.)
highway: via 4 iter 6 Appian 8 itiner-
  es(pl.)
hill: 7 Caelian, Viminal 8 Aventine, Palatine, Quirinal 9 Esquiline 10 Capitoline
historian: 4 Livy 5 Nepos
holiday: 5 feria 6 feriae(pl.)
judge: 5 edile 6 aedile
jurist: 5 Gaius
king: 5 Romulus, Servius, Tullius 12 An-
  cus Martius 13 Numa Pompilius 15
  Tullus Hostilius 18 Tarquinius Super-
  bus
lake: 4 Nemi
language: 5 Latin
law: fas, lex 4 cern
leader: dux
magistrate: 5 edile 6 aedile, censor, pretor
  7 praetor, tribune
marble: 7 cipolin
measure: pes, urn 4 mile, pace, urna 5 actus, clima, cubit, juger 6 culeus, dolium,
  gradus, hemina, modius, palmus, passus, saltus, versus 7 amphora, congius,
  cyathus, digitus, stadion, stadium 8
  centuria, hereduim, quadrant 9 decem-
  peda, millarium, sextarius 10 acetabulum, quartarius
measure of weight: bes 4 pood 5 assis(pl.),

libra, uncia 6 duella 7 dodrans, sextula,
  solidus 8 sicilium 9 scrupulus, scrupu-
  lum
military formation: ala 6 alares(pl.) 7
  phalanx
military machine: 7 terebra
military unit: 6 cohort, legion 7 maniple
military vessel: 6 bireme 7 trireme
naturalist: 5 Pliny
nymph: 6 Egeria
official: 5 augur, edile 6 aedile, lictor 7
  prefect, tribune 8 irenarch 9 nestorian
ox: 4 urus
palace: 5 chigi 7 lateran
palace troops: 9 palatines
people: 5 Laeti 7 Sabines 8 plebians 10
  patricians
pert. to: 9 classical
philosopher: 4 Cato 6 Seneca
physician: 9 archiater 11 Aesculapius
pillager: 6 Alaric
pin: 4 acus
poet: 4 Ovid 5 Cinna, Lucan 6 Horace,
  Vergil, Virgil 7 Juvenal, Terence 8 Ca-
  tullus, Tibullus 10 Propertius
port: 5 Ostia
praenomen: 5 Aulus, Caius, Gaius, Titus
  6 Appius 7 Quintus, Spurius 8 Tiberius
priest: 5 epulo 6 flamen 7 luperci
priestess: 6 vestal   \
procurator: 5 Felix 6 Pilate
province: 5 Dacia 7 Cilicia
queen of goddesses: 4 Juno
racecourse: 6 circus
regulator: 6 censor
religious law: fas
river: 5 Tiber
road: 4 iter
room: ala 5 atria(pl.) 6 atrium 7 tablin-
  a(pl.) 8 fumarium, tablinum
rural deity: 6 Faunus
saint: 4 Neri
senate division: 5 curia
senate emblem: 9 laticlave
senate house: 5 curia
shield: scuta(pl.) 6 ancile, scutum 7 anci-
  lia(pl.), clypeus
slave: 9 Spartacus
spirits of dead: 5 manes
standard: 7 labarum, vexilla(pl.) 8 vexillum
standard-bearer: 9 vexillary
statesman: 4 Cato 5 Pliny 6 Caesar, Cicero, Seneca 7 Agrippa 8 Maecenas
tax gatherer: 8 publican
temple: 4 naos 5 cella 8 pantheon
treasurer: 8 quaestor
veteran: 7 emeriti(pl.) 8 emeritus
weight: see measure of weight above
writing tablet: 7 diptych
Romeo: 7 gallant
beloved: 6 Juliet

enemy: 6 Tybalt

father: 8 Montague

friend: 8 Mercutio

rival: 5 Paris

romp: 4 hoit, play, roil 6 cavort, frolic, gambol, hoiden, hoyden 7 carouse, courant, gammock 8 carousal, courante 9 cut capers

Romulus: *brother:* 5 Remus

father: 4 Mars

rondure: orb 4 ball 5 globe, round 6 circle, sphere 9 plumpness, roundness

rood: 5 cross 7 measure 8 crucifix

roodebok: 6 impala

roof: top 5 cover 6 harbor 7 palate, shelter 8 covering

border: 4 eave

of mouth: 6 palate

style: hip 4 dome, flat, nave, sark 5 gable, spire 6 cupola 7 cricket, gambrel, mansard 9 penthouse pyramidal 10 jerkinhead

support: 6 rafter

window: 6 dormer

roofing material: tar, tin 4 tile 5 paper, slate, straw, terne 6 copper, gravel, shakes, thatch 7 pantile 8 shingles

rook: 4 bird, crow 5 cheat, raven, steal 6 castle, fleece 7 defraud, sharper, swindle 8 swindler

rookery: 5 roost 8 building

rookie: 4 tyro 6 novice 7 recruit, trainee 8 beginner 10 apprentice

rooky: 5 foggy 6 untidy 10 disheveled

room: ala, ben, den 4 aula, cell, digs, hall, loge, play, sala(Sp.), seat 5 atria(pl.), aulae(pl.), cubby, divan, kiosk, lodge, place, salle(F.), salon, scope, space 6 atrium, casino, harbor, leeway, margin, reside, saloon, scouth 7 boudoir, cabinet, chamber, cubicle, expanse, gallery, lodging, rotunda, theater 9 apartment, garderobe 10 auditorium

conversation: 6 exedra 7 exedrae(pl.) 9 drawing room

eating: 4 nook 7 cenacle, kitchen 8 cenacula(pl.) 9 cenaculum, refectory

on a ship: 5 cabin 6 galley

private: 7 boudoir

provision: 4 ewry 5 ewery 6 larder 7 pantry 8 cupboard

reading: den 5 study 7 library 8 Atheneum

sleeping: 5 lodge 6 dormer 7 barrack, bedroom 8 roomette 9 dormitory

storage: 4 loft, shed 5 attic 6 cellar 9 storeroom

room and board: 14 accommodations

roomer: 5 guest 6 lodger, tenant 7 boarder

rooms: 4 flat 5 suite 9 apartment

roomy: 5 ample, broad, spacy 8 spacious 9 capacious 10 commodious

roorback, roorbach: lie 4 hoax 6 canard 7 fiction 9 falsehood

roose: 5 boast, extol, vaunt 6 praise

Roosevelt, F. D.: *dog:* 4 Fala

mother: 4 Sara

wife: 7 Eleanor

roost: sit 4 nest, pole, rest 5 abode, perch, sleep 6 alight, garret 7 lodging, support

rooster: 4 cock 5 gallo(Sp.) 11 chanticleer

root: dig 4 base, bulb, core, grub, moot, rout, stem 5 basis, cheer, grout, plant, radix, shout, tuber 6 bottom, center, etymon, ground, origin, settle 7 applaud, essence, radical, radices(pl.), rootlet, support 8 entrench 9 beginning, establish 10 foundation

dyeing: 6 madder

edible: oca, roi, rue, uva, yam 4 beet, eddo, taro 5 orris, tania 6 carrot, ginger, orrice, radish, turnip 7 parsnip 8 rutabaga 9 sassafras

fragrant: 4 khus 5 orris

medicinal: 5 jalap, lappa 7 ginseng

outer layer: 7 exoderm

pert. to: 7 radical

principal: 7 taproot

pungent: 11 crinkleroot

starch: 4 arum

root out: 4 stub 6 evulse 7 destroy 8 demolish 9 eradicate, extirpate 10 annihilate, deracinate

rooted: 10 inveterate

rooter: fan 10 enthusiast

rootlet: 7 radicle, rhizoid

rootstock: 5 orris 6 ginger, pannum, stolon 7 rhizome

rope: gad, guy, tie, tow 4 bind, cord, hemp, line, stay 5 cable, longe, riata, sheet, widdy 6 binder, fasten, halter, hawser, lariat, shroud, tether 7 aweband, binding, bobstay, bollard, cordage, halyard, marline, painter 8 inveigle, prolonge

animal's: 5 leash 6 halter, tether

fiber: 4 coir, flax, jute 5 istle, sisal 6 cotton, Manila

holder: 6 becket

loop: 5 bight, noose 6 becket, parral, parrel

restraining: 6 tether

ship's: tye 4 colt, lift, rode, stay, vang 5 brace, braid, sheet 6 hawser, inhaul, parral, parrel, ratlin, shroud 7 halyard, lanyard, painter, ratline

splice pin: fid

throwing: 5 lasso, reata, riata 6 lariat

ropedancer: 7 acrobat 9 funambulo 11 funambulist

roper: 6 cowboy, packer

ropery: 6 banter 7 roguery

ropes: 8 minutiae 10 ins and outs

roque: 7 croquet

roric: 4 dewy

rosary: 4 bede 5 beads 7 chaplet, garland 8 beadroll

rose (see also **rise**): ris 5 blush, delta, flush 6 flower, nozzle 7 rambler, rosette 9 hellebore
    family: 8 rosaceae
    kind of: dog 4 moss, musk
    oil: 4 atar, otto 5 attar, ottar
    part: 5 petal

Rose City: 8 Pasadena, Portland

rose of Sharon: 6 althea 11 shrubby plant

rose parakeet: 7 rosella

rose pogonia: 10 snakemouth

rosebay: 8 oleander

rosemary: 4 herb, mint 8 moorwort

rosette: 4 chou, knot 7 cockade 8 ornament

rosilla: 9 rockbrush 10 sneezeweed

rosin: See resin

Rosinante: nag 4 jade, plug 5 horse, steed

rosiness: 5 blush, flush

ross: 4 bark, peel 5 waste 8 exterior

roster: 4 list, roll, rota 5 slate 6 muster 7 catalog

rostrum: 4 beak, dais 5 snout, stage 6 pulpit 7 lectern, tribune 8 platform 9 proboscis

rosy: red 4 pink 5 ruddy 6 bright, florid 7 auroral, flushed, hopeful, roseate 8 blooming, blushing, cheerful, rubicund 9 favorable, promising, rosaceous 10 favourable, optimistic

rot: ret 4 bosh, dote, doze, joke 5 chaff, decay, spoil, tease, trash 6 banter, fester, perish 7 corrupt, putrefy, rubbish, twaddle 8 nonsense 9 decompose, poppycock 10 degenerate 13 decomposition

rota: 4 list, roll 5 court, round 6 course, roster 8 register

rotate: 4 pass, roll, spin, turn 5 twirl, wheel, whirl 6 gyrate 7 perform, revolve, trundle 8 rotiform 9 alternate, take turns

rotation: 4 eddy 6 torque, vortex 9 pirouette 10 revolution
    part: cam 4 axle 5 rotor, wheel

rote: 4 list 5 learn 6 course, custom, memory, repeat, system 7 routine 8 practice 9 automatic 10 memorizing, repetition

rotiform: 6 rotate 11 wheel-shaped

rotor: 7 spinner 8 impeller

rotten: bad 4 evil, foul 5 fetid, nasty 6 putrid 7 carrion, corrupt, decayed, spoiled, tainted, unsound, vicious 8 depraved, unstable 9 offensive, putrefied 10 abdominable, decomposed, putrescent, undermined 12 disagreeable 13 disintegrated 14 unsatisfactory

rotter: cad 7 shirker, slacker 10 blackguard

rotula: 5 round 6 troche 7 kneepan, lozenge, patella

rotund: 5 beefy, chunky, obese, plump, round, stout 6 chubby, portly 7 rounded 8 rolypoly, sonorant, sonorous 9 spherical

roturier: 7 freeman, upstart 8 commoner

roué: rip 4 rake 9 debauchee, libertine

rouge: red 5 blush, color, flush, paint, score 6 redden, ruddle 8 cosmetic

rough: 4 hard, rude, wild 5 acrid, brute, crude, gross, hairy, harsh, husky, lumpy, raggy, rowdy, seamy, stern, surly, tight, tough, uncut 6 abrupt, broken, choppy, coarse, crabby, craggy, hoarse, jagged, rugged, severe, shaggy, uneven 7 austere, boorish, bristly, brusque, grating, hirsute, inexact, jarring, raucous, ruffian, ruffled, uncivil 8 churlish, clownish, gangster, impolite, obdurate, unplaned 9 imperfect, inclement, turbulent, unrefined 10 boisterous, discordant, incomplete, indecorous, tumultuous, unpleasant, unpolished 11 approximate, tempestuous

rough-and-ready: 9 makeshift 10 unpolished

roughen: 4 chap, fret, shag 5 feaze 7 engrail 10 exasperate

roughneck: 4 boor 5 rowdy, tough

roughness: 7 crudity 8 acrimony, asperity, inequality

rough out: 6 sketch

rough up: 9 manhandle

rouky: 5 foggy, misty

roulade: 8 arpeggio, division, flourish

roulette: 10 epicyloid 11 epitrochoid 12 gambling game, hypotrochoid
    bet: bas 4 noir 5 carre, rouge 6 milieu 7 dernier, encarre, enplein

rounceval: 5 giant, large 6 virago 7 monster 8 gigantic 9 termagant

round: 4 ball, beat, bout, full, rung 5 group, large, orbed, plump 6 circle, curved, nearly, period, polish, rotund 7 bulbous, circuit, liberal, through 8 circular, complete, globular, resonant, rolypoly 9 outspoken, spherical 11 cylindrical

round clam: 6 quahog

round dance: hay, ray 5 polka, waltz 7 roundel 9 roundelay, schottish 11 schottische

round robin: 6 letter, series 7 contest 8 document, petition, sequence 9 cigarfish 10 tournament

Round Table knight: Kay 4 Bors, Owen 6 Gawain 7 Caradoc, Cradock, Gaheris, Galahad 8 Lancelot, Tristram 9 Percivale

roundabout: 4 tour 5 dance 6 detour 7 devious 8 circular, indirect, tortuous, verbiage 9 excursion 10 circuitous, far-fetched 13 approximately 14 circumlocution, circumlocutory

rounded: 4 oval 5 bombe, ovate 6 convex, curved, rotund 7 arrondi, bunting, gibbous 8 circular 10 curvaceous, labialized

roundel: 4 guze, hurt 5 plate 6 circle, pellet, shield

rounder: 4 roue 5 sport 7 wastrel 8 criminal, drunkard, preacher 11 spendthrift

roundhead: 5 Swede 7 Puritan

roundup: 5 rodeo 7 summary 9 gathering

roundworm: 4 nema 7 ascaris 8 nematode

roup: 4 sale 6 clamor 7 auction 8 shouting

rouse: daw, hie 4 call, move, stir, wake, whet 5 alarm, awake, raise, rally, start, toast, upset, waken 6 arouse, awaken, bestir, excite, foment, frolic, revive, stir up 7 actuate, agitate, animate, disturb, enliven, provoke, startle 8 inspirit 9 intensify, stimulate

Rousseau hero: 5 Emile

roussette: 5 shark 7 dogfish

roust: 4 roar, stir, tide 5 rouse 6 bellow, tumult 7 current, provoke, roaring 9 bellowing

roustabout: 4 hand 6 worker 7 laborer 8 floorman

rout: mob 4 band, beat, bray, dart, fuss, roar, root 5 crowd, drive, expel, knock, noise, scoop, shout, snore, snort, troop 6 bellow, clamor, defeat, furrow, rabble, search, strike, throng, tumult, uproar 7 company, confuse, debacle, repulse, retinue, retreat, rummage, slumber, trouble 8 assemble, assembly, confound, disperse, reversal, shouting, stampede, vanquish 9 discomfit, multitude, overpower, overthrow, overwhelm 11 disturbance, put to flight 12 discomfiture

route: way 4 gest, lane, line, path, road, send 5 guide, guide, march, trail 6 course, skyway 7 circuit, journey 9 direction, itinerary

circuitous: 6 detour

ocean: 4 lane

straight: 7 beeline

routh: 6 plenty 8 abundant 9 abundance, plentiful

routine: rut 4 pace, rote 5 grind, habit, round, troll, usual 6 course, groove, system 8 habitual, ordinary 9 treadmill

rove: gad 4 move, part, pass, plow, roam, turn 5 prowl, range, stray 6 maraud, pierce, ramble, stroll, wander 8 straggle

rover: 5 nomad 6 pirate 7 corsair, drifter, floater, Ishmael, migrant, vagrant 8

gadabout 9 itinerant

roving: 6 errant 7 cursory, devious 9 desultory, itinerant 10 discursive

row: air, oar 4 bank, dust, file, fuss, line, list, pull, rank, sail, scud, spat, tier 5 align, aline, brawl, broil, garry, mouth, noise, scold, scull, swath 6 barney, clamor, paddle, pother, propel, rumpus, swathe 7 dispute, quarrel, ruction 8 argument, squabble 9 catalogue, commotion, excursion 11 disturbance 13 collieshangie

form in: 4 line 5 align, aline

rowan tree: ash 4 sorb

rowboat: cog, gig 4 dory, skif 5 canoe, cobil, coble, scull, skiff, skift 6 caique, galley, randan, wherry

stern: 7 transom

rowdy: 4 b'hoy, punk, rude 5 rough, tough 6 roarer, trickly 7 hoodlum, vicious 8 larrikin, plug-ugly 9 obstinate, roughneck 10 boisterous

rowel: 4 spur 5 wheel 6 circle

rowen: 4 crop 5 field 9 aftermath

rower: oar 6 punter 7 oarsman

rowing: 6 randan 8 sculling

royal: 4 easy, real, rial, stag, true 5 basil, grand, regal 6 august, kingly, superb 7 stately 8 imperial, imposing, majestic, princely, splendid 9 excellent, sovereign 11 magnificent, monarchical

royal agaric: 8 mushroom

Royal Canadian Mounted Police: 7 Mountie

royal rock snake: 6 python

royal standard: 4 flag 6 banner, emblem

royalist: 4 Tory 8 Cavalier 11 reactionary

royalty: 5 share 6 emblem 7 kingdom 8 dividend, kingship, nobility 10 kingliness, percentage 11 sovereignty

denoting: 5 crown 6 ermine, purple 7 scepter

symbol: 6 ermine

rub: irk, vex 4 bark, bray, buff, fret, rasp, wear, wipe 5 chafe, dight, feeze, grind, peeve, scour, smear 6 abrade, anoint, fridge, nettle, polish, scrape, smooth, stroke 7 burnish, massage 8 friction, irritate, obstacle 9 hindrance, triturate 10 difficulty, impediment

rub down: 4 comb, wipe 5 curry, groom 7 massage

rub elbows: 6 jostle 9 associate 10 fraternize

rub out: 4 kill 5 elide, erase 6 cancel, efface, murder 7 expunge 10 obliterate

rubber: 4 band 5 brick 6 caucho, cutter, eraser 7 ebonite, masseur 8 busybody, masseuse, overshoe, polisher 9 vulcanite 10 caoutchouc

juice: 6 achete

source: 5 latex
substitute: 7 factice
synthetic: 4 buna 5 butyl
tree: 7 seringa

Rubber City: 5 Akron

rubberneck: 4 gape 5 stare 6 butt-in 7 meddler, tourist 8 busybody, kibitzer, quidnunc

rubber tree: ule 4 para 6 caucho 7 seringa 10 caoutchouc

rubbish: ket(Sc.), pap 4 flam, gear, junk, mull, pelf, pelt, raff, rose 5 crawm, dross, offal, trash, waste, wrack 6 colder, debris, garble, litter, refuse, rubble, trashy 7 baggage, beggary, mullock, rummage 8 nonsense, trumpery 9 worthless 10 clamjamfry 11 foolishness

rube: 4 hick, jake 6 rustic 7 bumpkin, hayseed 9 hillbilly 10 countryman

rubellite: 10 tourmaline

rubeola: 7 measles, rubella

rubescent: red 4 pink 8 blushing, flushing 9 reddening 10 erubescent

rubicund: red 4 rosy, ruby 5 ruddy 6 florid 7 flushed, reddish, redness 8 sanguine 11 fullblooded

rubor: 9 hyperemia

rubric: red 4 name 5 title 6 redden 7 concept, heading 8 category
book: 4 ordo 7 ordines(pl.)

ruby: gem, red 5 balas, jewel, stone 6 spinel 7 rubasse

ruck: rut, sit 4 fold, heap, mass, pile, rake, rick 5 cower, crowd, squat, stack 6 crease, crouch, furrow, pucker 7 crumple, wrinkle 9 gathering, multitude

ruckus: ado, row 6 rumpus, uproar 7 ruction 9 confusion 11 disturbance

ruction: 4 fray 5 fight, melee 6 uproar 7 quarrel 8 fraction, outbreak 11 disturbance

rudder: *control:* 4 helm 6 tiller
edge: 8 bearding
part: 4 yoke

ruddle: 5 rouge 6 redden

ruddy: red 4 rosy 5 fresh 6 florid, tanned 7 reddish 8 blushing

rude: 4 bold, curt, lewd 5 bluff, crude, harsh, rough, rowdy 6 bloody, borrel, brutal, clumsy, coarse, crusty, fierce, rugged, rustic, savage, severe, vulgar 7 artless, boorish, brutish, country, jarring, loutish, uncivil, uncouth, violent 8 churlish, clownish, homespun, ignorant, impolite, impudent, insolent, ungentle, untaught 9 barbarian, barbarous, dissonant, ferocious, imperfect, impetuous, inclement, inelegant, insulting, makeshift, truculent, turbulent, unskilled, untrained 10 boisterous, discordant, tumultuous, uncultured, ungracious, un-

mannerly, unpolished 11 acrimonious, impertinent, uncivilized 12 contumelious, discourteous 13 inexperienced

rudeness: 4 gaff 6 ferity

rudiment: 4 germ 7 vestige 9 beginning

rudimentary: 5 basic 7 initial 9 elemental, vestigial 10 elementary 11 abecedarian, fundamental

rue: rew 4 pity, rake 5 dolor, grief, mourn 6 bewail, grieve, lament, regret, repent, sorrow, street, suffer 7 afflict, deplore, remorse, sorrow 8 penitent 10 bitterness, compassion, repentance 14 disappointment

rueful: 5 sorry 6 woeful 8 penitent, wretched 10 despondent, melancholy

ruff: ree 4 bird, fish 5 perch, plait, reeve, stamp, trump 6 collar, fraise, hackle, pigeon, rabato, rebato, ruffle, tippet 7 applaud, sunfish 8 disorder, drumbeat 9 sandpiper
female: ree 5 reeve

ruffian: 4 hood, pimp, rage, thug 5 bully, cruel, rowdy, tough 6 brutal, cutter, cuttle, pander, roarer, stormy 7 lawless, lustful, violent 8 assassin, gangster, hooligan, paramour 9 cutthroat, desperado

ruffle: vex 4 beat, blow, fret, roil, rool 5 annoy, crimp, frill, jabot, ruche, shake 6 abrade, nettle, riffle, ripple, tousel, tousle, tumult 7 agitate, derange, disturb, flounce, flutter, panuelo, roughen, wrinkle 8 brandish, dishevel, disorder, drumbeat, furbelow, irritate 9 balayeuse, carfuffle, commotion, confusion 10 disarrange, discompose, intimidate 12 irregularity
neck: 5 jabot, ruche

ruffler: 5 bully, tramp 6 beggar 7 boaster, ruffian 8 braggart 9 swaggerer 10 attachment

rufous: 5 color, rusty, tawny 7 reddish

rug: dog, mat, tug 4 Agra, cozy, haul, pull, snug, tear, wrap 5 Herat 6 afghan, carpet, frieze, kaross, liquor, runner, wrench 7 bargain, blanket, drugget, laprobe 8 Akhissar, Amritsar, covering, portiere 9 Samarkand 11 comfortable
Persian: See Oriental rug

ruga: 4 fold 6 crease 7 wrinkle 8 membrane

rugby: 8 football
formation: 5 scrum
player: 6 center, hooker, winger 8 standoff 9 scrum half
score: try 4 goal 10 conversion

rugged: 4 hard, rude, sour 5 asper, hardy, harsh, rough, stern, surly, tough 6 craggy, fierce, horrid, robust, seamed, severe, shaggy, stormy, strong, sturdy, uneven 7 arduous, austere, crabbed, gnarled, uncivil, unkempt 8 obdurate, vigorous, wrinkled 9 difficult, irregular, turbulent 10 ungracious, unpolished 11 tempestuous

rugose: 6 ridged 8 wrinkled 10 corrugated

ruin: gin 4 bane, bust, dash, do in, doom, fall, fate, fell, harm, loss, undo 5 blast, break, decay, exile, fordo, havoc, spoil, waste, wrack, wreck 6 beggar, blight, damage, deface, defeat, diddle, dismay, foredo, impair, injure, perish, ravage 7 decayed, despoil, destroy, pervert, ruinate, subvert 8 bankrupt, calamity, demolish, desolate, disaster, downfall 9 confusion, crumbling, decadence, desecrate, disfigure, overthrow, perdition, ruination 10 bankruptcy, desolation, subversion 11 destruction, devastation, dissolution, ecrouelone, play hob with 12 dilapidation

ruined: 4 dead 5 kaput 6 shabby, forlorn 8 bankrupt, desolate 10 tumbledown 11 dilapidated

ruinous: 5 fatal 10 pernicious 11 destructive

rule: law 4 lead, lord, norm, sway 5 axiom, by-law, canon, guide, maxim, order, regle, reign 6 course, decide, decree, direct, domine, empire, govern, manage, method, regime, screed 7 alidade, brocard, command, conduct, control, counsel, formula, precept, prevail, regency, regimen, theorem 8 behavior, decision, doctrine, domineer, dominion, persuade, practice, regulate, standard 9 authority, criterion, direction, enactment, influence, principle 10 convention, government, regulation 11 aristocracy, be number one, predominate 12 prescription 14 administration

absolute: 8 autarchy

pert. to: 5 rutic

rule out: bar 5 debar 6 forbid, refuse 7 exclude, prevent, scratch 8 preclude, prohibit

ruler: dey, min 4 amir, czar, emir, king, lord, tsar, tzar 5 alder, ameer, emeer, prior, queen 6 archon, author, despot, dynast, ferule, gerent, prince, regent, satrap, sultan, tyrant 7 emperor, monarch, regulus, viceroy 8 autocrat, dictator, governor, hierarch, interrex 9 dominator, governail, imperator, matriarch, potentate, sovereign, yardstick 10 interreges(pl.) 12 straightedge

family: 7 dynasty

former: Nhu 4 czar, Diem, tsar, tzar 5 Lenin 6 Fuhrer, Hitler, Stalin 7 Batista, Fuehrer, Leopold 8 Napoleon, Nicholas 9 Alexander, Mussolini

one of three: 7 triarch 8 triumvir

one of two: 6 duarch

wife: 4 rani 5 queen, ranee 7 czarina, empress, tsarina

rules: 4 code

infraction: 4 foul 8 cheating

ruling: law 5 edict 7 average, central, current, inkling, regnant, statute 8 decision, dominant 9 ascendant, ascendent, hegemonic, prevalent 10 prevailing 11 predominant 13 predominating

rum: bad, odd 4 good, grog, poor 5 queer, tafia 6 liquor 7 Bacardi, cachaca, strange 8 beverage, peculiar 9 excellent

rumal: 8 kerchief(Ind.)

Rumania: *capital:* 9 Bucharest

coin: ban, lei, leu, ley 4 bani(pl.)

Communist leader: 9 Ceausescu

conservative: 5 boyar

king: 5 Carol 7 Michael

mountain: 5 Negoi 10 Carpathian

old name: 5 Dacia

queen: 5 Marie

river: Alt, Jiu 4 Prut 5 Aluta, Arges, Schyl, Siret 6 Danube, Sereth

river port: 6 Galati, Galatz

town: 4 Arad, Iasi 5 Bacau, Jassy, Neamt, Turnu 6 Braila, Brasov, Galati, Galatz 7 Craiova, Focsani, Ploesti, Severin 8 Cernauti, Irongate, Kishenef, Kolsovar, Temesvar

rumble: 4 clap, peal, roll, seat 5 crack, crash, growl, rumor 6 murmur, polish, ramble, report, ripple, uproar 7 grumble 9 complaint 11 disturbance

rumbo: 4 grog 6 liquor

rumen: cud 6 paunch 7 stomach

ruminant: yak 4 deer, goat 5 bison, camel, llama, moose, okapi, sheep, steer 6 alpaca, cattle, vicuna 7 buffalo, chewing, giraffe 8 antelope 10 meditative, thoughtful

female: cow, doe, ewe 5 nanny

genus: bos 5 capra

male: ram 4 buck, bull

stomach: 4 read, reed 5 rumen 6 omasum 8 abomasum, abomasus, roddikin 9 reticulum

ruminate: 4 chaw, chew, mull, muse 5 think, weigh 6 ponder 7 reflect 8 cogitate, consider, meditate

rummage: 4 grub, rout, stow 6 gather, litter, search 7 clutter, collect, derange, examine, fossick, ransack, rubbish, stowage, turmoil 8 disorder, upheaval 9 confusion, ferret out, searching 10 disarrange 11 derangement

rummer: cup 5 glass

rummy: 4 chap, game 5 drunk 7 bizarre, strange 8 drunkard

rumor: 4 buzz, sugh, talk, tell, word 5 bruit, noise, sough, story, voice 6 clamor, furphy, gossip, murmur, norate, report, spread, uproar 7 hearsay, message, tidings, whisper 9 grapevine, statement 10 reputation 11 scuttlebutt

personification: 4 Fama

rump: 4 dock 6 behind, insult 7 hurdies, plunder, remnant 8 bankrupt, buttocks 11 legislature

rump bone: 6 sacrum 8 edgebone 9 aitchbone

rumple: 4 fold, muss, rool, rump, tail 5 plait, touse 6 crease, frowse, tousle 7 crinkle, crumple, wrinkle

rumpus: row 5 brawl 6 barney, fracas, hubbub, uproar 8 argument 9 commotion, confusion 11 disturbance

rumshop: bar 6 saloon, tavern 7 barroom, taproom

run: fly, gad, ply, rin(Sc.), sew 4 butt, cast, dart, dash, emit, flow, fuse, gait, grow, hare, hunt, melt, mold, move, pass, pour, race, roam, rove, sail, scud, tear, tend, trip, trot, turn, work 5 blend, brook, carry, climb, cover, creek, creep, dog it, drive, enter, going, hurry, range, ravel, reach, recur, river, route, scoot, score, scour, speed, stand, trace, treat 6 ascend, become, bicker, career, charge, course, elapse, extend, gallop, govern, hasten, manage, output, pursue, refine, resort, rotate, scurry, spread, spring, sprint, stream, thrust 7 conduct, contend, descend, develop, diffuse, journey, liquefy, make off, migrate, operate, proceed, process, roulade, scamper, scutter, scuttle, smuggle, stretch, trickle 8 continue, dissolve, duration, function, sequence, stampede, traverse 9 discharge, suppurate, take flight, transport 11 watercourse

run across: 4 meet 8 discover 9 encounter 10 transverse

run aground: 7 founder

run away: 4 bolt, flee 5 elope 6 decamp, desert, escape

run down: hit 4 kill, sink, stop 5 crush, decry, seedy 6 pursue 7 capture, decline, traduce 8 overbear 9 disparage, exhausted, overthrow 11 dilapidated

run for office: 5 stand

run-in: 4 tiff 5 fight 7 quarrel 11 altercation

run-of-the-mill: 6 common, medium 7 average, general 8 ordinary

run off: 5 print, waste 7 impress

run out: 4 fail, flow 5 expel, lapse, peter, spill, spilt, waste 6 banish, elapse, expire, spread 8 squander

run over: 6 exceed, strike 8 overflow, rehearse

run through: 4 stab 5 use up 6 browse, pierce 7 examine, inspect, pervade 8 transfix

run up: 4 grow, rise 5 erect 7 enlarge, throw up 8 increase 9 construct 10 accumulate

runagate: 7 runaway 8 apostate, deserter, fugitive, renegade, vagabond, wanderer

runaway: 7 escapee 8 fugitive, runagate

rundle: 4 ball, drum, rung, step 5 orbit, round 6 circle, sphere

rundlet: keg, tun 4 cask 6 barrel

rune: wen 5 charm, magic 6 secret 7 mystery

rung: rod 4 spar, step 5 round, spoke, staff, stair, stake, stave, tread 6 cudgel, degree, rundle 7 girdled

runnel: 4 rill 5 brook, creek, rhine 6 runlet, stream 7 channel, rivulet 9 streamlet 11 watercourse

runner: rug, ski 5 agent, miler, racer, ravel, scarf 6 cursor, stolon 8 operator, smuggler, sprinter 9 collector, detective, messenger, solicitor

running: 4 care, easy, trip 6 active, attack 7 contest, current, cursive, journey 8 skirmish, together 9 oversight 10 management, successive

running birch: 9 snowberry

running board: 9 footboard

running knot: 5 noose

running toad: 10 natterjack

runt: 4 chit, wrig 5 dwarf, pygmy 6 durgan, durgen, titman

runty: 4 puny 5 small 7 stunted 8 dwarfish 10 diminutive, undersized 12 contemptible

runway: 4 file, path, ramp, road 5 chute, strip, track, trail 6 bridge, groove, trough 7 channel 8 platform 10 passageway

rupia: 8 eruption

rupture: 4 open, part, rend, rent 5 break, burst, split 6 breach, hernia, rhexis 7 divorce, parting, ruction, ruption 8 division, fraction, fracture 10 disruption, separating

rural: 6 rustic 7 bucolic, country, idyllic, outland 8 agrestic, Arcadian, geoponic, pastoral 11 countrified

life: 7 bucolic, georgic 8 pastoral

ruse: 4 fall, hoax, slip, wile 5 dodge, feint, fraud, shift, trick 6 deceit 8 artifice 9 stratagem 10 subterfuge

rush: sag 4 birr, dart, dash, flow, junk, race, rout, scud, tear 5 break, brook, chute, feeze, haste, hurry, onset, press, sally, scoot, spate, sprat, sprot, straw, surge 6 attack, bustle, charge, combat, course, defeat, fescue, hasten, hurtle, hustle, plunge, runlet, sortie, trifle 7 assault, bulrush, cattail, destroy, rampage, repulse, tantivy 8 eruption, stampede, vanquish 9 overthrow 11 undergrowth 13 precipitation *family:* 9 juncaceae

rush hour: 4 peak

rush nut: 5 chufa

rush toad: 10 natterjack

rusk: 4 cake 5 bread, crisp, toast 7 biscuit 8 zwieback

Russia (Soviet Union): 4 USSR 6 Soviet 7 Muscovy

administrative committee: 9 presidium

alcoholic beverage: 5 kvass, quass, vodka 9 slivovitz

antelope: 6 saiga

apple: 9 astrachan

aristocrat: 5 Boyar 6 Boyard

automobile: Zis

beer: 4 kvas 5 kvass

bondman: 4 serf

braid: 8 soutache

cabinet member: 9 commissar

cactus: 7 thistle

calendar: 6 Julian

cap: 4 aska

capital: 6 Moscow

carriage: 6 drosky, troika 8 tarantas

cathedral: 5 sobor

caviar: 4 ikra 5 ikary

citadel: 7 Kremlin

city: 4 Kiev, Omsk, Orel, Perm 5 Gomel, Kasan, Kazan, Minsk, Pensa, Pskov 6 Kertch, Moskva, Nizhni, Odessa, Rostov, Samara, Sartov 7 Bataisk, Ivanovo, Kalinin, Rybinsk 8 Kostroma, Orenburg, Smolensk, Taganrog, Tashkent, Vladimir, Voronezh, Yaroslaf 9 Archangel, Astrakhan, Kuibishev, Petrograd

coal area: 6 Donets

coin: 5 altin, copec, kopek, ruble 6 copeck, grivna, kopeck 9 altininck, poltinnik 10 chervonets

collective farm: 6 kolhoz 7 kolkhos

commune: 6 kolhoz 7 kolkhos, kolkhoz

composer: Cui 9 Prokofiev 10 Stravinsky 12 Tschaikovsky 13 Shostakovitch 14 Rimsky-Korsakov

cossack: 6 Tartar

council: 4 Duma

country house: 5 dacha

dance: 7 ziganka

decree: 5 ukase

delicacy: 6 caviar 7 caviare

despot: 4 czar, tsar

devil: 5 chort

diplomat: 5 Malik, Zorin 6 Stalin 7 Gromyko, Molotov, Sobolev 8 Malenkov 9 Kuznetzov, Tsarapkin, Vishinsky 11 Shcherbakov

district: 7 Karelia

dog: 4 alan 6 borzoi 7 owtchah 9 wolfhound

dress; 7 sarafan

emperor: 4 czar, Ivan, tsar, tzar 5 Peter

empress: 7 czarina, tsarina, tzarina 8 tsaritza, tzaritza

exclamation: 7 nichevo 8 nitchevo

farmer: 5 kulak

fish: 6 beluga

flax: 6 bobbin

folk song: 6 bylina

forest: 6 tundra

former ruler: 4 czar, tsar

fortress: 7 Kremlin

fox: 6 corsac 7 karagan

gambling game: 6 coocoo

general: 10 Timoshenko 14 Tukhashchevski

government farm: 7 sovkhos, sovkhoz

government group: 4 duma, rada, tsik 6 soviet 7 zemstvo 9 Comintern, Politburo, Presidium 10 Praesidium 11 Politbureau

grandmother: 8 babushka

gulf: 4 Azov

hood: 7 bashlik, bashlyk

horse: 6 tarpan

house: 4 isba 5 dacha

image: 4 icon, ikon 5 ikono

imperial order: 5 ukase

kerchief: 6 analav

labor association: 5 artel

lagoon: 6 liman

lake: 4 Aral, Neva, Sego 5 Elton, Ilmen, Onega

leader: 5 Lenin 6 Stalin 7 Molotov 8 Andropov, Brezhnev 10 Khrushchev

measure: fut, lof 4 duim, fass, loof, stof 5 duime, foute, korec, ligne, osmin, pajak, stoff, vedro, verst 6 arshin, charka, liniya, osmina, paletz, sagene, tchast, versta, verste 7 arsheen, botchka, chkalik, garnetz, verchoc, verchok 8 boutylka, chetvert, krouchka, kroushka 9 chetverik 10 dessiatine 11 polugarnetz

mile: 5 verst

money: 5 ruble

monk: 7 starets 8 Rasputin

mountain range: 4 Alai, Ural 8 Caucasus

musical instrument: 5 gudok, gusla, gusle 9 balalaika

name: 4 Igor, Ivan, Olga 5 Peter, Sonya

naval academy: 6 Frunze

negative: 4 nyet

news agency: 4 Tass

newspaper: 6 Pravda 8 Izvestia

novelist: 5 Gorki 7 Chekhov, Tolstoy 10 Dostoevsky

peasant: 5 kulak 6 muzhik, muzjik

peninsula: 4 Kola 6 Crimea 7 Karelia

people: Red 4 Lett, Russ, Slav 5 Ersar 7 Cossack, Russine 9 Muscovite 12 Byelorussian

plain: 6 steppe

poet: 6 Jehuda 7 Pushkin 9 Aleksandr, Pasternak, Sholokhov 11 Sergyeevich,

Voznesensky, Yevtushenko
port: 4 Eisk 5 Anapa 6 Odessa 9 Archangel 10 Sebastopol, Sevastopol 11 Vladivostok
prince: 4 knez 5 knais, knyaz
republic: 5 Uzbek 6 Latvia 7 Armenia, Georgia, Kirghiz, Turkmen, Ukraine
revolutionist: 5 Lenin, Rykov 6 Stalin, Tomsky 7 Trotsky
river: Don, Ili, Ner, Oka, Ros, Ufa 4 Amur, Duna, Kara, Lena, Neva, Orel, Sura, Svir, Ural 5 Dnepr, Dvina, Onega, Terek, Tobol, Volga 6 Donets, Irtish, Irtysh 7 Dnieper
saint: 4 Olga 8 Vladimir
satellite: 7 sputnik
sea: 4 Aral, Azof, Azov 6 Baikal
secret police: KGB 4 NKVD, OGPU
soup: 5 shchi 6 borsch 7 borscht
spa: Ems
stockade: 5 etape
tavern: 6 caback
tax: 5 obrok
urn: 7 samovar
villa: 5 dacha
village: mir
violinist: 5 Elman
weight: 4 dola, pood
whip: 5 knout
wind: 5 buran
worker: 7 dvornik 12 Stakhanovite
youth organization: 8 Comsomol, Komsomol
russud: 5 grain 6 forage
rust: eat 5 erode 6 aerugo, blight, canker, patina 7 corrode, erosion, oxidize 9 corrosion, oxidation, verdigris
rustic: hob 4 boor, carl, dull, hick, hind, jake, rube, rude 5 bacon, carle, chuff, churl, clown, doric, hodge, plain, rough, rural, swain, yokel 6 coarse, gaffer, honest, simple, sturdy, sylvan 7 artless, awkward, boorish, bucolic, bumpkin, bushman, Corydon, country, georgic, hayseed, peasant, plowboy, plowman, uncouth 8 agrestic, churlish, clownish, pastoral 9 agrestian, campesino, chawbacon, greenhorn, unadorned 10 clodhopper, countryman, unaffected, unpolished 12 backwoodsman
rustle: 5 haste, steal 6 fissle, fistle, scroop 7 crinkle
Rustum: *father:* Zal
son: 6 Sohrab
rut: rat, rit 4 brim 5 ditch, grind, track 6 furrow, groove, strake 7 channel, routine, wrinkle
rutabaga: 6 turnip
ruth: woe 4 pity 5 grief, mercy 6 regret, sorrow 7 remorse, sadness 8 penitence 10 compassion, repentance, tenderness 17 compassionateness
Ruth: *husband:* 4 Boaz
mother-in-law: 5 Naomi
son: 4 Obed
ruthless: 4 grim 5 cruel 6 savage 8 pitiless 9 cutthroat, ferocious
rutter: 4 plow 5 guide 7 trooper 8 horseman
ruttle: 6 gurgle, rattle
Rwanda: *capital:* 6 Kigali
former name: 12 Ruanda-Urundi
lake: 4 Kivu
language: 7 Swahili 11 Kinyarwanda
monetary unit: 5 franc
mountain: 7 Virunga 9 Karisimbi
rye: ree, rie 5 grain, grass 6 whisky 7 whiskey 9 gentleman
disease: 5 ergot
ryot, raiyat (Ind.): 6 farmer, tenant 7 peasant 10 cultivator
Ryukyu island: 7 Okinawa

S

S-shaped: 4 ogee 7 sigmate, sigmoid

sabana: See **savanna**

sabbat: 8 assembly

sabbath: 6 Sunday 7 sabaoth, shabbat, shabbos

saber, sabre: 8 scimitar, scimiter, yataghan

Sabine: *goddess:* 6 Vacuna
   people: 7 Vestini

sable: sad 4 dark, ebon 5 black, brush, saber 6 dismal, gloomy, marten, pellet 8 antelope, darkened 10 mysterious 11 threatening
   genus of: 7 mustela
   pert. to: 8 zibeline 9 zibelline

sablefish: cod 6 beshow 10 candlefish

sabot: 4 shoe

sabotage: 5 block, wreck 7 destroy, subvert 9 undermine 10 impairment 11 destruction

sabre: See **saber**

Sabrina River: 6 Severn

sabulous: 5 dusty, sandy 6 floury, gritty 10 arenaceous

sabutan: 5 fiber, straw

sac: bag, pod 4 cyst, sack 5 ascus, bursa, pouch, theca 6 cavity 7 cistern, utricle, vesicle

Sacar's son: 5 Ahiam

saccadic: 5 jerky 9 twitching

saccharine: 5 sweet 7 gluside 10 sweetening 12 ingratiating

saccos: See **sakkos**

sacculated: 7 pouched

sacerdotal: 8 clerical, hieratic, priestly

sachem: 4 boss 5 chief 8 sagamore

sachet: bat, pad 4 oris 5 pouch, scent 8 reticule

sack: (see also **sac**): bag, bed 4 base, fire, loot, poke, ruin 5 bursa, gunny, harry, pouch, purse, waste 6 budget, burlap, jacket, ravage, wallet 7 boucher, dismiss, musette, pillage, plunder, ransack 8 desolate 9 container, discharge, dismissal 11 send packing
   fiber: 4 jute 5 gunny 6 burlap

sackbut: 8 trombone

sackless: 4 weak 7 bashful 8 harmless, innocent 9 guiltless, peaceable 10 dispirited, unmolested

sacque: 6 jacket

sacrament: 4 sign 5 token 6 pledge, symbol 7 baptism, mystery, penance, promise, unction 8 ceremony, covenant 9 communion, Eucharist, matrimony 12 confirmation

sacrarium: 5 ambry 6 chapel, shrine 7 oratory 9 sanctuary 10 tabernacle

sacred: 4 holy 5 godly, huaca, santo 6 divine 7 blessed, saintly 8 hallowed, reverend 9 cherished, geistlich(G.), inviolate, venerated 10 inviolable, sacrosanct 11 consecrated 13 sanctimonious
   make: 8 enshrine
   most: 10 sacrosanct

sacred bean: 5 lotus

sacred beetle: 10 scarabaeus

sacred fig: 5 pipal

sacred place: 6 chapel, church 7 sanctum

sacred weed: 7 vervain

sacrifice: 4 host, loss 5 forgo 6 corban, homage, korban, victim 8 hecatomb, immolate, oblation, offering, part with 9 holocaust, martyrdom, privation, surrender 10 immolation 11 destruction, kiss goodbye

sacrilege: 9 blasphemy 11 desecration, profanation

sacristy: 6 vestry
   pert. to: 7 vestral

sacrosanct: 6 sacred 8 esteemed, regarded 9 respected

sad: bad 4 blue, dark, dram(Sc.), dull 5 dusky, grave, sober, sorry, trist 6 dismal, dreary, gloomy, solemn, somber, sombre, triste(F.), wicked, woeful 7 doleful, dolente(It.), pensive, serious, unhappy 8 dejected, desolate, dolorous, downcast, grievous, mournful, pathetic, pitiable 9 afflicted, cheerless, depressed, plaintive, sorrowful 10 calamitous, deplorable, despondent, lugubrious 11 distressing, melancholic 12 disconsolate, heavyhearted

sadden: 7 attrist, depress 8 make blue

saddle: 4 load 5 ridge 6 burden, howdah 7 aparejo, pillion, restrict 8 encumber
   blanket: 6 corona, tilpah
   bow: 6 pommel
   maker: 7 knacker, saddler
   pad: 5 panel 7 housing
   part: 4 horn, tore 5 arson, cinch, croup,

girth, panel, pilch, skirt **6** cantle, corona, crutch, latigo, pommel **7** stirrup **8** sudadero **9** saddlebow
rear part: **6** cantle

saddle horse: **4** pony **5** mount

saddle rock: **6** oyster

saddle strip: **5** cindi, girth **6** latigo **7** harness

saddleback: **4** hill **5** ridge

saddlebag: sag(Sc.) **4** jagg(Sc.) **7** alforja, pannier

saddlecloth: **5** panel **7** housing **8** shabrack **9** shabraque

saddler: **4** seal **5** horse **7** cobbler, knacker, lorimer, loriner **9** shoemaker **11** saddlemaker

sadness: **4** funk **5** blues, dumps **7** anguish, megrims

saeter: **4** meadow **7** pasture

safari: **4** hunt, trek **7** caravan, journey **9** excursion **10** expedition

safe: box **4** sure **5** chest, siker, sound, vault **6** armory, closet, coffer, holder, secure, sicker, unhurt **8** cautious, cupboard, harmless, unharmed **9** strongbox, untouched **10** depository **11** gardeviance, trustworthy

safe-conduct: **4** pass **5** cowle, guard **6** convoy **10** permission, protection

safecracker: **4** yegg **7** peteman

safeguard: **4** pass **5** guard **6** convoy, escort, safety **7** defense, protect **10** protection

safekeeping: **4** care **7** custody, storage **10** protection **12** preservation

safety: **8** security **9** assurance, touchback
place of: **4** ark **4** port **5** haven **6** asylum, refuge **7** retreat, sanctum
zone: **6** island

safety lamp: **4** Davy

safety pin: **5** clasp **6** fibula

safety rail: **9** guardrail

safety zone: **5** islet **6** island, refuge

saffron: **6** crocus, yellow **9** safflower

sag: **4** bend, flag, reed, rush, sink, wilt **5** drift, droop, sedge, slump **6** settle, weaken **7** deflate

saga: **4** edda, epic, myth, tale **5** story **6** legend **7** history, recital **9** narrative
narrator: **7** sagaman

sagaciate: **4** fare **6** thrive

sagacious: **4** sage, wise **5** acute, quick **6** argute, astute, shrewd **7** knowing, politic, prudent, sapient **9** far-seeing, judicious **10** discerning, farsighted, hardheaded **11** clairvoyant, penetrating, wise as an owl **13** perspicacious

sagacity: **6** acumen, wisdom **8** sapience

sagamore: **5** chief **6** sachem

sage: **4** herb, mint, seer, wise **5** clary, grave, rishi(Ind.), solon, spice **6** pundit, salvia, savant, shrewd, solemn **7**

learned, prudent, sapient, wise man **8** sagebush **9** counselor, judicious, venerable **10** counsellor, discerning, perceptive **11** philosopher

Sage: *of Chelsea:* **13** Thomas Carlyle
of Concord: **17** Ralph Waldo Emerson
of Emporia: **17** William Allen White
of Ferney: **8** Voltaire
of Monticello: **15** Thomas Jefferson
of Pylos: **6** Nestor

sage cheese: **7** cheddar

sage cock: **6** grouse

sage hen: **6** grouse **7** Nevadan

Sagebrush State: **6** Nevada

saginate: **6** fatten, pamper

Sagittarius: **6** archer, bowman **13** constellation

sago: **6** starch

sago palm: **7** coontie

sagoin: **8** marmoset

saguaro: **6** cactus

sagum: **5** cloak

Sahara: **6** desert
people: **4** Arab **5** nomad **6** Berber, Tuareg
plateau: **6** hamada **7** hammada
wind: **5** leste **6** gibleh

saic: **4** boat **5** ketch

said (see also **say**): dit(F.) **4** such **5** quoth **6** spoken, stated **7** reputed, uttered **8** supposed

saiga: **4** coin **8** antelope

sail: awe, awn, fly, rig, van **4** dart, duck, haul, keel, luff, move, scud, skim, soar, swim, trip **5** fleet, float, glide, sheet **6** canvas, depart, embark, voyage **7** journey **8** go easily, navigate **9** excursion **11** get underway
nearer wind: **4** luff
part: **4** bunt, clew, yard **5** leach, leech, sheet **6** earing **7** earring, yardarm
pert. to: **5** velic
prepare to: **4** trim
triangular: jib

sailboat: **4** bark, yawl **5** ketch, skiff, sloop, yacht **7** caravel **9** caravelle

sailcloth: **4** duck **6** canvas

sailfish: **6** woohoo **9** billfish

sailing: **4** asea

sailing ship: cog, **4** bark, brig, saic, yawl **5** sloop **6** barque, cutter, galley, sampan, vessel **7** frigate, galleon **8** schooner **10** barkentine, brigantine **11** barquentine

scoop: **5** skeet

sailor: gob, hat, tar, tot **4** salt, swab **5** Jacky **6** hearty, lascar, ratiny, seaman **7**

mariner **8** coxswain, seafarer, waterman **10** bluejacket, lobscouser

assent: aye

associate: **8** messmate

British: **5** limey

call: **4** ahoy

carving: **9** scrimshaw

chapel: **6** bethel

fictional: **6** Sinbad

group: **4** crew **5** hands

jacket: **6** reefer

mess tub: kid

old: **4** salt

patron saint: **4** Elmo

patroness: **11** Mother Carey

potion: **4** grog

song: **6** chanty **7** chantey **9** barcarole

saint (see also **patron saint**): Sao(Port.), Ste. **4** holy **5** santa(Sp.), santo **6** hallow **7** beatify **8** canonize, enshrine

biography: **11** hagiography

image: **5** santo

invocation of: **10** hagiolatry

worship: **10** hagiolatry, hierolatry

Saint Andrew's cross; 7 saltier, saltire

Saint Anthony's cross: tau **4** ankh

Saint Catherine's home: 5 Siena

Saint Elmo's fire: 5 flame **6** furole **9** corposant

Saint John's bread: 5 carob

Saint Paul: *birthplace:* **6** Tarsus

companion: **4** Luke

Saint Peter: 5 Simon **7** apostle

Saint-Saens opera: 16 Samson and Delilah

Saint Vitus' dance: 6 chorea

saintly: 4 holy **5** godly, pious **6** devout **7** angelic **9** angelical **10** God-fearing **13** sanctimonious

sake: end **4** good **5** cause, drink **6** behalf, motive, regard **7** account, benefit, concern, purpose **8** beverage **9** advantage, intention **13** consideration

saker: 6 falcon

saki: 5 drink, yarke **6** monkey, yarkee **8** beverage **9** cup bearer

sakkos, saccos: 7 tunicle **8** vestment

sal: 4 salt

sala: 4 hall

salaam, salâm: bow **4** bend **6** salute **8** greeting **9** obeisance **10** compliment, salutation

salacious: 4 lewd **7** lustful, obscene **8** scabrous **9** lecherous **10** licentious **12** pornographic

salad: 5 aspic **6** Caesar, tossed **7** melange

ingredient: **5** cress **6** celery, endive, greens, tomato **7** cabbage, lettuce, parsley, romaine **8** scallion **9** dandelion **10** watercress

meal-size: **5** chef's

Saladin's foes: 9 Crusaders

salamander: eft, olm **4** evet, newt **6** spirit, triton **7** axoloti, axolotl, caudata, urodela, urodele **9** amphibian, fireplace **10** hellbender

order: **7** caudata, urodela

salami: 7 sausage

Salammbo author: 8 Flaubert

salary: fee, pay **4** hire **5** wages **6** reward **7** stipend **8** pittance **9** allowance, emolument **10** exhibition, honorarium, recompense **12** compensation, remuneration **13** consideration

sale: net **4** deal, hall, vend **5** bower **6** market, palace, vendue, willow **7** auction, bargain, rummage **8** contract, transfer **9** utterance, vendition **10** conveyance **11** transaction

kind: **4** yard **5** white **6** garage

sales talk: 4 line **5** pitch, spiel **6** patter

salesman: 5 agent, clerk **6** hawker, pedlar, seller, sutler, vendor **7** drummer, hustler, peddler **8** pitchman, vendeuse (fem.) **9** solicitor **14** representative

salience: 5 point **7** agility **8** emphasis **9** high-light **10** notability, prominence · **12** protuberance

salient: 4 line **5** redan **6** marked, moving, signal, trench **7** jumping, leaping **8** bounding, extended, striking **9** arresting, important **10** noticeable **11** conspicuous

salient angle: 5 arris

salient point: 5 heart **6** detail, source **7** feature

salientia: 5 anura, frogs, toads **7** aglossa, costata **8** Amphibia, linguata

salina: 4 lake, pond **5** marsh **9** saltworks

saline: 4 tear **5** briny, salty **8** brackish **10** saliferous

Salisbury steak: 9 hamburger

saliva: 4 spit **5** water **7** spittle

salix: 5 genus **6** osiers **7** sallows, willows

salle: 4 room

sallet: 6 helmet

sallow: wan **4** pale, twig **5** muddy, osier, shoot **6** pallid, willow **9** colorless, yellowish

sally: 4 leap, quip, rush, trip **5** dance, issue, jaunt, start **6** attack, emerge, escape, retort, sortie, spring **7** darting, journey, rushing **8** escapade, outbreak, outburst **9** excursion, witticism **10** liveliness

salmagundi: 4 hash, olio **5** salad **6** medley **7** mixture **9** potpourri **10** hodgepodge

salmi: 6 ragout

salmon: gib **5** chum, kelt, keta, pike, pink **5** color, haddo, holia, smolt, tecon **6** jumper, laurel, sauqui, taimen **7** gilling, saumont, shedder **8** schoodic, springer, weakfish **9** ceratodus **10** barramunda

enclosure: 4 weir, yair
female: 4 raun 6 baggit
male: 6 kipper
pool: 5 stell
silver: 4 coho
smoked: lox
trap: 4 slap
young: 4 parr
salmon trout: 5 sewen 9 steelhead
Salome: *mother:* 8 Herodias
  stepfather: 5 Herod
salon: 4 hall, room 5 group 6 museum 7
  gallery 9 apartment, reception 10 assemblage, exhibition 11 drawing room
saloon: bar 4 hall, room 5 cabin, coach,
  cuddy, divan, sedan 6 tavern 7 barroom, cantina(Sp.) 8 alehouse, groggery
salpa, salp: 8 tunicate
salse: 7 volcano
salt: sal, tar, wit 4 alum, corn, cure 5
  brine, briny, ester, salic, sharp, witty 6
  alkali, flavor, halite, harden, lively, sail-
  or, saline, seaman, season 7 bromate,
  piquant, pungent, seadust 8 brackish,
  halinous 9 seasoning
  deposit: 6 saline
  oleic acid: 6 oleate
  resembling: 5 halid 6 halide, haloid
  rock: pig
  working: 7 halurgy
salt-like: 6 haloid
salt marsh: 6 salina 9 grassland
salt pit: vat
salt tree: 4 atle 8 tamarisk
salt water: 5 brine
saltate: 4 jump, leap 5 bound, dance
saltcellar: 5 saler
salted: 4 alat 5 cured 6 corned
saltpeter, saltpetre: 5 niter, nitre
saltworks: 7 saltern, saltery
salty: 4 racy 5 witty 8 indecent, nautical
salubrious: 4 good 7 bracing, healthy 8
  salutary 9 benignant, healthful, wholesome 10 beneficial
salutary: 4 good 6 benign 7 healthy,
  helpful 8 curative 9 desirable, healthful,
  medicinal, wholesome 10 beneficial 11
  restorative
salutation: ave, bow 4 beck, hail 5 aloha,
  hello, howdy, skoal 6 curtsy, kowtow,
  Mizpah, Mizpeh, prosit, salaam, salute
  7 address, welcome, slainte 8 accolade,
  chin-chin, encomium, farewell, greeting
salute: nod 4 hail 5 greet, halse, salvo 6
  accost, praise, signal 7 address 9 obeisance 11 pay homage to
salvage: 4 save 6 rescue 7 reclaim 12
  compensation
salvation: 6 rescue 10 redemption 12
  conservation, preservation
  pert. to: 8 soterial 9 soterical
salve: 4 balm, nard 6 anoint, cerate,

soothe 7 assuage, unguent 8 flattery,
  gratuity, ointment, palliate 9 alleviate
salver: 4 tray
salvo: 4 shot 6 excuse, salute 7 gunfire,
  pretext, proviso, quibble 9 exception
  11 reservation, testimonial
samadh: 4 tomb 6 shrine
samaj: 6 church 7 society 12 congregation
samaritan: 6 helper, 8 welldoer 10 benefactor
Samaritan: *alphabet:* jud, mim, nun, phi,
  sen, tav, tit 4 alaf, bith, goph, kaph,
  rish, sadi, shan 5 dalat, gaman, labad 6
  simcat
  god: 6 Tartak
  people: 8 Assyrian 9 Israelite
sambar, sambur: elk 4 deer, maha, rusa
same: ilk, one 4 ibid, idem, like, meme(F.),
  self, very 5 alike, ditto, equal, exact 7
  identic 9 identical, unchanged 10 invariable
sameness: 8 identity, monotony 10 similarity 11 equivalence, resemblance 14
  correspondence
Samhain Eve: 9 Halloween
Samian philosopher: 10 Pythagoras
samisen: 5 banjo
samlet: 4 parr 6 salmon 10 fingerling
sammy: 5 ninny 6 clammy, sodden, watery 9 simpleton
Samoa (see also **Polynesia**): *capital:* 4
  Apia 8 Pago Pago
  fish: 6 ataata, sesele
  hostess: 5 taupo 6 taupou
  island: 5 Upolu 6 Savaii
  mollusk: asi
  mudworm: ipo
  owl: 4 lulu
  red: 4 mumu
  spirit: 4 aitu
  warrior: toa
samovar: urn 6 teapot
samp: 4 meal, mush, soup 6 cereal, hominy 8 porridge
sampaloc: 8 tamarind
sampan: 4 boat 5 skiff
sample: 4 test 5 taste 6 swatch 7 example, pattern 8 instance, specimen 12 illustration
sampleman: 6 taster 12 demonstrator
sampler: 5 model 6 taster 7 example,
  hanging, pattern 8 original, specimen 9
  archetype
Samson: *betrayer:* 7 Delilah
  deathplace: 4 Gaza
  vulnerable place: 4 hair
Samuel: *home:* 5 Ramah
  mentor: Eli
  parent: 6 Hannah 7 Elkanah
  son: 5 Abiah
  victim: 4 Agag, Agog

Samurai: 7 soldier, warrior
   ostracized: 5 Ronin
San Francisco hill: Nob
San Simeon name: 6 Hearst
sanative: 6 curing 7 healing 8 curative 9
   healthful
sanatorium: spa 8 hospital
Sancho Panza: *island:* 9 Barataria
   master: 10 Don Quixote
   mule: 6 Dapple
sanctify: 8 dedicate 10 consecrate
sanctimonious: 4 holy 5 pious 6 devout,
   sacred 7 prudish, saintly, zealous 10
   sanctified 12 hypocritical
sanction: 4 amen, fiat 5 allow 6 assent,
   avouch, permit, placet, ratify 7 approve, confirm, consent, endorse, indorse, support 8 accredit, approval, legalize 9 allowance, approbate,
   authority, authorize, encourage, subscribe 10 imprimatur 11 approbation,
   countenance, countersign, endorsement
   12 ratification 13 authorization, encouragement
sanctity: 5 piety, rites 6 purity 7 halidom
   8 halidome, holiness, recesses 9 godliness, solemnity 10 sacredness 11 obli-
   gations, saintliness 13 inviolability
   place of: 4 fane 5 altar, hiera 6 chapel,
   church, hieron, shrine, temple 7 chaitya
   9 synagogue
sanctuary: ark 4 bema, fane, holy, naos 5
   abbey, adyta(pl.), bamah, grith, haven 6
   adytum, asylum, bemata, chapel,
   church, haikal, priory, refuge, shrine,
   temple 7 alsatia, chancel, convent, halidom, preserve, retreat, sanctum, shelter
   8 cloister, halidome, holiness 9 monastery 10 penetralia, protection, tabernacle 11 hiding place, reservation 12 holy
   of holies
sanctum: den 5 study 6 adytum, office 7
   retreat 9 sanctuary
sand: rub 4 grit 5 nerve 6 abrade, desert,
   gravel, smooth 7 courage 8 alluvium,
   asbestic
   and clay: 4 loam
   particle: 5 grain
   particles: 4 silt
   resembling: 7 arenoid
sand dune: 4 hill, sand 5 towan
sand eel: 4 grig 5 lance 6 launce
sand flea: 6 chigoe 7 chigger
sand flounder: 5 fluke 10 windowpane
sand hill: 4 dune
sandal (see also **moccasin**)**:** 4 clog, shoe,
   zori 6 buskin, caliga, charuk 7 rullion,
   slipper, talaria 8 huarache 9 alpargata
   10 espadrille
   winged: 7 talaria(pl.)
   wooden: 6 patten
sandalwood: 5 algum, almug, maire

Sandalwood Island: 5 Sumba
sandarac: 4 tree 5 resin 7 realgar
   tree: 4 arar
   wood: 6 alerce, alerse
sandbank: 4 dune, meal
sandbar: 4 dene, dune, reef, spit 5 beach,
   shelf, shoal
sandpiper: ree 4 bird, knot, ruff 5 reeve,
   terek 6 dunlin, teeter, tiltup 7 brownie,
   chorook, fiddler, haybird 8 triddler,
   redshank 10 canderling
sandstone: 4 grit 5 hazel 6 arkose 8 ganister 9 gritstóne
   block: 6 sarsen
   pert. to: 10 arenilitic
sandy: dry 6 gritty, plucky 7 arenose 8
   granular, sabuline, shifting, unstable 13
   uninteresting
   pert. to: 6 eremic
sane: 4 wise 5 lucid, sober, sound 6 normal 7 healthy, sapient 8 all there, rational, sensible 10 reasonable
sangfroid: 8 calmness, coolness 9 composure, stability 16 imperturbability 10
   equanimity
Sangraal: See **Holy Grail**
sanguinaria: 6 yarrow 9 bloodroot
sanguine: red 4 fond, gory, warm 5 cruel,
   ruddy 6 ardent, bloody, crayon, savage,
   yarrow 7 buoyant, hopeful 8 cheerful,
   hematite 9 confident, expectant, ferocious, murderous 10 bloodstone, ensan-
   guine, optimistic, sanguinary 12 bloodthirsty
sanitarium: See **sanatorium**
sanitary: 5 clean 8 hygienic
sanitize: 8 clean out
sanity: 6 reason 7 balance 8 lucidity,
   saneness 9 soundness 13 wholesome-
   ness
sans: 7 without
Sanskrit: *dialect:* 4 Pali
   dictionary: 10 amara-kosha
   division of literature: 5 Sruti 6 Shruti
   epic: 8 Ramayana
   epic character: 4 Sita
   school: tol
   soul: 5 atman
   verse: 5 sloka
sans souci: 12 free from care
Santa Barbara island: 8 Catalina
Santa Claus's reindeer: 5 Comet, Cupid, Vixen 6 Dancer, Dasher, Donder,
   Donner 7 Blitzen, Prancer
santon: 4 monk 5 image, saint 6 hermit 7
   dervish
sap: lac 4 dupe, fool, milk, mine, seve(F.),
   upas 5 drain, fluid, juice, latex, lymph,
   vigor 6 energy, impair, trench, weaken
   7 exhaust, saphead 8 enervate, knock
   out, vitality, weakling 9 exudation,
   schlemiel, schlemihl, screwball, under-

mine 10 debilitate, devitalize
dried: gum
lose: 5 bleed
spout: 5 spile
sapajou: 6 monkey
sapanwood, sappanwood: 4 tree 10 brazilwood
saphead: See sap
saphie: 5 charm 6 amulet 8 talisman
sapid: 5 tasty 6 savory 7 savoury 8 engaging 9 palatable 10 flavorable 11 fit for a king
sapient: 4 sage, sane, wise 6 shrewd 7 erudite, knowing, learned 9 sagacious 10 discerning
sapiutan: 4 anoa
sapless: dry 7 insipid 8 withered 9 exsuccous 11 devitalized
sapling: 5 plant, youth
sapo: 4 soap 8 toadfish
sapodilla: 5 chico 7 nispero 9 naseberry
saponaceous: 6 soapy 7 elusive 8 slippery
sapor: 5 gusto, savor, taste 6 flavor, relish 7 flavour
sapper: 5 miner 6 digger
Sappho: 7 poetess
consort: 5 Phaon
home: 6 Lesbos
sappy: 5 juicy, moist, pithy, plump, silly 6 sodden 7 fatuous, foolish 8 vigorous 9 energetic, succulent 11 sentimental
sapsago: 6 cheese
sapsucker: 10 woodpecker
sapwood: 8 alburnum
Saracen: 4 Arab 5 nomad 6 Moslem, Muslim 7 infidel
knight: 6 Rogero 8 Ruggiero
leader: 7 Saladin
Sarah: *husband:* 7 Abraham
slave: 5 Hagar
son: 5 Isaac
sarcasm: 4 gibe, jeer 5 fling, humor, irony, taunt 6 attack, rebuke, satire 7 mockery 8 acerbity, acridity, reproach, ridicule 9 criticism
pert. to: 8 ironical
sarcastic: dry 6 biting 7 cutting, mordant 8 incisive, sardonic 9 corrosive, trenchant
sarcenet, sarsenet: 4 silk, soft 6 gentle, smooth 8 tempered
sarcina: 8 bacteria
sarcophagus: 4 tomb 6 coffin, cooler
sardine: 4 bang, sild 8 pilchard
Sardinia: 6 island
capital: 8 Cagliari
language: 7 Catalan
sardonic: 8 derisive 9 sarcastic
sargo: 5 grunt 7 pinfish 10 sheepshead
sarkinite: 8 arsenate
sarong: 5 skirt 6 comboy 7 garment
sarrazin: 9 buckwheat

sarsen: 5 block 8 monument 9 sandstone
sartor: 6 tailor
sash: obi 4 band, belt, benn(Sc.) 5 scarf 6 fascia, girdle 8 casement 9 waistband 10 cummerbund
sasin: 8 antelope 9 black buck
Saskatchewan: *capital:* 6 Regina
city: 8 Moose Jaw 9 Saskatoon 12 Prince Albert
Indian: 4 Cree
lake: 5 Rouge 8 Reindeer 9 Athabaska, Wollaston
national park: 12 Prince Albert
province of: 6 Canada
provincial bird: 6 grouse
provincial flower: 4 lily
river: 7 Red Deer 9 Qu'Appelle 11 Assiniboine
sasquatch: 4 omah 7 big boot 13 manlike animal
sassaby: 8 antelope
sassafras: tea 6 saloop
Satan: 4 liar, Nick 5 demon, devil, eblis, fiend 6 Belial 7 Lucifer, tempter 8 diabolus 9 archenemy, archfiend 14 Mephistopheles
associate: 9 Beelzebub
son: Imp
satanic: 4 evil 5 cruel 6 wicked 8 devilish, diabolic, infernal, terrible 10 diabolical
satchel: bag 4 case, grip 5 cabas 6 valise
sate: 4 cloy, cram, glut 5 gorge, stuff 7 gratify, surfeit
satellite (see also **Jupiter, Saturn** and **Uranus**): 4 luna, moon, vein 6 minion, planet 7 Iapetus, Japetus 8 follower, hanger-on 9 attendant, dependent 11 concomitant
man-made: Oso 4 Anna, Echo, Luna, Mars, Zond 5 Ariel, Faith, Lunik, Midas, Relay, Samos, Tiros 6 Cosmos, Flight, Ranger, Skylab, Syncom, Venera, Viking, Vostok 7 Courier, Mariner, Pioneer, Sputnik, Telstar, Transit, Voyager 8 Alouette, Explorer, Telestar, Vanguard 9 Vela-Hotel 10 Discoverer 12 Mercury-Atlas, Project-Score
pert. to: 9 aerospace
weather: 5 Tiros
satiny: 5 sleek 6 glossy, smooth 8 lustrous
satire: 5 grind, irony, spoof 6 banter, parody 7 lampoon, mockery, sarcasm 8 ridicule, travesty
satiric: dry 6 bitter, ironic 7 abusive, atellan, caustic, cutting, mocking 8 ironical, poignant, spoofing 10 censorious, lampooning 11 reproachful
satirize: 4 lash, mock 5 grind, spoof 6 attack, expose 7 lampoon 8 denounce, ridicule 9 criticize
satisfaction: 4 ease, gree 6 amends 7 content, payment 8 pleasure 9 atone-

ment, enjoyment 10 bloodmoney, recompense, reparation, settlement 11 complacence, contentment, restitution 12 compensation, propitiation, remuneration 13 gratification 15 indemnification.

combat for: 4 duel

payment for killing: cro

satisfactory: pat 4 good, okay 5 valid 6 decent, enough 8 adequate 9 allowable, expiatory 10 acceptable, sufficient

satisfied: fed 4 paid, smug 5 proud 9 contented, gratified 10 complacent

satisfy: pay 4 cloy, feed, fill, free, meet, sate, suit 5 appay, atone, clear, repay, serve, slake 6 assure, defray, please, supply 7 appease, assuage, content, expiate, fulfill, gratify, requite, satiate, suffice, surfeit 8 convince, make good, reparate 9 discharge 10 compensate, remunerate

satrap: 5 ruler 6 prince, tyrant 7 viceroy 8 governor, official, overlord

sattva: 5 truth 6 purity, wisdom 8 goodness 12 tranquillity

saturate: ret, sog, sop, wet 4 fill, glut, soak 5 imbue, souse, steep 6 dampen, drench, imbibe, imbrue, seethe, sodden 7 ingrain, satiate, satisfy 8 permeate 9 penetrate 10 impregnate

Saturday: 7 Sabbath

pert. to: 9 sabbatine

Saturday night special: 7 handgun

Saturn: 6 Cronus, planet

in alchemy: 4 lead

ring part: 4 ansa 6 ansae(pl.)

satellite: 4 Rhea 5 Dione, Mimas, Titan 6 Phoebe, Tethys 7 Iapetus, Japetus 8 Hyperion 9 Enceladus

temple treasury: 8 aerarium

wife: Ops

saturnalia: 4 orgy 5 feast 7 revelry 8 carnival, festival

saturnine: 4 dull 5 grave, heavy, staid 6 gloomy, morose, silent, somber, sullen 8 sluggish, taciturn

satyr: 4 faun, idol 5 deity 7 demigod 9 butterfly

sauce: dip 5 gravy 6 flavor, liquor, relish 8 back talk, dressing, matelote 9 condiment

kind: soy 4 alec, hard, lear 5 garum 6 catsup 7 catchup, gascony, ketchup, mustard 8 chawdron, remolade 9 genevoise, matelote, remoulade 10 Bordelaise, mayonnaise 11 Hollandaise, vinaigrette

thickener: 4 roux

saucy: 4 bold, coxy, pert, rude 5 brash, fresh 6 bantam, cocket 7 defiant, forward 8 impudent, malapert 9 audacious, sprightly 11 impertinent

Saudi Arabia (see also **Arabian**): *capital:* 6 Riyadh

city: 5 Jidda, Mecca 6 Jeddah

coin: 5 qursh, riyal

desert: 5 Nefud

gulf: 5 Aqaba

port: 5 Jidda 6 Jeddah

religious center: 5 Mecca 6 Medina

state: 4 Asir, Nejd

sauger: 4 fish 5 perch

Saul: *concubine:* 6 Rizpah

daughter: 6 Michal

father: 4 Kish

grandfather: Ner

herdsman: 4 Doeg

son: 8 Jonathan

successor: 5 David

uncle: Ner

wife: 7 Ahinoam

Saul of Tarsus: 4 Paul

Sault Sainte Marie: Soo

saumont: 6 salmon

sauna: 4 bath 9 bathhouse 12 bathing place

saunter: lag 4 idle, roam, rove, walk 5 amble, mosey, range, shool, stray 6 dander, dawdle, go slow, loiter, lounge, potter, ramble, stroll, wander 8 ruminate

saurel: 4 fish, scad 5 xurel

saurian: 6 lizard 8 dinosaur

saury: 4 fish

sausage: 5 gigot, wurst 6 salami, wiener 7 balloon, baloney, bologna, saveloy 8 cervelate, drisheen, rollejee, rolliche 9 andouille, bratwurst, rollichie 11 wienerwurst 12 andouillette

casing: 4 bung

poisoning: 11 allantiasis

sausage-shaped: 9 allantoid 10 botuliform

savage: 4 fell, grim, rude, wild 5 brute, crude, cruel, feral, rabid, rough 6 brutal, ferine, fierce 7 brutish, furious, howling, inhuman, untamed 8 pitiless, ruthless, work evil 9 aborigine, atrocious, barbarian, barbarous, ferocious, merciless, murderous, primitive, truculent 10 unpolished 11 uncivilized 12 uncultivated, unrestrained

Savage Island people: 5 Niuan

savanna, savannah: 5 plain 9 grassland

savant: 4 sage 5 Solon 6 expert, pedant 7 scholar, wise man 9 scientist

savarin: 7 brioche 10 coffeecake

save: aid, bar, but 4 hain, keep, only 5 amass, catch, guard, hoard, salve, spare, store 6 defend, except, redeem, rescue, retain, scrimp, unless 7 deliver, husband, protect, reclaim, reserve, salvage 8 conserve, maintain, preserve 9 economize, excepting 10 accumulate

savin, savine: 7 juniper 9 evergreen

saving: 6 frugal, rescue, thrift 7 thrifty 9 frugality 10 economical

savings: 7 account, addlins 8 addlings

savoir faire: 4 tact 7 know-how 10 adroitness 11 worldliness 12 mannerliness 14 sophistication

savor, savour: eat 4 odor, zest 5 sapor, scent, smack, smell, taste, tinge 6 degust, fervor, flavor, relish, season 9 degustate

savory: 5 gusty, salty, sapid, tasty 7 piquant 8 delicacy, flavored, fragrant, pleasing 9 agreeable, palatable 10 appetizing, delightful

saw: cut, hew 4 talk, word 5 adage, axiom maxim, motto, rumor, sever 6 cliche, saying 7 proverb 8 aphorism, apothegm 9 platitude 10 apophthegm

kind: 5 briar, edger, serra 6 stadda, trapan, trepan 8 trephine

part: 4 tine 5 redan, tooth

surgical: 6 trapan, trepan 8 trephine

saw-like: 8 serrated

sawbelly: 7 alewife

sawbones: 7 surgeon

sawbuck: 7 ten spot 13 ten-dollar bill

sawder: 7 flatter

sawfish: ray

sawhorse: 4 buck 7 sawbuck

sawyer: 6 beetle, logman 9 lumberman 10 woodcutter

saxhorn: 4 alto, tuba

Saxon: 9 Sassenach

chief: 5 Horsa

city: Ave

king: Ine 6 Harold

lady: 6 Godiva, Rowena

serf: 5 Esne

swineherd: 5 Gurth

warrior: 5 Thane

Saxony city: 7 Dresden

say: 4 aver, call, deem, show, silk, tell 5 put it, speak, state, utter, voice 6 advise, allege, answer, assert, bucket, direct, fabric, nearly, recite, relate, remark, repeat, report 7 declare, dictate, express, iterate, speak up, testify 8 announce, indicate 9 pronounce 10 asseverate, put in words

again: 6 repeat 9 reiterate

further: add

saying: mot, saw 4 quip, word 5 adage, axiom, logia, maxim, motto 6 byword, phrase 7 epigram, proverb 8 aphorism, apothegm 9 statement 11 declaration

apt: 6 bon mot

collection: ana 9 gnomology

distinguishing: 10 shibboleth

scab: 4 sore 5 crust, mange 6 eschar, ratter 7 blemish 8 blackleg 9 scoundrel 13 strike-breaker

scabbard: 4 case 6 sheath, tsubas 7 holster

put in: 7 sheathe

tip: 7 crampit

scabby: low 4 base, mean 5 flaky, mangy 6 scurvy, shabby, stingy 7 blotchy 9 blemished 12 contemptible

scabies: 4 itch 5 mange 11 skin disease

scads: 4 lots 6 oodles

scaffold: 4 cage, loft 5 easel, stage 7 gallery, support 8 platform

scalar: 10 ladderlike

scalawag, scallawag: 4 pony, runt 5 scamp 6 rascal 10 scapegrace

scald: vex 4 burn 5 worry 6 blanch, excite, scorch 7 inflame, torment

scale: cup, hut 4 bowl, film, husk, peel, rate, rule, scut, shed, size, skin 5 climb, flake, gamut, lepis, palea, scute, shive, weigh 6 ascend, degree, lamina, rament, spread, vessel, weight 7 balance, clamber, coating, compare, lamella, measure, scatter, vernier 8 covering, disperse, flake off, separate 9 gradation, steelyard 12 incrustation

bony: 6 scutum

earthquake: 7 Richter

graduated: 7 Vernier

having: 7 leprose, scutate

temperature: 6 Kelvin 7 Celsius 10 centigrade, Fahrenheit

scale-like: 6 scurfy 7 leprose

scallion: 4 leek 5 onion 7 shallot

scallop: 4 quin 5 crena, notch, twist 7 crenate, mollusk

scalp: rob 4 peel, skin 5 cheat 6 defeat, denude, profit, trophy 9 speculate

disease: 5 favus, scurf 8 dandruff

scalpel: 5 knife 6 lancet 8 bistoury

scalper: 6 punter, trader 10 speculator

scaly: low 4 mean 5 flaky 6 stingy 7 powdery 8 squamous 10 despicable

scam: 7 swindle 11 con man's ploy

scamble: 6 sprawl 7 collect, shamble, trample 8 scramble

scamp: imp 5 cheat, knave, rogue 6 rascal 8 scalawag, spalpeen, widdifow 9 scallawag, scoundrel 10 highwayman 13 mischief-maker

scamper: run 4 race 5 speed 6 frolic, hasten, scurry 7 brattle, skitter 9 hurry away, skedaddle

scan: eye 5 study, watch 6 behold, peruse, survey 7 examine, observe, poetize 8 skim over 10 scrutinize 11 contemplate

scandal: 5 eclat, odium, shame 6 gossip, malign 7 calumny, outrage, slander 8 disgrace, ignominy, iniquity 9 discredit 10 backbiting, defamation, detraction, opprobrium

scandalize: 5 shock 6 malign, offend, vilify

scandalous: 6 unholy 8 libelous, shocking

9 offensive 10 flagitious, outrageous 11 furciferous

scandent: 13 climbing plant

Scandinavian (see also Norse, Teutonic): 4 Dane, Lapp 5 Norse, Swede 8 Norseman, Suigoth 9 Icelandic, Norwegian

alphabetical character: 4 rune

bard: 5 scald 9 sagaman

country: 6 Norway, Sweden 7 Denmark, Finland, Iceland

division: amt

drink: 4 glog 7 aquavit

explorer: 4 Eric

hero's place: 8 Valhalla

king: 4 Atli

land: 4 odal

legend: 4 edda, saga

legendary creature: nis 5 nisse, troll 8 Kraken

measure: ass, lod, ort, vog 4 last, mark, pund, sten, untz 5 carat 6 nylast 7 centner, lispund 8 lispound, skalpund, skeppund, skippund 9 shippound, skaalpund, skibslast 10 bismerpund

minstrel: See *bard* above

money: 5 krone

navigator: 4 Eric

nobleman: 4 jarl

pert. to: 5 Norse

plateau: 5 fjeld

rulers: Ros 10 Varangians

ship: 4 aesc

small bay: 5 fjord

trumpet: 4 lure

scant: few 4 lean 5 chary, short, stint 6 geason, meager, meagre, narrow, scrimp, slight, sparse 7 limited, sparing, wanting 9 not enough 12 parsimonious

scantling: 4 beam, size, stud 5 grade 6 timber 7 caliber 8 standard

scape: 4 slip, stem, view 5 fault, shaft 7 picture 8 escapade, peduncle

scapegoat: 4 dupe 6 victim 9 sacrifice 10 substitute

scapegrace: 5 rogue, scamp 6 madcap, rascal 7 wastrel 8 scalawag 9 reprobate, scallawag 10 profligate

scar: arr, mar, shy 4 mark, rock, seam, slit, wild 5 chink, cliff, crack, wound 6 cinder, damage, deface, scared 7 blemish, catface, clinker 8 cicatrix, mountain, pockmark 9 disfigure, precipice 13 disfigurement

pert. to: 5 uloid

tissue: 6 keloid

scarab: 5 charm 6 beetle

scaramouch: 4 fool 5 scamp 6 rascal 7 buffoon 8 braggart, poltroon

scarce: few, shy 4 dear, just, rare 5 scant, short 6 geason, meager, meagre, scanty, sparse 8 uncommon 9 deficient 10 infrequent 12 insufficient

scarcely: 6 barely, hardly, merely

scarcity: 4 lack, need, want 6 dearth, famine, penury, rarity 7 failure, paucity, poverty 8 rareness, sparsity 9 parsimony 10 deficiency, scarceness 11 infrequency, sparingness 12 uncommonness 13 insufficiency, niggardliness

scare: awe, shy 4 fear, fleg 5 alarm, dread, gliff, gloff, panic, spook 6 fright 7 scarify, startle, terrify 8 affright, frighten

scarecrow: 5 bogle 6 figure 10 frightener

scarf: boa, tie 4 gand, sash, wrap 5 adorn, ascot, barbe, cloud, cover, orale, shawl, stole, unite 6 cravat, groove, rebozo, runner, tapalo, tippet 7 dopatta(Ind.), muffler, necktie 8 liripipe, neckwear 9 comforter, cormorant 10 fascinator 11 comfortable, neckerchief

feathered: boa

head: 8 babushka

scarfskin: 7 cuticle 9 epidermis

scarify: See scare

scarlet: red 4 lewd 5 bawdy 8 flagrant 10 prostitute

Scarlett O'Hara: *home:* 4 Tara

husband: 5 Rhett

scarp: cut 5 cliff, slope 7 descent, incline 8 fragment 9 declivity, precipice

scary: 4 eery 5 eerie, timid, weird 6 spooky 7 fearful, ghostly, uncanny 8 alarming 11 frightening

scat: bop, tax 4 beat, riff, shoo 5 smash 6 begone, go away, rebuff, shower 7 getaway, scatter, tribute, vamoose 8 nonsense

scathe: 4 harm, hurt, sear 5 blast 6 assail, damage, injure, scorch, wither 8 denounce, lash into, work evil 9 castigate

scathing: 6 biting, severe 7 mordant 8 blasting, injuring, wounding 9 scorching, truculent, withering

scatological: 5 fecal 7 obscene, raunchy

scatter: sow, ted 4 cast, deal, rout 5 fling, spray, strew, waste 6 dispel, shower, splash, spread 7 bestrew, confuse, diffuse, disband, fritter, radiate 8 dishevel, disperse, distract, separate, sprinkle, squander 9 bespatter, circulate, discomfit, dissipate 10 disconnect, distribute 11 disseminate

scatter-gun: 7 shotgun

scatterbrained: 6 giddy 7 flighty 9 frivolous

scattered: 6 sparse 7 erratic, strawed 8 rambling, sporadic 9 irregular 10 straggling

scatula: 7 pill box

scaup: 4 duck 8 grayback 10 canvasback

scavage: tax 4 duty, toll

scavenger: rat 7 sweeper, vulture

scenario: 4 plot 6 script 7 outline 10 continuity

scend: 4 lift 5 heave, pitch

scene: act 4 site, view 5 arena, sight, vista 6 blow-up, locale 7 diorama, display, episode, picture, quarrel, setting, tableau 8 prospect 9 landscape, spectacle, way of life

last: 6 finale

scenery: 4 view 5 decor, props 8 stage set 9 landscape 14 representation

sceneshifter: 4 grip

scenic: 8 dramatic 9 panoramic 10 theatrical 11 picturesque

scenite: 5 nomad

scent: 4 clue, nose, odor 5 aroma, odour, savor, smell, sniff, spoor, track 6 breath, flavor 7 bouquet, essence, flavour, inkling, perfume 8 effluvia 9 emanation, fragrance

scented: 5 olent 8 perfumed

scepter, sceptre: rod 4 mace 5 baton, staff 6 emblem 7 trident 8 caduceus 9 authority 11 sovereignty

schedule: 4 card, list, plan, time 5 slate, table 6 tariff 7 catalog, program, routine, writing 8 calendar, document, register, tabulate 9 catalogue, inventory, timetable

schefferite: 8 pyroxene

schelm: 5 rogue 6 rascal

schema: 4 plan 6 figure 7 diagram, outline

scheme: aim, gin, web 4 dart, list, plan, plot 5 angle, cabal, cadre, draft, drift, table, trick 6 design, device, devise, figure, racket 7 concoct, diagram, epitome, outline, program, project, purpose 8 conspire, contrive, forecast, gimcrack, intrigue, maneuver 9 statement, stratagem 10 concoction, conspiracy 11 contrivance, machination, proposition

schemer: 7 plotter, traitor 9 con artist

scheming: 6 artful, crafty, tricky 8 fetching 9 designing 10 intriguing

schism: 4 rent 5 split 6 breach, heresy 8 division 10 separation

schist: 5 slate

schizocarp: 5 fruit, regma

schizophrenia: 8 catatony, insanity 9 psychosis 16 split personality

schlemiel: dub, oaf 4 clod, goof 5 chump 7 saphead

schlepp: 4 jerk, drag, pull

schmaltz: 4 corn 14 sentimentality

scholar: 4 sage 5 clerk, pupil 6 pedant, savant 7 bookman, learner, student 8 disciple 11 academician, philologist

day: 6 extern

servant: 7 famulus

scholarly: 7 erudite, learned 8 studious 10 scholastic

scholarship: 7 bursary 8 learning 9 allowance, education, erudition, knowledge 10 fellowship 11 instruction

scholiast: 6 critic 9 annotator 10 glossarist 11 commentator 13 glossographer

school: gam, pod 4 cult, lead, sect 5 drill, ecole(F.), flock, group, lycee(F.), shoal, teach, train 6 manege 7 academy, advance, college, company, convent, educate, seminar 8 atheneum, document, exercise, instruct, seminary 9 athenaeum, cultivate 10 realschule(G.), university 11 institution

grounds: 6 campus

group: PTA

kind: 4 high, prep 5 grade 7 primary 8 military 9 finishing, secondary 10 elementary, vocational 11 preparatory

of fish: 5 shoal

of whales: gam

official: 9 principal, scholarch 10 headmaster 14 superintendent

pert. to: 8 academic

religious: 5 heder 6 cheder 8 seminary

riding: 6 manege

task: 6 lesson 7 problem 10 assignment 11 composition

term: 7 quarter 8 semester 9 trimester

schoolbook: 4 text 5 atlas 6 primer, reader 7 speller 9 geography

schoolmaster: 4 caji, head 7 dominie, manager, pedagog 8 pedagogue

schooner: 4 boat, brig, tern 5 glass 6 vessel 7 measure

builder: 14 Andrew Robinson

schottische: 5 dance, polka

schout: 7 bailiff, sheriff

schrik: 5 panic 6 fright

science: art, sci 5 ology 9 education, knowledge 10 technology

of agriculture: 8 agronomy

of animals: 7 zoology

of crop production: 8 agronomy

of enviroment: 7 ecology

of healing: 9 iatrology

of heredity: 8 genetics

of human behavior: 6 ethics 10 psychology

of motion: 8 kinetics

of mountains: 7 orology

of plants: 6 botany

of projectiles: 10 ballistics

of words: 9 semantics

principle: 5 logic

sciential: 4 able 7 capable 9 competent

scientific: 5 exact 8 skillful 9 practical, technical

scilicet: 5 to wit 6 namely 9 videlicet

scimitar, scimiter: 4 snee 5 saber, sword 8 billhook

scintilla: 4 atom, iota 5 spark, trace 8 particle 10 least trace

scintillate: 5 flash, gleam, spark 7 glitter, sparkle, twinkle 9 coruscate

scion, cion: bud, son 4 heir, twig 5 shoot, sprig 6 sprout 8 offshoot 9 offspring 10 descendant

scissor: cut 4 clip, trim 5 shear

scleroid: 4 hard 8 hardened 9 indurated

scoff: 4 food, gibe, gird, jeer, leer, meal, mock, rail 5 fleer, flout, gleek, scout, sneer, steal, taunt 6 deride 7 mockery, plunder 8 ridicule 9 indignity

scoffer: 5 clown 6 jester, mocker 10 unbeliever

scold: nag, yap 4 haze, jump, rail, rant, rate 5 abuse, barge, boast, brawl, chide, score, shrew, slate 6 berate, bounce, rebuff, rebuke, revile, virago 7 bawl out, chew out, reprove, upbraid 8 chastise, lambaste 9 criticize, objurgate 10 vituperate

scolding: 6 dirdum, rating, rebuke 7 combing, hearing, reproof 8 dressing 9 complaint

scombroid fish: 4 tuna 6 bonito 8 mackerel

sconce: 4 fine, fort, head 5 cover, skull 7 bracket, bulwark, lantern, penalty, shelter 8 entrench 10 protection 11 candlestick

scone: 4 farl 5 farle 7 biscuit

scoop: dig 4 bail, beat, lade, news 5 didle, empty, gouge, ladle, skeet, spoon 6 bucket, chisel, dipper, dredge, gather, hollow, shovel, vessel 7 curette 8 excavate

scoot: run 4 bolt, dart, dray, scud 5 hurry, scram, shoot, slide 6 begone, decamp, scurry 9 skedaddle

scooter: toy 4 boat, plow 6 glider

scop: 4 bard, poet

scope: 4 area, goal, room 5 range, reach, theme, tract 6 domain, extent, import, intent, length, object, sphere, target 7 breadth, liberty 8 distance, latitude 9 dimension, extension, intention
   having: 13 comprehensive
   large: 7 general

scopic: 6 visual 9 extensive

scorch: cut, dry 4 burn, char, flay, sear, skin 5 adust, be hot, parch, score, singe, slash, speed, sting, toast 6 birsle, scathe, wither 7 blister, scratch, shrivel 8 lambaste

score: cut, run, tab, taw 4 goal, line, mark, rate 5 chalk, chase, corge, count, judge, notch, scold, slash, tally 6 abrade, barter, berate, furrow, grudge, number, reason, record, scotch, twenty, weight 7 account, arrange, scratch, upbraid 8 incision 9 criticize, grievance, reckoning 10 obligation 11 enumeration, orchestrate 12 indebtedness

scoria: 4 lava, rock, slag 5 ashes, dross 6 refuse 7 residue

scoring point: ace, hit, run 4 down, goal 5 tally 6 basket

scorn: 4 geck, jeer, mock 5 flout, scoff 6 deride, reject, slight 7 condemn, despise, despite, disdain 8 contempt, derision 9 contumely

scornful: 5 aloof 7 haughty, stuckup 8 arrogant, insolent 9 rejecting 10 disdainful, fastidious

scorpion: 4 nepa 6 onager, weapon 7 scourge, stinger 8 arachnid, catapult 10 vinegaroon
   stinger: 6 telson

Scorpion's Heart: 7 Antares

scot: tax 4 levy 6 assess 7 payment 9 reckoning 10 assessment 12 contribution

Scot (see also **Scotland**): 4 Gael, Pict 10 Caledonian, Highlander

scotch (see also **Scotland**): cut 4 stop 5 check, chock, notch, score, wedge 6 hinder, stingy, whisky 7 scratch, scruple, sparing 8 hesitate 9 frustrate

Scotchman: Mac 4 Gael, Scot 7 bluecap, Scottie 10 Highlander

scoter: 4 coot, duck, fowl
   genus: 7 oidemia 9 melanitta

scot-free: 4 safe 5 clear 6 unhurt 7 untaxed

Scotland: *accent:* 4 birr, burr
   askew or awry: 4 agee 5 agley
   at all: ava
   author: 5 Scott 6 Barrie
   bay: 5 Scapa
   beg: 4 sorn
   bird: gae 4 hern 6 grouse, snabby 7 snabbie 8 throstle 9 swinepipe
   blessing: 6 rebuke 8 scolding
   blood money: cro
   boat: 4 zulu 6 scaffy, sexern 7 coracle, skaffie
   bonfire: 6 tandle
   brain: 4 harn
   bread: 5 briar 6 tammie 7 bannock
   bread dish: 4 saps
   briar: 4 rose
   brook: 4 sike
   broth: 4 soup
   bucket: 5 stoop, stoup
   bull: 4 stot
   bushel: fou
   buxom: 6 sonsie
   cake: 5 scone
   camp follower: 6 gudget
   cap: tam 6 bonnet, tassel, toorie 8 Balmoral 9 Glengarry 11 Tam O'Shanter
   capital: 9 Edinburgh
   cap tassel: 6 toorie
   cascade: lin 4 linn 5 force
   cat: 6 malkin

cattle: 8 Ayrshire
celebration: 4 kirn
chafing dish: 7 choffer
chair: 5 regal
chief: 5 thegn
child: 4 dalt 5 bairn 6 scuddy 8 smatchet
church: 4 kirk
city: Ayr 5 Alloa, Leith, Perth, Troon 6 Dundee 7 Glasgow, Grunock, Paisley 8 Aberdeen, Stirling 9 Edinburgh, Inverness, St. Andrews 10 Kilmarnock
cloth: 4 kelt 6 tartan
coin: 4 demy 5 bodle, groat 6 baubee, bawbee
colt: 4 stag
congress: Mod
corner: 4 neuk
county: Ayr 4 Bute, Fife, Ross 5 Angus, Banff, Moray, Nairn, Perth 6 Argyll, Lanark, Orkney 7 Berwick, Kinross, Peebles, Renfrew, Selkirk, Wigtown 8 Aberdeen, Ayrshire, Dumfries, Roxburgh, Shetland, Stirling
court officer: 5 macer
cross: 8 crantara 9 crostarie
cuddy: 6 draper 7 peddler
cup: 4 tass
curlies: 4 kale
dagger: 5 skean
dance: bob 4 reel 7 walloch 9 ecossaise 10 strathspey 13 Highland-fling
destiny: 5 weird
devil: 4 deil
district: Ayr 5 Rinns 6 Atholl 7 Lothian 8 Galloway 9 Tweeddale 11 Breadalbane
donkey: 5 cuddy
drapery: 4 pand
drinking bout: 6 screed
drinking vessel: 4 tass 6 quaich, quaigh
duck: 10 bufflehead
elm: 4 wych
ember: 5 aizle
endure: 4 dree
excuse: 6 sunyie
explorer: Rae
eye: ee
fairy: 4 fane
farmer: 6 cottar, cotter 7 crofter
fashion: 7 Scotice
festival: Mod 7 Uphelya
fiddle: 4 itch
fingering: 4 wool, yarn
fireplace: 5 ingle
firth: Tay 4 Loch, Lorn 5 Clyde, Forth, Moray 6 Linnhe 8 Cromarty
fish: 4 sile 7 sillock 8 spalding
fish trap: 4 yare 5 yaire
fishing expedition: 5 drave
fog: 4 haar
fool: 4 gype
fort: 4 dune 10 roundabout

game: 6 shinty
garment: tam 4 kilt, maud 5 toosh 6 fecket, tartan 7 arisard 8 Balmoral 11 Tam o' Shanter
garter: 8 wooer-bab
ghost: 6 taisch
girl: 4 jill, lass 5 quean 6 lassie, towdie 7 winklot
give: gie
grandchild: oe, oy; oye
grandfather: 8 gudesire
grandmother: 6 gudame
granite: 5 gowan
guess: 4 rede
gutter: 5 siver
hands: 8 paddling
have: hae
hazelnut: nit
heater: 7 choffer
heath: 7 heather
heavy: 5 tharf
hill: 4 brae 6 strone
hillside: 4 brae
historian: 4 Hume 5 Skene
hoppers: 9 hopscotch
icicle: 7 shoggle
inlet: gio
island: 4 Iona 5 Arran 6 Orkney 8 Hebrides, Shetland
kale: 8 borecole
kelp: 8 bellware
king: 6 Robert
kiss: 8 smoorich
lake: dee 4 loch
lament: 6 ochone
land: 6 carses
land tax: 4 cess
landholder: 5 laird, thane
language: 4 Erse 6 Lallan 7 Lalland
liquor: 5 scour 6 athole 8 whittier
lord: 5 laird
loyal: 4 leal
marauder: 7 cateran
measure: cop 4 cran, fall, mile, peck, pint, rood, rope 5 crane, crans, lippy 6 firlot, lippie 7 auchlet, chalder, choppin 8 mutchkin, stimpart, stimpert 9 particate, shaftmont, shaftmont
mist: ure
money: 6 siller
monk: 6 culdee
mountain: 8 Ben Nevis 9 Grampians
music festival: Mod
musical instrument: 5 pipes 7 bagpipe
muscian: 5 piper
must: 4 maun
native: 4 Gael, Pict, Scot
naval base: 9 Scapa Flow
negative: nae
oath: 4 aith
odd: 4 orra

pastry: 5 scone 7 carcake

patron saint: 6 Andrew

payment: cro

peasant: 6 cottar, cotter

peninsula: 5 Rinns

people: 8 Damnonii 9 Dammonian

physicist: 4 Watt

plaid: 4 maud

poet: 4 Hogg, Moir 5 Burns

pole: 5 caber

pool: lin 4 linn

porridge: 5 brose

proprietor: 5 laird

pouch: 6 sporan 7 sporran

pudding: 6 haggis

queen: 4 Mary

refuge: 6 bilbie

ridge: run

river: Ayr, Dee, Don, Esk, Tay 4 Doon, Find, Norn, Nith, Spey 5 Afton, Annan, Clyde, North, Tweed 6 Teviot 7 Deveron

sausage: 9 whitehass 10 whitehawse

schoolmaster: dux

scurvy grass: 8 seabells

seaport: 4 Leth 5 Alloa 6 Dundee

sect: 9 Buchanite

self: sel

servant: 5 gilly 6 gillie

sheepfold: ree

small: sma

snow: sna 4 snaw

soldier: 7 cateran

song: 6 strowd

student: 5 bejan 6 nejant

sweetheart: 4 jill

tenure: 6 sorren 7 sorehon

tinker: 5 caird

tithe: 5 teind

title: 5 laird

to: tae

toad: ted 4 taed

tobacco: 5 elder

toe: tae

toil: 4 darg

topaz: 6 tassel 9 cairngorm

tourist resort: 4 Oban

tower: 7 toorock

town hall: 8 tolbooth 9 tollbooth

tree: arm

trousers: 5 trews

uncle: eme

unit: ane

vigor: vir

warrior: 4 kemp

water spirit: 5 kelpy 6 kelpie

waterfall: lin 4 linn 5 force

weakling: 4 ribe 5 shilp 7 shilpit

weapon: 5 skean 8 claymore, skeandhu

weight: 4 boll, drop 5 trone 6 bushel

whine: 4 yirn

whirlpool: 7 swilkie 8 swelchie

whisky: 6 athole 9 Glenlivat, Glenlivit 10 Usquebaugh

whitefish: 7 vendace

window: 7 winnock

woman: 4 burd

woodcock: 4 eggs

world: 4 warl

yell: 4 gowl

youth: 5 chiel 7 callant

Scott: *character:* 5 Norma 7 Ivanhoe 9 Lochinvar

novel: 6 Rob Roy 7 Ivanhoe 8 Talisman 10 Kenilworth

poem: 7 Marmion

Scottish: See Scotland

scoundrel: cad 4 scab 5 cheat, filth, knave, scamp 6 rascal, varlet 7 glutton, villain, warlock 8 bezonian 9 miscreant, reprobate 10 blackguard

scour: eat, rub, run 4 beat, rake, rush, wash 5 clean, hurry, purge, scrub, sweep 6 decamp, polish, punish, remove 7 cleanse, roister 8 brighten, traverse

scourge: 4 bane, flay, flog, lash, whip 5 harry, shoot, slash 6 plague, punish, ravage, swinge, switch 7 afflict, torment 8 chastise, epidemic, lambaste 9 devastate 10 affliction, discipline, flagellate, infliction, punishment

Scourge of God: 6 Attila

scout: guy, spy 4 chap, jeer, look 5 scoff, spurn, watch 6 fellow, search 7 despise, explore, lookout, observe 8 emissary, informer, ridicule, watchman 9 search out 11 reconnoiter, reconnoitre

unit: den 4 pack 5 troop

scouth: 4 room 5 range, scope 6 plenty

scow: 4 acon(F.), boat 5 barge, float 6 garvey 7 lighter

scowl: 5 frown, glare, glout, lower 6 glower

scraggly: 6 jagged, ragged 7 unkempt 9 irregular 10 splintered

scraggy: 4 bony, lean, thin 5 rough, weedy 6 meager, rugged, skinny 7 knotted, scrawny 8 slovenly

scram: 4 flee, shoo 6 beat it, benumb, depart, go away 7 vamoose 8 paralyze, withered

scramble: mix 4 push 5 climb, crowd, crush, fight, haste 6 hustle, jostle, sprawl, spread, strive 7 clamber, pushing, scatter 8 struggle

scrambled: 4 pied 5 mixed 11 meaningless

scrap: bit, end, jag, ort, rag 4 chip, item, junk 5 brawl, fight, grain, piece, shred, waste 6 cullet, morsel, refuse 7 cutting, discard, extract, oddment, quarrel, remnant 8 fraction, fragment 11 small amount

scrape: bow, hoe, row, rub, saw 4 claw, grit, harl, rake, rasp, scud, trap 5 claut, erase,

grate, graze, gride, hoard, order, shave 6
abrade, dredge, fiddle, gather, harass,
refine, remove, sclaff 7 collect, corrode,
scratch 9 situation 10 difficulty 11
predicament 12 touch lightly

scraper: 4 tool 6 barber, rasper, xyster 7
fiddler, strigil 8 grattoir

scraping: 6 rasion, rasure

scrapper: 5 boxer 7 fighter 8 pugilist 9
combatant

scratch: dig, mar, rat, rit, rub, wig 4 claw,
draw, feed, heap, line, mark, race, rake,
rist, tear 5 break, claut, clawk, erase,
expel, flush, money, score, wound
6 cancel, furrow, gather, injury, rasure,
scotch, scrape, scrawl 7 expunge, rough-
en, scarify 8 abrasion, incision, scribble, scrobble, withdraw

scratchy: 6 uneven 10 irritating

scrawl: 4 teem 5 crawl 7 scratch, writing
8 scribble

scrawny: 4 lean, poor, thin 6 meager 7
scraggy, scranny, scrubby 8 rawboned

screak: 4 rasp 5 creak, grate

scream: cry 4 wail, yarm, yaup, yawl, yell,
yowt 6 shriek, squall, yammer 7
screech 10 funny story

screamer: 5 chaja, error 7 caption

scree: 5 stone, talus 6 pebble 7 deposit

screech: cry 4 yell 5 quawk 6 outcry,
scream, shriek 7 ululate

screed: say 4 land, rend, rent, tear 5
board, shred, strip 6 scrape, smooth, tirade 7 leveler 8 diatribe, fragment, harangue 9 discourse

screen: 4 cage, hide, mask, mesh, reja,
sept, sift, veil 5 arras, blind, chick-
(Ind.), cloak, cover, grill, purda, scarf,
shade, sieve, speer, spier 6 defend, filter, grille, purdah, settle, shield 7 conceal, curtain, protect, reredos, shelter,
shut out 8 block out, covering, separate
9 breakwind, partition

architectural: 5 spier

chancel: 4 jube 7 reredos

chimney: 6 bonnet

Japanese: 5 shoji

mesh: 4 laun 5 sieve

wind: 8 paravent

screw: key, pay 4 turn, wind, worm 5
cheat, guard, horse, miser, twist 6 extort, gimlet, keeper, salary, scrimp, spiral 7 contort, crumple, distort, robbery,
squeeze, tighten, turnkey 9 bargainer,
propeller, skinflint 10 contortion, crustacean, instructor

screw pine: 5 vacoa 6 vacona, vacoua 8
pandanus

screw-pine family: 11 pandanaceae

screwball: nut, sap 5 crank, crazy, dippy,
goose 6 galoot 7 fanatic, saphead 8
crackpot, dumbbell 9 blockhead, eccen-

tric 10 crackbrain, muttonhead

screwed: 5 drunk 11 intoxicated

screw up: 5 spoil 6 fasten

screwy: 5 crazy, wacky 6 absurd, insane,
whacky 7 winding 8 freakish, peculiar
9 eccentric, fantastic 10 irrational,
misleading, unbalanced 11 impractical
12 crackbrained, preposterous

scribble: 5 write 6 scrawl 7 jot down,
scratch 8 scrabble

scribe: 5 clerk, write 6 author, copier,
doctor, notary, penman, writer 7 copyist, graffer, teacher 9 draftsman, sce-
narist, scrivener, secretary 10 amanuensis, journalist 11 transcriber 13
bibliographer

scriggle: 5 twist 6 squirm, wiggle 7 wriggle 8 curlicue

scrimmage: 4 play 5 fight 6 battle,
splore, tussle 8 football, practice 10
free-for-all

scrimp: 4 save 5 stint 6 meager, save up,
scanty 9 economize 12 pinch pennies

scrimping: 7 miserly, sparing 9 niggardly

scrip: 4 list 5 token 7 writing 8 currency,
schedule 10 paper money 11 certificate

script: 5 ronde 8 scenario 10 penmanship
11 chirography, handwriting

Arabic: 5 neski

round: 5 ronde

Syriac: 5 serta

scriptor: See **scribe**

scriptural: 8 Biblical

scrivello: 4 tusk

scrivener: 6 notary, writer 8 recorder

scrofula: 4 evil 6 struma 9 king's evil

scrofulous: 7 corrupt 10 degenerate 12
contaminated

scroll: 4 curl, list, roll 5 draft 6 amulet,
legend, record, scrawl, spiral, volute 7
outline, papyrus, writing 8 enscribe, inscribe, schedule, streamer

Hebrew: 6 mezuza 7 mezuzah

writing: 8 makimono

scrouge: 5 crowd, press 7 squeeze

scrounge: beg 5 cadge, steal 6 pilfer,
search, sponge

scrub: mop, rub 4 mean, poor, runt, stop,
wash 5 clean, dwarf, scour, small 6
drudge, paltry, shabby 7 call off, cleanse
8 inferior 10 brushwood, shrubbery,
undersized 14 undernourished

scrub turkey: 6 leipoa 8 megapode

scrubby: 5 runty, small 6 shabby 7 stunted 8 inferior

scruff: 4 film, nape, scum 5 crust, dross 6
refuse 7 coating 8 covering, dandruff

scrumptious: 4 fine, nice 5 dandy, tasty
7 capital, elegant 8 splendid 9 delicious, excellent

scrunch: 5 crush 6 crunch, huddle 7
squeeze

scruple: 4 part 5 demur, doubt, qualm 6 amount, boggle, weight 7 anxiety, portion 8 question 9 disbelief, misgiving 10 uneasiness 11 compunction

scrupulous: 4 nice 5 chary, exact 6 honest, proper, strict 7 careful, correct, precise, upright 8 accurate, cautious 9 honorable, reluctant 11 punctilious 13 conscientious

to excess: 7 finicky, prudish 10 fastidious

scrutinize: eye, pry 4 scan, sift 5 probe 6 survey 7 examine, inspect, observe 8 look over

scrutiny: 4 gaze, look 8 overview

scryer: 4 seer

scuba diver: 7 frogman 8 aquanaut

scud: ale, fly, run 4 beer, gust, mist, move, skim 5 cloud, hurry, spray 6 scrape, shower 10 crustacean

scuff: 4 blow, cuff, drag, gust, toss, wipe 5 brush, evade, graze, rowdy, slare, touch, tread 6 buffet, rabble, scrape, scruff, shower, slight 7 scatter, shuffle, slipper 8 scramble 9 roughened, scratched

scuffle: row 4 cuff 5 amble, fight, melee, set-to 6 affray, bustle, clinch, combat, sclaff, strive, tussle 7 contend, shamble, shuffle 8 struggle

scug: 4 shade 6 shadow 7 protect, shelter 8 pretense, squirrel 9 schoolboy

scull: oar, row 4 boat 6 basket, propel, wherry 7 rowboat 8 scullion

scullion: 6 menial 7 servant

sculptor: 6 artist, graver, imager

famous: Arp 4 Gabo 5 Moore, Rodin, Smith 6 Calder, Robbia, Zorach 7 Cellini, daVinci, Epstein, Maillol, Noguchi, Pevsner, Phidias, Picasso, Zadkine 8 Brancusi, Hepworth, Nevelson 9 Lipschitz, Mestrovic 10 Giacometti, Praxiteles 11 Polycleitus 12 Michelangelo

tool: 6 graver

sculpture: 4 bust, form, head 5 carve, grave, torso 6 clusel, emboss, relief, statue 7 engrave, relievo

framework: 7 armature

pert. to: 7 glyphic, glyptic 9 glyptical

slab: 6 metope

scum: 4 brat, foam, scud, silt, skim 5 dregs, dross, froth, range, scour, slime, sperm, spume, sweep 6 bubble, rabble, refuse, scoria 10 impurities 12 offscourings

scumfish: 5 choke 9 discomfit, overpower, suffocate

scup: 4 fish 5 bream, porgy

scuppernong: 4 wine 5 grape 9 muscadine

scurrilous: low 4 foul, vile 5 gross 6 ribald, vulgar 7 abusive, obscene 8 indecent 9 insulting, offensive 11 disparaging, foulmouthed, opprobrious

scurry: hie, run 4 race, rush 5 harry, scoot, scour, skirr, speed 6 flurry, hasten 7 scamper, scuttle, skelter 9 skedaddle

scurvy: bad, low 4 mean 6 shabby, vulgar 7 disease 8 scorbute 12 contemptible, discourteous

preventative: 6 citrus 13 antiscorbutic

scutage: fee, tax 4 levy 6 impost

scuttle: hod, run 4 dish, ruin, rush, sink, veto 5 scoot 6 basket, bucket, scotch, scurry, shovel 7 octopus, platter 8 bankrupt, hatchway 10 cuttlefish

scuttlebutt: 5 rumor 6 gossip 7 hearsay

scutum: 5 plate, scute 6 shield

Scylla: 4 rock

father: 5 Nisus

lover: 5 Minos

scythe: 6 sickle

handle: 5 snath, thole 6 snathe

sweep: 5 swath

sea: mer(F.) 4 blue, deep, meer(G.), much 5 ocean

anemone: 5 polyp 7 actinia

approach: 7 seagate

arm: bay 4 gulf 5 bayou, firth, fjord, frith, inlet, lough 7 estuary

at: 4 asea

bottom: bed

current: 4 tide 8 undertow

deity: Ler, Ran 5 Aegir, Doris 6 Nereus, Triton 7 Neptune, Phorcus, Phorcyn, Phorcys, Phorkys, Proteus 8 Palaemon, Poseidon

delicacy: roe 4 nori

description: 11 haliography

god: 7 Neptune, Proteus 8 Poseidon

goddess: Ran 4 Nina 8 Eurynome 9 Leucothea 10 Amphitrite

king: Ler 5 chief 6 pirate, viking

land in: 6 island

life of: 8 halibios

little: 6 sealet

mammal: 4 seal 5 whale

open: 6 midsea

periodic motion: 4 tide

pert. to: 4 vast 5 naval 6 marine 7 oceanic, pelagic 8 maritime, nautical 9 aequoreal, thalassic

plant: 6 enalid

roughness: 5 swell, waves 6 lipper

route: 4 lane

spray: 9 spindrift 10 spoondrift

swell: 4 surf

term: 4 ahoy 5 avast, belay, trice

sea cow: 6 dugong, rytina, walrus 7 manatee 8 sirenian 12 hippopotamus

sea cucumber: 6 pedata 7 trepang 11 holothurian

sea dog: tar 4 seal 6 pirate, sailor 7 breaker, dogfish 9 privateer

sea duck: 5 eider 6 scoter

sea eagle: ern 4 erne, tern 6 osprey

sea-ear: 7 abalone

sea-foam: 5 froth 9 sepiolite 10 meer-schaum

sea hog: 8 porpoise

sea horse: 6 walrus 8 whitecap 11 hippocampus

sea kale: 4 cole 7 potherb

sea lettuce: 5 algae, laver 7 seaweed

sea nettle: 6 medusa 9 jellyfish

sea nymph: 5 siren 6 Nereid 7 Galatea, Oceanid

sea raven: 7 sculpin 9 cormorant 10 squaretail

sea robber: 6 jaeger, pirate 7 corsair 9 buccaneer, privateer

sea rover: 6 pirate, viking 7 scummer

sea slug: 6 trepan 8 cucumber 10 nudibranch

sea soldier: 6 marine 10 hermit crab

sea squirt: 5 salpa 8 ascidian, tunicate

sea swallow: 4 tern 6 petrel

sea unicorn: 7 narwhal

sea urchin: 6 repkie 7 echinid, echinus 8 echinoid 10 echinoderm

rock hole: 5 geode

sea wall: 7 bulwark 10 embankment

sea wolf: 4 seal 6 pirate 9 privateer, submarine

seabird: auk, ern 4 duck, erne, gull, smew, tern 5 solan, yager 6 gannet, petrel 7 pelican 9 albatross 10 shearwater

seaboard: 5 coast 9 coastland, tidewater

seafarer: gob, tar 4 salt 6 sailor, seaman 7 mariner 9 navigator

seagoing: 8 maritime, nautical 9 seafaring 13 weatherbeaten

seal: cap, fix, hem, set, wax 4 bind, bull, cere, lute, rope, shut, sign 5 bulla, chain, close, sigil, stamp, token, wafer 6 attest, cachet, clinch, fasten, pledge, ranger, ratify, scarab, secure, signet 7 closure, confine, confirm, leather, sticker 8 breloque, document, guaranty, imprison, sealskin, validate 9 assurance, carnivore, guarantee, sigillate, wax wafer 10 obligation 12 authenticate 14 authentication

bearded: 5 ursuk 6 makluk

decorated with: 9 sigillate

eared: 5 otary

eared genus: 8 zalophus

female fur: 5 matka

letter: 6 cachet

limb: 7 flipper

official: 6 signet

pelt: 5 sculp

pert. to: 7 phocine

place: 7 rookery

polar: 5 otary, phoca, Ross's, ursal, ursuk 6 makluk 8 bedlamer, seecatch 9 sterrinck

school: pod

young: pup 6 beater, hopper 7 quitter, saddler 11 flipperling, holluschick

sealing wax: lac

seam: sew 4 bond, fash, fold, join, line, load, mark, scar 5 cleft, joint, layer, raphe, ridge, strip, unite 6 groove, streak, suture 7 crevice, fissure, stratum, wrinkle 8 cicatrix 10 packsaddle

pert. to: 7 sutural, suturic

seaman: See **sailor, seafarer**

seamark: 6 beacon 8 landmark 10 lighthouse

seamer: 5 sewer 8 stitcher 10 dressmaker, seamstress

seamless: 5 whole 7 unsewed 12 araphorostic

seamy: 5 rough 6 sordid 8 degraded, wrinkled 12 disreputable

seance: 7 meeting, session, sitting

holder: 6 medium

seaport: 4 port 6 habor

sear (see also **sere**): dry 4 burn, cook, mark, scar 5 brand, brown, catch, parch, singe 6 braise, deaden, scorch, sizzle, wither 9 cauterize

search: 4 comb, grub, hunt, look, nose, rout, seek 5 delve, frisk, probe, quest, scour 6 brevit, ferret, forage, pierce, sphere, survey 7 canvass, examine, explore, inquire, inquiry, inspect, ransack, rummage 8 research, scrounge, scrutiny 9 penetrate, shake down 10 scrutinize 11 exploration, investigate

searching: 4 hard, keen 5 acute, sharp 6 shrewd 7 groping 10 discerning

seascape: 4 view 7 picture

seashell: 4 clam 5 conch, snail 7 scallop

seashore: 5 beach, coast, shore 7 seaside 8 seabeach, seacoast

pert. to: 8 littoral

season: age, dry, tid, ver 4 beek, fall, salt, sele, tide, time 5 devil, imbue, inure, ripen, savor, spice, taste, tinge, train 6 autumn, embalm, flavor, harden, mature, period, school, soften, spring, summer, temper, winter 7 condite, flavour, weather 8 accustom, marinate 9 habituate 10 impregnate 11 acclimatize, opportunity

religious: 4 Lent 6 careme

seasonable: apt, pat 4 ripe 6 timely 7 apropos 8 suitable 9 opportune 11 appropriate

seasonal: 8 periodic

seasoned: 7 veteran 8 finished, flavored 11 experienced

seasoning: 4 herb, mace, sage, salt 5 cumin, onion, spice, thyme 6 celery, cloves, cummin, garlic, nutmeg, pepper, relish 7 caraway, cuminos, mustard, oregano, paprika, vinegar 8 allspice, cardamom, marjoram, rosemary, turmeric 9 condiment, coriander 10 experience

seat: fix, pew, put, see 4 apse, bank, base, form, hold, home, loge, room, site 5 asana, bench, chair, floor, place, sella(L.), siege, stool, usher 6 exedra, center, grange, howdah, locate, sedile, settee, settle, throne 7 capital, install, ottoman, situate, station, taboret, tendoor, tendour 8 bleacher, buttocks, locality, location, tabouret 9 banquette, establish, residence, situation 10 foundation 11 nerve center

chancel: 6 sedile

high: 5 roost

of judgment: 8 tribunal

of justice: 4 banc

on elephant: 6 houdah; howdah

tier of: 6 gradin

seat bone: 7 ischium

seat worm: 7 pinworm

seaweed: ore 4 agar, alga, kelp, nori 5 algae, dulse, laver, varec, vraic, wrack 6 delisk, desmid, fucoid, varech 7 oreweek 8 agar-agar, hempweed, sargasso 9 desmidian

culture medium: 4 agar

edible: 4 limu, ulva 5 dulse

extract: 4 agar

genus of: 6 alaria

pert. to: 6 algous

purple: 4 nori 5 laver 9 carrageen, Irish moss

red: 5 dulse 6 delisk

study: 6 algology

sebaceous: 5 fatty

sec: dry

secant: 5 chord 7 cutting 12 intersecting

secede: 5 leave 6 desert 7 dissent 8 withdraw

secern: 11 distinguish 12 discriminate

seckel: 4 pear

seclude: bar 4 deny, hide 5 debar, expel 6 recess, remove, retire, screen 7 exclude, isolate, protect, retreat 8 cloister, prohibit, separate, withdraw 9 segregate, sequester 10 quarantine

secluded: 5 aloof, apart 6 remote, secret 7 private, retired 8 excepted, solitary 9 quiescent

second: aid 4 abet, back, echo, time 5 other 6 assist, attend, backer, handle, moment, ratify 7 another, confirm, endorse, forward, further, instant, succeed, support, sustain 8 inferior 9 assistant, encourage, imperfect, prototype, reinforce, secondary, supporter, viscosity 10 additional 11 corroborate, subordinate 13 supplementary

second childhood: 6 dotage 8 senility

second-rate: 6 shabby 8 inferior, mediocre

second sight: ESP 9 intuition 12 clairvoyance

second-story man: 5 thief 7 burglar

second team: 6 scrubs 9 yannigans 11 substitutes

secondary: bye 5 minor 6 deputy 8 delegate, inferior 9 auxiliary, satellite 10 accidental 11 subordinate, unessential

color: 5 green 6 orange, purple

proposition: 5 lemma

secondary school: 4 high, prep 5 lycee(F.) 7 academy 10 realschule(G.), vocational

secondhand: old 4 used, worn 6 resold 7 derived 8 borrowed 10 unoriginal

dealer: 6 ragman 7 junkman

secret: 4 dark, dern, hide, rune 5 blind, cabal, close, inner, privy 6 arcane, arcana, closet, covert, hidden, occult, remote, stolen 7 arcanum, cryptic, furtive, mystery, obscure, privacy, private, privity, retired, unknown 8 discreet, esoteric, eyes-only, intimate, mystical, reticent, secluded, stealthy 9 clancular, concealed, intrinsic, recondite, seclusion, secretive, underhand 10 confidence 11 clandestine, concealment 12 confidential, hugger-mugger 13 surreptitious, under-the-table

secret agent: spy 8 emissary, saboteur 10 counterspy

secret place: 6 adytum 7 retreat, sanctum

secretaire: 4 desk 10 escritoire

secretary: 4 desk 5 clerk 8 recorder 9 confidant 10 amanuensis

secrete: 4 bury, hide, ooze, stow 5 exude 7 conceal, store up

secretion: 3 gum, sap 4 bile, laap, lerp, milk 5 juice, latex, mucus, resin, sudor, sweat 6 saliva 9 exudation

sect: 4 clan, cult, part 5 class, group, order, party 6 school 7 faction 8 religion 9 following 10 philosophy 12 denomination

distinguishing word: 10 shibboleth

sectarian: 7 bigoted, heretic 8 apostate 9 dissenter 12 narrow-minded 13 nonconformist 17 denominationalist

section: 4 area, pane, part 5 piece, slice 6 canton 7 portion, segment 8 division 9 signature 11 subdivision

concluding: 8 epilogue

section hand: 6 worker 7 crewman, laborer

sector: 4 area, part 8 division 10 semicircle

secular: lay 4 laic 5 civil 6 carnal, laique(F.), vulgar 7 earthly, profane, worldly 10 temporal 9 temporary 17 nonecclesiastical

secure: buy, get, pot, tie 4 bail, bind, bolt,

easy, fast, firm, gird, moor, nail, safe, sure, tape 5 chain, guard, siker, spike, trice, truss 6 anchor, assure, clinch, defend, fasten, obtain, sicker, stable, strong 7 acquire, assured, certain, procure, protect 8 à couvert, conserve 9 confident, constrain, guarantee 10 batten down, dependable 11 trustworthy, undisturbed 13 overconfident

security: 4 bail, bond, ease, gage 5 guard 6 pledge, safety, surety 7 defense, hostage, shelter 8 guaranty, warranty 9 assurance, certainty, guarantee, insurance, stability 10 confidence, protection

sedan: car 4 auto, limo 5 chair 10 automobile

sedate: 4 calm, cool, dope, drug 5 douce, grave, quiet, sober, staid 6 demure, proper, serene, solemn 7 earnest, serious, settled 8 composed, decorous 9 dignified, unruffled 10 put to sleep 12 tranquillize 13 contemplative, dispassionate, imperturbable

sedative: 6 remedy 7 aconite, bromide, chloral, nervine 8 barbital, lenitive 9 paregoric 10 palliative 12 sleeping pill 13 tranquillizer, sleep-inducing

sedent: 6 seated 7 sitting
opposite: 9 analeptic

sedentary: 5 inert 7 settled, sitting 8 inactive, slothful, tranquil 10 deliberate, motionless, stationary

sederunt: 7 session, sitting 8 assembly

sedge: sag 5 brood, flock 7 bulrush, hassock
genus of: 5 carex 7 scirpus

sediment: lee 4 crap, silt 5 dregs, magma, waste 6 bottom, refuse 7 deposit, grounds, residue 8 settling

sedition: 4 coup 6 revolt, strife, tumult 7 treason 9 coup d'etat, rebellion 10 dissension, dissention, turbulence 12 insurrection

seduce: 4 lure 5 charm, decoy, tempt 6 allure, betray, enamor, entice 7 corrupt, debauch, mislead 8 inveigle

seducer: 4 beau 7 Don Juan 8 Casanova, Lothario 11 philanderer

sedulous: 4 busy 8 diligent, untiring 9 assiduous, laborious, unwearied 10 persistent 11 industrious, painstaking, persevering, unremitting

see: spy 4 espy, hear, ibid, look, meet, rank, scry, seat, view 5 chair, power 6 attend, behold, descry, detect, escort, notice, office, throne 7 diocese, discern, examine, inspect, observe, undergo, witness 8 cathedra, consider, discover, perceive 9 accompany, apprehend, authority, bishopric, encounter, interview, visualize 10 comprehend, experience,

scrutinize, understand

seed: ben, egg, pea, pip, pit, sow 4 germ, milt, tare 5 acorn, drupe, grain, ovule, plant, spore, sperm, stock 6 acinus, bubble, kernel, origin, samara, source 7 capsule, progeny, seedlet 8 ancestry 9 beginning, inoculate, offspring, posterity 10 descendant
apple: pip
aromatic: 5 anise 6 fennel, nutmeg
cell: 4 cyst
coat: pod 4 aril, bran, burr 5 testa
container: bur, pod 6 carpel, legume, loment
flavoring: 5 anise, cumin 6 sesame 7 caraway
immature: 5 ovule
organ: 6 pistil
part: pod 4 aril 5 testa 6 tegman, tunica 9 endosperm
part with: 4 core
poisonous: 7 calabar 9 jequirity 10 castor bean
remove: gin, pit 5 picul
scar: 4 hila(pl.) 5 hilum
vessel: pod 6 carpel, legume

seed leaf: 9 cotyledon

seedless: 7 agamous

seedy: 4 worn 5 tacky 6 shabby 7 scruffy 8 slovenly 11 debilitated

seek: beg, sue try, woo 4 busk, fand, hunt, sick 5 court, crave, essay, probe, quest, scout, trace 6 aspire, follow, fraist, pursue, search 7 attempt, beseech, entreat, examine, explore, inquire, request, solicit 8 endeavor 9 cast about, importune, search out 11 investigate

seeker: 6 hunter, prober, tracer 7 pursuer, zetetic 9 applicant 10 petitioner

seel: 5 blind 8 hoodwink

seem: 4 look 5 feign 6 appear 7 pretend 8 manifest

seeming: 5 false 8 apparent, illusory

seemingly: 5 quasi 10 apparently, supposedly

seemly: fit 5 right 6 comely, decent, proper, rather, suited 7 fitting 8 decently, decorous, graceful, handsome, passably, suitable, suitably 10 becomingly 13 appropriately

seen (see also see): 7 visible

seep: run 4 leak, ooze 5 exude 7 trickle 8 transude 9 percolate 10 infiltrate

seer: 4 sage 5 augur, sybil 6 mystic, oracle, scryer 7 augurer, diviner, prophet, wise man 9 predictor, spectator 10 forecaster, foreteller, soothsayer 11 clairvoyant, Nostradamus 14 prognosticator

seesaw: 6 teeter, tilter, totter 9 alternate, crossruff, vacillate 10 reciprocal

seethe: hum 4 boil, fume, soak, stew, teem

5 steep 6 bubble, buller, decoct 7 blubber 8 saturate

segment: arc 4 part 5 piece, tmema 6 cantle, divide, set off, somite 7 isomere, portion, section 8 division, fragment, metamere, separate
body: 8 somatome
of crustacean: 6 telson

segregate: 4 part 5 sever 6 divide, select 7 exclude, isolate, seclude 8 classify, separate

seine: net 5 trawl

Seine tributary: 4 Aube, Eure, Oise 5 Marne

seism: 10 earthquake

seity: 8 selfhood 13 individuality

seize: bag, cap, cly, cop, hap, nab, net 4 bind, bite, claw, fang, grab, grip, hent, hook, prey, take, trap 5 annex, catch, clink, grasp, reave, ravin, usurp, wrest 6 affect, arrest, attach, attack, betake, clinch, clutch, collar, fasten, kidnap, ravene, snatch, strike 7 afflict, capture, grabble, grapnel, possess, prehend 8 arrogate 9 apprehend, deprehend, lay hold of, raptorize 10 comprehend, confiscate, understand 11 appropriate
for debt: 6 attach 8 distrain 9 garnishee

seizure: fit 6 attack, stroke 10 androlepsy 11 androlepsia, manucapture

Sekhet's husband: 4 Ptah

seladang: 4 gaur 6 animal 7 buffalo

seldom: 4 rare 6 rarely 10 infrequent 12 infrequently

select: opt 4 cull, draw, name, pick, wale 5 allot, elect, elite 6 assign, choice, choose, chosen, exempt, picked, prefer 7 the best 8 eximious 9 excellent, exclusive, segregate 10 fastidious, particular 11 outstanding

selection: 5 piece 7 analect, excerpt, passage 10 collection

selective: 6 fussy, picky 6 choosy 8 eclectic 9 demanding

Selene: 4 Luna, moon

selenium: *compound:* 7 selenid 8 selenide
soft acid: 8 selenate

self: ego, own, sel(Sc.), soi(F.) 4 same, very 5 being 6 myself 7 himself 8 personal 9 identical 10 particular 11 personality
killing of: 7 suicide 8 felo-de-se
pert. to: 8 personal

self-acting: 9 automatic

self-assertion: 6 egoism, vanity

self-centered: 8 stable 7 selfish 8 egotistic 10 egocentric

self-confidence: 5 poise 6 aplomb 8 presence 9 composure

self-contained: 4 calm, cool 8 composed, reserved 9 collected 11 independent 15 uncommunicative

self-control: 4 will 8 calmness 10 equanimity, moderation 11 forbearance

self-defense: 4 judo 6 boxing, karate 7 fencing, j(i)ujitsu, j(i)ujutsu 8 fighting

self-denial: 10 abstinence, asceticism, puritanism 11 forbearance

self-esteem: 5 pride 6 egoism, vanity 7 egotism 9 assurance

self-evident: 5 clear 7 certain, obvious 8 truistic 9 axiomatic

self-examination: 13 introspection

self-generated: 11 spontaneous

self-government: 8 autonomy 11 self-control 12 independence

self-important: 7 pompous

self-love: 6 vanity 7 conceit, egotism

self-possessed: 4 calm, cool 6 cooler 8 composed 11 undisturbed 12 strong-willed

self-reproach: rue 6 regret 7 remorse 9 penitence 10 contrition

self-respect: 5 pride 6 vanity

self-righteous: 11 pharisaical

self-satisfied: 4 smug, vain 6 jaunty 10 complacent

self-subsistence: 12 independence

selfish: 6 stingy 7 hoggish 9 dissocial, egotistic 10 egocentric, egomaniacal 12 self-centered

selfsame: 9 identical

sell: 4 bilk, cant, deal, dump, dupe, give, gull, hand, hawk, hoax, vend 5 cheat, trade, trick, yield 6 barter, betray, impose, market, peddle, retail 7 auction, bargain, deceive, deliver, dispose 8 convince, persuade, transfer 9 negotiate, wholesale
out: 6 desert, betray 8 inform on
over official rate: 5 scalp

seller: 6 dealer, seller, sutler, trader, vender, vendor 7 peddler 8 salesman 9 tradesman 10 saleswoman, saltcellar

selling place: See market

selvage: 4 edge, list 5 gouge 6 border, margin 8 sticking

semblance: air 4 copy, face, form, look, mask 5 guise, image 6 aspect, figure 7 pretext 8 likeness, pretense 10 apparition, appearance, conformity, likelihood, similarity, similitude, simulacrum 11 countenance, presumption, resemblance 14 representation

Semele: *brother:* 9 Polydorus
father: 6 Cadmus
sister: 3 Ino 5 Agave
son: 7 Bacchus 8 Dionysos 9 Dionysius

semester: 4 half, term 6 course, period

semi: 4 half

semiape: 5 lemur

semidiameter: 6 radius

seminar: 6 course, school 7 meeting 10 conference, discussion

seminary: 6 school 7 academy, college 11 institution

Seminole Indian chief: 7 Osceola

Semiramis: *husband:* 5 Ninus
kingdom: 7 Babylon

Semite: Jew 4 Arab 6 Hebrew 7 Moabite 8 Aramaean, Assyrian 9 Canaanite 10 Babylonian, Phoenician
god: 4 Baal 5 Anath, Hadad 6 Moloch 7 Shamash
language: 4 Geez 6 Arabic, Hebrew, Syrian 7 Hebraic, Maltese
people: 6 Shagia 7 Shaigia 9 Shaikiyeh

semolina: 4 meal, suji 5 flour, sujee 6 groats

semper: 6 always

semper fidelis: 14 always faithful

sempiternal: 4 ever 7 endless, eternal 11 everlasting

senate: 5 boule, divan 7 council 8 assembly 11 legislature

senator: 5 solon 8 lawmaker 10 legislator

send: 4 haul, mail, ship 5 drive, grant, impel, issue, relay, speed, thrill 6 bestow, commit, convey, depute, ordain, propel 7 address, consign, delight, deliver, dismiss, forward, inflict, project 8 delegate, dispatch, transmit 9 broadcast, discharge, vouchsafe 10 commission
back: 5 remit 6 remand, return
down: 5 demit
for: 5 order 6 summon
forth: 4 emit 6 effuse 7 emanate
out: 4 beam, emit 5 exile 6 depot, export
to obscurity: 8 relegate
packing: 7 dismiss 9 discharge
up: 4 jail 6 parody, satire 7 take-off 8 imprison

Senegal: *capital:* 5 Dakar
gazelle: 5 korin
language: 5 Serer, Wolof 6 French
monetary unit: 5 franc
mountain: 6 Gounou
religion: 5 Islam
river: 6 Gambia 7 Senegal
timber: 9 cailcedra

senescent: 5 aging

senile: old 4 aged, weak 5 aging 6 daffle, dotard, infirm 7 ancient, elderly, rickety 8 decrepit 9 doddering 12 feeble-minded 13 deteriorating

senility: 6 dotage 8 caducity

senior: 4 aine, dean 5 doyen, elder, older 7 ancient, student 8 alderman, superior 13 undergraduate

senior citizen: 10 golden-ager

seniority: age 5 state 6 status 7 quality 8 priority 9 authority 10 precedence
by birth: 13 primogeniture

Sennacherib: *father:* 6 Sargon
son: 8 Sharezer

sensation: 5 sense 6 marvel, thrill 7 emotion, feeling 8 interest 10 appearance, experience, perception 11 sensibility 12 great success
lacking: 4 numb

sensational: 5 lurid 6 superb, yellow 8 eloquent, exciting 9 emotional, startling, thrilling 12 melodramatic

sense: 4 feel, mind, pith 5 touch 6 import, intuit, reason, sanity, wisdom 7 feeling, meaning 8 judgment, perceive, prudence 9 apprehend, awareness, sensation, sentience, soundness, substance 10 appreciate, brainpower, cognizance, comprehend, perception 11 sensibility 12 intelligence 13 consciousness, sensitiveness, understanding 14 susceptibility

Sense and Sensibility author: 6 Austen

sense organ: 3 ear, eye 4 nose, skin 5 nerve 6 tongue 8 receptor

senseless: mad 4 dumb, numb 5 blind, inane 6 simple, stupid, unwise 7 foolish, idiotic 9 insensate, unfeeling 10 half-witted, insensible, irrational 11 meaningless, nonsensical, purposeless, unconscious 12 unreasonable 13 unintelligent

sensible: 5 aware, privy 7 prudent 8 rational 10 reasonable, responsive 11 cognizant of

sensitive: raw 4 nice, sore 5 acute, alive 6 pliant, tender, touchy 8 delicate 9 receptive 10 compatible, responsive 11 susceptible 14 impressionable
plant: 6 mimosa

sensual: 4 lewd 5 alive, gross 6 carnal, coarse, fleshy, sexual 7 bestial, brutish, fleshly, lustful, worldly 9 seductive 10 lascivious, licentious, voluptuous 11 materialistic

sentence: rap 4 doom 5 award, axiom, maxim, motto 6 decide, decree, saying 7 adjudge, condemn, opinion, passage, proverb 8 aphorism, decision, judgment 9 destinate, proscribe, statement 12 adjudication, pass judgment 13 determination
consisting of one word: 7 monepic
construction: 6 syntax
describe: 5 parse
part: 6 clause, phrase, object 7 subject 9 predicate
same backwards and forwards: 10 palindrome
type: 6 simple 7 complex 8 compound

sententious: 5 pithy, short, terse 7 compact, concise, laconic 10 meaningful, moralistic, proverbial

sentient: 5 alive, aware 6 living 7 feeling 8 sensible 9 conscious

sentiment: 4 idea, love 5 maxim, toast 6 lyrics, saying 7 emotion, feeling, leaning, meaning, opinion 9 sensation, substance 10 perception 11 sensibility 14 susceptibility

sentimental: 5 gushy, loving 7 maudlin, mawkish, schmalz 8 romantic, schmaltz 9 fantastic 10 idealistic, lovey-dovey, moonstruck 11 susceptible, tear-jerking 13 lackadaisical

sentinel: 5 guard, vedet(Sp.), videt(Sp.), watch 6 bantay(P.I.), sentry, warder 7 soldier 8 watchman 10 factionary, watchtower

sepal: 4 leaf

separate: 4 bolt, cull, deal, free, know, part, rend, rift, shed, sift, slay, sley, sort 5 alone, aloof, apart, aside, break, hedge, ravel, sever, space, strip 6 assort, breach, cleave, decide, deduct, depart, detach, divide, refine, remove, secede, single, sleave, sleeve, sunder, winnow 7 break up, disjoin, dispart, diverse, divorce, expanse, isolate, segment 8 abstract, alienate, detached, discrete, disperse, dissolve, distinct, disunite, secluded, solitary, withdraw 9 demarcate, different, discharge, disengage, dismember, disparate, eliminate, segregate, withdrawn 10 disconnect, dispossess, dissociate, distribute, individual, quarantine, sejunctive 11 disembodied, distinctive, distinguish, fractionate, independent, part company, precipitate, unconnected 12 disassociate, disconnected, disintegrate

separation: 4 gulf 6 schism, tmesis 7 diacope, divorce 8 distance 9 apartheid, cessation, partition 14 discontinuance

separatist: 8 apostate 9 dissenter

separatists: 8 Pilgrims, Zoarites 9 Bimmelers

Sephardim: 4 Jews

country of origin: 5 Spain 8 Portugal

dialect: 6 Ladino

sepia: dun 5 color 7 pigment 9 red-yellow 10 cuttlebone, cuttlefish

sepiment: 5 hedge 7 defense 9 enclosure

sepiolite: 10 meerschaum

sepoy: 9 policeman

seps: 5 snake 6 lizard 7 serpent

sept: 4 clan, fine 5 seven, tribe 8 ancestry

septic: 5 putrid, rotten 8 diseased 9 infective

septum: 4 wall 9 partition

sepulcher: 4 bury, tomb 5 grave, inter, vault 6 entomb 8 monument 10 repository

subterranean vault: 8 catacomb

sepulchral: 4 deep 6 gloomy, hollow 7 charnel 8 funereal

sequacious: 6 pliant 7 ductile, servile 9 attendant, compliant, dependent, following, malleable

sequel (see also **sequence**): 4 next 5 issue 6 effect, result, upshot 7 outcome 8 follower, follow up, sequitur 9 aftermath, following, inference 10 conclusion 11 consequence, continuance 12 continuation

sequence (see also **sequel**): run, set 5 gamut, order, suite 6 course, series, tenace 8 straight 10 succession 11 progression

sequential: 9 following 10 continuous, processive, succeeding 11 consecutive

sequester: 5 seize 6 enisle 7 isolate, seclude 8 separate 10 appropriate 11 confiscate

sequestered: 5 alone 6 lonely, seized 7 private, recluse, removed, retired 8 isolated, secluded, solitary, withdrew 9 concealed, renounced, separated, withdrawn 10 cloistered, disclaimed, segregated 11 confiscated 12 appropriated

sequin: 4 disk 7 spangle

sequoia: 7 redwood

serac: 5 block 11 ice pinnacle

seraglio: 5 harem, serai 6 zenana 7 brothel 8 lodgings 9 enclosure, warehouse

serai: 8 lodgings, seraglio 9 rest house 11 caravansary 12 caravanserai

serape: 5 cloak, shawl 7 blanket

seraph: 5 angel 6 cherub

seraphic: 4 pure 5 pious 7 angelic, lovable, refined, sublime 8 beatific, cherubic 9 unworldly

Serb: 4 Slav

Serbia: See **Yugoslavia**

sere, sear: dry, wax 4 worn 5 dried, talon 6 yellow 7 parched, several, various 8 scorched, separate, withered 10 desiccated, threadbare

serenade: 6 aubade 8 nocturne, serenata

burlesque: 8 shivaree 9 charivari 10 callithump

serene: 4 calm, cool, damp 5 clear, light, quiet 6 bright, placid, sedate, serein, steady 7 pacific 8 composed, decorous, peaceful, tranquil 9 collected, impassive, unruffled 10 unobscured 11 undisturbed 13 dispassionate, imperturbable

serenity: 4 calm 5 peace 6 repose 7 balance 10 equanimity

serf: 4 esne, peon 5 churl, helot, slave 6 servus, thrall, vassal 7 bondman, peasant, villein 8 bondsman, hireling

female: 5 neife 6 colona

serge: 7 worsted

sergeant: 6 chiaus, noncom 7 topkick 9 attendant

sergeant fish: 5 cobia 6 robalo

series: set 4 list 5 chain, gamut, suite, train 6 catena, course 8 beadroll, category, sequence, seriatim 9 gradation 10 continuity, succession

arranged in: 6 serial 7 seriate 11 installment

serious: 4 deep, grim, hard, keen 5 grave, heavy, sober, staid 6 demure, sedate, severe, solemn 7 austere, capital, earnest, weighty 9 important, momentous 10 no-nonsense, poker-faced, thoughtful 11 considerate

serment: 4 oath 9 sacrament

sermon: 4 talk 5 psalm, speak 6 homily 7 address, lecture 8 harangue 9 collation, discourse, preaching 10 admonition

study of: 10 homiletics

subject: 4 text

sermonic: 5 grave 8 didactic

sermonize: 6 advise, preach 8 admonish, moralize 9 discourse

seroon: 4 bale 7 package

serotine: bat

serous: 4 thin 6 watery

serow: 5 goral, jagla 8 antelope

serpent (see also **snake**): 5 devil, fiend 7 entwine, reptile

elapine: 4 naia, naja

mythological: Ahi 5 Apepi, Dahak, Hydra 6 ellops, dragon 8 basilisk 11 Amphisbaena

nine-headed: 5 Hydra

pert. to: 5 anguine

thousand-headed: 5 Sesha 6 Ananta

victim: 7 Laocoon

worship of: 6 ophism

serpentine: 4 file, wily, worm 5 snaky 7 devious, sinuous, turning, winding 8 fiendish, tempting 10 circuitous, convoluted, meandering

variety: 10 antigorite

serpigo: 5 tinea 6 herpes, tetter 8 ringworm

serrate: 7 notched, toothed 11 denticulate

serried: 5 dense 6 massed, packed 7 compact, crowded 10 continuous

serum: 4 whey 5 fluid 9 antitoxin

servable: 6 usable 10 functional

servant: 4 amah, bata, cook, dasi, esne, girl, help, hewe, hind, maid, maty, mozo, syce 5 alila, biddy, boots, chela, gilly, groom, hamal, nurse, scout, slave, usher, valet 6 batman, bearer, bildar, butler, chakar, ewerer, flunky, garcon, gillie, hamaul, hammal, harlot, helper, khamal, menial, tenant, varlet, vassal 7 bondman, famulus, flunkey, footman, hummaul 8 chasseur, domestic, retainer, sergeant, servitor 9 atriensis 11 chamberlain, subordinate

female: 4 amah, maid 5 wench 6 slavey

garment: 5 apron 6 livery 7 uniform

head: 6 butler

male: 5 valet 6 butler, lackey

of God: 4 monk, pope 5 friar, rabbi 6 bishop, priest 8 chaplain, minister, preacher 10 Holy Father, missionary

of nobleman: 7 equerry

pert. to: 8 famulary

retired: 8 emeritus

serve: act, aid 4 abet, give, help, mess, pass, suit, tend, wait 5 avail, cater, frame, ladle, treat 6 answer, assist, attend, do good, succor 7 advance, benefit, be of use, bestead, deliver, forward, further 8 do a hitch, function, minister 9 officiate 10 distribute

server: urn 4 tray 6 salver, waiter 7 caterer 9 assistant, lazy-Susan

Servia: See Serbia

service: use 4 mass, rite 5 favor, throw 6 employ, repair, supply 7 chakari, retinue, utility 8 ceremony, kindness, ministry 11 maintenance 12 installation, ministration

military: 4 duty 5 hitch 7 stretch 10 enlistment 12 conscription

public: 7 utility

service charge: fee, tip

serviceable: 4 kind 6 useful 7 durable, helpful, lasting 8 obliging 9 available, practical 10 beneficial, commodious

serviette: 6 napkin

servile: 4 base, bond, mean 6 abject, menial, sordid 7 fawning, slavish 8 cringing, enslaved 9 dependent, parasitic, truckling 10 obsequious, sequacious, submissive 11 subservient, sycophantic

Servite: 5 friar 9 mendicant

servitor: 6 beadle, menial, squire 7 servant, soldier 8 adherent, follower 9 assistant, attendant 10 apprentice 12 exhibitioner

servitude: 4 yoke 7 bondage, peonage, serfdom, service, slavery 8 sentence 9 captivity, vassalage 10 subjection

sesame: til 4 herb, teel 5 benne 7 passkey 8 ajonjoli, password

seed: 7 gingili, tilseed

session: 4 term 6 assize 7 meeting, sitting 8 sederunt 10 assemblage, conference

set: fix, gel, lay, put, sit 4 bent, clan, club, cock, crew, gang, jell, laid, park, port, pose, prim, ring, seat, stud, suit 5 align, aline, brood, elect, elite, embed, fixed, group, imbed, place, plant, posit, range, ready, rigid, scene, staid, stake, stand, suite 6 adjust, assign, cement, circle, clique, define, direct, formal, harden, impose, impost, ordain, series, settle 7 appoint, arrange, bearing, company, confirm, congeal, coterie, decline, deposit, dispose, instate, platoon, station, stiffen 8 attitude, decorate, exchange, immobile, moveless, regulate, solidify 9

coagulate, collocate, designate, determine, establish, immovable, obstinate,
prescribe, stabilize 10 assortment, collection, constitute, stationary

about: 5 begin, start

afloat: 6 launch

apart: 5 elect 6 exempt 7 isolate, reserve,
seclude 8 allocate, dedicate, separate 9
segregate, sequester

aside: 4 void 5 annul, table 6 except, reject 7 discard, dismiss, earmark, exclude, reserve 8 overrule, separate

at naught: 4 defy 7 despise 9 disregard

back: 4 loss 5 check, delay 6 defeat, hinder 7 relapse, reverse, setback

down: fix 4 land, seat 5 abase, enter,
place, write 6 alight, depose, encamp,
ordain, reckon, record, regard, relate 7
appoint, descend, resolve, slacken 8
consider, estimate, register 9 attribute,
determine, establish, humiliate, prescribe

forth: 5 adorn, offer, state 6 expone, expose 7 arrange, commend, display,
enounce, exhibit, explain, expound, present, promote, propone, publish 8 announce, decorate, manifest 9 interpret,
translate 10 promulgate

free: See **liberate**

fresh: 5 relay

in motion: 5 start 6 excite 8 activate

in operation: 4 jump, move, skip 5 slide,
start 6 launch, plunge, spring

in order: 4 file, tidy 5 align, aline 6 adjust
7 arrange

of players: 4 team 5 squad

of rules: 4 code

off: 5 start 8 mobilize 10 compensate

on end: 5 upend 10 topsyturvy

on fire: 4 tind 5 light 6 kindle

out: 4 head, plan 5 adorn, allot, equip, extol, issue, limit, start 6 design, embark,
escort, outfit, recite 7 present, publish
8 describe, proclaim 9 embellish 10
promulgate

right: 4 file 5 align, aline, amend, order 6
adjust, repair 7 arrange, correct, redress, take off 11 systematize

thickly: 4 stud

to: 4 bout 5 fight 6 fracas 7 contest 8
struggle

TV: box 8 boob tube

up: 4 post 5 build, erect, exalt, found,
hoist, raise, treat 7 appoint, arrange, elevate 8 organize 9 establish

Set: 5 deity 9 god of evil

brother: 6 Osiris

father: Geb

mother: Nut

victim: 6 Osiris

wife: 8 Nephthys

seta: 6 chaeta 7 bristle

setaceous: 7 bristly

seth: 6 banker 8 merchant

Seth: *brother:* 4 Abel, Cain

descendant: 4 Enos 7 Sethite

father: 4 Adam

son: 4 Enos

seton: 6 suture

setout: 4 fuss 5 get-up 6 outfit 7 costume,
display, exhibit 9 beginning 10 excitement 13 entertainment

settee: 4 seat, sofa 5 bench, divan

setter: dog 5 Irish 6 Gordon 7 English 10
compositor

setting: 4 eggs, trap, pave 5 decor, scene,
snare, scena(It.) 6 locale 7 scenery 8
mounting 9 hardening 10 background,
thickening 11 environment, mise-en-
scene 12 surroundings

settle: fix, pay, sag, set 4 calm, firm, lend,
nest, root, seat, sink, toit 5 affix, agree,
audit, bench, clear, couch, lodge, order,
perch, plant, quiet, serve, solve 6 accord, adjust, alight, assign, decide, locate, purify, reduce, render, secure,
soothe, wind up 7 appoint, arrange,
clarify, compone, compose, confirm,
conform, deposit, depress, dispose, pri-
vide, resolve, silence, subside 8 colonize, compound, conclude, ensconce,
regulate 9 designate, determine, establish, habituate, liquidate, touch down
10 adjudicate, administer, strengthen
11 accommodate, tranquilize

strike: 7 mediate

settled: 4 alit, fast, firm 5 ended, fixed,
staid 6 formed, sedate 7 certain, decided, peopled, statary, testate 8 decorous
9 inerratic, sedentary, steadfast 10
consistent, contracted, determined, inveterate, unchanging 11 established

in advance: 13 predetermined

settlement: dos 4 camp, lees 5 abode,
dregs 6 colony, hamlet 7 payment, village 8 decision, disposal, fixation, sediment 9 aldeament, community, residence 10 adjustment, compromise,
conclusion, habitation, occupation, regulation 11 arrangement 12 coloniza-
tion, satisfaction 13 clarification, determination, establishment

arrange: 9 negotiate

study of: 8 ekistics

settler: 6 sooner, vessel 7 planter, pioneer
8 colonist, emigrant 9 colonizer, immigrant 10 forehearth, receptacle

American: 7 Pilgrim, Puritan

seven: 4 zeta

days and nights: 8 sennight

deadly sins: 4 envy, lust 5 anger, pride,
sloth 8 gluttony 12 covetousness

dice roll: 7 natural

group of: 6 heptad, septet 8 hebdomad

Seven Against Thebes: 6 Tydeus 8 Adrastus, Capaneus, Eteocles 10 Amphiaraus, Hippomedon, Polyneices 13 Parthenopaeus

Seven Churches: 6 Sardis, Smyrna 7 Ephesos 8 Laodicea, Pergamos, Thyatira 12 Philadelphia

Seven Dwarfs: Doc 5 Dopey, Happy 6 Grumpy, Sleepy, Sneezy 7 Bashful

seven-fold: 8 septuple

seven hills: See *Rome: hill*

seven-sided: 10 heptagonal

seventh heaven: 7 ecstasy

sever: cut 4 deal, know, part, rend, slit 5 break 6 breach, cleave, depart, detach, divide, sunder 7 dispart, divorce 8 disunite, separate 9 dismember 10 disconnect, dissociate 12 disassociate

from neck: 6 behead 9 decollate 10 decapitate

several: few 4 many, some 6 divers, single, sundry 7 diverse, not a few, various 8 distinct, peculiar 9 different 10 individual, respective

minimum: 5 three

severe: bad 4 cold, dear, dere, dour, dure, grim, hard, keen, sore, tart 5 acute, cruel, grave, gruff, harsh, rethe, rigid, rough, sharp, sober, stark, stern, stiff 6 biting, bitter, chaste, coarse, sedate, simple, solemn, strict, trying, unkind 7 ascetic, austere, caustic, chronic, condign, crucial, cutting, drastic, extreme, intense, painful, serious, spartan, violent 8 captious, exacting, grievous, rigorous, scathing 9 difficult, draconian, inclement, strenuous, stringent, unsparing 10 afflictive, astringent, censorious, forbidding, iron-willed, methodical, oppressive, restrained 12 unornamented

severity: 8 acerbity, acrimony, asperity 10 simplicity, unkindness

Seville cathedral tower: 7 Giralda

sew: hog, sow 4 bind, darn, join, mend, seam 5 baste, broth, drain, sewer, shirr, smock, unite 6 fasten, needle, stitch, suture 7 pottage

up: end 6 settle 7 exhaust 8 conclude 10 monopolize

with gathers: 4 full 5 shirr

sewan: 5 beads, money 6 wampum

Seward's Folly: 6 Alaska

sewer: 5 drain 6 tunnel 7 channel, conduit, servant 10 seamstress

opening: 7 manhole

sewing machine: *inventor:* 9 Elias Howe

part: 8 plicator 10 zipperfoot

sex: 6 gender 10 copulation

hormone: 7 steroid

sexless: 6 neuter 7 epicene

sexton: 6 shamus, verger, warden 7 sa-

crist 9 sacristan 12 underofficer

sextuplet: 7 sestole 8 sestolet

sexual: 5 gamic 6 carnal, erotic, loving 7 amatory 10 lascivious

continence: 8 chastity

inclination: 4 urge 6 libido

sexy: 4 racy 5 spicy 6 carnal, erotic 7 amatory, earthly

Seychelles Islands: 4 Mahe 7 La Digue, Praslin

capital: 8 Victoria

sha: 5 sheep, urial 6 nahoor, oorial

shabby: old 4 base, mean, worn 5 dowdy, faded, seedy 6 paltry, ragged, scurvy 7 outworn, unkempt 8 beggarly, dog-eared, shameful, tattered, unworthy 10 despicable, gone to seed, threadbare 11 disgraceful 12 contemptible, deteriorated

shack: coe 4 plug 5 cabin, catch, chase, hovel 6 lean-to, refuse, wander

shackle: tie 4 band, bind, bolt, bond, curb, gird, gyve, idle, iron, loaf, ring 5 chain, gyves 6 fetter, hamper, hinder, hobble, pinion, secure 7 confine, manacle, trammel 8 coupling, restrain 10 fetterlock

shad: 4 fish 5 alose 6 allice 7 crappie, herring, mojarra

shaddock: 5 fruit 6 pomelo 10 grapefruit

shade: bar, dim, hue 4 dark, dull, hint, tint, tone, veil 5 color, cover, ghost, hatch, tinge, trace, umbra, vault 6 awning, canopy, darken, degree, nuance, screen, shadow, spirit, sprite, shield 7 curtain, eclipse, foliage, obscure, parasol, phantom, protect, shelter, specter, shutter, umbrage, vestige 8 clearing, darkness, ornament, penumbra 9 adumbrate, gradation, variation 10 apparition, difference, overshadow, protection, silhouette 11 small amount

light: 6 pastel

lines: 5 hatch

of cap: 5 visor

of meaning: 6 nuance

shaded: 7 shadowy 8 screened 10 umbrageous

shaded walk: 4 mall 6 arcade 8 cloister

shadetail: 8 squirrel

shadow (see also shade): dog 4 blot, lurk, omen, tail 5 cleek, cloud 6 attend, follow, shroud, symbol 7 remnant, suggest, vestige 8 penumbra 9 adumbrate 10 apparition, indication, overspread 13 prefiguration

dark cone of: 5 umbra

dispelling: 9 scialytic

figure: 10 silhouette

of death: 5 gloom, Sheol

outline: 10 silhouette

person without: 6 ascian

shadowbox: 4 spar

shadowy: dim 5 faint, vague 6 opaque, umbral, unreal 7 ghostly, obscure, retired 8 adumbral 9 imaginary 10 impalpable, indistinct, overspread, transitory 12 inaccessible 13 unsubstantial

Shadrach: *companion:* 7 Meshach 8 Abednego

persecutor: 14 Nebuchadnezzar

shady: 6 risque 7 shadowy, umbrous 9 dishonest 11 underhanded 12 disreputable, questionable

shaffle: 4 limp 5 shirk 6 hobble, loiter 7 shuffle

shaft: bar, pit, ray, rod 4 axle, beam, bolt, cone, fust, hole, pole, stem, tige, tole 5 arbor, arrow, helve, heuch, heugh, irony, lance, scape, shank, spear, spire, stalk, stele, thill, trunk 6 arbour, column, groove, handle, pillar, tongue, upcast 7 chamber, chimney, Maypole, missile, obelisk, spindle 8 gatepost, monolith 9 flagstaff 10 air passage

column: 4 fust 5 scape, verge

feather: 5 scape

part: 4 orlo

plant: 4 axis

vehicle: 5 thill

shag: mat, nap 4 hair, mane, mass, pile, toss, wool 5 chase, fetch, fiber, shake 6 follow, rascal, refuse 7 garment, thicket, tobacco 9 cormorant 10 blackguard

shaggy: 5 bushy, furry, hairy, nappy, rough 7 hirsute, scrubby, unkempt, villous 8 straggly, textured 10 unpolished

shagreen: 4 skin 7 leather, rawhide 8 galuchat

shaitan, sheitan: 5 devil, fiend

shake: bob, jar, jog, wag 4 free, jolt, move, pass, rese, rock, shog, stir, sway, toss, wave 5 churn, drink, eject, greet, quake, shock, steal, swing, trill 6 depart, dither, dodder, goggle, hustle, joggle, quaver, quiver, rattle, shiver, totter, tremor, weaken 7 agitate, chatter, concuss, disturb, fluster, tremble, unnerve, vibrate 8 brandish, convulse, dislodge, enfeeble, flourish 10 earthquake

down: bed, con 5 dance 6 extort, search, settle, try out 9 blackmail

off: 4 shed 6 excuss 8 disagree

up: 6 jumble 7 agitate 10 clean-sweep

Shaker: 4 sect

founder: Lee

Shakespeare: *actor:* 4 Ward 5 Booth 6 Burton 7 Garrick, Gielgud, Olivier, Sothern 8 Modjeska 9 Barrymore

alternate author: 5 Bacon

character: 4 Bone, Iago, Iras, Lear, Snug 5 Biron, Cleon, Henry, Regan, Romeo, Speed, Timon 6 Banquo, Hamlet, Juliet, Oberon, Portia, Simple 7 Antonio, Cassius, Othello, Richard, Salerio, Shylock, Silence, Slender, Titania 8 Falstaff

elf: 4 Puck

forest: 5 Arden

home: 4 Avon

play: 4 Lear 6 Hamlet 7 Macbeth, Othello 9 Cymbeline 10 The Tempest 11 As You Like It 12 Julius Caesar, Twelfth Night

theater: 5 Globe

wife: Ann

shaking: 4 ague 7 jittery 9 tremulant, tremulous 10 concussion

shako: cap 9 headdress

decoration: 6 pompon

shakti: 5 force, power

shaky: 4 weak 6 groggy, infirm, wabbly, wobbly 7 rickety, unsound 8 insecure 9 tottering, trembling, tremulous, uncertain 10 unreliable 12 questionable

shale: 4 bone, husk, rock 5 metal, slate 8 impurity

shall: may 4 must, will 5 would 7 obliged

shallop: 4 boat 6 dinghy, vessel

shallot: 4 herb, tube 5 onion 8 eschalot

shallow: hat 4 cart, idle, tray, vain, weak 5 shoal 6 basket, flimsy, slight 7 cursory, trivial 9 depthless, frivolous 11 superficial

shalom: 5 peace 8 farewell, greeting

sham: 4 fake, hoax, mock 5 bogus, cheat, dummy, false, feign, fraud, trick 6 assume, bunyip, chouse, deceit, delude, device, duffer, humbug, shoddy 7 deceive, feigned, forgery, grimace, mockery, pretend 8 imposter, pretense, trickery 9 brummagem, deception, hypocrisy, imitation, imposture, pretended, trickster 10 artificial, fictitious, simulacrum, substitute 11 counterfeit, make-believe

shamal: 4 wind

shaman: 4 monk 6 beggar, priest 8 conjurer 11 medicine man

Shamash: 6 sun god

consort: Aya

messenger: 6 Bunene

worship center: 5 Larsa 6 Sippar

shamble: 5 stall, table 7 bauchle, butcher, shuffle 9 malformed, slaughter

shambles: 4 mess 5 mix-up 8 wreckage 9 confusion

shame: 5 abase, abash 6 assume, bemean, bismer 7 degrade, mortify 8 contempt, disgrace, dishonor 9 embarrass, humiliate 10 repentance 11 degradation, shortcoming 12 illegitimacy 13 embarrassment, mortification

shamefaced: shy 6 humble, modest 7 bashful 9 diffident, regretful

shameful: 4 base, mean 5 gross, wrong 7 ignoble 8 flagrant, improper, indecent, infamous **9** degrading, dishonest **10** outrageous, scandalous, slanderous **11** disgraceful, ignominious, opprobrious **12** contumelious, dishonorable, disreputable, vituperative **13** dishonourable

shameless: 6 arrant, brazen **8** immodest, impudent **9** abandoned, audacious, barefaced **10** unblushing **11** bold as brass

shampoo: 4 lave, wash **5** clean

shamrock land: 4 Eire, Erin **5** Irena **7** Ireland

Shang dynasty: Yin

shanghai: 4 drug, ship **5** seize **6** abduct, coerce, kidnap

Shangri-la: 6 utopia **8** paradise

shank: leg **4** gamb, meat, shin, stem, tang **5** gambe, knife, ladle, ridge, tibia
pert. to: **6** crural

shantung: 4 silk **6** fabric, pongee, tussah

Shantung's capital: 6 Tsinan

shanty: hut **5** cabin, hovel, hutch, lodge, shack **6** leanto **8** chantier, dwelling

shape: fit, hew **4** bend, cast, form, knap, make, mold, plan, tool, trim **5** block, boast, build, carve, feign, frame, guise, image, model, mould, order, state, torus **6** create, decree, design, devise, figure, format, happen, ordain **7** appoint, arrange, conform, contour, fashion, incline, phantom, posture, whittle **8** attitude, contrive **9** condition, determine, structure **10** apparition, appearance, figuration **11** arrangement **13** configuration
different: **8** variform
garden: **7** topiary
in: **4** trim
up: **9** get better

shapeless: 6 deform **8** deformed, formless **9** amorphous, contorted, distorted, misshapen, unshapely

shapely: fit **4** neat, trim **6** decent, gainly **8** suitable **9** beautiful **10** curvaceous **11** symmetrical

shaping machine: 5 edger, lathe **6** shaper

shard: 5 scale, shell **8** fragment, potsherd

share: cut, lot **4** cant, deal, dole, hand, part, rent **5** divvy, enter, quota, ratio, shear, split **6** cleave, divide, impart, moiety, ration **7** partake, portion **8** dividend, division, interest **9** allotment, allowance, apportion, communion, plowshare **10** distribute **11** participate
widow's: **5** dower, dowry, terce, third **6** dowery

sharecropper: 7 metayer **12** tenant farmer

Shari River: See **Cameroon**

shark: 4 gata, haye, mako, tope **5** adept **6** expert, lawyer, usurer **7** dogfish, sharper, sponger **8** drunkard, hybodont, man-

eater, parasite, predator, swindler, thrasher, thresher **9** porbeagle, selachian, trickster **10** hammerhead
blue pointer: **4** mako
genus of: **11** carcharodon
nurse: **4** gata
pilot: **6** remora
small: **4** tope **5** lamia
young: **8** sharklet

sharkskin: 12 cotton fabric

sharp: 4 acid, cold, cute, edgy, fell, gash, gnib, high, keen, nice, sour, tart, wise **5** acrid, acute, adept, alert, brisk, crisp, eager, edged, fiery, harsh, salty, steep, tangy, witty **6** abrupt, active, acuate, astute, barbed, biting, bitter, clever, crafty, crispy, expert, peaked, severe, shrewd, shrill, snelly(Sc.) **7** angular, austere, caustic, cunning, cutting, gingery, grating, intense, lyncean, nipping, painful, piquant, pointed, pungent, rasping, violent, waspish **8** aculeate, distinct, handsome, incisive, piercing, poignant, vigilant, vigorous **9** attentive, beautiful, designing, impetuous, merciless, penetrant, sagacious, sarcastic, trenchant **10** discerning, ungracious **11** acrimonious, intelligent, penetrating, quick-witted, underhanded
to taste: **4** acid **5** acrid

sharp-sighted: 6 astute

sharpen: nib, ted **4** edge, hone, whet **5** grind, point, reset, strop **6** acuate **7** enhance, quicken **9** aggravate, intensify, stimulate **10** cacuminate

sharper: gyp **4** bite **5** cheat, rogue **6** cogger, keener **7** cheater, gambler **8** deceiver, swindler **9** trickster **12** double-dealer

sharpness: 4 edge **6** acumen **8** acrimony, keenness

sharpshooter: 9 sniper **8** marksman

shastra class: 5 sruti **6** purana, smriti, tantra

shatter: 4 blow, dash **5** blast, break, burst, crash, smash, split, wreck **6** batter, damage, impair **7** clatter, derange, destroy, disable, scatter **8** demolish, disorder, disperse, splinter **9** dissipate

shattered: 6 broken **7** damaged **8** broozled, doddered

shave: ace, cut **4** pare, poll, trim **5** cheat, graze, skive **6** glance, rasure, reduce, scrape **7** tonsure, whittle

shaveling: boy **4** monk **5** youth **6** priest **9** hypocrite, stripling **10** cut it close

shavetail: 4 mule **10** lieutenant

shaving: 5 flake, piece **8** ramentum

shawl (see also **vestment**): **4** maud, wrap **5** manta, orale **6** serape(Mex.) **7** amlikar, paisley **8** epiblema

Shawnee Indian chief: 8 Tecumseh, Tecumtha

Shea player: Met

sheaf: 5 bunch 6 bundle 7 cluster

shear: cut 4 clip, gnaw, reap, rend, snip, trim 5 carve, force, mince, prune, sever, shave, strip 6 cleave, divest, fleece, nibble, pierce, remove 7 deprive, scissor, whittle 10 circumcise

shearing machine: 7 cropper

shears: 6 forfex 8 scissors, secateur

sheartail: 4 tern 11 hummingbird

shearwater: 4 crew 6 hagdon, haglet, petrel, puffin

sheatfish: 4 wels 7 catfish

sheath: cot 4 boot, case, skin 5 dress, ocrea, theca, stall 6 forrel, spathe 8 covering, envelope, scabbard

sheathe: 4 bury, case, ceil, dull 5 blunt, cover, glove 6 clothe 7 enclose, envelop

sheave: 5 wheel 6 pulley 9 back water

sheaves: See sheaf

shebang: hut 4 deal 6 affair, outfit 7 concern 8 business 11 contrivance 13 establishment

shed: cut, hut 4 abri(F.), byre, cast, cote, drop, emit, hull, lair, molt, nest, part, pour 5 booth, cabin, hovel, repel, scale, spill, tease 6 belfry, dingle, divest, divide, effuse, hangar, hemmel, impart, lean-to, slough 7 cast off, cottage, diffuse, emanate, radiate, scatter, shelter, testudo, take off 8 disperse, jettison, outhouse, separate, sprinkle, throw out, workshop 9 irradiate, penthouse 11 intersperse, out-building
    skin: 7 ecdysis

shedder: 4 crab 5 peeler, salmon 7 lobster

sheen: 4 fair 5 gleam, gloss, shine, shoes 6 bright, finish, glossy, luster 7 exalted, glisten, glitter, radiant, shimmer, shining 8 lustrous, splendid, splendor 9 beautiful, shininess 10 brightness, glittering 11 illustrious, resplendent

sheep: mug, sha 5 argal, dumba, ovine, urial 6 aoudad, argali, wether 7 bighorn, bleater, karakul, mouflon 8 karakule, moufflon, ruminant 9 blackface
    breed: 4 Horn 6 Dorset, Exmoor, Merino, Romney 7 Cheviot, Delaine, Lincoln, Suffolk 8 Cotswold, Dartmoor 9 Leicester, Southdown, Teeswater 10 Corriedale, Oxford Down, Shropshire
    caretaker: 8 shepherd
    coat: 4 wool 6 fleece
    cry: maa 5 bleat
    dead: 5 braxy, traik
    disease: coe, gid, rot 5 braxy 6 sturdy
    feed: 5 graze 7 pasture
    female: ewe
    male: ram, tup 6 wether 10 bellwether
    mark: 4 smit 5 brand
    meat: 6 mutton
    pathway: 6 roddin 7 rodding

    pen: 5 bught(Sc.) 6 bought(Sc.)
    pert. to: 5 ovine
    wild: sha 4 arui, udad 5 argal, audad, urial 6 aoudad, argali, bharal, nahoor, nayaur 7 mouflon 8 moufflon
    young: hog, teg 4 lamb, tegg 5 heder 6 bident, gimmer, hogget, sheder 7 twinter 8 hoggerel, shearhog 9 four-tooth, shearling

sheep dog: 6 collie 8 shepherd

sheep-like: 4 meek 5 ovine 6 docile

sheepfaced: See sheepish

sheepheaded: 5 silly 6 stupid 12 simpleminded

sheepish: shy 4 meek 5 blate, silly, timid 7 abashed, awkward, bashful, daffish 11 embarrassed

sheepskin: 4 bond, cape 5 basil 6 mouton 7 diploma 9 parchment
    leather: 4 roan

sheepwalk: run 5 range, slait 7 pasture

sheer: 4 fine, mere, pure, thin, turn 5 brant, clear, steep, utter 6 abrupt, bright, swerve 7 deviate, shining, unmixed, utterly 8 absolute, outright 9 deviation, downright, undiluted 10 diaphanous 11 transparent, unqualified 12 change course 13 perpendicular

sheet: air 4 fine, page, rope, sail 5 chain, daily, linen, paper, plate, white 6 expand, lamina, shroud 7 tabloid 8 handbill, pamphlet 9 baking tin, newspaper
    twelvemo: 9 duodecimo

sheeting: 5 linen 6 cotton 7 percale

shelf: 4 bank, berm, bink, reef, sill 5 altar, berme, layer, ledge, shoal 6 gradin, mantel 7 bedrock, bracket, gradine, retable, sandbar, stratum 8 credence, credenza, sandbank 9 banquette 10 pigeonhole

shell: hud, pod 4 boat, bomb, coin, hull, husk, lyre, shot, swad, test 5 balat, cameo, conch, cowry, crust, frame, money, murex, scale, shuck, spoon, testa, troca 6 coffin, concha, cowrie, crusta, dolite, dugout, lamina, lorica, strafe 7 abalone, admiral, bombard, capsule, caracol, dariole, grenade 8 caracole, carapace, covering, exterior, frustule 9 cartridge 10 open fire on, projectile, schoolroom
    beads: 4 peag 6 wampum
    casing: 5 gaine
    defective: dud
    explosive: 4 bomb 7 grenade
    hole: 6 crater
    large: 5 conch
    measuring device: 11 conchometer
    money: 4 peag 5 cowry, peage, sewan, uhllo 6 cowrie, seawan, wampum
    protected with: 8 loricate
    ridge: 4 lira 5 varix 7 varices(pl.)

unexploded: dud
shellac: lac 4 whip 5 resin 6 defeat 7 trounce
shellacking: 6 defeat 7 beating 8 flogging, whipping
Shelley: 4 poet
alias: 5 Ariel
poem: 7 Adonais, Alastor 8 Queen Mab 10 Ozymandias, To a Skylark
shellfire: 6 strafe 7 barrage
shellfish: 5 nacre 6 limpet 7 mollusk 10 crustacean
shell out: pay 4 give 5 spend 8 disburse
shelter: cot, hut, lee 4 abri, barn, camp, cote, fold, gite(F.), herd, howf, port, roof, shed, skug, tent 5 benab, bield, boist, bower, cloak, cover, embay, haven, house, hovel, howff, hutch, shack 6 asylum, burrow, covert, defend, garage, hangar, harbor, hostel, refuge, sconce, sconse, screen, shield, trench 7 carport, cottage, defense, embosom, foxhole, harbour, hospice, imbosom, nacelle, pillbox, protect, retreat, trailer, umbrage 8 bescreen, ensconce, mantelet, quarters, security 9 coverture, harbinger, harborage, sanctuary 10 harbourage, protection
sheltered side: 7 leeward
on: 4 alee
shelve: tip 4 tilt 5 defer, ledge, shelf, table 6 mantel, retire 7 dismiss, project, put away 8 overhang, platform, postpone 10 pigeonhole
Shem: *father:* 4 Noah
son: Lud 4 Aram, Elam 6 Asshur
shenanigan: 5 prank, trick 7 evasion, foolery 8 goings-on, mischief, nonsense, trickery 12 clownishness
Sheol: 4 hell 5 grave, Hades 10 underworld
shepherd: 4 herd, lead, tend 5 drive, guard, guide, watch 6 attend, escort, feeder, gather, herder, leader, pastor, shadow 7 care for 8 guardian, minister
band of: 10 pastoureau
dog: 6 Collie 8 Cebalrai
god: Pan 5 Pales
pert. to: 8 pastoral
pipe: 4 reed 7 musette 11 flageolette
purse: 4 herb 9 blindweed
staff: 4 kent 5 crook
shepherdess: 7 bergere 9 Amarillis, Amaryllis
sherbet: ice 5 glace
sherd: See **shard**
Sheridan play: 6 Critic, Rivals
sheriff: 6 grieve 7 bailiff, marshal, officer
aides: 5 posse
deputy: 6 elisor 7 bailiff
jurisdiction: 9 bailiwick
Sherlock Holmes: *companion:* 6 Watson

creator: 5 Doyle
sherry: 4 wine 5 tokay 6 Solera 7 oloroso 11 amontillado
Shetland Island: *capital:* 7 Lerwick
inlet: voe
land: 4 odal, udal 6 udaler 7 udalman
measure: ure
musical instrument: gue
ounce: ure
tax: 4 scat
shibboleth: 4 test 6 phrase 8 password 9 criterion, watchword
shield: ecu(F.), rim 4 egis, hide, umbo 5 aegis, armor, avert, badge, board, cloak, cover, guard, pavis, shade, targe 6 blazon, brooch, canopy, defend, forbid, screen, target 7 buckler, clypeus, conceal, defense, lirelle, prevent, protect, rotella, shelter, testudo 8 conserve, rondache 9 protector, safeguard 10 escutcheon, protection
band across: 4 fess
boss: 4 umbo
Minerva's: 4 egis 5 aegis
part of: 4 boss, ente, orle, umbo 6 pointe 7 bordure, impresa
rim: 4 orle
small: ecu
strap: 6 enarme
shield-bearer: 8 escudero
shield-shaped: 7 peltate, scutate 9 clypeolar
shift: yaw 4 deal, eddy, fend, jibe, move, quit, ruse, stir, tour, turn, veer 5 avoid, dodge, evade, feint, hours, order, shunt, slide, spell 6 assign, bestir, change, device, divide, period 7 arrange, convert, dispose, evasion, replace, shuffle 8 artifice, clothing, exchange, mutation, transfer 9 apportion, expedient, vacillate 10 equivocate, subterfuge, transition, transplant 11 contrivance 12 redistribute 13 transposition
shifting: 8 ambulant, drifting, floating 9 deviation
shiftless: 4 lazy 8 feckless, indolent 10 thriftless 11 inefficient
shifty: 4 haft 6 fickle, tricky 7 cunning, devious, evasive, hangdog 8 sneaking 9 faithless, underhand 10 changeable
shikar: 4 hunt 5 sport 7 hunting
shikari, shikaree: 5 guide 6 hunter 9 sportsman
shill: 5 decoy 10 accomplice 11 confederate
shillelagh: 4 club 6 cudgel 7 sapling
shillibeer: 6 hearse 7 omnibus
shilling: bob
shilly-shally: 5 hedge, waver 6 dawdle, trifle 8 hesitate 9 fluctuate, vacillate
shim: hoe 5 image, level, wedge 6 streak, washer 7 glimpse, shingle

Shimeil's father: 4 Gera
Shimel's father: Ela
shimmer: 5 flash, light 7 glimmer, glisten
shimmy: 5 dance, shake 6 quiver 7 chemise, tremble, vibrate
shin: run 4 kick, walk 5 climb, ridge, shank, tibia 6 ascend
  pert. to: 7 cnemial
shindig: 4 basli, fete 6 shiono 7 shebang
shindy: row 4 jump, lark, orgy, romp 5 brawl, dance, noise, party, revel, spree 6 fracas, frolic, rumpus, uproar 7 quarrel, wassail 8 carousal 9 commotion 11 disturbance, merrymaking
shine: ray, rub 4 beek(Sc.), glow, star 5 black, blaze, blink, excel, glaik, gleam, glent, glint, gloss, gloze, light, prank, sheen 6 liking, polish 7 glimpse, glisten, glister, glitter, radiate, touch up 8 fondness, illumine 9 coruscate, irradiate
shiner: hat 4 chub 6 bruise 8 blackeye 9 bootblack
shingle: 4 sign, whip, wood 7 haircut 9 hair style, signboard
  splitting tool: 6 prower
shingles: 4 zona 6 herpes 11 skin disease
shining: 4 glad, gold 5 aglow, glary, lucid, nitid, sleek 6 ardent, argent, bright, fulgid, glossy, lucent 7 beaming, eminent, fulgent, glowing, radiant 8 flashing, gleaming, gorgeous, luminous, lustrous, radiance, splendid 9 brilliant, effulgent, refulgent, sparkling, unclouded 10 glistening, glittering, remarkable 11 illustrious, irradiating, resplendent
shinplaster: 5 scrip
Shinto: *deity:* 8 Hachiman
  gateway: 5 torii
  temple: sha 5 Jinja 6 Jinsha 7 Yashiro
shiny: See **shining**
ship: 4 boat, pink, send 5 shift 7 hagboat 8 balinger
  abandoned: 8 derelict
  ancient: 5 knorr 7 galleon, trireme
  Arabian: 6 boutre
  arctic: 6 sealer
  Argonaut's: 4 Argo
  armored: 7 carrack, cruiser 9 destroyer, ironsides, submarine
  ascent: 5 scend
  attendant: 7 steward
  auxiliary: 6 tender
  beak: bow, ram 4 prow
  beam: 7 carling, keelson
  berth: 4 dock, slip
  boarding device: 6 ladder 9 gangplank
  boat: 4 dory, life 5 barge, dingy 6 dingey, dinghy, tender 7 pinnace
  body: 4 hull
  breadth of: 4 beam
  brutally disciplined: 8 hell ship

  burden: 5 cargo
  cabin: 9 stateroom
  canvas: 4 sail
  capacity: 7 tonnage
  capacity unit: ton
  cargo: 7 gaiassa
  cargo invoice: 8 manifest
  carpenter: 5 Chips
  channel: gat 5 canal 6 narrow, strait
  clean: 6 careen
  clock: nef
  coast guard: 6 cutter
  coastal: hoy 4 dhow, grab 6 droger, trader 7 drogher
  codfishing: 6 banker 8 walloper
  commercial: 6 trader
  company of: 4 crew 5 fleet, hands 6 armada
  compass housing: 8 binnacle
  cook: 6 slushy
  course: 7 sealane
  crane: 5 davit
  crew member: 4 hand, mate 5 bosun 6 purser, sailor
  curved planking: sny
  desert: 5 camel
  deserter: rat
  drain: 7 scupper
  enemy watching: 7 vedette
  employee: 5 oiler 6 purser, sailor 7 steward 8 deckhand, engineer, helmsman, steerman 9 navigator
  fishing: 5 smack 6 hooker, lugger 7 trawler
  flat-bottom: 4 keel 5 barge
  fleet of: 6 armada
  floor: 4 deck
  fuel: 5 barge, oiler 6 coaler, tanker 7 collier
  fur-hunting: 6 sealer
  group: 4 navy 5 fleet 6 armada
  hoist: 4 boom 5 crane, davit 7 capstan
  jail: 4 brig
  kitchen: 6 galley
  lateral movement: 6 leeway
  left side: 4 port
  line: 7 marline, ratline
  merchant: 6 argosy
  middle: 9 amidships
  mortgage: 8 bottomry
  movement: 6 leeway
  oar: 6 bireme, galley, sampan 7 pinnace, rowboat, trireme
  officer: 4 mate 5 bosun 6 purser 7 steward 9 boatswain
  part: bow 4 beam, brig, deck, helm, hold, hull, keel, mast, prow 5 bilge, stern, waist, wheel 6 bridge, galley, rudder, steven 7 lazaret, scupper 8 binnacle 9 lazarette, lazaretto, sternpost
  partition: 7 bulwark 8 bulkhead
  personnel: 4 crew 5 hands

pirate: 8 gallivat

planking: sny 6 strake

prison: 4 brig

privateer: 10 brigantine

prow: 5 prore

quarters: 6 fo'c'sle 8 steerage 10 forecastle

record: log

repair: 6 careen

repairing device: 7 drydock

rescue: ark

riglet side: 9 starboard

room: 4 brig 5 cabin, salon 6 galley 7 caboose 10 forecastle

rope: 4 line 6 hawser 7 halyard, lanyard, painter, ratline

sailing: 4 brig, buss, dhow, proa, yawl 5 ketch, sloop, smack, xebec 6 caique, chebec, hooker, lugger, mistic, saltie 7 caravel, galleon, Geordie, polacre 8 schooner

shovel: 5 skeet

side: 5 abeam

station: 5 berth

structure frame: 7 carcass

table frame: 6 fiddle

tender: 7 collier, pinnace

tiller: 4 helm

timber: rib 4 bitt, keel, mast, spar 5 stick 7 bollard

twin-hulled: 9 catamaran

unseaworthy: 4 hulk 5 wreck 8 ballahoo, ballahou, derelict

upward movement: 5 scend

Venetian: 9 frigatoon

voyage record: log

war (see also **warship**): sub 7 cruiser, flattop 8 corvette 9 destroyer, submarine 11 dreadnaught

wheel: 4 helm

windlass: 7 capstan

window: 4 port 8 porthole

wood for: 4 teak

worm: 5 borer 6 teredo

Ship of Fools author: 5 Brant 6 Porter

ship out: 6 enlist, export

shipment: 5 cargo 7 carload, freight 8 delivery

shipping center: 7 seaport

shipshape: 4 neat, taut, tidy, trim 7 orderly

shipwright: 6 fairer, plater, shorer, wayman 10 woodworker

shire: 5 derby, horse 6 county, region 8 district, province 11 subdivision

shirk: 4 duck, funk 5 avoid, dodge, evade, slack 6 desert 7 neglect 9 fainaigue 11 leave undone

shirker: 6 loafer, truant 7 slacker 8 embusque

shirr: 4 cook 6 gather 7 wrinkle

shirt: tee 4 jupe, polo, sark 5 dress, haire, kamis, parka, sport 6 camisa, camise, cilice, parkee

button: 4 stud

hair: 6 cilice

shirtfront: 5 dicky 6 dickey

shirtwaist: 6 blouse 9 garibaldi

shiver: 4 grue 5 chill, quake, shake 6 dither, quiver, tremor, twitch 7 flicker, frisson, shatter, shudder, tremble, vibrate 8 fragment, splinter

fit: 4 ague 6 chills 10 goosebumps

shivoo: 7 banquet, shindig 9 gathering 13 entertainment

shoal: bar 4 bank, fish, mass, reef 5 barra, crowd, flock 6 school, throng 7 shallow 9 coral reef, multitude

shoat: hog, pig

shock: jar, lot 4 blow, bump, heap, jolt, pile, stun 5 appal, brunt, bunch, bushy, gliff, gloff, scare, shake 6 excite, fright, impact, offend, parcel, shaggy, stroke, trauma 7 astound, collect, disgust, horrify, startle, terrify 8 paralyze 9 agitation, collision 10 assemblage, concussion, head of hair

mental: 6 trauma

to reality: 5 sober

shock absorber: 6 spring 7 snubber

shocking: 5 awful, lurid 6 horrid, unholy 7 fearful, ghastly, hideous 8 dreadful, horrible 9 egregious, revolting 10 disgusting, outrageous

shod: 5 soled 6 booted 7 ensoled

shoddy: 4 bad 4 poor 5 cheap 6 shabby 8 inferior, slovenly

shoe (see also **overshoe**): 4 boot, clog, flat, pump 5 gilly, sabot, scuff 6 brogan, brogue, buskin, caliga, crakow, gaiter, galosh, gillie, loafer, oxford, patten, sandal 7 blucher, flattie, slipper, sneaker 8 colonial, Congress, mocassin, mocasin, solleret 9 brodequin, pampootee 10 clodhopper, veldschoen

aid: 4 horn

baby: 6 bootee

form: 4 last, tree

grip: 5 cleat

gym: 7 sneaker

house: 4 mule 7 slipper

mule's: 6 planch

part: box, cap, tip, toe, top 4 heel, lace, lift, pull, rand, vamp, welt 5 shank, strap 6 insole, tongue 7 counter, outsole 8 backstay, slipsole

paste: 7 clobber

piked: 6 cleats, crakow

repair: tap 5 retap 6 reheel, resole, stitch

rolling: 5 skate

rubber: 6 arctic, galosh 7 galoshe 8 overshoe

winged: 7 talaria

wooden: 5 sabot 6 patten

worker: 6 laster 7 cobbler
worn: 7 bauchle
shoebill: 5 stork
shoelace: tie 5 lacet 7 latchet
tip: 5 aglet 6 aiglet
shoemaker: 5 soler, sutor(L.) 7 cobbler, crispin, farrier 10 cordonnier(F.)
apprentice: 4 snob
patron saint: 7 Crispin
tool: 4 butt 5 elsin 6 elshin
shoeshine: 9 bootblack
shofar, shophar: 4 horn
shog: jog 4 jerk, jolt, push, rock 5 shake 6 jostle
shole: 5 plank, plate
shoneen: 4 snob 5 toady
shoo: 4 scat 10 do away with
in: 6 victor 9 sure thing 11 sure success
shooi: 4 bird, skua 6 jaeger
shook: See shake
shoot: bud, pot 4 bine, cast, chit, cion, dart, emit, film, fire, grow, hunt, move, plug, push, rush, twig 5 bough, chute, drive, eject, plant, scion, snipe, spear, spout, spray, sprig, spurt, throw, tuber, utter, wound 6 branch, inject, propel, sprout, stolon, strike, thrust, twinge 7 burgeon, project 9 discharge 10 photograph 11 inject a drug, precipitate
objective: 6 target
shooting match: tir(F.) 5 skeet 6 affair
shooting star: 5 comet 6 meteor 8 fireball
shop: 5 store 6 market, office, prison, tienda 6 bottega, factory 8 boutique, emporium, workshop 9 workplace
coffee: 4 cafe 6 bistro 9 estaminet
dairy: 8 cremerie
kind: 6 smithy, stithy 7 mercery 8 saddlery, smithery 12 haberdashery
meat: 7 shamble 10 rotisserie 11 charcuterie
wine: 4 cafe 6 bistro
shopkeeper: cit 8 merchant, retailer 9 tradesman 11 businessman, storekeeper
shoplift: cop 5 boost, pinch, steal, swipe 6 rip off
shopper: 5 buyer 8 customer
shopworn: 5 trite 6 cliche 8 overused 9 hackneyed
shore: 4 bank, edge, land, prop, side 5 beach, brink, coast, drain, offer, scold, sewer 6 border, rivage, strand 7 seaside, support 8 buttress, threaten 9 foreshore
pert to: 8 littoral
poetic: 6 strand
recess: bay 4 cove 5 bayou, inlet
shore up: 4 prop 7 bolster, support 10 strengthen
shorebird: ree 4 ruff 5 snipe 6 curlew, plover 9 sandpiper

shorn: See shear
short: 4 curt, rude 5 bluff, brief, brusk, crisp, harsh, scant, spare, terse 6 abrupt, scanty, scarce 7 briefly, brusque, concise, crisply, curtail, friable, summary 8 abruptly, succinct, unawares 9 concisely, crumbling, deficient, shortstop 10 to the point 11 compendious 12 insufficient
and stout: 5 bunty, dumpy 6 stocky, stodgy, stubby 8 rolypoly, thickset
short-breathed: 5 pursy 6 winded 7 puffing
short-lived: 9 ephemeral, transient
short-spoken: 4 curt 5 gruff 7 laconic
shortage: 4 need 7 deficit, failure 10 deficiency 13 insufficiency
shortcoming: 4 flaw 5 fault 6 defect, foible 7 failure 9 weak point 10 deficiency, inadequacy 12 imperfection
shortcut: 5 alley, route 6 byroad 8 diagonal
shorten: bob, cut, lop 4 clip, furl, reef 5 check 6 lessen, reduce 7 abridge, curtail, curtate, deprive 8 condense, contract, decrease, diminish 9 apocopate, decurtate 10 abbreviate 11 encapsulate
short fuse: 11 quick temper
shorthand: 11 stenography 12 brachygraphy, speedwriting
system: 5 Gregg 6 Pitman
shortly (see also short): 4 soon 7 quickly 9 presently
shortness: 7 brevity
shortsighted: 4 dull 6 myopic, obtuse 11 nearsighted 12 narrow-minded 13 opportunistic
Shoshone Indian: Ute 4 Hopi, Otoe, Utah 5 Piute 6 Paiute 8 Comanche
shot (see also shoot): pop, try 4 dram 5 blank, carom, drink, fling, guess, masse, photo, range, reach, sally, tired, weary 6 bullet, pellet, stroke 7 attempt, missile 8 marksman, snapshot 9 exhausted, reckoning 10 conjecture, projectile 11 intoxicated, opportunity
size: BBB 4 dust 8 air-rifle, buckshot
should: 4 want 5 ought
shoulder: 4 berm, edge, push 5 bough, elbow, raise 6 axilla, hustle, jostle 7 bulwark, support
angle: 6 epaule
belt: 4 sash 7 baldric
bone: 7 scapula 8 clavicle
muscle: 7 deltoid
ornament: tab 7 epaulet 9 epaulette
pain: 7 omalgia
pert to: 4 alar 7 humeral 8 scapular
protection for: 8 pauldron
to shoulder: 7 serried
shoulder blade: 7 scapula 8 acromion
shout: boo, cry, hoy, hue 4 bark, bawl, call,

crow, hoot, howl, roar, root, scry, yell, yelp 5 cheer, huzza, noise, whoop, yodel, yodle 6 clamor, halloo, hurrah, outcry, yammer 7 acclaim 10 vociferate 11 acclamation

hunting: 5 hallo, holla 6 yoicks 7 tallyho 9 view-haloo

shove: 4 cast, push 5 drive, eject, elbow, hunch, shunt 6 hustle, jostle, propel, thrust

shovel: dig 4 pale, peel 5 scoop, skeet, spade 7 shuffle 8 excavate

shoveler: 9 broadbill, river duck

shovelfish: 9 spadefish 10 paddlefish

shovelhead: 5 shark 7 catfish 8 flathead, sturgeon

show: 4 bosh, come, dash, fair, lead, look, mask, pomp 5 coach, farce, gloss, guide, movie, plead, prove, raree, revue, stage, teach, train 6 accuse, afford, allege, appear, assign, bestow, blazon, cinema, circus, confer, denote, detect, escort, evince, expose, flaunt, gaiety, gayety, inform, locate, parade, reveal, tinsel, turn up, unveil, veneer 7 bespeak, betoken, bravura, declare, display, divulge, exhibit, explain, perform, present, produce, trot out 8 ceremony, disclose, evidence, flourish, indicate, instruct, manifest 9 barnstorm, burlesque, designate, establish, rareeshow, represent, semblance 10 appearance, exhibition, exposition, expression 11 countenance, demonstrate, opportunity, performance 12 motion picture 13 demonstration

false: 9 tinsel

forth: 7 publish 8 manifest, proclaim 9 publicize

stylized: 4 mime 6 parade 7 pageant 9 cavalcade, pantomime

way: 5 guide, usher 6 direct, escort 7 conduct

show up: 5 strip 6 appear, arrive, expose 7 display

showcase: 7 vitrine, cabinet, exhibit

shower: wet 4 bath, rain, sump, wash 5 bathe, party, spray, water 6 bestow, deluge 7 barrage, drizzle, scatter 8 revealer, sprinkle 9 exhibitor

meteor: 6 Leonid

showery: wet 4 damp 5 moist 7 tearful

showing: 4 sign 6 aspect 7 account 10 apocalypse, appearance

first: 8 premiere

showy: gay 4 arty, loud 5 dashy, gaudy, grand 6 flashy, garish, ornate, swanky 7 dashing, gallant, pompous 8 gorgeous, splendid, striking 9 brilliant, flaunting, sumptuous 10 pretensive 11 pretentious 12 ostentatious 13 grandiloquent

shrapnel: 8 fragment 10 projectile

shred: bit, cut, hew, jag, rag 4 fell, jagg, snip, tear, twig, wisp 5 blype, grate, piece, prune, rip up, scrap, sever, shard, strip 6 divide, screed, sliver, tailor, tatter 7 fritter, parings, vestige 8 fragment, particle 9 pulverize, tear apart 12 make confetti

shrew: 5 curse, harpy, scold, vixen 6 mammal, tartar, virago 7 muskrat, villain 9 scoundrel, termagant, Xanthippe

long-tailed: 5 sorex

shrewd: bad, sly 4 cagy, cute, evil, foxy, hard, keen, sage, wily, wise 5 acute, canny, harsh, sharp, smart, stern 6 argute, artful, astute, biting, clever, crafty, subtle, wicked 7 abusive, cunning, gnostic, hurtful, knowing, parlous, politic, sapient 8 depraved, grievous, piercing, shrewish 9 gnostical, ingenious, injurious, sagacious 10 discerning, farsighted, hardheaded 11 distressing, intelligent, mischievous, penetrating, sharpwitted 13 perspicacious

shrewish: 7 nagging 8 vixenish 9 termagant 10 ill-humored 11 quarrelsome

shriek: cry, yip 4 yell 6 holler, outcry, scream, squeal 7 screech

shrift (see also **shrive**): 10 absolution, confession, disclosure 12 confessional 14 acknowledgment

shrill: 4 high, keen 5 acute, sharp 6 argute, biting, piping, shriek, squeak 7 screech 8 piercing, poignant, strident 9 dissonant 11 highpitched, penetrating

shrimp: kid 5 dwarf 6 shaver 7 seafood 9 stripling 10 crustacean

large: 5 prawn

shrine: box 4 case, naos, tomb 5 altar, caaba, chest, kaaba, huaca 6 abaton, adytum, chapel, chasse, dagaba(Ind.), dagoba(Ind.), entomb, hallow, temple 7 chaitya, enciana, memoria 8 canonize, enshrine, memorial 9 container, holy place, reliquary, sanctuary 10 receptacle

goddesses: 9 anaktoran

visitor: 7 pilgrim

shrink: shy 4 fawn, funk, shun, wane 5 cling, cower, quail, rivel, shrug, wizen 6 blench, boggle, cotter, cringe, flinch, gizzen, huddle, humble, lessen, recoil, retire, wither 7 atrophy, dwindle, retract, shrivel 8 condense, contract, decrease, pull back, withdraw 9 constrict 10 depreciate 15 psychotherapist

shrinking: shy 5 timid 6 afraid, modest 8 reticent 9 diffident

shrive: rob 4 free 5 purge 6 acquit, pardon 7 absolve, confess 8 disclose 9 reconcile

shrivel: age 5 blast, crine, parch, rivel, wizen 6 cotter, scrump, shrink, weazen, wither 9 deteriorate

shroff: 6 banker, expert 7 changer, inspect 8 separate 12 moneychanger

shroud: lop 4 hide, trim, veil, wrap 5 array, cloak, cover, crypt, dress, shade, sheet, vault 6 branch, clothe, enfold, screen, shadow 7 conceal, curtain, envelop, foliage, garment, plumage, protect, shelter 8 cerement, clothing, covering, envelope 9 cerecloth 10 protection

shrub: lop, tea, tod 4 bago, bush, cade, coca, gumi, majo, nabo, olea, sida, sola 5 elder, lilac, prune, punch, salal 6 cudgel, frutex 7 arboret, buckeye, chamise, chamiso, heather, scratch, tarbush 8 abelmosk, barberry, beverage, huisache, 9 chaparral, manzanita

  aromatic: tea 4 mint, sage 5 batis, thyme 8 rosemary

  bean family: 4 ulex

  collection: 10 fruticetum

  desert: 5 retem 6 alhagi, raetam

  evergreen: box 4 ilex, moss, titi 5 furze, heath, salal, savin 6 laurel, myrtle 7 jasmine, juniper 8 oleander 9 mistletoe

  fence: box 5 hedge

  flowering: 5 lilac, tiara, wahoo 6 azalea, laurel, myrtle, spirea 7 lantana, rhodora, spiraea, syringa 8 japonica, oleander, oleaster 9 mistletoe 10 mignonette

  fruit: 5 salal

  genus of: 4 inga 5 erica, ledum 6 aralia

  hardy: 7 althaea, heather

  indigo: 4 anil

  Mexican: 8 bluebush

  myrtle-like: 7 cajeput, cajuput

  ornamental: 6 privet

  parasitic: 9 mistletoe

  pert. to: 9 fruticose, fruticous

  poisonous: 5 sumac 6 sumach

  prickly: 4 whin 5 briar, brier, caper, gorse 7 bramble 8 allthorn, hawthorn

  rubber: 7 guayule

  stunted: 5 scrag, scrub

  tea-like: kat 4 coca

  tropical: 5 henna 6 olacad 7 lantana 10 frangipani

shruff: 5 dross 7 rubbish

shrug: don, tug 5 hitch 6 fidget, shiver, shrink 7 gesture, shudder 8 contract, hitching 9 handshake 10 convulsion

  off: 7 dismiss, not care 13 underestimate

shrunken (see also **shrink**): 4 lank 9 atrophied, shriveled

Shu: *parent:* Ra 6 Hathor

  sister: 6 Tefnut

  wife: 6 Tefnut

shuck: pod 4 husk, sham 5 fraud, shell, strip 6 recoil, remove 7 discard, mislead, swindle

shudder: 4 grue 5 quake, shake 6 quiver,

    shiver 7 frisson, tremble

shuffle: mix 4 gait, plod, walk 5 dance, scuff 6 huddle, juggle, jumble, mingle, remove, sclaff 7 evasion, quibble, scuffle, shamble 8 artifice 9 confusion 10 equivocate 11 prevaricate 12 equivocation

shuffling: 6 shifty 7 evasive 9 deceitful 13 opportunistic

shun: 4 balk, flee, hide, snub 5 avert, avoid, evade, evite 6 eschew 7 abstain, forbear, forsake 8 restrain 9 forbear

shunt: 4 push 5 shift, shove 6 divert, remove, switch 9 conductor, rechannel, sidetrack, turn aside

shut: bar, rid 4 free 5 close 6 climax, fasten, forbid 7 confine, exclude, turn off 8 prohibit 10 portcullis

  in: hem, pen 4 cage, pent, wall 5 embar, embay, fence 6 bottle, hemmed 7 bottled, confine, enclose, impound 8 imprison 10 quarantine, surrounded

shut-in: 7 invalid, recluse 12 convalescent

shut out: bar 6 screen 7 exclude 8 preclude

shut up: end, gag 7 seclude 8 be silent, conclude 9 terminate

shutter: 5 blind, cover 6 screen 7 buckler 8 jalousie

shuttle: 4 loom 5 shunt, train 6 looper 9 air travel

shuttlecock: 4 bird 6 birdie

shy: coy, mim 4 balk, jump, shun, wary 5 aloof, avoid, chary, dodge, scant, start, throw, timid 6 boggle, demure, escape, modest, recoil, shrink 7 bashful, lacking, potshot 8 farouche, hesitant, reserved, retiring, secluded, sheepish, skittish 9 diffident, reluctant, shrinking 10 incomplete, shamefaced, suspicious, unassuming 11 distrustful, unobtrusive 13 self-conscious 14 unostentatious

Shylock: 6 usurer 9 loan shark 11 money lender

  coin: 5 ducat

  daughter: 7 Jessica

  friend: 5 Tubal

shyster: 11 pettifogger

si: yes

Siam: See **Thailand**

Siamese twin: Eng 5 Chang

sib: kin 4 akin 5 ayllu 6 allied, sister 7 brother, kindred, kinship, kinsman, related 8 friendly, relation, relative 9 congenial, kinswoman 12 well-disposed

Siberia: *antelope:* 5 saiga

  carnivore: 5 sable

  city: 4 Enna, Omsk 5 Chita, Tomsk 7 Barnaul, Irkutsk

  dog: 7 Samoyed 8 Samoyede

  Eskimo: 4 Yuit

  fish: 5 nelma

forest: 5 Urman

fur: 7 calabar

hunters and fishers: 6 Giliak, Gilyak 7 Samoyed 8 Samoyede

hut: 8 barabara, barabora

leopard: 5 ounce

mountains: 4 Ural 5 Altai

peninsula: 6 Taimir 9 Kamchatka

people: 5 Sagai, Tatar, Yakut 6 Kirgiz, Tartar 7 Kirghis, Kirghiz, Yukagir 8 Yukaghir 9 Mongolian

plain: 6 steppe, tundra

region: 5 taiga

river: Ili, Tom 4 Amur, Lena, Maya, Onon, Yana 5 Sobol, Tobol 6 Anadyr, Olenek 7 Yenisei

squirrel: 7 miniver

squirrel-skin: 7 calabar

storm: 5 buran

tanning plant: 5 badan

tent: 4 yurt 5 yurta

wild cat: 5 manul

wild sheep: 6 argali

sibilant: ess 7 hissing

sibling (see also **sib**): 6 sister 7 brother

sibyl: 4 seer 5 witch 6 Libyan, Samian, Trojan 7 Cumaean, prophet, seeress 8 Delphian, Phrygian 9 Cimmerian, Erythrean, sorceress, Tiburtine 10 prophetess 13 fortuneteller, Hellespontine

sibylline: 6 occult 7 cryptic, obscure 8 oracular 9 ambiguous, equivocal, prophetic 10 exorbitant, mysterious 11 prophetical

sic: set 4 seek, thus, urge 5 chase, egg on 6 attack, incite

Sicilian: 10 Trinacrian

Sicily: *cape:* 4 Boeo, Faro 7 Passaro

capital: 7 Palermo

city: 4 Gela 5 Aetna, Bidis, Nakos 6 Alcamo, Modica, Ragusa 7 Catania, Marsala, Messina, Trapani 8 Girgenti, Monreale, Taormina 9 Agrigento 13 Caltanissetta

composer: 7 Bellini

crime society: 5 Mafia

god: 7 Adranus

harbor: 7 Palermo

island: 11 Pantelleria

king: 4 Eryx

measure: 5 salma 7 caffiso

mountain: 4 Etna

people: 5 Elymi, Sicel

river: 5 Salso 6 Belice, Simeto 7 Platani

seaport: Aci 7 Messina

secret society: 5 Mafia

volcano: 4 Etna

whirlpool: 9 Charybdis

youth: 4 Acis

sick: bad, ill, set, wan 4 abed, pale, seek, urge, weak 5 badly, chase, crank, cronk,

fed-up, unfit, weary 6 ailing, attack, incite, insane, unwell 7 unsound 8 impaired 9 corrupted, crapulous, depressed, disgusted, instigate, nauseated, surfeited, unhealthy 10 indisposed 11 exasperated 12 disconsolate

deathly: 5 amort 7 alamort

person: 7 invalid, patient

sickbay: 6 clinic 8 hospital 9 infirmary 10 dispensary

sicken: 5 upset 6 affect 8 get worse, languish

sickening: 7 fulsome 9 offensive, revolting 10 disgusting, nauseating

sickle: 6 scythe

sickly: ill, wan 4 fue, pale, puny, weak cothy, faint, frail 6 ailing, cranky, feeble, infirm, morbid, weakly 7 cothish, insipid, invalid, languid, mawkish, queechy 8 diseased 9 colorless, sickening, unhealthy 10 unwholesome

sickness: 6 malady, nausea 7 ailment, disease, disgust, illness, insanity 9 distemper, infirmity, weariness 12 qualmishness 13 indisposition

feign: 8 malinger

mental: See **mental disorder**

side: far 4 edge, face, line, part, team, wall, wide 5 agree, ample, costa, facet, flank, latus, party, phase, place, proud, shore, slope, space, width 6 aspect, behalf, border, margin, region, severe 7 conceit, distant, faction, lateral, sheathe, support, surface 8 district, position, spacious 9 declivity, direction, outskirts, viewpoint 10 collateral, occasional 15 pretentiousness

on the: 5 apart

pain in: 6 stitch

pert. to: 7 lateral

piece: rib 5 stave

sheltered: lee

side arm: 5 sword 6 pistol, weapon 7 bayonet 8 revolver

side by side: 8 parallel, together 12 cheek to cheek

side view: 7 profile

sideboard: 6 buffet 8 credence, credenza, cupboard

sidekick: pal 4 chum 6 friend 7 partner 8 follower 9 assistant, companion, satellite 11 confederate

sideline: 5 bench 7 put away 9 avocation

sidepiece: rib 6 border

sidereal: 6 astral, starry 7 stellar 8 starlike

siderite: ore

sideroad: 5 byway 10 digression

siderolite: 9 meteorite

sideshow: 10 attraction

attraction: 5 freak

sideslip: 4 skid 5 slide 10 digression

sidestep: 4 duck 5 avoid, dodge, evade
sidetrack: 4 spur 5 shunt 6 divert, switch
sidewalk: 6 causey 9 banquette, boardwalk
  part: 4 curb, kerb 5 crack 6 paving
sideways: 5 aside 6 askant 7 askance, athwart, lateral 8 indirect 9 laterally, obliquely
Sidi's wife: 5 Amine
sidle: 4 edge 6 loiter 7 saunter
Sidon's modern name: 5 Saida
siege: see 4 bout, rank 5 bench, beset, flock, place, privy 6 attack 7 sitting 8 blockade 9 onslaught 13 beleaguerment
Siegfried: *mother:* 9 Sieglinde
  slayer: 5 Hagen
  sword: 7 Balmung
  vulnerable spot: 4 back 8 shoulder
  wife: 9 Kriemhild
sierra: 4 fish 5 range, ridge
Sierra Leone: *capital:* 8 Freetown
  coin: 5 leone
  language: 5 Mende, Temne 6 Creole
Sierra Nevada: *fog:* 7 pogonip
  peak: 4 Dana 7 Whitney
siesta: nap 4 lull, rest 5 sleep
sieve: 4 lawn, sift 5 tamis, temse 6 basket, bolter, filter, gossip, ranger, riddle, screen, sifter, strain 7 chaffer, cribble, measure 8 colander, separate, strainer
  for clay: 4 laun
sift: 4 bolt, cull, scry, sort 5 sieve, temse 6 dredge, filter, refine, riddle, screen, strain, winnow 7 analyze, canvass, examine, inspect, scatter 8 look into, separate 10 scrutinize
sifter: 5 sieve 6 bolter 8 strainer
sigh: sob 4 moan, wail 5 mourn, sough, yearn 6 bemoan, grieve, lament 7 deplore 11 respiration
sight: aim, ken, see 4 espy, gaze, look, mess, show, vane, view 5 scene 6 behold, descry, glance, vision 7 discern, display, eyesore, glimpse 9 spectacle 10 exhibition, inspection, perception 11 examination, observation
  defect: 7 anopsia
  gun: 4 bead
  loss: 9 amaurosis
  obscurity: 6 caligo
  offending: 7 eyesore
  out of: 11 disappeared
  pert. to: 6 ocular, visual
  second: ESP, fey 7 psychic
sightless: 5 blind 6 unseen 9 invisible
sightseer: 7 tourist 10 rubberneck
sigil: 4 seal, sign, word 6 device, signet 9 signature
sigmoid: ess
Sigmund: *father:* 7 Volsung
  son: 6 Sigurd
  sword: 4 Gram

  wife: 7 Hiordis
sign (see also **signal**): cue, nod 4 hint, hire, mark, note, omen 5 badge, image, segno(It.), sigil, spoor, token, trace 6 banner, beacon, beckon, effigy, emblem, engage, ensign, figure, motion, notice, poster, signet, symbol, wigwag 7 auspice, endorse, gesture, initial, message, picture, portent, prodigy, vestige, warning 8 evidence, password, pretense, standard 9 autograph, character, semaphore, semblance, subscribe, watchword 10 denotation, expression, forerunner, indication, prognostic, suggestion, underwrite 11 countersign 13 advertisement, constellation, demonstration, foreshadowing
  diacritical: 5 hamza, tilde 6 hamzah, tittle, umlaut 7 cedilla
  direction: 5 arrow
  illuminated: 4 neon 6 lights
  liturgical: 5 selah 6 shelah
  magic: 5 sigil
  music: 5 presa, segno
  pert. to: 5 semic 8 semantic
  Zodiac: See zodiac sign
sign language: 11 dactylology
sign off: end, out 6 thirty 8 withdraw
sign on: 4 hire, ship 6 engage, enlist, enroll 8 register
signal (see also **sign**): 4 flag 5 alarm, siren 6 buzzer, ensign, notify, sennet, tocsin 7 betoken, eminent, lantern, notable, presage, signify 9 memorable, prominent, semaphore, symbolize 10 noticeable, remarkable 11 communicate, conspicuous 13 extraordinary
  distress: SOS 6 mayday
  electric: 8 teleseme
  system: 4 code
  warning: 5 alarm, alert, flare, siren 6 alarum, beacon, tocsin 7 blinker
signature: ink 4 hand, mark, name, sign, visa, vise 5 sigil, stamp 9 allograph, autograph 10 directions, impression 11 bookbinding, countersign
signet: 4 mark, seal, sign 5 sigil, stamp 10 impression 12 authenticate
significance: 6 repute 7 bearing, meaning, purport 13 signification
significant: 4 sign 5 grave, token 6 symbol 7 ominous, weighty 8 eloquent, sinister 9 important, momentous, prominent 10 expressive, indicative, meaningful, portentous, suggestive 13 consequential
signify: nod 4 mean, show, sign 5 augur, imply, spell, utter 6 amount, denote, import, inform, matter, signal 7 add up to, betoken, compare, declare 8 announce, foreshow, indicate, intimate, manifest 11 communicate

signor: man 4 lord 5 title 9 gentleman

signpost: 5 guide 6 beacon 7 pointer 9 guidepost

signum: 4 bell, mark, sign 9 signature

Sigurd: *father:* 7 Sigmund
foster father: 5 Regin 6 Reginn
horse: 5 Grani
slayer: 5 Hogni
victim: 6 Fafnir
wife: 6 Gudrun

Sigyn's husband: 4 Loki

Sikkim (see also India): *capital:* 7 Gangtok
people: 4 Rong 6 Bhotia, Lepcha

silage: 4 feed, fodder

Silas Marner author: 5 Eliot

silence: gag 4 hush, mute, rest, stun 5 choke, death, floor, quiet, still, tacet 6 muffle, refute 7 confute, destroy, repress, secrecy 8 muteness, suppress 9 obscurity, reticence, stillness 10 silentness
goddess: 8 Angerona
music: 5 tacet

silencer: 4 mute 5 gavel 7 muffler 8 sourdine

silene: 7 campion 8 catchfly

silent: mum 4 dumb, flat, mute 5 quiet, still, tacit 8 inactive, overcome, reserved, reticent, taciturn, unspoken 9 noiseless, secretive, uttered 10 flavorless, speechless, unrecorded 11 unexpressed, unmentioned 15 uncommunicative

silex: 5 flint 6 quartz, silica 7 mineral

silhouette: 6 shadow 7 outline 9 lineation 10 figuration

silicate: 4 mica 6 cerite, iolite 7 epidote 8 calamine, severite, wellsite

silk: 5 pekin, surah, tulle 6 fabric 7 foulard 8 florence, sarcenet, sarsenet
corded: 6 faille
embroidery thread: 5 floss 8 arrasene
fabric: 4 gros 5 caffa, China, crepe, moire, ninon, pekin, satin, surah, tabby, tulle 6 cendal, faille, mantua, pongee, samite, sendal, tussah, tusser, tussur 7 alamode, marabou, sarsnet, taffeta, tsatlee, tussore 8 sarcenet, sarsenet
fishline: 4 gimp
hank: 4 hasp
hat: 6 topper
Indian moth: 4 muga
raw: 5 grege 8 marabout
refuse: 6 strass
source: 6 cocoon
thread: 4 filo
unspun: 6 sleave
waste: 4 noil 5 floss 6 frison
watered: 5 moire
wild: 6 tussah 7 tussore
worker: 7 thrower 9 throwster
yarn: 4 tram 7 schappe

yarn size: 6 denier

silk-stocking: 5 elite 7 elegant, wealthy 9 exclusive, luxurious 10 Federalist 12 aristocratic

silken: 4 fine, soft 5 quiet, silky, sleek, suave, sweet 6 gentle, glossy, smooth, tender 7 elegant 8 delicate, lustrous, silklike 9 luxurious, sericeous 10 effeminate 12 ingratiating

silkworm: eri 4 eria 6 bombyx, tussah 8 bombycid

silkworm rot: 7 calcino

sill: 4 beam, seat, sile 5 bench, frame, ledge, shelf, stone 6 timber 9 threshold 10 foundation

silliness: 5 folly 6 betise(F.) 11 foolishness

silly: mad 4 bete, daft, fond, fool, idle, simp, weak 5 anile, apish, barmy, dazed, dense, frail, giddy, goofy, goose, inane, plain 6 absurd, cranky, cuckoo, dotard, dottle(Sc.), feeble, footle, humble, infirm, paltry, rustic, sickly, simple, stupid, unwise 7 asinine, fatuous, foolish, foppish, shallow, trivial, witless 8 childish, fopperly, ignorant, imbecile, innocent 9 brainless, childlike, ludicrous, pointless, senseless, simpleton 10 half-witted, indiscreet 12 simpleminded 15 unsophisticated

silt: 4 scum 5 dregs 7 deposit, moraine, residue 8 sediment 9 percolate

silver: 4 coin, pale 5 money, plate, sweet 6 argent, gentle 7 bullion 8 argentum, eloquent, lustrous, peaceful, precious, sterling 9 tableware 11 resplendent 13 argentiferous
containing: 5 lunar
lace: 8 filigree
pert. to: 9 argentine, argentous
reducing kettle: 4 cazo(Sp.)

silver thaw: 10 glitter ice

silver thistle: 8 acanthus

silver-tongued: 4 glib 8 eloquent 10 persuasive

silverfish: 6 insect, tarpon

silversmith: 5 sonar 9 artificer

silverware: 5 vases 6 dishes 8 platters 9 ornaments, tableware
ornament: 7 gadroon

silverweed: rue 5 tansy 9 jewelweed 10 cinquefoil

silvery: 7 frosted 9 artentine 10 argenteous, shimmering

silviculture: 8 forestry

s'il vous plait: 6 please

simar: 4 robe 6 jacket 7 garment 12 undergarment

Simeon: *father:* 5 Jacob
mother: 4 Leah
son: 4 Ohad 6 Nemuel

simian: ape 6 monkey 7 apelike 10 anthropoid

similar: sib 4 akin, like, such 5 alike 6 evenly 7 uniform 8 analogic, parallel 9 semblance 9 analogous, resembling 11 approximate, counterpart, homogeneous, resemblance 13 correspondent

simile: 10 comparison 14 figure of speech

similitude: 4 form 5 image 6 simile, symbol 7 analogy, parable, replica 8 allegory, likeness 9 facsimile, semblance 10 similarity 11 counterpart, resemblance 14 representation

similize: 5 liken 7 compare

simmer: 4 boil, stew 6 braise

simmon: 9 persimmon

simnel: 5 bread 7 biscuit 8 cracknel 9 fruitcake

Simon: 5 Peter 7 apostle

Simon Legree: 10 taskmaster 11 slave driver

simon-pure: 4 real, true 6 simple 7 genuine 9 authentic 11 unqualified

simony: 8 barratry

simoom, simoon: 4 wind 5 storm 6 tebbad 9 dust storm

simper: 5 mince, smile, smirk 7 whimper

simple: 4 bald, bare, dull, easy, fond, mere, poor, pure, real, true, weak 5 folly, lowly, naive, naked, plain, Roman, silly 6 common, Dorian, homely, humble, oafish, rustic, severe, single, stupid 7 artless, austere, babyish, foolish, genuine, idyllic, natural, onefold, sincere, Spartan, unmixed 8 absolute, arcadian, childish, complete, gullible, homemade, ignorant, innocent, modestly, ordinary, retarded, tailored, trifling 9 childlike, elemental, ingenuous, primitive, unadorned 10 elementary, unaffected, uninvolved 11 homogeneous, undesigning, unimportant 12 inartificial, uncompounded, unpretending 13 insignificant, plain speaking, uncomplicated, unconstrained, unembellished 15 straightforward, undistinguished, unsophisticated

simple-minded: 6 simple, stupid 7 artless 12 feeble-minded, moronic, unsuspecting 13 simple-hearted 15 unsophisticated

simpleton: ass, daw 4 boob, dolt, fool, gaby, gawk, gawp, gowk, lout, simp, tony, zany 5 dunce, goose, idiot, ninny, noddy, sammy 6 dawkin, gander, gawney, gulpin, nincom, nincum, nitwit, noodle 7 gomeral, gomerel, gomeril, muggins, widgeon 8 Abderite, fondling, numskull, omadhaun 10 changeling, nincompoop 11 ninnyhammer

simplify: 6 clean up, cut down 7 clarify, expound 9 elucidate, interpret

simulacrum: 4 copy, fake, sham 5 image 6 aspect 7 phantom 8 likeness, pretense, travesty 9 imposture, semblance 11 assemblance, counterfeit

simulate: act, ape 4 fake, mock, sham 5 feign, feiut 6 affect, assume 7 feigned, imitate, pretend 8 make like, resemble 9 dissemble, personate, pretended 10 fictitious 11 counterfeit

simulation: 9 hypocrisy 10 sanctimony

simurg, simurgh: roc

sin: err 4 debt, envy, evil, lust, vice 5 anger, blame, crime, error, fault, folly, guilt, pride, sloth, wrong 6 acedia, felony 7 do wrong, offense, violate 8 gluttony, iniquity, peccancy 9 deviation 10 immorality, peccadillo, transgress, wickedness, wrongdoing 11 misdemeanor, ungodliness, viciousness 12 covetousness 13 transgression

canonical: 6 heresy, murder 8 adultery, idolatry

deadly: 4 envy, lust 5 anger, pride, sloth 8 gulttony 12 covetousness

Sinai mountain: 5 Horeb

sinapis: 4 herb 7 mustard

Sinbad's bird: roc

since: ago, for, fro, now 4 ergo, gone, past, sith, syne(Sc.) 5 after, hence, later 7 already, because, whereas 8 inasmuch, until now 9 afterward, therefore, thereupon 11 considering 12 continuously, subsequently

sincere: 4 open, pure, real, true 5 frank, whole 6 candid, devout, hearty, honest 7 artless, cordial, correct, earnest, genuine, unmixed, upright 8 faithful, truthful, virtuous 9 authentic, blameless, heartfelt, unfeigned, veracious 10 unaffected 11 unvarnished 12 wholehearted 13 unadulterated 15 straightforward

sinciput: 8 forehead

sind: 5 rinse 6 drench, quench

sine qua non: 13 indispensable

sinecure: 4 pipe, snap 5 cinch, gravy

sinew: 5 power, snare 6 tendon 8 potency

sinewy: 4 firm, wiry 5 thewy, tough 6 brawny, robust, strong 7 fibrose, nervous stringy 8 forceful, muscular, powerful, vigorous 9 tendinous

sinful (see also **sin**): bad 4 evil 5 wrong 6 wicked 7 immoral, ungodly, vicious 10 iniquitous 11 blameworthy, unrighteous

sing: hum 4 cant, lilt, pipe, ring, talk 5 carol, chant, chirl, croon, ditty, yodel, yodle 6 betray, inform, intone, warble 7 chortle, confess, descant, divulge, rejoice, roulade, tweedle

as a round: 5 troll

softly: hum 5 croon

with trills: 6 warble 7 roulade

singable: 7 lyrical, melodic, tuneful 9 cantabile

singe: 4 burn, char, sear 6 scorch 7 blemish
fiber: 6 genapp
singer: 4 alto, bard, bass, diva 5 basso, buffa, buffo, tenor 6 krant, cantor 7 artiste, chanter, crooner, soloist, songman, soprano 8 baritone, minstrel, vocalist 9 chanteuse, chorister, contralto, descanter 10 cantatrice 11 entertainer 12 mezzo-soprano
comic opera: 5 buffa
female: 9 chanteuse 10 cantatrice
opera: 4 diva
singerie: 6 design 7 picture 10 decoration 11 monkeyshine
singing: 4 cant 5 charm 9 cantation
group: 4 duet, trio 5 choir, octet 6 chorus, sextet 7 octette, quartet 8 chanters, sextette 9 quartette
pert. to: 6 choral 9 cantative
trio: 9 tricinium
voice: 4 alto, bass 5 tenor 7 soprano 8 baritone 9 contralto 12 mezzo-soprano
single: one 4 lone, only, part, sole, unit 5 alone, unwed 6 unique 7 base hit, onefold, unusual 8 celibate, separate, singular, solitary, withdraw 9 sequester, unmarried 10 individual, particular 11 unsupported
single out: 6 choose
singlet: 5 shirt 6 jersey 9 waistcoat 10 undershirt
singly: 4 once 5 alone, apart 6 merely, solely 7 unaided 8 honestly 9 severally, sincerely 12 individually, particularly, single-handed
singsong: 5 chime 7 tedious 11 repetitious
singular: odd, one 4 each, rare, sole 5 queer 6 single, unique 7 eminent, private, several, unusual 8 isolated, peculiar, separate, superior, uncommon 9 eccentric, fantastic, whimsical 10 individual, one and only, remarkable, unexampled 11 exceptional 12 unparalleled 13 extraordinary, unprecedented
singultus: 7 hiccups
sinister: car(Sc.) 4 dark, dire, evil, grim, left 7 adverse, baleful, corrupt, ominous 9 dishonest, injurious, malicious, underhand 10 disastrous, portentous 11 apocalyptic, prejudicial, unfortunate 12 inauspicious
sink: bog, dip, ebb, sag, pet 4 cave, drop, fail, fall, ruin, wane 5 avale, drain, droop, embog, heald, hield, lower, plump, sewer, slope, stoop 6 debase, dolina, doline, drench, extend, gutter, humble, plunge, settle, thrust 7 decline, degrade, depress, descend, destroy, immerse, relapse, subside 8 decrease, diminish, submerge, suppress 9 penetrate 11 come to grief

below horizon: set
ship: 7 scuttle
sinker: 5 pitch 6 weight 8 doughnut
Sinkiang: *capital:* 7 Urumchi
river: 5 Tarim
sinking: 7 descent 10 depression
sinless: 4 pure 7 perfect 8 innocent 9 righteous
sinner: 5 scamp 8 evildoer, offender, penitent 9 bad person, reprobate, wrongdoer 10 backslider, trespasser 12 transgressor
sinning: 7 peccant
sinuous: 4 wavy 5 snaky 7 bending, crooked, curving, devious, winding 9 deviating, intricate 10 circuitous, serpentine 11 anfractuous
sinus: bay 4 bend, fold 5 bosom, curve 6 cavity, hollow, recess 7 channel, opening 10 depression
pert. to: 5 sinal 7 sinusal
Sioux: Kaw, Oto 4 Crow, Iowa, Otoe 5 Brule, Omaha, Osage, Sioux 6 Dakota, Santee, Tuteo 8 Catawba 9 Winnebago
division: 5 Teton
sip: bib, lap, sup 5 draft, drink, quaff, taste 6 tipple 8 toothful 11 small amount
sipper: 4 tube 5 straw
sir: 4 lord 5 title 6 knight, master 9 gentleman
sirdar: 5 chief, noble 6 bearer 7 officer, servant
sire: 4 lord 5 title 6 father, master, parent 8 ancestor, begetter, generate 10 forefather, procreator, progenitor
siren: 5 alarm, lurer 7 charmer, foghorn, Lorelei, mermaid 8 water god 9 Cleopatra 10 attractive, bewitching 11 fascinating, femme fatale
Siren: 5 Ligea 8 Leucosia 10 Parthenope
siriasis: 9 sunstroke
Sirius' master: 5 Orion
sirocco: 4 wind
sisal: 4 hemp 5 fiber
Sisera: *enemy:* 5 Barak
murderer: 4 Jael
siskin: 5 finch, tarin 9 small bird
sissy: 6 coward 7 girlish 8 weakling 10 effeminate 11 mollycoddle
sister: nun, sis 4 girl 5 soror(L.) 7 sibling
murder: 10 sororicide
pert. to: 5 soral 8 sororate, sororial
younger: 7 cadette(F.)
Sister Superior: 6 abbess
sisterhood: 8 sorority
sistrum: 6 rattle 10 noisemaker
sit: lie, set 4 meet, pose, rest, seat 5 brood, dwell, model, perch, press, roost, squat 6 occupy, remain, repose 7 convene 8 incubate
carelessly: 4 loll 6 sprawl

sit in: 6 attend, object 7 protest 11 participate

sit on: 6 confer, hush up, rebuke 7 repress, squelch 8 suppress, siege 9 reprimand 11 appropriate, investigate

site: 4 ruin, seat, spot 5 arena, locus(L.), place, scene, venue 6 locale, locate 8 location, position 9 situation

sitfast: 5 fixed, stone 8 crowfoot 9 immovable 10 stationary

sithe: lot 6 chance, mishap

Sitsang: 5 Tibet

sitting: 4 seat 5 abode, place 6 clutch, posing, seance, sedent, sejaul 7 meeting, sejeant, session 8 sederunt

  court: 6 assize 7 session

Sitting Bull: *enemy:* 6 Custer

  tribe: 5 Sioux

sitting duck: 4 dupe 5 decoy 6 target

situated: 4 seat 5 basal 6 nether, placed, plight 7 located, station 8 marginal 13 circumstanced

  between folds: 11 interplical

  in the middle: 6 medial, median

  on membrane enveloping the brain: 8 epidural

  on right: 6 dexter

  toward rear: 6 astern 7 postern 9 posterior

situation: job 4 case, need, post, seat, site 5 berth, place, siege, situs(L.), state 6 estate, locale, morass, plight, scrape, strait 7 bargain, dilemma, station, vantage 8 locality, location, position, quandary 9 condition, emergency, imbroglio, pregnancy 11 predicament, whereabouts 12 circumstance

situla: 4 pail, vase 6 bucket 10 receptacle

situs: 5 place 8 location, position 9 situation

Siva: 8 Hindu god

  consort: Uma 4 Devi

  son: 6 Skanda

  trident: 6 trisul 7 trisula

  wife: 4 Sati

six: 6 senary, sestet 7 digamma, sestole 8 senarius

  group: 5 hexad 6 hexade, senary, sextet 8 sextette

  pert. to: 6 senary

  series of: 5 hexad 6 hexade

  six on dice: 4 sice

six sheets: 7 sextern

six-eyed: 9 senocular

sixfold: 8 sextuple

six-footed: 7 hexaped 9 hexapodal, hexapodan

six-line stanza: 6 sestet

six-shooter: gun 6 weapon 8 revolver

size: 4 area, bore, bulk, mass 5 cover, glaze, grade 6 adjust, amount, candle, extent, format, volume 7 arrange, examine, measure, stiffen 8 classify, standard 9 dimension, magnitude 11 measurement

  book page: 9 duodecimo

  indefinite: nth

  paper: cap 4 copy, demi, demy, pott 5 atlas, crown, felic, folio, legal 6 bagcap 7 bastard, emperor 8 foolscap, imperial 9 colombier

  separation device: 6 grader

  type: 4 pica, ruby 5 agate, canon, elite, pearl 6 minion, primer 7 brevier, diamond, English, paragon 9 bourgeois, columbian, nonpareil

  yarn: lea 5 forty 6 denier

sizing: 4 glue 6 starch 9 allotment

sizy: 7 viscous 9 glutinous

sizz: 4 hiss

sizzle: fry 4 burn, sear, siss 7 shrivel

sizzling: hot 6 torrid

sjambok: 4 flog, whip

skate: jag, man, ray 4 fish, plug, shoe, skid 5 flair, glide, horse

  kind: 6 figure, hockey

skate blade: 6 runner

skating arena: 4 rink

skean: 4 dirk 5 sword 6 dagger

skedaddle: 4 bunk, flee 5 leave, scoot 6 go away, scurry 7 scamper 8 clear out, hightail

skeesicks: 6 rascal 9 skinflint 14 good-for-nothing

skeet: 12 trapshooting

skegger: 4 fish, parr 6 salmon

skein: rap 4 hank, maze, wind 5 flock 6 flight, hurdle, sleeve 7 spireme, thimble 8 filament, wild fowl

skelder: 5 cheat 7 vagrant 9 panhandle

skeletal: 4 bony 9 emaciated

skeleton: 4 past 5 atomy, bones, coral, ilium, mummy 6 sketch 7 outline, remains 9 framework

  disease: 7 rickets

  hiding place: 6 closet

  organization: 5 cadre

  sea animal: 5 coral, shell 6 sponge

skeleton key: 4 gilt 5 screw 7 twirler

skelly: 4 chub 6 squint 9 chaffinch

skelp: say 4 beat, blow, kick, pare, push, rain, slap, walk 5 write 6 basket, colony, squall, stride, strike 7 beehive, measure, perform, quickly, scratch, scuttle 8 splinter, suddenly

skeppist: 8 apiarist 9 beekeeper

skeptic, sceptic: 7 doubter, infidel 10 pyrrhonist, unbeliever 11 disbeliever, freethinker, nullifidian

skeptical, sceptical: 8 doubting 9 faithless 11 incredulous, questioning

skerry: 4 isle, punt, reef, rock 6 potato

sketch: dot, jot, map 4 draw, limn, plan, play, skit 5 draft, paint, skate, story, trace 6 apercu, design, layout, pastel 7 cartoon, croquis, drawing, outline, schizzo(It.) 8 describe 9 delineate, summarize 10 compendium 11 composition, delineation, description

sketchy: 5 rough, vague 10 inadequate, unfinished 11 superficial

skew: cup, cut, set 4 awry, fail, make, shun, slip, turn 5 askew, avoid, flunk, slant, stone, throw, twist 6 coping, escape, eschew, gauche, glance, offset, squint, swerve 7 blunder, distort, drizzle, oblique, pervert 8 slanting 9 deviating, distorted 12 misrepresent

skewer: pin, rod 5 prick, truss 6 fasten, pierce 7 hairpin 8 puncture 9 brochette

ski: 5 glide, slide

fall marker: 8 sitzmark

lift: 4 j-bar, t-bar 5 chair 7 gondola

race: 6 slalom 8 down-hill

run: 6 schuss

skid: bar 4 clog, curb, drag, hook, rail, scud, shoe, slip, trig 5 brake, check, slide 6 fender, runner, timber, twitch 7 plummet, protect, skidpan, support 8 platform, sideslip

skid row: 4 slum 6 bowery

skiff: 4 boat, skim 5 canoe, glide, graze, touch 6 caique, flurry 7 currane, rowboat

skiing salutation: 4 heil

skill: art, can 5 craft, haunt, knack, virtu 6 ability, address, aptness, cunning, finesse, justice, mastery, science 8 artifice, capacity, deftness, facility, industry, rhetoric, training 9 adeptness, dexterity, knowledge, readiness 10 adroitness, artfulness, astuteness, capability, cleverness, competence, efficiency, experience, expertness 11 information, proficiency 12 skillfulness

skillet: 6 spider 9 frying pan

skillful: apt 4 able, deft, fine, good, hend 5 adept, handy 6 adroit, artful, aufait, clever, crafty, daedal, expert, habile 7 capable, cleanly, cunning 8 dextrous, tactical 9 daedalian, dexterous, ingenious, righteous 10 proficient 11 intelligent 12 accomplished

skim: cut 4 film, flit, sail, scud, scum, skip 5 clear, cover, fleet, float, glide, graze, ready, study, throw 6 browse, glance, refuse 7 examine

skim over: 5 skirr 6 passim

skimp: 6 meager, scanty, scrimp 7 neglect 9 economize

skimpy: 5 chary, spare 6 scanty, stingy 9 niggardly 12 parsimonious

skin: 4 bark, best, derm, dole, fell, film, flay, hide, pare, peel, pell, pelt, rack, rind, scum 5 bate, cheat, cutis, derma, fraud, layer, plica, purse, scalp, shell, strip, sweep 6 abrade, callus, dermis, escape, fleece, scrape, spoils 7 callous, coating, cuticle, defraud, plating, profits, sharper, sheathe, surface, swindle 8 covering, exterior, membrane, pellicle, planking 9 epidermis, skinflint 10 integument, overcharge, pocketbook 11 decorticate, outdistance

animal: fur 4 coat, hide, pelt, plew, rack, robe, vair 5 coney, sculp 6 hackle, peltry

beaver: 4 plew

blemish: wen 4 mole, wart 7 freckle

burning sensation: 5 uredo

decoration: 6 tattoo

deeper layer: 5 cutis

depression: 6 dimple

disease: 4 acne 5 hives, mange, psora, rupia, tinea 6 eczema, tetter

dressed: fur

dryness: 7 xerosis

excessive pigment: 8 melanism

exudation: 5 sudor, sweat 12 perspiration

fold: 5 plica 7 dewlaps

fruit: 7 epicarp

layer: 4 derm 5 cutis, derma

oil: 5 sebum

opening: 4 pore

pert. to: 5 deric 6 dermal 9 cuticular, epidermal

piece: 5 blype

prepare: 5 taw

presser: 7 sammier

protuberance: 4 mole, wart 6 pimple

remover: 5 parer

resembling: 7 dermoid

sensitive layer: 5 cutis 7 enderon

spot: 7 freckle

tan: taw

tumor: wen

unsheared pelt: 8 woolfell

without: 8 apellous

skin-deep: 7 shallow 9 cutaneous 13 insignificant

skin game: 5 bunco, bunko, fraud 7 swindle

skinflint: 5 miser 6 huddle 7 niggard

skink: 4 adda, draw, hock, shin 5 drink, serve 6 liquor, lizard

skinker: 7 tapster

skinned: *dark:* 7 melanic, swarthy

thick: 9 pachyderm 11 pachydermic

thin: 9 sensitive

skinner: bet, gyp 5 cheat 6 driver 8 swindler

skinny: 4 bony, lean, thin 5 scant, spare 6 meanly, stingy 9 emaciated, niggardly 10 membranous

dip: 8 nude swim

skip: dap, hip, hop 4 balk, flee, gait, jump, leap, miss, omit, trip 5 bound, caper, elide, frisk, leave, scout, vault 6 basket, bucket, escape, gambol, glance, lackey, spring **7** abscond, captain, footman, servant **8** be absent, ricochet

along a surface: **7** skitter

school: tib **9** play hooky

skip over: **5** elide

lightly: **4** skim

water: dap

skipjack: fop **4** dish **6** bonito, elater **7** upstart **8** sailboat **9** stripling **10** butterfish **11** V-bottom boat

skipper: ihi **5** saury **6** leader, master **7** captain **9** butterfly, commander

East Indian: **6** serang

skippet: box **4** boat **5** skiff **8** envelope

skirl: fly **4** pipe, rain, snow **5** sweep, whirl **6** scream, shriek

skirling: **5** trout **6** salmon

skirmish: **5** brush, clash, fence, fight, melee **6** action, battle, bicker, combat, effort **7** contend, contest **8** conflict, flourish **9** encounter **10** velitation

skirr: fly, run **4** move, skim, tern **5** scour, whirr **6** scurry

skirt: lie, rim **4** edge, flap, girl, maxi, mini, slit **5** dress, evade, trend, woman **6** border, fringe **8** envelope, environs, go around **9** outskirts, periphery, petticoat **10** wraparound

ballet: **4** tutu

coat: **6** lappet

divided: **7** culotte

hoop: **6** peplum **9** crinoline, krinoline **11** farthingale

section: **4** gore **5** panel

short: **4** kilt, mini

steel: **5** tasse **7** lamboys

velvet: **4** base

skit: act **4** gibe, girl, gust, hoax, jeer, jest, slap **5** caper, pound, revue, story, taunt, trick **7** parody, shower, sketch, splash **7** asperse, flounce **8** ridicule **9** enclosure, stage show **10** caricature, reflection

skitter: hop **4** pass, skim, skip **5** glide **7** scamper, scatter **8** sprinkle

skittish: coy, shy **5** jumpy **6** fickle, frisky, lively **7** nervous, playful, restive **8** spirited **9** excitable, frivolous, sensitive **10** capricious **12** undependable

skittle: **4** play **5** trash **7** ninepin **8** nonsense, squander **9** enjoyment

skive: **4** dart, pare, skim **5** shave, wheel

skiver: **6** impale, skewer **7** leather, scatter

skivvy: **9** underwear **10** undershirt

skoal: **5** drink, toast **10** salutation **11** exclamation

skua: **4** gull **5** jager **6** jaeger

skulduggery: **8** foul play, trickery **10** craftiness, wickedness

skulk: **4** hide, lurk **5** dodge, evade, hedge, shirk, slink, sneak **8** malinger

skull: **4** bean, head, mind **5** brain **6** cobbra, crania(pl.) **7** cranium, harnpan

back part: **7** occiput

bone: **5** vomer **6** zygoma **7** frontal, maxilla **8** mandible, sphenoid, temporal

cavity: **5** fossa **7** foramen

pert. to: **5** inial **7** cranial

protuberance: **5** inion

soft spot: **8** fontanel

skullcap: **5** calot **6** beanie **7** calotte **8** capeline, yarmelke, yarmulke **9** zucchetto

Arabian: **7** chechia

cardinal's: **10** berrettino

defensive: **4** coif **9** coiffette

ecclesiastical: **6** callot **7** calotte **9** zucchetto

felt: **6** pileus

Jewish: **8** yarmelke, yarmulke

skunk: **5** snipe **6** putois(F.) **7** polecat, stinker **8** betrayer **9** overwhelm

skunk-like animal: **5** civet **7** zorillo

sky: **4** blue **5** azure, ether **6** summit, welkin **7** heavens **9** firmament

god: Anu **4** Anat **5** Dyaus

goddess: **5** Frigg **6** Frigga

highest point: **6** zenith

pert. to: **6** coelar **9** celestial

sky-blue: **5** azure **7** celeste **8** cerulean

sky pilot: **5** padre **8** chaplain, preacher **9** clergyman **10** missionary

skylark: run **4** bird, jump, lark, play, skip, yerk **5** yirpt **6** frolic

genus: **6** alauda

skylight: **6** dormer, window **8** abatjour(F.)

skyline: **7** horizon

skyscraper: **5** tower **8** building **9** structure

slab: **4** tile, wood **5** dalle, plate, slice, stela, stele **6** tablet

slab-like: **6** stelar **7** stelene

slack: lax **4** dull, idle, lull, slow, soft **5** chaff, evade, loose, relax, shirk, slake, tardy **6** abated, ease up, loosen, remiss **8** careless, dilatory, inactive, listless, sluggish, unsteady **9** dissolute, impudence, looseness, negligent **10** diminished, inadequate, neglectful **11** inattentive, indifferent

slacken: **4** ease, slow **5** abate, delay, relax **6** loosen reduce, relent, retard **8** decrease, moderate

slackening: **7** detente(F.), slowing

slacker: **4** spiv **7** coucher, shirker **8** embusque **9** goldbrick

slacks: **8** trousers

slade: den **4** cave, glen **5** glade, glide, slide **6** ravine, valley **7** peat bog **8** hillside

slag: **4** lava **5** ashes, dross, waste **6** cinder, debris, refuse, scoria **7** residue, scoriae(pl.) **9** recrement **11** agglomerate

slain: **4** dead **6** fallen, killed **8** murdered **11** slaughtered **12** assassinated

slainte: 5 toast 6 health 8 greeting 10 salutation

slake: mud, wet 4 cool, daub, flag, free, lick, mire, sate 5 abate, algae, allay, gully, loose, relax, slack, slime, smear, yield 6 aslake, deaden, lessen, quench, ravine, reduce 7 appease, assuage, crumble, gratify, refresh, relaxed, release, relieve, satisfy, slacken 8 decrease, mitigate, moderate 10 extinguish 12 disintegrate

slam: hit 4 bang, beat, blow, cuff, dash, gibe, push, shut, vole 5 abuse, clash, close, noise, throw 6 impact 7 collide, flounce 9 criticize

in cards: 4 vole

slammer: 4 jail 6 prison

slander: 4 tale 5 belie, libel, shame 6 defame, malign, report, vilify 7 asperse, blacken, distort, scandal, traduce 8 derogate, disgrace, dishonor, reproach, tear down 10 defamation, depreciate, detraction, scandalize 12 misrepresent

slang: 4 cant 5 abuse, argot 6 jargon, rakish, vulgar 7 dialect, license, swindle 10 vernacular

slant: tip 4 bend, bias, cant, skew, slab, tilt, turn, view 5 aside, bevel, point, slope 6 biased, breeze, falsify, glance, sklent 7 incline, opinion 8 attitude, diagonal, occasion 9 prejudice, viewpoint 10 hypotenuse 11 inclination, opportunity

slanted angle: 5 bevel

slap: box, hit, lap 4 blow, clap, cuff, nick, scud, snub, spat 5 break, click, clink, cluff, plump, skelp, smack 6 buffet, insult, rebuff, slight, strike 7 attempt 8 haymaker 9 castigate

slapdash: 5 abuse, hasty 8 careless, reckless 9 impetuous, roughcast 10 abruptness 11 haphazardly 12 carelessness 13 precipitately

slapjack: 7 pancake 11 griddlecake

slapstick: 4 joke 5 farce 6 comedy

slash: cut 4 dash, gash, lash, slit 5 crack, slosh, wound 6 attack, defeat, lessen, reduce, splash, strike, stripe 7 censure, scourge, slitter 8 diagonal, mark down 9 criticize, light into

slasher: 5 knife, sword 6 dagger 8 billhook 9 swordsman 12 swashbuckler

slashing: 4 huge 6 severe 7 dashing, driving, immense, violent 8 spirited 9 merciless 10 tremendous 11 criticizing

slat: bar, dab, rib 4 blow, flap, hide, hurl, lath, slap 5 strip, throw 6 louver 8 fragment, splinter

slate: rag 4 gray, list, rock, tile 5 board, color, flesh, hound, plank, scold 6 ballot, berate, pummel, punish, pursue, record, roster, tablet, thrash, ticket 7 censure, roofing 8 nominate, register, schedule 9 criticize, reprimand, thrashing

clean: 10 tabula rasa

tool: sax, zax

slater: 6 critic 9 wood louse

slath: 6 basket

slattern: daw 4 drab, frow, slut 5 dolly, idler, moggy, waste 6 blowze, faggot, sloppy 7 trifler, trollop 8 careless, slovenly

slatternly: 5 dirty, dowdy 6 blowzy, sordid, untidy 8 slovenly

slaty: 6 clayey 7 grayish 9 argillous 12 argillaceous

slaughter: 4 gash, kill, slay 6 battue, murder, pogrom, reduce 7 butcher, carnage, destroy, killing 8 butchery, hecatomb, massacre, violence 9 bloodshed, reduction 10 butchering 11 destruction

slaughterhouse: 8 abattoir, butchery, matadero(Sp.)

waste: 7 tankage

Slav: 4 Pole, Serb, Sorb, Wend 5 Croat, Czech 6 Slovak 7 Russian, Servian 8 Bohemian, Croatian, Moravian, Silesian 9 Bulgarian, Ukrainian 12 Czechoslovak

slave: 4 bond, esne, neif, peon, serf, toil 5 chela, helot, thane 6 addict, cumhal, drudge, penest(Gr.), thrall, toiler, vassal, wretch 7 bondman, captive, chattel, enslave, odalisk, servant, work hard 9 gallerian, hierodule, odalisque, sycophant

block: 7 catasta

comedy: 5 Davus(L.)

dealer: 5 bichy

fugitive: 6 maroon

pen: 5 crawl

ship: 6 slaver

The Tempest: 7 Caliban

traveling group: 6 coffle

slave driver: 6 despot, tyrant 8 martinet 11 Simon Legree

Slave States: 5 Texas 7 Alabama, Florida, Georgia 8 Arkansas, Delaware, Kentucky, Maryland, Missouri, Virginia 9 Carolinas, Louisiana, Tennessee 11 Mississippi 13 North Carolina, South Carolina

slaver: 5 drool, smear 6 drivel, saliva 7 flatter, slabber, slobber 8 be insane

slavery: 7 bondage, service 8 drudgery 9 captivity, servitude thralldom, vassalage 10 subjection 11 enslavement 12 enthrallment

release from: 7 manumit 8 liberate 10 emancipate 11 affranchise, enfranchise

Slavic: See Slav

slavish: low 4 base, bond, hard, vile 6 abject, menial 7 servile 8 despotic, enslaved 9 barbarous, dependent, imitative **10** oppresive, tyrannical **11** down-trodden, subservient

slay: 4 do in, kill 5 amuse, smite 6 murder, strike 7 butcher, delight, destroy, execute 9 slaughter 10 annihilate 11 assassinate, exterminate

by suffocation: 5 burke

slayer: 4 bane 6 killer 8 criminal, genocide, murderer, regicide, vaticide 9 matricide, patricide, regicidal 10 fratricide, sororicide

sleazy: 4 mean, thin 5 tacky 6 flimsy

sled: 4 pung 6 jumper, sleigh 7 clipper, coaster, travois, vehicle 8 toboggan 10 conveyance

Russian: 6 troika

sledge: 4 dray, sled 5 break 6 hammer, hurdle, sleigh, strike

sleek: nap 4 chic, oily 5 gloss, preen, shiny, slick, smart, suave 6 finish, glossy, polish, smooth, soigne 7 flatter, mollify, soignee 8 polished, unctuous 10 flattering 11 insinuating

sleep: nap 4 doss, doze 5 death, sopor 6 drowse, repose, snooze, stupor 7 bed down, slumber 8 lethargy 10 somnipathy 11 hibernation 15 unconsciousness

deep: 4 coma 5 sopor 6 stupor

god: 4 Soma 6 Hypnos 8 Morpheus

inability to: 8 insomnia

inducer of: 6 opiate 7 sandman, sopient 8 sedative

midday: 6 siesta

pert. to: 7 somnial

sleeper: bet, tie 4 beam 5 horse, shark 6 rafter, rester, timber 7 dormant, earmark, Pullman, reposer 8 dormouse, long shot 9 dowitcher, slumberer 11 stringpiece

sleepiness: 10 drowsiness, somnolence

sleeping: 4 abed 6 latent 7 dormant 8 inactive 9 quiescent

place: bed 4 bunk, doss 5 berth, couch 6 pallet 7 cubicle 9 cubiculum, dormitory

sickness: 12 encephalitis

sleepless: 5 alert 7 unquiet, wakeful 8 restless, vigilant, watchful 9 ceaseless 11 industrious, persevering

sleepwalker: 12 noctambulist, somnambulist

sleepy: 4 dull 5 tired 6 drowsy 7 languid 8 sluggish, soporose, soporous 9 lethargic, somnolent 10 phlegmatic, slumberous

Sleepy Hollow author: 6 Irving

sleet: ice 5 glaze

sleeve: 6 armlet, moggan 7 bushing, cathead

bar on: 7 chevron

leg-of-mutton: 5 gigot

sleigh: 4 pung, sled 6 cutter 7 cariole 8

carriole, toboggan

runner: 4 shoe

sleight: sly 5 craft, knack, skill, trick 6 crafty, wisdom 7 address, agility, conjure, cunning 8 artifice, deftness, prudence, trickery 9 chicanery, deception, dexterity, dexterous, quickness, stratagem 10 nimbleness

sleight-of-hand: 11 legerdemain

performer: 4 mage 8 conjurer, magician 15 prestidigitator

slender: 4 lean, slim, thin, weak 5 exile, guant, lanky, lithe, petit, reedy, short, small, sylph, wispy 6 feeble, lissom, meager, narrow, slight, svelte 7 gracile, lissome, tenuous, trivial, willowy 8 ethereal 9 attenuate, elongated 10 abstemious

slenderize: 4 slim 6 reduce

slenderness: 7 exility, tenuity

sleuth: tec 6 tracer 7 gumshoe, tracker, trailer 9 detective, operative 10 private eye 12 investigator

slew (see also **slough**): lot 4 much, slue, turn 5 bunch, twist 6 slough

sley: 4 reed 8 guideway

slice: cut, saw 4 jerk, part 5 carve, piece, share, shave, slash, whang 6 cantle, divide, rasher, shiver, sliver 7 portion 8 separate, splinter

of bacon: 6 rasher

of meat: 6 collop

slick: mag 4 fine, neat, oily, tidy 5 alert, preen, sleek, slide 6 adroit, chisel, clever, crafty, glossy, paddle, polish, smooth 7 cunning, dress up, smarten, thicket 8 slippery 9 enjoyable, excellent, ingenious 10 attractive, glistening 12 accomplished

slicker: 4 dude 5 cheat 6 gypper 7 gambler 8 raincoat, swindler 9 trickster

slide: 4 fall, skid, sled, slew, slip, slue 5 chute, coast, creep, glide, hurry, scoot, steal 6 sledge 7 decline, incline, slither, sluther 8 glissade, ornament 9 avalanche, backslide, landslide

fastener: 6 zipper

slideway: 8 guideway

slight: cut 4 fine, slap, snub, thin 5 flout, frail, leger(L.), light, minor, scant, scorn, sleek, small 6 flimsy, ignore, meager, remote, scanty, simple, slight, smooth 7 distain, fragile, gracile, neglect, nominal, shallow, slender, trivial 8 careless, delicate 9 disesteem, disparage, disregard, indignity 10 immaterial 11 discourtesy, superficial, unimportant 12 contemptuous 13 disparagement, imperceptible, insignificant, unsubstantial

sound: 4 peep

variation: 6 nuance 7 shading

slightest: 5 least

slighting remark: 4 slur

slim: sly 4 lean, slur, thin 5 gaunt, small, spare 6 adroit, crafty, meager, meagre, scanty, slight, sparse, svelte 7 cunning, slender, tenuous 9 worthless 10 slenderize

slime: mud 4 gore, ooze, slop 5 cover, filth, gleet, smear 6 mucous

slimer: 8 toadfish

slimy: 4 vile 6 filthy, vulgar 7 viscous 9 glutinous, offensive, repulsive 10 disgusting

sling: 4 cast, hurl 5 drink, fling, throw 6 weapon 7 bandage 9 slingshot

slink: 4 lurk 5 cower, crawl, sneak, steal

slip: err, imp 4 balk, clay, fall, omit, pier, quay, shed, skid, slue 5 chute, elude, error, fault, glide, lapse, leash, scion, shoot, slide 6 elapse, harbor, miscue 7 blunder, cutting, delapse, descend, faux pas, illapse, misstep, mistake, neglect, slither, sluther 8 lingerie, pinafore 9 anchorage, gaucherie 12 undergarment 13 transgression

slip away: die 4 pass 5 steal 6 elapse, escape

slip back: 6 revert 7 relapse 8 get worse

slip by: 4 pass 6 elapse

slip-up: 5 error 6 miscue 7 failure 9 oversight

slipknot: 5 noose

slipper: 4 mule, shoe 5 moyle, scuff 6 juliet, pliant, sandal 7 bauchle, scuffer, shuffle, willowy 8 babouche, slippery

slippery: 4 eely, glib, oily 5 slick 6 crafty, shifty, tricky, wanton 7 elusive, evasive, glidder 8 glibbery, unstable 9 deceitful, uncertain 10 unreliable 11 treacherous 13 untrustworthy

slipshod: 8 careless, slommack, slovenly, slummock 10 disorderly

slipslop, slip-slop: 5 inane, slops 6 gabble 7 blunder, twaddle 10 wishy-washy 11 malapropism

slit: cut, rit 4 fent, gash, kerf, nick, open, race, rent, tear 5 break, crack, sever, slash, split, unrip 6 cleave 7 fissure, opening 8 aperture, incision

slither: 4 slip 5 glide, slide 6 rubble 7 rubbish 8 slippery

sliver: cut 5 shred, slice, slops, split 6 strand 7 slobber 8 fragment, splinter

slob: ice, mud 4 mire, ooze, snow 5 slime 6 sloven, sludge 7 bungler

slobber: 4 gush, kiss 5 drool, slime, smarm 6 drivel, slaver, sloven 7 blubber, moisten, slabber

sloe: haw 4 plum 10 blackthorn

slog: hit 4 blow, plod, plug, slam, slug, toil, work 5 drive 6 drudge, strike 9 persevere

slogan: cry 4 word 5 motto 6 phrase 9 catchword

sloop: 4 boat, dray 8 sailboat

slop: mud 4 gulp, gush, mash, plod 5 slush, smock, spill, swill, waste 6 puddle, refuse, splash 7 cassock, clothes, garment, slobber 8 breeches, clothing, trousers

slope: dip, lie 4 bank, brae(Sc.), brow, cant, hang, ramp, rise, tilt 5 bevel, cliff, grade, scarp, slant, talus 6 ascent, aslant, aslope, bajada, depart, escarp, glacis 7 descent, incline, terrace, versant 8 gradient, hillside 9 acclivity, declivity, obliquely 10 declension 11 inclination

angle-measuring device: 10 clinometer

protective: 6 glacis

sloping: 6 aslant 7 oblique 8 downhill, inclined, slanting 9 declivous, inclining

sloppy: 5 messy 6 slushy 7 splashy 8 careless, effusive, slipshod, slovenly 11 intoxicated 12 disagreeable

slosh: mud 4 blow, gulp 5 slime, slush, spill, throw 6 splash, wallow 8 flounder

slot: bar, cut 4 bolt, slat, stab 5 crack, track, trail 6 course, hollow, keyway, spline 7 keyhole, opening 8 aperture, guideway 10 depression

sloth: ai 4 idle, lazy, pack, slow, unau 5 delay 6 acedia, animal, apathy, torpor 7 accidie, inertia, neglect 8 edentate, idleness, laziness, slowness 9 indolence, tardiness 11 sleuthhound 12 sluggishness, wastefulness

two-toed: 4 anau

slothful: 4 argh, idle, lazy 5 inert 8 inactive, indolent, sluggish 9 sedentary

slouch: hat 4 gait, idle, loll, lout, pipe 5 droop 6 bonnet, loafer, lubber 7 posture 8 drooping, laziness 9 pendulous 13 shiftlessness

slough, slew, slue: bog, mud 4 fall, hull, husk, mire, molt, ooze, plod, road, shed, skin, turn, veer 5 bayou, inlet, pivot, swamp, swing, twist 6 sheath, strike, swerve 7 channel, discard, mudhole 8 imprison

of despond: 7 despair 10 depression

sloughing: 7 ecdysis

sloven: 4 slob 5 besom, clart 6 loafer 7 hallion 9 scoundrel 11 undeveloped 12 uncultivated

slovenly: 4 lazy 5 dowdy, messy 6 blowzy, frouzy, frowsy, frowzy, grubby, sloppy, untidy 7 unkempt 8 careless, slattern, slipshod, sluttish 9 negligent 10 disorderly, slatternly

slow: lax 4 dull, late, poky 5 brosy, delay, grave, hooly, inert, pokey, slack, tardy 6 boring, hamper, hinder, retard, stolid, strike, stupid 7 dronish, gradual, laggard, slacken 8 boresome, dilatory, diminish, inactive, retarded, sluggard, sluggish 9 leisurely, lingering, slowgoing, unhurried 10 decelerate, deliberate, phlegmatic, retrograde 13 unprogressive

music: 5 largo, lento, tardo 6 adagio

slow down: lap 4 idle 5 delay, relax 6 retard 7 decline 10 decelerate, deliberate

slow loris: 5 kokam

slow-witted: 4 bull 6 stupid

slowness: 5 delay 6 lentor

slowpoke: 5 snail 7 dawdler 9 straggler

sludge: ice, mud 4 mire, ooze, slob 5 slime, snag 6 gulch 7 draught, limax, snail 8 bullet, hinder, loiter, nugget, strike 7 draught, mollusk, trepang 9 gastropod 11 caterpillar

slue: See **slough**

sluff: 7 discard

slug: bat, hit 4 blow, dose, dram, slam, slow, snag, stud 5 delay, drink, limax, snail 6 bullet, hinder, loiter, nugget, strike 7 draught, mollusk, trepang 9 gastropod 11 caterpillar

genus of: 4 doto 5 limax 6 elysia

pert. to: 8 limacine

sea: 7 trepang 10 nudibranch

sluggard: daw 4 idle, lazy, slug 5 drone, idler 8 faineant

slugger: bat 4 goon 5 boxer 6 hitter, mauler 7 batsman 8 operator

sluggish: 4 dull, lazy, logy, slow 5 brosy, faint, heavy, inert 6 bovine, drowsy, leaden, supine, torpid 7 dronish, languor, lumpish 8 dilatory, inactive, indolent, slothful, sluggard, stagnant 9 apathetic, lethargic 10 tardigrade 15 procrastinating

sluice: 4 gash, gote, gout, pipe, pour, race 5 flume, flush, swill, valve 6 breach, stream, trough 7 channel, launder, opening, passage 8 irrigate 9 floodgate

sluit: 5 ditch, gulch, gully

slum: 4 dump, junk, room 5 alley 6 barrio, ghetto 7 skid row

slumber: 4 coma, doze 5 sleep 6 drowse, repose 8 lethargy

slumberous: 4 calm 5 quiet 6 drowsy, sleepy 8 peaceful, tranquil 9 lethargic, somnolent, soporific

slump: sag 4 drop, fall, sink, slip 5 droop 6 cave in, slouch 7 decline 8 collapse 10 depreciate, depression

slur: 4 blot, blur, slip, soil 5 cheat, decry, elide, glide, slare, slide, smear, stain, sully, trick 6 insult, macule, slight, smirch, stigma 7 blemish, calumny, dimness, traduce 8 besmirch, disgrace, innuendo, reproach 9 aspersion, criticize, discredit, disparage, indignity 10 calumniate 11 contaminate 12 imperfection

slush: mud, wet 4 gush, mire, pulp, slud,

wash 5 grout 6 drench, drivel, sluice, splash 7 mixture, sludder 14 sentimentality

slut: 4 jade, minx 5 bitch, filth, quean 6 harlot, wanton 8 slattern 9 dratchell

sluttish: 4 lewd 5 gross 6 filthy, sordid 8 slovenly 10 disorderly

sly: 4 arch, cagy, foxy, ruse, slee, wily 5 coony, snaky, sneak 6 artful, clever, crafty, feline, secret, shrewd, slinky, sneaky, subtle, tricky 7 cunning, evasive, furtive, roguish 8 skillful, sneaking 9 cautelous, deceitful, secretive, underhand 10 fallacious 11 clandestine, dissembling, mischievous, underhanded 12 hugger-mugger

look: 4 leer, ogle

slyly spiteful: 5 catty

smack: bit, hit 4 bash, belt, blow, boat, buss, kiss, slap, tang 5 crack, savor, sloop, taste, touch, trace 6 cutter, flavor, heroin, strike, vessel 7 vestige 8 mouthful, sailboat 10 suggestion

smacking: 5 brisk, sharp 6 lively 8 spanking, vigorous

small: dab, sma(Sc.), tot, wad, wee(Sc.) 4 base, cute, lite, mean, puny, thin, tiny, whit, wisp 5 dawny, minim, minor, petty, scant 6 atomic, dapper, grubby, humble, little, mignon, minute, modest, petite(F.), remote, slight 7 minimal, selfish, slender, trivial 8 atomical, picayune, trifling 9 miniature, minuscule, thumbnail 10 diminutive 12 narrowminded 13 insignificant

amount: mot 4 atom, chip, drop, iota, mote, tate 5 speck 6 detail, morsel 7 driblet, handful, modicum, morceau(F.), snippet 8 modecule

bunch: 4 wisp

coin: 4 mite

small-fry: 4 kids, tots 8 children 10 youngsters

small-minded: 4 mean 5 petty 6 narrow 7 bigoted, selfish 10 prejudiced, ungenerous, vindictive

small talk: 6 babble 7 prattle 8 badinage, chitchat

smallage: 6 celery 7 parsley

smallness: 7 elixity, paucity

smallpox: 7 variola

smaragd: 7 emerald

smarm: 4 gush 7 slobber

smarmy: 8 unctuous

smart: 4 bite, braw, chic, neat, pain, posh, smug, tidy, trig, wily, wise 5 acute, alert, brisk, clean, fresh, natty, nifty, quick, sharp, sting, witty 6 active, astute, bright, cheesy, clever, dressy, jaunty, lively, shrewd, spruce, suffer, swanky 7 capable, elegant, knowing, pungent, stylish 8 spirited, talented, vigorous 9 competent, dexterous **10** precocious, suffer pain **11** fashionable, intelligent

smarten: **6** spruce **7** improve **8** brighten, titivate

smash: hit **4** bash, blow, bung, dash, ruin **5** break, crash, crush, stave, wreck **6** defeat, impact **7** destroy, shatter, smash-up, success **8** collapse, stramash(Sc.) **9** collision, pulverize **10** bankruptcy

smashed: **5** drunk **11** intoxicated

smashup: **4** ruin **5** wreck **6** defeat, impact **7** failure **8** collapse **9** collision **10** bankruptcy **11** destruction

smatter: **5** break **6** babble, dabble **7** chatter, clatter, crackle, shatter **9** fragments, small bits

smatterer: **7** dabbler **8** sciolist

smear: dab, rub **4** blot, blur, daub, gaum, soil, spot, stop, whip **5** clart, cleam, slake, slare, stain, sully, taint **6** anoint, bedaub, blotch, defame, defeat, defile, grease, malign, smirch, smudge, spread, stigma, thwart **7** besmear, plaster, pollute, slander, splatch **8** besmirch, ointment, slaister **9** overwhelm **10** overspread

smearcase: **6** cheese

smectic: **9** detergent, purifying

smell: **4** funk, fust, odor, olid, reek **5** aroma, fetor, flair, scent, sniff, trace **6** breath **7** hircine, noisome, perfume **9** fragrance **10** suggestion **11** get a whiff of, graveolence

having a disagreeable: bad **4** foul, olid, **5** fetid **10** malodorous

loss of sense: **7** anosmia

offensive: **4** reek **5** fetor, nidor, stink **6** stench

pert. to: **9** olfactory

pleasant: **5** aroma **7** perfume

stale: **5** fusty, musty

smell-feast: **7** sponger **8** parasite

smeller: **4** nose **6** feeler **7** antenna, bristle

smelling salts: **9** hartshorn

smelt: **4** fish, flux, fuse, melt, prim **5** iuanga(N.Z.), reduce, refine **7** process, scorify

smelting: *by-product:* **4** slag

cone: **4** pina

smew: **4** duck **9** merganser

smidge, smidgen: bit **4** mite **8** particle

smile: **4** beam, grin **5** smirk, sneer **6** arride, simper

smirch: **4** blot, soil **5** smear, stain, sully, taint **6** blotch, smudge, smutch **7** begrime, blacken, blemish, tarnish **8** besmirch, discolor, dishonor

smirk: **4** leer, trim, yirn **5** quick, smart, smile, sneer **6** simper, spruce **7** grimace, smiling

smite: hit **4** blow, clap, cuff, dash, gird,

hurl, kill, pass, slap, slay, swat **5** blast, knock, skite **6** attack, buffet, defeat, hammer, pierce, punish, strike **7** afflict, chasten, clobber, collide, destroy, disease, impress, inspire **8** distress

smith: **6** forger **7** farrier **10** blacksmith **11** metalworker

smithereens: **4** bits **5** atoms **6** pieces **8** flinders **9** fragments, particles

smithy: **6** forger **7** farrier **10** blacksmith

smitten: **6** fond of **8** affected, enamored, stricken **9** afflicted, enamoured

smock: **5** kamis, shift, tunic **6** camise **7** chemise **11** overgarment

smog: fog **4** mist

smoke: **4** floc, fume, funk, haze, mist, pipe, smog **5** cigar, cubeb, segar, smook(Sc.), vapor **6** smudge **7** cheroot, cigaret **9** cigarette

fragrant: **7** incense

outlet: **7** chimney **8** fumeduct, fumiduct

wisp: **4** floc

smoke out: **5** flush **6** reveal **8** discover

smokejack: **4** flue **6** funnel

smoker: car **4** stag **5** party

smokestack: **4** pipe **6** funnel **7** chimney

smoky: **4** hazy **5** dingy, fumid **6** fumish, smudgy **9** fumacious

smolder, smoulder: **5** choke, smoke **6** smudge **7** smother **9** fulminate, suffocats

smooth: **4** calm, ease, easy, even, gleg, glib, iron, lene, mild, pave, sand **5** bland, brent, furry, glace, glary, glaze, level, plane, preen, press, quiet, silky, sleek, slick, soapy, suave **6** creamy, evenly, fluent, gentle, glassy, glossy, mangle, serene, sleeky **7** amiable, equable, erugate, flatten, plaster **8** explicit, friendly, glabrous, hairless, levigate, palliate, pleasant, polished, soothing **9** courteous, unruffled **10** flattering **11** alabastrine **12** frictionless, ingratiating **13** mellifluently, uninterrupted

phonetically: **4** lene

smoother: **7** abraser

smorgasbord: **8** mishmash **9** appetizer **10** restaurant **12** hors d'oeuvres

smother: **5** choke **6** stifle, welter **7** overlie, repress, smolder, turmoil **8** suppress **9** suffocate

smudge: **4** blot, blur, smug, smut, soil, soot **5** laugh, prink, smear, smile, stain **6** smutch **7** begrime, chuckle, smolder **10** blackening

smug: dig **4** neat, prig, tidy, trim, vain **5** clean, grind, smart, steal, suave **6** pilfer, spruce **7** correct **9** confident **10** blacksmith, complacent **13** selfsatisfied

smuggler: **6** runner **10** bootlegger

smurr, smur: **4** mist **5** cloud **7** drizzle

smut: **4** bunt, coom, mark, soil, spot **5**

coomb, grime, stain, sully, taint 6 blight, defile, smudge 8 besmirch, discolor 9 obscenity

smutch: 4 blot, dirt, smut, soot, spot 5 grime, stain, sully, taint, tinge, touch, trace 6 defile, smudge 7 blacken

smutty: 5 dirty, dusky, sooty 6 soiled, sordid 7 obscene, spoiled, tainted 8 indecent

Smyrna: 5 Izmir

fig: 5 eleme, elemi

snack: bit, sip 4 ball, bite, jibe, nosh, part, snap 5 acute, alert, chack, lunch, quick, seize, share, smack, taste 6 adroit, morsel, repast, snatch 7 portion, quickly, sharply, teatime 8 grasping, snappish 9 light meal

snaffle: bit 4 loot 5 check, steal 6 pilfer 7 saunter, snuffle 8 restrain 9 bridle bit, restraint

snafu: 4 awry 5 mix-up 6 muddle 8 disorder, entangle 9 confusion

snag: cut, hew, nag, nub 4 base, carp, knot, part, slug, tear, tine, tree, trim, unit 5 break, catch, fault, point, snail, stump, tooth 6 branch, damage, hazard, tongue 8 obstacle 9 hindrance 10 difficulty, impediment 11 obstruction 12 protuberance

snagger: 8 billhook

snail: 4 slug, snag, wilk 5 drone, mitra 6 dodman, tritou, winkle 7 driller, mollusk, testudo 8 escargot, neritine, sluggard 9 gastropod 10 hoddy-doddy

clam-killing: 6 winkle

genus of: 5 fusus 6 nerita 9 clausilia

pond: 6 coret

shell: 7 cochlea

snailflower: 7 caracol

snake: asp, boa, nag 4 bind, curl, drag, draw, naga, skid, snot, tail, turn, wind, worm 5 aboma, adder, arrow, braid, cobra, coral, crawl, creep, cribo, filch, kriat, mamba, racer, sneak, steal, viper 6 katuka, python 7 bokadam, camoodi, elapine, hagworm, ingrate, meander, rattler, reptile, serpent, slither 8 anaconda, bungarum, camoodie, moccasin, ophidian, ringhals 9 whipsnake 10 blacksnake, bushmaster, copperhead, massasauga, sidewinder 11 cottonmouth, rattlesnake 12 schaapsteker

big: boa 6 python 8 anaconda 11 constrictor

expert: 13 herpetologist

genus of: boa 7 ophidia

horned: 8 cerastes

killer: 7 mongoos 8 mongoose

marine: 6 chital

movement: 7 slither

mythological: See serpent

poison: 5 venom

resembling: 8 viperine

sea: 6 kerril

sound: 4 hiss 6 rattle

snake charmer's flute: 5 pungi

snake dancers: 4 Hopi, Taos 5 Moqui

snake-haired woman: 6 Gorgon, Medusa, Stheno 7 Euryale

snake in the grass: 4 evil 7 traitor 12 hidden danger

snake killer: 8 mongoose 10 road runner

snake-shaped: 9 anguiform

snakeberry: 6 byrony 9 baneberry 11 bittersweet 14 partridge-berry

snakebird: 6 darter 7 anhinga, wryneck

snakebite antidote: 5 guaco

snakeflower: 7 campion 8 blueweed 10 starflower, stitchwort

snakehead: 7 figwort 10 turtlehead

snakelike: 8 ophidian 9 colubrine 10 anguineous

fish: eel

snakemouth: 6 orchid 7 pogonia

snakeroot: 6 seneca, senega 7 bugbane, sangrel 9 birthwort 10 bitter-bush

snakeskin: 6 exuvia

snaky: sly 4 evil, wavy 5 angry 6 touchy 7 anguine, sinuous, winding, wriggly 8 spiteful, twisting, venomous 9 snakelike 10 perfidious, serpentine 11 exasperated, treacherous

snap: rod 4 bark, easy, knap, pass, shut 5 break, catch, chack, cheat, cinch, clap, crack, filip, flask, flick, ganch, grasp, hanch, quick, seize, sever, smart, snack, spell, stamp, steal, vigor, wafer 6 biting, cookie, energy, fillip, report, retort, snatch 7 capture, crackle, project, sharper, sparkle 8 interval, particle, puncheon, sinecure, snapshot 9 crackling, crispness, elasticity, fastening, handcuffs, interrupt, smartness, snatching 10 photograph 11 scintillate

with finger: 6 fillip

snap back: 7 rebound, recover

snape: nip 4 snub 5 bevel, check, stint, taper 6 rebuke 8 beveling 10 disappoint

snapper: 4 bean 5 error 6 beetle, bonbon, turtle 7 cosoque, stumble, whopper 8 cachucho, fastener 9 castanets 10 stitchwort, woodpecker 11 firecracker, glassworker, phainopepla

snappish: 4 edgy, tart 5 cross, short, testy 7 cutting, peevish, uncivil 8 petulant 9 fractious, irascible, irritable 12 sharp-tongued

snappy: 4 cold 5 brisk, quick, sharp, smart 6 spiffy, strong, sudden 7 pungent, stylish 9 energetic, copacetic

snapshot: 7 picture, tintype 10 photograph

snare: bag, gin, net, pit, web 4 fang, grin,

lure, mesh, toil, trap 5 benet, brake, catch, grasp, noose, steal 6 ambush, cobweb, entice, entoil, entrap, gilder, tangle, trapan, trepan 7 involve, overnet, pitfall 8 entangle, inveigle 9 deception 12 entanglement

snark: 5 snore 6 boojum

snarl: arr 4 carl, girn, gnar, harl, hurr, knot, maze, snap, yarr, yirr 5 anvil, catch, ganch, gnarl, gnarr, growl, scold 6 hamper, tangle 7 confuse, grizzle, grumble, involve, quarrel 8 complain, entangle 9 confusion 10 complicate 12 complication

snarly: 5 cross, surly 7 peevish, snarled, tangled 8 confused, snarling 10 illnatured 11 bad-tempered

snash: 5 abuse 6 gibing 9 insolence

snatch: bit, get, hap, nab 4 grab, snap, take, trap, yerk 5 braid, catch, clawk, cleek, erept, grasp, gripe, nip up, pluck, seize, snare, spell, stint, swipe, wrest 6 abduct, clutch, kidnap, remove, twitch 7 excerpt, grabble 8 fragment

snatchy: 9 irregular, spasmodic 11 interrupted 12 disconnected

snath, snathe: lop 5 prune, shaft, snead 9 handle

sneak: 4 lurk 5 cower, creep, filch, miche, peach, skulk, slink, snoop, steal 6 coward, cringe, pilfer, rascal, secret, snudge, tattle 9 fefnicute

sneaking: sly 4 mean, poor 6 craven, hidden, paltry, secret 7 furtive, hangdog 8 cowardly, stealthy 9 dastardly, niggardly, underhand 12 contemptible 12 surreptitious

sneap: spy 5 sneak 7 reprove

sneb: bar 4 bolt, snub 6 fasten, rebuke 9 reprimand

sneer: 4 gibe, gird, grin, jeer, mock, snub 5 fleer, fling, flird, flout, flurn, scoff, slare, snirl, snort 7 disdain, grimace, snicker 8 belittle, ridicule

sneeze: 5 neese(Sc.) 7 kerchoo 12 sternutation

pert. to: 7 errhine 12 sternutatory

sneezewort: 8 ptarmica, ptarmite

snell: 4 hard, keen 5 acute, eager, harsh, sharp, smart, snood, swift 6 active, biting, clever, leader, severe 7 caustic, extreme, pungent, quickly, swiftly 8 piercing 10 vigorously

snick: cut, hit 4 blow, draw, kink, knot, move, nick, snip 5 click, notch, share, shoot, snack 6 pierce, strike

snicker: 5 knife, laugh, neigh, sneer, snirl 6 giggle, hee-haw, titter, whinny 7 chortle, chuckle

snide: low, sly 4 base, mean 6 tricky 7 crooked 8 inferior, spurious 9 malicious 11 counterfeit

sniff: 4 nose 5 scent, smell, snuff 6 detect, inhale 7 sniffle 8 perceive, sibilate 9 recognize

sniffy: 8 scornful 10 disdainful 12 contemptuous, supercilious

snifter: 4 blow, dram, good 5 drink, sniff, snort, storm 6 goblet, moment, snivel 7 dilemma, reverse 9 excellent

snit: eel, lop 4 chop, drag, jerk 5 snake, sneak 6 pilfer

sniggle: 4 trap 5 catch 7 broggle

snip: bit, cut 4 clip, curb, minx, snap 5 check, filch, notch, piece, shred, snack 6 snatch, stripe, stroke, tailor 8 fragment, incision, particle 9 disfigure

snipe: 4 bird, butt, fool 5 skunk 8 fire upon 9 criticize 10 sharp-shoot

cry: 5 scape

flock: 5 whisp

snipe hawk: 7 harrier

sniper: 8 ambusher

snippy: 4 curt, mean, tart 5 bluff, brief, gruff, sharp 6 sniffy, stingy 8 snappish, snippety 11 closefisted, fragmentary 12 supercilious

snit: 5 pique 8 angry fit

snitch: 4 nose, tell 5 catch, peach, pinch, steal, thief 6 betray, inform, pilfer, smitch, snatch 8 informer, inform on, particle

snivel: cry 4 cant, fret, weep 5 sniff, whine 6 pathos 7 emotion, snuffle 8 complain

snob: cut, sob 4 aper, scab 5 toady 6 flunky, poseur 7 cobbler, cricket, flunkey, parvenu, plebian, shoneen, upstart 8 blackleg, bluenose, commoner, parvenue, townsman 9 pretender, shoemaker 10 fivestones

snobbish: 7 high-hat 11 overbearing

snood: hat, tie 4 bind 5 braid 6 fasten, fillet, ribbon 7 hairnet

snook: pry 5 smell, sneak, sniff 6 follow, robalo, search 7 snuffle 9 barracuda

snoop: pry 4 look, nose, peek, peep 5 sneak 6 search 8 busbody

snooper: 7 marplot, meddler 8 busybody

snoot: 4 face, nose, snub 7 grimace

snooty: 7 haughty, upstage 8 snobbish 10 hoity-toity 12 contemptuous, supercilious

snooze: nap 4 doze 5 sleep 6 drowse, siesta 7 snoozle

snoozle: 4 doze 5 sleep 6 cuddle, nuzzle 7 snuggle

snore: 4 rout 5 snork, snort 7 saw wood

snoring: 5 stiff 7 roaring, stertor 10 stertorous

snork: pig 5 grunt, snore, snort

snort: 4 rout 5 drink, grunt, laugh, snirl, snore, snork 11 inhale a drug

snotty: 5 dirty, nasty, slimy 6 offish,

snooty **7** haughty, viscous **8** impudent, snotlike **9** offensive **12** contemptible, supercilious

snout: neb **4** mull, nose **5** groin, spout, trunk **6** nozzle **7** conduit, rostrum, tobacco

snout-nose: **7** gruntle **9** proboscis

snow: ice, sna **4** grue, snaw(Sc.) **5** blizz, cover, opium **6** heroin **7** cocaine, deceive **8** obstruct **9** whiteness

glacial: **4** firn, neve

granular: **4** corn

half-melted: **5** slush

house: **4** iglu **5** igloo

living in: **5** neval

mushy: **4** slob

pellet: **7** graupel

resembling: **7** niveous

slide: **8** glissade **9** avalanche

vehicle: **4** pung, sled **6** sleigh

wedding: **4** rice

snow and rain: **5** sleet

snow flurry: **5** skirl

snow goose: **4** chen **5** brant, wavey

snow grouse: **9** ptarmigan

snow mass: **9** avalanche

snow ridges: **8** sastrugi, zastrugi

snow runner: ski **4** skee

snowflake: **4** bird **5** finch **7** crystal

snowshoe: pac, ski **4** skee

snowstorm: **8** blizzard

snowy: **4** pure **5** nival, white **6** chaste **8** spotless, unsoiled

snub: cut, nip **4** chip, curb, slap, stop **5** check, frump, quell, scold, snool, snoot **6** hinder, ignore, rebuff, rebuke, remark, retort, slight, tauten **7** affront, neglect, repress, upbraid **8** restrain, send away **9** interrupt, ostracize, reprimand

snuff: **4** odor **5** pinch, pique, scent, smell, sniff, snort **6** detect, inhale **7** offense, tobacco, umbrage **8** sibilate **10** extinguish

kind of: **5** musty **6** rappee **8** bergamot, Maccaboy **10** blackguard, Copenhagen

snuffbox: **4** mill, mull **9** tabatiere

snuffy: **5** dirty, sulky, vexed **6** horrid **7** annoyed **10** displeased **12** disagreeable, unattractive **13** short-tempered

snug, **4** bein, bien, cosh, cozy, neat, safe, tidy, trim, warm **5** close, quiet, tight **6** modest, secure, silent **7** compact, snuggle **8** reticent, secreted, taciturn **9** concealed, seaworthy, secretive **10** prosperous **11** comfortable

snuggery: den **4** nook **7** cottage

snuggle: **4** nest **6** cuddle, nestle

snugly: **6** cosily

so: sae, sic, sua **4** ergo, thus, very **5** hence **7** because **9** in this way, similarly, therefore **11** accordingly **12** consequently

so be it: **4** amen

so far: yet **4** thus

soak: dip, hit, ret, sog, sop, sot, wet **4** bate, blow, bowk, buck, hurl, ooze, pawn, sock **5** binge, drink, drouk, imbue, punch, souse, spree, steep **6** drench, engage, imbibe, imbrue, seethe, tipple **8** drunkard, macerate, permeate, saturate **9** distemper, percolate **10** impregnate, instructor, overcharge

flax: ret

in brine: **4** corn, salt **8** marinate

soaked: wet **6** sodden **7** drenched

soap: **4** sape, sapo, wash **5** money, savon **6** lather **7** cleanse, flatter **9** flattery detergent **14** television show

convert into: **8** saponify

frame bar: **4** sess

ingredient: lye

mottled: **7** castile **8** eschwege

parmaceutical: **4** sapo

plate: **4** sess

substitute: **5** amole, borax

soap plant: **5** amole

soapstone: **4** talc **8** steatite

full of: **7** talcose

soapy: **4** oily, soft **5** suave **6** smooth **7** saponic **8** lathered, unctuous **9** soapsuddy **10** latherable **11** saponaceous **12** ingratiating

soar: fly **4** lift, rise, sail **5** float, glide, hover, mount, plane **6** ascend, aspire **7** take off **9** transcend

Soave: **12** dry white wine

sob: cry **4** sigh, wail, weep **5** boohoo **7** whimper **8** frighten

sober: **4** calm, cool, dark, gray, poor, sane **5** douce, grave, quiet, staid **6** ailing, feeble, gentle, humble, sedate, severe, simple, solemn, somber, steady, subdue, temper **7** chasten, earnest, regular, serious, subdued, weighty **8** composed, decorous, moderate, peaceful, rational **9** abstinent, collected, realistic, temperate **10** abstemious **11** indifferent **13** unimpassioned, unpretentious

sobol: **5** sable **6** marten

soboles: **5** shoot **6** stolen, sucker

sobriety: **7** gravity **9** restraint, soberness, solemnity, soundness **10** abstinence, moderation, sedateness, temperance **11** seriousness **14** reasonableness

sobriquet, soubriquet: **4** name **5** alias, chuck, title **6** byname **7** affront, epithet **8** nickname **11** appellation

so-called: **7** alleged, nominal **10** ostensible

soccer player: **6** booter, goalie, kicker, winger

sociability: **10** affability

sociable: **4** cozy, sofa **6** chummy, social **7** affable **8** carriage, familiar, friendly, informal, tricycle **9** aeroplane, agreeable, reception, talkative **10** accessible, gregarious **13** communicative, companionable

social: tea **4** stag **5** party **6** genial, smoker **9** agreeable, convivial, gathering **10** gregarious **13** companionable

affair: tea **4** ball **6** soiree **9** reception

career beginning: **5** debut

climber: **4** snob **7** parvenu, upstart

gathering: bee, tea **4** club, stag **5** party **6** smoker **7** reunion **9** reception

group: **4** clan, club **5** caste, class, lodge, tribe **6** estate, family, jet set **7** coterie **8** sorority **9** fraternity

insect: bee

outcast: **5** leper **6** pariah

person: **4** host **5** mixer **7** hostess

system: **6** feudal, modern, regime, tribal **11** traditional

worker: **7** almoner, analyst **8** do-gooder **9** clinician

socialism: **7** etatism **9** Communism **10** utopianism

socialist: Red **6** Fabian **9** anarchist, Bolshevik, communist **10** Bolshevist **11** nationalist **12** collectivist

socialize: mix **6** mingle **9** associate

society (see also **organization**): **4** bund, clan, gild **5** guild, order, union **6** menage, jet set **7** academy, company, hetaera, hetaira **8** academie, alliance **9** accademie, community **10** connection, upper crust **11** aristocracy, association, cooperation, intercourse, partnership **12** denomination, relationship **13** companionship, confederation, confraternity, participation

girl: deb

high: **9** beau monde, haut monde

low (member): **4** raff **5** riff-raff

kind of: **4** SPCA, frat, tong **5** elite, order, choir **7** societe **8** sorority **10** fraternity

secret: Hui **4** tong, egbo **5** mafia, lodge **6** mafia, ogboni **7** Camorra **9** Carbonari

symbol: **7** regalia

Society Islands: **5** Tahaa **6** Moorea, Tahiti **7** Huahine, Maupiti, Raiatea **8** Bora Bora

capital: **7** Papeete

explorer: **4** Cook

people: **10** Polynesian

Society of Friends: **7** Quakers

founder: Fox

sociology: **8** demotics

sock: hit, sew **4** beat, blow, hurl, shoe, sigh, vamp **5** drive **6** anklet, buskin, comedy, sandal, strike **7** hosiery, slipper socking **8** drainage, stocking **9** plowshare

sockdolager: **4** oner **8** finisher

socket: **5** lance, spear **6** cavity, collet, hollow **7** opening **9** plowshare

kind of: pan **4** birn **5** orbit **8** alveolus

Socrates: *biographer:* **5** Plato

birthplace: **6** Athens

dialogue: **4** Meno **6** Phaedo **8** Apologia

escape plotter: **5** Crito

love: **10** philosophy, Alcibiades

method: **8** maieutic

poison: **7** hemlock

wife: **8** Xantippe **9** Xanthippe

sod: **4** delf, dove, flag, peat, soak, soil, turf **5** delft, divot, glebe, soggy, sward **6** saddle, sodden **7** stratum **9** fermented

pert. to: **8** alkaline

soda: sal **8** beverage **9** saleratus

sodalite: **5** lenad **7** mineral

sodality: **5** union, unity **6** chapel **10** fellowship, fraternity **11** association, brotherhood **13** companionship

sodden: wet **5** drunk, heavy, moist, sammy, soggy **6** boiled, dulled, soaked, stewed, stupid **7** bloated, drunken, steeped **8** spirited **9** saturated **11** intoxicated

sodium: **7** natrium

carbonate: **4** soda **5** borax, trona **6** natron **7** salsoda

chlorate: **5** NaClO₃

chloride: sal, tar **4** NaCl, salt **7** saltcat

compound: **4** soda

nitrate: **5** niter

tetraborate: **5** borax

Sodom: *king:* **4** Bera

neighbor: **8** Gomorrah

sodomite: **6** bugger

sofa: **5** boist, couch, divan **6** lounge, settee **7** bergere, dosados, ottoman **8** causeuse **9** banquette, davenport **12** chesterfield

soft: coy, low **4** easy, feil, fine, limp, mild, waxy, weak **5** bland, cushy, downy, dolce, dulce, faint, givey, hooly, light, mushy, piano, sooth **6** clammy, dreamy, fluffy, gentle, gently, placid, silken, simple, smooth, tender **7** clement, ductile, lenient, lightly, quietly, squashy, subdued **8** delicate, feminine, flexible, tranquil **9** temperate, tractable, untrained **10** effeminate, peacefully **11** comfortable, sympathetic **12** nonalcoholic **13** compassionate

and smooth: **5** furry, silky, soapy **6** mellow, supple **7** cottony

and sweet: **5** dolce **6** dulcet

and wet: **5** mushy **7** squashy

food: pap

mass: **4** pulp

music: **5** dulce, piano

palate: **4** cion **5** uvula, velum

pedal: **6** hush-up **7** silence **8** play down

soap: **4** gush **5** blarney, flatter, wheedle **8** flattery, sweet-talk, wheedling

soft drink: ade, pop **4** soda **5** tonic

softa: 7 student 8 beginner

soften: 4 ease, melt 5 allay, malax, relax, yield 6 affect, anneal, gentle, pacify, relent, soother, subdue, temper, weaken 7 amolish, appease, assuage, mollify 8 attemper, enervate, enfeeble, lenitive, macerate, mitigate, modulate 9 alleviate, emolliate, meliorate 10 emasculate, depreciate, intenerate 11 tranquilize

softening: 7 lenient 8 emulsive 9 demulcent 10 moderation 11 melioration

of brain: 8 dementia

of decayed fruit: 4 blet

soft-spoken: 4 mild 5 bland, suave 6 gentle, smooth 12 ingratiating

softhearted: 6 tender 13 compassionate

soft touch: 4 snap 6 sucker 8 easy mark, pushover

sog: 4 doze, soak 6 drowse 8 saturate

soggy: wet 4 damp 5 heavy, humid 6 soaked, sodden, watery 9 saturated

soigne, soignee: 4 chic, neat, tidy 5 sleek 7 stylish 9 dressed up 11 well-groomed

soil: 4 blot, daub, dirt, foil, grit, land, moil, mool, slur, spot 5 dirty, earth, filth, glebe, grime, smear, solum, stain, sully, taint 6 assoil, bedaub, befile, befoul, bemire, defile, grease, ground, refuse, sewage, smirch, smudge, vilify 7 begrime, benasty, besmear, corrupt, country, pollute, tarnish 8 alluvium, besmirch, disgrace 9 bedraggle, bespatter, droppings, excrement 11 contaminate

claylike: 4 marl

goddess of: 7 Demeter

kind of: 4 clay, loam, marl, lair, malm, moss 5 adobe, loess, groot, humus

organic: 5 humus

soiled: 4 foul 5 dingy, grimy 6 smeary 7 sullied 8 unchaste 9 blemished

soilure: 5 satin 6 smirch

soiree: 5 party 6 affair

sojourn: 4 bide, howf, rest, stay, stop 5 abide, abode, delay, dwell, howff, lodge, tarry, visit 6 reside, travel 7 allodge, mansion 8 abidance 9 residence, tarriance 11 peregrinate

sojourner: 7 boarder 8 comeling, resident 9 transient

sol: sun 4 gold 6 sun-god 7 Phoebus

solace: 5 allay, amuse, cheer 6 lessen, relief, soothe 7 assuage, comfort, console 9 alleviate, diversion, entertain 10 recreation, relaxation 11 alleviation, consolation

solan: 4 fowl 5 goose 6 gannet

solar, soler, sollar: 4 loft, roof, room 5 floor, story 6 garret, heliac, tropic 7 chamber 8 heliacal 9 apartment

excess over lunar year: 5 epact

solar system: *member:* 6 planet

beyond: 9 deep space

model: 6 orrery

sold (see also **sell**): 8 marketed

solder: 4 fuse, heat, join, mend, weld 5 braze, patch, unite 6 cement 9 sculpture

soldering: *flux:* 5 resin, rosin

piece: lug

soldier: man, vet 4 fogy, swad 5 fogey, guffy, poilu, sammy, shirk 6 galoot, marine, Zouave 7 brigand, feedman, fighter, hobbler, hotspur, palikar, private, regular, trooper, veteran, warrior 8 bear arms, buffcoat, cavalier, gendarme, malinger, servitor, tolpatch, shackman 9 grenadier, musketeer 10 serviceman

cavalry: 6 hussar 8 chasseur

detachment: 4 file

drinking flask: 7 canteen

female: 4 WAAC

foreign: 4 peon, kern 5 nezam, poilu, sepoy, kerne, spahi 6 askari, lascar, sapper 7 cateran, hoplite, Billjim 8 grognard, miquelet 10 base wallah, carmagnole, carabineer

group of: 4 band, file 5 corps, force, squad, troop 7 brigade, caterva, company, platoon 8 division 9 battalion

irregular: 9 guerrilla

mercenary: 7 Hessian, Swisser, Switzer

newly trained: 5 cadet, plebe, rooky 6 rookie 7 chicken, recruit, trainee 8 bezonian 11 replacement

of fortune: 10 adventurer

old: vet 7 veteran 8 grognard

overcoat: 6 capote

quarters: 7 billets 8 barracks

special functions: 6 lancer, sapper 7 velites, dragoon, trooper 8 fencible, fugleman 9 fantassin, targeteer, flugelman 10 cuirassier, velitation, carabineer, carabinier 12 antesignanus

trenching tools: 8 burgoyne

vacation: 4 pass 5 leave, R and R 8 furlough

soldierly: 5 brave 6 heroic 7 martial

sole: one 4 dish, fish, foot, lone, mere, only, yoke 5 afald, alone, floor, plate, slade 6 bottom, entire, furrow, halter, hearth, lonely, single, unique, valley 7 outsole, subsoil 8 desolate, flatfish, isolated, solitary, unshared 9 exclusive, threshold, unmarried, unmatched 10 foundation, one and only, underframe, unsharable, windowsill

foot: 4 vola 5 pelma

part: 5 shank

pert. to: 7 plantar

solecism: 5 error 9 barbarism, deviation 11 impropriety

solely: all 4 only 5 alone 6 merely, simply, singly 8 entirely 9 allenarly 11 exclusively

solemn: sad 5 budge, grave, sober, usual 6 august, devout, formal, gloomy, ritual, sacred, severe, somber 7 earnest, serious, stately, weighty 8 eloquent, funereal, splendid 9 customary, dignified, sumptuous 10 ceremonial, devotional, noteworthy 11 reverential 13 distinguished

solemnize: 5 exalt, marry 7 dignify, glorify, observe 9 celebrate 11 commemorate

soler: 7 cobbler 8 shoemaker

solicit: ask, beg, woo 4 bark, plea, seek, tout 5 court, crave, mooch, tempt 6 accost, demand, entice, incite, invite, manage 7 beseech, canvass, entreat, forward, implore, request 8 campaign, disquiet, petition 9 importune, panhandle, prosecute 10 supplicate 12 make advances

solicitor: 4 tout 6 barker, lawyer 8 attorney 10 petitioner

chambers: 4 inns

solicitous: 5 eager 7 anxious, careful 8 desirous, troubled 9 attentive, concerned 10 thoughtful 11 considerate 12 apprehensive

solicitude: 4 care, coda, ease, fear, heed, yeme 7 anxiety, concern 8 business 11 carefulness 12 apprehension 13 consideration

solid: 4 cone, cube, firm, full, hard 5 cubic, dense, level, sound, stiff, valid 6 bodily, sphere, stable, strong 7 bedrock, compact, uniform, weighty 8 constant, reliable, sterling, unbroken 9 estimable, unanimous 10 consistent, dependable, inflexible 11 homogeneous, responsible, substantial, trustworthy

geometrical: 4 cone, cube 5 prism 7 pyramid 8 cylinder 11 heptahedron, pentahedron 12 dodecahedron

solidify: gel, set 4 cake 6 cement, cohere, harden 7 compact 8 concrete, condense, contract 9 coagulate 11 consolidate, crystallize

solidity: 5 unity 8 firmness, hardness 9 solidness, soundness, stability 11 compactness, consistency 13 dependability

solidum: sum 4 dado

soliloquy: 4 poem 9 discourse, monologue, utterance

solitaire: 4 game 6 hermit 7 diamond, recluse 8 Canfield, patience 9 neckcloth

solitary: 4 hole, lone, monk, only, sole 5 alone 6 hermit, lonely, remote, simple, single 7 dungeon, eremite, recluse 8 derelict, desolate, lonesome, solitary 9 withdrawn 10 antisocial, individual 12 unfrequented

solitude: 6 dearth, desert 7 expanse, privacy, retreat 8 soleness 9 isolation, seclusion 10 loneliness, quarantine, remoteness, retirement, uniqueness, wilderness 12 solitariness

solo: air 4 aria 5 alone, scena, radel 6 strain 9 monologue 13 unaccompanied

accompaniment: 8 obligato 9 obbligato

soloist: 6 cantor, singer 7 aviator

Solomon: 7 wise man

ally: 5 Hiram

father: 5 David

gold obtained from: 5 Ophir

mother: 9 Bathsheba

son: 8 Rehoboam

temple: 6 shamir

Solomon Islands: 4 Buka, Gizo, Savo 7 Malaita 10 New Georgia 11 Guadalcanal

capital: 7 Honaira

discoverer: 9 de Mendana

gulf: 4 Huon, Kula

monetary unit: 6 dollar

volcano: 5 Balbi

Solon: 4 sage 7 senator 8 lawmaker 9 publicist, statesman 10 legislator

soluble: 4 frim 6 solute 11 liquefiable

solus: 5 alone

solute: 4 free 5 loose, solve 7 arrange, soluble 8 dissolve, separate 9 dissolved 13 disintegrated

solution: key 6 answer, result 8 analysis 9 discharge, releasing 10 denouement, resolution 11 deliverance, explanation 14 disintegration 15 disentanglement

kinds of: lye 5 brine, eusol, iodin, titer, sirup/syrup 6 iodine, phenol

strength of: 5 titer

solve: 4 free, undo 5 break 6 assoil, fathom, have it, unfold 7 explain, resolve, unravel, work out 8 dissolve 9 interpret 11 disentangle

solvent: 8 solution 9 detergent

Somalia: *capital:* 9 Mogidishu

division: 6 Hawiya

measure: top 4 caba 5 chela, darat, tabla 6 cubito

monetary unit: 8 shilling

river: 4 Juba 7 Shebeli

somatic: 6 bodily, carnal 8 parietal, physical 9 corporeal 13 somatopleuric

somber, sombre: sad 4 dark, dern, dull 5 dusky, gloom, grave, sober 9 dismal, gloomy, lenten, severe, solemn 7 austere, ominous 9 depressed 10 depressing, lackluster, melancholy

sombero: hat 8 headgear, sunshade

some: any, few, one 4 part 5 about 6 nearly 7 certain, portion, several 13 approximately

somersault: 4 flip

something: 5 drink 6 entity, liquor 7 aliquid, whatnot 8 beverage, somewhat

sometime: 4 late, once 6 former, whilom 7 quondam 8 formerly 12 occasionally

somewhat: 6 rather 7 aliquid 9 something, to a degree 10 moderately

Somme city: 6 Amiens 9 Abbeville

sommelier: 6 butler 9 cellarman 11 wine steward

somnambulism: 12 noctambulism, sleepwalking

somnolent: 6 drowsy, sleepy 7 languid

son: ben, boy 4 fils 5 child, scion 6 filius, Jesuit, native 8 disciple, follower, relative 9 offspring 10 descendant

pert. to: 6 filial

Scot.: Mac

youngest: 5 cadet

son-in-law: 5 gener 8 beau-fils

Son of God: 6 Savior 7 Saviour

sonance: 4 tune 5 sound

sonant: 4 oral 5 tonic, vocal 6 voiced 8 sounding 9 intonated

sonata: *closing:* 4 coda

part: 5 rondo 7 scherzo

song: dit, lay, uta 4 aria, call, cant, dite, duan, fuss, glee, hymn, lied, lilt, noel, poem, tune 5 blues, canto, carol, chant, charm, ditty, lyric, melos, music, psalm, verse 6 ballad, cantic, cantus, canzon, carmen, chanty, clamor, himene, himine, melody, poetry, shanty, sonnet, strain, trifle 7 cancion, cantion, canzone, chantey, descant, shantey 8 canticle, pittance 9 cabaletta 11 composition

baby's: 7 lullaby

choral muse: 11 Terpsichore

Christmas: 4 noel 5 carol

college: 4 glee

collection: 9 anthology 10 cancionero

evening: 6 vesper 8 serenade

folk: 5 blues 6 ballad

funeral: 5 dirge, elegy, elogy 6 elegie, lament, threne 7 elogium, epicede 8 epicedia, threnody 9 epicedium

gay: 4 lilt

German: 4 lied 6 lieder(pl.)

gypsy: 10 zingaresca

love: 6 amoret, ballad, serena 8 serenade

mountaineeer's: 5 yodel

mourning: see *funeral* above

obscure: 4 rune

of joy: 5 paean

operatic: 4 aria

part: 5 canon, round 8 madrigal

pert. to.: 5 melic

sacred: 4 hymn 5 chant, motet, psalm 6 anthem 7 polymny

sailor's: 6 chanty, shanty 7 chantey, shantey 8 rumbelow 9 barcarole 10 barcarolle

simple: 5 ditty

solo: 4 glee

triumphal: 5 paean

wedding: 5 hymen

song-like: 6 ariose, arioso 7 lyrical

Song of Bernadette author: 6 Werfel

songbird: 4 lark, wren 5 mavie, mavis, robin, veery, vireo 6 canary, linnet, mocker, oriole, oscine, thrush 7 mocking, warbler 8 redstart, vocalist

songman: 6 singer 7 gleeman 8 minstrel

songwriter: 8 composer, lyricist

sonnet: 4 poem, song 5 octet, verse 6 sestet

conclusion: 6 sestet

sonority: 8 loudness 9 resonance

sonorous: 7 ringing 8 imposing, resonant 10 impressive, rhetorical

sook: 4 call 5 booth 6 market

soon: ere 4 anon, fast, yern 5 early, later, quick, yerne 6 belive, rather, speedy 7 betimes, by-and-by, erelong, quickly, readily, shortly 8 directly, promptly, speedily 9 presently, willingly 10 beforetime 11 immediately, in the future

sooner: 4 erst 6 before 9 Oklahoman 10 preferably

Sooner State: 8 Oklahoma

soot: 4 coom, smut, stup 5 black, colly, coomb, grime, sweet, smoke 6 carbon, gentle, smudge 7 blacken, residue 9 melodious

particle: 4 isel, izle

pert. to: 10 fuliginous

sooth: 4 fact, real, soft, true 5 being, sweet, truly 6 augury, in fact, smooth 7 comfort, genuine, present, proverb, pleasing, pleasure, soothing, truthful 10 delightful 11 soothsaying, trustworthy

soothe: coy, pat, pet 4 balm, calm, dill, ease, lull 5 accoy, allay, charm, dulce, quiet 6 pacify, soften, solace, stroke 7 appease, assuage, comfort, compose, console, demulce, flatter, mollify, placate, relieve 8 mitigate, palliate 9 alleviate, attempter 10 demulceate 11 tranquilize

soother: 4 balm 5 salve 7 anodyne 9 emollient, flatterer

soothing: 4 mild 5 balmy, downy, dulce 6 dreamy, dulcet, gentle 7 anodyne, calming 8 lenitive, sedative 9 appeasing, assuasive, demulcent 13 tranquilizing

soothsay: 4 omen 7 portent, predict, proverb 8 foretell

soothsayer: 4 seer 5 augur, weird, vates 6 ariole, mantis 7 augurer, diviner, prophet, seeress 8 haruspex, chaldean 10 forecaster, hariolizer 14 prognosticator

sooty: 4 dark 5 black, colly, dingy, dirty, dusky 6 brokie 9 blackened 10 fuliginous

sop: wet 4 dunk, gift, heap, lump, mass, mess, soak, tuft 5 bribe, cloud, clump, steep 7 advance, milksop 8 saturate, weakling

sophist: 7 casuist, teacher, thinker 8 reasoner 10 paralogist 11 philosopher

sophistical: 7 cunning 8 captious 9 deceptive, insincere 11 adulterated

sophisticate: 5 alter, spoil 6 debase, garble 7 corrupt, falsify, mislead 10 adulterate 11 disillusion

sophisticated: 4 chic, wise 7 amended, refined, worldly 8 tasteful 11 adulterated, worldly-wise

sophistry: 6 deceit 7 fallacy, quibble 8 argument, trickery 9 deception 11 insincerity

Sophocles play: 4 Ajax 7 Electra, Oedipus 8 Antigone

sopor: 5 sleep 6 apathy, stupor

soporific: 5 dwale 6 drowsy, opiate, sleepy 8 hypnotic, narcotic 9 apathetic 11 somniferous 12 somnifacient, somnivolency

soppy: wet 5 rainy 6 soaked 7 mawkish 8 drenched 11 sentimental

soprano: 6 singer, treble 9 high voice

operatic: 4 Lind, Pons 5 Freni, Melba, Moffo, Patti, Price, Sills 6 Arroyo, Callas, Peters, Resnik, Scotto 7 Crespin, Farrell, Kirsten, Lehmann, Nilsson, Stevens, Tebaldi, Traubel 8 Flagstad, Ponselle 10 Sutherland, Tetrazzini 11 Schwarzkopf 12 de los Angeles

sora: 4 bird, rail

sorcerer: 4 mage, magi 5 boyla, brujo, Goeta 6 boolya, wizard 7 charmer, warlock 8 conjurer, magician 9 occultist 11 necromancer, thaumaturge 13 thaumaturgist

sorceress: hag, hex 5 Circe, Lamia, sibyl, witch 6 Gorgon 11 enchantress

sorcery: 5 magic, obeah, spell 6 fetich, fetish, voodoo 7 pishogue, prestige 9 diablerie, diabolism 10 necromancy, witchcraft 11 enchantment

sordellina: 7 bagpipe

sordid: low 4 base, mean, vile 5 dirty, gross 6 chetif, filthy, greedy, menial 7 ignoble, selfish, servile, squalid 8 churlish, covetous, grasping, grewsome, gruesome, sluttish, wretched 9 mercenary, niggardly 10 avaricious, despicable, slatternly 12 contemptible

sordor: 5 dregs 6 refuse 10 sordidness

sore: raw 4 boil, buck, evil, harm, kibe, pain, sair 5 angry, blain, botch, grief, ulcer, vexed, wound, wrong 6 bitter, bruise, fester, severe, sorrel, sorrow, tender, touchy 7 angered, annoyed, disease, extreme, grieved, hostile, painful, penance, trouble, violent 8 abrasion, grievous, inflamed, offended, sickness 9 detriment, irritated, sensitive, suffering, ulcerated, vexatious 10 affliction, afflictive, contrition, difficulty, distressed, unpleasant 11 disgruntled, distressing 13 temperamental, oversensitive

sorehead: 5 loser 6 griper, grouch 10 malcontent

sorely: 7 greatly 8 severely, urgently 9 extremely, painfully, violently 10 grievously 12 distressingly 13 unpleasantly

soreness: 4 ache, pain 8 severity, vexation, violence 10 bitterness 11 painfulness 12 irritability

sorghum: 4 cush, dura, milo 5 batad, darso, durra, sorgo 7 shallu 8 feterita

sorite: 4 heap 10 collection

sorority: 4 club 7 society 10 sisterhood

sorrel: oca 5 brown, color, horse, plant 6 oxalis 7 roselle

sorrow: rue, woe 4 bale, care, dole, harm, loss, sigh, teen, weal 5 devil, dolor, grief, mourn, rogue, scamp 6 grieve, lament, misery, plague, regret 7 sadness, trouble, waeness 8 calamity, distress, egrimony, mourning 9 adversity, penitence, suffering 10 affliction, compassion, contrition, discomfort, melancholy 11 lamentation, tribulation, unhappiness 12 wretchedness

over: 6 bemoan, bewail, lament 7 deplore

sorrowful: sad 4 teen 5 drear, sadly 6 dismal, dolent, dreary, rueful, woeful 7 doleful, grieved, unhappy 8 contrite, dolesome, dolorous, grievous, mournful 9 afflicted, plaintive 10 lamentable, melancholy 11 distressing 12 disconsolate

sorry: bad, sad 4 hurt, mean, poor 5 vexed 6 dismal, gloomy, regret, repent, vulgar 7 chagrin, painful, pitiful, unhappy 8 contrite, grievous, mournful, penitent, wretched 9 afflicted, chagrined, miserable, mortified, regretful, worthless 10 apologetic, melancholy, remorseful 12 contemptible, disappointed

sort: ilk, set, way 4 cull, gere, kind, part, race, rank, sift, suit, type 5 adapt, allot, batch, befit, breed, class, genus, grade, group, order 6 adjust, assign, garble, gender, manner, nature, punish, screen, select 7 arrange, conform, fashion, quality, species, stripes, variety 8 classify, separate 9 character 10 collection, distribute 11 accommodate, description

sorted: 6 chosen 8 assorted, selected 9 separated 10 classified

sortie: 4 knot 5 foray, sally 6 attack

sortilege: 7 sorcery 8 witchery 11 enchantment

sosh: jag 4 dash 5 drunk 11 intoxicated

soso: bad 4 poor 6 medium, unwell 8 mediocre, middling, passable 9 tolerable 11 indifferent

sot: 4 fool, lush 5 fixed, toper, waste 6 befool, guzzle, tipple 7 dastard, stupefy, tippler, tosspot 8 drunkard, squander, stubborn 9 immovable, inebriate, obstinate, simpleton, swillbowl 10 winebibber

sottish: 4 dull 6 stupid 7 doltish, drunken, foolish 9 senseless

sotto: 5 below, under

sotto voce: 5 aside 6 weakly 7 faintly 9 privately 13 in an undertone

soubise: 5 sauce

soubrette: 4 maid, role 7 actress 11 entertainer, maidservant

soucar: 6 banker 8 merchant, straight 9 honorable

souchong: tea

sough: die, sob 4 moan, sigh, whiz 5 chant, ditch, drain, rumor, whizz 6 murmur, report 7 breathe, moaning, whistle 8 singsong 9 murmuring

soul: ame, God, ker 4 alma 5 atman, being, force, heart, human, psyche, saint 6 dibbuk, esprit, fervor, leader, pneuma, spirit 7 courage, essence 8 inspirer 10 embodiment, heartiness, individual 11 anilopyrine 15 personification

   loss: 9 perdition

   personification: 6 Psyche

soulless: 5 brute

sound: cry, din 4 birr, blow, bray, firm, good, hail, hale, rime, safe, sane, seem, test, tone, true 5 alarm, blare, bruit(F.), chang, clang, fresh, grope, hoddy, inlet, legal, loyal, noise, plumb, probe, rhyme, solid, valid, whole 6 bedlam, bratte, clamor, entire, fathom, hearty, honest, hubbub, intact, measure, outcry, racket, report, robust, secure, stable, steven, strong, sturdy, tumult, uproar 7 bluster, clamour, clangor, clatter, clitter, clutter, declare, earshot, examine, explore, feel out, healthy, hearing, measure, perfect, sonance, sputter 8 complete, flawless, orthodox, profound, rational, reliable, shouting, splutter, thorough 9 honorable, undamaged 10 dependable, hullabaloo, scrutinize 11 arm of the sea, trustworthy, undisturbed

   amorous: coo

   atonic: 4 surd

   beating drum: 8 rataplan

   bell-like: 4 ding 5 clang, knell 6 tinkle

   breathing: 4 rale 5 snore

   bullet: zip 4 ping

   buzzing: 4 whiz 5 whirr, whizz

   cat's: mew 4 meow, mewl, purr

   contemptuous: 5 snort

   contented: 4 purr

   derisive: boo 7 catcall

   detection instrument: 10 hydrophone

   discordant: 6 jangle 9 cacophony

   distinctive: 6 timbre

   donkey's: 4 bray 6 heehaw

   dove's murmuring: 4 curr

   drum: 4 roll, tuck

   dry leaves: 6 rustle

   dull: 4 thud 5 clonk

   elephant's: 4 roar 7 trumpet

   engine: 4 chug, ping

   explosive: pop 4 bang, boom, clap, roar 5 blast 6 report

   guttural: 4 burr 5 grunt

   harsh: 4 bray 5 creak, twang 9 cacophony

   high-pitched: 4 ping, ting

   hissing: zip 4 siss

   hoarse: caw 4 bray

   in doctrine: 8 orthodox

   in mind: 4 sane

   insect's: 5 chirr

   jingling: 16 tintinnabulation

   light: 5 swish 7 pitapat

   loud: 4 boom, peal 5 blare, clang

   magnifying device: 9 megaphone 11 loudspeaker

   measurement of: bel

   menacing: 5 growl, snarl

   mentally: 4 sane 5 lucid 6 normal

   metallic: 4 ping, ting 5 clang, clank 6 tinkle

   monotonous: hum 4 moan 5 drone

   mournful: sob

   murmuring: 4 purr 5 groan

   musical: note

   nasal: 5 snore, whine 7 stridor

   of bell: 4 ding

   of disapproval: bah, boo 4 hiss 7 catcall

   of drinking: 4 glub

   of hoofbeat: 4 clop

   of horn: 7 tantara

   of pain: 4 moan, ouch, yell 5 groan

   or rising birds: 5 whirr

   of surf: 4 rote

   pert. to: 5 tonal 6 sonant 10 acoustical

   pleasing in: 8 euphonic

   repeated: 4 echo

   respiratory: 4 rale

   ringing: 5 clang 8 tinnitus

   rustling: 8 froufrou

   shallow: 6 lagoon, laguna, lagune

   shrill: 5 reedy, skirl

   sibilant: 4 hiss, siss

   small: 4 peep

   solemn: 4 peal

   speech: 5 vowel 8 phonetic

   splashing: 5 swash

   syllabic: 6 sonant

   throat: 8 guttural

   transposition: 10 spoonerism

   trumpet: 5 blare 7 clarion

unvaried: 8 monotone
vibrant: 4 birr
vocal: 4 tone 6 hiccup 8 hiccough
warning: 5 alarm 6 alarum, tocsin
water: 4 klop, rote 5 plash, swish 6 splash
whispering: 8 susurrus
whizzing: 4 ping 5 swish
yelping: yip
sounded: 4 blew, rang, rung 5 oaten 6 tooted 7 clanged 8 syllabic
sounding: 6 sonant 8 plangent, resonant, snorous, strident 9 bombastic 11 mellisonant 12 grandisonant, grandisonous
soundless: 4 deep 5 quiet 6 silent 9 noiseless 10 bottomless 12 unfathomable
soundly: 6 deeply 7 healthy 8 securely 9 violently 10 completely, forcefully, profoundly, thoroughly
soundness: wit 5 truth 6 sanity 8 lucidity, solidity, strength 9 integrity, rectitude, stability 10 heartiness 11 healthiness
sound off: 7 speak up 8 speak out
sound out: 5 study 7 explore 11 investigate
sounds: *having melody and rhythm:* 5 music
  succession of: 4 peal
  vocal symbols: 6 sonant
soup: 5 broth, puree, shchi, slash, stchi 6 borsch, borsht, oxtail 7 chowder, garbure, shtchee 8 consomme, gazpacho 11 predicament 12 mulligatawny 13 bouillabaisse
dish: 6 tureen
ingredient: 4 lalo, okra 7 noodlrs
spoon: 5 ladle
thick: 4 bisk 5 hoosh, puree 6 bisque, burgoo 7 burgout, pottage 8 minestra 10 minestrone
thickener: 7 tapioca
thin: 5 broth 8 consomme
soupcon: 4 hint 5 taste, trace 7 modicum, portion 8 particle 9 suspicion 10 suggestion
sour: bad, wry 4 acid, dour, grim, hard, tart 5 acerb, acrid, cross, eager, gruff 6 acetic, bitter, cruety, morose, sullen 7 acetose, acetous, acidify, austere, crabbed, painful, peevish 8 acerbate, acescent, embitter 9 acidulate, acidulent, acidulous, fermented 10 afflictive, astringent, ill humored, unpleasant 11 distasteful 12 disagreeable
source: 4 fons, font, germ, head, rise, root, seed 5 fount 6 ascent, origin, parent, spring 7 edition 8 fountain, wellhead 9 beginning 10 wellspring 12 fountainhead
of contrary action: 7 reagent
of gum arabic: 6 acacia

of income: 7 revenue
of indigo: 4 anil
of inspiration: 4 Muse
of iodine: 4 kelp
of knowledge: 7 organon
of metal: ore
of phosphorus: 7 apatite
of vitamin C: 6 citrus, orange
of vitamin E: 5 grain
primary: 4 root 5 radix
sourdine: 5 muted 7 subdued
sourdough: 6 leaven 7 settler 10 prospector
sourness: 7 acidity 8 acerbity, acrimony, asperity 10 moroseness 16 disagreeableness
sourpuss: 5 crank 6 grouch 8 sorehead 10 complainer
soursop: 4 tree 9 guanabana
souse, souce, sowce, sowse: ear, jag, wet 4 blow, cuff, duck, fall, prop, soak, wash 5 bathe, brine, douse, drink, swoop, thump 6 drench, pickle, plunge, pounce, strike, thwack 7 heavily, immerse, tippler 8 clumsily, drunkard, saturate, steeping, submerge 9 drenching
soutache: 5 braid 8 trimming
soutane: 5 cloak 7 cassock, zimarra
South: (see also **Confederacy**): 5 Dixie
crop: 6 cotton 7 tobacco
dish: 4 okra 5 gumbo 7 hoecake
inlet: 5 bayou
novelist: 5 Welty 8 Faulkner
South Africa: *animal:* das 5 nenta 8 suricate
antelope: gnu 5 eland, leche, oribi, peele 6 lechee, lechwe, rhebok 7 blaubok, blesbok, boshbok, grysbok, rheeboc, rheebok, sassaby 8 blesbuck, bontebok, boschbok
armadillo: 4 para
ass: 6 quagga
assembly: 4 raad
aunt: 5 tanta
bay: 5 Algoa, False
blaubok: 5 etaac
breastwork: 6 scherm
bushman: 4 Qung
camp: 5 lager 6 laager
capital: 8 Cape Town, Pretoria
caterpillar: 6 risper
cattle enclosure: 5 kraal
city: 6 Durban 9 Germiston 12 Bloemfontein, Johannesburg
cliff: 4 klip
club: 10 knobkerrie
coin: 4 cent, pond, rand 6 florin
colonist: 4 Boer
conference: 6 indaba
cony: 4 das
corn: 5 mealy 6 mealie
council: 4 raad

criminal: 8 amalaita
desert: 8 Kalahari
dialect: 4 Taal
diamond: 4 jager 9 schlenter
Dutch: 4 Boer, Taal
Dutch speech: 9 Afrikaans
ferry: 4 pont
foreigner: 9 uitlander
fox: 4 asse 5 caama
garment: 6 caross, kaross
gazelle: 9 springbok
goldfield: 4 rand
government: 8 republic
grass country: 4 veld 5 veldt
greenhorn: 5 ikona
gully: 5 donga
gun: 4 roer
hill: kop 8 spitzkop
hillock: 5 kopje
hippopotamus: 6 zeekoe
hog: 9 boschvark
hut: 8 rondavel, rondawel
javelin: 7 assagai
laborer: 4 togt
leader: 5 Botha, Smuts 7 Vorster 8 Verwoerd
legislative assembly: 4 raad
lowland: 4 vlei, vley
monetary unit: 4 rand
monkey: 4 vervet 8 talapoin
mountain: kop 9 Swartberg
native: 5 Bantu 7 Swahili 9 Hottentot
pass: nek
pasture: 5 veldt
people: 4 Xosa 5 Bantu, Namas, Pondo 6 Damara 7 Swahili 8 Bechuana 9 Hottentot
plain: 5 veldt
plant: 4 aloe
plot: erf
polecat: 6 musang
policeman: 4 zarp
province: 4 Cape 5 Natal 9 Transvaal
race: see *people* above
racial policy: 9 apartheid
region: 5 congo
river: 4 Vaal 6 Molopo, Orange 7 Limpopo
rodent: 5 ratel
settler: 4 Boer
shrub: 6 protea
simpleton: 5 ikona
snake: 5 elaps 8 eggeater
spirit: 8 tikolosh
starling: 5 sprew 7 spreeuw
stream: aar
sumac: 6 karree
throng: 4 reim 7 riempie
tick: 6 tampan
tract: 9 zuurveldt
trader: 7 Swahili
tree: 5 tenio 7 assagai 8 gamdeboo

tribe: see *people* above
village: 5 kraal
warrior: 4 impi
weaverbird: 4 taha
whip: 7 sjambok
South African: 4 Boer 9 Afrikaner 10 Afrikander
South America: *animal:* 4 paca 5 coati, coypu, llama, sloth, tapir 6 alpaca, jaguar, nutria, vicuna 8 anteater 9 armadillo
ant: 5 sauba, sauva
anteater: 7 tamandu
arbor: 6 ramada
armadillo: 4 apar 7 tatouay 10 pichiciago
arrow poison: 6 curara, curare
balsam: 4 tolu
beast of burden: 5 llama
beef: 6 tasajo
beverage: 4 mate
bird: 4 aura, guan, mitu, myna, rara, taha, yeni 5 agami, arara, chaja, mynah 6 barber, barbet 7 aracari, jacamar, oilbird, seriema, tinamou 8 bellbird, boatbill, curassow, guacharo, puffbird, screamer, terutero
blanket: 6 serape
boat: 6 cayuco
cactus: 7 airampo
catfish: 5 dorad
cattle ranch: 8 estancia 9 estantion
country: 4 Peru 5 Chile 6 Brazil, Guyana 7 Bolivia, Ecuador, Surinam, Uruguay 8 Colombia, Paraguay 9 Argentina, Patagonia, Venezuela
cowboy: 6 gaucho 7 llanero, planero
cowboy's weapon: 5 bolas
dance: 5 mambo, samba 6 cha-cha
deer: 6 guemal, guemul
dove: 9 talpacoti
duck: 7 muscovy
estuary: 4 para 5 Plata
fish: 4 paru 6 aimara, carbie 7 scalare 8 arapaima
fox: 4 asse
game: 6 pelota
garment: 6 serape
gold: oro
griddle cake: 5 arepa
hare: 6 tapeti
hawk: 8 caracara
herb: 9 romerillo
herdsman: 7 llanero
Indian: Ges, Ona 5 Auca, Inca, Tama 5 Carib, Tapas 6 Arawak, Jivaro 7 Cayapos, Goyanas, Guatoan, Pampero, Tapuyan 8 Camacans, Coroados, Timbiras 9 Caingangs, Chavantes 10 Patagonian
Indian hut: 5 toldo
Indian medicine man: 4 peai 6 shaman
Indian poison: 6 curara, curare, curari
island: 5 Aruba

knife: 7 machete 8 machette
language: Ona 7 Spanish 9 Portugese
lapwing: 8 terutero
liberator: 7 Bolivar
limestone: 5 tosca
liquor: 6 chicha
lizard: 4 teju 5 coati
lowlands: 6 llanos, pampas, selvas
mammal: ai 4 paca 5 coati, llama, tapir 6
   alpaca, guanco 8 kinkajou, pacarana 10
   coati-mondi, coati-mundi
marmoset: 7 tamarin
measure: 4 vara 7 manzana
mineral: 5 urso
monkey: sai 4 saki, titi 5 acari, araba 6
   grison, teetee 7 ouakari, sapajou 8 marmoset, orabassu 9 barrigudo, beelzebub
mountains: 5 Andes 6 Acarai, Parima
native: 5 Carib
oppossum: 5 quica 7 sarigue
ostrich: 4 rhea
palm: 5 assai, bussu, datil, troly 6 tooroo,
   ubussu 7 troolie
parrot: 5 macaw
plain: 5 llano, pampa
plains dweller: 7 llanero
plant: 6 ipecac 8 crassula 10 tillandsia
porridge: 5 atole
rabbit: 5 tapeti
raccoon: 5 coati 10 coatimundi
rain forest: 5 selva
rancher: 10 estanciero
river: 4 Para 5 Plata 6 Amazon 7 Orinoco
rodent: 4 degu, mara, paca 5 coypu 6
   agouti, agouty 8 viscacha, vizcacha 10
   chinchilla
root: oca
rubber tree: 4 para
ruminant: 5 llama 6 alpaca
scarf: 5 manta
serpent: 5 aboma
shrub: 4 coca
slaughterhouse: 11 frigorifico
snake: bom 4 lora 5 aboma 8 anaconda
   10 bushmaster
sorrel: oca
stock: Ona
strait: 8 Magellan
tapir: 5 danta
tiger cat: 5 chati
toucan: 4 toco 7 aracari
tree: 4 fotu, lana, mora, para, vera 5 balsa, cacao, cebil, couma, pekea 6 chicha,
   simaba, yachan 7 bebeeru, quayabi 9
   balaustre, couvatari 11 chichicaste
tribe: Ona
trumpeter: 5 agami
tuber: oca
turtle: 8 matamata
vulture: 6 condor
walnut: 9 conacaste

weapon: 4 bola 5 bolas
wild cat: 4 eyra
wind: 7 pampero
South American: 5 Latin
South Australia: See Australia
South Carolina: capital: 8 Columbia
   city: 8 Rock Hill 10 Charleston, Green-
      ville 11 Spartanburg
   county: Lee 4 York 5 Horry, Union 6
      Dillon, Oconee
   dam: 6 Santee 9 Pinopolis
   fort: 6 Sumter
   island: 4 Bull 6 Edisto, Klawah, Parris
      10 Hilton Head
   motto: 13 Dum spiro spero (While I
      breathe, I hope)
   mountain: 9 Sassafras
   nickname: 8 Palmetto
   resort: 10 Hilton Head
   river: 6 Peedee, Saluda, Santee
   state bird: 4 wren
   state flower: 7 jasmine
   state tree: 8 palmetto
South Dakota: capital: 6 Pierre
   city: 8 Aberdeen 9 Rapid City 10 Sioux
      Falls
   county: Day 4 Clay, Hand, Hyde, Lake,
      Todd 5 Bruel, Deuel, Tripp
   Indian: 5 Brule, Sioux 6 Dakota
   lake: 4 Oahe 8 Bigstone, Traverse
   mine: 9 Homestake
   mountain: 10 Black Hills
   national monument: 10 Mt. Rushmore
   river: 5 James 7 Big Bend, Randall 8
      Missouri
   state bird: 8 pheasant
   state flower: 12 pasqueflower
   state tree: 6 spruce
South India: See India
South Korea: capital: 5 Seoul
   city: 5 Pusan, Taegu 6 Inchon
   monetary unit: Won
South Pacific: See South Sea
South Pole: See Antarctica
South Sea: canoe: 4 proa
   island: 4 Bali, Fiji, Sulu 5 Samoa, Tonga
      6 Tahiti 7 Society 8 Pitcairn 9 New
      Guinea
   island drink: ava
   island money: 6 wakiki
   islander: 5 Maori 6 Kanaka, Samoan 10
      Melonesian, Polynesian 11 Microne-
      sian
   plant: 4 taro
   product: 5 copra
   sea: 5 Coral 6 Tasman
   staple: 4 taro
South Vietnam (see also Vietnam): capital: 6 Saigon
   guerillas: 8 Vietcong
   holiday: Tet
   monetary unit: 7 piastre

river: 6 Mekong
woman's garb: 5 aodai
south wind: 5 notus 6 auster
South Wind author: 7 Douglas
Southeast Asia (see also **Asia**): 4 Laos, Siam 5 Burma 6 Ceylon 7 Vietnam 8 Cambodia, Malaysia, Pakistan, Thailand 9 Indonesia 10 Bangladesh 11 Philippines
southeast wind: 5 eurus
southern: 7 austral
Southern dish: See **South:** *dish*
Southern France: 4 Midi
Southwest: *cowboy:* 7 llanero
  Indian: 4 Cree
southwest wind: 8 libeccio
southwester: hat 4 gale 5 squam, storm
souvenir: 5 curio, relic 6 memory 7 memento 8 keepsake, reminder 11 remembrance 12 recollection
sovereign: 4 coin, free, king 5 chief, liege, queen, royal, ruler 6 couter, Mikado, prince 7 emperor, empress, highest, monarch, supreme 8 autocrat, greatest, princely, reigning, superior, suzerain 9 effectual, excellent, governing, paramount, potentate 10 omnipotent 11 controlling, efficacious, independent
  petty: 8 tetrarch
sovereign power: 6 throne
sovereign prerogative claim: 11 seigniorage
sovereignty: 4 rule, sway 5 realm 6 diadem, empery, empire, status, throne 7 dynasty, majesty, scepter, sceptre 8 dominion 9 supremacy 10 ascendancy, ascendency, domination
  absolute: 8 autarchy
  joint: 11 condominium
soviet: 7 council, Russian 9 committee
Soviet Union (see also **Russia**): 4 USSR
  administrative committee: 9 presidium
  founder: 5 Lenin
  government farm: 7 sovkhos, sovkhoz 8 sovkhose
  hero: 5 Lenin 6 Stalin
  money: 5 ruble
  news agency: 4 Tass
  newspaper: 5 Pravda 8 Izvestia
  republic: 5 Uzbek 6 Latvia 7 Armenia, Georgia, Kirghiz, Turkmen, Ukraine
  secret police: KGB 4 NKVD, OGPU
sow: hog, pig 4 heap, seed, shed 5 ditch, drain, drill, plant, stack, strew, swine 6 runner, sluice, spread 7 channel, furnish, grumphy, implant, scatter 8 disperse, grumphie 9 broadcast, inoculate 10 salamander 11 disseminate
  wild: 8 javelina
  young: elt 4 gilt
sower: 7 seedman
  of dragon's teeth: 6 Cadmus

soy bean: 4 soja, soya
soya: 4 dill 6 fennel 7 soybean
spa: 5 oasis, oases 6 resort, spring 8 Saratoga 10 sanatorium 12 health resort
  place: Ems 4 Bath 5 Baden 8 Karlsbad
space: gap 4 area, path, rank, roam, room, rove, void, walk 5 ambit, plena(pl.), range, track 6 course, divide, extent, plenum, region 7 areolae, arrange, expanse 8 capacity, distance, duration, interval, quantity 11 reservation 14 accommodations
  agency: 4 NASA
  architectural: 8 pediment
  between eyes: 4 lore
  between two intersecting lines: 5 angle
  between two points: 8 distance
  blank: 6 lacuna 7 lacunae(pl.)
  breathing: 6 recess
  cleared: 5 glade
  coin: 7 exergue
  docking: 6 linkup
  empty: 4 void 5 blank, inane 6 vacuum
  forest: 5 glade
  hallowed: 7 mortice, mortise
  included: 8 contents
  limitless: 8 infinite
  occupied: 6 volume
  of time: 8 interval
  on surface: 4 area
  partitioned: 4 room
  pert. to: 5 areal
  portion of: 5 place
  safekeeping: 7 storage
  secluded: 6 alcove
  small: 6 areola, areole 7 aerolae
  storage: 4 shed 5 attic 6 cellar 9 storeroom, warehouse
  void: 5 chasm 7 inanity
  wall: 5 niche
  white: 6 margin
space full of matter: 6 plenum
space theory: 7 plenism
spacecraft: 6 rocket 9 satellite
  decision: 6 go-no-go
  first: 7 Sputnik
  part: 6 module 7 capsule
  to moon: 6 Apollo
  slowdown: 7 deboost
spaced out: 4 high 5 doped 6 stoned, zonked 7 drugged
spaceman: 9 astronaut, cosmonaut
spacer: bar
spacious: 4 vast 5 ample, broad, great, large, rangy, roomy 9 capacious, expansive, extensive 13 comprehensive
spad: 4 nail
spadassin: 5 bravo 7 duelist 9 swordsman
spade: dig 5 graft 6 shovel 11 playing card
  Irish: 5 slane
  kind of: 6 scavel

narrow: loy
plasterer's: 6 server
sharp: 4 spud
triangular: 5 didle
turf: 5 slane
spaghetti: 5 pasta
spahi, spahee: 7 cavalry
Spain: 6 Espana, Iberia
  adventurer: 9 almogaver
  ancient name: 8 Hispania
  article: las, los, una
  aunt: tia
  author: 9 Cervantes
  bayonet: 5 yucca
  beach: 5 playa
  belle: 4 maja
  blanket: 6 serape
  boat: 5 aviso
  brandy: 11 aguardiente
  bull: 4 toro
  cape: 9 Trafalgar
  capital: 6 Madrid
  cart: 7 carreta 8 carretta
  cathedral city: 7 Seville
  cedar: 6 acajou
  celery: 4 apio
  cellist: 6 Casals
  champion: Cid
  channel: 4 Cano
  chaperone: 6 duenna
  cheer: ole
  city: 6 Bilbao, Malaga 7 Granada, Seville
    8 Valencia 9 Barcelona, Saragossa
  clerk: 11 escribiente
  cloak: 4 capa 5 manta 6 mantle
  coat: 7 zamarra, zamarro
  coin: 5 dobla 6 cuarto, doblon, peseta 7
    Alfonso, centimo, piaster 8 cuartino 9
    cuartillo
  conqueror: Cid 7 Pizarro 12 conquistador
  contract: 7 asiento 8 assiento
  council: 5 junta
  count: 5 conde
  dance: 4 jota 5 danza, tango 6 bolero, gi-
    tano 8 fandango, saraband 9 zapateado
    10 seguidilla
  dish: 6 posole
  district: 5 Xeres
  dollar: 4 duro, peso, pezo 7 piaster, pias-
    tre
  dumpling: 6 tamale
  earth: 6 tierra
  exclamation: 6 carajo 7 caramba
  execution: 7 garotte, garrote 8 garrotte
  explorer: 7 Mendoza 8 Coronado
  fabric: 5 tiraz
  fleet: 6 armada
  former leader: 6 Franco
  friend: 6 amigo
  frigate: 5 zabra
  game: 5 omber 6 pelota 7 jai-alai
  gentleman: don 5 senor 9 caballero

god: 4 dios
goddess: 5 Diosa
gold: oro
governor: 10 idelantado
grass: 5 spart 7 esparto
greeting: 4 hola
griddlecake: 5 arepa
gunboat 5 barca
gypsy: 7 zincalo
hall: 4 sala
head covering: 8 mantilla
herdsman: 8 ranchero
hero: Cid 8 Palmerin
hill: 5 cerro, morro
holiday: 6 fiesta
horse: 7 caballo
hotel: 5 venta 6 posada
house: 4 casa
instrument: 8 castanet, zambomba
island: 5 Ibiza 7 Majorca, Minorca
island group: 6 Canary 8 Balearic
judge: 7 alcalde
kettle: 4 cazo
king: rey
kingdom: 4 Leon 6 Aragon 7 Castile
lady: 4 dona 6 senora
lagoon: 6 laguna
lake: 4 lago
lariat: 5 reata, riata
leather: 8 cordovan
legislature: 6 cortes
letter: 5 carta
letter carrier: 6 correo
linen cloth: 4 crea
lute: 7 vihuela
magic: 8 brujeria
man: don 6 hombre
mausoleum: 8 Escorial
mayor: 6 alcade 7 alcalde
measure: pie 4 codo, copa, dedo, moyo,
  paso, vara 5 aroba, braza, cafiz, cahiz,
  legua, linea, medio, milla, palmo, sesma
  6 cordel, cuarta, estado, fanega, league,
  racion, yugada 7 azumbre, cantara, celemin, estadel, pulgada 8 aranzada, fanegada 9 cuarteron, cuartilla, cuartillo
  10 caballeria
miss: 8 senorita
monetary unit: 6 peseta
monk: 5 padre
mountain: 8 Asturian, Pyrenees 9 Mula-
  hacem 10 Cantabrian, Guardarrama,
  Pic de Netou 11 La Maladetta 12 Sierra Morena, Sierra Nevada 14 Sierra de
  Toledo
mouth: 4 boca
muleteer: 8 arriero
native: 7 Catalan, Iberian
nobleman: don 7 grandee, hidalgo
now: 5 ahora
nun: 6 Teresa
officer: 8 alguacil, alguazil

operetta: 8 zarzuela
other: 4 otro
oyster: 5 pinna
painter: 4 Cano, Dali, Goya, Miro, Sert 6 Ribera 7 El Greco, Murillo, Picasso, Zuloaga 9 Velasquez
palace: 8 Escorial
pancake: 5 arepa
parliament: 6 cortes
pear: 7 avocado
peasant: 7 paisano
peninsula: 6 Iberia
pepper: 5 chili 7 pimento
pickpocket: 6 ratero
plant: aji
poet: 6 Encina
porridge: 5 atole
port: 5 Palos
post office: 6 correo
pot: 4 olla
priest: 4 cura 5 padre
promenade: 5 paseo
pronunciation mark: 5 tilde
province: 4 Jaen, Leon, Lugo, Vigo 5 Alava, Avila, Cadiz, Soria 6 Burgos, Coruna, Cuenca, Gerona, Huelva, Huesca, Lerida, Madrid, Malaga, Murcia, Orense, Oviedo, Teruel, Toledo, Zamora 7 Almeria, Badajoz, Caceres, Cordoba, Granada, Logrono, Navarra, Segovia, Seville, Vizcaya 8 Albacete, Alicante, Palencia, Valencia 9 Barcelona, Guipuscoa, Salamanca, Santander, Saragossa, Tarragona 10 Ciudad Real, Pontevedra, Valladolid 11 Guadalajara 15 Balearic Islands 18 Castellon de la Plana
raisin: 4 pasa
rice: 5 arroz
rider: 8 herisson
river: ria, rio 4 Ebro 5 Douro, Tagus 8 Guadiana 12 Guadalquivir
road: 6 camino
room: 4 sala
seaport: 4 Adra 5 Palos
sentinel: 5 vedet, videt 7 vedette, vidette
shawl: 5 manta 6 serape
sherry: 5 Xeres 11 Amontillado
silk: 5 tiraz
sorcerer: 5 brujo
south: sur
stanza: 10 seguidilla
street: 5 calle
sword: 5 bilbo
tax: 8 alcabala
title: don 5 senor 6 senora 7 hidalgo 8 senorita
tomorrow: 6 manana
town: 4 Irun, Jaen, Leon, Olot 5 Cadiz, Gijon, Lorca, Ronda, Siero, Xeres 6 Murcia, Toledo 7 Cordoba, Cordova, Granada 8 Zaragoza 9 Cartagena, Sala-

manca, Santander 10 Carthagena, Valladolid 17 Jerez de la Frontera
trail: 6 camino
trefoil: 7 alfalfa, lucerne
uncle: tio
vase: 4 urna
vehicle: 7 tartana
very: muy
victory cry: ole
watchword: 6 alerta
water: 4 agua
watercourse: 6 arroyo
weight: 4 onza 5 frail, grano, libra, marco, tomin 6 adarme, arroba, dinero, dracma, ochava 7 arienzo, quilate, quintal 8 caracter, tonelada 9 escrupulo 10 castellano
white: 6 blanco
wind: 6 solano
window: 7 ventana
witchcraft: 8 brujeria
woman: 6 senora
spalpeen: boy, fop, lad 5 scamp 6 rascal 7 laborer, workman 8 braggart 9 youngster
spall: 4 chip, fall 5 break 6 reduce 7 breakup, crumble 8 fragment, shoulder
spalt: 4 chip, tear 5 crisp, split 7 brittle
span: 4 arch, cock, pair, rope, swim, team, time 5 cover, grasp, reach, seize 6 attach, bridge, extend, fasten, fetter, hobble, length, period, spread 7 confine, matched, measure, stretch 8 distance, duration, encircle 9 encompass, perfectly 10 completely
spancel: tie 4 clog 6 fetter, hobble
spang: 4 bang, hurl, jump, kick, leap, yoke 5 clasp, crack 6 stride 7 spangle 8 abruptly, directly, ornament, straight
spangle: set 4 boss 5 adorn, aglet, gleam, plate 6 aiglet, sequin, zequin 7 glisten, glitter, sparkle 8 ornament, sprinkle, zecchino
Spaniard: 5 Latin 7 Espanol 9 Castilian
imaginary: 9 Espriella
spaniel: 5 trasy 6 cocker, punish 8 springer 9 sycophant
spank: 4 prat, slap, whip 6 strike 7 reprove 8 chastise
spanker: 4 sail
spanking: new 4 fine 5 brisk, fresh, large, stout 6 lively, strong 7 dashing 8 vigorous
spanner: 6 wrench
spar: bar, box, rod 4 beam, bolt, boom, gaff, mast, pole, raft, rung, shut, yard 5 close, fight, lever, lunge, sprit, steve 6 barite, bicker, charge, fasten, rafter, strike, thrust, timber 7 contend, contest, dispute, enclose, quarrel, wrangle, yardarm 8 dolomite, lazulite
end: 7 yardarm

spare: 4 bear, free, gain, hain, lean, part, save, slim, slit, slow, stop, thin 5 avoid, chary, extra, favor, gaunt, grant, lanky, stint 6 desist, endure, exempt, favour, frugal, let off, meager, scanty, scrimp 7 deprive, forbear, forgive, haggard, leisure, opening, placket, refrain, relieve, reserve, sparing 8 dilatory, forebear, preserve, tolerate 9 duplicate, parsimony 10 substitute 11 replacement, superfluous 12 parsimonious

spare time: 7 leisure

sparge: 6 splash 7 moisten 8 sprinkle 9 bespatter

sparing: 5 chary, gnede, scant 6 frugal, meager, saving, scanty 7 careful, limited, thrifty 8 merciful, reticent, stinting 9 scrimping 11 tightfisted 12 parsimonious

spark: arc, woo 4 beau, funk, soil 5 aizle, belle, blade, court, flash, grain, light, lover 7 diamond, gallant, sparkle, spatter 8 motivate, sparklet 9 scintilla 10 sweetheart 11 scintillate

igniting property: 11 incendivity

sparked: 5 arced 7 courted, spotted 8 streaked 10 variegated

sparker: 5 lover 7 gallant 8 firework

sparkle: 5 blink, flash, gleam, glent, glint, shine, spark, strew, trace 6 bubble 7 diffuse, glisten, glitter, radiate, reflect, scatter, showing, spangle 8 disperse, sprinkle, vivacity 9 coruscate 10 effervesce, illuminate, liveliness 11 coruscation, scintillate 13 scintillation

sparkling: 4 dewy 5 crisp, witty 6 bright, lively, starry 7 shining 8 animated, eloquent, flashing, gleaming 9 brillante, brilliant, twinkling 10 glittering, reflecting 12 effervescent, effervescing

sparoid fish: 4 scup 5 porgy 10 sheepshead

sparrer: 5 boxer 7 sparrow

sparrow: 7 chanter

sparse: 4 thin 5 scant 6 meager, meagre, scanty 7 scatter 8 disperse 9 scattered 10 distribute, infrequent

Sparta: *army:* 4 mora
bondman: 5 helot
commander: 7 lochage
country: 7 Laconia
dog: 10 bloodhound
enemy: 6 Athens
festival: 6 Carnea 7 Carneia
governor: 7 harmost
king: 5 Leonidas, Menelaus 9 Tyndareus
lawgiver: 8 Lycurgus
magistrate: 5 ephor
method of cipher writing: 7 scytale
native: 8 Laconian
queen: 4 Leda 5 Helen
serf: 5 helot

tyrant: 5 Nabis

spartan: 5 brave, hardy 6 frugal, heroic, severe 7 laconic 9 undaunted 10 courageous

spasm: fit, tic 4 grip 5 crick 6 frenzy 7 seizure 8 paroxysm 10 convulsion 11 contraction
muscle: 5 cramp
of distress: 4 pang
of pain: 5 throe

spasmodic: 6 fitful, sudden 7 snatchy, violent 9 excitable 12 intermittent
disease: 7 tetanus

spat: row 4 blow, clap, fuss, slap, tiff 5 eject 6 gaiter, oyster, splash, strike 7 dispute, legging, quarrel

spate: 4 gush, rain 5 flood 6 throng 7 freshet, outflow, torrent 8 cataract 9 overwhelm, rainstorm 10 waterspout

spatial: 5 areal 6 steric 8 sterical

spatter: jet 4 dash, drop, soil, spot 5 slart, spurt 6 dabble, defame, injure, splash, spread 7 scatter, spatule, sputter 8 splutter, sprinkle

spatterdash: 6 gaiter 7 legging

spatula: 4 tool 5 spade 6 thible

spatulate: 6 lyrate 11 spoon-shaped

spawn: roe 4 eggs, germ, seed, sire, spot 5 fungi 6 bulbis, source 7 cormels, deposit, produce 8 generate, mycelium 9 procreate

ascending river to: 10 anadromous

spay: 4 geld 8 castrate 9 sterilize

speak: say 4 carp, chat, hail, talk, tell 5 extol, honor, orate, utter 6 remark, reveal 7 address, bespeak, declaim, declare, deliver, express, publish 8 converse, harangue, manifest, proclaim 9 celebrate, discourse, pronounce 10 articulate
affectedly: 4 mimp 5 mince
against: 6 oppose
at length: 7 dissert 9 expatiate
curtly: 4 snap, birk
evasively: 5 hedge, stall
for: 6 defend 7 testify
foolishly: 5 prate 6 drivel
from memory: 6 recite
hesitantly: 7 stammer
imperfectly: 4 lisp 7 stutter
impulsively: 5 blurt
in undertone: 6 mumble, murmur
inability to: 6 alalia, mutism 7 aphasia 8 aglossia
incoherently: 6 gabble, gibber
noisily: 4 fume, rant, rave
of: 4 call 7 mention
offhand: 11 extemporize
oracularly: 11 pontificate
out: 6 affirm
pert. to: 10 oratorical
profusely: 6 dilate 7 palaver

rapidly: 5 troll 6 patter 8 splutter

rhetorically: 5 orate 7 declaim

slightingly: 8 backbite 9 disparage

slowly: 5 drawl

softly: 7 whisper

thoughtlessly: 4 blat 8 splutter

through nose: 9 nasillate

to: 5 greet 6 accost 7 address

under breath: 6 mumble, mutter

with interruption: haw, hem

speaker: 5 drone, sayer 6 lisper, orator, proser, ranter, talker 7 demagog, utterer 8 lecturer 9 demagogue, spokesman 10 mouthpiece, prolocutor 11 entertainer, spellbinder

inspired: 7 prophet

of many languages: 8 linguist, polyglot

speaker's hammer: 5 gavel

speaking: *style:* 8 staccato, fluently

without preparation: 13 extemporizing

spear: gad, rod 4 dart, fram, reed, shut, spar, stab 5 apine, blade, lance, shoot, stalk 6 aprout, glaive, impale, pierce, strike 7 feather, harpoon, javelin, missile, trident 9 penetrate

grass: 5 blade

kind of: 4 gaff 5 gidia, gidya 6 bident, fizgig, gidgea, gidgee, gidjee, gidyea 7 assagai, assegai, bourdon, harpoon, leister, trident

three-pronged: 7 trident

spear-shaped: 7 hastate

spearfish: 8 billfish 9 swordfish

spearhead: 4 gaff, lead 6 direct 7 advance, precede

spearwort: 8 crowfoot

special: 4 dear, rare 5 chief, extra, local 6 unique 7 express, limited, notable, unusual 8 concrete, detailed, favorite, intimate, paramour, peculiar, personal, specific, uncommon 9 specially 10 especially, individual, noteworthy, particular, restricted 11 distinctive, exceptional 12 particularly 13 distinguished, extraordinary

ability: 6 talent

edition: 5 extra

specialist: *atomic:* 9 physicist

city planning: 8 urbanist

medical: (see also **doctor**): 7 oculist, surgeon 9 internist, otologist 11 neurologist, orthopedist 12 gynecologist, obstetrician, pediatrician 15 ophthalmologist

mineral: 12 mineralogist

money management: 9 economist

surgical: see **doctor**

specialty: bag 5 forte, skill 8 aptitude 13 particularity

specie: 4 cash, coin 5 money

species: 4 kind, race, sort, type 5 breed, brood, class, genre, image 7 mankind, variety 8 category, humanity 9 spectacle 10 exhibition, reflection

modified by environment: 4 ecad

spider: 5 acera

various: 5 genus 6 genera

specific: 5 exact 7 precise, special 8 clearcut, concrete, definite, detailed, explicit, peculiar 10 particular, restricted, specifying 11 determinate

specifically: 6 namely 9 expressly, specially

specify: 4 name, tell 5 allot, state 6 assign, define, detail 7 itemize, mention 8 describe, nominate 9 designate, stipulate, enumerate 10 articulate

specimen: 4 mark 5 model, relic, token 6 cotype, sample, swatch 7 example, pattern 8 instance 11 examination 12 illustration

specious: gay 4 fair 5 false, showy 6 glossy, hollow 7 colored 8 coloured, illusory 9 colorable, plausible 10 ostensible 12 hypocritical

speck: bit, dot, nit 4 blot, iota, mark, mite, mote, spot, whit 5 glebe, stain 7 blemish, blubber 8 impurity, particle

speckle: dot 5 fleck 7 stipple

speckled: 6 menald 7 bracket

specs: 10 eyeglasses, spectacles

spectacle: 4 show 5 bysen, model, scene, sight 6 marvel, mirror 7 display, diorama, example, pageant, pattern 8 panorama, spyglass 9 cyclorama 10 exhibition 14 representation

structure for: 5 arena 7 stadium, theater, theatre 8 coliseum

spectacles: 7 glasses

part of: 6 bridge, temple

spectator: 4 eyer 6 espier 7 witness 8 beholder, kibitzer, looker-on, observer, onlooker

specter, spectre: 4 bogy 5 bogey, bogie, bogle, ghost, shade, spook 6 boggle, spirit, wraith 7 boggard, boggart, bugaboo, bugbear, phantom 8 boggle-bo, guytrash, illusion, phantasm, revenant 10 apparition

spectral: 6 ghosty, spooky 7 ghostly, phantom 12 apparitional 13 insubstantial

spectrum: 8 infrared 11 ultraviolet

colors: red 4 blue 5 green 6 indigo, violet, yellow

speculate: 5 guess, think 6 gamble, mirror, ponder, wonder 7 predict 8 consider, meditate, ruminate, theorize 10 conjecture, deliberate, philosophy 11 contemplate

speculation: 4 risk 6 bubble, vision 7 surmise 8 decision 9 guesswork, intuition 10 conclusion, conjecture

speculative: 5 risky 9 uncertain 11 theoretical

speculator: 7 gambler, lookout, scalper 8 explorer, observer, theorist 12 contemplator, investigator

speculum: 6 mirror 7 diopter

speech: 4 talk 5 idiom, voice, slang 6 dilogy, epilog, orison, steven, tongue 7 address, dialect, oration, oratory, vinegar 8 colloquy, epilogue, harangue, language 9 utterance 12 vocalization

abusive: 6 tirade
art: 8 rhetoric
bitter: 8 diatribe
blunder: 8 solecism
boastful: 7 bluster
bombastic: 8 harangue
conclusion: 10 peroration
defect: 4 lisp 6 alogia 7 stammer, stutter
denunciation: 5 frump 6 tirade 8 filippic 9 philippic
difficulty: 9 baryphony 10 baryphonia
element: 4 surd
expert: 9 phonetist
figure of: 5 irony, trope 6 aporia, simile 7 imagery 8 metaphor
goddess: Vac
hesitation: haw 7 stammer, stutter
impassioned: 6 tirade 9 dithyramb
insane: 9 bedlamism
local: 6 patois 7 dialect
long: 5 spiel
loss: 6 alalia 7 aphasia 8 muteness
part: 4 noun, verb 6 adverb 9 adjective 11 conjunction, preposition 12 interjection
peculiar: 5 idiom
provincial: 6 patois 7 dialect
readiness: 9 fecundity
religious: 6 sermon 9 preaching
representing: 8 phonetic
reserved: 8 reticent
summary: 5 notes
violent: 6 tirade
voiceless element: 4 surd 7 spirate
world language: 7 volapuk 9 esperanto

speechless: mum 4 dumb, mute 6 silent 9 voiceless

speed: hie, rip 4 drug, fare, flee, help, race, rate 5 haste, hurry 6 assist, career, gallop, hasten, profit, succor 7 execute, prosper 8 celerity, dispatch, expedite, rapidity, velocity 9 advantage, discharge, quickness, swiftness 10 accelerate, expedition, facilitate 12 precipitance

full: 5 amain
great: 4 zoom 5 haste, spurt, amain 6 career 9 posthaste
measuring device: 5 radar 8 odometer 10 tachymeter 11 speedometer, velocimeter
note: 4 time 5 clock
rate of: RPM 4 pace 5 tempo
ratio: 4 Mach

up: 6 hasten 8 catalyze

speeder: 5 racer 6 driver 11 accelerator

speedily: 4 fast, soon 5 apace 6 presto 7 betimes, hastily, quickly, rapidly 8 promptly 13 expeditiously

speedy: 4 fast 5 fleet, hasty, quick, rapid, swift 6 active, prompt 7 helpful 11 expeditious

spell: bar, peg 4 chip, form, lath, mean, rest, rung, save, tale, talk, tell, trap, turn, snap 5 brief, charm, curse, magic, relay, shift, spare, speak, spell, story, utter, weird, while 6 glamor, gospel, import, period, relate, relief, splint, trance, voodoo 7 bewitch, cantrip, compose, glamour, relieve, shaving, signify, sorcery, drought, syncope 8 pishogue, splinter 9 discourse 10 constitute, demonifuge 11 abracadabra, conjuration, enchantment, fascination 12 entrancement 13 orthographize, prognosticate, substitute for

in another alphabet: 13 transliterate
out: 7 clarify, develop, explain 9 interpret

spellbind: 5 orate 7 enchant, engross 8 enthrall 9 fascinate

speller *(according to pronunciation):* 9 phonetist 11 phoneticist

poor: 11 cacographer

spelt: 5 grain, wheat 6 cereal

spelter: 4 zinc

spencer: wig 4 coat 6 butler, jacket, pantry 7 buttery, steward, trysail

spend: run, use 4 blow, dash, flow, give, jump, pass, span 5 beset, exert, grasp, waste 6 attach, bestow, beware, devote, elapse, expend, fasten, lavish, lay out, manage, spread, spring, weaken 7 consume, exhaust, fatigue, perform 8 confound, disburse, squander 9 dissipate, sacrifice 10 distribute

wisely: 7 husband

spend the summer: 8 estivate

spendthrift: 6 waster 7 wastrel 8 prodigal, wasteful 10 dingthrift, profligate, squanderer

Spenserian character: Una

spent: 4 beat, paid, used 5 all in, weary 6 effete, wasted 7 worn out 8 lavished 9 exhausted 10 squandered

speos: 4 cave, tomb 6 grotto, temple

sperm: 4 germ, seed 5 semen

sperm whale: 8 cachalot

spet: 9 barracuda

spew, spue: bog 4 gush, ooze, spit 5 eject, exude, strew, vomit 7 extrude, flow out, scatter 8 disgorge

sphacelate: 7 decayed, mortify 8 withered

sphenic: 11 wedge-shaped

spheral: 7 perfect 10 harmonious 11 symmetrical

sphere: orb, sky 4 ball, rank, star 5 ambit,

arena, class, field, globe, orbit, order, range, scope 6 domain, orblet, planet 7 circuit, compass, heavens, stratum, station, theatre, terella 8 idiosome, position, province 9 idioblast 10 atmosphere, department, occupation 12 jurisdiction

of action: 5 arena

of influence: 5 orbit 14 balance of power

perforated: 4 bead

spheric: 8 globular 11 globe-shaped

spherical: 5 orbic, round 6 rotund 7 globate, globose, spatial 8 globated, globular, obrotund 9 globulous, orbicular

spheroid: 4 ball 5 earth

spherule: 7 globule, variole

sphinx: 6 enigma 7 monster, prophet 8 colossus, hawkmoth

land of: 5 Egypt

mother: 7 Echidna

query of: 6 riddle

site of: 4 Giza 5 Luxor

sphinxian: 10 mysterious 11 enigmatical, inscrutable

sphygmus: 5 pulse

spica: 4 star 7 bandage

spice: 4 dash, hint, kind, mace, mull, nard, odor, sort, vein 5 aroma, taste, touch 6 embalm, flavor, relish, season 7 modicum, perfume, portion, species, variety 8 quantity, specimen 9 admixture, condiment, fragrance, seasoning 10 appearance

kind of: 4 mace, mull, sage 5 anise, cumin, curry, thyme 6 cloves, fennel, ginger, nutmeg, pepper, stacte, tamara 7 caraway, cayenne, mustard, oregano, paprika, pimento 8 allspice, cinnamon, marjoram, pimiento, turmeric

mill: 5 quern

package for: 6 robbin

Spice Islands: See Molucca islands

spick-and-span: 4 neat, trim 5 clean, fresh 6 spruce 8 brand-new 11 well-groomed

spicknel: mew 8 bearwort

spicule: rod 4 dart, nail, toxa 5 aster, spine 6 actine 7 prickle, rhabdus 8 sclerite, spikelet

sponge: 5 cymba

spicy: hot 4 keen, racy 5 balmy, natty, showy, smart, sweet 6 active, risque 7 gingery, peppery, piquant, pungent 8 aromatic, fragrant, spirited 11 interesting

spider: bug, cob, cop, hub, pan 5 arain 6 eresid, epeira, snarer, tripod, trivet 7 pokomoo, skillet, retiary 8 arachnid, attercop, telarian 9 frying pan, tarantula 12 candleholder

family of: 7 attidae 9 drassidae 10 citigradae

genus of: 6 aranea, epeira

three-legged: 6 trivet

venomous: 9 tarantula 10 black widow

web-spinning organ: 9 spinneret

spider bug: 5 emesa

spider crab: 4 maia

spider monkey: 9 belzebuth

spider nest: web 5 nidus

spider web: 8 attercop

resembling: 9 arachnoid

spinner: 9 spinneret

spiel: 5 pitch

spieler: 5 crier 6 barker, talker 7 sharper, showman, speaker 8 lecturer, swindler 9 announcer 11 spellbinder

spiffy: 4 chic, neat 5 smart 6 spruce

spifflicate, spifflicate: 4 beat, kill 6 stifle 8 astonish, bewilder, confound

spigot: peg, pin, tap 4 cock, plug 5 spile, spout 6 dossil, faucet, pierce 7 stopper

spike: cut, cob, ear, gad 4 brob, chat, nail, stab, tine, umbo 5 ament, block, prong 6 antler, cereal, earlet, fasten, finish, impale, pierce, secure, thwart 7 bayonet, disable, fortify, trenail 8 mackerel, puncture 9 frustrate, merganser 10 spadix-tine 13 inflorescence

spikenard: 4 nard 8 ointment

spile: pin, rod, tap 4 bung, heap, pile, plug, rule, tube 5 spill, spout, stake 6 spigot 7 stopper 8 forepole, splinter

spill: die, mar, peg, pin 4 rod 4 disk, fail, fall, flow, kill, roll, ruin, shed, slip, slop, tell 5 flosh, spile, spoil, spool, waste 6 betray, injure, perish, punish, reveal, sheath, tumble, wasted 7 confess, correct, destroy, divulge, scatter 8 chastise, downpour, gratuity, overflow, spillway, splinter, squander 11 deteriorate

Spillane's detective: 6 Hammer

spiloma: 5 nevus 9 birthmark

spin: 4 birl, burl, gyre, pirl, reel, ride, turn 5 drive, spurt, swirl, twirl, twist, whirl 6 gyrate, rotate 7 prolong, revolve 8 protract

spin a yarn: 7 narrate

spina: 4 wall 5 backbone

spinach: 7 epinard, potherb

spinal: 5 balas

area: 6 dorsal, lumbar, sacral 8 cervical

column: 6 rachis 8 backbone 9 vertebrae

cord: 4 alba 6 myelon

disease: 5 polio 8 myelitis

layer: 4 dura

muscle: 5 psoas

spindle: pin, rod 4 axis, axle, hasp, stem 5 arbor, fusee, shaft, stalk, xeres 6 arbour, broach, fuseau, rachis 7 mandrel

spindling: 4 weak 5 leggy 7 slender 11 ineffectual

spine (see also **spinal**): awn 4 back, seta 5 chine, ridge, thorn 6 chaeta, needle, spirit 7 acantha, acicula, courage, prickle, spicule 8 backbone, spiculum 9 vertebrae

spine bone: 6 sacrum

spineless: 4 weak 7 slavish 11 ineffectual

spine-tingling: 4 eery 5 eerie 7 ghostly

spinet: 5 piano 7 giraffe 11 harpsichord

spinnaker: 4 sail

spinner: cap, top 5 spoon 6 spider, weaver 8 narrator 10 goatsucker

spinney: 5 copse, grove 7 thicket

spinning: 5 areel 6 rotary 8 whirling 9 revolving

device: 7 distaff

machine: 4 mule 5 jenny 8 throstle

rod: 7 distaff

spinning wheel: 6 charka 7 charkha

spin-off: 6 byproduct, outgrowth

Spinoza work: 6 Ethics

spinster: 7 old maid 10 maiden lady

spiny: 6 picked, thorny 7 prickly 9 acanthoid, difficult

spiny-footed: 10 acanthopod 13 acanthopodous

spiny shrub: 4 ulex

spiracle: 4 hole, pore, vent 6 breath 7 orifice 8 aperture, blowhole

spiral: 4 coil, curl 5 curve, helix 7 coiling, curving, helical, winding 8 circling, helicoid 9 corkscrew 11 anfractuous

spire: 4 coil, curl 5 blade, stalk, tower, twist, whorl 6 fleche, sprout 7 sapling, steeple

finial: epi 4 epis

ornament: 6 finial

spirit: hag, pep, vim 4 aitu, alma, dash, dook, elan, fire, gimp, life, mood, soul, wind 5 angel, ardor, bugan, dhoul, ethos, fairy, fling, ghost, haunt, metal, pluck, shade, spook, verve, vigor 6 ardour, asuang, breeze, elixir, energy, esprit, ginger, mettle, morale, pneuma, temper, yaksha (mas.), yakshi(fem.) 7 animate, bravery, courage, entrain, hearten, loyalty 8 folletto, phantasm, vivacity 9 animation, encourage 10 apparition, enterprise, enthusiasm, get-up-and-go 11 disposition, inspiration 12 cheerfulness, entrainement

air: 5 Ariel

animating: 6 animus

animation: pep 4 dash

avenging: Ate 6 alecto, erinys 7 megaera, nemesis 9 tisiphine

away: 6 abduct, kidnap; snatch

evil: Ate, imp, Ker 4 baka, beng, boko, drow, gyre 5 bugan, demon, devil 6 animus, asuang, daemon, daitya, dibbuk, Erynes, Lilith 9 cacodemon 10 cacodaemon

female: 6 undine 7 banshee, banshie

fire: 4 Agni

good: 5 genie, genus 7 eudemon 8 eudaemon

heralding death: 7 banshee, banshie

kinds of: akh, imp, lar, nat 4 arac, gimp, Kuei, Kwei, soul 5 angel, Ariel, duffy, duppy, dusio, ethos, genie, jinni, manes, rakee, shade 6 animus, fulgja, jinnee, mammon, tangie, Undine 7 banshee

lose: 7 despond

mischievous: imp 4 Puck 6 goblin 7 gremlin 11 poltergeist

of censure: 5 Momus

of people: 5 ethos

spirit-land: 9 fairyland

spirit-leaf: 8 manyroot

spirited: gay 4 fell, gamy, bold 5 brisk, eager, fiery 6 active, audace, birkie, ginger, lively, spunky 7 animato, dashing, zealous 8 animated, desirous, eloquent, frampoid, generous, vigorous 9 audacious, energetic, spiritoso, sprightly 10 mettlesome

horse: 5 steed 7 charger

spiritless: 4 cold, dead, meek 5 amort, blate, vapid 6 flashy 7 daviely, hilding, languid 8 dejected, feckless, flagging, lifeless, listless, thewless 9 apathetic, depressed, exanimate, heartless 10 dispirited

spiritlike: 8 ethereal

spirits: 4 mood 5 booze 6 liquor 7 alcohol

dash of: 5 lacer

dead: 5 manes

dwelling place of: Po 5 Hades 7 Elysium

kinds of: 6 furies, uplift 7 elation, Sammael 9 firewater 13 aquacaelestis

lift: 5 elate 7 gladden

low: 5 blues, dumps, gloom 6 gloomy 8 doldrums

spirits and water: 4 grog

spiritual: 4 holy, pure, song 6 devout, divine, sacred 7 ghostly 8 churchly, internal, platonic, spirited 9 animastic, geistlich, unworldly 10 devotional, immaterial 11 animastical, disembodied, incorporeal 14 ecclesiastical

apathy: 6 acedia

being: ens 5 angel, entia(pl.) 6 seraph

darkness: 4 Hell 5 tamas

spiritualistic meeting: 6 seance

spiritualize: 5 endow 6 purify, refine 7 animate 8 idealize 11 etherealize

spirituous: gay 4 airy, hard 5 vivid 6 active, ardent, lively 7 tenuous 8 ethereal 9 alcoholic 10 immaterial 11 incorporeal

spiry: 4 tall 6 coiled, curled, spiral 7 slender 8 tapering, wreathed 10 serpentine

spit: dig, fix, rod 4 emit, hang, rain, reef, snow 5 eject, image, light, plant, reach, retch, shoal, spade, stick, sword, utter 6 broach, dagger, impale, saliva, skewer, sputum, thrust 7 spindle, spittle, sputter 8 broacher, likeness, sandbank, spadeful, sprinkle 9 brochette, secretion 11 counterpart, expectorate

spital: den 6 refuge, resort 7 shelter 8 hospital 9 lazaretto

spite: vex 4 hate, hurt, mood 5 annoy, depit, pique, shame, venom 6 enmity, grudge, hatred, injury, malice, mauger, maugre, rancor, thwart 7 chagrin, despite, dislike, ill-will, mortify 8 disgrace, dishonor 9 animosity, frustrate, hostility, humiliate 10 resentment 11 disposition, malevolence 12 spitefulness 13 mortification

spiteful: 4 mean 5 catty, snaky 6 sullen 7 hostile, waspish 8 annoying, venomous 9 malicious, malignant 10 dispiteous, irritating, malevolent, vindictive 11 troublesome

spitfire: 6 virago 7 sulphur 9 brimstone

spitter: 4 deer 5 spade 7 brocket 8 spitball 9 expectorator

spitting: 6 saliva 10 exspuition

spitting image: 4 twin 6 double, ringer

spittle: 4 peel, spit 6 saliva

spittle insect: 10 froghopper

spittoon: 8 crachoir, cuspidor

spiv: 7 slacker 8 parasite

splash: lap 4 dash, daub, gout, lave, mark, plop, pond, pool, spot 5 bathe, blash, slart, slash, spray 6 blotch, dabble, flouse, floush, strike 7 display, feature, scatter, spatter 8 splatter 9 dashingly 10 appearance, excitement 14 ostentatiously

splashboard: 4 gate, trap 5 board, plank 6 fender, screen 8 mudguard

splashy: wet 5 muddy, showy 6 blashy, slushy, watery 8 striking 11 sensational, spectacular 12 ostentatious

splat: 4 open, plot, spot 5 patch 6 blotch 7 flatten

splatter: dab 4 dash, rush 6 hubbub, splash 7 cluster

splay: hem 4 awry, turn 5 adorn, bevel, carve, slant, slope 6 clumsy, expand, spread 7 awkward, display, diverge, sloping 8 ungainly 9 dislocate, expansion, obliquely, slopingly, spreading 10 slantingly 11 enlargement

spleen: 4 fire, milt 5 anger, ardor, freak, mirth, organ, spite 6 malice 7 dislike, impulse 8 ill-humor, laughter 9 lienculus, merriment 10 melancholy 11 impetuosity

pert. to: 6 lienal

spleeny: 5 angry 7 fretful, peevish 9 irritable 10 melancholy

splendent: 6 glossy 7 beaming, shining 8 lustrous, splendid 9 brilliant 11 conspicuous, illustrious, magnificent, resplendent

splendid: gay 4 braw, fine, good, rial 5 grand, regal, showy, tinny 6 bright, candid, costly, superb 7 gallant, ripping, shining, sublime 8 glorious, gorgeous 9 brilliant, excellent, grandiose, sumptuous 11 illustrious, magnificent, resplendent

splendor, splendour: 4 gite, pomp 5 blaze, eclat, gleam, glory, sheen 6 bright, fulgor, luster, parade 7 display, fulgour 8 elegance, grandeur, radiance, richness 9 pageantry, showiness 10 brightness, brilliance, brilliancy, effulgence 12 gorgeousness, magnificence, resplendence 14 impressiveness

splenetic: 6 sullen, vapory 7 fretful, peevish, splenic 8 spiteful 9 depressed, irritable, malicious, spleenful 10 melancholy

splice: 4 join 5 marry, unite 6 fasten 7 wedding 8 marriage 10 interweave

splint: 4 coal, lath, tace, scob 5 brace, plate, split, strip, tasse 6 fasten 7 confine

splinter: 4 chip, rend 5 break, broom, slice, smash, spale, split 6 fasten, shiver, sliver 7 confine, flinder, shatter 8 fragment

split: cut, rit 4 chap, rend, rent, rive, ruin, tear 5 break, burst, clave, cleft, crack, peach, reave, riven, share, wedge 6 betray, bisect, bottle, breach, broken, cleave, cloven, dilute, divide, rifted, schism, sliver, sunder 7 destroy, dispart, divided, fissure, portion, rupture, shatter 8 fragment, informer, separate, splinter 9 fractured, separated 10 separation

in two parts: 5 bifid 6 cloven, halved 8 bisected 9 bipartite

up: 10 separation

split pea: dal

splitting: 5 funny 6 severe 7 comical, fission, rending 8 piercing

of mind: 13 schizophrenia

splotch: dab 4 blob, blot, daub, mark, spot 5 smear, stain 6 blotch, mottle, splash 7 blemish

splurge: 5 spend 6 effort, splash 7 display 11 ostentation 13 demonstration

splutter: 4 fuff 5 hurry, noise, stuff 6 bustle, splash 7 dispute, glutter, quarrel, scatter, spatter, stammer 8 nonsense 9 confusion

Spode: 5 china 9 porcelain

Spohr opera: 8 Jessonda

spoil: mar, rob, rot 4 baby, blad, boot, loot, pelf, prey, rape, ruin, swag 5 bitch, blend, booty, carve, cheat, decay, harry, prize, seize, strip, taint, waste 6 coddle, damage, deface, divest, forage, impair, infuse, injure, pamper, perish, ravage, thwart 7 connach, corrupt, estrepe, deprive, despoil, destroy, indulge, pillage, plunder, violate, vitiate 8 confound, unclothe 10 chevisance, corruption, impairment

eggs: 5 addle

spoiled: bad 5 dazed, musty 6 addled, marred, molded, petted, preyed, rotted 7 botched, decayed, damaged, tainted 8 pampered, pillaged 9 plundered

spoiler: 6 robber 7 marplot 8 marauder, pillager 9 despoiler, plunderer 10 depredator

spoilsport: 7 killjoy 10 wet-blanket

spoke: bar 4 clog, grip, rung, tale, talk 5 block, check, drone, round, spake, stake, stick 6 radius, speech 7 mention, uttered 8 handhold 10 impediment 11 enchantment

spoken: 4 oral, said 5 parol, vocal 7 uttered 9 declaimed

spoliate: rob 6 ravage 7 despoil, pillage, plunder

spoliation: 4 loss 6 rapine 7 pillage, plunder, robbery 8 pillaged 11 destruction 12 despoliation

spondyl: 8 vertebra

sponge: bum, wet 4 form, swab, wipe 5 ascon, cadge, dough, erase, mooch 6 absorb, ascula, efface, rhagon 7 badiaga, cleanse, destroy, drinker, scrunge, zimocca 8 drunkard, parasite, scrounge 10 freeloader

calcareous: 6 leucon

orifice: 6 oscula(pl.) 7 osculum

pen: 5 kraal

pert. to: 9 poriferal

spicle: 4 toxa

vegetable: 4 loofa, luffa 6 loofah

sponge tree: 8 huisache

sponger: 5 leech 6 cadger 8 parasite

spongewood: 4 sola

spongy: 4 fozy, soft 5 rainy 6 porous, quaggy 9 absorbent

sponsor: 4 back 5 angel 6 backer, gossip, patron, surety 9 godfather, godmother, introduce

sponsorship: 4 egis 5 aegis 7 backing 8 auspices

spontaneous: 4 free, wild 6 native 8 careless, untaught 9 automatic, impulsive 10 indigenous, self-acting 11 instinctive, involuntary, unpremeditated

spontoon: 4 club, pike 6 cudgel 7 halberd, pantoon 9 truncheon

spoof: guy 4 fool, hoax, joke 5 trick 7 deceive, swindle 8 nonsense 9 deception

spook: spy 4 fool, hoax, joke 5 annoy, ghost, haunt 6 spirit, wraith 7 specter, startle 8 frighten 9 hobgoblin 10 apparition, make nervous

spooky: 4 eery 5 eerie, weird 6 creepy 7 ghostly, haunted, uncanny 8 spectral

spool: 4 reel, wind 6 bobbin, broach, holder 7 spindle 8 cylinder

spoon: pet, woo 4 neck 5 ladle, labis, lover, ninny 6 nestle, shovel, spoony 7 student 8 cochlear, golf club, make love 9 simpleton

spoon-fed: 7 coddled 8 pampered

Spoon River poet: 7 Masters

spoon-shaped: 8 cochlear, spatular

spoonbill: 5 ajaja 8 shoveler 10 paddlefish

spoor: 4 clue, hint, odor 5 piste, scent, trace, track, trail

spore: 4 cyst, germ, seed

spore sac: 5 ascus 7 capsule

sport (see also **game:** *official*): bet, fun, gig, toy 4 game, gaud, glee, jest, joke, mock, play, polo, romp 5 dally, freak, mirth, wager 6 frolic, gamble, racing, shikar 7 contest, gambler, jesting, mockery, pastime 8 derision, raillery 9 amusement, diversion, plaything 10 pleasantry, recreation 13 entertainment

attendance: 4 gate

event: 4 game, meet, race 5 match

shirt: tee 4 polo

shoe: 6 loafer 7 sneaker

site: gym 4 grid, oval, pool, ring, rink 5 arena, court, field, links, track 6 course 7 diamond, stadium 8 coliseum 10 hippodrome

summer: 6 diving, hiking, quoits, rowing, skiing 7 fishing, sailing 8 swimming

water: 6 diving, rowing 7 sailing, surfing 8 canoeing, swimming, yachting

winter: 6 hockey, skiing 7 curling, skating 8 sledding 11 tobogganing

sportive: gay 5 merry 6 frisky, lusory, wanton 7 amorous, festive, jocular, playful 8 frolicky, gamesome, playsome, pleasant 9 lecherous 10 frolicsome

sportiveness: 7 devilry, roguery, waggery

sportsman: 6 hunter 7 shikari 8 shikaree

sportula: 4 gift 7 largess, present

sporty: 4 loud 5 showy 6 casual, flashy

spot: bit, dab, dot, job, see 4 blot, blur, find, fish, flaw, mark, site, soil 5 blaze, fault, fleck, nevus, patch, place, point, ready, speck, stain, sully, tache, taint 6 blotch, defect, detect, locate, macula, macule, naevus, random, remove, stigma 7 asperse, blemish, freckle, splotch 8 discolor, disgrace, handicap, identify, locality, location, maculate, particle, position, quantity, reproach 9 bespatter, recognize 11 predicament

kinds of: ace, dot, pip, tee 4 blet, fret, gall, rone, spil, wems 5 macle, oasis 6 alcove, bethel, mascle, mottle, mouche 7 freckle 8 bethesda, fenestra, fontanel *on animal's face:* 4 star 5 blaze

on playing card: pip

spotless: 5 clean, snowy 6 chaste 9 blameless, unspotted, unsullied 10 immaculate 11 unblemished, untarnished 14 irreproachable

spotlight: arc 4 beam 9 emphasize, publicity 10 illuminate

spotted: 6 bauson, calico, espied, marked, notate, sanded, ticked 7 bracket, dappled, guttate, mottled, noticed, stained, sullied 9 blemished, suspected, tarnished

animal: 4 paco, pard 6 chital, ocelot 7 cheetah, leopard

fever: 6 typhus

spotter: 7 watcher 9 detective

spotty: few 5 dotty 6 uneven 9 irregular

spousal: 7 wedlock 8 ceremony, marriage, nuptials

spouse: 4 mate, wife 5 bride 6 fiance 7 consort, fiancee, husband, partner 9 companion 10 bridegroom

spout: jet, jut, lip 4 dale, flow, geat, gush, lift, pawn, pipe, rant 5 chute, eject, issue, orate, shoot, speak, spile, spurt, utter 6 pledge, recite, spigot, spring, squirt, stream, trough 7 conduit, declaim 8 downpour, gargoyle 9 discharge, waterfall 10 waterspout

sprack: 4 deft 5 alert 6 active, lively, nimble, shrewd

sprag: 4 prop 6 billet

sprain: 4 pull, tear, turn 5 chink 6 weaken, wrench 10 overstrain

sprat: 5 bleak 6 garvie 7 herring 8 sixpence

sprattle: 6 sprawl 8 scramble, struggle

sprawl: 4 loll 5 slump 7 grabble 8 struggle 9 sprauchie

spray: jet 4 chap, hose, twig 5 bough, shoot, spree, sprig, water 6 boquet, branch, sparge, spread, volley 7 atomize, bouquet, scatter 8 sprinkle 9 aspersion, discharge, sprindrift

spread: fan, jam, ted 4 emit, meal, oleo, open, span, taft 5 cover, feast, flare, jelly, reach, smear, splay, strew, widen 6 anoint, dilate, dinner, expand, extend, extent, ramify, unfold, unfurl 7 broaden, compass, diffuse, distend, diverge, divulge, enlarge, exhibit, expanse, overlay, overrun, prolong, protect, publish, radiate, scatter, slather, stretch 8 coverlet, diffused, dispense, disperse, expanded, extended, increase, multiply, permeate, straddle 9 broadcast, circulate, dispersed, displayed, expansion, expatiate, propagate 10 distribute, generalize 11 disseminate

abroad: 4 toot 5 bruit, noise, libel, rumor 6 delate, rumour, spring 7 divulge, radiate 9 broadcast, publicize 11 disseminate

as plaster: 4 teer

for drying: ted

loosely: 5 strew 7 scatter

on: 5 apply

out: fan, lap, ted 4 bray, open, span 5 flare, widen 6 deploy, flange, sprawl, unfold

spreader: 5 knife 6 tedder

spreading of light: 8 halation

spreading out: 6 radial

spree: bat, jag 4 bout, bust, gell, lark, orgy, romp, toot, jagg 5 beano, binge, booze, revel 6 bender, buster, bust-up, frolic, high-go, shindy 7 carouse, debauch, wassail 8 carousal 10 indulgence

sprig: 4 brad, nail, trim, twig 5 bough, scion, shoot, smart, spray, youth 6 active, branch, sprout, spruce 7 tendril 9 stripling, youngster

sprightly: gay, tid 4 airy, pert 5 agile, alive, antic, brisk, canty, crank, desto, elfin, peart 6 active, blithe, clever, lively 7 briskly, buoyant, chipper, ghostly, quickly 8 animated, vigorous 10 enlivening, spiritedly, spiritlike 11 incorporeal, quick-witted

spring: ain, fly, hop, spa 4 bend, dart, font, head, jump, leap, lilt, rise, warp, well 5 arise, begin, bound, flirt, issue, lymph, shoot, spurt, start, therm, tower, vault 6 accrue, bounce, emerge, season, therme, venero 7 estuary, thermae 8 fountain 10 intoxicate

abruptly: 4 bolt

back: 6 recoil, resile 7 rebound

deposit: 4 urao 5 trona

hot: 7 balneum, thermae, gipsies

kind of: ain, cee, spa, ver, hop, ojo 4 font 5 lymph 6 geyser, charco, source, saline 7 gambado 9 Castalian

pert. to: 6 vernal

up: 5 arise 6 sprout

spring-like: 6 vernal

springboard: 5 wagon 6 batule 8 tremplin 10 trampoline

springbok: 7 gazelle

springe: gin, set 4 trap 5 agile, catch, noose, snare 6 supple 7 pitfall 9 booby trap

springer: 5 fryer 7 grampus, spaniel 9 springbok

springing back: 7 elastic 9 renascent

springtime: May 8 germinal

springy: wet 6 pliant, spongy 7 elastic 8 flexible 9 resilient

sprinkle: deg, dot, wet 4 dart, rain, spot 5 color, flour, spray, strew, twist, water 6 affuse, bedrop, dabble, dredge, sparge 7 asperge, asperse, baptize, drizzle, moisten, scatter, spairge, sparkle, spatter,

speckle 8 disperse 9 bespangle, bespatter 10 besprinkle, intoxicate
with flour: 6 dredge
with grains of mustard: 8 sinapize
with grit: 4 sand
with moisture: 5 bedew
with mud: 9 bespatter
with powder: 4 dust
with water: deg
sprinkler: 7 dredger 11 aspergillum 12 extinguisher
sprinkling: 4 seme 7 baptism 9 aspersion
sprint: run 4 dash, race 5 snare, speed 6 bicker 7 springe
sprinter: 5 racer 6 runner 7 athlete
sprit: bud 4 dart, rush, spar 5 shoot, speck, sprat 6 sprint, sprout, squirt 8 bowsprit 9 germinate
sprite: elf, fay, hob, imp 4 elve, life, mind, mood, peri, soul 5 Ariel, bucca, fairy, genie, ghost, gnome, nisse, pixie, shade, vital 6 goblin, person, spirit 7 essence 9 germinate, hobgoblin 10 apparition, woodpecker 11 disposition, inspiration
kind of: nix 5 ariel, demon, Holda, naiad, nixie 6 Kelpie 8 coltpixy 9 coltpixie 10 leprechaun, shoopiltie
sprocket: cam 5 tooth, whelp
sproil: 6 active, energy 7 agility 8 activity 9 energetic
sprout: bud, eye, son 4 brod, chit, chun, cion, germ, malt 5 achar, brode, chine, shoot, spire, spout, sprig, spurt 6 braird, expand, germen, growth, ratoon 7 burgeon 8 offshoot, seedling 9 germinate
spruce: gim 4 chic, deft, neat, posh, smug, tidy, trig, trim 5 compt, fussy, natty, Picea, smart, sprig 6 dapper, picked 7 dandify, dress up, finical, smarten 8 overnice, titivate 11 well-groomed
tree: 5 larch 8 epinette
spruce: 4 hole 5 dross 7 opening 8 psilosis 9 asparagus
sprunt: 4 hill, leap 5 steep 6 spring 8 struggle
spry: 5 agile, brisk, quick, smart 6 active, clever, lively, nimble, spruce 7 knowing 8 vigorous 9 sprightly
spud: dig, man 4 hand 5 child, dough, drill, money, spade, tater 6 paddle, potato, reamer, remove, shovel 10 projection
spume: 4 foam, scum 5 froth 6 lather
spun: See spin
spunk, sponk: vim 4 punk 5 anger, flame, gleam, match, nerve, pluck, spark 6 kindle, mettle, spirit, sponge, tinder 7 courage, passion 9 fortitude, touchwood 10 doggedness
spunky: 4 game 5 brave, quick 6 plucky, touchy 8 spirited 9 irritable 10 coura-

geous, mettlesome
spur: egg 4 calk, gaff, goad, move, peak, prod, prop, urge 5 arete, brace, drive, hurry, impel, press, prick, range, ridge, rowel, spine, spoor, strut, tower 6 arouse, broach, calcar, digger, excite, foment, griffe, hasten, incite, motive, urge on 7 gablock, provoke, publish 8 buttress, stimulus 9 incentive, instigate, stimulate 10 blockhouse 11 publication
having: 7 spicate
of mountain: 5 arete
on gamecock: 4 gaff
railroad: 6 siding
wheel: 5 rowel
spur wheel: 5 rowel
spurge: 4 weed 6 balsam, purify 8 milkweed 9 euphorbia
spurious: 4 fake 5 bogus, false, phony, snide 6 forced 7 bastard 10 adulterate, apocryphal, artificial, fictitious, fraudulent 11 counterfeit, superficial 12 illegitimate 14 suppositious
spurn: hit 4 blow, dash, kick, rush, snub, spur 5 flout, haste, scorn 6 affray, incite, pillar, rebuff, refuse, reject, scrape, strike 7 contemn, decline, despise, disdain, scratch, stumble 10 engagement
spurt: jet, jut 4 dart, gush 5 expel, spell, spout 6 sprout, squirt 8 increase, outbreak
Sputnik: 9 satellite
dog: 5 Laika
sputter: ado 4 fuss, spit 7 bluster
sputum: 4 spit 6 saliva 7 spittle
spy: pry, see 4 case, espy, keek, note, tout 5 scout, sneak, snoop, spook, watch 6 behold, descry, detect, espial, gaycat, mouton, search 7 discern, examine, hicarra, inspect, observe, snooper 8 discover, emissary, hi-carrah, informer, perceive, stake out 10 discoverer, scrutinize 11 secret agent 13 intelligencer
famous: 4 Hari 5 Andre, Caleb, Fuchs 6 Arnold, Cavell 8 Mata Hari
spying: 9 espionage 12 surveillance 16 counter-espionage
Spyri's heroine: 5 Heidi
squab: coy, fat, shy 4 drop, sofa 5 couch, piper, plump, press, short, spill, thick 6 callow, pigeon, stocky 7 cushion, ottoman 8 nestling 9 fledgling, unfledged, upholster
squabble: 5 argue, brawl 6 bicker, jangle 7 bobbery, contend, dispute, quarrel, wrangle 13 collie-shangie
squad: 4 team 5 group, troop
leader of: 8 sergeant
squadron: 6 armada 10 escadrille
squalid: 4 base, foul, mean, poor, ugly, vile 5 dirty, nasty 6 filthy, shabby, sor-

did **7** unclean **8** wretched **9** miserable, repellant, repellent, repulsive **10** broken-down

squall: cry, pet **4** bawl, dear, drow, gush, gust, wawl **5** storm **6** flurry, scream, shower, squawk, wretch **7** borasca, borasco, dispute, quarrel, trouble **8** borasque **9** windstorm **11** disturbance

squalor: mud **4** dirt, mire **5** filth **9** roughness **10** filthiness **11** squalidness **12** wretchedness

squander: **4** burn, lash **5** spend, waste **6** befool, lavish, wander **7** consume, debauch, dispend, scatter **8** disperse, embezzle, misspend **9** dissipate **10** trifle away **12** extravagance

squanderer: **5** loser **7** wastrel

square: **4** even, parc, park, true **5** agora, carre, clear, exact, hunky, plaza **6** dinkum, direct, honest, settle **7** commons, quarrel, upright **8** justness, quadrate, **9** carre-four, criterion, principle **11** unequivocal **12** conventional **13** parallelogram **15** straightforward

public: **5** plaza **6** common

square dance: **4** reel **7** hoedown, lancers **9** quadrille

squared circle: **4** ring **5** arena

squarehead: **4** dolt **5** dunce, Swede **6** German **8** numskull **9** screwball **12** Scandinavian

squaring tool: **5** edger

squarish: **4** boxy

squarrose: **5** rough, scaly

squash: **4** beat, fall, ooze, pepo, stop **5** crowd, crush, press **6** stifle **7** cymling, flatten, pumpkin, squeeze, squelch **8** suppress **9** discomfit **10** disconcert

kind of: **5** acorn **6** banana, cushaw, simnel, summer, turban **7** cymling, Hubbard, Italian **8** cymbling, patty pan, zucchini **9** crookneck

squashy: wet **4** soft **5** boggy, muddy, mushy, pulpy **8** overripe

squat: sit **5** cower, dumpy, pudgy, stoop **6** bruise, crouch, fodgel, hurkle, settle, splash, stocky, stubby **8** thickset

squatter: **4** flap **5** squat **6** crouch, nester, plunge **7** bywoner, confuse, flutter, nestler, scatter, settler **8** bewilder, squander **9** sandpiper

Squatter State: **6** Kansas

squaw: **4** wife **5** woman **6** mahala, coween **10** klootchman

husband: **4** buck **6** sannup

squawbush: **5** sumac **6** shoval

squawfish: **4** chub **8** chappaul **9** surfperch

squeak: cry, wee **4** peep, talk **5** cheep, creak, noise, speak **6** betray, escape, inform, shrill **7** confess, disturb **11** opportunity

squeal: yip **4** blab, sing **5** broil, frail, weary **6** betray, inform, scream **7** dispute, protest, quarrel **8** complain

squealer: **4** duck, fink **5** quail, swift **6** grouse, pigeon, plover **7** traitor **8** informer **9** partridge

squeamish: shy **4** helo, nice, stir **5** dizzy, heloe **6** bustle, dainty, dauncy, modest, queasy **7** finical, prudish **8** overnice, qualmish **9** dizziness, giddiness, nauseated, reluctant, sensitive **10** fastidious, scrupulous **13** oversensitive

squeeze: eke, hug, jam **4** gain, mull, neck, silk **5** chirt, creem, crowd, crush, force, pinch, press, wring **6** corner, eke out, escape, extort, scrump, scruze, thrust, twitch **7** embrace, extract, oppress, procure, scrunch, scrunge **8** compress, condense, pressing, pressure, scrounge **9** constrict, influence **10** commission, constraint **11** compression, predicament

squeezer: **5** drier, noose **6** juicer, reamer **7** wringer **8** squeegee **9** extractor

squeezy: **7** cramped **8** confined

squelch: **4** blow, fall **5** crush, quash, quell, stamp **6** rebuke, subdue **7** silence **8** suppress **9** discomfit **10** disconcert

squib: jet **4** ball, bomb, mote, pipe, skit, tube **5** candy, match, throw **6** filler, squirt, writer **7** dispute, explode, lampoon, pasquil, torpedo, writing **9** bespatter **10** pasquinade **11** firecracker

squid: **6** loligo **7** mollusk, octopus **8** calamary **10** cuttlefish

arm: **8** tentacle

pen: **5** quill

secretion: ink

shell: pen

squiffer (Br.): **10** concertina

squiggle: **4** curl, line **5** shake, twist **6** squirm, writhe **7** wriggle **8** curlicue, scribble

squilla: **5** prawn **6** shrimp **8** sea onion

squinch: **4** arch **5** twist **6** lintel, quince, recoil, squint, wrench **7** squeeze, squench **9** corbeling

squint: **4** bent, cast, glee, gleg, skew **5** glent, trend **6** gledge, goggle **7** deviate **10** hagioscope, strabismus

squint-eyed: **5** gleed, gleyd

squire: **4** beau **5** lover, title **6** donzel, escort **7** gallant **8** henchman, servitor **9** accompany, attendant, gentleman, landowner

squirrel: bun **5** hoard, sisel, stash, xerus **6** chippy, gyrate **7** assapan **8** archilla, jelerang **9** assapanic, chickaree, shadetail

burrowing: **6** gopher

flying: **7** assapan

genus of: **7** sciurus

nest: **4** dray, drey

shrew: 4 tana

skin: 4 vair

squirrellike: 8 sciuroid

animal: 8 dormouse

squirt: jet 5 chirt, eject, skite, slirt, spout, spurt 14 whippersnapper

sri: 4 holy 7 Lakshmi 8 glorious, reverend 9 fortunate

Sri Lanka: See Ceylon

stab: dab, jab, jag, try 4 gore, jagg, pink, yerk 5 chive, drive, knife, knive, lunge, prick, sound, stake, stick, stool, stump, wound 6 attack, broach, dagger, pierce, strike, stroke, thrust 7 attempt, poniard, roughen 8 puncture 9 penetrate

in fencing: 4 pink 8 stoccado

stability: 5 poise 7 balance 8 firmance, firmness, strength 9 constancy, fixedness 10 permanence, stableness, steadiness 12 immovability, immutability 13 steadfastness 15 indissolubility

stabilize: fix, set 4 calm 5 poise 6 steady 8 regulate

stabilizer: 7 ballast

stable: 4 barn, fast, firm, mews, shed, sure 5 fixed, set-up, solid, sound, stall 6 hangar, secure, steady, strong, sturdy 7 durable, equerry, lasting 8 constant, enduring, immobile 9 confirmed, establish, permanent, resistant, steadfast, unabashed, unvarying 10 stationary, unwavering 11 established, trustworthy 12 unchangeable

royal: 4 mews

stableman: 5 groom 6 ostler 7 hostler

stack: set 4 bike, flue, heap, peak, pile, rick, stow, tier 5 group, hovel, mound, scroo, shock 7 chimney, conduit 9 fireplace

stacked: 10 curvaceous

stad: 4 town 7 village

staddle: row 4 tree 5 stain, swath 7 sapling, support

stadium: 4 oval 5 arena, stade, stage 7 furlong 8 coliseum

staff: bar, gad, rod 4 cane, club, line, mace, maul, pole, prod, rung, wand 5 aides, baton, crook, equip, lance, pedum, perch, spear, stave, stick, suite 6 baston, cudgel, stanza 7 attache, bailiff, caducei(pl.), scepter, sceptre, support 8 caduceus 9 constable, entourage, personnel 10 assistants, associates 12 quarter-staff

bearer: 5 macer

kinds of: 4 kent, wand 5 filch 6 croche, muleta 7 baculus, bourdon, cambuca, crosier, crozier, distaff, rhabdos 10 alpenstock

officers: 5 aides, cadre

staff of life: 5 bread

stag: 4 colt, deer, hart 5 party 7 pollard,

shorten 8 informer

horn: 4 rial 9 bezantler

stage: era 4 dais, gest, step, tier 5 arena, board, coach, floor, grade, level, phase, shelf, stair, story 6 degree, stadia 7 display, exhibit, produce, rostrum, stadium, theater 8 platform, scaffold 9 condition, dramatize, gradation 10 proscenium, stagecoach 11 subdivision

extra: 4 supe 5 super

hanging: 7 scenery 8 backdrop

on: 7 en scene

part: 4 role

pert. to: 6 scenic

raised: 4 dais 7 estrade

signal: cue

stage direction: 4 exit, sola 5 aside, enter, manet, omnes, solus 6 exeunt, sennet 8 loquitur

stage whisper: 5 aside

stagger: 4 reel, rock, stun, sway 5 lurch, shake, waver 6 hobble, totter, wintle (Sc.) 7 startle, tremble, vibrate 8 flounder, hesitate, titubate, unsettle

stagnant: 4 dull, foul 5 inert, stale, still 7 languid 8 sluggish, standing 10 motionless 13 unprogressive

stagnate: 4 dull 5 inert 8 vegetate 10 motionless

stagnation: 6 stases, stasis, torpor 10 depression

stagy: 8 affected 10 theatrical 12 ostentatious

staid: set 5 fixed, grave, sober 6 demure, sedate, solemn, steady 7 earnest, serious, settled 8 decorous 9 dignified, steadfast 10 coolheaded

stain: dye 4 blot, blur, soil, spot, tint 5 cloud, color, paint, smear, sully, tache, taint, tinge, trace 6 blotch, debase, infamy, macula, smirch, smudge, stigma, vilify 7 blemish, corrupt, tarnish 8 discolor, disgrace, dishonor, maculate, tincture 9 bespatter, pollution 10 attainture 11 contaminate

stainless: 4 pure 6 chaste, honest

stair: 4 step 5 stage, stile 6 degree

face: 5 riser

post: 5 newel

series of: 6 flight

staircase: 5 grece, grice 6 griece, ladder

handrail: 8 banister 9 bannister

moving: 9 escalator

on ship: 12 companionway

outdoor: 6 perron

part of: 4 rung 5 newel, riser, tread

portable: 6 ladder

spiral: 8 caracole

stake: bet, peg, pin, pot, set 4 ante, back, gage, pale, pile, pole, pool, post, risk, spit, stob 5 anvil, prize, spile, stick, teest, wager 6 chance, gamble, hazard, picket **7** venture **8** interest **9** horse race **10** capitalize

driver: **4** maul

pert. to: **5** palar

stale: old **4** flat, hoar, lure, rung, worn **5** banal, blown, corny, decoy, frowy, moldy, musty, shaft, trite, vapid, waugh(Sc.) **7** insipid, tainted **9** hackneyed, tasteless **10** flavorless, prostitute **11** commonplace, overtrained **13** uninteresting

stalemate: **4** draw **7** impasse **8** deadlock, standoff **10** standstill

stalk: bun **4** axis, halm, hunt, mote, prey, risp, seta, stem **5** chase, haulm, spear, stipe, straw **6** pursue, ratoon, stride **7** pedicel, petiole **8** peduncle

having: **9** petiolate

remove: **5** strig

stalker: **6** hunter

stalking-horse: **4** mask **5** blind, decoy **7** pretext **8** pretense

stalkless: **7** sessile

stall: bin, cot, pew **4** crib, loge, mire, seat, stop **5** boose, boosy, booth, check, crame, decoy, delay, stand **6** manger, stable **7** pretext, station **8** hesitate **9** enclosure **10** dilly-dally **11** compartment, confederate **13** procrastinate

stallion: **5** horse **6** cooser(Sc.)

stalwart: **4** firm **5** brave, stout **6** brawny, robust, strong, sturdy **7** valiant **8** partisan, resolute **10** unyielding

stamina: gut **4** grit **5** vigor **7** courage, essence **8** backbone, capacity, strength **9** endurance, fortitude

stammer: **6** falter, hacker, jabber **7** stumble, stutter **8** hesitate

stamp: die **4** beat, coin, form, kind, mark, seal, tool, type **5** brand, class, crush, drive, label, pound, press, print, stomp **6** signet, strike, thresh **7** impress, imprint, postage, sticker, trample **8** inscribe **9** character **10** impression **11** distinguish

collecting: **9** philately

fencing: **5** appel

madness for: **11** timbromania

paper: **6** pelure

space: **8** spandrel

stampede: **4** bolt, rout, rush **5** blitz, panic **6** flight **7** debacle

stamping plate: die

stance: **4** pose **7** posture, station **8** position

stanch, staunch: **4** firm, stem, stop, true **5** allay, check, close, loyal, quell, sound **6** hearty, quench, steady, strong, trusty **7** zealous **8** constant, faithful, resolute, suppress **9** steadfast **10** extinguish, unswerving, unwavering, watertight **11** substantial, trustworthy

stanchion: bar **4** beam, post, prop **5** brace, piton **7** confine, support, upright

stand: set **4** bear, dais, ease, halt, hold, last, rack, stop **5** abide, arise, booth, cease, erect, pause, table **6** afford, endure, hault it, podium, remain, resist, tripod, trivet **7** etagere, station, sustain, support, taboret, undergo **8** attitude, continue, hesitate, maintain, position, tabouret, tolerate **9** withstand **10** resistance

candles: **7** epergne **10** candelabra

cuplike: **4** zarf

for: **4** mean **8** tolerate **9** represent

for election: run

in awe of: **4** fear **5** dread **7** respect

on end: **5** upend

on hind legs: **4** ramp, rear

opposite: **4** face

ornamental: **7** atagere, etagere

out: jut **6** beetle **7** project **8** overhang, protrude

painter's: **5** easel

small: **7** taboret **8** tabouret

still: **4** stop, whoa

three-legged: **6** tripod, trivet

stand-in: **9** surrogate **10** substitute

standard: cup, par, set **4** fiar(Sc.), flag, mark, norm, suit, type, unit **5** canon, gauge, grade, ideal, level, model **6** assize, banner, beacon, ensign, goblet, normal, sample, signal **7** classic, example, labarum(L.), pattern, support, upright **8** accepted, brattach(Sc.), gonfalon, orthodox, vexillum **9** criterion, oriflamme, yardstick **10** touchstone **11** candlestick, rule of thumb

bearer: **11** gonfalonier

of measurement: **6** metric

Turkish: **4** alem, toug

standardize: **9** calibrate, normalize

standing: **4** rank, term **5** being, erect, fixed **6** estate, stable, stance, status **7** lasting, settled, statant, station, upright **8** constant, duration, location, position, stagnant **9** permanent, situation **10** reputation, stationary

upright: **11** orthostatic

standing room only: S.R.O.

standoff: tie **4** draw **10** unsociable

standstill: **4** halt, rest, stop **5** state **8** deadlock **9** cessation, stalemate

stanhope: **5** buggy

stank: **4** pond, pool **5** ditch **9** reservoir

stanze: **5** envoi, stave, verse **7** strophe **8** division **9** apartment

eight line: **6** huitan, octave **7** triolet

five line: **8** cinquain

four line: **8** quatrain

irregular: **13** alloeostropha

six line: **6** sestet

ten line: **6** dizain **7** dizaine

three line: 8 tristich

staple: 4 city, town 5 chief, fiber, shaft 6 fasten 7 chaplet, support 8 fastener 9 commodity, principal 10 foundation

star (see also **constellation**): ace, orb, sun 4 hero, lead 5 actor, badge, chief, shine 6 etoile 7 actress, estoile, heroine, ingenue, stellar 8 asterisk, luminary, pentacle, twinkler 9 bespangle, headliner, principal 10 preeminent, topnotcher

apple: 7 caimito

brightest in constellation: 5 alpha

difference in direction: 8 parallax

divination: 9 astrology

evening: 5 Venus 6 Hesper, Vesper 7 Evestar 8 Hesperus

evil: 8 sidereal

exploding: 4 nova

five-pointed: 8 pentacle

group: 6 galaxy 13 constellation

in Aquila: 8 Altair

in Bootes: 8 Arcturus

in Canis Major: 6 Sirius

in Carina: 7 Canopus

in Centaurus: 5 Agena

in Cetus: 4 Mira

in Cygnus: 5 Deneb 7 Albireo

in Draco: 6 Alsafi 7 Al Rakis, Eltanin

in Gemini: 5 Wasat 6 Alhena, Castor, Pollux

in Leo: 7 Regulus

in Lyra: 4 Vega

in Orion: 5 Rigel, Saiph

in Perseus: 5 Algol

in Scorpius: 7 Antares

in Taurus: 8 Pleiades

in Ursa Major: 5 Alcor, Mizar 6 Alkaid

in Ursa Minor: 7 Polaris

in Virgo: 5 Spica

morning: 4 Mars 5 Venus 6 Saturn 7 Daystar, Jupiter, Mercury 8 Phosphor

north: 7 polaris 8 loadstar, lodestar, polestar

pert. to: 6 astral 7 astrean, stellar 8 sidereal, stellate

representation: 6 etoile

shooting: 5 comet 6 Leonid, meteor

six-pointed: 8 hexagram

suddenly flaring: 4 nova

two: 9 bistellar

variable: 4 Mira

worshiper: 7 sabaist

star cluster: 6 nebula

star-crossed: 7 unlucky 11 unfortunate

star facet: 4 pane

star-like: 8 stellate

Star-Spangled Banner author: 15 Francis Scott Key

Star Wars: 5 force

characters: Han 4 C3PO, Ewok, Jedi, Leia, Luke, R2D2, Solo, Yoda 5 Jabba 7 Han Solo 8 Boba Fett 9 Chewbacca 10 Darth Vader 12 Obi-Wan Kenobi, Princess Leia 13 Luke Skywalker

starch: vim 4 arum, sago 5 tikor, vigor 6 amylum, energy, farina, strong 7 cassava, precise, stiffen 8 activity, glycogen, strength, vitality 9 arrowroot, formality, stiffness 12 carbohydrate

starchy: 5 rigid, stiff 6 formal 7 precise 9 unbending

stare: 4 gape, gaup, gawk, gawp, gaze, gouk, gowk, gype, look, ogle, peer 5 glare, glaze, glore 6 glower, goggle 7 bristle 8 starling 10 rubberneck

starfish: 7 sun star 8 asteroid

limb: ray

stargazer: 4 fish 10 astrologer, astronomer

staring: 6 gazing 7 glaring 8 wide-eyed

stark: 4 bare, firm, hard, nude, pure 5 bleak, harsh, plain, quite, rigid, rough, sheer, stern, stiff, tense, utter 6 barren, severe, strong, wholly 7 violent 8 absolute, complete, desolate, entirely, metallic, obdurate, powerful, stalwart, stripped, vigorous 9 downright, unadorned 10 absolutely, unyielding 11 intractable

starnose: 4 mole

starry: 6 astral, bright 7 shining, stellar 8 luminous, sidereal, starlike, stellate 9 celestial, sparkling

start: fit, run, shy 4 dart, head, jerk, jump, lead, rush 5 alarm, begin, dodge, enter, flush, found, glent, lever, onset, rouse, sally, shock, wince 6 boggle, broach, flinch, fright, loosen, recoil, outset, spring, twitch 7 disturb, get away, impulse, kickoff, provoke, retreat, startle 8 commence, displace, draw back, embark on, handicap, outburst 9 advantage, dislocate, introduce, originate 10 inaugurate

starter: 5 drill, punch 7 entrant 8 official 10 controller

startle: 5 alarm, rouse, scare, shock, start 6 excite 8 affright, frighten, surprise 9 electrify

startling: 7 rousing 8 alarming, restless, skittish 10 surprising 11 astonishing

starvation: 4 lack 6 famine

starve: 4 fast 6 famish, hunger

starveling: 4 lean 6 hungry, pining, wasted

starwort: 5 aster 9 chickweed, colicroot

stash: end 4 hide, stop 5 hoard, store 7 secrete

state: say 4 acme, aver, etat(F.), mode, pomp, rank, seat, tell, term, weal 5 chair, posit, style, utter 6 affirm, allege, assert, avouch, degree, empire, estate, height, nation, polity, recite, relate, report, status, throne 7 account, country, declare, dignity, enounce, express, narrate 8 ceremony, eminence, grandeur, position, property, propound, set forth, standing 9 community, condition, enunciate, pronounce, situation, territory 10 asseverate, possession 11 body politic, stateliness 12 circumstance, commonwealth

based on honor: 9 timocracy

bound by treaty: 4 ally

emotional: 5 fever 7 feeling

explicitly: 6 define 7 itemize, specify 13 particularize

ideal: 6 Utopia

member: 7 citizen

of balance: 9 equipoise

of excitement: 7 ferment

of mind: 4 mood 5 humor 6 fettle, morale

office of: 11 secretariat

pert. to: 7 federal

relating to: 6 statal

subdivision: 6 county

under foreign control: 12 protectorate

State Fair author: 5 Stong

state police: 7 trooper

stated: 4 firm 5 fixed 6 avowed 7 regular 8 declared 10 formulated 11 established

statehouse: 7 capitol

stately: 5 grand, lofty 6 august, formal, superb 7 courtly, gallant, haughty 8 imperial, imposing, majestic 9 dignified 10 deliberate 11 ceremonious, magisterial, magnificent

music: 5 largo

woman: 4 Juno

statement: 4 bill, word 5 audit, dicta 6 dictum, precis, remark, report, resume 7 account, address, article, bromide, epitome, invoice, recital, summary 8 abstract, averment(law), relation, sentence, schedule 9 affidavit, agreement, manifesto, narrative 10 abridgment, allegation, deposition, expression 11 abridgement, affirmation, assertion, certificate, declaration 12 presentation 13 prevaricán 14 circumspection

assumed true: 7 premise

authoritative: 6 dictum

defamatory: 5 libel

false: lie

financial: 6 budget 12 balance-sheet

formal: 9 affidavit 10 deposition

introductory: 5 proem 7 preface, prelude 8 foreword, prologue

mathematical: 7 theorem

of belief: 5 credo, creed

of facts: 4 case

self-contradictory: 7 paradox

self-evident: 6 truism

stateroom: 5 cabin

statesman: 7 statist 8 minister, diplomat 10 politician

static: 7 resting 8 inactive 9 quiescent 10 stationary 11 electricity

station: fix, run, set 4 camp, halt, post, rank, seat, spot, stop 5 berth, depot, field, place, serai, siege 6 assign, church, degree, region, stance, status 7 appoint, calling, cuartel(Sp.), dignity, habitat, posture 8 attitude, location, position 9 condition, homestead, situation 10 constitute 11 equilibrium, institution

stationary: set 4 fast 5 fixed 6 stable, static 8 immobile, inactive, moveless 9 immovable, permanent, sedentary 10 motionless, stock-still, unchanging

stationer: 9 publisher 10 bookseller

stationery: ink, pen 5 blank, paper 6 pencil 10 blank book, papeteries

statist: 9 statesman 10 politician

statistician: 7 analyst, statist

statue: 4 bust, icon, ikon, nude 5 image, orant 6 bronze 7 Madonna 8 Colossus, figurine, likeness, monument 9 sculpture

at Thebes: 6 Memnon

base: 6 plinth

gigantic: 8 colossus

in London Guildhall: Gog 5 Magog

praying: 5 orant

primitive: 6 xoanon

small: 8 figurine

that came to life: 7 Galatea

upper part of: 4 bust 5 torso

weeping: 5 Niobe

Statue of Liberty: *poet:* 7 Lazarus

sculptor: 9 Bartholdi

statuesque: 4 tall 7 shapely, stately 8 graceful

statuette: 8 figurine

stature: 6 height 8 prestige

status: 4 rank 5 state 6 aspect, classe(F.) 8 position, relation, standing 9 condition

status quo: 4 as is 13 existing state

statute: act, law 4 rule 5 edict 6 assize, decree 9 enactment, ordinance 10 regulation

heading of: 5 title

volume of: 4 code 6 codex 7 codices

staunch: See **stanch**

stave: bar 4 rung, slat, stap(Sc.) 5 break, lathi, staff, stick 6 stanza, verse 7 baculus 8 puncture

bundle of: 5 shook

off: 7 ward off 8 postpone 9 drive away

stavesacre: 8 larkspur

stay: dam, guy, lie, rib 4 base, bide, calm, curb, halt, hold, live, prop, rely, rest, rope, stem, stop, tack, wait 5 abide, allay, avast, await, brace, cable, cease, check, defer, delay, demur, dwell, pause, quell, stand, stare, tarry, visit 6 arrest,

staying power: 7 stamina 9 endurance

stead: 4 farm, help, lieu, site, spot 5 avail, beset, place, track 6 assist, behalf 7 benefit, bestead, impress, involve, replace, service, support 8 bedstead, locality, position 9 advantage, farmstead, situation, successor 10 substitute

steadfast, stedfast: 4 fast, firm, sure, true 5 fixed, staid 6 stable, stanch, steady 7 certain, settled, staunch 8 constant, enduring, faithful, resolute 9 immovable 10 inflexible, unchanging, unswerving 11 established, unalterable

steadiness: 5 nerve 7 balance 8 firmness 9 constancy, stability

steading: 4 site 9 farmhouse, homestead

steady: 4 calm, even, firm, sure 5 fixed, grave, sober, staid 6 direct, stable, sturdy 7 assured, equable, regular, uniform 8 constant, diligent, faithful, reliable, resolute 9 boyfriend, incessant, stabilize, steadfast 10 continuous, controlled, girlfriend, invariable, sweetheart, unswerving, unwavering 11 unfaltering, unmitigated 13 unfluctuating, uninterrupted

steak: 4 club 5 chuck, flank, round, shell, t-bone 7 griskin, New York, sirloin 9 entrecote, hamburger 10 tenderloin 11 porterhouse 13 chateaubriand

steal: 4 bag, cly, cop, gyp, nim, rap, rob 4 crib, gain, glom, hook, lift, stem, take 5 bribe, creep, fetch, filch, harry, pinch, poach, shaft, sneak, stalk, swipe, theft 6 abduct, burgle, convey, divert, extend, handle, kidnap, pilfer, pirate, rustle, snitch 7 bargain, purloin 8 embezzle, peculate 9 condiddle 10 plagiarize 11 appropriate 14 misappropriate

stealer: 5 thief 6 robber 7 burglar 10 plagiarist 11 biblioklept

cattle: 7 abactor, rustler

stealthy: sly 6 artful, secret 7 catlike, cunning, furtive 11 clandestine 13 surreptitious

walk: 5 stalk

steam: 4 boil, fume, heat, reek 5 force, power, smoke, vapor, water 6 energy 8 vaporize, vexation 10 exhalation, irritation

bath: 5 sauna

jet: 5 stufa 8 soffione

pipe: 5 riser

steamer: 4 boat, clam, ship 5 liner 6 vessel 9 steamship

cabin: 5 texas

steamroller: 4 whip 5 crush 8 override

steamship: 5 liner 7 steamer

route: 4 lane

smokestack: 6 funnel

steatite: 4 talc 9 soapstone

steed: 4 Arab 5 horse 7 charger, courser

steel: 4 gird, rail 5 acier(F.), inure, press 6 damask, harden, smooth, toledo 8 Bessemer, Damascus 9 encourage 10 strengthen

process: 8 Bessemer 11 cementation

steelhead: 5 trout

steely: 10 unyielding

steelyard: 7 balance

steep: ret 4 bate, bath, bold, bowk, brew, buck, high, soak, stew, tall 5 bathe, brant, brent, heavy, hilly, imbue, lofty, proud, sharp, sheer 6 abrupt, bright, clifty, decoct, drench, imbibe, imbrue, infuse, seethe 7 arduous, extract, extreme, immerse 8 elevated, headlong, macerate, saturate, solution 9 difficult, distemper, excessive, expensive, precipice 10 exorbitant, impregnate 11 precipitous 12 perpendicular

steeper: vat 6 teapot, vessel 7 cistern

steeple: 5 spire, tower 6 cupola 8 pinnacle 9 campanile

steer: con, tip 4 bull, conn, helm, lead, stot 5 guide, pilot 6 bovine, direct, govern, manage 7 bullock, control, operate, oversee

close to wind: 4 luff

steerage: 8 guidance 9 direction 10 management, regulation

steering: aim 9 direction 10 government, management

apparatus: 4 helm 6 wheel 6 rudder, tiller

part: 10 rudderhead

superintend: con 4 conn

steeve: 4 pack, stow 5 store, stuff

stein: mug 4 toby

steinbock: 8 antelope

stela, stele: 4 slab 6 pillar 8 monument 10 gravestone

stelar: 10 columnlike

stellar: 5 chief 6 astral, major, starry 7 leading 8 starlike, stellate 9 principal 10 preeminent 11 outstanding

Steller's sea cow: 6 rytina

stem: bow, bum, dam, leg, ram 4 axis, base, body, bole, cane, culm, halt, load, prow, race, reed, risp, root, stop, tamp 5 check, haulm, orise, shaft, stalk, stipe, stock, trunk 6 branch, derive, oppose, spring, stanch 7 lineage, pedicel, petiole, spindle 8 ancestry, contract, peduncle, restrain 9 originate, petiolule 10 derive from

bulblike: 4 corm 5 tuber 7 rhizome
climbing: 4 bine 7 tendril
fungus: 5 stipe
joint: 4 node
part: 4 pith 5 stele
pert. to: 7 cauline 8 stipular
sheath: 5 ocrea
stemma: 7 descent, lineage 8 ancestry, pedigree 9 genealogy
stemmer: bar
stench: 4 fogo, odor, reek 5 fetor, smell, stink 6 foetor
Stendhal hero: 5 Sorel
stenographer: 9 recorder
stenography: 9 shorthand 12 brachygraphy
stent: 5 tight 6 extend, extent 7 stretch 12 outstretched
stentor: 6 roarer
stentorian: 4 loud 10 resounding
step: act, sty, way 4 gait, pace, rank, rest, rung, walk 5 break, crush, dance, grade, ledge, level, plane, round, shelf, space, stage, stair, stalk, strut, stufe(G.), tread 6 action, degree, manner, squash, stride 7 advance, deprive, measure 8 distance, footfall, foothold, footrest, footstep, movement 9 footprint, gradation, procedure, promotion 10 proceeding, stepladder 11 translation
dance: pas 5 coule 6 chasse 8 glissade
introductory: 8 rudiment 10 initiative
ladder's: 4 rime, rung
measuring device: 10 passimeter
over fence: 5 stile
part: 5 riser, tread 6 nosing
recording device: 8 odograph
rope ladder: 7 ratline
series of raised: 6 gradin 7 gradine
step up: rev 8 increase 10 accelerate
step-by-step: 7 in order, gradual 9 piecemeal
step-in: 4 shoe 7 slipper
step-ins: 10 underpants
stepbrother: 9 beau-frere(F.) 11 beaux-freres
stepdame: 10 stepmother
steppe: 5 plain, space 7 prairie 9 grassland, wasteland
storm: 5 buran
stepper: 5 horse 6 dancer
steps: See step, staircase
stepson: 8 beau-fils(F.) 9 beaux-fils
stere: 9 kiloliter
stereotyped: 5 trite 7 routine 9 hackneyed
sterile: dry 4 arid, dead, geld 6 barren, meager, meagre, otiose 7 aseptic, useless 8 impotent, sanitary 9 fruitless, infertile 10 unfruitful, unoriginal 11 ineffective 12 unproductive
sterility: 7 asepsis 10 barrenness

sterilize: fix 4 geld, spay 5 unsex 6 change, neuter 9 disinfect
sterling: 5 penny 7 genuine 9 excellent
stern: 4 back, dour, firm, grim, hard, helm, rear 5 harsh, rough, steer, stout 6 fierce, gloomy, mighty, rudder, savage, severe, strict, strong, sturdy, sullen, tiller, unkind 7 austere, massive, tail end 8 buttocks, exacting, resolute, rigorous 9 unbending, unfeeling 10 astringent, forbidding, inexorable, inflexible, relentless, uninviting, unyielding 11 hardhearted 14 uncompromising
toward: aft 5 abaft 6 astern
Sterne character: 4 Slop, Toby, Trim 6 Shandy, Yorick 8 Tristram
sternforemost: 7 awkward 8 backward
sternness: 5 rigor 7 cruelty 8 hardness, severity 9 austerity, harshness, rigidness, stiffness 10 strictness 12 exactingness 13 inflexibility
sternum: 8 skeleton 10 breastbone
sternutation: 6 sneeze 8 sneezing
sterol: 7 alcohol
stertor: 5 snore
stertorous: 5 snore
stevedore: 6 loader, stower 8 cargador 12 longshoreman
Stevenson: *character:* 4 Hyde 6 Jekyll 10 Jim Hawkins 14 Long John Silver
home: 5 Samoa
novel: 5 Kidnapped 14 Treasure Island
stew: 4 boil, cook, dive, fret, mess, olio, slum, snit 5 anger, cloud, imbue, steep, study, sweat, worry 6 burgoo, dither, ragout, seethe, simmer 7 brothel, goulash, haricot, swelter 8 hothouse 9 Brunswick, commotion, confusion 10 capilotade, excitement, hodgepodge, hotchpotch, miscellany 11 predicament
steward: 5 dewan, diwan, graff, grave 6 factor, grieve, waiter 7 bailiff, curator, foreman, granger, manager, officer, proctor 8 bhandari, employee, guardian 9 custodian, dispense, seneschal 10 magistrate 11 chamberlain
monastery: 8 cellarer
ship: 6 flunky 7 flunkey
stewed: 5 drunk 10 inebriated 11 intoxicated
sthenic: 6 active, strong
stib: 6 dunlin 9 sandpiper
stich: 4 line 5 verse
stick: bar, bat, bow, cue, gad, gum, put, rod, set 4 bind, cane, clag, clam, club, fife, glue, kill, mast, poke, pole, push, spit, stab, stem, stop, twig, wand 5 affix, baton, cheat, cleam, cling, decoy, delay, demur, flute, mount, paste, place, prick, shoot, shove, staff, stalk, stall, stave, trunk 6 adhere, attach, baffle, ballow, billet, branch, cement, cleave, cohere, cudgel, endure, ferule, fescue,

fleece, impale, mallet, pierce, puzzle, rammer, strike, thrust **7** defraud, drummer, nonplus **8** bludgeon, clarinet, hesitate, puncture, revolver, tolerate **9** crabstick, drumstick **10** overcharge

bamboo: **5** lathi **6** lathee

bundle of: **5** fagot **6** fasces **7** fascine

conductor's: **5** baton

crooked: **5** caman **7** cammock, gambrel

jumping: **4** pogo

measuring: **5** ruler **7** ellwand **8** yardwand **9** yardstick

mountain climbing: **10** alpenstock

stick out: 7 extrude **8** protrude

stick up: 7 rob **10** hold up **7** plunder, ransack

sticker: bur **4** burr, seal **5** knife, label, poser, stamp, thorn **6** paster, puzzle, weapon **7** bramble

sticking: 6 viscid **8** adhering, cohesive **12** stonewalling

stick-in-the-mud: 4 fogy **6** square **10** fuddy-duddy

stickleback: 4 fish **6** bandie(Sc.)

stickler: 6 purist, second, umpire **7** arbiter, meddler **8** mediator

sticky: 4 clit, hard **5** gluey, gooey, humid, messy **6** claggy, clammy, clarty, slushy, viscid, wooden **7** viscous **8** adhesive **9** difficult, glutinous **10** saccharine **11** sentimental **13** uncomfortable

stiff: bum **4** dead, deep, firm, hard, high, hobo, taut **5** brave, budge, clung, dense, drunk, fixed, grave, harsh, horse, miser, rigid, steep, tense, thick, tramp, woody **6** clumsy, corpse, formal, loafer, proper, robust, severe, stanch, strong, sturdy **7** awkward, buckram, cadaver, precise, starchy **8** absorbed, drunkard, exacting, resolute, rigorous, stalwart, starched, stubborn **9** difficult, excessive, laborious, obstinate, unbending **10** ceremonial, consistent, inflexible, unyielding **11** intoxicated **12** pertinacious **14** uncompromising

stiff-necked: 5 proud **8** stubborn **9** obstinate **12** contumacious

stiffen: set **5** brace **6** benumb, harden, starch **10** inspissate

stiffness: 5 rigor **8** rigidity **10** constraint **11** starchiness

stifle: gag **4** stop **5** check, choke **6** muffle, quench **7** repress, silence, smother **8** strangle, stultify, suppress, throttle **9** suffocate **10** extinguish

stigma: 4 blot, mark, scar, spot **5** brand, cloud, odium, stain, taint **6** defect **7** blemish **9** disgrace, dishonor

stigmatize: 5 brand **7** censure **8** denounce

stile: 4 post, step **8** entrance **9** turnstile

stiletto: 4 kill, stab **6** bodkin, dagger, stylet **9** eyeleteer

still: but, een, low, mum, tho, yet **4** also, calm, cosh, drip, even, ever, hush, lull, stop **5** allay, check, inert, quiet **6** always, distil, gentle, hushed, pacify, serene, soothe **7** appease, however, silence, subdued **8** habitual, inactive, restrain, suppress, tranquil **9** noiseless, uniformly **10** constantly, distillery, motionless, photograph, stationary, uneventful **11** continually **12** nevertheless

stillicide: 4 drip, drop **9** eavesdrop

stilt: 4 bird, limp, pile, pole, post **5** shaft **6** crutch **8** longlegs

stilted: 6 formal, wooden **7** awkward, pompous **8** affected **9** bombastic, dignified **10** rhetorical **11** sententious

Stilton: 6 cheese

feature: **4** mold

Stilwell's nickname: 10 Vinegar Joe

stimulant: kat **4** drug **5** drink, tonic **6** bracer **8** beverage **9** incentive, sassafras

heart: **8** cardiant, thialdin **9** digitalis, thialdine **10** adrenaline, epinephrin **11** epinephrine

in coffee: **7** caffein **8** caffeine

in tea: **5** thein

stimulate: fan, jog, pep **4** goad, move, spur, stir, urge, whet **5** brace, elate, filip, impel, rouse, sting **6** affect, arouse, excite, fillip, incite **7** animate, enliven, inspire, provoke, quicken **8** irritate, motivate **9** encourage, galvanize, instigate **10** exhilarate, invigorate

stimulating: 5 brisk **7** pungent **8** exciting **9** innerving **12** invigorating

stimulus: 4 goad, spur **5** cause, filip, sting **6** fillip, motive **7** impetus **9** incentive

threshold: **5** limen

sting: gyp **4** bite, dupe, goad, mast, pain, pike, pole, post, tang, urge **5** cheat, prick, shaft, smart, wound **6** impale, incite, nettle, pierce, tingle **7** stimuli **8** irritate, stimulus **9** stimulate **10** incitement **11** double cross

stinger: 4 blow **5** drink

stinginess: 9 closeness, frugality, parsimony **13** niggardliness

stinging: 6 biting, bitter **7** caustic, piquant, pungent **8** piercing **10** irritating **11** acrimonious

stingo: ale, vim, zip **4** beer, zest **6** energy

stingy: 4 dree(Sc.), hard, mean **5** cheap, light, sharp, stint, tight **6** biting, greedy, meager, scanty **7** miserly, niggard, nipping, selfish **8** covetous **9** illiberal, penurious **10** avaricious **11** closefisted **12** parsimonious **13** pennypinching

stinking: bad **4** foul, rank **5** drunk, fetid **6** putrid, rancid **7** noisome **8** unsavory **9** offensive **10** malodorous

stint, stent: 4 duty, stay, stop, task **5**

bound, cease, check, chore, limit, scant, serve, spare, speil, stunt 6 assign, desist, divide, scrimp 7 confine 8 quantity, restrain, restrict 9 economize, restraint 10 assignment, limitation, proportion 11 restriction

stipe: 4 stem 5 stalk 6 caudex 7 petiole

stipend: ann, fee, pay 4 hire, wage 5 annal 6 income, salary 7 payment, prebend 9 allowance, emolument 12 compensation, remuneration

stipendiary: 4 beak 7 soldier, teacher 9 clergyman, mercenary 10 magistrate 11 beneficiary

stipple: dot 5 fleck 6 render 7 engrave, speckle

stipulate: 5 agree 7 bargain, provide, specify 8 contract, covenant

stipulation: 4 bond, item 6 clause, demand, detail 7 article, bargain, compact, proviso 8 contract, covenant 9 agreement, condition, situation 11 arrangement, undertaking

stir: ado, fan, gog, jog, mix, sir 4 busk, fuss, jail, move, plow, poke, roil, to-do 5 awake, budge, churn, doing, hurry, rally, rouse, shake, shift, shove, stoke, waken 6 arouse, awaken, bestir, bustle, excite, flurry, foment, hubbub, incite, motion, muddle, pother, prison, quetch, seethe, tumult 7 agitate, animate, blunder, disturb, flutter, inflame, provoke, trouble 8 activity, brandish, displace, movement 9 commotion, stimulate 10 manipulate 12 penitentiary

stirabout: 8 porridge

stirk: cow 4 bull 6 heifer 7 bullock

stirless: 10 motionless

stirps: 4 race 5 stock 6 branch, family

stirring: 5 afoot, astir 6 moving, tumult, uproar 7 rousing 8 activity, eloquent, exciting, movement 9 agitation, animating, inspiring, thrilling 10 incitement 11 stimulating

stirrup: bar 4 ring, rope 5 clamp, strap 6 stapes 7 support 8 footrest

hood: 8 tapadera(Sp.)

straps: 8 chapelet

stitch: bit, hem, sew 4 loop, pain, purl 5 baste, picot, ridge, unite 6 feston, suture, tailor 8 distance 9 embroider

knitting: 4 purl 6 feston

zigzag: 8 bargello

stitchbird: ihi

stitcher: 5 sewer 6 seamer 10 dressmaker

stitchwort: 9 chickweed

stithy: 5 anvil, forge 6 smithy 8 smithery

stive: 5 pen up 6 stifle 9 suffocate

stiver: 4 coin 5 money 7 bristle, stagger 8 struggle

stivy: 5 close 8 stifling

stoa: 7 portico 9 colonnade

stoat: 6 ermine, weasel 8 clubster 9 club-start

stob: 4 post, stab 5 stake 6 pierce

stock: cop, log 4 band, bond, butt, fund, hive, line, post, race, rail, soup, stem 5 banal, block, blood, brace, breed, broth, flesh, frame, hoard, stake, stick, store, stump, swell, trite, trunk, trust 6 budget, common, cravat, family, handle, holder, pillar, strain, supply 7 capital, descent, extract, lineage, provide, reserve, rhizome, support 8 ancestry, bitstock, colewort, material, ordinary 9 hackneyed, livestock, provision, replenish 10 estimation, foundation 11 commonplace, certificate 12 accumulation

framed on: 5 ramed

of food: 5 foray

of goods: 4 line

preliminary: 5 scrip

racial: 8 pedigree

stockade: pen 4 jail 5 etape, pound 6 corral, kennel, prison 7 barrier, fortify, protect 8 hoosegow, poundage 9 enclosure

Africa: 4 boma 5 kraal 6 keddah, zareba 7 zareeba

stock exchange: 6 bourse(F.)

business: 9 arbitrage

patron: 5 buyer 6 seller, trader

stockfish: cod 4 hake, ling 5 torsk 7 haddock

stock-in-trade: 4 tool, ware 5 goods 7 capital 8 material 9 equipment 11 merchandise

stocked: 7 replete

stockholder: 8 investor, stockman

stocking: bas(F.) 4 hose 7 hosiery

bishop's: 6 buskin, caliga

cotton: 5 lisle

footless: 7 hushion

ornament: 5 clock

run: 6 ladder

soleless: 7 traheen

worsted: 7 scogger

stockjobbing: 8 agiotage

stockman: 6 herder 7 rancher 8 beastman

stockpile: 5 amass, hoard, lay up 7 backlog, reserve 9 inventory, reservoir

stocky: fat 4 stub 5 cobby 6 chumpy, stubby, sturdy 7 bunting, defiant 8 thickset 9 corpulent 10 boisterous, headstrong

stodge: 4 plod 6 trudge 7 satiate, satisfy

stodgy: 4 dull 5 bulky, heavy, tacky, thick 6 packed, sticky 7 crammed, lumpish, stuffed, tedious 8 thickset 9 out-of-date, satiating 10 uninspired 13 uninteresting

stogy: 4 boot, shoe 5 cigar 6 brogan, clumsy, coarse

stoic: 5 porch 6 stolid 7 ascetic, passive, patient 9 impassive 10 phlegmatic 11 unconcerned

stoicism: 6 apathy 8 patience 11 impassivity 13 impassiveness

founder of: 4 Zeno

stoke: 4 feed, fire, fuel, poke, tend 5 stick 6 supply

stoker: 5 firer 7 fireman, greaser

glassworks: 6 teaser

stole: fur 5 scarf 7 garment, orarion 8 vestment 13 epitrachelion

stolen property: 4 loot, pelf

buyer of: 5 fence

stolid: 4 dull, firm, slow 5 beefy 6 stupid 7 brutish, clumpse, clumpst, passive 9 impassive, inanimate, unfeeling 10 impassable 12 unexciteable

stolon: 5 shoot 6 branch, runner 7 rhizome

stoma: 4 pore 5 mouth 7 opening, orifice

stomach: gut, maw 6 bear, craw, crop, kyte, vell 5 belly, bingy, brook, pride, rumen 6 bingey, desire, endure, gebbie(Sc.), resent, spirit 7 abdomen, gizzard, gizzern 8 appetite, tolerate 9 arrogance 11 inclination

acidity: 4 acor

bird's maw 4 craw, crop

enzyme: 6 pepsin, rennin

lower opening of: 7 pylorus

muscle: 7 pylorus

pert. to: 7 gastric

ruminant's first: 5 rumen

ruminant's fourth: 4 read, reed 8 abomasum, roddikin(Sc.)

ruminant's second: 6 bonnet 9 reticulum

ruminant's third: 6 omasum 9 manyplies 10 psalterium

used as food: 5 tripe

stomach-ache: 5 colic 7 gullion 12 collywobbles

stomacher: 4 gimp 7 echelle 8 forepart

stomachy: 5 proud 8 paunched, spirited 9 irascible, irritable, obstinate, resentful 10 potbellied

stomp: See **stamp**

stone (see also **rock**): gem, pit, rub 4 bone, buhr, pelt, rock 5 block, brick, lapis(L.), scour, scrub 6 chaton, cobble, domino, marble 7 diamond, dornick, scruple, sharpen 8 lapidate, memorial, monolith, testicle 9 hailstone, hemachate, milestone, millstone, whetstone 10 gravestone, grindstone

abrasive: 5 emery

and clay: 4 sere

artificial: 8 albolite, albolith 9 granolith

base: 6 plinth

Biblical: 4 ezel

broken: 6 rubble

carved: 5 cameo

chip of: 5 spall 6 gallet

convert into: 7 petrify

druid: 6 sarsen

drupe: 6 nutlet

eagle: 5 etite

engraving: 8 intaglio

famous: 4 Hope, Pitt 5 Green, Mogul, Sancy, Scone 6 Jonker, Nassak, Orloff, Regent, Vargas 7 Blarney, Dresden, Jubilee, Kohinur, Rosetta, Stewart, Tiffany 8 Braganza, Cullinan, Kohinoor 9 Excelsior, Polar Star 10 Florentine, Great Mogul 12 Plymouth Rock, Star of Africa 14 Star of the South

fruit: pit 4 paip 5 drupe 6 pyrene 7 putamen

gem cutting: 6 adamas

granitic: 6 gneiss

grave: 5 stela, stele 6 marker, stelae, steles 8 memorial, monument

grinding: 6 metate

hammering: 8 lapstone

hand grinding: 4 mano

hard: 5 flint 6 quartz 7 adamant 9 chatoyant

heap: 4 karn 5 cairn

hoist: 5 lewis

hollow: 5 druse, geode

hurling device: 9 trebucket

implement: 4 celt 5 arrow 7 neolith

kidney: 8 calculus

loose: 6 gibber

maize grinding: 4 mano

meteoric: 8 aerolite, aerolith

monumental: 4 lech 6 menhir 8 megalith

of arch: 8 keystone

paving: 4 flag, slab, slat

pert. to: 7 lithoid

philosopher's: 6 carmot, elixir

precious: gem 4 keas, onyx, opal, ruby 5 beryl, pearl, topaz 6 garnet, jasper, lazuli, ligure 7 diamond, peridot 8 astroite, sapphire, tigereye 9 aromatite

pyramid-shape: 6 benben

shaped into pillars: 7 obelisk 9 monoliths

sharpening: oil 4 hone, whet

seam: dry

semiprecious: 4 jade, onyx, sard 5 agate, lapis 6 garnet, lazule, lazuli 7 olivine 8 murrhine 11 lapis lazuli

small: 6 pebble

squared: 6 ashlar

to death: 8 lapidate

uncut: 4 naif

upright: 5 bauta 6 menhir

used for cameos: 4 onyx

woman turned into: 5 Niobe

worker: 5 mason 6 slater

writing: 5 slate

Stone Age tool: 4 celt 6 eolith 7 neolith 10 palaeolith

stonecrop: 5 orpin, sedum 6 orpine

stonecutter: 6 jadder
chisel: 5 drove
disease: 9 silicosis
wooden receptacle of: 7 sebilla
stoned: 5 doped, drunk 6 zonked 7 drugged 8 turned on 9 spaced-out 11 intoxicated
stonelike: 7 lithoid
stoneman: 5 cairn
stonewall: 5 evade 8 obstruct, stubborn 9 obstinate 10 determined, filibuster
stoneware: 4 gres 7 ceramic, pottery 11 earthenware
stonework: 7 masonry
stoneworker: 5 mason
stony: 4 cold, card, poor 5 fixed, rigid, rocky, rough, still 7 adamant 8 obdurate, pitiless 9 petrified, unfeeling 10 inexorable, inflexible, petrifying, relentless, stupefying, unyielding 14 expressionless 15 uncompassionate
stood: 5 arose 7 endured
stooge: 4 foil, tool
stookie: 4 fool
stool: 4 base, mora, pole, seat, thew 5 bench, decoy, morae, stand, stump 6 buffet, growth, tiller, tripod 7 commode, creepie, taboret, trestle 8 kingship, platform, standard, tabouret 9 footstool 10 foundation 11 chieftaincy
stoolpigeon: spy 4 fink, sing 5 decoy, narks, shill 6 inform, snitch, squeal 7 peacher 8 betrayer, informer, observer
stoop: bow, lay 4 bend, bode, duck, lean, post, sink, tilt 5 deign, lower, porch, slant, souse, stake, stump, swoop, yield 6 alight, boggle, coorie, crouch, debase, gamble, huckle, humble, patron, pillar, pounce, submit 7 decline, degrade, descend, subject, succumb, veranda 8 overcome, platform, stairway 9 prostrate, supporter 10 condescend 11 humiliation 13 condescension
stop: bar, dam, end, inn, pug 4 bait, bode, bung, call, calk, clog, drop, fill, halt, mend, pawl, plug, quit, stay, stem, stum, wear, weir, whoa 5 avast, basta, block, break, catch, caulk, cease, check, choke, close, delay, embar, estop, holla, hollo, parry, pause, point, repel, stall, tarry 6 alight, anchor, arrest, behold, boggle, defeat, desist, detain, draw up, finish, gravel, hinder, period, reside, scotch, stanch, stench 7 caesura, counter, prevent, sojourn, station, staunch, stopper, suspend 8 caesurae(pl.), obstacle, obstruct, obturate, pinblock, preclude, prohibit, restrain, stoppage, suppress, withhold 9 barricade, cessation, hindrance, intercept, interrupt, punctuate 11 countermand, discontinue, obstruction 12 intermis-

sion, interruption, lodginghouse
blood: 6 stanch
legally: 5 estop
organ: 5 orage, viola 7 posaune 8 dulciana, gemshorn 9 rohrflote
short: 5 delay, pause 7 respite 8 interval 9 cessation 12 intermission
temporary: 5 pause
up: 4 cork, plug 7 occlude
stop watch: 5 timer
stopcock: 5 valve 6 faucet
stope: 8 excavate 10 excavation
stopgap: 4 plug 5 shift 6 resort 9 expedient, makeshift 10 substitute
stoppage: end 4 halt 5 block, choke, hitch 6 arrest, devall, strike 7 embargo, seizure 9 cessation, detention 10 arrestment, congestion 11 obstruction
body fluid: 6 stasis
debate: 7 cloture
temporary: 5 delay, pause 6 arrest, recess 10 arrestment 12 interception, intermission, interruption
stopper: wad 4 bung, cork, fill, plug 7 bouchon
stopping: 4 halt 5 block, check 7 seizure 9 detention 11 obstruction, punctuation
device: 5 brake
stopple: 4 bung, cork, plug 7 stopper
storage: 4 dump 11 safekeeping
battery plate: 4 grid
bin: mow 4 loft 7 granary 8 elevator
charge: 9 demurrage
place: bin 4 shed, silo 5 attic, depot 6 cellar, closet 7 arsenal, granary 8 cupboard, elevator 9 blood bank, reservoir, warehouse
prepare for: can
room: 6 closet, larder 7 lastage, lazaret 9 lazarette, lazaretto
storax: 5 resin 6 balsam
store: bin 4 cave, deck, deep, dose, fond, fund, hold, mass, save, shop, stow 5 amass, breed, cache, depot, hoard, stock 6 amount, budget, garner, market, repair, shoppe, supply 7 bhandar, collect, deposit, furnish, husband, provide, put away, reserve, restore 8 emporium, reserves, supplies, treasure 9 abundance, chandlery, livestock, replenish, reservoir, resources, sweetshop, warehouse 10 accumulate, collection, provisions, storehouse 12 accumulation
candle: 9 chandlery
fodder: 6 ensile 8 ensilate
food: 6 market 9 sweetshop 12 delicatessen
fruit: 12 greengrocery
hidden: 5 cache
Hindu: 7 bhandar
in ground: 5 cache

in silo: 6 ensile

military: 7 canteen 10 commissary

milk: 5 dairy

shoe: 7 bootery

slang: 5 stash

up: 4 hive 6 garner 8 squirrel

storehouse: 4 barn, bike, crib, shed, silo 5 cache, depot, etape 7 arsenal, bhandar, camalig, camarin, granary 8 building, magazine, treasury 9 repertory, warehouse 10 commissary 11 chalkotheke

military: 5 depot 7 arsenal 10 commissary

public: 5 depot, etape

rural: mow 4 barn, crib, shed, silo 7 granary

wool: 6 lanary

storekeeper: 6 grocer 8 bhandari, merchant, storeman 10 shopkeeper 11 almacenista, stockkeeper

storeroom: 4 cave, gola, loft 5 attic 6 bodega, cellar, pantry 7 buttery, genizah, granary 8 basement 10 repository

stork: 4 ibis 6 simbil 7 marabou 12 xenorhynchus

kin of: 4 ibis 5 heron 10 hammerhead

storken: 6 thrive 7 congeal, stiffen

storklike: 8 pelargic

storm: wap 4 birr, blow, bura, fume, gale, gust, hail, rage, raid, rain, rand, rant, rave, snow, wind 5 anger, blizz, brash, buran, orage 6 attack, expugn, shamal, shower, simoom, simoon, tumult, Wester 7 assault, barrage, bluster, borasca, borasco, bravado, cyclone, rampage, tempest, tornado, trouble 8 calamity, eruption, outburst, upheaval, violence 9 agitation, bourasque, commotion, hurricane 10 hurly-burly 11 disturbance

dust: 6 simoom

god: 5 Rudra

revolving: 7 cyclone

sand: 6 tebbad

snow: 5 buran

stormcock: 6 petrel, thrush 9 fieldfare 10 woodpecker

stormy: 4 dark, foul, wild 5 dirty, gusty 6 raging 7 furious, riotous, violent 8 agitated, cluttery 9 inclement, turbulent 10 blustering, passionate, tumultuous 11 tempestuous

story: fib, lie 4 myth, news, plot, saga, tale, tier, yarn 5 etage, fable, floor, rumor, solar, soler 6 fabula, gossip, legend, record, report, solar 7 account, article, episode, history, narrate, parable, recital 8 anecdote, intrigue 9 falsehood, happening, narration, narrative, statement, tradition 11 description

complication in: 4 node 5 nodus

continued: 6 serial, sequel

correspondent's: 8 dispatch

exclusive: 4 beat 5 scoop

heroic: 4 gest, saga 5 geste

involved: 8 megillah

kind of: 4 epic, saga, tale, yarn 5 conte, fable 6 canard, legend, script 7 mystery, novella, parable, romance 8 allegory, scenario, whodunit

short: 5 conte 8 anecdote

traditional: 4 myth 6 legend

upper: 5 attic 6 garret

storyteller: 4 liar 5 Aesop 6 disour, fibber 8 narrator 9 raconteur

stot: 4 bull 5 bound, lurch, steer 6 bounce 7 rebound, stagger, stammer, stumble, stutter

stound: 4 ache, beat, blow, pain, pang, stun, time 5 grief, shock, sight, smart, swoon, throb 6 attack, benumb, bruise, moment, period, season, sorrow, thrill, twinge 7 assault, instant, stupefy 8 astonish, occasion 12 apparition 12 astonishment, stupefaction

stoup: cup 4 cask, font, pail 5 basin 6 bucket, flagon, vessel 7 measure, tankard 10 aspersoria 11 aspersorium

holy water: 8 benitier, canthari(pl.) 9 cantharus, kantharos, kantharoi(pl.)

stoush: 4 beat, blow 6 attack, strike, tirade 7 assault

stout: ale, fat 4 beer, bold, firm, gnat, hard 5 brave, bulky, burly, cobby, frack, freck, hardy, heavy, obese, plump, proud, shock, solid, tough 6 active, flagon, fleshy, liquor, porter, portly, robust, rotund, stable, stanch, stocky, stouty, strong, sturdy 7 defiant, haughty, violent, weighty 8 arrogant, bouncing, enduring, forceful, forcible, horsefly, insolent, powerful, resolute, stalwart, stubborn, thickset, vigorous 9 corpulent, energetic, obstinate 10 courageous, overweight 11 substantial

and rough: 5 burly

and short: 6 stocky 8 thickset

stout-hearted: 4 bold, good 5 brave 7 doughty 8 unafraid 9 dauntless 10 courageous

stove: 4 dent, etna, kiln 5 grate, plate, range, stave 6 cockle, heater 7 furnace 8 potbelly 10 calefactor, glasshouse 12 conservatory

alcohol: 4 etna

charcoal: hod

grated: 8 chauffer

part: 4 oven 7 firebox, griddle

stovepipe: hat 4 flue 7 silk hat

stow: box, cut 4 cram, crop, hide, hold, mass, pack, stop, trim 5 cease, crowd, douse, dowse, lodge, place, shoot, slice, stack, store, stump 7 arrange, contain, secrete *cargo:* 5 steve 6 steeve

stowage: 6 charge 7 packing

Stowe novel: 14 Uncle Tom's cabin

character: 5 Topsy 8 Little Eva, Uncle Tom 11 Simon Legree

stower: 9 stevedore

strabismus: 6 squint 8 cock-eye, cross-eye

Strad, Stradivarius: 6 violin

straddle: 5 hedge 6 option, sprawl 7 astride, bracket 8 bestride 11 noncommital, spread-eagle

strafe: 5 shell 6 punish 7 bombard 8 fire upon 9 castigate

straggle: 4 rove 5 stray 6 ramble, sprawl, wander 7 meander

straight: 4 neat 5 brant, erect, euthy, frank, ortho, plain, recti, rigid, stern 6 aright, candid, direct, graith, honest, severe 7 rightly, sincere, stretch, through, unmixed, upright 8 accurate, directly, honestly, reliable, rigorous, sequence, unbroken, virtuous 9 correctly, honorably, undiluted 10 continuous, conventional, methodical, unmodified 11 immediately, straightway, undeviating, unqualified 12 continuously, heterosexual, unswervingly 13 unaccompanied, uninterrupted

straight course: 7 beeline

straight edge: 5 ruler

straight-faced: 7 deadpan 9 impassive

straight-haired: 12 leiotrichous 13 lissotrichous

straight man: 4 foil 6 stooge

partner: 8 comedian

straight-out: 5 utter 6 direct 8 outright 11 unqualified 12 unrestrained 13 thorough-going

straight up and down: 15 perpendicularly

straighten: 5 align, aline, level, order, plumb 7 compose, rectify, unravel 11 disentangle

up: 4 tidy

straightforward: 4 even, open 5 apert, frank, aright, candid, dexter, direct, honest, simple 7 sincere 8 directly, outright, straight 9 foreright, outspoken 10 forthright, unaffected 11 undeviating

straightway: 4 anon 6 aright, bedene 8 directly 9 downright, forthwith 10 forthright 11 immediately

strain: air, hug, sie, sye, tax, try 4 balk, barb, bend, bind, curb, dash, gain, heft, kind, line, mood, note, ooze, race, sift, solo, sort, tone, tune, turn, urge, vein 5 breed, clasp, class, demur, exert, force, music, press, raise, shade, sieve, stock, style, tenor, touch, trace, track, trail, wield 6 burden, colate, effort, extend, extort, family, fasten, filter, injure, manner, melody, obtain, sprain, strand, streak, stress, strive, temper, thread, weaken, wrench 7 anxiety, confine, descent, element, embrace, lineage, overtax, progeny, quality, squeeze, stretch, strophe, tension, trickle, variety 8 ancestry, brandish, compress, eliquate, exertion, restrain, tendency 9 begetting, character, constrain, constrict, percolate 10 distortion, generation 11 deformation, disposition

blood: 4 race 5 breed, stock 6 family 7 lineage

chief: 5 brunt

great: tax, tug 5 tense 6 stress 7 tension 8 exertion, overbear 11 tenterhooks

measuring device: 9 telemeter

strained: 4 taut 5 tense, tight 6 forced 7 intense 8 weakened, wrenched 9 distorted, laborious 10 farfetched

strainer: 4 cage, sile 5 sieve, strum, tamis 6 filter, milsey, milsie, sifter 8 colander, colature, huckmuck 10 colatorium

strait: 4 area, bind, neck, pass 6 crisis, narrow 7 channel, isthmus 11 predicament

between Labrador and Newfoundland: 9 Belle Isle

Strait of Gibraltar: 17 Pillars of Hercules

Strait of Messina rock: 6 Scylla

straiten: 5 hem in, limit 6 hamper 7 confine, enclose 8 contract, distress, restrict 9 embarrass

strait-jacket: 8 camisole 9 restraint

strait-laced: 4 prim 5 stiff 6 severe, strict 8 stubborn 9 obstinate, puritanic 10 restricted 11 constrained 12 narrow-minded 14 overscrupulous

straits: 5 pinch, rigor 7 narrows, poverty 8 extremes 10 difficulty

Straits Settlement: 6 Penang 8 Malacca 9 Singapore

island: 5 Cocos 6 Labuan 9 Christmas

native state: 5 Perak 6 Johore, Pahang 8 Selangor 11 Sungei Ujong 13 Negri Sembilan

strake: rut 4 band 5 crack 6 loiter, streak, stripe, stroll, trough, wander 7 stretch

strand: sea 4 bank, quay, wire 5 beach, fiber, shore, wharf 6 gutter, maroon, region, stream, thread 7 channel, current 8 filament 9 shipwreck

stranded: 6 ashore 7 aground, beached 8 castaway, marooned 10 high and dry

strange: new, odd 4 fell, rare, unco 5 alien, droll, eerie, fremd, novel, queer 6 exotic, quaint 7 bizarre, curious, distant, erratic, foreign, oddball, uncanny, unknown, unusual 8 abnormal, estrange, fanciful, peculiar, reserved, singular, uncommon 9 couthless, different, eccentric, unnatural, wonderful 10 mysterious, outlandish, unfamiliar, unfriendly 11 exceptional 12 unaccustomed, unacquainted 13 extraordinary, inexperienced, preternatural

language: 4 cant 5 lingo 6 jargon 7 dialect

stranger: 5 alien, guest, odder 6 ganger, novice 7 comical, visitor 8 emigrant, estrange, intruder, newcomer, outsider 9 auslander, foreigner, outlander 10 tramontane 12 intermeddler

strangle: 4 kill, slay 5 choke, grane 6 stifle 7 garrote, repress 8 garrotte, suppress, throttle 9 constrict, suffocate

stranglehold: 4 grip 8 chancery, monopoly

strangulate: 5 choke 8 compress, obstruct, 9 constrict

strap: bar, fit, tie 4 band, beat, belt, bind, hang, rein, riem 5 girth, groom, strip, strop, thong 6 billet, chaser, credit, enarme, fillet, halter, latigo, ligule, punish, secure 7 furnish, laniard, lanyard, sharpen 8 chastise

kind of: 4 jess, taws 5 guige, leash, strop, tawse, thong 6 chaser, enarme 8 bretelle 10 boondoggle

strap-shaped: 6 lorate 7 ligular 8 ligulate

strapping: 6 robust, strong 7 beating 9 thrashing

strass: 5 glass, paste

strata (see also **stratum**): *geological:* 4 lias

later: 7 neozoic

social: 7 classes

stratagem: 4 coup, ruse, wile 5 cheat, fetch, fraud, trick 6 blench, device, humbug, scheme 7 finesse 8 artifice, intrigue, maneuver 9 chicanery, deception, execution, expedient, slaughter 10 artfulness

smart: 8 liripipe, liripoop

strategic: 9 favorable 12 advantageous

strategy: 8 artifice, game plan, intrigue, maneuver

stratification: 7 bedding

stratum: bed 5 class, layer, level 6 couche 7 section 8 division

thin: 4 seam

Strauss opera 6 Salome 7 Electra 10 Fledermaus 13 Rosenkavalier

Stravinsky work: 8 Firebird 10 Petrouchka

straw: hat, wap 4 gloy, mote, pipe, rush 5 chaff 6 fescue, litter, trifle 9 worthless, yellowish 11 meaningless 12 churchwarden

bed: 6 pallet

bundle of: 6 batten 8 windling

coat: 4 mino

color: 6 flaxen

colored: 11 stramineous

for hats: 6 sennit 7 leghorn, sabutan

half rotten: 5 mulch

load of: 5 barth

man: 9 scarecrow

plaited: 6 sennit

threshing floor: 6 bhossa

to protect plants: 5 mulch

waxed: 6 strass

weaving: 5 rafia

straw in the wind: 4 clue, omen, sign 7 portent, warning

straw vote: 4 poll

strawberry: 6 fraise, runner 8 fragaria

strawlike: 11 stramineous

stray: err, gad, odd 4 cavy, roam, rove, waif 5 range 6 casual, course, errant, random, stroll, swerve, wander 7 decline, deviate, digress, forlorn, go wrong, habitat, runaway, saunter 8 detached, distract, isolated, straggle 9 straggler, unrelated 10 incidental, occasional 12 unenumerated

calf: 4 dogy 5 dogie

straying: 6 astray, errant 7 erratic 8 aberrant 9 deviation, erroneous

streak: 4 hint, line, vein, wale 5 fleck, freak, garle, hurry, layer, lined, round, spell, trace, trait 6 period, smooth, strain, strake, stripe, stroke 7 stratum, striped 8 discolor 10 suggestion

mottled: roe

narrow: 5 stria 6 striae

regular: 6 stripe

streaked: 4 liny 6 marked 7 alarmed, brindle, striped, worried 8 brindled 10 variegated

streaking: 12 frosted hair

streaky: 4 liny 5 liney, mixed 6 uneven 8 variable

stream: run 4 burn, flow, flux, ford, gote, gush, pour, rill, rush 5 bache, bayou, bourn, brook, creek, fleam, floss, flume, fluor, force, issue, river, speed, trend 6 amount, bourne, course, fluent, runnel 7 channel, current, rivulet 8 affluent 9 anabranch 11 watercourse

diminutive: run 4 race 5 brook 6 rillet 7 rivulet 9 streamlet

dry bed: 6 arroyo

lava: 6 coulee

living in: 9 amphibian, rheophile

ravine: 4 ghyl, gill

rushing: jet 7 torrent

small: run 4 rill, sike 5 brook, siket 6 rillet, runlet

sound: 4 purl 6 murmur

underground: aar

upper part of: 6 source 9 headwater

streamer: jet 4 flag 5 strip 6 guidon, ribbon 7 feather, pendant, pennant 8 banderol, headline 9 banderole

streamlet: 4 rill 5 brook 6 rillet, runlet, runnel 7 freshet, rivulet

streamlined: 6 modern 8 straight 10 simplified

street: rew(Sc.), way 4 lane, road 5 calle, chare 6 avenue, causey, ruelle, spread 7 highway, roadway, strasse(G.) 8 chaussee, contrada 9 boulevard 12 thoroughfare

Chinese: 6 hutung

degraded: 4 slum

ditch: 6 gutter

India: 5 chawk, chowk

narrow: 4 wynd 5 alley, place

street urchin: 4 arab 5 gamin

streetcar: 4 tram 7 trolley

driver: 8 motorman

streetwalker: 5 whore 6 hooker, wanton 7 cruiser 10 prostitute

strength: arm 4 beef, iron, thew 5 brawn, force, might, power, vigor 6 energy, foison 7 ability, potency, stamina, sthenia 8 capacity, firmness, solidity, validity 9 coherence, endurance, fortitude, intensity, lustiness, puissance, stability, stoutness, substance, toughness, vehemence 10 heartiness, robustness 14 impregnability

deprive of: 7 unnerve 8 enervate

diminish: 6 dilute

electric current: 8 amperage

liquor: 5 proof

loss: 8 asthenia

military: 7 armament

of character: 4 guts, sand 9 fortitude

of will: 8 backbone

poetic: 9 puissance

regain: 5 rally

solution: 5 titer, titre

source of: 5 asset

strengthen: add 4 back, bind, frap, gird, help, prop 5 brace, nerve, steel 6 clench, deepen, endure 7 afforce, comfort, confirm, fortify, nourish, support, sustain, toughen 8 roborate 9 encourage, reinforce 10 invigorate 11 consolidate

with alcohol: 5 spike 7 fortify

strenuous: 4 hard 5 eager 6 active, ardent, severe 7 arduous, zealous 8 vigorous 9 energetic

strepitant: 5 noisy 9 clamorous

stress: try 4 pain 5 brunt, force, labor, press 6 accent, strain 7 afflict, amplify, overtax, tension, urgency 8 ampliate, distrain, distress, emphasis, exertion, pressure 9 emphasize, intensity 10 constraint, importance, overstrain, resistance 12 significance 13 inconvenience

free from: 4 calm 6 anneal

mechanical: 8 erossure

metrical: 5 ictus

music: 6 accent

voice: 5 arsis 6 accent

stretch: run 4 span, walk 5 range, reach, retch, space, tract, while 6 course, dilate, eke out, effort, expand, extend, period, spread, strain 7 distend, elastic, enlarge, expanse, tension 8 distance, elongate, sentence 9 direction, embroider, extension 10 exaggerate

injuriously: 6 sprain

out: lie 4 rest 6 repose

the neck: 5 crane

the truth: lie 10 exaggerate

stretched: 6 craned 7 porrect 8 extended, prolated 9 elongated

tight: 4 taut 5 tense

while drying: 8 tentered

stretcher: 5 dooly 6 litter, racker 8 ringhead

neck: 6 craner

strew: 6 litter, spread 7 diffuse, scatter 8 disperse, sprinkle 9 bespatter, broadcast 10 besprinkle 11 disseminate

strewing: 4 seme

stria: 4 band, line, vein 5 ridge 6 fillet, furrow, groove, hollow, streak, stripe 7 channel

stricken (see also strike): 7 smitten, worn out, wounded 13 incapacitated

strickle: 5 rifle 7 pattern 8 template

strict: 4 blue, hard, true 5 close, exact, harsh, rigid, stern, tense, tight 6 entire, severe 7 ascetic, austere, binding, correct, perfect, precise 8 absolute, acurate, intimate, limiting, rigorous, straight 9 confining, puritanic, stringent 10 compressed, forbidding, hardboiled, inexorable, inflexible, iron-handed, relentless, scrupulous 11 punctilious, puritanical, restricting, straitlaced, undeviating 14 uncompromising

disciplinarian: 8 martinet

discipline: 13 regimentation

strictness: 5 rigor 9 closeness

in law: 8 legalism

stricture: 4 sign 5 spark, touch, trace 7 binding, censure, closing 9 criticism 11 contraction 13 animadversion

strid: 5 gorge 6 ravine

stride: 4 step, walk 5 stalk 7 advance 8 bestride, progress, straddle 11 advancement

strident: 5 harsh 6 shrill 7 grating, raucous, yelling 11 acrimonious, cacophonous

stridulate: 5 cheep, chirk, chirp, creak, crick 7 clitter

strife: war 4 bait, bate, feud 5 fight, flite, flyte, noise, strow 6 combat, debate, estrif 7 contest, discord, hurling, quarrel

8 conflict, endeavor, exertion, struggle 9 emulation 10 contention 11 altercation, competition, controversy

about mere words: 9 logomachy

civil: 6 stasis

striffen: 6 membrane, thin skin

strigil: 7 scraper

strigose, strigous: 5 rough, sharp 6 hispid 7 bristly

strike: bat, bob, box, cob, cop, dab, dad, hew, hit, lam, pat, ram, rap, wap 4 baff, bang, bash, bean, beat, biff, bill, bump, bunt, chap, cope, coup, cuff, dash, daub, daud, dint, dunt, fist, flap, flog, frap, gird, give, gowf, hurl, hurt, knap, lash, pelt, rout, slam, slap, slay, swat 5 clash, clink, clout, douse, dowse, dunch, filch, gowff, impel, knock, occur, punch, skelp, skite, slash, smear, smite, spank, swipe, trend, whang 6 assail, attack, attain, bounce, buffet, fettle, hammer, hartal, punish 7 afflict, collide, impress, walkout 8 discover, struggle

a balance: 5 agree 6 settle 10 compromise

a mean: 7 average

against: ram 4 bump 5 crash 7 assault, collide

and rebound: 5 carom 6 carrom 9 carambole

demonstrator: 6 picket

down: 4 fell, kill 5 floor 7 disable

dumb: 4 stun

feature: 7 lockout

gently: dab, pat 4 bump, putt

heavily: lam, ram 4 bash, slog, slug

obliquely: 5 carom

on head: 4 bean

out: fan 4 dele, head 5 elide, erase 6 cancel, delete 9 eliminate

prepare to: 4 coil

producing musical sound: 5 chime

series of blows: 4 pelt

settler: 8 mediator

together: 5 clash, crash 7 collide

up: 5 begin, start 8 commence

violently: ram 4 bash, slam

with fist: 4 plug 5 pound, punch

with head: 4 butt

with wonder: awe 7 astound 8 surprise

strikebreaker: rat 4 fink, goon, scab 8 blackleg(Br.)

striker: 4 tern 6 batman, batter, helper, hitter, smiter 7 batsman, clapper, mobster 9 assistant, harpooner

striking: 4 dint 5 showy 6 cogent 7 salient, telling 8 stunning 9 arresting, effective 10 noticeable, remarkable, surprising 11 conspicuous

effect: 5 eclat

string: 4 band, cord, hoax, josh, line 5 bound, braid, chain, jolly, strip, twine 6 series, thread 8 resource 10 conditions, succession 14 qualifications

course: 6 guidon

kinds of: 4 wire 5 lacet, snare 6 amenta, hypate, lachet 7 amentum, langate

of beads: 6 rosary 8 necklace

up: 4 hang, lace 5 lynch, scrab, gibbet

string along: toy 4 fool 5 dally 6 lead on 7 deceive, flatter

string instrument: uke 4 harp, lute, lyre 5 banjo, cello, piano, viola 6 fiddle, guitar, spinet, violin, zither 7 ukelele, ukulele 8 mandolin 11 harpsichord

old: 4 lute, lyre 6 spinet 8 psaltery 11 harpsichord

stringent: 4 grim, hard, ropy 5 rigid, tense, tight 6 cogent, severe, strict 7 binding, extreme 10 convincing 11 restrictive

stringer: tie 4 rope, vein 6 timber 8 filament

stringy: 4 ropy 5 gluey 6 sinewy, viscid 7 fibrous, viscous 8 muscular 11 filamentous

strip: bar, rob, tab, tag, top 4 band, bare, bark, belt, doff, flay, hull, husk, peel, pull, skin, tear 5 clear, flake, fleck, pluck, shred, spoil, swath, unrig 6 border, denude, devest, divest, expose, flense, length, ravage, reduce, remove, runway, swathe 7 bandage, bandeau, bereave, degrade, deprive, despoil, disrobe, pillage, plunder, uncloak, uncover, undress, unleave 8 bandeaux(pl.), denudate, disarray, headland, separate 9 dismantle, excoriate 10 disfurnish, dispossess 11 debenzolize, decorticate

blubber: 6 flense

kinds of: 4 came, cove, lead, rand, riem, tirr 5 cleat, ridge, stave 6 inwale, reglet 7 gunwale

leather: 4 welt 5 thong 6 latigo 7 belting

narrow: 4 slat, tape 5 reeve, strap 7 bandeau 8 bandeaux(pl.)

wooden: rib 4 lath, slat 5 stave 6 reglet

strip tease dancer: 9 ecdysiast

stripe: bar, ilk, roe 4 band, beat, belt, blow, kind, lash, line, mark, sort, type, wale, weal, welt, zone 5 chest, stria 6 border, frenum, streak, strike, stroke 7 chevron, lineate, pattern, rivulet 8 division 9 character

striped: 5 bandy 6 banded, barred 7 lineate, vittate 8 bayadere, streaked

animal: 5 bongo, zebra

cloth: 6 madras

stripling: boy, lad 5 chiel, youth 6 chield

stripped: 4 bare, nude 6 picked 10 deprived of

by trickery: 7 buncoed, bunkoed, fleeced

strive: aim, hie, tew, try, tug, vie 4 seek, toil 5 bandy, ensue, fight, labor, rival 6 battle, buffet, resist, strain 7 attempt, compete, contend, contest, emulate 8 contrast, endeavor, struggle

striving: 5 nisus 7 attempt, contest

strobile: 4 chat 8 pine cone

strockle: 6 shovel

stroke: bat, coy, fit, hew, hit, pat, pet, rub 4 baff, beat, blow, chap, coup, dash, ding, dint, flip, gowf, hurt, lash, mark, milk, oner, shot, walk, whet 5 chare, douse, dowse, flack, fluke, gowff, ictus, knock, power, pulse, rower, strut, throb, trait 6 attack, caress, effort, fondle, ictuse, impact, injury, soothe, stride 7 seizure, sharpen, whample 8 apoplexy, disaster 9 influence

brilliant: ace 4 coup

cutting: 4 chop 5 slice

kinds of: 5 eagle, cerif, serif, wedge 6 birdie 7 virgule

of luck: hit 5 fluke 6 strike 8 windfall

short: 4 flip, putt 5 whisk

stroll: 4 gait, mosy, roam, rove, walk 5 mosey, range, stray, tramp 6 dacker, daiker, dander, ramble, soodle, wander 7 saunter

stroller: 4 cart, pram 5 actor, sulky, tramp 6 beggar, gocart, player, shuler 7 peddlar, pedler, shuiler, vagrant 8 bohemian, carriage, wanderer 9 saunterer

Stromboli: 6 island 7 volcano

stromming: herring

strong: fit, hot 4 able, bold, dure, elon, fere, firm, fort, hale, hard, rank, sure, warm, wiry 5 bonny, clear, eager, frack, freck, fresh, great, gross, hardy, heavy, large, lusty, solid, sound, stout, tough, yauld 6 active, ardent, bonnie, brawny, c⸎rent, feckle, mighty, potent, robust, r⸎ged, sinewy, stable, sturdy 7 buirdly, c⸎rable, fertile, greatly, humming, in-⸎nse, sthenic, violent, zealous 8 ac-⸎ented, athletic, distinct, flagrant, forceful, forcible, muscular, powerful, puissant, resonant, severely, stalwart, strongly, vehement, vigorous 9 Atlantean, difficult, effective, impetuous, important, strapping, tenacious, violently 10 boisterous, forthright, malodorous, nourishing, outrageous, passionate, persuasive, productive, pronounced, remarkable, spirituous 11 excessively 12 concentrated

upward movement: 5 surge

strong man: 6 tyrant 10 powerhouse

Biblical: 6 Samson 7 Sampson

legendary: 5 Atlas 8 Herakles, Hercules

strong point: 5 forte

strong-arm: rob 4 beat, thug 5 force, power 7 assault 8 violence 9 terrorize 10 intimidate

man: 4 goon 7 bouncer

strongbox: 4 case, safe 5 chest, vault 6 coffer

stronghold: 4 fort, hold, keep 5 tower 6 castle 7 citadel, fortify, redoubt 8 fast-hold, fastness, fortress 13 fortification

strong-smelling: 4 foul, rank 5 fetid 8 mephitic, stinking

strop: 4 hone, whet 7 sharpen

strophe: 6 stanza 10 heptastich

stroygood: 7 wastrel 11 spendthrift

struck: 4 smit 5 smote 7 shocked, smitten 8 punished

with amazement: 6 aghast

with small missiles: 6 pelted

with sudden fear: 7 alarmed

with terror: 6 aghast 7 shocked

with wonder: 6 aghast

struck out: 5 deled 6 elided, erased, fanned 7 deleted

structural quality: 7 texture

structure: dam 4 form 5 frame, house 6 bridge, format, make-up, syntax 7 edifice, texture 8 building, bulkhead 9 formation, framework 11 arrangement, composition, fabricature 12 constitution, construction

abnormal: 12 malformation

calcareous: 5 coral

conical: 7 pyramid

crown-like: 6 corona

curved: 4 arch

filamentous: 4 hair

floating: 4 roar

funeral: 10 catafalque

grammatical: 6 syntax

hallowed: 6 bethel, chapel, church, temple 8 basilica 9 cathedral, synagogue 10 tabernacle

high: 5 tower

human: 8 physique

keel-like: 6 carina

latticework: 7 trellis

looplike: 4 ansa

monumental: 5 pylon 7 pyramid

on roof: 6 cupola, dormer 9 penthouse

Oriental: 6 pagoda

original: 6 isogen

osseous: 4 bone

over obstacles: 6 bridge

pergola-like: 6 ramada

pert. to: 8 tectonic

projecting into water: 4 jiti 5 jetty 6 jettee

raised: 4 dais 5 altar, stage 8 platform

sacrificial: 5 altar

sheltering: cot 4 cote

supporting: 4 pier

tall: 5 tower 7 steeple 9 campanile

tent-like: 10 tabernacle

white: 6 albedo

strudel: 6 pastry

struggle: try, tug, vie 4 agon, cope, frab, wade 5 fight, heave, labor 6 battle, buckle, bustle, combat, effort, Peniel, strife, strike, strive, throes, tussle, widdle 7 attempt, bargain, barrace, contend, contest, flounce, scuffle, warfare, wrestle 8 conflict, endeavor, exertion, flounder, scraffle, scramble 10 contention, difficulty

a deux: 4 duel

helplessly: 8 flounder

struma: 6 goiter, goitre

strummed: 8 thrummed

strumpet: 4 brim 5 belie, wench 6 blowen, harlot, wanton 7 cocotte, debauch, slander 8 harridan 10 prostitute

strung: 6 beaded

highly: 5 tense 7 nervous

strut: 4 brag, cock, gait, step, walk 5 brace, bulge, swell 6 flaunt, parade, sashay, stride, strife, strunt, thrust 7 distend, peacock, provide, stiffen, stretch, support, swagger, wrangle 8 protrude 10 contention 11 protuberant

struthious: 4 emus 5 rheas 6 ratite 9 ostriches

stub: 4 pen 5 beat, dolt, snag 5 crush, drive, guard, hinge, squat, stumb 6 coupon, nubbin, stocky 7 feather, remnant 8 thickset 9 blockhead, extirpate 11 counterfoil

stubble: bun 6 strunt 8 eelgrass

field: 5 rowen

stubborn: set 4 rude 5 fixed, hardy, harsh, rough, tough 6 coarse, dogged, mulish, sturdy 7 restive 8 obdurate, perverse, resolute, starkish, vigorous 9 camsteary, camsteery, difficult, obstinate, pigheaded 10 bullheaded, calcitrant, determined, hardheaded, headstrong, inflexible, refractory, unyielding 11 intractable, persevering 12 pertinacious

stubby: 5 squat 6 stocky, stumpy 8 thickset

stuck: See stick

stuck in the mud: 7 bemired

stuck-up: 4 vain 7 haughty 8 arrogant, snobbish 9 conceited 12 supercilious 13 self-important

stud: dot, pin, rod 4 boss, knob, male, spot, stub 5 adorn, aglet, beset, brace haras, study, stump 6 aiglet, button, pillar 7 chaplet, sprinkle, support 9 studhorse

farm: 5 haras

for shoe: 7 hobnail

with jewels: 5 engem

with radiating bodies: 6 enstar

student: 5 eleve(F.), pupil 6 bursar 7 educand, learner 8 disciple, observer

according to grade: 6 termer

agricultural college: 5 Aggie

college: 4 soph 6 junior, senior 7 protege, scholar 8 freshman 9 sophomore 13 undergraduate

divinity: 9 theologue 10 theologian

fellow: 9 classmate

first-year: 5 Fuchs(G.) 8 freshman

former: 7 dropout 8 graduate

fourth-year: 6 senior

girl: 4 coed

group: 5 class

hall: 5 burse 9 dormitory

in charge: 7 monitor

law: 8 stagiary

medical: 6 intern 7 interne

military: 5 cadet, plebe

naval academy: 5 cadet 10 midshipman

of birds: 13 ornithologist

of crime: 10 penologist 13 criminologist

of heavens: 9 uranographist

of proverbs: 14 paroemiologist

of punishment: 10 penologist

of relics: 13 archaeologist

of reptiles: 13 herpetologist

of spiders: 13 arachnologist

Oxford: 8 commoner

probationary: 8 stibbler

residence: 5 house 6 hostel 9 dormitory

room: 7 seminar

second-year: 9 sophomore

stipend paid: 6 bursar

talmudic: 5 bahur

third-year: 6 junior

West Point: 5 cadet, plebe

studied: 5 pored 6 intent 7 learned, planned 8 affected, designed, inclined, reasoned 10 ceremonial, deliberate 12 premeditated

studies: *academic:* 4 arts 7 science 10 humanities

advanced: 7 seminar 8 graduate

chosen by students: 9 electives

series of: 6 course

studio: 7 atelier, bottega 8 workshop 11 ergasterion

studious: 5 booky 7 bookish, devoted, studied 8 diligent, sedulous 9 assiduous, scholarly 10 deliberate 13 contemplative

study: con, den, mug 4 bone, muse, muzz, pore, read, scan 5 grind 6 lesson, peruse, ponder 7 analyse, analyze, canvass, croquis, examine, reverie 8 consider, exercise, meditate 9 attention 10 scrutinize 11 contemplate 13 consideration, contemplation

animals: 9 zoography

bees: 8 apiology

Bible: 9 isagogics

by lamplight: 9 lucubrate

closely: con 4 pore 7 examine

course: 7 seminar

fingerprints: 13 dactylography

fixed course: 4 rote

flowers: 12 anthoecology

group: 7 seminar

handwriting: 10 graphology

hard: 4 bone, cram

horses: 9 hippology
human generations: 15 anthropogenesis
insect's habits: 10 entomology
laborious: 11 lucubration
mountains: 7 orology
musical: 5 etude
optional: 8 elective
population: 10 larithmics
preliminary: 6 sketch
punishment: 8 penology
sacred edifices: 7 naology
sacred images: 9 iconology
sermons: 10 homiletics
wines: 7 enology
words: 9 etymology

stuff: jam, pad, ram, wad 4 copy, cram,
   fill, gaum, junk, pang 5 crowd, farce,
   force, grain, pulse, steve 6 fabric,
   graith, matter, refuse, stifle 7 bombast,
   element, essence, filling, mixture, portion 8 material, medicine, nonsense,
   overload 9 character, principle, substance, suffocate
   full: 4 glut 5 gorge 6 stodge 7 satiate
   harvested grain: 7 stubble
   sticky: goo
   worthless: 4 gear 7 hogwash
stuffed: 6 bourre, stodgy 7 bombast, replete 8 farctate
stuffing: 7 padding, viscera 8 dressing 9
   forcemeat
stuffy: fat 4 dull, prim 5 angry, close,
   fubsy, fuggy, humid, stout, sulky 6
   froust, frowst, stodgy 7 airless, pompous 8 resolute, stifling 9 obstinate 10
   mettlesome, old-fogyish 11 strait-laced
   12 conservative, old-fashioned
Stuka: 6 bomber
stulm: 4 adit 8 entrance 10 passageway
stultiloquy: 6 babble 11 foolish talk
stumble: err 4 fall, slip, trip 5 lurch 6
   boggle, chance, faffle, falter, happen, offend, puzzle, teeter, wallow 7 blunder,
   failure, founder, perplex, scrupple, stagger, stammer 8 confound, flounder
stumbling block: 7 obstacle 9 hindrance
   10 impediment 11 obstruction
stump: cob, end, lop 4 butt, dare, foil,
   grub, plod, snag, stab, stub 5 block,
   clump 6 baffle, corner, hobble, lumber,
   pillar, puzzle, strunt, thwart, travel 7
   blunted, canvass, nonplus, perplex, rostrum, stumble 8 defiance, platform 9
   challenge 11 electioneer
stumps: 4 legs
stumpy: 5 bunty, money 6 stubby 8
   thickset
stun: 4 bowl, daze, tear 5 amaze, daunt,
   daver, dizzy, dover, shock 6 appall, benumb, bruise, crease, deaden, deafen 7
   astound, dammish, scratch, startle, stupefy 8 astonish, bewilder 9 dumbfound,

overpower, overwhelm 10 strike dumb
stunned: 10 astonished
stunning: 7 stylish 8 dazzling, gorgeous 9
   beautiful, excellent 10 foudroyant
stunt: act 4 feat 5 angry, blast, blunt,
   check, cramp, crowl, dwarf, stamp,
   trick, whale 6 abrupt, hinder 7 curtail,
   exploit, shorten 8 stubborn, suppress
   10 undersized 11 performance
   gymnastic: kip 4 kipp 10 handspring
stunty: 5 short 6 flashy, stocky 7 dwarfed
stupa: 5 mound, tower 6 shrine
   lamaism: 7 chorten
stupefacient: 4 drug 8 narcotic
stupefy: fox, sot 4 baze, daze, dope, doze,
   drug, dull, dunt, numb, stun 5 amaze,
   aston, besot, blunt, daunt, daver, deave,
   shock 6 astone, bedaze, bemuse, benumb, muddle 7 astound, confuse 8 astonish, bewilder, confound 11 incrassate
   with drink: 6 fuddle
stupendous: 4 huge 5 great, large 7 amazing, immense 8 enormous 9 marvelous,
   monstrous, wonderful 10 astounding
   11 astonishing 12 overpowering, overwhelming 13 extraordinary
stupid: 4 bete, clod, dull, dumb, dunt,
   guam, lewd, slow 5 besot, blunt, booby,
   crass, dazed, dense, dizzy, dunce, goosy,
   heavy, inane, sumph 6 assish, barren,
   beetle, boring, bovine, dawkin, doiled,
   doited, drowsy, goosey, hebete, lurdan,
   oafish, obtuse, simple, stolid, torpid 7
   asinine, brutish, buzzard, calvish, daffish, doldrum, doltish, duffing, dullard,
   fatuous, foolish, foppish, glaiket, glaikit,
   gomerel, goosish, gullish, lurdane, prosaic, stunned, vacuous, witless 8 anserine, anserous, backward, bayardly,
   blockish, boeotian, cloddish, deadened,
   footless, headless, retarded, sluggish 9
   blocklike, bourgeois, brainless, cod-
   headed, inanimate, insensate, insipient,
   lethargic, plumbeous, pointless, senseless, stupefied 10 hardwitted, hulver-
   head, irrational, slow-witted 11 claybrained, heavy-headed 12 buffleheaded
   13 unintelligent, uninteresting
   person: ass, sap 4 clod, clot, coot, dolt,
   dope, fool, jerk, loon 5 dunce, goose,
   idiot, moron, ninny 7 dullard, fathead 8
   numskull 9 blockhead
stupor: fog 4 coma, damp, dote 5 sopor 6
   apathy, trance 7 languor 8 lethargy
   pert. to: 7 carotic, narcose
sturdy: gid, set 4 buff, firm 5 felon, hardy,
   harsh, lusty, sound, stern, stiff, stout 6
   brawny, robust, rugged, rustic, stable,
   steady, strong 7 violent 8 obdurate, resolute, stalwart, stubborn, vigorous 9
   rigidness, obstinate 10 courageous, de-

termined, unyielding **11** substantial

sturdy and stout: 5 burly

sturgeon: 6 beluga
small: **7** sterlet
white: **6** beluga
roe: **6** caviar

Sturm and Drang: 6 unrest **7** ferment, turmoil

stutter: 7 stammer

stuttering: 8 psellism **9** psellisum

sty, stye: pen **4** boil, dump, sink **5** lodge, stair, steps, stile **6** ladder, pigpen **8** swelling **9** enclosure

stygian: 6 gloomy **7** hellish **8** infernal

style: air, dub, pen, pin, ton, way **4** call, garb, gere, kind, mode, name, sort, term, tone, type **5** vogue **6** format, gnomon, graver, manner, method, needle, phrase, stylus **7** alamode, diction, entitle, fashion, variety **8** demeanor **9** designate, execution **10** denominate **12** characterize, construction
architecture: **5** Doric, Greek, Ionic, Roman, Saxon **6** Gothic, Norman **7** Italian **8** Colonial, Georgian, Monterey **9** Byzantine **10** Corinthian, Romanesque **11** Elizabethan, Renaissance **13** Mediterranean
art: **5** genre
artistic: **5** gusto
dress: **5** get-up, guise
fantastic: **6** rococo **7** baroque
furniture: **6** Empire
hair: **4** Afro, coif **8** coiffure
lofty: **4** epic
oratorical: **10** rhetorical
out of: **5** dated, passe
painting: **5** genre
penmanship: **4** hand
performance: **9** execution

stylet: pro **5** organ, probe **6** dagger **7** poniard **8** stiletto **9** appendage
surgical: **6** trocar

stylish: 4 chic, posh, tony **5** dashy, nifty, smart, swell **6** chichi, classy, dressy, jaunty, modish, spiffy, swanky **7** alamode, dashing, doggish, genteel, knowing, swagger **11** fashionable

stylist: 7 modiste

stylites: 7 hermits **8** ascetics

styloid: 8 belonoid

stymie, stymy: 5 block **6** hinder, impede **8** obstruct

styptic: 4 alum **10** astringent, tannic acid

Styx: 5 nymph, river
father: **7** Oceanus
ferryman: **6** Charon
locale: **5** Hades
mother: **6** Tethys
pert. to: **7** stygian

suant: 4 even **5** grave, quiet **6** demure, placid, smooth, steady **7** equable, regular **9** agreeable, following

suave: 4 easy, oily, smug **5** bland, civil, soapy, sweet **6** polite, smooth, urbane **7** fulsome **8** gracious, mannered, pleasant, polished, tactful, unctuous **9** agreeable **12** ingratiating

suavity: 6 comity **7** amenity **8** urbanity **10** politeness **12** complaisance

sub: 6 fill-in **9** alternate, auxiliary, submarine **11** replacement

sub rosa: 8 covertly, secretly

subbase: 6 plinth

subdivide: 5 carve, mince **8** separate

subdivision: 4 part **6** sector **8** category **10** department
lateral: **5** aisle
rocks: **5** range

subdue: cow **4** bend, quay, tame **5** accoy, allay, amate, atill, break, charm, crush, daunt, dompt, lower, quell, sober **6** adaunt, bridle, disarm, dismay, evince, master, mellow, reduce, soften, steady, subact **7** affaite, chasten, conquer, control, put down, repress, squelch **8** convince, diminish, overcome, suppress, surmount, vanquish **9** captivate, castigate, overpower, subjugate

suber: 4 cork **10** cork tissue

subjacent: 8 inferior **10** underlying

subject: try **4** text **5** basis, cause, prone, theme, topic **6** liable, motive, phrase, reason, submit, vassal **7** article, citizen, conquer, exposed, reality **8** disposed, incident, inferior, ordered **9** dependent, subjugate **10** contingent, predispose, submissive, substratum **11** conditional, subordinate
of discourse: **5** theme, topic
of disease: **4** case **7** patient
of lawsuit: res
of verb: **4** noun
to abuse: **6** revile
to argument: **4** moot
to authority: **6** master
to be taught: **10** didascalic
to change: **7** mutable
to choice: **8** elective
to control: **7** rulable
to death: **6** mortal
to depression: **5** moody
to discussion: **4** moot **9** debatable
to dislike: **8** aversion
to ill treatment: **6** misuse
to mistakes: **7** erratic
to taxation: **8** reteable
to whirling action: **11** centifugate

subjection: 7 slavery **8** thirling **9** captivity

subjoin: add **5** affix, annex **6** append, attach

subjugate: 6 compel, master, reduce, subdue **7** conquer, depress, overawe **8** overcome

sublate: 4 deny 5 annul 6 cancel, lift up, negate, remove 9 eliminate, take away

sublime: 5 exalt, grand, great, lofty, noble, proud 6 purify, refine 7 emotion, exalted, haughty, supreme 8 elevated, empyreal, heavenly, heighten, majestic, splendid, upraised

sublimity: 4 apex 7 majesty 8 grandeur 12 magnificence

submarine: 4 boat 5 diver 9 periscope 11 submersible

   detector: 5 sonar

   group: 8 wolf-pack

   projectile: 7 missile, Polaris, torpedo

submerge: dip 4 bury, dive, hide, sink 5 souse 6 deluge, drench, engulf, plunge 7 immerse 8 inundate, suppress

submerged: 4 sunk 5 awash, latent 6 sunken 10 underwater

   continent: 8 Atlantis

submission: 5 offer 8 meekness 9 deference, obedience, surrender 10 compliance, confession 11 resignation 12 acquiescence 13 nonresistance

   act of: 5 kneel 6 curtsy 7 curtsey

   to destiny: 8 fatalism

submissive: 4 meek, tame 5 buxom 6 docile, humble 7 dutiful, passive, servile 8 obedient, resigned, yielding 9 childlike, compliant

   to wife: 8 uxorious

submit: bow 4 bend, fall, obey 5 abide, agree, avale, defer, heald, hield, lower, stoop, yield 6 assent, comply, delate, hand in, resign, soften, subdue, suffer, temper 7 exhibit, knuckle, propose, succumb, suggest 8 moderate 9 acquiesce, surrender 10 condescend

   for consideration: 5 remit

   proposal to: 4 move

   to: 4 obey 6 suffer

subordinate: 5 minor, under 6 puisne, subdue 7 control, subject 8 inferior, obedient, servient 9 ancillary, assistant, auxiliary, dependent, secondary, underling 10 accidental, collateral, incidental, submissive 11 subservient •

   activity: 8 parergon

   adjunct: 9 appendage

   officer: 4 exon

suborn: 5 bribe, foist 6 father, incite, induce 7 procure 9 instigate

subpoena: 4 writ 6 summon 7 summons

subrogate: 10 substitute

subscribe: 5 agree, favor 6 adhere, assent, attest 7 ascribe, consent, support 8 sanction 10 contribute, underwrite

subscription to newspaper: 10 abonnement

subsequent: 5 after, later 6 puisne 7 ensuing 8 retainer 9 attendant, companion, following 11 consecutive

   to birth: 9 postnatal

subsequently: 5 after, later, since 10 afterwards, thereafter

subservient: 6 menial, vassal 7 duteous, servile 8 obeisant 9 accessory, ancillary, auxiliary, truckling 10 obsequious, submissive 11 subordinate

subside: ebb 4 bate, fall, lull, sink, wane 5 abate, cease, lower, quiet 6 settle 7 descend, flatten, relapse 8 decrease, withdraw

subsidiary: 6 back-up 7 reserve 9 accessory, assistant, auxiliary, tributary 10 collateral 12 nonessential 13 supplementary

subsidy: aid 4 gift, help 5 bonus, grant 6 bounty 7 pension, reserve, support, tribute 10 assistance, subvention 13 appropriation

subsist: 4 feed, hold, live, stay 5 abide, exist, stand 6 obtain, remain 7 support, survive 8 continue, maintain

subsistence: 6 living 9 allowance, inherency, substance 10 livelihood, provisions 11 persistence

subsoil: bed, pan 4 sole 7 stratum

   animal: 4 mole

substance: sum 4 body, core, gist, mass, meat 5 basis, meat, stuff, tenor, thing 6 estate, ground, import, matter, realty, spirit, supply, wealth 7 aliment, content, essence, meaning, purport 8 hardness, majority, material, property, solidity, sum total 9 actuality, affluence, resources, solidness 11 consistency

   amorphous: 5 resin, rosin 7 ferrite

   animal: 7 gelatin

   bitter: 4 acid 5 aloes, aloin, linin 6 ilicin 7 amarine, emetine 8 elaterin

   dissolving: 9 resolvent

   drying: 9 desiccant

   expansive: gas

   reaction-inducing: 7 reagent

   rubber-like: 5 gutta

   simple: 7 element

   sour: 4 acid 7 vinegar

   starch-like: 6 inulin, olivil 8 alantine

   sticky: goo, gum, tar 4 glue 5 paste

   transparent: 6 hyalin 7 hyaline 9 celluloid

   unctuous: oil 6 grease

   vegetable: 4 peat 5 resin, rosin

   white: 4 alba 6 inulin 7 alanine 8 elaterin

substantial: big 4 firm, real, true 5 ample, large, meaty, solid, sound, stout 6 actual, bodily, hearty, stable, strong, sturdy 7 genuine, wealthy 8 material, tangible 9 corporeal, important 10 meaningful 12 considerable

substantiality: See substance

substantiate: try 4 test 5 prove 6 assure, embody, verify 7 confirm 9 establish 11 corroborate

substantive: 4 noun 5 vital 6 actual, entity 7 pronoun 9 essential 13 self-contained

substitute: 5 extra, fill-in, fudge, proxy, vicar 6 backup, deputy, ersatz(G.), ringer 7 commute, replace 8 exchange, nominate, resource 9 alternate, makeshift, surrogate 10 understudy, viceregent 11 succedaneum 13 succenturiate

for a name: 6 dingus, doodad, widget 9 doohickey 11 thingamabob

temporary: 7 stopgap 9 expedient

substructure: 4 base 6 podium 10 foundation

subsume: 7 contain, include 8 classify 9 encompass

subterfuge: 4 plan, ruse 5 blind, trick 6 device, escape, refuge 7 evasion, secrecy 8 artifice, pretense 9 chicanery, deception 13 prevarication 14 tergiversation

subterranean: 4 cave 6 cavern, grotto, hidden, secret 11 underground

subtile: See subtle

subtilize: 5 exalt 6 rarefy, refine 9 sublimate

subtle: sly 4 deft, fine, keen, nice, thin wily 5 acute 6 artful, clever, crafty, expert, shrewd 7 cunning, elusive, logical, refined, tenuous 8 abstruse, analytic, delicate, rarefied, skillful 9 beguiling, designing, ingenious, intricate 10 mysterious, perceptive 11 penetrating 14 discriminating

emanation: 4 aura

variation: 6 nuance

subtlety: 7 exility, finesse 8 delicacy

subtract: 5 minus 6 deduct, remove 7 detract 8 withdraw, withhold

suburb: 7 purlieu 8 environs 9 outskirts, periphery

subvention: aid 4 help 5 grant 7 subsidy, support 8 endowment, provision 10 assistance 11 maintenance 13 appropriation

subvert: sap 4 ruin 5 evert, upset 6 change, uproot 7 corrupt, destroy, pervert 8 alienate, overturn, sabotage 9 overthrow, undermine

subway: 4 tube 5 metro 6 tunnel 11 underground

entrance: 5 kiosk

succeed: win 4 fare 5 fadge 6 attain, follow, make it, thrive 7 achieve, catch on, come off, inherit, prevail, prosper, replace 8 approach, flourish 10 accomplish

succeeding: 7 ensuing, sequent 10 subsequent, successful 11 consecutive

success: hit, wow 4 luck 7 arrival, fortune 8 accolade 9 happiness 11 consequence

succession: row, run 5 cycle, order 6 course, series 7 dynasty 8 sequence 9 gradation

next in line: 4 heir

succin: 5 amber

succinct: 4 curt 5 brief, short, terse 6 girded 7 compact, concise, laconic, summary 10 compressed

succor: aid 4 abet, cure, help 5 serve 6 assist, refuge, relief, rescue 7 comfort, deliver, provide, sustain 8 befriend, mitigate 9 alleviate 10 strengthen

succory: 7 chicory

succulent: 4 aloe, lush 5 fresh, juicy, sappy, tasty, vital 6 cactus, tender

fruit: uva

succumb: die 4 fall 5 yield 6 perish, submit 8 pass away 10 capitulate

succursal: 6 branch 8 offshoot 9 auxiliary 10 subsidiary

such: sic(L.) 4 kind, like, some 7 certain, similar

suck: rob, sip 4 draw, lick, swig 5 bleed, draft, drain, drink, nurse 6 absorb, imbibe, inhale, take in 7 consume, extract, suction

sucker: 4 dupe, fool 5 leech 6 victim 8 lollipop, parasite, pushover 9 simpleton

sucking fish: 6 remora 7 lamprey

suckle: 4 feed, rear, suck 5 nurse 6 foster 7 nourish 10 breast-feed 11 honeysuckle

sucrose: 5 sugar 10 saccharose

suction: 6 intake 7 drawing, lifting

Sudan: *animal:* 4 dama 6 oterop

beer: 4 dolo

capital: 8 Khartoum

city: 7 Kassala 8 Omdurman 9 Port Sudan

conqueror: 11 Mohammed Ali

desert: 6 Nubian

language: Ewe, Ibo, Kru 4 Efik, Mole, Tshi 6 Yoruba 8 Mandingo 10 Kordofaman

monetary unit: 5 pound

mountain: 4 Nuba

people: 4 Beri, Daza, Fula, Golo, Nuer, Sere 5 Fulah, Hausa, Mossi 7 Nubiyan

province: 6 Darfur 8 Kordofan

river: 4 Nile

stockade: 6 zareba 7 zareeba

stretcher: 7 angareb

weapon: 8 trombash, trumbash

weight: 5 habba

sudarium: 6 napkin 8 veronica 10 sweat cloth 12 handkerchief

sudden: 4 rash, soon 5 early, ferly, hasty, short, swift 6 abrupt, speedy 7 prerupt, violent 8 headlong, meteoric, unawares 9 alertness, impetuous, impromptu 10 unexpected, unforeseen, unprepared 11 precipitate, precipitous

suddenly: 6 presto

Sudra caste member: 5 palli

suds: bog **4** beer, foam **5** dregs, filth, froth **6** lather, refuse **7** bubbles, sadness

sue: beg, woo **4** seek, urge **5** chase, court, ensue, plead **6** appeal, guided **7** address, beseech, contest, entreat, proceed, request, solicit **8** litigate, petition, practice **9** prosecute

suer: 9 plaintiff

suet: fat **6** tallow

Suez Canal: *builder:* **9** de Lesseps

port: **4** Said **7** Ismalia

suffer: get, let **4** bear, bide, dree(Sc.), hurt **5** admit, allow, thole **6** endure, grieve, permit, submit **7** agonize, undergo **8** tolerate **10** experience

sufferance: 4 pain **6** misery **7** consent **8** patience, sanction **9** endurance **10** permission **11** forbearance

sufferer: 6 martyr, victim

suffering: ill **4** bale, dree(Sc.), loss, pain **5** agony **6** ailing, injury, misery **7** passion **8** distress, sickness **9** adversity **10** affliction **11** tribulation

reliever of: **9** Samaritan

suffice: 5 serve **6** answer **7** appease, content, satisfy

sufficiency: 4 fill **6** enough **7** ability, conceit **8** adequacy, capacity **9** abundance **10** capability, competency

sufficient: due, fit **4** able, enow, good **5** ample, valid **6** decent, enough, plenty **7** suffice **8** abundant, adequate **9** competent, effectual, efficient, qualified **11** responsible, substantial **12** satisfactory **13** well-qualified

suffix: See list page 826

suffocate: 4 kill **5** burke, choke, stive **6** stifle **7** destroy, smother **8** compress, strangle, suppress, throttle **10** asphyxiate, extinguish

suffrage: aid **4** help, vote **5** right, voice **6** assent, ballot, prayer **7** witness **8** petition **9** franchise, testimony **10** assistance **12** intercession, supplication

suffuse: 4 fill, pour **5** embay **7** diffuse **9** interject, introduce **10** overspread

sugar: gur, ose **4** cane **5** biose, candy, maple, money, oside **6** acrose, aldose, fucose, gulose, hexose, ketose, talose, triose, xylose **7** caramel, chitose, glucide, maltose, sucrose, sweeten, tetrose, threose **8** rhodeose **9** muscovado, raffinose, sweetness **10** digitoxose, endearment, piloncillo, saccharose, sweetening **12** carbohydrate, disaccharide **14** monosaccharide

artificial: **6** allose **7** glucose **9** saccharin

boiling kettle: **8** flambeau

burnt: **7** caramel

crystals: **5** candy

daddy: **4** beau **6** patron

fruit: **8** fructose, levulose

liquid: **5** sirup, syrup

lump: **4** cube, loaf

measure: **13** saccharimeter

milk: **7** lactose

mixture: **5** syrup

preparation device: **10** granulator

raw: **9** cassonade

source: sap **4** beet, cane, corn **5** maple

substitute: **5** honey **9** saccharin

syrup: **7** treacle **8** molasses

sugar apple: 6 biriba **8** sweetsop

sugarcane: *disease:* **5** sereh

pulp: **4** marc **6** megass **7** bagasse

refuse: **4** marc **7** bagasse

stalk: **6** ratoon

sugarloaf: 4 hill **8** conoidal, mountain

sugarplum: sop **6** bonbon **9** juneberry, sweetmeat

sugary: 5 sweet **7** honeyed **8** pleasant **10** flattering, saccharine **11** mellifluous

suggest: 4 hint, move **5** imply **6** advise, allude, broach, prompt **7** connote, inspire, mention, propose **8** indicate, intimate **9** adumbrate, insinuate **11** bring to mind

suggestion: 4 hint, idea **5** tinge, touch, trace **6** advice **7** inkling, remnant, soupcon **8** proposal **9** complaint **10** accusation, incitement, intimation, temptation **11** information

sui generis: 6 unique **8** peculiar

sui juris: 5 adult **11** responsible

suicidal: 4 rash **5** fatal **6** deadly, lethal **8** dejected, wretched

suidae: hog **5** swine

suing: 6 wooing **11** prosecution

suint: 5 sweat **6** grease **12** perspiration

suit: fit **4** case(law), plea **5** adapt, agree, apply, cards, dress, fadge, group, habit, match, serve, tally **6** accord, adjust, answer, appeal, attire, behove, outfit, please, prayer, series, trover, wooing **7** arrange, behoove, clothes, comport, conform, costume, flatter, request, satisfy, uniform **8** courting, entreaty, petition **9** harmonize **10** correspond, litigation **11** accommodate **12** solicitation

maker: **6** sartor, tailer

type: **4** zoot **6** monkey **9** paternity **10** pinstriped **11** class action

suitable: apt, due, fit, pat **4** able, fair, good, just, meet **5** right **6** comely, gainly, proper **7** a propos, seeming **8** adequate, apposite, becoming, coherent, eligible, feasible, idoneous, matching **9** competent, congruent, congruous, consonant, expedient **10** commodious, compatible, consistent, convenient, equivalent **11** appropriate **12** commensurate

render: **5** adapt **7** prepare

suitcase: bag 4 grip 6 valise 9 gladstone

suite: set 4 band 5 abode, group, music, staff, train 6 series 7 retinue 8 equipage 9 apartment, entourage 10 collection

member of: 7 attache

musical: See musical composition

suited: See suitable

suiting: 4 wool 5 serge 6 fabric 9 gabardine, gaberdine

suitor: 4 beau 5 lover, wooer 7 gallant 8 follower, litigant 10 petitioner

sulcate: 4 plow 6 fluted 7 grooved 8 furrowed

sulfate: 5 treat 7 convert, sulphur 9 brimstone 10 impregnate

kind: 4 alum 5 hepar, matte 6 barite, blende 7 ilesite, loweite

sulfur: 9 brimstone

substance containing: 5 hepar

sulfuric acid: 7 vitriol

sulk: 4 dort(Sc.), mope, pout 5 brood, frown, grump 6 glower, grouch

sulky: 4 cart, dull, weak 5 chuff, dorty, inert 6 gloomy, gocart, grouty, sullen 7 doggish, peevish 8 carriage, inactive 10 unyielding

sullage: mud 4 silt 5 filth 6 refuse, scoria, sewage 8 drainage 9 pollution 10 filthiness

sullen: sad 4 dour, dull, glum, grim, sour 5 alone, black, cross, felon, gruff, heavy, moody, pouty, stern, sulky, surly 6 crusty, dismal, dogged, gloomy, grouty, morose, silent, somber 7 baleful, boorish, crabbed, fretful, hostile, peevish, serious 8 churlish, lowering, petulant, solitary 9 obstinate, saturnine 10 depressing, ill-humored, ill-natured, refractory, unsociable 11 intractable, threatening 12 unpropitious

Sullivan's collaborator: 7 Gilbert

sully: See soil

sulphate: See sulfate, sulfur

sultan: 5 ruler 8 padishah 9 sovereign

decree: 5 irade

sultry: hot 5 close, fiery, humid, lurid 6 coarse, smutty, torrid 7 obscene, sensual 8 inflamed, stifling 10 oppressive, sweltering 13 uncomfortable

sum: add, end, tot 4 gist, host 5 count, gross, issue, total, whole 6 amount, degree, extent, height, number, result, summit 7 integer, numeral, problem, summary 8 addition, assembly, entirety, perorate, quantity 9 aggregate, calculate, epitomize, gathering, magnitude, substance, summarize, summation 11 epilogation 12 recapitulate

forfeited: 5 dedit

large: gob, pot

small: 4 drab 7 driblet, peanuts 8 pit-

tance 11 chickenfeed

subtracted: 9 deduction

unexpended: 7 savings

up: add 9 summarize 12 recapitulate

sumac: 4 rhus 8 shoemake 11 balinghasay

Sumatra: 6 island

animal: 4 balu, tanu 5 orang

ape: 5 orang 6 ourang 9 orangutan

city: 5 Achin, Jambi, Medan 6 Padang 8 Bonkulin 9 Bencoolen, Indrapoor, Palembang

country: 9 Indonesia

deer: 4 napu

fiber: 6 caloee

highest peak: 8 Kerintji

lake: 4 Toba

language: 4 Nias

measure: 4 paal

mountain: 7 Barisan

raft: 5 rakit

river: 4 Musi 5 Jambi, Rokan 9 Indragiri

wildcat: 4 balu

summarize: sum 5 recap 6 digest, review 7 abridge, shorten 8 abstract 9 epitomize

summary: sum 4 gist 5 brief, recap, short 6 digest, precis, resume, summit 7 concise, epitome, extract, general, medulla 8 abstract, argument, breviate, succinct, synopsis 9 condensed, inventory 10 compendium, run-through 11 abridgment 13 comprehension 14 recapitulation

summation: See sum

summer: ete(F.) 6 lintel 8 estivate

ailment: 8 heat rash

beverage: ade

pass: 8 estivate

pert. to: 7 estival

summerhouse: 5 kiosk 6 alcove, casino, gazebo 7 cottage, pagoda 8 pavilion 9 belvedere

summery: 4 warm 5 light 7 estival 8 delicate

summing up: See sum

summit (see also **mountain, peak**): bow, cap, tip, top, van 4 acme, apex, knap, roof 5 crest, crown, ridge 6 climax, comble, height, vertex, zenith 8 pinnacle 9 fastigium(L.) 10 conference 11 culmination

pert. to: 6 apical

summon: ban, bid 4 call, page 5 charm, evoke, rally, rouse 6 accite, appeal, arouse, compel, demand, gather, muster 7 call for, collect, command, convoke, provoke

to court: 4 cite, sist

summoner: 6 beadle 9 apparitor

summons: 4 call, writ 6 venire 7 command, warning 8 citation, subpoena 9 challenge 12 notification

sump: mud, pit 4 dirt, pool, pump, tank, well 5 drain, march, swamp 6 puddle, slough 7 cistern, depress 8 cesspool 9 reservoir 10 depression, excavation, receptacle

sumpter: 4 pack 6 burden 7 baggage

sumptuous: 4 rich 5 grand 6 costly, lavish, superb 8 splendid 9 expensive, grandiose, luxurious 11 magnificent

sun: orb, sol 4 bask, star 5 Titan 6 bleach 7 daystar, Phoebus 8 luminary 9 Harmachis

crossing equator: 7 equinox

god: Tem, Utu 4 Baal, Lleu, Llew, Utug 6 Apollo, Helios 7 Chepera, Khepara, Shamash, Sokaris 8 Hyperion

luminous envelope of: 6 corona

measuring device: 13 pyrheliometer

mock: 9 acronical

near: 6 heliac

outer layer: 6 corona

part: 6 corona

path: 8 ecliptic

pert. to: 5 solar 6 heliac

protective devices: 7 parasol 8 blindage, havelock

satellite: 6 planet

worshiper: 5 Parsi 6 Parsee 10 heliolater

sun disk: 4 Aten

sun dog: 4 halo 7 rainbow 9 parhelion

Sun King: 8 Louis XIV

sun room: 7 solaria(pl.) 8 solarium

sun watch: 7 sundial 9 timepiece

sunburn: tan 8 heliosis

sunburst: 6 brooch, ensign

sun-clock: 7 sundial

Sunda Island: 4 Bali, Java, Nias 6 Borneo, Lombok 7 Celebes, Sumatra

Sunday: *following Easter:* Low 9 Quasimodo

mid-Lent: 7 Laetare

pert. to: 9 dominical

special: 4 Palm 6 Easter

sunder: cut, rip 4 part, rend, rive 5 break, sever, split 6 divide 7 disjoin, disrupt, divorce 8 demolish, dissever, disunite, separate

sundial part: 6 gnomon

sundown: See sunset

sundowner: 5 drink, tramp 7 captain 8 nightcap

sundry: 4 many 5 apart 6 divers 7 asunder, diverse, several, various 8 distinct, frequent, manifold, numerous, separate, sundered 9 different, disunited 10 all sorts of, respective, separately 12 multifarious 13 miscellaneous

companion of: all

sunfall: See sunset

sunfish: 4 opah 5 bream 8 bluegill, pondfish

genus of: 4 mola

sunflower: 4 marigold, rockrose 10 balsamroot, heliotrope

maid turned into: 6 Clytie

Sunflower State: 6 Kansas

sunk (see also **sink**): pad 4 bank, seat, turf 5 couch 6 abject, hollow 8 absorbed, downcast, overcome 9 depressed

sunken: 6 hollow 9 depressed

fence: 4 ha-ha

sunless: 4 dark

sunny: gay 4 fair, warm 5 clear, happy, merry 6 bright, golden, sunlit 8 cheerful, luminous 9 sparkling, vivacious

sunrise: 4 dawn, east

song: 6 aubade

sunset: e'en, eve 4 dusk 7 evening 8 twilight

pert. to: 9 acronical

reflection: 9 alpenglow

Sunset State: 6 Oregon 7 Arizona

sunshade: 5 visor 6 awning 7 parasol 8 umbrella

sunshine: 5 cheer, light 6 warmth 8 daylight, sunburst 9 happiness, sunniness 11 fairweather 12 cheerfulness

Sunshine State: 9 New Mexico 11 South Dakota

sunspot: 4 flaw 6 facula 7 blemish, freckle

sunstroke: 8 siriasis 9 calenture

sunwise: 6 deasil 9 clockwise

Suomi: 7 Finland

sup: eat, sip 4 dine 5 drink, feast, taste 6 tipple 7 swallow 8 mouthful, quantity, spoonful

supawn: 4 mush 12 hasty pudding

super: 5 actor, watch 6 square 7 janitor 9 excellent, marvelous, first-rate

superable: 12 surmountable

superabundance: 5 flood 6 excess, plenty 8 plethora, quantity 10 exuberance 11 diffuseness, superfluity

superabundant: 4 rank 6 lavish 9 redundant 11 overflowing

superannuate: 6 retire 7 outdate, outlast 8 obsolete 9 antiquate, out-of-date 10 disqualify

superb: 4 fine, rich 5 grand, noble, proud 6 lordly 7 elegant, haughty, stately 8 enormous, majestic, opulent, splendid, very best 9 excellent, grandiose, luxurious, sumptuous 13 extraordinary

superbity: 5 pride 9 arrogance 11 haughtiness

supercilious: 5 lofty, proud 6 uppish 7 haughty 8 arrogant, cavalier, snobbish 9 arbitrary 10 disdainful 11 overbearing 12 contemptuous 13 hypercritical

superficial: 4 glib 5 hasty 6 casual, flimsy, slight 7 cursory, outward, shallow, surface 8 apparent, external

superfine: 4 luxe, nice, rich 5 extra, plush, prime 6 choice, subtle, superb 8 delicate, overnice 9 excellent, grandiose

superfluity: 6 excess, luxury 9 abundance, profusion 11 prodigality

superfluous: 4 over 5 spare 6 de trop(F.) 7 surplus, useless 8 abnormal, needless, wasteful 9 excessive, redundant, worthless 10 gratuitous, inordinate 11 extravagant, unnecessary 12 nonessential 13 superabundant

superhuman: 6 divine 7 demigod, uncanny 9 herculean 13 extraordinary

superhumeral: 5 amice, stole

superimpose: 7 overlay

superintend: 4 boss 5 guide 6 direct, manage 7 conduct, control, inspect, oversee 8 engineer 9 supervise 10 administer

superintendence: 4 care 8 guidance 9 authority, oversight 14 responsibility

superintendent: 4 boss 5 super 6 bishop 7 captain, curator, manager 8 director, minister, overseer 9 inspector 10 supervisor 11 chamberlain

superior: 4 fine, head, lord, over, peer 5 above, chief, eigne, extra, liege, upper 6 better, choice, higher, senior 7 exalted, greater, haughty, palmary, prelate, ranking 8 alderman, arrogant, assuming, dominant, elevated, masterly 9 ascendant, ascendent, excellent, marvelous, paramount, spiritual 10 preeminent, surpassing 11 predominant 12 supercilious, supernatural 13 comprehensive

superiority: 4 gree(Sc.) 8 priority 9 advantage, meliority, seniority 13 preponderance

position of: 10 domination

superlative: 4 acme, best, peak 6 utmost 7 supreme 8 peerless 9 excessive, consummate 11 exaggerated

absolute: 7 elative

Superman's friend: 8 Lois Lane

supernal: 4 high 6 divine 8 ethereal, heavenly 9 celestial

supernatural: 5 magic 6 divine, occult 7 ghostly 9 marvelous 10 miraculous, superhuman 13 preternatural

supernatural being: elf, god 4 atua 5 angel, deity, demon, fairy, gnome, nymph, troll 6 cherub, seraph, spirit 7 banshee, goddess 10 leprechaun

Moslem: 4 jinn

Persian: 4 peri

supernatural happening: 6 vision 7 miracle

supernumerary: 5 actor, extra

superpower: USA 4 USSR

superscribe: 5 write 6 direct 7 address, engrave

superscription: 5 title 7 caption 9 direction 11 description, inscription

supersede: 7 replace, succeed 8 displace, override, set aside, supplant

supersonic noise: 4 boom

superstition: 5 freet, freit, magic 6 fetish, voodoo 8 idolatry

supervene: 5 ensue 6 follow, happen 7 succeed

supervise: 4 boss, edit, read, scan 5 check 6 direct, govern, manage, peruse, revise 7 conduct, correct, inspect, oversee 11 superintend

supervisor: 7 foreman 8 alytarch(G.) 9 spectator 10 roadmaster

supine: 5 inert, prone 6 abject, drowsy 7 languid, leaning, passive, sloping, unalert 8 inactive, inclined, indolent, listless, sluggish 9 apathetic, negligent, reclining 10 submissive 11 inattentive, indifferent

supper: tea 4 meal

supplant: 4 oust 5 usurp 6 follow, remove, uproot 7 replace, succeed 8 displace 9 extirpate, supersede, undermine

supple: sly 4 bain, oily 5 agile, lithe 6 limber, lissom, nimble, pliant, swanky 7 cunning, elastic, fawning, lissome, plastic, pliable, servile 8 flexible, yielding 9 adaptable, compliant, resilient, versatile 10 obsequious, responsive 11 complaisant

supplement: add 8 addendum, addition, appendix 9 accessory 10 complement 13 reinforcement

supplemental: 7 special 12 adscititious 13 succenturiate

suppliant: 5 asker 6 beggar, suitor 10 beseeching, entreating, petitioner

supplicate: beg, sue 4 pray 5 crave, plead 6 appeal, invoke, obtest 7 beseech, conjure, entreat, implore, request, solicit 8 petition 9 importune, obsecrate

supplication: 6 litany, prayer 8 rogative

supply: aid, fit 4 feed, fill, fund, give, help, load 5 cache, cater, equip, hoard, relay, stock, store, yield 6 afford, employ, foison, purvey, relief, succor 7 fraught, furnish, granary, nourish, plenish, provide, replace, reserve, satisfy 8 minister, ordnance, turn over 9 profusion, provision, reinforce, replenish, reservoir, temporary 10 administer, assistance, compensate, contribute 14 accumulation

support: aid, arm, guy, leg, peg, rib 4 back, base, beam, bear, bibb, fend, help, keep, limb, pier, prop, stay 5 boost, brace, carry, cheer, cleat, easel, favor, found, hinge, shore, sling, staff, strut, truss 6 anchor, assent, behalf, better, defend, endure, lintel, living, pillar, second, shield, splint, spring, suffer, tripod, trivet, uphold, upkeep, verify **7** bolster, cherish, comfort, confirm, console, endorse, espouse, fulcrum, nourish, nurture, protect, provide, reserve, shore up, subsidy, sustain, trestle **8** advocate, approval, baluster, befriend, evidence, maintain, pedestal, sanction, tolerate, underlie **9** adminicle, encourage, financing, reinforce, stanchion, vindicate **10** assistance, foundation, strengthen **11** corroborate, countenance **12** alimentation, substantiate

for statue: **5** socle **8** pedestal

one-legged: **6** unipod

slab: **4** tray **6** planch

supporter: 4 ally, knee **5** brace **6** bearer, patron, rooter **7** abetter, abettor, booster, founder **8** adherent, advocate, asserter, exponent, follower, henchman, partisan **9** auxiliary, suspender

suppose: 4 deem, trow, ween **5** allow, imply, judge, opine, think **6** assume, expect, repute, theory **7** believe, imagine, incline, opinion, presume, suspect **8** conceive, conclude, consider, obligate, supposal **9** apprehend, intention **10** conjecture, presuppose, substitute, understand **11** expectation, supposition

supposed: 7 alleged, assumed

supposition: 4 idea **6** notion, theory **7** forgery, surmise **9** postulate **10** alteration, assumption, conjecture, estimation, hypothesis **11** expectation, implication, proposition, uncertainty

supposititious: 7 assumed, feigned **8** fabulous, putative, spurious, supposed **9** imaginary, pretended **10** artificial, chimerical, fictitious **11** counterfeit **12** hypothetical, illegitimate

suppress: 4 hide, keep, kill, stop **5** check, choke, crush, elide, quash, quell, stunt **6** arrest, bridle, censor, harass, hush up, ravish, retard, stifle, subdue **7** abolish, compose, conceal, destroy, exclude, oppress, prevent, refrain, repress, silence, smother, squelch **8** compress, prohibit, restrain, withhold **9** interdict, overpower, overthrow **10** dissolving, extinguish

suprarenal: 7 adrenal

supremacy: 4 sway **5** power **7** control, mastery **8** dominion **9** authority, autocracy, dominance, influence **10** ascendancy, domination **11** sovereignty **12** predominance **13** preponderance

supreme: 4 best, last **5** alone, chief, final **6** superb, utmost **7** crucial, highest, maximum **8** foremost, greatest, loftiest, peerless, ultimate **9** excellent, paramount **10** preeminent

supreme being: God **5** Allah, monad **7** creator, Jehovah

surcease: end **4** rest, stay, stop **5** defer, delay **6** desist, relief **7** refrain, respite, suspend **8** postpone **9** cessation

surcharge: tax **4** cost, fill, load **6** burden, impost **7** surfeit **8** overload, surprint **9** overcrowd, overprint, overstock **10** impregnate, overburden, overcharge

surcingle: 4 band, belt **6** girdle **8** cincture

surcoat: 5 jupon **6** cyclas **7** garment

surd: 4 deaf **7** radical **9** insensate, voiceless **10** irrational

sure: 4 fast, firm, safe, true **5** siker(Sc.) **6** indeed, secure, sicker(Sc.), stable, steady, strong **7** assured, certain **8** enduring, positive, reliable, unerring **9** authentic, betrothed, confident, convinced, steadfast, undoubted, unfailing **10** dependable, infallible, inevitable **11** indubitable, trustworthy, unfaltering **12** indisputable **13** incontestable **14** unquestionable

surely: 6 atweel(Sc.), really

sureness: 9 certitude

sure thing: 6 shoo-in, winner **9** certainty

surety: 4 bail **6** backer, pledge **7** engager, sponsor **8** bailsman, bondsman, security **9** assurance, certainty, guarantee, guarantor **10** confidence

post: **4** bond

surf: 4 foam, wave **5** spray, swell **7** breaker

sound of: **4** rote

surface: top **4** area, face, pave, side, skin **5** facet, plane **6** come up, facing, finish, patina **7** outside **8** boundary, exterior **11** superficial

flat: **4** area **5** plane, sheet **7** lateral

geometrical: **5** nappe **6** sphere, toroid

inclined: **4** cant, ramp **7** descent

mellowed: **6** patina

pert. to: **6** facial

rounded: **9** concavity, convexity

toward: **5** ectad

surfacing: 6 gravel **7** asphalt, macadam **8** emerging

surfeit: 4 cloy, feed, glut, sate **6** excess, nausea, supply **7** disgust, replete, satiate, satiety, satisfy **9** disorder **10** satiation **10** discomfort **11** extravagant, overindulge, superfluity **13** overabundance **14** overindulgence

surge: 4 pour, rise, rush, tide, wave **5** gurge, swell **6** billow **7** estuate, rolling **8** sweeping, swelling

surgeon: 8 sawbones **10** chirurgeon

surgeonfish: 4 tang

surgery: 9 operation, resection

appliance: **5** brace **6** crutch, splint

compress: **5** stupe

instrument: **5** fleam, lance, probe, scala **6** bilabe, gorget, lancet, splint, stylet, trapan, trepan, trocar, vectis **7** forceps, levator, ligator, rongeur, scalpel, trilabe,

trochar **8** bistoury, ecraseur, trephine, tweezers **9** goosebill, heart tenaculum, vulsellum **10** abaptiston, adaptistum, terebellum, tourniquet
perform: **7** operate
plug: **6** tampon
puncture: **8** centesis
roller: **6** fascia **7** fasciae
stitch: **5** seton **6** suture
thread: **6** catgut
Surinam, Suriname: *capital:* **10** Paramaribo
formerly: **11** Dutch Guiana
hut: **5** benab
language: **5** Dutch
measure: **7** ketting
monetary unit: **7** guilder
mountain: **10** Tumuc-Humac
river: **5** Itany **6** Maroni **8** Suriname **9** Corantijn
toad: **4** pipa **5** pipal
tribe: **4** Boni **5** Djuka
surly: **4** glum, grum, rude **5** bluff, chuff, cross, gruff, gurly **6** abrupt, grumpy, morose, sullen **7** boorish, crabbed, haughty, uncivil, waspish **8** arrogant, churlish, growling **9** fractious **10** illnatured **11** intractable
surmise: **4** deem **5** guess, infer, trace **6** charge **7** believe, imagine, presume, suppose **9** suspicion **10** allegation, assumption, conclusion, conjecture **11** supposition
surmount: top **4** pass, rise, tide **5** clear, climb, crown, excel, outdo, total **6** ascend, exceed, hurdle, subdue **7** conquer, surpass **8** overcome **9** negotiate, transcend
surmountable: **8** possible **9** superable
surmounting: **4** atop
surname: **6** byname **7** agnomen **8** cognomen **11** appellation
surpass: cap, cob, top **4** beat, flog **5** amend, excel, outdo **6** better, exceed, outvie **7** eclipse, outrank, outsoar **8** outclass, outreach, outstrip, surmount **9** transcend
surpassing: **4** fine **6** banner **7** supreme **9** excellent **10** inimitable, preeminent
surplice: **5** cotta, ephod **8** vestment
surplus: **4** over, rest **5** extra **6** excess **7** backlog, reserve **8** overplus **9** remainder **10** redundancy
surprise: awe, cap **5** alarm, amaze, catch, seize, shock **6** ambush, dazzle, detect, strike, waylay, wonder **7** astound, capture, gloppen, perplex, startle, uncover **8** astonish, bewilder, confound, dumfound, overcome **9** amazement, overwhelm **11** flabbergast
surprised: **5** agape
surprising: **6** sudden **9** startling **10** unex-

pected **13** extraordinary
surrender: **4** cede, fall, give **5** remit, yield **6** remise, resign, tender, waiver **7** abandon, cession, concede, deliver, forsake **8** dedition, remittal **9** rendition **10** abdication, capitulate, compromise, relinquish **11** divestiture **12** cancellation
surreptitious: sly **6** covert, secret **7** bootleg **8** sneaking, stealthy **9** underhand **11** clandestine
surrey: **8** carriage
surrogate: **6** deputy **8** delegate, resource **9** subrogate **10** substitute
surround: bar, hem **4** belt, fold, gird, ring, span, wrap **5** beset, embay, flood, hedge **6** border, circle, corral, encase, enring, invest **7** besiege, embosom, enclose, environ, imbosom **8** encircle, envelope, inundate, overflow **9** beleaguer, encompass **12** circumscribe **14** circumnavigate
with water: **4** isle **6** enisle
surrounded: **4** amid **5** among **6** amidst **7** between, bounded
surrounding: **5** about, midst **7** context, setting **8** ambiance **9** entourage **11** environment **12** circumjacent, circumstance
surtax: **4** agio, levy **5** extra
surtout: **4** coat, hood **7** garment **8** overcoat
survey: **4** pool, scan, view **5** study **6** regard, review, search **7** examine, history, inspect, oversee **8** consider, estimate, traverse **9** delineate, determine, supervise, treatment **10** compendium, exposition, scrutinize **11** description, examination, reconnoiter, superintend **13** triangulation **14** reconnaissance
surveyor: **6** gauger **9** arpenteur, inspector **14** superintendent
helper: **6** rodman **7** lineman, poleman **8** chainman
instrument: **11** stratameter
nail: **4** spad
tool: **6** alidad **7** alidade, transit **10** theodolite **12** perambulator
survival: **5** relic
survive: **6** endure **7** outlast, outlive **11** pull through
Susanna: *accusers:* **6** elders
husband: **7** Joachim
susceptible: **4** easy, open **6** liable **7** exposed, subject **8** allergic, sensible, sentient **9** receptive, sensitive **10** responsive, vulnerable **11** softhearted, unresistant **13** tenderhearted **14** impressionable
to error: **8** fallible
susceptibility: **5** sense **7** emotion, feeling **11** sensibility **13** affectibility
suscitate: **5** rouse **6** excite **7** animate,

provoke 9 stimulate

suslik: 5 sisel 8 squirrel 11 spermophile

suspect: 4 fear 5 doubt, guess 7 accused, believe, dubious, imagine, inkling, presume, suppose, surmise 8 conceive, distrust, doubtful, mistrust 9 discredit 10 disbelieve, intimation, suspicious, understand 12 apprehension

suspend: bar 4 hang, hold, oust, stop 5 cease, debar, defer, demur, expel 6 dangle, recess, repeal 7 adjourn, exclude 8 intermit, postpone, withhold 9 pretermit

suspended: 4 hung 6 latent 7 abeyant, pendent, pensile 8 dangling, inactive 11 inoperative

suspender: 5 brace 6 gallus, garter, hanger 9 supporter

suspense: 5 worry 6 unease 7 anxiety 8 cautious, hesitant, withheld 11 tenterhooks, uncertainty 12 apprehension 14 indecisiveness

in: 7 pending

suspension: 4 stop 5 delay, pause 7 failure 8 abeyance, buoyancy, stoppage 9 remission 11 withholding 12 intermission, interruption

in air: 5 vapor

of court sentence: 9 probation

of hostilities: 5 truce 9 armistice, ceasefire

suspicion: 4 hint 5 doubt, hunch, touch, trace 7 askance, caution, inkling 8 distrust, jealousy, mistrust 9 misgiving 10 diffidence, intimation, suggestion, uneasiness 11 expectation, uncertainty 12 apprehension

suspicious: 4 wary 5 fishy, leery 8 doubtful 9 equivocal 11 mistrustful 12 questionable

suspire: 4 sigh 7 long for, respire

sustain: 4 abet, back, bear, buoy, dure, feed, help, prop 5 abide, carry 6 assist, endure, foster, second, succor, suffer, supply, uphold 7 comfort, confirm, console, contain, nourish, prolong, provide, stand by, support, undergo 8 befriend, continue, maintain 9 encourage, withstand 10 experience, strengthen 11 corroborate

sustenance: 4 food, meat 5 bread, viand 6 living, upkeep 7 aliment, support 9 nutrition, provision 10 exhibition 11 maintenance, nourishment, subsistence 12 alimentation

susurrus: 7 murmur, rustle 9 whisper

sutler: 7 provant 9 vivandier 10 vivandiere

suttee: 7 suicide 10 immolation

suture: 4 line, seam 6 stitch 9 arthrosis 12 articulation

suzerain: 8 overlord 9 paramount, sovereign 10 feudal lord

svelte: 4 slim 5 lithe 6 lissome 7 lissome, slender 8 graceful

swab: gob, mop 4 lout, wash, wipe 5 brush, clean 7 epaulet, officer, plunger 8 medicate

swack: 4 blow, cuff 5 whack 6 nimble, pliant, supple

swaddle: 4 beat, bind, wrap 6 clothe, cudgel, swathe 7 bandage 8 restrict, surround

swag: pit, sag, tip 4 list, loot, sway 5 booty, lurch, money, spoil, swing, tramp 6 bundle, hollow 7 plunder 10 decoration

swagger: 4 brag, lord 5 bluff, boast, bully, lurch, strut, swank, swell 6 cuttle, hector, prance 7 bluster, gauster, panache, quarrel, roister, ruffler, stagger, stylish 8 vagabond 11 braggadocio, fanfaronade 16 ultrafashionable

swaggering: 6 gascon 7 huffcap

swagman: 5 fence 7 bushman 9 sundowner

bundle: 5 bluey

swain: boy 5 lover, youth 6 escort, rustic, suitor 7 admirer, gallant, peasant, servant 8 shepherd 9 attendant, boyfriend 10 countryman

swale: fen 4 moor, sway 5 marsh, shade, slash, sweal, swing, swirl 6 hollow, meadow, valley 8 coolness 10 depression

swallow: eat, sip, sup 4 bear, bolt, down, gaup, gawp, glut, gulp, take, tern 5 drink, merge, quilt, swift 6 absorb, accept, englut, engulf, go-down, gullet, imbibe, ingest, martin, mumble, recant, resorb, throat, vanish 7 believe, consume, engorge, retract 8 aperture, suppress, tolerate, withdraw 9 esophagus

swamp: bog, fen 4 mire, moor, muck, ruin, sink, slew, sloo, slue, thin, wham 5 clear, empty, flood, marsh 6 deluge, engulf, hollow, morass, slough 7 cienaga, pocosin, pocoson, slender 8 overcome, quagmire, submerge 9 marshland, overwhelm 10 Everglades

gas: 6 miasma 7 methane

grass: 5 sedge

pert. to: 7 miasmal, paludal

swan: cob, elk, pen 5 swear 6 cygnet 7 declare, whooper 8 surprise 9 trumpeter

female: pen

genus: 6 cygnus

male: cob

young: 6 cygnet

Swan river: 4 Avon

swank: 5 showy 6 active, lively 7 stylish, swagger 12 ostentatious

swanky: 4 chic 9 grandiose

Swann's Way author: 6 Proust

swap: 5 trade 6 barter, dicker 8 exchange

sward: sod 4 lawn, skin, turf 8 covering

swarm: 4 bike(Sc.), byke(Sc.), host, move, shin, swim, teem 5 climb, cloud, crowd, flock, group, horde, mount 6 abound, rabble, throng 7 migrate 8 assemble 9 multitude 10 congregate

swarming: 6 aswarm 10 emigration

swarthy: dun 4 dark 5 dusky 8 blackish

swash: bar 4 blow, move 5 noise, slosh, sound 6 splash, strike 7 bluster, channel, dashing, swagger 9 splashing

swashbuckler: 5 bravo 6 gascon 7 ruffian, slasher, soldier 9 combatant, daredevil, swaggerer

swashy: 4 weak 6 watery 7 insipid

swastika: 5 cross 6 fylfot 7 insignia 9 Gammadion

swat: bat, hit 4 blow 5 clout 6 strike

swatch: 5 swash 6 sample 7 channel

swath, swathe: row 4 band, bind, crop, wrap 5 strip, sweep 6 clothe, stroke 7 enfold, swaddle, windrow

sway: 4 bend, bias, lean, move, reel, rock, rule, veer 5 force, grace, guide, lurch, power, shake, swing, waver, wield 6 direct, divert, govern, swerve, totter, waddle 7 affect, command, control, deflect, shoggie 8 dominion, rotation 9 dominance, influence, oscillate, vacillate 10 ascendancy, ascendency 11 fluctuation, inclination, sovereignty 13 lithesomeness

Swaziland: *capital:* 7 Mbabane
  language: 7 Siswati
  monetary unit: 9 lilangeni
  people: 4 Zulu 5 Bantu
  river: 5 Usutu 6 Komati, Umbuluzi
  town: 7 Manzini, Mbabane

swear: vow 4 bind 5 curse, utter 6 adjure, affirm, assert, pledge, threat 7 declare, promise, testify 8 execrate 9 blaspheme 10 administer, asseverate, vituperate
  falsely: 7 perjure, slander
  to secrecy: 4 tile

sweat: dry 4 emit, ooze, work 5 bleed, exude, hoist, labor, sudor(L.) 6 drudge, fleece 7 excrete, extract, ferment, putrefy, soldier 8 condense, overwork, perspire, transude

sweater: 5 shell 8 cardigan, pullover, slipover

Sweden: *artist:* 4 Zorn
  botanist: 5 Fries 9 Bromelius
  bread: 10 knackebrod
  capital: 9 Stockholm
  city and town: 5 Boras, Edane, Falun, Gavle, Malmo, Ystad 6 Orebro, Upsala 7 Uppsala 8 Goteborg, Nykoping 9 Falkoping, Jonkoping, 10 Eskilstuna, Gothenburg, Norrkoping 11 Halsingborg
  clover: 6 alsike

  coin: ore 5 krona 8 skilling
  county: lan
  dance: 6 polska
  division: amt 4 Laen 5 Skane 8 Gotaland, Gothland, Norrland, Swealand
  dynasty: 4 Vasa
  explorer: 5 Hedin
  farm: 4 torp
  gulf: 7 Bothnia
  highest peak: 10 Kebnekaise
  island: 5 Oland 8 Gotaland
  king: 4 Eric, Wasa 5 Oscar 10 Bernadotte
  lake: 5 Asnen, Malar, Wener 6 Siljan, Vanern, Vatter, Wennen, Wetter 7 Hielmar, Malaren, Vattern
  manual training: 5 sloyd
  match: 12 taendstikker
  measure: aln, fot, mil, ref, tum 4 famn, last, stop 5 carat, foder, kanna, kappe, linje, nymil, spann, stang, tunna 6 fathom, jumfru 7 kollast, oxhuvud, tunland 8 fjarding, kappland, koltunna, tunnland
  monetary unit: 5 krona
  motion-picture director: 7 Bergman
  mountain: 6 Kjolen Sarjek
  noble title: 4 graf
  parliament: 7 Riksdag
  philologist: 5 Ihre
  physicist: 5 Dalen
  province: 6 Kalmar, Orebro, Upsala 7 Gotland, Halland 8 Blekinge, Elfsborg, Jamtland, Malmohus, Wermland
  river: Dal 4 Gota, Klar, Umea 5 Indal, Kalix, Lulea, Pitea, Ranea, Torne 6 Lainio, Ljusne, Tornea, Windel 7 Ljungan
  soprano: 7 Nilsson 9 Jenny Lind
  sour milk: 8 tatmjolk
  state religion: 8 Lutheran
  tribe: 6 Geatas
  weight: ass, lod, ort 4 last, mark, pund, sten, untz 5 carat 6 nylast 7 centner, lispund 8 lispound, skalpund, skeppund 9 ship pound
  writer: 6 Carlen 7 Bellman 8 Lagerlof 10 Strindberg

Swedish Nightingale: 4 Lind 5 Jenny

sweep: fly, oar 4 line 5 besom, broom, brush, clean, clear, drive, range, scope, scour, strip, surge, swath 6 extend, remove 7 contour, stretch 8 traverse

sweeping: 6 all-out 8 complete 9 extensive, out-and-out 13 comprehensive, thoroughgoing

sweepings: 6 fulyie(Sc.), fulzie(Sc.), refuse

sweet: 4 dear, fair 5 bonny, candy, dolce, douce(F.) 6 fresh, soave 6 dulcet, gentle, lovely, pretty, sugary, syrupy 7 beloved, caramel, darling, honeyed, musical, winning 8 aromatic, fetching, fragrant, pleasant, pleasing, preserve 9 agreeable, ambrosial, melodious 10 attractive, confection, harmonious 11 good-natured, mellisonant

sweet flag: 4 arum 7 calamus

sweet potato: yam 6 batata 7 ocarina

sweetbread: 4 meat, veal 9 ris de veau

sweetbrier: 4 rose 9 eglantine

sweeten: 4 mull 5 sugar 6 pacify, purify, refine, soften, solace 7 appease, cleanse, freshen, mollify, perfume, relieve 9 disinfect, sugarcoat 10 edulcorate

sweetfish: ayu

sweetheart: gra 4 agra, beau, dear, doll, doxy, gill, girl, jill, lass, love 5 bully, court, flame, leman, lover, 6 adorer, fellow, orpine 8 paramour, truelove 9 good thing

sweetmeat: 4 cake 5 candy, goody 6 comfit, dragee, pastry 7 caramel, dessert 8 confetti, conserve, hardbake, marzipan, preserve 9 marchpane, sugarplum 10 confection

sweetsop: 4 ates

swell: nob, sea 4 bell, bulb, bulk, grow, huff, lord, rise, surf, toff, wave 5 bloat, bulge, grand, surge 6 billow, dilate, expand, extend, roller, tiptop, tumefy 7 augment, distend, enlarge, inflate, seagate, stylish 8 increase 9 elevation, excellent, first-rate, intumesce, marvelous, wonderful 10 prominence, thickening 11 fashionable 12 protuberance 16 ultrafashionable

swelled head: 6 egoist 7 conceit

swellfish: 6 puffer 8 puff-fish

swelling: sty 4 bleb, bubo, node 5 blain, botch, bouge, bunch, edema, tumor 6 aswell, gather, growth 7 gibbous, turgent 8 windgall 9 gibbosity 10 rhetorical

on plants: 4 gall

pert. to: 5 nodal 9 edematose, edematous

swelter: 4 burn, fret, heat, rush 5 exude, faint, roast, sweat 6 wallow, welter 8 perspire

swerve: bow 4 skew, turn, veer 5 stray, yield 6 totter 7 deflect, deviate, digress

swift: 4 cran(Sc.), fast, reel 5 alert, fleet, hasty, quick, rapid, ready 6 lizard, prompt, speedy, winged

Swift: 8 Jonathan, satirist

brute: 5 Yahoo

flying island: 6 Laputa

hero: 8 Gulliver

lady friend: 6 Stella

pen name: 11 Bickerstaff

swig: 4 gulp, rock, sway 5 booze, draft, drink, hoist, snort, swash 6 guzzle, imbibe, tackle

swile: 4 seal

swill: 4 fill, wash 5 drink, flood, rinse, swash, waste 6 basket, drench, guzzle, refuse 7 garbage, hogwash

swim: 4 reel, spin 5 float, swoon, whirl 9 dizziness 13 forgetfulness 15 unconsciousness

pert. to: 8 natatory

swimmer: 7 natator

of the English Channel: 6 Ederle

of the Hellespont: 7 Leander

of Tiber river: 7 Cloelia

swimming: 6 filled, naiant, natant 7 flooded, vertigo 9 dizziness

swimming pool: 4 tank 10 natatorium

swimming stroke: 4 back, side 5 crawl 6 breast 7 trudgen 9 butterfly, dogpaddle

swindle: con, gyp 4 bilk, dupe, fake, mace, rook 5 bunco, bunko, cheat, foist, fraud, spoof, trick 6 diddle, trepan 7 defraud 8 flimflam 10 overcharge

swindler: fob 5 biter, cheat, crook, knave, rogue, shark 6 chiaus, chouse, shaver 7 sharper 8 blackleg

swine: hog, pig, sow 4 boar 7 peccary

breed of: 8 Cheshire, Tamworth 9 Berkshire, Hampshire, Yorkshire 11 Duroc-Jersey, Poland China 12 Chester White

feeding of: 7 pannage 8 slopping

female: sow 4 gilt

fever: 6 rouget 7 cholera

flesh: 4 pork

litter of: 6 farrow

male: 4 boar

pert. to: 7 porcine

young: pig 5 shoat 6 piglet

swing: 4 beat, bent, blow, hang, hurl, lilt, slew, slue, sway, turn, whip 5 fling, lurch, power, shake, throw, trend, waver 6 dangle, handle, manage, rhythm, stroke, totter 7 flutter, shoggie(Sc.), suspend, trapeze, vibrate 8 brandish, undulate 9 fluctuate, oscillate

swing around: jib 4 slue

swinger: 8 party man 9 bon vivant

swinish: 5 gross 6 coarse 7 beastly, boarish, brutish, piggish, sensual

swipe: cut, hit 4 blow, glom 5 draft, drink, lever, steal, swape, sweep 6 pilfer, snatch, strike

swirl: ess 4 curl, eddy, purl 5 curve, gurge, twist, whirl, whorl

swish: 4 cane, flog, hiss, lash, whip 5 birch, smart, sound 6 rustle, strike 9 exclusive

Swiss: See Switzerland

switch: gad, rod, wag 4 beat, flog, lash, turn, twig, wand, whip 5 shift, shunt, swing 6 change, divert, strike 7 scourge 8 exchange, transfer 10 disconnect, substitute

switchboard: 5 panel

switchman: 7 shunter

Switzerland: 6 Suisse(F.) 7 Schweiz(G.)
  8 Helvetia
  archer: 11 William Tell
  ax: 6 piolet
  bay: 3 Uri
  canton: Uri, Zug 4 Bern, Genf, Vaud 5
    Basel, Basle, Waadt 6 Aargau, Geneva,
    Geneve, Glaris, Glarus, Luzern, St.
    Gall, Schwyz, Tessin, Ticino, Valais,
    Wallis, Zurich 7 Grisons, Lucerne,
    Schwytz, Berne 6 Geneva, Thurgau 8 Freiberg
    9 Appenzell, Neuchatel, Neuenberg, So-
    lothurn 10 Graubunden 11 Sankt Gal-
    len, Schaffhouse, Unterwalden 12
    Schaffhausen
  capital: 4 Bern
  card game: 4 jass
  cheese: 7 Gruyere, sapsago 9 schweizer
    10 Emmentaler 13 schweizer-kase
  city: 4 Bale, Chur, Genf, Sion 5 Basel,
    Basle, Berne 6 Geneva, Schwyz, Zurich
    7 Fyzabad, Locarno, Lucerne 8 Faiz-
    abad, Lausanne, Montreux, St. Gallen
    9 Constance, Neuchatel 10 Farukha-
    bad, Winterthur
  coin: 5 franc, rappe 6 rappen 7 angster,
    centime, duplone 8 blaffert
  commune: Zug 4 Biel, Wald 5 Aarau,
    Morat
  composer: 4 Raff 5 Bloch 6 Martin
  district: 6 canton
  food: 12 bernerplatte
  herdsman: 4 senn
  hero: 11 Wilhelm Tell
  highest peak: 9 Monte Rosa 12 Dufour-
    spitze
  lake: Uri, Zug 4 Joux, Thon 5 Leman 6
    Bienne, Brienz, Geneva, Lugano, Sar-
    nen, Wallen, Zurich 7 Lucerne, Lun-
    gern 8 Viervald 9 Constance, Neucha-
    tel, Sarnersee, Thunersee 10 Stattersee
    11 Brienzersee
  language: 5 Ladin 6 French, German 7
    Italian, Romansh 8 Romansch, Rou-
    mansh 14 Switzerdeutsch
  legislature: 8 grossrat 9 grosserat, gross-
    rath
  measure: imi, pot 4 aune, elle, fuss, immi,
    muid, pied, saum, zoll 5 lieue, ligne,
    linie, maass, moule, pouce, schuh, staab,
    toise 6 perche, setier, strich 7 juchart,
    klafter, viertel 9 quarteron 11 holz-
    klafter
  monetary unit: 5 franc
  mountain: 4 Alps, Jura, Rigi, Rosa 5
    Blanc, Cenis, Genis 7 Pilatus 8 Jung-
    frau 10 Matterhorn, St. Gotthard 11
    Burgenstock
  mountain pass: 5 Furka 7 Grimsel, Sim-
    plon 8 Gotthard, Lotschen 13 Saint
    Gotthard
  officer: 5 amman

  painter: 4 Klee
  people: 4 muff 5 French, German 7 Ital-
    ian, Romansh 8 Rhaetian, Romansch,
    Roumansh 9 Helvetian
  pine: 6 arolla
  psychologist: 4 Jung
  river: Aar, Inn 4 Aare 5 Doubs, Reuss,
    Rhine, Rhone
  sled: 4 luge 5 luger
  song: 5 yodel
  tunnel: 5 Cenis 7 Simplon 8 Gotthard 11
    Loetschberg
  valley: Aar 7 Zermatt 8 Engadine
  weight: 5 pfund 7 centner, quintal
  wind: 4 bise
  wine: 7 Dezaley
swivel: 4 turn 5 swing
swollen: 4 blub 5 blown, pursy, tumid 6
  turgid 7 blubber, bulbous, bulging,
  pompous 8 enlarged, inflated, varicose
  9 distended, increased, tumescent 10
  rhetorical
swoon: fit 4 coma, dwam 5 dwalm(Sc.),
  faint, sleep, spell 6 attack, stupor 7 ecstasy, syncope 8 black out, languish
swoop: cut 5 seize, sweep 6 pounce 7 descend
sword: sax 4 dirk, epee, foil, pata 5 bilbo,
  brand, estoc, glawe, gully, kukri, saber,
  sabre 6 barong, creese, cutlas, Damask,
  dusack, espada, floret, parang, rapier,
  spatha, Toledo 7 ascalon, askelon, bas-
  lard, curtana, curtein, cutlass, espadon,
  estoque, shabble, simitar 8 acinaces,
  camplian, claymore, Damascus, fal-
  chion, flamberg, scimitar, schlager,
  whinyard 9 achiavone, flamberge
  blade of: 5 forte
  cross guard: 7 quillon
  curved: 5 saber, sabre 8 scimitar
  fencing: 4 epee, foil
  handle: 4 haft, hilt
  of the Cid: 6 Colada
  shaped: 6 ensate 8 ensiform
  short: 4 dirk
  two-edged: 4 pata
  two-handed: 7 espadon 8 claymore
sword lily: 9 gladiolus
swordfish: 6 espada 7 espadon 9 broadbill
swordlike: 5 xypho 6 ensate 8 ensiform,
  gladiate
swordsman: 6 fencer 7 epeeist 8 thruster
sworn: 6 avowed 7 devoted 8 affirmed,
  attested 9 confirmed 10 determined,
  inveterate
swot (see also **swat**): 4 cram 5 grind, labor, sweat
syagush: 7 caracal
sybarite: 7 epicure 8 hedonist 10 volup-
  tuary
Sybil: See sibyl

sycophant: 5 toady 6 lackey 7 fawning, spaniel 8 informer, parasite 9 charlatan, flatterer 10 footlicker, talebearer

syllable: bit 4 whit 5 shred 7 modicum 8 particle
added: 6 prefix, suffix
deletion: 7 apocope
final: 6 ultima
lacking at end: 10 catalectic
next to last: 6 penult
second before last: 10 antepenult
short: 4 mora 5 breve
shortening: 7 apocope, elision, systole
stressed: 6 arsis
unaccented: 6 atonic

syllabus: 6 digest, precis, sketch 7 outline, summary 8 abstract, headnote, synopsis 9 statement 10 compendium

sylloge: 10 collection, compendium

syllogism: 5 logic 7 Sorites 8 argument 9 reasoning 10 epichirema 11 epicheirema

sylph: elf, fay 5 fairy 6 spirit, undine

sylphlike: 4 thin 7 lissome, slender 8 graceful

sylvan: 5 woody 6 rustic, wooded 8 woodsman 10 forestlike

sylvan deity: Pan 4 faun 6 Faunus

symbol (see also **element**)**:** 4 icon, ikon, sign, type, word 5 badge, creed, crest, cross, image, token, totem 6 caract, emblem, ensign, figure, letter 7 diagram 9 character, hierogram, trademark 10 expression, indication, similitude, substitute 12 abbreviation, contribution
achievement: 5 medal 6 ribbon
comedy: 4 sock
early Christian church: 5 orant
immortality: 6 phenix 7 phoenix
mourning: 5 crepe 7 cypress
peace: 4 dove
put into: 6 notate
saintliness: 4 halo
servitude: 4 yoke
victory: 4 palm 6 laurel
wisdom: owl

symbolical: 7 typical 8 mystical 11 allegorical 12 emblematical, sacramental 14 representative

symbolize: 5 agree 6 concur, mirror, typify 7 betoken, combine, express, signify 9 harmonize, represent 10 illustrate

symmetrical: 5 equal 7 regular, spheral 8 balanced 13 commensurable

symmetry: 7 balance, harmony 9 congruity 10 conformity, consistency, proportion

sympathetic: 4 soft 6 humane, tender 7 pietoso, piteous 8 affected 9 condolent, congenial, consonant, expansive, sensitive 10 responsive 13 compassionate, understanding

sympathize: 4 pity 6 bemoan 7 condole, feel for 11 commiserate

sympathy: 4 pity 6 accord, liking 7 harmony 8 interest 9 agreement 10 compassion, condolence, kindliness, tenderness 13 commiseration, understanding
expression of: 8 clemency 10 condolence
lack of: 8 dyspathy

symphony: 5 music 7 concord, harmony 9 orchestra
division: 8 movement
for Napoleon: 8 Eroica
form: 6 sonata

symposium: 4 talk 7 banquet 8 dialogue, potation 10 conference, discussion 11 compotation

symptom: 4 mark, note, sign 5 token 8 evidence 10 indication

synagogue: 4 shul 5 group 8 assembly, building, religion 9 communion, community 12 congregation
officer: 6 parnas
platform: 7 almemar
pointer: yad
Sephardic: 5 anoga
singer: 6 cantor, chazan 7 chazzan

synaxis: 7 meeting, service 12 congregation

synchronize: 6 concur 7 arrange 8 coincide, regulate 12 contemporize

synchronous: 8 existing 10 concurrent 11 concomitant 12 contemporary, simultaneous 15 contemporaneous

syndetic: 10 connective

syndic: 5 agent, judge, mayor 7 manager, officer, trustee 8 advocate, official 10 magistrate

syndicate: 4 sell 5 chain, group, trust, union, unite 6 cartel 7 censure, combine, council 8 monopoly 9 committee 11 association 12 conglomerate, organization

syndrome: 6 malady 7 ailment, disease 8 disorder

synod: 4 body 5 court 7 council, meeting 8 assembly 10 convention 11 convocation

synonym: 7 metonym

synonymous: 4 like 5 alike 10 equivalent

synopsis: 4 plan 5 brief 7 summary 8 abstract 9 statement 10 compendium, conspectus 11 abridgement

syntax: 5 order 6 system 7 grammar 9 structure 11 arrangement
analyze: 5 parse
mistake: 8 solecism

synthesis: 5 blend, summa 7 complex 11 combination, composition 13 incorporation

synthetic: 6 ersatz 7 man-made 10 artificial, fabricated

syphilis: pox 4 lues 7 disease

lesion: 7 chancre
old remedy: 9 Salvarsan
Syracuse: *conqueror:* 4 Rome
founder: 7 Archias
tyrant: 5 Gelon
Syria: *ancient name:* 4 Aram
animal: 5 addax, daman
bear: 4 dubb
bishop: 4 abba
buried city: 4 Dura
capital: 8 Damascus
church plan: 8 triconch
city and town: 4 Homs 5 Calno, Derra 6
   Aleppo, Balbec, Calneh 7 Antioch, Latakia 8 Seleucia
coin: 6 talent 7 piaster
deity: 4 Baal 5 Allat 6 Mammon 7 Resheph
district: 6 Aleppo, Hauran
goat: 6 angora
grass: 7 Johnson
gypsy: 5 Aptal
lake: 5 Merom 7 Djeboid 8 Tiberias
mallow: 4 okra
measure: 5 makuk 6 garava
monetary unit: 5 pound
mountain: 6 Carmel, Hermon 7 Libanus
peasant: 6 fellah
people: 5 Druse 7 Ansarie, Saracen
plant: 5 cumin
religious sect: 5 Druse
river: Asi 6 Barada, Jordan 7 Orontes
script: 5 serta
silk: 4 acca
tetrarchy: 7 abilene
weight: oke 4 cola, rotl 5 artal, artel, ratel
   6 talent
wind: 6 simoon
syringa: 5 lilac, shrub 10 mock orange
syrup: 4 karo, sapa 6 orgeat 7 glucose,
   sarghum 10 sweetening
system: ism 4 code 5 group, setup, whole
   6 circle, method, regime, theory 7 regimen 8 religion, treatise, universe 9 procedure 10 assemblage, hypothesis, philosophy, regularity 11 aggregation,
   arrangement, orderliness
of rules: 4 code
of weights: 4 troy
of worship: 4 cult
of writing: 7 braille 8 alphabet
systematic: 4 neat 7 orderly, regular 9 organized 10 methodical
systematics: 8 taxonomy
systematize: 5 order 6 adjust 7 arrange,
   catalog, marshal 8 organize, regiment 9
   catalogue
Szechwan capital: 7 Chengtu

T

t-shaped: tau
taa: 6 pagoda
Taal: 9 Afrikaans
tab: eye, pan, tag 4 bill, drop, flap, loop 5
   aglet, check, index, label, price, score,
   strap, strip 6 aiglet, eartab, record 7 account, latchet, officer 9 appendage,
   reckoning 10 accounting
tabac: 5 snuff 7 tobacco
tabanid: 6 gadfly 8 horsefly
tabard: inn 4 cape, coat 5 cloak, tunic 6
   chimer, jacket, mantle 7 pendant
tabasco: 5 sauce
tabatiere: 8 snuffbox
tabby: cat, pad 4 gown, silk 5 dress 6 fabric, gossip, moreen 7 old maid, padding,
   taffeta 8 brindled, spinster
tabella: 6 tablet 7 lozenge
tabernacle: 4 tent 5 abode, dwell, hovel,
   niche 6 church, recess, reside, temple 7
   deposit, shelter, support 8 enshrine 9
   sanctuary, structure 10 habitation,
   house of God, receptacle 13 house of
   prayer
table: hem 4 fare, feed, food, slab, wash 5
   bench, board, canon, index, panel, plate,
   treat 6 indius, lamina, record, repast,
   tablet 7 console, counter, plateau, surface 8 credence, feasting, postpone,
   schedule, synopsis, tabulate 9 sideboard
   10 collection 11 concentrate 12 string-
   course
centerpiece: 7 epergne
communion: 5 altar 8 credence, credenza

cover: **5** baize, cloth, tapis

decorative cloth: **6** runner

d'hote: **6** dinner **12** complete meal

dish: **6** tureen

dressing: **6** toilet, vanity

game: **4** pool **8** Ping-Pong **9** billiards

linen: **5** napery **7** napkins **11** tablecloths

philosophers: **14** deipnosophists

small: **5** stand, wagon **6** teapoy **7** taboret, tendoor, tendour

working: **5** bench

writing: **4** desk **10** escritoire

tableau: **7** picture **8** register, schedule **14** representation

tableland: **4** mesa **5** karoo **6** karroo **7** plateau **8** balaghat, plateaus, plateaux **9** balaghaut **12** altiplanicie

tablet: pad **4** bred, pill, slab **5** facia, panel **6** troche **7** lozenge **10** receptacle

medicine: **4** disc **6** troche

sculptured: **5** stela, stele

stone: **4** slab **5** stele

three-leaved: **8** triptych

two-leaved: **7** diptych

writing: pad **5** slate

tableware: cup **4** bowl, dish, fork **5** china, glass, knife, plate, spoon **6** saucer **8** flatware

tabloid: **7** short **9** condensed **11** sensational **12** concentrated

taboo, tabu: ban **5** debar **6** forbid **8** prohibit **9** forbidden, ineffable **12** interdiction

opposed to: noa

tabor, tabour: **4** drum **6** atabal **7** attabal, eardrum, timbrel

taboret, tabouret: **4** drum, seat **5** stand, stool, tabor **6** tabour **7** cabinet

tabu: See taboo

tabulate: **4** list **7** arrange **8** schedule

tabulation: **5** table, tally

grammatical: **8** paradigm

of the year: **8** calendar

tache: tie **5** clasp **6** attach, buckle

tacit: **6** silent **7** implied **8** implicit, unspoken, wordless **9** noiseless **10** understood

taciturn: **6** silent **7** laconic **8** reserved, reticent **9** saturnine **15** uncommunicative

tack: **4** beat, busk, clap, gear, haul, join, link, nail, rope, slap, trim, turn **5** baste, catch, fetch, rider, shift, spell, strip, tying, unite **6** attach, course, fasten, handle, method, secure, tackle **7** clothes, connect, payment **8** contract, saddlery **9** agreement, endurance, fastening **10** deflection, digression, stickiness, supplement **12** adhesiveness

glazier: **4** brad

nautical: **5** board

to: **4** jibe

to windward: **4** trip

two pointed: **6** staple

tackle: rig **4** arms, food, gear, tack **5** angle, drink, seize, stuff **6** attack, collar, secure, take on **7** grapple, harness, rigging, weapons **8** mistress, windlass **9** apparatus, encounter, equipment, undertake **13** accoutrements, paraphernalia

football: **4** stop **5** throw

fishing: tew

single and double block: **6** burton

strong: cat

tacky: **5** crude, dowdy, seedy **6** frowsy, frumpy, shabby, sticky, untidy **8** adhesive, slovenly

tact: **5** poise, touch **6** stroke **7** address, feeling **8** delicacy, graceful **9** appendage, diplomacy **10** adroitness, cleverness, discretion, perception **11** discernment **14** discrimination

tactful: **8** discreet, graceful **10** diplomatic

tactical: **9** expedient

tactics: **6** method, system **9** procedure

tactless: **5** brash

tactlessness: **9** gaucherie

tad: bit, boy, lad, son **5** child **6** urchin

tadpole: **8** polliwog

taenia: **4** band **6** fillet **8** headband

taffy: **5** candy, gundy **7** glaggum **8** flattery

Taffy: **8** Welshman

tag: dog, end, tab **4** flap, game, join, lock **5** aglet, label, shred, strip, touch **6** aiglet, append, attach, eartab, fasten, follow, rabble, ticket **7** refrain, taglock **9** appendage, catchword, shibboleth **11** aiguillette, commonplace

metal: **5** aglet **6** aiglet

Tagalog (see also Philippines): **8** Filipino, Pilipino

taha: **4** baya, **10** weaverbird

Tahiti: canoe: **4** pahi

capital: **7** Papeete

centipede: **4** veri

coronation robe: **4** maro

food plant: **4** taro

god: Oro **6** Taaroa

loincloth: **4** malo, maro

mountain: **7** Orohena

mulberry: **4** aute

neighboring islands: **6** Moorea **7** Huahine, Maupiti, Raiatea **8** Bora Bora

old name: **8** Otaheite

people: **10** Polynesian

resident painter: **7** Gauguin

seaport: **7** Papeete

woman: **6** vahine, wahine

Tai, Thai: **7** Siamese

tail: bun, cue, end, eye **4** arse, back, bunt, last, rear **5** cauda **6** follow, pursue, shadow, switch **7** limited, pendant, reduced **8** abridged, buttocks, encumber,

entailed 9 appendage, curtailed, extremity, fundament
having a: 7 caudate
kinds of: bob, bun, fud 4 bunt, scut 5 cauda, plume, stern, twist 6 strunt, wreath 8 streamer 9 empennage
pert to: 6 caudal
plane: 10 stabilizer
short: bun 4 scut
tailed: 7 caudate
tailing: 5 chaff, waste 6 refuse
tailless: 7 acaudal, anurous 8 acaudate, ecaudate 9 excaudate
tailor: 4 snip 5 adapt, alter, style 6 darzee, draper, sartor 7 cabbage 9 bushelman 11 bushelwoman
goose: 8 flatiron
iron: 5 goose
lap board: 5 panel
pert to: 9 sartorial
tailspin: 7 flicker
taint: dip, dye, hue 4 blow, blur, evil, hogo, hurt, spot, tint 5 cloud, color, imbue, prove, spoil, stain, sully, tinge, touch, trace, wound 6 accuse, damage, defile, infect, poison, stigma 7 attaint, blemish, convict, corrupt, debauch, deprave, pollute, vitiate 8 disgrace, empoison, hautgout, tincture 10 conviction, corruption, impregnate 11 contaminate
tainted: bad 5 blown
taipo: 5 demon, devil 10 theodolite
tait: 9 marsupial
Taiwan: *capital:* 6 Taipei
city: 7 Chilung 8 Taichung
island group: 5 Matsu 6 Penghu, Quemoy
mountain: 6 Tzukao, Yushan
other name: 7 Formosa
river: 5 Wuchi 6 Tachia 7 Choshui, Tanshui
seat of: 10 Kuomintang (Chinese Nationalists)
taj: cap 8 Taj Mahal
Taj Mahal site: 4 Agra
take: act, buy, eat, get, hit, win 4 bear, doff, fang, glom, grip, haul, lead, trap 5 adopt, atone, avail, carry, catch, charm, cheat, check, fetch, glaum, grasp, infer, seize, snare, spell, steal, swear, touch, treat, trick 6 absorb, accept, affirm, amount, arrest, assume, attach, attack, borrow, choose, convey, deduce, deduct, derive, employ, endure, engage, number, obtain, profit, remove, secure, select, strike, submit, tenure 7 attract, capture, conduct, detract, extract, promise, receive, swallow, undergo 8 abstract, contract, proceeds, quantity, receipts, subtract 9 apprehend, interrupt 11 appropriate

aback: 5 check 7 startle 8 astonish, confound, surprise
account of: 6 notice, regard
advantage of: 5 abuse 6 misuse 7 exploit
advice: 4 hear, heed, mind 6 listen
after: 6 follow 8 resemble
aim: 4 bead 5 level
another's place: sub9 alternate 10 substitute
apart: 4 ruin 7 analyze, destroy, dissect 9 dismantle
as actual: 5 posit
as one's own: 5 adopt 6 borrow
away: 5 decry, reave 6 adempt, deduct, divest, recant, remove 7 deprive, detract, retract 8 derogate, diminish, subtract
back: 6 abjure, recall, recant 7 retract 8 withdraw 9 repossess
beforehand: 7 pre-empt
bold attitude: 5 brisk
by craft: 6 entoil
by force: 5 erept 8 ereption
by storm: 5 seize 6 attack
by stratagem: 4 trap
care: 4 mind, reck 5 nurse, watch 6 beware, cuidado
care of: fix 4 tend 5 nurse
chair: sit
cognizance of: 4 note 6 notice
comb from beehive: 4 geld
delight: 5 revel
direction: 5 steer
down: 5 abase, lower 6 escort, humble, record, reduce 7 swallow 8 dismount, emaciate, withdraw 10 distribute
evening meal: sup 4 dine
exception: 5 demur 6 object
fire: 5 spunk
first: 7 preempt
five: 4 rest
for granted: 6 assume 7 presume
forcibly: 5 seize
from: 5 wrest 6 deduct, divest 7 deprive, derived, detract 8 derogate, subtract
heed: 4 mind, reck, ware
hold: 5 grasp 6 obtain
in: 4 furl, open 5 admit, annex, brail, cheat, fence, trick, visit 6 absorb, attend, escort 7 deceive, embrace, enclose, explore, include, observe, receive 8 commence, comprise, contract 9 apprehend, encompass 10 comprehend, understand
in hand: 5 seize 7 attempt 9 undertake
in sail: 4 reef
into custody: 6 arrest 9 apprehend
it ill: 6 resent
it easy: 4 rest 5 relax
leave: 6 decamp, depart
legal possession of: 5 seise, seize
liberties: 7 presume

meals for pay: 5 board
no notice of: 9 disregard
notice: see 7 witness
off: 4 copy, doff, lift, soar 5 abate, begin, deter, mimic, start 6 deduct, depart, get out, lessen, remove 7 detract 8 discount, distract, subtract, withdraw 9 burlesque, calculate, determine, reproduce
off suspended list: 9 reinstate
offense of: 6 resent
on: add, don 4 hire 5 start 6 assume, employ, engage, oppose, tackle 7 consort, receive 8 arrogate 9 associate, undertake
on cargo: 4 lade
one's way: 4 wend
orders: 4 obey 5 yield
out: 4 copy, dele, kill, omit 5 elide 6 deduct, delete, efface, escort, except, remove 7 excerpt, extract, scratch, unhitch 8 airbrush, overall, separate 9 eliminate
out by roots: 9 extirpate
out curves and bends: 10 straighten
out of pawn: 6 redeem
over: 5 seize 6 assume, convey 7 relieve
part: 4 join 5 share 11 participate
part in contest: 7 compete
part of: 4 side 8 enact
place: 5 occur 6 happen
place again: 5 recur
place of: 4 else 8 supplant 9 supersede
pleasure in: 5 enjoy, fancy 6 admire
positive opinion: 4 side
possession of: 5 enter, seise, seize
root: 4 grow 6 settle
service as seaman: 4 ship
shape: 4 form, jell 11 cyrstallize
shelter: 6 nestle, shroud
some of: 7 partake
stock: 5 count 6 survey 8 appraise, estimate 9 inventory
the stick: 5 steer
to court: sue
turns: 9 alternate
umbrage at: 6 resent
unawares: 5 seize 7 astound, capture, startle 8 astonish, confound, overcome, surprise 9 overwhelm
unlawfully: rob 5 steal, usurp 6 pilfer
up: buy 4 fill, lift 5 adopt, allow, begin, check, enter, exact, mount, raise, seize, set to 6 absorb, accept, arrest, assume, borrow, employ, gather, occupy, remove, resume 7 collect, dissent, elevate, engross, receive 8 commence, initiate 9 extirpate, reprimand 10 comprehend, understand
up again: 5 renew 6 reopen, resume
up weapons: arm 4 rise

with: 4 like 5 brook 6 accept 7 confess 11 acknowledge
without authority: 5 usurp
taken: 8 occupied
in all: 7 overall 9 inclusive
taker: 5 thief 6 captor 7 catcher 8 pilferer, purveyor 10 plagiarist
of court action: 4 suer
of income or profits: 6 pernor
takin: 7 gazelle 8 antelope
relative of: 6 musk ox
taking: 4 take 5 catch, palsy 6 arrest, attack, blight, plight 7 capture, malefic, seizing, seizure 8 alluring, captious, catching, engaging, grasping, receipts 9 accepting, rapacious, receiving, reception 10 attachment, attractive, contagious, infectious 11 captivating 12 apprehension
different form: 7 protean 11 metamorphic
precedence: 7 ranking
unauthorized leave: 4 A.W.O.L.
takt: 4 beat 5 beats, pulse, tempo 7 measure
talapoin: 6 monkey
talc: 4 mica 6 powder, talcum 7 agalite 8 steatite 9 soapstone
tale: lie 4 gest, myth, saga, talk, tell, yarn 5 count, fable, geste, speak, story, tally, total, whole 6 esteem, gossip, legend, reckon, report, speech 7 account, fiction, history, parable, recital 8 anecdote, category, consider, counting, relation 9 discourse, falsehood, narration, narrative, numbering, reckoning 10 detraction 11 declaration, enumeration, information 12 conversation
adventure: 4 gest 5 geste
kind of: lai 4 epic, gest, saga, yarn 5 bourd, geste, roman 6 legend 7 romance 8 allegory, jeremiad 9 storiette
medieval: lai, lay
Tale of Two Cities: *author:* 7 Dickens
characters: 5 Lucie (Manette) 6 Carton (Sidney), Darnay (Charles)
talebearer: 6 buzzer, gossip 7 tattler 8 informer, talepyet, telltale 10 newsmonger 13 scandalmonger
talent: 4 gift 5 anger, dowry, flair, gifts, knack, money, skill, talon 6 custom, desire, flavor, genius, powers, riches, wealth 7 ability, betters, faculty, feature, longing, passion 8 appetite, aptitude, capacity, charisma, gamblers, property 9 abilities, abundance, attribute, expertise 10 endowments 11 disposition, inclination 14 accomplishment
special: 5 forte
talented: 4 able 5 smart 6 clever, gifted 8

addicted, disposed, inclined
talesman: 5 juror 8 narrator
taletelling: 4 blab
taliation: 5 tally 10 adjustment
taliera: 4 tara
talion: 11 retaliation
talipot: 4 palm
talisman: 4 tara 5 charm, saffi, safie 6 amulet, fetich, fetish, grigri, saphie, scarab, telesm 8 greegree 10 lucky piece
talk: yap 4 buck, bukh, carp, chat, gaff, knap, talk, word 5 bazoo, lingo, parle, prate, rumor, speak, theme, utter 6 confer, debate, gabble, gossip, reason, report, speech, steven, tongue 7 address, chatter, consult, council, dialect, express, meeting, mention, palabra 8 causerie, parlance, verbiage 9 dalliance, discourse 10 conference, discussion 11 communicate 12 conversation
about: 6 gossip 7 discuss
abusive: 5 hoker
back: 4 sass 6 retort, ripost 7 riposte 8 repartee
big: 4 brag 5 boast
boastful: 4 gaff, rant
ceremonious: 8 chin-chin
chatty: gab 6 gossip
common: 7 hearsay
complaining: 4 carp
confused: 10 galimatias
desultorily: 6 ramble
deliriously: 4 rave
down: 7 outtalk, silence
down to: 9 patronize 10 condescend
effusively: 4 gush, rave
familiar: 6 confab
fast and idly: 7 gnatter
flattering: 7 palaver
flippant: 10 persiflage
fluent: 7 verbose, voluble
foolish: gab, gas 4 bosh, bunk, gash 5 spiel 6 babble, bunkum, claver, fraise, patter 7 blabber, palaver, twaddle 8 buncombe, wishwash 9 poppycock, rigmarole 11 goosecackle, stultiloquy
formal: 7 address, lecture
from pulpit: 6 homily, sermon
glib: 6 patter 7 palaver
idly: gab, gas 5 prate 6 tattle 7 chatter, twaddle
imperfectly: 4 lisp 7 stutter
in sleep: 15 somniloquacious
indiscreetly: 4 blab
indistinctly: 6 mumble, mutter 7 sputter
into: 6 induce
irrationally: 4 rant, rave
light: 5 chaff 6 banter 8 raillery
over: 7 discuss
persuasively: 6 reason

pert: lip 4 sass
profuse: 4 chat 6 patter 7 palaver 10 persiflage
slowly: 5 drawl
small: gab 4 chat, chin 7 prattle 8 chitchat
table: ana 9 symposiac
tediously: 5 prose
to no purpose: 4 blat
together: 4 chat 8 converse
turgid; 4 cant, rant
unintelligible: 6 drivel, jargon, patter 9 gibberish
wildly: 4 rant, rave
talkative: 4 cozy, gash, glib 5 gabby 6 chatty, clashy, fluent 7 verbose, voluble 8 flippant 9 garrulous 10 babblative, loquacious
talker: 6 proser, ranter, rhetor 7 babbler, spieler 17 conversationalist
incessant: 6 gasbag, magpie 10 chatterbox 12 blabbermouth
talkfest: 6 confab 9 gathering 10 discussion, bull session
talking iron: gun 5 rifle
tall: 4 bold, deft, fine, high, lank, long 5 brave, grand, great, lanky, large, lofty, quick, rangy, ready, steep, tally 6 comely, docile, seemly 7 doughty, skyhigh, unusual 8 obedient, towering, yielding 9 excellent 10 courageous, incredible 11 exaggerated 13 grandiloquent
tallow: fat 4 suet 5 sevum, smear 6 fatten, grease
pert to: 7 stearic
pot: 7 fireman
refuse: 9 crackling
sediment: 7 greaves
tally: run, tab, tag 4 deal, goal, jibe, mark, mate, suit 5 agree, check, count, grade, label, match, notch, score 6 accord, reckon, record 7 account, compare, loftily 8 estimate, numerate 9 agreement, reckoning 10 correspond 11 counterpart
tallyho: cry 5 coach
crier of: 6 hunter
talma: 4 cape, coat 6 cloak
Talmud: 9 Jewish law
commentary: 6 Gemara
text: 6 Mishna
Talmudic academy: 7 Yeshiva 8 Yeshibah, Yeshivah 9 Yeshiboth
student: 5 bahur
talon: 4 claw, fang, heel, sere 6 clutch, hallux 7 molding 11 certificate
Talos' slayer: 8 Daedalus
talus: 5 ankle, scree, slope 6 debris 8 clubfoot 9 anklebone 11 knucklebone
tam: cap, hat 5 beret 8 headgear
tamarack: 5 larch
tamarind: 8 sampaloc

tamarisk: sal 4 atle, jhow 5 atlee

tambo: inn 6 corral, stable, tavern 7 station

tambour: cup 4 desk, drum 5 frame 7 drummer 8 buttress, ornament 9 embroider 10 embroidery, projection

tambourin: 4 drum 5 dance, tabor

tambourine: 4 dove, drum, taar 5 daira 7 timbrel, travale

tame: cut 4 bust, dead, dull, meek, mild 5 accoy, begin, break, daunt, prune 6 broach, docile, gentle, humble, soften, subdue 7 affaite, crushed, insipid, servile 8 amenable, cicurate, civilize, familiar, harmless 9 deficient, tractable 10 accustomed, cultivated, submissive 11 domesticate, housebroken, ineffectual 12 domesticated 13 pusillanimous
animal: pet 4 cade 6 cosset

tamed: 6 broken, gentle

tameness: 10 mansuetude

Tamil: 8 language
caste member: 7 Vellala
race: 9 Dravidian

Taming of the Shrew character: Sly 4 Kate 6 Bianca, Tranio 8 Baptista

tamis: 5 sieve, tammy 8 strainer

Tammany Society: *boss:* 5 Tweed
leader: 6 sachem
officer: 8 Wiskinky 9 Wiskinkie

Tammuz: *love:* 6 Ishtar
sister: 6 Belili

tamp: ram 4 cram 5 drive 6 plug up 11 concentrate

tamper: fix 4 fool, plot, tool 5 bribe 6 dabble, meddle, potter, scheme 7 machine 9 influence, interfere

Tampico fiber: 5 istle

tampon: 4 plug 6 tympan 9 drumstick
nasal: 9 rhinobyon

tan: dun, sun, taw 4 beat, camp, ecru, flog, tent, whip 5 brown, color, toast 6 almond, bronze, switch, tannin, thrash 7 embrown, imbrown, sunburn, tanbark
derived from: 6 tannic

tanager: 4 bird, yeni 8 cardinal
genus of: 7 piranga

tang: nip 4 bite, butt, capt, fang, foil, odor, pang, pike, ring, root, spur, tine, zest 5 aroma, knife, prick, prong, shank, smack, sting, taste, tinge, trace, twang 6 branch, flavor, pierce, tangle, tongue 7 flavour, seatang, seaweed 8 rockweed 10 suggestion 11 surgeonfish

Tanganyika: See **Tanzania**

tangelo: 4 ugli

tangent: 5 slope 8 adjacent, touching

tangible: 4 real 6 actual 7 tactile 8 definite, material, palpable 9 objective, touchable 11 perceptible, substantial

Tangiers: *feature:* 6 casbah

measure: 4 kula, mudd

tangle: bar, cot, mat 4 fank, harl, kink, knot, mesh, trap 5 catch, frame, gnarl, ravel, snare, snarl 6 balter, entrap, icicle, medley, muddle, sleave 7 ensnare, involve 8 obstruct, quandary, scrobble 9 embarrass 10 complicate, intertwine, perplexity
of thread: 5 snarl

tangle-foot: 5 drink 6 liquor, whisky

tangled: 11 complicated

tango: 5 bingo, dance

tania: 4 taro 6 yautia

Tanis: 4 Zoan

tank: hit, vat 4 bang, lake, pond, pool 5 basin, knock, trunk 7 cistern, cuvette, drinker, pachuca, piscina, stomach 9 container, reservoir
part: 5 tread 6 turret

tankard: mug 5 facer, hanap, stoup 6 flagon, pottle 7 goddard

tanked: 11 intoxicated

tanker: 4 ship 5 oiler

tanned: 5 brown, tawny 8 sixpence, sunburnt

tanner: 6 barker 8 sixpence

Tannhauser composer: 6 Wagner

tannic acid salt: 7 tannate

tannin: 10 astringent

tanning: 7 pasting 8 browning, flogging, whipping
extract: 5 cutch 7 amaltas, catechu
material: 5 sumac 6 sumach
method: 4 napa
pert to: 11 scytodepsic
plant: 5 alder, sumac 6 sumach

tansy: 4 weed 9 tanacetum

tantalize: 4 grig 5 taunt, tease 6 harass 7 torment

Tantalus: *children:* 5 Niobe 6 Pelops
father: 4 Zeus

tantamount: 4 same 5 equal 9 identical 10 equivalent

tantara, tantarara: 5 blare 7 fanfare

tantieme: 5 bonus, share 10 percentage

tantrum: fit, pet 4 rage

tantum: 5 stint 9 allowance

Tanzania: *capital:* 11 Dar es Salaam
island: 5 Pemba
lake: 5 Nyasa, Rukwa 8 Victoria 10 Tanganyika
language: 7 Swahili
monetary unit: 8 shilling
mountain: 4 Meru 11 Kilimanjaro
part: 8 Zanzibar 10 Tanganyika
people: 4 Goma 5 Bantu 6 Sukuma, Wagogo, Wagoma 7 Swahili, Wabinga
river: 6 Kagera, Rufija 7 Pangane
title: 5 sahid
town: 5 Moshi, Tanga 6 Arusha, Mwanza
weight: 8 farsalah

Taoism: 8 religion 12 cosmic reason

founder: 6 Lao Tzu

tap: bar, bob, cut, hit, hob, pat, rap, tit, vat 4 beat, blow, cock, flip, heat, hole, open, pipe, plug 5 break, fever, flirt, knock, leach, spile, touch, valve 6 broach, faucet, repair, signal, spigot, strike, tapnet 7 censure, connect, penance, reprove 8 nominate 9 designate

down: 4 tamp

tape: gin, tie 4 band, bind, mole 5 scale, strip 6 fillet, liquor, ribbon, secure 7 bandage, binding

kind of: 4 lear, wick 5 inkle 6 ferret

machine: 8 recorder

needle: 6 bodkin

taper: 4 ream, wick 5 light, point, snape 6 candle, cierge, lessen, narrow, trowel 7 conical, dwindle, trindle 8 decrease, diminish 9 acuminate 11 pyramidical

tapering: 5 conic 6 terete 7 conical 9 acuminate

blades: 6 spires

four-sided pillar: 7 obelisk

piece: 4 gore, shim 5 miter 6 gusset

tapestry: 5 arras 6 bayeux, dorser, dosser 7 dossier, gobelin 8 dossiere

hanging: 5 tapis

kind: 5 Arras 7 Gobelin 8 Aubusson

warp thread: 5 lisse

tapeworm: 6 taenia 8 parasite

embryonic form: 10 oncosphere

segments: 8 strobila

head: 6 scolex

taphouse: bar, inn 6 saloon, tavern 7 tap-room

tapioca-like food: 5 salep

source: 7 cassava

tapir: 4 anta 5 danta 8 anteater, ungulate

taproom: bar, pub 6 saloon, tavern

tapster: 8 barmaid, skinker 9 barkeeper, bartender

Tapuyan: 8 S.A. Indian

tribe: Ges 5 Gesan 6 Cayapo, Goyana, Timbra 7 Camacan, Coroado 8 Botocudo, Caingang, Chavante

tar: gob 4 brea, salt 5 black, pitch, taint, tease 6 cresol, incite, sailor, seaman 7 blacken, mariner, provoke 8 alkitran, irritate, seafarer, telegram 9 alchitran 10 bluejacket

tar and feathers: 12 plumeopicean

taradiddle: fib, lie 8 nonsense

Taranaki volcano: 6 Egmont

tarantula: 6 spider

tarboosh: cap, fez

tardigrade: 8 sluggish 9 slow-paced

tardy: lag, lax 4 late, slow 5 delay, slack 6 remiss, retard 7 belated, lagging, overdue 8 dilatory 10 behindhand, unprepared 11 cunctatious

tare: 4 weed 5 vetch, weigh 6 darnel 7

leakage 9 allowance 13 counterweight

target: cut, tee, use 4 butt, coin, mark, vane 5 shred, sight, slice 6 cymbal, object, shield, tassel, tatter 7 buckler, pendant 8 ambition, bullseye, ornament, ridicule 9 indicator, objective, criticism

center: eye 5 clout 8 bull's-eye

shotting gallery: 4 duck

target finder: 5 radar, sonar

Tarheel State: 13 North Carolina

tariff: tax 4 duty, list, rate 5 price, scale 6 charge, scheme, system 7 average, tribute 8 schedule

favorer: 13 protectionist

Tarkington title: 6 Penrod 9 Seventeen

tarn: 4 lake, pool

tarnish: dim 4 blot, dull, soil, spot 5 cloud, dirty, spoil, stain, sully, taint 6 canker, darken, defile, injure, smirch 7 asperse, blemish, destroy, distain, obscure 8 besmirch, diminish, discolor

taro: 4 coco, eddo, gabi 5 aroid, cocgo, eddoe, tania 7 dasheen 8 caladium

paste: poi

tarpaulin: hat, tar 4 coat 5 cover 6 sailor 7 sea-bred 10 sailorlike

tarpon: 6 sabalo 9 savanilla 10 silverfish

relative of: 5 chiro

tarriance: 5 delay 7 sojourn 8 awaiting, tarrying 9 hindrance, lingering

tarrock: 4 gull, tern

tarry: lag, vex 4 bide, loll, rest, stay, stop, wait 5 abide, await, black, dally, defer, delay, demur, dwell, lodge, pause, visit, weary 6 arrest, bundle, hinder, linger, loiter, remain, retard, soiled, tarred, tarrow 7 fatigue, outstay, sojourn, unclean 8 irritate

tarrying: 6 arrest

tarsus: 5 ankle

fore: 4 pala

tart: pie 4 acid, doxy, flan, girl, keen, sour 5 acerb, acrid, acute, bowla, sharp 6 pastry, pielet, severe, tender, tourte 7 caustic, cutting, painful, piquant, pungent 8 piercing, poignant, turnover 9 acidulous, endearing, sensitive 10 astringent, prostitute

tartan: 4 sett, ship 5 plaid

tartar: 4 argol 12 incrustation

Tartar: See Tatar

tartarean: 8 infernal

Tartarus: 4 hell 5 Hades

Tartary prince: 4 Agib

Tartuffe: 9 hypocrite, pretender

author: 7 Moliere

tarweed: 5 Madia

Tarzan's mate: 4 Jane

task: job, tax 4 busk, char, darg, duty, lade, load, test, toil, work 5 chare, chore, labor, stent, stint, study 6 amount, burden, dargue, devoir, effort, impost, lesson, strain 7 aufgabe, censure, oppress, overtax 8 quantity 10 accounting, assignment, employment 11 undertaking

easy: 4 pipe, snap 5 cinch 8 sinecure

taskmaster: 6 driver 8 overseer 11 slave driver

Tasmania: 6 island

animal: 6 wombat

cape: 4 Grim

capital: 6 Hobart

devil: 7 dasyure

discoverer: 6 Tasman

lake: 4 Echo 6 Sorell 12 Westmoreland

location: 12 South Pacific

mountain: 4 Grey 5 Brown, Drome, Nevis 6 Barrow 8 Humboldt 9 Ben Lomond 10 Wellington

original name: 14 Van Dieman's Land

phalanger: 5 tapoa

river: 4 Huon 5 Tamar 6 Arthur, Jordan 7 Derwent

thylacine: 5 tiger

town: 6 Hobart 9 Devontown 10 Launceston

wolf: 9 thylacine

tass: cup, mow 4 bowl, heap 5 draft 6 goblet 10 small draft

tassel: 4 tuft 5 adorn, label 6 fringe, toorie, zizith 7 pendant 8 ornament

taste: bit, eat, gab, goo, sip, try 4 bent, dash, feel, gout, gust, heed, hint, rasa, tang, test 5 drink, flair, gusto, prove, sapor, savor, scent, shade, smack, smell, spice, touch, trace 6 degust, flavor, liking, little, palate, relish, relush, ribbon, sample, savour 7 flavour, soupcon, thought 8 appetite, delicacy, elegance, fondness 9 attention, degustate, judgement 10 experience, suggestion 11 discernment, inclination 14 discrimination

absence of: 7 ageusia

fundamental: 4 acid, salt, sour 5 sweet 6 bitter

kind of: nip, sip 4 tang 5 prose, sapor, savor, smack 7 penchant

lacking in: 4 rude 8 ungentle 9 inelegant 10 unpolished 11 inaesthetic

pert. to: 7 palatal 9 gustative, gustatory

perversion: 7 malacia

refined: 7 elegant

strong: 4 tang

tasteful: 4 neat 5 tasty 6 savory 7 elegant

tasteless: 4 dull, flat 5 vapid 7 insipid 8 barbaric, lifeless 9 savorless 10 inartistic 11 unpalatable

tasty: 5 quiet, sapid 6 savory 7 palatal 9 flavorful, palatable, toothsome 10 delectable

tat: rag, tap 4 pony 5 touch 6 tangle 7 crochet 8 absolute

Tatar, Tartar: Hun 6 ataman, hetman 7 Cossack

dynasty: Kin, Wei

horseman: 7 Cossack

king: 4 khan

militiaman: 4 Ulan 5 Uhlan

mounted band: 4 ulan 5 horde, uhlan 7 chambul

nobleman: 5 murza

principality: 7 Khanate

republic capital: 5 Kazan

tribe: Hun 5 Alani, Alans 7 Shortzy

tatou, tatu: 9 armadillo

tatter: jag, rag, rip 4 jagg, stir, tear 5 hurry, scold, scrap, shred, testy 6 bustle, gabble, ribbon, tattle 7 chatter, flitter, peevish 8 guenille 14 tatterdemalion

tatterdemalion: 8 vagabond 10 ragamuffin

tattered: 4 torn 6 broken, jagged, ragged, shabby, shaggy 7 slashed 9 disrupted 10 disheveled 11 dilapidated

tattle: 4 blab, chat, gash, talk, tell 5 cheep, clash, clype, prate 6 gossip, report 7 chatter, clatter, prattle, stammer

tattler: 6 gossip 8 informer, telltale 9 sandpiper 10 talebearer

Taube: 9 monoplane

taught: See **teach**

taunt: bob 4 dare, gibe, jeer, jibe, mock, quip, tall, twit 5 check, fleer, glaik, reply, slare, slart, sneer, tease, tempt 6 banter, deride, flaunt, insult, offend, rejoin 7 provoke, upbraid 8 reproach, ridicule 9 aggravate

taurine: 4 bull 6 bovine

Taurus: 4 bull

taut: 4 firm, neat, snug, tidy, trim 5 rigid, stiff, tense, tight, tough 6 severe, strict 9 distended, shipshape

tauten: 5 tense 7 tighten

tautog: 9 blackfish 10 oysterfish

tautology: 8 pleonasm, verbiage 10 redundancy

tavern: bar, hut, inn, pub 4 bush, howf 5 booth, hotel, house, howff 6 saloon 7 cabaret, gasthof 8 alehouse, gasthaus, hostelry

tavert: (Sc.) 5 tired 6 stupid 8 confused

taw: tan, tew 4 beat, whip 5 agate, stake 6 harass, marble, shooter, torment, toughen

tawdry: 5 cheap, gaudy, showy 6 sleazy, tinsel

tawny, tawney: tan 5 brown, dusky, olive, swart, tenne 6 Indian, tanned 7 fulvous, tigrine 8 brindled 9 bullfinch

tawse, taws: 4 whip 5 strap

tax: 4 cess, duty, feel, fine, levy, load, rate,

scat, scot, task, toll 5 abuse, agist, exact, order, scatt, stent, stint, tithe, touch, value 6 accuse, assess, avania, burden, charge, demand, excise, extent, handle, hidage, impose, impost, settle, strain 7 censure, dispute, finance, gabelle, license, tailage, tallage, tollage, tribute 8 estimate, exaction, overtire, reproach 9 prescribe 10 assessment, imposition 12 contribution

agency: IRS
assessment: 7 doomage
church: 5 tithe
feudal: 7 scutage, tailage, tallage
gatherer: 7 catchpole, catchpoll
hide: 6 hidage
kind of: cro, soc 4 cess, geld, scat 5 finta, tithe 6 abkari, excise, pavage, surtax, taille, vinage 7 boscage, chevage, patente, prisage, scewing, tailage 8 auxilium, carucage 9 surcharge 10 chaukidari
rate: 10 assessment
salt: 7 gabelle
taxable: 10 assessable, censurable
taxation: tax 6 charge 7 finance, reproof, revenue 9 valuation 10 accusation, assessment
degree of: 5 ratal
taxi: cab 4 hack 5 jixie 6 litter 7 vehicle
parking place: 5 stand
taximeter: 5 clock
taxing: 5 tough 6 trying 7 onerous 9 demanding 10 accusation
taxman: 8 publican
taxpayer: 9 ratepayer
tazza: cup 4 bowl, vase
tea: 5 party 6 repast, supper 8 beverage, function 9 collation, decoction, marijuana, reception
black: 5 bohea, oopak, pekoe 8 souchong
cake: 5 scone 6 cookie
constituent: 8 caffeine
container: 8 canister
drug: see *stimulant* below
expert: 6 taster
family: 8 Theaceae
genus: 4 thea
Indian: 10 Darjeeling
kind of: cha 4 chaa, chia, tsia 5 assam, black, bohea, congo, chias, Emesa, green, hyson, Ledum, oopak, pekoe, salop 6 congue, oolong, saloop 7 cambric 8 bouillon, go-widdie 9 gunpowder
plant: 4 thea
receptacle: 8 canister
room: 5 kiosk
serve: 4 pour
stimulant: 5 thein 6 theine
table: 5 tepoy 6 teapoy
urn: 7 samovar
weak: 5 blash

Tea House location: 4 Naha 7 Okinawa
teach: 4 show 5 coach, edify, endue, guide, point, train, tutor 6 commit, direct, lesson, preach, school 7 apprise, apprize, beteach, conduct, educate 8 accustom, amaister, document, instruct 9 enlighten 10 discipline 11 demonstrate 12 indoctrinate
teachable: apt 6 docile, pliant 7 fitting 8 amenable
teacher: 4 guru, prof 5 coach, guide, Plato, tutor 6 docent, doctor, mentor, pedant, pundit, reader, regent 7 adjunct, edifier, maestro, sophist, trainer 8 civilian, director, educator, gamaliel, moralist, preacher 9 pedagogue, preceptor 10 instructor 12 schoolmaster
Alexandria: 6 Origen
association: NEA
fee: 8 minerval
Hindu: 5 swami
Indian religion: 4 guru
Jewish: 5 rabbi
Mohammedan: pir 5 molla, mulla 6 mollah, mullah
of eloquence: 6 rhetor 7 sophist
of the deaf: 7 oralist
Russia: 7 starets
teaching: 5 moral 6 docent 7 precept 9 education 10 discipline 11 instruction
of a fable: 5 moral
of the Twelve: 7 Didache
pert. to: 9 pedagogic
teak: 4 wood 5 djati
teakettle: 4 suke, suky 5 sukey, sukie
teal: 4 duck 8 garganey
team: 4 crew, gang, join, pair, race, span, yoke 5 brood, chain, flock, group, wagon 6 convey, couple, number 7 lineage, progeny, vehicle 8 carriage 9 associate
baseball: 4 nine
basketball: 4 five
football: 6 eleven
kinds of: duo 4 crew 6 jayvee, scrubs 7 varsity
supporter: fan 6 rooter
two animals: 4 pair, yoke
teamster: 6 carter, driver 7 carrier
tear: ram, rip, rit, run 4 claw, drag, fine, pull, rage, rend, rent, rive, rush, skag, snag, weep 5 binge, break, claut, larme, reave, split, spree, touse, unrip, waste 6 cleave, course, dainty, damage, divide, flurry, lament, pierce, remove, screed, tatter, wrench 7 agitate, chatter, consume, destroy, disrupt, extract, fritter, passion, shatter, torment 8 carousal, delicate, lacerate, lachryma, separate
apart: 4 rend 9 dismember
down: 4 rase, raze 6 malign 7 destroy 8 demolish 10 scandalize 11 disassemble
into: rip 6 attack

limb from limb: 9 dismember
 off: rip, run 4 rush 5 start
 to pieces: 6 tatter 10 dilacerate
 up by the roots: 6 arache 9 eradicate, extirpate
teadrop design: 5 larme
tearful: sad 6 watery 7 flebile, snively, weeping 8 lacrimal 10 lachrymose
 mother: 5 Niobe
tearing: 4 rage 5 hasty, hurry 7 furious, violent 8 splendid 9 furiously, harrowing, impetuous 10 impressive 12 excruciating
tear-jerking: 5 mushy 6 sticky 7 maudlin 8 bathetic
tearpit: 7 larmier
tears: 5 grief
 inducing: 9 rheumatic
 pert. to: 8 lacrimal
 poetic: 5 rheum
tease: beg, guy, irk, nag, rag, tew, vex 4 card, coax, comb, drag, fret, hare, razz, stir, tear, twit 5 annoy, chevy, chivy, devil, taunt, worry, wrack 6 badger, bother, caddle, chivvy, harass, heckle, molest, pester, plague, teasel 7 disturb, hatchel, provoke, scratch, torment 8 irritate, separate 9 aggravate, importune, tantalize 11 disentangle
 wool: tum 4 comb, toom
teasel: 4 comb 5 plant
teaser: 4 gull 6 carder, curler, sniper, stoker, willow 7 curtain, fireman, problem 8 operator, pesterer, willower
teasing: 6 chaff 6 banter 11 importunate
teaty: 5 cross 7 fretful, peevish
tebbad: 6 simoom 9 sandstorm
tebeldi: 6 baobab
teched: 4 daft 5 batty 6 insane 7 cracked 8 demented
technology of agriculture: 10 agrotechny
techy: 4 spot 5 habit 6 touchy, vexing 7 blemish, fretful, peevish, quality 9 irascible, irritable
teck: 6 cravat 10 four-in-hand
tectonic: 7 builder, plastic 9 carpenter 10 structural 13 architectural
ted: 4 toad, turn 5 waste 6 spread 7 scatter
tedge: 6 ingate, runner
tedious: dry 4 arid, dead, dree, dull, long, slow 5 bored, prosy 6 boring, borish, elenge, prolix 7 irksome, noxious, peevish, prosaic 8 dilatory, slowness, tiresome 9 exhausted, irritable, laborious, prolixity, wearisome 10 monotonous 11 displeasing, everlasting 13 uninteresting
tedium: 5 ennui 7 boredom, doldrum 8 monotony 11 irksomeness, tediousness 13 wearisomeness

tee: 5 mound
 off: 5 drive, scold 9 reprimand
teem: 4 bear, fill, gush, lead, pour, rain, swim 5 bring, drain, empty, fetch, swarm 6 abound, resort, seethe, summon 7 produce 8 abundant, conceive, generate, prolific
teeming: 4 full 5 agush, alive 7 pouring, replete 8 crowding, prolific 9 abounding, bristling 11 overflowing 13 overabounding
teeny: wee 4 tiny 5 small 7 fretful, peevish 9 malicious
teeny-weeny: 4 tiny 5 small 6 minute
teeter: 4 rock, sway 5 lurch, waver 6 jiggle, quiver, seesaw 7 rocking, rolling, tremble 9 sandpiper, vacillate
teeter board: 6 seesaw
teeth: 5 tines 7 canines 8 choppers, crackers, grinders
 decay of: 6 caries
 false: 5 plate 8 dentures
 grinding of: 7 bruxism
 hard tissue: 7 dentine
 having all alike: 7 isodont
 incrustation on: 6 tartar
 large: 4 buck 5 snags
 long: 5 fangs 6 tushes
 outer covering of: 6 enamel
 pert. to: 5 molar 6 dental
 serpent: 5 fangs
 socket: 7 alveoli (pl.) 8 alveolus
 sower of dragon's: 6 Cadmus
 without: 10 edentulate, edentulous
teethy (Sc.): 5 cross 6 biting 7 crabbed 9 irritable
teeting: 7 titlark
teetotal: dry 6 entire 7 abstain 8 complete
teetotaller: dry 7 nonuser 9 abstainer, rechabite, refrainer
teetotum: top, toy
teg: doe 4 deer 5 sheep, woman 6 fleece
tegmen: 5 cover, plate 6 elytra 7 tympani 8 covering, fore-wing
tegua: 6 sandal
tegula: 4 tile
tegument: 4 coat 5 cover, testa 6 thatch
tegurium: hut 5 cabin 6 shrine
tehee: 5 laugh 6 giggle, titter 7 snicker
Tehuantepec Gulf Indian: 5 Huave
teiidae: 4 teju 7 lizards
teju: 6 lizard 8 teguexin
tekke: rug 6 carpet 7 convent 9 monastery
tela: web 6 tissue 7 bristle 8 membrane
telamon: 8 atlantes, caryatid
Telamon: 5 Atlas
 brother: 6 Peleus
 father: 6 Aeacus
 friend: 8 Heracles, Hercules
 son: 4 Ajax 6 Teucer

teledu: 6 badger

telega: 4 cart 5 wagon

telegraph: 4 wire 5 cable

code: 5 Morse

inventor: 5 Morse

key: 6 tapper

signal: dot 4 dash 9 semaphore

telegraphic communication: 10 letter-gram

Telemachus: *father:* 7 Ulysses 8 Odysseus

mother: 4 Penelope

teleost fish: eel 5 apoda

telephone: 4 buzz, call, dial, ring 6 ring up

book: 9 directory

inventor: 4 Bell

receiver: 8 cymaphen

Telephus: *father:* 8 Hercules

mother: 4 Auge

telescope: jam 5 glass 7 shorten 8 collapse, condense, simplify

object seen with: 11 debilissima

site: 7 Palomar

telescopic: 9 farseeing

television: TV 4 tube 5 telly, video 8 boob tube, idiot box

award: 4 Emmy

broadcast: 8 telecast

cable: 7 coaxial

camera platform: 5 dolly

commercial: 4 spot 7 message

commercial cat: 6 Morris

dragon: 5 Ollie

frequency: UHF, VHF

interference: 4 snow 5 ghost

lens: 4 zoom

network: ABC, CBS, NBC, NET, PBS

picture tube: 9 kinescope

type of show: 4 live, news, quiz, talk 5 movie, panel, rerun 6 serial, sitcom, sudser 9 soap opera

telic: 9 purposive 10 purposeful 12 teleological

tell: bid, say 4 chat, deem, hill, know, tale, talk, tole, toll 5 aread, areed, breve, count, mound, order, speak, state, utter, value, weigh 6 decide, direct, impart, inform, number, recite, reckon, regard, relate, repeat, report, reveal, tattle 7 account, command, dictate, discern, divulge, express, mention, narrate, publish, recount, request 8 acquaint, announce, disclose, rehearse 9 calculate, discourse, enumerate, recognize 11 communicate 12 discriminate

confidentially: 7 confide

in advance: 4 warn

on: 4 sing 5 peach 6 snitch, squeal

revelatory facts: 6 debunk

romances: 4 gest 5 geste

secrets: 5 clype

stories: 4 yarn 6 tattle

thoughtlessly: 4 blab, blat

without authority: 5 rumor

Tell's home: Uri

teller: 4 blow 5 shoot 6 remark, sprout 7 cashier 8 informer, narrator 9 bank clerk, describer 11 annunciator

telling: 5 valid 6 cogent 8 forceful, relation, striking 9 effective, pertinent 10 convincing, satisfying

telltale: 4 blab, hint 6 gossip 7 tattler 8 betrayer, informer 9 betraying, indicator 10 indication, talebearer

telltruth: 7 honesty 9 frankness

telluride: 7 altaite

telson: 6 somite 7 segment

of king crab: 5 pleon

temblor: 5 shake, shock 6 tremor 10 earthquake

temerarious: 4 rash 6 chance 8 heedless, reckless 9 venturous 10 fortuitous, headstrong 11 adventurous, venturesome

temerity: 4 gall 5 cheek, nerve 8 audacity, boldness, rashness 9 assurance, hardihood 10 effrontery 12 recklessness 13 foolhardiness 15 venturesomeness

temper: fit, ire, mix 4 bait, bate, coll, curb, cure, ease, heal, mean, mood, neal, rage, tone 5 adapt, anger, birse, blend, delay, humor 6 adjust, animus, anneal, attune, church, dander, dilute, direct, govern, harden, manage, medium, mingle, modify, puddle, reduce, season, soften, soothe, steady 7 assuage, chasten, control, moisten, mollify, passion, qualify, restore, toughen 8 chastise, compound, mitigate, moderate, modulate, regulate, restrain 9 composure 10 equanimity, irritation 11 accommodate, disposition, state of mind

display: 5 scene 7 tantrum

even: 4 calm 5 staid 6 sedate

kind of: ire 4 huff, mood 6 choler, spleen

temperament: 4 mood 5 gemut, humor 6 crasis, nature 7 caprice, climate, emotion 10 adjustment 11 disposition, temperature 12 constitution

temperance: 7 measure 8 sobriety 10 abstinence, continence, moderation

temperate: 4 calm, cool, mild 5 sober 6 soften 8 moderate 9 continent 10 abstemious, restrained 12 conservative 13 dispassionate

temperature: 4 heat 5 fever, state 6 temper, warmth 7 mixture 8 compound, mildness 9 intensity 10 moderation, proportion 11 disposition, temperament 12 constitution

tempest: 4 gale, rage, wind 5 orage, storm 6 tumult 7 agitate, borasca, borasco, turmoil 9 agitation, bourasque, commotion, hurricane 12 thunderstorm

Tempest characters: 5 Ariel 7 Caliban, Miranda 8 Prospero

tempestuous: 4 wild 5 galey, gusty 6 stormy 7 violent 9 turbulent

template, templet: 4 beam, lute, mold 5 bezel, bezil, gauge 7 pattern

temple: 4 fane, naos, rath 5 candi, cella, edile, huaca, kovil, ratha, speos 6 aedile, chandi, church, haffet, haffit, hieron 10 house of God, tabernacle

basin: 5 laver

for all gods: 8 pantheon

kind of: sha, taj, wat 4 deul, Rath 5 jinjua, Ratha 6 church, jinsha, pagoda 7 capitol 8 pantheon 9 Parthenon

part: 5 cella

sanctuary: 10 penetralia

tempo: 4 pace, rate, time 5 speed 6 rhythm, timing

pert. to: 6 agogic

rapid: 6 presto 7 allegro

slow: 5 lento 6 adagio

very slow: 5 grave

temporal: 4 laic 5 civil, scale 6 carnal, muscle 7 earthly, profane, secular, worldly 9 ephemeral, political, temporary 10 transitory 11 impermanent 13 chronological, materialistic

temporary: 6 acting, pro tem, timely 7 interim, secular, topical 8 temporal 9 ad interim, ephemeral, transient 10 transitory 11 provisional

contrivance: 9 makeshift

temporize: 5 delay, humor, yield 6 demand, parley, soothe 9 negotiate 13 procrastinate

tempt: try 4 defy, fand, lead, lure, test 5 decoy, probe, prove, taunt 6 allure, assail, entice, incite, induce, seduce 7 assault, attempt, attract, provoke 8 endeavor, persuade 9 endeavour, seduction 10 inducement

temptation: 4 bait 5 trial 7 testing 9 seduction 10 allurement, enticement, inducement

tempter: 5 devil, Satan 6 baiter

tempting: 8 alluring, enticing, inviting 9 seductive 10 attractive

temptress: 4 vamp 5 Circe, siren 7 Delilah, Lorelei, mermaid 10 Parthenope 11 enchantress

tempus fugit: 9 time flies

ten: 4 iota (Gk.) 5 decad 6 decade, denary

ares: 6 decare

decibels: bel

dollars: 7 sawbuck

group of: 6 decade

prefix: dec 4 deca

Ten Commandments: 9 Decalogue

ten-footed: 7 decapod

ten-gallon hat: 8 sombrero

ten-sided figure: 7 decagon

ten-stringed: 9 decachord

ten-year periods: 7 decades 9 decenniad, decennium

tenable: 8 credible 9 plausible 10 defensible 11 justifiable 12 maintainable

tenacious: 4 fast, firm 5 tough 6 cledgy, dogged, grippy, sticky, strong 7 gripple, miserly, viscous 8 adhesive, cohesive, holdfast, sticking, stubborn 9 glutinous, niggardly, retentive 10 persistent 11 closefisted 12 pertinacious

tenacity: 7 courage 8 firmness 9 toughness 11 miserliness, persistence 12 adhesiveness, cohesiveness, perseverance

tenancy: 6 estate, tenure 7 holding 9 occupancy 10 possession

tenant: 4 leud 5 ceile, dreng 6 border, drengh, geneat, holder, leaser, lessee, occupy, renter, vassal 7 chakdar, cottier, dweller, inhabit 8 occupant 9 bordarius, collibert 10 inhabitant

feudal: 4 leud 6 vassal 7 socager

tend: 4 burn, care, lead, mind, move, till, wait, work 5 apply, await, guard, nurse, offer, reach, see to, serve, swing, treat, watch 6 attend, direct, expect, extend, foster, intend, kindle, listen, manage, supply 7 care for, conduce, hearken, incline, oversee, provide, purpose, stretch, tending 8 minister, tendency 9 accompany, attentive, co-operate, cultivate, gravitate, look after 10 contribute

a fire: 5 stoke

to rise: 8 levitate

toward one point: 8 converge

tendency: run, set 4 bent, bias, tide 5 drift, drive, tenor, trend 6 course, effect, object, result 7 aptness, bearing, leaning 8 appetite, movement, relation 9 affection, direction, proneness, readiness 10 proclivity, propension, propensity 11 disposition, inclination

structural: 7 peloria

tender: bid, tid 4 boat, dear, fond, gift, keen, kind, mild, nice, soft, sore, thin, warm, weak 5 chary, frail, light, offer, young 6 delate, feeble, gentle, humane, loving, submit, touchy, vessel, waiter 7 amabile, amatory, amorous, careful, fragile, pitiful, present, proffer, slender, sparing, steamer, subdued, suggest, tenuous, vehicle 8 delicate, feminine, immature, merciful, precious, proposal, ticklish, tolerant 9 brotherly, sensitive, succulent 10 charitable, effeminate, scrupulous 11 considerate, kindhearted, softhearted, susceptible, sympathetic, warmhearted 12 affectionate 13 compassionate 14 impressionable

animals: 6 herder 10 husbandman

cattle: 6 cowboy, herder 7 byreman 8

neatherd 9 byrewoman

for cloth: 9 stenterer

horse: 5 groom 6 ostler 7 hostler, stabler

music: 7 amoroso

ship: gig 5 barge 6 dingey, dinghy 7 collier, pinnace

tenderfoot: 6 novice 7 greenie 8 beginner, neophyte, newcomer 9 cheechaco, cheechako, greenhorn

tenderhearted: 6 humane 11 sympathetic

tenderloin: 5 steak 11 filet mignon

tenderness: 4 love, pity 6 cherte 8 kindness, softness, sympathy, weakness 9 affection 10 compassion, gentleness 13 sensitiveness

tendon: 4 band, cord 5 chord, nerve, sinew 11 aponeurosis

Achilles: 9 hamstring

tendril: 4 curl 5 clasp, sprig 6 branch, cirrus 7 ringlet, stipule

tenebrous: 4 dark 5 dusky 6 gloomy 7 obscure 8 darkness

tenement: 5 abode 8 building, dwelling 9 apartment 10 habitation

tenet: ism 4 view 5 adoxy, canon, creed, dogma, maxim 6 belief, decree 7 opinion, paradox 8 doctrine 9 principle

tenfold: 6 denary 7 decuple

tengere: sky 7 heavens

teniente: 6 deputy 7 headman 10 lieutenant

tenne: 5 brown, color, tawny

Tennessee: *capital:* 9 Nashville

city: 7 Jackson, Memphis 9 Knoxville 11 Chattanooga

county: 4 Clay, Dyer, Knox, Lake, Polk, Rhea 6 Blount, Greene, Shelby 8 Davidson, Hamilton, Sullivan

dam: 6 Norris

explorer: 6 de Soto, Joliet 7 Jolliet, La-Salle 9 Marquette

federal agency: TVA

lake: 8 Reelfoot

mountain 5 Unaka 7 Lookout 12 Great Smokies

national park: 6 Shiloh

nickname: 9 Volunteer

pioneer: 12 Davy Crockett

plateau: 10 Cumberland

state bird: 11 mockingbird

state flower: 4 iris

state tree: 11 tulip poplar

tennis: *between four persons:* 7 doubles

between two persons: 7 singles

champion: 4 Ashe (Arthur), Betz (Pauline), Borg (Bjorn), Hard (Darlene), Hart (Doris), King (Billie Jean), Wade (Virginia) 5 Budge (Don), Bueno (Maria), Court (Margaret Smith), Evert (Chris), Laver (Rod), Lloyd (Chris Evert), Perry (Fred), Riggs (Bobbie),

Vilas (Guillermo), Wills (Helen) 6 Austin (Tracy), Fraser (Neale), Gibson (Althea), Kramer (Jack), Marble (Alice), Parker (Frank), Tilden (Bill) 7 Connors (Jimmy), Emerson (Roy), Lacoste (Rene), McEnroe (John), Nastase (Ilie), Sedgman (Frank) 8 Connolly (Maureen), Gonzalez (Pancho), Newcombe (John), Rosewall (Ken)

game series: set

no score: 4 love

old form: 5 bandy

points: 4 aces

prize cup: 5 Davis

racket: bat

related game: 6 squash 8 handball 9 badminton

score: ace 4 love 5 deuce

shoe: 7 sneaker

shot: cut, lob 4 chop, dink 8 backhand, forehand

term: ace, cut, let, lob, set 4 love 5 deuce, fault, serve 6 volley 7 receive, service 9 advantage

Tennyson: 11 English poet

character: 4 Enid 5 Arden 6 Hallam

poem: 4 Maud 10 In Memoriam 11 The Princess 12 Locksley Hall

tenon: cog 4 coak 8 dovetail

tenor: 4 body, copy, feck, gist 5 drift, stamp, trend 6 course, intent, nature, singer 7 holding, meaning, purport, writing 8 tendency 9 character, condition, direction, discourse, procedure, substance 10 transcript

falsetto: 8 tenorino

tens of thousands: 7 myriads

tense: 4 edgy, rapt, taut, time 5 rigid, stiff, tight 6 intent, queasy, tauten 7 intense, uptight 8 strained 9 stretched 10 breathless

past: 9 preterite

verb: 4 past 6 aorist, future 7 perfect, present 9 preterite 10 pluperfect 11 conditional

tensile: 6 pliant 7 ductile, elastic

tension: 4 bent 6 strain, stress 7 closure 8 pressure

releasing of: 7 detente

tent: hut 4 camp, care, heed, show, stop, tend, test, wine 5 cover, crame, frame, lodge, probe, teach, tempt 6 attend, beware, encamp, hinder, intent, pulpit, tender 7 observe, prevent, proffer, shelter 9 attention, attentive 10 habitation

dweller: 4 Arab 5 nomad 6 camper, Indian 7 scenite, tourist

flap: fly

kind: pup 4 pawl, yurt 5 darry, shoo!, tepee, toldo, yurta 6 abbacy, teepee, tienda, wigwam 7 balagan, kibitka, marquee, sparver 8 pavilion 9 pretor-

ium 10 praetorium
large: 8 pavilion
maker: 4 Omar
tentacle: 6 feeler 7 tendril
animal with: 5 squid 7 octopus 10 cuttle-fish
without: 7 acerous
tentage: 5 camps
tentamen: 5 trial 7 attempt
tentative: 9 temporary 11 conditional, impermanent, provisional, vacillating 12 experimental
tenter: 5 frame
tenterhooks: 4 nail 6 strain 8 suspense
tenth: 5 tithe 6 decima 7 decimae 8 decimate
part: 5 tithe
tenuity: 6 rarity 7 exility, poverty 8 delicacy, fineness, rareness, thinness 9 faintness, indigence 10 meagerness, slightness 11 slenderness
tenuous: 4 fine, rare, slim, thin, weak 6 flimsy, slight, subtle 7 gaseous, slender, subtile 8 delicate, ethereal 11 implausible 13 insignificant, unsubstantial
tenure: 4 hold, term 5 lease 6 manner 8 courtesy 9 condition
tepee, teepee: 6 wigwam
tepid: 4 mild, warm 8 lukewarm 11 half-hearted
tequila: 5 drink 6 liquor, mescal
tera: 6 church 9 monastery
Terah: *father:* 5 Nahor
son: 5 Haran 7 Abraham
teraph: 4 idol 5 image 8 talisman
teras: 7 monster
tercet: 5 rhyme 7 triplet
terebene: 9 deodorant 10 antiseptic 12 disinfectant
terebra: 5 auger, drill
terebrate: 4 bore 9 perforate
teredo: 4 mollusk 8 shipworm
terete: 7 centric, tapered 8 columnar 11 cylindrical
Tereus: *sister-in-law:* 9 Philomela
son: 4 Itys 6 Itylus
wife: 6 Procne
tergal: 4 back 6 dorsal
tergiversate: lie 5 shift 6 defect, weasel 7 shuffle 10 apostatize, equivocate
tergiversation: 6 deceit 7 evasion 8 apostasy 10 subterfuge
tergum: 4 back
term: end 4 call, date, half, name, span, time, word 5 bound, limit, state 6 period, tenure 7 article, entitle, epithet, session 8 boundary, duration, semester 9 condition, extremity 10 definition, expression 11 appellation, termination
cricket: off, ons 6 yorker
fencing: hai, hay 4 bind 5 coupe 6 touche 8 tacautac

golf: lie, par, tee 4 baff, fore, hook 5 bogey, bogie, divot, eagle, green, slice 6 birdie, stroke, stymie 7 gallery
grammar: 6 phase, simile, syntax
heraldry: 4 ente, urde
Hindu, of respect: sri
jail: lag 4 jolt 7 stretch
Jewish, of reproach: 4 raca
mathematics: 4 nome, root, sine 6 cosine
of address: sir 4 sire 6 milady, milord, sirrah
of endearment: 5 astor 8 ashtore
of life: age 5 sands
of office: 6 regime, tenure
printer: 4 dele, stet
rugby: try 5 scrum
school: 7 quarter 8 semester 9 trimester
science: ame, azo 4 beta 5 stoss
sea: 4 ahoy 5 avast, belay
termagant: 5 shrew 6 Amazon, tartar, virago 7 furious 8 scolding 9 turbulent 10 boisterous, tumultuous 11 quarrelsome
termed: 5 named 6 called, styled, yclept
terminable: 6 finish, finite 9 limitable 12 determinable 13 discontinuing
terminal: end 4 last 5 anode, depot, final, limit 6 finish 7 cathode, closing, limital, station 8 desinent, ultimate 9 electrode, extremity 10 concluding
negative: 7 cathode, kathode
positive: 5 anode
terminate: end 4 call, halt, quit, stop 5 bound, cease, close, limit 6 define, direct, expire, finish, result 7 achieve, adjourn, confine, destine, dismiss, perfect 8 complete, conclude, restrict
terminating: 5 final 6 ending
distinct point: 9 apiculate
trefoil: 6 botone
termination: end 4 amen 5 bound, close, event, limit 6 ending, expiry, finale, finish, period, result, upshot 7 outcome, purpose 8 boundary, decision, finality, terminus 9 extremity 10 completion, concluding, conclusion, expiration 13 determination
malady: 5 lysis
terminative: 8 absolute, bounding, definite 10 concluding 11 determining
termite: ant 4 anai, anay
termless: 8 infinite, nameless, unending 9 boundless, limitless 13 indescribable, inexpressible, unconditional
terms: 9 agreement 10 conditions, provisions 11 limitations 12 propositions 13 circumstances
come to: 5 agree
make: 5 treat 9 negotiate
tern: 4 darr, gull 10 sea swallow
genus: 5 anous 6 sterna
ternary: 6 treble, triple 7 ternion, trinity 9 threefold

ternate: 12 trifoliolate

terra: 5 earth

terra alba: 4 clay 6 gypsum, kaolin 8 magnesium

terra cotta: 4 clay 6 statue 7 pottery 11 earthenware

terra firma: 5 earth 6 estate 8 mainland 11 solid ground

terrace: 4 bank, dais, mesa, step 5 bench 7 balcony, gallery, portico 8 chabutra, platform 9 colonnade

in series: 8 parterre

wall: 6 podium

terrain: 4 form, turf 5 tract 6 milieu, region 7 contour, demesne 11 environment

terrapin: 4 emyd, emys 6 coodle, heifer, potter, slider, turtle

terrestrial: 6 earthy, layman, mortal 7 earthly, mundane, terrene, worldly 9 planetary

terret: 4 ring 7 cringle

terrible: 4 dire, gast, hard 5 awful, lurid 6 severe, tragic 7 direful, extreme, fearful, ghastly, hideous, intense, painful, very bad 8 almighty, dreadful, horrible, terrific 9 appalling, atrocious, excessive, frightful 10 formidable, terrifying, tremendous, unpleasant 12 disagreeable

Terrible one: 4 Ivan

terrier: dog, fox 4 Bull, Skye 5 cairn, Irish, Welsh 6 Boston 8 Airedale, Scottish, Sealyham 9 Yorkshire 10 Bedlington, Clydesdale

terrific: 7 extreme, fearful 8 dreadful, exciting, terrible 9 appalling, excessive, frightful, marvelous 10 terrifying, tremendous

terrified: 4 awed 6 afraid, aghast, frozen 7 ghastly

terrify: awe, cow, hag 4 bree, fray, stun 5 alarm, annoy, appal, daunt, deter, drive, haunt, impel, scare, shock, tease 6 affirm, afread, agrise, appall, bother, dismay, injure 7 stupefy, torment 8 affright, frighten 9 importune

terrifying: 6 horrid 7 ghastly, hideous 8 terrible

terrigenous: 9 earthborn 13 autochthonous

terrine: jar 4 dish, stew 6 ragout

territorial division: amt 6 canton 7 commune 10 department 14 arrondissement

territory: 4 area, land 5 field, scope, state, tract 6 extent, ground, region, sphere 7 country, portion, terrain 8 district, environs, province 9 bailiwick 12 neighborhood

kind of: 5 banat 6 canton 7 banlieu, enclave 8 banlieue, Pashalic 10 palatinate

shut in: 7 enclave

terror: awe 4 fear, fray, pest 5 alarm, dread, panic 6 affray, dismal, fright, horror 8 dreddour 11 trepidation 12 terribless 13 consternation

terrorism: 11 subjugation 12 intimidation

terrorist: 5 rebel 6 bomber 8 alarmist 11 scaremonger

terrorize: awe 5 abash, appal, scare 6 appall, coerce 8 frighten 9 embarrass 10 intimidate

terry: 4 loop 5 cloth

terse: 4 curt, neat 5 brief, pithy 6 abrupt, claret, rubbed, smooth 7 compact, concise, laconic, pointed, refined 8 clearcut, incisive, polished, succinct, unprolix 11 sententious, tightlipped 12 accomplished

tertiary period: 5 third 7 neocene

tertulia: 4 club 5 party 7 meeting

terzina: 6 tercet 7 triplet

tessellated: 5 tiled 6 mosaic 9 checkered

tessera: 4 cube, tile 5 glass, label, token 6 billet, marble, pledge, tablet, ticket 7 voucher 8 password 9 rectangle 11 certificate

test: pot, try 4 exam, fand, feel, will 5 assay, check, cupel, grope, proof, prove, shell, taste, testa, trial, weave 6 ordeal, refine, sample 7 approof, approve, examine, witness 8 cupeling, evidence, potsherd, standard 9 construct, criterion, determine, testament, testimony 10 experience, experiment, touchstone 11 examination, performance 12 authenticate

in fineness and weight: pyx

kind: 4 acid

operation: 9 shakedown

ore: 5 assay

series: 7 gantlet

testa: 7 coating 8 covering, episperm, tegument 10 integument

testament: Job 4 will 8 covenant, landbook 9 testimony 12 confirmation

testator: 7 legator, witness 9 testatrix

beneficiary of: 4 heir 7 heiress, heritor 9 inheritor

tester: 5 crown, frame 6 canopy, conner, helmet, prover, teston 7 assayer, candler, sparver 8 denierer 9 chauffeur, headpiece

testicle: cob 6 testis, testes(pl.) 7 genitor

deer: 6 doucet, dowcet, dowset

testified under oath: 7 deponed

testifier: 7 witness 8 deponent

testify: 5 swear 6 affirm, attest, depone, depose 7 declare, express, profess, protest 8 indicate, manifest, proclaim

testimonial: 4 sign 5 salvo, token 7 tribute, warrant, writing 8 evidence 9 testimony 10 credential 11 certificate

testimony: say 6 attest, avowal 7 witness

8 evidence 10 deposition, profession 11 affirmation, attestation, certificate, declaration 14 recommendation

testudo: 4 lyre, shed 5 cover, talpa, tumor, vault 6 screen 7 ceiling

testy: 6 touchy 7 crabbed, fretful, grouchy, peevish, waspish 8 petulant, snappish 9 impatient, irascible, irritable, obstinate 10 headstrong

tetanus: 7 lockjaw 9 holotonia

tetchy: 6 touchy 7 peevish 9 irascible, irritable, sensitive

tête-a-tête: 4 chat, seat, sofa 7 vis-a-vis 8 causeuse 12 conversation

tetel: 5 torah

tether: tie 4 band, rope 5 cable, chain, leash, limit, noose 6 fasten, picket 7 confine 8 restrain

Tethys: 5 Titan 8 Titaness
brother: 6 Cronus
father: 6 Uranus
husband: 7 Oceanus

tetrad: 4 four 7 quartet 8 fourfold

tetragon: 6 square 7 rhombus 10 quadrangle

tetric: 5 harsh 6 gloomy, sullen 7 austere

tetter: 4 fret 6 eczema, herpes, lichen

Teutonic: 5 Dutch 6 German, Gothic 7 English 12 Scandinavian
alphabet character: 4 rune
barbarian: 4 Goth
deity: Eir, Hel, Tiu, Tyr, Ull 4 Erda, Frea, Frig, Norn, Odin, Thor 5 Aesir, Baldr, Brage, Bragl, Donar, Othin, Tiwaz, Wodin, Wotan 6 Balder, Frigga, Saeter 7 Forseti 8 Heimdall
homicide: 5 morth
land: 4 odal
law: 5 Salic
legendary hero: 4 Offa
race: 4 Ubii 5 Danes, Goths, Jutes 6 Angles, Franks, Saxons 7 Germans, Vandals 8 Lombards 10 Norwegians 11 Burgundians 13 Scandinavians
water nymph: nis

tew: taw, tow, vex 4 beat, fuss, pull, work 5 knead, tease, tools 6 incite, strive, tackle, tuyere 7 fatigue 8 struggle

tewit: 7 lapwing

Texas: *battle:* 5 Alamo 10 San Jacinto
bronco, broncho: 7 mustang
capital: 6 Austin
city: 4 Waco 6 Dallas, El Paso, Laredo, Odessa 7 Abilene, Denison, Houston, Lubbock 8 Amarillo 9 Fort Worth 10 San Antonio
cottonwood: 5 alamo
county: Bee 4 Leon, Polk, Rusk 5 Nolan, Starr, Tyler 6 Harris, Sutton, Walker 7 Houston, Madison, Navarro, Trinity 8 Anderson, Angelina, Cherokee 9 Freestone, Limestone

cowboy jacket: 8 chaqueta
fever carrier: 4 tick
fortress: 5 Alamo
founder: 6 Austin
island: 5 Padre 9 Galveston, Matagorda
massacre site: 5 Alamo
motto: 10 Friendship
national park: 7 Big Bend
nickname: 8 Lone Star
river: Red 5 Pecos 6 Brazos, Neches, Nueces 9 Rio Grande
shrine: 5 Alamo
shrub: 6 anagua, anaqua
state bird: 11 mockingbird
state flower: 10 bluebonnet
state police: 6 ranger
state tree: 5 pecan
U.S. president: LBJ 10 Eisenhower 14 Lyndon B. Johnson

text: 4 copy 5 theme, topic 7 passage, subject 11 handwriting 13 subject matter
operatic: 8 libretto
pen: 5 ronde
pert. to: 7 textual
revision: 9 recension
set to music: 8 oratorio
variation: 7 lection

textbook: 6 manual, primer

textile: 6 fabric
dealer: 6 mercer
goods: 7 mercery
ornament: 8 fagoting
plant refuse: 5 hurds
ring device: 6 poteye
worker: 4 dyer 6 reeder

texture: web 4 wale 5 fiber, grain 6 cobweb, fabric, tissue 7 essence, textile 9 structure 11 composition, fabrication
cloth: 4 wale, warp, woof

tez: 7 pungent, violent

tezkirah: 7 license 8 passport 11 certificate

Thackeray: 8 novelist
novels: 9 Pendennis 10 Vanity Fair 11 Henry Esmond

Thailand: 4 Siam
cab: 5 samlo 6 samlaw, samlor
canal: 5 klong
capital: 7 Bangkok
city: 7 Ayuthia, Ayuthya, Bangkok 9 Sukhothai
coin: att 4 baht 5 fuang, tical 6 pynung, salung, satang
demon: nag
dialect: Lao
dress: 6 panung
fabric: 8 siamoise
island: 6 Phuket
isthmus: Kra
king: 4 Rama
measure: ken, niu, nmu, rai, sat, sen, sok,

wah, yot 4 keup, ngan, tang, yote 5 kwien, laang, sesti, tanan 6 kabiet, kam meu 6 kanahn 7 chai meu, roeneng 8 chang awn 9 anukabiet

monetary unit: 4 baht

mountain: 5 Khies 8 Maelamun

native: Lao

people: Tai 4 Thai 7 Siamese

provincial capital: 5 Muang

river: 6 Mekong, Meping 7 Meklong 10 Chaophraya

spirit: nat

state: 6 Patani

temple: wat

town: 5 Puket 7 Ayuthia, Bangkok, Lop-buri, Singora, Songkla 8 Kiangmai 9 Chiengmai

weight: hap, pai, sen, sok 4 baht, haph, klam, klom 5 catty, chang, coyan, picul, tical 6 fluang, salung, sompay 7 tam-lung

Thais composer: 8 Massenet

thalassic: 6 marine 7 oceanic, pelagic 8 maritime

Thalia: See **Grace, Muse**

thalidomide: 8 sedative 12 hypnotic drug

Thames: 4 Isis 5 river

city and town: 4 Eton 6 Henley, London, Oxford

tributary: 6 Tyburn

Thanatopsis author: 6 Bryant

Thanatos: 5 death

brother: 6 Hypnos

mother: Nyx

thane: 5 churl 7 servant, warrior 8 fol-lower 9 attendant

estate: 9 manor

thank: 5 blame 11 acknowledge

thankful: 8 grateful 11 meritorious 12 appreciative

thankless: 10 ungrateful 13 unappreci-ated

person: 7 ingrate

thanks: 7 cumshaw 8 gramercy 9 because of, gratitude 11 gratulation 12 appreci-ation 15 acknowledgement

that: yon 4 such 6 yonder 7 because

that is: 5 id est, to wit 6 namely

that not: 4 lest

thatch: 4 nipa, roof 5 cover

peg: 4 scob

support: 6 wattle

thatcher: 6 reeder 7 crowder, hellier

thaumaturgists: 6 Goetae 7 wizards 9 magicians, sorcerers

thaumaturgy: 5 magic 11 legerdemain

thaw: 4 melt 6 unbend 7 liquefy 8 dis-solve

the: 7 article

French: les

German: der, die, das

Italian: 4 egli, ella

Spanish: las, los

the same: 4 idem 5 ditto 8 likewise 9 identical

theater, theatre: 5 arena, drama, house, odeon, odeum, stage 8 coliseum 9 play-house

audience: 5 house

award: 4 Tony

box-office sign: SRO

curtain: 4 drop 6 teaser

district: 6 Rialto

Elizabethan: 5 Globe

entrance hall: 5 foyer, lobby

full: SRO

Greek: 5 odeon, odeum

group: 4 ANTA

low-class: 4 gaff

motion-picture: 5 movie 6 cinema 8 bio-scope 13 cinematograph, kinemato-graph

outdoor: 5 arena 7 drive-in, open-air

part: box, pit 4 loge 5 foyer, stage 7 bal-cony, gallery, parquet 8 parterre 9 or-chestra 10 proscenium

pit: 6 circle 7 parquet 8 parterre

sports: 5 arena

theater-in-the-round: 5 arena

theatrical: 5 showy, stagy 6 scenic 7 pompous 8 affected, dramatic 10 artifi-cial, histrionic 11 declamation 12 melodramatic

company: 6 troupe

extra: 4 supe 5 super

profession: 5 stage

sign: SRO

spectacle: 7 pageant

star: 4 hero, lead 7 heroine

valet: 7 dresser

Thebes: *acropolis:* 6 Cadmea

blind soothsayer: 8 Tiresias

deity: 4 Amon 5 Ament

district: 7 Thebiad

founder: 6 Cadmus

king: 5 Laius 7 Amphion, Oedipus 8 Eteocles, Pentheus

poet: 6 Pindar

prince: 7 Oedipus

queen: 5 Aedon, Niobe 7 Jocasta

statue: 6 Memnon

wicked queen: 5 Dirce

theca: sac, sad 4 case 7 capsule

theft: 5 pinch, steal 6 furtum, piracy 7 bribery, larceny, robbery 8 burglary 9 pilferage 10 conveyance, plagiarism 12 embezzlement

theft-like: 7 piratic

thelium: 6 nipple 7 papilla

them: 5 hemen

thema: 5 topic 6 thesis 7 subject 12 dis-sertation

theme: 4 base, text 5 ditty, essay, motif, topic 6 matter, theses, thesis 7 subject

9 discourse 11 composition, proposition 12 dissertation 13 subject matter

hackneyed: 6 cliche

literary: 5 motif

musical: 4 tema

title: 5 lemma

Themis: *concern of:* law 7 harmony

father: 6 Uranus

mother: 4 Gaea

then: 4 next 5 again, alors(F.) 6 before 7 besides 8 formerly, moreover 9 therefore 11 accordingly

music: poi

then too: 5 again

thence: 4 away 9 elsewhere, therefore, therefrom 10 henceforth 11 thenceforth

theodolite: 7 alidade

theologian: 6 cleric, divine 9 churchman

authority: 4 imam 5 ulema

famous: 5 Arius 6 Calvin, Luther 7 Erasmus 13 Thomas Aquinas

study of unity: 7 irenics

theorbo: 4 lute

theorem: 4 rule 5 axiom 9 principle

theoretical: 5 ideal 8 abstract, platonic 11 speculation, speculative, unpractical 12 hypothetical

theorist: 10 ideologist

theorize: 7 suggest 9 postulate, speculate

theory: ism 4 plan 5 guess 6 scheme 7 formula 8 analysis, doctrine 9 principle 10 assumption, conjecture, hypothesis 11 explanation, speculation 13 contemplation

kind of: 7 plenism 9 Platonism 13 phenomenalism

therapy: 9 treatment 10 psychiatry

there: ibi(L.), yon 4 able 5 ready, voila 6 yonder 7 thither 8 equipped, reliable 10 dependable

thereafter: 9 afterward 11 accordingly 12 subsequently

therefore: 4 ergo, then, thus 5 hence, since 6 frothy, thence 9 wherefore 11 accordingly 12 consequently

therewith: mit 6 withal 7 besides, threat 8 moreover 9 forthwith, thereupon

therm, therme: 4 bath, pool 7 calorie

thermal: hot 4 warm

thermal unit: btu 6 degree 7 calorie

thermometer: 7 Celsius, Reaumur 8 pyrostat 9 pyrometer 10 Centigrade, Fahrenheit

thesaurus: 5 Roget 7 lexicon 8 treasury 10 dictionary, repository, storehouse 12 encyclopedia

Thesaurus compiler: 5 Roget

Theseus: 12 King of Athens

father: 6 Aegeus

lover: 7 Ariadne

mother: 6 Aethra

slayer of: 8 Minotaur

wife: 7 Antiope, Phaedra 9 Hippolyte

thesis: 5 essay, point, theme 7 premise 9 discourse, postulate, statement 10 assumption, conception 11 affirmation, proposition 12 dissertation

opposed to: 5 arsis

thespian: 5 actor 6 player 7 actress 8 dramatic 9 tragedian

Thessaly: *king:* 7 Admetus

mountain: Ida, Osa 4 Ossa 6 Othrys, Pelion, Pindus 7 Olympus 9 Psiloriti

valley: 5 Tempe

witch: 7 Aganice

thetic: 8 positive 9 arbitrary 10 prescribed

Thetis: 6 Nereid

husband: 6 Peleus

son: 8 Achilles

theurgy: 5 magic 7 miracle, sorcery 9 occultism

thew: 4 form, mode 5 habit, power, press, sinew, stool, trait 6 custom, manner, muscle, virtue 7 oppress, pillory, quality 8 strength 10 discipline, resolution

thewless: 4 lazy 6 feeble 10 spiritless

thick: fat 4 dull, hazy 5 broad, brosy, burly, close, crass, dense, gross, heavy, husky, plump, solid 6 coarse, filled, greasy, hoarse, obtuse, shaggy, stodgy, stupid 7 blubber, compact, crowded, grumous, muffled, thicket, viscous 8 abundant, familiar, friendly, guttural, intimate, profound, thickset 9 excessive, luxuriant 10 indistinct 11 inspissated, marticulate, thickheaded 12 impenetrable

and short: 5 squat 6 chunky

soup: 5 puree 7 pottage

thick-skinned: 4 cold 7 callous 9 pachyderm 11 pachydermic

thicken: gel 4 clot, crud, curd 5 cloud, crowd, flock 6 curdle, deepen, harden 7 confirm, congeal, stiffen 8 condense 9 intensify 10 incrassate, inspissate, strengthen

thicket: 4 bosk, bush, rone, shaw 5 brake, clump, copse, grove, hedge, shola 6 bosket, covert, greave 7 boscage, boskage, bosquet, coppice, spinney 9 brushwood 10 underbrush

kind: 5 brake, hedge, shola 7 chamise, chamiso, coppice, spinney 8 chamisal 9 chaparral

thickheaded: 4 dull 5 dense 6 stupid 7 doltish 11 blockheaded

thickness: ply 5 layer, sheet 8 diameter 9 curdiness, denseness, dimension, heaviness 10 corpulence 11 consistency

thickset: 4 stub 5 squat, stout 6 chumpy, chunky, fleshy, portly, stocky, stodgy, stubby

thickskulled: 4 dull, slow 5 heavy 6 obtuse, stupid 11 thickheaded

thief (see also **stealer**): 4 chor, gilt, prig 5 budge, scamp 6 ackman, arrant, bandit, cannon, cloyer, hooker, looter, nimmer, rascal, robber, sucker, waster 7 bramble, brigand, burglar, filcher, grifter, sneaker, stealer 8 cutpurse, gangster, larcener 9 larcenist, scoundrel 10 cat burglar, depredator, freebooter, highwayman, plagiarist

crucified beside Christ: 6 Desmas, Dismas, Dysmas

kind of: gun 5 ganef, ganof, gonof, snoop 6 ackman, angler, gonoph, pirate, swiper 7 gorilla, mercury, rustler 9 drawlatch 10 pickpocket

thieveless(Sc.): 4 cold 5 bleak 6 frigid 7 aimless 8 bootless, listless 10 forbidding

thieves' Latin: 5 slang

thievish: sly 7 furtive, kleptic 8 stealthy 9 larcenous

thigh: ham 4 hock 5 carve, femur, flank, meros, merus 6 femora(pl.), gammon

armor: 5 cuish

bone: 5 femur, ilium

muscle: 9 sartorius

pains: 8 sciatica

pert. to: 6 crural

thill: 4 sill 5 plank, shaft 6 thwart 8 planking, wainscot

thimble: cup 5 cover

conjurer: 6 goblet

machine: 6 sleeve

thimblerigger: 5 cheat 8 imposter, swindler

thin: dim 4 bony, flue, lank, lean, pale, poor, rare, slim, weak 5 acute, exile, faint, gaunt, lanky, lathy, scant, sheer, spare, washy, wizen 6 dilute, flimsy, hollow, meager, meagre, papery, rarefy, reduce, scanty, scarce, skinny, slight, slinky, sparse, watery, weaken, weazen 7 gracile, haggard, scrawny, slender, tenuous 8 araneous, gossamer, rarefied, scantily 9 attenuate, emaciated, extenuate, infertile, subtilize 10 inadequate 11 high-pitched, transparent, watered down 12 unbelievable, unconvincing 13 unsubstantial

and delicate: 8 araneous

and haggard: 5 gaunt

and slender: 4 lean 5 lanky

and vibrant: 5 reedy

and weak: 6 watery

and withered: 5 wizen 6 weezen

coating or layer: 4 film 6 veneer

disk: 5 wafer

out: 5 peter

plate: 4 leaf, shim 5 wedge 6 lamina, tegmen

scale: 5 flake 6 lamina 7 lamella

Thin Man: *dog* 4 Asta

wife: 4 Nora

thin-skinned: 6 tender, touchy 9 sensitive

thine: 4 tuum

thing: act 4 deed, idea, item 5 cause, chose, court, event, point, stuff 6 action, affair, detail, entity, matter, notion, object, reason, wealth 7 article, council 8 assembly, incident, property 9 happening 10 occurrence 11 transaction 12 circumstance

accomplished: 4 acta, deed 5 actum, actus

added: ell 6 insert 7 addenda(pl.) 8 addendum, addition, appendix 9 insertion 10 additament, complement, supplement

admitted: 4 fact 5 datum 7 element 9 principle

aforesaid: 5 ditto

assumed: 7 premise, premiss 9 postulate 11 implication, stipulation 14 presupposition

brought into existence: 8 creation

capable of spontaneous motion: 8 automata 9 automaton

complete in itself: 5 unity

consecrated to a deity: 6 hieron, sacrum 8 anathema

cursed: 8 anathema

extra: 5 bonus 6 bounty, lanyap 7 premium 8 lagnappe 9 lagniappe

following: 6 sequel

forfeited to crown: 7 deodand

found: 5 trove

given as security: 4 gage 6 pledge

indefinite, unnamed: 7 so and so 11 nondescript

invariable: 8 constant

known by reasoning: 7 noumena 8 noumenon

known by senses: 9 phenomena 10 phenomenon

of no value: 4 bean, junk 5 nihil, waste 6 fillip, nought, stiver, trifle 7 bauchle, nothing, pinhead, trinket 8 picayune 9 nonentity, resnihili 10 resnullius

of remembrance: 5 token

personal property law: 5 chose

precious: 4 oner 5 curio, relic 6 pippin, rarity 8 treasure

small: dot, jot 4 atom, iota, whit 6 tittle 8 particle, scuddick

to be done: 5 chore 6 agenda 7 agendum

unusual: 5 freak 6 oddity 11 monstrosity 12 malformation

thingamajig: 6 device, doodad, gadget, widget 9 doohickey, doohickus, doohinkey, doohinkus, thingummy 10 thingumbob

things: res 4 duds, gear, togs 5 goods,

point 6 fetish 7 clothes, effects 10 belongings 13 appurtenances
between extremes: 13 intermediates
done: 9 res gestae
for sale: 5 goods, wares 8 services 11 merchandise
gained by purchase: 10 acquirenda 12 acquisitions
hidden: 10 penetralia
holy: 5 hagia
jumble of: 4 mess, muss 14 conglomeration
linked in nature: 8 cognates
movable: 8 chattels 10 resmobiles
obtained from other things: 11 derivatives
prohibited: 7 vetanda
suitable for eating: 9 esculents
to see: 5 sights
worth remembering: 11 memorabilia
thingumbob: See thingamajig
think: wis 4 deem, feel, muse, seem, trow, ween 5 judge, opine 6 appear, esteem, expect, intend, reason, repute, scheme 7 believe, bethink, concoct, imagine, purpose, reflect, resolve, suppose, surmise, suspect 8 cogitate, conceive, consider, meditate, ruminate 9 calculate, determine, speculate 10 conjecture, deliberate, reconsider, understand 11 contemplate
alike: 5 agree
logically: 6 reason
out: 4 plan 5 solve 6 devise 7 develop, perfect 8 cogitate, contrive, discover 10 excogitate
over: 5 brood 10 reconsider
think tank: 14 research center
thinker: 4 mind 5 brain 7 sophist, student 9 meditator 11 philosopher
Thinker sculptor: 5 Rodin
thinking: 7 opinion 9 judgement 10 cogitation, reflection 13 ratiocination 17 intellectualizing
marked by exact: 13 ratiocinative
thinly: 6 airily 8 sparsely 14 insufficiently
metallic: 5 tinny
scattered: 6 sparse
thinner: 5 rarer 7 sheerer 10 turpentine
thinness: 6 rarity 7 exility, tenuity 11 attenuation
third: *figure mood:* 7 ferison
in number: 8 tertiary
music: 6 tierce
power of number: 4 cube
third estate: 10 commonalty 11 rank and file
Third Man author: 6 Greene
third world: 17 nonaligned nations
thirlage: fee, pay 4 dues 5 right 7 multure, service 8 mortgage 9 servitude, thralldom

thirling: 7 bondage 10 subjection
thirst: 4 long, wish 5 covet, crave, dryth 6 desire 7 aridity, craving, longing
absence of: 7 adipsia
excessive: 9 anadipsia
thirsty: dry 4 adry, arid, avid 5 eager 6 desire, drouth 7 athirst, craving, drought, longing, parched, wild for 8 droughty
thirty: end 6 lambda(Gr.), trente(F.)
thirty-nine and thirty-seven hundredths inches: 5 meter
this: yis 4 esta(Sp.), haec(L.)
this and that: 8 sundries 11 odds and ends
this way: 4 here
Thisbe's love: 7 Pyramus
thistle: 4 weed 7 bedegar, caltrop 8 bedeguar 10 acanaceous
genus of: 5 layia
thistle-like plants: 7 carlina
thistledown: 6 pappus
thither: end, yon 5 hence, there 6 yonder 7 farther, thereat 8 ulterior
tho: 5 still
thole: peg, pin 4 bear 5 allow 6 endure, remain, suffer 7 oarlock, undergo 8 tolerate
Thomas' opera: 6 Mignon
thong: 4 lace, lash, rein, riem 5 lasso, leash, romal, strap, strip, whang 6 twitch 7 amentum, laniard, lanyard, latchet 8 whiplash
thong-shaped: 6 lorate
Thor: *father:* 4 Odin
god of: 7 thunder
hammer: 8 Mjollnir
stepson: Ull
wife: Sif
thorax: 5 chest, trunk 6 breast
thorn: 4 brod, goad 5 briar, brier, spine, worry 7 acantha 8 vexation 9 annoyance 10 irritation
apple: 5 metel 6 datura
Egyptian: 5 babul 6 gonake 7 gonakie
full of: 6 briery
small: 7 spinule
thorny: 5 sharp, spiny 6 spinal 7 brambly, bristly, prickly 8 spinated 9 acanthoid, difficult, vexatious 10 nettlesome 11 contentious
thorough: 4 deep, full 5 utter 6 arrant 7 through 8 absolute, accurate, complete, finished 9 downright, intensive 10 exhaustive, throughout 11 painstaking 13 thoroughgoing
thoroughbred: 5 horse 7 trained 8 cultured, educated, pedigree, purebred, well-bred 11 full-blooded
thoroughfare: way 4 road 5 alley 6 artery, avenue, street 7 highway, passage, transit 8 waterway 9 boulevard

thoroughgoing: 6 arrant 7 radical 13 dyed-in-the-wool

thoroughly: all 4 inly, well 6 deeply 9 downright, intensive 10 absolutely, altogether

thoroughwort: 7 boneset 9 hoarhound

thorp, thorpe: 4 dorp 6 hamlet 7 village 9 community

Thoth: god 6 Tehuti
head: 4 ibis

though: 4 when 5 while 7 however, whereas 12 nevertheless

thought: 4 care, hope, idea, mind, view 5 trace 6 deemed, musing, opined 7 anxiety, concept, judging, opinion 9 brainwork, cogitated, reasoning 10 cogitation, conception, meditation, melancholy, reflection 11 cerebration, expectation, imagination, speculation 12 deliberation, recollection 13 concentration, consideration, ratiocination 16 intellectualized
continuous: 10 meditation
deep in: 10 cogitabund
form: 6 ideate
inability to express: 6 asemia
reader: 8 telepath
transference: 9 telepathy

thoughtful: 4 kind 5 moody 7 careful, earnest, heedful, mindful, pensive, prudent, serious 9 attentive, designing, regardful 10 cogitabund, meditative, melancholy, reflective, ruminative, solicitous 11 circumspect, considerate

thoughtless: 4 dull, rash 5 hasty, short 6 remiss, stupid 7 glaiket, glaikit 8 careless, heedless, reckless 9 brainless 10 unthinking 11 harum-scarum, inadvertent, inattentive, lightheaded 13 inconsiderate

thousand: *dollars:* 5 grand
one: mil 5 grand 7 chiliad
years: 10 millennium

thousand-headed snake: 5 Sesha 6 Shesha

thousandth: 10 millesimal
of an inch: mil

Thrace: *goddess:* 6 Bendis
king: 6 Tereus
modern name: 8 Bulgaria
mountaineers: 5 Bessi
musician: 7 Orpheus
people: 6 Satrae 8 Bisaltae
river: 6 Hebrus 7 Maritsa
town: 6 Sestos

thrall: 4 esne, serf, thew 5 slave 7 bondage, bondman, captive, enslave, slavery, subject 8 enslaved, enthrall 9 servitude, suffering 10 oppression, subjugated

thrash: lam, tan 4 bang, beat, bray, ding, drub, flax, flog, lash, rush, sail, whip, yerk 5 array, baste, bless, flail, pound, swing, threp, whang 6 anoint, defeat, fettle, raddle, strike, threap, threep, threip, threpe, thresh, thwack 7 trounce 8 belabour, blathery, vanquish 9 triturate 10 flagellate
out: 5 argue 6 debate 7 discuss 10 kick around

thrashing: 4 bean 6 defeat 7 beating, milling 8 drubbing, flogging, whipping

thrave: 4 bind 5 crowd 6 bundle, number, throng 8 quantity

thread: ray 4 filo, line, vein, yarn 5 fiber, reeve, weave 6 strata, stream, string 7 quality, stratum 8 filament, fineness, raveling 9 ravelling 11 composition
a needle: 5 reeve
ball of: 4 clew, clue
bits of: 4 lint 9 ravelings
cell: 5 cnida
cone: cop
dental: 5 floss
division of: 4 beer
holder: 6 bobbin
in weaving shuttle: 4 weft
inserted beneath skin: 5 seton
kind of: 4 bast, bave, film, silk, yarn 5 floss, linen, lisle, rayon, seton, trame 6 cotton, lingel, lingle 8 arrasene
knot in: 4 burl
like: 6 filose
on spindle: cop
pert. to: 5 filar
raveled: 6 sleave
shoemaker's: 6 lingel
silk: bur 4 bave, burr 5 floss, trame 9 filoselle
skein of: 4 hasp
surgical: 5 seton 6 catgut, suture
tape: 5 inkle
tester: 9 serimeter
used as core for tinsel: 4 poil
winding tube: cop

threadbare: 4 bare, sere, worn 5 banal, corny, stale, trite 6 frayed, pilled, shabby 7 napless 9 hackneyed

threads: 4 beer, weft, woof 6 filler 8 clothing

threadworm: 7 filaria 8 nematode

threat: vex 4 fail, lack, urge, want, warn 5 chide, crowd, peril, press, troop 6 compel, menace, misery, throng 7 oppress, reprove, trouble, warning 8 maltreat, threaten 10 compulsion

threaten: cow 4 brag 5 augur, boast, lower, utter 6 charge, menace 7 portend, promise 8 denounce 10 intimidate

threatening: big 6 greasy, lowery 7 ominous 8 lowering, menacing 9 impending 10 formidable

three: 4 drei(G.) 5 crowd, gamma(Gr.), trias 7 Trinity

combination of: **7** triplet, ternary

consisting of: **7** ternate

group of: tre **4** trio **5** triad, trine **7** ternion **8** triumvir

months: **7** quarter **9** trimester

ruling group: **11** triumvirate

Three B's (in music): **4** Bach **6** Brahms **9** Beethoven

three-card monte: 9 montebank

three-cleft: 6 trifid

three-dimensional: 5 cubic **6** stereo **7** cubical

three-flowered: 9 trifloral

Three Graces: job **5** bloom **6** Aglaia, Thalia **10** brilliance, Euphrosyne

three-headed goddess: 6 Hecate

three-hundredth anniversary: 13 tercentennial, tricentennial

three in one: 6 triune **7** trinity

Three Kingdoms: Wu, Shu, Wei

three-layered: 10 trilaminar

three-legged stand: 6 tripod, trivet

three-lined: 9 trilinear

three L's: 4 lead **7** lookout **8** latitude

three-masted vessel: 5 xebec **8** schooner

Three Musketeers: 5 Athos **6** Aramis **7** Porthos

author: **5** Dumas

friend: **9** D'Artagnan

three-piled: 4 best **6** costly **11** extravagant

three-pointed: 11 tricuspidal

three-score: 5 sixty

three-seeded: 11 trispermous

three-sided figure: 6 trigon **8** triangle

three-spot: 4 trey

three-square: 5 cross **9** irritable, threefold

three-styled: 10 trystylous

Three Wise Men: 6 Gaspar **8** Melchior **9** Balthasar

threefold: 4 tern **5** trine **6** ternal, thrice, treble, trinal, triple, triply

threescore: 5 sixty

threesome: 4 trio **5** triad **11** triumvirate

threnody: 4 song **5** dirge **6** hearse

thresh (see also **thrash**): cob **4** beat, flog, lump, rush **5** berry, flail

thresh out: 5 argue **6** debate **7** discuss

threshed grain husks: 5 straw

thresher: 5 flail, shark **6** beater **7** combine

thresher shark: 6 sea fox **7** foxfish **7** whiptail

genus: **7** alopias

threshold: eve **4** gate, sill **5** limen, verge **6** outset **8** doorsill, entrance **9** beginning

thribble: 6 triple **9** threefold

thrice: 4 very **6** highly **7** greatly **9** threefold

thrift: 4 work **5** labor **7** economy **9** austerity, frugality, husbandry, parsimony

10 employment, occupation, prosperity, providence **14** forehandedness

thriftless: 6 lavish **8** prodigal, wasteful **11** extravagant, improvident

thrifty: 4 near **5** fendy, small **6** frugal, narrow, proper, saving, useful, worthy **7** careful, sparing **8** thriving **9** befitting, estimable, provident **10** economical, forehanded, prospering **11** flourishing, serviceable

thrill: 4 bang, bore, cast, dirl, girl, hurl, kick **5** drill, elate, flush, thirl, throw **6** dindle, pierce, quiver, tremor, wallop **7** frisson, tremble, vibrate **8** fremitus, transfix **9** penetrate, perforate, throbbing, vibration

thrilly: 8 stirring **11** sensational

thrive: dow **4** boom, gain, grow **5** addle, moise **6** batten, fatten **7** improve, prosper, succeed **8** flourish, increase

in shade: **11** sciophilous

thrivingly: 5 gaily, gayly **7** bravely

throat: maw **4** crag, crop, gowl, hals, lane, tube **5** halse **6** groove, gullet, guzzle, weason **7** channel, orifice, weasand **8** guttural

armor: **6** gorget

covering: **4** barb

infection: **5** croup **6** angina, quinsy **8** cynanche **9** squinancy **10** laryngitis **11** strep throat

irritation: **4** frog

lozenge: **6** pastil, troche **7** pastile **8** pastille

part: **7** glottis

pert. to: **5** gular **7** jugular **8** guttural

protector: **5** scarf **7** muffler

sore: **6** housty

swelling: **6** goiter

to clear: hem **5** hawk

upper: **4** gula

warmer: **5** scarf

throat skin: 6 dewlap

throaty: 5 husky **6** hoarse **8** guttural **9** voracious

throb: 4 ache, beat, drum, pant **5** flack, pulse, thump **7** flacker, pulsate, vibrate **8** resonate **9** palpitate, pulsation

throbbing: 4 beat **7** pitapat

throe: 4 pain, pang **5** agony **6** attack, effort **7** anguish **8** struggle **10** convulsion

thrombus: 4 clot **6** fibrin

throne: see **4** apse, seat **5** asana, chair, exalt, gaddi, gadhi, power, siege **6** toilet **7** anguish, dignity **8** cathedra, enthrone **11** sovereignty

remove from: **6** depose

throng: 4 busy, crew, heap, host, push, rout **5** bunch, close, crowd, flock, group, horde, peril, press, swarm **6** busily, bustle, strain, stress **7** company, hurried **8** distress, familiar, hardship, intimate **9**

confusion, frequency, multitude 10 assemblage

thronged: 5. alive 7 peopled 8 crawling 10 celebrious

throttle: gun 5 check, choke 6 throat 7 garrote 8 compress, garrotte, strangle, suppress, windpipe 9 suffocate 11 accelerator

open: gun

through, thru: per, via 4 over 5 about, athro, ended 6 across, coffin, direct 7 by way of, perpend 8 athrough, finished, washed-up 9 completed, tombstone 11 sarcophagus 12 thoroughfare, unobstructed

the agency of: per

the mouth: 7 peroral

throughgan(Sc.): 5 labor 6 energy 11 overhauling 12 thoroughfare

throughgoing: 9 reprimand 11 examination, overhauling 12 thoroughfare

throughout: 5 about 6 bedene, during, sempre 7 perfect 8 thorough 10 completely, everywhere

throw: boa, cob, don, hit, lob, pat, peg, put, shy, wap 4 bail, bear, blow, bung, cast, dash, fall, form, hike, hove, hurl, pelt, rack, risk, shed, time, toss, turn, yerk 5 check, chuck, chunk, crank, drive, exert, flick, fling, flirt, force, frame, heave, impel, pitch, place, scarf, sling, start, strip, trice, twist, whang, while, whirl 6 change, defeat, divest, hinder, retard, sprain, spread, spring, strike, stroke, thrust, thwart, wrench, writhe 7 address, advance, discard, fashion, present, produce, project, revolve, venture 8 catapult, coverlet, distance, obstruct 9 prostrate 10 flagellate

a fit: 5 angry 7 excited 9 disturbed, irritated

a scare into: 5 scare 7 terrify

about: 4 tack 5 slosh 6 thrash

at quoits: 6 leaner, ringer

away: 5 waste 6 refuse, reject 7 discard, leaflet 8 handbill, squander

back: 5 check, delay, repel 6 refuse, reject, retort, revert 8 reversal 9 reversion

dice: 4 cast, main, roll

double one at dice: 7 ambsace

down: 4 cast, fell 5 fling 6 defeat, reject 7 refusal, subvert 9 overthrow, rejection 11 precipitate

down the gauntlet: 4 defy 9 challenge

dust in one's eyes: 7 deceive, mislead

from saddle: 7 unhorse

in: add 4 join 6 inject 9 introduce 10 contribute

in the towel: 4 cede, quit 5 yield 6 give up 9 surrender

into confusion: 4 riot 5 snafu 7 disturb 8 stampede 10 demoralize

into disorder: pif 4 pied 7 derange

into ecstasy: 6 enrapt

into shade: 7 eclipse

lazily: lob

light upon: 6 illume

lightly: 4 toss

obliquely: 4 deal, skew, toss

off: rid 4 cast, emit, free, molt, shed 5 abate, expel, moult, shake 6 reject 7 abandon, deflect, discard 8 discount 10 disconnect

off the track: 6 derail

one's weight around: 4 push, urge 8 domineer

out: say 4 emit, lade 5 egest, eject, evict, expel, utter 6 extend, reject 7 confuse, discard, excrete, project 8 distance 9 eliminate

out of order: 7 derange

over: 4 jilt 7 abandon

overboard: 8 jettison

six at dice: 4 sise 5 sises

stones at: 8 lapidate

together: 7 collect 8 assemble

underhand: lob

up: 4 rise 5 demit, vomit 10 jerry-build, relinquish

water upon: 5 douse

with force: 4 bung

throwing rope: 5 lasso, reata, riata 6 lariat

throwing-stick: 6 atlatl 9 boomerang

thrown: 4 cast 6 hurled 7 twisted 8 unseated

thrum: bit 4 birr, drum, lout, purr, tuft 5 strum, waste 6 fringe, recite, repeat, tangle, thatch 8 particle 10 threepence

thrush: 5 mavie, mavis, ouzel, robin, veery 6 missel, oriole, shrike 7 bearing 8 bluebird, throstle 9 blackbird

disease: 4 soor 5 aptha 6 aphtha

European: 4 osel 5 mavis, ossel, ousel, ouzel 6 missel, shrike

ground: 5 pitta

migratory: 5 robin

thrust: dig, jab, ram, run 4 bear, birr, bore, butt, dush, gird, jerk, pelt, poke, prop, push, stab 5 barge, clash, crowd, drive, force, hunch, impel, longe, lunge, onset, press, shove 6 attack, detude, extend, hustle, pierce, plunge, repost, ripost, spread, stress, throng 7 allonge, assault, collide, extrude, intrude, riposte 8 estocade, pressure, protrude 9 interject, interpose, substance

against the wall: 5 crush, mured

aside: 5 shove, shunt

back: 4 rout 6 defeat 7 repulse

thud: 4 baff, blow, gust, move, push 5 clonk, clunk, press, thump 6 strike 7 tempest 9 windstorm

thug: 4 hood 5 rough 6 attack, cuttle,

gunman 7 gorilla, hoodlum, ruffian 8 assassin, gangster 9 cutthroat

thumb: 6 pollex, thenar 9 hitchhike, peachwort

part: 6 thenar

through: 6 browse 7 dip into 8 glance at

Thummim's partner: 4 Urim

thump: cob, dad, dub, hit 4 bang, beat, blow, bump, daud, ding, dird, drub, dunt, polt, whip, yerk 5 blaff, bunch, clour, crump, knock, pound, throb 6 bounce, cudgel, hammer, pummel, strike, thrash, thunge

thumping: 5 large 6 tattoo 7 bumping 8 whopping

thunder: 4 bang, peal, rage, roar 6 bronte 7 fouldre 9 fulminate

god: 4 Thor, Zeus

witch: 4 baba

thunder and lightning: 8 ceraunic 9 fulminous

thunder-smitten goddess: 6 Semele

thunderbolt: 6 fulmen 7 fouldre 9 fulminant, lightning

thunderhead: 4 omen 5 cloud 7 warning

thundering: 5 large 8 thumping, whopping 10 foudroyant

thunderstorm: *Cuba:* 6 bayamo

West Indies: 7 houvari

thunge: 4 bang 5 sound, thump

thurible: 6 censer

Thuringia: *castle:* 8 Wartburg

city: 4 Gera, Jena 5 Gotha 6 Erfurt, Weimar

Thursday: *god of:* 4 Thor

Holy: 5 Skire

thus: sae, sic 4 fiat 5 hence 9 therefore 12 consequently

thwack: rap 4 bang, blow, pack 5 crump, crush, drive, force, knock, whack 6 defeat, strike, thrash 7 belabor 8 belabour

thwart: 4 balk, foil, pert, seat 5 bench, block, brace, clash, cross, parry, saucy, spite, zygon 6 across, baffle, defeat, hinder, oppose, outwit, resist 7 athwart, oblique, prevent, quarrel 8 contrair, obstruct, perverse, stubborn, thwarty 9 frustrate, interpose 10 contravene, disappoint, opposition, transverse 11 intractable, obstruction

Thyestes: *brother:* 6 Atreus

father: 6 Pelops

mother: 10 Hippodamia

son: 9 Aegisthus

thylacine: 4 wolf 5 tiger, yabbi

thyme: 8 hillwort

thymus: 5 gland

thyroid enlargement: 6 goiter

thyrsus: 5 staff, stick

tiara: 5 crown, miter 6 diadem, fillet 7 cidares, cidaris, coronet 8 frontlet 9 headdress

Tibet: 7 Sitsang

animal: 5 panda

antelope: goa, sus

ass: 5 kiang

banner: 5 tanka

beast of burden: yak

beer: 5 chang

capital: 5 Lassa, Lhasa

coin: 5 tanga

deer: 4 shou

dialect: 9 Bhutanese

ecclesiastic: 4 lama 5 dalai

food: 6 tsamba

gazelle: goa

goat fleece: 5 pashm

kingdom: 5 Nepal

lama: 5 Dalai

language: 7 Bodskad

leopard: 5 ounce

monastery: 8 lamasery

monk: 4 lama

mountain range: 5 A-ling 6 Kunlun 8 Himalaya

ox: yak

oxlike animal: 4 zebu

people: 6 Bhotia 7 Bhotiya

pony: 6 tangum, tangun 7 tanghan

priest: 4 lama

religion: Bon

river: 5 Indus 7 Salween

ruminant: 5 takin

sheep: sha 6 bharal, nahoor, nayaur

town: Noh 5 Ka-erh

wild ass: 5 kiang

wildcat: 5 manul

Tibetan: 6 Tangut

tibia: 5 flute 6 cnemis 8 shinbone

pert. to: 7 cnemial

tiburon: 5 shark

Tiburon Island Indian: 4 Seri

tic: 4 jerk 5 spasm 8 fixation 9 twitching 11 vellication

tick: dot, fag, ked, pat, tag, tap 4 beat, case, dash, kade, mark, mite, note, pest 5 acari, chalk, click, count, cover, flirt, speck, touch, trust 6 acarid, acarus, credit, fondle, insect, moment, record, second, tampon, talaje 7 acarina, instant 8 acaridan, arachnid, garapata, indicate, mattress, parasite 10 pajahuello, pajaroello

fowl: 5 argas

genus of: 5 argas

sheep: ked

ticker: 4 bomb 5 clock, heart, watch

ticket: bid, tag 4 book, card, list, note, slip, tick 5 check, ducat, fiche, label, score, sight, slate, token 6 ballot, billet, notice, permit, record 7 license, placard, voucher, warrant 8 document, passport 9 cardboard, discharge, etiquette 10 memorandum 11 certificate *complimentary:* 4 comp, pass 11 Annie Oakley

of leave: 6 parole

receiver of free: 8 deadhead

season: 6 abonne 10 abonnement

sell above cost: 5 scalp

speculator: 7 scalper

tickle: 4 beat, nice, play, stir, take, whip 5 amuse, annoy, frail, tease, touch 6 arouse, cuitle, divert, excite, kittle, please, thrill, tingle, touchy, wanton 7 capture, cuittle, delight, gratify, operate, passage, portray, provoke, tickler 8 chastise, delicate, insecure, tickling, ticklish, unstable, unsteady 9 difficult, squeamish, titillate, vellicate 10 insecurely

tickled: 4 glad 6 amused 7 pleased 9 gratified

tickler: pad, sip 4 book, cane, file 5 flask, knife, prong, strap 6 pistol, puzzle, record, weapon 7 problem

tickling: 7 craving 13 gratification

ticklish: 4 nice 5 risky 6 fickle, queasy, touchy 7 comical 8 critical, delicate, unstable, unsteady 9 uncertain 10 changeable, inconstant, precarious, unreliable 13 oversensitive

tick off: 4 list 6 rebuke 8 reproach 9 make angry

tidal: *creek:* 5 firth 6 estero

current: 8 tiderace

flow: 4 bore 5 eagre

wave: 4 bore 5 aigre, eagre

tidbit, titbit: 5 goody 7 saynete 8 beatille, delicacy

tide: sea 4 fair, flow, hour, pass, time 5 carry, drift, drive, flood, point, space, surge, tidal 6 befall, betide, endure, happen, moment, period, stream 7 current, freshet, proceed 8 continue, festival, occasion, surmount, tendency 11 anniversary, opportunity

lowest: 4 neap

type: ebb, low 4 high 5 flood 6 spring

tidewater: 5 shore 6 strand 8 seaboard

tidily: 5 fitly 7 smartly 8 cleverly, suitable 9 shipshape

tiding, tidings: ebb 4 flow, news 5 event 6 advice, gospel 7 account, message 9 happening 11 information 12 intelligence

tidy: 4 cosh, fair, good, meet(obs.), neat, redd, smug, tosh, trig, trim 5 clean, douce, great, groom, large, natty, plump, sleek 6 comely, fettle, sleeky, spruce, tidily, timely, worthy 7 healthy, orderly, upright 8 diligent, pinafore, skillful 9 shipshape 10 receptacle, seasonable 12 antimacassar, considerable, satisfactory

cot, brace, cadge, chain, equal, hitch, marry, nexus, sheaf, trice, union, unite 6 attach, cement, connex, couple, cravat, enlace, fasten, hamper, pledge, string, tether, tiewig 7 confine, connect, necktie, oxfords, sleeper 8 alligate, restrain, restrict, shoelace 9 constrain, constrict, influence, stalemate 10 allegiance, obligation

down: 7 confine 8 restrain, restrict

fast: 5 belay

off: 4 snub 5 belay

ornament: pin 4 clip

securely: 4 lash 5 truss 7 shackle, trammel

tightly: 4 bind, lash

up: 4 bind, moor, stop 5 truss 6 hinder, tether 8 obstruct

tie-up: 5 delay 6 strike 7 mooring 10 connection

tied: 4 even 5 bound 8 knotted

up: 5 busy 8 occupied 10 encumbered

tier: row 4 bank, line, rank 5 class, layer, place, stack, story 6 degree 7 antenna, arrange 8 pinafore

tierce: 4 cask 5 lunge, parry, third 7 measure 8 sequence

Tierra del Fuego Indian: Ona 4 Agni

tiff: fit, pet, row, sip 4 huff, mood, spat 5 draft, dress, drink, humor, lunch, order, run-in, scent, smell, sniff, spell, state, taste 6 liquor 7 quarrel 8 outburst 9 condition 11 altercation

tiffin: 5 lunch 6 eating, repast 8 drinking

tiger: cat, cub 4 howl, rake, yell 5 bully, groom 6 feline, jaguar 7 leopard 9 carnivore, swaggerer, thylacine 12 organization

family: 7 felidae

young: cub

tiger finch: 8 amadavat

tiger-hunting dog: 5 dhole

tigerish: 5 cruel 6 fierce, flashy 9 ferocious 10 swaggering 12 bloodthirsty

tigers-mouth: 8 foxglove, toadflax 10 snapdragon

tight: 4 fast, firm, hard, held, neat, snug, taut, tidy, trim 5 alert, bound, cheap, close, dense, drawn, drunk, fixed, ready, smart, solid, tense, tipsy 6 climax, comely, firmly, packed, severe, steady, stingy, strait, strict 7 capable, compact, concise, quickly, shapely, soundly, unmoved 8 constant, exacting, faithful 9 competent, condensed, energetic, mercenary, niggardly 10 impervious, vigorously 11 close-fisted, intoxicated, restraining 12 parsimonious

tight-fisted: 6 stingy 12 parsimonious

tight-laced: 4 prim

tight-lipped: 5 terse 6 silent 8 taciturn 9 secretive

tighten: 5 tense 6 tauten 9 constrict

tie: rod, sag, wed 4 band, beam, beat, bind, bond, cord, draw, duty, even, join, knot, lace, link, post, rope, teck 5 angle, as-

ropes: 4 frap

tightwad: 4 fist 5 miser, piker 7 niggard 9 skinflint 10 cheapskate

Tigris River city: Kut 5 Ashur, Calah 7 Nineveh

til: 5 plant 6 sesame

tile: hat 5 brick, drain, plate, slate 6 tegula 7 carreau, quarrel

  composed of: 7 tegular 9 tessellar

  curved: 7 pantile

  malting floor: 6 pament 7 pamment

  mosaic: 7 tessera 8 abaculus

  pert. to: 7 tegular

  roofing: 7 pantile

  used in game: 6 domino

tiler: cat 4 kiln 5 field, thief 7 hellier 10 doorkeeper

tilery: 4 kiln

tiles: 8 ceramics

till: box, far, for, get, hoe, sow 4 draw, earn, farm, gain, plow, tend, tray, up to, work 5 charm, dress, labor, train, while 6 casket, drawer, entice, strive, whilst 7 develop, prepare 9 cultivate 10 concerning

tillable: 6 arable 7 earable

tillage: 4 farm, land 7 aration, culture 11 cultivation

  fit for: 6 arable

tilled land: 5 arada

tiller: bar, bow 4 helm, hoer 5 lever, stalk, stick 6 farmer, handle, rudder, sprout 7 husband, rancher 10 cultivator, husbandman

tilt: tip 4 cant, duel, heel, lean, list, rush, tent 5 argue, fight, forge, heald, hield, joust, pitch, poise, slant, slope, speed, upend, upset 6 awning, canopy, careen, combat, hammer, oppose, seesaw, stroke, thrust, topple 7 contest, dispute, incline 8 covering, tiltyard 10 tournament 1 altercation

  hammer: 6 oliver

  skyward: 5 upend

tilter: 5 sword 6 avocet, seesaw 7 jouster 9 sandpiper

tilting: 5 alist 7 swaying 8 inclined, jousting, slanting

timbal: 10 kettledrum

timber: log, rib 4 balk, beam, fuel, gate, land, raff, stay, wood 5 build, cahuy, cover, fence, frame, gripe, spile, stile, trees 6 forest, girder, lumber, rafter 7 support 8 building, contrive 9 construct, structure, underpier

  bend: sny 6 camber, rafter

  central portion: 7 duramen 9 heartwood

  cut: 4 bunk 6 lumber 7 fallage 8 teakwood

  decay: 4 conk, dote, doze

  end: 5 tenon

  estimator: 6 scaler 7 cruiser

  joining peg: 7 trenail, trunnel 8 treenail

  parts of building: rib 4 sill 5 joist, spale 6 purlin, rafter 7 purline 8 stringer

  peg: 4 coak

  ship: bao, rib 4 bibb, bitt, keel, mast, spar, wale 5 snape, spale 7 stemson 8 sternson

  sloping: 6 rafter

  standing: 4 stud 5 spile 6 forest, purlin 8 puncheon, studding, stumpage

  tree: ash, fir 4 pine 5 birch, cedar, maple 6 walnut 7 redwood 8 mahogany

  wolf: 4 lobo

timberman: 6 sawyer 7 cruiser 8 woodsman 9 carpenter, lumberman

timbre: 4 mood, tone 5 crest, miter 6 spirit, temper 7 coronet, quality, timbrel 9 character

timbrel: 4 tabor 5 tabor 10 tambourine

time: age, day, eld, era, tid 4 book, date, fuss, hint, hour, sele, term, week, year 5 clock, epoch, month, set up, spell, tempo, tense, watch 6 during, indeed, minute, moment, period, season, second, steven 8 duration, occasion, regulate, schedule, yuletide 11 opportunity 13 demonstration

  ahead of: 5 early 9 premature

  allowed for payment: 6 usance

  and again: 5 often 10 frequently

  another: 5 again

  at no: 5 never 9 nevermore

  before: eve

  blossom: 9 blutezeit

  break in: 6 hiatus

  brief: 4 span 6 moment

  Christmas: 8 yuletide

  devoted to religion: 8 holytide

  error in order of: 11 anachronism

  fast: 4 Lent

  gone by: 4 past, yore 10 yesteryear

  granted: 4 stay 5 delay, frist 8 reprieve

  happy: 4 bust, lark 5 revel, spree 6 soiree 8 jamboree

  intervening: 7 interim 8 meantime 9 meanwhile

  length: age, eon, era 6 moment, period

  long ago: 4 yore

  music: 6 presto

  music marker: 9 metronome

  of great depression: 5 nadir

  of highest strength: 6 heyday

  olden: eld 4 syne (Sc.), yore

  period of: age, day, eon, era 4 aeon, date, hour, span, term, week, year 5 epoch, month, spell, trice 6 decade, ghurry, minute, moment, recess, season, second 7 century, instant 8 azoic age 9 fortnight

  pert. to: 4 eral 8 temporal

  present: 5 nonce

  right: tid (Sc.)

  single: 4 once

  to come: 5 tabor 6 future

waste: 4 idle, loaf 5 dally 6 dawdle, diddle, loiter 8 flanerie
wrong: 13 anachronistic
time being: 5 nonce
time clock: 8 recorder
Time Machine author: 5 Wells
time out: 5 break 6 recess 10 rest period
timeless: 4 true 5 valid 6 eterne 7 ageless, eternal, undated 8 dateless, unending, untimely 9 co-eternal, continual, premature 11 everlasting 12 interminable
timely: apt, pat 4 soon 5 early 6 prompt, proper 8 relevant, temporal 9 favorable, opportune, pertinent 10 auspicious, forehanded, seasonable
timepiece: 4 dial 5 clock, watch 8 sunwatch 9 horologue 11 chronometer 17 chronothermometer
water: 9 clepsydra
times: many: oft 5 often 10 frequently
olden: eld 9 yesterday 10 yesteryear
prosperous: ups 5 booms
timetable: 7 program 8 schedule
timid: shy 4 argh, eery 5 arghe, bauch, blate, eerie, faint, mousy, pavid, scary 6 afraid 7 bashful, fearful, gastful, nervous 8 cowardly, fearsome, ghastful, hesitant, retiring, timorous, undaring 9 diffident, shrinking 11 vacillating 12 fainthearted 13 pusillanimous 14 chicken-hearted
timor: 5 dread
Timor: *capital:* 4 Dili
coin: avo 6 pataca
island: 4 Leti
language: 5 Tetum
part of: 9 Indonesia
timorous: 5 faint, timid 6 afraid, cowish, sheepy 7 fearful 8 fearsome, hesitant, quailing, terrible 9 shuddering 10 shuddering 12 fainthearted
timpani: 11 kettledrums
tin: box, can, pan 5 metal, money, terne 6 latten 7 element, stannic, stannum 8 preserve, prillion 9 container
pert. to: 7 stannic, stranic
rubbish: 8 stent
sheet: 6 latten
symbol: Sn
tin and copper alloy: 6 pewter
Tin Can Island: 7 Niuafoo
tin foil: 4 tain
Tin Pan Alley group: 5 ASCAP
tin-pot: 4 poor 6 paltry 8 inferior, wretched
tinamou: 4 bird, yutu 6 ynambu 7 ostrich
tincal: 5 borax
tincture: or 4 cast, tint 5 color, gules, imbue, myrrh, smack, stain, taint, tenne, tinge, trace 6 elixir, imbrue 7 pigment, vestige 8 coloring 9 admixture, suspicion 10 extraction 12 modification

for sprains: 6 arnica
of opium: 9 paregoric
tinder: 4 punk 6 amadou 8 kindling
tine: tub, vat 4 fork, lose, pain, teen 5 grief, point, prong, spike, tooth 6 harrow, perish 7 destroy, trouble
tinea: 8 ringworm 11 skin disease
tinean: 4 moth
tineoidea: 5 moths
tinge: dye, hue 4 cast, hint, odor, tint 5 color, imbue, savor, shade, smack, stain, touch, trace 6 affect, flavor 7 glimpse, quality 8 coloring, discolor, tincture 9 influence 10 suggestion
tinged with purple: 10 violaceous
tingle: 4 dirl, girl, nail, ring, tack 5 alive, chime, patch, sting 6 dindle, jingle, tinkle 7 support, tremble, vibrant 9 fastening, sensation, stimulate
tinker: auk 4 fuss, mend, work 5 caird, gypsy, murre, patch, rogue, skate, tramp 6 fiddle, mender, mugger, potter, putter, rascal, repair, wander 7 botcher, bungler, vagrant 8 mackerel 10 play around 11 silversides
tinkle: 5 clink 6 dindle, dingle, tingle
tinner: 6 canner 8 tinsmith
tinny: 4 hard, rich, thin 5 cheap, harsh 6 bright 7 brittle, wealthy 8 metallic, tinsmith
tinplate: 5 terne
tinsel: 4 sham 5 gaudy, showy 6 tawdry 8 specious, splendor 9 clinquant 10 forfeiture, glittering
tinstone: 11 cassiterite
tint: dye, hue 5 blush, color, stain, taste, tinge, trace 6 nuance 9 foretaste 10 complexion
cheeks: 5 rouge
tinter: 4 dyer
tintinnabulum: 4 bell 5 rhyme 6 rhythm 8 rhymster
tintype: 9 ferrotype
tiny: wee 5 small, teeny 6 atomic, infant, minute 9 miniature 10 diminutive, pocket-size 11 lilliputian, microscopic 13 infinitesimal
tip: cap, cue, end, fee, neb, tap, toe, top 4 apex, barb, blow, cant, cave, clue, dump, fall, heel, hint, keel, lean, list, pile, tilt, vail 5 aglet, alist, chape, crown, drink, empty, point, slant, snick, spire, steer, touch, upset 6 aiglet, apices, arista, careen, corona, nozzle, summit, topple, unload 7 crampit, crumshaw, ferrule, incline 8 bakshish, bonamano, gratuity, overturn 9 baksheesh, buona-mano, buona-mani, extremity, overthrow, pourboire, protector 10 intoxicate
near to: 6 apical
off: 4 hint, tell, warn 5 alarm 8 forewarn 10 indication

over: 5 upset 8 overturn

tippet: boa, fur 4 barb, cape, hood, rope, ruff 5 amice, scarf, snell 6 almuce, sindon 7 hanging, muffler, patagia(pl.) 8 liripipe, liripoop, palatine, patagium 9 comforter, victorine

tipping: 5 alist 7 ripping, topping

up: 5 atilt

tipple: bib, nip, sip, tip 4 drip, gill, lose, suck, whet 5 drink, spend, upset 6 fuddle, liquor, sipple, tumble 8 overturn

tippled: 5 drank 6 beered

tippler: sot 4 lush, soak 5 souse, toper, winer 6 boozer, bubber 7 drinker, whetter 8 drunkard 9 draftsman 11 draughtsman

tippy: 4 smart 6 wobbly 7 stylish 8 unsteady

tipstaff: 7 bailiff 9 attendant, constable

tipster: 4 tout 8 dopester, informer 10 forecaster

tipsy: ree 4 awry 5 bosky, drunk, shaky 6 bungfu, groggy 7 crooked, ebriose, ebrious, foolish, fuddled, muddled, puddled 8 unsteady 10 staggering 11 intoxicated

tiptoe: 5 alert, eager, steal 6 roused, warily 7 eagerly, exalted, gumshoe, quietly 8 cautious, stealthy 9 pussyfoot 10 cautiously 11 expectantly

tiptop: 4 best 9 first-rate 11 galumptious

tirade: 6 screed, speech 7 censure 8 diatribe, harangue, jeremiad 9 philippic

tirailleur: 5 tease 8 skirmish 12 sharpshooter

tire: fag, lag, rim 4 band, bore, gnaw, hoop, jade, pall, prey, pull, shoe, tear, tier 5 recap, seize, spare, weary 6 casing, harass, satiate, tucker 7 exhaust, fatigue, frazzle, vesture 8 decorate, enervate, enfeeble, enginery, overwork, pinafore, wear down

burst: 4 flat 7 blowout

casing: 4 shoe

kind: 4 bias, snow 6 radial 7 retread 9 whitewall

saver: 5 recap 7 retread

tired: 5 all in, blown, spent, weary 6 aweary, fagged, sleepy 7 wearied 8 fatigued 9 exhausted 10 tuckered out

out: 5 jaded, spent

tireless: 4 busy 6 active 8 untiring 10 unwearying 12 enthusiastic 13 indefatigable

Tiresias: 4 seer 10 soothsayer

blinded by: 6 Athena, Athene

home: 6 Thebes

tiresome: dry 4 dull, tame 6 boring, borish, dreary, prolix 7 irksome, onerous, prosaic, tedious 8 annoying, ennuyant 9 fatiguing, wearisome 10 irritating, monotonous 13 uninteresting

tiro: See **tyro**

tissue: gum, web 4 mesh, tela 5 cloth, gauze, sheer, telae, weave 6 girdle, ribbon 7 network 8 meshwork 9 embroider, gauzelike 10 interweave

animal: fat, gum 4 bone, seur, suet 6 paxwax 7 keratin 8 gelatine

connective: 6 stroma, tendon 9 cartilage

horny: 7 keratin

human: fat, gum 4 suet, tela 5 fiber 6 albedo, diploe, keloid, stroma, tendon 7 tonsils 8 ligament, stromata 10 aerenchyma

layer of: 6 dermis, strata 7 stratum

nerve: 8 ganglion

oily: fat

pert. to: 5 telar

resembling: 7 histoid

vegetable: 4 bast 5 xylem 6 lignin 7 endarch 8 meristem

wasting away of: 8 phthisis

tit: nag, pap, pin, tap, tee, tug 4 bird, blow, draw, girl, hade, jerk, plug, pull, teat, tite, twit 5 horse, woman 6 nipple, twitch

Titan: 4 Bana, Leto, Maia, Rhea 5 Atlas, Coeus, Creus, Dione, giant, Theia 6 Cronus, Kronos, Pallas, Phoebe, Tethys, Themis 7 Iapetus, Oceanus 8 gigantic, Hyperion 9 extensive, Mnemosyne

father: 6 Uranus

mother: 4 Gaia

Titania's husband: 6 Oberon

titanic: 4 huge 5 great 7 immense 8 colossal, gigantic

titanite: 6 sphene 7 ijolite

tite: 4 soon 7 quickly 8 promptly 11 immediately

tithe: tax 4 levy 5 tenth 6 decima

pert. to: 7 decimal

titi: 6 monkey 8 marmoset

titillate: 6 excite, tickle 9 stimulate, vellicate

titlark: 4 bird 5 pipit

title: Bey, sir 4 Czar, dame, deed, Duke, Earl, Emir, Khan, King, name, Raja, Shah 5 Baron, claim, Count, friar, Major, Mayor, Noble, right 6 assign, Ensign, Kaiser, Knight, legend, madame, Mikado, notice, Prince, record, squire, Sultan 7 Admiral, ascribe, Baronet, Captain, caption, Emperor, epithet, Esquire, General, heading, Justice, Khedive, Marquis, placard, Viceroy 8 Archduke, cognomen, document, Governor, Viscount 9 Commander, Commodore, designate, President 10 appellation, capitulate, Lieutenant 11 designation 12 championship, denomination 13 Generalissimo

ecclesiastic: dom, fra 4 abba 8 reverend

10 excellency 11 monseigneur

feminine: 4 dame, lady 5 hanum, madam 6 hanoum, milady, missis, missus 8 mistress

foreign: aga, aya, Dan, don, mir, sha, sri 4 baba, Herr, lars, sidi, shri 5 basha, mirza, mpret, pasha, sayid, senor, shree, sieur 6 bashaw, madame, shogun, squire 7 dominus, effendi, mynheer 8 monsieur

holder. 4 peer 5 noble 8 champion

of Athena: 4 Alea

pert. to: 7 titular

royal: hon., sir 4 sire 5 Grace 8 banneret 9 honorable

titmouse: mag, nun, tit 4 bird 6 fuffit, puffer, titmal, tomtit, verdin 7 jacksaw, titmall, tomnoup 8 heckimal 9 chickadee, mumruffin

pert. to: 6 parine

titter: 5 laugh 6 giggle, rather, seesaw, sooner, totter, wobble 7 tremble

tittered: 7 giggled, teeheed 9 snickered

tittle: dot, jot 4 iota, sign, whit 5 fleck, point, tilde 6 accent, gossip, tattle 7 cedilla, snippet, whisper 8 particle

tittup: 5 caper, frisk

titubate: 4 reel 6 totter 7 stagger 8 unsteady 11 vacillating

titular: 7 nominal 8 so-called

Titus Andronicus: *daughter:* 7 Lavinia

queen: 6 Tamora

Tivoli's ancient name: 5 Tibur

tizzy: 4 snit 6 dither 7 anziety

TNT: 6 trotyl 8 dynamite 14 trinitrotoluol 15 trinitrotoluene

to (see also next entries): tae 4 till, unto 5 until 6 before, toward 7 against, ahead of, forward

a conclusion: out

a place on: 4 onto

a point on: 4 onto

an end: out

be: 4 esse(L.), etre(F.), sein(G.) 5 einai(Gk.) 6 essere(It.)

be sure: 4 even 6 indeed 9 certainly

no extent: not

one side: 5 abeam

position into: 4 into

sheltered side: 4 alee

that time: 5 until

the left: haw 5 aport

the opposite side: 6 across

the point that: 5 until

the rear: 5 abaft 6 astern

the victor: 4 aboo

this: 6 hereto

this place: 4 here 6 hither

which: 7 whereto

wit: viz. 6 namely 8 scilicet 9 videlicet

your health: 5 skoal 6 prosit

to-do: ado 4 fuss, stir 6 bustle 9 commotion

toa: 7 warrior

toad: ted 4 agua, bufo, hyla, pipa, scum, snot, tade 6 anuran, peeper 7 crapaud, paddock, quilkin 9 amphibian, spadefoot, sycophant

genus of: 4 bufo, hyla 6 alytes

larva: 7 tadpole 8 polliwog

tongueless suborder: 7 aglossa

toadfish: 4 sapo 6 angler, grubby, puffer, slimer 8 frogfish 10 midshipman

toadflax: 8 gallwort, ramstead 13 butter-and-eggs

toady: 4 fawn, snob, ugly, zany 6 flunky 7 flunkey, hideous, shoneen, truckle 8 bootlick, hanger-on, parasite, truckler 9 dependent, flatterer, repulsive, sycophant, toadeater

toast: dry, tan 4 soak, warm 5 brede, brown, drink, melba, parch, roast, skoal, worst 6 birsle, pledge, prosit, salute 7 bristle, carouse, drinker, propose, swindle, tippler, wassail 8 cinnamon

kind of: 4 rusk 5 melba 8 zwieback

toasted bread: 6 sippet

toastmaster: 5 emcee

tobacco: leaf, weed

chewing: 4 quid

coarse: 7 caporal

disease: 6 calico 8 walloon

flavor mixture: 6 petune

holder: 4 pipe 7 humidor

hookah smoking: 7 goracco

ingredient: 8 nicotine

in pipe-bowl: 6 dottel, dottle

juice: 6 ambeer, ambier

kind of: 4 capa, shag 5 bogie, fogus, tabac 6 Burley, cowpen 7 caporal, henbane, Latakia, perique, Turkish 8 domestic, Virginia 9 salvadora

leaf moistener: 5 caser

low grade: 4 shag

paste: 7 goracco

pile: 4 bulk

pulverized: 5 snuff

receptacle: 4 pipe 7 humidor

roll: 5 cigar, segar 7 carotte 9 cigarette

small portion: cud, fid, fig 4 quid 6 dottel, dottle 7 carotte

Tobacco Road: *author:* 8 Caldwell

character: 5 Pearl 6 Jeeter

tobacco smoke hater: 11 misocapnist

Tobias: *father:* 5 Tobit

wife: 4 Sara

toboggan: 4 sled 7 coaster, decline

toby: cup, jug, mug, way 5 cigar, stein 6 street 7 highway, pitcher, robbery

toby-man: 6 robber 10 highwayman

tocology: 9 midwifery 10 obstetrics

tocsin: 4 bell, sign 5 alarm 6 alarum, signal

tod: fox, mat 4 bush, load, pack 5 clump, shrub 6 bundle, weight

today: now 4 here, oggi(It.) 7 present 8 nowadays
pert. to: 7 diurnal 9 hodiernal
toddle: 4 walk 5 dance 6 daddle, diddle, stroll, waddle 7 saunter
toddler: tot 4 trot 5 child
toe: paw, tip 5 digit, pivot, reach, touch 7 journal 10 projection
great: 6 hallux
little: 7 minimus
pert. to: 7 digital
thickening of skin: 4 corn 6 callus
without: 10 adactylous
toehold: 7 footing
toga: 4 gown, robe 5 tunic 7 garment
togated: 7 stately 9 dignified
together: mix 5 along, chain, on end, union 6 at once, bedene, fasten, unison 7 alongst, concert, contact, harmony, jointly 8 ensemble 9 cojointly, collision, courtship 11 association 12 cohabitation 13 companionship, consecutively 14 coincidentally, simultaneously
toggle, toggel: pin, rod 4 bolt, mend 5 screw 6 cotter 10 crosspiece
Togo: *capital:* 4 Lome
language: Ewe 4 Mina 6 French
tribe: Ewe 4 Mina 6 Cabrai
togs: 6 attire 7 clothes, raiment 8 clothing
togue: 9 namaycush
toil: fag, net, tug 4 drag, mesh, moil, plod, pull, rend, roll, task, trap, work 5 broil, cloth, graft, labor, slave, snare, sweat 6 battle, drudge, effort, entrap, harass, strife 7 contend, ensnare, travail, turmoil 8 distress, drudgery, industry, overwork, struggle 10 accomplish, contention, employment, occupation
toiler: 5 slave 7 laborer, plodder, workman
toilet: can 4 head, john 5 cloth, dress 6 attire 7 costume, latrine 8 bathroom, grooming, toilette 9 cleansing
case: 4 etui 5 etwee
toilsome: 4 hard 7 arduous 9 laborious, wearisome
toise: eye 4 look 6 extend 7 stretch
toit: 6 dawdle, settle, totter 7 saunter
Tokay: 4 wine 5 grape
token: 4 gift, mark, omen, sign 5 badge, check, medal, merit, proof 6 amulet, emblem, hansel, ostent, pledge, signal, symbol 7 betoken, betroth, feature, handsel, memento, portent, presage, signify 8 accolade, evidence, forbysen, keepsake, souvenir, tessella 9 character, symbolize 10 denotation, expression, indication, prognostic 11 remembrance 14 characteristic
affection: 6 amoret, mascot 7 handsel 8 accolade
officer: 5 badge

servitude: 4 yoke
victory: 4 palm 6 laurel
tokus: 8 buttocks
Tokyo: Edo 4 Yedo
tolbooth, tollbooth: 4 city, hall, jail, town 5 burgh 6 prison 9 tollhouse 11 customhouse
toldo: hut 4 tent
tole: 5 decoy 6 allure, entice
tolerable: gey 4 fair, so-so 6 decent 8 bearable, passable 9 allowance, endurable 10 good enough, sufferable 11 comportable, respectable, supportable, translation 13 entertainment
tolerance: 7 stamina 9 allowance, endurance, variation 10 indulgence 11 forbearance 13 understanding
tolerant: 5 broad 7 lenient, liberal, patient 8 enduring 9 indulgent 10 ecumenical, open-minded 11 forebearing
tolerate: 4 bear, bide 5 abide, allow, broad, brook, stand 6 accept, endure, permit, resist, suffer
Tolkien creature: Ent 7 Hobbit
toll: due, tax 4 chum, drag, draw, duty, lure, peal, pull, rent, ring 5 annul, decoy, knell, sound 6 allure, charge, custom, entice, excise, impost, invite, vacate 7 expense, scatter, trewage 8 announce, exaction 10 assessment 12 compensation
gatherer: 8 customer, publican 9 collector
kind of: 6 caphar 7 tronage 9 chiminage 10 ballastage
weight: 7 tronage
tolls: 4 dues
tolly: 4 cane 5 spire 6 candle
Toltec: 7 Nahuatl 9 Nahuatlan
site of ruins: 4 Tula 6 Mexico
tolu: 6 blasam
tolypeutine: 4 apar 9 armadillo
Tom Sawyer: *aunt:* 5 Polly
author: 5 Twain 7 Clemens
brother: Sid
girl friend: 5 Becky
pal: 15 Huckleberry Finn
Tom Thumb: 4 runt 5 dwarf 6 midget, peewee
Tom Tulliver's river: 5 Floss
tomahawk: ax; axe, cut 4 kill 6 assail, attack, strike 7 hatchet 9 criticize
toman: 4 coin 6 weight 8 division
tomato: 9 loveapple 10 prostitute
relish: 6 catsup 7 ketchup
sauce: 6 catsup 7 ketchup
soup: 6 bisque 8 gazpacho
tomb: 4 bury 5 grave, house, huaca, speos, vault 6 burial, hearse 7 chamber 8 catacomb, cenotaph 9 mausoleum, sepulcher
empty: 8 cenotaph
for bones: 7 ossuary

kind of: 4 cist 7 tritaph 8 cistvaen, kist-
vaen 9 mausoleum 11 sarcophagus
saint's: 6 shrine
tombe: 4 drum
tomboy: meg 5 rowdy 6 gamine, harlot,
hoyden 8 strumpet
tombstone: 5 stele 8 memorial, monument 11 grave marker
Tombstone marshal: 4 Earp 5 Wyatt
tomcat: gib
tome: 4 book 5 atlas 6 ledger, letter, volume 12 encyclopedia
tomfool: ass 5 clown 6 stupid 7 buffoon,
doltish, foolish, half-wit 8 rainbird 9
blockhead 10 flycatcher, nincompoop
11 harebrained
tomfoolery: 5 prank 8 nonsense 9 silliness
tommyrot: 7 hogwash, rubbish 8 nonsense 9 silliness
tomorrow: 6 domani(It.), manana(Sp.)
ton: 4 lots, mode 5 heaps, style, tunny,
vogue 6 weight 7 fashion
tonant: 7 blatant 10 boisterous
tone: 4 mood, note, tint, vein 5 color,
pitch, shade, sound, trend, vigor 6 accent, effect, intone, modify, temper,
timbre 7 quality 8 coloring, mitigate,
modulate, strength 9 character, harmonize 10 atmosphere, elasticity, inflection, intonation, modulation 12 modification
down: 4 mute, tame 6 soften, subdue 8
modulate
nasal: 5 twang
of cord: 8 concento
quality: 6 timbre
rapid: 7 tremolo
sharp: 4 tang
single: 8 monotone
singsong: 4 sugh 5 sough
succession: 5 melos
system of: 6 tonart
thin: 7 sfogato
third of diatonic scale: 7 mediant
vibrant: 5 twang
tone arm: 6 pickup
tone color: 6 timbre
toneless: 5 atony
tones: *combination of:* 5 chord
series of: 5 scale
Tonga: *also called:* 15 Friendly Islands
capital: 9 Nukualofa
island group: 5 Vavau 6 Haajai 9 Tonga-
tapu
monetary unit: 6 paanga
town: 6 Neiafu
tongs: 5 clamp 6 tenail 7 forceps, pincers,
tueiron 8 scissors, tenaille
tongue: gab 4 bark, chib, fame, flap, howl,
pole, sole, vote 5 chide, clack, lingo,
prate, scold, speak, utter 6 report 7

beeweed, dialect, feather, lingula 8 language, lingulae, reproach 9 pronounce
bone: 5 hyoid
classical: 5 Greek, Latin 6 Hebrew
click of: tch
disease: 5 agrom 9 lichenoid
Jesus': 7 Aramaic
mother: 10 vernacular
of land: 4 spit 5 reach
oxcart: 4 cope
pert. to: 7 glossal, lingual
pivoted: 4 pawl
projection: 7 papilla 8 papillae(pl.)
sacred: 4 Pali
seam: 5 raphe
serpent: 4 fang
tied: 4 dumb, mute 5 quiet 8 taciturn 12
inarticulate
tip of: 6 corona
wagon: 4 neap, pole 5 shaft
tongue-lash: 5 baste, scold 6 berate 7 tell
off
tongue-like: 7 lingual
tongued: 6 prated
tongueless: 4 dumb, mute 10 speechless
tonic: 5 aloes 6 bracer 7 bracing 8 medicine, pick-me-up, roborant 9 sassafras,
stimulant 10 astringent, refreshing 11
corroborant 12 invigorating
kind of: 4 dope 6 catnip 7 boneset, nervine
tonic leaf: 4 coca
tonsil: 5 gland 8 amygdala
inflammation: 6 quinsy
operation: 13 tonsillectomy
tonsorialist: 6 barber
tonsure: 5 crown, shave 7 haircut
tonsured: 4 bald 5 shorn 6 pilled, shaven
7 clipped
tony: 5 smart 7 stylish
too: and, tae 4 also, ever, over, very 6 as
well, overly 7 besides 8 likewise 9 extremely 11 exceedingly, excessively,
furthermore 13 superfluously
bad: 4 alas
late: 5 tardy 7 belated 8 untimely
little: 6 scanty, skimpy 12 insufficient
much: 7 nimiety
small to matter: 13 inappreciable
soon: 9 premature
tool (see also **instrument**): adz, axe, saw,
zax 4 adze, draw, dupe, file, form, ride
5 drive, plane, shape, sword 6 convey,
device, finish, hammer, manage, puppet, weapon 7 cat's-paw, hatchet, utensil 8 ornament 9 appliance, implement
10 manipulate
abrading: 4 file
biting edge: bit
bookbinding: 5 gouge
boring: awl, bit 5 auger, drill 6 gimlet,
reamer 7 bradawl

box: see *chest* below

bricklayer: 4 hock 5 float, level 6 hammer, trowel

butcher: saw 5 knife, steel 6 skewer, skiver 7 cleaver

carpenter: bit, saw 4 rasp 5 auger, level, plane, punch 6 chisel, gimlet, hammer, pliers, square 7 handsaw, hatchet, scriber

chest: kit

chopping: 7 dolabra

cobbler's: awl 6 hammer

cultivating: 4 plow 6 harrow, plough 7 leveler

cutting: adz, axe, bit, hob, saw 4 adze 5 bezel, knife, gouge, knife, plane, razor 6 chisel, graver, reamer, shears

edged: axe 4 adze 5 knife, razor 6 chisel, reamer

engraver's: 5 burin 7 scouper

excavating: 4 pick 6 pickax, shovel

flat: 7 spatula

garden: hoe 4 rake 5 edger, mower, spade 6 sickel, trowel, weeder

gripping: 4 vise 5 clamp, tongs 7 pincers 8 tweezers

hole-making: 6 dibble

kind of: awl, fid, fro, loy, tap, zax 4 celt, file, lute, sley 5 burin, edger, flail, lathe, loper, peavy, peevy, punch 6 chisel, cranny, eolith, flange, lifter, peavey, peevey, pommel, taster, trepan, trowel 7 setiron 8 burgoyne 12 straightedge

marble worker's: 6 fraise

mason's: 6 chisel

mining: gad 4 pick

molding: die

pointed: awl, fid, gad 4 barb, brod, brog, pick 6 gimlet, stylet

pounding: 6 hammer, mallet, pestle

prehistoric: 4 celt 5 flint 6 eolith 9 paleolith 10 palaeolith

set: kit

shaping: 5 lathe, swage

slate-measuring: 7 scantle

smoothing: 4 file 5 plane 7 sleeker

splitting: axe 4 frow 7 hatchet

temperer: 8 hardener

trimming: ax; axe, saw 6 shears 8 clippers, scissors

woodworking: adz 4 adze 7 edgeman, grainer, scauper, scriber 10 spokeshave

tool handle: *end* 4 butt

fitted part: 4 tang

tools: tew 4 gear 7 gibbles(Sc.)

toot: pry, spy 4 blow, fool, gaze, peep 5 binge, blast, draft, drink, shout, sound, spree 6 bender, spread, sprout 7 carouse, declare, trumpet, whistle 8 carousal, eminence, proclaim 9 elevation

tooter: spy 7 lookout 8 watchman 9 trumpeter

tooth (see also **teeth**): cog, jag 4 bite, dent, fang, jagg, snag, tine, tusk 5 molar, point, prong 6 cuspid, indent 7 consume, grinder, incisor, snaggle 10 projection

canine: 4 tush 6 cuspid, holder 7 laniary

cap: 5 crown

coat: 6 enamel

diminutive: 8 denticle 13 denticulation

doctor: 7 dentist

edge: 7 dentate

fore: 5 biter 6 cutter

gear wheel: cog 4 dent, tine

grinding surface: 5 mensa

having but one: 8 monodont

tooth decay: 6 caries 8 cavities 11 saprodontia

tooth for tooth: 6 talion

toothache: 4 worm(Sc.) 8 dentagra 10 odontalgia

toothed: *irregularly:* 5 erose

on edge: 8 serrated

toothless: 4 weak 6 futile 7 edental 8 decrepit, edentate 9 infantile 10 agomphious, edentulate

toothsome: 5 sapid, tasty 6 savory 8 pleasing 9 agreeable, delicious, palatable

top: ace, cap, fid, lid, tip, toy 4 acme, apex, crop, head, knap, lead, peak, pick, tent, tilt, tuft 5 caput, cream, crest, crown, drain, drink, equal, excel, outdo, prune, ridge, upset 6 apices(pl.), better, capote, culmen, exceed, finial, summit, swells, topple, tumble, upside, vertex, zenith 7 gyrator, highest, maximum, surpass, topmost 8 covering, dominate, forelock, foremost, pinnacle, surmount, vertexes(pl.), vertices(pl.) 9 excellent, uppermost 10 pre-eminent 11 aristocrats

altar: 5 mensa

head: 4 pate 5 scalp

of card suit: ace

of wave: 5 crest

toy: 8 teetotum

wooden stand: 5 criss

top-drawer: 7 exalted

top-hole: 6 tiptop 9 excellent, first-rate 10 first-class

top kick: 8 sergeant

top-notch: 4 best 6 tiptop 7 highest 9 excellent, first-rate 11 unsurpassed

topaz: gem 5 stone 7 pycnite 11 hummingbird

symbol of: 8 fidelity

topcoat: 6 reefer 8 siphonia 12 chesterfield

tope: 4 butt, wren 5 clump, drink, grove, shark, stupa 6 guzzle 7 dogfish, orchard

topee, topi: cap, hat 6 helmet

toper: sot 5 shark 6 boozer, bouser 7 tippler, tosspot 8 drunkard

tophaceous: 5 rough, sandy, stony 6 gritty

tophet, topheth: 4 hell 5 chaos 8 darkness 9 confusion

topic: 4 item, text 5 issue, theme 6 reason, remedy 7 heading, subject, themata 8 argument 11 proposition 13 consideration

topical: 5 local 9 temporary

topknot: 4 hair, head, tuft 5 crest, onkos 7 commode 8 flounder 9 headdress

toplofty: 5 proud 7 haughty 8 inflated 9 egotistic 10 disdainful 12 contemptuous, supercilious

topmost: 6 apical 7 highest, maximum 9 uppermost

topnotcher: ace 4 hero, star 8 jimdandy, knockout

topography: 7 terrain

topper: 4 hat 5 cover, float 6 stower 7 cheater, snuffer, topcoat 10 high-rigger 11 high-climber

toppiece: 4 head 6 toupee 11 masterpiece

topping: 4 bran, fine, good 5 icing, proud 6 refuse, tiptop 7 forlock, gallant, highest, topknot, topmost 8 arrogant, pleasant, superior 9 excellent, first-rate, skimmings 11 pretentious

topple: tip 4 fall, tilt 5 pitch, upset 6 teeter, totter, tumble 7 overset 8 overhang, overturn 9 overthrow 10 somersault 11 overbalance

tops: 5 A-one, aces, best 7 supreme 8 topnotch

topsman: 5 chief 6 drover 7 hangman, headman

topsy-turvy: 8 cockeyed, confused 10 disordered, upside-down 11 withershins

toque: hat 6 bonnet 9 headdress

tor: 4 taw 4 crag, hill, peak 5 mound 8 pinnacle

tora, torah: law 5 tetel 7 precept 10 hartebeest, Pentateuch, revelation 11 instruction

torch: 4 lamp 5 blaze, brand, flare, fusee 7 lucigen 8 flambeau 9 flambeaux(pl.) 10 flashlight, incendiary

frame: 7 cresset

tore: 4 knob, plod 5 grass 6 pommel 9 persevere

toreador: 6 torero 7 matador 11 bullfighter

torii: 7 gateway

torment: rib, vex 4 bait, hurt, pain, rack 5 agony, annoy, chevy, chivy, devil, force, grill, harry, tease, wrack 6 badger, chivvy, harass, harrow, hector, misery, molest, pester, plague, strain 7 afflict, agitate, anguish, bedevil, crucify, distort, hagride, hatchel, tempest, torture, travail 8 distress, vexation 9 martyrdom, suffering, tantalize 10 cruciation 11 persecution

tormenting: 6 plaguy, vexing 9 harassing 11 troublesome 12 excruciating

tormina: 5 colic, pains 6 cramps, gripes

torn: 4 rent 5 riven 6 broken, ripped 7 mangled 9 lacerated

tornado: 4 wind 6 squall 7 cyclone, thunder, twister 9 hurricane, whirlwind, windstorm 12 thunderstorm

Tornado Junction: 8 Trinidad

toro: 4 bull, tree 7 cavalla, cowfish

torous, torose: 6 brawny 7 bulging, knobbed, swollen 8 muscular 11 protuberant

torpedinous: 9 benumbing 10 stupefying

torpedo: 4 mine, ruin 5 wreck 6 attack, benumb, damage, gunman 7 destroy, explode, shatter 8 assassin, firework, gangster, numbfish, paralyze 9 crampfish, detonator

front end: 4 nose

torpedo fish: ray

torpid: 4 boat, dull, numb 5 inert 6 leaden, static, stupid 7 dormant 8 benumbed, inactive, lifeless, sluggish 9 apathetic, lethargic

torpor: 4 coma 5 sleep 6 acedia, apathy, stupor 7 accidie 8 dormancy, dullness, lethargy 10 inactivity, stagnation 12 sluggishness 13 insensibility

torque: bee 5 chain, sarpe, twist 6 collar 8 necklace

torrefy, torrify: dry 5 parch, 6 scorch

torrent: 4 flow, rush 5 flood, parch, roast, spate 6 stream 7 burning, channel consume, current, niagara, roaring, rushing 8 downpour 9 impetuous

torrential: 10 outpouring 12 overwhelming

torrid: hot 4 arid 5 dried 6 ardent, sultry 7 burning, parched, zealous 8 inflamed, parching, scorched 9 scorching 10 oppressive, passionate 11 impassioned

tort: 4 evil 5 libel, wrong 6 damage, injury 8 iniquity

tortoise: 6 turtle 8 terrapin 9 chelonian

genus: 4 emys

kind: 4 emyd 5 giant 9 Galapagos

marsh: 6 gopher 7 elodian

shell: 8 carapace

tortuous: 5 snaky 6 cranky, spiral 7 crooked, devious, immoral, sinuate, sinuous, winding, wriggly 8 wrongful 9 deceitful, injurious, twisting 10 circuitous, roundabout 11 anfractuous 12 labyrinthine

torture: 4 hurt, maim, pain, rack 5 agony, twist, wheel 6 deform, punish, wrench 7 afflict, agonize, anguish, crucify, distort, torment 8 distress, mutilate, twisting 9 martyrdom 10 affliction, cruciation, distortion, excruciate, perversion, punishment *device:* 4 rack

torus: 6 baston 7 ʌnolding 9 elevation 10 anchor ring, receptacle 12 protuberance

torvous: 4 grim 5 stern 6 severe

tory: 6 Papist 8 loyalist, marauder, Royalist 11 reactionary 12 conservative

Tosca's love: 5 Mario

tosh: 4 bath, bosh, neat, tidy 5 souse, trash 6 drench, neatly 7 bathtub 8 familiar, intimate, nonsense 10 intimately

toss: cob, cup, lob 4 cast, cave, flip, hike, hurl, rear, roll 5 chuck, flick, fling, flirt, heave, pitch, raise, serve, throw, wager 6 buffet, chance, fillip, harass, tossup, totter, uplift 7 agitate, disturb 8 disquiet 9 agitation, commotion 10 excitement

a coin: 4 flap, flip

about: 5 bandy 6 thrash, thresh 7 discuss

carelessly: 4 flip

head in derision: 4 geck

side to side: 6 careen

together confusedly: 8 scramble

tosspot: sot 5 toper 7 drinker 8 drunkard

bottle: 6 flagon

tosticate: 6 harass 8 distract 10 intoxicate

tosto: 4 fast 5 quick

tosy: 4 snug 10 comforting 11 intoxicated

tot: add, cup 4 dram, item, note 5 child, count, drink, total, totum 6 amount, toddle, totter 7 jotting, toddler

tota: 6 grivet, monkey

total: add, all, sum, tot 4 full 5 gross, run to, utter, whole 6 abrupt, all-out, amount, entire 7 concise, overall, perfect, plenary, summary 8 absolute, complete, entirety 9 aggregate, full-scale, undivided 10 accumulate

totalitarian: 7 fascist 8 absolute, despotic 9 arbitrary 10 tyrannical 13 authoritarian

tote: all, lug, tot 4 bear, haul, lead, load 5 carry, count, total 6 handle, reckon 7 conduct 9 abstainer, transport

totem: 6 emblem, fetich, fetish, figure

totem pole: xat

toto: all 4 baby 5 young

totter: 4 fall, hang, reel, rock, sway, toss 5 lurch, pitch, shake, swing, waver 6 dodder, falter, quiver, seesaw, staver(Sc.), toddle 7 fribble, stagger, tremble 8 titubate, unstable, unsteady 9 vacillate

tottle: 4 boil, purl 5 count, total 6 reckon, simmer, toddle, topple

toty(Ind.): 7 laborer 9 messenger

toucan: 4 bird, toco 7 aracari 8 hornbill 13 constellation

touch: dab, hit, paw, rap, rob, tag, tap, tig, toe, use 4 abut, blow, feel, hint, meet, rape 5 equal, reach, rival, steal, taste, trait 6 accuse, adjoin, affect, amount, attain, border, borrow, extend, handle, molest, rebuke, strike, stroke 7 attinge, censure, contact, impinge, palpate, partake 8 perceive 9 mishandle, tactility

boundary line: 4 abut

closely: 8 osculate

clumsily: paw

for medical diagnosis: 7 palpate

lightly: 5 brush, graze 7 attinge, twiddle

measuring device: 10 haptometer

off: 4 fire 5 start

organ of: 4 palp 6 feeler 7 antenna

perceptible by: 7 tactile 8 palpable

pert. to: 6 haptic 7 tactile, tactual

touching: 4 upon 6 moving 7 against, apropos, contact, meeting, piteous, tangent 8 adjacent, pathetic 9 affecting, attingent, conjoined 10 contacting, contiguous, contingent, responsive 13 compassionate

a single point: 7 tangent

touchstone: 4 test 8 basanite, standard 9 barometer, criterion

touchwood: 4 funk, punk 5 sponk, spunk 6 amadou, tinder 8 punkwood

touchy: 4 sore 5 cross, risky, snaky, techy, testy 7 peevish 8 ticklish 9 irascible, irritable, sensitive 10 precarious 11 inflammable 13 over-sensitive

tough: 4 thug, wiry 5 bully, hardy, rigid, rough, rowdy, stiff 6 brutal, flinty, robust, rugged, sinewy, sticky, strong 7 hickory, onerous, ruffian, violent, viscous 8 cohesive, enduring, hardened, hard-line, leathery, rowdyish, stubborn, sturdily, toilsome, vigorous 9 difficult, glutinous, obstinate, ruffianly 10 aggressive, unyielding

and lean: 5 scrag 6 sinewy

tough-minded: 6 shrewd 7 willful 8 stubborn 9 practical, realistic 10 hardheaded 13 unsentimental

toughen: 5 inure 6 anneal, endure, harden, temper

toupee: rug, wig 5 doily 6 peruke 7 periwig

tour: 4 trip, turn 5 cover, drive, range, round, shift, spell, trick, watch 6 course, travel 7 circuit, compass, journey, proceed 9 barnstorm, excursion 10 appearance, revolution

tourbillion: 5 whirl 6 vortex 8 firework, karrusel 9 whirlwind

tour de force: 4 feat 7 classic, exploit 11 masterpiece

tourelle: 5 tower 6 turret

tourist: 8 traveler 9 sightseer 10 rubberneck

tourmaline: 6 schorl 7 mineral 8 achroite, siberite 9 rubellite

tournament: 4 tilt 5 joust, sport, trial 6

battle 7 contest, tourney 9 encounter

tournure: pad 5 poise 6 bustle 7 contour, outline

touse: 4 pull, rack, tear 5 worry 6 handle, rumple 8 dishevel

tousle, tousel: 4 drag, muss, pull, tear 5 touse 6 ruffle, rumple, tussle 7 rummage 8 dishevel, disorder 9 mop of hair

tout: spy, vex 4 peep, peer, puff, toot 5 tease, thief, watch 6 herald, praise 7 canvass, lookout, solicit, tipster, touting, trumpet 8 ballyhoo, informer, proclaim, smuggler 9 importune, recommend

tout a fait: 5 quite 10 altogether

tow: tew, tug 4 drag, draw, flax, haul, lead, pull, rope 5 barge, chain 6 hawser, propel 7 towboat, towrope, tugboat 8 cordelle

tow-row: 6 rumpus, uproar 9 racketing

toward: tae(Sc.) 4 near 5 anent 6 coming, facing, future, onward 7 apropos, forward, willing 8 imminent, obliging 9 compliant, promising, regarding, tractable 10 concerning 11 approaching

center: 5 entad

exterior: 5 ectad

mouth: 4 orad

stern: aft 5 abaft 6 astern

towardly: 6 docile, gentle, kindly 7 affable 9 compliant, favorable, friendly, tractable 10 propitious

towel: dry, rub 5 cloth 6 napkin 8 vesperal 9 handcloth

fabric: 4 huck 5 linen, terry

tower: 4 rise, silo, soar 5 broch, exalt, mount, pylon, raise, reach, sikar, spire, stupa 6 ascend, belfry, castle, donjon, pagoda, prison, turret 7 bastile, bulwark, citadel, clocher, defense, elevate, mansion, minaret, mirador, overtop, shikara, steeple, surpass, zikurat 8 bastille, domineer, fortress, look down, overlook, ziggurat, zikkurat 9 campanile 10 protection, stronghold

bell: 6 belfry 8 carillon 9 campanile

castle: 6 donjon

church: 5 spire 7 steeple

famous: 4 Pisa 5 Babel, Minar 6 Eiffel, London

glacier ice: 5 serac

kind of: 5 ivory

mosque: 7 minaret

over: 5 dwarf 7 command 8 dominate

signal: 6 beacon

small: 6 turret

towering: 4 high, tall 5 great, lofty, steep 7 eminent, intense, supreme, violent 9 monstrous 11 overweening

towhee: 7 bunting, chewink

town: 4 burg, city, dorp, farm, stad, vill, yard 5 bourg, burgh, court, derby, house, manor, ville(F.), voter 6 ciudad(Sp.), garden, hamlet, parish, podunk, staple 7 borough, village 8 bourgade 9 enclosure, farmstead

Attica: 4 deme

official: 5 mayor 6 grieve 8 alderman

pert. to: 5 civic, urban 7 oppidon

plan: 4 plat

small: 8 one-horse 10 dullsville 11 whistle-stop

witch: 5 Salem

townsman: cit 7 burgher, citizen, oppidan

township: 4 area, dorp 8 district

toxic: 9 poisonous

toxophilite: 6 archer

toy: pet, top 4 ball, daff, doll, fool, play, whim 5 antic, dally, fancy, flirt, panda, sport 6 bauble, cosset, finger, frolic, gewgaw, hoople, rattle, trifle 7 caprice, conceit, disport, pastime, trinket 8 aversion, flirting, gimcrack, interest, mistress, ornament, teetotum, weakling 9 bandalore, dalliance, headdress, plaything, rattlebox, teddybear 10 knickknack

toyish: 6 wanton 7 playful, trivial, useless 8 sportive, trifling 9 fantastic, frivolous, whimsical 13 unsubstantial

trabant: 9 attendant, bodyguard

trabea: 4 toga

trabeation: 11 entablature

trabuco: 5 cigar 11 blunderbuss

trace: 4 clew, clue, copy, draw, fall, file, hint, line, mark, nose, path, road, seek, sign, step, tang, walk 5 grain, march, probe, route, shade, spoor, tinge, token, track, trail, tread 6 amount, deduce, derive, detect, follow, locate, ramble, sketch, trudge 7 conduct, glimpse, impress, imprint, inquire, outline, remnant, soupcon, uncover, vestige 8 discover, evidence, quantity, traverse 9 ascertain, attribute, delineate, establish, footprint, scintilla 10 indication, procession 11 investigate

tracer: 5 horse 6 bullet, gilder, seeker, stylus 7 stainer 8 outliner, searcher 9 draftsman

trachea: 4 duct 8 windpipe

trachyte: 4 rock 6 domite

tracing: 4 copy 6 record 8 ergogram 10 cardiogram

track: rut, way 4 drag, draw, hunt, line, mark, oval, path, rail, road, wake 5 march, route, scent, sight, spoor, trace, trail, tread 6 course, follow, infuse, pursue, shadow, teapot, travel 7 circuit, conduct, vestige 8 guideway, sequence, speedway, trackage, traverse 9 ascertain, footprint, spectacle 10 beaten path, cinder path, succession

animal: run 4 slot 5 spoor

down: 4 hunt 6 pursue, search
official: 5 judge, timer 7 referee, starter
race: 4 mile 5 relay 6 sprint
running: 4 fiat 7 cinders
ship: 4 wake
train: 4 rail, spur 6 siding

tracker: 5 guide, tower 7 tugboat

tract (see also **land**): lot 4 area, mark, path, zone 5 campo, clime, essay, lapse, range, trace, track 6 course, estate, extent, region 7 country, expanse, leaflet, portion, quarter, stretch 8 brochure, district, duration, pamphlet, sequence, treatise 9 lineament, narrative, territory 10 exposition 11 subdivision 12 dissertation

tractable: 4 easy 5 buxom 6 docile, gentle, pliant 7 ductile, flexile, pliable 8 amenable, flexible, obedient, workable 9 adaptable, complaint, malleable 10 governable

tractate: 5 essay, tract 8 handling, treatise 9 discourse, treatment 10 discussion 12 dissertation

tractile: 6 pliant 7 ductile, tensile

traction 5 power 7 drawing, utility 8 friction 9 influence 10 attraction

tractor: rig 9 agrimotor

trade: buy, way 4 chap, chop deal, fuss, path, sell, swap, work 5 cheap, craft, habit, track, trail, tread 6 action, barter, bother, course, employ, manner, method, metier, scorse 7 bargain, calling, dealing, pursuit, traffic 8 activity, business, commerce, exchange, practice, purchase 9 patronage 10 handicraft, occupation, profession 11 intercourse, nundination

association: NAM 5 hansa, hanse

combination: 4 gild 5 guild, hanse 6 cartel, merger

pert. to: 10 emporeutic

unlawful: 10 contraband 11 black market

votes: 7 logroll

trademark: 4 logo 5 brand 8 logotype

trader: 4 ship 6 dealer, monger, seller, slaver, sutler 7 chapman 8 barterer, merchant 9 tradesman 10 shopkeeper 11 stockbroker

tradesman: 5 buyer 7 artisan, workman 8 merchant 9 craftsman 10 shopkeeper 11 storekeeper

supply: 4 line 5 stock 9 inventory

tradition: 4 code, lore 5 belief, custom, legend 8 heritage, practice 9 surrender 10 convention

traduce: 4 slur 5 abuse, belie 6 debase, defame, malign, vilify 7 asperse, blacken, detract, pervert, slander 8 disgrace 10 calumniate

traffic: buy 4 coup, sell 5 trade 6 barter, market 7 chaffer, dealing 8 business,

commerce, exchange 9 patronage 11 intercourse

in holy offices: 6 simony

violator: 7 speeder 9 jaywalker

trafficker: 6 dealer, trader 8 merchant

in narcotics: 6 pusher

tragacanth: gum 4 tree 5 shrub

tragedy: lot, woe 6 buskin, misery 8 calamity, disaster 10 misfortune

Muse: 9 Melpomene

tragic: sad 4 dire 5 fatal 7 doleful 8 dreadful, mournful, pathetic, terrible

tragopan: 8 pheasant

tragule: 4 deer 10 chevrotain

trail: lad 4 drag, draw, halt, hang, hunt, mark, path, plod, slot, tail, wake 5 blaze, delay, drail, piste, route, scent, spoor, trace, track, train, tramp, troll 6 camino(Sp.), course, follow, trapse, trudge 7 draggle, dwindle, traipse 8 footpath, straggle

blazer: 7 pioneer

marker: 5 cairn

trailer: 4 vine

truck: 4 semi

train: row 4 bait, drag, draw, file, form, gait, lead, line, lure, rack, rank, rear, tail, trap 5 breed, coach, decoy, drawl, drill, flier, guide, local, seine, shape, snare, suite, teach, trace, trail 6 allure, coffle, convoy, cradle, direct, entice, ground, harden, scheme, school, season, series, shaped 7 caravan, conduct, cortege, educate, prepare, retinue 8 accustom, artifice, equipage, instruct protract, rehearse, sequence, trickery 9 condition, cultivate, entourage, following, stratagem, treachery 10 attendants, conveyance, discipline, procession, succession 11 streamliner 13 accommodation

end car of: 7 caboose

fast: 7 express, limited

horses: 6 manege

men: 4 crew

of attendants: 5 suite 7 cortege, retinue 9 entourage

overhead: 8 elevated, monorail

slow: 5 local

underground: 4 tube 5 metro(F.) 6 subway

trained: 4 bred 5 aimed 8 educated

trainee: 4 boot 5 cadet, pupil 6 novice 10 apprentice

trainer: 5 tamer 7 lanista 11 gymnasiarch

training: 4 diet 5 drill 8 breeding, exercise 9 education 10 background, discipline 11 supervision

lack of: 11 inappetence

manual: 5 sloid, sloyd

traipse, trapes: gad 4 drag, walk 5 trail,

tramp, tread 6 trudge, wander 8 gadabout, slattern

trait: 4 line, mark, note, thew 5 touch 6 streak, stroke 7 feature, quality 9 attribute, lineament, mannerism 11 peculiarity 14 characteristic

traitor: 5 Judas 8 betrayer, Iscariot, renegade

Norwegian: 8 Quisling

traitorous: 5 false 9 faithless, felonious 11 disaffected, treacherous, treasonable

traject: way 4 cast 5 ferry, route, throw 6 course, trajet 7 conduct, passage 8 transmit

tralatitious: 10 handed down 12 metaphorical

tram: car, leg 4 beam, haul, limb 5 bench, shaft, wagon 6 thread 7 tramcar, trammel, tramway, trolley 9 streetcar 10 conveyance

tier: 4 deck

trammel: net, tie 4 clog, lock 5 check, gauge 6 braids, fasten, fetter, hamper, impede 7 compass, confine, pothook, prevent, shackle, tresses 8 entangle, restrain, stultify 9 intercept, plaitings 1 instrument

tramontane: 4 boor 5 alien 7 foreign 8 stranger 9 barbarous 10 outlandish 11 transalpine

tramp: bo; boe, bum, vag 4 hike, hobo, hoof, plod, prog, step, tart, vamp, walk 5 caird, jaunt, tread 6 gaycat, trapes, travel, trudge, waffie, wander, wanton 7 steamer, traipse, vagrant 8 vagabond 9 excursion 10 prostitute 11 bindle stiff

baggage: 6 bindle

offering to: 7 handout

trample: 4 foil, hurt 5 crush, stamp, stomp, tread 6 injure 7 destroy, tread on, violate

trance: 4 coma, daze 5 spell, swoon 6 prance, raptus, stupor 7 ecstasy, enchant, passage, reverie 8 entrance 9 catalepsy, enrapture, transport

tranquil: 4 calm, cool, easy, even, mild 5 equal, quiet, still 6 gentle, placid, serene, steady 7 equable, pacific, restful 8 composed, peaceful 9 sedentary 10 motionless 11 undisturbed 13 imperturbable

tranquility, tranquillity: kef, kif 5 peace, quiet 8 ataraxia, serenity 10 equanimity 12 peacefulness

tranquilize: 4 calm, lull 5 allay, quiet 6 sedate, settle, soften, soothe, subdue 7 appease, assuage 10 alleviate

transact: 5 treat 7 conduct, perform 8 complete, transfer 9 negotiate

transaction: 4 deal, sale 6 affair 7 bargain 8 business, contract, covenant 10 proceeding 11 proposition

unlawful: 10 chevisance

Transcaspian capital: 9 Ashkhabad

Transcaucasia: See **Armenia, Azerbaijan**

transcend: 4 pass, soar 5 climb, excel, mount, raise 6 ascend, exceed 7 elevate, surpass 8 outstrip, overstep, surmount 9 rise above

transcendent: 8 superior 13 extraordinary

transcendental: 5 ideal 7 eternal, supreme 8 abstract, ethereal 10 superhuman 12 metaphysical, otherworldly, supersensual, supranatural

transcribe: 4 copy 5 write 6 impute, record 7 ascribe, imitate 9 reproduce, translate 10 paraphrase

transcript: 6 record 8 apograph 9 duplicate 12 reproduction

transfer: 4 cede, deed, give, move, pass, sale, send 5 carry, grant, shift 6 assign, attorn, change, convey, decant, demise, depute, remove 7 dispose 8 alienate, delegate, make over, sign over, transmit 9 transform, translate, transport 10 abalienate 12 transmission 13 transposition

bus or train: 6 ticket 8 add-a-ride

design: 5 decal

of court suit: 7 remover

property: 4 deed 5 grant 6 convey

transference: 7 passage 10 conveyance

transfigure: 5 exalt 7 glorify 8 idealize 9 transform 12 metamorphose

transfix: fix, pin 5 spear, stick 6 fasten, impale, pierce, thrill 11 transpierce

transform: 4 turn 5 alter 6 change 7 convert 9 transmute 11 transfigure 12 metamorphose, transmogrify

into human form: 16 anthropomorphize

transfuse: 5 imbue 6 infuse 7 instill 8 permeate, transfer, transmit

transgress: err, sin 5 break, cross 6 offend 7 disobey, violate 8 overstep, trespass

transgression: 5 crime, fault 6 breach 7 misdeed 8 trespass 10 infraction 12 infringement 13 contravention

transient: 7 flighty, passing 8 fleeting, fugitive 9 ephemeral, itinerant, migratory, momentary, temporary, transeunt 10 evanescent, shortlived, transitory 11 impermanent

transit: 6 change 7 passage 9 transport 10 conveyance, transition 12 thoroughfare

coach: bus

transition: 5 phase, shift 7 passage 9 metabasis 10 alteration, conversion

transitive: 7 flowing 12 transitional

transitory: 5 brief, fleet 8 caducous, temporal 9 ephemeral, short-term, temporary **10** evanescent

translate: put **4** read, rede **6** change, decode, remove, render **7** convert **8** construe, decipher, entrance, transfer **9** enrapture, interpret **10** paraphrase

translation: 4 pony, trot **7** version **9** rendition **10** paraphrase **14** interpretation **15** transliteration

translucent: 5 clear **6** limpid **7** obvious **9** alabaster **11** perspicuous, transparent

transmigration: 7 samsara

transmit: 4 emit, hand, send **5** carry, relay **6** convey, render **7** conduct, devolve, forward **8** bequeath, dispatch **9** pass along **11** communicate

transmutation: 9 evolution

transom: 5 trave **6** louver, window

transparent: 4 open **5** clear, filmy, frank, gauzy, lucid, plain, sheer **6** candid, limpid, lucent **7** obvious, pelucid **8** luminous, lustrous **9** colorless **10** diaphanous **11** crystalline, perspicuous, translucent **12** clear as glass

transpierce: 6 impale **8** transfix **9** penetrate

transpire: 6 get out, happen, result **9** eventuate

transport: dak **4** bear, boat, buss, haul, move, send, ship, tote **5** bring, carry, ferry, flute, truck **6** banish, convey, deport, ravish **7** convict, ecstasy, emotion, fraught, freight, passion, portage, rapture, smuggle, transit, vehicle **8** entrance, horsecar, overcome, palander, transfer **9** captivate, enrapture, happiness

transportation: *business:* **4** mail **7** air line, express **8** shipping, trucking **9** steamship **11** railroading

transpose: 5 shift **6** change, remove **7** convert, disturb, reverse **8** exchange, transfer **9** rearrange, transform, translate, transmute **11** interchange

transposition: 7 anagram **10** spoonerism **11** permutation

Transvaal: *capital:* **8** Pretoria

city: **12** Johannesburg

goldfield: **13** Witwatersrand

native: **4** Zulu **7** Bushman **9** Hottentot

province of: **11** South Africa (which also see)

resource: **4** gold

transverse: bar, way **4** bank, over, pass, rung, turn **5** argue, cross, pivot, route, shift, trace **6** across, denial, stripe, survey, swivel, thwart, travel **7** barrier, discuss, examine, impeach, oblique, pervade, quarrel **8** diagonal **9** alternate, crossbeam, crosswise **10** crosspiece

Transylvania: *city:* **4** Cluj

fabled resident: **7** Dracula, vampire

trap: bag, get, gin, net, pit **4** cage, lure, nail, snag **5** brake, buggy, catch, goods, mouth, rocks, snare, steps, trick **6** ambush, corner, detect, enmesh **7** capture, cunning, ensnare, luggage, pitfall, springe **8** carriage, confound, covering, deadfall, separate, trapball **9** caparison, detective, policeman, stratagem **10** belongings, stepladder

animal: pot, web **4** weir **5** creel **6** bownet, eelpot **8** deadfall

police: **7** dragnet **9** roadblock

trapdoor: 4 drop, slot

trapes: See **traipse**

trapeze: bar

trapping: 4 gear **5** cloth **7** harness **8** catching, covering, ornament **9** adornment, caparison, coverture **10** decoration **12** accouterment, accoutrement **13** embellishment, paraphernelia

theatrical: **4** prop **7** scenery **8** property

Trappist: 4 monk

cheese: oka

writer: **6** Merton

traps: 5 bells, drums **7** cymbals

trapshooting: 5 skeet

target: **10** clay pigeon

trash: jog, lop **4** bosh, clog, crop, dirt, jade, pelf, plod, raff, tosh **5** leash, money, tramp, waste, wrack **6** bushwa, debris, halter, hinder, rabble, refuse, retard, rubble, trudge **7** baggage, beggary, blather, rubbish **8** encumber, flummery, nonsense, restrain, riffraff, trumpery, vandalize **10** balderdash **11** sleuthhound

trashy: 4 mean **5** cheap **6** common **9** worthless

trauma: 5 shock, wound **6** injury, stress **8** collapse

travail: 4 pain, pang, task, toil, work **5** agony, drive, labor **6** effort, travel **7** journey, torment, trouble **8** exertion **9** suffering **10** birth throe **11** parturition

trave: 9 crossbeam

travel: run **4** fare, move, mush, post, ride, tour, trek, trip, walk, wend **5** coast **6** motion **7** commute, journey, migrate, passage, proceed, sojourn, travail **8** traverse **9** gallivant, itinerate **10** locomotion **11** peregrinate

company: **7** caravan

pert. to: **6** viatic

schedule: **9** itinerary

yen for: **10** wanderlust

traveler: 5 farer, tramp **6** viator **7** drummer, pilgrim, swagman, tourist, voyager **8** salesman, vagabond, wanderer, wayfarer **9** intinerant **12** globe-trotter

aid of: **5** guide **7** courier **8** cicerone

commercial: **5** agent **6** bagman **7** drummer **8** salesman

refuge: inn **5** oasis, motel **7** hospice

travels: 7 odyssey

traverse: 4 deny, ford, pass 5 cross, range, rebut 6 oppose, patrol, refute, swivel, thwart

travesty: 4 mimic 6 parody, satire 8 disguise 9 burlesque, imitation 10 caricature

writer: 8 parodist

trawl: net 4 fish, line 5 seine 7 boulter, dragnet

tray: hod 4 font 6 hurdle, salver, server 7 coaster

treacherous: 5 false, punic, snaky 6 fickle, hollow, tricky 8 disloyal, insecure, plotting, unstable 9 dangerous, faithless, insidious 10 fraudulent, perfidious, precarious, traitorous, unreliable 11 disaffected 12 Machiavelian 13 Machiavellian, untrustworthy

treachery: 5 guile 6 deceit 7 perfidy, treason, untruth 8 betrayal 9 dirty pool 10 infidelity

treacle: 4 cure 5 syrup 6 remedy 7 claggum 8 molasses

treaclewort: 4 herb 10 pennycress

tread: rut 4 gait, mark, pace, rung, step, volt, walk 5 clump, crush, dance, labor, march, press, stair, stamp, trace, track, trail, tramp 6 balter, course, quench, stride, subdue, traps 7 conquer, repress, traipse, trample 8 copulate, footfall 9 footprint 10 employment, occupation

treadle: 5 pedal 7 chalaza

treason: 7 perfidy 8 betrayal, sedition 9 treachery

treasure: 4 find, plum, roon 5 cache, hoard, pearl, prize, store, trove, value 6 gersum, riches, supply, wealth 7 cherish, finance 8 hold dear 9 thesaurus(L.) 10 appreciate, collection 12 accumulation

Treasure State: 7 Montana

treasured: 4 dear 5 chary 7 precious

treasurer: 7 cashier, curator 8 bhandari, cofferer, deftedar, guardian, receiver 11 chamberlain

college: 6 bursar

treasury: 4 fisc, fund 5 chest, hoard 6 coffer 7 bonanza, bursary, revenue 9 exchequer 10 repository, storehouse

Roman: 9 fiscus

treat: use 4 blow, deal, dose, lead, urge 5 argue, besee, Dutch, feast, guide, serve, stand, touch 6 attend, confer, demean, doctor, govern, handle, parley, regale, regard, repast 7 address, bargain, control, discuss, entreat, expound 8 consider, deal with, delicacy, transact, treatise 9 discourse, entertain, negotiate 10 manipulate

improperly: 4 snub 5 flout, scout, spite 6 ill-use, misuse 8 dishonor

leather: tan, taw 7 chamois

tenderly: 5 spare 6 coddle, pamper

treatise: 5 essay, tract 6 thesis, treaty 7 account, grammar 8 brochure 9 discourse, narration, treatment 10 commentary, discussion, exposition 11 description 12 dissertation

elementary: 6 primer 7 grammar

opening part: 8 exordium

preface: 7 isagoge

treatment: 4 care 5 usage 7 therapy 8 demeanor, entreaty, handling 10 management 13 entertainment

before doctor's arrival: 8 first aid

compassionate: 5 mercy

harsh: 5 abuse 8 misusage, severity

treaty: 4 pact 7 article, concord, entente 8 contract, treatise 9 agreement, discourse 10 convention, discussion 11 arrangement, negotiation 13 understanding

treaty-bound: 6 allied

treble: 4 high 5 acute 6 shrill, triple 7 soprano 9 threefold 11 high-pitched

tree (see also next entry): ach, ber, dal, dao, ebo, elm, fir, hur, iba, kou, lin, mee, oak 4 acle, alan, alof, anam, asak, asok, ates, ausu, bael, biti, bogo, bola, dali, dhak, dita, ipil, mabi, mora, odal, palm, pole, post, ship, toon, trap, wood, yaya 5 areca, asoka, betis, bongo, bulak, bumbo, cacao, carob, catch, cebil, couma, dadap, dalli, fulwa, genip, ligas, mahua, neeba, nepal, niepa, nitta, oodal, rohan, roman, salai, sassy, shaft, shift, siman, sissu, spade, staff, stake, stick, tikur, yacca 6 bahera, banyan, barbas, bariba, brauna, bucare, cativo, cedron, chalta, chogak, chupon, cocuyo, colima, corner, cudgel, design, gibbet, gomart, illupi, jarrah, locust, marane, marara, ramoon, sabino, simaba, sissoo, stemma, tikoor, timber 7 anubing, araraba, arboret, assagai, assegai, azarole, capture, champac, champak, cocullo, dhamnoo, diagram, gallows, guaraba, gumihan, hautboy, hollong, madrona, madrono, malpaho, mamborg 8 ahueuete, cockspur, gamdeboo, ironbark, magnolia, mangrove, mokihana, phulwara, seedling, tamarack 9 bandoline, betel-palm, bitanhole, canadulce, couratari, currajong genealogy, sassywood 10 bunyabunya, chaulmugra 11 balinghasay, chaulmaugra, chaulmoogra, guachipilin, hursinghair

alder: arn 5 alnus, birch 12 ament-bearing

algarroba: 5 carob 6 calden

allspice: 7 pimento

apple: 4 sorb

aromatic: 9 sassafras
balsam: fir 9 torch-wood
bark: 4 ross, tapa
basswood: 6 linden
bead: nim
bean: 5 sapan
bearing samara: ash
beefwood: 5 belah, belar
betel: 5 areca
bignoniacious: 7 catalpa
blinding sap: 7 alipata
boxwood: 5 seron
breadnut: 6 capomo
buckthorn: 7 cascara
buckwheat: 4 titi 6 teetee
Buddha's: 6 botree
bully: see *gum* below
burned, broken: 7 rampick, rampike
buttonball: 5 plane 8 sycamore
cabbage: 7 angelin
camphor: 5 kapur
candlenut: ama
caoutchouc: ule 6 rubber
caucho-yielding (see also *rubber* below):
  ule
cemetery: yew
chestnut: 10 chinqua pin
chocolate: 5 cacao
cinchona: 7 quinine 9 quinidine
cinnamon family: 6 cassia
citrus: 4 lime 5 lemon 6 orange 8 bergamot 10 calamondin
clump: 4 tump 5 motte
coconut: 4 coco
coffee: 6 chicot
conebearing: fir, yew 4 pine 5 alder, cedar, larch 6 spruce 7 conifer, cypress,
  hemlock, juniper, redwood 8 gnetales
coral: 6 gabgab
cottonwood: 5 alamo
covering: 4 bark
cranberry: 7 pembina
derivative: 5 pinic
devil: 4 dita
drumstick: 11 canafistolo, canafistula,
  canafistulo
drupe bearing: 4 bito
dwarf: 5 scrub 7 abuscle 10 chinquapin
dwelling: 4 nest
dye yielding: tua, tui 4 mora 7 annatto
  10 hursinghar
ebony: 9 diospyros
elder: 7 trammon
eucalyptus: 4 yati 6 mallee
evergreen: fir, yew 4 pine, tawa, titi 5 carob, cedar, holly, larch, ocote, olive 6
  balsam, carobe, cazaba, coigue, tarata 7
  bebeery, juniper, madrona, madrono,
  taratah
exudation: gum, lac, sap, tar 5 resin, rosin, xylan
fabacious: 5 agati

fiber: 5 bulak, simal, terap 7 bentang
fig family: 4 upas 5 pipal 6 botree 7 gondang
flowering: 5 agati, elder, sumac, titis 6
  mimosa, redbud 7 dogwood 8 cleaster,
  oleaster
fodder: 5 mahoe 9 tagasaste
food: 4 akee
fruit: bel, fig, gab 4 gaub, lime 5 araca,
  lemon, mahis, olive, papaw, topes 6 annona, banana, bearer, biriba, litchi,
  medlar, pawpaw, sapota 7 avocado, capulin, genipap, tangelo 8 bakupari, tamarind 9 tangerine 12 custard apple
gaucho: ule
group: 4 bosk 5 copse, grove, woods 6 forest 7 coppice, orchard
grower: 8 arborist
gum: 5 babul, balta 6 balata, sapota, sapote, tupelo, zapote 8 banildad 9 sapodilla, sapotilha, sapotilla 10 bansalague,
  eucalyptus
gum genus: 6 owenia
hardwood: 4 poon 5 aalii, gidia, gidya,
  mabee, maple, narra, ngaio 6 gidgea,
  gidgee, gidjee, gidyea, walnut 7 hickory,
  tindalo 8 macaasin, mahogany 9 quebracho
heartwood: 7 duramen
health: 5 briar, brier
hickory: 5 pecan
holly: 4 ilex
honeberry: 5 genip
horseradish: 4 behn 5 behen
jobber: 10 woodpecker
juniper: 4 cade 5 cedar
kino: 4 bija
koranic: 6 zaggum
laurel: bay 7 tarairi
limb: 5 bough 6 branch
lime: lin 4 linn, teil 6 linden 9 tilicetum
linden: 4 lime, teil 8 basswood
locust: 6 acacia 9 courbaril
lotus: sad 6 jujube
mafurra: 6 elcaja
magnolia: 5 yulan
mahogany: 4 toon
maple: 4 acer
margosa: 4 neem
marmalade: 6 mammee, mammey, sapote
medicinal: 5 sumac 6 sumach, wahahe
mimosaceous: 5 siris
monkeybread: 6 baobob
mountain ash: 4 sorb 5 rowan 7 service
mulberry: 5 osage 8 sycamine
nut: 4 cola 5 hazel, pecan, pinon 6 akhrot, chicha 9 almendron, pistachio
nymph turned into: 6 Daphne
oil: 5 mahua, mahwa 9 candlenut
oil-yielding: bel, ben 4 eboe, shea
olive: 4 olea
olive family: ash

palm: tal 4 coco, nipa 5 ratan 6 arengs
paradise: 8 aceituna
part: 4 bark, bole, knot, leaf, root, twig 5 trunk 6 branch
pert. to: 8 arboreal
pine: see *evergreen* above
plane: 8 sycamore 10 buttonwood
plantain: 4 pala
pod-bearing: 7 catalpa
poisonous: 4 upas 5 ligas 7 tanquen
poon: 4 dilo 5 keena
poplar: 5 abele, alamo, aspen, tulip 10 cottonwood
pottery: 7 caraipe, caraipi
rain: 5 saman, zaman 6 zamang 7 genisaro 9 algarroba
rare: 6 Joshua
resin: 4 arar
ribbon: 6 akaroa 7 houhere
rowan: see *mountain ash* above
rubber: ule 4 para 6 caucho 7 seringa 10 caoutchouc
rutaceous: 4 lime
salt: 4 atle 5 atlee
sandarac: 4 arar
sandbox: 6 assacu
science: 7 silvics
shade: ash, elm, oak 5 guama, maple 6 linden, poplar 7 catalpa 8 sycamore
smoke: 6 fustet 9 zante-wood
soft-wood: lin 5 ambay, balsa, linde
sour gum: 5 nyssa 6 tupelo
sprout: 5 sprig 7 sapling
streaked wood: 5 baria
stunted: 5 scrub
tallow: 4 cera
tamarisk: see *salt* above
tea: 6 manuka
teak: 4 teca
thorny: bel 4 bael, bito, brea 7 colorin 8 barriguda 11 chichicaste
timber: ash, dar, eng, koa, saj, sal, yew 4 coco, cuya, ipil, pelu, pine, poon, rata, tala, teak, toon, ulmo 5 acana, almon, amate, balao, balau, bayok, beech, birch, cedar, culla, dalli, ebano, fotui, guijo, icica, kauri, kaury, maple, narra, pekea, penda, rauli, tenio, timbo, uadal, yacal, zorro 6 alerce, alerse, alfaje, ausubo, bacury, banaba, banago, banaki, bancal, banuyo, bataan, batino, dagame, dungon, lanete, molave, satine, totara, walnut 7 batulin, becuiba, billian, camagon, capulin, cypress, gateado, gomavel, guacimo, hapiton, redwood 8 flindosa, flindosy, mahogany, zapetero 9 balaustre, guaraguao 10 batikuling
treatise: 5 silva
tropical genus: 8 bauhinia
trunk: 4 bole 5 shaft
tulip: 6 poplar
Turkey oak: 6 cerris

turpentine: 6 tarata 7 taratah 9 terebinth
walnut see *nut* above: 6 akhrot
wattle: 5 boree
wide-spreading: 5 cedar 7 juniper
willow: 5 osier, saugh 6 poplar
worship: 11 dendrolatry
yellow alder: 8 sagerose
young: 7 sapling
tree: For trees of specific countries or regions, see under that country or region.
tree bear: 7 raccoon
tree runner: 8 nuthatch
tree toad: 4 hyla 6 peeper
treeless: 6 barren
plain: 5 llano, pampa 6 steppe 7 prairie, savanna 8 savannah
treelike: 11 arborescent
treen: 6 wooden
treenail: nog, peg, pin 5 spike 7 trunnel
trefoil: 4 leaf 6 clover
treillage: 5 grill 7 trellis 8 espalier 11 laticework
trek: 4 draw, pull 5 march 6 travel 7 journey, migrate 10 expedition
trellis: 5 bower, cross 7 lattice, pergola 8 espalier 10 interweave 11 latticework
trematode: 6 cercaria, flatworm, parasite
tremble: 5 bever, quake, shake 6 didder, dither, dodder, falter, quaver, quiver, shiver, totter, tremor 7 flacker, flicker, shudder, vibrate 9 trepidate
trembling: 7 fearful, twitter 9 tremulous
tremendous: big 4 huge 5 awful, giant, great, large 7 amazing, fearful 8 dreadful, enormous, great big, horrible, powerful, terrific 9 frightful, momentous, monstrous 10 terrifying 13 extraordinary
tremolo: 6 quaver 7 vibrato
tremor: 5 quake, shake 6 quiver, shiver, thrill 7 tremble 9 vibration 10 earthquake
tremplin: 11 springboard
tremulous: 5 aspen, timid 7 aquiver, fearful, nervous, palsied 8 timorous, unsteady, wavering 9 quavering, sensitive 11 palpitating
trench: cut, gaw 4 bury, gash, moat, sike 5 carve, ditch, drain, fosse, fossa(L.), graff, graft, slash, slice 6 border, furrow, groove, gutter 7 acequia 8 encroach, entrench, infringe 10 excavation
digger: 6 sapper
digging: sap
trenchant: 4 keen 5 acrid, acute, sharp 6 biting, caustic 7 cutting 8 clear-cut, distinct, forceful, incisive, vigorous 9 energetic 11 penetrating
trencher: 5 board, plate 7 platter 9 parasitic 11 sycophantic
trencherman: 7 glutton, gormand, sponger 8 gourmand, hanger-on, parasite 11

gormandizer 12 gourmandizer

trend: run 4 bend, bent, tone, turn, vein 5 drift, swing, tenor 6 extend, strike 7 fashion, incline 8 movement, tendency 9 direction 11 inclination

trepan: 4 lure, tool, trap 5 snare, trick 7 entrap 7 deceive, ensnare, swindle 9 perforate, stratagem

trepang: 8 teatfish 10 beche-de-mer 22 holothurian-sea-cucumber

trepid: 7 quaking 8 timorous 9 trembling

trepidation: 4 fear 5 alarm, dread 6 dismay, tremor 7 quaking 9 agitation, confusion 11 disturbance 12 perturbation 13 consternation

trespass: sin 5 poach 6 breach, invade, offend 7 intrude 8 encroach, entrench, infringe 9 do wrong by, interlope 10 infraction, transgress 11 misfeasance

tress: 4 curl, hair, lock 5 braid, plait 7 ringlet, wimpler

treasure: 4 band, caul 6 border, fillet, ribbon 9 headdress

trestle: leg 5 bench, horse, stand, stool 6 tripod, trivet 7 support, viaduct 8 sawhorse 9 framework

tret: 9 allowance

trews: 8 breeches, trousers 9 stockings

triad: 5 three, trine 6 triune 7 trinity 9 threesome, trivalent 11 triumvirate

trial: try 4 bout, case, pain, test 5 assay, cross, essay, grief, proof 6 assize, effort, ordeal, sample 7 approof, attempt, calvary, contest, hearing, inquiry 8 crucible, endeavor, evidence, hardship 10 affliction, experience, experiment, tournament, visitation 11 examination, tribulation 13 investigation

and error: 10 experiment
inconclusive: 8 mistrial
pert. to: 7 empiric
scene of: 5 court

trial balloon: 4 kite, test 6 feeler

triangle: 5 delta 6 trigon 7 scalene, trigone 9 isosceles 11 equilateral
draw circle touching: 7 escribe
in heraldry: 5 giron
side: leg 10 hypotenuse
unequal sided: 7 scalene

triangular: 7 cunate, deltoid, hastate 13 three-cornered
piece: 4 gore 5 miter, mitre, wedge 6 gusset
sail: jib 6 lateen 9 spinnaker

triangular muscle: 7 deltoid

triarchy: 11 triumvirate

tribe: (for tribe of specific country see *tribe, native* or *people* under that country) rod 4 band, clan, kind, race, sept 5 class, firca(Ind.), group 6 family 9 community
emblem: 5 totem

head: 5 chief 9 patriarch

tribulation: 5 agony, trial 6 misery, sorrow 8 distress 9 suffering 10 affliction, oppression, wrongdoing 11 persecution

tribunal: bar 4 banc, seat 5 bench, court, forum 7 tribune 8 assembly 10 consistory

tribune: 4 dais 6 throne 8 platform 10 magistrate

tributary: 5 ruler, state 6 feeder 7 subject 9 auxiliary 10 subsidiary 11 subordinate 12 contributory

tribute: fee, tax 4 cain, dues, duty, gift, levy, rent, scat 5 grant 6 assign, eulogy, impost, praise, tariff 7 chevage, ovation, payment, respect 8 encomium 9 attribute, gratitude, laudation, panegyric 10 obligation 11 testimonial

trice: 4 bind, gird, haul, lash, pull 5 jiffy 6 moment, secure 7 instant 9 twinkling

trichome: 4 hair 7 bristle, prickle

trichord: 4 lyre

trick: bob, boy, cog, dor, fob, fox, fub, gag, gum, toy 4 bilk, dupe, feat, flam, fool, gaff, gaud, girl, gull, hoax, jest, joke, prat, ruse, trap, turn, wile 5 catch, child, cully, dodge, feint, fraud, gleek, guile, hocus, knack, prank, shift, skite, spell, stunt 6 begunk, chouse, delude, humbug, palter, trepan, trifle 7 beguile, cantrip, deceive, defraud, finesse, gimmick, pretext, sleight, swindle 8 artifice, flimflam, illusion, maneuver 9 bamboozle, capriccio, chicanery, diablerie, imposture, mannerism, stratagem 10 subterfuge 11 hornswoggle, legerdemain

trickery: art 5 fraud, hocus 6 cautel, deceit, japery 7 knavery, roguery, slyness 8 cheating, trumpery 9 deception, duplicity 10 hanky-panky 11 doublecross

trickle: 4 drip, flow, sipe(Sc.) 5 exude 6 distil 7 distill, dripple

trickster: 5 cheat 6 rascal 7 slicker 8 swindler 9 gyp artist

tricksy: 5 smart, tight 6 spruce 7 evasive, playful, quirksy, roguish 8 prankish, sportive 9 deceiving, deceptive, uncertain 11 embellished, mischievous

tricky: sly 5 dodgy 6 artful, catchy 7 devious 8 delicate, ticklish, unstable 9 deceitful, intricate

tricycle: 6 tricar

trident: 5 spear 7 scepter
bearer: 7 Neptune

tried: 6 ettled(Sc.), proved, select, tested 7 staunch 8 faithful, reliable 9 steadfast 11 trustworthy

trier: 5 judge 7 refiner 8 examiner, renderer 12 experimenter, investigator

trifle: bit, fig, rap, sou, toy 4 bean, doit,

fike, hint, jest, mock, mote, play 5 dally, flirt, straw, trick, use up, waste 6 bauble, burn up, coquet, dabble, dawdle, delude, dibble, doodle, fiddle, fidget, footer, footle, frivol, gewgaw, misuse, potter 7 deceive, dessert, fribble, nothing, traneen 8 flimflam, gimcrack, raillery 9 bagatelle 10 equivocate, knickknack, triviality

trifling: 4 airy, idle, mere 5 banal, inane, petty 6 futile, little 7 shallow, wasting 8 badinage, frippery 9 dalliance, small talk 10 immaterial 11 unimportant 13 insignificant

trifolium: 6 clover 8 shamrock

trig: run 4 chic, cram, deck, fill, firm, full, line, neat, prim, prop, stop, tidy, trim, trot 5 brisk, dandy, natty, smart, sound, stiff, stone, stuff, wedge 6 active, lively, spruce, steady, strong, trench 7 distend, foppish, precise, stylish, support 10 methodical

triggerman: gun 6 hit man 8 assassin

trigo: 5 wheat

trigon: 4 harp, lyre 5 trine 8 triangle

trigonometry function: 4 sine 6 cosine, secant 7 tangent

Trilby: *author:* 9 du Maurier
  character: 8 Svengali

trill: 4 drip, flow, move, turn 5 shake, twirl 6 gruppo, quaver, quiver, warble 7 mordent, trickle, vibrate

trim: bob, cut, gay, lop 4 beat, chic, clip, crop, deft, dink, edge, fine, firm, neat, nice, snod(Sc.), snug, tidy, trig, whip 5 adorn, braid, cheat, chide, dress, equip, fitty, natty, nifty, order, preen, prune, ready, shave, shear, whack 6 adjust, dapper, defeat, modify, petite, punish, spruce, thrash 7 balance, compact, defraud, furnish, orderly, shapely 8 chastise, decorate, ornament, pleasant, tailored 9 condition, embellish, excellent, shipshape 10 commission, compromise 11 disposition
  a tree: 5 prune 7 pollard
  coin: nig
  dress: 4 gimp 5 ruche 6 sequin
  lace: 5 jabot 6 ruffle

trimmer: 5 finer

trimming: 4 gimp, lace 5 braid, ruche 6 frieze, fringe, piping 7 falbala, ruching 8 furbelow, ornament, rick-rack 9 garniture 10 decoration 13 passementerie

trindle: 4 roll 5 wheel 7 trundle

trine: 4 hang 5 march, triad 6 trigon, trinal, triple, triune 7 Trinity 9 favorable, threefold 10 auspicious

Trinidad-Tobago: *capital:* 11 Port-of-Spain
  gulf: 5 Paria
  music: 7 calypso, goombay

point: 6 Galera
  seaport: 11 San Fernando

trinitrotoluene: TNT 6 trotyl 13 high explosive

trinity: 5 three, triad 6 triune 9 threeness 10 spiderwort

trinket: toy 4 bead, gaud, ring 5 bijou, jewel 6 bangle, bauble, gewgaw, tinsel, trifle 7 bibelot 8 gimcrack, intrigue, ornament 9 plaything, showpiece 10 knick-knack

trio: 5 triad 9 threesome

trip: run 4 gait, halt, hike, pawl, skip, slip, spin, tour 5 brood, caper, catch, danse, drive, error, flock, jaunt, lapse, tread, wedge 6 cruise, error, falter, voyage 7 blunder, failure, journey, misstep, mistake, release, stumble 8 obstruct 9 excursion 10 expedition

tripe: 5 trash 7 rubbish 8 nonsense

triple: 5 triad, trine 6 treble 9 threefold

triplet: 4 trin, trio

tripletail: 9 berrugate, spadefish

triplicate: 6 treble, triple 9 threefold

tripod: cat 5 easel, stand 6 trivet

Tripoli ruler: dey

trippet: cam

tripping: 5 quick 6 nimble 7 walking

triptych: 7 picture 10 altarpiece
  wing: 5 volet

trismus: 7 lockjaw, tetanus

Tristram, Tristan: *beloved:* 5 Isolt 6 Iseult, Isolde
  uncle: 4 Mark
  villain: 5 Melot

Tristram Shandy author: 6 Sterne

triste: sad 4 dull 6 dismal 8 mournful 9 sorrowful 10 depressing, melancholy

trite: 4 dull, flat, hack, worn 5 banal, corny, stale, vapid 6 common, jejune, old hat 7 bromide, trivial 9 hackneyed 10 threadbare, unoriginal, warmed-over 11 commonplace, stereotyped 12 conventional 13 platitudinous

trite expression: 6 cliche 7 bromide

triton: eft 4 newt 7 demigod 10 salamander

triturate: rub 5 crush, grind 6 bruise 9 comminute, pulverize

triumph: win 4 gain 5 exult, glory 6 defeat, hurrah 7 conquer, prevail, rejoice, success, victory 8 flourish 10 exultation 11 achievement, celebration

triumvirate: 5 junta 6 troika
  first: 6 Caesar, Pompey 7 Crassus
  second: 6 Antony 7 Lepidus 8 Octavius

trivet: 4 rack 5 stand 6 tripod 7 support

trivial: 5 banal, fluff, inane, petty, small, trite 6 common, little, paltry, slight 7 nominal, piperly 8 doggerel, ordinary, trifling 9 frivolous 10 negligible 11 unimportant 13 insignificant, no great shakes **14** inconsiderable

troche: **4** pill **6** pastil, rotula, tablet **7** lozenge, pastile **8** pastille **9** small ball

trochilus: **7** warbler **9** goldcrest **11** hummingbird

trod: **4** path, walk **5** trace, track, tread **8** footpath, footstep

trogon: **4** bird **7** quetzal

troika: **5** triad **8** carriage **11** triumvirate

Troilus: *beloved:* **8** Cressida

father: **5** Priam

mother: **5** Hecuba

slayer: **8** Achilles

Trojan: **9** Dardanian

epic: **5** Iliad

king: **5** Priam

prince: **5** Eneas, Paris **6** Aeneas, Hector

prisoner: **5** Sinon

serpent victim: **7** Laocoon

soothsayer: **7** Helenus **9** Cassandra

Trojan horse: **4** ruse, trap **6** ambush **8** saboteur **10** subversive

builder: **5** Epeus

Trojan War: *cause:* **5** Helen

hero: **4** Ajax **5** Eneas **6** Aeneas, Agenor, Hector **9** Agamemnon, Palamedes

troll: run, wag **4** bowl, fish, lure, reel, roll, sing, song, turn **5** angle, catch, chant, dwarf, giant, gnome, round, spoon **6** trolly **7** revolve, trolley, trollop **9** circulate

trolley: car **4** cart, tram **5** block **6** barrow, sledge **8** handcart **9** streetcar

trollop: **4** hang **5** slump **6** dangle, slouch, wanton **8** slattern **10** bedraggled, prostitute

trombone: **7** sackbut

trommel: **5** sieve **6** screen

troop: lot **4** army, band, ging, line, rout, walk, wave **5** crowd, group **6** number, troupe **7** battery, cavalry, company, echelon, militia, phalanx **8** quantity, soldiers **9** associate, gathering **10** combatants, congregate **11** armed forces

Anglo-Indian: **6** risala **7** ressala, risalah

arrangement: **7** echelon

assembling: **6** muster

concealed: **6** ambush

German: **6** Panzer

quarters: **4** camp **5** etape **8** barracks

raise: **4** levy **5** draft **9** conscript

sellers to: **6** sutler **10** vivandiere

trooper: **6** hussar **7** soldier **9** policeman, troopship **10** cavalryman

trop: too **4** many

trope: **5** irony **6** simile **8** metaphor

trophy: cup **4** palm **5** prize **6** laurel, reward **7** memento **8** memorial, ornament **11** remembrance

tropic: **5** limit **8** boundary

tropical: hot **6** steamy, torrid

animal: **4** alco, eyra **5** agama, coati, potto **6** agouti, iguana **7** peccary

bird: ani **4** tody **5** jalap **7** jacamar

fish: **4** toro **6** salema **7** squetee

fruit: **4** date **5** guava, mango, papaw **6** banana, papaya **8** tamarind

genus of herb: **4** evea, sida **5** tacca, urena **8** laportea

helmet: **4** topi

plant: **4** dal **5** aloe, arum, sida, taro **5** agave **6** alacad **7** cowhage, lantana **8** gardenia

plant genus: **5** rhoeo **6** cannas **7** bomarea, geonoma, hamelia

storm: **7** typhoon

tree: ebo **4** ceba, coco, dali, eboe, etua, guao, mabi, palm **5** acapu, amate, artar, assai, balsa, banak, bongo, cacao, dalli, guama, guava, icica, nepal, nitta, njave, papaw, seron, zorro **6** baboen, bacury, banana, barbas, cazaba, chupon, dagame, espave, mammee, pawpaw, sapota **7** anubing, gateado, guacimo **8** amarillo, mangrove, sweetsop, tamarind **9** huamuchli, quebracho, sapodilla, sapotilha, sapotilla **10** frangipane, frangipani, manchineel **11** guachipilin

trot: hag, jog, run, tot **4** gait, pony **5** child, hurry **6** hasten **7** toddler **11** translation

trot out: **4** show **6** expose **7** display, show off

troth: **5** certy, faith **6** certie, pledge **8** fidelity **9** betrothal **10** engagement

trottoir: **8** footpath, pavement, sidewalk

troubadour, troubador: **4** bard, poet **6** rhymer, singer **8** minstrel, musician

trouble: ado, ail, irk, try, vex, woe **4** busy, care, cark, fike, fuss, harm, pain, sore, stir **5** anger, annoy, grief, labor, tease, upset, worry **6** bother, burble, caddle, cumber, dither, effort, harass, impair, matter, mishap, molest, pester, plague, pother, sorrow, unrest **7** afflict, agitate, anxiety, chagrin, concern, disease, disturb, embroil, illness, perturb, travail **8** aggrieve, calamity, disorder, disquiet, distress, exertion **9** adversity, incommode, interfere **10** difficulty, disarrange, discomfort, discommode, misfortune, perplexity, uneasiness **11** displeasure, encumbrance **13** inconvenience

troubled: **6** queasy **10** distraught **12** heart-scalded

troublemaker: **6** gossip **8** agitator, bad actor

troublesome: **4** mean, ugly **5** pesky **6** wicked **8** fashious **9** pestilent, turbulent, wearisome **10** burdensome, oppressive

troublous: **6** stormy, turbid **7** unquiet **8** restless **9** unsettled

trough: bin **4** bosh, bowl, dale, tank, tomb **5** bakie, basin, chute **6** buddle, coffin, dugout, gutter, sluice 7 channel, conduit

between waves: 6 valley

inclined: 5 chute

trounce: sue 4 beat, flog, whip 5 scold, tramp 6 cudgel, defeat, indict, punish, ramble, thrash 7 censure, journey 11 walk all over

troupe: 4 band 5 group 7 company 9 cuadrilla(Sp.)

trouper: 5 actor 11 entertainer

troupial: 6 oriole 7 cacique, cowbird 9 blackbird 10 meadowlark

trousers: 5 pants 6 skilts, slacks 8 breeches, culottes 9 pantalets, shintiyan 10 pantaloons

foreign: 7 shalwar 9 shaksheer, shulwaurs 10 calzoneras(Sp.)

trout: sea 4 char, peal 5 brook, brown, river, sewen 6 finnac, grilse 7 gilaroo, rainbow 8 finnacle, speckled 9 steelhead 10 squeteague

lake: 9 namaycush

trovatore: 10 troubadour

trove: 9 discovery 12 accumulation

trow: 4 boat, hope 5 faith, fancy, smack, think, troll, trust 6 belief, expect 7 believe, imagine, suppose 8 covenant 9 catamaran

Troy (see also **Trojan, Trojan horse, Trojan War**): 5 Iliac, Ilian, Ilion, Ilium, Troad, Troas 8 Teucrian

defender: 6 Aeneas

excavator: 10 Schliemann

founder: 4 Ilus, Tros

king: 5 Priam

mountain: Ida

pert. to: 5 Iliac 6 Trojan

region: 5 Troad

troy weight: 5 grain, ounce, pound 11 pennyweight

truant: 4 idle 5 stray 6 beggar, errant 7 shirker, vagrant 8 straying, vagabond, wanderer 9 shiftless

play: 5 miche

truce: 5 pause, treve(F.) 7 respite 9 armistice, cease-fire, cessation 12 intermission

truck: van 4 deal, dray 5 lorry, trade, trash 6 barrow, barter, camion, peddle, potter 7 bargain, rubbish, traffic, trundle 8 business, commerce, exchange, handcart 9 negotiate, transport, vegetable 10 handbarrow 11 association, intercourse

with trailer: 4 semi

truckle: 4 fawn 5 toady, wheel 6 caster, cheese, cringe, submit 7 trundle 8 bootlick 11 apple-polish 12 knuckle under

truckling: 7 servile

truculent: 4 mean, rude 5 cruel, harsh 6 fierce, savage 7 abusive 8 ruthless,

scathing 9 barbarous, ferocious 11 belligerent, destructive

trudge: pad 4 plod, slog, trek, walk 5 stoge, tramp 6 trapes 7 traipse

true: 4 just, leal(Sc.), pure, real, vera(L.), vrai(F.) 5 align, aline, exact, level, loyal, plumb, right, valid 6 actual, adjust, honest, lawful, proper, steady 7 certain, correct, devoted, factual, genuine, germane, precise, sincere, staunch, upright 8 accurate, bonafide, constant, faithful, reliable, unerring, virtuous 9 authentic, steadfast, truepenny, unfeigned, veracious, veritable 10 legitimate 11 unfaltering

true blue: 5 loyal 7 staunch 8 faithful

truelove: 10 girl friend, sweetheart

truffle: 5 tuber 8 earthnut

truism: 5 axiom, maxim 8 veracity 11 commonplace

Truk island: Tol 4 Moen, Udot, Uman 6 Dublon

trull: 4 dell, girl, lass 5 demon, fiend, giant, wench 6 blowze, callet, wanton 7 trollop 8 strumpet 10 prostitute

truly: 4 iwis, very, well 6 atweel, dinkum, indeed, verily 13 realistically

trump: cap, pam 4 beat, ruff 5 outdo, pedro 7 nonplus, surpass 9 jew's-harp

trumpery: 5 fraud, showy, trash, weeds 6 deceit, paltry 7 rubbish 8 gimcrack, nonsense, trickery 9 worthless

trumpet: 4 horn, tout 5 blare 6 bucina(L.), funnel, kerana, summon 7 begonia, clarion, publish 8 denounce, proclaim

belt: 7 baldric

blare: 6 sennet 7 fanfare, tantara

caller: 7 Gabriel

muffler: 4 mute

ram's horn: 6 shofar

stage direction: 6 sennet

trumpet creeper: 5 plant 6 tecoma

trumpet shell: 6 triton

trumpeter: 4 bird, swan 6 herald, pigeon, tooter 7 yakamik

truncate: cut, lop, top 6 lessen 7 shorten 10 abbreviate

truncheon: 4 club, stem 5 baton, staff 6 cudgel 8 fragment, splinter 9 billy club 10 nightstick

trundle: bed 4 bowl, cart, hoop, roll 5 truck, twirl, wheel, whirl 6 barrow, caster, pinion, rotate 7 revolve 11 wheelbarrow

trunk: box 4 body, bole, pipe, runt, stem, tank, tube 5 chest, snout, stock, torso 6 caudex, coffer, corpse, thorax 7 baggage, carcass 9 proboscis

animal: 4 soma 5 torso, snout

truss: tie, wap 4 bind, furl, gird, hang, lade, pack 6 bundle, fasten 7 arrange, bracket, enclose, package, support, tighten 10 strengthen

trust: 4 affy, care, duty, hope, task 5 faith 6 belief, cartel, charge, credit, depend, merger, rely or. 7 believe, confide, consign, custody, keeping, loyalty 8 affiance, commenda, credence, reliance, security 9 assurance, coalition, fiduciary, syndicate 10 commission, confidence 11 combination

trustee: 6 bailee 7 sindico 8 director, guardian 9 fiduciary, garnishee 13 administrator

trustful: 7 devoted 9 confiding 13 unquestioning

trustworthy: 4 safe, true 5 siker, solid, tried 6 honest, sicker 7 certain 8 credible, fiducial, reliable 9 authentic, confiding 10 dependable 12 confidential

trusty: 8 faithful 9 confiding 12 tried and true

truth: 4 fact 5 sooth, troth 6 certes, verity 7 honesty, loyalty 8 accuracy, fidelity, veracity 9 agreement, constancy, integrity, principle, sincerity, veracity 11 correctness, genuineness, uprightness 12 faithfulness 14 verisimilitude
goddess: 4 Maat
personification of: Una
seeming: 14 verisimilitude
self-evident: 5 axiom 6 truism

truthful: 6 honest 7 correct 9 veracious, veridical

try: vex 4 cull, sift, test 5 annoy, assay, essay, ettle(Sc.), fling, found, prove, trial 6 choose, effort, hansel, harass, purify, refine, render, sample, screen, select, strain, strive 7 adjudge, afflict, approve, attempt, contest, extract, handsel, subject, torment, venture 8 audition, endeavor, irritate, separate, struggle 9 ascertain, undertake 10 experience, experiment 11 demonstrate, investigate

trying: 5 tight 6 severe 7 irksome, onerous, painful 8 annoying 12 exasperating

tryst: 4 fair 5 visit 6 market 7 bespeak, meeting 9 agreement, gathering 10 engagement, rendezvous 11 appointment, assignation

tsar: 4 czar, Ivan, tzar 5 Peter 6 despot 8 autocrat

tsetse fly: 4 kivu 6 muscid 8 glossina

tsine: 6 wild ox 7 banteng

tuatara, tuatera: 6 iguana, lizard

tub (see also **barrel, cistern, vat, vessel):** box, kid, soe, vat 4 bath, boat, cask, cool, ship, tram 5 barge, bathe, bowie(Sc.), eshin, fatty, keeve, skeel 6 bucket, pulpit, vessel 7 bathtub, cistern, tubfish 9 container

wooden: soe

tuba: 7 helicon
mouthpice: 5 bocal

tubal: 8 pipelike

Tubalcain's father: 6 Lamech

Tubal's father: 7 Japheth

tubber: 6 cooper, pickax

tubby: 5 plump, squat 6 chubby, portly, rotund

tube: 4 duct, hose, lull, pipe 5 chute, diode 6 cannon, siphon, tremie, triode, tunnel 7 cannula, conduit, fistula, pipette, tetrode 8 adjutage, bombilla(Sp.), cylinder 9 telescope
anatomical: 7 salpinx
flexible: 4 hose
for winding silk: cop
glass: 6 sipper 7 pipette
remove by: 6 siphon, syphon
system of: 6 pipage
underground: 6 subway, tunnel

tuber: oca, yam 4 beet, bulb, clog, eddo, root, taro, yamp 5 jalap, salep 6 potato 8 swelling 9 tubercule 10 tuberosity 12 protuberance
orchid: 5 salep

tubercle: 6 nodule 10 prominence

tuberculosis: 8 phthisis 11 consumption

Tubuai island: 4 Rapa 6 Rurutu 8 Rimatara

tubular: 4 pipy 5 round 11 cylindrical

tuck: eat, nip 4 draw, fold, hang, poke 5 cramp, feast, pinch, scold, stuff, sword 6 energy, gather, hamper, rapier 7 consume, shorten, tighten

tucked up: 7 cramped, worn out 8 hampered 9 exhausted

tucker: bib 4 food, meal, tire, wilt 5 board, weary 6 ration 7 fatigue 10 chemisette

Tuesday: 5 mardi(F.)
god of: Tiu, Tyr
Shrove: 9 Mardi Gras

tuft: 4 beat, coma, disk 5 beard, bunch, clump, crest, mound 6 button, comose, dollop, goatee, pompon, tassel 7 cluster, fetlock, scopula 8 imperial
of feathers: 7 panache
of hair: 4 tate
ornamental: 6 pompon
vascular: 6 glomus

tuft-hunter: 4 snob

tug: lug, tit, tow 4 drag, draw, haul, maul, pull, rope, toil, yank 5 chain, exert, hitch, labor, strap, trace 6 drudge, effort, strain, strife, strive, tussle 7 contend, contest, tugboat, wrestle 8 struggle 11 counterpull

tuition: 4 care 5 watch 6 charge 7 custody 8 teaching 10 protection 11 instruction 12 guardianship

tule: 7 bulrush

tumble: 4 fall, leap, roll, trip, veer 5 pitch, slope, spill, whirl 6 happen, rumple, spring, tousle 7 clutter, plummet, stumble 8 collapse, discover, dishevel, disorder 9 confusion, overthrow 10 disarrange, handspring, somersault 11 precipitate

down: 10 dilapidate

tumbler: dog 4 cart, pupa 5 glass 6 dunker, pigeon, roller, vessel 7 acrobat, gymnast, tippler, tumbrel

tumbrel, tumbril: 4 cart 5 wagon 8 dumpcart

tumefy: 4 puff 5 swell 7 inflate

tumid: 6 turgid 7 bloated, bulging, fustian, pompous, swollen, teeming 8 bursting, enlarged, inflated 9 bombastic, distended, plethoric, 10 rhetorical 11 protuberant

tumor: wen 4 beal, wart 5 edema, gumma 6 ambury, anbury, glioma, lipoma 7 bombast 8 blastoma, ganglion, hepatoma, neoplasm, papiloma, sarocele, swelling 10 distending 12 adamantinoma, protuberance

benign: 7 fibroid, fibroma

brain: 6 glioma

hard: 8 scirrhus

operation: 8 ancotomy

small: wen 7 papilla

soft: 5 gumma

study of: 8 oncology

tumult: din, mob 4 fray, fuss, riot 5 babel, brawl, broil, noise 6 affray, babble, bedlam, bustle, dirdum(Sc.), emeute, hubbub, uproar 7 bluster, bobbery, ferment, tempest, turmoil 8 disorder, outbreak, outburst, paroxysm, uprising 9 agitation, commotion, distemper, hurlement, maelstrom 10 convulsion, excitement, hullabaloo, turbulence 11 disturbance

tumultuous: 4 high, wild 5 rough 6 stormy 7 furious, violent 9 termagant, turbulent 10 boisterous, hurly-burly

tumulus: 4 tump 5 mound 6 barrow 7 hillock

tun: cup, jar, tub, vat 4 cask 5 drink 6 barrel, guzzle, vessel 7 chimney

tuna: 8 albacore, skipjack 11 prickly pear

tune: air, fix, key, pat 4 lilt, port, song, tone 5 dirge, drant, sound 6 choral, draunt, melody, string 7 chorale, concord, harmony, sonance 8 anglaise, regulate 9 agreement 10 adjustment

in: 4 dial

out: 6 detune

tuneful: 7 musical, tunable 9 melodious 10 concordant, euphonious, harmonious

tungsten 7 wolfram 8 scheelin

alloy: 8 carboloy

tunic: 4 coat, jamah, jupe, robe, toga, vest 5 acton, frock, gippo, jamah 6 kirtle 8 colobium 10 cote-hardie, sticharion 11 houppelande

tunicate: 4 salp 5 salpa 12 marine animal

Tunisia: *cape:* bon

capital: 5 Tunis

gulf: 5 Gabes, Tunis 8 Hammamet

island: 6 Djerba

lake: 7 Bizerte 10 Sida al-Hani

measure: saa, sah 4 saah 5 cafiz, whiba 6 mettar 9 millerole

mettar 9 millerole

monetary unit: 5 dinar

mountain range: 5 Atlas

river: 8 Medjerda

ruins: 8 Carthage

ruler: bey, dey

town: 4 Sfax 6 Sousse 7 Bizerte 8 Kairouan

weight: saa 4 rotl 5 artal, artel, ratel, uckia 6 kantar

tunk: rap, tap 5 thump

tunnel: net 4 adit, bore, flue, tube 6 burrow, funnel 10 smokestack

long: 5 Otira 6 Hoosac, Severn, Spiral 7 Arlberg, Detroit, Holland, Lincoln, Mont D'Or, St. Clair, Simplon 8 Gotthard, Gunnison 9 Baltimore, Cascade Mt., Connaught, Gallitzin, Montcenis, Mt. Roberts 10 Bitterroot, Cumberland, Lotschberg, St. Gotthard, Wasserfluh 11 Busk-Ivanhoe, Loetschberg, Trans-Andine

tunny: 4 tuna 7 bluefin 8 albacore

tupelo: gum 4 tree 5 nyssa

tur: pea 4 goat

turban: cap, fez, hat 4 pata 5 scarf 6 fillet, mandil 7 bandana 9 headdress

turbid: 4 dark, dull 5 dense, gumly(Sc.), muddy, riley, roily, thick 6 cloudy, grumly(Sc.), impure 7 muddled, obscure 8 confused, polluted 9 perplexed

render: 4 roil

turbine: 6 engine

part: 6 stator

wheel: 5 rotor

turbot: 5 brill 8 flatfish

turbulence: 4 fury 5 babel, fight 6 fracas, tumult, uproar 7 bluster, ferment, rioting 8 disorder 9 agitation, commotion 11 disturbance, pandemonium

turbulent: 4 wild 5 rough 6 stormy, unruly 7 furious, violent 9 clamorous 10 boisterous, rip-roaring, tumultuous 11 tempestuous

turdine bird: 6 thrush

turf: sod 4 area, flag, peat, vell 5 divot, grass, sward 6 region, sphere 7 terrain

Turgenev character: 5 Elena

turgid: 5 tumid 7 bloated, pompous, swollen, turgent 8 inflated, swelling 9 bombastic, distended, flatulent, grandiose, tumescent 10 rhetorical 12 magniloquent 12 grandiloquent

Turk: aga 5 Tatar 7 Osmanli, Ottoman 9 Kizilbash

Turkestan: See **Turkistan**

turkey: tom 4 flop 5 poult 7 bustard, failure, gobbler
- *buzzard:* 7 vulture
- *young:* 5 poult

Turkey: *agent:* 6 Kehaya
- *army corps:* 4 ordu 8 seraglio
- *army regiment:* 4 alai
- *bath:* 6 hamman
- *boat:* 4 sail 6 mahone
- *cabinet:* 5 divan
- *camp:* 7 palanka
- *cap:* 6 calpac
- *capital:* 6 Ankara
- *cavalryman:* 5 spahi 6 spahee
- *chief* (see also *ruler* below): aga 6 kehaya 7 chambul
- *city:* bir 4 Homs, Sert, Urfa 5 Adana, Bursa, Izmir, Konya, Siirt, Sivas 6 Aintab, Edessa, Edirne, Elaziz, Marash, Samsun, Smyrna 7 Broussa, Erzurum, Kayseri, Scutari, Skutari, Uskudar 8 Istanbul, Stamboul 9 Eskisehir 10 Adrianople, Diyarbekir
- *coin:* (see *money* below)
- *commander:* 4 amir, emir 5 ameer, emeer, pacha, pasha 6 sirdar 9 seraskier
- *council:* 5 divan, diwan
- *court:* 5 porte
- *decree:* 5 irade 11 hatti-sherif 12 hattihumaiun, hatti-humayun
- *deputy:* 6 kahaya
- *dignitary:* 5 pasha
- *district:* 4 Pera 7 Beyoglu, Cilicia
- *division:* 4 caza 5 adana 6 eyalet 7 vilayet 8 villayet
- *drink:* 5 airan
- *dynasty:* 6 seljuk
- *empire:* 7 Ottoman
- *fig:* 5 eleme, elemi
- *flag:* 4 alem, toug 9 horsetail
- *general:* 5 kamal
- *gold coin:* 4 lira 6 mahbub
- *gulf:* Cos 7 Antalya
- *hat:* fez 6 calpac
- *infidel:* 6 giaour
- *inn:* 6 imaret 7 cafenet
- *javelin:* 5 jerid 6 jeered
- *judge:* 4 cadi
- *liquor:* 4 raki 5 rakee 6 mastic
- *man-of-war:* 6 carvel 7 caravel 9 caravelle
- *measures:* dra, oka, oke, pic, pik 4 alma, draa, hatt, khat, kile, zira 5 almud, berri, donum, kileh, zirai 6 almude, arshin, chinik, djerib, fotin, halebi, parmak 7 arsheen, arshine, nocktat, parmack 9 pik halebi

military camp: 4 ordu
military rank: 6 chiaus 7 chaoush 8 bimbashi, binbashi
minister: 5 vizir 6 vizier
money: 4 lira, lire, para 5 akcha, asper, atun, pound, rebia 6 akcheh, sequin, zequin 7 altilik, beshlik, chequin, chiquin, pataque, piaster 8 medjidie, zecchino 9 medjidieh
mosque: 4 jami
mountain: 6 Ararat
mountain range: 6 Taurus
musical instrument: 5 canum, kanum 7 kussier
musket: 8 tophaike
oak: 6 cerris
official: 4 amir, emir 5 ameer, emeer 6 vizier 7 osmanli, subashi 8 subbassa
palace: 5 serai
policeman: 7 zaptiah, zaptieh
prayer rug: 5 kulah, melas, meles
province: 4 Sert 5 Bursa, Siirt 6 Angora, Eyalet
religious war: 11 crescentade
reservist: 5 redif
river: Gok 5 Mesta, Sarus 6 Delice, Seihun, Seyhan, Tigris 7 Maritsa
rug: 5 riconia 6 Smyrna 9 Kurdistan (see also **Oriental rug**)
ruler: bey, dey 4 khan 5 mudir 6 sultan 7 chambul 9 president
saber: 6 odolus
sailor: 8 galionji 9 galiongee
seaport: 4 Enos
slave: 8 mameluke
soldier: 6 nizami 8 janizary 9 janissary 11 bashi-bazouk
statue: 8 tanzimat
storage place: 5 ambar
sultan: Ali 5 Ahmed, calif, Selim 6 caliph 7 Ilderim, Saladin
sword: 7 yatagan 8 yataghan
tambourine: 5 daira
tax: 5 vergi 6 caphar, avania
title: ali 4 amir, baba 5 ameer, basha, pasha 6 bashaw 7 effendi
tobacco: 7 chibouk, Latakia 9 chibouque
treasurer: 8 deftedar
tribe: 4 Kurd
veil: 7 yashmac, yashmak 8 maharmah
weight: oka, oke 4 dram, kile, ocha, rotl 5 artal, artel, cequi, cheke, kerat, kileh, maund, obolu, ratel 6 batman, dirhem, kantar, miskal 7 drachma, quintal, yusdrum
wheat: 6 bulgar
woman's clothing: 6 jelick 8 charshaf

turkey buzzard: 4 aura 9 gallinazo

Turkish: 7 Osmanli

toweling: 10 terrycloth

Turkistan: *cities:* 6 Kokand 7 Andijan, Bukhara 8 Tashkent 9 Samarkand

highland: 6 Pamirs
land: 5 takyr
moslem: 5 salar
mountain: 4 Alai
peoples: 4 Sart 5 Tatar, Uigur, Usbeg, Usbek, Uzbeg, Yakut 6 Tartan
regiment: 4 alai
river: Ili
salt lake: 4 Shov
sea: 4 Aral

Turkmen: *capital:* 9 Ashkhabad
carpet: 5 Tekke, Yomud 6 Afghan 7 Bokhara
tribe: 5 Ersar 7 Viddhal

turmeric: rea 4 herb 5 spice 7 curcuma 9 bloodroot

turmoil: ado, din 4 hurl, toil, toss 5 hurly, labor, touse, upset, worry 6 harass, tumult, unrest, uproar, welter 7 ferment, quarrel, tempest, trouble 8 disquiet, drudgery 9 agitation, commotion, confusion 10 turbulence 11 disturbance 12 perturbation

turn: bow, lap, rev 4 airt, bend, bent, bout, cant, char, head, plow, roll, slew, slue, spin, veer, vert 5 alter, avert, cramp, crook, curve, hinge, pivot, quirk, screw, shunt, spell, tarve, upset, wheel, whirl, whorl 6 bought, change, curdle, direct, divert, gyrate, invert, ponder, rotate, sprain, swerve, swivel, wimple(Sc.), zig-zag 7 convert, derange, ferment, meander, rebound, reverse, revolve 8 exchange, nauseate, persuade 9 cinclamen, influence, pirouette, transform, translate 11 disposition 12 metamorphose
about: 9 alternate
another way: 6 obvert
inside out: 5 evert 6 invert
inward: 9 introvert
left: haw 4 port, wynd, wyne
outward: 5 evert, splay 8 extrorse 9 extrovert
rapidly: 4 spin 5 twirl, whirl
right: gee 9 starboard
sour: 5 blink, spoil 8 acescent
to one side: 4 awry, skew
to stone: 8 lapidify

turn around: 4 gyre, slue, spin 9 about-face, volte-face

turn aside: 4 skew, veer 5 shunt 6 detour, divert, swerve

turn away: shy 5 avert, avoid, deter, evade, repel, shunt 6 depart, desert, divert 7 abandon, decline, deflect, deviate, dismiss, diverge, swerve

turn back: 4 fold 5 repel 6 return, revert 7 evolute, retrace 9 inversion 10 recrudesce, retroverse

turn down: 4 fold, veto 6 invert, refuse, reject 7 decline 9 repudiate

turn in: 5 rat on 6 betray, retire 7 deliver, produce 8 hand over, inform on

turn off: 4 hang 5 marry, shunt 6 detour, divert 7 consign, deflect, dismiss, putrefy 9 discharge

turn out: 4 bear, oust, trig 5 array, evert, expel, prove 6 outfit, output, siding 7 abandon, costume, dismiss, produce, reverse, striker 8 equipage, withdraw 9 discharge, equipment, eventuate 12 lose interest

turn over: 4 keel 5 spill, upset 6 invert, ponder, reform 7 evolute 8 delegate, overturn, transfer 10 relinquish

turn up: 6 appear, arrive

turnabout: 8 reversal 9 about-face, volteface

turncoat: 8 apostate, renegade 10 changeling

turned up: 9 retrousse

turner: 7 gymnast, tumbler

turning point: 6 crisis 8 decision, juncture, landmark

turnip: 4 neep(Sc.) 5 dunce, watch 8 rutabaga 9 blockhead

turnip-shaped: 8 napiform

turnkey: 5 screw 6 jailer, warder

turnover: 4 tart 8 shake-up

turnpike: 4 road 7 highway 8 tollgate
gatekeeper: 7 pikeman

turnstile: 4 tirl 5 stile

turnstone: 4 bird 6 pover, redleg

turpentine: 4 thus 5 resin, rosin 7 galipot 9 oleoresin
residue: 5 resin, rosin
tree: 4 pine 6 tarata 9 terebinth

turpitude: 6 fedity 8 baseness, vileness 9 depravity

turquoise: 5 color, stone 10 chalchuite 12 greenish-blue

turret: 5 tower 8 gunhouse, turricle

turtle: 5 arrau, caret, torup 6 cooter, emydea, jurara 7 snapper 8 chelonia, matamata, shagtail, terrapin, tortoise 10 loggerhead, thalassian 11 leatherback
genus of: 4 emys 7 caretta, testudo 9 chelodina
giant: 5 arrau
part: 7 calipee
shell: 8 carapace

Tuscany: *city:* 4 Pisa 8 Florence
commune: 5 Greve
island: 4 Elba
river: 4 Arno
wine: 7 chianti

tusk: 4 fang 5 ivory, tooth 9 scrivello

tussis: 5 cough

tussle: 4 spar 5 fight 6 tousel, tousle 7 contend, contest, scuffle, wrestle 8 skirmish, struggle 9 scrimmage

tussock: 4 tuft 5 bunch, clump 7 hassock

tut: 4 hush 6 rebuke

tutelage: 7 nurture 8 guidance, teaching 9 tutorship 11 instruction 12 guardianship

tutelary: 10 protecting
gods: 5 Lares

tutor: 5 coach, drill, guide, teach, train, watch 6 ground, mentor, school 7 grinder, pedagog, teacher 8 guardian, instruct 9 pedagogue, preceptor 10 discipline

tutta: all 5 whole 6 entire

tuyere: tew 4 pipe 5 tewel 6 nozzle

TV: See television

twaddle: rot 4 bunk, chat 5 haver, prate 6 babble, drivel, fottle, gabble 8 nonsense 9 poppycock 10 balderdash

twangy: 5 nasal

tweak: 4 jerk, pull 5 pinch, twist 6 twitch

tweet: 4 peep 5 chirp 7 chirrup

tweezers: 7 pincers 9 merganser

twenty: 5 corge, kappa, score

twenty-faced: 11 icosahedral

twerp: 4 brat, jerk 5 sprat 6 squirt 7 big shot

twibil: axe 6 chisel 7 mattock

twice: bis(L.) 6 doubly 7 twofold

twig: see 4 beat, mode, pull 5 birch, bough, scion, shoot, spray, sprig, style, tweak, withe 6 branch, fescue, notice, sallow, switch, twitch, wattle 7 fashion, observe 8 perceive 9 apprehend 10 comprehend, understand
bundle: 5 fagot 6 barsom

twiggy: 4 thin 6 slight 7 slender 8 delicate

twilight: 4 dusk 5 gloam 6 dimmet 7 decline, evening 8 gloaming, glooming 9 cocklight 10 crepuscule
of the Gods: 8 Ragnarok 17 Goetterdaemmerung
pert. to: 11 crepuscular

twill: rib 5 cloth, quill, weave

twin: two 4 dual, pair, part 5 gemel, sever, twain 6 couple, double, sunder 7 twofold 8 didymous 11 counterpart
crystal: 5 macle
kind of: 9 fraternal, identical
one: 5 gemel
Siamese: Eng 5 Chang
stars: 6 Castor, gemini, Pollux

twinge: 4 ache, pain, pang 5 pinch, qualm, tweak 6 stitch, twitch

twine: ran 4 coil, turn, vine, warp, wind, wrap 5 braid, snarl, twist 6 encurl, enfold, enlace, infold, string, tangle, thread 7 anamite, embrace, wreathe 8 encircle, undulate 9 interlace 10 interweave 11 convolution, intermingle

twink: 6 punish, thrash 9 chaffinch

twinkle: 4 wink 5 blink, flash, gleam, shine 7 flicker, flutter, glimmer, glitter, instant, light up, sparkle 11 scintillate

twinkler: 4 star 8 sparkler

twirl: 4 coil, curl, gyre, move, spin, turn 5 querl, twist, whirl 6 gyrate 7 revolve, twizzle 8 flourish, rotation 9 pirouette, whirligig 11 convolution

twist: 4 bend, coil, cord, curl, skew, slew, slue, spin, tirl(Sc.), turn, wind, yarn 5 crink, crook, curve, gnarl, hinge, quirk, screw, tweak, twine, wring 6 hankle, spiral, sprain, squirm, thread, torque, wrench, writhe 7 confuse, contort, distort, entwine, flexure, meander, perplex, pervert, revolve, scatter, tendril, torment, torsion, torture 8 appetite, squiggle 9 constrain, corkscrew, deviation, insinuate 10 intertwine, interweave 11 convolution, misrepresent, peculiarity

twisted: cam, wry 6 warped 7 complex, tortile

twister: 4 roll, turn 7 cruller, cyclone, mallard, tornado 8 doughnut 10 somersault, waterspout

twit: guy 4 gibe, jive, josh 5 blame, chirp, taunt, tease 7 upbraid 8 reproach, ridicule

twitch: nip, tic, tie, tug 4 draw, jerk, pick, pull, skid, yank 5 grasp, pluck, start, thong, tweak 6 clutch, fasten, snatch 9 vellicate 11 contraction

twitter: 4 chat 5 chirp, run on, shake 6 giggle, titter, tremor 7 chatter, chitter, flutter, tremble 9 agitation

two: duo, twa(Sc.) 4 beta(Gr.), both, duet, dyad, pair 5 twain, twins 6 couple 7 twosome
chambered: 9 bicameral
edged: 5 sharp 9 ancipital
handed: 8 bimanual 12 ambidextrous
headed: 11 dicephalous
metrical feet: 6 dipody
months: 8 bi-mester
parts: 6 bident 9 bifurcate 11 dichotomous
pert. to: 4 dual 6 dyadic
winged: 7 bialate 8 dipteral 9 dipterous

two-bit: 5 cheap

two-faced: 5 false 9 deceitful 11 treacherous 12 hypocritical
god: 5 Janus

two-fisted: 6 virile 8 vigorous

two-foot: 5 biped 7 bipedal

two-pronged: 6 bident

two-sided: 9 bilateral

two-spot: 5 deuce

two-time: 5 cheat 7 deceive 11 doublecross

two-tone: 7 bicolor

twofold: 4 dual 5 duple 6 bifold, binary, double, duplex 9 bifarious, duplicate

twopenny: ale 4 mean 5 cheap 9 worthless

twosome: 4 duet, pair 6 couple

tycoon: 7 magnate 9 financier 13 industrialist

tydie: 4 bird, wren 8 titmouse

tyee: 5 chief

tyke, tike: cur, dog 5 child 6 shaver 7 bumpkin

tylopod: 5 camel

tympan: 4 drum

tympanum: 6 tympan 7 eardrum 10 kettledrum

tympany: 7 bombast, conceit 9 inflation 10 distention, turgidness

Tyndareus: *kingdom:* 6 Sparta
  wife: 4 Leda

typal: 8 symbolic

type: gem, ilk, lot 4 font, form, kern, kind, mark, mold, norm, pica, sign, slug, sort 5 agate, class, doric, elite, genre, group, ideal, ionic, metal, model, order, pearl, roman, stamp, token 6 emblem, italic, minion, nature, rubric, stripe, symbol 7 brevier, example, impress, paragon, pattern, species 8 boldface, classify 9 bourgeois, character, condensed, nonpareil 10 persuasion 11 Baskerville
  block: 4 quad 7 quadrat
  frame: 5 chase
  line: 4 slug
  mold: 6 matrix
  size: 4 pica, ruby 5 elite, pearl 6 minion 7 brevier, diamond 9 nonpareil
  slanting: 6 italic
  stroke: 5 serif
  tray: 6 galley

typeset: 7 compose

typesetter: 8 linotype, monotype 10 compositor

typewriter part: key 6 platen, spacer 9 tabulator

typhoon: 4 wind 5 storm 7 cyclone 9 hurricane

typical: 5 ideal, model, typal 6 classic, normal 7 regular 9 exemplary, schematic 10 emblematic, figurative 13 prefigurative 14 characteristic, representative

typify: 6 embody 9 epitomize, prefigure, represent, symbolize

typographer: 7 printer 10 compositor

tyrannical: 5 cruel, harsh 6 brutal, lordly, unjust 7 slavish 8 absolute, despotic 9 arbitrary, imperious 10 oppressive 11 domineering

tyrannosaurus: 8 dinosaur

tyranny: 5 rigor 7 fascism 8 iron heel, severity 9 despotism, harshness

tyrant: 4 czar, tsar, tzar 6 despot 7 fuehrer, monarch, usurper 8 dictator, martinet 9 oppressor, strong man
  murder: 11 tyrannicide

Tyre: *king:* 5 Belus, Hiram
  noble: 7 Acerbas
  prince: 8 Pericles
  princess: 4 Dido

tyro: 4 tiro 5 pupil 6 novice 7 amateur 8 beginner, neophyte 9 commencer 10 apprentice 11 abecedarian

tzar, czar, tsar: 4 king 5 ruler 6 tyrant

tzigane: 5 gypsy

U

U-boat: sub 9 submarine

ubermensch: 8 superman

uberous: 7 copious 8 abundant, fruitful

ubiety: 8 location, position, relation 9 whereness

ubiquitous: 10 everywhere 11 omnipresent

uca: 4 crab

udder: bag 5 gland

Uffizi site: 8 Florence

Uganda: *capital:* 7 Kampala
  cattle: 6 ankoli

lake: 5 George, Kyoga 6 Edward 8 Victoria
language: Luo 5 Atero 7 Luganda, Swahili
leader: 5 Obote 7 Idi Amin, Muwanga
monetary unit: 8 shilling
mountain: 5 Elgon 9 Ruwenzori
people: 5 Lango 7 Bunyoro
river: 4 Aswa, Kafu 5 Pager
town: 5 Jinja, Mbale 7 Entebbe

ughten: 4 dawn, dusk 7 evening, morning 8 twilight

ugli: 5 fruit 7 tangelo

ugliness symbol: 4 toad

ugly: bad 4 base, vile 5 awful, cross, grave, snivy, toady 6 cranky, homely, snivey, sullen 7 crabbed, hideous, ominous 8 grewsome, gruesome, horrible, terrible, unlovely 9 dangerous, fractious, frightful, graceless, loathsome, offensive, repulsive, unsightly 10 ill-favored, ill-natured, unpleasant 11 ill-tempered, quarrelsome, threatening, troublesome 12 cross-grained, disagreeable 13 objectionable

Ugrian: *language:* 6 Ostyak

   people: 4 Avar

ugsome: 6 horrid 9 abhorrent, frightful, loathsome

uhlan: 6 lancer 7 soldier 10 cavalryman

uitlander: 5 alien 9 foreigner, outlander

ukase: 5 edict, order 6 decree 7 command 12 proclamation

ukelele, ukulele: uke

Ukraine: *assembly:* 4 rada

   capital: 4 Kiev

   coin: 6 grivna 7 schagiv

   dance: 5 gopak

   holy city: 4 Kiev

   Mother of Cities: 4 Kiev

   river: Bug 6 Donets 7 Dnieper

   seaport: 6 Odessa

   town: 7 Donetsk, Kharkov

Ualume author: Poe

ulcer: 4 noma, sore 7 egilops 8 aegilops, fossette 9 cacoethes

   kind of: 6 peptic 8 duodenal

ulceration: 7 bedsore 8 helcosis

ule: 4 tree 6 caucho 10 rubber ball

uliginous: wet 4 oozy 5 moist, muddy 6 swampy

ullage: 7 wantage 8 shortage 10 deficiency

ulna: 4 bone 5 elbow 7 cubitus, forearm

   end of: 5 ancon

ulster: 8 overcoat

ulterior: 5 later, privy 6 future 7 further, guarded, remoter 9 concealed 10 subsequent, succeeding, under wraps 11 undisclosed

ultimate: end 4 dire, last 5 final, telos(Gr.) 6 remote 7 extreme, maximum, primary 8 eventual, eventual, farthest 9 elemental 10 apotheosis, conclusive 11 fundamental

ultimatum: 5 order 6 demand, threat

ultra: 5 kinky, outré 6 beyond 7 extreme, forward, radical 9 excessive, extremist, fanatical 10 outlandish 11 extravagant 14 uncompromising

ulu: 5 knife

ululate: bay 4 hoot, howl, wail, yelp 6 lament 7 screech

Ulysses: 8 Odysseus

   antagonist: 4 Irus

   author: 5 Joyce

   character: 5 Bloom, Molly 7 Dedalus

   dog: 5 Argos

   enchantress of: 5 Circe

   enemy: 8 Poseidon

   father: 7 Laertes

   friend: 6 Mentor

   kingdom: 6 Ithaca

   mother: 8 Anticlea

   plant: 4 moly

   son: 9 Telegonus 10 Telemachus

   swineherd: 7 Eumaeus

   temptress: 5 Circe

   voyage: 7 odyssey

   wife: 8 Penelope

umber: 5 brown, shade, visor 6 darken, shadow 7 protect, umbrere 8 grayling, umbrette

umbilicus: 4 core 5 heart, navel

umbra: 4 fish 5 ghost, shade 6 shadow 7 phantom, vestige 10 apparition

umbrage: 5 anger, cloak, doubt, pique, shade, trace 6 offend, shadow 7 foliage, offense, pretext, shelter 8 disfavor, disgrace, disguise 9 disesteem, semblance, suspicion 10 overshadow, protection, resentment 11 displeasure

umbrageous: 5 shady 6 shaded

umbrella: 4 gamp 5 blind, guard, shade 6 brolly, chatta, payong, pileus, screen 7 parasol, protect, shelter 8 disguise 11 bumber-shoot

umbrella tree: 8 magnolia

umbrette: 9 hammerkop 10 hammerhead

umbrous: 5 shady

umiak: 4 boat 6 oomiac, oomiak

umpire: 5 judge 6 decide, oddman 7 arbiter, daysman, oddsman, referee 9 supervise 10 arbitrator

Una boat: 7 catboat

unable: 6 cannot 7 disable 8 helpless, impotent 9 incapable 11 incompetent, inefficient, unqualified 13 incapacitated

unaccented: 4 lene 6 atonic

unaccompanied: 4 bare, solo 5 alone

unaccountable: 7 strange 9 countless 10 mysterious 12 inexplicable, unfathomable 13 irresponsible

unaccustomed: new 7 strange 8 uncommon, unwonted 10 unfamiliar

unacquainted: 7 strange, unusual 8 ignorant 10 unfamiliar 13 inexperienced

unadorned: 4 bald, bare 5 naked, plain, stark 6 rustic 7 austere

unadulterated: 4 pure 5 clean 6 honest 7 genuine, sincere, unmixed 8 straight 9 immutable

unaffected: 4 easy, naif, real 5 naive, plain 6 rustic, simple 7 artless, genuine, natural, sincere, unmoved 8 unbiased 9 ingenuous, unaltered, untouched 12 uninfluenced

Unalaska native: 5 Aleut
unalike: 9 different
unalleviated: 4 hard
unalloyed: 4 pure 7 genuine, unmixed 11 unqualified
unambiguous: 5 clear 8 explicit
unanchored: 6 adrift
unanimous: 5 solid 6 united 8 agreeing 9 of one mind 11 consentient
unanimously: 7 una voce
unanswerable: 5 final 10 conclusive
unappeasable: 10 implacable
unapproachable: 5 aloof 7 distant 10 unsociable 12 inaccessible
unarmed: 4 bare 5 inerm 11 defenseless
unaspirated: 4 lene
unassailable: 10 invincible 12 invulnerable
unassuming: shy 6 humble, modest 7 natural 8 retiring 9 diffident 14 unostentatious
unattached: 4 free 5 loose 6 single 9 unmarried 11 independent 13 noncollegiate
unattractive: 4 rude, ugly 5 plain 10 ungracious
unau: 5 sloth
unavailing: 6 futile 8 bootless, gainless
unavowed: 6 secret 8 ulterior
unaware: 6 unwary 8 heedless, ignorant 11 thoughtless
unbalanced: 6 insane, uneven 8 deranged, lopsided, one-sided
unbecoming: 4 rude 5 inept 6 clumsy, gauche 8 improper, unseemly, unworthy 10 indecorous, unsuitable 11 disgraceful 12 unattractive
unbefitting: 5 below 8 improper 10 unsuitable
unbelief: 10 skepticism 11 agnosticism, incredulity
unbelievable: 4 thin, weak 5 thick 8 fabulous 9 fantastic 10 incredible 11 implausible 13 inconceivable
unbeliever: 5 pagan 7 atheist, doubter, heretic, infidel, scoffer, skeptic 8 agnostic 11 freethinker
unbend: 4 rest, thaw 5 relax, untie, yield 6 loosen, uncock 7 slacken 8 unfasten
unbending: 5 rigid, stern, stiff 8 obdurate, resolute 10 inexorable, inflexible, unsociable
unbiased: 4 fair, just 8 detached 9 impartial 12 unprejudiced
unbind: 4 free, undo 5 untie 6 detach, loosen 7 absolve, deliver, release 8 dissolve, unfasten
unbleached: 4 blae, ecru 5 beige 7 natural
unblemished: 4 pure 5 whole 6 chaste 8 spotless

unblushing: 9 shameless
unbolt: 4 open 5 unbar, unpin 6 unlock 8 unfasten
unbosom: 4 tell 6 reveal
unbound: 4 free 5 loose 10 unconfined
unbounded: 4 open 9 limitless, unchecked, unlimited 11 measureless 12 uncontrolled, unrestrained
unbrace: 4 free, undo 5 carve, relax 6 loosen, reveal, weaken 8 disjoint, enfeeble
unbridled: 4 free 5 loose 7 violent 9 dissolute, unchecked 10 licentious, ungoverned 12 uncontrolled, unrestrained
unbroken: one 4 flat 5 undug, whole 6 entire, intact 7 untamed 8 unplowed 9 continual, undivided, unsubdued 10 continuous 13 uninterrupted
unburden: rid 4 ease 5 empty, untax 6 unload 7 disload, relieve
unbury: 6 exhume
uncanny: 4 eery 5 eerie, scary, weird 6 spooky 7 awkward, ghostly, strange 8 careless 9 dangerous, unnatural 10 mysterious 11 supernatural
uncanonical: 10 apocryphal
unceasing: 6 eterne 7 endless, eternal 9 continual, incessant, perennial 11 everlasting 14 unintermittent
unceremonious: 4 curt 5 bluff, blunt, short 6 abrupt 8 familiar, informal 14 unconventional
uncertain: 4 asea, dark, hazy, moot 5 fluky, vague 6 chancy, fitful, queasy 7 at a loss, dubious 8 aleatory, doubtful, unsteady, variable 9 ambiguous, equivocal, hazardous, undecided 10 changeable, inconstant, indefinite, precarious 11 vacillating 12 questionable 13 indeterminate, problematical, untrustworthy
uncertainty: 4 were 5 doubt, query 6 gamble, wonder 7 dubiety 8 suspense 9 dubiosity 10 skepticism
unchanging: 4 same 6 steady 7 eternal, forever, settled, uniform 9 immutable, steadfast, unvarying 10 invariable, stationary
unchaste: 4 lewd 5 bawdy 6 coarse, impure 7 haggard, obscene 8 immodest
unchecked: 4 free 5 loose 7 rampant 9 unbounded, unbridled
uncia: 4 coin, inch 5 ounce 7 twelfth
uncivil: 4 rude 5 bluff, crass, crude 7 ill-bred 8 clownish, impolite 9 barbarous 10 indecorous, ungracious, unsuitable 11 uncivilized 12 discourteous 13 disrespectful
uncivilized: 4 rude, wild 5 feral 6 brutal, ferine, savage 7 boorish 8 barbaric 9 barbarian, barbarous, primitive 10 outrageous, unmannerly 13 unenlightened

uncle: eme, oom 10 pawnbroker
pert. to: 9 avuncular
Uncle Remus: *author:* 6 Harris
rabbit: 4 Brer
Uncle Tom's Cabin author: 5 Stowe
character: 5 Eliza, Topsy 6 Legree 9 Little Eva
unclean: 4 foul, tref, vile 5 black, dirty 6 common, filthy, impure 7 defiled, obscene 8 polluted, unchaste 11 unwholesome
unclose: ope 4 open 6 reveal 10 unreserved
unclothe: 5 spoil, strip 6 divest, expose 7 despoil, uncover, undress
unclothed: 4 bare, nude 5 naked
unclouded: 4 fair, open 5 clear, sunny
uncoil: 6 unlink, unwind
uncombined: 4 free 5 frank, loose 10 elementary
uncomfortable: 5 harsh 6 uneasy 7 prickly 8 scratchy
uncommon: odd 4 rare 5 extra, novel 6 choice, scarce, unique 7 special, strange, unusual 8 especial, unwonted 10 infrequent, remarkable 11 exceptional 12 unaccustomed 13 extraordinary, preternatural
uncommunicative: 6 silent 8 reserved, reticent 10 unsociable
uncompassionate: 5 stony 9 unfeeling
uncomplaining: 5 stoic 7 patient, stoical
uncomplicated: 5 plain 6 honest, simple
uncompromising: 4 firm 5 rigid, stern, tough 6 strict 9 unbending 10 determined, inflexible, unyielding 12 intransigent
unconcealed: 4 bare, open 5 frank, overt
unconcerned: 4 cool, easy 8 careless, detached 9 apathetic 10 insouciant, nonchalant 11 indifferent 12 uninterested
unconditional: 4 free 5 frank 8 absolute, explicit
unconfined: 4 free 5 loose 9 boundless, limitless, unlimited
unconfused: 4 calm 5 clear 6 steady
unconnected: 5 gappy 6 abrupt 8 detached, rambling, separate 10 incoherent 12 disconnected
unconscionable: 5 undue 7 extreme 9 excessive 10 outrageous
unconscious: out 6 asleep, torpid 7 stunned, unaware 8 comatose, ignorant, mindless 9 inanimate, lethargic 10 insensible
render: 4 stun
state: 5 swoon 8 apsychia
unconsciousness: 4 coma 5 faint 6 torpor
unconstrained: 4 easy, free 7 natural 8 familiar 9 easygoing 11 spontaneous 12 unrestrained 13 demonstrative

uncontrollable: 4 wild 5 unruly 11 intractable
uncontrolled: 4 free, wild 5 loose 9 irregular, unbounded, unmanaged 10 hysterical, licentious, ungoverned 11 unregulated 12 unrestrained
unconventional: 5 loose, outre, queer 6 casual 7 devious, offbeat 8 Bohemian, informal 13 unceremonious
uncooked: raw
uncorrupted: 4 pure 5 naive 6 virgin 8 pristine 9 unspoiled
uncouple: 5 loose 6 detach 8 unfasten 10 disconnect
uncouth: odd 4 rare, rude 5 crude 6 clumsy, coarse, dismal, rugged 7 awkward, boorish, loutish, strange, uncanny, unknown 8 derelict, desolate, dreadful, ignorant, uncommon, ungainly, yokelish 9 unrefined 10 mysterious, outlandish, uncultured, unpolished 11 comfortless 12 discourteous, uncultivated
uncouth person: oaf 4 boor, lout 5 yokel 6 bumkin, rustic 7 bumpkin
uncover: 4 bare, open, tirl(Sc.), tirr(Sc.) 6 denude, detect, divest, expose, remove, reveal, unveil 7 display, divulge, undrape, unearth 8 disclose, discover
uncovered: 4 bald, nude, open 5 naked 6 cuerpo 9 developed 10 bareheaded
uncrystallized: 9 amorphous
unction: oil 7 suavity, unguent 8 ointment
give extreme: 5 anele
unctuous: fat 4 oily 5 bland, fatty, soapy, suave 6 fervid, greasy 7 fulsome, gushing, pinguid, plastic 10 oleaginous
uncultivated: 4 arid, wild 5 feral 6 coarse, desert, fallow 7 deserty 9 barbarous
uncultured: 4 rude 6 coarse 7 artless, boorish 9 unrefined
uncurbed: 9 audacious 12 uncontrolled
undamaged: 5 whole 6 intact
undaunted: 4 bold 5 brave 7 spartan 8 fearless, intrepid, undashed 9 confident, turbulent, unbridled, unchecked 10 courageous, undismayed 11 unconquered
undecayed: 5 fresh, green
undeceive: 8 disabuse 11 disillusion
undecided: 4 moot, pend 7 pending 8 doubtful, wavering 9 unsettled 10 inconstant, irresolute, unresolved 13 problematical
undefiled: 4 pure 6 chaste 8 innocent, virtuous 9 unlimited 10 immaculate
undemonstrative: 4 calm, cold, cool 7 aseptic, laconic 8 reserved 10 restrained
undeniable: 4 true 7 certain 12 indisputable 13 incontestable

undependable: 5 trick 6 unsafe 7 erratic 10 fly-by-night 13 irresponsible

under: 4 alow 5 below, neath, sotto(It.) 6 nether 7 beneath 8 inferior 10 underneath 11 subordinate

cover: 9 sheltered

obligation: 5 owing 8 beholden, indebted

the weather: 4 sick 5 drunk 6 ailing

under-set: 4 prop 6 sublet 7 provide, support 8 maintain, underlet 10 strengthen

undercover: 6 secret 13 surreptitious

man: spy 5 agent 9 detective 10 counterspy

underdog: 6 victim 9 dark horse

underdone: 4 rare

underestimate: 8 minimize 9 underrate 10 undervalue

undergarment: bra 4 slip 5 teddy 6 bodice, briefs 6 cilice, corset, flimsy, shorts, stepin 7 chemise, panties, step-ins 9 brassiere, chemilonn, hairshirt, petticoat, teddybear, underwear 10 foundation 11 camiknicker, combination

undergo: bow 4 bear, pass 5 carry, defer, yield 6 endure, suffer 7 sustain 8 tolerate 10 experience

undergraduate: 4 coed 6 junior, senior 7 student 8 freshman 9 sophomore

underground: 5 train 6 hidden, secret, subway 7 beneath 10 undercover 12 subterranean 13 surreptitious

burial place: 5 crypt 8 catacomb

dweller: 5 dwarf, gnome, troll

fighter: 6 marquis 8 partisan

fungus: 7 truffle 8 earthnut

railway: 6 subway

worker: 5 miner 6 mucker, pitman, sapper

undergrowth: 4 rush 5 brush 10 hypotrophy, underbrush

underhanded: sly 4 dern, mean 5 shady 6 byhand, secret, sneaky, unfair 8 sneaking, unfairly 9 deceitful 10 circuitous, fraudulent 11 clandestine, shorthanded, unobtrusive 13 unobtrusively 15 surreptitiously

underlie: 4 bear 7 support

underline: 4 mark 6 stress 9 emphasize

underling: 6 menial, minion 8 inferior 11 subordinate

underlying: 5 basic 7 obscure 8 cardinal 9 elemental 11 fundamental

undermine: sap 4 cave 5 drain, erode 6 impair, weaken 7 corrupt, founder, subvert 8 discover, enfeeble, excavate, sabotage 10 demoralize

underneath: 5 below, under 6 bottom, secret 8 beneath 13 surreptitious

underpin: 7 justify, support 8 maintain 9 vindicate 12 substantiate

underprop: 6 uphold 7 support 8 underpin

underrate: 5 decry 7 devalue 8 discount 9 extenuate 10 depreciate, undervalue 13 underestimate

underscore: 9 emphasize, italicize

undersea boat: sub 5 U-boat, wreck 9 submarine 11 submersible

eye: 9 periscope

undershirt: 4 vest 7 chemise

undershrub: 4 bush 7 heather

undersized: 4 puny 5 runty, small 7 scrubby

underskirt: 4 slip 9 petticoat

understand: con, dig, get, ken, see 4 know, sabe, twig 5 grasp, infer, sabby, savey, savvy, sense 6 follow, reason, savvey 7 discern, realize 8 conceive, perceive 9 apprehend, interpret, penetrate 10 comprehend, conjecture 12 get the hang of

understandable: 5 clear, lucid 6 simple 8 exoteric

understanding: ken 4 feet, idea, news 5 amity, brain 6 humane, kindly, reason, treaty 7 compact, concept, empathy, entente, knowing, meaning 8 attitude, contract, footwear, judgment, skillful, sympathy 9 agreement, diagnosis, knowledge, tolerance 10 acceptance 11 intelligent, sympathetic 12 intelligence

understatement: 7 litotes

understood: 5 clear, lucid, tacit 8 implicit

undertake: try 4 dare, fand, fang 5 chide, grant, seize 6 accept, assume, engage, incept, take on 7 attempt, emprise, emprize, execute, perform, promise, receive, reprove 8 contract, covenant, endeavor, overtake 9 guarantee

undertaker: 5 cerer 6 surety 7 rebuker, sponsor 8 embalmer 9 mortician 12 entrepreneur

undertaking: 4 task 6 charge, pledge 7 attempt, calling, project, promise, venture 8 covenant 9 adventure, guarantee 10 enterprise 11 proposition

written: 6 cautio

undertone: 5 aside 6 murmur 11 association

undertow: 4 eddy 6 vortex 7 current, riptide

undervalue: 5 decry 8 disprize, disvalue 10 depreciate

underwater: *apparatus:* 6 tremie 7 caisson

breathing equipment: 5 scuba

captain: 4 Nemo

chamber: 4 cave 7 caisson

craft: sub 5 U-boat 7 pigboat 9 submarine

missile: torpedo

sound detector: 5 sofar, sonar

underwear: 6 skivvy 7 dessous(F.), step-ins 8 lingerie, skivvies 12 underclothes

(see also **undergarment**)

underwood: 5 frith 7 boscage, coppice 8 gangland 10 underbrush 11 under-growth

underworld: 4 hell 5 Hades, Orcus, Sheol 6 Amenti, Erebus 7 xibalba 8 gangland 9 antipodes

boatman: 6 Charon

deity: Dis 4 Bran 5 Hades, Pluto 6 Osiris 8 Dispater 9 Enmeshara 11 Ningish-zida

goddess: 6 Allatu, Belili, Hecate, Trivia

organization: 5 Mafia

pert. to: 8 chthonic 9 chthonian

river: 4 Styx 5 Lethe 7 Acheron

watchdog: 8 Cerberus

underwrite: 4 sign 6 insure 7 assure, endorse, finance, sponsor 9 subscribe

undesigning: 6 simple 7 artless, genuine, sincere

undetermined: 5 vague 7 dubious, pending 8 aoristic, doubtful 9 equivocal

undeveloped: 5 crude 6 latent 8 backward, immature, primitive

undeviating: 4 even 6 direct 8 straight

undigested: 5 crude

undiluted: 4 neat, pure 8 straight

undiminished: 6 entire

undine: nix 4 wave 5 nymph 11 water spirit

undisciplined: 4 wild 6 unruly, wanton 9 untrained

undisclosed: 6 hidden, sealed, secret 8 ulterior 12 confidential

undisguised: 4 bald, open 5 frank, plain, overt 9 barefaced

undisturbed: 4 calm 5 quiet, sound 6 placid, secure, serene 8 tranquil 9 unruffled

undivided: one 5 total, whole 6 entire, intact 8 complete, unbroken 10 continuous

undo: 4 open, ruin 5 annul, fordo, loose, solve, untie 6 betray, cancel, defeat, diddle, foredo, outwit, unlash, unwrap 7 abolish, defease, destroy, disjoin, explain, nullify, release, uncover, unravel 8 unfasten 9 bring down 10 disappoint, disconnect, invalidate

undoing: 4 ruin 8 downfall 9 overthrow

undomesticated: 4 wild 5 feral 6 ferine

undone: raw 6 ruined 9 disgraced, neglected 10 defeasible

undoubted: 4 sure 7 certain 8 accepted, admitted 9 authentic 11 indubitable

undraped: 4 bare, nude

undress: 4 doff 5 strip 6 devest, divest, expose 7 disrobe 8 unclothe 10 dishabille

undressed skin: kip 4 pelt

undue: 7 extreme 8 improper 9 excessive 10 exorbitant, immoderate, inordinate,

unsuitable 11 unwarranted 12 unreasonable 13 inappropriate

undulant: 7 aripple, sinuous

fever: 11 brucellosis

undulate: 4 roll, wave 5 swell, swing 6 billow 9 fluctuate

undutiful: 7 impious

undying: 6 eterne 7 ageless, endless, eternal 8 immortal, unending 9 continual, deathless 10 continuing, persistent 12 imperishable

unearth: dig 4 show 5 learn 6 exhume, expose 7 uncover 8 disclose, discover

unearthly: 4 eery 5 eerie, weird 7 awesome, foolish, uncanny, ungodly 8 terrific 9 appalling, fantastic 10 mysterious, outlandish 12 preposterous, supernatural 13 preternatural

uneasiness: 4 care 5 worry 6 unrest 7 anxiety, disease, trouble 8 disquiet 10 constraint, discomfort, discontent 11 displeasure, disturbance 12 apprehension 13 embarrassment, inconvenience 15 dissatisfaction

uneasy: 5 stiff, tense 7 anxious, awkward, fidgety, unquiet, restive 8 doubtful, restless 9 difficult, perturbed, unsettled 13 uncomfortable

uneducated: 8 ignorant 10 illiterate, unlettered, unschooled

unemotional: 4 cold 5 stony, stoic 7 stoical 9 unfeeling 10 phelgmatic

unemployed: 4 idle 6 otiant, otiose 7 jobless, laid off 8 inactive, leisured 9 at liberty

unencumbered: 4 free

unending: 7 endless, eternal, undying 8 timeless 9 ceaseless, continual 11 everlasting 12 interminable

unendurable: 10 impassible, unbearable 11 intolerable 12 insufferable

unenthusiastic: 4 cool 5 tepid 9 apathetic 12 uninterested

unequal: 6 uneven, unfair, unjust 8 lopsided, variable 9 different, disparate, irregular 11 fluctuating 16 disproportionate

condition: 4 odds

unequaled: 5 alone 7 supreme 9 matchless, unmatched, unrivaled 10 surpassing 12 unparalleled

unequivocal: 5 clear, plain 7 sincere 8 definite, explicit, positive 9 certainly 11 categorical 15 straightforward

unerring: 4 sure, true 5 exact 7 certain 8 inerrant 9 inerrancy, unfailing 10 infallible

unethical: 5 wrong 6 amoral 7 corrupt

uneven: odd 5 erose, gobby, haggy, rough 6 hobbly, rugged, spotty, unfair, unjust, unlike 7 unequal, varying 8 lopsided 9 disparate, irregular 10 ill-matched 11 fluctuating, ill-assorted 12 inconsistent

unexamined: 7 apriori

unexcelled: 8 champion, superior, top-notch

unexceptional: 6 usual 6 common, decent 7 regular 8 ordinary

unexcited: 4 calm 5 level 7 stoical

unexciting: 4 dead, dull, tame 6 boring 7 prosaic 13 uninteresting

unexpected: 5 eerie 6 abrupt, sudden 9 inopinate, unguarded 10 accidental, unforeseen

unexpended: 6 saving 7 reserve, surplus 8 left over

unexpired: 5 alive, valid 9 operative, remaining

unexpressed: 5 tacit 6 silent 7 implicit

unfadable: 4 fast 9 memorable

unfaded: 5 fresh 6 bright

unfading flower: 8 amaranth

unfailing: 4 same, sure 7 certain 8 reliable, unerring 10 infallible, unflagging, unyielding 13 inexhaustible

unfair: 4 foul, hard 5 wrong 6 biased, uneven, unjust 8 unseemly, wrongful 9 dishonest, unethical 11 inequitable, underhanded, unfavorable 12 dishonorable

unfaithful: 7 infidel, traitor 8 derelict, disloyal, recreant, turncoat 9 dishonest, faithless 10 adulterous, inaccurate, traitorous 13 untrustworthy

unfaltering: 4 sure, true 5 brave 6 steady

unfamed: 5 lowly 6 humble 7 obscure

unfamiliar: new 7 strange, unknown 8 ignorant 12 unaccustomed

unfashionable: 5 dated 9 distorted, unshapely

unfasten: 4 free, open, undo 5 loose, unbar, unfix, unpin, untie 6 detach, loosen, unlace, unlock 8 untether

unfathomable: 10 bottomless 12 impenetrable

unfavorable: bad, ill 4 evil, foul 6 averse 7 adverse 8 contrary 15 disadvantageous

unfeeling: 4 dull, hard, numb 5 cruel, harsh, stern, stony 6 brutal, marble, stolid 7 callous 8 numbness, obdurate, pitiless 9 apathetic, bloodless, heartless, insensate, senseless 10 impassible, insensible 11 cold-blooded, hardhearted, insensitive 13 unsusceptible 16 unimpressionable

unfeigned: 4 real, true 6 hearty 7 genuine, natural, sincere

unfermented grape juice: 4 stum

unfertile: 4 arid 6 barren

unfettered: 4 free 5 broad, loose

unfilled: 5 blank, empty 6 vacant 7 vacuous

unfilled cavity: 4 vugg

unfinished: raw 4 rude 5 crude, rough 7 sketchy 8 immature 9 imperfect 10 amateurish, incomplete

unfit: bad 4 sick 5 inept, pasul(Heb.) 6 faulty 8 disabled, improper 9 ill-suited, maladroit 10 out of place, unsuitable 11 handicapped, incompetent, unqualified 12 disqualified 13 incapacitated

unfix: 6 detach, loosen 8 dissolve, unfasten, unsettle

unflagging: 6 steady 8 constant, tireless

unflappable: 4 calm, cool 7 relaxed

unflattering: 4 open 5 blunt, frank 6 candid 10 derogatory, unbecoming

unfledged: 5 green, young 6 callow 8 immature 11 undeveloped, unfeathered

bird: 5 eyas 8 nestling

unflinching: 4 firm, grim 6 stanch 8 resolute 9 steadfast 10 unwavering, unyielding

unfold: ope 4 open 5 break, solve 6 deploy, evolve, expand, explat, flower, reveal, spread, unfurl, unwrap 7 develop, display, divulge, evolute, explain, explate, release 8 disclose 9 explicate

unforced: 4 easy 7 natural, willing 9 voluntary

unforeseen: 6 casual, sudden 10 accidental

unformed: 4 rude 6 callow 9 shapeless, uncreated 11 undeveloped

unfortunate: bad, ill, sad 4 poor 5 worst 6 dismal, wretch 7 hapless, malefic, unhappy, unlucky 8 luckless, wretched 9 graceless, miserable 10 calamitous, deplorable, prostitute, ungracious 12 inauspicious, infelicitous, unsuccessful

unfounded: 4 idle, vain 8 baseless 10 chimerical, groundless

unfrequented: 6 lonely 8 isolated, solitary

unfriendly: 4 cool 6 remote 7 asocial, hostile 8 inimical, unsocial 9 dissocial

terms: 4 outs

unfruitful: 5 blunt 6 barren, wasted 7 sterile, useless 8 impotent, infecund 9 fruitless, infertile 12 unproductive, unprofitable

unfurl: 4 open 5 enrol 6 enroll, expand, spread, unfold, unroll 7 develop

unfurnished: 4 bare 6 vacant

ungainly: 5 lanky 6 clumsy 7 awkward, boorish, uncouth 8 clownish, slammock, slummock 9 maladroit 11 elephantine

ungenerous: 4 mean 5 harsh, nasty, petty 6 stingy

ungirt: 5 loose, slack 7 unbound

ungodly: 6 impure, sinful, wicked 7 impious, profane 8 dreadful 9 atheistic, atrocious, unearthly 10 indecorous, outrageous 11 unbelieving 12 hypocritical

ungovernable: 4 wild 6 unruly 7 froward

9 unbridled **10** disorderly, headstrong, licentious, rebellious **11** intractable **13** irrepressible **14** uncontrollable

ungraceful: 6 clumsy **7** angular, awkward **9** inelegant

ungracious: 4 hard, rude **5** short **8** churlish, impolite **9** offensive **10** unmannerly, unpleasant **11** unfortunate **12** discourteous, unattractive

ungrateful: 9 offensive, thankless

ungrounded: 8 baseless **9** unfounded **10** uninformed **12** uninstructed

ungrudging: 8 cheerful

unguarded: 6 unwary **8** careless **9** imprudent **10** incautious **11** defenseless, thoughtless, unprotected

unguent: 4 balm **5** salve **6** cerate, ceroma, chrism **8** ointment **9** lubricant

ungula: 4 claw, hoof, nail

ungulate: hog, pig **4** deer **5** horse, tapir **6** hoofed **8** elephant **10** rhinoceros

unhallowed: 6 impure, unholy, wicked **7** impious, profane **10** desecrated

unhandsome: 4 mean, rude **5** plain **6** homely, stingy **10** unbecoming

unhandy: 6 clumsy **7** awkward **12** inconvenient

unhappiness: woe **5** blues, dolor, grief, worry **6** misery, unrest **7** sadness

unhappy: sad **4** evil **6** dismal **7** unlucky **8** dejected, ill-fated, wretched **9** miserable, sorrowful, woebegone **10** calamitous **11** melancholic, mischievous, unfavorable, unfortunate **12** inauspicious, unsuccessful **13** inappropriate

unharmed: 4 safe **6** unhurt **8** harmless **10** scatheless

unharmonious: 9 dissonant

unharness: 6 disarm, divest, ungear **7** unhitch, unhorse

unhealthy: ill **4** sick **6** sickly **7** vicious **9** dangerous **11** unwholesome

unheard of: 7 obscure, strange, unknown **13** unprecedented

unheated: 4 cold

unheeding: 4 deaf **8** careless **11** inattentive **12** disregarding

unhesitating: 5 ready

unhidden: 5 overt

unholy: See **ungodly**

unhorse: 5 throw **8** dislodge, dismount **9** overthrow, unharness

unhurried: 4 easy, slow **10** deliberate

unhurt: 4 safe **5** whole **8** unharmed **9** uninjured

unicellular animal: 5 ameba **6** amoeba **9** protozoan **10** paramecium

unicellular plant: 5 spore

unicorn: 4 reem

unicorn fish: 4 unie **7** narwhal **8** filefish

unidentified flying object: UFO

uniform: 4 even, flat, like, suit **5** equal, level **6** livery, outfit, steady **7** orderly, regular, similar **8** constant, equiform **9** continual, equitable, unvarying **10** compatible, consistent, equiformal, invariable, monotonous, unchanging **11** homogeneous

cord: **11** aiguillette

in color: **4** flat, flot

prisoner's: **7** stripes

servant's: **6** livery

shoulder ornament: **7** epaulet **9** epaulette

uniformly: 6 always, evenly

unify: 5 merge, unite **8** coalesce **9** correlate, harmonize, integrate **11** consolidate

unimaginative: 4 dull **7** literal, prosaic **10** pedestrian

unimpaired: 4 free **5** fresh, whole **6** entire, intact

unimpassioned: 6 steady **10** phlegmatic **12** matter-of-fact

unimpeachable: 6 decent **9** blameless, faultless **14** irreproachable, unquestionable **15** unexceptionable

unimpeded: 4 free **8** expedite

unimportant: 5 minor, petty, small **6** little, paltry **7** trivial **10** negligible

uninformed: 8 ignorant

uninhabited: 5 empty **6** vacant **8** deserted, desolate

uninspired: 4 dull **9** stodgy **9** ponderous

unintelligent: 4 dumb **5** brute **6** obtuse, simple, stupid, unwise **7** foolish **8** ignorant **9** senseless **10** irrational

unintentional: 9 haphazard, unwitting **10** accidental **11** inadvertent

uninteresting: dry **4** arid, drab, dull, flat **5** stale **6** boring, jejune, prolix, stupid **7** humdrum, insipid, prosaic, tedious **8** tiresome **9** colorless **10** unexciting

uninterrupted: 6 direct **7** endless, eternal **9** continual **10** continuous **11** everlasting

unio: 6 mussel

union: AFL, CIO, one, UAW **4** bloc **5** artel, joint, ILGWU, unity **6** accord, copula, fusion, gremio(Sp.), league, merger, unicum **7** amalgam, concord, contact, entente, meeting, oneness, society **8** alliance, junction, marriage **9** coalition, coherence, composure **10** connection, copulation, federation, fellowship **11** association, coalescence, combination, concurrence, confederacy, conjunction, consistency, unification

political: **4** bloc **9** coalition

trade: **5** guild, hanse

union jack: 4 flag

Union of South Africa: See **South Africa**

Union of Soviet Socialist Republics (see also **Russia, Soviet Union**): **4** USSR **6** Russia, Soviet

unique: odd, one **4** only, rare, sole **5** alone,

queer 6 single 7 notable, special, unequal, unusual 8 peculiar, singular 9
matchless 11 exceptional 13 extraordinary

unison: 5 union 6 accord 7 concord, harmony 9 agreement, consonant, ho-
mophony, identical, unanimity, unisonous 10 concordant, consonance

unit: ace, one 4 item 5 digit, group, monad, whole 6 entity 10 individual

conductivity: mho

discord: 4 word

fluidity: rhe

flux density: 5 gauss

force: 4 dyne, volt 5 kinit, tonal 6 newton
7 poundal

hypothetical: 4 idant 6 pangen 7 pangene

illumination: 4 phot

inductance: 5 henry

light: lux, pyr 5 lumen

magnetic: 5 weber

measure: are, mil, rod 4 pint 5 meter,
stere

measuring sound: 7 decibel

metrical: 4 dyne, mora 5 liter, morae

military: 4 army 5 corps, squad 7 brigade,
company, platoon 8 division, regiment
9 battalion

physical: erg 7 atomerg

power: bel 4 watt 5 dynam, horse

pressure: 5 barad, barye 10 atmosphere

reluctance: rel

resistance: ohm

social: 4 clan, sect 5 tribe 6 family 7
chapter

speed: 4 velo

stellar: 6 parsec

tale: 4 rees

telegraphic: 4 baud

thermal: 6 calory 7 calorie

time: day 4 bell, hour, week, year 5
month 6 minute, season, second

ultimate: 5 monad

velocity: kin 4 kine, velo

volume: cwt, ton 5 ounce, pound 13 hundredweight

weight: ton 4 dram, gram, tael 5 carat,
grain, ounce, pound

work: erg 5 ergon, joule 6 kilerg

unite: ass, fay, mix, pan, sew, tie, wed 4
ally, band, bind, club, fuse, hasp, join,
knit, link, meld, pair, seam, weld 5 affix, annex, blend, graft, hitch, marry,
merge, piece, rally, unify 6 adhere, adjoin, attach, cement, cohere, concur,
couple, embody, mingle, solder, splice 7
combine, conjoin, connect, consort,
convene 8 assemble, coalesce, compound, concrete, condense, conspire,
continue, federate, regulate 9 affiliate,
aggregate, associate 10 amalgamate,
articulate, consociate, federalize, hook

up with, join forces 11 concentrate,
consolidate, incorporate 12 congluti-
nate

united: one 9 concerted, conjugate, corporate

United Nations Organization: UNO

United Provinces: 7 Holland, Utrecht,
Zeeland 9 Friesland, Groningen 10
Gelderland, Overijssel

United States: *coin:* bit 4 cent, dime 5
eagle, penny 6 dollar, nickel 7 quarter

falls: 7 Niagara 8 Yosemite 9 Multnomah

flagmaker: 9 Betsy Ross

frontiersman: 4 Cody 5 Boone, Clark,
Lewis 8 Crockett

measure: lea, mil, rod, ton, tub, vat 4 acre,
bolt, cord, drum, foot, gill, hand, hank,
heer, inch, iron, last, line, link, mile,
nail, pace, palm, peck, pint, pipe, pole,
pool, roll, sack, span, typp, vara, yard 5
block, carat, chain, labor, minim, perch,
point, prime, quart, skein, stran 6 barrel, basket, bushel, fathom, gallon,
league, pottle, square, strand, thread 7
quarter, section, spindle 8 hogshead,
quadrant, standard, township 9 board
foot, decillion, fluid dram 10 fluid
ounce 11 teaspoonful 13 tablespoonful
16 Winchester bushel

measure of weight: bag, keg, kip, ton 5
carat, flask, grain, ounce, pound 6 denier 7 long ton, quarter, quintal 9 troy
ounce, troy pound 11 metric carat 13
hundredweight

mountain: 4 Hood 5 Rocky 6 Cumbre,
Elbert, Helena, Shasta 7 Massive,
Rainier, Whitney 8 Katahdin, McKin-
ley 10 Laurentian 11 Appalachian

pioneer: see frontiersman above

President: see **President (U.S.)**

racetrack: 5 Bowie 6 Goshen, Laurel 7
Hialeah, Jamaica, Pimlico 8 Aqueduct
10 Meadowland, Santa Anita

river: see under individual states

Vice President: see **Vice President
(U.S.)**

unity: one 5 union 6 accord 7 concord,
harmony, oneness 8 alliance, identity 9
agreement, communion, congruity 10
singleness, solidarity, uniformity 11
conjunction, unification

universal: all 5 local, total, whole 6
common, cosmic, entire, public 7 general 8 catholic, constant 9 continual, unlimited 11 omnipresent 12 all-pervad-
ing

language: ido 9 Esperanto

military training: 5 draft

universe: 5 earth, monad, world 6 cosmos, nature, system 8 creation, mega-
cosm

controlling principle: 4 tien 5 logos

pert to: 6 cosmic

science: 9 cosmology

university (see also **college**): 7 academy, college 8 academie 9 accademie

division: 6 school 7 college

grounds: 6 campus

Ivy League: 4 Yale 5 Brown 7 Cornell, Harvard 8 Columbia 9 Dartmouth, Princeton 12 Pennsylvania

official: 4 dean 6 regent

rank: 9 professor 10 instructor

team: 7 varsity

univocal: 5 clear 7 uniform 9 unanimous, unisonous 11 indubitable 12 unmistakable

unjust: 5 cruel 6 unfair 8 improper, wrongful 9 dishonest, faithless 10 inaccurate, iniquitous, unfaithful 11 inequitable

unkempt: 5 crude, messy, rough 6 frouzy, frowsy, frowzy, shaggy, untidy 7 ruffled, squalid, tousled 8 slovenly 9 unrefined 10 disarrayed, disheveled, unpolished

unkind: bad, ill 4 mean, vile 5 cruel, harsh, rough, stern 6 severe, wicked 7 foreign, strange 8 ungenial 9 inclement, undutiful, unnatural 10 degenerate, ungenerous, ungracious, ungrateful, unsuitable 11 unfavorable

unknit: 4 undo 5 ravel, relax, untie 6 unknot 7 unravel 8 disperse, dissolve, disunite

unknowable: 6 sealed 8 mystical 9 enigmatic

unknown: 4 unco 7 inconnu(F.), obscure, strange 9 anonymous, incognito 10 unfamiliar 12 incalculable 13 inexpressible

unlace: 4 undo 5 loose 6 carver 7 undress, unravel 8 unfasten, untangle

unlawful: 4 bastard, illegal, illicit 8 criminal, wrongful 9 irregular 10 contraband 12 illegitimate

hunting: 8 poaching

intrusion: 8 trespass

unlearned: 4 lewd 5 gross 6 borrel 7 natural 8 ignorant, untaught 9 untutored 10 illiterate, uneducated 11 instinctive, instinctual, unscholarly

unleashed: 4 free 5 loose 8 released

unleavened: 4 flat 7 azymous

bread: 4 azym 5 azyme, matzo 7 matzoth(pl.)

unless: 4 lest, nisi(L.), save 6 except 9 excepting

unlettered: 4 lewd 8 ignorant 9 barbarian 10 illiterate, uneducated

unlike: 6 uneven 7 difform, diverse 8 unlikely 9 different, irregular 10 dissimilar, improbable 13 heterogeneous

unlikely: 5 unfit 10 improbable, unsuitable 11 unpromising 12 disagreeable,

unattractive 13 objectionable

unlikeness: 8 contrast 12 disagreement 13 dissimilarity

unlimited: 4 vast 5 total 9 boundless, limitless, unbounded, undefined, universal 10 indefinite, unconfined 11 illimitable, untrammeled 12 immeasurable, unrestricted 13 indeterminate

unload: 4 dump, land 5 empty, trash 6 decant, remove 7 deplete, discard, lighten, relieve 9 disburden, discharge, jettison, liquidate, sacrifice

unlock: ope 4 open 5 solve 6 reveal

unlooked for: 6 chance 10 unexpected

unlucky: bad, fey, ill 7 hapless 8 ill-fated 9 ill-omened 11 apocalyptic, star-crossed unfortunate

unman: 5 crush 7 monster, unnerve 8 castrate

unmanageable: 5 randy 6 unruly 8 churlish 10 disorderly

unmanly: 8 childish

unmannerly: 4 rude 7 boorish, uncivil 8 impolite 10 ungracious 12 discourteous

unmarried: one 4 lone 6 chaste, single

in law: 4 sole

woman: 7 old maid 8 spinster 12 bachelorette

unmask: 6 expose, reveal, unface 7 uncloak 8 disclose 9 dismantle

unmatched: odd 5 alone 9 matchless

unmeasured: 4 huge, vast 7 immense 9 boundless 12 incalculable, unrestrained

unmelodious: 9 dissonant 11 cacophonous

unmerciful: 5 cruel 8 pitiless, ruthless 9 inclement 10 relentless

unmethodical: 7 cursory, erratic 9 desultory

unmindful: 8 careless, heedless 9 forgetful, negligent 10 neglectful

unmistakable: 4 open 5 clear, plain 6 patent 7 evident, obvious 8 apparent, definite

unmitigated: 4 mere, pure 5 sheer, utter 6 arrant 8 absolute, clearcut 10 unmodified

unmixed: 4 deep, mear, mere, pure 5 blank, sheer, utter 7 sincere 8 straight

unmoved: 4 calm, cool, firm 5 stony 6 serene 7 adamant 8 obdurate, stubborn, unshaken 9 apathetic

unmoving: 5 inert 6 static

unnatural: 4 eery 5 eerie 7 strange, uncanny 8 abnormal, affected, farcical 9 irregular 10 artificial, factitious 11 counterfeit 12 supernatural

unnecessary: 6 excess 7 useless 8 needless 9 prodigal 9 redundant 10 gratuitous 11 superfluous, uncalled-for

unnerve: 5 unman 6 weaken, castrate 8 enervate 10 dishearten, emasculate

unobservant: 8 heedless 11 inattentive

unobstructed: 4 free, open 9 panoramic

unobtrusive: 5 quiet 6 modest 8 retiring

unobtrusively: 9 underhand

unoccupied: 4 free, idle, void 5 empty 6 vacant 7 leisure 10 unemployed

unofficial: 7 private 8 informal

unorganized: 5 messy 7 chaotic 10 disorderly, incoherent

unoriginal: 4 arid, copy 5 trite 7 sterile 10 secondhand

unorthodox: 9 heretical

unostentatious: 5 plain, quiet 6 lenten, modest 10 restrained

unpaid: due 6 arrear 10 unrevenged 11 outstanding

unpaired: odd

unpalatable: 4 flat, thin, weak 8 nauseous 10 unpleasant 11 distasteful

unparalleled: 5 alone 6 unique 7 unequal 8 peerless 9 matchless, unmatched 10 inimitable

unpleasant: bad 7 irksome 9 offensive 10 abominable, forbidding, ill-favored, ungracious 11 displeasing, distasteful 12 disagreeable

  most: 5 worst

unplowed: lea 6 fallow 8 untilled

unpolished: 4 rude 5 bruit, crude, rough 6 coarse, rugged 7 boorish 8 agrestic, impolite 9 barbarous 10 agrestical

unpopularity: 6 odium

unprecedented: new 5 novel 9 unheard-of 10 unexampled

unprejudiced: 4 fair 9 impartial 13 dispassionate

unpremeditated: 6 casual 9 extempore 10 accidental 11 spontaneous

unprepared: raw 5 unfit 6 asleep 11 unorganized

unprepossessing: 4 ugly 5 plain 6 homely 11 unappealing 12 unattractive

unpretentious: 5 plain 6 homely, humble, modest, simple 10 unaffected

unprincipled: 4 lewd 7 corrupt 9 abandoned 10 perfidious 12 unscrupulous

unprocessed: raw 5 crude

unproductive: 4 arid, dead, lean 6 barren, futile, geason 7 sterile 8 impotent 10 unfruitful

unprofessional: lay 6 laical 7 amateur 9 unskilled 15 nonprofessional

unprofitable: dry 4 dead 6 barren 7 inutile, useless 8 bootless, gainless 9 fruitless, frustrate 10 unfruitful 12 frustraneous 15 disadvantageous

unpropitious: 4 evil 7 adverse, counter, ominous, opposed 12 antagonistic, inauspicious

unprotected: 6 unsafe 7 exposed 8 helpless, insecure 9 unguarded

unqualified: 4 bare, mear, meer, mere, sure 5 sheer, unfit, utter 6 entire, unable 7 plenary 8 absolute, complete, definite 9 categoric, downright, incapable 11 categorical, incompetent

unquestionable: 7 certain, decided, evident 8 implicit, positive 9 authentic, downright 12 indisputable

unravel: 4 undo 5 feaze, ravel, solve 6 unfold, unlace 8 disorder, disunite, separate, untangle 9 disengage, extricate, figure out 11 disentangle

unready: 4 slow 5 unfit 6 clumsy 7 awkward 8 hesitant 9 undressed 10 unprepared

unreal: 5 false, ideal 6 aerial 7 fancied, fatuous, nominal 8 aeriform, fanciful, illusive, illusory, spurious 9 deceptive, fantastic, imaginary, pretended, visionary 10 apocryphal, artificial, barmecidal, fictitious, mendacious 11 counterfeit, imaginative 13 insubstantial, unsubstantial

unreasonable: mad 6 absurd 9 excessive, illogical, senseless 10 exorbitant, immoderate, irrational 11 extravagant, impractical

unrecognized: 6 unsung 7 unknown 13 unappreciated

unrefined: raw 4 dark, loud, rude 5 broad, crass, crude, gross 6 coarse, common, earthy, native, vulgar 7 uncouth 8 ungraded 12 uncultivated

unregenerate: 6 carnal, sinful 9 obstinate, shameless 10 impenitent 11 unrepentant 12 recalcitrant

unrelated: 5 fremd 8 separate 9 disjoined

unrelaxed: 4 taut 5 tense

unrelenting: 4 grim, hard, iron 5 cruel, stern 6 severe 8 rigorous 9 merciless 10 inexorable, inflexible, relentless, unyielding

unreliable: 5 fishy 6 fickle, shifty, unsafe 7 casalty 10 capricious, fly-by-night 12 undependable 13 irresponsible, untrustworthy

unremitting: 4 busy, hard 9 assiduous, continual, incessant 10 persistent 11 persevering

unrepentant: 10 impenitent 11 remorseless 12 unregenerate

unreserved: 4 free 5 frank 6 candid 9 outspoken, unlimited 13 demonstrative

unresponsive: 4 cold, cool 6 frigid

unrest: 5 alarm 6 bustle, motion 7 anarchy, ferment 8 disquiet 9 commotion 10 uneasiness

unrestrained: lax 4 free, wild 5 bluff, blunt, broad, loose 6 wanton 7 riotous 9 abandoned, audacious, dissolute, excessive, expansive, unbounded, unbridled, unlimited 10 licentious, unmeasured 11 extravagant 12 uncontrolled

unrestraint: 7 abandon, license 8 immunity 11 spontaneity

unrevealed: 6 hidden, latent, masked, untold 7 covered 9 concealed

unripe: 5 crude, green, young 6 callow 7 uncured, unready 8 immature 9 premature 10 precocious, unseasoned 12 unseasonable 13 inexperienced

unroll: 6 evolve, unfold 7 develop, display, open out 8 disclose

unruffled: 4 calm, cool 5 quiet 6 placid, poised, sedate, serene, smooth 8 decorous 11 undisturbed 13 dispassionate, philosophical

unruly: 6 haunty, ramage 7 froward, lawless, restive 8 fractious, obstinate, out of hand, turbulent 10 disorderly, headstrong, licentious, refractory 11 disobedient, intractable 12 recalcitrant, ungovernable, unmanageable

unsafe: 5 risky, shaky 7 exposed 8 insecure, perilous 9 dangerous, hazardous 10 unreliable

unsatisfactory: bad 9 defective, imperfect 10 inadequate 11 inefficient

unsavory: 7 insipid 9 offensive, tasteless 10 unpleasant 11 distasteful, unpalatable 12 disagreeable, unappetizing

unscrupulous: 5 shady, venal 6 crafty 7 corrupt 8 rascally 9 dishonest, miscreant 12 unprincipled 13 untrustworthy

unseal: 4 open 8 disclose

unseasonable: 6 unripe 8 ill-timed, improper, untimely 9 premature 11 inopportune

unseasoned: raw 5 bland, green 8 untimely

unseat: 6 depose, remove 7 unhorse 9 overthrow

unseemly: 5 crude, inept 6 coarse 8 improper, indecent, unworthy 10 indecorous, unbecoming 13 inappropriate

unseen: 9 invisible, unnoticed 10 unobserved 11 unperceived 12 undiscovered

unselfish: 6 heroic 8 generous 10 altruistic, benevolent

unserviceable: 7 useless 11 impractical

unsettle: 5 upset 7 commove, derange, disturb 8 disorder, displace, disquiet 10 disarrange, discompose

unsettled: 4 back, moot 6 fickle, queasy, unpaid 7 dubious, pending 8 restless, unstable 9 ambiguous, desultory, itinerant, uncertain, unquieted 10 changeable, precarious, unoccupied 11 unpopulated 12 undetermined 13 problematical

unshaken: 4 firm, sure 6 steady

unshapely: 8 deformed

unsheathe: 4 draw 6 remove 7 pull out

unsightly: 4 drab, ugly 5 messy 6 homely

unskilled: 4 rude 5 green 6 puisne 7 artless 8 ignorant, malapert 10 amateurish

unskillful: 5 inept 6 bungly, clumsy 7 awkward 10 inexpertly 13 inexperienced

unskillfully: 5 badly

unsociable: shy 4 cool 5 aloof 6 sullen 8 reserved 9 withdrawn 11 standoffish

unsoiled: 5 clean 10 immaculate

unsophisticated: 4 naif, pure 5 frank, green, naive 6 callow, simple 7 artless, genuine, natural 8 bona fide, innocent 9 ingenious, untutored

unsound: bad 4 evil, sick, weak 5 crazy, dotty, false, frail, risky, shaky 6 addled, fickle, flawed, hollow, insane, rotten, weakly 7 decayed, wracked 8 diseased, impaired, insecure, weakened 9 dangerous, defective, imperfect, tottering 10 ill-founded

unspeakable: bad 4 vile 6 wicked 7 heinous 9 ineffable 10 outrageous 11 unutterable

unspoiled: 4 racy 5 fresh 6 virgin

unspoken: 4 mute 5 tacit 6 silent 9 ineffable, unuttered

unspotted: 5 clear 8 spotless 10 immaculate

unstable: 5 loose, sandy 6 fickle, fitful, flitty, labile 7 astatic, dwaible, dwaibly, erratic, flightly, mutable, plastic 8 doubtful, insecure, ticklish, unhinged, unsteady, variable 9 eccentric, faithless, irregular, unsettled 10 changeable, inconstant, precarious, unreliable 11 fluctuating, vacillating

unsteady: 5 dizzy, fluky, shaky, tippy 6 fickle, flicky, fluffy, groggy, wabbly, wobbly 7 erratic, movable, quavery, rickety, unsound, wayward 8 titubate, unstable, variable, wavering 9 desultory, irregular, uncertain 10 capricious, changeable, flickering, inconstant 11 fluctuating, lightheaded, vacillating

unstinted: 5 ample 6 lavish 7 endless 8 generous

unstudied: 7 natural 8 careless, unforced, unversed 9 unlearned 10 colloquial, unaffected 11 extemporary, spontaneous

unsubstantial: 4 airy, slim, thin, weak 5 filmy, light, paper 6 aerial, flimsy, papery, slight, unreal 7 folious, gaseous, nominal, shadowy, tenuous 8 filigree, footless 9 visionary 10 immaterial 11 implausible

unsuccessful: 6 losing 7 failing, unlucky 8 abortive 9 fruitless 10 disastrous 11 ineffectual, unfortunate

unsuitable: bad 5 inapt, inept, undue, unfit 8 improper 10 unbecoming 13 inappropriate

unsullied: 4 pure 5 clean 6 chaste 8 spotless 10 immaculate

unsure: 4 weak 5 timid 6 infirm 8 doubtful 9 dangerous, hazardous 10 precarious, unreliable 11 vacillating 13 untrustworthy

unsusceptible: 6 immune 8 obdurate

unsweetened: dry, sec 4 sour

unswerving: 4 firm, true 5 fixed, loyal 6 steady 8 straight 9 steadfast

unsymmetrical: 8 lopsided 9 irregular 15 disproportional

unsympathetic: 4 cold, cool, hard 5 stony 6 frozen 7 hostile 9 heartless, unfeeling, unlikable 11 hardhearted 12 unresponsive

untainted: 4 free, good, pure 8 innocent 9 unsullied

untalented: 8 mediocre 11 incompetent

untamed: 4 wild 5 feral 6 ferine, ramage, ramish, savage 9 unsubdued

untangle: 4 free 6 sleave, unlace 9 extricate 11 disentangle

untanned skin: kip 4 hide, pelt 8 shagreen

untarnished: 5 clean 8 spotless

untaught: 5 naive 7 natural 8 ignorant 9 unlearned 10 illiterate, uneducated 11 spontaneous 12 uninstructed

untenanted: 5 empty 6 vacant

untended: 7 run-down 9 neglected

untested: new 5 green 9 untried

unthinking: 4 rash 5 brute 6 casual 8 careless, feckless, heedless 9 impetuous 11 thoughtless 13 inconsiderate

unthrifty: 6 wanton 7 foolish, profuse 8 prodigal 9 profitless, profligate 11 extravagant, improvident

untidy: 5 dowdy, messy 7 bunting 8 careless, littered, slipshod, slovenly 10 disheveled, disordered, slatternly 11 disarranged

untidy person: pig 4 slob 6 sloven 8 slattern

untie: 4 free, undo 5 loose 6 loosen, unbind, unlash 8 disunite, unfasten 9 disengage, extricate

until: til 4 till, unto

now: 5 as yet

untimely: 5 early 8 immature 9 premature 11 inopportune 12 unseasonable

untiring: 4 busy 8 sedulous, tireless 13 indefatigable

untold: 4 huge, vast 9 boundless, unrelated 10 uninformed, unrevealed 11 innumerable 12 immeasurable, incalculable

untouchable: 7 outcast 8 chandala, déclassé 10 intangible

untouched: 5 whole 6 intact, virgin 9 insensate

untoward: 6 unruly 7 awkward, froward,

unlucky 8 improper, perverse, stubborn, unseemly 9 vexatious 10 indecorous, ungraceful 11 troublesome, unfavorable, unfortunate 12 inconvenient, unpropitious

untrained: raw 4 wild 5 green 7 awkward, untamed 8 undocile 9 unskilled 10 amateurish, unprepared

untrammeled: 4 free 5 loose 9 audacious, unlimited 10 unhampered

untransferable: 11 inalienable

untraversed: 6 untrod

untried: new 5 fresh, green 8 immature, untested 13 inexperienced

untrue: 4 flam 5 false, wrong 8 disloyal, perjured 9 erroneous, faithless, incorrect 10 fallacious, unfaithful 11 disaffected

untrustworthy: 6 tricky, unsafe 8 slippery 9 dishonest, uncertain 10 perfidious, unreliable 12 undependable

untruth: lie 5 fable 7 fallacy, falsity 9 falsehood, mendacity, treachery 11 fabrication, tarradiddle

untutored: 5 naive 6 simple 7 artless, natural 8 clownish, ignorant, untaught 9 barbarian, unlearned 10 illiterate 15 unsophisticated

untwine: 4 free, undo 5 frese, untie 6 unwind 9 extricate 11 disentangle

unused: new 4 idle 5 fresh 6 vacant 8 unwonted 9 unaccustomed

unusual: odd 4 rare 5 novel, queer, weird 6 quaint, unique 7 strange 8 abnormal, uncommon, unwonted 9 anomalous, different, eccentric 10 remarkable 11 exceptional 12 illegitimate 13 extraordinary

unusual person or thing: 4 oner

unutterable, inutterable: 7 extreme 9 ineffable 11 unspeakable 13 inexpressible 15 unpronounceable

unvaried: 5 alike 7 uniform 10 monotonous

unvarnished: 4 bald 5 frank, plain 6 simple 8 unglazed 9 unadorned, unglossed 13 unembellished

unveil: 4 open 6 reveal 7 uncover 8 disclose

unvoiced: 4 surd 5 tacit 6 secret 8 unspoken 9 unuttered

unwarranted: 5 undue 8 baseless 11 unjustified 12 unreasonable

unwary: 4 rash 7 unaware 8 careless, heedless 9 credulous, unguarded 10 groundless, incautious 11 precipitate

unwavering: 4 firm, pure 5 solid 6 stable 8 constant 9 steadfast

unwearied: 4 busy 8 tireless 9 assiduous 13 indefatigable

unweave: 4 undo 5 ravel 6 unfold

unwed: 6 single

unwelcome: 8 non grata, unwanted 9 intruding, intrusive 13 objectionable

unwell: ill 4 evil, sick 5 badly 6 ailing 8 off-color 9 squeamish 10 out-of-sorts

unwholesome: 4 evil 6 impure 7 corrupt, harmful, immoral, noisome, noxious, unclean 9 offensive 11 unhealthful

unwieldy: 5 bulky, heavy 6 clumsy 7 awkward, hulking 8 cumbrous, ungainly 9 ponderous 10 cumbersome 12 hippopotamic, unmanageable

unwilling: 4 loth 5 loath 6 averse, mauger, maugre 7 loathly 8 backward 9 eschewing, reluctant 11 disinclined

unwind: 5 ravel, relax 6 uncoil 8 untangle 11 disentangle

unwise: 5 inane, naive 6 simple 7 foolish, witless 9 brainless, impolitic, imprudent, senseless 10 indiscreet, irrational 11 injudicious 12 undiplomatic 13 unintelligent

unwonted: 4 rare 6 unused 7 unusual 8 uncommon 10 infrequent 11 exceptional 12 unaccustomed

unworldly: 4 eery 5 eerie, naive, weird 6 dreamy, natural 9 spiritual, unearthly

unworthy: 4 base 7 beneath 8 shameful, unseemly 9 no-account, worthless 10 despicable, unbecoming 12 contemptible, dishonorable

unwrinkled: 5 brent(Sc.) 6 smooth

unwritten: 4 oral 5 blank, vocal 6 verbal 11 word-of-mouth

unwrought: 8 unworked

unyielding: set 4 fast, firm, grim, hard, iron 5 fixed, rigid, stern, stiff, stith, stony, tough 6 frozen, steely 7 adamant 8 obdurate, stubborn 9 inelastic, obstinate, unbending 10 determined, inexorable, inflexible, relentless 11 immalleable 12 contumacious, unsubmissive 14 uncompromising

unyoke: 4 free, part 5 loose 6 remove 7 disjoin, release 8 separate 10 disconnect

up: 4 busy, rise 5 aloft, astir, raise 6 active 7 success 8 familiar 9 according

up and down: 5 erect 6 direct, uneven 7 upright 8 vertical 9 downright, irregular 10 thoroughly, undulating 13 perpendicular

up to: 4 able 5 until

date: new 6 modern 7 stylish 11 fashionable

this time: 6 hereto 8 hitherto

upas tree gum: 6 antiar 11 arrow poison

upbeat: 5 arsis 10 optimistic

upbraid: 4 draw, rail, twit 5 abuse, blame, braid, chide, scold, score, taunt, twist 6 accuse, charge 7 censure, reprove 8 denounce, reproach 9 exprobate 10 denunciate

upbuilding: 8 increase 11 edification

update: 5 renew 7 restore 9 modernize

upgrade: 5 raise, slope 6 ascent 7 incline

upheaval: 5 storm 6 revolt 7 rummage 9 agitation, cataclysm, commotion

upheave: 4 lift, rear, rise

uphill: 4 hard 6 rising, tiring 7 arduous, labored 9 ascending, difficult, laborious

uphold: aid 4 abet, back, bear, lift, stay 5 favor, raise 6 assert, defend, favour, second 7 confirm, support, sustain 8 conserve, maintain 9 encourage, vindicate 11 countenance

upholder: 6 dealer 8 adherent 9 tradesman 10 undertaker 11 upholsterer

upholstered: fat 9 cushioned, luxurious

upkeep: 4 cost 6 repair 7 support 8 overhead 11 maintenance

upland: 4 wold 6 coteau 7 plateau

uplift: 4 head, lift, rock 5 erect, raise, tower 7 collect, elevate, ennoble, improve 8 upheaval 9 elevation 10 illuminate

Upolu: *city:* 4 Apia

island group: 5 Samoa

upon: oer, sur(law) 4 atop, over 5 about, above 8 touching 10 concerning

that: 7 thereat 9 thereupon

which: 7 whereat 9 whereupon

upper: 4 bunk, drug, over, vamp 5 above, berth 8 superior 9 stimulant 11 amphetamine

upper case: 7 capital

upper crust: 5 elite 7 segment, society

upper lips part: 5 flews

upperclassman: 6 junior, senior

uppermost: top 5 first 6 apical 7 highest, topmost 8 farthest, foremost, loftiest 9 outermost 11 predominant

uppish: 5 brash, proud 6 elated 7 haughty, peevish 8 arrogant, assuming, snobbish 12 presumptuous

upraised: 5 atilt 6 lifted, raised 7 erected 8 elevated, extolled, improved 10 encouraged

uprear: 5 build, erect, exalt, raise

upright: 4 good, just, true 5 erect, moral, piano, right, stela, stele, stile 6 honest, square 7 endwise, sincere 8 straight, vertical, virtuous 9 elevation, equitable, honorable, righteous 10 pianoforte, scrupulous 11 unambiguous 13 perpendicular

support: 4 jamb, stud

uprightness: 6 equity 7 probity 9 rectitude

uprising: 4 riot 6 ascent, mutiny, putsch, revolt, tumult 7 ensuing 8 reaction 9 ascending, commotion, rebellion 10 increasing, insurgency, revolution 12 insurrection 17 counterrevolution

uproar: din 4 riot, rout 5 brawl, chaos,

hurly, melee, noise 6 bedlam, bustle, clamor, dirdum, fracas, habble, hubble, hubbub, rattle, tumult 7 clamour, ferment, turmoil 8 outbreak 9 commotion, confusion 10 convulsion, donnybrook, hurlyburly, rumbullion, tintamarre 11 disturbance, pandemonium

uproot: 4 move 5 shift 7 destroy 8 supplant 9 eradicate, extirpate 10 annihilate, transplant 11 exterminate

upset: irk 4 cave, coup, keel, rile, turn 6 defeat, refund, topple 7 capsize, confuse, derange, disturb, outcome, pervert, quarrel, reverse, subvert 8 capsized, overturn 9 discomfit, embarrass, overthrow, perturbed 10 debilitate, discompose, disconcert, disordered, distressed, overturned 11 disorganize

upshot: end 5 issue, limit 6 effect, finish, result, sequel 7 outcome 9 aftermath, substance 10 conclusion 11 termination 12 consummation

upside-down: 7 chaotic, jumbled 8 inverted 10 topsy-turvy

upstage: shy 5 aloof 6 offish 8 backward, outshine, snobbish 9 conceited 12 supercilious

upstart: 4 snob 6 origin 7 dalteen, parvenu, saffron 8 parvenue 9 cockhorse

upstir: 6 incite 7 agitate 9 stimulate

upsurge: 4 boom 9 inflation

upstake: 4 flue, tube 5 shaft 6 upcast 10 collection, comprehend 13 comprehension, understanding

uptight: 4 edgy 5 tense 6 uneasy

up-to-date: 6 modern 7 abreast 9 au courant

upupoid bird: 6 hoopoe

upward: 4 more, over 5 above, aloft, lofty 7 airward, skyward 8 airwards 9 ascending

uraeus: asp 6 symbol 8 ornament 10 decoration

uralite: 9 amphibole

Urania's son: 5 Hymen

uranian: 8 heavenly 9 celestial, homosexual 12 astronomical

uranium: 15 chemical element
  dioxide: 10 ianthinite
  source: 11 pitchblende

Uranus: *children:* 4 Rhea 5 Titan 7 Cyclops
  moon: 5 Ariel 6 Oberon 7 Titania, Umbriel
  mother: 4 Gaea, Gaia
  satellite: 5 Ariel 6 Oberon 7 Miranda, Titania, Umbriel
  wife: 4 Gaea, Gaia

urban: 5 civic 7 oppidan 8 citified 9 inner city

urban division: 4 ward

urbane: 5 bland, civil, suave 6 poised, po-

lite, smooth 7 affable, elegant, genteel, refined 8 polished 9 courteous 12 cosmopolitan 13 sophisticated

urchin: boy, cub, elf, imp, tad 4 arab, brat 5 child, elfin, gamin 8 cylinder, hedgehog, hurcheon 9 hunchback, youngster 10 ragamuffin, street arab

ure: 4 haze, mist

urease: 6 enzyme

uredo: 5 hives 9 urticaria 11 burning itch

urge: dun, egg, ert(Sc.), hie, ply, sue 4 brod, coax, goad, prod, push, spur 5 broad, drive, filip, force, hurry, impel, plead, press 6 allege, compel, demand, desire, excite, exhort, fillip, incite, induce, insist, motive, needle 7 animate, augment, entreat, impulse, provoke, solicit 8 advocate, persuade 9 flagitate, importune, incentive, influence, stimulate 10 exasperate

urgency: 4 need 5 haste, hurry 6 crisis, stress 8 exigency, pressure 10 insistence 11 importunity

urgent: hot 5 grave 7 clamant, driving, exigent 8 critical, pressing 9 demanding, impelling, important 10 solicitous 11 importunate

Uriah's wife: 9 Bathsheba

urial, oorial: sha 5 sheep

Uriel: 5 angel 9 archangel

Urim's partner: 7 Thummim

Uris novel: 5 QBVII 6 Exodus

urisk: 7 brownie

urn: jar, run 4 bury, ewer, urna, vase 5 grave, inurn, steen, theca 6 spring 7 capsule, cistern, pitcher, samovar, vaselet 8 fountain 9 container 10 jardiniere 11 watercourse
  for bones: 7 ossuary
  tea: 7 samovar

urn-shaped: 9 urceolate

urodela: 5 newts, order 7 Caudata 8 amphibia 10 salamander

Ursa: 4 Bear
  Major: 9 Great Bear
  Minor: 10 Little Bear

ursine: 7 arctoid 8 bearlike

urticaria: 5 hives, uredo

urubu: 7 vulture

Uruguay: *capital:* 10 Montevideo
  city: 4 Melo 5 Minas 6 Rivera
  discoverer: 5 Solis
  estuary: 5 Plata
  lake: 5 Merin, Mirim
  measure: 4 vara 6 cuadra, suerte
  monetary unit: 4 peso
  river: 4 Malo 5 Negro 6 Ulimar 7 Uruguay 9 Cebollary 10 Tacarembo
  weight: 7 quintal

urus: tur 7 aurochs

us: uns(Gr.) 4 nous(Fr.)

usable: fit 4 open 8 servable 9 available,

practical 10 convenient, functional 11 serviceable, utilitarian

usage: use 4 form, wont 5 habit, haunt, idiom 6 custom, method 7 conduct, manners, utility 8 behavior, interest, practice 9 treatment 10 convention, employment, experience

use: try 4 boot, duty, hire, vail, wont 5 apply, avail, guide, habit, right, spend, stead, treat, trope, usage, value, wield 6 behoof, custom, employ, expend, handle, hansel, occupy, target 7 benefit, consume, exhaust, exploit, utility, utilize 8 accustom, deal with, exercise, frequent, function, handling, practice 9 habituate, privilege, treatment 10 employment, fall back on, manipulate 11 application, consumption, utilization
   as example: 4 cite
   refrain from: 7 boycott
   to be of: 5 avail
   up: eat 4 tire 5 drain, spend 7 consume, deplete, exhaust, outwear
   wastefully: 5 spill 7 fritter 8 squander 9 dissipate

used: 8 shopworn 10 secondhand 11 experienced

useful: 4 good 5 utile 7 helpful, thrifty 8 practical 10 beneficial, commodious, profitable 11 serviceable 12 advantageous

usefulness: 5 avail, value 6 profit 7 utility

useless: 4 idle, null, vain 6 futile, otiose 7 inutile 8 bootless, hopeless 9 fruitless, worthless 11 ineffectual, inefficient, superfluous 12 unprofitable 13 impracticable, unserviceable 14 good-for-nothing

user: 6 addict 7 pothead 8 consumer

usher: 4 lead, page 5 guide 6 beadle, escort, herald 7 chobdar, conduct, officer, precede, preface, servant, teacher 9 announcer, assistant, attendant, harbinger, introduce, precursor 10 doorkeeper, forerunner, inaugurate
   in: 6 launch 9 introduce 10 inaugurate

usings: 8 property 10 belongings

U.S.S.R.: See **Union of Soviet Socialist Republics**

usual: 4 rife 6 common, normal, wonted 7 average, chronic, general, regular, routine, typical 8 familiar, frequent, habitual, ordinary, orthodox 9 customary 10 accustomed, prevailing 11 stereotyped 12 conventional

usurer: 5 shark 6 loaner 9 loan shark 11 moneylender

usurp: 4 take 5 seize, wrest 6 assume 8 accroach, arrogate

usury: 7 gombeen

Utah: *canyon:* 5 Bryce

capital: 12 Salt Lake City
city: 4 Orem 5 Logan, Ogden, Provo 6 Murray
county: 4 Juab 5 Cache, Davis, Wayne, Weber 6 Uintah
highest peak: 5 Kings
Indian: Ute
lake: 4 Swan, Utah 6 Sevier 9 Great Salt
motto: 8 Industry
mountain range: 5 Uinta
national park: 4 Zion
nickname: 6 Mormon 7 Beehive
people: 6 Mormon
plateau: 7 Wasatch
river: 5 Grand, Green, Weber 6 Jordan, Sevier 8 Colorado
state bird: 7 seagull
state flower: 8 sego lily
state tree: 6 spruce
town: 4 Lehi 5 Delta, Heber, Kanab 6 Beaver, Eureka, Payson, Tooele 7 Milford

utensil: pan, pot, wok 4 tool 5 sieve 6 grater, vessel 7 skillet 8 strainer 9 colander, implement 10 instrument
   cleaning: mop 5 broom, brush 6 Hoover, ramrod, vacuum 7 Bissell, sweeper

Uther's son: 10 King Arthur

utile: 6 useful 9 practical 10 profitable 12 advantageous

utilitarian: 5 plain 6 useful 8 economic 9 practical, realistic 10 functional 12 matter-of-fact

utility: use 5 avail 6 profit 7 benefit, service

utilize: use 6 employ, enlist 7 consume, exploit, harness, husband 9 economize

utmost: end 4 best, last 5 final 7 extreme, maximum 8 farthest, greatest 9 uttermost

Uto-Aztecan Indian: 4 Pima 7 Nahuatl 8 Shoshone

Utopia: 4 Eden 9 Shangri La
   author: 4 More
   Harrington's: 6 Oceana

Utopian: 5 ideal 8 idealist, Quixotic 9 visionary 10 chimerical

utricle: sac 7 vesicle

Uttar Pradesh: *capital:* 7 Lucknow
   country: 5 India

utter: add, say 4 blat, bray, dang, darn, emit, gasp, pipe, pray, rail, roar, tell, vent 5 blurt, clack, croak, drawl, final, issue, mince, sheer, speak, spill, spout, stark, state, total, trill, voice 6 assert, direct, entire, mumble, reveal, warble 7 bluster, deliver, divulge, enounce, express, extreme, iterate, publish 8 abnormal, absolute, complete, disclose 9 downright, enunciate, out-and-out, pronounce 10 articulate, peremptory 11 unqualified 13 unconditional

utterance: gab 4 osse, word 5 aside, dicta,
   ditty 6 dictum, oracle, speech 7 calling
   8 effusion, monotone, phonesis, rhapsody 9 phonation 10 expression, forthgoing 12 articulation, vocalization
   soft: 6 breath, murmur 7 whisper
   voiced: 6 sonant
   voiceless: 4 surd 7 spirate
uttered: 4 oral 6 spoken
utterly: all 4 well 5 fully, stark 6 in toto,
   merely 7 totally 8 entirely 10 absolutely, allutterly, completely 11 diametrally
   13 diametrically 17 straightforwardly
uttermost: 5 final 6 utmost 7 extreme,
   outmost
utu: 6 reward 12 compensation, satisfaction
uva: 5 fruit, grape
uxorial: 6 wifely
Uzbek: *capital:* 8 Tashkent
   country: 4 USSR

V

V: vee 4 five
   symbol of: 7 victory
V-shaped piece: 5 wedge
vacancy: gap 5 break, chasm, space 6
   cavity, hollow 7 interim, vacuity 10
   hollowness, interstice 11 vacuousness
vacant: 4 free, idle, open, void 5 blank,
   empty, fishy, inane, silly 6 barren, devoid, hollow, lonely 7 foolish, lacking,
   leisure, vacuous, wanting 8 unfilled 9
   destitute 10 disengaged, unemployed,
   unoccupied, untenanted 12 unencumbered, unreflecting 14 expressionless
vacate: 4 quit, void 5 annul, avoid, clear,
   empty, leave 6 repeal 7 abandon, abolish, rescind 8 abdicate, abrogate, evacuate
vacation: 4 rest 5 leave, spell 6 outing,
   recess 7 holiday, leisure, nonterm, respite, time off 8 furlough 9 justitium
   12 intermission
   place: spa 4 city, lake, park 5 beach,
   ocean 6 forest, resort 7 seaside 9
   mountains
vaccinate: 9 inoculate
vaccination: *inventor:* 6 Jenner
vaccine: 4 sera, shot 5 serum
   discoverer of: 4 Salk 6 Jenner
vacillate: 4 sway 5 dally, waver 6 dacker,
   daiker, dawdle, seesaw, teeter, totter 7
   flutter, stagger 8 hesitate, titubate 9
   fluctuate, hem and haw, oscillate
vacillation: 5 doubt 7 halting, swaying 8
   wavering 9 faltering, hesitancy, infirmity 10 fickleness, indecision, unsureness
11 uncertainty 12 irresolution 13 dillydal-
   lying 14 changeableness
vacuity: 4 hole, void 6 hollow 7 inanity,
   vacancy 11 nothingness
vacuous: 4 dull, idle 5 blank, empty 6
   stupid 8 unfilled 9 evacuated, senseless
   11 purposeless 13 unintelligent
vacuum: 4 void 5 space 9 emptiness
   opposite of: 6 plenum
vacuum pump: 10 pulsometer
vacuum tube: 5 diode 7 tetrode 9 electrode
vade mecum: 6 manual 8 handbook
vadimonium: 4 bond 6 pledge 8 bail-
   ment, contract, security
vadium: 4 bail, pawn 6 pledge
vagabond: bum 4 rove 5 scamp, stray,
   tramp 6 beggar, canter, jockey, rascal,
   rogue, wander 7 erratic, gadling, nomadic, vagrant, wayward 8 bohemian,
   brodyaga, drifting, fugitive, wanderer 9
   itinerate, shiftless, straggler, wandering, worthless 10 blackguard, ne'er-do-
   well 11 bindle stiff 12 hallanshaker 14
   good-for-nothing
vagarious: 5 kinky 7 erratic 9 arbitrary
   13 unpredictable
vagary: 4 roam, whim 5 caper, fancy,
   freak, jaunt, prank, quirk, stray, trick,
   waver 6 action, breach, notion, oddity,
   ramble, totter, whimsy 7 caprice, conceit 8 flagarie, rambling 9 departure,
   excursion, procedure, wandering 10 digression, divergence 12 passing fancy
   13 manifestation

vagrant: See **vagabond**

vague: dim 4 dark, hazy 5 faint, loose, misty, stray 6 bleary, blurry, dreamy, vagary 7 obscure, shadowy, sketchy, unfixed, vagrant 8 confused, nebulous, vagabond, wanderer 9 ambiguous, uncertain, unsettled, wandering 10 ill-defined, indefinite, indistinct, intangible 13 indeterminate

vail: tip, use 4 doff, dole 5 bribe, lower, yield 6 humble, submit 7 benefit, subside 8 gratuity 9 advantage 10 beneficial

vain: 4 idle 5 empty, flory, petty, proud, silly 6 flimsy, futile, hollow, otiose, snooty 7 foolish, foppish, stuckup, trivial, useless 8 gorgeous, hopeless, ignorant, nugatory, peacocky 9 conceited, fruitless, worthless 10 chimerical, evanescent, unavailing, unrewarded 11 empty-headed, ineffectual, overweening, unimportant 12 unprofitable, vainglorious

vain boasting: 11 fanfaronade

vain person: fop 5 dandy 7 coxcomb

vainglorious: 8 boastful, insolent 9 conceited

vair: fur

Vaishnavas: *deity:* 6 Vishnu
priest: 6 gosain, gusain

Vaisya caste: 6 Aroras

vakass: 5 amice

valance: 5 drape 6 pelmet 7 curtain, drapery, hanging

vale: 4 dale, dean, dell, dene, glen 5 bache, combe, glade 8 dingle, valley 8 farewell

valediction: 5 adieu 7 address, good-bye 8 farewell

Valence's river: 5 Rhone

valence: 5 power, value 7 atomism 10 importance

valentine: 4 card, gift, love 8 greeting 10 sweetheart

valerian: 4 drug 5 plant 7 allheal, panacea, setwall

valet: man 4 goad 5 stick 6 andrew, tartar 7 dresser 9 attendant, cameriere, chamberer 10 manservant

Vali's parents: 4 Odin, Rind 5 Rindr

valiant: 4 bold, prow 5 aught, brave, proud, stout 6 heroic, robust, strong, sturdy 7 doughty 8 galliard, intrepid, powerful, stalwart, vigorous, virtuous 9 bounteous, excellent, steadfast 10 chivalrous, courageous 11 meritorious 12 stouthearted

valid: 4 good, just, true 5 legal, solid, sound 6 cogent, lawful, robust, strong 7 binding, healthy, telling, weighty 8 forcible, powerful 9 authentic, effective, efficient 10 conclusive, convincing, sufficient 11 efficacious 12 satisfactory, well-grounded

opposite of: 4 null, void

validate: 7 confirm 9 establish 11 rubber-stamp

valise: bag 4 case, grip 7 baggage, satchel 8 suitcase

valium: 4 drug 12 tranquilizer

Valjean: *pursuer:* 6 Javert
friend: 6 Marius
protege: 7 Cosette

Valkyrie: 6 maiden 8 Brynhild 10 Brunnhilde

vallecula: 6 furrow, groove 7 channel 10 depression

Valletta people: 7 Maltese

valley: dip 4 brae, comb, coom, cove, dale, dean, dell, dene, ghyl, gill, glen, rill, vale, wadi, wady 5 atrio, basin, combe, coomb, dhoon, glack, gorge, goyal, goyle, gully, kloof, swale, waddy 6 bolson, canada, canyon, clough, coombe, coulee, dingle, gutter, hollow, ravine, rincon, strath, trough 7 blowout 10 depression

between volcanic cones: 5 atrio

deep: 5 canon 6 canyon

vallum: 4 wall 7 rampart

valor, valour: 4 guts, sand 5 arete, merit, value, worth 6 bounty, spirit, virtue 7 bravery, courage, heroism, prowess 8 position 9 valuation 10 importance 11 distinction 12 fearlessness

valuable: 4 dear 5 asset 6 costly, prized, useful, worthy 8 precious 9 estimable, excellent, expensive, respected, treasured 10 worthwhile 11 serviceable

valuable discovery: 4 find

value: use 4 cost, feck(Sc.), rate 5 avail, cheap, price, prize, worth 6 assess, assize, esteem, extend, moment 7 account, apprise, apprize, care for, cherish, compute, opinion, quality, respect, utility 8 appraise, estimate, evaluate, treasure 9 inventory, valuation 10 appreciate, estimation, importance

anything of little: 5 plack(Sc.) 6 trifle

equal: 6 parity

full: 11 money's worth

mathematical limit of: 8 derivate

mean: 7 average

net: 7 reserve

nominal: par

reduction: 12 depreciation

relative: 9 ad valorem

without: 5 waste 6 trashy 7 useless 9 worthless

valve: tap 4 cock, gate 6 faucet, outlet, piston, spigot 7 petcock

heart: 6 mitral 8 bicuspid

sliding: 6 piston

vamoose: lam 4 scat 5 leave, scram 6 decamp, depart, get out

vamp: 4 hose, mend, plod, sock 5 fix up,

flirt, patch, tramp 6 invent, repair, seduce 7 beguile, concoct, fireman 8 contrive 9 fabricate, improvise

vampire: bat 5 lamia 6 alukah, corpse, usurer 7 seducer 11 blackmailer, bloodsucker, extortioner 12 extortionist

famous: 7 Dracula

van: fan 4 fore, lead, wing 5 front, truck, wagon 6 shovel, summit, winnow 7 fourgon, vehicle 9 forefront

Van Gogh town: 5 Arles

vandal: hun 6 looter 7 hoodlum, ruffian, wrecker 8 hooligan 9 plunderer

vandalize: mar 6 deface, rip off 7 destroy

Vandyke: 5 beard 6 artist 7 picture

vane: arm 5 blade 7 feather 9 indicator 11 weathercock

feather: web 8 vexillum

vanguard: 9 forefront 10 avantgarde

vanilla: 5 bland 7 extract

vanilla substance: 8 coumarin

vanish: 4 fade, melt 5 clear 8 disperse, evanesce 9 disappear

vanity (see also **vain**): 4 airs 5 pride 6 egoism 7 compact, conceit, egotism, falsity, foppery 8 futility, idleness 9 dizziness, emptiness 10 hollowness 11 fatuousness, foolishness, self-conceit

symbol of: 7 peacock

vanity case: 4 etui 7 compact

Vanity Fair: *author:* 9 Thackeray

character: 10 Becky Sharp

vanquish: get, win 4 beat, best, rout 5 expel, floor 6 defeat, expugn, humble, master, subdue 7 confute, conquer, subvert 8 confound, overcome, suppress, surmount 9 overthrow

vanquisher: 6 victor 8 champion

vantage: See **advantage**

vapid: dry 4 dull, flat, pall, weak 5 inane, stale, trite 7 insipid, mawkish 8 lifeless 9 milk-toast, pointless, tasteless 10 flavorless, spiritless, unanimated, unexciting 13 uninteresting

vapor: fog, gas 4 fume, haze, idea, mist 5 boast, brume, cloud, ewder, fancy, humor, smoke, steam 6 breath, bubble, humour, nimbus, notion 7 halitus 8 contrail, humidity, phantasm 9 evaporate 10 blustering 11 braggadocio

frozen: 4 hail, rime, snow 5 frost, sleet

pressure indicator: 9 tonometer

vaporize: 5 steam 7 boil off 9 evaporate

vaporous: 4 hazy 8 fleeting, volatile 13 unsubstantial

vaquero: 6 cowboy 8 herdsman, horseman 10 equestrian

varec, varech: 4 kelp 5 ashes, wrack 7 seaweed

variable (see also **vary**): 6 fickle, fitful 7 mutable, protean, unequal, variant, varying 8 floating, unstable, unsteady 9 irregular, uncertain 10 capricious, changeable, inconstant

variance (see also **vary**): 7 discord, dispute 10 contention, difference 11 discrepancy

variation (see also **vary**): 8 heterism, mutation 9 tolerance 10 aberration, deflection 11 distinction

varicose: 7 dilated, swollen 8 enlarged

varied: 6 daedal 7 several 13 miscellaneous

variegated: 4 pied, shot 5 lyard(Sc.), lyart(Sc.) 6 daedal, menald, motley, varied 7 dappled, flecked, mottled, painted, piebald, tissued 8 speckled 9 different, enamelled 11 diversified

variety: 4 kind, sort, type 5 breed, class 7 species 9 diversity, variation 10 assortment, difference

variola: 6 cowpox 8 horsepox, smallpox

various: 4 many 6 divers, sundry 7 certain, diverse, several 8 distinct, manifold, variable 9 different, uncertain, versatile 10 changeable, inconstant

varlet: boy 4 page 5 gippo, knave, noble, youth 6 menial, rabble, rascal, vassal 7 bailiff, footman, servant 8 coistrel, coistril 9 attendant, scoundrel

varnish: 4 spar 5 japan 7 lacquer 8 brighten, palliate 9 embellish

ingredient: lac 5 copal, elemi, resin, rosin 6 dammar

vary: 4 part 5 alter, range, shift 6 change, depart, differ, divide, modify, swerve 7 deviate, dispute, dissent, diverge, qualify, quarrel, variate 8 disagree, modulate, separate 9 alternate, diversify, fluctuate, oscillate

vas: 4 duct 6 pledge, surety, vessel

vase: jar, urn 4 asci, olla, vaso 5 ascus, askos, echea, tazza 6 crater, deinoi, deinos, krater 7 amphora, urceole 8 lekythose 10 cassolette, jardiniere

handle: 4 ansa

vasectomy: 13 sterilization

vassal: man 4 bond, esne, lend, rule, serf 5 ceile, helot, liege, slave 6 geneat, varlet 7 bondman, feedman, feodary, homager, peasant, servant, servile, subject 8 dominate 9 dependent, feudatory 11 beneficiary, subordinate

pert. to: 6 feudal

vast: 4 huge 5 ample, broad, great, large, vasty 6 cosmic, lonely, mighty, untold 7 immense 8 colossal, enormous, farflung, gigantic, spacious 9 boundless, capacious, cyclopean, extensive 11 farreaching, illimitable

vastness: 7 expanse 8 enormity, grandeur 9 magnitude

vat (see also **barrel, tub, vessel**): bac, fat, pit, tub, tun, wit 4 back, beck, cask, coom, gyle, keel, kier, tank 5 coomb, keeve, kieve, press 6 barrel, kettle, vessel 7 caldron, chessel, cistern 8 cauldron, chessart

bleaching: 4 kier

cheese: 7 chessel

vatic: 8 inspired, oracular 9 prophetic

Vatican: *basilica:* 8 St. Peter's

chapel: 7 Sistine

guards' nationality: 5 Swiss

official: 6 datary

palace: 7 Lateran

ruler: 4 Pope

site: 4 Rome

vaticinate: 5 augur 7 predict 8 foretell

vaudeville: 5 revue

act: 4 skit, song, turn 5 dance

vaudevillian: 5 actor 6 dancer, hoofer, singer 7 acrobat, juggler 9 performer

vaudy: gay 5 gaudy, showy 6 elated, sturdy 8 cheerful

vault: box, pit 4 arch, bend, cave, cope, dome, jump, leap, over, roof, room, safe, soar, tomb 5 bound, clear, croft, crypt, curve, floor, groin, mount, shade 6 cavern, cellar, crater, cupola, curvet, flaunt, grotto, hurdle, spring, welkin 7 ceiling, chamber, dungeon, glorify, testudo 8 flourish 9 concavity, staircase 10 depository, repository, testudines(pl.)

vaunt: van 4 brag, font 5 boast, roose 6 avaunt 7 display, exhibit, show off 11 ostentation

veal: 4 calf, meat, veau(F.)

cutlet: 9 schnitzel

larded: 8 fricando 10 fricandeau

shank: 8 osso buco

vector: 4 host 7 carrier 8 gradient

opposite of: 6 scalar

vedette: 5 vigil, watch 8 sentinel

Vedic: *artisans of gods:* 6 Ribhus

cosmic order: 4 Rita

fire god: 4 Agni

god: 6 Aditya

hymn: 6 mantra

language: 4 Pali 8 Sanskrit

sky serpent: ahi

sun god: 7 Savitar

text: 5 Sakha, Shaka

veer: yaw 4 slue, sway, turn 5 alter, shift 6 broach, career, change, depart, swerve 8 deviate, digress 8 angle off 9 fluctuate

veery: 6 thrush

vega: 5 tract 6 meadow

Vega's constellation: 4 Lyra

vegetable: pea, yam 4 bean, beet, corn, kale, leek, ocra, okra, soya 5 onion, plant 6 carrot, celery, lentil, pepper, radish, squash, tomato, turnip 7 brocoli, cabbage, lettuce, parsley, parsnip,

peascod, rhubarb, spinach 8 broccoli, cucumber, eggplant, peascod, rutabaga 9 artichoke 11 cauliflower 14 Brussels sprout

dealer: 8 huckster 11 greengrocer 12 costermonger

decayed: 4 duff 5 humus

dish: 6 zimmis 10 chiffonade

exudation: lac, sap 5 resin

ferment: 5 yeast

green: 5 sabzi

onionlike: 4 leek 7 shallot

pepsin: 6 caroid

pod: 4 hull 8 peasecod

purple: 8 eggplant

salad: 4 leek 5 chard 6 endive 7 cabbage, lettuce, romaine, shallot 8 scallion

sponge: 5 loofa, luffa 6 loofah

spread: 4 oleo 9 margarine

stunted: 5 scrub

vegetable caterpillar: 5 aweto

vegetable pear: 7 chayote

vegetate: 4 idle 8 languish, stagnate 9 hibernate

vegetation: 6 growth 7 verdure

floating: 4 sadd, sudd 8 pleuston

god: 4 Atys, Esus 5 Attis

vegete: 6 lively 7 healthy 11 flourishing

vehement: hot 4 wild 5 angry, eager, fiery, hefty, irked, rabid, yeder 6 ardent, fervid, flashy, heated, raging, urgent 7 animose, animous, fervent, furioso, furious, intense, violent 8 emphatic, forceful, vigorous 9 impetuous, pronounced 10 boisterous, passionate

vehicle (see also **aircraft, ship**): ark, bus, car, van 4 auto, shay, taxi, tool, wain 5 araba, brake, break, buggy, dilly, means, sedan, sulky, wagon 6 barrow, charet, device, hansom, landau, troika, vector 7 chariot, kibitka(Russ.), tallyho 8 carriage, charette 9 buckboard, implement, velociman 10 automobile, conveyance

army: 4 jeep, tank 9 ambulance

child's: 4 pram 5 buggy 6 walker 7 scooter 8 carriage, stroller, tricycle 10 velocipede

display: 5 float

hauling: van 4 dray, lory, sled 5 truck 7 tractor, trailer

parade: 5 float

passenger: bus, cab 4 hack, taxi, tram 5 train 6 hansom 7 minibus, omnibus, tramcar, trolley 9 charabanc

public: bus, cab, car 4 taxi, tram 5 train 7 omnibus, ricksha 8 rickshaw 10 jinricksha, jinrikisha

snow: 4 pung, sled 6 sleigh

two-wheeled: 4 cart 5 sulky, tonga 6 cisium 7 bicycle, caleche 9 carromata (Fil.) 11 vinaigrette *wheelless:* 4 ship, sled 6 cutter, sledge, sleigh

veil: dim 4 caul, film, hide, mask 5 cloak, cover, orale, velum, volet 6 bumble, enfold fannel, masque, screen, shroud, soften 7 conceal, cover up, curtain, secrete, watcher 8 calyptra, disguise, headrail 11 amphithyron

in botany: 9 velum

Moslem: 7 yashmak

veiling: 5 tulle, voile 6 purdah 7 curtain 10 obvelation

vein: bed, rib 4 dash, hilo, hint, lode, mood, seam, tang, tone, vena, wave 5 costa, crack, scrin, shade, smack, spice, style, tinge, touch, trend, venae 6 cavity, costae, manner, nature, strain, streak 7 bonanza, channel, crevice, fashion, fissure, stratum 8 tendency 9 character 11 inclination, variegation

arrangement of: 9 neuration

enlarged: 5 varix

fluid: 4 icor 5 blood, ichor

inflammation: 9 phlebitis

leaf: rib 5 costa

mining: 4 lode

pert. to: 6 veinal, venous

small: 6 venule

throat: 7 jugular

veinstone: 6 gangue, matrix 9 lodestuff

velamen: 5 velum 8 membrane

velar: 7 palatal 8 guttural

velarium: 8 awning 9 covering

veldt, veld: 6 meadow, plains 9 grassland

velitation: 5 brush, run-in 7 contest, dispute 8 skirmish 9 encounter

velleity: 4 hope, will, wish 6 desire 8 volition 11 inclination

vellicate: nip 4 jerk, pull 5 pinch, pluck 6 fidget, tickle, twitch 9 titillate

velocious: 4 fast 6 speedy

velocipede: 4 bike 7 bicycle, dicycle 8 tricycle 11 quadricycle

velocity: 4 pace 5 speed 7 headway, impetus 8 celerity, rapidity 9 quickness, swiftness

instrument: 11 cinemograph

velum: 4 veil 6 awning, palate 8 membrane

velutinous: 7 velvety

velvet: 4 gain 5 drink 6 birodo(Jap.), profit 7 surplus 8 winnings

fabric like: 6 panne 6 velour, velure

velvetbreast: 9 merganser

velvet dock: 6 mullen 7 mullein 10 elecampane

venal: 6 venous 7 corrupt, crooked, salable 8 infamous, saleable, vendible 9 mercenary

vend: 4 hawk, sell 5 utter 6 market, peddle 7 declare, publish 8 transfer

vendetta: 4 feud

vendeuse: 9 salesgirl 10 saleswoman

vendible: 5 venal 7 salable 8 saleable 9 mercenary 10 marketable

vendition: 4 sale

vendor, vender: 5 seller 7 alienor, butcher, peddler 8 merchant, salesman

vendue: 4 sale 7 auction

veneer: lac 4 coat, face, mask, show 5 glaze, gloss, layer, plate 6 enamel, facing 7 overlay 8 palliate

venerable: old 4 aged, hoar, sage 5 hoary 6 august 7 ancient, antique, classic 8 honorable

veneration: awe 4 fear 6 esteem 7 respect, worship 8 devotion, idolatry 9 adoration, reverence

of saints and angels: 5 dulia

venerer: 6 hunter 8 huntsman

venery: 5 chase 7 coition, hunting

Venetian: See Italy, Venice

Venezuela: *capital:* 7 Caracas

city: 7 Cabimas 8 Valencia 9 Maracaibo

coin: 4 real 5 medio 6 fuerte 7 bolivar, centimo 8 morocota 10 venezolano

dam: 4 Guri

fiber: 5 erizo

gulf: 5 Paria

Indian: 6 Timote

island: 9 Margarita

lake: 7 Valencia 9 Maracaibo, Tacarigua

language: 4 Pume 7 Spanish

liberator: 7 Bolivar

measure: 5 galon, milla 6 fanega 7 estadel

measure of weight: bag 5 libra

monetary unit: 7 bolivar

mountain: 5 Andes, Icutu 6 Concha, Cuneva, Parima 7 Imutaca, Roraima

people: 5 Carib 6 Timote 7 Timotex 8 Guarauno

plain: 5 llano

port: 8 La Guaira, La Guayra 9 Maracaibo 13 Ciudad Bolivar, Puerto-Cabello

revolutionist: 7 Miranda

river: 4 Meta 5 Apure, Caura 6 Arausa, Caroni 7 Orinoco, Ventuar

snake: 4 lora

state: 4 Lara 5 Apure, Sucre, Zulia 6 Aragua, Falcon, Merida, Zamora 7 Bolivar, Cojedes, Guarico, Monagas, Tachira, Yaracuy 8 Carabobo, Trujillo

town: 4 Aroa, Coro 6 Atures, Cumana, Merida 7 Barinas, Guaware, Maracay, Maturin

tree: 6 balata

vengeance: 5 wrack 6 wanion 7 revenge 8 reprisal, requital 10 punishment 11 retaliation, retribution

god of: 6 Erinys 7 Alastor

goddess of: Ara, Ate 7 Nemesis

venial: 7 trivial 9 allowable, excusable, tolerable 10 forgivable, pardonable 13 insignificant

Venice: *beach:* 4 Lido

boat: 7 gondola 9 bucentaur

bridge: 6 Rialto

coin: 5 betso, bezzo, ducat 6 sequin 8 bagatino, gazzetta

court: 8 quaranty

district: 6 Rialto

island: 6 Rialto 8 San Marco 9 San Giorgio

magistrate: 4 doge

medal: 5 osela, osele 6 osella, oselle 7 oscella

old silver coin: 5 betso

painter: 6 Titian 7 Bellini 8 Veronese 9 Giorgione 10 Tintoretto

resort: 4 Lido

river: 6 Brenta

traveler and writer: 5 Conti 9 Marco Polo

wine measure: 6 anfora

Venice of the North: 9 Stockholm

venin: 6 poison

venireman: 5 juror

venison: 4 deer

venomous: 5 snaky, toxic 6 attern, deadly 7 baleful, baneful, noxious 8 poisoned, spiteful, virulent 9 malicious, malignant, poisonous, rancorous 11 mischievous

vent: 4 draw, emit, exit, hole, slit 5 brand, eject 6 go into, outlet 7 cast out, express, fissure, opening, release 8 aperture, disgorge, emission 9 discharge, embrasure 10 escapement, expression

ventilate: air, fan 6 aerate, aerify, broach, winnow 8 talk over 9 broadcast, oxygenate

ventilation: 6 aerage 9 breathing 10 conference

ventilator: 6 blinds, funnel, louver 8 airshaft

ventral: 7 sternal

ventriloquist: 12 engastrimyth 13 gastriloquist

venture: hap, try 4 dare, face, luck, risk, wage 5 brave, essay, stake 6 chance, danger, feeler, gamble, hazard 7 attempt, courage, flutter, fortune, risking 8 trespass 9 adventure, speculate 10 enterprise 11 contingency, presumption, speculation, undertaking

venturesome: 4 bold, rash 5 hardy, risky 6 heroic 8 fearless, heedless, reckless 9 audacious, dangerous, foolhardy, hazardous, venturous 11 adventurous, furthersome, temerarious

venue: hit 4 bout, site 5 lunge, match, onset, place 6 coming, ground, locale, thrust 7 arrival, assault 9 encounter

Venus (see also Aphrodite): 6 Hesper, planet, Vesper 8 Hesperus

as morning star: 7 Lucifer

girdle: 6 cestus

island: 5 Melos

mother: 5 Dione

son: 5 Cupid

sweetheart: 6 Adonis

tree sacred to: 6 myrtle

Venus flytrap: 5 plant 7 dionaea 10 swamp plant

venust: 6 comely 7 elegant 8 graceful 9 beautiful

veracious: 4 true 6 direct 8 truthful 9 measuring, veridical

veracity: 5 truth 6 gospel, truism 7 honesty 8 accuracy, trueness 9 judgement, precision, sincerity 11 correctness 12 faithfulness, truthfulness

veranda: 5 lanai, porch, stoop 6 loggia, piazza 7 gallery, portico

verb: *auxiliary:* can, had, has, may, was 4 hast, have, must, will 5 might, shall, shalt, would

form: 5 tense

table: 8 paradigm

tense: 4 past 6 aorist 7 present 11 conditional

verbal: 4 oral 5 wordy 7 verbose 9 talkative 10 articulate

verbatim: 6 orally 7 literal 8 verbally 11 word for word

verbena: 4 tree 5 plant 7 aloysia, lantana

verbiage: 4 talk 7 chatter, diction, fustian, wording 9 verbosity, wordiness 10 redundancy 11 purple prose

verbose: 5 windy, wordy 6 prolix 7 diffuse 9 redundant 10 long-winded 11 tautologous

verboten: 4 tabu 5 taboo 6 banned 9 forbidden 10 prohibited

verdant: raw 5 fresh, green 6 grassy 8 immature, innocent 13 inexperienced 15 unsophisticated

Verdi: *opera:* 4 Aida 6 Ernani, Otello 7 Othello 8 Falstaff, Traviata 9 Rigoletto 9 Trovatore

verdict: 4 word 6 ruling 7 finding, opinion 8 decision, judgment

verdigris: 4 rust 6 aerugo

Verdun river: 5 Meuse

verdure: 4 odor 5 scent, smell 6 flavor 7 foliage 8 greenery, strength, tapestry, tartness 9 freshness, greenness

verecund: shy 6 modest 7 bashful

Verein: 7 society 11 association 12 organization

verge: lip, rim, rod 4 edge, tend, twig, wand 5 bound, brink, limit, marge, range, scope, shaft, staff, stick, watch 6 border, margin, point 7 incline, touch on, virgate 8 approach, boundary, yardland 9 extremity, threshold, timepiece 13 circumference

verger: 4 dean 6 garden 7 justice, orchard 8 official 9 attendant

Vergil: See **Virgil**
veridical: 4 real, true 7 genuine 8 accurate, truthful 9 veracious 12 truthtelling
verification: 5 proof 7 checkup 8 averment 12 confirmation 14 authentication
verify: 4 aver, back, test 5 audit, check, prove 6 affirm, ratify, second 7 certify, collate, confirm, support 8 maintain 9 establish 11 certificate 12 authenticate, substantiate
verily: yea 4 amen, even 5 parde, pardi, pardy, truly 6 certes, indeed, pardie, really 9 certainly 11 confidently
verisimilitude: 5 color, truth 10 likelihood 11 probability
veritable: 4 real, true 6 actual, gospel, honest 7 factual, genuine 9 authentic, veracious
verity: 8 veracity 12 faithfulness
verjuice: 7 acidity 8 sourness, tartness
vermiform: 4 long, thin 7 sinuous, slender 8 wormlike 10 vermicular
vermifuge: 4 drug 12 anthelmintic
vermilion: red 8 cinnabar
vermin: 4 lice, mice, rats 5 filth, fleas, flies 7 bedbugs, rodents, weasels
verminous: 5 dirty 6 filthy 7 noxious 9 offensive
Vermont: *capital:* 10 Montpelier
  city: 5 Barre 7 Rutland 10 Bennington, Burlington, Montpelier 11 Brattleboro
  county: 5 Essex 6 Orange 7 Addison, Windsor 8 Lamoille
  explorer: 9 Champlain
  highest peak: 11 Mt. Mansfield
  island: 5 Grand 7 LaMotte 9 North Hero
  lake: 7 Caspian, Dunmore, Seymour 9 Champlain
  motto: 15 Freedom and Unity
  mountain range: 5 Green 7 Taconic
  nickname: 13 Great Mountain
  river: 8 Lamoille, Poultney, Winooski 10 Otter Creek
  ski resort: 5 Stowe 9 Sugarbush
  state bird: 6 thrush
  state flower: 6 clover
  state tree: 5 maple
vernacular: 4 cant 5 argot, idiom, lingo 6 jargon, patois 7 dialect
vernal: 4 mild, warm 5 fresh, young 6 spring 8 youthful 10 springlike
Verne: *character:* 4 Fogg (Phileas), Nemo 12 Passepartout
  submarine: 8 Nautilus
verneuk: 5 cheat 6 humbug 7 swindle
versatile: 5 handy 6 mobile 7 flexile 8 flexible, variable 9 all-around, many-sided 10 changeable, reversible
verse (see also **poem**)**:** 4 turn 5 meter, stave, stich 6 stanza 7 revolve, stichos

8 consider 11 familiarize
  Bible: 4 text
  foot: 4 iamb
  pert. to: 6 poetic
  stress: 5 ictus
versed: 5 adept 6 beseen 7 abreast, erudite, learned, skilled 8 familiar 9 au courant, competent, practiced 10 acquainted, conversant, proficient 11 experienced
versifier: 4 poet 5 rimer 6 verser 7 poetess 9 poetaster
versify: 6 berime 7 berhyme
version: 7 account, edition, turning 9 rendition 10 conversion, paraphrase 11 translation 14 interpretation, transformation
versipel: 8 werewolf
versus: con 6 contra 7 against, vis-a-vis
vertebra: 4 axis, bone 7 spondyl
vertebrae: 4 back 5 spine
vertebrate: ray 7 animal 9 backboned
  class: 4 aves
  division: 6 somite
  feathered: 4 bird
  group: 9 amnionata
vertex: top 4 apex 6 apogee, summit, tiptop, zenith 11 culmination
vertical: 4 acme 5 apeak, erect, plumb, sheer 6 abrupt, height, summit, vertex 7 upright 9 up-and-down 10 straight-up 13 perpendicular
verticil: 5 whorl
vertiginous: 5 dizzy, giddy 6 rotary 8 rotating, spinning, unstable, whirling 9 dizziness, giddiness, revolving 10 inconstant 11 vacillating
vertigo: 6 megrim 9 dizziness, giddiness
verve: pep 4 dash, elan, fire, zest 5 ardor, gusto, vigor 6 bounce, spirit, talent 7 ability 8 aptitude, vivacity 9 animation 10 enthusiasm, resiliency
vervet: 6 monkey
very: too 4 bare, fell, mere, real, same, tres(F.), true, unco(Sc.) 5 assai(It.), molto(It.), truly, utter 6 actual, lawful, mighty, really 7 dimolto(It.), exactly, genuine, precise 8 absolute, complete, especial, peculiar, rightful, truthful 9 authentic, extremely, identical, precisely, veracious, veritable 10 legitimate, mortacious 11 exceedingly
  French: 4 tres
  German: 4 sehr
vesicle: sac 4 bleb, cell, cyst 5 bulla 6 cavity, vessel 7 bladder, blister, utricle
  air: 8 aerocyst
Vesper: 4 star 5 Venus 8 Hesperus
vespers: 6 prayer 7 service 8 ceremony, evensong
vessel (see also **aircraft, boat, container, pail, ship**)**:** can, cog, cup, jar, pan,

tub, urn, vas 4 bell, cadi, drum, duct, ewer, olla, olpe, tank, tube, vase 5 bocal, cadus, canoe, cogue, craft, cruse, laver, liner, paten 6 aftaba, aludel, barrel, cootie, crater, cutter, firkin, funnel, goblet, goulah, holmos, krater, patera, situla, yetlin 7 aleyard, blickey, blickie, cistern, cresset, gabbard, gabbart, paterae, pinnace, pitcher, situlae, steamer, utensil, yetling 8 aiguiere, ciborium 9 alcarraza 10 receptacle

anatomical: vas 4 vasa(pl.), vein 6 artery

assaying: 5 cupel

drinking: cup, mug 4 toby 5 flask, glass, gourd, jorum, stein, stoup 6 dipper, flagon, seidel 7 tankard, tumbler 8 schooner

earthen: 5 crock

oil: 5 cruse, cruet

pert. to: 5 vasal

sacred: ama, pix, pyx

small: nog 4 pony, shot 6 dinghy, jigger, noggin,

wooden: soe 5 cogue, skeel 6 barrel, piggin

vest: 4 robe 5 dress, endow, gilet 6 accrue, clothe, jacket, jerkin, linder, weskit 7 furnish, garment 9 waistcoat 10 undershirt

Vesta: 5 match 6 Hestia

vestal: nun 4 pure 6 chaste, virgin

vestibule: 4 hall 5 entry, foyer, lobby, porch 7 chamber, narthex, passage 8 anteroom, entrance, vestible 10 antechapel

vestige: bit 4 mark, path, sign 5 relic, scrap, shred, smack, trace, track, umbra 8 footstep, tincture 9 vestigium

vesture: 4 garb 5 dress 8 clothing

vestment (see also **dress**): 4 garb, gear, gown, hood, robe 5 cotta, dress, orale 6 chimer, chimre, gloves, rochet, tippet 7 cassock, garment, sandals 8 cincture, clothing, covering 10 habiliment

ecclesiastical: alb, cap 4 alba, cope 5 albae, amice, ephod, fanon, miter, orale, stole 6 lappet, palium, saccos 7 cassock, maniple, tunicle 8 chasuble, dalmatic, surplice

pert. to: 8 vestiary

vestry: 4 room 7 meeting 8 sacristy

vesture: 4 corn 5 cover, crops, grass 6 clothe, seizin 7 apparel, envelop, raiment, stubble, wrapper 8 garments, vestment 9 underwood 11 investiture

vesuvian: 5 fusee, match 8 volcanic

vetch: ers 4 akra, tare, weed 5 fetch 7 arvejon

bitter: ers 5 ervil

veteran: old 7 oldster 8 old-timer, seasoned 9 practiced 10 past master 11 experienced

veterinarian: 7 farrier 12 animal doctor

vetiver: 5 grass 6 cuscus 8 khuskhus

veto: nix 4 kill 6 forbid 7 message 8 disallow, document, negative, overrule, prohibit 11 disapproval, forbiddance, prohibition 12 interdiction

vettura: 5 coach 8 carriage

veuve: 4 bird 5 widow 6 whydah

vex: ire, irk, tew 4 cark, chaw, fret, fuss, gall, miff, rile, roil, toss 5 anger, annoy, chafe, harry, shake, spite, tease, worry, wrack 6 bother, cumber, harass, madden, molest, nettle, offend, plague, pother, ruffle 7 afflict, agitate, discuss, dispute, disturb, perplex, provoke, torment, trouble 8 disquiet, irritate, vexation 9 annoyance, displease, infuriate 11 disturbance

vexation: 5 pique, thorn 7 fatigue 9 annoyance, weariness 13 mortification

vexatious: 4 chaw, sore 5 pesky 8 annoying, cumbrous, frampoid, untoward 9 disturbed, pestilent 10 afflictive 11 contrarious, troublesome

vexed: 5 sorry 7 grieved

vexillum: web 4 flag, vane 6 banner 8 standard

via: way 4 road 5 right 7 by way of, passage, through 9 by means of

viable: 6 doable 8 feasible, possible, workable 11 practicable

viaduct: 6 bridge 7 trestle

vial: 5 ampul, cruet, phial 6 bottle, caster, vessel 7 ampoule

viand: 4 fare, food 6 edible 7 aliment 8 victuals 10 provisions

choice: 4 cate

viaticum: 5 money 8 supplies 9 allowance 10 provisions

viator: 8 traveler, wayfarer

Viaud's pen name: 5 Loti

vibrant: 5 alive, ringy 8 resonant, sonorous, vigorous 9 vibrating

vibrate: jar, wag 4 beat, cast, dirl, rock, whir 5 pulse, quake, shake, swing, throb, throw, trill, waver, whirr 6 dindle, launch, quaver, quiver, shimmy, shiver, thrill 7 agitate, resound, tremble 8 brandish, flichter(Sc.), resonate 9 fluctuate, oscillate, vacillate

vibration: 4 dirl(Sc.), tirl(Sc.) 5 thirl(Sc.) 6 dingle, quaver, quiver, thrill, tremor 7 flutter 8 fremitus, stirring 9 trembling 11 oscillation, vacillation

musical: 5 trill 7 sonance, tremolo, vibrato 8 overtone

point without: 4 node

vicar: 5 proxy 6 deputy, priest 8 minister 9 clergyman 10 substitute, vicegerent

assistant: 6 curate

of christ: 4 Pope

Vicar of Wakefield author: 9 Goldsmith

vicarage: 4 dues 5 house 6 salary, tithes 8 benefice 9 household, pastorate, rectorate, residence

vice: sin 4 evil, grip, hold, turn 5 crime, fault, force, grasp, place, proxy, stead, taint 6 defect 7 blemish, failing, squeeze, stopper 8 iniquity, stairway 9 deformity, depravity 10 corruption, immorality, wickedness 11 harmfulness, viciousness 12 imperfection

Vice President (U.S.): 4 Burr, Ford, King 5 Adams, Agnew, Dawes, Gerry, Nixon, Tyler 6 Arthur, Colfax, Curtis, Dallas, Garner, Hamlin, Hobart, Morton, Truman, Wilson 7 Barkley, Calhoun, Clinton, Johnson, Sherman, Wallace, Wheeler 8 Coolidge, Fillmore, Marshall, Tompkins, Van Buren 9 Fairbanks, Hendricks, Jefferson, Roosevelt, Stevenson 11 Rockefeller 12 Breckinridge

Adams, J.: 9 Jefferson
Adams, J.Q.: 7 Calhoun
Arthur: none
Buchanan: 12 Breckinridge
Carter: 7 Mondale
Cleveland: 9 Hendricks(1), Stevenson(2)
Coolidge: 5 Dawes
Eisenhower: 5 Nixon
Fillmore: none
Ford: 11 Rockefeller
Garfield: 6 Arthur
Grant: 6 Colfax(1), Wilson(2)
Harding: 8 Coolidge
Harrison, B.: 9 Morton
Harrison, W.H.: 5 Tyler
Hayes: 7 Wheeler
Hoover: 6 Curtis
Jackson: 7 Calhoun(1) 8 Van Buren(2)
Jefferson: 4 Burr(1) 7 Clinton(2)
Johnson, A.: none
Johnson, L.B.: 8 Humphrey
Kennedy: 7 Johnson
Lincoln: 6 Hamlin(1) 7 Johnson(2)
Madison: 5 Gerry(2) 7 Clinton(1)
McKinley: 6 Hobart(1) 9 Roosevelt(2)
Monroe: 8 Tompkins
Nixon: 4 Ford(2) 5 Agnew(1)
Pierce: 4 King
Polk: 6 Dallas
Reagan: 4 Bush
Roosevelt, F.D.: 6 Garner(1), Truman(3) 7 Wallace(2)
Roosevelt, T.: 9 Fairbanks
Taft: 7 Sherman
Taylor: 8 Fillmore
Truman: 7 Barkley
Tyler: none
Van Buren: 7 Johnson
Washington: 5 Adams
Wilson: 8 Marshall

viceroy: 5 nabob, nazim 6 exarch, satrap 7 khedive, provost 8 governor 9 butterfly

vice versa: 5 again 10 conversely

vicinity: 6 region 8 locality, nearness 9 proximity 11 propinquity, resemblance 12 neighborhood

vicious: bad, ill 4 evil, foul, lewd, mean, vile 5 wrong 6 faulty, savage, severe, wicked 7 corrupt, immoral, intense, noxious 8 debasing, depraved, infamous, spiteful 9 dangerous, defective, dissolute, malicious, malignant, nefarious, perverted 10 corrupting, iniquitous, villainous

vicissitude: 6 change 8 mutation, reversal 10 difficulty, revolution, succession 11 alternation, interchange

victim: 4 dupe, fool, goat, gull, prey 6 sucker 8 easy mark, offering, underdog 9 sacrifice
list: 4 toll

victor: 6 captor, master, winner 7 conquer 8 bangster, unbeaten 9 conqueror 10 vanquisher, victorious

victory: win 7 mastery, success, triumph 8 conquest 9 landslide, supremacy 11 superiority
celebrating: 9 epinician
crown: bay 6 laurel
easy: 6 breeze
goddess: 4 Nike
memorial: 4 arch 6 spoils, trophy
ruinous: 7 Pyrrhic
sign: vee
song: 9 epinicion
symbol: 4 palm 5 scalp 6 trophy
unexpected: 5 upset

Victory heroine: 4 Lena

victrola: 9 turntable 10 phonograph 12 record player

victualler: 6 sutler 9 innkeeper

victuals: bit 4 bite, chow, eats, food, grub, meat 6 viands 7 vittles 11 comestibles, nourishment

videlicet: viz 5 to wit 6 namely 8 scilicet

vie: bet, run 4 cope 5 bandy, rival, stake, wager 6 endure, hazard, oppose, strive 7 compete, contend, contest, emulate 8 panorama, prospect, struggle 9 challenge

Vienna: 4 Wien
palace: 10 Schonbrunn
park: 6 Prater

Vietnam (See also North Vietnam and South Vietnam): *capital:* 5 Hanoi
city: Hue 6 Da Nang 8 Haiphong, Nha Trang 13 Ho Chi Minh City (formerly Saigon)
Communist leader: 9 Ho Chi Minh
former division: 5 North, South
French defeated at: 11 Dien Bien Phu
independence movement: 8 Vietminh

monetary unit: 4 dong

region: 5 Annam 6 Tonkin 11 Cochin-China

river: Red 6 Mekong

view: aim, eye, ken, see, vue(F.) 4 goal, look, scan 5 aview, scape, scene, sight, slant, tenet, vista, watch 6 admire, apercu(F.), aspect, behold, belief, object, regard, sketch, survey, vision 7 concept, examine, inspect, observe, opinion, picture, profile, summary, thought, witness 8 attitude, consider, panorama, prospect, scrutiny, synopsis 9 apprehend 10 appearance, inspection, perception, photograph, scrutinize, standpoint 11 contemplate, examination, expectation 13 contemplation

extended: 8 panorama

mentally: 8 envision

obstruct: 4 hide 7 conceal

open to: 4 bare 5 overt 6 expose

pleasing: 6 eyeful

viewer: 9 spectator 11 eyewitness, stereoscope

viewing instrument: 5 scope 9 telescope 10 binoculars

viewy: 5 showy 8 fanciful 9 visionary 11 spectacular, unpractical 12 ostentatious

vigil: eve 4 wake 5 guard 7 lookout, prayers, service 8 devotion, watchman

vigilant: 4 agog, wary 5 alert, awake, aware 7 careful, wakeful 8 cautious, watchful 9 attentive, observant, sharp-eyed, sleepless, wide-awake 11 circumspect, on one's guard

vigilant person: 5 Argus

vigilantes: 5 posse

vigneron: 10 winegrower 13 viticulturist

vignette: 5 scene 6 sketch 7 picture

vigor, vigour: pep, vim, vir(Sc.), vis 4 bang, birr, zeal 5 drive, flush, force, nerve, power 6 energy, foison, growth, health, spirit 7 impetus, potency, stamina 8 activity, boldness, strength, virility, vitality 9 animation, fraicheur, hardihood, intensity, vehemence 10 get-up-and-go, invigorate

deprive of: sap 6 deaden 8 enervate

lose: fag, sag 4 fail, flag, pine 6 weaken 7 decline

period of: 6 heyday

vigoroso: 8 vigorous 9 direction, energetic

vigorous: yep 4 able, cant, fell, hale, spry, yepe 5 eager, frank, hardy, hefty, lusty 6 florid, hearty, lively, robust, rugged, strong, sturdy 7 cordial 8 athletic, muscular 9 effective, energetic, strenuous 11 efficacious, hard-hitting 13 rough-and-ready

Viking: 4 Dane, Eric 5 rover 6 pirate 8 Norseman, Northman 12 Scandinavian

vile: bad, low 4 base, evil, foul, mean 5 cheap, lowly, nasty 6 abject, coarse, drasty, filthy, impure, odious, sinful, sordid, wicked 7 bestial, carrion, corrupt, debased, ignoble, unclean, vicious 8 baseborn, befouled, depraved 9 abandoned, degrading, loathsome, nefarious, obnoxious, offensive, repulsive, worthless 10 abominable, despicable, disgusting, flagitious 12 contaminated

vileness: 6 fedity 9 turpitude

vilify: 5 abuse, avile, libel 6 bemean, berate, debase, defame, malign, revile, slight 7 asperse, blacken, cheapen, debauch, degrade, despise, detract, slander, traduce 8 belittle, disgrace, dishonor, mistreat, reproach, vilipend 9 blaspheme, disparage 10 calumniate, depreciate

villa: 5 aldea, dacha(Russ.), house 6 castle, estate 8 villakin 9 residence, villaette 10 villanette

village: gav, mir(Russ.), rew(Sc.) 4 burg, dorp, home, stad(African), town, vici 5 aldea, bourg, kraal, thorp, vicus 6 bustee, castle, hamlet, pueblo, thorpe 7 borough, caserio(Sp.), endship 8 bourgade 9 aldeament 10 settlement 11 aggregation 12 municipality

villain: 4 boor, heel, Iago, lout, serf 5 churl, demon, devil, heavy, knave, rogue, scamp 6 rascal 8 scelerat 9 miscreant, scoundrel 10 blackguard, villainous

mythological: 4 ogre 5 giant 6 dragon

nemesis of: 4 hero

villainous: bad, low 4 base, evil, mean, vile 6 common, slight, vulgar, wicked 7 boorish, vicious 8 clownish, criminal, depraved, flagrant, wretched 9 dastardly, dissolute, felonious 10 detestable, flagitious, iniquitous, outrageous 12 disagreeable 13 objectionable

villainy: 5 crime 7 knavery 9 depravity

villatic: 5 rural 6 rustic

villein: 4 carl, serf 5 ceorl, churl 7 bondsman, cottier

vim: zip 4 gimp, kick, push 5 force, vigor 6 energy, ginger, pepper, spirit 8 strength

vina: 10 instrument

vinaigrette: box 5 sauce 6 bottle 7 vehicle 8 carriage

vincible: 11 conquerable 12 surmountable

vinculum: tie 4 band, bond 5 brace, union 6 frenum

vindicate: 4 free 5 clear 6 acquit, assert, avenge, defend, excuse, uphold 7 absolve, bear out, deliver, justify, propugn, revenge, support, sustain 8 advocate, maintain, plead for 9 exculpate, exonerate

vindication: 7 apology

vindictive: 7 hostile 8 punitive, spiteful, vengeful 10 revengeful 11 retaliatory, retributive

vine: hop, ivy 4 akas, bine, gogo, odal, soma 5 betel, buaze, bwazi, guaco, liana, liane 6 maypop 7 creeper, cupseed, trailer 8 clematis 9 grapevine 10 chilicothe

covered with: 5 ivied 7 lianaed

fruit-bearing: 5 grape 7 cupseed

parasite: 5 aphid, aphis

twining: 4 bine

vinegar: vim 4 acid 5 eisel 6 acetum, alegar, eisell 8 vinaigre(F.)

bottle: 5 cruet

dregs: 6 mother

ester: 7 acetate

pert. to: 6 acetic

preserve in: 6 pickle

salt: 7 acetate

spice: 8 tarragon

vinegary: 4 sour 7 acetose, crabbed 9 unamiable 11 ill-tempered 12 cantankerous

vineyard: cru

protector: 7 Priapus

vinous: 4 winy 9 vinaceous

vintage: 4 crop, wine 5 cuvee, yield 6 demode, classic 7 antique 12 old-fashioned

vintner: 8 merchant

viol: 5 gigue, rebec 6 fiddle, rebeck, vielle 7 quinton 9 violaalta

progenitor: 7 rebec

violate: err, sin 4 flaw, rape 5 abuse, break, force, harry, spoil, wrong 6 betray, broach, defile, defoil, defoul, injure, insult, invade, offend, ravage, ravish 7 corrupt, debauch, disturb, falsify, outrage, pollute, profane 8 deflower, dishonor, infringe, mistreat, trespass 9 constrain, desecrate, disregard 10 contravene, transgress

violation: 5 crime, error 6 breach 10 infraction 11 delinquency, profanation 13 nonobservance

sentence structure: 11 anacoluthon

violence: 4 fury 5 ardor, force 6 bensel, bensil, fervor, frenzy, hubris, hybris 7 assault, bensail, bensall, bensell, outrage 8 ferocity, foul play 9 bloodshed 11 desecration, profanation 12 infringement

violent: 4 high, loud 5 acute, fiery, great, heady, heavy, hefty, rabid, rough, sharp, vivid 6 fierce, mighty, raging, savage, severe, stormy, strong 7 extreme, furious, hotspur, intense, rammish 8 flagrant, forceful, forcible, frenetic, vehe-

ment 9 atrocious, explosive, impetuous, phrenetic, turbulent 10 headstrong, hotspurred, immoderate, inordinate, passionate, tumultuous 11 tempestuous

violently: 4 hard 5 amain 8 like fury, slambang

violet: 5 mauve 6 blaver, flower, purple

perfume: 5 irone

violet root: 5 orris 6 iridin

violet tip: 9 butterfly

violin: kit 4 alto, bass 5 Amati, cello, Rocta, Strad 6 fiddle 7 Cremona 8 Guarneri 10 Guadagnini, Guarnerius, Stradivari 11 violincello 12 Stradivarius

city: 7 Cremona

direction: 4 arco 9 pizzicato

forerunner: 5 rabab

part: peg 4 hole, neck 6 string 7 eclisse

rare: 5 Amati, Strad 10 Guarnerius

violin-shaped: 7 waisted

violinist (first): 13 concertmaster 14 concertmeister

comic: 5 Benny

fabled: 4 Nero

famous: 4 Auer 5 Elman, Stern, Ysaye 7 Heifetz, Milstein, Menuhin 8 Kreisler, Spalding 9 Zimbalist

V.I.P.: 4 lion 6 bigwig 7 big shot, notable

viper: asp 5 adder, snake 8 cerastes 10 bushmaster, copperhead, fer-de-lance 11 rattlesnake

genus of: 5 echis

viperish: 8 spiteful, venomous 9 malicious

virago: 5 harpy, randy, scold, vixen, woman 6 Amazon, beldam, callet 7 beldame 8 fishwife 9 brimstone, termagant

vireo: 7 grasset 8 greenlet, songbird

Virgil: 9 Roman poet

birthplace: 6 Mantua

character: 5 Amata, Damon 7 Corydon

family name: 4 Maro

friend: 8 Maecenas

hero: 6 Aeneas

language: 5 Latin

poem: 4 epic 6 Aeneid

queen: 4 Dido

virgin: new 4 maid, pure 5 first, fresh 6 chaste, intact, maiden, modest, vestal 7 initial 8 maidenly, spinster 9 unalloyed, undefiled, unsubdued, unsullied, untouched 10 uncaptured 11 undisturbed 12 uncultivated, unfertilized 13 unadulterated

Virgin Islands (of U.S.): 6 St. John 7 St. Croix 8 St. Thomas

Virgin Mary: *flower:* 7 cowslip 8 marigold

image: 5 Pieta

Virgin Queen: 10 Elizabeth I

virginal: 6 spinet 11 harpsichord

Virginia: *aristocracy:* FFV
capital: 8 Richmond
city: 7 Hampton, Norfolk 8 Richmond 10 Chesapeake 11 Newport News
colonist: 7 Fairfax
county: 4 Bath 5 Bland, Floyd 7 Bedford, Fairfax, Henrico 9 Arlington
estuary: 12 Hampton Roads
highest point: 8 Mt. Rogers
Indian: 6 Tutelo 7 Monacan 8 Powhatan
lake: 7 Claytor 8 Drummond 13 Smith Mountain
motto: 17 Sic semper tyrannis
mountain: 9 Allegheny, Blue Ridge
mountain range: 11 Appalachian
national park: 10 Shenandoah
nickname: 11 Old Dominion
river: Dan 5 James 9 Potomac, Rapidan, Roanoke 9 Shenandoah
state bird: 8 cardinal
state flower: 7 dogwood
state tree: 7 dogwood
surrender site: 8 Yorktown 10 Appomattox
swamp: 6 Dismal
town: 5 Luray 8 Danville
Virginia creeper: ivy 5 plant 8 woodbine 10 ampelopsis
Virginia goat's rue: 6 catgut
Virginia snakeroot: 7 sangrel 9 birthwort 11 sangree-root
Virginia willow: iva 4 itea
Virginian author: 6 Wister
virgularian: 6 searod
viridity: 5 youth 7 verdure 8 verdance 9 freshness, greenness 10 liveliness
virile: 4 male 5 manly 6 potent, robust 7 lustful 8 forceful, powerful, vigorous 9 masculine, masterful
virose: 5 fetid 6 virulent 9 poisonous 10 malodorous
virtu: 5 curio 7 antique
virtually: 6 almost, nearly 7 morally, totally 8 in effect 9 in essence 11 practically
virtue: 4 thew 5 arete, grace, piety, power 6 bounty, purity 7 probity, quality 8 chastity, efficacy, goodness, morality 9 rectitude, excellence 11 uprightness 13 righteousness
cardinal: 4 hope 5 faith 7 charity, justice 8 prudence 9 fortitude 10 temperance
paragon of: 5 saint
virtuoso: 4 whiz 6 expert, savant 7 scholar 8 aesthete, esthetic 10 dilettante, empiricist 11 connoisseur, philosopher 12 professional
virtuous: 4 good, pure 5 brave, moral 6 chaste, honest, potent 7 goddard, thrifty, upright, valiant 8 valorous 9 effective, righteous 11 efficacious, industrious

virulent: 5 acrid, rabid 6 bitter, deadly, potent 7 cutting, hateful, hostile, noxious 8 spiteful, venomous 9 festering, injurious, malignant, poisonous 10 infectious 12 antagonistic
virus: 5 taint, venom 6 poison 8 acrimony 10 corruption
vis: 5 force, power, vigor 7 potency 8 strength
vis-a-vis: 4 seat, sofa 6 versus 7 against 8 carriage, opposite 9 tete-a-tete 10 face to face
visage: 4 face, look, show 5 image 6 aspect 8 features, portrait 9 semblance 10 appearance, expression 11 countenance
viscera: 4 guts 6 vitals 8 entrails 10 intestines
visceral: gut 5 inner 9 intuitive 11 instinctive
viscid: 7 viscous
viscount: 4 peer 6 deputy 7 sheriff 8 nobleman
viscous: 4 limy, ropy, sizy 5 gobby, gummy, tarry, thick, tough 6 mucous, sirupy, sticky, viscid 7 stringy 8 adhering, sticking 9 glutinous, semisolid, tenacious
vise: 5 clamp, winch
part: jaw
Vishnu: *bearer:* 6 Garuda
consort: Sri 7 Lakshmi
epithet: 8 Bhagavat
incarnation: 4 Rama 6 avatar 7 Krishna 8 Balarama 11 Ramachandra
serpent: 4 Naga
visible: 4 seen 6 extant 7 evident, glaring, obvious 8 apparent, manifest 9 available 11 conspicuous, discernible, perceivable, perceptible
Visigoth king: 6 Alaric
vision: eye 5 dream, fancy, image, sight, think 6 beauty, seeing 7 fantasy, imagine 9 nightmare 10 apparition, revelation
defect: 6 anopia, myopia 14 metamorphopsae, metamorphopsia
double: 8 diplopia
illusory: 6 mirage
instrument of: 6 retina
lacking in: 8 purblind
measuring device: 9 optometer
pertaining to: 5 optic 6 ocular, visual
without: 5 blind
visionary: fey 4 aery, airy, wild 5 ideal, lofty, noble 6 unreal 7 dreamer, fantast, laputan, utopian 8 delusive, idealist, quixotic, romantic 9 fantastic, imaginary 10 chimerical, ideologist 11 imaginative, impractical, speculative
visit: gam, see, vis 4 call, chat, hawk, slum, stay 5 apply, haunt 6 assail, at-

tend, avenge 7 afflict, ceilidh(Sc.), inflict, sojourn 8 converse 10 inspection, visitation 12 conversation

visitation: 5 trial 7 calvary 8 disaster 9 migration 10 affliction

visitor: 5 guest 6 caller 7 company

vison: 4 mink

visor: 4 bill, peak 8 eyeshade

vista: 4 view 5 scene 7 outlook 8 long view, panorama, prospect

Vistula tributary: Bug, San

visual: 5 optic 6 ocular, scopic 7 optical, visible 11 perceptible

visualize: 5 think 6 ideate 7 foresee, imagine, picture 8 envisage 13 conceptualize

vita: 4 life 9 biography

Vita Nuova author: 5 Dante

vital: 4 live 5 basic, chief, fatal 6 deadly, lively, living, needed, souled, viable 7 animate, capital, exigent, supreme 8 integral, vigorous 9 breathing, elemental, energetic, essential, important, necessary, requisite 10 imperative 11 fundamental 13 indispensable

vital fluid: sap 5 blood, lymph

vital signs: 5 pulse 11 respiration, temperature

vitality: sap, vim 5 vigor 6 foison

vitalize: 5 pep up 7 animate 8 activate 11 put life into

vitals: 7 viscera

vitamin: 6 citrin, niacin 7 choline 8 ascorbic, carotene, inositol, thiamine 10 calciferol, pyridoxine, riboflavin, tocopherol

vitellus: 4 yolk 7 egg yolk

vitiate: 5 pical, spoil, taint 6 debase, faulty, impair, impure, injure, poison, weaken 7 abolish, corrupt, deprave, envenom, pervert, pollute 9 defective 10 adulterate, invalidate, neutralize 11 contaminate

viticulturist: 8 vigneron 9 winegrower

vitrella: 11 retinophore

vitrify: 5 glaze

vitrine: 8 showcase

vitriol: 4 acid, sory 5 venom 7 caustic

vitriolic: 5 sharp 6 biting, bitter 7 caustic 8 scathing, virulent 9 sarcastic

vituperate: 4 rail 5 abuse, curse, scold 6 berate, revile, rip into 7 censure, chew out 8 lambaste

vituperative: 7 abusive 8 critical 10 scurrilous 11 opprobrious

vivacious: gay 4 airy 5 brisk, merry 6 active, breezy, lively, vivace(It.) 7 buoyant, zestful 8 animated, cheerful, spirited, sportive 9 exuberant, long-lived, sprightly 12 lighthearted

vivacity: 4 fire, zeal 5 ardor, force, verve, vigor 6 esprit, gaiety, gayety 7 gayness, sparkle 9 longevity 10 liveliness

vivarium: box, zoo 4 cage 6 warren 9 enclosure

viva voce: 5 vocal 6 orally 11 word of mouth

vive: 5 brisk, vivid 6 lively, living 8 forcible, lifelike 9 perceived

vivid: 4 keen, live, rich 5 clear, fresh, sharp 6 active, bright, lively, living, strong 7 eidetic, flaming, glaring, glowing, graphic, intense 8 animated, colorful, distinct, dramatic, spirited, striking, vigorous 9 brilliant

vivificate: 7 quicken

vivify: 5 endue 6 revive 7 animate, enliven, quicken 10 give life to, invigorate

vivres: 9 foodstuff 10 provisions

vixen: fox, nag 4 fury 5 scold, shrew, woman 6 virago 9 termagant

viz: 5 to wit 6 namely 9 videlicet

vizard: 4 mask 5 guise, visor 8 disguise

vizcacha, viscacha: 6 rodent

vocabulary: 5 words 7 diction, lexicon 8 glossary, wordbook 10 dictionary 11 terminology

vocabulist: 13 lexicographer

vocal: 4 oral 5 vowel 9 outspoken, unwritten 10 articulate

vocalist: 4 alto 5 basso, tenor 6 artist, singer 7 soprano 8 baritone, songster 9 performer 10 coloratura

vocalization: 6 speech 7 diction 11 melismatics

vocation: 4 call 5 trade 6 career 7 calling, mission, summons 8 business 9 following 10 employment, occupation, profession

vociferate: cry 4 bawl, call, roar 5 shout, utter 6 assert, bellow, clamor, holler 7 clamour

vociferous: 4 loud 5 noisy 7 blatant 8 brawling, strident 9 turbulent 10 boisterous 11 loud-mouthed, openmouthed 12 obstreperous

voe: bay 5 creek, inlet

vogue: cut, ton(F.) 4 mode 5 style 6 bon ton, custom 7 fashion 8 practice 10 dernier cri, popularity

in: 4 chic 5 smart 10 prevailing

voice: say, vox(L.) 4 emit, voce(It.), vote, wish 5 rumor, say-so, speak, utter 6 choice, report, speech, steven, tongue 7 divulge, express, opinion 8 announce, falsetto, proclaim 9 utterance 10 articulate, expression

handicap: 4 lisp 7 stutter

loss of: 7 anaudia, aphonia

loud: 12 megalophonic 13 megalophonous

male: 4 bass 5 basso, tenor 8 baritone, barytone 12 countertenor

natural singing: 7 dipetto

pert. to: 5 vocal 8 phonetic

principal: 6 cantus

quality: 5 pitch 6 timbre

quiet: 5 sotto 7 whisper

sound: 5 vowel 6 symbol

stop: 9 affricate

stress: 5 arsis

voice box: 6 larynx

voiced: 4 oral 6 sonant, spoken 11 articulated

voiceless: mum 4 dumb, mute, surd 6 atonic, flated, silent 7 aphonic, spirate 8 aphonous 10 speechless

void: gap 4 free, hole, idle, lack, null, vain, want 5 abyss, annul, blank, drain, egest, eject, empty, leave, space 6 devoid, hollow, remove, vacant, vacate, vacuum 7 invalid, lacking, leisure, nullify, opening, useless, vacuity, wanting 8 evacuate, throw out 9 destitute, discharge, emptiness, frustrate 10 unemployed, unoccupied 11 ineffective, ineffectual

voila tout: 8 that's all

voile: 5 ninon

voir dire: 10 juror's oath

voiture: 5 wagon 8 carriage

volage: 5 giddy 6 fickle 7 flighty 8 fleeting

volant: 5 agile, light, quick 6 flying, nimble 7 flounce 8 volitant

volary: 4 cage 6 aviary 8 bird cage

volatile: 4 airy, bird 5 ether 6 fickle, figent, flying, lively, volage, volant 7 alcohol, ammonia, buoyant, elastic, essence, gaseous, volatic 8 fleeting, fugitive, vaporous 9 excitable, fugacious, transient 10 capricious, changeable, inconstant, transitory 11 hairbrained 12 lighthearted

volcano: Apo, Aso 4 Etna 5 Askja, Pelee 6 Ranier, Shasta 8 Cotopaxi, Krakatao, Krakatau, Mauna Loa, Vesuvius 9 Stromboli 10 Mt. St. Helens 12 Popocatepetl

matter: ash 4 lava, tufa 6 pumice, scoria

mud from: 5 salse

opening: 5 mouth 6 crater 8 fumarole

rock: 5 trass 6 dacite 8 tephrite

slag: 6 cinder, scoria

steam from: 5 stufa

vole: 6 craber, rodent

Volga: Rha

volition: 4 will 6 choice desire, option 13 determination

volley: 6 shower 7 barrage 8 blizzard, drumfire

volplane: 5 coast, glide

Volsunga Saga: *dragon:* 6 Fafnir

characters: 4 Atli 6 Sigurd 7 Gunther 8 Brunhild 9 Siegfried

Voltaire: *character:* 8 Pangloss

estate: 6 Ferney

novel: 5 Zadig 7 Candide

real name: 6 Arouet

volte face: 8 reversal 9 about-face

voluble: 4 glib 5 wordy 6 fickle, fluent 8 rotating, unstable 9 garrulous, revolving, talkative 11 changeable, loquacious

volume: 4 body, book, bulk, coil, mass, roll, tome, turn 6 amount, cubage, scroll 7 content 8 capacity, document, fullness, loudness, quantity, strength 9 aggregate 10 crassitude 11 convolution

large: 4 tome

measure: 11 stereometer

voluminous: 4 lush, many 5 bulky, large

Volund's brother: 4 Egil 5 Egill

voluntary: 4 free 6 freely 7 willful, willing 8 elective, optional, unforced 9 volunteer, willingly 10 deliberate, unimpelled 11 intentional, spontaneous 13 unconstrained

volunteer: 5 offer 6 enlist, worker 7 proffer

Volunteer State: 9 Tennessee

voluptuous: 4 lush 6 wanton 7 sensual 8 sensuous 9 luxurious 11 pleasurable

volute: 4 turn 5 whorl 6 cilery, scroll, spiral 7 cillery

volution: 4 coil, turn 5 twist, whorl 7 rolling 9 revolving 11 convolution

vomit: 4 barf, boke, bolk, puke, spew 5 braid, brake, reach, retch 6 emetic 7 throw up 8 disgorge 10 egurgitate 11 regurgitate

voodoo: obe, obi 5 Jonah, magic, obeah 6 fetish 7 bewitch 8 magician, sorcerer

charm: 4 mojo

voracious: 5 eager 6 greedy, hungry 8 esurient, ravening, ravenous 9 cormorant, rapacious 10 gargantuan, gluttonous, immoderate, insatiable

voracity: 7 edacity 10 greediness 12 ravenousness

vorago: 4 gulf 5 abyss, chasm

vortex: 4 apex, eddy, gyre 5 spout, whirl 6 spiral 7 tornado 9 waterpool, whirlpool, whirlwind 10 waterspout

votary: 5 freak 6 addict, zealot 7 amateur, devoted, devotee 8 adherent, follower, promised 10 enthusiast

vote: aye, con, nay, pro, vow, yes 4 anti, poll, wish 5 elect, grant 6 assign, ballot, choice, confer, prayer 7 declare, opinion 8 dedicate, suffrage 10 plebiscite, referendum

group: 4 bloc

method: 4 hand 5 proxy, straw, voice 6 ballot, secret 7 write-in 10 plebiscite, referendum

of assent: aye, nod, yea 6 placet

of dissent: nay

receptacle: 6 situla 7 situlae

right to: 8 suffrage 9 franchise

solicitation of, for bill: 5 lobby

voter: 6 poller 7 elector 8 balloter, chooser 11 constituent

kind: 8 absentee

illegal: 8 repeater, underage 11 nonresident

voters (body of): 10 electorate

vouch: vow 4 aver, back, bail, call, pray 6 affirm, allege, assure, attest, second, summon 7 certify, confirm, declare, resolve, support, warrant 8 accredit, maintain, sanction 9 assertion, establish, guarantee 11 attestation 12 authenticate

voucher: 4 chit 7 receipt 9 debenture, statement 10 credential

vouchsafe: 4 give 5 design, grant, yield 6 assure, bestow, beteem 7 concede 9 guarantee 10 condescend

voussoir: 5 wedge 8 keystone

projection: ear

vow: vum 4 bind, hote, oath, wish 5 swear 6 behest, devote, pledge, plight 7 behight, declare, promise 8 dedicate 9 assertion 10 consecrate, obligation 12 asseveration, supplication

dedicated by: 6 votive

vowel: 5 vocal 6 letter

contraction: 6 crases, crasis 9 diphthong

gradation: 6 ablaut

group of two: 6 digram 7 digraph

mark: 5 breve, tilde 6 umlaut 8 dieresis 10 circumflex

omission: 7 aphesis

sound: 6 dental, labial 7 palatal

unaspirated: 4 lene

vox: 5 voice

voyage: 4 tour, trip 6 cruise, travel 7 journey, passage, passing, project 8 proceeds 9 excursion 10 enterprise, expedition, pilgrimage 11 undertaking

voyageur: 7 boatman, trapper 8 traveler, woodsman

voyaging: 4 asea

vraic: 7 seaweed

vrouw: 4 frow 5 woman 8 mistress 9 housewife

vug, vugg, vugh: 6 cavity, hollow

Vulcan: 5 smith 10 blacksmith, Hephaestus

consort: 4 Maia 5 Venus

epithet: 8 Mulciber

parents: 4 Juno 7 Jupiter

son: 5 Cacus 8 Caeculus

workshop: 4 Etna

vulcanite: 7 ebonite

vulcanize: 4 burn, cure

vulgar: 4 base, lewd, rude 5 crude, gross 6 coarse, common, public, slangy 7 boorish, general, obscene, popular, profane 8 barbaric, churlish, ordinary 9 customary, earthbred, inelegant, unrefined

vulgarism: 4 cant 9 barbarism

vulgate: 6 patois 10 colloquial, vernacular

vulnerable: 6 liable 7 exposed 9 pregnable, untenable 10 assailable 11 defenseless, susceptible

point: 12 Achilles heel

vulpine: fox, sly 4 foxy 6 artful, clever, crafty, tricky 7 cunning 9 alopecoid

vulture: 4 papa 5 arend, grape, gripe, griph, urubu 6 condor, griphe 8 aasvogel, zopilote 9 gallinazo 11 lammergeier

W

waag: 6 grivet, monkey

wabble: See wobble

wabby: 4 loon

wabeno: 7 shaman 8 magician

wachna: cod 7 codfish

wacky, whacky: 5 crazy 6 insane, screwy 7 erratic, foolish 9 eccentric 10 irrational

wad: bat, gag, pad, ram 4 cram, heap, lead, line, lump, mass, plug, roll, tuft 5 crowd, money, stuff, trace, track, would 6 bundle, insert, pledge, wealth 7 fortune, stopper 8 bankroll, compress, graphite

of paper money: 4 roll

Wadai Muslim: 4 Maba

wadding: 4 hemp 5 kapok 6 cotton

waddle: 5 tread 6 hoddle, toddle, widdle 7 trample

waddy: peg 4 beat, cane, club 5 stick 6

attack, cowboy 7 rustler

wade: 4 ford, pass, plod 6 paddle 7 proceed 8 struggle

wader: 4 boot, coot, hern, ibis, rail 5 crane, heron, snipe, stork 6 jacana 9 sandpiper

wadi, wady: bed 4 wash 5 gully, oasis, river 6 ravine, stream, valley 7 channel 11 watercourse

wading bird: See bird: *wading*

wadset: 4 pawn 6 pledge 8 mortgage

wafer: 4 cake, disk, ring, seal, snap 5 close 6 fasten, matzoh 7 biscuit, cracker

container for: pix, pyx

waffle: 4 cake 6 babble 10 equivocate

waft: 4 blow, buoy, flag, gust, odor, puff, turn, wave, weft 5 carry, drift, float, gleam, sound, taste, whiff 6 beckon, breath, direct, propel, signal, wraith 7 glimpse, pennant 9 transport

wag: wit 4 card, move, stir, sway, zany 5 joker, leave, nudge, rogue, shake, swing 6 beckon, depart, signal 7 farceur, vibrate 8 brandish, flourish, humorist, jokester 9 comedian, oscillate, prankster

wage (see also **wager**): fee, pay, utu 4 hire, levy, pawn 5 bribe, fight, incur 6 employ, engage, reward, salary 7 attempt, conduct, contend, stipend 9 emolument 10 recompense 12 compensation

deduct: 4 dock

insurance: 7 chomage

wage earner: 6 worker 7 laborer 8 employee, mechanic 11 proletarian

wager: bet, bid, lay, vie 4 gage, risk 5 prize, sport, stake 6 gamble, hazard, parlay, pledge 7 venture

made in bad faith: 6 levant

waggery: 4 jest, joke 7 foolery 10 pleasantry 11 waggishness

waggish: 4 arch, pert 5 droll, merry, saucy 7 jesting, jocular, parlous, playful, roguish 8 humorous, sportive 10 frolicsome 11 mischievous

waggle: 4 sway 6 switch, waddle, wobble

Wagner: *character:* Eva 4 Elsa, Erda 5 Hagen, Senta, Wotan 8 Parsifal

father-in-law: 5 Liszt

opera: 6 Rienzi 9 Lohengrin 10 Tannhauser 12 Das Rheingold 15 Gotterdammerung

wife: 6 Cosima

wagon: bin, van 4 cart, dray, tram, wain 5 araba, aroba, dilly, gilly, lorry, lurry, tonga 6 camion, telega 7 caisson, chariot, fourgon, vehicle 8 carryall 12 perambulator

maker: 10 wainwright

part: 4 neap, pole, rave 5 thill 6 tongue

shaft: 5 thill

wagon-lit: 7 sleeper

wagonload: 5 cargo 6 fother

wah: 5 panda

wahine: 4 wife 5 woman 8 mistress 10 girl surfer, sweetheart

wahoo: elm 4 fish, peto, tree 8 nonsense, tommyrot 9 buckthorn, guarapucu

waif: 4 flag 5 stray 7 pennant, vagrant, wastrel 8 castaway, homeless, wanderer 9 foundling

wail: cry, wow 4 bawl, howl, moan, waul, weep, yarm 5 croon, mourn 6 bemoan, bewail, grieve, lament, plaint 7 deplore, ululate 8 complain 9 complaint 11 lamentation

wain: 4 cart 5 fetch, wagon 6 convey 7 chariot, vehicle

wainscot: 4 ceil, dado, line 6 lining 7 ceiling 8 paneling 10 wall lining

waist: 4 belt, wasp 5 shirt 6 basque, blouse, bodice, camisa, girdle 7 corsage 8 camisole 10 mid-section

circumference: 5 girth

waistband: obi 4 sash 6 girdle 8 ceinture, cincture

waistcoat: 4 vest 5 benjy, gilet 6 fecket, jacket, jerkin, weskit

wait: 4 bide, rest, stay, stop, tend 5 await, cater, court, dally, defer, delay, guard, serve, tarry, watch 6 ambush, attend, escort, expect, follow, harken, linger, remain 7 hautboy, hearken, observe 8 hesitate, inactive, postpone 9 accompany 10 anticipate, minister to 11 stick around 12 watchfulness

waiter: spy 4 tray 6 garcon, salver, server, vessel 7 messboy, messman, servant, steward, watcher 8 servitor, watchman, waylayer 9 attendant

waive: put 4 cast, turn 5 allow, cease, defer, forgo, grant, leave, swing, yield 6 desert, forego, refuse, reject, vacate 7 abandon, forbear, forsake, neglect 8 postpone 9 disregard 10 relinquish

waka: 5 canoe

wake: 4 call, stir, wauk(Sc.) 5 guard, revel, rouse, track, trail, vigil, waken, watch 6 arouse, awaken, excite, revive 7 passage

wakeful: 5 alert 8 restless, vigilant 9 sleepless

Walden author: 7 Thoreau

Waldensian: 7 Leonist

wale: rib 4 best, flog, mark, pick, weal, welt 5 ridge, wheal 6 choice, choose, select, streak, strip 7 timber 8 choicest

Wales (see also **Welsh**): 5 Cymru 7 Cambria

bard: 5 ovate

boat: 7 coracle

capital: 7 Cardiff

city: 6 Amlweh, Bangor 7 Rhondda, Swansea 8 Hereford, Holyhead, Pem-

broke 9 Carnarvon, Worcester
cheese: 10 Caer-philly
county: 5 Clwyd, Dyfed, Gwent
deity: 4 Bran 5 Dylan
dog: 5 corgi
emblem: 4 leek
fine: 6 saraad
island: 8 Anglesey
lake: 4 Bala
language: 6 Cymric, Kymric 7 Cymraeg
law: 7 galanas
legendary prince: 5 Madoc
marriage fee: 6 amober
measure: 5 cover 7 cantred, cantref, les-
   trad, listred 8 crannock
mountain: 6 Berwyn 7 Snowdon 8 Cambrian
musical instrument: 7 pibcorn
patron saint: 5 David
people: 5 Cymry, Kymry
person: 5 Taffy 8 Welshman
poet: 5 Thomas
port: 7 Cardiff
river: Dee, Wye 4 Teme 5 Teifi 6 Conway, Severn
walk: mog, pad, wag 4 foot, gait, hike,
   hoof, limp, mall, pace, path, plod, ramp,
   reel, roam, roll, step, turn, wade 5 allee,
   amble, field, haunt, mince, scuff, stalk,
   stram, stray, strut, stump, trail, tramp,
   tread 6 airing, arcade, foot it, hobble,
   loiter, lumber, pasear, prance, ramble,
   resort, stride, stroll, toddle, totter,
   trapes, trudge, wander 7 alameda, saunter, shuffle, stretch, traipse 8 ambulate,
   frescade, traverse 9 esplanade, promenade, tilicetum 11 perambulate 12
   somnambulate 14 constitutional
a beat: 6 patrol
affectedly: 5 mince
inability to: 6 abasia
lamely: 5 limp
public: 4 mall 6 arcade 7 alameda 9 esplanade, promenade
reeling: 5 lurch
walk off: 5 leave 6 depart
walk off with: win 5 steal
walk-out: 6 strike
walk out on: 5 leave 6 desert 7 abandon
walkaway: 4 rout 7 victory
walker: 6 ganger 7 footman 8 stroller 10
   pedestrian
walking: 7 passant(her.) 8 ambulant 10
   ambulation 11 peripatetic
like a bear: 11 plantigrade
walking meter: 9 pedometer
walking stick: 4 cane 5 kebby, staff,
   stilt, waddy 6 kebbie
walkway: 4 path 7 catwalk, passage 8
   sidewalk
wall: bar 4 dike, ha-ha 5 fence, levee, redan, scarp 6 bailey, cashel, escarp, haw-

haw, paries, podium, septum 7 barrier,
   bastion, curtain, defense, enclose, parapet, rampart 9 barricade, enclosure, encompass, partition, revetment 13 fortification
bracket: 6 corbel, sconce
covering: 4 tile 5 cloth, paint, paper 8
   paneling 9 calcimine, draperies, kalsomine
dividing: 5 septa(pl.) 6 septum 9 partition
enclose within: 4 mure 6 immure
hanging: 5 arras
lining: 8 wainscot
masonry: 9 revetment
on: 5 mural
opening: 4 bole, door 6 window 7 scupper
ornament: 4 dado 6 mirror, plaque 7
   hanging, molding, picture, placque 8
   moulding, tapestry
part: 4 dado, pier 5 bahut, gable 6 coping,
   plinth 7 cornice
pert. to: 5 mural 8 parietal
plug: 6 outlet
protective: 7 parapet
up: 6 immure
wallaba tree: apa
wallaby: 8 kangaroo
wallah, walla: 5 agent, owner 6 fellow,
   master, person, worker 7 servant
wallet: bag, jag 4 jagg, pack, poke, sack 5
   purse, scrip 6 budget 8 billfold, knapsack 10 pocketbook
wallop: 4 beat, blow, flog, lick, whip,
   whop 6 defeat, impact, strike, thrash,
   thrill
walloping: 5 large 6 strong 8 enormous
wallow: pit 4 bask, fade, mire, roll 5 surge
   6 billow, grovel, hollow, trough, welter,
   wither 7 founder, stumble 8 flounder,
   kommetje 10 depression
wallowish: 4 flat 7 insipid
wallpaper measure: 4 bolt
walnut: 6 bannut
skin: 4 hull, zest 5 shell
walrus: 5 morse 6 mammal, seacat 8
   mustache 9 rosmarine
flock: pod
limb: 7 flipper
order: 5 bruta
tooth: 4 tusk
waltz: zip 5 dance, valse 6 breeze
kind of: 6 Boston, Vienna
wampum: 4 peag 5 beads, money, shells 7
   roanoke
wamus: 6 jacket 7 doublet 8 cardigan
wan: dim, one, sad 4 dark, fade, pale, sick,
   weak, worn 5 dusky, faint, livid 6 anemic, dismal, feeble, gloomy, pallid, pallor, peaked, sickly 7 ghastly, haggard,
   languid, wanness 8 paleness 9 bloodless, colorless, sorrowful, washed out 10
   lusterless

wand: rod 4 pole, twig 5 baton, shoot, staff, stick 6 switch 7 pointer, rhabdos, scepter, sceptre 8 caduceus 9 horsewhip
royal: 4 mace 7 scepter

wand-shaped: 7 virgate

wander: bat, err, gad 4 haik, hake, prog, rave, roam, roil, rove, wind 5 amble, drift, mooch, prowl, range, shift, stray 6 cruise, dander, depart, ramble, stroll, trapes, travel 7 deviate, digress, meander, saunter, traipse 8 divagate, straggle, traverse 11 peregrinate
aimlessly: gad 5 slosh, stray 7 meander traipse

wanderer: vag 4 Arab, waif 5 gypsy, nomad, rover 6 truant 7 migrant, pilgrim, vagrant 9 itinerant, meanderer 11 extravagant
religious: 6 palmer

wandering: 5 vagus(anat.) 6 astray, errant 7 devious, erratic, journey, odyssey 8 aberrant 9 aberrance, delirious, planetary 10 circuitous, incoherent 11 noctivagant, perambulant

wandering Jew: ivy 5 plant 7 zebrina 10 spiderwort

wanderlust: 8 nomadism 9 itchy-foot 12 restlessness

wane: ebb 4 fail, lack, sink, want 5 abate, decay, peter 6 absent, defect, repine 7 decline, dwindle, subside 8 decrease, diminish 10 defervesce
opposite of: wax

wang: 4 king 5 ruler 6 prince

wanga: 5 charm, spell 6 voodoo 7 philter, sorcery

wangle: 4 fake 5 shake 6 adjust, change, juggle, totter, wiggle 7 falsify, finagle, wriggle 8 contrive, engineer 9 extricate 10 manipulate

want: gap 4 hole, lack, lose, miss, mole, must, need, void, wish 5 crave, fault, ouglet 6 besoin, choose, dearth, desire, forget, hunger, penury 7 absence, beggary, blemish, craving, lacking, missing, poverty, require, straits, vacancy 8 exigency, scarcity, shortage 9 deficient, fall short, indigence, necessary, necessity, privation 10 deficiency, inadequacy 11 deprivation, destitution, requirement 12 difficulties

wanting: 4 less 5 minus, short 6 absent, devoid 7 without, witless 9 deficient 12 feeble-minded

wanton: gay 4 fast, lewd 5 cadgy, dally, frisk, merry, revel 6 frisky, frolic, giglet, harlot, lavish, trifle, unruly 7 fulsome, haggard, ill-bred, immoral, lustful, playful, sensual, wayward 8 arrogant, flagrant, inhumane, insolent, prodigal, spiteful, sportive, unchaste 9 dissolute, lecherous, luxuriant, luxurious, mali-

cious, merciless 10 capricious, effeminate, frolicsome, gratuitous, lascivious, licentious, prostitute, refractory, voluptuous 11 extravagant, mollycoddle 12 disregardful, supererogant, unmanageable, unrestrained 13 undisciplined, unjustifiable

wantwit: 4 fool 5 dunce

wap: 4 beat, bind, blow, whop, wrap 5 blast, fight, knock, storm, truss 6 bundle, strike 8 wrapping

wapiti: elk 4 deer, stag 8 wampoose

war: 4 feud 5 blitz, fight 6 battle, combat, strife 7 contend, crusade 8 struggle
alarm: 4 flap
club: 4 mace 5 nulla 6 nullah
fleet: 6 armada
god of: Ira, Tyr 4 Ares, Coel, Mars, Odin, Thor 5 Woden 6 Nergal
goddess: 4 Alea 5 Anath, Bella 6 Anunit, Ishtar 7 Bellona
instrument: 7 caltrap, caltrop 9 relocator
machine: ram 4 bomb, tank 6 rocket 7 missile 8 catapult
religious: 5 jehad, jihad 7 crusade
restriction: 8 blockade
trophy: 4 star 5 medal, scalp 6 ribbon
vehicle: 4 jeep, tank
vessel: sub 6 corvet 7 cruiser 8 corvette 9 destroyer, submarine 11 dreadnaught

War and Peace author: 7 Tolstoy

war chest: 8 treasury

war hawk: 5 jingo

war-horse: 5 steed 6 leader 7 charger, standby, veteran 8 partisan 10 campaigner, politician

warbird: 7 aviator, tanager 8 airplane

warble: 4 sing 5 carol, chant, chirl, shake, trill, yodel 6 melody 7 descant, twitter, vibrate

warbler: 4 wren 5 pipit, robin 6 singer, thrush 8 blackcap, grosbeak, redstart, songbird, songster 9 beccafico 10 bluethroat 11 whitethroat

ward: 4 care, jail, warn 5 guard, parry, watch 6 charge, defend, govern, prison, warden, warder 7 counsel, custody, defense, deflect, enclose, fortify, keeping, protege 8 district, garrison, guardian, watchman 9 safeguard 10 protection 11 confinement 12 guardianship 14 arrondissement(F.)
pert. to: 9 pupillary

ward off: end 4 fend 5 avert, guard, parry, repel 7 forfend, prevent

warden: 4 caid 5 guard, nazir 6 disdar, dizdar, jailer, keeper, ranger, regent, sexton 7 alcaide, alcayde, turnkey, viceroy 8 director, governor, guardian, overseer, watchman 9 castellan, concierge, constable, custodian 10 doorkeeper, gatekeeper, supervisor

warder (see also **warden**): 5 staff 7 bulwark 8 sentinel 9 caretaker, truncheon 10 stronghold

wardrobe: 4 room 5 privy, trunk 6 closet 7 apparel, armoire, bedroom, cabinet, chamber, clothes 8 costumes 9 garderobe 12 clothespress

ware: 4 host, sage, shun, wary, wise 5 avoid, aware, china, goods, ready, spend, stuff, waste 6 people, shrewd 7 careful, chaffer, heedful, pottery, prudent, seaweed 8 cautious, products, squander, vigilant 9 cognizant, commodity, porcelain

warehouse: 4 silo, stow 5 depot, etape, guard, store 6 fonduk, godown 7 almacen, fondouk, funduck, protect, shelter, storage 8 elevator, entrepot, magazine 10 storehouse 11 accommodate

fee: 7 storage

warfare: See war

warily (see also **wary**): 6 tiptoe 8 gingerly

warlike: 7 hostile, martial 8 militant, military 9 bellicose, Bellonian, soldierly 10 battalious, pugnacious 11 belligerent

warlock: 6 wizard 8 conjuror, magician, sorcerer 9 enchanter

warm (see also **hot**): 4 avid, beek, heat, keen, kind, mild 5 angry, brisk, calid, chafe, eager, fiery, fresh, tepid, toast 6 ardent, devout, genial, hearty, heated, kindly, lively, loving, strong, tender, toasty 7 affable, amorous, clement, cordial, earnest, enliven, excited, fervent, glowing, irksome, sincere, thermal, zealous 8 animated, friendly, generous, gracious, grateful, vehement, vigorous 9 harassing, irascible, irritated, sprightly, strenuous 10 overheated, passionate, responsive 11 sympathetic 12 affectionate, disagreeable, enthusiastic 13 uncomfortable

warmth: 4 elan, glow, heat, zeal, zest 6 spirit 7 passion

pert. to: 7 thermal

warn: tip 4 rede 5 alarm, alert 6 advise, exhort, inform, notify 7 apprise, apprize, caution, counsel 8 admonish, threaten 9 reprehend

warning: 4 omen 5 knell 6 alarum, beware, caveat, lesson, signal 7 caution, sematic 10 admonition 13 animadversion

sound of: 4 bell 5 alarm, siren 6 alarum, tocsin

warp: abb, end, hit, mud, wry 4 beat, bend, bias, cast, emit, hurl, kink, line, rope, silt, sway, turn, warf 5 eject, expel, fling, quirk, throw, twist 6 buckle, debase, deform, devise, fasten, swerve 7

contort, deflect, distort, falsify, pervert 8 sediment 9 fabricate 10 aberration, intertwine 12 misinterpret, misrepresent

thread for loom: 6 stamen

warragal, warrigal: 5 dingo, horse

warrant: act 4 earn, save, write 5 berat, guard, merit, order, right 6 assert, defend, ensure, ground, permit, reason, refuge, safety 7 behight, command, defense, justify, precept, protect, voucher, writing 8 document, guaranty, maintain, mittimus, sanction 9 authority, authorize, guarantee, protector, safeguard 10 commisssion, foundation, instrument, obligation, protection 11 certificate, stand behind 13 authorization, justification

warranty: 8 guaranty, sanction, security, 9 assurance, guarantee 13 authorization, justification

warren: 5 hutch 8 rabbitry, tenement

warrior: toa 4 hero, impi 5 brave 6 Amazon 7 fighter, martial, soldier 10 serviceman

group: 4 army

mythical: 6 Amazon 7 Aslauga

professional: 7 Hessian 9 gladiator, mercenary

Trojan: 6 Agenor, Hector

warship: sub 5 razee 6 bireme 7 cruiser, dromond, frigate, onebank, trireme 8 corvette 9 destroyer, submarine 10 battleship 11 dreadnaught

deck: 5 orlop

fleet: 6 armada

pert. to: 5 naval

quarters: 7 gunroom

squadron: 10 escadrille

three-bank: 7 trireme

two-bank: 6 bireme

wart: 5 tumor 7 verruca 9 subaltern 10 midshipman

wary: shy 5 alert, cagey, canny, chary, leery 7 careful, guarded, knowing, prudent, sparing 8 cautious, discreet, stealthy, watchful 9 cautelous, provident 10 economical 11 circumspect, on one's guard

wase: pad 4 wisp 6 bundle

wash: lap, mud, pan 4 lave, silt, soap 5 bathe, clean, creek, drift, float, leach, rinse, scour, scrub, slosh 6 buddle, debris, purify, sperge 7 cleanse, launder, shampoo 8 ablution, alluvium 9 lixiviate

away: 5 erode, purge

out: 4 fail 5 elute, erase, flush 7 discard, launder

up: 6 finish 7 discard, dismiss

washbowl: 4 sink 5 basin 6 lavabo 8 lavatory 9 aljofaina

washed-out: wan 4 pale 5 all in, faded, tired 6 effete 8 depleted 9 exhausted 10 dispirited, spiritless

washer: 4 rove 5 clove

washing: 8 ablution, lavation

chemical: 6 eluate

Washington, D.C.: 7 capital

art gallery: 5 Freer 8 National 8 Corcoran

nickname: 11 Foggy Bottom

original planner: 7 L'Enfant

river: 7 Potomac

Washington, George: *home:* 11 Mount Vernon

portraitist: 6 Stuart

wife: 6 Martha

Washington, State of: *capital:* 7 Olympia

city: 6 Tacoma, Yakima 7 Everett, Seattle, Spokane 10 Walla Walla

county: 4 King 5 Adams, Clark, Ferry, Lewis 6 Pierce

dam: 11 Grand Coulee

explorer: 4 Gray 6 Hecate 9 Vancouver 13 Lewis and Clark

Indian: 4 Chinook 8 Sahaptin

island: 5 Orcas 7 San Juan

motto: 4 Alki (By and By)

mountain peak: 5 Adams, Baker 7 Rainier 8 St. Helens

mountain range: 6 Kettle 7 Cascade, Olympic

nickname: 7 Chinook 9 Evergreen

river: 5 Snake 6 Yakima 8 Columbia

sound: 5 Puget

state bird: 9 goldfinch

state flower: 12 rhododendron

state tree: 7 hemlock

strait: 4 Haro 7 Georgia, Rosario 10 Juan de Fuca

washout: 4 flop 5 gulch, gully 6 fiasco 7 erosion, failure

washy: 4 oozy, thin, weak 5 loose 6 feeble, watery 7 diluted, insipid 8 slippery 9 frivolous, worthless

wasp: 5 whamp 6 dauber, hornet, insect, vespid 12 hymenopteron, yellow jacket

genus of: 5 sphex

pert. to: 6 vespal 7 vespine

waspish: 5 testy 7 peevish, slender 8 choleric, petulant, snappish, spiteful 9 fractious, irascible, irritable 11 bad-tempered 12 cantankerous

wassail: 4 lark, orgy, romp 5 binge, drink, revel 6 frolic, shindy 7 carouse 8 carousal 9 festivity, high jinks, merriment 10 salutation 11 celebration

waste (see also **refuse, wasteland**)**:** 4 bush, fail, idle, loss, pine, ruin, sack 5 decay, dwine, havoc 6 barren, bezzle, devour, molder, ravage, refuse 7 atrophy, badland, consume, corrode, destroy, dwindle, exhaust, fritter 8 confound, decrease, demolish, desolate, emaciate, enfeeble, misspend, squander 9 condiddle, devastate, dissipate 11 consumption, destruction, devastation, dissipation, fritter away, prodigality, superfluous, uninhabited 12 extravagance, improvidence, uncultivated

allowance: 4 tret

from a mine: 7 mullock

lay: 4 sack 5 havoc, spoil 6 ravage

waste away: age, rot 4 pine, wilt 5 decay 6 molder 7 atrophy

waste matter: 5 ashes, dregs, dross 6 debris 7 garbage

wasted: 7 haggard, wizened 8 impaired phthisic 9 emaciated, shriveled

wasteful: 6 lavish 8 prodigal 10 thriftless 11 extravagant, improvident

wasteland: fen 4 burn, moor 5 heath, marsh, swamp, wilds 6 desert, morass 8 badlands

wastrel: 4 rake, roué, waif 5 idler 6 waster 8 vagabond 9 profligate 11 spendthrift 13 good-for-nothing

wat: 6 temple

watch: eye, see, spy 4 espy, glom, heed, look, mark, mind, tend, view, wait 5 await, guard, timer, vigil 6 ambush, behold, defend, patrol, police, regard, sentry 7 bivouac, lookout, observe 8 horologe, meditate, sentinel 9 ambuscade, timepiece 11 keep an eye on, observation 13 sleeplessness

crystal rim: 5 basil, bezel, bezil

maker: 10 horologist

part: fob 7 crystal

watchdog: 6 keeper, warden 8 guardian 9 custodian

Hel's: 4 Garm 5 Garmr

underworld: 8 Cerberus

watcher: spy 5 scout 8 observer, watchman 9 spectator

watchful: 4 wary 5 alert, aware 7 careful, wakeful 8 cautious, open-eyed 9 attentive, wide-awake 10 unsleeping 11 circumspect

watchman: 5 guard, scout 6 sentry, warder 8 sentinel 10 gatekeeper

watchtower: 6 beacon, garret 7 lookout, mirador 8 bantayan 10 lighthouse, widow's walk

watchword: 5 motto 6 ensign, signal, parole 8 consigne 10 shibboleth 11 countersign

watchworks: 8 movement

arrangement: 7 caliper

mechanism: 10 escapement

water: eau(F.), wet 4 agua(Sp.), aqua(L.), brim, broo, burn, hose, pani 5 brine, fluid, flume, laver, lough, lymph, spray 6 dilute, liquid 7 moisten 8 calender, beverage, irrigate, sprinkle 10 citronelle *body:* (see also **watercourse**): bay, sea 4 deep, gulf, lake, mear, mere, pind, pool, tank, well 5 oasis, ocean 6 lagoon, strait 7 springs 9 reservoir

carrier: 4 duct, pipe 5 barge, canal, flume, zanja 7 aguador 8 aqueduct

congealed: ice 5 glace 6 icicle

covered by: 5 awash 7 flooded

down: 4 thin

draw: 4 lade

element: 6 oxygen 8 hydrogen

French: eau

goddess: 4 Nina 7 Anahita, Anaitis

hog: 8 capybara

hole: 5 oasis 7 alberca

Latin: 4 aqua

living in: 9 amphibian

mineral: 5 Vichy 6 selter, Shasta 7 seltzer

neck: 6 strait

obstruction: bar, dam 4 reef

pert. to: 6 marine 7 aquatic

play in: 5 plash

pure: 8 aqua pura(L.)

raising apparatus: 4 pump 5 sweep 6 siphon 7 shadoof 10 water wheel

rough: rip, sea 4 eddy 5 waves 6 rapids 8 breakers

search for: 5 dowse

soapy: 4 suds 6 graith

sound: 4 drip 5 plash 6 murmur, splash

Spanish: 4 agua

still: 6 lagoon

surface: 4 ryme

vessel: jug 4 cowl, ewer, lota, pail 5 cruse, flask, lotah 6 bottle, bucket, goglet 7 pitcher, stamnos 8 decanter

Water Bearer: 8 Aquarius

water bird: 4 coot, loon 5 diver 8 alcatras 9 waterfowl

water bottle: 4 lota, olla 6 tinaja

water buffalo: ox 7 carabao

water carrier: 4 pipe 7 aguador(Sp.), bheesty(Ind.), channel 8 bheestie(Ind.)

water cavy: 6 rodent 8 capybara

water centipede: 11 hellgrammite

water chicken: 9 gallinule

water clock: 6 ghurry 9 clepsydra

water cooler: 4 icer, olla, tank 11 refrigerant

water cow: 7 manatee

water crow: 4 coot 9 snakebird

water crowfoot: 4 herb 9 buttercup

water cure: 10 hydropathy 12 hydrotherapy 17 hydrotherapeutics

water deer: 10 chevrotain

water eagle: 6 osprey

water elephant: 12 hippopotamus

water gate: 6 sluice 9 floodgate 11 watercourse

water germander: 4 mint

water glass: 6 goblet 7 tumbler 9 clepsydra

water grampus: 12 hellgrammite

water hog: 7 bushpig 8 capybara

water hole: pit 4 lake, pond, pool 5 oasis 7 alberca

water horse: 6 kelpie 11 hippocampus 12 hippopotamus

water ice: 7 sherbet

water lily: 5 lotos, lotus 6 bobbin, nuphar 7 nelumbo 8 nenuphar

water meter: 7 venturi

water moccasin: 5 snake, viper

water mole: 6 desman 8 duckbill, platypus

water nymph: nix 4 lily 5 Ariel, naiad, nixie 6 flower, kelpie, nereid, Undine 7 goddess, hydriad, Oceanid 9 dragonfly

water on the brain: 13 hydrocephalus

water ouzel: 4 bird 6 dipper, thrush

water pig: 7 gourami 8 capybara

water pipe: 4 duct, hose, tube 6 hookah 8 nargileh

water plant: 7 aquatic 10 hydrophyte

water plug: tap 6 spigot 7 hydrant

water pocket: 6 tinaja

water rat: 4 vole 6 rodent 7 muskrat

water sprite: See **water nymph**

water thief: 6 pirate

watercourse (see also **water**: *body):* run 4 dike, dyke, race, wadi, wady 5 brook, canal, chute, creek, drain, gully, river 6 arroyo(Sp.), course, gutter, nullah, ravine, sluice, stream 7 channel, trinket 8 barranca(Sp.)

watercraft: See **boat, ship**

watercress: 9 brooklime

watered: 5 moire

waterfall: lin 4 linn 5 force 7 cascade, chignon, Niagara 8 cataract, Victoria, Yosemite 9 multnomah

waterfowl: 4 coot, loon 5 diver 8 game bird

waterfront worker: 4 navvy 9 stevedore

Watergate judge: 6 Sirica

waterhead: sap 5 booby 6 source 9 headwater 12 fountainhead 13 hydrocephalus

watering device: 4 hose, pump 5 spray 6 nozzle

watering place: bar, spa 4 pool 5 oasis 6 aguada(Sp.), battis, resort, spring 9 nightclub

waterless: dry 4 arid

waterlog: 4 soak 5 swamp 8 saturate

watermelon: 5 gourd 6 citrul, sandia 7 anguria

waters: See **watering place**

primeval: 4 Apsu

watershed: 5 ridge 6 divide

waterspout: 5 canal, spate 7 tornado 8 gargoyle 9 hurricane, whirlwind

waterwheel: 5 noria, sakia 6 sakieh 7 sakiyeh 8 tympanum watery: wet 4 pale, soft, thin, weak 5 fluid, sammy, soggy 6 blashy, dilute, serous, soaked, sweaty 7 aqueous, insipid, tearful, weeping 8 humorous 11 transparent

wattle: rod 4 beat, bind, flog, gill, jowl, twig, wand 5 cooba, fence, stick, twist, withe 6 acacia, coobah, dewlap, hurdle, lappet 9 boobyalla, framework, hackthorn 10 interwine, interweave

wave: ola(Sp.), sea, set, wag 4 bore, curl, flap, surf, sway, tide, vein 5 bless, crimp, curve, eager, eagre, float, flood, ridge, shake, surge, swell, swing, tilde, water, waver 6 beckon, billow, comber, fickle, flaunt, marcel, ripple, roller, signal 7 breaker, flutter, ripplet, seagate, tsunami, vibrate, wavelet 8 brandish, flourish, undulate, whitecap 9 fluctuate, permanent, vibration 10 undulation, unevenness

largest: 7 decuman
top: 5 crest
upward motion: 5 scend

waver: 4 reel, sway, trim, twig 5 quake, swing 6 change, falter, seesaw, teeter, totter, wiggle 7 flicker, flitter, flutter, sapling, stagger, tremble, vibrate 8 hesitate 9 fluctuate, hem and haw, oscillate, vacillate 11 back and fill

wavering: 4 weak 6 fickle 7 lambent 8 doubtful, flexuous, unsteady 9 desultory 10 hesitating, irresolute 11 vacillating

wavy: 4 ente(her.), onde(her.), unde(her.), undy(her.) 5 crisp, curly, snaky, undee(her.) 6 flying 7 billowy, sinuate, sinuous 8 squiggly, undulant 9 undulated 10 undulating

wax: 4 cere, grow, pela, rise 5 putty 6 become 7 cerumen, suberin 8 adhesive, increase, paraffin 11 zietriskite

candle: 4 taper 6 cierge
cobbler's: 4 code
figure: 9 ceroplast
match: 5 vesta
mixture: 6 cerate
myrtle: 8 bayberry
ointment: 6 cerate
opposite of: 4 wane
pert. to: 5 ceral
preparation: 6 cerate
substance: 5 cerin
used for skis: 7 klister
yellow: 7 ceresin

waxbill: 9 astrild

waxen: 4 ashy, pale 6 pallid, viscid 7 cerated, pliable 8 yielding 11 impressible 14 impressionable

waxwing: 9 cedarbird 10 weaverbird

waxy: 5 angry, vexed 7 pliable 8 yielding

way: via 4 cost, door, drag, fore, gait, lane, mode, path, plan, road, room 5 alley, going, habit, milky, route, space, style, track 6 ambage, arcade, artery, avenue, career, causey, chemin, course, detour, device, manner, method, scheme, street 7 advance, fashion, highway, opening, passage 8 causeway, contrada, distance, progress 9 banquette, boulevard, direction, procedure 12 idiosyncrasy

in: 7 contact 8 entrance
on: 7 en route
open: 7 pioneer
out: 4 exit 6 egress, escape

waybill: 8 manifest 9 itinerary

wayfarer: 6 viator 8 traveler 9 itinerant

waygate: 4 path 9 departure 10 passageway

waylay: 5 awiat, belay, beset, prowl, skulk, slink 6 ambush 7 forelay 8 surprise 9 ambuscade

waymark: ahu 5 arrow 9 guidepost, milestone

wayward: 6 fickle, unruly 7 erratic, froward, naughty, willful 8 contrary, perverse, stubborn, unsteady, untoward 9 arbitrary, irregular 10 capricious, headstrong, inconstant, refractory, selfwilled 11 disobedient, fluctuating, intractable 13 unpredictable

we: nos(L.) 8 ourselves

weak: wan 4 puny, soft, thin, worn 5 anile, bauch, chirp, crank, crimp, dicky, faint, frail, seely, washy, waugh, young 6 caduke, debile, dickey, dilute, dotish, faulty, feeble, flabby, flaggy, flimsy, foible, infirm, sickly, squeak, tender, unwise, watery 7 brittle, dwaibly, fragile, pliable, rickety 8 asthenic, childish, decrepit, feckless, flagging, helpless, impotent 9 childlike, dissolute, enfeebled, nerveless, powerless, spineless 10 effeminate, inadequate 11 implausible, ineffective 12 unconvincing

weaken: sap 4 thin, tire 5 appal, blunt, break, craze, delay 6 appall, deaden, defeat, dilute, impair, lessen, rebate, reduce, soften 7 cripple, decline, depress, disable, exhaust, unnerve 8 enervate, paralyze 9 attenuate, extenuate, undermine 10 debilitate, demoralize

weakling: 5 puler, sissy 6 softie, sucker 7 crybaby, sad sack 8 mama's boy, pushover 10 weak sister

weakness: 4 flaw 6 defect, foible 7 acratia, ailment, failing 8 appetite, debility, fondness 9 inability 11 attenuation 12 imperfection

of organ or muscle: 5 atony

weal: 4 line, mark, pomp, wale, welt 5 ridge, state 6 choice, choose, riches, stripe, wealth 7 welfare 9 happiness, wellbeing 10 commonweal, prosperity

wealth: 4 dhan, gear, gold, good, mean,

pelf, weal 5 goods, money 6 assets, graith, mammon, riches 7 capital, fortune, welfare 8 opulence, property, treasure 9 abundance, affluence, wellbeing 10 prosperity 11 possessions

gained: 8 chevance 9 chievance

god of: 6 Plutus

income from: 6 usance

person of: 5 Midas, nabob 7 Croesus, magnate 9 moneybags, plutocrat

wealthy: 4 full, rich 5 ample, pursy

wean: 4 baby 5 child 6 detach, infant 8 alienate, estrange 9 reconcile

weapon: arm, dag, gun 4 beak, bola, bolo, celt, claw, dart, dirk, epee, foil, pike 5 arrow, bolas, glave, knife, lance, rifle, saber, sabre, shaft, sling, spear, sword, talon, vouge 6 bomber, dagger, eolith, glaive, mortar, pistol, poleax, rapier 7 bayonet, bazooka, carbine, gisarme, halberd, hatchet, machete, missile, poleaxe, trident 8 catapult, crossbow, fauchard, leeangle, revolver, stiletto, tomahawk 9 artillery, derringer 11 blunderbuss

lay down: 6 disarm 9 surrender

storage place: 7 arsenal

without: 7 unarmed

wear: don, rub 4 fray, tire 5 chafe, erode, grind, sport, weary 6 abrade, attire, batter, endure, impair 7 apparel, clothes, consume, corrode, display, exhaust, exhibit, fatigue, frazzle 8 diminish 11 deteriorate

away: eat 5 erode 6 abrade 7 corrode

down: 4 tire 5 drain 7 exhaust, fatigue

out: 4 whip 6 tucker 7 exhaust 8 knock out

weariness (see also **weary**): 4 arid 5 ennui 6 tedium 7 fatigue 8 vexation 9 lassitude

weary: bad, fag, irk, sad 4 bore, jade, puny, tire, weak, worn 5 annoy, bored, curse, spent, timid, tired 6 harass, plague, sickly 7 exhaust, fatigue, irksome, tedious 8 fatigued, grievous, tiresome 9 forjaskit, forjesket, surfeited 10 defatigate, disastrous 11 unfortunate

Weary Willie: 5 tramp 7 shirker, vagrant 8 vagabond 13 featherbedder

weasand: 6 gullet, throat 7 trachea 8 windpipe 9 esophagus

weasel: 4 cane, stot, vare 5 ratel, sneak, stoat 6 ermine, ferret 9 pussyfoot 10 equivocate

family: 6 ermine, ferret, marten 9 musteline

weather: dry 4 hail, rain, snow, wind 5 erode, sleet 7 climate 8 discolor, windward 12 disintegrate

weather map line: 6 isobar

weather satellite: 5 Tiros

weathercock: 4 fane, vane

weathered: 5 faded 6 tanned 7 bronzed, stained 8 bleached, hardened 9 roughened, toughened

weatherman: 13 meteorologist

weave: 4 darn, knit, lace, spin 5 braid, drape, lurch, plait, unite 6 devise, enlace, wattle 7 canille, entwine, fashion, stagger 8 cannelle, contrive 9 fabricate, interlace, interwind 10 intertwine, intertwist

twigs: 6 wattle

weaverbird: 4 baya, taha 5 finch 6 whidah

weaver's tool: 4 loom, reed, sley

weaving: *cylinder:* 4 beam

goddess: 6 Ergane

machine: 4 loom 6 carder 8 jacquard

product: 5 cloth 7 textile

weazen: See **wizen**

web: 4 mat, net, ply 4 caul, maze, mesh, trap, veil, warp 5 snare 6 fabric, morass, tangle, tissue 7 ensnare, network, texture, webbing 8 entangle, gossamer, membrane, vexillum 9 labyrinth 11 fabrication 12 entanglement

pert. to: 6 telary 7 retiary

web-footed: 7 palmate 11 totipalmate

web-like: 4 lacy 7 spidery

half: 11 semi-palmate

webbing: 7 binding

Weber opera: 6 Oberon 13 Der Freischutz

wed: 4 join 5 elope, marry, mated, unite 6 joined, pawned 7 espouse, pledged, spliced 9 mortgaged

pert. to: 7 marital

wedding: 6 splice 8 ceremony, espousal, marriage, nuptials 11 anniversary

anniversary: see **wedding anniversary**

attendant: 5 usher 10 bridesmaid

canopy: 5 chupa 6 huppah 7 chuppah

celebration: 8 shivaree

party: 9 breakfast, reception

proclamation: 5 banns

ring: 4 band

wedding anniversary: *fifteenth:* 7 crystal

fifth: 4 wood

fiftieth: 6 golden

first: 5 paper

kind of: tin 4 ruby 5 candy, china, coral, linen, paper, pearl, straw 6 floral, golden, silver, wooden 7 crystal, diamond, emerald, leather

seventy-fifth: 7 diamond

tenth: tin

thirtieth: 5 pearl

twentieth: 5 china

twenty-fifth: 6 silver

wedge: jam 4 club, heel, lump, shim, shoe 5 cleat, crowd, ingot, piece, split 6 cleave, sector, wedgie 7 niblick 8 separate, triangle, voussoir 9 formation

wedge-shaped: 6 cuneal 7 cuneate, sphenic 8 cuneated, cuniform 9 cuneiform

wedgie: 4 shoe

wedlock (see also **wedding**): 4 wife 8 marriage 9 matrimony 11 conjugality

Wednesday (source of name): 5 Woden

wee: 4 tiny 5 bitty, small, teeny 6 little, minute 9 miniature 10 diminutive 11 lilliputian

weed: 4 band, garb, loco, milk, sida, tare 5 armor, cheat, dress, horse, vetch 6 darnel, datura, nettle, remove, sarcle, spurge 7 allseed, clothes, costume, garment, illness, mallows, purloin, ragweed, relapse, thistle, tobacco 8 clothing, plantain, purslane, sealwort, toadflax, trumpery 9 alfilaria, dandelion, eradicate, marijuana 11 undergrowth

weed killer: 8 paraquat 9 herbicide

weeds: 8 mourning

weedy: 4 foul, lean 5 lanky 7 scraggy 8 ungainly 9 overgrown

week: 8 hebdomad

weekday: 5 feria

weekly: 5 aweek 10 hebdomadal, periodical 11 hebdomadary, publication

weeks (two): 9 fortnight

weel: 4 eddy, pool, trap 6 basket 9 whirlpool

ween: 4 hope 5 fancy, think 6 expect 7 believe, imagine, suppose 8 conceive

weep: cry, sob 4 drip, leak, tear, wail 5 exude, greet, mourn 6 bewail, beweep, boohoo, lament 7 blubber, deplore

Weeping Philosopher: 10 Heraclitus

weeping statue: 5 Niobe

weepy: 5 moist, seepy 6 oozing 7 tearful, weeping 9 mournful

weevil: 4 boll, lota 7 billbug 8 circulio

weft: web 4 film, warp, woof, yarn 5 shoot, shute 7 filling 12 crossthreads

weigh: tax 4 bear, lift, tare, test 5 carry, hoist, poise 6 burden, esteem, matter, ponder, regard 7 balance, examine, measure, portion, support 8 consider, dispense, meditate, militate 9 apportion 14 counterbalance

weigh down: sit 4 lade, load, sway 5 beset 7 depress, oppress 8 encumber

weigher: 5 trone 6 potdar, scaler 7 balance, trutine 8 computer 9 steelyard

weighing machine: 5 scale, trone 7 balance 9 steelyard

weight: bob, CWT, keg, lot, mol, tod, ton, ton, tup 4 beef, dram, gram, heft, lade, last, load, mina, onus, pari, rati, shot, tola 5 carat, clove, flask, grain, ounce, pfund, poise, pound, power, ratti, rider, scale, stein 6 barrel, burden, cental,

charge, denier, fother, fotmal, gramme, grivna, import, moment 7 centner, drachma, gravity, oppress, plummet, quarter, quintal, scruple, tonnage 8 decagram, encumber, kilogram, pressure, vamfront, vammazsa, vierling 9 authority, centigram, heaviness, hectogram, influence, liespfund, microgram, milligram, myriagram, quentchen, zollpfund 10 importance 11 consequence 12 significance 13 hundredweight, ponderability

allowance: 4 bias, tret 7 scalage

gem: 5 carat

inspector: 6 sealer

of container: 4 tare

of 100 pounds: 6 cental

of 2000 pounds: ton

official: 6 metage

pert. to: 5 baric 8 ponderal

system of: net 4 troy 5 avoir 6 metric 8 jeweler's 11 avoirdupois 12 apothecaries

weighted: 4 bias 5 laden 6 loaded 8 burdened 9 evaluated, oppressed

weightiness: 4 pomp 7 dignity, gravity 9 solemnity 10 importance

weighty: fat 5 bulky, heavy, hefty, large, massy, obese, solid 6 severe, solemn 7 capital, massive, onerous, serious, telling 8 forcible, grievous, powerful 9 corpulent, important, momentous, ponderous 10 burdensome, chargeable, cumbersome, impressive, oppressive

weir: dam 4 bank 5 fence, garth, levee 7 barrier, milldam 11 obstruction

weird: lot, odd 4 eery, fate, unco, wild 5 charm, eerie, queer, scary, spell 6 creepy, kismet, spooky 7 awesome, curious, destine, destiny, fortune, ghostly, macabre, predict, strange, uncanny, unusual 8 foretell, prophecy 9 unearthly 10 mysterious, prediction, soothsayer

weka: 4 bird, rail

welcome: 4 hail 5 adopt, greet 7 acclaim, cordial, embrace 8 greeting, pleasant 9 agreeable, bienvenue, desirable 10 acceptable, salutation, satisfying

weld: 5 unite 6 solder 11 consolidate

welding gas: 9 acetylene

welfare: 4 dole, good, sele, weal 7 benefit 10 prosperity

goddess: 5 Salus

welkin: air, sky 10 atmosphere

well: fit, pit 4 bene(It., L.), bien (F.), fair, flow, gush, hole, sump 5 aweel(Sc.), fitly, fount 6 gusher, hearty, indeed, justly, source, spring 7 cistern, gaylies, geylies, gradely, healthy 8 artesian, expertly, fountain 9 correctly 10 gratifying, prosperous 11 excellently 12 satisfactory

drill device: jar
lining: 5 steen
pit: 4 sump
pole: 5 sweep
well-behaved: 4 good
well-being: 4 good, weal 6 health 7 comfort, welfare 8 eucrasia, felicity 9 eudaemony, happiness 10 prosperity
well-bred: 5 civil 6 polite 7 genteel, refined 8 cultured, wellborn 9 pedigreed 10 cultivated 11 gentlemanly 12 thoroughbred
well-defined: 8 distinct 11 distinctive
well-developed: 5 curvy 7 rounded 10 curvaceous
well-founded: 4 firm, good, just 6 cogent
well-groomed: 4 neat 5 clean, sleek 6 dapper, soigne 7 soignee
well-grounded: 4 firm 5 valid
well-heeled: 4 rich 7 moneyed 10 prosperous
well-known: 5 noted 6 famous 7 eminent, leading 8 familiar 9 notorious
well-liked: 7 popular 8 favorite 9 preferred
well-made: 5 solid 6 sturdy 9 affabrous
well-nigh: 6 almost, nearly
well-off: 5 lucky 8 thriving 10 prosperous
well-timed: 6 timely 9 opportune 10 propitious
well-versed: 7 erudite 13 knowledgeable
Welland: 4 city 5 canal, river
wellaway: woe 4 alas 5 alack 6 regret 9 alackaday
wellborn: 4 rich 5 noble 7 eugenic
wellhead: 6 source, spring 8 fountain 12 fountainhead
welsh, welch: 5 cheat, evade, renig 6 renege 7 swindle 8 back down
Welsh, Welch (see also **Wales**): 6 Cymric 8 Cambrian
welsh drake: 7 gadwall
welsh onion: 5 cibol
Welsh Rabbit: 7 rarebit
welt: 4 blow, mark, turn, wale 5 ridge, upset, wheal 6 stripe, thrash 8 overturn
welter: 4 reel, roll, toss, wilt 5 upset 6 grovel, tumble, wallow, wither 7 stagger, turmoil 8 overturn 9 confusion
wem: 4 flaw, scar, spot 5 stain
wen: 4 cyst, rune 5 tumor 6 growth 7 blemish 11 excrescence 12 imperfection, protuberance
wench: 4 dell, doxy, drab, gill, girl 5 child, gouge, trull, woman 6 blowen, blowze, damsel, maiden, wanton 7 consort, servant 8 strumpet 11 maidservant
wend: bow 4 fare, pass 5 alter, shift 6 depart, push on, travel 7 circuit, journey, proceed
Wend: 4 Slav, Sorb 7 Sorbian

wenzel: 4 jack 5 knave
werewolf: 8 turnskin, versipal 11 lycanthrope
West: 8 frontier, Occident
West Africa: See Africa
West Germany capital: 4 Bonn
West Indies: 7 Bahamas 8 Antilles
bird: 4 arar, tody 6 mucaro
boat: 7 drogher 9 catamaran
dance: 5 limbo
fiber: 5 cajun
fish: 4 paru, pega, sesi 5 pelon 6 testar 7 pegador 8 scirenga 9 picudilla
fleas: 7 chigoes
fruit: 4 tuna 5 papaw 6 papaya, pawpaw 7 genipap
handkerchief: 7 malabar
herb: 4 ocra 6 vanglo 7 vangloe
island: 4 Cuba 5 Aruba, Haiti, Nevis 6 Bahama 7 Grenada, Jamaica 8 Antilles, Barbados, Trinidad 10 Martinique, Puerto Rico, Santa Lucia 13 Virgin Islands
language: 6 Creole, French 7 English, Spanish
liquor: 5 mobby, tafia 6 mobbie, taffia
lizard: 6 arbalo
mistletoe: 7 gadbush
palm: 5 yagua, yaray 6 grigri, grugru
people: Ebo 4 Eboe 5 Cuban 6 Creole
pert. to: 9 Antillean
plum: 4 jobo
republic: 5 Haiti
rodent: 5 hutia, jutia 6 agouti
shrub: 4 anil 7 joewood
snuff: 8 maccaboy, maccoboy
sorcery: obe, obi 6 voodoo
sugar work: 5 usine
taro: 5 tania
tortoise: 7 hicatee 8 hiccatee
tree: 4 ausu, cera 5 acana, acapu, ebony, genip, papaw, yacca 6 aralie, ausubo, balata, cocuyo, gomart, pawpaw, ramoon 7 cocullo 8 aceituna, cockspur, drumwood 9 cocuswood, sapodilla
treewood: 5 galba
volcano: 5 Pelee
West Point: *mascot:* 4 mule
student: 4 pleb 5 cadet, plebe 8 yearling
West Virginia: *capital:* 10 Charleston
chief product: 4 coal
city: 7 Weirton 8 Wheeling
county: 4 Clay, Wood 5 Mingo, Roane 6 Cabell 7 Fayette, Kanawha
highest point: 10 Spruce Knob
nickname: 8 Mountain 9 Panhandle
river: Elk 4 Ohio
state bird: 8 cardinal
state flower: 12 rhododendron
state tree: 5 maple
western: 5 oater 10 horse opera
Western Samoa: *capital:* 4 Apia

monetary unit: 4 tala
Western treaty alliance: 4 NATO
Westminster clock: Ben
Westphalian city: 7 Munster
wet: lax, off 4 damp, dank, dewy, dram, lash, mire, rain, soak 5 bedew, bewet, dabby, foggy, humid, leach, misty, moist, mushy, rainy, soggy, soppy, sweat, wrong 6 clashy, dampen, drench, humect, imbrue, jarble, liquor, shower, soaked, sodden, watery 7 flotter, moisten, splashy, squashy 8 dampened, irrigate, moisture, sprinkle 9 misguided 11 intoxicated 18 anti-prohibitionist
wet blanket: 6 dampen 7 depress, killjoy 8 deadhead, dispirit 10 discourage, spoilsport
wet flax: ret
wet one's whistle: 5 drink
weta: 6 insect, locust
wetbird: 9 chaffinch
wether: ram 4 wool 5 sheep 6 eunuch 7 dinmont
whack: hit, try 4 bang, beat, belt, blow 5 fling, share, thump, trial, whang 6 chance, strike, stroke, thwack 7 attempt, portion 8 division 9 allowance, condition
whacking: 4 huge, very 5 large 8 whopping 10 tremendous
whale: hit, orc 4 beat, cete, drub, lash, orca, wale, whip, whop 5 giant, poggy, sperm, whack 6 baleen, beluga, blower, killer, strike, thrash 7 Cetacea, grampus, marwheel, rorqual, ripsack 8 cachalot, hardhead 9 blackfish, mysticete, mysticeti, zeuglodon 10 bottlehead, zeuglodont 13 sulphur-bottom
blue: 9 sibbaldus
carcass: 5 kreng
constellation: 5 Cetus
fat: 7 blubber
female: cow
food: 4 brit
iron: 7 harpoon
order: 4 cete 7 Cetacea
pert. to: 5 cetic
school: gam, pod
secretion: 9 ambergris
skin: 6 muktuk
strip blubber from: 6 flense
tail part: 5 fluke
young: 4 calf 5 stunt 9 shorthead
whale oil: 10 spermaceti
cask: 4 rier
whaleback: 9 steamship 10 turtleback 12 grain-carrier
whalebird: 4 gull 6 petrel 9 phalarope, turnstone
whalebone: 5 stiff 6 baleen, severe 10 inflexible
whalehead: 8 shoebill

whaler: 4 ship 7 bushman, swagman, whopper 8 whaleman 9 sundowner, whaleboat
visit: gam
whaling: 4 huge 8 whopping
cask: 4 rier 6 cardel
profit: lay
spear: 7 harpoon
whaling ship: 6 Pequod, whaler
wham: 4 bang 5 crack, smash
whammy: hex 4 jinks 6 hoodoo, voodoo 10 Indian sign
whang: 4 bang, blow, chop 5 chunk, slice, thong, throw, whack 6 assail, strike 7 leather, rawhide
whangee, wanghee: 4 cane 5 stick 6 bamboo
wharf: 4 dock, pier, quai(F.), quay 5 jetty, levee 7 landing
space: 7 quayage
worker: 9 stevedore
whatnot: 7 etagere 10 knickknack
wheal: 4 mark, mine, wale, weal 5 whelk 6 strake, streak, stripe 7 pustule 9 suppurate
wheat: 5 durum, spelt, trigo 6 imphee 7 einkorn, semoule
beard: awn
chaff: 4 bran
disease: 4 bunt, rust, smut 5 ergot 6 aecium, fungus
gritty part: 8 semolina
head: ear
outer coal: 4 bran
processed: 4 suji 5 grits 6 bulgur 9 middlings
repository: bin 8 elevator
state: 4 Ohio 5 Idaho 6 Dakota, Kansas 7 Indiana, Montana 8 Illinois, Missouri, Nebraska, Oklahoma 9 Minnesota 10 Washington 12 Pennsylvania
stubble: 6 arrish
wheat duck: 7 widgeon 8 baldpate
wheat louse: 5 aphid
wheat smut: 4 bunt 8 colbrand
wheatbird: 4 lark 9 chaffinch
wheater: 4 bird 5 chack 8 chickell 10 gorsehatch
wheedle: cog 4 cant, coax 5 carny, tease, whine 6 banter, butter, cajole, carney, fleech, whilly 7 blarney, cuittle, flatter 8 persuade, soft-soap 9 influence, sweet-talk
wheel (see also **gear**): cam, cog 4 bike, disk, helm, reel, roll, turn 5 cycle, drive, pivot, rotor, rowel, skeif, skive 6 caster, circle, league, roller, rotate, sheave 7 bicycle, chukkar, chukker, pedrail, revolve 10 revolution, waterwheel
furniture: 6 caster
part: cam, cog, hub, rim 4 tire 5 felly, spoke, sprag 6 felloe 8 sprocket

pert. to: 5 rotal

potters: see potter's wheel

rim: 5 felly 6 felloe

shaft: 4 axle

spinning: see spinning wheel

spoke: 6 radius

spurred: 5 rowel

stopper: 5 brake

toothed: cog 4 gear

water-raising: see waterwheel

wheel-shaped: 6 rotate 8 circular, rotiform

wheelbarrow: hod 10 hurlbarrow

wheeler (see also **wheelman**): 7 cyclist, vulture 11 wheelwright

wheeler-dealer: 7 shrewdy 8 go-getter, operator, promoter

wheelman: 5 pilot 7 cyclist, steerer, wheeler 8 helmsman, pedalist 9 bicyclist

wheeze: gag 4 hint, hiss, joke 5 adage, dodge, hoose, hooze, prank, trick 6 cliche, coghle(Sc.), device, saying 9 witticism

relative of: 4 rale

wheezy: 9 asthmatic

whelk: 4 acne 5 snail 6 papule, pimple, winkle 7 pustule

whelm (see also **overwhelm**): 5 cover, crush 9 deluge 9 drainpipe

whelp: cub, dog, pup 4 bear, fawn, lion, wale, welt, wolf 5 child, puppy, tiger, youth 7 leopard 11 give birth to

when: 5 until 6 though 7 whereas 8 although, whenever

where: 5 place 7 whither

whereas: 5 since 7 because

wherefore: 5 cause 6 reason 9 therefore 11 accordingly

whereness: 6 ubiety

wherewithal: 5 funds, means, money 9 resources

wherry: 4 boat 5 barge, carry, scull 7 lighter, rowboat, vehicle 9 transport

whet: 4 hone, stir 5 grind, rouse, strop 6 excite 7 quicken, sharpen 9 appetizer, stimulate

whetstone: bur 4 buhr, burr, hone 8 strickle 9 sharpener

whey: 4 pale 5 serum 6 watery

which: who 4 that, whom

which was to be shown: QED

whicker: 5 neigh 6 whinny

whiff: fan 4 flag, fuff, guff, gust, hint, odor, puff, waft, wave 5 expel, fluff, jiffy, smell 6 breath, exhale, inhale, stench 7 instant 10 inhalation

whiffle: 4 blow, emit, idle, turn, veer, wave 5 expel, shake, shift 6 change, trifle 7 flicker, flutter, scatter 9 disperse, hesitate 9 vacillate

while: yet 5 until 6 albeit, effort 7 where-

as 8 although, occasion

whilom: 4 erst, once, past 6 former 8 erewhile

whim: fad, fit, gig 4 idea, mood 5 fancy, humor, winch 6 megrim, notion, trifle, vagary, vision, whimsy 7 boutade, caprice, capstan, fantasy, whimsey 8 crotchet

whimper: cry, sob 4 mewl, moan, pule, weep 5 whine 6 murmur, yammer 7 grizzle, sniffle

whimsical: odd 5 droll, queer 6 cockle 7 bizarre, comical 8 fanciful, freakish, notional 9 arbitrary, conceited, eccentric, fantastic, grotesque, uncertain 10 capricious 11 fantastical

whimsy: See whim

whin: 4 rock 5 furze, gorse

whinchat: 8 songbird 9 gorsechat, grasschat

whine: wow 4 cant, girn, moan, pule 5 croon, whewl 6 snivel, yammer 7 whimper 8 complain

whinny: 4 bray 5 hinny, neigh

whinyard: 5 sword

whip: cat, gad, tan 4 beat, cane, crop, flay, flog, hide, jerk, lace, lash, urge, wind, wrap 5 birch, flick, knout, outdo, quirt, spank, strap, swish 6 defeat, punish, stitch, strike, swinge, switch, thrash 7 belabor, chicote, conquer, overlay, rawhide, scourge, sjambok 8 chawbuck, coachman, huntsman 9 bullwhack, flagellum 10 discipline, flagellate 13 cato-nine-tails

mark: 4 wale, weal, welt

part: 4 crop 5 snead 6 handle, socket

whippersnapper: 6 squirt 9 nonentity

whir: bur, fly 4 birl, burr, move, whiz, zizz 5 hurry, skirr, swirl, whizz 6 bustle, hurtle 7 revolve, vibrate 9 commotion

whirl: 4 eddy, reel, spin, stir, tirl, turn 5 drill, fling, hurry, swirl, twirl 6 bustle, circle, gyrate, rotate, swinge, tumult, uproar, vortex 7 revolve 9 commotion, pirouette 10 hurly-burly, revolution

whirlbone: 7 kneepan, patella 10 hucklebone

whirlpool: 4 eddy 5 gorce, swirl 6 gurges, vortex 9 Charybdis, maelstrom

whirlwind: 4 dust, fuss, stir 7 cyclone, tornado 9 hurricane, maelstrom

whirr: See whir

whisk: 4 tuft, whip, wisp 5 flisk, hurry

whiskers (see also **beard**): 6 growth 7 stubble 9 sideburns, vibrissae 11 muttonchops

fish: 7 barbels

whiskey, whisky: rye 4 corn 6 poteen, redeye, rotgut, Scotch 8 blockade, busthead 9 moonshine 10 usquebaugh

maker: 9 distiller

punch: 5 facer

whisper: 4 buzz, hint 5 rumor 6 breeze, murmur 7 confide

whisperer: 7 tattler 9 backbiter, slanderer 10 talebearer

whist: 4 game, hush, mute 5 cards, quiet, still 6 silent 7 silence 8 silently
declaration: 6 misere
dummy: 4 mort
hand: 6 tenace 10 Yarborough

whistle: 4 hiss, pipe, sugh, toot 5 flute, siren, sough 6 signal

whistle duck: 9 goldeneye

whistlewing: 9 goldeneye

whit: bit, jot 4 atom, doit, haet, hate, iota 5 speck 8 particle

white: wan 4 ashy, bawn, hoar, pale, pure 5 ashen, happy, hoary, ivory 6 albino, argent, blanch, chalky, grayed, honest, pallid, pearly 7 ivorine, silvery 8 harmless, innocent, palliate, spotless 9 colorless, fortunate, honorable 10 auspicious
becoming: 9 canescent
egg's: 5 glair 7 albumen
with age: 4 hoar 5 hoary

white ant: 4 anai, anay 7 termite

white cell: 9 leucocyte

white cliffs' site: 5 Dover

white-collar: 6 clerk 6 typist 8 salesman 9 secretary 10 bookkeeper

white crow: 7 vulture

white elephant (land of): 4 Siam 5 Burma, India 6 Ceylon 8 Thailand

white feather: 4 fear 9 cowardice

white flag: 5 truce 9 surrender

white gentian: 9 feverroot

white-haired: 5 favorite

white heat: 13 incandescence

White House: designer: 5 Hoban
first resident: 5 Adams

white Indian hemp: 8 milkweed

white iron pyrites: 9 marcasite

white jade: 9 alabaster

white lead: 6 ceruse

white lead ore: 9 cerussite

white-lightning: 9 moonshine

white livered: 8 cowardly 13 pusillanimous

white merganser: 4 smew

white mica: 9 muscovite

White Monk: 10 Cistercian

White Mountain: 5 Adams

white mule: gin 6 liquor, whisky 7 whiskey 9 moonshine

white mundic: 12 arsenopyrite

white nun: 4 smew

white plague: 8 phthisis 11 consumption 12 tuberculosis

white plantain: 9 pussytoes

white pyrite: 9 marcasite

white sanicle: 9 snakeroot

white snipe: 6 avocet 10 sanderling

white walnut: 8 shagbark, sycamore 9 butternut

white whale: 6 beluga

white widgeon: 4 smew

whitebelly: 6 grouse, pigeon

whitecap: 4 wave 5 crest

whitefish: 5 cisco 6 beluga 8 menhaden

whiten: 4 pale 5 chalk 6 blanch, bleach 8 etiolate, palliate

whitetail: 4 deer

whitewash: 6 blanch, defeat, parget 7 absolve, conceal, palliate

whiteweed: 5 daisy

whitewing: 4 sail 6 scoter 7 sweeper 9 chaffinch

whither: 5 where 8 wherever

whiting: 4 fish, hake 5 chalk

whitlow: 4 sore 5 felon 6 fetlow 12 inflammation

Whitsunday: 9 Pentecost

whitterick: 6 curlew

whittle: cut 4 pare, whet 5 carve, knife, shape, shave 6 reduce, remove

whiz: hum 4 buzz, hiss, pirr, whir 5 hurry 6 corker, expert, rotate 7 bargain

who: quo(L.), Wer(G.), wha(Sc.) 4 what 5 which 13 interrogative

whoa: 4 halt, stop

whole: all, sum 4 full, hail, hale, sole, unit 5 gross, total 6 entire, healed, intact, wholly 7 perfect 8 absolute, complete, ensemble, entirely, entirety, integral, thorough, totality, unbroken 9 aggregate, unanimous, undamaged, undivided 10 unimpaired

whole note: 9 semibreve

whole number: 7 integer

wholehearted: 6 hearty 7 devoted, earnest, sincere 8 bona fide, complete 10 unreserved 11 unmitigated

wholesale: 4 bulk, lots 7 massive 8 abundant, sweeping 9 extensive

wholesome: 4 safe 5 sound 6 benign, hearty, robust 7 healthy 8 benedict, clean cut, curative, halesome, salutary, vigorous 9 favorable, healthful 10 beneficial, healthsome, propitious, salubrious

wholly: all 4 well 5 quite 7 algates 10 altogether 11 exclusively

whoop: 4 hoot, urge, yell 5 cheer, shout 6 halloo

whooping cough: 9 pertussis

whop: 4 beat, blow, bump, flop 5 knock, throw 6 strike, stroke

whopper: lie 5 story 6 bender, bumper 7 bouncer

whopping: 4 huge, much, very 5 great, large 7 banging

whore: 4 drab 5 wench 6 harlot 8 strumpet 9 courtesan 10 prostitute

whorl: 5 spire, swirl

why: 5 proof 6 enigma, reason 7 mystery 9 wherefore

whyo: 6 robber 7 footpad 8 gangster

wick: bay 4 bend, town 5 creek, inlet 6 corner, hamlet 7 borough 9 farmstead

wicked: bad, ill 4 evil, vile, wrong 6 fierce, guilty, horrid, risqué, sinful, unjust 7 beastly, harmful, heinous, hellish, painful, playful, profane, vicious 8 criminal, depraved, devilish, diabolic, felonous, fiendish, flagrant, indecent, skillful, spiteful 9 atrocious, dangerous, difficult, malicious, nefandous, nefarious, perverted 10 diabolical, flagitious, impassable, iniquitous, outrageous, villainous 11 mischievous, troublesome

wicker: 4 twig 5 osier, withe

wicket: 4 arch, door, gate, hoop 5 hatch 6 window 7 guichet, opening

wickiup: hut 7 shelter

wide: 5 ample, broad, loose, roomy 6 opened 7 liberal 8 expanded, spacious 9 capacious, distended, expansive, extensive 12 farspreading 13 comprehensive

wide-awake: hat 4 keen, tern 5 alert, aware 7 knowing 8 watchful 10 interested

widely: far 4 afar 6 abroad

widen: 4 ream 5 dilate, expand, extend, spread 7 amplify, broaden, enlarge 10 generalize

widespread: 4 rife 7 allover, diffuse, general 8 diffused, sweeping 9 extensive, pervasive, prevalent, universal 10 prevailing 13 comprehensive

widgeon: 4 duck 5 goose 8 baldpate 9 simpleton
genus: 6 mareca

widow: 5 widdy 6 relict 7 dowager 8 bereaved
in cards: 4 skat
in printing: 9 short line
right: 5 dower 10 quarantine
suicide: 6 suttee

widow monkey: 4 titi

widowhood: 7 viduage

widowman: 7 widower

width: 5 girth, range 7 breadth 8 diameter, latitude, wideness

wield: ply 4 bear, cope, deal, rule 5 exert, power, swing 6 direct, employ, handle, manage, ordain 7 conduct, control 8 brandish 9 determine 10 manipulate

wife: ux(L.); hen 4 frau, frow, mate, uxor(L.) 5 donna, mujer, squaw 6 gammer, spouse 7 consort 8 helpmate, helpmeet 10 better half
bequest to: dot 5 dowry
clergyman's: 8 curatess
killer: 9 uxoricide
lord's: 4 lady
pert. to: 7 uxorial

rajah's: 4 rani 5 ranee

slave's: 9 broadwife

wig: 4 gizz 5 busby, caxon, jasey, judge, scold 6 baguio, peruke, rebuke, toupee 7 censure, periwig, spencer 8 Chedreux 9 dignitary, Gregorian, reprimand
repair: 6 careen

wiggle: 5 shake 6 waggle, wobble 7 stagger, wriggle

wight: man 4 loud 5 brave, human, swift, witch 6 active, nimble, strong 7 swiftly, valiant 8 creature, powerful, strongly

wigwag: 6 signal

wigwam: 4 home, tipi 5 tepee

wild: mad, ree 4 daft, wowf(Sc.) 5 feral, rough, waste, weird 6 desert, ferine, native, ramage, savage, stormy, unruly 7 bestial, furious, haggard, riotous, untamed, wilsome 8 aberrant, agrestal, desolate, dramatic, farouche, frenetic, reckless, untilled 9 agrestial, barbarian, barbarous, dissolute, disturbed, ferocious, hellicate, imprudent, primitive, turbulent, unbridled, visionary 10 chimerical, dissipated, irrational, licentious, tumultuous, wilderness 11 extravagant, harumscarum, uncivilized, uninhabited 12 obstreperous, uncontrolled, uncultivated 13 irresponsible 14 uncontrollable

wild alder: 8 goutweed

wild arum: 10 cuckoopint

wild ass: 5 kiang 6 onager

wild banana: 5 papaw 6 pawpaw

wild coffee: 9 buckthorn, feverroot

wild crocus: 12 pasqueflower

wild dog: 5 dhole, dingo

wild flower: See flower

wild goat: 4 ibex

wild goose: 7 greylag 8 Jacobite

wild hog: 4 boar

wild horse: 7 mustang

wild Irishman: 10 tumatakura

wild kale: 6 radish 8 charlock

wild masterwort: 8 goutweed

wild musk: 9 alfilaria

wild mustard: 8 charlock

wild passionflower: 6 maypop

wild pineapple: 7 penguin

wild plum: 4 sloe

wild pumpkin: 11 calabazilla

wild sage: 5 clary

wild sago: 7 coontie

wild sheep: See sheep

wild succory: 7 chicory

wild sweet potato: 7 manroot

wild turnip: 6 radish 8 rutabaga 9 breadroot

wildcat: cat 4 balu, eyra, lynx 6 ocelot, serval 7 panther 9 promotion

wildbeest: gnu

wilderness: 5 waste 6 desert, forest 10

hinterland **12** back of beyond

wildfowl: 4 duck **6** goose, quail **8** pheasant **9** partridge

flock: **5** skein

wildness: 5 waste **6** ramage **8** ferocity **12** extravagance

wile: art **4** lure, ruse **5** fraud, guile, trick **6** allure, deceit, entice **7** attract, beguile, cunning **8** artifice, trickery **9** stratagem

will: 4 lust, wish **5** elect, fancy **6** animus, choose, decree, desire, devise, prefer, see fit **7** command, longing **8** appetite, pleasure, volition **9** intention, testament **11** disposition, inclination, self-control **13** determination

appendix: **7** codicil

having no: **9** intestate

maker of: **8** testator **9** testatrix

proof of: **7** probate

valid: **7** testacy

willful: mad **4** rash **5** heady **7** wayward **8** stubborn **9** camsteary, camsteery, impetuous, obstinate, voluntary **10** hardheaded **11** intentional

willies: 6 creeps **7** jitters

William Tell: *canton:* Uri

composer: **7** Rossini

hero: **4** Egil

William the Conqueror's burial place:
4 Caen

willing: apt **4** fair **5** prone, ready **6** minded **7** tending **8** desirous, disposed, unforced **9** agreeable, voluntary **10** volitional

willingly: 4 fain, lief **5** lieve **6** freely, gladly

willingness: 7 consent **8** alacrity

willow: iva **4** itea **5** osier, salix **6** teaser

willow wren: 10 chiffchaff

willowy: 5 lithe **6** pliant, supple **7** slender **8** flexible, graceful

willpower: 7 purpose **10** resolution **11** self-control **12** resoluteness **13** determination

loss of: **6** abulia **7** aboulia

willy-nilly: 8 perforce **11** whether or no

Wilson's thrush: 5 veery

wilt: sag **4** fade, flag **5** droop, quail **6** wither **8** collapse, anguish

wily: sly **4** foxy **5** canny, smart **6** artful, astute, crafty, shrewd, subtle **7** cunning, subtile **9** cautelous, sagacious

wimble: awl **4** bore **5** auger, brace, scoop, twist **6** active, gimlet, pierce **9** penetrate, sprightly, whimsical

Wimbledon event: 6 tennis

wimple: 4 bend, fold, turn, veil, wind **5** curve **6** ripple **7** meander, wriggle **9** headdress

ture, conquer, prevail, succeed, triumph, victory **8** vanquish **9** captivate, influence **10** accomplish, conciliate

all tricks: **4** slam

back: **7** recover **8** retrieve

over: **6** defeat, disarm, induce **8** persuade, talk into **10** conciliate

wince: 4 crab, reel **5** start **6** cringe, flinch, recoil, shrink **8** windlass

wind: air **4** birr, bise, blow, bora, coil, flaw, gale, gust, hint, kona, reel, wend, wrap **5** belay(naut.), blast, buran, crank, curve, foehn, noser, reeve, samum, siroc, storm, trade, twine, twist, wield **6** boreas, bought, breath, breeze, buster, deform, gibleh, simoom, simoon, solano, squall, writhe, zephyr **7** chamsin, chinook, cyclone, entwine, entwist, etesian, gregale, khamsin, meander, monsoon, nothing, pampero, revolve, sirocco, tempest, tornado, typhoon, wreathe, wriggle, wulliwa **8** blizzard, entangle, khamseen, libeccio, williwaw, willywaw **9** harmattan, hurricane, libecchio, noreaster **10** euroclydon, tramontana, tramontane

desert: **6** simoon **7** sirocco

down: **5** relax **10** deescalate

god of: **4** Adad, Adda, Vayu **5** Eolus **6** Aeolus, Eecatl

periodic: **7** etesian, monsoon

personification: **6** Caurus **7** Caecias **8** Favonius

pert. to: **6** eolian **7** aeolian

scale: **8** Beaufort

summer: **6** breeze, zephyr

wind gauge: 4 vane **10** anemometer **11** weathercock

wind instrument: sax **4** fife, horn, oboe, tuba **5** flute, organ **6** cornet **7** hautboy, trumpet **8** clarinet, trombone

wind up: end **4** coil **5** close **6** finish, settle **8** conclude

windbreaker: 6 jacket

windfall: 4 boon, vail **5** manna **7** bonanza, fortune **8** buckshee

windflower: 7 anemone

windhover: 7 kestrel

windiness: 7 conceit **9** puffiness, verbosity **11** verboseness **12** boastfulness

winding: 4 wily **6** screwy, spiral, tricky **7** coiling, crinkle, devious, pliable, sinuous, twining, wriggly **8** flexible, rambling, tortuous, twisting **9** deceitful, intricate, meandrous, sinuosity **10** anfracyure, circuitous, convoluted, meandering, serpentine **11** amortisseur, anfractuous

winding device: 4 reel **7** capstan **8** windlass

winding sheet: 6 shroud

windjammer: 4 ship **6** bugler, sailor,

win: get, pot **4** beat, earn, gain, take **5** charm **6** allure, attain, defeat, entice, obtain, secure **7** achieve, acquire, cap-

talker 8 musician 9 trumpeter

windlass: 4 crab, reel 5 hoist, winch 7 capstan

windle: 7 measure, redwing

windmill: blade: 4 vane
fighter of: 7 Quixote
pump: gin
sail: awe, ban

window: bay 5 gable, glaze, oriel 6 dormer 7 balcone, fenetre, lucarne, mirador, opening, winnock(Sc.) 8 aperture, casement, fenestra, jalousie
arrangement: 12 fenestration
bay: 5 oriel
frame: 4 sash
leading: 4 came
ledge: 4 sill
part: 4 came, sill
pert. to: 9 fenestral
recess: 6 exedra
roof: 6 dormer 8 skylight
sash weight: 5 mouse
ship's: 4 port 8 porthole
ticket: 6 wicket 7 guichet
worker: 7 glazier

windpipe: 6 artery, gullet, throat, weason 7 trachea, weasand, weazand 9 esophagus
pert. to: 8 trachean

windrow: 4 pile 5 swath 6 furrow, swathe

windshake: 8 anemosis

windstorm (see also **storm, wind**): 4 gale 7 cyclone, typhoon 9 hurricane

windward: 5 aloof 8 aweather

Windward Island: 7 Grenada 9 Martinique

windy: 4 airy 5 blowy, empty, gusty, huffy, swift, wordy 6 breezy, stormy 7 gustful, pompous, verbose 8 boastful, skittish 9 aeolistic, bombastic, inflated 10 boisterous, changeable, intangible 11 harebrained, tempestuous 13 unsubstantial

Windy City: 7 Chicago

wine: vin(F.) 4 alac, Asti, Bual, cote, deal, port, tent 5 Baden, Casel, drink, liane, Medoc, merum(L.), Rhine, tinta, tokay, Yquem 6 Barolo, Barsac, Beaune, canary, claret, Malaga, Massic, Muscat, Saumur, sherry 7 Alicant, Banyals, Bastard, Chablis, chacoli, Chateau, Chianti, Conthey, Dezaley, Falerno, hollock, Madeira, Margaux, Marsala, Medeira, Moselle, Orvieto 8 Alicante, Ambonnay, beverage, Bordeaux, Bucellas, Burgundy, Florence, Marsalla, muscadel, Muscatel, Riesling, Ruchelle, Rulander, sauterne 9 Gladstone, hermitage, teneriffe, Zeltinger, zinfandel 10 Beaujolais, Calon-Segur, Hockheimer, Roussillon 11 Niersteiner,

scuppernong 12 Geisenheimer 15 scharlachberger
apple: 5 cider
bag: 8 wineskin
bibber: sot 5 toper 7 tippler 8 drunkard
bottle: 6 fiasco, magnum 8 decanter, jeroboam
cask: tun, vat 4 pipe
cask deposit: 6 tartar
cellar: 6 bodega
comb. form: oen 4 oeno
cruet: 7 burette
cup: ama 5 amula 6 goblet 7 chalice
deposit: 6 tartar
discoverer: 4 Noah
disorder: 5 casse
drink: kir 5 clary, mulse, negus, punch
dr: sec 4 brut
film: 8 beeswing
fragrance: 7 bouquet
god: 4 Soma 7 Bacchus 8 Dionysus
list: 4 card
lover: 11 oenophilist
maker: 6 abkari, abkary 7 vintner
measure: aam, aum 4 orna, orne
medicinal preparation: 5 mosto
merchant: 6 bistro(F.) 7 vintner 8 gourmand
new: 4 must
pert. to: 5 vinic 6 vinous
pitcher: 4 olpe 5 olpae 8 oenochoe
punch: 7 sangria
residue: 4 marc
rice: 4 sake
scene of miracle: 4 Cana
shop: 6 bistro, bodega
spiced: 9 hippocras
steward: 9 sommelier
stock: 6 cellar
study of: 7 enology 8 oenology
strength: 4 seve
sweet: 4 port 5 lunel, tokay 7 malmsey, Moselle 8 Alicante, muscatel
unfermented: 4 must
vessel: ama 5 amula 7 chalice
year: 7 vintage

wine and dine: 4 fete 6 regale

wineberry: 5 grape 7 currant 8 billberry, makomako 9 raspberry 10 gooseberry

winegrower: 8 vigneron 13 viticulturist

Winesburg Ohio author: 8 Anderson

wineshop: bar 6 bistro, bodega

wineskin: 5 askos

wing: ala, arm, ell, fin, fly, van 4 limb 5 aisle, alula, annex, pinna, shard, speed, volet, wound 6 hasten, pennon, pinion 7 flutter
arrangement: 7 alation
building: ell
pert. to: 4 alar 6 pteric
under: 8 subalary
vestigial: 5 alula

wing cover: 7 elytron

wing-footed: 5 fleet, swift 6 aliped 9 mercurial

wing-like: 4 alar 5 alary, alate 6 pteric 7 aliform, pteroid

part: ala 4 alae 7 aileron

winged: 4 aile, alar 5 alary, alate, lofty, rapid, swift 6 alated 7 bialate, sublime, wounded 9 aliferous, aligerous, feathered

in heraldry: 4 aile

Winged Horse: 7 Pegasus

wingless: 7 apteral 8 apterous

wingless locust: 4 weta

wink: bat, nap, nod 4 hint 5 blink, flash, gleam, prink, sleep 6 signal 7 connive, flicker, instant, nictate, slumber, sparkle, twinkle 9 nictation, nictitate, twinkling 10 periwinkle

winking: 13 blepharospasm

winks (forty): nap 6 catnap

winner: 6 earner, reaper, victor 7 faceman, sleeper 8 bangster 9 conqueror

Winnie-the-Pooh: *author:* 5 Milne

character: Owl, Roo 5 Kanga 6 Piglet, Rabbit, Tigger

winning (see also **win, winsome**): 5 shaft, sweet 6 profit 7 victory

winning three numbers: 4 tern

winnow: fan, van 4 beat, blow, flap, sift, sort 5 dight 6 assort, select 7 analyze, examine, scatter 8 brandish, disperse, separate 9 eliminate, screen out

winsome: gay 5 bonny, merry, sweet 6 blithe, bonnie 7 likable, lovable, winning 8 adorable, charming, cheerful, engaging, pleasant 9 agreeable 10 attractive 11 captivating 12 lighthearted

winter: 9 hibernate

French: 5 hiver

pear: 6 seckel, warden

pert. to: 6 brumal, hiemal

Spanish: 8 invierno

winter quarters: 10 hibernacle 12 hibernaculum

winter teal: 9 greenwing

winterbloom: 6 azalea

wintergreen: 10 pipsissewa

Winter's Tale character: 4 Dion 5 Mopsa 6 Dorcas 7 Camillo, Leontes, Perdita

wintle: 4 reel, roll 7 stagger, wriggle

wintry: icy 4 aged, cold 5 hoary, snowy, white 6 frigid, hiemal, stormy 8 chilling, hibernal, wintered 9 cheerless

wipe: dry, hit, mop, rub 4 beat, blow, draw, gibe, jeer, pass 5 brand, cheat, clean, dight, erase, stain, swipe, towel, trick 6 defeat, remove, sponge, strike, stroke 7 abolish, defraud, exhaust, sarcasm 8 disgrace 10 annihilate, obliterate 11 exterminate 12 handkerchief

off: 4 dust 5 scuff

out: 5 erase, scrub 6 cancel 7 destroy

up: 4 swab, swob

wire: 4 coil 5 cable 6 fasten 8 telegram 9 cablegram, telegraph

bundle of: 5 cable

cutters: 6 pliers

for teeth: 6 braces

measure: mil 5 stone

system: 7 network, reticle

wire cutter: 6 pliers 8 secateur

wiredraw: 4 thin 5 wrest 7 distort, prolong, spin out 8 protract 9 attenuate 10 overrefine

wireless: 5 radio

wirework: 7 netting 8 filigree

wireworm: 8 myriapod 9 millepede

wiry: 4 lean 5 hardy, stiff, tough 6 sinewy, strong 8 muscular

wis: 4 deem, know 5 think 7 believe, imagine, suppose

Wisconsin: *capital:* 7 Madison

city: 6 Racine 7 Kenosha 8 Green Bay 9 Milwaukee

county: 4 Dane, Polk, Rusk, Sauk 5 Brown, Dodge, Pepin, Vilas 6 Barron 7 Ozaukee 8 Bayfield, Walworth, Waushara

explorer: 7 Nicolet

falls: 10 Big Manitou

lake: 7 Mendota 9 Winnebago

motto: 7 Forward

native: 6 Badger

nickname: 6 Badger

river: 4 Wolf 5 Black 7 St. Croix 8 Chippewa 9 Wisconsin 11 Mississippi

state bird: 5 robin

state flower: 6 violet

state tree: 5 maple

wisdom (see also **wise**): 4 lore 5 sense 8 judgment, sagacity 9 knowledge

god of: 4 Nabu, Nebo 6 Ganesa 7 Ganesha

goddess of: 6 Athena, Pallas 7 Minerva

man of: 6 Nestor

wisdom tooth: 5 molar

wise: hep 4 mind, sage, sane, show, wary 5 aware, canny, smart, sound, witty 6 advise, crafty, direct, inform, manner, method, shrewd, subtle, versed, witful 7 beguile, cunning, erudite, explain, fashion, gnostic, heedful, knowing, learned, politic, prudent, sapient, skilled 8 discreet, informed, instruct, persuade, profound, sensible, skillful 9 cognizant, dexterous, expedient, judicious, on the beam, provident, sagacious 10 discerning, omniscient 11 calculating, circumspect, enlightened, intelligent, well-advised 13 sophisticated *infinitely:* 10 omniscient

up: 5 learn 6 advise, inform

wise man: 4 sage 5 magus, solon 6 Casper, Gasper, Nestor, savant, wizard 7 scholar 8 magician, Melchior 9 Balthasar, Balthazar, councilor

Wise Men: 4 Magi

wise saying: saw 5 adage, maxim

wiseacre: 5 dunce 7 prophet 9 simpleton 10 mastermind, smart aleck 11 wisenheimer

wisecrack: gag 4 joke, quip 9 witticism

wiselike: 6 decent 7 fitting 8 becoming, sensible 9 judicious 11 appropriate

wish: 4 hope, long, want 5 crave, fancy, yearn 6 behest, desire, expect, impose, invoke 7 longing, propose, request 8 petition, yearning 10 aspiration, invocation 11 imprecation

grammatical mood expressing: 8 optative

wishbone: 8 furculum 10 fourchette

wishful: 7 longing 8 desirous 9 desirable 10 attractive

wishy-washy: 4 pale, sick, thin, weak 5 tepid 6 feeble, trashy, watery 7 insipid 13 unsubstantial

wisp: 4 band, lock, ring, wase 5 broom, brush, bunch, clean, flock, shred, torch, whisk 6 bundle, parcel, rumple, strand, wreath 7 crumple, handful 8 fragment

wispy: 5 filmy, frail 6 slight 7 slender 8 gossamer, nebulous

wisteria: 4 bush, fuji 6 purple, violet

wistful: 6 intent 7 longing, pensive 8 yearning 9 attentive, nostalgic

wistfulness: rue 6 regret

wit: wag 4 know, mind 5 humor, irony, learn 6 acumen, esprit(F.), namely, reason, satire, widsom 7 cunning, faculty, punster 8 comedian, drollery, funnyman, prudence, repartee 9 intellect 12 intelligence, perspicacity 13 understanding

low form of: pun

witch: hag, hex 4 baba 5 biddy, bruja, charm, crone, lamia, woman 6 cummer, kimmer, wizard 8 magician, sorcerer 9 fascinate, sorceress

cat: 9 grimalkin

city: 5 Endor, Salem

doctor: 6 goofer

famous: 5 Circe 6 Lilith

gathering: 5 coven

male: 7 warlock

means of transportation: 5 broom

witch hazel: 4 tree 5 shrub 6 lotion 8 hornbeam 10 astringent

witchcraft: 5 charm, magic 7 cunning, hexerei, sorcery 8 brujeria(Sp.), pishogue, witchery, wizardry 9 sortilege 11 enchantment, fascination 12 invultuation

goddess of: 5 Obeah 6 Hecate

practice: hex 7 bewitch

witchman: 6 shaman, wizard 8 sorcerer

with: wi(Sc.); con(It.), cum(L.), mit(G.) 4 avec(F.), near 5 along 7 against 9 alongside 12 accompanying

with respect to: 4 as to 5 as for 7 apropos

withdraw: 4 void 5 avoid 6 absent, abjure, depart, detach, divert, recall, recant, recede, remove, retire, secede, shrink 7 abscond, decline, detract, extract, forbear, forsake, give way, refrain, retract, retreat, subduce, subside 8 abstract, alienate, derogate, distract, evacuate, fall back, renounce, restrain, withhold 9 disengage, sequester 10 relinquish, retrograde

from reality: 6 autism

withdrawn: shy 5 aloof 6 remote 8 detached 10 unsociable 11 indifferent

withe: 4 band, bind, herb, rope, twig 5 osier, snare, withy 6 branch, fasten, halter, wattle, willow

wither: age, die, dry 4 fade, pine, sear, sere, wilt 5 blast, cling, daver, decay, wizen 6 blight, cotter, shrink, weaken 7 shrivel, wrinkle 8 languish

withered: 4 arid, sere 7 sapless 10 marcescent 11 sphacelated

withershins: 10 topsy-turvy 12 contrariwise

withhold: 4 curb, deny, hide, keep 5 check 6 desist, detain, refuse, retain 7 abstain, forbear, prevent, refrain, repress, reserve 8 maintain, postpone, restrain

within: in, on; ben 4 inly, into 5 among 6 during, herein, inside 7 indoors 8 interior, inwardly 10 underneath

without: 4 bout, sans, sine(L.) 6 beyond 7 lacking, outside 9 outwardly 10 externally, out-of-doors

without this: 7 sine hoc

withstand: 4 bear, bide, defy 5 abide 6 combat, endure, oppose, resist 7 gainsay 8 confront, tolerate 9 gainstand 10 contradict, controvert

withy: 4 turn, twig, wind, wiry 5 agile, braid, tough 6 branch, willow 8 flexible

witless: mad 5 crazy, gross 6 insane, simple, stupid 7 foolish, unaware 8 heedless 9 brainless, pointless, unknowing 10 dullwitted, indiscreet

witness: eye, see, wit 4 know 5 teste 6 attest, beheld, behold, martyr 7 certify, endorse, observe, sponsor, testify 8 beholder, evidence, indicate, observer, onlooker 9 spectator, subscribe, testifier, testimony 11 attestation 13 understanding

witticism: mot, pun 4 gibe, jeer, jest, joke,

quip 5 sally 11 gauloiserie

witting: 5 aware 7 tidings 8 judgment 9 knowledge, voluntary 10 deliberate 11 information, intentional 12 intelligence

witty: 4 gash, wise 5 comic 6 bright, clever, facete, jocose, jocund, versed 7 amusing, comical, jocular, knowing 8 humorous, informed 9 facetious 11 intelligent

witty reply: 7 riposte 8 repartee

wivern: 6 dragon

wizard: 4 mage, sage 5 fiend 6 expert, genius, Merlin 7 magical, prodigy, warlock 8 charming, conjurer, magician, sorcerer 10 enchanting 11 necromancer, thaumaturge

wizardry: art 5 magic 7 sorcery 10 witchcraft

wizen, weazen: dry 6 whither 7 shrivel

woad: 6 indigo 8 dyestuff

wobble, wabble: 4 boil 5 lurch, shake, waver 6 quaver, teeter 7 tremble 9 vacillate

wobbly: 5 loose, shaky 7 rickety

woe: 4 bale, bane 5 grief 6 misery, sorrow 7 trouble 8 calamity, disaster 9 dejection 10 affliction, desolation, melancholy, misfortune

tale of: 8 jeremiad 11 lamentation

woebegone: 4 worn 6 gloomy, shabby 8 downcast 10 lugubrious, melancholy

woeful: sad 4 dire 6 paltry 7 direful, pitiful, unhappy 8 mournful, wretched 9 miserable, sorrowful, woebegone 10 deplorable, dispirited 12 disconsolate

wolaba: 8 kangaroo

wold: lea 5 plain 6 meadow

wolf: 4 lobo 6 canine, chanco, coyote 7 Don Juan 8 Casanova 9 thylacine 10 ladykiller 11 philanderer, skirt chaser

cry: 4 howl

gait: 4 lope

genus: 5 canis

pert. to: 6 lupine

timber: 4 lobo

young: pup 5 whelp

wolf-like: 6 lupine 9 rapacious

wolfhound: 4 alan 6 borzoi

wolfsbane: 7 aconite 9 monkshood

Wolsey's birthplace: 7 Ipswich

wolverine: 7 glutton 8 carcajou

genus of: 4 gulo

Wolverine State: 8 Michigan

woman (see also **girl, mother**): gin, hen 4 bint, dame, dona, lady, maid, rani, wife 5 begum, broad, chick, donna, femme, madam, mujer, ranee, skirt, squaw 6 calico, cummer, domina, female, heifer, kimmer, maness, senora 7 alewife, servant, signora 8 mistress, senorita 10 klootchman, sweetheart 11 gentlewoman

advisor: 6 egeria

attractive: 4 doll, peri 5 belle, filly, pin-up, siren, sylph, Venus 6 beauty, looker 7 charmer, Zenobia 8 Musidora

beloved: 9 inamorata

brave: 7 hellcat, heroine

celibate: 7 agapeta

domain: 7 distaff

dowdy: 5 frump

kept: 8 mistress 9 concubine 12 demimondaine

lawyer: 6 Portia

learned: 4 blue 7 basbleu(F.), seeress 12 bluestocking

little: Mrs. 4 wife 7 ladykin

loose: tib 4 drab, flap, jilt, slut 5 hussy, quean, queen 6 chippy, giglet, giglot, harlot, wanton 7 cocotte, Jezebel, trollop 9 courtesan, courtezen, dratchell

married: 4 frau, frow, wife 5 vrouw 6 matron

mythical: 6 Gorgon, Medusa

objectionable: hag 5 fagot, shrew, witch 6 faggot, gorgon, virago 8 harridan 9 grimalkin, termagant

old: gib, hag 4 baba, dame, trot 5 crone, frump 6 carlin, gammer, granny 7 carline, dowager, grandam 8 grandame, spinster 9 cailleach, cailliach

organization: DAR, WAC, WSP 4 AMVS, WAAC, WAVE, Wren 5 Ebell 6 circle 7 sorosis 8 sorority 10 sisterhood

pert. to: 7 gynecic 8 gynaecic 9 muliebral

patient: 8 Griselda

physicist: 5 Curie 7 Meitner

pregnant: 9 gravida

ruler: 5 queen 9 matriarch

sailor: 4 Spar, Wave

serving: see servant

single (see also **maiden**): 6 virgin 8 mistress, spinster

soldier: Wac 4 Waac

staid: 4 lady 6 beldam, matron 7 beldame

state of: 10 muliebrity

strong: 6 Amazon, virago 8 titaness

suffragist: 4 Mott 5 Stone 7 Anthony, Stanton

talkative: cat, gad, hen 5 dolly, flirt, scold, shrew, vixen 6 fizgig, virago 7 hellcat 9 termagant

theater: 6 dancer 7 actress, chorine, ingenue 9 soubrette

unattractive: bag, dog 4 drab 5 crone, dowdy, witch 8 slattern

young (see also **girl**): tib 4 burd, dell, drab, lass 5 filly, trull, wench 6 lassie 7 damozel 10 demoiselle

woman chaser: 4 wolf 8 lothario 10 sheepbiter 11 philanderer

woman hater: 10 misogynist

womanish: 5 anile 6 effete, female 8 feminine 10 effeminate

womb: bag 5 belly 6 uterus

wombat: 6 badger 9 marsupial

won (see also **win**): 4 live 5 abide, dwell 7 inhabit

wonder: awe 4 evil, fear, harm, sign 5 grief, shock, wrong 6 esteem, marvel 7 curious, miracle, prodigy 8 surprise 9 amazement, reverence, speculate, uncertain 10 admiration, wonderment 11 destruction, uncertainty 12 astonishment

of the world: 6 Pharos 8 pyramids, Colossus

performance: see **magic**

worker of: see **wizard**

Wonder State: 8 Arkansas

wonderful: 4 fine, good 5 super 6 lovely 7 amazing, amusing, corking, mirific, strange 8 wondrous 9 admirable, excellent, marvelous 10 miraculous, surprising 11 astonishing, interesting 13 extraordinary

wonky: off 4 awry 5 shaky 6 feeble 7 tottery 8 unsteady 9 tottering

wont: use 5 dwell, habit, usage, usual 6 custom, reside 8 inclined, practice 10 accustomed

woo: beg, sue 4 coax, seek 5 court, spark 6 assail, invite, splunt(Sc.) 7 address, beseech, entreat, solicit 9 importune 10 bill and coo

wood: hag, keg, mad 4 bois(F.), bosk, bowl, cask, holt, wold 5 angry, cahuy, grove, hurst, trees, xylem 6 forest, insane, lumber, timber 7 enraged, furious, violent 8 woodland

ash: 6 potash

black: 5 ebony

bundle of: 5 fagot

burned: ash 4 brae 8 charcoal

core: ame

dealer: 10 xylopolist

decayed: 4 punk

derivative: tar 5 turps 6 balsam 10 turpentine

distillation from: tar 5 turps 10 turpentine

eater: 7 termite

edge: 8 woodrime, woodside

fine-grained: yew 6 brauna

firing easily: 4 punk 5 sponk, spunk 6 tinder 8 kindling, punkwood 9 touchwood

flexible: 5 edder, osier 6 willow

fragrant: 5 aloes, cedar

god: see **woodland:** *deity*

growth: 7 coppice

gum: 5 resin, xylan

hard: ash, elm, eng, oak 4 lana, poon, rata, teak 5 ebony, maple, zante 6 walnut 7 hickory 8 mahogany

juice: sap

kind: see **tree**

knot: nur 4 burl, knag, knar 5 gnarl

light: 4 cork 5 balsa

overlaying: 6 veneer

part: fid, nog, peg, rib 4 lath, shim, slat 5 dowel, spile, sprag, stave, tenon 6 batten, billet, reglet, splint 7 dingbat

pert. to: 5 treen 6 xyloid

steward: 9 woodreeve

strip: 4 lath, slat 6 batten, spline

striped: roe

supporting: 5 cleat

valuable: sal 4 teak

worker: 6 joiner, sawyer 7 paneler 9 carpenter

wood alcohol: 6 methyl 8 methanol

wood-ash salt: 6 potash

wood nymph: 4 moth 5 dryad 8 grayling 11 hummingbird

wood pigeon: 4 dove 6 cushat 8 ringdove

wood pussy: 5 skunk

wood sorrel: oca 6 oxalis 7 begonia 8 haremeat

wood stork: 4 ibis

woodbine: 11 honeysuckle

woodchuck: 6 marmot 9 groundhog

woodcock: 4 dupe, fool 5 pewee 7 becasse(F.) 9 simpleton 10 woodpecker

woodcutter: 6 axeman, logger, sawyer 7 chopper 8 woodsman 9 lumberman

wooded: 5 bosky 7 sylvan

wooden: dry 4 dull, wood 5 heavy, oaken, stiff, treen 6 clumsy, stolid 7 awkward 8 lifeless 9 ponderous 10 spiritless 11 insensitive 14 expressionless

wooden-headed: 4 dull 6 stupid 8 blockish

Wooden Horse: See **Trojan Horse**

wooden shoe: 4 clog, geta 5 sabot 6 patten

woodland: 5 weald 6 forest 10 timberland

burnt over: 6 brulee

deity: Pan 4 faun 5 Diana, satyr, Silen 7 Silenus 8 Seilenos

landscape: 7 boscage

woodpecker: 4 chab 5 picus 6 picule, yaffle, yockel, yuckle, yukkel 7 flicker, piculet, whetile, wryneck, yaffler 8 hickwall, woodcock, woodhack 9 sapsucker, woodchuck, woodspite 10 carpintero, woodhacker, woodjobber 11 hickoryhead, woodknacker

genus: 5 picus

type: 5 downy, hairy 8 imperial, pileated 9 redheaded

pert. to: 6 picine 8 piciform

woodsman: 5 scout 6 hunter 7 bushman, trapper 8 forester

woodwind: 4 oboe 5 flute 7 bassoon, piccolo 8 clarinet 9 saxophone

woodworker: 6 joiner, turner 9 carpenter 12 cabinetmaker *machine:* saw 5 edger, lathe 6 planer, router, shaper 7 sticker

tool: adz, saw 4 adze 5 plane 6 hammer

woody: 4 bosky 6 sylvan, xyloid 8 ligneous

woody fiber: 4 bast, hemp 5 xylem

wooer: 4 beau 6 suitor 8 courtier, paramour

woof: abb 5 cloth, weave 6 fabric 7 filling, texture 9 essential

wool: fur 4 coat, hair, lamb 5 llama, sheep 6 fleece, mohair 8 barragan, barragon 9 cordillas

blemish: 4 mote

clean: 7 garnett

cloth: 5 baize, duroy, tweed 6 alpaca, angora, baline, duffel, frieze, hodden, kersey, melton, merino, mohair, vicuna 7 flannel, ratteen, stammel 8 cashmere, casimire 9 cassimere, gabardine, hauberget 10 broadcloth, fearnaught, fearnought 11 dreadnaught, dreadnought

fat: 5 suint 7 lanolin 8 lanoline

fibers: nep 4 noil

grower: 5 sheep 7 rancher

implement: 6 carder, shears, teaser 7 distaff, spindle

inferior: 7 cleamer

kind: 4 noil, shag 8 mortling 9 downright, shearling

lock: 5 flock

mixed hues: tum

nap-raising plant: 5 tease

package: 5 fadge

piece: 4 frib, tate(Sc.) 7 cleamer

pulled: 5 slipe

reclaimed: 5 mungo 6 shoddy

refuse: 6 pinion 7 backing

source: 4 goat, lamb 5 camel, llama, sheep

spun: 4 yarn

tease: tum 4 card

texture: nap

twisted roll: 4 slub

unravel: 5 tease

waste: fud

weight: tod 5 clove

worker: 8 shedhand

yarn: abb, eis 7 eiswool

wool-colored: 5 beige, camel

wool-dryer: 5 fugal

woolly: 5 hairy 6 fleecy, lanate, lanose 7 lanated 8 peronate

woozy: 5 dazed, dizzy, drunk, shaky 7 muddled, sickish, strange, trembly 9 befuddled

word: 4 fame, news, talk, term 5 adage, couch, honor, maxim, motto, order, parol, state, voice 6 assent, avowal, phrase, pledge, remark, report, repute, saying, signal, speech 7 account, adjunct, command, comment, dispute, express, message, promise, proverb, tidings 8 acrostic, language, password 9 direction, discourse, statement, watchword 10 expression 11 affirmation, declaration, information 12 intelligence 13 communication

battle: 9 logomachy

colorful: 5 slang

complex of ideas: 10 holophrase 11 holophrasis

connective: 11 conjunction

containing all vowels: 6 oiseau(F.) 7 eulogia, miaoued, sequoia 12 ambidextrous 14 undiscoverably 15 uncopyrightable

containing all vowels in reverse sequence: 10 duoliteral

containing all vowels in sequence: 8 caesious

containing four letters: 9 tetragram

containing no vowels: cwm, nth 5 crwth

containing uu: 6 mutuum, vacuum 7 duumvir, triduum 8 residuum 9 continuum, menstruum, perpetuum, zuurveldt 10 duumvirate

contraction: 9 haplology

corresponding: 8 analogue

derived from another: 7 paronym

figurative use: 5 trope 7 metonym

group: 6 clause, phrase 8 sentence

hard to pronounce: 10 jawbreaker

imitative: 9 onomatope

improper use: 8 solecism

inventor: 6 coiner 9 neologist

last sound omitted: 7 apocope

longest: 45 pneumonoultramicroscopicsilicovolcanokoniosis

magical: 6 presto, sesame 11 abracadabra

meaning: 9 semantics

misuse of: 11 catachresis, malapropism

mystical: 7 anagoge

new: 9 neologism, neoterism

of action: 4 verb

of naming: 4 noun

of opposite meaning: 7 antonym

of same meaning: 7 synonym

pretentious: 10 lexiphanic

root: 6 etymon

sacred: 5 selah 6 sesame, shelah

same backward and forward: 10 palindrome

same sound: 7 homonym 9 homophone

same spelling: 9 homograph

scrambled: 7 anagram

separation: 6 tmesis 7 diacope

square: 10 palindrome

substituted: 5 trope 7 metonym

transposition: 7 anagram

use of imitative: 12 onomatopoeia

use of new: 7 neology

use of unnecessary: 8 pleonasm

very long: 13 sesquipedalia(pl.)

word blindness: 6 alexia

word for word: 7 exactly 8 verbatim 9 literally

Word of God: 5 Logos

word of honor: 4 oath 6 parole 7 promise

word puzzle: 5 rebus 7 anagram, charade 8 acrostic 9 crossword

word-sign: 8 ideogram, logogram 10 hieroglyph, pictograph

wordbook: 7 lexicon, speller 8 libretto 9 thesaurus 10 cyclopedia, dictionary, vocabulary

wordiness: 8 verbiage

wording: 8 phrasing 9 wrangling 10 expression

wordless: 5 tacit 6 silent 8 unspoken

words: 4 text 6 lyrics 7 quarrel 8 libretto
depiction in: 8 vignette
excessive interest in: 10 verbomania
meaningless: 6 drivel 9 gibberish
misuse: 11 catachresis, heterophemy
put into: 5 state 6 phrase 7 express
written: 4 copy, text

wordy: 6 prolix 7 diffuse, verbose 9 garrulous, redundant 10 long-winded

wore: See wear

work: act, job, tew 4 beat, duty, feat, move, opus, plan, task, till, worm 5 chore, craft, draft, ergon, exert, graft, grind, knead, labor, solve, stint, trade 6 arbeit(G.), design, effort, puddle, strive 7 belabor, ferment, operate, pattern, perform, travail 8 activity, belabour, business, drudgery, exertion, function, industry, struggle 10 accomplish, employment, manipulate, occupation, profession 11 achievement, performance, undertaking
agreement: 4 code, pact 8 contract
aimlessly: 6 fiddle, potter, putter
aversion to: 10 ergophobia
by day: 4 char 5 chare
defensive: see **fortification**
divine: 7 theurgy
excess: 6 overdo
evade: 4 snib 9 goldbrick
hard: peg, ply 4 char, moil, plod, plug, toil 5 chare, delve, drill, labor, sweat 6 drudge 7 travail 8 scrabble 9 lucubrate
incomplete: 7 ebauche
labored: 11 lucubration
lover of: 9 ergophile
musical: see **musical composition**
period: day 4 hour, turn, week 5 month, shift, spell, trick, watch 8 schedule
steadily: ply
together: 4 team 5 co-act 9 co-operate 11 collaborate
unit: erg 5 ergon, joule 7 calorie
women's: 7 distaff

work-a-day: 7 prosaic 8 everyday, ordinary 11 commonplace

work for: 4 earn 5 serve 7 benefit

work of art: 4 song 6 statue 7 classic, etching, picture 8 painting

work on: 6 affect 9 influence

work out: fix 5 erase, solve 6 efface 7 arrange, develop, exhaust 8 exercise 9 calculate, elaborate 10 accomplish

work over: 4 redo 6 recast, rehash, revamp, revise 8 persuade 9 brainwash, elaborate, influence

work up: irk 5 raise, rouse 6 arouse, excite, expend 7 advance, develop 8 generate 9 elaborate 10 manipulate

workable: 4 ripe 6 mellow, pliant 8 feasible, possible 9 practical 11 practicable

workaholic: 5 grind

workbag: 8 reticule

worker: 4 arry, doer, hand, hind 5 navvy 6 earner, toiler 7 artisan, laborer 8 operator 9 artificer, craftsman, operative, performer 11 breadwinner
fellow: 5 buddy 7 comrade 8 confrere 9 colleague
group: 4 crew, gang, team 5 corps, shift, staff, union 9 personnel
hard: 6 beaver, drudge, fagger
head: 4 boss 5 super 6 ganger 7 foreman, manager 8 employer, overseer 10 supervisor 14 superintendent
kind: 5 diver, mason, miner, smith, tuner 6 barman, cocker, hopper, joiner, laster, sapper, sawyer, slater, smithy, tanner, warper, wright 7 analyst, cobbler, collier, geordie, glazier, paneler, plumber, reedman, riveter, sandhog, spinner 8 chaffman, chuckler, enameler, mechanic, shedhand, strapper 9 carpenter, groundhog, machinist, stevedore
migrant: 4 hobo, Okie 5 Arkie 6 boomer 7 floater, wetback
objectionable: 4 scab 7 botcher, bungler 11 scissorbill 13 featherbedder
skilled: 7 artisan
unskilled: 4 peon 6 coolie 7 laborer

workhorse: 4 peon, serf 5 slave 6 drudge, toiler 7 trestle 8 sawhorse

workhouse: 6 prison 8 workshop 9 almshouse, poorhouse

working (see also **work**): 4 busy 5 alert 6 active, decree, effort 7 halurgy 8 employed, endeavor 9 ordinance, practical 10 contortion
not: off 4 idle 5 kaput 6 broken 10 unemployed

working class: 7 laborer 11 proletariat

workman: See **worker**

workman-like: 4 deft 5 adept 8 skillful 10 proficient

workroom: den, lab 4 mill, shop 5 plant, study 6 studio 7 atelier, bottega, factory, library 10 laboratory 11 ergasterion

works: 5 plant

worktable: 5 bench

world: 5 earth, globe, realm 6 cosmos, domain, people, public 7 kingdom, mankind 8 creation, humanity, universe
antedating creation of: 10 premundane

bearer of: 5 Atlas
external: 6 nonego
lower: see underworld
miniature: 9 microcosm
pert. to: 7 mundane, secular 11 terrestrial
World War I: *battle:* 5 Marne, Somme, Ypres 6 Verdun 7 Jutland
general: 8 Pershing
hero: 5 York 12 Rickenbacker
marshal: 4 Foch
treaty: 10 Versailles
World War II: *alliance:* 4 Axis 6 Allies
battle: 4 Orel 5 Anzio, Bulge 6 Bataan, Sicily, Tarawa, Warsaw 7 Cassino, Iwo Jima, Okinawa 8 Normandy
general: 6 Patton, Rommel 7 Bradley 10 Eisenhower, Montgomery
worldly: 6 carnal, laical 7 earthen, earthly, mundane, secular, sensual, terrene 11 terrestrial 13 materialistic, sophisticated
worldwide: 6 global 8 ecumenic, pandemic 9 planetary, universal 10 ecumenical 13 international
worm: bob, eel, eri, ess ipo, loa, lug, pin 4 grub, nais, nema 5 borer, larva, tinea 6 looper, maggot, palolo, teredo, wretch 7 annelid, ascarid, ipomoea, reptile, sagitta, serpent, tagtail, wriggle 8 cercaria, helminth 9 angleworm, earthworm, insinuate, nemertina, nemertine, nemertini, trematode 10 nemertinea, serpentine 13 platyhelminth
aquatic: sao 4 nais, nema 5 cadew, leech 6 nereis 7 achaeta, annelid
bait: mad 4 lurg 7 tagtail
eye-infecting: loa
genus of: 6 nereis 8 geoplana
parasitic: 5 fluke, leech 7 ascarid, cestode, pinworm 8 tapeworm, trichina 9 roundworm
segment: 6 somite 8 metamere
threadlike: 7 filaria
worm-eaten: old 6 pitted, ragged, shabby 7 decayed, worn-out 8 decrepit 9 out-of-date, worthless 10 antiquated
worm-eating mammal: 4 mole
wormlike: 7 vermian 11 helminthoid
wormweed: 8 pinkroot
wormwood: 4 moxa 7 cudweed 8 mingwort
wormy: 6 earthy, rotten 8 diseased, crawling
worn: See wear
worn down: 5 erose, tired 6 eroded 7 abraded, attrite 8 attrited
worn-out: 4 sere, used 5 jaded, passe, seedy, spent, stale, trite 6 effete, frayed, shabby 7 haggard 8 consumed, decrepit, impaired, weakened 9 enfeebled, exhausted, hackneyed 10 bedraggled, threadbare 11 commonplace
worry: dun, hox, nag, vex 4 bait, care,

cark, faze, fear, fike, fret, fuss, gnaw, hare, stew 5 annoy, brood, choke, gally, harry, hurry, touse, trial, upset 6 badger, bother, caddle, fidget, harass, hatter, hector, pester, plague, pother 7 anxiety, bedevil, chagrin, concern, despair, disturb, perturb, torment, trouble 8 distress, strangle 9 worriment 10 disconcert, uneasiness
without: 8 carefree
worsen: 8 pejorate 7 decline, descend 10 retrogress 11 deteriorate
worship: 4 cult, fame, love 5 adore, dulia, honor, worth 6 credit, homage, latria, renown, repute, revere 7 dignity, idolism, idolize, liturgy, respect 8 blessing, devotion, hierugy, idolatry, venerate 9 adoration, deference, monolatry, reverence, theolatry 10 admiration, allotheism, hagiolatry, hierolatry, hyperdulia, reputation, veneration, worthiness
form of: 4 rite 6 ritual
house of: dom 6 chapel, church, mosque, shrine, temple 9 cathedral, synagogue 10 tabernacle
nature: 11 physiolatry
of angels and saints: 5 dulia
object of: 4 icon, idol 5 totem 6 fetich, fetish
pert. to: 8 liturgic 10 liturgical
place of: 5 altar
system of: 4 cult 6 cultus
worshiper: 6 adorer, bhakta, votary 7 devotee 8 disciple, idolater
worshipful: 4 good 5 proud 7 notable 8 esteemed 9 honorable, respected 10 venerating 11 worshipping 13 distinguished
worst: bad 4 beat, best 6 defeat 9 discomfit, overthrow
worsted: 4 garn, yarn 5 serge 6 fabric, tamine 8 whipcord 9 gabardine
yarn: 6 caddis, crewel 7 caddice, genappe 9 fingering
wort: 4 herb, root 8 fleabane
worth: 4 mark, note 5 merit, price, value 6 bounty, desert, esteem, riches, virtue, wealth 7 account, fitting, quality, stature 8 eminence 9 deserving, desirable, substance 10 excellence, importance, possession, usefulness
sense of: 5 pride 7 dignity, respect
thing of little: rap 6 stiver, trifle
worthless: bad, rap 4 base, evil, idle, vain, vile 5 inane 6 cheesy, drossy, futile, hollow, no-good, paltry, putrid, rotten, trashy 7 fustian, inutile, useless 8 feckless, unworthy 9 frivolous, no-account, valueless 11 undeserving 12 contemptible 14 good-for-nothing
worthy: 4 dear, good 7 condign 8 deserved, eligible, laudable, meriting, valuable 9 competent, deserving, estimable,

excellent, honorable, qualified 11 appropriate, meritorious

wound: cut 4 gore, harm, hurt, pain, stab, wing 5 break, ganch, sting 6 breach, damage, grieve, harrow, injury, trauma 7 afflict, attaint 8 distress, puncture
discharge from: pus 5 ichor, serum
dressing: 7 bandage, pledget
in heraldry: 4 vuln
lint to dilate: 4 tent
mark: 4 scab, scar, welt 7 blister

woundwort: 6 betony 7 allheal

wove: See weave

woven (see also **weave**): 4 lacy 7 damasse
raised figures: 6 broche 7 brocade

wow: hit, mew 4 howl, rave, wail 5 smash, whine 7 success

wrack: 4 kelp, rack, ruin 5 goods, trash, weeds, wreck 6 avenge, defeat, injury 7 destroy, seaweed, torment, unsound 8 calamity, mischief, wreckage 9 overthrow, shipwreck, vengeance 10 punishment 11 destruction, persecution

wraith: 5 ghost, spook 7 phantom, specter 10 apparition

wrangle (see also **quarrel**): 4 spar 5 argue, brawl, chide 6 bicker, debate, haggle 7 contend, dispute, quarrel 11 altercation, controversy 12 disagreement

wrangler: 4 cowboy, hafter 7 student 8 herdsman, opponent 9 disputant 10 antagonist

wrap: hap, rug, wap 4 cere, coil, fold, furl, hide, mask, roll, wind 5 cloak, cover, nubia, twine 6 afghan, encowl, enfold, infold, invest, swathe 7 blanket, conceal, enclose, envelop, package 8 enshroud, enswathe, surround 9 encompass 10 camouflage

wrapper: 4 gown 5 cover 6 fardel 8 galabeah

wrapping: wap 8 cerement, covering

wrasse: 4 fish 6 ballan

wrath: ire 4 fury, rage 5 anger 6 choler, felony 7 offense, passion 8 acerbity, violence 10 turbulence 11 indignation 12 exasperation

wrathful: 5 wroth 8 choleric, incensed 9 malignant

wreak: 5 exact 6 avenge, punish 7 gratify, indulge, inflict, revenge 9 vengeance

wreath, wreathe: lei 4 bank, coil, orle, roll, turn 5 crown, drift, torse(her.), twine, twist, whorl 6 anadem, corona, crants, crease, laurel, spirea, wrench 7 chaplet, contort, coronet, crownal, entwine, festoon, garland, spiraea, wrinkle 8 encircle, surround
in heraldry: 5 torse

wreck: 4 hulk, ruin 5 crash, ruins, smash, total, wrack 6 damage, defeat, jalopy, thwart 7 destroy, disable, founder, shat-

ter 8 collapse, demolish, derelict, sabotage 9 overthrow, shipwreck, vandalize 11 destruction

wreckage: 7 flotsam 8 driftage 9 driftwood

wrench (see also **wrest**): wry 4 jerk, pipe, pull, rack, tear, tool, turn 5 twist, wring 6 injury, monkey, sprain, strain, twinge 7 distort, spanner 8 Stillson 9 alligator, epitonion 10 distortion

wrest: 4 rend, ruse 5 exact, force, fraud, seize, trick, usurp, wring 6 elicit, extort, snatch 7 pervert, wrestle 10 confiscate

wrestle: tug 6 squirm, strive, tussle, wraxle 7 contend, grapple, wriggle 8 struggle

wrestler: 6 mauler

wrestling: *ceremonial:* 4 sumo
hold: 6 nelson 8 headlock, scissors
pad: mat
place: 4 ring 5 arena 8 palestra 9 palaestra
score: 4 fall
term: pin 8 takedown
throw: 4 hipe

wretch: bum, dog 4 worm 5 exile, loser 6 beggar, pauper 7 hilding, ingrate, sad sack, scroyle 8 derelict, recreant 9 miscreant 11 rapscallion

wretched: 4 base, foul, lewd, mean, poor 5 dawny 6 abject, dismal, paltry, pilled, woeful 7 baleful, caitiff, forlorn, unhappy 8 dejected, grievous, inferior, pitiable 9 afflicted, execrable, miserable, niggardly 10 calamitous, deplorable, depressing, despicable, distressed 11 unfortunate 12 contemptible, parsimonious 14 unsatisfactory

wriggle: 4 frig, turn, wind 5 dodge, evade, snake, twist 6 fitter, squirm, widdle, wintle, writhe 7 meander 10 equivocate

wring: 4 fret, rack 5 press, twist 6 elicit, extort, squirm, wrench 7 afflict, extract, squeeze, wrestle 8 compress, struggle

wrinkle: fad, rut 4 fold, idea, knit, line, lirk, ruck, ruga, seam 5 crimp, fancy, knack, reeve, ridge, rivel 6 cockle, crease, device, furrow, notion, pucker, rimple 7 crimple, crinkle, crumple, frumple, novelty, winding 8 contract 9 crow's foot, corrugate 10 prominence

wrinkled: 6 crepey, rugate, rugose, rugous 7 savoyed 8 rugulose
free from being: 6 smooth 7 erugate

wrist: 5 joint 6 carpus
bone: 4 ulna 6 carpal 7 carpale
mark: 7 rasceta
ornament: 4 band 8 bracelet
pert. to: 6 carpal

wristlet: 4 band 5 strap 8 bracelet, handcuff 9 wristband

writ: 5 breve, brief, tales 6 capias, elegit, extent, venire 7 exigent, process, writing 8 detainer, document, mittimus, replevin, subpoena 10 certiorari, distringas, injunction, instrument 11 fierifacias

of execution: 5 outre 6 elegit

write: pen 4 note 5 chalk, clerk, enrol 6 direct, enface, enroll, indite, record, scrawl, scribe 7 compose, engross, scratch 8 inscribe, scribble 9 character

letters: 10 correspond

write down: 4 list, note 6 record 10 deprecate

write off: 4 drop 5 decry 6 cancel, deduct, remove

writer: 4 hack, poet 5 clerk, odist 6 author, critic, glozer, lawyer, penman, scribe 7 copyist, glosser, hymnist, penster, realist, tropist 8 annalist, composer, essayist, gazeteer, literate, lyricist, novelist, parodist, prefacer, reviewer, scriptor 9 annotater, columnist, craftsman, dramatist, glossator, scrivener, solicitor 10 amanuensis, chronicler, glossarist, journalist 12 calligrapher, epistolarian 13 glossographer

inferior: 4 hack 8 rhymster 9 poetaster, scribbler

prose: 8 prosaist

unscrupulous: 10 plagiarist

verse: 4 bard, poet 5 odist 7 elegist 9 sonneteer

writhe: 4 bend, bind, curl, toss, turn 5 twist, wrest, wring 6 squirm 7 agonize, contort, distort, shrivel, wriggle 8 encircle, enswathe 9 convolute, insinuate 10 contortion, intertwine

writhing: 4 eely 9 wriggling

writing: ola 4 book, deed, olla, poem, writ 5 diary, essay, print, prose, verse 6 script 7 epistle, pothook 8 contract, covenant, document, makimono, pleading, spelling 9 allograph, cerograph, enrolment, esoterics 10 enrollment, instrument, literature, penmanship 11 chirography, composition, handwriting, inscription, orthography, pornography, publication

alternate: 13 boustrophedon

ancient manuscript: 6 uncial

character: (see also **word-sign**): 4 sign 6 letter, symbol 9 cuneiform 10 hieroglyph

desk: 9 secretary 10 escritoire

excessive interest in: 11 graphomania

inferior: 9 potboiler

master: 7 stylist

material: pad 5 board, paper, slate 6 tablet 7 papyrus 9 parchment 10 stationery

on the wall: 4 mene 5 tekel 8 upharsin

pert. to: 7 scribal

sacred: 5 Bible, Koran 6 psalms, Talmud 9 hagiology, testament 10 scriptures

secret: 4 code 6 cipher 10 cryptogram 12 cryptography

tool: pen 5 chalk, stick 6 pencil, stylus 8 computer 9 ballpoint 10 typewriter

wrong: bad, car, ill, off, out, sin 4 awry, evil, harm, tort 5 abuse, agley, amiss, crime, error, false, grief, malum, unfit 6 astray, faulty, injure, injury, malign, seduce, sinful, unfair, unjust, wicked 7 crooked, defraud, immoral, misdeed, twisted, vicious, violate 8 dishonor, improper, iniquity, mistaken, tortuous, wrongful, wrongous 9 erroneous, incorrect, injurious, injustice, reprobate, violation 10 dispossess, inaccurate, iniquitous, unsuitable 11 malfeasance, misfeasance 12 illegitimate 13 inappropriate 14 unsatisfactory

civil: 4 tort

wrongdoer: 5 felon 6 sinner 8 criminal, violator 9 miscreant 10 malefactor, tort-feasor, trespasser 12 transgressor

wroth: 5 angry, irate 7 violent 8 incensed, wrathful 9 turbulent

wrought (see also **work**): 4 agog, made 5 eager 6 formed, shaped, worked 7 excited, operose 9 decorated, disturbed, fashioned, processed 10 elaborated, ornamented, stimulated 11 embroidered 12 manufactured

up: 7 excited, stirred

wrung: See **wring**

wry: 4 awry, bend, bias, sour, tend, turn 5 avert, pinch, twist, wring 6 swerve, warped, wrench 7 contort, crooked, cynical, deflect, deviate, distort, incline 8 contrary, perverse, sardonic

wryneck: 5 loxia 9 snakebird 10 woodpecker 11 torticollis

genus: 4 jynx

Wurttemberg: *capital:* 9 Stuttgart

city: Ulm 9 Esslingen, Heilbronn

river: 6 Danube, Neckar

Wuthering Heights author: 6 Bronte

Wycliffe disciple: 7 Lollard

Wyoming: *capital:* 8 Cheyenne

city: 6 Casper 7 Laramie 8 Sheridan 11 Rock Springs

county: 4 Park 5 Teton 6 Albany, Carbon 7 Fremont

highest point: 11 Gannett Peak

Indian: 4 Crow 7 Arapaho

motto: 11 equal rights

mountain range: 8 Absaroka 9 Wind River

national park: 10 Grand Teton 11 Yellowstone

nickname: 8 Equality

river: 5 Green, Snake 6 Powder 7 Bighorn 11 North Platte

state bird: 10 meadowlark

state flower: 16 Indian paintbrush

state tree: 10 cottonwood

X

X: chi, ten 4 mark 5 cross, error 7 mistake 9 signature
X-shaped: 8 cruciate
Xanadu's river: 4 Alph
xanthic: 6 yellow 9 yellowish
Xanthippe: 5 scold, shrew 6 nagger, virago 9 termagant
  husband: 8 Socrates
xanthous: 6 yellow 9 Mongolian
xebec: 4 boat, ship 6 vessel
xema: 4 gull
xenium: 4 gift 7 present 8 delicacy
xenogamy: 13 fertilization
xenon: 7 element
Xenophanean: 7 eleatic
Xenophon: 14 Greek historian
  teacher: 8 Socrates
  work: 8 Anabasis 9 Hellenica
Xeres: 4 wine 5 Jerez 6 sherry
xerophyte: 6 cactus
xerosis: 7 dryness
xerotic: dry, sec
Xerox: 4 copy 6 copier 9 duplicate, reproduce
xerus: 8 squirrel

Xerxes: *composer:* 6 Handel
  kingdom: 6 Persia
  parent: 6 Atossa, Darius
  wife: 6 Esther
Xhosa, Xosa: 5 Bantu, tribe 8 language
xiphoid: 8 ensiform 9 sword-like
Xmas: 4 Noel, Yule 9 Christmas
X-ray: *inventor:* 8 Roentgen
  measuring device: 11 quantimeter
  science: 9 radiology 13 roentgenology
  source: 6 target
  treatment: 11 radiotherapy
  type: 8 grenzray
xurel: 4 scad 6 saurel
xylograph: 5 print 7 woodcut 9 engraving 10 impression
xyloid: 5 woody 8 ligneous
Xylonite: 9 celluloid
xylophone: 5 saron 6 gender 7 gambang, gamelan, marimba 8 gamalang, gigelira, sticcado
xyrid: 4 iris
xyst, xystos, xystus: 4 stoa, walk 5 porch 7 portico, terrace

Y

yabber: 4 talk 6 jabber 8 language 12 conversation
yabby, yabbie: 8 crayfish
yacht: 4 boat, race, sail. ship 5 craft 6 cruise, sonder
yacht basin: 6 marina
yacht flag: 6 burgee
yaffle: 10 woodpecker
yahoo: 4 lout 5 brute, tough 6 savage 7 bumpkin 9 roughneck
  creator: 5 Swift

Yahweh: God 4 YHVH, YHWH 5 Yahwe 7 Jehovah
yak: 4 joke, zobo 6 sarlak, sarlyk 7 buffalo, chatter
yakamik: 9 trumpeter
yaksha: god 4 jinn, ogre 5 angel, demon, dryad, fairy, gnome 6 spirit
Yakut river: 4 Lena
Yale: Eli 4 lock 10 University
Yalta: *conference member:* 6 Stalin 9 Churchill, Roosevelt

location: 6 Crimea

yam: ube, ubi 5 tugui 6 buckra, igname, potato, uviyam 7 boniata 8 cush-cush 9 posthouse 11 sweet potato

yamen: 6 office 7 mansion 9 residence 12 headquarters

yammer: cry 4 chat, yell 5 crave, gripe, shout, whine, yearn 6 clamor, desire, lament, scream 7 chatter, grumble, stammer, whimper 8 complain

yamp: 5 tuber

yang: cry 4 honk

yang-kin: 8 dulcimer

Yangtze River tributary: Han, Kan, Min

yank: tug 4 blow, jerk, pull 5 hoick 6 snatch, twitch 7 extract

Yank, Yankee: 8 American 10 Northerner

yap: apt, cur, dog, gab 4 bark, keen, talk, yelp 5 cheep, clown, eager, mouth, quick, ready, rowdy, scold 6 active, hungry, jabber, rustic 7 bumpkin, chatter, hoodlum 9 greenhorn

Yap Island money: fei 5 stone

yapock, yapok: 6 monkey 7 opossum

Yaqui: 5 river 6 Indian

yard: rod 4 lawn, spar, wand 5 court, garth, staff, stick 7 confine 9 courtyard, curtilage, enclosure 10 correction, playground, quadrangle
  enclosed: 5 garth, patio
  part of: 4 foot, inch
  sixteenth of: 4 nail

yards: five and one-half: rod
  119.6 square: ar
  600: 4 heer
  two hundred twenty: 7 furlong

yardage: 6 length 8 distance

yardland: 7 virgate

yardstick: 5 gauge 7 measure 8 standard

yarn: abb, eis, tow 4 chat, garn, sley, tale 5 fiber, story 6 caddis, crewel 7 caddice, eiswool, genappe, schappe 8 converse 9 fingering
  ball: 4 clew
  holder: cop
  quantity: cop, lea 4 clew, clue, hank, hasp 5 skein 7 spangle
  reel: 4 pirn
  size: 6 denier
  spindle: 4 hasp
  waste: 5 thrum

yarr: 5 growl, snarl 7 spurrey

yarrow: 4 herb 7 allheal, milfoil

yashmak, yasmak: 4 veil

yataghan: 5 knife, saber 8 scimitar

yaupon: 5 holly 7 cassena, cassina 9 evergreen

yaw: 4 turn, veer 5 steer 6 seesaw, swerve 7 deviate

yawl: 4 boat, howl 6 scream, vessel

yawn: nap 4 galp, gant(Sc.), gape, yaup, yawp 5 chasm 6 tedium 7 opening 8 oscitate

yawp: bay, cry, yap 4 bawl, call, gape, yelp 5 gripe 6 bellow, scream, squall 8 complain

yaws: 7 disease 9 frambesia

yawweed: 7 rhubarb

yclept: 5 named 6 called

ye: you 4 thee, thou

yea: aye, yes 4 also, even 5 truly 6 assent, indeed, verily 11 affirmative

yean: ean 4 bear, lamb 7 produce

yeanling: kid 4 lamb 7 newborn

year: 5 annus(L.)
  designation: 4 leap 5 lunar, solar 6 fiscal 7 natural 8 calendar, sidereal, tropical 12 astronomical
  difference between lunar and solar: 5 epact
  division: 5 month, raith(Sc.) 6 season
  of plenary indulgence: 7 jubilee
  one-fourth of calendar: 9 trimester
  one-half of academic: 8 semester
  one-third of academic: 9 trimester
  record: 5 annal 8 calendar

yearbook: 6 annual 7 almanac

yearling: 4 colt 9 hornotine

Yearling: author: 8 Rawlings
  boy: 4 Jody

yearly: 6 annual 7 etesian 8 annually

yearn: beg, vex, yen 4 ache, long, pine, sigh, wish 5 covet, crave 6 desire, grieve, hanker, yammer 7 request

yearning: 4 wish 5 eager 7 anxious 8 ambition 10 aspiration

years: age, eon, era 4 time
  eight: 9 octennial
  fifteen: 9 indiction
  five: 6 pentad 7 lustrum
  four: 11 quadrennial
  hundred: 9 centenary 10 centennial
  ninety: 10 nonagenary
  seventy: 12 septuagenary
  ten: 6 decade 8 decenary 9 decennary, decenniad, decennium
  thousand: 7 chiliad 10 millennium
  two: 8 biennium

yeast: bee 4 barm, foam, rise 5 froth 6 leaven 7 ferment 9 agitation
  brewer's: 4 barm

yeasty: 5 giddy, light 8 restless 9 frivolous, unsettled 11 superficial

yegg: 5 thief 6 robber 7 burglar 8 criminal 11 safebreaker, safecracker

yell: cry 4 call, gowl, howl, roar, yarm, yowl 5 cheer, shout, whoop 6 outcry, scream, shriek, yammer 7 yelloch

yelling: 8 strident 9 clamorous

yellow: 4 gull, mean, sere, turn, yolk 5 amber, blake, color, favel, lemon, ochre, tinge 6 butter, canary, fallow, flavic, flavid, flaxen, golden, sallow 7 unmanly, xanthic **8** cowardly, recreant **9** flavicant, jaundiced, lutescent **10** flavescent, melancholy **11** lily-livered, sensational, treacherous **12** contemptible, dishonorable **13** dishonourable, untrustworthy

brown: dun **4** bran **5** aloma, amber, pablo, straw **6** manila

dyestuff: **5** morin **6** orlean **7** annatto, annotto, arnatto

egg's: **4** yolk

gray: **4** drab

green: **5** olive **6** acacia, privet **8** glaucous, tarragon **10** chartreuse, serpentine

lemon: **8** generall

orange: **9** grenadine

red: **4** lava, roan **5** sandy **6** orange **7** nacarat

yellow alloy: 5 brass

yellow bird: 6 canary **7** warbler **9** goldfinch

yellow copper ore: 12 chalcopyrite

yellow copperas: 9 copiapite

yellow jacket: 4 wasp **6** hornet **8** eucalypt

yellow mustard: 8 charlock

yellow ocher: sil

yellow pigment: 7 etiolin **8** orpiment

yellow race: 6 Mongol **9** Mongolian

Yellow River: 7 Hwang Ho

yellow star: 10 sneezeweed

yellow starwort: 10 elecampane

yellowback: 9 dime novel

yellowbelly: rat **4** funk **6** coward

yellowhammer: 4 bird, yite **5** ammer, finch, skite **6** gladdy **7** yeldrin **8** yeldrine, yeldring, yeldrock, yoldring **10** woodpecker

Yellowhammer State: 7 Alabama

yellowlegs: 4 bird **7** tattler **8** redshank **9** sandpiper

Yellowstone Park attraction: 4 deer **5** bears **6** geyser **11** Old Faithful

yelp: cry, yip **4** bark, brag **5** boast, cheep, shout **6** greedy, outcry, shriek, squeal **7** ululate **9** criticize

Yemen (People's Democratic Republic of): *capital:* **4** Aden

gulf: **4** Aden

island: **5** Perim **7** Kamaran, Socotra

monetary unit: **5** dinar

town: **7** Mukalla

Yemen Arab Republic: *capital:* **4** San'a

desert: **10** Rub 'al-Khali

monetary unit: **4** rial

seaport: **4** Moka **5** Mocha **7** Hodeida

town: **5** Damar, Ta'izz **6** Dhamar

yen: 4 coin, long, urge **5** yearn **6** desire **7** longing **9** propensity

one-hundredth: sen

yenta (Yid.): **6** gossip

yeoman: 5 clerk **6** butler **8** retainer **9** assistant, attendant **10** freeholder, journeyman, manservant **11** subordinate

of guard officer: **4** exon

U.S. Navy: **12** petty officer

yes: aye, iss, oui(F.), yeh, yep **4** okay, yeah **5** agree **6** assent **7** exactly **8** all right **9** assuredly **11** affirmation, affirmative

yet: but **4** also **5** still **6** even so, though **7** algates, besides, further, however **9** after all, sometime **10** eventually **11** nonetheless **12** nevertheless **15** notwithstanding

yeti: 7 monster, snowman

yew: 4 tree **5** shrub **7** conifer **9** evergreen

genus: **5** taxus

Yiddish: 6 Jewish **8** language

prayer: **5** daven

synagogue: **4** shul

yield: bow, net, pay, sag **4** bear, bend, cave, cede, cess, elde, fold, give, obey, vail **5** addle, admit, agree, allow, avale, defer, grant, heald, hield, repay, stoop, waive **6** accede, afford, comply, impart, output, profit, relent, render, return, reward, soften, submit, supply **7** abandon, bring in, concede, consent, deliver, produce, revenue, succumb **9** acquiesce, surrender **10** capitulate, recompense, relinquish **11** acknowledge **12** knuckle under

yielding: 4 meek, soft, waxy **5** buxom **6** feeble, flabby, pliant, supple **7** flaccid, passive **8** flexible, recreant **9** tractable **10** manageable

yip: 4 yell, yelp

Ymer, Ymir: 5 giant

slayer: **4** Odin, Vili

yodel: 4 call, sing **5** carol, shout **6** warble **7** refrain

yogi: 5 fakir, yogin **6** fakeer **7** ascetic

sitting posture: **5** asana

yoke: tie **4** bail, bond, join, link, pair, span, team **5** bangy, fight(Sc.), hitch, marry, seize(Sc.) **6** attack(Sc.), banghy, couple, inspan, tackle(Sc.) **7** bondage, carrier, enslave, harness, oppress, service, slavery **8** restrain **9** associate, servitude

yoked: 9 conjugate

yokefellow: 4 mate, wife **6** spouse **7** husband, partner **9** associate, companion

yokel: oaf **4** boor, clod, lout, rube **6** obtuse, rustic **7** bumpkin, hayseed, plowboy **8** Abderite, gullible **10** countryman, slowwitted

yolk: 4 center, yellow **7** essence **8** vitellus

yon: See **yonder**

yonder: 4 away **5** there **6** beyond **7** distant, farther, further, thither

yore: 4 past **7** long ago

Yorkshire: *district:* **5** Otley, Selby

river: Ure

town: **5** Leeds

you: sie(G.), yez **4** thee, thou

young: fry, raw 4 tyro, weak 5 brood, fetus, fresh, green 6 active, callow, foetus, litter, strong, tender 7 pliable 8 childish, ignorant, immature, juvenile, newcomer, vigorous, workable, youthful 9 offspring, succulent 13 inexperienced
bring forth: ean 4 yean 5 calve, whelp
with: 6 gravid 8 pregnant
young animal: cub, kid, pup 4 calf, colt, fawn, joey 5 chick, puppy 6 kitten 7 tadpole
young hare: 7 leveret
young herring: 4 brit
younger: 6 junior
younger son: 5 cadet
youngster (see also **child**): boy, cub, lad, tad, tot 4 baby, calf, colt, girl, lass, tike 5 chick, child, filly, youth 6 moppet, shaver, urchin 9 stripling 10 midshipman
youth: bud 4 chap 5 chiel(Sc.), chabo 6 hoiden, hoyden 7 callant(Sc.), ephebos, ephebus, gossoon, puberty 8 teenager 9 youngster 10 adolescent 11 adolescence, hobbledehoy
goddess of: 4 Hebe
mythological: 5 Etana 6 Adonis, Apollo, Icarus
time of: 9 salad days
youth shelter: 6 hostel
youthful: new 5 early, fresh, young 6 active 7 puerile 8 immature, juvenile, vigorous, virginal
yowl: cry 4 bawl, howl, wail, yell
yo-yo: top 9 fluctuate, vacillate
Yucatan: 12 Mexican state
capital: 6 Merida
people: 4 Maya 5 Mayan
tree: 5 yaxche
yucca: 5 palma

Yugoslavia: *capital:* 8 Belgrade
city: 6 Skopje, Zagreb 7 Skoplje 8 Sarajevo
island: Rab, Vis 4 Cres, Hvar 5 Solta, Susak
language: 10 Macedonian
leader: 4 Broz, Tito 10 Mihajlovic
measure: rif 4 akov, ralo 5 donum, khvat, lanaz, stopa 6 motyka, palaze, ralico
monarch: 5 Peter 9 Alexander
monetary unit: 5 dinar
mountain: 7 Triglav 8 Durmitor
mountain range: 6 Julian 7 Dinaric, Velebit
people: 4 Serb 5 Croat 7 Slovene
plateau: 5 Karst
republic: 6 Serbia 7 Croatia 8 Slovenia 9 Macedonia 10 Montenegro
river: 4 Sava 5 Drava, Tisza 6 Marava, Vardar
seaport: 5 Split 7 Spalato 9 Dubrovnik
town: Pec 4 Stip 5 Veles
weight: oka, oke 5 dramm, tovar, wagon 7 satlijk
Yukon Territory: *capital:* 10 Whitehorse
explorer: 4 Bell (John) 9 Campbell (Robert)
flower: 8 fireweed
gold rush region: 8 Klondike
gold rush town: 10 Dawson City
highest peak: 7 Mt. Logan
lake: 6 Kluane
mountain range: 5 Rocky 7 St. Elias, Ogilvie, Stikine 9 Mackenzie
river: 5 Lewes, Liard, Pelly, White, Yukon 8 Klondike
territory of: 6 Canada
town: 4 Faro, Mayo
yule: 9 Christmas 13 Christmastide

Z

Z: zed 6 izzard

zac: 4 goat, ibex

zacate: hay 5 grass 6 forage

Zacchaeus, Zaccheus: 4 pure 8 innocent

Zadok: 4 just 9 righteous
son: 7 Ahimaaz

zaftig: 5 buxom, juicy, plump 10 full-bodied

Zagreb: See Yugoslavia

zaguan: 4 gate 8 entrance 11 entranceway

Zaire: *animal:* 5 okapi
capital: 8 Kinshasa
city: 7 Kananga 10 Luluabourg
cool season: 7 cacimba
formerly: 12 Belgian Congo
lake: 5 Tumba
official language: 6 French
people: 5 Bantu, Pygmy 7 Hamitic, Nilotic 8 Sudanese
river: 4 Uele 5 Congo, Dengi, Zaire 6 Likati 7 Aruwimi
snake: 8 amphiuma
wet season: 6 kundey

Zambia: *capital:* 6 Lusaka
falls: 8 Victoria
former name: 15 Northern Rhodesia
lake: 5 Niveru 9 Bangweulu
leader: 6 Kuanda
monetary unit: 6 kwacha
religion: 5 Hindu, Islam 7 animist
town: 5 Kitwe, Ndola 8 Chingola

zamia: 4 tree 5 cycad, shrub

zampogna: 7 bagpipe, panpipe

zanja: 5 canal, ditch, gully 6 arroyo

zanni: 5 clown

zany: wag 4 dolt, fool 5 clown, crazy, dotty, nutty, toady 7 acrobat, buffoon, idiotic 8 clownish, follower, imitator 9 simpleton 11 merry-andrew

Zanzibar: See Tanzania

zap: hit, pep 4 kill 5 verve 6 defeat, energy

zarf: cup 5 stand 6 holder

zarzuela: 11 seafood stew

zati: 6 monkey 7 ascetic, devotee

zeal: 4 fire 5 ardor, gusto 6 desire, fervor, spirit 7 passion 8 devotion, interest 9 eagerness 10 enthusiasm, fanatacism

Zealand: *city:* 10 Copenhagen

zealot: bug, nut 5 bigot 6 votary 7 devotee, fanatic 8 disciple, partisan, votaress 10 enthusiast

zealous: 4 warm 5 rabid 6 ardent, fervid, hearty 7 devoted, earnest, fervent 8 frenetic, vigorous, wild-eyed 9 phrenetic, strenuous 12 enthusiastic

Zebedee's son: 4 John 5 James

zebra: 4 dauw 9 butterfly
extinct: 6 quagga
resembling: ass 5 horse

zebrawood: 7 arariba 9 nakedwood 10 marblewood

zebu: 12 Brahmany bull

Zebulon, Zebulun: *brother:* 4 Levi 5 Judah 6 Simeon
father: 5 Jacob
mother: 4 Leah

zecchino: 6 sequin

Zelus: *brother:* Bia 6 Cratus
father: 6 Pallas
mother: 4 Styx
sister: 4 Nike

zemi: 5 charm

zenana: 5 harem 8 seraglio

zenith: 4 acme, apex, peak 6 summit 11 culmination
opposite of: 5 nadir

Zeno: *city:* 4 Elea
follower: 5 Stoic

Zenobia: *country:* 7 Palmyra
husband: 9 Odenathus

zephyr: 4 aura, wind 6 breeze

zeppelin: 5 blimp 7 balloon 9 dirigible

zero: nil 5 aught, zilch 6 cipher, naught, nought 7 nothing 9 nonentity

Zeruiah's son: 7 Abishai

zest: 4 tang 5 gusto, savor, taste 6 flavor, relish 8 piquancy 9 enjoyment 10 enthusiasm

zestful: 4 racy 6 hearty 7 pungent

Zeus: 7 Alastor, Jupiter
attendant: 4 Nike
beloved of: Io 6 Europa
brother: 5 Hades 8 Poseidon
cupbearer: 4 Hebe 8 Ganymede
daughter: Ate 4 Hebe, Kore 5 Irene 6 Athena, Athene 7 Artemis, Astraea 8 Despoina 9 Aphrodite 10 Persephone, Proserpina, Proserpine 11 Persephassa
epithet: 7 soter 7 Alastor
form assumed by: 4 bull, swan
messenger: 4 Iris 6 Hermes
nurse: 4 goat 8 Amalthea, Cynosura
oracle: 6 Dodona

parent: 4 Rhea 6 Cronus, Kronos
shield: 5 aegis
sister: 4 Hera
son: Gad 4 Ares 5 Arcas, Argus 6 Aeacus, Apollo, Hermes, Tityus 7 Perseus 8 Dardanus, Dionysos, Dionysus, Heracles, Herakles, Hercules, Tantalus 10 Hephaestus
victim: 4 Idas
wife: 4 Hera, Juno 5 Danae, Metis 6 Semele
ziarat, ziara: 4 tomb 6 shrine
ziggurat: 5 tower 7 pyramid
zigzag: 4 tack, turn 5 angle, crank, weave 8 flexuous
zilch: 4 zero 7 nothing 8 goose egg
Zillah: *husband:* 6 Lamech
son: 9 Tubal-cain
Zilpah's son: Gad 5 Asher
zimarra: 5 cloak 7 cassock, soutane
zimb: bug, fly 6 insect
Zimbabwe: *capital:* 6 Harare (formerly Salisbury)
former name: 8 Rhodesia
language: 5 Shona 7 Ndebele
leader: 5 Nkomo 6 Mugabe
monetary unit: 6 dollar
town: 6 Bulawayo
zinc: 7 adamine, adamite, spelter, tutenag 9 galvanize, tutenague
ore: 6 blende 10 splialerite
sulphate: 7 ilesite
zing: pep, vim, zip 4 dash, snap 5 force, vigor 6 energy, spirit, stingo 9 animation, eagerness 10 enthusiasm
zingaro: 5 gypsy, nomad
zingel: 4 fish 5 perch
zinger: 6 retort 9 punch line
zinnia: 5 aster 6 flower
Zion: 4 hill 6 heaven 7 Utopia
Zionism founder: 5 Herzl
zip: 4 zing 5 hurry 6 breeze
zipper: 8 fastener
Zipporah's kin: 5 Moses, Reuel 6 Jethro 7 Eliezer, Gershom
zippy: 5 agile, brisk 6 snappy
zizith: 7 fringes, tassels
zizz: 4 whir, whiz
Zoan: 5 Tanis
zodiac sign: Leo Ram 4 Bull, Crab, Fish, Goat, Lion 5 Aries, decan, Libra, Scale, Twins, Virgo 6 Archer, Cancer, Fishes, Gemini, Pisces, Taurus, Virgin 7 Balance, Scorpio 8 Aquarius, Scorpion 9 Capricorn 11 Capricornus, Sagittarius, Waterbearer
Zola: *defender of:* 7 Dreyfus
work: 4 Nana 6 Verite 7 J'accuse 8 Germinal
zombie: 5 drink, dunce, snake 9 eccentric
zone: 4 area, band, belt, path, zona (L.) 5 layer, tract 6 course, girdle, region, sector, stripe 7 circuit, segment 8 cincture, encircle, engirdle
geological succession: 6 assise
marked by: 6 zonate
zonked: 4 high 5 doped 6 stoned 7 drugged 8 turned on 9 spaced-out 11 intoxicated
zoom: 5 speed 9 chandelle
zoo: 8 vivarium 9 menagerie
floating: ark
zoophyte: 5 coral 9 ectoproct
zoril: 5 skunk 6 weasel 7 polecat
Zoroaster's works: 6 Avesta
Zoroastrian: 5 Parsi 6 gheber, ghebre, Parsee
demon: 4 deva
god: 5 Ahura, Mazda 10 Ahura-Mazda
zoster: 4 belt 6 girdle
Zouave: 4 Zuzu 7 soldier
zounds: 4 egad 8 mild oath
zoysia: 5 grass
zucchetto: 7 calotte 8 skullcap
zucchini: 5 gourd 6 squash
zufolo: 5 flute 9 flageolet
zuisin: 4 duck 7 widgeon 8 baldplate
Zulu: *boy:* 6 umfaan
headman: 6 induna
language: 5 Bantu
regiment: 4 impi
spear: 7 assegai
Zuni: 6 Indian, Pueblo
zwieback: 4 rusk 5 toast 7 biscuit
zygomatic bone: 5 malar 9 cheekbone
zygote: 7 oosperm
zymase: 6 enzyme
source: 5 yeast
zymogen activating substance: 6 kinase
zymosis: 7 disease 12 fermentation
zythum: 4 beer

Prefixes, Suffixes and Combining Forms

Prefixes, suffixes and combining forms are listed alphabetically rather than by number of letters. The endings given in parentheses may be added on to the affix given, or the affix may be used on its own. For example, the prefix for **accessory** may be either *par* or *para*.

PREFIXES

abnormal: dys
about: ambi
above: hyper, super, supra, sur
accessory: par(a)
across: di(a), trans
additional: super
advocating: pro
after: meta, post
again: an(a)
against: ant(h) (i), cat(a) (h) (o), contra, kat(a) (h) (o)
ahead: pre
almost: pen(e)
alongside: par(a)
alternate: counter
among: inter
anew: an(a)
apart: dis
around: ambi, circum, peri
asunder: dis
at the front: pre
away from: ap(h) (o)
back: an(a), retro
before: ante, pre, pro
beforehand: pre
beside: par(a)
between: inter, intra
beyond: extra, praeter, preter, sur, trans, ultra
both: ambi
chemical: ox(a)
chief: arch(i)
combating: ant(h) (i)
complementary: counter

corresponding: counter
deprived of: dis
detached: ap(h) (o)
different: ap(h) (o)
difficult: dys
diseased: dys
down: cat(a) (h) (o), kat(a) (h) (o)
dwarf: nan(o)
earlier: ante
excess: hyper
excessive: sur
extreme: arch(i)
faulty: par(a)
forward: ante
front: pro
great: arch(i)
half: hemi, semi
higher: super, supra
improper: mis
in advance: pre
incorrect: mis
later: meta
less than: hypo
low-pitched: contra
lower: hypo
mistaken: mis
near: pros
nearer: cis
near to: ep(h) (i)
negative: dis
not: non
one: uni
opposed: dis
opposing: ant(h) (i)
opposite: counter
outer: ep(h) (i)

outside: extra
over: ep(h) (i), extra, hyper, super, supra, sur
partial: demi, semi
prime: arch(i)
principal: arch(i)
prior: ante, pro
resembling: par(a)
retaliatory: counter
reverse: dis, dys
rival: ant(h) (i)
round: peri
ruler: arch
secondary: sub
single: uni
subsequent: post
substituting: pro
succeeding: meta
surrounding: circum, peri
through: di(a), per
throughout: per
together: co(l) (m) (n) (r), sy(m) (n), sym(n)
toward: pros
transcending: meta, supra
transformation: meta
two: twi
under: hypo, sub
underneath: intra
unfavorable: dys
up: an(a), sur
upon: ep(h) (i)
upward: ano
with: co(l) (m) (n) (r), sym(n)
within: intra
wrong: mis

SUFFIXES

abundance: ose
accomplishing: ive
act: ade, ance, ion, ure
act (upon): ate
action: age, ance, ence, ing, ization
adherent: ist, ite
adjective: ular
agency: ator, eer
agent: ator, eer, facient, fic, ier
alcohol: itol
approximately: ish
art: ery
becoming: escence, escent
beginning: escent
being: ant, ent, ical, ure
belonging to: an, ean, ian, ish
capable of: ile
capable: able, ible
caused by: ical
causing: able, facient, fic, ible
character: ery
characteristic: ism
characteristic of: ical, ish, ist, istic(al)
characterized by: ful, ial, ical, in(a) (e), ory, ous
chemical: ane, ein(e), ene, idin, ile, ine, ite, ole, olic, ose, ylene
citizen: ese, ian, ist, ite
city: polis
collection: ery
collection of: age
compound: ate
condition: ance, ate, ence, ency, hood, ile, ism, ment, osis
cult: ism
degree: ity
descendant: ite
diminutive: cle, cular, ette, ole, ule
direction: ling
disease: itis, oma
doctrine: ism

doer: ast, ator, eer, facient, ier, ist, ster
existing: ent
expert: ician, ist
female: ine
feminine: ette
fit: able, ible
form: ify
formation: osis
full of: ous
function: ate, ure
group: ery, ome
group of: ette
imitation: ette
inferior: ling
inflammation: itis
inhabitant: ese, ite
instrument: tron
language: ese
like: ose
little: ette
little one: el, elle, ium, kin(s), ock
make: ify
marked by: ling
mineral: ite
musical instrument: in(a) (e)
native: ite
object: ment
office: ate, dom, ship, ure
offspring: ite
old: ster
ordinal: eth, th
participant: ster
pertaining to: ese, ile
place: arium, ary, ery, orium
place for: ory
place of: age
places: aria
plant: acea
plants: aceae, ales
practice: ery, ics, ism
practitioner: ician
process: age, ence, ing, ion, ization, ment, osis, ure
product: ade

profession: ship
quality: ance, ancy, ence, ency, hood, ice, ity, ness, ship
rank: ate
realm: dom
reflecting: escent
related to: in(a) (e)
relating to: ative, ean, ese, ial, ical, ile, ine, ist, istic(al), itious, ory
resembling: ular
result: ization, ment
serving for: ory
skill: ics, ship
small: ling
small one: ula, ule, ulum, ulus
specialists: ician
specialized in: an, ean, ian
state: age, ance, ancy, ate, ation, dom, ence, ency, ery, hood, ion, ism, ity, ization, ment, ness, osis, ship
stem: ome
study: ics
style: esque
substitute: ette
sugar: ose, ulose
superlative: est
supporter: ite
sweet drink: ade
system: ism
tendency: itis
tending toward: ive
theory: ism
thing: ant, orium
things: oria
trace of: ish
trade: ery
trait: ism
tumor: oma
user: ster
vacuum tube: tron
worthy: able, ible
young: ster
youngster: ling

COMBINING FORMS

abdomen: ventr(i) (o)
abounding: poly
above: supero
accelerating: auxo
acid: acet(o), oxy
acorn: balan(o)

action: praxia
adhesion: anchyl(o), ancyl(o), ankyl(o)
affinity: phily
again: pali
against: cat(h) (a), kat(a)

agricultural: agro
air: atm(o), pneumo
aldehyde: ald(o)
alike: hom(o), is(o)
all: omn(i), pan(o)
alone: mon(o), soli

alternative: allelo
amber: succin(o)
ancient: archae(o), archeo, palae(o), pale(o)
angle: anguli, angulo, gon
animal: zoic
ankle: tars(o)
ant: myrmec(o)
antimony: stib(i) (o)
ape: pithec(o) (us)
apex: apic(i) (o)
appear: phaner(o)
appearance: phany
appetite: orexia
archetypal: prot(o)
arising: genous
arm: brachi(o)
armed: hoplo
around: amph(i)
arrangement: tax(i) (o)
art: techn(o)
ass: ono
asunder: dich(o)
atlas: atlant(o), atlo
aviation: aer(o)
avoidance: phob(o)
back: dors(i) (o), not(o) (us), opisth(o)
bad: cac(o), mal
balance: stato
beautiful: cali(o), calli(o)
bed: clin(o)
bee: api, avi
beginning: acr(o), akr(o)
berry: bacci, cocc(i) (o)
best: aristo
billionth: nano
bitter: picr(o)
black: atro, mel(a) (o), melan(o)
blind: typhl(o)
blood: haem(o), hem(a) (i) (o)
blue: cyan(o)
boat: scaph(o)
body: dema, soma, somat(o)
bone: oste(o)
book: biblio
both: amph(i) (o), bis
brain: cerebr(i) (o)
branched: cladous
breast: mast(o)
brief: brevi
bright: lampro
bristle: chaet(o), seti
broad: lati
broom: scopi
brush: scopi
bud: blast(o)
bulk: onc(h) (o)

bulky: hadr(o)
bull: taur(i) (o)
butter: butyr(o)
cat: aelur(o), ailur(o)
cattle: bovi
caudal: ur(o)
cause: aetio, aitio, etio
cavity: antr(o)
cecum: typhl(o)
cell: blast, cyt(e) (o), gamet(o), phag(e)
cement: lith
chain: strept(o)
chamber: thalam(o)
cheek: bucco, mel(o)
cheese: case(o), tyr(o)
chemical: amid(o), amin(o)
chest: stern(o), steth(o), thorac(i) (o)
chief: prot(o)
child: paed(o), ped(o)
chin: genio, mento
China: sino
Chinese: sinic(o)
church: ecclesi(o)
clay: argill(i) (o), argillaceo, pel(o)
cleft: fissi, schisto, schiz(o)
climate: meteor(o)
close: sten(o)
closed: cleist(o), clist(o)
closure: cleisis, clisis
clot: thromb(o)
cloud: cirr(hi) (i) (o) (ho), nephel(o), nepho, nimbo
cluster: cym(o), kym(o)
coal: anthrac(o)
cold: cry(o), frigo, psychro
color: chrom(o)
colorless: leuc(o), leuk(o)
combination: hapt(o)
compact: pycn(o)
complete: hol(o), tel(e) (o)
concealed: adel(o)
condition: ance, ancy, blasty
contact: hapt(o)
contemporary: ne(o)
contest: machy
copper: chalc(o), chalk(o), cupr(o)
correct: orth(o)
counterfeit: pseud(o)
counterpart: pseud(o)
covered: crypt(o), krypt(o)
craft: techn(o)
creeping: herpet(o)

crooked: anchyl(o), ancyl(o), ankyl(o)
crown: corono, stephan(o)
crystal: hedron
cup: cotyl(i) (o), cyath(o), scyph(i) (o)
current: rheo
dark: melan(o), nyct(i) (o)
dead: abio
decomposition: lysis
deep: bathy
deer: cervi
defective: atel(o)
deficiency: penia
deficient: privic
dense: pycn(o)
depth: bath(o)
descendant: ite
desire: orexia
development: plasia
devouring: vorous
diaphragm: phren(i) (o)
difficult: mogi
disease: agra, pathia, pathic, pathy
diseased: cac(o)
disintegration: lysis
dislike: mis(o)
distant: tel(e) (o)
distinct: idio
diver: dyt(a) (es)
diverse: vari(o)
divided: fid, fissi, schisto
doctrine: logy
doer: ist
dog: cyn(o)
donkey: ono
double: bis
down: cat(h) (a), kat(a)
dream: oneir(o), onir(o)
drug: pharmaco
dry: xer(o)
dull: ambly(o), brady
dwarf: nano
eagle: aet(o)
ear: aur(i), ot(o)
earnest: serio
earth: geo
earthquake: seismo
eat: phag(o)
eating: vore
egg: ov(i) (o)
empty: ken(o)
end: acr(o), akr(o), tel(e) (o)
entire: hol(o), integri, toti
environment: ec(o), oeco, oiko
equal: aequi, equi, is(o), pari

era: zoic
eruption: anthema
even: homal(o)
everywhere: omni
evil: mal
examination: opsy
existence: ont(o)
external: ect(o), exo
extremity: acr(o), akr(o)
eye: irid(o), ocul(o), opto, opy
eyelid: blephar(o)
false: pseud(o)
fat: adip(o), lip(o), seb(i) (o), steat(o)
fatty: lipar(o)
fear: phob(o)
fearful: din(o)
feather: penn(i) (o), pinn(i), pter(o)
feeling: pathia, pathy
feigned: pseud(o)
female: gyn(e) (o)
few: olig(o), pauci
fewer: meio, mi(o)
fictitious: pseud(o)
fifth: quint(i)
fight: machy
fin: pinn(i)
fine: lept(o)
finger: dactyl(o), digit(i)
fire: igni, pyr(o)
first: prot(o)
fish: ichthy(o), pisci
fixed: aplano, stato
flagellum: mastig(o)
flat: homal(o), plan(i)
flute: aul(o)
fondness: phily
food: sito, troph(o)
foot: ped(i) (o), pod(e) (o)
footprint: ichn(o)
foreign: xen(o)
forest: hyl(o)
form: morph(o)
four: tessar(a), tesser(a), tetr(a)
freezing: cry(o)
front: antero
fruit: carp(ia) (ium) (us), fructi
fungus: myc(o), mycete(e) (o)
gas: aer(o), pneumo
gate: pyl(e) (o)
ghost: sci(a) (o), skia
giant: megal(o)
gill: branch
gilled: branchia
gland: aden(o), adren(o)
glandular: aden(o)
glass: hyal(o), vitr(o)

glue: coll(o)
gnat: culic(i)
goat: capri
gold: auro
good: agath(o)
goose: chen(o)
government: archy, cracy
grain: cocc(i) (o), sito
grape: botry(o)
grave: serio
grease: seb(i) (o)
great: macr(o), meg(a), megal(o)
growth: auxo
guest: xen(o)
guiding: agogue
gums: ulo
habitat: ec(o), oeco, oiko
hand: cheir(o), chir(o), man(i) (u)
hard: scler(a) (o), stere(o)
hardening: scler(a) (o)
hare: lag(o)
hatred: mis(o), phobia
head: cephal(o) (us), crani(o)
healing: iatric(s), iatro(y)
heap: cumul(i) (o)
hearing: acou(o), acousia, audio, oto
heart: cardi(a) (o)
heavens: uran(o)
heavy: bary, gravi, hadr(o)
heel: calcaneo
height: acr(o), akr(o), alt, hyps(o)
hidden: adel(o), crypt(o), krypt(o)
hide: derm(a) (o)
high: alti
hollow: cel(o), coel(o)
holy: hagi(o), hier(o), sacr(o)
homogeneous: is(o)
honey: meli, mell(i)
horn: cerat(o), corn, kerat(o)
horned: cera
horse: equi, hipp(o)
human: anthrop(o)
hundred: centi, hect(o)
hundredth: centi
idea: ideo
illness: agra
image: eidolo, idolo, typ(o)
imperfect: atel(o)
incomplete: atel(o)
increase: auxo
individual: idio
inner: ent(o)
insect: entom(o)
instrument: labe

intermediate: mes(o)
intestine: enter(o)
iris: irid(o)
iron: ferr(i) (o), sider(o)
irregular: anom(o), anomal(i) (o)
irregularly: mal
jackass: ono
jaw: gnath(o)
joint: arthr(o), condyl(o)
juice: opo
kernel: cary(o), kary(o)
key: cleid(o)
kidney: nephr(o), ren(i) (o)
killer: cide
kind: gen(o)
knee: gon
knob: tyl(o)
knowledge: gnosia, gnosis, gnosy, ics
lake: limn(i) (o)
land: chor(o), gaea, geo
language: gloss(o), glott(o), lingua(i) (i) (o)
large: macr(o), meg(a), megal(o)
law: nom(o)
layer: cline
lead: molybd(o), plumb(o)
leaf: phyll(o)
level: plan(i) (o)
lifeless: abio
ligament: desm(o)
light: luci, lumin(i) (o), phos, phot(o)
like: home(o), homoe(o), homoi(o)
lily: crinus
line: lineo, stich
lip: labio
listening: acou(o)
living: ont(o), vivi
lizard: saur(o)
local: top(o)
love: eroto
loving: phil(e) (o)
lung: pneum(o), pulmo
maiden: partheno
male: andr(o)
man: anthrop(o)
manifest: phaner(o)
many: mult(i), pluri, poly
marriage: gamy
marrying: gamous
mass: onc(h) (o)
master: arch
matter: hyl(o)
measuring: metry
medical treatment: iatric(s), iatro(y)
memory: mnem(o)

middle: mes(o)
milk: lact(i) (o)
million: meg(a)
millionth: micr(o)
mind: menti, noo, phren(i) (o), psych(o)
mineral: lite, lyte
mite: acar(i) (o)
modern: ne(o)
moisture: hygr(o)
monster: terat(o)
moon: selen(i) (o)
mosquito: culic(i)
mother: matr(i) (o)
motley: part(i) (y)
mouse: my(o) (s)
mouth: or(i) (o), stom(a) (e) (o)
mouths: stomat(a) (o)
much: mult(i), poly
mud: pel(o)
muscle: my(o)
name: omato, onym
narrow: sten(o)
native: ite
navel: omphal(o)
near: juxta
neck: cervic(i) (o)
nerve: neur(o)
nerve tissue: gangli(o)
new: ne(o)
night: nyct(i) (o)
nine: ennea
ninth: non(a)
nipple: mast(o), papilli(o)
nitrogen: az(a) (o)
nose: nas(i) (o), rhin(o) (us)
novel: caen(o), cen(o)
nucleus: cary(o), kary(o)
number: arithmo
nut: cary(o), kary(o)
nutrition: troph(o)
occult: crypt(o), krypt(o)
odd: azygo
offspring: gen(o), ped(o)
oil: elaeo, elaio, eleo, ole(i) (o)
oily: lipar(o)
old age: geront(o)
one: mon(o)
opening: pora, pore, pyle, stom(a) (o)
organ (internal): viscer(i) (o)
organism: ont(o)
other: all(o), heter(o)
out of: ect(o)
outside: ect(o), exo
ox: bovi
oyster: ostre(i) (o)
pain: agra, alg(o), algia

paralysis: plegia, plegy
part: mer(o)
particle: plast
parturition: toky
path: ode
peak: acr(o), akr(o)
peculiar: idio
people: dem(o), ethn(o)
perfect: tel(e) (o)
person: idio
phenomena: ics
physician: iatrist, iatro(y)
picture: picto, pinac(o)
pig: choerus
pillar: styl(o)
pipe: aul(o), siphon(i) (o), solen(o)
pit: bothr(o)
place: chor(o), gaea, gea, loco, top(o)
plant: chore, phyt(a)
pleasant: hedy
poem: stich
poison: toxic(o)
pond: limn(i) (o)
pool: limn(i) (o)
pouch: cyst(i) (is) (o)
poverty: penia
power: dynam(o)
practice: ics
practitioner: path
pressure: baro, piezo, tono
prickly: echin(o)
primary: prot(o)
producer: gen(e)
producing: genetic
qualities: ics
quinine: chin(o)
race: ethn(o), gen(o), phyl(o)
radiating: actin(i) (o)
rain: hyet(o), ombro, pluvi(a) (o)
rainbow: irid(o)
raven: corax
ray: actin(i) (o)
recent: caen(o), cen(o), ne(o)
reciprocal: allelo
recital: logue
recognition: gnosia, gnosis, gnosy
record: gram, graph
recurring: ennial
red: erythr(o), pyrrh(o), rhod(o)
reduction: lysis
remote: dist(i) (o), palae(o), pale(o), tel(e) (o)
repetition: pali
representation: graphy

reptile: herpet(o)
resembling: form
respiration: pneumo
resting: stato
rib: cost(i) (o), pleur(i) (o)
ribbon: taen(i) (o)
rice: oryz(i) (o)
right: dextr(o), orth(o), rect(i)
river: potam(o)
rock: clast, ite, lite, lith, lyte, petr(i) (o), phyre
rod: rhabd(o)
roof: steg(o)
root: rhiz(o)
rose: rhod(o)
rotten: sapr(o)
rough: trachy
round: globo, troch(o), ventr(i) (o)
rule: archy
ruler: arch
running: drom(o), dromous
sac: cyst(i) (o)
sacred: hagi(o), sacr(o)
saints: hagi(o)
salt: hal(o), ite, sali
same: hom(o), is(o)
saw: serri
science: ics, logy, ology, onomy, sophy
sea: mer, pelag(o)
second: deuter(o), deut(o)
seed: sperm(a) (i) (o), spermat(o)
seizure: agra
self: aut(o)
separate: idio
serpent: ophi(o)
seven: hept(a), sept(i)
sex: gen(o)
shadow: sci(a) (o), skia
shaggy: dasy
shape: morph(o)
sharp: oxy
sheet: pallio
shell: conch(o), oeco, ostrac(o)
shield: aspid(o), aspis, scut(i)
shoot: blast(o), thall(i) (o)
short: brachy, brevi
shoulder: om(o)
shrub: thamn(o)
side: ali, later(i) (o), pleur(i) (o)
sides: ali
sight: opsia, opsy
silver: argent(i) (o), argyr(o)

similar: hol(o), home(o), hom(o), homoe(o), homoi(o)

simple: apl(o), hapl(o)

single: apl(o), hapl(o), mon(o)

six: hex(a), sex(i), sexti

skill: ics, techn(o)

skin: derm(a) (o), dermis

slant: clin(o)

sleep: hypn(o)

slope: cline

slow: brady

small: lept(o), micr(o), olig(o), parv(i) (o)

smaller: meio, mi(o)

smell: brom(o)

smooth: leio, lio, liss(o)

snake: ophi(o)

snow: chio, chion(o)

sodium: natr(o)

soil: agro, geo

solid: stere(o)

solitary: erem(o)

song: melo

soul: psych(o), thym(o)

sound: audio, phon(e) (o) (y), phonia

south: austr(o), not(o)

sow: choerus

specialist: ician, ist, logue

speech: lalo, log(o), phon(o)

spherical: globo

spider: arachn(o)

spiral: helic(o)

spirit: psych(o), thym(o)

spot: macul(i) (o)

spring: cren(o)

sprout: blast(o), clad(o)

sprouting: blastic

stain: macul(i) (o)

star: astr(o)

starch: amyl(o)

steam: atmid(o)

stem: caul(i) (o)

stick: rhabd(o)

stomach: gaster(o), gastr(i) (o)

stone: lith(o)

stoppage: stasis

straight: lineo, orth(o), rect(i)

strain: tono

strange: xen(o)

stranger: xen(o)

stream: fluvio

stroke: plegia

structure: morph(o)

stupor: narc(o)

substance: hyl(o), phane, state

suffering: path(o), pathia, pathy

sugar: gluc(o), glyc(o), sacchar(i) (o), sucr(o)

sulfur: thi(o)

summit: acr(o), akr(o), apic(i) (o)

sun: heli(o)

supporter: crat, ist, ite

surface: hedron

surgical removal: ectomy

sweat: hidr(o)

sweet: glyc(o)

swine: hyo

swollen: phys(o)

tablet: pinac(o), plac(o)

talk: logue

tallow: seb(i) (o), stear(o), steat(o)

tapeworm: taen(i) (o)

taste: geusia

teeth: odontia

ten: dec(a), decem, dek(a)

tendency: philia, phily

tendon: teno

tenth: deci

terrible: din(o)

theft: klept(o)

theory: logy

therapy: pathia, pathic, pathy

thick: dasy, hadr(o), pachy

thigh: mer(o), merus

thin: lept(o)

third: tri, trit(o)

thorn: acanth(o) (us), spini(o)

thought: ideo, log(o)

thousand: kilo

thread: nem(a) (o), nemat(o)

three: ter, tri

throat: bronch(o)

thunder: bront(o), ceraun(o), kerauno

tick: acar(i) (o)

time: chron(o), chronous

tin: stann(i) (o)

tip: acr(o), akr(o), apic(i)(o)

tissue: hist(o), hypho

toe: dactyl(o)

tone: phon(o)

tongue: gloss(o), lingu(a) (i) (o)

tooth: dent(i) (o), odont(o)

top: acr(o), akr(o), apic(i)(o)

total: hol(o)

touch: hapt(o), thigmo

track: ichn(o)

translucent: hyal(o)

transmission: phoresis

transparent: hyal(o)

treatise: logy

tree: dendr(o), dendron

trench: bothr(o)

triangular: trigon(o)

tribe: phyl(o)

trillion: treg(a)

trillionth: pico

trough: bothr(o)

true: orth(o)

tube: siphon(i) (o), solen(o), syring(o)

tumor: cele, gangli(o), myom(o), onc(h) (o)

twice: bis

twin: didym(o)

twist: spir(i) (o)

twisted: strept(o)

two: bin, duo

twofold: diphy(o), dipl(o)

type: morph(o)

umbilicus: omphal(o)

unarmed: anopl(o)

unequal: anis(o)

uniform: is(o)

union: gamous, gamy, zyg(o)

united: gam(o)

universal: cosm(o), omni

universe: cosm(o)

unpleasant: cac(o)

unreal: pseud(o)

untrue: pseud(o)

unusual: anom(o)

upright: orth(o)

urchin: echin(o)

usage: nom(o)

vapor: atm(o)

variation: all(o)

various: part(i) (y)

vehicle: mobile

vein: phleb(o), ven(i) (o)

vertebra: spondyl(o) (us)

vessel: angi(o), arteri(o), vas(i) (o), vascul(o)

viewing instrument: scope

vine: ampel(o), viti

vinegar: acet(o)

virgin: parthen(o)

viscera: splanchn(o)

visible: phaner(o)

vision: opia, opsy, opto, opy

voice: phon(e) (o) (y)
war: machy
water: hydr(o)
wave: cym(o), kym(o)
wax: cer(o)
way: ode
weak: asthen(o), lept(o)
wealth: plut(o)
weather: meteor(o)
web: hypho
weight: bar(o)
well: agath(o)
wet: hygr(o)
whale: cet(o)
wheel: troch(o)
whip: mastig(o), mastix
white: alb(o), cali(o),
   calli(o), leuc(o), leuk(o)

whole: hol(o), integri,
   pan(o), toti
wholly: toti
wide: eury, lati
wild: agrio
wild beast: ther(o)
wind: anem(o), venti,
   vento
windpipe: bronchi(o),
   trache(o)
wing: ali, pter(o)
within: end(o), ent(o), eso
wolf: lyc(o)
woman: gyn(e) (o),
   gynaec(o), gynec(o)
womb: hyster(o), metr(a)
   (o), uter(o)
wood: hyl(o), lign(i) (o),

   xyl(o)
wool: erio, lan(i) (o)
word: log(o)
work: erg(o) (y)
worker: ergat(o)
world: cosm(o)
worm: helminth(o), vermi
worship: latry
wound: traumat(o)
wrist: carp(o)
writer: grapher
writing: grapho
year: ennial
yellow: chrys(o), flav(o),
   lute(o), xanth(o)
yoke: zyg(o)
yolk: vitell(o)